THE ROUGH GUIDE TO
GREAT BRITAIN

This tenth edition updated by

Rob Andrews, Tim Burford, Samantha Cook, Greg
Dickinson, Matthew Hancock, Rob Humphreys,
Phil Lee, David
MacEacheran,
Claire Saunders,
Amanda Tomlin

ROUGH GUIDES

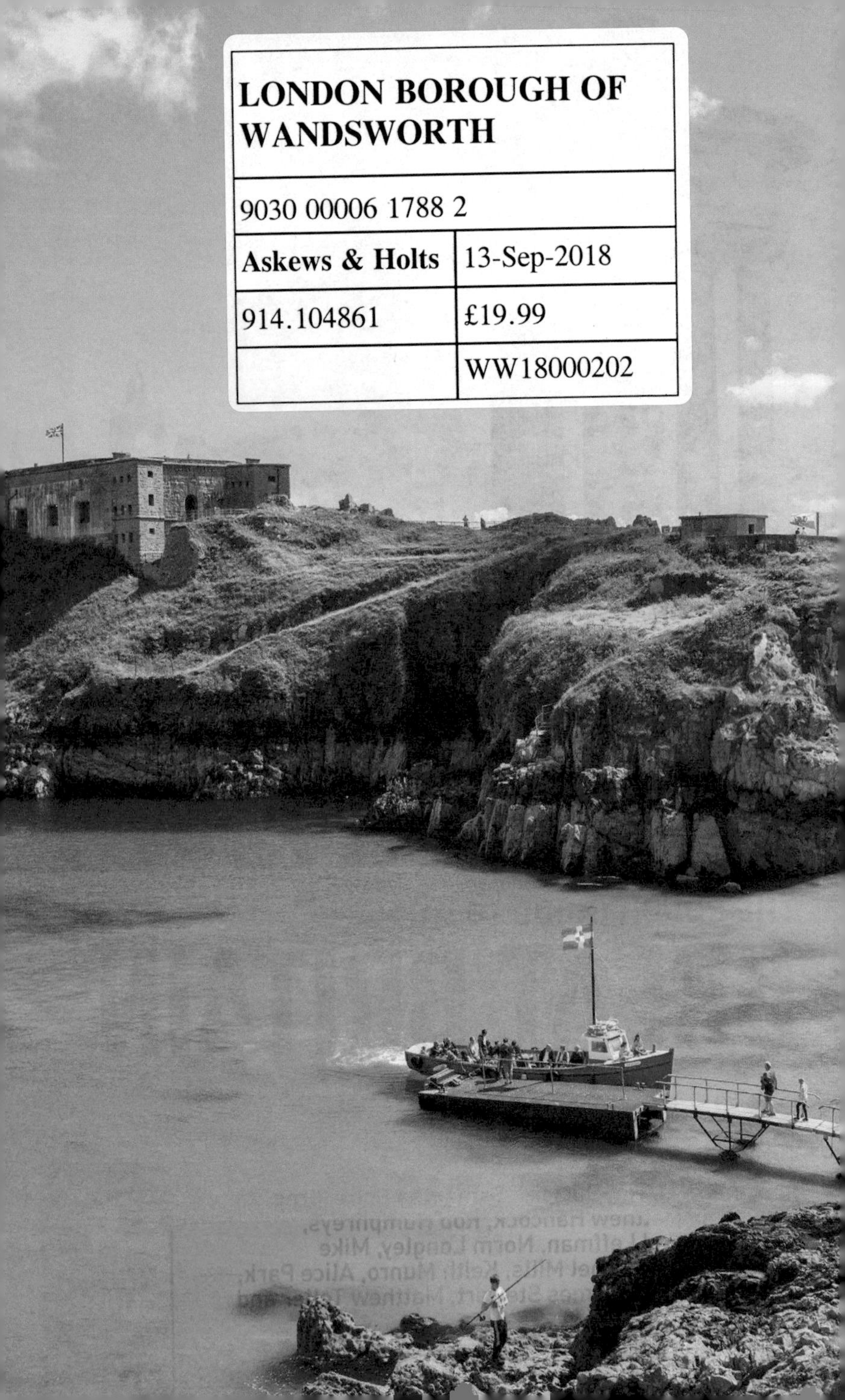

Contents

Introduction to
Great Britain

If you didn't know that the "Great" in Great Britain was strictly a geographical term (it refers to the largest island – containing England, Scotland and Wales – of the British Isles), you'd be tempted to give Britain the accolade anyway. It's hard to think of another country that's given so much to the world – railways to royalty, shipbuilding to Shakespeare, football to fish and chips – and there are few holiday destinations suffused with as much history, based on more than five thousand years of settlement and a proud record of stability, democracy and invention. From dynamic London to misty Scottish mountains, fishing villages to futuristic cityscapes – and whether you're looking for urban adventures, pagan festivals, cutting-edge galleries, world-class museums, wilderness hikes or majestic buildings – Britain is undoubtedly great.

Of course, the kind of time you have here depends on which Britain you visit – which sounds odd until you take on board that we're talking about three different countries and three distinct national identities, all wrapped up in a relatively modest-sized "United Kingdom" on the western edge of Europe. England, Scotland and Wales have had centuries to get used to each other, but even so there are sharp reminders of past conflicts and present politics at every turn – from mighty border castles to proud, devolved parliaments – while you'll find separate "national" cultural collections in the three very different capital cities of London, Cardiff and Edinburgh. You're not walking into any kind of vicious separatist clamour, but it's as well to remember that England (by far the dominant country) is not the same thing as Britain – even if the English sometimes act that way.

As well as the national variations that spice up any visit, there's also huge regional diversity in Britain – from the myriad accents and dialects that puzzle foreigners to the dramatically diverse landscapes. Bucolic Britain is still easy to find, be it in gentle

WORCESTER AND BIRMINGHAM CANAL, BIRMINGHAM

rolling farmland or alpine peaks and lakes, and tradition and heritage still underpins much that is unique about the great British countryside. But increasingly it's Britain's urban culture – innovative arts and music, challenging architecture, trend-setting nightlife – that the tourist authorities choose to promote.

In recent years Britain has showcased its international hosting skills with gusto, not least with the staging of the London 2012 Olympics and Glasgow 2014 Commonwealth Games, each of which went above and beyond the nation's ever-modest expectations – in terms of both execution and medal count – and placed the British Isles on the podium of global attention once again.

Britain has also been at the heart of some seismic political happenings in recent times: in 2014 the Scottish public voted in an independence referendum, opting to remain part of the union but only by an unexpectedly fine margin; then, in 2016, a UK-wide referendum on European Union membership resulted in a majority vote to leave (again, by the slimmest of margins). Despite these uncertain times, and with the full ramifications of Brexit yet to be played out, there's no doubt that Blighty is still a hugely rewarding place to visit.

Where to go

There's enough to see and do in Britain to swallow up months of travel. The rundown of country-by-country highlights over the following pages will help you plan an itinerary – or remind you of how much you've yet to see.

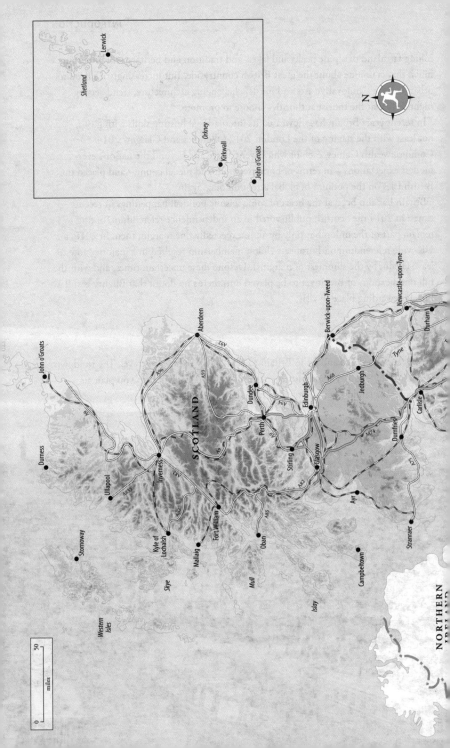

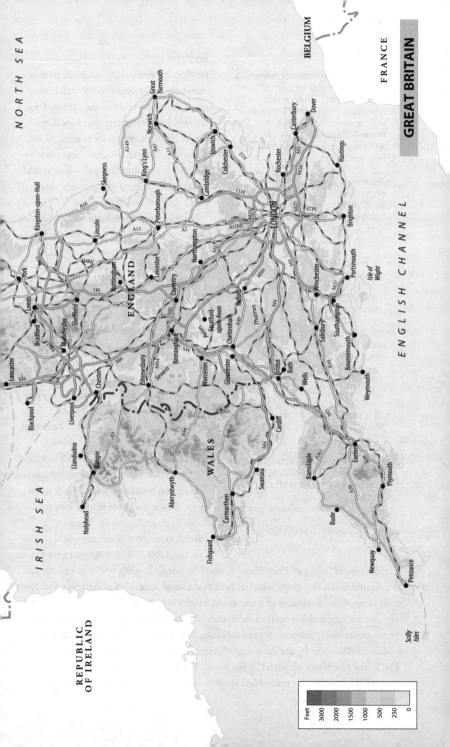

FACT FILE

- Britain is a **constitutional monarchy**, whose head of state is Queen Elizabeth II. **Parliament** is composed of the directly elected House of Commons and the unelected House of Lords. The **Prime Minister** is the head of the largest political party represented in the House of Commons.

- The **lowest point** is in the Fens of eastern England, at 13ft below sea level; the **highest mountain** is Ben Nevis, in Scotland, at 4406ft. The **longest river** is the Severn (220 miles), which flows through England and Wales.

- The **population** of Britain is about 63 million: 55 million in England, 5 million in Scotland and 3 million in Wales. The biggest city is London, with over 8 million inhabitants.

- The **distance** between the two extreme points of the British mainland – a journey beloved of charity fundraisers – is the 874 miles, from Land's End (Cornwall, England) to John O'Groats (in the Scottish Highlands).

- You can always plan a day out at the **seaside** – nowhere in Britain is more than 75 miles from the coast.

- Cary Grant, Stan Laurel, Robert Pattinson, Christian Bale and Guy Pearce? They're all **Brits** – oh, and Gregory House, MD (Hugh Laurie) too. But London-girl Bridget Jones (Renée Zellweger) and Mary Poppins' Cockney chimney sweep Bert (Dick van Dyke)? Definitely not.

England

London is emphatically the place to start. Nowhere in the country can match the scope and innovation of the capital. It's a colossal, dynamic city that is perhaps not as immediately pretty as some of its European counterparts, but does have Britain's – arguably Europe's – best spread of nightlife, cultural events, museums, pubs, galleries and restaurants.

The other large **English cities** – Birmingham, Newcastle, Leeds, Manchester and Liverpool – each have their strengths and admirers. Among much else, Birmingham has a resurgent arts scene, Leeds is the north's prime shopping city, and Newcastle's nightlife is legendary. Manchester can match the capital for glamour in terms of bars, clubbing and indie shopping, and also boasts two of the world's best-known football teams, while its near-neighbour Liverpool is successfully reinventing itself as a top cultural destination.

History runs deepest in England's oldest urban settlements. The glorious **cathedral cities**, like Lincoln, York, Salisbury, Durham and Winchester, form a beautiful national backbone of preserved churches, houses and buildings, while you're never more than a few miles from a spectacular castle, a majestic country house, or a ruined monastery. There are world-famous, UNESCO-recognized sites galore, from Blenheim Palace to Canterbury Cathedral, but all English towns can rustle up an example of bygone glory, whether medieval chapel, Georgian mansion or Victorian mill. Meanwhile, reminders of more **ancient times** are ubiquitous – and reveal quite how central England has been to thousands of years of European development. In the southwest there are remnants of an indigenous Celtic culture that was all but eradicated elsewhere by the Romans, who in turn left their mark from Hadrian's Wall in the north to Colchester in the south. Even more dramatic are the surviving traces of the very earliest **prehistoric** settlers – most famously the megalithic circles of Stonehenge and Avebury.

MICHELDEVER FOREST, WINCHESTER

For many visitors, it's not the towns or monuments that are most beguiling, but the long-established **villages** of England, hundreds of which amount to nothing more than a pub, a shop, a gaggle of cottages and a farmhouse or two. Traditional rural life may well be on the wane – though that's been said of England since the Industrial Revolution, over two hundred years ago – but in places like Devon, Cornwall, the Cotswolds, Cumbria and Yorkshire there are still villages, traditions and festivals that seem to spring straight from a Constable canvas or a Wordsworth poem. Indeed, the English **countryside** has been an extraordinarily fecund source of inspiration for writers and artists, and the English themselves have gone to great lengths to protect their natural heritage. Exmoor, Dartmoor, the North York Moors, the Lake District and the Peak District are the most dramatic of the country's ten **national parks**, each offering a mix of picturesque villages, wild landscapes and wonderful walks.

Scotland

The Scottish capital, **Edinburgh**, is – whisper it to the English – a far more handsome city than London, famous for its magnificent setting, majestic castle and ancient royal quarter of Holyrood, not to mention an acclaimed international arts festival and some excellent museums. A short journey west is the larger city of **Glasgow**, a sprawling postindustrial metropolis on the banks of the River Clyde that's an upbeat

destination with great bars, clubs and restaurants. Its museums and galleries are some of the best in Britain, while the city's impressive architecture reflects the wealth of its eighteenth- and nineteenth-century heyday.

Scotland's other towns and cities are only fitfully enticing, though central destinations like **Stirling**, **Perth** and **Dundee**, and **Aberdeen** in the northeast, make a valiant tilt at tourists, and, in the university town of **St Andrew's** (Prince William and Kate Middleton's alma mater) Scotland has a college town to rank with Oxford and Cambridge. However, what usually resonates most with visitors is Scotland's great outdoors, whether it's the well-walked hills of the **Trossachs** in central Scotland – home of Loch Lomond – or the **Highlands**, whose mountains, sea cliffs, shadowy glens and deep lochs cover the entire northern two-thirds of the country. In Highland Scotland in particular, famous destinations trip off the tongue – Loch Ness, Culloden, Cape Wrath and John O'Groats – while Ben Nevis has Britain's highest mountain.

Some of the most fascinating journeys are to be had on the **Scottish islands**, the most accessible of which extend in a long rocky chain off the Atlantic coast. Whether it's mooching around Mull, investigating the early Christian heritage of Iona, whisky-tasting on Islay, or touring the Isle of Arran – the most visited of the Hebrides – there are unique experiences on every inch of the Inner Hebridean archipelago. The outer Western Isles, meanwhile – from Lewis and Harris in the north to Barra in the south – feature some of Britain's most dramatic scenery, from towering sea cliffs to sweeping sandy beaches.

At Britain's northern extreme lie the sea- and wind-buffeted **Orkney** and **Shetland** islands, whose rich Norse heritage makes them distinct in dialect and culture from mainland Scotland, while their wild scenery offers some of Britain's finest birdwatching and some stunning Stone Age archeological remains.

THE CALL OF THE WILD

Despite the crowded motorways and urban sprawl, Britain can still be an astonishingly wild place. Natural habitats are zealously guarded in fifteen national parks, from the far southwest to the distant north – a jaw-dropping number of protected areas for a nation of Britain's size.

Even in the most popular parks – the almost Alpine **Lake District** (see page 510), say, or the rugged **Peak District** (see page 425) – it's never a problem to escape the day-tripper crowds, while true wilderness awaits in the **Cairngorms** of Scotland (see page 924) or **Snowdonia** in Wales (see page 722).

Outside the parks, too, every corner of Britain has its own wild charm – whether it's tracking Northumberland's **wild cattle** (see page 614), seal-spotting at **Blakeney Point** (see page 378), dolphin-watching on the **Moray Firth** (see page 924) or hiking across windswept **Lundy Island** (see page 328) to see its famous puffins.

Wales

It's **Cardiff**, of course, the vibrant capital, that boasts most of Wales's major institutions – the National Assembly, Principality Stadium, Millennium Centre, National Museum – and is the best place to get the feel of an increasingly confident country. The second city, **Swansea**, is grittier by far, a handy base for the sandy bays, high cliffs and pretty villages of the wonderful **Gower peninsula**. Meanwhile, in the postindustrial **Valleys** – once a byword for coal mining – a superb sequence of heritage parks, memorials and museums illuminates the period when South Wales produced a third of the world's coal.

Castles are everywhere in Wales, from the little stone keeps of the early Welsh princes to Edward I's ring of doughty fortresses, including Beaumaris, Conwy and Harlech. Religion played its part too – the cathedral at **St Davids** was founded as early as the sixth century AD, and the quiet charms of the later, medieval monastic houses, like ruined **Tintern Abbey**, are richly rewarding. Much older relics also loom large – **stone circles** offer a link to the pre-Roman era when the priestly order of Druids ruled over early Celtic peoples.

If England glories in its villages, perhaps it's the **small towns** of Wales that appeal most – New Age Machynlleth and lively Llangollen, the foodie centre of Abergavenny and festival-fuelled Llanwrtyd Wells. You could concoct a delightful tour that goes from one attractive, idiosyncratic town to another, but even so, you wouldn't want to miss Wales's other great glory – the wild countryside. The Cambrian mountains form the country's backbone, between the soaring peaks of **Snowdonia National Park** and the angular ridges of the **Brecon Beacons**. These are the two best places for a walking holiday – though you can get up Snowdon, Wales's highest mountain, by railway if you prefer. Mountainous Wales also offers world-class mountain biking – Coed-y-Brenin in Mid-Wales is the name all bikers know. As for the Welsh seaside, don't miss the magnificent clifftops of the rippling **Pembrokeshire** coast or the sandy beaches of the western **Cambrian** shore. Most of the coast remains unspoiled, and even where the long sweeps of sand have been developed they are often backed by enjoyable, traditional **seaside resorts**, such as Llandudno in the north, Aberystwyth in the west or Tenby in the south.

BRITAIN ON A PLATE

You might think of roast beef or fish and chips – but, only half-jokingly, **chicken tikka masala** is by now well accepted as a national dish, a reflection of the extent to which Britain's postwar immigrant communities have contributed to the country's dining scene. Even the smallest town will have an Indian restaurant (more properly, Bangladeshi or Pakistani), with Chinese (largely Cantonese) and Thai restaurants common too – not to mention countless Italian trattorias and pizza places and Spanish tapas bars. For the most authentic food, there are a few ethnic enclaves you need to know about – **Chinatown** in London (see page 74) and Manchester's "curry mile" in **Rusholme** (see page 479) are probaby the best-known, but there are all kinds of treats in store in the lesser-touristed parts of the country. Pakistani grills, Turkish meze or Polish pierogi in London's unheralded suburbs, a Kashmiri balti in **Birmingham** (see page 404) or **Bradford** (see page 565), or South Indian snacks in **Leicester** (see page 450) – all are as British as can be.

When to go

Considering the temperate nature of the **British climate**, it's amazing how much mileage the locals get out of the subject: a two-day cold snap is discussed as if it were the onset of a new Ice Age, and a few days around 25°C start rumours of a drought. The fact is that summers rarely get very hot and the winters don't get very cold, except in the north of Scotland and the highest points of the English, Welsh and Scottish uplands. **Rainfall** is fairly even, though again mountainous areas get higher quantities throughout the year (the west coast of Scotland is especially damp, and Llanberis, at the foot of Snowdon, gets more than twice as much rainfall as Caernarfon, seven miles away).

In general, the south is warmer and sunnier than the north, but the bottom line is that it's impossible to say with any degree of certainty what the weather will be like when you visit. May might be wet and grey one year and gloriously sunny the next; November stands an equal chance of being crisp and clear or foggy and grim. If you're planning to lie on a beach, or camp in the dry, you'll want to visit **between June and September** – though don't blame us if it pours down all August, as it might well do. Otherwise, if you're balancing the clemency of the weather against the density of the crowds, the best months to explore are April, May, September and October.

AVERAGE DAILY MAXIMUM TEMPERATURES

	Jan	Feb	Mar	Apr	May	Jun	Jul	Aug	Sep	Oct	Nov	Dec
CARDIFF												
°F	45	45	50	56	60	68	69	69	64	58	51	46
°C	7	7	10	13	16	20	21	21	18	14	11	8
EDINBURGH												
°F	42	43	46	51	56	64	65	64	61	54	48	44
°C	5	6	8	11	13	18	18	18	16	12	9	7
LONDON												
°F	43	44	50	56	62	69	71	71	65	58	50	45
°C	6	7	10	13	17	21	22	22	19	14	10	7

Author picks

Our indefatigable authors are always on the lookout for the best in Britain – start here for some truly wonderful British travel experiences…

Glorious gardens No one tends their gardens like the British, whether it's the Lost Gardens of Heligan in Cornwall (see page 332), the intriguing "poison garden" at Alnwick in Northumberland (see page 617), or the recently discovered historic walled gardens at Aberglasney (see page 665).

Remote beaches Head to the extremities: to Par Beach, Isles of Scilly (see page 345), the lonely beaches of North Uist (see page 971) or Barafundle Bay, Pembrokeshire (see page 670).

Wacky festivals The Welsh "capital of wackiness", Llanwrtyd Wells (see page 694), combines festive fun and British idiosyncrasy, as does Hastings' Jack in the Green shindig (see page 166).

Best views We simply can't choose – London from the Shard (see page 96), dramatic Hartland Point in Devon (see page 328), the stunning Scottish coast from Wester Ross (see page 937) or the views from the summit of Snowdon (see page 728).

Incredible industry From Ironbridge (see page 419) to Manchester (see page 466), Blaenavon (see page 653) to the Clyde (see page 833), Britain invented the stuff the world wanted.

Modern masterpieces Visit one of the superb Tate galleries in London (see page 94), St Ives (see page 343) and Liverpool (see page 492), or rub shoulders with Lichtenstein and Warhol in the Scottish National Gallery of Modern Art in Edinburgh (see page 768).

Classic journeys The Settle to Carlisle Railway (see page 558) and the West Highland Railway (see page 920) take some beating; walkers, meanwhile, should make for the magnificent Wales Coast Path (see page 650), a whopping 870 miles (1400km) long.

Proper pubs You can't beat an evening by the fire in a crooked-ceilinged British pub. The *Felin Fach* in Brecon (see page 688), *Bitter End* in Cockermouth (see page 533) and *Old Forge* in Knoydart (see page 936) are a few of our favourite spots for a tipple.

Our author recommendations don't end here. We've flagged up our favourite places – a perfectly sited hotel, an atmospheric café, a special restaurant – throughout the Guide, highlighted with the ★ symbol.

BARAFUNDLE BAY, PEMBROKESHIRE

OLD FORGE PUB, KNOYDART

30

things not to miss

It's not possible to see everything that Britain has to offer in one trip – and we don't suggest you try. What follows, in no particular order, is a selective taste of the highlights of England, Wales and Scotland, including stunning scenery, awe-inspiring architecture, thrilling activities and incomparable urban experiences. All highlights are colour-coded by chapter and have a page reference to take you straight to the Guide, where you can find out more.

1 THE GOWER PENINSULA
See page 661
A stunning stretch, fringed by glorious bays and dramatic cliffs, and dotted with prehistoric remains and castle ruins.

2 HAMPTON COURT PALACE
See page 112
With its yew-hedge maze and restored State Apartments, Henry VIII's extravagant Thames-side palace is the most revered of England's royal abodes.

3 STONEHENGE
See page 226
An ancient, still unexplained, ring of monoliths, Stonehenge attracts sun-worshippers in their thousands over the summer solstice.

4 THE LAKE DISTRICT
See page 510
England's largest national park is also one of its favourites, with sixteen lakes, scores of mountains and strong literary connections.

5 WEST HIGHLAND RAILWAY
See page 920
Take one of the great railway journeys of the world, the setting of the "Hogwarts Express" route in the *Harry Potter* movies.

6 WHALE- AND DOLPHIN-WATCHING
See page 924
Boat trips in the Moray Firth get you a great view of these beautiful marine creatures.

7 SOUTHWOLD
See page 369
Fine Georgian buildings, a long sandy beach and open heathland await in this charming East Anglian seaside town.

8 WHITBY
See page 587
Irresistible seaside town with a picturesque port, atmospheric ruined abbey, and dramatic Count Dracula connections.

9 OXFORD AND CAMBRIDGE COLLEGES
See pages 232 and 385
Two of the world's oldest and most esteemed academic institutions, whose colleges boast all the dreaming spires and perfectly tended lawns you could ask for.

10 THE BRITISH MUSEUM
See page 76
In parts controversial, and generally not British, the collections of the BM are still the greatest in the world.

9

10

11 EDINBURGH FESTIVAL

See page 772

One of the world's great arts festivals – in fact, several festivals – transforms the handsome old city each year into a swirling cultural maelstrom.

12 SHAKESPEARE'S GLOBE THEATRE, LONDON

See page 95

It's a genuine thrill to watch Shakespeare performed in this reconstruction of the famous Elizabethan theatre.

13 RENNIE MACKINTOSH ARCHITECTURE, GLASGOW

See page 820

The visionary architect's remarkable legacy is manifest in masterpieces such as The Lighthouse and the Scotland Street School.

14 EDEN PROJECT, CORNWALL

See page 331

Spectacular and ungimmicky display of the planet's plant life, housed in vast geometric biomes.

15 WALKING IN THE PEAK DISTRICT

See page 425

From inhospitable, windswept plains to deep-forested dales, the Peaks offer some of Britain's best walking trails.

11

12

16 IONA, ARGYLL
See page 878
The home of Celtic Christian spirituality, and an island of pilgrimage since antiquity.

17 THERMAE BATH SPA
See page 273
Heated by Bath's naturally hot, mineral-rich springs, Thermae Bath Spa's rooftop pool is a lovely spot for a dip.

18 SURFING IN NORTH DEVON
See page 327
The beaches along the north coast of Devon offer some truly great breaks.

19 MANCHESTER'S NORTHERN QUARTER
See pages 474
Manchester's bohemian Northern Quarter is a hive of music venues, cutting-edge street art and lively bars.

20 HADRIAN'S WALL PATH, NORTHUMBERLAND
See page 607
You can walk or cycle the length of this atmospheric Roman wall, once the frontier against Britain's northern tribes.

18

19

20

21

22

23

21 CURRY IN BRADFORD
See page 565
Bradford's famed curry houses offer everything from cheap-and-cheerful baltis to slick contemporary dining.

22 LIVE MUSIC IN LONDON
See page 129
Whether it's a sweat-soaked gig at the magnificent Roundhouse or a night at the Proms, London's music scene has few equals anywhere in the world.

23 SHOPPING IN THE LANES, BRIGHTON
See page 173
A warren of pedestrianized thoroughfares, Brighton's Lanes are lined with antiques shops, designer outlets and intimate pubs.

24 HAY-ON-WYE LITERARY FESTIVAL
See page 692
The prestigious literary festival at this bibliophile border town brings in all the bookish great and good.

25 BLAENAVON
See page 653
Head down a mine, if you dare, in this fascinating Welsh ironworks town.

26 EDWARD I'S IRON RING
See pages 713, 736, 738 and 742
Edward's fearsome Iron Ring of fortresses in North Wales includes Conwy, Caernarfon, Harlech and Beaumaris.

27 SEAFOOD IN CORNWALL
See page 348
Feast on the fresh catch in Padstow, where chef Rick Stein rules the roost.

28 DURHAM CATHEDRAL
See page 623
England's greatest Norman building perches on a peninsula overlooking Durham's lovely old town.

29 WHISKY IN SCOTLAND
See page 912
Sip a wee dram or two along Speyside's Malt Whisky Trail, or head for beautiful Islay and one of the island's eight distilleries.

30 PORTMEIRION
See page 732
Decidedly un-Welsh architecture makes this odd Italianate village a unique attraction; it also hosts the marvellously eclectic Festival no.6 in September.

29

30

Itineraries

The following itineraries plan routes through Britain in all its huge variety, from the wave-lashed Cornish coast to the misty hills of northern Scotland. Whether you want to survey the remnants of ancient cultures *in situ*, follow in the footsteps of some of the world's most famous writers, or feast on the best of British dining, these will point the way.

A HERITAGE TOUR

If there's one thing the Brits do brilliantly, it's heritage. Take a couple of weeks to travel back through the millennia.

❶ Hampton Court Palace, London You could spend days exploring this Tudor palace, famously pinched from Cardinal Wolsey by Henry VIII. Head straight for the State Apartments, and try not to lose yourself in the yew-hedge maze. See page 112

❷ Salisbury Plain, Wiltshire Salisbury Plain is littered with the remnants of Stone, Bronze and Iron Age settlements. Stonehenge is the most famous, but you should also make time for nearby Avebury, another stone circle built soon after 2500 BC. See page 223

❸ Blenheim Palace, Oxfordshire This sumptuous residence is England's grandest example of Baroque civic architecture, more a monument than a house. See page 247

❹ Ironbridge Gorge, Shropshire The gorge, home to the world's first iron bridge (1781), is now a UNESCO World Heritage Site, with an array of fascinating museums and industrial attractions. See page 419

❺ Conwy Castle, North Wales The most spectacular of Edward I's Iron Ring of monumental fortresses is in a lovely town on the Conwy Estuary. See page 742

❻ Chatsworth House, Derbyshire Chatsworth House, built in the seventeenth century, is one of Britain's finest – and most familiar – stately homes, in a lovely Peak District location. See page 435

❼ Holy Island, Northumberland Atmospheric tidal island where the illuminated Lindisfarne Gospels were created. See page 620

❽ Edinburgh Castle Perched imposingly atop an extinct volcanic crag, Edinburgh Castle dominates not only the city but the history of Scotland itself. See page 753

THE LITERARY TRAIL

You could spend two or three weeks on this tour, which takes in visits to birth- and burial places and dedicated museums, and allows you to explore the landscapes that inspired so many great books.

❶ Thomas Hardy country, Dorset Dorset will be forever linked with the wildly romantic works of Thomas Hardy. The town of Dorchester (or "Casterbridge") is the obvious focus, but the surrounding countryside and the coast to the south feature heavily in his novels too. See page 214

❷ Chawton, Hampshire The modest but elegant home where Jane Austen lived and wrote her most celebrated works is a delight; you can also visit her brother's house, which now holds a library of women's writing. See page 202

❸ Stratford-upon-Avon, the Midlands
Britain's most celebrated playwright defines this otherwise unextraordinary market town; don't miss Anne Hathaway's Cottage, and be sure to catch an RSC performance. See page 405

❹ Laugharne, South Wales Laugharne is saturated with the spirit of Welsh poet, Dylan Thomas; visit his boathouse and his grave, and have a drink in his favourite boozer, Brown's Hotel. See page 666

❺ Hay-on-Wye, Mid-Wales Browse antiquarian bookshops and join fellow bibliophiles at the literary festival at this appealing Welsh/English border town. See page 692

❻ Haworth, Yorkshire Get a glimpse of the Brontë sisters' lives in the pretty Yorkshire village of Haworth, and take a romantic Wuthering Heights-style stroll on the wild surrounding moors. See page 563

❼ The Lake District The Lake District has had a huge influence on writers as diverse as Beatrix Potter, William Wordsworth and John Ruskin – tour their homes, but be sure to explore the stunning natural surroundings that inspired them, too. See page 510

❽ Dumfries and Alloway, Southern Scotland Born in Alloway and laid to rest in Dumfries, Robert Burns is Scotland's most treasured poet. Both towns have a number of Burns-related sights. See pages 799 and 807

A FOODIE ODYSSEY

Long having lurked in the shadow of its more flamboyant European neighbours, British food is no longer the poor relation – this two-week-long trail focuses on offbeat destinations that offer memorable gastronomic experiences.

❶ Islay's whisky distilleries, Inner Hebrides Sample a wee dram and get behind the scenes at Islay's fascinating whisky distilleries. See page 887

❷ Baltis in Brum This delicious sizzling curry, which travelled with Pakistani immigrants to Birmingham, is an unmissable Brummie treat. See page 404

❸ Abergavenny, Mid-Wales Some of Britain's finest restaurants are to be found in and around the appealing market town of Abergavenny, along with a mouthwatering food festival in mid-September. See page 690

❹ Michelin-starred dining in Bray Splash out on a gastronomic experience at one of the two triple-Michelin-starred restaurants in Bray – Heston Blumenthal's *The Fat Duck* and Michael Roux Jr's *The Waterside Inn*. See page 249

❺ Street food in London From food trucks and pop-up stalls to traditional farmers' markets, the capital's streets offer an eclectic introduction to flavours from around the world. See page 120

❻ Whitstable, Kent This charming little Kentish seaside town has been farming oysters since classical times. You can tuck into freshly shucked bivalves year-round – head for *Wheelers* first of all – or head out of town to *The Sportsman*, one of the nation's best gastropubs. See page 145

❼ Seafood feasts in Padstow, Cornwall A stay on the Cornish coast warrants a fresh seafood extravaganza. Head to one of Rick Stein's restaurants for the very best in fish suppers. See page 348

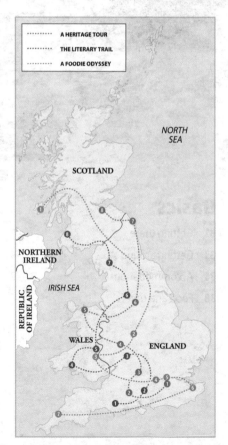

.... **A HERITAGE TOUR**

.... **THE LITERARY TRAIL**

.... **A FOODIE ODYSSEY**

NORTH SEA

SCOTLAND

NORTHERN IRELAND

IRISH SEA

REPUBLIC OF IRELAND

WALES

ENGLAND

FULLER'S BEER ON TAP, LONDON

Basics

Getting there

London is one of the world's busiest transport hubs, and there are good deals from around the world on flights into the UK's capital. However, if you're planning to tour the southwest or north of England, North Wales or Scotland, consider flying directly to more convenient international airports such as Manchester, Birmingham or Glasgow.

London's biggest and best-known airports – **Heathrow** and **Gatwick** – take the bulk of transatlantic and long-haul flights into the UK, though there are also several smaller London airports (notably **Stansted**, **Luton** and **City**) and a host of useful regional British airports, many of which are served by low-cost airlines from mainland Europe and Ireland. Principally, in England these are **Manchester** and **Liverpool** in the northwest; **Birmingham** in the West Midlands; **Bristol**, Newquay and Exeter in the West Country; **Leeds-Bradford** and Doncaster-Sheffield in Yorkshire; **Newcastle** and Durham Tees Valley in the northeast; **East Midlands**; and Bournemouth and Southampton in the south; plus **Edinburgh**, **Glasgow** and **Aberdeen** in Scotland, and **Cardiff** and **Swansea** in Wales. The cheapest deals need to be booked well in advance and tend to have little or no flexibility.

Overland routes from mainland Europe include high-speed trains into London (with onward connections) via the Channel Tunnel – either passenger-only **Eurostar** services or the drive-on drive-off **Eurotunnel** train. There's also a range of useful **ferry** routes.

Visas and red tape

At the time of writing citizens of all European countries – except Albania, Bosnia and Herzegovina, Macedonia, Montenegro, Serbia and all the former Soviet republics (other than the Baltic states) – can enter the UK with just a **passport**, for up to three months (and indefinitely if you're from the EU, European Economic Area or Switzerland). Americans, Canadians, Australians and New Zealanders can stay for up to six months, providing they have a return ticket and funds to cover their stay. Citizens of most other countries require a **visa**, obtainable from their British consulate or mission office. Check with the **UK Border Agency** (Ⓦ ukvisas.gov.uk) for up-to-date information about visa applications, extensions and all aspects of residency.

The 2016 referendum, when the UK voted **to leave the European Union**, has, in theory, put many visa and entry requirements to the UK in flux. The UK is set to leave the EU by March 2019, at which point new arrangements will need to be in place. In reality, the status quo will most likely continue for short-term visits, when visas are unlikely to be required, but check in advance. Work, study and longer-term visa requirements may change. Until 2019, EU, EEA and Swiss citizens can work in the UK without a permit (other nationals need a permit in order to work legally in the UK).

Even without potential Brexit complications, visa regulations are subject to frequent changes, so it's always wise to contact your nearest British embassy or High Commission or check Ⓦ www.gov.uk/check-uk-visa.

Flights from the US and Canada

Many airlines fly nonstop to London, Manchester and other British airports – flight time is around seven hours from the east coast, ten hours from the west. Flights on European airlines might be cheaper but tend to route through their respective European hubs, adding to the journey time.

From the US, low-season round-trip fares from New York are most competitive, starting at US$500–700; from Chicago they start at around US$1000 direct (cheaper non-direct). There are good deals from New York with Iceland's WOW air (Ⓦ wowair.us), changing at Reykjavik, and direct with Norwegian Air Shuttle (Ⓦ norwegian.com). Fares from the west coast can start from between US$700 (with Norwegian offering cheap deals from LA) and US$1000.

From Canada, the best deals involve flying to London out of Toronto or Montreal: flights from Toronto are around Can$750, while from Vancouver they start around Can$1000.

There are nonstop flights from North America to Glasgow and Edinburgh, though cheaper fares often route through London or Manchester. Return fares start from around US$800/Can$800. There are no direct flights to Wales from outside Europe.

Flights from Australia, New Zealand and South Africa

Flight time from **Australia** and **New Zealand** to Britain is at least 22 hours. Flights via Southeast Asia or the Middle East to London are generally the cheapest. Return **fares** start at Aus$1200 from Sydney. From Auckland to London return fares start at around NZ$1800.

There are direct flights from Johannesburg (11hr) in **South Africa** to London Heathrow with South African Airways (Ⓦflysaa.com), British Airways (Ⓦba.com) and Virgin Atlantic (Ⓦvirginatlantic.com); single flights cost around ZAR8000. BA also run more expensive flights from Cape Town (12hr; around ZAR11,500). Savings are available with indirect flights via a Western European or Middle Eastern hub, when a single fare can start at around ZAR4500.

Flights from Ireland

You can get a one-way flight between **Ireland** and England for around €40–70. There are routes out of Dublin, Cork, Knock, Kerry and Shannon to many English, Scottish and Welsh airports; airlines include Aer Lingus (Ⓦaerlingus.com), British Airways (Ⓦba.com), Flybe (Ⓦflybe.com) and Ryanair (Ⓦryanair.com). The cheapest options **from Belfast** and Derry are usually easyJet (Ⓦeasyjet.com), Flybe and Ryanair.

Ferries

There are several ferry routes from mainland Europe and Ireland to Britain. The quickest, cheapest services to England are on the traditional cross-Channel routes **from the French ports** of Calais and Dunkirk to **Dover** in Kent and Dieppe to Newhaven in East Sussex, plus routes to Portsmouth from Le Havre, Cherbourg and St Malo and from Spain (Santander and Bilbao). From Zeebrugge (Belgium) and Rotterdam (the Netherlands) ferries go to Hull; from the Hook of Holland they go to Harwich, while from Amsterdam they arrive in Newcastle.

Ferry services **from Ireland** (Dublin, Rosslare and Belfast) run to England's northwest (Liverpool and the Isle of Man) and **Wales** (Holyhead, Fishguard and Pembroke). There are also services from Belfast to Cairnryan in Scotland.

Fares vary considerably, according to time of year, and time and type of crossing – some high-speed ferry services can cut journey times on the same route by up to half – while accommodation is often obligatory (and welcome) on night crossings from the continent.

For **information** on routes and operators, see Ⓦaferry.co.uk or Ⓦdirectferries.com.

Trains

Direct **Eurostar trains** (Ⓦeurostar.com) run roughly hourly to London St Pancras International from Calais (1hr 10min), Lille (1hr 20min), Brussels (2hr) and Paris (2hr 20min), with connections into those cities from across Europe and direct seasonal services from southern France (Lyon, Avignon and Marseille in summer and over Christmas; Bourg St Maurice, Aime La Plagne and Moutiers in winter), as well as Disneyland Paris, and a direct Amsterdam–London service as of 2018. Fares start from around €50 one-way, though you'll have to book well in advance. There are discounts on standard fares for travellers under 26 and over 60.

For drivers, the fastest and most convenient cross-Channel option is the **Eurotunnel** (Ⓦeurotunnel.com) drive-on-drive-off shuttle train from Calais to Folkestone (around 75 miles southeast of London), which runs 24 hours and takes 35–45 minutes. Booking is advised, especially at weekends or if you want the best prices. The standard fare for a car and all its passengers is from €85 one way (with cheap deals available for short trips); more if booked at short notice. **Irish Ferries** (Ⓦirishferries.com) offer SailRail return fares of around €100 to London (via Holyhead) from anywhere in the Republic; journey time is around eight hours from Dublin. For the best train information online, check the **Man in Seat 61** at Ⓦseat61.com and Ⓦloco2.com for journey planning.

Buses

Eurolines (Ⓦeurolines.co.uk) coordinates international bus services to London (with connections onwards) from dozens of **European cities**. This is the cheapest way of travelling, but you really do have to ask yourself how long you want to spend cooped up in a bus. Only routes from northern European cities are anything like bearable: the journey from Paris, for example, which takes around six hours to London Victoria Coach Station and costs from €18 one-way.

Tours and organized holidays

Package tours of Britain, where all flights, accommodation and ground transport are arranged for you, can be worthwhile if you want to cover several destinations in a limited time, and are a good option for travellers with a particular interest. Some operators specialize in **activity holidays** (see page 45).

AGENTS AND OPERATORS

STA Travel UK ☎ 0333 321 0099, US ☎ 1800 781 4040, Australia ☎ 134 782, New Zealand ☎ 0800 474 400, South Africa ☎ 0861 781 781; Ⓦstatravel.co.uk. Worldwide specialists in independent travel; also student IDs, travel insurance, car rental, rail passes and more. Good discounts for students and under-26s.

Trailfinders UK ☎ 020 7368 1200, Ireland ☎ 01 677 7888; Ⓦ trailfinders.com. One of the best-informed and most efficient agents for independent travellers.

Travel CUTS Canada ☎ 1800 667 2887, Ⓦ travelcuts.com. Canadian youth and student travel firm.

PACKAGE TOURS

Abercrombie & Kent US ☎ 1800 554 7016, Ⓦ abercrombiekent.com. Classy travel specialist, with no-expense-spared escorted and independent holidays, from London highlight trips to ten days visiting the historic abbeys and country homes of Cornwall, the Welsh borders and the Cotswolds.

Contiki Holidays UK ☎ 0808 281 1120, Ⓦ contiki.com. Lively, reasonably priced, budget-accommodation adventure tours for 18–35s, including London trips and a nine-day England and Scotland tour.

Martin Randall Travel UK ☎ 020 8742 3355, Ⓦ martinrandall.com. Wide-ranging all-inclusive historical and cultural tours led by experts – for example, seven days walking Hadrian's Wall, nine days exploring England's cathedrals or four days soaking up the Arts and Crafts heritage of the Cotswolds, plus one-day lecture tours in London.

Getting around

Almost every town and larger villages in Britain can be reached by train or – if you have time and flexibility – bus, but public transport costs are among the highest in Europe and travel can eat up a large part of your budget. Rural destinations are often poorly served, too. It pays to investigate all the special deals and passes, some of which are only available outside the UK and must be bought before you arrive. It may be cheaper and easier to drive, especially if you're in a group, though traffic can be bad in the cities and on the motorways. If you want to find if a particular route is feasible by public transport, Ⓦ traveline.info is a good first port of call.

By plane

Given the time it takes getting to and from many airports (particularly London, if not flying from City), there are few domestic journeys where **flying** is worthwhile. There are exceptions, however – if you're travelling from the southwest to the north of England, say (flights from Newquay to Newcastle take 1hr 30min compared to 9hr 30min on the train, though there aren't flights every day), or considering flights to places like the Isle of Man or the Scottish islands. In addition, airfares can be competitive compared with

expensive on-the-spot train tickets for journeys such as London to Newcastle or Edinburgh.

Domestic **airlines** include British Airways (Ⓦ ba.com), easyJet (Ⓦ easyjet.com), Ryanair (Ⓦ ryanair.com), flybe (Ⓦ flybe.com) and Cityjet (Ⓦ cityjet.com) and – in Scotland – Loganair (Ⓦ loganair.co.uk). Fares on popular routes such as London to Newcastle, with journey times of around an hour, can cost as little as £75 return.

By train

Despite grumbles about the rail network and the high cost of travel compared to other European rail systems, getting around Britain by train is still the best, most scenic and – usually – most painless way to travel.

Most major towns in **England** have rail links (though coverage of small towns is woeful compared with other European countries), and mainline routes out of London in particular are **fast and frequent** – the 200-mile trips to York and Exeter, for instance, are covered in two hours. The fastest journeys head north from London on east- and west-coast mainline routes (to Birmingham, Manchester, Leeds and Newcastle, among others), and there are high-speed services to Kent from King's Cross St Pancras; other journeys, however, can be more complicated, particularly if you're travelling east–west, which might involve a train change or two.

Scotland has a more modest rail network, densest in the central belt between Edinburgh and Glasgow, and most skeletal in the Highlands. **ScotRail** (Ⓦ scotrail.co.uk) runs the majority of train services, sometimes on lines rated among the great scenic routes of the world. One appealing option is the overnight Caledonian Sleeper from London to Edinburgh and beyond. Travelling to **Wales**, most people use the fast, frequent service from London Paddington to **Newport**, **Cardiff** and **Swansea**. Within Wales, services cover the main towns and many rural towns and wayside halts.

Britain's trains are run by myriad **operators**, but all are required to work as a single network with integrated ticketing. The **National Rail Enquiries** website (Ⓦ nationalrail.co.uk) is a useful first call for timetable, route and fare information; it lists all the regional operators and offers ticket-buying links from its journey planner. For an exhaustive rundown of train travel in the UK, check the excellent **Man in Seat 61** website (Ⓦ seat61.com).

Buying tickets

As a rule, the earlier you book, the less you will pay. Always look out for **online offers** with **booking** sites like the user-friendly ⓦloco2.com, ⓦtick-etclever.com, which are good for route planning, and ⓦmegatrain.com, which is frustrating to use, but can help you find low fares on a few routes. It's also worth checking the websites of the individual operators, as usually their fares will match those offered by the booking sites. A **seat reservation** is usually included with the ticket. Just turning up and buying a ticket at the station is always the most expensive way to go (sometimes phenomenally so); it's always worth asking at the ticket desk about the options, as you may get discounts on groups or couples travelling together. If the ticket office is closed, or the automatic machines aren't working, you may buy your ticket on board from the inspector. In some cases, though, buying a ticket on the train when you had the opportunity to buy one beforehand could lead to a penalty of £20 – the stations from which penalty fares apply will have large posters advertising that fact.

Cheapest are **advance tickets**, which are only available several weeks ahead of time and sell out quickly. They can only be used on the specified train booked – miss it, and you pay a surcharge or have to buy another ticket. Off-peak fares can be bought in advance or on the day of travel, but are only valid for travel at quieter times (generally outside Mon–Fri 5–10am & 3–8pm). Most expensive are the fully flexible anytime tickets.

Rail passes

For overseas visitors planning to travel widely by train, a **BritRail England pass** could be a wise investment (ⓦbritrail.net). It gives unlimited travel throughout England, Scotland and Wales (there are also separate regional and Scotland passes) and is valid for varied periods from two to fifteen days in two months (not necessarily consecutive). There are first- and second-class versions, discounted Youth Passes and Senior Passes, and for every adult buying a full-priced ticket one child (ages 5 to 15) receives the same pass for free. Note that BritRail passes have to be bought before you enter the UK.

If you've been resident in a European country other than the UK for at least six months, an **InterRail pass** (ⓦinterrail.eu), allowing unlimited train travel in England, Wales and Scotland (for three, four, six or eight days within one month), might be worth it – but note that you can't use the pass for travel in your country of residence. **Eurail** passes are not valid in the UK, though they do provide discounts on Eurostar trains to England and on some ferry routes.

National Rail Enquiries (ⓦnationalrail.co.uk) details the many regional rail passes that can be bought by locals and visitors in Britain itself. **Rover and Ranger passes** offer unlimited travel in single, multi-day or flexi-day formats – the Ride Cornwall Ranger, for example, which costs £13 for one day of off-peak train travel in that county. The **All-Line Rail Rover** offers unlimited travel on almost the entire network throughout England, Scotland and Wales for seven consecutive days (£492, discounts available with certain railcards; some time restrictions apply).

There are numerous options when it comes to **annual railcards** (ⓦrailcard.co.uk), including the 16–25 Railcard for full-time students and people aged between 16 and 25; the Senior Railcard for travellers over 60; the Two Together card for a couple travelling together; and the Family & Friends Railcard for groups of up to four adults and four children travelling together. Each costs £30 for the year and gives up to a third off most adult fares in Britain (more for children's fares).

By bus

Travel by bus – long-distance services are known as "coaches" – is usually much cheaper than by train, though less comfortable, and traffic congestion can make the same journey much longer. The biggest **intercity** bus operators in England are **National Express** (ⓦnationalexpress.com) and **Megabus** (ⓦmegabus.com); north of the border, **Scottish Citylink** is the main operator (ⓦwww.citylink.co.uk). On busy routes, and on any route at weekends and holidays, it's advisable to book ahead to get the best deal. Fares are generally very reasonable, with discounts for under-26s, over-60s and families, plus various advance-purchase fares and special promotions. **Regional and urban** bus services are run by a huge array of companies. Check **Traveline** (ⓦtraveline.info), which covers the whole of Britain, and Traveline Scotland (ⓦtravelinescotland.com) for information and routes. In many cases, timetables and routes are well integrated, but more remote, rural spots are neglected.

By car

Your British driving experience will depend very much on where you drive. Slogging through the traffic from major city to major city is rarely an illuminating way to see the nation – motorways ("M" roads) and main "A" roads may have up to four lanes in each direction, but even these can get very congested, with long traffic jams, especially at peak travel times and on public holidays. Driving in the countryside is far more agreeable, though on "B" roads and minor roads there might only be one lane (single track) in both directions. Keep your speed down, and be prepared for abrupt encounters with tractors, sheep and other hazards in remote spots.

Don't underestimate the British **weather**, either. Snow, ice, fog and wind can cause havoc – and there has been major flooding in the past few years – and driving conditions, on motorways as much as in rural areas, can deteriorate quickly. Local radio stations feature regularly updated traffic bulletins, as does the **Highways Agency** (W highways.gov.uk or W trafficengland.com).

Britain has a few toll roads, namely the M6 in the Midlands and the Dartford Thames crossing east of London, plus various local bridges and tunnels; the Severn Bridge tolls into Wales will cease at the end of 2018. Note, too, that **congestion charges** apply in London (see page 115). **Fuel** is pricey – unleaded petrol (gasoline) and diesel in particular. Out-of-town supermarkets usually have the lowest prices, while the highest prices are charged by motorway service stations.

Parking in towns, cities and popular tourist spots can be a nightmare and often costs a small fortune. A yellow line along the edge of the road indicates **parking restrictions**; check the nearest sign to see exactly what they are. A double-yellow line means no parking at any time, though you can stop briefly to unload or pick up people or goods, while red lines signify no stopping at all. Fines for parking illegally are high – as much as £130 (though reduced if you pay within fourteen days) – and if you're wheel-clamped it will cost you £200 or so to have your vehicle released.

Rules and regulations

Drive on the left. **Seatbelts** must be worn by everyone in a vehicle, front and back, while motorcyclists and their passengers must wear a helmet. You are not permitted to make a kerbside turn against a red light and must always give way to traffic (circulating clockwise) on a **roundabout** – this applies even for mini-roundabouts, which may be no more than a white circle painted on the road. **Speed limits** are 20mph in many residential streets, 30mph in built-up areas, 70mph on dual carriageways and motorways and 60mph on most other roads – as a rule, assume that in any area with street lighting the speed limit is 30mph unless otherwise stated. Be alert to the signs, as **speed cameras** are everywhere.

Most foreign nationals can get by with their **driving licence** from home, but if you're in any doubt, obtain an **international driving permit** from a national motoring organization. Anyone bringing their own vehicle into the country should also carry vehicle registration, ownership and insurance documents.

The AA (W theaa.com), RAC (W rac.co.uk) and Green Flag (W greenflag.com) all operate **24-hour emergency breakdown** services, and offer useful online route planners. You may be entitled to free assistance through a reciprocal arrangement with a motoring organization in your home country – check before setting out. You can make use of these emergency services if you are not a member, but you will need to join at the roadside and will incur a hefty surcharge.

Vehicle rental

Car rental is best booked online through one of the large multinational chains – Avis (W avis.co.uk), Budget (W budget.co.uk), easyCar (W easycar.com), Hertz (W hertz.co.uk) or National (W nationalcar.co.uk), for example – or through a site such as W auto-europe.co.uk.

If you rent a car from a company in the UK, expect to pay around £30 per day, £50 for a weekend, or £100–160 per week. Few companies will rent to drivers with less than one year's experience and most will only rent to people aged between 21 (or 23) and 70. Rental cars will be manual (stick shift) unless you specify otherwise – if you want an **automatic transmission**, book well ahead and expect to pay at least £170 a week. **Motorbike rental** is more expensive – around £80 a day or £400 a week. Try London-based Raceways (W raceways.net) or RoadTrip in Woking, near Heathrow (W roadtrip.uk).

When considering touring some of Brtain's wilder areas, a motorhome or **camper van** can be a great way to choose your own adventure while saving money. Rates start at around £400–500 a week in high season, but you'll save on accommodation. Try W bunkcampers.com, which has depots in London, Belfast, Birmingham, Glasgow and Edinburgh.

By bike

Cycling around Britain can be a pleasant option, as long as you stick to the quieter "B" roads and country lanes – or, best of all, follow one of the **traffic-free trails** of the extensive National Cycle Network (see page 45).

Cycle helmets are not compulsory – but you're well advised to wear one, especially if you're hell-bent on tackling the congestion, pollution and aggression of city traffic. You do have to have a **rear reflector** and front and back **lights** when riding at night, and you are not allowed to carry children without a special **child seat**. It is also illegal to cycle on pavements and in most public parks (unless designated), while **off-road** cyclists must stick to bridleways and by-ways designated for their use.

Bike rental is available at cycle shops in most large towns, and at villages within National Parks and other scenic areas. Expect to pay around £20–25 per day, or more for specialist mountain bikes and less for multi-day rents; you may need to provide credit card details or leave a passport as a deposit.

Accompanied bikes are allowed free on mainline trains, but you usually need to book the space in advance; check Ⓦ nationalrail.co.uk for individual company regulations. Bus and coach companies rarely accept cycles, and even then only if they are dismantled and boxed.

Accommodation

Accommodation in Britain ranges from corporate chain hotels to crumbling castles, from budget backpacker hostels to chic boutique hotels. Often they're in interesting old buildings – former coaching inns, converted mansions and manor houses – which offer heaps of historic atmosphere. Accommodation does tend to be quite expensive, but there are bargains to be had.

A nationwide **grading system**, annually upgraded, awards **stars** to hotels, guesthouses and B&Bs. There's no hard and fast correlation between rank and price, but the system does lay down minimum levels of standards and service. However, not every establishment participates, and you shouldn't assume that a particular place is no good simply because it doesn't. In the rural backwaters in particular some of the best accommodation is to

be found in **farmhouses** and other simple properties whose facilities may technically fall short of official standards.

When it comes to **costs**, single occupancy rates vary widely: though they're typically around three-quarters of the price of a double, some places charge almost the full double rate and others charge only a little over half that. Rates in hotels and B&Bs may well drop between Sunday and Thursday, or if you stay more than one night, and some places will require a minimum stay of two or more nights at the weekend and/or in high season; we indicate in the Guide when an establishment has a general rule on this.

Breakfast is generally included in rates –except in pricer places – and free **wi-fi** is usually available. Reviews in the Guide note when that isn't the case.

Hotels

British **hotels** vary wildly in size, style, comfort and price. The starting price for a basic hotel is around £80 per night for a double or twin room, breakfast usually included; anything more upmarket, or with a bit of boutique style, will be around £100 a night, while at the top-end properties the sky's the limit, especially in London or in resort or country-house hotels. Note that in comparison to the cheaper places, many of the pricier hotels – especially those in the cities – may charge extra for breakfast.

Budget hotel chains – including Premier Inn (Ⓦ premierinn.com) and its cooler offshoot Hub by Premier Inn (currently in London and Edinburgh only; Ⓦ hubhotels.co.uk), Holiday Inn Express (Ⓦ hiexpress.com), Jurys Inn (Ⓦ jurysinns.com), Travelodge (Ⓦ travelodge.co.uk), Ibis (Ⓦ ibishotel. com) and Comfort/Quality/Sleep Inns (Ⓦ choice hotelsuk.co.uk) – have properties across the country. With no frills (and with breakfast charged extra), they are not always automatically the cheapest option, but they can be a good deal for families and small groups, and rates can get down to a bargain £40–50

ACCOMMODATION PRICES

Throughout this Guide we give a headline price for every accommodation reviewed, which indicates the lowest price you could expect to pay per night for a **double or twin room in high season** (prices fluctuate a lot depending on demand, with high-season rates generally guaranteed in July and August, plus during school holidays between Easter and the end of September, though local variations apply). We also give the high-season price for a dorm bed, and double rooms where they exist, in **hostels** – note that for YHA hostels, prices quoted are for non-members (members get a £3/night discount). Prices given for **self-catering** options indicate the minimum per-night price in high season. For **campsites** we quote the cost of a pitch for two people bringing their own tent, unless otherwise stated.

per night if booked ahead. Point A Hotels (London and Glasgow; Ⓦpointahotels.com) and easyHotel (London, Liverpool, Manchester, Birmingham, Glasgow and Edinburgh; Ⓦeasyhotel.com) can be even cheaper, offering a simple "add-on" system whereby you book a minimal room online with the option of adding niceties including cleaning, windows, TVs, wi-fi and baggage storage.

B&Bs, guesthouses and pubs

At its most basic, the typical English **bed-and-breakfast** (**B&B**) is an ordinary private house with a couple of bedrooms set aside for paying guests. Larger establishments with more rooms, particularly in resorts, style themselves as **guesthouses**, but they are pretty much the same thing.

At the extreme budget end of the scale – basic B&Bs under £70 a night, a little less in Wales – you'll normally experience small rooms, fairly spartan facilities and shared bathrooms (though there are some fantastic exceptions). Many top-notch B&Bs – say around £100–120 or more per night – offer more luxury and far better value pound for pound than more impersonal hotels. In this category you can also count **pubs** (or inns), and the increasingly popular "**restaurants with rooms**".

Hostels

Between them, the **Youth Hostels Association** (Ⓦyha.org.uk) of England and Wales, and the **Scottish Youth Hostels Association** (Ⓦsyha.org. uk), have hundreds of hostels across Britain, ranging from lakeside mansions to thatched country cottages. There are still shared bathrooms and traditional single-sex bunk-bed dormitories in most, though the majority now also offer smaller rooms (sometimes en-suite) of two to six beds for couples, families and groups. Some hostels have been purpose-built, or have had expensive refurbishments, and in cities, resorts and National Park areas the facilities are often as good as budget hotels. Most offer kitchens, laundry facilities and lounges, while wi-fi access, cafés, bars, tour bookings and bike rental and storage are common. The hostel will usually provide bed linen, pillows and duvet; towels and other necessities can often be rented.

You don't have to be a member to stay at a YHA hostel but non-members are charged an extra £3 a night. One year's membership, which is open only to residents of the EU, costs £15 per year (for either YHA or SYHA membership) and can be bought online or at any YHA or SYHA hostel. Members gain automatic

TOP 5 SEASIDE SLEEPS
Belle Tout Beachy Head. See page 168
Bournemouth Beach Lodges See page 207
Horgabost Campsite Harris. See page 970
Hotel Portmeirion North Wales. See page 734
Millers at the Anchor Porlock Weir, Somerset. See page 298

membership of the hostelling associations of the ninety countries affiliated to **Hostelling International** (HI; Ⓦhihostels.com).

Prices are calculated according to season, location and demand, with adult dorm beds usually £15–30 per night – rates can get higher than that in London and at peak holiday periods. A private twin room in a hostel goes for around £40–80, and family rooms sleeping four start from around £75 (much more in London). **Meals** are good value – breakfast or a packed lunch for around £5–7, or £9–13 for dinner. Advance **booking** is recommended, and essential at Easter, Christmas and from May to August.

A large number of **independent hostels** offer similar prices. With no membership fees, more relaxed rules, mixed dorms and no curfew, many of them, in the cities at least, tend to attract a predominantly young, keen-to-party crowd, but there are family-friendly options, too. For news and reviews, check Ⓦindependenthostelguide.co.uk or Ⓦhostel-scotland.co.uk, which also lists primitive bunkhouses, bunk barns and camping barns in the most rural locations.

Camping

England has hundreds of **campsites**, ranging from small, family-run places to large sites with laundries, shops and sports facilities. Prices start at around £5 per adult in the simplest sites, though at larger, more popular locations you can pay far more, and sometimes there are separate charges per car and tent. Many campsites also have accommodation in permanently fixed, fully equipped caravans, or in wooden cabins or similar. Perhaps in part due to the unreliable weather, Brits have taken **glamping** to their hearts, with more tipis, yurts, bell tents and camping pods than you can shake a billycan at. Ⓦcoolcamping. co.uk, Ⓦcampingandcaravanningclub.co.uk and Ⓦukcampsite.co.uk are useful online resources.

In Britain's wilder places you will find **camping barns** and **bunkhouses** (known as bothies in

Scotland), many administered by the YHA and SYHA, though with plenty of others operated by individual farmers and families. They are pretty basic – often in converted agricultural buildings, old crofters' cottages and the like – but they are weatherproof and cheap (from around £8 a night). **Farmers** may offer field-and-tap pitches for around £3 per night, but setting up a tent without asking first is counted as trespassing and not recommended. In England and Wales **camping wild** is illegal even in in most National Parks and nature reserves, though Dartmoor is one exception; check ⓦnationalparks.gov.uk/visiting/camping for more information. There are also places in Scotland where you can camp wild; check ⓦoutdooraccess-scotland.com.

Self-catering

Holiday self-catering properties range from city penthouses to secluded cottages. **Studios and apartments**, available by the night in an increasing number of cities, offer an attractive alternative to hotels, with prices from around £90 a night (more in London). Rural **cottages and houses** work out cheaper, though the minimum rental period may be a week. Depending on the season and location, expect to pay from around £350 for a week in a small cottage.

ACCOMMODATION CONTACTS

B&BS, FARMS AND STUDENT ROOMS

Cool Places ⓦ coolplaces.co.uk. Good selection of unusual places to stay, from hostels and glamping to farmhouse B&Bs.

Farm Stay ⓦ farmstay.co.uk. The UK's largest network of farm-based accommodation – B&B, self-catering and camping.

University rooms ⓦ universityrooms.co.uk. Student halls of residence in university towns from Cornwall to Aberdeen, offering good-value rooms (mostly single) or apartments over the summer (July–Sept), Easter and Christmas holidays.

Wolsey Lodges ⓦ wolseylodges.com. Superior B&B in grand properties throughout Britain, from Elizabethan manor houses to Victorian rectories.

SELF-CATERING

Airbnb ⓦ airbnb.com. A huge variety of properties – seaside cottages to farmhouses, canal barges to warehouse apartments, and rooms in private houses.

Landmark Trust ⓦ landmarktrust.org.uk. A preservation charity that lists pricey, rather special accommodation in distinctive historic properties – castles, ruins, follies, towers and cottages.

National Trust Holiday Cottages ⓦ nationaltrustcottages.co.uk and ⓦ nts.org.uk. Self-catering holiday cottages, houses and farmhouses, most of which are set in the gardens or grounds of National Trust (in England and Wales) and National Trust for Scotland properties.

Rural Retreats ⓦ ruralretreats.co.uk. Upmarket accommodation in restored historic buildings.

Scottish Country Cottages ⓦ scottish-country-cottages.co.uk. Superior cottages with character scattered across Scotland.

Under the Thatch ⓦ underthethatch.co.uk. A select choice of self-catering cottages and cabins, many beautifully restored, from traditional thatched cottages to Romany caravans and yurts; particularly focused on Wales.

Wales Cottage Holidays ⓦ walescottageholidays.co.uk. A varied selection of hundreds of properties all over Wales.

Food and drink

The British culinary scene is going from strength to strength. Along with an insatiable appetite for trying new foods from around the world, increasing importance has been placed on good-quality and sustainable eating – not only sourcing products locally, but also using free-range, organic, humanely produced ingredients. London continues to be the main centre for all things foodie and fashionable, though great restaurants, gastropubs, farmers' markets, street food markets and local suppliers can be found throughout Britain.

British cuisine

For some visitors the quintessential British meal is **fish and chips** (known in Scotland as a "fish supper", even at lunchtime), a dish that can vary from the succulently fresh to the indigestibly greasy: local knowledge is the key, as most towns, cities and resorts have at least one first-rate fish-and-chip shop ("chippie") or restaurant. Other **traditional British dishes** (Scotch eggs, pies, bacon sandwiches, roast dinners, sausage and mash) have largely discarded their stodgy image and been poshed up to become restaurant, and particularly gastropub, staples – comfort food still, but often cooked with the best ingredients and genuinely tasty. Many hitherto neglected or previously unfashionable British foods – from brawn to brains – are finding their way into top-end restaurants, too, as inventive restaurateurs, keen on using good, seasonal produce, reinvent the classics. The principles of this "nose to tail" eating cross over with the tenets of **Modern British** cuisine, which marries local produce with ingredients and techniques from around the world. **Vegetarians** need not worry, either – veggie restaurants are fairly easy to find in towns and cities, and practically every

THE GREAT BRITISH BREAKFAST

The traditional **British breakfast** (aka the "Full English", "Full Scottish", etc) will keep you going all day. As a rule it includes eggs, bacon, sausage, tomatoes, mushrooms, baked beans and toast – generally they're all fried, though the eggs may be scrambled or poached. It might also include black pudding (ie, blood sausage). Veggie alternatives are commonly available. A traditional **Scottish breakfast** includes oatmeal porridge (eaten with salt or sugar), oatcakes (plain savoury biscuits) or potato scones; in **Wales** breakfast might also feature laverbread (edible seaweed). Though less common, you may also be served kippers (smoked herring) for a traditional breakfast. B&Bs and hotels will also serve cereals, toast, and many other breakfast standards. A **"continental" breakfast** usually means cereal, toast and preserves, though often croissants, fruit and yoghurt too. Though the staple early morning drink is tea, drunk strong, hot and with cold milk, coffee is just as popular.

restaurant and pub will have at least one vegetarian option. As **veganism** becomes more popular (though still fairly niche) vegan-friendly places are popping up, too, in the big cities at least.

The wealth of **fresh produce** varies seasonaly and regionally, from hedgerow herbs to fish landed from local boats. Restaurants are increasingly making use of seasonal ingredients – and in rural areas many farms offer "Pick Your Own" sessions, when you can come away with armfuls of delicious berries, orchard fruits, beetroot and the like. Check out the growing profusion of **farmers' markets** and farm shops to enjoy the best local goodies and artisan products. For a directory of markets in Britain see ⓦfarma.org.uk/members-map.

Cafés, tearooms and coffee shops

Though traditionally a nation of tea-heads, Brits have also become bona fide **coffee** addicts, and international chain outlets such as *Starbucks*, *Costa* and *Caffè Nero* line every high street. However, there will usually be at least one independent coffee shop, even in the smallest places, and artisan coffee, brewed with obsessive care, can be found in many towns and cities. Despite the encroaching grip of the coffee chains, every town, city and resort in Britain should also have a few cheap **cafés** offering all-day breakfasts, snacks and meals. Most are only open during the daytime, and have few airs and graces; the quality is not guaranteed, however. A few more genteel **teashops** or **tearooms** serve sandwiches, cakes and light meals throughout the day, as well, of course, as tea – the best of them will offer a full afternoon tea, including sandwiches, cakes and scones with cream and jam.

Pubs and gastropubs

The old-fashioned British **pub** remains an enduring social institution, and is often the best introduction to town or village life. In some places, it might be your only choice for food. While occasionally the offerings can be terrible, Britain's foodie renaissance, and a commercial need to diversify, means that many have had to up their game. The umbrella term **gastropub** can refer to anything from a traditional country inn with rooms and a restaurant to a slick city-centre pub with upmarket dining room, but generally indicates a pub that puts as much emphasis on the food as the drink. Some are really excellent – and just as expensive as a regular restaurant, though usually with a more informal feel – while others simply provide a relaxed place in which to enjoy a gourmet pork pie or cheese platter with your pint.

Restaurants

Partly by dint of its size, London has the broadest selection of **top-class restaurants**, and the widest choice of cuisines, but there are some seriously fine dining options in most major cities and in many rural spots. Indeed, wherever you are in Britain you're rarely more than half an hour's drive from a really good meal. Heston Blumenthal's Michelin-star-studded *Fat Duck*, for example, touted as one of the world's best restaurants, is in the small Berkshire village of Bray, where you will also find the equally lauded *Waterside Inn*.

While you can eat well in cheap restaurants and cafés for just £15–20 a head, the going rate for a meal with drinks in most modest restaurants is more like £25–30 per person. If a restaurant has any sort of reputation, you can expect to be spending £40–60 each, and much, much more for the services of a top chef – tasting menus (excluding drinks) at the best-known Michelin-starred restaurants cost upwards of £80 per person. However, **set meals** can be a steal, even at the poshest of restaurants, where a limited-choice two- or three-course lunch or "pre-the-atre" menu might cost less than half the usual price.

TOP 5 DESTINATION RESTAURANTS

Clove Club London. See page 124
The Kitchin Edinburgh. See page 778
L'Enclume Cartmel. See page 514
Three Chimneys Skye. See page 959
Waterside Inn Bray. See page 249

Drink

Originating as wayfarers' hostelries and coaching inns, **pubs** – "public houses" – have outlived the church and marketplace as the focal points of many a British town and village. They are as varied as the townscapes: in larger market towns you'll find huge oak-beamed inns with open fires and polished brass fittings; in remoter villages there are stone-built pubs no larger than a two-bedroomed cottage. In towns and cities corner pubs still cater to local neighbourhoods, the best of them stocking an increasingly varied list of local beers and craft brews, while chain pubs, cocktail bars, independent music venues and wine bars all add to the mix. Most pubs and bars serve food, in some shape or form (see page 39).

Most pubs are officially open from around 11am to 11pm, though cities and resorts have a growing number of places with extended licences, especially at weekends. The legal **drinking age** is 18, and although many places will allow, or even encourage, families – particularly in places that also serve food, or have a beer garden – young children may not always be welcome in pubs or bars after 8 or 9pm.

Beer and cider

Beer, sold by the pint (generally £3.20–5) and half pint (often just a touch over half the price), is Britain's staple drink, which has been a mainstay of the local diet for centuries, dating back to times when water was too dangerous to drink. Ask simply for a "beer", though, and you'll cause no end of confusion.

While lager is sold everywhere, in recent years there's been a huge resurgence in regional brewing, and England's unique glory is its **real ale** or **cask ale**, a refreshing beer brewed with traditional ingredients, without additional carbonation, pumped by hand from a cask and served at cellar temperature (not "warm", as foreign jibes have it). If it comes out of an electric pump it isn't real ale (though it might be a craft beer). The most common ale is known as **bitter**, with a colour ranging from straw-yellow to dark brown, depending on the brew. Other real ales include golden or **pale ales**, plus darker and maltier **milds**, **stouts** and **porters**. For more on cask ales, check the website of the influential **Campaign for Real Ale** (Ⓦcamra.org.uk), who remain the bastions of this traditional brewing scene.

Traditionally, Scottish beer is graded by a shilling mark (/-), and includes distinctive styles like the Scottish "Heavy", which is typically a darker, sweeter brew; however lighter, hoppier styles are now also produced by Scottish breweries.

Complementary to real ale – and with the distinction between them contentious – are the **craft beers** produced by hundreds of small, independent breweries that have flourished in recent years, influenced by the American craft-brewing scene. Though hoppy pale ales predominate – generally carbonated and served chilled from kegs, not casks – the range of craft beers is overwhelming. They cover everything from German-style lagers to IPAs (Indian Pale Ales) and Belgian-influenced sour saisons – name a beer style and an independent British brewer will have tried making it, in small batches, probably in a shed in the suburbs or under the railway arches in a former industrial zone. Scotland's BrewDog (Ⓦbrewdog.com) were at the forefront and are now going global, while London's Kernel (Ⓦthekernelbrewery.com), Manchester's Cloudwater Brew Co (Ⓦcloudwaterbrew.co) and Newport's Tiny Rebel (Ⓦtinyrebel.co.uk) are just a few names to look out for.

The resurgence of independent breweries – both real ale traditionalists and craft brewers – means that, unlike a decade ago, in many pubs across the country you'll see a row of quirky hand pumps and keg clips lined up along the bar, boasting local provenance and unusual names. It's always worth asking if there's a good local brewery whose beers you should try – and a good pub will always let you taste first.

Though many pubs are owned by large breweries who favour their own beers, this beer revolution has increased the choice in most places. Still best, however, is a **free house** – an independently run pub that can sell whichever beer it pleases.

In England and Wales the other traditional pint is **cider**, made from fermented apple juice and usually sparkling, with most brewers based in the west of England. There's also a variant made from pears, called **perry**, and, particularly in England's West Country, **scrumpy**, a potent and cloudy beverage, usually flat, dry and very apple-y. In recent years "real" cider – which CAMRA defines as containing a minimum of ninety percent fresh apple juice – has been gaining popularity.

Whisky and gin

Scotland's national drink is **whisky** – *uisge beatha*, the "water of life" in Gaelic (and almost never referred to as "scotch"). Despite the dominance of the blended whiskies such as Johnnie Walker, Bell's and The Famous Grouse, single malt whisky is infinitely superior, though more expensive. Single malts vary in character enormously depending on the amount of peat used for drying the barley, the water used for mashing and the type of oak cask used in the maturing process, with, for example, the distilleries of Islay producing distinctive, peaty flavours (see page 887).

The latest traditional tipple to have been given a "craft" makeover is the most English of ruins, **gin**. Long a stalwart of the British drinks cabinet, usually drunk as a gin and tonic, the juniper-flavoured spirit is enjoying a renaissance as part of the cocktail and craft drinks scene. Dozens of craft distillers have popped up across the region, often including local botanicals to create distinctive variations, such as Wales' Dyfi (Ⓦ dyfidistillery. com), which adds local bog myrtle and seasonal botanicals to the juniper.

Wine

Now is the time for English (and to a lesser extent Welsh) **wine**. It has firmly shucked off its image as inferior to its longer-established European counterparts, with nearly five hundred small-scale vineyards producing delicious tipples, mainly in southern England, where the conditions – and rising temperatures – are favourable. The southwest has a couple of notable wineries, including Sharpham, outside Totnes in Devon, but most are in the southeast; there are several excellent vineyards for visiting in Kent, Sussex and Surrey. The speciality is sparkling wine, and the best of these have beaten French champagnes in international blind-tasting competitions. For more, see Ⓦ englishwineproducers.co.uk, which also lists the twenty or so vineyards in Wales.

Festivals and events

Britain's showpiece events – from the military pageant of Trooping the Colour to the jolly bombast of the Last Night of the Proms and the Edinburgh Military Tattoo – portray one side of Britain: formal, patriotic, royal… and stuck in the past.

However, that typifies just a fraction of the festivities you'll find. There are quirky village fêtes that date back centuries with customs that defy explanation; major music festivals that transform the countryside into tent cities each summer; popular book festivals and other cultural soirées; and large, loud and fabulous street parties like Notting Hill's carnival and the LGBT+ Pride festivals of London, Manchester, Brighton and Glasgow. All are different, but if there's music, drink and a touch of the absurd – cheese rolling, bog-snorkelling? – so much the better.

A festival calendar

This list just scratches the surface – most regions will have major arts and cultural festivals, a music festival or two, plus country shows, food and drink fairs and sporting events. Check with the local tourist office, or see Ⓦ visitengland.com/things-to-do/upcoming-events; Ⓦ visitwales.com/things-to-do/whats-on; and Ⓦ visitscotland.com/see-do/events/ for more information.

JANUARY–MARCH

London New Year's Day Parade (Jan 1) Ⓦ lnydp.com; admission charge for grandstand seats in Piccadilly, otherwise free. A procession of floats, marching bands, cheerleaders and clowns wends its way from Parliament Square to Green Park.

Celtic Connections (last 2 weeks Jan) Ⓦ celticconnections.com. A major celebration of Celtic, folk and world music, with concerts and events held in venues across Glasgow.

Burns Night (Jan 25). Scots worldwide get stuck into haggis, whisky and vowel-grinding poetry to commemorate Scotland's greatest poet.

Up-Helly-Aa, Lerwick, Shetland (last Tues in Jan) Ⓦ uphellyaa. org. Spectacular Norse festival culminating in the burning of a Viking longship.

Chinese New Year (Late Jan/Early Feb). Processions, fireworks and festivities in Britain's three main Chinatowns – London, Liverpool and Manchester.

Shrove Tuesday (47 days before Easter Sun). The last day before Lent is also known as "Pancake Day" – it's traditional to eat thin pancakes, usually with sugar and lemon; public events include pancake races.

Rye Bay Scallop Week (10 days end Feb/early March) Ⓦ scallop. org.uk. Ten days of foodie events in the pretty English town of Rye: scallop tastings, cookery demos, barrow races and special menus.

Six Nations Rugby tournament (Feb & March) Ⓦ rbs6nations. com. Tournament between England, Scotland, Wales, Ireland, France and Italy, with fixtures held in all the countries' home stadiums.

St David's Day (March 1) Wales's national day, with *hwyrnos* (late nights) and celebrations nationwide, including a carnival in Cardiff.

APRIL & MAY

St George's Day (April 23). The day that commemorates England's patron saint is also, by chance, the birthday of William Shakespeare, so in addition to Morris dancing and other traditional festivities in towns and villages – with celebrations in London's Trafalgar Square and at other major destinations – there are also Bard-related events at Stratford-upon-Avon (Ⓦ shakespeare.org.uk).

Padstow 'Obby 'Oss (May 1) Ⓦ padstowlive.com. Processions, music and May Day dancing in Padstow, Cornwall, centring on the 'oss itself, a curious costumed and masked figure with obscure origins. See page 348

Jack-in-the-Green Festival (May Day weekend) Ⓦ hastingsjitg. co.uk. Rumbustious May Day celebration that fills the streets with parades, drumming bands and cavorting, greenery-swathed locals. The climax sees the ritual "slaying" of the "Jack" –a mysterious, pagan and very leafy figure – to release the spirit of summer.

Exeter Festival of South West Food and Drink (early May) Ⓦ exeterfoodanddrinkfestival.co.uk. See page 305

Glyndebourne Opera Festival (mid-May to late Aug) Ⓦ glyndebourne.com. One of the classiest arts festivals in the country, in East Sussex.

Bath Festival (late May) Ⓦ bathfestivals.org.uk. Top-class, ten-day music and literature jamboree, ranging from orchestral, jazz and world music to author talks, workshops and debates.

Hay Festival (late May to early June) Ⓦ hayfestival.com. Bibliophiles descend on this Welsh border town for a big literary shindig and its offshoot HowTheLightGetsIn, a festival of philosophy and music.

Highland Games (end May to mid-Sept) Ⓦ shga.co.uk. Celebrating a tradition dating back over a thousand years, more than sixty Games take place across the Scottish Highlands, northeast Scotland and Argyll – all including traditional sports, piping and Highland dance.

JUNE & JULY

Trooping the Colour (Second Sat in June) Ⓦ householddivision.org.uk. Massed bands, equestrian pageantry, gun salutes and fly-pasts for the Queen's Official Birthday on Horse Guards Parade, London.

Aldeburgh Festival (mid- to end June) Ⓦ snapemaltings.co.uk. Suffolk festival of classical music, established by Benjamin Britten.

Cardiff Singer of the World competition (mid-June) Ⓦ bbc. co.uk/cardiffsinger. Huge, week-long festival of music and song held in odd-numbered years, with a star-studded list of international opera and classical singers.

Glastonbury (late June) Ⓦ glastonburyfestivals.co.uk. This five-day music and performing arts festival, taking place over the last weekend in June on a beautiful site in Somerset, has grown from its hippie roots to become the greatest music festival on the planet. No festival in 2018, returning 2019.

Pride London (end June/early July) Ⓦ prideinlondon.org. England's biggest LGBT+ event, with parade, music and parties, plus two weeks of events preceding the parade. Brighton (Ⓦ brighton-pride.org), Manchester (Ⓦ manchesterpride.com), Cardiff (Ⓦ pridecymru.co.uk) and Glasgow, Scotland's largest (Ⓦ pride.scot), have big Pride events of their own in Aug. Edinburgh's is in June (Ⓦ prideedinburgh.org.uk).

TRNSMT (early July) Ⓦ trnsmtfest.com. Inaugurated in 2017 and run by the people behind Scotland's biggest music festival, T in the Park, which is currently on hold, TRNSMT puts on three nights of big-name acts on Glasgow Green.

Llangollen International Eisteddfod (early July) Ⓦ international-eisteddfod.co.uk. "The world's greatest folk festival" attracts more than twelve thousand international participants, including choirs, folk singers, groups and instrumentalists.

Latitude (mid-July) Ⓦ latitudefestival.com. Set near the lovely Suffolk seaside town of Southwold, Latitude festival is laidback and family-friendly with a good mix of music stages, comedy, talks and other performances, and attracts some pretty big names.

Liverpool International Music Festival (mid-July) Ⓦ limfestival.com. Four days of free events in Sefton Park, with an eclectic line up of music, plus other gigs around the city.

The Proms (mid-July to mid-Sept) Ⓦ bbc.co.uk/proms. Top-flight international classical music festival at the Royal Albert Hall, London, ending in the famously patriotic Last Night of the Proms.

WOMAD (late July) Ⓦ womad.org. Renowned four-day world music festival outside Malmesbury, Wiltshire.

Cambridge Folk Festival (end July/early Aug) Ⓦ cambridgefolkfestival.co.uk. Superb festival encompassing folk music in its broadest sense, with a good mix of big names and interesting newcomers.

AUGUST & SEPTEMBER

Edinburgh Festivals (Aug) Ⓦ eif.co.uk, Ⓦ edfringe.com. One of the world's great arts festivals, with an "official" festival, Military Tattoo and a huge "fringe" festival, which includes high-profile comedy performances, that all run for a month. Book and art festivals run concurrently to these, while immediately preceding this cultural extravaganza, Scotland's capital also hosts a film festival and jazz and blues festival, both in July. See Ⓦ edinburghfestivalcity.com for an overview of all of them.

National Eisteddfod (1st week Aug) Ⓦ eisteddfod.org.uk. The "National Eisteddfod of Wales" is Wales's leading festival and the largest travelling cultural festival in Europe – a week-long annual culture, music and arts bash, almost entirely in Welsh, and held at a different Welsh location each year (traditionally alternating between North and South Wales).

Cowes Week (1st week Aug) Ⓦ cowesweek.co.uk. Sailing extravaganza in the Isle of Wight, with partying and star-studded entertainment.

Boardmasters, Newquay (five days in early Aug) Ⓦ boardmasters.co.uk. Cornish seaside music and surfing festival.

Sidmouth FolkWeek (1st week Aug) Ⓦ sidmouthfolkweek. co.uk. The country's longest-running folk festival, with events throughout the town.

Green Man Crickhowell, mid-Aug; Ⓦ greenman.net. In a gorgeous site nestled below the peaks of the Brecon Beacons, this is Wales' most appealing music festival. Held over four days (though you can camp for the week), there's an eclectic mix of folk, rock and dance acts, plus spoken word and film, all washed down with lashings of local beer and cider. Entertainment areas for kids and teenagers, too.

WEIRD AND WONDERFUL FESTIVALS

National nuttiness and general British barminess is displayed at dozens of local festivals every year. The Highlands and islands of Scotland offer rich pickings when it comes to ancient traditions: at New Year, for example, when the **Kirkwall Boys' and Men's Ba' Games**, in Orkney, sees a mass, drunken football game through the streets of the town, with the players jumping into the harbour as a grand finale.

Easter is also particularly big on eccentricity, from the **Hare Pie Scramble and Bottle-Kicking** (Easter Mon), a chaotic village bottle-kicking contest at Hallaton, Leicestershire, to Gawthorpe in Yorkshire's **World Coal-Carrying Championship** (Easter Mon; Ⓦ gawthorpemaypole.org.uk), an annual race to carry 50kg of coal a mile through the village. May brings a host of ancient spring rites, including the **Helston Furry Dance** (May 8), a courtly procession and "Floral Dance" through the Cornish town (see page 337). There's more odd racing at the **Brockworth Cheese Rolling** (late May, bank hol Mon; Ⓦ cheese-rolling.co.uk) when crowds of daredevils chase a large cheese wheel down a murderous Gloucestershire incline. Perhaps the British capital of bonkers festivities is Wales's Llanwrtyd Wells. Among the many events in the "World Alternative Games" held every other August (Ⓦ worldalternativegames.co.uk) are gravy wrestling and wife-carrying; later in the month you can enjoy the **World Bog Snorkelling Championships** (Ⓦ www.green-events.co.uk).

In autumn, thousands flock to Northamptonshire to watch modern-day gladiators fight for glory armed only with a nut and twelve inches of string, in the **World Conker Championship** (mid-Oct; Ⓦ worldconkerchampionships.com).

Great British Beer Festival (mid-Aug) Ⓦ gbbf.org.uk. Colossal booze-fest in London, featuring more than nine hundred real ales and ciders from around the world.

Notting Hill Carnival (last Sun & bank hol Mon Aug) Ⓦ thelondonnottinghillcarnival.com. Vivacious two-day carnival led by London's Caribbean community with parades and floats, thumping soundsystems, food stalls and huge crowds taking over the whole neighbourhood.

Blackpool Illuminations (late Aug or early Sept to early Nov) Ⓦ visitblackpool.com. Initiated to extend the traditional Blackpool holiday season, the Blackpool lights have been a tourist attraction for more than a century. Switch-on weekend is celebrated with free events and music (register for wristband).

Heritage Open Days (2nd week Sept) Ⓦ heritageopendays.org.uk. Annual opportunity to peek inside hundreds of buildings in England that don't normally open their doors to the public, from factories to Buddhist temples. Scotland's **Doors Open Days** (Ⓦ doorsopendays.org.uk) and Wales's **Open Doors** (Ⓦ cadw.gov.wales) offer the same, over several weekends in Sept.

Ludlow Food Festival (mid-Sept) Ⓦ foodfestival.co.uk. High-profile fest in this foodie Shropshire town, with local producers, Michelin-starred chefs, events and masterclasses.

St Ives September Festival (2 weeks mid-Sept) Ⓦ stivesseptemberfestival.co.uk. Eclectic Cornish festival of art, poetry, literature, jazz, folk, rock and world music.

Great Welsh Beer & Cider Festival (late Sept) Ⓦ gwbcf.org.uk. Huge three-day event highlighting hundreds of ales and ciders (the majority from Welsh breweries) in Cardiff.

Wigtown Book Festival (end Sept–early Oct) Ⓦ wigtownbookfestival.com. Scotland's "national book town" celebrates its literary leanings with a ten-day book fest.

OCTOBER–DECEMBER

Swansea International Festival (early to mid-Oct) Ⓦ swanseafestival.org. Two superb weeks of concerts, drama, opera, ballet and art.

Battle of Hastings re-enactment (weekend in mid-Oct) Ⓦ www.english-heritage.org.uk. Annual re-enactment of the famous 1066 battle in Battle, featuring more than one thousand soldiers and living history encampments.

Halloween (Oct 31). Last day of the Celtic calendar and All Hallows Eve: pumpkins, plus a lot of ghoulish dressing-up, trick-or-treating and parties.

Guy Fawkes Night/Bonfire Night (Nov 5). Nationwide fireworks and bonfires commemorating the foiling of the Gunpowder Plot in 1605 – atop every bonfire is hoisted an effigy known as the "guy" after Guy Fawkes, one of the conspirators. Many events stick to fireworks nowadays, but notable traditional events include those in York (Fawkes' birthplace), Ottery St Mary in Devon, Lewes in East Sussex and Machynlleth in Wales.

Lord Mayor's Show (2nd Sat in Nov) Ⓦ lordmayorsshow.org. Held annually in the City of London since 1215, and featuring a daytime cavalcade and night-time fireworks to mark the inauguration of the new Lord Mayor.

Hogmanay (New Year's Eve) and Ne'er Day (Dec 31 & Jan 1). Traditionally New Year's Eve – or Hogmanay – is more important in Scotland where it is marked with the custom of "first-footing", when revellers visit neighbours at midnight bearing gifts. More popular these days are huge, organized street parties, most notably in Edinburgh, but also in Inverness, Glasgow and other Scottish towns and cities, where you can expect fire-lit processions in places like Stonehaven. There are also big New Year's Eve parties in the rest of Britain; in London, there's a massive fireworks display over the Thames, centred on the London Eye (tickets required for riverside locations).

Sports and outdoor activities

As the birthplace of football, cricket, rugby and tennis, Britain boasts a series of sporting events that attract a world audience. For those who wish to participate, the UK caters for numerous outdoor activities – in particular walking, cycling and watersports, but with opportunities for anything from rock climbing to pony trekking.

Spectator sports

Football (soccer) is the national game in England and Scotland, with a wide programme of professional league matches taking place every Saturday afternoon from early August to mid-May, with plenty of Sunday and midweek fixtures too. It's very difficult to get tickets to Premier League matches involving the most famous teams (Chelsea, Arsenal, Manchester United, Liverpool and Celtic), but tours of their grounds are feasible. You could also try one of the lower-league games.

Rugby comes in two codes – 15-a-side **Rugby Union** and 13-a-side **Rugby League**, both fearsomely brutal contact sports that can make entertaining viewing even if you don't understand the rules. In England, rugby is much less popular than football, but Rugby League has a loyal and dedicated fan base in the north – especially Yorkshire and Lancashire – while Union has traditionally been popular with the English middle class. Rugby Union is popular in the Scottish Borders and is effectively the **national sport in Wales**. Key Rugby Union and League games are sold out months in advance, but ordinary fixtures present few ticketing problems. The Rugby Union season runs from September to just after Easter, Rugby League February to September.

Cricket is English idiosyncrasy at its finest. People from non-cricketing nations – and most Brits for that matter – marvel at a game that can last several days and still end in a draw, while many people are unfamiliar with its rules. International, five-day "Test" matches, pitting the English national side against visiting countries, are played most summers at grounds around the country, and tickets are usually fairly easy to come by. The domestic game traditionally centres on four-day County Championship matches between English county teams, though there's far bigger interest – certainly for casual watchers – in the "Twenty20" (T20) format, designed to encourage flamboyant, decisive play in three-hour matches.

Finally, if you're in Britain at the end of June and early July, you won't be able to miss the country's annual fixation with **tennis** in the shape of the Wimbledon championships. It's often said that no one gives a hoot about the sport for the other fifty weeks of the year, though the success of Scottish champion Andy Murray (who has won the men's singles twice), has changed that somewhat, and has meant the crowds at Wimbledon and watching on screens across the country are no longer rooting for an underdog. Advance tickets for main courts are hard to come by, but you can join the queue for ground passes (Ⓦwimbledon.com).

Walking

Walking routes track across many of Britain's wilder regions, amid landscapes varied enough to suit any taste. Turn up in any National Park area and local information offices will be able to advise on anything from a family stroll to a full day out on the mountains. For shorter walks, you could check out the **National Trust** and **National Trust for Scotland**'s websites (Ⓦnationaltrust.org.uk and Ⓦnts.org.uk), which detail picturesque routes of varying lengths that weave through or near their properties. If you're travelling on public transport, consult the user-generated site **Car Free Walks** (Ⓦcarfreewalks.org), which details hundreds of routes that set off and finish at train stations and bus stops, providing OS map links and elevation profiles for each. Various **membership associations**, including the Ramblers Association (Ⓦramblers. org.uk) and Walkers are Welcome (Ⓦwalkersarewelcome.org.uk) also provide information and route ideas online.

Even for short hikes you need to be **properly equipped**, follow local advice and listen out for local weather reports – British weather is notoriously changeable and increasingly extreme. You will also need a good **map** – in most cases one of the excellent and reliable Ordnance Survey (OS) series (see page 49), usually available from local tourist offices or outdoor shops.

Hiking trails

Britain's finest **walking areas** include the granite moorlands and spectacular coastlines of Devon and Cornwall in southwest England; the highlands of North England – notably the Yorkshire Dales, North York Moors and the Lake District – the Welsh coastlines, particularly of Pembrokeshire; the peaks of Snowdonia National Park in North Wales; and pretty much all of highland Scotland.

Keen hikers might want to tackle one of England and Wales' fifteen **National Trails** (Ⓦ nationaltrail. co.uk). The most famous – certainly the toughest – is the **Pennine Way** (268 miles; usual walking time 16–19 days), stretching from the Derbyshire Peak District to the Scottish Borders (see page 432), while the challenging **South West Coast Path** (630 miles; from thirty days) through Cornwall, Devon, Somerset and Dorset tends to be tackled in shorter sections (see page 297). Other English trails are gentler, like the **South Downs Way** (100 miles; eight days) following the chalk escarpment and ridges of the South Downs (see page 168) or the fascinating **Hadrian's Wall footpath** (84 miles; seven days).

In Wales, the spectacular **Pembrokeshire Coast Path** (186 miles; twelve to fifteen days; see page 608) reveals some of the most beautiful coastal scenery in Britain (see page 670), while **Glyndŵr's Way** (135 miles; nine days) takes you through the moorland, farmland, woods and forests of mid-Wales and **Offa's**

Dyke Path (177 miles; twelve to fourteen days) traces the England–Wales border (see page 700).

Scotland is covered by 29 **Great Trails** (Ⓦ scotlands greattrails.org.uk), which cover more than 1900 miles between them. Of these, the **Southern Upland Way** crosses the country from coast to coast in the south, and is the longest at 212 miles (twelve to sixteen days). The best known, and busiest, is the **West Highland Way** (see page 847), a 96-mile hike from Glasgow to Fort William via Loch Lomond and Glen Coe (five to eight days).

Cycling

The **National Cycle Network** is made up of 14,500 miles of signed cycle route, mainly on traffic-free paths (including disused railways and canal towpaths) and country roads. You're never far from one of the numbered routes, all of which are detailed on the **Sustrans** website (Ⓦ sustrans.org. uk), a charitable trust devoted to the development of environmentally sustainable transport. Sustrans also publishes an excellent series of waterproof cycle maps (1:100,000) and regional guides.

ACTIVITY TOUR OPERATORS

There are numerous activity tours available taking in the best of the British outdoors.

BOATING AND SAILING

Blakes Holiday Boating ☎ 0345 498 6184, Ⓦ blakes.co.uk. Cruisers, yachts and narrowboats on the Norfolk Broads, the River Thames and various English and Scottish trips, including "whisky, wildlife and waves" sails around Jura and Islay.

Classic Sailing ☎ 01872 580022, Ⓦ classic-sailing.co.uk. Hands-on sailing holidays on traditional wooden boats and tall ships, including Cornwall, Scotland's Western Isles and the Isles of Scilly.

CYCLING

The Carter Company ☎ 01296 631671, Ⓦ the-carter-company.com. Gentle self-guided cycling and walking tours, including in London, Kent, Oxford and the Cotswolds, Devon, Cornwall, Dorset, Wales and Scotland, in simple or luxury accommodation.

Saddle Skedaddle ☎ 01912 651110, Ⓦ skedaddle.co.uk. Biking adventures and classic road rides – including guided, self-guided and tailor-made tours in Cornwall, the Cotswolds, Northumberland and the New Forest, Wales and Scotland, lasting from a weekend to a week, or a 22-day Land's End to John O'Groats tour.

SWIMMING

Swim Trek ☎ 01273 739 713, Ⓦ swimtrek.com. Guided wild-swimming holidays and trips, including one day on the Thames or along the Dorset coast, and Lake District trips.

SURFING

Surfers World ☎ 07540 221089, Ⓦ surfersworld.co.uk. Short breaks with surfing courses in Woolacombe, Croyde, and on the north Cornwall coast, as well as coasteering and paddle-boarding and group holidays.

WALKING

Contours Walking Holidays ☎ 01629 821900, Ⓦ contours. co.uk. Excellent short breaks or longer walking holidays and self-guided hikes in every region of Britain.

English Lakeland Ramblers US ☎ 1800 724 8801, Ⓦ ramblers.com. Escorted and self-guided walking tours in the Lake District and the Cotswolds, either inn-to-inn or based in a country hotel.

Ramblers Worldwide Holidays ☎ 01707 331133, Ⓦ ramblersholidays.co.uk. Sociable guided walking tours all over Britain, on a variety of themes, and for various fitness levels.

Walkabout Scotland ☎ 0131 243 2664, Ⓦ walkaboutscotland.com. Hiking in Scotland, with guided hillwalking holidays, including a thirteen-day Highlands trip and weekend walks.

Walkabout Wales UK ☎ 07775 444176, Ⓦ walkabout-wales. com. Can arrange half-day and day-walks, as well as bespoke guided treks of the Brecon Beacons, Welsh coast paths and Snowdonia.

BRITAIN'S NATIONAL PARKS

Britain has fifteen National Parks (W www.nationalparks.gov.uk), from Dartmoor in the southwest to the Cairngorms in the north.

- **The Broads** See page 376. The best place for a boating holiday – the rivers, marshes, fens and canals of Norfolk (and stretching into Suffolk) make up one of the most important wetlands in Europe, and are also ideal for birdwatching. Cyclists and walkers have the best of it. Don't miss: the long-distance footpath, Weavers' Way (see page 376).
- **Brecon Beacons** See page 686. In southern Wales, this range of grassy hills covers 520 square miles, with a striking sandstone scarp, and cave-riddled limestone valleys. Don't miss: the climb up Pen y Fan (see page 687).
- **Cairngorms** See page 924. In the Scottish Highlands, this is Britain's biggest national park, which includes its highest mountain massif. It includes some marvellous walking around Aviemore. Don't miss: the RSPB Reserve at Loch Garten (see page 925).
- **Dartmoor** See page 315. Southern England's largest wilderness attracts back-to-nature hikers and is famous for its standing stones, Stone Age hut circles and hill forts. Don't miss: Grimspound Bronze Age village (see page 316).
- **Exmoor** See page 295. Exmoor straddles the Somerset/Devon border and on its northern edge overlooks the sea. Crisscrossed by trails and also accessible from the South West Coast Path, it's ideal for walking and pony trekking. Don't miss: the four-mile hike to Dunkery Beacon (see page 296).
- **Lake District** See page 510. The Lake District (in Cumbria) is an almost alpine landscape of glacial lakes and rugged mountains. It's great for hiking, rock climbing and watersports, and has strong literary connections. Don't miss: Honister's hard-hat mine tour and Via Ferrata mountain traverse (see page 528).
- **Loch Lomond and the Trossachs** See page 846. Scotland's first national park incorporates a stretch of the West Highland Way along the loch. The wild glens of the Trossach range are also highly scenic. Don't miss: the ascent of Ben Lomond (see page 849).
- **New Forest** See page 202. England's best surviving example of a medieval hunting forest can be surprisingly wild. The majestic woodland is interspersed by tracts of heath, and a good network of paths and bridleways offers plenty of scope for biking and pony rides. Don't miss: camping in one of the stunning New Forest sites (see page 203).
- **Northumberland** See page 611. Remote Northumberland, in England's northeast, is adventure country. The long-distance Pennine Way runs the length of the park, and the Romans left their mark in the shape of Hadrian's Wall, along which you can hike or bike. Don't miss: the Chillingham cattle wildlife safari (see page 614).
- **North York Moors** See page 580. A stunning mix of heather moorland, gentle valleys, ruined abbeys and wild coastline. Walking and mountain biking are the big outdoor activities here. Don't miss: a day out at Ryedale Folk Museum (see page 583).
- **Peak District** See page 425. England's first National Park (1951), in the Midlands, is also the most visited. It's rugged outdoors country, with some dramatic underground caverns, tempered by stately homes and spa and market towns. Don't miss: a trip down Treak Cliff Cavern (see page 431).
- **Pembrokeshire Coast** See page 667. Some 170 miles of Wales's southwestern peninsula make up this park, best explored along the Pembrokeshire Coast Path that traverses the clifftops, often dipping down into secluded coves. Don't miss: the hike round St Bride's Bay (see page 672).
- **Snowdonia National Park** See page 722. Occupying almost the whole of the northwestern corner of Wales, this park incorporates a dozen of the country's highest peaks separated by dramatic glacial valleys. Don't miss: a ride on the Snowdon Mountain Railway (see page 728).
- **South Downs** See page 179. England's newest National Park (established 2010) might not be as wild as the others – about 85 percent is farmland – but it offers an easy rural escape into West and East Sussex. Don't miss: a walk along the South Downs Way, which covers more than 100 miles of the chalk uplands between Winchester and Beachy Head (see page 168).
- **Yorkshire Dales** See page 553. The best choice for walking, cycling and pony trekking, Yorkshire's second National Park spreads across twenty dales, or valleys, while caves, waterfalls and castles provide the backdrop. Don't miss: the walk to dramatic Malham Cove (see page 557).

Major routes include the **C2C** (Sea-to-Sea), which runs for 140 miles between Whitehaven/Workington on the English northwest coast and Tynemouth/Sunderland on the northeast; the **Cornish Way** (123 miles), from Bude to Land's End; the **Celtic Trail** (220 miles) across South Wales and the Pembrokeshire coast; and the classic cross-Britain route from **Land's End to John O'Groats**, the far southwest of England to the northeast tip of Scotland – roughly 1000 miles, which can be covered in two to three weeks, depending on which route you choose.

Britain's biggest cycling organization, **Cycling UK** (Ⓦcyclinguk.org), provides lists of tour operators and rental outlets, and supplies members with touring and technical advice, as well as insurance.

Watersports

Sailing and **windsurfing** in England are especially popular along the south coast (particularly the Isle of Wight and Solent) and in the southwest (around Falmouth in Cornwall, and around Salcombe and Dartmouth in Devon). Here, and in the Lake District, you'll be able to rent dinghies, boats and kayaks, either by the hour or for longer periods of instruction – from around £30 for a couple of hours of kayaking to about £150 for a two-day nonresidential sailing course. Opportunities for sailing around Scotland (Ⓦsailscotland.co.uk) are great, but changeable conditions combined with tricky tides and rocky shores demand good skills. If you want to learn to sail in Wales, contact Plas Menai: The National Watersports Centre (Ⓦplasmenai.co.uk), which offers sailing courses in a beautiful location on the Menai Strait. Scotland also has some top spots for windsurfing and kitesurfing, including Troon on the Ayrshire coast, St Andrews and Tiree.

Newquay in Cornwall is England's undisputed **surfing** centre, whose main break, Fistral, regularly hosts international contests. But there are quieter spots all along the north coast of Cornwall and Devon, as well as a growing scene on the more isolated northeast coast from Yorkshire up to Northumberland, with lots of action at the pretty seaside Teesside town of Saltburn. For more information on surfing in England, including a directory of surf schools and an events calendar, check Ⓦsurfing england.org.

Scotland is fast gaining a reputation for the high quality of its breaks, with many people heading for Thurso on the north coast (largely in winter) and Isle of Tiree. Other good breaks lie within easy reach of large cities (such as Pease Bay, near Edinburgh, and

Fraserburgh, near Aberdeen), while the west coast has numerous possibilities.

Surfing in Wales (Ⓦwsfsurfschool.co.uk) tends to be concentrated on the south coast, around the Gower Peninsula.

Wales has led the way for **coasteering**, a thrilling extreme sport that involves climbing, swimming, scrambling and cliff-jumping – with a guide – along the more spectacular stretches of rocky coast; other coasteering centres include Cornwall and the Scottish Highlands. Finally, if you can brave the often chilly temperatures, **wild swimming** is a wonderful way to experience Britain's many beautiful rivers, lakes, waterfall pools and sea caves. Check Ⓦwildswimming.co.uk for a run-down of good places plus safety tips – you should always heed local advice.

Travel essentials

Climate

Though it has seen some extreme storms, flooding and snowfall in recent years, Britain has a generally temperate, maritime climate, which means largely moderate temperatures (see page 14) and a decent chance of at least some rain whenever you visit. If you're attempting to balance the clemency of the weather against the density of the crowds, even given regional variations and microclimates the best months to come to Britain are April, May, September and October.

Costs

Faced with another £4 pint, a £40 theatre ticket and a £20 taxi ride back to your £100-a-night hotel, Britain might seem like the most expensive place in Europe – though the decline in the value of the pound since the 2016 EU referendum has made it increasingly attractive for non-domestic visitors. As a rule of thumb, if you're camping or hostelling, using public transport, buying picnic lunches and eating in pubs and cafés your minimum expenditure will be around £40 per person per day. Couples staying in B&Bs, eating at local pubs and restaurants and sightseeing should expect to splash out £70 per person, while if you're renting a car, staying in hotels and eating at fancier places, budget for at least £120 each. Double that last figure if you choose to stay in stylish city or grand country-house hotel, while on any visit to London work on the basis that you'll need an extra £30 per day.

TIPPING

Although there are no fixed rules for **tipping**, a ten to fifteen percent gratuity is anticipated by restaurant waiters. Tipping taxi drivers ten percent or so is optional, but most people at the very least round the fare up to the nearest pound. Some restaurants levy a "discretionary" or "optional" **service charge** of 10 or 12.5 percent, which must be clearly stated on the menu and on the bill. However, you are not obliged to pay it, and certainly not if the food or service wasn't what you expected. It is not normal to leave tips if you order at the bar in pubs, though more likely if there's table service in bars, when some people choose to leave a few coins. The only other occasions when you might be expected to tip are at the hairdressers, and in upmarket hotels where porters and bell boys expect and usually get a pound or two per bag or for calling a taxi.

Discounts and admission charges

Many of Britain's **historic attractions** – from castles to stately homes – are owned and/or operated by either the **National Trust** (W nationaltrust.org.uk; denoted as NT in the Guide) covering England and Wales, or the **National Trust for Scotland** (W nts.org.uk; NTS). Many other historic sites are operated by **English Heritage** (W english-heritage.org.uk; EH), **Historic Scotland** (W historic-scotland.gov.uk; HS), and **CADW Welsh Historic Monuments** (W cadw.gov.wales; CADW). All these organizations usually charge entry fees, though some sites are free. If you plan to visit more than half a dozen places owned by one of them, it's worth considering an annual membership (£65 for the National Trust; £54 for English Heritage; £47.25 for Historic Scotland; £44 for CADW) – you can join on your first visit to any attraction. For non-UK visitors, English Heritage's nine- or sixteen-day **overseas visitors passes** (£31/£37; family passes available) are good value if you are planning on visiting more than two of their properties. The National Trust touring pass is similar (seven days £29; fourteen days £34; buy online in advance), though some NT properties are not included. US members of the **Royal Oak Foundation** (W royal-oak.org) get free admission to all National Trust properties.

Municipal art galleries and museums across Britain often have free admission, as do the world-class **state museums** in London, Cardiff, Edinburgh and elsewhere, from the British Museum (London) and the National Gallery of Scotland (Edinburgh) to York's National Railway Museum. Private and municipal museums and other collections rarely charge more than £10 admission. Some **cathedrals** and churches either charge admission or ask for voluntary donations.

The admission charges given in the Guide are the full adult rate, unless otherwise stated. Concessionary rates – generally a few pounds less – for **senior citizens** (over 60), under-26s and **children** (generally from 5 to 17) apply almost everywhere, from tourist attractions to public transport. Family tickets are often available, and children under 5 are usually free.

Full-time students can benefit from an International Student ID Card (ISIC; W isic.org), and those under 30 from an International Youth Travel Card (IYTC), while **teachers** qualify for the International Teacher Identity Card (ITIC). Available from STA Travel (see page 32), all cost £12 and are valid for special air, rail and bus fares, and discounts at museums and other attractions.

Crime and personal safety

Terrorist attacks in Britain – and particularly in London – may have changed the general perception of how safe the region feels, but it's still extremely unlikely that you'll be at any risk as you travel around, though you will be aware of heightened **security** at airports, major train stations and high-profile attractions. You can walk more or less anywhere without fear of harassment, though the big cities can have their edgy districts and it's always better to err on the side of caution, especially late at night. Leave your passport and valuables in a hotel or hostel safe (carrying **ID** is not compulsory, though if you look particularly youthful and intend to drink in a pub or buy alcohol in a shop it can be a good idea to carry it, and some clubs require ID for entry), and exercise the usual caution on public transport. If you're taking a taxi, always make sure it's officially licensed and never pick one up in the street – unless it's an official black taxi in London (see page 116), for example. Bar or restaurant staff can usually provide a reliable recommendation or direct you to the nearest taxi rank.

Other than asking for directions, most visitors rarely come into contact with the **police**, who as a rule are approachable and helpful. Most wear chest guards and carry batons, though regular street officers do not carry guns. If you are robbed, report it straight away to the police; your insurance company will require a **crime report number**. For **police**, **fire** and **ambulance** services phone ☎ 999.

Electricity

The **current** is 240V AC. North American appliances will need a transformer and adaptor; those from Europe, South Africa, Australia and New Zealand only need an adaptor.

Health

No vaccinations are required for entry into Britain. Citizens of all EU and EEA countries and Switzerland are entitled to free medical treatment within the National Health Service (**NHS**), which includes the vast majority of hospitals and doctors, on production of their **European Health Insurance Card** (EHIC) or, in extremis, their passport or national identity card. However, this could change when the UK leaves the EU, estimated for 2019, so check in advance. Some Commonwealth countries also have reciprocal healthcare arrangements with the UK – for example Australia and New Zealand. If you don't fall into either of these categories, you will be charged for all medical services – except those administered by accident and emergency (units at NHS hospitals – so health insurance is strongly advised.

Pharmacists (known as **chemists** in Britain) can advise you on minor conditions but can dispense only a limited range of drugs without a doctor's prescription. Most are open standard shop hours, though there are also late-night branches in large cities and at 24-hour supermarkets. For generic pain relief, cold remedies and the like, the local super-market is usually the cheapest option.

Minor complaints and injuries can be dealt with at a **doctor's (GP's) surgery** – your hotel should be able to point you in the right direction, where you can register as a temporary patient, though you may not be seen immediately. For serious injuries, go to the 24-hour **Accident and Emergency (A&E)** depart-ment of the nearest **hospital**, and in an **emergency**, call an ambulance on ☎ 999. If you need medical help fast but it's not a 999 emergency you can also get free advice from the NHS's 24-hour **helpline** on ☎ 111.

Insurance

It's a good idea to take out an **insurance policy** before travelling to cover against theft and loss, as well as illness or injury if not covered by reciprocal arrangements with your home country (see above). Most exclude so-called dangerous sports unless an extra premium is paid: in Britain this can mean most watersports, rock climbing and mountaineering, though hiking, kayaking and jeep safaris would probably be covered.

Internet

Most hotels and hostels in Britain have free **wi-fi** (we indicate in the Guide if they do not). In addition, many museums, public buildings, tourist offices and some train stations provide free wi-fi, as do numerous cafés, restaurants and bars. Less common are dedicated internet cafés, but some public libraries also offer free access.

LGBT+ travellers

England offers one of the most diverse and acces-sible **LGBT+** scenes anywhere in Europe. Nearly every sizeable town has some kind of organized LGBT+ life – from bars and clubs to community groups – with the major scenes found in London, Manchester, Brighton Edinburgh, Glasgow, Cardiff and Swansea. Listings, news and reviews can be found at *Gay Times* (Ⓦ gaytimes.co.uk) and *Pink News* (Ⓦ pinknews.co.uk). The campaigning organization Stonewall's website (Ⓦ stonewall.org.uk) is also useful, with directories of local groups and advice on reporting hate crimes, which unfortunately continue to be a concern. The age of consent is 16.

Maps

Petrol stations in England stock large-format **road atlases** produced by the AA, RAC, Collins, Ordnance Survey and others, which cover all of Britain, at a scale of around 1:250,000, and include larger-scale plans of major towns. The best of these is the **Ordnance Survey** road atlas, which handily uses the same grid reference system as their folding maps. Overall the Ordnance Survey (OS; Ⓦ ordnancesurvey.co.uk) produces the most comprehensive maps, renowned for their accuracy and clarity. Their 1:50,000 (pink)

DISTANCES, WEIGHTS AND MEASURES

Distances (and speeds) on British signposts are in miles, and beer is still served in pints. For everything else – money, weights and measures – a confusing mixture of the **metric and imperial** systems is used: fuel is dispensed by the litre, while meat, milk and vegetables may be sold in either or both systems. Throughout this Guide distances are given in feet, yards and miles.

ROUGH GUIDES TRAVEL INSURANCE

Rough Guides has teamed up with WorldNomads.com to offer great **travel insurance** deals. Policies are available to residents of over 150 countries, with cover for a wide range of adventure sports, 24-hour emergency assistance, high levels of medical and evacuation cover and a stream of travel safety information. Roughguides.com users can take advantage of their policies online 24/7, from anywhere in the world – even if you're already travelling. And since plans often change when you're on the road, you can extend your policy and even claim online. Roughguides.com users who buy travel insurance with WorldNomads.com can also leave a positive footprint and donate to a community development project. For more information go to ⓦ roughguides.com/travel-insurance.

Landranger series shows enough detail to be useful for most walkers and cyclists, and there's more detail still in the full-colour 1:25,000 (orange) *Explorer* series – both cover the whole of Britain. The full OS range is only available at a few big-city stores or online; you can also download high-resolution maps via their app.

The media

For television, radio and online news, the **British Broadcasting Corporation** (**BBC**; ⓦ bbc.co.uk), paid for by a licence fee levied on viewers, remains the biggest media provider, with national and regional coverage, with Welsh and Scottish divisions that broadcast some separate content, including the Scottish Gaelic BBC Alba. The BBC's website is useful for news headlines and weather forecasts. Two terrestrial channels, **BBC1** and **BBC2**, plus digital **BBC4**, cover the full swathe of television broadcasting from international, national and local news and in-depth documentaries to world-famous drama and entertainment.

The BBC's **radio network** (ⓦ bbc.co.uk/radio) has five nationwide stations: **Radio 1** (chart and dance music); **Radio 2** (light pop and rock for an older audience); **Radio 3** (classical and jazz); **Radio 4** (current affairs, arts and drama); and **5 Live** (sports, news, discussions and phone-ins). Digital-only BBC stations include the alternative-music 6 Music, and the BBC Asian Network, and there are stations for all regions. You can find many of the BBC's best radio shows as **podcasts**.

Beyond the BBC, there are three terrestrial TV channels: ITV (ⓦ itv.com), Channel 4 (ⓦ channel4.com) and Channel 5 (ⓦ channel5.com), plus dozens of digital and satellite options. In Wales, Channel 4 also produces Welsh-language digital channel S4C. Live sport is often shown on satellite provider Sky, whose 24-hour rolling Sky News programme rivals that of CNN. Most homes and hotels get around forty "freeview" channels spread across the networks, including dedicated news, film, sports, arts and entertainment channels.

The major **newspapers**, providing print and online news, include the higher-end traditional papers, *The Times* (ⓦ thetimes.co.uk; paywall), the staunchly Conservative *Daily Telegraph* (ⓦ telegraph.co.uk; paywall), the left-of-centre *Guardian*, with its Sunday sister paper the *Observer* (ⓦ theguardian.com), and the *Independent* (ⓦ independent.co.uk; online only). Of the **tabloids**, the most popular across Britain is *The Sun* (ⓦ thesun.co.uk), a muck-raking right-wing paper whose chief rival is the traditionally left-leaning *Mirror* (ⓦ mirror.co.uk). The middlebrow daily tabloids – the *Daily Mail* (ⓦ dailymail.co.uk) and the *Daily Express* (ⓦ express.co.uk) – are particularly partisan and noticeably xenophobic.

The **Scottish print press** is distinct, with the main quality newspapers the *Scotsman* (ⓦ scotsman.com), the *Herald* and *Sunday Herald* (ⓦ heraldscotland.com) and *Sunday Post* (ⓦ sundaypost.com). The biggest-selling dailies are the tabloid *Daily Record* (ⓦ dailyrecord.co.uk). Most of the main UK newspapers produce specific Scottish editions, but are often seen as being "London" papers. In November 2014, The National (ⓦ thenational.scot) was launched – a daily paper (Mon–Sat) with a specifically pro-Scottish-independence remit.

In **Wales**, the only quality Welsh daily is the *Western Mail*, and its Sunday edition, *Wales on Sunday* (ⓦ walesonline.co.uk). In the north of the country, the *Daily Post* (ⓦ dailypost.co.uk) has a decent spectrum of news and features that marks it out from other local dailies.

Money

Britain's currency is the **pound sterling** (£), divided into 100 pence (p). Coins come in denominations of 1p, 2p, 5p, 10p, 20p, 50p, £1 and £2. Bank of England notes are in denominations of £5, £10, £20 and £50. Scottish and Northern Irish banknotes are legal tender throughout the UK, though some traders in England and Wales may be unwilling to accept them. For current **exchange rates**, visit ⓦ xe.com.

The easiest way to get hold of cash is to use your **debit card** at an **ATM**; there's usually a daily withdrawal limit, which varies depending on the money issuer, but starts at around £250. You'll find ATMs outside banks, at all major points of arrival and motorway service areas, at large supermarkets, petrol stations and even inside some pubs, post offices and shops (though a charge of a few pounds may be levied on cash withdrawals at small, standalone ATMs – the screen will tell you).

Credit cards are widely accepted in hotels, shops and restaurants – MasterCard and Visa are almost universal, charge cards like American Express and Diners Club less so.

Contactless payments, where you simply hold your credit or debit card on or near a card reader without having to key in a PIN, can be used for transactions for up to £30. Note that the same overseas transaction fees will apply to contactless payments as to those made with a PIN. Contactless has increased the number of establishments that take cards – even market stalls may do so nowadays – though some smaller places, such as B&Bs and shops, may accept cash only, and occasionally there's a minimum amount for card payments (usually £5 or £10).

You can change currency or cheques at **post offices** and **bureaux de change** – the former charge no commission, while the latter tend to be open longer hours and are found in most city centres and at major airports and train stations – and can charge high commission; it is cheaper to order currency online in advance to pick up later.

Opening hours and public holidays

Though traditional office hours are Monday to Saturday from around 9am to 5.30 or 6pm, many businesses, shops and restaurants throughout Britain will open earlier – or later – and close later. The majority of shops are open daily, and in the towns some at least might stay open late on a Thursday evening, but some places – even the so-called "24hr supermarkets" – are closed or have restricted hours on Sunday, and businesses in remote areas and villages might even have an "early closing day" – often Wednesday – when they shut at 1pm. Banks are not open at the weekend. We have given full **opening hours** for everything we review – museums, galleries and tourist attractions, cafés, restaurants, pubs and shops – throughout

the Guide, noting where they're especially complex or prone to change; it's always worth checking to confirm beforehand.

While many local shops and businesses close on **public holidays**, few tourist-related businesses observe them, particularly in summer. However, nearly all museums, galleries and other attractions are closed on Christmas Day and New Year's Day, with many also closed on Boxing Day (Dec 26). Britain's public holidays are usually referred to as **bank holidays** (though it's not just the banks who have a day off).

Phones

Every British landline number has a prefix, which, if beginning ⓣ 01 or 02, represents an **area code**. The prefix ⓣ 07 is for mobile phones/cellphones. A variety of ⓣ 08 prefixes relate to the cost of calls – some, like ⓣ 0800, are free to call from a landline, others (like ⓣ 0845 and ⓣ 0870) are more expensive than landlines, the actual price depending on your phone or phone operator. ⓣ 03 numbers are charged at local rates. Beware, particularly, of **premium-rate ⓣ 09 numbers**, common for pre-recorded information services (including some tourist authorities), which can be charged at anything up to £3.60 a minute.

Numerous companies offer a **directory enquiries** service, all with six-figure numbers beginning with ⓣ 118, but charges are extortionate (minimum £5-plus, with costs quickly escalating) and are best avoided.

Most hotel rooms have telephones, but there is almost always an exorbitant surcharge to use them. The odd public **payphone** – telephone box – still exists, though with the ubiquity of mobile phones, they're seldom used.

PUBLIC HOLIDAYS
Jan 1 (New Year's Day)
Jan 2 Scotland only
Good Friday
Easter Monday Not in Scotland
First Mon in May ("May Day")
Last Mon in May
Last Mon in Aug
Nov 30 (St Andrew's Day) Scotland only
Dec 25 (Christmas Day)
Dec 26 (Boxing Day)
Note that if January 1, December 25, December 26 or St Andrew's Day falls on a Saturday or Sunday, the next weekday becomes a public holiday.

CALLING ABROAD FROM BRITAIN

Australia ☎0061 + area code minus the initial zero + number.

New Zealand ☎0064 + area code minus the initial zero + number.

US and Canada ☎001 + area code + number.

Republic of Ireland ☎00353 + area code minus the initial zero + number.

South Africa ☎0027 + area code + number.

Mobile phone access is universal in towns and cities, and rural areas are well served too, though coverage can be patchy. To use your own phone, check with your provider that international roaming is activated – and that your phone will work in the UK. Any EU-registered phones will be charged the same rates for calls, text messages and data as your home tariff (at least until March 2019, when the UK is set to leave the EU). Calls using non-EU phones are still unregulated and can have prohibitively expensive roaming charges. If you're staying in Britain for any length of time, it's often easiest to **buy a mobile** and local SIM card in the UK – basic pre-pay ("pay as you go") models start at around £30, usually including some calling credit.

Post

The postal service (**Royal Mail**) is reasonably efficient. First-class **stamps** to anywhere in the UK currently cost 65p and post should arrive the next day; if the item is anything approaching A4 size, it will be classed as a "Large Letter" and will cost 98p; if you want to guarantee next-day delivery, ask for Special Delivery (from £6.45). Second-class stamps cost 56p, taking up to three days; airmail to the rest of Europe and beyond costs £1.17 and should take three days within Europe, five days further afield. Stamps can be bought at post offices, singly or in books of four, six or twelve; books of stamps are also often available from newsagents, many gift shops and supermarkets.

Post offices are typically open Monday to Friday 9am–5.30pm and Saturday 9am–12.30pm, occasionally till 5.30pm for larger branches. To find your nearest branch, see ⓦpostoffice.co.uk.

Smoking

Smoking is banned in all public buildings and offices, restaurants and pubs, and on all public transport. In addition, the vast majority of hotels and B&Bs no longer allow it. **Vaping** – the use of e-cigarettes – is not allowed on public transport and is generally prohibited in museums and other public buildings; for restaurants and bars it depends on the individual proprietor.

Time

Greenwich Mean Time (GMT) – equivalent to Co-ordinated Universal Time (UTC) – is used from the end of October to the end of March; for the rest of the year Britain switches to **British Summer Time** (BST), one hour ahead of GMT.

Tourist information

Britain's tourism authority, VisitBritain (ⓦvisitbritain.com), promotes the nation as a destination overseas. The three national tourism websites – ⓦvisitengland.com, ⓦvisitscotland.com and ⓦvisitwales.com – cover popular activities, festivals, accommodation advice and so on, and there are also many regional tourist websites.

Tourist offices exist in major destinations, though local cuts have led to closures over recent years, and services may depend on volunteers. We've listed opening hours in the Guide.

The **National Parks** usually have their own dedicated information centres, which offer similar services to tourist offices but can also provide expert guidance on local walks and outdoor pursuits.

Travellers with disabilities

On the whole, Britain has good facilities for travellers with disabilities. All new public buildings – including museums, galleries and cinemas – are obliged to provide **wheelchair access**; airports and (generally) train stations are accessible; many buses have easy-access boarding ramps; and dropped kerbs and signalled crossings are the rule in every city and town. However, old buildings and Victorian infrastructure still creates problems for accessibility in some places (not all of London's tube system is wheelchair accessible, for example). The number of accessible hotels and restaurants is growing, and reserved parking bays are available almost everywhere, from shopping centres to museums. If you have specific requirements, it's always best to talk first to your chosen hotel or tour operator.

Wheelchair-users and blind or partially sighted people are automatically given thirty to forty percent reductions on train fares, and people with other disabilities are eligible for the Disabled Persons Railcard (£20/year; ⓦdisabledpersons-railcard.co.uk), which gives a third off the price of most tickets for you and someone accompanying you. There are no bus discounts for disabled tourists. In addition to the resources listed below, for detailed reviews of some of Britain's leading attractions – museums, markets, theatres – written by and for disabled people, download the free **Rough Guide to Accessible Britain** (Ⓦ accessibleguide.co.uk).

CONTACTS FOR DISABLED TRAVELLERS

Open Britain Ⓦ openbritain.net. Accessible travel-related information, from accommodation to attractions.

Tourism For All Ⓦ tourismforall.org.uk. Listings, guides and advice for access throughout Britain.

Travelling with children

Facilities in Britain for travellers with children are similar to those in the rest of Europe. Breast-feeding is officially permitted in all public places, including restaurants and cafés, and **baby-changing** rooms are widely available, including in shopping centres and train stations (where you may have to pay). Children aren't allowed in certain **licensed (alcohol-serving) premises**, though this doesn't apply to restaurants, and many pubs and inns, particularly if they serve food, welcome children, (sometimes with restricted times, or limiting kids to certain areas within the pub). Some **B&Bs and hotels** won't accept children under a certain age (usually 12). Under-5s generally travel free on public transport and get in free to attractions; 5- to 16-year-olds are usually entitled to concessionary rates. Many public museums and attractions have kids' activity packs, family events, play areas and so on, and you can generally find a playground in most neighbourhoods.

London

TOWER BRIDGE

1 London

For the visitor, London is a thrilling place. Monuments from the capital's glorious past are everywhere, from medieval banqueting halls and the great churches of Christopher Wren to eclectic Victorian architecture. You can relax in the city's quiet Georgian squares, explore the narrow alleyways of the City of London, wander along the riverside walkways, and uncover the quirks of what is still identifiably a collection of villages. The largest capital in Europe, stretching for more than thirty miles from east to west, and with a population just short of nine million, London is also incredibly diverse, ethnically and linguistically, offering cultural and culinary delights from right across the globe.

The capital's great historical **landmarks** – Big Ben, Westminster Abbey, Buckingham Palace, St Paul's Cathedral, the Tower of London and so on – draw in millions of tourists every year. Things change fast, though, and the regular emergence of new attractions ensures there's plenty to do even for those who've visited before. With Tate Modern and the Shard, the city boasts the world's most popular modern art museum and Western Europe's tallest building. And the city continues to grow, its cultural, nightlife and culinary scenes pushing ever onwards into neighbourhoods once well beyond the tourist radar – into East London in particular.

You could spend days just **shopping** in London, mixing with the upper classes in the "tiara triangle" around Harrods, or sampling the offbeat weekend markets of Portobello Road, Brick Lane and Camden. The city's **pubs** have always had heaps of atmosphere, and **food** is now a major attraction too, with more than fifty Michelin-starred restaurants and the widest choice of cuisines on the planet. The **music**, **clubbing** and **LGBT+** scenes are second to none, and mainstream **arts** are no less exciting, with regular opportunities to catch outstanding theatre companies, dance troupes, exhibitions and opera.

London's special atmosphere comes mostly, however, from the life on its streets. A cosmopolitan city since at least the seventeenth century, when it was a haven for Huguenot immigrants escaping persecution in Louis XIV's France, today it is truly **multicultural**, with over half its permanent population originating from overseas. The last hundred years has seen the arrival of thousands from the Caribbean, the Indian subcontinent, the Mediterranean, the Far East and Eastern Europe, all of whom play an integral part in defining a metropolis that is unmatched in its sheer diversity.

Brief history

The Romans founded **Londinium** in 47 AD as a stores depot on the marshy banks of the Thames. Despite frequent attacks – not least by Queen Boudica, who razed it in 61 AD – the port became secure in its position as capital of Roman Britain by the

COLUMBIA ROAD FLOWER MARKET

Highlights

HIGHLIGHTS ARE MARKED ON THE MAPS ON PAGES 58 AND 62

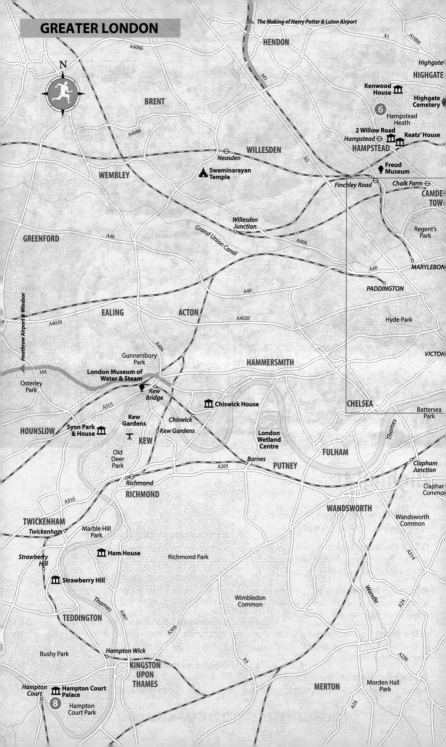

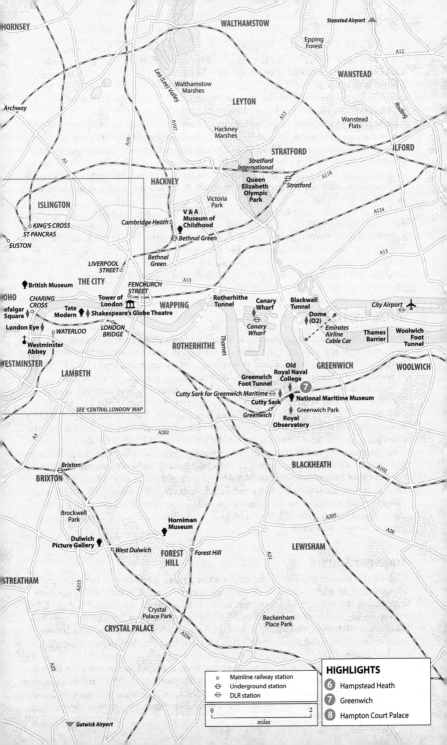

1

end of the century. London's expansion really began, however, in the eleventh century, when it became the seat of the last successful invader of Britain, the Norman duke who became **King William I of England** (aka "the Conqueror"). Crowned in Westminster Abbey, William built the White Tower – centrepiece of the Tower of London – to establish his dominance over the merchant population, the class that was soon to make London one of Europe's mightiest cities.

Little is left of medieval or Tudor London. Many of the finest buildings were wiped out in the course of a few days in 1666 when the **Great Fire of London** annihilated more than thirteen thousand houses and nearly ninety churches, completing a cycle of destruction begun the year before by the Great Plague, which killed as many as a hundred thousand people. Chief beneficiary of the blaze was Christopher Wren, who was commissioned to redesign the city and rose to the challenge with such masterpieces as St Paul's Cathedral and the Royal Naval Hospital in Greenwich.

Much of the public architecture of London was built in the Georgian and Victorian periods of the eighteenth and nineteenth centuries, when grand structures were raised to reflect the city's status as the financial and administrative hub of the **British Empire**. And though postwar development peppered the city with some undistinguished Modernist buildings, more recent experiments in high-tech architecture, such as the Gherkin, the Cheesegrater and the Shard, have given the city a new gloss.

Westminster

Political, religious and regal power has emanated from **Westminster** for almost a millennium. It was Edward the Confessor (1042–66) who first established Westminster as London's royal and ecclesiastical power base, some three miles west of the City of London. The embryonic English parliament used to meet in the abbey and eventually took over the old royal palace of Westminster. In the nineteenth century, Westminster – and Whitehall in particular – became the "heart of the Empire", its ministries ruling over a quarter of the world's population. Even now, though the UK's world status has diminished, the institutions that run the country inhabit roughly the same geographical area: Westminster for the politicians, Whitehall for the civil servants.

The monuments and buildings in and around Westminster also span the millennium, and include some of London's most famous landmarks – **Nelson's Column**, **Big Ben** and the **Houses of Parliament**, **Westminster Abbey**, plus two of the city's finest permanent art collections, the **National Gallery** and **Tate Britain**. This is a well-trodden tourist circuit since it's also one of the easiest parts of London to walk round, with all the major sights within a mere half-mile of each other, linked by one of London's most majestic streets, **Whitehall**.

Trafalgar Square

Despite the persistent noise of traffic, **Trafalgar Square** is still one of London's grandest architectural set pieces. John Nash designed the basic layout in the 1820s, but died long before the square took its present form. The Neoclassical National Gallery filled up the northern side of the square in 1838, followed five years later by the central focal point, **Nelson's Column**, topped by the famous admiral; the very large bronze lions didn't arrive until 1868, and the fountains didn't take their present shape until the late 1930s.

As one of the few large public squares in London, Trafalgar Square has been both a tourist attraction and a focus for **political demonstrations** since the Chartists assembled here in 1848 before marching to Kennington Common. Since then, countless demos and rallies have taken place, and nowadays various free events, commemorations and celebrations are staged here.

1

Stranded on a traffic island to the south of the column, and predating the entire square, is an **equestrian statue of Charles I**, erected shortly after the Restoration on the very spot where eight of those who had signed the king's death warrant were disembowelled. Charles's statue also marks the original site of the thirteenth-century **Charing Cross**, from where all distances from the capital are measured – a Victorian imitation now stands outside Charing Cross train station.

St Martin-in-the-Fields

Trafalgar Square, WC2N 4JH · Mon, Tues, Thurs & Fri 8.30am–1pm & 2–6pm, Wed 8.30am–1.15pm & 2–5pm, Sat 9.30am–6pm, Sun 3.30–5pm; concerts Mon, Tues & Fri 1pm · Free · ☎ 020 7766 1100, ⓦ stmartin-in-the-fields.org · ⊖ Charing Cross

The northeastern corner of Trafalgar Square is occupied by James Gibbs's church of **St Martin-in-the-Fields**, fronted by a magnificent Corinthian portico. Designed in 1721, the interior is purposefully simple, though the Italian plasterwork on the barrel vaulting is exceptionally rich; it's best appreciated while listening to one of the church's free lunchtime **concerts**. There's a licensed café (see page 120) in the roomy **crypt**, along with a shop, gallery and brass-rubbing centre.

National Gallery

Trafalgar Square, WC2N 5DN · Daily 10am–6pm, Fri till 9pm · Guided tours daily 11.30am & 2.30pm, plus Fri 7pm · Free · ☎ 020 7747 2885, ⓦ nationalgallery.org.uk · ⊖ Charing Cross

The **National Gallery** was begun in 1824 by the British government. The gallery's canny acquisition policy has resulted in more than 2300 paintings, but the collection's virtue is not so much its size as its range, depth and sheer quality. To view the collection chronologically, begin with the **Sainsbury Wing**, to the west. With more than one thousand paintings on display, you'll need real stamina to see everything, so if time is tight your best bet is to home in on your areas of special interest or join one of the gallery's free **guided tours**, which set off from the Sainsbury Wing foyer.

LONDON ORIENTATION: WHERE TO GO

Although the majority of the city's sights are situated north of the **River Thames**, which loops through the centre of the city from west to east, there is no single focus of interest. That's because London hasn't grown through centralized planning but by a process of agglomeration. Villages and urban developments that once surrounded the core are now lost within the amorphous mass of Greater London.

Westminster, the country's royal, political and ecclesiastical power base for centuries, was once a separate city. The grand streets and squares to the north of Westminster, from **St James's** to **Covent Garden**, were built as residential suburbs after the Restoration in 1660, and are now the city's shopping and entertainment zones known collectively as the **West End**, with **Soho** long the seedy heart of London after dark, now packed with restaurants, pubs and bars. To the east is the original City of London – known simply as **The City** – founded by the Romans, with more history than any other patch of the city, and now one of the world's great financial centres.

East of the City, the neighbourhoods of **East London** draw in visitors for the markets and nightlife of Brick Lane, Spitalfields and Shoreditch, with the creative scene spreading ever outwards to places like Bethnal Green, Hackney and Dalston. In its far reaches, East London is home to the **Olympic Park**, and the second financial centre of Canary Wharf.

The **south bank** of the Thames is perfect for exploring on foot, from the London Eye, in the west, to Tate Modern and the pubs and markets of Borough beyond, with the Shard looming overhead. To the west, the **museums** of South Kensington are a must, as is Portobello Road market in trendy Notting Hill. Literary Hampstead and Highgate in north London are refined neighbourhoods to wander, standing either side of half-wild **Hampstead Heath**. To the southeast, **Greenwich**, downstream of central London, with its nautical associations, royal park and observatory, makes a great day out – especially if visited by boat. Finally, there are plenty of rewarding day-trips in west London along the Thames, most notably to **Hampton Court Palace** and Windsor Castle.

1

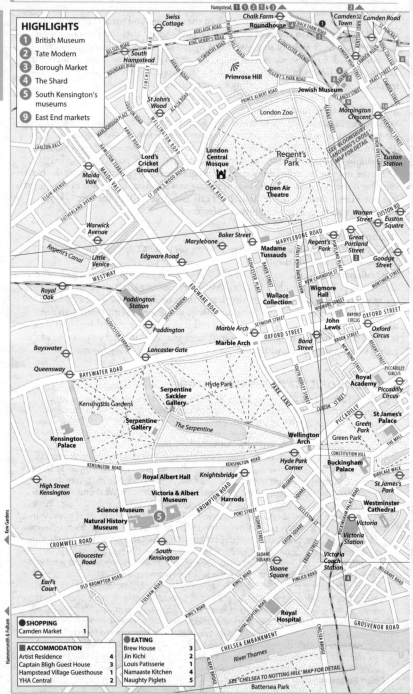

HIGHLIGHTS

1 British Museum
2 Tate Modern
3 Borough Market
4 The Shard
5 South Kensington's museums
9 East End markets

● **SHOPPING**
Camden Market 1

■ **ACCOMMODATION**
Artist Residence 4
Captain Bligh Guest House 3
Hampstead Village Guesthouse 1
YHA Central 2

◆ **EATING**
Brew House 3
Jin Kichi 2
Louis Patisserie 1
Namaaste Kitchen 4
Naughty Piglets 5

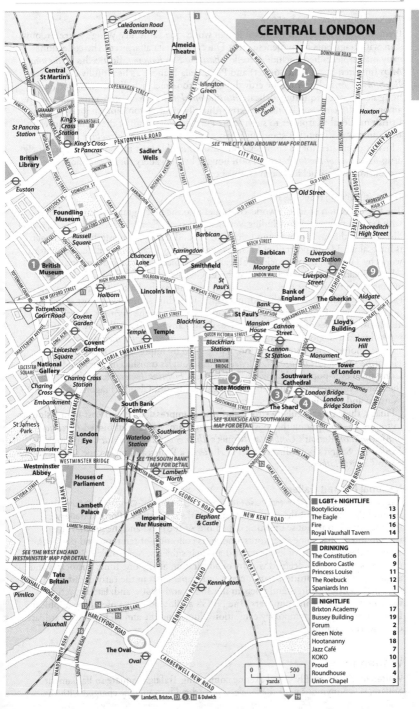

1

CENTRAL LONDON

N

Caledonian Road & Barnsbury

Almeida Theatre

Central St Martin's

Islington Green

Regent's Canal

Hoxton

Angel

St Pancras Station

King's Cross Station

King's Cross-St Pancras

Sadler's Wells

SEE 'THE CITY AND AROUND' MAP FOR DETAIL

British Library

Euston

Shoreditch High Street

Foundling Museum

Russell Square

Barbican

Old Street

Shoreditch High Street

1 British Museum

Chancery Lane

Farringdon

Barbican

Moorgate

Liverpool Street Station

9

Smithfield

St Paul's

Liverpool Street

Holborn

Lincoln's Inn

Bank of England

The Gherkin

Aldgate

Tottenham Court Road

Covent Garden

Blackfriars

St Paul's

Mansion House

Cannon Street

Lloyd's Building

Leicester Square

Covent Garden

Temple

Temple

Blackfriars Station

Cannon St Station

Monument

Tower Hill

National Gallery

Charing Cross Station

Victoria Embankment

MILLENNIUM BRIDGE

Tower of London

River Thames

Charing Cross

Embankment

South Bank Centre

2 Tate Modern

Southwark Cathedral

London Bridge

London Bridge Station

St James's Park

London Eye

Waterloo

Southwark

3 The Shard **4**

SEE 'BANKSIDE AND SOUTHWARK' MAP FOR DETAIL

Westminster

Waterloo Station

SEE 'THE SOUTH BANK' MAP FOR DETAIL

Lambeth North

Borough

12

Westminster Abbey

Houses of Parliament

3

Lambeth Palace

ST GEORGE'S ROAD

SEE 'THE WEST END AND WESTMINSTER' MAP FOR DETAIL

Imperial War Museum

Elephant & Castle

NEW KENT ROAD

Tate Britain

Pimlico

Kennington

Vauxhall

13 **14**

15

The Oval

Oval

0   500
yards

■ LGBT+ NIGHTLIFE	
Bootylicious	13
The Eagle	15
Fire	16
Royal Vauxhall Tavern	14

■ DRINKING	
The Constitution	6
Edinboro Castle	9
Princess Louise	11
The Roebuck	12
Spaniards Inn	1

■ NIGHTLIFE	
Brixton Academy	17
Bussey Building	19
Forum	2
Green Note	8
Hootananny	18
Jazz Café	7
KOKO	10
Proud	5
Roundhouse	4
Union Chapel	3

▼ Lambeth, Brixton, **17**, **5**, **18** & Dulwich   ▼ **19**

1

The Sainsbury Wing (1200–1500)

Predominantly filled with medieval Italian works, the Sainsbury Wing's sixteen rooms start with fragments from Sienese artist Duccio's *Maestà* altarpiece. The collection's early masterpieces here include Uccello's *Battle of San Romano*, Botticelli's *Venus and Mars* (inspired by a Dante sonnet) and Piero della Francesca's beautifully composed *Baptism of Christ*. Drawing the crowds is Leonardo's melancholic *Virgin of the Rocks*, hung next to the exquisitely delicate *Burlington House Cartoon* preparatory sketch. In among the Italians, you'll find the extraordinarily vivid **Wilton Diptych**, one of the few British medieval altarpieces to survive the Puritan iconoclasm of the Commonwealth, while in room 56 another standout is Jan van Eyck's intriguing *Arnolfini Portrait*, which is celebrated for its complex symbolism. Finally, don't miss the small, pristinely crisp *Madonna of the Pinks* (room 60), bought by the gallery for £22 million, once its attribution to Raphael had been established.

The main building (1500–1930)

The fine collection of Italian works continues into the much grander main building with large-scale paintings including Veronese's lustrous *Family of Darius before Alexander* displayed in the vast Wohl Room (room 9). Beyond, Holbein's masterful *Ambassadors* is hung alongside his portrait of Erasmus and works by Cranach the Elder. Numerous works by Titian on display include his early masterpiece *Bacchus and Ariadne*.

From **Spain** there are dazzling pieces by El Greco, Goya, Murillo and Velázquez, among them the provocative *Rokeby Venus*, while from the Dutch Golden Age, the gallery owns numerous Rembrandt paintings, including some of his most searching portraits – two of them self-portraits – and a typically serene Vermeer, as well as abundant examples of Rubens' expansive, fleshy canvases. The gallery owns several works by Caravaggio, including *Salome receives the head of John the Baptist*.

There's home-grown **British** art, too, represented by important works such as Hogarth's satirical *Marriage à la Mode*, Gainsborough's translucent *Morning Walk*, Constable's ever-popular *Hay Wain*, and Turner's *Fighting Temeraire*. Highlights of the **French** contingent include superb works by Poussin, Claude, Fragonard, Boucher, Watteau and David.

Finally, there's a particularly strong showing of **Impressionists** and **Post-Impressionists** in rooms 43–46. Among the most famous works are Manet's unfinished *Execution of Maximilian*, Renoir's *Umbrellas*, Monet's *Thames below Westminster*, Van Gogh's *Sunflowers*, Seurat's pointillist *Bathers at Asnières*, a Rousseau junglescape and Cézanne's proto-Cubist *Bathers*.

National Portrait Gallery

St Martin's Place, WC2H 0HE • Daily 10am–6pm, Thurs & Fri till 9pm • Free • ☏ 020 7306 0055, ⊚ npg.org.uk • ⊖ Charing Cross

Around the east side of the National Gallery lurks the **National Portrait Gallery**, founded in 1856 to house uplifting depictions of the good and the great. Though it undoubtedly has some fine works among its collection of ten thousand portraits, many of the studies are of less interest than their subjects. Nevertheless, it's fascinating to trace who has been deemed worthy of admiration at any one time: aristocrats and artists in previous centuries, warmongers and imperialists in the early decades of the twentieth century, writers and poets in the 1930s and 1940s, and, latterly, retired footballers, and film and pop stars. The NPG's **audioguide** gives useful biographical information, and the temporary exhibitions, including the annual portrait award, are often worth catching.

Whitehall

Whitehall, the unusually broad avenue connecting Trafalgar Square to Parliament Square, is synonymous with the faceless, pinstriped bureaucracy charged with the

day-to-day running of the country, who inhabit the governmental ministries which line
the street. During the sixteenth and seventeenth centuries, however, Whitehall was the
permanent residence of the kings and queens of England.

The statues dotted about recall the days when Whitehall stood at the centre of an
empire on which the sun never set. Halfway down, in the middle of the road, stands
Edwin Lutyens' **Cenotaph**, a memorial to the war dead, erected after World War I and
the centrepiece of the Remembrance Sunday ceremony in November. Close by are the
gates of Downing Street, home to London's most famous address, **Number 10 Downing
Street**, the seventeenth-century terraced house that has been the official residence of
the prime minister since it was presented to Sir Robert Walpole, Britain's first PM, by
George II in 1732.

Banqueting House

Whitehall, SW1A 2ER • Daily 10am–5pm but frequent early closures so ring or check website before visiting; last entry 4.30pm • £6.50 •
☎ 020 3166 6154, ⓦ hrp.org.uk • ⊖ Charing Cross

Whitehall Palace was originally the London seat of the Archbishop of York, confiscated
and greatly extended by Henry VIII after a fire at Westminster forced him to find
alternative accommodation. The chief section of the old palace to survive the 1698
fire was the **Banqueting House** begun by Inigo Jones in 1619 and the first Palladian
building to be built in England. The one room open to the public has no original
furnishings, but features superlative Rubens ceiling paintings glorifying the Stuart
dynasty, commissioned by Charles I in the 1630s. Charles himself walked through the
room for the last time in 1649 when he stepped onto the executioner's scaffold from
one of its windows.

Horse Guards and the Household Cavalry Museum

Whitehall, SW1A 2AX • Daily: April–Oct 10am–6pm (part-day closures through May & June); Nov–March 10am–5pm • £7 • ☎ 020 7930
3070, ⓦ householdcavalrymuseum.co.uk • ⊖ Charing Cross or Westminster

Two mounted sentries of the Queen's Household Cavalry and two horseless colleagues
are posted to protect **Horse Guards**, originally the main gateway to St James's Park
and Buckingham Palace. Round the back of the building, you'll find the **Household
Cavalry Museum** where you can learn about the regiments' history. With the stables
immediately adjacent, it's a sweet-smelling place, and – horse-lovers will be pleased
to know – you can see the beasts in their stalls through a glass screen. Don't miss the
pocket riot act on display, which ends with the wise warning: "must read correctly:
variance fatal".

Churchill War Rooms

King Charles St, SW1A 2AQ • Daily 9.30am–6pm; June–Aug till 7pm • £19 • ☎ 020 7416 5000, ⓦ iwm.org.uk • ⊖ Westminster

In 1938, in anticipation of Nazi air raids, the basements of the civil service buildings
on the south side of King Charles Street, south of Downing Street, were converted into
the **Cabinet War Rooms**. It was here that Winston Churchill directed operations and

---

CHANGING THE GUARD

The Queen is Colonel-in-Chief of the seven **Household Regiments**: the Life Guards and the
Blues and Royals are the two Household Cavalry regiments; while the Grenadier, Coldstream,
Scots, Irish and Welsh Guards make up the Foot Guards.

Changing the Guard takes place at two London locations: the Foot Guards march with a
band to Buckingham Palace (May–July daily 11.30am; Aug–April alternate days; no ceremony
if it rains; ⓦ royal.gov.uk) – they're best sighted coming down the Mall around 11.15am. The
Household Cavalry have a ceremony at Horse Guards on Whitehall (Mon–Sat 11am, Sun 10am,
with an elaborate inspection at 4pm), and they don't care if it rains or shines. A ceremony also
takes place regularly at Windsor Castle (see page 249).

1

THE WEST END AND WESTMINSTER

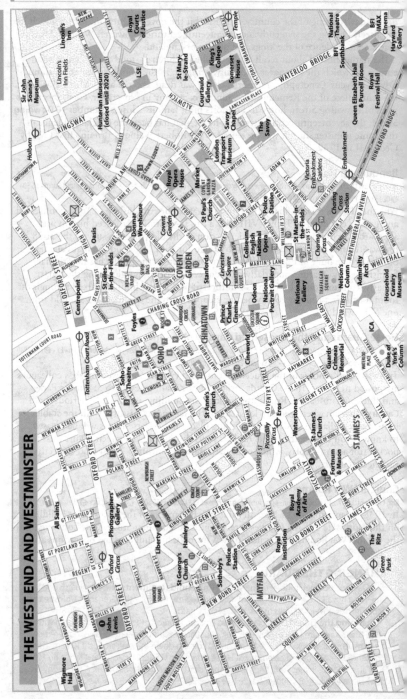

1

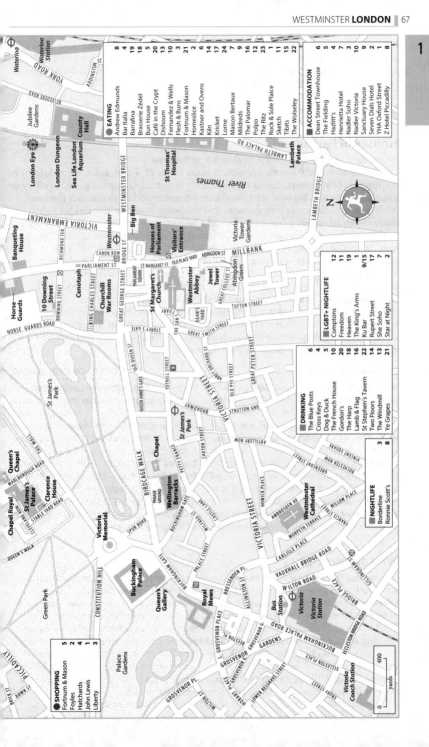

● **SHOPPING**
Fortnum & Mason — 5
Foyles — 2
Hatchards — 4
John Lewis — 1
Liberty — 3

● **EATING**
Andrew Edmunds — 8
Bar Italia — 4
Barrafina — 19
Brasserie Zédel — 18
Bun House — 15
Café in the Crypt — 20
Dishoom — 13
Fernandez & Wells — 10
Flesh & Buns — 21
Fortnum & Mason — 2
Homeslice — 6
Kastner and Ovens — 14
Kiln — 17
Kricket — 24
Lorne — 7
Maison Bertaux — 9
Mildreds — 16
The Palomar — 12
Polpo — 23
The Ritz — 1
Rock & Sole Plaice — 11
Sketch — 15
Tibits — 3
The Wolseley — 22

■ **ACCOMMODATION**
Dean Street Townhouse — 6
The Fielding — 5
Hazlitt's — 4
Henrietta Hotel — 7
Nadler Soho — 3
Nadler Victoria — 10
Sanctuary House — 3
Seven Dials Hotel — 9
YHA Oxford Street — 2
Z Hotel Piccadilly — 8

■ **LGBT+ NIGHTLIFE**
Comptons — 12
Freedom — 11
Heaven — 19
The King's Arms — 1
Ku Bar — 9/15
Rupert Street — 17
She Soho — 14
Star at Night — 13
Two Floors — 22

■ **DRINKING**
The Blue Posts — 6
Cross Keys — 4
Dog & Duck — 10
The French House — 20
Gordon's — 5
The Harp — 18
Lamb & Flag — 16
St Stephen's Tavern — 22
Two Floors — 14
The Windmill — 13
Ye Grapes — 21

■ **NIGHTLIFE**
Borderline — 3
Ronnie Scott's — 8

1

held Cabinet meetings for the duration of World War II, and the rooms have been left pretty much as they were when they were finally abandoned on VJ Day 1945, making for an atmospheric underground trot through wartime London. Also in the basement is the excellent **Churchill Museum**, where you can hear snippets of Churchill's most famous speeches and check out his trademark bowler, spotted bow tie and half-chewed Havana, not to mention his wonderful burgundy zip-up "romper suit".

Houses of Parliament

Parliament Square, SW1A 0AA • ☎ 020 7219 4114, ⓦ parliament.uk • ⊖ Westminster

Perhaps London's best-known monument is the Palace of Westminster, better known as the **Houses of Parliament**, thanks to its instantly recognizable, ornate, gilded clocktower popularly known as **Big Ben**, after the thirteen-tonne main bell that strikes the hour. Such is its national status that the news that the bongs would be silenced for four years during essential repairs to the tower brought howls of protest from traditionalist MPs (repairs are due to be completed in 2021, though it will still ring out at New Year and for other major occasions). The original medieval palace burned down in 1834, and everything you see now – save for Westminster Hall – is the work of **Charles Barry**, who created an orgy of honey-coloured pinnacles, turrets and tracery that attempts to express national greatness through the use of Gothic and Elizabethan styles. It's undoubtedly the city's finest Victorian Gothic Revival building, and the Victorian love of mock-Gothic detail is as apparent throughout the interior, where the fittings were largely the responsibility of Barry's assistant, **Augustus Pugin**. Tours start with the eleventh-century **Westminster Hall**, with its huge oak hammer-beam roof: one of the most magnificent secular medieval halls in Europe.

INFORMATION AND TOURS

HOUSES OF PARLIAMENT

Tours Saturday year-round, plus Mon–Fri during parliamentary recess (usually 9.20am–4.30pm; 1hr 15min self-guided audio tours £18.50 advance/£20.50 on the day; 1hr 30min guided tours £25.50 advance/£28 on the day; ☎ 020 7219 4114; ⓦ parliament.uk/visiting). Advance booking is recommended and cheaper, or buy tickets on the day from the ticket office at the front of Portcullis House, on Victoria Embankment. UK residents are entitled to a free guided tour of the palace, which needs to be organized through your local MP's office.

Public galleries To watch proceedings in either the House of Commons – the livelier of the two – or the House of Lords,

join the queue for the public galleries at the Cromwell Green visitor entrance during sitting times. For a full schedule of debates phone ☎ 020 7219 4272, or visit ⓦ parliament. uk. For the House of Commons, regular sitting times are Mon 2.30–10.30pm, Tues & Wed 11.30am–7.30pm, Thurs 9.30am–5.30pm and occasionally Fri 9.30am–3pm.

Question Time UK citizens can attend Prime Minister's Question Time (Wed noon–12.30pm) – when the House of Commons is at its liveliest – and ministerial Question Times (Mon 2.30pm, Tues 11.30am, Thurs 9.30am); book in advance with your MP's office, though members of the public will be let in if there's space.

Westminster Abbey

Parliament Square, SW1P 3PA • **Abbey** Mon–Sat 9.30am–4.30pm, Wed until 7pm, last admission on any day 1hr before closing • £20 in advance or £22 on the day, including audioguide • **Verger tours** Mon–Sat times vary • £5 • **Great Cloisters** Daily 9.30am–4.30pm • **College Garden** Tues–Thurs: April–Sept 10am–6pm; Oct–March 10am–4pm • Entry to cloisters and garden included in cost of ticket to abbey but free on Sundays when entry is via Dean's Yard • ☎ 020 7222 5152, ⓦ westminster-abbey.org • ⊖ Westminster

The Houses of Parliament dwarf their much older neighbour, **Westminster Abbey**, yet this single building embodies much of the history of England: it has been the venue for all coronations since the time of William the Conqueror, and the site of more or less every royal burial for some five hundred years between the reigns of Henry III and George II. Scores of the nation's most famous citizens are honoured here, too; and the interior is crammed with hundreds of monuments and statues.

Entry is via the north transept, which is cluttered with monuments to politicians and traditionally known as **Statesmen's Aisle**, beyond which is the main **nave**: narrow, light and, at over 100ft in height, one of the tallest in the country. The most famous monument in this section is the **Tomb of the Unknown Soldier**, near the west door. Passing through the choir, you reach the central sanctuary, site of the coronations, and the wonderful **Cosmati floor mosaic**, constructed in the thirteenth century by Italian craftsmen.

Henry VII's Chapel and Shrine of Edward the Confessor

The abbey's most dazzling architectural set piece, the **Lady Chapel**, is better known as **Henry VII's Chapel**, after the Tudor monarch who added it in 1503 as his future resting place. With its intricately carved vaulting and fan-shaped gilded pendants, the chapel represents the last spectacular gasp of English Perpendicular Gothic.

As you leave Henry VII's Chapel, look out for Edward I's **Coronation Chair**, a decrepit oak throne dating from around 1300 and used in every coronation since 1308. Behind the high altar, the **Shrine of Edward the Confessor** is the sacred heart of the building, now only accessible on a guided tour.

Poets' Corner

Nowadays, the abbey's royal tombs are upstaged by **Poets' Corner**, in the south transept, though the first occupant, Geoffrey Chaucer, was in fact buried here not because he was a poet, but because he lived nearby. By the eighteenth century this zone had become an artistic pantheon; those buried here include Charles Dickens and Thomas Hardy, while there are memorials to Shakespeare, Oscar Wilde and William Blake.

Great Cloisters

Doors in the south choir aisle (plus a separate entrance from Dean's Yard) lead to the **Great Cloisters**. On the east side lies the octagonal Chapter House, where the House of Commons met from 1257, boasting thirteenth-century apocalyptic wall paintings. Also worth a look is the museum, filled with generations of royal funereal effigies.

Tate Britain

Millbank, SW1P 4RG · Daily 10am–6pm; usually first Fri of month until 10pm · Free; charge for some temporary exhibitions (around £16–18) · ☎ 020 7887 8888, ⓦ tate.org.uk · ⊖ Pimlico

A purpose-built gallery half a mile south of Parliament, founded in 1897 with money from sugar baron Henry Tate, **Tate Britain** is devoted to British art. The collection covers 1500 to the present, and the gallery also puts on large-scale temporary exhibitions that showcase British artists.

The pictures are largely hung chronologically, so you begin with the richly bejewelled portraits of the Elizabethan nobility, before moving on to Britain's most famous artists – Hogarth, Constable, Gainsborough, Reynolds – plus foreign-born artists like Van Dyck who spent much of their career in Britain. The ever-popular **Pre-Raphaelites** are always well represented, as are established twentieth-century greats such as Stanley Spencer and Francis Bacon alongside living artists such as David Hockney and Bridget Riley. Lastly, don't miss the Tate's outstanding **Turner collection**, displayed in the Turner Wing, and the room dedicated to William Blake on its upper floor.

Westminster Cathedral

Victoria St, SW1P 1LT · **Cathedral** Mon–Fri 7am–7pm, Sat 8am–7pm, Sun 8am–8pm · Free · **Tower** Mon–Fri 9.30am–5pm, Sat & Sun 9.30am–6pm · £6 · ☎ 020 7798 9055, ⓦ westminstercathedral.org.uk · ⊖ Victoria

Begun in 1895, the stripy neo-Byzantine concoction of the Roman Catholic **Westminster Cathedral** was one of the last and wildest monuments to the Victorian era. It's constructed from more than twelve million terracotta-coloured bricks, decorated with hoops of Portland stone – "blood and bandages" style, as it's known – and culminates in a magnificent tapered tower which rises to 274ft, served by a lift. The

1

interior is only half finished, so to get an idea of what the place will look like when it's finally completed, explore the series of **side chapels** whose rich, multicoloured decor makes use of more than one hundred different marbles from around the world.

St James's

St James's, the exclusive little enclave sandwiched between St James's Park and Piccadilly, was laid out in the 1670s close to St James's Palace. Regal and aristocratic residences overlook Green Park, gentlemen's clubs cluster along Pall Mall and St James's Street, while jacket-and-tie restaurants and expense-account gentlemen's outfitters line Jermyn Street, giving the area an air of exclusivity that's rare in London. Open to all, though, is **St James's Park**, with large numbers heading for the Queen's chief residence, **Buckingham Palace**, and the adjacent Queen's Gallery and Royal Mews.

The Mall

Laid out as a memorial to Queen Victoria, the tree-lined sweep of **The Mall** is at its best on Sundays, when it's closed to traffic. The bombastic **Admiralty Arch** was erected to mark the entrance at the Trafalgar Square end of The Mall, while at the Buckingham Palace end stands the ludicrous **Victoria Memorial**, Edward VII's overblown 2300-ton marble tribute to his mother, which is topped by a gilded statue of Victory. Four outlying allegorical groups in bronze confidently proclaim the great achievements of her reign.

St James's Park

SW1A 2BJ · Daily 5am–midnight · Free · ☎ 0300 061 2350, ⓦ royalparks.org.uk

Flanking nearly the whole length of the Mall, **St James's Park** is the oldest of the royal parks, having been drained and enclosed for hunting purposes by Henry VIII. It was landscaped by Nash in the 1820s, and today its lake is a favourite picnic spot. Pelicans – originally a gift from the Russians to Charles II – can still be seen at the eastern end of the lake, and there are exotic ducks, swans and geese aplenty.

Buckingham Palace

The Mall, SW1A 1AA · Late July to late Aug 9.30am–7.30pm, last admission 5.15pm; Sept 9.30am–6.30pm, last admission 4.15pm · State Rooms: £23, including garden highlights: £32.50 · ☎ 030 3123 7300, ⓦ royalcollection.org.uk · ⊖ Green Park or Victoria

The graceless colossus of **Buckingham Palace** has served as the monarch's permanent London residence only since the accession of Victoria. Bought by George III in 1762, the building was overhauled in the late 1820s by Nash and again in 1913, producing a palace that's as bland as it's possible to be.

For a few months a year, the hallowed portals are grudgingly nudged open. The interior, however, is a bit of an anticlimax: of the palace's 750 rooms you're permitted to see twenty or so, and there's little sign of life, as the Queen decamps to Scotland every summer. For the rest of the year the only draw is to watch **Changing the Guard** (see page 65), in which a detachment of the Queen's Foot Guards marches to appropriate martial music from St James's Palace and Wellington Barracks to the palace forecourt (unless it rains, that is).

TOP 5 QUIRKY MUSEUMS

Dennis Severs' House Spitalfields. See page 88
Horniman Museum Forest Hill. See page 109
Old Operating Theatre and Herb Garret Borough. See page 96
Sir John Soane's Museum Holborn. See page 80
Wellcome Collection Euston. See page 78

Queen's Gallery

Buckingham Palace Rd, SW1A 1AA • Daily: Aug & Sept 9.30am–5.30pm; Oct–July 10am–5.30pm • £11 • ☎ 030 3123 7301, ⓦ royalcollection.org.uk • ⊖ Victoria

A Doric portico on the south side of Buckingham Palace forms the entrance to the **Queen's Gallery**, which puts on temporary exhibitions drawn from the **Royal Collection**, a superlative array of art that includes works by Michelangelo, Raphael, Holbein, Reynolds, Gainsborough, Vermeer, Van Dyck, Rubens, Rembrandt and Canaletto, as well as the world's largest collection of Leonardo drawings, the odd Fabergé egg and heaps of Sèvres china.

Royal Mews

Buckingham Palace Rd, SW1W 1QH • April–Oct daily 10am–5pm; Feb, March & Nov Mon–Sat 10am–4pm • £10; combined ticket with Queen's Gallery £19 • ☎ 030 3123 7302, ⓦ royalcollection.org.uk • ⊖ Victoria

Royal carriages are the main attraction at the Nash-built **Royal Mews**, in particular the Gold State Coach, made for George III in 1762 and used in every coronation since. It's smothered in 22-carat gilding and weighs four tonnes, its axles supporting four life-sized figures.

St James's Palace

Marlborough Rd, SW1A 1BS • **Chapel Royal** Oct–Good Friday services Sun 8.30am & 11.15am • **Queen's Chapel** Easter Sun–July services Sun 8.30am & 11.15am • ⊖ Green Park

St James's Palace's main red-brick gate-tower is pretty much all that remains of the Tudor palace erected here by Henry VIII in the 1530s. When Whitehall Palace burned down in 1698, St James's became the principal royal residence and, in keeping with tradition, every ambassador to the UK is still accredited to the "Court of St James's", even though the court has since moved down the road to Buckingham Palace. The modest, rambling, crenellated complex is off limits to the public, with the exception of the **Chapel Royal**, situated within the palace, and the **Queen's Chapel**, on the other side of Marlborough Road, both of which are open for services only.

Clarence House

The Mall, SW1 1BA • Aug Mon–Fri 10am–4.30pm, Sat & Sun 10am–5.30pm, last admission 1hr before closing; visits (by guided tour) must be booked in advance • £10 • ☎ 020 7766 7303, ⓦ royalcollection.org.uk • ⊖ Green Park

Clarence House, connected to the palace's southwest wing, was home to the Queen Mother, and now serves as the official London home of Charles and his second wife, Camilla, but a handful of rooms can be visited over the summer when the royals are in Scotland. The interior is pretty unremarkable, so apart from a peek behind the scenes in a working royal palace, or a few mementos of the Queen Mum, the main draw is the twentieth-century British paintings on display by the likes of Walter Sickert and Augustus John.

Mayfair

Piccadilly, which forms the southern border of swanky **Mayfair**, may not be the fashionable promenade it started out as in the eighteenth century, but a whiff of exclusivity still pervades **Bond Street** and its tributaries, where designer clothes emporia jostle for space with jewellers, bespoke tailors and fine art dealers. **Regent Street** and **Oxford Street**, meanwhile, are home to the flagship branches of the country's most popular chain stores.

1

OXFORD STREET: THE BUSIEST STREET IN EUROPE

As wealthy Londoners began to move out of the City in the eighteenth century in favour of the newly developed West End, so **Oxford Street** – the old Roman road to Oxford – gradually became London's main shopping thoroughfare. Today, despite successive recessions and sky-high rents, Oxford Street remains Europe's busiest street, simply because this two-mile hotchpotch of shops is home to (often several) flagship branches of Britain's major retailers. The street's only real architectural landmark is **Selfridges** (see page 136), which opened in 1909 and has a facade featuring the Queen of Time riding the ship of commerce and supporting an Art Deco clock.

Regent Street

Regent Street, drawn up by John Nash in 1812 as both a luxury shopping street and a triumphal way between George IV's Carlton House and Regent's Park, was the city's earliest attempt at dealing with traffic congestion, slum clearance and planned social segregation, something that would later be perfected by the Victorians. The increase in the purchasing power of the city's middle classes in the last century brought the tone of the street "down" and heavyweight stores now predominate. Among the best known are **Hamley's**, reputedly the world's largest toyshop, and **Liberty**, the upmarket department store that popularized Arts and Crafts designs.

Piccadilly

Piccadilly apparently got its name from the ruffs or "pickadills" worn by the dandies who used to promenade here in the late seventeenth century. It's not much of a place for promenading today, however, with traffic nose to tail most of the day and night. Infinitely more pleasant places to window-shop are the various **nineteenth-century arcades** that shoot off to the north and south, grandest of which is the Burlington Arcade, built to protect shoppers from the mud and horse dung on the streets, but now equally useful for escaping exhaust fumes.

Royal Academy of Arts

Piccadilly, W1J 0BD • Daily 10am–6pm, Fri till 10pm • Special exhibitions from £12 • Regular guided tours of building (check online) • ☎ 020 7300 8000, ⓦ royalacademy.org.uk • ⊖ Green Park

The **Royal Academy of Arts** occupies one of the few surviving aristocratic mansions that once lined the north side of Piccadilly. Rebuilding in the nineteenth century destroyed the original curved colonnades beyond the main gateway, but the complex has kept the feel of a Palladian *palazzo*. The country's first-ever formal art school, founded in 1768, the RA hosts a wide range of art exhibitions, and an annual **Summer Exhibition** whereby anyone can enter paintings in any style, and the lucky winners get hung, in rather close proximity, and are for sale. RA "Academicians" are allowed to display six of their own works – no matter how awful. The result is a bewildering display, which gets panned annually by highbrow critics, but enjoyed happily by everyone else. Other temporary exhibitions range from Rubens to Ai Weiwei, while the **Collections Gallery** in the rear building – connected by a David Chipperfield-designed concrete bridge and opening in 2018 – displays highlights from the Royal Academy's eclectic permanent collection, including Michelangelo's marble relief, the *Taddei Tondo*.

Bond Street

Bond Street, which runs parallel with Regent Street and is lined with designer shops, art galleries and auction houses, carefully maintains its exclusivity. It is, in fact, two streets rolled into one: the southern half, laid out in the 1680s, is known as Old Bond Street; its northern extension, which followed less than fifty years later, is known as New Bond Street. They are both pretty unassuming streets architecturally, yet the shops that line them are among the flashiest in London, dominated by perfumeries, jewellers and designer clothing stores. In addition to fashion, Bond Street is also renowned for its fine art galleries and its **auction houses**, the oldest of which is Sotheby's, 34–35 New Bond St, whose viewing galleries are open free of charge.

Marylebone

Marylebone, which lies to the north of Oxford Street, is, like Mayfair, another grid-plan Georgian development. Marylebone High Street retains a leisurely, village-like ambience, and has some good independent shops. The area boasts a very fine art gallery, the **Wallace Collection**, and, in its northern fringes, one of London's biggest tourist attractions, **Madame Tussauds**, plus the ever-popular **Sherlock Holmes Museum**.

Wallace Collection

Manchester Square, W1U 3BN • Daily 10am–5pm • Free • Free guided tours daily 2.30pm, Sat & Sun also 11.30am • ☎ 020 7563 9500, ⓦ wallacecollection.org • ⊖ Bond Street

Housed in a well-preserved, eighteenth-century manor, incongruously situated not far from the hubbub of Oxford Street, the splendid **Wallace Collection** is best known for its eighteenth-century French paintings, Franz Hals' *Laughing Cavalier*, Titian's *Perseus and Andromeda*, Velázquez's *Lady with a Fan* and Rembrandt's affectionate portrait of his teenage son, Titus. It was bequeathed to the nation in 1897 by the widow of Richard Wallace, an art collector and the illegitimate son of the fourth Marquess of Hertford, and the museum has preserved the feel of a grand stately home, its exhibits piled high in glass cabinets, and paintings covering almost every inch of wall space. The fact that these exhibits are set amid priceless Boulle furniture – and a bloody great armoury – makes the place even more remarkable.

Madame Tussauds

Marylebone Rd, NW1 5LR • Times vary, but generally: Sept–June Mon–Fri 9am–4pm, Sat & Sun 9am–5pm; July, Aug & peak times daily 8.30am–6pm • Advance booking online £29/on the day £35 • ⓦ madametussauds.com • ⊖ Baker Street

Madame Tussauds has been pulling in the crowds ever since the good lady arrived in London from Paris in 1802 bearing the sculpted heads of guillotined aristocrats. The entrance fee might be extortionate and the waxwork likenesses of the famous occasionally dubious, but you can still rely on finding London's biggest queues here (book online to avoid waiting). Inside, they change exhibits regularly, but one of the more original experiences is the **Spirit of London**, an irreverent five-minute romp through the history of London in a miniaturized taxicab.

Sherlock Holmes Museum

239 Baker St, NW1 6XE • Daily 9.30am–6pm • £15 • ☎ 020 7224 3688, ⓦ sherlock-holmes.co.uk • ⊖ Baker Street

Baker Street is synonymous with Sherlock Holmes, the fictional detective who lived at no. 221b (the number on the door of the museum, though it's actually at no. 239). Unashamedly touristy, the **Sherlock Holmes Museum** is stuffed full of Victoriana and life-size models of characters from the books. It's an atmospheric and competent exercise in period reconstruction, though it won't take you long to see everything.

Soho

Bounded by Regent Street to the west, Oxford Street to the north and Charing Cross Road to the east, **Soho** is very much the heart of the West End. It was the city's premier red-light

1

district for centuries and, even as major developments encroach, it retains an unorthodox and slightly raffish air that's unique in central London. It has an immigrant history as rich as that of the East End and a louche nightlife that has attracted writers, musicians and revellers of every sexual persuasion since the eighteenth century. Conventional sights are few, yet, away from the big tourist junctions of Piccadilly Circus and Leicester Square, there's probably more interesting street life here than anywhere in the city centre, whatever the hour. Today it's London's most high-profile LGBT+ quarter, especially around **Old Compton Street**, with Greek, Frith and Dean streets, which cut across it, home to a mix of old-style Soho venues, such as *Ronnie Scott's* on Frith Street – London's longest running jazz club – cellar bars and some good restaurants. At the north end is Soho Square, the area's main green space. Dividing Soho in two is busy **Wardour Street**, with nearby **Berwick Street** known for its street market, record and fabric stores. At the western end, near Regent Street, you'll find **Carnaby Street**, made famous as the place to buy your miniskirts in the swinging 1960s, when Mary Quant had a shop here. Nowadays, it has a decent mix of chain stores, while you can find some more interesting one-off boutiques and places to eat just off it along **Foubert's Place** and **Newburgh Street** and in **Kingly Court**.

Piccadilly Circus

Anonymous and congested, **Piccadilly Circus** is a much-altered product of Nash's grand 1812 Regent Street plan and now a major traffic interchange. It may not be a picturesque place, but thanks to its celebrated aluminium statue, popularly known as **Eros**, it's prime tourist territory. The fountain's archer is one of the city's top attractions, a status that baffles all who live here. Despite the bow and arrow, the figure is not the god of love at all but his lesser-known brother, Anteros, god of requited love, commemorating the selfless philanthropic love of the Earl of Shaftesbury, a Bible-thumping social reformer who campaigned against child labour.

Leicester Square

When the big cinemas and nightclubs are doing good business, and the buskers are entertaining the crowds, **Leicester Square** is one of the most crowded places in London, particularly on a Friday or Saturday when huge numbers of tourists and half the youth of the suburbs seem to congregate here. It wasn't until the mid-nineteenth century that the square actually began to emerge as an entertainment zone; cinema moved in during the 1930s, a golden age evoked by the sleek black lines of the Odeon on the east side.

Chinatown

Chinatown, hemmed in between Leicester Square and Shaftesbury Avenue, is a self-contained jumble of shops, cafés and restaurants. Only a minority of London's Chinese live in these three small blocks, but it remains a focus for the community, a place to do business or the weekly shop, celebrate a wedding, or just meet up for meals, particularly on Sundays, when the restaurants overflow with Chinese families tucking into *dim sum*. **Gerrard Street** is the main drag, where you'll see telephone kiosks rigged out as pagodas and fake Chinese gates or *paifang*.

Old Compton Street

If Soho has a main road, it would be **Old Compton Street**, which runs parallel with Shaftesbury Avenue. The shops, boutiques and cafés here are typical of the area and a good barometer of the latest fads. Soho has been a permanent fixture on the **LGBT+ scene** for the better part of a century, and you'll find a profusion of gay bars, clubs and cafés jostling for position here and at the junction with Wardour Street.

Photographers' Gallery

16–18 Ramillies St, W1F 7LW • Mon–Sat 10am–6pm, Thurs till 8pm, Sun 11–6pm • £4, free before noon • ☎ 020 7087 9300, ⓦ thephotographersgallery.org.uk • ⊖ Oxford Circus

Established in 1971, the **Photographers' Gallery** was the first independent gallery devoted to photography in London, and is now the city's largest public photographic gallery. This former warehouse hosts three floors of exhibitions that change regularly and are invariably worth a visit, as are the bookshop and café. There's also a **camera obscura** in the third-floor studio (open when the studio isn't in use).

Covent Garden and Strand

More sanitized and commercial than neighbouring Soho, the shops and restaurants of **Covent Garden** today are a far cry from the district's heyday when the piazza was the great playground (and red-light district) of eighteenth-century London. The buskers in front of St Paul's Church, the theatres round about, and the **Royal Opera House** on Bow Street are survivors of this tradition, and on a balmy summer evening, **Covent Garden Piazza** is still an undeniably lively place to be, while the streets to the north, around Neal Street, and the Seven Dials junction, including Monmouth Street and the tucked-away **Neal's Yard**, are better for browsing and people-watching. On the area's southern edge, the **Strand**, a busy thoroughfare connecting Westminster to the City, was once famous for its riverside mansions, though only **Somerset House**, on the north side of Waterloo Bridge, remains.

Covent Garden Piazza

London's oldest planned square, laid out in the 1630s by Inigo Jones, **Covent Garden Piazza** was initially a great success, its novelty value alone attracting a rich and aristocratic clientele, but over the next century the tone of the place fell as the fruit and vegetable market expanded, and theatres, coffee houses and brothels began to take over the peripheral buildings. When the market closed in 1974, the piazza narrowly survived being turned into an office development. Instead, the elegant Victorian market hall and its environs were restored to house shops, restaurants and arts-and-crafts stalls. Of Jones's original piazza, the only remaining parts are the two rebuilt sections of north-side arcading, and **St Paul's Church**, to the west.

London Transport Museum

Covent Garden Piazza, WC2E 7BB • Daily 10am–6pm, Fri opens 11am • Adults £17.50, under-16s free; tickets are valid for unlimited entries for a year • ☎ 020 7379 6344, ⓦ ltmuseum.co.uk • ⊖ Covent Garden

A former flower-market shed on Covent Garden Piazza's east side is home to the **London Transport Museum**, a sure-fire hit for families. To follow the displays chronologically, head for Level 2, where you'll find a reconstructed 1829 Shillibeer's Horse Omnibus, which provided the city's first regular horse-bus service. Level 1 tells the story of the world's first underground system and contains a lovely 1920s Metropolitan Line carriage in burgundy and green with pretty, drooping lamps. On the ground floor, one double-decker **tram** is all that's left to pay tribute to the world's largest tram system, dismantled in 1952. Look out, too, for the first **tube** train, from the 1890s, whose lack of windows earned it the nickname "the padded cell".

Royal Opera House

Bow St, WC2E 9DD • Backstage tours (booked in advance): usually Mon–Sat 10.30am, 12.30pm & 2.30pm • ☎ 020 7304 4000, ⓦ roh.org.uk • ⊖ Covent Garden

The arcading on the northeast side of the piazza was rebuilt as part of the redevelopment of the **Royal Opera House**, whose main Neoclassical facade dates from 1811 and opens onto Bow Street. The adjoining Victorian wrought-iron-and-glass

1

structure is the Floral Hall, once home to Covent Garden's flower market and now the **Paul Hamlyn Hall**, a spectacular setting for the theatre's champagne bar (open 1hr 30min before performances). Some areas of the Opera House are closed for limited periods for refurbishment, which, once complete, will create more public spaces looking out onto the piazza and Bow Street.

Somerset House

The Strand, WC2R 1LA • **Fountain Court** Daily 7.30am–11pm • Free • **Riverside terrace** Daily 8am–11pm • Free • **Guided tours** Thurs 1.15pm & 2.45pm, Sat 12.15pm, 1.15pm, 2.15pm & 3.15pm • Free • **Embankment Galleries** Mon, Tues, Sat & Sun 10am–6pm, Wed–Fri 11am–8pm • £6 • **East and West Wing Galleries** Daily 10am–6pm during exhibitions • Usually free • ☎ 020 7845 4600, Ⓦ somersethouse.org.uk • ⊖ Temple or Covent Garden

Somerset House is the sole survivor of the grandiose river palaces that once lined the Strand. Although it looks like an old aristocratic mansion, the present building was purpose-built in 1776 to house government offices. Nowadays, Somerset House's granite-paved courtyard, which has a 55-jet **fountain** that spouts little syncopated dances straight from the cobbles, is used for open-air performances, concerts, installations and, in winter, an ice rink.

The interior is a network of corridors and exhibition spaces, also housing half a dozen cafés and restaurants. The south wing has a lovely riverside terrace with a café/restaurant and the **Embankment Galleries**, which host special exhibitions on contemporary art and design. You can also admire the Royal Naval Commissioners' superb gilded eighteenth-century barge in the **King's Barge House**, below ground level in the south wing.

Courtauld Gallery

Somerset House, The Strand, WC2R 1LA • Daily 10am–6pm, last entry 5.30pm, Thurs occasionally open until 9pm • £8, more during temporary exhibitions • ☎ 020 7848 2526, Ⓦ courtauld.ac.uk • ⊖ Temple or Covent Garden

In the north wing of Somerset House is the **Courtauld Gallery**, chiefly known for its dazzling collection of Impressionist and Post-Impressionist paintings. Among the most celebrated is a small-scale version of Manet's *Déjeuner sur l'herbe*, Renoir's *La Loge*, and Degas' *Two Dancers*, plus a whole heap of Cézanne's canvases, including one of his series of *Card Players*. The Courtauld also boasts a fine selection of works by the likes of Rubens, Van Dyck, Tiepolo and Cranach the Elder, as well as top-notch twentieth-century paintings and sculptures by, among others, Kandinksy and Matisse.

Bloomsbury and King's Cross

Bloomsbury was built over in grid-plan style from the 1660s onwards, and the formal bourgeois Georgian squares laid out then remain the area's main distinguishing feature. In the twentieth century, Bloomsbury acquired a reputation as the city's most learned quarter, dominated by the dual institutions of the **British Museum** and **London University**, but perhaps best known for its literary inhabitants, among them T.S. Eliot and Virginia Woolf. Today, the British Museum is clearly the star attraction, but there are other minor sights, such as the **Charles Dickens Museum**. Only in its northern fringes does the character of the area change dramatically, as you near the hustle and bustle of **Euston**, **St Pancras** and **King's Cross** train stations, beyond which one section of the Regent's Canal is the focus for an imaginatively designed new quarter that has adapted former industrial structures – gasholders and warehouses – into galleries, parks and luxury apartments.

British Museum

Great Russell St, WC1B 3DG • Daily 10am–5.30pm, Fri till 8.30pm • Free; special exhibitions £12–17; audioguides £6 • **Eye-opener tours** Numerous each day, ask at information desks; 30–40min • Free • **Highlights tour** Fri–Sun 11.30am & 2pm; 1hr 30min • £12 • ☎ 020 7323 8181, Ⓦ britishmuseum.org • ⊖ Tottenham Court Road, Russell Square or Holborn

The **British Museum** is one of the great museums of the world. With more than seventy thousand exhibits ranged over several miles of galleries, it boasts a huge collection of antiquities, prints and drawings. Its assortment of Roman and Greek art is unparalleled, its Egyptian collection is the most significant outside Egypt, and there are fabulous treasures from Anglo-Saxon and Roman Britain, and from China, Japan, India and Mesopotamia.

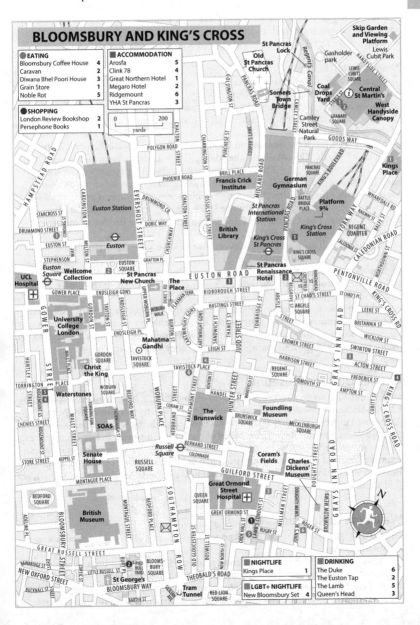

BLOOMSBURY AND KING'S CROSS

EATING

Bloomsbury Coffee House	4
Caravan	2
Diwana Bhel Poori House	3
Grain Store	1
Noble Rot	5

SHOPPING

London Review Bookshop	2
Persephone Books	1

ACCOMMODATION

Arosfa	5
Clink 78	4
Great Northern Hotel	1
Megaro Hotel	2
Ridgemount	6
YHA St Pancras	3

NIGHTLIFE

Kings Place	1

LGBT+ NIGHTLIFE

New Bloomsbury Set	4

DRINKING

The Duke	6
The Euston Tap	2
The Lamb	5
Queen's Head	3

1

The building itself, begun in 1823, is the grandest of London's Greek Revival edifices, dominated by the giant Ionian colonnade and portico that forms the main entrance. At the heart of the museum is the **Great Court**, with its remarkable, curving glass-and-steel roof, designed by Norman Foster. At the centre stands the copper-domed former **Round Reading Room**, built in the 1850s to house the British Library, where Karl Marx penned *Das Kapital* (unfortunately currently closed to the public).

The museum is vast, immensely popular and, on first visit, overwhelming, so it's worth focusing on one or two sections. There are **information desks** in the Great Court, where you can get audioguides and find out about **tours**: the Eye-opener tours, which concentrate on just one or two rooms, are particularly recommended.

The collections

To get a sense of the origins of the collection, start at the ground-floor **Enlightenment gallery** (room 1). Originally the King's Library, this imposing 300ft Neoclassical room was built to house George III's library (now at the British Library), and looks like a very large cabinet of curiosities, full of unusual items that formed the nucleus of the collection.

The most famous of the **Roman and Greek antiquities** are the Parthenon sculptures, better known as the **Elgin Marbles**, after the British aristocrat who acquired the reliefs in 1801. There's a splendid series of **Assyrian reliefs**, depicting events such as the royal lion hunts of Ashurbanipal, in which the king slaughters one of the cats with his bare hands. The **Egyptian collection** of monumental sculptures is impressive, with the ground-floor centrepiece the **Rosetta Stone**, which finally unlocked the secret of Egyptian hieroglyphs. On the first floor, it's the remarkable collection of **mummies** that draws the biggest crowds.

The leathery half-corpse of the 2000-year-old **Lindow Man**, discovered in a Cheshire bog, and the Anglo-Saxon treasure from the **Sutton Hoo** ship burial, are among the highlights of the prehistoric and Romano-British section. The medieval and modern collections, meanwhile, include the exquisite twelfth-century **Lewis chessmen**, carved from walrus ivory.

Further rooms cover European Renaissance treasures, Mexico and North America, plus Africa, Islamic art, Japan, Korea and China – including a remarkable collection of Chinese porcelain. There are also changing exhibits from the museum's large collection of prints and drawings, and rooms devoted to money and clocks.

Charles Dickens Museum

48 Doughty St, WC1N 2LX • Tues–Sun 10am–5pm, last admission 4pm • £9 • ☎ 020 7405 2127, ⓦ dickensmuseum.com • ⊖ Russell Square

Charles Dickens moved to Doughty Street in 1837, shortly after his marriage to Catherine Hogarth, and they lived here for two years, during which time he wrote *Nicholas Nickleby* and *Oliver Twist*. Much of the house's furniture belonged, at one time or another, to Dickens. Also on display are numerous portraits, including the earliest known portrait of the writer (a miniature painted by his aunt in 1830), and original, heavily annotated manuscripts. The museum puts on special exhibitions, and you'll also find a café here.

Wellcome Collection

183 Euston Rd, NW1 2BE • Tues–Sat 10am–6pm, Thurs till 10pm, Sun 11am–6pm • Free • ☎ 020 7611 2222, ⓦ wellcomecollection.org • ⊖ Euston or Euston Square

The **Wellcome Collection** is the foundation established by American-born pharmaceutical magnate Henry Wellcome (1853–1936). It puts on thought-provoking scientifically themed exhibitions, and has various permanent displays, the one unmissable one being **Medicine Man**, which showcases the weird and wonderful collection of historical and scientific artefacts amassed by Henry Wellcome. These range from Florence Nightingale's moccasins to a mummified human body from the Chima people of Peru (1200–1400). Don't leave without taking a look at the top-floor **reading room** – a fantastically quirky library and gallery, where you could happily spend a few hours perusing the exhibits. A café, bookshop and restaurant are all on site.

British Library

96 Euston Rd, NW1 2DB • Building Mon–Thurs 9.30am–8pm, Fri 9.30am–6pm, Sat 9.30am–5pm, Sun 11am–5pm; Treasures Gallery closes 6pm on Mon • Free; charge for some special exhibitions • ☎ 0330 333 1144 or ☎ 020 7412 7332, ⓦ bl.uk • ⊖ King's Cross

As one of the country's most expensive public buildings, the **British Library** took flak from all sides during its protracted construction, and finally opened in 1998. Yet while it's true that the building's uncompromising red-brick edifice is resolutely unfashionable, the library's interior has met with general approval, and the exhibition galleries are superb. At its centre, a huge multistorey glass-walled tower houses the vast **King's Library**, collected by George III.

With the exception of the reading rooms, the library is open to the public and puts on a wide variety of exhibitions and events, and has several cafés, a restaurant and free wi-fi. In the **Treasures Gallery** is a selection of the BL's ancient manuscripts, maps, documents and precious books, including the richly illustrated Lindisfarne Gospels and the Magna Carta, along with changing displays of early literary editions and manuscripts.

King's Cross and St Pancras stations

Euston Rd, N1C 4QP • ⊖ King's Cross St Pancras

The area around King's Cross and St Pancras stations is always buzzing with buses, cars, commuters, tourists and, with the massive development behind, construction workers. Architecturally, the area is dominated by **St Pancras Station**, the most glorious of London's red-brick Victorian edifices, with the neo-Gothic former *Midland Grand Hotel* designed by George Gilbert Scott, now the *St Pancras Renaissance*, forming its facade. It overshadows neighbouring **King's Cross Station**, opened in 1852, a mere shed in comparison, albeit one that has been beautifully restored. It is, of course, the station from which Harry Potter and his wizarding chums leave for school aboard the *Hogwarts Express* from platform 9¾. The film scenes were shot between platforms 4 and 5, and a station trolley is now embedded in the new concourse wall, providing a perfect photo opportunity for Potter fans (expect to queue), next to a Harry Potter-themed shop.

Granary Square and the canal

Granary Square, N1C 4AA • **King's Cross Visitor Centre** Stable St • Mon–Fri 10am–5pm, Sat 10am–4pm • Free • ☎ 020 3479 1795, ⓦ kingscross.co.uk • **Camley Street Natural Park** 12 Camley St, N1C 4PW • Daily: April–Sept 10am–5pm; Oct–March 10am–4pm • Free • ☎ 020 7833 2311, ⓦ wildlondon.org.uk • ⊖ King's Cross St Pancras

From King's Cross station, walk north up King's Boulevard and you reach the Regent's Canal and the district that once serviced the industries dependent on the canal and railways. The relocation of Eurostar to St Pancras kick-started redevelopment here, which is now well underway, transforming 67 acres into a new city quarter. It will ultimately include twenty new streets and ten new public squares, with around twenty venerable former industrial structures, mostly designed by Lewis Cubitt, surviving. Beyond the canal is the centrepiece **Granary Square**, a large open space almost entirely taken over by a grid of playful dancing fountains that are irresistible to children on hot days. The former Granary building itself is home to **Central Saint Martins**, part of the University of the Arts.

1

To find out more about the development, visit **King's Cross Visitor Centre** to the side of the Granary building, which has a model of the development and from where you can take a guided tour (1hr 30min; free; book online). Largely car-free, with plenty of green spaces and frequent pop-up markets and events, the whole area is fun to explore. Walk along the canal, past the picturesque **St Pancras Lock**, and you reach a cluster of brooding Victorian gasholders, one framing a landscaped park with mirrored pergola, **Gasholder Park**. On the other side of the canal, connected by a pedestrian bridge, is **Camley Street Natural Park**, which was transformed into a wildlife haven of woodland sand ponds in the 1980s.

Holborn

Holborn, on the periphery of the financial district of the City, has long been associated with the law, and its **Inns of Court** make for an interesting stroll, their archaic, cobbled precincts exuding the rarefied atmosphere of an Oxbridge college, and sheltering one of the city's oldest churches, the twelfth-century **Temple Church**. Holborn's gem, though, is the **Sir John Soane's Museum**, one of the most memorable and enjoyable of London's small museums, packed with architectural illusions and an eclectic array of curios.

Temple

Temple is the largest and most complex of the Inns of Court, where every barrister in England must study (and eat) before being called to the Bar. A few very old buildings survive here and the maze of courtyards and passageways are still redolent of Dickens's London, as described in *Bleak House*.

Middle Temple Hall

Middle Temple Lane, EC4Y 9AT · **Hall** Mon–Fri 10am–noon & 3–4pm, though sometimes closed for events · Free · **Gardens** May–July & Sept Mon–Fri noon–3pm· Free · ☎ 020 7427 4800, ⓦ middletemplehall.org.uk · ⊖ Temple or Blackfriars

Medieval students ate, attended lectures and slept in the **Middle Temple Hall**, still the Inn's main dining room. The present building, constructed in the 1560s, provided the setting for many great Elizabethan masques and plays – probably including Shakespeare's *Twelfth Night*, which is believed to have been premiered here in 1602. The hall is worth a visit for its fine hammer-beam roof, wooden panelling and decorative Elizabethan screen.

Temple Church

Temple, EC4Y 7HL · Mon, Tues, Thurs & Fri 10am–4pm, Wed usually term time 2–4pm & summer 10am–4pm, but times and days vary; check online · £5 · ☎ 020 7353 3470, ⓦ templechurch.com · ⊖ Temple or Blackfriars

The complex's oldest building is **Temple Church**, built in 1185 by the Knights Templar, and modelled on the Church of the Holy Sepulchre in Jerusalem. The interior features striking Purbeck marble piers, recumbent marble effigies of medieval knights and tortured grotesques grimacing in the spandrels of the blind arcading. The church makes an appearance in both the book and the film of Dan Brown's *The Da Vinci Code*.

Sir John Soane's Museum

12–14 Lincoln's Inn Fields, WC2A 3BP · Tues–Sat 10am–5pm, candlelit eve first Tues of month 6–9pm (very popular, so you may have to queue) · Free · **Guided tours** (including the private apartment) Tues & Sat 11am & noon, Thurs & Fri noon; book ahead · £10 · **Private apartment tours** Tues–Sat 1.15pm & 2pm; no advance booking, sign up ahead of time on the day · Free · ☎ 020 7405 2107, ⓦ soane.org · ⊖ Holborn

A trio of buildings on the north side of Lincoln's Inn Fields houses the fascinating **Sir John Soane's Museum**. Soane (1753–1837), a bricklayer's son who rose to be architect of the Bank of England, was an avid collector who designed this house not only as a

1

home and office, but also as a place to show his large collection of art and antiquities. Arranged much as it was in his lifetime, the ingeniously planned house – with mirrors, domes and skylights creating space and light as if out of nowhere – reveals surprises in every alcove. Standouts among the thousands of objects and artworks are the Egyptian sarcophagus of Seti and Hogarth's mercilessly satirical series *Election* and *The Rake's Progress* (in the picture room, the latter hung hidden behind the former; the room guides will show you). To get a real sense of the man and architect who created this curious place, take one of the private apartment tours of the upper floor.

The City

Stretching from Temple Bar in the west to the Tower of London in the east, **The City** is where London began. It was here, nearly two thousand years ago, that the Romans first established a settlement on the Thames; later the medieval City emerged as the country's most important trading centre and it remains one of the world's leading financial hubs. However, in this Square Mile (as the City is sometimes referred to), you'll find few leftovers of London's early days, since four-fifths burnt down in the Great Fire of 1666. Rebuilt in brick and stone, the City gradually lost its centrality as London swelled westwards. What you see now is mostly the product of three fairly recent building phases: the Victorian construction boom; the postwar reconstruction following World War II; and the building frenzy that began in the 1980s and has continued ever since, most recently adding a cluster of dizzingly high skyscrapers.

When you consider what has happened here, it's amazing that anything has survived to pay witness to the City's 2000-year history. Wren's spires still punctuate the skyline and his masterpiece, **St Paul's Cathedral**, remains one of London's geographical pivots. At the City's eastern edge, the **Tower of London** still boasts some of the best-preserved medieval fortifications in Europe. Other relics, such as Wren's **Monument** to the Great Fire and London's oldest synagogue and church, are less conspicuous, and even locals have problems finding modern attractions like the **Museum of London** and the **Barbican** arts complex.

St Paul's Cathedral

St Paul's Churchyard, EC4M 8AD • Cathedral Mon–Sat 8.30am–4.30pm, last admission 4pm; galleries Mon–Sat 9.30am–4.15pm • £18; £16 online • ☎ 020 7236 4128, ⓦ stpauls.co.uk • ➔ St Paul's

Designed by Christopher Wren and completed in 1710, **St Paul's Cathedral** remains a dominating presence in the City, despite the encroaching tower blocks. Topped by an enormous lead-covered dome, its showpiece west facade is particularly magnificent.

The best place from which to appreciate St Paul's is beneath the **dome**, decorated (against Wren's wishes) with Thornhill's trompe-l'oeil frescoes. The most richly decorated section of the cathedral, however, is the **chancel**, where the gilded mosaics of birds, fish, animals and greenery, dating from the 1890s, are spectacular. The intricately carved oak and limewood **choir stalls**, and the imposing organ case, are the work of Wren's master carver, Grinling Gibbons.

The galleries

A series of stairs, beginning in the south aisle, lead to the dome's three **galleries**, the first of which is the internal **Whispering Gallery**, so called because of its acoustic properties – words whispered to the wall on one side are distinctly audible over 100ft away on the other, though the place is often so busy you can't hear much above the hubbub. The other two galleries are exterior, with suitably breathtaking views: the wide **Stone Gallery**, around the balustrade at the base of the dome, and, ultimately, the tiny **Golden Gallery**, below the golden ball and cross which top the cathedral.

1

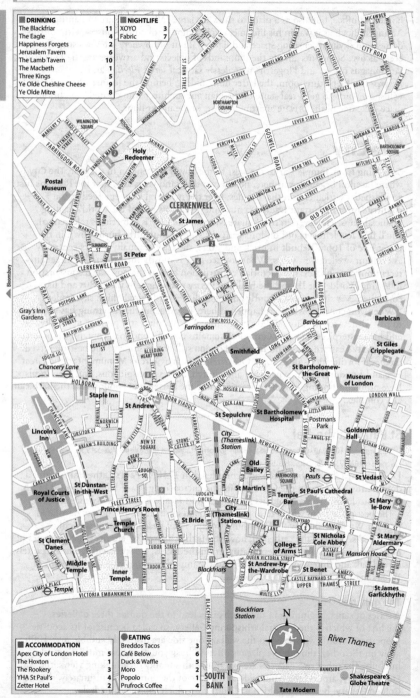

■ DRINKING
The Blackfriar	11
The Eagle	4
Happiness Forgets	2
Jerusalem Tavern	6
The Lamb Tavern	10
The Macbeth	1
Three Kings	5
Ye Olde Cheshire Cheese	9
Ye Olde Mitre	8

■ NIGHTLIFE
XOYO	3
Fabric	7

■ ACCOMMODATION
Apex City of London Hotel	5
The Hoxton	1
The Rookery	3
YHA St Paul's	4
Zetter Hotel	2

● EATING
Breddos Tacos	3
Café Below	6
Duck & Waffle	5
Moro	2
Popolo	1
Prufrock Coffee	4

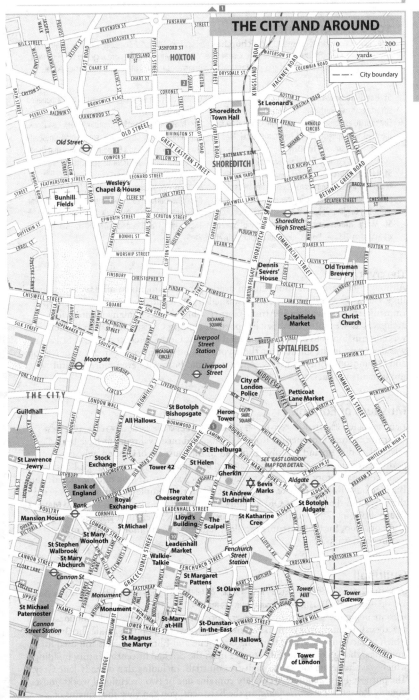

THE CITY AND AROUND

0 — 200
yards

– – – City boundary

HOXTON

FANSHAW STREET
BEVENDEN ST
HABERDASHER ST
BUTTESLAND ST
ASHFORD ST
PITFIELD STREET
HOXTON STREET
WATERSON ST
COLUMBIA ROAD
KINGSLAND ROAD
HACKNEY ROAD
DRYSDALE ST
AUSTIN ST
VIRGINIA ROAD
ARNOLD ROAD

St Leonard's
CALVERT AVENUE
ARNOLD CIRCUS

Shoreditch Town Hall

Old Street

SHOREDITCH

BATEMAN'S ROW
OLD NICHOL ST
REDCHURCH ST
BETHNAL GREEN ROAD
BACON ST
SLATER STREET
CHESHIRE ST

Wesley's Chapel & House

Bunhill Fields

Shoreditch High Street

COMMERCIAL STREET
QUAKER ST
BUXTON ST

Dennis Severs' House

Old Truman Brewery

Spitalfields Market

Christ Church

SPITALFIELDS

Liverpool Street Station

Moorgate

Liverpool Street

City of London Police

Petticoat Lane Market

THE CITY

Guildhall

St Botolph Bishopsgate

All Hallows

Heron Tower

Aldgate

St Lawrence Jewry

Stock Exchange

Tower 42

St Ethelburga

St Helen

The Gherkin

Bevis Marks

Bank of England

Royal Exchange

The Cheesegrater

St Andrew Undershaft

St Botolph Aldgate

Mansion House

St Michael

Lloyd's Building

The Scalpel

St Katharine Cree

St Stephen Walbrook

St Mary Woolnoth

Leadenhall Market

Walkie-Talkie

Fenchurch Street Station

St Mary Abchurch

Cannon St

St Margaret Pattens

St Olave

Tower Hill

Tower Gateway

St Michael Paternoster

Monument

St-Mary-at-Hill

St-Dunstan-in-the-East

Cannon Street Station

St Magnus the Martyr

All Hallows

Tower of London

SEE "EAST LONDON" MAP FOR DETAIL

1

TOP 5 CITY CHURCHES

The City of London is crowded with **churches** (⊕ london-city-churches.org.uk), the majority of them built or rebuilt by Wren after the Great Fire. Weekday lunchtimes are a good time to visit, when many put on free concerts of classical and chamber music; others have branched out and host cafés during the week.

St Bartholomew-the-Great Cloth Fair; ⊕ great stbarts.com; ⊖ Barbican. The oldest surviving pre-Fire church, established in 1123, in the City and by far the most atmospheric, with a Norman chancel. Mon–Fri 8.30am–5pm, Sat 10.30am–4pm, Sun 8.30am–8pm; mid-Nov to mid-Feb Mon–Fri closes 4pm; £5.

St Mary Abchurch Abchurch Lane; ⊖ Cannon Street or Bank. Unique among Wren's City churches for its huge, painted, domed ceiling, plus the only authenticated reredos by Grinling Gibbons. Mon–Fri 11am–3pm.

St Mary Aldermary Bow Lane/Watling Street; ⊖ Mansion House. Wren's most successful stab at

Gothic, with fan vaulting in the aisles and a panelled ceiling in the nave. Mon–Fri 9am–4.30pm.

St Mary Woolnoth Lombard St; ⊖ Bank. Hawksmoor's only City church, sporting an unusually broad, bulky tower and a Baroque clerestory that floods the church with light from its semicircular windows. Mon–Fri 7.30am–5.15pm.

St Stephen Walbrook Walbrook; ⊖ Bank. Wren's dress rehearsal for St Paul's, with a wonderful central dome and plenty of original woodcarving. Mon, Tues & Thurs 10am–4pm, Wed 11am–3pm, Fri 10am–3.30pm.

The crypt

Although the nave is crammed full of overblown monuments to military types, burials in St Paul's are confined to the whitewashed **crypt**, reputedly the largest in Europe. Immediately to your right is Artists' Corner, which boasts as many painters and architects as Westminster Abbey has poets, including Christopher Wren himself, who was commissioned to build the cathedral after its Gothic predecessor, Old St Paul's, was destroyed in the Great Fire. The crypt's two other star tombs are those of **Nelson** and **Wellington**, both occupying centre stage and both with even more fanciful monuments upstairs.

Museum of London

150 London Wall, EC2Y 5HN • Daily 10am–6pm • Free • ☎ 020 7001 9844, ⊕ museumoflondon.org.uk • ⊖ Barbican or St Paul's

Over the centuries, numerous Roman, Saxon and medieval remains have been salvaged or dug up and are now displayed in the **Museum of London**, whose permanent galleries provide an educational and imaginative trot through London's past, from prehistory to the present day. Specific exhibits to look out for include the Bucklersbury Roman mosaic, marble busts from the Temple of Mithras (uncovered in the City) and the model of Old St Paul's, but the prize possession is the **Lord Mayor's Coach**, built in 1757 and rivalling the Queen's in sheer weight of gold decoration. Look out, too, for the museum's excellent temporary exhibitions, gallery tours, lectures and walks.

Guildhall

Gresham St, EC2V 5AE • Great Hall May–Sept daily 10am–4.30pm; Oct–April Mon–Sat 10am–4.30pm; gallery Mon–Sat 10am–5pm, Sun noon–4pm • Free • ☎ 020 7332 1313, ⊕ cityoflondon.gov.uk • ⊖ Bank

Despite being the seat of the City governance for over 800 years, **Guildhall** doesn't exactly exude municipal wealth. Nevertheless, it's worth popping inside the **Great Hall**, which miraculously survived both the Great Fire and Blitz. The hall is still used for functions, though only the walls survive from the original fifteenth-century building, which was the venue for several high-treason trials, including that of Lady Jane Grey. The purpose-built **Guildhall Art Gallery** contains one or two exceptional works, most notably Rossetti's *La Ghirlandata*. In the basement, you can view the remains of a

Roman amphitheatre, dating from around 120 AD, which was discovered when the gallery was built in 1988.

Bank

Bank is the finest architectural arena in the City. Heart of the finance sector and the busy meeting point of eight streets, it's overlooked by a handsome collection of Neoclassical buildings – among them, the **Bank of England**, the **Royal Exchange** (now a shopping mall) and **Mansion House** (the Lord Mayor's official residence) – each one faced in Portland stone.

Bank of England

Threadneedle St, EC2R 8AH · Mon–Fri 10am–5pm · Free · ☎ 020 7601 5545, Ⓦ bankofengland.co.uk · ⊖ Bank

Established in 1694 by William III to raise funds for the war against France, the **Bank of England** wasn't erected on its present site until 1734. All that remains of the building on which Sir John Soane spent the best part of his career from 1788 onwards is the windowless, outer curtain wall. However, you can view a reconstruction of Soane's Bank Stock Office, with its characteristic domed skylight, see a virtual tour of the bank, and touch a real gold bar, in the **museum**, which has its entrance on Bartholomew Lane.

Bevis Marks Synagogue

Bevis Marks, EC3A 7LH · Mon, Wed & Thurs 10.30am–2pm, Tues & Fri 10.30am–1pm, Sun 10.30am–12.30pm · £5 · **Guided tours** Wed & Fri 11.30am, Sun 11am · Included in entry fee · ☎ 020 7626 1274, Ⓦ sephardi.org.uk/bevis-marks · ⊖ Aldgate

Hidden away behind a red-brick office block in a little courtyard is the **Bevis Marks Synagogue**. Built in 1701 by Sephardic Jews who had fled the Inquisition in Spain and Portugal, this is the country's oldest surviving synagogue, and its roomy, rich interior gives an idea of just how wealthy the community was at the time. Nowadays, the Sephardic community has dispersed across London and the congregation has dwindled, though the magnificent array of chandeliers makes it popular for candlelit Jewish weddings.

The Monument

Fish St Hill, EC3R 8AH · April–Sept daily 9.30am–6pm; Oct–March 9.30am–5.30pm · £5; joint ticket with Tower Bridge £12 · ☎ 020 7403 3761, Ⓦ themonument.org.uk · ⊖ Monument

The Monument was designed by Wren to commemorate the Great Fire of 1666. Crowned with spiky gilded flames, this plain Doric column stands 202ft high; if it were laid out flat it would touch the bakery where the Fire started, east of Monument. The bas-relief on the base, now in very bad shape, depicts Charles II and the Duke of York in Roman garb conducting the emergency relief operation. Views from the gallery, accessed by 311 steps, are somewhat dwarfed nowadays by the buildings springing up around it.

LONDON BRIDGE

Until 1750, **London Bridge** was the only bridge across the Thames. The medieval bridge achieved world fame: built of stone and crowded with timber-framed houses, a palace and a chapel, it became one of the great attractions of London – there's a model in the nearby church of **St Magnus the Martyr** (Tues–Fri 10am–4pm). The houses were finally removed in the mid-eighteenth century, and a new stone bridge, erected in 1831, lasted until the 1960s; that one was bought by an American industrialist and now stands reconstructed in the Arizona desert. It was transported there to be the focus of a new settlement, where it remains, now a curious centrepiece in a sprawling desert town. The present concrete structure dates from 1972.

1

AIMING HIGH: CITY SKYSCRAPERS

Throughout the 1990s, most people's favourite modern building in the City was Richard Rogers' **Lloyd's Building**, on Leadenhall Street – a vertical version of his Pompidou Centre in Paris – an inside-out array of glass and steel piping. Lloyd's was upstaged in 2003 by Norman Foster's 590ft-high glass diamond-clad **Gherkin**, which endeared itself to Londoners with its cheeky shape. In recent years, the City skyline has sprouted yet more skyscrapers, with the **Cheesegrater** (officially the Leadenhall Building), Richard Rogers' 737ft wedge-shaped office block, opposite the Lloyd's Building, and the **Scalpel**, a 620ft angular shard of glass, clustering near the Gherkin. Set away from this tight grouping and so more controversial is Rafael Viñoly's ugly, unsympathetic 525ft **Walkie Talkie**, on Fenchurch Street, which features a public **Sky Garden** on the top floor (20 Fenchurch St, EC3M 8AF; Mon–Fri 10am–6pm, Sat & Sun 11am–9pm; book free tickets in advance; ☎020 7337 2344, ⓦ skygarden.london), and several restaurants and bars.

More are planned, with the vast block of the 219ft **22 Bishopsgate** currently under construction and, tallest of all, **1 Undershaft**, planned for completion in the 2020s, which will be the tallest construction in the Square Mile, at 951ft. It'll remain second tallest in London (and Europe) to Renzo Piano's 1016ft **Shard**, by London Bridge (see page 96).

Tower of London

EC3N 4AB • Mon & Sun 10am–5.30pm, Tues–Sat 9am–5.30pm; Nov–Feb closes 4.30pm; last admission 30min before closing • £28; £24.80 online in advance • **Guided tours** Every 30min; 1hr • Included in entry fee • ☎ 0844 482 7799, ⓦ hrp.org.uk • ⊖ Tower Hill

One of Britain's main tourist attractions, the **Tower of London** overlooks the river at the eastern boundary of the old city walls. Despite all the hype, it remains one of London's most remarkable buildings, site of some of the goriest events in the nation's history, and somewhere all visitors and Londoners should explore at least once. Chiefly famous as a place of imprisonment and death, it has variously been used as a royal residence, armoury, mint, menagerie, observatory and – a function it still serves – a safe-deposit box for the Crown Jewels.

The lively free **guided tours** given by the Tower's **Beefeaters** (officially known as Yeoman Warders) are useful for getting your bearings. Visitors enter the Tower by the Middle Tower and the Byward Tower, in the southwest corner, but in times gone by most prisoners were delivered through **Traitors' Gate**, on the waterfront. Immediately, they would have come to the **Bloody Tower**, which forms the main entrance to the Inner Ward, and which is where the 12-year-old Edward V and his 10-year-old brother were accommodated "for their own safety" in 1483 by their uncle, the future Richard III, and later murdered. It's also where **Walter Raleigh** was imprisoned on three separate occasions, including a thirteen-year stretch.

Tower Green and the White Tower

At the centre of the Inner Ward is village-like **Tower Green**, where, over the years, seven highly placed but unlucky individuals have been beheaded, among them Anne Boleyn and her cousin Catherine Howard (Henry VIII's second and fifth wives). The **White Tower**, which overlooks the Green, is the original "Tower", begun in 1078, and now home to displays from the **Royal Armouries**. Even if you've no interest in military paraphernalia, you should at least pay a visit to the **Chapel of St John**, a beautiful Norman structure on the second floor that was completed in 1080 – making it the oldest intact church building in London.

Crown Jewels

The **Waterloo Barracks**, to the north of the White Tower, hold the **Crown Jewels**; queues can be painfully long, however, and you only get to view the rocks from moving walkways. The vast majority of exhibits post-date the Commonwealth (1649–60), when many of the royal riches were melted down for coinage or sold off. Among the jewels are some of the largest cut diamonds in the world, plus the legendary **Koh-i-Noor**, which was set into the Queen Mother's Crown in 1937.

Tower Bridge

SE1 2UP • Daily: April–Sept 10am–5.30pm; Oct–March 9.30am–5pm • £9.80; joint ticket with Monument £12 • ☎ 020 7403 3761, ⓦ towerbridge.org.uk • ⊖ Tower Hill

Tower Bridge ranks with Big Ben as the most famous of all London landmarks. Completed in 1894, its neo-Gothic towers are clad in Cornish granite and Portland stone, but conceal a steel frame, which, at the time, represented a considerable engineering achievement, allowing a road crossing that could be raised to give tall ships access to the upper reaches of the Thames. The raising of the bascules remains an impressive sight (check the website for times). If you buy a ticket, you get to walk across the elevated walkways that link the summits of the towers, and which have glass-floor sections, and visit the Tower's Victorian Engine Rooms, on the south side of the bridge, where you can see the now defunct giant coal-fired boilers which drove the hydraulic system until 1976, and play some interactive engineering games.

East London

Few places in London have engendered so many myths as the **East End**, an area long synonymous with slums, sweatshops and crime, its dark mythology surrounding the likes of Jack the Ripper and the Kray twins. It was also the first port of call for wave after wave of **immigrants**, including the French Huguenots, Jewish eastern Europeans and those from the Indian subcontinent. Now, however, visitors arriving here are most likely to be those in search of the next London scene. Art previews, experimental cocktail bars and edgy nightlife all find a space in the sprawl of neighbourhoods – Spitalfields, Whitechapel, Bethnal Green, Shoreditch, Hoxton, Dalston, Hackney – that make up the wider East London.

For day-time visitors, Sunday morning is the best time to visit for the network of famous **Sunday markets** – clothes and crafts in Spitalfields, hip vintage gear around Brick Lane and flowers on Columbia Road – while further afield the **Olympic Park** has some fun spots for families.

THE EVOLUTION OF EAST LONDON

Since the 1990s, the northern fringe of the City has been colonized by artists, designers and architects. This has evolved into a distinctive look, scene and attitude found across East London – think vintage markets, revamped old pubs, speakeasy-style bars, hipster coffee shops and street art. You'll find a swathe of neighbourhoods where cheap Turkish, Bangladeshi or Vietnamese restaurants, plus the occasional traditional East End café (such as *E. Pellicci* in Bethnal Green), sit alongside high-end boutique hotels, art galleries and street fashion stores. **Hoxton** (to the north of Old Street) and **Shoreditch** (to the south) kicked off the East End transformation, but they have since been upstaged by **Dalston** (up Kingsland Road) and **Hackney** beyond. To get a taste of the area try these East London favourites:

AN EAST LONDON TOP 5

Bethnal Green Working Men's Club See page 130
Columbia Road Flower Market See page 136
Culpeper See page 118
E. Pellicci See page 123
First Thursdays at Whitechapel Gallery See page 90

1

Spitalfields

Spitalfields, within sight of the sleek tower blocks of the financial sector, lies at the old heart of the East End, where the French Huguenots settled in the seventeenth century, where the Jewish community was at its strongest in the late nineteenth century, and where today's Bengali community eats, sleeps, works and prays. If you visit just one area in the East End, it should be this, which preserves mementos from each wave of immigration. The focal point of the area is **Spitalfields Market**, the red-brick and green-gabled market hall built in 1893; the west end has been extensively remodelled and holds glass-fronted chain stores and restaurants, but the original facades survive on the northern and eastern sides. Within, you can find a daily changing mix of crafts, arts and food stalls (see page 137).

Dennis Severs' House

18 Folgate St, E1 6BX • Mon noon–2pm (last admission 1.15pm), Sun noon–4pm (last admission 3.15pm); Mon, Wed & Fri "Silent Night" visits 5–9pm • £10; "Silent Night" visits £15 • ☎ 020 7247 4013, ⓦ dennissevershouse.co.uk • ⊖ Shoreditch High Street or Liverpool Street

You can visit one of Spitalfields' characteristic eighteenth-century terraced houses at 18 Folgate St, where the American artist **Dennis Severs** lived until 1999. Eschewing all modern conveniences, Severs lived under candlelight, decorating his house as it would have been two hundred years ago. The public were invited to share in the experience that he described as like "passing through a frame into a painting". Today visitors are free to explore the cluttered, candlelit rooms, which resonate with the distinct impression that the resident Huguenot family has just popped out, not least due to the smell of cooked food and the sound of horses' hooves on the cobbles outside.

Brick Lane

Truman Brewery, Brick Lane, E1 6QL • Various markets Sat 11am–6pm, Sun 10am–5pm • ⓦ trumanbrewery.com • ⊖ Aldgate East, Shoreditch High Street, Liverpool Street

Brick Lane gets its name from the brick kilns situated here after the Great Fire to help rebuild the City. By 1900, this was the high street of London's unofficial Jewish ghetto, but from the 1960s, Brick Lane became the heart of the Bangladeshi community; latterly it has gentrified into a mix of hip vintage shops and music venues, intermingled with the Bangladeshi curry houses. The Sunday flea market (8am–3pm) occupies the northern stretch of the road, while craft, vintage and food markets fill every corner of the **Old Truman Brewery** complex, halfway up Brick Lane, at weekends.

QUEEN ELIZABETH OLYMPIC PARK

The focus of the 2012 Olympics was the **Olympic Park**, laid out over a series of islands formed by the River Lee and various tributaries and canals. Since the Olympics, it has been renamed the **Queen Elizabeth Olympic Park** and the whole area has been replanted with patches of grass, trees and flowers, with waterways meandering through it, and it's peppered with cafés, making it a great new park in which to hang out on a sunny day (ⓦ queenelizabetholympicpark.co.uk; ⊖ Stratford). The centrepiece is the **Olympic Stadium**, now home to West Ham United football club and UK Athletics; it also serves as a major events venue. Standing close to the stadium is the **ArcelorMittal Orbit** tower (daily: April–Sept 10am–6pm; Oct–March 10am–5pm, sometimes later during peak periods; tower £11.50, tower and slide £16.50; book online in advance; ⓦ arcelormittalorbit.com), a 377ft-high continuous loop of red recycled steel designed by Anish Kapoor, with the world's longest tunnel slide spiralling down it. But the most eye-catching venue is Zaha Hadid's wave-like **Aquatics Centre**, where a swim costs under £5. To the north of the site, you can try out track, BMX and mountain biking at the **Velodrome** (ⓦ visitleevalley.org.uk).

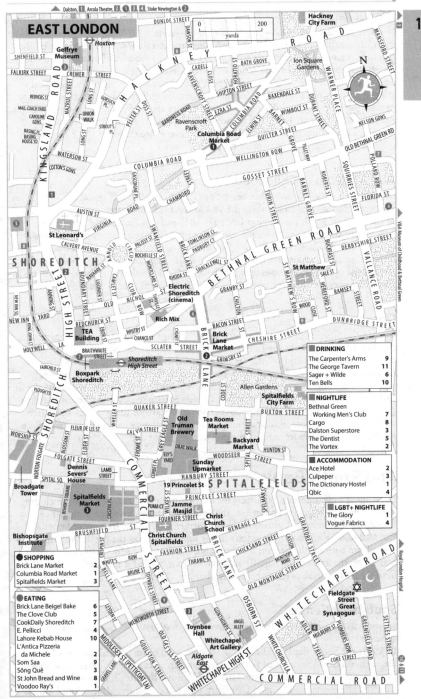

EAST LONDON

▲ Dalston, **1**, Arcola Theatre, **2**, **1**, **3**, **4**, Stoke Newington & **2**

N

0   200
yards

Geffrye Museum 3
Hoxton

Columbia Road Market 1

St Leonard's

SHOREDITCH

Electric Shoreditch (cinema)

Rich Mix

TEA Building

Shoreditch High Street

Boxpark Shoreditch

Brick Lane Market 2

St Matthew

Spitalfields City Farm

Old Truman Brewery

Tea Rooms Market

Backyard Market

Sunday Upmarket

Dennis Severs' House

Broadgate Tower

Spitalfields Market 3

19 Princelet St

Jamme Masjid

Christ Church School

Christ Church Spitalfields

Bishopsgate Institute

Fieldgate Street Great Synagogue

Toynbee Hall

Whitechapel Art Gallery

Aldgate East

V&A Museum of Childhood & Bethnal Green

Royal London Hospital

DRINKING

The Carpenter's Arms	9
The George Tavern	11
Sager + Wilde	6
Ten Bells	10

NIGHTLIFE

Bethnal Green Working Men's Club	7
Cargo	8
Dalston Superstore	3
The Dentist	5
The Vortex	2

ACCOMMODATION

Ace Hotel	2
Culpeper	3
The Dictionary Hostel	1
Qbic	4

LGBT+ NIGHTLIFE

The Glory	1
Vogue Fabrics	4

SHOPPING

Brick Lane Market	2
Columbia Road Market	1
Spitalfields Market	3

EATING

Brick Lane Beigel Bake	6
The Clove Club	5
CookDaily Shoreditch	7
E. Pellicci	4
Lahore Kebab House	10
L'Antica Pizzeria da Michele	2
Som Saa	9
Sông Quê	3
St John Bread and Wine	8
Voodoo Ray's	1

1

Whitechapel Gallery

77–82 Whitechapel High St, E1 7QX • Tues–Sun 11am–6pm, Thurs until 9pm • Free • ☎ 020 7522 7888, ⓦ whitechapel.org • ⊖ Aldgate East

Near the south end of Brick Lane, the **Whitechapel Art Gallery** is housed in its original beautiful, crenellated 1899 Arts and Crafts building by Charles Harrison Townsend, its facade embellished with a smattering of gilded leaves by the sculptor Rachel Whiteread, and an extension into a former library next door. Founded by one of the East End's many Victorian philanthropists, Samuel Barnett, the gallery has an illustrious history of showing innovative exhibitions of contemporary art. There's also a great bookshop, reading room and café-bar. Its **First Thursdays** initiative is a perfect way to soak up the East London buzz: on the first Thursday of every month, some 150 East London galleries, small and large, stay open till 9pm.

V&A Museum of Childhood

Cambridge Heath Rd, E2 9PA • Daily 10am–5.45pm • Free • ☎ 020 8983 5200, ⓦ vam.ac. uk/moc • ⊖ Bethnal Green

The wrought-iron hall that houses the **V&A Museum of Childhood** was originally part of the V&A in South Kensington (see page 101) and was transported here in the 1860s to bring art to the East End. On the ground floor you'll see clockwork **toys** – everything from classic robots to a fully functioning model railway – marionettes and puppets, teddies and Smurfs, and even Inuit dolls. The most famous exhibits are the remarkable antique **dolls' houses** dating back to 1673, displayed upstairs, where you'll also find a play area for very small kids, and the museum's special exhibitions.

Docklands

Built in the nineteenth century to cope with the huge volume of goods shipped along the Thames from all over the Empire, **Docklands** was once the largest enclosed cargo-dock system in the world. When the docks closed in the 1960s the area was generally regarded as having died forever, but regeneration in the 1980s brought luxury flats and, on the Isle of Dogs, a huge high-rise office development. Here, at **Canary Wharf**, César Pelli's landmark stainless steel tower **One Canada Square** remains an icon on the city's eastern skyline. The excellent **Museum of London Docklands** (daily 10am–6pm; free; ⓦ museumoflondon.org.uk/docklands), in an old warehouse in Canary Wharf, charts the history of the area from Roman times to the present day.

The South Bank

Drawing in huge numbers of visitors for its high-profile tourist attractions, including the enormously popular **London Eye**, the **South Bank** forms a waterside cluster of London's finest cultural institutions, while further south is the impressive **Imperial War Museum**. With most of London's major sights sitting on the north bank, the views from here are the best on the river, and, thanks to the wide, traffic-free riverside boulevard, the area can be happily explored on foot, while for much of the year outdoor festivals take place along the riverbank.

Southbank Centre

Belvedere Rd, SE1 8X • Foyers daily 10am–11pm; occasional closures for events • ☎ 020 3879 9555, ⓦ southbankcentre.co.uk • ⊖ Waterloo

In 1951, the South Bank Exhibition, on derelict land south of the Thames, formed the centrepiece of the national **Festival of Britain**, an attempt to revive postwar morale by celebrating the centenary of the Great Exhibition. The site's most striking features were the saucer-shaped Dome of Discovery (inspiration for the Millennium Dome), the Royal Festival Hall (which still stands) and the cigar-shaped steel-and-aluminium Skylon tower (yet to be revived).

The Festival of Britain's success provided the impetus for the creation of the **Southbank Centre**, home to a string of venerable artistic institutions: the Royal Festival Hall and Queen Elizabeth Hall concert venues; the Hayward Gallery, known for its large temporary exhibitions of modern art; the BFI Southbank arts cinema, and the National Theatre (see page 132). Its uncompromising concrete brutalism is softened by its riverside location, its avenue of trees, its buskers and skateboarders, the weekend food stalls behind the RFH, and the busy secondhand bookstalls outside the BFI. In summer, the roof garden tucked away above the Queen Elizabeth Hall is a delightful spot, while there are often free events and live music in the Festival Hall's main public spaces, plus seasonal outdoor bars and pop-up venues that host summer-long festivals of cabaret and theatre.

London Eye

County Hall, SE1 7PB • Daily: Jan–May & Sept–Dec 11am–6pm; Easter holidays & June–Aug 10am–8.30pm; closed two weeks in Jan for maintenance • £26; £23.45 online • ☎ 0871 781 3000, ⓦ londoneye.com • ⊖ Waterloo or Westminster

Having graced the skyline since the start of the twenty-first century, the **London Eye** is one of the city's most famous landmarks. Standing an impressive 443ft high, it's the

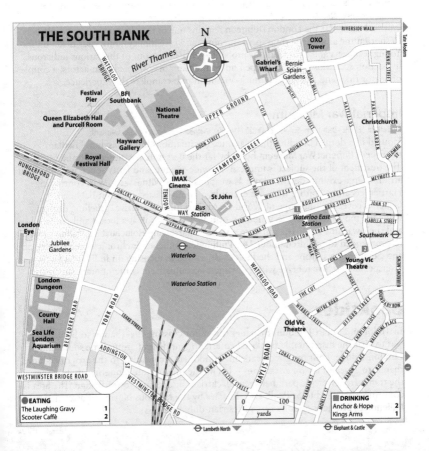

1

largest Ferris wheel in Europe, weighing over two thousand tonnes, yet as simple and delicate as a bicycle wheel. It's constantly in slow motion, which means a full circuit in one of its 32 pods (one for each of the city's boroughs) should take around thirty minutes. Booking online is cheaper, but note that unless you've paid extra you'll still have to queue to get on. Tickets are sold from the box office at the eastern end of County Hall.

Sea Life London Aquarium

County Hall, SE1 7PB • Mon–Fri 10am–6pm, last entry 5pm; Sat, Sun & school holidays 9.30am–7pm, last entry 6pm • £26; £20.40 online • ⓦ visitsealife.com • ⊖ Waterloo or Westminster

The most popular attraction in County Hall – the giant building beside the London Eye – is the **Sea Life London Aquarium**, spread across three subterranean levels. With some super-large tanks, and everything from sharks in the biggest tank and eerie large rays that glide over the walk-through glass tunnel, to turtles and Gentoo penguins, this is an attraction that is almost guaranteed to please kids, albeit at a price (book online; multi-attraction tickets, including the London Eye and Madame Tussauds, are also available).

London Dungeon

County Hall, SE1 7PB • Mon–Wed & Fri 10am–5pm, Thurs 11am–5pm, Sat & Sun 10am–6pm; school holidays closes 7pm or 8pm • £30; £21–28.50 online • ⓣ 020 7654 0809, ⓦ thedungeons.com • ⊖ Waterloo or Westminster

Gothic horror-fest the **London Dungeon** remains one of the city's major crowd-pleasers – to shorten the amount of time spent queuing (and save money), buy your ticket online. Young teenagers and the credulous probably get the most out of the various ludicrous live-action scenarios, each one hyped up by the team of costumed ham-actors; a couple of horror rides and a drink at a mock-Victorian pub complete the experience.

Imperial War Museum

Lambeth Rd, SE1 6HZ • Daily 10am–6pm • Free • ⓣ 020 7416 5000, ⓦ london.iwm.org.uk • ⊖ Lambeth North

Housed in a domed building that was once the infamous lunatic asylum "Bedlam", the superb **Imperial War Museum** holds by far the best military museum in the capital. The treatment of the subject is impressively wide-ranging and fairly sober, with the main atrium's large exhibits described not as weapons but as **Witnesses to War**, contrasting Harrier jets and a Spitfire with, for example, a bomb-blasted car from Baghdad. Galleries cover the full scope of World War I, in a fully immersive, gruelling display, while the most interesting section on World War II is a look at a local Lambeth family and their wartime lives. The museum also has a harrowing **Holocaust Exhibition** (not recommended for children under 14). Pulling few punches, it chronicles the history of anti-Semitism in Europe and the Holocaust, as well as focusing on individual victims, interspersing archive footage with eyewitness accounts from contemporary survivors.

Bankside

In Tudor and Stuart London, the chief reason for crossing the Thames to Bankside was to visit the disreputable Bankside entertainment district around the south end of London Bridge. Four hundred years on, Londoners are heading to the area once more, thanks to a wealth of top attractions – led by the mighty **Tate Modern** – that pepper the traffic-free riverside path between Blackfriars Bridge and Tower Bridge. The area is conveniently linked to St Paul's and the City by the fabulous Norman Foster-designed **Millennium Bridge**, London's first pedestrian-only bridge.

1

Tate Modern

Bankside, SE1 9TG • Daily 10am–6pm, Fri & Sat till 10pm • Free; special exhibitions around £17–18 • ☎ 020 7887 8888, ⓦ tate.org.uk • ⊖ Southwark or Blackfriars

Bankside is dominated by the awesome **Tate Modern**. Designed as an oil-fired power station by Giles Gilbert Scott, this austere, brick-built "cathedral of power" was converted into a splendid modern art gallery in 2000. Such was its phenomenal success that in 2016 Tate opened a vast new extension, the **Blavatnik Building**, a distorted prism of latticed bricks that rises to 215ft, above the power station's three original circular tanks; this extension is topped by a superb, open-air, tenth-floor **viewing level**. At the centre of this huge art complex is the original, stupendously large **Turbine Hall**, used for large installations. The original building, the riverside **Boiler House**, and the extension are connected at the Turbine Hall at Level 0 and via bridges on levels 1 and 4.

Initially, Tate Modern can overwhelm in its size and scope. To ease yourself in, go to the **Start Display** at the centre of Boiler House's Level 2. Here, three modest rooms hold some of the Tate's most illustrious works, including Matisse's late work *The Snail* (1953), in order to introduce you to key ideas in modern art. Beyond here you'll find permanent displays on levels 2 and 4 of the Boiler House and levels 2, 3 and 4 of the Blavatnik Building, where the focus is specifically on the post-1960s period.

The Tate's **permanent collection** dates back to 1900, but the curators have largely eschewed a chronological approach and have instead displayed work thematically. They also re-hang spaces regularly, so even big names may not be on show. The Tate has growing collections by artists from Africa, Latin America, the Middle East and across the globe; women artists also tend to be well represented. The consequence is that many names will be unfamiliar, but one of the joys of Tate Modern is coming across surprising juxtapositions of instantly recognizable artworks – a Monet water lily, Warhol's Marilyn or one of the gallery's numerous Picassos – next to artists about whom you know very little. Several artists get rooms to themselves, among them **Mark Rothko**, whose abstract "Seagram Murals", originally destined for a posh restaurant in New York, have their own shrine-like room in the heart of the collection.

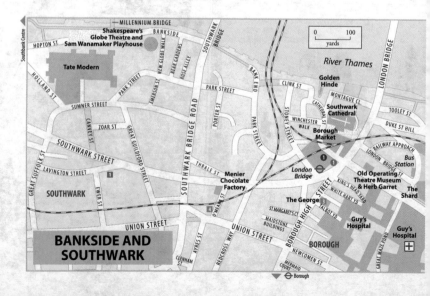

Shakespeare's Globe

21 New Globe Walk, SE1 9DT • Exhibition and tours daily 9am–5pm; tours every 30min (no Globe tours summer Tues–Sat after 12.30pm) • £15; £11.50 with Bankside tour • ☎ 020 7902 1500, ⓦ shakespearesglobe.com • ⊖ Southwark or London Bridge

Dwarfed by Tate Modern, but equally remarkable in its own way, **Shakespeare's Globe** is a reconstruction of the open-air polygonal playhouse where most of the Bard's later works were first performed. The theatre, which boasts the first new thatched roof in central London since the Great Fire of 1666 – and the first candlelit indoor theatre since the advent of electricity – puts on plays by Shakespeare and his contemporaries, both outside and in the indoor Sam Wanamaker Playhouse. To find out more about Shakespeare and the history of Bankside, the Globe's stylish **exhibition** is well worth a visit. You can have a virtual play on medieval instruments such as the crumhorn or sackbut, prepare your own edition of Shakespeare, and see some exquisitely authentic costumes up close. Included in the ticket is an informative half-hour **guided tour** of the theatre; during the summer season, if you visit in the afternoon, you'll be taken on a tour of the Bankside area instead.

Southwark Cathedral

London Bridge, SE1 9DA • Mon–Fri 8am–6pm, Sat & Sun 8.30am–6pm • Free • ☎ 020 7367 6700, ⓦ cathedral.southwark.anglican.org • ⊖ London Bridge

Built as the medieval Augustinian priory church of St Mary Overie, **Southwark Cathedral** was given cathedral status only in 1905. Of the original thirteenth-century church, only the choir and retrochoir now remain, separated by a tall and beautiful stone Tudor screen, making them probably the oldest Gothic structures left in London. The nave was entirely rebuilt in the nineteenth century, but the cathedral contains numerous interesting monuments, from a thirteenth-century oak effigy of a knight to an early twentieth-century memorial to Shakespeare.

Borough Market

Borough High St & Stoney St, SE1 1TL • Mon & Tues some stalls 10am–5pm, Wed & Thurs 10am–5pm, Fri 10am–6pm, Sat 8am–5pm • ☎ 020 7407 1002, ⓦ boroughmarket.org.uk • ⊖ London Bridge

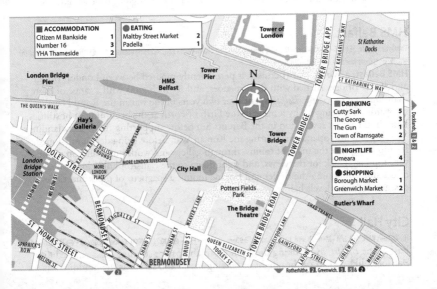

1

There has been a produce market near the southern end of London Bridge since medieval times. **Borough Market**, beneath the railway arches between Borough High Street and Southwark Cathedral, and now sprawling out over a fairly large area, is now best known for its busy specialist food market (see page 136), with stalls selling top-quality produce from around the world – pungent cheeses, unusual wild mushrooms, oysters, game, charcuterie and far more besides – along with hot food stalls (some of which operate Mon–Sat). It's very popular on Friday and Saturday so get there early.

The Shard

Railway Approach, SE1 9QU • April–Oct daily 10am–10pm; Nov–March Mon–Wed & Sun 10am–7pm, Thurs–Sat 10am–10pm • £30.95; £25.95 online in advance • ☎ 0844 499 7111, ⓦ theviewfromtheshard.com • ⊖ London Bridge

London's – and the country's – tallest building, Renzo Piano's 1016ft, tapered, glass-clad tower **the Shard** rises directly above the remodelled and expanded London Bridge station. In the years since it topped out in 2012, it has become a favourite city landmark, not least because it's considerably more elegant than some of the towers that have shot up since. Though pricey to visit, the view from the two public galleries at the top is sublime, the highest one open to the elements. From up here everything else in London looks small, from the unicycle of the London Eye to the tiny box that is St Paul's Cathedral, while the model railway of London Bridge is played out below you.

Old Operating Theatre Museum and Herb Garret

9a St Thomas St, SE1 9RY • Daily 10.30am–5pm; closed mid-Dec to early Jan • £6.50; NT members half-price • ☎ 020 7188 2679, ⓦ oldoperatingtheatre.com • ⊖ London Bridge

By far the most educative and the strangest of Southwark's museums is the **Old Operating Theatre Museum and Herb Garret**. Built in 1821 in a church attic, where the hospital apothecary's herbs were stored, this women's operating theatre, reached via a narrow spiral staircase, was once adjacent to the women's ward of St Thomas' Hospital (now in Lambeth). Despite being gore-free, the museum is a stomach-churning place: the surgeons would have concentrated on speed and accuracy (most amputations took less than a minute), but there was still a thirty percent mortality rate. The instruments on display are gruesome, while the apothecary's supplies include snail water and other intriguing concoctions.

HMS Belfast

The Queen's Walk, SE1 2JH • Daily: March–Oct 10am–6pm; Nov–Feb 10am–5pm • £16, including audioguide • ☎ 020 7940 6300, ⓦ iwm. org.uk/visits/hms-belfast • ⊖ London Bridge

HMS Belfast, a World War II cruiser, is permanently moored between London Bridge and Tower Bridge. Armed with six torpedoes, and six-inch guns with a range of more than fourteen miles, the *Belfast* spent over two years of the war in the Royal Naval shipyards after being hit by a mine in the Firth of Forth at the beginning of hostilities. Later in the war it saw action in the Barents Sea before supporting the D-Day landings. The ship was also operational during the Korean War, before being decommissioned. It's fun to explore the maze of cabins, through galleys and workrooms and up to the very top Flag Deck for the views, and right down to the claustrophobic lowest reaches of the ship containing the Boiler and Engine rooms, a spaghetti of pipes and valves that descend for three levels below water level.

City Hall

The Queen's Walk, SE1 2AA • Mon–Thurs 8.30am–6pm, Fri 8.30am–5.30pm • Free • ☎ 020 7983 4000, ⓦ london.gov.uk • ⊖ London Bridge

East of the *Belfast*, overlooking the river, Norman Foster's startling glass-encased **City Hall** looks like a giant car headlight or fencing mask, and serves as the headquarters for the Greater London Authority and the Mayor of London. Visitors are welcome to stroll up the helical walkway, visit the café and watch proceedings from the second floor.

Kensington and Chelsea

Hyde Park and **Kensington Gardens** cover a distance of a mile and a half from Oxford Street in the northeast to Kensington Palace, set in the Royal Borough of **Kensington** and **Chelsea**. Other districts go in and out of fashion, but this area has been in vogue ever since royalty moved into **Kensington Palace** in the late seventeenth century.

The most popular tourist attractions lie in **South Kensington**, where three of London's top **museums** – the Victoria and Albert, Natural History and Science museums – stand on land bought with the proceeds of the 1851 Great Exhibition. Chelsea, to the south, once had a slightly more bohemian pedigree. In the 1960s, the **King's Road** carved out its reputation as London's catwalk, while in the late 1970s it was the focus for the city's punk explosion, though nothing so rebellious could be imagined in Chelsea now.

Hyde Park and Kensington Gardens

Hyde Park Daily 5am–midnight • **Kensington Gardens** Daily 6am–dusk • **Lido** May Sat & Sun 10am–6pm; June–Aug daily 10am–6pm • £4.80 • **Memorial fountain** Daily: March & Oct 10am–6pm; April–Aug 10am–8pm; Sept 10am–7pm; Nov–Feb 10am–4pm • **Playground** Daily: Feb & late Oct 10am–4.45pm; March & early Oct 10am–5.45pm; April & Sept 10am–6.45pm; May–Aug 10am–7.45pm; Nov–Jan 10am–3.45pm • ☎ 0300 061 2114, ⓦ royalparks.org.uk • ⊖ Hyde Park Corner, Marble Arch, Knightsbridge or Lancaster Gate

Hangings, muggings, duels and the 1851 Great Exhibition are just some of the public events that have taken place in **Hyde Park**, which remains a popular spot for political demonstrations and pop concerts. For most of the time, however, the park is simply a lazy leisure ground – a wonderful open space that allows you to lose all sight of the city beyond a few persistent tower blocks.

The park is divided in two by the **Serpentine**, which has a pretty upper section known as the **Long Water**, which narrows until it reaches a group of four fountains. In the southern section, you'll find the popular **Lido** on its south bank and the **Diana Memorial Fountain**, less of a fountain and more of a giant oval-shaped mini-moat. The western half of the park is officially **Kensington Gardens**. In the northwest is the **Diana Memorial Playground**, featuring a ship stuck in sand and other imaginative playthings; at busy times you may have to queue to get in. The other two most popular attractions are the **Serpentine Galleries** and the overblown **Albert Memorial**.

Marble Arch

At Hyde Park's treeless northeastern corner is **Marble Arch**, erected in 1828 as a triumphal entry to Buckingham Palace, but now stranded on a busy traffic island at the west end of Oxford Street. This is a historically charged piece of land, as it marks the site of **Tyburn gallows**, the city's main public execution spot until 1783. It's also the location of **Speakers' Corner**, a peculiarly English Sunday-morning tradition, featuring an assembly of ranters and hecklers.

Wellington Arch

Hyde Park Corner, W1J 7JZ • Daily: April–Sept 10am–6pm; Oct 10am–5pm; Nov–March 10am–4pm • £5; EH • ⊖ Hyde Park Corner

At the southeast corner of Hyde Park, the **Wellington Arch** stands in the midst of **Hyde Park Corner**, one of London's busiest traffic interchanges. Erected in 1828, the arch was originally topped by an equestrian statue of the Duke himself, later replaced by Peace driving a four-horse chariot. Inside, you can view an exhibition on the history of the arch, and the Battle of Waterloo, and take a lift to the top of the monument where the exterior balconies offer a bird's-eye view of the swirling traffic.

1

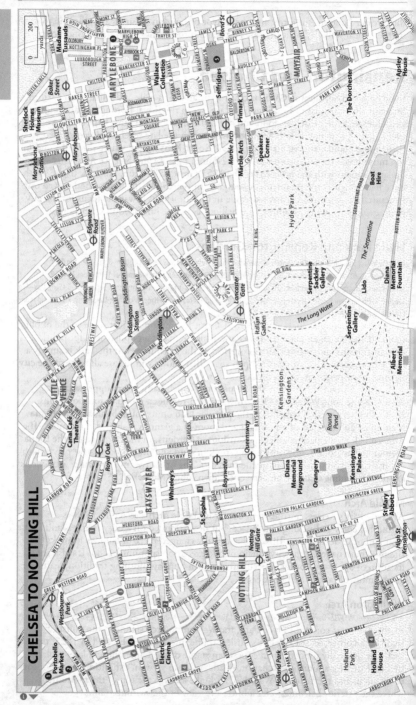

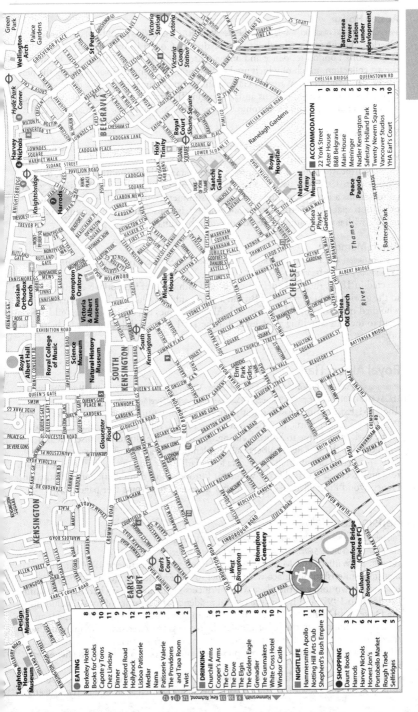

■ ACCOMMODATION	
22 York Street	1
Aster House	9
B&B Belgravia	8
Main House	2
Meininger	6
Nadler Kensington	5
Safestay Holland Park	7
Twenty Nevern Square	4
Vancouver Studios	3
YHA Earl's Court	10

● EATING	
Berkeley Hotel	8
Books for Cooks	6
Capote y Toros	10
Chez Lindsay	11
Dinner	9
Hereford Road	7
Hollyhock	12
Lisboa Patisserie	1
Medlar	13
Nama	3
Patisserie Valerie	5
The Providores and Tapa Room	4
Twist	2

■ DRINKING	
Churchill Arms	6
Cooper's Arms	13
The Cow	9
The Dove	1
The Elgin	8
The Golden Eagle	3
Grenadier	8
The Gunmakers	10
White Cross Hotel	7
Windsor Castle	2

■ NIGHTLIFE	
Hammersmith Apollo	11
Notting Hill Arts Club	5
Shepherd's Bush Empire	12

■ SHOPPING	
Daunt Books	3
Harrods	7
Harvey Nichols	6
Honest Jon's	1
Portobello Market	4
Rough Trade	2
Selfridges	5

1

Apsley House

149 Piccadilly, W1J 7NT · April–Oct Wed–Sun 11am–5pm; Nov–March Sat & Sun 10am–4pm · £9.30; EH · ⊖ Hyde Park Corner

Overlooking the traffic whizzing round Hyde Park Corner is **Apsley House**, Wellington's London residence and now a museum to the "Iron Duke". The highlight is the **art collection**, much of which used to belong to the King of Spain. Among the best pieces, displayed in the Waterloo Gallery on the first floor, are works by de Hooch, Van Dyck, Velázquez, Goya, Rubens and Correggio. The famous, more than twice life-size, nude statue of Napoleon by Antonio Canova stands at the foot of the main staircase.

Serpentine Galleries

Kensington Gardens, W2 3XA · Tues–Sun 10am–6pm; Pavilion mid-June to mid-Oct · Free · ☎ 020 7402 6075, ⓦ serpentinegalleries.org · ⊖ Knightsbridge or South Kensington

In the southeast corner of Kensington Gardens stands the **Serpentine Gallery**, built as a tearoom in 1908, but used as a contemporary art gallery since the 1960s. The gallery commissions a leading architect to design a summer pavilion each year. A second exhibition space, the **Serpentine Sackler Gallery**, is housed in a former munitions depot nearby, with a restaurant on the side designed by Zaha Hadid.

Albert Memorial

Kensington Gardens, W2 2UH · Guided tours March–Dec first Sun of month 2pm & 3pm; 45min · £9 · ☎ 020 8969 0104 · ⊖ Knightsbridge or South Kensington

Erected in 1876, the richly decorated, High Gothic **Albert Memorial** is as much a hymn to the glorious achievements of Britain as to its subject, Queen Victoria's husband, who died in 1861, possibly of typhoid. Albert occupies the central canopy, gilded from head to toe and clutching a catalogue for the 1851 Great Exhibition that he helped to organize.

Royal Albert Hall

Kensington Gore, SW7 2AP · Guided tours depart from Door 12 every 30min: April–Oct 9.30am–4.30pm; Nov–March 10am–4pm · £12.25 · ☎ 0845 401 5045, ⓦ royalalberthall.com · ⊖ South Kensington or High Street Kensington

The 1851 Exhibition's most famous feature – the gargantuan glasshouse of the Crystal Palace – no longer exists, but the profits were used to buy a large tract of land south of the park, now home to South Kensington's remarkable cluster of museums and colleges, plus the vast **Royal Albert Hall**, a splendid iron-and-glass-domed concert hall with an exterior of red brick, terracotta and marble that became the hallmark of South Ken architecture. The hall is the venue for Europe's most democratic music festival, the Henry Wood Promenade Concerts, better known as the **Proms** (see page 133).

Kensington Palace

Kensington Gardens, W8 4PX · Daily: March–Oct 10am–6pm; Nov–Feb 10am–5pm; last admission 1hr before closing · £17 March–Oct; £16.50 Nov–Feb · ☎ 020 3166 6000, ⓦ hrp.org.uk · ⊖ Queensway or High Street Kensington

Bought by William and Mary in 1689, the modestly proportioned Jacobean brick mansion of **Kensington Palace** was the chief royal residence for the next fifty years. It's best known today as the place where Princess Diana lived from her marriage until her death in 1997, and is now the official residence of a number of royals including the Duke and Duchess of Cambridge (William and Kate). **Queen Victoria** spent an unhappy childhood in the palace, under the steely gaze of her strict German mother. According to her diary, her best friends were the palace's numerous "black beetles". Victoria's apartments have not been preserved, but the permanent **Victoria Revealed** exhibition traces and examines her life.

The palace is home to the **Royal Ceremonial Dress Collection**, which means you usually get to see a few of the frocks worn by Diana, as well as several of the Queen's dresses. The highlights of the **King's State Apartments** are the trompe-l'oeil ceiling paintings by William Kent, particularly those in the Cupola Room, and the paintings in the King's Gallery by, among others, Tintoretto. The more modest **Queen's State Apartments** are lined with royal portraits, all part of the Royal Collection and rotated periodically.

Victoria and Albert Museum (V&A)

Entrances on Cromwell Rd and Exhibition Rd, SW7 2RL • Daily 10am–5.45pm, Fri till 10pm • Free; charge for some exhibitions • **Guided tours** Daily 10.30am, 12.30pm, 1.30pm & 3.30pm; meet at main entrance • Free • ☎ 020 7942 2000, ⓦ vam.ac.uk • ⊖ South Kensington

For sheer variety and scale, the **Victoria and Albert Museum** is the greatest museum of applied arts in the world. Beautifully displayed across a seven-mile, four-storey maze of rooms, the V&A's treasures are impossible to survey in a single visit; get hold of a floor plan to help you decide which areas to concentrate on, or join a free tour. And if you're flagging, head for the edifying café in the museum's period-piece **Morris, Gamble & Poynter Rooms.**

Perhaps the most precious of the V&A's many exhibits are the **Raphael Cartoons** (room 48a, level 1), from the Italian *cartone* meaning a large piece of paper. They comprise seven vast, full-colour paintings in distemper, which are, in fact, designs for tapestries ordered in 1515 by Pope Leo X for the Sistine Chapel. Also on the ground floor, you'll find one of the more disorientating sights in the museum, the two enormous **Cast Courts**, filled with plaster casts of famous sculptural works, created to allow Victorian Londoners to experience the glories of ancient art and including the colossal Trajan's Column, sliced in half to fit in the room, and a life-sized replica of Michelangelo's *David.*

Beyond these, you'll find the finest collection of Italian sculpture outside Italy, the world's largest collection of Indian art outside India, plus extensive Chinese, Islamic and Japanese galleries. Among the other highlights are the justifiably popular jewellery section, the beautifully designed Medieval and Renaissance galleries, the British Galleries and the costume and fashion collections. In addition, the V&A's temporary shows on art, photography and fashion are among the best in Britain, and are now housed in new subterranean gallery spaces built below the gleaming porcelain-tiled Sackler Courtyard, separated from Exhibition Road by the museum's original Portland stone screen.

Science Museum

Exhibition Rd, SW7 2DD • Daily 10am–6pm; school holidays 10am–7pm • Free; charge for some activities; Wonderlab £8, £6 under-17s • ☎ 0870 870 4868, ⓦ sciencemuseum.org.uk • ⊖ South Kensington

With galleries large enough to display jet planes and a phenomenal range of interactive exhibits that appeal to all ages, the **Science Museum** is impressive in its scope, covering every conceivable area of science. Major refurbishments have created some fantastic new displays, including the Zaha Hadid-designed Maths Gallery, though with redesigns ongoing at the time of research, some areas are closed for the foreseeable future.

On the ground floor, **Exploring Space** follows the history of rockets and space, with a full-size replica of the Apollo 11 landing craft which deposited US astronauts on the moon in 1969. **Making the Modern World** displays iconic inventions of modern science and technology, including Robert Stephenson's *Rocket* of 1829. Other galleries cover flight – including flight simulators and a vast gallery of flying machines – energy and materials. One of the most popular galleries is the **Wonderlab** on floor 3, also known as **The Statoil Gallery**; aimed at 5- to 15-year-olds, it's packed with dozens of hands-on activities and experiments with magnetism, electric circuits, light and sound.

1

Natural History Museum

Cromwell Rd, SW7 5BD • Daily 10am–5.50pm • Free • ☎ 020 7942 5000, ⓦ nhm.ac.uk • ⊖ South Kensington

Alfred Waterhouse's purpose-built mock-Romanesque colossus ensures the status of the **Natural History Museum** as London's most handsome museum, both an important resource for serious zoologists and a major tourist attraction.

The central **Hintze Hall** is dominated by a full-size, 25m blue-whale skeleton, dramatically suspended from the ceiling. The rest of the museum is divided into four colour-coded zones. The **Blue Zone** includes the ever-popular Dinosaur gallery, with its fossils and grisly life-sized **animatronic dinosaurs**. Popular sections over in the **Green Zone** include the Creepy-Crawlies, and the excellent **Investigate** centre, where children aged 7 to 14 get to play at being scientists (you need to obtain a timed ticket; reserved for school groups in term-time mornings).

Less visited, the **Darwin Centre** – also known as the **Orange Zone** – is dominated by the giant concrete **Cocoon**, home to more than twenty million specimens, where visitors can learn more about the scientific research and specimen collections. In the nearby **Zoology spirit building**, you can view a small selection of bits and bobs pickled in glass jars.

If you enter the museum via the side entrance on Exhibition Road, you start at the **Red Zone**, a visually exciting romp through the earth's evolution, with the solar system and constellations writ large on the walls and the most intact Stegosaurus skeleton ever found. Boarding the central escalator will take you through a partially formed globe to the top floor and an exhibition on volcanoes and earthquakes, including the slightly tasteless Kobe earthquake simulator.

Design Museum

224–238 Kensington High St, W8 6AG • Daily 10am–6pm • Free; charge for some temporary exhibitions (up to £16) • ☎ 020 3862 5900, ⓦ designmuseum.org • ⊖ High Street Kensington

One of the most striking 1960s buildings in London, a concrete-framed structure with a sweeping hyperbolic paraboloid roof clad in copper, the former home of the Commonwealth Institute next to Holland Park has been, appropriately enough, taken over by the **Design Museum**, which moved in at the end of 2016. It hosts numerous temporary exhibitions and events, along with a slightly cramped permanent exhibition, **Designer Maker User**, which features highlights from the museum's collection of design classics and everyday objects.

Leighton House Museum

12 Holland Park Rd, W14 8LZ • Mon & Wed–Sun 10am–5.30pm • £9 • ☎ 020 7602 3316, ⓦ rbkc.gov.uk • ⊖ High Street Kensington

Several wealthy Victorian artists rather self-consciously founded an artists' colony in the streets that lay to the west of Kensington Gardens. "It will be opulence, it will be sincerity", Lord Leighton opined before starting work on the remarkable **Leighton House** in the 1860s – he later became President of the Royal Academy and was ennobled on his deathbed. The big attraction here is the domed **Arab Hall**, decorated with Saracen tiles, gilded mosaics and latticework drawn from all over the Islamic world. The other rooms are hung with paintings by Lord Leighton and his Pre-Raphaelite chums, and there's even a Tintoretto.

Chelsea

From the Swinging Sixties up until the era of Punk, **Chelsea** had a slightly bohemian pedigree; these days, it's just another wealthy west London suburb. Among the most nattily attired of all those parading down the King's Road nowadays are the scarlet- or navy-blue-clad Chelsea Pensioners, army veterans from the nearby **Royal Hospital**.

Saatchi Gallery

Duke of York's HQ, King's Rd, SW3 4RY • Daily 10am–6pm • Free • ⓦ saatchigallery.com • ⊖ Sloane Square

1

On the south side of the King's Road, a short stroll from Sloane Square, the former **Duke of York's HQ**, built in 1801, is now the unlikely home of the **Saatchi Gallery**, which puts on changing exhibitions of contemporary art in its whitewashed rooms. Charles Saatchi, the collector behind the gallery, was the man who promoted the Young British Artists (YBAs) beyond the art world, though these days you'll find a global roster of contemporary artists represented, along with commercial photography exhibitions.

Royal Hospital

Royal Hospital Rd, SW3 4SR • **Grounds** Daily: May–Sept 10am–8pm; Oct–April 10am–4.30pm • Free • **Great Hall & Chapel** Mon–Sat 10am–noon & 2–4.40pm, Sun 2–4pm • Free • **Museum** Mon–Fri 10am–4pm • Free • ⓣ 020 7881 5516, ⓦ chelsea-pensioners.co.uk • ⊖ Sloane Square

Founded as a retirement home for army veterans by Charles II in 1682, and designed by Christopher Wren, the **Royal Hospital**'s majestic red-brick wings and grassy courtyards became a blueprint for institutional and collegiate architecture all over the English-speaking world. The public are welcome to view the austere hospital chapel, and the equally grand, wood-panelled dining hall opposite, where three hundred or so uniformed Pensioners still eat under the royal portraits and the vast allegorical mural of Charles II. On the east side of the hospital, a small **museum** displays Pensioners' uniforms, medals and two German bombs.

National Army Museum

Royal Hospital Rd, SW3 4HT • Daily 10am–5.30pm; open until 8pm on first Wed of the month • Free • ⓣ 020 7730 0717, ⓦ nam.ac.uk • ⊖ Sloane Square

The concrete bunker next door to the Royal Hospital, on Royal Hospital Road, houses the **National Army Museum**. After a complete redesign, the coverage and range of army exhibits is wide-ranging and thoughtful, considering army life and subjects like the ethics of warfare alongside a plethora of historical artefacts, including a huge scale model of the Battle of Waterloo and interactive exhibits such as strategy games.

North London

Stretching north from the Regent's Canal and **Regent's Park**, home to **London Zoo**, North London's neighbourhoods are a historically rich, attractive and eclectic series of villages, now subsumed into the general mass of the city, and with a reputation for a certain sort of wealthy liberal bohemianism. Drawing the tourist hordes, **Camden Town** has its markets, pubs and live music. The highlights, however, are the village-like suburbs of **Hampstead** and **Highgate**, on the edge of London's wildest patch of greenery, **Hampstead Heath**.

Regent's Park

Daily 5am–dusk • Free • ⓣ 0300 061 2300, ⓦ royalparks.org.uk • ⊖ Regent's Park, Baker Street, Great Portland Street, St John's Wood or Camden Town

Regent's Park is one of London's smartest parks, with a boating lake, ornamental ponds, waterfalls and some lovely gardens. Under the reign of the Prince Regent (later George IV), the park was to be girded by a continuous belt of terraces, and sprinkled with a total of 56 villas, including a magnificent royal palace. Inevitably, the plan was never fully realized, but enough was built to create something of the idealized garden city that Nash and the Prince Regent had envisaged. Within the Inner Circle, the **Queen Mary's Gardens** are by far the prettiest section of the park. Prominent on the

1

skyline is the shiny copper dome of **London Central Mosque** at 146 Park Road, an entirely appropriate addition given the Prince Regent's taste for the Orient.

London Zoo

Outer Circle, Regent's Park, NW1 4RY • **Zoo** Daily: April–Aug 10am–6pm (5pm during Sunset Safaris); March, Sept & Oct 10am–5.30pm; Nov–Feb 10am–4pm • March–Oct £27.04; £24.30 online; Nov–Feb £22.73; £20.45 online • **Sunset Safaris** June to mid-July Fri 6–10pm • £20.80 online; buy in advance • ☎ 020 7722 3333, ⓦ zsl.org/zsl-london-zoo • ⊖ Camden Town

The northeastern corner of Regent's Park is occupied by **London Zoo**. Founded in 1826 with the remnants of the royal menagerie, the enclosures here are as humane as any inner-city zoo could make them. In recent years, many of the animals have been moved from their classic, architecturally listed homes, such as the famous penguin pool, into more spacious, modern enclosures. Among the biggest hits is the impressive 2500-square-metre **Land of the Lions**, a scaled-down recreation of an Indian village, that allows for surprisingly close encounters with the big cats. Likewise, **Gorilla Kingdom** has large viewing areas, while for smaller animals there are some imaginative walk-through enclosures, such as **Rainforest Life**, with its sleepy sloths, **Meet the Monkeys** and **In with the Lemurs**.

Camden Market

Off Chalk Farm Road, NW1 8A • Camden Lock Market and Stables Market daily 10am–7pm • ⓦ camdenmarket.com • ⊖ Camden Town or Chalk Farm

For all its tourist popularity, **Camden Market** remains a genuinely offbeat place. It began life in the 1970s, as a small craft market in the cobbled courtyard by Camden Lock, and now encompasses several sections; the sheer variety of what's on offer – from jewellery to furniture, along with a mass of street fashion and clubwear, and plenty of food stalls – is what makes Camden Town so special. More than 100,000 shoppers turn up here each weekend, and most parts of the market now stay open week-long, alongside a crop of shops, cafés and bistros.

Jewish Museum

129–131 Albert St, NW1 7NB • Daily 10am–5pm, Fri until 2pm • £8.50 • ☎ 020 7284 7384, ⓦ jewishmuseum.org.uk • ⊖ Camden Town

Camden is home to London's purpose-built **Jewish Museum**. On the first floor, there's an engaging exhibition explaining Jewish practices, illustrated by cabinets of Judaica.

REGENT'S CANAL

The **Regent's Canal**, completed in 1820, was constructed as part of a direct link from Birmingham to the newly built London Docks in the East End, covering nine miles, with 42 bridges, twelve locks and two tunnels. The lock-less stretch **between Little Venice and Camden Town** is the busiest, most attractive section, tunnelling through to Lisson Grove, skirting Regent's Park, offering back-door views of the aviary at London Zoo and passing straight through the heart of Camden Market. You can walk, jog or cycle along the towpath, but this section of the canal is also served by scheduled narrowboats.

Three companies run daily **boat services** between Camden and Little Venice, passing through the Maida Hill tunnel. The narrowboat *Jenny Wren* (March Sat & Sun; April–Oct daily; 2–3 daily; £14 return; ☎020 7485 4433, ⓦ walkersquay.com) starts off at Camden, goes through a canal lock (the only company to do so) and heads for Little Venice (with live commentary) before returning; while you can embark on *Jason's* narrowboats (April–early Nov 3–4 daily; £9.50 one-way, £14.50 return; ⓦ jasons.co.uk) at either end (live commentary to Camden); the London Waterbus Company (April–Sept daily; Oct Thurs–Sun; Nov to mid-Dec & Jan–March Sat & Sun, weather permitting; up to 8 daily; £9 one-way, £14 return; with zoo visit £25 from Camden, £27 from Little Venice; ☎020 7482 2550, ⓦ londonwaterbus.com) sets off from both places and calls at London Zoo. Journey times are around 45 minutes one-way.

1

On the second floor, there's a special Holocaust gallery which tells the story of Leon Greenman (1920–2008), one of only two British Jews who suffered and survived Auschwitz. The museum also puts on a lively programme of special exhibitions, discussions and concerts, and has a café on the ground floor.

Hampstead

Perched on a hill to the west of Hampstead Heath, **Hampstead** village developed into a fashionable spa in the eighteenth century, and was not much altered thereafter. Later, it became one of the city's most celebrated literary *quartiers* and even now it retains its reputation as a bolthole of the high-profile intelligentsia and discerning pop stars. Proximity to **Hampstead Heath** is, of course, the real joy of Hampstead; this mixture of woodland, smooth pasture and landscaped garden is quite simply the most exhilarating patch of greenery in London.

Keats' House

10 Keats Grove, NW3 2RR • March–Oct Wed–Sun 11am–5pm; Nov–Feb Fri–Sun 1–5pm; tours 3pm (30min) • £6.50 (including tour); garden free • ☎ 020 7332 3868, ⓦ cityoflondon.gov.uk/keats • Hampstead Heath Overground or ⊖ Hampstead

The English Romantic poet John Keats is celebrated at **Keats' House**, an elegant, whitewashed Regency double villa off Downshire Hill at the bottom of the High Street. Inspired by the tranquillity of Hampstead and by his passion for girl-next-door Fanny Brawne (whose house is also part of the museum), Keats wrote some of his most famous works here before leaving for Rome, where he died of consumption in 1821, aged just 25. The neat, simple interior contains books, letters and Fanny's engagement ring, as well as listening posts and a film of Keats' life.

2 Willow Road

2 Willow Rd, NW3 1TH • March–Oct Wed–Sun 11am–5pm; note that before 3pm, visits are by hourly guided tour • £6.50; NT • ☎ 020 7435 6166, ⓦ nationaltrust.org.uk/2-willow-road • Hampstead Heath Overground or ⊖ Hampstead

An unassuming red-brick terraced house built in the 1930s by the Hungarian-born architect **Ernö Goldfinger** (1902–87), **2 Willow Road** gives a fascinating insight into the Modernist mindset. This was a state-of-the-art pad when Goldfinger moved in, and as he changed little during the following fifty years, what you see today is a 1930s avant-garde dwelling preserved in aspic, a house both modern and old-fashioned. An added bonus is that the rooms are packed with works of art by the likes of Bridget Riley, Duchamp, Henry Moore and Man Ray.

Freud Museum

20 Maresfield Gardens, NW3 5SX • Wed–Sun noon–5pm • £8; fifty percent discount for NT • ☎ 020 7435 2002, ⓦ freud.org.uk • ⊖ Finchley Road

The **Freud Museum** is one of the most poignant of London's house museums. Having lived in Vienna for his entire adult life, the psychotherapist, by now semi-disabled and with only a year to live, was forced to flee the Nazis, arriving in London in the summer of 1938. The ground-floor study and library look exactly as they did when Freud lived here; the collection of erotic antiquities and the famous couch, sumptuously draped in Persian rugs, were all brought here from Vienna. Upstairs, home movies of family life are shown continually, and a small room is dedicated to Freud's daughter, Anna, herself an influential child analyst, who lived in the house until her death in 1982.

Hampstead Heath

Daily 24hr • Free • **Hill Garden** Daily 8.30am–dusk • ☎ 020 7332 3322, ⓦ cityoflondon.gov.uk • **Men's and women's bathing ponds** Daily year-round from 7am, closing time varies • **Mixed pond** Mid-May to mid-Sept daily 7am–6.30pm • £2 • Hampstead tube and Hampstead Heath or Gospel Oak Overground; bus #210 from ⊖ Hampstead or Golders Green or #24 from central London, including Tottenham Court Rd and Camden

1

Hampstead Heath may not have much of its original heathland left, but it packs a wonderful variety of bucolic scenery into its eight hundred acres. At its southern end are the rolling green pastures of **Parliament Hill**, north London's premier spot for kite flying, and with unrivalled views over the London skyline. On either side are numerous **ponds**, three of which – one for men, one for women and one mixed – you can swim in. The thickest woodland is to be found in the **West Heath**, beyond Whitestone Pond, also the site of the most formal section, **Hill Garden**: a secluded and romantic little gem with eccentric balustraded terraces and 800ft pergola, which create an alluring sense of faded grandeur. Beyond lies **Golders Hill Park**, where you can gaze at pygmy goats and fallow deer, and inspect the impeccably maintained aviaries, home to flamingos, cranes and other exotic birds.

Kenwood House

Hampstead Lane, NW3 7JR • Daily: April–Oct 10am–5pm; Nov–March 10am–4pm • Free • ☎ 020 8348 1286, ⓦ english-heritage.org.uk • Bus #210 from ⊖ Archway or Golders Green

Hampstead Heath's most celebrated sight is the whitewashed Neoclassical mansion of **Kenwood House**, set within landscaped grounds dotted with sculptures. The house is home to a collection of seventeenth- and eighteenth-century art, including a handful of real masterpieces by Vermeer, Rembrandt, Boucher, Gainsborough and Reynolds. Of the period interiors, the most spectacular is Robert Adam's sky-blue and pink library.

Highgate Cemetery

Swain's Lane, N6 6PJ • **East Cemetery** March–Oct Mon–Fri 10am–5pm, Sat & Sun 11am–5pm; Nov–Feb closes 4pm • £4 • **Guided tours** Sat 2pm • £8 • **West Cemetery** Guided tours only: March–Oct Mon–Fri 1.45pm, Sat & Sun every 30min 11am–3pm; Nov–Feb Sat & Sun hourly 11am–3pm • £12; no under-8s • ☎ 020 8340 1834, ⓦ highgatecemetery.org • ⊖ Archway

Highgate Cemetery, ranged on both sides of Swain's Lane, is London's best-known graveyard. The most illustrious incumbent of the **East Cemetery** is **Karl Marx**. Marx himself asked for a simple grave topped by a headstone, but by 1954 the Communist movement decided to move his grave to a more prominent position and erect the hulking bronze bust that now surmounts a granite plinth. To visit the more atmospheric and overgrown **West Cemetery**, with its spooky Egyptian Avenue and sunken catacombs, you must take a guided tour. Among the prominent graves usually visited are those of artist Dante Gabriel Rossetti, and lesbian novelist Radclyffe Hall.

The Swaminarayan temple

105–119 Brentfield Rd, NW10 8LD • **Temple** Daily 9am–6pm • Free • **Exhibition** Mon–Fri 9am–5pm, Sat & Sun 9am–6pm • £2 • ☎ 020 8965 2651, ⓦ londonmandir.baps.org • ⊖ Neasden

Perhaps the most remarkable building in the whole of London lies just off the North Circular, in the glum suburb of Neasden. Here, rising majestically above the surrounding semi-detached houses, is the **Shri Swaminarayan Mandir**, a traditional Hindu temple topped with domes and *shikharas*, erected in 1995 in a style and scale unseen outside of India for over a millennium. You enter through the Haveli (cultural complex) and, after taking off your shoes, proceed to the Mandir (temple) itself, carved entirely out of Carrara marble, with every possible surface transformed into a honeycomb of arabesques, flowers and seated gods. Beneath the Mandir, an **exhibition** explains the basic tenets of Hinduism, details the life of Lord Swaminarayan, and includes a video about the history of the building.

South London

Spreading out from the river that marks the city's great divide – both real and imagined – South London is formed by a series of distinctive, often underrated neighbourhoods, villages subsumed into the city with the railways and industrialization. It includes one outstanding area for sightseeing, **Greenwich**, with its fantastic ensemble of the Royal Naval College, the *Cutty Sark*, the National Maritime Museum, the Royal Observatory and the beautifully landscaped royal park. Other standouts are the **Dulwich Picture Gallery**, a superb public art gallery older than the National Gallery, and the eclectic **Horniman Museum** in neighbouring Forest Hill, plus a few diverse, busy neighbourhoods worth exploring, **Brixton** chief among them.

Greenwich

Greenwich draws tourists out from the centre in considerable numbers. At its heart is the outstanding architectural set piece of the **Old Royal Naval College** and the **Queen's House**, courtesy of Christopher Wren and Inigo Jones respectively. Most visitors, however, come to see the **Cutty Sark**, the **National Maritime Museum** and Greenwich Park's **Royal Observatory**. With the added attractions of its parkland, covered market of crafts, antiques and food stalls (see page 136), riverside pubs and walks – plus startling views across to Canary Wharf and Docklands – it makes for one of the best days out in the capital. To reach Greenwich, you can take a **train** from London Bridge (every 30min) or the **DLR** to Cutty Sark station (every 4–10min), but by far the most scenic option is by **boat** from one of the piers in central London (every 20–30min), with Thames Clippers (see page 115).

Cutty Sark

King William Walk, SE10 9HT • Daily 10am–5pm • £13.50; combined ticket with Observatory £18.50 • ☎ 020 8312 6608, ⓦ rmg.co.uk • Cutty Sark DLR

Wedged in a dry dock by the river is the majestic **Cutty Sark**, the world's last surviving tea clipper. Launched in 1869, the *Cutty Sark* was actually more famous in its day as a wool clipper, returning from Australia in just 72 days. The vessel's name comes from Robert Burns' *Tam O'Shanter*, in which Tam, a drunken farmer, is chased by Nannie, an angry witch in a short Paisley linen dress, or "cutty sark"; the clipper's figurehead shows her clutching the hair from the tail of Tam's horse. After a devastating fire in 2007, the ship has been beautifully restored, and you can explore the bunks, officers' quarters and below-deck storage, where there are interactive displays.

Old Royal Naval College

SE10 9NN • Daily: grounds 8am–11pm; buildings 10am–5pm • Free • ☎ 020 8269 4747, ⓦ ornc.org • ⊖ Cutty Sark DLR

Making the most of its riverbank location, the **Old Royal Naval College** is a majestic Baroque ensemble designed, for the most part, by Wren. Initially built as a royal palace, but eventually converted into the Royal Hospital for Seamen, the complex was later home to the Royal Naval College, but now houses the University of Greenwich and the Trinity Laban. The two grandest rooms, situated underneath Wren's twin domes, are open to the public and well worth visiting. The **Chapel**, in the east wing, has exquisite pastel-shaded plasterwork and spectacular, decorative detailing on the ceiling, all designed by James "Athenian" Stuart after a fire in 1799 destroyed the original interior. Opposite the chapel is the magnificent **Painted Hall** in the west wing, which is dominated by James Thornhill's gargantuan allegorical ceiling painting, and his trompe-l'oeil fluted pilasters (reopening after renovation in 2019). Over in the Pepys Building, you can get a good overview of Greenwich's history in **Discover Greenwich**, where there's an information desk and historical displays.

1

National Maritime Museum

Romney Rd, SE10 9NF • Daily 10am–5pm; Ahoy! and All Hands: Tues, Sat, Sun & hols 10am–5pm, Mon & Wed–Fri 2–5pm, open other times if no school groups • Free; charge for special exhibitions • ☎ 020 8312 6608, 🖥 rmg.co.uk • ⊖ Cutty Sark DLR

The main building of the **National Maritime Museum** is centred on a glass-roofed courtyard, which houses the museum's largest artefacts, among them the splendid 63ft-long gilded **Royal Barge**, designed in Rococo style by William Kent for Prince Frederick, the much unloved eldest son of George II. The various themed galleries are superb, and stuffed full of model ships and curious artefacts, including Nelson's coat. Several well-designed sections are just for kids: **Ahoy!** is a nautically themed play area for under-7s on the ground floor; while the second-floor **All Hands** gallery gives older kids a taste of life on the seas.

Inigo Jones's **Queen's House**, originally built amid a rambling Tudor royal palace, is now the focal point of the Greenwich ensemble, and is part of the Maritime Museum. As royal residences go, it's an unassuming country house, but as the first Neoclassical building in the country, it has enormous architectural significance. You enter via the beautiful **Tulip Staircase**, Britain's earliest cantilevered spiral staircase – its name derives from the floral patterning in the wrought-iron balustrade – which takes you to the Great Hall, a perfect cube. The rooms here show the museum's **art collection**, ranging from royal portraits and scenes of Greenwich to nautical scenes, plus a few navigational instruments.

Royal Observatory

Greenwich Park, SE10 9NF • **Flamsteed House** Daily 10am–5pm • £9.50, including audioguide; combined ticket with Cutty Sark £18.50 • **Astronomy Centre** Daily 10am–5pm • Free • **Planetarium** Shows every 45min • £7.50; combined ticket with Flamsteed House £12.50 • ☎ 020 8312 6565, 🖥 rmg.co.uk • Greenwich DLR/train station

Perched on the crest of Greenwich Park's highest hill – and so with sublime views over to Canary Wharf – the **Royal Observatory** was established by Charles II in 1675. It's housed in a rather dinky Wren-built red-brick building, whose northeastern turret sports a bright-red time-ball that climbs the mast at 12.58pm and drops at 1pm GMT precisely; it was added in 1833 to allow ships on the Thames to set their clocks.

Greenwich's greatest claim to fame, of course, is as the home of **Greenwich Mean Time** (GMT) and the **Prime Meridian**. Since 1884, Greenwich has occupied zero longitude, the **Meridian Line** marked by the strip in the observatory's main courtyard. The observatory housed the first Astronomer Royal, John Flamsteed, whose chief task was to study the night sky in order to discover an astronomical method of finding the longitude of a ship at sea. Beyond the Octagon Room, where the king used to show off to his guests, are the Time galleries, which display four of the clocks designed by **John Harrison**, including "H4", which helped win the Longitude Prize in 1763.

The free **Astronomy Centre** galleries give a brief rundown of some of the big questions of the universe, and you can also watch one of the thirty-minute presentations in the **Planetarium**.

Brixton

Market stalls Mon–Sat 8am–6pm, Wed till 3pm • **Brixton Village and Market Row** Mon 8am–6pm, Tues–Sun 8am–11.30pm (shops shut earlier; check individual café and restaurant times) • **Farmers' market** Sun 9.30am–2.30pm • 🖥 brixtonmarket.net • **Pop Brixton** Mon–Wed & Sun 9am–11pm, Thurs–Sat 9am–midnight • 🖥 popbrixton.org • ⊖ Brixton

Brixton is a classic Victorian suburb, transformed from open fields into bricks and mortar in a couple of decades following the arrival of the railways in the 1860s. The viaducts dominate central Brixton, with shops and arcades hidden under their arches, but it's the West Indian community, who arrived here in the 1950s and 1960s, who define the character of the place. These days the area's revived indoor markets attract increasing numbers of visitors to a plethora of small restaurants and bars, making this always busy, noisy neighbourhood even more frenetic. As you leave the tube, directly opposite, you'll see the bright mural of **David Bowie**, who was born in Brixton in 1947; it became a shrine to Bowie on his death in January 2016.

The main axis for the market is **Electric Avenue**, which runs behind the tube station, so called as it was one of the first London shopping streets to be lit by electricity in the 1880s. From here you can find the arcades of **Market Row** and **Brixton Village**, which create a maze of activity. Nearby, **Pop Brixton**, on the corner of Pope's Road and Brixton Station Road, is a shipping-container-built mini village of shops and street-food traders, plus a couple of tiny but excellent restaurants, outdoor bars and an events space.

Dulwich Picture Gallery

Gallery Rd, SE21 7AD • Tues–Fri 10am–5pm, Sat & Sun 11am–5pm • Permanent collection £7; exhibitions (including entry to permanent collection) around £15.50 • ☎ 020 8693 5254, ⓦ dulwichpicturegallery.org.uk • West Dulwich (from Victoria) or North Dulwich (from London Bridge) train stations

Dulwich Picture Gallery, the nation's oldest public art gallery, was designed by John Soane in 1814, who created a beautifully spacious building, awash with natural light. The collection was acquired on behalf of the King of Poland, who lost his kingdom before he could take possession of it; it was then bequeathed to the foundation of Dulwich, and is crammed with superb paintings: elegiac landscapes by Cuyp, one of the world's finest Poussin series, and splendid works by Gainsborough, Van Dyck, Canaletto and Rubens, plus **Rembrandt**'s beautiful *Girl at a Window*. At the centre of the museum, look out for the tiny mausoleum designed by Soane for the sarcophagi of the gallery's founders. The temporary exhibitions are often excellent and there's a good café, overlooking the museum's well-tended gardens.

Horniman Museum

100 London Rd, SE23 3PQ • Daily 10.30am–5.30pm • Free; aquarium £4; butterfly house £5.40; charge for temporary exhibitions (around £7) • ☎ 020 8699 1872, ⓦ horniman.ac.uk • Forest Hill train station from Victoria or London Bridge

The wonderful **Horniman Museum** was purpose-built in 1901 by Frederick Horniman, a tea trader with a passion for collecting. In addition to the museum's natural history collection of stuffed birds and animals – with a majestic, overstuffed walrus its centrepiece – there's an eclectic ethnographic collection, and a music gallery with more than 1500 instruments from Chinese gongs to electric guitars. The gardens, with animal trail, butterfly house, bandstand and glasshouse, and with views over South London, are charming, and there's an aquarium in the basement.

West London

Running through the swathes of green, suburban West London is the **River Thames**, once the "Great Highway of London" and still the most pleasant way to travel in these parts during summer. Boats plough up the Thames all the way from central London via the **Royal Botanic Gardens** at **Kew** and the picturesque riverside at **Richmond**, as far as **Hampton Court**. In among the commuter-belt suburbs are several picturesque former country retreats. The Palladian villa of **Chiswick House** is perhaps the best known, as well as popular **Syon House**, a showcase for the talents of Robert Adam.

Chiswick House

Burlington Lane, W4 2RP • **House** April–Oct Mon–Wed & Sun 10am–6pm; Oct closes 5pm; March Sat & Sun 10am–4pm • £7.20; EH • **Gardens** Daily 7am–dusk • Free • ☎ 020 8995 0508, ⓦ chgt.org.uk • Chiswick train station from Waterloo or ⊖ Turnham Green

Chiswick House is a perfect little Neoclassical villa, designed in the 1720s by the Earl of Burlington, and set in one of the most beautifully landscaped gardens in London. Like its prototype, Palladio's Villa Rotonda near Vicenza, the house was created as a "temple

1

to the arts" where, amid his fine art collection, Burlington could entertain artistic friends such as Swift, Handel and Pope. Entertaining took place on the **upper floor**, a series of cleverly interconnecting rooms, each enjoying a wonderful view out onto the gardens – all, that is, except the Tribunal, the domed octagonal hall at the centre of the villa, where the earl's finest paintings and sculptures are displayed.

London Museum of Water and Steam

Green Dragon Lane, TW8 0EN • Daily 11am–4pm • £12.50 • ☎ 020 8568 4757, ⓦ waterandsteam.org.uk • Bus #237 or #267 from ⊖ Gunnersbury or Kew Bridge train station (from Waterloo)

Difficult to miss, thanks to its stylish Italianate standpipe tower, the **Museum of Water and Steam** occupies a former Victorian pumping station, 100 yards west of Kew Bridge. At the heart of the museum is the Steam Hall, which contains a triple expansion steam engine and four gigantic nineteenth-century Cornish beam engines. The museum also has a hands-on **Waterworks** gallery in the basement, devoted to the history of the capital's water supply, and **Splash Zone**, ideal for younger kids. The best time to visit is at weekends, when each of the museum's industrial dinosaurs is put through its paces, and the small narrow-gauge steam **Waterworks Railway** runs back and forth round the yard.

Syon House

London Rd, TW8 8JF • **House** Mid-March to Oct Wed, Thurs & Sun 11am–5pm • £12.50 (includes gardens) • **Gardens** Mid-March to Oct daily 10.30am–5pm • £7.50 • ☎ 020 8560 0882, ⓦ syonpark.co.uk • Bus #237 or #267 from ⊖ Gunnersbury or Kew Bridge train station (from Waterloo)

From its rather plain castellated exterior, you'd never guess that **Syon House** contains the most opulent eighteenth-century interiors in London. The splendour of Robert Adam's refurbishment is immediately revealed, however, in the pristine **Great Hall**, an apsed double cube with a screen of Doric columns at one end and classical statuary dotted around the edges. There are several more Adam-designed rooms to admire in the house, in particular the **Long Gallery** – 136ft by just 14ft – plus a smattering of works by Lely, Van Dyck and others.

While Adam beautified Syon House, Capability Brown laid out its **gardens** around an artificial lake, surrounding it with oaks, beeches, limes and cedars. The gardens' chief focus now, however, is the crescent-shaped **Great Conservatory**, an early nineteenth-century addition which is said to have inspired Joseph Paxton, architect of the Crystal Palace.

Kew Gardens

Kew Green or Kew Road, TW9 3AE • Jan & Nov daily 10am–4.15pm; March daily 10am–5.45pm; April–Sept Mon–Thurs 10am–6.30pm, Fri–Sun 10am–7.30pm (till 9pm June; till 8.30pm mid-July to Aug); Oct daily 10am–6pm; Dec daily 10am–3.30pm • £16.50; £15.50 online • ☎ 020 8332 5655, ⓦ kew.org • ⊖ Kew Gardens, then a short walk down Lichfield Rd to Victoria Gate

---

RIVER TRANSPORT: HEADING WEST

From April to October **Westminster Passenger Services** runs a scheduled service from Westminster Pier to Kew, Richmond and Hampton Court (departure times vary, but the first boat from Westminster usually leaves around 10.30am and the last around 2pm; your last chance to get back from Kew to Westminster is usually 5.30pm; 1hr 30min to Kew, around 3hr to Hampton Court; £13 single to Kew, £20 return; £17 to Hampton Court, £25 return; ☎ 020 7930 2062, ⓦ wpsa.co.uk). In addition, **Turks** runs a regular service from Richmond to Hampton Court (around 3 daily; to mid-Sept Tues–Sun; Aug daily; £9 single, £10.80 return; 1hr 45min; ☎ 020 8546 2434, ⓦ turks.co.uk). For the latest on boat services on the Thames, see ⓦ tfl.gov.uk.

1

Established in 1759, Kew's **Royal Botanic Gardens** manage the extremely difficult task of being both a world leader in botanic research and an extraordinarily beautiful and popular public park. There's always something to see, whatever the season, but to get the most out of the place come some time between spring and autumn, bring a picnic and stay for the day.

Of all the glasshouses, by far the most celebrated is the **Palm House**, a curvaceous mound of glass and wrought iron, designed by Decimus Burton in the 1840s. Its drippingly humid atmosphere nurtures most of the known palm species. Elsewhere in the gardens, you'll find the **Treetop Walkway**, which lifts you 60ft off the ground, and gives you a novel view of the tree canopy, a 163ft-high **Pagoda**, an art gallery, and various follies and semi-wild areas. The newest addition is the **Hive**, a 17m-high honeycomb structure that takes you inside the world of honeybees using 900 LED lights and the sound of 40,000 bees.

The three-storey red-brick mansion of **Kew Palace** (April–Oct only), to the northwest of the Palm House, was bought by George II as a nursery and schoolhouse for his umpteen children. Later, George III was confined to the palace and subjected to the dubious attentions of doctors who attempted to find a cure for his "madness".

Richmond

Richmond, upriver from Kew, basked for centuries in the glow of royal patronage, with Plantagenet kings and Tudor monarchs frequenting the riverside palace. Although most of the courtiers and aristocrats have gone, it is still a wealthy district, with two theatres, riverside walks and spacious, leafy upmarket residential streets.

Richmond Park

Daily: March–Sept 7am–dusk; Oct–Feb 7.30am–dusk • Free • ☎ 0300 061 2200, ⓦ royalparks.org.uk • Bus #371 from ⊖ Richmond to Richmond Gate or #65 from ⊖ Richmond to Petersham Gate

Richmond's greatest attraction is the enormous **Richmond Park**, at the top of Richmond Hill – 2500 acres of undulating grassland and bracken, dotted with coppiced woodland and as wild as anything in London. Eight miles across at its widest point, this is Europe's largest city park, famed for its red and fallow deer, which roam freely, and for its ancient oaks. For the most part untamed, the park does have a couple of deliberately landscaped plantations that feature splendid springtime azaleas and rhododendrons.

Ham House

Ham St, TW10 7RS • House April–Oct daily noon–4pm; Jan–March visits by guided tour only (Mon–Fri hourly noon–3pm, Sat & Sun noon–4pm); gardens daily 10am–5pm • £10.80; NT • ☎ 020 8940 1950, ⓦ nationaltrust.org.uk/ham-house-and-garden • Bus #371 or #65 from ⊖ Richmond

Leave the rest of London far behind at **Ham House**, home to the earls of Dysart for nearly three hundred years. Expensively furnished in the seventeenth century, but little altered since then, the house is blessed with one of the finest Stuart interiors in the country, from the stupendously ornate Great Staircase to the Long Gallery, featuring six "Court Beauties" by Peter Lely. Elsewhere, there are several fine Verrio ceiling paintings, some exquisite parquet flooring and works by Van Dyck and Reynolds. Also glorious are the formal seventeenth-century **gardens**, especially the Cherry Garden, laid out with an aromatic lavender parterre. The Orangery, overlooking the original kitchen garden, serves as a tearoom.

Strawberry Hill

268 Waldegrave Rd, TW1 4ST • **House** March–Oct Mon–Wed & Sun hours vary but generally 11am–5pm • £12.50 • **Garden** Daily 10am–6pm • Free • ☎ 020 8744 1241, ⓦ strawberryhillhouse.org.uk • Strawberry Hill train station from Waterloo

In 1747 writer, wit and fashion queen Horace Walpole, youngest son of former prime minister Robert Walpole, bought this "little play-thing house … the prettiest

1

bauble you ever saw … set in enamelled meadows, with filigree hedges", renamed it **Strawberry Hill** and set about inventing the most influential building in the Gothic Revival. Walpole appointed a "Committee of Taste" to embellish his project with details from other Gothic buildings: screens from Old St Paul's and Rouen cathedrals, and fan vaulting from Henry VII's Chapel in Westminster Abbey. Walpole wanted visits of Strawberry Hill to be a theatrical experience, and, with its eccentric Gothic decor, it remains so to this day.

Hampton Court

Hampton Court Rd, KT8 9AU • **Palace** Daily: April–Oct 10am–6pm; Nov–March closes 4.30pm; last entry 1hr before closing • £20.90 (tickets £1–3 cheaper online) • **Magic Garden** April–Oct daily 10am–6pm, last admission 5.15pm • £7.70, kids aged 3–15 £5.50 (includes Maze) • ☎ 020 3166 6000, ⓦ hrp.org.uk • Hampton Court train station from Waterloo

Hampton Court Palace, a sprawling red-brick ensemble on the banks of the Thames thirteen miles southwest of London, is the finest of England's royal abodes. Built in 1516 by the upwardly mobile **Cardinal Wolsey**, Henry VIII's Lord Chancellor, it was purloined by Henry himself after Wolsey fell from favour. In the second half of the seventeenth century, Charles II laid out the gardens, inspired by what he had seen at Versailles, while William and Mary had large sections of the palace remodelled by Wren a few years later.

Audioguides are available and free guided tours are led by period-costumed historians who bring the place to life. It's worth taking a day to explore fully – Hampton Court is huge – but the most rewarding sections are: **Henry VIII's Apartments**, which feature the glorious double-hammer-beamed Great Hall and Chapel Royal, with vaulted ceiling adorned with gilded cherubs; **William III's Apartments**, covered in militaristic trompe-l'oeil paintings; **Henry VIII's Kitchens**; and the **Cumberland Art Gallery**, which display a superb selection of works from the Royal Collection.

Overlooked by Wren's magnificent South Front is the formal **Privy Garden**, laid out as it would have been under William III. Here is the palace's celebrated **Great Vine**, whose grapes are sold at the palace each year in September. Close by is the gallery housing *The Triumphs of Caesar*, a series of heroic canvases by **Andrea Mantegna** from around 1486. To the west, the magnificent **Broad Walk** runs north for half a mile from the Thames. Halfway along lies the indoor **Royal Tennis Court**, used for real tennis, an arcane precursor of the modern game.

To the north of the palace the informal **Wilderness** area contains the famous trapezoidal **Maze**, laid out in 1714. Also on this side of the palace grounds is the gorgeous **Rose Garden** and an elaborate adventure playground for kids called the **Magic Garden**.

ARRIVAL AND DEPARTURE

BY PLANE

The capital's five international airports – Heathrow, Gatwick, Stansted, Luton and City Airport – are all less than an hour from the city centre.

HEATHROW

Some 15 miles west of central London, Heathrow (ⓦ heathrow airport.com) has five terminals and three train/tube stations: one for terminals 1, 2 and 3, and separate ones for terminals 4 and 5; Oyster and contactless can be used on the Underground and Elizabeth Line, and Heathrow Express (as of mid-2018).

Heathrow Express High-speed trains travel nonstop to Paddington Station (Mon–Sat 5.15am–11.20pm, Sun 6.20am–11.20pm; every 15min; journey 15min; £22–25

one-way off-peak, £37 return, more if you purchase your ticket on board; ⓦ heathrowexpress.com).

Elizabeth Line Formerly Heathrow Connect, the new Elizabeth Line (Crossrail) service will run four trains an hour from terminals 2, 3 and 4 to Paddington from May 2018 (with a service from terminal 5 from December 2019 onwards), with several stops on the way.

Underground The Piccadilly tube line runs directly into central London (daily 5am–11pm; Fri & Sat 24hr from terminals 1, 2, 3 & 5 only; every 5min; 50min–1hr); £3.10 off-peak, £5.10 peak (Mon–Fri 6.30–9.30am) with Oyster card (see page 114).

National Express Bus services run direct to Victoria Coach Station (daily 4.20am–10.10pm; every 20min–1hr;

journey 40min–1hr; £6–£13.50 one-way; Ⓦ national express.com).

GATWICK

Around 30 miles south of London, Gatwick Airport (Ⓦ gatwickairport.com) has good transport connections; you can pay by Oyster and contactless on train services (though it's cheaper to buy returns in advance).

Gatwick Express Nonstop service between the airport's South Terminal and Victoria Station (daily 5.50am–11.20am; every 15min; journey 30min; £17.80 one-way, £31.60 return, if bought online; group savings and other discounts available; Ⓦ gatwickexpress.com).

Southern and Thameslink trains Other train options include Southern services to Victoria (daily 5.40am–11pm, roughly every 15min; Fri & Sat hourly night service; 35min) and Thameslink services to various stations (24hr; every 15–30min; journey 30–45min), including Blackfriars and St Pancras; one-way tickets with Oyster: peak £16.50, off-peak £10.30; return £19.80.

National Express Buses run from Gatwick direct to central London (daily 24hr; 1–2 hourly; 1hr 30min; £6–£10 one-way).

STANSTED

Roughly 35 miles northeast of the capital, Stansted (Ⓦ stanstedairport.com) is mainly used by the budget airlines.

Stansted Express The most convenient way to get into town is by train on the Stansted Express to Liverpool Street (daily 5.30am–12.30am; every 15–30min; journey 45min; £16.60 one-way, £28 return; Ⓦ stanstedexpress.com).

National Express Buses to Liverpool Street, Stratford, Waterloo, Victoria Coach Station and Paddington (daily 24hr; every 20–30min; journey 1hr–1hr 45min), with tickets around £8–13 one-way.

CITY AIRPORT

London's smallest airport, City Airport, which handles almost entirely domestic and European flights (Ⓦ london cityairport.com), is in Docklands, 10 miles east of central London. Docklands Light Railway (DLR) will take you straight to Bank in the City (Mon–Sat 5.30am–12.15am, Sun 7am–11.15pm; every 8–15min; journey 20min); pay by Oyster or contactless (see opposite).

LUTON

Around 30 miles north of London, Luton (Ⓦ london-luton.co.uk) handles mostly charter flights.

Luton Airport Parkway A free shuttle bus (every 10min; 5min) transports passengers to Luton Airport Parkway train station, connected to St Pancras (daily 24hr; every 15–30min; journey 25–45min; one-way £14) and other stations in central London.

Buses Green Line runs the #757 coach from Luton Airport to Victoria Coach Station (daily 24hr; every 20min–1hr; journey 1hr–1hr 30min; one-way £10, return £17; Ⓦ www.greenline.co.uk), stopping at several locations en route. National Express runs buses to Victoria Coach Station (daily 24hr; every 20min–1hr; journey 1hr 5min–1hr 20min; £6–12 one-way).

BY TRAIN

From Europe Eurostar (Ⓦ eurostar.com) trains arrive at St Pancras International, next door to King's Cross.

From Britain Arriving by train from elsewhere in Britain, you'll come into one of London's mainline stations, all of which have adjacent Underground stations. As a rough guide, Charing Cross handles services to Kent; Euston to the Midlands, northwest England and Glasgow; Fenchurch Street to south Essex; King's Cross to northeast England and Scotland; Liverpool Street to eastern England; Marylebone to the Midlands; Paddington to west and southwest England, including Oxford, Bath and Bristol; St Pancras for Eurostar and the southeast, plus trains to the East Midlands and South Yorkshire; Victoria to destinations south, including Brighton; and Waterloo directly southwest of London, including Southampton and Salisbury.

Information National Rail Enquiries (☎ 0345 748 4950, Ⓦ nationalrail.co.uk).

DESTINATIONS

Charing Cross to: Canterbury West (hourly; 1hr 40min); Dover Priory (every 30min; 1hr 40min–2hr); Hastings (every 30min; 1hr 35min–1hr 50min); Rochester (every 30min; 1hr 15min).

Euston to: Birmingham New Street (every 20min; 1hr 25min); Carlisle (hourly; 3hr 25min); Lancaster (hourly; 2hr 30min); Liverpool Lime Street (hourly; 2hr 10min); Manchester Piccadilly (every 20min; 2hr 5min).

King's Cross to: Cambridge (every 30min; 45min); Durham (hourly; 2hr 55min); Leeds (every 30min; 2hr 15min); Newcastle (every 30min; 2hr 50min–3hr 15min); York (every 20–30min; 1hr 50min–2hr 30min).

Liverpool Street to: Cambridge (every 30min; 1hr 15min); Norwich (every 30min; 1hr 45min–1hr 55min).

London Bridge to: Brighton (every 30min; 1hr).

Paddington to: Bath (every 30min; 1hr 30min); Bristol (every 15–30min; 1hr 20min–1hr 40min); Cheltenham (every 2hr; 2hr 15min); Exeter (every 30min–1hr; 2hr 15min–2hr 50min); Gloucester (every 2hr; 2hr); Oxford (every 30min; 55min); Penzance (every 1–2hr; 5hr 30min); Plymouth (hourly; 3hr 15min–3hr 40min); Worcester (hourly; 2hr 20min–2hr 50min).

St Pancras to: Brighton (every 30min; 1hr 15min); Canterbury (every 30min–1hr; 55min); Dover Priory (every 30min–hourly; 1hr 5min); Leicester (every 15–30min; 1hr–1hr 35min); Nottingham (2 hourly; 1hr 40min–2hr); Rochester (every 30min; 35min); Sheffield (every 30min; 2hr–2hr 20min).

Victoria to: Arundel (Mon–Sat every 30min, Sun hourly; 1hr 30min); Brighton (every 30min; 50min); Canterbury East (every 30min–1hr; 1hr 40min); Chichester (1–2 hourly; 1hr 30min); Dover Priory (Mon–Sat every 30min; 2hr–2hr 15min); Lewes (Mon–Sat every 30min, Sun hourly; 1hr–1hr 10min); Rochester (every 30min; 40min–1hr).

Waterloo to: Portsmouth Harbour (every 15–30min; 1hr 40min–2hr 15min); Southampton Central (every 30min; 1hr 15min); Winchester (every 30min; 1hr).

BY BUS

Victoria Coach Station Coming into London by coach, you're most likely to arrive at Victoria Coach Station, a couple of hundred yards south down Buckingham Palace Rd from the train and Underground stations of the same name. Journey times leaving London can vary considerably: maximum times are given, but avoid travelling by coach during the afternoon rush hour if at all possible.

Information Traveline (☎ 0871 200 2233, ⊛ traveline.info) or National Express (☎ 0871 781 8181, ⊛ nationalexpress.com).

Destinations Bath (hourly–every 1hr 30min; 3hr 15min); Birmingham (every 30min; 3hr 20min); Brighton (every 30min–1hr 30min; 3hr); Bristol (every 2hr; 3hr); Cambridge (every 30min–1hr 30min; 2hr); Canterbury (hourly–every 1hr 30min; 2hr 40min); Dover (8 daily; 3hr–3hr 30min); Exeter (every 2–3hr; 4hr 30min); Gloucester (every 1–2hr; 3hr 25min); Liverpool (every 1–2hr; 6hr 15min); Manchester (every 1hr 30min; 6hr 25min); Newcastle (4 daily; 7hr 55min); Oxford (every 20min; 2hr); Plymouth (5 daily; 6hr 20min); Stratford (3 daily; 3hr 45min).

GETTING AROUND

London's **transport network** is complex and expensive, but will get you wherever you want at most hours of the day or night. Avoid travelling during the **rush hour** (Mon–Fri 8–9.30am & 5–7pm), when tubes become unbearably crowded, and some buses get so full that they won't let you on. You're best using Oyster or a contactless payment card.

INFORMATION

Transport for London (TfL) For maps, route planning and information see ⊛ tfl.gov.uk, or call ☎ 0343 222 1234.

Visitor Centres TfL has Visitor Centres, where you can buy Oyster cards and get information, at: Piccadilly Circus (daily 9.30am–4pm); Liverpool Street (daily 9am–5pm); Victoria (daily 8am–6pm); Euston, King's Cross Underground and Paddington (all Mon–Sat 8am–6pm, Sun 8.30am–6pm); Heathrow terminals 2 & 3 Underground station (daily 7.30am–8.30pm); and Gatwick North and South Arrivals (daily 9.15am–4pm).

Apps The best mobile phone app for route planning, including finding live bus times, is Citymapper (⊛ citymapper.com).

GETTING ABOUT: OYSTER CARDS AND CONTACTLESS PAYMENT

For all London transport, the cheapest, easiest ticketing option is an **Oyster card**, London's transport smartcard, available from all tube stations and TfL Visitor Centres. Use it either to store a weekly/monthly **travelcard**, or as a **pay-as-you-go** card. As you enter the tube or bus, simply touch in your card at the card reader. On a tube or train, you need to touch out again, or a maximum cash fare of up to £7.80 will be deducted; on a bus, you only touch in. A pay-as-you-go Oyster operates daily and weekly price-capping; you will stop being charged when you have this (£6.60 for zones 1–2 for a day; £33 for a week, running Mon–Sun), but you still need to touch in (and out). Unless you're buying a monthly or yearly Oyster card, it costs £5 for the card (refundable on return), or visitors can buy a Visitor Oyster card for £3, plus the amount of credit you want.

If you have a debit or credit card or smart phone with a **contactless payment** function, you can use this in the same way as a pay-as-you-go Oyster card, with the same fares and price-capping (make sure that you use the same card all day). British Visa, MasterCard and American Express cards work; for cards issued outside the UK, American Express and most but not all MasterCard and Visa with contactless payment should work. However, any **overseas bank charges** will apply to each use.

Children under 11 travel for free; children aged 11–15 travel free on all buses and at child rate on the tube; children aged 16 or 17 can travel at half the adult rate on all forms of transport. Children 11 years old and over must have a Zip Oyster photocard; apply in advance online (£15 for 11–15 year olds; £20 for 16–17 year olds). Visitors from outside the UK will need to pick this up from a TfL Visitor Centre (see above).

Other travelcards and passes are available, too; check ⊛ tfl.gov.uk for details.

THE CONGESTION CHARGE

All vehicles entering central London on weekdays between 7am and 6pm are liable to a **congestion charge** of £11.50 per vehicle (£10.50 if you sign up online to pay automatically each time you travel in the zone; vehicles that don't meet certain emission standards have to pay an additional £10/day emissions surcharge). Pay the charge online or over the phone (lines open Mon–Fri 8am–10pm, Sat 9am–3pm; ☎0343 222 2222, Ⓦtfl.gov.uk), before midnight; paying the following day costs £14; 24 hours later, you'll be liable for a £130 Penalty Charge Notice (reduced to £65 if you pay within fourteen days). Disabled travellers, motorcycles, minibuses and some alternative-fuel vehicles are exempt from the charge, but you must register in order to qualify. For more details, visit Ⓦtfl.gov.uk.

BY TUBE

Except for very short journeys, the Underground – or tube – is by far the quickest way to get about.

Tube lines Eleven different lines cross much of the metropolis, although south of the river is not very well covered. Each line has its own colour and name – all you need to know is which direction you're travelling in (northbound, eastbound, southbound or westbound), and the final destination (plus sometimes which branch).

Services Frequent Mon–Sat 5.30am–12.30am, Sun 7.30am–11.30pm; you rarely have to wait more than 5min for a train between central stations.

Night Tube The 24hr Night Tube service runs every 10–20min on Friday and Saturday on five main lines: Central, Jubilee, Piccadilly, Victoria and Northern (Charing Cross branch), plus an East London section of the Overground.

Fares An Oyster card or contactless payment (touched in and out at the barrier at each station) is by far your best option (see page 114); one-way fares with paper tickets are never the best choice – a journey in zone 1 costs £4.90 with a paper ticket, £2.40 with an Oyster or contactless card.

BY BUS

London's red buses – most, but not all, of them, double-deckers – are fun to ride on and a cheap way of sightseeing. For example, the #11 bus from Victoria station will take you past Westminster Abbey and the Houses of Parliament, up Whitehall, round Trafalgar Square, along the Strand and on to St Paul's Cathedral. You can also take an old-fashioned double-decker Routemaster, on "heritage" route #15 (daily 9.30am–6.30pm; every 20min) from Trafalgar Square to Tower Hill. At many stops you need to stick your hand out to get the bus to stop, and press the bell in order to get off.

Services Some buses run a 24hr service, but most run between about 5am and midnight, with a network of night buses (prefixed with the letter "N") operating outside this period (every 20–30min).

Fares A one-way fare is £1.50, any time and for any distance travelled, including if you transfer to another bus within an hour (the Hopper fare). You must touch in every time you alight (though you don't touch out); cash is not accepted – you need an Oyster card, contactless debit card or travelcard.

BY OVERGROUND AND DLR

Overground The orange Overground line is a large network that connects with the tube system and stretches out to Richmond in the west, Stratford in the east, forming an orbital railway, a sort of outer Circle Line. It's particularly useful for reaching parts of East London (every 5–15min roughly). From New Cross Gate to Dalston Junction there's a night service (Fri & Sat), with plans to extend it to Highbury & Islington.

DLR The Docklands Light Railway is a network of driverless trains from Bank in the City, and from Tower Gateway (close to Tower Hill tube and the Tower of London) above ground to the financial centre of Docklands, plus other areas in the East End, and also below ground to Greenwich. It's integrated with the tube; pay by Oyster.

BY TRAIN

Large areas of London's outskirts are best reached by the suburban train network, departing from one of the main central termini (see page 113); they all accept Oyster, and main routes generally run every 15–30min.

BY BOAT

Boat trips on the Thames are a fun way of sightseeing, and there are several tours and speedboats as well as Thames Clippers.

Thames Clipper Runs a regular commuter service between the London Eye and Greenwich (every 15–30min Mon–Fri 7am–10.30pm, Sat & Sun 8.30am or 9.30am–10.30pm, then one final eastbound service around 11.30pm; Ⓦthamesclippers.com). There are piers on both sides of the river, including Embankment, Bankside, Blackfriars, London Bridge and Tower. You can buy tickets at a pier, but there is a discount if you buy online in advance or use an Oyster card. Typical fares are £6.30 for a central zone single with a pay-as-you-go Oyster card or online (£8.10 otherwise), with an unlimited hop-on hop-off day River Roamer costing £16.30 online, £18.50 from the pier.

1

BY TAXI

Black cabs Compared to most cities, London's metered black cabs are expensive unless there are three or more of you, though black-cab drivers have unparalleled knowledge of the city's streets. The minimum fare is £2.60, and a ride from Euston to Victoria, for example, costs around £15–20 (Mon–Fri 5am–8pm). After 8pm on weekdays and all day during the weekend, a higher tariff applies, and after 10pm it's higher still. A yellow light over the windscreen tells you if the cab is available – just stick your arm out to hail it. To order a black cab in advance (£2 extra), phone ☎ 0871 871 8710.

Minicabs and apps Private minicabs are much cheaper than black cabs, but cannot be hailed from the street. They must be licensed and able to produce a TfL ID on demand. Apps like Hailo and Uber can come in handy, too, though

at the time of going to print TfL had decided not to renew Uber's licence to operate in London; check for updates before you travel.

BY BIKE

Boris bikes The city's cycle rental scheme – or Boris bikes, as they're universally known, after former Mayor of London Boris Johnson – has over 700 docking stations across central London. With a credit or debit card, you can buy 24hr access for just £2. You then get the first 30min on a bike free, so if you hop from docking station to docking station you don't pay another penny. Otherwise, it's £2 for each additional 30min. For more details see ⓦ tfl.gov.uk.

Bike rental London Bicycle Tour Company, 1a Gabriel Wharf on the South Bank (☎ 020 7923 6838, ⓦ londonbicycle.com), has bikes for rent (£3.50–4/hr; £20–24/day).

INFORMATION AND TOURS

Visit London The official tourist information body, though they don't run any tourist offices. Check ⓦ visitlondon.com for information.

City of London Information Centre The City's central information office, situated on the south side of St Paul's Cathedral (Mon–Sat 9.30am–5.30pm, Sun 10am–4pm; ⓦ cityoflondon.gov.uk; ⊖ St Paul's); several walking tours of the City run daily from here (most £7).

London Pass and discounts The London Pass (ⓦ londonpass.com) covers a hop-on hop-off bus tour, Thames river cruise and entry to around 70 of London's top charging attractions, including Hampton Court Palace, London Zoo, St Paul's Cathedral, the Tower of London, Westminster Abbey and Windsor Castle. The pass costs £62 for one day (£42 for kids), rising to £139 for six days (£96 for kids), with all-zone Oyster card options available too. Buy online or from a TfL Visitor Centre and other outlets. If you've travelled to London by National Rail train (not Eurostar) you can get two-for-one tickets on numerous attractions

(see ⓦ daysoutguide.co.uk).

Bus tours Standard sightseeing tours are run by several rival bus companies, with open-top double-deckers every 30min from Victoria station, Trafalgar Square, Piccadilly and other tourist spots. You can hop on and off several different routes with the Original Tour for £29 (daily 8.20am–6pm; every 15–30min; ☎ 020 8877 1722, ⓦ theoriginaltour.com). Golden Tours' (ⓦ goldentours.com) bus tour is included in the London Pass.

Boat tours City Cruises run from Westminster to Greenwich (every 40min; tickets £10–16, one-day ticket included in London Pass, if bought online; ☎ 020 7928 3132, ⓦ citycruises.com).

Walking tours Numerous walking tours are offered, including those departing from the City of London information centre (see above). They normally cost around £10 and take around 2hr; often you can simply show up at the starting point. Original London Walks (☎ 020 7624 3978, ⓦ www.walks.com) are a well-established company.

ACCOMMODATION

London **accommodation** is expensive. The **hostels** are among the costliest in the world, while venerable institutions such as the *Ritz*, the *Dorchester* and the *Savoy* charge the very top international prices – from £300 per luxurious night. For a decent **hotel** room, don't expect much change out of £110 a night, and even **B&Bs** struggle to bring their tariffs down to £90 for a double with shared facilities. The **chain hotels** are a safe bet – but they'll offer less character than the places that we've reviewed below and, depending on the season or location, may not always be that much cheaper. Premier Inn (ⓦ premierinn.com), Travelodge (ⓦ travelodge.co.uk), easyHotel (ⓦ easyhotel.com) and Point A (ⓦ pointahotels.com) all have properties in central locations. Whatever the time of year, you should book as early as possible if you want to stay within a couple of tube stops of the West End. Among the many price comparison sites and booking portals, ⓦ londontown.com often offers good discounts.

HOTELS, GUESTHOUSES AND B&BS

When choosing your area, bear in mind that the West End – Soho, Covent Garden, St James's, Mayfair and Marylebone – and the western districts of Knightsbridge and Kensington are dominated by expensive, upmarket hotels; for central

hotels at a good price, Bloomsbury remains a safe bet, while a number of less expensive options are popping up on the fringes. Free wi-fi is almost universally standard, and is free in all the establishments we review. While anywhere categorized as a B&B automatically includes

1

LONDON POSTCODES

A brief word on **London postcodes**: the name of each street is followed by a letter giving the geographical location (E for "east", WC for "west central" and so on) and a number that specifies the postal area. However, this is not a reliable indication of the remoteness of the locale – W5, for example, lies beyond the more remote-sounding NW10 – so it's always best to check a map before taking a room in what may sound like a fairly central area.

breakfast, our reviews specify where breakfast is included in hotel rates (which is unusual) and guesthouses (which is less so).

WESTMINSTER AND ST JAMES'S

★ **Artist Residence** 52 Cambridge St, SW1V 4QQ ☎ 020 7828 6684, ⓦ artistresidence.co.uk; ⊖ Pimlico; map p.62. Boutique guesthouse offering relaxed luxury and cool style. The ten rooms – exposed brick, bare wood, stylish prints and upcycled furnishings – feature lots of extras, but the cheapest are small. There's a Modern British restaurant and a cocktail bar on site. **£265**

B&B Belgravia 64–66 Ebury St, SW1W 9QD ☎ 020 7259 8570, ⓦ bb-belgravia.com; ⊖ Victoria; map p.98. Welcoming B&B near Victoria train and coach stations. The small, simple, en-suite rooms are comfortable, with some original features; those on the ground floor can get street noise. There's a lounge with hot drinks and a guest laptop, plus a garden and bike loan. **£160**

Nadler Victoria 10 Palace Place, SW1E 5BW ☎ 020 3540 8800, ⓦ nadlerhotels.com; ⊖ Victoria; map p.66. One of a sophisticated mini-chain – well-designed, comfortable rooms with kitchenettes, plus friendly service – very near Buckingham Palace. The cheapest rooms are small, but still prove excellent value in this part of town. Branches in Soho (see below) and Earl's Court (see page 119). **£195**

Sanctuary House 33 Tothill St, SW1H 9LA ☎ 020 7799 4044, ⓦ sanctuaryhousehotel.co.uk; ⊖ St James's Park; map p.66. Fuller's Brewery runs a number of hotels in London; this one has a terrific location by St James's Park. The 34 smart rooms, despite being above the drinking action, are quiet enough, and kitted out in an uncontroversially contemporary style. **£166**

Z Hotel Piccadilly 2 Orange St, WC2H 7DF ☎ 020 3551 3700, ⓦ thezhotels.com; ⊖ Piccadilly Circus; map p.66. While this modern hotel is convenient for Piccadilly, it's also a hop away from Trafalgar Square. With properties all over London, the Z chain specializes in well-designed, teeny rooms – they're en suite, with storage space, but the cheapest don't have windows (rooms with windows cost £15 more). Free nightly wine and cheese buffets. **£164**

MARYLEBONE

22 York Street 22 York St, W1U 6PX ☎ 020 7224 2990, ⓦ 22yorkstreet.co.uk; ⊖ Baker Street; map p.98. This ten-

room B&B, in a family house, delivers a home from home with heart. The Georgian building is antique-bedecked, with comfortable public spaces for reading and board games. Breakfasts are communal. **£150**

SOHO

Dean Street Townhouse 69–71 Dean St, W1D 3SE ☎ 020 7434 1775, ⓦ deanstreettownhouse.com; ⊖ Tottenham Court Road; map p.66. One of a set of hotels owned by the Soho House members' club, this 1730s beauty is in a great location. The split-level "broom cupboard" is OK for one night – after that rooms increase in size up to the relatively capacious "bigger" (£470). All are luxurious, with nice touches including home-made biscuits; many have standalone tubs. **£220**

★ **Hazlitt's** 6 Frith St, W1D 3JA ☎ 020 7434 1771, ⓦ hazlittshotel.com; ⊖ Tottenham Court Road; map p.66. This early eighteenth-century building, off Soho Square, is a hotel of character and charm. Creaky, crooked old stairs lead up to romantic en-suite rooms, decorated with period furniture and antique books. Continental breakfast (not included) is served in your room; there's also a small library with real fire and honesty bar. **£299**

Nadler Soho 10 Carlisle St, W1D 3BR ☎ 020 3697 3697, ⓦ thenadler.com; ⊖ Tottenham Court Road; map p.66. Attention to detail, lovely service and good prices for this location. The smart, modern rooms are businesslike (the cheapest are small), with a microwave, fridge, coffee machine and kettle, so you could effectively self-cater. There are (cheaper) branches in St James's (see above) and near Earl's Court (see page 119). **£209**

COVENT GARDEN

The Fielding 4 Broad Court, Bow St, WC2B 5QZ ☎ 020 7836 8305, ⓦ thefieldinghotel.co.uk; ⊖ Covent Garden; map p.66. In an old building (there's no lift) on a pedestrianized court behind the Royal Opera House, this little hotel offers simple, en-suite rooms – a little tired in places, but clean, comfortable and great value for this location, with tea- and coffee-making facilities. Rates increase by £20 at the weekend. **£140**

Henrietta Hotel 14–15 Henrietta St, WC2E 8QH ☎ 020 3794 5313, ⓦ henriettahotel.com; ⊖ Covent Garden; map p.66. Opulent boutique hotel spread across two historic townhouses, with an on-site restaurant helmed by star chef Ollie Dabbous. With a hipster-boudoir feel, the rooms include a minibar stocked with cocktails created by the mixologists at *Experimental Cocktail Club*. **£238**

Seven Dials Hotel 7 Monmouth St, WC2H 9DA ☎ 020 7240 0823, ⓦ sevendialshotel.com; ⊖ Covent Garden; map p.66. Welcoming, eighteen-room guesthouse on one of Covent Garden's nicest streets. It's in no way fancy: the staircase is narrow and steep (no lift) and the basic en-suite rooms are very small, but all are clean and comfy, and rates include breakfast. **£110**

BLOOMSBURY AND KING'S CROSS

Arosfa 83 Gower St, WC1E 6HJ ☎ 020 7636 2115, ⓦ arosfalondon.com; ⊖ Goodge Street; map p.77. The fifteen en-suite rooms in this popular, friendly guest-house aren't big, but they're clean and comfortable. There's a homely guest lounge/bar and a walled garden – and breakfasts (Full English and buffet) are included. **£160**

Great Northern Hotel King's Cross St Pancras Station, Pancras Rd, N1C 4TB ☎ 020 3388 0800, ⓦ gnhlondon. com; ⊖ King's Cross St Pancras; map p.77. Gussied-up station hotel with a vaguely Deco feel and lots of extras – Nespresso coffee, pastries and fresh fruit offered on each floor. The boutique rooms are bijou; the smallest, called "couchettes", evoke the romance of a train sleeper, while others are tucked beneath the eaves. **£230**

Megaro Hotel Belgrove St, WC1H 8AB ☎ 020 7843 2222, ⓦ hotelmegaro.co.uk; ⊖ King's Cross St Pancras; map p.77. Unfussy contemporary choice opposite the train station. The rooms – fifty or so, including family options – are relatively spacious, with good bathrooms and espresso machines. **£200**

★ **Ridgemount** 65–67 Gower St, WC1E 6HJ ☎ 020 7636 1141, ⓦ ridgemounthotel.co.uk; ⊖ Goodge Street; map p.77. Old-fashioned, friendly and popular family-owned guesthouse, faded but clean. Around half of the 32 rooms have washbasins but share facilities, which are spotless, and are sizeable; en-suites cost about £20 more. Full breakfast included. **£95**

THE CITY

Apex City of London Hotel 1 Seething Lane, EC3N 4AX ☎ 020 7702 2020, ⓦ apexhotels.co.uk; ⊖ Tower Hill; map p.82. Sleek and nicely appointed modern hotel on a secluded street near the Tower of London. It's geared towards a corporate clientele, but welcoming to all – and every guest gets a free rubber duck. Book early for the best rates. **£152**

The Rookery 12 Peter's Lane, Cowcross St, EC1M 6DS ☎ 020 7336 0931, ⓦ rookeryhotel.com; ⊖ Farringdon; map p.82. Rambling Georgian townhouse, all panelled walls, flagstoned floors and creaky timeworn floorboards. The rooms, some of which are a little dark, offer faded Baroque glam. There's a comfy conservatory and an honesty bar, but breakfast, not included in the price, is served in your room. **£240**

★ **Zetter Hotel** 86–88 Clerkenwell Rd, EC1M 5RJ ☎ 020 7324 4567, ⓦ thezetter.com; ⊖ Farringdon; map p.82. In a stylishly converted warehouse, the *Zetter* epitomizes good-value boutique style. Rooms are colourful and bold, with extras such as hot-water bottles and vintage paperbacks. Free bike rental. Their more expensive sister hotels *Zetter Townhouse* (opposite, on St John's Square) and *Zetter Townhouse Marylebone* are even more whimsical. **£145**

EAST LONDON

Ace Hotel 100 Shoreditch High St, E1 6JQ ☎ 020 7613 9800, ⓦ acehotel.com/london; ⊖ Liverpool Street; map p.89. This branch of the US hipster hotel chain is a party-animal choice. Hosting exhibitions, talks, gigs and DJ nights, it also has various artisan coffee and snack bars and a Modern British restaurant, with a club in the basement and a rooftop bar. Rooms are as cool as you'd expect, all subdued dark colours, retro styling and quirky touches – deluxe options include turntables and vinyl. **£219**

Culpeper 40 Commercial St, E1 6LP ☎ 020 7247 5371, ⓦ theculpeper.com; ⊖ Aldgate East; map p.89. Simple, artfully distressed en-suite rooms above a gastropub near Brick Lane (don't expect peace and quiet during pub hours). There's a plant-filled terrace on the roof, where you can sit with a drink overlooking the City, and a good hot breakfast is included. **£120**

The Hoxton 81 Great Eastern St, EC2A 3HU ☎ 020 7550 1000, ⓦ hoxtonhotels.com; ⊖ Old Street; map p.89. "The Hox" was one of the first hotels in this nightlife neighbourhood, and despite a change in ownership it remains a stalwart, with buzzy communal areas and two hundred or so attractive rooms. Downstairs, the *Hoxton Grill* and the DJ bar are popular hangouts – ask for a quiet room if you value your sleep. A light breakfast is delivered to your room. **£199**

★ **Qbic** 42 Adler St, E1 1EE ☎ 020 3021 2644, ⓦ london. qbichotels.com; ⊖ Aldgate East; map p.89. Bright, youthful hotel – the eye-popping colour blocks and kitschy photos are not for everyone. Rooms feature fab bathrooms and comfortable beds; the cheapest are very small, though, with no windows, for which you'll pay around £15 more. Bikes for loan, free hot drinks, and a Modern British restaurant/bar hosting monthly gigs and DJ sets. **£130**

SOUTH BANK

★ **Captain Bligh Guest House** 100 Lambeth Rd, SE1 7PT (no phone), ⓦ captainblighhouse.co.uk; ⊖ Lambeth North; map p.62. Captain Bligh's former residence can be your home from home – a cosy Georgian building, opposite the Imperial War Museum, run by a friendly, unobtrusive couple. The five en-suite rooms each have kitchenettes stocked with simple breakfast provisions. The three-night minimum may be the only snag. No cards. **£100**

1

BANKSIDE

Citizen M Bankside 20 Lavington St, SE1 0NZ ☎ 020 3519 1680, ⓦ citizenm.com; ⊖ Southwark; map p.94. One of a slick European chain that also has branches near Tower Hill and Shoreditch. The modern rooms are pod-like, but well designed, with big windows, big beds and touch-tablet controls, and the buzzy canteen/bar is handy. **£160**

KENSINGTON AND CHELSEA

Aster House 3 Sumner Place, SW7 3EE ☎ 020 7581 5888, ⓦ asterhouse.com; ⊖ South Kensington; map p.98. Set on a white-stuccoed South Ken street, this upmarket B&B has thirteen rooms, all en suite but of varying sizes, decorated in a chintzy, traditional style. One opens out onto the pretty back garden. A copious buffet breakfast is served in a sunny conservatory. **£240**

★ **Main House** 6 Colville Rd, W11 2BP ☎ 020 7221 9691, ⓦ themainhouse.co.uk; ⊖ Notting Hill Gate; map p.98. Homely, and a tad bohemian, this guesthouse offers huge suites (one with two bedrooms), covering a floor each. No breakfast, but there's a fridge for guests' use (along with all manner of extras) and you can have tea/coffee brought to your room. Three-night minimum. **£130**

Nadler Kensington 25 Courtfield Gardens, SW5 0PG ☎ 020 7244 2255, ⓦ thenadler.com/kensington.shtml; ⊖ Earl's Court; map p.98. Good-value contemporary accommodation, with attention to detail but no fussy extras. The 65 rooms range from bijou singles via "luxury bunks" to deluxe; all have mini-kitchens and a choice of pillows. A good choice for families. There are two more Nadlers, in St James's (see page 117) and Soho (see page 117). **£165**

Twenty Nevern Square 20 Nevern Square, SW5 9PD ☎ 020 7565 9555, ⓦ 20nevernsquare.mayflowercollection.com; ⊖ Earl's Court; map p.98. In an area of bog-standard B&Bs, this small hotel is a more interesting alternative, strewn with Oriental and European antiques. Rooms are en suite; some, however, are teeny, and others can be noisy. Buffet breakfast included. **£150**

Vancouver Studios 30 Prince's Square, W2 4NJ ☎ 020 7243 1270, ⓦ vancouverstudios.co.uk; ⊖ Bayswater; map p.98. Good-value self-catering suites (some with balconies) in a grand old Victorian townhouse with maid service, a walled garden and a resident cat. Those at the back are quietest. **£149**

NORTH LONDON

Hampstead Village Guesthouse 2 Kemplay Rd, NW3 1SY ☎ 020 7435 8679, ⓦ hampsteadguesthouse.com; ⊖ Hampstead; map p.62. Prettily located on a quiet residential street between Hampstead Village and the Heath, this is an unconventional guesthouse in a

family home. Rooms (most en suite) are full of character, crammed with books, pictures and personal mementos. Breakfast costs £10. One-night bookings cost £5 (Mon–Fri) or £10 (Sat) more. **£105**

SOUTH LONDON

Number 16 16 St Alfege Passage, SE10 9JS ☎ 020 8853 4337, ⓦ st-alfeges.co.uk; ⊖ Cutty Sark DLR; map p.94. Behind Hawksmoor's St Alfege church, this Greenwich B&B – owned by a flamboyant ex-antique dealer/actor – offers a warm welcome, offbeat flair and the feel of being in a slightly eccentric home from home. **£140**

HOSTELS

Youth Hostel Association (YHA) hostels (ⓦ yha.org.uk) are generally the cleanest, most efficiently run in the capital. However, they often charge more than private hostels, and tend to get booked up months in advance. Independent hostels are cheaper and more relaxed, but can be less reliable in terms of facilities – some are noisy, not that clean, and essentially little more than places to flop after partying all night. A good website for booking independent places online is ⓦ hostelworld.com/hostels/London.

YHA HOSTELS

★ **Central** 104 Bolsover St, W1W 5NU ☎ 0345 371 9154, ⓦ yha.org.uk/hostel/london-central; ⊖ Great Portland Street; map p.77. Secure, clean 300-bed hostel, in a surprisingly quiet West End location, with a kitchen, 24hr café and bar. Most dorms, and some doubles, are en-suite; others have showers next door. Dorms **£35**, doubles **£89**

Earl's Court 38 Bolton Gardens, SW5 0AQ ☎ 0345 371 9114, ⓦ yha.org.uk/hostel/london-earls-court; ⊖ Earl's Court; map p.98. Buzzy, busy 186-bed hostel with kitchen, café, lounge and patio garden. Some doubles are en suite. Dorms **£32**, doubles **£79**

Oxford Street 14 Noel St, W1F 8GJ ☎ 0345 371 9133, ⓦ yha.org.uk/hostel/london-oxford-street; ⊖ Oxford Circus; map p.66. The Soho location and modest size (around 105 beds) mean this hostel tends to be full year-round. The atmosphere can be party central, but it's pretty family-friendly. There's a café, kitchen, dining room and bar. No en suites. Dorms **£35**, doubles **£85**

St Pancras 79–81 Euston Rd, NW1 2QE ☎ 0345 371 9344, ⓦ yha.org.uk/hostel/london-st-pancras; ⊖ King's Cross St Pancras; map p.77. This hostel, near the train station on the busy Euston Rd, has nearly two hundred beds. Dorms and private rooms are clean, bright and double-glazed, and some are en suite. No kitchen, but there's a café. Dorms **£34**, doubles **£85**

St Paul's 36 Carter Lane, EC4V 5AB ☎ 0345 371 9012, ⓦ yha.org.uk/hostel/london-st-pauls; ⊖ St Paul's; map p.82. A 213-bed hostel in a grand old school building

1

opposite St Paul's Cathedral. Dorms sleep up to eleven; all facilities are shared, including for the private rooms. Café, but no kitchen. Dorms **£30**, doubles **£79**

Thameside 20 Salter Rd, SE16 5PR ☎ 0345 371 9756, ⊛ yha.org.uk/hostel/london-thameside; ⊖ Rotherhithe; map p.94. Huge purpose-built hostel in a quiet spot near the river. A 15min walk from the tube, it often has space when more central places are full. All dorms (sleeping up to eleven) and private rooms are en suite. Self-catering is available, and there's a simple café-bar. Dorms **£25**, doubles **£69**

INDEPENDENT HOSTELS

Clink 78 78 King's Cross Rd, WC1X 9QG ☎ 020 7183 9400, ⊛ clinkhostels.com; ⊖ King's Cross St Pancras; map p.77. Occupying a Victorian magistrates' court, this huge party hostel has plenty of jazzed-up period features (you can even stay in one of the tiny old prison cells). It can get noisy – and there's a lively DJ bar – but it's fun if you're feeling sociable. Dorms (four to fourteen beds; some pods; some en suite) include women-only options, and there are private singles/twins (some en suite). Kitchen facilities (not for breakfast), internet lounge and travel shop, plus continental breakfast for £1. They have a smaller, quieter sister property, *Clink 261*, down the road. Dorms **£25**, twins **£90**

The Dictionary Hostel 10–20 Kingsland Rd, E2 8DA ☎ 020 7613 2784, ⊛ thedictionaryhostel.com; ⊖ Old Street; map p.89. This is a friendly, party hostel, as you'd expect from its Shoreditch location. There's a café, bar, kitchen and roof terrace, plus a good free breakfast. The dorms (four to sixteen beds, some women-only) and doubles (with TVs and tea- and coffee-making facilities) look good, with whitewashed walls and timber floors – most options are en suite. Dorms **£22**, doubles **£70**

Meininger 65–67 Queen's Gate, SW7 5JS ☎ 020 3318 1407, ⊛ meininger-hotels.com; ⊖ Gloucester Road; map p.66. Secure, family-friendly hostel, one of a German chain, near the South Ken museums. The 48 rooms include dorms (four to twelve beds), some en suite and some women-only, plus singles and doubles (some en suite, with TV). No kitchen, but there's a bar/bistro, laundry and table tennis. Minimum two-night stay in summer. Dorms **£27**, doubles **£200**

★ **Safestay Holland Park** Holland Walk, W8 7QU ☎ 020 7870 9629, ⊛ safestay.com; ⊖ Holland Park; map p.66. This bright hostel, within Holland Park, is a smart choice. The unisex dorms, which sleep four to 33, are clean, with good beds (with curtains and reading lights) and showers; the private twins (some en suite) have TVs. There's a garden, lounge and pool room, a café-bar and laundry, but no self-catering. Families welcome. Dorms **£23**, twins **£80**

EATING

London is a great city for eating out. You can sample any kind of **cuisine** here, from Pakistani to Japanese, Modern British to fusion. And it needn't be expensive – even in the fanciest restaurants, set menus (most often served at lunch) can be a great deal, and sharing plates can be a godsend if you want to cut costs. The city's dynamic **street food** scene, meanwhile, with food trucks, carts and pop-up stalls dishing up artisan food at low prices, offers an amazing diversity. Keep track of the ever-shifting scene on ⊛ kerbfood.com, ⊛ streetfeastlondon.com and ⊛ realfoodfestival.co.uk. Bear in mind also that many pubs serve food, from simple pub grub to haute cuisine – check out the **gastropubs** in our Drinking section (see page 126).

WESTMINSTER
CAFÉ

Café in the Crypt St Martin-in-the-Fields, Trafalgar Square, WC2N 5DN ☎ 020 7766 1158, ⊛ stmartin-in-the-fields.org; ⊖ Charing Cross; map p.66. This handy café – below the church, in the eighteenth-century crypt – is a nice spot at which to fill up. The daily-changing selection focuses on home-made British comfort food, plus soups, salads and puds. Live jazz Wed 8pm. Mon & Tues 8am–8pm, Wed 8am–10.30pm (jazz ticket holders only after 6.30pm), Thurs–Sat 8am–9pm, Sun 11am–6pm.

RESTAURANT

★ **Lorne** 76 Wilton Rd, SW1V 1DE ☎ 020 3327 0210, ⊛ lornerestaurant.co.uk; ⊖ Victoria; map p.66. Modern British food made with farm-fresh seasonal ingredients; the intriguing menu lists dishes such as cod with curried peas, sea herbs, mussels and onion rings. Mains from £19; one-/two-course lunch menus £15/£22. Mon 6.30–9.30pm, Tues–Sat noon–2.30pm & 6.30–9.30pm.

MAYFAIR AND MARYLEBONE
CAFÉS

Patisserie Valerie 105 Marylebone High St, W1U 4RS ☎ 020 7935 6240, ⊛ patisserie-valerie.co.uk; ⊖ Bond Street; map p.66. Founded as Swiss-run *Maison Sagne* in the 1920s, and preserving its glorious decor, the café is now run by Soho's fab patissiers. They do light lunches and brunch dishes (£6–14), but the plump, creamy cakes are the stars. Mon–Fri 7am–8pm, Sat 8am–8pm, Sun 8.30am–7pm.

Tibits 12–14 Heddon St, W1B 4DA ☎ 020 7758 4112, ⊛ tibits.co.uk; ⊖ Piccadilly Circus; map p.66. Rather glam veggie/vegan café (Tues is totally vegan) in a restaurant-packed lane, offering self-service salads, soups, hot dishes and desserts from around the world. Pay by weight (£2.40/100g before 6pm, £2.70 after). There's another branch in Southwark. Mon–Wed 9am–10.30pm, Thurs & Fri 9am–midnight, Sat 11.30am–midnight, Sun 11.30am–10.30pm.

The Wolseley 160 Piccadilly, W1J 9EB ☎ 020 7499 6996,

ⓦthewolseley.com; ⊖Green Park; map p.66. The 1920s interior is a major draw at this opulent brasserie, which started its days as the showroom for Wolseley cars. The European comfort food is good, if pricey – come for a big breakfast, a bowl of chicken soup with dumplings (£8.75), a half-dozen oysters (from £17), or afternoon tea. Mon–Fri 7am–midnight, Sat 8am–midnight, Sun 8am–11pm.

RESTAURANTS

The Providores and Tapa Room 109 Marylebone High St, W1U 4RX ☎020 7935 6175, ⓦtheprovidores.co.uk; ⊖Baker Street; map p.66. New Zealand chef Peter Gordon serves elegant fusion cuisine at *Providores* (mains from £16 at lunch; £23 at dinner) and, downstairs, anything from cheese platters to beef pesto (£5–22) at the casual *Tapa Room* (no reservations). Providores: Mon–Fri noon–2.45pm & 6–10pm, Sat 10am–2.30pm & 6–10pm, Sun 10am–2.30pm & 6–9.45pm; Tapa Room: Mon–Fri 8am–10.30pm, Sat 9am–3pm & 4–10.30pm, Sun 9am–3pm & 4–10pm.

★ **Twist** 42 Crawford St, W1H 1JW ☎020 7723 3377, ⓦtwistkitchen.co.uk; ⊖Edgware Road; map p.66. Superb, rustic-chic restaurant where the Mediterranean/Eastern/Latin American fusion tapas menu (£10–13), lists such dishes as black-ink gnocchi with langoustine cream or ricotta-stuffed courgette flowers. Charcuterie, cheeses and Josper-grilled meats are also on offer. Mon–Thurs noon–3pm & 6–11pm, Fri noon–3pm & 6–11.30pm, Sat noon–3pm & 6pm–midnight.

SOHO
CAFÉS

★ **Bar Italia** 22 Frith St, W1D 4RF ☎020 7437 4520, ⓦbaritaliasoho.co.uk; ⊖Leicester Square; map p.66. Tiny espresso bar that's been a Soho institution since the 1950s, keeping many of its original features. Check out the Gaggia coffee machine and the iconic neon sign. Daily 7am–5am.

★ **Bun House** 24 Greek St, W1D 4DZ ☎020 8017 9888, ⓦbun.house; ⊖Leicester Square; map p.66. Pretty corner spot for fresh steamed Cantonese buns (all £2.50). Most are filled with umami-packed meats, but there's one veggie option and a couple of decadent dessert buns. Mon–Wed 11am–11pm, Thurs 11am–midnight, Fri & Sat 11am–late, Sun noon–10pm.

Fernandez & Wells 43 Lexington St, W1F 9AL ☎020 734 1546, ⓦfernandezandwells.com; ⊖Piccadilly Circus; map p.66. With its hanging hams and urban-rustic ambience, this café is popular for coffee, breakfasts and cakes to take away or eat in, plus small plates/sandwiches piled high with the best Iberian ingredients. There are four more branches around Central London. Mon–Fri 7.30am–11pm, Sat 9am–11pm, Sun noon–6pm.

★ **Maison Bertaux** 28 Greek St, W1D 5DQ ☎020 7437 6007, ⓦmaisonbertaux.com; ⊖Leicester Square; map p.66. Open since 1871, this charming, ramshackle and *très* French patisserie is an unmissable Soho experience. The decor is simple, bohemian and a little dog-eared; the cakes, tarts and croissants are to die for. No cards. Mon–Sat 9am–10pm, Sun 9am–8pm.

RESTAURANTS

★ **Andrew Edmunds** 46 Lexington St, W1F 0LP ☎020 7437 5708, ⓦandrewedmunds.com; ⊖Piccadilly Circus; map p.66. Romantic, though usually packed, dining room in a Regency townhouse, candlelit at night, with a neighbourhood feel and simple food – roast pigeon with Swiss chard, say, or fennel, butterbeans and roast tomato. Mains £14–25. No mobile phones. Mon–Fri noon–3.30pm & 5.30–10.45pm, Sat 12.30–3.30pm & 5.30–10.45pm, Sun 1–4pm & 6–10.30pm.

Brasserie Zédel 20 Sherwood St, W1F 7ED ☎020 7734 4888, ⓦbrasseriezedel.com; ⊖Piccadilly Circus; map p.66. Huge, opulent Art Deco brasserie offering French classics – onion soup, cassoulet, choucroute – in

---

MORE THAN JUST A CUPPA: AFTERNOON TEA

The capital's most popular venues for a classic **afternoon tea** – sandwiches and scones and cream, cakes and tarts, and, of course, pots of leaf tea – are the top hotels and swanky department stores, though many restaurants offer their own version. Wherever you go, you should book well in advance. Most hotels will expect at least "smart casual attire"; only *The Ritz* insists on jacket and tie. Prices quoted here are for the standard teas; champagne teas, or more substantial high teas, are more expensive.

Berkeley Hotel Wilton Place, SW1X 7RL ☎020 7235 6000, ⓦthe-berkeley.co.uk; ⊖Knightsbridge; map p.98. Daily 1.30–5.30pm. £52.

Fortnum & Mason 181 Piccadilly, W1A 1ER ☎020 7734 8040, ⓦfortnumandmason.com; ⊖Green Park; map p.66. Mon–Sat 11am–7pm, Sun 11.30am–6pm. £44.

The Ritz 150 Piccadilly, W1J 9BR ☎020 7300 2345, ⓦtheritzlondon.com; ⊖Green Park; map p.66. Daily 11.30am, 1.30pm, 3.30pm, 5.30pm & 7.30pm. £54.

Sketch 9 Conduit St, W1S 2XG ☎020 7659 4500, ⓦsketch.london; ⊖Oxford Circus; map p.66. Daily noon–4.30pm. £58.

1

an irresistibly Gallic atmosphere. There's a street-level café, too, which opens at 8am (Sat and Sun 9am) for coffee and patisserie. Mains from £13; all-day menus £9.75/£12.75/£19.95. Mon–Sat 11.30am–midnight, Sun 11.30am–11pm.

★ **Kiln** 58 Brewer St, W1F 9TL ⓦ kilnsoho.com; ⊖ Piccadilly Circus; map p.66. Sophisticated Thai food with twists – a dash of Myanmar here, a little Yunnan there – and amazingly fresh ingredients. Typical dishes (£6–22) on the small-plates menu include jungle curry of turbot and snake beans or five-spice duck and offal with aged soy. Reservations taken for parties of four or more only. Mon–Sat noon–2.30pm & 5–10.30pm, Sun 1–8pm.

Kricket 12 Denman St, W1D 7HH (no phone) ⓦ kricket. co.uk; ⊖ Piccadilly Circus; map p.66. Born from a pop-up, this terrific Indian place now has a permanent Soho home, all exposed pipes, bare brick and open kitchen. Mix and match creative dishes (£5.50–12) like Keralan fried chicken with curry leaf mayonnaise or smoked aubergine with sesame raita. Reservations are only accepted for groups of four or more. Mon–Sat noon–2.30pm & 5.30–10.30pm.

Mildreds 45 Lexington St, W1F 9AN ⓣ 020 7494 1634, ⓦ mildreds.co.uk; ⊖ Piccadilly Circus; map p.66. This veggie restaurant, serving tasty, home-made world cuisine – Sri Lankan curries, burritos, stir-fried Asian veg, burgers – is a Soho standby. It's petite, and can get busy, but takes no bookings. Mains £7–12. Branches in Camden and King's Cross. Mon–Sat noon–11pm.

The Palomar 34 Rupert St, W1D 6DN ⓣ 020 7439 8777, ⓦ thepalomar.co.uk; ⊖ Piccadilly Circus; map p.66. Contemporary Jerusalem food in a noisy, slick space, with counter seating around the busy kitchen and a dining room at the back. It's a sociable sharing-plate experience, full of hefty flavours – octopus with burnt courgette, labneh and chimichurri, for example. Dishes £4–15. Mon–Sat noon–2.30pm & 5.30–11pm, Sun 12.30–3.30pm & 6–9pm.

★ **Polpo** 41 Beak St, W1F 9SB ⓣ 020 7734 4479, ⓦ polpo.co.uk; ⊖ Piccadilly Circus; map p.66. The first in what has become a mini-chain, this branch of Polpo serves delicious *cicheti* (bar snacks) and small plates from £3 to £10 – try the crab and chilli linguine or any of the meatballs. Reservations are taken for lunch; dinner bookings are limited. The other London Polpos – in Covent Garden (two branches), Chelsea, Notting Hill and Smithfield – along with, from the same team, *Polpetto* on Berwick St, and *Spuntino*, a hip take on American diner food on Rupert St, are also recommended. Mon–Thurs 8am–11pm, Fri 8am–midnight, Sat 11.30am–midnight, Sun 11.30am–10pm.

COVENT GARDEN
CAFÉS

Homeslice 13 Neal's Yard, WC2H 9DP ⓣ 020 3151 7488, ⓦ homeslicepizza.co.uk; ⊖ Covent Garden; map

p.66. Rustic-cool pizza joint offering thin-crust, wood-fired gourmet pizzas – pig cheek, collard greens and crackling, say – plus sparkling wine on tap; £4/slice (some varieties only) or £20 for a 20-inch pizza. Branches in Shoreditch and Fitzrovia. Daily noon–11pm.

★ **Kastner and Ovens** 52 Floral St, WC2E 9DA ⓣ 020 7836 2700, ⓦ facebook.com/kastnerandovens; ⊖ Covent Garden; map p.66. Tiny takeaway turning out home-made fresh salads and heart-warming pies, quiches, soups and hot specials, and an irresistible selection of cakes. Around £7 for three salads. Mon–Fri 8am–4pm.

Rock & Sole Plaice 47 Endell St, WC2H 9AJ ⓣ 020 7836 3785, ⓦ rockandsoleplaice.com; ⊖ Covent Garden; map p.66. This venerable fish-and-chip shop is an appealing, no-nonsense place, but it's not cheap – cod and chips costs around £15. Eat in or at a pavement table, or take away. Mon–Sat 11.30am–10.30pm, Sun noon–10pm.

RESTAURANTS

★ **Barrafina** 10 Adelaide St, WC2N 4HZ ⓦ barrafina. co.uk; ⊖ Charing Cross; map p.66. This terrific tapas bar has won bucketloads of accolades for doing simple food impeccably well. It's fairly meaty – suckling pig, braised ox tongue and herb-crusted rabbit shoulder are typical. Branches in Drury Lane and Soho. No reservations; no groups larger than four. Mon–Sat noon–3pm & 5–11pm, Sun 1–3.30pm & 5.30–10pm.

Dishoom 12 Upper St Martin's Lane, WC2H 9FB ⓣ 020 7420 9320, ⓦ dishoom.com; ⊖ Leicester Square; map p.66. Re-creating the atmosphere of the Persian cafés of Old Bombay, *Dishoom* is buzzy and stylish but, most importantly, serves great food – don't miss the black dhal. Mains from £6.50. Very limited reservations. Branches in Shoreditch, King's Cross and near Carnaby Street. Mon–Thurs 8am–11pm, Fri 8am–midnight, Sat 9am–midnight, Sun 9am–11pm.

Flesh & Buns 41 Earlham St, WC2H 9LX ⓣ 020 7632 9500, ⓦ bonedaddies.com; ⊖ Covent Garden; map p.66. The boozy, rock'n'roll vibe at this noisy Japanese *izakaya*-style basement restaurant belies the quality of the food: the rice buns are the stars, served with succulent toppings (crispy duck leg £14.20; miso-grilled aubergine £9.70). Mon & Tues noon–3pm & 5–10pm, Wed–Fri noon–3pm & 5–11pm, Sat noon–11pm, Sun noon–9.30pm.

BLOOMSBURY AND KING'S CROSS
CAFÉS

Bloomsbury Coffee House 20 Tavistock Place, WC1H 9RE ⓣ 020 7837 2877, ⓦ bloomsburycoffeehouse. co.uk; ⊖ Russell Square; map p.77. Cosy basement café, a popular student haunt, serving breakfasts, home-made savoury dishes, Allpress coffee and cakes. Mon–Fri 8am–4.30pm, Sat & Sun 8am–1.30pm.

Caravan 1 Granary Square, N1C 4AA ☎ 020 7101 7661, ⓦ caravanrestaurants.co.uk; ➔ King's Cross; map p.77. A trailblazer on the King's Cross dining scene, this buzzy spot, occupying a huge old grain store, serves tempting Modern European/fusion breakfasts, brunches, small plates (from £6.50), gourmet pizza (from £9) and larger mains (from £17.50) to a lively crowd. Expect to see anything from molasses-roasted beets to chaat-masala-braised oxtail. There are branches in Exmouth Market and near Bankside. Mon–Fri 8am–10.30pm, Sat 10am–10.30pm, Sun 10am–4pm.

Diwana Bhel Poori House 121–123 Drummond St, NW1 2HL ☎ 020 7387 5556, ⓦ diwanabph.com; ➔ Euston; map p.77. On a street lined with cheap Indian restaurants, this South Indian veggie diner wins for its enormous all-you-can-eat lunchtime buffet (£7) – dinners are not nearly as good value. Mon–Sat noon–11.30pm, Sun noon–10.30pm.

RESTAURANTS

Grain Store Granary Square, N1C 4AB ☎ 020 7324 4466, ⓦ grainstore.com; ➔ King's Cross; map p.77. Warehouse-style restaurant with a strong focus on fresh veg; try oyster mushrooms in vegan XO sauce with wasabi pea coulis and herb tofu. Mains from £13.50; small plates (£3.50–16) served all day. Mon–Fri noon–10.30pm, Sat 10am–10.30pm, Sun 10.30am–3.30pm.

★ **Noble Rot** 51 Lamb's Conduit St, WC1N 3NB ☎ 020 7242 8963, ⓦ noblerot.co.uk/wine-bar; ➔ Russell Square; map p.77. Superlative seasonal food served in a cosy wine bar in a lovely old townhouse. Many dishes have a European accent (Auvergne guinea fowl with sweetcorn and girolles, say). Small plates from £9; mains from £18. Mon–Sat noon–2.30pm & 6–9.30pm.

THE CITY
CAFÉS

★ **Breddos Tacos** 82 Goswell Rd, EC1V 7DB ☎ 020 3535 8301, ⓦ breddostacos.com; ➔ Barbican; map p.82. High-spirited fusion taqueria, born from an East London food shack, that uses the best British produce in everything from crunchy sweetbread tacos to chanterelle mushroom tostadas. Tacos £2.50–4.50; tostadas around £7; grills £7–20. No reservations. Mon–Sat noon–3pm & 5–10.30pm.

Café Below St Mary-le-Bow Church, Cheapside, EC2V 6AU ☎ 020 7329 0789, ⓦ cafebelow.co.uk; ➔ St Paul's; map p.82. A rare City gem: a cosy, family-owned café in a Norman church crypt, serving home-cooked bistro-style dishes with creative veggie choices and good hot breakfasts. Lunch mains from £11. Mon–Fri 7.30–10am & 11.30am–2.30pm.

Prufrock Coffee 23–25 Leather Lane, EC1N 7TE ☎ 020 7242 0467, ⓦ prufrockcoffee.com; ➔ Chancery Lane; map p.82. This pared-down shrine to the coffee bean pioneered London's artisan coffee craze. The coffee is great, of course – and there's a short menu of breakfast, lunch and pastries. Mon–Fri 8am–6pm, Sat & Sun 10am–5pm.

RESTAURANTS

Duck & Waffle Heron Tower, 110 Bishopsgate, EC2N 4AY ☎ 020 3640 7310, ⓦ duckandwaffle.com; ➔ Aldgate; map p.82. Forty floors up, this smart place offers amazing City views and hipster comfort food (the signature dish features waffles, duck confit, fried duck egg and mustard maple syrup; £17). Small plates £8–13. Daily 6am–5am.

★ **Moro** 34–36 Exmouth Market, EC1R 4QE ☎ 020 7833 8336, ⓦ moro.co.uk; ➔ Angel; map p.82. This lovely, lively and warmly decorated restaurant is a place of pilgrimage for disciples of Sam and Sam Clark's Moorish/Mediterranean/Middle Eastern cuisine. The changing menus are outstanding, especially the lamb dishes and the yoghurt cake. Mains £17.50–24; tapas (from £3.50) are served at the bar all day Mon–Sat. Mon–Sat noon–2.30pm & 5.15–10.45pm (tapas all day), Sun 12.30–3pm.

EAST LONDON
CAFÉS

Brick Lane Beigel Bake 159 Brick Lane, E1 6SB ☎ 020 7729 0616, ⓦ facebook.com/beigelbake; ➔ Shoreditch High Street; map p.89. Fresh bagels baked on the spot in a basic, much-loved takeaway. They're delicious, and cheap; by far the priciest is the hot salt beef (£4.10), and even smoked salmon and cream cheese is a mere £1.90. Daily 24hr.

★ **CookDaily Shoreditch** 2–10 Bethnal Green Rd, E1 6GY ☎ 07498 563168, ⓦ cookdaily.co.uk; ➔ Shoreditch High Street; map p.89. Among many good eating options in the Boxpark shipping container complex, this cool vegan place is a massive hit for its big, flavour-packed bowls of global food (all £9), served over a half rice/half quinoa mix. Mon–Wed & Sat noon–9pm, Thurs & Fri noon–9.30pm, Sun noon–7pm.

★ **E. Pellicci** 332 Bethnal Green Rd, E2 0AG ☎ 020 7739 4873, ⓦ epellicci.com; ➔ Bethnal Green; map p.89. *Pellicci's* caff (open since 1900) is an iconic, family-owned and jubilantly friendly East End institution with its stunning 1940s decor intact, serving hefty fry-ups and good home-made Anglo-Italian grub. Mon–Sat 7am–4pm.

Voodoo Ray's 95 Kingsland High St, E8 2PB ☎ 020 7249 7865, ⓦ voodoorays.com; ➔ Dalston Junction; map p.89. Grungy late-night drinking dens come and go in Dalston, but *Voodoo Ray's* seems set to stay – a post-party pizza/Margarita joint where the pizzas (from £3.50/ slice) are huge and the Margaritas are strong. Branches in Shoreditch, Camden and Peckham. Mon–Wed 5pm–midnight, Thurs 5pm–1am, Fri & Sat noon–3am, Sun noon–midnight.

1

RESTAURANTS

The Clove Club 380 Old St, EC1V 9LT ☎ 020 7729 6496, ⓦ thecloveclub.com; ⊖ Old Street; map p.89. This relatively relaxed, Michelin-starred restaurant offers flawless set menus (lunch five courses, £75; dinner five/nine courses, £75/£110; veggie menus same price), listing innovative British dishes with Scottish accents – the buttermilk-fried chicken with pine salt is a hit. Small plates are served at the bar from 6pm (£5–50), and you can go a la carte at lunch (mains £18–35). Beware, though: the "ticketing" system requires you to pay in advance. Mon 6–10.30pm, Tues–Sat noon–2.15pm & 6–10.30pm.

Lahore Kebab House 2–10 Umberston St, E1 1PY ☎ 020 7481 9737, ⓦ lahore-kebabhouse.com; ⊖ Aldgate East; map p.89. Legendary Pakistani kebab house. Go for the lamb cutlets and roti, and turn up hungry. BYOB. Mains £8–16. Daily noon–1am.

★ **L'Antica Pizzeria da Michele** 125 Stoke Newington Church St, N16 0UH ☎ 020 7687 0009, ⓦ facebook.com/damichelelondon; ⊖ Stoke Newington; map p.89. In 2016 the best pizza restaurant in Naples (for which read the best pizza restaurant in the world) made its second home in a simple little Stoke Newington space. Just two pizzas are served: the Margherita and the Marinara (without cheese, but with lashings of garlic). In both, the smoky, blistered base perfectly balances that terrific, nuanced tomato sauce. From £8. No reservations; arrive early. Tues–Sat noon–11pm, Sun noon–10.30pm.

Popolo 6 Rivington St, EC2A 3DU ☎ 020 7729 4299, ⓦ popoloshoreditch.com; ⊖ Old Street; map p.89. Convivial spot dishing up gutsy Italian tapas with Spanish and Moorish influences – fresh pasta or risotto, Dorset crab and bottarga salad, labneh with deep-fried olives – around a busy open kitchen or in an upstairs dining room. Plates £4–14. No reservations. Tues & Wed noon–3pm & 5.30–10.30pm, Thurs–Sat noon–3pm & 5.30–11pm.

★ **Som Saa** 43a Commercial St, E1 6BD ☎ 020 7324 7790, ⓦ somsaa.com; ⊖ Aldgate East; map p.89. The short menu of regional Thai food served in this revamped warehouse is outstanding (and spicy): try the jungle curry of guinea fowl with garlic and kajron flowers. Sharing plates £7.50–14.50 at lunch, more at dinner. Reservations only for groups larger than four. Mon 6–10.30pm, Tues–Fri noon–2.30pm & 6–10.30pm, Sat noon–3pm & 6–10.30pm.

Sông Quê 134 Kingsland Rd, E2 8DY ☎ 020 7613 3222, ⓦ songque.co.uk; ⊖ Hoxton; map p.89. In a street heaving with budget Vietnamese restaurants, this basic place is a favourite for steaming phở (from £9) and spicy seafood. Mon–Fri noon–3pm & 5.30–11pm, Sat noon–11pm, Sun noon–10.30pm.

St John Bread and Wine 94–96 Commercial St, E1 6LZ ☎ 020 7251 0848, ⓦ stjohngroup.uk.com/spitalfields; ⊖ Liverpool Street; map p.89. A simpler offshoot of the famed St John, serving the same superlative British food on a regularly changing menu – featuring offal, pig's cheek and the like, but also wonderful veg and fish dishes, and simple breakfasts. Sharing plates £5–21. Mon 8–11.30am, noon–4pm & 6–10pm, Tues–Fri 8–11.30am, noon–4pm & 6–11pm, Sat 8.30am–noon, 1–4pm & 6–11pm, Sun 8.30am–noon, 1–4pm & 6–10pm.

THE SOUTH BANK AND BANKSIDE

CAFÉS

Maltby Street Market Maltby St, SE1 3PA ⓦ maltby.st; ⊖ London Bridge; map p.94. Within walking distance of Borough Market (see page 95), this smaller foodie hotspot huddles under the railway arches south of Tower Bridge. The stalls – plus some good bars and restaurants – spread along Maltby and Druid streets (ⓦ druid.st) down to the Spa Terminus (ⓦ www.spa-terminus.co.uk); most action is on the Ropewalk. Sat 9am–4pm, Sun 11am–4pm.

Scooter Caffè 132 Lower Marsh, SE1 7AE ☎ 020 7620 1421, ⓦ facebook.com/scootercaffe; ⊖ Waterloo; map p.91. This quirky little coffee house, filled with bric-a-brac, vintage furniture and scooter memorabilia, is a relaxed spot to drink good coffee and linger. At night it morphs into a boho bar. Mon–Thurs 8.30am–11pm, Fri 8.30am–midnight, Sat 10am–midnight, Sun 10am–11pm.

RESTAURANTS

Laughing Gravy 154 Blackfriars Rd, SE1 8EN ☎ 020 7998 1707, ⓦ thelaughinggravy.co.uk; ⊖ Southwark; map p.91. There's a cosy neighbourhood vibe at this upmarket brasserie, which serves bistro food – braised duck pappardelle; pan-fried cod; roast dinners – in a brick-walled dining room. Mains £12.50–25. Mon–Thurs noon–3pm & 5–10pm, Fri noon–3pm & 5–10.30pm, Sat noon–4pm & 5–10.30pm, Sun noon–4.30pm.

★ **Padella** 6 Southwark St, SE10 1TQ ⓦ padella.co; ⊖ London Bridge; map p.94. The open kitchen at this bright, contemporary pasta place by Borough Market turns out wonderful, authentic fresh pasta. A small plate of gnocchi with sage and butter costs just £4, while tagliarini with crab, chilli and lemon is one of the most expensive dishes at £11.50. BYOB; no reservations. Mon–Sat noon–4pm & 5–10pm, Sun noon–5pm.

KENSINGTON AND CHELSEA

CAFÉS

★ **Books for Cooks** 4 Blenheim Crescent, W11 1NN ☎ 020 7221 1992, ⓦ booksforcooks.com; ⊖ Ladbroke Grove; map p.98 There's a cute dining area inside this excellent cookery bookshop. Get there early to grab a seat for the three-course set lunch (£7). Tues–Sat 10am–6pm; food noon–1.30pm.

Capote y Toros 157 Old Brompton Rd, SW5 0LJ ☎ 020 7373 0567, ⓦ cambiodetercio.co.uk; ⊖ Gloucester

Road; map p.98. The emphasis at this tapas bar is on Spain's sherries, with 125 on offer, along with modern tapas (£6–29). Nightly flamenco guitar. Tues–Sat 6–11.30pm.

Lisboa Patisserie 57 Golborne Rd, W10 5NR ☎020 8968 5242; ⊖Ladbroke Grove; map p.98. Authentic Portuguese *pastelaria*, a perfect post-Portobello Rd pit stop, with coffee, croissants and the best *pasteis de nata* (custard tarts) this side of Lisbon. Daily 7.30am–7.30pm.

RESTAURANTS

Dinner Mandarin Oriental Hotel, 66 Knightsbridge, SW1X 7LA ☎020 7201 3833, ⓦdinnerbyheston.com; ⊖Knightsbridge; map p.98. Though this is a Heston Blumenthal restaurant, he doesn't actually cook here – the head chef worked with him at the *Fat Duck* – and there is less emphasis on flashy molecular cuisine. However, the creative food, using old English recipes, is as intriguing as you'd expect; try the salamagundy or the "meat fruit". Mains £28–90; three-course weekday lunch menu £45. Mon–Fri noon–2pm & 6–10.15pm, Sat & Sun noon–2.30pm & 6.30–10.30pm.

Hereford Road 3 Hereford Rd, W2 4AB ☎020 7727 1144, ⓦherefordroad.org; ⊖Bayswater; map p.98. The contemporary dining room, with bustling open kitchen, is a smart setting for accomplished English cooking – beetroot, sorrel and boiled egg; braised duck leg with turnips, and such like. Mains £12–16.50; two-/three-course weekday lunch menus £13.50/£15.50. Mon–Sat noon–3pm & 6–10.30pm, Sun noon–4pm & 6–10pm.

★ **Medlar** 438 Kings Rd, SW10 0LJ ☎020 7349 1900, ⓦmedlarrestaurant.co.uk; ⊖Fulham Broadway; map p.98. Superlative Modern European food – roast stone bass with palourde clams and pancetta, for example – served in a relaxed, elegant dining room. It's prix fixe, and excellent value: one-/two-/three-course lunch menus £25/£30/£35, two-/three-course dinner £41/£49 (£35 on Sun). Mon–Fri noon–3pm & 6.30–10.30pm, Sat noon–3pm & 6–10.30pm, Sun noon–3pm & 6–9.30pm.

Nama 110 Talbot Rd, W11 1JR ☎020 7313 4638, ⓦnamafoods.com; ⊖Westbourne Park; map p.98. Creative raw vegan food with global accents – raspberry gazpacho; truffle pasta; kohlrabi ravioli – with lots of juices, smoothies and infusions. Mains £9–16.50. Tues & Wed noon–10pm, Thurs noon–11pm, Fri & Sat 9am–11pm, Sun 9am–6pm.

NORTH LONDON

CAFÉS

Brew House Kenwood House, Hampstead Lane, NW3 7JR ☎020 8348 4073, ⓦsearcyskenwoodhouse.co.uk; ⊖Highgate; map p.62. The food isn't amazing – though they do a good line in cakes – but the location, in the huge, sunny garden courtyard of Kenwood House, more than compensates. Daily: spring & summer 9am–6pm; rest

of year 9am–4pm.

Louis Patisserie 32 Heath St, NW3 6TE ☎020 7435 9908; ⊖Hampstead; map p.62. For more than fifty years this tiny tearoom/patisserie has been serving sticky cakes, tea and coffee to a local crowd. They may now play background music, and some Hungarian specialities have dropped off the menu, but it's still a refreshingly uncorporate choice. Daily 8am–6pm.

RESTAURANTS

Jin Kichi 73 Heath St, NW3 6UG ☎020 7794 6158, ⓦjinkichi.com; ⊖Hampstead; map p.62. Book ahead for this tiny, homely and busy neighbourhood Japanese diner, which specializes in charcoal-grilled *yakitori* (skewers). The sushi, noodles and other Japanese staples are good, too. Skewers from £2; other dishes from £4. Tues–Sat 12.30–2.10pm & 6–11pm, Sun 12.30–2.10pm & 6–10pm.

Namaaste Kitchen 64 Parkway, NW1 7AH ☎020 7485 5977, ⓦnamaastekitchen.co.uk; ⊖Camden Town; map p.62. You'll find unusual dishes, including wild rabbit *achari* with aubergine compote, at this superb contemporary Indian and Pakistani restaurant. Mains £12–23; one-/two-/three-course lunch menus £8.50/£10/£12.50. Mon–Thurs noon–3pm & 5.30–11.30pm, Fri & Sat noon–11.30pm, Sun noon–11pm.

SOUTH LONDON
RESTAURANT

Naughty Piglets 28 Brixton Water Lane, SW2 1PE ☎020 7274 7796, ⓦnaughtypiglets.co.uk; map p.62. Small, convivial restaurant with a cosy local vibe, dishing up flavour-packed small plates (£7–16) – pork belly with Korean spices, say, or sardine lasagne with black olives – and "low intervention" wines. Tues & Wed 6–10pm, Thurs noon–2.30pm & 6–10pm, Fri & Sat noon–3pm & 6–10pm, Sun noon–3pm.

WEST LONDON
CAFÉ

Hollyhock Terrace Gardens, Petersham Rd, TW10 6UX ☎020 8948 6555; ⊖Richmond; map p.98. This laidback fairtrade vegetarian café, hidden away in Richmond's flower-filled Terrace Gardens, is perfect for light lunches or coffee and cakes on the shady terrace overlooking the river. Daily 9am–dusk.

RESTAURANT

Chez Lindsay 11 Hill Rise, Richmond, TW10 6UQ ☎020 89487473, ⓦchezlindsay.co.uk; ⊖Richmond; map p.98. Small, bright, riverside Breton restaurant, serving *galettes*, crêpes and French mains including steak frites and oysters. *Galettes* from £5.25, mains £12.50–25; two-/three-course menus (Mon–Fri noon–7pm) £12.75/£15.75. Mon–Sat noon–11pm, Sun noon–10pm.

1

DRINKING

WESTMINSTER

St Stephen's Tavern 10 Bridge St, SW1A 2JR ☎020 7925 2286, ⓦststephenstavern.co.uk; ⊖Westminster; map p.66. Opulent Victorian pub opposite the Houses of Parliament and wall to wall with civil servants and MPs. Good real ales, plus fish and chips and pies. Mon–Sat 10am–11pm, Sun 10am–10pm.

MAYFAIR AND MARYLEBONE

The Golden Eagle 59 Marylebone Lane, W1U 2NY ☎020 7935 3228; ⊖Bond Street; map p.98. Proper old one-room neighbourhood pub – a delight in this swanky area – with a good range of real ales, and regular singalongs around the piano (Tues, Thurs & Fri). Mon–Sat 11am–11pm, Sun noon–10pm.

The Gunmakers 33 Aybrook St, W1U 4AP ☎020 7487 4937, ⓦthegunmakersmarylebone.co.uk; ⊖Bond Street; map p.98. This place is all wood panelling, Churchill memorabilia and an awful lot of framed bullets. Decent range of ales (including a few crafts), plus a brief menu of dirty burgers. Mon–Sat 10am–11pm, Sun noon–10pm; kitchen Mon–Sat noon–9pm, Sun noon–5pm.

The Windmill 6–8 Mill St, W1S 2AZ ☎020 7491 8050, ⓦwindmillmayfair.co.uk; ⊖Oxford Circus; map p.98. Convivial pub just off Regent St, a perfect retreat for exhausted shoppers. The Young's beers are good, as are the award-winning pies. Mon–Fri 11am–11pm, Sat noon–11pm, Sun noon–6pm.

Ye Grapes 16 Shepherd Market, W1J 7QQ ☎020 7493 4216; ⊖Green Park; map p.98. Located in Shepherd Market, a charming corner of Mayfair, it's the location that really makes this pub. If it's too busy, try the *King's Arms*, also in Shepherd Market. Mon–Sat 11am–11pm, Sun noon–10pm.

SOHO

The Blue Posts 22 Berwick St, W1F 0QA ☎020 7437 5008; ⊖Tottenham Court Road; map p.66. Real old-school Soho – the "governor" wears a tie, pulls pints from a relatively small selection of ales and lagers, and offers only the finest selection of peanuts and crisps. Popular with the local media crowd. Mon–Fri 11am–11pm.

Dog & Duck 18 Bateman St, W1D 3AJ ☎020 7494 0697, ⓦbit.ly/DogDuck; ⊖Tottenham Court Road; map p.66. Tiny Nicholson's pub that retains much of its old character, beautiful Victorian tiling and mosaics, a range of real ales and a loyal clientele. If it gets too busy downstairs, head upstairs to the George Orwell Bar (he used to drink here). Daily 10am–11pm.

★ **The French House** 49 Dean St, W1D 5BG ☎020 7437 2799, ⓦfrenchhousesoho.com; ⊖Leicester Square; map p.66. This cosy pub has been a boho-Soho institution since Belgian Victor Berlemont bought the place shortly

before World War I. Strictly no music or TV, but plenty of classic Soho barflies and no end of Free French and literary associations. Beer – lager only – famously comes by the half pint; wine and champagne a speciality. Mon–Sat noon–11pm, Sun noon–10pm.

Two Floors 3 Kingly St, W1B 5PD ☎020 7439 1007, ⓦtwofloors.com; ⊖Oxford Circus; map p.66. An unlikely combo: craft ales and cocktails in the pubby street-level bar and a dimly lit tiki bar in the basement – yet this place pulls it off with aplomb. Mon–Thurs noon–11pm, Fri & Sat noon–midnight, Sun noon–10pm.

COVENT GARDEN AND THE STRAND

Cross Keys 31 Endell St, WC2H 9BA ☎020 7836 5185, ⓦcrosskeyscoventgarden.com; ⊖Covent Garden; map p.66. You'll do well to find a seat in this cosy, foliage-drenched Covent Garden favourite, which is stuffed with copper pots, brass instruments, paintings and memorabilia. Most beer is from Brodie's in Leyton. Mon–Sat 11am–11pm, Sun noon–10pm.

Gordon's 47 Villiers St, WC2N 6NE ☎020 7930 1408, ⓦgordonswinebar.com; ⊖Charing Cross; map p.66. Cavernous, shabby, atmospheric old wine bar, open since 1890 and specializing in ports, sherries and Madeiras; the cheese platters are legend. It's a favourite with local office workers, who spill outdoors in the summer. Mon–Sat 11am–11pm, Sun noon–10pm.

★ **The Harp** 47 Chandos Place, WC2N 4HS ☎020 7836 0291, ⓦharpcoventgarden.com; ⊖Leicester Square; map p.66. For such a sliver of a pub, they pack in an excellent array of ales and ciders. The tiny bar is invariably packed; there's more room in the comfortably battered upstairs. Mon–Thurs 10am–11pm, Fri & Sat 10am–midnight, Sun noon–10pm.

Lamb & Flag 33 Rose St, WC2E 9EB ☎020 7497 9504, ⓦlambandflagcoventgarden.co.uk; ⊖Leicester Square; map p.66. More than three hundred years old, this agreeably tatty Fuller's pub, tucked down an alley between Garrick and Floral streets, is perennially popular. Mon–Sat 11am–11pm, Sun noon–10pm.

BLOOMSBURY AND KING'S CROSS

The Duke 7 Roger St, WC1N 2PB ☎020 7242 7230, ⓦdukepub.co.uk; ⊖Russell Square; map p.77. Lovely little neighbourhood pub with an unusual, unforced Art Deco flavour and lots of interwar design details. Its discreet location keeps the crowd in the small bar manageable. Mon–Sat noon–11pm.

★ **The Euston Tap** 190 Euston Rd, NW1 2EF ☎020 3137 8837, ⓦeustontap.com; ⊖Euston; map p.77. A pleasingly peculiar set-up, the *Euston Tap* comprises two of the station's original entrance lodges, separated by a bus lane. A pair of taprooms are tucked within these somewhat tomb-like little spaces, serving cask and keg ales plus ciders and perries. Daily noon–11pm.

The Lamb 94 Lamb's Conduit St, WC1N 3LZ ☎020 7405 0713, ⓦthelamblondon.com; ⊖Russell Square; map p.77. Well-preserved Victorian pub with mirrors, polished wood, leather banquettes and etched-glass "snob" screens. Rather peaceful, as there's no music or TV. Mon–Wed 11am–11pm, Thurs–Sat 11am–midnight, Sun noon–10pm.

Queen's Head 66 Acton St, WC1X 9NB ☎020 7713 5772, ⓦqueensheadlondon.com; ⊖King's Cross; map p.77. Attractive and laidback local offering cheese, chunky pies and charcuterie alongside craft beers and ciders. Occasional live jazz and piano. Mon & Sun noon–11pm, Tues–Sat noon–midnight.

HOLBORN

Princess Louise 208 High Holborn, WC1V 7EP ☎020 7405 8816, ⓦprincesslouisepub.co.uk; ⊖Holborn; map p.77. This Sam Smith's pub features six rooms of gold-trimmed mirrors, gorgeous mosaics and fine moulded ceilings – even the toilets are listed. Mon–Fri 11am–11pm, Sat noon–11pm, Sun noon–6pm.

Ye Olde Mitre 1 Ely Court, EC1N 6SJ ☎020 7405 4751, ⓦyeoldemitreholborn.co.uk; ⊖Chancery Lane; map p.82. Hidden down a tiny alleyway off Hatton Garden, this Fuller's pub dates back to 1546, although it was rebuilt in the eighteenth century. The low-ceilinged, wood-panelled rooms are packed with history and the ales are good. Mon–Fri 11am–11pm.

THE CITY

The Blackfriar 174 Queen Victoria St, EC4V 4EG ☎020 7236 5474; ⊖Blackfriars; map p.82. Quirky, relaxing Nicholson's pub, with Art Nouveau marble friezes of boozy monks and a highly decorated alcove – all original, dating from 1905. Mon–Fri 10am–11pm, Sat 9am–11pm, Sun noon–10pm.

★ **The Eagle** 159 Farringdon Rd, EC1R 3AL ☎020 7837 1353, ⓦtheeaglefarringdon.co.uk; ⊖Farringdon; map p.82. The original and still arguably the best of London's gastropubs. They offer a fairly limited selection of beers – but, wow, the food. Prepared in the tiny kitchen behind the bar, the Mediterranean-tinged dishes come out perfect time after time. Mon–Sat noon–11pm, Sun noon–5pm.

★ **Jerusalem Tavern** 55 Britton St, EC1M 5UQ ☎020 7490 4281, ⓦstpetersbrewery.co.uk; ⊖Farringdon; map p.82. Tiny converted Georgian coffee house – the frontage dates from 1810 – with a raffish, sociable character. The excellent draught beers are from St Peter's Brewery in Suffolk. Mon–Fri 11am–11pm.

The Lamb Tavern 10–12 Leadenhall Market, EC3V 1LR ☎020 7626 2454, ⓦlambtavernleadenhall.com; ⊖Monument; map p.82. In Leadenhall Market, this

historic Young's pub is almost exclusively standing room only (both inside and out) for a suited local crowd. The basement bar, *Old Tom's*, is a little more on trend, serving London beers and artisan cheese and meat platters. Mon–Fri 11am–11pm.

Three Kings 7 Clerkenwell Close, EC1R 0DY ☎020 7253 0483, ⓦbit.ly/ThreeKingsClerk; ⊖Farringdon; map p.82. Perennial favourite north of Clerkenwell Green, with an eclectic interior, big windows and two small rooms upstairs perfect for lingering. Interesting craft beers and food, too. It's next to *The Crown*, which is also worth a trip. Mon–Fri noon–11pm, Sat 5–11pm.

Ye Olde Cheshire Cheese 145 Fleet St, EC4A 2BU ☎020 7353 6170, ⓦbit.ly/YeOldeCheshire; ⊖Temple; map p.82. This seventeenth-century watering hole – famous for its historic literary associations, with patrons including Dickens and Dr Johnson – is now a Sam Smith's pub. Its dark-panelled bars and real fires make it a cosy maze, popular – some would say too popular – with tourists and locals alike. Mon–Fri 11am–11pm, Sat noon–11pm.

EAST LONDON AND DOCKLANDS

The Carpenter's Arms 73 Cheshire St, E2 6EG ☎020 7739 6342, ⓦcarpentersarmsfreehouse.com; ⊖Shoreditch High Street; map p.89. Iconic East End pub – the Kray twins bought it for their dear old mum – with an excellent range of craft lagers and ales and home-made food. A friendly, relaxed, low-lit place that feels wonderfully set apart. Mon–Wed 4–11pm, Thurs & Sun noon–11pm, Fri & Sat noon–midnight.

★ **The George Tavern** 373 Commercial Rd, E1 0LA ☎020 7790 7335, ⓦbit.ly/GeorgeTav; ⊖Whitechapel; map p.89. Arty, shabby, dilapidated pub, packed with history and lovely period detail. There's a bohemian theatre space, and regular, very cool, live music. Mon–Thurs & Sun 4pm–midnight, Fri & Sat 4pm–3am.

The Gun 27 Coldharbour, E14 9NS ☎020 7515 5222, ⓦthegundocklands.com; ⊖Canary Wharf DLR; map p.94. Legendary dockers' pub, once the haunt of Lord Nelson, *The Gun* is now a classy Fuller's gastropub, with a cosy back bar and a deck offering unrivalled views. Mon–Sat 11am–midnight, Sun 11am–11pm.

Happiness Forgets 8–9 Hoxton Square, N1 6NU ☎020 7613 0325, ⓦhappinessforgets.com; ⊖Old Street; map p.89. Candlelit, bare-brick bar with a Hoxton-via-New York vibe, serving fashionably obscure, serious cocktails to a cool crowd. Has an excellent sister bar in Stoke Newington (ⓦoriginalsin.bar). Daily 5–11pm.

Sager + Wilde 193 Hackney Rd, E2 8JL ☎020 8127 7330, ⓦsagerandwilde.com; ⊖Hoxton; map p.89. Gentrification doesn't get much starker. What was formerly an England flag-draped, locals-only boozer is now this sleek wine bar that makes a lovely stop post-Columbia Road

1

flower market. Across the road, *The Marksman* has won plaudits for its food. Mon–Wed 5pm–midnight, Thurs & Fri 5pm–1am, Sat noon–1am, Sun noon–midnight.

Ten Bells 84 Commercial St, E1 6LY ☎ 020 7247 7532, ⊛ tenbells.com; ⊖ Shoreditch High Street; map p.89. Stripped-down pub with Jack the Ripper associations, great Victorian tiling and a hip, young crowd. Meat and cheese plates are on offer, and there's a cocktail bar upstairs. Pub Mon–Wed noon–midnight, Thurs–Sat noon–1am, Sun 1–9pm; bar Tues & Wed 5pm–midnight, Thurs & Fri 5pm–1am, Sat 1pm–1am, Sun 1–9pm.

Town of Ramsgate 62 Wapping High St, E1W 2PN ☎ 020 7481 8000; ⊖ Wapping; map p.94. Narrow, medieval pub by Wapping Old Stairs, which once led down to Execution Dock. Captain Blood was discovered here with the Crown Jewels under his cloak. Mon–Sat noon–midnight, Sun noon–10pm.

SOUTH BANK AND BANKSIDE

★ **Anchor & Hope** 36 The Cut, SE1 8LP ☎ 020 7928 9898, ⊛ anchorandhopepub.co.uk; ⊖ Southwark; map p.91. Superb gastropub dishing up excellent, comforting grub – slow-roasted meats, terrines, soufflés, heritage veggies and mouth-watering puds. You can't book (except on Sun), so the bar is basically the waiting room. Mon 5–11pm, Tues–Sat 11am–11pm, Sun 12.30–3.15pm; kitchen Mon 6–10.30pm, Tues–Sat noon–2.30pm & 6–10.30pm, Sun 12.30–3.15pm.

The George 77 Borough High St, SE1 1NH ☎ 020 7407 2056, ⊛ george-southwark.co.uk; ⊖ Borough; map p.94. London's only surviving galleried coaching inn, dating from the seventeenth century and owned by the National Trust. Managed by Greene King, it serves a decent range of real ales (stick to drinks), and is usually mobbed by tourists. Mon–Sat 11am–11pm, Sun noon–10pm.

★ **Kings Arms** 25 Roupell St, SE1 8TB ☎ 020 7207 0784, ⊛ thekingsarmslondon.co.uk; ⊖ Waterloo; map p.91. Set on one of Waterloo's impossibly cute terraced Georgian backstreets, this terrific local has a traditional drinking area with an excellent range of beers at the front, and a conservatory-style space with a large open fire and long wooden tables at the rear, where they also serve Thai food. Mon–Sat 11am–11pm, Sun noon–10pm.

The Roebuck 50 Great Dover St, SE1 4YG ☎ 020 7357 7324, ⊛ theroebuck.net; ⊖ Borough; map p.62. Big, airy pub with distressed walls covered with colourful prints. There's an excellent range of beers and a real mix of drinkers; the upstairs room – where Charlie Chaplin performed as a boy – hosts lively events. Above-average pub grub (£10–15) and lots of pavement seating. Mon–Thurs noon–midnight, Fri & Sat noon–1am, Sun noon–11pm; kitchen Mon–Fri noon–2pm & 5–10pm, Sat noon–4pm & 5–10pm, Sun noon–9pm.

KENSINGTON AND CHELSEA

Churchill Arms 119 Kensington Church St, W8 7LN ☎ 020 7727 4242, ⊛ churchillarmskensington.co.uk; ⊖ Notting Hill Gate; map p.98. Justifiably popular, flower-festooned local serving Fuller's beers and passable Thai food in a quirky, eclectic space. Mon–Wed 11am–11pm, Thurs–Sat 11am–midnight, Sun noon–10pm.

Cooper's Arms 87 Flood St, SW3 5TB ☎ 020 7376 3120, ⊛ coopersarms.co.uk; ⊖ Sloane Square; map p.98. This revamped pub is bright and airy, with Mediterranean tiles behind the bar, ornithological paintings everywhere and gramophone horns for light shades. There's a decent range of ales and ambitious pub grub. Mon–Sat 11pm, Sun noon–10pm.

★ **The Cow** 89 Westbourne Park Rd, W2 5QH ☎ 020 7221 0021, ⊛ thecowlondon.co.uk; ⊖ Royal Oak; map p.98. This handsome gastropub pulls in a cool, slightly raffish crowd. Tasty British food, including shellfish platters, is served both in the bar and in a more formal dining room. Mon–Thurs noon–11pm, Fri & Sat noon–midnight, Sun noon–10pm (kitchen closes 3pm Sun).

The Elgin 96 Ladbroke Grove, W11 1PY ☎ 020 7229 5663, ⊛ theelginnottinghill.co.uk; ⊖ Ladbroke Grove; map p.98. Enormous pub with a riot of original features and modish decorative touches. Buzzy, with regular events, from comedy and live music to life drawing. Mon–Thurs 11am–11pm, Fri & Sat 11am–midnight, Sun noon–10pm.

Grenadier 18 Wilton Row, SW1X 7NR ☎ 020 7235 3074, ⊛ bit.ly/GrenadierSW1X; ⊖ Hyde Park Corner; map p.98. Hidden in a private mews, this charming little Greene King pub was Wellington's local and his officers' mess; the original pewter bar survives, and there's plenty of military paraphernalia on display. Daily noon–11pm.

Windsor Castle 114 Campden Hill Rd, W8 7AR ☎ 020 7243 8797, ⊛ thewindsorcastlekensington. co.uk; ⊖ Notting Hill Gate; map p.98. A country pub in the backstreets of one of London's poshest neighbourhoods, this is a pretty, popular, early Victorian wood-panelled place with a great beer garden. They serve craft beers and grub with ideas above its station. Mon–Sat noon–11pm, Sun noon–10pm.

NORTH LONDON

The Constitution 42 St Pancras Way, NW1 0QT ☎ 020 7380 0767, ⊛ conincamden.com; ⊖ Camden Town; map p.62. Light seems to pour into this canal-side pub, while the beer garden overlooking the water is ideal for fine weather. Its lovely location makes it ripe for gentrification but, for now, it's very much a locals' haunt. Mon–Sat 11am–midnight, Sun noon–10pm.

Edinboro Castle 57 Mornington Terrace, NW1 7RU ☎ 020 7255 9651, ⊛ edinborocastlepub.co.uk; ⊖ Camden Town; map p.62. The main draw at this big, high-ceilinged pub is the leafy beer garden, which hosts

NOTTING HILL CARNIVAL

Notting Hill's three-day free **festival** (Ⓦ thelondonnottinghillcarnival.com), held over the August bank holiday weekend, is the longest-running street party in Europe. Dating back to 1959, the Caribbean carnival is a tumult of elaborate parade floats, eye-catching costumes, chest-thumping sound systems, live bands, irresistible food and huge crowds. Bringing revellers from all over London – it can become unbelievably crowded – it is still at heart a major celebration of Notting Hill's West Indian community, with steel bands, calypso and soca to the fore.

summer-weekend barbecues and hog roasts. Mon–Fri noon–11pm, Sat 11am–11pm, Sun noon–10pm.

Spaniards Inn Spaniards Rd, NW3 7JJ ☎ 020 8731 8406, Ⓦ thespaniardshampstead.co.uk; ⊖ Hampstead; map p.62. Rambling sixteenth-century coaching inn near the Heath, once frequented by everyone from Dick Turpin to John Keats. With a garden of heath-rivalling proportions and good food, it really draws the crowds at weekends, especially Sun afternoons. Mon–Sat noon–11pm, Sun 11am–10pm.

SOUTH LONDON

Cutty Sark Ballast Quay, off Lassell St, SE10 9PD ☎ 020 8858 3146, Ⓦ cuttysarkse10.co.uk; ⊖ Cutty Sark DLR; map p.94. This three-storey Georgian pub, not too touristy, is a good place for a riverside pint – food, however,

is overpriced. Mon–Sat 11am–11pm, Sun noon–10pm.

WEST LONDON

★ **The Dove** 19 Upper Mall, W6 9TA ☎ 020 8748 9474, Ⓦ dovehammersmith.co.uk; ⊖ Ravenscourt Park; map p.98. Very old, low-beamed Fuller's pub with literary associations, the smallest bar in the UK (4ft by 7ft), popular Sunday roasts and a riverside terrace. Mon–Sat 11am–11pm, Sun noon–10pm.

White Cross Hotel Water Lane, Richmond, TW9 1TH ☎ 020 8940 6844, Ⓦ thewhitecrossrichmond.com; ⊖ Richmond; map p.98. With a longer pedigree and more character than its rivals, the *White Cross* has a large, popular garden overlooking the river, and an open fire in winter. It's a hub for rugby fans. Mon–Sat 10am–11pm, Sun 10am–10pm.

NIGHTLIFE

LIVE MUSIC

LARGE VENUES

Brixton Academy 211 Stockwell Rd, SW9 9SL ☎ 020 77713000, Ⓦ o2academybrixton.co.uk; ⊖ Brixton; map p.62. The Academy has seen them all, from mods and rockers to Chase and Status. The 4900-capacity Victorian hall's sound quality isn't immaculate, but it remains a cracking place to see bands.

Hammersmith Apollo 45 Queen Caroline St, W6 9QH ☎ 020 8563 3800, Ⓦ eventimapollo.com; ⊖ Hammersmith; map p.98. The former Hammersmith Odeon is a cavernous space (downstairs can be seating or standing), hosting everyone from Sigur Ros to Regina Spektor and nostalgia acts.

Shepherd's Bush Empire Shepherd's Bush Green, W12 8TT ☎ 020 8354 3300, Ⓦ o2shepherdsbushempire. co.uk; ⊖ Shepherd's Bush; map p.98. Great mid-league bands play here. Views from the vertigo-inducing balconies are great, but downstairs lacks atmosphere if you're not at the front.

SMALL AND MID-SIZED VENUES

Borderline Orange Yard, Manette St, W1D 4JB ☎ 020 3871 7777, Ⓦ borderline.london; ⊖ Tottenham Court Road; map p.66. One of the last central venues still standing, with a guitar-infused music rota, some indie

club nights and good sound.

Cargo 83 Rivington St, EC2A 3AY ☎ 020 7739 3440, Ⓦ cargo-london.com; ⊖ Old Street; map p.89. Small, popular venue in what was once a railway arch. Hosts a variety of live acts, including jazz, hip-hop, indie and folk, and excellent club nights.

★ **The Dentist** 33 Chatsworth Rd, E5 0LH (no phone) Ⓦ theolddentist.com; ⊖ Homerton; map p.89. Tasteful guitars, experimental music, cool crowds and a laidback atmosphere in a barely renovated old surgery that puts you and the musicians face to face.

Forum 9–17 Highgate Rd, NW5 1JY ☎ 020 7428 4080, Ⓦ o2forumkentishtown.co.uk; ⊖ Kentish Town; map p.62. The programming at this mid-sized venue has moved towards a reliance on nostalgia acts, but it still occasionally surprises with special events.

Green Note 106 Parkway, NW1 ☎ 020 7485 9899, Ⓦ greennote.co.uk; ⊖ Camden Town; map p.62. Bijou music venue that punches way above its weight with its excellent line-up of roots, folk, acoustic and world music.

Hootananny 95 Effra Rd, SW2 1DF ☎ 020 7737 7273, Ⓦ hootanannybrixton.co.uk; ⊖ Brixton; map p.62. Charismatic world music, ska, reggae, folk and dancehall merge in this once-grand, raucous venue. Over-21s only.

Jazz Café 5 Parkway, NW1 7PG ☎ 020 7485 6834, Ⓦ thejazzcafelondon.com; ⊖ Camden Town; map p.62.

There's the odd cheesy pop night, but a combination of big names (at big prices) and clubbier acts from jazz, soul and beyond keep the dancefloor and balcony buzzing.

Kings Place 90 York Way, N1 9AG ☎020 7520 1490, ⓦkingsplace.co.uk; ⊖ King's Cross St Pancras; map p.77. Two halls host sophisticated classical, jazz and world music gigs at this rather swish development – the acoustics are excellent.

KOKO 1a Camden High St, NW1 7JE ☎020 7388 3222, ⓦkoko.uk.com; ⊖Mornington Crescent; map p.77. An atmospheric Camden institution, hosting gigs and weekend club nights, with a cracking assortment of Radio 1-friendly hit-makers dominating proceedings for young crowds.

★ **The Macbeth** 70 Hoxton St, N1 6LP ☎020 7749 0600, ⓦthemacbeth.co.uk; ⊖Old Street; map p.89. Beautiful venue, good sound system and a great schedule, from buzzing rock and indie gigs to imaginative club nights. Try the roof terrace if you need a break from the dancefloor.

Omeara 6 O'Meara St, SE1 1TE ☎020 3179 2900, ⓦomearalondon.com; ⊖London Bridge; map p.94. Fantastic under-arch venue with a lively atmosphere, high-profile DJs and cutting-edge indie acts.

Ronnie Scott's 47 Frith St, W1D 4HT ☎020 7439 0747, ⓦronniescotts.co.uk; ⊖Leicester Square; map p.66. London's most famous jazz club, this small, smart Soho stalwart hosts the really big names as part of its ambitious programme. The Sun jazz lunches are a hit.

★ **Roundhouse** Chalk Farm Rd, NW1 8EH ☎0300 678 9222, ⓦroundhouse.org.uk; ⊖Chalk Farm; map p.62. This magnificent listed Victorian steam engine shed is one of London's premier performing arts centres, pulling in huge names like Bob Dylan and John Cale alongside more eclectic acts.

★ **Union Chapel** Compton Terrace, N1 2UN ☎020 7226 1686, ⓦunionchapel.org.uk; ⊖Highbury & Islington; map p.62. Handsome, intimate venue in a beautiful old church (seating is on pews); acts range from contemporary folk via comedy to world music, r'n'b and indie legends. Free Sat lunchtime sessions.

The Vortex 11 Gillett Square, N16 8AZ ☎020 7254 4097, ⓦvortexjazz.co.uk; ⊖Dalston Kingsland; map p.89. This small venue is a serious player on the contemporary jazz scene, combining a touch of urban style with a cosy, friendly atmosphere.

CLUBS

Disco tunnels, sticky-floored rock clubs and epic house nights: London has it all. While the capital has lost most of its superclubs, the spread of mid-sized venues gives more choice than ever. Places tend to open between 10pm and midnight – check online. All-nighters and anywhere with a dress code will be pricey, but elsewhere £5–10 is standard, and finding a place to dance for free midweek isn't hard (though prices at the bar may be outrageous).

★ **Bethnal Green Working Men's Club** 42–44 Pollard Row, E2 6NB ☎020 7739 7170, ⓦworkersplaytime. net; ⊖Bethnal Green; map p.89. Postwar kitsch sets the backdrop for some serious playtime: choose from Fifties dress-up, burlesque, disco, rock'n'roll and high-camp gay nights. Thurs–Sat 9pm–2am, check listings for other days.

★ **Bussey Building** 133 Rye Lane, SE15 4ST ☎020 7732 5275, ⓦclfartcafe.org; ⊖Peckham Rye; map p.62. The very heart of Peckham's cool scene, with three floors of mixed bills – lots of afrobeat and disco – with a friendly crowd and loads of space to dance. The fortnightly Soul Train is big fun. Usually Thurs 5pm–2.30am, Fri & Sat 5pm–6am.

★ **Dalston Superstore** 177 Kingsland High St, E8 2PB ☎02072542273, ⓦdalstonsuperstore.com; ⊖Dalston Kingsland; map p.89. Dalston's nightlife hub, with picky door staff, fashionable straight/gay clientele and a hedonistic mix of disco, house and party tunes. Bar daily, club usually Wed–Sun 9pm–2.30am.

Fabric 77a Charterhouse St, EC1M 6HJ ☎020 7336 8898, ⓦfabriclondon.com; ⊖Farringdon; map p.82. Despite long queues (buy tickets online) and a maze-like layout, this 1600-capacity club gets in the big names. Music booming from the devastating sound system includes drum'n'bass, techno and house. Fri 11pm–7am, Sat 11pm–8am, Sun 11pm–5.30am.

Notting Hill Arts Club 21 Notting Hill Gate, W11 3JQ ☎02074604459, ⓦnottinghillartsclub.com; ⊖Notting Hill Gate; map p.98. Groovy dressed-down basement club-bar playing everything from funk through to soul and guitar music. Usually Wed–Sun 7pm–2am.

Proud Camden Stables Market, Chalk Farm Rd, NW1 8AH ☎020 7482 3867, ⓦproudcamden.com; ⊖Camden Town; map p.62. Crossing the dance/rock spectrum, the club nights at this former horse hospital have an endfor lingly student vibe. Club usually 10pm–2.30am.

XOYO 32–37 Cowper St, EC2A 4AP ☎020 7608 2878, ⓦxoyo.co.uk; ⊖Old Street; map p.89. This nine-hundred-capacity venue and club has an annoying layout, with convoluted corridors, but the programming is big-time fun, often delivered by Radio 1's roster of dance DJs. Club nights 9pm–4am.

LGBT+ NIGHTLIFE

London's **queer scene** is so huge, diverse and well established that it's easy to forget just how much – and how fast – it has grown over the last couple of decades. **Soho** remains its spiritual heart, with a mix of traditional gay pubs, designer café-bars and a range of gay-run services, while Vauxhall and Shoreditch/Dalston are also good stomping grounds. The major **outdoor event** of the year is **Pride** (ⓦprideinlondon.org) in late June, a colourful, whistle-blowing parade that takes over central London and features a massive rally in Trafalgar Square; the newer July event **UK Black Pride** (ⓦukblackpride.org.uk) also has a large following, with a star-studded rally in Vauxhall Pleasure Gardens.

BARS AND CLUBS

Many LGBT+ venues act as pubs by day and transform into raucous parties by night. Lots have cabaret or disco nights and are open until the early hours, making them an affordable alternative to clubs. Admission can be free or fairly cheap, though a few levy a charge after 10pm or 11pm (usually £5–10) for music, cabaret or a disco. We use "mixed" below to mean places for both gay men and lesbians, though most are primarily frequented by men.

MIXED BARS

Freedom 66 Wardour St, W1F OTA ☎020 7734 0071, ⓦfreedombarsoho.com; ⊖Piccadilly Circus; map p.66. Hip, metrosexual place, popular for cheap afterwork drinks and a fun dance spot at the weekend. Mon–Thurs 4pm–3am, Fri & Sat 2pm–3am, Sun 2–10.30pm.

Ku Bar 30 Lisle St, WC2H 7BA ☎020 7437 4303; 25 Frith St, W1D 5LB ☎020 7437 4303, ⓦku-bar. co.uk; ⊖Leicester Square; map p.66. The Lisle St original is one of Soho's largest and best-loved gay bars, serving a scene-conscious yet attitude-free clientele. Ruby Tuesdays are for lesbians only. The Frith St sister bar is a calmer cocktail spot. Lisle St: Mon–Sat noon–3am, Sun noon–midnight; Frith St: Mon–Thurs noon–11.30pm, Fri & Sat noon–midnight, Sun noon–10.30pm.

New Bloomsbury Set 76 Marchmont St, WC1N 1AG ☎020 7383 3084, ⓦnewbloomsburyset.net; ⊖Russell Square; map p.77. Hit happy hour at the right time and get cheap and cheerful cocktails in this tasteful basement bar; secure a cute and cosy snug to enjoy its speakeasy vibe. Mon–Sat 4–11.30pm, Sun 4–10.30pm.

★**Royal Vauxhall Tavern** 372 Kennington Lane, SE11 5HY ☎020 7820 1222, ⓦvauxhalltavern.com; ⊖Vauxhall; map p.62. This iconic, disreputable, divey drag and cabaret pub is home to legendary alternative club night Duckie on Sat. The rest of the week brings a changing calendar of performance that attracts a varied, often older crowd. Mon–Thurs 7pm–midnight, Fri 7pm–3am, Sat 9pm–2am, Sun 2pm–2am.

Rupert Street 50 Rupert St, W1D 6DR ⓦrupert-street. com; ⊖Piccadilly Circus; map p.66. See and be seen at this smart, mainstream bar with a mixed after-work crowd and more of a pre-club vibe at weekends. The ideal place to start a Soho night out; happy hour lasts until 8pm. Mon–Thurs noon–11pm, Fri & Sat noon–11.45pm, Sun noon–10.30pm.

LESBIAN BARS

★**She Soho** 23a Old Compton St, W1D 5JL ☎020 7437 4303, ⓦshe-soho.com; ⊖Tottenham Court Road; map p.66. Remarkably, this is Old Compton Street's only lesbian bar, relatively smart and with DJs at the weekend. Mon–Thurs 4–11.30pm, Fri & Sat noon–midnight, Sun noon–10.30pm.

Star at Night 22 Great Chapel St, W1F 8FR ☎020 7494 2488, ⓦthestaratnight.com; ⊖Tottenham Court Road; map p.66. Mixed, female-led venue, popular with a slightly older crowd who want somewhere to sit, a decent glass of wine and good conversation. Tues–Fri 4–11.30pm, Sat noon–11.30pm.

GAY MEN'S BARS

Comptons 51–53 Old Compton St, W1D 6HN ☎020 7096 5470; ⊖Leicester Square; map p.66. This large, traditional-style pub attracts a butch, cruising yet relaxed 25-plus crowd. Upstairs is more chilled and draws younger drinkers. Mon–Sat noon–11.30pm, Sun noon–10.30pm.

The King's Arms 23 Poland St, W1F 8QL ☎020 7734 5907, ⓦkingsarms-soho.co.uk; ⊖Oxford Circus; map p.66. London's best-known and perennially popular bear bar, with a traditional pub atmosphere. Sun is (raucous) karaoke night. Mon & Tues noon–11pm, Wed & Thurs noon–11.30pm, Fri & Sat noon–midnight, Sun 1–10.30pm.

CLUBS

Bootylicious Club Union, 66 Albert Embankment, SE1 7TP ☎07973 628585, ⓦbootylicious-club.co.uk; ⊖Vauxhall; map p.62. Despite having a large black community, London offers just one dedicated gay and lesbian urban music/BME night, held monthly and featuring r'n'b, hip-hop, dancehall, house and classic vibes. Last Sat of the month 11pm–4am.

★**The Eagle** 349 Kennington Lane, SE11 5QY ☎02077930903, ⓦeaglelondon.com; ⊖Vauxhall;map p.62. Home to the excellent Sunday-night Horse Meat Disco, this club's vibe is a loose, friendly re-creation of late 1970s New York, complete with facial hair, checked shirts and a pool table. Mon–Wed 4pm–midnight, Thurs 4pm–2am, Fri 4pm–4am, Sat 9pm–4am, Sun 8pm–3am.

Fire South Lambeth Rd, SW8 1RT ☎020 3242 0040, ⓦfirelondon.net; ⊖Vauxhall; map p.62. London's superclub of choice for disco bunnies and hardboyz, with all-nighters – and often all-dayers if you're making a proper weekend of it. Fri, Sat & occasionally Sun from 10pm or 11pm.

1

★ **The Glory** 281 Kingsland Rd, E2 8AS ⓦ theglory. co; ⊖ Haggerston; map p.89. Drag legend Jonny Woo's meld of lip-syncingly excellent performance, booze and a basement club for disco queens. Days and hours vary.

Heaven Villiers St, WC2N 6NG ☎ 020 7930 2020, ⓦ heavennightclub-london.com; ⊖ Charing Cross; map p.66. Said to be the UK's most popular gay club, this two thousand-capacity venue is home to G-A-Y (Thurs–Sat), with big-name DJs and PAs – expect lots of Drag

Race rejects – and Popcorn Monday, which prolongs the weekday fun till 5.30am. Thurs–Sat & Mon hours vary.

★ **Vogue Fabrics** 66 Stoke Newington Rd, N16 7XB ⓦ vfdalston.com; map p.89. Dalston's favourite disco basement offers an array of arts events and disco fun for a fashion crowd. Highlights include genderqueer performance night Icy Gays and the mega all-nighter Anal House Meltdown. Days and hours vary.

THEATRE AND COMEDY

London has enjoyed a reputation for quality **theatre** since the time of Shakespeare and, along with huge popular hits, still provides platforms for innovation and new writing. The **West End** is the heart of "Theatreland", with Shaftesbury Avenue its main drag, but the term is more conceptual than geographical. Less mainstream work is performed in **Off-West End** theatres and **fringe** venues, where ticket prices are lower and quality more variable. The capital's **comedy** scene is lively, too, whether you want to keep things low-key in an intimate pub or pay top dollar for big-name shows.

INFORMATION AND COSTS

Websites Good starting points for comedy gigs include ⓦ rabbitrabbitcomedy.com, ⓦ alwaysbecomedy.com, ⓦ amusedmoose.com and ⓦ laughoutlondoncomedyclub. co.uk. Consult *Time Out* for weekly, citywide listings (ⓦ timeout.com/london/comedy). For details and news about West End shows, along with tickets and promotions, see ⓦ officiallondontheatre.co.uk and ⓦ londontheatre.co.uk. And for weekly listings for theatre of all stripes, check *Time Out* (ⓦ timeout.com/london/theatre).

Prices Most comedy shows cost around £5–15, but there's plenty of free comedy to be found – often upstairs at pubs. Tickets for O2 and Wembley Arena tours cost anything from £35 up to £125 and beyond. For West End shows the box-office average is around £25–40, with £50–110 the usual top price, but bargains can be found. If you want to buy from the theatre direct it's best to go to the box office; you'll probably be charged a fee for booking over the phone or online. Ticket agencies such as Ticketmaster (ⓦ ticketmaster. co.uk) get seats for West End shows well in advance, but can add hefty booking fees.

Discounts Whatever you do, avoid the touts and the ticket agencies that abound in the West End – there's no guarantee that they are genuine. The Society of London Theatre (ⓦ officiallondontheatre.co.uk) offers online discounts on West End shows; their booth in Leicester Square, "tkts" (Mon–Sat 10am–7pm, Sun 11am–4.30pm; ⓦ tkts.co.uk), sells on-the-day tickets for the big shows at discounts of up to fifty percent. These tend to be in the top end of the price range and are limited to four/person; there's a service charge of £3/ticket. Cheap standby, "first look" and standing tickets can be very good value, and some major theatres sell a few on the door on the day; check the venue's website, and be prepared to put up with a restricted view.

THEATRES

Almeida Almeida St, N1 1TA ☎ 020 7359 4404, ⓦ almeida.co.uk; ⊖ Highbury & Islington. Popular little Islington venue that premieres excellent new plays and excitingly reworked classics from around the world. It often attracts big names, including Benedict Cumberbatch and Ben Whishaw.

★ **Arcola** 24 Ashwin St, E8 3DL ☎ 020 7503 1646, ⓦ arcola theatre.com; ⊖ Dalston Junction. Exciting fringe theatre in an old Dalston factory and a tent space. Politically charged plays – classics and contemporary – with shows from young, international companies and cabaret in the tent.

Barbican Silk St, EC2Y 8DS ☎ 020 7638 8891, ⓦ barbican.org.uk; ⊖ Barbican. Theatre, dance and performance by leading international companies and emerging artists, with excellent post-show talks.

The Bridge Theatre 1 Tower Bridge, SE1 2SD ☎ 0333 3200052, ⓦ bridgetheatre.co.uk; ⊖ London Bridge. Major new venue masterminded by Nicholas Hytner, formerly director at the National. The innovative performance space can be moulded to suit the performance.

Donmar Warehouse 41 Earlham St, WC2H 9LX ☎ 0844 871 7624, ⓦ donmarwarehouse.com; ⊖ Covent Garden. Long home to excellent writing, the Donmar has also garnered attention with big-name performers.

Menier Chocolate Factory 53 Southwark St, SE1 1RU ☎ 020 7378 1713, ⓦ menierchocolatefactory.com; ⊖ London Bridge. Great name, great venue, with a decent bar; the restaurant's food is inconsistent. Plays tend towards showy casting but interesting works do appear here.

★ **National Theatre** South Bank, SE1 9PX ☎ 020 7452 3000, ⓦ nationaltheatre.org.uk; ⊖ Waterloo. The country's top actors and directors produce an ambitious programme in the three NT theatres: the raked, 1150-seat Olivier, the classic "proscenium" Lyttelton and the experimental Dorfman. Cheap deals are available; on

"Travelex" performances seats can cost just £15. Some shows sell out months in advance, but £15/£18 day tickets go on sale on the morning of each performance – get there early (two tickets/person).

Open Air Theatre Inner Circle, Regent's Park, NW1 4NU ☏ 0844 826 4242, ⓦ openairtheatre.com; ⊖ Baker Street. Lovely alfresco space in Regent's Park hosting a tourist-friendly summer programme of Shakespeare, musicals, plays and concerts, many of which are geared towards children.

Roundhouse Chalk Farm Rd, NW1 8EH ☏ 0300 678 9222, ⓦ roundhouse.org.uk; ⊖ Chalk Farm. Camden's most exciting cultural venue, in an old – round – engine repairs shed, the Roundhouse puts on cutting-edge theatre, circus, cabaret and spoken word.

Royal Court Sloane Square, SW1W 8AS ☏ 020 7565 5000, ⓦ royalcourttheatre.com; ⊖ Sloane Square. The Royal Court's programme includes arguably the most ambitious

and radical new writing in town; £12 tickets on Mon.

★ **Shakespeare's Globe** 21 New Globe Walk, SE1 9DT ☏ 020 7401 9919, ⓦ shakespearesglobe.com; ⊖ London Bridge. This open-roofed replica Elizabethan theatre stages superb Shakespearean shows as they were originally conceived, as well as works from the Bard's contemporaries and new writing. Seats £20–45, with seven hundred standing tickets for around a fiver. The Globe Theatre season runs April–Oct, but the site's indoor Jacobean theatre, the Sam Wanamaker Playhouse, hosts a candlelit winter theatre season Oct–April, plus concerts and events in summer.

★ **Soho Theatre** 21 Dean St, W1D 3NE ☏ 020 7478 0100, ⓦ sohotheatre.com; ⊖ Tottenham Court Road. Great central theatre featuring new writing from around the globe at affordable prices. It's renowned for its comedy and cabaret, too, and has a popular, starry bar.

CINEMA

There are a lot of cinemas in London, especially the **West End**, with the biggest on and around Leicester Square. A few classy independent chains show more offbeat screenings, in various locations – check the **Picturehouse** (ⓦ picturehouses.co.uk), **Curzon** (ⓦ curzoncinemas.com) and **Everyman** (ⓦ everymancinema.com). **Tickets** at the major screens cost at least £13, although concessions are offered for some shows at virtually all cinemas, usually off-peak.

★ **BFI Southbank** Belvedere Rd, South Bank, SE1 8XT ☏ 020 7928 3232, ⓦ bfi.org.uk; ⊖ Waterloo. Eclectic themed seasons, showing between seven and fourteen films daily on four screens. The BFI, in association with Odeon, also runs the nearby IMAX (☏ 0330 333 7878, ⓦ bfi.org.uk/imax), a huge glazed drum where the colossal screen is not recommended for anyone with vertigo.

Electric 191 Portobello Rd, W11 2ED ☏ 020 7908 9696, ⓦ electriccinema.co.uk; ⊖ Notting Hill Gate. The Notting Hill Electric – quirky mainstream hits and offbeat offerings – is one of the oldest cinemas in the country (opened 1911). Its current, luxurious incarnation even includes a few double

beds. There's a second branch in Shoreditch.

ICA Cinema Nash House, The Mall, SW1Y 5AH ☏ 020 7930 3647, ⓦ ica.org.uk; ⊖ Charing Cross. Shows avant-garde, world, underground movies and docs on two screens in the seriously hip HQ of the Institute of Contemporary Arts, some with talks. There's a bar, too.

★ **Prince Charles** 7 Leicester Place, WC2H 7BY ☏ 020 7494 3654, ⓦ princecharlescinema.com; ⊖ Leicester Square. Two screens in the heart of the West End, with great prices (from £8.50) and a daily changing, lively programme of newish movies, classics and cult favourites, plus all-nighters and sing-a-long romps.

CLASSICAL MUSIC

On most days you should be able to attend a **classical concert** in London for around £15 (the usual range is about £12–50). During the week there are also numerous **free concerts**, often at lunchtimes, in London's churches or given by the city's two leading conservatoires, the Royal College of Music (ⓦ rcm.ac.uk) and Royal Academy of Music (ⓦ ram.ac.uk).

THE PROMS

The **Proms** (Royal Albert Hall; ☏ 0845 401 5040, ⓦ bbc.co.uk/proms; ⊖ South Kensington) provide a summer-season feast of classical music, much of it at bargain prices; uniquely, there are up to 1350 **standing places** available each evening, which cost just £6, even on the famed last night. They're sold from 9am each day; a few are available online but most are at the door. Promming **passes**, which guarantee you entrance up to thirty minutes before a show, cost from £11 (for two proms) up to £240 (for the entire season). **Seated tickets** are £7.50–100; those for the **last night**, which start at £62, are largely allocated by ballot. While the magnificence of the Royal Albert Hall is undeniable, the acoustics aren't the best – OK for orchestral blockbusters, less so for small-scale pieces – but the performers are outstanding, the atmosphere is uplifting and the hall is so vast that everyone has a good chance of getting in.

1

Barbican Silk St, EC2Y 8DS ☎020 7638 8891, ⓦbarbican.org.uk; ⊖Barbican. With the outstanding resident London Symphony Orchestra (ⓦlso.co.uk) and the BBC Symphony Orchestra (ⓦbbc.co.uk/symphony orchestra) as associate orchestra, plus top foreign orchestras and big-name soloists in regular attendance, the Barbican is an excellent venue for classical music.

Kings Place 90 York Way, N1 9AG ☎020 7520 1490, ⓦkingsplace.co.uk; ⊖King's Cross St Pancras. Modern, purpose-built venue, by the canal behind King's Cross, featuring new and interesting work in its two performance spaces.

Southbank Centre Belvedere Rd, South Bank, SE1 8XX ☎020 7960 4200, ⓦsouthbankcentre.co.uk; ⊖Embankment. Three spaces: the 2500-seat Royal Festival Hall (RFH), home to the Philharmonia (ⓦphilharmonia. co.uk) and the London Philharmonic (ⓦlpo.co.uk), is tailor-made for large-scale choral and orchestral works, while the Queen Elizabeth Hall (QEH) and intimate Purcell Room are used for chamber concerts, solo recitals, opera and choirs.

Wigmore Hall 36 Wigmore St, W1U 2BP ☎020 7935 2141, ⓦwigmore-hall.org.uk; ⊖Bond Street. With its near-perfect acoustics, the Wigmore Hall – built in 1901 as a hall for the adjacent Bechstein piano showroom – is a favourite, so book well in advance. It's brilliant for piano recitals, early music and chamber music, but best known for its song recitals by some of the world's greatest vocalists.

OPERA

In addition to the major venues below, a number of **fringe companies**, including Size Zero (ⓦsizezerooperera.com), Erratica (ⓦerratica.org), Diva Opera (ⓦdivaopera.com) and Opera Up Close (ⓦoperaupclose.com), produce consistently interesting work.

English National Opera London Coliseum, St Martin's Lane, WC2N 4ES ☎02078459300, ⓦeno.org; ⊖Leicester Square. The ENO is committed to keeping opera accessible, with operas sung in English, an adventurous repertoire, dazzling new productions, non-prohibitive pricing (£12–150) and various discount options.

Royal Opera House Bow St, WC2E 9DD ☎020 7304 4000, ⓦroh.org.uk; ⊖Covent Garden. The ROH, one of the world's leading opera houses, puts on lavish productions, performed in the original language with surtitles. Most tickets are more than £40 (reaching as high as £270), though there is some restricted-view seating (or standing room), which isn't at all bad, from around £10, and various special offers.

DANCE

London's biggest dance festival is **Dance Umbrella** (Oct; ⓦdanceumbrella.co.uk), a season of new work. For a **roundup** of all the major dance events, check ⓦlondondance.com.

The Place 17 Duke's Rd, WC1H 9PY ☎020 7121 1100, ⓦtheplace.org.uk; ⊖Euston. The Place, home to a conservatoire and a touring company, presents the work of contemporary choreographers and student performers.

Royal Opera House Bow St, WC2E 9DD ☎020 7304 4000, ⓦroh.org.uk; ⊖Covent Garden. Based at the Opera House, the world-renowned Royal Ballet puts on the very best in classical dance; tickets (£10–150) may be slightly cheaper than for opera. Book early.

Sadler's Wells Rosebery Ave, EC1R 4TN ☎020 7863 8000, ⓦsadlerswells.com; ⊖Angel. With resident dance companies including Matthew Bourne's New Adventures and the ZooNation hip-hop outfit, Sadler's Wells also hosts many international troupes and celebrates everything from flamenco to Bollywood. The Lilian Baylis Theatre, around the back, stages smaller productions, while the Peacock Theatre in Holborn adds populist shows to the mix.

SHOPPING

DEPARTMENT STORES

Fortnum & Mason 181 Piccadilly, W1A 1ER ☎020 7734 8040, ⓦfortnumandmason.com; ⊖Piccadilly Circus; map p.66. Beautiful 300-year-old store that started out as a humble grocer. It's famous for its pricey food, luxury hampers and fancy afternoon teas (see page 121), but is also good for designer clothes, furniture, luggage and stationery. Mon–Sat 10am–9pm, Sun noon–6pm.

Harrods 87–135 Brompton Rd, SW1X 7XL ☎020 7730 1234, ⓦharrods.com; ⊖Knightsbridge; map p.98. Vast, expensive and a little stuffy, Harrods is most notable for its Art Nouveau tiled food hall – and of course, its memorial statue of Princess Diana and Dodi, erected by Mohamed Al-Fayed, the store's previous owner and Dodi's father. Mon–Sat 10am–9pm, Sun noon–6pm.

Harvey Nichols 109–125 Knightsbridge, SW1X 7RJ ☎020 7235 5000, ⓦharveynichols.com; ⊖Knightsbridge; map p.98. Absolutely fabulous, sweetie, "Harvey Nicks" has eight floors of designer collections and casual wear, with a renowned cosmetics department and luxury food hall. Mon–Sat 10am–8pm (July & Aug closes 9pm), Sun noon–6pm.

LIBERTY

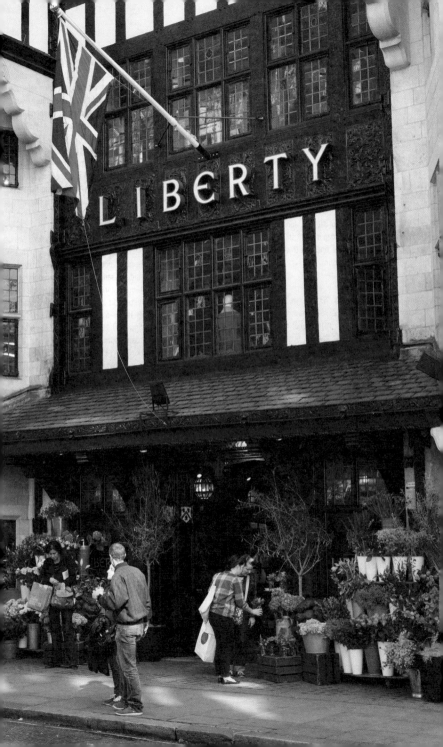

1

John Lewis 300 Oxford St, W1C 1DX ☎ 020 7629 7711, ⓦ johnlewis.co.uk; ⊖ Oxford Circus; map p.66. "Never knowingly undersold", this much-loved institution can't be beaten for basics. Mon–Wed, Fri & Sat 9.30am–8pm, Thurs 9.30am–9pm, Sun noon–6pm.

★ **Liberty** 210–220 Regent St, W1B 5AH ☎ 020 7734 1234, ⓦ liberty.co.uk; ⊖ Oxford Circus; map p.66. A glorious emporium of luxury infused with a dash of Art Nouveau bohemia, this exquisite store, with its mock-Tudor exterior, is most famous for its fabrics, designer goods and accessories, but also has an excellent reputation for mainstream and high fashion. Mon–Sat 10am–8pm, Sun noon–6pm.

★ **Selfridges** 400 Oxford St, W1A 1AB ☎ 0800 123 400, ⓦ selfridges.com; ⊖ Bond Street; map p.98. This huge, airy palace of clothes, food and furnishings was London's first great department store and remains its best. The food hall is the finest in town. Mon–Sat 9.30am–10pm, Sun noon–6pm.

BOOKS

★ **Daunt Books** 83 Marylebone High St, W1U 4QW ☎ 020 7224 2295, ⓦ dauntbooks.co.uk; ⊖ Baker Street; map p.98. Inspirational range of travel writing, guidebooks, maps, literary fiction and more, in the galleried interior of this famous Edwardian store. Other branches. Mon–Sat 9am–7.30pm, Sun 11am–6pm.

Foyles 107 Charing Cross Rd, WC2H 0DT ☎ 020 7437 5660, ⓦ foyles.co.uk; ⊖ Tottenham Court Road; map p.66. It may have moved down the road, but this huge and famous store continues to offer a splendid selection of titles – including antiquarian books – on all subjects across its four miles of shelves. Smaller branches under the RFH on the South Bank and in Waterloo Station. Mon–Sat 9.30am–9pm, Sun noon–6pm.

Hatchards 187 Piccadilly, W1J 9LE ☎ 020 7439 9921, ⓦ hatchards.co.uk; ⊖ Piccadilly Circus; map p.66. A little overshadowed by the colossal Waterstones down the road, and actually part of the Waterstones group, the venerable Hatchards holds its own when it comes to quality fiction, biography, history and travel. Mon–Sat 9.30am–8pm, Sun noon–6.30pm.

London Review Bookshop 14 Bury Place, WC1A 2JL ☎ 02072699030, ⓦ lrbshop.co.uk; ⊖ Tottenham Court Road; map p.77. All the books reviewed in the august literary journal and many more are available in this excellent Bloomsbury store. Nice little coffee (and cake) shop, too. Mon–Sat 10am–6.30pm, Sun noon–6pm.

Persephone Books 59 Lamb's Conduit St, WC1N 3NB ☎ 020 7242 9292, ⓦ persephonebooks.co.uk; ⊖ Russell Square; map p.77. Lovely bookshop offspring of a publishing house that specializes in neglected early and mid-twentieth-century writing, mainly by women. Mon–Fri 10am–6pm, Sat noon–5pm.

MUSIC

★ **Honest Jon's** 278 Portobello Rd, W10 5TE ☎ 020 8969 9822, ⓦ honestjons.com; ⊖ Ladbroke Grove; map p.98. West London stalwart offering a choice selection of reggae, blues, soul, jazz, funk, R&B, rare groove, world music and more, with current releases, secondhand finds and reissues. Mon–Sat 10am–6pm, Sun 11am–5pm.

Rough Trade 130 Talbot Rd, W11 1JA ☎ 020 7229 8541, ⊖ Ladbroke Grove; ⓦ roughtrade.com; map p.98. This historic indie specialist has a dizzying array – not all of it obscure – from electronica to hardcore and beyond. A second branch, in East London's Truman Brewery, hosts big-ticket live bands. Mon–Sat 10am–6.30pm, Sun 11am–5pm.

MARKETS

★ **Borough** 8 Southwark St, SE1 1TL ☎ 020 7407 1002, ⓦ boroughmarket.org.uk; ⊖ London Bridge; map p.94. Gourmet suppliers from all over the UK converge to sell organic and artisan goodies from around the world at this bustling, historic and utterly enjoyable food market, while street trucks and restaurants do a roaring trade. Mon & Tues 10am–5pm (some stalls only), Wed & Thurs 10am–5pm, Fri 10am–6pm, Sat 8am–5pm, sometimes Sun 10am–4pm.

Brick Lane Brick Lane, E1 6QL ⓦ visitbricklane.org, ⓦ trumanbrewery.com/cgi-bin/markets.pl; ⊖ Shoreditch High Street; map p.82. Sprawling and frenzied, the famous East End market, spreading through Dray Walk, Cygnet and Sclater streets, has become a must-do for hipsters and tourists both – it's hard to say what you can't find here. The coolest gear is sold in and around the Old Truman Brewery (with various markets open Thurs–Sun). Sun 10am–5pm.

Camden Camden High St to Chalk Farm Rd, NW1 ⓦ camdenmarket.com; ⊖ Camden Town; map p.62. Once beloved of hippies, punks and goths, and still a firm favourite with young European tourists, this huge, sprawling mass of stalls, including excellent vintage/antique stuff, segues into one enormous shopping district. Daily, roughly 10am–7pm, with more stalls at the weekend.

Columbia Road Columbia Rd, E2 ⓦ columbiaroad.info; ⊖ Hoxton; map p.82. This pretty East End street spills over in a profusion of blooms and resounds with the bellows of Cockney barrow boys during its glorious market. Come late for the best bargains, or early to enjoy a coffee and brunch in one of the groovy local cafés. It's an excellent shopping area, abounding in indie, arty and vintage stores. Sun 8am–3pm.

Greenwich Greenwich Church St, SE10 9HZ ⓦ greenwichmarketlondon.com; ⊖ Cutty Sark DLR; map p.94. Sprawling set of covered flea markets selling everything from bric-a-brac to board games, with antiques and crafts, food and vintage clothes. The surrounding streets, and the shops inside the market, offer more treasures. Daily 10am–5.30pm.

1

THE MAKING OF HARRY POTTER

Kids and Harry Potter fans will love **The Making of Harry Potter** tour in the Warner Bros studios in Leavesden (20 miles northwest of London); but impressively, they've managed to keep it interesting for everyone else, too. The self-guided **tour** (typically Mon–Fri 8.30/10.30am–6/10pm, Sat & Sun 8.30am–10pm; closed late Jan to early Feb, mid-Nov & around Christmas; last tour 3–4hr before closing; check website for latest hours and tour times; £39, under-16s £31; book far in advance; ☏ 0345 084 0900, ⊛ wbstudiotour.co.uk) takes you around the studios where much of the footage for the eight Harry Potter movies was shot, and every space is crammed with paraphernalia from filming. You can geek out over individual characters' wands and original costumes, or marvel at the films' creature technology – like the giant animatronic spiders – and the hand-drawn, hyper-detailed architectural plans.

Allow a few hours to get the most out of the tour and avoid rushing at the end – they save the best for last. If you can, time your visit to coincide with one of the **seasonal events**; these include Dark Arts at the end of October, and Hogwarts in the Snow, when the sets are decked out with fake snow and Christmas trees.

To get to the studios, take the train to Watford Junction from Euston (around 8/hr; 15–45min), then shuttle bus (around every 30min; 15min; £2.50, cash only).

Portobello Portobello and Golborne rds, W10 and W11 ⊛ shopportobello.co.uk; ⊖ Ladbroke Grove/Notting Hill Gate; map p.98. Probably the best way to approach this enormous market, or rather markets – beloved of tourist crowds – is from the Notting Hill end, winding your way through the antiques (Fri & Sat) and bric-a-brac down to the fruit and veg, and then via the fashion stalls under the Westway to the vintage (Fri & Sun) and fashion scene (Sat) at Portobello Green (⊛ portobellofashionmarket.com). The Golborne Rd market is cheaper and less crowded, with antique and retro furniture on Fri and Sat (food Mon–Thurs). Roughly 8am–6pm, till 1pm on Thurs; Golborne Rd closed Sun.

Spitalfields Commercial St, between Brushfield and Lamb sts, E1 6AA ⊛ spitalfields.co.uk; ⊖ Liverpool Street; map p.82. The East End's Victorian fruit and veg hall feels more like an upmarket mall nowadays, but there are interesting things to be found among its crafts, gifts and clothes stalls. Plenty of bars and restaurants, too, plus independent shops and street food. Mon–Fri 10am–5pm, Sat 11am–5pm, Sun 9am–5pm.

DIRECTORY

Hospitals Central A&Es include: St Thomas' Hospital, Westminster Bridge Rd, SE1 7EH (⊖ Westminster); and University College London Hospital, 235 Euston Rd, NW1 2BU (⊖ Euston Square or Warren Street).

Left luggage Left luggage is available at all airports and major train terminals; the Excess Baggage Company (⊛ excess-baggage.com) runs many of them. All facilities cost around £10–12/24hr.

Police Central 24hr Metropolitan Police stations include Charing Cross, Agar St, WC2N 4JP (⊖ Charing Cross) and West End Central, 27 Savile Row, W1S 2EX (⊖ Oxford Circus). The City of London has its own police force, and a 24hr station at 182 Bishopsgate, EC2M 4NP (⊛ cityoflondon.police.uk; ⊖ Liverpool Street).

Post offices Conveniently near Trafalgar Square is the post office at 24–28 William IV St, WC2N 4DL (Mon & Wed–Fri 8.30am–6.30pm, Tues 9.15am–6.30pm, Sat 9am–5.30pm).

The Southeast

COBBLED STREETS IN RYE, EAST SUSSEX

The Southeast

The southeast corner of England was traditionally where London went on holiday. In the past, trainloads of East Enders were shuttled to the hop fields and orchards of Kent for a working break from the city; boats ferried people down the Thames to the beaches of north Kent; while everyone from royalty to cuckolding couples enjoyed the seaside at Brighton, a blot of decadence in the otherwise sedate county of Sussex. Although many of the old seaside resorts have struggled to keep their tourist custom in the face of ever more accessible foreign destinations, the region still has considerable charm, its narrow country lanes and verdant meadows appearing, in places, almost untouched by modern life.

The proximity of **Kent** and **Sussex** to the continent has dictated the history of this region, which has served as a gateway for an array of invaders. **Roman remains** dot the coastal area – most spectacularly at Fishbourne in Sussex – and many roads, including the main A2 London to Dover, follow the arrow-straight tracks laid by the legionaries. When Christianity spread through Europe, it arrived in Britain on the Isle of Thanet – the northeast tip of Kent, then an island but since rejoined to the mainland by silting. In 597 AD Augustine moved inland and established a monastery at **Canterbury**, still the home of the Church of England and the county's prime historic attraction.

The last successful invasion of England took place in 1066, when the Normans overran King Harold's army near **Hastings**, on a site now marked by Battle Abbey. The Normans left their mark all over this corner of the kingdom, and Kent remains unmatched in its profusion of medieval castles, among them **Dover**'s sprawling clifftop fortress guarding against continental invasion and **Rochester**'s huge, box-like citadel, close to the old dockyards of **Chatham**, power base of the formerly invincible British navy. Gentler reminders of history can be found in pretty **Sandwich** and **Rye**, two of the best-preserved medieval towns in the country.

You can spend unhurried days in elegant old towns such as **Tunbridge Wells**, **Arundel**, **Midhurst** and **Lewes**, or enjoy the less elevated charms of the traditional resorts. **Whitstable** is an arty getaway famed for its oysters, **Deal** has a laidback vibe, and cheeky **Margate** goes from strength to hipster strength, but chief among them all is **Brighton**. The rolling chalk uplands of the **South Downs National Park** get you away from it all, with the soaring white cliffs of the **Sussex Heritage Coast** the unmissable scenic highlight. Kent and Sussex also harbour some of the country's finest **gardens** – ranging from the lush flowerbeds of Sissinghurst in the **High Weald** to the great landscaped estate of Petworth House – and a string of excellent **galleries**, among them the Pallant Gallery in **Chichester**, the Turner Contemporary in Margate, the Towner in **Eastbourne** and the tiny Ditchling Museum of Art + Craft just outside Brighton. **Folkestone**, meanwhile, with its high-profile triennial art show, is building a strong cultural reputation.

THE SEVEN SISTERS, SOUTH DOWNS WAY

Highlights

❶ The Sportsman, Seasalter Savour the impeccable, locally sourced, Michelin-starred food at this simple gastropub by the sea. See page 146

❷ Margate With its quirky Old Town, its broad sandy beach and the fabulous Turner Contemporary gallery, this brash old resort is an increasingly hip destination. See page 146

❸ Canterbury Cathedral The destination of the pilgrims in Chaucer's *Canterbury Tales*, with a magnificent sixteenth-century interior that includes a shrine to the murdered Thomas Becket. See page 150

❹ The White Cliffs of Dover Immortalized in song, art and literature, the famed chalky

cliffs offer walks and vistas over the Channel. See page 156

❺ Rye Ancient hilltop town of picturesque cobbled streets, with some great places to eat, shop and sleep. See page 162

❻ Walking the South Downs Way Experience the best walking in the southeast – and some fantastic views – on this national trail, which spans England's newest National Park. See page 168

❼ The Lanes and North Laine, Brighton Explore the café- and shop-crammed streets of the maze-like Lanes and the buzzy, hip North Laine: Brighton at its best. See page 173

HIGHLIGHTS ARE MARKED ON THE MAP ON PAGE 142

GETTING AROUND THE SOUTHEAST

By train Southeastern (w southeasternrailway.co.uk) covers Kent and the easternmost part of Sussex, and also the high-speed services which run from London St Pancras to the north Kent coast and Chichester. The rest of Sussex is served instead by Southern Rail (w southernrailway.com).

By bus National Express services from London and other main towns are pretty good, though local bus services are less impressive, and tend to dry up almost completely on Sundays outside of the major towns. Traveline (w travelinesoutheast.org.uk) has route details and timetables. The Discovery Ticket (£8.50, family

ticket £16) allows a day's unlimited travel across most bus services in the southeast; see w southdowns.gov.uk/discovery-ticket.

By car Outside of the main towns, driving is the easiest way to get around, although commuter traffic in this corner of England is very heavy. The A2, M2 and M20 link the capital with Dover and Ramsgate, and the M23/A23 provides a quick run to Brighton. The A27 runs west–east across the Sussex coast, giving access to Chichester, Arundel, Brighton, Lewes, Eastbourne and Hastings, but can be slow-going.

North Kent

North Kent has a good share of appealing destinations, all easily accessible from London. The attractive little town of **Rochester** has historic and literary interest, but it's the seaside resorts that really pull in the visitors: arty **Whitstable**; appealingly old-fashioned **Broadstairs**; and **Margate**, which combines a dash of offbeat bucket-and-spade charm with the big-name Turner Contemporary gallery and a thriving vintage scene.

Rochester and around

The handsome town of **ROCHESTER** was settled by the Romans, who built a fortress on the site of the existing castle. The town's most famous son is **Charles Dickens** – mischievously, it appears as "Mudfog" in *The Mudfog Papers*, and "Dullborough" in

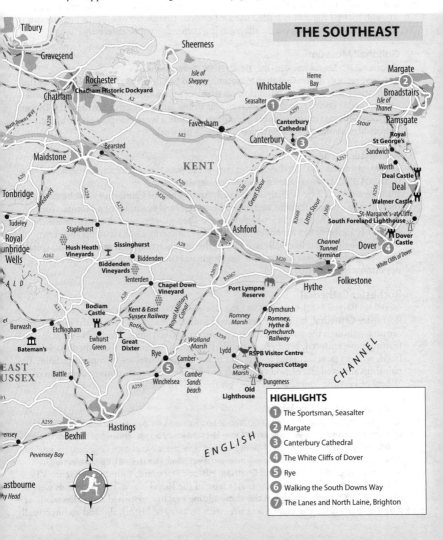

THE SOUTHEAST

HIGHLIGHTS

1. The Sportsman, Seasalter
2. Margate
3. Canterbury Cathedral
4. The White Cliffs of Dover
5. Rye
6. Walking the South Downs Way
7. The Lanes and North Laine, Brighton

The Uncommercial Traveller as well as featuring in *The Pickwick Papers* and *The Mystery of Edwin Drood*. Many of the buildings Dickens described can still be seen today. In neighbouring Chatham, the colossal **Chatham Historic Dockyard** records more than four hundred years of British maritime history – even if ships don't float your boat, it is well worth a trip.

Huguenot Museum

95 High St, ME1 1LX • Wed–Sat 10am–5pm; bank hol Mon 10am–4pm; last admission 30min before closing • £4 • ☎ 01634 789347, ⓦ huguenotmuseum.org

Above the tourist office on Rochester's historic High Street, the **Huguenot Museum** makes interesting connections between the fifty thousand French Protestants who fled France for Britain between 1685 and 1700 and modern-day refugees. The small display focuses on the dire religious persecution that drove them to flee their homes, the hostility they faced on arrival, and the huge contribution they made to British culture. Though many Huguenots settled in east London, there were significant populations in Kent – including an important silk-weaving community in Canterbury.

Guildhall Museum

17 High St, ME1 1PY • Tues–Sun 10am–5pm • Free • ☎ 01634 332900, ⓦ medway.gov.uk

The best section in the **Guildhall Museum**, in two buildings at the riverside end of the High Street, is its chilling exhibition on the decommissioned prison ships – or hulks – used to house convicts and prisoners of war in the late eighteenth century. The **Dickens Discovery Rooms**, in the adjoining building, include a wordy display about his life, and a short film about the locations that feature in his work.

Rochester Castle

Northwest end of the High St, ME1 1SW • Daily: April–Sept 10am–6pm; Oct–March 10am–4pm; last entry 45min before closing • £6.40; EH • ☎ 01634 335882, ⓦ www.english-heritage.org.uk/visit/places/rochester-castle

Built around 1127 by William of Corbeil, Archbishop of Canterbury, **Rochester Castle**, though now ruined, remains one of the best-preserved examples of a Norman fortress in the country. The stark 113ft-high ragstone keep glowers over the town, while the interior is all the better for having lost its floors, allowing clear views up and down the dank shell. The outer walls and two of the towers retain their corridors and spiral stairwells, allowing you to scramble up rough and uneven damp stone steps to the uppermost battlements.

Rochester Cathedral

Boley Hill, ME1 1SX • Mon–Fri 7.30am–6pm, Sat & Sun 7.30am–5pm • Free • ☎ 01634 843366, ⓦ rochestercathedral.org

Rochester Cathedral, built on Anglo-Saxon foundations, dates back to the eleventh century – though the structure has been much modified since. Plenty of Norman features have endured, however, particularly in the nave and on the cathedral's west front, with its pencil-shaped towers and richly carved portal and tympanum. Some fine paintings survived the Dissolution; look out for the thirteenth-century depiction of the Wheel of Fortune (only half survives) on the walls of the quire.

Chatham Historic Dockyard

About 1 mile north of Chatham along Dock Rd, ME4 4TE • Daily: mid-Feb to end March & Nov 10am–4pm; end March to Oct 10am–6pm; Victorian Ropery and *Ocelot* tours by timed ticket only • £24; under-15s £14; tickets valid for a year • ☎ 01634 823800, ⓦ thedockyard.co.uk • Bus #190 runs to the docks from Rochester (every 7–20min; 5min); there are also trains to Chatham station from Rochester (see below) and St Pancras International (every 30min; 40min) – from the station you can walk (30min), catch a bus (#101; 15min) or take a taxi (£7)

Two miles east of Rochester, the **Chatham Historic Dockyard**, founded by Henry VIII, was by the time of Charles II the major base of the Royal Navy. The dockyards were closed in 1984, with the end of the shipbuilding era, but reopened soon afterwards as a tourist attraction. The eighty-acre site, with its array of historically and architecturally fascinating ships and buildings, is too big to explore in one trip. Highlights include the interactive **Command of the Oceans** displays, the Victorian sloop **HMS Gannet**, the **Victorian Ropery** and the **Ocelot submarine**, the last warship to be built at the yard.

ARRIVAL AND INFORMATION ROCHESTER AND AROUND

By train Trains arrive in the heart of town just east of the High St, opposite the back entrance of the tourist office.
Destinations Canterbury (every 20–45min; 40–50min); Chatham (every 5–25min; 3min); London Charing Cross (Mon–Fri every 30min; 1hr 20min); London St Pancras (every 30min; 35–40min); London Victoria (every 10–

20min; 45min–1hr 20min); Ramsgate (every 5–40min; 1hr 10min).
Tourist office 95 High St (April–Sept Mon–Sat 10am–5pm, Sun 10.30am–5pm; Oct–March Mon–Sat 10am–5pm; ☎ 01634 338141, ⓦ visitmedway.org).

ACCOMMODATION

Golden Lion 147–151 High St, ME1 1EL ☎ 01634 405402, ⓦ jdwetherspoon.com. Rochester's most central option, with nine well-equipped en-suite rooms above a busy Wetherspoons pub. Breakfast is available in the pub (for an extra fee). **£80**

Ship & Trades Maritime Way, Chatham, ME4 3ER ☎ 01634 895200, ⓦ shipandtradeschatham.co.uk. Fifteen contemporary B&B rooms in a great location above a waterside brasserie-bar near the dockyard. Many rooms have marina views and some have terraces. **£100**

EATING

The Deaf Cat 83 High St, ME1 1LX ⓦ thedeafcat.com. A hop away from the cathedral, this coffee shop, dedicated to the memory of Dickens's deaf cat, is a laidback place serving espresso drinks, cookies, cakes and sandwiches to tourists and locals. Mon–Sat 9am–5pm, Sun 10am–5pm.
Topes 60 High St, ME1 1JY ☎ 01634 845270, ⓦ topes restaurant.com. Rochester's best restaurant, near the

cathedral, in a wood-panelled dining room with sloping ceilings. Lunch sees gourmet burgers (£8) and inventive dishes (from £12) – basil gnocchi with Jerusalem artichoke and salsify, perhaps – with a two-/three-course set menu on Sun (£19.50/25); dinner is also prix fixe (£28/£35). Afternoon tea Wed–Sat 3–4pm (from £12.50). Wed–Fri & Sun noon–4pm, Sat noon–4pm & 6.30–9pm.

Whitstable

Fishermen, artists, yachties and foodies rub along in lively, laidback **WHITSTABLE**. The **oysters** for which the town is famed have been farmed here since Roman times, and there is no shortage of places to enjoy them, from the tourist-friendly joints around the harbour to the wonderful *Wheelers*, a Whitstable institution. Indeed, Whitstable is a great place to eat all year round, with seasonal, local food to the fore –and the incomparable *Sportsman* gastropub just along the coast at **Seasalter**.

Formal sights are few, which is part of the appeal. Follow the signs from the lively **High Street** and trendy **Harbour Street**, with its delis, restaurants and boutiques, to reach the **seafront**, a quiet shingle beach punctuated by weathered groynes and backed for most of its length by seaside houses and colourful beach huts in varying states of repair.

The Victorian **harbour**, a mix of pretty and gritty that defines Whitstable to a tee, bustles with a fish market, whelk stalls and a couple of seafood restaurants, and offers plenty of places to sit outside and watch the activity. The handsome 1892 Thames sailing barge, **Greta** (☎ 07711 657919, ⓦ greta1892.co.uk), offers boat trips around the estuary.

ARRIVAL AND INFORMATION WHITSTABLE

By train From the train station it's a 15min walk to the centre, along Cromwell Rd to Harbour St, the northern continuation of High St.
Destinations Broadstairs (every 10–45min; 25min); London St Pancras (hourly; 1hr 15min); London Victoria (hourly; 1hr 30min); Margate (every 10–45min; 20min); Ramsgate (every 10–45min; 35min).

By bus Buses to Canterbury (every 15min; 30min) stop on the High St.
Tourist information The Whitstable Shop, 34 Harbour St (Jan–March Mon–Sat 10am–4pm, Sun 11am–4pm; April–Dec Mon–Fri 10am–4pm, Sat 10am–5pm, Sun 11am–5pm; ☎ 01227 770060).

2

ACCOMMODATION

★ **Duke of Cumberland** High St, CT5 1AP ☎ 01227 280617, ⓦ thedukeinwhitstable.co.uk. Eight comfortable, good-value en-suite B&B rooms above a friendly, boho music pub. It can be noisy on weekend nights, when they have live bands, but the music (which is invariably excellent) usually winds up around midnight. On sunny mornings breakfast in the garden is a treat. **£80**

Fishermen's Huts Near the harbour ☎ 01227 280280, ⓦ whitstablefishermanshuts.com. Thirteen two-storey weatherboard cockle-farmers' stores (sleeping 2–6 people), offering cute, characterful accommodation near the harbour. Most have sea views, and some have basic self-catering facilities. Rates include breakfast, served at the nearby *Continental Hotel*, and drop considerably out of season. Mon–Thurs & Sun **£125**, Fri & Sat (two-night minimum) **£195**

EATING

★ **The Sportsman** Faversham Rd, Seasalter, CT5 4BP ☎ 01227 273370, ⓦ thesportsmanseasalter.co.uk. The drab exterior belies the Michelin-starred experience inside this fabulous gastropub, in a lonesome seaside spot four miles west of town. The deceptively simple food takes local sourcing to the extreme: fresh seafood, marsh lamb, seaweed from the beach, bread and butter made right here – even the salt comes from the sea outside. Mains from £21 – roast gurnard with bouillabaisse and green olive tapenade, say. Reservations essential. Tues–Sat noon–2pm & 7–9pm, Sun noon–2.30pm.

★ **Wheelers Oyster Bar** 8 High St, CT5 1BQ ☎ 01227 273311, ⓦ wheelersoysterbar.com. A Whitstable institution dating back to 1856, this is one of the best restaurants in Kent. It's an informal, friendly little place, with just four tables in a back parlour and a few stools at the fish counter, but the inventive, super-fresh seafood is stunning, whether you choose raw oysters or more substantial mains (from £16) like roasted bass with coriander mash in a prawn and mussel broth with samphire. Delicious quiches available from the counter, too. BYO; cash only; reservations essential. Mon & Tues 10.30am–9pm, Thurs 10.15am–9pm, Fri 10.15am–9.30pm, Sat 10am–10pm, Sun 11.30am–9pm.

Windy Corner Stores 110 Nelson Rd, CT5 1DZ ☎ 01227 771707, ⓦ facebook.com/windycornerstoresandcafe. Homely neighbourhood café with a couple of outdoor tables on the quiet residential street. The home-made food includes breakfasts (£3–7) from a full veggie to a bacon sarnie, creative salads, sandwiches and daily specials (lasagne, perhaps, or vegetable gratin; from £7), and good coffee and cakes. Daily 8am–4.30pm.

DRINKING

Black Dog 66 High St, CT5 1BB ⓦ facebook.com/TheBlackDog13. Don't be deceived by the vaguely Goth exterior – this quirky micropub is a cheery place, with (mainly) Kentish ales, ciders and wines, inexpensive local snacks, and a friendly regular crowd. No cards, no vaping, no children. Mon–Wed noon–11pm, Thurs–Sun noon–midnight.

Old Neptune Marine Terrace, CT5 1EJ ☎ 01227 272262, ⓦ thepubonthebeach.co.uk. A white weatherboard landmark standing alone on the beach, the "Neppy" is the perfect spot to enjoy a sundowner at a picnic table on the shingle, or to hunker down with a pint after a bracing beach walk. Some real ales, plus live music on Sat & Sun. Mon–Wed 11.30am–10.30pm, Thurs–Sat 11.30am–11.30pm, Sun noon–10.30pm.

Margate

After a few decades in decline, the tide in **MARGATE** is undoubtedly turning. It may not be the prettiest town on the Kent coast, but its energetic combination of eccentricity, nostalgia and cheery seaside fun give it a definite appeal. With the splendid **Turner Contemporary** gallery, the retro-cool **Dreamland** amusement park, a cluster of **vintage shops** and indie galleries in the Old Town and some superb places to eat and stay – not to mention the big, sandy **beach** – Margate is a must-see.

Dreamland

Marine Terrace/Belgrave Rd, CT9 1XG • Days and hours vary widely, depending on school holidays and special events: check website • Free entry; attractions £1.50–3.50 – buy an unlimited wristband (£13.50/children £9.50) or load cash onto a rechargeable "Dream Pass" and pay as you go • ☎ 01843 295887, ⓦ dreamlandmargate.com

Dreamland, which grew from Victorian pleasure gardens to become a wildly popular theme park in the 1920s, stood derelict on the seafront for nearly ten miserable years following its closure in 2003. Restored in 2015 under the guiding eye of designers Wayne and Geraldine Hemingway, it's become the flagbearer for the new, improved

Margate – a hit with hipsters and hen dos alike. There's more here than knowing vintage cool, though. Certainly the look of the place – old-school **roller disco** and **pinball machines**, jaunty **helter skelter** and wooden **rollercoaster** – plays on beloved memories of the traditional British seaside, but there's lots for today's kids, too, from the Octopus's Garden playground to the gravity-defeating Barrel of Laughs ride. It also hosts a lot of cool music events.

Turner Contemporary

Rendezvous, CT9 1HG • Tues–Sun 10am–6pm • Free • ☎ 01843 233000, ⓦ turnercontemporary.org

Rearing up on the east side of the harbour, the opalescent **Turner Contemporary** is a seafront landmark. Named for J.M.W. Turner, who went to school in the Old Town in the 1780s, and who returned frequently as an adult to take advantage of the dazzling light, the gallery is built on the site of the lodging house where he created some of his famous sea paintings. Offering fantastic views of the ever-changing seascape through its enormous windows, the gallery hosts temporary exhibitions of contemporary art – previous shows have featured Yinka Shonibare and Grayson Perry.

Shell Grotto

Grotto Hill, CT9 2BU • Easter–Oct daily 10am–5pm; Nov–Easter Sat & Sun 11am–4pm • £4 • ☎ 01843 220008, ⓦ shellgrotto.co.uk

Discovered, or so the story goes, in 1835, Margate's bizarre **Shell Grotto** has been captivating visitors ever since. Accessed via a damp subterranean passageway, the grotto's hallways and chambers are covered with mosaics made from shells – more than 4.5 million of them, tinted silvery grey and black by the fumes of Victorian gas lamps. The origins of the grotto remain a mystery – some believe it to be an ancient pagan temple, others a Regency folly – which only adds to its offbeat charm.

ARRIVAL AND INFORMATION   MARGATE

By train The station is near the seafront on Station Rd. Destinations Broadstairs (every 5–30min; 5min); Canterbury (hourly; 30min); London St Pancras (every 25min–1hr; 1hr 30min); London Victoria (Mon–Sat hourly; 1hr 50min); Ramsgate (every 5–30min; 15min); Whitstable (every 10–45min; 20min).
By bus Buses pull in at the clocktower on Marine Terrace.

Destinations Broadstairs (every 10–30min; 30min); Canterbury (every 30min; 1hr); Herne Bay (hourly; 50min); London (7 daily; 2hr–2hr 30min); Ramsgate (every 10–15min; 45min).
Tourist office Droit House, Harbour Arm (April–Oct daily 10am–5pm; Nov–March Tues–Sat 10am–5pm; ☎ 01843 577577, ⓦ visitthanet.co.uk).

ACCOMMODATION

Sands Hotel 16 Marine Drive, CT9 1DH ☎ 01843 228228, ⓦ sandshotelmargate.co.uk. This airy boutique refurb of an old seafront hotel has twenty luxe rooms, some with little balconies and sea views. The swanky restaurant has glorious sunset views, and there's a roof terrace for relaxing. £200
★ **Walpole Bay Hotel** Fifth Ave, Cliftonville, CT9 2JJ ☎ 01843 221703, ⓦ walpolebayhotel.co.uk. This

family-run hotel has changed little since Edwardian times, and exudes an air of shabby gentility from its pot-plant-cluttered dining room to its clanky vintage elevator. Don't miss the museum of, well, everything – including a collection of napery (household linen) art. Rooms vary, but most have sea views, many have small balconies and all are comfy, clean and well equipped. £85

EATING

Cheesy Tiger 7–8 Harbour Arm, CT9 1AP ☎ 01843 448550, ⓦ facebook.com/cheesytigermargate. Rickety, boho little deli/café/wine bar offering small plates (pea and wild garlic risotto, for example) and cheese dishes made with the finest ingredients. Choose a sinfully unctuous toastie – or just sit with a simple cheese platter and glass of red gazing across at the sands. Dishes from £6. Hours vary; usually Mon & Wed 6–9pm, Thurs 6–10pm, Fri & Sat noon–10pm, Sun noon–9pm.

GB Pizza Co 14 Marine Drive, CT9 1DH ☎ 01843 297700, ⓦ greatbritishpizza.com. A buzzing contemporary pizza joint on the seafront, with smiley staff and a lively vibe, dishing up gourmet crispy pizza (£5–9.50) made with ingredients from small producers. Mon–Fri 11.30am–9.30pm, Sat & Sun 10am–9.30pm; shorter hours in autumn/winter.
★ **Hantverk & Found** 18 King St, CT9 1DA ☎ 01843 280454, ⓦ hantverk-found.co.uk. Tiny Old Town gallery

café serving fabulous, inventive fish. It's hard to choose – prawn and squid ink croquettes? Plaice with seaweed and caper butter? Clams in dashi miso? – but you simply can't go wrong. Starters/small plates from £7, large plates £13–20. Thurs & Fri noon–4pm & 6.30–11pm, Sat noon–4pm & 6–11pm, Sun noon–4pm.

DRINKING

Fez 40 High St, CT9 1DS. Relaxed and eccentric pub, stuffed with recycled vintage memorabilia – young mods and old soulboys alike perch on Waltzer ride carriages, barber chairs or cinema seats to enjoy a good chat and a pint of real ale or speciality cider. Mon–Sat noon–10.30pm, Sun noon–10pm.

Harbour Arms Harbour Arm, CT9 1JD ☎07776 183273, ⓦthe-harbour-arms.co.uk. This cosy, cluttered micropub, with a nautical, sea-salty atmosphere, serves cask ales and ciders to a loyal local crowd. In warm weather the outside benches are at a premium, especially at sunset. Daily from noon; closing hours vary.

Broadstairs

Overlooking its golden sandy beach – Viking Bay – from its clifftop setting, **BROADSTAIRS** is the smallest and most immediately charming of the resort towns in northeast Kent. A fishing village turned Victorian resort, it's within walking distance of several sandy **bays** and has an excellent **folk festival**. It also has strong **Charles Dickens** connections: the author stayed here frequently, and rented an "airy nest" overlooking the sea, where he finished writing *David Copperfield*. A small **museum** and, in June, the **Dickens Festival** (ⓦbroadstairsdickensfestival.co.uk), play up the associations.

Dickens House Museum

2 Victoria Parade, CT10 1QS • Easter to mid-June & mid-Sept to mid-Oct daily 1–4.30pm; mid-June to mid-Sept daily 10am–4.30pm; Nov Sat & Sun 1–4.30pm • £3.75 • ☎01843 861232, ⓦdickensmuseumbroadstairs.co.uk

The broad, balconied cottage that houses the **Dickens House Museum** was once the home of Miss Mary Pearson Strong, on whom Dickens based the character of Betsey Trotwood in *David Copperfield*. Its small rooms are crammed with memorabilia, including Dickens' correspondence, illustrations from the original novels and a reconstruction of Betsey Trotwood's parlour.

ARRIVAL AND DEPARTURE   BROADSTAIRS

By train Broadstairs station is at the west end of the High St, a 10min walk to the seafront.
Destinations Canterbury (hourly; 25min); London St Pancras (every 25min–hourly; 1hr 20min–1hr 45min); London Victoria (Mon–Sat hourly; 1hr 50min); Margate (every 5–30min; 5min); Ramsgate (every 5–30min; 6min); Whitstable (every 10–45min; 25min).

By bus Buses stop along the High St.
Destinations Canterbury (hourly; 1hr–1hr 30min); London (7 daily; 2hr 45min–3hr 20min); Margate (every 10–30min; 30min); Ramsgate (every 5–20min; 15min).

Tourist information There's a small information kiosk on the Promenade by the *Royal Albion* hotel terrace (ⓦvisitthanet.co.uk).

ACCOMMODATION

★ **Belvidere Place** 43 Belvedere Rd, CT10 1PF ☎01843 579850, ⓦbelvidereplace.co.uk. This stylish, quirky boutique B&B earns extra points for its warm, friendly management and gourmet breakfasts. The five lovely rooms feature sleek bathrooms, contemporary art and one-off vintage furniture finds. **£160**

EATING AND DRINKING

Tartar Frigate Harbour St, CT10 1EU ☎01843 862013, ⓦtartarfrigate.co.uk. In an unbeatable location right on the harbour, this eighteenth-century flint pub is a relaxed, friendly hangout, with regular folk bands. Book ahead for the restaurant, which offers classic seafood dishes from £17. Sun lunch sees things go off-piste, with a traditional four-course roast (£19). Pub Mon–Sat 11am–11pm, Sun 11am–10.30pm; restaurant Mon–Sat noon–1.45pm & 7–9.45pm, Sun seatings 12.30pm & 3.30pm.

★ **Wyatt & Jones** 23–27 Harbour St, CT10 1EU ☎01843 865126, ⓦwyattandjones.co.uk. Stylish, airy restaurant a pebble's throw from the beach, dishing up superb Modern British food – try roasted hake with cauliflower, crab, shredded ham hock and beans – using mainly Kentish ingredients. Mains from £14 at lunch (small plates also available from £6), a little more in the evening.

Wed & Thurs 9–11am, noon–3pm & 6.30–9pm, Fri & Sat 9–11am, noon–3pm & 6–10pm, Sun 9–11am & noon–4pm.

Ramsgate

RAMSGATE is the largest of the northeast Kent resorts, its Victorian red-brick architecture and elegant Georgian squares set high on a cliff linked to the seafront by broad, sweeping ramps. Down by the **harbour** (ⓦportoframsgate.co.uk) cafés and bars overlook bobbing yachts, while small, busy **Ramsgate Sands** lies just a short stroll away. Sights include the **Maritime Museum**, on the quayside, which chronicles local maritime history (Easter–Sept Tues–Sun 10.30am–5.30pm; £2.50; ⓦramsgatemaritimemuseum. org) and the **Ramsgate Tunnels**, on Marina Esplanade (tours Wed–Sun 10am, noon, 2pm & 4pm; 1hr; £6.50; ☎01843 588123, ⓦramsgatetunnels.org), a subterranean warren of air-raid shelters – with bunk beds, electric lights and lavatories – that saved thousands of lives in World War II.

ARRIVAL AND DEPARTURE   RAMSGATE

By train Ramsgate's station lies about 1.5 miles northwest of the centre, at the end of Wilfred Rd, at the top of the High St.

Destinations Broadstairs (every 5–30min; 6min); Canterbury (every 20–40min; 20min); London St Pancras (every 10min–1hr; 1hr 15min–1hr 45min); London Charing Cross (hourly; 2hr 10min); London Victoria (Mon–Sat hourly; 2hr); Margate (every 5–30min; 15min); Whitstable (every 10–45min; 35min).

By bus Buses pull in at the harbour.

Destinations Broadstairs (every 5–20min; 15min); Canterbury (hourly; 45min); London (7 daily; 2hr 30min–3hr); Margate (every 10–15min; 45min).

ACCOMMODATION AND EATING

Albion House Albion Place, CT11 8HQ ☎01843 606630, ⓦalbionhouseramsgate.co.uk. Boutique hotel in an elegant clifftop Regency house. Most of the fourteen rooms, decorated with soothing contemporary syle, offer sea views and some have balconies. *Townleys*, their brasserie/ bar, is good, too, serving anything from afternoon tea to cheeseboards or Modern British mains. Two-night minimum stay at weekends. **£155**

Belgian Café 98 Harbour Parade, CT11 8LP ☎01843 587925, ⓦwww.belgiancafe.co.uk. Big, brash, casual place near the seafront, its outside tables spilling over with an eclectic crowd enjoying breakfasts, brunches, Belgian beers, real ales and marina views. Mon–Thurs & Sun 7am–2am, Fri & Sat 7am–3am.

Vinyl Head Café 2 The Broadway, Addington St, CT11 9JN ☎07901 334653, ⓦfacebook.com/ vinylheadramsgate. Cool, chilled-out neighbourhood café offering home-made cakes, crêpes and veggie food, plus interesting events, from haircuts to live music – and vinyl for sale, of course. Mon–Thurs & Sun 9am–5pm, Fri & Sat 9am–10pm.

Canterbury

The fine old city of **CANTERBURY** offers a rich slice through two thousand years of English history, with Roman and early Christian remains, a ruined Norman **castle** and a famous **cathedral** that looms over a medieval warren of time-skewed Tudor buildings. Its compact centre, partly ringed by ancient **walls**, is virtually car-free, but this doesn't stop the High Street seizing up in high summer with the milling crowds.

Brief history

The city that began as a Belgic settlement was known as **Durovernum Cantiacorum** to the Romans, who established a garrison here, and was renamed **Cantwaraburg** by the Saxons. In 597 King Ethelbert welcomed the monk Augustine, sent by the pope to Christianize England; one of the two Benedictine monasteries Augustine founded – Christ Church, raised on the site of the Roman basilica – was to become England's first cathedral.

After the Norman invasion, a power struggle ensued between the archbishops, the abbots from the nearby monastery – now **St Augustine's Abbey** – and King Henry II. This culminated in the assassination of Archbishop **Thomas Becket** in the cathedral in 1170, a martyrdom that created one of Christendom's greatest shrines and made Canterbury one of the country's richest cities. Believers flocked to see Becket's tomb – ribald events portrayed to great effect in Chaucer's fourteenth-century **Canterbury Tales**.

Becket's tomb was later destroyed on the command of Henry VIII, who also ordered the dissolution of St Augustine's Abbey, and the next couple of centuries saw a downturn in Canterbury's fortunes. The city suffered extensive damage from German bombing in 1942 during a "**Baedeker Raid**" – a Nazi campaign to destroy Britain's most treasured historic sites as identified in the eponymous German travel guides. The cathedral survived, however, and today, along with St Augustine's Abbey and St Martin's Church (at the corner of B. Holmes Rd and St Martin's Lane), has been designated a **UNESCO World Heritage Site**.

Canterbury Cathedral

Buttermarket, CT1 2EH • April–Oct Mon–Sat 9am–5.30pm (crypt from 10am), Sun 12.30–2.30pm; Nov–March Mon–Sat 9am–5pm (crypt from 10am), Sun 12.30–2.30pm; last entry 30min before closing • £12 • ☎ 01227 762862, ⓦ canterbury-cathedral.org

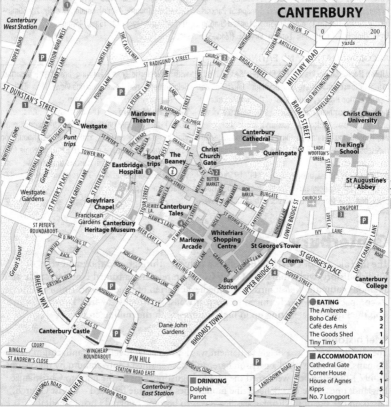

CANTERBURY

	EATING	
	The Ambrette	5
	Boho Café	3
	Café des Amis	2
	The Goods Shed	1
	Tiny Tim's	4

	ACCOMMODATION	
	Cathedral Gate	2
	Corner House	4
	House of Agnes	1
	Kipps	5
	No. 7 Longport	3

	DRINKING	
	Dolphin	1
	Parrot	2

Mother Church of the Church of England, **Canterbury Cathedral** dominates the northeast quadrant of the city. A cathedral has stood here since 602, established by Augustine, but the structure you see today owes most to the **Normans**, who rebuilt it in 1070 after a huge fire. Modified over successive centuries, today it is characterized by the puritanical lines of the late medieval Perpendicular style.

The spot where Thomas Becket was murdered, known as the **Martyrdom**, is just off the nave in the northwest transept, marked by a modern-day flagstone etched with the name "Thomas". Next to it, the **Altar of the Sword's Point** – where, in medieval times, the shattered tip of the sword that hacked Becket's scalp was displayed as a relic – is marked by a modern sculpture of the assassins' weapons. From the Martyrdom you descend to the low, Romanesque **crypt**, one of the few surviving parts of the Norman cathedral and the finest of its type in the country. Becket's original shrine stood down here until 1220, when it was moved to a more resplendent position in the **Trinity Chapel**, beyond the Quire. The new shrine, far more ornate than the earlier tomb, studded, according to the writer Erasmus in 1513, with jewels as big as goose eggs, was demolished during the Dissolution of the Monasteries in 1538; a candle marks where it once stood. You can get a sense of what the shrine looked like in the thirteenth-century stained-glass **Miracle Windows**, on the north side of the chapel.

The Beaney

18 High St, CT1 2RA • Tues–Sat 10am–5pm, Sun noon–5pm • Free • ☎ 01227 862162, ⓦ canterburymuseums.co.uk/beaney

A sturdy terracotta, brick and mock-Tudor ensemble built in 1898, the **Beaney** – officially the **Beaney House of Art and Knowledge** – has the not unlikeable feel of a Victorian collection. The stuffed animals, pinned beetles and cases of **antiquities and archeological finds** are intriguing, but make sure to spend time with the **paintings**. Highlights include the Van Dyck portrait of Kent MP Sir Basil Dixwell (1638), a Walter Sickert landscape (1936) painted during his four-year stay on the Kent coast, and the vigorous images of 1930s Kentish hop-pickers by English Impressionist Dame Laura Knight.

Roman Museum

Butchery Lane, CT1 2JR • Daily 10am–5pm • £8; joint ticket with Canterbury Heritage Museum (see page 152) £12 • ☎ 01227 785575, ⓦ canterburymuseums.co.uk/romanmuseum

Following the devastating bombings of 1942, excavations of the destroyed Longmarket area, off the High Street, exposed the foundations of a Roman townhouse complete with mosaic floors. These are now preserved *in situ* in the subterranean **Roman Museum**, but it's the rich haul of **artefacts**, domestic and military, that proves to be the big attraction.

Canterbury Tales

St Margaret's St, CT1 2TG • April–Aug daily 10am–5pm; Sept & Oct daily 10am–4pm; Nov–March Wed–Sun 10am–4pm • £9.95 • ☎ 01227 696002, ⓦ canterburytales.org.uk

Based on Geoffrey Chaucer's medieval stories, the **Canterbury Tales** is a quasi-educational, and fun, attraction. Costumed guides set you on your way through odour-enhanced galleries depicting a series of fourteenth-century tableaux as you follow the progress of a group of pilgrims (or rather, suitably scrofulous mannequins) from London to Becket's fabulously ornate shrine. Each space provides a setting for one of the famous tales.

Canterbury Heritage Museum

Stour St, CT1 2NR • 11am–5pm: April–Sept Wed–Sun; Oct & some hol weeks daily • £8; joint ticket with Roman Museum (see page 151) £12 • ☎ 01227 475202, ⓦ canterburymuseums.co.uk/heritagemuseum

The **Canterbury Heritage Museum** provides a lively jaunt through local history, with particularly strong sections on the Roman city, the medieval pilgrimage era and the Tudors and Stuarts – and interesting sections on local literary figures Christopher Marlowe, Joseph Conrad and Oliver Postgate (originator, in the 1970s, of children's television programmes *Bagpuss* and *The Clangers*).

St Augustine's Abbey

Longport, CT1 1PF • April–Sept daily 10am–6pm; Oct daily 10am–5pm; Nov–March Sat & Sun 10am–4pm • £6.20; EH • ☎ 01227 767345, ⓦ www.english-heritage.org.uk/visit/places/st-augustines-abbey

St Augustine's Abbey, founded as a monastery by Augustine in 598, was vastly altered and enlarged by the Normans before being destroyed in the Dissolution. Today, it is an atmospheric site, with more to see than its ruinous state might suggest. Ground plans, delineated in stone on soft carpets of grass, along with scattered semi-intact chapels, altar slabs and tombstones, powerfully evoke the original buildings, while illustrated information panels recount the abbey's changing fortunes.

ARRIVAL AND INFORMATION   CANTERBURY

By train Canterbury has two train stations: Canterbury East (in the south) and Canterbury West (in the north), each a 15min walk from the cathedral. Canterbury West is used by the high-speed train from London St Pancras. Destinations from Canterbury East Chatham (every 20–40min; 45min); Dover (every 30min–1hr; 15–30min); London Victoria (every 30–40min; 1hr 35min); Rochester (every 20–40min; 40min–1hr). Destinations from Canterbury West Ashford (every 10–30min; 15–25min); Broadstairs (hourly; 25min); London Charing Cross (Mon–Sat hourly; 1hr 45min); London St Pancras (hourly; 55min); Margate (hourly; 30min); Ramsgate (every 20–40min; 20min).

By bus National Express services and local Stagecoach East Kent buses use the station just inside the city walls on St George's Lane beside the Whitefriars shopping complex. Destinations Broadstairs (hourly; 1hr–1hr 30min); Deal (Mon–Sat every 30min–1hr; 45min–1hr 20min); Dover (every 15min–1hr; 45min); Folkestone (every 15min–1hr; 45min); London Victoria (hourly; 2hr); Margate (every 30min; 1hr); Ramsgate (hourly; 45min); Sandwich (every 20min; 40min); Whitstable (every 15min; 30min).

Tourist office In the Beaney, 18 High St (Mon–Wed & Fri 9am–6pm, Thurs 9am–8pm, Sat 9am–5pm, Sun 10am–5pm; ☎ 01227 862162, ⓦ canterbury.co.uk).

ACCOMMODATION

Cathedral Gate 36 Burgate, CT1 2HA ☎ 01227 464381, ⓦ cathgate.co.uk; map p.150. Built in 1438 in a fantastic location next to the cathedral, this ancient pilgrims' hostelry – all crooked, creaking floors and narrow, steep staircases – is in no way fancy, but it's comfortable, with cathedral views from many of the rooms and a simple continental breakfast. The cheapest rooms share toilets and showers, but have basins and tea- and coffee-making facilities. **£81.50**

Corner House 1 Dover St, CT1 3HD ☎ 01227 780793, ⓦ cornerhouserestaurants.co.uk; map p.150. Set on a busy corner just outside the city wall, these three gorgeous B&B rooms combine rustic charm and contemporary cool. The same people run the superb Modern British restaurant downstairs. **£99**

★ **House of Agnes** 71 St Dunstan's St ☎ 01227 472185, ⓦ houseofagnes.co.uk; map p.150. You can't fail to be charmed by the crooked exterior of this quirky B&B, which has eight individually designed rooms in the main fifteenth-century house (mentioned in *David*

Copperfield), and another eight options in the old stable block in the walled garden (£95). **£115**

★ **Kipps** 40 Nunnery Fields, CT1 3JT ☎ 01227 786121, ⓦ kipps-hostel.com; map p.150. A 10min walk from Canterbury East station, this excellent self-catering hostel – with mixed en-suite dorms plus single and double rooms – is clean and very friendly, with homely touches and a large cottage garden. Regular events mean you can be sociable, but it's more a home from home than a party place. No curfew. Breakfast £3.50. Dorms **£24**, doubles **£75**

No. 7 Longport 7 Longport, CT1 1PE ☎ 01227 455367, ⓦ 7longport.co.uk; map p.150. This fabulous little hideaway – a tiny, luxuriously decorated fifteenth-century cottage with a double bedroom, wet room and lounge – is tucked away in the courtyard garden of the friendly owners' home, opposite St Augustine's Abbey. Breakfasts are wonderful, with lots of locally sourced ingredients, and can be eaten in the main house, in the cottage or in the courtyard. **£100**

EATING

The Ambrette 14–15 Beer Cart Lane, CT1 2NY ☎01227 200777, ⓦtheambrette.co.uk; map p.150. Smart nouvelle Indian cuisine with a strong focus on local produce, with delicious flavours infusing everything from quinoa and mushroom biryani to goat stew with jasmine rice. Mains £17–30; two-/three-course lunch menus (Mon–Sat) £21.95/£24.95. Mon–Thurs 11am–2.30pm & 6–9.30pm, Fri & Sat 11am–2.30pm & 5.30–10pm, Sun noon–2.30pm & 5.30–10pm.

Boho Café 27 High St, CT1 2AZ ☎01227 458931, ⓦbohocafecanterbury.co.uk; map p.150. This funky café-bar, with its paintbox-bright, mismatched decor, has an informal feel. The Mediterranean-accented menu (mains from £8) ranges from big breakfasts via tapas to home-made burgers, with coffee and cake all day. There's a little suntrap garden at the back. Mon–Thurs 9am–6pm, Fri & Sat 9am–9pm, Sun 10am–5pm.

Café des Amis 95 St Dunstan's St, CT2 8AD ☎01227 464390, ⓦcafedez.com; map p.150. Lively Mexican/Tex-Mex/South American place with eclectic, carnivalesque decor and delicious food. Try the paella (£26.95 for two)

followed by a bubbling chocolate *fundido*. Mon–Thurs noon–10pm, Fri noon–10.30pm, Sat 11am–10.30pm, Sun 11am–9.30pm.

★ **The Goods Shed** Station Rd West, CT2 8AN ☎01227 459153, ⓦthegoodsshed.co.uk; map p.150. It doesn't get any more locally sourced than this – a buzzing, shabby-chic Modern British restaurant in the fabulous Goods Shed farmers' market, where most of the ingredients are provided by the stalls themselves. The regularly changing menu might feature dishes such as pressed leek and goat curd with herb salad (£7) or steamed hake with wilted chard (£17.50). Great breakfasts, too. Tues–Fri 8–10.30am, noon–2.30pm & 6–9.30pm, Sat 8–10.30am, noon–3pm & 6–9.30pm, Sun 9–10.30am & noon–3pm.

★ **Tiny Tim's** 34 St Margaret's St, CT1 2TG ☎01227 450793, ⓦtinytimstearoom.com; map p.150. This incongruously named, elegant, 1930s-inspired tearoom offers some thirty blends of tea as well as all-day breakfasts, light lunches (from £7), cakes and filling afternoon teas (all day, from £18.50). In good weather sit in the cute back garden. Tues–Sat 9.30am–5pm, Sun 10.30am–4pm.

DRINKING

Canterbury is a nice place for a drink, with a number of pubs serving **real ales** in cosy, historic buildings. The Kentish Shepherd Neame-owned places are in the majority, but look out, too, for beers from Canterbury's own Wantsum, Canterbury Brewers and Canterbury Ales breweries.

Dolphin 17 St Radigund's St, CT1 2AA ☎01227 455963, ⓦthedolphincanterbury.co.uk; map p.150. Likeable, unpretentious 1930s-built pub with a good selection of local real ales, a roaring fire in winter and a big, grassy beer garden. Tasty modern pub grub, too (mains from £9). Mon–Wed noon–11pm, Thurs–Sat noon–midnight, Sun noon–10pm; kitchen Mon–Wed noon–2pm & 6–9pm, Thurs & Fri noon–2pm & 6–10pm, Sat noon–

10pm, Sun noon–3pm & 6–9pm.

Parrot 1–9 Church Lane, CT1 2AG ☎01227 454170, ⓦtheparrotonline.com; map p.150. Ancient hostelry – among the oldest in Canterbury – in a quiet location, with loads of character, a decent selection of ales and a gastropub menu (mains from £9). There's a beer terrace at the back. Daily noon–11pm; kitchen Mon–Sat noon–10pm, Sun noon–9.30pm.

Sandwich

SANDWICH, one of the best-preserved medieval towns in England, is a sleepy, picturesque place, with some fine half-timbered buildings lining its narrow streets and a lovely location on the willow-lined banks of the River Stour. Sandwich's riverfront **quayside**, peaceful today, was once the heart of a great medieval port. While the river estuary began silting up in the sixteenth century, and the sea is now miles away, the waterfront gives the place a breezily nautical atmosphere, with small boats moored by the toll bridge, open countryside stretching out across the river and the cry of seagulls raking the air. Seal- and bird-spotting **boat trips** (£7–35; ☎07958 376183, ⓦsandwichriverbus.co.uk) run from the toll bridge over the Stour.

ARRIVAL AND INFORMATION   SANDWICH

By train Sandwich station is off St George's Rd, from where it's a 10min walk north to the town centre and the quay. Destinations Deal (every 30min–1hr; 6min); Dover (every

30min–1hr; 25min); Ramsgate (hourly; 15min).
By bus Buses pull in and depart from outside the tourist office.

Destinations Canterbury (every 20min–1hr; 45min); Deal (every 20min–1hr; 25–35min); Dover (every 45min–1hr; 45min–1hr); Ramsgate (hourly; 45min–1hr).

Tourist office Guildhall, Cattle Market (April–Oct Mon–Sat 10am–4pm; ☎01304 613565, ⓦsandwich towncouncil.gov.uk or ⓦ whitecliffscountry.org.uk).

ACCOMMODATION AND EATING

Bell Hotel The Quay, CT13 9EF ☎01304 613388, ⓦbellhotelsandwich.co.uk. Rambling hostelry that has stood here since Tudor times; today's buildiing is largely Edwardian. Rooms are comfy, in a contemporary style; the priciest have balconies overlooking the Stour. There's a good restaurant serving Modern European food (mains from £13). Minimum two-night stay on summer weekends. __£130__

★**George and Dragon** 24 Fisher St, CT13 9EJ ☎01304 613106, ⓦgeorgeanddragon-sandwich.co.uk. A fifteenth-century inn and unpretentious gastropub, with

delicious Modern British food (mains £11–18), cask ales, roaring fires in winter and a courtyard. Booking advised for dinner. Mon–Sat 11am–11pm, Sun 11am–4pm; kitchen Mon–Sat noon–2pm & 6–9.15pm, Sun noon–2pm.

No Name 1 No Name St, CT13 9AJ ☎01304 612626, ⓦnonameshop.co.uk. For picnic supplies, look no further than this excellent French deli near the Guildhall. You can also eat in, from a daily-changing menu (£7–14) of light dishes – salads, soups, quiches – and heartier mains such as confit de canard or *tartiflette*. Mon–Sat 8am–5pm, Sun 9am–4pm.

Deal

The low-key seaside town of **DEAL**, six miles southeast of Sandwich, was the site of Julius Caesar's first successful landfall in Britain in 55 BC. Today it's an appealing place, with a broad, steeply shelving shingle **beach** backed by a jumble of faded Georgian townhouses, a picturesque **Old Town** redolent with maritime history and a striking concrete **pier** lined with hopeful anglers casting their lines. Henry VIII's two seafront **castles**, linked by a seaside path, are the main attractions, and there are enough good places to eat, drink and stay to make the town an appealing weekend destination.

Deal Castle

Marine Rd, CT14 7BA • April–Sept daily 10am–6pm; Oct daily 10am–5pm; Nov–March Sat & Sun 10am–4pm • £6.60; EH • ☎01304 372762, ⓦwww.english-heritage.org.uk/visit/places/deal-castle

Diminutive **Deal Castle**, at the south end of town, is one of the most striking of Henry VIII's forts. Its distinctive shape – viewed from the air it looks like a Tudor rose – owes less to aesthetics than to sophisticated military engineering: the squat rounded walls were good at deflecting missiles. Self-guided **audio tours** outline every detail of the design, with the bare rooms revealing how the castle changed over the years and giving a good sense of how the soldiers lived.

THE CINQUE PORTS

In 1278 Dover, Hythe, Sandwich, Romney and Hastings – already part of a long-established, unofficial confederation of defensive coastal settlements – were formalized under a charter by Edward I as the **Cinque Ports** (pronounced "sink", despite the name's French origin). In return for providing England with maritime support, they were granted trading privileges and other liberties – including self-government, exemption from taxes and tolls and "possession of goods thrown overboard" – that enabled them to prosper while neighbouring ports struggled.

Rye, Winchelsea and seven other "**limb**" **ports** on the southeast coast were later added to the confederation. The ports' privileges were revoked in 1685; their maritime services had become increasingly unnecessary after Henry VIII had founded a professional navy and, due to a shifting coastline, several of their harbours had silted up anyway, stranding some of them miles inland. Today, of all the Cinque Ports, only Dover is still a major working port.

Walmer Castle

Kingsdown Rd, 1 mile south of Deal, CT14 7LJ • Jan to mid-Feb Sat & Sun 10am–4pm; mid-Feb to March Wed–Sun 10am–4pm;
April–Sept daily 10am–6pm; Oct daily 10am–5pm; Nov & Dec Sat & Sun 10am–6pm • £10.70; EH • ☎ 01304 364288, ⊛ www.english-
heritage.org.uk/visit/places/walmer-castle-and-gardens • Hourly buses (#82/#82A) from Deal; also accessible from Walmer train station,
a mile away

Walmer Castle is another of Henry VIII's Tudor-rose-shaped defences, built to protect
the coast from its enemies across the Channel. Like Deal Castle it saw little fighting,
and changed use when it became the official residence of the Lords Warden of the
Cinque Ports in 1708. Adapted over the years, today the castle resembles a heavily
fortified stately home; the best-known resident was the Duke of Wellington, who was
given the post of Lord Warden in 1828 and who died here in 1852. You can see the
armchair in which he expired and a pair of original Wellington boots.

2

ARRIVAL AND INFORMATION   DEAL

By train The station is on Queen St, 10min from the sea.
Destinations Dover (every 15min–1hr; 15min); Ramsgate
(every 30min–1hr; 20min); Sandwich (every 30min–1hr;
6min); Walmer (every 30min–1hr; 3min).
By bus Buses run from South St, Queen St and Victoria Rd,
all near each other in the centre.
Destinations Canterbury (hourly; 1hr 15min); Dover (every

30min–1hr; 45min); London Victoria (2 daily; 2hr 50min–
3hr 45min); Sandwich (every 20min–1hr; 25–35min);
Walmer (every 15min–1hr; 15–30min).
Tourist office Town Hall, High St (April–Sept Mon–
Fri 10am–2pm, Sat 10am–2pm; Oct–March Mon–Fri
10am–2pm; ☎ 01304 369576, ⊛ deal.gov.uk or
⊛ whitecliffscountry.org.uk).

ACCOMMODATION AND EATING

Bear's Well 10 St George's Rd, CT14 6BA ☎ 01304
694144, ⊛ bearswell.co.uk. In a central but peaceful
Old Town house, this airy boutique B&B has three lovely
en-suite rooms with views of the church or the pretty
back garden. Breakfasts, made using local produce, are
great. __£120__
★ **Frog and Scot** 86 High St, CT14 6EG ☎ 01304
379444, ⊛ frogandscot.co.uk. Delightful neighbourhood
haven serving superlative French-inspired dishes, from
sea bass with bouillabaisse to chestnut soup with goose

confit, and a fabulous wine list. Mains from £15; two- and
three-course lunch menus £13.95 and £16.95. Wed–Sat
noon–2.30pm & 6.15–9.15pm, Sun noon–3.30pm.
Poppy's Kitchen 119 High St, CT14 6BB ☎ 01304
371719, ⊛ poppyskitchen.co.uk. Simple, fresh and
delicious food, with a focus on organic ingredients. Dishes
(from £5.50) might include chard and Cheddar tart or kale,
apple, spelt and hazelnut salad, while breakfasts range
from home-made granola to a Full English. Gorgeous cakes,
too. Mon–Sat 9am–5.30pm, Sun 10am–3pm.

Dover and around

Given its importance as a travel hub – it's the busiest ferry port in Europe – **DOVER**
is surprisingly small and, badly bombed during World War II, the town centre is
unprepossessing. The nearby attractions, however, are big ones: **Dover Castle**, looming
proudly above town, and the iconic **White Cliffs**.

Dover Castle

Castle Hill, CT16 1HU • Mid-Feb to March Wed–Sun 10am–4pm; April–July & Sept daily 10am–6pm; Aug daily 9.30am–6pm; Oct daily
10am–5pm; Nov to mid-Feb Sat & Sun 10am–4pm • £19.40, under-16s £11.60; EH • ☎ 0370 333 1181, ⊛ www.english-heritage.org.uk/
visit/places/dover-castle • Buses #15, #15X, #80, #80A & #93 from Dover town centre (hourly; 20min)

No historical stone goes unturned at **Dover Castle**, an astonishingly imposing
defensive complex that has protected the English coast for more than two thousand
years. In 1068 **William the Conqueror**, following the Battle of Hastings, built over
the earthworks of an Iron Age hillfort here; a century later, the Normans constructed
the handsome **keep**, or Great Tower, that now presides over the heart of the complex.
The grounds also include a **Roman lighthouse**, a **Saxon church** – with motifs graffitied
by irreverent Crusaders still visible near the pulpit – and all manner of later additions,

including a network of **tunnels** dug during the Napoleonic Wars and extended during World War II.

You should allow a **full day** for a visit. If time is short, head first for the **Operation Dynamo tunnel tours** (at regular intervals; 40min), which are affecting immersive experiences that, accompanied by the muffled sound of anti-aircraft guns and screaming Spitfires, shed light on the build-up to the war and the Dunkirk evacuation. From there, make your way to Henry II's **Great Tower**. Here the opulent medieval royal court has been painstakingly re-created, with everything from the pots and pans in the kitchen to the richly coloured furniture in the King's Chamber.

White Cliffs of Dover

Stretching sixteen miles along the coast, a towering 350ft high in places, the vast **White Cliffs of Dover** are composed of chalk plus traces of quartz, shells and flint. A large area of the cliffs lies within the Kent Downs Area of Outstanding Natural Beauty, and with their grasslands home to rare plants, butterflies and migrant birds, have been designated a Site of Special Scientific Interest. A **walk** along the cliffs affords you amazing views of the Straits of Dover – and on a clear day you may well even see France.

A significant stretch is owned by the **National Trust**, which has a visitor centre on Upper Road, Langdon Cliffs (daily: March–June, Sept & Oct 10am–5pm; July & Aug 10am–5.30pm; Nov–Feb 11am–4pm; parking £3.50; ⍟nationaltrust.org.uk/white-cliffs-dover). The NT manages two clifftop attractions: **Fan Bay Deep Shelter**, an underground labyrinth that housed troops during World War II (tours every 30min April–Oct Mon & Fri–Sun 11am–3pm; 45min; £10); and the **South Foreland lighthouse**, above St Margaret's Bay (regular tours 11am–5pm: mid-March to mid-July, Sept & Oct Mon & Fri–Sun; mid-July to Aug daily; 30min; £6; ⍟nationaltrust.org.uk/south-foreland-lighthouse).

ARRIVAL AND INFORMATION   DOVER AND AROUND

By train Dover Priory station is off Folkestone Rd, a 10min walk west of the centre.
Destinations Canterbury (every 30min–1hr; 15–30min); Deal (every 15min–1hr; 15min); London Victoria (every 30min–1hr; 2hr); Sandwich (every 30min–1hr; 25min).
By bus The town-centre bus station is on Pencester Rd.
Destinations Canterbury (every 15min–1hr; 45min);

Deal (every 30min–1hr; 45min); London Victoria (11 daily; 1hr 55min–3hr 20min); Sandwich (every 45min–1hr; 45min–1hr).
Tourist office Dover Museum, Market Square (April–Sept Mon–Sat 9.30am–5pm, Sun 10am–3pm; Oct–March Mon–Sat 9.30am–5pm; ☎01304 201066, ⍟whitecliffscountry.org.uk).

ACCOMMODATION

Maison Dieu 89 Maison Dieu Rd, CT16 1RU ☎01304 204033, ⍟maisondieu.co.uk. Welcoming, central guesthouse with six spotless single, double, twin and family rooms, most of which are en suite. A few have views over the garden to Dover Castle. Optional breakfast £6.50 extra. **£85**
White Cliffs Hotel High St, St-Margaret's-at-Cliffe, 4 miles northeast of Dover, CT15 6AT ☎01304 852229,

⍟thewhitecliffs.com. Friendly place – a hit with walkers and cyclists – with a sociable restaurant/bar. The seven rooms tucked away in the main building – a sixteenth-century weatherboard house – come in all shapes and styles, from rustic and cosy to glamorous and huge; there are nine less expensive options (£90) in outbuildings around the spacious beer garden. Tasty full breakfast included. **£120**

EATING AND DRINKING

★ **Allotment** 9 High St, CT16 1DP ☎01304 214467, ⍟facebook.com/allotmentdover. The best option on Dover's high street, this bistro serves tasty, unpretentious food in a light space. Try a simple breakfast or lunch (wild boar sausages in Kentish cider; baguettes), or fancier dinner mains

including Whitstable fish stew or partridge in perry sauce. Mains £10–16. Tues–Thurs 10.30am–9.30pm, Fri 9am–9.30pm, Sat 9am–10pm, Sun noon–4pm.
The Coastguard St Margaret's Bay, 4 miles northeast of Dover, CT15 6DY ☎01304 853051, ⍟thecoastguard.

co.uk. This nautically themed beachside pub/restaurant, at the bottom of the White Cliffs, is a good spot for a Kentish cask ale, either on the large terrace or in the small beer garden. They serve traditional English dishes (fish and chips, burgers, pies) and interesting daily specials (razor clams with garlic and toasted nuts, say); mains £10–20. Mon–Sat 10am–11pm, Sun 10am–10pm; kitchen Mon–Sat noon–2.45pm & 6–8.45pm, Sun noon–2.30pm & 6–8pm.

Folkestone

In the early 2000s, depressed after the demise of its tourist industry and the loss of its ferry link to France, **FOLKESTONE** was a doleful place. Thus began a concerted effort to start again, with hopes pinned on the arts and the creative industries. Cue Folkestone's **Triennial** (Ⓦfolkestonetriennial.org.uk), a contemporary art show that since its premier in 2008 has been gradually bringing Folkestone out of its extended limbo. With the regenerating **Creative Quarter** and the salty little fishing **harbour**, the gloriously landscaped **Lower Leas Coastal Park**, a sandy town **beach**, and the wild **Warren** cliffs and beach nearby, Folkestone has plenty to offer.

ARRIVAL AND INFORMATION   FOLKESTONE

By train Folkestone Central station is off Cheriton Rd, just under a mile northwest of the Creative Quarter.
Destinations Dover (every 10–50min; 20min); London Charing Cross (every 30min–1hr; 1hr 40min); London St Pancras (every 30min–1hr; 55min).

By bus The bus station is in the centre of town.
Destinations Dover (every 20–30min; 30min); London Victoria (4 daily; 2hr 10min–3hr).
Tourist office 1–2 Guildhall St (Mon–Fri 9am–5pm; Ⓣ01303 257946, Ⓦdiscoverfolkestone.co.uk).

ACCOMMODATION AND EATING

★ **Rocksalt Rooms** 1–3 Back St, CT19 6NN Ⓣ01303 212070, Ⓦrocksaltfolkestone.co.uk. Four "boutique bolt holes" (they're small) in an unbeatable harbourside location. It's run by the people who own the excellent *Smokehouse* chippy downstairs, and the sophisticated *Rocksalt* restaurant, footsteps away. Rooms at the front are the best, with French windows and water views, but they're all chic and super-comfy. Continental breakfast is delivered to your room in a hamper. **£85**

Steep Street 18–24 Old High St, CT10 1RL Ⓣ01303 247819, Ⓦsteepstreet.co.uk. This gorgeous coffee house, lined ceiling to floor with books, buzzes with a Creative Quarter crowd. They serve simple, good food, from sandwiches to salads, quiches to cakes (cakes from £2; savoury tarts £4). Mon–Fri 8.30am–6pm, Sat 9am–6pm, Sun 9am–5pm.

Romney Marsh

In Roman times, what is now the southernmost chunk of Kent was submerged beneath the English Channel. Lowering of sea levels in the Middle Ages and later reclamation created **Romney Marsh**, a hundred-square-mile area of shingle and marshland. Once home to important Cinque and limb ports (see page 154), and villages made wealthy from the wool trade, this rather forlorn expanse now presents a melancholy aspect, given over to agriculture and with few sights – unless you count the sheep, the birdlife and several curious medieval **churches**. While it makes good walking and cycling country, its salt-speckled, big-skied strangeness can also be appreciated on the dinky **Romney, Hythe & Dymchurch Railway** (mid-March to Oct daily; Nov to mid-March Sat & Sun; £18 Hythe–Dungeness return; Ⓣ01797 362353, Ⓦrhdr.org.uk), a fifteen-inch-gauge line whose miniature steam trains run the 13.5 miles between the lonesome shingle spit of **Dungeness** and the seaside town of **Hythe**. Around five miles west of the latter, **Port Lympne Reserve**, working on a conservation and breeding programme for wild and endangered species, is home to more than seven hundred animals, including spectacled bears, Western Lowland gorillas and black rhino (daily: April–Oct 9.30am–6.30pm, last admission 3.30pm; Nov–March 9.30am–5pm, last admission 2.30pm; £25, under-16s £21; Ⓣ01303 264647, Ⓦaspinallfoundation.org/port-lympne).

Dungeness

An end-of-the-earth eeriness pervades **DUNGENESS**, the windlashed shingle headland at the marsh's southernmost tip. Dominated by two hulking nuclear power stations (one of them disused), "the Ness" is not conventionally pretty, but there's a strange beauty to this lost-in-time spot, where a scattering of weatherboard shacks and disused railway carriages houses fishermen, artists and recluses drawn to the area's bleak, otherworldly allure. The late Derek Jarman, artist and filmmaker, made his home here, at **Prospect Cottage** – on Dungeness Road, a twenty-minute walk from the RH&DR station – and the shingle garden he created from beachcombed treasures and tough little plants remains a poignant memorial. Panoramic views over the headland can be had from the decommissioned **Old Lighthouse** (10.30am–4.30pm: March–May & late Sept to Oct Sat & Sun; June Tues–Thurs, Sat & Sun; July to late Sept daily; £4; ⓦdungenesslighthouse.com), built in 1904.

The unique ecology around here attracts huge colonies of gulls, terns, smews and gadwalls; you can see them, and all manner of waterbirds, waders and wildfowl, from the **RSPB visitor centre** (daily: March–Oct 10am–5pm; Nov–Feb 10am–4pm; free; ⓦrspb.org.uk) on the Lydd road three miles from Dungeness.

The High Weald

The **Weald** stretches across a large area between the North and South Downs and includes parts of both Kent and Sussex. The central part, the **High Weald**, is epitomized by gentle hills, sunken country lanes and somnolent villages as well as some of England's greatest gardens. The Weald also offers a wealth of picturesque historical sites, including a couple of picture-book castles – **Hever** and **Bodiam** – as well as stately homes at **Penshurst** and **Knole**, the home of Winston Churchill at **Chartwell** and Rudyard Kipling's countryside retreat at **Bateman's**. **Tunbridge Wells**, set in beautiful High Weald countryside, is a good base.

Royal Tunbridge Wells

The handsome spa town of **ROYAL TUNBRIDGE WELLS** was established after a bubbling ferrous **spring** discovered here in 1606 was claimed to have curative properties, and reached its height of popularity during the Regency period when restorative cures were in vogue. It remains an elegant place, with some smart places to stay and eat and three lovely urban parks: the **Grove** and **Calverley Grounds** offer formal gardens, while the wilder **Common**, spreading out to the west, is laced with historic pathways.

The Pantiles

Tucked off the southern end of the High Street, the colonnaded **Pantiles** – named for the clay tiles, shaped in wooden pans, that paved the street in the seventeenth century – is a pedestrianized parade of independent shops, delis and cafés that exudes a faded elegance. Here, at the original **Chalybeate Spring**, outside the 1804 Bath House, a costumed "dipper" will serve you a cup of the iron-rich waters (Easter–Sept Wed–Sun 10.30am–3.30pm; £1), a tradition dating back to the eighteenth century.

ARRIVAL AND INFORMATION · ROYAL TUNBRIDGE WELLS

By train The train station stands where the High St becomes Mount Pleasant Rd.

Destinations Hastings (every 30min–1hr; 40–50min); London Charing Cross (every 15–30min; 55min); Sevenoaks (every 20min; 20–25min).

By bus Buses set down and pick up along the High St and Mount Pleasant Rd.

Destinations Brighton (every 30min–1hr; 1hr 50min); Hever (Mon–Sat 2 daily; 40–50min); Lewes (every 30min–1hr; 1hr 20min); London Victoria (1 daily; 1hr 40min); Sevenoaks (every 30min–2hr; 45min).

Tourist office Corn Exchange, The Pantiles (10am–3pm: April–Sept Mon–Sat; Oct–March Tues–Sat 3pm; ☏01892 515675, ⓦvisittunbridgewells.com).

ACCOMMODATION AND EATING

The Black Pig 18 Grove Hill Rd, TN1 1RZ ☎01892 523030, ⓦtheblackpig.net. Smart gastropub, where locally sourced dishes (mains from £11) might include slow-roast pork belly, crispy squid or honey-roast squash risotto. On a sunny day, settle down with a sandwich in the beer garden. Daily noon–11pm; kitchen Mon–Thurs noon–2.30pm & 6.30–9.30pm, Fri noon–2.30pm & 6.30–10pm, Sat noon–3pm & 6–10pm, Sun noon–3pm.

Hotel du Vin Crescent Rd, TN1 2LY ☎01892 320749, ⓦhotelduvin.com. Elegantly set in a Georgian mansion overlooking Calverley Grounds, this member of the luxe *Hotel du Vin* chain is quietly classy, with a cosy bar, romantic French restaurant and a beautifully sloping old staircase leading up to the rooms. **£175**

Mount Edgcumbe The Common, TN4 8BX ☎01892 618854, ⓦthemountedgcumbe.com. Hidden away in an old Georgian house, this food pub has a deliciously rural feel, with a nice garden. It makes a cosy, offbeat place for a Modern British meal – from veggie sharing plates to fish and chips – or a pint of local ale. Check out the real cave in the bar area, strewn with fairy lights. Mains from £12. Mon–Wed 11am–11pm, Thurs–Sat 11am–11.30pm, Sun noon–10.30pm; kitchen Mon–Thurs noon–3pm & 6–9.30pm, Fri & Sat noon–9.30pm, Sun noon–8pm.

Sankey's 39 Mount Ephraim, TN4 8AA ☎01892 511422, ⓦsankeys.co.uk. Lively pub, decked out with enamel signs, squishy sofas and a wood-burning stove. It has a host of specialist beers and a good pub-grub menu (burgers, bangers, salads) but is best known for its seafood. Mains from £7. Mon–Wed & Sun noon–11pm, Thurs–Sat noon–1am; kitchen Mon noon–3pm, Tues–Fri noon–3pm & 6–9pm, Sat noon–9pm, Sun noon–8pm.

Sissinghurst

Biddenden Rd, 15 miles east of Tunbridge Wells, TN17 2AB • Gardens mid-March to Oct daily 11am–5.30pm, last admission 45min before closing; estate daily dawn–dusk • Mid-March to Oct £12.50; Nov & Dec £9; NT • ☎01580 710700, ⓦnationaltrust.org.uk/sissinghurst

When she and her husband took it over in 1930, writer **Vita Sackville-West** described the neglected Tudor estate of **Sissinghurst** as "a garden crying out for rescue". Over the next thirty years they transformed the five-acre plot into one of England's greatest gardens, the romantic abundance of flowers, spilling onto narrow brick pathways, defying the formality of the great gardens that came before. Don't miss the magical **White Garden**, with its pale blooms and silvery foliage, and, in summer, the lush, overblown **Rose Garden**. From the Tudor **tower** that Vita used as her quarters you get a bird's-eye view of the gardens and the ancient surrounding woodlands; halfway up, peep into Vita's study, which feels intensely personal, with rugs on the floor and a photo of her lover, Virginia Woolf, on her desk.

Great Dixter

Near Northiam, TN31 6PH, 22 miles southeast of Tunbridge Wells • April–Oct Tues–Sun & bank hols: gardens 11am–5pm; house 2–5pm • £11, gardens only £9 • ☎01797 252878, ⓦgreatdixter.co.uk • Stagecoach bus #2 passes through Northiam on its way from Hastings to Tenterden (Mon–Sat hourly; 45min from Hastings)

One of the best-loved gardens in the country, **Great Dixter** was the creation of gardener and writer **Christopher Lloyd**, who lived here until his death in 2005. Exuberant and informal, the gardens – now maintained by Lloyd's friend and head gardener **Fergus Garrett** – spread around a splendid medieval half-timbered house in a series of intimate garden "rooms" and sweeps of wildflower-speckled meadow.

Bodiam Castle

Bodiam, TN32 5UA, 18 miles southeast of Tunbridge Wells • Daily 10.30am–5pm, or dusk if earlier • £9.30; NT • ☎01580 830196, ⓦnationaltrust.org.uk/bodiam-castle • Bus #349 from Hastings (Mon–Fri every 2hr; 40min); steam train from Tenterden (April–Sept up to 5 services a day; ☎01580 765155, ⓦkesr.org.uk)

One of the country's most picturesque castles, **Bodiam** is a classically stout square block with rounded corner turrets, battlements and a wide moat. It was state-of-the-art military architecture when it was built in 1385, but during the Civil War, a company of Roundheads breached the fortress and removed its roof, and over the following centuries Bodiam fell into neglect. Inside the castle walls there are plenty of nooks and crannies to explore, and steep spiral staircases leading up to the crenellated battlements; look out for the castle's portcullis, claimed to be the oldest in the country.

Bateman's

Bateman's Lane, Burwash, TN19 7DS, 13 miles southeast of Tunbridge Wells off the A265 • Daily: garden 10am–5pm or dusk; house April–Oct 11am–5pm, Nov–March 11am–3pm • £10.40; NT • ☎ 01435 882302, ⓦ nationaltrust.org.uk/batemans

Near the picturesque village of Burwash, **Bateman's** was the idyllic home of writer **Rudyard Kipling** from 1902 until his death in 1936. The house is set amid attractive gardens, which feature a still-working watermill converted by Kipling to generate electricity. Inside, the house displays Kipling's letters, early editions of his work and mementos from his travels.

Penshurst Place

Penshurst, TN11 8DG, 5 miles northwest of Tunbridge Wells • April–Oct daily: house noon–4pm; gardens noon–6pm • £11, gardens only £9 • ☎ 01892 870307, ⓦ penshurstplace.com • Bus #231 or #233 from Tunbridge Wells (Mon–Sat); Penshurst train station is 2.5 miles north (no taxis)

Tudor timber-framed buildings line the pretty main street of **Penshurst**, presided over by fourteenth-century **Penshurst Place**, home to the Sidney family since 1552 and birthplace of the Elizabethan soldier and poet, Sir Philip Sidney. The jaw-dropping Baron's Hall, with its 60ft-high chestnut-beamed roof, is the glory of the interior. The 48 acres of grounds offer good walks, while the **walled garden** is a beautiful example of Elizabethan garden design.

Hever Castle

Hever, TN8 7NG, 10 miles northwest of Tunbridge Wells • Daily: castle April–Oct noon–6pm, Nov noon–4.30pm; gardens April–Oct 10.30am–6pm, Nov 10.30am–4.30pm; last entry 1hr 30min before closing • £16.90, gardens only £14.20 • ☎ 01732 865224, ⓦ hevercastle.co.uk • Hever train station is a mile west (no taxis)

The moated **Hever Castle** was the childhood home of Anne Boleyn, second wife of Henry VIII, and where Anne of Cleves, Henry's fourth wife, lived after their divorce. In 1903, having fallen into disrepair, the castle was bought by William Waldorf Astor, who had it assiduously restored in mock-Tudor style. Today, Hever has an intimate feel, and though it does display some intriguing Elizabethan artefacts it tells you more about the aspirations of American plutocrats than the lifestyle of Tudor nobles. **Anne Boleyn's room** is the most affecting; small and bare, dominated by a wooden chest carved with the words "Anne Bullen". You can also see the book of prayers she carried to the executioner's block, inscribed in her own writing and with references to the pope crossed out. Outside is the beautiful **Italian Garden**, decorated with statues, some more than two thousand years old, as well as a yew-hedge maze, adventure playground, water maze and boating lakes.

Chartwell

Mapleton Rd, Westerham, TN16 1PS, 17.5 miles northwest of Tunbridge Wells • **House** March–Oct Mon–Fri 11.30am–5pm, Sat & Sun 11am–5pm; Dec (some rooms only) Sat & Sun 11am–3pm • **Studio** Daily: March–Oct noon–4pm; Nov & Dec noon–3.30pm • **Gardens** Daily: March–Oct 10am–5pm; Nov–Feb 10am–4pm • £13.50; studio & gardens only £6.75; NT • ☎ 01732 868381, ⓦ nationaltrust.org.uk/chartwell

Packed with the wartime prime minister's possessions – including his rather contemplative paintings – there is something touchingly intimate about **Chartwell**, the country residence of **Winston Churchill** from 1924 until his death in 1965. The house

is set up to look as it would have in the 1920s and 1930s, revealing the personal side of this gruff statesman; don't miss the sweet series of notes between him and his wife, and a letter from his father written when he was a young man, expressing his fears that he was to become "a social wastrel". In the rolling **gardens**, dotted with lakes and ponds and shaded by mature fruit trees, you can see Churchill's **studio**, which is lined with over one hundred canvases.

2 Knole

Sevenoaks, entered from the south end of Sevenoaks High St, TN15 0RP · **House** March–Oct Tues–Sun noon–4pm · £8.15; NT · **Gatehouse tower** Daily: mid-March to Oct 10am–5pm; Nov–Feb 10am–4pm · £3.15; NT · **Parkland** Daily dawn–dusk · Free; NT · ☎ 01732 462100, ⊛ nationaltrust.org.uk/knole · The High St entrance is a mile south of Sevenoaks train station and half a mile south of the bus station; it's a 15min uphill walk from the entrance through the estate to the house

Covering a whopping four acres, **Knole** palace, in the commuter town of **Sevenoaks**, is an astonishingly handsome ensemble. Built in 1456 as a residence for the archbishops of Canterbury, it was appropriated in 1538 by Henry VIII, who loved to hunt in its thousand acres of **parkland** (still home to several hundred wild deer). Elizabeth I gave the estate to her Lord Treasurer, Thomas Sackville, who remodelled the house in 1605; it has remained in the family's hands ever since. Bloomsbury Group writer and gardener Vita Sackville-West was raised here, and her lover Virginia Woolf derived inspiration for her novel *Orlando* from frequent visits. Highlights of this endlessly fascinating treasure-trove range from the lustrous **Venetian Ambassador's Room** with its staggering carved and gilded eighteenth-century bed, to the **Gatehouse tower**, filled with the private possessions of Eddy Sackville-West, a Bloomsbury Group stalwart, who lived here from 1926 to 1940. A **major restoration** project was started in 2012, finishing in 2019; check prices before you go, as they were lowered at the time of writing to account for the disruption.

Rye and around

Perched on a hill overlooking Romney Marsh, the pretty, ancient town of **RYE** was added as a "limb" to the original Cinque Ports (see page 154), but subsequently marooned two miles inland by the retreat of the sea and the silting-up of the River Rother. It is one of East Sussex's most-visited places – half-timbered, skew-roofed and quintessentially English, with interesting independent shops to poke around in and some excellent places to eat.

Rye's most picturesque – and frequently photographed – street is the sloping, cobbled **Mermaid Street**, the town's main thoroughfare in the sixteenth century. At the top of the road, just around the corner in West Street, is **Lamb House** (mid-March to Oct Tues, Fri & Sat 11am–5pm; £5.85; NT; ☎ 01580 762334, ⊛ nationaltrust.org.uk/lamb-house), home of the authors Henry James and (subsequently) E.F. Benson. Just a few yards away is the peaceful oasis of Church Square, where **St Mary's Church** boasts the oldest functioning pendulum clock in the country; the church tower (£3.50) offers fine views over the rooftops. In the far corner of the square stands **Ypres Tower** (daily: April–Oct 10.30am–5pm; Nov–March 10.30am–3.30pm; £4; ☎ 01797 227798, ⊛ ryemuseum. co.uk), built to keep watch for cross-Channel invaders; it now houses a number of relics from Rye's past, including paraphernalia from the town's smuggling heyday.

Rye Harbour Nature Reserve

Rye Harbour Rd, TN31 7TU · Nature Reserve open access; Information centre most days 10am–4/5pm · Free · ☎ 01797 227784, ⊛ sussexwildlifetrust.org.uk · Bus #313 runs from Rye station to Rye Harbour (roughly hourly)

A few miles south of town is **Rye Harbour Nature Reserve**, by turns bleak and beautiful. Miles of footpaths meander around the shingle ridges, salt marsh and reed beds; you can download walks from the website, or pick up a map from the **information centre** situated down the path opposite the car park.

Camber Sands

Around three miles east of Rye, on the other side of the River Rother estuary, **Camber Sands** is a two-mile stretch of gorgeous dune-backed sandy beach that has become a renowned centre of wind- and watersports. The nicest way to reach it from Rye is by bike, on the three-mile dedicated **cycle path**.

2

ARRIVAL AND GETTING AROUND

RYE AND AROUND

By train Rye's station is at the bottom of Station Approach, off Cinque Ports St; it's a 5min walk up to High St.
Destinations Ashford (hourly; 20min); Hastings (hourly; 20min); London St Pancras (hourly; 1hr 25min).
By bus Bus #100 runs into the centre of Rye from Hastings (Mon–Sat every 30min, Sun hourly; 40min), passing

through Winchelsea en route. Bus #101 (Mon–Sat hourly, Sun every 2hr; 15min) runs from Rye station to Camber Sands (Mon–Sat hourly, Sun every 2hr; 15min).
By bike Rye Hire, 1 Cyprus Place (Mon–Fri 8am–5pm, Sat 8am–noon, Sat afternoon & Sun by appointment only; £13/half-day, £18/day; ☎01797 223033, �🌐 ryehire.co.uk).

INFORMATION

Rye Heritage and Information Centre Strand Quay, TN31 7AY (daily 10am–5pm; check website for winter hours; ☎01797 226696, �🌐 ryeheritage.co.uk). This privately run information centre sells town maps (30p)

and rents out walking tour audioguides (£4). Its excellent sound-and-light show (every 30min; 20min; £3.50) gives you a potted history of Rye using a model of the town as it would have looked in the early nineteenth century.

ACCOMMODATION

The George 98 High St, TN31 7JT ☎01797 222114, �🌐 thegeorgeinrye.com. This luxurious small hotel manages to get everything just right, from the cosy, wood-beamed bar and excellent restaurant to the tasteful, individually furnished rooms: there are 34 to choose from, ranging from an Arts and Crafts-styled room decked out in William Morris textiles to a Miami-themed hangout with circular bed. **£145**
★ **Hayden's** 108 High St, TN31 7JE ☎01797 224501, �🌐 haydensinrye.co.uk. Friendly, popular B&B with seven

elegant, contemporary rooms set above a restaurant in the heart of town. Rooms at the back have lovely views out over Romney Marsh. **£125**
Rye Windmill Off Ferry Rd, TN31 7DW ☎01797 224027, �🌐 ryewindmill.co.uk. Great value for Rye, this 300-year-old Grade II listed smock windmill contains eight smart en-suite rooms, plus two suites in the windmill itself; splash out on the Windmill Suite (£170) for panoramic views over Rye. Minimum two-night stay at weekends. **£90**

EATING AND DRINKING

★ **Knoops** Tower Forge, Hilders Cliff, Landgate ☎01797 225838, �🌐 facebook.com/KnoopsChocolateBar. This little place only offers one thing – hot chocolate – but it does it with style. Choose your chocolate (from 27 to 80 percent solids; £3), add your extras (various spices, peppers, fruits, even flowers – all 50p, or a shot of something stronger for £1) and wait to be presented with your own bowl of made-to-order chocolately loveliness. Mon & Fri–Sun 10am–6pm, plus Tues & Wed same hours in school hols.
Landgate Bistro 5–6 Landgate, TN31 7LH ☎01797 222829, �🌐 landgatebistro.co.uk. Perhaps the best restaurant in Rye, this small, intimate place – housed

in two interconnected Georgian cottages – is known for its traditionally British food: there's plenty of fish from the local fishing fleet, Romney Marsh lamb and game in season (mains £11–20). Wed–Fri 7–11pm, Sat noon–3.30pm & 6.30–11pm, Sun noon–3.30pm.
Standard Inn The Strand, TN31 7EN ☎01797 225231, �🌐 thestandardinnrye.co.uk. Beautifully restored inn, with bare brick walls and beams. There's a good selection of craft beer and local ale, including the pub's own Standard Inn Farmer's Ale, plus excellent food (mains £10–16). Mon–Thurs noon–11pm, Fri & Sat noon–midnight, Sun noon–10pm; kitchen daily noon–3/4pm & 6–9/9.30pm.

Hastings and around

The seaside town of **HASTINGS** has all the ingredients for a perfect break: a picturesque Old Town crammed with independent shops and cafés; a seafront that combines plenty of tacky seaside amusements with a sleek modern art gallery and a splendid new pier; a still-working fishing quarter supplying a multitude of excellent fish and seafood restaurants; and miles of lovely countryside right on its doorstep.

Just inland is the town of **Battle**, where William, Duke of Normandy, marched to meet King Harold's army in the famous battle of 1066. Bexhill's striking **De La Warr Pavilion** lies a few miles west of Hastings along the coast.

2 Old Town

The pretty **Old Town** is the nicest part of Hastings. **High Street** and pedestrianized **George Street** are the focus, lined with antiques shops, galleries, restaurants and pubs. Running parallel to the High Street is **All Saints Street**, punctuated with the odd timber-framed dwelling from the fifteenth century. Midway along George Street, the **West Hill Cliff Railway** (March–Sept daily 10am–5.30pm; Oct–Feb Sat & Sun 11am–4pm; return ticket £2.60) ascends West Hill, depositing you a short walk from **Hastings Castle** (hours vary, but generally April–Oct daily 10am–4pm; £4.75; ☎01424 422964, ⓦsmugglersadventure.co.uk/hastings-castle-experience), of which very little remains bar a few crumbling walls.

The Stade

Down by the seafront, the area known as **The Stade** is characterized by its tall, black weatherboard **net shops**, most dating from the mid-nineteenth century, and still in use today. The Stade is home to the town's fishing fleet – the largest beach-launched

---

WINE IN THE SOUTHEAST: A SPARKLING SUCCESS STORY

With almost identical soil and geology to the Champagne region, and increased temperatures due to global warming, the Southeast is home to many of the country's best **vineyards**, several of which offer **tours** and **tastings**; see their websites for information. For more details of vineyards throughout Kent and Sussex – including a downloadable wine routes **map** – check the website of the Southeastern Vineyard Association, ⓦseva.uk.com.

KENT

Biddenden Gribble Bridge Lane, Biddenden, TN27 8DF ☎01580 291726, ⓦbiddendenvineyards.com. Kent's oldest commercial vineyard, producing wines from eleven varieties of grape, plus traditional ciders and juices. Short, self-guided tours and occasional themed tours are all free.

Chapel Down Small Hythe, Tenterden, TN30 7NG ☎01580 763033, ⓦchapeldown.com. Multi-award-winning winemaker – they do a great lager, too. Pop in for a wander, or take a guided tour.

Hush Heath Five Oak Lane, Staplehurst, TN12 0HT ☎01622 832794, ⓦhushheath.com. Family-owned estate famed for its sparkling wines, made using traditional methods, and in particular the Balfour Brut Rosé. The free self-guided trail through the glorious estate is stunning, as are the free tastings.

SUSSEX

Bolney Wine Estate Foxhole Lane, Bolney, RH17 5NB ☎01444 881894, ⓦbolneywineestate.co.uk. This small, family-run vineyard has a lovely setting and offers a variety of tours. The vineyard has won awards for its sparkling wines, but is also known for its red wines.

Ridgeview Wine Estate Fragbarrow Lane, Ditchling Common, BN6 8TP ☎01444 241441, ⓦridgeview.co.uk. Award-winning vineyard, known for its sparkling wines. Try one of the tours (pre-booking essential), or just turn up at the cellar door and taste before you buy.

Tinwood Estate Tinwood Lane, Halnaker, PO18 0NE ☎01243 537372, ⓦtinwoodestate.com. Smart vineyard near Chichester producing sparkling wines from classic Champagne-variety grapes. There are tours (pre-booking essential) in summer, plus there's a stylish, modern tasting room.

fleet in Europe – and many of the net shops sell fresh-off-the-boat fish. Just west of the net huts, the wide expanse of the **Stade Open Space** is used for various events throughout the year.

Jerwood Gallery

Rock-a-Nore Rd, TN34 3DW • Feb–Dec Tues–Sun & bank hols 11am–5pm; first Tues of month open until 8pm • £9, free first Tues of month 4–8pm • ☎ 01424 425809, ⓦ jerwoodgallery.org

Adjacent to the fishing quarter, the sleek **Jerwood Gallery**, covered in shimmering dark-glazed tiles, provides a home for the Jerwood Foundation's modern art collection, which includes works by Stanley Spencer, Walter Sickert and Augustus John. A **café** up on the first floor overlooks the fishing boats on the beach.

2

East Hill and Hastings Country Park

Just behind the net shops, the venerable **East Hill Cliff Railway** (March–Sept daily 10am–5.30pm; Oct–Feb Sat & Sun 11am–4pm; return ticket £2.60) climbs up to **East Hill**, for wonderful views over the town and access to **Hastings Country Park** (ⓦhastingscountrypark.org.uk), a beautiful expanse of heathland, sandstone cliffs and ancient woodland ravines which spreads east for three miles.

Hastings Pier

Open daily; hours vary depending on season, weather and events – check website • Free • ⓦ hastingspier.org.uk

West of The Stade, the beautifully restored **Hastings Pier** has risen phoenix-like from the ashes of an arson attack in 2010. Wide expanses of bare deck allow it to be used for everything from markets to concerts to open-air film screenings – check the website to see what's on. The centrepiece is The Deck, a beautifully designed visitor centre and café.

St Leonards-on-Sea

Shabby, arty, quirky and a bit rough around the edges, **St Leonards** – once a separate town but now more or less absorbed into Hastings – lies at the western end of the seafront. It's worth spending a morning or afternoon checking out some of the cool art galleries, shops, cafés and restaurants along **Norman Road** and **Kings Road**.

Battle Abbey and Battlefield

At the south end of High St, Battle, TN33 0AD • Feb half term daily 10am–4pm; mid-Feb to March Wed–Sun 10am–4pm; April–Sept daily 10am–6pm; Oct daily 10am–5pm; Nov to mid-Feb Sat & Sun 10am–4pm • £11.20; EH • ☎ 01424 775705, ⓦ www.english-heritage.org. uk/visit/places/1066-battle-of-hastings-abbey-and-battlefield • Buses #304 and #305 from Hastings (Mon–Sat hourly; 15min), or regular trains from Hastings and London Charing Cross to Battle station, a 10min walk away

Six miles inland from Hastings in the small town of Battle, the remains of **Battle Abbey** occupy the site of the most famous land battle in British history. Here, or hereabouts, on October 14, 1066, the invading Normans swarmed up the hillside from Senlac Moor and overcame the army of King Harold, spelling an end to Anglo-Saxon England. Before the battle, William vowed that, should he win, he would build a religious foundation on the very spot of Harold's slaying to atone for the bloodshed; true to his word, Battle Abbey was built four years later and subsequently occupied by a fraternity of Benedictines.

The abbey, once one of the richest in the country, was partially destroyed in the Dissolution and much rebuilt and revised over the centuries. The magnificent 1330s gatehouse (topped by a rooftop viewing platform) still survives, along with the thirteenth-century rib-vaulted dormitory range, but all that remains of William's original

2

HASTINGS FESTIVALS

The year's biggest event is the **Jack-in-the-Green Festival** (May Day weekend; Ⓦhastingsjitg.co.uk), three days of festivities culminating in a parade of dancers, drummers and leaf-bedecked revellers through the streets of the Old Town up to Hastings' hilltop castle, where "the Jack" – a garlanded figure whose origins date back to the eighteenth century – is ritually slain and the spirit of summer released. Other events include three **food festivals** celebrating Hastings' fishing industry; **Hastings Week** in October; and **Fat Tuesday** (Ⓦhastingsfattuesday.co.uk) held over four days in February or March, which sees hundreds of gigs taking place around town, many of them free.

abbey church is an outline on the grass, with the site of the high altar – the spot where Harold was supposedly killed – marked by a memorial stone. An excellent **visitor centre** shows a film about the battle and the events leading up to it. Audioguides (40min) take you round the site of the **battlefield**, vividly re-creating the battle and its aftermath.

De La Warr Pavilion

Marina, Bexhill-on-Sea, TN40 1DP • Daily: April–Oct 10am–6pm; Nov–March 10am–5pm • Free • ☏ 01424 229111, Ⓦdlwp.com • Bus #98 from Hastings (Mon–Sat every 30min, Sun hourly; 40min); train from Hastings (every 20min; 10min); or seafront cycle path from Hastings to Bexhill

The seaside town of Bexhill-on-Sea, five miles west of Hastings, is home to the iconic **De La Warr Pavilion**, a sleek Modernist masterpiece overlooking the sea. Built in 1935 by architects Erich Mendelsohn and Serge Chermayeff, the Pavilion slid gradually into disrepair after World War II, but today it has been restored to its original glory, hosting contemporary art **exhibitions** and **live performances**.

ARRIVAL AND INFORMATION
HASTINGS AND AROUND

By train Hastings station is a 10min walk from the seafront along Havelock Rd. There's another station, St Leonards Warrior Square, at the north end of Kings Rd.

Destinations Ashford (hourly; 40min); Battle (every 30min; 15min); Brighton (every 30min; 1hr 5min); Eastbourne (every 20min; 25min); Lewes (every 20min; 55min); London Victoria (hourly; 2hr–2hr 15min); Rye (hourly; 20min); Tunbridge Wells (every 30min; 35–50min).

By bus Bus services operate from outside the train station.

Destinations Battle (Mon–Sat hourly; 15min); Dover (Mon–Sat every 30min, Sun hourly; 2hr 50min); Eastbourne (Mon–Sat every 20–30min, Sun hourly; 1hr 15min); London Victoria (1 daily; 2hr 35min); Rye (Mon–Sat every 30min, Sun hourly; 40min).

Tourist office On the seafront at Aquila House, Breeds Place (April–Oct Mon–Fri 9am–5pm, Sat 9.30am–5.30pm, Sun 10.30am–4pm; Nov–March Mon–Fri 9am–5pm, Sat 9.30am–4.30pm, Sun 11am–3pm; ☏01424 451111, Ⓦvisit1066country.com).

ACCOMMODATION

★ **The Laindons** 23 High St, TN34 3EY ☏01424 437710, Ⓦthelaindons.com. Set in a Georgian townhouse, this friendly boutique B&B has five gorgeous rooms, all with a crisp Scandi vibe. Breakfast includes coffee which they roast themselves. **£120**

Senlac Guesthouse 46–47 Cambridge Gardens, TN34 1EN ☏01424 435767, Ⓦsenlacguesthouse.co.uk. Stylish yet affordable, this friendly guesthouse with smart rooms and a good location near the station, is fantastic

value. The cheapest rooms share bathrooms. Breakfast £8.50 extra. **£60**

Swan House 1 Hill St, TN34 3HU ☏01892 430014, Ⓦswanhousehastings.co.uk. Beautiful B&B in a half-timbered fifteenth-century building on one of the Old Town's most picturesque streets. Rooms are luxurious and tasteful, and there's a pretty decked patio garden where you can enjoy a sunny breakfast. Minimum two-night stay at weekends. **£120**

EATING AND DRINKING

The Crown 64–66 All Saints St, TN34 3BN ☏01424 465100, Ⓦthecrownhastings.co.uk. Great pub with a lovely ambience and a trendy crowd. There's plenty of local produce on the menu (Hastings fish, Bodiam ice cream,

Rye Bay coffee, and so on) and behind the bar (Sussex ales, gins and ciders). Mon–Sat 11am–11pm, Sun 11am–10.30pm; kitchen Mon–Fri noon–5pm & 6–9.30pm, Sat & Sun 11am–5pm & 6–9.30pm.

Maggies Above the fish market, Rock-a-Nore Rd ☎01424 430205. The best fish and chips in town can be found at this first-floor café, right on the beach. It's open for lunch only, and is very popular, so book ahead. Mon–Sat noon–2pm.

Webbe's 1 Rock-a-Nore Rd, TN34 3DW ☎01424 721650, Ⓦwebbesrestaurants.co.uk. Good seafood restaurant opposite the Jerwood Gallery. Mains such as steamed panache of Hastings fish cost around £15, or you can pick and choose from tasting dishes at £3.75 each. There's plenty of outside seating in summer. Mon–Fri noon–2pm & 6–9pm, Sat & Sun noon–9.30pm.

Eastbourne

Like so many of the southeast's seaside resorts, **EASTBOURNE** was kick-started into life in the 1840s, when the Brighton, Lewes and Hastings Rail Company built a branch line from Lewes to the coast. Nowadays Eastbourne has a solid reputation as a retirement town by the sea, and though the contemporary **Towner Gallery** has introduced a splash of modernity, the town's charms remain for the most part sedate and old-fashioned. The Towner Gallery lies in the **Cultural Quarter**, centred on Devonshire Park; three theatres sit on the park's fringes, while the park itself is home to **lawn tennis courts**, which play host to big-name players during the Aegon International Eastbourne in June. The focus of the elegant seafront is the Victorian **pier**; just to the west is the splendid **bandstand** (Ⓦeastbournebandstand.co.uk), which hosts various musical events throughout the year. Continue west to the end of the seafront and you'll come to the start of the steep two-mile-long path climbing up to Beachy Head (see page 168), one of the scenic splendours of the South Downs National Park.

Towner Art Gallery and Museum

Devonshire Park, BN21 4JJ • Tues–Sun & bank hols 10am–5pm • Free • ☎ 01323 434670, Ⓦ townereastbourne.org.uk

Housed in a sleek modern edifice by Devonshire Park, the excellent **Towner Art Gallery and Museum** puts on four or five exhibitions a year, which are shown alongside rotating displays of modern and contemporary art from its own permanent collection; it's especially well known for its modern British art.

ARRIVAL AND INFORMATION

EASTBOURNE

By train Eastbourne's splendid Italianate station is a 10min walk from the seafront up Terminus Rd.
Destinations Brighton (every 20min; 35min); Hastings (every 20min; 30min); Lewes (every 20min; 30min); London Victoria (Mon–Sat 4 hourly, Sun 2 hourly; 1hr 20min–1hr 50min).

By bus The National Express coach station is on Junction Rd, right by the train station. Most local bus services are run by Stagecoach.

Destinations Brighton (every 10–15min; 1hr 15min); Hastings (Mon–Sat every 20min, Sun hourly; 1hr 10min); London Victoria (2 daily; 3hr 15min); Tunbridge Wells (Mon–Sat hourly; 50min).

Tourist office 3 Cornfield Rd, just off Terminus Rd (March, April & Oct Mon–Fri 9am–5.30pm, Sat 9am–4pm; May–Sept Mon–Fri 9am–5.30pm, Sat 9am–5pm, Sun 10am–1pm; Nov–Feb Mon–Fri 9am–4.30pm, Sat 9am–1pm; ☎ 01323 415415, Ⓦvisiteastbourne.com).

ACCOMMODATION AND EATING

Beach Deck Royal Parade, BN22 7AE ☎01323 720320, Ⓦthebeachdeck.co.uk. The perfect spot for an alfresco lunch, with a big suntrap deck overlooking the beach. Food (including gluten-free options) ranges from burgers to fresh fish. Summer Mon–Wed & Sun 8.30am–6pm, Thurs–Sat 8.30am–late; winter hours vary – check website.

Fusciardi's 30 Marine Parade, BN22 7AY ☎01323 722128, Ⓦfusciardiicecreams.co.uk. This ice-cream parlour is an Eastbourne institution, with piled-high sundaes that are a work of art. Daily 9am–7pm; June &

Aug generally open until 10/10.30pm.

Pebble Beach 53 Royal Parade ☎01323 431240, Ⓦpebblebeacheastbourne.com. Boutique B&B at the eastern end of town, with six stylish, good-value rooms set across three floors of a Victorian seafront townhouse. **£80**

Urban Ground 2a Bolton Rd, BN21 3JX ☎01323 410751, Ⓦurbanground.co.uk. Fab little independent coffee shop with great coffee and a range of tasty sandwiches, soups and cakes. There's a second branch in the Towner Gallery. Mon–Sat 7.30am–6pm, Sun 9am–5pm.

Sussex Heritage Coast and around

Just west of Eastbourne lies the most dramatic stretch of coastline in the South Downs National Park, the **Sussex Heritage Coast**, where the chalk uplands are cut by the sea into a sequence of splendid cliffs that stretch for nine pristine miles. The most spectacular of these is **Beachy Head** (575ft high), the tallest chalk sea-cliff in the country. A couple of miles to the west of here the cliffs dip down to **Birling Gap**, where's there's access to the beach, and a National Trust-run café and information centre. Birling Gap marks the eastern end of a series of magnificent undulating chalk cliffs known as the **Seven Sisters**, which end three miles further west at the meandering River Cuckmere – an area encompassed by the **Seven Sisters Country Park**. This stretch of coast provides some of the most impressive walks in the region; head to one of the visitor centres (see below) for advice and route maps.

Alfriston and around

Three miles inland from the Seven Sisters Country Park along the River Cuckmere is the picture-perfect village of **ALFRISTON**, with plenty of creaky old smuggling inns, a picturesque village green ("The Tye") and some lovely riverside walks. On The Tye sits the fourteenth-century timber-framed and thatched **Clergy House** (mid-March to Oct Mon–Wed, Sat & Sun 10.30am–5pm; Nov & Dec Sat & Sun 11am–4pm; £5.35; NT; ☎01323 871961, ⓦnationaltrust.org.uk/alfriston-clergy-house), the first property to be acquired by the National Trust, in 1896. At the other end of the green is the Gun Room (daily 10am–4pm; ☎01323 870 022, ⓦrathfinnyestate.com), the shop-cum-cellar door of the **Rathfinny Wine Estate**, which sprawls over the hillsides on the southern outskirts of Alfriston; tours of the vineyard are available.

ARRIVAL AND INFORMATION   SUSSEX HERITAGE COAST AND AROUND

By bus Bus #13X runs from Eastbourne and Brighton via Beachy Head, Birling Gap and the Seven Sisters Country Park Visitor Centre (late April to mid-June Sat & Sun hourly; mid-June to mid-Sept Mon–Fri 3 daily, Sat & Sun hourly; 35min). The Cuckmere Valley Ramblerbus operates an hourly circular service (50min) from Berwick train station – with hourly connections to Eastbourne, Lewes and Brighton – to the Seven Sisters Country Park via Alfriston (April–Oct Sat, Sun & bank hols; ⓦcuckmerebuses.org.uk).
Tourist information Beachy Head Countryside Centre, Beachy Head (Easter–Oct Mon 1–4pm, Tues–Sun 10am–

4pm; Nov Sat & Sun 11am–3pm; volunteer-run, so opening times can vary, especially in winter; ☎01323 737273, ⓦbeachyhead.org). Birling Gap Information Centre, Birling Gap (daily 10am–5pm, or 4pm in winter; ☎01323 423197, ⓦnationaltrust.org.uk/birling-gap-and-the-seven-sisters). Seven Sisters Country Park Visitor Centre, Exceat, on the A259 between Seaford and Eastbourne (March & Nov Sat & Sun 11am–4pm; April–Sept daily 10.30am–4.30pm; Oct daily 11am–4pm; volunteer-run, so opening times can vary, especially in winter; ☎0345 608 0194, ⓦsevensisters.org.uk).

ACCOMMODATION

Belle Tout Beachy Head ☎01323 423185, ⓦbelletout. co.uk. For a real treat book into this fabulous lighthouse, perched high up on the dramatic cliffs just west of Beachy Head. The cosy rooms boast stupendous views,

there's a snug residents' lounge and – best of all – there's unrestricted access to the lamproom at the top of the lighthouse, where you can sit and watch the sun go down. **£190**

THE SOUTH DOWNS WAY

The long-distance **South Downs Way** rises and dips over one hundred miles along the chalk uplands between the city of Winchester and the spectacular cliffs at Beachy Head, and offers the southeast's finest walks. The OS *Explorer* **maps** OL11 and OL25 cover the eastern end of the route; you'll need OL10, OL8, OL3 and OL32 as well to cover the lot. Several **guidebooks** are available (some covering the route in just one direction); you can also check out the **website** ⓦnationaltrail.co.uk/south-downs-way.

Lewes and around

LEWES, the county town of East Sussex, straddles the River Ouse as it carves a gap through the South Downs on its final stretch to the sea. Though there's been some rebuilding, the core of Lewes remains remarkably good-looking: replete with crooked older dwellings, narrow lanes – or "twittens" – and Georgian houses. With numerous traces of its long history still visible (not least a medieval castle), plus a lively cultural scene, plenty of independent and antiques shops, and some of England's most appealing chalkland on its doorstep, Lewes makes a great Sussex base. Nearby are the Bloomsbury Group's country home at **Charleston**, Virginia Woolf's former home **Monk's House**, and the **Ditchling Museum of Art + Craft** – all a short hop by car.

2

Lewes Castle

169 High St • Mon & Sun 11am–5.30pm (dusk in winter), Tues–Sat 10am–5.30pm (dusk in winter); closed Mon in Jan • £7.70, joint ticket with Anne of Cleves House £12.30 • ☎ 01273 486290, ⓦ sussexpast.co.uk

Both **Lewes Castle** and St Pancras Priory (see below) were the work of William de Warenne, who was given the land by William I following the Norman Conquest. Inside the castle complex – unusual for being built on two mottes, or mounds – the shell of the eleventh-century keep remains, and can be climbed for excellent views over the town to the surrounding Downs. Tickets include admission to the **museum** (same hours as castle) by the entrance, where exhibits include archeological artefacts and a town model.

Southover

From the High Street, the steep, cobbled and much photographed **Keere Street** leads to **Southover**, the southern part of town. At the foot of Keere Street, tranquil **Grange Gardens** (daily dawn–dusk; free) sprawl around Southover Grange, childhood home of the diarist John Evelyn. Nearby on Southover High Street is the timber-framed **Anne of Cleves House** (Feb–Nov Mon & Sun 11am–5pm, Tues–Sat 10am–5pm; closes 4pm in Feb & Nov; sometimes closed for private functions – call to check; £5.60, joint ticket with Lewes Castle £12.30; ☎ 01273 474610, ⓦ sussexpast.co.uk), a fifteenth-century hall house laid out as it would have looked in Tudor times. Cross the road and head down Cockshut Lane to reach the evocative ruins of **St Pancras Priory** (open access; free); in its heyday it was one of Europe's principal Cluniac institutions, with a church the size of Westminster Abbey.

Monk's House

Rodmell, BN7 3HF, 3 miles south of Lewes • Easter–Oct Wed–Sun & bank hols: house 1–5pm; garden 12.30–5.30pm • £5.75; NT • ☎ 01273 474760, ⓦ nationaltrust.org.uk/monks-house

The pretty, weatherboard **Monk's House** was the home of novelist **Virginia Woolf** and her husband, Leonard. Like nearby Charleston (see below), where Virginia's much-loved sister Vanessa Bell lived, Monk's House hosted gatherings of the Bloomsbury Group, and the house is unmistakably "Bloomsbury" in style, with painted furniture and artworks by Vanessa and her partner Duncan Grant in every room. The real highlight, though, is the tranquil **garden**, with its beautiful views over the Ouse Valley.

Charleston

BN8 9LL • March–June, Sept & Oct Wed–Sun & bank hols noon–5pm; July & Aug Wed–Sat 11.30am–5.30pm, Sun & bank hols noon–5.30pm; note that Wed–Sat entry is by 1hr guided tour only; garden open same hours as house (not part of tour); last entry 1hr before closing • House and garden £12.50, garden only £4.50 • ☎ 01323 811626, ⓦ charleston.org.uk

Six miles east of Lewes lies **Charleston**, the country home and gathering place of the writers, intellectuals and artists known as the Bloomsbury Group. Virginia Woolf's

LEWES BONFIRE NIGHT

Each November 5, while the rest of Britain lights small domestic bonfires or attends municipal firework displays, Lewes puts on a more dramatic show, whose origins lie in the deaths of the Lewes Martyrs, the seventeen Protestants burned here in 1556 at the height of Mary Tudor's militant revival of Catholicism. Members of the town's six tightly knit **bonfire societies** dress up in traditional costumes and parade through the narrow streets carrying flaming torches and flares, before marching off to the outskirts of town for their society's individual bonfire and fireworks display. Boisterous and anarchic, the **Lewes Bonfire Night** experience is brilliant, but it does get packed, especially on years when November 5 falls on a weekend. With loud bangs, flying sparks and lots of open flames, the event is definitely not suitable for small children. For more, see ⓦ lewesbonfirecouncil.org.uk.

sister Vanessa Bell, Vanessa's husband, Clive Bell, and her lover, Duncan Grant, moved here during World War I so that the men, both conscientious objectors, could work on local farms. Almost every surface of the farmhouse interior is painted and the walls are hung with paintings by Picasso, Renoir and Augustus John, alongside the work of the residents. Elsewhere on the site, the purpose-built **Wolfson Gallery** hosts changing exhibitions exploring the Bloomsbury Group's artistic and literary heritage.

Ditchling Museum of Art + Craft

Lodge Hill Lane, BN6 8SP • Tues–Sat 10.30am–5pm, Sun & bank hols 11am–5pm • £6.50 • ☎ 01273 844744, ⓦ ditchlingmuseumartcraft.org.uk

The pretty village of **DITCHLING** lies eight miles west of Lewes at the foot of the Downs, overlooked by Ditchling Beacon – one of the highest spots on the escarpment. On the village green, the beautifully designed two-room **Ditchling Museum of Art + Craft** houses a fascinating assortment of prints, paintings, weavings and sculptures from the artists and craftspeople who lived in Ditchling in the last century, among them typographer and sculptor Eric Gill, printer and writer Hilary Pepler, weaver Ethel Mairet and calligrapher Edward Johnson, who designed the iconic London Underground typeface.

ARRIVAL AND INFORMATION

LEWES AND AROUND

By train The station is south of High St down Station Rd. Destinations Brighton (every 10–20min; 15min); Eastbourne (every 20min; 30min); London Victoria (Mon–Sat every 30min, Sun hourly; 1hr 10min).
By bus The bus station is on Eastgate St, by School Hill. Destinations Brighton (Mon–Sat every 15min, Sun every 30min; 30min); Tunbridge Wells (Mon–Sat every 30min,

Sun hourly; 1hr 10min).
Tourist office At the junction of High St and Fisher St (April–Sept Mon–Fri 9.30am–4.30pm, Sat 9.30am–4pm, Sun 10am–2pm; Oct–March Mon–Fri 9.30am–4.30pm, Sat 10am–2pm; ☎ 01273 483448, ⓦ staylewes.org). They hold copies of the excellent free monthly magazine *Viva Lewes* (ⓦ vivalewes.com).

ACCOMMODATION

The Corner House 14 Cleve Terrace, BN7 1JJ ☎ 01273 567138, ⓦ lewescornerhouse.co.uk. Super-friendly B&B on a quiet Edwardian terrace, close to Grange Gardens. The two en-suite rooms have lovely homely touches such as patchwork quilts and plenty of books, and the owner is a great source of information on the town and area. **£85**
YHA South Downs Itford Farm, Beddingham, 5 miles from Lewes ☎ 0870 371 9574. The nearest hostel to

Lewes is a gem, newly renovated from an old farm, and in a fabulous location right on the South Downs Way footpath, with great transport connections (Southease station – with regular connections to Lewes – is under 200m away). Camping pods (sleeping 3) and bell tents (sleeping 5) are available, and there's a café and licensed bar too. Dorms **£25**, doubles, **£55**, camping pods **£49**, bell tents **£89**

EATING AND DRINKING

Bus Club Eastgate, BN7 2LP ☎ 01273 470755, ⓦ thehearth.co. Down-to-earth pizzeria above Lewes bus station, serving excellent wood-fired pizzas (£7–10). The

downstairs *Bakehouse* sells pizza by the slice, along with other snacks. Mon & Tues 5–10pm, Wed–Fri noon–2pm & 5–10pm, Sat noon–10pm.

Flint Owl 209 High St, BN7 2DL ☎01273 472769, ⓦflintowlbakery.com. The café of the Glynde-based Flint Owl Bakery – which supplies its pastries and artisan bread around Sussex – is a stylish space with a small courtyard garden out the back, and counters piled high with freshly baked goodies. Mon–Sat 9am–5pm.

Lewes Arms Mount Place, BN7 1YH ☎01273 473252, ⓦlewesarms.co.uk. This characterful local is a good spot to sample a pint of Sussex Best, produced down the road at Harvey's brewery. The home-cooked pub food is great value, too. Mon–Thurs 11am–11pm, Fri & Sat 11am–midnight, Sun noon–11pm; kitchen Mon–Fri & Sun noon–8.30pm, Sat noon–9pm.

2

Brighton

Vibrant, quirky and cool, **BRIGHTON** (or **Brighton & Hove**, to give it its official name) is one of the country's most popular seaside destinations. The essence of the city's appeal is its faintly bohemian vitality, a buzz that comes from a mix of holiday-makers, foreign-language students, a thriving **LGBT+ community**, and an energetic local student population from the art college and two universities.

Any trip to Brighton inevitably begins with a visit to its two most famous landmarks – the exuberant **Royal Pavilion** and the wonderfully tacky **Brighton Pier** – followed by a stroll along the seafront promenade or the pebbly beach. Just as fun, though, is an exploration of Brighton's car-free **Lanes** – the maze of narrow alleys marking the old town – or a meander through the more bohemian streets of **North Laine**. Brighton's other great draw is its **cultural life**: you're spoilt for choice when it comes to live music, theatre, comedy and concerts.

The Royal Pavilion

4/5 Pavilion Buildings, BN1 1EE • Daily: April–Sept 9.30am–5.45pm; Oct–March 10am–5.15pm; last entry 45min before closing • £13, audioguides £2 • ☎0300 029 0900, ⓦbrightonmuseums.org.uk/royalpavilion

In any survey to find England's most loved building, there's always a bucketful of votes for Brighton's exotic extravaganza, the **Royal Pavilion**. The building was the south-coast pied-à-terre of the fun-loving Prince Regent (the future George IV), who first visited the seaside resort in 1783 and spent much of the next forty years partying, gambling and frolicking with his mistress here. The building you see today is the work of John Nash, architect of London's Regent Street, who in 1815 redesigned the Prince's original modest dwelling into an extraordinary confection of slender minarets, twirling domes, pagodas, balconies and miscellaneous motifs imported from India and China. The result defined a genre of its own – Oriental Gothic.

Inside, the **Banqueting Room** erupts with ornate splendour and is dominated by a one-tonne chandelier hung from the jaws of a massive dragon cowering in a plantain tree. The stunning **Music Room**, the first sight of which reduced George to tears of joy, has a huge dome lined with more than 26,000 individually gilded scales and hung with exquisite umbrella-like glass lamps. After climbing the famous cast-iron staircase with its bamboo-look banisters, you can go into Victoria's sober and seldom-used bedroom and the **North-West Gallery**, where the king's portrait hangs, along with a selection of satirical cartoons. More notable, though, is the **South Gallery**, decorated in sky-blue with trompe l'oeil bamboo trellises and a carpet that appears to be strewn with flowers.

Brighton Museum

Royal Pavilion Gardens, BN1 1EE • Tues–Sun & bank hols 10am–5pm • £5.20 • ☎0300 029 0900, ⓦbrightonmuseums.org.uk/brighton

Across the gardens from the Pavilion stands the **Brighton Museum** – once part of the royal stable block – which houses a wonderful and eclectic mix of modern fashion and design, archeology, painting and local history. Among the highlights are Dalí's famous

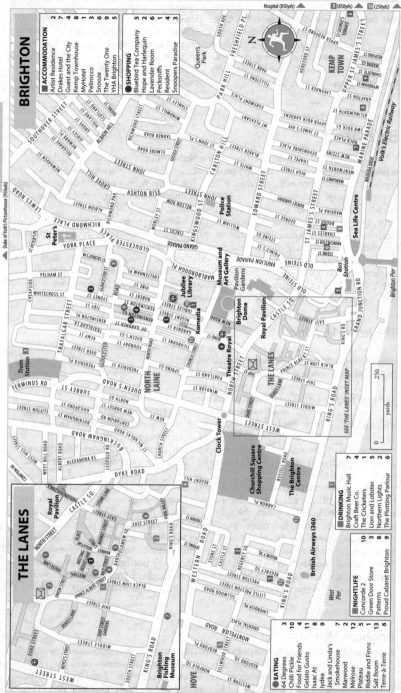

BRIGHTON

■ **ACCOMMODATION**
Artist Residence	2
Drakes Hotel	7
Guest and the City	4
Kemp Townhouse	8
MyHotel	1
Pelirocco	3
Snooze	6
The Twenty One	9
YHA Brighton	5

● **SHOPPING**
Bluebird Tea Company	5
Hope and Harlequin	2
Lavender Room	6
Pecksniffs	1
Resident	4
Snoopers Paradise	3

■ **DRINKING**
Brighton Music Hall	7
Craft Beer Co.	4
The Cricketers	1
Lion and Lobster	5
Northern Lights	2
The Plotting Parlour	6

■ **NIGHTLIFE**
Concorde 2	10
Green Door Store	3
Patterns	8
Proud Cabaret Brighton	9

● **EATING**
64 Degrees	3
Chilli Pickle	10
Food for Friends	4
Gelato Gusto	11
Isaac At	9
Iydea	7
Jack and Linda's Smokehouse	12
Marwood	1
Melrose	5
Plateau	8
Riddle and Finns	13
Salt Room	6
Terre-à-Terre	2

THE LANES

sofa (1938) based on Mae West's lips, the 13,000-object ethnographic collection, and the mummified animals and painted coffins of the Ancient Egypt galleries.

The Lanes

Tucked between the Pavilion and the seafront is a warren of narrow, pedestrianized alleyways known as **The Lanes** – the core of the old fishing village from which Brighton evolved. Long-established jewellers' shops, boutiques and several cafés, pubs and restaurants make this a great place to wander.

North Laine

Vibrant, buzzy **North Laine** (ⓦnorthlaine.co.uk), which sprawls west and north of the Royal Pavilion as far as Trafalgar Street, bordered by Queens Road to the west and the A23 to the east, is more offbeat than the Lanes. Here the eclectic shops, selling secondhand records, vintage gear, homeware, upmarket fashion and New Age objects, mingle with cool coffee shops and pavement cafés and bars.

The seafront

To soak up the tackier side of Brighton, head down to the **seafront** and take a stroll along **Brighton Pier** (daily: April–Oct 10am–10pm; Nov–March 11am–5pm; opening hours can vary depending on weather; free; ☎01273 609361, ⓦbrightonpier.co.uk), completed in 1899, its every inch devoted to cacophonous fun.

The busiest section of the seafront is between Brighton Pier and the derelict **West Pier**, half a mile west; here, down at beach level underneath the old fishermen's arches, the **Lower Esplanade** is lined with cafés, shops, galleries, bars and clubs. By the West Pier, there's no missing the 162m-high **British Airways i360** (daily, check website for hours; £15; ☎0333 772 0360, ⓦbritishairwaysi360.com), the world's tallest moving observation tower.

East of Brighton Pier, the 300m-long twin zipwires of **Brighton Zip** (daily 10am–9pm; £16; ⓦbrightonzip) whisk thrill-seekers along the seafront. If you prefer a more sedate form of transport, try the antiquated locomotives of **Volk's Electric Railway** (Easter–Sept open daily; trains run every 15min; £3.60 return; ⓦvolkselectricrailway.co.uk) – the world's oldest electric railway – which trundle east to **Brighton Marina** (ⓦbrightonmarina.co.uk), stopping off en route at the fabulous **Yellowave** beach sports venue (☎01273 672222, ⓦyellowave.co.uk).

Kemp Town

East of the city centre, **Kemp Town** is the heart of the city's LGBT+ community and one of Brighton's liveliest, most colourful neighbourhoods. From the Old Steine, head along busy, bustling **St James's Street** (Brighton's "Gay Village"), and its quieter continuation, **St George's Road**, where you'll find a clutch of antique and vintage shops, cosy pubs and laidback coffee shops.

Hove

West of the city centre, **Hove** – which started life as a separate resort in the 1820s and only merged with Brighton in 1997 – is a stylish neighbourhood, with some beautiful Regency architecture and an elegant, lawn-backed seafront. The main sight is **Hove Museum** (19 New Church Rd; Mon, Tues & Thurs–Sat 10am–5pm, Sun & bank hols 2–5pm; free; ☎0300 029 0900, ⓦbrightonmuseums.org.uk/hove), which houses an eclectic collection covering everything from contemporary crafts to a 3500-year-old Bronze Age cup.

2

ARRIVAL AND DEPARTURE

By train Brighton train station is at the top of Queen's Rd, which descends to the clocktower and then becomes West St, eventually leading to the seafront, a 10min walk away.
Destinations Arundel (hourly; 1hr 10min); Chichester (every 30min; 45–55min); Eastbourne (every 20min; 35min); Hastings (every 30min; 1hr 5min); Lewes (every 10–20min; 15min); London Bridge (Mon–Sat 2 hourly; 1hr); London St Pancras (every 30min; 1hr 15min); London Victoria (1–2 hourly; 55min); Portsmouth Harbour (Mon–

Sat every 30min, Sun hourly; 1hr 30min).
By bus The long-distance bus station is just in from the seafront on the south side of the Old Steine.
Destinations Arundel (Mon–Sat every 30min, Sun hourly; 2hr); Chichester (every 20–30min; 1hr 45min); Eastbourne (every 10–15min; 1hr 15min); Lewes (Mon–Sat every 15min, Sun every 30min; 30min); London Victoria (hourly; 2hr 20min); Tunbridge Wells (Mon–Sat every 30min, Sun hourly; 1hr 50min).

GETTING AROUND

By bus A one-day CitySaver ticket (£5) allows you unlimited travel on the city bus network (ⓦ buses.co.uk). Short-hop journeys cost £2.20.
By taxi For a city taxi, call ☎ 01273 202020 or ☎ 01273 204060. There are central ranks at Brighton station, East St, Queens Square near the clocktower and outside St Peter's Church.
By tour For details of city tours, which range from ghost walks to food tours to a "Piers and Queers" tour, see ⓦ visitbrighton.com/things-to-do/tours-and-sightseeing.

The Brighton Greeters scheme pairs up visitors with a volunteer Brighton resident tour guide for a free two-hour tour; see ⓦ visitbrighton.com/greeters for more information.
By bike There's a downloadable cycling map of the city at ⓦ brighton-hove.gov.uk/content/cycle-facilities-map. Bike rental is available from Brighton Cycle Hire, Unit 8, under the station, off Trafalgar Street (£7/3hr, £10/24hr; ☎ 01273 571555, ⓦ brightoncyclehire.com); and Brighton Beach Bike Hire, Madeira Drive, by Yellowave (£12 for 3hr, £16 for 4+ hours; ☎ 07917 753794, ⓦ brightonbeachbikes.co.uk).

INFORMATION

Visitor information There are fifteen staffed Visitor Information points (☎ 01273 290337, ⓦ visitbrighton. com) throughout the city, including at Brighton Pier, the Royal Pavilion shop and Jubilee Library in the North Laine.
Apps, magazines and websites VisitBrighton produces

a free app (ⓦ visitbrighton.com/apps). The best listing magazine is *Source* (ⓦ brightonsource.co.uk), but *XYZ* (ⓦ xyzmagazine.co.uk) and *BN1* (ⓦ bn1magazine.co.uk) are also worth a look, as is *Viva Brighton* (ⓦ vivabrighton. com) a free monthly magazine of articles and reviews.

ACCOMMODATION

Brighton's **accommodation** is pricey. The listings below quote weekend, high-season rates; at many places these prices will fall dramatically out of season and midweek, so it pays to check around. Note that at weekends there's generally a two-night-minimum stay. Much of the city's nicest B&B accommodation is found in **Kemp Town**.

Artist Residence 33 Regency Square, BN1 2GG ☎ 01273 324302, ⓦ artistresidencebrighton.co.uk; map p.172. Cool and quirky, this uber-stylish hotel has 23 rooms – some of them decorated by local and international artists – plus a cocktail bar and two very good restaurants. **£170**
Drakes Hotel 33–34 Marine Parade, BN2 1PE ☎ 01273 696934, ⓦ drakesofbrighton.com; map p.172. The unbeatable seafront location is the big draw at this chic boutique hotel. The most expensive rooms come with freestanding baths by floor-to-ceiling windows. There's an excellent restaurant, too. Breakfast £7.50–15 extra. **£160**
★ **Guest and the City** 2 Broad St, BN2 1TJ ☎ 01273 698289, ⓦ guestandthecity.co.uk; map p.172. Lovely B&B in a great central location a minute from the pier, with stylish rooms (the two feature rooms – £140 – come with stained-glass windows of classic Brighton scenes), and super-friendly owners. **£90**
Kemp Townhouse 21 Atlingworth St, BN2 1PL ☎ 01273 681400, ⓦ kemptownhouse.com; map p.172. Stylish

five-star B&B with excellent service and nine chic rooms decked out with black-and-white photos of the city. A complimentary carafe of port in the room is a nice touch. **£155**
MyHotel 17 Jubilee St ☎ 01273 900300, ⓦ myhotels. com/my-hotel-brighton; map p.172. Hip boutique hotel in the heart of North Laine, with rooms designed along feng shui lines, and a great bar, *Merkaba*, downstairs. Rates fluctuate with demand, so check online for last-minute bargains. **£120**
Pelirocco 10 Regency Square ☎ 01273 327055, ⓦ hotelpelirocco.co.uk; map p.172. "England's most rock'n'roll hotel" is a real one-off, featuring extravagantly themed rooms inspired by pop culture and pin-ups. There's a Fifties-style boudoir, a Pop Art "Modrophenia" room featuring bedside tables made from scooters, and even a twin room styled as Lord Vader's Quarters, complete with lightsaber, Darth Vader costume and Star Wars DVDs. **£145**
★ **Snooze** 25 St George's Terrace, BN2 1JJ ☎ 01273 605797, ⓦ snoozebrighton.com; map p.172. Quirky,

characterful guesthouse in Kemp Town, with eight funky rooms that range in style from "Brighton Bollywood" or French flea market to full-on 1970s glamour. **£140**

The Twenty One 21 Charlotte St, BN2 1AG ☎01273 686450, ⓦthetwentyone.co.uk; map p.172. Popular Regency townhouse B&B, with stylish rooms and super-friendly owners. Rooms come with iPads, bathrobes and a well-stocked hospitality tray. **£135**

YHA Brighton Old Steine, BN1 1NH ☎01273 738674, ⓦyha.org.uk/hostel/brighton; map p.172. Less than a minute's walk from the pier, this hostel has 51 en-suite rooms (including 20 doubles, some with roll-top baths), plus a self-catering kitchen and a good café-bar. Prices drop midweek and out of season; book well ahead for weekend stays. Breakfast £5.75 extra. Dorms **£33**, doubles **£80**

EATING

Brighton has the greatest concentration of **restaurants** in the southeast after London and a thriving **café** culture, especially in the buzzy North Laine area. There are plenty of good **coffee shops** in the city, including those belonging to Brighton-based chains Ground and the Small Batch Coffee Company; the latter has its own roastery in Hove.

THE SEAFRONT

Jack and Linda's Smokehouse 197 Kings Arches; map p.172. This tiny beachfront smokehouse is run by a lovely couple who've been traditionally smoking fish here for over a decade. Grab a fresh crab sandwich or hot mackerel roll (£4.40) to eat on the beach for a perfect summer lunch. April–Sept daily 10am–5pm; Oct Sat & Sun 10am–5pm; March & Nov weather dependent.

Melrose 132 King's Rd, BN1 2HH ☎01273 326520, ⓦmelroserestaurant.co.uk; map p.172. Traditional seafront establishment that's been serving up tasty, excellent-value fish and chips (£7.25), local seafood, roasts and custard-covered puddings for over forty years. The next-door *Regency Restaurant* is smaller and similar. Daily 11.30am–10.30pm.

Salt Room 106 King's Rd, BN1 2FU ☎01273 929488, ⓦsaltroom-restaurant.co.uk; map p.172. One of the city's best fish and seafood restaurants, with a stylish exposed-brick interior, sea views and fantastic charcoal-grilled fish and seafood (mains £20 and up). Daily noon–4pm & 6–10pm.

THE LANES

★ **64 Degrees** 53 Meeting House Lane, BN1 1HB ☎01273 770115, ⓦ64degrees.co.uk; map p.172. The best seats in the house at this tiny restaurant in the Lanes are up at the counter of the open kitchen: the idea is that you choose several small plates of food (£6–12) and share them, to create your own tasting menu. The food's inventive, delicious and prepared in front of you, and the whole experience is brilliant fun. Daily noon–3pm & 6–9.45pm.

Food for Friends 18 Prince Albert St, BN1 1HF ☎01273 202310, ⓦfoodforfriends.com; map p.172. Brighton's original vegetarian restaurant – on this spot for over 35 years – serves up sophisticated veggie dishes (mains £12–14) that are imaginative enough to please die-hard meat-eaters too. Mon–Thurs & Sun noon–10pm, Fri & Sat noon–10.30pm.

Marwood 52 Ship St, BN1 1AF ☎01273 382063, ⓦthemarwood.com; map p.172. Quirky, laidback café with great coffee and food (mains around £7) and splendidly bonkers decor that runs from stuffed animals and skateboards on the walls to Star Wars spaceships dangling from the ceiling. Mon 8am–7pm, Tues–Fri 8am–11pm, Sat 9am–11pm, Sun 10am–7pm.

Plateau 1 Bartholomews, BN1 1HG ☎01273 733085, ⓦplateaubrighton.co.uk; map p.172. Laidback little restaurant-cum-wine bar serving cocktails, organic beers and biodynamic wine, and food that ranges from small "bites" (£5–9) to bigger "plats" (from £11), so you can stop by for a nibble and a drink, or a full-blown meal. Daily noon–late; kitchen noon–3.30pm & 6–10pm.

Riddle and Finns 12b Meeting House Lane, BN1 1HB ☎01273 721667, ⓦriddleandfinns.co.uk; map p.172. Bustling champagne and oyster bar where you can tuck into a huge range of shellfish and fish (mains £13–19) at communal marble-topped tables in a white-tiled, candle-lit dining room with an open kitchen. No bookings. Sat 11.30am–11pm, Mon–Fri & Sun noon–10pm.

★ **Terre-à-Terre** 71 East St, BN1 1HQ ☎01273 729051, ⓦterreaterre.co.uk; map p.172. One of the country's best vegetarian restaurants, serving up inventive global veggie cuisine (mains around £15/16). The taster plate for two (£30) is a good place to start if you're befuddled by the weird and wonderful creations on offer. Mon–Fri noon–10.30pm, Sat 11am–11pm, Sun 11am–10pm.

NORTH LAINE

Chilli Pickle 17 Jubilee St, BN1 1GE ☎01273 900383, ⓦthechillipickle.com; map p.172. Buzzing restaurant in North Laine serving sophisticated, authentic Indian food – everything from masala dosas to Chennai seafood stew (mains £10–17). At lunchtimes they offer a range of thalis and street food. Daily noon–3pm & 6–10.30pm.

★ **Gelato Gusto** 2 Gardner St, BN1 1UP ☎01273 673402, ⓦgelatogusto.com; map p.172. Splendid *gelateria*, with regularly changing flavours that run from Turkish Delight to blood-orange *sorbetto*. Mon–Fri 11.30am–6pm, Sat & Sun 11am–6pm.

2

★**Isaac At** 2 Gloucester St, BN1 4EW ☎07765 934740, ⓦisaac-at.com; map p.172. A fun fine-dining experience, with food – inspired by Sussex and all sourced locally – prepared in front of you in the open kitchen: for the full experience, opt for the six-course tasting menu (£50) paired with Sussex wines or juices (£29/22 respectively). Tues–Fri 6.30–10.30pm, Sat 12.30–2.30pm & 6.30–10.30pm.

Iydea 17 Kensington Gardens, BN1 4AL ☎01273 667992, ⓦiydea.co.uk; map p.172. Good-value, tasty veggie food served up cafeteria-style. What's on offer changes every day, but there tends to be a quiche, a lasagne, a curry and enchiladas, alongside half a dozen other dishes (£4.70–7.70). Daily 9.30am–5.30pm; lunch served Mon–Thurs & Sun 11.30am–4.30pm, Fri & Sat 11.30am–5pm.

DRINKING

Brighton Music Hall 127 King's Rd Arches, BN1 2FN ☎01273 747287, ⓦbrightonmusichall.co.uk; map p.172. Beachfront bar with a huge open-air heated terrace, and free live music when the sun shines. Hours vary but generally summer daily 9/10am–late; winter most days from noon.

Craft Beer Co. 22–23 Upper North St, BN1 3FG ☎01273 723736, ⓦthecraftbeerco.com; map p.172. One for beer lovers, this friendly pub has nine daily-changing cask ales and over 200 bottled varieties. The house Craft Pale Ale is brewed for them by Kent Brewery. Mon–Thurs noon–11pm, Fri & Sat noon–1.30am, Sun noon–11pm.

The Cricketers 15 Black Lion St BN1 1ND ☎01273 329472, ⓦcricketersbrighton.co.uk; map p.172. Brighton's oldest pub, immortalized by Graham Greene in *Brighton Rock*, has a traditional feel, with good daytime pub grub, real ales and a cosy courtyard bar. Mon–Thurs 11am–midnight, Fri & Sat 11am–1am, Sun 11am–11pm.

Lion and Lobster 24 Sillwood St, BN1 2PS ☎01273 327299, ⓦthelionandlobster.co.uk; map p.172. One of the city's best pubs, with a traditional feel but a young, fun atmosphere. Pub quiz on Mon nights, and live jazz on Sun. Good food is served until late. Mon–Thurs 11am–1am, Fri & Sat 11am–2am, Sun noon–midnight.

Northern Lights 6 Little East St, BN1 1HT ☎01273 747096, ⓦnorthernlightsbrighton.co.uk; map p.172. Laidback, ever-popular bar with a Scandinavian theme: choose from two dozen different flavoured vodkas, aquavit, and beers from Denmark, Sweden and Finland. The Nordic menu features reindeer, Smörgåsbord and pickled herring. Mon–Thurs 5pm–midnight, Fri 3pm–2am, Sat noon–2am, Sun noon–midnight.

★**The Plotting Parlour** 6 Steine St BN2, 1TE ☎01273 621238, ⓦtheplottingparlour-brighton. co.uk; map p.172. This dimly lit, snug cocktail bar is a real treat, with exquisite cocktails (£8 and up), table service and stylish decor. Mon–Thurs & Sun 3pm–midnight, Fri & Sat 3pm–1am.

NIGHTLIFE

Concorde 2 Madeira Shelter, Madeira Drive, BN2 1EN ☎01273 673311, ⓦconcorde2.co.uk; map p.172. A Victorian tearoom in a former life, this intimate live music venue features up-and-coming acts, big names and varied club nights.

Green Door Store Trafalgar Arches, Lower Goods Yard ⓦthegreendoorstore.co.uk; map p.172. Uber-cool club and live music venue in the arches under the train station, playing anything from psych to blues, punk or powerdisco. The bar is free entry; live gig entry varies.

Patterns 10 Marine Parade, BN2 1TL ☎01273 894777, ⓦpatternsbrighton.com; map p.172. Trendy seafront hangout that boasts a terrace with sea views and a basement club. The range of club nights is broad but specializes in electronic music and attracts internationally renowned DJs.

Proud Cabaret Brighton 83 St Georges Rd, BN2 1EF ☎01273 605789, ⓦproudcabaretbrighton.com; map p.172. Opulent venue in a former ballroom hosting dinner and cabaret/burlesque shows, plus diverse club nights.

ENTERTAINMENT

Brighton Dome 29 New Rd, BN1 1UG ☎01273 709709, ⓦbrightondome.org. Home to three venues – Pavilion Theatre, Concert Hall and Corn Exchange – offering theatre, concerts, dance and performance.

Duke of Yorks Picturehouse Preston Circus, BN1 4NA ☎0871 704 2056, ⓦpicturehouses.co.uk. Grade II listed cinema with a licensed bar showing art-house, independent and classic films. Dukes at Komedia is its sister cinema, based at the Komedia arts centre (see below).

★**Komedia** 44–47 Gardner St, BN1 1UN ☎0845 293 8480, ⓦkomedia.co.uk/brighton. A Brighton institution, this highly regarded arts venue hosts stand-up comedy, live music and cabaret, as well as fun club nights.

Theatre Royal New Rd, BN1 1SD ☎01273 764400, ⓦatgtickets.com/venues/theatre-royal-brighton. Venerable old theatre – going since 1807 – offering predominantly mainstream plays, opera and musicals.

SHOPPING

Most of Brighton's high street chains are found in and around **Churchill Square** (ⓦ churchillsquare.co.uk) and **East Street**. The best areas for independent shops are the **Lanes** and **North Laine** (ⓦ northlaine.co.uk); it's also worth wandering over to **Kemp Town** for a browse around its antiques shops.

Bluebird Tea Company 41 Gardner St, BN1 1UN ☏ 01273 325523, ⓦ bluebirdteaco.com; map p.172. The UK's only tea mixologist, selling a huge variety of fine leaf teas from Gingerbread Chai to Enchanted Narnia (with Turkish Delight). Mon–Fri 10.30am–6pm, Sat 10am–6.30pm, Sun 10.30am–5.30pm.

Hope and Harlequin 31 Sydney St, BN1 4EP ☏ 01273 675222, ⓦ hopeandharlequin.com; map p.172. Upmarket vintage shop, stocking clothes and collectables up to the 1970s, with a special emphasis on the 1930s and 1940s. Mon & Wed–Sat 10.30am–6pm, Sun 11am–5pm; call ahead to check Tues opening.

Lavender Room 16 Bond St, BN1 1RD ☏ 01273 220380, ⓦ lavender-room.co.uk; map p.172. Stylish boutique selling fragrances, lingerie, jewellery and vintage-inspired home accessories. Mon–Sat 10am–6pm, Sun 11am–5pm.

Pecksniffs 45–46 Meeting House Lane, BN1 1HB ☏ 01273 723292, ⓦ pecksniffs.com; map p.172. Independent British fragrance house in the Lanes, selling a range of perfumes, bespoke blends and body products. Mon–Sat 11am–5pm, Sun 10.30am–4pm.

Resident 28 Kensington Gardens, BN1 4AL ☏ 01273 606312, ⓦ resident-music.com; map p.172. Award-winning independent record shop in North Laine; it also sells tickets for local venues. Mon–Sat 9am–6.30pm, Sun 10am–6pm.

Snoopers Paradise 7–8 Kensington Gardens ☏ 01273 602558; map p.172. Huge North Laine flea market containing over ninety different stalls over two floors; don't miss Snoopers Attic (ⓦ snoopersattic.co.uk), a "vintage makers' boutique" up on the first floor. Mon–Sat 10am–6pm, Sun 11am–4pm.

Arundel

The hilltop town of **ARUNDEL**, eighteen miles west of Brighton, has for seven centuries been the seat of the dukes of Norfolk, whose fine **castle** looks over the valley of the River Arun. The medieval town's well-preserved appearance and picturesque setting draws in the crowds on summer weekends, but at any other time a visit reveals one of West Sussex's least spoilt old towns. The main attraction is the castle, but the rest of Arundel is pleasant to wander round, with some good independent shops, cafés and restaurants on the High Street and Tarrant Street.

Arundel Castle

Mill Rd, BN18 9AB • April–Oct Tues–Sun & bank hols: keep 10am–4.30pm; Fitzalan Chapel & grounds 10am–5pm; castle rooms noon–5pm • Castle rooms, keep, grounds & chapel £18; keep, grounds & chapel £13; grounds & chapel £11 • ☏ 01903 882173, ⓦ arundelcastle.org

Despite its medieval appearance, much of **Arundel Castle** is comparatively new, the result of lavish reconstructions from 1718 onwards, after the original Norman structure was badly damaged in the Civil War. One of the oldest parts is the twelfth-century **keep**, from which you can peer down to the current duke's spacious residence. Inside the main castle, highlights include the impressive **Barons Hall** and the **library**, which has paintings by Van Dyck, Gainsborough and Holbein. On the edge of the grounds, the fourteenth-century **Fitzalan Chapel** houses tombs of past dukes of Norfolk, including twin effigies of the seventh duke – one as he looked when he died, and one of his emaciated corpse.

Arundel Cathedral

Corner of Parson's Hill & London Rd, BN18 9AY • Daily 9am–6pm or dusk • Free • ☏ 01903 882297, ⓦ arundelcathedral.net

The flamboyant **Arundel Cathedral** was constructed in the 1870s by the fifteenth duke of Norfolk over a former Catholic church; its spire was designed by John Hansom, inventor of the hansom cab. Inside are the enshrined remains of St Philip Howard, the thirteenth earl, who was sentenced to death in 1585, accused of Catholic conspiracy against Elizabeth I's Protestant court. He died of dysentery in the Tower of London ten years later.

WWT Arundel Wetland Centre

Mill Rd, BN18 9PB • Daily: April to mid-Oct 9.30am–5.30pm; mid-Oct to March 9.30am–4.30pm • £11, under-17s £5.50 • ☎ 01903 883355, ⓦ wwt.org.uk/visit/arundel

The **WWT Arundel Wetland Centre**, a mile out of town, is home to endangered waterfowl from around the world, but a wander around the scenic 65-acre site can also turn up sightings of native wildlife, including water voles, kingfishers, sand martins, dragonflies and peregrines. Don't miss the tranquil, rustling **reedbed boardwalks** or the boat trips, probably your best chance of spotting water voles.

ARRIVAL AND INFORMATION   ARUNDEL

By train Arundel's station is half a mile south of the town centre over the river on the A27.

Destinations Brighton (hourly; 1hr 10min); Chichester (Mon–Sat 2 hourly, Sun hourly; 30–50min); London Victoria (every 30min; 1hr 20min).

By bus Buses from Brighton (Mon–Sat every 30min, Sun hourly; 2hr) arrive on either the High St or River Rd.

Tourist information There's a Visitor Information Point at Arundel Museum, opposite the castle entrance on Mill Road (daily 10am–4pm; ⓦ sussexbythesea.com).

ACCOMMODATION AND EATING

Bay Tree 21 Tarrant St, BN18 9DG ☎ 01903 883679, ⓦ thebaytreearundel.co.uk. Cosy and relaxed little restaurant squeezed into three low-beamed rooms, with a small terrace out the back. Mains such as pheasant breast wrapped in bacon cost £16–18 at dinner; lunch features simpler dishes. Mon–Fri 11.30am–2.45pm & 6.30–9.30pm, Sat & Sun 10.30am–4.30pm & 6.30–9.30pm.

George and Dragon Inn Burpham ☎ 01903 883131, ⓦ georgeatburpham.co.uk. Three miles from Arundel (a lovely walk up the east bank of the river), this seventeenth-century pub has bags of character, plenty of Sussex ales on tap and a seasonal, local menu that runs from ciabattas (£6.50) to burgers (£12.50), fish, salads and steaks. Mon–Fri 10.30am–3pm & 6–11pm, Sat 10.30am–11pm, Sun 10.30am–10pm; kitchen Mon–Fri noon–2.30pm & 6–9pm, Sat noon–3pm & 6–9.30pm, Sun noon–4pm & 6–8.30pm.

Swan Hotel 27–29 High St, BN18 9AG ☎ 01903 882314, ⓦ swanarundel.co.uk. Fifteen smart rooms above a pub, decked out in shabby-chic style, with shutters and bare boards or coir carpets, and seaside prints on the wall. Prices fluctuate according to demand. **£99**

Midhurst and around

Lying right in the centre of the South Downs National Park, and home to the park's headquarters, the small market town of **MIDHURST** has plenty of charm and a lovely location, surrounded by swathes of gorgeous countryside. Midhurst grew up around the medieval market in **Market Square**, still the most attractive corner of town. If you're visiting on a summer weekend, don't miss the atmospheric **Cowdray Ruins** at the northern end of town (June–Aug Sat, Sun & bank hols 11am–4pm; £6.50; ☎ 01730 810781, ⓦ cowdray.org.uk); before it was gutted by fire in 1793, the house was one of the grandest homes in the country.

Petworth House

Petworth, GU28 9LR • **House** Mid-March to early Nov daily 11am–5pm; rest of year opening hours vary – check website • **Pleasure Ground** Daily: Feb 10am–4pm; early March 10am–4.30pm; mid-March to Oct daily 10am–5pm; Nov–Jan 10am–3.30pm • House and Pleasure Ground mid-March to early Nov £13.50, rest of year £7.20; NT • ☎ 01798 342207, ⓦ nationaltrust.org.uk/petworth • Train to Pulborough, then Stagecoach Coastline #1 bus (Mon–Sat hourly, Sun every 2hr)

Seven miles east of Arundel, the pretty little town of Petworth is dominated by **Petworth House**, one of the southeast's most impressive stately homes. Built in the late seventeenth

---

THE SOUTH DOWNS NATIONAL PARK

The **South Downs National Park** came into being in 2010. Covering over six hundred square miles, it stretches for 70 miles from eastern Hampshire through to the chalk cliffs of East Sussex, encompassing rolling hills, heathland, woodland and coastline. More than 112,000 people live and work in the national park – more than in any other – and it is crisscrossed by a dense network of over 1800 miles of footpaths and bridleways. The park's headquarters and visitor centre, the South Downs Centre, is in Midhurst. ⓦ **southdowns.gov.uk** has comprehensive information on public transport, walks, cycling, horseriding and other activities, plus an events calendar.

2

---

century, the house is stuffed with treasures – including the 1592 Molyneux globe, believed to be the earliest terrestrial globe in existence – and contains an outstanding art collection, with paintings by Van Dyck, Titian, Gainsborough, Bosch, Reynolds, Blake and Turner (the last a frequent guest here). The 700-acre **grounds**, home to a large herd of fallow deer, were landscaped by Capability Brown and are considered one of his finest achievements.

ARRIVAL AND INFORMATION

By train and bus The closest stations are at Haslemere (connected by bus #70 to Midhurst: Mon–Sat hourly; 25min), Petersfield (bus #92: Mon–Sat hourly; 25min) and Chichester (bus #60: Mon–Sat every 30min, Sun hourly; 40min).

South Downs Centre Capron House, North St, GU29 9DH (Mon–Thurs 9am–5pm, Fri 9am–4.30pm; May–Sept

MIDHURST AND AROUND

also Sat 9am–1pm; ⓣ 01730 814810, ⓦ southdowns. gov.uk). The visitor centre of the South Downs National Park contains a small exhibition about the National Park, and has plenty of leaflets and information on walks and public transport. There's also information on Midhurst (ⓦ visitmidhurst.com), including town maps and trails.

ACCOMMODATION AND EATING

The Church House Church Hill, GU29 9NX ⓣ 01730 812990, ⓦ churchhousemidhurst.com. A great location by Market Square, five gorgeous rooms, and home-made cake on arrival are just some of the things to love about this B&B. **£140**

★ **Horse Guards Inn** Upperton Rd, Tillington, GU28 9AF ⓣ 01798 342332, ⓦ thehorseguardsinn.co.uk. Lovely little gastropub between Midhurst and Petworth; in summer you can grab a deckchair (or hay-bale) in the idyllic garden. Harveys and guest ales on tap, plus excellent

seasonal food (mains around £15). Daily noon–midnight; kitchen Mon–Thurs noon–2.30pm & 6.30–9pm, Fri noon–2.30pm & 6–9.30pm, Sat noon–3pm & 6–9.30pm, Sun noon–3.30pm & 6.30–9pm. **£100**

The Olive & Vine North Street, GU29 9DJ ⓣ 01730 859532, ⓦ theoliveandvine.co.uk. Popular, contemporary restaurant-bar that covers all bases, from morning coffee through to evening meals (burgers, salads, *moules frites*) and late-night cocktails. Daily 9am–late; kitchen daily noon–9pm.

Chichester and around

The handsome city of **CHICHESTER** has plenty to recommend it: a splendid twelfth-century **cathedral**, a thriving cultural scene and the outstanding **Pallant House Gallery**. The city began life as a Roman settlement, and its Roman cruciform street plan is still evident in the four-quadrant symmetry of the town centre. The main streets lead off from the Gothic **Market Cross**, a bulky octagonal rotunda topped by ornate finials and a crown lantern spire, built in 1501 to provide shelter for the market traders. The big attraction outside Chichester is **Fishbourne Roman Palace**, the largest excavated Roman site in Britain.

Chichester Cathedral

West St, PO19 1RP • Mon–Sat 7.15am–6.30pm, Sun 7.15am–5pm; tours (45min) Mon–Sat 11.15am & 2.30pm • Free • ⓣ 01243 782595, ⓦ chichestercathedral.org.uk

The city's chief attraction is the fine Gothic **Chichester Cathedral**. Building began in 1076, but the church was extensively rebuilt following a fire a century later and has

2

been only minimally modified since about 1300, except for the slender spire and the unique, freestanding fifteenth-century bell tower. The **interior** is renowned for modern devotional art, which includes a stained-glass window by Marc Chagall and an altar-screen tapestry by John Piper. Older treasures include a sixteenth-century painting in the north transept of the past bishops of Chichester, and the fourteenth-century Fitzalan tomb that inspired Philip Larkin to write *An Arundel Tomb*. However, the highlight is a pair of carvings created around 1140, the **Chichester Reliefs**, which show the raising of Lazarus and Christ at the gate of Bethany; originally brightly coloured, with semiprecious stones set in the figures' eyes, the reliefs are among the finest Romanesque stone carvings in England.

Pallant House Gallery

9 North Pallant, PO19 1TJ • Tues, Wed, Fri & Sat 10am–5pm, Thurs 10am–8pm, Sun & bank hols 11am–5pm • £10, Tues £5, Thurs 5–8pm permanent collection free (£5 for temporary exhibitions) • ☎ 01243 774557, ⓦ pallant.org.uk

Off South Street, in the well-preserved Georgian quadrant of the city known as the Pallants, you'll find **Pallant House Gallery**, a superlative collection of twentieth-century British art housed in a Queen Anne townhouse and award-winning contemporary extension. Artists whose works are on display in the permanent collection include Henry Moore, Lucian Freud, Walter Sickert, Barbara Hepworth and Peter Blake, and there are also excellent temporary exhibitions.

Fishbourne Roman Palace

Salthill Rd, Fishbourne, PO19 3QR, 2 miles west of Chichester • Daily: Feb & Nov to mid-Dec 10am–4pm; March–Oct 10am–5pm • £9.20 • ☎ 01243 789829, ⓦ sussexpast.co.uk • Train from Chichester to Fishbourne (hourly; 3min); turn right from the station and the palace is a few minutes' walk away

Fishbourne is the largest and best-preserved Roman dwelling in the country. Roman relics have long been turning up hereabouts, and in 1960 a workman unearthed their source – the site of a depot constructed by the invading Romans in 43 AD, which is thought later to have become the vast, hundred-room palace of a Romanized Celtic aristocrat. The one surviving wing, the north wing, displays floor mosaics depicting Fishbourne's famous dolphin-riding cupid as well as the more usual geometric patterns. An audiovisual programme portrays the palace as it would have been in Roman times, and the extensive gardens attempt to re-create the palace grounds.

ARRIVAL AND INFORMATION   CHICHESTER AND AROUND

By train Chichester's train station lies on Stockbridge Rd; it's a 10min walk north to the Market Cross.

Destinations Arundel (Mon–Sat 2 hourly, Sun hourly; 30–50min); Brighton (2 hourly; 45–55min); London Victoria (Mon–Sat 2 hourly, Sun hourly; 1hr 35min); Portsmouth Harbour (Mon–Sat every 15min, Sun every 30min; 25–40min).

By bus The bus station is across the road from the train station, on Southgate.

Destinations Brighton (every 20–30min; 1hr 45min); Midhurst (Mon–Sat every 30min, Sun hourly; 40min); Portsmouth (hourly; 55min).

Tourist information At the Novium Museum, Tower St (April–Oct Mon–Sat 10am–5pm, Sun 10am–4pm; Nov–March Mon–Sat 10am–5pm, Sun 10am–4pm; ☎ 01243 775888, ⓦ visitchichester.org).

ACCOMMODATION AND EATING

4 Canon Lane 4 Canon Lane, PO19 1PX ☎ 01243 813586, ⓦ chichestercathedral.org.uk. Eight-bedroom Victorian house owned by the cathedral and located in its grounds. Rooms are big and comfortable, with art on the walls lent by Pallant House Gallery. Breakfast costs extra (£8.95). **£99**

Field & Fork 4 Guildhall St, PO19 1NJ ☎ 01243 789915,

ⓦ fieldandfork.co.uk. One of the best places to eat in the city, serving imaginative, locally sourced food, such as wild sea trout with local broad beans or maple-glazed short rib of beef (£12–19). Tues–Sat 11.30am–3pm & 5pm–late.

★ **Musgrove House B&B** 63 Oving Rd, PO19 7EN ☎ 01243 790179, ⓦ musgrovehouse.co.uk. Great-value boutique B&B, just a short walk from the centre, with three lovely rooms and super-friendly owners. **£90**

Park Tavern 11 Priory Rd ☎01243 785057, ⓦpark tavernchichester.co.uk. Overlooking Priory Park, this is one of the city's nicest pubs. Good-value home-made food (around the £10 mark), plus sandwiches and ploughman's. Fuller's on tap, plus a guest ale. Live music on Sun afternoons. Mon–Sat 11am–11pm, Sun noon–10.30pm; kitchen Mon noon–3pm, Tues–Fri noon–3pm & 6–9pm, Sat 11am–9pm, Sun noon–4pm.

2

Hampshire, Dorset and Wiltshire

SIKA DEER, ISLE OF PURBECK, DORSET

Hampshire, Dorset and Wiltshire

The distant past is perhaps more tangible in Hampshire (often abbreviated to "Hants"), Dorset and Wiltshire than in any other part of England. Predominantly rural, these three counties overlap substantially with the ancient kingdom of Wessex, whose most famous ruler, Alfred, repulsed the Danes in the ninth century and came close to establishing the first unified state in England. And even before Wessex came into being, many earlier civilizations had left their stamp on the region. The chalky uplands of Wiltshire boast several of Europe's greatest Neolithic sites, including Stonehenge and Avebury, while in Dorset you'll find Maiden Castle, the most striking Iron Age hillfort in the country, and the Cerne Abbas Giant, source of many a legend.

3

The Romans tramped all over these southern counties, leaving the most conspicuous signs of their occupation at the amphitheatre at **Dorchester** – though that town is more closely associated with Thomas Hardy and his vision of Wessex. None of the landscapes of this region are grand or wild, but the countryside is consistently seductive, not least the crumbling fossil-bearing cliffs around **Lyme Regis**, the managed woodlands of the **New Forest** and the gentle, open curves of Salisbury Plain. The area's historic towns such as **Sherborne**, **Shaftesbury** and **Bridport** are generally modest and slow-paced, with the notable exceptions of the two major maritime bases of **Portsmouth** and **Southampton**, a fair proportion of whose visitors are simply passing through on their way to the more genteel pleasures of the **Isle of Wight**. The two great cathedral cities in these parts, **Salisbury** and **Winchester**, and the seaside resorts of **Bournemouth** and **Weymouth** see most tourist traffic, while the great houses of Wilton, Stourhead, Longleat and Kingston Lacy also attract the crowds. You don't have to wander far off the beaten track, however, to find attractive villages such as **Lacock** and the appealing town of **Bradford-upon-Avon** – and, of course, some of the region's most dramatic coastal scenery around the **Isle of Purbeck**.

Portsmouth and around

Britain's foremost naval station, **PORTSMOUTH** occupies the bulbous peninsula of Portsea Island, on the eastern flank of a huge, easily defended harbour. Billing itself as Britain's only island city, it is also its most densely populated, with over 15,000 people per square mile. The ancient Romans raised a fortress on the northernmost edge of this inlet, but the strategic location wasn't fully exploited until Tudor times, when Henry VII established the world's first dry dock here and made Portsmouth a royal dockyard. It has flourished ever since and nowadays Portsmouth is a large industrialized city, its harbour clogged with naval frigates, ferries bound for the continent or the Isle of Wight, and swarms of tugs.

Boats to Gosport p.189
The Isle of Wight Steam Railway
    p.194
The Watercress Line p.200

The Real Downton Abbey p.201
Lyme's Jurassic coast p.222
Stonehenge – a brief history
    p.226

DURDLE DOOR, DORSET

Highlights

❶ Osborne House Wander around the stunning gardens and get an insight into royal family life at Queen Victoria's former seaside home. See page 197

❷ The New Forest William the Conqueror's old hunting ground, home to wild ponies and deer, is ideal for walking, biking and riding. See page 202

❸ Sea kayaking in Studland View the rugged Old Harry Rocks up close on a guided kayak tour through sea arches and below towering chalk cliffs. See page 212

❹ Durdle Door Famous natural arch at the end of a splendid beach, accessed by a steep cliff path – a great place for walkers and swimmers alike. See page 214

❺ Seaside Boarding House, Burton Bradstock Down a Daiquiri on the terrace while watching the sun set over this stunning stretch of coast. See page 221

❻ Lyme Regis Enjoy one of the most historic and picturesque villages on the south coast. See page 221

❼ Stonehenge Marvel at one of Britain's most iconic sites, which is now much enhanced by an informative, environmentally friendly visitor centre. See page 226

HIGHLIGHTS ARE MARKED ON THE MAP ON PAGE 186

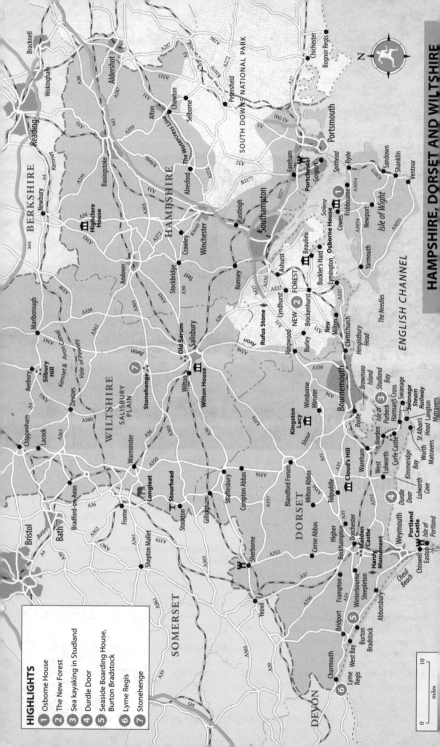

Due to its military importance, Portsmouth was heavily bombed during World War II, and bland tower blocks now give the city an ugly profile. Only **Old Portsmouth**, around the original harbour, preserves some Georgian and a little Tudor character. East of here is **Southsea**, an attractive suburb of terraces facing a large common and a shingle beach.

Portsmouth Historic Dockyard

Victory Gate, HM Naval Base, PO1 3LJ • Daily: April–Oct 10am–5.30pm; Nov–March 10am–5pm; last entry 1hr before closing • All-inclusive ticket £35, under-16s £15 (online £28/£12); individual attraction tickets £18; all tickets valid for one year • ☎ 023 9283 9766, ⓦ historicdockyard.co.uk

For most visitors, a trip to Portsmouth begins and ends at the **Historic Dockyard**, in the **Royal Naval Base** at the end of Queen Street. The complex comprises three ships and several museums. In addition, the Dockyard Apprentice exhibition gives insights into the working of the docks in the early twentieth century, while Action Stations provides interactive activities and simulators, plus the UK's tallest indoor climbing tower.

HMS Warrior

Portsmouth Historic Dockyard's youngest ship, **HMS Warrior**, dates from 1860. It was Britain's first armoured (iron-clad) battleship, complete with sails and steam engines. The ship displays a wealth of weaponry, including rifles, pistols and sabres, though the *Warrior* was never challenged nor even fired a cannon in her 22 years at sea.

Mary Rose Museum

The impressive **Mary Rose Museum** was built around Henry VIII's flagship, the **Mary Rose**, and houses not only the ship itself, but also thousands of objects retrieved from the wreck, including guns, gold and the crew's personal effects. The ship capsized before the king's eyes off Spithead in 1545 while engaging French intruders, sinking with almost all her seven-hundred-strong crew. In 1982 a massive conservation project raised the remains of the hull, which silt had preserved beneath the seabed, and you can now view the world's only remaining sixteenth-century warship through protective glass windows.

HMS Victory

Currently undergoing restoration (though still open to the public), **HMS Victory** was already forty years old when she set sail from Portsmouth for Trafalgar on September 14, 1805, returning in triumph three months later, but bearing the corpse of Admiral Nelson. Shot at the height of the battle, Nelson expired three hours later, having been assured that victory was in sight. A plaque on the deck marks the spot where Nelson was fatally wounded and you can also see the wooden cask in which his body was preserved in brandy for the return trip to Britain. Although badly damaged in the battle, the *Victory* continued in service for a further twenty years, before being retired to the dry dock where she rests today.

National Museum of the Royal Navy

Opposite the *Victory*, various buildings house the exhaustive **National Museum of the Royal Navy**. Tracing naval history from Alfred the Great's fleet to the present day, the collection includes some jolly figureheads, Nelson memorabilia, including the only surviving sail from HMS *Victory*, and nautical models, though there's scant coverage of more recent conflicts. The Trafalgar Experience is a noisy, vivid re-creation of the battle itself, with gory bits to thrill the kids.

Royal Navy Submarine Museum

Haslar Jetty, Gosport, PO12 2AS • Daily: April–Oct 10am–5.30pm; Nov–March Wed–Sun 10am–4.30pm (daily in school hols); last HMS *Alliance* tour 1hr before closing • £13.50 • ☎ 023 9251 0354, ⓦ submarine-museum.co.uk

Portsmouth's naval theme persists throughout otherwise humdrum Gosport, where the **Royal Navy Submarine Museum** displays, unsurprisingly, submarines – four in total, some of which you can enter. Allow a good couple of hours to explore these slightly creepy vessels – a guided **tour** inside HMS *Alliance* (the only remaining World War II-era submarine) gives you a gloomy insight into how cramped life on board would have been, and the museum elaborates evocatively on the history of submersible craft.

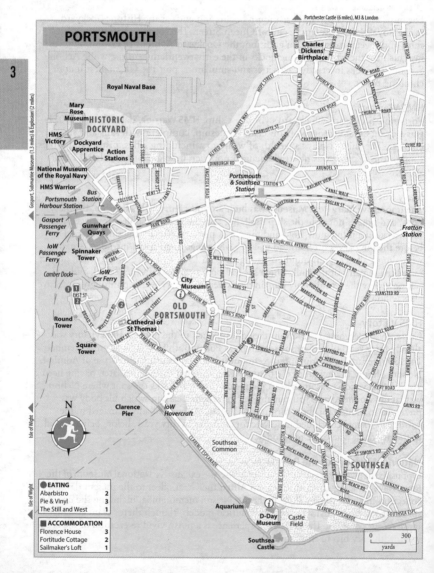

PORTSMOUTH

Portchester Castle (6 miles), M3 & London

Charles Dickens' Birthplace

Royal Naval Base

HISTORIC DOCKYARD

Mary Rose Museum

HMS Victory

Dockyard Apprentice   Action Stations

National Museum of the Royal Navy

HMS Warrior

Portsmouth Harbour Station   Bus Station

Gosport Passenger Ferry

Gunwharf Quays

IoW Passenger Ferry   Spinnaker Tower

Camber Docks   IoW Car Ferry

Round Tower

Square Tower

Portsmouth & Southsea Station

City Museum

OLD PORTSMOUTH

Cathedral of St Thomas

Clarence Pier   IoW Hovercraft

Southsea Common

Aquarium

D-Day Museum   Castle Field

Southsea Castle

SOUTHSEA

Gosport, Submarine Museum (1.3 miles) & Explosion! (2 miles)

Isle of Wight

Isle of Wight

N

0   300   yards

EATING

Ababistro	2
Pie & Vinyl	3
The Still and West	1

ACCOMMODATION

Florence House	3
Fortitude Cottage	2
Sailmaker's Loft	1

3

BOATS TO GOSPORT

Gosport can be reached on the **passenger ferry** from Harbour train station jetty between the historic dockyard and Gunwharf Quays (daily 5.30am–midnight every 10–15min; 5min; £3.40 return; ☎ 023 9252 4551, ⓦ gosportferry.co.uk). If you have an all-inclusive ticket for Portsmouth Historic Dockyard, you can take the hourly **Waterbus** shuttle (Nov–March Sat & Sun 10.15am–4.15pm) between the Historic Dockyard, Gunwharf Quays, the Submarine Museum and Explosion!

Explosion! The Museum of Naval Firepower

Priddy's Hard, Gosport, PO12 4LE • April–Oct daily 10am–5pm; Nov–March Sat & Sun 10am–4pm; last entry 1hr before closing • £10.80 • ☎ 023 9250 5600, ⓦ explosion.org.uk

Near the Royal Submarine Museum, housed in an old armaments depot, **Explosion!** tells the story of naval warfare from the days of gunpowder to the present, with weapons of all descriptions, including mines, big guns and torpedoes, all backed up by vivid computer animations.

3

Spinnaker Tower

Gunwharf Quays, PO1 3TT • Daily 10am–5.30pm; open from 9.30am in the school summer hols • £10.50, or £8.90 online • ☎ 023 9285 7520, ⓦ www.spinnakertower.co.uk

From Portsmouth Harbour train station, it's a short walk along the historic waterfront to the sleek modern **Gunwharf Quays** development, where you'll find a multitude of cafés, restaurants, nightspots and shops. Here you'll find **Spinnaker Tower**, an elegant, 557ft-high sail-like structure, offering **views** of up to twenty miles over land and sea. Its three viewing decks can be reached by a high-speed lift, the highest one being open to the elements, though most people stick to View Deck 1, which has one of Europe's largest glass floors.

Old Portsmouth

It's a well-signposted fifteen-minute walk south of Gunwharf Quays to what remains of **Old Portsmouth**. Along the way, you pass the simple **Cathedral of St Thomas** on the High Street (ⓦ portsmouthcathedral.org.uk), whose original twelfth-century features have been obscured by rebuilding after the Civil War and again in the twentieth century. The High Street ends at a maze of cobbled Georgian streets huddling behind a fifteenth-century wall protecting the **Camber**, or old port, where Walter Raleigh landed the first potatoes and tobacco from the New World. Nearby, the Round and Square towers are popular vantage points for observing the comings and goings of the boats.

D-Day Museum

Clarence Esplanade, Southsea, PO5 3NT • Daily: April–Sept 10am–5.30pm; Oct–March 10am–5pm; last entry 30min before closing • £6.80 • ☎ 023 9282 6722, ⓦ ddaymuseum.co.uk

Located in the suburb of **Southsea**, southeast of Old Portsmouth, the **D-Day Museum** focuses on Portsmouth's role as the principal assembly point for the Normandy beach landings in World War II, code-named "Operation Overlord". The most striking exhibit is the 295ft-long Overlord Embroidery, a sort of twentieth-century Bayeux Tapestry, which took five years to complete. The museum was undergoing substantial refurbishment at the time of going to press, so check the website for the latest details.

Southsea Castle

Clarence Esplanade, Southsea, PO5 3PA • March–Oct Tues–Sun & bank hols 10am–5pm • Free • ☎ 023 9282 6722, ⓦ southseacastle.co.uk

Next door to the D-Day Museum, Southsea's most historic building, marked by a little lighthouse, is the squat **Southsea Castle**, built from the remains of Beaulieu Abbey (see page 204). You can go inside the keep and learn about Portsmouth's military history, and can climb up to the spot from where Henry VIII is said to have watched the *Mary Rose* sink in 1545 (see page 187). There's also an appealing café inside the castle walls and courtyard.

Charles Dickens' Birthplace

393 Old Commercial Rd, PO1 4QL • April–Sept Fri–Sun 10am–5.30pm, last entry 5pm • £4.20, free for Portsmouth residents • ☎ 023 9282 7261, ⓦ charlesdickensbirthplace.co.uk

Just over a mile northeast of Old Portsmouth, **Charles Dickens' Birthplace** is set up to look much as it would have been when the famous novelist was born here in 1812. Charles's father, John, moved to Portsmouth in 1809 to work for the Navy Pay Office before he was recalled to London in 1815, so Charles only lived here for three years, but nevertheless he is said to have returned often and set parts of *Nicholas Nickleby* in the city. The modest house not only contains period furniture (including the couch on which he died) but also a wealth of information about the time when Dickens lived here.

Portchester Castle

Church Rd, Portchester, PO16 9QW • April–Sept daily 10am–6pm; Oct daily 10am–5pm; Nov–March Sat & Sun (daily in Feb half term) 10am–4pm • £6.20; EH • ☎ 02392 378291, ⓦ www.english-heritage.org.uk/visit/places/portchester-castle • Bus #3 stops a quarter of a mile from the castle and Portchester train station is a mile away

Six miles northwest of the centre, just past the marina development, **Portchester Castle** was built by the Romans in the third century, and boasts the finest surviving example of Roman walls in northern Europe – still over 20ft high and incorporating twenty bastions. The Normans felt no need to make substantial alterations when they moved in, but Henry II later built a keep within Portchester's precincts, which Richard II extended and Henry V used as his garrison when assembling the army that was to fight the Battle of Agincourt.

ARRIVAL AND INFORMATION

PORTSMOUTH AND AROUND

By train Portsmouth's main station is in the city centre, but the line continues to Harbour Station, the most convenient stop for the dockyard sights and old town.

Destinations Brighton (every 30min; 1hr 20min–1hr 30min); London Waterloo (every 15–20min; 1hr 35min–2hr 15min); Salisbury (hourly; 1hr 15min); Southampton (every 20min; 45min–1hr); Winchester (hourly; 1hr).

By bus National Express buses stop at The Hard Interchange, right by Harbour Station.

Destinations London Victoria (hourly; 1hr 50min–2hr 30min); Southampton (hourly; 40min–1hr).

By ferry Wightlink passenger catamarans leave from the jetty at Harbour Station for Ryde (see page 193), while car ferries depart from the ferry port off Gunwharf Rd, just south of Gunwharf Quays, for Fishbourne (see page 193). Hovercraft link Southsea with Ryde (see page 193), while ferries run regularly from the Harbour Station to Gosport, on the other side of Portsmouth Harbour (see page 189).

Tourist offices There are two tourist offices in Portsmouth (☎ 023 9282 6722, ⓦ visitportsmouth.co.uk), one in the City Museum, 2 Museum Rd (daily 10am–5.30pm), the other in the D-Day Museum (see page 189).

ACCOMMODATION

Florence House 2 Malvern Rd, Southsea, PO5 2NA ☎ 023 9200 9111, ⓦ florencehousehotel.co.uk; map p.188. Tasteful boutique B&B in an Edwardian townhouse with a range of rooms over three floors, all spick and span and with flatscreen TVs. There's a tiny downstairs bar and communal lounge, and parking permits can be provided.

If it's full, check out the other boutique-style hotels in the area run by the same group (the Mercer Collection). **£95**

Fortitude Cottage 51 Broad Street, PO1 2JD ☎ 023 9282 3748, ⓦ fortitudecottage.co.uk; map p.188. Stylish B&B in Portsmouth Old Town overlooking the ferry terminal and Gunwharf Quays. The top-floor room has its

own roof terrace with fantastic views, and three others have harbour views (though not all do). Free parking. **£170**
Sailmaker's Loft 5 Bath Square, PO1 2JL ☎ 023 9282 3045, ⓦ sailmakersloft.org.uk; map p.188. Recently renovated, this modern B&B is set just back from the waterfront, right opposite *The Still* pub, with top-floor rooms overlooking the water. Most rooms have their own bathroom. **£70**

EATING

Abarbistro 58 White Hart Rd, PO1 2JA ☎ 023 9281 1585, ⓦ abarbistro.co.uk; map p.188. Lively bar/restaurant with an outside terrace on the edge of Old Portsmouth. The menu features popular classics such as pork belly (£16.50) and steaks (£22.50), plus daily-changing fish specials. Mon–Sat 11am–11pm, Sun noon–10pm.

Pie and Vinyl 61 Castle Road, Southsea, PO5 3AY ☎ 023 9275 3914 ⓦ pieandvinyl.co.uk; map p.188. Part café, part hip shop selling – as the name suggests – records and pies. It's a great space for browsing and chilling, with

a wide range of tasty pies on offer (from £6; extra for mash, peas and gravy) – there are also vegan options. Mon–Sat 11am–9pm, Sun 11am–5pm.

The Still and West 2 Bath Square, Old Portsmouth, PO1 2JL ☎ 023 9282 1567, ⓦ stillandwest.co.uk; map p.188. A waterfront terrace and cosy interior with harbour views make this pub worth stopping by. Food ranges from fish and chips (£13.50) to thyme-roasted chicken (£14). Mon–Sat 9.30am–11pm, Sun 9.30am–10.30pm; kitchen Mon–Fri noon–9pm, Sat noon–10pm, Sun noon–8pm.

Southampton

A glance at the map gives some idea of the strategic maritime importance of **SOUTHAMPTON**, which stands on a triangular peninsula formed at the place where the rivers Itchen and Test flow into Southampton Water, an eight-mile inlet from the Solent. Sure enough, Southampton has figured in numerous stirring events: it witnessed the exodus of Henry V's Agincourt-bound army, the Pilgrim Fathers' departure in the *Mayflower* in 1620 and the maiden voyages of such ships as the *Queen Mary* and the *Titanic*. Despite its pummelling by the Luftwaffe and some disastrous postwar urban sprawl, the thousand-year-old city has retained some of its medieval charm in parts and has reinvented itself as a twenty-first-century shopping centre in others, with the giant glass-and-steel **West Quay** as its focus. A short stroll north of here, Southampton's new **Cultural Quarter** is worth a visit, with its open squares, excellent art gallery and superb Sea City Museum.

City Art Gallery

Civic Centre, Commercial Rd • Mon–Fri 10am–3pm, Sat 10am–5pm • Free • ☎ 02380 833007, ⓦ southamptoncitygallery.com

Core of the modern town is the Civic Centre, a short walk east of the train station and home to the excellent **City Art Gallery**. Though not always on show at the same time, its collection is particularly strong on contemporary British artists, with works by Gilbert and George, Chris Ofili and Lucian Freud. You can also see works by older masters: Gainsborough, Joshua Reynolds and the Impressionists – Monet and Pissarro included.

Sea City Museum

Civic Centre, Havelock Rd, SO14 7FY • Daily 10am–5pm • £8.50, joint ticket with Tudor House £12 • ☎ 02380 833007, ⓦ seacitymuseum.co.uk

The purpose-built **Sea City Museum** is a triumph of design that succeeds in being both moving and fun. Opened on April 10, 2012, the hundredth anniversary of the day that the *Titanic* sailed from Southampton's Town Quay on its maiden voyage, the museum provides a fascinating insight into the history of the ship, its crew, its significance to Edwardian Southampton and, of course, its fateful journey, which started in high excitement and ended only four days later in tragedy. Impressive **interactive displays** give you the chance to steer the *Titanic* around the icebergs, while re-creations of a second-class cabin and the boiler room allow you to imagine life as both crew and passenger. **Interviews with survivors** of the disaster are particularly moving, with tales of children being put into hessian sacks and hauled up from the lifeboats onto the rescue ship, the *Carpathia*.

ARRIVAL AND INFORMATION   SOUTHAMPTON

By train Southampton's central station is in Blechynden Terrace, west of the Civic Centre.
Destinations Bournemouth (every 15–20min; 30min–1hr 10 min); London Waterloo (every 15–20min; 1hr 20min–1hr 35min); Portsmouth (every 20min; 45min–1hr); Salisbury (every 30min; 30–40min); Weymouth (every 30min; 1hr 20min–1hr 40min); Winchester (every 15min; 15–30min).
By bus National Express buses run from the coach station on Harbour Parade.

Destinations Bournemouth (roughly hourly; 45min–1hr); London Victoria (15 daily; 2hr–2hr 20min–2hr 45min); Portsmouth (13 daily; 50min–1hr); Salisbury (1 daily; 45min); Weymouth (3 daily; 2hr 40min–3hr) and Winchester (10 daily; 25–45min).
Tourist information The main tourist information point is in the Central Library of the Civic Centre, 8 Civic Centre Rd (Mon–Thurs 10am–6pm, Fri 10am–5pm, Sat 10am–4pm; ☎02380 833333, ⓦdiscoversouthampton.co.uk), where you can pick up leaflets, maps and guides to the city.

ACCOMMODATION

Ennios Town Quay Rd, SO14 2AR ☎02380 221159, ⓦennios.co.uk. In a former warehouse right on the waterfront, this boutique-style hotel has plush rooms with comfortable beds and smart bathrooms. The stylishly decorated rooms come with L'Occitane toiletries, and there's an excellent Italian restaurant downstairs. **£120**
★ **Pig in the Wall** 8 Western Esplanade, SO14 2AZ ☎02380 636900, ⓦthepighotel.com. Built into the city walls, Southampton's most stylish boutique hotel has been

cleverly renovated and beautifully decorated in a shabby-chic style. All the rooms have powerful showers and top-of-the range coffee machines – the large (pricier) rooms boast glamorous roll-top baths in the rooms themselves. There's a great bar/lounge/deli downstairs, or you can jump in one of the hotel Land Rovers, which will take you to their sister hotel/restaurant in the New Forest for dinner (see page 206). **£145**

EATING AND DRINKING

The Arthouse Gallery Café 178 Above Bar St, SO14 7DW ☎02380 238582, ⓦthearthousesouthampton. org. Friendly, community-run café which serves delicious home-made vegan and vegetarian dishes, such as sharing platters and Greek meze (both £9), as well as organic rum and craft beers. The café also hosts workshops, art exhibitions, knitting circles and live music; upstairs, there's a piano, comfy sofas and plenty of board games. Tues–Sat 10.30am–10pm, Sun noon–5pm.
Kuti's Royal Thai Pier Gate House, Royal Pier, SO14 2AQ ☎02380 339211, ⓦroyalthaipier.co.uk. Choose from the Thai tapas menu (mains from £9), the set menus or, best of all, the excellent five-course Sun lunch buffet (£12) at this superbly ornate waterside restaurant. The building was once a pier opened by the then Princess

Victoria in 1833, and has fine views over the water from the outside deck on summer evenings. Mon–Thurs noon–2.30pm & 5–10pm, Fri & Sat noon–2.30pm & 5pm–11pm, Sun noon–3pm & 5–10pm.
The Dancing Man Brewery Wool House, Town Quay, SO14 2AR ☎02380 836666, ⓦdancingmanbrewery. co.uk. The atmospheric fourteenth-century Wool House, a medieval warehouse, now houses a lively pub and micro-brewery, with the beers brewed on site in vast stills. The food is good – pies, burgers, steaks (£11–18) plus tasty sandwiches at lunch (£5–8) – with waiter service upstairs and bar service downstairs. There are tables outside and dogs are welcome too. Mon–Wed & Sun noon–11pm, Thurs–Sat noon–midnight; kitchen Mon–Sat noon–3pm & 6–9pm, Sun noon–5pm.

The Isle of Wight

The lozenge-shaped **ISLE OF WIGHT** has begun to shake off its old-fashioned image and attract a younger, livelier crowd, with a couple of major annual **rock festivals** and a scattering of fashionable hotels. Despite measuring less than 23 miles at its widest point, the island packs in a surprising variety of landscapes and coastal scenery. Its **beaches** have long attracted holiday-makers, and the island was a favourite of such eminent Victorians as Tennyson, Dickens, Swinburne, Julia Margaret Cameron and Queen Victoria herself, who made **Osborne House**, near Cowes, her permanent home after Albert died.

ARRIVAL AND DEPARTURE

THE ISLE OF WIGHT

There are three **ferry** departure points from the mainland – Portsmouth, Southampton and Lymington. **Fare** structures and **schedules** on all routes are labyrinthine, from £16 for a day-return foot-passenger ticket on the Southampton–West Cowes route in low season to over £100 for a high-season return for a car and four passengers on the Lymington–Yarmouth route: check the companies' websites for full details of current fares and schedules.

From Portsmouth Wightlink (ⓦwightlink.co.uk) runs car ferries from the Gunwharf Terminal to Fishbourne (45min), and a high-speed catamaran from the Harbour to Ryde (passengers only; 20min). Hovertravel (ⓦhovertravel. co.uk) runs hovercraft from Clarence Esplanade in Southsea to Ryde (passengers only; 10min).

From Southampton Red Funnel (ⓦredfunnel. co.uk) operates a high-speed catamaran to West Cowes (passengers only; 25min) and a car ferry to East Cowes (1hr).
From Lymington Wightlink (ⓦwightlink.co.uk) runs car ferries to Yarmouth (40min).

INFORMATION

Tourist information The helpful Visit Isle of Wight (ⓞ01983 521555, ⓦvisitisleofwight.co.uk) is a good source of information and runs the island's only tourist office; it's in The Guildhall, High St, Newport (Mon–Fri 10am–3pm).

GETTING AROUND

By train There are two train lines on the island: the seasonal Isle of Wight Steam Railway (ⓞ01983 882204, ⓦiwsteamrailway.co.uk) runs from Wootton Bridge to Smallbrook Junction, where it connects with the east-coast Island line from Ryde to Shanklin (every 20–40min; 25min; ⓦislandlinetrains.co.uk).
By bus Local buses are run by Southern Vectis (ⓞ01983 827000, ⓦislandbuses.info), who sell good-value tickets offering unlimited travel on their network (£10/day, £24/week).
By bike Cycling is a popular way of getting around the island, though in summer the narrow lanes can get very busy. For bike rental, contact Wight Cycle Hire (ⓞ01983 761800, ⓦwightcyclehire.co.uk, from £12/half-day, £16/day): its office is in Yarmouth, but it can deliver bikes anywhere on the island (minimum hire fee £50).

Ryde

As a major ferry terminal, **RYDE** is the first landfall many visitors make on the island, but one where few choose to linger, despite some grand nineteenth-century architecture and a fine sandy town **beach**.

Donald McGill Postcard Museum

The Royal Victoria Arcade, Union St, PO33 2LQ • Mon–Sat 11am–4pm • £3 • ⓞ01983 717435, ⓦsaucyseasidepostcards.com

Ryde's quirky little **Postcard Museum** crams in a good proportion of the twelve thousand saucy postcards created by artist Donald McGill. The cards, produced throughout the first half of the twentieth century, reached their peak of popularity in the 1930s. Packed with daft double entendres, the collection here also shows how far things have moved since the Obscene Publications Act regularly tried to have McGill's cards banned.

ARRIVAL AND DEPARTURE

RYDE

The **bus station**, **hovercraft** terminal and Esplanade **train station** are all near the base of the pier, while **catamarans** from Portsmouth dock at the Pier Head.

ACCOMMODATION AND EATING

The Boathouse Springvale Rd, Seaview, PO34 5AW, 2 miles east of Ryde ⓞ01983 810616, ⓦtheboat houseiow.co.uk. It's a pleasant 2-mile walk along the coast to this classy gastropub, whose garden boasts fantastic views across the Solent. A great spot for a drink, it also serves scampi and chips (£12), seafood platters (£10.50) and fresh fish of the day. It also has spacious en-suite rooms decorated in a contemporary style with iPod docks; superior rooms have sea views. Mon–Sat 9am–11pm, Sun 9am–10.30pm; kitchen Mon–Sat 9–11am & noon–9.30pm, Sun 9–11am & noon–9pm. **£130**
Olivo 32–33 Union St, PO33 2LE ⓞ01983 611118, ⓦolivorestaurant.co.uk/ryde. Tasty Italian dishes in a buzzy, stylish restaurant with bare-brick walls and an

THE ISLE OF WIGHT STEAM RAILWAY

The seasonal **Isle of Wight Steam Railway** (T 01983 882204, W iwsteamrailway.co.uk) makes the delightful ten-mile return trip from Smallbrook Junction (where it connects with the Island line) to Wootton Bridge, between Ryde and Newport. Its impeccably restored carriages in traditional green livery run through lovely unspoilt countryside, stopping at Ashey and Havenstreet, where there's a small museum of railway memorabilia. The adult return fare (£13, or £11.50 online) is valid for any travel on that day.

open kitchen. There are decent pizzas (£10–13) and pasta dishes (£10–15), plus some less usual main courses, such as seared duck breast (£17). Daily 9am–9pm.

Sorrento Lodge 11 The Strand PO33 2LG T 01983 812813 W sorrentolodge.co.uk. Very well kept B&B in a large townhouse with a seafront garden, run by a helpful couple. Some of the rooms have sea views, all are en suite, and the breakfasts are good. **£80**

Three Bouys Appley Lane, PO33 2DU T 01983 811212, W threebuoys.co.uk. Excellent food in a lovely setting in this upstairs restaurant with a large balcony overlooking Ryde beach. The decor is contemporary, with wooden floors and tables and big picture windows giving fantastic views over the Solent, and the food is well-cooked and -presented. Dishes include seared scallops (£9) and St Austell mussels (£15), and there are good vegetarian options. Mon–Fri noon–2.30pm & 6–9pm, Sat noon–3pm & 6–9.30pm, Sun noon–9pm.

Brading Roman Villa

Morton Old Rd, PO36 0PH • Daily 10am–5pm; last entry 4pm • £9.50 • T 01983 406223, W bradingromanvilla.org.uk • Bus #3 from Ryde or Sandown

Just south of the ancient village of **Brading**, on the busy Ryde to Sandown A3055, are the remains of **Brading Roman Villa**, which are renowned for their **mosaics**. This is the more impressive of two such villas on the island, both of which were probably sites of bacchanalian worship. The Brading site is housed in an attractive modern museum and its superbly preserved mosaics include intact images of Medusa and depictions of Orpheus. There's also a good café here.

Sandown

The traditional seaside resort of **SANDOWN** merges with Shanklin across the sandy reach of Sandown Bay, representing the island's holiday-making epicentre. This traditional 1960s bucket-and-spade resort has the island's only surviving pleasure **pier**, bedecked with traditional amusements and a large theatre, with nightly entertainment in season.

ARRIVAL AND DEPARTURE — SANDOWN

By train The Island line train station, served by trains from Ryde and Shanklin, is on Station Ave, about a 10min walk inland from the pier.

By Bus Buses #2 from Newport via Shanklin, or #3 & #8 from Ryde.

ACCOMMODATION AND EATING

The Belmore 101 Station Avenue PO36 8HD T 01983 404189, W belmorebandb.com. On a quiet street a short walk from the beach, this large Victorian house has been converted into a smart B&B. The comfortable rooms are decorated with stylish furnishings and have a marine vibe. Two-night minimum stay in summer. **£80**

The Reef The Esplanade, PO36 8AE T 01983 403219, W thereefsandown.co.uk. A bright bar/restaurant right on the seafront, with great views. It serves up a range of mid-priced dishes including pizzas, pasta and burgers (from £10), steaks (£18) and fresh fish (from £11). Daily 11am–11pm; kitchen daily noon–9pm.

Shanklin

SHANKLIN, with its auburn cliffs, Old Village and scenic Chine, has a marginally more sophisticated aura than its northern neighbour. The rose-clad, thatched **Old Village**

may be syrupy, but the adjacent **Shanklin Chine** (daily: April to late May 10am–5pm; late May to Sept 10am–10pm; late Oct 10am–8pm; £4.50 single visit, £5.50 return ticket valid for a week; ☎01983 866432, ⓦshanklinchine.co.uk), a twisting pathway descending a mossy ravine and decorated on summer nights with fairy lights, is undeniably picturesque; former resident John Keats once drew inspiration from the environs.

ARRIVAL AND DEPARTURE   SHANKLIN

By train The final stop on the Island Line from Ryde, Shanklin train station is about half a mile inland at the top of Regent St.

By bus The bus station (buses #2 & #3 from Ryde and Newport) is a little south of the train station, on Landguard Rd.

ACCOMMODATION, EATING AND DRINKING

Fisherman's Cottage Southern end of the Esplanade, at the bottom of Shanklin Chine, PO37 6BN ☎01983 863882, ⓦfishermanscottageshanklin.co.uk. An atmospheric nineteenth-century thatched pub right on the seafront, with outside tables: it's child-friendly and serves wholesome pub food, such as fish pie and cod and chips (mains around £11). Mid-March to Oct daily: pub 11am–10pm; kitchen noon–9pm.

Pendleton's 85 High Street, PO37 6NR ☎01983 868727, ⓦpendletons.org. Well-regarded restaurant serving local produce where possible, in dishes such as duck leg with champ mash, pork medallions (around £16) and pasta (from £12). Tues–Sat 6pm–11pm.

Rylstone Manor Rylstone Gardens, PO37 6RG ☎01983 862806, ⓦwww.rylstone-manor.co.uk. This superb Victorian pile, with period decor, sits right in the middle of the leafy public gardens at the top of the cliff. It has its own bar and dining room, though children under 16 are not allowed and in high season there is a 3-night minimum stay. **£145**

Ventnor

The seaside resort of **VENTNOR** and its two village suburbs of **Bonchurch** and **St Lawrence** sit at the foot of St Boniface Down, the island's highest point at 787ft. The Down periodically disintegrates into landslides, creating the jumbled terraces known as the **Undercliff**, whose sheltered, south-facing aspect, mild winter temperatures and thick carpet of undergrowth have contributed to the former fishing village becoming a fashionable health spa. Thanks to these unique factors, the town has rather more character than the island's other resorts, its Gothic Revival buildings clinging dizzily to zigzagging bends.

The floral terraces of the Cascade curve down to the slender Esplanade and narrow beach, where some of the former boat-builders' cottages now house shops, cafés and restaurants. From the Esplanade, it's a pleasant mile-long stroll to Ventnor's rolling **Botanical Gardens**, filled with exotic plants and impressive glasshouses (daily 10am–5pm; £9.50, valid for one week; ☎01983 855397, ⓦbotanic.co.uk).

ACCOMMODATION   VENTNOR

Hambrough Hotel Hambrough Rd, PO38 1SQ ☎01983 856333, ⓦthehambrough.com. Small, stylish, modern hotel with a chic bar. The comfortable rooms come with all the luxuries, including flatscreen TV and espresso machines; most have sea views, and some have balconies. **£150**

★ **The Leconfield** 85 Leeson Rd, Upper Bonchurch, PO38 1PU ☎01983 852196, ⓦleconfieldhotel.com. Friendly and comfortable B&B in attractive grounds overlooking the sea. The well-kept rooms are spacious, light and airy, and many have free-standing baths and sea views. The breakfast's delicious, and there's a heated pool in summer in the lovely garden. **£90**

EATING AND DRINKING

El Toro Contento 2 Pier St, PO38 1ST ☎01983 857600, ⓦeltorocontento.co.uk. A cosy restaurant dishing up home-made tapas, such as chorizo in cider and spicy mussels, most for under a fiver. Also serves Spanish hams and cheeses and will cook paella (around £11 a head, minimum 4 people) with 24hr notice. Summer daily 5–10pm; winter Thurs–Sun 4–10pm.

Spyglass Inn Ventnor Esplanade, PO38 1JX ☎01983 855338, ⓦthespyglass.com. Lively pub, with a terrace, in a great location on the seafront. You can eat giant portions of pub grub, such as fisherman's pie (most mains £10–12). Frequent live music, too. Daily 10am–11pm; kitchen daily noon–9.30pm.

★ **Wheelers Crab Shed** Steephill Cove, PO38 1AF ☎01983 855819. Delicious home-made crab pasties, sandwiches and mackerel ciabattas served from a pretty shack on the seashore. Also tasty local lobster salads and daily fish specials. Easter to October Mon & Wed–Sun (plus sunny weekends & hols in other months) noon–3pm.

The southwest coast

The western Undercliff begins to recede at the village of Niton, where a path continues to the most southerly tip of the island, **St Catherine's Point**, marked by a modern lighthouse. A prominent landmark on the downs behind is **St Catherine's Oratory**, known locally as the "Pepper Pot": originally a lighthouse, it reputedly dates from 1325. Seven miles northwest along the coast, Military Road ascends the flank of Compton Down before descending into Freshwater Bay. If you're walking this way, stop off at National Trust-owned **Compton Bay**, a splendid spot for a swim or picnic that's frequented by local surfers and accessed by a steep path from the dark red cliffs. On the coastal road at Freshwater Bay is **Dimbola Lodge** (April–Oct daily 10am–5pm, Oct–March Tues–Sun 10am–4pm; £5; ☎01983 756814, ⓦdimbola.co.uk), home to pioneer photographer **Julia Margaret Cameron**, who settled here after visiting Tennyson in 1860. The building now houses a gallery of her work plus changing exhibitions, and a room of memorabilia from the Isle of Wight festival. There's also a bookshop and tearoom/restaurant.

ACCOMMODATION

THE SOUTHWEST COAST

Tom's Eco Lodge Tapnell Farm, Newport Rd, PO41 0YJ ☎07717 666346, ⓦtomsecolodge.com. Set next to the Tapnell Farm animal park and activity centre (ⓦtapnellfarm.com) with stunning views over the distant Solent, these ready-erected, upmarket tents are the ultimate in glamping – they come complete with fridges, electricity, private hot-water showers and flushing toilets. Great for families. Minimum three-night stay. From **£192**

The Needles and Alum Bay

The breezy four-mile ridge of **Tennyson Down** running from Freshwater Bay to **The Needles** is one of the island's most satisfying walks, with vistas onto rolling downs and vales. On top of the Down, there's a monument to the eponymous poet, who lived on the island for forty years from 1853 until his death. At its western tip sits the **Needles Old Battery**, a gun emplacement built 250ft above the sea in 1863 (April–Oct daily 10.30am–5pm; fort may be closed in bad weather; £6.50, NT; ☎01983 754772, ⓦnationaltrust.org.uk/the-needles-old-battery-and-new-battery). There are fabulous views from here over the three tall chalk stacks known as **The Needles**, which jut out into the English Channel. Needles Pleasure Cruises runs **boat trips** round the Needles (April–Oct; £6; ☎01983 761587, ⓦwww.needlespleasurecruises.co.uk) from **Alum Bay**, a twenty-minute walk away. To catch the boat, you can take the cliff path or the chairlift (daily 10am–4pm; £6 return; ⓦwww.theneedles.co.uk), which descends the polychrome cliffs to ochre-hued sands.

Yarmouth

Four miles east of the Needles and linked to Lymington in the New Forest by car ferry, the pleasant north-coast town of **YARMOUTH** makes a lovely entrance to the island and is the best base for exploring its western tip. Although razed by the French in 1377, the port prospered after **Yarmouth Castle** (Easter–Oct daily 10am–4pm; £5.20, EH; ☎01983 760678, ⓦwww.english-heritage.org.uk/visit/places/yarmouth-castle), tucked between the quay and the pier, was commissioned by Henry VIII. Some of the rooms re-create life in a sixteenth-century castle, and there's also a display on the many wrecks that floundered here in the Solent, while the battlements afford superb views over the estuary. Yarmouth's only other sight is the Grade II listed **pier**, England's longest wooden pier still in use.

ACCOMMODATION AND EATING   YARMOUTH

The Blue Crab High St, PO41 0PL ☎01983 760014, ⓦthebluecrab.co.uk. A simply decorated restaurant, with cosy booths, that offers fish and shellfish dishes such as hake with mussel and leek sauce (£15). Also does top-quality fresh fish and chips from £8. Mon–Wed, Fri & Sat 11am–3pm & 6–11pm, Thurs 10am–3pm & 6–11pm, Sun 6–11pm.

The George Hotel Quay St, PO41 0PE ☎01983 760331, ⓦthegeorge.co.uk. In a great position right by the ferry dock, with a lovely garden overlooking the Solent, this seventeenth-century hotel has hosted the likes of Charles II in its time. The rooms are comfortable and elegantly furnished, some with balconies looking out over the water, and there are two excellent restaurants downstairs, specializing in local produce. Minimum two-night stay at weekends. £200

Off the Rails Station Rd, PO41 0QT ☎01983 761600, ⓦofftherailsyarmouth.co.uk. In the former station on a disused railway line that is now a popular cycle path, this cosy café has train-style banquettes and a wood-burner inside, while outside there are tables on the platform overlooking the River Yar. The food is good, if slightly pricey, with breakfasts such as smoked salmon and scrambled eggs (£10.50), tasty burgers (£12), and more unusual options for dinner such as duck cassoulet (£16). Wed, Thurs & Sun 9am–4pm, Fri & Sat 9am–10pm.

Cowes

COWES, at the island's northern tip, is associated with sailing and boat building: Henry VIII installed a castle to defend the Solent's expanding naval dockyards from the French and Spanish, and in the 1950s the world's first hovercraft made its test runs here. In 1820 the Prince Regent's patronage of the yacht club gave the port its cachet, and the Royal Yacht Squadron is now one of the world's most exclusive sailing clubs. The first week of August sees international yachting festival **Cowes Week** (ⓦlendycowesweek.co.uk), where serious sailors mingle with royalty, and most summer weekends have some form of nautical event.

The town is bisected by the River Medina, with **West Cowes** being the older, more interesting half. At the bottom of the meandering High Street, **boat trips** around the harbour and the Solent leave from Thetis Wharf, near the Parade (☎01983 564602, ⓦsolentcruises.co.uk). The more industrial **East Cowes**, where you'll find Osborne House, is connected to West Cowes by a "floating bridge", or chain ferry (approx every 10–15min, Mon–Sat 5–12.30am, Sun 6.30–12.30am; pedestrians £1.50 return, cars £2.60 single; ⓦiwfloatingbridge.co.uk, ☎01983 293041).

Osborne House

East Cowes, PO32 6JX · April–Sept daily 10am–6pm; Oct daily 10am–5pm; Nov–March Sat & Sun 10am–4pm · £16.20; EH · ☎01983 200022, ⓦwww.english-heritage.org.uk/visit/places/osborne · Bus #4 from Ryde or #5 from Newport, or either from East Cowes

The only place of interest in East Cowes is Queen Victoria's family home, **Osborne House**, a mile southeast of town. It was built in the late 1840s by Prince Albert and Thomas Cubitt in the style of an Italianate villa, with balconies and large terraces looking over the gardens to the Solent. The **state rooms**, used for entertaining visiting dignitaries, exude formality as one would expect – the Durbar Room, clad almost entirely in ivory, is particularly impressive – while the **private apartments** feel homely in a manner appropriate to the affluent family holiday residence that Osborne was. Following Albert's death, the desolate Victoria spent much of her time here, and it's where she eventually died in 1901. Since then, according to her wishes, the house has remained virtually unaltered, allowing an intimate glimpse into Victoria's family life. In the **grounds**, you can see the remains of a barracks with its own drawbridge, built by Prince Albert as a place where the boys could play soldiers, and Queen Victoria's original bathing machine, next to her private beach.

ACCOMMODATION

Albert Cottage York Ave, East Cowes, PO32 6BD ☎01983 299309, ⓦalbertcottagehotel.com. Adjacent to and once part of the Osborne estate, this lovely mansion has a country house feel. Rooms are very comfortable, and have flatscreen TVs; it has its own highly rated restaurant, too. **£140**

★ **Into the Woods** Lower Westwood, Brocks Copse Rd, Wootton, PO33 4NP ☎07769 696464, ⓦisleof wighttreehouse.com. Luxury treehouse (sleeps 4) and shepherds' huts (sleep 6) to rent on a farm three miles south of East Cowes. Both are beautifully finished and eco-friendly, with wood-burning stoves, en-suite showers,

and wi-fi. The location is peaceful, with chickens and geese, rope swings to play on and woods to run around in – the perfect combination of nature and home comforts. Two-night minimum stay off-season, up to seven nights minimum in Aug. Treehouse **£175**, huts **£150**

Villa Rothsay Baring Rd, West Cowes, PO31 8DF ☎01983 295178, ⓦvilla-rothsay.co.uk. Upmarket boutique hotel that's maintained its Victorian roots with period decor throughout – think curtains, ornate stairways and stained-glass windows. Some of the rooms have sea views and balconies (£10 extra) and there are great views from the grounds and raised patio area. **£145**

EATING AND DRINKING

The Coast Bar & Dining Room 14–15 Shooters Hill, West Cowes, PO31 7BG ☎01983 298574, ⓦthecoastbar. co.uk. Light and airy bar/restaurant with wooden floors and a lively, informal vibe. The menu features wood-fired pizzas (£9–12), plus the likes of seafood linguine (£14) and a good selection of steaks (from £19). Daily 9am–1am.

Folly Inn Folly Lane, Whippingham, PO32 6NB ☎01983 297171. A mile from Osborne House, this attractive waterside pub has the river lapping at its decks and is said to have replaced a French smuggler's barge that sold produce here in the 1700s. It serves decent pub food such as beef and ale pie (£11), plus tasty fajitas (£12). The

Folly Waterbus (☎07974 864627) runs a taxi service from Cowes to the jetty next to the pub. Daily 9am–10pm.

The Mess Canteen & Bar 63 High St, West Cowes, PO31 7RL ☎01983 280083. Completely decorated with recycled materials, this lively place serves great burgers – try tempura soft-shell crab or halloumi – and unusual salads like calamari or goats' cheese, all around £9–12. There's a good range of cocktails – the Isle of Wight jam-jar tea is tasty – the service is friendly and the vibe is fun. Mon–Thurs 11am–2.30pm & 6–9pm, Sat 11am–9.30pm, Sun 11am–3.30pm.

Newport

The capital of the Isle of Wight, **NEWPORT**, sits in the centre of the island at a point where the River Medina's commercial navigability ends. Though worth a visit to see the hilltop fortress of **Carisbrooke Castle**, the town itself isn't particularly engaging.

Carisbrooke Castle

Castle Hill, southwest of Newport, PO30 1XY • Feb half term daily 10am–4pm; late Feb & March Wed–Sun 10am–4pm; April–Sept daily 10am–6pm; Oct daily 10am–5pm; Nov to early Feb Sat & Sun 10am–4pm • £9.40; EH • ☎01983 523112, ⓦwww.english-heritage.org. uk/visit/places/carisbrook-castle • Bus #7 from Newport

The most famous resident of **Carisbrooke Castle**, a rather austere Norman pile, was Charles I, detained here (and caught one night ignominiously jammed between his room's bars while attempting escape) before his execution in London. The **museum** features relics from his incarceration, as well as those of the last royal resident, Princess Beatrice, Queen Victoria's youngest daughter. There's also a sixteenth-century well-house, where you can watch donkeys trudge around a huge treadmill to raise a barrel 160ft up the well shaft.

Winchester and around

Nowadays a tranquil, handsome market town, **WINCHESTER** was once one of the mightiest settlements in England. Under the Romans it was Venta Belgarum, the fifth-largest town in Britain, but it was **Alfred the Great** who really put Winchester on the map when he made it the capital of his Wessex kingdom in the ninth century. For the next two hundred years or so Winchester ranked alongside London, its status affirmed by William the Conqueror's coronation in both cities and by his commissioning of the local monks to prepare the **Domesday Book**. It wasn't until after the Battle of Naseby in 1645, when Cromwell took the city, that Winchester began its decline into provinciality.

Hampshire's county town now has a scholarly and slightly anachronistic air, embodied by the ancient almshouses that still provide shelter for senior citizens of "noble poverty" – the pensioners can be seen walking round the town in medieval black or mulberry-coloured gowns with silver badges. It also makes a good base from which to explore the nearby towns of **Chawton** and **Selborne**, homes, respectively, to Jane Austen and the eminent naturalist, Gilbert White.

Winchester Cathedral

9 The Close, SO23 9LS • Mon–Sat 9.30am–5pm, Sun 12.30–3pm • £8, including a guided tour of cathedral, treasury and crypt (ticket valid for one year) • **Tower tours** Jan–May, Oct & Nov Wed 2.15pm, Sat 11.30am & 2.15pm; June–Sept Mon, Wed & Fri 2.15pm, Sat 11.30am & 2.15pm; 1hr 30min • £6.50 • ☎ 01962 857275, ⊕ winchester-cathedral.org.uk

The first minster to be built in Winchester was raised by Cenwalh, the Saxon king of Wessex in the mid-seventh century, and traces of this building have been unearthed near the present **cathedral**, which was begun in 1079 and completed some three hundred years later. The exterior is not its best feature – squat and massive, it crouches stumpily over the tidy lawns of the Cathedral Close. The interior is rich and complex, however, and its 556ft **nave** makes this Europe's longest medieval church. Outstanding features include the carved Norman font of black Tournai marble, the fourteenth-century misericords (the choir stalls are the oldest complete set in the country) and some amazing monuments – **William of Wykeham's Chantry**, halfway down the nave on the right, is one of the most ornate.

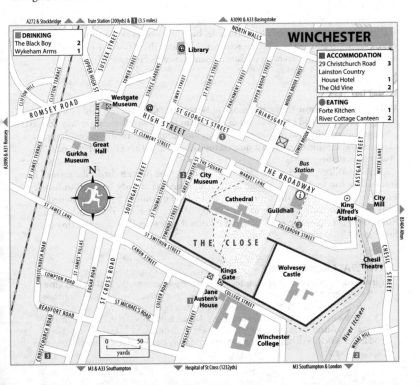

Jane Austen, who died in Winchester, is commemorated close to the font by a memorial brass and slab beneath which she's interred, though she's recorded simply as the daughter of a local clergyman. Above the high altar lie the mortuary chests of pre-Conquest kings, including **Cnut** (though the bones were mixed up after Cromwell's Roundheads broke up the chests in 1645); **William Rufus**, killed while hunting in the New Forest in 1100, lies in the presbytery.

Behind the impressive Victorian screen at the end of the presbytery, look out for the memorial shrine to **St Swithun**. Originally buried in the churchyard, his remains were later interred inside, where the "rain of heaven" could no longer fall on him, whereupon he took revenge and the heavens opened for forty days – hence the legend that if it rains on St Swithun's Day it will do so for another forty. His exact burial place is unknown.

Accessible from the north transept, the Norman **crypt** – often flooded – is home to Antony Gormley's contemplative figure *Sound II*, which is frequently ankle-deep in the waters. The cathedral's original foundations were dug in marshy ground, and at the beginning of the last century a steadfast diver, William Walker, spent five years replacing the rotten timber foundations with concrete.

Great Hall

At the top of the High St on Castle Ave, SO23 8UJ • Daily 10am–5pm • Free, donation requested • ☎ 01962 846476, ⓦ hants.gov.uk/greathall

The **Great Hall** is all that remains of a thirteenth-century castle destroyed by Cromwell. Sir Walter Raleigh heard his death sentence here in 1603, though he wasn't finally dispatched until 1618, and Judge Jeffreys held one of his Bloody Assizes (see page 1013) in the castle after Monmouth's rebellion in 1685. The main interest now is a large, brightly painted disc slung on one wall like some curious antique dartboard. This is alleged to be King Arthur's Round Table, but the woodwork is probably fourteenth-century, later repainted as a PR exercise for the Tudor dynasty – the portrait of Arthur at the top of the table bears an uncanny resemblance to Henry VIII.

College Street

College Street is home to the buildings of **Winchester College**, England's oldest public school – set up in 1382 by William of Wykeham for "poor scholars", it now educates few but the wealthy and privileged. You can look round the medieval buildings, cloisters and Gothic chapel on a **guided tour** (2–4 daily; 1hr; £8; ☎ 01962 621209, ⓦ winchestercollege.org).

At no.8 College Street stands the house where **Jane Austen** died. She moved here from Chawton in 1817 (see page 202), when she was already ill with Addison's Disease, and died later the same year, aged 42. The house is privately owned, though, so you can't look round. At the top of the street, the thirteenth-century **Kings Gate** is one of the city's original medieval gateways, housing the tiny St Swithun's Church.

THE WATERCRESS LINE

Alresford, six miles east of Winchester, is the departure point for the **Watercress Line** (Feb–July, Sept & Oct days vary; Aug & school hols daily; call or check website for details; £16; ☎ 01962 733810, ⓦ watercressline.co.uk), a steam-powered railway so named because it passes through the former watercress beds that once flourished here. The train chuffs ten miles to **Alton**, with gourmet dinners served on board on Saturday evenings, plus traditional Sunday lunches, and Real Ales Trains serving ales from local breweries on some Saturday evenings.

THE REAL DOWNTON ABBEY

Tucked away in the northern reaches of Hampshire, twenty miles north of Winchester, **Highclere Castle** (9.30am–5pm: Easter, early April & May bank hol weekends daily, mid-July to mid-Sept Mon–Thurs & Sun; castle, exhibition and gardens £22, castle and gardens £15, gardens £7; ☎01635 253210, ⓦhighclerecastle.co.uk) will be very familiar to fans of ITV's hit period drama, **Downton Abbey**, which was filmed here. Home to Lord Carnarvon and his family, the house is approached via a long drive that winds through a stunning 5000-acre estate, and is surrounded by beautiful **gardens** designed by Capability Brown. Inside, *Downton Abbey* aficionados will enjoy loitering in the **Drawing Room** and **Library**, scene of many a quivering stiff-upper-lip of Lord Grantham and family, while upstairs you can peer into the Crawley girls' rooms. In the castle cellars, an **Egyptian Exhibition** celebrates the real-life fifth Earl of Carnarvon, who, in 1922, discovered the tomb of Tutankhamun with Howard Carter, and who funded many of Carter's expeditions. Since the house is still a family home and is sometimes closed for filming, hours vary; call ahead or check online.

3

Wolvesey Castle

Entrance off College St, SO23 9NB • April–Sept daily 10am–5pm • Free; EH • ⓦwww.english-heritage.org.uk/visit/places/wolvesey-castle-old-bishops-palace

East of the cathedral, the remains of Winchester's Saxon walls bracket the twelfth-century **Wolvesey Castle** – actually the palace for the Bishops of Winchester, who once wielded great clout over England's religious and political affairs. As a result, this was once one of the most important buildings in Winchester, with its own stables, prison, chapel and gardens. Today, the castle ruins remain impressive, dwarfing the current dwelling of the Bishop of Winchester, a relatively modest house built in 1680, which sits alongside it.

ARRIVAL AND INFORMATION   WINCHESTER

By train The station is about a mile northwest of the cathedral, on Stockbridge Rd.
Destinations Bournemouth (every 15–20min; 45min–1hr); London Waterloo (every 15–20min; 1hr–1hr 10min); Portsmouth (hourly; 1hr); Southampton (every 15min; 15–30min).
By bus National Express buses pull in at and depart from the conveniently located bus station on the Broadway,

opposite the tourist office.
Destinations Bournemouth (8 daily; 1hr 20min–1hr 55min); London (8 daily; 1hr 55min–2hr 30min); Southampton (10 daily; 25–45min).
Tourist office In the imposing Guildhall, High St (May–Sept Mon–Sat 10am–5pm, Sun & bank hols 11am–4pm; Oct–April Mon–Sat 10am–5pm; ☎01962 840500, ⓦvisitwinchester.co.uk).

ACCOMMODATION

29 Christchurch Road 29 Christchurch Rd, SO23 9SU ☎01962 868 661, ⓦbedbreakfastwinchester. co.uk; map p.199. Well-furnished, comfortable B&B in a charming Regency house located in a quiet, residential part of town. No smoking. **£100**
Lainston Country House Hotel Woodman Lange, Sparshot, SO21 1LT ☎01962 776088, ⓦexclusive.co.uk/lainston-house; map p.199. Around a 10min drive from Winchester towards Stockbridge, this seventeenth-century

mansion sits in 63 acres of grounds – it's luxurious and comfortable, with huge bedrooms and friendly staff. It has its own quality restaurant, specializing in local produce. **£175**
The Old Vine 8 Great Minster St, SO23 9HA ☎01962 854616, ⓦoldvinewinchester.com; map p.199. Lovely, big rooms that combine period decor with modern touches such as widescreen TVs, above a fine bar/restaurant, and right opposite the cathedral. The street can be noisy at night. **£120**

EATING

Forte Kitchen 78 Parchment St SO23 8AT ☎01962 856840, ⓦfortekitchen.co.uk; map p.199. The best place in town for lunch. There's a good selection of sandwiches plus hearty mains such as smoked mackerel with spinach, poached eggs and sourdough, or Hampshire beef burger

(both £11.50). Attracts a lively, arty clientele. Mon–Fri 8am–4pm, Sat 9am–5pm, Sun 9am–4pm.
★ **River Cottage Canteen** Abbey Mill, Abbey Mill Gardens, The Broadway, SO23 9GH ☎01962 457747, ⓦrivercottage.net/canteens; map p.199. Located in a

converted mill building, this is a great venue spread over several floors, with outside seating by the millstream. The menu features local ingredients, such as pan-fried gurnard (£16), and plenty of veggie options like roasted squash and spinach curry (£14). The cocktails are good, too. Mon–Fri 11am–10.30pm, Sat 10am–10pm, Sun 10am–4pm.

DRINKING

The Black Boy Wharf Hill, SO23 9NP ☎01962 861754, ⓦtheblackboypub.com; map p.199. Fantastic old pub with log fires, book-lined walls and low ceilings hung with old coins and miniature bottles. Good local cask ales are on draught and there's reasonable pub grub from around £10, as well as a small outdoor terrace. Mon–Thurs noon–

11pm, Fri & Sat noon–midnight, Sun noon–11.30pm.
Wykeham Arms 75 Kingsgate St, SO23 9PE ☎01962 853834, ⓦwykehamarmswinchester.co.uk; map p.199. This highly atmospheric eighteenth-century pub has a warren of cosy rooms, with open fireplaces, good bar snacks and decent beers. Daily 11am–11pm.

Chawton

A mile southwest of Alton and sixteen miles northeast of Winchester, the village of **CHAWTON** was home to Jane Austen from 1809 to 1817, during the last and most prolific years of her life – it was here that she wrote or revised almost all of her six books, including *Sense and Sensibility* and *Pride and Prejudice*.

Jane Austen's House Museum

Winchester Road, GU34 1SD · Daily: March–May & Sept–Dec 10.30am–4.30pm; June–Aug 10am–5pm · £8 ☎01420 83262, ⓦwww.jane-austens-house-museum.org.uk

A plain red-brick building in the centre of the village, **Jane Austen's House** contains first editions of some of her greatest works and provides a fascinating insight into her daily life. You can see a lock of her hair, pieces of her jewellery and the desk where she wrote her books. The gardens include a learning centre that shows a short film about her life.

Chawton House

GU34 1SJ · Late March to Oct Mon–Fri noon–4.30pm, Sun 11am–5pm; last entry 30mins before closing · £8 · ☎01420 541010, ⓦwww.chawtonhouse.org

A short walk from Jane Austen's house is **Chawton House**, which belonged to Jane's brother, Edward Austen Knight. It remained in the Austen family until 1987, when it was bought by American IT millionaire Sandy Lerner. She opened the **Chawton House Library**, which contains an impressive collection of women's writing in English from 1600 to 1830; it also hosts frequent events.

ARRIVAL AND DEPARTURE

CHAWTON

By train The village is accessible on the Watercress Line steam train (see page 200).
By bus From Winchester or Alton train station, take the #64 to Chawton roundabout (1–2 hourly; 15min from Alton; 40min from Winchester), then it's a 12min walk.

The New Forest

Covering about 220 square miles, the **NEW FOREST** is one of southern England's favourite rural playgrounds, with some 13.5 million day-visits annually. The land was requisitioned by William the Conqueror in 1079 as a hunting ground, and the rights of its inhabitants became subservient to those of his precious deer. Fences to impede their progress were forbidden and terrible punishments were meted out to anyone caught poaching – hands were lopped off, eyes put out. Later monarchs less passionate about hunting gradually restored the commoners' rights, and today the New Forest enjoys a unique patchwork of ancient laws and privileges alongside the regulations applying to its National Park status.

The **trees** here are now much more varied than they were in pre-Norman times, with birch, holly, yew, Scots pine and other conifers interspersed with the ancient oaks and beeches. One of the most venerable trees is the much-visited **Knightwood Oak**, just a few hundred yards north of the A35, three miles southwest of Lyndhurst, which measures about 22ft in circumference at shoulder height. The most conspicuous species of **fauna** is the New Forest **pony** – you'll see them grazing nonchalantly by the roadsides and ambling through some villages. The local deer are less visible now that some of the faster roads are fenced, although several species still roam the woods, including the tiny **sika deer**, descendants of a pair that escaped from nearby Beaulieu in 1904.

ARRIVAL AND DEPARTURE   THE NEW FOREST

By train The main London to Weymouth line passes through the New Forest, with fast trains stopping at Brockenhurst (see page 206); slower trains also stop at Ashurst, Sway and New Milton. From Brockenhurst a branch line runs to Lymington (every 30min; 10min) to link with the Isle of Wight ferry.

GETTING AROUND

Though the southern forest stretches have a reasonably efficient bus network, to get the best from the New Forest, you need to walk or ride through it, avoiding the places cars can reach.

By bus Useful routes through the forest include the #6 from Southampton to Lymington via Lyndhurst and Brockenhurst; the coastal routes #X1 and #X2 from Bournemouth and Christchurch to Lymington; and in summer the hop-on hop-off open-top New Forest Tour bus which runs on three different circular routes around the forest, taking in all the main settlements, and can carry up to four bikes for free (July to mid-Sept; £14.40 for a one-day ticket, valid on all three routes; ⓦthenewforesttour.

info). Other services are run by More Buses (☎01202 338420, ⓦmorebus.co.uk) and Blue Star (☎01202 338421, ⓦbluestarbus.co.uk).

By bike There are 150 miles of car-free gravel roads in the forest, making cycling an appealing prospect – pick up a book of route maps from tourist offices or bike rental shops. Bikes can be rented in several places: for details of cycle routes and bike-hire outfits, check ⓦwww.new-forest-national-park.com/bike-hire-in-the-new-forest.html.

INFORMATION

Information offices There are two information centres in the forest, one in Lyndhurst (see below), and the other in Lymington (see page 205), in the St Barbe Museum, New St, off the High St (Mon–Sat 10am–5pm, Sun 11am–4pm;

☎01590 689000, ⓦlymington.org).

Maps The Ordnance Survey Leisure Map 22 of the New Forest is best for exploring. Shops in Lyndhurst sell specialist walking books and natural history guides.

ACCOMMODATION

Camping There are ten campsites throughout the forest run by Camping in the Forest (☎024 7642 3008, ⓦcampingintheforest.co.uk); most are open from Easter to late Sept, though some are open year-round. Some are very simple, with few or no facilities, others have electricity and hot shower blocks, but they all have open access to the forest. Many even have streams and fords running through them, with ponies and donkeys wandering freely.

Lyndhurst

LYNDHURST, its town centre skewered by an agonizing one-way system, isn't a particularly interesting place, though the brick **parish church** is worth a glance for its William Morris glass and the grave of Mrs Reginald Hargreaves, better known as Alice Liddell, Lewis Carroll's model for Alice. The town is of most interest to visitors for the **New Forest Museum and Visitor Centre** in the central car park off the High Street (daily: April–Oct 10am–5pm; Nov–March 10am–4pm; ☎023 8028 3444, ⓦnewforestcentre.org.uk), and the adjoining **museum** (free, donations welcome), which focuses on the history, wildlife and industries of the New Forest. The forest's most visited site, the **Rufus Stone**, stands three miles northwest of Lyndhurst. Erected in 1745, it marks the putative spot where the Conqueror's son and heir, **William II** – aka William Rufus, after his ruddy complexion – was killed by a crossbow bolt in 1100.

3

ACCOMMODATION
LYNDHURST

Forest Lodge Hotel Pikes Hill, Romsey Rd, SO43 7AS ☎ 023 8028 3677, ⊛ newforesthotels.co.uk/forest-lodge-hotel. Attractive Georgian building in a good location – a short walk from Lyndhurst High St but away from the main road, so there's less traffic noise. The rooms are comfortable and there's an indoor pool and sauna. **£150**

Rufus House Southampton Rd, SO43 7BR ☎ 023 8028 2930, ⊛ rufushouse.co.uk. A couple of minutes out of town on the Ashurst road, opposite some fine New Forest countryside, this good-value place has plenty of character. Its tower room has a four-poster bed (£15 extra), though front rooms face a busy road. Minimum two-night let in high season. **£95**

EATING AND DRINKING

★ The Oak Inn Pinkney Lane, Bank, SO43 7FD ☎ 023 8028 2350, ⊛ oakinnlyndhurst.co.uk. Fantastic little country pub a mile out of Lyndhurst, with low wooden ceilings, a roaring fire for winter and a garden for the summer. It's popular with walkers and cyclists and there's decent food (mains from £14.50), featuring local ingredients – it's best to book in advance. Mon–Sat 11.30am–11pm, Sun noon–10.30pm; kitchen Mon–Fri noon–5pm & 6–9pm,

Sat noon–5pm & 6–9.30pm, Sun noon–5pm & 6–8pm.

La Pergola Southampton Rd, SO43 7BQ ☎ 023 8028 4184, ⊛ la-pergola.co.uk. Lively Italian restaurant in an attractive building with its own garden. Sizzling meat and fish dishes cost around £15–20, and there's tasty pasta and pizza from £10 and superb home-made desserts, as well as daily specials. Tues–Sun & bank hols 11am–2.30pm & 6–10.30pm.

Beaulieu

The village of **BEAULIEU** (pronounced "Bewley"), in the southeast corner of the New Forest, was the site of one of England's most influential monasteries, a Cistercian house founded in 1204 by King John – in remorse, it is said, for ordering a group of supplicating monks to be trampled to death. Built using stone ferried from Caen in northern France and Quarr on the Isle of Wight, the **abbey** managed a self-sufficient estate of ten thousand acres, but was dismantled soon after the Dissolution. Its refectory now forms the parish church, which, like everything else in Beaulieu, has been subsumed into the Montagu family estate – they have owned a large chunk of the New Forest since one of Charles II's illegitimate progeny was named duke of the estate.

Beaulieu House and the National Motor Museum

Beaulieu, SO42 7ZN • Daily: June–Sept 10am–6pm; Oct–May 10am–5pm • £24.75, or £19.50 online • ☎ 01590 612435, ⊛ beaulieu.co.uk

Beaulieu estate comprises **Palace House**, the family home of the Montagus, a ruined Cistercian **abbey** and the main attraction, the **National Motor Museum**, plus fine grounds. The museum's collection of over 250 vehicles includes spindly antiques, recent classics and Formula I cars rubbing shoulders with land-speed racers, Ferraris and a Sinclair C5, as well as some of *Top Gear*'s more outlandish vehicles. A monorail runs through the museum and grounds, towards Palace House, formerly the abbey's gatehouse, which contains masses of Montagu-related memorabilia. The undercroft of the abbey houses an exhibition on medieval monastic life.

ACCOMMODATION AND EATING
BEAULIEU

The Montagu Arms Lyndhurst Rd, SO42 7ZL ☎ 01590 612324, ⊛ montaguarmshotel.co.uk. You can stay in smart and comfortable rooms, some with four-poster beds, in this seventeenth-century building with open fires and a lovely garden. There's good-quality pub food at the on-site *Monty's Inn*, or you can push the boat out for a meal

at *The Terrace*, one of the New Forest's top restaurants. The three-course *Terrace* lunch menu is good value at £23, while the full tasting menu costs £90 a head. Monty's: Mon–Fri 11am–3pm & 6–11pm, Sat 11am–11pm, Sun 11am–10.30pm; The Terrace: Tues 7–9.30pm, Wed–Sun noon–2.30pm & 7–9.30pm. **£190**

Buckler's Hard

Daily: April–Sept 10am–5pm; Oct–March 10am–4.30pm • Free (if you walk or cycle), £6.90 (covers parking and Maritime Museum entrance) • ☎ 01590 616203, ⊛ bucklershard.co.uk

The hamlet of **BUCKLER'S HARD**, a couple of miles downstream from Beaulieu, has a wonderful setting. A row of picturesque thatched shipwrights' cottages, some of which are inhabited, leads down to the Beaulieu River; it doesn't look much like a **shipyard** now, but from Elizabethan times onwards dozens of men o' war were assembled here from giant New Forest oaks. Several of Nelson's ships were launched here, to be towed carefully by rowing boats past the sandbanks and across the Solent to Portsmouth. The largest house in the hamlet, which forms part of the Montagu estate, belonged to Henry Adams, the master builder responsible for most of the Trafalgar fleet; it's now a hotel, pub and restaurant (see below).

At the top of the village is the **Maritime Museum**, which traces the history of the great ships and incorporates buildings preserved in their eighteenth-century form. The hamlet is also the starting point for a bucolic **river cruise** down the Beaulieu River (Easter to Oct daily, roughly hourly 11am–4.30pm; 30min; £5, or £4.50 if booked online).

ACCOMMODATION AND EATING

The Master Builder's Hotel SO42 7XB ☎ 0844 815 3399, ⊛ hillbrookehotels.co.uk/the-master-builders. Picturesque and peaceful, this wonderful quirky hotel is in a sixteenth-century building with open fires and a superb location overlooking the river. The rooms are a mixed bunch; some have east Asian flourishes and individually designed furniture, and some have views of the river. There's also a decent restaurant and pub – the *Yachtsman's Bar* menu features standard pub grub, with sandwiches (£6.50), pizzas (£12–14) and fish and chips (£13), while the *Riverview Restaurant* is a more upmarket affair, serving starters such as salt-fired Solent mackerel (£7), followed by roast sea bass with Lymington crab risotto (£19.50). You can take drinks and food from the bar menu outside onto the lawns in nice weather. Bar daily noon–9pm; restaurant Mon–Sat noon–2.30pm & 7–9pm, Sun 12.30–3pm & 7–9pm. **£120**

Lymington

The most pleasant point of access for ferries to the Isle of Wight (see page 192) is **LYMINGTON**, a sheltered haven that's become one of the busiest leisure harbours on the south coast. Rising from the quay area, the cobbled street of the old town is lined with Georgian houses. At the top of the High Street (opposite Church Lane) is the partly thirteenth-century **Church of St Thomas the Apostle**, which has a cupola-topped tower built in 1670.

ARRIVAL AND DEPARTURE LYMINGTON

By train A branch line runs from Brockenhurst to Lymington (every 30min; 10min). Trains call first at Lymington Town station, a short walk from the High St, then run onto Lymington Pier to link with the Isle of Wight ferry.

By bus Bus #6 runs roughly hourly from Southampton to Lymington (1hr 15min) via Lyndhurst (40min) and Brockenhurst (55min); the coastal routes #X1 and #X2 (1–2 hourly) run here from Christchurch (1hr 10min) and Bournemouth (1hr 45min).

ACCOMMODATION AND EATING

Britannia House Mill Lane, SO41 3BA ☎ 01590 672091, ⊛ britannia-house.com. A well-kept, friendly and central B&B, right by the train station. The comfortable rooms are on the small side but there's a fine sitting room commanding views over the waterfront. **£99**

Lanes Ashley Lane, SO41 3RH ☎ 01590 672777, ⊛ lanesoflymington.com. Set in an old chapel and former school, with some tables on an internal balcony, this bright buzzy restaurant and bar serves locally sourced fish and meats (£16–24) including halibut steak, rack of lamb and less pricey burgers (£13). Tues–Sat 11.30am–2.30pm & 6.30–9.30pm.

The Haven King Saltern Rd, SO41 3QD ☎ 01590 679971, ⊛ havenrestaurant.co.uk. Wedged among the luxury yachts in Lymington harbour, this is, not surprisingly, a favoured haunt for the local sailing fraternity. The smart but laidback café-restaurant has a nautical-themed bar area, tables inside and a great raised terrace with views across the Solent. Fresh fish is the speciality, with dishes such as seafood bouillabaisse (£18.50), or swordfish steaks (£19.50), though it also does burgers and steaks. Daily 8am–midnight (food served until 9.30pm).

Stanwell House 14–15 High St, SO41 9AA ☎ 01590 677123, ⊛ stanwellhousehotel.co.uk. The most

3

upmarket choice in town, this handsome boutique-style hotel has an array of individually designed rooms boasting roll-top baths, flatscreen TVs and the like. Its main restaurant, Burcher & Co, is also the top spot to eat, in a dining room with a distinctly colonial feel (mains from around £16); there is also a less formal bistro serving modern European cuisine, and light snacks and afternoon teas are also available. Daily 7am–9pm. **£135**

Brockenhurst

You'll frequently find New Forest ponies strolling down the High Street of **BROCKENHURST**, undoubtedly the most attractive and liveliest town in the forest. Surrounded by idyllic heath- and woodland and with a ford at one end of the High Street, it's a picturesque spot and a useful travel hub.

ARRIVAL AND DEPARTURE BROCKENHURST

By train The station is on the eastern edge of town – from here, turn left and left again onto Brookley Rd, and you'll find the bulk of shops, banks and places to eat and drink. Mainline services run every 15–20min from/ to Southampton (15–20min), Winchester (30min) and London Waterloo (1hr 30min). In addition, a branch line runs to Lymington (every 30min; 10min) to link with the Isle of Wight ferry.

ACCOMMODATION AND EATING

★ **The Pig** Beaulieu Rd, SO42 7QL ☎ 01590 622354, ⓦ thepighotel.co.uk. Brockenhurst's best restaurant by a mile is in a fabulous New Forest country house with chic rooms, set in stunning grounds. The innovative menu uses ingredients from its gardens or from the surrounding area – fish is smoked on site, eggs come from its own chickens, and the herbs and vegetables are home-grown. All the ingredients are sourced from within 25 miles and the results, such as New Forest wood pigeon with locally foraged mushrooms (around £16), are delicious. Daily 12.30–2.30pm & 6.30–9.30pm. **£185**

Rosie Lee 6 Brookley Rd, SO42 7RBA ☎ 01590 622797. Lovely tearoom serving delicious and inexpensive home-made cakes and tasty sandwiches on vintage china. You can sit outside – they provide blankets and hot water bottles when it's cold – or at one of the cosy tables inside; dogs welcome. Daily 9am–4.30pm.

Bournemouth and around

Renowned for its pristine sandy beach (one of southern England's cleanest) and its gardens, the resort of **BOURNEMOUTH** dates from 1811, when a local squire, Louis Tregonwell, built a summerhouse on the wild, unpopulated heathland that once occupied this stretch of coast, and planted the first of the pine trees that now characterize the area. The mild climate, sheltered site and glorious beach encouraged the rapid growth of a full-scale family-holiday resort, complete with piers, cliff railways and boat trips. Today Bournemouth has a rather genteel image, counterbalanced by a thriving university scene.

Bournemouth's beach spreads either side of the Victorian **pier**, which was built in 1880, then extended in 1894 and 1909 to more than 300m long, and used as a landing stage for steamers. Today, it's home to the usual arcades and amusements plus the world's first pier-to-shore **zipwire**, a quick but exhilarating ride with dual wires so you can race down with a friend (April–Sept £18; Oct–March £15; ⓦ rockreef.co.uk/pier).

Russell-Cotes Art Gallery and Museum

Russell-Cotes Rd, East Cliff, BH1 3AA • Tues–Sun & bank hols 10am–5pm • April–Sept £6; Oct–March free • ☎ 01202 451858, ⓦ russellcotes.com

Surrounded by lovely gardens on a clifftop, the **Russell-Cotes Art Gallery and Museum** has one of the UK's best collections of Victoriana, collected from around the world by the wealthy Russell-Cotes family. The quirky assortment of artworks, Asian souvenirs and curios, such as the ornate loo used by royal mistress Lily Langtry, are displayed in an ornately decorated mansion, once the family home. Highlights of the collection are Rossetti's *Venus Verticordia* (1864) and England's most important collection of Victorian nudes, which scandalized much of society at the time.

St Peter's Church

Hinton Rd, BH1 2EE • ☎ 01202 290986, ⓦ stpetersbournemouth.org.uk

In the centre of town, the graveyard of **St Peter's Church** is where **Mary Shelley**, author of Gothic horror tale *Frankenstein*, is buried, together with the heart of her husband, the Romantic poet Percy Bysshe Shelley. The tombs of Mary's parents – radical thinker William Godwin and early feminist **Mary Wollstonecraft** – are also in the graveyard.

ARRIVAL AND INFORMATION

BOURNEMOUTH

By train The station is about a mile inland, connected to the town centre and seafront by frequent buses, or you can walk there in around 15–20min.

Destinations Brockenhurst (every 15–20min; 15–25min); Dorchester (every 30min–1hr; 45min); London Waterloo (every 30min; 2hr); Poole (every 20min; 10min); Southampton (every 15–20min; 30min–1hr 10min); Weymouth (hourly; 55min); Winchester (every 15min; 45min–1hr).

By bus Opposite the train station (see above). Destinations Direct National Express buses run to London (hourly; 2hr 30min); Southampton (hourly; 45min–1hr); Weymouth (5 daily; 1hr 15min–1hr 20min); and Winchester (8 daily; 1hr 20min–1hr 55min).

Tourist office Pier Approach (Jan–March & Nov–Dec daily 10am–4pm; April–June & Sept–Oct daily 10am–5pm; July–Aug Mon–Sat 9am–6pm, Sun 9am–5pm; ☎ 01202 451734, ⓦ bournemouth.co.uk).

ACCOMMODATION

★ **Beach Lodges** Seafront Promenade, Boscombe, BH5 1BN ☎ 01202 451781, ⓦ bournemouthbeach lodges.co.uk. If you want to sleep right on the beach, opt for these deluxe beach huts which sleep up to six and come complete with hot showers, loos, fridges and kitchens. Set back slightly from the promenade, they boast terrific views. There are good low-season discounts, and with their own heating, they're magical even in winter. Minimum three-night stay. **£210**

★ **The Greenhouse Hotel** 4 Grove Rd, BH1 3AX ☎ 01202 498900, ⓦ thegreenhousehotel.co.uk. Boutique-style, eco-friendly hotel in a Grade II listed Victorian villa a short

walk from the town centre. The stylish rooms come with all the latest mod cons, ultra-comfy beds, and free home-made biscuits. The environmental standards are very high – water is solar-heated, and much of the electricity is generated on site. There's also an excellent bar and restaurant. **£160**

Urban Beach Hotel 23 Argyll Rd, Boscombe, BH5 1EB ☎ 01202 301509, ⓦ urbanbeachhotel.co.uk. A short (but steep) walk from Boscombe's beach, and close to the shops, this old Victorian townhouse has been given a boutique makeover. There's a variety of rooms, all of them stylish with designer furniture, comfy beds and DVDs. The downstairs bar/restaurant serves great cocktails. **£145**

EATING AND DRINKING

Koh Thai Tapas Daimler House, 38–40 Poole Hill, BH2 5PS ☎ 01202 294723, ⓦ koh-thai.co.uk. Lively restaurant done out with stylish Thai decor – all dark-wood furniture, comfy sofas and fresh orchids. The Thai food is beautifully presented and can be ordered in tapas size (£6–8.50) or full portions. Mains (£8–18) include Thai curries, stir fries and noodles. The cocktails are great too. Mon 5.30–10pm, Tues–Sun 12.30–3pm & 5.30–10pm.

★ **Sixty Million Postcards** 19–21 Exeter Rd, BH2 5AF ☎ 01202 292697, ⓦ sixtymillionpostcards.com. One of Bournemouth's best bars, attracting an unpretentious but trendy student crowd. There are board games, various alcoves for cosy chats and comfy sofas. Offers a good range of beers, drinks and good-value burgers, with occasional DJs and live music. Mon–Thurs noon–midnight, Fri & Sat noon–2am, Sun 11am–midnight.

★ **Urban Reef** Undercliff Drive, Boscombe, BH5 1BN

☎ 01202 443960, ⓦ urbanreef.com. Art Deco-style restaurant/bar/café in a fabulous position on Boscombe seafront. Designed to give great sea views from both floors, its quirky decor features a mock-up beach hut hanging on the wall, and there's a large deck for drinks on the front and an adjacent takeaway serving wood-fired pizzas (£10). Food varies from cooked breakfast (£8.50) to New Forest mushroom risotto (£12) and pan-seared salmon (£17). Daily 8am–10pm.

West Beach Pier Approach, BH2 5AA ☎ 01202 587785, ⓦ west-beach.co.uk. Close to the pier, this seafood restaurant has a prime position on the beach, with decking out on the promenade. It's smart and stylish, and you can watch the chefs at work in the open kitchen. Fish and seafood dishes start at around £18, and there are also some meat and veg dishes. Daily 9am–10pm; closed Mon eves in winter.

Wimborne Minster

An ancient town on the banks of the River Stour, just a few minutes' drive north from the suburbs of Bournemouth, **WIMBORNE MINSTER** is an attractive little town, worth an hour or two's wander around its narrow alleys, or along the riverbank. It's home to southern England's largest covered **market** (Fri–Sun; ⓦwimbornemarket.co.uk), though its main point of interest is the great **church**, the Minster of St Cuthberga.

Minster of St Cuthberga

High St, BH21 1HT • Mon–Sat 9.30am–5.30pm, Sun 2.30–5.30pm; Chained Library Easter–Oct Mon 2–4pm, Tues–Fri 10.30am–12.30pm & 2–4pm; phone for winter opening times • Free • ☎ 01202 884753, ⓦ wimborneminster.org.uk

Built on the site of an eighth-century monastery, the **Minster of St Cuthberga**'s massive twin towers of mottled grey and tawny stone dwarf the rest of town. At one time the church was even more imposing – its spire crashed down during morning service in 1602. What remains today is basically Norman with later additions, such as the Perpendicular west tower; this bears a figure dressed as a grenadier of the Napoleonic era, who strikes every quarter-hour with a hammer. The **Chained Library** above the choir vestry, dating from 1686, is Wimborne's most prized possession and one of the oldest public libraries in the country. Its collection of ancient books includes a manuscript written on lambskin dating from 1343.

Kingston Lacy

2 miles northwest of Wimborne Minster; BH21 4EA • **House** Mid-March to Oct Wed–Sun 11am–5pm; Nov to mid-March 11am–4pm • £12.70 (includes grounds); NT • **Grounds** Daily: mid-March to Oct 10am–6pm; Nov to mid-March 10am–4pm • £7 • ☎ 01202 883402, ⓦ nationaltrust.org.uk/kingston-lacy

The glorious seventeenth-century mansion of **Kingston Lacy** stands in 250 acres of parkland grazed by a herd of Red Devon cattle. Designed for the Bankes family, who were exiled from Corfe Castle (see page 211) after the Roundheads reduced it to rubble, the brick building was clad in grey stone during the nineteenth century by Sir Charles Barry, co-architect of the Houses of Parliament. William Bankes, then owner of the house, was a great traveller and collector, and the **Spanish Room** is a superb scrapbook of his Grand Tour souvenirs. Kingston Lacy's **picture collection** is also outstanding, featuring Titian, Rubens, Velázquez and many other old masters.

Christchurch

CHRISTCHURCH, five miles east of Bournemouth, is best known for **Christchurch Priory** (Mon–Sat 9.30am–5pm, Sun 2.15–5.30pm; donation requested; ☎01202 485804, ⓦchristchurchpriory.org), England's longest parish church at 311ft. The oldest parts date back to 1094, and its fan-vaulted North Porch is impressively large. Fine views can be gained from the top of the 120ft-high **tower** (£3; call ahead to book).

The area round the old town quay has a carefully preserved charm, with the **Red House Museum** on Quay Road (Tues–Fri 10am–5pm, Sat 10am–4pm; free; ☎01202 482860, ⓦwww.hampshireculturaltrust.org.uk) containing an affectionate collection of local memorabilia. **Boat trips** (Easter–Oct daily; ☎01202 429119, ⓦbournemouthboating. co.uk) leave from the grassy banks of the riverside quay, heading east to the sandspit at Mudeford (30min; £8 return) or upriver to Tuckton (15min; £3 return).

ARRIVAL AND INFORMATION   CHRISTCHURCH

By train Christchurch is on the main London Waterloo to Weymouth line; the train station is on Stour Rd, a mile north of the town centre.

By bus Local buses from Bournemouth in the east, Lymington in the west and Ringwood in the north pull up at the bus stop close to the tourist office.

Tourist office Regent Centre, 51 High St (Mon 9am–4.30pm, Tues–Sat 10am–4.30pm; ☎01202 499199, ⓦvisitdorset.com).

EATING AND DRINKING

The Boathouse 9 Quay Rd, BH23 1BU ☎01202 480033, ⓦ boathouse.co.uk. This modern café-bar/restaurant is in a lovely location overlooking the river with a large outdoor terrace, and a modern wood-burner inside. Main courses include salmon and monkfish skewers with couscous (£16.50) or Cornish mussels and chips (£15.50), as well as a selection of tasty stone-baked pizzas (£11–13). Mon–Thurs & Sun 9am–9pm, Fri & Sat 9am–10pm.

The Jetty Christchurch Harbour Hotel, 95 Mudeford, BH23 3NT ☎01202 400950, ⓦ thejetty.co.uk. Renowned chef Alex Aitken uses local seasonal produce in this contemporary wooden restaurant with stunning views of Christchurch harbour. Interesting main courses include a

mixed fish grill served with garlic and seaweed mayonnaise (£24.50), and the local-produce lunch/early-evening menu is good value at £25 for three courses. Mon–Sat noon–2.30pm & 6–10pm, Sun noon–8pm.

Ye Olde George Inn 2a Castle St, BH23 1DT ☎01202 479383, ⓦ yeoldegeorgeinnchristchurch. co.uk. Christchurch's oldest pub, the *George* is an attractive former coaching inn with a great courtyard garden, and a warren of small rooms inside. Serves reasonably priced pub grub (from £11), tasty pizzas (£7–10) and a selection of real ales. Mon–Thurs & Sun 11am–11pm, Fri & Sat 11am–midnight; kitchen daily noon–10pm.

Poole

West of Bournemouth, **POOLE** is an ancient seaport on a huge, almost landlocked harbour. The town developed in the thirteenth century and was successively colonized by pirates, fishermen and timber traders. The old quarter by the quayside contains more than one hundred historic buildings, as well as the contemporary Poole Museum.

Poole Museum

4 Old High St, BH15 1BW • Easter–Oct daily 10am–5pm; Nov–Easter Mon–Sat 10am–4pm, Sun noon–4pm • Free • ☎01202 262600, ⓦ poolemuseum.co.uk

Poole Museum traces the town's development through the centuries, with displays of local ceramics and a rare Iron Age log boat that was dug out of the harbour in 1964: carved out of a single tree trunk, the 33ft-long boat dates from around 300 BC. Look out, too, for the fascinating footage of the flying boats that took off from Poole harbour during the 1940s for east Asia and Australia.

Brownsea Island

BH13 7EE • Feb & March Sat & Sun 10am–4pm; April–Oct daily 10am–5pm • £6.75; NT • ☎01202 707744, ⓦ nationaltrust.org.uk/brownsea-island • Access by boat: Feb & March from Sandbanks only (Sat & Sun 10am–4pm, every 30min); April–Oct from Sandbanks and Poole Quay (daily 10am–5pm, every 30min); from Sandbanks £6.50 return, from Poole Quay £10.75 return

Brownsea Island is famed for its red squirrels, wading birds and other **wildlife**, which you can spot on themed trails. The landscape is surprisingly diverse for a small island, much of it heavily wooded, though with areas of heath and marsh, and narrow, shingly beaches too. It's pretty easy to escape from the boat-trippers and find a peaceful corner to picnic.

Compton Acres

164 Canford Cliffs Rd, BH13 7ES • Daily: Easter–Oct 10am–6pm; Nov–Easter 10am–4pm; last entry 1hr before closing • £8.45 • ☎01202 700778, ⓦ comptonacres.co.uk • Bus #50 from Bournemouth and #52 from Poole

One of the area's best-known gardens, **Compton Acres**, lies on the outskirts of Poole. Spectacularly sited over ten acres on steep slopes above Poole Harbour, the five gardens are internationally theme, including a formal Italian garden and an elegantly understated Japanese one, its meandering streams crossed by stone steps and wooden bridges.

ARRIVAL AND INFORMATION

POOLE

By train Poole's train station is on Serpentine Rd, about a 15min walk from the waterfront along the High St.
Destinations Bournemouth (every 20min; 10min); London

Waterloo (every 30min; 2hr–2hr 10min); Weymouth (every 30min; 35–45min).

By bus The bus station is in front of the Dolphin Centre

3

on Kingland Rd, with regular National Express services to London Victoria (11 daily; 3–4hr).
Tourist office At Poole Museum, 4 High St (April–Oct daily 10am–5pm; Nov–March Mon–Sat 10am–4pm, Sun noon–4pm; ☎01202 262600 ⍟pooletourism.com).

ACCOMMODATION

★**Hotel du Vin** Thames St, BH15 1JN ☎01202 685666, ⍟hotelduvin.com. Inside a fine old mansion with a double staircase, this stylish hotel has plush, comfortable rooms, an atmospheric restaurant and wine cellar, and a very cosy bar with its own log fire – great in winter. The location is ideal, in the pretty old town, a minute's walk from the Quay. **£160**

The Old Townhouse 7 High St, BH15 1AB ☎01202 670950, ⍟theoldtownhouse.co.uk. Attractive little Victorian-style B&B in a great location opposite the museum, with a wood-panelled tearoom/breakfast room on the ground floor. The decor in the four rooms may be rather traditional, but they are spotless and comfortable – one has its own terrace – and the owners go out of their way to be helpful. **£95**

EATING AND DRINKING

Deli on the Quay Unit D17 Dolphin Quays, The Quay, BH15 1HH ☎01202 660022, ⍟delionthequay. com. Bright, light harbourfront café-deli stacked with delicious preserves, wines and the like. The café serves fresh croissants, sandwiches and decent coffee. Mon & Wed–Fri 8.30am–5pm, Tues 8.30am–8pm, Sat & Sun 9am–5pm; Nov–March closes 4pm Mon–Fri.

★**The Guildhall Tavern** 15 Market Street, BH15 1NB, ☎01202 671717, ⍟guildhalltavern.co.uk. Fantastic French seafood restaurant with marine-themed decor and a small patio at the back, serving local fish and shellfish – scallops, crab, lobster and oysters among them – as well as traditional French dishes such as snails in garlic butter (six for £7) and boeuf bourguignon (£18). There's a very reasonable lunchtime set menu (two courses for £17, three for £20.50). Tues–Thurs 11.30am–3.30pm & 6–9.30pm,

Fri & Sat 11.30am–3.30pm & 5.30–10pm.
Karma 22 High St, BH15 1BP ☎01202 6701818, ⍟karma-mediterranean.co.uk. Atmospheric dining room with quirky decor, bare brick arches and wooden tables. The food is Mediterranean/Middle Eastern; the tasty meze include aubergine dip and falafel (starter platter to share £16), and there are mains such as hearty grills (chicken or lamb kebab and rice), moussaka and kleftiko (£14–16). Tues–Thurs 5.30–9pm, Fri & Sat 5.30–10pm.
Poole Arms 19 The Quay, BH15 1HJ ☎01202 673450 ⍟poolearms.co.uk. Completely covered with green tiles, this wonderfully atmospheric sixteenth-century pub is reassuringly old-fashioned, with decent beers and great fish dishes (£11–15). There's outdoor seating facing the waterfront, too. Mon–Sat 11am–11pm, Sun noon–11pm; kitchen daily noon–9pm.

The Isle of Purbeck

Though not actually an island, the **ISLE OF PURBECK** – a promontory of low hills and heathland jutting out beyond Poole Harbour – does have an insular and distinctive feel. Reached from the east by the ferry from Sandbanks at the narrow mouth of Poole Harbour, or by a long and congested landward journey via the bottleneck of **Wareham**, Purbeck can be a difficult destination to reach, but its villages are immensely pretty, none more so than **Corfe Castle**, with its majestic ruins. From **Swanage**, a low-key seaside resort, the Dorset Coast Path provides access to the oily shales of **Kimmeridge Bay**, the spectacular cove at **Lulworth** and the much-photographed natural arch of **Durdle Door**.

The whole coast from Purbeck to Exmouth in Devon – dubbed the **Jurassic Coast** (⍟jurassiccoast.org) – is a World Heritage Site on account of its geological significance and fossil remains; walkers can access it along the South West Coast Path.

ARRIVAL AND GETTING AROUND   THE ISLE OF PURBECK

By ferry There are regular ferries from Sandbanks (7am–11pm every 20min; pedestrians & bikes £1, cars £4.30; ☎01929 450203, ⍟sandbanksferry.co.uk).
By train Wareham is the only place served by mainline trains, though a steam train also runs between Swanage and Norden (see page 212). The train track has now been fully restored between Swanage and Wareham,

with a trial diesel service running the full route (see ⍟swanagerailway.co.uk for details of schedule).
By bus The Purbeck Breezer (⍟morebus.co.uk) runs two services around the Purbecks – route #40 from Poole to Swanage via Wareham and Corfe Castle, and route #50 from Bournemouth to Swanage via the Sandbanks ferry and Studland. In summer, some services are open-top.

By bike Cycling is a great way to get around, though be prepared for steep hills; bikes can be rented from Cycle Experience at Norden Car Park, Corfe Castle (☎01929 481606, ⓦpurbeckcyclehire.co.uk) and Charlie the Bikemonger, 5 Queen's Rd, Swanage (☎01929 475833, ⓦcharliethebikemonger.com).

Wareham

The grid pattern of its streets indicates the Saxon origins of **WAREHAM**, and the town is surrounded by even older earth ramparts known as the Walls. A riverside setting adds greatly to its charms, though the place gets fairly overrun in summer. Nearby lies an enclave of quaint houses around **Lady St Mary's Church**, which contains the marble coffin of Edward the Martyr, murdered at Corfe Castle in 978 (possibly by his stepmother, to make way for her son Ethelred).

St Martin's Church, at the north end of town, dates from Saxon times and contains a faded twelfth-century mural of St Martin offering his cloak to a beggar. The church's most striking feature, however, is a romantic effigy of T.E. Lawrence in Arab dress, which was originally destined for Salisbury Cathedral, but was rejected by the dean there who disapproved of Lawrence's sexual proclivities. Lawrence was killed in 1935 in a motorbike accident on the road from Bovington (six miles west); his simply furnished cottage is at **Clouds Hill**, seven miles northwest of Wareham (late May to Oct daily 11am–5pm; £6.30, NT; ☎01929 405616, ⓦnationaltrust.org.uk/clouds-hill). The small **Wareham Town Museum**, next to Wareham's town hall on East Street (Easter–Oct Mon–Sat 10am–4pm; free; ☎01929 553448, ⓦgreenacre.info/WTM) focuses on local history and Lawrence memorabilia.

3

ARRIVAL AND INFORMATION
WAREHAM

By train Wareham station, a 15min walk north of the town, sees regular trains from London (every 30min; 2hr 20min) and Weymouth (every 20–40min; 25–35min), with a limited train service to Swanage (see page 212).

Tourist office Wareham Library, South St (Easter–Oct Mon 10am–5pm, Tues–Sat 9.30am–5pm; Nov–Easter Mon 10am–4pm, Tues–Sat 9.30am–4pm; ☎01929 552740, ⓦvisit-dorset.com).

Corfe Castle

The Square, Corfe Castle, BH20 5EZ · Daily: March & Oct 10am–5pm; April–Sept 10am–6pm; Nov–Feb 10am–4pm · £9; NT · ☎01929 481294, ⓦnationaltrust.org.uk/corfe-castle · A few minutes' walk from Corfe Castle station (on the Swanage Steam Railway)

The romantic ruins of **Corfe Castle**, crowning the hill behind the village of the same name, are perhaps the most evocative in England. The family seat of Sir John Bankes, Attorney General to Charles I, this Royalist stronghold withstood a Cromwellian siege for six weeks, gallantly defended by Lady Bankes. One of her own men, Colonel Pitman, eventually betrayed the castle to the Roundheads, after which it was reduced to its present gap-toothed state by gunpowder. Apparently the victorious Roundheads were so impressed by Lady Bankes' courage that they allowed her to take the keys to the castle with her – they can still be seen in the library at her subsequent home, Kingston Lacy (see page 208).

ACCOMMODATION
CORFE CASTLE

Mortons House 45 East St, BH20 5EE ☎01929 480988, ⓦmortonshouse.co.uk. In a sixteenth-century manor house with a beautiful walled garden and log fires in winter, this award-winning small hotel has snug rooms, some with four-poster beds and stone fireplaces. The restaurant offers top local cuisine. **£160**

Norden Farm Norden, BH20 5DS, 1 mile from Corfe Castle ☎01929 480098, ⓦnordenfarm.com. Tucked into a tranquil valley, this working farm has extensive fields for tents and caravans, good facilities, its own shop and a menagerie of animals. Closed Nov–Feb. **£14.50**

EATING AND DRINKING

The Greyhound The Square, BH20 5EZ ☎01929 480205, ⓦgreyhoundcorfe.co.uk. One of England's oldest coaching inns, with frequent live music and a pleasant garden at the back with views of the castle.

The food is good, with simple dishes such as pulled pork sandwiches or fish and chips (£9–14), and more elaborate meals like langoustine risotto (£16). Daily 11am–11pm; kitchen Mon–Sat noon–9pm, Sun noon–8pm.

★ **The Scott Arms** West St, Kingston, BH20 5LH, 2 miles from Corfe Castle ⊕01929 480270, ⊛thescottarms.com. In the neighbouring village, a steep climb above Corfe Castle, this is a wonderful old inn with a warren of cosy rooms at the front and a large, modern-looking back room that doubles as its restaurant. The biggest draw is its garden, which commands a stupendous view over Corfe Castle in the valley below. The food is substantial, varied and good value at around £13 for mains; in summer the *Jerk Shak* sells fantastic Caribbean food in the garden. Daily 11am–11pm; kitchen Mon–Fri noon–2.30pm & 6–8.30pm, Sat & Sun noon–2.45pm & 6–8.45pm.

Swanage and around

3

Purbeck's largest town, **SWANAGE**, is a traditional seaside resort with a pleasant sandy beach and an ornate town hall. The town's station is the southern terminus of the **Swanage Steam Railway** (April–Oct daily; Nov– March Sat, Sun & school hols; £12.50 return; ⊕01929 425800, ⊛swanagerailway.co.uk), which runs for six miles to Norden, just north of Corfe Castle. There are plans to extend the service to Wareham. West of Swanage, you can pick up the coastal path to **Durlston Country Park**, (daily sunrise–sunset; free) around a mile out of town. Set in 280 acres of coastal woodland and crisscrossed with clifftop paths, it's a great place for a picnic or for wind-blown walks.

ACCOMMODATION — SWANAGE AND AROUND

The Swanage Haven 3 Victoria Rd, BH19 1LY ⊕01929 423088, ⊛swanagehaven.com. Good-value boutique guesthouse: the smart rooms have flatscreen TVs and the decked garden has a great outdoor hot tub. Breakfasts are made from locally sourced ingredients. No children. £90

★ **Tom's Field Campsite** Langton Matravers, BH19 3HN, a couple of miles west of Swanage ⊕01929 427110, ⊛tomsfieldcamping.co.uk. Wonderfully sited and well run, this is the best campsite in the region, with sea views from some pitches and direct access to the coast path. It also lets out bunks in a converted Nissen hut (the Walker's Barn) and pigsty (the Stone Room) and there's a well-stocked shop. Only takes reservations for longer stays – turn up early to bag a pitch. Walker's Barn £13, camping £16, Stone Room £30

EATING AND DRINKING

Gee Whites The Old Stone Quay, 1 High St, BH19 2LN ⊕01929 425720, ⊛geewhites.co.uk. Fashionable seafood bar right on the quay serving local lobster, crabs, mussels and oysters. The menu changes daily according to what's been caught (most dishes £7–10), but usually features the likes of *moules marinières*, tempura prawns and dressed crab. Summer daily 9am–9.30pm; rest of year hours are weather dependent.

★ **Seventh Wave** Durlston Castle & Country Park, Lighthouse Rd, BH19 2JL ⊕01929 421111, ⊛7eventhwave.com. Inside Durlston Castle with stunning coastal views, this is an unmissable stop – either for a coffee, snack or full meal. There are paninis and sandwiches for around £7.50, fresh fish or mains for £11–15, and cream teas for £10. Easter–Sept Mon–Thurs & Sun 9.30am–4pm, Fri & Sat 9.30am–4pm & 6–9pm; Oct–Easter daily 9.30am–4pm.

★ **Square and Compass** Worth Matravers, BH19 3LF, 4 miles west of Swanage ⊕01929 439229, ⊛squareandcompasspub.co.uk. In a quintessential Purbeck village, with views over the surrounding Downs and sea, this is one of England's finest pubs: the bar is a tiny hatch, the interior is a winter fug of log fires, walkers and dogs (and the occasional live band), while outside there's a motley collection of stone seats and wooden benches. Regularly winning CAMRA awards for its local ales and ciders, and with its own little fossil museum, it also serves delicious home-made pies. April–Sept daily noon–11pm; Oct–March Mon–Thurs noon–3pm & 6–11pm, Fri–Sun noon–11pm.

Studland

East of Swanage, you can follow the South West Coast Path over Ballard Down to descend into the pretty village of **STUDLAND** at the southern end of **Studland Bay**. The most northerly stretch of the beach, **Shell Bay**, is a magnificent strand of icing-sugar sand backed by a remarkable heathland ecosystem, home to all six British species of reptile –

adders are quite common, so be careful. On Middle Beach, you can **hire kayaks** from the **Studland Sea School** (☎01929 450430, ⓦstudlandseaschool.co.uk), or take one of their excellent guided kayak or snorkelling tours round Old Harry Rocks, through rock arches.

ACCOMMODATION AND EATING
STUDLAND

★ **Bankes Arms** Manor Rd, BH19 3AU ☎01929 450225, ⓦbankesarms.com. Lovely location, good food, and a great range of real ales, some from local breweries and others from its own on-site Purbeck Brewery. The pub food costs slightly more than average, but the portions are big, and frankly it's worth it for the joy of sitting in the grassy front garden with fantastic bay views, or by the roaring log fire in the cosy Purbeck stone interior. Daily 11am–11pm; kitchen May–Sept Mon–Sat noon–9.30pm & Sun noon–9pm, Oct–April daily noon–9pm.

The Pig on the Beach Studland Bay, BH19 3AU ☎01929 450288, ⓦthepighotel.com. An eighteenth-century manor house in a fantastic location, renovated in *The Pig*'s signature shabby-chic style, with lovely gardens leading down to the sea. Stay in the very comfortable rooms – some have sea views, all have luxurious showers – or a converted shepherd's hut in the grounds (£240). The restaurant is great too, specializing in locally caught or foraged ingredients, plus herbs and veg grown here – expect dishes such as south coast hake with marsh samphire (£18); it's very popular, so book ahead. Daily noon–2.30pm & 6.30–9.30pm. **£180**

Lulworth Cove and around

The quaint thatch-and-stone villages of **EAST LULWORTH** and **WEST LULWORTH** form a prelude to **Lulworth Cove**, a perfect shell-shaped bite formed when the sea broke through a weakness in the cliffs and then gnawed away at them from behind, forming a circular cave that eventually collapsed to leave a bay enclosed by sandstone cliffs. West of the cove is **Stair Hole**, a roofless sea cave riddled with arches that will eventually collapse to form another Lulworth Cove. The mysteries of local geology are explained at the **Lulworth Heritage Centre** (daily 10am–5pm; free) by the car park at the top of the lane leading down to the cove.

Durdle Door

A mile west of Lulworth Cove, the iconic limestone arch of **Durdle Door** can be reached via the steep uphill path starting at Lulworth Cove's car park. The arch itself sits at the end of a long shingle beach (accessed via steep steps), a lovely place for catching the sun and swimming in fresh, clear water. There are further steps to a bay just east of Durdle Door, **St Oswald's Bay**, with another shingle beach and offshore rocks that you can swim out to.

ACCOMMODATION AND EATING
LULWORTH COVE AND AROUND

Castle Inn 8 Main Rd, West Lulworth, BH20 5RN ☎01929 400311, ⓦthecastleinn-lulworthcove.co.uk. This sixteenth-century thatched pub has a lovely terraced garden, a range of local real ales and a selection of traditional pub games. High-quality pub grub features home-made steak and ale pie (£14) and salmon steaks (£13). Very dog-friendly. Daily noon–10pm; kitchen daily noon–9pm.

Durdle Door Holiday Park West Lulworth, BH20 5PU ☎01929 400200, ⓦlulworth.com. Superbly positioned up on the cliffs above Durdle Door, this campsite has fabulous views from its touring field, while tents can be pitched in the more sheltered wooded field. It's a 20min walk across fields to Lulworth Cove and there's also a shop and café-bar on site. **£42**

Lulworth Cove Inn Main Rd, Lulworth Cove, BH20 5RQ ☎01929 400333, ⓦlulworth-coveinn.co.uk. With a great location right on the main street leading down to the cove and overlooking the duck pond, this is the first choice in Lulworth itself – try to bag one of the front rooms, with their own cove-view terraces (£10 extra). The pub downstairs offers local Blandford ales, real fires, a pleasant garden and decent food, including steak and ale pie (£13.50) and smoked mackerel (£11.50). Daily 11am–11pm; kitchen noon–9pm. **£110**

Dorchester and around

For many, **DORCHESTER**, county town of Dorset, is essentially **Thomas Hardy**'s town; he was born at Higher Bockhampton, three miles east, his heart is buried in Stinsford, a couple of miles northeast (the rest of him is in Westminster Abbey), and he spent much of his life in Dorchester itself. The town appears in his novels as Casterbridge, and the local countryside is evocatively depicted, notably the wild heathland of the east (Egdon Heath) and the eerie yew forest of Cranborne Chase. The real Dorchester – liveliest on Wednesday, market day – has a pleasant central core of mostly seventeenth-century and Georgian buildings, though the town's origins go back to the Romans, who founded "Durnovaria" in about 70 AD. The Roman walls were replaced in the eighteenth century by tree-lined avenues called "Walks", but some traces of the Roman period have survived. On the southeast edge of town, **Maumbury Rings** is where the Romans held vast gladiatorial combats in an amphitheatre adapted from a Stone Age site.

In addition to its Hardy connections, Dorchester is associated with the notorious **Judge Jeffreys**, who, after the ill-fated rebellion of the Duke of Monmouth (one of Charles II's illegitimate offspring) against James II, held his "**Bloody Assizes**" in the Oak Room of the former Antelope Hotel on Cornhill in 1685. A total of 292 men were sentenced to death; most got away with a flogging and transportation to the West Indies, but 74 were hung, drawn and quartered, their heads stuck on pikes throughout Dorset and Somerset.

Shire Hall

58–60 High St, DT1 1UZ • Daily 10am–5pm • £8, ticket valid for one year • ☎ 01305 267992

Shire Hall, also known as the **Old Crown Courts**, are where the **Tolpuddle Martyrs** (see page 216), were sentenced to transportation for forming what was in effect Britain's first trade union. The room in which the Martyrs were tried (and where Thomas Hardy later served as a magistrate) has been preserved almost unchanged from when it first opened in 1796; it is now the centrepiece of a fascinating courthouse museum, with changing exhibitions and events linked to the history of justice. You can also visit the original cells.

Dorset County Museum

High West St, DT1 1XA • April–Oct Mon–Sat 10am–5pm (daily in school summer hols); Nov–March Mon–Sat 10am–4pm • £6.35 • ☎ 01305 262735, ⓦ dorsetcountymuseum.org

The best place to find out about Dorchester's history is the engrossing Victorian **Dorset County Museum**, where archeological and geological displays trace Celtic and Roman history, including a section on nearby Maiden Castle and a Jurassic Coast gallery, complete with fossils and animated flying dinosaurs. Pride of place goes to the re-creation of Thomas Hardy's study – his pens are inscribed with the names of the books he wrote with them. In early 2018, the museum was the first venue to host London's Natural History Museum's diplodocus skeleton (aka Dippy) on its nationwide tour, in advance of a substantial renovation project. Parts of the museum will be closed during the construction of a £13 million extension, including new galleries, a library and a café, due to open in 2020.

Maiden Castle

Around 2 miles southwest of Dorchester, DT2 9EY • Daily 24hr • Free; EH • ⓦ www.english-heritage.org.uk/visit/places/maiden-castle

One of southern England's finest prehistoric sites, covering about 115 acres, is **MAIDEN CASTLE**. It was first developed around 3000 BC by a Stone Age farming community and then used during the Bronze Age as a funeral mound. Iron Age dwellers expanded it into a populous settlement and fortified it with a daunting series of ramparts and ditches, just in time for the arrival of Vespasian's Second Legion. The ancient Britons' slingstones were no match for the more sophisticated weapons of the Roman invaders, however, and

Maiden Castle was stormed in a massacre in 43 AD. What you see today is a massive series of grassy concentric ridges about 60ft high, creasing the surface of the hill. The main finds from the site are displayed in the Dorset County Museum (see page 215).

Cerne Abbas giant

Cerne Abbas, 7 miles north of Dorchester, DT2 7AL • Daily 24hr • Free; NT • ☎ 01297 489481, ⓦ nationaltrust.org.uk/cerne-giant

The village of **CERNE ABBAS** has bags of charm, with gorgeous Tudor cottages and abbey ruins, but its main attraction is the enormously priapic **Cerne Abbas giant** carved in the chalk hillside just north of the village, standing 180ft high and brandishing a club over his disproportionately small head. The age of the monument is disputed, though it is likely that the giant originated as some primeval fertility symbol. Folklore has it that lying on the outsize member will induce conception, but the National Trust, who now own the site, do their best to stop people wandering over it and damaging the 2ft-deep trenches that form the outlines. Although you can walk round the giant, the carving itself is fenced off to avoid erosion and you don't get the full impact when you are so close – for the best view, follow signs to the car park and **viewpoint** on the hillside opposite.

Tolpuddle Martyrs Museum

Tolpuddle, DT2 7EH, 8 miles east of Dorchester • April–Oct Tues–Sat 10am–5pm, Sun 11am–5pm; Nov–March Thurs–Sat 10am–4pm, Sun 11am–4pm • Free • ☎ 01305 848237, ⓦ tolpuddlemartyrs.org.uk

The delightful Dorset village of **TOLPUDDLE** is of interest principally because of the **Tolpuddle Martyrs**. In 1834, six villagers, George and James Loveless, Thomas and John Standfield, John Brine and James Hammett, were sentenced to transportation for banding together to form the Friendly Society of Agricultural Labourers, in order to petition for a small wage increase on the grounds that their families were starving. The men spent three years in Australia's penal colonies before being pardoned following a public outcry – and the Martyrs passed into history as founders of the **trade union** movement. Six memorial cottages were built in 1934 to commemorate the centenary of the Martyrs' conviction. The middle one has been turned into the little **Tolpuddle Martyrs Museum**, which charts the story of the men, from their harsh rural lives before their conviction to the horrors of transportation in a convict ship and the brutal conditions of the penal colonies.

ARRIVAL AND INFORMATION

By train Dorchester has two train stations, Dorchester South and Dorchester West, both south of the centre.
Destinations (Dorchester South) Bournemouth (every 30min; 40–45min); London Waterloo (every 30min; 2hr 35min–2hr 50min); Weymouth (every 15–30min; 10–15min).
Destinations (Dorchester West) Bath (5 daily; 2hr); Bristol (5 daily; 2hr 10min–2hr 25 min).
By bus Most local buses stop around the car park on Acland Rd, to the east of South St, though long-distance

DORCHESTER AND AROUND

buses pull in next to Dorchester South train station.
Destinations Bournemouth (4 daily; 1hr–1hr 45min); London Victoria (1 daily; 4hr); Weymouth (at least hourly; 25min–1hr).
Tourist Information Centre Dorchester Library, South Walks House, Charles St (April–Oct Mon 10am–5.30pm, Tues & Fri 9.30am–7pm, Wed 9.30am–1pm, Thurs 9.30am–5.30pm, Sat 9am–4pm; Nov–March Mon 10am–4pm, Tues, Thurs & Fri 9.30am–4pm, Wed 9.30am–1pm, Sat 9am–4pm; ☎ 01305 267992, ⓦ visit-dorset.com).

ACCOMMODATION

The Old Rectory Winterbourne Steepleton, DT2 9LG, 4 miles west of Dorchester ☎ 01305 889468, ⓦ theold rectorybandb.co.uk. A lovely former rectory from 1850 in a tiny, pretty village. The B&B has four comfortable en-suite rooms, one with a four-poster, and attractive gardens. **£80**

Westwood House 29 High West St, DT1 1UP ☎ 01305 268018, ⓦ westwoodhouse.co.uk. Comfortable Georgian townhouse on the busy high street, with well-furnished rooms complete with flatscreen TVs. The breakfasts are great, and there's an inexpensive car park nearby. **£100**

EATING AND DRINKING

Potters Café 19 Durngate St, DT1 1JP ☎ 01305 260312. Very appealing café/restaurant with a log fire in winter and a small garden. It serves a range of inexpensive dishes such as fish soup, quiche and salads, as well as the likes of tempura red mullet (£10). Mon–Sat 9.30am–4pm, Sun 10am–2.30pm.

Sienna 36 High West St, DT1 1UP ☎ 01305 250022, ⓦ siennadorchester.co.uk. Former Masterchef contestant Marcus Wilcox is the chef at this small upmarket restaurant which specializes in locally sourced British cuisine, with innovative dishes such as sea trout with artichoke and lamb with aubergine and yoghurt (£17–20). Wed–Fri noon–2pm & 7–9pm, Sat 10am–2pm & 7–9pm, Sun noon–3pm.

Yalbury and Yvons Café & Wine Bar Dukes Auction House, Brewery Square, DT1 1GA ☎ 01305 260185, ⓦ ycscafe.com. In the modern cultural quarter of Brewery Square, this friendly café-restaurant serves a good range of sandwiches and pastries by day, and evening meals at weekends such as wild boar and faggots and Portland crab (mains £10–14). Mon–Thurs 8.30am–5pm, Fri & Sat 8.30am–11pm, Sun 9am–3pm.

Sherborne

3

Tucked away in the northwest corner of Dorset, ten miles north of Cerne Abbas, the pretty town of **SHERBORNE** was once the capital of Wessex, its church having cathedral status until Old Sarum (see page 225) usurped the bishopric in 1075.

Abbey Church

3 Abbey Close, ST9 3LQ • Daily: April–Oct 8am–6pm; Nov–March 8am–4pm • Free, but donation welcome • ☎ 01935 812452, ⓦ sherborneabbey.com

Sherborne's former historical glory is embodied by the magnificent **Abbey Church**, founded in 705 and later becoming a Benedictine abbey. Most of its extant parts date from a rebuilding in the fifteenth century. Among the abbey church's many tombs are those of Alfred the Great's two brothers, Ethelred and Ethelbert, and the Elizabethan poet Thomas Wyatt, all in the northeast corner.

The castles

Sherborne boasts two "castles", both associated with Sir Walter Raleigh. Queen Elizabeth I first leased, then gave, Raleigh the twelfth-century **Old Castle**, on Castletom (April–June, Sept & Oct daily 10am–5pm; July & Aug daily 10am–6pm; £4.30, EH; ☎ 03703 331181, ⓦ www.english-heritage.org.uk/visit/places/sherborne-old-castle), but it seems that he despaired of feudal accommodation and built himself a more comfortably domesticated house, **Sherborne Castle**, in adjacent parkland accessed from New Road (April–Oct Tues–Thurs, Sat & Sun 11am–5pm, gardens 10am–6pm; castle and gardens £12, gardens only £6.50; ☎ 01935 812072, ⓦ sherbornecastle.com). When Sir Walter fell from the queen's favour by seducing her maid of honour, the Digby family acquired the house and have lived here ever since. The Old Castle fared less happily, and was pulverized by Cromwellian cannon fire for the obstinately Royalist leanings of its occupants.

ARRIVAL AND INFORMATION   SHERBORNE

By train The station is 5min south of the town centre, and is served by hourly trains between London and Exeter, with some services continuing on to Plymouth.

By bus Buses from Dorchester, Yeovil and Blandford Forum pull in outside the train station.

Tourist office 3 Tilton Court, Digby Rd (Mon–Sat: Easter–Aug 9am–5pm; Sept–Nov 9.30am–4pm; Dec–Easter 10am–3pm; ☎ 01935 815341, ⓦ sherbornetown.com).

ACCOMMODATION AND EATING

The Eastbury Long St, DT9 3BY ☎ 01935 813131, ⓦ theeastburyhotel.co.uk. In a fine Georgian house, with its own highly regarded restaurant, bar and lovely walled gardens. The front rooms are on the small side; it's worth paying extra for one of the executive rooms, which are spacious and boutique in feel, overlooking the gardens. The restaurant specializes in seasonal and locally sourced ingredients. Daily noon–2pm & 6.30–9pm. **£150**

★ **Oliver's** 19 Cheap St, DT9 3PU ☎01935 815005,

ⓦoliverscoffeehouse.co.uk. With long wooden benches laid out in a former Victorian butcher's, adorned with the original tiles, this friendly café-deli serves great cakes and coffee, accompanied by oodles of atmosphere. Mon–Fri 9am–5pm, Sat 9.30am–5pm, Sun 10am–4pm.

Shaftesbury

Fifteen miles east of Sherborne on the A30, **SHAFTESBURY** perches on a spur of lumpy hills, with severe gradients on three sides of the town. On a clear day, views from the town are terrific – one of the best vantage points is **Gold Hill**, quaint, cobbled and very steep. At its crest, the **Gold Hill Museum and Garden** (April–Oct daily 10.30am–4pm; free; ☎01747 852157, ⓦgoldhillmuseum.org.uk) displays items ranging from locally made buttons, for which the area was once renowned, to a mummified cat.

Pilgrims used to flock to Shaftesbury to pay homage to the bones of Edward the Martyr, which were brought to the **abbey** in 978, though now only the footings of the abbey church survive, just off the main street on Park Walk (April–Oct daily 10am–5pm; £3; ☎01747 852910, ⓦshaftesburyabbey.org.uk). **St Peter's Church** on the marketplace is one of the few reminders of Shaftesbury's medieval grandeur, when it boasted a castle, twelve churches and four market crosses.

ARRIVAL AND INFORMATION

SHAFTESBURY

By bus There are services from Salisbury (Mon–Sat 2–3 daily; 1hr 15min) and Blandford Forum (Mon–Sat 4 daily; 45min).

Tourist office 8 Bell St (Mon–Sat 10am–4pm; ☎01747 853514, ⓦshaftesburydorset.com).

ACCOMMODATION AND EATING

The Grosvenor Arms The Commons, SP7 8JA ☎01747 850580, ⓦgrosvenorarms.co.uk. This former coaching inn in the centre of town has had a successful makeover into a buzzy, boutique-style hotel. The rooms are stylish, with comfy beds, coffee machines and flatscreen TVs, and the downstairs restaurant is good too, with a wood-fired pizza oven, plus local fish and meat dishes (£10–15). Daily noon–3pm & 6–10pm. **£90**

Number 5 Bimport 5 Bimport, SP7 8AT ☎01747

228490, ⓦfivebimport.co.uk. Small, friendly B&B in an attractive, classily renovated Georgian townhouse in the centre of Shaftesbury. There are just two rooms – the larger one opens onto the garden. **£135**

★ **The Salt Cellar** Gold Hill, SP7 8JW ☎01747 851838. Right at the top of the hill itself and with great views, this place serves inexpensive snacks and daily specials from around £8, including home-made pies, in the pillar-lined interior or at outdoor tables on the cobbles. Mon–Sat 9am–5pm.

Weymouth and around

Whether George III's passion for sea bathing was a symptom of his eventual madness is uncertain, but it was at **WEYMOUTH** in 1789 that he became the first reigning monarch to follow the craze. Sycophantic gentry rushed into the waves behind him, and soon the town, formerly a busy port, took on the elegant Georgian stamp that it bears today. Weymouth's highlight, of course, is its long sandy beach, and it makes a lively family holiday destination in summer, reverting to a more sedate rhythm out of season.

The Esplanade

Weymouth's most imposing architectural heritage stands along the **Esplanade**, a dignified range of bow-fronted and porticoed buildings gazing out across the graceful bay. At the far southern end of the Esplanade, the Quay juts out into the sea, housing the town's ferry terminals and its newest attraction, the 173ft-high **Jurassic Skyline** (daily: April, May & late Oct 11am–3pm; June to late July & mid-Sept to mid-Oct 11am–5pm; late July to early Sept 11am–6pm; check website for half-term and bank hol hours; £7.50, £6.50 online; @jurassicskyline.com), which provides stunning views over the town and coastline. At the northern end of the promenade, in Lodmoor Country Park, the excellent **Sea Life Park** (daily March–Oct 10am–5pm, Nov–Feb 10am–4pm; last admission 1hr before closing; £23.50, £16.50 online, includes entry to Jurassic Skyline; @visitsealife.com/weymouth) is home to turtles, penguins, otters and seals, as well as a seahorse breeding centre, and water play areas.

The Old Harbour

The pedestrianized **St Mary's Street** heads south from the Esplanade to the Town Bridge, beyond which is the more intimate quayside of the **Old Harbour**. Here, a few buildings survive from pre-Georgian times, including the restored **Tudor House** at 3 Trinity Street (Feb–April, Nov & Dec first Sun of month 2–4pm; May–Oct Tues–Fri 1–4pm, Sun 2–4pm; £4; ☎01305 779711).

3

ARRIVAL AND INFORMATION   WEYMOUTH AND AROUND

By train Weymouth is served at least hourly by trains from London (2hr 45min–3hr), Southampton (1hr 20min–1hr 40min), Bournemouth (50min) and Poole (35–45min), with less regular services from Bristol (2hr 30min) and

Bath (2hr 10min). Trains arrive at the station on King St, a short walk back from the seafront.
By bus Buses from Dorchester (at least hourly; 25min–1hr) pull in at the stops by King George III's statue.

ACCOMMODATION

★**Bay View House** 35 The Esplanade, DT4 8DH ☎01305 782083, @bayview-weymouth.co.uk. Clean, friendly and well-kept guesthouse right on the seafront. All the rooms are comfortable, but the front ones overlooking the sea are particularly great value, at £65. Also has family rooms and free private garage parking. **£60**

Old Harbour View 12 Trinity Rd, DT4 8TJ ☎01305 774633, @oldharbourview.co.uk. Cosy guesthouse in a great harbourfront location. It consists of just two rooms in a Georgian townhouse, but it's worth paying a few pounds extra for the one at the front with a harbour view. The breakfasts are great, using locally sourced and free-range ingredients. **£98**

EATING AND DRINKING

Enzo 110 The Esplanade, DT2 7EA ☎01305 778666, @enzo-ristorante.co.uk. Traditional Italian restaurant with clean, contemporary decor, tiled floors and modern furnishings; it's right on the seafront, but away from the main drag. It serves a range of pasta dishes (£9–12) and pizzas (£8–13), plus other main courses such as veal escalope (£15.50). Excellent value and friendly service. Daily 12.30–2.30pm & 5.30–10.30pm.

Manbo's Bistro 46 St Mary St, DT4 8PU ☎01305 839839, @manbosbistro.com. They serve good-value fish, pasta and meat dishes, such as prawn and pesto linguine (£10) and fish chowder (£13), plus tasty daily fish and game specials, at this friendly family-run bistro. The dining area is

narrow with an open kitchen at the back, and there are a few tables on the pedestrianized street in front. Mon 6–9pm, Tues–Thurs noon–2.30pm & 6–9pm, Fri noon–2.30pm & 6–9.30pm, Sat noon–3pm & 6–9.30pm.

★**The Hive Café** 20 Park St, DT4 7DQ ☎07867 898498. Great veggie and vegan café with friendly service, a little courtyard at the back and a cosy upstairs room with a wood-burner. The food is fantastic – home-made quiche and filo pastries, falafel and a great-value meze plate with a pasty and a selection of salads for £6. Tasty cakes are made with honey from their own hives, and the hot lemon, ginger and honey drink (£2) is delicious. Wed–Sat 10.30am–4pm, Sun 11am–3.30pm.

Isle of Portland

Just south of Weymouth stretch the giant arms of Portland Harbour, where a long causeway links the mainland to the stark, wind-battered and treeless **Isle of Portland**. It's famed for its hard white limestone, which has been quarried here for centuries – Wren used it for St Paul's Cathedral, and it clads the UN headquarters in New York. It was also used for the 6000ft breakwater that protects Portland Harbour – the largest artificial harbour in Britain, built by convicts in the nineteenth century and the main centre for the 2012 Olympic Games sailing events. It is still surveyed by **Portland Castle** (daily: April–Sept 10am–6pm; Oct 10am–5pm; £5.70, EH; ☎01305 820539, ⍵www.english-heritage.org.uk/visit/places/portland-castle), which was commissioned by Henry VIII. Southeast of here, the craggy limestone of the Isle rises to 496ft at Verne Hill. At **Portland Bill**, the southern tip of the island, you can climb the 153 steps of **Portland Lighthouse** (10am–5pm: Easter–Oct daily; Nov–Easter Sat & Sun; £7; ☎01305 821050, ⍵trinityhouse.co.uk), which dates from 1906, for superb views in all directions.

ARRIVAL AND DEPARTURE   **ISLE OF PORTLAND**

By bus First Bus service #1 runs every 20–30min from Weymouth King's Statue to Portland (30–40min).

EATING AND DRINKING

Cove House Inn 91 Chiswell, DT5 1AW ☎01305 820895, ⍵thecovehouseinn.co.uk. A good spot for food or a quick drink, with pub staples such as burgers (£9.25) as well as a daily local fish menu, featuring such treats as scallops with chorizo and garlic (£13). It's cosy inside, with its wood-burner and big windows with sea views, while the outside tables look over Chesil Beach. Mon–Sat 11am–11pm, Sun noon–10.30pm; kitchen daily noon–2.30pm & 6–9pm.

Crab House Café Ferrymans Way, Portland Rd at the entrance to the Portland causeway, DT4 9YU ☎01305 788867, ⍵crabhousecafe.co.uk. In a great location overlooking Chesil Beach, this upmarket beach shack is renowned for its locally caught fresh fish and seafood (from £14), including oysters from its own beds. The menu changes daily according to the catch, but expect dishes like turbot steak with samphire. There are tables outside; reservations advised. Wed & Thurs noon–2.30pm & 6–9pm, Fri & Sat noon–2.30pm & 6–9.30pm, Sun noon–3.30pm.

Chesil Beach

Chesil Beach is the strangest feature of the Dorset coast, a 200yd-wide, 50ft-high bank of pebbles that extends for eighteen miles, its component stones gradually decreasing in size from fist-like pebbles at Portland to "pea gravel" at Burton Bradstock in the west. This sorting is an effect of the powerful coastal currents, which make this one of the most dangerous beaches in Europe – churchyards in the local villages display plenty of evidence of wrecks and drownings. Though not a swimming beach, Chesil is popular with sea anglers, and its wild, uncommercialized atmosphere makes an appealing antidote to the south-coast resorts. Behind the beach, **The Fleet**, a brackish lagoon, was the setting for J. Meade Faulkner's classic smuggling tale, *Moonfleet*.

ACCOMMODATION

★ **East Shilvinghampton Farm** Portesham, DT3 4HN ☎01420 80804, ⍵featherdown.co.uk. A lovely farm in a beautiful valley, a couple of miles inland from the Fleet Lagoon. It has various spacious, luxurious tents to rent – ready-erected, with running water, a toilet, a wood-burning stove and comfortable beds – in an idyllic field that looks down the valley, with horses, goats and chickens in the paddock next door. Three-night minimum stay. From £145

Abbotsbury

At the point where Chesil Beach attaches itself to the shore is the pretty village of **ABBOTSBURY**, all tawny ironstone and thatch. The village has three main attractions, which can be visited individually or on a combined "Passport" ticket for £18 (☎01305 871130, ⍵abbotsbury-tourism.co.uk). The most absorbing is the **Swannery** (daily mid-March to Oct 10am–5pm; £12.50), a wetland reserve for mute swans dating back to medieval times, when presumably it formed part of the abbot's larder. If you visit in late May or June, you'll see baby cygnets waddling around. The eel-grass reeds through which the swans paddle were once harvested to thatch roofs in the region. One example can be seen on the fifteenth-century Tithe Barn, the last remnant of the abbey and today housing the **Children's Farm** (10am–5pm: mid-March to early Sept daily; late Sept & Oct Sat & Sun; £11, under-16s £9.50), whose highlights include goat-racing and pony rides. Lastly, in the **Subtropical Gardens** (daily: Nov–March 10am–4pm; April–Oct 10am–5pm; closed over Christmas period; £12.50) delicate species thrive in the microclimate created by Chesil's stones, which act as a giant radiator to deter all but the worst frosts.

Bridport and around

Ten miles west of Abbotsbury is pretty **BRIDPORT**, mentioned in the Domesday Book of 1086 and an important port before the rivers silted up in the early 1700s. It's a pleasant old town of solid brick buildings with very wide streets, a hangover from its days as a rope-making centre when cords were stretched between the houses to be twisted and dyed. Today, it's a lively **market** town (Wed & Sat) with an arty, alternative vibe. The harbour lies a mile or so south at **West Bay**, which has a fine sandy beach sheltered below majestic red cliffs – the sheer East Cliffs are a tempting challenge for intrepid walkers – and it made a suitably brooding location for the ITV murder series, *Broadchurch*.

3

ACCOMMODATION AND EATING

BRIDPORT AND AROUND

The Bull 34 East St, DT6 3LF ☎ 01308 422878, ⓦ thebullhotel.co.uk. Friendly, boutique-style hotel in a former seventeenth-century coaching inn in the centre of town. The rooms are comfortable and modern, some with roll-top baths: there are also some family rooms. The restaurant and bar are good, too: try *moules marinières* (£9) to start, followed by an 8oz rib-eye steak (£22). Daily noon–3pm & 6.30–9.30pm. **£135**

★ **Seaside Boarding House** Cliff Rd, Burton Bradstock, DT6 4RB ☎ 01308 897205, ⓦ theseasideboardinghouse. com. Smart and stylish, this beachside bolthole has a relaxed vibe, great cocktails, and comfortable contemporary rooms, with lovely sea or countryside views. Set up by the founders of London's Groucho Club, it's a wonderful place to chill out and the location is hard to beat – a short walk from the beach, with a large terrace giving fantastic coast views. The restaurant is highly recommended for its tasty Modern British dishes, such as halibut with shellfish bisque (mains £14–20), with plenty of fresh fish and local, seasonal produce. Daily 10am–10pm. **£195**

The Riverside West Bay, DT6 4EZ ☎ 01308 422011, ⓦ thefishrestaurant-westbay.co.uk. Reservations are recommended for this renowned restaurant which offers fresh, sumptuous fish and seafood and fine river views. There is a daily changing menu, but expect the likes of lemon sole fillets with sea salt and lemon (£22.25). There are also meat and vegetarian options. Tues–Thurs noon–2.30pm & 6.30–8.30pm, Fri & Sat noon–2.30pm & 6.30–9pm, Sun noon–2.30pm.

★ **Watch House Café** West Bay, DT6 4EL ☎ 01308 459330, ⓦ hivebeachcafe.co.uk/watch-house-caf. Nestled into a bank of shingle right on the beach, and with an appealing outdoor terrace, this rightly popular café-restaurant is a must-visit. You can just have a coffee and cake or ice cream, but the real draw is the fresh fish and seafood, including a superb fish soup (£12) and Lyme Bay hake fillets with samphire (£17). There is also a wood-fired oven which churns out good-sized pizzas (£10–15). July & Aug Mon–Wed & Sun 10am–5pm, Thurs–Sat 10am–5pm & 6–8pm; Sept–June daily 10am–5pm.

Lyme Regis

LYME REGIS, Dorset's most westerly town, shelters snugly between steep, fossil-filled cliffs. Its intimate size and photogenic qualities make this a popular spot in summer, with some upmarket literary associations – Jane Austen summered in a seafront cottage and set part of *Persuasion* in Lyme (the town appears in the 1995 film version), while novelist John Fowles lived here until his death in 2005 (the film adaptation of *The French Lieutenant's Woman* was also shot here). Colourwashed cottages and elegant Regency and Victorian villas line its seafront and flanking streets, but Lyme's best-known feature is a practical reminder of its commercial origins: **the Cobb**, a curving harbour wall originally built in the thirteenth century. It has suffered many alterations

LYME'S JURASSIC COAST

The cliffs around Lyme are made up of a complex layer of limestone, greensand and unstable clay, a perfect medium for preserving **fossils**, which are exposed by landslips of the waterlogged clays. In 1811, after a fierce storm caused parts of the cliffs to collapse, 12-year-old **Mary Anning**, a keen fossil-hunter, discovered an almost complete dinosaur skeleton, a 30ft ichthyosaurus now displayed in London's Natural History Museum.

Hands-off inspection of the area's complex **geology** can be enjoyed all around the town: as you walk along the seafront and out towards The Cobb, look for the outlines of ammonites in the walls and paving stones. To the west of Lyme, the **Undercliff** is a fascinating jumble of overgrown landslips, now a nature reserve, where a great path wends its way through the undergrowth for around seven miles to neighbouring Seaton in Devon. East of Lyme is **Charmouth** (Jane Austen's favourite resort), from where you can take the coastal path to the headland of **Golden Cap**, whose brilliant outcrop of auburn sandstone is crowned with gorse.

3

since, most notably in the nineteenth century, when its massive boulders were clad in neater blocks of Portland stone.

On Bridge Street, the excellent **Lyme Regis Museum** (daily 10am–5pm; £4.95; ☎01297 443370, ⓦlymeregismuseum.co.uk) displays artefacts related to the town's literary connections, including John Fowles' office chair; the new Mary Anning Wing tells the story of Anning's life and her incredible fossil finds (see above). **Dinosaurland** on Coombe Street (late Feb to late Oct daily 10am–5pm; sporadic openings at other times; £5; ☎01297 443541, ⓦdinosaurland.co.uk) fills out the story of ammonites and other local fossils. The town is also a foodie destination, with lots of superb fish restaurants and good pubs, plus the **Town Mill Complex** (ⓦtownmill.org.uk) in Mill Lane, with a fantastic cheese shop, local brewery and café, as well as a working mill, pottery and art gallery.

ARRIVAL AND INFORMATION
LYME REGIS

By train Lyme's nearest station is in Axminster, 5 miles north, served by regular trains from London Waterloo and Exeter: bus #X54 runs from the station to Lyme.

By bus First Buses (ⓦfirstgroup.com) runs a daily #X52 bus service from Exeter (1hr 45min) and Bridport (25min).

Tourist office Church St (April–July & Sept–Oct Mon–Sat 10am–5am; Aug Mon–Sat 10am–5am, Sun 10am–4pm; Nov–March Mon–Sat 10am–3pm; ☎01297 442138, ⓦlymeregis.org).

ACCOMMODATION

★ **Alexandra Hotel** Pound St, DT7 3HZ ☎01297 442010, ⓦhotelalexandra.co.uk. Popular with honeymooners and good for families, this is the town's top hotel, located inside an eighteenth-century manor house with bleached wood floors and lovely gardens overlooking the sea. Many of the comfortable rooms have sea views, and there is also a highly rated restaurant. **£180**

Old Lyme 29 Coombe St, DT7 3PP ☎01297 442929, ⓦoldlymeguesthouse.co.uk. Guesthouse right in the town centre in a lovely 300-year-old stone former post office. There are six smallish but spruce bedrooms – one of them is a triple room and all are en suite, or with a private bathroom. **£90**

EATING AND DRINKING

Hix Oyster and Fish House Cobb Rd, DT7 3JP ☎01297 446910, ⓦhixoysterandfishhouse.co.uk. In a lovely location overlooking the town and sea, this airy restaurant, owned by acclaimed chef Mark Hix, specializes in local fish and seafood: sublime main courses include Torbay cod with shrimps (£21.50), though there are cheaper options, like huss curry (£13.50). April–Oct daily noon–10pm; Nov–March Tues–Sat noon–10pm, Sun noon–4pm.

Royal Standard 25 Marine Parade, DT7 3JF ☎01297 442637, ⓦtheroyalstandardlymeregis.co.uk. Lovely beachside inn dating back four hundred years, with a log fire inside, and a great sea-facing beer garden that leads onto the beach. There are real ales on tap, brewed by Palmers in nearby Bridport, and decently priced pub grub (from £11). Daily 10am–11pm; kitchen April–Sept daily noon–9pm, Oct–March daily noon–3pm &

5.50–9pm.

★ **Tierra Kitchen** 1a Coombe St, DT7 3PY ☎01297 445189, ⓦtierrakitchen.co.uk. Overlooking the millstream, *Tierra Kitchen* is a bright vegetarian restaurant serving a wide range of seasonal lunches such as courgette-flower fritters or vegetable tagine (around £10), plus more substantial evening meals like goat's cheese and beetroot tarte tatin, with delicious desserts (two courses £20). Tues 6–9pm, Wed–Sat noon–2.15pm & 6–9pm.

Town Mill Bakery 2 Coombe St, DT7 3PY ☎01297 444754, ⓦtownmillbakery.wordpress.com. A wonderful bakery/café serving a superb array of breads and cakes freshly baked on the premises. The ingredients are mostly local and largely organic, with sublime breakfasts of home-made jam, boiled eggs and local honey – choose your bread and toast it yourself, then sit at the communal long wooden tables. Lunch includes home-made soup and pizzas (from £7.50). Daily: Aug 8.30am–8pm; Sept–July 8.30am–5pm.

Salisbury and around

SALISBURY, huddled below Wiltshire's chalky plain in the converging valleys of the Avon and Nadder, sprang into existence in the early thirteenth century, when the bishopric was moved from nearby **Old Sarum** (see page 225). Today, it looks from a distance very much as it did when Constable painted his celebrated view of it, and though traffic may clog its centre, this prosperous and well-kept city is designed on a pleasantly human scale, with no sprawling suburbs or high-rise buildings to challenge the supremacy of the cathedral's immense spire. The city's inspiring silhouette is best admired by taking a twenty-minute walk through the water meadows southwest of the centre to the suburb of **Harnham**.

North of Salisbury stretches a hundred thousand acres of chalky upland, known as **Salisbury Plain**; it's managed by the Ministry of Defence, whose presence has protected it from development and intensive farming, thereby preserving species that are all but extinct elsewhere in England. Though largely deserted today, in previous times Salisbury Plain was positively overrun with communities. Stone, Bronze and Iron Age settlements left hundreds of scattered burial mounds, as well as major complexes like **Old Sarum**, and, of course, the great circle of **Stonehenge**, England's most famous historical monument. To the west, Salisbury's hinterland also includes one of Wiltshire's great country mansions, **Wilton House**, as well as **Stourhead** and **Longleat Safari Park**.

Salisbury Cathedral

The Close, SP1 2EJ • Cathedral daily Mon–Sat 9am–5pm, Sun noon–4pm; chapter house April–Oct Mon–Sat 9.30am–5pm & Sun 11am–4pm, Nov–March Mon–Sat 10am–4.30pm & Sun 11am–4pm • £7.50 suggested donation • **Tower tours** April–Sept Mon–Sat at least 2 daily, usually at 11.15am & 1.15pm, up to 5 a day at busy times; 1hr 45min; book ahead • £12.50 • ☎01722 555120, ⓦsalisburycathedral.org.uk

Begun in 1220, **Salisbury Cathedral** was mostly completed within forty years and is thus unusually consistent in its style, with one prominent exception – the **spire**, which was added a century later and, at 404ft, is the highest in England. Its survival is something of a miracle, for the foundations penetrate only about six feet into marshy ground, and when Christopher Wren surveyed it he found the spire to be leaning almost two and a half feet out of true. He added further tie rods, which finally arrested the movement.

The interior is over-austere, but there's an amazing sense of space and light in its high nave, despite the sombre pillars of grey Purbeck marble, which are visibly bowing beneath the weight they bear. Monuments and carved tombs line the walls. Don't miss the octagonal **chapter house**, which displays a rare original copy of the Magna Carta, and whose walls are decorated with a frieze of scenes from the Old Testament.

The Close

Surrounding the cathedral is the **Close**, a peaceful precinct of lawns and mellow old buildings. Most of the houses have seemly Georgian facades, though some, like the Bishop's Palace and the deanery, date from the thirteenth century. **Mompesson House** (mid-March to Oct daily 11am–5pm; £6.50, garden only £1, NT; ☎01722 420980, ⓦnationaltrust.org.uk/mompesson-house), built by a wealthy merchant in 1701, contains some beautifully furnished eighteenth-century rooms and a superbly carved staircase. Also in the Close is the **King's House**, home to the **Salisbury and South Wiltshire Museum** (Oct–May Mon–Sat 10am–5pm; April–Oct Mon–Sat 10am–5pm & Sun noon–5pm; £7.50; ☎01722 332151, ⓦsalisburymuseum.org.uk) – an absorbing account of local history.

Around the Market Square

The Close's **North Gate** opens onto the centre's older streets, where narrow pedestrianized alleyways bear names like Fish Row and Salt Lane, indicative of their trading origin. Many half-timbered houses and inns have survived, and the last of four market crosses, **Poultry Cross**, stands on stilts in Silver Street, near the Market Square. The market (Tues & Sat) still serves a large agricultural area, as it did back when the city grew wealthy on wool. The nearby **Church of St Thomas** – named after Thomas Becket – is worth a look inside for its carved timber roof and "Doom painting" over the chancel arch, depicting Christ presiding over the Last Judgement. Dating from 1475, it's the largest of its kind in England.

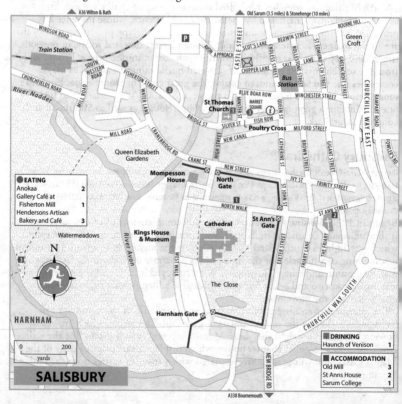

EATING
Anokaa	2
Gallery Café at Fisherton Mill	1
Hendersons Artisan Bakery and Café	3

DRINKING
Haunch of Venison	1

ACCOMMODATION
Old Mill	3
St Anns House	2
Sarum College	1

SALISBURY

ARRIVAL AND DEPARTURE

By train Trains from London arrive half a mile west of Salisbury's centre, on South Western Rd.
Destinations Bath (2–4 daily; 1hr); Bradford-Upon-Avon (2–4 daily; 45min); Bristol (2–4 daily; 1hr 10min); London Waterloo (every 30min; 1hr 30min); Portsmouth (hourly;

SALISBURY AND AROUND

1hr 15min); Southampton (every 30min; 30min–40min).
By bus Buses stop at various sites around the city centre.
Destinations Bournemouth (Mon–Sat every 30min, Sun hourly; 1hr 15min); London (5 daily; 3hr 15min–4hr); Southampton (Mon–Sat every 1–2hr; 1hr 10min).

INFORMATION AND TOURS

Tourist office Fish Row, just off Market Square (Mon–Fri 9am–5pm, Sat 10am–4pm, Sun & bank hols 10am–2pm; ☎01722 3428606, ⓦvisitwiltshire.co.uk). It's also the starting point for informative, inexpensive guided walks.

Bus tours Tours to Stonehenge and Old Sarum depart from the train station (bus only £14, with entry to Old Sarum and Stonehenge £29; ☎01722 336855, ⓦthestonehengetour. info) every 30min in summer, and hourly at other times.

ACCOMMODATION

★ **Old Mill** Town Path, Harnham, SP2 8EU ☎01722 512139, ⓦoldmillhotelsalisbury.co.uk; map p.224. The fully equipped rooms of this riverside pub in a sixteenth-century papermill have great views across the meadows to the cathedral. The location feels really rural but is just a short walk from the city centre. Real ales are on tap in the bar, and there's an adjoining restaurant serving good local food. **£125**

St Anns House 32–34 St Ann St, SP1 2DP ☎07715 213146, ⓦstannshouse.co.uk; map p.224. A well-restored Georgian

townhouse with stylish, comfortable rooms in a quiet street a short walk from the cathedral. **£110**

★ **Sarum College** 19 The Close, SP1 2EE ☎01722 424800, ⓦsarum.ac.uk; map p.224. By no means luxurious but in the best location in Salisbury, this friendly ecumenical college (with parts designed by Sir Christopher Wren) rents out simple en-suite doubles with views over The Close, plus others without private facilities (£45). There's also a decent common room, and breakfast is included. **£105**

EATING

Anokaa 60 Fisherton Street, SP2 7RB ☎01722 341717, ⓦanokaa.com; map p.224. Attractive Indian restaurant with smart decor – fresh orchids and contemporary painting on the walls – and waiters in traditional, brightly coloured Indian dress. The food is a cut above the average too, with unusual dishes such as rum-soaked wild venison starter (£8) and main courses including Chardonnay-soaked duck breast (£16) and marinated Portobello mushrooms with masala mash (£11.25). Daily noon–2pm & 5.30–11pm.

★ **Gallery Café at Fisherton Mill** 108 Fisherton St, SP2 7QY ☎01722 500200, ⓦfishertonmill.co.uk; map p.224. Great café within a renovated mill/art gallery serving delicious soups (£4.50), sandwiches on sourdough

(£6) and main courses such as lemon roast chicken (£13.50), as well as tasty home-made cakes. Upstairs, you can watch artists at work in their studios, weaving and making jewellery. Mon–Fri 10am–5pm, Sat 9.30am–5pm.

Hendersons Artisan Bakery and Café 19 Oatmeal Row, SP1 1TH ☎01722 341717; map p.224. Lovely bakery/café, which makes its own breads, quiches and pastries on site. They use local and seasonal ingredients, so you may find specials such as beetroot bread, rosemary and sea-salt focaccia and wild garlic tart on the menu (tart with salad £5). There's plenty of space upstairs, or you can sit at the tables outside in the square with a made-to-order sandwich and coffee for lunch. Mon–Sat 8am–5pm.

DRINKING

★ **Haunch of Venison** 1 Minster St, SP1 1TB ☎01722 411313 ⓦhaunchpub.co.uk; map p.224. One of the city's most atmospheric and historic pubs, with a wonderful warren of rooms, a fireplace dating from 1588,

and a former bread oven containing a mummified hand. The quirky, sloping-floored restaurant serves interesting dishes such as pulled haunch of venison burgers (£16) and Wiltshire pork belly (£15). Daily 11am–11pm.

Old Sarum

Castle Rd, SP1 3SD, 2 miles north of Salisbury • Daily: April–Sept 10am–6pm; Oct 10am–5pm; Nov–March 10am–4pm • £4.80; EH • ☎01722 335398, ⓦwww.english-heritage.org.uk/visit/places/old-sarum

The ruins of **Old Sarum** occupy a bleak hilltop site. Possibly occupied up to five thousand years ago, then developed as an Iron Age fort, it was settled by Romans and Saxons before the Norman bishopric of Sherborne was moved here in the 1070s.

Within a couple of decades a new **cathedral** had been consecrated at Old Sarum, and a large religious community was living alongside the soldiers in the central castle. Old Sarum was an uncomfortable place, parched and windswept, and in 1220 the dissatisfied clergy appealed to the pope for permission to decamp to Salisbury (still known officially as New Sarum). When permission was granted, the stone from the cathedral was commandeered for Salisbury's gateways, and once the church had gone the population waned. By the nineteenth century Old Sarum was deserted, and today the dominant features of the site are huge earthworks, banks and ditches, with a broad trench encircling the rudimentary remains of the Norman palace, castle and cathedral.

Stonehenge

Near Amesbury, SP4 7DE, 9 miles north of Salisbury • Daily: mid-March to May & Sept to mid-Oct 9.30am–7pm; June–Aug 9am–8pm; mid-Oct to mid-March 9.30am–5pm; last entry 2hr before closing; advance booking of timed tickets essential • £16.50; EH • ☎ 0870 333 1181, ⓦ www.english-heritage.org.uk/visit/places/stonehenge • Shuttle buses to the site (every 10min; 10min) leave from the visitor centre

No ancient structure in England arouses more controversy than **Stonehenge**, a mysterious ring of monoliths. While archeologists argue over whether it was a place of ritual sacrifice and sun-worship, an astronomical calculator or a royal palace, the guardians of the site have struggled for years to manage its enormous visitor numbers, particularly at the summer **solstice**, when crowds of 35,000 or more gather to watch the sunrise.

Access to the stones themselves is via a **shuttle-bus service** from the sleek **visitor centre**. This low-rise, environmentally sensitive pair of buildings includes a shop, café and

---

STONEHENGE – A BRIEF HISTORY

Some people may find **Stonehenge** underwhelming, but understanding a little of its history gives an insight into its mystical appeal. What exists today is only a small part of the original prehistoric complex, as many of the outlying stones were probably plundered by medieval and later farmers for building materials. The **construction** of Stonehenge is thought to have taken place in several stages. In about 3000 BC the outer circular bank and ditch were built, just inside which was dug a ring of 56 pits, which at a later date were filled with a mix of earth and human ash. Around 2500 BC the first stones were raised, approximately forty great blocks of dolerite (bluestone), whose ultimate source was Preseli in Wales. Some archeologists have suggested that these were found lying on Salisbury Plain, having been borne down from the Welsh mountains by a glacier in the last Ice Age, but the lack of any other glacial debris on the plain seems to disprove this theory. The most likely explanation is that the stones were cut from quarries in Preseli and dragged or floated here on rafts, a prodigious task that has defeated recent attempts to emulate it.

The crucial phase in the creation of the site came during the next six hundred years, when the incomplete bluestone circle was transformed by the construction of a circle of 25 **trilithons** (two uprights crossed by a lintel) and an inner horseshoe formation of five trilithons. Hewn from Marlborough Downs sandstone, these colossal stones (called sarsens), ranging from 13ft to 21ft in height and weighing up to thirty tons, were carefully dressed and worked – for example, to compensate for perspectival distortion the uprights have a slight swelling in the middle, the same trick as the builders of the Parthenon employed hundreds of years later. More bluestones were arranged in various patterns within the outer circle over this period. The purpose of all this work remains baffling, however. The symmetry and location of the site (a slight rise in a flat valley with even views of the horizon in all directions) as well as its alignment towards the points of sunrise and sunset on the summer and winter solstices tend to support the supposition that it was some sort of observatory or time-measuring device. The site ceased to be used at around 1600 BC, and by the Middle Ages it had become a "landmark". Recent excavations have revealed the existence of a much larger settlement here than had previously been thought (the most substantial Neolithic village of this period to be found on the British mainland, in fact), covering a wide area.

exhibition space combining archeological remains with high-tech interactive displays explaining their significance and history. Outside, you can look round a cluster of re-created Neolithic houses, and try pulling a life-size Preseli bluestone. Perhaps a more fitting way to approach the site, however, is on foot – the stones are a pleasant thirty-minute walk from the visitor centre across fields (once part of a World War I airfield).

Wilton House

Wilton, SP2 0BJ, 5 miles west of Salisbury • **House** Easter & May–Aug Mon–Thurs, Sun & bank hols Sat 11.30am–5pm • £15 (includes grounds) • **Grounds** Easter to mid-Sept daily 11am–5.30pm • £6.25 • ☎ 01722 746714, ⓦ wiltonhouse.co.uk

The splendid **Wilton House** dominates the village of **WILTON**, renowned for its carpet industry. The original Tudor house, built for the first earl of Pembroke on the site of a dissolved Benedictine abbey, was ruined by fire in 1647 and rebuilt by Inigo Jones, whose classic hallmarks can be seen in the sumptuous Single Cube and Double Cube rooms, so called because of their precise dimensions. The easel **paintings** are what makes Wilton really special, however – the collection includes works by Van Dyck, Rembrandt, two of the Brueghel family, Poussin, Andrea del Sarto and Tintoretto. In the grounds, the famous **Palladian Bridge** has been joined by various ancillary attractions including an adventure playground and restaurant. Note, too, that the grounds host frequent events which can restrict access; check the website for details.

Stourhead

Near Mere, BA12 6QF, 25 miles west of Salisbury • **House** Mid-Feb to mid-March Sat & Sun 11am–3pm; mid-March to Oct daily 11am–4.30pm; first two weeks of Nov & Dec daily 11am–3.30pm • **Gardens** Daily: mid-April to Oct 9am–6pm; Nov to mid-April 9am–5pm • House and gardens £16; NT • **King Alfred's Tower** Aug daily noon–4pm • £4.20; NT • ☎ 01747 841152, ⓦ nationaltrust.org.uk/stourhead

Landscape gardening was a favoured mode of display among the grandest eighteenth-century landowners, and **Stourhead** is one of the most accomplished examples of the genre. The Stourton estate was bought in 1717 by Henry Hoare, who commissioned Colen Campbell to build a new villa in the Palladian style. Hoare's heir, another Henry, returned from his Grand Tour in 1741 with his head full of the paintings of Claude and Poussin, and determined to translate their images of well-ordered, wistful classicism into real life. He dammed the Stour to create a lake, then planted the terrain with blocks of trees, domed temples, stone bridges, grottoes and statues, all mirrored vividly in the water. The **house** itself is of minor interest, with the stunning **gardens** the highlight. At the entrance, you can pick up a map detailing a lovely two-mile walk around the lake. The estate itself is vast and includes a pub, a church and a farm shop, plus **King Alfred's Tower**, about three miles from the main entrance. Built in 1772, it is one of England's oldest follies, and you can climb the two hundred or so steps up to the top for fine views stretching into neighbouring counties.

Longleat

Warminster, BA12 7NW, 27 miles west of Salisbury • Opening hours and closing days vary throughout the season, but are generally 10am–5pm, 6pm or 7pm; check website for exact times and days • House and grounds only £18.95, all attractions £33.95; discounts available online • ☎ 01985 844400, ⓦ longleat.co.uk

The African savanna intrudes into the bucolic Wiltshire countryside at **Longleat** safari and adventure park. In 1946 the sixth marquess of Bath became the first stately-home owner to open his house to the public on a regular basis, and in 1966 he caused more amazement by turning Longleat's Capability Brown landscapes into England's first drive-through **safari park**, with lions, tigers, giraffes and rhinos on show, plus monkeys clambering all over your car. Other attractions followed, including boat trips on a lake full of sea lions and a large hedge maze. Beyond the razzmatazz, there's an exquisitely furnished Elizabethan **house**, with an enormous library and a fine collection of pictures, including Titian's *Holy Family*.

Avebury

The village of **AVEBURY** stands in the midst of a **stone circle** (daily 24hr; free) that rivals Stonehenge – the individual stones are generally smaller, but the circle itself is much wider and more complex. A massive earthwork 20ft high and 1400ft across encloses the main circle, which is approached by four causeways across the inner ditch, two of them leading into wide avenues stretching over a mile beyond the circle. It was probably built soon after 2500 BC, and presumably had a similar ritual or religious function to Stonehenge. The structure of Avebury's diffuse circle is quite difficult to grasp, but there are plans on the site, and the **Alexander Keiller Museum** provides further details and background. Further prehistoric sites can be seen at nearby **Silbury Hill** and **West Kennet Long Barrow**, making the sixteenth-century **Avebury Manor** seem youthful in comparison.

Alexander Keiller Museum

SN8 1RF • Daily 10am–6pm • £4.40; NT • ☎ 01672 539250, ⓦ nationaltrust.org.uk/avebury

The nearby **Alexander Keiller Museum** provides an excellent overview of the Avebury stones and their significance, plus information about the role of Keiller himself. A Scottish archeologist and heir to a marmalade fortune, Keiller was responsible for restoring the stones and excavating the surrounding site. The museum is housed in two separate buildings: the **Stables Gallery** houses some of Keiller's original finds, while the seventeenth-century **Barn Gallery** has exhibits on local archeology, interactive displays plus activities for children.

Silbury Hill and West Kennet Long Barrow

Just outside Avebury, the neat green mound of **Silbury Hill** is disregarded by the majority of drivers whizzing by on the A4. At 130ft it's no great height, but when you realize that it's the largest prehistoric artificial mound in Europe, and was made using nothing more than primitive spades, it commands more respect. It was probably constructed around 2600 BC, and though no one knows quite what it was for, the likelihood is that it was a burial mound. You can't actually walk on the hill – having admired it briefly from the car park, cross the road to the footpath that leads half a mile to the **West Kennet Long Barrow** (daily 24hr; free; NT & EH). Dating from about 3250 BC, this was definitely a chamber tomb – nearly fifty burials have been discovered here.

ACCOMMODATION AND EATING   AVEBURY

Circles Café Next to the Barn Gallery, SN8 1RF ☎ 01672 539250. This National Trust café is your best bet for an inexpensive lunch, offering good meals and snacks, plenty of veggie options and, of course, tasty cakes and cream teas. There's indoor seating in a converted farm building, plus outdoor tables in the courtyard. Daily 10am–5.30pm.

The Lodge High St, SN8 1RF ☎ 01672 539023, ⓦ averburylodge.co.uk. An attractive Georgian and vegetarian B&B with just two rooms, one en suite, but both comfortable and overlooking the Stone Circles. Breakfast is served in a grand dining room filled with antiques. Free parking for guests. **£195**

Lacock

LACOCK, twelve miles west of Avebury, is the perfect English feudal village, albeit one gentrified by the National Trust and besieged by tourists all summer, partly due to its fame as a location for several films and TV series – the later *Harry Potter* films and the BBC's *Wolf Hall*, among others. The village's most famous son is photography pioneer **Henry Fox Talbot**, a member of the dynasty that has lived in the local abbey since it passed to Sir William Sharington on the Dissolution of the Monasteries in 1539. The opulent tomb of Sir William Sharington, buried beneath a splendid barrel-vaulted roof, can be seen in the village church of **St Cyriac** (daily 24hr; free).

Lacock Abbey and the Fox Talbot Museum

SN15 2LG • Abbey Jan Sat & Sun 11am–5pm, Feb–Dec daily 11am–5pm; museum, cloisters and grounds Feb–Dec daily 10.30am–5.30pm
• £12.70; NT • ☎ 01249 73045, ⓦ nationaltrust.org.uk/lacock

William Henry Fox Talbot was the first person to produce a photographic negative, and the **Fox Talbot Museum**, in a sixteenth-century barn by the gates of Lacock Abbey, captures something of the excitement he must have experienced as the dim outline of an oriel window in the abbey imprinted itself on a piece of silver nitrate paper. The museum also houses the **Fenton Collection**, featuring photos and cameras from the birth of photography to the 1980s, which was donated by the British Film Institute. The **abbey** itself boasts a medieval cloister and a few monastic fragments amid the eighteenth-century Gothic.

3

ARRIVAL AND DEPARTURE **LACOCK**

By bus The #X34 runs hourly from Chippenham and Frome, stopping outside the *George Inn* (ⓦ faresaver.co.uk).

ACCOMMODATION AND EATING

Beechfield House Hotel Beanacre, SN12 7PU, 2 miles south of Lacock ☎ 01225 703700, ⓦ beechfieldhouse. co.uk. This lovely country-house hotel has comfortable rooms, an excellent restaurant and a heated outdoor pool, all set in attractive grounds. It has family rooms and the service is friendly but professional. **£125**

George Inn 4 West St, SN15 2LH ☎ 01249 730263 ⓦ georgeinnlacock.co.uk. A rambling, partly fourteenth-century pub with roaring fires and a dog-wheel (the dog powered the wheel to turn a spit over the fire). Good

for a drink, with a variety of guest ales, plus decent pub food, such as fish of the day with chips (£13). Mon–Fri 11am–3pm & 6–11pm, Sat 11am–11pm, Sun 11am–10.30pm; kitchen Mon–Sat noon–2.30pm & 6–9pm, Sun noon–2.30pm & 6–8pm.

Lacock Pottery The Tanyard, Church St, SN15 2LB ☎ 01249 730266, ⓦ lacockbedandbreakfast.com. Three comfortable B&B rooms in a lovely old building overlooking the church and the village. Breakfasts are good, featuring home-made bread and jams. Weekdays **£90**, weekends **£100**

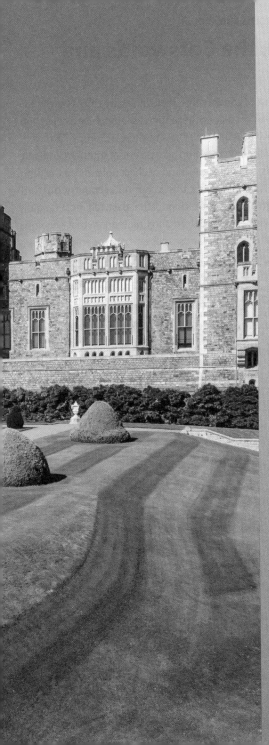

Oxford-shire, the Cotswolds and around

WINDSOR CASTLE, BERKSHIRE

Oxfordshire, the Cotswolds and around

About sixty miles northwest of London, the small university city of Oxford is one of England's great urban set pieces, presenting as impressive a collection of Gothic, Classical and Revival architecture as anywhere in Europe. Oxford anchors a diverse swathe of terrain reaching across central southern England, straddling the Chiltern Hills, a picturesque band of chalk uplands on the fringes of the capital. Close to the M25 motorway, this is commuter country, but further out a rural spirit survives from England's pre-industrial past, felt most tangibly in the Cotswolds, rolling hills between Oxford and Cheltenham that encompass some of the country's most celebrated landscapes and photogenic villages.

Covering much of **Oxfordshire** and **Gloucestershire**, the picture-postcard **Cotswolds** region sports old churches and handsome stone mansions, with scenic drives galore and plenty of walking opportunities, not least on the long-distance Cotswolds Way. Highlights include the engaging market town of **Chipping Campden**, the delightful village of Northleach and bustling **Cirencester**. Within striking distance of Oxford are handsome Woodstock, a little town that lies alongside one of England's most imposing country homes, Blenheim Palace, and further south, Henley-on-Thames, an attractive spot on the river famous for its regatta. To the west lies **Cheltenham**, an appealing Regency spa town famous for its horse-racing, that serves as a base for visits to **Gloucester** and its magnificent cathedral. Bordering south Oxfordshire, Berkshire has the royal residence of **Windsor Castle** as its focus, but can also offer a fine gallery in the Thames-side village of Cookham. Striking west from the Chilterns across the North Wessex Downs is the 85-mile-long Ridgeway, a prehistoric track – and now a national trail with a string of prehistoric sites, most notably the gigantic chalk horse that gives the Vale of White Horse its name.

GETTING AROUND   OXFORDSHIRE, THE COTSWOLDS AND AROUND

By train Mainline services from London Paddington serve Reading, Oxford, Cheltenham and Gloucester, also stopping at Cotswolds villages including Kingham, Moreton-in-Marsh and Kemble. There are also fast trains from London Marylebone, Birmingham, Reading and Southampton to Oxford, and from Birmingham and Bristol to Cheltenham.

By bus Long-distance buses stick mostly to the motorways, providing an efficient service to the larger towns, but local services between the villages are patchy, or nonexistent.

By car The Cotswolds are enclosed by the M5, M4 and M40, which, along with the M1 and A1(M) to the east, provide easy access.

Oxford

When visitors think of **OXFORD**, they almost always imagine its **university**, revered as one of the world's great academic institutions, inhabiting honey-coloured stone buildings set around ivy-clad quadrangles. The image is accurate enough, but although the university dominates central Oxford both physically and spiritually, the wider city has an entirely

Highlights

❶ Oxford One of Britain's most captivating cities, with dozens of historic colleges, memorable museums and an enjoyably lively undergraduate atmosphere. See page 232

❷ Windsor Castle The oldest and largest inhabited castle in the world – still an important ceremonial residence of the Queen – in the Berkshire countryside near London. See page 249

❸ Chipping Campden Perfectly preserved medieval wool town, with honey-coloured houses lining its historic main street. See page 257

❹ Cirencester Self-styled "Capital of the Cotswolds", with a bustling marketplace overlooked by the superb Gothic church of St John the Baptist. See page 260

❺ Festivals in Cheltenham Alongside its fixtures on the British horse racing calendar, the upmarket spa town of Cheltenham also boasts lively festivals dedicated to folk, jazz, classical music, literature and science. See page 263

❻ Gloucester Cathedral The earliest – and one of the finest – examples of English Perpendicular architecture, topped by a magnificent tower. See page 266

HIGHLIGHTS ARE MARKED ON THE MAP ON PAGE 234

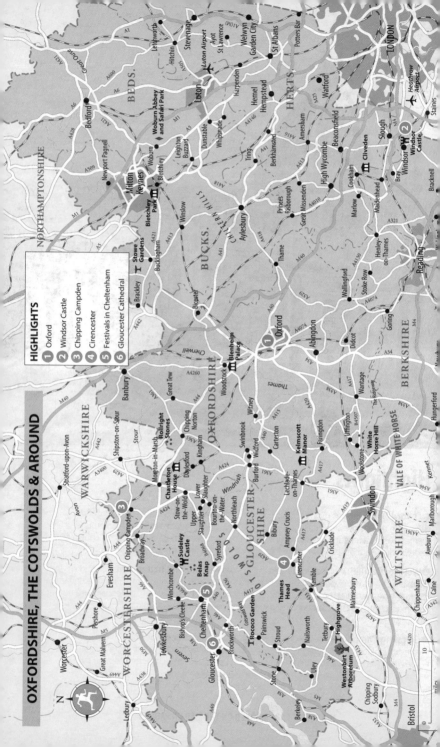

different character, its economy built chiefly on the **factories** of Cowley, south of the centre. It was here that Britain's first mass-produced cars were made in the 1920s and, although there have been more downs than ups in recent years, the plants are still vitally important to the area. Oxford should be high on anyone's itinerary, and can keep you occupied for several days. The **colleges** include some of England's finest architecture, and the city also has some excellent **museums** and a good range of bars and restaurants.

Christ Church College

St Aldates, OX1 1DP • Mon–Sat 10am–5pm, Sun 2–5pm; last entry 4.15pm • July & Aug £9, rest of year £7–8; discounts apply if you visit at times when the hall and/or cathedral are closed • ☎ 01865 276492, ⓦ www.chch.ox.ac.uk

Stretching along the east side of St Aldates is the main facade of **Christ Church College**, whose distinctive Tom Tower was added by Christopher Wren in 1681 to house the weighty "Great Tom" bell. The tower lords it over the main entrance of what is Oxford's largest and arguably most prestigious college, but visitors have to enter from the south, a signed five-minute walk away – just beyond the tiny War Memorial Garden and at the top of Christ Church Meadow. Don't be surprised if you have to queue to get in. This is the most touristy of all the Oxford Colleges, particularly popular thanks to its Harry Potter connections: many scenes from the films were shot here, while a studio recreation of the college's hall provided the set of Hogwarts' Great Hall.

From the entrance it's a few steps to the striking **Tom Quad**, the largest quad in Oxford – so large in fact that the Royalists penned up their mobile larder of cattle here during the Civil War. Guarded by Tom Tower, the quad's soft, honey-coloured stone makes a harmonious whole, but it was actually built in two main phases, with

4

OXFORD'S COLLEGES

So where, exactly, is **Oxford University**? Everywhere – and nowhere. The university itself is nothing more than an administrative body, setting examinations and awarding degrees. Although it has its own offices (on Wellington Square), they are of no particular interest. What draws all the attention are the university's constituent **colleges** – 38 of them (plus another six religious foundations known as Permanent Private Halls), most occupying historic buildings scattered throughout the city centre. It is these that hold the 800-year-old history of the university, and exemplify its spirit.

The origins of the university are obscure, but it seems that the reputation of **Henry I**, the so-called "Scholar King", helped attract students in the early twelfth century. The first **colleges**, founded mostly by rich bishops, were essentially ecclesiastical institutions and this was reflected in collegiate rules and regulations – until 1877 lecturers were not allowed to marry, and women were not granted degrees until 1920.

There are common **architectural features** among the colleges, with the students' rooms and most of the communal areas – chapels, halls (dining rooms) and libraries – arranged around quadrangles (**quads**). Each, however, has its own character and often a label, whether it's the richest (St John's), most left-wing (Wadham) or most public-school-dominated (Christ Church). Collegiate rivalries are long established, usually revolving around sports, and tension between the city and the university – "Town" and "Gown" – has existed as long as the university itself.

EXPLORING THE COLLEGES

All the more popular colleges have restricted **opening hours** – and may close totally during academic functions. Most now also impose an **admission charge**, while some (such as University and Queens) are out of bounds to outsiders. Regardless of published rules, it's always worth asking at the **porter's lodge**, at the main entrance of each college: porters have ultimate discretion and if you ask they may let you look around. One nice way to gain access is to attend choral evensong, held during term time and offering the chance to enjoy superb music in historic surroundings for free. New College choir is generally reckoned to be the best, but Queen's College and Merton are also good. Some colleges also **rent out student rooms** in the holidays (see page 243).

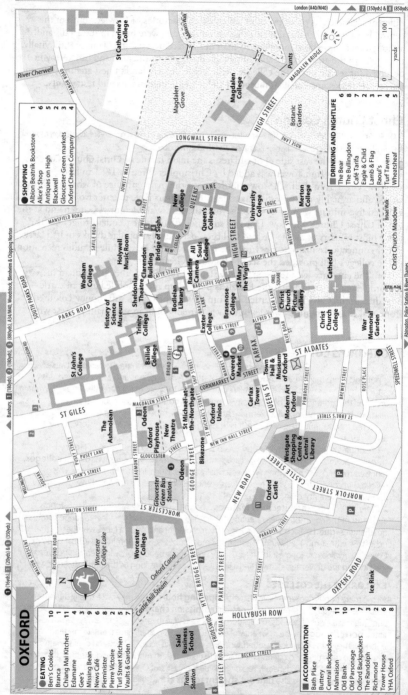

OXFORD

● **SHOPPING**

Albion Beatnik Bookstore	1
Alice's Shop	6
Antiques on High	5
Blackwell	3
Gloucester Green markets	2
Oxford Cheese Company	4

● **DRINKING AND NIGHTLIFE**

The Bear	6
The Bullingdon	8
Café Tarifa	7
Eagle & Child	2
Lamb & Flag	3
Raoul's	1
Turf Tavern	4
Wheatsheaf	5

● **EATING**

Ben's Cookies	10
Branca	1
Chiang Mai Kitchen	11
Edamame	4
Gee's	3
Missing Bean	9
News Café	6
Pieminister	8
Pierre Victoire	2
Turf Street Kitchen	5
Vaults & Garden	7

■ **ACCOMMODATION**

Bath Place	4
Buttery	5
Central Backpackers	9
Malmaison	11
Old Bank	10
Old Parsonage	1
Oxford Backpackers	7
The Randolph	3
Richmond	2
Tower House	6
YHA Oxford	8

the southern side dating back to Wolsey, and the north finally finished in the 1660s. A wide stone staircase in the southeast corner beneath a stupendous fan-vaulted ceiling leads up to the **Hall**, the grandest refectory in Oxford, with its fanciful hammer-beam roof and a set of stern portraits of past scholars by a roll call of famous artists, including Reynolds, Gainsborough and Millais. As well as Albert Einstein, William Gladstone and no fewer than twelve other British prime ministers were educated here.

Oxford Cathedral

Christ Church's college chapel is otherwise known as **Oxford Cathedral**. The Anglo-Saxons built a church on this site in the seventh century as part of the priory of St Frideswide (Oxford's patron saint), although the present building dates mainly from 1120–80. The priory was suppressed in 1524, but the church survived. It's unusually discordant, with all sorts of bits and bobs from different periods, but fascinating all the same. The dominant features are the sturdy circular columns and rounded arches of the Normans, but there are also early Gothic pointed arches, and the chancel ceiling is a particularly fine example of fifteenth-century stone vaulting.

Christ Church Picture Gallery

June Mon & Wed–Sat 10.30am–5pm, Sun 2–5pm; July–Sept Mon–Sat 10.30am–5pm, Sun 2–5pm; Oct–May Mon & Wed–Sat 10.30am–1pm & 2–4.30pm, Sun 2–4.30pm • £4, or £2 with a Christ Church admission ticket • **Tours** Mon 2.30pm • Free with admission • ☎ 01865 276172, ⓦ www.chch.ox.ac.uk/gallery

Hidden away in Christ Church's pocket-sized Canterbury Quad is the college's **Picture Gallery**. The extensive collection comprises around three hundred paintings and two thousand drawings, with fine works by artists from Italy and the Netherlands including paintings by Tintoretto, Van Dyck and Frans Hals and drawings by da Vinci, Dürer, Raphael and Michelangelo.

Christ Church Meadow

Christ Church Meadow fills in the tapering gap between the rivers Cherwell and Thames. If you decide to delay visiting Christ Church College, you can take a stroll east along Broad Walk for the Cherwell, or keep going straight down tree-lined (and more appealing) New Walk for the Thames.

Merton College

Merton St, OX1 4JD • Mon–Fri 2–5pm, Sat & Sun 10am–5pm • £3 • ☎ 01865 276310, ⓦ www.merton.ox.ac.uk

Merton College is historically the city's most important. Balliol and University colleges may have been founded earlier, but it was Merton – opened in 1264 – which set the model for colleges in both Oxford and Cambridge, being the first to gather its students and tutors together in one place. Furthermore, unlike the other two, Merton retains some of its original medieval buildings, with the best of the thirteenth-century architecture clustered around **Mob Quad**, a charming courtyard with mullioned windows and Gothic doorways to the right of the Front Quad. From the Mob Quad, an archway leads through to the **Chapel**, dating from 1290, inside which you'll find the funerary plaque of Thomas Bodley, founder of Oxford's famous Bodleian Library (see page 239).

Magdalen College

High St, OX1 4AU • Daily: July & Aug 10am–7pm; Sept noon–7pm; Oct–June 1–6pm or dusk • £6 • ☎ 01865 276000, ⓦ www.magd.ox.ac.uk

At the east end of the High Street stands **Magdalen College** (pronounced "maudlin"), whose gaggle of stone buildings is overshadowed by its chunky medieval bell tower. Steer right from the entrance and you reach the **chapel**, which has a handsome reredos, though you have to admire it through the windows of an ungainly stone screen. The adjacent **cloisters** are adorned by standing figures, some biblical and others folkloric,

---

TAKING TO THE WATER

Punting is a favourite summer pastime among both students and visitors, but handling a punt – a flat-bottomed boat ideal for the shallow waters of the Thames and Cherwell rivers – requires practice. The punt is propelled and steered with a long pole, which beginners inevitably get stuck in riverbed mud: if this happens, let go of it and paddle back, or you may be dragged overboard.

There are two central **boat rental** places: Magdalen Bridge Boathouse (☎01865 202643, ⊚oxfordpunting.co.uk), beside the Cherwell at the east end of the High Street; and Salter's Steamers (☎01865 243421, ⊚salterssteamers.co.uk) at Folly Bridge, south of Christ Church. Opening times vary: call for details, or arrive early (around 10am) to avoid the queues which build up on sunny summer afternoons. At either, expect to **pay** £20–22 per hour plus a deposit of about £50; ID is required. Punts can take a maximum of five or six people, including the person punting.

Salter's Steamers also runs **passenger boats** downstream along the Thames from Folly Bridge, including to Iffley Lock (April–Oct 7 daily; 40min return; £8). Oxford River Cruises (☎01865 987147, ⊚oxfordrivercruises.com) also run short cruises from Folly Bridge, including upstream as far as Godstow on Port Meadow (April–Oct 2 daily; 2hr 30min; £29).

---

most notably a tribe of grotesques. Magdalen also boasts better **grounds** than most other colleges, with a bridge – at the back of the cloisters – spanning the River Cherwell to join **Addison's Walk**. You can hire punts from beneath **Magdalen Bridge**, beside the college.

4 Botanic Garden

Rose Lane, OX1 4AZ • March, April, Sept & Oct Mon noon–5pm, Tues–Sun 9am–5pm; May Mon noon–6pm, Tues–Sun 9am–6pm; June–Aug daily 9am–6pm; Nov–Feb Mon noon–4pm, Tues–Sun 9am–4pm • £5 • ⊚www.botanic-garden.ox.ac.uk

Bounded by a curve of the River Cherwell, Oxford's **Botanic Garden** is the oldest of its kind in England, established in 1621. Still enclosed by its original high wall, it comprises several different zones, from a lily pond, a bog garden and a rock garden through to borders of bearded irises and variegated plants. There are also six large **glasshouses** containing tropical and carnivorous species.

New College

New College Lane, OX1 3BN • Daily: Easter–Oct 11am–5pm, rest of year 2–4pm • Easter–Oct £4, rest of year free • ☎01865 279555, ⊚new.ox.ac.uk

Founded in 1379, **New College** is entered via the large but rather plain **Front Quad**. On the left side of the quad rises the magnificent Perpendicular **chapel**, arguably the finest in Oxford. The ante-chapel contains some superb fourteenth-century stained glass and the west window – of 1778 – holds an intriguing Nativity scene based on a design by Sir Joshua Reynolds. Beneath it stands the wonderful 1951 sculpture *Lazarus* by Jacob Epstein. Immediately past the chapel lies the college's peaceful **cloisters**.

An archway on the east side of the Front Quad leads through to the modest **Garden Quad**, with the thick flowerbeds of the **College Garden** beckoning beyond. The north side of the garden is flanked by the largest and best-preserved section of Oxford's medieval **city wall**. The conspicuous earthen **mound** in the middle is a later decorative addition, not medieval.

Bridge of Sighs

Spanning **New College Lane** a few paces off Catte Street is the iconic **Bridge of Sighs**, an archway completed in 1914 to link two Hertford College buildings. In truth it bears little resemblance to its Venetian namesake, but it does haves a certain Italianate elegance. It was designed, so the story goes, to give residents of Hertford's older buildings a way to reach the newfangled flushing toilets across the road without having to venture outdoors.

Bodleian Library

Broad St, OX1 3BG · Closed to the public; some rooms accessible on tours (see page 239) · ☎ 01865 287400, ⓦ www.bodleian.ox.ac.uk

Christopher Wren's pupil Nicholas Hawksmoor designed the **Clarendon Building**, a domineering, solidly symmetrical edifice at the east end of Broad Street, completed in 1713. It now forms part of the **Bodleian Library**. Founded by scholar Sir Thomas Bodley in 1602, the Bodleian is the UK's largest library after the British Library in London, with an estimated 117 miles of shelving. It includes the Modernist 1930s **Weston Library** (formerly known as the **New Bodleian**) directly opposite the Clarendon, designed by Sir Giles Gilbert Scott and linked to the main building by tunnels. As one of the UK and Ireland's six copyright libraries, the Bodleian must find room for a copy of every book, pamphlet, magazine and newspaper published in Britain.

Old Schools Quadrangle

Mon–Fri 9am–5pm, Sat 9am–4.30pm, Sun 11am–5pm · Free

Behind the Clarendon Building you enter the Bodleian's beautifully proportioned **Old Schools Quadrangle**, completed in 1619 in an ornate Jacobean-Gothic style and offering access to all of the university's academic faculties, or schools: the name of each is lettered in gold above the doorways which ring the quad. On the east side rises the handsome **Tower of the Five Orders**, its tiers of columns in ascending order Tuscan, Doric, Ionic, Corinthian and Composite.

The Divinity School

Mon–Sat 9am–5pm, Sun 11am–5pm · £1 · Tours available (see below)

Entered from the quad, the **Divinity School** is a highlight. Begun in 1424, this exceptional room is a masterpiece of late Gothic architecture, featuring an extravagant vaulted ceiling adorned with a riot of pendants and 455 decorative bosses. Built to house the university's theology faculty, it was, until the nineteenth century, also where degree candidates were questioned about their subject by two interlocutors, with a professor acting as umpire. Few interiors in Oxford are as impressive.

4

The Sheldonian Theatre

Broad St, OX1 3AZ · Jan & Dec Mon–Sat 10am–3pm; Feb–April & Oct–Nov Mon–Sat 10am–4.30pm; May–Sept daily 10am–4.30pm · £3.50 · ⓦ www.admin.ox.ac.uk/sheldonian

At the east end of Broad Street, the **Sheldonian Theatre** is ringed by railings topped with a line of glum-looking, pop-eyed classical busts. The Sheldonian was Christopher Wren's first major work, a reworking of the Theatre of Marcellus in Rome, semicircular

---

TOURS OF BODLEIAN LIBRARY

An **audioguide** is available for self-guided tours of the Bodleian Library quad and Divinity School (40min; £2.50) – or there's a host of **guided tours** around those few areas of the Bodleian open to the public. It's always advisable to **book in advance** with the tours office (Mon–Sat 9am–4pm, Sun 11am–4pm; ☎ 01865 287400, ⓦ www.bodleian.ox.ac.uk), located inside the Great Gate on Catte Street. Tours also cover atmospheric Duke Humfrey's Library and sometimes Convocation House, which aren't otherwise accessible to the public.
Mini tour 30min; £6. Divinity School and Duke Humfrey's Library. Mon–Sat 3.30pm, 4pm & 4.40pm, Sun 12.45pm, 2.15pm, 2.45pm, 3.15pm, 4pm & 4.40pm.
Standard tour 1hr; £8. Divinity School, Duke Humfrey's Library, Convocation House. Mon–Sat 10.30am, 11.30am, 1pm & 2pm, Sun 11.30am, 2pm & 3pm.
Extended tour "Upstairs Downstairs" 1hr 30min; £14. Divinity School, Duke Humfrey's Library, Convocation House, Gladstone Link, Radcliffe Camera. Wed & Sat 9.15am.
Extended tour "Reading Rooms" 1hr 30min; £14. Divinity School, Duke Humfrey's Library, Convocation House, Upper Reading Room. Sun 11.15am & 1.15pm.

at the back and rectangular at the front. It was conceived in 1663, when the 31-year-old Wren's main job was as professor of astronomy. Designed as a stage for university ceremonies, nowadays it also functions as a concert hall, but the interior lacks much sense of drama, and even the views from the cupola are disappointing.

Museum of the History of Science

Broad St, OX1 3AZ • Tues–Sun noon–5pm • Free • W www.mhs.ox.ac.uk

The classical heads that shield the Sheldonian Theatre continue along the front of the fascinating **Museum of the History of Science**, whose two floors display an amazing clutter of antique microscopes and astrolabes, sundials, quadrants and sextants. The highlights are Elizabeth I's own astrolabe and a blackboard used by Einstein in 1931, still covered with his scribbled equations.

Trinity College

Broad St, OX1 3BH • Daily 10am–noon & 2–6pm • £3 • T 01865 279900, W www.trinity.ox.ac.uk

Trinity College is fronted by three dinky lodge-cottages. Behind them the manicured lawn of the Front Quad stretches back to the richly decorated **chapel**, awash with Baroque stuccowork. Its high altar is flanked by an exquisite example of the work of Grinling Gibbons – a distinctive performance, with cherubs' heads peering out from delicate foliage. Behind the chapel stands **Durham Quad**, an attractive ensemble of old stone buildings begun at the end of the seventeenth century.

The Radcliffe Camera

Radcliffe Sq, OX1 3BG • Closed to the public; accessible only on Bodleian Library's extended tour (see page 239) • T 01865 287400, W www.bodleian.ox.ac.uk

The mighty rotunda of the **Radcliffe Camera**, built between 1737 and 1748 by James Gibbs, architect of London's St Martin-in-the-Fields church, displays no false modesty. Dr John Radcliffe, royal physician (to William III), was, according to a contemporary diarist, "very ambitious of glory": when he died in 1714 he bequeathed a mountain of money for the construction of a library. Gibbs was one of the few British architects of the period to have been trained in Rome and his design is thoroughly Italian in style, its limestone columns ascending to a delicate balustrade, which is decorated with pinprick urns and encircles a lead-sheathed dome. Taken over by the Bodleian Library in 1860, it now houses a reading room.

All Souls College

High St, OX1 4AL • Mon–Fri 2–4pm; closed Aug • Free • T 01865 279379, W www.asc.ox.ac.uk

Running the entire east side of Radcliffe Square, its immense chapel windows the epitome of the Perpendicular Gothic style, **All Souls College** is one of the quietest places in central Oxford – because it has no undergraduates. Uniquely, it admits only "fellows" (that is, distinguished scholars) either by election of existing fellows, or by an exam reputed to be the hardest in the world. The result is that All Souls is generally silent. Sightseers gather at the elaborate gates on Radcliffe Square, wondering how to gain access to the lovely quad beyond: turn right and walk around the corner onto High Street to reach the **college entrance**. This gives onto the modest Front Quad, location of the spectacular fifteenth-century **chapel**, with its gilded hammer-beam roof and neck-cricking reredos (though all its figures are Victorian replacements). Move through to the spacious **North Quad**, the object of all that admiration: Hawksmoor's soaring Gothic twin towers face the Radcliffe Square gates, while ahead, the Codrington Library – also Hawksmoor – sports a conspicuous, brightly decorated sundial designed by Wren.

Church of St Mary the Virgin

High St, OX1 4BJ • Mon–Sat 9am–5pm, Sun noon–5pm (July & Aug until 6pm) • Free; tower £4 • ☎01865 279111,
Ⓦuniversitychurch.ox.ac.uk

Mostly dating from the fifteenth century, **St Mary the Virgin** is a hotchpotch of
architectural styles. The church's saving graces are its elaborate, thirteenth-century
pinnacled spire and its distinctive Baroque **porch**, flanked by chunky corkscrewed
pillars. The interior is disappointingly mundane, though the carved poppy heads on
the choir stalls are of some historical interest: the tips were brusquely squared off when
a platform was installed here in 1555 to stage the heresy trial of Cranmer, Latimer
and Ridley, leading Protestants who had run foul of Queen Mary. The church's other
diversion is the **tower**, with wonderful views.

Covered Market

High St, OX1 3DZ • Mon–Sat 8am–5pm, Sun 10am–4pm • Ⓦ oxford-coveredmarket.co.uk

For refreshment on the hoof – as well as a fascinating glimpse into the life of Oxford
away from the colleges – drop into the **Covered Market**, wedged between High and
Market streets. Opened in 1774, it remains full of atmosphere, home to butchers, bakers,
fishmongers, greengrocers and cheese sellers, plus cafés, clothes boutiques and shoe shops.

Carfax Tower

Carfax, OX1 1ET • Daily: March 10am–4pm; April–Oct 10am–4.30pm; Nov–Feb 10am–3pm • £3

The busy **Carfax** crossroads is a fulcrum, where chiefly "gown" architecture along the
High Street to the east is balanced by the distinctly "town" atmosphere of Cornmarket
and Queen Street to the west. This has been a crossroads for more than a thousand
years: roads met here in Saxon times, and the name "Carfax" derives from the Latin
quadrifurcus ("four-forked"). The junction is overlooked by a square thirteenth-century
tower, adorned by a pair of clocktower jacks. You can **climb** it for wide views over the
centre, though other vantage points – principally St Mary's (see above) – have the edge.

St Michael-at-the-Northgate

Cornmarket, OX1 3EY • Daily: April–Oct 10.30am–5pm; Nov–March 10.30am–4pm • Free; tower £2.50 • ☎01865 240940, Ⓦ www.smng.org.uk

North of Carfax is **Cornmarket**, now a busy pedestrianized shopping strip lined with
familiar high-street stores. There's precious little here to fire the imagination until you
reach **St Michael-at-the-Northgate**, a church recorded in the Domesday Book, with a
late fourteenth-century font where Shakespeare's godson was baptized in 1606. The
church's Saxon **tower**, built in 1050, is Oxford's oldest surviving building; enter for
rooftop views and to see an eleventh-century sheela-na-gig.

Ashmolean Museum

Beaumont St, OX1 2PH • Tues–Sun 10am–5pm • Free • ☎ 01865 278000, Ⓦ www.ashmolean.org

Second only to the British Museum in London, the **Ashmolean Museum** occupies a
mammoth Neoclassical building on the corner of Beaumont Street and St Giles. It
grew from the collections of the magpie-like **John Tradescant**, gardener to Charles I and
an energetic traveller, and today it possesses a vast and far-reaching collection covering
everything from Minoan vases to Stradivarius violins.

Light and airy modern galleries cover four floors (pick up a **plan** at reception). The
"orientation" gallery in the basement provides a thematic overview of the museum,
while the ground floor houses the museum's "ancient world" exhibits, including
its superb Egyptology collection and an imposing room full of Greek sculptures.
Floor 1 is dedicated to Mediterranean, Indian and Islamic artefacts (Hindu bronzes,

---

FIRST FOR COFFEE

East of St Mary's church, two cafés face each other across the High Street, both claiming to be **England's oldest coffee house**. To the south, the *Grand Café* occupies the site of a coffee house opened by a Lebanese Jew named Jacob in or just after 1650. Opposite, the *Queen's Lane Coffee House* stands where a Syrian Jew named Cirques Jobson launched a competing enterprise at roughly the same time. Whichever was first, Oxford's gentlefolk were drinking coffee – and also hot chocolate – several years ahead of London.

Iranian pottery and so on) while floor 2 is mainly European, including the museum's wide-ranging collection of Dutch, Flemish and Italian paintings. Floor 3 focuses on European art since 1800, including works by Sickert, Pissarro and the Pre-Raphaelites.

Oxford University Museum of Natural History

Parks Rd, OX1 3PW · Daily 10am–5pm · Free · ☎ 01865 272950, ⓦ www.oum.ox.ac.uk

From the Ashmolean, it's a brief walk north up St Giles to the *Lamb & Flag* pub (see page 245), beside which an alley cuts east through to the **Oxford University Museum of Natural History**. The building, constructed under the guidance of John Ruskin, looks like a cross between a railway station and a church – and the same applies inside, where a High Victorian-Gothic fusion of cast iron and glass features soaring columns and capitals decorated with animal and plant motifs. Exhibits include some impressive dinosaur skeletons, models of exotic beasties, a four-billion-year-old meteorite, and so on.

Pitt Rivers Museum

Parks Rd, OX1 3PP · Mon noon–4.30pm, Tues–Sun 10am–4.30pm; tours (20min) Tues & Wed 2.30pm & 3.15pm; object handling Sat 11am–1pm · Free · ☎ 01865 270927, ⓦ www.prm.ox.ac.uk

Oxford's eye-popping **Pitt Rivers Museum** is housed in the same building as the University Museum of Natural History, accessed via a door at the rear of the ground-floor level. Founded in 1884, this is one of the world's finest ethnographic museums and an extraordinary relic of the Victorian age, arranged like an exotic junk shop with each intricately crammed cabinet labelled meticulously by hand. The exhibits – brought to England by, among others, Captain Cook – range from totem poles and mummified crocodiles to African fetishes and gruesome shrunken heads. Set aside an hour or two to roam the dark corners of this three-storey wonder: look out especially for the brilliant puppets on level 1 and blood-curdling swords and knuckle-dusters on level 2.

Modern Art Oxford

30 Pembroke St, OX1 1BP · Tues–Sat 10am–5pm, Sun noon–5pm · Free · ☎ 01865 722733, ⓦ www.modernartoxford.org.uk

Just south of Carfax, narrow Pembroke Street heads west to the outstanding **Modern Art Oxford** gallery, founded in 1965 and hosting an excellent programme of temporary exhibitions. It's worth stopping by, whatever happens to be showing.

Oxford Castle Unlocked

New Rd, OX1 1AY · Tours daily 10am–5pm, every 20min; last tour starts 4.20pm; 1hr · £10.95; discounted joint tickets with other attractions available, see website · ☎ 01865 260666, ⓦ oxfordcastleunlocked.co.uk

West of Carfax is the site of what was **Oxford Castle**, built in 1071. **Oxford Castle Unlocked** offers memorable **guided tours**, during which costumed warders lead you up the Saxon-era **St George's Tower**, show you medieval prison cells and take you down into the Romanesque crypt beneath **St George's Chapel**, telling tales of wars, executions and hauntings along the way.

ARRIVAL AND DEPARTURE

OXFORD

By train Oxford station is on the west side of the city centre, a 10min walk along Hythe Bridge St. It's served by direct trains from around the country, including London Paddington and – slightly slower but often cheaper – London Marylebone.

Destinations Bath (2 hourly; 1hr 20min–1hr 40min); Birmingham (2 hourly; 1hr 10min); Bristol (hourly; 1hr 40min); Cheltenham (every 30min; 2hr–2hr 15min); Gloucester (every 30min; 1hr 40min–2hr 20min); London (2–3 hourly; 1hr); Winchester (2 hourly; 1hr 10min–1hr 30min); Worcester (2 hourly; 1hr 15min–1hr 35min).

By bus Most buses are operated by Oxford Bus (☎01865 785400, ⓦoxfordbus.co.uk) and Stagecoach (☎01865 772250, ⓦstagecoachbus.com). Long-distance routes terminate at Gloucester Green bus station, in the city centre adjoining George St. Most county buses terminate on Magdalen St, St Giles or St Aldates – the #853 service (Mon–Sat 2–4 daily, Sun daily) covers Burford (45min), Northleach (1hr) and Cheltenham (1hr 30min).

Destinations (from Gloucester Green) London Victoria coach station (Oxford Tube and X90 express coaches daily every 10–30min; 1hr 40min); Heathrow Airport (Airline coach daily every 20–30min; 1hr 30min); Gatwick Airport (Airline coach daily hourly; 2hr).

By car Five big park-and-ride sites (ⓦparkandride. oxfordbus.co.uk) are signposted around the ring road. All offer cheap parking (around £2/day) as well as frequent buses into the centre (usually every 8–15min: Mon–Sat 6am–11pm, Sun 8am–7pm; £2.80 return). Central Oxford is not car-friendly: many streets are pedestrianized and parking is limited. The largest car park is at the Westgate shopping mall, accessed off Thames St (£28 for up to 24hr).

GETTING AROUND

On foot From the rail station to Magdalen Bridge it's roughly a mile and a quarter, and you pass almost everything of interest on the way.

By bike Bainton Bikes at Walton Street Cycles, 78 Walton St (☎01865 311610, ⓦbaintonbikes.com) rents bikes from £10/day.

By taxi There are taxi ranks at Carfax, Gloucester Green, St Giles and the railway station. Otherwise, call Radio Taxis (☎01865 242424, ⓦradiotaxisoxford.co.uk).

4

INFORMATION AND TOURS

Tourist office 15 Broad Street (July & Aug Mon–Sat 9am–5.30pm, Sun 9.30am–4pm; rest of year Mon–Sat 9.30am–5pm, Sun 10am–3.30pm; ☎01865 686430, ⓦexperience oxfordshire.org). Staff also sell discounted tickets for a range of nearby attractions, including Blenheim Palace, as well as tickets for coaches to London.

Listings information *Daily Info* (ⓦdailyinfo.co.uk) is the continually updated online version of Oxford's student news sheet. You'll spot the twice-weekly paper version (Tues & Fri) pinned up in colleges and cafés around town.

Guided tours The tourist office offers excellent guided walking tours of the city centre (daily 10.45am & 2pm, plus extra slots if there's sufficient demand; 2hr; £14). Many guides tout for business along Broad St, offering daytime walks and evening ghost tours. A literary walk starts from Carfax Tower (Wed 2pm; 1hr 30min; £15; ⓦoxfordwalkingtours.com).

ACCOMMODATION

As well as the places listed below, another good source of accommodation is the **university**. Outside term time, many colleges let out rooms on a B&B basis at often bargain rates. Expect little or no hotel-style service, but you are free to soak up the college ambience and may score a view over a historic quad. For more information, visit ⓦoxfordrooms.co.uk.

HOTELS

★ **Bath Place** 4 Bath Place, OX1 3SU ☎01865 791812, ⓦbathplace.co.uk; map p.236. This unusual hotel is tucked away down an old cobbled courtyard flanked by ancient buildings in an unbeatable central location. The sixteen creaky rooms are each individually decorated in attractive antique style with canopied beds and bare stone walls. **£135**

Malmaison Oxford Castle, 3 New Rd, OX1 1AY ☎01865 268400, ⓦmalmaison.com/locations/oxford; map p.236. Classy designer hotel in what was a Victorian prison, part of the Oxford Castle complex. Rooms – which take up three cells, knocked through – are nothing short of glamorous, featuring contemporary bathrooms and high-tech gadgets. Head through to C wing for the bigger, mezzanine suites. **£173**

Old Bank 92 High St, OX1 4BJ ☎01865 799599, ⓦoldbank-hotel.co.uk; map p.236. Great location for a slick hotel in a shiny conversion of an old bank. All 42 bedrooms are decorated in crisp, modern style, some with great views over All Souls College opposite. **£209**

★ **Old Parsonage** 1 Banbury Rd, OX2 6NN ☎01865 310210, ⓦoldparsonage-hotel.co.uk; map p.236. This lovely, centrally located hotel occupies a charming, wisteria-clad building from 1660, with 35 tasteful, modern rooms. Free parking, and free walking tours for guests on request. **£195**

The Randolph 1 Beaumont St, OX1 2LN ☎0344 879 9132, ⓦrandolph-hotel.com; map p.236. Oxford's most famous hotel, long the favoured choice of the well-heeled visitor, occupies a neo-Gothic brick building with a distinctive, nineteenth-century interior. It's now part of the Macdonald chain, still with traditional service, well-appointed bedrooms and a distinguished club atmosphere. **£151**

GUESTHOUSES AND B&BS

Buttery 11 Broad St, OX1 3AP ☎01865 811950, ⓦthebutteryhotel.co.uk; map p.236. This friendly sixteen-room guesthouse/hotel has a slap-bang central location, and modest rooms, plain but decent. Choose a back room to avoid the noise of carousing students. **£125**
Richmond 25 Walton Crescent, OX1 2JG ☎01865 311777, ⓦthe-richmond-oxford.co.uk; map p.236. Quiet B&B attached to the excellent *Al-Shami* Lebanese restaurant. Rooms are simple but prices are low – and you can opt for a delicious Lebanese breakfast (hummus, olives, white cheese, pitta bread etc). **£85**
★ **Tower House** 15 Ship St, OX1 3DA ☎01865 246828, ⓦtowerhouseoxford.co.uk; map p.236. This lovely

guesthouse in a 300-year-old building overlooks Jesus College. The eight doubles (five en suite) sport fresh, modern decor. Breakfast is at the affiliated *Turl Street Kitchen* (see page 245) next door. Profits support local charities. **£115**

HOSTELS

Central Backpackers 13 Park End St, OX1 1HH ☎01865 242288, ⓦcentralbackpackers.co.uk; map p.236. Independent hostel with fifty beds (including female-only dorms), 24-hour access and a friendly attitude. On a busy street: expect noise from nearby bars. Dorms **£22**
Oxford Backpackers 9a Hythe Bridge St, OX1 2EW ☎01865 721761, ⓦhostels.co.uk; map p.236. Independent hostel with 120 beds in bright, modern dorms (including female-only) and 24-hour access – but just a touch scruffy. Dorms **£15**
YHA Oxford 2a Botley Rd, OX2 0AB ☎0345 371 9131, ⓦyha.org.uk/hostel/oxford; map p.236. Located in a modern block behind the train station, this popular YHA hostel has 187 beds in four- and six-bedded dorms, plus nine doubles, some en suite. There's 24-hour access, with good facilities and a decent café. Dorms **£18**, doubles **£49**

4   EATING

With so many students and tourists, Oxford has a wide choice of places to eat. Lunchtimes tend to be very busy, though there's no shortage of options. The **restaurant** scene ranges from fine dining to more affordable outlets offering seasonal cooking. The best choice lies on the edge of the centre, along Walton Street and Little Clarendon Street in easygoing Jericho, or southeast on the grungier Cowley Road, buzzing with after-work lounge bars.

CAFÉS

★ **Ben's Cookies** 108 Covered Market, OX1 3DZ ☎01865 247407, ⓦbenscookies.com; map p.236. This hole in the wall – the first outlet in a now-global chain – has been churning out the best cookies in Oxford, perhaps England (and some say the world) since 1984, from ginger to peanut butter to triple chocolate chunk. Mon–Sat 9.15am–5.30pm, Sun 10am–4pm.
Missing Bean 14 Turl St, OX1 3DQ ☎01865 794886, ⓦwww.themissingbean.co.uk; map p.236. Plate-glass windows look out onto this pleasant old street, as conversation swirls and Oxford's finest coffee – or so they say – goes down. Mon–Fri 8am–6pm, Sat 9am–6.30pm, Sun 10am–5.30pm.
News Café 1 Ship St, OX1 3DA ☎01865 242317; map p.236. Breakfasts, bagels and daily specials, plus beer and wine, in this brisk and efficient café. Plenty of local and international newspapers are on hand too. Mon–Thurs & Sun 9am–5pm, Fri & Sat 9am–6pm.
★ **Vaults & Garden** Radcliffe Sq, OX1 4AH ☎01865 279112, ⓦthevaultsandgarden.com; map p.236. In atmospheric stone-vaulted chambers attached to St Mary's church, this busy café serves up good-quality organic, local wholefood, plus coffee and cake. The small terrace gazes up at the Radcliffe Camera. Cash only. Daily 8am–6pm.

RESTAURANTS

Branca 111 Walton St, OX2 6AJ ☎01865 556111, ⓦbranca.co.uk; map p.236. Large, buzzy bar-brasserie dishing up well-prepared Italian food, from simple pastas, pizzas and risottos through to more elaborate meat and fish mains (£11–18). Mon–Wed & Sun 10am–10pm, Thurs–Sat 10am–10.30pm.
Chiang Mai Kitchen 130a High St, OX1 4DH ☎01865 202233, ⓦchiangmaikitchen.co.uk; map p.236. An authentically spicy blast of Thai cooking in a homely little timber-framed medieval building tucked down an alleyway off the High St. All the traditional classics are done well, and there's a good vegetarian selection. Mains around £8–10. Mon–Sat noon–10.30pm, Sun noon–10pm.
★ **Edamame** 15 Holywell St, OX1 3SA ☎01865 246916, ⓦedamame.co.uk; map p.236. Voted one of the best Japanese restaurants in Britain, this tiny canteen-style place enjoys a flawless reputation. No bookings are taken, so you may have to queue (and then share a table). Tuck into ramen noodles with pork, chicken or tofu, for instance, or salmon teriyaki. There's plenty for vegetarians. Thurs is sushi night. Mains £6–11; cards not accepted at lunchtime. Wed 11.30am–2.30pm, Thurs–Sat 11.30am–2.30pm & 5–8.30pm, Sun noon–3.30pm.
Gee's 61 Banbury Rd, OX2 6PE ☎01865 553540,

@ gees-restaurant.co.uk; map p.236. Formal restaurant occupying chic Victorian conservatory premises. The inventive menu takes in British seasonal dishes such as asparagus and locally reared spring lamb, alongside steaks, fish dishes and more continental cuisine – crab linguine, bouillabaisse, burrata. Mains £15–26; two-course express menu (Mon–Fri noon–6pm) £13.50. Book ahead. Daily 10am–10.30pm.

Pieminister 56 Covered Market, OX1 3DX @01865 241613, @ pieminister.co.uk; map p.236. Your nose will lead you to this pie shop inside the Covered Market. The wide choice includes deerstalker pie (venison and red wine), moo pie (beef and ale), heidi pie (goats' cheese and spinach), and so on, all accompanied by mashed potato, gravy and minty peas, for just £7.50. Gluten-free options, too. Mon–Sat 10am–5pm, Sun 11am–4pm.

Pierre Victoire 9 Little Clarendon St, OX1 2HP @01865 316616, @ pierrevictoire.co.uk; map p.236. Much-loved French bistro in a buzzy little Jericho street behind St Giles. The two-course lunch menu (Mon–Sat only) is a steal: £11.50 for great cooking – trout fillet, coq au vin, stuffed peppers – warm service and pleasant ambience. Or go for the dinner menu of steak frites, mussels, duck breast or calves' liver (mains £12–19). Two-course pre-theatre menu £12.50 (6–7pm; not Sat). Mon–Sat noon–2.30pm & 6–11pm, Sun noon–10pm.

★ **Turl Street Kitchen** 16 Turl St, OX1 3DH @01865 264171, @ turlstreetkitchen.co.uk; map p.236. Much-loved hideaway on a charming backstreet, one of Oxford's top spots for a quiet battery-recharge over coffee and cake. Food is seasonal and hearty – parsnip soup, braised free-range chicken with chickpeas, fennel and wild garlic gratin – served in a cosy setting of sofas and grained wood. Mains £8–15. All profits support local charities. Mon–Thurs & Sun 8am–midnight, Fri & Sat 8am–1am.

DRINKING AND NIGHTLIFE

PUBS AND BARS

The Bear 6 Alfred St, OX1 4EH @01865 728164, @ bearoxford.co.uk; map p.236. Tucked away down a narrow side street, this tiny old pub (the oldest in Oxford, founded roughly 800 years ago) offers a wide range of beers and quirkily traditional decor, which includes a collection of ties. Mon–Thurs 11am–11pm, Fri & Sat 11am–midnight, Sun 11.30am–10.30pm.

Café Tarifa 56 Cowley Rd, OX4 1JB @01865 256091, @ cafe-tarifa.co.uk; map p.236. Atmospheric lounge bar decked out in Arabian style, with cocktails and cushions, also hosting a variety of generally chilled live music and DJ nights and cult movie screenings. Mon–Thurs 10am–midnight, Fri 10am–12.30am, Sat 10am–1am, Sun 10am–11pm.

Eagle & Child 49 St Giles, OX1 3LU @01865 302925, @ nicholsonspubs.co.uk; map p.236. Dubbed the "Bird & Baby", this was once the haunt of J.R.R. Tolkien and C.S. Lewis. The beer is still good and the old wood-panelled rooms at the front are great, but the pub is no longer independently owned – and feels a bit corporate. Mon–Sat 11am–11pm, Sun noon–11pm.

★ **Lamb & Flag** 12 St Giles, OX1 3JS @01865 515787; map p.236. Generations of university types have relished this quiet old tavern, owned by St John's College, which comes with low-beamed ceilings and cramped but cosy rooms in which to enjoy hand-drawn ale and genuine pork scratchings. Cash only. Mon–Sat noon–11pm, Sun noon–10.30pm.

Raoul's 32 Walton St, OX2 6AA @01865 553732, @ raoulsbar.com; map p.236. Famed Jericho cocktail bar, with a retro Seventies theme, great tunes and a devoted clientele. Navigate the mammoth menu of cocktails to choose a fave or three. Mon, Tues & Sun 4pm–midnight, Wed–Sat 4pm–1am.

★ **Turf Tavern** 4 Bath Place, OX1 3SU @01865 243235, @ turftavern-oxford.co.uk; map p.236. Small, atmospheric medieval pub, reached via a narrow passageway off Holywell St, with a fine range of beers, and mulled wine in winter. Daily 11am–11pm.

CLUBS AND LIVE MUSIC

The Bullingdon 162 Cowley Rd, OX4 1UE @01865 434998, @ thebullingdon.co.uk; map p.236. Popular East Oxford venue for comedy, live music and DJ nights, from punk to grime. The cheap drinks for students pull in a predictable crowd, but the atmosphere rarely disappoints. Mon–Thurs & Sun noon–1am, Fri & Sat noon–3am.

Wheatsheaf 129 High St, OX1 4DF @01865 721156, @ facebook.com/wheatsheaf.oxford; map p.236. Cramped music pub in a great central location, mainly showcasing local indie and punk bands. Also hosts the Spin Jazz Club (Thurs from 8.30pm; @ spinjazz.net). Mon–Wed & Sun noon–11pm, Thurs–Sat noon–midnight.

ENTERTAINMENT

Holywell Music Room 32 Holywell St, OX1 3SD @01865 766266, @ www.music.ox.ac.uk. This small, plain, Georgian building was opened in 1748 as the first public music hall in England. It offers a varied programme, from straight classical to experimental, with occasional bouts of jazz. Popular Sun morning "coffee concerts" (@ coffeeconcerts.com) run year-round.

Sheldonian Theatre Broad St, OX1 3AZ @01865 277299, @ www.admin.ox.ac.uk/sheldonian. Seventeenth-century edifice that is Oxford's top concert hall, despite rather dodgy acoustics, with the Oxford Philomusica symphony orchestra in residence (@ oxfordphil.com).

4

SHOPPING

Albion Beatnik Bookstore 34 Walton St, OX2 6AA ☎07737 876213, ⓦalbionbeatnik.co.uk; map p.236. Quirky independent bookshop in Jericho that focuses on twentieth-century literature (and jazz). Also has a good secondhand selection, lots of readings and events, and plenty of tea. Mon & Tues 3–8pm, Wed–Fri 1–8pm, Sat 11am–7pm; also Sun 3–6pm in university term time.

Alice's Shop 83 St Aldates, OX1 1RA ☎01865 723793, ⓦaliceinwonderlandshop.com; map p.236. Tiny Victorian shop that featured in Lewis Carroll's "Through The Looking Glass" – staffed by a sheep – that is now a mini-emporium of all things Alice: books, souvenirs, toys, ornaments, home furnishings and more. July & Aug daily 9.30am–6.30pm; Sept–June Mon–Fri & Sun 10.30am–5pm, Sat 10am–6pm.

Antiques On High 85 High St, OX1 4BG ☎01865 251075, ⓦantiquesonhigh.co.uk; map p.236. A group of outlets for antiques, prints, books and vintage fashion, as well as an affiliated gallery selling contemporary pieces by the Oxfordshire Craft Guild and Oxford Art Society. Mon–Sat 10am–5pm, Sun 11am–5pm.

Blackwell 48 Broad St, OX1 3BQ ☎01865 792792, ⓦblackwell.co.uk; map p.236. Oxford's leading university bookshop, a behemoth of a place that seems to extend for miles, above and below ground, stocking huge general ranges as well as academic titles. Mon–Sat 9am–6.30pm, Sun 11am–5pm.

Gloucester Green markets Gloucester Green, OX1 2BN ⓦlsdpromotions.com/oxford; map p.236. This city-centre square hosts vibrant open-air food and craft markets: great for browsing and some of the city's best street food on Sat. Food Wed 9am–4pm; food, antiques & crafts Thurs 9am–4pm; food, arts & textiles Sat 10am–5pm; farmers' market 1st & 3rd Thurs of month 9am–3pm.

Oxford Cheese Company 17 Covered Market, OX1 3DZ ☎01865 721420, ⓦoxfordcheese.co.uk; map p.236. Fantastically aromatic deli in the Covered Market. The perfect place to pick up all sorts of delicious nibbles, including their very own creation: Oxford Blue soft cheese, mellow, creamy and delicious. Mon–Sat 9am–5pm.

4

Around Oxford

From Oxford, a short journey west brings you into the Cotswolds; your first stop could be Burford (see page 251) or Moreton-in-Marsh (see page 254) – but make time, on the way, for the charming little town of **Woodstock** and its imperious country-house neighbour **Blenheim Palace**, birthplace of Winston Churchill. South of Oxford you'll find the pleasantly old-fashioned riverside haunt of **Henley-on-Thames** and open walking country around the **Vale of White Horse**. plus genteel **Windsor** and **Cookham** further afield.

Woodstock

WOODSTOCK, eight miles northwest of Oxford, has royal links going back to Saxon times, with a string of kings attracted by its excellent hunting. The Royalists used Woodstock as a base during the Civil War but, after their defeat, Cromwell never got round to destroying the town or its manor house: the latter was ultimately given to the Duke of Marlborough in 1704, who razed it to build Blenheim Palace. Long dependent on royal and then ducal patronage, Woodstock is now both a well-heeled commuter town for Oxford and a base for visitors to Blenheim. It is also an extremely pretty little place, its handsome stone buildings gathered around the main square, at the junction of Market and High streets.

Oxfordshire Museum

Park St, OX20 1SN • Tues–Sat 10am–5pm, Sun 2–5pm • Free • ☎01993 814106, ⓦwww.tomocc.org.uk

In an eighteenth-century house in the centre of Woodstock, the rather good **Oxfordshire Museum** offers an engaging take on the county's archeology, social history and industry. Its café overlooks the rear garden, which shelters original megalosaurus footprints, recovered from a local quarry and displayed i a Jurassic garden of ferns, pines and redwoods.

ARRIVAL AND INFORMATION

By bus #S3 for Oxford (every 20min; 30min) and Chipping Norton (hourly; 20min); #500 for Oxford Parkway station (every 30min; 20min); #233 for Burford (Mon–Sat hourly; 55min).

Websites ⓦwakeuptowoodstock.com and ⓦwww.oxfordshirecotswolds.org.

ACCOMMODATION AND EATING

The Bear Park St, OX20 1SZ ☎01993 811124, ⓦbear hotelwoodstock.co.uk. Behind the ivy-clad walls of this thirteenth-century coaching inn lurks a stylish, modern chain hotel – oak-carved four-poster, roaring log fires and all. Grab a table by the bay window for upscale, country-house food: Gressingham duck, Scottish beef and the like. Two-course menu £32. Mon–Thurs noon–2.30pm & 7–9.30pm, Fri & Sat noon–2.30pm & 7–10pm, Sun noon–2.30pm & 7–9pm. **£110**

King's Arms Market St, OX20 1SU ☎01993 813636, ⓦwww.kingshotelwoodstock.co.uk. Chic little hotel, with fifteen contemporary-styled rooms. The fine restaurant (mains £12–17) specializes in Modern British cuisine – leg of lamb or local goats' cheese salad. The bar/restaurant can remain busy until after 11pm: if you want an early night, choose a room at the back. Mon–Fri noon–2.30pm & 6.30–9.30pm, Sat & Sun noon–9pm. **£110**

Blenheim Palace

Woodstock, OX20 1PS • Daily: palace & gardens 10.30am–5.30pm; park 9am–6.30pm or dusk • Palace, park and gardens £24.90; park and gardens £15.30 • ☎01993 810530, ⓦblenheimpalace.com

In 1704, as thanks for his victory over the French at the Battle of Blenheim, Queen Anne gave John Churchill, **Duke of Marlborough** (1650–1722), the royal estate of Woodstock, along with the promise of enough cash to build himself a gargantuan palace. Work started on **Blenheim Palace** with Sir John Vanbrugh, who was also responsible for Castle Howard in Yorkshire (see page 548), as principal architect. However, the duke's formidable wife, Sarah Jennings, who had wanted Christopher Wren, was soon at loggerheads with Vanbrugh, while Queen Anne had second thoughts, stifling the flow of money. Construction halted and the house was only finished after the duke's death at the instigation of his widow, who ended up paying most of the bills and designing much of the interior herself. The result is England's grandest example of Baroque civic architecture, an Italianate palace of finely worked yellow stone that is more a monument than a house – just as Vanbrugh intended.

The **interior** of the house is stuffed with paintings and tapestries, plus all manner of objets d'art, including furniture from Versailles and carvings by Grinling Gibbons. The **Churchill Exhibition** on the ground floor provides a fascinating introduction to Winston (1874–1965), born at Blenheim as grandson of the seventh Duke of Marlborough, and buried alongside his wife in the graveyard of Bladon church just outside the estate.

Start your exploration of Blenheim's **gardens** by riding the narrow-gauge **miniature train** (March–Oct every 30min; 50p) on a looping journey to the **Pleasure Gardens** a few hundred yards to the east of the palace (also an easy walk). Here, as well as a café, you'll find a butterfly house, lavender garden, maze and other diversions. On the west side of the house, fountains spout beside the terrace of the palace café and paths lead down to the lake past the vivid **Rose Garden**. A path from the front of the house leads you across Blenheim's open **park** down to Vanbrugh's **Grand Bridge** and up to the hilltop **Column of Victory**, topped by a heroic statue of the 1st Duke.

ARRIVAL AND DEPARTURE

Entrances The estate has two entrances: the Hensington Gate lies just south of Woodstock on the A44 Oxford Rd, a few minutes on foot from town; the quieter Woodstock Gate is in the centre of town, at the far end of Park St.

By bus All of Woodstock's main buses (see above) stop at the Hensington Gate.

TOURS

Blenheim Palace tours Free guided tours (35min) inside the palace depart about every quarter-hour, though you're free to opt out and stroll at your own pace. On Sun or when the palace is very busy, tours are replaced by guides stationed in every room, who give details as you move through.

Henley-on-Thames

Three counties – Oxfordshire, Berkshire and Buckinghamshire – meet at genteel **HENLEY-ON-THAMES**, long a favourite stopping place for travellers between London and Oxford. Nowadays, Henley is a good-looking, affluent commuter town at its prettiest among the old brick and stone buildings that flank the short main drag, **Hart Street**. At one end of Hart Street is the Market Place and its fetching **Town Hall**, while at the other stand the easy Georgian curves of **Henley Bridge**. Overlooking the bridge is the parish church of **St Mary**, whose square tower sports a set of little turrets worked in chequerboard flint and stone.

River and Rowing Museum

Mill Meadows, RG9 1BF · Daily 10am–5pm · £12.50 · ☏ 01491 415600, ⊛ rrm.co.uk

A five-minute walk south along the riverbank from the foot of Hart Street lies Henley's imaginative **River and Rowing Museum**. Three galleries explore the wildlife and ecology of the Thames along with the history of rowing and the regatta, from ancient triremes to the modern Olympics. A fourth gallery is devoted to models illustrating scenes from the children's classic *Wind in the Willows* by Kenneth Grahame (1859–1932), set near Henley.

ARRIVAL AND DEPARTURE

HENLEY-ON-THAMES

By train Trains arrive from London Paddington (every 30min; 1hr – change at Twyford) and Reading (every 30min; 30min). From the station, it's a 5min walk north to Hart St.

By bus Bus #800/850/X80 from High Wycombe (every 15min; 40min) and Reading (hourly; 40min) stops on Hart St.

INFORMATION AND TOURS

Tourist office In the Town Hall (Mon–Sat 9am–4pm; ☏ 01491 578034, ⊛ visit-henley.com and ⊛ experience oxfordshire.org).

Boat trips Just south of the bridge, Hobbs of Henley offers boat trips along the Thames (Easter–Sept; 1hr; £9.75; ☏ 01491 572035, ⊛ hobbsofhenley.com), and has rowing boats and motor-launches for rent.

ACCOMMODATION AND EATING

★ **The Angel** Thameside, RG9 1BH ☏ 01491 410678, ⊛ theangelhenley.com. Of Henley's many pubs, this one stands out for its prime riverside location, with a fine outside deck overlooking the water. Decent food, too: light bites £6–9, mains £11–15. Mon–Sat 11.30am–10pm, Sun 11.30am–7pm; kitchen same hours.

Chocolate Café 13 Thameside, RG9 1BH ☏ 01491 411412, ⊛ thechocolatecafe.info. Lovely local café on the water, serving posh all-day breakfasts (eggs benedict £7.50), lunchtime light bites (£6–9), cream teas (from £6.50) and a massive range of hot chocolates, dark and white, with options for nougat, chilli, cinnamon, peppermint and more. Mon–Thurs 8am–5.30pm, Fri–Sun 8am–6pm.

Hotel du Vin New St, RG9 2BP ☏ 0330 016 0390, ⊛ hotelduvin.com. This slick central hotel occupies the creatively revamped old Brakspear Brewery. Rooms are in contemporary boutique style; a few on the top floor have river views. The restaurant serves sumptuous modern European cuisine using local produce. Two-course menu £17.95. Mon–Sat noon–2.30pm & 5.30–10pm, Sun noon–4pm & 6–9.30pm. **£129**

Windsor and Eton

The main reason to visit **WINDSOR**, a royally associated town 21 miles west of London, is to join the human conveyor belt ogling **Windsor Castle**. If you've got the energy and inclination, it's also worth crossing the river to visit **Eton College**, which grew from a fifteenth-century free school for impoverished scholars to become one of the most elitist schools in the world (for guided tours contact ☏ 01753 370100, ⊛ etoncollege.com). Download details of the **Eton Walkway**, a two-mile circular walk, at ⊛ outdoortrust.com.

Windsor Castle

Windsor, SL4 1NJ • Daily: March–Oct 9.30am–5.30pm; Nov–Feb 9.45am–4.15pm; last entry 1hr 30min before closing • £20.50 • ☎ 0303 123 7304, ⓦ royalcollection.org.uk/visit/windsorcastle

Towering above the town on a steep chalk bluff, **Windsor Castle** is an undeniably imposing sight, its chilly grey walls, punctuated by mighty medieval bastions, continuing as far as the eye can see. Inside, most visitors just gape in awe at the monotonous, gilded grandeur of the **State Apartments**, while the real highlights – the paintings from the Royal Collection that line the walls – are rarely given a second glance. More impressive is **St George's Chapel**, a glorious Perpendicular structure ranking with Henry VII's chapel in Westminster Abbey (see page 68), and the second most important resting place for royal corpses after the Abbey. On a fine day, you should put aside some time for exploring **Windsor Great Park**, which stretches for several miles south of the castle.

ARRIVAL AND DEPARTURE WINDSOR AND ETON

By train London Paddington to Windsor & Eton Central station via Slough (every 30min; 40min) or London

Waterloo to Windsor & Eton Riverside station (every 30min; 55min). From Oxford and Reading, change at Slough.

Cookham and around

Tiny **COOKHAM**, a prosperous Berkshire village five miles northwest of Windsor on the border with Buckinghamshire, was home to **Stanley Spencer** (1891–1959), one of Britain's greatest – and most eccentric – artists. Much of his work was inspired by the Bible, and many of his paintings depict biblical tales transposed into Cookham – which he once famously described as "a village in Heaven". There's a fine sample of his work at the **Stanley Spencer Gallery** (April–Sept Tues–Sun 10.30am–5.30pm; Oct–March Thurs–Sun 11am–4.30pm; £6; ☎ 01628 471885, ⓦ stanleyspencer.org.uk), which occupies the old Methodist Chapel on the High Street. Three prime exhibits are *View from Cookham Bridge*, the unsettling *Sarah Tubb and the Heavenly Visitors*, and the wonderful (unfinished) *Christ Preaching at Cookham Regatta*. Download details of an hour-long walk round Cookham, visiting places with which Spencer is associated, from the gallery website.

About three miles south of Cookham, on the banks of the Thames, the even smaller village of **BRAY** has the unlikely distinction of hosting two of Britain's four triple-Michelin-starred restaurants – the other two are in London.

ARRIVAL AND DEPARTURE COOKHAM AND AROUND

By train First get to Maidenhead, served by trains every 15min from London Paddington (40min) and Reading

(15min). Change at Maidenhead for hourly trains to Cookham (7min). Bray is a mile or so from Maidenhead station.

EATING AND DRINKING

Bel & The Dragon High St, Cookham, SL6 9SQ ☎ 01628 521263, ⓦ belandthedragon-cookham. co.uk. This historic half-timbered pub is a nice place for a pint, while the airy modern cuisine offers excellent upmarket international cuisine (mains £9–33), with a more affordable bar menu, backed by an extensive wine list. Also five comfortable rustic-style rooms. Mon–Fri noon–11pm, Sat noon–11.30pm, Sun noon–10.30pm; kitchen Mon–Sat noon–3pm & 6–10pm, Sun noon–9pm. **£140**

Fat Duck High St, Bray, SL6 2AQ ☎ 01628 580333, ⓦ thefatduck.co.uk. Regularly voted one of the world's top restaurants, showcasing chef Heston Blumenthal's uniquely inventive culinary style. The menu might feature

such classic creations as snail porridge and egg-and-bacon ice cream, with whisky wine gums to finish. Reservations (bookable up to four months in advance) are like gold dust. From £265 a head. Tues–Sat noon–1.15pm & 7–8.15pm.

Waterside Inn Ferry Rd, Bray, SL6 2AT ☎ 01628 620691, ⓦ waterside-inn.co.uk. Part of the Roux family's culinary empire, this lovely restaurant has been wowing diners with its idiosyncratic take on French cuisine since 1972. Signature dishes include sumptuous soufflé Suissesse (cheese soufflé with double cream) and *tronçonnette de homard* (pan-fried lobster with white port sauce). Lunchtime menus £50–80; six-course tasting menu £168. Reserve well in advance. Wed–Sun noon–2pm & 7–10pm.

THE RIDGEWAY NATIONAL TRAIL

The Iron Age inhabitants of Britain developed the **Ridgeway** (ⓦ nationaltrail.co.uk/ridgeway) as a major thoroughfare, a fast route that beetled across the chalky downs of modern-day Berkshire and Oxfordshire, negotiated the Thames and then traversed the Chiltern Hills. It was probably once part of a longer route from the Dorset coast to the Wash in Norfolk. Today, the Ridgeway is a National Trail, running from **Overton Hill**, near Avebury in Wiltshire, to **Ivinghoe Beacon**, 87 miles to the northeast near Tring. Crossing five counties, it keeps to the hills and avoids densely populated areas, except where the Thames slices through the trail at **Goring Gap**, marking the transition from the open Berkshire–Oxfordshire downs to the wooded valleys of the Chilterns.

It's fairly easy hiking, and most of the route is accessible to cyclists. The prevailing winds mean that it is best walked in a northeasterly direction. The trail is strewn with prehistoric monuments, though the finest archeological remains are on the downs edging the **Vale of White Horse** and around **Avebury** (see page 228).

Vale of White Horse

In the southwestern corner of Oxfordshire lies the pretty **Vale of White Horse**, a shallow valley whose fertile farmland is studded with tiny villages a striking collection of prehistoric remains. The **Ridgeway National Trail**, running along – or near – the top of the downs, links several of these ancient sites and offers wonderful, breezy views. The Vale is an easy day-trip from Oxford or elsewhere, but you might opt to stay locally in one of the Vale's quaint villages – tiny **Woolstone** is perhaps the most appealing.

White Horse Hill

Uffington, SN7 7UK • Open access • Free • ☎ 01793 762209, ⓦ nationaltrust.org.uk/white-horse-hill • 10min walk from signposted car park. Or, from Oxford, take a bus to Wantage (45min) then change for a Swindon-bound bus to Woolstone (35min), 15min walk away

White Horse Hill, overlooking the B4507 six miles west of the unexciting market town of Wantage, follows close behind Stonehenge (see page 226) and Avebury (see page 228) in the hierarchy of Britain's ancient sites, though it attracts nothing like the same number of visitors. Carved into the north-facing slope of the downs, the 374ft-long **Uffington White Horse** looks like something created with a few swift strokes of an immense brush. The first written record of the horse's existence dates from the time of Henry II, but it was cut much earlier, probably in the first century BC, making it one of the oldest chalk figures in Britain. There's no lack of weird and wonderful theories concerning its origins, but burial sites excavated in the surrounding area point to the horse having some kind of sacred function, though no one knows quite what.

Just below the horse is **Dragon Hill**, a small flat-topped hillock that has its own legend. Locals long asserted that this was where St George killed and buried the dragon, a theory proved, so they argued, by the bare patch at the top and the channel down the side, where blood trickled from the creature's wounds. Here also, at the top of the hill, is the Iron Age earthwork of **Uffington Castle**, which provides wonderful views over the Vale.

The Ridgeway trail (see above) runs alongside the white horse and continues west to reach, after one and a half miles, **Wayland's Smithy**, a 5000-year-old burial mound encircled by trees. It is one of the best Neolithic remains in the area, though heavy restoration has rather detracted from its mystery.

ACCOMMODATION AND EATING   VALE OF WHITE HORSE

Fox and Hounds Uffington, SN7 7RP ☎ 01367 820680, ⓦ uffingtonpub.co.uk. Friendly local pub in this quiet village a mile and a half north of White Horse Hill. Four well-kept en-suite rooms for B&B, and decent food; mains £10–12. Kitchen Mon–Fri noon–2pm & 6–9pm, Sat noon–3pm & 6–9pm, Sun noon–3pm. **£105**

White Horse Inn Woolstone, SN7 7QL ☎ 01367 820726, ⓦ whitehorsewoolstone.co.uk. A mile north of White Horse Hill, this half-timbered, partly thatched old inn offers swanky accommodation, mostly in a modern annexe, and upmarket pub food (mains £11–15). Kitchen daily noon–2.30pm & 6–9pm. **£90**

The Cotswolds

The limestone hills that make up the **Cotswolds** are preposterously photogenic, dotted with a string of picture-book villages, many of them built by wealthy cloth merchants between the fourteenth and sixteenth centuries. Largely bypassed by the Industrial Revolution, which heralded the area's commercial decline, the Cotswolds is characterized by handsomely preserved traditional architecture. Numerous churches are decorated with beautiful carving, for which the local limestone was ideal: soft and easy to carve when first quarried, but hardening after long exposure to the sunlight.

For their beauty and ease of access the Cotswolds are a major tourist attraction, with many towns afflicted by plagues of tearooms, antiques shops and coach parties. To see the region at its best, avoid the main towns and instead escape into the countryside. If you have a car, almost any minor road between Oxford and Cheltenham will deliver views, thatched cottages and oodles of rural atmosphere; otherwise, plan day-walks from one of the more attractive centres – **Chipping Campden** is the number-one choice, or opt for **Northleach**, foodie hub **Kingham** or the walkers' haven of **Winchcombe**.

This might be a tamed landscape, but there's good scope for exploring the byways, either in the gentler valleys that are most typical of the Cotswolds or along the dramatic escarpment that marks the western boundary with the Severn Valley. The **Cotswold Way** national trail runs for a hundred miles along the edge of the Cotswold escarpment from Chipping Campden in the northeast to Bath in the southwest, with a number of prehistoric sites providing added interest along the route. The section around Belas Knap is particularly rewarding, offering superb views over Cheltenham and the Severn Valley to the distant Malvern Hills.

4

By train Hourly trains from London Paddington via Oxford serve Kingham (1hr 25min) and Moreton-in-Marsh (1hr 35min), access points for the central and northern Cotswolds between Stow and Chipping Campden. Hourly trains on a different line from London Paddington via Swindon serve Kemble (1hr 15min), useful for Cirencester and southerly stretches around Tetbury.

By bus Local buses do a reasonable job connecting the larger towns and villages, but few buses run on Sun; smaller villages are rarely served more than once a week, if at all. Local tourist offices will be able to advise on travel plans – or you can check the public transport info at ⓦ escapetothecotswolds.org.uk.

On foot The Cotswolds is prime walking country: wherever

you are there's likely to be a marked trail nearby for anything from an hour's rural stroll to a multi-day epic. Loads of routes are downloadable for free from tourism websites (see page 44), with full descriptions and maps.

Travel pass The one-day "Cotswold Discoverer" (£10) allows unlimited travel on trains (Mon–Fri after 8.50am, Sat & Sun all day) between Oxford, Kingham and Moreton, and between Swindon, Kemble, Cheltenham and Gloucester, and on many of the buses covering main routes in and around Cotswold villages, from Oxford and Stroud in the south to Stratford-upon-Avon in the north. Buy it from local bus drivers or any train station. Details at ⓦ escapetothecotswolds.org.uk.

Websites ⓦ cotswolds.com, ⓦ www.oxfordshirecotswolds. org and ⓦ escapetothecotswolds.org.uk.

Burford

Twenty miles west of Oxford you get your first real taste of the Cotswolds at **BURFORD**, where the long, wide High Street, which slopes down to the bridge over the River Windrush, is simply magnificent, despite the traffic. The street is flanked by a remarkable line of old buildings that exhibit almost every type of classic Cotswolds feature, from wonky mullioned windows and half-timbered facades with bendy beams, through to spiky brick chimneys, fancy bow-fronted stone houses and grand horse-and-carriage gateways.

Church of St John the Baptist

Church Green, near the river, OX18 4RY • Daily 9am–5pm • Free, but donation welcomed • ⓦ burfordchurch.org

Of all the Cotswold churches, **St John the Baptist** has the most historical resonance, with architectural bits and pieces surviving from every phase of its construction, beginning

TOP 5 COTSWOLDS CHURCHES

St James Chipping Campden. See page 257
St John the Baptist Burford. See page 251
St John the Baptist Cirencester. See page 260
St Mary Tetbury. See page 261
St Peter and St Paul Northleach. See page 256

with the Normans and ending in the wool boom of the seventeenth century – the soaring Gothic spire built atop the old Norman tower is particularly eye-catching. Thereafter, it was pretty much left alone and, most unusually, its clutter of mausoleums, chapels and chantries survived the Reformation. A plaque outside commemorates three "Levellers" – a loose coalition of political thinkers that blossomed during the English Civil War – who were executed here in 1649 and whose aims are commemorated on **Levellers Day** in May (ⓦlevellersday.wordpress.com).

ARRIVAL AND INFORMATION
BURFORD

By bus #853 (Mon–Sat 3–4 daily, Sun daily) stops by the A40 at the top of Burford, from Northleach (15min), Cheltenham (45min) and Oxford (45min). #233 (Mon–Sat hourly) from Woodstock (55min) and #X10 from Chipping Norton (Mon–Sat hourly; 30min) stop on the High St.
Tourist office 33a High St (Mon–Sat 9.30am–5pm, Sun 10am–4pm; ☎01993 823558, ⓦwww.oxfordshire cotswolds.org).

ACCOMMODATION AND EATING

★ **Angel** 14 Witney St, OX18 4SN ☎01993 822714, ⓦtheangelatburford.co.uk. This sixteenth-century inn is highly regarded for its lively, creative menu – black pudding enlivening calves' liver, apricots and salsa adding zip to aubergine tagine. Mains £15–18. Also three traditional, tasteful en-suite rooms. Kitchen daily noon–9.30pm. **£110**
Bay Tree Sheep St, OX18 4LW ☎01993 822791, ⓦcotswold-inns-hotels.co.uk. First-class hotel in a lovely location off the High St, occupying a wisteria-clad stone house dating from the sixteenth century. Its twenty-odd rooms, in the main house and a couple of annexes, are done up in a lavish rendition of period character. Bar meals

are excellent (light bites £8–10, mains £13–20), featuring anything from tiger prawns to local pork sausages. Kitchen daily noon–2pm & 7–9.30pm. **£125**
Bull 105 High St, OX18 4RG ☎01993 822220, ⓦbullatburford.co.uk. This venerable old inn has been hosting guests for more than three hundred years – Charles II dallied here with Nell Gwynne, as did Lord Nelson with Lady Hamilton. Traditionally styled rooms feature panelling and four-poster beds, while the restaurant grafts French and Mediterranean influences onto local ingredients, with emphasis on fish and seafood. Mains £15–23. Kitchen daily noon–2.30pm & 6.30–9pm. **£110**

Kelmscott Manor

Kelmscott, GL7 3HJ • April–Oct Wed & Sat 11am–5pm • £9.50; timed tickets, so call ahead to confirm arrangements • ☎01367 252486, ⓦkelmscottmanor.org.uk • No public transport. The car park is a 10min walk from the house

Kelmscott Manor, amid the Thames-side water meadows about eight miles south of Burford, is a place of pilgrimage for devotees of **William Morris**, who used this Tudor house as a summer home from 1871 to his death in 1896. The simple beauty of the house is enhanced by the furniture, fabrics and wallpapers created by Morris and his Pre-Raphaelite friends, including Burne-Jones and Rossetti.

Kingham and around

When *Country Life* magazine calls you "England's favourite village", it could easily prompt a downward spiral. But for **KINGHAM**, set in the Evenlode Valley between Chipping Norton (the highest town in Oxfordshire) and Stow-on-the-Wold (the highest town in the Cotswolds), everything's looking up. There's still nothing to do in this cheery, noticeably upmarket village, other than eat well, walk well and sleep well… but that's the point. The stroll in from the railway station is lovely, marked by the Perpendicular tower of **St Andrew's Church**.

ARRIVAL AND DEPARTURE

By train Kingham has hourly trains from London Paddington (1hr 25min), Oxford (25min), Moreton (10min) and Worcester (50min). The station is a mile west of the village.

ACCOMMODATION AND EATING

Daylesford Organic Daylesford, GL56 0YG ☎01608 731700, ⓦdaylesford.com. This super-sleek farm complex a mile north of Kingham includes a spectacularly well-stocked deli and café, where light lunches (£10–16) are filled out by cream teas and informal suppers of wood-fired pizza or chicken teriyaki (£13–19). An absurdly expensive, but very good, glimpse of Chelsea in the Cotswolds. Booking essential. Mon–Sat 8am–8pm, Sun 10am–4pm.

★ Kingham Plough Kingham, OX7 6YD ☎01608 658327, ⓦthekinghamplough.co.uk. The epitome of a Cotswold gastropub. Book ahead for one of Oxfordshire's most atmospheric, upmarket and welcoming restaurants. Local, seasonal produce of all kinds, expertly prepared, is

served off a short, daily-changing a la carte menu (mains £18–25) or a less ambitious bar menu: see twebsite for specific menu times. They also have seven comfortable, country-style rooms. Kitchen Mon–Sat noon–9pm, Sun 11.30am–3pm & 6–8pm. **£145**

Kings Head Bledington, OX7 6XQ ☎01608 658365, ⓦthekingsheadinn.net. Just west of Kingham, this sixteenth-century inn with regulars popping up the bar serves local, ethically sourced Modern British fusion dishes – potted shrimps, steak and ale pie, Cotswold lamb (mains £14–22). The rooms, some floral, some designer-chic, are a snip. Kitchen Mon–Thurs noon–2pm & 6.30–9pm, Fri noon–2pm & 6.30–9.30pm, Sat noon–2.30pm & 6.30–9.30pm, Sun noon–2.30pm & 7–9pm. **£100**

Moreton-in-Marsh

A key transport hub and one of the Cotswolds' more sensible towns, **MORETON-IN-MARSH** is named for a now-vanished wetland nearby. It has always been an important access point for the countryside and remains so with its **railway station**, which is on the line between London, Oxford and Worcester. It also sits astride the A429 Fosse Way, the former Roman road that linked Exeter with Lincoln. On the broad, handsome **High Street**, enhanced with Jacobean and Georgian facades, stands the nineteenth-century **Redesdale Hall**, named for Lord Redesdale, father of the infamous Mitford sisters (among them Diana, wife of British wartime fascist leader Oswald Mosley; and Unity, a close companion of Adolf Hitler), who as children lived at Batsford House near the town.

ARRIVAL AND INFORMATION

By train Moreton has hourly trains from London Paddington (1hr 35min), Oxford (35min), Kingham (10min) and Worcester (40min). The station is a 2min walk from the High St.

By bus #1 (Mon–Sat 4 daily) to/from Broadway (25min), Chipping Campden (45min) and Stratford-upon-Avon (1hr 15min); #2 (Mon–Sat 4 daily) to/from Chipping Campden (30min) and Stratford-upon-Avon (1hr 10min); #801

(Mon–Sat every 1–2hr; June–Sept also 2–3 on Sun) to/from Stow-on-the-Wold (15min), Bourton-on-the-Water (25min) and Cheltenham (1hr 10min), some also via Northleach (55min).

Tourist office High St (Mon 8.45am–4pm, Tues–Thurs 8.45am–5.15pm, Fri 8.45am–4.45pm, Sat 10am–1pm; Nov–March Sat closes 12.30pm; ☎01608 650881, ⓦcotswolds.com).

ACCOMMODATION AND EATING

Acacia Guest House 2 New Rd, GL56 0AS ☎01608 650130, ⓦacaciainthecotswolds.co.uk. Decent little B&B on the short street connecting the station to the High St – very handy for arrivals and departures by train or bus. **£65**

★ Horse and Groom Bourton-on-the-Hill, GL56 9AQ ☎01386 700413, ⓦhorseandgroom.info. Occupying a Georgian building of honey-coloured Cotswold stone two miles west of Moreton, this free house has a reputation for good beer and excellent food. The menu changes frequently, focused on meat sourced from local farmers and seasonal veg. It's popular: book ahead. Mains £13–18. Also

five appealing rooms, one with French doors opening onto the garden. Mon–Sat noon–11pm, Sun noon–10.30pm; kitchen Mon–Sat noon–3pm & 6.30–9.30pm, Sun noon–3pm & 6.30–8.30pm. **£120**

Manor House High St, GL56 0LJ ☎01608 650501, ⓦcotswold-inns-hotels.co.uk. Pleasant four-star hotel occupying a sixteenth-century former coaching inn, with a nice garden and stylish rooms. Its posh restaurant, with muted contemporary styling, serves Modern British cuisine (mains £11–17), with good vegetarian options available. Daily noon–2.30pm & 7–9.30pm. **£120**

Stow-on-the-Wold

Ambling over a steep hill seven hundred feet above sea level, **STOW-ON-THE-WOLD**, five miles south of Moreton, draws in a quantity of visitors disproportionate to its size and attractions, which essentially comprise an old **marketplace** surrounded by pubs, antique and souvenir shops, and an inordinate number of tearooms. The narrow alleyways, or "tchures", running into the square were designed for funnelling sheep to the market, which is itself dominated by an imposing Victorian hall. **St Edward's Church** has a photogenic north porch, where two yew trees flanking the door appear to have grown into the stones.

ARRIVAL AND INFORMATION   STOW-ON-THE-WOLD

By bus Buses stop just off the main square, including #801 (Mon–Sat every 1–2hr; May–Sept also 2–3 on Sun) to/from Bourton-on-the-Water (10min), Moreton (15min) and Cheltenham (1hr 10min), some also via Northleach (30min); and #802 (Mon–Sat 4–6 daily) to/from Kingham station (15min).

Tourist office In the library on the main square (April–Oct Mon & Wed 10am–5pm, Tues & Fri 10am–7pm, Thurs 10am–2pm, Sat 10am–4pm; ☎01451 870998, ⓦstowinfo.co.uk and ⓦcotswolds.com).

ACCOMMODATION AND EATING

★ **Jaffe & Neale** 8 Park St, GL54 1AQ ☎01451 832000, ⓦjaffeandneale.co.uk. Outpost for this much-loved Chipping Norton bookshop/café, which has brought a fresh, contemporary feel to the interior of this old building. Come for the carrot cake, stay for the literary inspiration. Mon–Sat 9.30am–5pm, Sun 10am–4pm.

Number Nine 9 Park St, GL54 1AQ ☎01451 870333, ⓦnumber-nine.info. Pleasant old house offering quality B&B just down from the town square. The three bedrooms feature low beams but contemporary styling – and the rates are a bargain. **£75**

Porch House Digbeth St, GL54 1BN ☎01451 870048, ⓦporch-house.co.uk. Purportedly the oldest inn in Britain, with parts of the building dated at 947 AD (though the interiors have been freshly modernized). The thirteen hessian-floored rooms look good, but are on the small side. The restaurant is a comfortably posh affair (mains £13–18), with cheaper nosh in the wonky-beamed pub. Mon–Sat 8am–11pm, Sun 8am–10.30pm; kitchen Mon–Fri noon–3pm & 6–9.30pm, Sat noon–9.30pm, Sun noon–8.30pm. **£115**

★ **Queen's Head** The Square, GL54 1AB ☎01451 830563, ⓦqueensheadstowonthewold.com. Traditional old pub that provides good beer, good service and a pleasant chatty atmosphere. Food is a level above standard pub grub (mains £11–15), and they have a few simple, stylish rooms nearby. Mon–Sat 11am–11pm, Sun noon–10.30pm; kitchen daily noon–2.30pm & 6.30–9pm. **£79**

SHOPPING

Borzoi Bookshop Church St, GL54 1BB ☎01451 830268, ⓦborzoibookshop.co.uk. Lovely little independent bookshop in the centre of town, with a great range of stock and knowledgeable staff. Mon–Sat 9.30am–5pm.

Fosse Gallery The Square, GL54 1AF ☎01451 831319, ⓦfossegallery.com. Long-established, privately owned gallery devoted to contemporary British art. Whatever's showing, it's worth popping in. Mon–Sat 10.30am–5pm.

Bourton-on-the-Water

BOURTON-ON-THE-WATER is the epicentre of Cotswold tourism. By the village green – flanked by photogenic Jacobean and Georgian facades in yellow Cotswold stone – five picturesque **bridges** span the shallow River Windrush, dappled by shade from overhanging trees. It looks lovely, but its proximity to main roads means it's invariably packed: coaches cram in all summer and the **High Street** now concentrates on souvenirs and teashops, interspersed with everything from a Model Village to a Dragonfly Maze and Bird Park.

Lower Slaughter

A mile outside Bourton-on-the-Water, **LOWER SLAUGHTER** (as in *slohtre*, Old English for a marshy place, cognate with "slough") is a more enticing prospect, though still on the day-trippers' circuit. Pop by to take in some of the most celebrated village scenery in the

4

Cotswolds, as the River Eye snakes its way between immaculate honey-stone cottages. There is a small **museum** (and souvenir shop) signposted in a former mill, but the main attraction of the stroll through the village is to stop in for a little something at one of the grand hotels occupying gated mansions on both sides of the street.

Northleach

Secluded in a shallow depression, **NORTHLEACH** is one of the most appealing and atmospheric villages in the Cotswolds – a great base to explore the area. Despite the fact that the A40 Oxford–Cheltenham road and A429 Fosse Way cross at a large roundabout nearby, virtually no tourist traffic makes its way into the centre. Rows of immaculate late medieval cottages cluster around the **Market Place** and adjoining **Green**.

The Old Prison

Fosse Way, GL54 3JH · May–Oct daily 10am–5pm; Nov–April Mon, Tues & Thurs–Sun 9.30am–4pm · Free · ☎ 01451 861563, ⓦ escapetothecotswolds.org.uk

Just outside town is the Georgian **Old Prison**, which has interesting displays on the history of crime and punishment, along with the **Cotswolds Discovery Centre**, a visitor centre explaining the work of the Cotswolds Conservation Board in maintaining the Cotswolds Area of Outstanding Natural Beauty.

Church of St Peter and St Paul

Mill End, GL54 3HL · Daily 9am–5pm · Free · ☎ 01451 861132, ⓦ northleach.org

One of the finest of the Cotswolds "wool churches", **St Peter and St Paul** is a classic example of the fifteenth-century Perpendicular style, with a soaring tower and beautifully proportioned nave lit by wide clerestory windows. The floors of the aisles are inlaid with an exceptional collection of memorial **brasses**, marking the tombs of the merchants whose endowments paid for the church. On several, you can make out the woolsacks laid out beneath the owner's feet – a symbol of wealth and power that survives today in London's House of Lords, where a woolsack is placed on the Lord Chancellor's seat.

ARRIVAL AND DEPARTURE

NORTHLEACH

By bus Buses stop by the Green.

Destinations #801 (Mon–Sat 5 daily) to/from Cheltenham (40min), Bourton-on-the-Water (15min), Stow-on-the-Wold (30min) and Moreton-in-Marsh (40min); #853 (Mon–Sat 3–4 daily, 1 on Sun) to Burford (15min), Cheltenham (30min) and Oxford (1hr); #855 (Mon–Sat 5–6 daily) to/from Cirencester (20–40min) and Bibury (20min).

ACCOMMODATION AND EATING

Cotswold Lion Café Old Prison, GL54 3JH ☎ 01451 861563, ⓦ escapetothecotswolds.org.uk. Friendly café on the edge of the town, serving up teas, coffees, cakes and light lunches (under £10). Daily 10am–4.30pm.

Wheatsheaf West End, GL54 3EZ ☎ 01451 860244, ⓦ cotswoldswheatsheaf.com. Excellent former coaching inn, remodelled in a bright modern style softened by period furniture, bookcases and etchings. Its restaurant has upscale Mediterranean cuisine – polenta with nettles and peas, spiced lamb pie with sultanas, and so forth. Mains £13–19. It also has fourteen comfortable, en-suite rooms. Mon–Sat noon–3pm & 6–9pm, Sun noon–3.30pm & 6–9pm. **£120**

Bibury

A detour between Northleach and Cirencester passes through **BIBURY**, dubbed "the most beautiful village in England" by William Morris. Bibury draws attention for **Arlington Row**, originally built around 1380 as a wool store and converted in the seventeenth century into a line of cottages to house weavers. Their hound's-tooth gables, warm yellow stone and wonky windows stole William Morris's heart – and are now immortalized in the British passport as an image of England.

ARRIVAL AND DEPARTURE BIBURY

By bus The #855 (Mon–Sat 5–6 daily) runs to Northleach (20min) and Cirencester (20min).

Chipping Campden

Situated on the northern edge of the Cotswolds, near Stratford-upon-Avon (see page 405), **CHIPPING CAMPDEN** gives a better idea than anywhere else in the area of how a prosperous wool town might have looked in the Middle Ages. Its name derives from the Saxon term *campadene*, meaning cultivated valley, and the Old English *ceapen*, or market. The elegant **High Street** is hemmed in by mostly Tudor and Jacobean facades – an undulating line of weather-beaten roofs above twisted beams and mullioned windows. The evocative seventeenth-century **Market Hall** has survived too, an open-sided pavilion propped up on sturdy stone piers in the middle of the High Street, where farmers once gathered to sell their produce.

The Old Silk Mill

Sheep St, GL55 6DS • Daily 10am–5pm; Hart Silversmiths Mon–Fri 9am–5pm, Sat 9am–noon • Free • ☎ 01386 841100, ⓦ hartsilversmiths.co.uk

Just off the High Street is the **Old Silk Mill**, where designer Charles Ashbee relocated the London Guild of Handicraft in 1902, introducing the Arts and Crafts movement to the Cotswolds. Today, as well as housing galleries of local art, the building rings with the noise of chisels from the resident stone carvers. Upstairs, you're free to wander into the workshop of **Hart**, a silversmith firm – it's like stepping into an old photograph, with metalworking tools strewn everywhere under low ceilings, and staff perched by the windows working by hand on decorative pieces.

Court Barn Museum

Church St, GL55 6JE • Tues–Sun 10am–5pm; Oct–March closes 4pm • £5 • ☎ 01386 841951, ⓦ courtbarn.org.uk

The history of the Guild of Handicraft, and its leading exponents, is explained at the superb **Court Barn Museum**. Sited opposite a magnificent row of seventeenth-century Cotswold stone **almshouses**, the museum displays the work of Charles Ashbee and eight Arts and Crafts cohorts, placing it all in context with informative displays and short videos. Featured works include the bookbinding of Katharine Adams, the stained-glass design of Paul Woodroffe and furniture by Gordon Russell.

St James' Church

Church St, GL55 6JG • March–Oct Mon–Sat 10am–4.30pm, Sun noon–4pm; Nov–Feb Mon–Sat 11am–3pm, Sun noon–3pm • Free • ☎ 01386 841927, ⓦ stjameschurchcampden.co.uk

At the top of the village rises **St James' Church**. Built in the fifteenth century, the zenith of Campden's wool-trading days, this is the archetypal Cotswold wool church, beneath a magnificent 120ft tower. Inside, the airy nave is bathed in light from the clerestory windows. The South Chapel holds the ostentatious **funerary memorial** of the Hicks family, with fancily carved marble effigies lying on a table-tomb.

Dover's Hill

Panoramic views crown the short but severe hike up the first stage of the Cotswold Way, north from Chipping Campden to **Dover's Hill** (which is also accessible by car). The highest point, 740ft above sea level, affords breathtaking vistas over to the Malvern Hills and beyond. This is where, in 1612, local lawyer Robert Dover organized competitions of running, jumping, wrestling and shin-kicking that rapidly became known as the **Cotswold Olimpicks**, still staged here annually (see ⓦ olimpickgames.co.uk).

ARRIVAL AND INFORMATION

CHIPPING CAMPDEN

By train Moreton-in-Marsh station (see page 254) is 8 miles away, connected by bus #1 or #2.

By bus Buses stop on the High St, including routes #1 & #2. Destinations Broadway (Mon–Sat 4 daily; 20min); Moreton-in-Marsh (Mon–Sat every 1–2hr; 45min); Stratford-upon-Avon (Mon–Sat every 1–2hr; 40min).

Tourist office High St (March–Oct daily 9.30am–5pm; Nov–Feb Mon–Thurs 9.30am–1pm, Fri–Sun 9.30am–4pm; ☎ 01386 841206, ⓦ campdenonline.org and ⓦ cotswolds.com).

ACCOMMODATION AND EATING

Badgers Hall High St, GL55 6HB ☎ 01386 840839, ⓦ badgershall.com. This tearoom in an old stone house has won awards for its traditional English teas and cakes, all freshly made daily. It also does light lunches (under £10). En-suite guest rooms upstairs feature period detail – beamed ceilings and antique pine furniture. Mon–Sat 10am–4.30pm, Sun 11am–4.30pm. **£115**

Bakers Arms Broad Campden, GL55 6UR ☎ 01386 840515, ⓦ bakersarmscampden.com. From the archway under the *Noel Arms* on the High St, walk a mile or so south to find this gem, named a North Cotswolds Pub of the Year for its ales, its atmosphere and its solid food – fish pie, gammon and good veggie options (mains £10–15). Mon 5–11pm, Tues–Fri noon–3pm & 5–11pm, Sat noon–11pm, Sun noon–10.30pm; kitchen Tues–Thurs noon–2pm & 6–8pm, Fri & Sat noon–2pm & 6–9pm, Sun noon–4pm.

★ **Eight Bells** Church St, GL55 6JG ☎ 01386 840371, ⓦ eightbellsinn.co.uk. Much-loved old inn with a first-rate restaurant – pheasant with mushrooms, pork with apricots and chestnuts, lamb's liver on bubble and squeak. Mains £13–22. It also has seven individually done-up bedrooms, smartly modern without boutique pretension. Kitchen Mon–Thurs noon–2pm & 6.30–9pm, Fri & Sat noon–2.30pm & 6.30–9.30pm, Sun noon–3pm & 6–9pm. **£120**

Volunteer Inn Lower High St, GL55 6DY ☎ 01386 840688, ⓦ thevolunteerinn.net. There are nine budget rooms at this lively pub, often used by walkers and cyclists (you can rent bikes from £12/day; ⓦ www.cyclecotswolds.co.uk). The on-site *Maharaja* restaurant serves unusual Bangladeshi fish and chicken curries and fruity Kashmiri dishes (mains £8–17). Pub daily 11am–11pm; restaurant Mon–Thurs & Sun 6–10.30pm, Fri & Sat 6–11pm. **£50**

Broadway

BROADWAY, five miles west of Chipping Campden, is a handsome little village at the foot of the steep escarpment that rolls along the western edge of the Cotswolds. It seems likely that the Romans were the first to settle here, but Broadway's high times were as a stagecoach stop on the route from London to Worcester. Its long, broad main street, framed by honey-stone cottages and shaded by chestnut trees, attracts more visitors than is comfortable, but things do quieten down in the evening.

Gordon Russell Design Museum

Russell Square, WR12 7AP • Tues–Sun: Feb, Nov & Dec 11am–4pm; March–Oct 11am–5pm • £5 • ☎ 01386 854695, ⓦ gordonrussellmuseum.org

Just off the village green, the absorbing **Gordon Russell Design Museum** is dedicated to the work of this local furniture-maker (1892–1980), whose factory formerly stood next door. Influenced both by the Arts and Crafts movement but also by modern technology, Russell's stated aim was to "make decent furniture for ordinary people" through "a blend of hand and machine". The museum showcases many of his classic furniture designs, alongside other period artefacts ranging from metalware to mirrors.

Broadway Museum

65 High St, WR12 7DP • Tues–Sun 10am–5pm • £5 • ☎ 01386 859047, ⓦ broadwaymuseum.org.uk

A former coaching inn now holds the **Broadway Museum**, run in partnership with Oxford's mighty Ashmolean Museum. Objects across four floors of displays include embroidered tapestries and furniture in the panelled ground-floor rooms, Worcester porcelain, glass, examples of William Morris tiles, and Cotswold pottery on the upper levels, as well as paintings by Gainsborough and Reynolds.

Broadway Tower

Fish Hill, WR12 7LB • Daily 10am–5pm; shorter hours in bad weather • Tower £5, bunker £4, joint ticket £8 • ☎ 01386 852390, Ⓦ broadwaytower.co.uk

A mile southeast of the village, **Broadway Tower**, a turreted folly built in 1798, has become an icon of the Cotswolds, perched at more than 1000ft above sea level with stupendous views that purportedly encompass thirteen counties. Now privately owned, it stands alongside a family activity park with café. The historical displays in the tower are a bit limp: visit to climb the 71 steps to the roof, for those views. Nearby you can venture down into a Cold War-era **nuclear bunker**. A circular **walk** from Broadway heads up to the tower (4 miles; 3hr).

ARRIVAL AND INFORMATION   BROADWAY

By bus #1 (Mon–Sat 4 daily) to/from Chipping Campden (20min), Moreton-in-Marsh (25min) and Stratford-upon-Avon (1hr); #606 (Mon–Sat 4 daily, 2 on Sun) to/from Winchcombe (25min) and Cheltenham (1hr).

Tourist office Russell Square (Feb, March, Nov & Dec Mon–Sat 10am–4pm, Sun 11am–3pm; April–Oct Mon–Sat 10am–5pm, Sun 11am–3pm; ☎ 01386 852937, Ⓦ broadway-cotswolds.co.uk).

ACCOMMODATION AND EATING

Crown and Trumpet 14 Church St, WR12 7AE ☎ 01386 853202, Ⓦ cotswoldholidays.co.uk. This cheery, historic local tavern has decent beers, a lively atmosphere, quality Sun roasts and regular sessions of live blues and jazz. Mains £6–13. Also has five simple en-suite rooms. Kitchen Mon–Fri 11am–3pm & 5–11pm, Sat 11am–11pm, Sun noon–4pm & 6–10.30pm. **£75**

Lygon Arms High St, WR12 7DU ☎ 01386 852255, Ⓦ lygonarmshotel.co.uk. A grand coaching inn that hosted Charles I (in 1645) and Oliver Cromwell (in 1651) in rooms which still retain their original panelling and fittings today. In 2017, they had a top-to-toe refit, which injected much-needed freshness into both the rooms and restaurant, now serving good, upmarket Modern European cuisine (mains £13–21), including in the majestic Great Hall. Food served Mon–Fri

11am–3pm & 5–10pm, Sat & Sun 11am–10pm. **£170**

Olive Branch 78 High St, WR12 7AJ ☎ 01386 853440, Ⓦ theolivebranch-broadway.com. Award-winning guesthouse in an old stone house – a touch pastel-and-chintz, but cosy and well run. Some rooms have king-size beds and access to the garden. **£117**

Russell's 20 High St, WR12 7DT ☎ 01386 853555, Ⓦ russellsofbroadway.co.uk. This relaxed, stylish restaurant serves Modern British cooking: Cotswold lamb chops with lemon & caper-crumbed kidney, honey & thyme-glazed duck breast, monkfish with bulgur wheat, and so on. Mains £15–32, or two-course set menu £20. Seven boutique rooms feature mood lighting, designer furniture and huge stand-alone bathtubs and showers-for-two. Food served Mon–Sat noon–2.15pm & 6–9.15pm, Sun noon–2.30pm. **£130**

Winchcombe and around

About eight miles southwest of Broadway – and nine miles northeast of Cheltenham – **WINCHCOMBE** has a long main street flanked by a fetching medley of stone and half-timbered buildings. Placid today, it was an important Saxon town and one-time capital of the kingdom of Mercia, and flourished during the medieval cloth boom, one of the results being **St Peter's** church, a mainly fifteenth-century structure distinguished by forty alarming gargoyles that ring the exterior. On Winchcombe's southern edge is **Sudeley Castle** (March–Oct daily 10am–5pm; £14.95; ☎ 01242 604244, Ⓦ sudeleycastle.co.uk), which combines ravishing good looks with a fascinating history. In its magnificent estate stands **St Mary's Church**, housing a beautiful Victorian tomb that marks the final resting place of Katherine Parr, Henry VIII's sixth wife.

Belas Knap

2 miles south of Winchcombe, GL54 5AL • Open access • Free; EH • Ⓦ www.english-heritage.org.uk/visit/places/belas-knap-long-barrow • On foot from Winchcombe, the path strikes off to the right near the entrance to Sudeley Castle. When you reach the country lane at the top, turn right and then left for the 10min hike to the barrow

The Neolithic long barrow of **Belas Knap** occupies one of the Cotswolds' wildest summits. Dating from around 3000 BC, this is the best-preserved burial chamber in England, stretched out like a strange sleeping beast cloaked in green velvet, more than fifty metres long. The best way to get there is to **walk**.

4

By bus #606 from Broadway (Mon–Sat 4 daily; 35min) and Cheltenham (Mon–Sat 4 daily, 5 on Sun; 20min).

Tourist office High St (April–Oct daily 10am–4pm; Nov–

March Sat 10am–4pm, Sun 10am–3pm; ☏ 01242 602925, ⓦ winchcombe.co.uk and ⓦ cotswolds.com).

Cirencester

Self-styled "Capital of the Cotswolds", the affluent town of **CIRENCESTER** lies on the southern fringes of the region, midway between Oxford and Bristol. As Corinium, it became a provincial capital and a centre of trade under the **Romans**, in Britannia second in size and importance only to "Londinium" (London). The Saxons destroyed almost all of the Roman city, and the town only revived with the wool boom of the Middle Ages. Few medieval buildings have survived, however, and the houses along the town's most handsome streets – Park, Thomas and Coxwell – date mostly from the seventeenth and eighteenth centuries. Cirencester's heart is the delightful **Market Place**, packed with traders' stalls every Monday and Friday, and for the fortnightly Saturday farmers' market (ⓦ cirencester.gov.uk/markets).

Church of St John the Baptist

Market Place, GL7 2NX · Daily 10am–5pm; Oct–March closes 4pm · Free · ☏ 01285 659317, ⓦ cirenparish.co.uk

The magnificent parish church of **St John the Baptist**, built during the fifteenth century, dominates the market place. The church's most notable feature is its huge **porch**, so big that it once served as the local town hall. The flying buttresses that support the tower had to be added when it transpired that the church had been built over the filled-in Roman ditch that ran beside the Gloucester–Silchester road. Inside the church is a colourful wineglass **pulpit**, carved in stone around 1450, and the **Boleyn Cup**, a gilded silver goblet made in 1535 for Anne Boleyn.

Corinium Museum

Park St, GL7 2BX · Mon–Sat 10am–5pm, Sun 2–5pm; Nov–March closes 4pm · £5.40 · ☏ 01285 655611, ⓦ coriniummuseum.org

West of the Market Place, the sleek **Corinium Museum** is devoted to the history of the town from Roman to Victorian times. The collection of Romano-British antiquities is particularly fine, including some wonderful **mosaic pavements**. Other highlights include a trove of Bronze Age gold and an excellent video on Cotswold life in the Iron Age.

New Brewery Arts Centre

Brewery Court, off Cricklade St, GL7 1JH · Mon–Sat 9am–5pm; April–Dec also Sun 10am–4pm · Free · ☏ 01285 657181, ⓦ newbreweryarts.org.uk

Just south of the Market Place, the **New Brewery Arts Centre** is occupied by more than a dozen resident artists whose studios you can visit and whose work you can buy in the shop. It's worth popping by to see who is working and exhibiting – and, perhaps, to catch some live music.

By train From Kemble station, about 5 miles southwest – served by hourly trains from London Paddington (1hr 15min) and Cheltenham (1hr) – take bus #882 (Mon–Fri 5 daily, 2 on Sat; 15min) or a taxi (about £10).

By bus National Express coaches from London Victoria and Heathrow Airport stop on London Rd, while local buses stop in or near Market Place.

Destinations Bibury (#855; Mon–Sat 4 daily; 15min); Cheltenham (#51; Mon–Sat hourly; 40min); Gloucester

(#882; Mon–Fri every 1–2hr, 2 on Sat; 45min); Heathrow Airport (National Express; 5 daily; 1hr 30min); London Victoria (National Express; 5–8 daily; 2hr 20min); Northleach (#855; Mon–Sat every 2hr; 20min); Tetbury (#882; Mon–Sat 3 daily; 45min).

Tourist office At Corinium Museum, Park St (Mon–Sat 10am–5pm, Sun 2–5pm; Nov–March closes 4pm; ☏ 01285 654180, ⓦ cotswolds.com).

ACCOMMODATION

Corinium 12 Gloucester St, GL7 2DG ☎ 01285 659711, ⓦ coriniumhotel.com. Decent three-star family-run hotel in a historic property a short walk northwest of the centre. Only fifteen rooms, modestly priced and adequately furnished. **£105**

Fleece Market Place, GL7 2NZ ☎ 01285 658507, ⓦ the fleececirencester.co.uk. This old town-centre inn has been freshly updated to a smart, contemporary look. The 28 rooms, all beams and low ceilings, feature swanky en-suite bathrooms. **£99**

Ivy House 2 Victoria Rd, GL7 1EN ☎ 01285 656626, ⓦ ivyhousecotswolds.com. One of the more attractive of a string of B&Bs along this road, a high-gabled Victorian house with four en-suite rooms. **£90**

YHA Cotswolds New Brewery Arts Centre, GL7 1JH ☎ 01285 657181, ⓦ yha.org.uk/hostel/cotswolds. Converted in 2016 from a long-closed brewery warehouse, this new hostel known as the Barrel Store sits alongside a buzzing arts centre, with keenly priced dorms, doubles and family rooms. No food served, but there's a café next door. Dorms **£23**, doubles **£68**

EATING AND DRINKING

Indian Rasoi 14 Dollar St, GL7 2AJ ☎ 01285 644822, ⓦ indianrasoi.org. An up-to-date, contemporary styled restaurant serving excellent Indian food. Go for one of the chef's specials – fiery Naga chilli lamb or coconutty Mangalore chicken – or one of the great vegetarian options, such as Bengali aubergine. Mains £9–14. Mon–Sat noon–2pm & 5.30–11.30pm, Sun noon–2pm & 5.30–11pm.

★ **Jesse's Bistro** The Stableyard, 14 Black Jack St, GL7 2AA ☎ 01285 641497, ⓦ jessesbistro.co.uk. Wonderful little hideaway, in a courtyard near the museum. The speciality here is fish and seafood, freshly caught and whisked over directly from Cornwall. Expect crab salad or *moules marinière*, oven-roasted mackerel or pepper-crusted bream alongside meaty favourites such as rump steak. Mains £14–23; two-course lunch £19.50. Mon noon–2.30pm, Tues–Sat noon–2.30pm & 7–9.30pm, Sun noon–4pm.

Made By Bob The Corn Hall, 26 Market Place, GL7 2NY ☎ 01285 641818, ⓦ foodmadebybob.com. Buzzy, hip daytime café/restaurant. Opens for breakfast (Bircher muesli, kippers, eggs Benedict, full English; £6–11), and stays open after lunch for posh tea. Watch the chefs prepare anything from fish soup with gruyère or linguine with cockles to grilled sardines or rib-eye steak (mains £9–21) – or visit the deli section for swanky sandwiches (£6–8). Booking essential for "Bob's Bar" (Wed–Fri 5–11pm), where nibbles (£4–8) accompany drinks. Mon, Tues & Sat 7.30am–6pm, Wed–Fri 7.30am–11pm.

Tetbury and around

With Prince Charles's Highgrove estate and Princess Anne's Gatcombe Park nearby, **TETBURY** is the Cotswolds' most royal town – but this attractive, engaging place has plenty going for it with or without the Windsors. Scenic countryside, good shopping and excellent food make a fine combination. Just down from the central crossroads, marked by the seventeenth-century **Market House**, Tetbury's **church** (daily 10am–4pm; ⓦ tetburychurch.co.uk) – curiously dedicated to both St Mary the Virgin and St Mary Magdalene – is one of England's finest examples of **Georgian Gothic**: the view along the eighteenth-century nave, with its dark box pews, candle chandeliers, slender wooden columns and enormous windows, is breathtaking.

Westonbirt: the National Arboretum

3 miles southwest of Tetbury, GL8 8QS • Daily 9am–5pm • £10 (Dec–Feb £7) • Guided walks March–Oct Mon, Wed & Fri 11am, Sat & Sun 11am & 2pm; 2hr • Free with admission • ☎ 0300 067 4890, ⓦ forestry.gov.uk/westonbirt • From Tetbury take bus #27 or #69 (Mon–Sat 2/3 daily; 8min)

Everything about **Westonbirt: the National Arboretum** relies on superlatives, from its role as protector of some of the oldest, biggest and rarest trees in the world to the stunning display of natural colours it puts on in autumn. With seventeen miles of paths to roam, across six hundred acres, the best advice is to make a day of it. There are **guided walks**, **self-guided trails** and lots for kids and families.

ARRIVAL AND INFORMATION   TETBURY AND AROUND

By train From Kemble station, about 7 miles northeast – served by hourly trains from London Paddington (1hr 15min) and Cheltenham (1hr) – take bus #882 (Mon–Fri 5 daily, 3 on Sat; 20min).

THAMES HEAD

Between Cirencester and Tetbury, **Kemble** is surrounded by water meadows regarded as the **source of the River Thames**. From Kemble station – served by hourly trains from London Paddington (1hr 15min) and Cheltenham (1hr) – walk half a mile north to the *Thames Head Inn* (☎01285 770259, ⓦthamesheadinn.co.uk), by the railway bridge on the A433. At the pub, bar staff and a sketch-map hanging in the porch can point you towards the stroll of about fifteen minutes to **Thames Head**, a point by a copse in open fields, where a stone marker declares a shallow depression to be the river's source. However, the Thames is fed by groundwater, and since the water table rises and falls, the river's source shifts: don't be disappointed if Thames Head is dry when you visit. The **Thames Path** (ⓦnationaltrail.co.uk) starts here: you can follow it all the way to Greenwich in southeast London, 184 miles away.

By bus Buses drop off in the centre, including #882 to/from Cirencester (Mon–Fri 5 daily, 3 on Sat; 35min).
Tourist office 33 Church St (Mon–Sat: April–Oct 10am–4pm; Nov–March 10am–2pm; ☎01666 503552, ⓦvisittetbury.co.uk and ⓦcotswolds.com).

Painswick

PAINSWICK is a beautiful old Cotswolds wool town easily accessible from Cheltenham. The fame of Painswick's **church** stems not so much from the building itself as from the surrounding **graveyard**, where 99 yew trees, trimmed into bulbous lollipops, surround a collection of eighteenth-century table-tombs unrivalled in the Cotswolds.

Rococo Garden

Half a mile north of Painswick, off Gloucester Rd, GL6 6TH • Mid-Jan to Oct daily 10.30am–5pm • £7.20 • ☎01452 813204, ⓦwww.rococogarden.org.uk

Created in the early eighteenth century, the **Rococo Garden** has been restored to its original form with the aid of a painting from 1748. This is England's only example of Rococo garden design, a short-lived fashion typified by a mix of formal geometrical shapes and more naturalistic, curving lines. With a vegetable patch as an unusual centrepiece, it spreads across a sheltered gully. For the best views, walk around anti-clockwise.

ARRIVAL AND INFORMATION — PAINSWICK

By bus #61 runs to/from Cheltenham (hourly; 40min).
Tourist office Painswick's summer-only tourist office (March–Oct Mon & Wed–Fri 10am–4pm, Tues 10am–1pm, Sat 10am–1pm; ☎01452 812278, ⓦpainswicktouristinfo.co.uk and ⓦcotswolds.com) is in the gravedigger's hut in the corner of the churchyard.

ACCOMMODATION AND EATING

Cardynham House Tibbiwell St, GL6 6XX ☎01452 814006, ⓦcardynham.co.uk. Lovely guesthouse with nine modern, themed rooms, most with four-posters and all en suite. The bistro has simple, well-cooked nosh – cod loin, lamb cutlets, beef stroganoff and the like (mains £13–17). Tues–Sat noon–3pm & 6.30–9.30pm, Sun noon–3pm. **£110**

★ **Olivas** Friday St, GL6 6QJ ☎01452 814774, ⓦolivas.moonfruit.com. Brilliant deli and café that does delicious Mediterranean-style lunches – Spanish soups and stews of chicken, chickpeas and chorizo, stuffed aubergines, loads of tapas including calamari, whitebait, olives, and more, all around £12. Daily 10am–5pm.

Cheltenham

Until the eighteenth century **CHELTENHAM** was a modest Cotswold town like any other, but the discovery of a spring in 1716 transformed it into Britain's most popular **spa**. During Cheltenham's heyday, a century or so later, royalty and nobility descended in droves to take the waters, which were said to cure anything from constipation to worms. These days, the town – still lively, still posh – has lots of good restaurants and some of England's best-preserved Regency architecture.

Cheltenham also has excellent **arts festivals** (ⓦcheltenhamfestivals.com) – **jazz** (May), **science** (June), **classical music** (July) and **literature** (Oct), plus a separately run **folk** festival (Feb) – as well as world-class **horse racing** (main events March & Nov, plus smaller meetings throughout the season, late Oct to early May).

Promenade

Cheltenham's main street, **Promenade**, sweeps majestically south from the High Street, and is lined with some of the town's grandest houses and smartest shops. It leads into Imperial Square, whose greenery is surrounded by proud Regency terraces that herald the handsome squares of the Montpellier district, which stretches south in a narrow block to Suffolk Road, making for a pleasant urban stroll.

The Wilson

Clarence St, GL50 3JT • Mon–Sat 9.30am–5.15pm, Sun 11am–4pm • Free • ☎ 01242 237431, ⓦ thewilson.org.uk

Just off the Promenade stands **The Wilson**, formerly known as the **Cheltenham Art Gallery and Museum**, now housing the tourist office, a shop selling beautiful work by the Gloucestershire Guild of Craftsmen (ⓦguildcrafts.org.uk) and four floors

of exhibitions. The rebranding honours Edward Wilson, a Cheltonian who was on Scott's ill-fated Antarctic expedition of 1912. Photographs and some of his Antarctic gear are displayed alongside a collection focused on the Arts and Crafts movement, ranging from superb furniture to ceramics, jewellery, pottery and exquisitely hand-illustrated books.

Holst Birthplace Museum

4 Clarence Rd, GL52 2AY • Tues–Sat 10am–5pm, Sun 1.30–5pm • £5 • ☎ 01242 524846, ⓦ holstmuseum.org.uk

Housed in a refined Regency terrace house, the **Holst Birthplace Museum** was where the composer of *The Planets* was born, in 1874. Its intimate rooms hold plenty of Holst memorabilia – including his piano in the ground-floor music room – and give a good insight into Victorian family life.

Pittville Pump Room

Pittville Park, GL52 3JE • Wed–Sun 10am–4pm • Free • ☎ 01242 523852, ⓦ cheltenhamtownhall.org.uk/visit-us/pittville-pump-room

About ten minutes' walk north of the centre along handsome Evesham Road brings you into the **Pittville** district, where local chancer Joseph Pitt began work on a grand spa in the 1820s, soon afterwards running out of cash, though he did manage to complete the domed **Pump Room** before he hit the skids. A lovely Classical structure with an imposing colonnaded facade, it is now used mainly as a concert hall, but you can still sample the pungent **spa waters** from the marble fountain in the main auditorium for free.

ARRIVAL AND INFORMATION

CHELTENHAM

By train Cheltenham Spa station is on Queen's Rd, southwest of the centre. Local buses run into town every 10min; otherwise it's a 20min walk.

Destinations Birmingham New Street (2–3 hourly; 40min); Bristol (every 30min; 40min); London Paddington (hourly, some change at Swindon; 2hr 15min).

By bus National Express coaches for London and Heathrow stop on Royal Well Rd. Local buses stop on Promenade.

Destinations #46 to/from Painswick (hourly; 40min); #51 to/from Cirencester (Mon–Sat hourly; 40min); #94 to/from Gloucester (every 10min; 35min); #606 to/from Winchcombe

(Mon–Sat 4 daily, 5 on Sun; 20min) & Broadway (Mon–Sat 4 daily, 2 on Sun; 1hr); #801 to/from Northleach (Mon–Sat 5 daily; 40min), Stow-on-the-Wold (Mon–Sat every 1–2hr; June–Sept also 2–3 on Sun; 55min) & Moreton-in-Marsh (Mon–Sat every 1–2hr; June–Sept also 2–3 on Sun; 1hr 10min); #853 (Mon–Sat 3–4 daily, 1 on Sun) to/from Northleach (30min), Burford (45min) & Oxford (1hr 30min).

Tourist office In The Wilson, Clarence St (Mon–Wed 9.30am–5.15pm, Thurs 9.30am–7.45pm, Fri & Sat 9.30am–5.30pm, Sun 10.30am–4pm; ☎ 01242 237431, ⓦ visitcheltenham.com and ⓦ cotswolds.com).

ACCOMMODATION

Cheltenham has plenty of **hotels** and **guesthouses**, many of them in fine Regency buildings, but you should book well in advance during the races and festivals.

Abbey 14 Bath Parade, GL53 7HN ☎ 01242 516053, ⓦ abbeyhotel-cheltenham.com; map p.263. There are thirteen individually furnished rooms at this centrally located B&B, with wholesome breakfasts taken over-looking the garden. £101

Big Sleep Wellington St, GL50 1XZ ☎ 01242 696999, ⓦ thebigsleephotel.com; map p.263. Contemporary budget hotel with 59 rooms including family rooms and suites, all with a retro designer feel and high-tech gadgetry but no frills – and unusually low prices. £49

George St George's Rd, GL50 3DZ ☎ 01242 235751, ⓦ stayatthegeorge.co.uk; map p.263. This Grade II listed building bang in the centre, built in the 1840s, now hosts a

stylishly designed 31-room hotel, with contemporary flair to the interiors. Prices are surprisingly competitive. £89

Hotel du Vin Parabola Rd, GL50 3AH ☎ 0330 016 0390, ⓦ hotelduvin.com; map p.263. Occupying a splendid old Regency mansion, this glam boutique-style hotel in the sought-after Montpellier district has 49 jazzy rooms and suites and a reputation for excellence. £109

Lypiatt House Lypiatt Rd, GL50 2QW ☎ 01242 224994, ⓦ lypiatt.co.uk; map p.263. Splendid, four-square Victorian villa set in its own grounds a short walk from the centre, with spacious rooms, open fires and a conservatory with a small bar. £111

EATING

★ **Daffodil** 18–20 Suffolk Parade, GL50 2AE ☎01242 700055, ⊛www.thedaffodil.com; map p.263. Eat in the circle bar or auditorium of this breathtakingly designed 1922 Art Deco ex-cinema, where the screen has been replaced with a hubbub of chefs. Great atmosphere and first-class British cuisine (mains £15–28), as well as cocktails and a swish of style. Two-course set menu (Mon–Sat 5–6.30pm, plus Fri & Sat noon–2.30pm) from £12. Mon–Thurs 5–11pm, Fri & Sat noon–midnight.

Le Champignon Sauvage 24 Suffolk Rd, GL50 2AQ ☎01242 573449, ⊛lechampignonsauvage.co.uk; map p.263. Cheltenham's highest-rated restaurant, whose sensitively updated French cuisine has been awarded two Michelin stars, and a welter of other awards. The ambience is chic and intimate, the presentation immaculately artistic. The full menu is £53 (two courses) or £67 (three courses), and there's a smaller set menu at £27 (two courses). Book

well ahead. Tues–Sat 12.30–1.15pm & 7.30–8.30pm.

Lumière Clarence Parade, GL50 3PA ☎01242 222200, ⊛lumiere.cc; map p.263. Upscale, contemporary, seasonal British food in a genial ambience of informality, recently named England's Restaurant of the Year. Cornish scallops or sexed-up corned beef prelude mains such as Gloucester Old Spot pork done two ways, partridge or local venison. Three-course menu £65 (or £35 at lunch), with six- and nine-course tasting menus available. Wed & Thurs 7–8.30pm, Fri & Sat noon–1.30pm & 7–8.30pm.

Scandinavian Coffee Pod Royal Well Place, GL50 3DN ⊛thescandinaviancoffeepod.com; map p.263. Eye-catching little coffee house, in architecturally converted premises, that roasts its own beans and offers exquisitely prepared espressos and lattes, along with cakes and light bites (£4–6). Mon–Fri 8am–5pm, Sat 8.30am–5pm, Sun 9.30am–4pm.

DRINKING AND NIGHTLIFE

Beehive 1–3 Montpellier Villas, GL50 2XE ☎01242 702270, ⊛thebeehivemontpellier.com; map p.263. Popular, easy-going pub with good beer – including locally brewed ales – a friendly ambience and excellent food in the atmospheric restaurant upstairs (mains £10–15). Mon–Thurs & Sun noon–11.30pm, Fri & Sat noon–1am.

Deya Brewing Units 33/34, Lansdown Industrial Estate, Gloucester Rd, GL51 8PL ☎01242 269189, ⊛deyabrewing.com; map p.263. Every Fri & Sat this craft brewery, a 2min walk behind the station, opens up its taproom to serve its range of beers on draught – it's a unique way to sample unique beers. Fri 4–9pm, Sat 2–8pm.

★ **John Gordons** 11 Montpellier Arcade, GL50 1SU

☎01242 245985, ⊛johngordons.co.uk; map p.263. Lovely little independent wine bar, hidden off Montpellier's fanciest street. Take a seat in the shop or outside in the old Victorian covered arcade to watch the world go by while sampling a glass or two of wine, alongside a plate of charcuterie, cheeses and/or antipasti (£6–14), or a range of tapas (£2–5). Mon–Wed 11am–10pm, Thurs 10.30am–11pm, Fri & Sat 10.30am–1am.

Montpellier Wine Bar Bayshill Lodge, Montpellier St, GL50 1SY ☎01242 527774, ⊛montpellierwinebar. co.uk; map p.263. Stylish wine bar and restaurant with lovely bow-fronted windows on a busy little corner. Hang out at the bar with a glass of something smooth, or drop in mid-morning for brunch. Mon–Thurs & Sun 9.30am–11pm, Fri & Sat 9.30am–1am.

SHOPPING

Cheeseworks 5 Regent St, GL50 1HE ☎01242 255022, ⊛thecheeseworks.co.uk; map p.263. Posh, aromatic cheesemonger's in the centre of town, selling from local farm cheeses to European varieties, plus ports, chutneys and accessories. Mon–Sat 9.30am–5.30pm.

The Guild at 51 51 Clarence St, GL50 3JT ☎01242 245215, ⊛guildcrafts.org.uk; map p.263. Showroom and shop beside the Wilson gallery for the Gloucestershire Guild of Craftsmen – professional designers working in

jewellery, ceramics, textiles, leatherwork, glass, basketry and more. Quality is excellent, which nudges prices up, but these are unusual items. Tues–Sat 10am–5pm, Sun 11am–4pm.

Proud Lion 8 St George's Place, GL50 3JZ ☎01242 525636, ⊛proudlion.co.uk; map p.263. Geeky outlet for comics, graphic novels and gaming, with a wealth of knowledge and enthusiasm to boot. Mon & Sun noon–5.30pm, Tues & Thurs–Sat 10am–5.30pm, Wed 10am–6.30pm.

Gloucester

For centuries life was good for **GLOUCESTER**, ten miles west of Cheltenham. The Romans chose this spot for a garrison to guard the River Severn, while in Saxon and Norman times the Severn developed into one of Europe's busiest trade routes. The city became a major religious centre too, but from the fifteenth century onwards a combination of fire, plague, civil war and increasing competition from rival towns sent Gloucester into a decline from which it never recovered – even the opening of a new canal in 1827 between Gloucester and Sharpness failed to revive the town's dwindling fortunes. Today, the **canal** is busy once again, though this time with pleasure boats, and the Victorian **docks** have undergone a facelift, offering a fascinating glimpse into the region's industrial past. The main reason for a visit, however, remains Gloucester's magnificent **cathedral**, one of the finest in the country.

Gloucester Cathedral

College Green, GL1 2LX • Daily 7.30am–6pm • Free • ☎ 01452 528095, ⓦ gloucestercathedral.org.uk

The superb condition of **Gloucester Cathedral** is striking in a city that has lost so much of its history. The Saxons founded an abbey here, but four centuries later Benedictine monks arrived intent on building their own church; work began in 1089. As a place of worship it shot to importance after the murder of King Edward II in 1327 at nearby Berkeley Castle: Gloucester took his body, and the king's shrine became a place of pilgrimage. The money generated helped finance the conversion of the church into the country's first example of the **Perpendicular style**: the magnificent 225ft tower crowns the achievement.

Beneath the fourteenth- and fifteenth-century construction, some Norman aspects remain, and these are best seen in the **nave**, which is flanked by sturdy pillars and arches adorned with immaculate zigzag carvings. The **choir** provides the best vantage point for admiring the **east window**, completed in around 1350 and – at almost 80ft tall – the largest medieval window in Britain, a stunning cliff face of stained glass. Beneath it to the left is the **tomb of Edward II**, immortalized in alabaster and marble, while below it lies the **Lady Chapel** (closed at the time of writing for restoration), whose delicate carved tracery holds a staggering patchwork of windows. The innovative nature of the cathedral's design can also be appreciated in the beautiful **cloisters**, completed in 1367 and featuring the first fan vaulting in the country – used to represent the corridors of Hogwarts in the *Harry Potter* films.

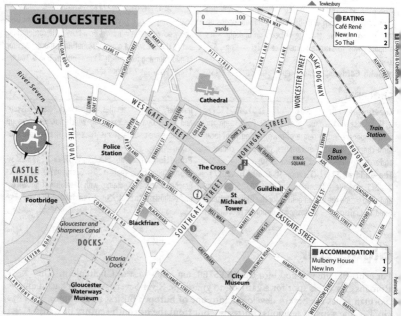

Gloucester Waterways Museum

Gloucester Docks, GL1 2EH • April–Oct daily 10am–5pm; Nov–March Tues–Sun 11am–3pm • £8.50 • **Boat trips** July, Aug & school hols daily noon, 1.30pm & 2.30pm; rest of year Sat & Sun 1.30pm; 45min • £6.50 • ☎ 01452 318200, ⓦ canalrivertrust.org.uk/gloucester-waterways-museum

Less than half a mile southwest of the city centre, **Gloucester Docks** holds fourteen warehouses that were built to store grain following the opening of the Sharpness canal to the River Severn in 1827. Most have been turned into offices and shops, but the southernmost Llanthony Warehouse is now occupied by the **Gloucester Waterways Museum**, which delves into every nook and cranny of the area's watery history, from the engineering of the locks to the lives of the horses that trod the towpaths, along with plenty of interactive displays. The museum runs regular **boat trips** out onto the Sharpness canal, with commentary.

ARRIVAL AND INFORMATION
GLOUCESTER

By train Gloucester station is on Bruton Way, a 5min walk east of the centre.
Destinations Birmingham New Street (hourly; 50min); Bristol (hourly; 40min); London Paddington (hourly, some change at Swindon; 1hr 55min).
By bus Local buses and National Express coaches for London and Heathrow Airport stop opposite the train station.

Destinations #94 for Cheltenham (every 10min; 35min); #882 for Cirencester (Mon–Fri every 1–2hr, 2 on Sat; 45min); #853 (Mon–Sat 2 daily, 1 on Sun) for Northleach (50min), Burford (1hr 5min) & Oxford (2hr).
Tourist office 28 Southgate St (Mon 10am–5pm, Tues–Sat 9.30am–5pm; ☎ 01452 396572, ⓦ thecityofgloucester.co.uk and ⓦ cotswolds.com).

ACCOMMODATION

Mulberry House 2a Heathville Rd, GL1 3DP ☎ 01452 720079, ⓦ the-mulberry-house.co.uk; map p.266. Decent B&B in a modern family home roughly 10min walk northeast of the centre. Two en-suite doubles are enhanced with quality breakfasts. Cash only. **£60**

New Inn 16 Northgate St, GL1 1SF ☎ 01452 522177, ⓦ newinn.relaxinnz.co.uk; map p.266. Though this inn's 33 rooms are pretty basic, with bland decor and corporate furniture, their location above an impressively historic pub (see below) is a big plus. **£55**

EATING

Café René 31 Southgate St, GL1 1TS ☎ 01452 309340, ⓦ caferene.co.uk; map p.266. This lively, fancifully decorated central pub serves decent burgers and steaks, with plenty for vegetarians (mains £9–14), plus lighter lunches and great barbecues in summer (Sun). Live blues, jazz and acoustic music twice a week, and after 11pm on weekend nights the cellar bar turns into a club (£2 admission), with loud local DJs. Mon–Thurs & Sun 11am–midnight, Fri & Sat 11am–4am.
New Inn 16 Northgate St, GL1 1SF ☎ 01452 522177, ⓦ newinn.relaxinnz.co.uk; map p.266. Pop into this fourteenth-century pub in the city centre to sup a pint of one of their several cask ales and have a gander at

the preserved interior – this is Britain's most complete surviving medieval courtyard tavern, ringed by galleries (and, reputedly, haunted). You can stay here, too (see above). Mon–Thurs 11am–11pm, Fri & Sat 11am–midnight, Sun noon–10.30pm. **£55**
So Thai Longsmith St, GL1 2HJ ☎ 01452 535185, ⓦ so-thai.co.uk; map p.266. This Thai restaurant is holding onto its reputation for quality and authenticity. The decor features vaulted brickwork, service is attentive and the food – including unusual northern Thai pork curry with pineapple, and lamb massaman curry – is expertly prepared. Mains £10–16, two-course lunch menu £10. Tues–Sun noon–3pm & 6–11pm.

Bath, Bristol and Somerset

THE ROMAN BATHS, BATH

5 Bath, Bristol and Somerset

Ranging from tidy cricket greens and well-kept country pubs to limestone gorges and windswept moorland, Somerset makes a fitting introduction to England's Southwest. The Georgian, honey-toned terraces of Bath lie at the eastern end of the county, and offers a beautifully preserved set of Roman baths, some first-class museums and a mellow café culture that makes it an unmissable stop on any tour of the region. Just a few miles away, the main city hereabouts is Bristol, one of the most dynamic and cosmopolitan centres outside London, its medieval old quarter and revitalized waterfront supplemented by a superb range of pubs, clubs and restaurants.

Within easy reach to the south lie the exquisite cathedral city of **Wells** and the ancient town of **Glastonbury**, a site steeped in Christian lore, Arthurian legend and New Age mysticism. Nearby, **the Mendips** are fine walking territory and are pocked by cave systems, as at Wookey Hole and Cheddar Gorge. The county town of **Taunton** is a useful base for exploring the **Quantock Hills**, while further west, straddling the Devon border, the heathery slopes of **Exmoor** offer a range of hikes, with wonderful views from its cliffy seaboard.

Bath

A graceful succession of urban set pieces, **BATH** is a visual feast: harmonious, compact and perfectly complemented by the softly undulating hills that surround it. The city's elegant crescents and Georgian buildings are studded with plaques naming Bath's eminent inhabitants from its heyday; it was here that Jane Austen set *Persuasion* and *Northanger Abbey*, and Gainsborough established himself as a portraitist and landscape painter.

Bath owes its name and fame to its **hot springs** – the only ones in the country – which made it a place of reverence for the local Celtic population, though it took Roman technology to turn it into a fully fledged bathing establishment. The baths fell into decline with the Romans' departure, but the town regained its importance under the Saxons, its abbey seeing the coronation of the **first king of all England**, Edgar, in 973. A new bathing complex was built in the sixteenth century, popularized by the visit of Elizabeth I in 1574, and the city reached its zenith in the eighteenth century, when it acquired its ranks of Palladian mansions and Regency townhouses, all built in the local **Bath stone**. The legacy is a city whose streets are a joy simply to wander along, with their pale gold architecture and sweeping vistas.

The Roman Baths

Abbey Churchyard, BA1 1LZ • Daily: March to mid-June, Sept & Oct 9am–6pm; mid-June to Aug 9am–10pm; Nov–Feb 9.30am–6pm; last entry 1hr before closing • £15.50, £17 in July & Aug, £21.50 combined ticket with Fashion Museum & Victoria Art Gallery • **Tours** Daily, on the hour; 1hr • Free • ☎ 01225 477785, ⓦ romanbaths.co.uk

There are hours of entertainment in Bath's premier attraction, the **Roman Baths**, which comprises the baths themselves and an informative museum – highlights include the

GLASTONBURY FESTIVAL

Highlights

❶ Roman Baths Thermal waters still bubble up in this beautifully restored complex of baths from the Roman era in the UK's original spa town. See page 270

❷ Royal Crescent, Bath In a city famous for its graceful arcs of Georgian terraces, this is the granddaddy of them all, an architectural tour de force with a magnificent view. See page 275

❸ ss Great Britain, Bristol Moored in the dock in which she was built, the iconic ship is now a museum, an interactive insight into life aboard a nineteenth-century steamer. See page 283

❹ Wells Cathedral A gem of medieval masonry, this richly ornamented Gothic

masterpiece is the centrepiece of England's smallest city. See page 286

❺ Cheddar Gorge Impressive rockscape with a network of illuminated caves at its base; it's an excellent starting point for wild walks in the Mendip Hills. See page 289

❻ Glastonbury Festival Pack your tent, dust off your wellies and enjoy the ride that is simply Britain's biggest, boldest and best music festival. See page 291

❼ Exmoor Whether you ride it, bike it or hike it, the rolling wilderness of Exmoor offers fine opportunities to experience the great outdoors. See page 295

HIGHLIGHTS ARE MARKED ON THE MAP ON PAGE 272

BATH, BRISTOL & SOMERSET

Sacred Spring, part of the temple of the local deity Sulis Minerva, where water still bubbles up at a constant 46.5°C; the open-air (but originally covered) Great Bath, its vaporous waters surrounded by nineteenth-century pillars, terraces and statues of famous Romans; the Circular Bath, where bathers cooled off; and the Norman King's Bath, where people were taking a restorative dip right up until 1978. The free **audioguide** is excellent.

Among a quantity of coins, jewellery and sculpture exhibited are the bronze head of Sulis Minerva and a grand, Celtic-inspired gorgon's head from the temple's pediment. Models of the complex at its greatest extent give some idea of the awe which it must have inspired, while the **graffiti** salvaged from the Roman era – mainly curses and boasts – offer a personal slant on this antique leisure centre.

You can get a free glimpse into the baths from the next-door **Pump Room**, the social hub of the Georgian spa community and still redolent of that era, which houses a formal tearoom and restaurant.

Bath Abbey

Abbey Churchyard, BA1 1LT • April–Oct Mon 9.30am–5.30pm, Tues–Fri 9am–5.30pm, Sat 9am–6pm, Sun 1–2.30pm & 4.30–5.30pm (Sun till 6pm in Aug); Nov–March Mon–Sat 9am–4.30pm, Sun 1–2.30pm & 4.30–5.30pm • Free, but £4 donation requested • **Tower tours** From 10/11am: Mon–Fri on the hour, Sat every 30min; 45min • £6 • ⓦ bathabbey.org

Although there has been a church on the site since the seventh century, **Bath Abbey** did not take its present form until the end of the fifteenth century, when Bishop Oliver King began work on the ruins of the previous Norman building, some of which were incorporated into the new church. The bishop was said to have been inspired by a vision of angels ascending and descending a ladder to heaven, which the present facade recalls on the turrets flanking the central window. The west front also features the founder's signature in the form of carvings of olive trees surmounted by crowns, a play on his name.

The **interior** is in a restrained Perpendicular style, although it does boast splendid fan vaulting on the ceiling, which was not completed until the nineteenth century. The floor and walls are crammed with elaborate monuments and memorials, and traces of the grander Norman building are visible in the Gethsemane Chapel.

On most days, you can join a **tower tour** to see the massive bells, clock and bell-pulling machinery, and can enjoy a bird's-eye view of Bath – but be prepared for the 212 spiral steps.

Thermae Bath Spa

Hot Bath St, BA1 1SJ • **Baths** Daily: New Royal Bath 9am–9.30pm, last entry 7pm; Cross Bath 10am–8pm, last entry 6pm • £35/2hr (Sat & Sun £38), £10/hr extra • **Visitor centre** April–Sept Mon–Sat 10am–5pm, Sun 11am–4pm • Free • ☎ 01225 331234, ⓦ thermaebathspa.com

At the bottom of the elegantly colonnaded Bath Street, **Thermae Bath Spa** allows you to take the waters in much the same way that visitors to Bath have done throughout the ages, but with state-of-the-art spa facilities. Heated by the city's thermal waters, the spa includes two open-air pools, one on the roof of its centrepiece, the New Royal Bath, Sir Nicholas Grimshaw's futuristic "glass cube". Treatments offered range from massages to hot-stone therapies, and a small **visitor centre** has displays on Bath's thermal waters.

Queen Square and around

North of Hot Bath Street, Sawclose is presided over by the **Theatre Royal** (see page 279), opened in 1805 and one of the country's finest surviving Georgian theatres; Beau Nash had his first house in Bath here from 1743, in what is now the theatre's foyer. Barton Street leads north of Sawclose to **Queen Square**, the first Bath venture of the architect **John Wood the Elder** (1704–54), champion of Neoclassical Palladianism,

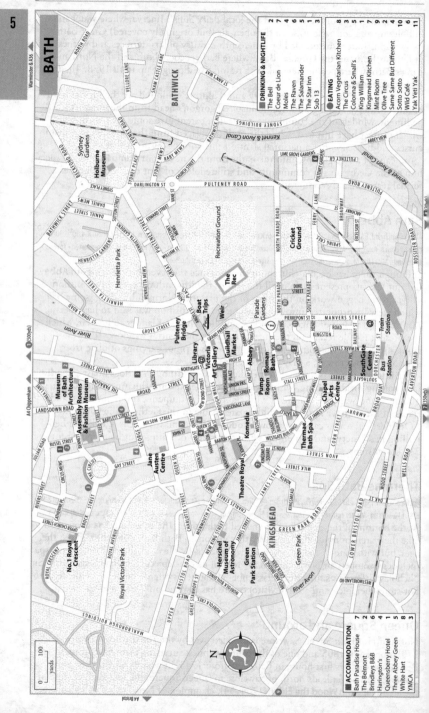

BATH

◄ Warminster & A36

◄ A4 Chippenham

◄ A4 Bristol

■ DRINKING & NIGHTLIFE
The Bell	2
Coeur de Lion	7
Moles	4
The Raven	6
The Salamander	5
The Star Inn	1
Sub 13	3

● EATING
Acorn Vegetarian Kitchen	8
The Circus	3
Colonna & Small's	5
King William	1
Kingsmead Kitchen	7
Mint Room	9
Olive Tree	2
Same Same But Different	4
Sotto Sotto	10
Wild Café	6
Yak Yeti Yak	11

■ ACCOMMODATION
Bath Paradise House	7
The Belmont	2
Brindleys B&B	6
Harington's	4
Queensberry Hotel	1
Three Abbey Green	5
White Hart	8
YMCA	3

N

> ## BEAU NASH
>
> Bath's social renaissance in the eighteenth century was largely due to one man: **Richard "Beau" Nash** (1674–1761), an ex-army officer, ex-lawyer, dandy and gambler, who became Bath's Master of Ceremonies in 1704, conducting public balls of unprecedented splendour. Wielding dictatorial powers over dress and behaviour, Nash orchestrated the social manners of the city and even extended his influence to cover road improvements and building design. In an early example of health awareness, he banned smoking in Bath's public rooms at a time when pipe-smoking was generally enjoyed among men, women and children. Less philanthropically, he also encouraged gambling and even took a percentage of the bank's takings. According to his rules, balls were to begin at 6pm and end at 11pm, and each had to open with a minuet "danced by two persons of the highest distinction present". White aprons were banned, gossipers and scandalmongers were shunned, and, most radical of all, the wearing of swords in public places was forbidden. Nash's fortunes changed when gambling restrictions were introduced in 1739, greatly reducing his influence; he died in poverty aged 87, but was treated to a suitably lavish send-off.

who lived at no. 15 (not no. 24, as a tablet there asserts). East of the square is the wide shopping strand of **Milsom Street**, which was designed by Wood as the main thoroughfare of Georgian Bath.

Herschel Museum of Astronomy

19 New King St, BA1 2BL • Mid-Jan to mid-Dec Mon–Fri 1–5pm, Sat & Sun 11am–5pm • £6.50 • ☎ 01225 446865, ⓦ herschelmuseum.org.uk

A few minutes west of the centre is the small **Herschel Museum of Astronomy**, former home of the musician and astronomer Sir William Herschel and his sister Caroline, who together discovered the planet Uranus here in 1781. Among the furnishings, musical instruments and knick-knacks from the Herschels' era, you can see a replica of the telescope with which Uranus was identified.

Jane Austen Centre

40 Gay St, BA1 2NT • April–June, Sept & Oct daily 9.45am–5.30pm; July & Aug daily 9.30am–6pm; Nov–March Mon–Fri & Sun 11am–4pm, Sat 9.45am–5.30pm • £11 • ☎ 01225 443000, ⓦ janeausten.co.uk

The **Jane Austen Centre** provides a superficial overview of the author's connections with Bath, illustrated by extracts from her writings, contemporary costumes and household items; visits start with a talk (every 20min). Austen herself, who wasn't entirely enamoured of the city, lived down the road at 25 Gay Street, and at a number of other places in Bath.

The Circus

Situated at the top of Gay Street, the elder John Wood's masterpiece, **The Circus**, consists of three crescents arranged in a tight circle of three-storey houses, with a carved frieze running round the entire circle. Wood died soon after laying the foundation stone, and the job was finished by his son, **John Wood the Younger** (1728–82), who was as instrumental as his father in defining Bath's elegant Georgian appearance. The painter Thomas Gainsborough lived at no. 17 from 1760 to 1774.

The Royal Crescent and around

No. 1 Royal Crescent BA1 2LR • Mid-Feb to Dec Mon noon–5.30pm, Tues–Sun 10.30am–5.30pm • £10, or £12.50 with Museum of Bath Architecture • ☎ 01225 428126, ⓦ no1royalcrescent.org.uk

The Circus is connected by Brock Street to the **Royal Crescent**, grandest of Bath's crescents, begun by the younger John Wood in 1767. The stately arc of thirty houses –

5

said to be the country's first – is set off by a spacious sloping lawn from which a magnificent vista extends to green hills and distant ribbons of honey-coloured stone. The interior of **No. 1 Royal Crescent**, on the corner with Brock Street, has been restored to reflect as nearly as possible its original Georgian appearance at the end of the eighteenth century.

At the bottom of the Crescent, Royal Avenue leads onto **Royal Victoria Park**, the city's largest open space, containing an aviary and nine acres of botanical gardens.

The Fashion Museum

Assembly Rooms, Bennett St, BA1 2QH • Daily: March–Oct 10.30am–6pm; Nov–Feb 10.30am–5pm; last admission 1hr before closing • £9, or £21.50 with the Roman Baths & Victoria Art Gallery • ☎ 01225 477789, ⓦ fashionmuseum.co.uk

The younger John Wood's **Assembly Rooms**, east of the Circus, were, with the Pump Room, the centre of Bath's social scene. The building was virtually destroyed by bombing during World War II, but it has since been perfectly restored and houses the **Fashion Museum**, an entertaining collection of clothing from the Stuart era to the latest Milanese designs.

Museum of Bath Architecture

The Vineyards, The Paragon, BA1 5NA • Mid-Feb to Nov Tues–Fri 2–5pm, Sat & Sun 10.30am–5pm • £6, or £12.50 with No. 1 Royal Crescent • ☎ 01225 333895, ⓦ museumofbatharchitecture.org.uk

The Georgian-Gothic Countess of Huntingdon's Chapel houses the **Museum of Bath Architecture**, a fascinating exploration of the construction and architecture of the city and a great place to start your visit. Everything is covered, from the kind of facades associated with the two John Woods to balustrades, door designs and such aspects of interior ornamentation as marbling, stencilling and japanning.

Holburne Museum

Great Pulteney St, BA2 4DB • Mon–Sat 10am–5pm, Sun 11am–5pm • Free • ☎ 01225 388569, ⓦ holburne.org

The River Avon is crossed by the graceful, shop-lined **Pulteney Bridge**, an Italianate structure designed by Robert Adam, from the other side of which a lengthy vista stretches along Great Pulteney Street to the imposing classical facade of the **Holburne Museum**. The building, with a startlingly modern extension at the back, holds an impressive range of decorative and fine art, mostly furniture, silverware, porcelain and paintings, including several works by Gainsborough, notably the famous *Byam Family*, his largest portrait.

ARRIVAL AND INFORMATION   BATH

By train Bath Spa station is a short walk south of the centre at the bottom of Manvers St.

Destinations Bristol (every 15–30min; 15min); London Paddington (every 30min–1hr; 1hr 30min); Salisbury (every 30min–1hr; 1hr).

By bus The bus station (ⓦ firstgroup.com) lies next to the train station on Dorchester St.

Destinations Bristol (3–6 hourly; 45min); London (14 daily; 2hr 30min–3hr 15min); Salisbury (Mon–Sat 4 daily;

1hr 35min–2hr 50min); Wells (Mon–Sat every 30min, Sun hourly; 1hr 25min).

By bike/on foot The 13-mile Bristol & Bath Railway Path (ⓦ bristolbathrailwaypath.org.uk) connects the two cities along the route of a disused railway line and the course of the River Avon.

Tourist office Bridgwater House, 2 Terrace Walk (March–Sept Mon–Sat 9am–5.30pm, Sun 10am–4pm; Oct–Feb Mon–Sat 9am–5.30pm; ☎ 01225 322442, ⓦ visitbath.co.uk).

GETTING AROUND AND TOURS

By car Cars are a hindrance and parking is expensive; if you must drive, use a Park-and-Ride car park on the edge of town.

Bike rental Nextbike (☎ 020 8166 9851, ⓦ nextbike. co.uk) operates a rental service for up to 24hr, with bikes available at stands scattered around the city. To use it, you must first register (via the website or on a free app) and pay a £10 deposit; charges are £1/30min or £10 for up to 24hr. Alternatively, there's Bath Bike Hire, Sydney Wharf, Bathwick Hill (£15/day; ☎01225 447276, ⓦbath-narrowboats.co.uk); they also rent narrowboats (from £80/ half-day).

Boat tours Hour-long river trips run from Pulteney Bridge; operators include Pulteney Cruisers (Easter–Oct 6–12 daily; £9; ☎01225 312900, ⓦpulteneycruisers.com) and Avon Cruising (April–Oct 6 daily; £9; ⓦpulteneyprincess.co.uk).

Walking tours Mayor's Guides run free 2hr walking tours, starting outside the Pump Room in Abbey Churchyard (ⓦbathguides.org.uk; Mon–Fri & Sun 10.30am & 2pm, Sat 10.30am, May–Aug also Tues & Thurs 7pm).

ACCOMMODATION

Bath is full of **hotels** and **B&Bs**, but most of the latter are small. It's worth booking early, especially at weekends, when most places have a two-night minimum and prices rise; rates quoted below are midweek. There are central **hostels**, but the nearest **campsites** are out of town. The centre can get noisy at night, so choose a room away from the street for a good night's sleep.

Bath Paradise House 86–88 Holloway, BA2 4PX ☎01225 317723, ⓦparadise-house.co.uk; map p.274. Georgian villa an uphill trudge from the centre, but with wonderful views. Open fires in winter, elegant four-posters in some of the rooms, and three rooms opening straight onto the award-winning gardens. **£92**

The Belmont 7 Belmont, Lansdown Rd, BA1 5DZ ☎01225 423082, ⓦbelmontbath.co.uk; map p.274. Large doubles, some with tiny, clean, modern en-suite bathrooms, in a centrally located B&B in a house designed by John Wood. No credit cards. **£85**

Brindleys B&B 14 Pulteney Gardens, BA2 4HG ☎01225 310444, ⓦbrindleysbath.co.uk; map p.274. Half a dozen light, airy, elegantly decorated bijou rooms that have more than a hint of a French country manor about them, a feeling that extends to the stylish communal areas. It's set in a quiet residential area just a 5min walk from the centre. **£115**

Harington's Queen St, BA1 1HE ☎01225 461728, ⓦharingtonshotel.co.uk; map p.274. Central hotel in a converted townhouse with friendly service and modern, well-equipped rooms – most are quite small, and some at the top of steep steps. Breakfasts are superlative, and food is available throughout the day. **£130**

Queensberry Hotel Russel St, BA1 2QF ☎01225 447928, ⓦthequeensberry.co.uk; map p.274. Spread across four Georgian townhouses, the *Queensberry* combines a clubhouse feel with a boutique vibe. Rooms are tastefully minimalist – most with a fabulous bathroom – and there's a peaceful garden and superb restaurant (see page 278). **£155**

★**Three Abbey Green** 3 Abbey Green, BA1 1NW ☎01225 428558, ⓦthreeabbeygreen.com; map p.274. Top-notch B&B in a superbly renovated Georgian house just steps from the abbey. The airy, spotless rooms are beautifully done; the larger ones overlooking a peaceful square are more expensive. **£120**

★**White Hart** Widcombe Hill, BA2 6AA ☎01225 313985, ⓦwhitehartbath.co.uk; map p.274. The comfiest of Bath's hostels has a kitchen, a first-class bar/ restaurant and a spacious courtyard. There are clean doubles and twins available, some en suite. Accommodation not available Sun. Dorms **£15**, doubles **£50**

YMCA International House, Broad St, BA1 5LH ☎01225 325900, ⓦbathymca.co.uk; map p.274. Clean, central and spacious, this friendly place has dorms, singles and doubles. No curfew, but no kitchen, either. All rates include breakfast (cooked £3.50 extra). Dorms **£16**, singles **£32**, doubles **£56**

EATING

CAFÉS

Colonna & Small's 6 Chapel Row, BA1 1HN ☎07766 808067, ⓦcolonnaandsmalls.co.uk; map p.274. The highbrowed but helpful brewmasters at this stripped-back coffee specialist serve a serious cup of Joe. Choose from a range of weekly changing single-origin espresso beans and filter coffees. Just don't ask for milk. Or sugar. Mon–Fri 8am–5.30pm, Sat 8.30am–5.30pm, Sun 10am–4pm.

Kingsmead Kitchen 1 Kingsmead Square, BA1 2AA ☎01225 329002, ⓦkingsmeadkitchenbath.co.uk; map p.274. Big breakfasts, snack fodder and dishes such as meze with warm pitta bread (£9) are served at this café tucked away in a corner of one of Bath's most attractive squares. There are beers and wines, and outside seating to boot. Mon–Sat 8.30am–6pm, Sun 9am–5pm.

★**Wild Café** 10a Queen St, BA1 1HE ☎01225 448673, ⓦwildcafe.co.uk; map p.274. Hidden down a cobbled side street behind Queen Square, the open kitchen at this popular café does burgers, salads (£8–10) and sandwiches (including an excellent BLT; £6), which can also be bought to take away. Mon–Fri 8am–4.30pm, Sat 9am–6pm, Sun 10am–5pm.

RESTAURANTS

★**Acorn Vegetarian Kitchen** 2 North Parade Passage, BA1 1NX ☎01225 446059, ⓦacornvegetariankitchen. co.uk; map p.274. Classy veggie restaurant offering dishes such as butternut squash terrine with pine-nut

5

risotto in an unruffled, arty environment. Set-price lunches are £18 or £23 for two and three courses respectively, while dinners cost £27 or £35 (£20 or £25 before 6.30pm). Mon–Fri & Sun noon–3pm & 5.30–9.30pm, Sat noon–3.30pm & 5.30–10pm.

The Circus 34 Brock St, BA1 2LN ☎01225 466020, ⓦthecircusrestaurant.co.uk; map p.274. There's a refined but relaxed atmosphere at this family-run spot, just a stroll from the Royal Crescent. It specializes in Modern European dishes like Sicilian-style braised globe artichokes (£17.50) and tagine of kid goat on saffron couscous (£19.70) – both around £6.50 cheaper at lunch. Mon–Sat 10am–late.

★ **King William** 36 Thomas St, BA1 5NN ☎01225 428096, ⓦkingwilliampub.com; map p.274. North of the centre, the upstairs dining room at the *King William* pub regularly receives accolades for its locally sourced dishes, such as confit pork belly (£19) and gnocchi with Jerusalem artichoke (£14), but the beer and wine list is top-drawer, too. Bar Mon–Fri noon–3pm & 5–11pm, Sat noon–midnight, Sun noon–11pm; restaurant Wed–Fri 6–9pm, Sat 6–10pm, Sun noon–3pm.

Mint Room Longmead Gospel Hall, Lower Bristol Rd, BA2 3EB ☎01225 446656, ⓦthemintroom.co.uk; map p.274. Indian food but not as you know it: innovative yet authentic regional cuisine ranging from South Indian king prawn *moilee* (£17) to biryanis served under a pastry crust (£10–12). Mon–Thurs & Sun noon–2pm & 6–11pm, Fri & Sat noon–2pm & 6–11.30pm.

★ **Olive Tree** Queensberry Hotel, Russel St, BA1 2QF ☎01225 447928, ⓦolivetreebath.co.uk; map p.274. One of Bath's top restaurants, with inventively prepared dishes, a relaxed, contemporary ambience and attentive,

friendly service. Whether you order from the tasting menus (£58–80) or opt for individual dishes (mains £19.50–28.50), you can sample such dishes as lobster lasagne, pan-fried turbot and pigeon with asparagus and hazelnut (a vegetarian menu is also available). There are set-price lunch menus Fri & Sat for £26.50 or £32. Mon–Thurs 7–9.30pm, Fri & Sat 12.30–2pm & 6.30–10pm, Sun 12.30–2pm & 7–9.30pm.

Same Same But Different 7a Prince's Buildings, Bartlett St, BA1 2ED ☎01225 466856, ⓦsame-same.co.uk; map p.274. Excellent café/restaurant that mixes a laidback ambience with quality food – try some of the unusual tapas dishes (from £4.50), or go for something a bit more substantial, such as smoked haddock kedgeree with duck egg (£10). Mon 8am–6pm, Tues–Fri 8am–11pm, Sat 9am–11pm, Sun 10am–5pm.

Sotto Sotto 10 North Parade, BA2 4AL ☎01225 330236, ⓦsottosotto.co.uk; map p.274. Authentic Italian restaurant in cave-like, brick-vaulted subterranean rooms. The simple but heavenly dishes include orecchiette with spinach and sausage (£9.75) and *pesce spada alla griglia* (grilled swordfish; £16.25). Make sure you sample the excellent antipasti too (around £7.50). Service is superb. It's usually packed, so booking is essential. Daily noon–2pm & 5–10pm.

Yak Yeti Yak 12 Pierrepont St, BA1 1LA ☎01225 442299, ⓦyakyetiyak.co.uk; map p.274. Quality Nepalese restaurant in a series of cellar rooms with a choice of chairs or floor cushions. Meat dishes are stir-fried or spicily marinated, and there's a good vegetarian selection (dishes all £5–9). Mon–Thurs noon–2pm & 6–10.30pm, Fri & Sat noon–2pm & 5–10.30pm, Sun noon–2pm & 6–10pm.

DRINKING AND NIGHTLIFE

★ **The Bell** 103 Walcot St, BA1 5BW ☎01225 460426, ⓦthebellinnbath.co.uk; map p.274. Easy-going, slightly grungy tavern with a great jukebox, live music (Mon & Wed eve, plus Sun lunchtime) and DJs (Fri & Sat). There's bar billiards and a beer garden with table footy. Mon–Sat 11.30am–11pm, Sun noon–10.30pm.

Coeur de Lion 17 Northumberland Place, BA1 5AR ☎01225 463568, ⓦcoeur-de-lion.co.uk; map p.274. Bath's smallest boozer serves local Abbey Ales, and is a regular tourist stop, with good lunchtime snacks (baguettes £6.50). Mon–Thurs 11am–11pm, Fri & Sat 11am–midnight, Sun noon–10.30pm.

★ **Moles** 14 George St, BA1 2EN ☎01225 437537, ⓦmoles.co.uk; map p.274. Much-loved Bath institution which features a mix of good live music, DJs and club nights. The cramped basement can get pretty hot and sweaty, though – not for claustrophobes. Mon–Sat 5pm–late.

The Raven 6–7 Queen St, BA1 1HE ☎01225 425045, ⓦtheravenofbath.co.uk; map p.274. A civilized spot with

first-rate local ales, which occasionally holds storytelling nights. Food available, including renowned pies (£9.80). Mon–Thurs 8.30am–11pm, Fri & Sat 8.30am–midnight, Sun 8.30am–10.30pm.

The Salamander 3 John St, BA1 2JL ☎01225 428889, ⓦbathales.com; map p.274. Local brewer Bath Ales' pub, with a traditional, dark-wood interior, relaxed atmosphere and tasty dishes available at the bar or in the upstairs restaurant (mains £10–15). Mon–Thurs 11am–midnight, Fri & Sat 11am–1am, Sun 11am–11pm.

★ **The Star Inn** 23 The Vineyards, The Paragon, BA1 5NA ☎01225 425071, ⓦabbeyales.co.uk; map p.274. First licensed in 1760, this Abbey Ales pub has a classic Victorian interior, and beers that include the award-winning Bellringer and draught Bass served from a jug. Mon–Thurs noon–2.30pm & 5.30pm–midnight, Fri & Sat noon–1am, Sun noon–midnight.

Sub 13 4 Edgar Buildings, George St, BA1 2EE ☎01225 466667, ⓦsub13.net; map p.274. Settle into a white leather booth in the Champagne Lounge or chill out on the backyard terrace at this trendy basement bar, boasting the best cocktails in town. Mon–Wed 5pm–midnight, Thurs 5pm–2am, Fri & Sat 5pm–3am, Sun noon–11pm.

5

ENTERTAINMENT

Chapel Arts Centre St James's Memorial Hall, Lower Borough Walls, BA1 1QR ☎01225 461700, ⓦchapelarts.org. Nice little venue for all kinds of performing arts, including jazz, folk and comedy. Arrive early to get one of the cabaret-style tables.

Komedia 22–23 Westgate St, BA1 1EP ☎0845 293 8480, ⓦkomedia.co.uk/bath. Cabaret and burlesque, comedy, punk and ska bands, tribute acts and more are all staged at this venue. The popular Krater Comedy Club is held on Sat, after which you can stay on for club nights. Meals are available.

Theatre Royal Sawclose, BA1 1ET ☎01225 448844, ⓦtheatreroyal.org.uk. Theatre fans should check out what's showing at this historic venue, if only for the atmosphere. More experimental productions are staged in its Ustinov Studio, with family shows at the egg.

Bristol

Just twelve miles from Bath, on the borders of Gloucestershire and Somerset, **BRISTOL** has a very different feel from its sedate neighbour. The city's mercantile roots are overlaid with an innovative, modern culture, fuelled by technology-based industries, a large student population and a lively arts and music scene. As well as its vibrant **nightlife**, the city's sights range from medieval churches to cutting-edge attractions highlighting its maritime and scientific achievements. Weaving through its centre, the River Avon forms part of a system of waterways that made Bristol a great inland port, in later years booming on the transatlantic trafficking of rum, tobacco and slaves. In the nineteenth century, **Isambard Kingdom Brunel** laid the foundations of a tradition of engineering, creating two of Bristol's greatest monuments: the *ss Great Britain* and lofty Clifton Suspension Bridge.

Bristol Cathedral

College Green, BS1 5TJ • Mon–Fri 8am–5pm, Sat & Sun 8am–3.15pm; evensong Mon–Fri 5.15pm, Sat & Sun 3.30pm • Free • **Tours** Usually Sat 11.30am & 1.30pm; up to 1hr • Free • ⓦbristol-cathedral.co.uk

Founded as an abbey around 1140 on the supposed spot of St Augustine's convocation with Celtic Christians in 603, venerable **Bristol Cathedral** became a cathedral church with the Dissolution of the Monasteries in the mid-sixteenth century. The two towers on the west front were erected in the nineteenth century in a faithful act of homage to Edmund Knowle, architect and abbot at the start of the fourteenth century. The interior offers a unique example among Britain's cathedrals of a German-style "hall church", in which the aisles, nave and choir rise to the same height. Abbot Knowle's immense **choir** offers one of the country's most exquisite illustrations of the early

---

BANKSY AND BRISTOL STREET ART

An integral part of Bristol's cultural profile, the street artist known as **Banksy** has (more or less) managed to maintain his anonymity, with exhibitions pulling crowds from London to LA. It was in Bristol, though, a city known since the 1980s for its **graffiti**, that he first made his mark, leaving his stencilled daubs and freehand murals on inner city walls. Websites such as ⓦbristol-street-art.co.uk allow you to track down his surviving murals, though it's easy enough to locate his more iconic works such as *The Mild Mild West* on Stokes Croft and *The Naked Man* off the bottom of Park Street.

Banksy's global celebrity has led to his works becoming accepted and even protected by city supremos, and the council has given its blessing to **Upfest** (ⓦupfest.co.uk), Europe's largest street-art and graffiti festival; it takes place in Bedminster, South Bristol, over a weekend in late July.

5

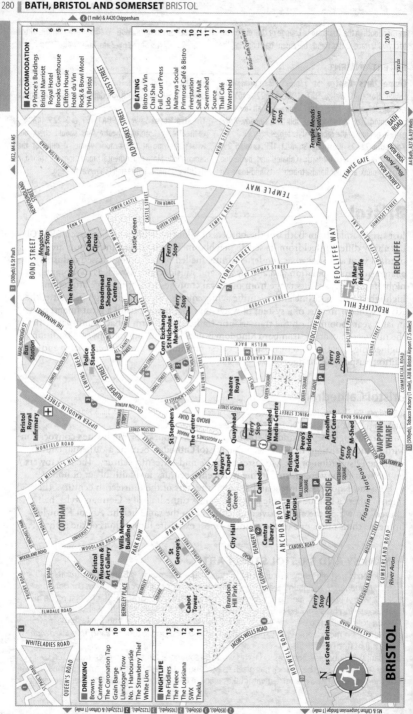

▲ ④ (1 mile) & A420 Chippenham

■ ACCOMMODATION	
9 Prince's Buildings	2
Bristol Marriott	6
Royal Hotel	5
Brooks Guesthouse	1
Clifton House	3
Hotel du Vin	4
Rock & Bowl Motel	4
YHA Bristol	7

■ EATING	
Bistro du Vin	5
Chai Shai	8
Full Court Press	6
Lido	1
Maitreya Social	4
Primrose Café & Bistro	2
riverstation	10
Salt & Malt	12
Severnshed	11
Source	7
Thali Café	3
Watershed	9

■ DRINKING	
Browns	5
Canteen	1
The Coronation Tap	2
Grain Barge	10
Llandoger Trow	8
No. 1 Harbourside	9
The Strawberry Thief	6
White Lion	3

■ NIGHTLIFE	
The Fiddlers	13
The Fleece	7
The Louisiana	12
SWX	4
Thekla	11

BRISTOL

N

0   200
         yards

▲ M5 & Clifton Suspension Bridge (1 mile)
▼ (1 mile) (850yds) (1050yds) (1232yds) (1232yds) & Clifton (1 mile)
◄ (500yds) & St Paul's
◄ (500yds), Tobacco Factory (1 mile), A38 & Bristol Airport (7.5 miles)
► A4 Bath, A37 & A39 Wells

5

THE SLAVE TRADE IN BRISTOL

Over two hundred years after the abolition of the **British slave trade**, Bristol is still haunted by the instrumental part it played in the trafficking of African men, women and children to the New World – indeed, according to some interpretations, it was Bristol-born Sir John Yeamans, a Barbados planter, who effectively introduced slavery to North America.

Throughout the eighteenth century, Bristol's merchants participated in the "**triangular trade**" whereby brass pots, glass beads and other manufactured goods were traded for slaves on the coast of West Africa, who were then shipped to plantations in the Americas, the vessels returning to Europe with cargoes of sugar, cotton, tobacco and other slave-labour-produced commodities. By the 1730s, Bristol had become – along with London and Liverpool – one of the main beneficiaries of the trade; in 1750 alone, Bristol ships transported some eight thousand of the twenty thousand slaves sent to colonies in the Caribbean and America. The direct profits, together with the numerous spin-offs, helped to finance some of the city's finest Georgian architecture.

The British slave trade was finally abolished in 1807, but its legacy is still felt strongly in the city, particularly in the divisive figure of **Edward Colston**. The eighteenth-century sugar magnate is revered by many as a great philanthropist – his name given to numerous buildings, streets and schools in Bristol – but also reviled as a leading light in the Royal African Company. His statue in The Centre has more than once been the subject of graffiti attacks and calls for its removal, and famous Bristol band Massive Attack refused to play the Colston Hall because of the connotations of its name, which is scheduled to be changed for the venue's reopening in 2020.

Decorated style of Gothic, while the adjoining thirteenth-century **Elder Lady Chapel** contains some fine tombs and eccentric carvings of animals, including (between the arches on the right) a monkey playing the bagpipes accompanied by a ram on the violin. The **Eastern Lady Chapel** has some of England's finest examples of heraldic glass. From the south transept, a door leads to the **Chapter House**, a richly carved piece of late Norman architecture.

Bristol Museum and Art Gallery

Queen's Rd, BS8 1RL • Tues–Sun 10am–5pm, daily in hols • Free • ☎ 0117 922 3571, ⓦ bristolmuseums.org.uk/bristol-museum-and-art-gallery

Housed in a grandiose Edwardian-Baroque building, the **Bristol Museum and Art Gallery** has sections on local archeology, geology and natural history, as well as an important collection of Chinese porcelain and some magnificent Assyrian reliefs carved in the eighth century BC. Artworks by Banksy, the Bristol School and French Impressionists are mixed in with some choice older pieces, including a portrait of Martin Luther by Cranach the Elder and Giovanni Bellini's unusual *Descent into Limbo*.

St Stephen's

21 Stephen's St, off Corn St, BS1 1EQ • Mon–Fri 9.30am–3pm • Free • ☎ 0117 927 7977, ⓦ saint-stephens.com

Hemmed in by characterless modern buildings just east of The Centre (as the elongated traffic intersection northeast of the cathedral is known), **St Stephen's** is one of Bristol's oldest and most graceful churches. It dates from the thirteenth century, was rebuilt in the fifteenth, and was thoroughly restored with plenty of neo-Gothic trimmings in 1875. The church has some flamboyant tombs inside, mainly of various members of the merchant class who were the church's main patrons.

Corn Exchange

Corn St, BS1 1JQ • Mon–Sat 9.30am–5pm • Free

The Georgian **Corn Exchange**, designed by John Wood the Elder, now contains the covered **St Nicholas Markets**, a lively spot for a bite to eat. The engraved brass pillars

5

outside the entrance date from the sixteenth and seventeenth centuries and originally served as trading tables – thought to be the "nails" that gave rise to the expression "pay on the nail".

The New Room

36 The Horsefair, BS1 3JE • Mon–Sat 10am–4pm, Sun 1–4pm • Chapel free, museum £6 • ☎ 0117 926 4740, ⓦ newroombristol.org.uk

Hidden within **Broadmead** shopping centre is the world's first Methodist chapel, **the New Room**. Established by John Wesley in 1739, it looks very much as he left it, with a double-deck pulpit in the chapel, beneath a hidden upstairs window from which the evangelist could observe the progress of his trainee preachers. The rooms where Wesley stayed are now a **museum** illustrating the Bristol connections of John and his brother Charles.

King Street and around

King Street, a short walk southeast from The Centre, was laid out on marshland in 1663 and still holds a cluster of historic buildings, among them the **Theatre Royal**, the oldest working theatre in the country, opened in 1766 and preserving many of its original Georgian features. Further down, and in a very different architectural style, stands the timber-framed **Llandoger Trow** pub (see page 285), once the haunt of seafarers, and reputed to have been the meeting place of Daniel Defoe and Alexander Selkirk, the model for Robinson Crusoe. South of King Street is the elegant, grassy **Queen Square**.

St Mary Redcliffe

Redcliffe Way, Redcliffe, BS1 6RA • Mon–Sat 9am–4.30pm, Sun 8am–8pm • Free • ☎ 0117 231 0060, ⓦ www.stmaryredcliffe.co.uk

Described by Elizabeth I as "the fairest, goodliest and most famous parish church in England", the richly decorated **St Mary Redcliffe**, across Redcliffe Bridge from The Centre, was largely paid for and used by merchants and mariners. The present building was begun at the end of the thirteenth century, though it was added to in subsequent centuries and its tall spire – a distinctive feature on the city's skyline – dates from 1872. Above the church's north porch is the muniment room, where **Thomas Chatterton** claimed to have found a trove of medieval manuscripts; the poems, distributed as the work of a fifteenth-century monk, were in fact dazzling fakes.

We the Curious

Anchor Rd, BS1 5DB • Daily 10am–5pm, Sat, Sun & hols 10am–6pm • £13.90, under-15s £8.95 • ☎ 0117 915 1000, ⓦ wethecurious.org

Occupying a corner of the sleekly modern Millennium Square, marked out by the spherical, stainless-steel planetarium attached to one side, **We the Curious** deals with all things science. It's chiefly aimed at children, but there's enough interactive wizardry here to entertain everyone, with opportunities to view the blood in your veins, freeze your shadow and create your own short films (with input from Aardman Animations). The **planetarium** has up to eight shows daily; book when you buy your entry ticket (from £2.50 extra).

M-Shed

Princes Wharf, Wapping Rd, BS1 4RN • Tues–Sun & hols 10am–5pm • Free • Boat, train and crane rides on selected days throughout the year; £2–6 • ☎ 0117 352 6600, ⓦ bristolmuseums.org.uk/m-shed

Housed in an old harbourside transit shed, the superb **M-Shed** is dedicated to Bristol itself, past and present. It's an enjoyable, unashamedly populist survey, full of memorabilia and anecdotes and casting light on everything from the city's mercantile history to its festivals and street life. On the ground floor, Bristol Places charts the city's changing face, taking in its development as a port and the hardships of World War II. On the floor above, Bristol People and the adjoining Bristol Life look at the (often ordinary) folk who have shaped the city, with the former including a small display on Bristol's links with the transatlantic slave trade (see page 281). Afterwards, head out to the long terrace for fantastic harbour views.

ss Great Britain

Great Western Dockyard, BS1 6TY • Daily: April–Oct 10am–5.30pm; Nov–March 10am–4.30pm • £14 • ☎ 0117 926 0680, ⓦ ssgreatbritain.org

Harbourside's major draw, and one of Bristol's iconic sights, the **ss Great Britain** was the first propeller-driven, ocean-going iron ship in the world, built by **Isambard Kingdom Brunel** in 1843. She initially ran between Liverpool and New York, then Liverpool and Melbourne, circumnavigating the globe 32 times and chalking up over a million miles at sea. Her ocean-going days ended in 1886 when she was caught in a storm off Cape Horn, and she was eventually recovered and returned to Bristol in 1970. On board, you can see restored cabins and peer into the immense engine room, while the adjoining museum gives the background of the vessel and of Bristol's long shipbuilding history.

Clifton

On the western side of the city, **Clifton**, once an aloof spa resort, is now Bristol's stateliest neighbourhood. At the top of Blackboy Hill, the wide green expanses of **Durdham Down** and **Clifton Downs** stretch right up to the edge of the Avon Gorge, a popular spot for picnickers, joggers and kite-flyers. On the southern edge of the Downs is the select enclave of Clifton Village, centred on the Mall, where **Royal York Crescent**, the longest Georgian crescent in the country, offers splendid views over the steep drop to the River Avon below.

Clifton Suspension Bridge

Bridge Rd, BS8 3PA • Free, £1 for motor vehicles • **Visitor Centre** Daily 10am–5pm • Free • **Guided tours** Easter–Oct Sat & Sun 3pm; 45min • Free • ⓦ cliftonbridge.org.uk

A few minutes' walk from Clifton Village is Bristol's most famous symbol, **Clifton Suspension Bridge**, 702ft long and poised 245ft above high water. Money was first put forward for a bridge to span the Avon Gorge by a Bristol wine merchant in 1754, though it wasn't until 1829 that a competition was held for a design – won by **Isambard Kingdom Brunel** in a second round – and not until 1864 that the bridge was completed, five years after Brunel's death. Hampered by financial difficulties, the bridge never quite matched the engineer's original ambitious design, which included Egyptian-style towers topped by sphinxes at each end. You can see copies of his plans in the **Visitor Centre** at the far side of the bridge, alongside designs proposed by Brunel's rivals, some of them frankly bizarre.

ARRIVAL AND DEPARTURE

BRISTOL

By train Temple Meads train station is a 20min walk east of the city centre.
Destinations Bath (every 15–30min; 15min); Birmingham (every 30min; 1hr 25min); Cheltenham (every 30min; 40min); Exeter (1–2 hourly; 1hr); Gloucester (Mon–Sat hourly, Sun every 2hr; 55min); London Paddington (2–3 hourly; 1hr 45min); Taunton (2–4 hourly; 30min–1hr); Yeovil (Mon–Sat 7 daily, Sun 4 daily; 1hr 30min).

By bus Bristol's bus station (ⓦ firstgroup.com) is centrally located off Marlborough St; at the time of writing, Megabus (ⓦ megabus.com) services to and from London stop outside Black's camping shop on Bond St (near the bus station), though check the website as this may change.
Destinations Bath (3–6 hourly; 40min); Glastonbury (every 30min; 1hr 40min); London (every 30min–1hr; 2hr 30min–3hr); Wells (every 30min; 1hr).

5

GETTING AROUND

By ferry A ferry, setting off from the Quayhead, just south of The Centre, connects various parts of the Floating Harbour, including Temple Meads station and the *ss Great Britain* (every 40min; 10am–6.15pm; from £1.70 single, £2.90 return, £6.50 all-day ticket; ☎0117 927 3416,

ⓦbristolferry.com).

By bus Local buses are useful for getting to Clifton's upper reaches; take #8 or #9 from Temple Meads station or The Centre, which also connects the city's train and bus stations.

INFORMATION AND TOURS

Tourist office E-Shed, Canon's Rd (daily 10am–5pm; ☎0906 711 2191, ⓦvisitbristol.co.uk).

Tours Bristol In-Sight (☎0117 971 9279, ⓦbristolinsight. co.uk) runs a hop-on, hop-off, open-top bus tour of the

city's key sights (£15, £13 online), while Bristol Packet (☎0117 926 8157, ⓦbristolpacket.co.uk) offers cruises around the harbour, in the Avon Gorge and along the river to Bath (from £6.50).

ACCOMMODATION

With a few notable exceptions, good accommodation in Bristol is surprisingly thin on the ground. Hotels and B&Bs in the centre can suffer from traffic noise and the sound of late-night drinkers; for quieter and more traditional lodgings, choose **Clifton**.

★ **9 Prince's Buildings** 9 Prince's Buildings, Clifton, BS8 4LB ☎0117 973 4615, ⓦ9princesbuildings.co.uk; map p.280. A short walk from the Clifton Suspension Bridge and within staggering distance of several real-ale pubs, this five-storey Georgian B&B, lovingly cared for by its easy-going owners, enjoys a grand view over the Avon Gorge from its antique-filled rooms. Great breakfasts, too. Singles from £72. No credit cards. **£105**

Bristol Marriott Royal Hotel College Green, BS1 5TA ☎0117 925 5100, ⓦbristolmarriottroyal.co.uk; map p.280. Right next to Bristol Cathedral, this Italianate-style Victorian hotel is by far the more attractive of the city's two *Marriotts*, with spacious rooms, two restaurants, a Champagne bar and a lovely swimming pool. **£110**

★ **Brooks Guesthouse** Exchange Ave, off St Nicholas St, BS1 1UB ☎0117 930 0066, ⓦbrooksguesthousebristol. com; map p.280. Set in the midst of bustling St Nicholas Markets, this boutique B&B has small but comfortable rooms. The airy, modern breakfast room gives onto a spacious courtyard for relaxing with a book or a drink. You can also stay in an airstream trailer on the roof (£99). **£79**

Clifton House 4 Tyndall's Park Rd, Clifton, BS8 1PG ☎0117 973 5407, ⓦcliftonhousebristol.com; map

p.280. This handily sited B&B at the bottom of Clifton and near the centre offers fairly plush rooms with big windows, modern bathrooms and plenty of space. There's parking, too. **£85**

Hotel du Vin The Sugar House, Narrow Lewins Mead, BS1 2NU ☎0330 016 0390, ⓦhotelduvin.co.uk; map p.280. Chic conversion of an old dockside warehouse, centrally located, with dark, contemporary decor. Rooms have big beds and grand bathrooms, and there's an excellent restaurant to boot (see below). **£129**

Rock'n'Bowl Motel 22 Nelson St, BS1 2LA ☎0117 325 1980, ⓦthelanesbristol.co.uk/hostel; map p.280. Clean and efficient hostel in an ex-dole office above a busy bowling alley. Single- and mixed-gender dorms (4- to 20-person) and a few en-suite doubles and twins, plus a self-catering kitchen and laundry. Can be noisy. Dorms **£15**, doubles **£65**

YHA Bristol 14 Narrow Quay, BS1 4QA ☎0345 371 9726, ⓦyha.org.uk/hostel/bristol; map p.280. In a refurbished grain house on the quayside, this warm and friendly hostel has mostly four-bed dorms, plus (smallish) private doubles. There's a decent kitchen, and prices include an abundant breakfast. Dorms **£15**, doubles **£39**

EATING

CAFÉS

Full Court Press 59 Broad St, BS1 2EJ ☎07794 808552, ⓦfcpcoffee.com; map p.280. The select menu of superb speciality coffees at this dinky joint near St Nick's Markets have made it an instant hit with local connoisseurs. Mon–Fri 7.30am–5pm, Sat 9am–5pm, Sun 10am–4pm.

Primrose Café 1 Clifton Arcade, Boyces Ave, Clifton, BS8 4AA ☎0117 946 6577, ⓦprimrosecafe.co.uk; map p.280. Homely café in Clifton Village serving a good range of teas, fruit juices and wines, as well as a choice of breakfasts, sandwiches, salads, burgers and pancakes. There's a roof

garden open in summer, too. Daily 9/9.30am–5pm.

Watershed 1 Canon's Rd, BS1 5TX ☎0117 927 5101, ⓦwatershed.co.uk; map p.280. Cool café-bar overlooking the boats in a long-established arts complex. Good coffee and local beers are supplemented by an appetizing menu, and there's a tiny (non-smoking) terrace. Mon–Fri 9.30am–11pm, Sat 10am–11pm, Sun 10am–10.30pm.

RESTAURANTS

Bistro du Vin Hotel du Vin, The Sugar House, Narrow Lewins Mead, BS1 2NU ☎0117 925 5577, ⓦhotelduvin.

com; map p.280. Fine French bistro-style dining, using good seasonal West Country produce in its Modern European menu; most mains around £16. Mon–Sat noon–2.30pm & 5.30–10pm, Fri & Sat noon–2.30pm & 5.30–10.30pm, Sun noon–4pm & 6–9.30pm.

Chai Shai 4 Jacobs Well Rd, BS8 1EA ☎0117 925 0754; map p.280. Friendly, laid-back Indian restaurant with an open kitchen and a small menu of light and tasty dishes such as *saag ghosht* (mutton and spinach), *achari* chicken and fish *khata* (all around £8). Book ahead, or wait in the neighbouring pub for a table to become free. Bring your own beers. Takeaways available. Mon–Sat 11.30am–3pm & 4–11pm.

★ **Lido** Oakfield Place, Clifton, BS8 2BJ; restaurant entrance on Southleigh Rd ☎0117 332 3970; Ⓦlidobristol.com; map p.280. The glass-walled restaurant at this pool/spa complex overlooks the outdoor pool, and dining on dishes like seafood stew (£21) while others exercise makes them somehow tastier. There are set-price menus (£12–20), while in the poolside bar, breakfast is available until 11.30am and tapas from noon. Daily: restaurant noon–2.45pm & 6–9.45pm; poolside bar 8/9am–10pm.

Maitreya Social 89 St Mark's Rd, BS5 6HY ☎0117 951 0100, Ⓦcafemaitreya.co.uk; map p.280. Tucked away in the multicultural Easton neighbourhood, this easy-going place serves delicious, inventive vegetarian dishes like falafel with charred aubergine, or smoked shallot tart (both £12). The early-bird menu is great value (£15–17). Tues–Fri 6–11.30pm, Sat 10am–11.30pm, Sun 10am–3pm.

riverstation The Grove, BS1 4RB ☎0117 914 4434, Ⓦriverstation.co.uk; map p.280. Two-storey former river-police station, with all-day brunches, tapas and flatbreads at the relaxed ground-floor bar and more refined Modern European dining upstairs, where mains cost £15–

24 and set-price meals £15–19. Bag a table by the window for dockside views. Restaurant Mon–Sat noon–2.30pm & 6–10pm, Sun noon–3pm; bar Mon–Sat 10am–11pm (kitchen until 10pm), Sun 10am–10pm (kitchen until 8pm).

Salt & Malt Cargo 2, Museum St, BS1 6WD ☎01275 333 345, Ⓦsaltmalt.com; map p.280. Housed in a shipping container, this smart little fish bar has lightly fried cod, haddock and plaice and crispy chips. It's ideal for mooching along the harbourfront, or you can eat at small tables within view of the boats. Cod and chips is £7.50 to take away, £11.50 at table. Alternatives include battered halloumi . Tues–Sat noon–10pm, Sun noon–8pm.

Severnshed The Grove, BS1 4RB ☎0117 925 1212, Ⓦsevernshedrestaurant.co.uk; map p.280. *Severnshed*, which has a waterside terrace, serves pastas and pizzas (from £8) and grills, including meat and fish firesticks (£17–21), as well as cocktails until late. DJs provide the soundtrack on Sat evenings. Mon–Thurs 10am–11pm, Fri 10am–1am, Sat 9am–1am, Sun 9am–11pm.

★ **Source** 1–3 Exchange Ave, off St Nicholas St, BS1 1JW ☎0117 927 2998, Ⓦsource-food.co.uk; map p.280. Almost all the food in this relaxed deli and canteen next to St Nick's Markets is from the West Country, and much of it is organic – for example, fish soup, spiced aubergine and charcuterie-style cold meats (£7–11). Breakfasts, teas and cakes are also available. Mon–Sat 8am–4pm.

Thali Café 1 Regent St, Clifton, BS8 4HW ☎0117 974 3793, Ⓦthethalicafe.co.uk; map p.280. *Dhaba*-style South Asian food in vibrant surroundings. This Clifton branch – there are four others across Bristol – has the trademark deep-pink decor and range of tasty thalis, a balanced selection of dishes served on a stainless-steel platter (from £9.50). Daily 5–10pm, Sat & Sun noon–10pm.

DRINKING

Browns 38 Queen's Rd, BS8 1RE ☎0117 930 4777, Ⓦbrowns-restaurants.com; map p.280. Spacious and relaxed place, housed in the Venetian-style former university refectory. The wide choice of tipples includes a range of beers, wines, Champagnes and cocktails. Mon–Thurs 9am–11pm, Fri & Sat 9am–midnight, Sun 9am–10.30pm.

Canteen Hamilton House, 80 Stokes Croft, BS1 3QY ☎0117 923 2017, Ⓦcanteenbristol.co.uk; map p.280. Overlooked by one of Banksy's most famous murals, a drab 1960s office block now accommodates this popular collective-style bar. Take a seat at a graffitied table for a coffee or a pint, accompanied most nights from 9.30pm by live music (but Sun 4–6pm) and DJs. Mon–Thurs 10am–midnight, Fri & Sat 10am–1am, Sun 10am–11pm.

★ **The Coronation Tap** 8 Sion Place, Clifton, BS8 4AX ☎0117 973 9617, Ⓦthecoronationtap.com; map

p.280. A proper cider house, the *Cori Tap* produces its own Exhibition "apple juice", which is sold by the half-pint only, and stocks a wide range of locally produced ciders. Excellent live music, too. Daily 5.30–11.30pm, Sat & Sun 7–11.30pm.

Grain Barge Mardyke Wharf, Hotwell Rd, BS8 4RU ☎0117 929 9347, Ⓦgrainbarge.com; map p.280. Floating pub, café and restaurant near the mouth of the harbour, with a tranquil ambience and half a dozen real ales brewed at the Bristol Beer Factory. Interesting calendar of events, including occasional live music on Thurs evenings. Daily noon–11pm, Thurs–Sat noon–11.30pm.

Llandoger Trow 1–3 King St, BS1 4ER ☎0117 926 1650, Ⓦbrewersfayre.co.uk; map p.280. Seventeenth-century drinking den full of history (see page 282), with cosy nooks and armchairs, benches outside and a

5

restaurant upstairs. Snacks and full meals available. Gets very busy on summer evenings. Mon–Sat 7.30am–11pm, Sun 8am–10.30pm.

No.1 Harbourside 1 Canon's Rd, BS1 5UH ☎0117 929 1100, ⓦno1harbourside.co.uk; map p.280. Laidback spot for drinks, snacks (including veggie and vegan choices) and live music (Wed–Sun) until late. Sun evenings are for dancing, from flamenco to swing. Mon & Sun 10am–11pm, Tues–Thurs 10am–midnight, Fri & Sat 10am–1am.

The Strawberry Thief 26 Broad St, BS1 2HG ☎0117 925 6925, ⓦstrawberrythiefbar.com; map p.280. Boasting the West Country's largest selection of Belgian beers (around fifty), as well as a good twenty UK craft beers, this place has a mellow vibe, with small tables and William Morris wallpaper. Food (including brunches and waffles) is gluten-free, mostly vegan and served until 9.30pm. Tues–Thurs 4–11pm, Fri 4pm–midnight, Sat noon–midnight.

White Lion Avon Gorge Hotel, Sion Hill, Clifton, BS8 4LD ☎0117 403 0210, ⓦtheavongorgehotel.com; map p.280. Attached to a hotel perched on the edge of the Gorge in Clifton Village, this modern bar draws in the crowds thanks to its broad terrace, affording magnificent views of the gorge and suspension bridge. Food available. Mon–Sat 11am–11pm, Sun 11am–10.30pm.

NIGHTLIFE

The Fiddlers Willway St, Bedminster, BS3 4BG ☎0117 987 3403, ⓦfiddlers.co.uk; map p.280. Mainly roots bands, good-time retro acts and niche artists perform at this relaxed, family-run venue (formerly a prison) south of the river.

The Fleece 12 St Thomas St, BS1 6JJ ☎0117 945 0996, ⓦthefleece.co.uk; map p.280. Stone-flagged ex-wool warehouse, now a loud, sweaty pub staging everything from acoustic blues and alt-country to punk and deathcore.

The Louisiana Wapping Rd, BS1 6UA ☎0117 926 5978, ⓦwww.thelouisiana.net; map p.280. Established music pub with a well-earned reputation for helping break bands (The White Stripes, Florence + the Machine) and promoting local artists. It's a mite cramped, but the acoustics and atmosphere are excellent.

SWX 15 Nelson St, BS1 2JY ☎0117 945 0325, ⓦswx bristol.com; map p.280. A real super-club, one of the largest in Bristol, and home to various club nights, as well as live music and comedy.

Thekla The Grove, BS1 4RB ☎0117 929 3301, ⓦthekla bristol.co.uk; map p.280. Ex-cargo boat, now a much-loved venue staging a varied line-up of live bands plus indie, house and club nights.

ENTERTAINMENT

Bristol Old Vic King's St, BS1 4ED ☎0117 987 7877, ⓦbristololdvic.org.uk. Britain's oldest working theatre, dating from the 1760s, retains its Georgian interior but has modern facilities. It lays on a full programme of mainstream and more experimental productions in its main auditorium and the Studio.

★ **St George's** Great George St, BS1 5RR ☎0845 402 4001, ⓦstgeorgesbristol.co.uk. Elegant Georgian church with superb acoustics, staging a packed programme of lunchtime and evening concerts covering classical, world, folk and jazz music.

Tobacco Factory Raleigh Rd, Southville, BS3 1ET ☎0117 902 0344, ⓦtobaccofactorytheatres.com. South of the river, this theatre offers a broad spectrum of drama, dance, comedy and other performing arts on two stages.

Wells

The miniature cathedral city of **WELLS**, 21 miles south of Bristol and the same distance southwest from Bath, has not significantly altered in eight hundred years. Charming and compact, it is eminently walkable, and a stroll around its tightly knit streets reveals a cluster of medieval buildings, archways and almshouses.

Wells Cathedral

Cathedral Green, BA5 2UE • Daily: April–Sept 7am–7pm; Oct–March 7am–6pm • Free, but suggested donation £6 • **Tours** Usually Mon–Sat: April–Oct 11am, noon, 1pm, 2pm & 3pm; Nov–March 11am, noon & 2pm; 1hr • Free • ☎01749 674483, ⓦwellscathedral.org.uk

Hidden from sight until you pass into its spacious close from central Market Place, **Wells Cathedral** presents a majestic spectacle. The west front teems with some three hundred thirteenth-century figures of saints and kings, once brightly painted and gilded, though their present honey tint has a subtle splendour of its own. The

BANKSY MURAL, BRISTOL

5

sensational facade was constructed about fifty years after work on the main building was begun in 1180.

The **interior** is a supreme example of early English Gothic, the long nave punctuated by a dramatic and very modern-looking "scissor arch", one of three that were constructed in 1338 to take the extra weight of the newly built tower. Beyond the arches, there are some gnarled old tombs to be seen in the aisles of the **Quire**, at the end of which is the richly coloured stained glass of the fourteenth-century **Lady Chapel**. The capitals and corbels of the transepts hold some amusing narrative carvings, and in the north transept there's a 24-hour astronomical clock dating from 1390. Opposite the clock, a well-worn flight of steps leads to the **Chapter House**, an octagonal room elaborately ribbed in the Decorated style.

Wells & Mendip Museum

8 Cathedral Green, BA5 2UE • Mon–Sat: Easter–Sept 10am–5pm; Oct–Easter 10am–4pm • £3 • ☏ 01749 673477, ⓦ wellsmuseum.org.uk

The row of clerical houses on the north side of Cathedral Green mainly dates from the seventeenth and eighteenth centuries. The chancellor's house is now the **Wells & Mendip Museum**, displaying some of the cathedral's original statuary as well as a good geological section with fossils from the Mendip area. There are also changing exhibitions, with a focus on World War I until late 2018, then on the history of Wells itself.

Bishop's Palace

Market Place, BA5 2RA • Daily: Early Jan to March & Nov to late Dec 10am–4pm; April–Oct 10am–6pm • £7.25 • **Tours** Daily 11am & 2pm (palace), noon & 3pm (grounds); palace 30min, grounds 45min • Included in entry fee • ☏ 01749 988111, ⓦ bishopspalace.org.uk

The tranquil grounds of the **Bishop's Palace**, residence of the Bishop of Bath and Wells since 1206, are reachable through the Bishop's Eye archway from Market Place. The palace was walled and moated as a result of a rift with the borough in the fourteenth century, and the imposing gatehouse still features the grooves of the portcullis and a chute for pouring oil and molten lead on would-be assailants. The gardens contain the springs from which the city takes its name and the scant but impressive remains of the **Great Hall**, built at the end of the thirteenth century and despoiled during the Reformation. Across the lawn stand the square **Bishop's Chapel** and **Bishop Jocelyn's Hall**, a few state rooms holding displays relating to the history of the site, and the *Undercroft* café.

ARRIVAL AND INFORMATION
WELLS

By bus Buses (☏ 0345 602 0121, ⓦ firstgroup.com/somerset) pull in at the station off Market St. Destinations Bath (Mon–Sat 2 hourly, Sun hourly; 1hr 25min); Bristol (every 30min; 1hr); Glastonbury (Mon–Sat every 15min, Sun every 30min; 15min); Taunton (Mon–Sat every 2hr; 1hr 40min); Wookey Hole (Mon–Sat 1–2 hourly, Sun 4 daily; 5–10min); Yeovil (Mon–Sat hourly; 1hr 20min).

Tourist office Wells & Mendip Museum, 8 Cathedral Green (Mon–Sat: Easter–Sept 10am–5pm; Oct–Easter Mon–Sat 10am–4pm; ☏ 01749 671770, ⓦ wellssomerset.com).

ACCOMMODATION AND EATING

Beryl Hawkers Lane, BA5 3JP, 1 mile northeast of Wells ☏ 01749 678738, ⓦ www.beryl-wells.co.uk. Luxury country-house B&B, a former hunting lodge, set in lovely gardens with a children's play area and pool (May–Sept). Decor varies between the fourteen rooms – some are quite twee, others stylishly understated – though all enjoy good views. **£100**

The Crown Market Place, BA5 2RP ☏ 01749 673457,

ⓦ crownatwells.co.uk. Fifteenth-century coaching inn where William Penn was arrested in 1695 for illegal preaching; it's got a suitably old-fashioned flavour that verges on the fusty and faded. Rooms can be noisy from the bar and bistro below and/or the Wed and Sat markets. **£95**

★ **The Good Earth** 4 Priory Rd, BA5 1SY ☏ 01749 678600, ⓦ thegoodearthwells.co.uk. Excellent wholefood restaurant that was making a name for itself with its delicious home-made quiches long before eco food was in vogue. Soups, salads, veggie pizzas and other organic goodies (mains from £7) available to eat in or take away. Mon–Fri 9am–4.30pm, Sat 9am–5pm.

Square Edge Café 2 Town Hall Buildings, Market Place, BA5 1SE ☎01749 671166, ⓦsquare-edgecafe. co.uk. Close to the sights, this retro café makes a cosy spot for a cup of first-rate coffee and a slice of cake. You can also opt for a full breakfast or a snack lunch, such as a hummus

platter (£10.50) or a bun stuffed with beef brisket (£11). The atmospheric interior has two fireplaces and a range of ancient radios among other curios, and there's an equally quirky courtyard. Mon–Sat 9am–5pm, Sun 10am–4pm.

Swan Hotel Sadler St, BA5 2RX ☎01749 836300, ⓦswanhotelwells.co.uk. This swanky and rambling inn has plenty of antique character, plus friendly service and a rated restaurant (for which booking is essential). Pricier rooms have cathedral views. **£148**

The Mendips

Northwest of Wells, the ancient woodland, exposed heaths and limestone crags of the **Mendip Hills** are chiefly famous for **Wookey Hole** – the most impressive of many caves in this narrow limestone chain – and for **Cheddar Gorge**, where a walk through the narrow cleft makes a starting point for more adventurous hikes across the Mendips.

Wookey Hole

Two miles northwest of Wells, BA5 1BB • Tours daily every 10–30min: April–Oct 10am–6pm; Nov–March 10am–5pm; last tour 1hr before closing; 1hr • £19, online £17.10 • ☎01749 672243, ⓦwookey.co.uk

It's folklore rather than geology that takes precedence at **Wookey Hole**, a stunning cave complex of deep pools and intricate rock formations hollowed out by the River Axe. Highlight of the **tour** is the alleged petrified remains of the Witch of Wookey, a "blear-eyed hag" who was said to turn her evil eye on crops, young lovers and local farmers. To finish off, there's a functioning Victorian paper mill and rooms containing speleological exhibits, plus a melange of family "attractions" that range from King Kong to a Clown Museum.

Cheddar Gorge

The nondescript village of **CHEDDAR**, six miles west of Wookey on the A371, has given its name to Britain's best-known cheese – most of it now mass-produced far from here – and is also renowned for **Cheddar Gorge**, lying about a mile to the north. Cutting a jagged gash across the Mendip Hills, the limestone gorge is an amazing geological phenomenon, though its natural beauty is compromised by Lower Gorge's mile of trinket shops and parking. Few venture further than the first few curves of the gorge, which hold its most dramatic scenery – at its narrowest, the road squeezes between cliffs towering almost 500ft above – though each turn of the two-mile length presents new, sometimes startling vistas.

Up the 274 steps of **Jacob's Ladder** is a clifftop tower with views to Glastonbury Tor (daily 10am–5pm; £5.50, free to Cheddar Caves ticket-holders). From the tower, there's a circular three-mile clifftop Gorge Walk, and you can branch off along marked paths to spots including **Black Down** and Beacon Batch, at 1068ft the Mendips' highest point.

Cheddar Caves

BS27 3QF • Daily 10am–5pm • £17.95, online £15.25 • ☎01934 742343, ⓦcheddargorge.co.uk

Beneath the towering Cheddar Gorge, the **Cheddar Caves** were scooped out by underground rivers in the wake of the Ice Age, and subsequently occupied by primitive communities. Today, the caves are floodlit to pick out the subtle tones of the rock, and the array of rock formations that resemble organ pipes, waterfalls and giant birds.

5

By bus Public transport is essentially limited to #67 from Wells to Wookey Hole (Mon–Fri 7 daily; 10min), and #126 from Wells to Cheddar (Mon–Sat hourly, 4 on Sun; 25min).
By car The Mendips are best explored on your own wheels.

Tourist information There's an information desk at the National Trust shop in Cheddar Gorge (Easter to late Oct daily 10am–5pm; late Oct to Christmas & late Feb to Easter Sat & Sun 10am–4pm; ☎ 01934 744689).

ACCOMMODATION AND EATING

Chedwell Cottage 59 Redcliffe St, Cheddar, BS27 3PF ☎ 01934 743268, ⓦ chedwellcottage.co.uk. The charming owners of this homely B&B, in a quiet lane a 10min walk from the gorge, provide three simple en-suite rooms and delicious breakfasts which include home-made bread. No cards. **£75**
The Wookey Hole Inn Wookey Hole, BA5 1BP ☎ 01749 676677, ⓦ wookeyholeinn.com. Very close to the caves, this is a great place to stay, with funky, fully equipped

guest rooms and a restaurant (booking essential) serving expensive but memorable dishes (mains from £13). Mon–Sat noon–2.30pm & 6.30–9pm, Sun noon–3pm. **£75**
YHA Cheddar Hillfield, Cheddar, BS27 3HN ☎ 0345 371 9730, ⓦ yha.org.uk. Clinically refurbished Victorian house with clean, spacious rooms – four- to six-bed dorms, en-suite doubles and family rooms – and a decent kitchen. Dorms **£13**, doubles **£29**

Glastonbury

On the southern edge of the Mendips and six miles south of Wells, **GLASTONBURY**, famed for its annual music festival, is built around the evocative set of ruins belonging to its former abbey. The town lies at the heart of the so-called **Isle of Avalon**, a region rich with mystical associations, and for centuries it has been one of the main Arthurian sites of the West Country – today, it's an enthusiastic centre for all manner of New Age pursuits.

Glastonbury Abbey

Magdalene St, BA6 9EL • Daily: March–May, Sept & Oct 9am–6pm; June–Aug 9am–8pm; Nov–Feb 9am–4pm • £7.50, online £6.67 • ☎ 01458 832267, ⓦ glastonburyabbey.com

Aside from its mythological origins, **Glastonbury Abbey** can claim to be the country's oldest Christian foundation, dating back a least to the seventh century. Enlarged by St Dunstan in the tenth century, it became the country's richest Benedictine abbey, and three Anglo-Saxon kings (Edmund, Edgar and Edmund Ironside) were buried here.

GLASTONBURY TALES

At the heart of the complex web of **myths surrounding Glastonbury** is the early Christian legend that Jesus once visited this site – not quite as far-fetched as it sounds. The Romans had a heavy presence in the area, mining lead in the Mendips, and one of these mines was owned by **Joseph of Arimathea**, who is said to have been related to Mary. It's not completely unfeasible that he took his kinsman along on one of his many visits, in a period of Christ's life about which nothing is recorded. William Blake was referring to this possibility in his *Glastonbury Hymn*, better known as *Jerusalem*: "And did those feet in ancient times/Walk upon England's mountains green?"

Another legend relates how Joseph was imprisoned for twelve years after the Crucifixion, miraculously kept alive by the **Holy Grail**, the chalice of the Last Supper, in which the blood was gathered from the wound in Christ's side. The Grail, along with the spear that had caused the wound, were later taken by Joseph to Glastonbury, where he built the "First Church", around which the abbey later grew, and commenced the conversion of Britain.

Glastonbury is also popularly identified with the mythical **Avalon**. The story goes that King Arthur, having been mortally wounded, sailed to Avalon where he was buried in the abbey's choir, alongside his queen – somehow Glastonbury was taken to be the best candidate for the place.

GLASTONBURY FESTIVAL

Glastonbury Festival of Contemporary and Performing Arts (Ⓦglastonburyfestivals. co.uk) takes place most years over four days in late June, with happy campers braving the predictable mudfest at Worthy Farm, six miles east of Glastonbury. Having started as a small hippy affair in the 1970s, "Glasto" has become the biggest and best-organized festival in the country, without shedding too much of its alternative feel. Much more than just a music festival, large parts of the sprawling site are given over to themed "lifestyle" areas, from the meditation marquees of Green Fields to campfire-filled Strummerville and futuristic Arcadia. Bands cover all musical spectrums – recent headliners have included Foo Fighters, Radiohead and Ed Sheeran. Despite the steep price (£243), tickets are invariably snapped up within hours of going on sale around October of the previous year.

The abbey was the longest in Europe by the time it was destroyed in the Dissolution of the Monasteries in 1539, and the ruins, now hidden behind walls and among parkland, only hint at its former extent. The most complete set of remains is the shell of the **Lady Chapel**, with its carved figures of the Annunciation, the Magi and Herod.

The abbey's **choir**, announced by the striking transept piers, holds what is alleged to be the tomb of **Arthur and Guinevere**. The discovery of two bodies in an ancient cemetery by the abbey in 1191 was taken to confirm that here was, indeed, the mystical Avalon. Elsewhere in the grounds, the fourteenth-century **abbot's kitchen** is the only monastic building to survive intact, with four huge corner fireplaces and a great central lantern. Behind the main entrance to the grounds, look out for the thorn tree that is supposedly a descendant of the original **Glastonbury Thorn** on Wearyall Hill, said to have sprouted from the staff of Joseph of Arimathea.

Glastonbury Lake Village Museum

9 High St, BA6 9DP • Mon–Sat 10am–3pm • £3.50; EH • ☎ 01458 832954, Ⓦ www.english-heritage.org.uk/visit/places/glastonbury-tribunal

The fifteenth-century **Glastonbury Tribunal** makes an atmospheric setting for the small but interesting **Glastonbury Lake Village Museum**, with displays from the Iron Age settlements that fringed the former marshland below the Tor. The villages' wattle houses were rebuilt on layers of clay as they slowly submerged into the marshes, and the perfectly preserved finds include jewellery made from animal bones and a 3000-year-old wooden canoe.

Somerset Rural Life Museum

Chilkwell St, BA6 8DB • 10am–5pm; Easter–Oct Tues–Sun; Nov–Easter Tues–Sat • £5.45 • ☎ 01458 831197, Ⓦ somersetrurallifemuseum. org.uk

Centred around the fourteenth-century Abbey Barn, the engaging **Somerset Rural Life Museum** has historically focused on a range of local rural occupations, from cider-making and peat-digging to the unusual practice of mud-horse fishing, named after the sledge shrimpers used to navigate the mud flats of Bridgwater Bay.

Glastonbury Tor

Just east of town, BA6 8BG • Free; NT • Ⓦ nationaltrust.org.uk/glastonbury-tor

Towering over the Somerset Levels, the 521ft-high conical hill of **Glastonbury Tor** commands stupendous views as far as the Welsh mountains on very clear days. It is topped by the dilapidated **St Michael's Tower**, sole remnant of a fourteenth-century church, and pilgrims once embarked on the stiff climb up here with hard peas in their shoes as penance – nowadays, people come to picnic, fly kites or feel the vibrations of crossing ley lines.

5

By bus Frequent buses (ⓦfirstgroup.com) #29, #75, #77 and #376 connect Glastonbury with Wells; #376 also goes to Bristol and #29 to Taunton.

Destinations Bristol (every 30min; 1hr 25min); Taunton (Mon–Sat every 2hr; 1hr 15min); Wells (Mon–Sat 3–4 hourly, Sun every 30min; 15min).

Tourist office Glastonbury Tribunal, 9 High St (Mon–Sat 10am–3.15pm; ⓣ01458 832954, ⓦglastonburytic.co.uk).

GETTING AROUND

By bus The Glastonbury Tor Bus (April–Sept daily 10am–5pm; £3, valid all day) runs from the abbey car park to the base of the Tor every 30min, and stops at the Somerset Rural Life Museum (when open) and Chalice Well.

By bike Lintells Garage, 140 Wells Rd (ⓣ01458 832117, ⓦlintellsgarage.co.uk), rents bikes for £15/day.

ACCOMMODATION

George & Pilgrim Hotel 1 High St, BA6 9DP ⓣ01458 831146, ⓦgeorgeandpilgrim.relaxinnz.co.uk. This fifteenth-century oak-panelled inn with mullioned windows brims with medieval atmosphere. It's tired and worn in parts and some of the rooms are a bit ordinary – go for one of the older ones, which include frilly four-posters. **£86**

Isle of Avalon Godney Rd, BA6 9AF ⓣ01458 833618, ⓦavaloncaravanpark.co.uk. Convenient campsite a 10min walk from Northload St and within sight of the Tor. The pitches are spacious, and there's a well-stocked shop, plus decent washing facilities and a freezer for cool-box ice packs. **£18**

★ **Magdalene House** Magdalene St, BA6 9EJ ⓣ01458

830202, ⓦmagdalenehouseglastonbury.com. In a former convent directly abutting the abbey grounds, this B&B has three stylish, spacious en-suites (one overlooking the abbey, the others with views to Wearyall Hill) with comfy beds. The generous breakfasts use local and organic products. No children under 7. No debit/credit cards. **£95**

Middlewick Holiday Cottages Wick Lane, BA6 8JW, 1.5 miles north of Glastonbury ⓣ01458 832351, ⓦmiddlewickholidaycottages.co.uk. A dozen self-catering cottages plus cabins (£81) in rural surroundings, the former with stone walls, oak floors and, in some, cosy wood burners. There's a steam room, indoor pool, BBQ and pizza oven. **£90**

EATING AND DRINKING

Blue Note Café 4a High St, BA6 8DU ⓣ01458 832907. A relaxed place to hang out over coffees and cakes with some courtyard seating. It's vegetarian and mostly organic, with nourishing soups, salads and halloumi burgers (mains from £6; three tapas for £10). Mon–Thurs & Sun 9am–5pm, Fri & Sat 9am–11pm.

Hawthorns 8–12 Northload St, BA6 9JJ ⓣ01458 831255, ⓦhawthornshotel.co.uk. Homely bar and restaurant whose main draws are its curries (£13) and music sessions (Tues, Thurs, Fri from about 8pm; Sun 5–7pm). Mon–Wed 6–11pm, Thurs noon–3pm & 6–11pm, Fri & Sat noon–11pm, Sun noon–10.30pm; kitchen daily till 9pm.

★ **Hundred Monkeys** 52 High St, BA6 9DY ⓣ01458 833386, ⓦhundredmonkeyscafe.com. Mellow contemporary café/restaurant whose wholesome offerings include seafood stew (£11.50) and aubergine and tamarind curry (£10), as well as gourmet salads (from £9) and some great cakes. You can sit outdoors at the back. Mon–Thurs & Sun 9am–5pm, Fri 9am–9pm, Sat 8am–9pm.

King Arthur 31–33 Benedict St, BA6 9NB ⓣ01458 831442. Wood-floored freehouse near St Benedict's Church, serving snacks, burgers (from £7) and a great Sunday roast (£9), plus there's live music most nights and a garden. Mon & Tues 3pm–midnight, Wed–Sun noon–midnight; kitchen Mon–Sat till 10pm, Sun till 4.30pm.

Taunton

West of Glastonbury, the county town of **TAUNTON** makes a handy starting point for excursions into the Quantock Hills, and is home to the excellent **Museum of Somerset**. While in town, take a look at the pinnacled and battlemented towers of its two most important churches – **St James** on Coal Orchard and **St Mary Magdalene** on Church Square – both fifteenth-century structures remodelled by the Victorians.

Museum of Somerset

Taunton Castle, Castle Green, TA1 4AA • Tues–Sat 10am–5pm • Free • ⓣ01823 255088, ⓦmuseumofsomerset.org.uk

Started in the twelfth century, **Taunton Castle** staged the trial of royal claimant Perkin Warbeck, who in 1490 declared himself to be the Duke of York, the younger of the

5

SOMERSET CIDER FARMS

Nothing is quite so synonymous with Somerset as **cider**, a drink ingrained in the regional identity. Most pubs across the region stock one or two local ciders, but for the real deal it's hard to beat a visit to a working cider farm itself, where you can sample traditional ciders (around £4.10 for 2 litres) and learn more about the cider-making process.

Burrow Hill Cider Farm Pass Vale Farm, Burrow Hill, TA12 6BU ☎01460 240782, ⓦciderbrandy.co.uk. Tastings are done in an old, dark cider house dripping with atmosphere – try one of their single-variety, bottle-fermented sparkling ciders. Tours by arrangement.

Perry's Cider Mills Dowlish Wake, TA19 0NY ☎01460 55195, ⓦperryscider.co.uk. Archetypal cider farm and orchards, with a dozen farmhouse and single-variety ciders, plus a small rural museum.

Sheppy's Cider Three Bridges, Bradford-on-Tone, TA4 1ER ☎01823 461233, ⓦsheppyscider.com. Complex combining a shop, tearooms, museum, and orchards complete with resident herd of longhorn cattle. Tours available (Fri & Sat 2pm; 1hr 30min; £10).

Wilkins Lands End Farm, Wedmore, BS28 4TU ☎01934 712385, ⓦwilkinscider.com. Legendary cider-maker Roger Wilkins offers generous tastings in his Banksy-decorated barn up on the Isle of Wedmore.

"Princes in the Tower" – the sons of Edward IV, who had been murdered seven years earlier. Parts of the structure were pulled down in 1662 and much of the rest has been altered, and it now houses the **Museum of Somerset**, a wide-ranging display that includes finds from Somerset's Lake Villages; the "Frome Hoard", the second-largest collection of Roman coins ever discovered in Britain; and a superb fragment of Roman mosaic found near Langport in the Somerset Levels. The ground-floor Great Hall was where Judge Jeffreys held one of his "Bloody Assizes" following the Monmouth Rebellion of 1685, at which 144 prisoners were sentenced to be hanged, drawn and quartered.

ARRIVAL AND INFORMATION
TAUNTON

By train The station lies a 20min walk north of town. There's also the West Somerset Railway (ⓦwest-somerset-railway.co.uk), which terminates at Bishops Lydeard.
Destinations Bristol (2–3 hourly; 30min–1hr); Exeter (2–3 hourly; 25min).

By bus Taunton's bus station (ⓦfirstgroup.com) is off Castle Green.
Destinations Bishops Lydeard (Mon–Sat every 30min, Sun hourly; 25min); Combe Florey (Mon–Sat every 30min, Sun hourly; 35min); Dulverton (Mon–Sat every 2hr; 1hr 25min); Dunster (Mon–Sat every 30min, Sun hourly; 1hr 15min); Glastonbury (Mon–Sat every 2hr; 1hr 20min); London Paddington (4 daily; 3hr 25min–4hr 20min); Minehead (Mon–Sat every 30min, Sun hourly; 1hr 25min); Wells (Mon–Sat 6 daily; 1hr 40min); Yeovil (Mon–Sat hourly, Sun 2 daily; 1hr–1hr 20min).

Tourist office Market House, Fore St (Mon–Sat 9.30am–4.30pm; ☎01823 340470, ⓦvisitsomerset.co.uk/taunton). Provides information and publications on the whole area, including the Quantocks.

ACCOMMODATION AND EATING

Brookfield House 16 Wellington Rd, TA1 4EQ ☎01823 272786, ⓦbrookfieldguesthouse.uk.com. This B&B close to the centre makes for a clean and comfortable stay, though light sleepers should choose rooms at the back. Evening meals can be arranged, and there's limited off-road parking. No under-8s. **£93**

The Castle Castle Green, TA1 1NF ☎01823 272671, ⓦthe-castle-hotel.com. A wisteria-clad, three-hundred-year-old mansion next to Taunton Castle, this hotel has atmospheric public rooms, though some of the bedrooms are fairly ordinary, with dated decor. **£130**

The Cosy Club Hunts Court, Corporation St, TA1 4AJ ☎01823 253476, ⓦcosyclub.co.uk. In a converted Victorian arts college, this bar-restaurant has several rooms across two floors, with comfy chairs and delightfully quirky decor. Coffees, teas and meals are available; burgers cost from £9 and tapas are £12 for three. Mon–Wed & Sun 9am–11pm, Thurs–Sat 9am–12.30am; kitchen daily 9am–10pm.

The Quantock Hills

Extending for some twelve miles north of Taunton, the **Quantock Hills** offer some marvellous hiking opportunities off the beaten track. Its snug villages, many of them

5

boasting beautifully preserved churches, are connected by steep, narrow lanes and set in scenic wooded valleys or "combes" that are watered by clear streams and grazed by red deer.

Nether Stowey and around

The pretty village of **NETHER STOWEY** is best known for its association with **Samuel Taylor Coleridge**, who in 1796 walked here from Bristol to join his wife and child at their new home. Coleridge drew inspiration for some of his best-known works while rambling in the countryside here, and you can pick up a leaflet at his former abode for the **Coleridge Way** (ⓦ coleridgeway.co.uk), a walking route supposedly following the poet's footsteps between Nether Stowey and Lynmouth (see page 298); waymarked with quill signs, the 51-mile hike passes through some of the most scenic tracts of the Quantocks and Exmoor.

Coleridge Cottage

35 Lime St, TA5 1NQ • March–Oct Mon & Thurs–Sun 11am–5pm; early to mid-Dec Sat & Sun 11am–3pm • £6.20; NT • ☎ 01643 821314, ⓦ nationaltrust.org.uk/coleridgecottage

At this "miserable cottage", as Sara Coleridge rather harshly called what is now **Coleridge Cottage**, you can see the poet's parlour, reading room and bedroom, plus an exhibition containing letters and first editions. Rooms are laid out as they would have been in the eighteenth century, and there's a re-creation of the poet's "lime-tree bower" in the garden.

The western Quantocks

On the southwestern edge of the Quantocks, the village of **BISHOPS LYDEARD**, terminus of the restored West Somerset Railway line, is worth a wander, not least for **St Mary's** church, which has a splendid tower and carved bench-ends inside. A couple of miles north, pretty **COMBE FLOREY** is almost exclusively built of the pink-red sandstone characteristic of Quantock villages. For over fifteen years (1829–45), the local rector was the unconventional cleric Sydney Smith, called "the greatest master of ridicule since Swift" by the essayist Macaulay; more recently the village was home to Evelyn Waugh.

A little over three miles further north along the A358, **CROWCOMBE** is another typical cob-and-thatch Quantock village, with a well-preserved Church House from 1515 and a lovely old church with a superb collection of pagan-looking carved bench-ends. A minor road from here winds up to **Triscombe Stone**, in the heart of the Quantocks, from where a footpath leads for about a mile to the range's highest point at **Wills Neck** (1260ft).

Stretching between Wills Neck and the village of Aisholt, the moorland plateau of **Aisholt Common** is best explored from **West Bagborough**, where a five-mile path starts at Birches Corner. Lower down the slopes, outside Aisholt, the banks of **Hawkridge Reservoir** make a lovely picnic stop.

GETTING AROUND   THE QUANTOCK HILLS

By public transport The West Somerset Railway (ⓦ west-somerset-railway.co.uk) stops near some of the villages along the west flank of the range, but public transport actually in the Quantocks is minimal.

ACCOMMODATION AND EATING

★ **The Blue Ball Inn** Triscombe, TA4 3HE ☎ 01984 618242, ⓦ blueball.pub. This secluded inn below Wills Neck has two tastefully decorated B&B rooms, plus meals sourced from neighbouring farms (evening mains £12–16), good local ales and a nice pub garden. Mon–Sat

noon–11pm, Sun noon–7pm; kitchen Mon–Sat noon–2.30pm & 6.30–9pm, Sun noon–4pm. __£75__

Carew Arms Crowcombe, TA4 4AD ☎ 01984 618631, ⓦ thecarewarms.co.uk. Don't be put off by the stags' heads covering the walls and the riding boots by the fire –

this is a delightful rustic pub with a skittles alley and a spacious garden. Local ales complement the top-notch nosh, with mains from £9.50. Half a dozen rooms also available. Easter–Sept daily noon–11pm; Oct–Easter Mon–Sat noon–2.30pm & 5–11pm, Sun noon–6pm. **£50**

Mill Farm Caravan and Camping Park Fiddington, TA5 1JQ, a couple of miles east of Nether Stowey ☎ 01278 732286, ⓦ millfarm.biz. This family-friendly campsite has indoor and outdoor pools (open summer only), a boating lake, a gym and pony rides. Advance booking essential at peak times. Closed Dec to mid-March. **£13.50**

The Old House St Mary St, Nether Stowey, TA5 1LJ ☎ 01278 732392, ⓦ theoldhouse-quantocks.co.uk. This large house in the centre of the village once accommodated Samuel Coleridge. The two rooms – Sarah's Room and the huge Coleridge Suite – are period-furnished, and there's an acre of garden. Self-catering cottages also available (from £350/week). **£85**

★ **Parsonage Farm** Over Stowey, TA5 1HA, a mile south of Nether Stowey ☎ 01278 733237, ⓦ parsonage farm.uk. In the shadow of a lovely old Quantock church, this homely B&B with its own orchard and walled kitchen garden has stone floors, brick fireplaces and heaps of character. Run organically and sustainably by a native of Vermont, it offers a Vermont breakfast among other options, and simple candlelit suppers (£12). **£70**

Exmoor

A high, bare plateau sliced by wooded combes and gurgling streams, **EXMOOR** (ⓦ www. exmoor-nationalpark.gov.uk) can present one of the most forbidding landscapes in England, especially when shrouded in a sea mist. On clear days, though, the moorland of this National Park reveals rich bursts of colour and an amazing diversity of wildlife, from buzzards to the unique **Exmoor ponies**, a breed closely related to prehistoric horses and now endangered; in the treeless heartland of the moor in particular, it's not difficult to spot these short and stocky animals. Much more elusive are the **red deer**, England's largest native wild animal, of which Exmoor supports the country's only wild population.

Endless **walking routes** are possible along a network of some six hundred miles of footpaths and bridleways, and **horseriding** is another option for getting the most out of Exmoor's desolate beauty. Inland, there are four obvious bases for walks, all on the Somerset side of the county border: **Dulverton** in the southeast, site of the main information facilities; **Simonsbath** in the centre; **Exford**, near Exmoor's highest point at Dunkery Beacon; and the attractive village of **Winsford**, close to the A396 on the east of the moor.

Exmoor's coastline offers an alluring alternative to the open moorland, all of it accessible via the **South West Coast Path**, which embarks on its long coastal journey at **Minehead**, though there is more charm to be found further west at the sister villages of **Lynton** and **Lynmouth**, just over the Devon border.

GETTING AROUND EXMOOR

In addition to the sketchy scheduled bus service (ⓦ www.filers.co.uk, ⓦ firstgroup.com & ⓦ quantockheritage.com), the **Moor Rover** provides on-demand transport anywhere within the National Park (and along the Coleridge Way; see page 294) for walkers and bikers – bikes are hitched on the back; call to book a ride at least a day prior to travel (☎ 01643 709701, ⓦ atwest.org.uk).

ACTIVITIES ON EXMOOR

Walking is the activity that draws most people to Exmoor, but there are plenty of other choices. Several operators arrange **nature safaris**, usually small-group 4WD trips taking in wildlife and local history; try Red Stag Safaris (☎ 01643 841831, ⓦ redstagsafari.co.uk; from £35pp). Exmoor Adventures (☎ 01643 863536, ⓦ exmooradventures.co.uk) runs rock climbing, kayaking and other group activities (from £35/person). See the National Park website (ⓦ www. exmoor-nationalpark.gov.uk) for other activity operators. While on the moor, bear in mind that over seventy percent of the National Park is privately owned and that access is theoretically restricted to public rights of way; special permission should certainly be sought before camping, canoeing, fishing or similar.

5

Dulverton and the eastern moor

The village of **DULVERTON**, on Exmoor's southern edge, is the Park Authority's headquarters and makes a good entry point. Five miles north, just west of the A396, **WINSFORD** lays justified claim to being the moor's prettiest hamlet. A scattering of thatched cottages ranged around a sleepy green, it is watered by a confluence of streams and rivers, giving it no fewer than seven bridges; it's a good stopover on the way to the famous beauty spot of **Tarr Steps**, a seventeen-span clapper bridge. Four miles northwest of Winsford, the village of **EXFORD**, an ancient crossing point on the River Exe, is popular with walkers for the four-mile hike to **Dunkery Beacon**, Exmoor's highest point (1704ft).

INFORMATION   DULVERTON AND THE EASTERN MOOR

National Park Visitor Centre 7–9 Fore St, Dulverton (daily: April–Oct 10am–5pm; Nov–March 10.30am–3pm; ☏ 01398 323841, ⊛ www.exmoor-nationalpark.gov.uk).

ACCOMMODATION AND EATING

Royal Oak Winsford, TA24 7JE ☏ 01643 851455, ⊛ royaloakexmoor.co.uk. This thatched and rambling old inn dominates the centre of charming Winsford and offers Exmoor ales, snacks and an extensive restaurant menu (mains from £12). The accommodation is plush (most rooms have four-posters) but does vary, so check first. Mon–Sat noon–2pm & 6.30–8.30pm, Sun (daily in winter) noon–2pm & 6.30–8pm. __£130__

Tongdam 26 High St, Dulverton, TA22 7DJ ☏ 01398 323397, ⊛ tongdam.com. Take a break from English country cooking at this quality Thai outpost (most dishes £12.50–16.50). There's also excellent, tastefully furnished accommodation: two doubles with shared bathroom, and a suite. Mon & Wed–Sun noon–3pm & 6–10.30pm. __£56__

Woods 4 Bank Square, Dulverton, TA22 9BU ☏ 01398

324007, ⊛ woodsdulverton.co.uk. Decorated with a scattering of antlers, boots and riding whips, this gastro-pub offers Gallic-inspired dishes such as confit duck and foie gras terrine, brill fillet and roast guinea fowl (mains £13.50–18.50). Excellent wine list, too. Mon–Sat noon–2pm & 6–9.30pm, Sun noon–2pm & 7–9.30pm.

YHA Exford Exe Mead, Exford, TA24 7PU ☏ 01643 831229, ⊛ yha.org.uk/hostel/exford. Exmoor's main hostel occupies a gabled Victorian house on the banks of the Exe. Camping is also possible, and camping pods (£69) and a bell tent (£95) are available June–Oct. The hostel is owned and operated by the *White Horse*, just across the bridge, where you should go to check in. Camping/person __£12__, dorms __£22__, doubles __£54__

Exmoor Forest and Simonsbath

At the heart of the National Park lies **Exmoor Forest**, the barest (and wettest) part of the moor, scarcely populated except by sheep and a few red deer – the word "forest" denotes simply that it was a king's hunting reserve. In its centre stands the village of **SIMONSBATH** (pronounced "Simmonsbath"), once home to the Knight family, who bought the forest in 1819 and, by introducing tenant farmers, building roads and importing sheep, brought systematic agriculture to an area that had never before produced any income.

ACCOMMODATION AND EATING   EXMOOR FOREST AND SIMONSBATH

★ **Simonsbath House** Simonsbath, TA24 7SH ☏ 01643 831259, ⊛ simonsbathhouse.co.uk. Cosy bolthole offering spacious and swanky rooms with glorious moorland views

and a quality restaurant (three-course meals £25). Self-catering cottages in a converted barn are also available (from £210 for 2 nights). Daily 7–9pm. __£120__

Minehead

The Somerset port of **MINEHEAD** quickly became a favourite Victorian getaway with the arrival of the railway, and it has preserved an upbeat holiday-town atmosphere ever since. Steep lanes link the two quarters of **Higher Town**, on the slopes of North Hill, containing some of the oldest houses, and **Quay Town**, the harbour area. Minehead is a terminus for the diesel and steam trains of the restored **West Somerset**

THE SOUTH WEST COAST PATH

Extending for some **630 miles**, the **South West Coast Path** starts at Minehead and tracks the coastline along the northern seaboard of Somerset and Devon, round Cornwall, back into Devon and on to Dorset, where it finishes close to the entrance to Poole Harbour. Much of the **route** runs on land owned by the National Trust, and all of it is well signposted.

The relevant Ordnance Survey **maps** can be found at most village shops en route, while Aurum Press (ⓦquartoknows.com) produces four *National Trail Guides* covering the route and the **South West Coast Path Association** (☎01752 896237, ⓦsouthwestcoastpath.org.uk) publishes an annual guide to the whole path, including accommodation lists, ferry timetables, tide times and transport details.

Railway (ⓦwest-somerset-railway.co.uk), which curves eastwards into the Quantocks as far as Bishops Lydeard (see page 294), and also for the South West Coast Path (see above), signposted by the harbour.

ARRIVAL AND INFORMATION

MINEHEAD

By bus Bus stops are on or around The Avenue, in the centre of town.

Destinations Bishops Lydeard (Mon–Sat every 30min, Sun hourly; 1hr); Dunster (Mon–Sat every 30min, Sun hourly; 10min); Lynmouth (mid-July to early Sept Mon–Fri & Sun 2 daily; 55min–1hr 5min); Porlock (mid-July to early Sept Mon–Fri & Sun 2 daily; 15–20min); Taunton (Mon–Sat every 30min, Sun hourly; 1hr 20min).

Tourist information The Beach Hotel, The Avenue (Easter–Oct Tues–Sat 10am–4pm, Sun 11am–4pm; Nov–Easter Sat & Sun noon–3pm; ☎01643 702624, ⓦvisit minehead.org).

ACCOMMODATION

Baytree 29 Blenheim Rd, TA24 5PZ ☎01643 703374, ⓦbaytreebandbminehead.co.uk. Victorian B&B facing the public gardens, offering roomy en-suites, including a

family unit (£120). Minimum two-night stay at weekends in July & Aug. No debit/credit cards. No children under 10. **£60**

Dunster

Three miles southeast of Minehead, the old village of **DUNSTER** is the area's major attraction. Its impressive castle rears above its well-preserved High Street, where the octagonal **Yarn Market**, dating from 1609, recalls Dunster's wool-making heyday.

Dunster Castle

TA24 6SL · **Castle** Daily: early March to Oct 11am–5pm; mid- to late Dec 2–7pm; Jan to early March & Nov to mid-Dec tours only (call for times) · £11 (includes grounds); NT · **Grounds** Daily 10am–5pm (or dusk if sooner) · £8; NT · ☎01643 821314, ⓦnationaltrust.org.uk/dunster-castle

A landmark for miles around with its towers and turrets, **Dunster Castle** has parts dating back to the thirteenth century, but most of its fortifications were demolished following the Civil War. The structure was subjected to a thorough Victorian restoration in 1868–72, though its interior preserves much from its earlier incarnations. Highlights include a bedroom once occupied by Charles II, a fine seventeenth-century carved staircase, a richly decorated banqueting hall, and various portraits of the Luttrells, owners of the house for six hundred years. The **grounds** feature terraced gardens and riverside walks, all overlooked by a hilltop folly, **Conygar Tower**, dating from 1775.

INFORMATION

DUNSTER

National Park Visitor Centre At the top of Dunster Steep, by the main car park (Easter–Oct daily 10am–5pm; Nov–Easter Sat & Sun 10am–2pm; ☎01643 821835).

5

ACCOMMODATION AND EATING

Luttrell Arms 36 High St, TA24 6SG ☎01643 821555, ⓦluttrellarms.co.uk. Traditional, atmospheric fifteenth-century inn with open fires and beamed rooms, some with four-posters (the cheaper rooms are smaller and plainer).

The bar and more formal restaurant (mains £15–19) offer decent food, and there's a pleasant garden. Bar daily 11am–11pm; restaurant daily noon–2.30pm & 6–9.30pm. **£140**

Porlock and around

Six miles west of Minehead, cupped on three sides by the hogbacked hills of Exmoor, the thatch-and-cob houses and distinctive charm of **PORLOCK** draw armies of tourists. Many come for the village's literary links: according to Coleridge's less-than-reliable testimony, it was a "man from Porlock" who broke the opium trance in which he was composing *Kubla Khan*, while the High Street's fourteenth-century *Ship Inn* features prominently in the Exmoor romance *Lorna Doone* and, in real life, sheltered the poet Robert Southey when he got caught in a storm. Just two miles west yet feeling refreshingly remote, the tiny harbour of **PORLOCK WEIR** is a tranquil spot for a breath of sea air and a drink.

ARRIVAL AND INFORMATION

By bus The main stop is by St Dubricius church, High St.
Destinations Lynmouth (mid-July to early Sept Mon–Fri & Sun 2 daily; 50min); Minehead (mid-July to early Sept Mon–Fri & Sun 2 daily; 20min).

Tourist information The Old School Centre, West End, High St (Easter–Oct Mon–Fri 10am–12.30pm & 2–5pm, Sat 10am–5pm; Nov–Easter Tues–Fri 10am–12.30pm, Sat 10am–1pm; ☎01643 863150, ⓦporlock.co.uk).

ACCOMMODATION AND EATING

★**Glen Lodge** Hawkcombe, TA24 8LN ☎01643 863371, ⓦglenlodge.net. At the top of Parson's Lane, running south from St Dubricius on the High St, this beautifully furnished Victorian B&B offers perfect seclusion, comfort and character. There are distant sea views from the rooms and access to the moor right behind. No credit cards. **£100**

Lorna Doone Hotel High St, TA24 8PS ☎01643 862404, ⓦlornadoonehotel.co.uk. This thoroughly Victorian lodging offers rooms of varying sizes (and prices), all clean, comfortable and en suite. The restaurant delivers well-prepared dishes ranging from pasta to steak and

ale pie (mains from £9). Mon–Sat 6–9pm, Sun noon–2.30pm. **£65**

★**Millers at the Anchor** Porlock Weir, TA24 8PB ☎01643 862753, ⓦmillersattheanchor.co.uk. This eccentric, curio-stuffed hotel, pitched as a "hunting lodge by the sea", enjoys a superb setting on tranquil Porlock Weir's miniature harbourfront. The rooms – it's worth paying more for the lovely harbour views – are great. In the equally atmospheric restaurant, sandwiches, pizzas (in summer) and full meals are served at lunchtime, dinners are available in the evening (mains around £15). Daily noon–3pm & 6.30–9pm. **£90**

Lynmouth and around

Eleven miles west of Porlock, at the junction and estuary of the East and West Lyn rivers and just inside Devon, **LYNMOUTH** is where the poet Percy Shelley spent his nine-week honeymoon with his 16-year-old bride Harriet Westbrook, writing his polemical *Queen Mab*. The village is linked to Lynton, some 500ft above, by an ingenious water-driven **cliff railway** (mid-Feb to mid-Nov daily, generally 10am–7pm, though closing times vary; £3.80 return; ⓦcliffrailwaylynton.co.uk), or walkable along an adjacent zigzagging path. At the top of the village, you can explore the walks and waterfalls and an exhibition on the uses of waterpower in the wooded **Glen Lyn Gorge** (Easter–Oct most days 10am–6pm; call for winter opening; £6; ☎01598 753207, ⓦwww.theglenlyngorge.co.uk), all the more poignant given that the village was almost washed away by flooding in August 1952, when 34 people lost their lives. The owners of the Gorge also run **boat trips** (April–Sept; £10; ☎01598 753207) from the harbour to Lee Bay and back – a great opportunity to view the cliffs and the birdlife that thrives on them.

A beautiful mile-and-a-half walk follows the river east from Lynmouth to where the East Lyn River joins Hoar Oak Water at the aptly named **Watersmeet**, one of Exmoor's most celebrated beauty spots, overlooked by two slender bridges.

ARRIVAL AND INFORMATION   LYNMOUTH AND AROUND

By bus The stop is in Lyndale coach park, next to the Gorge. Destinations Lynton (Mon–Sat 4–5 daily, Sun July & Aug 1 daily; 8min); Minehead (mid-July to early Sept Mon–Fri & Sun 2 daily; 55min–1hr 5min); Porlock (mid-July to early Sept Mon–Fri & Sun 2 daily; 35–50min).

National Park Visitor Centre Lynmouth Pavilion, The Esplanade (daily 10am–5pm; ☎01598 752509).

ACCOMMODATION AND EATING

Rising Sun Harbourside, EX35 6EG ☎01598 753223, ⓦrisingsunlynmouth.co.uk. The stylish rooms in this fourteenth-century harbourfront inn all have the requisite beams and sloping floors. The pub and restaurant are equally atmospheric, and attract crowds with their classic English dishes of steak and lamb, plus plenty of seafood (from £14) – there are few vegetarian options. Bar Mon–Sat 11am–11pm, Sun 11am–10.30pm; kitchen daily noon–2.30pm & 6–9pm in bar, 6.30–8.30pm in restaurant. **£160**

Lynton

The Victorian resort of **LYNTON** perches above a lofty gorge with splendid views over the sea. Almost completely cut off from the rest of the country for most of its history, the village struck lucky during the Napoleonic Wars, when frustrated Grand Tourists – unable to visit their usual continental haunts – discovered in Lynton a domestic piece of alpine landscape, nicknaming the area "Little Switzerland". Samuel Taylor Coleridge and William Hazlitt trudged over to Lynton from the Quantocks, but the greatest spur to the village's popularity came with the publication in 1869 of R.D. Blackmore's Exmoor melodrama *Lorna Doone*, based on the outlaw clans who inhabited these parts in the seventeenth century.

ARRIVAL AND INFORMATION   LYNTON

By bus Buses stop in Castle Hill car park and on Lee Rd. Destinations Barnstaple (Mon–Sat hourly; 50min–1hr 10min); Ilfracombe (early July to Aug Mon–Fri 2 daily, Sun 1 daily; 55min); Lynmouth (Mon–Sat 5–6 daily, Sun July & Aug 1 daily; 6min).

Tourist information Town Hall, Lee Rd (Tues–Thurs & Sat 10am–3pm; ☎01598 752225, ⓦlynton-lynmouth-tourism.co.uk).

ACCOMMODATION AND EATING

★ **North Walk House** North Walk, EX35 6HJ ☎01598 753372, ⓦnorthwalkhouse.co.uk. Top-quality B&B in a superb position overlooking the sea, and convenient for the coast path. The spacious, stylish rooms have wooden floors bedecked in rugs, and two have wrought-iron beds. Breakfasts are filling and delicious, and three-course organic dinners are available to guests for £30/person. Self-catering accommodation (from £203 for 3 nights) also available. **£136**

Sunny Lyn Lynbridge, EX35 6NS ☎01598 753384, ⓦsunnylyn.co.uk. You can camp next to the West Lyn River at this tranquil spot within a 20min walk from Lynton, with an on-site shop and café (limited opening in low season), and static caravans and lodges available for rent (minimum two-night stay, or four night in peak season). It's small, so booking is essential. Camping and caravans closed Nov to mid-March. Camping/person **£6.75**, lodges and caravans **£75**

Vanilla Pod 10–12 Queens St, EX35 6AA ☎01598 753706. Good, wholesome meals are served at this friendly place, which is both café-bar and restaurant, with Mediterranean and Middle Eastern leanings. Most mains, such as pork belly and grilled sea bass, cost £12–16. Daily 10am–4pm & 6pm–late; summer school hols daily 10am–late; reduced opening in winter.

Devon and Cornwall

EDEN PROJECT, CORNWALL

Devon and Cornwall

At England's western extremity, the counties of Devon and Cornwall encompass everything from genteel, cosy villages to vast Atlantic-facing strands of golden sand and wild expanses of granite moorland. The winning combination of rural peace and first-class beaches lends the peninsula a particular appeal to outdoors enthusiasts, and the local galleries, museums and restaurants provide plenty of rainy-day diversions. Together, these attractions have made the region perennially popular, so much so that tourism has replaced the traditional occupations of fishing and farming as the main source of employment and income. The authentic character of Devon and Cornwall may be obscured during the summer season, but avoid the peak periods and you can't fail to be seduced by their considerable charms.

If it's wilderness you're after, nothing can beat the remoter tracts of **Dartmoor**, the greatest of the West Country's granite massifs, much of which retains its solitude despite its proximity to the region's two major cities. Of these, **Exeter** is by far the more interesting, dominated by the twin towers of its medieval cathedral and offering a rich selection of restaurants and nightlife. As for **Plymouth**, much of this great naval port was destroyed by bombing during World War II, though some of the city's Elizabethan core has survived.

The coastline on either side of Exeter and Plymouth enjoys more hours of sunshine than anywhere else on the British mainland, and there is some justification in **South Devon**'s principal resort, Torquay, styling itself the capital of the "English Riviera". St Tropez it ain't, but there's no denying a certain glamour, alloyed with an old-fashioned charm that the seaside towns of **East Devon** and the cliff-backed resorts of **North Devon** share.

Cornwall too has its pockets of concentrated tourist development – chiefly at Falmouth, the main resort in **Southeast Cornwall**, and Newquay, a major draw for surfers on **Cornwall's Atlantic coast** due to its fine west-facing beaches. **St Ives** is another crowd-puller, though the town has a separate identity as an arts centre. Further up Cornwall's long north coast, Tintagel's ruined castle and the rock-walled harbour of Boscastle have an almost embattled character in the face of the turbulent sea. However, the full elemental power of the ocean can best be appreciated on the western headlands of Lizard Point and Land's End – on the **Lizard and Penwith peninsulas**, respectively – where the cliffs resound to the thunder of the waves, or offshore on Lundy Island and the distant **Isles of Scilly**.

Inland, the mild climate has enabled a slew of gardens to flourish, none quirkier than the **Eden Project**, with its science-fiction-style "biomes". You'll find nature in a rawer guise on **Bodmin Moor**, a great opportunity to escape the crowds.

GETTING AROUND   DEVON AND CORNWALL

Getting around the West Country by **public transport** can be a convoluted and lengthy process, especially in remoter areas.

Walking on Dartmoor p.317
Firing ranges on Dartmoor p.319
Sir Francis Drake p.324
The Tarka Line and the Tarka Trail p.326

Surfing in North Devon p.327
Lundy Island p.328
King Arthur in Cornwall p.350

HAYTOR, DARTMOOR

Highlights

❶ Hiking on Dartmoor Experience this bleakly beautiful landscape along a good network of paths. See page 317

❷ Surfing in North Devon The endless ranks of rollers pounding Devon's west-facing northern coast – above all at Woolacombe, Croyde and Saunton – draw surfers of every ability. See page 327

❸ The Eden Project Embark on a voyage of discovery around the planet's ecosystems at this disused clay pit, now home to a fantastic array of exotic plants and crops. See page 331

❹ St Ives Fine-sand beaches, a brace of renowned galleries and a maze of tiny lanes give this bustling harbour town a feel-good vibe. See page 342

❺ Cornish beaches Cornwall has some of the country's best beaches, mostly in fabulous settings. Beauties include Newquay, plus Whitesand Bay, the Isles of Scilly, Bude and, overlooked by dramatic black crags, Porthcurno. See page 347

❻ Seafood in Padstow The local catch goes straight into the excellent restaurants of the southwestern peninsula. Padstow, where celebrity chef Rick Stein owns a number of places, is a great culinary hotspot. See page 349

HIGHLIGHTS ARE MARKED ON THE MAP ON PAGE 304

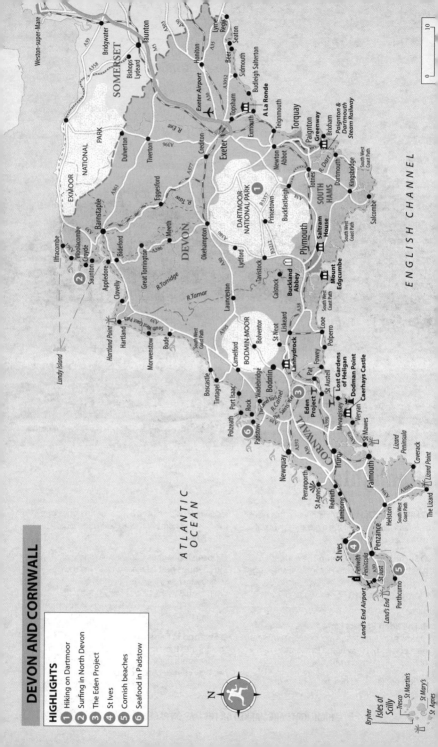

DEVON AND CORNWALL

HIGHLIGHTS

1. Hiking on Dartmoor
2. Surfing in North Devon
3. The Eden Project
4. St Ives
5. Cornish beaches
6. Seafood in Padstow

By train You can reach Exeter, Plymouth, Bodmin, Truro and Penzance by train on the main rail lines from London and the Midlands, with branch lines linking Falmouth (from Truro), Newquay (from Par) and St Ives (from St Erth). The frequent London Waterloo–Exeter service makes several useful stops in Devon, at Axminster, Feniton, Honiton and Pinhoe.

By bus Buses from the chief towns fan out along the coasts and into the interior, though the service can be rudimentary (or completely nonexistent) for the smaller villages.

South West Coast Path The best way of exploring the coast of Devon and Cornwall is on foot along the South West Coast Path (⟲ southwestcoastpath.org.uk; see page 297), England's longest waymarked trail (at least until the England Coast Path is completed).

6

Exeter

EXETER has more historical sights than any other town in Devon or Cornwall, legacies of an eventful existence dating from its Celtic foundation and the establishment here of the most westerly Roman outpost. After the Roman withdrawal, Exeter was refounded by Alfred the Great and by the time of the Norman Conquest had become one of the largest towns in England, profiting from its position on the banks of the River Exe. The expansion of the wool trade in the Tudor period sustained the city until the eighteenth century. Since then, Exeter has maintained its status as Devon's commercial and cultural hub, despite having much of its ancient centre gutted by World War II bombing.

Exeter Cathedral

Cathedral Close, EX1 1HS • Mon–Sat 9am–5.30pm, Sun 11.30am–5.30pm • £7.50 • **North Tower tours** Usually May–Sept twice weekly, check in advance; 30min • £3.50 • **Roof tours** Usually July–Sept Tues & Sat, check in advance; 1hr 30min–2hr • £5 • ☎ 01392 255573, ⟲ exeter-cathedral.org.uk

The most distinctive feature of the city's skyline, **Exeter Cathedral** is a stately monument with two great Norman towers flanking the nave. Close up, it's the façade's ornate Gothic screen that commands attention: its three tiers of sculpted (and very weathered) figures – including Alfred, Athelstan, Cnut, William the Conqueror and Richard II – were begun around 1360, part of a rebuilding programme which left only the towers from the original twelfth-century construction.

Entering the cathedral, you're confronted by the longest unbroken **Gothic ceiling** in the world, its **bosses** vividly painted – one, towards the west front, shows the murder of Thomas Becket. The **Lady Chapel** and **Chapter House** – at the far end of the building and off the right transept respectively – are thirteenth-century, but the main part of the nave, including the lavish rib vaulting, dates from a century later. There are many fine examples of sculpture from this period, including, in the minstrels' gallery high up on the left side, angels playing musical instruments, and, below them, figures of Edward III and Queen Philippa. In the **Choir** don't miss the 60ft **bishop's throne** or the **misericords** – decorated with mythological figures and dating from around 1260, they are thought to be the oldest in the country. Outside, a graceful statue of the theologian Richard Hooker surveys **Cathedral Close**, a motley mixture of architectural styles from Tudor to Regency, though most display Exeter's trademark red brickwork. For a glimpse of the cathedral's clock mechanism and spectacular views across the city, consider joining one of the guided **tours** of the roof.

The Guildhall

High St, EX4 3LN • Generally Mon–Fri 10.30am–1pm & 2–4pm, Sat 10.30am–1pm, but subject to change at short notice; call ahead • Free • ☎ 01392 665500

Some older structures still stand amid the banal concrete of the modern town centre, including, on the pedestrianized High Street, Exeter's finest civic building, the fourteenth-century **Guildhall**, which is claimed to be England's oldest municipal building still in regular use. It's fronted by an elegant Renaissance portico and merits a glance inside for its main chamber, whose arched roof timbers rest on carved bears holding staves, symbols of the Yorkist cause during the fifteenth-century Wars of the Roses.

RAMM (Royal Albert Memorial Museum)

Queen St, EX4 3RX • Tues–Sun 10am–5pm • Free • ☎ 01392 265858, ⓦ rammuseum.org.uk

RAMM is the closest thing in Devon to a county museum. Exuding the Victorian spirit of wide-ranging curiosity, it includes everything from a menagerie of stuffed animals to mock-ups of the various building styles used at different periods in the city. The collections of silverware, watches and clocks contrast nicely with the colourful ethnography section, and the picture gallery has some good specimens of West Country art.

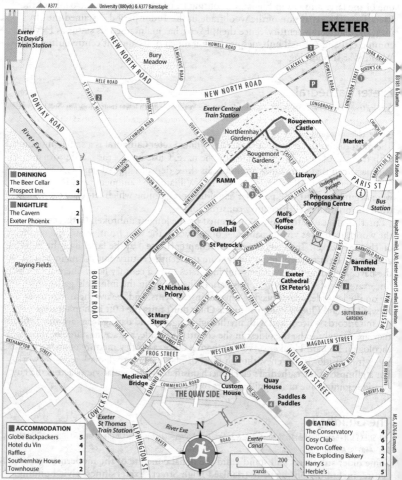

EXETER

DRINKING
The Beer Cellar	3
Prospect Inn	4

NIGHTLIFE
The Cavern	2
Exeter Phoenix	1

ACCOMMODATION
Globe Backpackers	5
Hotel du Vin	4
Raffles	1
Southernhay House	2
Townhouse	3

EATING
The Conservatory	4
Cosy Club	6
Devon Coffee	3
The Exploding Bakery	2
Harry's	1
Herbie's	5

Underground passages

Paris St, EX1 1GA • June–Sept & school hols Mon–Sat 9.30am–5.30pm, Sun 10.30am–4pm; Oct–May Tues–Fri 10.30am–4.30pm, Sat
9.30am–5.30pm, Sun 11.30am–4pm; last tour 1hr before closing • £6 • ☎ 01392 665887, Ⓦ exeter.gov.uk/passages

Off the top end of the High Street, the Princesshay shopping precinct holds the
entrance to a network of **underground passages**. First excavated in the fourteenth
century to bring water to the cathedral precincts, they're now visitable on a guided
tour – not recommended for claustrophobes.

The Quayside

The **River Exe** marks the old city's southwestern boundary; today, the **Quayside** is mostly
devoted to leisure activities. Pubs, shops and cafés share space with handsomely restored
nineteenth-century warehouses and the smart **Custom House**, built in 1681, its opulence
reflecting the former importance of the cloth trade. The area comes into its own at night,
but is worth a wander at any time; you can rent bikes and canoes here, too (see below).

ARRIVAL AND DEPARTURE   EXETER

By plane Exeter's airport is 6 miles east of the centre, just
off the A30. Stagecoach buses #56A and #56B connect
the airport with the bus station on Paris Street (roughly
hourly; 20min).

Destinations London City (1–3 daily; 1hr 5min);
Manchester (1–3 daily; 1hr 5min); St Mary's, Isles of Scilly
(mid-March to early Nov Mon–Sat 1–4 daily; 1hr).

By train Exeter has two main stations, Exeter Central and St
David's, the latter a 15min uphill walk or 10min bus ride from
the city centre. South West trains from Salisbury stop at both,
as do trains on the branch lines to Barnstaple and Exmouth,
but most long-distance trains stop at St David's only.

Destinations Barnstaple (Mon–Sat hourly, Sun 7 daily; 1hr

15min); Bodmin (every 30min–1hr 30min; 1hr 30min–2hr);
Liskeard (every 30min–1hr 30min; 1hr 25min–1hr 50min);
London (every 30min–1hr; 2hr 10min–3hr 30min); Par
(every 30min–1hr 30min; 2hr); Penzance (every 30min–
1hr 30min; 3hr–3hr 10min); Plymouth (every 30min–1hr
30min; 1hr); Torquay (1–3 hourly; 40min–1hr); Totnes (1–3
hourly; 35min); Truro (every 30min–1hr 30min; 2hr 30min).
By bus The bus station is on Paris St, one block north of
the tourist office.
Destinations Penzance (1 daily; 4hr 50min); Plymouth
(every 1–2hr; 1hr 15min–1hr 50min); Sidmouth (1–2
hourly; 55min); Torquay (roughly hourly; 1hr–1hr 15min);
Truro (2 daily; 3hr 15min).

INFORMATION AND ACTIVITIES

Tourist office Dix's Field, off Princesshay (Mon–Sat: April–
Sept 9am–5pm, Oct–March 9.30am–4.30pm; ☎ 01392
665700, Ⓦ visitexeter.com).
Saddles & Paddles On the quayside (☎ 01392 424241,

Ⓦ sadpad.com). You can rent bikes here (£16/day), as well
as kayaks (£10 for the first hour and £5/hr thereafter) to
explore the Exeter Canal, which runs 5 miles to Topsham
and beyond.

ACCOMMODATION

Globe Backpackers 71 Holloway St, EX2 4JD ☎ 01392
215521, Ⓦ exeterbackpackers.co.uk; map p.306. Clean
and central (though a bit of a hike from the stations), this
hostel has a kitchen with free tea and coffee. Dorms have
six to ten beds and there are a few private rooms too.
No check-in 1–3.30pm. Dorms __£17.50__, doubles __£45__
Hotel du Vin Magdalen St, EX2 4HY ☎ 01392 790120,
Ⓦ hotelduvin.com/locations/exeter; map p.306. A
red-brick former eye hospital has been jazzed up to create
a contemporary hotel with quirky details. Rooms are full of
funky charm – those higher up are bigger and better (and
rooms at the back are quieter). There's a French-inspired
bistro, a spa and a great indoor/outdoor pool. __£125__
Raffles 11 Blackall Rd, EX4 4HD ☎ 01392 270200,
Ⓦ www.raffles-exeter.co.uk; map p.306. The rooms
in this elegant Victorian B&B are furnished with Pre-

Raphaelite etchings and other items from the owner's
antiques business. Breakfasts make use of the B&B's
organic home-grown produce. __£85__
★ **Southernhay House** 36 Southernhay East, EX1
1NX ☎ 01392 435324, Ⓦ southernhayhouse.com;
map p.306. Attractive, individually themed rooms in
a renovated nineteenth-century townhouse, with plush
carpets and – in the best rooms – freestanding bathtubs.
Breakfast is included as standard, but cheaper room-only
rates are available. __£125__
Townhouse 54 St David's Hill, EX4 4DT ☎ 01392
494994, Ⓦ townhouseexeter.co.uk; map p.306. This
Edwardian guesthouse midway between the train stations
backs onto a churchyard and has a garden and generous
breakfasts. Rooms are modern but some bathrooms are
small. __£77__

6

EATING

The Conservatory 18 North St, EX4 3QS ☎01392 273858, ⓦtheconservatoryrestaurant.co.uk; map p.306. Centrally located, semiformal restaurant popular for its fresh fish dishes (including grilled sole from Cornwall) and Devon wine. The £10 two-course lunch is great value. Tues–Sat noon–2pm & 5.30–9pm.

Cosy Club 1 Southernhay Gardens, EX1 1SG ☎01392 848744, ⓦcosyclub.co.uk; map p.306. The institutional setting of this place in a former hospital wing is offset by the zany decor – a retro confection of flouncy lampshades, mismatched furniture, anatomical prints and animal skulls. It's a great spot for brunches, coffees, tapas (£12 for 3) and burgers (£9–14). Daily 9am–11pm; food until 10pm.

★ **Devon Coffee** 88 Queen St, EX4 3RP ☎07796 678559, ⓦfacebook.com/devoncoffeeshop; map p.306. Relaxed, independent coffee shop, all stressed wood and chalkboards. The brownies here (£2.80) are very good, as is the coffee. A second branch at 19 Heavitree Rd serves pizzas Fri & Sat eves. Mon–Sat 8am–6pm, Sun 10am–4pm.

★ **The Exploding Bakery** 1b Central Crescent, Queen St, EX4 3SB, next to Exeter Central station ☎01392 427900, ⓦexplodingbakery.com/cafe; map p.306. Slurp top-quality coffee (just £3 a cup) as you watch sweet-smelling cakes being pulled out of the ovens at this busy little wholesale bakery, which has plenty of art on the walls. Mon–Fri 8am–4pm, Sat 9am–4pm.

Harry's 86 Longbrook St, EX4 6AP ☎01392 202234, ⓦharrysrestaurants.co.uk; map p.306. In a converted Victorian stonemason's workshop, this place attracts a cheery crowd with its good-value Mexican and Italian staples (mains £10–15). Daily 9am–2.30pm & 6–11pm.

★ **Herbie's** 15 North St, EX4 3QS ☎01392 258473, ⓦfacebook.com/HerbiesVegetarian; map p.306. Friendly, dimly lit place serving up great vegan, vegetarian and wholefood dishes (most mains around £11) plus organic beers and wines and local ice cream. Mon 11am–2.30pm, Tues–Fri 11am–2.30pm & 6–9.30pm, Sat 11am–3.30pm & 6–9.30pm.

DRINKING

The Beer Cellar 2 South St, EX1 1DZ ☎01392 757570, ⓦfacebook.com/thebeercellarexeter; map p.306. This friendly corner bar near the cathedral does great local beer on tap and bottled from around the world. Look out for ales from Devon's Branscombe Vale Brewery. Daily 11am–11pm.

Prospect Inn The Quay, EX2 4AN ☎01392 273152, ⓦheavitreebrewery.co.uk; map p.306. You can eat and drink outside at this seventeenth-century riverside pub, which was the setting for TV drama *The Onedin Line*. Mon–Thurs & Sun 10am–11pm, Fri & Sat 10am–midnight.

NIGHTLIFE

The Cavern 83–84 Queen St, EX4 3RP ☎01392 495370, ⓦexetercavern.com; map p.306. A long-established hub of Exeter's music scene, this subterranean haunt is best known for its live bands (think indie, punk and metal) but it also has more diverse club nights and is open for daytime snacks. Daily 11am–5pm & 8pm–late.

Exeter Phoenix Bradlynch Place, Gandy St, EX4 3LS ☎01392 667080, ⓦexeterphoenix.org.uk; map p.306. Live music and comedy are among the cultural offerings at this arts centre, which also hosts films, exhibitions and readings and has a relaxed café-bar. Mon–Sat 10am–11pm, sometimes Sun for events.

East Devon

Quiet, coastal **East Devon** is best known for its elegant nineteenth-century resorts, prime among them **Sidmouth**. But there are plenty of other spots worth visiting along the fossil-rich Jurassic Coast (ⓦjurassiccoast.org), which stretches from the white sands of **Exmouth** via the smugglers' village of **Beer**, all the way to the Isle of Purbeck in Dorset (see page 210).

Exmouth and around

EXMOUTH, ten miles south of Exeter, started as a Roman port and went on to become the first of the county's resorts to be popularized by holiday-makers in the late eighteenth century. Overlooking lawns, rock pools and a respectable two miles of sandy **beach**, Exmouth's Georgian terraced houses once accommodated the wives of Nelson and Byron, installed at nos. 6 and 19 The Beacon respectively (on a rise overlooking the seafront, above the public gardens). Today it's a relaxed spot that attracts a steady stream of visitors – both from Exeter and, in the summer, from other beach resorts along the south coast.

A La Ronde

Off the A376, EX8 5BD, 2 miles north of Exmouth • Mid-Feb to Oct daily 11am–5pm • £8.90; NT • ☎ 01395 265514, ⓦ nationaltrust.org. uk/a-la-ronde • Take bus #57 from Exmouth or Exeter and get off at the Courtlands Cross stop

The Gothic folly of **A La Ronde** was the creation of two spinster cousins, Jane and Mary Parminter, who in the 1790s were inspired by their European Grand Tour to build a **sixteen-sided house**, possibly based on the Byzantine basilica of San Vitale in Ravenna. The end product is filled with mementos of the Parminters' travels as well as a number of their more offbeat creations, such as a frieze made of feathers culled from game birds and chickens. In the upper rooms are a gallery and staircase completely covered in shells, too fragile to be visited, though part can be glimpsed from the octagonal room on the first floor. Superb views over the Exe estuary extend from the second-floor dormer windows.

ARRIVAL AND DEPARTURE — EXMOUTH AND AROUND

By train Regular Exeter trains arrive at and leave from the station on Marine Way, a short walk north of the centre.
By bus Buses pull in by the train station; #57 links the town frequently with Exeter.

Destinations Budleigh Salterton (Mon–Sat 2 hourly, Sun hourly; 15–20min); Exeter (Mon–Sat every 15min, Sun every 30min; 40min); Sidmouth (Mon–Sat hourly, Sun 4 daily; 50min–1hr).

Sidmouth

Set amid a shelf of crumbling red sandstone, **SIDMOUTH** is the stately queen of East Devon's resorts. The cream-and-white town boasts nearly five hundred buildings listed as having special historic or architectural interest, among them the grand Georgian homes of **York Terrace** behind the Esplanade. Both the mile-long, pebbly main town beach and **Jacob's Ladder**, a cliff-backed shingle and sand strip to the west of town, are easily accessible and well tended. To the east, the coast path climbs steep Salcombe Hill to follow cliffs that give sanctuary to a range of birdlife. Further on, the path descends to meet one of the most isolated and attractive beaches in the area, **Weston Mouth**.

Sidmouth hosts what many consider to be the country's best **folk festival** over eight days in early August. It's an upbeat affair: folk and roots artists from around the country perform in marquees, pubs and hotels around town, and there are numerous ceilidhs and pavement buskers. For detailed information, see ⓦ sidmouthfolkweek.co.uk.

ARRIVAL AND INFORMATION — SIDMOUTH

By bus Most services depart from Sidmouth Triangle on Station Rd. From Exeter, take bus #9 or #9A (1–2 hourly; 50min).
Tourist office Ham Lane, off the eastern end of the

Esplanade (May–Sept Mon–Sat 10am–5pm, Sun 10am–4pm; Oct–April Mon–Sat 10am–1.30pm; ☎ 01395 516441, ⓦ visitsidmouth.co.uk). Head here for information on bay cruises and free guided walks around the area.

ACCOMMODATION

Cheriton Guest House 9 Vicarage Rd, EX10 8UQ ☎ 01395 513810, ⓦ cheriton-guesthouse.co.uk. This B&B has spotless, mostly spacious rooms (one with a balcony), those at the back overlooking a leafy garden leading down to the River Sid. There's a lounge and car park, and the seafront is less than a 10min walk away. **£80**

Oakdown Gatedown Lane, Weston, EX10 0PT ☎ 01297

680387, ⓦ oakdown.co.uk. Spacious, well-maintained campsite some three miles east of Sidmouth off the A3052 (there's some road noise). Camping pods (£50 for 2; max 4 people for £57) and "Shepherd Huts" (£90; max 2 people) are also available for two nights or more, and pubs are nearby. There's a three-night minimum stay on bank hols, or seven nights in Folk Week. Closed early Nov to mid-March. **£21**

EATING AND DRINKING

The Dairy Shop 5 Church St, EX10 8LY ☎ 01395 513018. Stacked wall to wall with chutneys, gooseberry wine, biscuits and the like, this shop and café is a good spot for soups (£5), savoury crêpes (£6–7) or an ice cream – try the knickerbocker glory. Mon–Sat: April–Sept 9am–5pm; Oct–March 10am–4pm.

Swan Inn 37 York St, EX10 8BY ☎ 01395 512849, ⓦ rampubcompany.co.uk. Close to the tourist office, this convivial but slightly run-down pub with a garden serves real ales, baguettes, plus meat and fish dishes (sirloin steak £14.95). Mon–Sat 11am–11pm, Sun noon–11pm; kitchen Mon–Sat noon–2pm & 6–9pm, Sun noon–2pm & 7–9pm.

Beer and around

Eight miles east of Sidmouth, the largely unspoilt fishing village of **BEER** lies huddled within a small sheltered cove between gleaming white headlands. A stream rushes along a deep channel dug into Beer's main street, and if you can ignore the crowds in high summer much of the village looks unchanged since the time when it was a smugglers' haven. While away a sunny afternoon here fishing for mackerel in the bay, for example on the *Lillie May* (£8/person; ☎ 01297 23455 or ☎ 07779 040491), or pull up a deckchair and tuck into a couple of fresh crab sandwiches on the beach.

The area around Beer is known for its quarries, which were worked from Roman times until the nineteenth century: **Beer stone** was used in many of Devon's churches and houses, and as far afield as London. You can visit **Beer Quarry Caves** (tours daily April–Sept 10am–4.30pm, Oct 10am–3.30pm, school hols closes 1hr later; £8; ☎ 01297 680282, ⓦ beerquarrycaves.co.uk), which includes an exhibit on pieces carved by medieval masons.

ARRIVAL AND DEPARTURE   BEER AND AROUND

By bus Beer is connected to Sidmouth by bus #899 (Mon–Sat 3–4 daily; 35min).

ACCOMMODATION AND EATING

Bay View Fore St, EX12 3EE ☎ 01297 20489, ⓦ bayview guesthousebeer.com. Close to the beach and harbour, most of the rooms in this bright B&B overlook the sea. Abundant breakfasts in the attached café, which does crab sandwiches to take away (£7), include smoked haddock and waffles with maple syrup. Closed Nov–Easter. **£80**

Steamers New Cut, EX12 3DU ☎ 01297 22922, ⓦ steamersrestaurant.co.uk. Family-run restaurant on a quiet alley just up from the harbour. The fresh fish dishes are the main reason to come here, with locally caught monkfish, plaice and brill (£16–18) featuring on the menu. Tues–Sat 10am–1.45pm & 6.45–9pm, Sun call ahead.

South Devon

Southwest of Exeter, the wedge of land that comprises **South Devon** is a mix of traditional seaside resorts, striking coastline and rich agricultural hinterland. With its marina and fairy lights, **Torquay** comes closest to living up to the self-styled "English Riviera" sobriquet of this stretch of coast, while **Brixham**, further south, is still essentially a fishing port, despite the tourist deluge every summer. Inland, things get quieter around **Totnes**, a historic river-port that makes an agreeable base for exploring the region. Eight miles downstream, the estuary town of **Dartmouth** retains its strong medieval flavour, while the sailing resort of **Salcombe** is a good starting point for exploring the dramatic coast to either side.

Torquay and around

Sporting a mini-corniche and promenades landscaped with palm trees and ornate flowerbeds, **TORQUAY** appealingly blends a quasi-continental flavour with its air of a classic English resort. The town's transformation from a fishing village began with its establishment as a fashionable haven for invalids, among them the consumptive

Elizabeth Barrett Browning, who spent three years here. The resort centres on the small **harbour** and marina, separated by limestone cliffs from **Abbey Sands**, its main beach.

Torre Abbey

The King's Drive, TQ2 5JE • Tues–Sun 10am–5pm • £8 • ☎ 01803 293593, ⓦ torre-abbey.org.uk

The Norman abbey that once stood here was razed by Henry VIII, though a gatehouse, tithe barn, chapter house and tower escaped demolition. **Torre Abbey** now contains a good museum, set in pretty ornamental gardens, with collections of silver and glass, window designs by Edward Burne-Jones, illustrations by William Blake, and nineteenth-century and contemporary works of art.

Living Coasts

Beacon Quay, TQ1 2BG • Daily: Easter to early July & early Sept to Oct 10am–5pm, last entry 4pm; early July to early Sept 10am–6pm, last entry 4.30pm; Nov–Easter 10am–4pm, last entry 3pm • £11.80 • ☎ 01803 202470, ⓦ livingcoasts.org.uk

At the northern end of Torquay harbour, **Living Coasts** is home to a variety of fauna and flora found on British shores, including puffins, penguins and seals. There are reconstructed beaches, cliff faces and an estuary, as well as underwater viewing areas and a huge meshed aviary. The rooftop café and restaurant have splendid panoramic views.

The beaches

East of Torquay's harbour, you can follow the shore round to some good sand beaches. **Meadfoot Beach**, one of the busiest, is reached by crossing Daddyhole Plain, named after a large chasm in the adjacent cliff caused by a landslide, but locally attributed to the devil ("Daddy"). North of the Hope's Nose promontory, the coast path leads to a string of less crowded beaches, including **Babbacombe Beach**, **Watcombe** and **Maidencombe**.

ARRIVAL AND INFORMATION

TORQUAY AND AROUND

By train Torquay's main station is off Rathmore Rd, southwest of Torre Abbey Gardens. There are regular trains to/from Exeter (1–3 hourly; 40min–1hr).

By bus Most buses stop on Lymington Rd (a short walk north of the centre), or on The Strand, close to the marina. Destinations Exeter (12–15 daily; 45min–1hr 10min);

Totnes (Mon–Sat every 30min, Sun hourly; 45min).

Tourist office Vaughan Parade, by the harbour (June–Sept & school hols Mon–Sat 10am–1pm & 1.30–5pm, Sun 10am–1pm & 1.30–3pm; Oct–May Mon–Wed, Fri & Sat 10am–1pm & 1.30–5pm, Sun 10am–1pm & 1.30–3pm; ☎ 0844 474 2233, ⓦ englishriviera.co.uk).

ACCOMMODATION

Exton House 12 Bridge Rd, TQ2 5BA ☎ 01803 293561, ⓦ extonhotel.co.uk. Small, clean and quiet B&B a 10min walk from the train station (free pick-up is usually offered), and just 15min from the centre. The guests' lounge has a balcony, and there's a licensed bar. Book direct for the best rates. **£60**

Torquay Backpackers 119 Abbey Rd, TQ2 5NP ☎ 01803 299924, ⓦ torquaybackpackers.co.uk. Friendly hostel a 15min walk northeast of the station, with free tea and coffee and convivial common areas (including space

outside for barbecues). Dorms have 4–6 beds. Dorms **£17**, doubles **£38**

★ **The 25 Boutique B&B** 25 Avenue Rd, TQ2 5LB ☎ 01803 297517, ⓦ the25.uk. Rooms in this B&B, a 10min walk from the seafront, feature zebra-striped or purple-hued walls, mood lighting, iPads, smarts TVs, rain showers and posh toiletries. The superb breakfasts include home-made yoghurt and smoothies. Book ahead. No under-18s. **£115**

EATING AND DRINKING

Hole in the Wall Park Lane, TQ1 2AU ☎ 01803 200755. This pub is supposed to be one of Torquay's oldest, and was Irish playwright Sean O'Casey's boozer when he lived here. There's a good range of beers, a separate restaurant (mains around £10) and live music on Tues, Thurs and Sun. Daily 11.30am–midnight; kitchen Mon–Sat noon–2.30pm & 6–9pm, Sun 12.30–2.30pm & 6–9pm.

★ **Number 7 Fish Bistro** Beacon Terrace, TQ1 2BH

☎ 01803 295055, ⓦ no7-fish.com. Just above the harbour, this place is a must for seafood fans, covering everything from fresh whole crab to grilled turbot – or whatever else the boats have brought in. Mains around £18. Mon, Tues & Sun 6.30–9.45pm, Wed–Sat 12.45–1.45pm & 6.30–9.45pm (closed Mon & Sun eves Nov–May, Sun eve June–Oct).

6

Brixham and around

BRIXHAM is a major fishing port and the prettiest of the Torbay towns. Among the trawlers on the quayside is moored a full-size reconstruction of the **Golden Hind** (Feb–Oct daily 10.30am–4pm; £7; ☎01803 856223, ⓦgoldenhind.co.uk), the surprisingly small vessel in which Francis Drake circumnavigated the world. The harbour is overlooked by an unflattering statue of William III, who landed in Brixham to claim the crown of England in 1688. From the harbour, climb King Street and follow Berry Head Road to reach the promontory at the southern limit of Torbay, **Berry Head**, now a conservation area attracting colonies of nesting seabirds. There are fabulous views, and you can see the remains of fortifications built during the Napoleonic Wars.

Greenway

Outside Galmpton, TQ5 0ES, 4 miles west of Brixham • Mid-Feb to Oct daily 10.30am–5pm; Nov & Dec Sat & Sun 11am–4pm • £11; NT • ☎01803 842382, ⓦnationaltrust.org.uk/greenway • Greenway Ferry (☎01803 882811, ⓦgreenwayferry.co.uk) offers services from Dartmouth (6–8/day; £8.50 return); Dartmouth Steam Railway (ⓦdartmouthrailriver.co.uk) runs trains from Paignton to Greenway Halt (up to 9 daily; 20min; £8.50 return), from where it's a 30min walk through woodland; car parking is free but must be booked a day in advance

The birthplace of Walter Raleigh's three seafaring half-brothers, the Gilberts, and later rebuilt for Agatha Christie, **Greenway** stands high above the Dart amid steep wooded grounds (the ascent from the river landing is challenging). As well as arriving by ferry or steam train, you can reach the house on foot on the waymarked "**Greenway walk**" from Brixham (around 1hr 30min) or via the Dart Valley Trail from Dartmouth or Kingswear (both around 1hr 20min) – Dartmouth's tourist office (see page 314) can supply route maps. Once here, you'll find a low-key collection of memorabilia belonging to the Christie family, including archeological scraps, silverware, ceramics and books, while the grounds afford lovely views over the river.

ARRIVAL AND INFORMATION
BRIXHAM AND AROUND

By bus Most buses arrive at and depart from Town Square and Bank Lane, in the upper town.
Destinations Exeter (2 daily; 1hr 40min); Torquay (every 10–15min; 45min).

Tourist office Hobb Nobs Gift Shop, 19 The Quay (daily 10am–5pm; ☎01803 211211, ⓦenglishriviera.co.uk).

ACCOMMODATION

Quayside Hotel King St, TQ5 9TJ ☎01803 855751, ⓦquaysidehotel.co.uk. Handsome 29-room hotel with superb harbour views, two bars and a good restaurant where meat and seafood dishes are £15–20. It's worth paying extra for a harbour-facing room. **£100**

Sampford House 57–59 King St, TQ5 9TH ☎01803 857761, ⓦsampfordhouse.com. Wake up to stunning views from the front-facing rooms at this B&B, which are smallish but tastefully decorated. Breakfasts include home-made yoghurt and jams. Self-catering is also available. **£80**

EATING AND DRINKING

Blue Anchor 83 Fore St, TQ5 8AH ☎01803 859373. A great spot for a relaxed pint of local ale, with open fires and low beams. They also offer (rather mediocre) bar food plus live music at weekends. Mon–Sat 11am–midnight, Sun 11am–11.30pm; kitchen daily noon–2.30pm & 6–9.30pm.

★ **Rockfish** Fish Market, TQ5 8AJ ☎01803 850872, ⓦtherockfish.co.uk. Set in an airy modern building at one end of the harbour, with lofty views from its curving deck, this place specializes in the freshest seafood, served with unlimited chips. Apart from the usual cod, haddock and scampi (£12–15), you can order devilled sprats (£7), calamari (£8.50) and roast scallops (£10). There's a takeaway at street level. Daily noon–9.30pm.

Totnes

On the west bank of the River Dart, **TOTNES** has an ancient pedigree, its period of greatest prosperity occurring in the sixteenth century when this inland port exported cloth to France and brought back wine. Some handsome buildings survive from that era, and there is still a working port down on the river, but these days Totnes has mellowed into a residential market town, popular with the alternative and New Age crowd.

The town centres on the long main street, which changes its name from Fore Street to High Street at the **East Gate**, a much-retouched medieval arch. On Fore Street, the town **museum**, occupying a four-storey Elizabethan house, illustrates how wealthy clothiers lived at the peak of Totnes's fortunes (April–Sept Tues–Fri 10am–4pm, also Sat 10am–4pm during summer school hols; free; ☎01803 863821, ⊚totnesmuseum. org). From the East Gate, **Ramparts Walk** trails off along the old city walls, curving round the fifteenth-century church of **St Mary**, a red sandstone building containing an exquisite rood screen. Looming over the High Street is **Totnes Castle**, a classic Norman motte-and-bailey structure (April–Sept daily 10am–6pm; Oct daily 10am–5pm; Nov–March Sat & Sun 10am–4pm; £4.30, EH; ☎01803 864406, ⊚www.english-heritage. org.uk/visit/places/totnes-castle).

6

ARRIVAL AND INFORMATION

TOTNES

By train Totnes train station lies just off Station Rd, a 10min walk north of the centre; it's served by trains to/from Exeter and Plymouth (both 1–3 hourly; 30min).

By bus Most buses stop on or around two central streets: The Plains and Coronation Rd.

Destinations Exeter (Mon–Sat 12 daily, Sun 5 daily; 1hr 10min–1hr 45min); Plymouth (Mon–Sat every 30min, Sun hourly; 1hr); Torquay (Mon–Sat every 30min, Sun hourly; 40min).

Website ⊚visittotnes.co.uk.

ACCOMMODATION

Great Grubb Fallowfields, Plymouth Rd, TQ9 5LX ☎01803 849071, ⊚thegreatgrubb.co.uk. Leather sofas, restful colours, healthy breakfasts and a patio are the main appeal of this friendly B&B a 10min walk from the centre. Work by local artists is displayed in the rooms. __£85__

Royal Seven Stars Hotel The Plains, TQ9 5DD ☎01803 862125, ⊚royalsevenstars.co.uk. This seventeenth-century coaching inn has had a modern makeover, giving it contemporary bedrooms and a stylish bar alongside the traditional *Saloon Bar* and more formal brasserie. The Sunday-night deal, including a carvery meal and breakfast for two, is great value at £100. __£110__

EATING AND DRINKING

★ Pie Street 26 High St, TQ9 5RY ☎01803 868674, ⊚piestreet.co.uk. A purveyor of "British soul food", this place specializes in pies (around £10) made on the premises, to eat in or take away. Choices include curry; chicken, ham and leek; and mushroom *au poivre* – all accompanied by mashed potatoes, chips or salad. Apart from pies, you'll find soup, pork baps and a selection of cheeses on the menu, Timothy Taylor's ale on tap, and a lounge upstairs with board games. Mon–Sat 11.30am–late, Sun noon–6pm; last food orders Mon 6pm, Tues–Thurs 8pm, Fri & Sat 9pm, Sun 3pm.

Totnes Brewing Company 59 High St, TQ9 5PB ☎01803 849290. This pub and microbrewery serves a range of craft ales and ciders from around the world, in addition to its own. It has an authentic, spit-and-sawdust feel, and the small garden occupies the former moat of Totnes Castle. Upstairs, an old ballroom with chandeliers and cinema seats is a venue for live music nights on Fri & Sat (⊚barrelhousetotnes.co.uk). Mon–Thurs 5pm–midnight, Fri & Sat noon–midnight, Sun noon–11.30pm.

Willow 87 High St, TQ9 5PB ☎01803 862605. Inexpensive vegetarian snacks, evening meals and organic drinks are served at this mellow café/restaurant. Main dishes are £10–11. There's a courtyard, and live acoustic music on Fri. No credit cards. Mon, Tues & Thurs 10am–5pm, Wed, Fri & Sat 10am–5pm & 6.30–9pm.

Dartmouth and around

South of Torbay, and eight miles downstream from Totnes, **DARTMOUTH** has thrived since the Normans recognized the trading potential of this deep-water port. Today its activities embrace fishing, freight and a booming leisure industry, as well as the education of the Senior Service's officer class at the Royal Naval College, on a hill overlooking the port. Regular ferries shuttle across the River Dart between Dartmouth and **Kingswear**, terminus of the Dartmouth Steam Railway (see page 312). **Boat cruises** from Dartmouth are the best way to view the deep creeks and grand houses overlooking the river, among them Greenway (see page 312).

6

The Butterwalk

Duke St, TQ6 9PZ • **Dartmouth Museum** April–Oct Mon & Sun 1–4pm, Tues–Sat 10am–4pm; Nov–March daily 1–3pm • £2 • ☎ 01803 832923, ⓦ dartmouthmuseum.org

Behind the enclosed boat basin at the heart of town, the four-storey **Butterwalk** was built in the seventeenth century for a local merchant. The timber-framed construction, richly decorated with woodcarvings, was restored after bombing in World War II – though it still looks precarious, overhanging the street on eleven granite columns. This arcade now holds shops and the small **Dartmouth Museum**, mainly devoted to maritime curios, including old maps, prints and models of ships.

Dartmouth Castle

Castle Rd, TQ6 0JN • April–Sept daily 10am–6pm; Oct daily 10am–5pm; Nov–March Sat & Sun 10am–4pm • £6.60 • EH • ☎ 01803 833588, ⓦ www.english-heritage.org.uk/visit/places/dartmouth-castle • By boat: Dartmouth Castle Ferry between Dartmouth Quay and castle, Easter–Oct continuous service 10am–4/5pm; £2.50; ⓦ dartmouthcastleferry.co.uk

A twenty-minute riverside walk southeast from **Bayard's Cove** – a short cobbled quay lined with eighteenth-century houses, where the Pilgrim Fathers stopped en route to the New World – brings you to **Dartmouth Castle**, one of two fortifications on opposite sides of the estuary dating from the fifteenth century. The castle was the first in England to be constructed specifically to withstand artillery, though was never tested in action, and consequently is excellently preserved.

Blackpool Sands

Two and a half miles southwest of Dartmouth, the coastal path brings you through the pretty hilltop village of Stoke Fleming to **Blackpool Sands**, the best beach in the area. The unspoilt cove, flanked by steep, wooded cliffs, was the site of a battle in 1404 in which Devon archers repulsed a Breton invasion force sent to punish the privateers of Dartmouth for their cross-Channel raiding.

ARRIVAL AND INFORMATION   **DARTMOUTH AND AROUND**

By ferry Coming from Torbay, visitors to Dartmouth can save time and a long detour through Totnes by using the frequent Higher Ferry (ⓦ dartmouthhigherferry.com) or Lower Ferry (ⓦ southhams.gov.uk) across the Dart from Kingswear (60p–£1.50 foot passengers; £5–5.60 for cars);

the last ones are at around 10.45pm.

Tourist office Mayor's Ave (Easter–Sept Mon, Tues & Thurs–Sat 10am–4pm, Wed 10am–2.30pm; Oct–Easter Mon, Tues & Thurs–Sat 10am–2.30pm; ☎ 01803 834224, ⓦ discoverdartmouth.com).

ACCOMMODATION AND EATING

Browns 27–29 Victoria Rd, TQ6 9RT ☎ 01803 832572, ⓦ brownshoteldartmouth.co.uk. Boutique-style hotel, with small, stylish rooms decorated with contemporary paintings. Good Mediterranean dishes are served in the bar and restaurant for £10 or less. Mon 10am–6pm, Tues–Sat 10am–11pm (last orders 9pm). **£120**

Café Alf Resco Lower St, TQ6 9AN ☎ 01803 835880, ⓦ cafealfresco.co.uk. Funky snack bar that's good for all-day breakfasts, crab sandwiches, steaming coffees and live music at weekends. There's decent accommodation available above the café. Daily 7am–2pm. **£95**

The Captain's House 18 Clarence St, TQ6 9NW ☎ 01803 832133, ⓦ captainshouse.co.uk. If you don't mind the

lack of both panoramic views and breakfast, this place offers excellent value for money. Bedrooms are simply decorated in white and pale grey, and you'll find plenty of breakfast venues within an easy walk. Parking available. **£72**

The Seahorse 5 South Embankment, TQ6 9BH ☎ 01803 835147, ⓦ seahorserestaurant.co.uk. Seafood restaurant facing the river, offering such Italian-inspired dishes as octopus salad and grilled John Dory. It's pricey, with mains costing £20 and up, but the two-course lunch and early-evening menu is more reasonable (£20). The same team also runs *Rockfish*, a couple of doors down (daily noon–9.30pm), which serves first-class fish and chips. Tues–Sat noon–2.30pm & 6–9.30pm.

Salcombe and around

The area between the Dart and Plym estuaries, the **South Hams**, holds some of Devon's comeliest villages and most striking coastline. The "capital" of the region,

Kingsbridge, is a useful transport hub but lacks the appeal of **SALCOMBE**, linked to Kingsbridge by a seasonal ferry (late July to Sept most days 2–4 daily; 35min; £7.50 one-way, £12 return; ⊚kingsbridgesalcombeferry.co.uk). Once a fishing village, Devon's southernmost resort is now a sailing and holiday centre, its calm waters strewn with small pleasure craft.

You can swot up on boating and local history at **Salcombe Maritime Museum** on Market Street (April–Oct daily 10.30am–12.30pm & 2.30–4.30pm; £2; ☎01548 843080, ⊚salcombemuseum.org.uk) or take a ferry down to South Sands (April–Oct 2 hourly; £3.70 one-way; ☎01548 561035, ⊚southsandsferry.co.uk) and climb up to the intriguing **Overbeck's** at Sharpitor (mid-Feb to Oct daily 11am–5pm; £8.80, NT; ☎01548 842893, ⊚nationaltrust.org.uk/overbecks), a house and museum that focuses on nineteenth-century curiosities and the area's natural history.

ARRIVAL AND INFORMATION

SALCOMBE AND AROUND

By bus Salcombe is served by regular buses from Kingsbridge (Mon–Sat hourly, Sun 2 daily; 20min), where you'll have to change if you're coming from Dartmouth and further afield.

Tourist office Market Street (Easter–Oct Mon–Sat 10am–5pm, Sun 10am–4pm; Nov–Easter Mon–Sat 10am–3pm; ☎01548 843927, ⊚salcombeinformation.co.uk).

ACCOMMODATION AND EATING

Higher Rew Caravan and Camping Park 2 miles west of town, TQ7 3BW ☎01548 842681, ⊚higherrew. co.uk. Large, grassy campsite on a slope surrounded by attractive farmland. The on-site facilities are good, and there are plenty of places for kids to play. No credit cards. Closed Nov–March. __£22__

Waverley Devon Rd, TQ8 8HL ☎01548 842633, ⊚waverleybandb.co.uk. With rooms in the main house or in a nautically themed annexe, this B&B offers excellent breakfasts (at a communal table), with lots of choice, and a lounge. It's less than a 10min steep walk from the centre. Self-catering also available. No credit cards. Closed Dec–Feb. __£85__

Winking Prawn North Sands, TQ8 8LD ☎01548 842326, ⊚winkingprawn.co.uk. Right on the beach, this is an alluring stop for a cappuccino, baguette or ice cream by day, or a chargrilled steak or Cajun chicken salad in the evening, from around 6pm, when booking is advised (mains £17–25). You don't need to book for the summer barbecues (May–Sept 4–8.30pm; £19). Mon–Thurs 9.30am–8.30pm, Fri & Sat 8.45am–8.30pm.

Dartmoor

Occupying the main part of the county between Exeter and Plymouth, **DARTMOOR** is southern England's greatest expanse of wilderness, some 368 square miles of raw granite, barren bogland, sparse grass and heather-grown moor. It was not always so desolate, as testified by the remnants of scattered Stone Age settlements and the ruined relics of the area's nineteenth-century tin-mining industry. Today desultory flocks of sheep and groups of ponies are virtually the only living creatures to be seen wandering over the central fastnesses of the National Park, with solitary birds – buzzards, kestrels, pipits, stonechats and wagtails – wheeling and hovering high above.

The core of Dartmoor, characterized by tumbling streams and high **tors** chiselled by the elements, has belonged to the Duchy of Cornwall since 1307, though there is almost unlimited public access today. However, camping should be out of sight of houses and roads, fires are strictly forbidden, no vehicles are permitted beyond fifteen yards from the road and overnight parking is only allowed in authorized places.

Postbridge and around

You can see one of Dartmoor's famed **clapper bridges** midway between Two Bridges and the village of **POSTBRIDGE**, while the largest and best preserved of these simple structures is in Postbridge itself, just over five miles northeast of Princetown on the

B3212. Used by tin miners and farmers since medieval times, clapper bridges are little more than huge slabs of granite supported by piers of the same material. From Postbridge, head south through **Bellever Forest** to the open moor, where **Bellever Tor** (1453ft) affords outstanding views.

Grimspound

3 miles northeast of Postbridge, PL20 6TB · Daily 24hr · Free

The Bronze Age village of **Grimspound** lies below Hameldown Tor (1735ft), about a mile off the road. Inhabited some three thousand years ago, this is the most complete example of Dartmoor's prehistoric settlements, consisting of 24 circular huts scattered within a four-acre enclosure. The site is thought to have been the model for the Stone Age settlement where Sherlock Holmes camped in Conan Doyle's *The Hound of the Baskervilles*, while **Hound Tor**, an outcrop three miles to the southeast, provided inspiration for the tale itself. According to local legend, phantom hounds were sighted racing across the moor to hurl themselves on the tomb of a hated squire following his death in 1677.

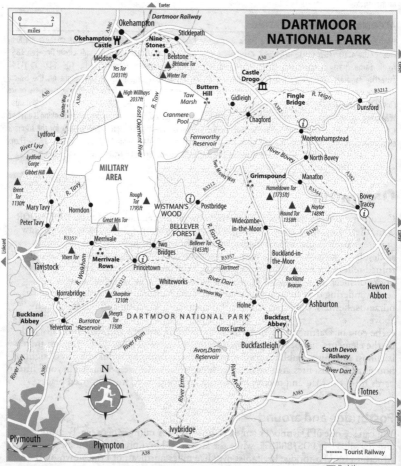

WALKING ON DARTMOOR

Walking is the best way to experience the moor, and a limited network of signposts and painted stones exists to guide **hikers**. Considerable experience is essential for longer distances, however, and map-reading abilities are a prerequisite for any but the shortest strolls (the 1:25,000 Ordnance Survey *Explorer* map OL28 should suffice). Waterproof clothing is also essential.

Broadly speaking, the gentler contours of the southern moor provide less strenuous rambles, while the harsher northern tracts require more skill and stamina. Several walking routes link up with some of Devon's long-distance trails, such as the **Dartmoor Way**, **Tarka Trail**, **Templer Way** and **Two Moors Way**. Information and downloads for these and a range of shorter hikes can be found at ⓦdartmoor.gov.uk and ⓦexploredevon.info, while more detailed itineraries are available from local bookshops, National Park visitor centres and tourist offices in Dartmoor's major towns and villages. An extensive programme of **guided walks** (2–6hr; £5–10) is also listed at ⓦmoorlandguides.co.uk. Beware of **firing schedules** in the northwest quadrant of the moor (see page 319).

INFORMATION

Postbridge National Park Visitor Centre Car park off the B3212 (April–Oct daily 10am–5pm; Nov–March

POSTBRIDGE AND AROUND

Thurs–Sun 10am–3pm, or daily 10am–3pm during school hols; ☎01822 880272, ⓦdartmoor.gov.uk).

ACCOMMODATION AND EATING

Warren House Inn 2 miles northeast of Postbridge, PL20 6TA ☎01822 880208, ⓦwarrenhouseinn.co.uk. Set in a bleak tract of moorland, this solitary pub offers fire-lit comfort and very basic meals, such as steak and ale pie with chips and veg (£13.50). Easter–Oct daily 11am–10pm, Nov–Easter Mon & Tues 11am–3pm, Wed–Sat 11am–10pm, Sun noon–10pm; kitchen Easter–Oct Mon–Sat noon–9pm, Sun noon–8.30pm, Nov–Easter

Mon & Tues noon–2.30pm, Wed–Sat noon–9pm, Sun noon–8.30pm.
YHA Dartmoor Bellever, PL20 6TU ☎0345 371 9622, ⓦyha.org.uk/hostel/dartmoor. One of Dartmoor's two YHA hostels lies a mile or so south of Postbridge on the edge of the forest and on the banks of the East Dart River. Take bus #98 from Tavistock or Princetown (Mon–Sat 1 daily) to Postbridge; it's a mile's walk from the bus stop. Dorms £19

The southeastern moor

Four miles east of the crossroads at Two Bridges, crowds home in on the beauty spot of **Dartmeet**, where the valley is memorably lush and you don't need to walk far to leave the car park and ice-cream vans behind. From here the Dart pursues a leisurely course, joined by the River Webburn near the pretty village of **BUCKLAND-IN-THE-MOOR**, one of a cluster of moorstone-and-thatch hamlets on this side of the moor. South of Buckland, the village of **HOLNE** is another rustic idyll, surrounded on three sides by wooded valleys. Two and a half miles north of Buckland, **WIDECOMBE-IN-THE-MOOR** is set in a hollow amid high granite-strewn ridges. Its church of **St Pancras** provides a famous local landmark, its pinnacled tower dwarfing the fourteenth-century main building, whose interior includes a beautiful painted rood screen.

ACCOMMODATION

Great Hound Tor Camping Barn Near Manaton, TQ13 9UW ☎01647 221202, ⓔgreathoundtor@gmail.com. This farmhouse on the eastern edge of Dartmoor offers a cooking area, a woodburner and hot water for showers, but no bedding is provided – you'll basically need all your camping gear except the tent. Per person £7

THE SOUTHEASTERN MOOR

Higher Venton Farm Half a mile south of Widecombe-in-the-Moor, TQ13 7TF ☎01364 621235, ⓦventonfarm.com. A peaceful sixteenth-century thatched longhouse that was once home to the Dartmoor writer Beatrice Chase. The bedrooms are fine (the cheapest double shares a bathroom), and it's close to a couple of good pubs. No wi-fi. £70

The northeastern moor

On Dartmoor's northeastern edge, the market town of **MORETONHAMPSTEAD** makes an attractive entry point from Exeter. Moretonhampstead has a historic rivalry with neighbouring **CHAGFORD**, a Stannary town (a chartered centre of the tin trade) that also flourished from the local wool industry. On a hillside overlooking the River Teign, Chagford has a fine fifteenth-century church and some good accommodation and eating options. Numerous **walks** can be made along the Teign and elsewhere in the vicinity.

Castle Drogo

2.5 miles northeast of Chagford, EX6 6PB · **House** Early March to Oct daily 11am–5pm; Nov to mid-Dec Sat & Sun noon–4pm · **Garden** Daily: early March to Oct 10am–5.30pm; Nov to early March 11am–4pm · House & garden £11; NT · **Grounds** Daily dawn–dusk · Free, but parking £2/2hr or £4/day; NT · ☎ 01647 433306, ⟨w⟩ nationaltrust.org.uk/castle-drogo · Bus #173 from Exeter stops at end of castle drive

The twentieth-century extravaganza of **Castle Drogo** is stupendously sited above the Teign gorge. Having retired at the age of 33, grocery magnate Julius Drewe unearthed a link that suggested his descent from a Norman baron, and set about creating a castle befitting his pedigree. Begun in 1910, to a design by **Edwin Lutyens**, it was not completed until 1930, but the result was an unsurpassed synthesis of medieval and modern elements. Paths lead from Drogo east to **Fingle Bridge**, a lovely spot where shaded green pools shelter trout and the occasional salmon. The castle is undergoing extensive renovation work until around 2019 but remains open to the public, giving visitors a rare chance to see rooms that had long been hidden from view.

ARRIVAL AND INFORMATION

THE NORTHEASTERN MOOR

By bus There are frequent services into Devon.
Destinations from Chagford Exeter (Mon–Sat 5 daily; 1hr); Moretonhampstead (Mon–Sat 3 daily; 15min); Okehampton (Mon–Sat 1 daily; 55min).
Destinations from Moretonhampstead Chagford (Mon–Sat 3 daily; 12min); Exeter (7 daily; 50min–1hr 20min);

Okehampton (Mon–Sat 1 daily; 1hr 10min).
Tourist office New St, Moretonhampstead (April–Oct daily 9.30am–5pm; Nov–March Thurs–Sat 10am–4pm, Sun 11am–3pm; ☎ 01647 440043, ⟨w⟩ visitmoreton hampstead.co.uk).

ACCOMMODATION AND EATING

Chagford Inn 7 Mill St, Chagford, TQ13 8AW ☎ 01647 433109, ⟨w⟩ thechagfordinn.com. Chic gastropub with slate floors and local art on the walls. Come by at lunchtime for roast-beef baguette (£8.50) or mushroom risotto (£13.50), or in the evening to sample local meat and seafood dishes (£13–17). There's even a separate beef menu, which offers different cuts of a locally reared steer. Three rooms available, too. Kitchen daily noon–2.30pm & 6–9pm. £80

Cyprian's Cot 47 New St, Chagford, TQ13 8BB ☎ 01647 432256, ⟨w⟩ cyprianscot.co.uk. Comfy, sixteenth-century cottage where you can warm your bones by an inglenook fireplace and, in fine weather, breakfast and take tea in the garden. No debit/credit cards. £75

Kestor Inn Manaton, TQ13 9UF ☎ 01647 221626, ⟨w⟩ www.kestorinn.com. A popular pub with walkers, serving hot food as well as local ales and ciders, and selling maps, provisions and walking guides. There are en-suite rooms available here too, some with good views. Daily 11am–11pm; kitchen Mon–Sat noon–2pm & 6.30–9pm, Sun noon–4pm & 6.30–9pm. £95

Sparrowhawk Backpackers 45 Ford St, Moretonhampstead ☎ 01647 440318, ⟨w⟩ sparrowhawkback packers.co.uk. Excellent, eco-minded hostel with fourteen beds in a light and spacious bunk room, plus a private room sleeping up to four. Good kitchen for self-catering. Dorm £19, double £40

Okehampton

The main centre on the northern moor, **OKEHAMPTON** grew prosperous as a market town for the medieval wool trade, and some fine old buildings survive between the two branches of the River Okement that meet here, among them the prominent fifteenth-century tower of the **Chapel of St James**. Across the road from the seventeenth-century town hall, a granite archway leads into the **Museum of Dartmoor Life** (April to early Dec Mon–Fri 10am–4.15pm, Sat 10am–1pm; £4; ☎ 01837 52295, ⟨w⟩ museumofdartmoorlife.org.uk), which offers an excellent overview of habitation on the moor since earliest times.

Okehampton Castle

1 mile southwest of Okehampton, EX20 1JA • Daily: April–June, Sept & Oct 10am–5pm; July & Aug 10am–6pm • £4.80; EH • ☎ 01837 52844, ⓦ www.english-heritage.org.uk/visit/places/okehampton-castle

Perched above the West Okement, **Okehampton Castle** is the shattered hulk of a stronghold laid waste by Henry VIII. The tottering ruins include a gatehouse, Norman keep, and the remains of the Great Hall, buttery and kitchens. Woodland walks and riverside picnic tables invite a gentle exploration of what was once the deer park of the earls of Devon.

FIRING RANGES ON DARTMOOR

A significant portion of northern Dartmoor, containing the moor's highest tors and some of its most famous beauty spots, is run by the **Ministry of Defence**, whose **firing ranges** are marked by red-and-white posts; when firing is in progress, red flags or red lights signify that entry is prohibited. Generally, if no warning flags are flying by 9am between April and September, or by 10am from October to March, there will be no firing on that day; alternatively, check at ☎ 0800 458 4868 or ⓦ mod.uk/access.

6

ARRIVAL AND DEPARTURE
OKEHAMPTON

By train Okehampton has a useful – if infrequent – link with Exeter (late May to mid-Sept Sun 4 daily; 45min). The station is a 15min walk south along Station Rd from Fore St.

By bus There are regular buses to Chagford (Mon–Sat 1 daily; 50min), Exeter (Mon–Sat hourly, Sun 6 daily; 1hr) and Tavistock (Mon–Sat every 1–2hr; 50min).

ACCOMMODATION

Meadowlea 65 Station Rd, EX20 1EA ☎ 01837 53200, ⓦ meadowleaguesthouse.co.uk. A short walk south of the centre, below the train station and within 550yd of the Granite Way cycling route, this bike-friendly B&B has seven rooms (four en suite) and cycle storage. **£66**

YHA Okehampton Klondyke Rd, EX20 1EW ☎ 01837 53916, ⓦ yha.org.uk/hostel/okehampton. Housed in a converted goods shed at the station, this well-run hostel offers a range of outdoor activities, plus camping and bike rental. Camping/person **£10**, dorms **£27**, doubles **£67**

The western moor

Southwest from Princetown, walkers can trace the grassy path of the defunct rail line to **Burrator Reservoir**, four miles away; flooded in the 1890s to provide water for Plymouth, this is the biggest stretch of water on Dartmoor. The wooded lakeside teems with wildlife, and is overlooked by craggy **Sharpitor** (1210ft) and **Sheep's Tor** (1150ft). For the best walk from here, strike northwest to meet the valley of the **River Walkham**, which rises in a peat bog at Walkham Head (5 miles north of Princetown), then scurries through moorland and woods to join the River Tavy at Double Waters (2 miles south of Tavistock).

Merrivale

The River Tavy crosses the B3357 four miles west of Princetown at **MERRIVALE**, a tiny settlement amounting to little more than a pub. It's another good starting point for walks, only half a mile west of one of Dartmoor's most important prehistoric sites, the **Merrivale Rows**. These upright stones form a stately procession for 850ft across the moor. Dating from between 2500 BC and 750 BC, they are probably connected with burial rites.

Lydford

Five miles southwest of Okehampton, the village of **LYDFORD** preserves the sturdy but small-scale **Lydford Castle** (daylight hours; free), a Saxon outpost, then a Norman keep and later used as a prison. The chief attraction here, though, is the one-and-a-half-mile **Lydford Gorge** (daily: March–Oct 10am–5pm; Nov–Feb restricted access 11am–3.30pm; £8.90, NT; ☎ 01822 820320, ⓦ nationaltrust.org.uk/lydford-gorge), overgrown with thick woods and alive with butterflies, spotted woodpeckers, dippers and herons.

Castle Inn Next to Lydford Castle, EX20 4BH ☎01822 820241, ⓦcastleinnlydford.com. Sixteenth-century inn with en-suite rooms, one with a roof terrace looking onto the castle. The oak-beamed, fire-lit bar provides local ales, and there's a beer garden and a restaurant (mains £10–20). Daily noon–11pm; kitchen daily noon–3pm & 6–9pm. **£70**

★ **Dartmoor Inn** A386, opposite Lydford turning,

EX20 4AY ☎01822 820221, ⓦwww.dartmoorinn.com. Three spacious guest rooms furnished with antiques are available above this popular gastropub. The restaurant features tasty options like mushroom risotto and slow-roasted confit of duck leg (£12–19), and there's a set-price Sun lunch (two courses £22). Booking advised. Daily 11am–3pm & 6–11pm; kitchen daily noon–2.30pm & 6–9.15pm. **£115**

Tavistock and around

The main town of the western moor, **TAVISTOCK** owes its distinctive Victorian appearance to the building boom that followed the discovery of copper deposits here in 1844. Originally, however, this market and Stannary town on the River Tavy grew around what was once the West Country's most important Benedictine abbey, established in the eleventh century. Some scant remnants survive in the churchyard of **St Eustachius** (ⓦtavistockparishchurch.org.uk), a mainly fifteenth-century building with stained glass from William Morris's studio in the south aisle.

North of Tavistock, a four-mile lane wanders up to **Brent Tor** (1130ft), which dominates Dartmoor's western fringes. Access is easiest along the path gently ascending through gorse on its southwestern side, leading to the small church of St Michael at the top.

By bus Tavistock has good connections with both Okehampton (Mon–Sat every 1–2hr; 50min) and Princetown (Mon–Sat 3 daily; 30min).

ACCOMMODATION

★ **Mount Tavy Cottage** Half a mile east of Tavistock on the B3357, PL19 9JL ☎01822 614253, ⓦmounttavy. co.uk. Set on a beautiful plot with its own lake, this B&B

in a former gardener's cottage has comfortable rooms, organic breakfasts, evening meals by prior arrangement (£20 for two courses) and self-catering options. **£85**

Plymouth and around

PLYMOUTH's predominantly bland and modern face belies its great historic role as a naval base and, in the sixteenth century, the stamping ground of such towering figures as John Hawkins and Francis Drake. It was from here that Drake sailed to defeat the Spanish Armada in 1588, and 32 years later the port was the last embarkation point for the Pilgrim Fathers, whose New Plymouth colony became the nucleus for the English settlement of North America. The importance of the city's Devonport dockyards made the city a target in World War II, when the Luftwaffe reduced most of the old centre to rubble. Subsequent reconstruction has done little to improve the place, though it would be difficult to spoil the glorious vista over **Plymouth Sound**, the basin of calm water at the mouth of the combined Plym, Tavy and Tamar estuaries, largely unchanged since Drake played his famous game of bowls on the Hoe before joining battle with the Armada.

One of the best local excursions from Plymouth is to **Mount Edgcumbe**, where woods and meadows provide a welcome antidote to the urban bustle. East of Plymouth, the aristocratic opulence of **Saltram House** includes fine art and furniture, while to the north you can visit Francis Drake's old home at **Buckland Abbey**.

Plymouth Hoe

A good place to start a tour of the city is **Plymouth Hoe**, an immense esplanade with glorious views over the water. Here, alongside various war memorials, stands a rather portly statue of Sir Francis Drake gazing grandly out to the sea. Appropriately, there's a bowling green back from the brow.

Smeaton's Tower

Plymouth Hoe, PL1 2NZ • Daily 10am–5pm; check winter times • £4 • ☎ 01752 304774, ⓦ plymhearts.org/smeatons-tower

One of the city's best-known landmarks, the red-and-white-striped **Smeaton's Tower** was erected in 1759 by John Smeaton on the treacherous Eddystone Rocks, fourteen miles out to sea. When replaced by a larger lighthouse in 1882, it was reassembled here, where it gives lofty views across Plymouth Sound.

Around the Barbican

At the old town's quay at **Sutton Harbour**, the **Mayflower Steps** commemorate the sailing of the Pilgrim Fathers, with a plaque listing the names and professions of the 102 Puritans on board. Edging the harbour, the **Barbican** district is the heart of old Plymouth; most of the buildings are now shops and restaurants.

National Marine Aquarium

Rope Walk, PL4 0LF • Daily 10am–5pm; last entry 4pm • £15.95, or £14.35 online • ☎ 0844 893 7938, ⓦ national-aquarium.co.uk

Across the footbridge from Sutton Harbour, the **National Marine Aquarium** has re-created a range of marine environments, from moorland stream to coral reef and deep-sea ocean. The most popular exhibits are the seahorses, the colourful reefs and the sharks, though some of the smaller tanks hold equally compelling exhibits – the anemones, for example.

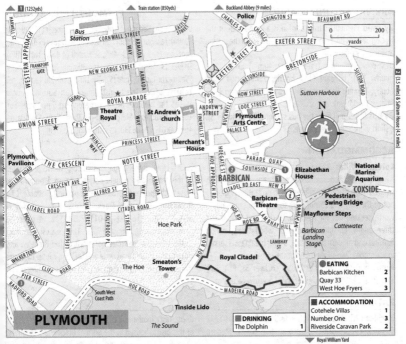

Mount Edgcumbe

2 miles southwest of the city, PL10 1HZ • **House & Earl's Garden** April–Sept Mon–Thurs & Sun 11am–4.30pm • £7.20 • **Lower gardens and country park** Daily 8am–8pm (winter 8am–6pm) • Free • ☎ 01752 822236, ⊛ mountedgcumbe.gov.uk • Plymouth Boat Trips runs ferries from Mayflower Steps to Mt Edgcumbe (April–Sept Sat & Sun, daily in school hols: 6–7 daily; ⊛ plymouthboattrips.co.uk). Bus #34 runs from Royal Parade to Admiral's Hard, Stonehouse, from where Plymouth Boat Trips operates a ferry to Cremyll (every 30min), just outside the park

Lying on the Cornish side of Plymouth Sound and visible from the Hoe is **Mount Edgcumbe house**, a reconstruction of the bomb-damaged Tudor original; inside, the predominant note is eighteenth-century, the rooms elegantly restored with authentic Regency furniture. Far more enticing are the impeccable **gardens** divided into the formal **Earl's Garden**, next to the house, and the **lower gardens**, including French, Italian and English sections – the first two a blaze of flowerbeds adorned with classical statuary, the last an acre of sweeping lawn shaded by exotic trees. The **park** gives access to the coastal path and the huge **Whitsand Bay**, the best bathing beach for miles around, though subject to dangerous shifting sands and fierce currents.

Saltram House

Near Plympton, 2 miles east of Plymouth, PL7 1UH • **House** Daily: March–Oct 11am–4.30pm; Nov–Feb 11am–3.30pm • **Garden** Daily: March–Oct 10am–5pm; Nov–Feb 10am–4pm • House & garden March–Oct £11, Nov–Feb £8; NT • **Park** Daily dawn–dusk • Free, but parking £3; NT • ☎ 01752 333500, ⊛ nationaltrust.org.uk/saltram • Buses #19, #21, #51 or #200 from Royal Parade to Marsh Mills roundabout, from where it's a walk of a mile (signposted)

The remodelled Tudor **Saltram House** is Devon's largest country house, featuring work by architect Robert Adam and fourteen portraits by **Joshua Reynolds**, who was born in nearby Plympton. The showpiece is the Saloon, a fussy but exquisitely furnished room dripping with gilt and plaster, set off by a huge Axminster carpet especially woven for it in 1770. The landscaped **garden** and **park** provide a breather from this riot of interior design.

ARRIVAL AND INFORMATION

PLYMOUTH AND AROUND

By train Plymouth's train station is a mile north of the Hoe off Saltash Rd. Frequent buses run between the station and the city centre.

Destinations Bodmin (every 1–2hr; 40min); Exeter (1–2 hourly; 1hr); Liskeard (1–2 hourly; 25min); Par (1–2 hourly; 50min); Penzance (1–2 hourly; 2hr); Truro (1–2 hourly; 1hr 15min).

By bus Buses pull in at the bus station off Mayflower St, a short walk from Royal Parade.

Destinations Bodmin (4 daily; 1hr 15min); Exeter (10 daily; 1hr 10min); Falmouth (3 daily; 2hr 30min); Newquay (5 daily; 2hr); Penzance (4–5 daily; 3–4hr); St Austell (4 daily; 1hr 15min); St Ives (3 daily; 2hr 50min–3hr 30min); Torquay (2 daily; 55min–2hr 15min); Truro (5 daily; 1hr 40min–2hr 10min).

Tourist office The tourist office is off Sutton Harbour at 3–5 The Barbican (April–Oct Mon–Sat 9am–5pm, Sun 10am–4pm; Nov–March Mon–Fri 9am–5pm, Sat 10am–4pm; ☎ 01752 306330, ⊛ visitplymouth.co.uk).

ACCOMMODATION

Cotehele Villas 217 Stuart Rd, PL1 5LQ ☎ 07877 474643, ⊛ cotehelevillas.com; map p.321. This smart, stylish place 10min from the train station is slightly out of the way – a 25min walk to the Barbican – but is worth seeking out for its fresh, uncluttered feel. It has three bright, en-suite rooms with wood floors, period features and modern bathrooms; a light breakfast is served in your room. Two-night minimum. **£75**

Number One 1 Windsor Villas, Lockyer St, PL1 2QD ☎ 01752 212981, ⊛ numberoneplymouth.co.uk; map

p.321. Light, airy and spacious en-suite rooms are offered in this refurbished Regency-style villa on a quiet street close to the Hoe and Barbican, with parking available. **£74**

Riverside Caravan Park Leigham Manor Drive, Marsh Mills, PL6 8LL ☎ 01752 344122, ⊛ riverside caravanpark.com; map p.321. The nearest campsite to the centre, three miles northeast of the Barbican and close to the Drake's Trail cycle and walking route. There are riverside walks, and an outdoor pool open in summer. **£16**

EATING

Barbican Kitchen 60 Southside St, PL1 2LQ ☎ 01752 604448, ⊛ barbicankitchen.com; map p.321. Modern

decor, tasty food and a casual ambience draw the crowds at this bistro, housed in the ancient Black Friars Distillery.

The varied menu runs from wild garlic risotto to slow-cooked lamb (£11–18). Decent set menus, too. Mon–Thurs noon–2.30pm & 6–9.30pm, Fri & Sat noon–2.30pm & 5–10pm.

Quay 33 33 Southside St, PL1 2LE ☎01752 229345, ⓦquay33.co.uk; map p.321. This elegant but informal harbourside spot is ideal at lunch for a plate of pasta or a doorstop sandwich (£10–11). The evening menu usually includes Exmouth mussels (£8), pork belly (£15) and fish

stew (£17). Sit upstairs for the view. Mon–Sat noon–2.30pm & 5pm–late, Sun noon–3pm & 6–8.30pm.

West Hoe Fryers 7 Radford Rd, PL1 3BY ☎01752 221409; map p.321. It doesn't get much simpler than this: an old-style fish shop with a queue for takeaway orders on one side and tables on the other. The fish and chips (from £5.80 to take away) might come with extras like pickled eggs and cockles. Mon–Sat noon–2pm & 5–9pm.

DRINKING

The Dolphin 14 The Barbican, PL1 2LS ☎01752 660876; map p.321. A local institution, this harbourside pub has an authentic atmosphere, and West Country ales

straight from the barrel. Look out for the pictures by Beryl Cook, who used to drink here. Mon–Sat 10am–midnight, Sun 11am–midnight.

Buckland Abbey

9 miles north of Plymouth, PL20 6EY • Jan to mid-Feb Sat & Sun 10am–4pm; mid-Feb to Oct daily 10am–5pm; Nov & Dec daily 10am–4pm • £11; NT • ☎01822 853607, ⓦnationaltrust.org.uk/buckland-abbey • From Plymouth, #1 or #X1 to Yelverton (4 hourly), then #55 (Mon–Sat 5 daily)

Close to the River Tavy and on the edge of Dartmoor, **Buckland Abbey** was once the most westerly of England's Cistercian abbeys. After its dissolution, Buckland was converted to a family home by privateer Richard Grenville (cousin of Walter Raleigh), from whom Francis Drake acquired the estate in 1582, after becaming mayor of Plymouth. It remained Drake's home until his death, though the house reveals few traces of his residence. There are, however, numerous maps, portraits and mementos of his buccaneering exploits on show, most famous of which is Drake's Drum, which was said to beat a supernatural warning of impending danger to the country. More eye-catching are the oak-panelled **Great Hall**, previously the nave of the abbey, a newly identified Rembrandt self-portrait, and, in the majestic grounds, a fine fourteenth-century **monastic barn**.

North Devon

Apart from a few pockets of more intense activity, **North Devon** is a tranquil, unhurried region, encompassing picture-postcard villages, wind-lashed cliffs and some of the county's finest beaches. The chief town, **Barnstaple**, is a good place to get started, close to some of Devon's best surf breaks at **Woolacombe** and nearby Croyde and Saunton Sands. **Ilfracombe**, on the other hand, is a traditional resort with a modern edge, while, on the coast west of the historic river-port of **Bideford**, the tourist honeypot of **Clovelly** clings to the steep slopes amid thick woods. You can escape the crowds by following the bay round to stormy **Hartland Point** at Devon's northwestern corner, though for remoteness you can't beat **Lundy Island**, a tract of wilderness in the middle of the Bristol Channel.

Barnstaple

BARNSTAPLE, at the head of the Taw estuary, makes an excellent North Devon base, well connected to the resorts of Bideford Bay, Ilfracombe and Woolacombe, as well as to the western fringes of Exmoor. The town's centuries-old role as a marketplace is perpetuated in the daily bustle around the huge timber-framed **Pannier Market** off the High Street, alongside which runs **Butchers Row**, its 33 archways now converted to a variety of uses. At the end of Boutport Street is the **Museum of Barnstaple and North**

6

SIR FRANCIS DRAKE

Born around 1540 near Tavistock, **Francis Drake** worked in the domestic coastal trade from the age of 13, but was soon taking part in the first English slaving expeditions between Africa and the West Indies, led by his Plymouth kinsman John Hawkins. Later, Drake was active in the secret war against Spain, raiding merchant ships in actions unofficially sanctioned by Elizabeth I. In 1572 he became the first Englishman to sight the Pacific, and soon after, on the *Golden Hinde*, became the first to **circumnavigate the world**, for which he received a knighthood on his return in 1580. The following year Drake was made mayor of Plymouth, settling in Buckland Abbey (see page 323), but he was back in action before long – in 1587 he "singed the king of Spain's beard" by entering Cadiz harbour and destroying 33 vessels that were to have formed part of Philip II's **Armada**. When the replacement invasion fleet appeared in the English Channel in 1588, Drake – along with Raleigh, Hawkins and Frobisher – played a leading role in wrecking it. The following year he set off on an unsuccessful expedition to help the Portuguese against Spain, but otherwise most of the next decade was spent in relative inactivity in Plymouth, Exeter and London. Finally, in 1596 Drake left with Hawkins for a raid on Panama, a venture that cost the lives of both captains.

Devon (Mon–Sat: April–Oct 10am–5pm; Nov–March 10am–4pm; free; ☎01271 346747), which holds a lively miscellany that includes a collection of the eighteenth-century pottery for which the region was famous. The museum lies alongside the Taw, where footpaths make for a pleasant riverside stroll, with the colonnaded eighteenth-century **Queen Anne's Walk** – built as a merchants' exchange – providing some architectural interest.

ARRIVAL AND INFORMATION
BARNSTAPLE

By train Barnstaple's train station is on the south side of the Taw, a 5min walk from the centre. There are good connections with Exeter on the Tarka Line (Mon–Sat hourly, Sun 7 daily; 1hr 10min).

By bus The bus station is centrally located between Silver St and Belle Meadow Rd.

Destinations Bideford (every 10–20min; 30min); Croyde (Mon–Sat hourly, Sun 5 daily; 35min); Ilfracombe (every 30min; 40min).

Tourist office The local tourist office is inside the Museum of North Devon on The Square (Mon–Sat 10am–5pm; ☎01271 346747, ⊛staynorthdevon.co.uk).

ACCOMMODATION

★ **Broomhill Art Hotel** Muddiford, EX31 4EX, 2 miles north of Barnstaple ☎01271 850262, ⊛broomhillart.co.uk. Striking combination of gallery, restaurant and hotel where the rooms look onto a sculpture garden. The *Terra Madre* restaurant alone is worth a visit (see below). **£75**

The Old Vicarage Barbican Terrace, EX32 9HQ ☎01271 328504, ⊛oldvicaragebarnstaple.co.uk. This well-kept Victorian house has modern double and twin rooms,

some with freestanding bathtubs and all with good-sized beds. Handily, there's on-site parking too. **£90**

Yeo Dale Hotel Pilton Bridge, EX31 1PG ☎01271 342954, ⊛yeodalehotel.co.uk. Clean B&B rooms in a converted Georgian merchant's house, just a short walk from the centre. The best ones (£120) are on the first floor, and there are cheaper doubles higher up – though these have steeply sloping ceilings. Room-only rates also available. **£85**

EATING

Monty's Caribbean Kitchen 19 Tuly St, EX31 1DH ☎01271 372985, ⊛montyscaribbeankitchen.co.uk. Patties, jerk chicken, and ackee and saltfish feature on the menu of this modern Jamaican restaurant with small wooden tables, off Boutport St. Most dishes are £10–15. Tues & Wed 11.30am–3pm, Thurs–Sat 11.30am–3pm & 6–11pm.

Old School Coffee House 6 Church Lane, EX31 1BH ☎01271 372793. This well-preserved building from 1659 now houses a no-frills café/restaurant – nothing fancy, but brimming with atmosphere. The meals are a bit hit

and miss but the coffee and cakes are good value (try a slice of the chocolate and raisin cake for 95p). Mon–Sat 9.15am–3pm.

Terra Madre Muddiford, EX31 4EX, 2 miles north of Barnstaple ☎01271 850262, ⊛broomhillart.co.uk. Part of the *Broomhill Art Hotel* (see above), this relaxed place specializes in Mediterranean-style cuisine in the form of lunchtime tapas or set-price three-course lunches (Wed–Sun; £17) and evening meals (Wed–Sat; £25). Mon, Tues & Sun 12.30–2.30pm, Wed–Sat noon–2.30pm & 7–8.30pm.

Ilfracombe and around

The most popular resort on Devon's northern coast, **ILFRACOMBE** is essentially little changed since its evolution into a Victorian and Edwardian tourist centre. The town has started to assume a hipper image in recent years, however, symbolized by the dramatic **Damien Hirst sculpture** *Verity*, installed at the end of the compact harbour, depicting a giant, half-flayed, pregnant woman, trampling on law tomes and with a sword upthrust – said to be an allegory of truth and justice.

In summer, if the crowds become oppressive, you can escape on a coastal tour, a fishing trip or the fifteen-mile cruise to Lundy Island (see page 328), all available at the small harbour. On foot, you can explore the attractive stretch of coast running east out of Ilfracombe and beyond the grassy cliffs of Hillsborough, where a succession of undeveloped coves and inlets is backed by jagged slanting rocks and heather-covered hills. There are sandy **beaches** here, though many prefer those beyond **Morte Point**, five miles west of Ilfracombe, from where the view takes in Lundy. Below the promontory, the pocket-sized **Barricane Beach**, famous for the tropical shells washed up by Atlantic currents from the Caribbean, is a popular swimming spot.

6

ARRIVAL AND INFORMATION

ILFRACOMBE AND AROUND

By bus Stagecoach bus #21 runs every 30min from/to Braunton (30min), Barnstaple (45min) and Bideford (1hr 30min), stopping at St James's Place Gardens in Ilfracombe, a short walk west of The Quay.

Tourist office At the Landmark Theatre, on the seafront (Easter–Oct Mon–Fri 9.30am–4.30pm, Sat & Sun 10.30am–4.30pm; Oct–Easter Mon–Fri 9.30am–4.30pm, Sat 10am–4pm; ☎ 01271 863001, ⊛ visitilfracombe.co.uk).

ACCOMMODATION

The Collingdale Larkstone Terrace, EX34 9NU ☎ 01271 863770, ⊛ collingdalehotel.co.uk. Attractive Victorian house with friendly owners, where six of the nine rooms look out over the harbour. There's also a small bar and a lounge to relax in. **£80**

Ocean Backpackers 29 St James Place, EX34 9BJ ☎ 01271 867835, ⊛ oceanbackpackers.co.uk. Excellent, central hostel that's popular with surfers. Dorms are mostly five- or six-bed, and there are doubles available and a well-equipped kitchen. Dorms **£18**, doubles **£48**

EATING AND DRINKING

Blacksands Bistro 3 St James Place, EX34 9BH ☎ 01271 523296. Cosy and welcoming restaurant with a small selection of thoughtfully prepared items. Try the baked blue cheesecake made with Stilton and leeks, or the rainbow trout, both around £14. There's a warm atmosphere and some tables outside on the heated terrace. June–Sept Tues–Sat 5–11pm, Sun noon–4pm; reduced hours in winter.

The Quay 11 The Quay, EX34 9EQ ☎ 01271 868090,

⊛ 11thequay.co.uk. By the harbour and with great sea views, this restaurant (co-owned by artist Damien Hirst, whose works are displayed) offers European-inspired dishes using local ingredients – seared scallops, for example, or Exmoor beef. Most mains are £15–20, and drinks and snacks are available in the relaxed ground-floor bar. Daily 10.30am–late, kitchen noon–2.30pm & 6–9pm; closed Sun eve, Mon & Tues in winter.

Woolacombe and around

Woolacombe Sands is a broad, west-facing beach much favoured by surfers and families alike. At the more crowded northern end of the beach, a cluster of hotels, villas and retirement homes makes up the summer resort of **WOOLACOMBE**. At the quieter southern end lies the choice swimming and surfing spot of **Putsborough Sands** and the promontory of **Baggy Point**, where gannets, shags, cormorants and shearwaters gather in September and November.

South of here is **Croyde Bay**, another surfers' delight, more compact than Woolacombe, with stalls on the sand renting surfboards and wetsuits. South again around the headland is **Saunton Sands**, a magnificent long stretch of wind-blown coast pummelled by seemingly endless ranks of classic breakers.

6

THE TARKA LINE AND THE TARKA TRAIL

North Devon is closely associated with Henry Williamson's **Tarka the Otter** (1927), which relates the travels and travails of a young otter, and is one of the finest pieces of nature writing in the English language. With parts of the book set in the Taw valley, it was perhaps inevitable that the Exeter to Barnstaple rail route – which follows the Taw for half of its length – should be dubbed the **Tarka Line**. Barnstaple itself forms the centre of the figure-of-eight traced by the **Tarka Trail**, which tracks the otter's wanderings for a distance of more than 180 miles. To the north, the trail penetrates Exmoor (see page 295) then follows the coast back, passing through Williamson's home village of **Georgeham** on its return to Barnstaple. South, the path takes in Bideford (see below), and continues as far as Okehampton (see page 318).

For 23 miles the trail follows a former rail line that's ideally suited to **bicycles**, and there are bike rental shops in Barnstaple and Bideford. You can pick up a *Tarka Trail* booklet and free leaflets on individual sections of the trail from tourist offices.

ARRIVAL AND INFORMATION

By bus Service #303 links Barnstaple and Woolacombe (Mon–Sat 4–6 daily; 45min), while bus #31 runs between Woolacombe and Ilfracombe (Mon–Sat roughly hourly; 30min).

WOOLACOMBE AND AROUND

Tourist office The Esplanade (Easter–Oct daily 10am–5pm; Nov–Easter Mon, Tues, Fri & Sat 10am–1pm, sometimes also Wed & Thurs; ☎01271 870553, ⓦwoolacombetourism.co.uk).

ACCOMMODATION

North Morte Farm Mortehoe, 1 mile north of Woolacombe, EX34 7EG ☎01271 870381, ⓦnorthmortefarm.co.uk. More peaceful than many of the campsites around here, with panoramic sea views and access to Rockham Beach, though not much shelter. Mortehoe's pubs are a short walk away. Closed Nov–Easter. Per person **£10**

Rocks Hotel Beach Rd, EX34 7BT ☎01271 870361, ⓦtherockshotel.co.uk. This surfer-friendly place close to the beach has smallish but smart, high-spec bedrooms

and bathrooms, and a breakfast room styled like a 1950s American diner. Sea-view rooms cost an extra £10. **£79**

Woolacombe Bay Hotel South St, EX34 7BN ☎01271 870388, ⓦwoolacombe-bay-hotel.co.uk. This grand building just up from the beach once housed American troops training for the Normandy landings, and is now a tidy hotel with comfortable rooms, good leisure facilities (including indoor and outdoor pools and a spa) and a restaurant overlooking the water. **£184**

EATING AND DRINKING

Bar Electric Beach Rd, EX34 7BP ☎01271 870429, ⓦbarelectric.co.uk. Friendly hangout that stays buzzing until late, with themed food nights and a long list of drinks and meals, including pizzas and pastas (all £10–12). Easter–Dec Mon–Thurs 11am–10pm, Fri 11am–midnight, Sat & Sun 10am–midnight; kitchen Easter–Dec Mon–Fri 12.30–3pm & 5–9pm, Sat & Sun (or daily in summer) 10am–3pm & 5–9pm.

Blue Groove Hobbs Hill, Croyde, EX33 1LZ ☎01271 890111, ⓦblue-groove.co.uk. As well as burgers, steaks and seafood, this modern restaurant/bar offers

a good range of international food, from enchiladas to prawn dhansak (most mains £13–15). Easter–Oct daily 9am–late; Nov & Dec Mon & Sun 10am–4pm, Fri & Sat 10am–late.

★**The Thatch** Hobbs Hill, Croyde, EX33 1LZ ☎01271 890349, ⓦthethatchcroyde.com. Perennially popular pub in the centre of Croyde, worth visiting for its ice-cold local cider and enormous stacks of nachos (£7–12). There's often live music on Fri nights, when the pub and its two beer gardens get especially busy. Mon–Thurs & Sun 8am–11pm, Fri & Sat 8am–midnight; kitchen daily 8am–10pm.

Bideford and around

Like Barnstaple, nine miles to the east, the handsome estuary town of **BIDEFORD** formed an important link in north Devon's trade network in the Middle Ages, mainly due to its **bridge**, which still straddles the River Torridge. Just northwest is the seafront village of **Westward Ho!**, which faces a broad, sandy beach blessed with fairly consistent swell. A couple of miles downstream from Bideford, the old shipbuilding port of

APPLEDORE, lined with pastel-coloured Georgian houses, is worth visiting for a wander and a drink in one of its cosy **pubs**.

ARRIVAL AND INFORMATION

By bus Route #21 (every 30min) handily links Bideford with Barnstaple (40min) and Westward Ho! (20min). Services #15A, #15C (Mon–Sat every 30min) and #21A (Sun hourly) connect Bideford with Appledore (15min).

BIDEFORD AND AROUND

Tourist office In the Burton Art Gallery and Museum, Kingsley Road (Mon–Sat 10am–4pm, Sun 11am–4pm; ☎01237 477676, ⓦburtonartgallery.co.uk).

6

ACCOMMODATION AND EATING

Beaver Inn Irsha St, Appledore, EX39 1RY ☎01237 474822, ⓦbeaverinn.co.uk. At Appledore's northern tip, this traditional pub has wonderful views from its outdoor tables, regular live music and a friendly mix of visitors and locals. Snacks under £10, seafood mains round £15. Daily 11am–11pm; kitchen daily noon–2.30pm & 6–9pm.

The Mount Northdown Rd, Bideford, EX39 3LP ☎01237 473748, ⓦwww.themountbideford.co.uk. Handsome Georgian guesthouse set in its own walled gardens, with elegantly furnished rooms and a separate guests' lounge. It's in a quiet area a few minutes outside the centre, linked by a footpath. **£90**

Clovelly

West along Bideford Bay, picturesque **CLOVELLY** was put on the map in the second half of the nineteenth century by two books: Charles Dickens' *A Message From the Sea* and *Westward Ho!* by Charles Kingsley, whose father was rector here for six years. The picture-postcard tone of the village has been preserved by strict regulations, but its excessive quaintness and the streams of visitors on summer days can make it hard to see beyond the artifice.

Beyond the **visitor centre**, where an entrance fee to the village is charged (£7.25), the cobbled, traffic-free main street plunges down past neat, flower-smothered cottages. The tethered sledges here are used for transporting goods, the only way to carry supplies up and down the hill since they stopped using donkeys. At the bottom, Clovelly's stony beach and tiny harbour snuggle under a cleft in the cliff wall.

ARRIVAL AND INFORMATION

By bus Bus #319 from Bideford Quay (Mon–Sat 4 daily; 45min) stops by the visitor centre, then continues to Hartland (15min).
Tourist office The visitor centre is at the top of the village

CLOVELLY

(daily: Easter–June, Sept & Oct 10am–5pm; July & Aug 9am–6pm; Nov–Easter 10am–4pm; ☎01237 431781, ⓦclovelly.co.uk).

GETTING AROUND

Land Rover service If you can't face the return climb to the top of the village, make use of the rLand Rover service that leaves from behind the *Red Lion* on the quayside (Easter–Oct 11am–5pm, roughly every 15min; £2.50).

SURFING IN NORTH DEVON

Devon's premier **surfing** sites are on the west-facing coast between Morte Point and the Taw estuary. While **Woolacombe Sands** and **Saunton Sands** can (and often do) comfortably accommodate armies of surfers, smaller **Croyde Bay** does get congested in summer. **Equipment** is available to rent from numerous places in the villages of Woolacombe and Croyde or from stalls on the beach (around £8–12 for 4hr or £10–15/day for a board, £8 for 4hr or £10/day for a wetsuit). You can see local surf reports and live webcams at ⓦmagicseaweed. com. If you find yourself without any waves, you can while away half an hour at the tiny **Museum of British Surfing** in Braunton, four miles east of Croyde (April–Sept Mon–Sat 11am–3pm; £2; ☎01271 815155, ⓦmuseumofbritishsurfing.org.uk), which uses interactive exhibits and old boards to tell the story of British board riding – from the early "surf bathers" of the 1920s to today's fearless big-wave surfers.

ACCOMMODATION AND EATING

★ **East Dyke Farmhouse** Higher Clovelly, EX39 5RU ☎ 01237 431216, ⊚ bedbreakfastclovelly.co.uk. Away from the old village, this 200-year-old building with a beamed and flagstoned dining room has guest rooms with fridges and private bathrooms. No credit cards. **£65**

Red Lion The Quay, EX39 5TF ☎ 01237 431237, ⊚ stay atclovelly.co.uk. Of the village's two luxurious and pricey hotels, this one enjoys the best position, right on the harbourside. It's got a congenial bar and the formal *Harbour Restaurant*, specializing in super-fresh seafood (£28 for two courses). Daily noon–3pm & 6.30–8.30pm. **£160**

Hartland and around

Three miles west of Clovelly, the inland village of **HARTLAND** holds little appeal, but the surrounding coastline is spectacular. You could arrive at **Hartland Point** along minor roads, but the best approach is on foot along the coast path. The jagged black rocks of the dramatic headland are battered by the sea and overlooked by a solitary lighthouse 350ft up. South of Hartland Point, the saw-toothed rocks and near-vertical escarpments defiantly confront the waves, with spectacular waterfalls tumbling over the cliffs.

Hartland Abbey

1.5 miles west of Hartland, EX39 6DT · **House** Easter to early Oct Mon–Thurs & Sun 2–5pm · £12 (includes grounds) · **Grounds** Easter to early Oct Mon–Thurs & Sun 11am–5pm · £8.50 · ☎ 01237 441496, ⊚ hartlandabbey.com

Surrounded by gardens and lush woodland, **Hartland Abbey** is an eighteenth-century mansion incorporating the ruins of an abbey dissolved in 1539. The Regency library

---

LUNDY ISLAND

There are fewer than thirty full-time residents on **Lundy**, a tiny windswept island twelve miles north of Hartland Point. Now a refuge for thousands of marine birds, Lundy has no cars, just one pub and one shop – indeed, little has changed since the Marisco family established itself here in the twelfth century, making use of the shingle beaches and coves to terrorize shipping along the Bristol Channel. The family's fortunes only fell in 1242 when one of their number, William de Marisco, was found to be plotting against the king, whereupon he was hung, drawn and quartered at Tower Hill in London. The castle erected by Henry III on Lundy's southern end dates from this time.

Today the island is managed by the **Landmark Trust**. Unless you're on a specially arranged diving or climbing expedition, **walking** along the interweaving tracks and footpaths is really the only thing to do here. The shores – mainly cliffy on the west side of the island, softer and undulating on the east – shelter a rich variety of **birdlife**, including kittiwakes, fulmars, shags and Manx shearwaters, which often nest in rabbit burrows. The most famous birds, though, are the **puffins** after which Lundy is named – from the Norse *Lunde* (puffin) and *ey* (island). They can only be sighted in April and May, when they come ashore to mate. Offshore, **grey seals** can be seen all year round.

ARRIVAL AND INFORMATION

By boat Between April and Oct, the *MS Oldenburg* sails to Lundy up to four times a week from Ilfracombe, less frequently from Bideford (around 2hr from both places; day returns £37, child £19, open returns £65). To reserve a place, call the shore office on ☎ 01271 863636 or visit ⊚ landmarktrust.org.uk/lundyisland/ ms-oldenburg (day returns can also be booked from local tourist offices).

ACCOMMODATION

Self-catering A number of idiosyncratic Landmark Trust properties are available for self-catering for a minimum of two nights (at around £170). These range from eighteenth-century hideaways for two in a castle keep to weathered fishermen's cottages. They're hugely popular, so book well in advance (☎ 01628 825925, ⊚ landmarktrust.org.uk/ Search-and-Book/landmark-groups/lundy).

B&B The shore office (☎ 01271 863636) can occasionally arrange accommodation on a bed and breakfast basis, with meals at the island's pub. **£75**

Camping Lundy has a small campsite, also run by the Landmark Trust (closed late Oct to late March; book two weeks ahead). Per person **£6**

has portraits by Gainsborough and Reynolds, George Gilbert Scott designed the vaulted Alhambra Corridor and outer hall, and fine furniture, old photographs and frescoes are everywhere. A path leads a mile from the house to cliffs and a small, sandy bay.

ARRIVAL AND DEPARTURE   **HARTLAND AND AROUND**

By bus The #319 (Mon–Sat 4–5 daily) links Hartland with Clovelly (15min), Bideford (1hr) and Barnstaple (1hr 30min).

ACCOMMODATION

2 Harton Manor The Square, off Fore St, EX39 6BL ☏ 01237 441670, ⓦ twohartonmanor.co.uk. Small, friendly B&B offering three rooms above an artist's studio – one en suite with a four-poster. Organic, locally sourced and Aga-cooked breakfasts are served in the flagstoned kitchen. No credit cards. **£100**

Stoke Barton Farm Stoke, EX39 6DU, half a mile west of Hartland Abbey ☏ 01237 441238, ⓦ westcountry-camping.co.uk. Right by the fourteenth-century church of St Nectan's, this working farm offers camping, plus basic "Pixie huts" (£45) and a B&B room in the farmhouse (£60). Closed Nov–Easter. Per person **£7.50**

Southeast Cornwall

The numerous estuaries strung along the seaboard of **Southeast Cornwall** shelter a succession of quaint old fishing ports, among them **Looe**, **Polperro**, **Fowey** and **Mevagissey**. The area is also noted for its china clay industry, and the conical spoil heaps left by the mines are a feature of the landscape around **St Austell Bay**; a short distance inland, a former clay pit is home to the **Eden Project**, a visionary celebration of environmental diversity and one of the region's biggest draws. West of here, bustling **Falmouth** and the pretty village of **St Mawes** on either side of the Carrick Roads estuary are both worth a wander, as is the laidback county capital, **Truro**.

Looe

In the southeast corner of Cornwall, **LOOE** was drawing crowds as early as 1800, when the first "bathing-machines" were wheeled out; it was the arrival of the railway in 1879, though, that really packed the beaches of this river-divided resort. The handiest stretch of sand lies in front of East Looe, but you'll find cleaner water and less congestion away from the river mouth, a mile eastwards at **Millendreath**.

ARRIVAL AND INFORMATION   **LOOE**

By train The station is on the river's east bank, on Station Rd. There's an hourly Liskeard train (not Sun in winter; 30min).

By bus Most buses to and from Looe stop on the eastern side of the bridge joining East Looe with West Looe. Destinations Liskeard (Mon–Sat hourly, Sun every 2hr; 25min); Plymouth (Mon–Sat every 2hr; 1hr 10min); Polperro (Mon–Sat 2–3 hourly, Sun hourly; 10–20min).

Tourist office The Guildhall, Fore St (Easter to mid-Sept Mon–Sat 10am–3pm; mid-Sept to Easter Mon–Fri 10am–1pm; ☏ 01503 262072, ⓦ www.looeguide.co.uk).

ACCOMMODATION AND EATING

Meneglaze House Shutta, East Looe, PL13 1LU ☏ 01503 269227, ⓦ looebedandbreakfast.com. Guests at this B&B near the station are greeted with fresh flowers and home-made biscuits. Rooms have fridges and Egyptian cotton bedding, and breakfasts include hog's pudding. No children. **£84**

Old Sail Loft The Quay, East Looe, PL13 1AP ☏ 01503 262131, ⓦ oldsailloftlooe.co. This oak-beamed warehouse offers the freshest seafood – seafood tagliatelle (£15), lemon sole (£24) – plus meat dishes like lamb shank (£18). Mon–Thurs 5.30–9pm, Fri & Sat 11.45am–2pm & 5.30–9pm.

Schooner Point 1 Trelawney Terrace, Polperro Rd, West Looe, PL13 2AG ☏ 01503 262670, ⓦ schoonerpoint. co.uk. Just 100yd from Looe Bridge, this family-run guesthouse has great river views from most of its good-value rooms, which include a single (£50) with a private shower. **£90**

Polperro

Linked to Looe by frequent buses, **POLPERRO** is smaller and quainter than its neighbour, but has a similar feel. From the bus stop and car park at the top of the village, it's a five- or ten-minute walk alongside the River Pol to the pretty harbour. The surrounding cliffs and the tightly packed houses rising on each side of the stream have an undeniable charm, and the tangle of lanes is little changed since the village's heyday of pilchard fishing and smuggling. However, the influx of tourists has inevitably taken its toll, and the straggling main street – the Coombes – is now an unbroken row of tacky shops and food outlets.

ARRIVAL AND DEPARTURE
POLPERRO

By bus Polperro is served by frequent buses from Looe (Mon–Sat 2–3 hourly, Sun hourly; 15–30min) and Plymouth (Mon–Sat every 2hr; 1hr 40min).

ACCOMMODATION AND EATING

★ **Blue Peter** The Quay, PL13 2QZ ☎01503 272743, ⓦthebluepeterinn.yolasite.com. Welcoming harbourside pub serving real ales and local scrumpy. The bar food is good (£11 for fish and chips) and there's live music at weekends. Mon–Sat 11am–11pm, Sun noon–10.30pm; kitchen daily noon–2.30pm & 6–8.30pm, school hols daily noon–8.30pm.

The House on the Props Talland St, PL13 2RE ☎01503 272310, ⓦhouseontheprops.co.uk. Staying at this quirky B&B right on the harbour is a bit like being on a boat, with snug rooms, wonky floors and awesome views; there's also a tearoom and restaurant on board. Closed mid-Nov to Easter. Mon & Tues 9am–4pm, Thurs–Sat 9am–8.30pm. **£85**

Penryn House The Coombes, PL13 2RQ ☎01503 272157, ⓦpenrynhouse.co.uk. Relaxed and friendly B&B with a country-house feel. The immaculately clean rooms are small but cosy – those at the back are quietest, but have no view. Parking available. **£75**

Fowey

The ten miles west from Polperro to Polruan are among south Cornwall's finest stretches of the coastal path, giving access to some beautiful, secluded **sand beaches**. There are frequent ferries across the River Fowey from Polruan, affording a fine prospect of **FOWEY** (pronounced "Foy"), a cascade of neat, pale terraces at the mouth of one of the peninsula's greatest rivers. The major port on the county's south coast in the fourteenth century, Fowey finally became so ambitious that it provoked Edward IV to strip the town of its military capability, though it continued to thrive commercially, becoming the leading port for china clay shipments in the nineteenth century.

Fowey's steep layout centres on the distinctive fifteenth-century church of **St Fimbarrus** (ⓦfoweyparishchurch.org). Below the church, the **Ship Inn**, which sports some fine Elizabethan panelling, held the local Roundhead HQ during the Civil War. From here, Fore Street, Lostwithiel Street and the Esplanade fan out, the last of which leads to a footpath that gives access to some splendid **coastal walks**. One of these passes Menabilly House, where **Daphne Du Maurier** lived for 24 years – it was the model for Manderley in her novel *Rebecca*. The house is not open to the public, but the path takes you down to the twin coves of **Polridmouth**, where Rebecca met her watery end. The tourist office can provide information on the eight-day **Fowey Festival** (☎01726 879500, ⓦfoweyfestival.com) which takes place each May, with talks, walks, workshops and concerts.

ARRIVAL AND INFORMATION
FOWEY

By bus Buses #24 and #25 run from Par (Mon–Sat every 30min, Sun every 1hr 30min; 15min) and St Austell (Mon–Sat every 30min, Sun every 1hr 30min; 45min).

By ferry Fowey can be reached by ferry every 10–15min daily from Bodinnick (foot passengers and vehicles) and Polruan (foot passengers only); tickets cost around £2 for a foot passenger, £5 for a car and passengers (☎01726 870232, ⓦctomsandson.co.uk).

Tourist office 5 South St (Mon–Sat 10am–5pm, Sun 11am–4pm; ☎0905 151 0262, ⓦfowey.co.uk).

ACCOMMODATION AND EATING

Coombe Farm Lankelly Lane, PL23 1HW, 1 mile southwest of Fowey ☏01726 833123, ⓦcoombe farmbb.co.uk. A 20min walk from town, this B&B provides perfect rural isolation – and there's a bathing area just 300yd away. **£75**

Old Quay House 28 Fore St, PL23 1AQ ☏01726 833302, ⓦtheoldquayhouse.com. Pricey harbourside hotel with eleven compact yet fresh-feeling rooms, some of which have balconies. The restaurant, *Q*, serves plenty of fresh seafood on set-price menus (£29 at lunch, £40 in

the evening for three courses). Mon & Tues 6.30–9pm, Wed–Sun 12.30–3pm & 6.30–9pm; reduced hours in winter. **£190**

Sam's 20 Fore St, PL23 1AQ ☏01726 832273, ⓦsams cornwall.co.uk. With a menu ranging from burgers (£10–16) to seafood (£7–16.50), this place has 1960s rock'n'roll decor and friendly service. It doesn't take bookings, so arrive early or be prepared to wait. There's a late-closing lounge/bar upstairs. Daily noon–9pm (last orders).

St Austell Bay

It was the discovery of china clay, or kaolin, in the downs north of **St Austell Bay** that spurred the area's growth in the eighteenth century. An essential ingredient in porcelain, kaolin had until then only been produced in northern China. Still vital to Cornwall's economy, the clay is now mostly exported for use in the manufacture of paper, paint and medicines, the green and white spoil heaps making an eerie sight in the local landscape.

The town of **ST AUSTELL** itself is fairly unexciting, but makes a useful stop for trips in the surrounding area. Its nearest link to the sea is at **CHARLESTOWN**, an easy downhill walk from the centre of town. This unspoilt port is still used for china clay shipments, and is a frequent filming location (including for *Poldark*). Behind the harbour, the **Shipwreck & Heritage Centre** (March–Oct daily 10am–5pm; £5.95; ☏01726 69897, ⓦshipwreckcharlestown.com) is entered through tunnels once used to convey clay to the docks, and shows a good collection of photos and relics as well as tableaux of historical scenes. On either side of the dock, the coarse sand and stone **beaches** have small rock pools, above which cliff walks lead around the bay.

ARRIVAL AND DEPARTURE   **ST AUSTELL BAY**

By train The station, off High Cross St, is one of the main rstops in southeast Cornwall, with regular Bodmin (every 30min–1hr; 20min) and Truro (every 30min–1hr; 20min) services, plus trains for Plymouth, Bristol and London.
By bus Buses pull in next to St Austell's train station, off High Cross St.

Destinations Bodmin (Mon–Sat hourly; 1hr); Charlestown (Mon–Sat every 10–20min, Sun 7 daily; 10–15min); Falmouth (2 daily; 1hr); Newquay (Mon–Sat 1–2 hourly, Sun every 1–2hr; 1hr–1hr 20min); Plymouth (3 daily; 1hr 20min); Truro (Mon–Sat hourly, Sun 4 daily; 30–40min).

ACCOMMODATION AND EATING

Rashleigh Arms Charlestown Rd, PL25 3NJ ☏01726 73635, ⓦrashleigharms.co.uk. Friendly inn with St Austell and guest ales, reasonably priced food (mains £10–16) including sandwiches and a Sunday carvery,

and outdoor seating. Rooms are available upstairs or in a Georgian annexe. Daily 11am–11pm; kitchen daily noon–9pm. **£125**

The Eden Project

4 miles northeast of St Austell, PL24 2SG • Jan to mid-Feb & early to late Nov Mon–Fri 10am–4pm, Sat & Sun 9.30am–6pm; mid-Feb to March daily 10am–4pm; April–July, Sept & Oct daily 9.30am–6pm; Aug Mon–Thurs 9.30am–8pm, Fri–Sun 9.30am–6pm; late Nov to mid-Dec Mon–Thurs 10am–4pm, Fri–Sun 9.30am–8pm; mid- to late Dec daily 9.30am–8pm; last entry 1hr 30min before closing • £27.50, or £25 in advance (under-17s £14/£12.60); £23.50 (£10) if arriving by bus, by bike or on foot; £38 (£18.45) combined ticket with Lost Gardens of Heligan (see page 332) • ☏01726 811911, ⓦedenproject.com • Bus #101 from St Austell station (roughly hourly; 20min)

Occupying a 160ft-deep crater whose awesome scale only reveals itself once you have passed the entrance at its lip, the **Eden Project** showcases the diversity of the planet's plant life in an imaginative way. Centre-stage are the geodesic "**biomes**" – vast conservatories made up of eco-friendly Teflon-coated, hexagonal panels. One holds groves of olive and citrus trees, cacti and other plants usually found in the warm, temperate zones of the Mediterranean, southern Africa and southwestern USA, while the larger one contains plants from the tropics, including teak and mahogany trees, with a waterfall and river gushing through. Equally impressive are the **grounds**, where plantations of bamboo, tea, hops, hemp and tobacco are interspersed with brilliant displays of flowers. In summer, the grassy arena sees **performances** of a range of music – from Van Morrison to Foals (ⓦedensessions.com) – and in winter they set up a skating rink.

Mevagissey and around

MEVAGISSEY was once known for the construction of fast vessels, used for carrying pilchards (officially) and contraband (less officially). Today the tiny port might display a few stacks of lobster pots, but the real business is tourism, and in summer the maze of backstreets is saturated with day-trippers, converging on the inner harbour and overflowing onto the large sand beach at **Pentewan** a mile to the north.

Four miles south of Mevagissey juts the striking headland of **Dodman Point**, cause of many a wreck and topped by a stark granite cross built by a local parson as a seamark in 1896. The promontory holds the remains of an Iron Age fort, with an earthwork bulwark cutting right across the point. Curving away to the west, elegant **Veryan Bay** holds a string of exquisite coves, such as **Hemmick Beach**, a fine place for a dip with rocky outcrops affording a measure of privacy, and **Porthluney Cove**, a crescent of sand whose centrepiece is the battlemented **Caerhays Castle** (house tours mid-March to mid-June Mon–Fri 11.30am, 1pm and 2.30pm; 45min; gardens mid-Feb to mid-June daily 10am–5pm; house tours £8.50, gardens £8.50, combined ticket £13.50; ☎01872 501310, ⓦwww.caerhays.co.uk), built in 1808 by John Nash and surrounded by beautiful gardens. A little further on is the minuscule whitewashed village of **Portloe**, fronted by jagged black rocks that throw up fountains of seaspray, giving it a poignant, end-of-the-road feel.

Lost Gardens of Heligan

Near Pentewan, PL26 6EN · Daily: April–Sept 10am–6pm; Oct–March 10am–5pm; last entry 1hr 30min before closing · £14.50, £38 combined ticket with Eden Project (see page 331) · ☎01726 845100, ⓦheligan.com · Bus #471 (Mon–Sat 4–8 daily) from Mevagissey (10min) and St Austell (30–40min)

A couple of miles north of Mevagissey lie the **Lost Gardens of Heligan**; these fascinating Victorian gardens had fallen into neglect and were resurrected by Tim Smit, the visionary instigator of the Eden Project, in the 1990s. A boardwalk takes you through a jungle and under a canopy of bamboo and ferns down to the Lost Valley, where there are lakes, woods and wildflower meadows.

ARRIVAL AND DEPARTURE   MEVAGISSEY AND AROUND

By bus From St Austell's station, the #24 and #471 services leave for Mevagissey (Mon–Sat 1–2 hourly; Sun 7 daily; 20min); #471 continues to the Lost Gardens of Heligan (10min).

ACCOMMODATION AND EATING

Alvorada 5 East Quay, PL26 6QQ ☎01726 842055. The chances are that if you choose a fish dish at this small, family-run Portuguese restaurant, it'll have been caught by the chef. Dishes include sardines, mussels with chorizo and *caldeirada* (fish casserole), with most mains around £17.50. Noon–2pm & 6.30pm–late; call for winter opening. **Wild Air** Polkirt Hill, PL26 6UX ☎01726 843302, ⓦwildair.co.uk. Away from the harbour crowds, this B&B has three tasteful rooms, all with en-suite or private

bathrooms, and all enjoying lofty views over the harbour and coast. There's also a panoramic patio, and parking. **£85** **YHA Boswinger** Boswinger, PL26 6LL, half a mile from Hemmick Beach and 3.5 miles southwest of Mevagissey ☎01726 844527, ⓦyha.org.uk/hostel/boswinger. Set in a former farmhouse, this is a remote spot a mile from the bus stop at Gorran Churchtown (Mon–Sat #471 or #G1 from St Austell and Mevagissey). Kitchen and meals available. Only groups can book Nov–Feb. Dorms **£19**, doubles **£59**

6

Truro

Cornwall's capital, **TRURO**, presents a mixture of different styles, from the graceful Georgian architecture that came with the tin-mining boom of the 1800s to its neo-Gothic cathedral and modern shopping centre (Lemon Quay). It's an attractive place, not overwhelmed by tourism and with a range of good-value facilities.

Truro Cathedral

St Mary's St, TR1 2AF • Mon–Sat 7.30am–6pm, Sun 9am–7pm; tours April–Oct Mon–Thurs 11am, 1hr • Free (£5 suggested donation) • T 01872 276782, W trurocathedral.org.uk

Truro's dominant feature is its faux-medieval **cathedral**, completed in 1910 and incorporating part of the fabric of the old parish church that previously occupied the site. In the airy interior, the neo-Gothic baptistry commands attention, complete with its emphatically pointed arches and elaborate roof vaulting.

Royal Cornwall Museum

River St, TR1 2SJ • Mon–Sat 10am–4.45pm, Sun 10am–4pm • £4.50 • T 01872 272205, W royalcornwallmuseum.org.uk

Truro's **Royal Cornwall Museum** offers a rich, wide-ranging hoard that takes in everything from the region's natural history to Celtic inscriptions. If time is tight you could confine yourself to the renowned collection of minerals on the ground floor and the upstairs galleries holding works by Cornish artists including members of the Newlyn School.

ARRIVAL AND INFORMATION — TRURO

By train The train station is just off Richmond Hill, a 10min walk west of the centre.

Destinations Bodmin (hourly; 35min); Exeter (every 1–2hr; 2hr 20min); Falmouth (Mon–Sat every 30min, Sun hourly; 25min); Liskeard (hourly; 50min); Penzance (hourly; 45min); Plymouth (hourly; 1hr 15min).

By bus Buses stop centrally at Lemon Quay, or near the train station.

Destinations Falmouth (Mon–Sat every 30min, Sun hourly; 45min); Newquay (Mon–Sat 3 hourly, Sun 1–2 hourly; 55min–1hr 30min); Penzance (Mon–Sat every 30min, Sun hourly; 1hr 40min); Plymouth (5 daily; 1hr 40min–2hr 20min); St Austell (Mon–Sat hourly, Sun 3 daily; 30–40min); St Ives (Mon–Sat every 30min, Sun hourly; 1hr 35min); St Mawes (Mon–Sat 7 daily, Sun 4 daily; 1hr 5min).

Tourist office Municipal Buildings, Boscawen St (Mon–Sat 9.30am–5pm T 01872 274555, W visittruro.org.uk).

ACCOMMODATION

Bay Tree 28 Ferris Town, TR1 3JH T 01872 240274, W baytree-guesthouse.co.uk. Homely, restored Georgian house between the station and town centre, with a friendly owner and shared bathrooms. Singles available. Rough Guide readers receive a discount if prebooked. No cards. **£65**

★ **Truro Lodge** 10 The Parade, TR1 1QE T 07813 755210, W trurolodge.co.uk. Relaxed B&B in a large, Georgian terraced house near the centre. Buffet breakfasts are available in the kitchen, which is accessible all day for guests' use, and there's a lounge and veranda. **£45**

EATING AND DRINKING

Charlotte's Teahouse 1 Boscawen St, TR1 2QU T 01872 263706. Upstairs in the old Coinage Hall, this is a gloriously old-fashioned spot for sandwiches (£6.50–8.50), muffins and cream teas. The setting is Victorian, with staff in period dress. Mon–Sat 10am–5pm.

Hooked! Tabernacle St, TR1 2EJ T 01872 274700, W hookedrestaurantandbar.co.uk. This relaxed restaurant sports banquettes, bare brick walls and a vaulted ceiling, and has a menu that's strong on seafood, including tapas (£3) and more substantial dishes like paella and seafood curry (both £15). Mon–Sat noon–2pm & 5.30–9pm (last orders).

Wig & Pen 1 Frances St, TR1 3DP T 01872 273028, W staustellbrewery.co.uk. The pick of Truro's pubs serves St Austell ales and bar food, as well as brunches and cream teas, with some tables outside. Simple bar meals such as pastas and burgers cost £7.50–10. Mon–Thurs 11am–11pm, Fri & Sat 11am–midnight, Sun 11am–6pm; kitchen Mon–Sat noon–3pm & 6–9pm, Sun noon–3pm.

Falmouth

Amid the lush tranquillity of the **Carrick Roads** estuary basin, the major resort of **FALMOUTH** is the site of one of Cornwall's mightiest castles, **Pendennis Castle**, and of one of the country's foremost collections of boats in the **National Maritime Museum Cornwall**. The town sits at the mouth of the Fal estuary, at the end of a rail branch line from Truro and connected by ferry to Truro and St Mawes. Round Pendennis Point, south of the centre, a long sandy bay holds a succession of sheltered **beaches**: from the popular **Gyllyngvase Beach**, you can reach the more attractive **Swanpool Beach** by cliff path, or walk a couple of miles further on to **Maenporth**, from where there are some fine clifftop walks.

National Maritime Museum Cornwall

Discovery Quay, TR11 3QY • Daily 10am–5pm • £12.95 • ☎ 01326 313388, ⓦ nmmc.co.uk

Vessels from all around the world are exhibited in Falmouth's **National Maritime Museum Cornwall**. Of every size and shape, the craft are arranged on three levels, many of them suspended in mid-air in the cavernous Flotilla Gallery. Smaller galleries examine specific aspects of boat-building, seafaring history and Falmouth's packet ships, and a lighthouse-like lookout tower offers excellent views over the harbour and estuary, with a lift descending to an underwater viewing room.

Pendennis Castle

Pendennis Head, TR11 4LP • Mid-Feb to late Feb daily 10am–4pm; late Feb to March Wed–Sun 10am–4pm; April–Sept daily 10am–6pm; Oct daily 10am–5pm; Nov to mid-Feb Sat & Sun 10am–4pm • £8.40; EH • ☎ 01326 316594, ⓦ www.english-heritage.org.uk/visit/places/pendennis-castle • Bus #367 from town centre

Under a mile southeast of Falmouth's harbour, **Pendennis Castle** stands sentinel at the tip of the promontory that separates the Carrick Roads estuary from Falmouth Bay. The extensive fortification shows little evidence of its five-month siege by the Parliamentarians during the Civil War, which ended only when half its defenders had died and the rest had been starved into submission. Though this is a less-refined contemporary of the castle at St Mawes (see page 336), its site wins hands down, the stout ramparts offering the best all-round views of Carrick Roads and Falmouth Bay.

ARRIVAL AND INFORMATION
FALMOUTH

By train The branch rail line from Truro (Mon–Sat every 30min, Sun hourly; 30min) stops at Falmouth Town, best for the centre, and Falmouth Docks, 2min away, near Pendennis Castle.

By bus Most buses stop on The Moor, close to the Prince of Wales Pier and just east of the High St.

Destinations Helston (Mon–Sat hourly, Sun 2 daily; 25– 50min); Penzance (Mon–Sat 6 daily, Sun 1 daily; 55min– 1hr 40min); St Austell (2 daily; 1hr); Truro (Mon–Sat every 30min, Sun hourly; 45min).

Tourist office Prince of Wales Pier (April–Oct Mon–Sat 9.45am–3.15pm, Sun 9.45am–1pm; Nov–March Mon–Thurs & Sat 10am–3pm; ☎ 01326 741194, ⓦ falmouth.co.uk).

ACCOMMODATION

★**Falmouth Lodge** 9 Gyllyngvase Terrace, TR11 4DL ☎ 01326 319996, ⓦ falmouthbackpackers.co.uk. Clean and friendly backpackers' hostel located a couple of minutes' walk from the beach, with a sociable lounge and kitchen. Dorms £19, doubles £52

Falmouth Townhouse 3 Grove Place, TR11 4AL ☎ 01326 312009, ⓦ falmouthtownhouse.co.uk. Chic boutique hotel in a Georgian building just across from the Maritime Museum. It's all highly designed, with spacious guestrooms,

quirky bathrooms and a buzzing bar, though some front-facing rooms suffer from street noise at night. £75

St Michael's Hotel and Spa Gyllyngvase Beach, TR11 4NB ☎ 01326 312707, ⓦ stmichaelshotel.co.uk. Sleekly luxurious seaside hotel, very close to the beach and with a range of spa facilities, including an indoor pool. Rooms are bright and contemporary, the cheapest being compact "cabin rooms" (£176). The *Flying Fish* bistro provides quality modern cuisine with sea views. £200

EATING AND DRINKING

★**Beerwolf Books** Bells Court, off Market St, TR11 3AZ ☎ 01326 618474, ⓦ beerwolfbooks.com. Here's a novel concept – a free house and bookshop combined. Set in a beautifully restored old building, with tables in a

secluded courtyard, it makes a relaxing spot for a drink, with a great selection of local beers. Mon–Sat 10am–midnight, Sun noon–11pm.

Fuel 35–37 Arwenack St, TR11 3JG ☎ 01326 314499,

6

ⓦfuelfalmouth.co.uk. This buzzy, colourful spot near the Maritime Museum on the main drag provides all-day breakfasts, coffees, cream teas, snack lunches and full meals, with friendly service and an upbeat atmosphere. Main courses such as moussaka, fishcakes and beef burgers cost around £10. Daily 8am–10pm.

Gylly Beach Café Gyllyngvase Beach, TR11 4PA

ⓣ01326 312884, ⓦgyllybeach.com. Cool beachside hangout serving everything from baguettes to monkfish curry. Breakfast is served until 11.30am, lunch dishes are £8–12, and evening mains start at £14. There are outdoor barbecues in summer from 4pm and live music on Sun eves. Daily 9am–late.

St Mawes and around

Situated on the east side of the Carrick Roads estuary, the two-pronged **Roseland Peninsula** is a luxuriant backwater of woods and sheltered creeks. The main settlement is **ST MAWES**, a tranquil old fishing port easily reached from ferries from Falmouth. Moving east from St Mawes, you could spend a pleasant afternoon poking around the southern arm of the peninsula, which holds the twelfth- to thirteenth-century church of **ST ANTHONY-IN-ROSELAND** and the **lighthouse** on St Anthony's Head, marking the entry into Carrick Roads. Two and a half miles north of St Mawes is the scattered hamlet of **ST JUST-IN-ROSELAND**, home to the strikingly picturesque **Church of St Just** (ⓦstjustandstmawes.org.uk/st-just-in-roseland), which is right next to the creek and surrounded by palms and subtropical shrubbery, its gravestones tumbling down to the water's edge.

St Mawes Castle

Half a mile west of the quay, TR2 5DE • Mid-Feb to late Feb daily 10am–4pm; late Feb to March Wed–Sun 10am–4pm; April–Sept daily 10am–6pm; Oct daily 10am–5pm; Nov to mid-Feb Sat & Sun 10am–4pm • £5.40; EH • ⓣ01326 270526, ⓦwww.english-heritage.org.uk/visit/places/st-mawes-castle

At the end of the walled seafront of St Mawes stands the sister fort of Pendennis Castle, the small and pristine **St Mawes Castle**, built during the reign of Henry VIII to a clover-leaf design. The castle owes its excellent condition to its early surrender to Parliamentary forces during the Civil War in 1646. The various rooms and gun decks contain artillery exhibits and historical background, and you can climb to the top of the tower and explore the grounds.

Trelissick

Feock, TR3 6QL, 6 miles north of St Mawes • **House** Mid-Feb to Oct daily 11am–5pm; Dec Fri–Sun 11am–7pm • **Garden** Daily: mid-Feb to Oct daily 10.30am–5.30pm; Nov to mid-Feb 10.30am–4.30pm; closes at dusk if earlier • £10.90; NT • ⓣ01872 862090, ⓦnationaltrust.org.uk/trelissick • The King Harry Ferry stops near here, as do ferries from Falmouth, St Mawes and Truro, and the #493 bus from Truro (Mon–Sat)

On a spectacular site that was first settled in the Iron Age, eighteenth-century **Trelissick House** displays Spode china, family portraits, and exhibitions relating to the place and the family, but the real attraction is **Trelissick Garden**, celebrated for its hydrangeas and other Mediterranean species. There are impressive vistas over the River Fal, and splendid woodland walks.

ARRIVAL AND GETTING AROUND   ST MAWES AND AROUND

By bus There are regular buses (#50 & #551) between Truro and St Mawes (Mon–Sat 7 daily, Sun 4 daily; 1hr), stopping off at St Just-in-Roseland (7min from St Mawes) en route.

By ferry St Mawes can be reached on frequent ferries from Falmouth's Prince of Wales Pier and Custom House Quay (£10 return). Passenger ferries from St Mawes also cross to Place on the southern arm of the peninsula (daily every 30min: April, May & Oct 9am–4.30pm; June–Sept

9.30am–5.30pm; £7 return).

By car The fastest road route from Truro, Falmouth and west Cornwall involves crossing the River Fal on the chain-driven King Harry Ferry (every 20min: April–Sept Mon–Sat 7.20am–9.20pm, Sun 9am–9.20pm; Oct–March Mon–Sat 7.20am–7.20pm, Sun 9am–7.20pm; cars £6 & bicycles £1 one-way, foot passengers free in exchange for a charity donation; ⓣ01872 862312, ⓦfalriver.co.uk).

ACCOMMODATION AND EATING

Little Newton Newton Rd, TR2 5BS ☎01326 270664, ⓦlittle-newton.co.uk. Two small but smart and modern en-suite rooms are available at this B&B just off Castle Rd, a steep 10min walk up from the seafront. No debit/credit cards. Closed Nov–Feb. **£65**

St Mawes Hotel Harbourside, TR2 5DW ☎01326 270170, ⓦstmaweshotel.com. Superbly sited overlooking the harbour, this place offers sober but stylish, airy rooms, a quirkily decorated restaurant offering delicious, modern European dishes (mains around £16), and a cosy street-level bar serving snacks and local beers. Daily noon–3pm & 6–9pm. **£195**

★ **Tresanton Hotel** 27 Lower Castle Rd, TR2 5DR ☎01326 270055, ⓦtresanton.com. Cornwall doesn't get much ritzier than this, a slice of Mediterranean-style luxury with bright, sunny colours and a yacht and speedboat available to guests in summer. There's a fabulous Italian-inspired restaurant, too; you can have lunch (£25 for two courses) or an evening meal (mains around £20). Daily noon–3pm & 6.30–10pm. **£280**

The Lizard Peninsula

The **Lizard Peninsula** – from the Celtic *lys ardh*, or "high point" – is mercifully undeveloped. If this flat and treeless expanse can be said to have a centre, it's **Helston**, a junction for buses running from Falmouth and Truro, and to the spartan villages of the peninsula's interior and coast. Other than that it's all deserted beaches and windswept downland – plus **Lizard Point**, the farthest south you can go on the British mainland.

Helston

The otherwise quiet and workaday inland town of **HELSTON** is best known for its **Furry Dance** (or Flora Dance), dating from the seventeenth century. Held on May 8 (unless this falls on Sun or Mon, when the procession takes place on the preceding Sat), it's a stately procession of top-hatted men and summer-frocked women performing a solemn dance through the town's streets and gardens. You can learn something about it and absorb plenty of other local history in the eclectic **Helston Folk Museum** (Mon–Sat 10am–4pm; free; ☎01326 564027, ⓦhelstonmuseum.co.uk), housed in former market buildings behind the Guildhall on Church Street.

Porthleven and around

Two and a half miles southwest of Helston, tin ore from inland mines was once shipped from **PORTHLEVEN**. Good **beaches** lie to either side: the best for swimming are around **Rinsey Head**, three miles north along the coast, including the sheltered **Praa Sands**. One and a quarter miles south of Porthleven, strong currents make it unsafe to swim at **Loe Bar**, a strip of shingle which separates the freshwater **Loe Pool** from the sea. The elongated Pool is one of two sites which claim to be the place where the sword Excalibur was restored to its watery source (the other is on Bodmin Moor). The path running along its western edge makes a fine walking route between here and Helston.

Mullion and around

The inland village of **MULLION**, five miles south of Porthleven, has a fifteenth- to sixteenth-century church dedicated to the Breton **St Mellanus** (or Malo), complete with a dog-door for canine churchgoers. A lane leads a mile and a quarter west to **Mullion Cove**, where a tiny beach is sheltered behind harbour walls and rock stacks, though the neighbouring sands at **Polurrian** and **Poldhu**, to the north, are better and attract surfers.

Lizard Point and around

Five miles south of Mullion, **Lizard Point** is the southern tip of the promontory and mainland Britain's southernmost point, marked by a plain lighthouse above a tiny cove and a restless, churning sea. If you're not following the coast path, you can reach the point via the road and footpath leading a mile south from the nondescript village called simply **THE LIZARD**, where you'll find several places to stay and eat. A little more than a mile northwest, the peninsula's best-known beach, **Kynance Cove**, has sheer 100ft cliffs, stacks and arches of serpentine rock and offshore outcrops. The water quality here is excellent – but take care not to be stranded by the tide.

The east coast

In the north of the peninsula, the snug hamlets dotted around the **River Helford** are a complete contrast to the rugged character of most of the Lizard. On the river's south side, **Frenchman's Creek**, one of a splay of serene inlets, was the inspiration for Daphne Du Maurier's novel of the same name. From Helford Passage you can take a ferry (Easter–Oct 9.30am–5pm; £6 return; ☎01326 250770, ⓦhelford-river-boats.co.uk) to reach **HELFORD**, an agreeable old smugglers' haunt on the south bank.

South of here, on the B3293, the broad, windswept plateau of **Goonhilly Downs** is interrupted by the futuristic saucers of Goonhilly Satellite Station and the nearby ranks of wind turbines. As you head east, the road splits: left to **ST KEVERNE**, an inland village whose tidy square is flanked by two inns and a church; right to **COVERACK**, a fishing port in a sheltered bay. Following the coast path or negotiating minor roads south will bring you to the safe and clean swimming spot of **Kennack Sands**.

GETTING AROUND   THE LIZARD PENINSULA

By bus From Helston, bus #2 goes to Porthleven (Mon–Sat hourly, Sun every 2hr; 10min), #36 (Mon–Sat 5–6 daily) goes to Coverack (30–40min) and St Keverne (30–50min), and #37 (Mon–Sat 8–11 daily, Sun 3–5 daily) goes to Mullion (35min) and The Lizard (45–55min).

ACCOMMODATION AND EATING

★ **Blue Anchor** 50 Coinagehall St, Helston, TR13 8EL ☎01326 562821, ⓦspingoales.com. Deeply traditional West Country pub, once a fifteenth-century monastery rest house, now brewing its own Spingo beer on the premises. Four B&B rooms are available in an adjacent building. Mon–Thurs & Sun 10am–midnight, Fri & Sat 10am–1am. **£75**

Mounts Bay Inn On the B3296, Mullion, TR12 7HN ☎01326 240221, ⓦmountsbaymullion.co.uk. Mullion's best place for Cornish ales, snacks and meals (£6–8) with a beer garden and views over Mounts Bay. Live bands every fortnight and Cornish songs on the last Sun of the month. B&B also available. Mon–Thurs 11am–11pm, Fri & Sat 11am–midnight, Sun noon–11pm; kitchen Mon–Sat noon–2pm & 6–9pm, Sun noon–2.30pm &

6–8.30pm. **£80**

Poldhu Beach Café Poldhu Cove, near Mullion, TR12 7JB ☎01326 240530, ⓦpoldhu.com. The perfect beach café, with energizing breakfasts, burgers (from £4), good coffee and hot chocolate, and locally produced ice cream. Stays open late on Fri in summer for pizza nights. Daily 9.30am–4.30/5.30pm.

YHA Lizard Lizard Point, TR12 7NT ☎0345 371 9550, ⓦyha.org.uk/hostel/lizard. This hostel occupies a former Victorian hotel right on the coast, with majestic views. Camping is also possible, either in your own tent or the hostel's bell tent (July–Sept only; £59) that sleeps up to five, and there's a kitchen for self-catering. Only groups can book Dec–Feb. Camping/person **£13**, dorms **£19**, doubles **£39**

The Penwith Peninsula

Though more densely populated than the Lizard, the **Penwith Peninsula** is a more rugged landscape, with a raw appeal that is still encapsulated by **Land's End**, despite the commercialization of that headland. It also boasts some excellent beaches, chief among them **Porthcurno**, as well as the quaint-but-crowded fishing village of **Mousehole** and the fascinating **St Michael's Mount**, rising out of the sea near **Penzance**. The seascapes, the quality of the light and the slow tempo of the local fishing communities made this area a hotbed of artistic activity from the late nineteenth century onwards, when **Newlyn** became associated with a distinctive school of painting, quickly followed by **St Ives**, while **Zennor** is associated with one-time resident D.H. Lawrence.

Penzance and around

Occupying a sheltered position at the northwest corner of Mount's Bay, **PENZANCE** has always been a major port, but most traces of the medieval town were obliterated at the end of the sixteenth century by a Spanish raiding party. From the top of **Market Jew Street** (from *Marghas Jew*, meaning "Thursday Market"), which climbs from the harbour and the train and bus stations, turn left into **Chapel Street** to see some of the town's finest buildings, including the flamboyant **Egyptian House**, built in 1835 to contain a geological museum but subsequently abandoned until its restoration by the Landmark Trust (Ⓦlandmarktrust.org.uk) in 1973; you can now stay there. Across the street, the seventeenth-century **Union Hotel** originally held the town's assembly rooms, where news of Admiral Nelson's victory at Trafalgar and the death of Nelson himself was first announced in 1805.

Penlee House Gallery and Museum

Morrab Rd, TR18 4HE • Mon–Sat: April–Oct 10am–5pm; Nov–March 10.30am–4.30pm; last entry 30min before closing • £5 • Ⓣ01736 363625, Ⓦpenleehouse.org.uk

Long a centre of the local art movements, **Penlee House Gallery and Museum** holds the country's largest collection of Newlyn School artworks – impressionistic harbour scenes, frequently sentimentalized but often bathed in an evocatively luminous light. There are also displays on local archeology and history, and frequent exhibitions.

St Michael's Mount

Off Marazion, TR17 0HS, 5 miles east of Penzance • **House** Mon–Fri & Sun: mid-March to June, Sept & Oct 10.30am–5pm; July & Aug 10.30am–5.30pm; last entry 45min before closing • £9.50, £14 with garden; NT • **Garden** Mid-April to June Mon–Fri 10.30am–5pm; July & Aug Thurs & Fri 10.30am–5.30pm; Sept Thurs & Fri 10.30am–5pm • £7, £14 with house; NT • Ⓣ01736 710265, Ⓦstmichaelsmount.co.uk • At low tide you can approach on foot via a cobbled causeway (daily tide times on the website); at high tide there are boats from Marazion (£2–3)

Frequent buses from Penzance leave for **MARAZION**, the access point to **St Michael's Mount**, some four hundred yards offshore. A vision of the archangel Michael led to the building of a church on this granite pile around the fifth century, and within three centuries a Celtic monastery had been founded here. The present building derives from a **chapel** raised in the eleventh century by Edward the Confessor, who handed it over to the Benedictine monks of Brittany's Mont St Michel, whose island abbey was the model for this one. Following the Civil War, it became the residence of the St Aubyn family, who still inhabit the castle. Some of the buildings date from the twelfth century, but the later additions are more interesting, such as the battlemented **chapel** and the seventeenth-century decorations of the **Chevy Chase Room**, the former refectory. The lush **gardens** are also well worth exploring.

ARRIVAL AND DEPARTURE	PENZANCE AND AROUND
By train The station is on the seafront, on Station Rd. Destinations Bodmin (roughly hourly; 1hr 15min); Exeter (roughly hourly; 3hr 15min); Plymouth (roughly hourly; 2hr); St Ives (most with a change at St Erth; hourly; 30min–1hr 20min); Truro (roughly hourly; 40min). **By bus** The bus station is next to the train station, on the seafront. Destinations Falmouth (Mon–Sat 7 daily, Sun 1 daily;	55min–1hr 50min); Helston (Mon–Sat hourly, Sun 7 daily; 50min); Plymouth (4 daily; 2hr 50min–4hr); St Austell (2 daily; 1hr 35min–2hr); St Ives (Mon–Sat every 10–30min, Sun 2 hourly; 30min); Truro (Mon–Sat every 30min, Sun hourly; 1hr 40min). **By boat** From Easter to early Nov boats depart from Penzance Quay for the Isles of Scilly (Mon–Sat 4–6 weekly; 2hr 45min; Ⓣ01736 334220, Ⓦislesofscilly-travel.co.uk).

6

ACCOMMODATION

★ **Artist Residence** 20 Chapel St, TR18 4AW ☎01736 365664, ⓦartistresidencecornwall.co.uk. Artistic licence has been given free rein at this central hotel, where each room is designed by a different artist (some rooms are quite cramped). The staff are friendly and helpful, the breakfasts are superb and there's a popular bar and restaurant. **£130**

Penzance Backpackers Alexandra Rd, TR18 4LZ ☎01736 363836, ⓦpzbackpack.com. In a quiet neighbourhood 15min from the centre, this is a tidy, good-value hostel, with en-suite dorms, a well-equipped kitchen and a large lounge. Dorms **£17**, doubles **£38**

Warwick House 17 Regent Terrace, TA18 4DW ☎01736 363881, ⓦwarwickhousepenzance.co.uk. Located near the town centre and the harbour, this B&B has elegant rooms decorated in blue and white – the best ones have views of the water. Two- or three-night minimum stay in summer. **£95**

EATING AND DRINKING

Admiral Benbow 46 Chapel St, TA18 4AF ☎01736 363448. Characterful pub crammed with gaudy ships' figureheads and other nautical items. The bar meals are pretty standard, but this is really a drinking pub, and the atmosphere more than compensates. Mon–Sat 11am–11pm, Sun noon–11pm; kitchen daily noon–2.30pm & 6–9.30pm.

Archie Browns Bread St, TR18 2EQ ☎01736 362828, ⓦarchiebrowns.co.uk. Vegans, veggies and whole-foodies will be happy in this café above a health shop, with its relaxed, friendly vibe and local art on the walls. Dishes include quiches, curries, stews and homity pie (£6–9). Mon–Sat 9am–5pm.

Old Lifeboat House Wharf Rd, TR18 4AA ☎01736 369409, ⓦoldlifeboathouse.co.uk. On the seafront, this café-bistro delivers seafood dishes at reasonable prices (around £15 on the evening menu). Apart from the daily specials, you'll find bouillabaisse and fish pie, as well as a couple of meat and vegetarian options. You can also drop by for breakfast, a well-filled sandwich or coffee and cake. Tues–Sat 9.30am–9pm, Sun 9.30am–4pm.

★ **The Shore** 13–14 Alverton St, TR18 2QP ☎01736 362444, ⓦtheshorerestaurant.uk. Simple seafood dishes are expertly prepared at this friendly, semiformal restaurant, where starters might include red mullet with chana dal, and mains like hake and steamed sole cost around £19. The desserts are memorably good too. Tues–Thurs 6.30–9pm, Fri & Sat 12.30–1.30pm & 6.30–9pm.

Mousehole

Accounts vary as to the derivation of the name of **MOUSEHOLE** (pronounced "Mowzle"), though it may be from a smugglers' cave just to the south. In any case, the name evokes perfectly this minuscule fishing port cradled in the arms of a granite breakwater, three miles south of Penzance. The village attracts more visitors than it can handle, so hang around until the crowds have departed before exploring its tight tangle of lanes, where you'll come across Mousehole's oldest house, the fourteenth-century **Keigwin House**, a survivor of the sacking of the village by Spaniards in 1595.

ARRIVAL AND DEPARTURE   MOUSEHOLE

By bus The #M6 bus (every 20–30min) connects Mousehole's harbour with Newlyn (10min) and Penzance (15min).

ACCOMMODATION AND EATING

Ship Inn Harbourside, TR19 6QX ☎01736 731234, ⓦshipinnmousehole.co.uk. Overlooking the boats, this is a perfect spot for a pint, or a crab sandwich (£12) or grilled mackerel (£13). Accommodation is available in surprisingly modern en-suite rooms, some in an annexe (those with a view cost extra). Daily 11am–11pm; kitchen daily noon–2.30pm & 6–8.30pm. **£115**

Porthcurno

Eight miles west of Mousehole, one of Penwith's best **beaches** lies at **PORTHCURNO**, sandwiched between cliffs. On the shore to the east, a white pyramid marks the spot where the first transatlantic cables were laid in 1880. On the headland beyond lies an Iron Age fort, **Treryn Dinas**, close to the famous rocking stone called **Logan Rock**, a seventy-ton monster that was knocked off its perch in 1824 by a gang of sailors, among them a nephew of writer and poet Oliver Goldsmith. Somehow they replaced the stone, but it never rocked again.

Minack Theatre

South end of village, TR19 6JU • Exhibition Centre daily: March–Oct generally 9.30am–5.30pm, but may close at 12.30pm on Tues & Thurs when performances take place; Nov–Feb 10am–4pm • £5; performances cost £10–14 • ☎ 01736 810181, ⓦ www.minack.com

Steep steps lead up from the beach of tiny white shells to the **Minack Theatre**, hewn out of the cliff in the 1930s and since enlarged to hold 750 seats, though retaining the basic Greek-inspired design. The spectacular backdrop of Porthcurno Bay makes this one of the country's most inspiring theatres (providing the weather holds), where a range of plays, operas and musicals are presented from April to September – bring a cushion and a blanket. The attached **Exhibition Centre** gives access to the theatre during the day and explains the story of its creation.

6

ARRIVAL AND DEPARTURE   PORTHCURNO

By bus Only one bus service – #A1 – runs to and from Porthcurno, making hourly trips to Land's End (15min), Newlyn (30min) and Penzance (40min).

Land's End and around

The extreme western tip of England, **Land's End**, lies four miles west of Porthcurno. Best approached on foot along the coastal path, the 60ft turf-covered cliffs provide a platform to view the Irish Lady, the Armed Knight, Dr Syntax Head and the rest of the Land's End outcrops. Beyond, look out for the Longships lighthouse, a mile and a half out to sea; you can sometimes spot the Wolf Rock lighthouse, nine miles southwest, or even the Isles of Scilly, 28 miles away (see page 344).

Whitesand Bay

To the north of Land's End the rounded granite cliffs fall away at **Whitesand Bay** to reveal a glistening mile-long shelf of beach that offers the best swimming on the Penwith peninsula. The rollers make for good surfing and boards can be rented at **Sennen Cove**, the more popular southern end of the beach.

St Just-in-Penwith

Three miles north of Sennen Cove, the highly scenic headland of **Cape Cornwall** is dominated by the chimney of the Cape Cornwall Mine, which closed in 1870. Half a mile inland is the grimly grey village of **ST JUST-IN-PENWITH**, formerly a centre of the tin and copper industry, with rows of cottages radiating out from Bank Square. The tone is somewhat lightened by **Plen-an-Gwary**, a grassy open-air theatre where miracle plays were once staged; it was later used by Methodist preachers and Cornish wrestlers.

ARRIVAL AND DEPARTURE   LAND'S END AND AROUND

By bus The hourly #A1 and #A3 run to and from Land's End, providing easy connections to Penzance (55min) and St Ives (1hr 20min) respectively. Bus #A3 also runs between Sennen Cove and Land's End (10min), while bus #A17 runs to St Just from Penzance (Mon–Sat hourly, Sun every 2hr; 20–30min).

By plane Land's End Airport, around 1.5 miles south of St Just, handles flights to and from St Mary's in the Isles of Scilly (Mon–Sat: April–Oct 9–17 daily; Nov–March around 10 daily; 20min). For schedules call ☎ 01736 334220 or see ⓦ islesofscilly-travel.co.uk.

ACCOMMODATION

Kelynack Caravan and Camping Park Kelynack, TR19 7RE ☎ 01736 787633, ⓦ kelynackholidays. co.uk. Secluded campsite, one of the few sheltered ones on Penwith, about a mile south of St Just. There are also caravans (from £330/week) and self-catering rooms. Camping/person £8, doubles £70

Trevedra Farm 1 mile north of Sennen, TR19 7BE ☎ 01736 871818, ⓦ trevedrafarm.co.uk. Popular but

spacious campsite above Gwynver Beach (at the northern end of Sennen Cove), with level pitches and sea views. There's a modern block providing good facilities, a shop, and a restaurant serving breakfast and dinner. Closed Nov–Easter. Per person £8

YHA Land's End TR19 7NT ☎ 0345 371 9643, ⓦ yha.org. uk/hostel/lands-end. Less than a mile south of St Just and a half-mile from the coast path, this hostel offers a kitchen, meals and camping facilities with a bell tent to rent (June to mid-Sept; £59). Take the left fork past the post office in St Just to find it. Only groups can book late Oct to Easter. Camping/person **£13**, dorms **£16**, doubles **£39**

EATING

Kegen Teg 12 Market Square, St Just, TR19 7HD ☎01736 788562. Locally sourced ingredients go into the tasty breakfasts, home-made cakes and ice cream served here. You'll also find fresh juices, organic coffee and a range of snacks – try the falafel or Welsh rarebit (around £8). Mon–Sat 10am–5pm.

Old Success Inn Sennen Cove, TR19 7DG ☎01736 871232, ⓦoldsuccess.co.uk. Excellent seaside pub offering craft ales, baguettes (£6–7) and bar meals such as Korean spiced chicken (£13) and local mussels (£16). Rooms with sea views are also available (£110). Daily 11am–11pm; kitchen daily noon–9pm.

Zennor and around

Eight miles northeast of St Just, set in a landscape of rolling granite moorland, **ZENNOR** is where D.H. Lawrence came to live with his wife Frieda in 1916. "It is a most beautiful place," he wrote, "lovelier even than the Mediterranean". The Lawrences stayed a year and a half in the village – long enough for him to write *Women in Love* – before being given notice to quit by the local constabulary, who suspected them of unpatriotic sympathies (their Cornish experiences were later described in *Kangaroo*). At the top of the lane, the church of **St Sennen** displays a sixteenth-century bench carving of a mermaid who, according to local legend, was so entranced by the singing of a chorister that she lured him down to the sea, from where he never returned – though his song can still occasionally be heard.

Chysauster

2 miles inland from Zennor, TR20 8XA • Daily: April–June & Sept 10am–5pm; July & Aug 10am–6pm; Oct 10am–4pm • £4.60; EH • ☎ 07831 757934, ⓦ www.english-heritage.org.uk/visit/places/chysauster-ancient-village

On a windy hillside a couple of miles inland from Zennor, the Iron Age village of **Chysauster** is the best-preserved ancient settlement in the southwest. Dating from about the first century BC, it contains two rows of four buildings, each consisting of a courtyard with small chambers leading off it, and a garden that was presumably used for growing vegetables.

ARRIVAL AND DEPARTURE

ZENNOR AND AROUND

By bus The #A3 service from St Ives (hourly; 20min) and #16A from Penzance (Mon–Sat 4 daily; 20–40min) stop near the turn-off for Zennor. From here it's a short stroll into the village.

ACCOMMODATION AND EATING

Gurnard's Head Treen, TR26 3DE, a mile west of Zennor ☎01736 796928, ⓦgurnardshead.co.uk. This relaxed gastropub serves delicious meals (set-price menus, otherwise mains around £17 at lunchtime, £20 eves; booking advised) and a good selection of wines and beers. Smallish B&B rooms are also available. Daily 8am–11pm; kitchen daily noon–2.30pm & 6–9/9.30pm. **£120**

Zennor Chapel TR26 3DA ☎01736 798307, ⓦzennorchapelguesthouse.com. This guesthouse in a former Wesleyan chapel has five en-suite rooms, each with space for two to four people. The café downstairs turns out breakfasts 8–9.30am (£5, not included in rate), and sells snacks (£6.50–8), coffees and cakes throughout the day. **£80**

St Ives

East of Zennor, the road runs four hilly miles on to the steeply built town of **ST IVES**. By the time the pilchard reserves dried up around the early 1900s, the town was beginning to attract a vibrant **artists' colony**, precursors of the wave later headed by Ben Nicholson, Barbara Hepworth, Naum Gabo and the potter Bernard Leach, who in the 1960s were followed by a third wave including Peter Lanyon and Patrick Heron.

Tate St Ives

Porthmeor Beach, TR26 1TG • March–Oct daily 10am–5.20pm; Nov–Feb Tues–Sun 10am–4.20pm; closes for one week three times a year
• £9.50, £13 with Hepworth Museum • ☎ 01736 796226, ⓦ tate.org.uk/visit/tate-st-ives

The place to view the best work created in St Ives is the **Tate St Ives**, overlooking
Porthmeor Beach on the north side of town. Most of the paintings, sculptures and
ceramics displayed within the airy, gleaming-white building date from 1925 to 1975,
with specially commissioned contemporary works also on view as well as exhibitions.
The gallery's rooftop **café** is a splendid spot for a coffee.

6

Barbara Hepworth Museum

Barnoon Hill, TR26 1AD • March–Oct daily 10am–5.20pm; Nov–Feb Tues–Sun 10am–4.20pm; closes for one week three times a year •
£7.50, £13 with Tate • ☎ 01924 247360, ⓦ tate.org.uk/visit/tate-st-ives

Not far from the Tate, the **Barbara Hepworth Museum** provides further insight into the
local arts scene. One of the foremost nonfigurative sculptors of her time, Hepworth
lived in the building from 1949 until her death in a studio fire in 1975. Apart from the
sculptures, which are arranged in positions chosen by Hepworth in the house and garden,
the museum has background on her art, from photos and letters to catalogues and reviews.

The beaches

Porthmeor Beach dominates the northern side of St Ives, its excellent water quality
and surfer-friendly rollers drawing a regular crowd, while the broader **Porthminster
Beach**, south of the station, is usually less busy. A third town beach, the small and
sheltered **Porthgwidden**, lies in the lee of the prong of land separating Porthmeor and
Porthminster, while east of town a string of magnificent golden beaches lines **St Ives
Bay** on either side of the Hayle estuary.

ARRIVAL AND INFORMATION ST IVES

By train Trains from Penzance (most with a change at St Erth; roughly hourly; 30min–1hr) arrive at the train station on Trelyon Ave, off Porthminster Beach.

By bus The bus station is on Station Hill, just off The Terrace. Destinations Penzance (Mon–Sat 3 hourly, Sun 2 hourly; 35–55min); Plymouth (3 daily; 3hr–3hr 30min); Truro (Mon–Sat every 30min, Sun hourly; 1hr 35min).

Tourist office In St Ives library, Gabriel St (May & June daily 10am–4pm; July–Sept Mon–Sat 10am–5pm, Sun 10am–4pm; Oct–April Mon–Sat 10am–3pm; ☎ 01736 796297, ⓦ stives-cornwall.co.uk).

ACCOMMODATION

Cohort Hostel The Stennack, TR26 1FF ☎ 01736 791664, ⓦ stayatcohort.co.uk. Centrally located in a restored Wesleyan chapel school from 1845, this hostel has a clean, modern feel, with mixed or single-sex dorms, double and twin rooms, a bar and a kitchen. Only groups can book Nov–Feb. Dorms **£24**, doubles **£50**

Cornerways 1 Bethesda Place, TR26 1PA ☎ 01736 796706, ⓦ cornerwaysstives.com. Daphne du Maurier once stayed here; it's now a modern cottage conversion with friendly owners and small, bright rooms. Ask about complimentary tickets for the Tate and Hepworth galleries. No credit cards. **£100**

★ **Little Leaf** 16 Park Ave, TR26 2DN ☎ 01736 795427, ⓦ littleleafguesthouse.co.uk. With friendly young hosts and local art on the walls, this guesthouse has six en-suite rooms, two with fantastic views. Breakfasts are fresh and use locally sourced ingredients. Two- to three-night minimum stay March–Oct. **£85**

Primrose Valley Porthminster Beach, TR26 2ED ☎ 01736 794939, ⓦ primroseonline.co.uk. Relaxed boutique hotel, a level walk from the centre and close to the train station and Porthminster Beach (from which it's separated by the railway). The chic, contemporary rooms, some with balconies, are fresh and light, though some are small and viewless. Closed mid-Dec to mid-Feb. **£175**

EATING

Alba Wharf Rd, TR26 1LF ☎ 01736 797222, ⓦ alba-stives.co.uk. Sleekly modern harbourfront restaurant with top-class seafood, including a superb fish soup (£8). Set-price menus (£24 & £28) are available 6–7.30pm, otherwise mains are around £18. Daily 11am–2pm & 6–10pm.

Blas Burgerworks The Warren, TR26 2EA ☎ 01736 797272, ⓦ blasburgerworks.co.uk. This diminutive spot doles out extremely good burgers (£11–13), using local ingredients. There's just one small room with communal tables made from found or reclaimed wood. No reservations. Mid-Feb to Nov daily 5–9.30pm.

The Cornish Deli 3 Chapel St, TR26 2LR ☎01736 795100 ⓦcornishdeli.com. The tables fill up quickly at this cosy café and deli, which sells excellent sandwiches (using meat from the local butcher's shop), as well as wine, Cornish chocolate, West Country cheeses and the like. In summer, bistro-style meals are served in the evenings, including tapas (£6–7) and chorizo and squid (£13). No

credit cards. Mon–Sat 9.30am–4/5pm, school hols daily 9.30am–9.30pm.

★ **Porthminster Café** Porthminster Beach, TR26 2EB ☎01736 795352, ⓦporthminstercafe.co.uk. With its sun deck and beach location, this is an appealing venue for coffees, snack lunches and sophisticated seafood dinners (mains around £22; book ahead). Late Feb to Dec daily 9am–9.30pm; reduced hours in winter.

The Isles of Scilly

The **ISLES OF SCILLY** are a compact archipelago of about a hundred islands, 28 miles southwest of Land's End. None is bigger than three miles across, and only five of them are inhabited – St Mary's, Tresco, Bryher, St Martin's and St Agnes. In the annals of folklore, the Scillies are the peaks of the submerged land of Lyonnesse, a fertile plain that extended west from Penwith before the ocean broke in, drowning the land and leaving only one survivor to tell the tale. In fact they form part of the same granite mass as Land's End, Bodmin Moor and Dartmoor, and despite rarely rising above 100ft, they possess a remarkable variety of landscape. Points of interest include irresistible **beaches**, such as Par Beach on St Martin's; the southwest's greatest concentration of **prehistoric remains**; some fabulous **rock formations**; and the impressive **Tresco Abbey Gardens**.

Along with tourism, the main source of income is flower-growing, for which the equable climate and long hours of sunshine – their name means "Sun Isles" – make the islands ideal. The profusion of **wildflowers** is even more noticeable than the fields of narcissi and daffodils, and the heaths and pathways are often dense with marigolds, gorse, sea thrift, trefoil and poppies, not to mention a host of more exotic varieties introduced by visiting foreign vessels. The waters hereabouts are held to be among the country's best for **diving**, while between May and September, on a Wednesday or Friday evening, islanders gather for **gig races**, performed by six-oared vessels – some of them more than a hundred years old and 30ft long.

Free of traffic, theme parks and amusement arcades, the islands are a welcome respite from the tourist trail, the main drawbacks being the high cost of reaching them and the shortage of **accommodation**, most of which is on the main isle of St Mary's.

St Mary's

The majority of the resident population of just over two thousand is concentrated on the biggest island, **ST MARY'S**, which has the lion's share of facilities in its capital, **Hugh Town**, and the richest trove of prehistoric sites. The cove-fringed island is also home to **Star Castle**, a huge eight-pointed fortress that was originally built to deter Spanish invasions, and is now a four-star hotel.

Tresco

The second-largest island, **TRESCO**, presents an appealing contrast between the orderly landscape around the remains of its ancient abbey and the bleak, untended northern half. The exuberant **Abbey Garden** (daily 10am–4pm; £15; ☎01720 424108, ⓦtresco.co.uk) hosts an impressive collection of subtropical plants.

Bryher

West of Tresco, **BRYHER** has the smallest population, the slow routines of island life quickening only in the tourist season. The bracing, back-to-nature feel here is nowhere more evident than on the exposed western shore, where **Hell Bay** sees some formidable Atlantic storms.

St Martin's

East of Tresco, **ST MARTIN'S** has some of the archipelago's most majestic white-sand beaches – **Par Beach** deserves a special mention. There are stunning views from its cliffy northeastern end, and the surrounding waters are much favoured by scuba enthusiasts.

6

St Agnes

On the southwest rim of the main island group, the tidy lanes and picturesque cottages of **ST AGNES** are nicely complemented by the weathered boulders and craggy headlands of its indented shoreline. Many of the islanders still make their living by farming **flowers**, and you'll find plenty of tranquil spots even in summer.

The uninhabited isles

A visit to the Scillies would be incomplete without a sortie to the **uninhabited isles**, sanctuaries for seals, puffins and other marine birdlife. On the largest, **SAMSON**, you can poke around prehistoric and more recent remains that testify to former settlement. Some of the smaller islets are worth visiting for their delightfully deserted beaches, though the majority amount to no more than bare rocks. This chaotic profusion of rocks of all shapes and sizes, each bearing a name, is densest at the archipelago's extremities – the **Western Rocks**, lashed by ferocious seas and home to Bishop's Rock Lighthouse (Britain's tallest and most westerly lighthouse), and the milder **Eastern Isles**.

ARRIVAL AND DEPARTURE   THE ISLES OF SCILLY

Transport to the Isles of Scilly – by plane, boat and helicopter – is currently operated solely by **Isles of Scilly Travel** (☏ 01736 334220, ⓦ islesofscilly-travel.co.uk).

By plane Flights depart from Land's End Airport (near St Just; Mon–Sat 9–17 daily; 20min), Newquay (Mon–Sat 3–6 daily; 30min) and Exeter (Mon–Sat 3–5 daily; 1hr); in winter (usually Nov–Feb) there are departures only from Land's End and Newquay. A one-way flight from Land's End starts at £70.

By boat Boats to St Mary's depart from Penzance's South Pier between Easter and early Nov (2hr 45min). A one-way fare from Penzance costs from £45.

By helicopter Added to the roster in May 2018, the year-round helicopter service runs from Land's End Airport to St Mary's, with up to 8 flights per day Mon–Sat (fewer in winter). Flights take just 15min, but with fares starting at £215 return, it's an expensive option. An alternative route was also under consideration at the time of writing; check ⓦ penzanceheliport.co.uk for updates.

GETTING AROUND AND INFORMATION

By boat Boats link each of the inhabited islands, though services are sporadic in winter. The St Mary's Boatmen's Association (☏ 01720 423999, ⓦ scillyboating.co.uk) publishes up-to-date timetables and fares online. Ask the Association about trips to the uninhabited isles, or look out for boards advertising excursions.

By bike Cycling is the ideal way to get around (bikes can be taken on ferries from the mainland for £13 each way). Alternatively, you can rent bikes from St Mary's Bike Hire in Porthmellon Business Park, off Telegraph Rd just outside Hugh Town (£12.50/day; ☏ 07552 994709, ⓦ stmarysbikehire.co.uk).

Tourist office Schiller Shelter, Porthcressa beachfront, St Mary's (March–Oct Mon–Sat 9am–5pm, Sun 9am–2pm; Nov–Feb Mon–Fri 10am–2pm; ☏ 01720 424031, ⓦ visitislesofscilly.com).

ACCOMMODATION

St Mary's has the great majority of the **accommodation** on the islands; the smaller isles (excepting Tresco) each have two or three B&Bs only, and these are booked up early. Tresco and St Martin's have luxury hotels, and all the islands except Tresco have **campsites**, which usually close in winter. See ⓦ visitislesofscilly.com for complete accommodation lists.

6

Fuchsia Cottage Middle Town, St Martin's, TR25 0QN ☏01720 422023, ⓦscillyman.co.uk. This simple, white-washed cottage has two rooms with en-suite or shared facilities, and home-made bread for breakfast. No debit/credit cards. Closed Nov–Feb. **£70**

★ **Mincarlo** Carn Thomas, Hugh Town, St Mary's, TR21 0PT ☏01720 422513, ⓦmincarloscilly.com. With modern decor in a traditional building, this B&B has fantastic views. Most rooms have big windows, though the cheapest (on the ground floor) don't overlook the sea. The terrace is a great suntrap, and top-quality meals are available some evenings. **£92**

Old Chapel Old Town Lane, Old Town, St Mary's, TR21 0NN ☏01720 422100, ⓦtheoldchapelislesofscilly.co.uk. A 15min walk east of Hugh Town, this former Wesleyan meeting hall has two spacious rooms, one with a separate sun lounge. You can sit outside in the lush garden or in the conservatory. Minimum two-night stay. No debit/credit cards. **£100**

Polreath Higher Town, St Martin's, TR25 0QL ☏01720 422046, ⓦpolreath.com. Three smartly furnished rooms with sea views are available at this B&B, with a conservatory and garden. Daytime meals are served in the popular tearoom, as well as evening meals three times a week. The minimum stay is five days in April, one week (from Fri) at other times. No credit cards. Closed Oct–March. **£120**

EATING AND DRINKING

St Mary's has most of the **restaurants** and **pubs**. Each of the other inhabited islands has a pub serving food and one or two cafés, while all hotels and some B&Bs also provide meals.

Juliet's Garden Restaurant Porthloo, St Mary's, TR21 0NF ☏01720 422228, ⓦjulietsgardenrestaurant.co.uk. With garden terraces and panoramic sea views, this restaurant just outside Hugh Town serves snacks, cakes and teas by day, and in the evenings (for which booking is essential) dishes might include braised organic beef and pan-roasted bream fillets (mostly £13–19). Easter–Oct daily 10am–5pm, plus most eves until 9.30pm.

Seven Stones Inn Lower Town, St Martin's, TR25 0QW ☏01720 423777. This place boasts the best views of any Scillies pub, and offers a good selection of ales and meals – soups, salads, ciabattas, burgers (£11) and dishes like couscous with halloumi (£9.50). There's occasional live music and film screenings. April–Oct Mon–Sat 11am–11pm, Sun noon–10.30pm; Nov–March Wed & (sometimes) Fri 6–11pm, Sun noon–6pm.

★ **Turk's Head** Porth Conger, St Agnes, TR22 0PL ☏01720 422434. Sited just above the jetty, with plenty of outdoor seating, this pub serves superb St Agnes pasties (£4.75) as well as a range of meat, seafood and veggie dishes (around £11) to accompany local beers. Easter–Oct Mon–Sat 10.30am–11.30pm, Sun 10.30am–10.30pm; kitchen Easter–Oct daily noon–2/2.30pm & 6–8/9pm.

Vine Café Below Watch Hill, Bryher, TR23 0PR ☏01720 423168. Hot snacks, sandwiches and cakes are sold during the day, and there are twice-weekly set evening meals (£21; bookings only, BYOB). No debit/credit cards. Easter–Oct Mon & Thurs–Sat 10.30am–4pm, Wed & Sun 10.30am–4pm & 7–9.30pm.

Cornwall's Atlantic coast

The north Cornish coast is punctuated by some of the finest beaches in England, the most popular of which are to be found around **Newquay**, the surfers' capital, and **Padstow**, also renowned for its gourmet seafood restaurants. North of the Camel estuary, the coast features an almost unbroken line of cliffs as far as the Devon border; this gaunt, exposed terrain makes a melodramatic setting for **Tintagel Castle** and nearby **Boscastle**. There are more good beaches nearby, for instance at **Bude**.

Newquay

In a superb position on a knuckle of cliffs overlooking fine golden sands and Atlantic rollers, its glorious natural advantages have made **NEWQUAY** the premier resort of north Cornwall. The "new quay" in question was built in the fifteenth century in what was already a long-established fishing port, up to then more colourfully known as Towan Blistra. The town was given a boost in the nineteenth century when a railway was constructed across the peninsula for china clay shipments; with the trains came a swelling stream of seasonal visitors.

Today, the town centre is a tacky parade of shops, bars and restaurants from which lanes lead to ornamental gardens and clifftop lawns. The main attraction is the **beaches**. A number of **surfing competitions** and festivals run through the summer, when Newquay can get very crowded – it's also popular with stag and hen parties.

The beaches

All Newquay's beaches can be reached fairly easily on foot from the centre, otherwise take bus #A5 for Porth Beach and Watergate Bay, #85 for Crantock and Holywell Bay

Close to the centre of town, **Towan Beach**, **Great Western Beach** and **Tolcarne Beach** are the most sheltered of the seven miles of firm sand that line the coast around Newquay, and all are very busy with families in high season. Together with **Porth Beach**, with its grassy headland further east, these are popular with bodyboarders and novice and intermediate surfers all year. Experienced surfers are generally more partial to **Watergate Bay** to the north, and the more exposed **Fistral Bay**, west of Towan Head. Fistral is also the venue for national and international surfing competitions.

On the other side of East Pentire Head from Fistral, **Crantock Beach** – reachable over the Gannel River by ferry or upstream footbridge – is usually less crowded, and has a lovely backdrop of dunes and undulating grassland. South of Crantock, **Holywell Bay** and Perran Beach are also very popular with surfers.

ARRIVAL AND DEPARTURE
NEWQUAY

By plane Newquay's airport is at St Mawgan, 5 miles northeast of town, with connections to major British and Irish cities, and linked to town by bus #A5.
Destinations London Gatwick (1–3 daily; 1hr 10min); Manchester (1–2 daily; 1hr 20min); St Mary's, Isles of Scilly (Mon–Sat 3–6 daily; 30min).
By train Newquay is served by trains from Par (Mon–Sat 6–7 daily, Sun 3–5 daily; 50min); the train station is off

Cliff Rd, a short walk east of the centre.
By bus The bus station is on Manor Rd, near the tourist office.
Destinations Bodmin (4 daily; 30–55min); Padstow (hourly; 1hr 20min–1hr 30min); Plymouth (4–5 daily; 1hr 35min–2hr); St Austell (Mon–Sat hourly, Sun every 2hr; 1hr–1hr 15min); Truro (Mon–Sat 3 hourly, Sun 1–2 hourly; 55min–1hr 30min).

INFORMATION AND ACTIVITIES

Tourist office Marcus Hill (April–Sept Mon–Fri 9.15am–5.30pm, Sat & Sun 10am–4pm; Oct–March Mon–Fri 10am–4pm, Sat & Sun 10am–3pm; ☎01637 838516, ⓦvisitnewquay.org).

Surfing Newquay's surfing buzz is infectious enough to tempt scores of non-surfheads to try their hand every summer. Equipment is available to rent or buy from beach stalls and shops along Fore St, Tower Rd and

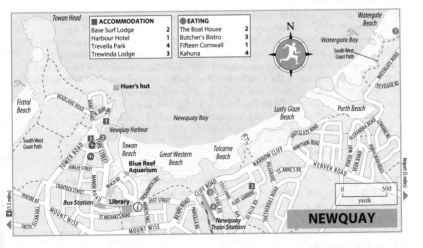

ACCOMMODATION		EATING	
Base Surf Lodge	2	The Boat House	2
Harbour Hotel	1	Butcher's Bistro	3
Trevella Park	4	Fifteen Cornwall	1
Trewinda Lodge	3	Kahuna	4

NEWQUAY

Cliff Rd (£5–15/day for board or wetsuit rental). Dozens of local outfits arrange surfing coaching and courses year-round. For surf reports and webcam images, see Ⓦ magicseaweed.com.

ACCOMMODATION

Base Surf Lodge 20 Tower Rd, TR7 1LR ☎ 07766 132124, Ⓦ basesurflodge.co.uk; map p.347. A good central option for small groups, with fresh, private bunk rooms sleeping 2–6 people. It's surfer-friendly, with board storage facilities and free hot drinks to warm you up post-surf. Beginners should ask about their surf and stay packages, which include lessons. No credit cards. Closed Oct–March. Dorms **£25**

Harbour Hotel North Quay Hill, TR7 1HF ☎ 01637 873040, Ⓦ harbourhotel.co.uk; map p.347. Small, luxurious hotel with stunning views from its stylish rooms, all with balconies. Some rooms are tiny, so check first. **£180**

Trevella Park Near Crantock, 1.5 miles southwest of town, TR8 5EW ☎ 01637 830308, Ⓦ trevella.co.uk; map p.347. It can feel crowded at peak times, but this remains one of the better holiday parks near Newquay, with good, clean facilities for campers and a heated outdoor pool. Apart from camping pitches, they offer "Ready Tents" sleeping four (three nights £221) and static caravans sleeping six (three nights £284), both self-catering, among other options. Camping **£21**

Trewinda Lodge 17 Eliot Gardens, TR7 2QE ☎ 01637 877533, Ⓦ trewinda-lodge.co.uk; map p.347. The owners of this B&B, close to Tolcarne Beach, can give informed advice to surfers (they also run Dolphin Surf School). Rooms are on the small side, but clean and comfortable. **£60**

EATING

The Boat House Newquay Harbour, TR7 1HT ☎ 01637 874062, Ⓦ the-boathouse-newquay.co.uk; map p.347. Seafood is the main event at this atmospheric bar/restaurant by the old harbour. The menu includes hake, haddock, crab (£11–17) and whatever else is on the specials board. Easter–Nov daily 10am–11pm; kitchen Easter–June & Oct daily noon–3pm & 6–10pm, July–Sept daily noon–10pm.

Butcher's Bistro 26 Cliff Rd, TR7 2ND ☎ 01637 874470, Ⓦ butchers-bistro.co.uk; map p.347. This small eatery is renowned for its steaks and seafood. For a real treat try the seafood *marinière* – a big, steaming bowl of prawns, crab claws, mussels and boneless fish (£20). Daily 6–9pm; Sept–June closed Wed.

★ **Fifteen Cornwall** Watergate Bay, TR8 4AA ☎ 01637 861000, Ⓦ fifteencornwall.co.uk; map p.347. Overlooking the beach, this contemporary restaurant set up by TV chef Jamie Oliver showcases the culinary talents of trainee chefs. The Italian-inspired but locally sourced dishes are inventive and delicious; set menus are £26–40 at lunchtime, £65 in the evening, and breakfasts are also worth tucking into. Daily 8.30–10am, noon–2.30pm & 6.15–9.15pm.

★ **Kahuna** Station Approach, TR7 2NG ☎ 01637 850440, Ⓦ kahunarestaurant.co.uk; map p.347. Mouthwatering Asian dishes from *tom yum* seafood soup to beef rendang are presented beautifully at this friendly, relaxed and modern restaurant. Mains are £12–15. Daily 6pm–late.

Padstow and around

PADSTOW attracts nearly as many holiday-makers as Newquay, but has a very different feel. Enclosed within the estuary of the Camel – the only river outlet of any size on Cornwall's north coast – the town has retained its position as North Cornwall's principal fishing port, and boasts some of the country's best seafood **restaurants**. The **harbour** is jammed with launches and boats offering cruises in the bay, while a **ferry** carries people across the river to **ROCK** – close to the isolated church of **St Enodoc** (John Betjeman's burial place) and to the good beaches around Polzeath. Padstow is also known for its annual **Obby Oss** festival, a May Day romp when locals in horse costumes prance through the town preceded by a masked and club-wielding "teaser", in a spirited reenactment of an old fertility rite.

Church of St Petroc

Church Lane, PL28 8BG • Daily 9.30am–5pm, closes 4pm in winter • ☎ 01841 533776, Ⓦ padstowparishchurch.org.uk

Set on the hill overlooking Padstow, the **Church of St Petroc** is dedicated to Cornwall's most important saint, a Welsh or Irish monk who landed here in the sixth century, died in the area and gave his name to the town – "Petrock's Stow". The building has a fine fifteenth-century font, an Elizabethan pulpit and some amusing carved bench ends – seek out the one to the right of the altar depicting a fox preaching to a congregation of geese.

Prideaux Place

Half a mile west of the quay, PL28 8RP • Easter to early Oct Mon–Thurs & Sun 1.30–4pm; grounds 12.30–5pm • £9 • ☎ 01841 532411, ⓦ prideauxplace.co.uk

Padstow's ancient Prideaux family – whose Cornish origins date back to the Normans – still occupy **Prideaux Place**, an Elizabethan manor house with grand staircases, richly furnished rooms full of portraits, fantastically ornate ceilings and formal gardens. You might recognize some parts of the house, which is used extensively for location filming and has appeared in a plethora of films, including *Oscar and Lucinda* (1997).

The beaches

The area immediately west of Padstow has some fine **beaches** – all within a short walk or drive of the town. On the west side of the estuary, round **Stepper Point**, you can reach the sandy and secluded **Harlyn Bay** and, turning the corner southwards, **Constantine Bay**, the best surfing beach hereabouts. The dunes backing the beach and the rock pools skirting it make this one of the most appealing bays on this coast, though the tides can be treacherous and bathing hazardous near the rocks. Three or four miles further south, the slate outcrops of **Bedruthan Steps** were traditionally held to be the stepping-stones of a giant; they can be readily viewed from the clifftop path and the B3276, with steps descending to the broad beach below (not safe for swimming).

ARRIVAL AND DEPARTURE   PADSTOW AND AROUND

By bus Buses #A5 from Newquay (hourly; 1hr 20min) and #11A from Bodmin (Mon–Sat hourly, Sun 6 daily; 50min) pull in on Station Rd, above the harbour.

GETTING AROUND AND INFORMATION

By ferry The ferry across the river to Rock operates daily year-round, roughly every 20min during the day (£4 return; ⓦ padstow-harbour.co.uk).

By bus Bus #A5 (hourly) connects Padstow with Harlyn Bay (10min) and Constantine Bay (15min). Every 1–2hr, the same bus calls at Bedruthan (40min).

Tourist office North Quay, by the harbour (April to late July, Sept & Oct Mon–Fri 10am–5pm, Sat & Sun 10am–4pm; late July & Aug Mon–Fri 9.30am–5.30pm, Sat & Sun 10am–4.30pm; Nov–March Mon–Sat 10am–4pm; ☎ 01841 533449, ⓦ padstowlive.com).

ACCOMMODATION

St Petroc's Hotel New St, PL28 8EA ☎ 01841 532700, ⓦ rickstein.com. Restaurateur Rick Stein has extended his Padstow empire to include classy accommodation, including this chic little lodging away from the harbour, with modern decor and outstanding breakfasts. But even the very small rooms are pricey. **£175**

Treverbyn House Treverbyn Rd, PL28 8DA ☎ 01841 532855, ⓦ treverbynhouse.com. A short walk up from the harbour, this elegant Edwardian B&B has large, beautifully furnished rooms. Breakfast is served in the dining room or on a terrace in the garden with views over the river. No debit/credit cards. **£130**

YHA Treyarnon Bay Treyarnon, PL28 8JR, 4.5 miles west of Padstow ☎ 345 371 9664, ⓦ yha.org.uk/hostel/treyarnon. Perfectly sited hostel in a 1930s summer villa right by the beach. Take bus #A5 from Padstow or Newquay to Constantine, then walk half a mile. Surf packages available. Camping/person **£15**, dorms **£15**, doubles **£39**, bell tents **£59**

EATING

Foodies know Padstow for its high-class **restaurants**, particularly those associated with star chef **Rick Stein**; the waiting list for a table at one of his establishments can be months long, though a weekday reservation out of season might mean booking only a day or two ahead. For something a little cheaper, try Stein's fish and chip shop or his deli, both on South Quay.

Prawn on the Lawn 11 Duke St, PL28 8AB ☎01841 532223, ⓦprawnonthelawn.com. Part fishmonger, part rough-and-ready bistro, this cheerful place is usually abuzz. Menus are based on what's on display: small plates such as marinated scallops and Szechuan prawns cost £7–10, larger platters are £16–30. Book ahead. Tues–Sat noon–10pm.

★**The Seafood Restaurant** Riverside, PL28 8BY ☎01841 532700, ⓦrickstein.com. The core of Rick Stein's culinary empire, this is one of Britain's top places for fish. Most mains – Singapore chilli crab, hake *en papillote*, seafood curry – cost £25–35. Daily noon–2.30pm & 6.30–9.30pm.

6 Tintagel

Despite its romantic name and its famous **castle** standing aloof on a promontory to the north, the village of **TINTAGEL** is for the most part a dreary collection of cafés and B&Bs. Apart from the castle, Tintagel has one other item of genuine interest: the **Old Post Office** on Fore Street (daily: mid-Feb, early March to early April & late Sept to Oct 11am–4pm; early April to late Sept 10.30am–5.30pm; £4, NT; ☎01840 770024, ⓦnationaltrust.org.uk/tintagel-old-post-office), a slate-built, rickety-roofed construction dating from the fourteenth century, now restored to its appearance in the Victorian era.

Tintagel Castle

Half a mile northwest of the village, PL34 0HE • Mid- to late Feb daily 10am–4pm; late Feb to March Wed–Sun 10am–4pm; April–Sept daily 10am–6pm; Oct daily 10am–5pm; Nov to mid-Feb Sat & Sun 10am–4pm • £8.40; EH • ☎01840 770328, ⓦwww.english-heritage.org.uk/visit/places/tintagel-castle

The wild and unspoilt coast around Tintagel provides an appropriate backdrop for the forsaken ruins of **Tintagel Castle**. It was the twelfth-century chronicler Geoffrey of Monmouth who first popularized the notion that this was the **birthplace of King Arthur**, son of Uther Pendragon and Ygrayne, though the visible ruins in fact belong to a Norman stronghold occupied by the earls of Cornwall. After sporadic spurts of rebuilding, the castle was allowed to decay, and most of it had been washed into the

---

KING ARTHUR IN CORNWALL

Did **King Arthur** really exist? It's more likely that he was an amalgam of two people: a sixth-century Celtic warlord who united the local tribes in a series of successful battles against the invading Anglo-Saxons, and a local Cornish saint. Whatever his origins, his role was recounted and inflated by poets and troubadours in later centuries. The Arthurian legends were elaborated by the medieval chroniclers Geoffrey of Monmouth and William of Malmesbury and in Thomas Malory's epic, *Morte d'Arthur* (1485), further romanticized in Tennyson's *Idylls of the King* (1859) and resurrected in T.H. White's saga, *The Once and Future King* (1958).

Although there are places throughout Britain and Europe that claim some association with Arthur, it's England's West Country, and **Cornwall** in particular, that has the greatest concentration of places boasting a link. Here, the myths, enriched by fellow Celts from Brittany and Wales, have established deep roots, so that, for example, the spirit of Arthur is said to be embodied in the Cornish chough – a bird now almost extinct. Cornwall's most famous Arthurian site is his supposed birthplace, **Tintagel**, where Merlin apparently lived in a cave under the castle (he also resided on a rock near Mousehole, south of Penzance, according to some sources). Nearby **Bodmin Moor** is littered with places with names such as "King Arthur's Bed" and "King Arthur's Downs", while Camlan, the battlefield where Arthur was mortally wounded fighting against his nephew Mordred, is associated with Slaughterbridge, on the northern reaches of the moor near **Camelford** (which is also sometimes identified as Camelot itself). At **Dozmary Pool**, the knight Bedivere was dispatched by the dying Arthur to return the sword Excalibur to the mysterious hand emerging from the water – though Loe Pool in Mount's Bay also claims this honour. Arthur's body was supposedly carried after the battle to **Boscastle**, on Cornwall's northern coast, from where a funeral barge transported it to Avalon, identified with Glastonbury in Somerset (see page 290).

sea by the sixteenth century. The remains of a sixth-century **Celtic monastery** on the headland have provided important insights into how the country's earliest monastic houses were organized.

ARRIVAL AND INFORMATION

By bus Buses pull in on Bossiney Rd, opposite the tourist office.
Destinations Boscastle (Mon–Sat 7 daily, Sun 5 daily; 15min); Bude (5–6 daily; 50min); Camelford (Mon–Sat 7 daily, Sun 5 daily; 20min).

Tourist office Bossiney Rd (daily: April–Oct 10am–4pm; Nov–March 10am–1pm; ☎01840 779084, ⓦ visit boscastleandtintagel.com); it also has a small exhibition about the region's cultural heritage.

ACCOMMODATION AND EATING

Avalon Hotel Atlantic Rd, PL34 0DD ☎01840 770116, ⓦ theavalonhotel.co.uk. Classy guesthouse at the eastern end of the village, mixing Victorian-Gothic details with a fresh, contemporary style. Some rooms are small, but all are spotless and most have amazing views. Breakfast choices include porridge brûlée. **£89**

★ **Bosayne** Atlantic Rd, PL34 0DE ☎01840 770514, ⓦ bosayne.co.uk. This solid Edwardian B&B has amiable, eco-aware owners and smallish rooms with sea views and mini-fridges. Breakfasts are mainly organic with home-made bread and cakes. **£75**

★ **Charlie's** Fore St, PL34 0DA ☎01840 779500, ⓦ charlies.cafe. Deli and café with outdoor seating and a bright, family-friendly feel. Choose from among the pies and Scotch eggs for a superlative picnic, or settle down for brunch, sandwiches (£4–7) or burgers (£7–9). Cakes and cream teas include gluten-free options. Mon–Sat 10am–5pm.

YHA Tintagel Dunderhole Point, PL34 0DW ☎0345 371 9145, ⓦ yha.org.uk/hostel/tintagel. Three-quarters of a mile south of Tintagel, the offices of a former slate quarry now house this hostel with great coastal views. There's a kitchen and BBQ area but no restaurant. Closed Nov–Easter. Dorms **£17**

Boscastle

Three miles east of Tintagel, the port of **BOSCASTLE** lies compressed within a narrow ravine drilled by the rivers Jordan and Valency, and ending in a twisty harbour. One of the lime-washed cottages bordering the tidy riverfront holds the **Museum of Witchcraft and Magic** (April–Oct Mon–Sat 10.30am–6pm, Sun 11.30am–6pm; £5; ☎01840 250111, ⓦ museumofwitchcraftandmagic.co.uk), an absorbing, non-gimmicky account of witchcraft and sorcery through the ages, displayed in themed galleries. Above and behind, you can see more seventeenth- and eighteenth-century cottages on a circular walk that traces the valley of the Valency for about a mile to reach Boscastle's graceful parish church of **St Juliot**, tucked away in a peaceful glen, where Thomas Hardy once worked as a young architect.

ARRIVAL AND INFORMATION

By bus There are bus stops at the car park and Boscastle Bridge, at the top of the harbour.
Destinations Bude (5–6 daily; 40min); Camelford (5 daily; 30min); Tintagel (5 daily; 10min).

Tourist office The Harbour (daily: March–Oct 10am–5pm; Nov–Feb 10.30am–4pm; ☎01840 250010, ⓦ visitboscastleandtintagel.com).

ACCOMMODATION AND EATING

Napoleon Inn High St, PL35 0BD ☎01840 250204, ⓦ napoleoninn.co.uk. Boscastle's excellent pubs include this traditional tavern in the upper town with tankards hanging off the ceiling, real ale, great food (mains £9–13) and Cornish singing every Tues. Daily noon–11pm; kitchen daily noon–2pm & 6–9pm.

Old Rectory St Juliot, PL35 0BT, 1.5 miles east of Boscastle ☎01840 250225, ⓦ stjuliot.com. For a real Thomas Hardy experience, head for this luxurious Victorian B&B, where you can stay in the author's bedroom and roam the extensive grounds. Minimum two-night stay. **£95**

★ **YHA Boscastle** Harbourside, PL35 0HD ☎0345 371 9006, ⓦ yha.org.uk/hostel/boscastle. Fine old hostel in a former stables right by the river. Rooms have two to six beds and there's a self-catering kitchen and a comfy lounge. Only groups can book Nov–Feb. Dorms **£18**, doubles **£69**

Bude and around

Just four miles from the Devon border, Cornwall's northernmost town of **BUDE** is built around an estuary surrounded by a fine expanse of sands. The town has sprouted a crop of hotels and holiday homes, though these have not unduly spoilt the place nor the magnificent cliffy coast surrounding it.

Of the excellent **beaches** hereabouts, the central **Summerleaze** is clean and spacious, but the mile-long **Widemouth Bay**, south of town, is the main focus of the holiday crowds (though bathing can be dangerous near the rocks at low tide). Surfers also congregate five miles down the coast at **Crackington Haven**, wonderfully situated between 430ft crags at the mouth of a lush valley. To the **north** of Bude, acres-wide **Crooklets** is the scene of **surfing** and life-saving demonstrations and competitions. A couple of miles further on, **Sandy Mouth** holds a pristine expanse of sand with rock pools beneath the encircling cliffs. It's a short walk from here to another surfers' delight, **Duckpool**, a tiny sandy cove flanked by jagged reefs at low tide, and dominated by the three-hundred-foot **Steeple Point**.

ARRIVAL AND INFORMATION   BUDE AND AROUND

By bus Buses stop on The Strand, running to Boscastle (5–6 daily; 40min) and Hartland (Mon–Sat 6 daily; 30–55min).

Tourist office The Crescent car park (Mon–Sat 10am–5pm, Sun 10am–4pm; summer school hols daily 10am–7pm; ☎01288 354240, ⊛visitbude.info).

ACCOMMODATION AND EATING

The Bank at Bude Pethericks Mill, EX23 8TF ☎01288 352070, ⊛thebankatbude.co.uk. A bit out of the way – unless you're a cyclist, as it's right on the cycle path – this place offers tapas (£5–9) as well as paellas and other meat and seafood dishes (£14–25). It's a 5min walk along the riverbank from the tourist office. Easter–June, Sept & Oct Tues & Wed 6–10pm, Thurs–Sat noon–10pm; July & Aug Tues, Wed & Sun 3–10pm, Thurs–Sat noon–10pm; Nov–Easter Tues–Sat 6pm–late.

The Beach Summerleaze Crescent, EX23 8HJ ☎01288 389800, ⊛thebeachatbude.co.uk. Chic hotel overlooking the beach, with modern, airy rooms, swish bathrooms and an excellent restaurant (mains £17–20). The bar has an outdoor terrace, perfect for soaking up the sunset. Daily noon–2.30/3pm & 6–9/9.30pm. **£175**

★**Cerenety** Lynstone Lane, EX23 0LR ☎01288 356778 or ☎07429 016962, ⊛cerenetycampsite. co.uk. Back-to-basics, eco-friendly camping a mile south of Bude, with grassy pitches, solar-powered showers and composting toilets. In summer, hot drinks and crêpes can be bought from a caravan on the site. **£14**

Life's a Beach Summerleaze Beach, EX23 8HN ☎01288 355222, ⊛lifesabeach.info. Right on the beach, this is a café by day, offering baguettes, burgers and drinks, and a seafood-focused bistro, with the accent on seafood (mains £18–26). Easter–Oct Mon–Sat 10.30am–3.30pm & 7–9pm, Sun 10.30am–3.30pm; reduced hours in winter, call to check.

North Shore 57 Killerton Rd, EX23 8EW ☎01288 354256, ⊛northshorebude.com. Friendly hostel 5min from the centre of town, with clean and spacious rooms – including en-suite doubles – a large garden and a kitchen. Dorms **£22**, doubles **£60**

Bodmin Moor

Bodmin Moor, the smallest of the West Country's great moors, has some beautiful tors, torrents and rock formations, but much of its fascination lies in the strong human imprint, particularly the wealth of relics left behind by its **Bronze Age** population. Separated from these by some three millennia, the churches in the villages of **St Neot**, **Blisland** and **Altarnun** are among the region's finest examples of fifteenth-century art and architecture.

Bodmin

BODMIN's position on the western edge of Bodmin Moor, equidistant from the north and south Cornish coasts and the Fowey and Camel rivers, encouraged its growth as a trading town. It was also an important ecclesiastical centre after the establishment of a priory by St Petroc, who moved here from Padstow in the sixth century.

St Petroc's Church
Priory Rd, PL31 2DT · Daily 9am–4pm · Free · ☎ 01208 73867

After Bodmin's priory had disappeared, the town retained its prestige through its **church of St Petroc**, built in the fifteenth century and still Cornwall's largest parish church. Inside, there's an extravagantly carved twelfth-century font and an ivory casket that once held the bones of the saint. The southwest corner of the churchyard holds a sacred well.

Bodmin Jail
Berrycoombe Rd, PL31 2NR · Daily: April–Sept 9.30am–8pm; Oct–March 9.30am–6pm · £10 · ☎ 01208 76292, 🌐 bodminjail.org

The notorious **Bodmin Jail** is redolent of the public executions that were guaranteed crowd-pullers until 1862, though it didn't finally close until 1927. You can visit part of the original eighteenth-century structure, including the condemned cell and "execution pit", and some grisly exhibits chronicling the lives of the inmates. *The Governors Hall* café/restaurant stays open until 9pm.

Lanhydrock
3 miles southeast of Bodmin, PL30 5AD · **House and garden** Daily: March & Oct 11am–5pm; April–Sept 11am–5.30pm · £13.55, Nov & Dec £7.50; garden only £8.25, Nov & Dec £4.35; NT · **Grounds** Daily dawn–dusk · Free, but parking £3; NT · ☎ 01208 265950, 🌐 nationaltrust.org.uk/lanhydrock · Less than 2 miles' walk from Bodmin Parkway train station

One of Cornwall's most celebrated country houses, **Lanhydrock** originally dates from the seventeenth century but was totally rebuilt after a fire in 1881. The most prominent survivor from its Jacobean past is the long picture gallery, whose plaster ceiling depicts scenes from the Old Testament, while the servants' quarters fascinatingly reveal the daily workings of a Victorian manor house. The grounds have magnificent **gardens** with lush beds of magnolias, azaleas and rhododendrons, and a huge area of wooded parkland bordering onto the River Fowey

Blisland

BLISLAND stands in the Camel valley on the western slopes of Bodmin Moor, three miles northeast of Bodmin. Georgian and Victorian houses cluster around a village green and a church whose well-restored interior has an Italianate altar and a startlingly painted screen.

The western moor

On **Pendrift Common** above Blisland, the gigantic **Jubilee Rock** is inscribed with patriotic insignia commemorating the jubilee of George III's coronation. From this 700ft vantage point you look east over the De Lank gorge and the boulder-crowned knoll of **Hawk's Tor**, three miles away. On the shoulder of the tor stand the Neolithic **Stripple Stones**, a circular platform once holding 28 standing stones, of which just four are still upright.

The northern tors

The northern half of the moor is dominated by its two highest tors, both of them easily accessible from **CAMELFORD**, an unassuming local centre known for its slate industry. Four miles southeast, **Rough Tor** is the second-highest peak on Bodmin Moor at 1311ft. A short distance to the east stand **Little Rough Tor**, where there are the remains of an Iron Age camp, and **Showery Tor**, capped by a prominent formation of piled rocks. Easily visible to the southeast, **Brown Willy** is, at 1378ft, the highest peak in Cornwall, as its original name signified – Bronewhella, or "highest hill". Like Rough Tor, Brown Willy shows various faces, its sugarloaf appearance from the north sharpening into a long multi-peaked crest as you approach. The tor is accessible by continuing from the summit of Rough Tor across the valley of the De Lank or, from the south, by footpath from Bolventor.

Bolventor and around

The village of **BOLVENTOR**, lying at the centre of the moor midway between Bodmin and Launceston, is an uninspiring place close to **Jamaica Inn**, one of the moor's chief focuses for walkers and literary sightseers alike.

Jamaica Inn

10 miles northeast of Bodmin, PL15 7TS • Museum daily 8am–9pm • £3.95 • ☎ 01566 86250, ⓦ jamaicainn.co.uk

A staging post even before the precursor of the A30 road was laid here in 1769, the inn was described as being "alone in glory, four square to the winds" by **Daphne Du Maurier**, who stayed here in 1930, soaking up inspiration for her smugglers' yarn, *Jamaica Inn*. There's a room inside devoted to the author, and the hotel also has an attached **Smugglers Museum**, illustrating the diverse ruses used for concealing contraband.

Dozmary Pool

The car park at *Jamaica Inn* is a useful place to leave your car and venture forth on foot. A mile south is **Dozmary Pool**, another link in the West Country's Arthurian mythologies – after Arthur's death, according to some versions of the story, Sir Bedivere hurled Excalibur into this pool, where it was seized by an arm raised from the depths. Despite its proximity to the A30, the diamond-shaped lake usually preserves an ethereal air, though it's been known to run dry in summer, dealing a bit of a blow to the legend that it is bottomless.

Altarnun

Four miles northeast of Bolventor, **ALTARNUN** is a pleasant, granite-grey village snugly sheltered beneath the eastern heights of the moor. Its prominent **church**, **St Nonna's**, contains a fine Norman font and 79 bench ends carved at the beginning of the sixteenth century, depicting saints, musicians and clowns.

St Neot and the southeastern moor

Approached through a lush wooded valley, **ST NEOT** is one of the moor's prettiest villages. Its fifteenth-century **church** contains some of the most impressive stained-glass windows of any parish church in the country, the oldest glass being the fifteenth-century **Creation Window**, at the east end of the south aisle.

Golitha Falls

One of the moor's most attractive spots lies a couple of miles east of St Neot, below Draynes Bridge, where the Fowey tumbles through the **Golitha Falls**, less a waterfall than a series of rapids. Dippers and wagtails flit through the trees, and there's a pleasant woodland walk to Siblyback Lake reservoir just over a mile away.

Kilmar and Stowe's Hill

North and east of Siblyback Lake are some of Bodmin Moor's grandest landscapes. The quite modest elevations of Hawk's Tor (1079ft) and the lower Trewartha Tor appear enormous from the north, though they are overtopped by **Kilmar**, highest of the hills on the moor's eastern flank at 1280ft. **Stowe's Hill** is the site of the moor's most famous stone pile, **The Cheesewring**, a precarious pillar of balancing granite slabs, marvellously eroded by the wind. A mile or so south down Stowe's Hill stands an artificial rock phenomenon, **The Hurlers**, a wide complex of three circles dating from about 1500 BC. The purpose of these stark upright stones is not known, though they owe their name to the legend that they were men turned to stone for playing the Celtic game of hurling on the Sabbath.

Minions and Trethevy

The Hurlers are easily accessible just outside **MINIONS**, Cornwall's highest village, three miles south of which stands another Stone Age survival, **Trethevy Quoit**, a chamber tomb nearly nine feet high, surmounted by a massive capstone. Originally enclosed in earth, the stones have been stripped by centuries of weathering to create Cornwall's most impressive megalithic monument.

ARRIVAL AND INFORMATION

BODMIN MOOR

By train 3 miles outside Bodmin, Bodmin Parkway station has a regular bus link (hourly; 15min) to the centre of town. Destinations Exeter (every 1–2hr; 1hr 40min); Penzance (every 30min–1hr; 1hr 25min); Plymouth (every 1–2hr; 40min).

By bus Most buses to and from Bodmin stop on Mount Folly, near the tourist office.

Destinations Newquay (4 daily; 35–50min); Padstow (Mon–Sat hourly, Sun 6 daily; 45min); Plymouth (4 daily; 1hr); St Austell (Mon–Sat hourly; 1hr).

Tourist office Mount Folly, Bodmin (March–May & Oct Mon–Fri 8.45am–4pm, Sat 10am–5pm; June–Sept Mon–Fri 8.45am–5pm, Sat 10am–5pm; Nov–Feb Mon–Fri 8.45am–2pm; ☎01208 76616, ⓦ bodminlive.com).

6

ACCOMMODATION AND EATING

★ **Bedknobs** Polgwyn, Castle St, Bodmin, PL31 2DX ☎01208 77553, ⓦ bedknobs.co.uk. Victorian villa in an acre of wooded garden, with three spacious and luxurious B&B rooms (the priciest with its own en-suite Airbath) and a self-catering apartment (£115). Friendly, eco-aware hosts and lots of extras. __£95__

Blisland Inn The Green, Blisland, PL30 4JK ☎01208 850739. Traditional village pub on the green, serving seven cask ales, including Blisland Bulldog, as well as Cornish fruit wine, bar snacks and full meals (£8–15). There are outdoor tables, and often live music on Sat. Mon–Sat 11.30am–11pm, Sun noon–10.30pm; kitchen Mon–Sat noon–2pm & 6.30–9pm, Sun noon–2pm.

Jamaica Inn Bolventor, PL15 7TS ☎01566 86250, ⓦ jamaicainn.co.uk. Despite its fame, this inn immortalized by Daphne du Maurier has lost any trace of romance since its development into a bland hotel and restaurant complex. It occupies a grand site, though, ideal for trips onto the moor. Mon–Sat 7.30am–midnight, Sun 7.30am–10.30pm; kitchen daily 7.30–10.30am, 11am–4pm & 5–9pm. __£89__

Roscrea 18 St Nicholas Rd, Bodmin, PL31 1AD ☎01208 74400, ⓦ roscrea.co.uk. Central, friendly B&B with tasteful Victorian rooms. Breakfasts include home-made bread, jams and muesli. __£90__

East Anglia

VIEW OF COLLEGES FROM THE BACKS, CAMBRIDGE

East Anglia

Strictly speaking, East Anglia is made up of just three counties – Suffolk, Norfolk and Cambridgeshire, which were settled in the fifth century by Angles from today's Schleswig-Holstein – but the term is now loosely applied to parts of Essex too. As a region it's renowned for its wide skies and flat landscapes, but there are a few surprises too: parts of Suffolk and Norfolk are decidedly hilly, with steep coastal cliffs; broad rivers cut through the fenlands; and Norfolk also boasts some wonderful sandy beaches. Fine medieval churches abound, built in the days when this was England's most progressive and prosperous region.

Heading into East Anglia from the south takes you through **Essex**, whose proximity to London has turned much of the county into an unappetizing commuter strip. Amid the suburban gloom, there are, however, several worthwhile destinations, most notably **Colchester**, once a major Roman town and now a busy place with an imposing castle, and the handsome hamlets of the bucolic **Stour River Valley** on the Essex–Suffolk border. Essex's Dedham is one of the prettiest of these villages, but the main attraction hereabouts is Suffolk's Flatford Mill, famous for its associations with the painter John Constable.

Further north, **Suffolk** boasts a string of pretty towns that enjoyed immense prosperity from the thirteenth to the sixteenth centuries, the wool trade's heyday, with Lavenham the prime example. Suffolk's county town is **Ipswich**, which has more to offer than it's given credit for, but really it's the **Suffolk coast** that is the main magnet, especially the delightful resort of Southwold and neighbouring Aldeburgh, with its prestigious music festival.

Norfolk, as everyone knows thanks to Noël Coward, is very flat. It's also one of the most sparsely populated counties in England, a remarkable turnaround from the days when it was an economic and political powerhouse – until the Industrial Revolution simply passed it by. Its capital, **Norwich**, is East Anglia's largest city, renowned for its Norman cathedral and castle; nearby are the Broads, a unique landscape of reed-ridden waterways that have been intensively mined by boat-rental companies. The **North Norfolk coast** holds a string of busy, very English seaside resorts, but for the most part it's charmingly unspoilt, its marshes, creeks and tidal flats studded with tiny flint villages.

Cambridge is much visited, principally because of its world-renowned university, whose ancient colleges boast some of the finest medieval and early-modern architecture in the country. The rest of **Cambridgeshire** is pancake-flat fenland, for centuries an inhospitable marshland, but now rich alluvial farming land. The cathedral town of **Ely**, settled on one of the few areas of raised ground in the fens, is an easy and popular day-trip from Cambridge, while farther up the River Ouse is the ancient port of **King's Lynn**.

GETTING AROUND   EAST ANGLIA

By train Trains from London are fast and frequent: one main line links Colchester, Ipswich and Norwich, another Cambridge and Ely. Among several cross-country services, there are trains between Peterborough, Ely, Norwich and Ipswich.

By bus Beyond the major towns you'll have to rely on local buses. Services are patchy, except on the north Norfolk coast, covered by the Norfolk Coasthopper bus (ⓦ stagecoachbus.com/promos-and-offers/east/coasthopper).

HOLKHAM BAY, NORFOLK

Highlights

❶ Orford Solitary hamlet with a splendid coastal setting that makes for a wonderful weekend away. See page 367

❷ The Aldeburgh Festival The region's prime classical music festival takes place every summer. See page 368

❸ Southwold Handsome and genteel seaside town, which is perfect for walking and bathing – with the added incentive of the most inventive Under the Pier Show in the country. See page 369

❹ Norwich Market This open-air market is the region's biggest and best for everything from whelks to wellies. See page 373

❺ Holkham Bay and beach Wide bay holding Norfolk's finest beach – acres of golden sand set against pine-dusted dunes. See page 381

❻ Ely Isolated Cambridgeshire town, with a true fenland flavour and a magnificent cathedral. See page 384

❼ Cambridge With some of the finest late medieval architecture in Europe, Cambridge is a must-see, its compact centre graced by dignified old colleges and their neatly manicured courts. See page 385

HIGHLIGHTS ARE MARKED ON THE MAP ON PAGE 360

Colchester

If you visit only one place in Essex, it should be **COLCHESTER**, a lively, medium-sized town with a **castle**, a university and an army base, just fifty miles or so northeast of London. Colchester prides itself on being England's oldest town, and there is indeed documentary evidence of a settlement here as early as the fifth century BC. Today, Colchester makes a good base for explorations of the surrounding countryside – particularly the **Stour Valley** towns of Constable Country, within easy reach a few miles to the north.

Brief history

By the first century AD, the original settlement was the region's capital under **King Cunobelin** – better known as Shakespeare's Cymbeline – and when the **Romans** invaded Britain in 43 AD they chose Colchester (Camulodunum) as their new capital, though it was soon eclipsed by London. Later, the conquering Normans built one of

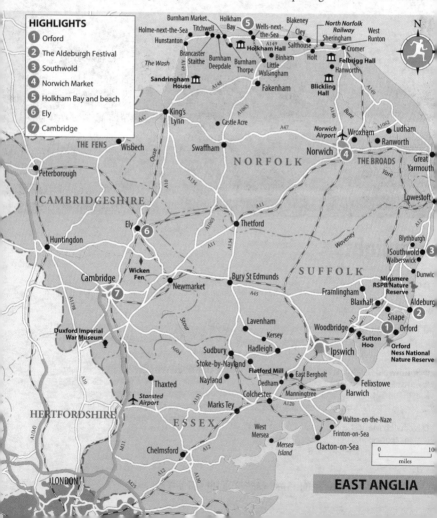

HIGHLIGHTS

1 Orford
2 The Aldeburgh Festival
3 Southwold
4 Norwich Market
5 Holkham Bay and beach
6 Ely
7 Cambridge

EAST ANGLIA

their mightiest strongholds here, but the conflict that most marked the town was the **Civil War**. In 1648, Colchester endured a gruelling siege by the Parliamentarian army; after three months, during which the population ate every living creature within the walls and then some, the town finally surrendered and the Royalist leaders were promptly executed for their pains.

Colchester Castle

Castle Park, CO1 1TJ • Mon–Sat 10am–5pm, Sun 11–5pm • £7.75 • **Tours** 3–4 daily; 45min–1hr • £3 • **Park** Daily dawn–dusk • Free • ☏ 01206 282939, Ⓦ www.cimuseums.org.uk

At the heart of the town is the remains of **Colchester Castle**, a ruggedly imposing, honey-coloured keep, set in attractive parkland stretching down to the River Colne. Begun less than ten years after the Battle of Hastings, the keep was the largest in Europe at the time, built on the site of the Temple of Claudius. Inside the keep, a **museum** holds an excellent collection of Romano-British archeological finds, notably a miscellany of coins and tombstones. The museum also runs regular **guided tours**, giving access to the Roman vaults and the castle roof, which are otherwise out of bounds. Outside, down towards the river in **Castle Park**, is a section of the old **Roman walls**, whose battered remains are still visible around much of the town centre. They were erected after Boudica had sacked the city and, as such, are a case of too little too late.

Firstsite Art Gallery

Lewis Gardens, High St, CO1 1JH • Daily 10am–5pm • Free • ☏ 01206 713700, Ⓦ firstsite.uk

In a new and stunningly handsome modern building near the castle, the **Firstsite Art Gallery** offers a varied and often challenging programme of contemporary art exhibitions. Recent exhibitors have included Ed Gold and Patrick Hough. The building itself has a lustrous metallic gold sheen and was designed by the Uruguayan architect **Rafael Viñoly**.

The High Street

Colchester's long and largely pedestrianized **High Street** follows pretty much the same route as it did in Roman times. The most arresting building is the flamboyant **Town Hall**, built in 1902 and topped by a statue of St Helena, mother of Constantine the Great and daughter of "Old King Cole" of nursery-rhyme fame – after whom, some say, the town was named. Looming above the western end of the street is the town landmark, "**Jumbo**", a disused nineteenth-century water tower, considerably more imposing than the nearby **Balkerne Gate**. Built in 50 AD, this is the largest surviving Roman gateway in the country, though with the remains at only a touch over 6ft high, it's far from spectacular.

ARRIVAL AND INFORMATION

COLCHESTER

By train Colchester has two train stations. Colchester station (a 20min walk north of the centre – follow the signs) covers mainline services, including for the Tendring peninsula. Colchester Town (on the southeast corner of the centre) is only for local services out along the Tendring.
Destinations (Colchester) Clacton (hourly; 30min); Ipswich (every 30min; 20min); London Liverpool Street (every 20min; 1hr); Norwich (every 30min; 1hr); Sudbury (change at Marks Tey; hourly; 40min).
Destinations (Colchester Town) Walton-on-the-Naze (hourly; 40min).

By bus The bus station is on Osborne St, on the southeast side of the centre, near Colchester Town train station.
Destinations Chambers bus #753 (Ⓦchambersbus.co.uk) links Colchester with Bury St Edmunds (Mon–Sat hourly; 2hr), Lavenham (Mon–Sat hourly; 1hr 30min) and Sudbury (Mon–Sat hourly; 50min). Other companies link Colchester with Dedham (every 1–2hr; 40min) – consult Ⓦtraveline.info.
Tourist office On the ground floor of the Hollytrees Museum, just off the High St in Castle Park (Mon–Sat 10am–5pm; ☏01206 282920, Ⓦvisitcolchester.com).

ACCOMMODATION AND EATING

The Company Shed 129 Coast Rd, West Mersea, CO5 8PA ☎01206 382700, ⓦthe-company-shed.co.uk. Colchester's oysters have been highly prized since Roman times and nowadays they are at their best among the oyster beds of Mersea Island, about 6 miles south of Colchester. It's here you'll find *The Company Shed*, where they serve the freshest of oysters at simple rickety tables in, to quote their own PR, a "romantically weatherbeaten shed". Romantic or not, the oysters are indeed delicious. Last orders for eating in 4pm. Tues–Sat 9am–5pm, Sun 10am–5pm.

Four Sevens Guesthouse 28 Inglis Road, CO3 3HU ☎01206 546093, ⓦfoursevens.co.uk. This is one of the best of the town's B&Bs, in an attractively remodelled Victorian house with six bright and breezy guest rooms decorated in an uncluttered modern style. Two of the rooms are en suite (£10 extra). It's on a leafy residential street, a brief walk southwest from the centre. **£65**

Il Padrino 11 Church St, CO1 1NF ☎01206 366699, ⓦilpadrinocolchester.co.uk. This excellent Italian café-restaurant, a few yards from the west end of the High St, serves all the classics for both lunch and dinner. There are daily specials, chalked up on a blackboard, and prices are very reasonable, with mains averaging £15 (£9 for pasta dishes), less at lunchtime. Cosy premises and attentive service. Mon noon–2.30pm, Tues–Sat noon–2.30pm & 6–10pm.

North Hill Hotel 51 North Hill, CO1 1PY ☎01206 574001, ⓦnorthhillhotel.com. Set within an intelligently revamped older building, this appealing, mid-range hotel has seventeen guest rooms with lots of original features – especially the exposed half-timbered walls and beams. Handy location too, just north of the High St, but North Hill can be noisy so you may prefer a room at the back. **£75**

The Stour Valley

Six miles or so north of Colchester, the **Stour Valley** forms the border between Essex and Suffolk, and signals the beginning of East Anglia proper. The river valley is dotted with lovely little villages, where rickety, half-timbered Tudor houses and handsome Georgian dwellings cluster around medieval churches, proud buildings with square, self-confident towers. The Stour's prettiest villages are concentrated along its lower reaches – to the east of the A134 – in Dedham Vale, with **Dedham** the most appealing of them all. The vale is also known as "**Constable Country**", as it was the home of John Constable, one of England's greatest artists, and the subject of his most famous paintings. Inevitably, there's a Constable shrine – the much-visited complex of old buildings down by the river at **Flatford Mill**. Elsewhere, the best-preserved of the old south Suffolk wool towns is **Lavenham**, while neighbouring **Sudbury** has a fine museum, devoted to the work of another outstanding English artist, Thomas Gainsborough.

Brief history

The villages along the River Stour and its tributaries were once busy little places at the heart of East Anglia's medieval **weaving trade**. By the 1480s, the region produced more cloth than any other part of the country, but in Tudor times production shifted to Colchester, Ipswich and Norwich and, although most of the smaller settlements continued spinning cloth for the next three hundred years or so, their importance slowly dwindled. Bypassed by the Industrial Revolution, **south Suffolk** had, by the late nineteenth century, become a remote rural backwater, an impoverished area whose decline had one unforeseen consequence: with few exceptions, the towns and villages were never prosperous enough to modernize, so the architectural legacy of medieval and Tudor times survived and now pulls in second-home owners and tourists alike.

By public transport Seeing the Stour Valley by public transport can be problematic – distances are small (Dedham Vale is only about ten miles long), but buses between the villages are patchy, especially on Sunday. The only local rail service is the short branch line between Marks Tey, on the London Liverpool Street to Colchester line, and Sudbury.

Flatford Mill

"I associate my careless boyhood with all that lies on the banks of the Stour," wrote **John Constable**, who was born in **EAST BERGHOLT**, ten miles northeast of Colchester, in 1776. The house in which he was born has long since disappeared, so it has been left to **FLATFORD MILL**, a mile or so to the south, to take up the painter's cause. The mill was owned by his father and was where Constable painted his most celebrated canvas, *The Hay Wain* (now in London's National Gallery), which created a sensation when it was exhibited in Paris in 1824. To the chagrin of many of his contemporaries, Constable turned away from the landscape painting conventions of the day, rendering his scenery with a realistic directness that harked back to the Dutch landscape painters of the seventeenth century.

The mill itself – not the one he painted, but a Victorian replacement – is not open to the public and neither is neighbouring **Willy Lott's Cottage**, which feature in *The Hay Wain*, but the National Trust has colonized several buildings, principally **Bridge Cottage**.

Bridge Cottage

Flatford Mill, CO7 6UL • Jan & early Feb Sat & Sun 10.30am–3.30pm; late Feb to March Wed–Sun 10am–4.30pm; April–Sept daily 10am–5pm; Oct daily 10am–4.30pm; Nov & early Dec Wed–Sun 10.30am–3.30pm • Free, but parking £4; NT • ☎ 01206 298260, ⊛ nationaltrust.org.uk/flatford • The nearest train station is at Manningtree, 2 miles away

Neat and trim and tidily thatched, **Bridge Cottage** was familiar to Constable and, although none of the artist's paintings are displayed here, it is packed with Constabilia alongside a small exhibition on the artist's life and times. The cottage also has a very pleasant riverside tearoom where you can take in the view.

Dedham

Constable went to school just upriver from Flatford Mill in **DEDHAM**, a pretty little village whose wide main street is graced by a handsome medley of old timber-framed houses and Georgian villas. The main sight is the **Church of St Mary** (daily 9am–dusk; free; ⊛ dedham-and-ardleigh-parishes.org.uk), a large, well-proportioned structure with a sweeping, sixteenth-century nave and attractive Victorian stained glass. Constable painted the church on several occasions, and today it holds one of his rare religious paintings, *The Ascension* – though frankly, it's a good job Constable concentrated on landscapes. Be aware that day-trippers arrive in Dedham by the coachload throughout the summer.

ARRIVAL AND DEPARTURE   DEDHAM

By bus There is a reasonably good bus service to Dedham from Colchester (every 1–2hr; 40min).

ACCOMMODATION AND EATING

The Sun Inn High St, CO7 6DF ☎ 01206 323351, ⊛ thesuninndedham.com. Among Dedham's pubs, the pick is *The Sun*, an ancient place that has been sympathetically modernized. The menu is strong on local ingredients and offers tasty Italian and British dishes, all washed down by real ales; mains average £15. They also have five en-suite rooms decorated in a creative blend of country-inn and boutique-hotel styles, from four-poster beds through to billowy, caramel-cream curtains. Kitchen Mon–Sat noon–2.30pm & 6.30–9.30pm, Sun noon–4pm & 6.30–9pm. **£145**

Sudbury

By far the most important town in this part of the Stour Valley, **SUDBURY** holds a handful of timber-framed houses that recall its days of wool-trade and **silk-weaving** prosperity. The town's most famous export, however, is **Thomas Gainsborough** (1727–88), the leading English portraitist of the eighteenth century. Although he left Sudbury when he was just 13, the artist is still very much identified with the town: his statue, with brush and palette, stands on Market Hill, the predominantly Victorian marketplace, while a superb collection of his work is on display inside the house in which he was born.

Gainsborough's House

46 Gainsborough St, CO10 2EU · Mon–Sat 10am–5pm, Sun 11am–5pm · £7 · ☎ 01787 372958, ⓦ gainsborough.org

Gainsborough's House has an outstanding collection of the artist's work distributed over a couple of main floors. Displayed here is the earliest of his surviving portraits – *Boy and Girl*, a remarkably self-assured work dated to 1744, though it's exhibited in two pieces as someone chopped up the original. Later, Gainsborough developed a fluid, flattering style that was ideal for his well-heeled subjects, posed in becoming postures and painted in soft, evanescent colours as in the striking *Portrait of Abel Moysey, MP* (1771). Look out also for one of Gainsborough's specialities, his wonderful "**conversation pieces**", so called because the sitters engage in polite chitchat – or genteel activity – with a landscape as the backdrop. In his last years, the artist also dabbled with romantic paintings of country scenes – as in *A Wooded Landscape with Cattle by a Pool* – a playful variation on the serious landscape painting he loved; the rest, he often said, just earned him a living.

ARRIVAL AND INFORMATION

SUDBURY

By train Sudbury station is a 5–10min walk from the centre via Station Rd, with services to Marks Tey, on the London to Colchester line (hourly; 20min).

By bus The bus station is on Hamilton Rd, just south of Market Hill. The main local bus company is H.C. Chambers (ⓦ chambersbus.co.uk).

Destinations Bury St Edmunds (Mon–Sat every 1–2hr; 1hr 10min); Colchester (Mon–Sat every 1–2hr; 50min); Lavenham (Mon–Sat hourly; 35min); Stoke-by-Nayland (Mon–Sat every 1–2hr; 40min).

Tourist office In the library, which is in the grand old Corn Exchange, near Market Hill (Mon–Thurs 9.30am–4.30pm, Fri 9.30am–4pm, Sat 10am–3.30pm; ☎ 01787 881320, ⓦ sudburytowncouncil.co.uk).

EATING AND DRINKING

Black Adder Brewery Tap 21 East St, CO10 2TP ☎ 01787 370876, ⓦ blackaddertap.co.uk. Enjoyable pub where the big deal is the beer – a rotating selection of draught ales, always including something from local brewer Mauldons. There's a patio and pub grub, too. Mon–Thurs 11am–11pm, Fri & Sat 11am–midnight, Sun noon–10.30pm.

David's 51 Gainsborough St, CO10 2ET ☎ 01787 373919, ⓦ davidsdelicatessen.co.uk. Neat and trim café-deli, where they turn out a tasty range of salads and light meals, mostly featuring local ingredients. Try, perhaps, the scrambled eggs and pancetta on toast. Sandwiches around £3.50. Mon–Sat 9am–4pm.

Lavenham

LAVENHAM, seven miles northeast of Sudbury, was once a centre of the region's wool trade and is now one of the most visited villages in Suffolk, thanks to its unrivalled ensemble of perfectly preserved half-timbered houses. In outward appearance at least, the whole place has changed little since the demise of the wool industry, owing in part to a zealous local preservation society, which has carefully maintained the village's antique appearance. Lavenham is at its most beguiling in the triangular **Market Place**, an airy spot flanked by pastel-painted, medieval dwellings whose beams have been warped into all sorts of wonky angles by the passing of the years.

Guildhall of Corpus Christi

Market Place, CO10 9QZ · Jan to late Feb Sat & Sun 11am–4pm; March–Oct daily 11am–5pm; Nov & Dec Thurs–Sun 11am–4pm · £6.50; NT · ☎ 01787 247646, ⓦ nationaltrust.org.uk/lavenham-guildhall

On the Market Place you'll find the village's most celebrated building, the lime-washed, timber-framed **Guildhall of Corpus Christi**, erected in the sixteenth century as the headquarters of one of Lavenham's four guilds. In the much-altered interior (used successively as a prison and workhouse), there are modest exhibitions on timber-framed buildings, medieval guilds, village life and the wool industry, though most visitors soon end up in the **walled garden**, or the teashop next door.

ARRIVAL AND INFORMATION

LAVENHAM

By bus Buses pull in at the corner of Water and Church streets, a 5min walk from Market Place. Among several services, perhaps the most useful is Chambers bus #753 (⚥ chambersbus.co.uk), which links Lavenham with Sudbury, Bury St Edmunds and Colchester.
Destinations Bury St Edmunds (Mon–Sat every 1–2hr;

40min); Colchester (Mon–Sat every 1–2hr; 1hr 30min); Sudbury (Mon–Sat every 1–2hr; 35min).
Tourist office Lady St, just south of Market Place (Jan to mid-March Sat & Sun 11am–3pm; mid-March to Oct daily 10am–4.45pm; Nov to mid-Dec daily 11am–3pm; ☎ 01787 248207, ⚥ heartofsuffolk.co.uk).

ACCOMMODATION AND EATING

★ **The Great House** Market Place, CO10 9QZ ☎ 01787 247431, ⚥ greathouse.co.uk. Delightful, family-run hotel bang in the centre of the village. Each of the five guest rooms is decorated in a thoughtful and tasteful manner, amalgamating the original features of the old – very old – house with the new. Deeply comfortable beds and a great breakfast round it all off. The hotel restaurant specializes in classic French cuisine, with both set meals and a la carte. Main courses start at £24. Tues 7–10.30pm, Wed–Sat noon–2.30pm & 7–10.30pm, Sun noon–2.30pm. **£180**
Swan Hotel High St, CO10 9QA ☎ 01787 247477,

⚥ theswanatlavenham.co.uk. This excellent hotel is a veritable rabbit warren of a place, its nooks and crannies dating back several hundred years. There's a lovely, very traditional, lounge to snooze in, a courtyard garden, an authentic Elizabethan Wool Hall and a wood-panelled bar. Just as appealing, most of the comfy guest rooms abound in original features, and the restaurant is first-rate too, serving imaginative British-based cuisine – roasted wood pigeon and puy lentils for example – with mains starting at around £18. Main restaurant daily noon–2pm & 7–9pm; brasserie daily noon–2.30pm & 6–9.30pm. **£180**

Ipswich

IPSWICH, situated at the head of the Orwell estuary, was a rich trading port in the Middle Ages, but its appearance today is mainly the result of a revival of fortunes in the Victorian era – give or take some clumsy postwar development. The two surviving reminders of old Ipswich – **Christchurch Mansion** and the splendid **Ancient House** – plus the renovated **waterfront** are all reason enough to spend an afternoon here, and there's also the **Cornhill**, the ancient Saxon marketplace and still the town's focal point, an agreeable urban space flanked by a bevy of imposing Victorian edifices – the Italianate town hall, old Neoclassical Post Office and grandiose pseudo-Jacobean Lloyds building.

Ancient House

30 Buttermarket, at corner of St Stephen's Lane, IP1 1BT • Lakeland store Mon–Sat 9am–5.30pm

From Cornhill, at the centre of town, it's just a couple of minutes' walk southeast to Ipswich's most famous building, the **Ancient House**, whose exterior was decorated around 1670 in extravagant style, a riot of pargeting and stuccowork that together make it one of the finest examples of Restoration artistry in the country. The house is now a branch of the Lakeland homewares chain, and as such you're free to take a peek inside to view yet more of the decor, including its hammer-beam roof.

Christchurch Mansion and Wolsey Gallery

Soane St, IP4 2BE • Mansion and Wolsey Art Gallery: March–Oct Tues–Sat 10am–5pm, Sun 11am–5pm; Nov–Feb Tues–Sat 10am–4pm, Sun 11am–4pm • Free • ☎ 01473 433554, ⚥ cimuseums.org.uk

Christchurch Mansion is a handsome if much-restored Tudor building, sporting seventeenth-century Dutch-style gables and set in 65 acres of parkland – an area larger than the town centre itself. The labyrinthine interior is worth exploring. There are period furnishings and an impressive collection of paintings by Constable and Gainsborough both in the main building and in the attached **Wolsey Art Gallery**.

The Waterfront

Neptune Quay, IP4 1AX, half a mile south of Cornhill

The **Waterfront** – or Wet Dock – was the largest dock in Europe when it opened in 1845. Today, after an imaginative refurbishment, it's flanked by apartments and offices, pubs, hotels and restaurants, many converted from the old marine warehouses. Walking around the Waterfront is a pleasant way to pass an hour or so – look out, in particular, for the proud Neoclassical **Customs House**.

ARRIVAL AND INFORMATION   IPSWICH

By train The train station is on the south bank of the River Orwell, a 10min walk from Cornhill along Princes St. Destinations Bury St Edmunds (hourly; 35min); Cambridge (hourly; 1hr 20min); Colchester (every 30min; 20min); Ely (every 2hr; 1hr); London Liverpool Street (every 30min; 1hr); Norwich (every 30min; 40min).

By bus There are several stops in the city centre, including the Cattle Market bus station, a 5min walk south of Cornhill on Turret Ln, and the Tower Ramparts bus station, just north of Cornhill. Timetables on ⓦ suffolkonboard.com.

Destinations Aldeburgh (Mon–Sat hourly; 2hr); Orford (Mon–Sat every 1–2hr; 1hr 50min; change at Rendlesham).

Tourist office St Stephen's Church, St Stephens Ln (Mon–Sat 9am–5pm; ☎ 01473 258070, ⓦ allaboutipswich.com).

ACCOMMODATION AND EATING

Aqua Eight 8 Lion St, IP1 1DQ ☎ 01473 218989, ⓦ aquaeight.com. Asian fusion restaurant in the heart of town. Most mains go for £10–15, but you can't go wrong with the superb steamed silver cod with ginger and spring onions (£21). It also has a great bar serving East Asian-style meze and finger food. Tues–Sun noon–3pm & 6–10pm.

Salthouse Harbour Hotel Neptune Quay, IP4 1AX ☎ 01473 226789, ⓦ salthouseharbour.co.uk. Housed in an imaginatively converted old warehouse on the quayside, this is the city's best choice, with seventy large, modern and minimalist rooms whose floor-to-ceiling windows look out over Ipswich's old harbour. The hotel restaurant lives up to the same high standards, with curvy banquettes and a low lighting. The food is hearty rather than healthy, but served with flourish and a good eye for detail. Mains £15–22. Daily noon–5pm & 6–10pm. **£150**

The Suffolk coast

The **Suffolk coast** feels detached from the rest of the county: the main road and rail lines from Ipswich to the seaport of Lowestoft funnel traffic a few miles inland for most of the way, and patches of marsh and woodland make the separation still more complete. The coast has long been plagued by erosion and this has contributed to the virtual extinction of the local fishing industry – and in the case of **Dunwich**, almost destroyed the whole town. What is left, however, is undoubtedly one of the most unspoilt shorelines in the country – if you set aside the Sizewell nuclear power stations. Highlights include the sleepy isolation of minuscule **Orford** and several genteel resorts, most notably **Southwold** and **Aldeburgh**, which have evaded the lurid fate of so many English seaside towns.

There are some delightful **walks** around here too, easy routes along the coast that are best followed with either the appropriate OS *Explorer* map or the simplified footpath maps available at most tourist offices. The Suffolk coast also hosts East Anglia's most compelling cultural gathering, the three-week-long **Aldeburgh Festival**, which takes place every June.

By public transport Getting around the Suffolk coast requires planning; check ⓦ traveline.info or ⓦ suffolkonboard. com in advance.

Sutton Hoo

Tranmer House, Sutton Hoo, IP12 3DJ · **Exhibition hall** Jan, Nov & early Dec Sat & Sun 10.30am–4pm; mid-Feb to Oct daily 10.30am–5pm · £8.50; NT · ☎ 01394 389700, ⓦ nationaltrust.org.uk/sutton-hoo · No public transport

In 1939, a local farmer/archeologist, Basil Brown, investigated one of a group of burial mounds on a sandy ridge at **Sutton Hoo**, on a remote part of the Suffolk coast east of Ipswich. Much to everyone's amazement, including his own, he unearthed the forty-oar burial ship of an Anglo-Saxon warrior king, packed with his valuable possessions, from a splendid iron and tinted-bronze helmet to intricately worked gold and jewelled ornaments.

Much of the Sutton Hoo treasure is now in the British Museum (see page 76), but a scattering of artefacts can be seen in the **Sutton Hoo exhibition hall**, which explains the history and significance of the finds. Afterwards, you can wander 500 yards to the burial site itself.

7

Orford

Some twenty miles from Ipswich, on the far side of the Tunstall Forest, two medieval buildings dominate the tiny, eminently appealing village of **ORFORD**. The more impressive is the twelfth-century **castle** (April–Oct daily 10am–5pm; Nov–March Sat & Sun 10am–4pm; £7.30, EH; ⓦ www.english-heritage.org.uk/visit/places/orford-castle), built on high ground by Henry II, and under siege by Henry's rebellious sons within months of its completion. Most of the castle disappeared centuries ago, but the lofty keep remains, its striking stature hinting at the scale of the original fortifications. Orford's other medieval edifice is **St Bartholomew's Church**, where Benjamin Britten premiered his most successful children's work, *Noye's Fludde*, as part of the 1958 Aldeburgh Festival.

Orford Ness National Nature Reserve

Orford Quay, IP12 2NU · **Boat trips** Outward boats 10am–2pm, last boat back 5pm: mid-April to late June & Oct Sat only; July to Sept Tues–Sat · £9; NT · ☎ 01728 648024, ⓦ nationaltrust.org.uk/orford-ness-national-nature-reserve

From the top of the castle keep, there's a great view across **Orford Ness National Nature Reserve**, a six-mile-long shingle spit that has all but blocked Orford from the sea since Tudor times. The National Trust offers **boat trips** across to the Ness from Orford Quay, 400 yards down the road from the church – and a five-mile **hiking trail** threads its way along the spit. En route, the trail passes a string of abandoned military buildings, where some of the pioneer research on radar and atomic weapons testing was carried out.

By bus Buses to and from Orford are poor and often need advance booking. Consult ⓦ traveline.info.

ACCOMMODATION AND EATING

Butley Orford Oysterage Market Hill, IP12 2LH ☎ 01394 450277, ⓦ pinneysoforford.co.uk. A local institution, this simple café/restaurant dishes up great fish and seafood, much of it caught and smoked locally. Hours vary, but core hours daily noon–2.15pm & 6.30–9pm.

Crown & Castle Market Hill, IP12 2LJ ☎ 01394 450205, ⓦ crownandcastle.co.uk. Orford's unhurried air is best experienced by staying overnight at this outstanding (albeit expensive) hotel, with eighteen stylish rooms. The excellent restaurant focuses on local, seasonal ingredients– rump of Suffolk lamb with broad-bean cream sauce for example. Mains around £20. Daily 12.15–2pm & 6.30–9pm. **£200**

Aldeburgh

Well-heeled **ALDEBURGH**, a small seaside town just along the coast from Orford, is best known for its annual **arts festival**, the brainchild of composer **Benjamin Britten** (1913–76), who is buried in the village churchyard alongside the tenor Peter Pears, his lover and musical collaborator. They lived by the seafront in Crag House on Crabbe Street – named after the poet, George Crabbe, who provided Britten with his greatest inspiration (see below) – before moving to a much larger house a few miles away.

Outside of June, Aldeburgh is a relaxed and low-key coastal resort, with a small fishing fleet selling its daily catch from wooden shacks along the pebbled shore. Aldeburgh's slightly old-fashioned-shop appearance is fiercely defended by its citizens, who caused an almighty rumpus – Barbours at dawn – when Maggi Hambling's 13ft-high *Scallop* sculpture appeared on the beach in 2003. Hambling described the sculpture as a conversation with the sea and a suitable memorial to Britten; many disgruntled locals compare it to a mantelpiece ornament gone wrong.

Aldeburgh's wide **High Street** and narrow side streets run close to the **beach**, but this was not always the case – hence their quixotic appearance. The sea swallowed much of the medieval town long ago and today Aldeburgh's oldest building, the sixteenth-century **Moot Hall** (daily: April, May, Sept & Oct 2.30–5pm; June–Aug noon–5pm), which began its days in the centre of town, is on the seashore. Several **footpaths** lead out from Aldeburgh, with the most pleasant heading southwest to the winding estuary of the **River Alde**.

ARRIVAL AND DEPARTURE
ALDEBURGH

By bus Buses to Aldeburgh pull in along the High St and on the south side of the resort at Fort Green, heading to Ipswich (Mon–Sat hourly; 2hr) and Saxmundham (Mon–Sat every 30min; 30min).

ACCOMMODATION

Brudenell The Parade, IP15 5BU ☎01728 452071, ⓦbrudenellhotel.co.uk. This bright and smart seafront hotel has something of a New England feel that sits very comfortably here in Aldeburgh. There's a pleasant sitting room downstairs with sea views and the bedrooms are thoughtfully furnished in a contemporary style. **£170**
★ **Ocean House B&B** 25 Crag Path, IP15 5BS ☎01728 452094, ⓦoceanhousealdeburgh.co.uk. Housed in

---

BENJAMIN BRITTEN AND THE ALDEBURGH FESTIVAL

Born in Lowestoft in 1913, **Benjamin Britten** was closely associated with Suffolk for most of his life. The main break was during World War II when, as a conscientious objector, Britten exiled himself to the US. Ironically enough, it was here that Britten first read the work of the nineteenth-century Suffolk poet, George Crabbe, whose *The Borough*, a grisly portrait of the life of the fishermen of Aldeburgh, was the basis of the libretto of Britten's best-known opera, *Peter Grimes*, which was premiered in London in 1945. Three years later, Britten launched the **Aldeburgh Festival** as a showpiece for his own works and those of his contemporaries. For the rest of his life he composed many works specifically for the festival, including his masterpiece for children, *Noye's Fludde*, and the last of his fifteen operas, *Death in Venice*.

By the mid-1960s, the festival had outgrown the parish churches in which it began, and moved into a collection of disused malt houses, five miles west of Aldeburgh on the River Alde, just south of the small village of **Snape**. The complex, the **Snape Maltings** (ⓦsnapemaltings.co.uk), was subsequently converted into one of the finest concert venues in the country and, in addition to the concert hall, there are now recording studios, galleries, a tearoom, and a pub, the *Plough & Sail*. The Aldeburgh Festival takes place every June for two and a half weeks. Core performances are still held at the Maltings, but a string of other local venues are pressed into service as well. Throughout the rest of the year, the Maltings hosts a wide-ranging programme of musical and theatrical events. For all programme information and bookings, go to ⓦsnapemaltings.co.uk or call the box office on ☎01728 687110. **Tickets** for the Aldeburgh Festival usually go on sale to the public towards the end of March, and sell out fast for the big-name recitals.

an immaculately maintained Victorian dwelling right on the seafront, *Ocean House* has just three traditional, en- suite guest rooms including a top-floor suite. The English breakfasts, with home-made bread, are delicious. **£100**

EATING AND DRINKING

★**Aldeburgh Fish & Chip Shop** 226 High St, IP15 5DB ☎01728 452250, ⑩aldeburghfishandchips. co.uk. One of Aldeburgh's two outstanding fish-and-chip shops – this is the original, serving takeaway only. Such is its reputation that there are often long queues at the weekend. Core hours: daily noon–2pm & 5/6–8/9pm.
The Golden Galleon 137 High St, IP15 5AR ☎01728 454685, ⑩aldeburghfishandchips.co.uk. Canteen-style, sit-down fish-and-chip restaurant, sister to the *Fish & Chip*

Shop along the road. Mon–Fri noon–2.30pm & 5–8pm, Sat & Sun noon–8pm.
★**The Lighthouse** 77 High St, IP15 5AU ☎01728 453377, ⑩lighthouserestaurant.co.uk. Aldeburgh's best restaurant, a relaxed, informal and busy place in cosy, split-level premises. The menu favours local ingredients, featuring everything from burgers and fish and chips to venison tagine with couscous. Mains average £13 at lunch, more in the evening. Daily noon–2pm & 6.30–10pm.

Dunwich and around

7

Tiny **DUNWICH**, about twelve miles up the coast from Aldeburgh, is probably the strangest and certainly the eeriest place on the Suffolk coast. The one-time seat of the kings of East Anglia, a bishopric and formerly a large port, Dunwich peaked in the twelfth century since when it's all been downhill: over the last millennium something like a mile of land has been lost to the sea, a process that continues at the rate of about a yard a year. As a result, the whole of the medieval city now lies underwater, including all twelve churches, the last of which toppled over the cliffs in 1919. All that survives today are fragments of the Greyfriars monastery, which originally lay to the west of the city and now dangles near the sea's edge. For a potted history of the lost city, head for the **museum** (April–Oct daily 11.30am–4.30pm; free, but donation requested; ☎01728 648796, ⑩www.dunwichmuseum.org.uk) in what's left of Dunwich – little more than one small street of terraced houses built by the local landowner in the nineteenth century.

Minsmere RSPB Nature Reserve

IP17 3BY • Reserve daily 9am–9pm or dusk; visitor centre daily 9am–5pm, 4pm in winter • £9 • ☎01728 648281, ⑩rspb.org.uk/minsmere

From Dunwich, it's about an hour's walk south along the coast to the **Minsmere RSPB Nature Reserve**, though there's a road here too – just watch for the sign on the more southerly of the two byroads into Dunwich. The reserve covers a varied terrain of marsh, scrub and beach, and in the autumn it's a gathering place for wading birds and waterfowl, which arrive here by the hundred. The reserve is also home to a small population of bitterns, one of England's rarest birds. You can rent binoculars from the **visitor centre** and strike out on the trails to the birdwatching hides.

ARRIVAL AND DEPARTURE   DUNWICH AND AROUND

By car There's no regular public transport to Dunwich, so driving is your best bet. A sprawling seashore car park gives ready access to both the village and this slice of coast.

EATING

Flora Tearooms Dunwich beach, IP17 3EN ☎01728 648433. Set right on the beach, this popular café is a large hut-like affair, where they serve steaming cups of tea and

piping hot fish and chips to an assortment of birdwatchers, hikers and anglers. Daily 11am–4pm.

Southwold

Perched on robust cliffs just north of the River Blyth, **SOUTHWOLD** is one of the region's most charming towns, its genteel delights attracting the well-heeled and well-spoken. It was not always so: by the sixteenth century Southwold was Suffolk's busiest fishing port, but thereafter it lost most of its fishery to neighbouring Lowestoft. Today, although a small fleet still brings in herrings, sprats and cod, the town is primarily a **seaside resort** – one with none of the crassness of many of its competitors. There are fine Georgian buildings, a long sandy beach, open heathland and even a little industry – in the shape of the Adnams brewery – but no burger bars or amusement arcades. This gentility was not to the liking of **George Orwell**, who lived for a time at his parents' house at 36 High Street, but he might well have taken a liking to Southwold's major music festival, **Latitude** (ⓦlatitudefestival.co.uk), which spreads over four days in the middle of July with happy campers grubbing down in Henham Park, about five miles west of town.

Market Place and around

The centre of Southwold is its triangular, pocket-sized **Market Place**, sitting at one end of the town's busy High Street and framed by attractive, mostly Georgian buildings. From here, it's a couple of hundred yards north along Church Street to **East Green**, one of the several greens that were left as firebreaks after the town was gutted by fire in 1659. On one side of East Green is **Adnams Brewery** (tours available; ⓦtours.adnams.co.uk), on the other a stumpy old lighthouse. Close by is Southwold's architectural pride and joy, the **Church of St Edmund** (daily 9am–4pm; free), a handsome fifteenth-century structure whose solid symmetries are balanced by its long and elegantly carved windows.

The Sailors' Reading Room

East Cliff, IP18 6EL • Daily 9am–dusk • Free • ⓦ www.southwoldsailorsreadingroom.co.uk

From Market Place, it's a short stroll along East Street to a clifftop vantage point, which offers a grand view over the beach. Also up there is the curious **Sailors' Reading Room**, where pensioners gather in the mornings to shoot the breeze in a room full of model ships, seafaring texts and vintage photos of local tars, all beards and sea boots: founded in 1864, it was designed to keep these very same men reading rather than drinking.

Under the Pier Show

Southwold pier, IP18 6BN • Daily: April–Sept 9am–7pm; Oct–March 10am–5pm • Free • ☎ 01502 7221055, ⓦ underthepier.com

Jutting out from the beach, **Southwold pier** is the latest incarnation of a structure that dates back to 1899. Revamped and renovated a decade ago, the pier houses the usual – if rather more polite than usual – cafés and souvenir shops, but its star turn is the **Under the Pier Show**, where a series of knowingly playful machines, handmade by Tim Hunkin, provide all sorts of arcade-style sensory surprises. Try the "Pirate Practice", the "Rent-a-Dog" and the mischievous (and emotionally rewarding) "Whack-a-banker".

The harbour

At the mouth of the River Blyth is **the harbour**, an idyllic spot where fishing boats rest against old wooden jetties and nets are spread out on the banks to dry. A footpath leads west from the river mouth to a tiny foot **ferry** (April–Oct Sat & Sun 10am–5pm, plus sometimes Mon–Fri 10am–12.30pm & 2–5pm; £1; ⓦexplorewalberswick.co.uk/ferry), which shuffles across the river to Walberswick. If you're heading back towards Southwold, keep going along the river until you pass the *Harbour Inn* and then take the path that leads back into town across **Southwold Common**. The whole walk takes about thirty minutes.

ARRIVAL AND DEPARTURE	**SOUTHWOLD**
By bus Buses pull in on Station Rd, just west of the centre. **Destinations** Halesworth (on the Ipswich to Lowestoft	train line; Mon–Sat hourly; 30min); Norwich (Mon–Sat every 1–2hr; 1hr 30min to 2hr).

ACCOMMODATION

The Crown 90 High St, IP18 6DP ☎01502 722275, ⓦ thecrownsouthwold.co.uk. The less upmarket (and less expensive) of Adnams' two hotels in Southwold, with a dozen or so rooms above a bar/restaurant (see below). Most of the rooms are large and have been decorated in a pleasant, contemporary style. **£170**

★ **Home@21** 21 North Parade, IP18 6LT ☎ 01502 722573, ⓦ homeat21.co.uk. Located near the pier, this seafront guesthouse occupies a well-maintained Victorian terraced house. There are three sympathetically updated guest rooms, two of which are en suite and two sea-facing. **£100**

The Swan Market Place, IP18 6EG ☎ 01502 722186, ⓦ theswansouthwold.co.uk. Delightful if pricey hotel occupying a splendid, recently refurbished Georgian building right at the heart of Southwold. The main building is a real period piece, its nooks and crannies holding all manner of Georgian details. Some of the guest rooms are here, others (the "Lighthouse Rooms") are in the more modern garden annexe at the back. **£200**

EATING AND DRINKING

The Crown 90 High St, IP18 6DP ☎ 01502 722275, ⓦ thecrownsouthwold.co.uk. Deluxe bar food featuring local, seasonal ingredients, all washed down with Adnams ales. Try, for example, the roast butternut squash with puy lentils. Mains £8–19. Tables are allocated on a first-come, first-served basis. Drinks daily noon–11pm; kitchen Mon–Sat noon–2pm & 6–9pm, Sun noon–3pm & 6–9pm.

Lord Nelson 42 East St, IP18 6EJ ☎ 01502 722079, ⓦ thelordnelsonsouthwold.co.uk. This lively neighbourhood pub, with its low-beamed ceilings, has a first-rate, locally inspired menu. Try, for example, the herring, Nelson smokes (smoked haddock and cod in sauce) or the dressed crab. Mains average £13. Drinks Mon–Sat 10.30am–11pm, Sun noon–10.30pm; kitchen daily noon–2pm & 7–9pm.

Sutherland House 56 High St, IP18 6DN ☎ 01502 724544, ⓦ sutherlandhouse.co.uk. There's a strong local emphasis to the menu at this classy Modern British restaurant, which is housed in one of Southwold's oldest buildings. Main courses are £12–20, and they have a helpful food-miles chart attached. Daily noon–2.30pm & 6.30–8.30pm; closed Mon in winter.

Norwich

One of the five largest cities in Norman England, **NORWICH** once served a vast hinterland of East Anglian **cloth producers**, whose work was brought here by river and then exported to the continent. Its isolated position beyond the Fens meant that it enjoyed closer links with the Low Countries than with the rest of England and, by 1700, Norwich was the second-richest city in the country after London. With the onset of the Industrial Revolution, however, Norwich lost ground to the northern manufacturing towns – the city's famous mustard company, Colman's, is one of its few industrial success stories – and this has helped preserve much of the ancient street plan and many of the city's older buildings. Pride of place goes to the beautiful **cathedral** and the sterling **castle**, but the city's hallmark is its **medieval churches**, thirty or so squat flint structures with sturdy towers and sinuous stone tracery decorating the windows. Many are no longer in regular use and are now in the care of the **Norwich Historic Churches Trust** (ⓦ norwich-churches.org), whose website describes each in precise detail.

Norwich's relative isolation has also meant that the population has never swelled to any great extent and today, with just 220,000 inhabitants, it remains an easy and enjoyable city to negotiate. Yet Norwich is no provincial backwater. In the 1960s, the foundation of the **University of East Anglia** (UEA) made it much more cosmopolitan and bolstered its arts scene, while in the 1980s it attracted new high-tech companies, who created something of a mini-boom, making the city one of England's wealthiest. As East Anglia's unofficial capital, Norwich also lies at the hub of the region's **transport** network, serving as a useful base for visiting the Broads and as a springboard for the north Norfolk coast.

The Cathedral

The Close, NR1 4EH • Daily 7.30am–6pm • Free, but donation requested • ☎ 01603 218300, ⓦ cathedral.org.uk

Of all the medieval buildings in Norwich, it's the **Cathedral** that fires the imagination, a mighty, sandy-coloured structure finessed by its prickly octagonal spire, which rises to a height of 315ft, second only to Salisbury Cathedral in Wiltshire. Entered via the Hostry, a glassy, well-proportioned visitor centre, the **interior** is pleasantly light thanks to a creamy tint in the stone and the clear glass windows of much of the **nave**, where the thick pillars are a powerful legacy of the Norman builders who began the cathedral in 1096. The nave's architectural highlight is the ceiling, a finely crafted affair whose delicate and geometrically precise fan vaulting is embellished by several dozen **roof bosses**. Accessible from the south aisle of the nave are the cathedral's unique **cloisters**. Built between 1297 and 1450, and the only two-storey cloisters left standing in England, they contain a remarkable set of sculpted **bosses**, similar to the ones in the main nave, but close enough to be scrutinized without binoculars. The dominant theme is the **Apocalypse**, but look out also for the bosses depicting green men, originally pagan fertility symbols.

Cathedral precincts

Outside, in front of the main entrance, stands the medieval **Carnary Chapel**. This is the original building of Norwich School, whose blue-blazered pupils are often visible during term time – the rambling school buildings are adjacent. A statue of the school's most famous boy, **Horatio Nelson**, faces the chapel, standing on the green of the **Upper Close**, which is guarded by two ornate and imposing medieval gates (**Erpingham** and, a few yards to the south, **Ethelbert**). Beside the Erpingham gate is a memorial to **Edith Cavell**, a local woman who was a nurse in occupied Brussels during World War I. She was shot by the Germans in 1915 for helping Allied prisoners to escape, a fate that

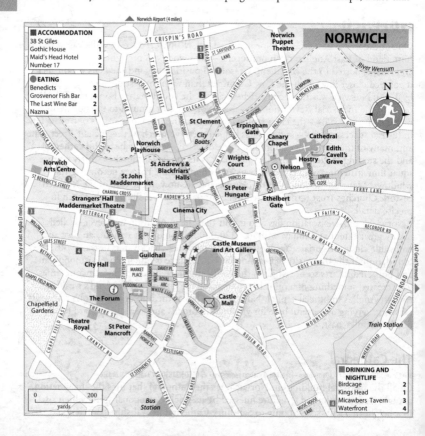

made her an instant folk hero; her grave is outside the cathedral ambulatory. Both gates lead onto the old Saxon marketplace, **Tombland**, a wide and busy thoroughfare whose name derives from the Saxon word for an open space.

Strangers' Hall

4 Charing Cross, NR2 4AL • Mid-Feb to May & Oct–Dec Wed 10am–4pm, Sun 1–4.30pm; June–Sept Wed–Fri 10am–4pm Sun 1–4.30pm • £5 • ☎ 01603 667229, ⓦ museums.norfolk.gov.uk

Strangers' Hall is the city's most unusual attraction. Dating back to the fourteenth century, it's a veritable rabbit warren of a place stuffed with all manner of bygones, including ancient fireplaces, oodles of wood panelling, a Regency music room and a Georgian dining room. Allow an hour or so to explore, though the most impressive room, the Great Hall, with its church-like Gothic windows, comes right at the beginning. The hall is named after the Protestant refugees who fled here from the Spanish Netherlands to avoid the tender mercies of the Inquisition in the 1560s; at the peak of the migration, these "Strangers" accounted for around a third of the local population.

Market Place

The city's **Market Place** is the site of one of the country's largest **open-air markets** (Mon–Sat), with stalls selling everything from bargain-basement clothes to local mussels and whelks. Four very different but equally distinctive buildings oversee the market's stripy awnings, the oldest of them being the fifteenth-century **Guildhall**, a capacious flint and stone structure begun in 1407. Opposite, commanding the heights of the marketplace, are the austere **City Hall**, a lumbering brick pile with a landmark clocktower that was built in the 1930s in a Scandinavian style, and **The Forum**, a large, flashy glass structure completed in 2001. The latter is home to the city's main library and tourist office (see page 374). On the south side of Market Place is the finest of the four buildings, **St Peter Mancroft** (Mon–Sat 10am–3pm; free; ⓦ stpetermancroft.org. uk), whose long and graceful nave leads to a mighty stone tower, an intricately carved affair surmounted by a spiky little spire, while inside slender columns reach up to the delicate groining of the roof.

Back outside and just below the church is **Gentlemen's Walk**, once the town's main promenade, which runs along the bottom of the marketplace and abuts the **Royal Arcade**, an Art Nouveau extravagance from 1899. The arcade has been beautifully restored to reveal its swirling tiling, ironwork and stained glass.

Castle Museum and Art Gallery

Castle Meadow, NR1 3JU • Late June to late Sept Mon–Sat 10am–5pm, Sun 1–5pm; late Sept to late June Mon–Sat 10am–4.30pm, Sun 1–4.30pm • £9.15 • ☎ 01603 493625, ⓦ museums.norfolk.gov.uk

Glued to the top of a grassy mound in the centre of town – and with a modern shopping mall drilled into its side – the stern walls of **Norwich Castle** date from the twelfth century. To begin with they were a reminder of Norman power and then, when the castle was turned into a prison, they served as a grim warning to potential lawbreakers. Today, much of the castle is occupied by the **Castle Museum and Art Gallery**, whose wide-ranging displays spread over two floors around a central rotunda. Pride of place goes to the **Colman Art galleries**, which boast an outstanding selection of work by the **Norwich School**. Founded in 1803, and in existence for just thirty years, this school of landscape painters produced – for the most part – richly coloured, formally composed land- and seascapes in oil and watercolour, paintings whose realism harked back to the Dutch landscape painters of the seventeenth century. The leading figures were **John Crome** (1768–1821) – aka "Old Crome" – and **John Sell Cotman** (1782–1842).

University of East Anglia

Earlham Rd, NR4 7TJ · **UEA Campus** Open access · Free · ☎ 01603 456161, ⓦ uea.ac.uk · **Sainsbury Centre for Visual Arts** Tues–Fri 10am–6pm, Sat & Sun 10am–5pm · Free, but admission charged for some exhibitions · ☎ 01603 593199, ⓦ scva.ac.uk · Among several services, bus #25 runs to the UEA campus from the train station and Castle Meadow

The **University of East Anglia** (UEA) occupies a sprawling campus on the western outskirts of the city. Its buildings are resolutely modern, an assortment of concrete-and-glass blocks of varying designs, some quite ordinary, others, like the prize-winning "ziggurat" halls of residence, designed by Denys Lasdun, eminently memorable. The main reason to visit is the **Sainsbury Centre for Visual Arts**, which occupies a large, shed-like building designed by Norman Foster. Well-lit and beautifully presented, the bulk of the permanent collection spreads out over the main floor, beginning with a substantial selection of non-European – particularly Asian and African – artefacts positioned close to some of the European paintings and sculptures they influenced and/or inspired.

ARRIVAL AND INFORMATION NORWICH

By plane Norwich Airport (ⓦ norwichairport.co.uk) serves national and international destinations and is about 4 miles north of the city centre along the A140. Park and Ride buses (ⓦ norwichparkandride.co.uk) run from the airport to the centre (Mon–Sat every 20min; 20min).

By train The station is on the east bank of the River Wensum, a 10min walk from the city centre along Prince of Wales Rd.

Destinations Cambridge (hourly; 1hr 20min); Cromer (hourly; 45min); Colchester (every 30min; 1hr); Ely (every 30min; 1hr); Ipswich (every 30min; 40min); London Liverpool Street (every 30min; 1hr 50min); Sheringham (hourly; 1hr).

By bus Long-distance buses mostly terminate at the main bus station between Surrey St and Queen's Rd, a 10min walk from the centre. Some services also stop on Castle Meadow.

Destinations King's Lynn (hourly; 1hr 50min with one change); London Victoria (every 2–3hr; 2hr 30min–3hr 45min).

Tourist office In the Forum building, overlooking Market Place (Mon–Sat 9.30am–5.30pm, plus early July to mid-Sept Sun 10.30am–3.30pm; ☎ 01603 213999, ⓦ visitnorwich.co.uk).

ACCOMMODATION

38 St Giles 38 St Giles St, NR2 1LL ☎ 01603 662944, ⓦ 38stgiles.co.uk; map p.372. Billing itself as a cross between a B&B and a hotel, this deluxe establishment has five en-suite guest rooms of varying size and description, but all top quality. Great home-made breakfasts too. It's in a handy location, just a few yards from the Market Place. **£120**

★ **Gothic House** King's Head Yard, 42 Magdalen St, NR3 1JE ☎ 01603 631879, ⓦ gothic-house-norwich.com; map p.372. This particularly charming B&B occupies a slender, three-storey Georgian house down a little courtyard off Magdalen Street. The interior has been meticulously renovated in a period style and the two salon-style bedrooms are reached via the most charming of spiral staircases. The guest rooms are not attached to their bathrooms, but this really is no inconvenience. **£105**

Maid's Head Hotel 20 Tombland, NR3 1LB ☎ 01603 209955, ⓦ maidsheadhotel.co.uk; map p.372. Not

everyone's cup of tea perhaps, but this chain hotel is delightfully idiosyncratic – a rabbit warren of a place with all sorts of architectural bits and pieces, from the mock-Tudor facade to the ancient, wood-panelled bar, though there is also a clumpy modern extension. The rooms are mostly large and very comfortable in a standard-issue sort of way, and the location, bang in the centre opposite the cathedral, can't be beat. If you are a light sleeper, you should avoid those rooms that overlook the street, especially at the weekend. **£120**

Number 17 17 Colegate, NR3 1BN ☎ 01603 764486, ⓦ number17norwich.co.uk; map p.372. Family-run guesthouse with eight en-suite guest rooms decorated in a brisk, modern style with solid oak flooring; there are two larger family rooms as well. Good location, in one of the nicest parts of the centre. **£90**

EATING

Benedicts 9 St Benedict's St, NR2 4PE ☎ 01603 926080, ⓦ restaurantbenedicts.com; map p.372. All simple lines and bright whites, this appealing, family-owned restaurant offers a well-considered Modern British menu: try, for example, the local sea bass or mullet with turnips, Jersey Royals and passion fruit. A two-course meal

costs £30, less at lunch. Tues 6–10pm, Wed–Sat noon–2pm & 6–10pm.

★ **Grosvenor Fish Bar** 28 Lower Goat Lane, NR2 1EL ☎ 01603 625855, ⓦ fshshop.com; map p.372. A fish-and-chip shop with bells on: the funky decor is inventive, but this plays second fiddle to the delicious fish and chips (from £6), not to mention the veggie burgers, meat pies and more distinctive dishes – tuna with wasabi beans, for one. Eat in or take away. Mon–Sat 11am–7.30pm.

The Last Wine Bar 76 St George's St, NR3 1AB ☎01603 626626, ⓦlastwinebar.co.uk; map p.372. Imaginatively converted old shoe factory, a couple of minutes' walk north of the river that has an unpretentious wine bar in one section and an excellent restaurant in the other. The food is firmly Modern British, with the

likes of braised lamb shank with carrots and parsnips in a rosemary jus (around £17). Mon–Sat noon–2.30pm & 6–10.30pm.

Nazma 15 Magdalen St, NR3 1LE ☎01603 618701, ⓦnazmaonline.co.uk; map p.372. The menu at this modern Indian restaurant covers all the classics, each prepared from scratch with the freshest of ingredients. Particularly strong on Bangladeshi cuisine. Eat in or take away. Mains around £11. Daily 5–11pm.

DRINKING AND NIGHTLIFE

Birdcage 23 Pottergate, NR1 1BA ☎01603 633534 ⓦthebirdcagenorwich.co.uk; map p.372. Idiosyncratic pub with a classic Art Deco exterior and a self-proclaimed "Bohemian" interior – take it all in, from the razzly furniture to the modern art and vintage postcards on the walls. It all works very well and the place casts a wide net, with light bites, board games, cocktails, cabaret and cupcakes. Mon–Wed & Sun noon–11pm, Thurs–Sat noon–midnight.

★ **Kings Head** 42 Magdalen St, NR3 1JE ☎01603 620468 ⓦkingsheadnorwich.com; map p.372. The perfect drinkers' pub, with precious little in the way of distraction – there are certainly no one-armed bandits here. The outstanding selection of real ales is supplemented by an equally impressive range of bottled beers, most notably Belgian. The pub has just two smallish

rooms, so you may need to be assertive to get served. Daily noon–11pm, sometimes later.

Micawbers Tavern 92 Pottergate, NR2 1DZ ☎01603 626627; map p.372. Lodged in an old beamed building on one of the city's prettiest streets, this friendly pub is a local par excellence, featuring an outstanding range of guest ales on draft. There's home-cooked food and sports TV too. Mon & Tues 5–11pm, Wed & Thurs 3–11pm, Fri 3pm–midnight, Sat noon–midnight, Sun noon–9pm.

Waterfront 139–141 King St, NR1 1QH ☎01603 632717, ⓦwaterfrontnorwich.webflow.io; map p.372. This happening club and alternative music venue, which occupies a one-time beer bottling plant, showcases some great bands, both big names and local talent, and offers club and DJ nights too. Schedule varies; see website.

ENTERTAINMENT

Cinema City Suckling House, St Andrew's St, NR2 4AD ☎0871 902 5724, ⓦpicturehouses.co.uk. Easily the best cinema in town, featuring prime new releases plus themed evenings and cult and classic films. Also live feeds, a Kids' Club and late-night horror films.

Norwich Arts Centre 51 St Benedict's St, NR2 4PG ☎01603 660352, ⓦnorwichartscentre.co.uk. Housed in a redundant church, this inventive and creative Arts Centre offers a wide range of media and performing arts plus an enterprising programme of participatory workshops and activities for both kids and adults.

Norwich Puppet Theatre Church of St James, Whitefriars, NR3 1TN ☎01603 629921, ⓦpuppet

theatre.co.uk. Housed in a deconsecrated medieval church beside the busy Whitefriars roundabout, this long-established puppet theatre company has an outstanding reputation for the quality of its puppets and the excellence of its shows. Some performances are aimed at young children – who are simply enraptured – while others are for adults.

Theatre Royal Theatre St, NR2 1RL ☎01603 630000, ⓦtheatreroyalnorwich.co.uk. This is the city's major performance venue, located in a clunky modern building with a capacious auditorium. It casts its artistic net wide, from world music to opera.

North Norfolk coast

About forty miles from one end to the other, the **north Norfolk coast** is a top tourist destination, attracting a wide cross section of the British population to its long sandy beaches and seaside resorts. This stretch of coast begins (or ends) at **Cromer**, perhaps the most appealing of the larger resorts on account of its handsome setting, perched on the edge of blustery cliffs. A few miles to the west is another well-established resort, Sheringham, but thereafter the shoreline becomes a beguiling patchwork of salt marshes, dunes and shingle spits trimmed by a string of charming villages, principally **Cley**, **Blakeney**, **Burnham Market** and **Wells-next-the-Sea**, all prime targets for an overnight stay.

7

THE NORFOLK BROADS

Three **rivers** – the Yare, Waveney and Bure – meander across the flatlands to the east of Norwich, converging on Breydon Water before flowing into the sea at Great Yarmouth. In places these rivers swell into wide expanses of water known as **broads** (ⓦvisitthebroads. co.uk), which for years were thought to be natural lakes. In fact they're the result of peat cutting – centuries of accumulated diggings made in a region where wood was scarce and peat a valuable source of energy. The pits flooded when sea levels rose in the thirteenth and fourteenth centuries to create what is now one of the most important wetlands in Europe – a haven for birds including kingfishers, grebes and warblers – and one of the region's major tourist attractions. Looking after the Broads, the **Broads Authority** (ⓦwww.broads-authority. gov.uk) has several information centres in the region.

The Norfolk Broads are crisscrossed by roads and rail lines, but the best – really the only – way to see them is **by boat**, and you could happily spend a week or so exploring the 125 miles of lock-free navigable waterways, visiting the various churches, pubs and windmills en route. Of the many **boat rental** companies, Norfolk Broads Direct (ⓣ01603 782207, ⓦbroads. co.uk), is one of the most reputable; they have an outlet at The Bridge in **Wroxham**. Prices for cruisers start at around £700 a week for four people in peak season, but less expensive, short-term rentals are widely available too. For something rather more adventurous, contact the Wroxham-based **Canoe Man** (ⓣ01603 783777, ⓦthecanoeman.com), who organizes a whole range of activities from guided canoe trips to bushcraft expeditions.

Trying to explore the Broads by car is pretty much a waste of time, but **cyclists** and **walkers** can take advantage of the region's network of footpaths and trails. There are **bike rental** points dotted around the region and walkers might consider the 62-mile **Weavers' Way**, a footpath that winds through the best parts of the Broads on its way from Cromer to Great Yarmouth.

GETTING AROUND
NORTH NORFOLK COAST

By train There are hourly Bittern Line trains (ⓦbitternline. com) from Norwich to Cromer (45min) and Sheringham (1hr).

By bus Easily the most useful bus is Stagecoach's Norfolk Coasthopper (ⓦstagecoachbus.com/promos-and-offers/east/coasthopper), which runs along the coast between Cromer and King's Lynn via a whole gaggle of coastal towns and villages, including Blakeney, Sheringham, Wells and Burnham Market; it generally sticks to the main coast road,

the A149. Frequencies vary on different stretches of the route and there are more services in the summer than in the winter, but on the more popular stretches buses appear every 30min or hourly (less frequently on Sun). There are lots of different tickets and discounts; perhaps most useful is the Coasthopper Rover, which provides unlimited travel on the whole route for either one day (£10), three days (£21) or seven days (£36); tickets can be bought from the driver.

Cromer

Dramatically poised on a high bluff, **CROMER** should be the most memorable of Norfolk's coastal resorts, but its fine aspect has long been undermined by a certain shabbiness. To be fair, however, things are at last on the mend, with new businesses arriving to add a touch of flair, and the town council keeps a string of clifftop parks and gardens in immaculate condition. It's no more than the place deserves: Cromer has a long history, first as a prosperous medieval port – witness the tower of **St Peter and St Paul**, at 160ft the tallest in Norfolk – and then as a fashionable seaside spot after the advent of the railway in the 1880s. There are three things you must do here: take a walk on the **beach**, stroll out onto the **pier**, and, of course, grab a **crab**: Cromer crabs are famous right across England and several places sell them, reliably fresh, and cooked and stuffed every which way.

ARRIVAL AND INFORMATION
CROMER

By train From Cromer station, with trains for Norwich (hourly; 45min) and Sheringham (hourly; 10min), it's a 5min walk to the centre.

By bus Buses to Cromer, including the Norfolk Coasthopper (see above), stop at the east end of Cadogan Rd, on the western side of the town centre.

Tourist office The North Norfolk Information Centre is on the south side of the town centre on Louden Rd (late May to Aug Mon–Sat 10am–5pm, Sun 10am–4pm; Sept to late May daily 10am–4pm; ☎01263 512497, ⓦvisitnorfolk.co.uk).

ACCOMMODATION

Cliftonville Hotel 29 Runton Rd, NR27 9AS ☎01263 512543, ⓦcliftonvillehotel.co.uk. Of the old mansions that line Runton Rd just west of the town centre facing out to sea, this is the smartest, its grand Edwardian foyer equipped with an impressive double staircase and oodles of wood panelling. After the foyer, the rooms beyond can't help but seem a tad mundane, but they are large and most have sea views. **£160**

Virginia Court Hotel 9 Cliff Ave, NR27 0AN ☎01263 512398, ⓦvirginiacourt.co.uk. This recently revamped, medium-sized hotel, arguably Cromer's best, has super-comfy beds, super-thick towels, and super-warm duvets. It dates back to Edwardian times, hence the capacious foyer with its wide, sweeping staircase, and the atmosphere is very much that of a traditional seaside hotel, friendly and relaxed. **£140**

EATING AND DRINKING

Mary Jane's Fish & Chip Shop 27 Garden St, NR27 9HN ☎01263 511208, ⓦmaryjanes.co.uk. Many Norfolk tourists are fastidious about their fish and chips, with allegiances strongly argued and felt. This simple, family-owned place is especially popular, for the lightness of the batter and the freshness of the fish. Eat in or take away. Takeaway May–Aug Mon–Sat 11.30am–10pm, Sun noon–9.30pm; Sept–April Mon–Thurs 11.30am–9pm, Fri & Sat 11.30am–10.30pm, Sun noon–8pm.

Rocket House Café RNLI building, The Gangway, NR27 9ET ☎01263 519126, ⓦrockethousecafe. co.uk. Offering sparkling views over the beach, pier and ocean from its giant windows – and from its blustery terrace – this café has the best location in town. The food lacks subtlety, though – stick to the crabs and the salads (which start at just £5). Mon–Fri 9am–5pm, Sat & Sun 10am–5pm.

Virginia Court Hotel 9 Cliff Ave, NR27 0AN ⓦvirginiacourt.co.uk. Excellent hotel restaurant, where the emphasis is on local, seasonal ingredients – try, for example, the roast duckling with an orange and redcurrant jus. Mains average £16. Accommodation and dinner deals available. Daily: afternoon teas 2–5pm; dinner 6–8.30pm.

Salthouse

The tiny hamlet of **SALTHOUSE** may look inconsequential today, but the wool from the flocks of sheep that once grazed here provided a rich living for the lord of the manor and funded the construction of the **Church of St Nicholas** (daily 10am–4pm; free), an imposing and strikingly beautiful edifice stuck on top of a grassy knoll; the church's prominent position was both a reminder to the faithful and a landmark for those at sea.

ARRIVAL AND DEPARTURE   SALTHOUSE

By bus The Norfolk Coasthopper (see page 376) pulls in by The Green, a small triangular piece of grass by the A149.

EATING

Cookie's Crab Shack The Green, NR25 7AJ ☎01263 740352, ⓦsalthouse.org.uk. *Cookie's* has something of a cult following, for the freshness and variety of the seafood. Crabs, prawns and smoked fish lead the maritime way, but there's lots more to choose from, including samphire, a local delicacy harvested from the surrounding mud flats and salt marshes from late June to mid-Sept. Daily: April–Sept 9am–6pm; Oct–March 10am–4pm.

Cley Marshes Nature Reserve

A149, NR25 7SA • Reserve daily dawn to dusk; visitor centre April–Oct daily 10am–5pm, Nov–March daily 10am–4pm • £5 • ☎01263 740008, ⓦnorfolkwildlifetrust.org.uk

Beside the A149, between Salthouse and Cley (see page 378), **Cley Marshes Nature Reserve**, with its conspicuous, roadside **visitor centre**, attracts birdwatchers like bees to a honey pot. Owned and operated by the Norfolk Wildlife Trust (NWT), the visitor centre issues permits for entering the reserve, whose saltwater and freshwater marshes, reed beds and coastal shingle ridge are accessed on several footpaths and overseen by half a dozen hides.

Cley beach to Blakeney Point

NT information centre Blakeney Point • April–Sept daily dawn to dusk • Free; NT • ⓦ nationaltrust.org.uk/blakeney-national-nature-reserve

On the west side of the Cley Marshes Nature Reserve – and about 400 yards east of Cley village – is the mile-long byroad (Beach Rd) that leads to the shingle mounds of **Cley beach**. This is the starting point for the four-mile hike west out along the spit to **Blakeney Point**, a nature reserve famed for its colonies of terns and seals. The seal colony is made up of several hundred common and grey seals, and the old lifeboat house, at the end of the spit, is now a **National Trust information centre**. The shifting shingle can make walking difficult, so keep to the low-water mark. The easier alternative is to take one of the **boat trips** to the point from Blakeney or Morston (see page 380).

Cley

Once a thriving wool port, **CLEY** (formally **Cley-next-the-Sea** and pronounced "cly") is one of the coast's most agreeable spots, beginning beside the main road with a row of flint cottages and Georgian mansions that stand beside a narrow, marshy inlet that (just) gives access to the sea. The sea once dipped further inland, which explains why the main part of the village, including the fine medieval **Church of St Margaret** (daily 9.30am–4.30pm or dusk; free), is located half a mile further inland beside an expansive green.

ARRIVAL AND DEPARTURE
CLEY

By bus The Norfolk Coasthopper (see page 376) stops outside the Picnic Fayre deli on Cley's main street (the A149).

ACCOMMODATION AND EATING

★ **Cley Windmill** NR25 7RP ☎ 01263 740209, ⓦ cleywindmill.co.uk. This outstanding B&B occupies a converted windmill that offers wonderful views over the surrounding marshes. The guest rooms, both in the windmill and the adjoining outhouses, are decorated in attractive period style and the best have splendid beamed ceilings; self-catering arrangements are possible as well. At peak times, there's a minimum two-night stay. The *Windmill*'s smart and very agreeable restaurant specializes in traditional, home-made English cooking (three-course set meal £32.50/person). Advance reservations – by 10am of the same day – are required. Daily from 7.30pm, plus Sun lunch Nov–Easter. £160

★ **Cley Smokehouse** High St, NR25 7RF ☎ 01263 740282, ⓦ cleysmokehouse.com. Superb smokehouse selling a wide range of freshly smoked shellfish, fish and cured meats. Their kippers are near impossible to beat. Mon–Fri 9am–5pm, Sat 8.30am–5pm, Sun 9.30am–4.30pm.

Blakeney and around

Delightful **BLAKENEY**, a mile or so west of Cley, was once a bustling port, but that was before its harbour silted up; nowadays it's a lovely little place of pebble-covered cottages with a laidback nautical air. Crab sandwiches are sold from stalls at the quayside, the meandering high street is flanked by family-run shops, and footpaths stretch out along the sea wall, allowing long, lingering views over the salt marshes. At low tide, the harbour is no more than a muddy creek (ideal for crabbing and mud sliding) and at high tide the waters rise just enough to allow for boat trips into the North Sea (see page 380). Blakeney is also close to the charming ruins of sixteenth-century **Binham Priory** (daily dawn–dusk; free; ☎ 01328 830362, ⓦ www.english-heritage.org.uk/visit/places/binham-priory).

ARRIVAL AND DEPARTURE
BLAKENEY

By bus Buses to Blakeney pull in at the Westgate bus shelter, a couple of minutes' walk from the harbour.

BINHAM PRIORY, NEAR BLAKENEY

7

BOAT TRIPS TO BLAKENEY POINT

Depending on the tides, there are **boat trips** to **Blakeney Point** (see page 378) from either Blakeney or **Morston quay**, a mile or so west. Passengers have a couple of hours at the point before being ferried back and also get the chance to see the seal colony just off the point; some boat trips just offer the seal colony. The main **operators** advertise departure times on blackboards by Blakeney quayside, or you can reserve in advance with Beans Boats (☎01263 740505, ⓦbeansboattrips.co.uk) or Bishop's Boats (☎01263 740753, ⓦbishopsboats.co.uk). All boat trips cost £12.

ACCOMMODATION AND EATING

King's Arms Westgate St, NR25 7NQ ☎01263 740341, ⓦblakeneykingsarms.co.uk. The best pub in Blakeney by far, this traditional boozer, with its low, beamed ceilings and rabbit-warren rooms, offers top-ranking bar food (mains average £13), largely English but with an international slant. They also have seven modest, en-suite bedrooms. Kitchen daily noon–2pm & 6–9pm. **£80**

★ **The Moorings** High St, NR25 7NA ☎01263 740054, ⓦblakeney-moorings.co.uk. Informal, cheerful little bistro where the creative menu is particularly strong on Norfolk meat, fish and shellfish. A typical main course might be sautéed lamb kidneys with pancetta, rosemary,

and a white-bean ragout (£17). Tues–Sun 10.30am–9.30pm.

The White Horse Blakeney 4 High St, NR25 7AL ☎01263 740574, ⓦwhitehorseblakeney.co.uk. This well-regarded inn has nine guest rooms kitted out in a bright and cheerful version of country-house style. The *White Horse* is also noted for its food: great play is made of local ingredients, the bread is baked here daily, and they offer lunchtime snacks and a la carte suppers. Mains average £15. Kitchen Mon–Sat noon–2.30pm & 6–9pm, Sun noon–2.30pm & 6–8.30pm. **£130**

Wells-next-the-Sea

Despite its name, **WELLS-NEXT-THE-SEA**, some eight miles west of Blakeney, is actually a good mile or so from open water. In Tudor times, before the harbour silted up, this was one of the great ports of eastern England, a major player in the trade with the Netherlands. Those heady days are long gone – the port is now a shadow of its former self – but Wells has reinvented itself as a popular coastal resort.

The town divides into three areas, starting with the **Buttlands**, a broad rectangular green on the south side of town, lined with oak and beech trees and framed by a string of fine Georgian houses. North from here, across Station Road, lie the narrow lanes of the town centre, with **Staithe Street** the main drag. Staithe Street leads to the **quay**, a somewhat forlorn affair inhabited by a couple of amusement arcades and fish-and-chip shops as well as the mile-long byroad that scuttles north to the **beach**, a handsome sandy tract backed by pine-clad dunes. Shadowing this beach road is the dinky, narrow-gauge **Wells Harbour Railway** (Easter to mid-Oct every 20min or so from 10.30am; £3 return).

ARRIVAL AND DEPARTURE

WELLS-NEXT-THE-SEA

By bus Buses stop on Station Rd, between Staithe St and the Buttlands; some also travel towards the quay.

ACCOMMODATION AND EATING

★ **The Crown** The Buttlands, NR23 1EX ☎01328 710209, ⓦcrownhotelnorfolk.co.uk. This enjoyable hotel occupies an attractive, three-storey former coaching inn with Georgian facade. Inside, the first batch of public rooms is cosy and quaint, all low ceilings and stone-flagged floors, and upstairs the dozen guest rooms are decorated in an imaginative and especially soothing style. The *Crown* also prides itself on its food, with splendid takes on traditional British dishes. Mains average around £19, less

at lunch times. Mon–Sat noon–2.30pm & 6.30–9.30pm, Sun noon–9pm. **£150**

The Merchant's House 47 Freeman St, NR23 1BQ ☎01328 711877, ⓦthe-merchants-house.co.uk. Occupying one of the oldest houses in Wells, parts of which date back to the fifteenth century, this deluxe B&B has just two cosy, en-suite guest rooms. It's handily located, just a couple of minutes' walk from the quayside. **£95**

Pinewoods Holiday Park Beach Rd, NR23 1DR

☎01328 710439, ⓦpinewoods.co.uk. Sitting pretty behind a long line of dunes and a splendid beach, *Pinewoods* has been welcoming holiday-makers for over sixty years. It's a sprawling complex that holds touring and static caravans, beach huts and cosy wooden lodges. It is located about 15min walk from the town quay and accessible on the narrow-gauge railway (see page 380). The caravan pitches are open from mid-March to late Oct, the lodges from mid-March to Dec. Tariffs vary widely, and minimum stays often apply. **£170**

Holkham Hall

A149, NR23 1AB, 3 miles west of Wells · **Hall** April–Oct Mon, Thurs & Sun noon–4pm · £15 · **Park** April–Oct daily 9am–5pm · Free, but parking £3/day · ☎01328 713111, ⓦ holkham.co.uk

One of the most popular outings from Wells is to neighbouring **Holkham Hall**, a grand and self-assured (or vainglorious) stately home designed by eighteenth-century architect William Kent for the first earl of Leicester – and still owned by the family. The severe Palladian exterior belies the warmth and richness of the interior, which retains much of its original decoration, notably the marble hall with its fluted columns and intricate reliefs. The rich colours of the state rooms are an appropriate backdrop for a fabulous selection of **paintings**, including canvases by Van Dyck, Rubens, Gainsborough and Gaspar Poussin.

The **grounds** are laid out on sandy, saline land, much of it originally salt marsh. The focal point is an 80ft-high **obelisk**, atop a grassy knoll, from where you can view both the hall to the north and the triumphal arch to the south. In common with the rest of the north Norfolk coast, there's plenty of **birdlife** – Holkham's lake attracts Canada geese, herons and grebes, and several hundred deer graze the open pastures.

Holkham Bay

The **footpaths** latticing the Holkham estate stretch to the A149, from where a half-mile byroad – **Lady Anne's Drive** – leads north across the marshes from opposite the *Victoria Hotel* to **Holkham Bay**, which boasts one of the finest beaches on this stretch of coast, with golden sand and pine-studded dunes flanking a tidal lagoon. Warblers, flycatchers and redstarts inhabit the drier areas, while waders paddle about the mud and salt flats.

ARRIVAL AND DEPARTURE   **HOLKHAM HALL**

By bus The Norfolk Coasthopper (see page 376) stops beside the *Victoria Hotel* on the A149. This is at the north entrance of the Holkham estate (about a mile from the house) and at the south end of Lady Anne's Drive.

The Burnhams

About five miles west of Wells is tiny **BURNHAM OVERY STAITHE**, the first of a handful of villages hereabouts that are collectively known as **the Burnhams**. A mile further is the pretty little village of **BURNHAM MARKET**, the leading player of the Burnhams, where a medley of Georgian and Victorian houses surrounds a dinky little green. The village attracts a wealthy, north London crowd, most of them here to enjoy the assorted comforts of the *The Hoste* (see page 382) and/or hunker down in their second homes.

Burnham Thorpe

Straggling **BURNHAM THORPE**, a mile or so southeast of Burnham Market, was the birthplace of **Horatio Nelson**, who was born in the village parsonage in 1758. The parsonage was demolished years ago, but Nelson is still celebrated in the village's **All Saints Church**, where the lectern is made of timbers taken from his last ship, the *Victory*, the chancel sports a Nelson bust, and the south aisle has a small exhibition on his life.

ARRIVAL AND DEPARTURE   **THE BURNHAMS**

By bus The Norfolk Coasthopper bus (see page 376) travels through Burnham Overy Staithe on the main road and stops beside the green on the Market Place in Burnham Market, but it does not pass through Burnham Thorpe.

7

ACCOMMODATION AND EATING

The Hoste The Green, Burnham Market PE31 8HD ☎ 01328 738777, ⊛ thehoste.com. One of the most fashionable spots on the Norfolk coast, this former coaching inn has been sympathetically modernized. The hotel's guest rooms are round the back and range from the small (verging on cramped) to the much more expansive (and expensive). At the front, the *Hoste*'s antique bar, complete with its wooden beams and stone-flagged

floor, is merely a foretaste of the several, chi-chi dining areas beyond. Throughout, the menu is a well-balanced mixture of "land and sea", anything from wood pigeon with strawberries to cod in beer batter. Main courses average around £18 in the evening, slightly less at lunch. Daily: brasserie noon–9.30pm; afternoon teas 3–5.30pm; dinner 6–9.30pm. **£165**

Brancaster and around

The last of the Burnhams – Burnham Deepdale – leads seamlessly into **BRANCASTER STAITHE** and then **BRANCASTER**, both of which spread along the main coastal road, the A149. Behind them, to the north, lies pristine coastline, a tract of lagoon, sandspit and creek that pokes its head out into the ocean, attracting an extravagant range of wildfowl. This is prime **walking** territory and it's best explored along the Norfolk Coast Path as it nudges its way through the marshes that back up towards the ocean. Push on west from Brancaster and it's a mile or so more to minuscule **TITCHWELL**, with its handful of flint-walled houses, old stone cross and bird reserve.

Titchwell Marsh RSPB Nature Reserve

Titchwell, PE31 8BB • Daily: reserve dawn to dusk; information centre March–Oct 10am–5pm Nov–Feb 10am–4pm • Free, but parking £5 • ☎ 01485 210779, ⊛ rspb.org.uk/titchwellmarsh

The old sea approaches to Titchwell harbour have now become **Titchwell Marsh RSPB Nature Reserve**, whose mix of marsh, reed bed, mud flat, lagoon and sandy beach attracts a wide variety of birds, including marsh harriers, bearded tits, avocets, gulls and terns. A series of footpaths explore this varied terrain, there are several well-positioned bird hides, including a super Parrinder hide, and a very helpful shop and **information centre**.

ARRIVAL AND DEPARTURE · BRANCASTER AND AROUND

By bus The Norfolk Coasthopper (see page 376) travels from the Burnhams through Brancaster Staithe, Brancaster and Titchwell.

ACCOMMODATION AND EATING

★ **Titchwell Manor Hotel** Titchwell, PE31 8BB ☎ 01485 472027, ⊛ titchwellmanor.com. Facing out towards the salt marshes that roll down to the sea, this large Victorian hotel is one of the most enjoyable on the Norfolk coast. There are nine rooms in the main building, with more in the courtyard complex. Everything is high spec, from the top-quality duvets to the bespoke furniture. The restaurant menu is very British with traditional dishes superbly prepared – anything from fish and chips with mushy peas (£13) to lobster thermidor with new potatoes. Daily noon–9.30pm. **£170**

White Horse Brancaster Staithe, PE31 8BY ☎ 01485 210262, ⊛ whitehorsebrancaster.co.uk. This hotel, pub and restaurant backs straight onto the coast – and, even better, the Norfolk Coast Path runs along the bottom of its car park. The hotel divides into two sections: there are seven en-suite rooms in the main building, and eight more at the back with grass roofs. Brancaster is famous for its mussels and oysters, which you can try in the restaurant; the local duck and beef are also good (main courses average £16). Restaurant daily noon–2pm & 6.15–9pm. **£110**

King's Lynn

Straddling the Great Ouse river just before it slides into The Wash, **King's Lynn** is an ancient trading port. The good times came to an end when the focus of maritime trade moved to the Atlantic seaboard, but its port struggled on until it was reinvigorated in the 1970s by the burgeoning trade between the UK and EU. Much of the old centre was demolished in the 1960s, so most of Lynn is not that enticing, but it has a cluster of handsome old **riverside buildings**, and its lively **markets** attract large fenland crowds.

Saturday Market Place and around

Behind the riverfront, the **Saturday Market Place** is a focal point of the old town. In addition to the Saturday market, it's home to Lynn's main parish church, **St Margaret's**, and the striking **Trinity Guildhall**, which has a wonderful, chequered flint-and-stone facade dating to 1421. Just across from the church is the former **Hanseatic Warehouse**, the most evocative of the medieval warehouses that survive along the quayside. Built around 1475, its half-timbered upper floor juts unevenly over the cobbles of St Margaret's Lane. A couple of minutes' walk north stands Lynn's finest building, the **Custom House**, which was erected beside Purfleet Quay in 1683. It's the dinky little cupola that catches the eye.

7

King Street and around

Beyond the Custom House, **King Street** is perhaps the town's most elegant thoroughfare, lined with beautiful Georgian buildings. On the left is **St George's Guildhall**, one of the oldest surviving guildhalls in England, now part of the popular King's Lynn Arts Centre. At the end of King Street, the **Tuesday Market Place** is a handsome square surrounded by yet more Georgian buildings and the plodding Neoclassical **Corn Exchange** (now a theatre); it hosts King's Lynn's main market on Fridays and, yes, Tuesdays.

Lynn Museum

Market St, PE30 1NL • April–Sept Tues–Sat 10am–5pm, Sun noon–4pm; Oct–March Tues–Sat 10am–5pm • £4.35 • ☎ 01553 775001, ⓦ museums.norfolk.gov.uk

Located in the old Union Chapel by the bus station, much of **Lynn Museum** is given over to **Seahenge**, a circle of 556 oak timbers, preserved in peat, that were found on the Norfolk coast. The timber circle is now housed in an atmospheric gallery that showcases the timbers themselves, their original position and their possible purpose.

ARRIVAL AND INFORMATION | **KING'S LYNN**

By train The station is 5min from the centre, via Waterloo St. Destinations Cambridge (hourly; 50min); Ely (hourly; 30min); London King's Cross (hourly; 1hr 40min). **By bus** The bus station is in the centre of town just off Market St. The Norfolk Coasthopper (see page 376) begins (and ends) its journey at King's Lynn, putting a string of Norfolk destinations within easy reach. **Tourist office** In the Custom House, Purfleet Quay (Mon–Sat 10am–5pm, Sun noon–5pm; Oct–March closes 4pm; ☎ 01553 763044, ⓦ visitnorfolk.co.uk).

A MYSTERIOUS LANDSCAPE: THE FENS

One of the strangest of all English landscapes, **the Fens** cover a vast area of eastern England from just north of Cambridge right up to Boston in Lincolnshire. For centuries, they were an inhospitable wilderness of quaking bogs and marshland, punctuated by clay islands on which small communities eked out a livelihood cutting peat for fuel, using reeds for thatching and living on a diet of fish and wildfowl. Piecemeal land reclamation took place throughout the Middle Ages, but it wasn't until the seventeenth century that the systematic draining of the Fens was undertaken – amid fierce local opposition – by the Dutch engineer **Cornelius Vermuyden**. Drained, the Fens now comprise some of the most fertile agricultural land in Europe – though at least **Wicken Fen** (see page 385) gives the flavour of what went before.

ACCOMMODATION AND EATING

★ **Bank House Hotel** King's Staithe Square, PE30 1RD ☎ 01553 660492, ⓦ thebankhouse.co.uk. A riverside boutique hotel in a lovely Georgian house in the heart of the town's oldest quarter. The twelve, period-style rooms are simply delightful, and there's also a wonderfully inviting bar and restaurant, whose Modern British menu features dishes like Lowestoft plaice and guinea fowl with bacon and cabbage. Mains average £12. Mon–Sat noon–9.30pm, Sun noon–8.30pm. £115

The Old Rectory 33 Goodwins Rd, off London Rd, PE30 5QX ☎ 01553 768544, ⓦ www.theoldrectory-kingslynn.com. Small, agreeable B&B in a substantial Victorian house on the southern side of town; bedrooms are decorated in a modern and reassuringly cosy style. £80

Ely and around

Perched on a mound of clay above the Great Ouse river about thirty miles south of King's Lynn, the attractive little town of **ELY** – literally "eel island" – was to all intents and purposes a true island until the draining of the surrounding fens in the seventeenth century. Before that, the town was encircled by treacherous marshland, which could only be crossed with the help of the local "fen-slodgers" who knew the firm tussock paths. In 1070, **Hereward the Wake** turned this inaccessibility to military advantage, holding out against the Normans and forcing William the Conqueror to undertake a prolonged siege – and finally to build an improvised road floated on bundles of sticks. Since then, Ely has been associated with that rebellious Englishman, which is more than a little ridiculous as Ely is, above all else, a Norman town: it was the Normans who built the **cathedral**, a towering structure visible for miles across the flat fenland landscape and Ely's principal sight. The rest of Ely is at its busiest to the immediate north of the cathedral on the **High Street**, a slender thoroughfare lined with old-fashioned shops, and at its prettiest down by the **river**, a relaxing spot with a riverside footpath and a tearoom or two. Ely is also within easy driving distance of an undrained chunk of fenland at **Wicken Fen**.

Ely Cathedral

The College, CB7 4DL • **Cathedral** June–Sept daily 7am–6.30pm; Oct–May Mon–Sat 7am–6.30pm, Sun 7am–5.30pm • Mon–Sat £8 (includes free ground-floor tour; 1hr), Sun free • **Tower tours** Mon–Sat 8/9 daily, Sun 5 daily (West Tower Sat & Sun only in winter); 1hr • Mon–Sat £7 (on top of cathedral admission), Sun £9; reserve in advance • ☎ 01353 667735, ⓦ elycathedral.org • **Stained Glass Museum** Mon–Sat 10.30am–5pm, Sun noon–4.30pm • £4.50 • ☎ 01353 660347, ⓦ stainedglassmuseum.com

Ely Cathedral is one of the most impressive churches in England, but the west facade, where visitors enter, has been an oddly lopsided affair ever since one of the transepts collapsed in a storm in 1701. Nonetheless, the remaining transept, which was completed in the 1180s, is an imposing structure, its dog-tooth windows, castellated towers and blind arcading possessing all the rough, almost brutal charm of the Normans.

The first things to strike you as you enter the **nave** are the sheer length of the building and the lively nineteenth-century painted ceiling, largely the work of amateur volunteers. The nave's procession of plain Norman arches leads to the feature that makes Ely so special, the **Octagon** – the only one of its kind in England – built in 1322 to replace the collapsed central tower. Its construction, employing the largest oaks available in England to support some four hundred tons of glass and lead, was a wonder of the medieval world, and the effect is breathtaking. You can take a **tour** of the Octagon, and of the taller **West Tower**, from which you can see the Octagon and take in the sweeping views.

When the central tower collapsed, it fell eastwards onto the **choir**, the first three bays of which were rebuilt at the same time as the octagon in the Decorated style – in contrast to the plainer Early English of the choir bays beyond. The other marvel is the **Lady Chapel**, a separate building accessible via the north transept. It lost its sculpture and stained glass in the Reformation, but its fan vaulting remains, an exquisite example of English Gothic. The south triforium near the main entrance holds the **Stained Glass Museum**, an Anglican money-spinner exhibiting examples of this applied art from 1200 to the 1970s.

Oliver Cromwell's House

29 St Mary's St, CB7 4HF • Daily: April–Oct 10am–5pm; Nov–March 11am–4pm • £4.90 • ☎ 01353 662062, ⊛ olivercromwellshouse.co.uk

Near the cathedral is **Oliver Cromwell's House**, a timber-framed former vicarage that holds a small exhibition on the Protector's ten-year sojourn in Ely, where he was employed as a tithe collector. The tourist office (see below) is here as well.

Wicken Fen Nature Reserve

Lode Lane, Wicken, CB7 5XP, 9 miles south of Ely • Reserve daily dawn to dusk; dragonfly centre late May to late Sept Sat & Sun 11am–4pm • £6.95; NT • ☎ 01353 720274 • ⊛ nationaltrust.org.uk/wicken-fen-nature-reserve

Wicken Fen National Nature Reserve is one of the few remaining areas of undrained fenland and as such is an important wetland habitat. It owes its survival to a group of Victorian entomologists who donated the land to the National Trust in 1899. The seven hundred acres are undrained but not uncultivated – sedge and reed cutting are still carried out to preserve the landscape as it is – and the reserve is easily explored by means of several clearly marked **footpaths**. The reserve holds about ten birdwatching hides and is also one of the best places in the UK to see **dragonflies**.

ARRIVAL AND INFORMATION

ELY AND AROUND

By train Ely is a major railway junction, with direct trains from as far afield as Liverpool, Norwich and London, as well as Cambridge. From the station, it's a 10min walk to the cathedral, straight up Station Rd and its continuation Back Hill before veering right along The Gallery.

Destinations Cambridge (every 15min; 15min); Ipswich (every 2hr; 1hr); King's Lynn (hourly; 30min); London King's Cross (every 30min; 1hr); Norwich (every 30min; 1hr).

By bus Most buses, including Stagecoach express services to Cambridge (hourly; 1hr), stop on Market St immediately north of the cathedral.

Tourist office In Oliver Cromwell's House, 29 St Mary's Street (daily: April–Oct 10am–5pm; Nov–March 11am–4pm; ☎ 01353 662062, ⊛ visitely.org.uk).

ACCOMMODATION AND EATING

Peacocks Tearoom 65 Waterside, CB7 4AU ☎ 01353 661100, ⊛ peacockstearoom.co.uk. This popular riverside tearoom serves a delicious range of cream teas and lunches with the odd surprise: try, for example, the chocolate courgette cake. There's also an enormous choice of teas from around the world. After the success of their tearoom, the owners ventured into B&B, offering two comfortable suites in the same premises. Both are kitted out in antique style – and very pleasant they are too.

Wed–Sun 10.30am–5pm. **£135**

29 Waterside B&B 29 Waterside, CB7 4AU ☎ 01353 614329, ✉ info@29waterside.org.uk. Ely is a tad short of places to stay, but this cosy B&B, in a pair of pretty brick cottages dating to the 1760s, helps remedy things. Several original features have been preserved, including the beamed ceilings, and the remainder sympathetically modernized. If the sun is out, breakfast can be taken in the garden. **£86**

Cambridge and around

On the whole, **CAMBRIDGE** is much quieter and more secluded than Oxford, though for the visitor what really sets it apart from its scholarly rival is "**The Backs**" – the green sward of land that straddles the languid River Cam, providing exquisite views over the backs of the old colleges. At the front, the colleges' handsome facades dominate the town centre. Most of the older frontages date back to the late thirteenth and early fourteenth centuries and are designed to a **similar plan**, with the main gate leading through to a series of "courts", typically a manicured slab of lawn surrounded by college residences or offices. Many of the buildings are extraordinarily beautiful, but the most famous is **King's College**, whose magnificent chapel is one of the great statements of late Gothic architecture. There are 31 colleges in total, each an independent, self-governing body, proud of its achievements and attracting – for the most part – a close loyalty from its students.

Note that most colleges have restricted opening times and some impose admission charges; during the **exam period** (late April to early June) most of them close their doors to the public at least some of the time.

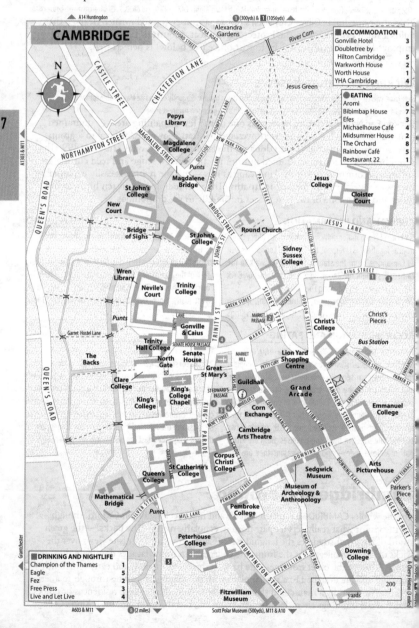

CAMBRIDGE

■ **ACCOMMODATION**
Gonville Hotel 3
Doubletree by
 Hilton Cambridge 5
Warkworth House 2
Worth House 1
YHA Cambridge 4

● **EATING**
Aromi 6
Bibimbap House 7
Efes 3
Michaelhouse Café 4
Midsummer House 2
The Orchard 8
Rainbow Café 5
Restaurant 22 1

■ **DRINKING AND NIGHTLIFE**
Champion of the Thames 1
Eagle 5
Fez 2
Free Press 3
Live and Let Live 4

0   200
yards

King's College

King's Parade, CB2 1ST • Term time Mon–Fri 9.30am–3.30pm, Sat 9.30am–3.15pm, Sun 1.15–2.30pm; rest of year daily 9.30am–4.30pm • £9 (includes chapel) • ☎ 01223 331100, ⓦ www.kings.cam.ac.uk

Henry VI founded **King's College** in 1441, but he was disappointed with his initial efforts. So, four years later, he cleared away half of the town to make room for a much grander foundation. His plans were ambitious, but the Wars of the Roses – and bouts of royal insanity – intervened and by the time of his death in 1471 very little had been finished and work on what was intended to be Henry's **Great Court** hadn't even started. This part of the site remained empty for three hundred years and today's Great Court complex – facing King's Parade from behind a long stone screen – is largely neo-Gothic, built in the 1820s to a design by William Wilkins. Henry's workmen did, however, start on the college's finest building, **King's College Chapel**, on the north side of the Great Court.

King's College once enjoyed an exclusive supply of students from Eton and until 1851 claimed the right to award its students degrees without their taking any examinations. The first non-Etonians were only accepted in 1873. Times have changed, and King's is now one of the more progressive colleges – it was among the first three to admit women, in 1972, and consistently has one of the highest intakes of state-school students.

King's College Chapel

Entrance either via the main gatehouse on King's Parade or the North Gate, at the end of Senate House Passage

Committed to canvas by Turner and Canaletto, and eulogized in no fewer than three sonnets by Wordsworth, **King's College Chapel** is now famous for its **boys' choir**, whose members process across the college grounds during term time in their antiquated garb to sing **evensong** (Tues–Sat at 5.30pm, plus choral services Sun 10.30am & 3.30pm) and carols on Christmas Eve. The setting for the choristers is supreme, the chapel impossibly slender, its streamlined buttresses channelling up to a dainty balustrade and four spiky turrets, though the exterior was, in a sense, a happy accident – its design predicated by the carefully composed interior. Here, the high and handsome **nave** has an exquisite ceiling, whose fantail tracery has a dense geometry of extraordinary complexity and delicacy. The nave is flooded with kaleidoscopic patterns of light that filter in through copious windows. Paid for by Henry VIII, the **stained glass** was largely the work of Flemish glaziers; the lower windows portray scenes from the New Testament and the Apocrypha, and the upper windows the Old Testament. Above the **altar** hangs Rubens' tender *Adoration of the Magi* and an exhibition in the side **chantries** puts more historical flesh on Henry's grand plans.

King's Parade and around

King's College dominates **King's Parade**, the town's medieval High Street, but the higgledy-piggledy shops and cafés opposite are an attractive foil to Wilkins' architectural screen. At the street's northern end is **Great St Mary's** (May–Aug Mon–Sat 9.30am–5pm, Sun 12.30–5pm; Sept–April closes 4pm; free; ☎ 01223 747272, ⓦ www.gsm.cam.ac.uk), the university's pet church, a sturdy Gothic structure whose **tower** (£4) offers a good view of the surrounding colleges. Opposite the church stands **Senate House**, an exercise in Palladian classicism by James Gibbs, and the scene of graduation ceremonies in late June, when champagne corks fly around the (faux) fur collars and black gowns. Behind the church is **Market Hill**, usually full of stalls selling books, records, flowers and food – make time for the Belgian waffle stand on the eastern edge, a student favourite.

Gonville and Caius College

Trinity St, CB2 1TA • Daily 9am–2pm • Free • ☎ 01223 332400, ⓦ cai.cam.ac.uk

The northern continuation of King's Parade is Trinity Street, a short way along which is the cramped main entrance to **Gonville and Caius College**, known as Caius (pronounced "keys") after the sixteenth-century co-founder John Keys, who latinized his name as was then the custom with men of learning. The design of the college owes much to Keys, who placed three gates on two adjoining courts, each representing a different stage on the path to academic enlightenment: at the main entrance is the **Gate of Humility**, through which the student enters the college; the **Gate of Virtue**, sporting the female figures of Fame and Wealth, marks the entrance to Caius Court; and the exquisite **Gate of Honour**, capped with sundials and decorated with classical motifs, leads onto Senate House Passage.

Clare College

Trinity Lane, CB2 1TL • No set opening hours • Summer £5; winter free • ☎ 01223 333200, ⓦ clare.cam.ac.uk

Senate House Passage continues west beyond Caius College's Gate of Honour en route to **Clare College**. Clare's plain period-piece courtyards, completed in the early eighteenth century, lead to one of the most picturesque of all the bridges over the Cam, **Clare Bridge**. Beyond lies the **Fellows' Garden**, one of the loveliest college gardens open to the public (same times as college). Back at the entrance to Clare, it's a few steps more to the North Gate of King's College, beside King's College Chapel (see page 387).

Trinity College

Trinity St, CB2 1TQ • **College** Daily 10am–4.30pm • £3 • **Wren Library** Mon–Fri noon–2pm, plus Sat during term 10.30am–12.30pm • Free • ☎ 01223 338400, ⓦ trin.cam.ac.uk

A statue of Henry VIII, who founded **Trinity College** in 1546, sits in majesty over Trinity's **Great Gate**, his sceptre replaced long ago with a chair leg – legend has it a student stole it for a prank, either switching it themselves or leaving it, only for a helpful college employee to come up with the ad hoc replacement. Beyond lies the vast asymmetrical expanse of **Great Court**, which displays a superb range of Tudor buildings, the oldest of which is the fifteenth-century clocktower. The centrepiece of the court is a delicate fountain, in which, so it's said, Lord Byron used to bathe naked with his pet bear – the college forbade students from keeping dogs.

On the far side of Great Court, walk through "**the screens**" – the narrow passage separating the Hall from the kitchens – to reach **Nevile's Court**, where Newton calculated the speed of sound. The west end of the court is enclosed by one of the university's most famous buildings, the **Wren Library** (access only from The Backs). From the outside, it's impossible to appreciate the scale of the interior due to Wren's clever device of concealing the internal floor level by means of two rows of stone columns. Light pours into the white, stuccoed interior, which contrasts wonderfully with the dark lime-wood bookcases.

St John's College

St John's St, CB2 1TP • Daily: March–Oct 10am–5pm; Nov–Feb 10am–3.30pm • £10 • ☎ 01223 338600, ⓦ www.joh.cam.ac.uk

Next door to Trinity, **St John's College** sports a grandiloquent Tudor gatehouse, which is distinguished by the coat of arms of the founder, Lady Margaret Beaufort, the mother of Henry VII. Beyond, three successive courts lead to the river, but there's an excess of dull reddish brickwork here – enough for Wordsworth, who lived on F staircase, to describe the place as "gloomy". The arcade on the far side of Third Court leads to the **Bridge of Sighs**, a chunky, covered bridge across the river built in 1831 but in most respects very unlike its Venetian namesake. The bridge is best viewed from the much older – and much more stylish – Wren-designed bridge a few yards to the south. The Bridge of Sighs links the old college with the fanciful nineteenth-century **New Court**, a crenellated neo-Gothic extravaganza topped by a feast of dinky stone chimneys and pinnacles.

Magdalene College

Magdalene St, CB3 0AG • **College** Daily 10am–6pm • Free • **Pepys Library** Late April to early Sept Mon–Fri 2–4pm, Sat 11.30am–12.30pm & 1.30–2.30pm; Oct to late March Mon–Sat 2–4pm • Free • ☎ 01223 332100, ⓦ www.magd.cam.ac.uk

Founded as a hostel by the Benedictines, **Magdalene College** (pronounced "maudlin") became a university college in 1542; it was also the last of the Oxbridge colleges to admit women, finally surrendering in 1988. Male students responded by wearing black armbands to symbolize the "death of education" – but, armbands or not, the college's academic results swiftly improved. The main focus of attention here is the **Pepys Library**, in the second of the college's ancient courtyards. Samuel Pepys, a Magdalene student, bequeathed his entire library to the college, where it has been displayed ever since in its original red-oak bookshelves. His famous diary is also parked here.

Jesus College

Jesus Lane, CB5 8BL • Daily 10am–5pm • Free • ☎ 01223 339339, ⓦ jesus.cam.ac.uk

The intimate cloisters of **Jesus College** are reminiscent of a monastery – appropriately, as the Bishop of Ely founded the college on the grounds of a suppressed Benedictine nunnery in 1496. Beyond the main red-brick gateway, much of the ground plan of the nunnery has been preserved, especially around **Cloister Court**, the first court on the right after the entrance and the prettiest part of the college, dripping with ivy and, in summer, overflowing with hanging baskets. Entered from Cloister Court, the college **chapel** occupies the former priory chancel and looks like a medieval parish church, though in fact it was imaginatively restored in the nineteenth century, using ceiling designs by William Morris and Pre-Raphaelite stained glass. The poet **Samuel Taylor Coleridge** was the college's most famously bad student, absconding in his first year to join the Light Dragoons, and returning only to be kicked out for a combination of bad debts and unconventional opinions.

Sidney Sussex College

Sidney St, CB2 3HU • No set opening times • Free • ☎ 01223 338800, ⓦ sid.cam.ac.uk

The sombre, mostly mock-Gothic facade of **Sidney Sussex College** glowers over Sidney Street. The interior is fairly unexciting too, though the long, slender **chapel** is noteworthy for its fancy marble floor, hooped roof and Baroque wood panelling, as well as for being the last resting place of the skull of its most famous alumnus, **Oliver Cromwell** – though the exact location remains a closely guarded secret. Incidentally, neighbouring **Hobson Street** is named after the owner of a Cambridge livery stable, who would only allow customers to take the horse nearest the door, hence "Hobson's choice".

Christ's College

St Andrew's St, CB2 3BU • Daily 9am–4pm • Free • ☎ 01223 334900, ⓦ christs.cam.ac.uk

Close to Cambridge's central shopping area, the turreted gateway of **Christ's College** features the coat of arms of the founder, Lady Margaret Beaufort, who also founded St John's. Passing through First Court you come to the Fellows' Building, attributed to Inigo Jones, whose central arch gives access to the **Fellows' Garden**. The poet **John Milton** is said to have either painted or composed here, though there's no definite proof that he did either; another of Christ's famous undergraduates was **Charles Darwin**, who showed little academic promise and spent most of his time hunting.

CAMBRIDGE: TAKING A PUNT

Punting is the quintessential Cambridge activity, though it is, in fact, a good deal harder than it looks. First-timers find themselves zigzagging across the water and in summer "punt jams" are very common on the stretch of the River Cam by The Backs. **Punt rental** is available at several points, including the boatyard at Mill Lane (beside the Silver Street bridge), at Magdalene Bridge, and at the Garret Hostel Lane bridge behind Trinity College. It's almost always possible to rent on spec, but you can save money if you book ahead – Scudamore's (☎01223 359750, ⓦscudamores.com) are as good as anyone. Hiring a punt costs around £27 per hour (and most places charge a deposit), for up to six people per punt.

Alternatively, you can hire a **chauffeured punt** from any of the rental places – either shared (with strangers) for about £12 per person per hour, or your own around £18 per person per hour.

Queens' College

Silver St, CB3 9ET, but visitors' gate on Queens' Lane • March–Oct daily 10am–4.30pm; Dec–Feb Mon–Fri 10am–3pm • £3.50 • ☎01223 335511, ⓦwww.queens.cam.ac.uk

Queens' College is particularly beautiful, boasting, in the **Old Court** and the **Cloister Court**, two dream-like, fairy-tale Tudor courtyards: the first of the two is a perfect illustration of the original collegiate ideal, with kitchens, library, chapel, hall and rooms all set around a tiny green. Flanking Cloister Court is the Long Gallery of the President's Lodge, the last remaining half-timbered building in the university, and the tower where Erasmus is thought to have beavered away during his four years here, probably from 1510 to 1514. Equally eye-catching is the wooden **Mathematical Bridge** over the River Cam (visible for free from the Silver Street Bridge), a copy of the mid-eighteenth-century original, which – so it was claimed – would stay in place even if the nuts and bolts were removed.

The Fitzwilliam Museum

Trumpington St, CB2 1RB • Tues–Sat 10am–5pm, Sun noon–5pm • Free • ☎01223 332900, ⓦfitzmuseum.cam.ac.uk

The **Fitzwilliam Museum** holds the city's premier fine and applied art collection in an imposing Neoclassical edifice, which was built to house the vast hoard bequeathed by Viscount Fitzwilliam in 1816. Since then, the museum has been gifted a string of private collections, most of which follow a particular specialism. The **Lower Galleries** contain a wealth of antiquities including Egyptian sarcophagi and mummies, fifth-century BC Greek vases, plus a bewildering display of early European and Asian ceramics and sections dedicated to armour, glass and pewterware. Temporary exhibitions are held here too. The **Upper Galleries** hold an eclectic assortment of mostly eighteenth- to early twentieth-century European paintings and sculptures, with more modern pieces by Lucian Freud, David Hockney, Henry Moore, Ben Nicholson, Jacob Epstein and Barbara Hepworth.

The Polar Museum

Lensfield Rd, CB2 1ER • Tues–Sat 10am–4pm • Free • ☎01223 336540, ⓦspri.cam.ac.uk

The pocket-sized **Polar Museum** at the Scott Polar Research Institute begins with a section devoted to the native peoples of the Arctic, with an especially good collection of Inuit soapstone sculptures. It continues with sketches of the European explorers who ventured to both poles with varying degrees of success; it's here you'll find a substantial set of documents – original letters, incidental artefacts and so on – relating to the fateful expedition to the South Pole led by **Captain Robert Falcon Scott** (1868–1912), after whom the institute is named.

Duxford Imperial War Museum

Duxford, CB22 4QR, 11 miles south of Cambridge • Daily: mid-March to late Oct 10am–6pm; late Oct to mid-March 10am–4pm • £16.35 • ☏ 01223 835000, ⓦ iwm.org.uk

The giant hangars of the **Duxford Imperial War Museum** dominate the eponymous airfield. In World War II, East Anglia was a centre of operations for the RAF and USAAF, with the region's flat, unobstructed landscape dotted with dozens of airfields, among which Duxford was one of the more important. In total, the museum holds nearly 200 historic aircraft, a wide-ranging collection of civil and military planes from the Sunderland flying boat to Concorde and the Vulcan B2 bombers, which were used for the first and last time in the 1982 Falklands conflict; the Spitfires, however, are the enduring favourites.

ARRIVAL AND INFORMATION

By train The station is a mile southeast of the centre, off Hills Rd. It's an easy 20min walk into the centre, or a short bus ride; take any one of several Citi buses to Emmanuel St. Destinations Bury St Edmunds (hourly; 40min); Ely (every 15min; 15min); Ipswich (hourly; 1hr 20min); King's Lynn (hourly; 45min); London King's Cross (every 30min; 50min); London Stansted Airport (every 30min; 30min); Norwich (hourly; 1hr 20min).

By bus Local buses use the Drummer St bus station. Long-

CAMBRIDGE AND AROUND

distance services, including to London Victoria (every 2hr; 2hr) pull in at Parkside, by Parker's Piece.

By car Much of the centre is closed to traffic, and on-street parking well-nigh impossible to find. Most visitors go for a park-and-ride car park, signposted on all major approaches.

Tourist office In the Guildhall, Peas Hill, just off King's Parade (April–Oct Mon–Sat 10am–5pm, Sun 11am–3pm; Nov–March Mon–Sat 10am–5pm; ☏ 01223 791500, ⓦ visitcambridge.org).

GETTING AROUND

By bike Popular with locals and students alike, cycling is a good way to get around the city. Among the small army of bike rental outlets, one of the more dependable is Rutland Cycling (☏ 01223 352728, ⓦ rutlandcycling.

com), with several branches, including one close to the train station at 155 Great Northern Rd and another in the Grand Arcade. Always lock your bike securely as bike theft is not uncommon.

ACCOMMODATION

Cambridge is light on central **accommodation** so vacant rooms are often thin on the ground, but the situation improves outside term time when many colleges let out rooms on a B&B basis, often at bargain rates. The rooms are pretty frugal, but visitors can enjoy the college atmosphere; for bookings, go to ⓦ visitcambridge.org/accommodation/college-rooms.

★ **Doubletree by Hilton Cambridge** Granta Place, Mill Lane, CB2 1RT ☏ 01223 259988, ⓦ doubletree3.hilton.com; map p.386. This is the city's most appealing hotel by a long chalk, occupying a stylishly designed 1960s building a short walk from the centre. The best rooms have balconies overlooking the river (though the views are hardly riveting) and breakfasts are first-rate – as you'd expect at this price. **£210**

Gonville Hotel Gonville Place, CB1 1LY ☏ 01223 366611, ⓦ gonvillehotel.co.uk; map p.386. One of the better mid-range choices in Cambridge, this pleasantly refurbished hotel occupies a long albeit somewhat undistinguished building just set back off a busy main road. Proficient, efficient lodgings with smart, modern guest rooms. **£140**

Warkworth House Warkworth Terrace, CB1 1EE ☏ 01223 363682, ⓦ warkworthhouse.co.uk; map p.386. Welcoming, family-run B&B with a handful of straight-

forward, bright and unfussy en-suite rooms. In a substantial Victorian property a shortish walk southeast of the bus station, off Parkside. **£95**

Worth House 152 Chesterton Rd, CB4 1DA ☏ 01223 316074, ⓦ worth-house.co.uk; map p.386. Friendly B&B in a pleasantly upgraded Victorian house a 20min walk from the centre. All the bedrooms are decorated in a bright modern style and have generous en-suite bathrooms. Great breakfasts too. **£120**

YHA Cambridge 97 Tenison Rd, CB1 2DN ☏ 0345 3719728, ⓦ yha.org.uk/hostel/cambridge; map p.386. This long-established hostel occupies a substantial Victorian house and a modern annexe near the train station. Facilities include a laundry and self-catering kitchen, cycle storage, a games room and a small courtyard garden. There are just over one hundred beds in two- to six-bedded rooms, some en suite; advance reservations advised. Dorms **£20**, doubles **£60**

7

EATING

With most Cambridge students and staff eating in college, good-quality restaurants are comparatively thin on the ground – whereas the **takeaway** and **café** scene is on a roll.

★ **Aromi** 1 Bene't St, CB2 3QN ☎ 01223 300117, ⓦ aromi.co.uk; map p.386. The furnishings and fittings may be standard-issue modern, but, oh my word, the food at this little café is superb: they offer authentic Sicilian dishes – pizza slices, focaccia and cannoli, plus a hatful of other delights. Eat in or takeaway. Expect queues at peak times. Thee are two other branches in the city, more focused on snacks and gelato. Mon–Thurs & Sun 9am–7pm, Fri & Sat 9am–8pm.

★ **Bibimbap House** 60 Mill Rd, CB1 2AS ☎ 01223 506800; map p.386. Tiny, family-run Korean restaurant, specializing in – you guessed it – bibimbap. Portions are huge, always served with an array of delicious side dishes. Slightly out of the centre, but worth the walk. Mains £12–15. Mon 5–10pm, Wed–Sun noon–3pm & 5–9/10pm.

Efes 78 King St, CB1 1LN ☎ 01223 500005; map p.386. Something of an institution, this Turkish restaurant may have uninspiring decor, but the chargrilled meats – the house speciality – are extremely tasty. Mains around £12. Mon–Fri noon–2.30pm & 6–11pm; Sat & Sun noon–11pm.

Michaelhouse Café Trinity St, CB2 1SU ☎ 01223 309147 ⓦ michaelhousecafe.co.uk; map p.386. Good-quality café food – snacks, salads and so forth – in an attractively renovated medieval church. Great, central location too. Mains for around £6. Mon–Sat 8am–5pm.

Midsummer House Midsummer Common, CB4 1HA ☎ 01223 369299, ⓦ midsummerhouse.co.uk; map p.386. This two-Michelin-starred restaurant delights with its inventive French cuisine and surprisingly unpretentious atmosphere. Everything is delicious, of course, but the

good-humoured, knowledgeable staff really set it apart. One for a major treat: a five-course lunch is £56.50, eight-course dinner £120. Book well ahead. Sittings Tues 7–8.30pm, Wed & Thurs noon–1.30pm & 7–8.30pm, Fri & Sat noon–1.30pm & 6.30–9.30pm.

The Orchard 47 Mill Way, Grantchester, CB3 9ND ☎ 01223 840230, ⓦ theorchardteagarden.co.uk; map p.386. Follow the river south out of Cambridge for a lovely 2-mile stroll or cycle through Grantchester Meadows, and reward yourself with a cream tea (£5.75) at *The Orchard*. This simple tearoom with deckchairs dotted around an orchard was a favourite haunt of Rupert Brooke, among many other famous alumni. It's still a popular escape for students today – many punt all the way here. Hours vary by season, but usually daily 9.30am–5/6pm.

Rainbow Café 9a King's Parade, CB2 1SJ ☎ 01223 321551, ⓦ rainbowcafe.co.uk; map p.386. Cramped but agreeable vegetarian restaurant with main courses – ranging from Jamaican roti cups to North African tagine – for around £10. Specializes in vegan and gluten-free food plus organic wines. Handy location, down an alley opposite King's College. Don't be surprised if there's a queue. Tues–Sat 10am–10pm, Sun 10am–3pm.

Restaurant 22 22 Chesterton Rd, CB4 3AX ☎ 01223 351880, ⓦ restaurant22.co.uk; map p.386. Well-regarded and long-established restaurant in cosy premises where they serve a Modern British menu with seafood at the fore. A three-course set meal will set you back about £40. Northeast of the centre, on the far side of Jesus Green and the river. Tues–Sat 7–11pm.

DRINKING AND NIGHTLIFE

Champion of the Thames 68 King St, CB1 1LN ☎ 01223 351464, ⓦ thechampionofthethames.com; map p.386. Gratifyingly old-fashioned central pub with oodles of wood panelling, decent beer and a student/academic crowd. Daily noon–11pm.

Eagle 8 Bene't St, CB2 3QN ☎ 01223 505020, ⓦ eagle-cambridge.co.uk; map p.386. Owned and operated by Greene King, this ancient city-centre inn, with its antique appearance and cobbled courtyard, is associated with Crick and Watson, two of the scientists who discovered DNA in 1953. It gets horribly crowded, but is still worth a pint of anyone's time – the ales are reliably good. Mon–Sat 10am–11pm, Sun 11am–10.30pm.

Fez 15 Market Passage, CB2 3PF ☎ 01223 519224, ⓦ cambridgefez.com; map p.386. Popular city-centre club with vaguely Middle Eastern decor, good drinks deals and the requisite sticky floor. It tends to have better DJs

than the competition, and some excellent one-off nights; check the website to see what's coming up. Tues & Thurs–Sat 10pm–3am, other days vary.

★ **Free Press** 7 Prospect Row, CB1 1DU ☎ 01223 368337, ⓦ freepresskitchen.co.uk; map p.386. Classic, traditional and superbly maintained backstreet local with a great selection of real ales and single malts. Walled garden, too. Just off Parkside. Daily noon–11pm.

Live and Let Live 40 Mawson Rd, CB1 2EA ☎ 01223 460261; map p.386. This smashing pub, in an old corner building among a battery of terrace houses, is the epitome of the traditional local – from the pot-pourri furnishings and fittings through to the wood-panelled alcoves. Mawson Rd leads off Mill Rd in between Parker's Piece and the train station. Mon, Tues & Fri 11.30am–2.30pm & 5.30–11pm, Wed & Thurs 5.30–11pm, Sat 11.30am–2.30pm & 6–11pm, Sun noon–3pm & 7–11pm.

ENTERTAINMENT

The **performing arts** scene is at its best in term time, with numerous student drama productions, classical concerts and gigs culminating in the "May Week" excesses following exam season. The most celebrated concerts are given by **King's College choir** (see page 387), while the four-day **Cambridge Folk Festival** (late July to early Aug; ⓦcambridgelivetrust.co.uk/folk-festival) takes place in neighbouring Cherry Hinton. The tourist office (see page 391) has free **listings** leaflets and brochures.

Cambridge Arts Picturehouse 38–39 St Andrew's St, CB2 3AR ⓣ0871 902 5720, ⓦpicturehouses. com. Arthouse cinema with an excellent, wide-ranging programme – and a decent bar.

Cambridge Arts Theatre 6 St Edward's Passage, off King's Parade, CB2 3PJ ⓣ01223 503333, ⓦcambridge artstheatre.com. The city's main rep theatre, founded by John Maynard Keynes, and launch pad of a thousand and one famous careers; offers a top-notch range of cutting-edge and classic productions.

Cambridge Corn Exchange Wheeler St, CB2 3QE ⓣ01223 357851, ⓦcambridgelivetrust.co.uk/cornex. Revamped nineteenth-century trading hall, now the main city-centre venue for opera, ballet, musicals and comedy as well as regular rock and folk gigs.

Cambridge Junction Clifton Way, CB1 7GX ⓣ01223 511511, ⓦjunction.co.uk. Rock, indie, jazz, reggae or soul gigs, plus theatre, comedy and dance at this popular arts venue. Out near the train station.

7

The West Midlands and the Peak District

IRONBRIDGE GORGE

The West Midlands and the Peak District

Birmingham, the urban epicentre of the West Midlands, is Britain's second city and was once the world's greatest industrial metropolis, its slew of factories powering the Industrial Revolution. Long saddled with a reputation as an ugly, unappealing city, Birmingham has broken free, redeveloping its central core with vim and architectural verve, its prestige buildings – especially Selfridges and the Symphony hall – helping to redefine and reshape its image. Within easy striking distance is Stratford-upon-Avon, famous as the birthplace of William Shakespeare and for the exemplary Royal Shakespeare Company (RSC). Beyond are the rural shires that stretch out towards Wales, with the bumpy Malvern Hills, one of the region's scenic highlights, in between; you could also drift north to the rugged scenery of the Peak District, whose surly, stirring landscapes enclose the attractive little spa town of Buxton.

Change was forced on **Birmingham** by the drastic decline in its manufacturing base during the 1980s; things were even worse in the Black Country, that knot of industrial towns clinging to the west of the city, where deindustrialization has proven particularly painful. The counties to the south and west of Birmingham – Warwickshire, Worcestershire, Herefordshire and Shropshire – comprise a rural stronghold that maintains an emotional and political distance from the conurbation. Of the four, Warwickshire is the least obviously scenic, but draws by far the largest number of visitors, for – as the road signs declare at every entry point – this is "Shakespeare Country". The prime target is **Stratford-upon-Avon**, Shakespeare's birthplace, but spare time also for the town of **Warwick**, which has a superb church and a whopping castle.

Neighbouring Worcestershire, which stretches southwest from the urban fringes of the West Midlands, holds two principal places of interest: **Worcester**, with its mighty cathedral, and Great Malvern, a mannered inland resort in the rolling contours of the **Malvern Hills**. From here, it's west again for **Herefordshire**, a large and sparsely populated county that's home to several amenable market towns, notably Hereford, where the remarkable medieval **Mappa Mundi** is displayed in the cathedral, and pocket-sized Ross-on-Wye, which is near a scenic stretch of the Wye River Valley. To the north is rural **Shropshire**, which has one of the region's prettiest towns, **Ludlow**, awash with antique half-timbered buildings, and the county town of Shrewsbury, close to the hiking trails of the Long Mynd. Shropshire has a fascinating industrial history, too, which you can explore in **Ironbridge Gorge**.

To the north of Birmingham and its sprawling suburbs is Derbyshire, its northern reaches dominated by the rough landscapes of the **Peak District National Park**. The park's many trails attract hikers by the thousand and one of the best bases is the appealing former spa town of **Buxton**. The Peak District is also home to the limestone caverns of Castleton, the "Plague Village" of Eyam and the grandiose stately pile of Chatsworth House.

ROYAL SHAKESPEARE THEATRE

Highlights

❶ Staying Cool, Birmingham Stay Cool and be cool by renting an apartment at the top of the Rotunda, a Birmingham landmark, and enjoy the panoramic views. See page 404

❷ RSC theatres, Stratford-upon-Avon Shakespeare's birthplace is quite simply the best place in the world to see the great man's plays, performed by the pre-eminent Royal Shakespeare Company. See page 409

❸ Mappa Mundi, Hereford Cathedral This glorious antique map, dating to around 1000 AD, provides a riveting insight into the medieval mind with all its quirks and superstitions. See page 416

❹ Ironbridge Gorge The first iron bridge ever constructed arches high above the River Severn – industrial poetry in motion. See page 419

❺ Ludlow A postcard-pretty country town with a castle, a platoon of half-timbered houses and some quality restaurants. See page 423

❻ Buxton Good-looking and relaxed former spa town with good hotels and restaurants; it's an ideal base for exploring the Peak District. See page 429

❼ Hiking in the Peak District The wonderful wilds of the Peak District are crisscrossed by hiking trails – start with an amiable stroll or two near Bakewell. See page 434

HIGHLIGHTS ARE MARKED ON THE MAP ON PAGE 398

GETTING AROUND

Birmingham has a major international **airport** and is readily accessible by **train** from all of England's big cities. It is also well served by the National Express **bus** network, with dozens of buses leaving every hour for destinations all over Britain. Furthermore, Birmingham acts as a public transport hub for the whole of the West Midlands, with trains fanning out into the surrounding counties. However, once you leave the rail network behind you'll find local buses thin on the ground, especially in the quieter parts of Worcestershire, Herefordshire and Shropshire. The main exception is the Peak District, where a dense network of bus services will take you most places on most days.

HIGHLIGHTS

1. Staying Cool, Birmingham
2. RSC theatres, Stratford-upon-Avon
3. Mappa Mundi, Hereford Cathedral
4. Ironbridge Gorge
5. Ludlow
6. Buxton
7. Hiking in the Peak District

0   10
miles

THE WEST MIDLANDS AND THE PEAK DISTRICT

Birmingham

If anywhere can be described as the first purely industrial conurbation, it has to be **BIRMINGHAM**. Unlike the more specialist industrial towns that grew up across the north and the Midlands, "Brum" – and its "Brummies" – turned its hand to every kind of manufacturing, gaining the epithet "the city of 1001 trades". It was here that the pioneers of the Industrial Revolution – James Watt, Matthew Boulton, Josiah Wedgwood, Joseph Priestley and Erasmus Darwin (grandfather of Charles) – formed the **Lunar Society**, an extraordinary melting pot of scientific and industrial ideas. They conceived the world's first purpose-built factory, invented gas lighting and pioneered both the distillation of oxygen and the mass production of the steam engine. Thus, a modest Midlands market town mushroomed into the nation's economic dynamo, with a population to match: in 1841 there were 180,000 inhabitants; just fifty years later that number had trebled.

Now Britain's second-largest city, with a population of over one million, Birmingham has long outgrown the squalor and misery of its boom years and today its industrial supremacy is recalled – but only recalled – by a crop of **recycled buildings**, from warehouses to old factories, and an extensive network of **canals**. This recent (and enforced) shift to a post-manufacturing economy has also been trumped by an intelligent and far-reaching revamp of the city centre that has included the construction of a glitzy **Convention Centre**, a talented reconstruction of the **Bull Ring**, the reinvigoration of the excellent **Birmingham Museum & Art Gallery**, and, at a time when other councils are nervously biting their nails, the building of a lavish, state-of-the-art **Library**. Birmingham has also launched a whole range of cultural initiatives – including the provision of a fabulous new concert hall for the **City of Birmingham Symphony Orchestra** – and boasts both a first-rate restaurant scene and a boisterous nightlife. While Birmingham doesn't have the density of attractions of a capital city, it's well worth at least a couple of days of anyone's time.

8

The Bull Ring and around

Most visitors to Birmingham arrive at **New Street Station**, formerly an unsightly modern building, but now transformed into an airy, billowing structure clad in bands of undulating stainless steel. From here, it's just a few steps to Rotunda Square, at the intersection of New and High streets, which takes its name from the soaring **Rotunda**, a handsome and distinctive cylindrical tower that is the sole survivor of the notorious **Bull Ring** shopping centre, which fulfilled every miserable cliché of 1960s town planning until its demolition in 2001. The new Bull Ring shopping centre, which replaced it, has two strokes of real invention: firstly, the architects' decision to split the shops into two separate sections, providing an uninterrupted view of the medieval spire of **St Martin's** in between; and secondly, the dramatic design of the **Selfridges'** store.

Selfridges

Bull Ring, B5 4BP • Mon–Wed 10am–8pm, Thurs & Fri 10am–9pm, Sat 9am–9pm, Sun 11am–5.30pm • ☎ 0800 123400, ⊛ selfridges.com

Birmingham's **Selfridges** is an extraordinary sight – a billowing organic swell protruding from the Bull Ring's east side, and seen to best advantage from the wide stone stairway that descends from Rotunda Square to St Martin's. Reminiscent of an inside-out octopus, Selfridges shimmers with an architectural chain mail of thousands of spun aluminium discs, an altogether bold and hugely successful attempt to create a popular city landmark.

Victoria Square

Busy **New St** stretches west from the Bull Ring to the handsomely refurbished **Victoria Square**, whose wide stone stairways and assorted statues serve as an attractive prelude

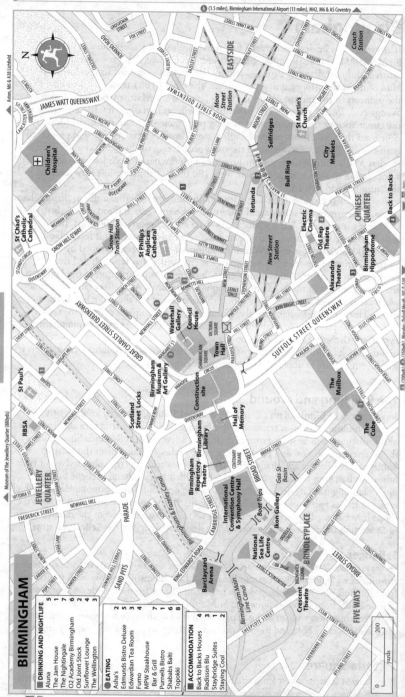

BIRMINGHAM

DRINKING AND NIGHTLIFE

Aluna	5
The Jam House	1
The Nightingale	7
O2 Academy Birmingham	6
Old Joint Stock	2
Sunflower Lounge	4
The Wellington	3

EATING

Asha's	2
Edmunds Bistro Deluxe	5
Edwardian Tea Room	3
Fumo	4
MPW Steakhouse Bar & Grill	7
Purnells Bistro	1
Shababs Balti	6
Topokki	8

ACCOMMODATION

Back to Backs Houses	4
Radisson Blu	3
Staybridge Suites	1
Staying Cool	2

to the **Council House**, whose gables and cupola, columns and tympana – completed in 1879 – witness the thrusting self-confidence of the Victorian bourgeoisie. Across the square is the **Town Hall** of 1834, whose classical design – by Joseph Hansom, who went on to design Hansom cabs – was based on the Roman temple in Nîmes. The building's simple, flowing lines and imposing size contrast with much of its surroundings, but it's a wonderful structure all the same, and now houses a performing arts venue.

The Birmingham Museum and Art Gallery

Chamberlain Square, B3 3DH • Mon–Thurs, Sat & Sun 10am–5pm, Fri 10.30am–5pm • Free • ☎ 0121 348 8000, ⓦ birminghammuseums. org.uk/bmag

The **Birmingham Museum and Art Gallery** (BM&AG), which occupies a grand Edwardian building and one of its neighbours, possesses a multifaceted collection running from fine and applied art through to archeological finds. The key paintings, including the museum's prime collection of **Pre-Raphaelites**, are spread over one long floor – Floor 2 – as is the **Staffordshire Hoard** of Anglo-Saxon treasures. That the museum's collection of paintings is too large to all be exhibited at once, and artworks are regularly rotated, so pick up a **plan** at reception. There's also a pleasant **café** on Floor 2 (see page 404).

The Pre-Raphaelites

The BM&AG holds a significant sample of **European** paintings and an excellent collection of eighteenth- and nineteenth-century British art, most notably a supreme muster of **Pre-Raphaelite** work. Founded in 1848, the Pre-Raphaelite Brotherhood consisted of seven young artists, of whom Rossetti, Holman Hunt, Millais and Madox Brown are the best known. Two seminal Pre-Raphaelite paintings on display are **Dante Gabriel Rossetti**'s stirring *Beata Beatrix* (1870) and **Ford Madox Brown**'s powerful image of emigration, *The Last of England* (1855). The Brotherhood disbanded in the 1850s, but a second wave of artists carried on in its footsteps, most notably **Edward Burne-Jones**, whose *Star of Bethlehem* is one of the largest watercolours ever painted, a mysterious, almost magical piece with earnest Magi and a film-star-like Virgin Mary.

The Staffordshire Hoard

Discovered by amateur detectorists in 2009, the **Staffordshire Hoard** is the largest collection of Anglo-Saxon treasure ever unearthed, consisting of nearly 4000 pieces, mostly related to warfare. Gold, silver and garnet are the three main materials, but it's the delicacy and intricacy of the work that inspires – and a selection of pieces, along with detailed explanations, is exhibited here to fine effect.

The Industrial Gallery, Gas Hall and the Waterhall Gallery

Sharing Floor 2 is the **Industrial Gallery**, which is set around an expansive atrium whose wrought-iron columns and balconies clamber up towards delicate skylights. The gallery holds a choice selection of ceramics, jewellery and stained glass retrieved from defunct churches all over Birmingham. Here also is the *Edwardian Tea Room*, one of the city's more agreeable places for a cuppa (see page 404). Elsewhere in the museum, the cavernous **Gas Hall** is an impressive venue for touring art exhibitions, while the **Waterhall Gallery**, inside the Council House, just across Edmund St from the main museum building, showcases temporary exhibitions of modern and contemporary art.

St Philip's Cathedral

Colmore Row, B3 2QB • Mon–Fri 7.30am–6.30pm, Sat & Sun 8.30am–5pm • Free • ☎ 0121 262 1840, ⓦ birminghamcathedral.com

The string of fancily carved, High Victorian stone buildings on Colmore Row provides a suitable backdrop for **St Philip's Anglican Cathedral**, a bijou example of

English Baroque. Consecrated in 1715, the church is a handsome affair, its graceful, galleried interior all balance and poise, its harmonies unruffled by the Victorians, who enlarged the original church in the 1880s, when four stained-glass windows were commissioned from local boy **Edward Burne-Jones**, a leading light of the Pre-Raphaelite movement. The windows are typical of his style – intensely coloured, fastidiously detailed and distinctly sentimental. Three – the *Nativity*, *Crucifixion* and *Ascension* – are at the east end of the church beyond the high altar, the fourth – the *Last Judgement* – is directly opposite.

Centenary Square

One of the city's centrepieces, the wide, pedestrianized expanse of **Centenary Square** is framed by several of Birmingham's key buildings. These begin on the left with the showpiece **International Convention Centre** (ICC) and **Symphony Hall**. Next up is the **Birmingham Repertory Theatre**, which is attached to the super-duper **Library** and in front of this – in architectural contrast – is the older **Hall of Memory**.

Birmingham Library

Centenary Square, B1 2ND • Mon–Fri 9am–9pm, Sat 11am–5pm • Free • ☎ 0121 242 4242, ⓦ libraryofbirmingham.com

At a time when many British libraries were under threat, it was a brave move for the City Council to fund the construction of the new **Birmingham Library**, a prestige structure completed in 2013 to a striking design, its cubic superstructure clad with a shimmering filigree of overlapping metal rings. Local opinion is divided as to whether it was a sound investment, but it's certainly a landmark, and its terraces offer views over the city centre.

Hall of Memory

Centenary Square, B1 2HF • Mon–Sat 10am–4pm • Free • ⓦ hallofmemory.co.uk

Erected in the 1920s, the distinctive **Hall of Memory** was built to commemorate the 12,320 citizens of Birmingham who died in World War I. An architectural hybrid, the Hall has a delightful mix of Art Deco and Neoclassical features rendered in Portland stone, its centrepiece a domed Remembrance chamber complete with a mournful inscription.

Gas Street Basin

Away2canal times & frequency vary; 1hr • £8 • ☎ 0121 647 7151, ⓦ away2canal.co.uk

Gas Street Basin is the hub of Birmingham's intricate canal system. There are eight canals within the city's boundaries – 32 miles' worth in total – with most dug in the late eighteenth century before the railways made them uneconomic. Much of the surviving network slices through the city's grimy, industrial bowels, but certain sections have been immaculately restored, with Gas Street Basin leading the way. The Basin, which is edged by a fascinating medley of old brick buildings, lies at the junction of the Worcester and Birmingham and Birmingham Main Line canals, and its dark waters almost invariably bob with a fleet of brightly painted narrowboats; from the periphery of the Basin, Away2canal organizes **narrowboat excursions** along Birmingham's canals.

Brindleyplace

Beside Gas Street Basin is the waterside **Brindleyplace**, which is named after James Brindley, the eighteenth-century engineer responsible for many of Britain's early canals. It's an aesthetically pleasing development, with an attractive central plaza that's popular with office staff at lunch times. The city's much-praised **Ikon Gallery** is just off the central square.

Ikon Gallery

1 Oozells Square, B1 2HS • Tues–Sun & bank hols 11am–5pm • Free • ☎ 0121 248 0708, ⓦ ikon-gallery.org

Housed in a substantial Victorian building, the **Ikon Gallery** is one of the country's most imaginative venues for touring exhibitions of contemporary art, with recent shows by the likes of Oliver Beer and Jean Painlevé. Perhaps even better, the gallery organizes all sorts of workshops, family days and special events plus guided **tours** of the gallery itself.

The Birmingham & Fazeley Canal

Just beyond Brindleyplace, in front of the massive dome of the Barclaycard Arena, the canal forks: the Birmingham Main Line Canal cuts west (to the left) and the more interesting **Birmingham & Fazeley Canal** leads northeast (to the right), running past a sequence of antique brick buildings en route to the quaint **Scotland St Locks**. Further on, the canal slides past a string of new apartment blocks as well as the (signed) flight of steps that clambers up to Newhall Street, about half a mile beyond the main canal junction, and a few minutes' walk from St Paul's church.

St Paul's church

St Paul's Square, B3 1QZ • Ring for opening times • ☎ 0121 236 7858, ⓦ stpaulsjq.church

On **St Paul's Square**, an attractive ensemble of old houses flank **St Paul's church**, whose rational symmetries, dating to the 1770s, are an excellent illustration of Neoclassical design. To the people who paid for it (by public subscription), though, there was much more to the building than aesthetics: gone were the mysteries of the medieval church, replaced by a church of the Enlightenment and one that proved popular with the new industrialists – both Matthew Boulton and James Watt had family pews here, though Watt never actually turned up.

8

ARRIVAL AND DEPARTURE   BIRMINGHAM

By plane Birmingham's airport is 8 miles east of the city centre off the A45 – and near the M42 (Junction 6). The terminal is beside Birmingham International train station, from where there are regular services into New St train station (every 10–15min; 10min).

By train Most intercity and many local services use New St station, in the heart of the city. There are two smaller stations – Snow Hill and Moor St, respectively a (signed) 10min walk north and 5min walk east of New St. Moor St, the quaintest of the three – with much of its Edwardian fabric intact – is used primarily by Chiltern Railways.

Destinations (New St) Birmingham International (every 10–15min; 10min); Derby (every 20min; 45min); Great Malvern (every 30min; 1hr); Hereford (every 30min; 1hr 30min); London Euston (every 30min; 1hr 25min); Shrewsbury (every 30min; 1hr); Telford (Mon–Sat every 30min, Sun hourly; 40min); Worcester Foregate (hourly; 45min).

Destinations (Snow Hill) Stratford-upon-Avon (hourly; 50min); Warwick (every 30min; 30min).

Destinations (Moor St) London Marylebone (every 30min; 1hr 50min); Stratford-upon-Avon (hourly; 45min); Worcester Foregate (hourly; 1hr).

By bus National Express long-distance buses arrive at the Birmingham Coach Station, in Digbeth, from where it's a 10min walk northwest to the Bull Ring. Regular services to London (hourly; 3hr 30min) and Manchester (hourly; 3–4hr).

INFORMATION AND GETTING AROUND

Public transport Birmingham's trains, buses and metro (a light railway/tram) delve into almost every urban nook and cranny. Various companies provide these services, but they are all coordinated by Transport for West Midlands, with journey planning available online (ⓦ networkwest midlands.com).

Tourist office There are currently no tourist offices in the city, but Visit Birmingham does operate an excellent and comprehensive website, ⓦ visitbirmingham.com.

ACCOMMODATION

To see Birmingham at its best, you really need to stay in the centre, preferably in the vicinity of **Centenary Square**, though chain hotels do monopolize the downtown core. A comprehensive list of options is available on Visit Birmingham's website (ⓦ visitbirmingham.com/where-to-stay).

Back to Backs Houses 52 Inge St, B5 4TE ☎ 0344 800 2070, ⓦ nationaltrustholidays.org.uk; map p.400. The most distinctive place to stay in town: the National Trust has refurbished a small block of nineteenth-century back-to-back workers' houses conveniently located just to the south of the city centre along Hurst St. Part of the complex now holds two small "cottages" – really terraced houses – kitted out in Victorian period style, but with the addition of en-suite and self-catering facilities. Each accommodates two guests. **£110**

Radisson Blu 12 Holloway Circus, Queensway, B1 1BT ☎ 0121 654 6000, ⓦ radissonblu.com/en/hotel-birmingham; map p.400. Smart hotel in a tall, sleek skyrise within a few minutes' walk of the centre. The interior is designed in routine modern-minimalist style, but the floor-to-ceiling windows of many of the bedrooms add more than a dash of élan. **£100**

Staybridge Suites Martineau Place, Corporation St, B2 4UW ☎ 0121 289 3636, ⓦ ihg.com; map p.400. Classic 1960s, city-centre office block that has been cleverly converted into a hotel, holding 179 smart, modern suites with fitted kitchenettes. Capacious breakfast area, too. **£85**

★ **Staying Cool** The Rotunda, 150 New St, B2 4PA ☎ 0121 285 1290, ⓦ stayingcool.com; map p.400. The top three floors of the Rotunda, right at the heart of the city, have been converted into fully furnished and serviced apartments. All the apartments are modern and spotless, and those on the top floor – Floor 20 – come with a balcony from where there are panoramic views over the city. The apartments can be rented for one night – no problem. **£140**

EATING

Central Birmingham has a bevy of first-rate **restaurants** with a string of smart new venues springing up in the slipstream of the burgeoning conference and trade-fair business. Birmingham's gastronomic speciality is the **balti**, a delicious Kashmiri stew cooked and served in a small wok-like dish called a *karahi*, eaten with naan bread instead of cutlery. The original balti houses are concentrated out in the suburbs of Balsall Heath, Moseley and Sparkhill to the south of the centre, which is where you should head if a balti whets your appetite.

Asha's 12 Newhall St, B3 3LX ☎ 0121 200 2767, ⓦ ashasrestaurant.co.uk; map p.400. Chic and polished Indian restaurant named after a Bollywood star – Asha Parekh – with a wide-ranging menu that covers all the classics and then some. Reservations strongly advised. Mains average £16 or £11 for a vegetarian dish. Mon–Fri noon–2.30pm & 5.30–10.30pm, Sat 5–11pm, Sun 5–10pm.

Edmunds Bistro Deluxe 6 Brindleyplace, B1 2JB ☎ 0121 633 4944, ⓦ edmundsrestaurant.co.uk; map p.400. High-life dining in smart, contemporary premises. An inventive, French-style menu features seasonal ingredients – venison with dauphinoise potato, duck liver, parsnip mousseline and hazelnut crumble is typical. Mains £16–28. Reservations well-nigh essential. Mon–Fri noon–2pm & 6–10pm, Sat 6–10pm.

Edwardian Tea Room BM&AG, Chamberlain Square, B3 3DH ☎ 0121 348 8082, ⓦ bmag.org.uk; map p.400. This canteen-style café has a great setting in one of the large and beautifully decorated halls of the museum's industrial section – check out the fancy ironwork and skylights. The food doesn't quite match up to the surroundings, but stick to the simpler dishes and you won't go far wrong: the soup and bread should hit the mark (£4.50). Mon–Thurs, Sat & Sun 10am–4.30pm, Fri 10.30am–4.30pm.

Fumo 1 Waterloo St, B2 5PG ☎ 0121 643 8979, ⓦ sancarlofumo.co.uk; map p.400. In smart modern premises, this fast-paced Italian restaurant serves up excellent and authentic Italian cuisine, from the basics (pizzas and pastas) through to more elaborate concoctions like monkfish and prawns marinated in garlic, parsley and lemon. Tapas-style mains cost around £9. Daily 11.30am–11.30pm.

★ **MPW Steakhouse Bar & Grill** The Cube, 200 Wharfside St, B1 1PR ☎ 0121 634 3433, ⓦ mpwsteakhousebirmingham.co.uk; map p.400. Amazingly popular Marco Pierre White-run cocktail bar and restaurant. A no-nonsense menu features steaks (as you would expect), but there are other offerings too – for example pork belly and bramley apple with bubble and squeak and mustard sauce. The location is excellent – on the top-floor of The Cube, a high-rise that has been creatively reconfigured, including the addition of a sculpture-like external casing/screen. Steaks from £20, other mains from £16. Daily noon–10pm.

Purnells Bistro 11 Newhall St, B3 3NY ☎ 0121 200 1588, ⓦ purnellsbistro-gingers.com; map p.400. A side venture by Michelin-starred chef Glynn Purnell, who already operates one of the city's best restaurants – Purnell's – this combined cocktail bar and upmarket bistro offers a menu inspired by "rustic British fare". Quite. A la carte mains average £17 and include such delights as pan-fried sea bass with olive tapenade and anchovy. Reservations recommended. Mon–Fri noon–2.30pm & 6–9.30pm, Sat noon–3.30pm & 5–9.30pm, Sun noon–4pm.

Shababs Balti 163 Ladypool Rd, Sparkbrook, B12 8LQ ☎ 0121 440 2893, ⓦ shababs.co.uk; map p.400. Long-established and much praised balti restaurant with strikingly garish decor in the so-called "Balti Triangle" to the south of the city centre. Reckon on £7 per balti. Daily noon–10pm.

Topokki Unit 1C, Hurst St, B5 4TD ☎ 0121 666 7200; map p.400. Informal, canteen-style restaurant serving up delicious and authentic Korean dishes at very affordable prices – *odeng guk* (fishcake soup), for example, at £6.80. Daily noon–9pm.

DRINKING AND NIGHTLIFE

Birmingham's **pub and club scene** is one of Britain's best, with the latter spanning everything from word-of-mouth underground parties to meat-market mainstream clubs. **Live music** is strong, too, with big-name concerts at several major venues and other (often local) bands appearing at some clubs and pubs. Birmingham's showpiece **Symphony Orchestra** and **Royal Ballet** are the spearheads of the city's **classical scene**, while the city also lines up a string of top-ranking **festivals**. For details of all upcoming events, performances and exhibitions, consult either ⓦ visitbirmingham. com/explore-birmingham or ⓦ livebrum.co.uk.

Aluna 128 The Mailbox, Wharfeside St, B1 1RQ ☎ 0121 633 9987, ⓦ aluna.uk.com; map p.400. There are no real-ale fans here in this popular cocktail bar, whose over-the-top decor (orange crushed-velvet banquettes, etc) wows its twenty-something customers. There's a small canalside terrace here too. Mon–Thurs & Sun noon–midnight, Fri & Sat noon–1.30am.

★ **The Jam House** 3 St Paul's Square, B3 1QU ☎ 0121 200 3030, ⓦ thejamhouse.com; map p.400. This jazz, funk, blues and swing club/pub pulls in artists from every corner of the globe. Great vibe; great gigs. Has a close relationship with Jools Holland. Tues & Wed 6pm–midnight, Thurs–Sat 6pm–1am.

The Nightingale 18 Kent St, B5 6RD ☎ 0121 622 1718, ⓦ nightingaleclub.co.uk; map p.400. The king/queen of Brum's gay clubs, popular with straight folks as well. Five bars, three levels, two discos, a café-bar and even a garden. Thurs–Sat from 10pm.

Old Joint Stock 4 Temple Row West, B2 5NY ☎ 0121 200 1892, ⓦ oldjointstocktheatre.co.uk; map p.400. This charming pub has the fanciest decor in town – with busts and a balustrade, a balcony and chandeliers, all dating from its days as a bank. There's a medium-sized theatre studio upstairs, mostly featuring improv comedy and musical theatre. Mon–Fri 8am–11pm, Sat 9am–11pm, Sun 10am–5pm.

★ **Sunflower Lounge** 76 Smallbrook Queensway, B5 4EG ☎ 0121 632 6756, ⓦ thesunflowerlounge.com; map p.400. Quirky pub-cum-bar in modern premises on the inner ring road near New St station. Attracts an indie/student crowd and covers many bases, with quizzes and big-screen TV plus resident DJs and live gigs. It really is cool without being pretentious – just as they say on their website. Mon, Tues & Sun noon–11.30pm, Wed–Sat noon–2am.

The Wellington 37 Bennetts Hill, B2 5SN ☎ 0121 200 3115, ⓦ thewellingtonrealale.com; map p.400. Specialist real-ale pub with a top-notch range of local brews, including those of the much-vaunted Black Country Brewery. A good selection of ciders, too. Daily 10am–midnight.

ENTERTAINMENT

Birmingham Hippodrome Hurst St, B5 4TB ☎ 0844 338 5000, ⓦ birminghamhippodrome.com. Lavishly refurbished, the Hippodrome is home to the Birmingham Royal Ballet. Also features touring plays and big pre- and post-West End productions, plus a splendiferous Christmas pantomime.

Birmingham Repertory Theatre Centenary Square, B1 2EP ☎ 0121 236 4455, ⓦ birmingham-rep.co.uk. Mixed diet of classics and new work featuring local and experimental writing.

The Electric Cinema 47 Station St, B5 4DY ☎ 0121 643 7879, ⓦ theelectric.co.uk. Britain's oldest working cinema, housed in a handsome Art Deco building, with an inventive programme of mainstream and art-house films. Sofas and waiter service too.

O2 Academy Birmingham 16–18 Horsefair, Bristol St, B1 1DB ☎ 0844 477 2000 (Ticketmaster ticket line), ⓦ o2academybirmingham.co.uk. State-of-the-art venue with three performance areas, hosting either gigs or club nights, though the big deal is the top-ranking artists who regularly appear here.

Symphony Hall ICC, Centenary Square, B1 2EA ☎ 0121 780 3333, ⓦ thsh.co.uk. Acoustically one of the most advanced concert halls in Europe, home of the acclaimed City of Birmingham Symphony Orchestra (CBSO; ⓦ cbso. co.uk), as well as a venue for touring music and opera.

Town Hall Victoria Square, B3 3DQ ☎ 0121 780 3333, ⓦ thsh.co.uk. The old Town Hall, with its magnificent interior fully renovated, offers a varied programme of popular, classical and jazz music through to modern dance and ballet.

Stratford-upon-Avon

Despite its fame, **STRATFORD-UPON-AVON**, thirty miles south of Birmingham, is at heart an unassuming market town with an unexceptional pedigree. A charter for Stratford's weekly market was granted in the twelfth century and the town later became a key stopping-off point for stagecoaches between London, Oxford and the north. Like all such places, Stratford had its clearly defined class system and within this milieu John and Mary **Shakespeare** occupied the middle rank, and would have been forgotten long ago had their first son, **William**, not turned out to be the greatest writer ever to use the English language. A consequence of their good fortune is that, in summer at least, this pleasant little town can seem overwhelmed by the number of visitors, but don't be deterred: the **Royal Shakespeare Company** offers superb theatre and if you are willing to forgo the busiest attraction – **Shakespeare's Birthplace** – you can largely avoid the crush. Stratford's key attractions are dotted around the centre, a flat and compact slice of land spreading back from the River Avon, and three of them – as well as two more on the edge of town – are owned and operated by the excellent **Shakespeare Birthplace Trust** (see page 409).

Shakespeare's Birthplace

Henley St, CV37 6QW • Daily: late March–Oct 9am–5pm; Nov to mid-March 10am–4pm • Shakespeare Birthplace Trust combination ticket £17.50/£26.25 (see page 409) • ☎ 01789 204016, ⓦ shakespeare.org.uk/visit/shakespeares-birthplace

Top of everyone's bardic itinerary is **Shakespeare's Birthplace**, comprising a modern visitor centre and the heavily restored, half-timbered building where the great man was born, or rather, where it is generally believed he was born. The visitor centre pokes into every corner of Shakespeare's life and times, making the most of what little hard evidence there is. Next door, the birthplace itself is actually two buildings knocked into one. The northern, much smaller and later part was the house of Joan, Shakespeare's sister; adjoining it is the main family home, bought by John Shakespeare in 1556 and now returned to something like its original appearance. Despite the many historical uncertainties, the house has been attracting visitors for centuries and upstairs one of the old mullioned windows, now displayed in a glass cabinet, bears the scratch-mark signatures of some of them, including Thomas Carlyle and Walter Scott.

Shakespeare's New Place and Nash's House

22 Chapel St, CV37 6EP • Daily: late March to Oct 9am–5pm, Nov to mid-March 10am–4pm • Shakespeare Birthplace Trust combination ticket £17.50/£26.25 (see page 409) • ☎ 01789 204016, ⓦ shakespeare.org.uk/visit/shakespeares-new-place

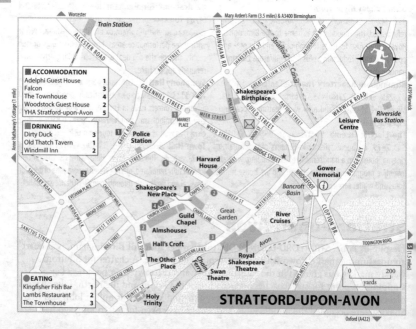

STRATFORD-UPON-AVON

WHO EXACTLY WAS SHAKESPEARE

Over the past hundred years or so, the deification of **William Shakespeare** (1564–1616) has been dogged by an eccentric backlash among a fringe of revisionist scholars and literary figures sometimes known as "**Anti-Stratfordians**", according to whom the famous plays and sonnets were not written by a glover's son from Stratford, but by someone else, and William Shakespeare was merely a nom de plume. A variety of candidates has been proposed for the authorship of Shakespeare's works, from the vaguely plausible (Christopher Marlowe, Francis Bacon, Ben Jonson, and the Earls of Rutland, Southampton and Oxford) to the manifestly whacko (Queen Elizabeth I, King James I and Daniel Defoe, who was born six years after publication of the first Folio).

Lying at the root of the authorship debate are several **unresolved questions** that have puzzled scholars for years. How could a man of modest background have such an intimate knowledge of royal protocol? How could he know so much about Italy without ever having travelled there? Why did he not leave a library in his will, when the author of the plays clearly possessed a detailed knowledge of classical literature? And why, given that Shakespeare was supposedly a well-known dramatist, did no death notice or obituary appear in publications of the day?

The lack of **definite information** about Shakespeare's life has only fuelled the speculation, and the few details that have been preserved come mostly from official archives – birth, marriage and death certificates and court records. From these we know that on April 22 or 23, 1564, John Shakespeare and his wife, Mary, had their first son, William. We also know that William attended a local grammar school and that, at the age of 18, he married a local woman, Anne Hathaway, seven years his senior, with whom he had three children. Several years later, probably in 1587, William was forced to flee Stratford after being caught poaching. Five companies of players passed through Stratford on tour that year and it is believed that he **absconded** with one of them to London, where a theatre boom was in full swing. *Henry VI*, Shakespeare's first play, appeared soon after, followed by the hugely successful *Richard III*. Over the next decade, Shakespeare's output was prodigious. Thirty-eight plays appeared and most were performed by his own theatre troupes based in London's **Globe** theatre (see page 95), in which he had a one-tenth share.

Success secured him the **patronage** of London's fashionable set and Queen Elizabeth I regularly attended the Globe, as did her successor, James I, whose Scottish ancestry and fascination with the occult partly explain the subject matter of *Macbeth* – Shakespeare knew the commercial value of appealing to the rich and powerful. This, as much as his extraordinary talent, ensured that his plays were the most acclaimed of the day, earning him enough money to buy the largest house in Stratford, where he lived with his family until his death. Ultimately, however, the sketchy details of Shakespeare's life are of far less importance than the plays, sonnets and songs he left behind. Whoever wrote them – and William almost certainly did – the body of work attributed to him comprises some of the most inspired and exquisite English ever written.

8

Kept in immaculate order by the Birthplace Trust, the gardens of **Shakespeare's New Place** are divided into three sections. The first displays a small selection of modern sculptures with Shakespearean references along with the ground plaques that mark the layout of what were the foundations of New Place, Shakespeare's family home for the last nineteen years of his life, long ago demolished. Beyond is a neat and trim Knot Garden and this leads to the **Great Garden**, decorated with an enjoyable set of sculptures by Gregg Wyatt and also home to the ancient mulberry tree that, legend asserts, was grown from a cutting off the tree that the great man himself had planted. Adjoining the gardens is **Nash's House**, an attractive Tudor building once owned by Thomas Nash, the first husband of Shakespeare's granddaughter, Elizabeth Hall. The house delves into the details of Shakespeare's family life by means of a "timeline" and among the supporting exhibits are the archeological bits and pieces retrieved during a recent excavation of the New Place site.

Hall's Croft

Old Town, CV37 6BG • Daily: late March to Oct 10am–5pm, Nov to mid-March 11am–4pm • Shakespeare Birthplace Trust combination ticket £17.50/£26.25 (see page 409) • ☎ 01789 204016, ⓦ shakespeare.org.uk/visit/halls-croft

Stratford's most impressive medieval building is **Hall's Croft**, the former home of Shakespeare's elder daughter, Susanna, and her physician husband, John Hall. This immaculately maintained house, with its beamed ceilings and rickety rooms, holds a good-looking medley of period furniture and paintings – and upstairs it exhibits a fascinating display on **Elizabethan medicine**. Hall established something of a reputation for his medical know-how and after his death some of his case notes were published in a volume entitled *Select Observations on English Bodies*. The best view of the building itself is at the back, in the neat walled garden.

Holy Trinity Church

Old Town, CV37 6BG • March & Oct Mon–Sat 9am–5pm, Sun 12.30–5pm; April–Sept Mon–Sat 8.30am–6pm & Sun 12.30–5pm; Nov–Feb Mon–Sat 9am–4pm & Sun 12.30–5pm • Free, but chancel £3 • ☎ 01789 266316, ⓦ stratford-upon-avon.org

Dating from the thirteenth century, the mellow stonework of **Holy Trinity Church** is enhanced by its riverside setting, though the dignified proportions of this quintessentially English church are the result of several centuries of chopping and changing, culminating in the replacement of the original wooden spire with today's stone version in 1763. Inside, the nave is flanked by a fine set of stained-glass windows, some of them medieval, and bathed in light from the clerestory windows up above. Quite unusually, you'll see that the nave is built on a slight skew from the line of the chancel – to represent Christ's inclined head on the cross. William Shakespeare lies buried in the **chancel**, his remains overseen by a sedate and studious memorial plaque and effigy added just seven years after his death.

Bancroft Basin

In front of the **Royal Shakespeare Theatre**, the manicured lawns of a small riverside park stretch north as far as **Bancroft Basin**, where the Stratford Canal meets the river. This is one of the prettiest parts of Stratford, with brightly painted narrowboats bobbing in the water and a fancy pedestrian bridge leading over to the finely sculpted **Gower Memorial** of 1888, where Shakespeare sits surrounded by characters from his plays.

Anne Hathaway's Cottage

22 Cottage Lane, Shottery, CV37 9HH • Daily: late March to Oct 9am–5pm; Nov to mid-March 10am–4pm • £10.25, Shakespeare Birthplace Trust combination ticket £26.25 (see page 409) • ☎ 01789 204016, ⓦ shakespeare.org.uk/visit/anne-hathaways-cottage • There's a mile-long signposted footpath from Evesham Place in the town centre (20min)

Anne Hathaway's Cottage is just over a mile west of the centre in the well-heeled suburb of Shottery. The cottage – actually an old farmhouse – is an immaculately maintained, half-timbered affair with a thatched roof and dinky little chimneys. This was the home of Anne Hathaway before she married Shakespeare in 1582, and the interior holds a comely combination of period furniture, including a superb, finely carved four-poster bed. The garden is splendid too, bursting with blooms in the summertime. The adjacent orchard features more than forty types of tree, shrub and rose mentioned in the plays, each bearing a plaque with the appropriate quotation.

Mary Arden's Farm

Station Rd, Wilmcote, CV37 9UN, 3 miles northwest of Stratford • Late March to Oct daily 9am–5pm • £13.25, Shakespeare Birthplace Trust combination ticket £26.25 (see page 409) • ☎ 01789 204016, ⓦ shakespeare.org.uk/visit/mary-ardens-farm

Mary Arden's Farm takes its name from Shakespeare's mother, who at the time of her father Robert's death in 1556 was his only unmarried daughter. Unusually for the

STRATFORD'S THEATRES

Sitting pretty beside the River Avon are the **Royal Shakespeare Company**'s two main **theatres**, the Swan and the Royal Shakespeare. There was no theatre in Stratford in Shakespeare's day and indeed the first hometown festival in his honour was only held in 1769 at the behest of London-based David Garrick. Thereafter, the idea of building a permanent home in which to perform Shakespeare's works slowly gained momentum, and finally, in 1879, the first Memorial Theatre was opened on land donated by local beer baron Charles Flower. A fire in 1926 necessitated the construction of a new theatre, and the ensuing architectural competition, won by Elisabeth Scott, produced the **Royal Shakespeare Theatre**, a red-brick edifice that has recently been remodelled and extended, its proscenium stage replaced by a thrust stage – to the horror of many and the delight of some. Attached to the main theatre is the **Swan Theatre**, a replica "in-the-round" Elizabethan stage that has also been refurbished; close by is the RSC's third theatre, formerly called The Courtyard Theatre and now The Other Place.

PERFORMANCES AND TICKETS

The RSC (☎01789 403493, ⓦrsc.org.uk) works on a repertory system, which means you could stay in Stratford for a few days and see three or four different plays, and not necessarily all by Shakespeare. The RSC does indeed focus on the Bard's plays, but it offers other productions too, from new modern writing through to works by Shakespeare's contemporaries – performed at three locations, the Royal Shakespeare, the Swan and The Other Place. **Tickets** start from as little as £14 and can be bought online, by phone and in person at the Royal Shakespeare Theatre's box office. Note that some performances are sold out months in advance; though there's always the off-chance of a last-minute return or stand-by ticket (for unsold seats), don't bet on it.

8

period, Mary inherited the house and land, thus becoming one of the neighbourhood's most eligible women – John Shakespeare married her within a year. The house is a well-furnished example of an Elizabethan farmhouse and costumed guides fill in the details of family life. Outside, several acres of farmland are presented as a working Tudor farm complete with rare-breed animals and a woodland area with nature trails and a wildflower meadow.

ARRIVAL AND DEPARTURE   STRATFORD-UPON-AVON

By train Stratford's main train station is on the northwest edge of town, a 10min walk from the centre.
Destinations Birmingham Snow Hill (every 30min; 1hr); London Marylebone (hourly, with one change; 2hr);

Warwick (every 2hr; 30min).
By bus Local buses arrive and depart from Bridge St; most long-distance buses pull into the Riverside bus station on the east side of the town centre, off Bridgeway.

INFORMATION

Tourist office Handily located by the bridge at the junction of Bridgeway and Bridgefoot (Mon–Sat 9am–5.30pm, Sun 10am–4pm; ☎01789 264293, ⓦdiscover-stratford.com). Among much else, they offer a last-minute accommodation booking service that can be especially handy at the height of summer.
Shakespeare Birthplace Trust (☎01789 204016, ⓦshakespeare.org.uk) cares for five properties – three in the town centre (Shakespeare's Birthplace,

Shakespeare's New Place and Hall's Croft) and two on the outskirts (Anne Hathaway's Cottage and Mary Arden's Farm). Tickets are not available for the three individual properties in the town centre – instead you have to buy a combined ticket for £17.50, or a ticket covering all five for £26.25. You can purchase individual tickets for the two outlying attractions. Tickets are on sale at all five and are discounted online.

ACCOMMODATION

At peak periods it's essential to book well ahead. The town has a dozen or so **hotels**, the pick in half-timbered buildings in the centre, but most visitors choose to stay in a **B&B**; they're concentrated west of the centre, around Grove Rd and Evesham Place.

Adelphi Guest House 39 Grove Rd, CV37 6PB ☎01789 204469, ⓦadelphi-guesthouse.com; map p.406. Extremely cosy B&B in a Victorian townhouse a short walk from the centre. The owners have accumulated all sorts of interesting curios – from vintage theatrical posters to ornate chandeliers – and the five double rooms are all en suite. The best, which has a four-poster, is in the attic and offers pleasing views. Top-notch home-cooked breakfasts, too. **£90**

Falcon Chapel St, CV37 6HA ☎01789 279953, ⓦfalconstratfordhotel.com; map p.406. Right in the centre of town, this chain hotel is a rambling affair whose front section, with its half-timbered facade and stone-flagged bar, dates from the sixteenth century. A corridor connects this to the modern block behind, where the rooms are neat, trim and rather well designed; the rooms in older parts of the hotel, however, are not nearly as appealing. **£110**

The Townhouse 16 Church St, CV37 6HB ☎01789 262222, ⓦstratfordtownhouse.co.uk; map p.406. Twelve deluxe, en-suite guest rooms decorated in a

smart and neat modern manner and equipped with king-size beds. Two-night minimum stay at peak periods. Convenient, central location and first-rate breakfasts, plus good food in the bar/restaurant (see below). **£100**

Woodstock Guest House 30 Grove Rd ☎01789 299881, ⓦwoodstock-house.co.uk; map p.406. A smart, neatly kept B&B just a 5min walk from the centre, by the start of the path to Anne Hathaway's Cottage. The five (extremely comfortable) rooms are all en suite, decorated in a fetching modern style. Minimum two nights at peak times. **£90**

YHA Stratford-upon-Avon Hemmingford House, Wellesbourne Rd, Alveston, CV37 7RG ☎0345 371 9661, ⓦyha.org.uk/hostel/stratford-upon-avon; map p.406. Occupying a rambling Georgian mansion about two miles east of Stratford on the B4086, this medium-sized hostel has dorms, doubles and family rooms, some en suite, plus car parking and self-catering facilities. Breakfasts and evening meals are on offer, too. Local bus from Stratford's Wood St. Dorms **£18**, doubles **£39**

EATING

Kingfisher Fish Bar 13 Ely St, CV37 6LW ☎01789 292513; map p.406. The best fish-and-chip shop in town, a 5min walk from the theatres. Takeaway and sit-down. Mon–Sat 11.30am–1.45pm & 5–9.30pm.

★**Lambs Restaurant** 12 Sheep St, CV37 6EF ☎01789 292554, ⓦlambsrestaurant.co.uk; map p.406. A mouth-watering range of English and continental dishes – such as slow-roasted lamb shank – in a smart restaurant with period features like beamed ceilings, and modern art on the walls. Mains £14–20;

specials around £12. Mon 5–9pm, Tues–Sat noon–2pm & 5–9.30pm, Sun noon–2pm & 6–9pm.

The Townhouse 16 Church St, CV37 6HB ☎01789 262222, ⓦstratfordtownhouse.co.uk; map p.406. Smart spot in one of the town's oldest premises. The menu is creative with emphasis on local ingredients – vegetable risotto, for instance, or pan-roasted turbot with braised oxtail. Mains £13–18. Rooms available, too (see above). Mon–Fri noon–3pm & 5–10pm, Sat noon–10pm, Sun noon–8pm.

DRINKING

Dirty Duck 53 Waterside, CV37 6BA ☎01789 297312, ⓦoldenglishinns.co.uk; map p.406. The archetypal actors' pub, albeit now one of a chain, which is stuffed to the gunwales every night with a vocal entourage of RSC thesps and admirers. Traditional beers in somewhat spartan premises plus a terrace for hot-weather drinking. Daily 11am–11pm.

Old Thatch Tavern Market Place, CV37 6LE ☎01789 295216, ⓦoldthatchtavernstratford.co.uk; map

p.406. Ancient pub with a convivial atmosphere and a good range of beers attracting a mixed bag of tourists and locals. Fuller's ales on tap. Mon–Sat 11.30am–11pm, Sun noon–11pm.

Windmill Inn Church St, CV37 6HB ☎01789 297687, ⓦwindmill-stratford-upon-avon.co.uk; map p.406. Popular pub with a rabbit-warren of rooms and low-beamed ceilings. Greene King beers, too. Daily 10am–11pm.

Warwick and around

Small-town **WARWICK**, just nine miles northeast of Stratford, is famous for its massive **castle**, but it also has several charming streetscapes, which arose in the aftermath of a great fire in 1694. An hour or two is quite enough time to see the centre, though you'll need the whole day if, braving the crowds and medieval musicians, you're set on exploring the castle and its extensive grounds; either way, Warwick is the perfect day-trip from Stratford.

Warwick Castle

CV34 4QU • Daily: core hours June–Sept 10am–5pm; Oct–May 10am–4pm • Various ticketing options from £18 in advance (£26 on the day) • ☎ 01926 495421; recorded info ☎ 0871 265 2000, ⓦ warwick-castle.com

Towering above the River Avon at the foot of the town centre, **Warwick Castle** is often proclaimed the "greatest medieval castle in Britain". This claim is valid enough if bulk equals greatness, but actually much of the existing structure is the result of nineteenth-century tinkering. It's likely that the Saxons raised the first fortress on this site, though things really took off with the Normans, who built a large motte and bailey here in the late eleventh century. Almost three hundred years later, the eleventh Earl of Warwick turned the stronghold into a stone castle, complete with gatehouses, turrets and a keep.

Today, the **entrance** to the castle is through the old stable block at the foot of Castle St. Beyond, a footpath leads round to the imposing moated and mounded **East Gate**. Over the footbridge – and beyond the protective towers – is the main **courtyard**. You can stroll along the ramparts and climb the towers, but most visitors head straight for one or other of the special, very touristy displays installed inside the castle's many chambers and towers. The **grounds** are perhaps much more enjoyable, acres of woodland and lawn inhabited by peacocks and including a large glass **conservatory**. A footbridge leads over the River Avon to **River Island**, the site of jousting tournaments and other such medieval hoopla.

Lord Leycester Hospital

60 High St, CV34 4BH • Tues–Sun & bank hols: April–Oct 10am–5pm; Nov–March 10am–4pm • £8.50 • ☎ 01926 491422, ⓦ lordleycester.com

The fascinating **Lord Leycester Hospital**, a tangle of half-timbered buildings leaning at fairy-tale angles against the stone remains of the West Gate, represents one of Britain's best-preserved examples of domestic Elizabethan architecture. It was established as a hostel for old soldiers by Robert Dudley, Earl of Leicester, and incorporates several beamed buildings, principally the Great Hall and the Guildhall, as well as a wonderful galleried courtyard and a chantry chapel. Retired servicemen still live here, so some areas are out of bounds, but you can visit a **tearoom**, the *Brethrens' Kitchen* (Feb–Nov; same hours).

St Mary's Church

Old Square, CV34 4RA • April–Sept Mon–Sat 10am–6pm, Sun 12.30–4.30pm; Oct–March Mon–Sat 10am–4.30pm, Sun 12.30–4.30pm • Free, but £2 donation suggested • ☎ 01926 403940, ⓦ stmaryswarwick.org.uk

Rebuilt in a weird Gothic-Renaissance amalgam after the fire of 1694, **St Mary's Church** may not look too exciting from the outside, but wander inside and you'll see that the flames spared the **chancel**, a simply glorious illustration of the Perpendicular style with a splendid vaulted ceiling of flying and fronded ribs. To the right of the chancel is the even more spectacular **Beauchamp Chantry Chapel**, which holds the beautiful tomb of Richard Beauchamp, Earl of Warwick, who is depicted in an elaborate, gilded-bronze suit of armour of Italian design from the tip of his swan helmet down to his mailed feet. A griffin and a bear guard Richard, who lies with his hands half-joined in prayer. The adjacent tomb of Ambrose Dudley is of finely carved and painted alabaster, as is that of Robert Dudley – who founded the Lord Leycester Hospital – and his wife.

ARRIVAL AND INFORMATION   WARWICK AND AROUND

By train Warwick station is on the northern edge of town, a 15min walk from the centre via Station and Coventry roads.

Destinations Birmingham Snow Hill or Birmingham Moor St (every 30min; 30min); Stratford-upon-Avon (every 2hr; 30min).

By bus The bus station is on Market St, yards from Market Place in the town centre.

Tourist office The old Courthouse, on the corner of Castle St and Jury St (Mon–Fri 9.30am–4.30pm, Sat 10am–4.30pm; ☎ 01926 492212, ⓦ visitwarwick.co.uk).

8

Catalan 6 Jury St, CV34 4EW ☎01926 498930, ⍵catalantapas.co.uk. This inviting café/restaurant has a wide-ranging, Mediterranean-inspired menu, but the tasty tapas are its speciality – try, for example, the sardines or the white beans, shallots and leeks in a tomato sauce. Tapas average around £7, a la carte mains £14, less at lunch times. Mon–Sat noon–2.30pm & 6–9.30pm.

Rose and Crown 30 Market Place, CV34 4SH ☎01926 411117, ⍵roseandcrownwarwick.co.uk. This centrally located, independently owned place offers thirteen attractive, competitively priced guest rooms, all en suite, five above the pub and eight just across the street. Each is decorated in a bright and breezy contemporary style. The first-rate pub/restaurant offers a lively, creative menu from breakfast through to dinner. Try, for example, the Cornish lamb with green bean and caper beurre noisette. A prime selection of guest beers and house wines, too. Mains average £16. Mon–Sat 7am–11pm, Sun 8am–10.30pm. **£90**

Worcester and around

In geographical terms, **Worcestershire** can be compared to a huge saucer, with the low-lying plains of the Severn Valley and the Vale of Evesham, Britain's foremost fruit-growing area, rising to a lip of hills, principally the Malverns in the west and the Cotswolds (see page 251) to the south. In character, the county divides into two broad belts. To the north lie the industrial and overspill towns that have much in common with the Birmingham conurbation, while the south is predominantly rural. Bang at the heart of the county is **WORCESTER**, an amenable county town, where a liberal helping of half-timbered Tudor and handsome Georgian buildings stand cheek by jowl with some fairly charmless modern developments. The biggest influence on the city has always been the **River Severn**, which flows along Worcester's west flank. It was the river that made the city an important settlement as early as Saxon times, though its propensity to breach its banks has prompted the construction of a battery of defences which tumble down the slope from the mighty bulk of the **cathedral**, easily the town's star turn. Worcester's centre is small and compact, with all the key sights and best restaurants clustered around the cathedral.

Worcester Cathedral

College Yard, WR1 2LA • Daily 7.30am–6pm • Free • ☎01905 732900, ⍵worcestercathedral.co.uk

Towering above the River Severn, the soaring sandstone of **Worcester Cathedral** comprises a rich stew of architectural styles dating from 1084. The bulk of the church is medieval, from the Norman transepts through to the late Gothic cloister, though the Victorians did have a good old hack at the exterior. Inside, the highlight is the thirteenth-century **choir**, a beautiful illustration of the Early English style, with a forest of slender pillars rising above the intricately worked choir stalls. Here also, in front of the high altar, is the **table-tomb** of England's most reviled monarch, **King John** (1167–1216), who certainly would not have appreciated the lion that lies at his feet biting the end of his sword – a reference to the curbing of his power by the barons when they obliged him to sign the Magna Carta. Just beyond the tomb – on the right – is **Prince Arthur's Chantry**, a delicate lacy confection of carved stonework erected in 1504 to commemorate Arthur, King Henry VII's son, who died at the age of 15. He was on his honeymoon with Catherine of Aragon, who was soon passed on – with such momentous consequences – to his younger brother, the future Henry VIII. A doorway on the south side of the nave leads to the **cloisters**, with their delightful roof bosses, and the circular, largely Norman **chapter house**.

Museum of Royal Worcester

Severn St, WR1 2ND • Mon–Sat: March–Oct 10am–5pm; Nov–Feb 10am–4pm • £6 • ☎01905 21247, ⍵museumofroyalworcester.org

There was a time when Severn Street, tucked away just south of the cathedral, hummed with the activity of one of England's largest porcelain factories, **Royal Worcester**. Those days ended when the company hit the skids and was finally rolled up in 2008 after more than one hundred and fifty years in production. Much of the old factory complex has been turned into apartments, but the **Museum of Royal Worcester** has survived, and exhibits a comprehensive collection of the ornate porcelain for which Royal Worcester was famous.

The Commandery

Sidbury, WR1 2HU • Feb–Dec Tues–Sat 10am–5pm, Sun 1.30–5pm • £5.50 • ☎ 01905 361 821, ⓦ www.worcestershire.gov.uk/museums

In Worcester's oldest building, a rambling, half-timbered structure from the early sixteenth century, the **Commandery**, beside the busy Sidbury dual carriageway, holds several displays tracing the history of the building and its assorted occupants. **King Charles II** used it as his headquarters during the Battle of Worcester in 1651, the endgame of his unsuccessful attempt to regain the throne from Cromwell and the Parliamentarians, who had executed his father in 1649. The high point of the interior is the medieval **painted chamber**, whose walls are covered with intriguing cameos recalling the building's original use as a monastery hospital. Each relates to a saint with healing powers – for example St Thomas Becket, the patron saint for headaches, shown being stabbed in the head by a group of knights.

Greyfriars' House and Garden

Friar St, WR1 2LZ • Mid-Feb to mid-Dec Tues–Sat 11am–4pm • £5.25; NT • ☎ 01905 23571, ⓦ nationaltrust.org.uk/greyfriars-house-and-garden

From the Commandery, it's a short step northwest along Sidbury to narrow Friar Street, whose hotchpotch of half-timbered houses and small, independent shops make it Worcester's prettiest thoroughfare. Among the buildings is **Greyfriars**, a largely fifteenth-century townhouse whose wonky timbers and dark-stained panelling shelter a charming collection of antiques. There's an attractive walled garden here too. From Greyfriars, it's a couple of minutes' walk west to the High Street, a couple more back to the cathedral.

8

ARRIVAL AND INFORMATION
WORCESTER AND AROUND

By train Worcester has two stations. The handiest for the city centre is Foregate St; the cathedral is 800yd south, along Foregate and its continuation The Cross and then High St. The other station, Shrub Hill, is a mile northeast of the cathedral.
Destinations (Foregate St) Birmingham Moor St (every 30min; 1hr); Great Malvern (every 30min; 15min); Hereford (hourly; 50min).

By bus The bus station is behind the sprawling Crowngate shopping centre, about 600yd north of the cathedral.
Destinations Great Malvern (2 hourly; 40min); Hereford (Mon–Sat every 2hr; 1hr 20min).
Tourist office Guildhall, towards the cathedral end of the High St (Mon–Fri 9.30am–5pm, Sat 10am–4pm; ☎ 01905 726311, ⓦ visitworcestershire.org).

ACCOMMODATION

The Cardinal's Hat 31 Friar St, WR1 2NA ☎ 01905 724006, ⓦ the-cardinals-hat.co.uk. In a great central location, this old inn with its mullioned windows and wooden panelling offers a handful of attractive rooms kitted out in lavish retro-meets-period style. Tasty breakfasts too. **£100**
Diglis House Hotel Severn St, WR1 2NF ☎ 01905

353518, ⓦ diglishousehotel.co.uk. Medium-sized hotel in an attractive Georgian villa by the river, about 5min walk south of the cathedral. Some rooms are in the main building, others in the modern annexe, and all are decorated in a pleasant if staid version of country-house style. The hotel's prime feature is the large conservatory overlooking the river. **£110**

EATING AND DRINKING

Mac & Jac's Café 44 Friar St, WR1 2NA ☎ 01905 731331, ⓦ macandjacs.co.uk. With a sister café in Great Malvern (see page 415), this family-run place occupies an old, half-

timbered building near the cathedral. Offers a tasty range of snacks and meals – try, for example, the pollack and salmon fishcake with green beans (£12). Tues–Sat 9am–5pm.

Saffrons Bistro 15 New St, WR1 2DP ☎01905 610505, ⓦsaffronsbistro.co.uk. One of Worcester's best restaurants, this cheerfully decorated little place near Greyfriars is strong on local ingredients – and the proof is in the eating. Try the slow-braised blade of beef with green beans, mushrooms and shallots in a red-wine sauce. Reservations advised in the evening. Mains hover around £15. Mon–Fri noon–2.15pm & 5.30–9.30pm, Sat noon–2.30pm & 5.30–10.30pm.

The Malvern Hills

One of the more prosperous parts of the West Midlands, **The Malverns** is the generic name for a string of towns and villages stretched along the eastern lower slopes of **THE MALVERN HILLS**, which rise spectacularly out of the flatlands a few miles to the southwest of Worcester. About nine miles from north to south and never more than five miles wide, the hills straddle the Worcestershire–Herefordshire boundary. Of ancient granite rock, they are punctuated by over twenty summits, mostly around 1000ft high, and in between lie innumerable dips and hollows. It's easy, if energetic, walking country, with great views, and there's an excellent network of **hiking trails**, most of which can be completed in a day or half-day, with **Great Malvern** being the obvious base.

Great Malvern

Of all the towns in the Malverns, it's **GREAT MALVERN** that grabs the attention, its pocket-sized centre clambering up the hillside with the crags of North Hill beckoning beyond. The grand old houses, which congregate around the top of the main drag, **Church Street**, mostly date from its nineteenth-century heyday as a spa town when the local **spring waters** drew the Victorians here by the trainload. You can still sample the waters at the gushing **Malvhina spring** in the mini-park at the top of Church Street – or venture further afield to the spring at St Ann's Well Café (see below) – but the town's principal sight is its splendid **Priory Church**, yards from the Malvhina spring (Mon–Sat 9am–5pm; free; ⓦgreatmalvernpriory.org.uk). The Benedictines built one of their abbeys here and, although Henry VIII closed the place down in 1538, the church's elaborate decoration and fabulous late medieval **stained-glass windows** proclaim the priory's former wealth.

ARRIVAL AND INFORMATION
GREAT MALVERN

By train From Great Malvern's rustic train station, with its dainty ironwork and quaint chimneys, it's about 800yd to the town centre – take Avenue Rd, which leads to Church St. Destinations Birmingham New St (hourly; 1hr); Hereford (hourly; 35min); Worcester Foregate (every 30min; 15min).

Tourist office At the top of Church St, metres from the Priory Church (daily 10am–5pm; ☎01684 892289, ⓦvisitthemalverns.org).

ACCOMMODATION

Abbey Hotel Abbey Rd, WR14 3ET ☎01684 892332, ⓦsarova-abbeyhotel.com. This is easily the most conspicuous hotel in Great Malvern, a few yards from the Priory Church, much of it occupying a rambling, creeper-

---

HIKING THE MALVERN HILLS

Great Malvern tourist office (see page 414) sells hiking maps and issues half a dozen free **Trail Guide leaflets**, which describe circular routes up to and along the hills that rise behind the town. The shortest trail is just a mile and a half, the longest four. One of the most appealing is the 2.5-mile hoof up to the top of – and back from – **North Hill** (1307ft), from where there are panoramic views over the surrounding countryside. This hike also takes in St Ann's Well Café (times vary; ☎01684 560285, ⓦstannswell.co.uk), a sweet little café in an attractive Georgian building where you can taste the local spring water; the signposted path begins beside the Mount Pleasant Hotel, on Belle Vue Terrace, just to the left (south) of the top of Church Street.

clad Victorian building executed in a sort of neo-Baronial style. It's part of a small chain, and the guest rooms, especially in the hotel's lumpy modern wing, can be a little characterless – but they are comfortable enough and many have attractive views back over town. **£110**

The Cottage in the Wood Holywell Rd, Malvern Wells, WR14 4LG ☎01684 588860, ⓦcottageinthewood.

co.uk. Family-run hotel with a dozen or so cheery, comfortable guest rooms in the main house and a brace of small annexes. The main house is not so much a cottage as a spacious villa built as a dower house to a neighbouring estate in the late 1700s. Wooded grounds surround the hotel and there are fine views. The rooms vary considerably in size and comfort. **£110**

EATING AND DRINKING

Mac & Jac's Café 23 Abbey Rd, WR14 3ES ☎01684 573300, ⓦmacandjacs.co.uk. This bright and cheery café does its level best to source things locally (with the exception of its teas, the house speciality). It offers a particularly good range of salads – for example, beef salad with salsa verde and rocket (£8). Tues–Sat 9am–6.30pm, Sun 10am–3.30pm.

The Morgan 52 Clarence Rd, WR14 3EQ ☎01684 578575, ⓦwyevalleybrewery.co.uk. Just beyond the train station, this is the best pub in town, where you can sample the assorted brews of Herefordshire's much-praised Wye Valley Brewery. Drink outside on the terrace if the sun is out, or inside in the wood-panelled bar. Mon–Wed noon–3pm & 5–11pm, Thurs–Sun noon–11pm.

Herefordshire

Over the Malvern Hills from Worcestershire, the rolling agricultural landscapes of **HEREFORDSHIRE** have an easy-going charm, but the finest scenery hereabouts is along the banks of the **River Wye**, which wriggles and worms its way across the county. Plonked in the middle of Herefordshire on the Wye is the county town, **Hereford**, a sleepy, old-fashioned place whose proudest possession is the cathedral's remarkable medieval map, the **Mappa Mundi**. Beyond Hereford, the southeast corner of the county has one especially attractive town, **Ross-on-Wye**, a genial little place with a picturesque setting that serves as a gateway to one of the wilder portions of the **Wye River Valley**, around **Symonds Yat**, where canoeists gather in their droves.

8

GETTING AROUND
HEREFORDSHIRE

By train Herefordshire has just one rail line, linking Hereford with points north to Shrewsbury and east to Great Malvern and Worcester.

By bus Local buses provide a reasonable service between

the county's villages and towns, except on Sun when there's very little at all. For timetable details, consult ⓦtraveline midlands.co.uk or pop into the nearest tourist office.

Hereford

A low-key county town with a spacious feel, **HEREFORD** was long a border garrison held against the Welsh, its military importance guaranteed by its strategic position beside the River Wye. It also became a religious centre after the Welsh murdered the Saxon king **Ethelbert** near here in 794. Today, with the fortifications that once girdled the city all but vanished, it's the **cathedral** – and its extraordinary medieval **Mappa Mundi** – which forms the focus of interest. The cathedral lies just to the north of the river at the heart of the city centre, whose compact tangle of narrow streets and squares is clumsily boxed in by the ring road. Taken as a whole, Hereford makes for a pleasant overnight stay.

Hereford Cathedral

Cathedral Close, HR1 2NG • Daily 9.15am–5.30pm • Free • ☎ 01432 374200, ⓦ www.herefordcathedral.org • **Mappa Mundi** Mon–Sat: April–Oct 10am–5pm; Nov, Dec, Feb & March 10am–4pm • £6 • ⓦ themappamundi.co.uk

Hereford Cathedral is a curious building, an uncomfortable amalgamation of styles, with bits and pieces added to the eleventh-century church by a string of bishops and culminating in an extensive – and not especially sympathetic – Victorian refit. From the outside, the sandstone **tower** is the dominant feature, constructed in the early fourteenth century to eclipse the Norman western tower, which collapsed under its own weight in 1786. The crashing masonry mauled the **nave** and its replacement lacks some of the grandeur of most other English cathedrals, though the forceful symmetries of the long rank of surviving Norman arches and piers more than hint at what went before. The **north transept** is, however, a flawless exercise in thirteenth-century taste, its soaring windows a classic example of Early English architecture.

The Mappa Mundi

In the 1980s, the cathedral's finances were so parlous that a plan was drawn up to sell its most treasured possession, the **Mappa Mundi**. Luckily, the government and John Paul Getty Jr rode to the rescue, with the oil tycoon stumping up a million pounds to keep the map here and install it in a new building, the New Library, which blends in seamlessly with the older buildings it adjoins at the west end of the cloisters.

The Mappa Mundi exhibit begins with a series of interpretative panels explaining the historical background and composition of the map. Included is a copy in English, which is helpful as the original, displayed in a dimly lit room beyond, is in Latin. Measuring 64 by 52 inches and dating to about 1300, the Mappa provides an extraordinary insight into the medieval mind. It is indeed a map (as we know it) insofar as it suggests the general geography of the world – with Asia at the top and Europe and Africa below – but it also squeezes in history, mythology and theology. In the same building as the Mappa Mundi is the **Chained Library**, a remarkably extensive collection of books and manuscripts dating from the eighth to the eighteenth centuries. A selection is always on display.

8

ARRIVAL AND INFORMATION

By train Hereford train station is about 800yd northeast of the main square, High Town, via Station Approach, Commercial Rd and its continuation Commercial St. Destinations Birmingham New St (hourly; 1hr 30min); Great Malvern (hourly; 30min); Ludlow (every 30min; 30min); Shrewsbury (every 30min; 1hr); Worcester Foregate (hourly; 50min).

By bus The long-distance bus station is on the north side of the town centre, just off Commercial Rd; most local and regional buses stop in the centre on High Town. Destinations Hay-on-Wye (Mon–Sat every 2hr; 1hr); Ross-on-Wye (Mon–Sat hourly; 1hr).

ACCOMMODATION

★**Castle House** Castle St, HR1 2NW ☎01432 356321, ⓦcastlehse.co.uk. Occupying an immaculately refurbished Georgian mansion and a neighbouring townhouse near the cathedral, it's hard to praise this medium-sized hotel too highly: the staff are obliging; the better, bigger rooms are simply delightful, with all sorts of period details; and the breakfast room has a lovely outside terrace. They have two smashing restaurants here too (see below). **£160**

No. 21 21 Aylestone Hill, HR1 1HR ☎01432 279897, ⓦ21aylestonehill.co.uk. In a substantial, half-timbered Edwardian house just northeast of the centre, this comfortable B&B has five, en-suite rooms decorated in soothing shades and complete with period flourishes. It's within easy walking distance of the centre, near the train station. **£70**

EATING AND DRINKING

The Barrels 69 St Owen St, HR1 2JQ ☎01432 274968, ⓦwyevalleybrewery.co.uk. A popular local just 5min southeast of High Town, *The Barrels* is the home pub of the local Wye Valley Brewery, whose trademark bitters are much acclaimed. Mon–Thurs 11am–11.30pm, Fri & Sat 11am–midnight, Sun noon–11.30pm.

Cafe@allsaints All Saints Church, High St, HR4 9AA ☎01432 370415, ⓦcafeatallsaints.co.uk. Near the cathedral, in the old church at the top of Broad St, this excellent café has become something of a local institution since it was founded in the late 1990s. Serves a range of well-conceived and tasty dishes – ricotta pie with salad leaves for instance – at around £7. Mon–Sat 8am–4pm.

★**Castle House** Castle St, HR1 2NW ☎01432 356321, ⓦcastlehse.co.uk. This superb hotel (see above) has two first-rate restaurants – one formal, the other casual. Both emphasize local ingredients, with Gloucestershire pork and Hereford beef being prime examples. Prices are reasonable too, with mains from £10. Mon–Sat noon–2pm & 6.30–9.30pm, Sun noon–2pm & 6.30–9pm.

Ross-on-Wye

Nestling above a loop in the river fifteen miles southeast of Hereford, **ROSS-ON-WYE** is a relaxed and easy-going market town with an artsy/New Age undertow. Ross's jumble of narrow streets converges on **Market Place**, shadowed by the seventeenth-century **Market House**, a two-storey sandstone structure sporting a bust of a bewigged Charles II. Veer right at the top of Market Place, then turn left up Church Street to reach Ross's other noteworthy building, the mostly thirteenth-century **St Mary's Church**, whose sturdy stonework culminates in a slender, tapering spire. In front of the church, at the foot of the graveyard, is a plain but rare **Plague Cross**, commemorating the three hundred or so townsfolk who were buried here by night during a savage plague outbreak in 1637.

ARRIVAL AND DEPARTURE   ROSS-ON-WYE

By bus Ross bus station is on Cantilupe Rd, a 4min-walk from Market Place.

Destinations Goodrich (Mon–Sat every 2hr; 20min); Hereford (Mon–Sat hourly; 1hr).

ACCOMMODATION AND EATING

★ **Linden Guest House** 14 Church St, HR9 5HN ☎ 01989 565373, ⓦ lindenguesthouse.com. In a fetching Georgian building opposite St Mary's Church, this B&B has three en-suite rooms, all cosily decorated. The cooked breakfasts are delicious too – both traditional and vegetarian. **£75**

Old Court House B&B 53 High St, HR9 5HH ☎ 01989 762275, ⓦ theoldcourthousebandb.co.uk. Unusual B&B in a rabbit warren of an old stone building, complete with open fires and exposed wooden beams. Has four en-suite rooms of varying sizes. Handily located in the centre of the town. **£80**

Pots and Pieces Teashop 40 High St, HR9 5HD ☎ 01989 566123, ⓦ potsandpieces.com. This appealing little café and gift shop behind the Market House sells a tasty range of snacks and light meals. The toasted teacakes are the best for miles around. Mon–Fri 9am–4.30pm, Sat 10am–4.30pm, plus June–Aug Sun 11am–3.30pm.

Yaks N Yetis 1 Brookend St, HR9 7EG ☎ 01989 564963. Not the prettiest of restaurants perhaps, but this is genuine Nepalese (Gurkha) cuisine – and the staff are more than willing to help explain its intricacies. It's delicious and, with mains from around £9, economically priced too. Tues–Sun noon–2.30pm & 6–11pm.

The Wye River Valley

Travelling south from Ross along the B4234, it's just five miles to the gaunt sandstone mass of **Goodrich Castle** (April–Oct daily 10am–5pm; Nov–March restricted hours; £7.60, EH; ⓦ www.english-heritage.org.uk/visit/places/goodrich-castle), which commands wide views over the hills and woods of the **Wye River Valley**. The castle's strategic location guaranteed its importance from the twelfth century onwards and today the substantial ruins incorporate a Norman keep, a maze of later rooms and passageways and walkable ramparts. The castle stands next to the tiny village of **GOODRICH**, from where it's around a mile and a half southeast along narrow country lanes to the solitary *YHA Wye Valley Hostel* (see below), with the **Wye Valley Walk** running past the front door.

From Goodrich, it's a couple of miles southwest along narrow lanes to a signed fork in the road – go straight on for the wriggly road up to the top of **Symonds Yat Rock**, one of the region's most celebrated viewpoints, rising high above a wooded loop in the River Wye. Down below is **SYMONDS YAT EAST** (which you reach if you veer right at the fork in the road), a pretty hamlet straggling along the east bank of the river. It's a popular spot and one that offers canoe rental and **river trips** (40min). The road to the village is a dead end, so you have to double back to regain Goodrich, though you can cross the river to **Symonds Yat West** on a hand-pulled rope **ferry**, which leaves from outside the *Saracens Head Inn*.

ACCOMMODATION AND EATING   THE WYE RIVER VALLEY

Saracens Head Inn Symonds Yat East, HR9 6JL ☎ 01600 890345, ⓦ saracensheadinn.co.uk. There are twelve en-suite rooms in this hotel by the River Wye, each

decorated in pleasant modern style with wooden floors and pastel walls. You can eat well in both the restaurant and the bar, with the menu featuring mostly English favourites. Mains average £14. Kitchen daily noon–2.30pm & 6.30–9pm. **£95**

YHA Wye Valley Hostel Near Goodrich, HR9 6JJ ☎ 0345 371 9666, ⓦ yha.org.uk/hostel/wye-valley. If you're after a remote location, this is the hostel to head for – in a Victorian rectory in its own grounds above the River Wye. There are eighty-odd beds here, in anything from two-bedded private rooms to ten-bed dorms, as well as camping and self-catering facilities. Advance booking is essential as the hostel is sometimes rented by groups. Evening meals on request. Open March to Oct. Camping/person **£13**, dorms **£15**, doubles **£40**

Shropshire

One of England's largest and least populated counties, **SHROPSHIRE** stretches from its long and winding border with Wales to the edge of the urban Black Country. The Industrial Revolution made a huge stride forward here, with the spanning of the River Severn by the very first iron bridge and, although the assorted industries that then squeezed into the **Ironbridge Gorge** are long gone, a series of museums celebrates their craftsmanship. Further west, the River Severn also flows through the county town of **Shrewsbury**, whose centre holds dozens of old half-timbered buildings, though **Ludlow**, further south, has the edge when it comes to handsome Tudor and Jacobean architecture. In between the two lie some of the most beautiful parts of Shropshire, primarily the **Long Mynd**, a hiking area that's readily explored from the attractive town of **Church Stretton**.

GETTING AROUND AND INFORMATION   SHROPSHIRE

By train There are frequent trains from Birmingham to Telford (for Ironbridge Gorge) and Shrewsbury, which is also linked to Church Stretton and Ludlow on the Hereford line.

By bus Services are patchy, but one small step forward has been the creation of the Shropshire Hills Shuttle service (mid-April to Sept Sat & Sun; every 1–2hr; ⓦ shropshirehillsaonb.co.uk) aimed at the tourist market. The shuttle noses round the Long Mynd as well as the Stiperstones and drops by Church Stretton. An adult Day Rover ticket, valid on the whole route and available from the driver, costs just £8. Timetables are available at most tourist offices and on the website.

Website ⓦ shropshiretourism.co.uk.

Ironbridge Gorge

IRONBRIDGE GORGE, the collective title for a cluster of small villages huddled in the Severn Valley to the south of new-town Telford, was the crucible of the Industrial Revolution, a process encapsulated by its famous span across the Severn – the world's first **iron bridge**, engineered by **Abraham Darby** and opened on New Year's Day, 1781. Darby was the third innovative industrialist of that name – the first Abraham Darby started iron-smelting here back in 1709 and the second invented the forging process that made it possible to produce massive iron beams. Under the guidance of such creative figures as the Darbys and Thomas Telford, the area's factories once churned out engines, rails, wheels and other heavy-duty iron pieces in quantities unmatched anywhere else in the world. Manufacturing has now all but vanished, but the surviving monuments make the Gorge the most extensive **industrial heritage site** in England – and one that has been granted UNESCO World Heritage Site status.

Ironbridge village

There must have been an awful lot of nail-biting during the construction of the **Iron Bridge** over the River Severn in the late 1770s. No one was quite sure how the new material would wear and although the single-span design looked sound, many feared that the bridge would simply tumble into the river. To compensate, Abraham Darby used more iron than was strictly necessary, but the end result still manages to appear stunningly graceful, arching between the steep banks with the river far below. The settlement at the north end of the span was promptly renamed **IRONBRIDGE**, and today its brown-brick houses climb prettily up the hill from the bridge.

8

Museum of the Gorge

Wharfage, TF8 7DQ · Daily 10am–4pm · £4.50, but covered by Passport Ticket (see page 421) · ☎ 01952 433424, ⓦ www.ironbridge.
org.uk/museum-of-the-gorge

Ironbridge village is also home to the **Museum of the Gorge**, in a church-like, neo-Gothic riverside warehouse about seven hundred yards west of the bridge along the main road. This provides an introduction to the Gorge's industrial history and gives a few environmental pointers too; it also houses the main visitor centre (see page 421).

Coalbrookdale Museum of Iron

Coach Rd, Coalbrookdale, TF8 7DQ · Daily 10am–4pm · £8.85, but covered by Passport Ticket (see page 421) · ☎ 01952 433424,
ⓦ www.ironbridge.org.uk/coalbrookdale-museum-of-iron

At the roundabout just west of the Museum of the Gorge, turn right for the half-mile trip to what was once the Gorge's big industrial deal, the **Coalbrookdale iron foundry**, which boomed in the eighteenth and early nineteenth centuries, employing up to four thousand. The foundry has been imaginatively converted into the **Museum of Iron**, with displays on iron-making in general and the history of the company in particular. There are superb examples of Victorian and Edwardian ironwork, including the intricate castings – stags, dogs and even camels – that became the house speciality. Also in the complex, across from the foundry beneath a protective canopy, are the ruins of the **furnace** where Abraham Darby pioneered the use of coke as a smelting fuel in place of charcoal.

Bedlam Furnace

TF8 7QY, about 600yd east of Ironbridge village on the B4373 · Open access · Free · ⓦ www.ironbridge.org.uk/bedlam-furnace

Heading east from the bridge along the north bank of the river, you soon pass the battered brick-and-stone remains of the **Bedlam furnace**, one of the first furnaces to use coke rather than charcoal. It was kept alight around the clock, and at night its fiery silhouette was said to have scared passers-by out of their wits – hence the name.

Blists Hill Victorian Town

Coalport Rd, TF7 5DU, about half a mile north of the River Severn – take the signed turning between the Bedlam Furnace and Coalport · Daily 10am–4.30pm · £16.25, but covered by Passport Ticket (see page 421) · ☎ 01952 433424, ⓦ www.ironbridge.org.
uk/blists-hill-victorian-town

The rambling **Blists Hill Victorian Town** is the Gorge's most popular attraction, enclosing a number of reconstructed Victorian buildings, most notably a school, a candle-maker's, a doctor's surgery, a pub and wrought-iron works. Jam-packed on most summer days, it's especially popular with school parties, who keep the period-dressed employees busy.

Tar Tunnel

Coalport High St, Coalport, TF8 7HT · On the north bank of the river, 500yd east of the turning to Blists Hill & on the west edge of Coalport · Daily 11am–3pm · £3.40, but covered by Passport Ticket (see page 421) · ☎ 01952 433424, ⓦ www.ironbridge.org.uk/tar-tunnel

Built to transport coal from one part of the Gorge to another, but named for the bitumen that oozes naturally from its walls, the **Tar Tunnel** may not be long, but it's certainly more than a tad spooky and you'll be issued with a hard hat for reassurance.

Coalport China Museum

Coalport High St, Coalport, TF8 7HT · Daily 10am–4pm · £8.85, but covered by Passport Ticket (see page 421) · ☎ 01952 433424,
ⓦ ironbridge.org.uk/coalport-china-museum

The most easterly of the industrial sites on the north bank of the River Severn, the former **Coalport China works** occupies a sprawling brick complex, which incorporates the **Coalport China Museum**, packed with gaudy Coalport wares. There's also a workshop, where potters demonstrate their skills, and two **bottle kilns**, those distinctive conical structures that were long the hallmark of the pottery industry.

Jackfield

From the north bank of the Severn, take the Jackfield Bridge just east of Bedlam Furnace or the footbridge beside the Tar Tunnel

Now a sleepy little village of pretty brown-brick cottages that string along the south bank of the River Severn, **JACKFIELD** was once a sooty, grimy place that hummed to the tune of two large tile factories, Maws and Craven Dunnill. Both were built in the middle of the nineteenth century to the latest industrial design, a manufacturing system that produced literally thousands of tiles at breakneck speed. The more easterly of the two is now the **Maws Craft Centre** (w mawscraftcentre.co.uk), which holds more than twenty arts, craft and specialist shops; the other, about half a mile west, boasts the Jackfield Tile Museum.

Jackfield Tile Museum

Salthouse Rd, TF8 7LJ · Daily 10am–4pm · £8.85, but covered by Passport Ticket (see below) · ☎ 01952 433424, w www.ironbridge.org. uk/jackfield-tile-museum

A small part of the expansive Craven Dunnill factory still produces Craven Dunnill tiles (w cravendunnill-jackfield.co.uk), but mostly it's home to the outstanding **Jackfield Tile Museum**. The exhibits here include the superb "Style Gallery" and "Tiles Everywhere Galleries", where room after room illustrates many different types of tile, by style – Art Deco and Art Nouveau through to Arts and Crafts and the Aesthetic Movement – and location, from a London underground station to a butcher's shop.

ARRIVAL AND DEPARTURE

IRONBRIDGE GORGE

By bus Arriva bus #96 (w arrivabus.co.uk) connects both Shrewsbury and Telford bus stations with Ironbridge village (Mon–Sat every 2hr; 40min/15min). There's also an Arriva bus service to Much Wenlock (Mon–Sat every 2hr; 30min).

GETTING AROUND AND INFORMATION

By bus Bus services are limited to Gorge Connect (late July to mid-Sept Sat & Sun 10am–5pm; every 30min; w telford. gov.uk), which links Coalbrookdale in the west with Coalport in the east, via Ironbridge village and Blists Hill.

Tourist information Ironbridge Gorge tourist information (daily 10am–4pm; ☎ 01952 433424, w ironbridge. org.uk) is in the Museum of the Gorge (see page 420). In addition to local maps and information, they sell the Passport Ticket.

Admissions and passes Each museum and attraction charges its own admission fee, but if you're intending to visit several, then buy a Passport Ticket (£25), which allows access to all ten as many times as you want for year. Available at all the main sights, and through tourist information. Does not cover parking, but charges are reasonable.

ACCOMMODATION

Buckatree Hall Hotel The Wrekin, Telford, TF6 5AL ☎ 01952 641821, w buckatreehallhotel.com. In a pleasant rural setting near the wooded slopes of The Wrekin, the distinctive 1334ft peak that rises high above its surroundings, the *Buckatree* comprises the original Edwardian house and a modern wing. Most of the rooms have balconies. Just south of the M54 and Wellington. **£65**

Coalbrookdale Villa Guesthouse 17 Paradise, Coalbrookdale, TF8 7NR ☎ 01952 433450, w www. coalbrookdalevilla.co.uk. This B&B occupies an attractive Victorian ironmaster's house set in its own grounds about half a mile up the hill from Ironbridge village in the tiny hamlet of Paradise. Rooms are sedately decorated, country-house-style, and en suite. **£75**

The Library House 11 Severn Bank, Ironbridge village, TF8 7AN ☎ 01952 432299, w libraryhouse.com. Enjoyable B&B, the village's best, in a charming Georgian villa yards from the Iron Bridge. Three doubles, decorated in a modern rendition of period style. **£100**

YHA Ironbridge Coalport High St, Coalport, TF8 7HT ☎ 0345 371 9325, w yha.org.uk/hostel/ironbridge-coalport. At the east end of the Gorge in the former Coalport China factory, this YHA hostel has around eighty beds in two- to six-bedded rooms (doubles all en suite), plus a shop and a café. Popular with school groups and for activity breaks. Dorms **£16**, doubles **£40**

EATING

Coalbrookdale Inn 12 Wellington Rd, Coalbrookdale, TF8 7DX ☎ 01952 432166, w facebook.com/Coalbrookdale Inn. On the main road across from the Coalbrookdale iron foundry, this traditional pub offers a top-notch selection of real ales plus filling pub grub. Mon–Thurs noon–2pm & 5–11.30pm, Fri–Sun noon–11.30pm.

8

Restaurant Severn 33 High St, Ironbridge village, TF8 7AG ☎01952 432233, ⊚restaurantsevern.co.uk. This smart little place, just yards from the bridge, has an inventive menu with mains such as venison in a cognac and cranberry sauce. In the evening, a two-course set meal is around £28. Wed–Sat noon–4.30pm & 6–10.30pm, Sun noon–6pm.

Shrewsbury

SHREWSBURY, the county town of Shropshire, sits in a tight and narrow loop of the River Severn. It would be difficult to design a better defensive site and predictably the Normans built a stone castle here, one which Edward I decided to strengthen and expand in the thirteenth century. In Georgian times, Shrewsbury became a fashionable staging post on the busy London to Holyhead/Ireland route and it's since evolved into a laidback, middling market town. It's the overall feel of the place that is its main appeal, rather than any specific sight, though to celebrate its associations with **Charles Darwin**, who was born here, the town is now in possession of a 40ft-high, concertina-like sculpture entitled **Quantum Leap**: it cost nigh-on half a million pounds, so many locals may well be rueing the cost rather than celebrating the artistic vision.

The obvious place to start an exploration of Shrewsbury is the 1840s **train station**, built in a fetching neo-Baronial-meets-country-house style. Looming overhead are the ramparts of the **castle**, a pale reminder of the mighty medieval fortress that once dominated the town – the illustrious Thomas Telford turned it into the private home of a local bigwig in the 1780s. **Castle Gates** and its continuation **Castle Street/Pride Hill** cuts up from the station into the heart of the river loop where the medieval town took root. Here, on St Mary's Place, you'll find Shrewsbury's most interesting church, **St Mary's** (no set opening hours), whose architecturally jumbled interior is redeemed by a magnificent east window. From St Mary's, it's only a few steps to **St Alkmund's Church**, with its charming view of the fine old buildings of **Fish Street**, which cuts its way down to the High Street. Near here is **The Square**, which stands at the very heart of town, its narrow confines inhabited by the **Old Market Hall**, a heavy-duty stone structure from 1596.

From The Square, High Street snakes down the hill to become **Wyle Cop**, lined with higgledy-piggledy ancient buildings and leading to the **English Bridge**, which sweeps across the Severn in grand Georgian style to the stumpy red-stone mass of the **Abbey Church**, on Abbey Foregate (daily: April–Oct 10am–4pm, Nov–March 10.30pm–3pm; free; ⊚shrewsburyabbey.com). This is all that remains of the Benedictine abbey that was a major political and religious force hereabouts until the Dissolution.

ARRIVAL AND INFORMATION
SHREWSBURY

By train The station is on the northeast edge of the centre. Destinations Birmingham (every 30min; 1hr); Church Stretton (hourly; 15min); Hereford (every 30min; 1hr); Ludlow (hourly; 30min); Telford (every 30min; 20min).
By bus Most buses pull into the Raven Meadows bus station, off Smithfield Rd, on the north side of the centre.

Destinations Ironbridge village (Mon–Sat every 2hr; 40min); Much Wenlock (Mon–Sat hourly; 30min); Telford (Mon–Sat every 2hr; 55min).
Tourist office In The Square (Mon–Sat 10am–4pm; ☎01743 258888, ⊚shropshiretourism.co.uk); shares premises with the Shrewsbury Museum & Art Gallery.

ACCOMMODATION

★ **Lion and Pheasant** 50 Wyle Cop, SY1 1XJ ☎01743 770345, ⊚lionandpheasant.co.uk. Excellent, medium-sized, town-centre hotel in the shell of a former coaching inn; rooms are in pastel shades with lots of period details. Delicious breakfasts too. **£120**
Prince Rupert Hotel Butcher Row, off Pride Hill, SY1

1UQ ☎01743 499955, ⊚princeruperthotel.co.uk. A smart and popular hotel, the *Rupert* occupies a cannily converted old building in the middle of the town centre. There are seventy comfortable guest rooms – including twelve suites – and the pick have a platoon of period details like wood panelling and exposed wooden beams. **£130**

EATING AND DRINKING

Admiral Benbow 24 Swan Hill, SY1 1NF ☎01743 244423. Popular and enterprising town-centre pub with a beer garden and a fine selection of real ales, Hereford farmhouse ciders and perry. Mon–Fri 5–11pm, Sat noon–

11pm & Sun 7–10.30pm.

Golden Cross 14 Princess St, SY1 1LP ☎01743 362507, ⊚goldencrosshotel.co.uk. This must be the best restaurant in Shrewsbury, a cosy, intimate spot (don't be deterred by the mullioned windows) with a select international menu – try, for example, the pan-roasted, crusted fillet of sea bass. In the city centre, a 2min walk from

The Square. Mains average a very reasonable £14. Tues–Sat noon–2.30pm & 5.30–9.30pm, Sun noon–2.30pm.

Good Life Coffee Shop & Restaurant Barracks Passage, SY1 1XA ☎01743 350455. Something of a local institution, this excellent café specializes in salads and vegetarian dishes from a daily menu. Locals swear by the quiches. Mains around £8. Mon–Sat 9am–4pm.

Long Mynd

Beginning about nine miles south of Shrewsbury, the upland heaths of the **Long Mynd**, some eight miles long and between two and four miles wide, run parallel to and just to the west of the A49. This is prime **walking** territory and the heathlands are latticed with footpaths, the pick of which offer sweeping views over the border to the Black Mountains of Wales. Also popular with hikers, and even more remote, are the **Stiperstones**, a clot of boggy heather dotted with ancient cairns and earthworks lying to the west of the Long Mynd.

Church Stretton

Nestled at the foot of the Mynd is **CHURCH STRETTON**, a tidy little village that makes an ideal base for hiking the area. The village also possesses the dinky parish **church of St Laurence**, parts of which – especially the nave and transepts – are Norman. Look out also for the (badly weathered) fertility symbol over the side door, just to the left of the entrance – it's a genital-splaying **sheela-na-gig**, whose sheer explicitness is eye-watering.

8

ARRIVAL AND INFORMATION

CHURCH STRETTON

By train The train station is beside the A49 about 600yd east of High St, which forms the heart of the village. Destinations Hereford (every 1hr–1hr 30min; 40min); Ludlow (every 1hr–1hr 30min; 15min); Shrewsbury (hourly; 15min).

By bus Most buses pull in beside the train station, but some also continue on to High St. There's also a useful Shropshire Hills Shuttle bus service (see page 419).

Tourist office The library, Church St (Mon–Sat 9.30am–1pm & 2–5pm; ☎01694 723133, ⊚churchstretton.co.uk).

ACCOMMODATION AND EATING

★ **Berry's Coffee House** 17 High St, SY6 6BU ☎01694 724452, ⊚berryscoffeehouse.co.uk. The dinkiest of cafés, squeezed into antique premises in the centre of the village. They serve delicious snacks and light meals, but the salads (around £9) are especially tasty – locally smoked salmon with *Berry's* dill sauce salad, for example. Daily 9am–5pm.

★ **Victoria House** 48 High St, SY6 6BX ☎01694 723823, ⊚victoriahouse-shropshire.co.uk. An extra-ordinarily cosy little place, the most central of several excellent B&Bs. The six guest rooms – all kitted out with heavy curtains, thick carpets and iron beds – are above

the owner's teashop, *Jemima's Kitchen*, which serves delicious home-made food including specialist teas and mouth-watering scones. Breakfast, as you would expect, is delicious. Wed–Sun 9.30am–4pm. £85

YHA Bridges Ratlinghope, SY5 0SP, 5 miles west of Church Stretton ☎01588 650656, ⊚yha.org.uk/hostel/bridges. On the edge of a tiny village, this hostel occupies a converted village school, has 38 beds in four- to eight-bedded rooms, a café, camping and a self-catering kitchen. It's an ideal base for hiking to the Long Mynd or the Stiperstones. Camping/person £8, dorms £19

Ludlow

Perched on a hill in a loop of the River Teme, **LUDLOW**, thirty miles from Shrewsbury, is one of the most picturesque towns in the West Midlands – a gaggle of beautifully preserved Georgian and black-and-white half-timbered buildings packed around a craggy stone castle, with rural Shropshire forming a drowsy backdrop. These are strong recommendations in themselves, but Ludlow earns bonus points by being something of a gastronomic hidey-hole with a clutch of outstanding **restaurants**, whose chefs gather at the much-vaunted **Ludlow Food Festival** (ⓦ foodfestival.co.uk), held over three days every September. The other notable knees-up is the **Ludlow Fringe Festival** (ⓦ ludlowfringe.co.uk), two weeks of music, art and theatre held in late June.

Ludlow Castle

Castle Square, SY8 1AY • Jan to mid-Feb Sat & Sun 10am–4pm; mid-Feb to March & Oct–Dec daily 10am–4pm; April–July & Sept daily 10am–5pm; Aug daily 10am–6pm • £5 • ☎ 01584 873355, ⓦ ludlowcastle.com

Ludlow's large and imposing **castle** dates mostly from Norman times, its rambling ruins incorporating towers and turrets, gatehouses and concentric walls as well as the remains of the 110ft Norman **keep** and an unusual **Round Chapel** built in 1120. With its spectacular setting high above the river, it also offers grand views over the surrounding countryside.

Castle Square and around

The castle entrance abuts **Castle Square**, an airy rectangle whose eastern side breaks into several narrow lanes; the one on the left leads to the gracefully proportioned **Church of St Laurence** (ⓦ stlaurences.org.uk), its interior distinguished by its stained-glass windows and exquisite misericords in the choir. From the church, it's a few paces to the **Butter Cross**, a Neoclassical extravagance from 1744, and a few more to the **Bull Ring**, home of the **Feathers Hotel**, a fine Jacobean building with the fanciest wooden facade imaginable.

Broad Street

South of Castle Square, the gridiron of streets laid out by the Normans has survived intact, though most of the buildings date from the eighteenth century. Steep **Broad Street** is particularly attractive, flanked by many of Ludlow's five hundred half-timbered Tudor and red-brick Georgian listed buildings. At the foot of the street is Ludlow's only surviving **medieval gate**, which was turned into a house in the eighteenth century.

ARRIVAL AND INFORMATION LUDLOW

By train Ludlow station is a 15min walk from the castle via Station Drive and Corve St – just follow the signs.
Destinations Church Stretton (hourly; 20min); Hereford (every 30min; 30min); Shrewsbury (hourly; 30min).
By bus Most long-distance buses pull in on Corve St, just north of its junction with Station Drive.
Destinations Church Stretton (Mon–Sat hourly; 30min); Shrewsbury (Mon–Sat hourly; 1hr 15min).
Tourist office Castle Square (Mon–Sat 10am–4pm; ☎ 01584 875053, ⓦ ludlow.org.uk).

ACCOMMODATION

Dinham Hall Hotel Dinham, SY8 1EJ ☎ 01584 876464, ⓦ dinhamhall.co.uk. Handily located near the castle, this deluxe, medium-sized hotel, with its thirteen appealing rooms, occupies a rambling, bow-windowed eighteenth-century mansion, which has previously seen service as a boarding house for Ludlow School. **£140**

Ludlow Bed & Breakfast 35 Lower Broad St, ☎ 01584 876912, ⓦ sawdays.co.uk. Near the bridge over the River Teme, a 5–10min walk from the castle, this extremely cosy B&B has just two doubles in a pair of Georgian terrace cottages, which have been carefully knocked into one. Great breakfasts. **£75**

EATING

Bistro 7 7 Corve St, SY8 1DB ☎ 01584 877412, ⓦ bistro7 ofludlow.co.uk. One of Ludlow's best restaurants, featuring a lively, varied menu – from tortillas to fish pie – mostly based on local ingredients. Superb vegetarian options, too. Mains average £19. Reservations advised. Tues–Sat noon–3pm & 6–10pm.

The Fish House 51 Bullring, SY1 1AB ☎ 01584 879790, ⓦ thefishhouseludlow.co.uk. First-class fishmonger's with a few tables where they serve sparkling wine and fresh seafood – anything from smoked mackerel (£5) through to dressed crabs, oysters and prawns. Wed–Sat 9.30am–4pm.

Mortimers 17 Corve St, SY8 1DA ☎ 01584 872325, ⓦ mortimersludlow.co.uk. Top-ranking restaurant with a strong French influence, where a two-course lunch costs a very reasonable £22. Try, for example, the halibut with white beans and crayfish ragout. Reservations essential. Tues–Sat noon–2pm & 6.30–9pm.

Derby

Resurgent **DERBY** may be close to the wilds of the Peak District (see below), but it has more in common with its big-city neighbours, Nottingham and Leicester – except that here the industrial base is thriving, with **Rolls-Royce** leading the charge. Furthermore, recent attempts to spruce up the place have proved particularly successful and there's one especially diverting attraction in the centre too, the **Derby Museum and Art Gallery**. From the gallery, it's the briefest of strolls along Derby's most boho street, **Sadlergate**, to the central **Market Place** and the **cathedral** (daily 8.30am–5.30pm; ⓦderbycathedral. org), the city's most impressive building, whose sturdy medieval tower rises high above its Victorian surroundings. A couple of hours will do to see the sights before you hightail it to the Peak District.

Derby Museum and Art Gallery

The Strand, DE1 1BS • Tues–Sat 10am–5pm, Sun noon–4pm • Free • ☎ 01332 641901, ⓦ derbymuseums.org/locations/museum-art-gallery

Among much else, **Derby Museum and Art Gallery** exhibits a splendid collection of Derby **porcelain**, several hundred pieces tracking through its different phases and styles from the mid-eighteenth century until today. There's also a room devoted to **Bonnie Prince Charlie**, whose march from Scotland to London to seize the crown during the Jacobite Rebellion of 1745 ended here – he turned round and headed back north, a dismal retreat that culminated in the battle of Culloden. The museum's star turn, however, is its collection of the work of **Joseph Wright** (1734–97), a local artist regarded as one of the most talented English painters of his generation. Wright was one of the few artists of his period to find inspiration in technology and his depictions of the scientific world were hugely influential – as in his *The Alchemist Discovering Phosphorus* and *A Philosopher Lecturing on the Orrery*.

ARRIVAL AND INFORMATION

By train The station is a mile southeast of the centre – just follow the signs – but it's a dreary walk, so you may as well take a bus; they leave from by the station every few minutes. Destinations Birmingham New Street (every 30min; 40min); Leicester (every 30min; 30min); London St Pancras (every 30min; 1hr 30min); Nottingham (every 30min; 25min).

By bus The bus station is on Morledge on the east side of the city centre. One useful service beginning here is High Peak

Buses' (ⓦ highpeakbuses.com) TransPeak service across the Peak District via Bakewell and Buxton to Manchester. Destinations Ashbourne (hourly; 40min); Bakewell (hourly; 1hr 20min); Buxton (hourly; 1hr 50min); Manchester (3 daily; 3hr 30min).

Tourist office Derby tourist information centre is in a part of the Assembly Rooms, on Market Place (Mon–Sat 9.30am–8pm; ☎ 01332 643411, ⓦ visitderby.co.uk).

EATING AND DRINKING

Brunswick Inn 1 Railway Terrace, DE1 2RU ☎ 01332 290677, ⓦ brunswickderby.co.uk. In a handsome Georgian terrace just a couple of minutes' walk from the train station, this traditional pub, with its garden and leather banquettes, offers an impressive range of ciders and real ales, some of which are brewed on the premises. Mon–Sat 11am–11pm, Sun noon–10.30pm.

Exeter Arms 47 Sadler Gate, DE1 3NQ ☎ 01332 608619, ⓦ exeterarms.co.uk. Occupying lovely old

premises and complete with a garden terrace, this first-rate gastropub has an excellent range of draft ales and a wide-ranging, top-ranking bar menu – try, for example, the lamb with sumac yoghurt (£7.75). It's on the east side of the city centre, a 5min walk from the Assembly Rooms across the River Derwent. Mon–Fri noon–11.30pm, Sat 11am–midnight & Sun noon–10.30pm; kitchen Mon–Sat noon–9pm, Sun noon–6pm.

The Peak District

In 1951, the hills and dales of the **PEAK DISTRICT**, at the southern tip of the Pennine range, became Britain's **first National Park**. Wedged between Derby, Manchester and Sheffield, it is effectively the back garden for the fifteen million people who live within

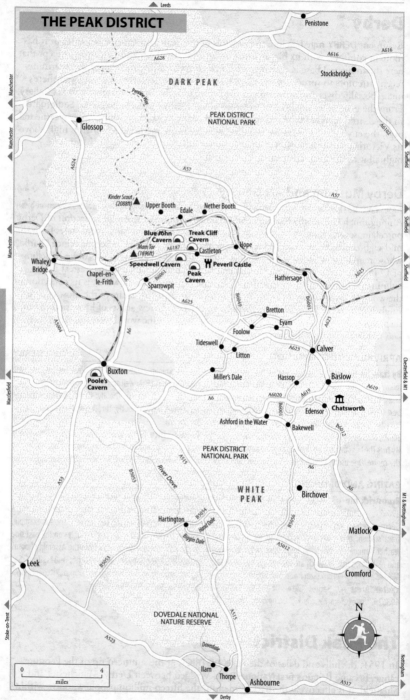

an hour's drive of its boundaries, though somehow it accommodates the huge influx with minimum fuss.

Landscapes in the Peak District come in two forms. The brooding high moorland tops of **Dark Peak**, to the east of Manchester, take their name from the underlying gritstone, known as millstone grit for its former use – a function commemorated in the millstones demarcating the park boundary. Windswept, mist-shrouded and inhospitable, the flat tops of these peaks are nevertheless a firm favourite with walkers on the **Pennine Way**, which meanders north from the tiny village of **Edale** to the Scottish border. Altogether more forgiving, the southern limestone hills of **White Peak** have been eroded into deep forested dales populated by small stone villages and often threaded by walking **trails**, some of which follow former rail routes. The limestone is riddled with complex cave systems around **Castleton** and on the periphery of **Buxton**, a pleasant former spa town lying just outside the park's boundaries. Elsewhere, one of the country's most distinctive manorial piles, **Chatsworth House**, stands near **Bakewell**, a town famed locally not just for its cakes but also for its **well-dressing**, a possibly pagan ritual of thanksgiving for fresh water that takes place in about thirty local villages each summer. The well-dressing season starts in May and continues through to mid-September (get exact dates and details on ⓦwelldressing.com).

As for a **base**, Buxton is perhaps your best bet, though if you're after hiking and cycling you'll probably prefer one of the area's villages – Edale or Castleton will do very nicely.

ARRIVAL AND DEPARTURE THE PEAK DISTRICT

By train Frequent trains run south from Manchester to end-of-the-line Buxton, and Manchester/Sheffield trains stop at Hathersage and Edale.

By bus One especially useful service is High Peak Buses' (ⓦhighpeakbuses.com) TransPeak service, which runs from Derby to Manchester (3 daily), with more frequent buses on parts of the route – Derby to Bakewell (hourly) and Buxton (hourly). There's also a reasonably good daily bus service from Sheffield to Castleton and Hathersage. See ⓦtraveline.info.

GETTING AROUND

By bus Within the Peak District, you'll find that local bus services are reasonably frequent (less so on Sun & in winter). Local tourist offices almost always have bus and train timetables, or see ⓦtraveline.info.

By bike The Peak District has a good network of dedicated cycle lanes and trails, sometimes along former railway lines, and the Peak District National Park Authority (see below) operates three cycle rental outlets: at Ashbourne (☎01335 343156); Derwent, Bamford (☎01433 651261); and Parsley Hay, Buxton (☎01298 84493).

INFORMATION

Visitor centres The Peak District National Park Authority (ⓦpeakdistrict.gov.uk) operates four visitor centres, including those at Bakewell and Castleton; these supplement a platoon of town and village tourist information offices.

Maps and guides A variety of maps and trail guides are widely available at most tourist information centres.

Useful websites ⓦvisitpeakdistrict.com; ⓦpeakdistrict.gov.uk.

ACCOMMODATION

There's a plethora of accommodation in and around the Peak District National Park, mostly **B&Bs** and cottages. There are also numerous **campsites** and half a dozen or so **YHA hostels** as well as a network of YHA-operated **camping barns**. These are located in converted farm buildings and provide simple, inexpensive self-catering facilities. For details, consult ⓦyha.org.uk.

Ashbourne and around

Sitting pretty on the edge of the Peaks thirteen miles northwest of Derby, **ASHBOURNE** is an amiable little town, whose stubby, cobbled **Market Place** is flanked by a happy ensemble of old red-brick buildings. Hikers tramp in and out of town, many wandering the popular **Tissington Trail**, which runs north from near Ashbourne for thirteen miles along an old railway line. Just down the hill from the Market

Place, a suspended **wooden beam** spans St John's Street. Once a common feature of English towns, but now a rarity, these **gallows** were not warnings to malcontents, but advertising hoardings.

Dovedale

Head north on Ashbourne along the A515, then follow the signs. The main car park is on a narrow country road just past the hamlet of Thorpe

The **River Dove** is at its scenic best four miles north of Ashbourne in the stirring two-mile gorge that comprises **Dovedale** – confusingly, other parts of the river are situated in different dales. The **hike** along the gorge is a real pleasure, and easy to boot, the only problem being the bogginess of the valley after rain, but be warned that the place heaves with visitors on summer weekends and bank holidays.

ARRIVAL AND INFORMATION
ASHBOURNE AND AROUND

By bus The bus station is conveniently located on King Edward St, off Dig St, a 3min walk from Market Place. Destinations Buxton (every 2hr; 1hr 20min); Derby (hourly; 40min); Hartington (every 2hr; 40min).

Tourist office Market Place (March–Oct daily 10am–5pm; Nov–Feb Mon–Sat 10.30am–4pm; ☎01335 343666, ⓦ visitpeakdistrict.com).

EATING AND DRINKING

Bennetts 19 St John St, DE6 1GP ☎01335 342982. Independent department store in the centre of Ashbourne with a particularly cosy café, where they do a good line in home-made cakes, scones and sandwiches. Mon–Sat 9.30am–3.30pm.

Bramhalls Deli & Café 22 Market Place, DE6 1ES ☎01335 342631, ⓦbramhallsdeli.co.uk. Pop into this first-rate deli to stock up on local cheeses, hams, terrines, etc. There's a small café too – try the local sausages and Derbyshire oatcakes. Mon–Sat 8am–4.30pm, Sun 9am–4.30pm.

Hartington

Best approached from the east, through Hand Dale's boisterous scenery, **HARTINGTON**, twelve miles north of Ashbourne, is one of the Peaks' prettiest villages, an easy ramble of stone houses zeroing in on a tiny duck pond. It's also within walking distance of the River Dove and some handsome limestone dales, **Biggin Dale** perhaps the pick. The other excitement is cheese – the village has its own specialist **cheese shop** (ⓦhartingtoncheeseshop. co.uk), which offers a raft of local and international cheeses and chutneys.

ARRIVAL AND DEPARTURE
HARTINGTON

By bus Buses stop on Mill Lane in the centre of the village, yards from the duck pond.

Destinations Ashbourne (every 2hr; 40min); Buxton (every 2hr; 40min).

ACCOMMODATION

The Hayloft Church St, SK17 0AW ☎01298 84358, ⓦhartingtonhayloft.co.uk. Perhaps the best of Hartington's B&Bs, in a sympathetically converted barn near the duck pond and part of a working farm. There are just four rooms – each decorated in a straightforward modern style. £80

YHA Hartington Hall Hall Bank, SK17 0AT ☎0345

371 9740, ⓦyha.org.uk/hostel/hartington-hall. Well-equipped hostel whose 130-odd beds – in one- to six-bunk dorms – are squeezed into a seventeenth-century manor house, Hartington Hall, about 300yd from the centre of the village. Facilities include a self-catering kitchen, a café and cycle storage. Dorms £15, doubles £40

Cromford Mills

Mill Lane, Cromford, DE4 3RQ • **Complex** Daily 9am–5pm • Free • **Arkwright Mill & visitor centre** Daily 10.30am–4pm • £5 • ☎01629 823256, ⓦ cromfordmills.org.uk • 15min walk from Cromford train station

Dating from the early 1770s, **Cromford Mills**, in a slender ravine eighteen miles north of Derby, held the world's first water-powered cotton-spinning mill – hence its UNESCO designation. The original mill, built at the instigation of formidable industrialist Sir Richard Arkwright (1732–92), has recently been returned to something like its original appearance and is flanked by several other stone buildings, mostly mills too. Arkwright ran his mill day and night in two twelve-hour shifts, employing mostly women and children – an early example of the industrialistion that was about to sweep the country. The mills closed in the nineteenth century and the complex was long neglected, but the process of restoration is now well under way. Today the original **Arkwright Mill** and attached **visitor centre** include an excellent museum and a peek into the dark and dank mill interior.

Buxton

BUXTON, twelve miles north of Hartington, has had more than its fair share of ups and downs, but with its centre revamped and reconfigured, it is without doubt the most agreeable town in the Peak District, and a perfect base for further explorations. Buxton has a long history as a **spa**, beginning with the Romans, who happened upon a spring from which 1500 gallons of pure water gushed every hour at a constant 28°C. Impressed by the recuperative qualities of the water, the Romans came here by the chariot-load, setting a trend that was to last hundreds of years. The spa's heyday came at the end of the eighteenth century with the **fifth Duke of Devonshire**'s grand design to create a northern answer to Bath or Cheltenham, a plan ultimately thwarted by the climate, but not before some distinguished buildings had been erected. Victorian Buxton may not have had quite the élan of its southern rivals but it still flourished, creating the rows of handsome stone houses that inhabit the town centre today. The town's **thermal baths** were closed in 1972, but Buxton has hung on, not least because of its splendid **festival**, held every July (wbuxtonfestival.co.uk).

8

The Crescent and around

The centrepiece of Buxton's hilly, compact centre is **The Crescent**, a broad sweep of Georgian stonework commissioned by the Duke of Devonshire in 1780 and modelled on the Royal Crescent in Bath. It was cleaned and scrubbed a few years ago, but has lain idle ever since. Facing The Crescent, and also currently empty, is the old **Pump Room**, an attractive Victorian building where visitors once sampled the local waters; next to it is a **water fountain**, supplied by St Ann's Well and still used to fill many a local water bottle. For a better view of The Crescent and the town centre, clamber up **The Slopes**, a narrow slice of park that rises behind the Pump Room, that is dotted with decorative urns. From here, it's impossible to miss the enormous **dome** of what was originally the Duke of Devonshire's stables and riding school, erected in 1789 and now part of Derby University.

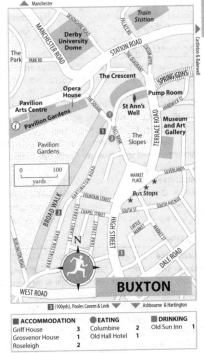

BUXTON

■ ACCOMMODATION		● EATING		■ DRINKING	
Griff House	3	Columbine	2	Old Sun Inn	1
Grosvenor House	1	Old Hall Hotel	1		
Roseleigh	2				

Pavilion Gardens and around

Next to The Crescent, the appealing old stone buildings of **The Square** – though square it isn't – nudge up to the grandly refurbished **Buxton Opera House**, an Edwardian extravagance whose twin towers date from 1903. Stretching back from the Opera House are the **Pavilion Gardens** (Feb–Dec daily 10/10.30am–4/5pm; free), a slender string of connected buildings distinguished by their wrought-iron work and culminating in a large and glassy dome, the **Octagon**, and the **Pavilion Arts Centre**. The adjoining **park** (daily dawn–dusk; free), also known as the Pavilion Gardens and cut across by the River Wye, is especially pleasant, its immaculate lawns and neat borders graced by a bandstand, ponds, dinky little footbridges and fountains.

Poole's Cavern

Green Lane, SK17 9DH • Daily: March–Oct 9.30am–5pm; Nov–Feb 10am–4pm • Tours March–Oct daily every 20min; Nov–Feb Mon–Fri 3 daily, Sat & Sun every 20min; 50min • £9.75 • ☎ 01298 26978, ⓦ poolescavern.co.uk • Half a mile southwest of central Buxton: take the A53 towards Macclesfield/Leek and watch for the sign

The Peaks are riddled with cave systems and half a dozen have become popular tourist attractions rigged up with underground lighting. One of the better examples is **Poole's Cavern**, whose network of caves culminates in a vast chamber dripping with stalactites and stalagmites. Visitors have been popping in for centuries – apparently, Mary, Queen of Scots, dropped by and was suitably impressed.

ARRIVAL AND INFORMATION

BUXTON

By train Buxton train station is on Station Rd, a 4min walk from the town centre, with regular services to Manchester Piccadilly (hourly; 1hr).

By bus Buses stop on Market Place, a 4min walk from the Opera House.

Destinations Ashbourne (every 2hr; 1hr 20min); Bakewell (hourly; 30min); Castleton (1 daily; 50min); Derby (hourly; 1hr 40min); Hartington (every 2hr; 40min).

Tourist office Pavilion Gardens, behind the Opera House (daily: Feb & March 11am–4pm; April–June & Sept 10.30am–5pm; July & Aug 10am–5pm; Oct & Nov 10.30am–4pm; ☎ 01298 25106, ⓦ visitbuxton.co.uk).

ACCOMMODATION

Buxton's centre is liberally sprinkled with **B&Bs** and finding somewhere to stay is rarely a problem, except during the Buxton Festival, when advance reservations are essential.

Griff House 2 Compton Rd, SK17 9DN ☎ 01298 23628, ⓦ griffhousebuxton.co.uk; map p.429. Cosy B&B in a sympathetically updated Victorian house with a handful of well-appointed, en-suite rooms. Local produce is served up at breakfast. A 5min walk south of the centre. **£85**

★ **Grosvenor House** 1 Broad Walk, SK17 6JE ☎ 01298 72439, ⓦ grosvenorbuxton.co.uk; map p.429. There are eight unfussy, en-suite guest rooms in this attractive B&B, which is located in a handsome Victorian townhouse.

The best rooms offer gentle views over the gardens. Delicious home-made breakfasts, too. **£75**

Roseleigh 19 Broad Walk, SK17 6JR ☎ 01298 24904, ⓦ roseleighhotel.co.uk; map p.429. This classic, three-storey gritstone Victorian townhouse, overlooking Pavilion Gardens, is an excellent place to stay. The trim public rooms are decorated in attractive Victorian style, and the en-suite bedrooms are well appointed. Family-run and competitively priced. **£75**

EATING

Columbine 7 Hall Bank, SK17 6EW ☎ 01298 78752, ⓦ columbinerestaurant.co.uk; map p.429. The menu at this small and intimate restaurant, right in the centre of Buxton, is short but imaginative; main courses, such as saddle of monkfish with crab risotto, average £17. Pre-theatre dinners, from about 5pm, can be reserved in advance. May–Oct Mon–Sat 7–10pm; Nov–April Mon & Wed–Sat 7–10pm.

Old Hall Hotel The Square, SK17 6BD ☎ 01298 22841, ⓦ oldhallhotelbuxton.co.uk; map p.429. A few steps from the Opera House, in a building that dates way back, the *Old Hall* offers good-quality, if sometimes inconsistent, food in both its (fairly formal) restaurant and in the bar. The menu is Modern British. Mains average £16. Pre-theatre dinners, from about 5pm, can be reserved in advance. Kitchen daily noon–2pm & 7–10pm.

DRINKING

Old Sun Inn 33 High St, SK17 6HA ☎ 01298 72375; map p.429. This fine old pub, with its maze of antique beamed rooms, is just south of Market Place. It's a good spot for a fine range of real ales and above-average bar food. Daily noon–11pm.

Castleton and around

A hikers' heaven, pocket-sized **CASTLETON**, a scenic ten miles northeast of Buxton via Sparrowpit and the dramatic **Winnats Pass**, lies on the northern edge of White Peak, its huddle of old stone cottages ringed by hills and set beside a babbling brook, all beneath a ruined **castle**. It's a distinctly unpretentious place – and none the worse for that – and the hikers are joined by platoons of cyclists and cavers, all of whom gather together to prepare for the off on **Market Place**, yards from the main drag. The limestone hills pressing in on Castleton are riddled with water-worn **cave systems**, four of which have been developed as tourist attractions complete with subterranean lighting. Peak Cavern (ⓦpeakcavern. co.uk) and Speedwell Cavern (ⓦspeedwellcavern.co.uk) are within easy walking distance of Castleton Market Place, but the more interesting are slightly further afield, these being the Blue John Cavern (ⓦbluejohn-cavern.co.uk) and, the pick of the bunch, **Treak Cliff Cavern**.

Peveril Castle

Off Market Place, S33 8WQ • April–Oct daily 10am–5pm; Nov–March Sat & Sun 10am–4pm • £5.60; EH • ☎ 01433 620613, ⓦ www. english-heritage.org.uk/visit/places/peveril-castle

Overseeing Castleton is **Peveril Castle**, from which the village takes its name. William the Conqueror's illegitimate son William Peveril raised the first fortifications here to protect the king's rights to the forest that then covered the district, but most of the remains – principally the ruinous square keep – date to the 1170s. After a stiff climb up to the keep, you can enjoy commanding views over the Hope Valley.

8

Treak Cliff Cavern

Buxton Rd, S22 8WP • Guided tours daily 10am–5pm; 40min • £9.75 • ☎ 01433 620571, ⓦ bluejohnstone.com • Take the signed minor road off the A6187 just west of Castleton; it's about 1 mile in total

Treak Cliff Cavern is a major source of a rare sparkling fluorspar known as **Blue John**. Highly prized for ornaments and jewellery since Georgian times, this semi-precious stone comes in a multitude of hues from blue through deep red to yellow, depending on its hydrocarbon impurities. The Treak Cliff contains the best examples of the stone *in situ* and is also the best cave to visit in its own right, dripping – literally – with ancient stalactites, flowstone and bizarre rock formations, all visible on an entertaining walking **tour** through the main cave system.

ARRIVAL AND INFORMATION

CASTLETON AND AROUND

By train There are no trains to Castleton – the nearest you'll get is Hope, a couple of miles or so east along the valley on the Manchester–Sheffield line. Regular buses run from very close to Hope train station to Castleton (every 1–2hr; 10min); walk down Station Rd to the bus stop on the main road. Destinations (from Hope) Edale (hourly; 7min); Hathersage (hourly; 7min); Manchester Piccadilly (hourly; 1hr); Sheffield (hourly; 30min).

By bus Castleton's main bus stop is on the main street, How Lane (the A6187).

Destinations Bakewell (3 daily; 2hr); Buxton (1 daily; 50min); Hope (every 1–2hr; 10min).

Tourist office A combined tourist office and Peak District exhibition centre is on the west side of the village, just off the main street (daily: April–Oct 10am–5pm; Nov–March 10.30am–4.30pm; ☎ 01629 816572, ⓦ peakdistrict.gov.uk).

Maps The tourist office sells hiking leaflets and maps, which are invaluable for a string of walking routes that take you up to the bulging hilltops and along the dales that surround Castleton.

ACCOMMODATION AND EATING

Castleton heaves with visitors throughout the summer, but especially on bank holidays and at the weekend, when accommodation should be booked in advance.

1530 The Restaurant Cruck Barn, Cross St, S33 8WH ☎ 01433 621870, ⓦ 1530therestaurant.co.uk. Located in an old stone building near the centre of the village, this bright and breezy restaurant specializes in Italian cuisine – from pizzas and pastas through to more ambitious dishes, like sea bass with artichokes and sun-dried tomatoes. Mains average £12. Mon & Wed–Fri 5.30–11pm, Sat & Sun 1–11pm.

Causeway House Back St, S33 8WE ☎ 01433 623291, ⓦ causewayhouse.co.uk. The cream of the crop, this B&B occupies a well-tended stone cottage just north of Market Place. There are five rooms, three en suite, all tastefully kitted out to make the most of the cottage's original features. **£75**

Ramblers' Rest Back St, S33 8WR ☎ 01433 620125, ⓦ ramblersrest-castleton.co.uk. Four spick and span, modern, en-suite guest rooms shoehorned into an old stone building just to the north of Market Place. Parking and a small garden for guests, too. **£80**

YHA Castleton Losehill Hall Castleton Rd, S33 8WB, signed off the A6187 just to the east of Castleton ☎ 0345 371 9628, ⓦ yha.org.uk/hostel/castleton-losehill-hall. The YHA has spent a bucket refurbishing this Victorian Neo-Gothic mansion set in its own grounds to the north of the village. It's a well-equipped hostel with a self-catering kitchen, café, laundry, cycle storage and drying room, and its many beds are parcelled up into two- to six-bedded rooms, most of which are en suite. Dorms **£18**, doubles **£30**

Edale village

There's almost nothing to **EDALE VILLAGE**, about five miles from Castleton, except for a slender, half-mile trail of stone houses, which march up the main street from the train station, with a couple of pubs, an old church and a scattering of B&Bs on the way – and it's this somnambulant air that is its immediate appeal. It's also extremely popular with walkers, who arrive in droves year-round to set off on the **Pennine Way** (see below) – the route's traditional starting point is the *Old Nag's Head* at the top of the village. If that sounds too daunting, try one of the more manageable alternatives, such as the excellent **circular walk** (9 miles; 5hr) that takes in the first part of the Pennine Way, leading up onto the bleak, gritstone tabletop of **Kinder Scout** (2088ft), below which Edale cowers.

ARRIVAL AND INFORMATION
EDALE VILLAGE

By train Located at the southern end of the village, Edale train station is on the Sheffield–Manchester line.
Destinations Hope, for Castleton (hourly; 7min); Hathersage (hourly; 15min); Manchester Piccadilly (hourly; 45min); Sheffield (hourly; 35min).

Tourist information From Edale train station, it's 400yd or so up the road to the Moorland Centre (Jan & Feb daily 9.30am–3.30pm; March & Oct Mon–Fri 10am–3.30pm, Sat & Sun 9.30am–4.30pm; April–Sept daily 9.30am–5pm; Nov Sat & Sun 9.30am–4.30pm; closed Dec; ☎ 01433 670207, ⓦ peakdistrict.gov.uk), who sell all manner of trail leaflets and hiking guides and can advise on local accommodation.

ACCOMMODATION AND EATING

Cheshire Cheese Inn Edale Rd, Hope, S33 6ZF ☎ 01433 620381, ⓦ thecheshirecheeseinn.co.uk. Two attractively renovated old stone cottages with a cosy/folksy bar downstairs and four pleasant en-suite guest rooms up

---

THE PENNINE WAY

When it was opened in 1965, the 268-mile-long **Pennine Way** (ⓦ nationaltrail.co.uk) was the country's first official long-distance footpath. A dramatic route by any standard, the trail stretches north from the boggy plateau of the Peak District's Kinder Scout (see above) to the Yorkshire Dales and then crosses Hadrian's Wall and the Northumberland National Park, before entering Scotland to fizzle out at the village of **Kirk Yetholm**. One of the most popular walks in the country, either taken in sections or completed in two to three weeks, the wild countryside of the Pennine Way is a challenge in the best of weather and you must certainly arrive properly equipped. Information centres along the route – like the one at Edale village (see above) – stock a selection of guides, maps and associated trail leaflets and can offer advice. Some hikers, however, stick to Wainwright's *Pennine Way Companion*, first published in 1968 and re-edited in 2012.

above. They serve the best food hereabouts – good-quality, very English dishes featuring local, seasonal ingredients with mains at about £12. Just north of Hope on the road to Edale. Tues–Fri noon–3pm & 6–11pm, Sat noon–11.30pm, Sun noon–10pm; kitchen Tues–Fri noon–2pm & 6–9pm, Sat noon–9pm, Sun noon–7.30pm. **£85**

Stonecroft S33 7ZA ☎01433 670262, ⓦ stonecroft guesthouse.co.uk. Arguably the pick of the several B&Bs here, this detached Edwardian house offers two en-suite doubles and one single, each of which is decorated in an unfussy traditional style. On the main street, just short of the Old Nag's Head. Caters well for dietary restrictions. **£100**

Upper Booth Camping West of Edale village on the way to Kinder Scout, S33 7ZJ ☎01433 670250,

ⓦ upperboothcamping.co.uk. This campsite and camping barn is a popular spot for walkers on the Pennine Way. Car parking £5 extra. Camping/person **£8**, camping barn/person **£10**

YHA Edale Rowland Cote, Nether Booth, S33 7ZH, 2 miles east of Edale ☎0345 371 9514, ⓦ yha.org.uk/hostel/edale. This large hostel has a good range of facilities, including a laundry, café and a self-catering kitchen, and also offers an extensive range of outdoor activities. These must be booked ahead – as must accommodation, which is parcelled up into two- to six-bedded rooms. The hostel is signed from the road into Edale, or you can hike across the fields from the nearby Moorland Centre (see above). Dorms **£18**, doubles **£60**

Eyam

Within a year of September 7, 1665, the lonely lead-mining settlement of **EYAM** (pronounced "Eem") had lost almost half of its population of 750 to the bubonic plague, a calamity that earned it the enduring epithet "**The Plague Village**". The first victim was one George Viccars, a journeyman tailor who is said to have released some infected fleas into his lodgings from a package of cloth he had brought from London. Acutely conscious of the danger to neighbouring villages, **William Mompesson**, the village rector, speedily organized a self-imposed quarantine, arranging for food to be left at places on the parish boundary. Payment was made with coins left in pools of disinfecting vinegar in holes chiselled into the old boundary stones – and these can still be seen at **Mompesson's Well**, half a mile up the hill to the north of the village along Edge Road. You can find out more at **Eyam Museum** (April–Oct Tues–Sun 10am–4pm; £2.50; ☎01433 631371, ⓦ eyam-museum.org.uk), whose several displays examine the course of the plague as it ripped through the village.

Church of St Lawrence

Church St, S32 5QH • Easter–Sept Mon–Sat 9am–6pm, Sun 1–5.30pm; Oct–Easter Mon–Sat 9am–4pm, Sun 1–5.30pm • Free • ☎01433 630930, ⓦ eyam-church.org

In the **graveyard** of the **Church of St Lawrence** – of medieval foundation but revamped in the nineteenth century – stands a conspicuous, eighth-century carved Celtic cross, and close by is the distinctive table-tomb of Mompesson's wife, Catherine, whose sterling work nursing sick villagers caused her early death. Rather more cheerful is the grave of one **Harry Bagshaw** (d. 1927), a local cricketer whose tombstone shows a ball breaking his wicket with the umpire's finger raised above, presumably – on this occasion – to heaven.

ARRIVAL AND DEPARTURE	EYAM

By bus Buses stop on The Square, beside the green at the east end of the village.

Destinations Baslow (every 2hr; 10min); Hathersage (Mon–Sat every 2hr; 30min); Sheffield (Mon–Sat every 2hr; 1hr).

ACCOMMODATION AND EATING

Village Green Café The Square, S32 5RB ☎01433 631293, ⓦ cafevillagegreen.com. The pick of the two cafés on The Square, a cosy, family-run place with pavement terrace. Home-made soups and sandwiches lead the gastronomic way. Mon & Thurs–Sun 9.15am–4pm.

YHA Eyam Hawkhill Rd, S32 5QP ☎0345 371 9738, ⓦ yha.org.uk/hostel/eyam. This well-equipped hostel

occupies an idiosyncratic Victorian house, whose ersatz medieval towers and turrets overlook Eyam from amid wooded grounds on Hawkhill Rd, a good, half-mile ramble up from Eyam Museum (see page 433). The hostel has a café, self-catering facilities, cycle storage and a lounge, with sixty-odd beds in two- to six-bed rooms; advance reservations are recommended. Dorms **£18**, doubles **£40**

8

Bakewell and around

Amenable **BAKEWELL**, flanking the banks of the River Wye about thirty miles north of Derby, is famous for both its **Bakewell Pudding** and its **Bakewell Tart**. The former is much more distinctive (and less commonplace), being a sweet and slippery almond-flavoured confection – now with a dab of jam – invented here around 1860 when a cook botched a recipe for strawberry tart. Almost a century before this fortuitous mishap, the Duke of Rutland set out to turn what was then a remote village into a prestigious spa, thereby trumping the work of his rival, the Duke of Devonshire, in Buxton. The frigidity of the water made failure inevitable, leaving only the prettiness of **Bath Gardens** at the heart of the town centre as a reminder of the venture. Bakewell is within easy striking distance of the big tourist attraction hereabouts, **Chatsworth House**.

Ashford in the Water

Minuscule **ASHFORD IN THE WATER**, just over a mile to the west of Bakewell along the River Wye, is one of the prettiest and wealthiest villages in the Peaks, its old stone cottages nuzzling up to a quaint medieval church. It was not always so. Ashford was once a poor lead-mining settlement with sidelines in milling and agriculture, hence the name of the (impossibly picturesque) **Sheepwash Bridge**. There was, however, a bit of a boom when locals took to polishing the dark limestone found on the edge of the village (and nowhere else), turning it into so-called **Ashford black marble** – much to the delight of Buxton's petrifactioners.

ARRIVAL AND INFORMATION

BAKEWELL AND AROUND

By bus Buses to Bakewell stop on – or very close to – central Rutland Square; there are no trains.
Destinations Baslow (hourly; 20min); Buxton (hourly; 30min); Castleton (3 daily; 2hr); Derby (hourly; 1hr 20min);

Hathersage (3 daily; 45min); Sheffield (hourly; 1hr).
Tourist office Handy location in the Old Market Hall, Bridge St (April–Oct daily 9.30am–5pm; Nov–March daily 10.30am–4.30pm; ☎01629 816558, ⌨peakdistrict.gov.uk).

ACCOMMODATION AND EATING

★**Hassop Hall** Hassop, DE45 1NS, 3 miles north of Bakewell on the B6001 ☎01629 640488, ⌨hassophall.co.uk. Hidden away in the heart of the Peaks, the solitary hamlet of Hassop is home to the wonderful *Hassop Hall*, a handsome stone manor house with just 13 guest rooms. The interior has kept faith with the Georgian architecture – modernization has been kept to a subtle minimum – and the views out over the surrounding parkland are delightful. The hotel restaurant is also first-class, with a two-course set meal costing £32. Daily noon–1.30pm & 7–8.30pm. **£110**

Old Original Bakewell Pudding Shop The Square, DE45 1BT ☎01629 812193, ⌨www.bakewellpudding

shop.co.uk. Bakeries all over town claim to make Bakewell Pudding to the original recipe, but the most authentic are served up here. They sell the pudding in several sizes. Mon–Sat 8.30am–6pm, Sun 9am–5pm.

Riverside House Hotel Fennel St, Ashford in the Water, DE45 1QF ☎01629 814275, ⌨riversidehousehotel.co.uk. The plush and lush *Riverside House* occupies a handsome Georgian building by the banks of the Wye. There are a dozen or so extremely well-appointed rooms here, each decorated in a full-blown country-house style, and the hotel takes justifiable pride in both its gardens and its restaurant. Daily noon–1.30pm & 7–9pm. **£150**

HIKING AROUND BAKEWELL

Bakewell is a popular starting point for short hikes out into the easy landscapes that make up the town's surroundings, with one of the most relaxing excursions a four-mile loop along the banks of the **River Wye** to the south of the centre. Chatsworth (see page 435) is also within easy hiking distance – about seven miles there and back – or you could try one of the best-known hikes in the National Park – the **Monsal Trail**, which cuts eight miles north through some of Derbyshire's finest limestone dales using part of the old Midland Railway line. The trail begins at Coombs viaduct, a mile southeast of Bakewell, and ends at Topley Pike Junction, three miles east of Buxton.

Chatsworth House

Bakewell, DE45 1PN • Daily: late March to late May & Sept–Dec 11am–5pm; late May to Aug 10.30am–5pm; gardens open until slightly later • £19.90; gardens only £12.90 • ☎ 01246 565300, ⓦ chatsworth.org

Fantastically popular, and one of the finest stately homes in Britain, **Chatsworth House** was built in the seventeenth century by the first Duke of Devonshire. It has been owned by the family ever since and though several of them have done a fair bit of tinkering it's still remarkably harmonious. The property is best seen from the B6012, which meanders across the estate to the west of the house, giving a full view of its vast Palladian frontage.

Many visitors forgo the **house** altogether, concentrating on the grounds – an understandable decision given the predictability of the assorted baubles accumulated by the family over the centuries. Nonetheless, among the maze of grandiose rooms and staircases there are several noteworthy highlights, including the ornate ceilings of the **State Apartments** and, in the State Bedroom, the four-poster bed in which George II breathed his last. And then there are the **paintings**. Among many, Frans Hals, Tintoretto, Veronese, Reynolds, Van Dyck and Lucian Freud all have a showing, and there's even a Rembrandt.

Back outside, the **gardens** are a real treat and owe much to the combined efforts of Capability Brown, who designed them in the 1750s, and Joseph Paxton (designer of London's Crystal Palace), who had a bash seventy years later. Among all sorts of fripperies, there are water fountains, modern sculptures, a rock garden, an artificial waterfall, a grotto and a folly as well as a nursery and greenhouses. Afterwards, you can wend your way to the **café** in the handsomely converted former stables.

8

ARRIVAL AND DEPARTURE
CHATSWORTH HOUSE

On foot The best way to approach is on one of the paths which network the estate; Bakewell (4 miles; see page 434) and Baslow (2 miles) make good starting points.

By bus Buses from several neighbouring towns, including Sheffield, Derby and Buxton, pull into the bus stop a 2min walk from Chatsworth House.

The East Midlands

LINCOLN CATHEDRAL

9 The East Midlands

Many tourists bypass the East Midlands' four major counties – Nottinghamshire, Leicestershire, Northamptonshire and Lincolnshire – on their way to more obvious destinations, an understandable mistake given that the region seems, at first sight, to be short of star attractions. Nevertheless, though the county towns of Nottingham, Leicester and Northampton are at heart industrial – sometimes post-industrial – cities, they each have enough sights and character to give them appeal, while Lincoln, with its superb cathedral, is in parts a fine old city. What's more, the countryside hereabouts is sprinkled with historic market towns, pretty villages and prestigious country homes.

Of the county towns, **Nottingham** has perhaps the most to offer, not least an enjoyable castle and a cutting-edge art gallery, while the rest of **Nottinghamshire** holds Byron's Newstead Abbey, the pleasing Harley Gallery and, even better, Elizabethan **Hardwick Hall** (just over the border in Derbyshire, but covered in this chapter). To the south, **Leicester** boasts an excellent art gallery and its county – **Leicestershire** – offers Market Bosworth, an amiable country town famous as the site of the Battle of Bosworth Field, and a particularly intriguing church at Breedon-on-the-Hill. Leicestershire also lies adjacent to the easy countryside of **Rutland**, where you'll find another pleasant county town, Oakham. Rutland and **Northamptonshire** benefit from the use of limestone as the traditional building material and rural Northamptonshire is studded with handsome stone villages and towns.

Lincolnshire is very different in character from the rest of the region, an agricultural hidey-hole that remains surprisingly remote, its landscapes at their prettiest in the rolling hills of the **Lincolnshire Wolds**. Locals sometimes call it the "forgotten county", but this was not always the case: throughout medieval times the county flourished as a centre of the wool trade, its merchants and landowners becoming some of the wealthiest in England. Reminders of the high times are legion, beginning with the majestic **cathedral** that rises above **Lincoln**; equally enticing is the splendidly intact stone town of **Stamford**. Out in the sticks, the county's most distinctive feature is the **Lincolnshire Fens**, whose pancake-flat fields, filling out much of the south of the county, have been reclaimed from the marshes and the sea. Fenland villages are generally short of charm, but their parish churches, whose spires regularly interrupt the wide-skied landscape, are simply stunning.

Very different again is the **Lincolnshire coast**, whose long sandy beach extends, with a few marshy interruptions, from Mablethorpe to Skegness, the region's main resort. The coast has long attracted holiday-makers from the big cities of the East Midlands and Yorkshire, but significant chunks of the seashore are now protected as nature reserves.

GETTING AROUND

THE EAST MIDLANDS

By train and bus Travelling between the cities of the East Midlands by train or bus is simple and most of the larger towns have good regional links, too. Things are very different in the country, however, where bus services are

Highlights

❶ Newstead Abbey One-time hideaway of Lord Byron, this intriguing old mansion has superb period rooms, with lots of Byron memorabilia, plus delightful gardens. See page 445

❷ Hardwick Hall A beautifully preserved Elizabethan mansion that was home to the formidable Bess of Hardwick, one of the leading figures of her age. The gardens and surrounding parkland are charming, too. See page 446

❸ Lincoln Cathedral One of the finest medieval cathedrals in the land, dominating this fine old city and seen to best advantage on a guided tour. See page 456

❹ Gibraltar Point National Nature Reserve Escape the crowds and enjoy the wonderful birdlife at this first-class coastal nature reserve. See page 459

❺ Stamford Lincolnshire's prettiest town, with its cobbled lanes, lovely old churches, and ancient limestone buildings, well deserves an overnight stay. See page 461

HIGHLIGHTS ARE MARKED ON THE MAP ON PAGE 440

distinctly patchy, nowhere more so than in Lincolnshire. **By plane** The region's international airport, East Midlands (wwweastmidlandsairport.com), is located just off the M1 between Derby, Nottingham and Leicester. There are buses from the airport to these three major cities – the operator is currently Trentbarton (wwwtrentbarton.co.uk/skylink247).

Nottingham

With a population of around 320,000, **NOTTINGHAM** is one of England's big cities. A one-time lace manufacturing and pharmaceutical centre (the Boots chain began here), today it's famous for its association with **Robin Hood**, the legendary thirteenth-century outlaw. Hood's bitter enemy was, of course, the **Sheriff of Nottingham**, but unfortunately his home and lair – the city's imposing medieval castle – is long gone, replaced by a handsome Palladian mansion that is still called, somewhat confusingly, **Nottingham Castle**. Nowadays, Nottingham is at its most diverting around both the castle and the handsome **Market Square**, which is also the centre of a heaving, teeming weekend nightlife scene.

Brief history
Controlling an important crossing point over the River Trent, the Saxon town of **Nottingham** was built on one of a pair of sandstone hills whose 130ft cliffs looked out over the river valley. In 1068, William the Conqueror built a castle on the other hill, and the Saxons and Normans traded on the low ground in between, the Market Square. The castle was a military stronghold and royal palace, the equal of the great castles of Windsor and Dover, and every medieval king of England paid regular visits. In August 1642, Charles I stayed here too, riding out of the castle to raise his standard and start the Civil War – not that the locals were overly sympathetic. Hardly anyone joined up, even though the king had the ceremony repeated on the next three days.

After the Civil War, the Parliamentarians slighted the castle and, in the 1670s, the ruins were cleared by the Duke of Newcastle to make way for a palace, whose continental – and, in English terms, novel – design he chose from a pattern book, probably by Rubens. Beneath the castle lay a handsome, well-kept market town until the second half of the eighteenth century, when the city was transformed by the expansion of the lace and hosiery industries. Within the space of fifty years, Nottingham's population increased from ten thousand to fifty thousand, the resulting slums becoming a hotbed of radicalism.

The worst of the slums were cleared in the early twentieth century, when the city centre assumed its present structure, with the main commercial area ringed by alternating industrial and residential districts. Crass postwar development, adding tower blocks, shopping centres and a ring road, ensconced and embalmed the remnants of the city's past.

The Market Square
One of the best-looking central squares in England, Nottingham's **Market Square** remains the heart of the city, an airy open plaza whose shops, offices and fountains are overlooked by the grand neo-Baroque **Council House**, completed as part of a make-work scheme in 1928. Just off the square there's also a statue honouring one of the city's heroes, the former manager of Nottingham Forest FC, **Brian Clough** (1935–2004), shown in his characteristic trainers and tracksuit. Clough won two European cups with Forest, a remarkable achievement by any standards, but his popularity came just as much from his forthright personality and idiosyncratic utterances. One quote will suffice to show the mettle of the man: "I wouldn't say I was the best manager in the business, but I was in the top one."

9

Nottingham Castle

Castle Place, NG1 6EJ • Mid-Feb to mid-Nov daily 10am–5pm; mid-Nov to mid-Feb Wed–Sun 10am–3pm; last entry 1hr before closing •
£8 • **Cave tours** Same days as castle: noon, 1pm, 2pm & 3pm; 45min • £5 • ☎ 0115 876 1400, ⓦ nottinghamcastle.org.uk

From the Market Square, it's a five-minute walk to **Nottingham Castle**, whose heavily restored medieval gateway edges the immaculately maintained gardens, whose lawns, flower borders and trees slope up to the squat, seventeenth-century ducal **palace**. Parts of the castle will be closed during **major renovation works** (2018–20), but the end result should feature a gallery exploring the city's radical, rebellious past – from its support for Parliament against the king through to its espousal of Chartism. There is also likely to be a display of the small but exquisite medieval **alabaster carvings** for which Nottingham once had an international reputation and, on the top floor, the capacious and handsome **picture gallery** will undoubtedly survive – and continue to display its enjoyable collection of mostly English nineteenth- and early twentieth-century paintings.

Just outside the main entrance, two sets of steps lead down into the maze of ancient **caves** that honeycomb the sandstone cliff below – one set being **King David's Dungeon**, the other **Mortimer's Hole**. Both are open for tours, but Mortimer's Hole is the more atmospheric, a 300ft shaft along which, so the story goes, the young Edward III and his accomplices crept in 1330 to capture his mother, Isabella, and her lover, Roger Mortimer. The two had staged a coup four years earlier in which Edward's hapless father, Edward II, was murdered, but they were unable to keep a firm hold on power,

with Edward III proving too shrewd for them. Edward had his revenge on Mortimer, who came to a grisly end, but the remarkable Isabella was allowed to simply step back from politics, living out her days in comfort (and probably acute boredom).

The Lace Market

Once key to the city's fortunes, Nottingham's lace industry boomed in the nineteenth century, its assorted warehouses and factories flanking the narrow streets of a compact area known as the **Lace Market**, beginning just to the east of the Market Square. The lace industry has pretty much disappeared but the buildings haven't, with **Stoney Street** the most architecturally striking, its star turn being the **Adams Building**, whose handsome stone-and-brick facade combines both neo-Georgian and neo-Renaissance features. Take a peek also at neighbouring **Broadway**, where a line of impressive red-brick buildings perform a neat swerve halfway along the street. The district grew up round a much older structure, the **church of St Mary's** (daily 9am–5pm; free; ⓦstmarysnottingham.org), an imposing, medieval Gothic building with Saxon origins. The church interior is fairly routine, but there is a particularly interesting memorial on the wall of the nave to a Lieutenant James Still, who died of yellow fever while serving in a British anti-slaving squadron off Sierra Leone in 1821 – the memorial's rant against slavery cheers the soul.

Nottingham Contemporary

Weekday Cross, NG1 2GB • Tues–Sat 10am–6pm, Sun 11am–5pm, bank hols 10am–5pm • Free • ☎ 0115 948 9750, ⓦ nottinghamcontemporary.org

In a handy, central location, **Nottingham Contemporary** is the city's premier art gallery, though from the outside it looks like something assembled from an IKEA flat pack. The gallery's temporary exhibitions are consistently strong; hit shows have included the early paintings of David Hockney, a wonderful, all-encompassing display on Haitian voodoo, and a solo exhibition by Wu Tsang.

ARRIVAL AND INFORMATION

By train Nottingham train station is on the south side of the city centre, a 10min walk (just follow the signs), or a tram ride, from Market Square.

Destinations Birmingham (every 30min; 1hr 20min); Leicester (every 30min; 20min); Lincoln (hourly; 1hr); London (every 30min; 1hr 45min); Newark (every 30min; 30min); Oakham (hourly; 1hr 15min, change at Leicester).

By bus Most long-distance buses pull in near the station while the Broad Marsh bus station is being rebuilt, but others – including services to north Nottinghamshire (see page 445) – pull in at the Victoria bus station, a 5min walk north of Market Square.

Tourist office Market Square, on the ground floor of the Council House, 1 Smithy Row (Mon–Sat 9.30am–5.30pm, plus selected Sun 11am–5pm; ☎ 0844 477 5678, ⓦ experiencenottinghamshire.com).

ACCOMMODATION

★**Harts Hotel** Standard Hill, Park Row, NG1 6GN ☎ 0115 988 1900, ⓦ hartsnottingham.co.uk; map p.442. Nottingham may be short of good places to stay, but this chic hotel does much to fill the gap. The thirty-odd stylish rooms feature ultramodern fixtures and fittings, Egyptian-cotton bed linen and contemporary paintings. Handy location, plus a smashing restaurant next door (see page 444). **£140**

The Walton Hotel 2 North Road, The Park, NG7 1AG ☎ 0115 947 5215, ⓦ thewaltonhotel.com; map p.442. Garners mixed reviews, but this 28-room hotel does occupy a good-looking nineteenth-century building and its annexe on the edge of the city centre – a 15min walk from Market Square, beside Derby Rd. The rooms vary considerably, though the best are cheered by a smattering of period furnishings and fittings. **£125**

EATING

Annie's Burger Shack 5 Broadway, NG1 1PR ☎ 0115 684 9920, ⓦ anniesburgershack.com; map p.442. This large and extremely busy burger joint has been a real local hit, attracting a young and lively crowd, who chomp

9

away at a wide range of top-ranking burgers, including the "Deathray" (with jalapeños, peppers and chilli paste). Craft ales, stouts and ciders too – but come early or expect to queue. Burgers average £10. Mon–Thurs noon–10pm, Fri & Sat noon–11pm, Sun 11am–10pm.

Edin's 15 Broad St, NG1 3AJ ☎ 0115 924 1112, ⓦ edins nottingham.co.uk; map p.442. This city-centre café-bar has a laidback vibe, with its pocket-sized open kitchen, boho furniture and jazzy, bluesy soundtrack. The menu is short, unpretentious and inexpensive; mains cost as little as £7, but there are also snacks such as the bread and cheese board. Mon–Sat 9.30am–11.30pm, Sun 9.30am–9pm.

Harts Restaurant Standard Hill, Park Row, NG1 6GN ☎ 0115 988 1900, ⓦ hartsnottingham.co.uk; map p.442. One of the city's most acclaimed restaurants, occupying a tastefully remodelled wing of the old general hospital and offering a creative international menu – try, for example, the sea bream bouillabaisse. Reservations recommended. Mains average £21. Daily noon–2.15pm

& 6–10pm, Sun till 9pm.

★ **Masala Junction** 301 Mansfield Road, NG5 2DA ☎ 0115 962 2366, ⓦ masalajunction.co.uk; map p.442. The best Indian restaurant in Nottingham, its menu featuring canny amalgamations of different regional cooking styles. It's in an attractively refurbished former bank, about a mile from the city centre up along Mansfield Road (buses from Lower Parliament St). Mains around £14. Mon–Thurs 5.30–10.30pm, Fri & Sat 5.30–11pm.

★ **World Service** Newdigate House, Castle Gate, NG1 6AF ☎ 0115 847 5587, ⓦ worldservicerestaurant.com; map p.442. Chic restaurant with bags of decorative flair in charming premises up near the castle, complete with a delightful terrace. A Modern British menu, including delights like rack of lamb with butternut squash, is prepared with imagination and flair. In the evenings, mains start around £20, but there are great deals at lunchtimes (two-course set menu £17). Mon–Fri noon–2pm & 7–10pm, Sat noon–2pm & 6.30–10pm, Sun noon–3.30pm.

DRINKING AND NIGHTLIFE

Central Nottingham's **pubs** literally heave on the weekend and are not for the faint-hearted – and anyone over thirty may well feel somewhat marooned. That said, there are several particularly engaging places amid all the argy-bargy.

★ **Boilermaker** 36 Carlton St, NG1 1NN ☎ 0115 986 6333, ⓦ boilermakerbar.co.uk; map p.442. Don't be deterred by the glum, anonymous exterior, this is Nottingham's coolest cocktail bar, set in a large, almost shed-like space with boho decor – and it has superb cocktails. First come, first served, so come early. Mon–Fri 5pm–1am, Sat 2pm–1am, Sun 7pm–1am.

Broadway Cinema Bar Broadway Cinema, 14 Broad St, NG1 3AL ☎ 0115 952 6611, ⓦ broadway.org.uk; map p.442. Informal, fashionable (in an arty sort of way) bar serving an eclectic assortment of bottled beers to a cinema-keen clientele. Filling, inexpensive bar food too. Much to its credit, Broadway has played a key role in boosting Nottingham's creative credentials – hence the city's clutch of artist-led collectives. Mon–Wed 9am–11pm, Thurs 9am–midnight, Fri & Sat 9am–1am, Sun 10am–11pm.

Lincolnshire Poacher 161 Mansfield Rd, NG1 3FR ☎ 0115 941 1584, ⓦ castlerockbrewery.co.uk/pubs/lincolnshire-poacher; map p.442. Popular and relaxed pub, where the decor is pleasantly traditional and the customers take their real ales (fairly) seriously. About half a mile from the Market Square. Mon–Wed 11am–11pm, Thurs & Fri 11am–midnight, Sat 10.30am–midnight, Sun noon–11pm.

★ **Ye Olde Trip to Jerusalem** Brewhouse Yard, NG1 6AD ☎ 0115 947 3171, ⓦ triptojerusalem.com; map p.442. Carved into the sandstone cliff below the castle, this ancient inn – said to be the oldest in England – may well have been a meeting point for soldiers gathering for the Third Crusade. Its cave-like bars, with their rough sandstone ceilings and antique furniture, are delightfully secretive and there's a good range of ales too. Mon–Thurs & Sun 11am–11pm, Fri & Sat 11am–midnight.

ENTERTAINMENT

Broadway Cinema 14 Broad St, NG1 3AL ☎ 0115 952 6611, ⓦ broadway.org.uk. The best cinema in the city, showing a mix of mainstream and avant-garde films.

Motorpoint Arena & National Ice Centre Bolero Square, Lace Market, NG1 1LA ☎ 0843 373 3000, ⓦ motorpointarenanottingham.com; ⓦ national-ice-centre.com. Major performance venue that seems to change its name (and sponsor) with surprising regularity. Big-name acts perform here – from music through to shows and comedy. The Arena is inside the National Ice Centre, with its prime ice-skating facilities.

Nottingham Playhouse Wellington Circus, NG1 5AF

☎ 0115 941 9419, ⓦ nottinghamplayhouse.co.uk. Long-established theatre which puts on a wide range of plays – Shakespeare through to Ayckbourn – plus dance, music and comedy, often with a local twist or theme. There's also a delightful piece of modern art beside the entrance – Anish Kapoor's whopping, reflective *Sky Mirror*.

Theatre Royal & Royal Concert Hall Theatre Square, NG1 5ND ☎ 0115 989 5555, ⓦ trch.co.uk. Two venues with one set of contact details: the Theatre Royal is an attractive, well-maintained Victorian theatre and the nearby Concert Hall dates from the 1980s. Many of the big names in live music, both popular and classical, play at one or the other.

SHOPPING

Five Leaves Bookshop 14a Long Row, NG1 2DH ☎ 0115 837 3097, ⓦ fiveleavesbookshop.co.uk; map p.442. UK bookshops may be having a bumpy ride, but this new and independent place bucks the trend, with a well-chosen selection of titles with a radical twist. Down an alley opposite the tourist office. Mon–Sat 10am– 5.30pm, Sun noon–4pm.

Paul Smith 20 Low Pavement, NG1 7DN ☎ 0115 968 5990, ⓦ paulsmith.co.uk; map p.442. Nottingham's Paul Smith (b.1946) worked in a clothing factory as a young man, but only developed a passion for art and design after a bike accident left him incapacitated for six months. He opened his first small shop on Byard Lane in 1970, since when he has become one of the major success stories of contemporary British fashion, his trademark multicoloured stripes proving popular on every continent. The Byard Lane shop closed in 2017 but the flagship store on Low Pavement is worth a visit. Mon–Sat 10am–6pm, Sun 11am–5pm.

Rough Trade 5 Broad St, NG1 3AJ ☎ 0115 896 4012, ⓦ roughtrade.com; map p.442. To have a Rough Trade outlet here in Nottingham is a real coup – take your pick from the stacks of vinyl and selected books on the ground floor or visit the dimly lit café up above. Mon–Sat 10am– 8pm, Sun 11am–7pm.

Northern Nottinghamshire

Rural **northern Nottinghamshire**, with its gentle rolling landscapes and large ducal estates, was transformed in the nineteenth century by **coal** – deep, wide seams of the stuff that spawned dozens of collieries, and colliery towns, stretching up across the county and on into Yorkshire. Today, the mines have all gone, their passing marked only by the occasional pithead winding wheel, left, bleak and solitary, to commemorate the thousands of men who laboured here.

The suddenness of the pit closure programme imposed by Thatcher and her Conservative cronies in the 1980s and 1990s knocked the stuffing out of the area, but one prop of its slow revival has been the tourist industry. The countryside in between these former mining communities holds several enjoyable attractions, the best known of which is **Sherwood Forest** – or at least the patchy remains of it – with one chunk of woodland preserved in the **Sherwood Forest National Nature Reserve**, supposedly where Robin Hood did his canoodling with Maid Marian. Byron is a pipsqueak in the celebrity stakes by comparison with Robin, but his family home – **Newstead Abbey** – is here too, as is **Hardwick Hall**, a handsome Elizabethan mansion built at the behest of one of the most powerful women of her day, Bess of Hardwick.

Newstead Abbey

Ravenshead, NG15 8NA, 10 miles north of Nottingham on the A60 • **House** Sat, Sun & some hols noon–4pm; last entry 1hr before closing • £8 • **Gardens & grounds** Daily 9am–5pm or dusk • Vehicles £6; pedestrians & cyclists £1 • ☎ 01623 455900, ⓦ newsteadabbey.org.uk • A regular Pronto bus (every 20min; 40min; ⓦ trentbarton.co.uk) leaves Nottingham's Victoria bus station for Mansfield, and stops at the abbey gates

In 1539, **Newstead Abbey** was granted by Henry VIII to Sir John Byron, who demolished most of the church and converted the monastic buildings into a family home. Much later, in 1798, **Lord Byron** (1788–1824) inherited the estate, but by then it was little more than a ruin; he restored part of the complex during his six-year residence (1808–14), but most of the present structure dates from later renovations, which maintained much of the shape and feel of the medieval original while creating the warren-like mansion that exists today.

Inside, a string of intriguing period rooms begins with the neo-Gothic Great Hall and Byron's bedroom (one of the few rooms to look pretty much like it did when he lived here) and then continues on into the Library, which holds a collection of the poet's possessions, from letters and an inkstand through to his pistols and boxing gloves. A further room contains a set of satirical watercolours entitled *The Wonderful History of Lord Byron & His Dog* by his friend Elizabeth Pigot – there's a portrait of the self-same dog, **Boatswain**, in the south gallery, and a conspicuous memorial bearing an absurdly

9

extravagant inscription to the mutt in the delightful walled garden at the back of the house. Beyond the house lie the main **gardens**, a secretive and subtle combination of lake, Gothic waterfalls, yew tunnels and Japanese-style rockeries, complete with idiosyncratic pagodas.

Sherwood Forest

The main entrance to the Sherwood Forest National Nature Reserve is half a mile north of Edwinstowe village, about 20 miles north of Nottingham via the A614 • Daily dawn–dusk • Free, but parking £3 (April–Dec only) • ☎ 01623 823202, ⓦ nottinghamshire.gov.uk • The Sherwood Arrow bus (ⓦ stagecoachbus.com) links Nottingham's Victoria bus station with Worksop via the visitor centre (hourly; 1hr)

Most of **Sherwood Forest**, once a vast royal woodland of oak, birch and bracken covering all of northern Nottinghamshire, was cleared in the eighteenth century. It's difficult today to imagine the protection all the greenery provided for generations of outlaws, the most famous of whom was of course **Robin Hood**. There's no "true story" of Robin's life – the earliest reference to him, in Langland's *Piers Plowman* of 1377, treats him as a fiction – but to the balladeers of fifteenth-century England, who invented most of Hood's folklore, this was hardly the point. For them, he was a symbol of yeoman decency, a semi-mythological opponent of corrupt clergymen and evil officers of the law; in the early tales, Robin may show sympathy for the peasant, but he has rather more respect for the decent nobleman, and he's never credited with robbing the rich to give to the poor. This and other parts of the legend, such as Maid Marian and Friar Tuck, were added later.

Robin Hood may lack historical authenticity, but it hasn't discouraged the county council from spending thousands of pounds sustaining the **Major Oak**, the creaky tree where Maid Marian and Robin are supposed to have plighted their troth. The Major Oak is on a pleasant one-mile woodland walk that begins beside the visitor centre at the main entrance to **Sherwood Forest National Nature Reserve**, which comprises 450 acres of ancient gnarled oak and silver birch crisscrossed with footpaths.

Hardwick Hall

Doe Lea, Chesterfield, Derbyshire, S44 5QJ • **Hardwick Hall & gardens** Wed–Sun: mid-Feb to Oct 11am–5pm; mid-Nov to mid-Dec 11am–3pm • Hall & gardens £14; gardens only £7; NT • **Parkland** Daily 9am–6pm (or dusk if sooner) • Free, but parking £4; NT • ☎ 01246 850430, ⓦ nationaltrust.org.uk/hardwick-hall • **Hardwick Old Hall** April–Sept Wed–Sun 10am–6pm; Oct Wed–Sun 10am–5pm; Nov–March Sat & Sun (daily in school hols) 10am–4pm • £6.50; EH • ☎ 01246 850431, ⓦ www.english-heritage.org.uk/visit/places/hardwick-old-hall

Elizabeth, Countess of Shrewsbury (1527–1608) – aka **Bess of Hardwick** – became one of the leading figures of Elizabethan England, renowned for her political and business acumen. She had a penchant for building and her major achievement, **Hardwick Hall**, begun when she was 62, has survived in amazingly good condition. The house was the epitome of fashion, a balance of symmetry and ingenious detail in which the building's rectangular lines are offset by line upon line of windows – there's actually more glass than stone – while up above, her giant-sized initials (E.S.) hog every roof line.

The highlights of the labyrinthine mansion are on its top floor (closed late Dec), home to the breathtaking **High Great Chamber**, where Bess received her most distinguished guests. The Chamber boasts an extraordinary, brightly painted plaster frieze celebrating the goddess Diana, the virgin huntress – designed, of course, to please the Virgin Queen herself. Next door, the **Long Gallery** features eye-catching furnishings and fittings, from splendid chimneypieces and tapestries through to a set of portraits, including one each of the queen and Bess. Bess could exercise here while keeping out of the sun – at a time when any hint of a tan was considered decidedly plebeian.

Outside, the **garden** makes for a pleasant wander and, beyond the ha-ha, rare breeds of cattle and sheep graze the **parkland**. Finally – and rather confusingly – Hardwick Hall is next to **Hardwick Old Hall**, Bess's previous home, but now little more than a broken-down if substantial ruin (combined tickets are available; £20).

Leicester

At first glance, **LEICESTER**, some 25 miles south of Nottingham, seems a resolutely modern city, but further inspection reveals traces of its medieval and Roman past as a settlement on the Fosse Way (now the A46) linking Exeter and Lincoln. In 2012, Leicester's national profile was boosted by the discovery of the remains of **Richard III** beneath a council car park in the centre – the body was originally brought here after the Battle of Bosworth Field (see page 451). There followed a prolonged legal battle with York as to who should keep the king's skeleton, but Leicester won and the body has now been reinterred in Leicester Cathedral. This was, however, small beer compared with Leicester's general delirium when their **football** team won the English Premier League title in 2016, at odds which started out at 5000/1.

Skeleton and football apart, it's probably fair to say that Leicester has a reputation for looking rather glum, but the centre is on the move, with the addition of **Highcross**, a

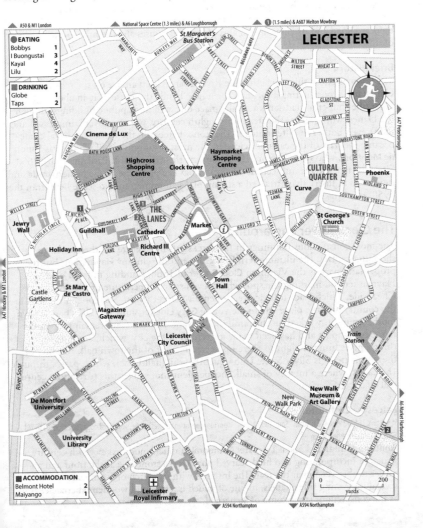

9

LEICESTER'S FINEST FESTIVALS

The crowded terraced streets on and around Belgrave Road are the hub for the city's principal Hindu festival, **Diwali** (ⓦvisitleicester.info), the Festival of Light, held in October or November, when thousands of lamps illuminate proceedings. In addition, the city's sizeable African-Caribbean community holds England's second-biggest street festival (after Notting Hill Carnival; see page 129). It's called the **Leicester Caribbean Carnival** (ⓦfacebook.com/LeicesterCaribbeanCarnival), and it's held on the first weekend in August.

large and glitzy shopping centre, and the creation of a Cultural Quarter equipped with both a flashy performance venue, **Curve Theatre**, and a first-rate independent cinema, the **Phoenix**. The star attractions are, however, the **New Walk Museum and Art Gallery**, which features an exemplary collection of German Expressionist paintings, and the intriguing **King Richard III Visitor Centre**. Leicester is also distinctive in its make-up: more than a third of the population is Asian and indeed the city elected England's first Asian MP, Keith Vaz, in 1987. The traditional focus of the Asian community is **Belgrave Road** and its environs, an area of terraced houses about a mile to the northeast of the centre.

Brief history

The **Romans** chose this site beside the River Soar to keep an eye on the rebellious Corieltauvi, constructing a fortified town here beside the Fosse Way in about 47 AD. Later, the Emperor Hadrian kitted the place out with huge public buildings, though the Danes, who overran the area in the eighth century, were not overly impressed and didn't even bother to pilfer much of the stone. Later still, the town's medieval castle became the base of the earls of Leicester, the most distinguished of whom was **Simon de Montfort**, who forced Henry III to convene the first English Parliament in 1265. Since the late seventeenth century, Leicester has been a centre of the **hosiery trade** and it was this industry that attracted a stream of Asian immigrants to settle here from the 1950s onwards.

The Clock Tower and around

The most conspicuous buildings in Leicester's bustling centre are the two large shopping centres, the ultramodern **Highcross** and the clumpy **Haymarket**, but the proper landmark is the Victorian **Clock Tower** of 1868, standing in front of the Haymarket and marking the spot where seven streets meet. One of the seven is Cheapside, which leads to Leicester's open-air **market** (Mon–Sat), one of the best in the country and the place where the young **Gary Lineker**, now the UK's best-known football pundit, worked on the family stall. Good-hearted Gary remains a popular figure hereabouts and has been made a freeman of the city, which, among other things, gives him the right to graze his sheep in front of the town hall. Another of the seven streets is Silver Street (subsequently Guildhall Lane), which passes through **The Lanes**, where a medley of small, independent shops gives this part of the centre real character.

Leicester Cathedral

St Martin's, LE1 5PZ • Mon–Sat 10am–5pm, Sun 12.30–2.30pm (dependent on services) • Free, suggested donation £3 • ☏0116 261 5200, ⓦleicestercathedral.org

Abutting Guildhall Lane is **Leicester Cathedral**, a much-modified eleventh-century structure incorporating two finely carved porches – a stone one at the front and an earlier timber version at the rear. The interior, with its clutch of Gothic arches, holds several interesting side chapels, in one of which is a splendid wooden tabernacle, as well as the conspicuous stone **tomb of Richard III**.

King Richard III Visitor Centre

4a St Martin's, LE1 5DB · Mon–Fri & Sun 10am–4pm, Sat & bank hols 10am–5pm · £8.95 · ☎ 0300 300 0900, ⓦ kriii.com

Across the street from the cathedral, Leicester's old Grammar School is a substantial Victorian redbrick that has been turned into the ambitious **King Richard III Visitor Centre** after the royal body was discovered in 2012 beneath the adjoining car park, where Greyfriars church had once stood. The Centre has four distinct sections. The first examines Richard's reign and the battle of Bosworth Field that ended it; the second explores the nature of Richard's disability – he suffered from curvature of the spine – and relates the story of how the body was discovered, a remarkable tale in itself. The third section comprises a replica of Richard's skeleton with the various wounds the king suffered at the Battle of Bosworth Field clearly observable. This is really intriguing stuff – and it's all immaculately presented. The fourth and final section gives visitors the chance to peer down into the makeshift grave where the body was found.

The Jewry Wall

A five-minute stroll from the cathedral, beside the large St Nicholas Circle roundabout, you'll spot the conspicuous **church of St Nicholas**; beside that, in a small dell, lie the foundations of Emperor Hadrian's public baths, which culminate in the **Jewry Wall**, a substantial chunk of Roman masonry some 18ft high and 73ft long. The baths were a real irritation to the emperor: the grand scheme was spoilt by the engineers, who miscalculated the line of the aqueduct that was to pipe in the water, and so bathers had to rely on a hand-filled cistern replenished from the river – not what Hadrian had in mind at all.

Castle Gardens and around

Near the Roman ruins, **Castle Gardens** is a narrow strip of a park that runs alongside a canalized portion of the River Soar. It's a pleasant spot and one that incorporates the overgrown mound where Leicester's Norman castle motte once stood. Beyond the motte, at the far end of Castle Gardens, you emerge on The Newarke; turn left and follow the road round, and in a jiffy you'll reach **Castle View**, a narrow lane spanned by the Turret Gateway, a rare survivor of the city's medieval castle. Just beyond the gateway is **St Mary de Castro**, a rambling old church with a chunky crocketed tower; curiously, Chaucer may well have got married here.

New Walk Museum and Art Gallery

53–55 New Walk, LE1 7EA · Mon–Sat 10am–5pm, Sun 11am–5pm · Free · ☎ 0116 225 4900, ⓦ visitleicester.info

The **New Walk** is a long and agreeable pedestrianized promenade that's home to the city's best museum, the **New Walk Museum and Art Gallery**. The museum covers a lot of ground, from dinosaurs to geology and beyond, but one highlight is its collection of Ancient Egyptian artefacts, featuring mummies and hieroglyphic tablets brought back to Leicester in the 1880s. The museum also holds an enjoyable collection of paintings and, although these are rotated regularly, you're likely to see a good range of works by British artists as well as an outstanding collection of German Expressionist works, mostly sketches, woodcuts and lithographs by artists such as Otto Dix and George Grosz.

ARRIVAL AND INFORMATION   **LEICESTER**

By train Leicester train station is on London Rd, on the southeast edge of the city centre.

Destinations Birmingham (every 30min; 1hr); Lincoln (hourly; 2hr); London (every 30min; 1hr 15min); Nottingham (every 30min; 30min); Oakham (hourly; 30min); Stamford (hourly; 40min).

By bus St Margaret's bus station is on the north side of the centre, just off Gravel St.

Destinations Ashby-de-la-Zouch (hourly; 1hr 20min); Market Bosworth (hourly; 1hr 10min).

Tourist office In the centre at 51 Gallowtree Gate (Mon– Sat 9.30am–5.30pm, Sun 10am–4pm; ☏ 0116 299 4444, ⓦ visitleicester.info).

ACCOMMODATION

★ **Belmont Hotel** 20 De Montfort Square, LE1 7GR ☏ 0116 254 4773, ⓦ belmonthotel.co.uk; map p.447. A particularly pleasant and proficient hotel in an attractively modernized Victorian property, about 300yd south of the train station via London Rd. Independently owned, it's popular with business folk and tourists alike, and the 74 rooms vary in size and character, though all are extremely well-appointed. **£100**

Maiyango 13–21 St Nicholas Place, LE1 4LD ☏ 0116 251 8898, ⓦ maiyango.com; map p.447. This small hotel has fourteen slick modern rooms, each with bespoke artwork and handmade furniture. Their "superior" rooms have rain showers, whereas the larger "deluxe" rooms opt for walk-in wet rooms and bathtubs – and both have king-size beds. The hotel is also in a handy location, a brief walk from Leicester's main sights and shopping centres. **£170**

EATING

Bobbys 154 Belgrave Rd, LE4 5AT ☏ 0116 266 0106, ⓦ eatatbobbys.com; map p.447. In operation for more than forty years, *Bobbys* is something of a local institution. It's an unpretentious, family-run place with simple decor, where they serve all things vegetarian; £15 will cover a meal for two. At the junction with MacDonald Road. Mon–Fri 11am–10pm, Sat & Sun 10am–10pm.

I Buongustai 82 Granby St, LE1 1DJ ☏ 0116 367 0511, ⓦ facebook.com/BuongustaiLeicester; map p.447. Unusual little café – with just three tables and takeaway – that specializes in Italian street food at bargain prices. The calzone, for instance cost just £3, and very tasty they are too. Mon–Fri 9am–5.30pm & Sat 9am–4pm.

★ **Kayal** 153 Granby St, LE1 6FE ☏ 0116 255 4667, ⓦ kayalrestaurant.com; map p.447. Outstanding South Indian restaurant offering a well-conceived menu covering all the classic dishes and then some – try the Kayal fish curry (£12), or the Njandu crab curry (£14), influenced by Portuguese seafarers. In a handy location near the train station. Mon–Fri noon–3pm & 6–11pm, Sat & Sun noon–10pm.

Lilu 76 Highcross St, LE1 4NN ☏ 0116 262 3119, ⓦ lilurestaurant.co.uk; map p.447. Modern, cosy and inviting restaurant serving a pan-Indian menu, though the key dishes reflect the Gujarati heritage of the family which owns the place. One of the house specials, on a menu strong on meat and fish dishes, is Tandoori-style rack of lamb. On a narrow side street in the heart of the city. Two-course set meal £35. Tues–Thurs 6–9.30pm, Fri & Sat 6–10pm.

DRINKING

Globe 43 Silver St, LE1 5EU ☏ 0116 253 9492, ⓦ www. eversosensible.com/globe; map p.447. Popular and traditional pub in an attractive old building at the heart of the city. Smashing range of real ales, and filling bar food too. Mon–Thurs & Sun 11am–11pm, Fri & Sat 11am–1am.

Taps 10 Guildhall Lane, LE1 5FQ ☏ 0116 253 0904, ⓦ taps-leicester.com; map p.447. Inventive bar and restaurant, whose main claim to fame is the beer taps at many of the tables – help yourself and pay later (yes, the taps are monitored as they dispense). Excellent range of bottled beers too, plus vaulted cellars that date back yonks, and an above-average menu – lamb shank with mash and apricot gravy, for example, for just £15. Mon–Sat noon–11.30pm.

ENTERTAINMENT

Curve Rutland St, LE1 1SB ☏ 0116 242 3595, ⓦ curveonline.co.uk. The heart of the Cultural Quarter, Curve is Leicester's leading performing arts venue, offering a varied programme from within its dramatic glass facade.

Phoenix 4 Midland St, LE1 1TG ☏ 0116 242 2800, ⓦ www.phoenix.org.uk. Just a couple of minutes' walk from Curve, the Phoenix is an outstanding art-house cinema, one of the best in the Midlands.

Leicestershire

Shaped rather like a fox's head, **Leicestershire** is perhaps one of the more anonymous of the English shires, its undulating landscapes comprising an apparently haphazard mix of the industrial, post-industrial and rural with Leicester itself (see page 447) plumb in the middle. The star turn is the pretty little village of **Market Bosworth**, or rather the neighbouring **Bosworth Battlefield Heritage Centre**, near where – at the Battle

---

THE PORK PIE: A GASTRONOMIC DELIGHT?

Melton Mowbray, some eighteen miles northeast of Leicester, is famous for its **pork pies**, an extraordinarily popular English delicacy made of compressed balls of meat and gristle encased in wobbly jelly and thick pastry. To many, the pie's appeal is unaccountable, but in 2009 the EU accorded it Protected Geographical Status, a coveted designation if ever there was one. Pork pies were the traditional repast of the foxhunting fraternity, for whom Melton Mowbray was a favourite haunt. The antics of some of the aristocratic huntsmen are legend – in 1837 the Marquis of Waterford literally painted the town's buildings red, hence the saying. Connoisseurs swear by Dickinson & Morris – visit their shop at 10 Nottingham St, just off the Market Place (Mon–Sat 8am–5pm; ⓦ porkpie.co.uk), to gawp at the full range, from the tiny to the enormous.

---

of Bosworth Field – Richard III met a sticky end in 1485. Less well known are the county's most intriguing church, **St Mary and St Hardulph**, and **Calke Abbey**, technically over the boundary in Derbyshire and not an abbey at all, but an intriguing country house whose faded charms bear witness to the declining fortunes of the landed gentry.

Market Bosworth and around

The thatched cottages and Georgian houses of pocket-sized **MARKET BOSWORTH**, thirteen miles west of Leicester, fan out from a dinky **Market Place**, which was an important trading centre throughout the Middle Ages. From the sixteenth to the nineteenth centuries, the dominant family hereabouts were the Dixies, merchant-landlords who were not universally admired: the young Samuel Johnson, who taught at the **Dixie Grammar School** – its elongated facade still abuts the Market Place – disliked the founder, Sir Wolstan Dixie, so much that he recalled his time there "with the strongest aversion and even a sense of horror". The Dixies mostly ended up at the **Church of St Peter** (daily 8.30am–dusk), a sturdy structure just north of Market Place, whose chancel holds the early eighteenth-century **tomb** of John Dixie, one-time rector, who is honoured by a long hagiographic plaque and the striking effigy of his weeping sister.

Bosworth Field

Sutton Cheney, Nuneaton, CV13 0AD, just south of Market Bosworth • **Heritage Centre** Daily: April–Oct 10am–5pm; Nov–March 10am–4pm • £8.95 • ⓣ 01455 290429, ⓦ bosworthbattlefield.org.uk • The Centre is clearly signed, but there is also an unsigned, 2km-long lane from the south side of Market Bosworth's Market Place

Market Bosworth is best known for the **Battle of Bosworth Field**, fought near the village in 1485. This was the last battle of the Wars of the Roses, an interminably long-winded and bitterly violent conflict for control of the English Crown. The victor was Henry Tudor, subsequently Henry VII, and he defeated Richard III (1452–85), who famously died on the battlefield. In desperation, Shakespeare's villainous Richard cried out "A horse, a horse, my kingdom for a horse," but in fact the defeated king seems to have been a much more phlegmatic character. Taking a glass of water before the fighting started, he actually said, "I live a king: if I die, I die a king". What happened to Richard's body after the battle was long a matter of conjecture, but in 2012 his skeleton was unearthed in the centre of Leicester beneath a council car park (see page 449).

The **Bosworth Battlefield Heritage Centre** features a lucid and well-illustrated description of the battle and explains its historical context in intriguing detail. There is also a section on recent archeological efforts to verify the actual site of the battle: when it was set up in the 1970s, the Heritage Centre followed eighteenth-century tradition in claiming that the battle took place on adjacent Ambion Hill; a circular 1.5-mile **Battle Trail** was laid out accordingly. In the event, it turns out that the battlefield was actually a couple of miles further west on what is now private land, so there has been

9

some tinkering; the Battle Trail now offers views over to the actual battlefield, and makes for an enjoyable ramble. On the way you'll pass **King Richard's Well**, a rough cairn where the king was supposed to have had his final drink. Pick up a trail map at the Heritage Centre before you set out.

ARRIVAL AND DEPARTURE
MARKET BOSWORTH AND AROUND

By bus There are regular services from Leicester to Market Bosworth's Market Place (hourly; 1hr 10min).

ACCOMMODATION AND EATING

Softleys 2 Market Place, CV13 0LE ☎01455 290464, ⓦsoftleys.com. In the centre of the village, this first-rate, family-run hotel has three well-appointed rooms decorated in homely country-house style. The rooms serve as an adjunct to the restaurant, where the menu is lively, creative and local where possible – the lamb is especially good. Mains around £19. Tues–Thurs noon–1.45pm & 6.30–9pm, Fri & Sat noon–1.45pm & 6.30–9.30pm, Sun noon–2.30pm. **£100**

Calke Abbey

Near Ticknall, DE73 7LE • **House** March–Oct daily 11am–5pm • £13.50 (inc. gardens and park); NT; timed tickets • **Gardens** Feb–Oct daily 10am–5pm • £9.10 (inc. park); NT • **Park** Daily 7.30am–7.30pm (dusk if sooner) • £3.60; NT • ☎01332 863822, ⓦnationaltrust.org.uk/calke-abbey

The eighteenth-century facade of **Calke Abbey**, set deep in the countryside about 25 miles northwest of Leicester, is all self-confidence, its acres of dressed stone and three long lines of windows polished off with an imposing Greek Revival portico. This all cost oodles of money and the Harpurs, and then the Harpur-Crewes, who owned the estate, were doing very well until the finances of the English country estate changed after World War I. Then they simply hung on, becoming the epitome of faded gentility and refusing to make all but the smallest of changes – though they did finally plump for electricity in 1962. In 1985, the estate was passed to the National Trust, who decided not to bring in the restorers and have kept the house in its dishevelled state – and this is its real charm.

Church of St Mary and St Hardulph, Breedon-on-the-Hill

DE73 8AJ • Daily 9.30am–4pm, sometimes later in summer • Free • ☎01530 564372, ⓦbreedonchurches.co.uk

Some 9km from Calke Abbey, the hamlet of **BREEDON-ON-THE-HILL** lies at the foot of the large, partly quarried hill from which it takes its name. A steep footpath and a winding, half-mile byroad lead up to the summit, from where there are commanding views over the surrounding countryside – a grand setting for the village's fascinating church. A sturdy edifice that mostly dates from the thirteenth century, the **Church of St Mary and St Hardulph** has an evocative interior with a finely preserved set of Georgian pews, a large and intricate seventeenth-century box-pew, and a trio of exquisite alabaster tombs. Even more rare, however, are a number of **Anglo-Saxon carvings** that include saints and prophets as well as panels in which a dense foliage of vines is inhabited by a tangle of animals and humans. The carvings are quite extraordinary, and the fact that the figures look Byzantine rather than Anglo-Saxon has fuelled much academic debate.

Rutland

To the east of Leicestershire lies **Rutland**, England's smallest county – at least when it's not high tide on the Isle of Wight – a well-heeled pocket of steeply rolling hills just eighteen miles from north to south. Rutland has a few places of note, chiefly **Oakham**, the amiable county town.

OUTDOORS AT RUTLAND WATER

The gentle waters and easy, green hills of **Rutland Water** (ⓦrutlandwater.org.uk) have made it a major centre for outdoor pursuits. There's **sailing** at Rutland Sailing Club (ⓦrutlandsc. co.uk); **cycle hire** with Rutland Cycling (ⓦrutlandcycling.com); and a **Watersports Centre** at Whitwell on the north shore (ⓦanglianwater.co.uk). Rutland Water also attracts a wide range of waterfowl, which prompted the establishment of a **nature reserve** with numerous hides and a **Birdwatching Centre** (ⓦrutlandwater.org.uk/awbc). The reserve is home to a successful Osprey breeding project.

Oakham

The prosperity of **OAKHAM**, twenty miles east of Leicester, is bolstered by Oakham School, one of the region's more exclusive private schools, and by its proximity to Rutland Water, a large reservoir whose assorted facilities attract cyclists, ramblers, sailors and birdwatchers by the hundred. Oakham's stone terraces and Georgian villas are too often interrupted to assume much grace, but the town does have its moments, particularly in the L-shaped **Market Place**, where a brace of sturdy awnings shelter the old water pump and town stocks, and where **Oakham School** is housed in a series of impressive ironstone buildings.

Oakham Castle

Market Place, LE15 6DR • Mon & Wed–Sat 10am–4pm, Sun noon–4pm • Free • ☎ 01572 757578, ⓦ oakhamcastle.org

Footsteps from the Market Place stands **Oakham Castle**, a large banqueting hall that was once part of a twelfth-century fortified house. The hall is a good example of Norman domestic architecture and surrounding the building are the grassy banks of the castle that once protected it. Inside, the whitewashed walls are covered with **horseshoes**, the result of an ancient custom by which every lord or lady, king or queen, is obliged to present an ornamental horseshoe when they first set foot in the town.

All Saints' Church

Church St, LE15 6AA • Daily dawn to dusk • Free • ☎ 01572 724007, ⓦ oakhamteam.uk/oakham

A narrow lane leads from the Market Place to **All Saints' Church**, whose heavy tower and spire rise high above the town. The thirteenth-century church is an architectural hybrid, its solemn interior distinguished by a handsome timber ceiling and intense medieval carvings, with Christian scenes and symbols set alongside dragons, grotesques, devils and demons.

ARRIVAL AND DEPARTURE   OAKHAM

By train Rutland's only station is in Oakham on Station Rd, on the northwest side of town, a 10min walk from Market Place.
Destinations Birmingham (hourly; 1hr 20min); Leicester (hourly; 30min); Melton Mowbray (hourly; 10min); Stamford (hourly; 15min).

By bus The bus station is on John St, 5min from Market Place.
Destinations Lyddington (Mon–Sat hourly; 25min); Uppingham (Mon–Sat hourly; 15min).

ACCOMMODATION AND EATING

Castle Cottage Café Church Passage, off Church St, LE15 6DR ☎01572 757952, ⓦcastlecottagecafe.co.uk. Cosy little café at the back of All Saints' Church featuring a tempting range of moderately priced home-made dishes. They do a particularly good line in cakes and salads. Mon–Fri 10am–4pm, Sat 8.30am–4.30pm, plus dinner specials.

Hambleton Hall Hambleton, LE15 7PL ☎01572 756991, ⓦhambletonhall.com. Just a couple of miles from Oakham, overlooking Rutland Water in tiny Hambleton, this opulent hotel occupies an imposing Baronial-Gothic mansion set in its own immaculate grounds. It's seriously expensive – and seriously luxurious. **£300**

9

Northampton

Spreading north from the River Nene, **NORTHAMPTON** is a workaday town whose modern appearance largely belies its ancient past. Throughout the Middle Ages, this was one of central England's most important towns, a flourishing commercial hub whose now demolished castle was a popular stopping-off point for travelling royalty. A fire in 1675 burnt most of the medieval city to a cinder, and the Georgian town that grew up in its stead was itself swamped by the Industrial Revolution, when Northampton swarmed with **boot- and shoemakers**, whose products shod almost everyone in the British Empire.

Church of All Saints

George Row, NN1 1DF • Mon–Sat 10am–5pm • Free • ☏ 01604 632845, ⓦ allsaintsnorthampton.co.uk

In the centre of town, the **Church of All Saints** is Northampton's finest building, its secular appearance stemming from its finely proportioned, pillared portico and towered cupola. A statue of Charles II in Roman attire surmounts the portico, a (flattering) thank-you for his donation of a thousand tonnes of timber after the Great Fire of 1675 had incinerated the earlier church. The handsome interior holds a sweeping timber gallery and a quartet of Neoclassical pillars, which lead the eye up to the fancy plasterwork decorating the ceiling.

Charles Rennie Mackintosh House

78 Derngate, NN1 1UH • Feb to mid-Dec Tues–Sun & bank hols 10am–5pm; last entry 4pm • £7.50 • ☏ 01604 603407, ⓦ 78derngate.org.uk

In 1916–17, the Scottish architect **Charles Rennie Mackintosh** (1868–1928), the most celebrated proponent of Art Nouveau in the UK, played a key role in the remodelling of this house on behalf of wealthy newlyweds Florence and Wenman Bassett-Lowke. Since the redesign, the **Charles Rennie Mackintosh House** has had a chequered history, but in recent years it has been painstakingly restored and now shows to fine effect many of the man's stylistic hallmarks, most notably the strong, almost stern, right angles which are set against the flowing lines of floral-influenced decorative motifs.

ARRIVAL AND INFORMATION   NORTHAMPTON

By train Northampton train station is on the western edge of the city centre, a 10min walk from All Saints' church.
Destinations Birmingham (every 30min; 1hr); London Euston (every 30min; 1hr).
By bus North Gate bus station is on Bradshaw St, a

short walk from All Saints, with regular Leicester services (every 30min; 1hr 20min).
Tourist office In the former county courthouse on George Row (Mon–Fri 8am–5.30pm, plus April–Sept Sat 10am–2pm; ☏ 01604 367997, ⓦ northamptonshire.gov.uk).

Northamptonshire

Running northeast to southwest and sliced by the M1, **Northamptonshire** holds four medium-sized, semi-industrial towns – Kettering, Corby, Wellingborough and **Northampton** (see above) and a scattering of stone villages set amid rolling countryside. Of the villages, one standout is tiny **Fotheringhay**, where Mary, Queen of Scots came to her untimely end.

Fotheringhay

Hard to believe today, but **FOTHERINGHAY**, a delightful hamlet nestling by the River Nene about thirty miles northeast of Northampton, was once an important centre of feudal power with both a weekly market and a castle. The castle was demolished long

THE GUNPOWDER PLOT

Many of England's Catholics were delighted when the Protestant **Queen Elizabeth I** died in 1603, but when her successor, **James I** (1603–25), proved even less sympathetic to their cause, a small group, under the leadership of a certain **Robert Catesby**, began to plot against the king. The conspirators met at **Ashby St Ledgers**, about 15 miles northwest of Northampton, where they hatched the simplest of plans: first they rented a cellar under Parliament and then they filled it with barrels of gunpowder – enough to blow Parliament sky high. The preparations were in the hands of **Guy Fawkes**, an ardent Catholic and experienced soldier, but the authorities discovered this so-called **Gunpowder Plot** on the eve of the attack, November 4, 1605, and the conspirators were soon rounded up and dispatched. It's quite possible that James's men knew of the plot long before November and allowed it to develop for political (anti-Catholic) reasons. Fawkes himself was tortured, tried and executed and he is still burnt in effigy across the UK on **Bonfire Night** (Nov 5).

ago, but the magnificent **Church of St Mary and All Saints**, rising mirage-like above the green riverine meadows, recalls Fotheringhay's medieval heyday.

Fotheringhay Castle ruins

Signposted down a short and bumpy lane on the bend of the road as you come into the village from Oundle • Daily 24hr • Free

Precious little remains of **Fotheringhay Castle**, but the fortress witnessed both the birth of Richard III in 1452 and the beheading of Mary, Queen of Scots, in 1587. On the orders of Elizabeth I, Mary was beheaded in the castle's Great Hall with no one to stand in her support, apart, that is, from her dog, which is said to have rushed from beneath her skirts as her head hit the deck. Thereafter, the castle fell into disrepair and nowadays only a grassy mound, the outline of earthen ramparts and a marshy ditch remain.

Church of St Mary and All Saints

Fotheringhay, PE8 5HZ • Daily 9am–5pm (4pm in winter) • Free • ⓦ friends-of-fotheringhay-church.co.uk

Begun in 1411 and 150 years in the making, Fotheringay's **Church of St Mary and All Saints** is a paradigm of the Perpendicular, its exterior sporting arching buttresses, its nave lit by soaring windows and the whole caboodle topped by a splendid octagonal lantern tower. The interior is a tad bare, but there are two carved medieval pieces to inspect – a painted pulpit and a sturdy stone font – and two cumbersome memorials to the Dukes of York.

Lincoln

Reaching to the sky from the top of a steep hill, the triple towers of **LINCOLN**'s magnificent **cathedral** are visible for miles across the surrounding flatlands. The cathedral, along with the neighbouring **castle**, are the city's main draws – although, for a smallish place, Lincoln also packs in several good places to eat and one outstanding hotel. The sights are best seen over a leisurely weekend, not least in December during the lively **Christmas market**. The **International Bomber Command Centre** (ⓦ internationalbcc.co.uk) on the southeast edge of town, which celebrates the Allied airmen of World War II, is also worth a visit.

Brief history

High ground is in short supply in Lincolnshire, so it's no surprise that the steep hill which is today surmounted by Lincoln Cathedral was fortified early, firstly by the **Celts**, who called their settlement Lindon, "hillfort by the lake". In 47 AD the **Romans** occupied Lindon and built a fortified town, which subsequently became

9

Lindum Colonia, one of the four regional capitals of Roman Britain. During the reign of William the Conqueror the construction of the **castle** and **cathedral** initiated Lincoln's medieval heyday – the town boomed, first as a Norman power base and then as a centre of the wool trade with Flanders, until 1369 when the wool market was transferred to neighbouring Boston. It was almost five hundred years before Lincoln revived, its recovery based upon the manufacture of agricultural machinery and drainage equipment for the neighbouring fens. As the nineteenth-century town spread south down the hill and out along the old Roman road – the Fosse Way – so Lincoln became a place of precise class distinctions: the **Uphill** area, spreading north from the cathedral, became synonymous with middle-class respectability, **Downhill** with the proletariat, a distinction which only disappeared with the development of **Lincoln University**, whose campus abuts the old city harbour, **Brayford Pool**.

Lincoln Cathedral

Minster Yard • July & Aug Mon–Fri 7.15am–8pm, Sat & Sun 7.15am–6pm; Sept–June Mon–Sat 7.15am–6pm, Sun 7.15am–5pm • Access restricted during services • £8 (includes tour; see page 457), free Sun • ☏ 01522 561600, ⓦ lincolncathedral.com

Lincoln Cathedral is best approached from the west, through the fancy stone arches of the medieval **Exchequergate**, beyond which soars the glorious main facade, a veritable

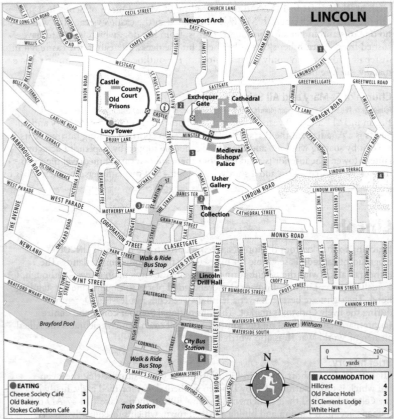

LINCOLN

EATING
Cheese Society Café	3
Old Bakery	1
Stokes Collection Café	2

ACCOMMODATION
Hillcrest	4
Old Palace Hotel	3
St Clements Lodge	1
White Hart	2

International Bomber Command Centre (1.7 miles)

GUIDED TOURS OF LINCOLN CATHEDRAL

The cathedral offers three types of **guided tour**. The first, the **Floor Tour** (Mon–Sat 2–3 daily; 30min; free with the price of admission), is a quick trot around the cathedral's defining features; the second, the **Roof Tour** (Mon–Sat 1–2 daily; 1hr 30min; £4), takes in parts of the church otherwise out of bounds, as does the third, the **Tower Tour** (March–Nov Sat 3 daily; 1hr 30min; £4). Advance reservations are advised for the Tower and Roof tours.

cliff face of blind arcading mobbed by decorative carving. The west front's apparent homogeneity is, however, deceptive, and further inspection reveals two phases of construction – the small stones and thick mortar of much of the facade belong to the original church, completed in 1092, whereas the longer stones and finer courses date from the early thirteenth century. These were enforced works: in 1185, an earthquake shattered much of the Norman church, which was then rebuilt under the auspices of **Bishop Hugh of Avalon**, the man responsible for most of the present cathedral, with the notable exception of the (largely) fourteenth-century central tower.

The mighty **interior** is a fine example of Early English architecture, with the nave's pillars conforming to the same general design yet differing slightly, their varied columns and bands of dark Purbeck marble contrasting with the oolitic limestone that is the building's main material. Looking back up the nave from beneath the **central tower**, you can also observe a major medieval cock-up: Bishop Hugh's roof is out of alignment with the earlier west front, and the point where they meet has all the wrong angles. It's possible to pick out other irregularities, too – the pillars have bases of different heights, and there are ten windows in the nave's north wall and nine in the south – but these are deliberate features, reflecting a medieval aversion to the vanity of symmetry.

Beyond the nave lies **St Hugh's Choir**, more jumbled architecturally but with some exquisite medieval misericords, and beyond that is the open and airy **Angel Choir**, completed in 1280 and famous for the tiny, finely carved **Lincoln imp** (see page 458), which embellishes one of its columns; helpfully, there's a light trained on it, but it costs 20p to switch it on. Finally, a corridor off the choir's north aisle leads to the wooden-roofed **cloisters** and the splendid, polygonal **chapter house**, where Edward I and Edward II convened gatherings that prefigured the creation of the English Parliament.

Lincoln Castle

Castle Hill, LN1 3AA • Daily: April–Sept 10am–5pm; Oct–March 10am–4pm • £13.80; prison & Magna Carta only £11.50; wall walkway only £6 • ☎ 01522 554559, ⓦ lincolncastle.com

Intact and forbidding, the gateway, walls and towers of **Lincoln Castle** incorporate bits and pieces from the twelfth to the nineteenth centuries with the **wall walkway** offering great views over town. The wall encloses a large central courtyard dotted around which are law courts, a heritage skills centre and two former **Victorian prisons**. The debtors' prison serves as the entrance to a newly constructed **vault**, which was built to display several rare documents, most memorably one of the four surviving copies of the **Magna Carta**.

Behind the vault is the old felons' prison, where you can wander several floors of cells and visit a truly remarkable **prison chapel**. Here, the prisoners were locked in high-sided cubicles designed so that they could see the pulpit but not each other. This approach was not only applied to the chapel: prisoners were kept in perpetual **solitary confinement**, even compelled to wear masks in the exercise yard. This so-called Pentonville System of "Separation and Silence", introduced here in 1846, was based on the pseudo-scientific theory that crime is a contagious disease, but unfortunately for the theorists it drove so many prisoners crazy that it had to be abandoned thirty years later; nobody ever bothered to dismantle the chapel.

9

THE LINCOLN IMP

The **Lincoln imp**, carved high on a column in Lincoln Cathedral, had long been a source of legend, but it was the entrepreneurial James Ward Usher who turned the wee beastie into a tidy profit in the 1880s, selling Lincoln imp tie-pins, cuff-links, spoons, brooches and beads. Usher also popularized the traditional legend of the imp, a tall tale in which a couple of imps are blown to Lincoln by a playful wind. They then proceed to hop around the cathedral, until one of them is turned to stone for trying to talk to the angels carved into the roof of the Angel Choir. His chum makes a hasty exit on the back of a witch, but the wind is still supposed to haunt the cathedral, awaiting its opportunity to be mischievous again.

The Collection

Danes Terrace, LN2 1LP • Daily 10am–4pm • Free • ☎ 01522 782040, ⓦ thecollectionmuseum.com

Occupying two contrasting buildings – a striking modern structure and a really rather grand 1920s edifice close by – **The Collection** is Lincoln's main museum. Pride of place in the more modern building is the city's extensive collection of archeological artefacts, from prehistoric times onwards, while the older building, aka the **Usher Gallery**, features a regularly rotated selection of fine and applied art, including English landscape paintings, sculptures, porcelain, watches and clocks.

ARRIVAL AND INFORMATION
LINCOLN

By train Lincoln train station is on St Mary's Street, on the south side of the centre.
Destinations Leicester (hourly; 2hr); Newark (1–2 hourly; 30min); Nottingham (hourly; 1hr); Stamford (hourly; 2hr–2hr 30min, min of one change).

By bus The new bus station is by the train station.
Tourist office 9 Castle Hill, between the cathedral and the castle (April–Sept Mon–Sat 10am–5pm, Sun 10.30am–4pm; Oct–March daily 11am–3pm; ☎ 01522 545458, ⓦ visitlincoln.com).

GETTING AROUND

By Walk & Ride From both the train and bus stations, it's a steep, 20min walk up to the cathedral, or you can take the Walk & Ride minibus (Mon–Sat 9am–2pm & 4–5pm, every 20min; single £1.50), which loops through the city centre. Another handy Walk & Ride stop is on Silver St, just off High St.

ACCOMMODATION

Hillcrest 15 Lindum Terrace, LN2 5RT ☎ 01522 510182, ⓦ hillcresthotel-lincoln.co.uk; map p.456. Traditional, very English hotel in a large red-brick house that was originally a Victorian rectory. Sixteen comfortable rooms with all mod cons plus a large, sloping garden. About 10min walk from the cathedral. **£100**

★ **Old Palace Hotel** Minster Yard, LN2 1PU ☎ 01522 580000, ⓦ theoldpalace.org; map p.456. Easily the best place to stay in Lincoln, this excellent hotel occupies a rambling, largely nineteenth-century mansion – once a bishops' palace – within earshot of the cathedral. The hotel has 32 rooms, half in the main building, including a tower suite, and the remainder in an immaculately reconfigured 1920s chapel. The hotel's grand drawing room is in the former library and most of the furniture has been made by local carpenters. Smashing views, too. **£90**

St Clements Lodge 21 Langworthgate, LN2 4AD ☎ 01522 521532, ⓦ stclementslodge.co.uk; map p.456. In a smart, modern house a short walk from the cathedral, this comfortable B&B has three cosy, en-suite rooms. Home-made breakfasts too – try the haddock or the kippers. **£85**

White Hart Bailgate, LN1 3AR ☎ 01522 526222, ⓦ whitehart-lincoln.co.uk; map p.456. Antique former coaching inn, whose public rooms have received a fairly humdrum revamp. The bedrooms are in a more traditional, country-house style and the pick overlook the cathedral. Curiously, it was here in an upstairs room during World War I that a local engineering firm set about designing a motorized gun at the behest of the government. To camouflage their intentions, the new behemoths were called water carriers – hence "tanks" – and the name stuck. **£100**

EATING

★ **Cheese Society Café** 1 St Martin's Lane, LN2 1HY ☎ 01522 511003, ⓦ thecheesesociety.co.uk; map p.456. This bright and breezy little café is something of a gastronomic landmark hereabouts, its menu featuring all things cheesy, from rarebits and raclettes – all with salads – through to an especially delicious stilton, red wine and walnut pâté. There are non-cheesy options, too, plus a good range of beers and ciders. Mains at £9. Mon–Fri 10am–4.30pm, Sat 10am–5pm.

★ **Old Bakery** 26 Burton Rd, LN1 3LB ☎01522 576057, ⓦtheold-bakery.co.uk; map p.456. Cosy, rural-chic restaurant, where the menu is both well considered and inventive – try, for example, the grilled polenta and cherry tomatoes with Gorgonzola and green olive purée. Has an excellent wine cellar, too. Reservations recommended. Mains average £18. Tues & Wed 7–8.30pm, Thurs–Sat

noon–1.30pm & 7–8.30pm, Sun noon–1.30pm.

Stokes Collection Café Danes Terrace, LN2 1LP ☎01522 523548, ⓦstokes-coffee.co.uk; map p.456. Attached to Lincoln's principal museum (see page 458), this cheerful modern café is a self-service affair where they do a tasty line in crêpes, sandwiches and salads. They also have a line-up of special musical events, mainly jazz and classical. The owners, the Stokes family, have been roasting coffee and blending tea in Lincoln for several generations. Daily 10am–4pm.

ENTERTAINMENT

Lincoln Drill Hall Free School Lane, LN2 1EY ☎01522 873891, ⓦlincolndrillhall.com. Lincoln's prime arts and

entertainment venue, featuring everything from stand-up and theatre to classical concerts, rock and pop.

The Lincolnshire Wolds and the coast

Northeast of Lincoln, the **Lincolnshire Wolds** are a narrow band of chalky land whose rolling hills and gentle valleys are particularly appealing in the vicinity of Louth, a trim little place where conscientious objectors were sent to dig potatoes during World War II. East of the Wolds lies the **coast**, with its bungalows, campsites and caravans parked behind a sandy **beach** that extends, with a few marshy interruptions, north from **Skegness**, the main resort, to Mablethorpe and ultimately Cleethorpes. At its worst, the coast's amusement-arcade commercialism can be hard to warm to, but small portions have been preserved and protected, most notably at the **Gibraltar Point National Nature Reserve**, just south of Skegness.

Skegness

SKEGNESS has been a busy resort ever since the railways reached the Lincolnshire coast in 1875. Its heyday was before the 1960s, when the Brits began to take themselves off to sunnier climes, but it still attracts tens of thousands of city-dwellers who come for the wide, sandy **beaches** and attractions ranging from nightclubs to bowling greens. Every inch the traditional English seaside town, Skegness outdoes its rivals by keeping its beaches sparklingly clean and its parks spick-and-span. That said, the seafront, with its rows of souvenir shops and amusement arcades, can be dismal, especially on a rainy day.

Gibraltar Point National Nature Reserve

Gibraltar Rd, PE24 4SU, 3 miles south of Skegness • Reserve daily dawn–dusk; visitor centre daily 10am–3pm • Free • ☎01754 898057, ⓦlincstrust.org.uk/gibraltar-point

At the **Gibraltar Point National Nature Reserve**, a network of clearly signed footpaths patterns a narrow strip of salt- and freshwater marsh, sand dune and beach that attracts an inordinate number of birds, both resident and migratory. There are numerous hides dotted around and a brand-new **visitor centre** has been built to replace an earlier version, which was badly damaged by floods.

ARRIVAL AND INFORMATION

SKEGNESS

By bus & train Skegness's bus and train stations are adjacent, about 10min walk from the seashore – cut across Lumley Square and head straight up the main street to the landmark clocktower.

Destinations (bus) Lincoln (2–4 daily; 2hr).

Destinations (train) Boston (hourly; 30min); Nottingham (hourly; 2hr).

Tourist office Inside the Embassy Theatre, close to the clocktower on Grand Parade (core hours: daily 9.30am–4pm; ☎01507 613100, ⓦvisitlincolnshire.com).

9

The Lincolnshire Fens

The Fens, that great chunk of eastern England extending from Boston in Lincolnshire right down to Cambridge, encompass some of the most productive farmland in Europe. Give or take the occasional hillock, this pancake-flat, treeless terrain has been painstakingly reclaimed, from the marshes and swamps which once drained into the intrusive stump of **The Wash**, an indentation of the North Sea, a process that has taken almost two thousand years. In earlier times, outsiders were often amazed by the dreadful conditions hereabouts, but they did spawn the distinctive culture of the so-called **fen-slodgers**, who embanked small portions of marsh to create pastureland and fields, supplementing their diets by catching fish and fowl and gathering reed and sedge for thatching and fuel. This local economy was threatened by the large-scale land reclamation schemes of the late fifteenth and sixteenth centuries, and time and again the locals sabotaged progress by breaking down new banks and dams. But the odds were stacked against the saboteurs, and a succession of great landowners eventually drained huge tracts of the fenland – and by the 1790s the fen-slodgers' way of life had all but disappeared.

Nonetheless, the **Lincolnshire Fens** remain a distinctive area, with a scattering of introverted little villages spread across the flatlands within easy striking distance of the A17. Several of these villages are distinguished by their imposing **medieval churches** – St Mary Magdalene's in **Gedney** and St Mary's in **Long Sutton** for example – and their soaring spires are seen to best advantage in the pale, watery sunlight and wide skies of the fenland evening. But it's above the rough-edged old port of **Boston**, Lincolnshire's second-largest settlement, that you'll find the most impressive church of all, mighty St Botolph's.

St Botolph's Church, Boston

Church St, PE21 6NW • **Church** Mon–Sat 8.30am–4pm, Sun 7.30am–4pm • Free • **Tower** Mon–Sat 10am–3.30pm & Sun 1–3.30pm • £5 • 📞 01205 354670, 🌐 parish-of-boston.org.uk • Regular trains from Lincoln, Skegness and Grantham, and buses from Lincoln

In the fourteenth century **BOSTON** became England's second-largest seaport, its flourishing economy dependent on the wool trade with Flanders, and it was rich local merchants who built the magnificent **St Botolph's**. The massive bulk of the church looms over the River Witham, its exterior embellished by the high-pointed windows and elaborate tracery of the Decorated style. Most of the building dates from the fourteenth century, but the huge and distinctive tower – whose lack of a spire earned the church the nickname the "**Boston Stump**" – is of later construction, and the octagonal lantern is later still. Down below, the light and airy **nave** is an exercise in the Perpendicular, all soaring columns and high windows, a purity of design that is simply stunning. Look out also for the **misericords** in the chancel (a 50p leaflet gives the lowdown on all sixty), which sport a charming mixture of vernacular scenes, from organ-playing bears and a pair of medieval jesters squeezing cats in imitation of bagpipes through to a schoolmaster birching a boy, watched by three more awaiting the same fate – or perhaps they are just watching and laughing. By the nave, a narrow and tortuous 365-step spiral staircase leads up the **tower** to a balcony, from where there are panoramic views over Boston and the fens.

Church of St Mary Magdalene, Gedney

Church End, PE12 0BU, 17 miles from Boston via the A17 • Daily dawn–dusk • Free

The scattered hamlet of **GEDNEY** is home to the remarkable **Church of St Mary Magdalene**. Seen from a distance the church seems almost magical, its imposing lines in striking contrast with its fen-flat surroundings. Up close, the triple-aisled nave is beautiful, its Norman arcade splendid, and a battery of windows lights the exquisite Renaissance alabaster effigies of husband and wife Adlard and Cassandra Welby, facing each other on the south wall near the chancel. Their tomb is decorated with a corn-on-the-cob motif – one of the earliest representations of this American import to be found in England.

Long Sutton

A modest farming centre a couple of miles from Gedney, **LONG SUTTON** limps along its main street to a trim Market Place. Here, the **church of St Mary** (daily dawn–dusk; free) has preserved many of its Norman features, with its arcaded tower supporting the oldest lead spire in the country, dating from around 1200. Long Sutton once lay on the edge of the mouth of the **River Nene**, where it emptied into The Wash. This was the most treacherous part of the road from Lincoln to Norfolk, and for centuries locals had to guide travellers across the mud flats on horseback. In 1831, the river was embanked and then spanned with a wooden bridge at **Sutton Bridge**, a hamlet just two miles east of Long Sutton. The present swing bridge, with its nifty central tower, was completed in 1894.

Stamford and around

Tucked away in the southwest corner of Lincolnshire, **STAMFORD**, 35 miles from Boston, is delightful, a handsome little limestone town of yellow-grey seventeenth- and eighteenth-century buildings, which slope up from the River Welland. The town's salad days were as a centre of the medieval wool and cloth trade, when wealthy merchants built its medley of stone churches and houses. Stamford was also the home of William Cecil, Elizabeth I's sagacious chief minister, who built his splendid mansion, **Burghley House**, close by.

The town survived the collapse of the wool trade, prospering as an inland port after the Welland was made navigable to the sea in 1570, and, in the eighteenth century, as a staging point on the Great North Road from London. More recently, Stamford escaped the three main threats to old English towns – the Industrial Revolution, wartime bombing and postwar development – and was designated the country's first Conservation Area in 1967. Its unspoilt streets lend themselves to period drama and filmmaking, and although it's the harmony of Stamford's architecture that pleases rather than any specific sight, there are still some buildings of special interest as well as an especially charming **High Street**.

Church of All Saints

All Saints' Place, PE9 2AG • Mon–Sat 9am–5pm, Sun 9am–7pm • Free • ⓦ stamfordallsaints.org.uk

A convenient place to start an exploration of Stamford, the **Church of All Saints** stands at the western end of the town centre, its beautiful facade a happy amalgamation of Early English and Perpendicular. Entry is via the south porch, an ornate structure with a fine – if badly weathered – crocketted gable. Beyond, though much of the interior is routinely Victorian, the nave's carved capitals are of great delicacy. Look out also for an engaging folkloric carving of the Last Supper behind the high altar that dates to the 1870s.

STAMFORD SHAKESPEARE COMPANY

One of the most enjoyable of Stamford's festivals is the **Stamford Shakespeare Company**'s (☎01780 756133, Ⓦ stamfordshakespeare.co.uk) open-air performances of the great man's works set in the grounds of **Tolethorpe Hall**, an Elizabethan mansion just outside town. The season lasts from June to August, with the audience protected from the elements by a vast canopy.

Browne's Hospital

Broad St, PE9 1PF · **Guided tours** Late May to Sept by arrangement; advance booking required · £3.50/person, but minimum £30/tour · **Open days** Two per year, spring & autumn, 11am–4pm · Free · ☎01780 763153, Ⓦ stamfordcivicsociety.org.uk

A stone's throw from All Saints, wide and good-looking Broad Street is home to **Browne's Hospital**, the most extensive of the town's surviving almshouses, a substantial complex dating from the late fifteenth century. The cottages and the green towards the rear are rarely open to the public, but the old **dormitory** at the front, with its splendid wood-panelled ceiling, is usually included on the guided tour as is the adjacent **chapel**, which holds some fine stained-glass windows and appealingly folksy misericords.

Church of St Mary

St Mary's St, PE9 2DS · No regular opening hours · Free · Ⓦ stamfordbenefice.com

A brief stroll from Broad Street, sitting pretty just above the main bridge over the River Welland, the **Church of St Mary** boasts a splendid spire. The interior is small but airy and incorporates an imposing reredos, a batch of Victorian stained glass and the **Corpus Christi** chapel, whose intricately embossed, painted and panelled ceiling dates back to the 1480s.

Church of St Martin

23 High St St Martin's, PE9 2NT · Daily 9.30am–4pm · Free · ☎01780 753356, Ⓦ achurchnearyou.com/stamford-baron-st-martin

The sombre, late fifteenth-century **Church of St Martin** shelters the magnificent tombs of the lords Burghley, beginning with a recumbent William Cecil (1520–98) carved beneath twin canopies, holding his rod of office and with a lion at his feet. Immediately behind are the early eighteenth-century effigies of John Cecil, the fifth Lord Burghley (1648–1700), and his wife, with the couple depicted as Roman aristocrats, propped up on their elbows, John to stare across the nave commandingly, Anne to gaze at him.

Burghley House

Barnack Rd, PE9 3JY · **House & gardens** Mid-March to Oct Mon–Thurs, Sat & Sun 11am–5pm · £18, £16 in advance · **Park** Daily 8am–6pm (dusk if sooner) · Free · ☎01780 752451, Ⓦ burghley.co.uk · The main entrance is signposted 1.5miles southeast of Stamford

Now famous for the prestigious Burghley Horse Trials, held over four days in late August or early September, **Burghley House** is an extravagant Elizabethan mansion standing in Capability Brown parkland. Completed in 1587 after 22 years in the making, the house sports a yellow ragstone exterior, embellished by dainty cupolas, a pyramidal clocktower and skeletal balustrading, all to a plan by **William Cecil**, long-time adviser to Elizabeth I. However, with the notable exception of the kitchen, little remains of Burghley's Tudor interior; instead, the house bears the heavy hand of John Cecil, who toured France and Italy in the late seventeenth century, buying paintings and commissioning furniture, statuary and tapestries. To provide a suitable setting for his old masters, John brought in Antonio Verrio and his assistant Louis

Laguerre, who covered many of Burghley's walls and ceilings with frolicking gods and goddesses. These gaudy and gargantuan murals are at their most engulfing in the **Heaven Room**, a classical temple that adjoins the **Hell Staircase**, where the entrance to the inferno is through the gaping mouth of a cat.

ARRIVAL AND INFORMATION

STAMFORD AND AROUND

By train Stamford's pretty station is on the south side of the River Welland, a 5–10min walk from the centre.
Destinations Cambridge (hourly; 1hr 10min); Leicester (hourly; 40min); Oakham (hourly; 15min).

By bus The bus station is on Sheepmarket, off All Saints' St.
Tourist office In the Stamford Arts Centre, 27 St Mary's Street (Mon–Sat 9.30am–5pm; ☎ 01780 755611, ⓦ south westlincs.com).

ACCOMMODATION AND EATING

★ **George Hotel** 71 High St St Martin's, PE9 2LB ☎01780 750750, ⓦ georgehotelofstamford.com. Stamford's most celebrated hotel by a country mile, *The George* is a sympathetically renovated old coaching inn; the most appealing of the plush rooms overlook a cobbled courtyard. The *Garden Room*, the less formal of the two excellent restaurants, serves everything from hamburgers to lobster spaghetti, all prepared to a high standard; mains average £18. Garden Room daily noon–10pm. **£200**
Hambleton Bakery 1 Ironmonger St, PE9 1PL ☎ 01780 754327, ⓦ hambletonbakery.co.uk. A small regional chain offering a first-rate range of breads – rye, sourdough and so forth – plus muffins and cakes. Takeaway only.

Mon–Sat 8am–5pm.
No.3 The Yard 3 Ironmonger St, PE9 1PL ☎01780 756080, ⓦ no3theyard.co.uk. Inside a creatively refurbished old building at the back of a scrappy courtyard, this spilt-level restaurant has an excellent Modern British menu – try the smoked haddock with pancetta. Mains around £16. Tues–Sat 11.30am–2pm & 6.30–9.30pm, Sun noon–3pm.
Stamford Lodge Guest House 66 Scotgate, PE9 2YB ☎01780 482932, ⓦ stamfordlodge.co.uk. In an attractive, Georgian stone house on the north side of the town centre, this smartly turned-out establishment has five, en-suite guest rooms decorated in a warm and cosy version of period style. **£95**

The Northwest

WHITWORTH ART GALLERY, MANCHESTER

The Northwest

Ask most Brits about northwest England and they'll probably mention football and rain – stereotypes that don't come close to summarizing this exciting region of dynamic urban centres, pretty countryside, iconic seaside resorts and historic towns. One of the world's great industrial cities, Manchester has transformed its cityscape in recent decades to place itself firmly in the vanguard of modern British urban design, and complements its top-class visitor attractions with lively cafés and an exciting music scene. Just thirty miles west, revitalized Liverpool has kept apace of the "northern renaissance", too, and is a city of great energy and charm.

The southern suburbs of Manchester bump into the steep hills of the **Pennine range**, and to the southwest the city slides into pastoral **Cheshire**, a county of rolling green countryside whose dairy farms churn out the famed crumbly white cheese. The county town, **Chester**, with its complete circuit of Roman walls and partly Tudor centre, is as alluring as any of the country's northern towns, capturing the essence of one of England's wealthiest counties.

The historical county of **Lancashire** reached industrial prominence in the nineteenth century primarily due to the cotton-mill towns around Manchester and the thriving port of Liverpool – although neither city is part of the county today. Resorts along the coast between Southport and Morecambe once formed the mainstay of the northern British holiday, though only **Blackpool** is really worth visiting for its own sake, a rip-roaring resort which has stayed at the top of its game by supplying undemanding entertainment with more panache than its neighbours. However, **Morecambe**, with its Art Deco *Midland Hotel*, is easily combined with a visit to the historically important city of **Lancaster** and its hilltop Tudor castle. Finally, the Crown dependency of the **Isle of Man**, just 25 miles off the coast, provides a rugged terrain almost as rewarding as that of the Lake District, but without the seasonal overcrowding.

GETTING AROUND   THE NORTHWEST

By train Both Manchester and Liverpool are well served by trains, with regular high-speed connections to the Midlands and London, and up the west coast to Scotland. The major east–west rail lines in the region are the direct routes between Manchester, Leeds and York, and between Blackpool, Bradford, Leeds and York. The Lancaster–Leeds line slips through the Yorkshire Dales and further south, the Manchester–Sheffield line provides a rail approach to the Peak District.

By bus The major cities, as well as Chester, are connected by frequent bus services.

Manchester

MANCHESTER has had a global profile for more than 150 years, since the dawn of the industrial revolution. But today's elegant core of converted warehouses and glass skyscrapers is a far cry from the smoke-covered sprawl George Orwell once described

GORMLEY STATUES, CROSBY BEACH

Highlights

❶ Manchester's Northern Quarter Lose yourself in chic shops, cafés and music venues in this vibrant warehouse district. See page 474

❷ Whitworth Art Gallery, Manchester An ambitious £15m transformation has created a light-filled gallery space that blends seamlessly with the surrounding park. See page 474

❸ City walls, Chester The handsome old town of Chester is best surveyed from the heights of its Roman walls. See page 483

❹ Culture in Liverpool From the artistic hub of the Baltic Triangle to Antony Gormley's Crosby Beach statues, this dynamic city pulses with creative energy. See page 485

❺ Blackpool Pleasure Beach Bright, bawdy and brash, Britain's cheekiest resort is constantly reinventing itself. See page 496

❻ Lancaster Castle From the dungeons to the ornate courtrooms, the castle is a historical tour de force. See page 499

❼ Sunset across Morecambe Bay Drink in one of the country's finest sunsets at the bar in the Art Deco *Midland Hotel*. See page 501

❽ Sea-kayaking, the Calf of Man Taking to the water in a kayak allows you to view local seal colonies, seabirds, and the Isle of Man's stunning, rugged coast from a unique perspective. See page 506

HIGHLIGHTS ARE MARKED ON THE MAP ON PAGE 468

as "the belly and guts of the nation". Its renewed pre-eminence expresses itself in various ways, most swaggeringly in its **football**, as home to the world's most famous and wealthiest clubs – Manchester United and Manchester City, respectively – but also in a thriving **music scene** that has given birth to world-beaters as diverse as the Hallé Orchestra and Oasis. Moreover, the city's celebrated concert halls, theatres, clubs and cafés feed off the cosmopolitan drive provided by the country's largest **student** population outside London and a high-profile **LGBT+** community.

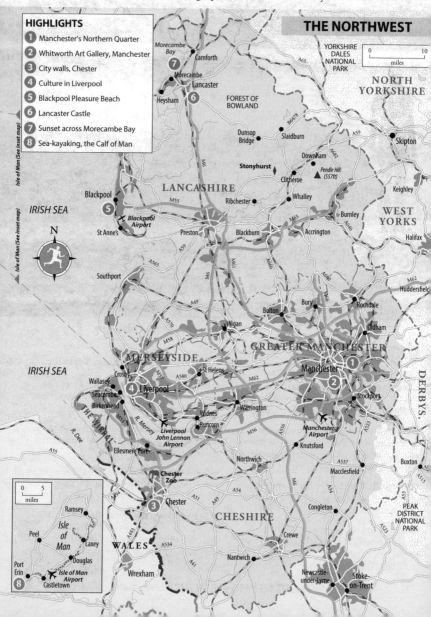

THE NORTHWEST

HIGHLIGHTS

1. Manchester's Northern Quarter
2. Whitworth Art Gallery, Manchester
3. City walls, Chester
4. Culture in Liverpool
5. Blackpool Pleasure Beach
6. Lancaster Castle
7. Sunset across Morecambe Bay
8. Sea-kayaking, the Calf of Man

10

MANCHESTER ORIENTATION

If Manchester can be said to have a centre, it's **Albert Square** and the cluster of buildings surrounding it – the Town Hall, the Central Library and the *Midland Hotel*, originally built in the railway age to host visitors to Britain's greatest industrial city. South of here, the former Central Station now functions as the **Manchester Central** convention centre, with the Hallé Orchestra's home, **Bridgewater Hall**, just opposite. **Chinatown** and the **Gay Village** are just a short walk to the east, while to the northeast, the revamped **Piccadilly Gardens** provides access to the hip **Northern Quarter**. To the southwest is the **Castlefield** district, site of the Museum of Science and Industry, and flashy **Spinningfields**, incongruous home of the People's History Museum. The central spine of the city is **Deansgate**, which runs from Castlefield to the cathedral and, in its northern environs, displays the most dramatic core of urban regeneration in the country, centred on the unalloyed modernity of **Exchange Square**.

There are plenty of sights, too: the centre possesses the **Manchester Art Gallery**, the **National Football Museum** and the fantastic **People's History Museum** as well as the **Museum of Science and Industry**, while further south is **The Whitworth Art Gallery**, and, to the west, the revamped **Salford Quays**, which are home to the prestigious **Lowry arts centre**, the stirring and stunning **Imperial War Museum North**, and **MediaCityUK**, the new northern base of the BBC.

Brief history

Despite a **history** stretching back to Roman times, and pockets of surviving medieval and Georgian architecture, Manchester is first and foremost a **Victorian manufacturing city**. Its rapid growth set the pace for the flowering of the Industrial Revolution elsewhere – transforming it in just a hundred years from little more than a village to the world's major cotton centre. The spectacular rise of **Cottonopolis**, as it became known, arose from the manufacture of vast quantities of competitively priced imitations of expensive Indian calicoes, using water and then steam-driven machines developed in the late eighteenth and nineteenth centuries.

Rapid industrialization brought immense wealth for a few but a life of misery for the majority. The discontent came to a head in 1819 when eleven people were killed at the **Peterloo Massacre**, in what began as a peaceful demonstration against the oppressive **Corn Laws**. Things were, however, even worse when the 23-year-old Friedrich Engels came here in 1842 to work in his father's cotton plant: the grinding poverty he recorded in his *Condition of the Working Class in England* was a seminal influence on his later collaboration with **Karl Marx** in the *Communist Manifesto*.

The **Manchester Ship Canal**, constructed in 1894 to entice ocean-going vessels into Manchester and away from burgeoning Liverpool, played a crucial part in sustaining Manchester's competitiveness. From the late 1950s, however, the docks, mills, warehouses and canals were in dangerous decline. The main engine of change turned out to be the devastating **IRA bomb** which exploded outside the Arndale shopping centre in June 1996, wiping out a fair slice of the city's commercial infrastructure. Rather than simply patching things up, the council embarked on an ambitious rebuilding scheme, which transformed the face of Manchester. In 2017, the resilience of the city was demonstrated once again as performers took to the stage for One Love, a benefit concert for those affected by the tragic suicide bombing at Manchester Arena on May 22, which killed 22 people.

Albert Square

Most of Manchester's panoply of **neo-Gothic** buildings and monuments date from the city's heyday in the second half of the nineteenth century. One of the more fanciful is the shrine-like, canopied **monument** to Prince Albert, Queen Victoria's husband, perched prettily in the middle of the trim little square that bears his name – **Albert Square**. The monument was erected in 1867, six years after Albert's death, supposedly because he had always shown an interest in industry, but perhaps more to curry favour with the grieving queen. Overlooking the prince is Alfred Waterhouse's magnificent, neo-Gothic **Town Hall** (Mon–Fri 9am–5pm; free), whose mighty clocktower, completed in 1877, pokes a sturdy finger into the sky, soaring high above its gables, columns and arcaded windows.

St Peter's Square and around

Just south of the Town Hall is **St Peter's Square**, home to the revamped **Central Library**. Footsteps away, over on Peter Street, the **Free Trade Hall** was the home of the city's Hallé Orchestra for more than a century – until Bridgewater Hall was completed in 1996. The Italianate facade survived intense wartime bombing and is now a protected part of the *Radisson Blu Edwardian Hotel*, whose modern tower block rises up behind at a (fairly) discreet distance.

■ ACCOMMODATION	
ABode	2
Arora	4
Great John Street	3
Hilton Chambers	1
Midland	7
Motel One	6
Radisson Blu Edwardian	5
YHA Manchester	8

● EATING			■ DRINKING		■ NIGHTLIFE		● SHOPPING	
Australasia	8	Richmond Tea Rooms 11	Big Hands	15	Albert Hall	7	Afflecks	5
Dimitri's	12	Rudy's Pizza 4	Britons Protection	11	Band on the Wall	1	Craft & Design Centre	1
Eighth Day	13	Sam's Chop House 6	Circus Tavern	8	The Castle Hotel	3	Oklahoma	3
Federal Café Bar	2	Takk 7	Cloud 23	9	The Deaf Institute	14	Piccadilly Records	4
Home Sweet Home	3	Trof NQ 1	Corbières	5	Matt & Phreds	2	Retro Rehab	2
The Koffee Pot	5	Yang Sing 10	Mr Thomas'		O2 Apollo Manchester	16		
Lime Tree	15	Yuzu 9	Chop House	6	O2 Ritz Manchester	12		
Mughli Charcoal Pit	14		Sand Bar	13	Soup Kitchen	4		
			The Temple	10				

Central Library

St Peter's Square, M2 5PD • Mon–Thurs 9am–8pm, Fri & Sat 9am–5pm • Free • ☎ 0161 234 1983, ⓦ manchester.gov.uk/centrallibrary • St Peter's Square Metrolink

The circular **Central Library** was built in 1934 as the world's largest municipal library, a self-consciously elegant, classical construction. After a four-year closure, it reopened, beautifully refurbished and extended, in 2014, with its showpiece domed **reading room** restored; check out the display case of sweet wrappers, found stuffed down the desks here over the last eighty years. The **children's library** is modelled on *The Secret Garden* by local author Frances Hodgson Burnett.

10

Manchester Art Gallery

Mosley St, M2 3JL • Daily 10am–5pm, till 9pm Thurs • Free • ☎ 0161 235 8888, ⓦ manchesterartgallery.org • St Peter's Square Metrolink

Manchester Art Gallery, as well as attracting big-name exhibitions by contemporary artists, holds an invigorating collection of eighteenth- and nineteenth-century art. Spread across **Floor 1**, these works are divided by theme – Face and Place, Expressing Passions and so on – rather than by artist (or indeed school of artists), which makes it difficult to appreciate the strength of the collection, especially when it comes to its forte, the Pre-Raphaelites. There's much else – views of Victorian Manchester, a Turner or two, a pair of Gainsboroughs, and Stubbs's famous *Cheetah and Stag with Two Indians* to name but a few. **Floor 2** features temporary exhibitions and crafts, while the **Ground Floor**'s Manchester Gallery is devoted to a visual history of the city. The **Clore Art Studio** is fun for kids.

Petersfield

South of St Peter's Square, on **Lower Mosley Street**, stands Britain's finest concert hall, **Bridgewater Hall**, balanced on shock-absorbing springs to guarantee the clarity of the sound. The apartment block at the corner of Lower Mosley Street and Whitworth Street West bears the name of the site's previous occupant, the infamous **Hacienda Club**, the spiritual home of Factory Records, an independent label that defined a generation of music through such bands as Joy Division, New Order and the Happy Mondays before closing down in 1997. Across the road on Tony Wilson Place is Manchester's glitzy new cultural hub, **HOME** (see page 480), a merger between Manchester heavyweights Cornerhouse and the former Library Theatre Company. It comprises two theatres, five cinema screens, gallery space, and production and broadcast facilities; each of the three floors has a low-key bar or restaurant with additional outdoor seating for when the sun shines.

Turn left along Whitworth Street West and you'll spot the string of café-bars and restaurants that have been shoehorned along the Rochdale canal's **Deansgate Locks**, a pattern repeated along and across the street in the old railway arches abutting Deansgate Station. Look up and you'll see the striking **Beetham Tower**, easily the tallest skyscraper in Manchester and home to a glitzy hotel.

Castlefield and St John's

Just west of Deansgate Station, the tangle of railway viaducts and canals that lie sandwiched between Water Street, Liverpool Road and Deansgate make up pocket-sized **Castlefield**. It was here that the country's first man-made canal, the Bridgewater Canal, brought coal and other raw materials to the city's warehouses throughout the eighteenth century. By the early 1960s, the district was an eyesore, but an influx of money cleaned it up, and it now boasts cobbled canalside walks, attractive café-bars and the **Castlefield Urban Heritage Park** (always open; free), centred on the excavated and partially reconstructed *Mamucium* Roman fort, from which the name "Manchester" is derived.

10

Exciting changes are afoot west of Lower Byrom St around the old ITV Granada studios; newly labelled **St John's** (ⓦstjohnsmanchester.com) is a neighbourhood to watch, particularly as **Factory**, an impressive arts space which will be a permanent home for the Manchester International Festival (see page 481), is slated to open in 2020.

Museum of Science and Industry

Liverpool Rd, M3 4FP • Daily 10am–5pm • Free, but admission charge for special exhibitions • ⓣ 0161 832 2244, ⓦ msimanchester.org.uk • Deansgate-Castlefield Metrolink

One of the country's most impressive museums of its type, the **Museum of Science and Industry** mixes technological displays and blockbuster exhibitions with trenchant analysis of the social impact of industrialization. Points of interest include the **Power Hall**, which trumpets the region's remarkable contribution to the Industrial Revolution by means of a hall full of steam engines, some of which are fired up daily. There's more steam in the shape of a working replica of Robert Stephenson's *Planet*. Built in 1830, the *Planet* reliably attained a scorching 30mph but had no brakes; the museum's version does, however, and it's used at weekends (noon–4pm; £2, children £1), dropping passengers a couple of hundred yards away at the **Station Building**, the world's oldest passenger railway station.

The **1830 Warehouse** features a sound-and-light show that delves into the history of the city's immense warehouses, and the **Air and Space Hall**, which barely touches on Manchester at all, features vintage planes, cutaway engines and space exploration displays.

Spinningfields

From the old to the uber-new, Castlefield blends into **Spinningfields**, a glitzy, corporate district that's home to law courts, designer shops and a crop of bars and restaurants, including a swanky rooftop terrace bar as the cherry on the top of shiny high-rise No. 1 Spinningfields. A couple of standout cultural attractions bookend the district.

People's History Museum

Left Bank, M3 3ER • Daily 10am–5pm, until 8pm second Thurs of the month • Free • ⓣ 0161 838 9190, ⓦ phm.org.uk • Deansgate-Castlefield Metrolink

The superb **People's History Museum** explores Britain's rich history of radicalism and the struggles of marginalized people for rights and suffrage – ideas that developed out of the workers' associations and religious movements of the industrial city and helped to shape the modern world. In a former pump house with an ultramodern, four-storey extension, the galleries use interactive displays – including coffins and top hats – to trace a compelling narrative from the 1819 Peterloo Massacre onwards. As the gallery shows, this moment became the catalyst for agitation that led to the 1832 Reform Act, and subsequent rise of the Chartist movement; the museum will play a big part in the 2019 two-hundred-year anniversary. The galleries go on to explore the struggle for female suffrage, the Communist party in Britain, Oswald Mosley's fascists, and the working-class origins of football and pop music, and include the country's finest collection of trade union banners.

John Rylands Library

Deansgate, M3 3EH • **Library** Mon & Sun noon–5pm, Tues–Sat 10am–5pm • **Tour and treasures** Rare books can be seen close up every third Thurs of month 3–4pm (booking required) • Free • ⓣ 0161 306 0555, ⓦ www.library.manchester.ac.uk/rylands • Metroshuttle #1, #2

Nestling between Spinningfields and the north end of Deansgate, **John Rylands Library** is the city's supreme example of Victorian Gothic – albeit with an unbecoming modern entrance wing. The architect who won the original commission, Basil Champneys, opted for a cloistered neo-Gothicism of narrow stone corridors, delicately crafted stonework, stained-glass windows and burnished wooden panelling. The library, which has survived in superb condition, now houses specialist collections of rare books and manuscripts.

Deansgate and around

Deansgate cuts through the city centre from the Rochdale canal to the cathedral, its architectural reference points ranging from Victorian industrialism to post-millennium posturing. The **Great Northern** mall flanks Deansgate between Great Bridgewater and Peter streets. This was once the **Great Northern Railway Company's Goods Warehouse**, a great sweep of brickwork dating back to the 1890s, originally an integral part of a large trading depot with road and rail links on street level and subterranean canals down below.

St Ann's Square

Slender **St Ann's Square** is tucked away off the eastern side of Deansgate, not far from the cathedral. On the square's southern side is **St Ann's Church** (Tues–Sat 10am–5pm; free), a trim sandstone structure whose Neoclassical symmetries date from 1709, though the stained-glass windows are firmly Victorian. At the other end of the square is the **Royal Exchange**, which houses the much-lauded **Royal Exchange Theatre**. Formerly the Cotton Exchange, this building employed seven thousand people until trading finished in 1968 – the old trading board still shows the last day's American and Egyptian cotton prices.

10

Manchester Cathedral and around

Exchange Station Approach, Victoria St, M3 1SX • Mon–Sat 8.30am–6.30pm, Sun 8.30am–7pm • Free • **Tours** Mon–Fri 11am & 2.30pm, Sat 1pm, Sun 2.30pm; 30min • Free, but £3 donation suggested • Ⓦ manchestercathedral.org • Victoria Metrolink

Manchester's **cathedral** dates back to the fifteenth century, though its Gothic lines have been hacked about too much to have any real architectural coherence. Actually, it's surprising it's still here at all: in 1940, a 1000lb bomb all but destroyed the interior, knocking out most of the stained glass, which is why it's so light inside today.

Exchange Square

A pedestrian high street – **New Cathedral Street** – runs north from St Ann's Square to **Exchange Square**, with its water features, public sculptures and massive department stores. On the southeast side of the square stands the whopping **Arndale Centre**, once a real Sixties eyesore, but now a modern shopping precinct, clad in glass.

Chetham's School of Music

Long Millgate, M3 1SB • Library Mon–Fri timed entry, 10am, 11am, noon, 1.30pm, 2.30pm & 3.30pm • Free • ☎ 0161 834 7961, Ⓦ chethamsschoolofmusic.com • Victoria Metrolink

Manchester Cathedral's choristers in are trained at **Chetham's School of Music**. This fifteenth-century manor house became a school and a free public library in 1653 and was turned into a music school in 1969. There are free recitals during term time, and you can visit the oak-panelled **Library** with its handsome eighteenth-century bookcases. Along the side corridor is the main **Reading Room**, where Marx and Engels beavered away on the square table that still stands in the windowed alcove. There's no public access to the rest of the complex, except to **Stoller Hall**, a 500-seat concert hall (see page 481) that opened in 2017.

National Football Museum

Urbis Building, Cathedral Gardens, M4 3BG • Mon–Sun 10am–5pm • Free except for special exhibitions • ☎ 0161 605 8200, Ⓦ nationalfootballmuseum.com • Victoria Metrolink

Manchester's **National Football Museum**, housed in a suitably spectacular structure – the sloping, six-storey glass Urbis building near Victoria train station – houses some true treasures of the world's most popular game. Here you can see the 1966 World Cup Final ball, Maradona's "Hand of God" shirt, and the only surviving version of the Jules Rimet world cup trophy. They also display the personal collection of Sir Stanley Matthews (1915–2000), considered one of the greatest English footballers of all time.

Piccadilly

Piccadilly is another area earmarked by developers for regeneration. Exciting projects in the pipeline include a four-storey food-and-drink venue at **Mayfield Depot** (Ⓦ mayfieldmanchester.co.uk) and renovation of the Grade I listed Fire Station on London Road. **Piccadilly Gardens** (Piccadilly Gardens Metrolink), historically the largest green space in the city, has also recently been spruced up; this family-friendly space has a fountain and water jets, and a pavilion at one end to screen off the traffic. Regular events, including a food **market** (Thurs–Sat 10am–5pm), keep the gardens lively.

10

The Northern Quarter and Ancoats

Oldham Street, which shoots off northeast from Piccadilly Gardens, is the shabby gateway to the hip **Northern Quarter**. Traditionally, this is Manchester's garment district and you'll still find old-fashioned shops and wholesalers selling clothes, mannequins and hosiery alongside the more recent designer shops, music stores and trendy café-bars. The side wall of iconic indie emporium Afflecks (see page 481) sports a colourful series of **mosaics** depicting Manchester legends – from stars of Coronation Street to the Stone Roses. As rents in the Northern Quarter rise, the arty types are spilling over into **Ancoats**, an area of conservation across busy Great Ancoats Street. It's here in the old red-brick factory buildings that you'll find the most innovative new restaurants and bars popping up (see page 478).

Chinatown

A short walk south of Piccadilly Gardens is **Chinatown**, whose grid of narrow streets stretches north–south from Charlotte to Princess streets between Portland and Mosley streets, dotted with Chinese restaurants, supermarkets and bakeries. The inevitable **Dragon Arch**, at Faulkner and Nicolas, provides the focus for Chinese New Year celebrations.

Along Oxford Road

A couple of blocks out of the Gay Village (see page 475), you'll come to the junction of Whitworth Street and **Oxford Road**, the latter cutting a direct route south through a string of impressive Manchester University buildings towards The Whitworth Art Gallery.

Manchester Museum

Oxford Rd, M13 9PL • Daily 10am–5pm • Free • ☎ 0161 275 2648, Ⓦ www.museum.manchester.ac.uk

The university's Gothic Revival **Manchester Museum** boasts a diverse collection spread over five floors, with displays on rocks, minerals and prehistoric life, meteorites, animal life, the human body and biomedical research. It also boasts one of the country's finest collections outside of the British Museum on **Ancient Egypt**. The **Vivarium** is dedicated to reptile and amphibian conservation, with plenty of frogs, snakes and lizards to handle, while new high-tech space **The Study** (Ⓦ thestudymcr.com) is an interactive learning and exhibition facility on the top floor of the museum's Grade II listed Alfred Waterhouse building.

Whitworth Art Gallery

Corner of Oxford Rd & Denmark Rd, M15 6ER • Mon–Wed & Fri–Sun 10am–5pm, Thurs 10am–9pm • Free • ☎ 0161 275 7450, Ⓦ www. whitworth.manchester.ac.uk

The university's **Whitworth Art Gallery** reopened in 2015 after a £15 million renovation project to double and extend its public space into the surrounding Whitworth Park. A lively rota of exhibitions showcases contemporary artists, designers and performers, as well as the gallery's fine collection of pre-1880s and modern art, and the country's

10

widest range of textiles outside London's Victoria and Albert Museum. The glass walls and walkways of the award-winning gallery space blends seamlessly with the park, and sculpture by the likes of Emily Young, Nathan Coley and Dorothy Cross have augmented the already spectacular collection that included work by Epstein, Hepworth and Moore.

Salford Quays

After the Manchester Ship Canal opened in 1894, **Salford docks** played a pivotal role in making the city one of Britain's busiest seaports. Following their closure in 1982, which left a post-industrial mess just a couple of miles west of the city centre, an extraordinarily ambitious redevelopment transformed **Salford Quays**, as it was rebranded, into a popular waterfront complex with its own gleaming apartment blocks, mall and arts centre, **The Lowry**. Also here is the splendid **Imperial War Museum North** and the **MediaCityUK** site.

The Lowry

Pier 8, Salford Quays, M50 3AZ • Galleries Mon–Fri & Sun 11am–5pm, Sat 10am–5pm • Free • ☎ 0843 208 6000, ⓦ thelowry.com • Harbour City/MediacityUK Metrolink

Perched on the water's edge, **The Lowry** is the quays' shiny steel arts centre. The **Galleries**, which host sixteen different exhibitions each year, are largely devoted to the paintings of **Lawrence Stephen Lowry** (1887–1976), the artist most closely associated with Salford. The earlier paintings – those somewhat desolate, melancholic portrayals of Manchester mill workers – are the most familiar, while later works, repeating earlier paintings but changing the greys and sullen browns for lively reds and pinks, can come as a surprise.

Imperial War Museum North

The Quays, Trafford Wharf North, M17 1TZ • Daily 10am–5pm • Free • ☎ 0161 836 4000, ⓦ iwm.org.uk • MediacityUK Metrolink

A footbridge across the Manchester Ship Canal links The Lowry with the startling **Imperial War Museum North**, which raises a giant steel fin into the air, in a building designed by Daniel Libeskind. The interior is just as striking, its angular lines serving as a dramatic backdrop to the displays, which kick off with the Big Picture, when the walls of the main hall are transformed into giant screens to show fifteen-minute, surround-sound films. Superb themed displays fill six separate exhibition areas – the "Silos" – focusing on everything from women's work in the World Wars to the 9/11 attacks (with a 23ft section of crumpled steel recovered from the World Trade Center).

MediaCityUK

Salford, M50 2EQ • BBC tours Mon–Thurs 10.30am, 12.30pm & 3pm (Thurs in school term time, radio studio tour only), Sat & Sun times vary; 1hr 30min • £11.75 • Book on ⓦ bbc.co.uk/showsandtours • MediaCityUK Metrolink

In 2011, the BBC moved 26 of its London-based departments up north to **MediaCityUK**, a vast, purpose-built workspace for creative and digital businesses. ITV followed suit in 2013, the *Coronation Street* set arrived in 2014, and the whole place has a certain pizzazz, with telly types buzzing about on Segway scooters, and trendy bars and restaurants open until the early hours. The BBC offer insanely popular though mildly underwhelming **tours** (the highpoint of which is the sound studio and its semi-anechoic chamber), but you don't have to join a tour to wander around the piazza and visit the **Blue Peter garden**, transplanted here from London complete with Shep's paw print.

The National Cycling Centre

10

Stuart St, M11 4DQ, 2 miles east of the city centre ☏ 0161 223 2244 option 3, ⊕ nationalcyclingcentre.com • Daily 7.30am–10pm • Tours 10am–4pm, £45 for up to 14 people, booking essential • From Piccadilly Gardens (Stop D) take bus #216 to Sport City; or Velopark Metrolink

Opposite Man City's football ground (see page 477), in an area being touted as "sports city", the **National Cycling Centre** is the home of British Cycling and one of the fastest and busiest velodromes in the world. Its stunning, Olympic-standard loop of Siberian pine track, angled at 42.5°, is in constant use, with hour-long taster sessions (bikes and coach provided) available to anyone aged nine and over; arrive early and you might well catch the end of a Team GB training session. Also on site is a world-class indoor **BMX track** and the start of 7.5 miles of **mountain-bike** trails. Elsewhere in the city, the centre's facilities include an outdoor BMX track and a mountain-bike skills zone.

ARRIVAL AND DEPARTURE

By plane Manchester International Airport (☏ 0161 489 3000, ⊕ manchesterairport.co.uk) is 10 miles south of the city centre. There's a train service to Piccadilly Station (£5 single; 20min); the new Metrolink (£4.20 single; 45min) runs daily to Deansgate-Castlefield; and taxis are around £25.

By train Piccadilly Station, southeast of the centre, sees the largest number of long-distance services, some of which continue south to the airport. Services to Lancashire, Liverpool and Yorkshire can leave from Piccadilly, Oxford Road (just west) and Victoria (on the city's north side) stations. All three are connected to the centre via the free Metroshuttle bus (see below); Piccadilly and Victoria are also on the Metrolink tramline (see below).

Destinations from Piccadilly Barrow-in-Furness (Mon–Sat 7 daily, Sun 3 daily; 2hr 15min); Birmingham (hourly; 1hr 30min); Blackpool (hourly; 1hr 10min); Buxton (hourly; 1hr); Carlisle (8 daily; 1hr 50min); Chester (every 30min; 1hr–1hr 20min); Lancaster (hourly; 1hr); Leeds (hourly; 1hr); Liverpool (every 30min; 50min); London (hourly; 2hr 20min); Newcastle (10 daily; 3hr); Oxenholme (4–6 daily; 40min–1hr 10min); Sheffield (hourly; 1hr); York (every 30min; 1hr 30min).

Destinations from Oxford Road Blackpool (hourly; 1hr 15min); Carlisle (8 daily; 1hr 50min); Chester (hourly; 1hr); Lancaster (8 daily; 1hr); Leeds (10 daily; 1hr); Liverpool (every 30min; 50min); Oxenholme (8 daily; 1hr 10min); Penrith (8 daily; 1hr 40min); Sheffield (hourly; 1hr); York (hourly; 1hr 30min).

Destinations from Victoria Blackpool (6 daily; 1hr 30min); Leeds (every 30min; 1hr 20min); Liverpool (hourly; 35min).

By bus Most long-distance buses use Chorlton Street Coach Station, about halfway between Piccadilly train station and Albert Square, though some regional buses also leave from Shudehill Interchange, between the Arndale Centre and the Northern Quarter.

Destinations Birmingham (6 daily; 3hr); Blackpool (5 daily; 1hr 40min); Chester (3 daily; 1hr); Leeds (6 daily; 2hr); Liverpool (hourly; 40min); London (every 1–2hr; 4hr 30min–6hr 45min); Newcastle (6 daily; 5hr); Sheffield (4 daily; 2hr 40min).

Travel information For information on train and bus services, contact TFGM (☏ 0871 200 2233, ⊕ tfgm.com).

GETTING AROUND

On foot About a 30min walk from top to bottom, central Manchester is compact enough to cover on foot.

By bus Three free Metroshuttle bus services (⊕ tfgm. com) weave across the centre of town, linking the city's train stations and NCP car parks with all the major points of interest; Metroshuttle #1 runs Mon–Fri every 10min 7am–7pm, Sat every 10min 8.30am–6.30pm, Sun & public hols every 12min 9.30am–6pm; Metroshuttle #2 runs every 10min Mon–Fri 6.30am–6.30pm, Sat 8.30am–6.30pm, Sun & public hols every 12min 9.35am–6pm; Metroshuttle #3 runs every 10min Mon–Fri 7.25am–7.20pm, Sat 8.35am–

6.25pm, Sun & public hols every 12min 9.40am–6.05pm.

By taxi Mantax (☏ 0161 230 3333) and Streetcars (☏ 0161 228 7878) are two reliable taxi firms.

By tram Metrolink trams (⊕ metrolink.co.uk) whisk through the city centre bound for the suburbs, along an ever-expanding network of routes. Services run from approximately 6am–12.30am (Mon–Thurs), with last trams running later on Fridays and Saturdays, and Sunday services between around 7am–10.30pm. Ticket machines are on the platform; single journeys cost from £1.20, while day and weekend Travelcards (from £5 off-peak) are good value.

MANCHESTER FOOTBALL TOURS

Manchester is, of course, home to two mega Premier League football teams. It's tough to get tickets for matches if you're not a season-ticket-holder, but **guided tours** placate out-of-town fans who want to gawp at the silverware and sit in the dug-out. You'll need to book in advance.

Old Trafford Sir Matt Busby Way, off Warwick Rd, M16 0RA ☎0161 868 8000, ⓦmanutd.com; Old Trafford Metrolink. The self-styled "Theatre of Dreams" is the home of Manchester United, arguably the most famous football team in the world. Stadium tours include a visit to the club museum. Tours daily (except match days) 9.40am–4.30pm; £18.

Etihad Stadium Sport City, off Alan Turing Way, M11 3FF ☎0161 444 1894, ⓦmcfc.co.uk; Etihad Campus Metrolink. United's formerly long-suffering local rivals, Manchester City, became the world's richest club in 2008 after being bought by the royal family of Abu Dhabi. They play at the revamped Etihad Stadium, east of the city centre. Tours daily 9am–5pm; £17.

10

INFORMATION AND TOURS

Tourist information Manchester Visitor Centre is at 1 Piccadilly Gardens, on the corner of Portland Street (Mon–Sat 9.30am–5.30pm, Sun 10.30am–4.30pm; ☎0871 222 8223, ⓦvisitmanchester.com); it has a useful blog.

Listings information In print, Thursday's *City Life* supplement in the *Manchester Evening News* (ⓦmanchester eveningnews.co.uk) covers popular events, while *The Skinny*, widely available in the Northern Quarter, is a hip and independent monthly freebie. Online, there's intelligent

and incisive guidance on ⓦcreativetourist.com, while ⓦconfidentials.com/manchester has informative restaurant and bar reviews.

Walking tours The Visitor Centre has details of the city's many walking tours, including a street art tour of the northern quarter (from £7). There's also a 3hr pay-what-you-can walking tour that leaves from the Alan Turing Memorial in Sackville Gardens (11am Tues, Fri, Sat & Sun; ⓦfreetour.com/manchester).

ACCOMMODATION

There are many city-centre **hotels**, especially budget chains, which means that you have a good chance of finding a smart, albeit generic, en-suite room in central Manchester for around £60–70 at almost any time of the year – except when City or United are playing at home. Less expensive **guesthouses** and **B&Bs** are concentrated some way out of the centre, mainly on the southern routes into the city. Prices often halve midweek.

HOTELS

ABode 107 Piccadilly, M1 2DB ☎0161 247 7744, ⓦabodemanchester.co.uk; Piccadilly Gardens Metrolink; map p.470. Part of a small chain of boutique hotels, this gem occupies a former cotton warehouse a stone's throw from Piccadilly Station. Rooms are light and elegant, with high ceilings and polished wooden floors. £85

Arora 18–24 Princess St, M1 4LG ☎0161 236 8999, ⓦmanchester.arorahotels.com; Piccadilly Gardens/St Peter's Square Metrolink; map p.470. Four-star with more than 100 neat, modern rooms in a listed building in a great central location opposite the Manchester Art Gallery. The convivial, obliging staff pride themselves on offering a "real Manchester welcome". Good online discounts. £99

★ **Great John Street** Great John St, M3 4FD ☎0161 831 3211, ⓦeclectichotels.co.uk/great-john-street; Deansgate-Castlefield Metrolink; map p.470. Deluxe hotel in an imaginatively refurbished old school building not far from Deansgate, with thirty individual, spacious and comfortable suites, some split-level. The on-site bar/restaurant has an open fire and deep sofas, with a gallery breakfast room above. Nice rooftop garden, too. They've

also recently opened sister hotel *King Street Townhouse*. £250

Midland Peter St, M60 2DS ☎0161 236 3333, ⓦqhotels. co.uk; St Peter's Square Metrolink; map p.470. Once the terminus hotel for the old Central Station – and where Mr Rolls first met Mr Royce – this building was the apotheosis of Edwardian style and is still arguably Manchester's most iconic hotel. The public areas today are returned to their former glory, with bedrooms in immaculate chain style. *Mr Cooper's House and Garden*, attached to the hotel, is wonderful for pre-theatre cocktails. £130

Motel One London Rd, M1 2PF ☎0161 200 5650, ⓦmotelone.com; Piccadilly Metrolink; map p.470. Not much to look at from the outside, but the location couldn't be more central and the stylish lobby leads to clean, modern rooms. The fixed room prices are higher at the weekend. £69

Radisson Blu Edwardian Peter St, M2 5GP ☎0161 835 9929, ⓦradissonblu-edwardian.com; St Peter's Square Metrolink; map p.470. The Neoclassical facade is all that's left of the Free Trade Hall; inside, this five-star hotel has a sleek modern interior full of natural light, tasteful rooms, and all the extras you'd expect – spa, gym and the trendy *Opus One* bar. **£120**

HOSTELS

Hilton Chambers 15 Hilton St, M1 1JJ ☎ 0161 236 4414 ⓦ hattersgroup.com/manchester-hilton-chambers; Piccadilly Gardens Metrolink; map p.470. Part of a small regional chain, this newish hostel is right in the heart of the Northern Quarter, and a great location for exploring the city's nightlife. A range of different rooms and some great

communal spaces, including an outdoor deck. Rates reduce considerably midweek. Dorms **£21**, doubles **£82**

YHA Manchester Potato Wharf, Castlefield, M3 4NB ☎ 0845 371 9647, ⓦ yha.org.uk/hostel/manchester; Deansgate-Castlefield Metrolink; map p.470. Excellent hostel overlooking the canal that runs close to the Museum of Science and Industry, with 35 rooms (three of them doubles). Good facilities, including a café. Dorms **£20**, doubles **£40**

EATING

Rivalling London in the scope of its **cafés** and **restaurants**, Mancunians are justly baffled at Michelin not awarding any restaurant in the city a star (yet). Most options are in the centre, with the vast majority of new openings in the Northern Quarter and Ancoats. If you have time, head a couple of miles along Wilmslow Road to **Didsbury**, a leafy suburb with several excellent places to eat, or to **Altrincham**, 8 miles outside the city, which has an outstanding food market (ⓦ altrinchammarket.co.uk).

CAFÉS AND CAFÉ-BARS

Eighth Day 107–111 Oxford Rd, M1 7DU ☎ 0161 273 1850, ⓦ 8thday.coop; Metroshuttle #2; map p.470. Manchester's oldest organic vegetarian café has a shop, takeaway and juice bar upstairs, with a great-value café/restaurant downstairs. Mon–Fri 9am–7pm, Sat 10am–5pm.

Federal Café Bar 9 Nicholas Croft, Northern Quarter, M4 1EY ☎ 0161 425 0974, ⓦ federalcafe.co.uk; Shudehill Metrolink; map p.470. Manchester's latest independent coffee shop-cum-bar has queues out of the door for its all-day brunch (try the smashed avo on sourdough toast with bacon for £8.50), strong coffee (flat white £2.60) and superb cocktails (around £8). Mon–Fri 7.30am–6pm, Sat 8am–6pm, Sun 8am–5pm.

Home Sweet Home 49–41 Edge St, Northern Quarter, M4 1HW ☎ 0161 224 9424, ⓦ homesweethomenq. com; Shudehill Metrolink; map p.470. Queues snake round the block for this gem, which serves huge portions of American/Tex Mex-influenced mains (from £8), luscious milkshakes and generous slices of the most extravagantly decorated cakes you will ever have seen. Mon–Thurs & Sun 9am–10pm, Fri 9am–11pm, Sat 9am–midnight.

The Koffee Pot 84–86 Oldham St, Northern Quarter, M4 1LE ☎ 0161 236 8918, ⓦ thekoffeepot.co.uk; Market St Metrolink; map p.470. Beloved by hungover hipsters, this is *the* place for a Full English (£5.80) or Veggie (£5.60) brekkie (served until 2pm) amid much Formica and red leatherette. Often packed. Mon 7.30am–4pm, Tues–Fri 7.30am–11pm, Sat 9am–11pm, Sun 9am–4pm; note the kitchen closes at 9pm Tues–Sat.

★ **Richmond Tea Rooms** Richmond St, Gay Village, M1 3HZ ☎ 0161 237 9667, ⓦ www.richmondtearooms. com; Metroshuttle #1; map p.470. Without question the most brilliantly conceived tearoom in Manchester, with an amazing Tim Burton-esque *Alice in Wonderland* theme.

The sumptuous afternoon teas (£6.50–23.50) are the stuff of local legend, while the adjoining cocktail lounge is a super-stylish place to kick off an evening. Mon–Thurs 11am–9pm, Fri 11am–10pm, Sat 10am–10pm, Sun 10am–9.30pm.

Takk 6 Tariff St, Northern Quarter, M1 2FF ⓦ takkmcr. com; Shudehill Metrolink; map p.470. Cool yet cosy Icelandic coffee bar with a living-room feel, home-made cakes, hipster brunch (blueberry pie porridge £4), a changing roster of sandwiches (£6), Nordic art and, of course, superior coffee. Mon–Fri 8am–5pm, Sat 9am–5pm, Sun 10am–5pm.

Trof NQ 8 Thomas St, Northern Quarter, M4 1EU ☎ 0161 833 3197, ⓦ trofnq.co.uk; Shudehill Metrolink; map p.470. Three storeys of cool, relaxed café-bar populated by trendy young things. It's ideal for a late breakfast or early afternoon drink, and hosts open-mic nights, poetry readings and DJ sets. Mon & Tues 10am–midnight, Wed & Thurs 10am–1am, Fri 10am–3am, Sat 9am–3am, Sun 9am–midnight.

RESTAURANTS

Australasia 1 The Ave, Spinningfields, M3 3AP ☎ 0161 831 0288, ⓦ australasia.uk.com; Metroshuttle #1 or #2; map p.470. A remarkable glass pyramid on street level leads down under (get it?) to *Australasia*, a buzzing, white-tiled restaurant that's arguably the star of the Spinningfield dining scene. Food is Modern Oz meets Pacific Rim and pricey but well-regarded (mains from £15, with the Australian Wagyu steak fillet a whopping £60). Daily noon–midnight.

★ **Dimitri's** 1 Campfield Arcade, Deansgate, M3 4FN ☎ 0161 839 3319, ⓦ dimitris.co.uk; Metroshuttle #1 or #2; map p.470. Long-established Manchester favourite: pick and mix from the Greek/Spanish/Italian menu (particularly good for vegetarians) and enjoy it at a semi-alfresco arcade table with a Greek coffee or Lebanese wine; you'll think you're in the Med. Mon–Thurs & Sun 11am–midnight, Fri & Sat 11am–2am.

★ **Lime Tree** 8 Lapwing Lane, West Didsbury, M20 2WS ☎0161 445 1217, ⓦthelimetreerestaurant. co.uk; West Didsbury Metrolink; map p.470. The finest local food, with a menu that chargrills and oven-roasts as if its life depended on it, using produce from its own smallholding. Main courses cost £14 and up, less at lunchtime. Reservations recommended. Mon & Sat 5.30–10pm, Tues–Fri noon–2.30pm & 5.30–10pm, Sun noon–8pm.

Mughli Charcoal Pit 30 Wilmslow Rd, M14 5TQ ☎0161 248 0900, ⓦmughli.com; map p.470. Out by the Whitworth Art Gallery, this stylish Indian restaurant is a standout in the area traditionally known as "curry mile". Mouth-watering meat, veggie and vegan dishes include butter paneer (£11) and charred lamb chops (£10.50) – there's even a mild "little mughal" for children (£6.50). Mon–Thurs 5pm–midnight, Fri 5pm–12.30am, Sat 4pm–12.30am, Sun 2–10.30pm.

Rudy's Pizza 9 Cotton St, Ancoats, M4 5BF ☎07931 162059, ⓦrudyspizza.co.uk; map p.470. Super-light handstretched pizza the Neapolitan way, this place gets rave reviews (and has long queues). On afternoons from Wed to Sat they stay open for drinks only as the chefs are busy making dough. Prices from £4.90 for a Marinara and you'll pay £15 for a bottle of the house wine. Tues 5–10pm, Wed–Sat noon–3pm & 5–10pm, Sun noon–6pm.

Sam's Chop House Chapel Walks, off Cross St, M2 1HN ☎0161 834 3210, ⓦsamschophouse.com; Market St Metrolink; map p.470. One of three good chop houses in the city, the restaurant attached to this wonderful old-world pub is a hidden gem. It has a Victorian gas-lit feel and a delightful menu of English food (mains £14–16) – and they really know their wine, too. Mon–Sat noon–3pm & 5.30–11pm, Sun noon–8pm.

Yang Sing 34 Princess St, M1 4JY ☎0161 236 2200, ⓦyang-sing.com; St Peter's Square Metrolink; map p.470. One of the best Cantonese restaurants in the country, with authentic dishes ranging from a quick-fried noodle plate to the full works. For the most interesting food, stray from the printed menu; ask the friendly staff for advice. Sister restaurant, the *Little Yang Sing* on George St, slightly cheaper, is also worth stopping by. Mains from £12. Mon–Sat noon–11.30pm, Sun noon–10.30pm.

★ **Yuzu** 39 Faulkner St, M1 4EE ☎0161 236 4159, ⓦyuzumanchester.co.uk; St Peter's Square Metrolink; map p.470. Outstanding Japanese in Chinatown with a shortish menu of exceptionally executed sashimi (from £10.50), tempura (from £5.90) dishes and more, plus a tempting range of sake. Tues–Sat noon–2pm & 5.30–10pm.

10

DRINKING

From Victorian boozers to designer cocktail bars, Manchester does **drinking** in style, while its musical heritage and large student population keep things lively and interesting.

★ **Big Hands** 296 Oxford Rd, M13 9NS ☎0161 272 7779, ⓦfacebook.com/BigHandsBar; map p.470. Right by the Academy venues, this intimate, uber-cool bar is popular with students, usually post-gig as it has a late licence. Mon–Fri 10am–2am, Sat noon–3am, Sun 6pm–1am.

Britons Protection 50 Great Bridgewater St, M1 5LE ☎0161 236 5895, ⓦfacebook.com/britonsprotection; map p.470. Cosy old pub with a couple of small rooms, a backyard beer garden and all sorts of Victorian detail – most splendidly the tiles and the open fires in winter. Boasts over 300 whiskies and a large mural depicting the Peterloo Massacre. Mon–Thurs 11am–11.30pm, Fri noon–12.30am, Sat 11am–midnight, Sun noon–11pm.

Circus Tavern 86 Portland St, M1 4GX ☎0161 236 5818; map p.470. Manchester's smallest pub, this Victorian drinking hole is a favourite city-centre pit stop. You may have to knock to get in; when you do, you're confronted by the landlord in the corridor pulling pints. Daily 11am–11pm.

Cloud 23 Beetham Tower, 301 Deansgate, M3 4LQ ☎0161 870 1670, ⓦcloud23bar.com; map p.470. Manchester's highest and most popular cocktail bar, with a 23rd-floor glass overhang. Expensive, but worth it for the view of the city and Pennines beyond. Mon–Thurs & Sun 11am–1am, Fri & Sat 11am–2am.

Corbières 2 Half Moon St, just off St Ann's Square, M2 7BS ☎0161 834 3381; map p.470. Look for the Gaudí-esque wall art flanking the door of this long-standing subterranean, slightly dank drinking cellar with arguably the best jukebox in Manchester. Mon–Thurs 11am–11pm, Fri & Sat 11am–midnight, Sun 2–10.30pm.

★ **Mr Thomas' Chop House** 52 Cross St, M2 7AR ☎0161 832 2245, ⓦtomschophouse.com; map p.470. Victorian classic with Dickensian nooks and crannies. Office workers, daytime drinkers, old goats and students all call it home, and there's good-value, traditional food too. Mon–Thurs 11am–11pm, Fri & Sat 11am–midnight, Sun noon–10.30pm.

Sand Bar 120 Grosvenor St, M1 7HL ☎0161 273 1552, ⓦwww.sandbarmanchester.co.uk; map p.470. Between the university and the city centre, this is a brilliant modern take on the traditional pub, where students, lecturers and workers shoot the breeze. There's a great selection of beers and wines. Mon–Wed & Sun noon–midnight, Thurs noon–1am, Fri & Sat noon–2am.

10

The Temple 100 Great Bridgewater St, M1 5JW ☎ 0161 228 9834; map p.470. Teeny-tiny subterranean boozer in an old public toilet, with an amazing jukebox and bags of atmosphere, if not much elbow room. It's run by the same people as *Big Hands* (see page 479) and shares its nonchalant, fun-time vibe. Mon–Thurs & Sun noon–midnight, Fri & Sat noon–1am.

NIGHTLIFE

Manchester has an excellent **live-music** scene, of course, and a mercurial roster of **clubs**; note too that many of the city's hip **café-bars** (see above) host regular club nights. See print and online listings (see page 477) for information.

Albert Hall 27 Peter St, M2 5QR ☎ 0844 858 8521, ⓦ alberthallmanchester.com; map p.470. Former Wesleyan chapel that's now an atmospheric live-music venue hosting a select programme of high-quality, slightly left-field artists. Hours vary.

★ **Band on the Wall** 25 Swan St, Northern Quarter, M4 5JZ ☎ 0161 834 1786, ⓦ bandonthewall.org; map p.470. This legendary Northern Quarter joint remains true to its commitment to "real music": it's one of the city's best venues to see live bands – from world and folk to jazz and reggae – and it hosts club nights to boot. Box office Mon–Sat 5–9pm. Mon–Thurs 9am–1am, Fri & Sat 9am–3am, Sun noon–5pm.

The Castle Hotel 66 Oldham St, Northern Quarter, M4 1LE ☎ 0161 237 9485, ⓦ thecastlehotel.info; map p.470. Genuinely good 200-year-old pub with cask and craft ales and an extremely intimate backroom gig space. Jake Bugg played to just seventy-odd people here months before hitting the big time. Hosts regular spoken word nights too. Mon–Thurs noon–1am, Fri noon–2am, Sun noon–midnight.

★ **The Deaf Institute** 135 Grosvenor St, M1 7HE ☎ 0161 276 9350 ⓦ thedeafinstitute.co.uk; map p.470. A mile down Oxford Rd, this bar and music hall sits in a funky makeover of the elegant Victorian former deaf institute. Mostly folk, indie and r'n'b, with lots of up-and-coming talent, and a raft of great club nights. Sister venue *Gorilla* (ⓦ thisisgorilla.com) on Whitworth Street is also excellent. Mon–Thurs & Sun 10am–midnight, Fri & Sat 10am–3am.

Matt & Phreds 64 Tib St, Northern Quarter, M4 1LW ☎ 0161 831 7002, ⓦ mattandphreds.com; map p.470. The city's finest jazz bar, offering everything from swing to gritty New Orleans blues. Mon–Thurs & Sat 6pm–late, Fri 5pm–late.

O2 Apollo Manchester Stockport Rd, M12 6AP ☎ 0844 477 7667, ⓦ academymusicgroup.com/o2apollomanchester; map p.470. Medium-sized theatre auditorium for all kinds of concerts; a brilliant place to see big names up close, with bags of atmosphere. Hours vary.

O2 Ritz Manchester Whitworth St West, M1 5NQ ☎ 0161 236 3234, ⓦ academymusicgroup.com/o2ritzmanchester; map p.470. This legendary dance hall has been around for decades (it's where The Smiths first played) and has a sprung dancefloor that really boings when things get going. Jumping live music and plenty of fun club nights, including a roller disco. Hours vary.

Soup Kitchen 31–33 Spear St, Northern Quarter, M1 1DF ☎ 0161 236 5100, ⓦ soupkitchenmcr.co.uk; map p.470. Soup-specializing canteen with a basement club/live-music venue that's among Manchester's finest. Mon–Wed & Sun noon–11pm, Thurs noon–1am, Fri & Sat noon–4pm.

ENTERTAINMENT

The artist-led **Manchester International Festival** (see page 481) is a biennial eighteen-day culture fest, but te city's many **theatres** also produce a lively year-round programme. As for **classical music**, Manchester is blessed with the North's most highly prized **orchestra**, the Hallé, resident at Bridgewater Hall. Other acclaimed names include the **BBC Philharmonic** and the **Manchester Camerata** chamber orchestra (ⓦ manchestercamerata.com), who perform at a variety of venues.

CLASSICAL MUSIC

Bridgewater Hall Lower Mosley St, M2 3WS ☎ 0844 907 9000, ⓦ bridgewater-hall.co.uk. Home of the Hallé Orchestra, the BBC Philharmonic and the Manchester Camerata; also a full programme of chamber, pop, classical and jazz concerts.

Royal Northern College of Music (RNCM) 124 Oxford Rd, M13 9RD ☎ 0161 907 5200, ⓦ rncm.ac.uk; Metroshuttle #2. Top-quality classical and modern jazz concerts.

THEATRE, CINEMA AND DANCE

The Dancehouse 10 Oxford Rd, M1 5QA ☎ 0161 237 9753, ⓦ thedancehouse.co.uk; Metroshuttle #2. Home to the Northern Ballet School and the eponymous theatre troupe; venue for dance, drama and comedy.

★ **HOME** 2 Tony Wilson Place, M15 4FN ☎ 0161 200 1500, ⓦ homemcr.org; Deansgate-Castlefield Metrolink. A new sleek centre for contemporary arts, with two theatres, five cinema screens, changing art exhibitions in a flexible gallery space, recitals and talks, plus a bookshop, café and

MANCHESTER INTERNATIONAL FESTIVAL

Manchester is well established as a leading light on the UK arts and music scene and the biennial **Manchester International Festival** (2018, 2020, etc) pulls together an impressive array of performers, directors and theatre companies to celebrate Manchester doing things a bit differently. Radical plays are premiered, new arty concepts trialled (opera for babies, anyone?) and big names – including Damon Albarn, Björk, New Order, Punchdrunk, Sir Kenneth Branagh and Jane Horrocks – collaborate with the industry's best directors and producers. Traditionally at various public venues across Manchester, the festival will have a permanent £110m state-of-the-art home once **The Factory** opens in St John's in 2020 (ⓦ stjohnsmanchester.com).

10

ground-floor bar.

The Lowry Pier 8, Salford Quays, M50 3UB ☏ 0843 208 6000, ⓦ thelowry.com; Harbour City Metrolink. This quayside venue hosts many of the biggest shows, including major National Theatre touring productions, most recently *La Strada* and *War Horse*.

Opera House 3 Quay St, M3 3HP ☏ 0844 871 3018, ⓦ manchesteroperahouse.com; Deansgate-Castlefield Metrolink. Major venue for touring West End musicals, drama, comedy and concerts.

Royal Exchange Theatre St Ann's Square, M2 7DH ☏ 0161 833 9833, ⓦ royalexchange.co.uk; Market St Metrolink. The theatre-in-the-round in the Royal Exchange is the most famous stage in the city, with a Studio Theatre (for works by new writers) alongside.

Stoller Hall Hunts Bank, M3 1DA ☏ 0333 130 0967, ⓦ stollerhall.com. Manchester's major new £8.7 million concert hall is attached to the world-renowned Chetham School of Music. With a focus on chamber music, the hall also hosts family concerts, workshops and masterclasses.

SHOPPING

As well as the out-of-town Trafford Centre, the high-end boutiques on **King Street**, and the **department stores** around Market Street and Exchange Square, the Northern Quarter has a plethora of smaller independent stores catering for all tastes. If you're around between mid-November and mid-December, make for the **Christmas Market**, when Albert Square is packed with nearly 350 stalls and a lot of Christmas cheer.

Afflecks 52 Church St, Northern Quarter, M4 1PW ☏ 0161 839 0718, ⓦ afflecks.com; Piccadilly Gardens Metrolink; map p.470. A Manchester institution, where more than fifty independent stalls are spread over four floors mixing everything from goth outfits to retro cocktail dresses and quirky footwear. Mon–Fri 10.30am–6pm, Sat 10am–6pm, Sun ground and first floors only 11am–5pm.

Craft & Design Centre 17 Oak St, Northern Quarter, M4 5JD ☏ 0161 832 4274, ⓦ craftanddesign.com; Shudehill Metrolink; map p.470. The city's best place to pick up ceramics, fabrics, earthenware, jewellery and decorative art – there's also a good little café. Mon–Sat 10am–5.30pm.

Oklahoma 74–76 High St, Northern Quarter, M4 1ES ☏ 0161 834 1136, ⓦ okla.co.uk; Shudehill Metrolink; map p.470. Hidden behind large wooden doors, this charming gift-shop-cum-veggie-café is packed

with fun knick-knacks and fripperies, with some pretty jewellery too. Mon–Thurs & Sun 10am–6pm, Fri & Sat 10am–7pm.

Piccadilly Records 53 Oldham St, Northern Quarter, M1 1JR ☏ 0161 839 8008, ⓦ piccadillyrecords. com; Piccadilly Gardens Metrolink; map p.470. The enthusiastic staff, many of them DJs themselves, are more than willing to navigate you through the shelves of collectibles and vinyl towards some special gem, whatever your taste. Mon–Sat 10am–6pm, Sun 11am–5pm.

Retro Rehab 91 Oldham St, Northern Quarter, M1 1JR ☏ 0161 839 2050, ⓦ retro-rehab.co.uk; Piccadilly Gardens Metrolink; map p.470. Gorgeously feminine dresses abound, be they reworked vintage styles or genuine 1950s pieces, in this wonderful little boutique that prides itself on the range of its fashions and accessories from across several decades. Mon–Sat 10am–6pm, Sun noon–4pm.

DIRECTORY

Hospital Manchester Royal Infirmary, Oxford Rd ☏ 0161 276 1234.

Left luggage Facilities at Piccadilly train station on platform 10 (Mon–Sat 7am–11pm, Sun 8am–11pm;

☏ 0161 236 8667, ⓦ left-baggage.co.uk).

Police There's a 24hr police counter in an extension of the town hall on the corner of Lloyd and Mount St.

Post office 26 Spring Gardens.

10

Chester

CHESTER, forty miles southwest of Manchester across the Cheshire Plain, is home to a glorious two-mile ring of medieval and Roman **walls** that encircles a kernel of Tudor and Victorian buildings, all overhanging eaves, mini-courtyards, and narrow cobbled lanes, which culminate in the raised arcades called the "**Rows**". The compact centre of this little city is full of easy charms that can be explored on foot, and taken altogether Chester has enough in the way of sights, restaurants and atmosphere to make it an enjoyable base for a day or two.

Though traditionally viewed as rather staid compared to its near neighbours Manchester and Liverpool, Chester is gradually acquiring a bit of an edge – the new cultural centre on Hunter Street, **Storyhouse** (ⓦstoryhouse.com), marks the city as one to watch.

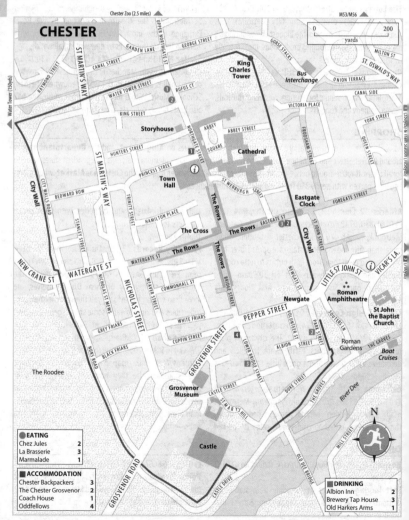

● EATING	
Chez Jules	2
La Brasserie	3
Marmalade	1

■ ACCOMMODATION	
Chester Backpackers	3
The Chester Grosvenor	2
Coach House	1
Oddfellows	4

■ DRINKING	
Albion Inn	2
Brewery Tap House	3
Old Harkers Arms	1

The Rows

Intersecting at **The Cross**, the four main thoroughfares of central Chester are lined by **The Rows**, galleried shopping arcades that run along the first floor of a wonderful set of half-timbered buildings with another set of shops down below at street level. This engaging tableau, which extends for the first 200 or 300 yards of each of the four main streets, is a blend of genuine Tudor houses and Victorian imitations. There's no clear explanation of the origin of The Rows – they were first recorded shortly after a fire wrecked Chester in 1278 – but it seems likely that the hard bedrock that lies underneath the town centre prevented its shopkeepers and merchants from constructing the cellars they required, so they built upwards instead. The finest Tudor buildings are on **Watergate Street**, though **Bridge Street** is perhaps more picturesque. From The Cross, it's also a brief walk along **Eastgate Street** to one of the old town gates, above which is perched the filigree **Eastgate Clock**, raised in honour of Queen Victoria's Diamond Jubilee.

10

Chester Cathedral

St Werburgh St, off Northgate St, CH1 2DY • Mon–Sat 9am–6pm, Sun 11am–4pm • Free, but £3 donation suggested • **Cathedral at Height tours** Regular, but check website for specific times; 1hr • £8, children (over-8s only) £6 • ☎ 01244 324756, ⓦ chestercathedral.com

North of The Cross, along **Northgate Street**, rises the neo-Gothic **Town Hall**, whose acres of red and grey sandstone look over to the **cathedral**, a much modified red sandstone structure dating back to the Normans. The **nave**, with its massive medieval pillars, is suitably imposing, and on one side it sports a splendid sequence of Victorian Pre-Raphaelite mosaic panels that illustrate Old Testament stories in melodramatic style. Close by, the **north transept** is the oldest and most Norman part of the church – hence the round-headed arch and arcade – and the adjoining **choir** holds an intricately carved set of fourteenth-century choir stalls with some especially beastly misericords. The atmospheric East Cloister leads to a gorgeously tranquil **garden**.

The **Cathedral at Height** tour, an enjoyable rootle around the building's previously hidden spaces, takes you up onto the roof for panoramic views over five counties – you'll even spot Liverpool's cathedrals.

Around the city walls

East of the cathedral, steps provide access to the top of the **city walls** – a two-mile girdle of medieval and Roman handiwork that's the most complete in Britain, though in places the wall is barely above street level. You can walk past all its towers, turrets and gateways in an hour or so, and most have a tale or two to tell. The fifteenth-century **King Charles Tower** in the northeast corner is so named because Charles I stood here in 1645 watching his troops being beaten on Rowton Moor, two miles to the southeast, while the earlier **Water Tower** at the northwest corner once stood in the river – evidence of the changes brought about by the gradual silting of the River Dee. South from the Water Tower you'll see the **Roodee**, England's oldest racecourse, laid out on a silted tidal pool where Roman ships once unloaded wine, figs and olive oil from the Mediterranean, and slate, lead and silver from their mines in North Wales. Races are still held here throughout the year.

The Grosvenor Museum

27 Grosvenor St, CH1 2DD • Mon–Sat 10.30am–5pm, Sun 1–4pm • Free; £3 donation requested • ☎ 01244 972197, ⓦ grosvenormuseum. westcheshiremuseums.co.uk

Scores of sculpted tomb panels and engraved headstones once propped up the wall to either side of the Water Tower, evidence of some nervous repair work undertaken when the Roman Empire was in retreat. Much of this stonework was retrieved by the Victorians and is now on display at the **Grosvenor Museum**, which also has interesting background displays on the Roman Empire in general and Roman Chester in particular. At the rear of the museum is **20 Castle Street**, a period house with nine rooms tricked out to represent domestic scenes from 1680 to 1925.

The Roman Gardens and around

Immediately to the east of one of the old city gates, **Newgate**, a footpath leads into the **Roman Gardens** (open access), where a miscellany of Roman stonework – odd bits of pillar, coping stones and incidental statuary – is on display. Footsteps away, along Little St John Street, is the shallow, partly excavated bowl that marks the site of the **Roman Amphitheatre** (open access); it is estimated to have held seven thousand spectators, making it the largest amphitheatre in Britain, but frankly it's not much to look at today.

Chester Zoo

CH2 1EU, 2 miles north of Chester • Daily: April–Sept 10am–5/6pm; Oct–March 10am–4/4.30pm; last admission 1hr before closing • £26, £24 in winter; under-16s £24/£20 • ⓦ chesterzoo.org • Buses #1 or #X8 from the new Chester Bus Interchange or opposite the train station

Chester's most popular attraction is **Chester Zoo**, one of the best in Europe. It is also the second largest in Britain (after London's), with over eleven thousand animals spread over a hundred landscaped acres. The zoo is well known for its **conservation projects** and has had notable success with its Asiatic lions and giant Komodo dragons. Animals are grouped by region in large paddocks viewed from a maze of pathways, from the monorail or the waterbus, with main attractions including the baby animals, the Tropical Realm and the Chimpanzee Forest, which has the biggest climbing frame in the country.

ARRIVAL AND INFORMATION

CHESTER

By train The station is a 10min walk northeast of the centre, down City Road and Foregate Street from the central Eastgate Clock. Bus #40 (Mon–Sat 7.30am–7pm, Sun 9.30am–5pm; every 12min) links the station with the city centre.

Destinations Birmingham (5 daily; 2hr); Liverpool (every 30min; 45min); London (hourly; 2–3hr); Manchester (every 30min; 1hr–1hr 20min).

By bus The new Bus Interchange opened at Gorse Stacks in the northeast of the city centre in June 2017. All long-distance and most local buses stop here, including the

free #200 Shopper Hopper running between here and the Town Hall (for Chester Market and Storyhouse; daily 8am–6pm, every 15min).

Destinations Liverpool (every 20min; 1hr 20min); Manchester (3 daily; 1hr).

Tourist information Chester's information centre (March–Oct Mon–Sat 9am–5.30pm, Sun 10am–5pm; Nov–Feb Mon–Fri 9.30am–4.30pm, Sat 10am–5pm, Sun 10am–4pm; ☏ 01244 405340, ⓦ visitchester.com) is in the Town Hall on Northgate St.

ACCOMMODATION

Chester is a popular tourist destination, with dozens of **B&Bs** and a slew of **hotels**. At the height of the summer and on high days and holidays – like Chester Races – advance booking is strongly recommended, directly or via the tourist office.

Chester Backpackers 67 Boughton, CH3 5AF ☏ 01244 400185, ⓦ chesterbackpackers.co.uk; map p.482. Close to the city walls and a 5min walk from the train station, in a typically Chester mock-Tudor building. En-suite doubles and two dorms (8- and 15-bed). Dorms **£20**, doubles **£38**

The Chester Grosvenor Eastgate St, CH1 1LT ☏ 01244 324024, ⓦ chestergrosvenor.co.uk; map p.482. Superb luxury hotel in an immaculate Victorian building in the

centre of town. Extremely comfortable bedrooms and a host of facilities, not least a full-blown spa (charges apply) and posh chocolatier Rococo on site. Continental breakfast is included, but it's an extra £7.50 for a cooked breakfast. Rack rates are vertiginous, but look for special offers online. **£280**

Coach House Chester 39 Northgate St, CH1 2HQ ☏ 01244 351900, ⓦ coachhousechester.co.uk; map p.482. All eight rooms at this city centre gastropub were fully renovated in 2017 – in time for the opening of nearby

Storyhouse. Cosy and contemporary, but with gorgeous period features, and all have en-suite bathrooms. **£100**

★ **Oddfellows** 20 Lower Bridge St, CH1 1RS ☎01244 895700, ⓦoddfellowschester.com; map p.482. Quirky boutique hotel packed with look-at-me touches – from

the typewriters climbing the reception walls to the neon "Good Night" sign en route to the eighteen comfortable, individually styled bedrooms. There's a buzzy bar scene – including the *Secret Garden* – and popular restaurant on site too. **£179**

EATING

★ **Chez Jules** 71 Northgate St, CH1 2HQ ☎01244 400014, ⓦchezjules.com; map p.482. There's a classic brasserie menu – salade nicoise to rib-eye steak – at this popular spot in an attractive half-timbered building. In the evenings, main courses begin at around £10, with a terrific-value, two-course prix fixe menu (Mon–Sat noon–6pm, Sun noon–5.30pm) for £12.95 and a two-course lunch for £9.95. Mon–Sat noon–10.30pm, Sun noon–9.30pm.

★ **La Brasserie** Chester Grosvenor, Eastgate St, CH1 1LT ☎01244 324024, ⓦchestergrosvenor.com; map p.482. In the same hotel as the Michelin-starred *Simon Radley's*, where the a la carte menu sits at a cool £75, this

is a much more affordable yet smart brasserie that serves inventive French and fusion cooking. Main courses average £20, and it's also a great place for a coffee and pastry. Light bites daily 11.30am–9pm; a la carte Mon–Thurs noon–2.30pm, 5.30–9pm, Fri & Sat noon–2.30pm, 5.30–9.30pm, Sun noon–8.30pm.

Marmalade 67 Northgate St, CH1 2HQ ☎01244 314565, ⓦmarmalade-chester.co.uk; map p.482. An amenable little licensed café with tasty food – filling breakfasts, sandwiches and salads (all around £5) are made using all local produce (and a lot of it is – or can be – gluten-free). Mon–Fri 8am–7.30pm, Sat 9am–7.30pm, Sun 10am–4pm.

10

DRINKING

Albion Inn Corner of Albion and Park streets, CH1 1RN ☎01244 340345, ⓦalbioninnchester.co.uk; map p.482. A Victorian terraced pub in the shadow of the city wall – no fruit machines, no muzak, just good old-fashioned decor (and a World War I theme), tasty bar food and a great range of ales. Hilariously unwelcoming signs outside – basically, if you're on a hen or stag do, or have a child in tow, forget it. Mon–Thurs & Sat noon–3pm & 5–11pm, Fri noon–11pm, Sun noon–2.30pm & 7–10.30pm.

Brewery Tap House 52–54 Lower Bridge St, CH1 1RU ☎01244 340999, ⓦthe-tap.co.uk; map p.482. Up the

cobbled ramp, this converted medieval hall, once owned by the royalist Gamul family and confiscated by Parliament after the English Civil War, serves a good selection of ales from local brewery Spitting Feathers in a tall, barn-like room with whitewashed walls. Mon–Sat noon–11pm, Sun noon–10.30pm.

★ **Old Harkers Arms** 1 Russell St, CH3 5AL ☎01244 344525, ⓦbrunningandprice.co.uk/harkers; map p.482. Canalside real-ale pub imaginatively sited in a former warehouse about 500 yards northeast of Foregate Street. Quality bar food too (until 9.30pm). Mon–Sat 10.30am–11pm, Sun noon–10.30pm.

Liverpool

Standing proud in the 1700s as the empire's second city, **LIVERPOOL** faced a dramatic change of fortune in the twentieth century, suffering a series of harsh economic blows and ongoing urban deprivation. The postwar years were particularly tough, but the outlook changed again at the turn of the millennium, as economic and social regeneration brightened the centre and old docks, and the city's stint as European Capital of Culture in 2008 transformed the view from outside. Today Liverpool is a dynamic, exciting place with a Tate Gallery of its own, a series of innovative museums and a fascinating social history. And of course it also makes great play of its musical heritage – as well it should, considering that this is the place that gave the world The Beatles.

The main sights are scattered throughout the centre of town, but you can easily walk between most of them. The **River Mersey** provides one focus, whether crossing on the famous ferry to the **Wirral** peninsula or taking a tour of the Albert Dock. **Beatles** sights could easily occupy another day. If you want a cathedral, they've "got one to spare" as the song goes; plus there's a fine showing of British art in the celebrated **Walker Art Gallery** and **Tate Liverpool**, a multitude of exhibits in the terrific **World Museum Liverpool**, a revitalized arts and nightlife urban quarter centred on **FACT**, Liverpool's

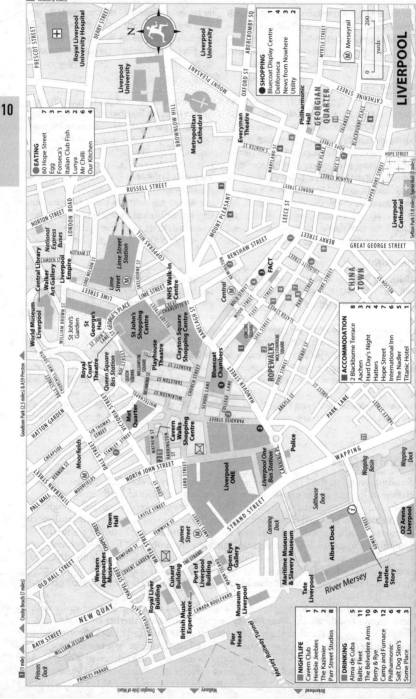

LIVERPOOL

Anfield (2 miles)

● SHOPPING
Bluecoat Display Centre	1
Delifonseca	4
News from Nowhere	3
Utility	2

● EATING
60 Hope Street	7
Egg	3
Fonseca's	1
Italian Club Fish	5
Lunya	2
Mr Chilli	6
Our Kitchen	4

■ ACCOMMODATION
2 Blackburne Terrace	8
Aachen	3
Hard Day's Night	7
Hatters	4
Hope Street	9
International Inn	6
The Nadler	5
Titanic Hotel	1

■ NIGHTLIFE
Cavern Club	7
Heebie Jeebies	1
The Kazimier	2
Parr Street Studios	8

■ DRINKING
Alma de Cuba	5
Baltic Fleet	11
The Belvedere Arms	10
Berry & Rye	9
Camp and Furnace	12
Philharmonic	6
Salt Dog Slim's	4
Some Place	3

Royal Liverpool University Hospital

Liverpool University

Liverpool University

Metropolitan Cathedral

Everyman Theatre

Philharmonic Hall

GEORGIAN QUARTER

Liverpool Cathedral

Sefton Park (1.8 miles); Spike Hall (7 miles)

Central Library
Walker Art Gallery
World Museum Liverpool
St George's Hall
St John's Shopping Centre
Clayton Square Shopping Centre
Playhouse Theatre
Bluecoat Chambers
ROPEWALKS
CHINA TOWN
FACT

Lime Street Station
Liverpool Empire
NHS Walk-in Centre

National Express Buses

Royal Court Theatre
Queen Square Bus Station
Met Quarter
Cavern Walks Shopping Centre

Moorfields

Town Hall

Liverpool ONE
Liverpool One Bus Station
Police

Western Approaches Museum
Cunard Building
Port of Liverpool Building
British Music Experience
Royal Liver Building
Museum of Liverpool

Tate Liverpool
Open Eye Gallery

Maritime Museum & Slavery Museum
Albert Dock
The Beatles Story
O2 Arena Liverpool

River Mersey

Pier Head

New Quay

Princes Dock

Goodison Park (2.5 miles) & A59 Preston
Crosby Beach (7 miles)

Mersey Railway Tunnel

Douglas (Isle of Man)
Wallasey
Birkenhead

M Merseyrail

0   200
yards

showcase for film and the media arts, and a whole new cutting-edge creative district known as the **Baltic Triangle**.

Brief history

Liverpool gained its charter from King John in 1207, but remained a humble fishing village for half a millennium until the booming slave trade prompted the building of the first dock in 1715. From then until the abolition of slavery in Britain in 1807, Liverpool was the apex of the **slaving triangle** in which firearms, alcohol and textiles were traded for African slaves, who were then shipped to the Caribbean and America where they were in turn exchanged for tobacco, raw cotton and sugar. After the abolition of the trade, the port continued to grow into a seven-mile chain of docks, not only for freight but also to cope with wholesale European emigration, which saw nine million people leave for the Americas and Australasia between 1830 and 1930. During the 1970s and 1980s Liverpool became a byword for British economic malaise, but the waterfront area of the city was granted **UNESCO World Heritage** status in 2004, spurring major refurbishment of the city's magnificent municipal and industrial buildings.

10

St George's Hall

St George's Place, off Lime St, L1 1JJ · Daily 10am–5pm · Free; walking tour £4.95 (booking essential) · ☎ 0151 233 3020, ⓦ liverpoolcityhalls.co.uk

Emerging from Lime Street Station, you can't miss **St George's Hall**, one of Britain's finest Greek Revival buildings and a testament to the wealth generated from transatlantic trade. Now primarily an exhibition venue, but once Liverpool's premier concert hall and crown court, its vaulted Great Hall features a floor tiled with thirty thousand precious Minton tiles (usually covered over, but open for a week or two in Aug), while the Willis organ is the third largest in Europe. You can take a self-guided tour, or call for details of the guided tours.

Walker Art Gallery

William Brown St, L3 8EL · Daily 10am–5pm · Free; audio tour £2.50 · ☎ 0151 478 4199, ⓦ liverpoolmuseums.org.uk/walker

Liverpool's **Walker Art Gallery** houses one of the country's best provincial art collections. The city's explosive growth in the eighteenth and nineteenth centuries, a time when British painting began to blossom, is illustrated by such luminaries as native Liverpudlian George Stubbs, England's greatest animal painter. Impressionists and Post-Impressionists, including Degas, Sickert, Cézanne and Monet, take the collection into more modern times and tastes, before the final round of galleries of contemporary British art. Paul Nash, Lucian Freud, Ben Nicholson, David Hockney and John Hoyland all have work here, much of it first displayed in the Walker's biennial John Moores Exhibition.

Although the paintings are up on the first floor, don't miss the ground-floor with its Sculpture gallery, excellent Big Art for Little Artists gallery (aimed at young children), and the Craft and Design gallery, which displays changing exhibits from a large applied arts collection – glassware, ceramics, fabrics, precious metals and furniture – largely retrieved from the homes of the city's early industrial businessmen.

Central Library

William Brown St, L3 8EW · Mon–Fri 9am–8pm, Sat 9am–5pm, Sun 10am–5pm · Free · ☎ 0151 233 3069, ⓦ liverpool.gov.uk/libraries/find-a-library/central-library

Next to the Walker Gallery, the city's spectacular **Central Library** had a £50 million facelift back in 2013. Approached via a "Literary Pavement" celebrating the city's considerable contribution to the written word, it centres on a stunning atrium crowned by an elliptical dome made of around 150 pieces of glass. Don't miss the beautiful circular **Picton Reading Room** and, in the **Oak Room**, a copy of John James Audubon's huge *Birds of America*.

World Museum Liverpool

William Brown St, L3 8EN • Daily 10am–5pm • Free • ☎ 0151 478 4393, ⓦ liverpoolmuseums.org.uk/WML

The **World Museum Liverpool** is a great family attraction. The dramatic six-storey atrium provides access to an eclectic series of themed exhibits of broad appeal – from natural history to ethnography, insects to antiquities, dinosaurs to space rockets. Excellent sections for children include the Bug House and the newly reopened Mummy Room, plus a hands-on discovery centre. The **planetarium** (£2.50, children £1.50) and theatre have daily shows, with times posted at the information desk.

Metropolitan Cathedral

On the hill behind Lime St, off Mount Pleasant, L3 5TQ • Daily 7.30am–6pm • Free; £3 admission to crypt • ☎ 0151 709 9222, ⓦ liverpoolmetrocathedral.org.uk

After an original grandiose project of Sir Edwin Lutyens to outdo St Peter's in Rome was left incomplete (and eventually demolished in the 1980s), the idiosyncratically shaped Catholic **Metropolitan Cathedral** of Christ the King was built to Sir Frederick Gibberd's spectacular Modernist design. Consecrated in 1967, and denigratingly known as "Paddy's Wigwam" or the "Mersey Funnel", the building is anchored by sixteen concrete ribs supporting the landmark stained-glass lantern. Ceremonial steps mark the approach from Mount Pleasant/Hope Street, with a café-bar at the bottom and four huge bells at the top.

Liverpool Cathedral

Hope St, L1 7AZ • Daily 8am–6pm • Free, but donation requested • **Tower** Daily 10am–5pm • £5.50 • ⓦ liverpoolcathedral.org.uk

The Anglican **Liverpool Cathedral** looks much older than the Metropolitan Cathedral, but was actually completed eleven years later, in 1978, after 74 years in construction. The last of the great British neo-Gothic structures, Sir Giles Gilbert Scott's masterwork claims a smattering of superlatives: Britain's largest and the world's fifth-largest cathedral, the world's tallest Gothic arches and the highest and heaviest bells. Contemporary art adds to its unique feel, including a neon sign by Tracey Emin: "I Felt You And I Knew You Loved me". On a clear day, a trip up the 330ft tower is rewarded by views to the Welsh hills.

Ropewalks and around

At the heart of Liverpool's regenerating city centre, **Ropewalks**, the former warehouse and factory district roughly between Bold Street and Duke Street, is anchored by **FACT** (Foundation for Art and Creative Technology; 88 Wood Street; galleries Tues–Sun 11am–6pm; free; ⓦ fact.co.uk), with its galleries, community projects, cinema, café and bar. Just north of Duke Street, in Wolstenholme Square, is *Penelope*, a huge modern sculpture of coloured plexiglass spheres on giant interwoven stalks, created by sculptor Jorge Pardo for the 2006 Biennial; it's especially striking when illuminated at night.

A short walk northwest over Hanover Street – almost in the shadow of the enormous **Liverpool ONE** shopping complex – is the beautifully proportioned Bluecoat Chambers on School Lane, built in 1717 as an Anglican boarding school for orphans. Today it houses **The Bluecoat** (ⓦ www.thebluecoat.org.uk), a mainstay of Liverpool's cultural life, complete with artists' studios and venues for exhibitions, courses and performances. There's also a fantastic **Bluecoat Display Centre** (see page 495), where contemporary crafts are for sale.

FERRY ACROSS THE MERSEY

Though the tumult of shipping which once fought the current in Liverpool has gone, the **Pier Head** landing stage remains the embarkation point for the **Mersey Ferry** (☎ 0151 330 1444, ⓦ merseyferries.co.uk) to Woodside (for Birkenhead) and Seacombe (Wallasey). Ferries (£2.80 return) run in the morning and evening rush hours. At other times there are circular "river explorer" **cruises** (hourly: Mon–Fri 10am–4pm, Sat & Sun 10am–6pm; 50min; £9), which you can combine with a visit to Seacombe's **Spaceport** space exploration visitor centre (Tues–Fri 10am–3pm; Sat, Sun & bank hols 10am–5pm; £9.50, with ferry £14.50; ☎ 0151 330 1444, ⓦ spaceport.org.uk).

Western Approaches Museum

1–3 Rumford St, off Chapel St, L2 8SZ • March–Oct Mon–Thurs & Sat 10.30am–4.30pm (closed Nov–Feb) • £8 • ⓦ liverpoolwarmuseum.co.uk

Not far from the waterfront, the **Western Approaches Museum** reveals an underground labyrinth of rooms, formerly headquarters for the Battle of the Atlantic during World War II. The massive Operations Room vividly displays all the technology of a 1940s nerve centre – wooden pushers and model boats, chalkboards and ladders.

The waterfront

Dominating the waterfront are the so-called **Three Graces** – namely the Port of Liverpool Building (1907), Cunard Building (1913) and, most prominently, the 322ft-high Royal Liver Building (1910), topped by the "Liver Birds", a couple of cormorants that have become the symbol of the city. As the waterfront has developed in the last decade or so it has sprouted a number of attractions, including **Tate Liverpool**, the **Maritime Museum**, the **Beatles Story**, the **Museum of Liverpool** and the marvellous **Open Eye** gallery.

Museum of Liverpool

Pier Head, L3 1DG • Daily 10am–5pm • Free • ☎ 0151 478 4545, ⓦ liverpoolmuseums.org.uk/mol

Huge and flashy, in a show-stopping Danish-designed building, the brilliant **Museum of Liverpool** opened in 2011. Spread over three floors, the galleries play on Liverpool's historic status as the "second city of Empire", exploring the complex political and life histories that have unfolded in a community whose wealth and social fabric were built on international trade. Children will enjoy "Little Liverpool", a gallery where they can design and build their own city, while anyone with any interest in popular culture will have an absolute ball at "Wondrous Place", a memorabilia-rich celebration of sports and music.

Open Eye Gallery

19 Mann Island, L3 1BP • Tues–Sun 10.30am–5.30pm; closed during exhibition takeovers, which take place four times a year and last approximately 12 days • Free • ☎ 0151 236 6768, ⓦ openeye.org.uk

On the new Mann Island development just by the Museum of Liverpool sits the **Open Eye Gallery**, dedicated to photography and related media. As well as presenting an impressive programme of international exhibitions, it contains a permanent archive of around 1600 prints from the 1930s onwards.

British Music Experience

Cunard Building, L3 1DS • Daily 9am–7pm, Thurs until 9pm • Last entry 1hr 30min before closing • £16, children £11 • ☎ 0344 3350655, ⓦ britishmusicexperience.com

The British Music Experience is an essential stop if you have an interest in British culture and pop music – or if you have children in tow. It's a fun and interactive experience with loads of memorabilia from 1945 onwards on display, plus a hands-on instrument studio.

10

THE BEATLES TRAIL

Mathew Street, ten minutes' walk west of Lime Street Station, is now a little enclave of Beatles nostalgia, most of it bogus – typified by the **Cavern Walks Shopping Centre**, with a bronze statue of the boys in the atrium. **The Cavern** club, where the band was first spotted by Brian Epstein, saw 275 Beatles' gigs in 1961–63; it closed in 1966 and was partly demolished in 1973, though a latter-day successor, the *Cavern Club* (10 Mathew St), complete with souvenir shop, was rebuilt on the original site. The *Cavern Pub*, across the way, boasts a coiffed Lennon mannequin and a "Wall of Fame" with the names of all the bands who appeared at the club in 1957–73, and brass discs commemorating every Liverpool chart-topper since 1952 – the city has produced more UK No. 1 singles than any other. There's more Beatlemania at **The Beatles Shop** (31 Mathew St; ⓦthebeatleshop.co.uk), which claims to have the largest range of Beatles gear in the world.

For a personal and social history, head to Albert Dock for **The Beatles Story** (daily: April–Oct 9am–7pm, Nov–March 10am–6pm; £15.95; ⓦbeatlesstory.com), which traces the band's rise from the early days to their solo careers. Then it's on to the two houses where John Lennon and Paul McCartney grew up. Both **20 Forthlin Road**, home to the McCartney family 1955–64, and the rather more genteel **Mendips**, where Lennon lived with his Aunt Mimi and Uncle George 1945–63, are only accessible on pre-booked **National Trust** minibus tours (£23, NT members £9.50; ☎0844 800 4791), which run from both the city centre and Speke Hall, seven miles south (tour times vary). The experience is disarmingly intimate, whether you're sitting in John Lennon's bedroom – which has its original wallpaper – on a replica bed looking out, as he would have done, onto the lawn, or simply entering Paul's tiny room and gazing at pictures of his childhood.

BEATLES TOURS

Phil Hughes ☎0151 228 4565 or ☎07961 511223, ⓦtourliverpool.co.uk. Small (eight-seater) minibus tours run daily on demand with a Blue Badge guide well versed in The Beatles and Liverpool life (4hr; £120 minimum tour price, £25/person for 5+). Includes city-centre pick ups/drop-offs and refreshments.

Magical Mystery Tour ☎0151 236 9091, ⓦcavernclub.org; or book at tourist offices. Tours on the multicoloured Mystery Bus (daily from 10am; 2hr; £17.95) leave from Albert Dock.

Albert Dock

Five minutes' walk south of Pier Head is **Albert Dock**, built in 1846 when Liverpool's port was a world leader. Its decline began at the beginning of the twentieth century, as the new deep-draught ships were unable to berth here, and the dock last saw service in 1972. A decade later the site was given a refit, and it is now one of the city's most popular areas, full of **attractions** – including the **Beatles Story** (see above) – and bars and restaurants.

Merseyside Maritime Museum

Albert Dock, L3 4AQ • Daily 10am–5pm • Free • ☎0151 478 4499, ⓦliverpoolmuseums.org.uk/maritime

The **Merseyside Maritime Museum** fills one wing of the Dock; there's lots to see, even if some of the exhibits are looking a little tired. The basement houses **Seized!**, giving the lowdown on smuggling and revenue collection, along with **Emigrants to a New World**, an illuminating display detailing Liverpool's pivotal role as a springboard for more than nine million emigrants. Other galleries tell the story of the Battle of the Atlantic and of the three ill-fated liners – the *Titanic*, *Lusitania* and *Empress of Ireland*.

International Slavery Museum

The unmissable **International Slavery Museum**, on the third floor of the Maritime Museum, manages to be both challenging and chilling, as it tells dehumanizing stories of slavery while examining contemporary issues of equality, freedom and racial injustice.

Tate Liverpool

Albert Dock, L3 4BB • Daily 10am–5.50pm • Free, except for special exhibitions • ⓦ tate.org.uk/liverpool

The country's national collection of modern art from the north, **Tate Liverpool** holds popular retrospectives of artists such as Mondrian, Dalí, Magritte and Calder, along with an ever-changing display from its vast collection, and temporary exhibitions of artists of international standing. There's also a full programme of events, talks and tours.

10 Crosby Beach

Mariners Rd, L23 6SX/Hall Rd West, L23 8TA, Crosby • Trains from Lime St to Hall Road Station; every 30min; 20min

Seven miles north of Liverpool city centre, **Crosby Beach** was an innocuous, if picturesque, spot until the arrival in 2005 of Antony Gormley's haunting **Another Place** installation, spread along more than two miles of the shore. An eerie set of a hundred life-size cast-iron statues, each cast from Gormley's own body, are buried at different levels in the sand, all gazing out to sea and slowly becoming submerged as high tide rolls in.

ARRIVAL AND DEPARTURE
LIVERPOOL

By plane Liverpool John Lennon Airport (☎0870 129 8484, ⓦ liverpoolairport.com) is 8 miles southeast of the city centre, connected by the Airlink #500 bus (5.45am–11.45pm; every 30min; £2.20). A taxi to Lime Street costs around £15.

By train Mainline trains pull in to Lime Street Station, northeast of the city centre.

Destinations Birmingham (hourly; 1hr 40min); Chester (every 30min; 45min); Leeds (hourly; 1hr 40min); London Euston (hourly; 2hr 20min); Manchester (hourly; 50min); Sheffield (hourly; 1hr 45min); York (11 daily; 2hr 15min).

By bus National Express buses use the station at Liverpool ONE, on Canning Place.

Destinations Chester (12 daily; 1hr); London (9 daily; 5hr 10min–6hr 40min); Manchester (hourly; 1hr).

By ferry Ferries for the Isle of Man (☎0872 299 2992, ⓦ steam-packet.com) dock at the terminals just north of Pier Head, not far from James Street Merseyrail station. From Belfast, Stena Line (☎0844 770 7070, ⓦ stenaline. co.uk) dock over the water on the Wirral at Twelve Quays, near Woodside ferry terminal (ferry or Merseyrail to Liverpool).

GETTING AROUND

By bus Local buses depart from Queen Square and Liverpool ONE bus station. The anti-clockwise circular CityLink service is a perfect way to see the sights (every 12min; day tickets from £3)

By train The suburban Merseyrail system (trains from Chester) calls at four underground stations, including Lime Street and James Street (for Pier Head and the Albert Dock).

By bike The largest public bicycle scheme outside of London, Citybike (☎0151 374 2034, ⓦ citybikeliverpool. co.uk) has bikes from £3 a day, with stations citywide.

INFORMATION AND TOURS

Tourist information The best online source of information is ⓦ visitliverpool.com. There are visitor centres at Albert Dock, Anchor Courtyard (daily 10am–4.30pm; ☎0151 707 0729, ⓦ albertdock.com) and Liverpool John Lennon Airport (daily 8am–6pm; ☎0151 907 1057). Merseytravel (☎0151 236 7676, ⓦ merseytravel.gov.uk) has travel centres at Queen Square and the Liverpool ONE Interchange.

Listings The Liverpool Echo's website (ⓦ liverpoolecho. co.uk/whats-on) is always current; while the hip ⓦ the doublenegative.co.uk and ⓦ creativetourist.com will see you right. The Skinny (ⓦ theskinny.co.uk) also publishes a useful, widely available monthly freebie.

Beatles tours Among the most popular jaunts in the city are those around the Fab Four's former haunts (see page 490).

Football tours You're unlikely to get a ticket for a Liverpool game, but there are daily tours around the museum, trophy room and dressing rooms (£17; museum only £10; ⓦ liverpoolfc.com). Everton, the city's other Premiership side, also offers tours (Mon, Wed, Fri 11am & 1pm, Sun 10am, noon & 2pm; ☎0151 530 5212; £12; ⓦ evertonfc.com).

Walking tours ⓦ visitliverpool.com has details of local guides (most Easter–Sept; from £5).

ACCOMMODATION

Budget chains are well represented in Liverpool, with Premier, Travel Inn, Ibis, Express (Holiday Inn) and others all with convenient city-centre locations, including down by Albert Dock and near Mount Pleasant.

2 Blackburne Terrace 2 Blackburne Terrace, L8 7PJ ☎0151 708 5474, ⓦwww.2blackburneterrace.com; map p.486. Beautiful B&B in a grand Georgian house set back from Blackburne Place, with just four elegant and individually designed rooms boasting high thread-count linens, original artworks and cutting-edge technology. With welcoming hosts and a sumptuous breakfast, this is a hidden, high-end gem. You'll save around £80 by staying midweek. **£270**

Aachen 89–91 Mount Pleasant, L3 5TB ☎0151 709 3477, ⓦaachenhotel.co.uk; map p.486. The best of the Mount Pleasant budget choices, with a range of good-value rooms (with and without en-suite showers), big "eat-as-much-as-you-like" breakfasts, and a bar. **£95**

Hard Day's Night North John St, L2 6RR ☎0151 668 0476, ⓦharddaysnighthotel.com; map p.486. Up-to-the-minute four-star close to Mathew Street. Splashes of vibrant colour and artful lighting enhance the elegant decor. The Lennon and McCartney suites (£950/750 respectively) are the tops. Breakfast not included. **£120**

Hatters 56–60 Mount Pleasant. L3 5SD ☎0151 709 5570, ⓦhattershostels.com/liverpool-hostel; map p.486. Though it's housed in the former YMCA building – with an institutional feel and gymnasium-size dining hall – *Hatters* has clean rooms, friendly staff and a great location. Standard facilities, including internet. Prices fluctuate wildly according to what's on. Dorms **£28**, doubles **£100**

★ **Hope Street** 40 Hope St, L1 9DA (entrance on Hope Place) ☎0151 709 3000, ⓦhopestreethotel.co.uk; map p.486. In an unbeatable location between the cathedrals, this former Victorian warehouse retains its original elegant brickwork and cast-iron columns but now comes with hardwood floors, huge beds and luxurious bathrooms. Fabulous breakfasts, too, served in the highly rated *London Carriage Works* restaurant. Flash sales, held three times a year, offer bargain rooms; register for the email newsletter to snap one up. **£152**

★ **International Inn** 4 South Hunter St, off Hardman St, L1 9JG ☎0151 709 8135, ⓦinternationalinn.co.uk; map p.486. Converted Victorian warehouse in a great location, with modern en-suite rooms sleeping two to ten people, and 32 new double and twin "Cocoon Pods". Dorms **£20**, doubles **£45**, pods **£55**

The Nadler 29 Seel St, L1 4AU ☎0151 705 2626, ⓦnadlerhotels.com/the-nadler-liverpool.html; map p.486. Smack in the heart of the Ropewalks is this converted warehouse, with more than 100 minimalist rooms that complement the building's original brickwork and well-appointed modern art pieces. Rooms include a "mini-kitchen". Prices are almost halved midweek. **£119**

★ **Titanic Hotel** Stanley Dock, Regent Rd, L3 0AN ☎0151 559 1444, ⓦtitanichotelliverpool.com; map p.486. This vast warehouse was converted into a designer hotel and spa for a cool £53million. Light-filled rooms have views of the next-door tobacco warehouse or the Mersey, all have exposed brick ceilings, classy decor and en-suite bathrooms with a drench shower. It's a long walk or short taxi ride into the city; free parking. **£165**

EATING

Many Liverpool venues morph from breakfast hangout to dinner spot to late-night live-music space, making categorization tricky. Most **eating** choices are in three distinct areas – at Albert Dock, around Hardman and Hope streets in the Georgian Quarter, and along Berry and Nelson streets, the heart of Liverpool's Chinatown. Alternatively, take a short taxi ride out to Lark Lane in Aigburth, close to Sefton Park, where a dozen eating and drinking spots pack into one short street.

★ **60 Hope Street** 60 Hope St, L1 9BZ ☎0151 707 6060, ⓦ60hopestreet.com; map p.486. The star of the Liverpool gastronomic scene, set in a Georgian terrace, serves British cuisine (mains around £22) with creative flourishes – roast rump of Cumbrian lamb with broccoli purée, for example – and an extensive wine list. It takes some nerve to offer, as a dessert, deep-fried jam sandwich with Carnation milk ice cream (£8.50), but the confidence is justified. Just around the corner on Falkner St, they also operate *The Quarter*. Mon–Sat noon–2.30pm & 5–10.30pm, Sun noon–8pm.

Egg 16–18 Newington, L1 4AD ☎0151 707 2755, ⓦeggcafe.co.uk; map p.486. Up on the third floor, this plant-strewn bohemian café serves excellent vegan and vegetarian food with good set-meal deals. Also a nice place for a chai. Mon–Fri 9am–10.30pm, Sat & Sun 10am–10.30pm.

★ **Fonseca's** 12 Stanley St, L1 6AF ☎0151 255 0808, ⓦdelifonseca.co.uk; map p.486. Bistro with a changing blackboard menu of Italian and British delights, including Welsh black beef braised in local Wapping ale, and crayfish and chicken pie (mains around £13). The small deli counter downstairs offers a sample of the wares at the newer *Delifonseca*, 30min away on the dockside (see page 495). Mon–Thurs noon–2.30 & 5–9pm, Fri & Sat noon–10pm.

Italian Club Fish 128 Bold St, L1 4JA ☎0151 707 2110, ⓦtheitalianclubfish.co.uk; map p.486. Proper Italian seafood place with a menu that adapts to what's fresh – try the *Sauté Di Maurizio* (£17.95). There are also a few token meat and vegetarian dishes, all around £13. Over the road is *Italian Club*, its slightly cooler, younger sister. Mon–Sat 10am–10pm, Sun noon–9pm.

Lunya 18–20 College Lane, L1 3DS ☎0151 706 9770, ⓦlunya.co.uk; map p.486. Gorgeous Catalan and Spanish deli-restaurant in the heart of Liverpool ONE, with

10

a vast tapas selection (from around £5) and menus running the gamut from suckling pig banquet to vegan. Mon & Tues 10am–9pm, Wed & Thurs 10am–9.30pm, Fri 10am–10pm, Sat 9am–10.30pm, Sun 10am–8.30pm.
Mr Chilli 92 Seel St, L1 4BL ☎0151 709 5772, ⓦmrchilli.co.uk; map p.486. *Mr Chilli* is widely held to be the best Sichuan restaurant in Liverpool, with dishes – many of them fiery – at around £8, and famous hot pots for £10/person (min two). Mon & Tues noon–midnight,

Wed–Sun noon–2am.
Our Kitchen 84b Bold St, L1 4HR ☎0151 709 0606, ⓦourkitchen.co.uk; map p.486. Brand-new Scandi-feel veggie & vegan restaurant on cool Bold St. Brunch is superb, with dishes like huevos rancheros with poached eggs or spicy tofu for £7.95; later in the day plump for an awesome Buddha Bowl filled with fresh organic produce. Juices, smoothies and tonics from £2.25. Mon–Fri 8am–10pm, Sat 9am–10pm, Sun 10am–8pm.

10

DRINKING

You'll enjoy a perfect evening's **bar-hopping** along Seel Street, while cutting-edge **Baltic Triangle**, the old industrial warehouse district south of Chinatown, has become the go-to quarter for the artsy crowd.

Alma de Cuba St Peter's Church, Seel St, L1 4BH ☎0151 702 7394, ⓦalma-de-cuba.com; map p.486. It may have far more candles now than when it was a church – and even more in the mezzanine restaurant – but the mirrored altar is still the focus of this bar's rich, dark Cuban-themed interior. Daily 11am–2am.
Baltic Fleet 33a Wapping, L1 8DQ ☎0151 709 3116, ⓦbalticfleetpubliverpool.com; map p.486. Restored, no-nonsense, quiet pub with age-old shipping connections and an open fire, just south of the Albert Dock. Beer brewed on site and good pub grub on offer. Mon–Thurs & Sun noon–11pm, Fri noon–midnight, Sat 11am–midnight.
The Belvedere Arms 5 Sugnall St, L7 7EB ☎0151 709 0303; map p.486. Teeny-tiny two-roomed backstreet pub; punters spill outside when the sun shines. Changing ales and a splendid selection of gin. Daily noon–11pm.
★ **Berry & Rye** 48 Berry St, L1 4JQ ⓔberryandrye@gmail.com; map p.486. You'll have to hunt hard – or ask a likely local – to find this unmarked bar, but once you're in it's a delight. An intimate, bare-brick gin and whiskey joint with knowledgeable bartenders, turn-of-the-twentieth-century music – often live – and well-crafted cocktails (from £6.50). Mon–Sat 5pm–2am, Sun 7pm–1am.
★ **Camp and Furnace** 67 Greenland St, L1 0BY ☎0151 708 2890, ⓦcampandfurnace.com; map p.486. The city's most creative and exhilarating venue is in the Baltic Triangle. Its huge warehouse spaces – one boasting the

city's biggest public screen, one with a mighty furnace at one end, a cosier bar area – host festival-style food slams (Fri), massive, communal Sunday roasts, all sorts of parties and pop-ups, art installations, live performances, the lot. Do not miss it. Mon–Thurs 9am–10pm, Fri & Sat 10am–2am, Sun 10am–midnight/1am.
★ **Philharmonic** 36 Hope St, L1 9BX ☎0151 707 2837, ⓦnicholsonspubs.co.uk; map p.486. Liverpool's finest traditional watering hole where the main attractions – beer aside – are the mosaic floors, tiling, gilded wrought-iron gates and the marble decor in the gents. Daily 11am–midnight.
Salt Dog Slims 79–83 Seel St, L1 4BB ☎0151 709 7172, ⓦsaltdogslims.com; map p.486. American-style bar that's a lot of fun, with a young, friendly crowd wolfing delicious hot dogs (from £3.50) washed down with plenty of beers, backed by a solidly indie soundtrack. Upstairs is the supposedly secret *81 Ltd*, which rocks a Prohibition-era speakeasy vibe, though perhaps a tad self-consciously. Mon–Fri 3pm–2am, Sat & Sun 1pm–2am.
★ **Some Place** 43 Seel St, L1 4AZ; map p.486. A green light above an unmarked doorway hints at what lies up the incense-heavy staircase – an utterly gorgeous absinthe bar that is every inch a bohemian fantasy. Savour an absinthe cocktail (from £4.50), drink in the meticulous decor and channel your inner Oscar Wilde. Wed, Thurs & Sun 9pm–late, Fri & Sat 8pm–late.

NIGHTLIFE

Liverpool's **club scene** is famously unpretentious, with posing playing second fiddle to drinking and dancing, and particularly rich in home-grown live music. Popular annual **festivals** include Beatles Week (last week of Aug; ⓦcavernclub.org/beatleweek) and the Liverpool International Music Festival (Aug bank hol; ⓦlimfestival.co.uk), with big-name acts playing across the city.

Cavern Club 10 Mathew St, L2 6RE ☎0151 236 1965, ⓦcavernclub.org; map p.486. The self-styled "most famous club in the world" has live bands, from Beatles tribute acts to indie pop and rock, at the weekends, plus occasional backstage tours and special events. The atmosphere is always high-spirited, and even though

this is not the *Cavern* club of the Beatles' days (see page 490), there's a certain thrill to it all. Entry fee Thurs–Sun nights. Daily from 10am.
Heebie Jeebies 80–82 Seel St, L1 4BH ☎0151 708 7001, ⓦfacebook.com/Officialheebiejeebies; map p.486. Student favourite in a huge brick-vaulted room.

Mainly indie and soul, with some live bands. Outdoor courtyard too. Daily 1pm–3am.

★ **The Kazimier** 4–5 Wolstenholme Square, L1 4BE ☎ 0151 324 1723, ⓦ thekazimier.co.uk; map p.486. A super-creative, split-level place with a magical garden space (entrance at 32 Seel St); *the* place to come for cabaret-style club nights, gigs and eclectic events. Hours vary but generally noon–midnight.

Parr Street Studios Parr St, L1 4JN ☎ 0151 707 1050, ⓦ parrstreet.co.uk; map p.486. Dynamic working recording studios – the UK's biggest outside London – hosting a long list of big names and home to bars/performance spaces Studio 2 and The Attic. Check website for details of what's on when.

ARTS AND ENTERTAINMENT

On the classical music scene, the **Royal Liverpool Philharmonic Orchestra** dominates; it's ranked with Manchester's Hallé as the best in the region. The **Liverpool Biennial** (July–Oct; free; ⓦ biennial.com) is a world-renowned contemporary arts festival that takes place in various public spaces and galleries across the city; the next Biennial is 2018.

CLASSICAL MUSIC AND THEATRE

Everyman Theatre Hope St, L1 9BH ☎ 0151 709 4776, ⓦ everymanplayhouse.com. Iconic, remodelled theatre staging a mix of classics with a twist, blockbusters and new writing. The theatre's stunning portrait wall – 105 aluminium shutters featuring life-size photographs of everyday people – is a celebration of its inclusive ethos.

Liverpool Empire Lime St, L1 1JE ☎ 0870 606 3536, ⓦ liverpooltheatres.com/empire.htm. The city's largest theatre, a venue for touring West End shows and large-scale opera and ballet productions.

Philharmonic Hall Hope St, L1 9BP ☎ 0151 709 3789, ⓦ liverpoolphil.com. Home to the Royal Liverpool Philharmonic Orchestra, and with a full programme of other concerts.

Playhouse Theatre Williamson Square, L1 1EL ☎ 0151 709 4776, ⓦ everymanplayhouse.com. Sister theatre to the Everyman, staging bold productions of great plays in the three-tier main house and new plays in the seventy-seat Studio.

Royal Court Theatre Roe St, L1 1HL ☎ 0870 787 1866, ⓦ royalcourtliverpool.co.uk. Art Deco theatre and concert hall, which sees regular plays, music and comedy acts.

CINEMA

Picturehouse at FACT Wood St, L1 4DQ ☎ 0871 704 2063, ⓦ picturehouses.co.uk. The city's only independent cinema screens new films, re-runs, cult classics and festivals.

SHOPPING

Liverpool is fabulous for shopping, with the brilliantly designed **Liverpool ONE** shopping complex holding pretty much all the names, a stretch of independent stores on **Bold Street** and arty originals in the **Baltic Triangle**.

Bluecoat Display Centre College Lane, L1 3BZ ☎ 0151 709 4014, ⓦ www.bluecoatdisplaycentre.com; map p.486. Established in 1959, this contemporary crafts and design gallery curates, exhibits and promotes jewellery, textiles, ceramics and more. Mon–Sat 10am–5.30pm, Sun noon–5pm.

Delifonseca Brunswick Dock, L3 4BN ☎ 0151 255 0808, ⓦ delifonseca.co.uk; map p.486. The new food hall of this acclaimed, two-site bistro offers a vast array of fine deli foods and wines. Daily 8am–9pm.

News From Nowhere 96 Bold St, L1 4HY ☎ 0151 708 7270, ⓦ newsfromnowhere.co.uk; map p.486.

Proper radical bookshop in the heart of Bold St, packed with left-leaning literature and music, plus an informative noticeboard. Mon–Sat 10am–5.45pm, Sun (Dec only) 11am–5pm.

Utility 8 Paradise Place, L1 8BQ ☎ 0151 702 9116, ⓦ utilitydesign.co.uk; map p.486. Stylish, design-led Liverpool store with three outlets across the city, two of them on Bold Street. This one, in Liverpool ONE, has the longest hours. Make a beeline for the quality Scouse souvenirs, particularly the brilliant wheelie-bin desk tidy. Mon–Fri 9.30am–8pm, Sat 9am–7pm, Sun 11am–5pm.

Blackpool

BLACKPOOL remains Britain's archetypal seaside resort. Alongside its Golden Mile, piers, amusement arcades, tram and donkey rides, fish-and-chip shops, candyfloss stalls and glitzy venues, it boasts six miles of beach – the tide ebb is half a mile, leaving plenty of sand at low tide – a revamped **prom** and an increasingly attractive, gentrified centre.

10

It was the coming of the railway in 1846 that made Blackpool what it is today: Blackpool's own "Eiffel Tower" on the seafront and other refined diversions were built to cater to the tastes of the first influx of visitors, but it was the Central Pier's "open-air dancing for the working classes" that heralded the crucial change of accent. Suddenly Blackpool was favoured destination for the "Wakes Weeks", when whole Lancashire mill towns descended for their annual holiday.

Where other British holiday resorts have suffered from the rivalry of cheap foreign packages, Blackpool has gone from strength to strength. Underneath the populist veneer there's a sophisticated marketing approach, which balances ever more elaborate rides and public art installations with well-grounded traditional entertainment. And when other resorts begin to close up for the winter, Blackpool's main season is just beginning, as more than half a million light bulbs create the **Illuminations** that decorate the prom from early September to early November.

The Blackpool Tower

Promenade, FY1 4BJ • **Tower** Mon–Fri 10am–4.45pm, Sat & Sun 10am–6.15pm • Free entry to tower, but charges for attractions; for multi-attraction all-day tickets from £30, book online 24hr in advance • **Circus** 1–3 shows daily; 2hr • £16.95, or included in package • ☏ 01253 622242, ⓦ theblackpooltower.com

Between Central and North piers stands the 518ft-high **Blackpool Tower**, erected in 1894 when it was thought that the northwest really ought not to be outdone by Paris. Ride up to the top for the stunning view and an unnerving walk on the see-through glass floor. The all-day ticket covers all the other tower attractions, including the gilt Edwardian ballroom (otherwise £7.95), with its Wurlitzer organ tea dances and big band evenings, plus dungeon, children's entertainers, adventure playground, cafés and amusements. From the earliest days, there's also been a Moorish-inspired **circus** held between the tower's legs.

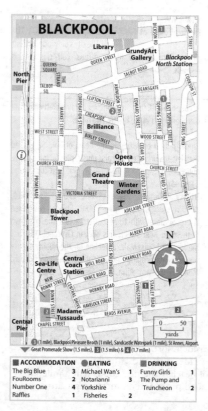

BLACKPOOL

The Comedy Carpet

Right outside Blackpool Tower, **The Comedy Carpet** is one of the country's most engaging pieces of public art – a 2200m-square, cross-shaped pavement comprising jokes and catchphrases from around a thousand comedians and writers, both old-school and new, in a dazzling typographic display that recalls a music hall playbill. Opened in 2011 by end-of-the-pier stalwart Ken Dodd, it's a unique celebration of British comedy and a marvellous way to spend an hour.

Blackpool Pleasure Beach

525 Ocean Blvd, FY4 1EZ • April–Nov daily from 10am • £6 (rides extra); wristband £32.50, cheaper online • ⓦ blackpoolpleasurebeach.com

The major draw in town is **Blackpool Pleasure Beach** on the South Promenade,

■ ACCOMMODATION		● EATING		■ DRINKING	
The Big Blue	3	Michael Wan's	1	Funny Girls	1
FouRooms	2	Notarianni	3	The Pump and	
Number One	4	Yorkshire		Truncheon	2
Raffles	1	Fisheries	2		

BLACKPOOL – BEHIND THE SCENES

There is, after all, an alternative Blackpool – one of history, heritage and even a spot of culture. Scene of party political conferences over the decades, the **Winter Gardens** (Coronation Street) opened to fanfares in 1878. Among the motley array of cafés, bars and amusements, seek out the extraordinary **Spanish Hall Suite** (in the form of a carved galleon), and the **Opera House** honours board – Lillie Langtry, George Formby and Vera Lynn are all present. From in front of the Opera House, follow Abingdon Street to Queen Street and the porticoed Central Library, next to which the **Grundy Art Gallery** (Mon–Sat 10am–5pm; free) might tempt you in to see its Victorian oils and watercolours, contemporary art and special exhibitions. **North Pier**, the first pier to be opened (1863) on the Blackpool seafront, is now a listed building. Head northbound from here on the tram to the **Imperial Hotel**, whose wood-panelled No. 10 Bar is covered with photographs and mementos of every British prime minister since Lloyd George.

10

just south of South Pier. Entrance to the amusement park is relatively cheap, but you'll have to fork out for the superb array of white-knuckle rides including the 235ft-high "Big One". The wonderful antique wooden roller coasters ("woodies" to aficionados) may seem like kids' stuff, but each is unique – the original "Big Dipper" was invented at Blackpool in 1923 and still thrills, as does the "Grand National" (1935). Caution: don't disregard the warning at the thrilling "Valhalla" ride – you will indeed get (very) wet, so maybe save it for the end of the day. Recuperate in the park's champagne and oyster bar, which adds a bit of class to the otherwise relentless barrage of fairground noise, shrieking, jangling and fast food.

Great Promenade Show

South of the Pleasure Beach, from the Sandcastle Waterpark down to Squire's Gate, FY4 1BB • Free

Perhaps nowhere sums up the "new" Blackpool better than the **Great Promenade Show**, a set of ambitious outdoor sculptures, installations and soundscapes set along a mile or so of the new promenade. All relating to some aspect of Blackpool's history or its natural environment, these include the mighty **High Tide Organ**, which gives off haunting music when "played" by the swell of the waves, a set of sculptures of circus characters by **Sir Peter Blake**, and the world's largest **disco ball**, named "They Shoot Horses, Don't They?"

ARRIVAL AND INFORMATION

BLACKPOOL

By train The town's main train station, Blackpool North, is just off Talbot Road, a few minutes' walk northeast of the town centre, with two smaller stations, Blackpool South, just north of the Pleasure Beach on Waterloo Road, and Blackpool Pleasure Beach. There are regular trains to Manchester (hourly; 1hr 10min).

By bus Blackpool Central Coach Station is behind the Coral Island arcade, where Central Drive meets New Bonny St.

Tourist office Festival House, on the Promenade (Mon & Tues 9am–6pm, Wed–Sat 9am–5pm, Sun 10am–4pm; ☎ 01253 478222, ⓦ visitblackpool.com). Excellent purpose-built information centre selling discounted admission tickets for all major Blackpool attractions (except the Pleasure Beach), and travel passes.

GETTING AROUND

By tram Electric trams (ⓦ blackpooltransport.com) cover the length of the promenade, from Fleetwood, north of Blackpool, to Starr Gate, south of the Pleasure Beach. Prices vary, but the cheapest option is to buy a travel pass online or from the tourist office (see above) that is valid for local buses and trams (1/3/7-day, £5/11/14); you'll pay more if you buy on board.

ACCOMMODATION

B&B **prices** are generally low (from £25/person, even less on a room-only basis or out of season), but rise at weekends and during the Illuminations. To avoid the noisy crowds in peak season, make for the North Shore, beyond North Pier (the grid west of Warbreck Hill Road has hundreds of options).

10

The Big Blue Ocean Blvd, Pleasure Beach, FY4 1ND ☎01253 400045, ⓦbigbluehotel.com; map p.496. Spacious family rooms with games consoles and separate children's area, plus boutique-style, dark-wood executive rooms. There's a bar and brasserie, parking and a gym. It's next to the Pleasure Beach (and Blackpool South train station), and most rooms look out on the rides. **£135**

★**FouRooms** 60 Reads Ave, FY1 4DE ☎01253 752171, ⓦfouroomsblackpool.co.uk; map p.496. One of Blackpool's best boutique hotels, a tastefully converted Victorian townhouse with airy rooms and original dark-wood fittings. The four suites are individually furnished, and staff are keen to help. **£129**

★**Number One** 1 St Luke's Rd, FY4 2EL ☎01253 343901, ⓦnumberoneblackpool.com; map p.496. There's no other B&B quite like this – an extraordinarily lavish experience hosted by the ultra-amiable Mark and Claire. There are just three extravagantly appointed rooms here, with more at *Number One South Beach* nearby. Parking available. **£100**

Raffles 73–77 Hornby Rd, FY1 4QJ ☎01253 294713, ⓦraffleshotelblackpool.co.uk; map p.496. Nice place back from Central Pier and away from the bustle, with well-kept rooms, a bar, and traditional tearooms attached. Winter rates are a good deal. **£84**

EATING

Michael Wan's Mandarin 27 Clifton St, FY1 1JD ☎01253 622687, ⓦmichaelwansmandarin.co.uk; map p.496. Delicious and authentic Asian food served up in contemporary surroundings by charming staff. Signature dishes include zesty lemon chicken (£11.90) and Szechuan twice-cooked pork (£11.50). Tues–Fri noon–3pm & 4.30pm–midnight, Sat noon–1.45pm & 5.30–11.45pm, Sun 5.30–10.15pm.

Notarianni 9 Waterloo Rd, FY4 1AF ☎01253 342510, ⓦnotarianni.co.uk; map p.496. Now with the third-

and fourth-generation of Italians at the helm, this ice-cream parlour is a Blackpool institution. No fancy flavours here; they only serve vanilla. The banana split (£4.50) is unmissable. Daily 10am–8pm.

Yorkshire Fisheries 14–16 Topping St, FY1 3AQ ☎01253 627739, ⓦyorkshirefisheries.co.uk; map p.496. Behind the Winter Gardens, this sit-down and takeaway fish-and-chip shop is commonly agreed to be the best in the centre of town. Mon–Sat 11.30am–7pm, Sun noon–6pm.

DRINKING AND NIGHTLIFE

Blackpool has a plethora of **theme bars** and any number of places for **karaoke** or **dancing**. Family-oriented fun revolves around musicals, veteran TV comedians, magicians, ice dance, tribute bands, crooners and stage spectaculars put on at a variety of end-of-pier and historic venues.

Funny Girls 5 Dickson Rd, off Talbot Rd, FY1 2AX ☎01253 649194, ⓦfunnygirlsonline.co.uk; map p.496. A Blackpool institution – a bar with nightly cabaret shows run by drag queens, attracting long (gay and straight) queues. It's a hen-party favourite, and the best place in town if you fancy some unabashedly bawdy Blackpool fun.

The Pump and Truncheon 13 Bonny St, FY1 4AR (behind Madame Tussauds) ☎01253 624099, ⓦbit.ly/Truncheon; map p.496. If you're after something a little more low-key, this traditional backstreet pub is a gem. Craft beers, cask ales and CAMRA discount – and they serve pizza for less than a tenner.

ENTERTAINMENT

The Grand Theatre Church St, FY1 1HT ☎01253 290190, ⓦblackpoolgrand.co.uk. Built in 1894 for the town's more refined audiences, the Grand has a tradition of distinguishing itself from other amusements, putting on performances of Shakespeare as well as more popular variety shows.

Opera House Winter Gardens, Church St, FY1 1HL

☎01253 625252, ⓦwintergardensblackpool.co.uk. Set in the Winter Gardens, the Opera House has a star-studded history that includes such populist greats as Charlie Chaplin, George Formby and Vera Lynn. These days you'll find a variety of shows on offer, including West End hits. Also in the Winter Gardens is the Empress Ballroom, which is a majestic gig venue (same contact details).

Lancaster

LANCASTER, Lancashire's county town, dates back at least as long ago as the Roman occupation, though only scant remains survive from that period. A Saxon church was later built within the ruined Roman walls as Lancaster became a strategic trading centre, and by medieval times a **castle** had been built on the heights above the river.

Lancaster later developed into an important port on the slave trade triangle, and it's the **Georgian buildings** from that time – especially those around the castle – that give the town much of its character. Many people choose to stay here on the way to the Lakes or Dales to the north; and it's an easy side-trip the few miles west to the resort of **Morecambe** and to neighbouring **Heysham village**, with its ancient churches, or east through the **Forest of Bowland**.

Lancaster Castle

10

Castle Park, LA1 1YJ • Daily 9.30am–5pm • £8 • **Tours** Every 30min Mon–Fri 10am–4pm, Sat & Sun 10.30am–4pm; 1hr 30min • Included in entry price • ☎ 01524 64998, ⓦ lancastercastle.com

The site of **Lancaster Castle** has been the city's focal point since Roman times. The Normans built the first defences here, at the end of the eleventh century – two hundred years later it became a **crown court**, a role it maintains today, and until 2011 it was a working prison. Currently, about a third of the battlemented building can be visited on an entertaining hour-and-a quarter-long tour, though court sittings sometimes affect the schedules.

Lancaster City Museum

Market Square, LA1 1HT • Tues–Sun 10am–5pm • Free • ☎ 01524 64637, ⓦ lancashire.gov.uk/leisure-and-culture/museums/lancaster-maritime-museum

Drop into the former Town Hall to peruse the **Lancaster City Museum**. While hardly groundbreaking, exhibits do a good job of illustrating the history of Lancaster. One of the rooms holds the **Kings Own Royal Regiment Museum**, and the landscapes and portraits on the stairway are a nice local touch.

Lancaster Maritime Museum

Custom House, St George's Quay, LA1 1RB • Daily: April–Oct 10am–5pm; Nov–March 12.30–4pm • £3 • ☎ 01524 382264, ⓦ lancashire.gov.uk/leisure-and-culture/museums/lancaster-maritime-museum

Down on the banks of the River Lune – which lent Lancaster its name – one of the eighteenth-century quayside warehouses is taken up by part of **Lancaster Maritime Museum**. The museum amply covers life on the sea and inland waterways of Lancashire, including the role of Lancaster's residents in the highly profitable slave trade.

Williamson Park

Quernmore Rd, LA1 1UX • Daily: April–Sept 10am–5pm; Oct–March 10am–4pm • Free; butterfly house £3.90, under-16s £2.90 • ☎ 01524 33318, ⓦ lancaster.gov.uk/parks-and-open-spaces/williamson-park

For a panorama of the town, Morecambe Bay and the Cumbrian fells, take a steep 25-minute walk up Moor Lane (or a taxi from the bus station) to the beautifully maintained **Williamson Park**, Lancaster's highest point. Funded by local statesman and lino magnate Lord Ashton, the park's centrepiece is the 220ft-high **Ashton Memorial**, a Baroque folly raised by his son in memory of his second wife. The revamped tropical **Butterfly House** is a must if you have children with you.

> ### ON YOUR BIKE
>
> Lancaster promotes itself as a **cycling centre**, and miles of canal towpaths, old railway tracks and riverside paths provide excellent traffic-free routes around the Lune estuary, Lancaster Canal and Ribble Valley, southeast of Lancaster. Typical is the easy riverside path to the **Crook O'Lune** beauty spot, where you can reward yourself with a bacon buttie and an Eccles cake at *Woodie's* famous snack bar. For bike hire, contact **Leisure Lakes Bikes** (from £10/4hr; 103–105 Penny St; ☎ 01524 844389, ⓦ leisurelakesbikes.com).

10

ARRIVAL AND DEPARTURE

By train Trains pull in at Meeting House Lane, a 5min walk from the town centre.

Destinations Carlisle (every 30min–1hr; 50min); Manchester (every 30min–1hr; 1hr); Morecambe (every 30min–1hr; 10min).

By bus The bus station is on Cable St, a 5min walk from the tourist office.

Destinations Carlisle (4–5 daily; 1hr 20min); Kendal (hourly; 1hr); Manchester (2 daily; 2hr); Windermere (hourly; 1hr 45min).

INFORMATION AND TOURS

Tourist office The Storey, Meeting House Lane (Mon–Sat 10am–5pm; ☏ 01524 582394, ⓦ visitlancaster.org.uk).

Canal cruises Contact Lancaster Canal Boats (☏ 01524 389410, ⓦ budgietransport.co.uk).

ACCOMMODATION

Toll House Penny St, LA1 1XT ☏ 01524 599900, ⓦ www.thwaites.co.uk/hotels-and-inns/inns/toll-house-at-lancaster. Recently refurbished, this elegant townhouse has 28 oddly shaped rooms, all with airy high ceilings and flatscreen TVs. It's worth popping in the bar for a pint of good local ale too. **£95**

★ **The Sun Hotel and Bar** 63 Church St, LA1 1ET ☏ 01524 66006, ⓦ thesunhotelandbar.co.uk. The city centre's only four-star hotel is in a handsome Georgian building, with sixteen contemporary rooms (some with king-sized beds, all with fine bathrooms) above a relaxed bar-restaurant. **£90**

EATING

The Borough 3 Dalton Square, LA1 1PP ☏ 01524 64170, ⓦ theboroughlancaster.co.uk. Great for informal dining, this roomy gastropub – in a refurbished 1824 building – has a rigorously sourced local, organic menu. Well-priced tapas platters include smoked fish and Lancashire cheese, while mains range from ostrich to salmon. Nine smart new rooms upstairs too (£95). Kitchen Mon–Thurs & Sun 8–11am & noon–9pm, Fri & Sat 8–11am & noon–9.30pm.

The Music Room Sun St, LA1 1EW ☏ 01524 65470, ⓦ facebook.com/themusicroomcafe. A quirky, stylish little place with a marvellous glass frontage, serving top-quality coffees (it has its own roaster), teas and melt-in-the-mouth cake. The best place in town to take a break.

Mon–Sat 10am–5pm.

Water Witch Canal towpath, Aldcliffe Lane, LA1 1SU ☏ 01524 63828, ⓦ waterwitchlancaster.co.uk. Relaxing canalside pub named after an old packet boat. There's a good range of real ales and continental lagers, and the food is a cut above pub grub (sharing platters from £10). Kitchen Mon–Fri noon–9pm, Sat noon–9.30pm, Sun noon–8pm.

★ **Whale Tail** 78a Penny St, LA1 1XN ☏ 01524 845133, ⓦ whaletailcafe.co.uk. Tucked away in a yard and up on the first floor, this cheery veggie and wholefood café serves good breakfasts, quiche, moussaka and baked potatoes. Mon–Sat 9am–4.30pm, Sun 10am–3pm.

DRINKING AND NIGHTLIFE

The Dukes Moor Lane, LA1 1QE ☏ 01524 598500, ⓦ dukes-lancaster.org. Lancaster's arts centre is the main cultural destination in town, with cinemas and stages for all manner of theatre and dance performances, exhibition space and a café-bar.

Yorkshire House 2 Parliament St, LA1 1DB ☏ 01524 64679, ⓦ bit.ly/YorkshireHouse. Down-to-earth real ale boozer with a cracking alternative live-music venue upstairs, pulling in a young crowd. Mon–Wed 7pm–midnight, Thurs 7pm–1am, Sat 2pm–1am, Sun 7–11.30pm.

THE FOREST OF BOWLAND

The remote **Forest of Bowland** (ⓦ forestofbowland.com), designated an Area of Outstanding Natural Beauty, is a picturesque drive east from Lancaster. The name forest is used here in its traditional sense of "a royal hunting ground" – it's a captivating landscape of remote fells and farmland with plenty of walks and is populated by rare birds like the golden plover, short-eared owl, snipe and merlin. Head east on the A683, turning off towards High Bentham; once at the village turn right at the sign for the station and you begin the fifteen-mile slog down an old drovers' track (now a very minor road) known as the **Trough of Bowland**. This winds through heather- and bracken-clad hills before ending up at the compact village of Slaidburn. If you've got time, it's worth pushing ahead to **Clitheroe**, a tidy little market town overlooked by a Norman keep.

Morecambe and Heysham

The seaside resort of **MORECAMBE** lies five miles west of Lancaster – there's a pleasant cycle path between the two, and bus and train services that can whizz you there in ten minutes. The sweep of the bay is the major attraction, with the Lake District fells visible beyond, while the **Stone Jetty** features bird motifs and sculptures – recognizing Morecambe Bay as Britain's most important wintering site for wildfowl and wading birds. A little way along the prom is a statue of one of Britain's most treasured comedians – Eric Bartholomew, who took the stage name **Eric Morecambe** when he met his comedy partner, Ernie Wise.

10

Heysham Village

Three miles southwest of Morecambe – you can walk here along the promenade – the shoreside **HEYSHAM VILLAGE** is centred on a group of charming seventeenth-century cottages and barns. Proudest relic is the well-preserved Viking hog's-back tombstone in Saxon **St Peter's Church**, set in a romantic churchyard below the headland. Don't miss the local **nettle beer**, brewed since Victorian times and served in the village tearooms.

ARRIVAL AND DEPARTURE   **MORECAMBE AND HEYSHAM**

By bus and train Morecambe's bus and train stations are close together near Central Drive; both receive regular services from Lancaster (10min). The train is by far the cheaper option.

ACCOMMODATION

Midland Hotel The Promenade, Marine Road West, LA4 4BU ☎ 0845 850 3502, ⓦ englishlakes.co.uk/the-midland. Lovely four-star Art Deco hotel whose comfortable rooms extend the Modernist theme. Even if you're not staying it's worth popping into the electric-blue bar, and taking a drink onto the terrace to watch the sunset. **£125**

The Isle of Man

The **Isle of Man** (locally called **Ellan Vannin**), almost equidistant from Ireland, England, Wales and Scotland, is one of the most beautiful spots in Britain, a mountainous, cliff-fringed island just 33 miles by 13. There's peace and quiet in abundance, walks around the unspoilt hundred-mile coastline, rural villages and steam trains straight out of a 1950s picture book – a yesteryear ensemble if ever there was one.

Many true Manx inhabitants, who comprise a shade under half of its 87,500 population, insist that the Isle of Man is not part of England, nor even of the UK. Indeed, although a Crown dependency, the island has its own government, **Tynwald**, arguably the world's oldest democratic parliament, which has run continuously since 979 AD. To further complicate matters, the island maintains a unique associate status in the EU (islanders were not allowed a vote in the recent Brexit referendum), and also has its own sterling currency (worth the same as the mainland currency), its own laws, an independent postal service, and a Gaelic-based language which is taught in schools and seen on dual-language road signs.

All roads lead to the capital, **Douglas**, the only town of any size. From the summit of **Snaefell**, the island's highest peak, you get an idea of the island's varied scenery, the finest parts of which are to be found in the seventeen officially designated National Glens. Most of these are linked by the 95-mile **Raad Ny Foillan** (Road of the Gull) coastal footpath, which passes several of the island's numerous hillforts, Viking ship burials and Celtic crosses. Scenery aside, the main tourist draw is the **TT (Tourist Trophy) motorcycle races** held in the two weeks around the late May bank holiday, a frenzy of speed and burning rubber that has shattered the island's peace annually since 1907.

10

By plane The cheapest way to arrive is by air. Several budget airlines, such as Flybe (ⓦ flybe.com); and easyJet (ⓦ easyjet. com), – offer flights from British and Irish regional airports. **By ferry** Ferries or the quicker fastcraft (Manannan), both run by the Isle of Man Steam Packet Company (ⓣ 0872 299 2992, ⓦ steam-packet.com), leave from Heysham (ferries; 1 or 2 daily; 3hr 30min) and Liverpool (fastcraft; 1 or 2 daily March–Nov; 2hr 30min).

GETTING AROUND

Travel passes "Island Explorer" tickets – sold at Douglas's Welcome Centre (see below) – give one (£16), three (£32), or seven (£47) days' unlimited travel on all buses and trains. **Car rental** Most rental outfits have offices at the airport or can deliver cars to the Sea Terminal in Douglas. Contact Athol (ⓣ 01624 820092, ⓦ athol.co.im); Mylchreests (ⓣ 0800 019 0335, ⓦ mylchreests.com); or 4Hire (ⓣ 01624 820820, ⓦ 4hire.co.im).
Transport website ⓦ gov.im/publictransport.

INFORMATION

Manx National Heritage (ⓦ manxnationalheritage. im) run thirteen heritage sites and museums around the Isle of Man including the Old House of Keys, the House of Manannan, Castle Rushen and the Laxey Wheel. They also offer money-saving passes including a 14-Day Holiday pass (£20, available from any attraction).

Tourist information The Welcome Centre in the Sea Terminal building at Douglas (Mon–Sat 8am–6pm, plus Sun 10am–2pm May–Sept only); ⓣ 01624 686766, is the best place for island-wide information.
Useful websites ⓦ gov.im, ⓦ visitisleofman.com and ⓦ www.iomguide.com.

Douglas

Dubbed "the Naples of the North" by John Betjeman, **DOUGLAS** has developed since its 1950s heyday of seaside holiday-making into a major offshore financial centre. The seafront has changed little since Victorian times, still trodden by heavy-footed carthorses pulling trams (April–Sept daily 9am–5.30pm; £3). On Harris Promenade the opulent Edwardian **Gaiety Theatre** sports a lush interior that can be seen on fascinating tours (Easter–Oct Sat 10am; 2hr; £8.50, call ahead; ⓣ 01624 600555, ⓦ www.villagaiety.com).

Further up Harris Promenade, approaching Broadway, the **Villa Marina gardens** display classic Victorian elegance with their colonnade walk, lawns and bandstand. The main sight, however, is the **Manx Museum**, on the corner of Kingswood Grove and Crellin's Hill (Mon–Sat 10am–5pm; free), which helps the visitor get to grips with Manx culture and heritage from the Vikings to the Victorians. Finally, out on **Douglas Head** – the point looming above the southern bay – the town's Victorian camera obscura has been restored for visits (May–Sept Sat 1–4pm, Sun & bank hols 11am–4pm; weather dependent, open when flag is flying; £2).

By plane Ronaldsway Airport (ⓣ 01624 821600, ⓦ gov. im) is 10 miles south of Douglas, close to Castletown. A regular bus runs into town, while a taxi costs around £20. Car hire is available at the airport.
By ferry The Isle of Man Steam Packet Company (ⓦ steam-packet.com) ferries from Liverpool, Heysham, Dublin, and Belfast arrive at the Sea Terminal (April–Oct 7am–8pm; Nov–March 8am–6/8pm), close to the centre of town, at the south end of the promenade.
By train The Steam Railway (March–Nov 9.50am–4.50pm; £5.20–12.40 return) extends for 15 miles and connects Douglas to Port Soderick, Santon, Castletown, Port St Mary and Port Erin. The Douglas station is alongside the river and fishing port, at the top end of the North Quay. Meanwhile, the Manx Electric Railway (March–Nov daily 9.40am–4.40pm; some later departures in summer; £4.40–14 return), which runs for 17.5 miles from Douglas to Snaefell, departs from the northern end of the seafront at Derby Castle Station.
By bus The Lord St terminal, the hub of the island's dozen or so bus routes, is 50yd west of the Sea Terminal's forecourt taxi rank.

GETTING AROUND AND TOURS

By bus Buses #1, #1H, #2, #2A, #11, #12 and #12A run along Douglas's promenade from North Quay; you can also take a horse-drawn tram.

Bike rental Eurocycles, 8a Victoria Rd, off Broadway (Mon–Sat 9am–5.30pm; ⓣ 01624 624909, ⓦ eurocycles. co.im).

Cruises Seasonal pleasure cruises on the *MV Karina* head out from Douglas Sea Terminal (daily April–Oct, weather permitting; ☎ 01624 861724 or ☎ 07624 493592, ⓦ iompleasurecruises.com).

ACCOMMODATION

The Claremont Hotel Loch Promenade, IM1 2LX ☎ 01624 617068, ⓦ claremonthoteldouglas.com. Recently renovated throughout, the centrally located 56-room *Claremont* boasts sea views and gym access for all guests. **£150**

The Mereside 1 Empire Terrace, IM2 4LE ☎ 01624 676355, ⓦ hqbar.im. Small, family-owned B&B just off the Central Promenade, with well-appointed if slightly old-fashioned rooms. There's a good bar/restaurant too. **£80**

The Sefton Harris Promenade, IM1 2RW ☎ 01624 645500, ⓦ seftonhotel.co.im. Next to the Gaiety Theatre, this four-star has spacious rooms – some of which have been modernized – offering either a sea view or a balcony overlooking the impressive internal water garden. Facilities include gym, an underground car park, a bar and restaurant. **£125**

The Town House Loch Promenade, IM1 2LX ☎ 01624 626125, ⓦ thetownhouse.im. This aparthotel is set over three floors and offers 15 individually designed suites with complimentary telephone calls. Service is excellent. **£120**

Welbeck Hotel Mona Drive, IM2 4LF ☎ 01624 675663, ⓦ welbeckhotel.com. A traditional, mid-sized, family-run seaside hotel, with well-maintained, comfortable rooms and friendly service. It lies just 100yd from the seafront, up the hill. **£90**

EATING

The food scene in Douglas is increasingly sophisticated and many of the independent cafés and restaurants are focusing on seasonal Manx produce. In the summer months, the places below get busy in the evenings, so always book ahead.

★ **Café Tanroagan** 9 Ridgeway St, IM1 1EW ☎ 01624 612355, ⓦ tanroagan.co.uk. The best fish and seafood on the island, straight off the boat, served simply or with an assured Mediterranean twist in a relaxed, contemporary setting. Dinner reservations essential. Mains around £20. Mon–Fri 12.30–2.30pm & 6–9.30pm, Sat 6–9.30pm.

L'Experience 1 Summer Hill, IM2 4PH ☎ 01624 623103, ⓦ lex.co.im. This seemingly unexceptional whitewashed shack is in fact a long-standing French bistro that serves up meat dishes as well as daily caught fish specials, and good lunchtime dishes; £18 average for a main. Mon & Wed–Sat noon–2pm & 7–11pm.

Little Fish Café 31 North Quay, IM1 4LB ☎ 01624 622518, ⓦ littlefishcafe.com. This stylish quayside eatery offers freshly brewed coffee and a breakfast, brunch and evening menu featuring locally sourced ingredients. Tues–Sat 11am–9pm, Sun 10am–3pm.

Noa Bakehouse Fort St, IM1 2LJ ☎ 01624 618063, ⓦ bit.ly/NoaBakehouse. An open-plan industrial space made cosy with eclectic decor and the smell of coffee and fresh baking. Locals descend for the delicious breakfasts (until 11am) and brunch and lunch (until 3pm). Daily specials such as Manx lamb burger with Moroccan spices are around £7.50. Mon–Sat 8am–4pm, Sun 10am–2pm.

The Ticket Hall Douglas Station, North Quay, IM1 1JE, ☎ 01624 627888, ⓦ ticket-hall.com. A very handy and pleasantly traditional café in the former ticket office at Douglas Station. Serving brunch 8–11am and hot lunches and daily specials noon–2.30pm, otherwise only drinks and snacks. Daily 8am–4pm, Fri & Sat 7–9.30pm.

DRINKING

The Bridge North Quay, IM1 4LQ ☎ 01624 675 268 ⓦ facebook.com/TheBridgeIOM. Cosy and comfortable quayside pub with a lovely patio. The food is good, staff are friendly and there's plenty of choice at the bar. Mon–Thurs noon–11pm, Fri & Sat noon–midnight, Sun noon–6pm.

Queen's Hotel Queen's Promenade, IM2 4NL ☎ 01624 674438, ⓦ facebook.com/thequeensisleofman. This old seafront pub at the top end of the promenade is the best place for alfresco drinks, with picnic tables looking out over the sweeping bay. Daily noon–1am.

Rovers Return 11 Church St, IM1 2AG ☎ 01624 611101, ⓦ facebook.com/TheRoversReturnPubIoM. Cosy old local where you can try the local Manx beers, including "Old Bushy Tail". Daily 11am–11pm.

Laxey

Filling a narrow valley, the straggling village of **LAXEY**, seven miles north of Douglas, spills down from its train station to a small harbour and long, pebbly beach, squeezed between two bulky headlands. The Manx Electric Railway from Douglas drops you at the station used by the Snaefell Mountain Railway (see page 504). Passengers

10

disembark and then head inland and uphill to Laxey's pride, the **"Lady Isabella" Great Laxey Wheel** (April–Nov daily 9.30am–5pm; £8), which is smartly painted in red and white. With a diameter of over 72ft it's said to be the world's largest working water wheel.

Snaefell

Every hour (30min in high season), the tramcars of the **Snaefell Mountain Railway** (April–Nov daily 10.15am–3.45pm; £12 return) begin their thirty-minute climb from Laxey through increasingly denuded moorland to the island's highest point, on **Snaefell** (2036ft), the Vikings' "Snow Mountain". At the summit, most people are content to pop into the café and bar and then soak up the views until the return journey – on a clear day, you can see England, Wales, Scotland and Ireland – but with a decent map and good weather, you could follow the trails back down to Laxey instead (around 5.5 miles).

Maughold

Bus #16 direct from Ramsey (Mon–Fri 6 daily)

The Manx Electric Railway trains stop within a mile and a half of **MAUGHOLD**, seven miles northeast of Laxey, a tiny hamlet just inland from Maughold Head's cliffside lighthouse. The isolation adds to the attraction of its **parish church**, with its outstanding collection of early Christian and Norse carved crosses – 44 pieces, dating from the sixth to thirteenth centuries, ranging from fragments of runic carving to a 6ft-high rectangular slab.

Peel

The main settlement on the west coast, **PEEL** (bus #4, #5 or #6 hourly from Douglas) is one of the most Manx of all the island's towns, with an imposing medieval **castle** rising across the harbour and a sandy **beach** running the length of its eastern promenade.

Peel Castle

IM5 1TB · April–Nov daily 10am–4/5pm · £6, audioguide £5

What probably started out as a flint-working village on a naturally protected spot gained significance with the foundation of a **monastery** in the seventh or eighth century, parts of which remain inside the ramparts of the red sandstone **Peel Castle**.

The site became the residence of the Kings of Mann until the mid-thirteenth century, when they moved to Castle Rushen in Castletown. It's a fifteen-minute walk from the town around the river harbour and over the bridge to the castle.

House of Manannan

IM5 1TA • Daily 10am–5pm • £10

The excellent harbourside **House of Manannan** heritage centre is named after the island's ancient sea god. You should allow at least two hours to get around this splendid three-floor participatory museum, where you can listen to Celtic legends in a replica roundhouse, wander through a replica kipper factory and even examine the contents and occupants of a life-sized Viking ship.

10

EATING AND DRINKING   PEEL

Cod and Castle 16 Shore Road, IM5 1QH ☎01624 840624, ⓦfacebook.com/thecodandcastle. Traditional seafront chippie with a few tables, or get takeaway and cross the road to the beach. Manx Queenies (lightly battered Queen scallops) are a local speciality (£4.50). Mon–Sat 11.30am–9pm, Sun 11.30am–8pm.

Creek Inn The Quayside, IM5 1AT ☎01624 842216, ⓦthecreekinn.co.uk. Popular quayside pub opposite the House of Manannan, serving real ale, with monthly guest beers, and a delicious array of specials. Live music at the weekends. Daily from 10am–midnight; food served noon–10pm.

Port Erin

The small, time-warped resort of **PORT ERIN**, at the southwestern tip of the island, a one-hour train ride from Douglas, has a wide, fine sand beach backing a deeply indented bay sitting beneath green hills. To stretch your legs, head up the promenade past the golf club to the entrance of Bradda Glen, where you can follow the path out along the headland to Bradda Head.

ARRIVAL AND DEPARTURE   PORT ERIN

By bus Buses #1 and #2 from Douglas/Castletown, and #8 from Peel/St John's, stop on Bridson St, across Station Rd and opposite the *Cherry Orchard* aparthotel.

By train Trains pull in on Station Rd, a couple of hundred yards above and back from the beach.

ACCOMMODATION

Rowany Cottier Spaldrick, IM9 6PE ☎01624 832287, ⓦrowanycottier.com. Port Erin's best B&B, in a detached house overlooking the bay, opposite the entrance to Bradda Glen. No credit cards. **£48**

Port St Mary and around

Two miles east of Port Erin, the fishing harbour still dominates little **PORT ST MARY**, with its houses strung out in a chain above the busy dockside. The best beach is away to the northeast, reached from the harbour along a well-worked Victorian path that clings to the bay's rocky edge.

From Port St Mary, a minor road runs out along the Meayll peninsula towards **CREGNEASH**, the oldest village on the island. The **Cregneash Village Folk Museum** (April–Nov daily 10am–4/5pm; £6) is a picturesque cluster of nineteenth-century thatched crofts populated by craftspeople in period costume; there's a tearoom and information centre. Local views are stunning, and it's just a short walk south to **The Chasms**, a headland of gaping rock cliffs swarming with gulls and razorbills. The footpath continues around Spanish Head to the turf-roofed **Sound Visitor Centre** (daily 10am–4/5pm; free), which also marks the end of the road from Port St Mary. There's an excellent café (see page 506), with windows looking out towards the **Calf of Man**.

10

THE CALF OF MAN

It is worth making the effort to visit the **Calf of Man**, a craggy, heath-lined nature reserve lying off the southwest tip of the Isle of Man, where resident wardens monitor the seasonal populations of kittiwakes, puffins, choughs, razorbills, shags, guillemots and others, and grey seals can be seen all year round basking on the rocks.

There are no scheduled tours but **boats** can be chartered (May–Sept, weather permitting) from Port St Mary (Gemini Charter; wildlife and fishing trips; ☎01624 832761, ⓦgeminicharter.co.uk) and Port Erin pier (Shona Boat Trips; Calf of Man round trips or drop off/pick up; ☎07624 322765 or ☎07624 480682, ⓦbit.ly/Shonaboat). You can also **sea-kayak** around this spectacular coast. **Adventurous Experiences** (☎01624 843034, ⓦadventurousexperiences.com) runs trips from evening paddles (£55) to full-day excursions (from £85) – no experience is required, but the location might change depending on sea conditions.

ARRIVAL AND DEPARTURE | **PORT ST MARY AND AROUND**

By train Regular steam trains run to Port Erin or back to Douglas from Port St Mary. The station is a 10min walk from the harbour along High St, Bay View Rd and Station Rd.

By bus Hourly buses from the harbour serve Port Erin and Douglas.

ACCOMMODATION AND EATING

★ **Aaron House** The Promenade, IM9 5DE ☎01624 835702, ⓦaaronhouse.co.uk. High up on the Promenade, this guesthouse lovingly re-creates a Victorian experience and features brass beds and claw-foot baths in some of the rooms, with home-made scones and jam in the parlour and splendid breakfasts. The bay views from the front are superb. **£40**

The Café at the Sound Sound Rd, IM9 5PZ, 2.5 miles south of Port St Mary ☎01624 838123, ⓦbit.ly/TheCafeAtTheSound. This incredible Modernist building has a hard-to-beat location overlooking the Calf of Man – weather permitting, nab a table outside. Sandwiches from £4.95 and fish and chips (£11.95) all day, with a fancier evening menu and daily specials. All local produce. April–Oct Mon–Thurs & Sun 9am–5pm, Fri & Sat 9am–9pm; Nov–March daily 10am–4/5pm.

Castletown and around

From the twelfth century until 1869, **CASTLETOWN** was the island's capital, but then the influx of tourists and the increase in trade required a bigger harbour and Douglas took over. Its sleepy harbour and low-roofed cottages are dominated by **Castle Rushen** (April–Nov, daily 10am–4/5pm; £8), formerly home to the island's legislature and still the site of the investiture of new lieutenant-governors.

Old House of Keys

Parliament Square, IM9 1LA • April–Nov daily 10am–4pm • Free • **Debates** Daily 11am & 2.45pm • £6 • ☎01624 648017

Across the central Market Square and down Castle Street in tiny Parliament Square you'll find the **Old House of Keys**. Built in 1821, this was the site of the Manx parliament, the Keys, until 1874 when it was moved to Douglas. The frock-coated Secretary of the House meets you at the door and shows you into the restored debating chamber, where visitors are included in a highly entertaining participatory session of the House, guided by a hologram Speaker.

Rushen Abbey

Ballasalla, IM9 3DB, 2 miles north of Castletown • Daily April–Nov 10am–4/5pm • £8 • Buses #1, #2, #8, #11, #12 from Castletown or steam railway

The island's most important medieval religious site, **Rushen Abbey** lies two miles north of Castletown at Ballasalla ("place of the willows"). A Cistercian foundation of 1134, it was abandoned by its "White Monks" in the 1540s and was subsequently used as a school. The excavated remains themselves – low walls, grass-covered banks and a sole church tower from the fifteenth century – would hold only specialist appeal were it not for the excellent interpretation centre, which explains much about daily life in a Cistercian abbey.

ARRIVAL AND DEPARTURE
CASTLETOWN AND AROUND

By bus Buses #8 (from Peel/Port Erin) and #1 (from Douglas) stop in the main square.

By train Castletown Station is a 5min walk from the centre, out along Victoria Rd from the harbour. Destinations include Ballabeg, Colby, Port St Mary and Port Erin to the south and Ballasalla, Santon, Port Soderick and Douglas to the north.

EATING AND DRINKING

The Abbey Restaurant Ballasalla, IM9 3DB, 2 miles north of Castletown ☎ 01624 822393 ⓦ theabbey.im. Located next to Rushen Abbey, this restaurant and café serves up modern European cuisine complemented by a predominately Southern European wine list. The venue is child-friendly and also boasts a spacious outdoor garden and a private dining room. Wed–Sat 10am–10pm, Sun noon–3.30pm.

10

Cumbria and the Lakes

WINDERMERE

Cumbria and the Lakes

The Lake District is England's most hyped scenic area, and for good reason. Within an area a mere thirty miles across, sixteen major lakes are squeezed between the country's highest mountains – an almost alpine landscape of glistening water, dramatic valleys and picturesque stone-built villages. Most of the region lies within the Lake District National Park (sightly expanded in 2016 to touch borders with the Yorkshire Dales National Park, and named a UNESCO World Heritage Site in 2017), which, in turn, falls entirely within the county of Cumbria. The county capital is Carlisle, a place that bears traces of a pedigree stretching back to Roman times, while both the isolated western coast and market towns like Kendal and Penrith counter the notion that Cumbria is all about its lakes.

Given a week you could easily see most of the famous settlements and lakes – a circuit taking in **Windermere**, with the towns of **Ambleside**, Windermere and **Bowness** dotted around it, **Coniston**, with its own lake and famous peak, the Wordsworth houses in **Grasmere**, the picture-postcard village of **Hawkshead**, and the more dramatic northern scenery near **Keswick** and **Ullswater** would give you a fair sample of the whole.

But it's away from the more obvious sights that the Lakes really begin to pay dividends, in the dramatic valleys of **Langdale**, **Wasdale** and **Eskdale**, villages such as the foodie haven of **Cartmel**, or over on the coast's less-visited destinations: **Ravenglass** – access point for the **Ravenglass and Eskdale Railway** – and the attractive Georgian port of **Whitehaven**.

ARRIVAL AND INFORMATION

By bus National Express coaches connect London and Manchester with Windermere, Ambleside, Grasmere and Keswick.

By train Trains (ⓦvirgintrains.co.uk/train-to/lake-district) leave the West Coast main line at Oxenholme, north of Lancaster, for the branch-line service to Kendal and Windermere (ⓦlakesline.co.uk).

Websites ⓦgolakes.co.uk and, for the National Park, ⓦlakedistrict.gov.uk.

GETTING AROUND

By train The Cumbrian Coast Line (ⓦcumbriancoastline.co.uk) and Furness Line (ⓦfurnessline.co.uk) between them offer a useful passenger service along the coast between Carlisle, Barrow-in-Furness, and Carnforth (on the main Lancaster–Carlisle line). Rail enthusiasts also shouldn't miss the short Ravenglass–Eskdale ride (see page 529).

By bus The North West 7-day megarider Gold (£27.30, family £55; ⓦstagecoachbus.com/northwest) allows unlimited travel for a week on the entire regional bus network. Note that some local services run only through the busy summer months.

By car Before deciding to explore the Lake District in your own vehicle, be aware that narrow roads, heavy holiday traffic and an almost total lack of free parking can make for a frustrating experience. You're better off – at least during the summer, when local buses are most abundant – leaving your car at your accommodation and using public transport where possible.

Windermere cruises p.517
Walks from Ambleside p.518
Coniston's speed king p.522

Ullswater lake services p.533
Climbing Helvellyn p.534
Potty Penrith p.535

WORDSWORTH HOUSE, COCKERMOUTH

Highlights

① Windermere Enjoy the changing seasons and serene views with a cruise on England's largest lake. See page 516

② Wray Castle Picnic in the grounds of this extraordinary Victorian holiday home on the shores of Windermere. See page 518

③ Old Dungeon Ghyll Hotel, Langdale The hikers' favourite inn – cosy rooms, stone-flagged floors and open fires – has England's most famous mountains on the doorstep. See page 520

④ Brantwood, Coniston Water John Ruskin's elegant home and inspiring garden are beautifully sited on Coniston Water. See page 522

⑤ Via Ferrata, Honister Pass The Lake District's biggest thrill sees you scrambling, climbing and hanging on for dear life along the old miners' route up Fleetwith Pike. See page 528

⑥ Ravenglass and Eskdale Railway It's a great day out on the narrow-gauge railway from coast to mountains. See page 529

⑦ Wordsworth House, Cockermouth Costumed staff and authentic surroundings bring the eighteenth century back to life at the birthplace of William Wordsworth. See page 532

⑧ Carlisle Castle Cumbria's mightiest castle dominates the county town. See page 536

HIGHLIGHTS ARE MARKED ON THE MAP ON PAGE 512

Kendal and around

The self-billed "Gateway to the Lakes" (though just outside the National Park and nearly ten miles from Windermere), **KENDAL** is the largest of the southern Cumbrian towns. It offers rewarding rambles around the "yards" and "ginnels" (courtyards and alleys) on both sides of Highgate and Stricklandgate, the main streets, and while the old Market Place long since succumbed to development, traditional stalls still do business outside the Westmorland Shopping Centre (Wed & Sat). Outside Kendal, the main trips are to the stately homes of **Sizergh Castle** and **Levens Hall**, both with beautifully kept gardens.

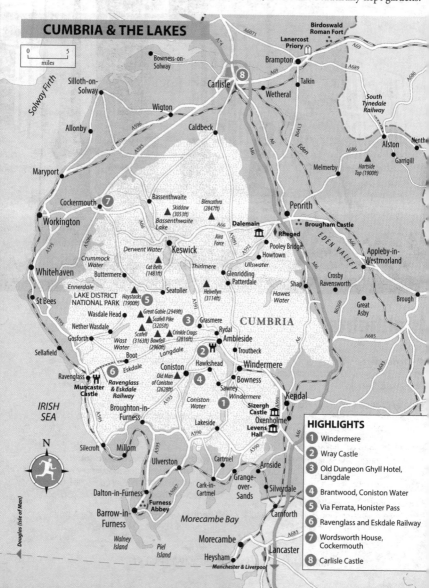

CUMBRIA & THE LAKES

0 — 5 miles

HIGHLIGHTS

1. Windermere
2. Wray Castle
3. Old Dungeon Ghyll Hotel, Langdale
4. Brantwood, Coniston Water
5. Via Ferrata, Honister Pass
6. Ravenglass and Eskdale Railway
7. Wordsworth House, Cockermouth
8. Carlisle Castle

Kendal Museum

Station Rd, LA9 6BT • Tues–Sat 10am–4pm; closed Christmas week • £2 • ☎ 01539 815597, ⓦ kendalmuseum.org.uk

The **Kendal Museum** holds the district's natural history and archeological finds, and town history displays. You'll also find collections related to **Alfred Wainwright** (1907–91), Kendal's former borough treasurer and honorary clerk at the museum. Wainwright moved to Kendal in 1941, and in 1952, dissatisfied with the accuracy of existing maps, he embarked on his series of painstakingly handwritten walking guides, with mapped routes and delicately drawn views. They have been hugely popular guidebooks ever since, which many treat as gospel in their attempts to "bag" ascents of the 214 fells he recorded.

Abbot Hall

LA9 5AL • Mon–Sat 10.30am–5pm (Nov–Feb closes at 4pm), plus July & Aug Sun noon–4pm • Joint ticket £9.90 • **Art Gallery** £7.70 • ☎ 01539 722464, ⓦ abbothall.org.uk • **Museum** £5.50 • ☎ 01539 722464, ⓦ lakelandmuseum.org.uk

The town's two main cultural attractions are at the Georgian **Abbot Hall**, by the river near the parish church. The principal hall houses the **Art Gallery**, concentrating in particular on the works of the eighteenth-century "Kendal School" of portrait painters, most famously George Romney. Across the way, the former stables contain the **Museum of Lakeland Life and Industry**, where reconstructed house interiors and workshops exhibit rural trades and crafts, from spinning and weaving to shoemaking and tanning.

11

Sizergh Castle

Off A591, LA8 8DZ, 3 miles south of Kendal • **House** Easter–Oct Tues–Sun & bank hols noon–4pm • £10.50 (includes gardens); NT • **House tours** Easter–Oct Tues–Fri & Sun 11am & 11.20am; 45min • £1 (on top of entry fee); NT • **Gardens** Daily: Easter–Oct 10am–5pm; Nov–Easter 10am–4pm • £6.50; NT • ☎ 01539 560951, ⓦ nationaltrust.org.uk/sizergh • Bus #555 from Kendal

Sizergh Castle owes its "castle" epithet to the fourteenth-century peel tower at its core, one of the best examples of the towers built as safe havens during the region's medieval border raids. The rooms themselves are largely Elizabethan, and aside from the informative **tours** you can wander around at will. On a sunny day, it's worth exploring the **gardens** too, with their rockeries and kitchen garden.

Levens Hall

Off A6, LA8 0PD, 6 miles south of Kendal • **House** Easter to mid-Oct Mon–Thurs & Sun noon–4pm • £13.50 (includes gardens) • **Gardens** Easter to mid-Oct Mon–Thurs & Sun 10am–5pm • £9.90 • ☎ 01539 560321, ⓦ levenshall.co.uk • Bus #555 from Kendal

The sturdy, fortress-like stone towers at **Levens Hall** date back to the fourteenth century, but the interior was refurbished in the classic Elizabethan manner – all heavy panels and ornate plaster – between 1570 and 1640. House stewards are on hand to point out the oddities and curios – for example, the dining room is panelled not with oak but with goat's leather, printed with a deep-green floral design. Outside are beautiful topiary **gardens**, featuring yews in the shape of pyramids, peacocks and top hats.

ARRIVAL AND DEPARTURE

KENDAL AND AROUND

By train Kendal's station is a 10min walk from the centre. **Destinations** Oxenholme (for Carlisle, Lancaster or Manchester; hourly; 5min); Windermere (hourly; 20min).

By bus The bus station is on Blackhall Road (off Stramongate), with main routes including the #599 (to Windermere, Ambleside and Grasmere) or #555 (to Keswick or Lancaster).

Destinations Ambleside (hourly; 40min); Grasmere (hourly; 1hr); Keswick (hourly; 1hr 30min); Lancaster (hourly; 1hr); Windermere/Bowness (hourly; 30min).

ACCOMMODATION

Bolt Hole 40 Greenside, LA9 4LD, ☎ 01539 720385, ⓦ beechhouse-kendal.co.uk. Self-contained self-catering apartments, complete with wood-burning stoves, richly coloured fabrics, and black-and-white bathrooms with gleaming roll-top baths. Per apartment **£100**

★ **Punch Bowl Inn** Crosthwaite, LA8 8HR, 5 miles west of Kendal ☎015395 68237, ⓦthe-punchbowl.co.uk. A super-stylish country inn – the earth-toned rooms have exposed beams and superb bathrooms, while the restaurant serves locally sourced food (from pot-roast woodpigeon to local lamb; mains £14–20). Rooms are individually priced, up to £310, with highest rates at weekends and holidays. **£170**

EATING AND DRINKING

★ **Grain Store** Brewery Arts Centre, 122 Highgate, LA9 4HE ☎01539 725133, ⓦbreweryarts.co.uk. The arts centre bistro has a mix-and-match menu of Mediterranean dishes – anything from local pork-and-chilli bangers to salmon skewers (£5–9) – plus a range of gourmet pizzas (£8–9.50). You can also get pizza, tapas and real ales in the adjacent *Vats Bar*, and there's often a weekday lunch service in holiday periods. Mon–Fri noon–2.30pm & 5.30–11pm, Sat noon–11pm, Sun 2–10.30pm.

Waterside Café Gulfs Rd, bottom of Lowther St, LA9 4DZ ☎01539 729743, ⓦwatersidekendal.co.uk. A handy place by the river for veggie and vegan wholefood snacks or meals (mains from £7.95), such as poached pear salad or falafel burgers. Mon–Sat 8.30am–4pm.

ENTERTAINMENT

Brewery Arts Centre 122 Highgate, LA9 4HE ☎01539 725133, ⓦbreweryarts.co.uk. Hub of everything that's happening in town, with cinema, theatre, galleries and concert hall, not to mention all-day café (closed Sun), bistro (see above) and the lively *Vats Bar*.

Cartmel and around

Around eighteen miles southwest of Kendal, the pretty village of **CARTMEL** is something of an upmarket getaway, with its Michelin-starred restaurant-with-rooms, winding country lanes and cobbled market square brimming with inns and antique shops. You're in luck if you're looking to buy a handmade doll's house or embroidered footstool, while in the **Cartmel Village Shop** on the square they sell the finest sticky-toffee pudding known to humanity. Quite what the original monks of Cartmel would have made of all this is anyone's guess – the village first grew up around its twelfth-century Augustinian priory and is still dominated by the proud **Church of St Mary and St Michael** (daily 9am–5.30pm; guided tours Wed April–Oct 11am & 2pm, £3; ⓦcartmelpriory.org.uk).

Holker Hall

Cark-in-Cartmel, LA11 6PU, 2 miles west of Cartmel • Easter–Oct Wed–Sun: house 11am–4pm, gardens 10.30am–5pm • £12.50, gardens only £8.50, house only £8; under-15s free • ☎01539 558328, ⓦholker.co.uk

West of Cartmel lies **Holker Hall**, one of Cumbria's most glorious country estates. The impressive 25-acre **gardens**, both formal and woodland, are the highlight for many, and a celebrated annual garden festival (June) is held here, as well as spring and winter markets. You don't have to pay the entrance fee to visit the excellent Food Hall and Courtyard Café.

ACCOMMODATION AND EATING   CARTMEL AND AROUND

L'Enclume Cavendish St, LA11 6PZ ☎01539 536362, ⓦlenclume.co.uk. One of England's most critically acclaimed dining experiences, overseen by the masterful Simon Rogan. Expect a succession of artfully constructed dishes, accompanied by intensely flavoured jellied cubes, mousses or foams, wild herbs, hedgerow flowers and exotic roots; lunch is £49, dinner £130. The dozen highly individual rooms and suites (up to £350, depending on location and size) mix antique French furniture and designer fabrics. Restaurant closed for two weeks in winter. Food served Tues–Sun noon–1.30pm & 6.30–8.30pm. **£170**

Windermere town

WINDERMERE TOWN was all but nonexistent until 1847 when a railway terminal was built here, making England's longest lake (after which the town is named) an easily accessible resort. Windermere remains a major gateway and transport hub for the lakes, but there's precious little else to keep you in the slate-grey streets. All the traffic pours a mile downhill to Windermere's older twin town – Bowness, actually on the lake – but you should stay long enough to make the twenty-minute stroll up through the woods to **Orrest Head** (784ft), from where you get a 360-degree panorama from the Yorkshire fells to Morecambe Bay. The path begins by the *Windermere Hotel* on the A591, across from Windermere train station.

Brockhole Lake District Visitor Centre

Brockhole, LA23 1LJ, 3 miles northwest of Windermere town • Daily: Easter–Oct 10am–5pm; Nov–Easter 10am–4pm • Free • ☎ 01539 446601, ⓦ brockhole.co.uk • Buses between Windermere and Ambleside run past the visitor centre, or you can take the cruise launch from Waterhead, near Ambleside (see page 517)

The Lake District National Park Authority has its main visitor centre at **Brockhole**, a late Victorian mansion set in lush grounds on the shores of Windermere, northwest of Windermere town. It's the single best place to get to grips with what there is to see and do in the Lakes, with some excellent natural history and geological displays, lovely gardens and a big range of activities (separate fees apply), including bike hire, adventure playground, watersports and high-ropes treetop adventures.

11

ARRIVAL AND INFORMATION

By train Windermere is as far into the Lakes as you can get by train, on the branch line from Oxenholme, via Kendal.
Destinations Kendal (hourly; 15min) and Oxenholme (for London, Carlisle, Lancaster, Manchester or Penrith; hourly; 20min).

By bus All buses (including National Express coaches from London and Manchester) stop outside Windermere train station.

WINDERMERE TOWN

Destinations Ambleside (hourly; 15min); Bowness (every 20–30min; 15min); Brockhole Visitor Centre (every 20–30min; 7min); Carlisle (3 daily; 2hr 20min); Grasmere (every 20–30min; 30min); Kendal (hourly; 25min); Keswick (hourly; 1hr).
Tourist office Brockhole aside, Windermere's local tourist office is on Victoria Street (daily: April–Oct 8.30am–5pm, Nov–March 9am–4.30pm; ☎ 01539 446499, ⓦ windermereinfo.co.uk), 100yd from the train station.

GETTING AROUND

Bike rental Country Lanes, at the train station (☎ 01539 444544, ⓦ countrylaneslakedistrict.co.uk), provides bikes (£20–30/day) plus route maps for local rides.

ACCOMMODATION

★ **Archway** 13 College Rd, LA23 1BU ☎ 01539 445613, ⓦ archwayguesthouse.co.uk. Four trim rooms in a Victorian house known for its breakfasts – traditional Full English or American, pancakes, kippers, home-made yoghurt and granola, smoked haddock and the like. £80
Brendan Chase 1–3 College Rd, LA23 1BU ☎ 01539 445638, ⓦ brendanchase.co.uk. Popular place with overseas travellers, providing a friendly welcome, a good breakfast and eight comfortable rooms (some en suite). £60
Holbeck Ghyll Holbeck Lane, LA23 1LU, 3 miles north of Windermere town ☎ 01539 432375, ⓦ holbeckghyll. com. Luxurious rooms either in the main house or in the lodge or suites in the grounds (with room-and-dinner prices up to £550/night). There's a sherry decanter in every

room, seven acres of gardens, and excellent food (dinner included in the price). £320
Lake District Backpackers High St, LA23 1AF, across from the tourist office ☎ 01539 446374, ⓦ lakedistrictbackpackers.co.uk. Nineteen backpackers' beds in small dorms, with a women-only room plus a couple of private rooms available on request. There's a kitchen too, though the price includes a tea-and-toast breakfast. No credit cards. Dorms £16.50, doubles £39
YHA Windermere High Cross, Bridge Lane, LA23 1LA, 2 miles north of Windermere ☎ 0845 371 9352, ⓦ yha.org. uk/hostel/windermere. The local YHA hostel is a revamped old mansion with magnificent lake views; you can camp here too. Camping/person £12, dorms £19, doubles £29

EATING

First Floor Lakeland Ltd, Alexandra Buildings, LA23 1BQ, behind the train station ☎ 01539 488100. Occupying a first-floor gallery, this superior café's snacks, lunches and high teas attract peak-period queues. Daily

filled baguettes, tortilla wraps, soups, meat and cheese platters, salads, cakes and puddings, plus a seasonally changing menu covering dishes such as salmon, rocket and radicchio salad. Most dishes £5–7.50. Mon–Fri

9.30am–5.30pm, Sat 9am–5pm, Sun 10.30am–4pm.

Francine's 27 Main Rd, LA23 1DX ☎ 01539 444088, ⓦ francinesrestaurantwindermere.co.uk. Drop in during the day for anything from a pain au chocolat or a sandwich to a big bowl of mussels (lunch dishes mostly £6–10). Dinner sees the lights dimmed for a wide-ranging continental menu, from pork belly confit to seafood casserole. Mains £12–16. Café Tues–Sun 10am–2.30pm, restaurant Tues–Sun 6–11pm.

Hooked Ellerthwaite Square, LA23 1BU ☎ 01539 448443, ⓦ hookedwindermere.co.uk. Fabulous contemporary seafood place serving fish straight from the Fleetwood boats.

Typical dishes include hake with chorizo, fava beans and garlic, or Thai-style sea bass. Starters are £6–8, mains around £22. Tues–Sun 5.30–10pm; check website for occasional closures.

Lamplighter Dining Rooms High St, LA23 1AF ☎ 01539 443547, ⓦ www.lamplighterdiningrooms.com. Very popular local choice for bistro meals, served in the hotel's bar/dining room. Expect classics (fish and chips, burgers, rack of lamb, steaks), and big portions; most dishes £15–20. There's also a cracking carve-your-own Sun lunch. April–Oct Mon–Thurs 4–9pm, Fri 4–9.30pm, Sat noon–9.30pm, Sun noon–9pm; check website for off-season hours.

Bowness and Windermere

BOWNESS-ON-WINDERMERE spills back from its lakeside piers in a series of terraces lined with guesthouses and hotels. There's been a village here since the fifteenth century and a ferry service across the lake for almost as long – these days, however, you could be forgiven for thinking that Bowness begins and ends with its best-known attraction, the **World of Beatrix Potter**. At ten and a half miles long, a mile wide in parts and a shade over 200ft deep, the **lake** itself – **Windermere**, incidentally, never "Lake" Windermere – is the heavyweight of Lake District waters. On a busy summer's day, crowds swirl around the trinket shops, cafés, ice-cream stalls and lakeside seats, but you can easily escape onto the water or into the hills, and there are lots of attractions around town to fill a rainy day.

The World of Beatrix Potter

Old Laundry, Crag Brow, LA23 3BX • Daily 10am–5.30pm • £7.50, children £3.95 • ☎ 01539 488444, ⓦ hop-skip-jump.com

You either like Beatrix Potter or you don't, but it's safe to say that the elaborate 3D story scenes, audiovisual "virtual walks", themed tearoom and gift shop here at the interactive **World of Beatrix Potter** find more favour with children than the more formal Potter attractions at Hill Top and Hawkshead.

Blackwell

LA23 3JT, 1.5 miles south of Bowness, off A5074 • Daily 10.30am–5pm • £8.80, under-16s free • ☎ 01539 446139, ⓦ blackwell.org.uk

Mackay Hugh Baillie Scott's **Blackwell** was built in 1900 as a lakeside holiday home, and boasts a superbly restored Arts and Crafts interior. Lakeland motifs – trees, flowers, birds and berries – abound, while temporary exhibits focus on furniture and decorative art. There's an informative introductory talk (usually weekdays at 2.30pm), plus a tearoom, craft shop and gardens. Parking is available; alternatively, you can walk from Bowness in about 25 minutes (although along a busy road).

Lakeside and Haverthwaite Railway

Haverthwaite station, LA12 8AL, on A590 • Easter–Oct 6–7 departures daily • £6.80 return; £16.20 including cruise boat from Bowness • ☎ 01539 531594, ⓦ lakesiderailway.co.uk

From Bowness piers, boats head to the southern reaches of Windermere at Lakeside. This is the terminus of the **Lakeside and Haverthwaite Railway**, whose steam-powered engines puff gently over four miles of track along the River Leven and through the woods of Backbarrow Gorge. Boat arrivals from Bowness connect with train departures throughout the day and, as well as the boat-and-train combination, there are also joint tickets for the Lakes Aquarium and the nearby Lakeland Motor Museum.

WINDERMERE CRUISES

Windermere Lake Cruises (ⓦwindermere-lakecruises.co.uk) operates services from Bowness to Lakeside ("Yellow Cruise"; return £11; 1hr 30min), Bowness to Ambleside via the Visitor Centre at Brockhole ("Red Cruise"; return £10.50; 1hr 10min), and a 45min Islands Cruise (return £8). There's also a service from Ambleside that calls at Wray Castle and Brockhole ("Green Cruise"; return £8; 45min). The **Freedom-of-the-Lake ticket** (one-day £19.50) is valid on all routes, while the **Walkers Ticket** (£10.50) allows you to catch a ferry from Ambleside to Wray Castle, walk four miles to Ferry House and then travel back by water via Bowness, Brockhole and Ambleside.

ARRIVAL AND DEPARTURE

By bus The open-top #599 bus from Windermere town train station stops at the lakeside piers (every 20–30min; 15min). For onward routes to Ambleside and Grasmere you have to return first to Windermere town station.

By ferry The traditional ferry service is the chain-guided contraption from Ferry Nab on the Bowness side (10min

BOWNESS AND WINDERMERE

walk from the cruise piers) to Ferry House, Sawrey (every 20min; Mon–Sat 7am–10pm, Sun 9am–10pm; 50p, bike and cyclist £1, cars £4.40), providing access to Hill Top and to Hawkshead. There's also a useful pedestrian launch service between Bowness piers and Ferry House, Sawrey, saving you the walk down to the car ferry.

11

GETTING AROUND

Cross Lakes Experience A connecting boat-and-minibus shuttle service (Easter–Oct, up to ten departures daily; ☏01539 448600, ⓦlakedistrict.gov.uk/crosslakes)

runs from Bowness pier 3 to Beatrix Potter's house at Hill Top (£10.40 return), and then to Hawkshead (£11.95) and Coniston Water (£21).

ACCOMMODATION

Angel Inn Helm Rd, LA23 3BU ☏01539 444080, ⓦtheangelinnbowness.com. A dozen chic rooms – all bright, with thick-pile carpets and patterned curtains – bring a bit of country style to Bowness. Snacks and sandwiches and posh pub food are served in the contemporary bar downstairs, back restaurant or terraced garden. **£95**

Linthwaite House Crook Rd, LA23 3JA, 1 mile south of Bowness ☏01539 488600, ⓦlinthwaitehouse.com. Contemporary boutique style grafted onto an ivy-covered

country house set high above Windermere. A conservatory and terrace offer fabulous views, and you can work up an appetite for dinner with a walk in the gardens to the hotel's private tarn. Suites run up to £460, dinner included. **£225**

★ **Number 80** 80 Craig Walk, LA23 2JS ☏01539 443584, ⓦnumber80bed.co.uk. Colin and Mandy's quiet townhouse offers quirky, stylish B&B in four rather dramatic, earth-toned double rooms – a grown-up space for couples (no pets, no children). **£90**

EATING AND DRINKING

Bowness has plenty of places offering pizza, fish and chips, a Chinese stir-fry or a budget café meal – a stroll along pedestrianized **Ash Street** and up **Lake Road** shows you most of the possibilities.

★ **Hole in t'Wall** Fallbarrow Rd, LA23 3DH ☏01539 443488, ⓦwww.robinsonsbrewery.com. For a drink and a bar meal (£9–12) you can't beat the town's oldest hostelry,

with stone-flagged floors, open fires and real ales, plus a terrace-style beer garden that's a popular spot on summer evenings. Mon–Sat 11am–11pm, Sun noon–10.30pm.

Ambleside and around

Five miles northwest of Windermere, **AMBLESIDE** town centre consists of a cluster of grey-green stone houses, shops, pubs and B&Bs (and the tiny landmark of **Bridge House**, a seventeenth-century cottage built over a stream) hugging a circular one-way system, which loops round just south of the narrow gully of stony Stock Ghyll. Huge car parks soak up the day-trip trade, but actually Ambleside improves the longer you spend here, with some enjoyable local walks and also the best selection of accommodation and restaurants in the area. The rest of town lies a mile south at **Waterhead**, where the cruise boats dock, overlooked by the grass banks and spreading trees of Borrans Park. Four miles away, Victorian neo-Gothic **Wray Castle** is a great place to visit for the day.

11

> ## WALKS FROM AMBLESIDE
>
> A couple of good walks are accessible straight from the town centre. First, from the footbridge across the river in Rothay Park you can strike up across **Loughrigg Fell** (1099ft). Dropping down to Loughrigg Terrace overlooking Grasmere, you then cut south at Rydal on the A591 and follow the minor road back along the River Rothay to Ambleside – a total of 6 miles (4hr).
>
> The walk over **Wansfell to Troutbeck** and back (6 miles; around 4hr) is a little tougher. Stock Ghyll Lane runs up the left bank of the tumbling stream to **Stock Ghyll Force** waterfall. The path then rises steeply to **Wansfell Pike** (1581ft) and down into Troutbeck village, where you can have lunch either at the *Mortal Man* or the nearby *Queen's Head* (recently rebuilt after a fire), both just a short walk from the village centre. The return cuts west onto the flanks of Wansfell and back to Ambleside.

The Armitt

Rydal Rd, LA22 9BL • Mon–Sat 10am–5pm, check website for winter hours • £5 • ☎ 01539 431212, ⓦ armitt.com

For some background on Ambleside's history, stroll a couple of minutes from the centre along Rydal Road to **The Armitt**, a library and gallery which catalogues the very distinct contribution to Lakeland society made by writers and artists from John Ruskin to Beatrix Potter.

Wray Castle

Low Wray, LA22 0JA, 4 miles south of Ambleside • Easter–Oct daily 10am–5pm, last admission 4pm • £10 • ⓦ nationaltrust.org.uk/wray-castle • Windermere Lake Cruises service from Waterhead or Brockhole (see page 517), or bus #505 to Low Wray turn-off and 1 mile walk

Take the boat across to Wray and walk up through the grounds to magnificent **Wray Castle**, a castellated, mock-Gothic mansion built in the 1840s by a wealthy couple as their retirement home. Appealingly, it's not presented as a period piece but rather a family-friendly attraction where you are positively begged to walk on the grass and sit on the chairs. House **tours** (every hour or so) are available to explain the finer points of the architecture and history, but in the end it's the freedom to play and picnic in lovely surroundings that's the real draw.

ARRIVAL AND INFORMATION

AMBLESIDE AND AROUND

By bus All buses in town stop on Kelsick Rd, opposite the library.
Destinations Windermere (every 30min–1hr; 14min); Grasmere (every 30min–1hr; 13min); Keswick (hourly; 45min); Hawkshead/Coniston (every 1–2hr; 20min/30min); and Langdale (5–6 daily; 30min) via Elterwater (17min).

By ferry There are ferry services from Bowness and Lakeside; it's a 15min walk into Ambleside from the piers at Waterhead.

Tourist office Central Buildings, Market Cross (Mon–Sat 9am–5.30pm, Sun 10am–5pm; ☎ 01539 432582, ⓦ lakelandgateway.net.

GETTING AROUND

Bike rental Ghyllside Cycles, The Slack (Mon–Sat 9.30am–5.30pm; ☎ 01539 433592, ⓦ ghyllside.co.uk), rents out bikes at around £25/day.

ACCOMMODATION

Lake Rd, running between Waterhead and Ambleside, is lined with **B&Bs**, as are Church St and Compston Road. Fancier places lie out of town, especially a mile to the south at Waterhead by the lake, which is also where you'll find Ambleside YHA. The nearest **campsite**, *Low Wray*, is three miles south and also right by the lake.

Compston House Compston Rd, LA22 9DJ ☎ 01539 432305, ⓦ compstonhouse.co.uk. There's a breezy New York vibe in this traditional Lakeland house, where the American style extends from the rooms to the breakfasts – home-made pancakes and maple syrup, fluffy omelettes and the like. **£95**

Low Wray Campsite Low Wray, LA22 0JA, 3 miles south of Ambleside ☎ 01539 463862, ⓦ ntlakescampsites. org.uk, ⓦ 4windslakelandtipis.co.uk or ⓦ luxury-yurt-holidays.co.uk. The beautiful National Trust site on the western shore of the lake is a glampers' haven. As well as tent pitches (prices vary according to location – some sites are bang on the water's edge), there are wooden camping pods for couples and families (from £35), tipis (part-week from £200, full week from £360) and bell tents (part-week from £199, full week from £385). Bike and kayak hire make it great for families too. Closed Nov–Easter. Per person **£8.50**

★ **Randy Pike** On B5286, LA22 0JP, 3 miles south of Ambleside ☎01539 436088, ⓦrandypike.co.uk. Two amazing, boutique B&B suites open out on to the gardens of what was once a Victorian gentleman's hunting lodge. It's a grown-up, romantic retreat, and you can either stay put with the snack larder, terrace and gardens, or be whizzed down to the owners' *Jumble Room* restaurant in Grasmere (see page 521) for dinner. Prices are £25 higher at weekends. **£200**

Riverside Under Loughrigg, LA22 9LJ ☎01539 432395, ⓦriverside-at-ambleside.co.uk. Charming guesthouse, half a mile from Ambleside across Rothay Park. Six large, light country-pine-style rooms available, including a river-facing four-poster (£140) with an en-suite spa bath. **£110**

YHA Ambleside Waterhead, LA22 0EU, 1 mile south of Ambleside ☎0845 371 9620, ⓦyha.org.uk/hostel/ambleside. The YHA's flagship regional hostel has an impressive lakeside location (most rooms have a water view), and 250 beds divided among neatly furnished small dorms, twins, doubles and family rooms (including 11 en-suites). Tour and activity bookings, and licensed bar and restaurant. Dorms **£25**, doubles **£56**

EATING AND DRINKING

11

★ **Apple Pie** Rydal Rd, LA22 9AN ☎01539 433679, ⓦapplepieambleside.co.uk. The best café and bakery in town has a secluded patio-garden and plenty of room inside for lounging around. Breakfast is served until 11am (with free tea/coffee refills); they also have BLTs, soup and quiche, along with trademark home-made pies that come savoury (say, broccoli and stilton or sausage and cider) or sweet (a luscious Bramley apple variety laced with cinnamon and raisins). Dishes around £8. Mon–Fri 9am–5.30pm, Sat & Sun 8.30am–5.30pm; winter hours may be reduced.

Doi Intanon Market Place, LA22 9BU ☎01539 432119, ⓦambleside-thai-restaurant.com. Ambleside's popular Thai restaurant makes a welcome change, with a standard stir-fry and curry menu bolstered by specials such as a fiery vegetable jungle curry or a grilled chicken appetizer wrapped in pandan leaves. Most mains £9–12. Daily 6–10pm.

Golden Rule Smithy Brow LA22 9AS ☎01539 432257, ⓦwww.robinsonsbrewery.com. The beer-lovers' and climbers' favourite pub – this is a cosy place for a post-hike pint (six real ales usually available) and a read of the Wainwright, with no jukebox, pool table or other

distractions besides the dart board. No meals. Daily 11am–midnight.

★ **Lucy's On A Plate** Church St, LA22 0BU ☎01539 432288, ⓦlucysofambleside.co.uk. Quirky, hugely enjoyable, informal bistro – if they know you're coming, you'll probably find yourself name-checked on the menu. Daytime café dishes (brunch, dips, pastas, salads, soup and sandwiches; £5–10) give way to a dinner menu (mains £14–19) that is "sourced locally, cooked globally". Mon–Fri 5–10.30pm, Sat & Sun 11am–10.30pm; last orders 9.30pm.

Zeffirelli's Compston Rd, LA22 9AD ☎01539 433845, ⓦzeffirellis.com. *Zeffirelli's* independent cinema has five screens at three locations in town. The restaurant attached to the Compston Road screens is famous for its wholemeal-base pizzas, plus Italian-with-a-twist pastas and salads, all vegetarian (pizzas and mains around £12). The menu is available at lunch and dinner, but *Zeff's* is also open from 10am as a café for tea, coffee and snacks. There's a great music-bar upstairs, plus an associated fine-dining veggie restaurant (*Fellini's*) elsewhere in town. Daily 10am–10pm.

Great Langdale

Three miles west of Ambleside along the A593, Skelwith Bridge marks the start of **Great Langdale**, a U-shaped glacial valley overlooked by the rocky summits of the **Langdale Pikes**, the most popular of the central Lakeland fells. You can get to the pretty village of **Elterwater** – where there's a tiny village green overlooked by the excellent *Britannia Inn* (see page 520) – by bus, which then continues on to the **Old Dungeon Ghyll Hotel** (see page 520) at the head of the valley. Three miles from Elterwater, at **Stickle Ghyll** car park, Harrison Stickle (2414ft), Pike of Stickle (2326ft) and Pavey Ark (2297ft) form a dramatic backdrop, though many walkers go no further than the hour-long climb to **Stickle Tarn** from Stickle Ghyll. Another car park, a mile further west up the valley road by the *Old Dungeon Ghyll Hotel*, is the starting point for a series of more hardcore hikes to resonant Lakeland peaks like Crinkle Crags (2816ft) or Bowfell (2960ft).

By bus From Ambleside, the #516 Langdale Rambler bus runs to Elterwater (5–6 daily; 17min) and the *Old Dungeon Ghyl* (5–6 daily; 30min).

ACCOMMODATION AND EATING

Britannia Inn Elterwater, LA22 9HP ☎ 01539 437210, ⓦ thebritanniainn.com. Halfway up the valley, this popular pub on Elterwater's green has nine recently refurbished, cosy rooms – cosy being the key word, since there's not a lot of space in a 500-year-old inn. Rates are at least £10 higher at weekends. A wide range of beers and good-value food – home-made pies and Cumberland sausage to beer-battered haddock (mains £12.50–16) – is served either in the dining room (booking advised) or front bar. Kitchen daily noon–2pm & 6–9pm. **£125**

Great Langdale Campsite LA22 9JU ☎ 01539 463862, ⓦ ntlakescampsites.org.uk, ⓦ luxury-yurt-holidays. co.uk, or ⓦ basecamptipi.co.uk. The National Trust's stupendously sited Langdale campsite has gone stellar since camping pods (from £35) and yurts (from £365 for 4 days) and nordic tipis (£50) were added into the mix. The bar at the *Old Dungeon Ghyll* is a 5min walk away. Per person **£8.50**

★ **Old Dungeon Ghyll** LA22 9JY ☎ 01539 437272, ⓦ odg. co.uk. The Lakes' most famous inn is decidedly old-school – well-worn oak, floral decor, four-poster beds – but walkers can't resist its unrivalled location. Dinner (£25, reservations essential) is served at 7.30pm in the dining room, though all the action is in the stone-flagged *Hikers' Bar*, which has real ales and hearty pub food (from £12). Daily noon–9pm. **£116**

Grasmere and around

Four miles northwest of Ambleside, **GRASMERE** consists of an intimate cluster of grey-stone houses on the old packhorse road that runs beside the babbling River Rothay. Pretty it certainly is, but in high summer its charms are submerged by the hordes who descend on the trail of the village's most famous former resident, **William Wordsworth** (1770–1850). The poet, his wife Mary, sister Dorothy and other members of his family are buried beneath the yews in **St Oswald's churchyard**, around which the river makes a sinuous curl. There's little else to the village, save its gift shops, galleries, tearooms and hotels, though the **lake** is just a ten-minute walk away; tremendous views unfold from **Loughrigg Terrace**, on its southern reaches. A four-mile circuit of Grasmere and adjacent **Rydal Water** takes around two hours, with the route passing Wordsworth haunts **Rydal Mount** and **Dove Cottage**.

Dove Cottage

Town End, LA22 9SH, half a mile southeast of Grasmere • Daily: March–Oct 9.30am–5.30pm; Nov–Feb 10am–4.30pm; check Jan opening hours for closures • £8.95 • ☎ 01539 435544, ⓦ wordsworth.org.uk • Buses #555 and #599

Dove Cottage, home to William and Dorothy Wordsworth from 1799 to 1808, was the place where Wordsworth wrote some of his best poetry. Guides, bursting with anecdotes, lead you around the cottage rooms, little changed now but for the addition of electricity and internal plumbing. In the adjacent **museum** are paintings, manuscripts and mementos of the so-called "Lake Poets" Robert Southey and Samuel Taylor Coleridge, as well as "opium-eater" Thomas De Quincey, who also lived in the cottage for several years.

Rydal Mount

Rydal, LA22 9LU, 2 miles southeast of Grasmere • March–Oct daily 9.30am–5pm; Nov–Feb Wed–Sun 11am–4pm; closed for 3 weeks in Jan • £7.50, gardens only £4.50 • ☎ 01539 433002, ⓦ rydalmount.co.uk • Buses #555 and #599

At Dove Cottage Wordsworth had been a largely unknown poet of straitened means, but by 1813 he'd written several of his greatest works (though not all had yet been published) and had been appointed Westmorland's Distributor of Stamps, a salaried position which allowed him to take up the rent of a comfortable family house. **Rydal Mount** remained Wordsworth's home from 1813 until his death in 1850, and the house is still owned by descendants of the poet. You're free to wander around what is essentially still a family home, as well as explore Wordsworth's cherished garden.

| ARRIVAL AND DEPARTURE | GRASMERE AND AROUND |

By bus The #555 (between Kendal and Keswick) and the #599 (from Kendal, Bowness, Windermere and Ambleside) stop on the village green.

ACCOMMODATION AND EATING

Daffodil Keswick Rd, LA22 9PR ☎01539 463550, ⓦdaffodilhotel.co.uk. This huge slate Victorian-era lakefront hotel, the landmark at the southern village entrance, has been given a complete contemporary makeover. Its lakeview rooms and suites, restaurant-with-a-view and up-to-the-minute spa add another string to Grasmere's increasingly boutique bow. **£175**

★**Grasmere Independent Hostel** Broadrayne Farm, LA22 9RU, 1.3 miles north of Grasmere ☎01539 435055, ⓦgrasmerehostel.co.uk. A stylish gem of a backpackers' hostel, with 24 beds in carpeted en-suite rooms – the price goes up a quid at weekends and two on bank holidays. There's an impressively equipped kitchen, and even a sauna, with the local pub just a few hundred yards away. Dorms **£22**

How Foot Lodge Town End, LA22 9SQ, half a mile southeast of Grasmere ☎01539 435366, ⓦhowfoot lodge.co.uk. You won't get a better deal on good-quality B&B accommodation than in this light-filled Victorian villa just a few yards from Dove Cottage. **£78**

★**Jumble Room** Langdale Rd, LA22 9SU ☎01539 435188, ⓦthejumbleroom.co.uk. Funky, relaxed dining spot, where the menu roams the world – blue swimmer crab risotto, Thai salmon salad, or fish in organic beer batter – and, once ensconced, no one's in any hurry to leave. Mains £15–25. Wed–Sun 5.30–9.30pm, plus Mon in summer; closed 2 weeks in Dec.

Moss Grove Organic Grasmere, LA22 9SW ☎01539 435251, ⓦmossgrove.com. Stunning, revamped Victorian-era hotel that's been designed along organic, low-impact lines – thus, handmade beds of reclaimed timber, wallpaper coloured with natural inks, and windows screened by natural wood blinds. **£159**

Thorney How Independent Hostel Off Easedale Rd, LA22 9QW, 0.75 miles north of Grasmere ☎01539 435597, ⓦthorneyhow.co.uk. This, the first-ever hostel bought by the YHA (back in 1931), now trades as an indie backpacker hostel, overseen by friendly owners. It's been spruced up recently, though a café-bar, film nights and bike hire already make it a great night's stay. Dorms **£23.50**, doubles **£47**

11

Coniston and around

Coniston Water is not one of the most immediately imposing of the lakes, yet it has a quiet beauty that sets it apart from the more popular destinations. The nineteenth-century art critic and social reformer John Ruskin made the lake his home, and today his isolated house, **Brantwood**, on the northeastern shore, provides the most obvious target for a day-trip. **Arthur Ransome** was also a frequent visitor, his local memories and experiences providing much of the detail in his *Swallows and Amazons* children's books.

Coniston village

The small, slate-grey village of **CONISTON** hunkers below the craggy and copper-mine-riddled bulk of **The Old Man of Coniston** (2628ft), which most fit walkers can climb in under two hours. In the village itself, **John Ruskin's grave** lies in St Andrew's original churchyard beneath a beautifully worked Celtic cross.

Ruskin Museum

Yewdale Rd, LA21 8DU • Easter to mid-Nov daily 10am–5.30pm; mid-Nov to Easter Wed–Sun 10.30am–3.30pm • £6 • ☎01539 441164, ⓦruskinmuseum.com

The highly entertaining local museum is named after Coniston's most famous resident but covers all aspects of local life, from pre-history to the exploits of Donald Campbell (see page 522). Ruskin's fascinating ideas are also given an airing – not to mention his socks, Oxford matriculation certificate, letters, manuscripts, sketchbooks and watercolours.

CONISTON'S SPEED KING

On January 4, 1967, **Donald Campbell** set out to better his own world water-speed record (276mph, set three years earlier in Australia) on the glass-like surface of Coniston Water. Just as his jet-powered *Bluebird* hit an estimated 320mph, however, a patch of turbulence sent it into a somersault. Campbell was killed immediately and his body and boat lay undisturbed at the bottom of the lake until they were retrieved in 2001. Campbell's grave is in the small village cemetery behind the *Crown Hotel*, while the *Bluebird* tailfin is displayed in a purpose-built gallery at the local museum, where you can find out more about Campbell and that fateful day.

Coniston Water

Lake Rd, LA21 8AN · **Steam Yacht Gondola** Easter–Oct, 4–5 times daily from 11am, weather permitting · £11 · ☎01539 432733, Ⓦnationaltrust.org.uk/steam-yacht-gondola · **Coniston Launch** Easter–Oct hourly 10.45am–5pm; Nov–Easter up to 5 daily · £11.25 (north route) or £16.95 (south) · ☎01768 775753, Ⓦconistonlaunch.co.uk

Coniston Water is hidden out of sight, half a mile southeast of the village. As well as boat and kayak rental from the pier, there are two lake cruise services, which both call at Ruskin's Brantwood as well as various other points around the lake. The National Trust's restored **Steam Yacht Gondola** is the historic choice, while the **Coniston Launch** runs the solar-powered wooden vessels "Ruskin" and "Ransome" on two routes around the lake, north and south. You can stop off at any pier en route, and local walking leaflets are available, as well as special cruises throughout the year.

Brantwood

Off B5285, LA21 8AD, 2.5 miles southeast of Coniston · Mid-March to Nov daily 10.30am–5pm; Dec to mid-March Wed–Sun 10.30am–4pm · £7.50, gardens only £5.20, under-16s free · ☎01539 441396, Ⓦbrantwood.org.uk

Sited on a hillside above the eastern shore of Coniston Water, **Brantwood** was home to John Ruskin from 1872 until his death in 1900. Ruskin was the champion of J.M.W. Turner and the Pre-Raphaelites and the foremost Victorian proponent of the supremacy of Gothic architecture. His **study** and **dining room** boast superlative lake views, bettered only by those from the **Turret Room** where he used to sit in later life in his bathchair. Exhibition rooms and galleries display Ruskin-related arts and crafts, while the excellent *Jumping Jenny Tearooms* has an outdoor terrace with lake views.

ARRIVAL AND GETTING AROUND

CONISTON AND AROUND

By bus The #505 "Coniston Rambler" (from Kendal, Windermere, Ambleside or Hawkshead) stops in Coniston. The "Ruskin Explorer" ticket (from £18) includes return travel on the #505 from Windermere, a return trip on the Coniston Launch to Brantwood and entry to Brantwood itself.

Cross Lakes Experience The boat-and-minibus service from Bowness (Easter–Oct daily; ☎01539 448600, Ⓦlakedistrict.gov.uk) runs as far as the *Waterhead Hotel* pier (for Brantwood and lake services), at the head of Coniston Water, half a mile out of the village.

ACCOMMODATION

Bank Ground Farm Coniston Water, LA21 8AA, 2 miles southeast of Coniston ☎01539 441264, Ⓦbankground. com. This lakeside farmhouse was the model for Holly Howe Farm in *Swallows and Amazons* and later used in the 1970s film. Seven traditionally furnished rooms have oak beams and carved beds, and there's also a farmhouse tearoom. **£90**

Black Bull Inn Coppermines Rd, LA21 8DU, by the bridge ☎01539 441335, Ⓦblackbullconiston.co.uk. The village's best pub has reasonable B&B rooms (£10 more at weekends). It also brews its own beer, while local lamb, sausage and trout are menu mainstays (bar meals £11–18). **£100**

Church House Inn Torver, LA21 8AZ, 2 miles south of Coniston ☎015394 49159, Ⓦthechurchhouseinn.com. Anyone after good food should drop by for a meal (mains £12–20; generous Sun roast £12.95), but there are also five comfortable, small and charming B&B rooms with a modern "country cottage" look, offering very good value (plus hook-ups for a few motorhomes out the back). **£79**

YHA Coniston Holly How Far End, LA21 8DD ☎0845 371 9511, Ⓦyha.org.uk/hostel/coniston-holly-how. Well-equipped hostel in a big old slate house (with some four-bed family rooms; £69) set in its own gardens just a

few minutes' walk north of the centre on the Ambleside road. It's popular with schools and families for its café, bar (with real ale), outdoor activities, and unusually spacious dorms. Good meals available too. Dorms **£21.50**

EATING

Bluebird Café Lake Rd, LA21 8AN ☎ 01539 441649, ⓦ thebluebirdcafe.co.uk. The big, covered outdoor terrace with lake views makes this the perfect place to watch the comings and goings of the boats. On the menu are Cumberland sausage butties, soups and sandwiches, jacket potatoes and salads (£3.50–8); also good for a decent coffee and a cake. Daily: Feb half term to Nov 9.30am–5.30pm; Dec to Feb half term 10am–4.30pm.

★ **Swallows & Amazons Tearoom** Bank Ground Farm, Coniston Water, LA21 8AA, 2 miles southeast of Coniston ☎ 01539 441264, ⓦ swallowsandamazons.net. For a drive, cycle or walk with a café at the end of it, this place is worth a special trip. Lunches, cakes and ice cream are served at the farmhouse associated with Arthur Ransome and his adventure stories; try the farmhouse taster, with locally sourced game terrine and lamb cutlet (£15) or a spinach pancake with smoked salmon (£11). 11am–5pm: Easter–Oct Thurs–Sun; daily during school hols.

11 Hawkshead and around

HAWKSHEAD, midway between Coniston and Ambleside, wears its beauty well, its handful of whitewashed eighteenth-century cottages and cobbles backed by woods and fells, all barely affected by modern intrusions. Seemingly oversized car parks at the edge of this little village take the strain, and when the crowds of day-trippers leave, Hawkshead regains its natural tranquillity. It's a major stop on both the **Beatrix Potter** and **Wordsworth** trails (Potter's house, Hill Top, is nearby, while William and his brother went to school here), and makes a handy base for days out in **Grizedale Forest**.

Beatrix Potter Gallery

Main St, LA22 0NS • Feb half term to Easter Mon–Thurs, Sat & Sun 10am–4pm; Easter–May Mon–Thurs, Sat & Sun 10am–5pm, June–Aug daily 10am–5pm, Oct Mon–Thurs, Sat & Sun 10am–5pm • £6.30, discount available for Hill Top visitors; NT • ☎ 01539 436355, ⓦ nationaltrust.org.uk/beatrix-potter-gallery-and-hawkshead

Hawkshead's **Beatrix Potter Gallery** occupies rooms once used by Potter's solicitor husband, William Heelis, and contains an annually changing selection of her original sketchbooks, drawings, watercolours, letters and manuscripts. Those less devoted to the "Tales" will find displays on Potter's life as a keen naturalist, conservationist and early supporter of the National Trust more diverting.

Hill Top

Near Sawrey, LA22 0NF, 2 miles southeast of Hawkshead • Mon–Thurs, Sat & Sun: Feb half term to May & Sept–Oct 10.30am–4.30pm, June–Aug 10am–5.30pm • £10.40, garden free; NT • ☎ 01539 436269, ⓦ nationaltrust.org.uk/hill-top

Beatrix Potter's beloved house, **Hill Top**, lies in the gorgeous hamlet of Near Sawrey. A Londoner by birth, Potter bought this farmhouse with the proceeds from her first book, *The Tale of Peter Rabbit*, and retained it as her study long after she moved out following her marriage in 1913. Entry is by timed ticket: you'll probably have to wait in line to enter the small house, and sell-outs are possible (you can't book in advance).

Grizedale Forest

LA22 0QJ, 2.5 miles southwest of Hawkshead • Daily 24hr; Grizedale Forest Centre Easter–Oct daily 10am–5pm, Nov–Easter daily 10am–4pm • Free • ☎ 0300 067 4495, ⓦ forestry.gov.uk/grizedale • Cross Lakes Experience bus from Hawkshead

Grizedale Forest extends over the fells separating Coniston Water and Hawkshead from Windermere, and the picnic spots, open-air sculptures, children's activities, cycle trails and treetop adventure course make for a great day out away from the main lakes. The best starting point is the **Grizedale Forest Centre**, where there's a café and information point.

Go Ape

LA22 0QJ • Sessions daily Feb half term & Easter–Oct, otherwise weekends only and closed certain other days in season • £33–45, advance booking essential • ☎ 0845 519 3342, ⓦ goape.co.uk

Go Ape, a high-ropes adventure course in the thick of Grizedale Forest, has you frolicking in the tree canopy for a couple of hours. You get a quick safety briefing and then make your own way around the fixed-ropes course – fantastic fun involving zipwires, Tarzan swings and aerial walkways.

HAWKSHEAD AND AROUND

ARRIVAL AND DEPARTURE

By bus The main Hawkshead service is the #505 Coniston Rambler between Windermere, Ambleside and Coniston.

GETTING AROUND

Cross Lakes Experience The shuttle bus service (Easter–Oct daily; ☎ 01539 448600, ⓦ lakedistrict.gov. uk) runs from Hawkshead to Grizedale and to Hill Top, and on to Sawrey for boat connections back to Bowness.

By bike Grizedale Forest Centre (ⓦ velobikes.co.uk/pages/hire, ☎ 01229 581116) rents bikes at £20/4hr, or £25/day.

ACCOMMODATION AND EATING

Ann Tyson's Guest House Wordsworth St, LA22 0PA ☎ 01539 436405, ⓦ anntysons.co.uk. Wordsworth briefly boarded at this quaint B&B on an old cobbled street, and now you can too. Two double bedrooms, plus space for an extra single bed. You can also rent the whole place on a self-catering basis. **£76**

★ **Drunken Duck Inn** Barngates crossroads, LA22 0NG, 2 miles north of Hawkshead off B5285 ☎ 01539 436347, ⓦ drunkenduckinn.co.uk. Stylish restaurant-with-rooms in a beautifully located 400-year-old inn. Smallish standard rooms are cheapest, weekend stays cost at least £140, and there's more deluxe accommodation too

(up to £325 a night). Bar meals at lunch (sandwiches, or dishes from belly pork to roast cod, £6–13) give way to more modish dining in the evening, with local sourcing a priority (mains £22; reservations essential). Daily noon–4pm & 6–9pm. **£105**

Yewfield Hawkshead Hill, LA22 0PR, 2 miles northwest of Hawkshead off B5285 ☎ 01539 436765, ⓦ yewfield.co.uk. Splendid vegetarian guesthouse set among organic vegetable gardens and wildflower meadows. The house is a Victorian Gothic beauty, filled with Oriental artefacts and art from the owners' travels. Closed Dec & Jan. **£105**

11

Keswick and around

Standing on the shores of **Derwent Water**, the market town of **KESWICK** makes a good base for exploring the northern Lake District, particularly delightful **Borrowdale** to the south of town or the heights of Skiddaw (3053ft) and Blencathra (2847ft), which loom over Keswick to the north. Granted its **market** charter by Edward I in 1276 – held in the main Market Place on Saturdays – Keswick was an important wool and leather centre until around 1500, when these trades were supplanted by the discovery of local graphite. Keswick went on to become an important pencil-making town; the entertaining **Derwent Pencil Museum**, (daily 9.30am–5pm; £4.95; ⓦ pencilmuseum. co.uk) tells the whole story.

Castlerigg Stone Circle

Castle Lane, CA12 4RN • Daily 24hr • Free

Don't miss Keswick's most mysterious landmark, **Castlerigg Stone Circle**, where 38 hunks of volcanic stone, the largest almost 8ft tall, form a circle 100ft in diameter set against a magnificent mountain backdrop. The array probably had an astronomical or timekeeping function when it was erected four or five thousand years ago, but no one really knows. Whatever its origins, it's a magical spot.

Take the Threlkeld rail-line path (signposted by the *Keswick Country House Hotel*) and follow the signs for around a mile and a half.

Derwent Water

Keswick Launch departures: Easter–Oct daily, Nov–Easter Sat & Sun only • £9.75 return, £2.10 per stage • ☎ 01768 772263, ⊛ keswick-launch.co.uk

The shores of **Derwent Water** lie five minutes' walk south of the town centre. It's ringed by crags and studded with islets, and is most easily seen by hopping on the **Keswick Launch**, which runs around the lake calling at several points en route. You can jump off the launch at any of the half a dozen piers on Derwent Water for a stroll, but if you've only got time for one hike, make it up **Cat Bells** (take the launch to Hawes End), a superb vantage point (1481ft) above the lake's western shore – allow two and a half hours for the scramble to the top and a return to the pier along the wooded shore.

Borrowdale

It is difficult to overstate the beauty of **Borrowdale**, a valley of river flats and yew trees, lying at the head of Derwent Water and overshadowed by Scafell Pike, the highest mountain in England, and Great Gable, reckoned as one of the finest-looking. At the straggling hamlet of **Rosthwaite**, seven miles south of Keswick, there are a couple of hotels with public bars, while another mile up the valley there's a café and a car park at Seatoller. From here, it's twenty minutes' walk down a minor road to the hamlet of **Seathwaite**, the base for walks up **Scafell Pike** (3205ft). The classic ascent is a tough eight-mile (6hr) loop walk from Seathwaite, heading up the thrilling Corridor Route then descending via Esk Hause.

ARRIVAL AND DEPARTURE

KESWICK AND AROUND

By bus Buses (including National Express services from Manchester and London) use the terminal in front of the large Booths supermarket, off Main Street. Some local services are seasonal.

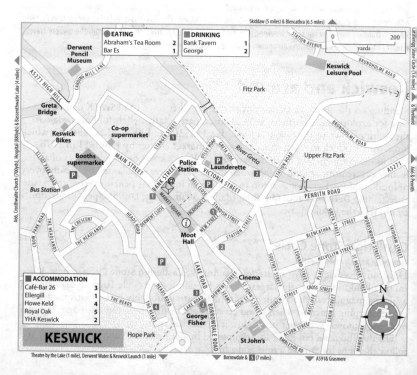

Destinations Ambleside (hourly; 50min); Buttermere (2 daily; 50min); Carlisle (3 daily; 1hr 10min); Cockermouth (every 30min–1hr; 30min); Grasmere (hourly; 40min); Honister (Easter–Oct 4 daily; 40min); Kendal (hourly; 1hr 30min); Rosthwaite (every 30min–1hr; 25min); Seatoller (every 30min–1hr; 30min); Windermere (hourly; 1hr).

GETTING AROUND

By bus Local services include the #77A (Easter–Oct only; down the west side of Derwent Water, via the access point for Cat Bells) and the scenic #78 "Borrowdale Rambler", which runs south down the B5289 to Seatoller. You can use either service all day with the "Honister Rambler" ticket (from £8).
By bike Keswick Bikes, 133 Main Street (daily 9am–5pm; ☏01768 775202, ⊚keswickbikes.co.uk), rents out bikes from £25/day.

INFORMATION AND TOURS

Tourist office National Park Information Centre, Moot Hall, Market Square (daily: April–Oct 9.30am–5.30pm; Nov–March 9.30am–4.30pm; ☏0845 901 0845, ⊚lake district.gov.uk).

Guided walks For a good walk in good company – lakeside rambles to mountain climbs – contact Pace the Peaks (regular walks Easter–Sept; £15; booking essential; ⊚pacethepeaks.co.uk).

ACCOMMODATION

11

B&Bs and **guesthouses** cluster around Southey, Blencathra, Church and Eskin streets, in the grid off the A591 (Penrith road). Smarter guesthouses and **hotels** line The Heads, overlooking Hope Park, a couple of minutes south of the centre on the way to Derwent Water, while nearby Borrowdale has several fine old inns and country-house hotels.

Café-Bar 26 26 Lake Rd, CA12 5DQ ☏01768 780863; map p.526. Four stylishly decorated rooms on the first floor offer a chintz-free B&B base right in the town centre, while downstairs is a funky café-bar. It's £95 at the weekend. **£75**
★ **Ellergill** 22 Stanger St, CA12 5JU ☏01768 773347, ⊚ellergill.co.uk; map p.526. Owners Robin and Clare have grafted a chic European feel onto their restored Victorian house, and offer classy B&B with five rooms. **£75**
★ **Howe Keld** 5–7 The Heads, CA12 5ES ☏01768 772417, ⊚howekeld.co.uk; map p.526. The Fishers' boutique guesthouse puts local crafts and materials centre stage, with furniture and floors handcrafted from Lake District trees, plus green-slate bathrooms and carpets of Herdwick wool. Breakfast is terrific, from the daily home-

baked bread to veggie rissoles and other specialities. **£115**
Royal Oak Rosthwaite, CA12 5XB, 7 miles south of Keswick ☏01768 777214, ⊚royaloakhotel.co.uk; map p.526. The Borrowdale hikers' favourite – rooms in a traditional inn with stone-flagged bar, where a hearty lakeland dinner (no choice, but vegetarian alternative available) is served at 7pm, and a bacon-and-eggs breakfast at 8.30am. Rates include dinner, bed and breakfast. **£134**
YHA Keswick Station Rd, CA12 5LH ☏0845 371 9746, ⊚yha.org.uk/hostel/keswick; map p.526. Once a riverside woollen mill, Keswick's YHA is more budget hotel than hostel these days, but still good value. It's big (84 beds in 21 rooms) but you're still advised to book, especially for a twin-bedded or family room. Dorms **£23.50**, doubles **£56**

EATING

Abraham's Tea Room George Fisher, 2 Borrowdale Rd, CA12 5DA ☏01768 772178, ⊚georgefisher.co.uk; map p.526. Keswick's celebrated outdoors store has a top-floor tearoom for home-made soups, big breakfasts, open sandwiches and other daily specials (£5–9). Mon–Fri 10am–5pm, Sat 9.30am–5pm, Sun 10.30am–4.30pm.
Bar Es 1 New St, CA12 5BH ☏01768 775222, ⊚esbar

keswick.co.uk; map p.526. On the right night *Bar Es* can be a real buzz (it's best to book at weekends in summer) – have a drink in the downstairs bar, munch "Mexican-inspired tapas" and then move upstairs for hearty portions of chorizo stew and beans, quesadillas, or their slow-cooked beef enchiladas (around £12 a head). Daily 5–11pm, kitchen closes 9pm.

DRINKING

Bank Tavern 47 Main St, CA12 5DS ☏01768 772663, ⊚banktavern.co.uk; map p.526. Resolutely traditional pub with a great range of beers (usually half a dozen real ales available), and a terrace at the back. Also enjoys a local reputation for its classic bar meals – bangers and mash to rib-eye steak (£9–14) – which can mean a crush at meal times. Daily 11am–11pm; kitchen daily noon–9pm.
George St John St, CA12 5AZ ☏01768 772076, ⊚george

hotelkeswick.co.uk; map p.526. If you're looking to down a pint or two of local Jennings ale at a traditional pub with bags of character, you won't do better than this 350-year-old inn. There's also a good bistro menu: slow-roast lamb to venison casserole, local trout to fish and chips (mains £11–16). Mon–Thurs & Sun 11am–11pm, Fri & Sat 11am–midnight; kitchen Mon–Thurs noon–2.30pm & 5.30–9pm, Fri–Sun noon–4.30pm & 5.30–9.30pm.

ENTERTAINMENT

There's a fair amount going on in Keswick throughout the year, including the **jazz festival** (ⓦkeswick.org) and **mountain festival** (ⓦkeswickmountainfestival.co.uk), both in May, a **beer festival** in June (ⓦkeswickbeerfestival.co.uk), and the **Keswick Agricultural Show** (Aug bank hol, ⓦkeswickshow.co.uk).

Theatre by the Lake Lake Rd, CA12 5DJ ☎01768 774411, ⓦtheatrebythelake.com. England's loveliest theatre hosts a full programme of drama, concerts, exhibitions, readings and talks. "Words By The Water", a literature festival, takes place here in the spring.

Honister Pass

Near the head of Borrowdale at Seatoller, the B5289 road cuts west, snaking up and over the dramatic **Honister Pass**, en route to Buttermere. At the top lie the unassuming buildings of **Honister Slate Mine** – an unexpectedly great place for daredevil adventurers with its deep mine tours and mountain activities. Come suitably clothed – it's wet or windy up here at the best of times.

Honister Slate Mine

Honister Pass, CA12 5XN • **Visitor centre, shop and café** Daily 9am–5pm • Free • **Tours** Daily 10.30am, 12.30pm & 3.30pm; 1hr 30min • From £13.50; reservations essential • ☎01768 777230, ⓦhonister.com

Slate has been quarried on Honister since the eighteenth century. **Honister Slate Mine**, the last remaining working slate mine in England, was rescued by local entrepreneurs in 1996 and is now operating again as a sustainable, commercial enterprise. To get an idea of what traditional mining entailed, you can don a hard hat and lamp to join one of the hugely informative guided **tours**, which lead you through narrow tunnels into illuminated, dripping caverns.

Via Ferrata

Daily departures from Honister Slate Mine • Classic £38, Xtreme £45; reservations essential • ☎01768 777714, ⓦhonister.com

Honister features England's first **Via Ferrata** – a dramatic Alpine-style three-hour mountain climb using a fixed cableway and harness, which allows visitors to follow the old miners' route up the exposed face of Fleetwith Pike (2126ft), the peak right above the mines. There are two options, labelled "Classic" and "Extreme"; both are terrifying and exhilarating in equal measure. Although you don't need climbing experience, check out the photos and videos on the website first to see what you're in for.

ARRIVAL AND DEPARTURE   HONSITER PASS

By bus The #77/77A runs up to Honister from Keswick on a circular route, coming either via Borrowdale (40min) or via Whinlatter and Buttermere (1hr). Buses run April–Sept only.

Buttermere

Ringed by peaks and crags, the tranquil waters and lakeside paths of **Buttermere** make a popular day-trip from Keswick, with the best approach being the sweeping descent into the valley from Honister Pass. There's no real village here – just a few houses and farms, a couple of hotels and a youth hostel, a café and large car park. The four-mile, round-lake stroll circling Buttermere shouldn't take more than a couple of hours. You can always detour up Scarth Gap to the peak known as **Haystacks** (1900ft) if you want more of a climb and views.

By bus The #77 from Keswick travels to Buttermere via Whinlatter Pass (1hr 15min), and the #77A travels via Honister Pass (1hr). Buses run April–Sept only.

Eskdale

Eskdale is perhaps the prettiest of the unsung Lake District valleys, reached from Ambleside on a long, twisting and alarmingly steep drive via the dramatic Hardknott Pass and **Hardknott Roman Fort** (daily 24hr; free), which commands a strategic and panoramic position. Eskdale can also be accessed less dramatically from the Cumbrian coast by road or the Ravenglass and Eskdale Railway (see below). However you arrive, you end up in the heart of superb walking country around the hamlet of **Boot**, where there's an old mill to explore and several local trails.

By car There's parking at Dalegarth station and at a couple of other designated areas in Eskdale, but the valley road is very narrow and side-of-the-road parking is impossible. Come by train if you can for a hassle-free day out.

By train There are year-round services on the Ravenglass and Eskdale Railway (see page 529), with stops at Eskdale Green (for *Stanley House*) and Dalegarth Station, the latter a short walk from Boot and around 1.5 miles from the *Woolpack Inn*.

ACCOMMODATION AND EATING

Eskdale Campsite Eskdale, Hardknott Pass road, CA19 1TF, just east of Boot ☎01946 723253, ⍟eskdalec amping.com. Small, beautifully sited campsite, just a short walk from the railway and the valley's pubs. For camping without canvas they also have ten heated "pods" (£45.50). Closed two weeks in Jan, and all of Feb. **£12.80**

★ **Stanley House** Eskdale Green, CA19 1TF ☎01946 723327, ⍟stanleyghyll-eskdale.co.uk. Self-catering/ B&B with a home-from-home feel and contemporary air. Accommodation is in a dozen spacious rooms, while downstairs is a huge open-plan kitchen-diner, plus lounge

with woodburner. The genial owners – who also run the *Woolpack Inn* – can arrange a lift to the pub. **£110**

★ **Woolpack Inn** Eskdale, Hardknott Pass road, CA19 1TH, 1 mile east of Boot ☎01946 723230, ⍟woolpack. co.uk. Friendly country inn whose weather-beaten facade conceals a cosy B&B and popular bar. Their seven rooms enjoy a smart urban chic feel, while downstairs the bar sports leather sofas and wood-fired pizza oven. It's strong on Cumbrian real ales, and the beer garden has spectacular fell views. Bar hours flexible but around 10am–10pm; bar meals noon–9pm, pizza noon–10pm. **£80**

Ravenglass and around

A sleepy coastal village at the estuary of three rivers, the Esk, Mite and Irt, **RAVENGLASS** is the starting point for the wonderful narrow-gauge **Ravenglass and Eskdale Railway**. It's worth taking some time to look around, though, before hopping on the train or heading out to **Muncaster Castle**, the other main local attraction. The single main street preserves a row of characterful nineteenth-century cottages facing out across the estuarine mud flats and dunes – the northern section, across the Esk, is a **nature reserve** where black-headed gulls and terns are often seen (get there by crossing over the mainline railway footbridge).

Ravenglass and Eskdale Railway

Ravenglass station, CA18 1SW • March–Oct, at least 5 trains daily (up to 15 daily in school summer hols); also most winter weekends, plus Christmas, New Year and Feb half-term hols • £13.90 return • ☎01229 717171, ⍟ravenglass-railway.co.uk

Opened in 1875 to carry ore from the Eskdale mines to the coastal railway, the 15-inch-gauge track of the **Ravenglass and Eskdale Railway** winds seven miles up through the Eskdale Valley to Dalegarth Station. The ticket lets you break your journey, get off and take a walk from one of the half-dozen stations en route (the full return journey, without a break, takes 1hr 40min). Alternatively, take your bike up on the train (prebooking essential; £3.50/bike) and cycle back from Dalegarth down the traffic-free **Eskdale Trail** (8.5 miles, 2hr; route guide available from Ravenglass and Dalegarth stations).

Muncaster Castle

A595, CA18 1RQ, 1 mile east of Ravenglass • Late March to late Oct; castle Mon–Fri & Sun noon–4pm; gardens and bird centre daily 10.30am–5pm; bird displays daily 2.30pm; check website for out-of-season openings • £14, £11 without castle entrance • ☎ 01229 717614, ⓦ muncaster.co.uk • There's a footpath (30min) from Ravenglass

The **Muncaster Castle** estate, a mile east of Ravenglass, provides one of the region's best days out. Apart from the ghost-ridden rooms of the castle itself, there are also seventy acres of well-kept **grounds and gardens**, at their best in spring and autumn, as well as an entertaining **hawk and owl centre** where they breed endangered species (including England's own barn owl).

ARRIVAL AND DEPARTURE RAVENGLASS AND AROUND

By train As well as the narrow-gauge line to Eskdale, Ravenglass is on the Cumbrian Coast line. There are hourly services to Barrow-in-Furness (50min), Carlisle (1hr 50min), Carnforth (1hr 50min) and Lancaster (2hr).

Wasdale

Wasdale is all about the mountains, which encircle three-mile long **Wast Water**, England's deepest lake. Awesome 1700ft screes plunge to its eastern shore, separating Wast Water from Eskdale to the south, while the highest peaks in England – Great Gable and the Scafells – frame **Wasdale Head**, the tiny settlement at the top of the lake. Apart from a few farms and cottages, and a single inn, the valley head is a remote yet starkly beautiful environment – mountain hikers know all about it, and can access some of the toughest, most rewarding lakeland peaks and circuits from here.

Wasdale has its softer side too, starting in the approach village of **Gosforth**, with its Viking-era cross, just off the A595. Beyond here, through forestry plantations and farmland, lie several scattered hamlets; the foot of the lake is just a mile and a half east of the village of **Nether Wasdale**, where there's overflow accommodation and places to eat. The drive in is a treat – bracken-covered walls hide the fields from view, while the roads cross little stone bridges and pass farm shops selling jars of bramble jelly or bags of new potatoes. Beyond Nether Wasdale the road hugs Wast Water's western shore, with occasional parking spots by bosky groves, stony coves and little promontories.

Wasdale Head

The road ends a mile beyond Wast Water at **Wasdale Head**, a clearing between the mountain ranges where you'll find the *Wasdale Head Inn*, one of the most celebrated in all the lakeland. British mountain climbing was born here in the days when the inn's landlord and champion liar was the famous Will Ritson (there's an annual **"World's Biggest Liar" festival** in his honour just down the road at Santon; ⓦ santonbridgeinn. com). Black-and-white photographs pinned to the panelled rooms inside show Victorian gents in hobnailed boots and flat caps scaling dreadful precipices with nonchalant ease. The inn's gone a bit upmarket since those days, but still attracts a genuine walking and climbing crowd, unfazed by the general lack of TV or mobile phone reception in the valley.

For a true measure of your own insignificance, take a walk down to Wast Water and along the eastern lakeshore path, approaching the unnerving, implacable screes – beware of tackling the tricky "footpath" across them, marked on some maps.

St Olaf's church

St Olaf's, reputedly **England's smallest church**, lies a couple of hundred yards from the *Wasdale Head Inn*, encircled by evergreens and dwarfed by the surrounding fells. The small cemetery contains graves and memorials to several of those killed while climbing them. Wasdale's had a church since medieval times and though no one knows quite how old this plain chapel is, its current appearance – moss-grown slate roof and all – dates from a complete overhaul in 1892. A path over Eskdale Moor, via Burnmoor Tarn, was the former "corpse road" along which the dead were carried for burying in Eskdale church, as St Olaf's had no consecrated churchyard until 1901.

ARRIVAL AND DEPARTURE
WASDALE HEAD

By car There's a public car park near the head of the lake and another close to the *Wasdale Head Inn*, but the spaces fill quickly with hikers, even on the grottiest of days. There are other parking places down the side of the lake.

INFORMATION

Information and supplies For everything you might need, from advance information to last-minute outdoor gear and supplies, contact the *Wasdale Head Inn* (☎01946 726229, ⓦwasdale.com). Their Barn Door Shop, next to the inn (daily: Easter–Oct 9am–5pm; Nov–Easter 9am– 4pm) is the only proper store for miles, and has a full range of outdoor clothes, equipment, camping gear, maps and guides – and the staff give great local walking advice. They also sell basic foodstuffs, including those crucial slabs of Kendal mint cake to get you up any mountain.

ACCOMMODATION

★ **Burnthwaite Farm** Wasdale Head, CA20 1EX ☎01946 726242, ⓦburnthwaite.co.uk. The last building in the valley – up a driveable track from the parking area near the inn – is a handsome old working sheep farm with six traditional B&B rooms (only two en suite, £76) inside a whitewashed farmhouse. All rooms have up-close-and-personal views of Lingmell, the adjacent mountain. There is also a self-catering apartment (sleeps four; from £395/week, or £60/night when available). A big farmhouse breakfast sets you up for the day. No credit cards. **£66**

Wasdale Campsite Wasdale Head, CA20 1EX ☎01946 726220, reservations on ☎01539 463862, ⓦnationaltrust.org.uk. The National Trust's Wasdale site is a mile from the pub, under glowering mountains at the head of the lake. There's a basic store, showers and a laundry room beneath the trees, and a couple of camping pods for softies (sleep two adults and a child; from £35). Open all year. Per person **£13.50**

★ **Wasdale Head Inn** Wasdale Head, CA20 1EX ☎01946 726229, ⓦwasdale.com. In addition to the excellent bar there are nine en-suite guest rooms in the main building of this famous inn; three "superior rooms" (£130) in the adjacent cottage conversion offer more space. The inn also runs six self-catering apartments in a converted barn (sleeping two to five; £470–540/week, short breaks and winter discounts available), a nearby B&B (£70), and another campsite (£5/person) with campers' toilets, hot showers (£1) and a wash-up area. **£118**

Whitehaven and around

Around twenty miles up the coast from Ravenglass, some fine Georgian houses mark out the centre of **WHITEHAVEN** – one of the few grid-planned towns in England and easily the most interesting destination on Cumbria's west coast. Whitehaven had a long history of trade in coal, but its rapid economic expansion was largely due to the booming slave trade – the town spent a brief period during the eighteenth century as one of Britain's busiest ports, importing sugar, rum, spices, tea, timber and tobacco.

The Beacon Museum

West Strand, on the harbour, CA28 7LY • Tues–Sun 10am–4.30pm, plus school and bank hols; last admission 3.45pm • £5 • ☎01946 592302, ⓦthebeacon-whitehaven.co.uk

The best place to swot up on Whitehaven's local history is the enterprising **Beacon Museum** on the harbour with interactive exhibitions covering a variety of themes from slaving and smuggling to the history of the nuclear industry at nearby Sellafield. You could easily spend a couple of hours here, teaching yourself how to build a ship, tie a sailor's knot or dress like a Roman centurion.

Rum Story

Lowther St, CA28 7DN • 10am–4.30pm: Easter–Sept daily; Oct–Easter Mon–Sat; closed 2nd week in Jan • £5.95 • ☎ 01946 592933, ⓦ rumstory.co.uk

Housed in the eighteenth-century shop, courtyard and warehouses of the Jefferson family, the **Rum Story** museum is where you can learn about rum, the navy, temperance and the hideousness of the slaves' Middle Passage, among other matters.

ARRIVAL AND DEPARTURE   WHITEHAVEN AND AROUND

By train From Whitehaven's train station (services to St Bees and Ravenglass, or north to Carlisle) you can walk around the harbour to The Beacon in less than 10min.

By bike Whitehaven is the start of the 140-mile C2C cycle route to Sunderland/Newcastle – a metal cut-out at the harbour marks the spot.

ACCOMMODATION

★**Lowther House** 13 Inkerman Terrace, CA28 7TY ☎ 01946 63169, ⓦ lowtherhouse-whitehaven.com. A highly personal, period restoration of an old Whitehaven house, with three charming rooms (one with harbour and sea views). You're welcomed with tea and cake, and breakfast is a chatty affair around your host's kitchen table. **£90**

St Bees

Five miles south of Whitehaven (and easily reached by train or bus), lie long sands, just west of the coastal village of **St Bees**. The steep, sandstone cliffs of **St Bees Head** to the north are good for windy walks and birdwatching, while the headland's lighthouse marks the start of Alfred Wainwright's 190-mile **Coast-to-Coast Walk** to Robin Hood's Bay.

Cockermouth

There's a lot to admire about the attractive small town and market centre of **COCKERMOUTH** – impressive Georgian facades, tree-lined streets and riverside setting – and there's no shortage of local attractions, not least the logical first stop on the **Wordsworth** trail, namely the house where the future poet was born. In the smartened-up Market Place (with monthly farmers' **markets**) there are more reminders of bygone days, including a pavement plaque teaching you the basics of talking Cumbrian.

Wordsworth House

Main St, CA13 9RX • Easter–Oct Mon–Thurs, Sat & Sun 11am–5pm, last admission 4pm • £7.50, admission by timed ticket on busy days; NT • ☎ 01900 824805, ⓦ nationaltrust.org.uk/wordsworth-house

The **Wordsworth House**, where William and sister Dorothy spent their first few years, is presented as a functioning eighteenth-century home – with a costumed cook sharing recipes in the kitchen and a clerk completing the ledger with quill and ink.

Jennings Brewery

Brewery Lane, CA13 9NE • Tours Feb, Nov & Dec Thurs–Sat 1.30pm; March–Oct Wed–Sat 1.30pm; 1hr 30min • £9 • ☎ 0845 129 7190, ⓦ www.jenningsbrewery.co.uk

Follow your nose in town, after the heady smell of hops, and you're likely to stumble upon **Jennings Brewery**, near the river. Jennings have been brewers in Cockermouth since 1874 and you don't have to step far to sample their product, available in any local pub. Or you can take the brewery **tour**, which ends with a free tasting in the bar.

ARRIVAL AND DEPARTURE   COCKERMOUTH

By bus All buses stop on Main Street, with the most useful service being the #X4/X5 (hourly, Sun every 2hr) from Penrith (1hr 30min) and Keswick (35min).

ACCOMMODATION AND EATING

★ **Bitter End** 15 Kirkgate, CA13 9PJ ☎ 01900 828993, ⓦ bitterend.co.uk. The cosiest pub in town also contains Cumbria's smallest brewery, producing ales like "Farmers", "Cockersnoot" and "Cuddy Lugs". Food ranges from steak and ale pie to cajun chicken (dishes £10–13). Mon–Fri 4–11pm, Sat & Sun 11am–11pm; kitchen Mon & Tues 4–9pm, Wed–Fri & Sun noon–2pm & 4–9pm, Sat noon–9pm.
Merienda 7a Station St, CA13 9QW ☎ 01900 822790, ⓦ merienda.co.uk. Bright and breezy café-bar offering breakfasts (from £3), light lunches (around £7) and evening meals (mains from £13). Also open Fri nights for tapas and music. Mon–Thurs & Sat 8am–9pm, Fri 8am–10pm, Sun 9am–9pm.

★ **Six Castlegate** 6 Castlegate, CA13 9EU ☎ 01900 826786, ⓦ sixcastlegate.co.uk. Period-piece house that retains its lofty Georgian proportions, impressive carved staircase and oak panelling, though the half-dozen B&B rooms are contemporary country in style. **£85**

Ullswater

Wordsworth declared **Ullswater** "the happiest combination of beauty and grandeur, which any of the Lakes affords", a judgement that still holds good. At almost eight miles, it's the second-longest lake in the National Park, with a dramatic serpentine shape that's overlooked by soaring fells, none higher than **Helvellyn** (3114ft), the most popular of the four 3000ft mountains in Cumbria. Cruises depart from the tiny village of **Glenridding**, at the south of the lake, and also call at lovely **Pooley Bridge**, the hamlet at the head of the lake. Meanwhile, at **Gowbarrow Park**, three miles north of Glenridding, the hillside still blazes green and gold in spring, as it did when the Wordsworths visited in April 1802; it's thought that Dorothy's recollections of the visit in her diary inspired William to write his famous "Daffodils" poem. The car park, tearooms and ferry dock here mark the start of a walk up to the 70ft falls of **Aira Force** (40min return).

ARRIVAL AND INFORMATION   ULLSWATER

By bus Buses from Penrith, Keswick and Bowness/Windermere) stop on the main road in Glenridding.
By boat The Glenridding steamer pier is a 5min walk from the centre. There's pay-and-display parking by the pier.
By car Parking along the lake is difficult, especially in summer, but it's easy to park in Glenridding and use the bus or boat to visit local attractions. Use the large pay-and-display car park by the visitor centre.
Tourist office National Park Information Centre, in the main car park at Glenridding (Easter–Oct daily 9.30am–5.30pm; Nov–Easter Sat & Sun 9.30am–3.30pm, weather dependent; ☎ 07769 956144, ⓦ lakedistrict.gov.uk).

ULLSWATER LAKE SERVICES

Ullswater steamer services started in 1859, and the lake still has a year-round ferry and cruise service provided by The Ullswater Navigation & Transit Company (☎ 01768 482229, ⓦ ullswater-steamers.co.uk). Services run from Glenridding to Howtown (45min; £6.60 single, £10.40 return), and from Howtown on to Pooley Bridge (1hr 5min; £9.30 each way) and back again. The one-day hop-on, hop-off "Round the Lake" pass (£13.50) also nets you a fifty percent discount on the Ravenglass and Eskdale Railway (see page 529). You can buy tickets at the piers or on board.

In school and summer holidays there are up to nine **daily departures** from Glenridding (basically an hourly service), down to between three and six a day at other times of the year – only Christmas Eve and Christmas Day have no sailings. The same company also runs a separate **Glenridding–Aira Force ferry** (June–Sept 6 daily; £5.20 each way; 20min).

11

CLIMBING HELVELLYN

The climb to the summit of **Helvellyn** (3114ft) forms part of a day-long circuit from Glenridding. The most frequently chosen approach is via the infamous **Striding Edge**, an undulating rocky crest offering the most direct access via a steep and dangerous scramble. The classic return is via the less demanding and less exposed **Swirral Edge**, where a route leads down to **Red Tarn** – the highest Lake District tarn – then follows the beck down to Glenridding past Helvellyn youth hostel. The Swirral Edge route is also the best way *up* Helvellyn if you don't fancy chancing Striding Edge (or you can try the even easier west face, from Thirlmere on the A591). Either approach from Glenridding makes for a seven-mile (5–6hr) round walk.

ACCOMMODATION AND EATING

★ **The Quiet Site** Watermillock, CA11 0LS ☎07768 727016, ⓦthequietsite.co.uk. The eco-friendly choice for cool campers is this hilltop site with sweeping views, around 2.5 miles north of Ullswater. Grassy camping pitches, a dozen camping pods (from £35) and a bar-in-a-barn (open most summer evenings) offer a bit of glamping comfort. Check website for seasonal rate hikes. **£20**

Sharrow Bay 2 miles south of Pooley Bridge, CA10 2LZ, on the Howtown road ☎01768 486301, ⓦsharrowbay. co.uk. Halfway down Ullswater's eastern shore, *Sharrow Bay* offers a breathtaking setting and excellent food. Needless to say, it's London prices in the country (rooms

up to £400 a night, suites up to £700) but there are few places in England that compare. The dining room is open to nonresidents (reservations essential); afternoon tea here (£25) is famous, while lunch and dinner (£65) are classy, formal affairs – and the desserts are renowned. Lunch noon–2pm, afternoon tea 4pm, dinner 7–9pm. **£165**

YHA Helvellyn Greenside, CA11 0QR ☎0845 371 9742, ⓦyha.org.uk/hostel/helvellyn. Walkers wanting an early start on Helvellyn stay at this basic hostel, dramatically sited 900ft up in the foothills around 1.5 miles from Glenridding. There are lots of beds (and private rooms; £50) while the nearest pub, the *Travellers Rest*, is a mile away. Dorms **£21.40**

Penrith and around

The nearest town to Ullswater – just four miles from the head of the lake – is **PENRITH**, whose deep-red buildings are constructed from the same rust-red sandstone used to build **Penrith Castle** in the fourteenth century; this is now a romantic ruin, opposite the train station. The town itself is at its best in the narrow streets, arcades and alleys off **Market Square**, and around **St Andrew's churchyard**, where the so-called "Giant's Grave" is actually a collection of pre-Norman crosses and "hogback" tombstones.

Dalemain

A592, CA11 0HB, 2 miles north of Pooley Bridge or 3 miles southwest of Penrith • **House** Easter–Oct Mon–Thurs & Sun 10.30am–3.30pm • £11.50 (includes gardens & tearoom) • **Gardens & tearoom** Mon–Thurs & Sun: Feb–Easter & Nov to mid-Dec 11am–3pm; Easter–Oct 10am–4.30pm • £8.50 • ☎01768 486450, ⓦdalemain.com • No public transport

Residence to the same family since 1679, the country house of **Dalemain** started life in the twelfth century as a fortified tower, but has been added to by successive generations, culminating with a Georgian facade grafted on to a largely Elizabethan house. Its grounds are gorgeous and, rather remarkably, inside you're given the run of the public rooms, which the Hasell family still use.

Rheged

Redhills, CA11 0DQ, 1.5 miles southwest of Penrith • Daily 10am–5.30pm • Free; admission to one film £6.50, each extra film £5 • ☎01768 868000, ⓦrheged.com • Bus #X4/X5 from Penrith or Keswick/Cockermouth

Rheged – a Cumbrian "visitor experience", just outside Penrith – is billed as Europe's largest earth-covered building, and blends in admirably with the surrounding

POTTY PENRITH

Potfest (ⓦpotfest.co.uk), Europe's biggest ceramics show, takes place in Penrith over two consecutive weekends (late July/early Aug). The first is **Potfest in the Park**, with ceramics on display in marquees in front of Hutton-in-the-Forest country house, as well as larger sculptural works laid out in the grounds.

This is followed by the highly unusual **Potfest in the Pens**, which sees potters displaying their creations in the unlikely setting of the covered pens at Penrith's cattle market, just outside town on the A66. Here, the public can talk to the artists, learn about what inspires them and sign up for free classes.

fells – from the main road you wouldn't know it was there. An impressive atrium-lit underground visitor centre fills you in on the region's history, and you'll also find souvenir shops, food outlets, galleries, workshops, demonstrations and play areas. The staple visit, though, is for the big-screen 3D **cinema**, which shows family-friendly movies.

11

ARRIVAL AND DEPARTURE
PENRITH AND AROUND

By train Penrith train station is 5min walk south of Market Square and the main street, Middlegate.
Destinations Carlisle (every 30min; 20min), with onward services to Glasgow/Edinburgh; Lancaster (every 30min; 40min), with onward services to London; Manchester (hourly; 1hr 40min).

By bus The bus station is on Albert St, behind Middlegate. Regular Ullswater, Keswick, Cockermouth and Carlisle services.

ACCOMMODATION AND EATING

Askham Hall Askham, CA10 2PF, 6 miles south of Penrith ⓣ01931 712350, ⓦaskhamhall.co.uk. Country-house living at its most gracious – the Lowther family's *Askham Hall* boasts stunning rooms, a heated outdoor pool and gorgeous gardens. There's both elegant restaurant dining (bookings essential) and the *Kitchen Garden Café*, which has an outdoor wood-fired oven for pizzas. Restaurant daily 7–9.30pm; café March & Nov Fri & Sun 11am–4pm, Easter to mid-Oct Mon–Fri & Sun 10am–5pm. **£190**

Brooklands 2 Portland Place, CA11 7QN ⓣ01768 863395, ⓦbrooklandsguesthouse.com. Handsome 1870s townhouse, whose colour-coordinated B&B rooms all have country pine furniture and small but snazzy bathrooms. **£95**

Crake Trees Manor Crosby Ravensworth, CA10 3JG, 15 miles southeast of Penrith ⓣ01931 715205, ⓦcraketreesmanor.co.uk. A gorgeous barn-conversion B&B in the nearby Eden Valley. Rooms have slate floors, antique beds, serious showers and fluffy, wrap-me-up towels; or consider the self-catering Brewhouse (sleeps two; from £260 for three nights), or the cosy Shepherds' Hut (sleeps two; £75–85). **£100**

★**George and Dragon** Clifton, CA10 2ER, 3 miles northeast of Askham/south of Penrith ⓣ01768 865381, ⓦgeorgeanddragonclifton.co.uk. This revamped eighteenth-century inn is a real class act – country-chic rooms (up to £160) feature big beds with brocade headboards and slate-floor bathrooms, while the informal downstairs bar and restaurant (around £35 for three courses) sources pretty much everything from the adjacent Lowther estate. Kitchen daily noon–2.30pm & 6–9pm. **£95**

Carlisle and around

The county capital of Cumbria, **CARLISLE** has been fought over for more than 2000 years, ever since the construction of Hadrian's Wall – part of which survives at nearby **Birdoswald Roman Fort**. The later struggle with the Scots defined the very nature of Carlisle as a border city: William Wallace was repelled in 1297 and Robert the Bruce eighteen years later, but Bonnie Prince Charlie's troops took Carlisle in 1745 after a six-day siege, holding it for six weeks before surrendering to the Duke of Cumberland. It's not surprising, then, that the city trumpets itself as "historic Carlisle", and it's well worth a night's stop.

Carlisle Cathedral

Castle St, CA3 8TZ · Mon–Sat 7.30am–6.15pm, Sun 7.30am–5pm · Free, £5 donation requested · ☏ 01228 548151, ⓦ carlislecathedral.org.uk

Carlisle Cathedral was founded in 1122 but embraces a considerably older heritage. Christianity was established in sixth-century Carlisle by St Kentigern (often known as St Mungo), who became the first bishop and patron saint of Glasgow. Parliamentarian troops during the Civil War caused much destruction, but there's still plenty to admire in the ornate fifteenth-century choir stalls and the glorious **East Window**, which features some of the finest pieces of fourteenth-century stained glass in the country.

Tullie House Museum and Art Gallery

Castle St, CA3 8TP · April–Oct Mon–Sat 10am–5pm, Sun 11am–5pm; Nov–March Mon–Sat 10am–4pm, Sun noon–4pm · £7.70, under-18s free · ☏ 01228 618718, ⓦ tulliehouse.co.uk

The wonderful **Tullie House Museum and Art Gallery** takes an imaginative approach to Carlisle's turbulent past, with special emphasis on life on the edge of the Roman Empire. Climbing a reconstruction of part of Hadrian's Wall, you learn about catapults and stone-throwers, while other sections elaborate on domestic life, work and burial practices.

Carlisle Castle

Bridge St, CA3 8UR · April–Sept daily 10am–6pm; Oct daily 10am–5pm; Nov–March Sat & Sun 10am–4pm · £6.80; EH · Guided tours Easter–Oct daily; ask at the entrance · ☏ 01228 591922, ⓦ www.english-heritage.org.uk/visit/places/carlisle-castle

With a thousand years of military occupation of the site, **Carlisle Castle** is loaded with significance – not least as the place where, in 1568, Elizabeth I kept Mary Queen of Scots as her "guest". Guided **tours** help bring the history to life; don't leave without climbing to the battlements for a view of the Carlisle rooftops.

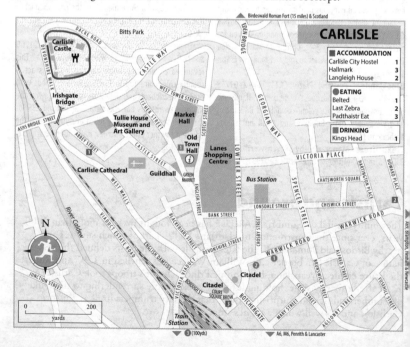

CARLISLE

ACCOMMODATION
Carlisle City Hostel	1
Hallmark	3
Langleigh House	2

EATING
Belted	1
Last Zebra	2
Padthaistr Eat	3

DRINKING
| Kings Head | 1 |

Birdoswald Roman Fort

Gilsland, Brampton, CA8 7DD, 15 miles northeast of Carlisle • April–Sept daily 10am–6pm; Oct daily 10am–5pm; Nov–March Sat & Sun 10am–4pm • £6.10; EH • ☎ 01697 747602, ⓦ www.english-heritage.org.uk/visit/places/birdoswald-roman-fort-hadrians-wall

One of sixteen major fortifications along Hadrian's Wall, **Birdoswald Fort** has all tiers of the Roman structure intact, while a drill hall and other buildings have been excavated. There's a tearoom and picnic area at the fort.

ARRIVAL AND INFORMATION

By train The station is in the town centre. Carlisle is on the West Coast mainline (for London–Manchester–Scotland services), and has services to Whitehaven and to Newcastle. The Settle to Carlisle Railway, the magnificent scenic railway through the Yorkshire Dales (see page 584), ends its run here.
Destinations Lancaster (every 30min–1hr; 1hr); Newcastle (hourly; 1hr 20min–1hr 40min); Whitehaven (hourly; 1hr 10min).
Tourist office Old Town Hall, Green Market (March, April, Sept & Oct Mon–Sat 9.30am–5pm; May–Aug Mon–Sat 9.30am–5pm, Sun 10.30am–4pm; Nov–Feb Mon–Sat 10am–4pm; ☎ 01228 598596, ⓦ discovercarlisle.co.uk).

11

ACCOMMODATION

Carlisle City Hostel 36 Abbey St, CA3 8TX ☎ 01228 545637, ⓦ carlislecityhostel.com; map p.536. Carlisle's indie hostel makes a great budget base, with four bright bunk rooms offering flexible accommodation for groups or families. One room is available as a private double/triple (£50), another as a family room (£74). There's a kitchen, free tea and coffee, bike storage and secure lockers, and the location is excellent. Dorms **£19**

Hallmark Court Square, CA1 1QY ☎ 01228 531951, ⓦ hallmarkhotels.co.uk; map p.536. Right by the train station, the boutique-style *Hallmark* has a chic look, sleek rooms with big beds, and a contemporary bar/brasserie. **£95**
Langleigh House 6 Howard Place, CA1 1HR ☎ 01228 530440, ⓦ langleighhouse.co.uk; map p.536. Nicely presented Victorian townhouse B&B – furnishings reflect the period, and original features abound. **£76**

EATING

Belted 20–34 Warwick Rd, CA1 1DN ☎ 01228 528941, ⓦ beltedburgers.co.uk; map p.536. The place to go if you're after a full-on burger experience (around £12 a head), with meat sourced from prime Scots beef, in a big, bustling, barn-like setting. Vegetarians can opt for the mushroom or beetburger instead. Good range of bottled craft beers, too. Tues–Sun 11am–11pm.
Last Zebra 6 Lowther St, CA3 8DA ☎ 01228 593600, ⓦ thelastzebra.co.uk; map p.536. Quirky lounge bar and grill serving cosmopolitan food at lunch and dinner – mussels to local lamb, burgers to piri-piri chicken (mains £10–28) – and good cocktails. Mon–Fri 11am–midnight, Sat 11am–1am, Sun noon–11pm.
Padthaistr Eat In the car park by Nelson Bridge, between the train station and the river, CA3 0BB ☎ 07970 030658; map p.536. Amazingly tasty Thai takeaway food at around £5 a portion, sold out of a red van; something of a local institution. Mon–Sat 11.30am–3pm.

DRINKING

Kings Head 31 Fisher St, CA3 8RF ⓦ kingsheadcarlisle. co.uk; map p.536. Recently given a much-needed facelift, this reliable, old-style pub right in the centre of town specializes in real ale; there are always a few guest beers on tap, plus local brews by Yates. Service can occasionally be surly. Mon–Thurs 10am–11pm, Fri 10am–midnight, Sat 11am–midnight, Sun noon–11pm.

MALHAM COVE

Yorkshire

Yorkshire

It's easy to be glib about Yorkshire – to outsiders it's the archetypal "up North" with all the clichés that implies, from flat caps to grim factories. For their part, many Yorkshire locals are happy to play up to these prejudices, while nursing a secret conviction that there really is no better place in the world to live. In some respects, it's a world apart, its most distinctive characteristics – from the broad dialect to the breathtaking landscapes – deriving from a long history of settlement, invention and independence. It's hard to argue with Yorkshire's boasts that the beer's better, the air's cleaner and the people are friendlier.

The number-one destination is undoubtedly **York**, established by the Vikings and for centuries England's second city; the region's **Norse heritage** is still evident in Yorkshire dialect words, such as -gate ("street", from the Norse *gata*), dale ("valley"), tarn ("pond") and force ("waterfall"). York's mixture of medieval, Georgian and Victorian architecture is repeated in towns such as **Beverley**, Richmond and **Ripon**, while the Yorkshire **coast**, too, retains something of its erstwhile grandeur – Bridlington and Scarborough boomed in the nineteenth century and again in the postwar period, though it's in smaller resorts like **Whitby** and Robin Hood's Bay that the best of the coast is to be found today. A renewed vigour has infused the maritime city of **Hull**, which hopes to emulate the remarkable city-centre transformations of once-industrial **Leeds** and **Sheffield** to the south and west of the county, where **Bradford** also makes a fine diversion on the way to **Haworth**, home of the Brontë sisters.

The **Yorkshire Dales**, to the northwest, form a patchwork of stone-built villages, limestone hills, serene valleys and majestic heights. The county's other National Park, the **North York Moors**, is divided into bleak upland moors and a tremendous rugged coastline between Robin Hood's Bay and Staithes.

GETTING AROUND
YORKSHIRE

By train Fast trains on the East Coast main line link York to London, Newcastle and Edinburgh. Leeds is served by trains from London, and is at the centre of the integrated Metro bus and train system that covers most of West and South Yorkshire. There are services to Scarborough (from York) and Whitby (from Middlesbrough), while the Settle to Carlisle line, to the southern and western Dales, can be accessed from Leeds, as can Hull.

Transport passes The North Country Rover ticket (🌐 northernrailway.co.uk/tickets/rail-rover-tickets), £93 for four days in eight) covers train travel north of Leeds, Bradford and Hull and south of Newcastle and Carlisle.

York and around

YORK is the North's most compelling city, a place whose history, said George VI, "is the history of England". This is perhaps overstating things a little, but it reflects the significance of a metropolis that stood at the heart of the country's religious and

12

WHITBY

Highlights

❶ Jorvik & Jorvik Dig, York Travel through time to Viking York, then seek out new discoveries at Jorvik Dig. See page 547

❷ Fountains Abbey Enjoy views of the atmospheric ruins of Fountains Abbey set in spectacular Studley Water Garden. See page 553

❸ Malham It's a breathtaking hike from Malham village to the glorious natural amphitheatre of Malham Cove. See page 557

❹ Haworth Visiting the moorland home of the talented and ultimately tragic Brontë sisters is an affecting experience, despite the crowds. See page 563

❺ Bradford curry houses Bradford's Indian restaurants provide wonderful opportunities for gastronomic exploration. See page 565

❻ National Coal Mining Museum A working coal mine until the mid-1980s, now a museum; you can even head underground, if you're brave enough. See page 572

❼ Ferens Art Gallery Hull's 2017 stint as European Capital of Culture marked the city's transformation into a hub for the arts. See page 576

❽ Whitby Follow in the footsteps of Count Dracula and Captain James Cook in this spectacularly pretty former whaling port. See page 587

HIGHLIGHTS ARE MARKED ON THE MAP ON PAGE 542

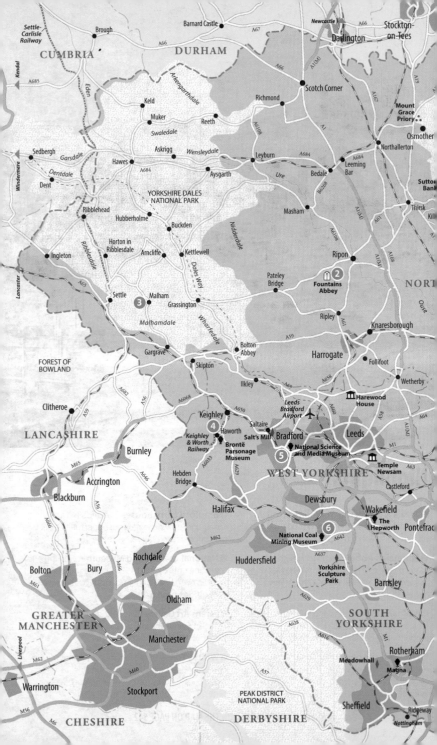

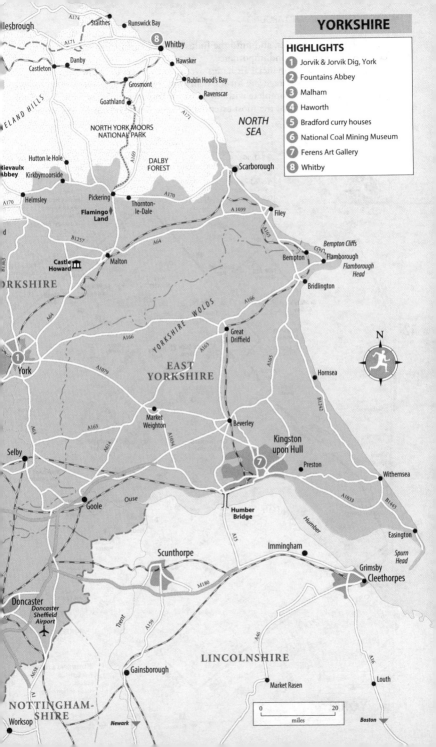

political life for centuries, and until the Industrial Revolution was second only to London in population and importance.

These days a more provincial air hangs over the city, except in summer when it comes to feel like a heritage site for the benefit of tourists. That said, no trip to this part of the country is complete without a visit to York, which is also well placed for any number of **day-trips**, the most essential being to **Castle Howard**, the gem among English stately homes.

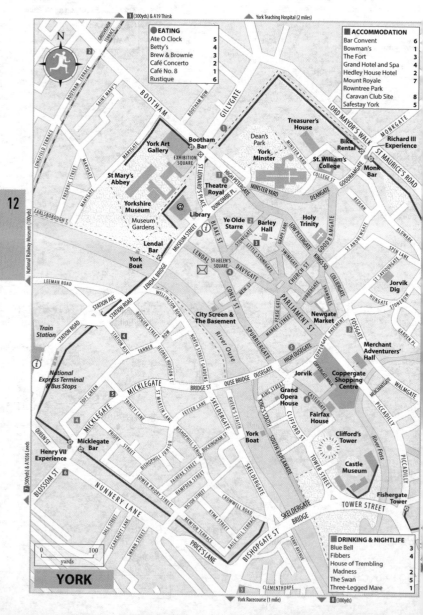

EATING

Ate O Clock	5
Betty's	4
Brew & Brownie	3
Café Concerto	2
Café No. 8	1
Rustique	6

ACCOMMODATION

Bar Convent	6
Bowman's	1
The Fort	3
Grand Hotel and Spa	4
Hedley House Hotel	2
Mount Royale	7
Rowntree Park Caravan Club Site	8
Safestay York	5

DRINKING & NIGHTLIFE

Blue Bell	3
Fibbers	4
House of Trembling Madness	2
The Swan	5
Three-Legged Mare	1

YORK

The **minster** is the obvious place to start, and you won't want to miss a walk around the old city **walls**. Standout historic buildings include the Minster's Treasurer's House, Georgian Fairfax House, the Merchant Adventurers' Hall, and the stark remnants of York's **Castle**; the medieval city is at its most evocative around the streets known as Stonegate and the **Shambles**. The city's favourite family attraction, **Jorvik Viking Centre**, isn't far from here. The two major museum collections are the incomparable **Castle Museum** and the **National Railway Museum** (where the appeal goes way beyond railway memorabilia), while the **Museum Gardens** (ⓦyorkmuseumgardens.org.uk) between Exhibition Square and the river are home to the evocative ruins and gardens of **St Mary's Abbey** and the child-friendly **Yorkshire Museum**. Recent redevelopment work has extended the gardens to the back of **York Art Gallery**.

Brief history

An early **Roman** fortress of 71 AD in time became a city – Eboracum, capital of the empire's northern European territories and the base for Hadrian's northern campaigns. Later, the city became the fulcrum of **Christianity** in northern England: on Easter Day in 627, Bishop Paulinus, on a mission to establish the Roman Church, baptized King Edwin of Northumbria in a small timber chapel here. Six years later the church became the first minster and Paulinus the first archbishop of York.

In 867 the city fell to the **Danes**, who renamed it **Jorvik**, and later made it the capital of eastern England (Danelaw). Later Viking raids culminated in the decisive **Battle of Stamford Bridge** (1066) six miles east of the city, where English King Harold defeated Norse King Harald – a pyrrhic victory in the event, for Harold's weakened army was defeated by the Normans just a few days later at the Battle of Hastings, with well-known consequences for all concerned.

The **Normans** devastated much of York's hinterland in their infamous "Harrying of the North". Stone walls were thrown up during the thirteenth century, when the city became a favoured Plantagenet retreat and commercial capital of the north, its importance reflected in the new title of Duke of York, bestowed ever since on the monarch's second son. Although Henry VIII's Dissolution of the Monasteries took its toll on a city crammed with religious houses, York remained wedded to the Catholic cause, and the most famous of the Gunpowder Plot conspirators, **Guy Fawkes**, was born here. During the **Civil War** Charles I established his court in the city, which was strongly pro-Royalist, inviting a Parliamentarian siege. Royalist troops, however, were routed by Cromwell and Sir Thomas Fairfax at the **Battle of Marston Moor** in 1644, another seminal battle in England's history, which took place six miles west of York.

The city's eighteenth-century history was marked by its emergence as a social centre for Yorkshire's landed elite. While the Industrial Revolution largely passed it by, the arrival of the **railways** brought renewed prosperity, thanks to the enterprise of pioneering "Railway King" George Hudson, lord mayor during the 1830s and 1840s. The railway is gradually losing its role as a major employer, as is the traditional confectionery industry, and incomes are now generated by new service and bioscience industries – not forgetting, of course, the 6.9 million annual tourist visits.

York Minster

Minster Yard, YO1 7HH • Mon–Sat 9am–5pm, Sun 12.45–5pm • £10 (including undercroft), combined ticket with tower £15; admission ticket valid for 12 months • **Tours** Mon–Sat 10am–3pm, on the hour; access to "Revealing York Minster" and the Orb included; 1hr • Included in entry price • ☎ 01904 557200, ⓦ yorkminster.org

York Minster ranks as one of the country's most important sights. Seat of the Archbishop of York, it is Britain's largest Gothic building and home to countless treasures, not least of which is an estimated half of all the medieval stained glass in England. The first significant foundations were laid around 1080 by the first Norman archbishop, Thomas of Bayeux, and it was from the germ of this Norman church that the present structure emerged.

The stained-glass windows

Nothing else in the minster can match the magnificence of the **stained glass** in the nave and transepts. The **West Window** (1338) contains distinctive heart-shaped upper tracery (the "Heart of Yorkshire"), while in the nave's north aisle, the second bay window (1155) contains slivers of the oldest stained glass in the country. The greatest of the church's 128 windows, however, is the majestic **East Window** (1405), at 78ft by 31ft the world's largest area of medieval stained glass in a single window.

The undercroft, treasury and crypt

The Minster's foundations, or **undercroft**, have been turned into a museum, featuring a new interactive gallery "Revealing York Minster". Among precious relics in the adjoining **treasury** is the eleventh-century *Horn of Ulf*, presented to the minster by a relative of the tide-turning King Canute. There's also access from the undercroft to the **crypt**, the spot that transmits the most powerful sense of antiquity, as it contains sections of the original eleventh-century church, including pillars with fine Romanesque capitals. Access to the undercroft, treasury and crypt is from the south transept, which is also the entrance to the **central tower**, which you can climb for exhilarating rooftop views over the city.

Around the walls

The city's superb **walls** date mainly from the fourteenth century, though fragments of Norman work survive, particularly in the gates (known as "bars"), and the northern sections still follow the line of the Roman ramparts. **Monk Bar** is as good a point of access as any, tallest of the city's four main gates and host to the small **Richard III Experience** (daily: April–Oct 10am–5pm; Nov–March 10am–4pm; £5; ☎01904 615505, ⓦrichardiiiexperience.com). For just a taste of the walls' best section – with great views of the minster and acres of idyllic-looking gardens – take the ten-minute stroll west from Monk Bar to Exhibition Square and **Bootham Bar**, the only gate on the site of a Roman gateway and marking the traditional northern entrance to the city. A stroll round the walls' entire two-and-a-half-mile length will also take you past the southwestern **Micklegate Bar**, long considered the most important of the gates since it marked the start of the road to London; it's now home to the Henry VII Experience (April–Oct 10am–4pm; Nov–March 10am–3pm; £5; ☎01904 615505).

York Art Gallery

Exhibition Square, YO1 7EW • Daily 10am–5pm • £7.50; free access to garden • ☎ 01904 687687, ⓦ yorkartgallery.org.uk

York Art Gallery houses an impressive collection of early Italian, British and northern European paintings, some of which are on display in the Burton Gallery. The gallery's extensive recent renovations made space for its notable British studio ceramics collection, which now has a permanent home in two of the first-floor state-of-the-art exhibition spaces. The ground floor hosts a year-round series of special exhibitions and events and a café (daily 10am–4.45pm); a second entrance leads directly from the Museum Gardens.

Yorkshire Museum

Museum Gardens, YO1 7FR • Daily 10am–5pm • £7.50 • ☎ 01904 687687, ⓦ yorkshiremuseum.org.uk

In the beautiful Museum Gardens, next to the romantic ruins of St Mary's Abbey, sits the majestic Grade I listed building of the **Yorkshire Museum**. Five exciting, hands-on galleries comprise the "History of York", a multiscreen, audiovisual display; "Extinct", which covers dinosaurs and more recently extinct creatures; "Meet the People of the Empire" (Roman York); the "Power and the Glory" (Medieval York); and "Enquiry", about how archeology and science can uncover the past.

Stonegate

One of York's most picturesque streets, **Stonegate** is as ancient as the city itself. Originally the Via Praetoria of Roman York, it's now paved with thick flags of York stone, which were once carried along here to build the minster (hence the name). The Tudor buildings that line it retain their considerable charm – **Ye Olde Starre Inne** at no. 40, one of York's original inns, is on every tourist itinerary (you can't miss the sign straddling the street).

Barley Hall

Off Stonegate, YO1 8AR • Daily: April–Oct 10am–5pm, Nov–March 10–4pm • £6, under-17s £3; joint ticket with Jorvik £14/£9.25 • ☎ 01904 615505, ⓦ barleyhall.co.uk

Step through an alley known as Coffee Yard (opposite *Ye Olde Starre Inne*) to find **Barley Hall**, a fine restoration of a late medieval townhouse with a lively museum where you can learn about fifteenth-century life by, among other things, playing period games and trying on costumes. Barley Hall is one of the Jorvik group of attractions.

The Shambles

12

York's most famous street, and one which appears regularly on its promotional brochures, **The Shambles** could be taken as the epitome of the medieval city. Almost impossibly narrow and lined with perilously leaning timber-framed houses, it was the home of York's butchers (the word "shambles" derives from the Old English for slaughterhouse) – old meat hooks still adorn the odd house.

Jorvik

Coppergate Shopping Centre, YO1 9WT • Daily: April–Oct 10am–5pm; Nov–March 10am–4pm • £10.25, under-17s £7.25; joint ticket with Jorvik Dig £14.45/£11; joint ticket with Barley Hall £14/£9.25 • ☎ 01904 615505, ⓦ jorvikvikingcentre.co.uk

Excavations of Coppergate in 1976 uncovered York's original Viking settlement, now largely buried beneath a shopping centre. But at adjacent **Jorvik**, visitors are propelled in "time capsules" on a ride through a reconstructed version of the tenth-century Viking city, immersing you in the sights, sounds and even the smells of the times. You also get to see how artefacts unearthed from the original site were used, and watch live-action domestic scenes on actual Viking-age streets, with constipated villagers, axe-fighting and other singular attractions.

Jorvik Dig

St Saviourgate, YO1 8NN • Daily 10am–5pm • £6.50, under-17s £6; joint ticket with Jorvik £14.45/£11; pre-booking advised • ☎ 01904 615505, ⓦ digyork.com

Where Jorvik shows what was unearthed at Coppergate, the associated attraction that is **Jorvik Dig** illustrates the science involved. Housed five minutes' walk away from the museum, in the medieval church of St Saviour, on St Saviourgate, a simulated dig allows children to take part in a range of excavations in the company of archeologists, using authentic tools and methods. There's an on-site exhibition **Looking Back at Hungate** (included in admission, or £2.50), which has some interesting artefacts from a five-year archeological excavation of local Roman, Viking and medieval remains.

Clifford's Tower

Tower St, YO1 9SA • Daily 10am–6pm • £5; EH • ☎ 01904 646940, ⓦ www.english-heritage.org.uk/visit/places/cliffords-tower-york

There's precious little left of **York Castle**, one of two established by William the Conqueror. Only the perilously leaning **Clifford's Tower** remains, a stark stone keep built between 1245 and 1262 to replace the original wooden keep burned down in 1190 AD when it was being used as a refuge by hundreds of Jews trying to escape anti-Semitic riots in the city. Of a rare quatrefoil (clove-leaf) design, perhaps an experiment to improve sight lines between the top of the keep and the base of the walls, it once had two floors with a supporting central column. Controversial plans are afoot to build a large visitor centre into the mound that the tower sits on.

Castle Museum

Eye of York, YO1 9WD • Daily 9.30am–5pm • £10 • ☎ 01904 687687, ⓦ yorkcastlemuseum.org.uk

Housed in what was once a couple of prisons, displays in the wonderfully inventive **Castle Museum** begin with a series of period rooms from the seventeenth century to the 1980s. There's a large room devoted to Victorian attitudes to birth, marriage and death, followed by a wonderful reconstruction of the sights and sounds of York's Kirkgate during the final years of the nineteenth century, often staffed by people dressed-in authentic costume. There are displays, too, of period kitchens, plus a superb re-creation of the fashion, music and news stories of the 1960s. Finally, the cells in the basement of the prison building contain an affecting series of real-life stories, told by video recordings of actors projected onto cell walls, gleaned from the prison's records.

The National Railway Museum

Leeman Rd, a 10min walk from the train station, YO26 4XJ • Daily 10am–6pm • Free • ☎ 0844 815 3139, ⓦ nrm.org.uk • A "road train" shuttles visitors here from Duncombe Place next to York Minster (April–Oct daily every 30min; £2)

The **National Railway Museum** is a must if you have even the slightest interest in railways, history, engineering or Victoriana. The Great Hall alone features some fifty restored locomotives dating from 1829 onwards, among them *Mallard*, at 126mph the fastest steam engine ever built. After a lengthy on-site £4.2 million restoration, the **Flying Scotsman** is back on the tracks as a working exhibit (ⓦ flyingscotsman.org.uk); it returns to the museum in winter. Engines aside, you can't help but love the sheer Britishness of the Station Hall with its Royal carriages, railway memorabilia and real-life stories.

Castle Howard

15 miles northeast of York off the A64, YO60 7DA • Late March to late Oct & late Nov to mid-Dec house daily 11am–4pm, grounds 10am–5pm; grounds also open Jan to late March & Nov to mid-Dec • £18.95; grounds only £11.95 • ☎ 01653 648333, ⓦ castlehoward. co.uk • Tours run from York (see page 549), or catch a Yorkshire Coastliner bus from York, Malton or Pickering, or summer-only Moorsbus (see page 580) from Helmsley

Immersed in the deep countryside of the Howardian Hills, **Castle Howard** is the seat of one of England's leading aristocratic families and among the country's grandest stately homes. The grounds especially are worth visiting, and you could easily spend the best part of a day here. The colossal main house was designed by **Sir John Vanbrugh** in 1699 and was almost forty years in the making – remarkable enough, even were it not for the fact that Vanbrugh was, at the start of the commission at least, best known as a playwright and had no formal architectural training. Shrewdly, Vanbrugh recognized his limitations and called upon **Nicholas Hawksmoor**, who had a major part in the house's structural design – the pair later worked successfully together on Blenheim Palace.

Vanbrugh also turned his attention to the estate's thousand-acre **grounds**, where he could indulge his playful inclinations – the formal gardens, clipped parkland, towers, obelisks and blunt sandstone follies stretch in all directions, sloping gently to two artificial lakes. The whole is a charming artifice of grand, manicured views – an example of what three centuries, skilled gardeners and pots of money can produce.

ARRIVAL AND DEPARTURE
YORK AND AROUND

By train Trains arrive at York Station, just outside the city walls, a 10min walk from the historic core.

Destinations Durham (every 10min; 50min); Harrogate (hourly; 30min); Hull (hourly; 1hr); Leeds (every 10–15min; 25min); London (every 30min; 2hr); Manchester (every 15min; 1hr 25min); Newcastle (every 15min; 1hr); Scarborough (hourly; 50min); Sheffield (every 15–30min; 45min).

By bus National Express buses and most other regional bus services drop off and pick up on Rougier St, 200yd north of the train station, or on Station Road itself. Companies include East Yorkshire (for Hull, Beverley and Bridlington; ⓦ eyms.co.uk) and Yorkshire Coastliner/City Zap (for Leeds, Castle Howard, Pickering, Scarborough and Whitby; ⓦ yorkbus.co.uk).

Destinations Beverley (Mon–Sat hourly, Sun 7 daily; 1hr 10min); Hull (Mon–Sat hourly, Sun 7 daily; 1hr 35min); Leeds (Mon–Sat every 15min, Sun every 30min; 50min–1hr 20min); Pickering (hourly; 1hr 8min); Scarborough (hourly; 1hr 40min); Whitby (4–6 daily; 2hr 13min).

GETTING AROUND

On foot The historic core is easily explored on foot; from the minster in the north, for example, to Castle Museum in the south is about a 10min walk. Indeed, one of the best ways to explore the city is to circumnavigate it atop the splendid city walls.

By taxi There are taxi ranks at Duncombe Place and the train station, or call Streamline Taxis on ☎ 01904 656565.

INFORMATION AND TOURS

Tourist office 1 Museum St, on the corner with Blake Street (Mon–Sat 9am–5pm, July & Aug to 5.30pm, Sun 10am–4pm; ☎ 01904 550099, ⓦ visityork.org). There is also a smaller tourist office at the train station.

Listings information The monthly *What's On York* (ⓦ whatsonyork.com) provides detailed entertainment, events, festival and exhibition listings for the city. Online guide YORK:PM (ⓦ york-pm.co.uk) is another useful local resource.

Bus tours City tours by bus – pick up details at the tourist office – cost around £10. Stephensons of Easingwold (☎ 01347 838990, ⓦ stephensonsofeasingwold.co.uk) operates services to Castle Howard for £10 return, along with several routes to the Dales.

Walking tours The York Association of Voluntary Guides (☎ 01904 550098, ⓦ avgyork.co.uk) offers a free historic guided tour of the city (daily: April–Oct 10.15am & 1.15pm, Nov–March 10.15am & 2.15pm, plus June–August 6.15pm; 2hr), from outside the York Art Gallery – just turn up. The tourist office has details of other tours, which start at around £6.

River cruises The best river operator is YorkBoat (☎ 01904 628324, ⓦ yorkboat.co.uk; Feb–Nov; cruises from £10, families £27; 45min–1hr), who run cruises with commentary from King's Staith and Lendal Bridge.

York Pass The York Pass (☎ 01904 550099, ⓦ yorkpass. com) gives free entry to over thirty attractions, not only in the city (eg Barley Hall, Clifford's Tower, Jorvik Dig and Fairfax House) but also elsewhere (Castle Howard and the North York Moors Railway); it costs £38/£50/£65 for one/two/three days respectively, with reductions if you buy it online.

ACCOMMODATION

The main **B&B** concentration is in the side streets off Bootham (immediately west of Exhibition Square), with nothing much more than a 10min walk from the centre.

★ **Bar Convent** 17 Blossom St, YO24 1AQ ☎ 01904 464902, ⓦ bar-convent.org.uk; map p.544. Unique opportunity to stay in a working convent. The grand Georgian building houses a museum and café as well as nine single rooms, twins, doubles and a family room (en-suite a little more expensive), self-catering kitchen and guest lounge. Single **£44**, double **£74**

Bowman's 33 Grosvenor Terrace, YO30 7AG ☎ 01904 622204, ⓦ bowmansguesthouse.co.uk; map p.544. Six spotless rooms in a friendly renovated Victorian terrace B&B off Bootham, within easy reach of the city centre. They provide a permit for free on-street parking. **£80**

The Fort Little Stonegate, YO1 8AX ☎ 01904 639573, ⓦ thefortyork.co.uk; map p.544. An interesting idea –

12

a "boutique hostel" in the city centre, offering rooms and dorms decorated on themes (log cabin, deep-sea creatures) at a knock-down price. Dorms £22, doubles £85

★ **Grand Hotel and Spa** Station Rise, YO1 6GD ☎01904 891949, ⓦthegrandyork.co.uk; map p.544. Splendid five-star hotel and spa a 2min walk from the train station, housed in what was the 1906 headquarters of the North Eastern Railway. Bags of character, with wonderful views of the walls and the minster, luxurious rooms, a fine-dining restaurant and relaxing bar. £180

Hedley House Hotel 3 Bootham Terrace, YO30 7DH ☎01904 637404, ⓦhedleyhouse.com; map p.544. Friendly, comfortable small hotel that is at its best in summer, when the outdoor area with jacuzzi comes into its own. There is a spa and hot-room yoga available on site. Free car parking on first-come, first served basis. £115

Mount Royale The Mount, YO24 1GU ☎01904 628856, ⓦwww.mountroyale.co.uk; map p.544. Lots of antiques, super garden suites (and cheaper rooms), and a heated outdoor pool in summer. Plus a hot tub, sauna and steam room, and a well-regarded restaurant. £125

Rowntree Park Caravan Club Site Terry Ave, YO23 1JQ ☎01904 658997, ⓦcaravanclub.co.uk; map p.544. A wonderful site, the best-located in the city, a 10min walk from the centre, with a back gate that opens onto a street of delis, gastropubs and shops. Open to non-members. Mainly for caravans and motorhomes, but with a small tent enclosure – those with tents must arrive on foot. Advance booking essential, especially at weekends. Motorhome plus two adults £26

Safestay York Micklegate House, 88–90 Micklegate, YO1 6JX ☎01904 627720, ⓦsafestayyork.co.uk; map p.544. In a handsome 1752 building in the centre of the city, with many impressive features. Beds are in dorms (sleeping 4 to 14) and private rooms, all en suite; prices drop during the week and for multi-night stays. Dorms £21, doubles £80

EATING

Ate O Clock 13a High Ousegate, YO1 8RZ ☎01904 644080, ⓦateoclockyork.co.uk; map p.544. The name is dreadful, but the – largely Mediterranean – food is excellent, and there's attentive service and a relaxed atmosphere. Lunch dishes such as risotto come in around £8.50, while main dishes are around £14–20. Music most Fri evenings. Tues–Thurs noon–3.30pm & 5.50–9.30pm, Fri noon–3.30pm & 5.50–10pm, Sat & Sun noon–10pm.

Betty's 6–8 St Helen's Square, YO1 8QP ☎01904 659142, ⓦbettys.co.uk; map p.544. Famous across Yorkshire, *Betty's* specializes in cakes and pastries like granny used to make (or not) – try a hot buttered pikelet (£2.95) or a Yorkshire fat rascal (£4.10) – plus hot dishes and puddings from around £6. No reservations. In the basement there's a mirror with the signatures of the hundreds of Allied airmen who used *Betty's* as an unofficial mess during World War II. Daily 9am–9pm.

Brew & Brownie 5 Museum St, YO1 7DT ☎01904 647420, ⓦbrewandbrownie.co.uk; map p.544. This buzzing café is usually busy with students and thirty-somethings enjoying strong coffee and stupendous home-made cakes. Brunch and light lunches not to be missed either – a stack of American pancakes for £6.25, or the Eeh Bah Gum sharing plate for £15. Yorkshire-sourced produce where possible. Mon–Sat 9am–5pm, Sun 9.30–4pm.

Café Concerto 21 High Petergate, YO1 7EN ☎01904 610478, ⓦcafeconcerto.biz; map p.544. Relaxed, belle epoque-style bistro facing the minster, with sheet-music-papered walls and waiting staff in robust aprons. Food is modern European; there are papers to browse. Daily 9am–9pm.

★ **Café No. 8** 8 Gillygate, YO31 7EQ ☎01904 653074, ⓦcafeno8.co.uk; map p.544. Limited menu using excellent locally sourced produce (Masham sausages, Yorkshire beef and lamb, Ryedale ice cream, beer from Masham) in unpretentious surroundings. Mains cost around £10 during the day, and £14–17 in the evening, or have two courses midweek for £12.50. Its heated garden is a popular spot, and they now have a café in the Art Gallery (see page 546). Mon–Fri noon–10pm, Sat & Sun 9am–10pm.

Rustique 28 Castlegate, YO1 9RP ☎01904 612744, ⓦrustiqueyork.co.uk; map p.544. French-style bistro serving excellent-value Gallic food and wine. There are a couple of set menus (two courses £14.95, three £17.95); a la carte features all the classics, including steak frites, moules marinière and confit de canard. Mon–Sat noon–10pm, Sun noon–9pm.

DRINKING AND NIGHTLIFE

Blue Bell Fossgate, YO1 9TF ☎01904 654904; map p.544. Built in 1798, the *Blue Bell* is a tiny, friendly local with two rooms, oak-panelling and good real ales. When landlord John took over in 2015, he upheld the traditional pub values: no mobile phones or swearing. Mon–Thurs 11am–11pm, Fri & Sat 11am–12.30am, Sun noon–10.30pm.

Fibbers 3 Toft Green, YO1 6JT ☎01904 651250, ⓦfibbers.co.uk; map p.544. York's primary live-music venue, *Fibbers* regularly puts on local and nationally known bands in a lively atmosphere. Hours changeable; check online.

★ **House of Trembling Madness** 48 Stonegate, YO1 8AS ☎ 01904 640009, ⓦ tremblingmadness.co.uk; map p.544. A wonderfully atmospheric attic pub (it's above their shop) with exposed beams and a medieval hall feel. Bar snacks are exceptional and so is the range of craft ales, lagers and ciders. Arrive early to avoid the queue. Mon–Sat 10am–midnight, Sun 11am–midnight.

★ **The Swan** 16 Bishopgate, YO23 1JH ☎ 01904 634968; map p.544. Proper local, a Tetley Heritage Inn that offers convivial surroundings, well-kept real ale and a really friendly atmosphere a few minutes from the city centre. Mon–Wed 4–11pm, Thurs 4–11.30pm, Fri 3pm–midnight, Sat noon–midnight, Sun noon–10.30pm.

Three-Legged Mare 15 High Petergate, YO1 7EN ☎ 01904 638246, ⓦ threeleggedmareyork.co.uk; map p.544. A converted shop provides an airy outlet for York Brewery's own quality beer. No kids, no jukebox, no video games. It's named after a three-legged gallows – it's there on the pub sign, with a replica in the beer garden. Mon–Sat 11am–midnight, Sun 11am–11pm.

ENTERTAINMENT

York has its fair share of theatres and cinemas, and **classical music concerts** and recitals are often held in the city's churches and York Minster. Major annual events include the **Viking Festival** (ⓦ jorvik-viking-festival.co.uk) every Feb and the **Early Music Festival** (ⓦ ncem.co.uk), perhaps the best of its kind in the country, held in July. The city is also famous for its **Mystery Plays** (ⓦ ympst.co.uk), traditionally held every four years – the next are planned for 2018.

The Basement 13–17 Coney St, below City Screen cinema, YO1 9QL ☎ 01904 612940, ⓦ thebasementyork.co.uk. An intimate venue with a variety of nights – from music to comedy to arts events. The first Wed of every month is "Café Scientifique" – a free evening of discussion surrounding current issues in science. Live music events are scattered through the week, along with cabaret, burlesque and club nights. Most nights 8–11pm.

City Screen 13–17 Coney St, YO1 9QL ☎ 0871 902 5726, ⓦ picturehouses.co.uk. The city's independent cinema is the art-house choice, with three screens, a riverside café-bar, and licensed restaurant.

Grand Opera House Cumberland St at Clifford St, YO1 9SW ☎ 0844 871 3024, ⓦ atgtickets.com. Musicals, ballet, pop gigs and family entertainment in all its guises.

The National Centre for Early Music St Margaret's Church, Walmgate, YO1 7TL ☎ 01904 632220, ⓦ ncem. co.uk. Not just early music, but also folk, world and jazz.

Harrogate

HARROGATE – the very picture of genteel Yorkshire respectability – owes its landscaped appearance and early prosperity to the discovery of Tewit Well in 1571. This was the first of more than eighty ferrous and sulphurous **hot springs** that, by the nineteenth century, were to turn the town into one of the country's leading spas. With this in mind, tours of the town should begin with the **Royal Baths**, facing Crescent Road, first opened in 1897 and now restored to their late Victorian finery. You can experience the beautiful Moorish-style interior during a session at the **Turkish Baths and Health Spa** (from £15.50, booking recommended especially at weekends; ☎ 01423 556746, ⓦ turkishbathsharrogate.co.uk).

The Royal Pump Room and around

Pump Room Crown Place, HG1 2RY • Mon–Sat 10.30am–4pm, Sun 2–4pm • £4 • ☎ 01423 556188 • **Mercer Art Gallery** • Tues–Sat 10am–5pm, Sun 2–5pm • Free • ☎ 01423 556188

Just along from the Royal Baths stands the **Royal Pump Room**, built in 1842 over the sulphur well that feeds the baths. Today it houses a small local museum with eclectic exhibits from Victorian bikes to an Egyptian collection. The town's earliest surviving spa building, the old Promenade Room of 1806, is just 100yd from the Pump Room on Swan Road – now housing the **Mercer Art Gallery** and its changing fine art exhibitions. The nearby 17-acre **Valley Gardens** are a delightful place to stretch your legs (entrance just over the zebra crossing).

12

RHS Harlow Carr

Crag Lane, 1.5 miles west of the centre, HG3 1QB • Daily March–Oct 9.30am–6pm, Nov–Feb 9.30am–4pm • £11 • ☎ 01423 565418, ⓦ rhs.org.uk • Bus #X6A (every 20min) or follow the path from Valley Gardens through Pinewoods

The botanical gardens at **Harlow Carr** are the northern showpiece of the Royal Horticultural Society. The woodland and wildflower meadow are a wonderful place to wander, but there are also formal rose gardens, an alpine house and kitchen gardens to explore. Year-round events are hosted, including **Live Music Sundays** in July and August (1–4pm), and **Betty's** (daily 9am–5.30pm) have a branch of their popular tearooms overlooking the grounds.

ARRIVAL AND INFORMATION

By train The station is on Station Parade, on the eastern edge of the town centre. There are regular services from/to Leeds (every 30min; 37min).

By bus The bus station is next to the train station on Station Parade and is served by #36 buses from/to Leeds (every

HARROGATE

15min–1hr; 40min) and Ripon (every 15min–1hr; 32min).

Tourist office In the Royal Baths on Crescent Road (April–Oct Mon–Sat 9am–5.30pm, Sun 10am–1pm; Nov–March Mon–Sat 9.30am–5pm; ☎ 01423 537300, ⓦ visit harrogate.co.uk).

ACCOMMODATION

Acorn Lodge Studley Rd, HG1 5JU ☎ 01423 525630, ⓦ acornlodgeharrogate.co.uk. A guesthouse with big-hotel aspirations (luxury fittings, individual decor, jacuzzi, in-room massages) but B&B friendliness (and tariffs). Well placed for the town centre (a 5min walk). **£94**

The Grafton 1–3 Franklin Mount, HG1 5EJ ☎ 01423 508491, ⓦ graftonhotel.co.uk. Just a 10min walk from town, and close to the International Conference Centre,

the hotel's thirteen stylish rooms all have drape curtains and tasteful decor. The helpful owners will lend you a permit for parking. Price drops £20 Sun–Thurs. **£135**

Studley Swan Rd, HG1 2SE ☎ 01423 560425, ⓦ studleyhotel.co.uk. Mid-sized independent hotel with attached Thai restaurant. The attractive rooms vary in size and cost, and service is good, though the restaurant can get very busy. You can find surprisingly good rates online. **£119**

EATING AND DRINKING

Betty's 1 Parliament St, HG1 2QU ☎ 01423 814070, ⓦ bettys.co.uk. *Betty's* has a uniquely old-fashioned air, with a wrought-iron canopy, large bowed windows, a light airy room and waiting staff in starched linen. While they are known for cakes (from £2.95), speciality teas and coffees, they also offer delicious breakfasts and mains – try the Swiss breakfast rösti (£11.85). No reservations (except for afternoon tea Fri–Sun), so you may have to wait. They have another outlet at RHS Gardens Harlow Carr (see page 550). Daily 9am–9pm.

10 Devonshire Place HG1 4AA ☎ 01423 202356. A bit of a walk east of town, but worth it. An old coaching inn with bags of character, it can get crowded (especially for the brill pub quiz on Sunday night), but always has a fantastic atmosphere. There's a bottle shop tucked away

as you walk in. Mon–Thurs 3pm–midnight, Fri–Sun noon–midnight.

Le D2 Bower Rd, HG1 1BB ☎ 01423 502700, ⓦ led2.co.uk. Quality French food and excellent service in unpretentious surroundings, and at affordable prices – one course for £9.95 at lunch and three courses for £19.95 in the evening (includes a drink). Tues–Thurs noon–2pm & 6pm–late, Fri & Sat noon–2pm & 5.30pm–late.

The Tannin Level 5 Raglan St, HG1 1LE ☎ 01423 560595, ⓦ tanninlevel.co.uk. Popular brasserie, smartly understated, with a Michelin-trained cook and super locally sourced food. Express two courses £13.95, a la carte mains around £15–25. Tues–Fri noon–2pm & 5.30–9pm, Sat noon–2pm & 5.30–9.30pm.

Ripon and around

The attractive market town of **RIPON**, eleven miles north of Harrogate, is centred upon its small **cathedral** (Mon–Sat 8.30am–6pm, Sun noon–5pm; donation requested; ☎ 01765 602072, ⓦ riponcathedral.info), which can trace its ancestry back to its foundation by St Wilfrid in 672; the original crypt below the central tower can still be reached down a stone passage. The town's other focus is its **Market Place**, linked by narrow Kirkgate to the cathedral (market day is Thurs, with a farmers' market on the third Sun of the month). Meanwhile, three restored buildings – prison, courthouse and workhouse (which was expanded in 2017) – show a different side of the local heritage, under the banner of the **Yorkshire Law and Order Museums** (all daily: Workhouse 11am–4pm; Prison & Police and Courthouse 1–4pm; combined ticket £12; ☎01765 690799, ⓦriponmuseums.co.uk). Just four miles away lies **Fountains Abbey**, the one Yorkshire monastic ruin you must see.

Fountains Abbey and Studley Royal Water Garden

4 miles southwest of Ripon off the B6265, HG4 3DY • Feb & March daily 10am–5pm; April–Oct daily 10am–6pm; Oct–Jan Sat–Thurs 10am–5pm; free guided tours of abbey April–Oct daily • £15; NT & EH • ☎ 01765 608888, ⓦfountainsabbey.org.uk • #139 bus from Ripon (Mon, Thurs & Sat 4 daily; 15min)

It's tantalizing to imagine how the English landscape might have appeared had Henry VIII not dissolved the monasteries, and the substantial ruins at **Fountains Abbey** gives a good idea of what might have been. The abbey was founded in 1133 by thirteen dissident Benedictine monks and formally adopted by the Cistercian order two years later. Within a hundred years, Fountains had become the wealthiest Cistercian foundation in England, supporting a magnificent **abbey church**. The almost-intact **Perpendicular Tower**, 180ft high, looms over the whole ensemble, while equally grandiose in scale is the undercroft of the **Lay Brothers' Dormitory** off the cloister, a stunningly vaulted space over 300ft long that was used to store the monastery's annual harvest of fleeces. Its sheer size gives some idea of the abbey's entrepreneurial scope; the estate produced some thirteen tons of wool annually, most of it sold to Venetian and Florentine merchants who toured the monasteries.

Studley Royal Water Garden

A riverside walk, marked from the visitor centre car park, takes you through Fountains Abbey to a series of ponds and ornamental gardens, harbingers of **Studley Royal Water Garden** (same times as the abbey), which can also be entered via the village of Studley Roger, where there's a separate car park. This lush medley of lawns, lake, woodland and **Deer Park** was laid out in 1720 to form a setting for the abbey, and there are some scintillating views from the gardens, though it's the cascades and water gardens that command most attention.

ARRIVAL AND INFORMATION
RIPON AND AROUND

By bus Ripon is served by #36 buses from/to Harrogate (every 10–25min; 35min) and Leeds (every 20–35min; 1hr 30min); the bus station is just off Market Place.

Tourist information Ripon Town Hall, Market Place (April–Oct Mon–Sat 10am–5pm, Sun 10am–1pm; Nov–March Thurs & Sat 10am–4pm; closes daily 1–1.30pm year-round; ☎ 01765 604625, ⓦvisitharrogate.co.uk).

ACCOMMODATION AND EATING

The Old Deanery Minster Rd, HG4 1QS ☎01765 600003, ⓦtheolddeanery.co.uk. Luxurious contemporary hotel opposite the cathedral with eleven charming rooms. The innovative menu (main courses from £15.95) features dishes such as belly of pork or fried stone bass. Mon–Sat noon–2pm & 7–9pm, Sun 12.30–2.30pm. **£125**

The Yorkshire Dales

The **Yorkshire Dales** – "dales" from the Norse word *dalr* (valley) – form a varied upland area of limestone hills and pastoral valleys at the heart of the Pennines. Protected as a National Park (or, in the case of Nidderdale, as an Area of Outstanding Natural Beauty), there are more than twenty main dales covering 680 square miles, crammed with opportunities for outdoor activities. Most approaches are from the south, via the superbly engineered **Settle to Carlisle Railway**, or along the main A65 road from towns such as **Skipton**, **Settle** and **Ingleton**. Southern dales like **Wharfedale** are the most visited, while neighbouring **Malhamdale** is also immensely popular due to the fascinating scenery squeezed into its narrow confines around **Malham** village. **Ribblesdale** is more sombre, its villages popular with hikers intent on tackling the famous **Three Peaks** – the mountains of Pen-y-ghent, Ingleborough and Whernside. To the northwest lies the more remote **Dentdale**, one of the least known but most beautiful of the valleys, and further north still **Wensleydale** and **Swaledale**, the latter of which rivals Dentdale as the most rewarding overall target. Both flow east, with Swaledale's lower stretches encompassing the appealing historic town of **Richmond**.

GETTING AROUND AND INFORMATION
THE YORKSHIRE DALES

On foot The Pennine Way cuts right through the heart of the Dales, and the region is crossed by the Coast-to-Coast Walk, but the principal local route is the 84-mile Dales Way (ⓦdalesway.org.uk). Shorter guided walks (5–13 miles; April–Oct Sun & bank hols; free) are organized by the National Park Authority and Dalesbus Ramblers (ⓦdalesbusramblers.org.uk).

By bike The Dales has a network of over 500 miles of bridleways, byways and other routes for mountain bikers (download routes on ⓦyorkshiredales.org.uk). The main touring cycle route is the circular 130-mile Yorkshire Dales

Cycle Way (ⓦwww.cyclethedales.org.uk), which starts and finishes in Skipton.

By public transport Bus timetables (ⓦdalesbus.org) are available at tourist offices across the region, as are *Dales Explorer* timetable booklets, or consult ⓦwymetro.com.

National Park Centres There are useful National Park Centres (ⓦyorkshiredales.org.uk) at Grassington, Aysgarth Falls, Malham, Reeth and Hawes (April–Oct daily 10am–5pm; Nov–March Sat & Sun 10am–4pm; Hawes is also open weekdays Feb & March, but all sites close in Jan).

Skipton

12

Skipton (Anglo-Saxon for "sheep town") sits on the Dales' southern edge, at the intersection of the two routes that cradle the National Park and Area of Outstanding Natural Beauty – the A65 to the western and the A59/61 to the eastern dales. A pleasant market town with a long history, it is defined by its **castle** and **church**, by its long, wide and sloping **High Street**, and by a **water system** that includes the Leeds and Liverpool Canal, its spur the Springs Canal and the Eller Beck.

ARRIVAL AND INFORMATION
SKIPTON

By train Trains run from/to Leeds (every 30min–2hr; 54min) and Bradford (every 30min; 49min), and there's a daily service to London (every 30min; 3hr 10min with one change). The train is by far the best way of getting to Dentdale/Ribblesdale: Dent (every 2hr; 46min); Settle (every 30min–1hr 25min; 30min–1hr).

By bus Buses run from Skipton up Wharfedale towards

Buckden (every 2hr; 1hr), to Malham (every 2–3hr; 35min) and Settle (every 2hr; around 40–50min). Links to the rest of the Dales are more difficult, and usually involve using trains and/or changing buses.

Tourist office Town Hall, High Street (Mon–Sat 9.30am–4pm; ☎01756 792809).

Useful website ⓦwelcometoskipton.com.

ACCOMMODATION AND EATING

Herriot's Hotel Broughton Rd, BD23 1RT ☎01756 792781, ⓦherriotsforleisure.co.uk. A short walk along the canal towpath from the centre of Skipton, in a Victorian listed building, the boutique-style hotel and its restaurant, *Rhubarb*, both offer cheerful decor and lots of original features. Rooms vary in size and price, and there are frequent packages available. **£125**

The Woolly Sheep Inn 38 Sheep St, BD23 1HY ☎01756

700966, ⓦwoollysheepinn.co.uk. Pleasant town-centre Timothy Taylor tavern which offers a good range of pub food (from £11) along with sandwiches, steaks and pasta dishes. The nine rooms are comfortable and well furnished, though some are small. Convivial, but pub noise can reach some of the rooms at weekends. Mon–Wed 10am–11pm, Thurs 10am–midnight, Fri & Sat 10am–1am, Sun noon–11pm; kitchen Mon–Sat 11.30am–9pm, Sun noon–8pm. **£80**

Ilkley

The small town of **ILKLEY** holds a special place in the iconography of Yorkshire out of all proportion to its size, largely because it's the setting of the county's unofficial anthem, *On Ilkley Moor baht 'at*. Vibrant and stylish, Ilkley has plenty to see, including an interesting church, a **toy museum** (@ilkleytoymuseum.co.uk) and enough top-end shops, bars and restaurants to keep even the visiting urbanites happy.

All Saints Church

Church St, LS29 9DS • Office hours Mon & Thurs 9.30am–2.30pm, Tues 9am–noon • ☎ 01943 816035

Ilkley's parish church, **All Saints**, was established in AD 627 by King Edwin of Northumbria and Bishop Paulinus of York, whose carved heads you can see in the entrance porch. Inside, highlights include three impressive eighth-century Saxon crosses, a family pew dating from 1633 and a Norman font made of Ilkley Moor stone with a seventeenth-century font cover complete with pulley and counterweight for raising and lowering it. Tucked in just behind the church, **Ilkley Manor House** (@manorhouse.ilkley.org) stands on the site of a Roman fort (you can see a section of the original Roman wall at the rear of the building).

Ilkley Moor

A 20min walk from the town centre

Dominating Ilkley's southern skyline is its famous **moor**, somehow smaller yet more forbidding than you might expect. Far from being a remote wilderness, it is very much part of the town's fabric: a place where people can walk, climb or ponder the immensities of time reflected in its ancient rock formations and prehistoric markings. Look out for the Swastika Stone, the Twelve Apostles, the famous Cow and Calf, and a host of cup-and-ring marked rocks. For a bite to eat or a dip in its eighteenth-century open-air plunge pool, you can also visit the **White Wells Spa Cottage Café** on Wells Road (pool open when the flag is flying, usually Sat & Sun 10am–5pm, plus school hols Mon–Fri 2–5pm; ☎01943 608035).

12

ARRIVAL AND INFORMATION   ILKLEY

By train Ilkley station, in Station Plaza in the town centre, is the terminus of a line which links the town to Leeds and Bradford (every 30min; 31min).

By bus The bus station is next to the train station. Destinations Bolton Abbey (Mon, Wed & Sat 3 daily; 17min); Harrogate (every 2hr; 55min), Leeds (every 30min; 1hr); Malham (6 daily; 1hr 10min); Skipton (hourly; 30min).

Tourist office Station Road (April–Sept Mon–Sat 9.30am–4.30pm; Oct–March Mon–Sat 10am–4pm, Tues from 10.30am; ☎01943 602319, @visitilkley.com).

EATING AND DRINKING

Bar t'at Ale and Wine Bar 7 Cunliffe Rd, LS29 9DZ ☎01943 608888, @markettowntaverns.co.uk. With an irresistible name, a huge selection of wines and beers and a good atmosphere, this place also offers a decent range of light lunches, sandwiches and main meals (£9.50–12.50), though service can be slow. Daily noon–11pm; kitchen Mon–Thurs noon–8pm, Fri & Sat noon–9pm, Sun noon–6pm.

The Box Tree 35–37 Church St, LS29 9DR ☎01943 608484, @theboxtree.co.uk. One of Yorkshire's handful of Michelin-starred restaurants, offering inventive modern French cuisine in mellow surroundings. There are fixed-price menus at £37.50 (lunch), £47.50 (dinner), £65 (called a la carte, though it's not) and £80 (gourmand). Wed & Thurs 7–9.30pm, Fri & Sat noon–2pm & 7–9.30pm, Sun noon–3pm.

The Flying Duck 16 Church St, LS29 9DS ☎01943 609587, @wharfedalebrewery.com. Occupying the town's oldest pub building, this real ale pub sports old stone walls, beamed ceilings and stone-flagged and wooden-floored rooms. Also has its own brewery in a barn at the rear. Mon–Thurs & Sun noon–11pm, Fri & Sat noon–12.30am.

Piccolino 31–33 Brook St, LS29 8AE ☎01943 605827, @individualrestaurants.com. Large Italian restaurant in the centre of Ilkley, one of a chain across the country. The star attraction is a roof terrace (with a retractable roof and heaters – this is England after all), which has terrific views across the town. Good food (mains around £16–23) and helpful staff. Mon–Sat 10am–11pm, Sun 10am–10.30pm.

Wharfedale

The River Wharfe runs south from just below Wensleydale, eventually joining the Ouse south of York. The best of **Wharfedale** starts just east of Skipton at **Bolton Abbey**, and then continues north in a broad, pastoral sweep scattered with villages as picture-perfect as any in northern England. The popular walking centre of **Grassington** is the main village.

Bolton Abbey

BOLTON ABBEY, five miles east of Skipton, is the name of a whole village rather than an abbey, a confusion compounded by the fact that the place's main monastic ruin is known as **Bolton Priory** (daily 8am–dusk; free; ☎01756 710238, ⍵boltonpriory.org.uk). The priory is the starting point for several popular riverside **walks**, including a section of the **Dales Way** footpath that follows the river's west bank to take in Bolton Woods and the **Strid** (from "stride"), an extraordinary piece of white water two miles north of the abbey, where softer rock has allowed the river to funnel into a cleft just a few feet wide. Beyond the Strid, the path emerges at **Barden Bridge**, four miles from the priory, where **Barden Tower** shelters The Priests House, a wedding venue which is sometimes open for Sunday lunch (⍵thepriestshouse.com).

ARRIVAL AND INFORMATION   BOLTON ABBEY

By train For a fun excursion, ride the Embsay & Bolton Abbey Steam Railway (late July and Aug five daily; rest of year schedule varies, check website; day rover £11; ☎01756 710614, ⍵embsayboltonabbeyrailway.org.uk). Trains run between Embsay, 1.5 miles east of Skipton, to Bolton Abbey station, around a mile from the abbey ruins – a journey of 15min.

Tourist information The main source of information is the estate office (Bolton Abbey, ☎01756 718009, ⍵boltonabbey.com).

ACCOMMODATION AND EATING

Cavendish Pavilion One mile north of Bolton Abbey along the river, D23 6AN ☎01756 710245, ⍵cavendishpavilion.co.uk. Restaurant and café on the Bolton Abbey estate serving roasts, casseroles and the like at good prices. Daily: March–Oct 10am–5pm; Nov–Feb 10am–4pm.

Grassington

GRASSINGTON is Wharfedale's main village, nine miles northwest of Bolton Abbey. The cobbled Market Square is home to several inns, a few gift shops and, in a converted lead-miner's cottage, a small **Folk Museum** (April–Oct daily 2–4.30pm; free; ☎01756 753287, ⍵grassingtonfolkmuseum.org.uk), which is filled with domestic equipment and artefacts relating to local crafts and farming.

ARRIVAL AND INFORMATION   GRASSINGTON

By bus #72/72R buses to Grassington run roughly hourly (X43 on Sun and bank hols) from Skipton (33min) and then, six times a day, on up the B6160 to Kettlewell, Starbotton and Buckden in upper Wharfedale.

National Park Centre Hebden Road, across from the bus stop (April–Oct daily 10am–5pm; for winter hours, check with the centre; ☎01756 751690, ⍵yorkshiredales.org.uk).

ACCOMMODATION AND EATING

★ **Angel Inn** Hetton, 4 miles southwest of Grassington, BD23 6LT ☎01756 730263, ⍵angelhetton.co.uk. The Dales' gastropub par excellence has nine immaculate rooms and suites that are either in the charming cottage next door to the inn, or just over the road in a converted barn. Main courses from £17.95. Kitchen Mon–Thurs noon–2.15pm & 6–8.30pm, Fri & Sat noon–2.15pm & 6–9.30pm, Sun noon–2.30pm & 6–8.30pm. **£150**

Grassington Lodge 8 Wood Lane, BD23 5LU ☎01756 752518, ⍵grassingtonlodge.co.uk. A splash of contemporary style – coordinated fabrics, hardwood floors, Dales photographs – together with a pleasant front terrace enhances this comfortable village guesthouse. **£90**

Upper Wharfedale

KETTLEWELL (a Norse/Old English compound name for "bubbling spring") is the main centre for **Upper Wharfedale**, and it has plenty of local B&B accommodation plus a youth hostel. It was also one of the major locations for *Calendar Girls*, the 2003 based-on-a-true-story film of doughty Yorkshire ladies who bared all for a charity calendar.

ARRIVAL AND DEPARTURE

UPPER WHARFEDALE

By bus There's a Sun and bank hol bus service (#800) from Leeds to Hawes, connecting the top end of Wharfedale with Wensleydale, via Ilkley, Grassington and Kettlewell, among other stops. It takes 3hr 10min for the whole trip, and 1hr 5min from Kettlewell to Hawes.

ACCOMMODATION AND EATING

Blue Bell Inn Kettlewell, BD23 5DX ☎01756 760230, ⓦbluebellkettlewell.co.uk. Pretty seventeenth-century coaching inn that's very much a traditional pub and serves good, no-nonsense pub grub (lasagne, steak and ale pie and the like; main courses £10–15). Daily specials are a cut above the usual fare. Daily noon–11pm; kitchen Mon–Fri noon–2.30pm & 5–8pm, Sat noon–9pm, Sun noon–8pm. **£85**

Racehorses Hotel Kettlewell, BD23 5QZ ☎01756 760233, ⓦracehorseshotel.co.uk. Comfortable, refurbished hotel in what was once the *Blue Bell Inn*'s stables. The food is a cut above your standard bar food (home-made paté, for example, or rare-breed belly pork); main courses start at £11. Daily noon–2pm & 6–9pm. **£90**

Malhamdale

A few miles west of Wharfedale lies **Malhamdale**, one of the National Park's most heavily visited regions, thanks to its three outstanding natural features of **Malham Cove**, **Malham Tarn** and **Gordale Scar**. All three attractions are within easy hiking distance of **Malham village**.

12

Malham

MALHAM village is home to barely a couple of hundred people who inhabit the huddled stone houses on either side of a bubbling river. Appearing in spectacular fashion a mile to the north, the white-walled limestone amphitheatre of **Malham Cove** rises 300ft above its surroundings. After a breath-sapping haul to the top, you are rewarded with fine views and the famous limestone pavement, an expanse of clints (slabs) and grykes (clefts) created by water seeping through weaker lines in the limestone rock. A simple walk (or summer shuttle-bus ride) over the moors abruptly brings **Malham Tarn** into sight, its waterfowl protected by a nature reserve on the west bank. Meanwhile, at **Gordale Scar** (also easily approached direct from Malham village), the cliffs are if anything more spectacular than at Malham Cove. The classic circuit takes in cove, tarn and scar in a clockwise **walk from Malham** (8 miles; 3hr 30min).

ARRIVAL AND INFORMATION

MALHAMDALE

By bus Malham village is served year-round by bus services from Skipton (3 daily; 35min) and the seasonal Malham Tarn shuttle (Easter–Oct Sun & bank hols 3 daily; 25min) which runs between Settle and the National Park Centre.

National Park Centre At the southern edge of the village (April–Oct daily 10am–5pm; for winter hours, check with centre; ☎01729 833200, ⓦyorkshiredales.org.uk).
Website A good online source of tourist information is ⓦmalhamdale.com.

ACCOMMODATION AND EATING

★**Buck Inn** Cove Road, BD23 4DA ☎01729 830317, ⓦthebuckmalham.co.uk. Pleasant pub that's popular with walkers. Given the good, locally sourced food – especially sausages, pies and steaks (main courses £10–22) – eleven comfortable rooms, and a relaxed attitude to muddy boots, this is the ideal base for a walking holiday. Daily noon–9pm. **£95**
Miresfield Farm Across the river from the Buck Inn and Lister Arms, BD23 4DA ☎01729 830414,

THE SETTLE TO CARLISLE RAILWAY

The 72-mile **Settle to Carlisle** line – hailed by some as "England's most scenic railway" – is a feat of Victorian railway engineering that has few equals in Britain. In particular, between Horton and Ribblehead, the line climbs 200ft in five miles, before crossing the famous 24-arched **Ribblehead viaduct** and disappearing into the 2629yd Blea Moor Tunnel. Meanwhile, the station at **Dent Head** is the highest, bleakest mainline station in England. The journey through the Yorkshire Dales and Eden Valley from Settle to Carlisle takes 1hr 40min, so it's easy to do the full **return trip** in one day (£20.90). If you're short of time, ride the most dramatic section between Settle and Garsdale (30min). There are connections to Settle from Skipton (20min) and Leeds (1hr); full **timetable** details are available from ⓦ settle-carlisle.co.uk.

ⓦ malhamdale.com/miresfield.htm. The first house in the village, by the river, with lovely rural views. The country-pine-bedecked rooms vary in size, and there's a small campsite with toilet and shower. Breakfast available. **£64**

YHA Malham Centre of village, next to the Lister Arms pub, BD23 4DB ☎ 0845 371 9529, ⓦ yha.org.uk/hostel/malham. A purpose-built and newly renovated hostel that's a good bet for families and serious walkers. Open all year with midweek prices often slashed by half. Check-in 5–10.30pm. Dorms **£30**, doubles **£69**

Ribblesdale

The river Ribble runs south along the western edges of the Yorkshire Dales, starting in the bleak uplands near the Ribblehead Viaduct, flowing between two of Yorkshire's highest mountains, **Ingleborough** and **Pen-y-ghent**, and through the village of **Horton in Ribblesdale** and on to **Settle**, the upper dale's principal town.

Settle

West of Malhamdale, Ribblesdale is entered from **SETTLE**, starting point of the **Settle to Carlisle Railway** (see page 558). The small town has a typical seventeenth-century market square (market day Tues), still sporting its split-level arcaded shambles, and the **Museum of North Craven Life** (April–Oct Tues 10.30am–4.30pm & Thurs–Sun 12.30–4.30pm; £2.50; ☎ 01524 251388), which contains odds and ends from the history of the town and of the construction of the railway. The museum is housed in the eccentric Folly, dating from the 1670s and earning its name from the strange combination of styles, and the curiously upside-down look created by the fact that there are far more windows on the ground floor than on the first and second – it seems surprising that it hasn't fallen down.

ARRIVAL AND INFORMATION

SETTLE

By train The train station, less than a 5min walk from Market Place, down Station Road, is served by the famous Settle to Carlisle railway (see page 558).

By bus #580 buses connect Settle with Skipton (Mon–Sat; every 2hr; 40min); #11 buses go north to Horton-in-Ribblesdale (Mon–Sat every 2hr; 21min); while #581 (every 2hr; 31min) runs to the western Dales. The Malham

Tarn shuttle (Dalesbus #881; Easter–Oct Sun & bank hols 3 daily) makes a stop at Settle en route to Malham (25min) and Ingleton (25min).

Tourist information In the town hall, just off Market Place (Mon, Tues, Thurs–Sat 9.30am–4pm, Wed & Sun 9.30am–1pm; closed Sun in winter; ☎ 01729 825192). They can provide hiking maps and pamphlets.

ACCOMMODATION AND EATING

The Lion Duke St, BD24 9DU ☎ 01729 822203, ⓦ thelionsettle.co.uk. The ground-floor inn offers a fantastic range of locally sourced fish, meats, cheese, pies and sausages (mains £10.50–21), and guest rooms are comfortable and contemporary. Mon–Thurs & Sun 8am–9pm, Fri & Sat 8am–10.30pm. **£95**

Ye Olde Naked Man Café Market Place, BD24 9ED ☎ 01729 823230. For non-alcoholic drinks and traditional hot food, cakes and scones, this unfussy tearoom is your best bet. They also have a takeaway sandwich bar and shop selling local produce. Daily 9am–5pm.

Horton in Ribblesdale

The valley's only village of any size is **HORTON IN RIBBLESDALE**, a noted walking centre which is the usual starting point for the famous **Three Peaks Walk**: namely a 25-mile, 12-hour circuit of Pen-y-ghent (2273ft), Whernside (2416ft) – Yorkshire's highest point – and Ingleborough (2373ft).

ARRIVAL AND INFORMATION

HORTON IN RIBBLESDALE

By bus The #11 service from Settle runs every 2hr (20min).

Tourist and hiking information The *Pen-y-ghent Café* (see below; ☎01729 860333) doubles as a tourist office and unofficial headquarters for the Three Peaks walk. They operate a clocking-in/clocking-out system; walkers who complete the route within a 12hr period become eligible

to join the Three Peaks of Yorkshire Club. Note that they do not provide automatic back-up should walkers fail to return, though can make arrangements for this if notified at least a day in advance. Opening hours are complicated, so phone to check.

EATING

Pen-y-ghent Café BD24 0HE ☎01729 860333. A local institution for more than forty years, not only supplying much-needed hot drinks, snacks and meals, but also information and advice to walkers. Phone in advance to

confirm hours. Roughly Feb half term to mid-Oct Mon & Wed–Sun 9am–5.30pm (Sat & Sun 8am in summer); Jan & Feb hours vary.

The western Dales

The **western Dales** is a term of convenience for a couple of tiny dales running north from **Ingleton**, and for **Dentdale**, one of the loveliest valleys in the National Park. Ingleton has the most accommodation, but **Dent** is by far the best target for a quiet night's retreat, with a cobbled centre barely altered in centuries.

12

Ingleton and around

The straggling slate-grey village of **INGLETON** sits upon a ridge at the confluence of two streams, the Twiss and the Doe, whose beautifully wooded valleys are easily the area's best features. The 4.5-mile **Waterfalls Trail** (daily Nov–March 9am–2.30pm, April–Aug 9am–7pm, Sept & Oct 9am–4pm; £6; ☎01524 241930, ⓦingletonwaterfallstrail. co.uk) is a lovely circular walk (2hr 30min) taking in both valleys, and providing viewing points over its waterfalls.

Just 1.5 miles out of Ingleton on the Ribblehead/Hawes road (B6255) is the entrance to the **White Scar Cave** (tours 10am–5pm: Feb–Oct daily, Nov–Jan weather permitting Sat & Sun; 1hr 20min; £9.95; ☎01524 241244, ⓦwhitescarcave.co.uk). It's worth every penny for the tour of dank underground chambers, contorted cave formations and glistening stalactites.

ARRIVAL AND INFORMATION

INGLETON AND AROUND

By bus Buses stop at the tourist office: the #80 runs from/ to Lancaster (every 30min; 1hr 10min) and the #581 and #881 from/to Settle (every 30min; 25min).

Tourist office Community Centre car park, Main St (daily:

Easter–Sept 10am–4.30pm; Nov–March 11am–3pm; ☎01524 241049).

Website ⓦvisitingleton.co.uk.

ACCOMMODATION AND EATING

The Inglesport Café Main St, LA6 3EB ☎01524 241146. On the first floor of a hiking supplies store, this café dishes up hearty breakfasts, soups, and potatoes with everything. Mon–Fri 9am–5pm, Sat & Sun 9am–5.30pm.

Riverside Lodge 24 Main St, LA6 3HJ ☎01524 241359, ⓦriversideingleton.co.uk. Clean and tidy, with eight bedrooms decorated individually (if a little fussily) and

named after flowers. There's a small sauna and play room, and an optional evening meal at £15. **£70**

YHA Ingleton Sammy Lane, LA6 3EG ☎015242 41444, ⓦyha.org.uk/hostel/ingleton. This YHA hostel is in an attractively restored Victorian stone house, set in its own gardens, close to the village centre. Reception 7–10am & 5–11pm. Dorms **£24**, doubles **£52**

Dentdale

In the seventeenth and eighteenth centuries, **Dentdale** supported a flourishing hand-knitting industry, later ruined by mechanization. These days, the hill-farming community supplements its income through tourism and craft ventures, and in **DENT** village itself the main road soon gives way to grassy cobbles.

ARRIVAL AND INFORMATION   DENTDALE

By train While the famous Settle to Carlisle railway (see page 558) might seem a good alternative to the bus, be warned that Dent station is over 4 miles from the village itself.

By bus Most of Dent's bus connections are with towns outside Yorkshire – Sedbergh (April–Oct 5 daily; 15min),

Kirkby Stephen and Kendal (Sat 1 daily; 50min) – though there is a service to Settle.

Tourist information Dentdale Heritage Centre, Dent (daily 11am–4pm; ☎ 01539 625800, ⓦ museumsinthe yorkshiredales.co.uk).

Website ⓦ dentdale.com.

ACCOMMODATION AND EATING

★ **George & Dragon** Dent, LA10 5QL ☎ 01539 625256, ⓦ thegeorgeanddragondent.co.uk. Opposite the fountain in the centre of the village, the *George & Dragon* is bigger and more expensive than the nearby *Sun*, with ten comfortable rooms (though some are small and all are a little tired),

good service and a convivial bar. There's an extensive menu of traditional pub food with a twist (try, for example, the terrine of Cumberland sausage and black pudding) – mains cost between £8.50 and £16.50. Daily 11am–11pm; kitchen daily noon–2pm & 6–8.30pm. **£80**

Wensleydale

The best known of the Dales, if only for its cheese, **Wensleydale** is also the largest. With numerous towns and villages, the biggest and busiest being **Hawes**, it has plenty of appeal to non-walkers, too; many of its rural attractions will be familiar to devotees of the **James Herriott** books and TV series.

Hawes

HAWES is Wensleydale's chief town, main hiking centre, and home to its tourism, cheese and rope-making industries. It also claims to be Yorkshire's highest market town; it received its market charter in 1699, and the weekly Tuesday market is still going strong. In the same building as the National Park Centre (see page 561), the recently revamped **Dales Countryside Museum** (April–Oct daily 10am–5pm; closed Jan; for winter hours phone ahead; £4.80; ☎ 01969 666210, ⓦ www.dalescountrysidemuseum. org.uk) focuses on local trades and handicrafts.

You'll find another attraction a 15min-walk south of the town centre; the **Wensleydale Creamery** on Gayle Lane has a café and restaurant, and of course a cheese shop – you only pay to enter the adjacent museum and cheese-making viewing gallery (daily 10am–4pm; £2.95; ☎ 01969 667664, ⓦ wensleydale.co.uk). The first cheese in Wensleydale was made by medieval Cistercian monks from ewes' milk; after the Dissolution local farmers made a version from cows' milk which, by the 1840s, was being marketed as "Wensleydale" cheese.

Askrigg

The mantle of "Herriot country" lies heavy on **ASKRIGG**, six miles east of Hawes, as the TV series *All Creatures Great and Small* was filmed in and around the village. Nip into the *King's Arms* on Main Street, where you can see stills from the programme.

Aysgarth

The ribbon-village of **AYSGARTH**, straggling along and off the A684, sucks in Wensleydale's largest number of visitors due to its proximity to the **Aysgarth Falls**, half a mile below. A marked nature trail runs through the surrounding woodlands and there's a big car park and excellent **National Park Centre** on the north bank of the River Ure (see page 561).

HERE FOR THE BEER

If you're a beer fan, the handsome Wensleydale market town of **Masham** (pronounced Mass'm) is an essential point of pilgrimage. At **Theakston brewery** (tours daily 11am–3pm; £7.75, reservations advised; ☎01765 680000, ⊛theakstons.co.uk), sited here since 1827, you can learn the arcane intricacies of the brewer's art and become familiar with the legendary Old Peculier ale. The **Black Sheep Brewery**, set up in the early 1990s by one of the Theakston family brewing team, also offers tours (four daily, evening tours Thurs & Fri, but call for availability; £9.50; ☎01765 680101, ⊛blacksheepbrewery.com). Both are just a few minutes' signposted walk out of the centre.

Bolton Castle

Castle Bolton village, DL8 4ET • Feb–March daily 10am–4pm; April–Oct 10am–5pm (restricted winter opening, call for details) • £8.50, gardens only £4 • ☎01969 623981, ⊛boltoncastle.co.uk

The foursquare battlements of **Bolton Castle** are visible from miles away. Completed in 1399, its Great Chamber, a few adjacent rooms and the castle gardens have been restored, and there's also a café that's a welcome spot if you've hiked here – a superb circular **walk** (6 miles; 4hr) heads northeast from Aysgarth via Castle Bolton village, starting at Aysgarth Falls and climbing up through Thoresby.

ARRIVAL AND GETTING AROUND   WENSLEYDALE

By bus The #156 route runs along Wensleydale from Leyburn to Hawes (every 2hr; 50 min), calling at Aysgarth and Bolton Castle. Less frequently, the #59 runs once a day along a similar route (1 daily; 47min). The Little White Bus runs from Hawes to Garsdale (2–4 daily; 23min). A post-bus service runs between Hawes and Northallerton (Mon–Fri 3 daily; 1hr 45min). There's also a summer Sun and bank holiday service (#800) connecting Hawes to Leeds (3hr).

INFORMATION

Tourist information There are National Park Centres at Hawes Dales Countryside Museum, Station Yard (daily 10am–5pm; closed Jan, for winter hours, check with centre; ☎01969 666210; ⊛yorkshiredales.org.uk) and at Aysgarth, by the river (April–Oct daily 10am–5pm; for winter hours check with centre; ☎01969 662910). **Useful website** ⊛wensleydale.org.

ACCOMMODATION AND EATING

Herriot's Main St, Hawes, DL8 3QW ☎01969 667536, ⊛herriotsinhawes.co.uk. Small, friendly guesthouse in an eighteenth-century building off the market square. There are just six rooms – some of which have fell views. Good hearty breakfasts are cooked to order. **£80**

Herriot's Kitchen Main St, Hawes, DL8 3QW ☎01969 667536, ⊛herriotsinhawes.co.uk. Light lunches, Yorkshire cream teas and cakes, plus preserves made on the premises. Mon, Tues & Fri–Sun 11am–3pm.

The Old Dairy Farm Widdale, 3 miles west of Hawes, DL8 3LX ☎01969 667070, ⊛olddairyfarm.co.uk. Once the home of the original Wensleydale dairy herd, this farm offers luxurious and contemporary accommodation, with fine dining available (main courses around £15). While nonresidents are welcome to dine, there are no fixed opening hours – it is essential to phone first. **£140**

Swaledale

Narrow and steep-sided in its upper reaches beyond the tiny village of Keld, **Swaledale** emerges rocky and rugged in its central tract around Thwaite and Muker before more typically pastoral scenery cuts in at **REETH**, the dale's main village and market centre (market day is Fri). Its desirable cottages sit around a triangular green, where you'll find a couple of pubs, a hotel, a **National Park Centre** (see page 563) and the **Swaledale Museum** (May–Oct daily 10am–5pm; £3; ☎01748 884118, ⊛swaledalemuseum.org), containing an interesting hotchpotch of material on the geology, industry, domestic life and people of the valley. Downriver, the dale opens out into broad countryside and the splendid historic town of **Richmond**.

Richmond

RICHMOND is home to the Dales' single most tempting destination, a magnificent **castle**, whose extensive walls and colossal keep cling to a precipice above the River Swale. Indeed, the entire town is an absolute gem, centred on a huge cobbled market square backed by Georgian buildings, hidden alleys and gardens. Market day is Saturday, augmented by a farmers' market on the third Saturday of the month.

Richmond Castle

Riverside Rd, DL10 4QW • April–Sept daily 10am–6pm; Oct daily 10am–5pm; Nov–March Sat & Sun 10am–4pm • £5.70; EH • ☎ 01748 822493, ⓦ www.english-heritage.org.uk/visit/places/richmond-castle

Most of medieval Richmond sprouted around its **castle**, which, dating from around 1071, is one of the oldest Norman stone fortresses in Britain. The star turn is, without doubt, the massive **keep** – which was built between 1150 and 1180 – with its stone staircases, spacious main rooms and fine battlements. From the top, the **views** down into the town, across the turbulent Swale and out across the gentle countryside, are out of this world. For more splendid views, with the river roaring below, take a stroll along Castle Walk, around the outside of the curtain walls.

Green Howards Museum

Trinity Church Square, DL10 4QN • Mon–Sat 10am–4.30pm (plus Sun July & Aug) • £4.50 • ☎ 01748 825561, ⓦ greenhowards.org.uk

Fully revamped in 2014, this regimental collection of 35,000 objects (not all on display) has some fascinating items including a key to Hitler's office and the first poppy to be laid on The Cenotaph in London. By focusing on the real-life stories, the **Green Howards Museum** avoids being just for those with a specialist interest; ask staff about the painting of Henry Tandey that Hitler used for propaganda, or the first footballer to be awarded the Victoria Cross.

Richmondshire Museum

Ryder's Wynd, off the Victoria Rd roundabout at the top of King St, DL10 4JA • April–Oct Mon–Sat 10.30am–4.30pm • £3.50 • ☎ 01748 825611, ⓦ richmondshiremuseum.org.uk

For a fascinating chunk of Richmond history, visit the charming **Richmondshire Museum**, off the northern side of the market square. It's full of local treasures, covering subjects as varied as lead mining and toys through the ages, with reconstructed houses and shops re-creating village life, and even the set from the TV series *All Creatures Great and Small*.

Theatre Royal

Victoria Rd, DL10 4DW • Tours on the hour mid-Feb to mid-Nov Mon–Sat 10am–4pm; £5 • ☎ 01748 825252, ⓦ georgiantheatreroyal.co.uk

Richmond's tiny Georgian **Theatre Royal** (1788) has the diminutive feel of a toy theatre made from a shoe box. One of England's oldest theatres, it features a sunken pit with boxes on three sides and a gallery above; it is open for both performances and tours.

Easby Abbey

1 mile southeast of town, DL10 7EU • April–Sept daily 10am–6pm; Oct daily 10am–5pm; Nov–March daily 10am–4pm • Free; EH • ⓦ www.english-heritage.org.uk/visit/places/easby-abbey

A signposted walk runs along the north bank of the River Swale out to the golden stone walls of **Easby Abbey**. The evocative ruins are extensive, and in places – notably the thirteenth-century refectory – still remarkably intact.

ARRIVAL AND INFORMATION SWALEDALE

By train There are regular services into Wensleydale and lower Swaledale on the heritage Wensleydale Railway from Leeming to Redmire, and to Darlington, 10 miles to the northeast, on the main east-coast train line.

By bus The main transport hub is Richmond, where buses stop in the market square. Bus #159 runs between Masham, Leyburn and Richmond, while bus #30 runs up the valley along the B6270 as far as Keld, 8 miles north of

Hawes and at the crossroads of the Pennine Way and the Coast-to-Coast path.

Destinations from Richmond Keld (Mon–Sat 4 daily; 1hr); Leyburn (hourly; 25 min); Masham (Mon–Sat hourly; 55min); Ripon (Mon–Sat hourly; 1hr 15min).

Tourist office Richmond Library, Queens Rd (Mon & Thurs 10am–6pm, Tues & Fri 10am–5pm, Wed 10am–noon, Sat 10am–1pm; ☎01609 532980, ⓦrichmond.org).

National Park Centre Hudson House, Reeth (April–Oct daily 10am–5pm; Nov, Dec, Feb & March Sat & Sun 10am–4pm; ☎01748 884059, ⓦhudsonhouse.org).

ACCOMMODATION AND EATING

Frenchgate Hotel 59–61 Frenchgate, Richmond, DL10 7AE ☎01748 822087, ⓦthefrenchgate.co.uk. Georgian townhouse hotel with eight rooms and walled gardens. Its food (set menu £39) has an excellent reputation – spiced loin of Yorkshire rabbit, for example, & Reg's duck breast. Mon–Fri 7.30–9.30am, noon–2pm & 6–9.30pm, Sat & Sun 8–10am, noon–2pm & 6–9.30pm. **£118**

Frenchgate House 66 Frenchgate, Richmond, DL10 7AG ☎01748 823421, ⓦ66frenchgate.co.uk. Eight immaculately presented rooms, plus breakfast with the best – panoramic – view in town. **£95**

King's Arms High Row, Reeth, DL11 6SY ☎01748 884259, ⓦthekingsarms.com. Attractive eighteenth-century inn on the green, offering a range of meals and snacks using locally sourced food, and rooms – all of which are en suite. Daily 11am–11pm; kitchen daily noon–2.30pm & 6–9pm. **£70**

★**Millgate House** Millgate, Richmond, DL10 4JN ☎01748 823571, ⓦmillgatehouse.com. Shut the big green door of this Georgian house and enter a world of books, antiques, embroidered sheets, handmade toiletries, scrumptious breakfasts and the finest (and least precious) hosts you could wish for. No credit cards. **£125**

Rustique Finkle St, Richmond, DL10 4QB ☎01748 821565, ⓦrustiqueyork.co.uk. The clue to *Rustique's* ambience lies in its name – it concentrates on rural French food and wine in a bistro setting. The atmosphere is busy and cheerful, and the food's lovely, and very reasonably priced (two courses £14.95, three for £17.95). Daily noon–9pm.

Whashton Springs Near Whashton, DL11 7JS, 3 miles north of Richmond on Ravensworth Rd ☎01748 822884, ⓦwhashtonsprings.co.uk. This working Dales farm offers a peaceful night in the country in rooms (in the main house or round the courtyard) filled with family furniture. **£80**

12

Haworth

Of English literary shrines, probably only Stratford sees more visitors than the quarter of a million who swarm annually into the village of **HAWORTH**, eight miles north of Bradford, to tramp the cobbles once trodden by the Brontë sisters. In summer the village's steep Main Street is lost under huge crowds, herded by multilingual signs around the various stations on the **Brontë trail**. The most popular local walk runs to **Brontë Falls** and **Bridge**, reached via West Lane (a continuation of Main St) and a track from the village, signposted "Bronte Falls"; and to **Top Withens**, a mile beyond, a ruin fancifully (and erroneously) thought to be the model for the manor, Wuthering Heights (allow 3hr for the round trip). The moorland setting beautifully evokes the flavour of the book, and to enjoy it further you could walk on another two and a half miles to **Ponden Hall**, claimed by some to be Thrushcross Grange in *Wuthering Heights*.

Brontë Parsonage Museum

Church St, BD22 8DR • Daily: April–Oct 10am–5.30pm; Nov–March 10am–5pm • £8.50 • ☎01535 642323, ⓦbronte.org.uk

Behind the parish church is the **Brontë Parsonage Museum**, a modest Georgian house bought by Patrick Brontë in 1820 and in which he planned to bring up his family. After the tragic early loss of his wife and two eldest daughters, the surviving four children – Anne, Emily, Charlotte and their dissipated brother, Branwell – spent most of their short lives in the place, which is furnished as it was in their day, filled with the sisters' pictures, books, manuscripts and personal treasures. Between 2016 and 2020, Brontë200 celebrates the bicentenary of the births of these four, and special events are taking place here and across the globe (see website for details). The **parish church** in front of the parsonage contains the family vault; Charlotte was married here in 1854.

ARRIVAL AND INFORMATION

HAWORTH

By train The nicest way of getting to Haworth is on the steam trains of the Keighley and Worth Valley Railway (Easter week, school hols, June, July & Aug daily; rest of the year Sat & Sun; day rover ticket £16; ☎ 01535 645214, ⓦ kwvr.co.uk); regular trains from Leeds or from Bradford's Forster Square station run to Keighley, from where the steam train takes 18min to Haworth.

By bus Bus #662 from Bradford Interchange runs to Keighley (every 10–30min; 50min); change there for the #663, #664 (not Sun) or #665 (every 20–30min; 16–24min).
Tourist office 2–4 West Lane (daily: April–Sept 10am–5pm; Oct–March Mon, Tues, Thurs–Sun 10am–4pm, Wed 10.30am–4pm; ☎ 01535 642329, ⓦ haworth-village.org.uk).

ACCOMMODATION

Apothecary 86 Main St, BD22 8DP ☎ 01535 643642, ⓦ theapothecaryguesthouse.co.uk. Traditional guesthouse opposite the church, in a seventeenth-century building with oak beams, millstone grit walls and quaint passages. The rear rooms, breakfast room and attached café have moorland views. **£60**
Wilsons of Haworth 15 West Lane, BD22 8DU ☎ 01535 643209, ⓦ wilsonsofhaworth.co.uk. Top-end B&B with all the bells and whistles you might expect in a quality

boutique hotel; its five luxurious rooms (four doubles and a single), are in a converted row of weavers' cottages within sight of the Brontë Parsonage Museum. **£79**
YHA Haworth Longlands Hall, Lees Lane, BD22 8RT, a mile from Haworth ☎ 0845 371 9520, ⓦ yha.org.uk/hostel/haworth. YHA hostel – a little in need of a refurb – overlooking the village; Bradford buses stop on the main road nearby. Only open to groups Mon–Fri Nov to mid-Feb. Dorms **£13**, doubles **£39**

Bradford and around

12

BRADFORD has always been a working town, booming in tandem with the Industrial Revolution, when just a few decades saw it transform from a rural seat of woollen manufacture to a polluted metropolis. In its Victorian heyday it was the world's biggest producer of worsted cloth, its skyline etched black with mill chimneys, and its hills clogged with some of the foulest back-to-back houses of any northern city. A look at the Venetian-Gothic **Wool Exchange** building on Market Street, or a walk through **Little Germany**, northeast of the city centre (named for the German wool merchants who populated the area in the second half of the 1800s) provides ample evidence of the wealth of nineteenth-century Bradford.

Contemporary Bradford, perhaps the most multicultural centre in the UK outside London, is valiantly rinsing away its associations with urban decrepitude, and while it can hardly yet be compared with neighbouring Leeds as a visitor attraction, it has two must-see attractions in the **National Science and Media Museum** and the industrial heritage site of **Saltaire**. The major annual event is the **Bradford Festival** (ⓦ bradfordfestival.org.uk), a three-day multicultural celebration of art, music, theatre and dance, held in late July.

National Science and Media Museum

Little Horton Ln, BD1 1NQ • Daily 10am–6pm • Free, screenings £9 • ☎ 0844 856 3797, ⓦ scienceandmediamuseum.org.uk

The main interest in the centre of Bradford is provided by the superb **National Science and Media Museum**, which wraps itself around one of Britain's largest cinema screens showing daily **IMAX** and 3D film screenings. Exhibitions are devoted to every nuance of film and television, including topics like digital imaging, light and optics, and computer animation, with fascinating detours into the mechanics of advertising and news-gathering.

Saltaire

4 miles northwest of Bradford towards Keighley, BD17 7EF • 1853 Gallery Mon–Fri 10am–5.30pm, Sat & Sun 10am–6pm • Free • ☎ 01274 531163, ⓦ saltmill.org.uk • Trains run from Bradford Forster Square, or take bus #678 from the Interchange

The city's extraordinary outlying attraction of **Saltaire** was a model industrial village built by the industrialist Sir Titus Salt. Still inhabited today, the village was constructed between 1851 and 1876, and centred on **Salt's Mill**, which, larger than London's St Paul's Cathedral, was the biggest factory in the world when it opened in 1853. The mill was surrounded by schools, hospitals, parks, almshouses and some 850 homes, yet for all Salt's philanthropic vigour the scheme was highly paternalistic: of the village's 22 streets, for example, all – bar Victoria and Albert streets – were named after members of his family, and although Salt's workers and their families benefited from far better living conditions than their contemporaries elsewhere, they certainly were expected to toe the management line. Salt's Mill remains the fulcrum of the village, the focus of which is the **1853 Gallery**, three floors given over to the world's largest retrospective collection of the works of Bradford-born **David Hockney**.

ARRIVAL AND DEPARTURE   BRADFORD AND AROUND

By train Bradford has two train stations: Bradford Forster Square, just north of the city centre, offers routes to suburbs, towns and cities to the north and west of the city, while Bradford Interchange, off Bridge St, south of the city centre, serves destinations broadly south and west of the city.
Destinations from Bradford Forster Square Ilkley (every 30min; 31min); Keighley (every 30min; 20min); Leeds (every 30min; 22min); Skipton (every 30min; 39min).
Destinations from Bradford Interchange Halifax (every 15min; 12min); Leeds (every 15min; 23min); Manchester

(every 30min; 1hr); Todmorden (every 30min; 35min).
By bus Bradford Interchange is the departure point for regional buses to the rest of West Yorkshire; as well as National Express coaches for long-distance services (travel centre Mon, Wed, Thurs & Fri 8.30am–5.30pm, Tues 9am–5.30pm, Sat 9am–4.30pm; ☏ 0113 245 7676).
Destinations Leeds (every 30min; 30–45min); Liverpool (every 30min–2hr; 3–4hr); London (every 25–90min; 5–6hr); Manchester (every 10min–2hr; 1–2hr).

GETTING AROUND AND INFORMATION

By bus Bradford's handy free citybus service (Mon–Fri 7am–7pm, every 10min) links the Interchange with Forster Square, Kirkgate, Centenary Square, the National Media Museum, the University and the West End (☏ 0113 245

7676, ⓦ wymetro.com).
Tourist office Britannia House, Broadway (April–Sept Mon–Sat 10am–5pm, Oct–March Mon 10.30am–4pm, Tues–Sat 10am–4pm; ☏ 01274 433678, ⓦ visitbradford.com).

12

EATING AND DRINKING

With nearly a quarter of its population having roots in south Asia, Bradford is renowned for its hundreds of **Indian restaurants**, and in 2016 was crowned "Curry Capital of Britain" for the sixth year in a row. Meanwhile, a burgeoning craft beer scene has seen an explosion of independent brew pubs opening along Westgate and North Parade.

Akbar's 1276 Leeds Rd, BD3 8LF ☏ 01274 773311, ⓦ akbars.co.uk. The original in a chain that now has branches across the north of England (and one in Birmingham). It's famed for the quality of its south Asian cuisine, offering a wide range of chicken, lamb and prawn curries, and is hugely

popular, so at weekends you may end up waiting, even when you've booked. Most dishes well under £10. Mon–Fri 5pm–midnight, Sat 4pm–midnight, Sun 2–11.30pm.
Bradford Brewery 22 Rawson Rd, BD1 3SQ ☏ 01274 397054, ⓦ bradfordbrewery.com. In a period building

---

HIP HEBDEN BRIDGE

Hebden Bridge's independent galleries, bookshops and boutiques give it more of an artsy vibe than might be expected from a small mill town set in a deep valley. Community spirit has ensured that the cooperative-run town hall got a £3.7 million development that repurposed the Grade II listed building into a hub for creative business (ⓦ hebdenbridgetownhall.org.uk); the 1921 picture house is civic-owned (ⓦ hebdenbridgepicturehouse.co.uk); and the 120-seat Little Theatre produces a range of independent plays (ⓦ hblt.co.uk). The annual **Hebden Bridge Arts Festival** (ⓦ hebdenbridgeartsfestival.co.uk) at the end of June sees open studios and gardens, live gigs at various venues and free street theatre.

Hebden Bridge is easily accessed by train from Manchester, Leeds or Bradford, or it's a beautiful drive over the moors from Haworth. Nearby **Heptonstall** is also worth a visit for its connections to poets Ted Hughes and Sylvia Plath – the latter is buried in the churchyard here.

with quirky decor, this is one of the craft beer places blazing a trail in Bradford. Great selection of ales and craft lagers, cheap and tasty pub grub (chilli and nachos £5), nice people, and a beer garden. Mon–Thurs & Sun noon–11pm, Fri & Sat noon–1am.

Mumtaz 386–410 Great Horton Rd, BD7 3HS ☎ 01274 522533, ⓦ mumtaz.co.uk. With its smart decor and delicious Kashmiri food – a range of *karahi* and biryani dishes, with meat, fish and vegetarian options – *Mumtaz* has won plaudits from everyone from Dawn French to Amir Khan. No alcohol. Around £30/person. Mon–Thurs & Sun 11am–midnight, Fri & Sat 11am–1am.

Prashad Vegetarian Cuisine 137 Whitehall Rd, Drighlington, BD11 1AT ☎ 0113 285 2037, ⓦ prashad. co.uk. Located five miles southeast of Bradford, this family-run vegetarian restaurant specialises in masterfully crafted Gujarat and Punjab dishes. The seven-course tasting menu (£46/person) shows off the very best of local produce and tantalizing spices. Tues–Fri 5–11pm, Sat noon–11pm, Sun noon–10pm.

Leeds

Yorkshire's commercial capital, and one of the fastest-growing cities in the country, **LEEDS** has undergone a radical transformation in recent years. There's still a true northern grit to its character, but any trace of grime has been removed from the impressive Victorian buildings and the city – along with its well-connected suburbs – is revelling in its new persona as a booming financial, commercial and cultural centre. The renowned **shops**, **restaurants**, **bars** and **clubs** provide one focus of a visit to contemporary Leeds – it's certainly Yorkshire's top destination for a day or two of conspicuous consumption and indulgence. Museums include the impressive **Royal Armouries**, which hold the national arms and armour collection, while the **City Art Gallery** has one of the best collections of British twentieth-century art outside London.

City Art Gallery

The Headrow, LS1 3AA • Mon & Tues 10am–5pm, Wed noon–5pm, Thurs–Sat 10am–5pm, Sun 1–5pm • Free • ☎ 0113 247 8256, ⓦ leeds.gov.uk

Sharing a recently restored Victorian building with the Central Library, the **City Art Gallery** has an important collection of largely nineteenth- and twentieth-century paintings, prints, drawings and sculptures, some on permanent display, others rotated. There's an understandable bias towards pieces by **Henry Moore** and **Barbara Hepworth**, both former students at the Leeds School of Art; Moore's *Reclining Woman* lounges at the top of the steps at the gallery entrance – near where you'll also find the ornate Art Nouveau café with its grand marble columns.

Henry Moore Institute

The Headrow, LS1 3AH • Tues–Sun 11am–5.30pm (8pm Wed) • Free • ☎ 0113 246 7467, ⓦ henry-moore.org

The City Art Gallery connects with the adjacent **Henry Moore Institute**, which, despite its misleading name, is devoted not to Moore himself but to temporary exhibitions of sculpture from all periods and nationalities.

Royal Armouries

Armouries Drive, LS10 1LT • Daily 10am–5pm • Free • ☎ 0113 220 1999, ⓦ armouries.org.uk • Bus #28, #70 from city centre or free water taxi in summer

On the south side of the riverbank beckons the spectacular glass turret and gunmetal grey bulk of the **Royal Armouries**, purpose-built to house the **arms** and **armour** collection from the Tower of London. One of the best museums of its type in the world, its five enormous galleries hold beautifully displayed weapons for war, tournaments and hunting, and armour and other artefacts dating from Roman times onwards. Particularly spectacular are the reconstruction of a tiger hunt; the Indian elephant armour (the heaviest armour in the world) consisting of 8500 iron plates; fabulously decorated ceremonial suits of full plate armour; a Sikh "quoit turban" which carried a blood-curdling array of throwing quoits; garrotting wires and knives; Samurai, Mongol and Indian armour and weapons; and many ornate guns, from a reconstruction of an enormously long Essex punt gun to an exquisite Tiffany-decorated Smith and Wesson .44 Magnum.

ARRIVAL AND INFORMATION

LEEDS

By train National and local Metro trains use Leeds Station in the city centre.

Destinations Bradford (every 20min; 20min); Carlisle (every 2hr; 2hr 40min); Harrogate (every 30min; 34min); Hull (hourly; 1hr); Knaresborough (every 30min; 45min); Lancaster (4 daily; 2hr); Liverpool (hourly; 1hr 50min); London (every 30min; 2hr 20min); Manchester (every 15min; 1hr); Scarborough (every 30min–1hr; 1hr 20min);

Settle (every 2hr; 1hr); Sheffield (every 10–15min; 40min–1hr 25m); Skipton (every 15–30min; 45min); Wakefield (Westgate & Kirkgate; every 10–15min; 12min); York (every 10–15min; 25min).

By bus The bus station is to the east of the centre behind Kirkgate Market, on St Peter's Street, though many buses stop outside the train station as well. Buses run from the bus station to all parts of the city, the suburbs, the rest of West

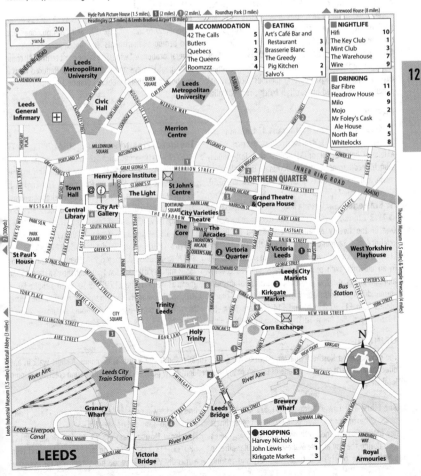

ACCOMMODATION
42 The Calls	5
Butlers	1
Quebecs	2
The Queens	3
Roomzzz	4

● EATING
Art's Café Bar and Restaurant	3
Brasserie Blanc	4
The Greedy Pig Kitchen	2
Salvo's	1

■ NIGHTLIFE
Hifi	10
The Key Club	1
Mint Club	3
The Warehouse	7
Wire	9

■ DRINKING
Bar Fibre	11
Headrow House	6
Milo	9
Mojo	2
Mr Foley's Cask Ale House	4
North Bar	5
Whitelocks	8

● SHOPPING
Harvey Nichols	2
John Lewis	1
Kirkgate Market	3

LEEDS

12

Yorkshire and, via National Express, the rest of the country. Destinations Bradford (10–30min; 25min); Halifax (every 30min; 1hr 16min); London (hourly; 4hr 25min); Manchester (every 30min–1hr; 1hr 5min–1hr 45min); Wakefield (every 10min; 31min); York (hourly; 1hr).
Public transport information The Metro Travel Centres

at the bus and train stations have up-to-date service details for local transport; information is also available from Metroline (☎0113 245 7676, ☯wymetro.com).
Tourist office Visit Leeds, City Art Gallery shop ☎0113 378 6977, ☯visitleeds.co.uk (Mon–Sat 10am–5pm, Sun 11am–3pm).

ACCOMMODATION

There's a good mix of **accommodation** in Leeds. Cheaper lodgings lie out to the northwest in the student area of Headingley, though these are a train, bus or taxi ride away.

★ **42 The Calls** 42 The Calls, LS2 7EW ☎0113 244 0099, ☯42thecalls.co.uk; map p.567. Converted riverside grain mill, where rooms come with great beds and sharp bathrooms. Being next to the Centenary footbridge, it can sometimes suffer from noisy passers-by. **£89**
Butlers Cardigan Rd, Headingley, LS6 3AG, 1.5 miles northwest of the centre ☎0113 274 4755, ☯butlers hotel.co.uk; map p.567. This hotel offers cosy and traditionally furnished rooms on a suburban street, breakfast is an extra £4. **£69**
Quebecs 9 Quebec St, LS1 2HA ☎0113 244 8989, ☯quebecshotel.co.uk; map p.567. The ultimate city-boutique lodgings, boasting glorious Victorian oak panelling and stained glass, offset by chic rooms. Online

deals can cut costs considerably. Limited parking. **£170**
The Queens City Square, LS1 4DY ☎0113 242 1323, ☯qhotels.co.uk; map p.567. This luxurious 4-star option sports an imposing Art Deco facade and is located bang in the centre of town, right next to the train station. Standard rooms are a little small, but smart. Valet parking £15.95/24hr. **£100**
Roomzzz 12 Swine Gate, LS1 4AG ☎0113 233 0400, ☯roomzzz.co.uk; map p.567. Self-catering, one- and two-bedroom apartments in contemporary style, at several locations – Swine Gate is the most central. All come with great kitchens and widescreen TVs. Reduced rates if you book more than a week in advance. **£88**

EATING

★ **Art's Café Bar and Restaurant** 42 Call Lane, LS1 6DT ☎0113 243 8243, ☯artscafebar.co.uk; map p.567. A relaxed hangout for drinks, dinner or a lazy Sunday brunch. Mediterranean flavours dominate the well-priced menu, and the wine list is excellent. Mains £10.95–16.50. Mon–Fri noon–11pm, Sat noon–late, Sun noon–9pm.
★ **Brasserie Blanc** Victoria Mill, Sovereign St, LS1 4BJ ☎0113 220 6060, ☯brasserieblanc.com; map p.567. One of the twenty restaurants established by French celebrity chef Raymond Blanc all over the country, the Leeds branch is a 5min walk from the train station. Housed in an old mill, with plain brick walls, vaulted ceilings and iron pillars, it offers good food in smart but unstuffy surroundings at unthreatening prices. Set two-course menus from £11.50 (lunch) and £14 (dinner). Mon–Fri 10am–10pm, Sat 9am–10.30pm, Sun 9am–9pm (bar

open all day).
The Greedy Pig Kitchen 58 North St, LS2 7PN ☎07477 834227, ☯thegreedypigkitchen.co.uk; map p.567. This little spot just outside the city-centre ring road is where those in the know go for brunch. Full English is £7 (they do a veggie version too) and all the ingredients are locally sourced. Small plate dining on Thurs, Fri & Sat evenings only. Tues & Wed 7am–3pm, Thurs & Fri 7am–3pm & 5.30–9pm, Sat 8.30am–1.30pm & 5.30–9pm.
Salvo's 115 Otley Rd, Headingley, LS6 3PX ☎0113 275 5017, ☯salvos.co.uk; map p.567. Mention pizza to Leeds locals and they'll think of *Salvo's*, though there's a classy Italian menu as well – mains £15.95–19.50 – and a choice list of daily specials. It really is worth the trek out from the centre. Mon–Thurs noon–2pm & 6–10pm, Fri noon–2pm & 5.30–10.30pm, Sat noon–10.30pm, Sun noon–9pm.

DRINKING

The newly coined Northern Quarter, north of the Grand Theatre and Opera House, is booming. A short walk in any direction and you'll stumble on one of Leeds's many independent brew pubs packed out with young creatives sipping local ales.

Bar Fibre 168 Lower Briggate LS1 6LY ☎0870 120 0888, ☯barfibre.com; map p.567. One of Leeds's finest gay-friendly bars comes with plenty of attitude. There's food during the day at *Café Mafiosa*, and regular alfresco parties in the courtyard outside (summer) and roaring

fires inside (winter). Mon–Wed & Sun noon–1am, Thurs & Fri noon–3am, Sat noon–4am.
Headrow House Bramleys Yd, 10 The Headrow, LS1 6PU ☎0113 245 9370; map p.567. Low-key and with a friendly vibe, this venue has something for everyone

(beer hall, decent restaurant, live music and a stunning roof terrace). Mon–Thurs noon–11pm/midnight, Fri noon–2am, Sat 11am–3am, Sun 11am–11pm.

Milo 10–12 Call Lane, LS1 6DN ☎0113 245 7101; map p.567. Unpretentious, intimate and offbeat bar, with DJs most evenings, ringing the changes from old soul and reggae to indie and electronica. Mon–Thurs 5pm–2am, Fri 4pm–3am, Sat noon–3am, Sun noon–2am.

★ **Mojo** 18 Merrion St, LS1 6PQ ☎0113 244 6387, ⓦmojobar.co.uk; map p.567. A great bar with classic tunes ("music for the people" – an eclectic mix with a swerve towards soul), American food, and a classy drinks menu with lots of cocktails. Mon–Wed 4pm–3am, Thurs, Fri & Sun 4pm–4am, Sat noon–3am.

Mr Foley's Cask Ale House 159 The Headrow, LS1 5RG ☎0113 242 9674, ⓦmrfoleysleeds.co.uk; map p.567. Super Victorian pub near the Town Hall, with several bars on

different levels, draught beers listed on a blackboard with strengths and tasting notes, and bottled beers from around the world. Food is served, too, from around a fiver. Mon–Thurs noon–11pm, Fri & Sat 11am–1am, Sun noon–10pm.

North Bar 24 New Briggate, LS1 6NU ☎0113 242 4540, ⓦnorthbar.com; map p.567. The city's beer specialist has a massive selection of guest beers (more Belgian than bitter) plus cold meats and cheeses to nibble on. This place is part of the hugely successful North Bar group, with great pubs popping up across the city. Mon & Tues 11am–1am, Wed–Sat 11am–2am, Sun noon–midnight.

Whitelocks Turk's Head Yard, off Briggate, LS1 6HB ☎0113 245 3950, ⓦwhitelocksleeds.com; map p.567. Leeds's oldest and most atmospheric pub retains its traditional Victorian decor and a good choice of beers. Mon–Thurs 11am–midnight, Fri & Sat 11am–1am, Sun 11am–11pm.

NIGHTLIFE

For information about **what's on**, your best bets are the fortnightly listings magazine *The Leeds Guide* (ⓦleedsguide. co.uk) or the daily *Yorkshire Evening Post* (ⓦyorkshireeveningpost.co.uk).

Hifi 2 Central Rd, LS1 6DE ☎0113 242 7353, ⓦthehifi club.co.uk; map p.567. Small club playing everything from Stax and Motown to hip-hop or drum 'n' bass. Live comedy from top comics.

The Key Club 66 Merrion St, LS2 8LW ☎0113 244 1573, ⓦslamdunkmusic.com/the-key-club; map p.567. Took on the mantle of best live music spot after closure of the renowned Cockpit, although the focus is strictly on rock. Cheap bar, young crowd, and club nights Tues, Fri & Sat.

Mint Club 8 Harrison St, LS1 6HD ☎0113 244 3168, ⓦthemintclub.com; map p.567. Up-to-the-minute

house tunes (there's a "no-cheese" policy), and the best chill-out space in the city.

The Warehouse 19–21 Somers St, LS1 2RG ☎0113 234 3535, ⓦwww.theleedswarehouse.com; map p.567. A mix of house, electro and techno – plus an epic sound system – brings in clubbers from all over the country, especially for Saturday's Technique night.

Wire 2–8 Call Lane, LS1 6DN ☎0113 234 0980, ⓦwire club.co.uk; map p.567. A good indie/alternative dance/ rock/electronic club associated with *Hifi* (see above) with weekly club nights and individual events.

ENTERTAINMENT

City Varieties Swan St, LS1 6LW ☎0113 243 0808, ⓦwww.cityvarieties.co.uk. One of the country's last surviving music halls, this place hosts a wide range of acts and was from 1953 to 1983 the venue for the TV series *The Good Old Days*.

Grand Theatre and Opera House 46 New Briggate, LS1 6NZ ☎0870 121 4901, ⓦleedsgrandtheatre.com. The regular base of Opera North (ⓦoperanorth.co.uk) – who organize programming in the first-floor Howard

Assembly Room – and Northern Ballet (ⓦnorthernballet. com), but also puts on a full range of theatrical productions.

Hyde Park Picture House Brudenell Rd, Headingley, LS6 1JD ☎0113 275 2045, ⓦhydeparkpicturehouse.co.uk. The place to come for classic cinema with independent and art-house shows alongside more mainstream films; get there on bus #56.

West Yorkshire Playhouse Quarry Hill, LS2 7UP ☎0113 213 7700, ⓦwyp.org.uk. The city's most innovative theatre has two stages, plus a bar, restaurant and café.

LEEDS CONCERTS AND FESTIVALS

Temple Newsam, four miles east of Leeds city centre (see page 566), hosts numerous events, from concerts and plays to rock gigs and opera. Roundhay Park is the other large outdoor venue for concerts, while Bramham Park, ten miles east of the city, hosts the annual **Leeds Festival** (ⓦleedsfestival.com) at the end of August with rock/indie music on five stages. August bank holiday weekend heralds the **West Indian Carnival** (ⓦleedscarnival. co.uk) in the Chapeltown area of Leeds.

SHOPPING

Leeds is one of the best cities outside the capital for **shopping**, with numerous independent shops, a throng of classy emporia in the beautifully restored **Victoria Leeds** (ⓦ victorialeeds.co.uk) – the "Knightsbridge of the North" which includes brand-new landmark Victoria Gate – and other arcades that open off **Briggate**. Other options include the shopping complex **The Light** (ⓦ thelightleeds.co.uk), the city-centre malls, such as the **Merrion Centre** (ⓦ merrioncentre.co.uk) off Merrion St and the **Trinity Leeds complex** (ⓦ trinityleeds.com) in Albion Street, not forgetting the eight hundred traders in Kirkgate.

Harvey Nichols 107–11 Briggate, LS1 6AZ ☎ 0113 204 8888, ⓦ harveynichols.com/leeds; map p.567. Harvey Nicks, who opened their first branch outside London here in the Victoria Quarter in 1996, are the lodestone for this chi-chi shopping district. Mon–Sat 10am–7pm, Sun 10.30am–5pm.

John Lewis Victoria Gate, Harewood St, LS2 7AR ⓦ johnlewis.com; map p.567. This extravagant five-storey flagship store opened at the end of 2016; most talked about for its impressive architecture and plush decor, it also stocks Yorkshire suppliers such as the Harrogate Candle Company. Mon–Fri 9.30am–7pm, Sat 9am–7pm, Sun 10.30am–5pm.

Kirkgate Market Vicar Lane, LS2 7HY ⓦ leeds.gov.uk; map p.567. The largest covered market in the north of England, housed in a superb Edwardian building. If you're after tripe, haberdashery or big knickers, this is the place to come. Mon–Sat 8am–5.30pm.

Around Leeds

Beyond the city, a number of major attractions are accessible by bus or train: north of town lies the stately home **Harewood House**, while south of Leeds, the neighbouring town of **Wakefield** is home to the stunning **Hepworth Gallery** and not far from the **National Coal Mining Museum** and the **Yorkshire Sculpture Park**.

Thackray Museum

Beckett St, LS9 7LN, 2 miles northeast of the centre • Daily 10am–5pm, last admission 3pm • £8 • ☎ 0113 244 4343, ⓦ thackraymedicalmuseum.co.uk • Bus #16 #42 #49 #50 #50A or #61 from the city centre (all around 15min, all stop outside the museum)

Essentially a medical history museum, and a hugely entertaining one, the **Thackray Museum**, next to St James's Hospital, has displays on subjects as diverse as the history of the hearing aid and the workings of the human intestine. It's gruesome, too, with a film of a Victorian limb amputation in a gallery called "Pain, pus and blood".

Leeds Industrial Museum

Off Canal Rd, between Armley and Kirkstall Rd, LS12 2QF, 2 miles west of the centre • Tues–Sat 10am–5pm, Sun 1–5pm • £3.80 • ⓦ leeds.gov.uk, ☎ 0113 263 7861 • Bus #15 from Leeds railway station

For Leeds's industrial past, visit the vast **Leeds Industrial Museum**. There's been a mill on the site since at least the seventeenth century, and the present building was one of the world's largest woollen mills until its closure in 1969. Although most of its displays naturally centre on the **woollen industry**, and famous offshoots like Hepworths and Burtons, the cinema and printing in the local area are also covered.

Kirkstall Abbey

Abbey Rd, LS5 3EH, about 3 miles northwest of the city centre • **Abbey** Tues–Sun: April–Sept 10am–4.30pm; Oct–March 10m–4pm Free • **Museum** Tues–Fri & Sun 10am–5pm, Sat noon–5pm • £4.50 • ☎ 0113 230 5492, ⓦ leeds.gov.uk • Buses #33, #33A or #757 from city centre

The bucolic ruins and cloisters of **Kirkstall Abbey**, which was built between 1152 and 1182 by Cistercian monks from Fountains Abbey (see page 553), are well worth a

visit. The former gatehouse now provides the setting for the family-friendly **Abbey House Museum**, which takes a look at Victorian Leeds.

Temple Newsam

Off Selby Rd, LS15 0AE, 4 miles east of Leeds • **House** Tues–Sun: April–Sept 10.30am–5pm; Oct–March 10.30am–4pm • £6 • **Rare breeds farm** Tues–Sun: April–Sept 10am–5pm; Oct–March 10am–4pm • £3.80 • ☎ 0113 264 7321, ⓦ leeds.gov.uk • On Sun bus #63a runs to the house from central Leeds and during the rest of the week #19 and #19a run to Whitkirk, from where it is a 1-mile walk; during hols (Easter to Oct half term), #10 bus runs directly to the house

The Tudor-Jacobean house of **Temple Newsam** shows many of the paintings and much of the decorative art owned by Leeds City Art Gallery. There are paintings from the sixteenth to the nineteenth centuries, furniture (including a number of Chippendale pieces), textiles and tapestries, silver, porcelain and pottery. The estate is over fifteen thousand acres and also contains Europe's largest **rare breeds farm**, where you can see four breeds of pigs, six of sheep, eight of poultry and no fewer than nine of cattle.

Harewood House

Harewood, LS17 9LG, 7 miles north of Leeds • Opening hours vary widely according to day and season; check website for full details • Freedom ticket, covering all parts of house and gardens £16.50 • ☎ 0113 218 1010, ⓦ harewood.org • Frequent buses run to Harewood from Leeds, including the #36 (Mon–Sat every 15min, Sun every 30min)

Harewood House – still the home of the Earl and Countess of Harewood – is one of the UK's greatest country mansions. It was created in the mid-eighteenth century by an all-star team: designed by John Carr of York, with interiors by Robert Adam, furniture by Thomas Chippendale, and paintings by Turner, Reynolds, Titian and El Greco, all sitting in beautiful **grounds** landscaped by Capability Brown. Tours take in the below-stairs kitchen and servants' quarters as well as innumerable galleries, halls, reception rooms and staircases, dripping with antiques and priceless art treasures, while added attractions include an adventure playground and gardens – including the famous bird garden. Numerous special events, special-interest tours and talks on things like beekeeping, photography and food keep things lively. Incidentally, the village is pronounced "Harewood" as it is spelt, while the house is pronounced "Harwood".

The Hepworth Wakefield

Gallery Walk, Wakefield, WF1 5AW • Tues–Sun 10am–5pm • Free; parking £5 • ☎ 01924 247360, ⓦ hepworthwakefield.org • From Leeds, take a train to Wakefield Westgate and walk, or a bus to Wakefield city centre, then a local bus to Bridge St (next to the gallery); alternatively, Wakefield's FreeCityBus (9.30am–3pm; ⓦ wymetro.com) links all major parts of town, including the Hepworth Gallery

Established in May 2011, **The Hepworth** was the largest new gallery to open outside London for decades. Inside a cuboid concrete riverside building designed by Sir David Chipperfield, it has ten display areas housing a wonderful collection of Dame Barbara Hepworth's work – not only finished sculptures, but also working models in plaster and aluminium, lithographs and screen prints. You can even see her original workbench and tools. Other contemporary artists are represented, too, and a flow of new exhibits is assured by close cooperation with the Tate. There's a café and shop, and a children's playground within its pleasant surroundings, which are set to be developed into a vast landscaped garden.

National Coal Mining Museum

Caphouse Colliery, Overton, WF4 4RH, about 10 miles south of Leeds, halfway between Wakefield and Huddersfield (on the A642, signposted from M1) • Tours daily 10am–5pm; last tour 3.15pm; 1hr 30min • Free • ☎ 01924 848806, ⓦ ncm.org.uk • Train from Leeds to Wakefield Westgate, then from the station the #128 bus goes right past the museum, while #232 passes nearby

While the gentry enjoyed the comforts of life in grand houses like Harewood (see above), just a few miles away generations of Yorkshiremen sweated out a living underground. Mining is now little more than a memory in most parts of Yorkshire, but visitors can get all too vivid an idea of pit life through the ages at the excellent **National Coal Mining Museum**. Based in a former pit, Caphouse Colliery, the highlight is an underground **mine tour** (warm clothes required; arrive early in school hols; no under-5s) with a former miner as your guide.

Yorkshire Sculpture Park

West Bretton, outside Wakefield, WF4 4LG, a mile from the M1 (junction 38) • Daily 10am–6pm (galleries, restaurant and café 10am–5pm) • Free, but parking £5 for 1–2hr, £8/day • ☎ 01924 832631, ⓦ ysp.co.uk • Train from Leeds to Wakefield Westgate, then bus #96 (Mon–Sat) – a fair bit of walking is necessary

The Yorkshire country estate at West Bretton now serves as the **Yorkshire Sculpture Park**. Trails and paths run across five hundred acres of eighteenth-century parkland, past open-air "gallery spaces" for some of Britain's most famous sculptors; there are also three indoor galleries for exhibitions. The two big local names represented here are Henry Moore (1898–1986), born in nearby Castleford, and his contemporary Barbara Hepworth (1903–75), from Wakefield. The **visitor centre** is the place to check on current exhibitions and pick up a map – the restaurant has great views over Moore's monumental pieces.

Sheffield and around

12

Yorkshire's second city, **SHEFFIELD** remains linked with its steel industry, in particular the production of high-quality cutlery. As early as the fourteenth century the carefully fashioned, hard-wearing knives of hard-working Sheffield enjoyed national repute, while technological advances later turned the city into one of the country's foremost centres of heavy and specialist engineering. Unsurprisingly, it was bombed heavily during World War II, and by the 1980s the steel industry's subsequent downturn had tipped parts of Sheffield into dispiriting decline. The subsequent revival has been rapid, however, with the centre utterly transformed by flagship architectural projects. Steel, of course, still underpins much of what Sheffield is about: museum collections tend to focus on the region's industrial heritage, complemented by the startling science-and-adventure exhibits at **Magna**, which was built in a disused steelworks at **Rotherham**, the former coal and iron town a few miles northeast of the city.

Sheffield's **city centre** is very compact and easily explored on foot. The hub of the city is the **Winter Garden**, as well as the attractive **Peace Gardens** (named in hope immediately after World War II) nearby, with their huge bronze water features and converging ceramic-lined rills that represent the rivers that gave Sheffield steel mills their power. Southeast of here, clubs and galleries exist alongside the arts and media businesses of the **Cultural Industries Quarter**. To the northeast, spruced-up warehouses and cobbled towpaths line the canal basin, **Victoria Quays**. The **Devonshire Quarter**, east of the Peace Gardens and centred on Division Street, is the trendiest shopping area.

Winter Garden

Surrey St, S1 2HH • Mon–Sat 8am–8pm, Sun 8am–6pm • Free • ☎ 0114 273 6895, ⓦ sheffield.gov.uk

A minute's walk east of the Peace Gardens, the stunning **Winter Garden** is a potent symbol of the city's regeneration. A twenty-first-century version of a Victorian conservatory on a huge scale (230ft long, and around 70ft high and wide), it's created from unvarnished, slowly weathering wood and polished glass, and filled with more than two thousand seasonally changing plants and towering trees.

Millennium Gallery

Arundel Gate, S1 2PP • Mon–Sat 10am–5pm, Sun 11am–4pm • Free • ☎ 0114 278 2600, ⓦ museums-sheffield.org.uk

Backing onto the Winter Garden are the **Millennium Galleries**, consisting of the **Metalwork Gallery**, which is devoted to the city's world-famous cutlery industry, including an introduction to the processes involved and a collection of fine silver and stainless steel cutlery, and the diverting **Ruskin Gallery**. Based on the cultural collection founded by John Ruskin in 1875 to "improve" the working people of Sheffield, this includes manuscripts, minerals, watercolours and drawings, all relating in some way to the natural world.

Sheffield Cathedral

Church St, S1 1HA • Visitor centre open Mon 8am–5pm, Tues–Fri 8.30am–6.30pm (5pm in school hols), Sat 9.30am–4pm, Sun 7.30am–5pm • Details of recitals and tours available on ☎ 0114 279 7412, ⓦ sheffieldcathedral.org

The **Cathedral Church of St Peter and St Paul**, to give **Sheffield Cathedral** its full title, was a simple parish church before 1914, and subsequent attempts to give it a more dignified bearing have frankly failed. It's a mishmash of styles and changes of direction, and you'd need a PhD in ecclesiastical architecture to make any sense of it. That said, the magnificent **Shrewsbury Chapel**, at the east end of the south aisle, is worth a look. Built around 1520, it contains the tombs of the fourth and sixth Earls of Shrewsbury, whose alabaster effigies adorn their tombs.

Kelham Island Museum

Alma St, S3 8RY • Mon–Thurs 10am–4pm, Sun 11am–4.45pm • £6 • ☎ 0114 272 2106, ⓦ simt.co.uk

Fifteen minutes' walk north of the cathedral, the **Kelham Island Museum** reveals the breadth of the city's **industrial output** – cutlery, of course, but also Barnes Wallis's 22ft-long Grand Slam bomb, the Sheffield Simplex roadster, and the gigantic River Don steam engine. Many of the old machines are still working, arranged in period workshops where craftspeople show how they were used.

Weston Park Museum

Weston Bank, S10 2TP • Mon–Sat 10am–5pm, Sun 11pm–4pm • Free • ☎ 0114 278 2600, ⓦ museums-sheffield.org.uk • Bus #51 or #52 from city centre, or Sheffield University tram

You can put the city's life and times into perspective a mile or so west of the centre at the **Weston Park Museum**. Here the imaginatively themed and family-friendly galleries draw together the city's extensive archeology, natural history, art and social history collections.

Magna

Magna Way, Rotherham, S60 1FD • Mon–Fri 10am–2pm, Sat & Sun 10am–5pm • £10.95, family ticket from £28.95 • ☎ 01709 720002, ⓦ visitmagna.co.uk • Bus #X1 (every 10min) from either Sheffield or Rotherham Interchanges, or a 15min taxi ride from Sheffield

Housed in a former steelworks building in **ROTHERHAM**, about six miles northeast of Sheffield and just off the M1, **Magna** is the UK's best science adventure centre. The vast internal space comfortably holds four gadget-packed **pavilions**, themed on the elements of earth, air, fire and water. You're encouraged to get your hands on a huge variety of interactive exhibits, games and machines – operating a real JCB, filling diggers and barrows, blasting a rock face or investigating a twister, for example. On the hour, everyone decamps to the main hall for the **Big Melt**, when the original arc furnace is used in a bone-shaking light and sound show that has visitors gripping the railings.

ARRIVAL AND DEPARTURE

By train Sheffield's train station is on the eastern edge of the city centre.

Destinations Leeds (every 12min; 40min–1hr 19min); London (hourly; 2hr 30min); York (every 30min; 53min).

By bus Sheffield Interchange bus and coach station lies

SHEFFIELD AND AROUND

about 200yd north of the train station. Buses run to and from most regional and national centres – including all the main South Yorkshire towns; London (hourly; 3hr 45min); Birmingham (every 30min; 2hr 5min); Liverpool (hourly; 2hr 50min) and Manchester (every 30min; 1hr).

GETTING AROUND AND INFORMATION

By bus Local buses depart from High Street or Arundel Gate.

By tram The Supertram system (⟨ℳ⟩supertram.com) connects the city centre with the Meadowhall shopping centre (see page 576), Halfway, Herdings Park, Malin Bridge and Middlewood, with the stations in between giving comprehensive access to most of the city and connections to the Park and Ride scheme.

Transport information For fare and timetable information, visit the Mini Interchange travel centre on Arundel Gate, behind the Crucible Theatre (Mon–Fri 7am–6pm, Sat 9am–5pm; ☎01709 515151, ⟨ℳ⟩sypte.co.uk).

Tourist office Unit 1, The Winter Garden (Mon–Fri 9.30am–1pm & 1.30–5pm, Sat 9.30am–1pm & 1.30–4pm; ☎0114 275 7754, ⟨ℳ⟩welcometosheffield.co.uk).

ACCOMMODATION

Houseboat Hotels Victoria Quays, S2 5SY ☎07776 144693, ⟨ℳ⟩houseboathotels.com. Something different – two moored houseboats, available by the night, with en-suite bathrooms and kitchens. You get exclusive use of your own boat, sleeping up to four people (£190) and priced accordingly. **£130**

Leopold Hotel 2 Leopold St, S1 2GZ ☎0114 252 4000, ⟨ℳ⟩leopoldhotel.co.uk. Once a boys' grammar school, this place is immaculately modernized but retains some

original features. Centrally located, the hotel backs onto remodelled Leopold Square, which has an appealing array of places to eat. **£99**

Mercure St Paul's Hotel 119 Norfolk St, S1 2JE ☎0114 278 2000, ⟨ℳ⟩mercure.com. Sandwiched between the Peace Gardens and Tudor Square, this modern hotel couldn't be more central. Comfortable rather than innovative, with understated (if a little anodyne) decor and fine views over the city the higher you go. **£94**

EATING

★ **Forum Kitchen + Bar** 127–129 Devonshire St, S3 7SB ☎0114 272 0569, ⟨ℳ⟩forumsheffield.co.uk. A vibrant and recently refurbed mixture of bar, café, music venue and boutique mall, with a lively clientele who use it as a breakfast stop, lunch spot, after-work bar, dinner venue, comedy club and night club. Mon–Wed 8am–1am, Thurs 8am–2am, Fri 8am–3am, Sat 9am–3am, Sun 10am–1pm.

Nonna's 535–541 Ecclesall Rd, S11 8PR ☎0114 268 6166, ⟨ℳ⟩nonnas.co.uk. Italian bar/restaurant with a great reputation and a family feel. Authentic Italian cuisine (menus have English descriptions). Evening mains £9.95 and up. Mon–Sat 8.30am–11pm, Sun 9am–10.30pm.

Silversmiths 111 Arundel St, S1 2NT ☎0114 270 6160, ⟨ℳ⟩silversmiths-restaurant.com. A "kitchen nightmare" turned around in 2008 by Gordon Ramsay in his TV show, city-centre *Silversmiths* supplies top-notch Yorkshire food from local ingredients – venison sausages and pies, spinach tart with Yorkshire Blue cheese – in a 200-year-old silversmith's workshop. Pre-theatre three-course menu for £18.95 or three-course seasonal Sunday roast for £25. Reservations recommended. Tues–Thurs 10am–9.30pm, Fri & Sat 10am–9.45pm, Sun noon–2.30pm.

DRINKING AND NIGHTLIFE

For the best insight into what makes Sheffield tick as a party destination take a night-time walk along **Division St** and **West St** where competing theme and retro bars go in and out of fashion. Locals and students also frequent the bars and pubs of **Ecclesall Rd** (the so-called "golden mile"), out of the centre to the southwest.

★ **Devonshire Cat** 49 Wellington St, Devonshire Green, S1 4HG ☎0114 279 6700, ⟨ℳ⟩devonshirecat.co.uk. Renowned ale house with wide variety of domestic and imported beers, plus good pub food (£7.75–14.25) with drinks matched to every selection. Daily noon–2am; kitchen Mon–Sat noon–9pm, Sun noon–8pm.

★ **Fat Cat** 23 Alma St, S3 8SA ☎0114 249 4801, ⟨ℳ⟩thefatcat.co.uk. Bought by real ale enthusiasts in

1981 after a brewery sell-off, the *Fat Cat* is now a Sheffield institution offering a wide range of bottled and draft beers, ciders and country wines, and a hearty pub-grub menu (meals around £4.50). With its open fires, polished mahogany bar and etched mirrors, and its total absence of flashing gaming machines and piped music, this is pub-going as it used to be. Mon–Thurs & Sun noon–11.30pm, Fri & Sat noon–midnight; kitchen Mon–Fri noon–3pm

& 6–8pm, Sat noon–7pm, Sun noon–3pm.

Leadmill 6–7 Leadmill Rd, S1 4SE ☎0114 221 2828, ⓦleadmill.co.uk. In the Cultural Industries Quarter, this venue hosts live bands and DJs most nights of the week, as well as screenings and comedy nights.

Plug 14 Matilda St, S1 4QD ☎0114 279 5039, ⓦthe plug.com. Mid-sized music venue featuring everythin from live acoustic folk to diverse club nights, including the award-winning "Jump Around". Check online for hours.

ENTERTAINMENT

Crucible, Lyceum and Studio 55 Norfolk St, S1 1DA ☎0114 249 6000, ⓦsheffieldtheatres.co.uk. Sheffield's theatres put on a full programme of theatre, dance, comedy and concerts. The *Crucible*, of course, has hosted the World Snooker Championships for thirty years. It also presents the annual Music in the Round festival of chamber music (May), and the Sheffield Children's Festival (late June or July).

Sheffield City Hall Barker's Pool, S1 2JA ☎0114 278 9789, ⓦsheffieldcityhall.com. Year-round programme of classical music, opera, mainstream concerts, comedy and club nights, in a magnificent, renovated concert hall.

Showroom 7 Paternoster Row, S1 2BX ☎0114 275 7727, ⓦshowroom.org.uk. The biggest independent cinema outside London, and also a popular workstation and meeting place, with a relaxed café-bar.

SHOPPING

Sheffield has all the national chain stores and other shops you'd expect in the city centre, with top-end shops concentrated particularly along **Fargate** and **High St** on one side of the Peace Gardens and budget alternatives along **The Moor** on the other. The trendiest shopping is to be found in the **Devonshire Quarter**, based on Division St, while due south there's an **indoor market** at 77 The Moor (Mon–Sat 8.30am–5.30pm).

Meadowhall Centre S9 1EP ☎0845 600 6800, ⓦmeadowhall.co.uk. Since it opened in 1990 on the site of a derelict steelworks, out-of-town Meadowhall has pulled in thirty million shoppers a year. Free parking is a boon, or it's an easy tram ride three miles east of the centre. Mon–Fri 10am–9pm, Sat 9am–8pm, Sun 11am–5pm.

Antiques Quarter A621 and surrounding roads ⓦsheffieldantiquesquarter.co.uk. To the south of the city centre, along Abbeydale and Broadfield roads and easily reached by bus, you'll find a horde of delightful independent antique dealers and an auction house. For exact shop locations and opening hours, check online.

Hull

HULL – officially **Kingston upon Hull** – dates back to 1299, when it was laid out as a seaport by Edward I. It quickly became England's leading harbour, and was still a vital garrison when the gates were closed against Charles I in 1642, the first serious act of rebellion of what was to become the English Civil War. Fishing and **seafaring** have always been important here, and today's city maintains a firm grip on its heritage with a number of superb visitor attractions, including the excellent **Museum Quarter** in the **Old Town**. The city's stint as **UK City of Culture** in 2017 saw a massive investment in arts and culture across the city; the revitalization is particularly noticeable in the burgeoning **Fruit Market** district between the Marina and river (ⓦfruitmarkethull. co.uk), where new galleries and cool cafés have opened.

Ferens Art Gallery

Queen Victoria Square, HU1 3RA • Mon–Sat 10am–5pm (Thurs 7.30pm), Sun 11am–4.30pm • Free • ☎01482 300300, ⓦhcandl.co.uk/ferens

When it reopened in April 2017 after a multi-million pound refurbishment, **Ferens Art Gallery** attracted more than 10,000 visitors in its first weekend. The world-class gallery has a permanent collection of paintings and sculpture with works by Frans Hals, David Hockney and Antonio Canaletto. Visiting exhibitions have included SKIN – major works by Lucian Freud, Ron Mueck and Spencer Tunick – and the prestigious Turner Prize.

The Maritime Museum

Queen Victoria Square, HU1 3DX • Mon–Sat 10am–5pm (Thurs 7.30pm), Sun 11am–4.30pm • Free • ☎ 01482 300300, ⓦ hullcc.gov.uk

The city's maritime legacy is covered in the **Maritime Museum**, housed in the Neoclassical headquarters of the former Town Docks Offices. With displays on fishing, whaling and sailing, this provides a valuable record of centuries of skill and expertise, not to mention courage and fortitude, now fading into the past. Highlights include the whaling gallery, with whale skeletons, fearsome exploding harpoons, the sort of flimsy boats in which whalers of old used to chase the leviathans of the deep, and oddities such as a whalebone seat and a blubber cauldron.

The Museums Quarter

Between High St & the River Hull, HU1 1NQ • All attractions Mon–Sat 10am–5pm, Sun 11am–4.30pm • Free • ☎ 01482 300300, ⓦ hullcc.gov.uk

Over towards the River Hull, you reach the **Museums Quarter** and **High Street**, which has been designated an "Old Town" conservation area thanks to its crop of former merchants' houses and narrow cobbled alleys. At its northern end stands **Wilberforce House**, the former home of William Wilberforce, which contains fascinating exhibits on slavery and its abolition, the cause to which he dedicated much of his life. Next door is **Streetlife**, devoted to the history of transport in the region and centred on a 1930s street scene. The adjoining **Hull and East Riding Museum** is even better, with attractions including vivid displays of Celtic burials and an impressive full-size model of a woolly mammoth.

The Deep

Tower St, HU1 4DP • Daily 10am–6pm, last entry 5pm • £12.50, children £10.50 (discount online) • ☎ 01482 381000 , ⓦ thedeep.co.uk

Protruding from a promontory overlooking the River Humber, Hull's splendid aquarium, **The Deep**, is just ten minutes' walk from the old town. Its educational displays and videos wrap around an immense 30ft-deep, 2.3-million-gallon viewing tank filled with sharks, rays and octopuses. There's an underwater tunnel along the bottom of the tank, together with a magical glass lift in which you can ascend or descend through the water.

12

ARRIVAL AND DEPARTURE   HULL

By train Hull's train station is situated in the Paragon Interchange off Ferensway. There are direct trains between London and Hull, while the city is also linked to the main London–York line via Doncaster as well as to the East Yorkshire coast.
Destinations Bempton (hourly; 55min); Beverley (Mon–Sat every 25min, Sun 6 daily; 13min); Bridlington (every 30min; 42min); Filey (around 10 daily; 1hr10min); (Leeds (hourly; 1hr); London (6 daily; 2hr 45min); Scarborough

(every 2hr; 1hr 30min); York (hourly; 1hr 10min).

By bus The bus station is near the train station in the Paragon Interchange off Ferensway. Buses run to all parts of the region including York (2hr) and the East Coast (1hr 40min to Bridlington; 2hr 30min to Scarborough).

By ferry Daily crossing to/from Rotterdam and Zeebrugge (Bruges) from the ferry terminal, 3 miles from the city centre (ⓦ poferries.com).

INFORMATION AND TOURS

Visitor information There's a volunteer-run hub in Hull railway station, where you can pick up the entertaining "Fish Trail" leaflet, a self-guided trail that kids will love. See also ⓦ visithullandeastyorkshire.com.
Walking tour Paul Schofield (☎ 01482 878535, ⓦ tour

hull.com) is an English Heritage-accredited guide who leads historic Old Town tours (from the tourist office; Mon, Fri & Sat 10am & 2pm, Sun 11am & 2pm; £4), as well as tours of some of Hull's best pubs.

ACCOMMODATION

Holiday Inn Hull Marina Castle St, HU1 2BX ☎ 0871 9422 9043, ⓦ hihullmarinahotel.co.uk. Rooms at the city's best central hotel overlook the marina, and there's a restaurant and bar, plus an indoor pool, gym, sauna and

plenty of parking. **£114**
Kingston Theatre Hotel 1–2 Kingston Square, HU2 8DA ☎ 01482 225828, ⓦ kingstontheatrehotel. com. This straightforward, good-value hotel on the city's

prettiest square, across from Hull New Theatre, is a 5min walk from the city centre, yet in a quiet neighbourhood. Street parking only (but there's a public car park nearby). **£110**

EATING AND DRINKING

Cerutti's 10 Nelson St, HU1 1XE ☎01482 328501, ⓦceruttis.co.uk. Facing the old site of the Victoria Pier (now replaced by a wooden deck overlooking the river), this first-floor Italian restaurant is especially good for fish dishes. The atmosphere is busy and friendly, and there are frequent special events including live jazz. Main courses are around £13–23, but look out for two- and three-course deals. Mon–Fri noon–2pm & 6.45–9.30pm, Sat 6.45–9.30pm.

The George The Land of Green Ginger, HU1 2EA ☎01482 226373. Venerable pub on Hull's most curiously named street – see if you can find England's smallest window. Mon noon–6pm, Tues–Thurs noon–11.00pm, Fri & Sat noon–midnight, Sun noon–10pm.

Pave Café-Bar 16–20 Princes Ave, HU5 3QA ☎01482 333181, ⓦpavebar.co.uk. Nice laidback atmosphere with lots going on – live jazz/blues and comedy nights, and readings by the likes of Alexei Sayle, Will Self and Simon Armitage – and a comprehensive menu of home-cooked food served till 7pm (most mains well under £10). Mon–Thurs & Sun 11am–11.00pm, Fri & Sat 11am–11.30pm.

Thieving Harry's 73 Humber St, HU1 1UD ☎01482 214141, ⓦthievingharrys.co.uk. A cornerstone of the Fruit Market regeneration, quirky *Thieving Harry's* "food + stuff" has mismatched chairs, a cool vibe, gorgeous views and tasty food (poached egg on toast with charred avocado and bacon £6). Mon–Thurs 10am–4pm, Fri & Sat 9am–midnight, Sun 9am–4pm.

ENTERTAINMENT

Hull Venue ⓦcityplanhull.co.uk. A major state-of-the-art music and events complex set to open in 2018. Check the website for updates.

Hull Truck Theatre Company 50 Ferensway, HU2 8LB ☎01482 323638, ⓦhulltruck.co.uk. Renowned theatre, where, among other high-profile works, many of the plays of award-winning John Godber see the light of day.

Beverley

With its tangle of old streets, cobbled lanes and elegant Georgian and Victorian terraces **BEVERLEY**, nine miles north of Hull, is the very picture of a traditional market town. More than 350 of its buildings are listed, and though you could see its first-rank offerings in a morning, it makes an appealing place to stay.

Beverley Minster

Minster Yard North, HU17 0DP • April–Oct Mon–Sat 9am–5.30pm, Sun noon–4.30pm; Nov–March Mon–Sat 9am–4pm, Sun noon–4.30pm; services Thurs & Sun (see website) • Free, but donation requested • Roof tours Thurs (by prior appointment only) & Sat 11am; 1hr • £10; advance booking only • ☎01482 868540, ⓦbeverleyminster.org.uk

The town is dominated by the fine, Gothic twin towers of **Beverley Minster**. The **west front**, which crowned the work in 1420, is widely considered without equal, its survival due in large part to architect Nicholas Hawksmoor, who restored much of the church in the eighteenth century. The carving throughout is magnificent, particularly the 68 misericords of the oak **choir** (1520–24), one of the largest and most accomplished in England. Much of the decorative work here and elsewhere is on a musical theme. Beverley had a renowned guild of itinerant minstrels, which provided funds in the sixteenth century for the carvings on the transept aisle capitals, where you'll be able to pick out players of lutes, bagpipes, horns and tambourines.

St Mary's

Corner of North Bar Within and Hengate, HU17 8DL • Mon–Sat 11.30am–3pm, Sun before and after services only • Free • ☎01482 869137, ⓦstmarysbeverley.org

Cobbled Highgate runs from the minster through town, along the pedestrianized shopping streets and past the main Market Square, to Beverley's other great church,

St Mary's, which nestles alongside the **North Bar**, sole survivor of the town's five medieval gates. Inside, the chancel's painted panelled ceiling (1445) contains portraits of English kings from Sigebert (623–37) to Henry VI (1421–71), and among the carvings the favourite novelty is the so-called "Pilgrim's Rabbit", said to have been the inspiration for the White Rabbit in Lewis Carroll's *Alice in Wonderland*.

ARRIVAL AND INFORMATION

BEVERLEY

By train Beverley's train station on Station Square is just a couple of mins' walk from the town centre and the minster. Destinations Bridlington (every 30min; 30min); Hull (every 30min; 15min); Sheffield (hourly; 1hr 40min).

By bus The bus station is at the junction of Walkergate and Sow Hill Road, with the main street just a minute's walk away. Destinations Bridlington (hourly; 1hr) Driffield (hourly;

25min); Hull (every 30min–1hr; hourly; 40min); Scarborough (hourly; 1hr 16min).

Tourist office 34 Butcher Row in the main shopping area (April–Sept Mon–Fri 9.30am–5.30pm, Sat 9.30am–4.30pm, Sun 10am–3.30pm; Oct–March Mon–Fri 10am–5pm, Sat 10am–4.30pm; ☏ 01482 391672, ⍉ visithull andeastyorkshire.com).

ACCOMMODATION AND EATING

★ **Cerutti 2** Station Square, HU17 0AS ☏ 01482 866700, ⍉ ceruttis.co.uk. Occupying what was once the station waiting rooms, *Cerutti 2*, run by the same family as *Cerutti's* in Hull, specializes in fish, though there are meat and vegetarian options too (mains around £12–23). Popular with locals, so it's as well to book, especially at weekends. Tues–Sat noon–2pm & 6.45–9.30pm.

King's Head Hotel 37–38 Saturday Market, HU17 9AH ☏ 01482 868103, ⍉ kingsheadpubbeverley.co.uk. Tucked into a corner of busy Saturday Market, this period building has contemporary decor inside. It's a Marston's

pub, with food from £7, and it can be noisy, especially at weekends, but the rear rooms are quieter, and earplugs are provided. Mon–Thurs 9am–11pm, Fri & Sat 9am–1am, Sun 11am–11pm; kitchen Mon–Sat 10am–9pm, Sun 10am–8pm. **£100**

YHA Beverley Friary Friar's Lane, HU17 0DF ☏ 0845 371 9004, ⍉ yha.org.uk/hostel/beverley-friary. Beautiful medieval monastic house in the shadow of the minster. What it lacks in luxury it makes up for in atmosphere, location and, of course, economy. Limited parking. Dorms **£18**, triples **£69**

12

The East Yorkshire coast

The **East Yorkshire coast** curves south in a gentle arc from the mighty cliffs of Flamborough Head to Spurn Head, a hook-shaped promontory formed by relentless erosion and shifting currents. There are few parts of the British coast as dangerous – indeed, the Humber lifeboat station at **Spurn Point** is the only one in Britain permanently staffed by a professional crew. Between the two points lie a handful of tranquil villages and miles of windswept dunes and mud flats. The two main resorts, **Bridlington** and **Filey**, couldn't be more different, but each has its own appeal.

Bridlington and around

The southernmost resort on the Yorkshire coast, **BRIDLINGTON** has maintained its harbour for almost a thousand years. The seafront promenade looks down upon the town's best asset – its sweeping sandy **beach**. It's an out-and-out family resort, which means plenty of candyfloss, fish and chips, rides, boat trips and amusement arcades. The historic core of town is a mile inland, where in the largely Georgian Bridlington Old Town the **Bayle Museum** (Easter–Oct Mon–Fri 11am–4pm; £2; ☏ 01262 674308) presents local history in a building that once served as the gateway to a fourteenth-century priory.

Around fourteen miles of precipitous 400ft-high cliffs gird **Flamborough Head**, just to the northeast of Bridlington. The best of the seascapes are visitable on the peninsula's north side, accessible by road from Flamborough village.

Bempton

From **BEMPTON**, two miles north of Bridlington, you can follow the clifftop path all the way round to Flamborough Head or curtail the journey by cutting up paths to Flamborough village. The **RSPB sanctuary** at **Bempton Cliffs**, reached along a quiet lane from Bempton, is the best single place to see the area's thousands of cliff-nesting birds.

RSPB Bempton Cliffs

1 mile from Bempton, YO15 1JF • Visitor centre daily 9.30am–5pm (4pm in winter) • £4 • ☎ 01262 4222212, ⓦ rspb.org.uk

A quarter of a million seabirds nest in these cliffs, including fifteen thousand pairs of gannets, and the second-largest **puffin colony** in the country, with several thousand returning to the cliffs each year. Late March and April is the best time to see the puffins, but the reserve's **visitor centre** can advise on other breeds' activities. There are six clifftop viewpoints (three of them wheelchair accessible), plus a beautiful picnic spot.

Filey

FILEY, half a dozen miles north up the coast from Bempton, is at the very edge of the Yorkshire Wolds (and technically in North Yorkshire). It has a good deal more class as a resort than Bridlington, retaining many of its Edwardian features, including some splendid panoramic gardens. It, too, claims miles of wide sandy beach, stretching most of the way south to Flamborough Head and north the mile or so to the jutting rocks of **Filey Brigg**, where a nature trail wends for a couple of miles through the surroundings.

12 | **ARRIVAL AND GETTING AROUND** | **THE EAST YORKSHIRE COAST**

By train Bridlington and Filey are linked by the regular service between Hull and Scarborough, and there are regular trains between York and Scarborough, further up the coast.

By bus There are buses from York to Bridlington (every 2hr; 2hr), plus a service from Hull to Scarborough (every 2hr; 2hr 50min) via Bridlington and Filey. There's also an hourly service between Bridlington, Filey and Scarborough.

The North York Moors

Virtually the whole of the **North York Moors**, from the Hambleton and Cleveland hills in the west to the cliff-edged coastline to the east, is protected by one of the country's finest National Parks. The heather-covered, flat-topped hills are cut by deep, steep-sided valleys, and views here stretch for miles, interrupted only by giant cultivated forests. This is great walking country; footpaths include the superb **Cleveland Way**, one of England's premier long-distance National Trails, which embraces both wild moorland and the cliff scenery of the North Yorkshire coast. Barrows and ancient forts provide memorials of early settlers, mingling on the high moorland with the battered stone crosses of the first Christian inhabitants and the ruins of great monastic houses such as **Rievaulx Abbey**.

GETTING AROUND | **THE NORTH YORK MOORS**

By train The steam trains of the North Yorkshire Moors Railway (see page 584) run between Pickering and Grosmont and on to Whitby. At Grosmont you can connect with the regular trains on the Esk Valley line, running either 6 miles east to Whitby and the coast, or west through more remote country settlements (and ultimately to Middlesbrough).

By bus The main bus approaches to the moors are from

Scarborough and York to the main towns of Helmsley and Pickering. There are two seasonal services that connect Pickering and Helmsley to everywhere of interest in the National Park. Moorsbus (☎ 01751 477216, ⓦ moorsbus.org) and the Moors Explorer from Hull (☎ 01482 592929 or ⓦ eyms. co.uk) both have several departures on summer weekends, fewer at other times (at least every Sun & bank hols).

INFORMATION

National Park Visitor Centres There are two National Park Visitor Centres for the North York Moors, one in Danby

(daily: April–July & Sept–Oct 10am–5pm; Aug 9.30am–5.30pm; for winter hours check with centre; ☎ 01439

72737), and the other in Sutton Bank (same hours; 01845 597426). Both offer exhibitions, pamphlets and maps, a café and a shop. The National Park's website is northyorkmoors.org.uk.

Cleveland Way Project Provides maps and information about the route, including an annual, downloadable accommodation guide (01439 770657, nationaltrail. co.uk/cleveland-way).

Thirsk

The market town of **THIRSK**, 23 miles north of York, made the most of its strategic crossroads position on the ancient drove road between Scotland and York and on the historic east–west route from dales to coast. Its medieval prosperity is clear from the large, cobbled **Market Place** (markets Mon & Sat), while well-to-do citizens later endowed the town with fine Georgian houses and halls. However, Thirsk's main draw is its attachment to the legacy of local vet Alf Wight, better known as James Herriott. Thirsk was the "Darrowby" of the Herriott books, and the vet's former surgery, at 23 Kirkgate, is now the hugely popular **World of James Herriott** (daily: March–Oct 10am–5pm; Nov–Feb 10am–4pm; £8.50; 01845 524234, worldofjamesherriot. org), and is crammed with period pieces and Herriott memorabilia.

ARRIVAL AND INFORMATION   **THIRSK**

By train The train station is a mile west of town on the A61 (Ripon road); minibuses connect the station with the town centre.

Destinations Middlesbrough (hourly; 44min); Manchester (hourly; 1hr 50min); London (every 2hr; 2hr 30min).

By bus Buses stop in the Market Place.

Destinations Northallerton (every 2hr; 25–30min); Ripon (every 2hr; 41min); York (every 1–2hr; 1hr).

Tourist office 93a Market Place (Mon–Sat 10am–4pm; 01845 522755, visit-thirsk.org.uk).

12

ACCOMMODATION AND EATING

Gallery 18 Kirkgate, YO7 1PQ   01845 523767, gallerybedandbreakfast.co.uk. An award-winning B&B with three comfortable rooms and excellent breakfasts in an eighteenth-century Grade II listed building. It's on a main street, and can get noisy when the pubs close. **£70**

Golden Fleece Market Place, YO7 1LL 01845 523108, goldenfleecehotel.com. There are good rooms and a pleasant busy atmosphere in this charming old coaching inn, nicely located on Thirsk's large cobbled square. They serve locally sourced food, too. Daily noon–9pm. **£95**

Osmotherley and around

Eleven miles north of Thirsk, the little village of **OSMOTHERLEY** huddles around its green. The pretty settlement gets by as a hiking centre, since it's a key stop on the **Cleveland Way** as well as starting point for the brutal 42-mile **Lyke Wake Walk** to Ravenscar, south of Robin Hood's Bay.

Mount Grace Priory

Half a mile off the A19, DL6 3JG · April–Sept daily 10am–6pm; Oct daily 10am–5pm; Nov–March Sat & Sun 10am–4pm · £6.60; NT & EH
01609 883494, nationaltrust.org.uk, english-heritage.org.uk · #80/#89 from Northallerton, then a 30min walk

An easy two-mile walk from Osmotherley via Chapel Wood Farm, the fourteenth-century **Mount Grace Priory** is the most important of England's nine Carthusian ruins. The Carthusians took a vow of silence and lived, ate and prayed alone in their two-storey cells, each separated from its neighbour by a privy, small garden and high walls. The foundations of the cells are still clearly visible, and one has been reconstructed to suggest its original layout.

Sutton Bank

The main A170 road enters the National Park from Thirsk as it climbs 500ft in half a mile to **Sutton Bank** (960ft), a phenomenal **viewpoint** from where the panorama extends across the Vale of York to the Pennines on the far horizon. While you're here, call in at the **National Park Visitor Centre** (see page 583) half a mile further up the road, to pick up information on the **walks** and off-road **bike rides** you can make from here.

Kilburn

To the south of the A170, the **White Horse Nature Trail** (2–3 miles; 1hr 30min) skirts the crags of Roulston Scar en route to the **Kilburn White Horse**, northern England's only turf-cut figure, 314ft long and 228ft high. You could make a real walk of it by dropping a couple of miles down to pretty **KILBURN** village (a minor road also runs from the A170, passing the White Horse car park), which has been synonymous with woodcarving since the days of "Mouseman" Robert Thompson (1876–1955), whose woodcarvings are marked by his distinctive mouse motif. The **Mouseman Visitor Centre** (Easter–Oct daily 10am–5pm; Nov & Dec Wed–Sun 11am–4pm; £4.50; ☎01347 869102, ⊛robertthompsons.co.uk) displays examples of Thompson's personal furniture.

Coxwold

Most visitors to the attractive village of **COXWOLD** come to pay homage to the novelist **Laurence Sterne**, who is buried by the south wall (close to the porch) in the churchyard of **St Michael's**, where he was vicar from 1760 until his death in 1768. **Shandy Hall**, further up the road past the church (house May–Sept Wed & Sun 11am–4.30pm; gardens May–Sept Mon–Fri & Sun 11am–4.30pm; tours Wed & Sun 2.45pm & 3.45pm, or by appointment; house & gardens £5, gardens only £3; ☎01347 868465, ⊛laurencesternetrust.org.uk), was Sterne's home, now a museum crammed with literary memorabilia. It was here that he wrote *A Sentimental Journey through France and Italy* and the wonderfully eccentric anti-novel *The Life and Opinions of Tristram Shandy, Gentleman*.

Helmsley and around

One of the moors' most appealing towns, **HELMSLEY** makes a perfect base for visiting the western moors and **Rievaulx Abbey**. Local life revolves around a large cobbled market square (market Fri), which is dominated by a boastful monument to the second earl of Feversham, whose family was responsible for rebuilding most of the village in the nineteenth century. The old **market cross** now marks the start of the 110-mile **Cleveland Way**. Signposted from the square, it's easy to find **Helmsley Castle** (April–Sept daily 10am–6pm; Oct–Nov daily 10am–5pm; Nov–March Sat & Sun 10am–4pm; £6.20, EH; ☎01439 770442, ⊛www.english-heritage.org.uk/visit/places/helmsley-castle), its unique twelfth-century D-shaped keep ringed by massive earthworks.

Rievaulx Abbey

Just over 2 miles northwest of Helmsley, YO62 5LB • April–Sept daily 10am–6pm; Oct to early Nov daily 10am–5pm; mid-Nov to March Sat & Sun 10am–4pm • £8.50; EH • ☎01439 798228, ⊛www.english-heritage.org.uk/visit/places/rievaulx-abbey

From Helmsley you can easily walk across country to **Rievaulx Abbey** on a signposted path (1hr 30min). Founded in 1132, the abbey became the mother church of the Cistercians in England, quickly developing into a flourishing community with interests in fishing, mining, agriculture and the woollen industry. At its height, 140 monks and up to five hundred lay brothers lived and worked here, though numbers fell dramatically once the Black Death (1348–49) had done its worst. The end came with the Dissolution, when many of the walls were razed and the roof lead stripped – the beautiful ruins, however, still suggest the abbey's former splendour.

Rievaulx Terrace

YO62 5LJ, 2 miles northwest of Helmsley • Feb–Oct daily 10am–5pm • £5.40; NT • ☎01439 798340 (summer) or ☎01439 748283 (winter), ⓦ nationaltrust.org.uk/rievaulx-terrace

Although they form some sort of ensemble with the abbey, there's no access between the ruins and **Rievaulx Terrace**. This half-mile stretch of grass-covered terraces and woodland was laid out as part of Duncombe Park in the 1750s, and was engineered partly to enhance the views of the abbey. The resulting panorama over the ruins and the valley below is superb, and this makes a great spot for a picnic.

ARRIVAL AND INFORMATION   HELMSLEY AND AROUND

By bus Buses from Scarborough (every 1hr 15min; 1hr 35min) and Pickering (every 1hr 15min; 35min) stop on or near the Market Place. In addition, seasonal Moorsbus

services (April–Oct; ☎01751 477217, ⓦ moorsbus.org), connect Helmsley to most places in the National Park.

ACCOMMODATION, EATING AND DRINKING

Black Swan Market Place, YO62 5BJ ☎01439 770466, ⓦ blackswan-helmsley.co.uk. An interesting Tudor/Georgian ex-coaching inn right on the main square, with a comfortable bar, airy restaurant, award-winning tearoom, refurbished rooms and charming, attentive staff. Daily: 11am–11pm, later at weekends; tearoom 10am–5.30pm; restaurant 7.30–9.30pm. **£144**

Feathers Hotel Market Place, YO62 5BH ☎01439 770275, ⓦ feathershotelhelmsley.co.uk. Pub serving restaurant food – all the staples, from £11.95 – and with a surprisingly large choice of rooms. Mon–Sat 11.30am–midnight, Sun 11.30am–11pm; kitchen Mon–Fri noon–2.30pm & 5.30–9pm, Sat noon–9pm, Sun noon–8.30pm. **£79**

★ **Feversham Arms** 1 High St, YO62 5AG ☎01439 770766, ⓦ fevershamarmshotel.com. One of Yorkshire's top hotels, multi-award-winning, luxurious yet unpretentious.

It has a pool, underground car park, spa and a terrific fine-dining restaurant. Look out for special deals. Mon–Sat noon–2.30pm & 6.45–9.30pm, Sun 12.30–2.30pm & 6.45–9.30pm. **£190**

Star Inn Harome, YO62 5JE, 2 miles southeast of Helmsley ☎01439 770397, ⓦ thestaratharome.co.uk. The *Star* is not only a spectacularly beautiful thatched inn, but a restaurant which regained its Michelin star in 2015. Food is classic British and surprisingly affordable (main courses around £19–30), and the atmosphere is blessedly unpretentious. Accommodation is available in a separate building, and there's an associated shop/deli across the road. Mon 6–11pm, Tues–Sat 11.30am–3pm & 6–11pm, Sun noon–11pm; kitchen Mon 6.15–9.30pm, Tues–Sat 11.30am–2pm & 6.15–9.30pm, Sun noon–6pm. **£180**

Hutton le Hole

Eight miles northeast of Helmsley, one of Yorkshire's quaintest villages, **HUTTON LE HOLE**, has become so great a tourist attraction that you'll have to come off-season to get much pleasure from its stream-crossed village green and the sight of sheep wandering freely through the lanes. Apart from the sheer photogenic quality of the place, the big draw is the family-oriented **Ryedale Folk Museum** (mid-Jan to March & Nov to early Dec daily 10am–4pm; April to Oct 10am–5pm; £7.50; ☎01751 417367, ⓦ ryedalefolkmuseum.co.uk), where local life is explored in a series of reconstructed buildings, notably a sixteenth-century house, a glass furnace, a crofter's cottage and a nineteenth-century blacksmith's shop.

ARRIVAL AND INFORMATION   HUTTON LE HOLE

By bus The #174 travels from/to Pickering once on Mon (30min).

National Park Information Centre At Ryedale Folk Museum (see above).

ACCOMMODATION AND EATING

The Barn Guest House Hutton-le-Hole, YO62 6UA ☎01751 417311, ⓦ thebarnguesthouse.com. Comfortable en-suite rooms, plus tearooms serving home-made cakes, scones, sandwiches and hot specials. Food served March–Oct daily 10.30am–4.30pm. **£79**

The Crown Hutton-le-Hole, YO62 6UA ☎01751 417343, ⓦ crownhuttonlehole.com. Spacious real ale pub where you can sit outside and enjoy the peace of the village. They serve traditional, freshly cooked food, too; you can eat well for under a tenner. Typically daily

12

THE NORTH YORKSHIRE MOORS RAILWAY

The **North Yorkshire Moors Railway** (☎01751 472508, ⓦnymr.co.uk) provides a double whammy of nostalgia: first there's the rolling stock, station furniture and smell of steam conjuring up images of bygone travel (especially to those who remember rail in the mid-twentieth century); and then the countryside through which the trains pass is reminiscent of an England which in many places has disappeared. Lately, the railway has been attracting a younger generation, too, as a result of its connection with the **Harry Potter films**: Goathland Station was used in the first of the Harry Potter films as **Hogsmeade**, where Harry and co disembarked from the *Hogwarts Express*.

The line, completed by George Stephenson in 1835 just ten years after the opening of the Stockton and Darlington Railway, connects **Pickering** with the Esk Valley (Middlesbrough–Whitby) line at **Grosmont**, eighteen miles to the north. Scheduled **services** operate year-round (limited to weekends and school hols Nov–March), and a **day-return ticket** costs £24. Daily services also run on the Esk Valley line from Grosmont to the nearby seaside resort of Whitby from April to early November, with a return fare from Pickering of £29.

11am–10pm (later when busy); kitchen Mon–Thurs 11.45am–2.15pm & 5.30–8.15pm, Fri & Sat 11.45am– 2.30pm & 5.30–8.30pm, Sun 11.45am–6pm; winter closed Mon & Tues.

Pickering

The biggest centre for miles around, **PICKERING** takes for itself the title "Gateway to the Moors", which is pushing it a bit, though it's certainly a handy halt if you're touring the villages and dales of the **eastern moors**. Its most attractive feature is its motte and bailey **castle** on the hill north of the Market Place (daily: April–Sept 10am–6pm; Oct–Nov 10am–5pm; £4.90, EH; ☎01751 474989, ⓦwww.english-heritage.org.uk/visit/places/pickering-castle), reputedly used by every English monarch up to 1400 as a base for hunting in nearby Blandsby Park. The other spot worth investigating is the **Beck Isle Museum of Rural Life** on Bridge Street (Feb–Nov daily 10am–5pm; £6; ☎01751 473653, ⓦwww.beckislemuseum.org.uk), which has reconstructions of a gents' outfitters and barber's shop, a case full of knickers, and a painting of two giant Welsh guardsmen produced by Rex Whistler for a children's party. **Market** day in town is Monday, and there's a farmers' market on the first Thursday of the month.

ARRIVAL AND DEPARTURE PICKERING

By train The steam trains of the North Yorkshire Moors Railway (see page 584) run between Pickering and Grosmont and on to Whitby. The station is a 5min signposted walk from the main street.

By bus Buses stop outside the library and tourist office, opposite the Co-op in the centre of town.
Destinations Helmsley (hourly; 35min); Scarborough (hourly; 53min); Whitby (4–6 daily; 1hr 4min); York (hourly; 1hr 10min).

ACCOMMODATION AND EATING

The White Swan Market Place, YO18 7AA ☎01751 472288, ⓦwhite-swan.co.uk. Delightful traditional coaching inn, fully refurbished and updated, with contemporary and traditional bedrooms, and fine Modern British food (mains from £13.95). Daily 7.30am–11pm; kitchen daily noon–2pm & 6.45–9pm. **£149**

The North Yorkshire coast

The **North Yorkshire coast** is the southernmost stretch of a cliff-edged shore that stretches almost unbroken to the Scottish border. **Scarborough** is the biggest resort, with a full set of attractions and a terrific beach. Cute **Robin Hood's Bay** is the most popular of the coastal villages, with fishing and smuggling traditions, while bluff **Staithes** – a fishing harbour on the far edge of North Yorkshire – has yet to tip over into a full-blown tourist trap. **Whitby**, between the two, is the best stopover, with its fine sands, good facilities, abbey ruins, Georgian buildings and maritime heritage – more than any other local place Whitby celebrates Captain Cook as one of its own. Two of the best sections of the **Cleveland Way** start from Whitby: southeast to Robin Hood's Bay (six miles) and northwest to Staithes (eleven miles), both along thrilling high-cliff paths.

Scarborough

The oldest resort in the country, **SCARBOROUGH** first attracted early seventeenth-century visitors to its newly discovered mineral springs. To the Victorians it was "the Queen of the Watering Places", but Scarborough saw its biggest transformation after World War II, when it became a holiday haven for workers from the industrial heartlands. All the traditional ingredients of a beach resort are still here, from superb, clean sands and kitsch amusement arcades to the more refined pleasures of its tight-knit old-town streets and a genteel round of quiet parks and gardens. Be sure to drop into the **Church of St Mary** (1180), below the castle on Castle Road, whose graveyard contains the tomb of Anne Brontë, who died here in 1849.

Rotunda Museum

Vernon Rd, YO11 2PS • Tues–Sun 10am–5pm • £3 • ☎ 01723 353665, ⓦ scarboroughmuseumstrust.com

The second-oldest purpose-built museum in the country (the oldest is in Oxford), the **Rotunda Museum** was constructed to the plans of William Smith, the founder of English geology, and opened in 1829. A fascinating building in its own right, it includes in its venerable shell some high-tech displays on geology and local history. The Dinosaur Coast Gallery is particularly child-friendly.

Art Gallery

The Crescent, YO11 2PW • Tues–Sun 10am–5pm • £3 • ☎ 01723 384503 ⓦ scarboroughartgallery.co.uk

Scarborough's **Art Gallery**, housed in an Italianate villa, contains the town's permanent collection – largely the work of local artists, and including paintings, posters and photography – which gives an insight into the way the town has been depicted over the centuries.

Scarborough Castle

Castle Rd, YO11 1HY • April–Sept daily 10am–6pm; Oct daily 10am–5pm; Nov to mid-Feb Sat & Sun 10am–4pm • £5.90; EH • ☎ 01765 608888, ⓦ www.english-heritage.org.uk/visit/places/scarborough-castle

There's no better place to acquaint yourself with the local layout than **Scarborough Castle**, mounted on a jutting headland between two golden-sanded bays. Bronze and Iron Age relics have been found on the wooded castle crag, together with fragments of a fourth-century Roman signalling station, Saxon and Norman chapels and a Viking camp, reputedly built by a Viking with the nickname of Scardi (or "harelip"), from which the town's name derives.

The bays

One fun way to explore **North Bay** is aboard the miniature **North Bay Railway** (Feb–Oct daily 10/11am–4pm; day return £3.90; ☎ 01723 368791, ⓦ nbr.org.uk), which runs for just under a mile between Scarborough's **Sea Life Centre and Marine Sanctuary** at Scalby Mills (daily 10am–5pm; £18, £9.50 online; ☎ 01723 373414, ⓦ visitsealife.com/scarborough) and Peasholme Park. For unique entertainment, head to the park for **naval warfare**, when miniature man-powered naval vessels battle it out on the lake (July & Aug Mon, Thurs & Sat; £4; details from the tourist office).

To explore the bays from the water, board one of the pleasure steamers that ply the coastline on one-hour **cruises** or zip across to Casty Rocks on a **speedboat** to view seals and seabirds. All boat tours depart from the harbourside throughout the day between Easter and October (ⓦ scarboroughboats.webs.com).

12

The **South Bay** is more refined, backed by the Valley Gardens and the Italianate meanderings of the South Cliff Gardens, and topped by an esplanade from which a **hydraulic lift** (Feb–Nov daily 9.30am–5pm; 90p) chugs down to the beach.

ARRIVAL AND DEPARTURE

SCARBOROUGH

By train The train station is at the top of town facing Westborough.
Destinations Hull (every 2hr; 1hr 30min); Leeds (hourly; 1hr 16min); York (hourly; 50min).
By bus Buses pull up outside the train station or in the surrounding streets. National Express services (direct from London) stop in the car park behind the station.

Destinations Bridlington (hourly; 1hr 18min); Filey (hourly; 30min); Helmsley (hourly; 1hr 30min); Hull (hourly; 1hr 30min); Leeds (hourly; 2hr 40min); Pickering (hourly; 1hr); Robin Hood's Bay (hourly; 38min); Whitby (hourly; 1hr); York (hourly; 1hr 35min).

GETTING AROUND AND INFORMATION

By bus Open-top seafront buses (Feb–Nov daily from 9.30am, every 12–20min; £2 single) run between North Bay to the Spa Complex in South Bay.
Tourist offices Scarborough has two tourist information points; one inside the Stephen Joseph Theatre (Mon–Sat 10am–6pm), and the other by the harbour in RNLI Scarborough (daily 9am–5pm).

ACCOMMODATION

Crescent Hotel The Crescent, YO11 2PP ☎ 01723 360929, ⓦ thecrescenthotel.com. A spacious, slightly old-fashioned hotel catering for both holiday-makers and business folk, with friendly, helpful staff, comprehensive facilities and a fine restaurant, all housed in mid-nineteenth-century splendour. **£107**
Crown Spa Hotel The Esplanade, YO11 2AG ☎ 01723 357400, ⓦ crownspahotel.com. On the south cliff, overlooking the town, this elegant and traditional hotel and spa brings a bit of luxury to Scarborough. Sea views are extra, but worth it. **£150**
YHA Scarborough Burniston Rd, YO13 0DA, 2 miles north of town ☎ 01723 361176, ⓦ yha.org.uk/hostel/scarborough. In an early seventeenth-century watermill a 15min walk from the sea, this is a good hostel for families with kids. Dorms **£13**, private rooms sleeping four **£60**

EATING AND DRINKING

Café Fish 19 York Place, at the intersection with Somerset Terrace, YO11 2NP ☎ 01723 500301, ⓦ cafefish.co.uk. More of a top-end fish restaurant than a fish-and-chip shop, where a two-course dinner with wine could feature fish curry, steamed mussels or Thai fishcakes, and will cost from about £30. Gets very busy at weekends. Daily 5.30–10pm.
Café Italia 36 St Nicholas Cliff, YO11 2ES ☎ 01723 501973. Enchanting, tiny, authentic Italian coffee bar. They stick to what they're good at: excellent coffee, ice cream and cakes. Daily 9am–9pm.
Golden Grid 4 Sandside, YO11 1PE ☎ 01723 360922, ⓦ goldengrid.co.uk. The harbourside's choicest fish-and-chip establishment, "catering for the promenader since 1883". Offers grilled fish, crab and lobster, a fruits-de-mer platter and a wine list alongside the standard crispy-battered fry-up. Decent portions of fish from £7.80. Easter–Oct Mon–Thurs 10am–8.30pm, Fri 10am–9pm, Sat 10am–9.30pm, Sun 11am–6.30pm; Nov–Easter opens daily 11am, closing varies.

ENTERTAINMENT

Scarborough Open Air Theatre Burniston Rd, YO12 6PF ☎ 01723 818111, ⓦ scarboroughopenairtheatre. com. Europe's largest open-air theatre, built in 1932, hosts a range of top-end concerts and gigs by the likes of Jessie J, Elton John and Status Quo.
Stephen Joseph Theatre Westborough, YO11 1JW ☎ 01723 370541, ⓦ sjt.uk.com. Housed in a former Art Deco cinema, this premieres every new play of local playwright Alan Ayckbourn and promotes strong seasons of theatre and film. There's a good, moderately priced café/restaurant and a bar open Mon–Sat.

Robin Hood's Bay

The most heavily visited spot on this stretch of coast, **ROBIN HOOD'S BAY** is made up of gorgeous narrow streets and pink-tiled cottages toppling down the cliff-edge site, evoking the romance of a time when this was both a hard-bitten fishing community

12

and smugglers' den par excellence. From the upper village, lined with Victorian villas, now mostly B&Bs, it's a very steep walk down the hill to the harbour. The **Old Coastguard Station** (Jan, March, Nov & Dec Sat & Sun 10am–4pm, Feb daily 10am–4pm, April–Oct daily 10am–5pm, late Dec Mon–Wed, Sat & Sun 10am–4pm; free; NT; ☎01947 885900; ⓦnationaltrust.org.uk/yorkshire-coast) has been turned into a visitor centre with displays relating to the area's geology and sealife. When the tide is out, the massive rock beds below are exposed, split by a geological fault line and studded with fossil remains. Robin's Hood's Bay is the traditional finishing point for Alfred Wainwright's 190-mile **Coast-to-Coast Walk** from St Bees, but you might prefer to take the much shorter circular walk (2.5 miles) to **Boggle Hole** and its youth hostel, a mile south, returning inland via the path along the old Scarborough–Whitby railway line.

ARRIVAL AND GETTING AROUND
ROBIN HOOD'S BAY

By bus Robin Hood's Bay is connected to Whitby by Arriva #93 buses (hourly; 20min) and to Scarborough by Arriva #93 buses (hourly; 40min).

By bike A couple of miles northwest of Robin Hood's Bay

at Hawsker, on the A171, Trailways (☎01947 820207, ⓦtrailways.info) is a bike rental outfit based in the old Hawsker train station, perfectly placed for day-trips in either direction along the disused railway line.

INFORMATION

Tourist information Though you can pick up a lot of information at the Old Coastguard Station (see above), the nearest official tourist office is in Whitby (see page 589).

ACCOMMODATION AND EATING

Bay Hotel On the harbour, YO22 4SJ ☎01947 880278, ⓦbayhotel.info. At the traditional start or end of the Coast-to-Coast Walk, this inn offers rooms and bar meals, with main courses at around £9–11. Mon–Sat 11am–11pm, Sun noon–11pm; kitchen daily noon–2pm & 6.30–9pm. <u>£70</u>

Swell Café Old Chapel, Chapel St ☎01947 880180, ⓦswellcafe.co.uk. A gift shop and café in an old Wesleyan Chapel, built in 1779, where John Wesley himself once preached. They serve a good range of snacks, sandwiches,

cakes, teas and coffees, and alcoholic drinks, and there are great coastal views from its terrace tables. Daily 9.30am–3.30pm, or later if busy.

YHA Boggle Hole Boggle Hole, Fylingthorpe, YO22 4UQ ☎0845 371 9504, ⓦyha.org.uk/hostel/boggle-hole. In a former mill in a wooded ravine about a mile south of Robin Hood's Bay at Mill Beck, this outstanding hostel has a great location practically on the beach. Dorms <u>£18</u>, doubles <u>£59</u>

12

Whitby

If there's one essential stop on the North Yorkshire coast it's **WHITBY**, with its historical associations, atmospheric ruins, fishing harbour, lively music scene and intrinsic charm. The seventh-century clifftop **abbey** here made Whitby one of the key foundations of the early Christian period, and a centre of great learning. Below, on the harbour banks of the River Esk, for a thousand years the local herring boats landed their catch until the great **whaling** boom of the eighteenth century transformed the fortunes of the town. Melville's *Moby Dick* makes much of Whitby whalers such as William Scoresby, and James Cook took his first seafaring steps from the town in 1746, on his way to becoming a national hero. All four of Captain Cook's ships of discovery – the *Endeavour, Resolution, Adventure* and *Discovery* – were built in this town.

Walking around Whitby is one of its great pleasures. Divided by the River Esk, the town splits into two halves joined by a swing bridge: the cobbled **old town** to the east, and the newer (mostly eighteenth- and nineteenth-century) town across the bridge, generally known as **West Cliff**. **Church Street** is the old town's main thoroughfare, barely changed in aspect since the eighteenth century, though now lined with tearooms and gift shops. Parallel **Sandgate** has more of the same, the two streets meeting at the small **marketplace** where souvenirs and trinkets are sold, and which hosts a farmers' market every Thursday.

Captain Cook Memorial Museum

Grape Lane, YO22 4BA • Daily: Feb–March 11am–3pm; April–Oct 9.45am–5pm • £5.70 • ☎ 01947 601900, ⓦ cookmuseumwhitby.co.uk

Whitby, understandably, likes to make a fuss of Captain Cook, who served an apprenticeship here from 1746–49 under John Walker, a Quaker shipowner. The **Captain Cook Memorial Museum**, housed in Walker's rickety old house, contains an impressive amount of memorabilia, including ships' models, letters and paintings by artists seconded to Cook's voyages.

Church of St Mary

Abbey Plain, YO22 4JT • Daily 10am–4pm

At the north end of Church Street, you climb the famous **199 steps** of the Church Stairs – now paved, but originally a wide wooden staircase built for pall-bearers carrying coffins to the **Church of St Mary** above. This is an architectural amalgam dating back to 1110, boasting a Norman chancel arch, a profusion of eighteenth-century panelling, box pews unequalled in England and a triple-decker pulpit – note the built-in ear trumpets, added for the benefit of a nineteenth-century rector's deaf wife.

Whitby Abbey

Abbey Lane, YO22 4JT • April–Sept daily 10am–6pm; Oct daily 10am–5pm; Nov–March Sat & Sun 10am–4pm • £7.60; EH • ☎ 01947 603568, ⓦ www.english-heritage.org.uk/visit/places/whitby-abbey

The clifftop ruins of **Whitby Abbey** are some of the most evocative in England. Its monastery was founded in 657 by St Hilda of Hartlepool, daughter of King Oswy of Northumberland, and by 664 had become important enough to host the **Synod of**

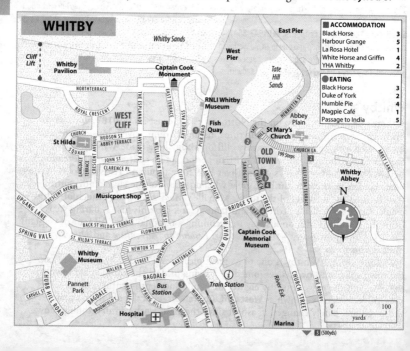

BRAM STOKER AND DRACULA

The story of **Dracula** is well known, but it's the exact attention to the geographical detail of Whitby – little changed since Bram Stoker first wrote the words – which has proved a huge attraction to visitors. Using first-hand observation of a town he knew well – he stayed at a house on the West Cliff, now marked by a plaque – Stoker built a story which mixed real locations, legend and historical fact: the grounding of Count Dracula's ship on Tate Hill Sands was based on an actual event reported in the local papers.

It's hardly surprising that the town has cashed in on its **Dracula Trail**. The various sites – Tate Hill Sands, the abbey, church and steps, the graveyard, Stoker's house – can all be visited, while down on the harbourside the Dracula Experience attempts to pull in punters to its rather lame horror-show antics. Keen interest has also been sparked among the **Goth** fraternity, who now come to town en masse a couple of times a year (in late spring and around Halloween) for a vampire's ball, concerts and readings.

Whitby, an event of seminal importance in the development of English Christianity. It settled once and for all the question of determining the date of Easter, and adopted the rites and authority of the Roman rather than the Celtic Church. You'll discover all this and more in the **visitor centre** (same hours), which is housed in the shell of the adjacent mansion, built after the Dissolution using material from the plundered abbey.

Whitby Museum

Pannett Park, YO21 1RE • Tues–Sun 9.30am–4.30pm • £5 • ☎ 01947 602908, ⓦ whitbymuseum.org.uk

The gloriously eclectic **Whitby Museum** features more Cook memorabilia, including various objects and stuffed animals brought back as souvenirs by his crew, as well as casefuls of exhibits devoted to Whitby's seafaring tradition, its whaling industry in particular. Some of the best and largest fossils of Jurassic period reptiles unearthed on the east coast are also preserved here.

ARRIVAL AND INFORMATION

WHITBY

By train Whitby's station is in the centre of town on Station Square, just south of the swing bridge, next to the bus station. Whitby is the terminus of the Esk Valley line, which runs from Middlesbrough and connects with the steam trains of the North Yorkshire Moors Railway at Grosmont, which run south to Pickering (see page 584).
Destinations Danby (4–5 daily; 40min); Great Ayton (4–5 daily; 1hr 5min); Grosmont (4–5 daily; 16min); Middlesbrough (4–5 daily; 1hr 30min).

By bus The bus station is next to the train station in the centre of town.
Destinations Robin Hood's Bay (hourly; 19min); Staithes (every 30min; 30min); York (4–6 daily; 2hr).
Tourist office On the corner of Langborne Rd and New Quay Rd, opposite the train station (May–Oct daily 9.30am–5pm; Nov–April Thurs–Sun 9.30am–4.30pm; ☎ 01723 383636, ⓦ discoveryorkshirecoast.com or ⓦ visitwhitby.com).

ACCOMMODATION

Black Horse 91 Church St, YO22 4BH ☎ 01947 602906, ⓦ the-black-horse.com; map p.588. Four simple en-suite guest rooms above this fine old pub (see below), each named after one of Captain Cook's ships. **£60**
Harbour Grange Spital Bridge, Church St, YO22 4BF ☎ 01947 600817, ⓦ whitbybackpackers.co.uk; map p.588. Backpackers' hostel right on the river (eastern side) with 24 beds from a double up to an eight-bed dorm. Self-catering kitchen and lounge; 11.30pm curfew. **£18**
★ **La Rosa Hotel** 5 East Terrace, YO21 3HB ☎ 01947 606981, ⓦ larosa.co.uk; map p.588. Eccentric B&B with

themed rooms done out in extravagantly individual style courtesy of auctions, eBay and car boot sales. Great fun, with terrific views of the harbour and the abbey. Breakfast picnic delivered in a basket to your door. Street parking. **£110**
White Horse and Griffin 87 Church St, YO22 4BH ☎ 01947 604857, ⓦ whitehorseandgriffin.com; map p.588. In the centre of Whitby's old town, with wonderful views of the harbour. Nicely renovated rooms with many original features. It's full of character, but can be noisy. **£120**

12

WHITBY MUSIC SCENE

Whitby has a strong **local music** scene, with an emphasis on folk and world music. During the annual **Whitby Folk Week** (wwhitbyfolk.co.uk), held the week preceding the August bank holiday, the town is filled day and night with singers, bands, traditional dancers, storytellers and music workshops. Not-for-profit Musicport (wmusicportfestival.com) put on gigs from big names in the world/folk scene and hold a renowned annual World Music Festival at Whitby Pavilion in October. The shop of the same name, Musicport (16 Skinner Street; 01947 603475, wmusicportshop.com), is a great spot to find out more about live music in the town.

YHA Whitby Abbey House, East Cliff, YO22 4JT 0845 371 9049, wyha.org.uk/hostel/whitby; map p.588. Flagship hostel in a Grade I listed building next to the Abbey Visitor Centre. Stunning views, good facilities and a Victorian conservatory, tearoom and restaurant. Rates include breakfast and entry to the abbey. Dorms __£15__, doubles __£59__

EATING

Black Horse 91 Church St, YO22 4BH 01947 602906, wthe-black-horse.com; map p.588. Lovely pub (parts date from the seventeenth century) in the old town, with real ales and food served all day, including tapas, Yorkshire cheeses and local seafood. Easter–Nov Mon–Sat 11am–11pm, Sun noon–11pm; Dec–Easter daily noon–4pm & 7–11pm.

★ **Duke of York** 124 Church St, YO22 4DE 01947 600324, wdukeofyork.co.uk; map p.588. In a great position at the bottom of the 199 steps, this is a warm and inviting pub, with beams, nautical memorabilia, church pews and views across to the harbour and West Cliff. Come for good real ales, modern pub food and music. Mon–Thurs & Sun 11am–11pm, Fri 11am–11.30pm, Sat 11am–midnight; kitchen daily noon–9pm.

★ **Humble Pie** 163 Church St, YO22 4AS 07919 074954, whumblepie.tccdev.com; map p.588. Tiny sixteenth-century building serving a range of pies, cooked fresh to order – steak, stout and leek, Romany, Homity, haggis and neep, and many more – with mash and peas. The decor is 1940s, with World War II background music. All pies £5.99; soft drinks only. Mon–Sat noon–8pm, Sun noon–4pm.

Magpie Café 14 Pier Rd, YO21 3PU 01947 602058, wwww.magpiecafe.co.uk; map p.588. Said by Rick Stein to be one of the best fish-and-chip shops in the country, the *Magpie* has served food from its 1750-built premises since the start of World War II. To call it a fish-and-chip shop is a bit disingenuous – although it provides the normal takeaway service, it also serves lesser-known fish like Woof and John Dory in its restaurant (from £10.95) and has an extensive wine list. Closed at time of writing because of a fire, but hoping to reopen for the 2018 season.

Passage to India 30–31 Windsor Terrace, YO1 1ET 01947 606500, wpassagetoindia.eu; map p.588. Stylish tandoori restaurant near the station, with bright red-and-black decor, great food, and friendly, efficient service. Mains £8–12; look out for the tandoori king prawn *karahi* or the Lam Kam. Mon–Thurs 5pm–midnight, Fri 5.30pm–1am, Sat noon–1am, Sun noon–midnight.

Staithes

At the northernmost border of the Yorkshire coast is the fishing village of **STAITHES**, an improbably beautiful grouping of huddled stone houses around a small harbour, backed by the severe outcrop of Cowbar Nab, a sheer cliff face that protects the northern flank of the village. James Cook worked here in a draper's shop before moving to Whitby, and he's remembered in the **Captain Cook and Staithes Heritage Centre**, on the High Street (Feb–Nov daily 10am–5pm; Dec & Jan Sat & Sun 10am–5pm; £3; 01947 841454, wcaptaincookatstaithes.co.uk), which recreates an eighteenth-century street, among other interesting exhibits. Other than this, you'll have to content yourself with pottering about the rocks near the harbour – there's no beach to speak of – or clambering the nearby cliffs for spectacular views. At **Boulby**, a mile and a half's trudge up the coastal path (45min), you're walking on the highest cliff (670ft) on England's east coast.

ARRIVAL AND DEPARTURE
STAITHES

On foot There's a fine coastal walk from Whitby, passing pretty Runswick Bay and the village of Sandsend (around 4hr).

By bus The X4 runs daily between Staithes and Whitby (every 30min; 30min).

ACCOMMODATION AND EATING

Endeavour House 1 High St, TS13 5BH ☎01947 841029 (rooms), ☎07969 054556 (restaurant), ⓦ endeavour-restaurant.co.uk. Three lovely doubles in this restaurant-B&B located in a two-centuries-old house by the harbour. Parking available in municipal (£6/ day) and private (Glen Vale, £5/day) car parks. There's also a restaurant, run separately from the B&B, currently operating as a pop-up. Opening times vary – phone for details. **£100**

The Northeast

HOLY ISLAND

13 The Northeast

Post-industrial Tyne and Wear is home to the Northeast's major metropolis, the dynamic and distinctive city of Newcastle upon Tyne. Crammed with cultural attractions, great shops and an exceptionally energetic nightlife, Newcastle is up there with the most exciting cities in England. The bulk of the Northeast is, however, formed by the remote and beautiful county of Northumberland, an enticing medley of delightful market towns, glorious golden beaches, wooded dells, wild uplands and an unsurpassed collection of historical monuments. South of Northumberland lies the county of Durham, famous for its lovely university town and magnificent twelfth-century cathedral.

While its most recent past is defined by industry and in particular post-industrial hardship, the Northeast has an eventful early history: Romans, Vikings and Normans have all left dramatic evidence of their colonization, none more cherished than the 84-mile-long **Hadrian's Wall**, built by the Romans in 122 AD to contain the troublesome tribes of the far north. Thousands come each year to walk along parts, or all, of the Wall, or to cycle the nearby National Route 72. Neighbouring Northumberland National Park also has plenty for outdoors enthusiasts, with the huge **Kielder Water** reservoir, and surrounding footpaths and cycleways.

As well as Roman ruins, medieval **castles** scatter the region, the best-preserved being Alnwick, with its wonderful gardens, and stocky Bamburgh, on the coast. The shoreline round here, from Amble past Bamburgh to the Scottish border town of Berwick-upon-Tweed – and officially the end of Northumberland – is simply stunning, boasting miles of pancake-flat, dune-backed beach and a handful of off-shore islands. Reached by a tidal causeway, the lonely little islet of **Lindisfarne** – Holy Island – where early Christian monks created the Lindisfarne Gospels, is the most famous, while not far away to the south, near Seahouses, the **Farne Islands** are the perfect habitat for large colonies of seabirds including puffins, guillemots and kittiwakes.

South of Northumberland, the counties of **Durham** and **Tyne and Wear** better illustrate the region's industrial heritage. It was here in 1825 that the world's first railway opened – the Darlington and Stockton line – with local coal and ore fuelling Tyneside's shipbuilding and heavy-engineering companies. The area's abandoned coalfields, train lines, quaysides and factories have been transformed into superb, child-friendly tourist attractions.

GETTING AROUND   THE NORTHEAST

By public transport The main East Coast train line runs along the coast from London King's Cross to Edinburgh, calling at Darlington, Durham, Newcastle and Berwick-upon-Tweed, while cross-country trains and buses serve smaller towns and villages inland. In the more remote areas public transport is spotty, so it's best to have your own car or bike.

BEAMISH MUSEUM

Highlights

❶ Newcastle nightlife From raucous clubs and chic wine bars to cosy boozers and chilled-out indie gigs, there's something for everybody. See page 604

❷ Hadrian's Wall Walk the length of the greatest Roman monument in England, built in 122 AD to contain the troublesome tribes of the far north. See page 607

❸ Northumberland castles Northumberland is littered with beautiful castles, telling of a violent past ridden with ferocious battles and embittered family feuds. See page 614

❹ Holy Island A brooding lump of rock reached by a tidal causeway, this is a cradle of Christianity,

where the splendid, illuminated Lindisfarne Gospels were created. See page 620

❺ Durham Cathedral Said to be the finest Norman building in Europe, this awe-inspiring cathedral soars above the River Wear. See page 623

❻ Beamish Museum Exceptional open-air museum that recreates the Northeast's industrial past. See page 627

❼ Killhope Lead Mining Museum Put on a hard hat and get down the pit to see what life was really like for the Weardale coal miners. See page 631

HIGHLIGHTS ARE MARKED ON THE MAP ON PAGE 596

THE NORTHEAST

HIGHLIGHTS
1 Newcastle nightlife
2 Hadrian's Wall
3 Northumberland castles
4 Holy Island
5 Durham Cathedral
6 Beamish Museum
7 Killhope Lead Mining Museum

N

0 miles 10

NORTH SEA

Edinburgh

SCOTLAND

Norham Castle
Coldstream
Cornhill-on-Tweed
Branxton
Kirk Yetholm
The Cheviot (2674ft)

Berwick-upon-Tweed
Edinburgh
Scremerston
Beal
Etal
Ford
Crookham
Heatherslaw Light Railway
Etal Castle

Holy Island
Fenwick Islands
Waren Mill
Bamburgh
Seahouses
Beadnell
Newton-by-the-Sea
Embleton
Dunstanburgh Castle
Craster

Belford
Chillingham Castle
Eglingham
Wooler

Alnwick
Alnmouth
Newton-on-the-Moor
Warkworth
Amble

Cragside
Rothbury
Morpeth
Ashington

Otterburn
NORTHUMBERLAND NATIONAL PARK
Wallington
Cambo

THE CHEVIOT HILLS
Byrness
REDESDALE
Greenhaugh
Tarset
Stannersburn
Falstone

KIELDER FOREST PARK
Kielder
Kielder Water
Kielder Waterside
Belvedere
Tower Knowe

B6525
A697
A1
B1340
A1
A697
A697
A1068
A189
A696
A68

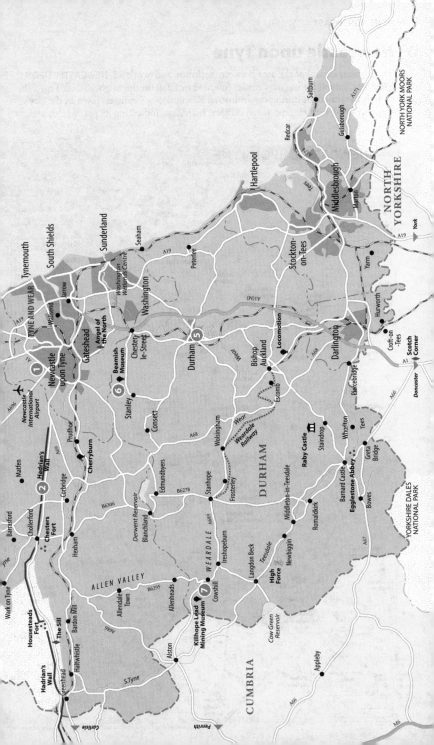

Newcastle upon Tyne

The de facto capital of the area between Yorkshire and Scotland, **NEWCASTLE UPON TYNE** was named for its "new castle" founded in 1080 on the mighty River Tyne. The city hit the limelight during the Industrial Revolution – Grainger Town in the city's centre is lined with elegant, listed classical buildings, indicating its past wealth and

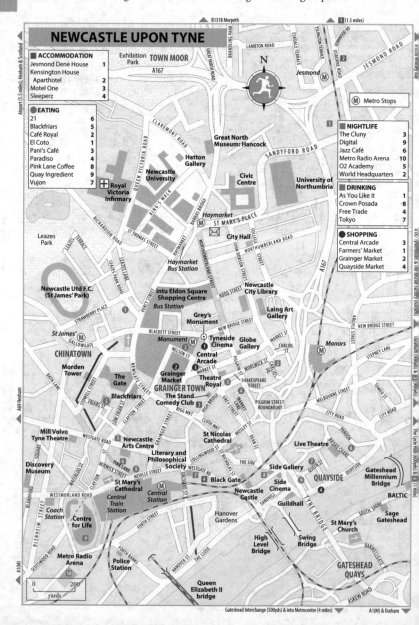

NEWCASTLE UPON TYNE

■ ACCOMMODATION
Jesmond Dene House	1
Kensington House Aparthotel	2
Motel One	3
Sleeperz	4

● EATING
21	6
Blackfriars	5
Café Royal	2
El Coto	1
Pani's Café	3
Paradiso	4
Pink Lane Coffee	8
Quay Ingredient	9
Vujon	7

■ NIGHTLIFE
The Cluny	3
Digital	9
Jazz Café	6
Metro Radio Arena	10
O2 Academy	5
World Headquarters	2

■ DRINKING
As You Like It	1
Crown Posada	8
Free Trade	4
Tokyo	7

● SHOPPING
Central Arcade	3
Farmers' Market	1
Grainger Market	2
Quayside Market	4

Ⓜ Metro Stops

13

importance as one of Britain's biggest and most important exporters of coal, iron and machinery. Although the decline of industry damaged Newcastle badly, today the city has emerged from its post-industrial difficulties with barely a smut on its face. Its reputation for lively nightlife is just the tip of the iceberg; visitors flock here for its collection of top-class art galleries, museums and flourishing theatre scene – not to mention the shopping – with 2018's huge **Great Exhibition of the North** showcasing its rich cultural offerings.

Newcastle Castle

Castle Garth, NE1 1RQ • Daily 10am–5pm • £6.50, purchased at the Black Gate • ☎ 0191 230 6300, ⓦ newcastlecastle.org.uk

Anyone arriving by train from the north will get a sneak preview of the **Castle**, as the rail line splits the keep from its gatehouse, the **Black Gate**, on St Nicholas Street. A wooden fort was built here over an Anglo-Saxon cemetery by Robert Curthose, illegitimate eldest son of William the Conqueror, but the present keep dates from the twelfth century. There's a great view from the rooftop over the river and city.

St Nicholas Cathedral

At the junction of St Nicholas St and Mosley St, NE1 1DF • Mon–Fri & Sun 7.30am–6pm, Sat 8am–4pm • Free, donation requested • ☎ 0191 232 1939, ⓦ stnicholascathedral.co.uk

St Nicholas Cathedral, dating mainly from the fourteenth and fifteenth centuries, is remarkable chiefly for its tower; erected in 1470, it is topped with a crown-like structure of turrets and arches supporting a lantern. Inside, behind the high altar, is one of England's largest funerary brasses, commissioned by Roger Thornton, the Dick Whittington of Newcastle, who arrived in the city penniless and died its richest merchant in 1429.

Quayside

From between the castle and the cathedral a road known simply as The Side – formerly the main road out of the city, and home to the excellent **Side Gallery** – descends to Newcastle's **Quayside**. The river is spanned by seven bridges in close proximity, the most prominent being the looming **Tyne Bridge** of 1928, symbol of the city. Immediately west is the hydraulic **Swing Bridge**, erected in 1876 by Lord Armstrong so that larger vessels could reach his shipyards upriver, while modern road and rail

---

NEWCASTLE ORIENTATION

Visitors are encouraged to think of the city as **Newcastle Gateshead**, an amalgamation of the two conurbations straddling the Tyne. On Gateshead Quays are the **BALTIC** contemporary arts centre and Norman Foster's **Sage** music centre, and on the opposite side, Newcastle's **Quayside** is where you'll find much of the city's nightlife. The city splits into several distinct areas, with just a few minutes' walk between them. The **castle** and **cathedral** occupy the heights immediately above the River Tyne, while north of here lies the city centre, **Grainger Town**. Chinatown and the two big draws of the **Discovery Museum** and **Centre for Life** are west of the centre, while east is the renowned **Laing Gallery** and, a short walk along the river, the old industrial **Ouseburn** area, home to an alternative cultural scene, interesting galleries, the excellent **Seven Stories** children's museum and some popular bars. In the north of the city, on the university campus, is the **Great North Museum: Hancock**; further north, through the landscaped Exhibition Park, is the **Town Moor**, 1200 acres of common land where freemen of the city – including Jimmy Carter and Bob Geldof – are entitled to graze cattle.

13

lines cross the river on the adjacent **High Level Bridge**, built by Robert Stephenson in 1849 – Queen Victoria was one of the first passengers to cross, promoting the railway revolution. Beyond the Tyne Bridge is an area of riverside apartments, landscaped promenades, public sculpture and pedestrianized squares, along with a series of fashionable bars and restaurants centred on the graceful **Gateshead Millennium Bridge**, the world's first tilting span, which pivots to let ships pass.

BALTIC

By the Millennium Bridge, Gateshead Quays, NE8 3BA • Mon & Wed–Sun 10am–6pm, Tues 10.30am–6pm • Free • ☎ 0191 478 1810, ⓦ balticmill.com

Fashioned from an old brick flourmill, **BALTIC** sits on the Gateshead riverbank, by the Millennium Bridge. Designed to be a huge visual "art factory", it's second only in scale to London's Tate Modern. There's no permanent collection here – instead there's an ever-changing calendar of exhibitions and local community projects, as well as artists' studios, education workshops, an art performance space and cinema, plus a rooftop restaurant with uninterrupted views of the Newcastle skyline.

Sage Gateshead

St Mary's Square, Gateshead Quays, NE8 2JR • Daily 9am–late • ☎ 0191 443 4666, ⓦ sagegateshead.com

Sitting on the riverbank, the **Sage Gateshead** is an extraordinary billowing steel, aluminium and glass concert hall complex, best seen at night when it glows with many colours. It's home to the Royal Northern Sinfonia orchestra and Folkworks, an organization promoting British and international traditional music, and there's something on most nights – from music concerts to workshops and lectures, as well as the Gateshead International Jazz Festival every April. The public concourse provides marvellous river and city views, and there are bars, a café and a brasserie.

Ouseburn

The **Ouseburn area**, fifteen minutes' walk up the River Tyne from Millennium Bridge, was once at the heart of Newcastle's industrial activities but became a derelict backwater in the mid-twentieth century. A jumble of old Victorian mills and warehouses, Ouseburn has seen a remarkable rejuvenation, as artists, musicians, businesses and even residents move in. Lime Street, home to quirky live-music venue, **The Cluny** (see page 605), artists' workshops and the nationally renowned **Seven Stories**, is the hub, but there are plenty of attractions nearby including Europe's biggest commercial art space, the **Biscuit Factory** (see page 602), plus an art-house cinema, riding stables and a small working farm.

Seven Stories

30 Lime St, NE1 2PQ • Tues–Sat 10am–5pm, Sun & bank hols 10am–4pm • £7.70, under-17s £6.60 • ☎ 0300 330 1095 ext 300, ⓦ sevenstories.org.uk

Housed in a beautifully converted Victorian riverside mill and spread over seven floors, **Seven Stories** celebrates the art of children's books through displays of original artwork, manuscripts and related documents. The bright, interactive exhibitions change regularly but highlights include original sketches taken from Noel Streatfield's *Ballet Shoes*, material from *Charlie and the Chocolate Factory* by Roald Dahl, Philip Pullman's early drafts, and the unpublished novel by Enid Blyton, *Mr Tumpy's Caravan*. Kids get the opportunity to dress up and create their own artworks; there is also a simple café.

Grainger Town

The heart of the city is known as **Grainger Town**, one of the best-looking city centres in Britain. Thrown up in a few short mid-nineteenth-century years by businessmen-

THE GEORDIE NATION

Tyneside and Newcastle's native inhabitants are known as **Geordies**, the word probably derived from a diminutive of the name "George". There are various explanations of who George was (King George II, railwayman George Stephenson), all plausible, none now verifiable. Geordies speak a highly distinctive dialect and accent, heavily derived from Old English. Phrases you're likely to come across include: haway man! (come on!), scran (food), a'reet (hello) and propa belta (really good) – and you can also expect to be widely addressed as "pet" or "flower".

builders and architects such as Richard Grainger, Thomas Oliver and John Dobson, the area is known for its classical stone facades lining splendid, wide streets and, in particular, **Grey Street**, named for the second Earl Grey (he of the tea), prime minister from 1830 to 1834. In 1832, Grey carried the Reform Act – which granted seats in the House of Commons to large cities that had developed during the Industrial Revolution, like Newcastle – through parliament, an act commemorated by **Grey's Monument** at the top of the street. The restored **Grainger Market** (Mon–Sat 9am–5.30pm, ⓦgraingermarket.org.uk), nearby, was Europe's largest covered market when built in the 1830s, and is today home to the smallest branch of Marks & Spencer, known as the Original Penny Bazaar.

Centre for Life

Times Square, NE1 4EP • Mon–Sat 10am–6pm, Sun 11am–6pm; last admission 4pm • £13, under-18s £7.50 • ☎ 0191 243 8210, ⓦ life.org.uk

A five-minute walk west of Central Station, the sleek buildings of the **Centre for Life** reach around the sweeping expanse of Times Square. This ambitious "science village" project combines bioscience and genetics research with a science visitor centre that aims to convey the secrets of life using the latest entertainment technology. Children find the whole thing enormously rewarding – from the sparkling Planetarium to the motion simulator – so expect to spend a good three hours here, if not more.

Discovery Museum

Blandford Square, NE1 4JA • Mon–Fri 10am–4pm, Sat & Sun 11am–4pm • Free • ☎ 0191 232 6789, ⓦ twmuseums.org.uk

The **Discovery Museum** concentrates on the maritime history of Newcastle and Tyneside, and their role in Britain's scientific and technological developments. Highlights include the *Turbinia* – the first ship to be powered by a steam turbine – which dominates the museum entrance, and the Newcastle Story, a walk through the city's past with tales from animatronic characters along the way.

Literary and Philosophical Society

23 Westgate Rd, NE1 1SE • Mon, Wed & Thurs 9.30am–7pm, Tues 9.30am–8pm, Fri 9.30am–5pm, Sat 9.30am–1pm • Free • ☎ 0191 232 0192, ⓦ litandphil.org.uk

Known as the **Lit and Phil**, this temple-like public library and learned society occupies one of the city's finest Georgian buildings: the domed roof, stucco ceilings and wrought-iron galleries are well worth a look. Established in 1825, it now runs a programme of recitals, jazz concerts, talks and exhibitions.

Laing Art Gallery

New Bridge St, NE1 8AG • Tues–Sat 10am–5pm, Sun 2–5pm • Free • ⓦ laingartgallery.org.uk

The **Laing Art Gallery**, in the east of the city, is home to the northeast's premier art collection: the permanent display is a sweep through British art from the seventeenth

13

century to today, featuring sculpture from Henry Moore and a large collection of John Martin's fiery landscapes, along with a smattering of Pre-Raphaelites, a group much admired by the English industrial barons. Another permanent display highlights a superb collection of Newcastle silver dating from the seventeenth century and some colourful 1930s glassware by George Davidson.

Newcastle University

Great North Museum: Hancock Barras Bridge, NE2 4PT • Mon–Fri 10am–5pm, Sat 10am–4pm, Sun 11am–4pm • Free • ☎ 0191 208 6765, ⓦ greatnorthmuseum.org.uk • **Hatton Gallery** Kings Rd, NE1 7RU • Mon–Sat 10am–5pm • Free • ☎ 0191 208 6059, ⓦ hattongallery.org.uk

A short walk north of Haymarket Metro are two sites of interest on the **Newcastle University** campus. The **Great North Museum: Hancock** has an engaging mishmash of natural history exhibits – there's a knobbly T-Rex skeleton, some stuffed animals and an aquarium – historical artefacts like a large-scale replica Hadrian's Wall, and a planetarium (£2.50). Across the road is the bijou **Hatton Gallery**, famous for housing the only surviving example of German Dadaist Kurt Schwitters' *Merzbau* (a sort of architectural collage).

ARRIVAL AND DEPARTURE
NEWCASTLE UPON TYNE

By plane Newcastle International Airport is 6 miles north of the city (☎ 0871 882 1121, ⓦ newcastleairport.com). It is linked by the Metro to Central Station (every 7–15min 5.45am–midnight; 22min; £4.70) and beyond. You can also take a taxi into the centre (around £18).

By train Central Station is a 5min walk from the city centre or Quayside, and has a Metro station.

Destinations Alnmouth (hourly; 25min); Berwick-upon-Tweed (hourly; 45min); Carlisle (hourly; 1hr 30min); Darlington (frequent; 35min); Durham (frequent; 15min); Hexham (every 30min; 40min); London (every 30min; 2hr 45min–3hr 15min); York (frequent; 1hr).

By bus National Express coaches stop on St James's Boulevard/Churchill St, not far from Central Station, while regional buses stop at Haymarket bus station (Haymarket

Metro). Gateshead Interchange is a big bus station served by local and national buses, linked by Metro to the city centre.

Destinations Alnmouth (every 30min; 1hr 30min); Alnwick (every 30min; 1hr 20min); Bamburgh (Mon–Sat 3 daily; Sun 2 daily; 2hr 30min); Beamish (April–Oct daily, Nov–March Sat & Sun; every 30min; 1hr); Berwick-upon-Tweed (Mon–Sat 8 daily; 2hr 30min); Carlisle (Mon–Sat hourly; 2hr 10min); Craster (Mon–Sat 7 daily, Sun 4 daily; 1hr 50min); Durham (Mon–Sat every 30min, Sun 4–6 daily; 50min); Hexham (hourly; 50min); Middlesbrough (Mon–Sat every 30min; 1hr); Rothbury (Mon–Sat hourly, Sun 2 daily; 1hr 30min); Seahouses (Mon–Sat 3 daily, Sun 2 daily; 2hr 10min); Warkworth (daily every 30min; 1hr 20min).

GETTING AROUND

By Metro The convenient, easy-to-use Tyne and Wear Metro (daily 5.30am–midnight, every 5–10min or 10–20min in the evening) connects the city centre with the

airport and runs out to the suburbs. You can buy a Metro Day Saver ticket for unlimited rides in all zones (£5).

By bus All city and local buses stop at Eldon Square

NEWCASTLE ART GALLERIES

Biscuit Factory 16 Stoddart St, Ouseburn, NE1 2NP ☎ 0191 261 1103, ⓦ thebiscuitfactory.com. Britain's largest commercial art gallery, displaying and selling anything from pendulum clocks and carved wooden tables to ceramic teapots and quirky necklaces. Free. Mon–Fri 10am–5pm, Sat 10am–6pm, Sun 11am–5pm.

Globe Gallery 47 Pilgrim St, NE1 6QE ☎ 0191 597 9377, ⓦ globegallery.org. Contemporary arts space that supports local, up-and-coming artists; it hosts a variety of exhibitions and one-off events.

Free. Wed–Sat noon–5pm.

Northern Print Stepney Bank, Ouseburn, NE1 2NP ☎ 0191 261 7000, ⓦ northernprint.org.uk. Little gallery that sells affordable prints by local artists. You can also learn how to make prints at the studio's workshop. Free. Wed–Sat noon–4pm.

Side Gallery 5–9 Side, NE1 3JE ☎ 0191 232 2208, ⓦ amber-online.com. A long-established, collectively run space with a strong specialism in social documentary photography. Free. Tues–Sun 11am–5pm.

shopping centre. Quaylink buses connect major attractions in Newcastle and Gateshead Quays with Newcastle Central Station, Haymarket Bus Station and Gateshead Interchange. Buses run frequently daily (day ticket from £5.10).

By bike Rent bikes at The Cycle Hub, Quayside (☎0191 276 7250, ⓦthecyclehub.org). Town bikes £10/2hr.

By taxi There are taxi ranks at Haymarket, Grey St (near the Theatre Royal) and outside Central Station. To book, contact Noda Taxis (☎0191 222 1888, ⓦnoda-taxis.co.uk).

INFORMATION AND TOURS

Tourist information Up-to-date visitor information is available online (ⓦnewcastlegateshead.com) and maps and brochures are available at hotels and attractions across Newcastle and Gateshead.

Public transport information Nexus Traveline has shops at the Central Station, Haymarket, Monument and Gateshead Metro stations (☎0191 202 0747, ⓦnexus.org.uk).

Tours City tours and various tours to Hadrian's Wall, Northumberland and Durham are run by Newcastle City Tours (from £40 per group of seven people max; ☎07780

958679, ⓦnewcastlecitytours.co.uk) while River Escapes Cruises' sightseeing boats (£6/10/12; ☎01670 785666, ⓦriverescapes.co.uk) depart most weekends throughout the year, and other days in summer, from the Quayside. A hop-on hop-off, open-top sightseeing bus departs from Central Station (April–June, Sept & Oct Sat & Sun only, July & Aug daily; every 30min–1hr; £8; ☎01789 299123, ⓦcity-sightseeing.com). Saddle Skedaddle (ⓦskedaddle. co.uk) organizes C2C (sea-to-sea) cycle tours and trips to Hadrian's Wall from £250/3 days.

ACCOMMODATION

Budget **hotel chains** offer plenty of good-value rooms in the city centre and down by the Quayside, while the biggest concentration of small hotels and guesthouses lies a mile north of the centre in popular, student-filled Jesmond, along and off Osborne Road: take bus #33 from Central Station or Haymarket.

★ **Jesmond Dene House** Jesmond Dene Rd, Jesmond, NE2 2EY ☎0191 212 3000, ⓦjesmonddenehouse. co.uk; map p.598. An imposing Arts and Crafts house in a very peaceful wooded valley. The sleek, boldly decorated rooms are decked out in decadent velvet and silk furnishings and have enormous bathrooms with underfloor heating. There's fine dining in the garden-room restaurant and breakfasts are particularly luxurious, with smoked salmon, a range of cooked meats and champagne on offer. Rates vary; book well in advance. **£110**

Kensington House Aparthotel 5 Osborne Rd, Jesmond, NE2 2AU ☎0191 281 8175, ⓦkensington aparthotel.com; map p.598. Twenty-three upmarket apartments of varying sizes, conveniently situated near Jesmond Metro. The decor is modern and sleek, with wood

floors, cream carpets and marble kitchen surfaces. Beds are kitted out with luxurious Egyptian cotton sheets and feather down duvets. Six apartments have wheelchair access. **£115**

Motel One 15–25 High Bridge, NE1 1EW ☎0191 211 1090, ⓦmotel-one.com/en; map p.598. This new 222-bed budget chain hotel has retained period features while embracing modern style. Rooms are small but perfectly formed and staff go the extra mile. Breakfast extra. **£59**

Sleeperz 15 Westgate Rd, NE1 1SE ☎0191 261 6171, ⓦsleeperz.com/newcastle; map p.598. A great-value option in the heart of town, part of a little chain that marries functionality with good design. Despite the city-centre location, the 98 compact but comfortable rooms provide a quiet respite from Saturday-night mayhem, and there's a funky breakfast bar/café downstairs. **£52**

EATING

Newcastle has a great variety of places to eat, from expensive, top-quality restaurants showcasing the talents of young and creative chefs, to fun, relaxed cafés and budget-friendly Chinese restaurants (mostly around Stowell Street in Chinatown). The popular chain restaurants are down by the Quayside.

21 Trinity Gardens, NE1 2HH ☎0191 222 0755, ⓦ21newcastle.co.uk; map p.598. Parisian-style bistro with crisp white tablecloths, leather banquettes, a classic French menu and slick service. Expect dishes like confit of duck with Lyonnaise potatoes (£20.50) or smoked haddock with softly poached hen's egg (£18.20), and delicious desserts – the Florentine doughnut with strawberry jam and crème Chantilly (£7.20) is particularly good. Mon–Sat noon–2.30pm & 5.30–10.30pm, Sun noon–8pm.

★ **Blackfriars** Friars St, NE1 4XN ☎0191 261 5945,

ⓦblackfriarsrestaurant.co.uk; map p.598. Housed in a beautiful stone building dating to 1239, *Blackfriars* offers superb traditional British dishes made with local ingredients. Mains (from £15) could include pork loin with a bacon and cheese floddie (potato cakes, originating from Gateshead, and traditionally eaten for breakfast) or a Doddington cheese and onion Wellington with chive cream sauce. For afters, dig into sticky toffee pudding with green grape ice cream and Brown Ale caramel (puddings from £6). Book ahead. Mon–Sat noon–2.30pm & 5.30pm–late, Sun noon–4pm.

13

Café Royal 8 Nelson St, NE1 5AW ☎0191 231 3000, ⓦsjf.co.uk; map p.598. Bright and buzzy café with great smoothies, coffees and delectable home-made breads and cakes – try the raspberry scones with clotted cream (£3.50) or hazelnut twists (£2). Mon–Sat 8am–6pm, Sun 10am–3.30pm.

El Coto 21 Leazes Park Rd, NE1 4PF ☎0191 261 0555, ⓦelcoto.co.uk; map p.598. Cute and cosy, this great tapas place has an extensive, good-value menu featuring all the usuals, such as *patatas bravas* and marinated sardines – dishes cost around £5, though paella goes for £10 per person. Daily noon–11pm.

Pani's Café 61–65 High Bridge St NE1 6BX ☎0191 232 4366, ⓦpaniscafe.co.uk; map p.598. On a side street below the Theatre Royal, this lively Sardinian café has won a loyal clientele for its good-value sandwiches, pasta and salads (mains around £8). Mon–Sat 10am–10pm.

Paradiso 1 Market Lane, NE1 6QQ ☎0191 221 1240, ⓦparadiso.co.uk; map p.598. Mellow café-bar hidden down an alley off Pilgrim Street – the snack food in the daytime becomes more substantial at night, with truffle risotto, salmon steaks and the like. There are set menus

throughout the day (two courses: lunchtime £9.95, evening £16.95) as well as a la carte. You can dine outdoors on the terrace in good weather. Mon–Thurs 11am–2.30pm & 5–10.30pm, Fri & Sat 11am–10.45pm.

Pink Lane Coffee 1 Pink Lane, NE1 5DW ☎07841 383085, ⓦpinklanecoffee.co.uk; map p.598. The best coffee in town: their beans are slow roasted and the milk is Northumbrian Pedigree. Exposed light bulbs, reclaimed furniture and brickwork tiling makes for an uber-hip interior. Mon–Fri 7.30am–6pm, Sat 9am–5pm, Sun 10am–4pm.

Quay Ingredient 4 Queen St, Quayside, NE1 3UG ☎0191 447 2327, ⓦquayingredient.co.uk; map p.598. Teeny tiny and popular, so it's best to get here early for brunch at weekends. Full English (£6.95) or eggs benedict (£5.95), plus sandwiches and salads (from £4.95) and delicious cakes (sweet muffin £1). Great coffee, too. Daily 8am–5pm.

Vujon 29 Queen St, NE1 3UG ☎0191 221 0601, ⓦvujon.com; map p.598. The city's classiest Indian restaurant, housed in an elegant building by the Quayside, serving dishes a cut above the ordinary, from venison Jaipur-style with chilli jam (£15.90) to the spicy duck *salan* (£14.90). Daily 5.30–11.30pm.

DRINKING

Newcastle's boisterous pubs, bars and clubs are concentrated in several areas: in the **Bigg Market** (between Grey St and Grainger St), around the **Quayside** and in the developing **Ouseburn** area, where bars tend to be quirkier and more sophisticated; in **Jesmond**, with its thriving student-filled strip of café-bars; and in the mainstream leisure-and-cinema complex known as **The Gate** (Newgate St). The main **LGBT+** area, known as the "Pink Triangle", focuses on the Centre for Life, spreading out to Waterloo Street and Westmorland and Scotswood roads.

As You Like It Archbold Terrace, NE2 1DB ☎0191 281 2277, ⓦasyoulikeitjesmond.com; map p.598. The top bar in the Jesmond area sits incongruously beneath an ugly tower block. This funky bar/restaurant has a relaxed vibe, exposed brick walls and a mishmash of furniture. The Supper Club, a club night on Fri & Sat (10pm–2am) features jazz, blues and soul. Mon–Thurs & Sun noon–midnight, Fri & Sat noon–2am.

Crown Posada 31 Side, NE1 3JE ☎0191 232 1269, ⓦsjf.co.uk; map p.598. A proper old man's boozer: local beers and guest ales in this small wood-and-glass-panelled Victorian pub. You might fancy the dark, malty Hadrian's Gladiator (£3.80) or opt for the golden, hoppy Tyneside Blonde (£3.80). Mon–Wed noon–11pm, Thurs 11am–11pm, Fri 11am–midnight, Sat noon–midnight, Sun noon–10.30pm.

★ **Free Trade** St Lawrence Rd, NE6 1AP ☎0191 265 5764; map p.598. Walk along the Newcastle Quayside past the Millennium Bridge and look for the shabby pub on the hill, where you are invited to "drink beer, smoke tabs" with the city's pub cognoscenti. Cask beer from local microbreweries, a great free juke box and superb river views from the beer garden. Mon–Thurs 11am–11pm, Fri & Sat 11am–midnight, Sun noon–11pm.

Tokyo 17 Westgate Rd, NE1 1SE ☎0191 232 1122, ⓦtokyonewcastle.co.uk; map p.598. The dark, sleek main bar is handsome enough, but follow the tealights up the stairs to the outdoor "garden" bar lined by plants and trees, giving the area a secret, exclusive feel. A pre-club favourite for Shindig (see below). Mon, Tues & Sun 5pm–midnight, Wed & Thurs 5pm–1am, Fri & Sat 5pm–2am.

NIGHTLIFE

Newcastle's biggest club night is **Shindig**, taking place on Saturdays and switching locations around the city. See ⓦshindiguk.com for the latest. Gigs, club nights and the LGBT+ scene are reviewed exhaustively in *The Crack* (monthly; free; ⓦthecrackmagazine.com), available in shops, pubs and bars.

CLUBS

Digital Times Square, NE1 4EP ☎0191 261 9755, ⓦyourfutureisdigital.com/newcastle; map p.598. The

city's top club, with an amazing sound system pumping out a variety of musical genres. If you like cheesy classics, look out for Born in the Sixties nights; while house, funk and disco fans will get their fix on Saturday's Love nights. Mon & Thurs 10.30pm–2.30am, Fri & Sat 11pm–3.30am.

World Headquarters Carliol Square, East Pilgrim St, NE1 6UF ☎0191 281 3445, ⓦwelovewhq.com; map p.598. Smallish, down-to-earth club that's always packed, playing a medley of house, hip-hop, soul and r'n'b and reggae. Downstairs there's a comfy lounge area with squashy sofas and a pool table. Entry fee around £10. Fri & Sat 10.30pm–3am.

LIVE MUSIC VENUES

★ **The Cluny** 36 Lime St, Ouseburn, NE1 2PQ ☎0191 230 4474, ⓦthecluny.com; map p.598. Based in an old whisky bottling plant, this is the best small music venue in the city, with something going on most nights, from quirky indie bands to contemporary punk-pop. *Cluny 2*, around the corner at 34 Lime Street (same hours), is its spacious sister

venue, with less frequent gigs. Mon–Fri noon–11pm, Fri & Sat noon–1am, Sun noon–10.30pm.

Jazz Café 23–25 Pink Lane, NE1 5DW ☎0191 232 6505, ⓦjazzcafe-newcastle.co.uk; map p.598. Slick and intimate jazz club in inauspicious surroundings, hosting top-quality jazz from 9.30pm on Friday and Saturday nights. Tues–Thurs 11am–11pm, Fri & Sat 11am–1am.

Metro Radio Arena Arena Way, NE4 7NA ☎0844 493 4567, ⓦmetroradioarena.co.uk; map p.598. The biggest concert and exhibition venue in the Northeast; star appearances have included Lady Gaga, Dolly Parton and The Killers. Book popular gigs well in advance.

O2 Academy Westgate Rd, NE1 1SW ☎0844 477 2000, ⓦo2academynewcastle.co.uk; map p.598. Housed in the former bingo hall, this mainstream venue hosts a variety of big names and local talent.

ENTERTAINMENT

Live Theatre 27 Broad Chare, NE1 3DQ ☎0191 232 1232, ⓦlive.org.uk. Enterprising theatre company that aims to find and develop local, and particularly young, talent – the attached *Caffe Vivo* is good for coffee by day and pre-theatre meal deals by night.

Mill Volvo Tyne Theatre 111 Westgate Rd, NE1 4AG ☎0844 493999, ⓦmillvolvotynetheatre.co.uk. Beautifully restored Victorian theatre with a wide range of plays, comedy shows and gigs.

Side Cinema 3 Side, NE1 3JE ☎0191 232 2000, ⓦamber-online.com. A quaintly dishevelled fifty-seat cinema: they run an imaginative programme combining art-house movies with live music.

The Stand Comedy Club 31 High Bridge, NE1 1EW

☎0191 300 9700, ⓦthestand.co.uk. Great venue for comedy downstairs, with great pub food and a lovely courtyard upstairs. Laidback and friendly, with something showing every night of the week.

Theatre Royal 100 Grey St, NE1 6BR ☎0844 811 2121, ⓦtheatreroyal.co.uk. Grand venue for drama, opera, dance, musicals and comedy; also hosts the annual RSC season in Nov.

Tyneside Cinema 10 Pilgrim St, NE1 6QG ☎0845 217 9909, ⓦtynesidecinema.co.uk. The city's premier art-house cinema, with coffee, light meals and movie talk in the Art Deco cinema café. The gorgeous restored decor includes Persian-inspired gilded stucco, stained glass and mosaic floors.

SHOPPING

Newcastle has two shopping centres, the central intu Eldon Square (ⓦintu.co.uk/eldonsquare) and the vast intu Metrocentre (ⓦintu.co.uk/metrocentre), 4 miles west of the city centre.

Central Arcade Grainger Town, NE1 6EG; map p.598. A classy Edwardian arcade with a barrel-vaulted roof. Several high-end chain stores here include Office, Jones, Space NK and JG Windows (with its lovely window display of musical instruments). Daily 9am–5pm.

Farmers' Market Grey's Monument, NE1 7AL; map p.598. Central market selling wonderful locally sourced fruit and veg, jams, meats and fish. First Fri of each month 9.30am–2.30pm.

Grainger Market Grainger Town, NE1 5JQ ⓦgrainger

market.org.uk; map p.598. One of the city's oldest and best shopping experiences: a centrally located Georgian market painted in pastel colours and featuring old-fashioned fishmongers, butchers and a hardware store, alongside delis, gift shops and a French café. Mon–Sat 9am–5.30pm.

Quayside Market NE1 3DE; map p.598. Busy, popular market down on the quayside selling locally produced food, clothes and arts and crafts including jewellery. Sun 9.30am–4pm.

DIRECTORY

Hospital Royal Victoria Infirmary, Queen Victoria Rd (☎0191 233 6161, ⓦwww.newcastle-hospitals.org.uk) has 24hr A&E services and a Minor Injuries Unit (daily 8am–9pm). The Westgate Walk-in Centre at Newcastle

General Hospital, Westgate Road, is open daily (8am–8pm).

Police Newcastle City Centre Police Station, Forth Banks ☎0191 214 6555.

13 Around Newcastle

There are a number of attractions near Newcastle, all accessible by Metro. The train runs east towards **Wallsend**, where **Segedunum** fort marks the beginning of Hadrian's Wall, while out at Jarrow, **Bede's Museum** pays homage to Christianity's most important historian. Further out again is the splendid **Washington Wildfowl Centre** near Sunderland, while the Angel and the Goddess of the North are two striking pieces of public art south and north of Newcastle respectively.

Wallsend and Segedunum

Budle St, Wallsend, NE28 6HR, 4 miles east of Newcastle • June to mid-Oct 10am–6pm • £5.95 • ☎ 0191 236 9347, ⓦ segedunumromanfort.org.uk • Metro to Wallsend

Wallsend was the last outpost of Hadrian's great border defence and **Segedunum**, the "strong fort" a couple of minutes' signposted walk from the Metro station, has been admirably developed as one of the prime attractions along the Wall. The grounds contain a fully reconstructed bathhouse, complete with heated pools and colourful frescoes, while the "wall's end" itself is visible at the edge of the site, close to the river and Swan Hunter shipyard. From here, the **Hadrian's Wall Path** (see page 608) runs 84 miles westwards to Bowness-on-Solway in Cumbria; you can get your walk "passport" stamped inside the museum.

Jarrow Hall

On the edge of Jarrow, NE32 3DY, 5 miles east of Newcastle • Daily: Feb & March 10am–4.30pm; April–Sept 10am–5.30pm • £5 • ☎ 0191 424 1585, ⓦ jarrowhall.org.uk • Newcastle Metro to Jarrow, from where it's a 20min walk through the industrial estate

Jarrow Hall sits at the edge of the town of **JARROW** – ingrained on the national consciousness since the 1936 **Jarrow Crusade**, when 201 people marched three hundred miles down to London to protest against the government's refusal to ease unemployment and poverty in the Northeast. The complex is made up of the eighteenth-century Jarrow Hall House; a reconstructed Anglo Saxon Farm and Village; and the **Bede Museum**, which explores the life of Venerable Bede (673–735 AD), who lived here as a boy. Bede grew up to become one of Europe's greatest scholars and England's first historian – his *History of the English Church and People*, describing the struggles of the island's early Christians, was completed at Jarrow in 731.

Angel of the North

6 miles south of Newcastle upon Tyne, off A167 (signposted Gateshead South), NE9 7TY • Bus #21 from Eldon Shopping Centre; there's car parking at the site

Since 1998, Antony Gormley's 66ft-high **Angel of the North** has stood sentinel over the A1 at Gateshead. A startling steel colossus that greets anyone travelling up from the south by rail or road, it's sited on top of a former coal-mining site, and has become both a poignant eulogy for the days of industry and a symbol of resurgence and regeneration.

Goddess of the North

Cramlington, NE23 8AU, 9 miles north of Newcastle upon Tyne • Daily dawn–dusk, café & visitor centre July & Aug 10am–4pm • ⓦ northumberlandia.com • Cramlington's train station is 2.5 miles from the site, or take bus #X13 from Newcastle

The Angel of the North (see above) has a rival in Charles Jencks' **Goddess of the North** (or *Northumberlandia*), a gigantic landscaped sculpture laid out as a park. Made out of 1.5 million tonnes of earth from Shotton mine and an epic 34m-high and 400m-long, the recumbent naked Goddess was unveiled in 2013.

Washington Wildfowl and Wetlands Centre

13

Pattinson, NE38 8LE, 10 miles east of Newcastle • Daily: April–Oct 9.30am–5.30pm; Nov–March 9.30am–4.30pm • £9.45 • ☎ 0191 416 5454, ⓦ wwt.org.uk • Bus #8 from Sunderland (Mon–Sat only) stops at the Waterview Park, a short walk from the wildfowl centre; from Newcastle, take the Metro to Washington

Taking up one hundred acres of the north bank of the River Wear in Pattinson, the popular **Washington Wildfowl and Wetlands Centre** is a lush conservation area of meadows, woods and wetlands that acts as a winter habitat for migratory birds, including geese, waders and ducks. In summer, you can watch fluffy ducklings hatch in the Waterfowl Nursery.

Sunderland

SUNDERLAND is fifteen miles southeast of Newcastle and shares that city's long history, river setting and industrial heritage – but can't match its architectural splendour. However, it's worth a trip to visit the museum, easily accessible by Metro from Newcastle.

Sunderland Museum

Burdon Rd, SR1 1PP • Mon–Sat 10am–4pm, Sun noon–4pm • Free • ☎ 0191 561 2323

The **Sunderland Museum** does a very good job of telling the city's history, relating how Sunderland ships were once sent around the world, and also has much to say about the city's other major trades, notably its production of lustreware and glass. The **Winter Gardens**, housed in a steel-and-glass hothouse, invite a treetop walk to view the impressive polished-steel column of a water sculpture.

ARRIVAL AND INFORMATION

SUNDERLAND

By Metro The main stop for Metros from Newcastle (30–35min) is in the central train station opposite The Bridges shopping centre.

Website ⓦ seeitdoitsunderland.co.uk is a great site for visitors; it also lists visitor information points around the city where you can pick up maps and brochures.

Hadrian's Wall

Hadrian's Wall (ⓦ hadrianswallcountry.co.uk) was constructed in 122 AD at the behest of the Roman emperor Hadrian. Keen for peace and safety within his empire, fearing attacks from Pictish Scotland, Hadrian commissioned a long wall to act as a border, snaking its way from the Tyne to the Solway Firth. It was built up to a height of 15ft in places and was interspersed by milecastles, which

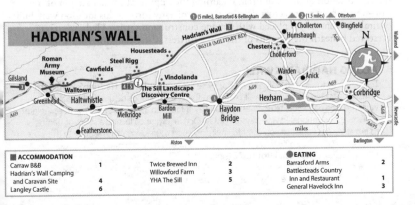

■ ACCOMMODATION				● EATING	
Carraw B&B	1	Twice Brewed Inn	2	Barrasford Arms	2
Hadrian's Wall Camping		Willowford Farm	3	Battlesteads Country	
and Caravan Site	4	YHA The Sill	5	Inn and Restaurant	1
Langley Castle	6			General Havelock Inn	3

13

functioned as gates, depots and mini-barracks. The best-preserved portions of the Wall are concentrated between **Chesters Roman Fort**, four miles north of Hexham, and Haltwhistle, sixteen miles to the west, which passes **Housesteads Roman Fort**, **Vindolanda** and the **Roman Army Museum**. Most people come to walk or cycle the length of the Wall, but if you're only planning to walk a short stretch, start off at Housesteads and head west for sweeping views. There are plenty of interesting places to stay and eat around and along the Wall, including the handsome market town of **Hexham** (see page 610).

Chesters Roman Fort

4 miles north of Hexham, NE46 4EU • April–Sept daily 10am–6pm; Oct & Nov daily 10am–5pm; Nov–April Sat & Sun 10am–4pm • £6.60; EH • ☎ 01434 681379, ⓦ www.english-heritage.org.uk/visit/places/chesters-roman-fort-and-museum-hadrians-wall

Beautifully sited next to the gurgling River Tyne, **Chesters Roman Fort**, otherwise known as Cilurnum, was built to guard the Roman bridge over the river. Enough remains of the original structure to pick out the design of the fort, but the highlight is down by the river where the vestibule, changing room and steam range of the garrison's **bathhouse** are still visible, along with the furnace and the latrines.

Housesteads Roman Fort

Around 8 miles west of Chesters, NE47 6NN • Daily: April–Sept 10am–6pm; Oct–March 10am–4pm • £7.50; EH & NT • ☎ 01434 344525, ⓦ www.english-heritage.org.uk/visit/places/housesteads-roman-fort-hadrians-wall

Housesteads Roman Fort is one of the most popular sites on the Wall. The fort is of standard design but for one enforced modification – forts were supposed to straddle the line of the Wall, but here the original stonework follows the edge of the cliff, so Housesteads was built on the steeply sloping ridge to the south. Enter via the tiny **museum**, and walk across to the south gate; next to this lies the ruins of a garrison of up to one thousand infantrymen. It's not necessary to pay for entrance to the fort if you're simply walking along the Wall west from here; the three-mile hike takes in wonderful views as it meanders past **Crag Lough** and over to **Steel Rigg** (which has a car park).

Vindolanda

13 miles west of Hexham, NE47 7JN, turn-off at Bardon Mill is signposted • Daily: mid-Feb to late March & Oct 10am–5pm; April–Sept 10am–6pm; Nov & Dec 10am–4pm • £7, combined ticket with Roman Army Museum £11 • ☎ 01434 344277, ⓦ vindolanda.com

The garrison fort of **Vindolanda** is believed to have been built and occupied before the construction of the Wall itself. Guarding the important central section of the east–west supply route across Britain, a series of early forts in this location were built of timber, eventually replaced with a stone construction during Hadrian's reign. Preserved beneath the remains of the stone fortress, these early forts are now being

---

ALONG HADRIAN'S WALL

The best way to visit the Wall is to walk or cycle the length of it. The **Hadrian's Wall Path** (ⓦ nationaltrail.co.uk/hadrians-wall-path) runs for 84 miles alongside the Wall itself from Wallsend (see page 606) to Bowness-on-Solway. It takes on average seven days to complete and there's an optional Passport system (May–Oct) involving collecting a series of stamps to prove you've done it. If you want to walk only short routes, you can link up with the AD122 bus (see page 609) that runs along Hadrian's Wall between mid-April and October. Alternatively, the **National Route 72** (signposted NCN 72; ⓦ www.sustrans.org.uk), shares some of the same route as the Hadrian Wall Path, and runs from South Shields to Ravenglass in Cumbria. There's bike hire in Newcastle (see page 603).

excavated – around three to four hundred volunteers take part every day. The museum contains the largest collection of Roman leather items ever discovered on a single site – sandals, purses, an archer's thumb guard – and a fascinating series of **writing tablets** dating to 90 AD. The earliest written records found in Britain, they feature shopping lists, duty rotas and even a birthday party invitation from one Claudia Severa to Sulpicia Lepidina.

Roman Army Museum

20 miles west of Hexham, CA8 7JB • Daily: mid-Feb to end March & Oct 10am–5pm; April–Sept 10am–6pm; Nov & Dec 10am–4pm • £5.75, combined ticket with Vindolanda £11 • ☎ 01434 344277, ⓦ vindolanda.com

The **Roman Army Museum** aims to illustrate how the Roman soldiers stationed here lived. There's everything from armour and weapons – including javelins, shields and swords – to a full-size chariot and a wagon. It's all very entertaining, and successfully brings to life the ruins you may just have seen at Vindolanda.

ARRIVAL AND GETTING AROUND   HADRIAN'S WALL

By train The nearest train stations are on the Newcastle–Carlisle line at Corbridge, Hexham, Bardon Mill and Haltwhistle.

By bus The little #AD122 (known as the "Hadrian's Wall bus"; Easter–Oct up to five times daily in each direction) runs from Newcastle to Corbridge, Hexham, and all the Wall sites and villages, before heading on to Carlisle and Bowness-on-Solway (the end of the Hadrian's Wall Path). There's also a year-round hourly service on the #685 bus between Newcastle and Carlisle, and other local services from Carlisle and Hexham, which provide access to various points along the Wall.

INFORMATION AND TOURS

Information The Sill Landscape Discovery Centre, Military Rd (☎ 01434 605555, ⓦ northumberlandnationalpark.org.uk) is a National Park hub that introduces visitors to the natural and human history of Hadrian's Wall. It has an exhibition centre and shop, a café and an 86-bed youth hostel.

Tours Wild Dog Outdoors (☎ 01434 688386, ⓦ wilddogoutdoors.co.uk) runs tours of the wall and forts suitable for all ages. Guides dress up as Celts or Romans and most of the walks set out from Cawfields, a lesser-known, but well-preserved section on the wall. From £20/2hr.

ACCOMMODATION

In addition to the B&Bs in the countryside around the Wall, Hexham (see page 610), Haltwhistle and Corbridge have a good selection of accommodation.

★ **Carraw B&B** Military Rd, Humshaugh, NE46 4DB ☎ 01434 689857, ⓦ carraw.co.uk; map p.607. It's not often you can say "I've slept on Hadrian's Wall", but here you can – this beautiful B&B, run by a friendly couple, is built right next to Hadrian's masterpiece and boasts stunning views. Lovely homely touches, like home-made shortbread and cake on arrival, hot-water bottles and luxurious toiletries make this place really special. Delicious breakfasts – the nutty granola is a winner. Supper £12.50. **£105**

Hadrian's Wall Camping and Caravan Site Melkridge Tilery, NE49 9PG, 2 miles north of Melkridge ☎ 01434 320495, ⓦ hadrianswallcampsite.co.uk; map p.607. Friendly, family-run site half a mile from the Wall, with showers, café, washing machine and dryer, and bike storage; breakfast and evening meals available. There's also a heated bunk room sleeping 10 people (£15/person). Open all year. Camping **£12**, camper van **£15**

Langley Castle A686, Langley-on-Tyne, 2 miles south of Haydon Bridge, NE47 5LU ☎ 01434 688888, ⓦ www.langleycastle.com; map p.607. There are suitably regal rooms – four-poster beds, sumptuous furnishings and beautiful bathrooms with saunas and spa baths – in this turreted medieval castle. The cheaper rooms are in the grounds, looking onto the castle. There's also an atmospheric restaurant, cocktail bar, lounge and gardens. **£195**, castle rooms **£245**

Twice Brewed Inn Military Rd, NE47 7AN ☎ 01434 344534, ⓦ twicebrewedinn.co.uk; map p.607. This friendly community pub close to new hub The Sill (see below) has simple en-suite rooms that have been recently redecorated. On site there's a microbrewery and beer garden; breakfast is included, but must be ordered the night before. **£85**

★ **Willowford Farm** Gilsland, CA8 7AA ☎ 01697 747962, ⓦ willowford.co.uk; map p.607. Strictly speaking just over the Northumbrian border in Cumbria, but this farmhouse B&B still makes a lovely, tranquil base to explore the Wall. Rooms are in converted farm buildings

13

and decked out with pretty wooden beams and large beds. Packed lunch £6. **£88**

★ **YHA The Sill** Military Road, Bardon Mill, NE47 7AN ☎ 0800 019 1700, ⓦ yha.org.uk/sill-hadrians-wall; map p.607. Opened in summer 2017, this 86-bed hostel, attached to The Sill information centre, has doubles, triples and four-bed rooms, some of them en suite. Dorms **£15**, doubles **£39**

EATING

★ **Barrasford Arms** Barrasford, NE48 4AA, 9 miles north of Hexham ☎ 01434 681237, ⓦ barrasfordarms. co.uk; map p.607. Endearingly local, welcoming and homely, this country pub serves great traditional British food with a French twist; dishes could include pan-roasted lamb rump with creamy mash, wilted spinach, onion gravy and onion rings (£16) and for pudding, sticky toffee pudding with butterscotch sauce (£6.50). Booking advisable. Tues–Sat noon–midnight, Sun noon–11pm; snacks served all day; kitchen Tues–Sat noon–2pm & 6–9pm, Sun noon–3pm.

Battlesteads Country Inn and Restaurant Wark-on-Tyne, NE48 3LS, 12 miles north of Hexham ☎ 01434 230209, ⓦ battlesteads.com; map p.607.

In a charming village by a trickling stream, this locally renowned restaurant with a lovely beer garden uses fresh produce sourced from within a 30-mile radius. Leave room for their famed whisky and marmalade bread-and-butter pudding (£5.75). Best to book. Food served daily noon–3pm & 6.30–9.30pm.

General Havelock Inn 9 Ratcliffe Rd, Haydon Bridge, NE47 6ER ☎ 01434 684376; map p.607. Eighteenth-century inn that specializes in tasty Modern British food, from crab cakes and Cumberland sausages to chocolate brûlée and ice-cream sundaes. Great locally brewed ales on offer, too. Main meals average around £17 (bar menu cheaper). Daily noon–3pm & 5pm–midnight; kitchen daily noon–3pm & 6–11pm.

Hexham

HEXHAM is the only significant stop between Newcastle and Carlisle, and however keen you are on seeing the Wall, you'd do well to spend a night at this handsome market town – or even make it your base. The focal point is the **abbey**, whose foundations were originally part of a fine Benedictine monastery founded by St Wilfrid in 671. Claimed, according to contemporary accounts, to be the finest this side of the Alps, the church – or rather its gold and silver – proved irresistible to the Vikings, who savaged the place in 876. It was rebuilt in the eleventh century as part of an Augustinian priory, and the town grew up in its shadow.

Hexham Abbey

NE46 3NB • Daily 9.30am–5pm • ⓦ hexhamabbey.org.uk

The stately exterior of **Hexham Abbey** dominates the west side of the central marketplace. Entry is through the south transept, where there's a bruised but impressive first-century tombstone honouring Flavinus, a standard-bearer in the Roman cavalry, who's shown riding down his bearded enemy. The memorial lies at the foot of the broad, well-worn steps of the canons' **night stair**, one of the few such staircases – providing access from the monastery to the church – to have survived the Dissolution. The chancel, meanwhile, displays the inconsequential-looking **frith-stool**, an eighth-century stone chair that was once believed to have been used by St Wilfrid.

The Old Gaol

Hallgate, NE46 1XD • Feb, March, Oct & Nov Tues & Sat 11am–4.30pm; April–Sept Tues–Sat 11am–4.30pm • £3.95 • ☎ 01434 652349, ⓦ hexhamoldgaol.org.uk

Britain's first purpose-built prison, **Hexham Old Gaol** occupies a solid sandstone building to the east of the abbey. It was commissioned by the powerful Archbishop of York in 1330, and constructed using stone plundered from the Roman ruins at Corbridge. Inside there's an entertaining museum extolling the virtues and pitfalls of medieval crime and punishment.

ARRIVAL AND INFORMATION

13

By train The train station sits on the northeastern edge of the town centre, a 10min walk from the abbey.
Destinations Carlisle (hourly; 50min); Haltwhistle (hourly; 20min); Newcastle (hourly; 50min).
By bus The bus station is Loosing Hill, a 10min stroll east of the abbey.

Destinations Bellingham (Mon–Sat hourly; 45min); Newcastle (hourly; 50min).
Tourist office In the library at Queens Hall, Beaumont St (Mon 9am–6pm, Tues–Thurs 9am–5pm, Friday 9am–6pm, Sat 9.30am–5pm; ☎ 01670 620250).
Websites ⓦ hadrianswallcountry.co.uk, ⓦ visithexham.net.

ACCOMMODATION

The County Hotel Priestpopple, NE46 1PS ☎ 01434 608444, ⓦ countyhotelhexham.co.uk. A refurbished pub with seven spacious and elegant en-suite rooms. The staff are incredibly welcoming and there's great food served here, too. Street parking. **£110**

Hallbank Hallgate, behind the Old Gaol, NE46 1XA ☎ 01434 605567, ⓦ hallbankguesthouse.co.uk. A restored house in a quiet town-centre location, with eight very comfortable rooms and an associated coffee shop/restaurant. Evening meals available on request. **£120**

EATING AND DRINKING

★ **Bouchon Bistrot** 4–6 Gilesgate, NE46 3NJ ☎ 01434 609943, ⓦ bouchonbistrot.co.uk. Very stylish restaurant in a handsome terraced townhouse, serving sophisticated French dishes such as crispy duck confit with gratin potatoes (£15.95) and crème brûlée (£5.50). Mon–Sat noon–2pm & 6–9.30pm.
Dipton Mill Inn Dipton Mill Rd, NE46 1YA, 2 miles south of Hexham ☎ 01434 606577, ⓦ diptonmill.co.uk. A lovely, traditional country pub covered in ivy. While the food is excellent – good pub grub like steak and kidney pie and vegetable casserole – it's most famous for the home-brewed ales, made at Hexhamshire Brewery. Try

Old Humbug, named after the landlord. Mon–Sat noon–2.30pm & 6–11pm, Sun noon–3pm; kitchen Mon–Sat noon–2.30pm & 6.30–8.30pm, Sun noon–2pm.
★ **Rat Inn** Anick, NE46 4LN, 2 miles northeast of Hexham ☎ 01434 602814, ⓦ theratinn.com. In a glorious hillside location overlooking Hexham, this quaint pub has a roaring fire in winter and a pretty summer garden. The food is all locally sourced – try the braised local beef in Allendale beer (£10.50). Booking essential for Sun lunch. Mon–Sat noon–11pm, Sun noon–10.30pm; kitchen Mon–Sat noon–2pm & 6–9pm, Sun noon–3pm.

Northumberland National Park

Northwest Northumberland, the great triangular chunk of land between Hadrian's Wall and the coastal plain, is dominated by the wide-skied landscapes of **Northumberland National Park** (ⓦnorthumberlandnationalpark.org.uk), whose four hundred windswept square miles rise to the **Cheviot Hills** on the Scottish border. The bulk of the park is taken up by **Kielder Water and Forest nature reserve**, a superb destination for watersports and outdoor activities; the small town of **Bellingham** on the eastern edge of the park makes a good base for the reserve, as do **Rothbury** and **Wooler**, both of which also provide easy access to some superb walking in the craggy Cheviots.

Kielder Water and Forest

Surrounded by 250 acres of dense pine forest, **Kielder Water and Forest** is the largest reservoir in England; the mass of woodlands and wetlands means that **wildlife** is abundant – you might spot badgers, deer, otters, ospreys and red squirrels. The road from Bellingham follows the North Tyne River west and skirts the forested edge of the lake, passing an assortment of visitor centres, waterside parks, picnic areas and anchorages that fringe its southern shore. Mountain biking, hiking, horseriding and fishing are some of the land-based activities on offer, and of course watersports (waterskiing, sailing, kayaking and windsurfing) are hugely popular, too.

13

The skies here are some of the darkest in Europe and star-gazing can be magical; award-winning **Kielder Observatory** (ⓦkielderobservatory.org) hosts over forty night-time events a month (booking essential). **Kielder Waterside**, on the western flank of the reservoir, is the best place to head to get your bearings.

Kielder Waterside

NE48 1BT • Birds of Prey Centre daily 10.30am–4pm • Flying demonstrations summer 1.30pm & 3pm, Oct–March 2pm • £7, children £4.50 • ☏ 01434 251000, ⓦ kielderwaterside.com

Kielder Waterside Park is a purpose-built hub of lodges with cafés and a restaurant, a visitor centre, bike hire (see below) and a Birds of Prey Centre where you can see a variety of handsome, sharp-taloned beasts, from owls and falcons to vultures and ospreys.

ARRIVAL AND INFORMATION

By bus The #880 from Hexham serves the visitor centres of Tower Knowe, Kielder Waterside (by request) and Kielder Castle via Bellingham (2 daily Tues & Sat). The #714 from Newcastle upon Tyne runs on Sun (1 daily) to Tower Knowe, Kielder Waterside (by request) and Kielder Castle.

Visitor centres Tower Knowe: from Bellingham, the first visitor centre you come to as you head anti-clockwise

KIELDER WATER AND FOREST

round the reservoir (daily: April–June & Sept 10am–5pm; July & Aug 10am–6pm; Oct 10am–4pm; ☏ 0845 155 0236). Kielder Waterside: western flank of the reservoir (Feb–Oct daily 9am–5pm; ☏ 01434 251000). Kielder Castle: at the northernmost point of the reservoir (daily 10am–5pm; ☏ 01434 250209).

GETTING AROUND

By bike The Bike Place (ⓦthebikeplace.co.uk) has two hire centres at Kielder Castle Visitor Centre (daily 9.30am–5.30pm; ☏ 01434 250457) and at Kielder Waterside (daily 9.30am–6pm; ☏ 01434 250144); rental from £15/2hr.

By car For parking, you can buy a ticket at your first stop

(£5) that's valid for all other car parks throughout the day.

By ferry The 60-seater Osprey Ferry (☏01434 251000) sails round the reservoir, with stops at Kielder Waterside, Tower Knowe and occasionally Belvedere. Tickets (from £4.40, day pass £6.75) are available at Tower Knowe; book in advance.

ACCOMMODATION AND EATING

Hollybush Inn Greenhaugh, NE48 1PW, 12 miles east of Kielder Water ☏01434 240391, ⓦhollybushinn.net. Super little pub in a remote village serving great ales and food, and with seven simple and attractive bedrooms upstairs or in the quiet cottage next door. **£85**

Kielder Lodges Kielder Waterside Park, NE48 1BT ☏0845 155 0236, or Hoseasons ☏0345 498 6060, ⓦhoseasons.co.uk. Scandinavian-style self-catering lodges, all with access to the park's pool, sauna, bar and restaurant. Bring plenty of midge repellent. Two-night

minimum stay; rates vary widely. From **£60**

★ **Pheasant Inn** Stannersburn, NE48 1DD ☏01434 240382, ⓦthepheasantinn.com. A traditional country pub on the road from Bellingham, the *Pheasant Inn* has eight very comfortable bedrooms (including one family room). The highlight is the food, though, served downstairs in the cosy restaurant; expect game pies, Northumbrian cheeses and plenty of fish (mains around £12 in the evening). Booking recommended. Food served noon–2pm & 6.30–8.30pm. **£110**

Rothbury and around

ROTHBURY, straddling the River Coquet thirty miles northeast of Hexham, prospered as a late Victorian resort because it gave ready access to the forests, burns and ridges of the **Simonside Hills**. The small town remains a popular spot for walkers, with several of the best local trails beginning from the **Simonside Hills** car park, a couple of miles southwest of Rothbury. Nearby, the estates of **Cragside** and **Wallington** are good options if you want to take a break from hiking.

Cragside

1 mile east of Rothbury, NE65 7PX • **House** March–Oct daily 11am–5pm • £17 (includes gardens); NT • **Gardens** March–Oct daily 10am–6pm; Nov–Feb Fri–Sun 11am–4pm • £11; NT • ☏ 01669 620333, ⓦnationaltrust.org.uk/cragside

Victorian Rothbury was dominated by Sir William, later the first Lord Armstrong, the wealthy nineteenth-century arms manufacturer, shipbuilder and engineer who built his country home at **Cragside**, a mile to the east of the village. He hired Richard Norman Shaw, one of the period's top architects, who produced a grandiose Tudor-style mansion entirely out of place in the Northumbrian countryside. Armstrong was an avid innovator, and in 1880 Cragside became the first house in the world to be lit by hydroelectric power. The surrounding **gardens**, complete with the remains of the original pumping system, are beautiful and there's a pleasant tearoom for a light snack.

Wallington

13 miles south of Rothbury, NE61 4AR • House March–Oct daily noon–5pm; gardens year-round daily 10am–dusk • £12.40; NT • ☎ 01670 773967, ⓦ nationaltrust.org.uk/wallington

South of Rothbury, down the B6342, stands **Wallington**, an ostentatious mansion rebuilt in the 1740s by Sir Walter Blackett, the coal- and lead-mine owner. The house is known for its Rococo plasterwork and William Bell Scott's Pre-Raphaelite murals of scenes from Northumbrian history. Children will love the collection of doll's houses, one of which has thirty-six rooms and was originally fitted with running water and a working lift. However, it's the magnificent **gardens and grounds** that are the real delight, with lawns, woods and lakes laced with footpaths. There are events, concerts and activities throughout the year, as well as a café and farm shop on site.

ARRIVAL AND INFORMATION
ROTHBURY AND AROUND

By bus Buses from Newcastle via Morpeth stop outside the *Queen's Head* pub in the centre (hourly; 1hr 20min).

Information Help and advice for visitors to Northumber-land National Park is available at the Coquetdale Centre near the cross on Church St (daily 9.30am–5pm; ☎ 01669 621462, ⓦ northumberlandnationalpark.org.uk).

ACCOMMODATION

★ **Hillcrest** Rothbury, NE65 7TL ☎ 01669 621944, ⓦ hillcrestbandb.co.uk. Superb B&B in a pretty Georgian house, with two beautifully decorated bedrooms – wooden floorboards, antique furniture, exposed walls and the like – with an intriguing past (the owner will explain). Wonderful breakfasts, too. **£85**

Thistleyhaugh Longframlington, NE65 8RG, 5 miles east of Rothbury ☎ 01665 570629. Gorgeous, ivy-smothered Georgian farmhouse with five luxurious chintzy

bedrooms. They serve delicious three-course dinners (7pm; £20) and hearty breakfasts. **£80**

★ **Tosson Tower** Great Tosson, NE65 7NW, 2 miles southwest of Rothbury ☎ 01669 620228, ⓦ tosson towerfarm.com. Seven lovely rooms on this little working farm in a quiet hamlet with spectacular views out over the Cheviot Hills. Four charming self-catering cottages also available for longer stays. **£90**

Wooler and around

Stone-terraced **WOOLER** – rebuilt after a terrible fire in the 1860s – is a one-street market town twenty miles north of Rothbury. It's the best base for climbs up **The Cheviot** (2674ft), seven miles to the southwest and the highest point in the Cheviot Hills. From *YHA Wooler* at 30 Cheviot St, it's four hours there and back; from Hawsen Burn, the nearest navigable point, it's two hours walking there and back. Wooler is also a staging post on the Pennine Way and the lovely **St Cuthbert's Way** (from Melrose in Scotland to Lindisfarne).

Chillingham Castle

6 miles southeast of Wooler, NE66 5NJ • April–Oct daily noon–5pm • £9.50 • ☎ 01668 215359, ⓦ chillingham-castle.com

Chillingham Castle started life as an eleventh-century tower. The castle was augmented at regular intervals until the nineteenth century, but from 1933 was largely left to the elements for fifty years, until the present owner set about restoring it in his own individualistic way: bedrooms, living rooms and even a grisly torture chamber (designed to "cause maximum shock") are decorated with historical paraphernalia.

13

Chillingham Wild Cattle

Between Alnwick and Belford, signposted The Wild White Cattle, NE66 5NP · Tours April–Oct Mon–Fri hourly 10am–noon & 2–4pm, Sun 10am–noon; winter by appointment · £16 · ⓦ chillinghamwildcattle.com

In 1220, Chillingham Castle's adjoining 365 acres of parkland were enclosed to protect the local wild cattle for hunting and food. And so the **Chillingham Wild Cattle** – a fierce, primeval herd with white coats, black muzzles and black tips to their horns – remained to this day, cut off from mixing with domesticated breeds. It's possible to visit these unique relics, who number around ninety, but only in the company of a warden, as the animals are potentially dangerous, and also need to be protected from outside infection. The visit takes about two hours and involves a short country walk before viewing the cattle at a safe distance – the closest you're likely to get to big-game viewing in England. Bring strong shoes or walking boots if it's wet.

ARRIVAL AND INFORMATION

WOOLER AND AROUND

By bus The bus station is set back off High St.
Destinations Alnwick (Mon–Sat 9 daily; 45min); Berwick-upon-Tweed (Mon–Sat 9 daily; 50min); Newcastle (Mon–Sat 2 daily; 1hr 15min).

Tourist office Cheviot Centre, Padgepool Place (Mon–Sat 10am–4.30pm, plus Sun 10am–2pm Easter to Oct; ☏ 01668 282123).

ACCOMMODATION AND EATING

Milan 2 High St, through the arch of the Black Bull hotel, NE71 6BY ☏ 01668 283692, ⓦ milan-restaurant.co.uk. Good-value Italian restaurant with exposed brick walls and a jolly ambience, serving large pizzas (from £7.50), pasta dishes (from £7.95) and plenty of meat and fish options. It's a very popular place, so book ahead. Daily 5–10pm.

Tilldale House 34 High St, NE71 6BG ☏ 01668 281450, ⓦ tilldalehouse.co.uk. Snug seventeenth-century stone cottage in the middle of town with three en-suite bedrooms. With enormous, soft beds, deep-pile carpets, an open fire and great breakfasts, it makes a very cosy and enticing base after a long day hiking in the hills. **£75**

The Northumberland coast

Stretching 64 miles north of Newcastle up to the Scottish border, the low-lying **Northumberland coast** is the region's shining star, stunningly beautiful and packed with impressive sights. Here you'll find mighty fortresses at **Warkworth**, **Alnwick** and **Bamburgh** and magnificent Elizabethan ramparts surrounding **Berwick-upon-Tweed**; in between there are glorious sandy beaches, the site of the Lindisfarne monastery on **Holy Island**, and the seabird and nature reserve of the **Farne Islands**, reached by boat from Seahouses.

Warkworth

WARKWORTH, a peaceful coastal hamlet set in a loop of the River Coquet a couple of miles from Amble, is best seen from the north, from where the grey stone terraces of the long main street slope up towards the commanding remains of **Warkworth Castle**. From the castle, the main street sweeps down into the village, flattening out at Dial Place and the Church of St Lawrence before curving right to cross the River Coquet; just over the bridge, a signposted quarter-mile lane leads to the **beach**, which stretches for five miles from Amble to Alnmouth.

Warkworth Castle

Castle Terrace, NE65 0UJ · April–Oct daily 10am–5pm; rest of the year usually Sat & Sun only, see website for details; Duke's Rooms April–Sept Mon, Sun & bank hols only · £6.20, combined ticket with hermitage £8.90; EH · ☏ 01665 711423, ⓦ www.english-heritage.org.uk/visit/places/warkworth-castle-and-hermitage

Ruined but well-preserved, **Warkworth Castle** has Norman origins, but was constructed using sandstone during the fourteenth and fifteenth centuries. Home to generations

13

of the Percy family, the powerful earls of Northumberland, it appears as a backdrop in several scenes of Shakespeare's *Henry IV, Part II*. The cross-shaped keep contains a great hall, a chapel, kitchens, storerooms and the Duke's Rooms, which are kitted out in period furniture and furnishings.

Warkworth Hermitage

Castle Terrace, NE65 0UJ • Weather permitting April–Oct Mon, Sun & bank hols (plus Fri & Sat in July & Aug) 11am–5pm; rest of the year limited opening hours, see website for details • £4.30, combined ticket with castle £8.90; EH • ☎ 01665 711423, ⊕ www.english-heritage.org.uk/visit/places/warkworth-castle-and-hermitage

A path from the churchyard heads along the right bank of the Coquet to the boat that shuttles visitors across to **Warkworth Hermitage**, a series of simple rooms and a claustrophobic chapel that were hewn out of the cliff above the river some time in the fourteenth century, but abandoned by 1567. The last resident hermit, one George Lancaster, was charged by the sixth earl of Northumberland to pray for his noble family, for which lonesome duty he received around £15 a year and a barrel of fish every Sunday.

ARRIVAL	WARKWORTH
By bus The #X18 (Newcastle to Berwick) stops here, but it's quicker to take the train to Alnmouth, then the bus.	Destinations Alnmouth (every 30min; 10min), Berwick (every 2hr; 2hr 10min), Newcastle (hourly; 1hr 30min).

Alnmouth

It's three miles north from Warkworth to the seaside resort of **ALNMOUTH**, whose narrow centre is strikingly situated on a steep spur of land between the sea and the estuary of the Aln. This lovely setting has been a low-key holiday spot since Victorian times, and is particularly popular with golfers: the village's nine-hole course, right on the coast, was built in 1869 (it's claimed to be the second oldest in the country) and dune-strollers really do have to heed the "Danger – Flying Golf Balls" signs which adorn Marine Road.

ARRIVAL AND DEPARTURE	ALNMOUTH
By train Trains pass through from Berwick (every 2hr; 20min) and Newcastle (hourly; 30min). **By bus** There are local bus services from Alnwick and	Warkworth, and the regular #X18 Newcastle–Berwick bus also passes through Alnmouth and calls at its train station, 1.5 miles west of the centre.

ACCOMMODATION AND EATING

Red Lion 22 Northumberland St, NE66 2RJ ☎ 01668 30584, ⊕ redlionalnmouth.com. Six spacious and modern rooms, with pine furniture, cream walls and fresh bathrooms, above a popular, traditional pub. The beer garden is perfect for sunny days, and the menu has everything from big open sandwiches (from £4.95) to sirloin steak (£17.50). Restaurant Mon–Sat noon–3pm & 4–9pm, Sun noon–8pm. **£85**

Alnwick

The appealing market town of **ALNWICK** (pronounced "Annick"), thirty miles north of Newcastle and four miles inland from Alnmouth, is renowned for its **castle** and **gardens** – seat of the dukes of Northumberland – which overlook the River Aln. It's worth spending a couple of days here, exploring the medieval maze of streets, the elegant gatehouses on Pottergate and Bondgate and the best **bookshop** in the north.

Alnwick Castle

NE66 1NQ • April–Oct daily 10am–5.30pm • £15.50; castle and garden £26.10 • ☎ 01665 511100, ⊕ alnwickcastle.com

The Percys – who were raised to the dukedom of Northumberland in 1750 – have owned **Alnwick Castle** since 1309. In the eighteenth century, the first duke had the interior refurbished by Robert Adam in an extravagant Gothic style – which in turn was supplanted by the gaudy Italianate decoration preferred by the fourth duke in the 1850s. There's plenty to see inside, including remains from Pompeii, though the **interior** can be crowded at times – not least with families on the *Harry Potter* trail, since the castle doubled as Hogwarts School in the first two films.

Alnwick Garden

NE66 1YU • April–Oct & late Nov to early Jan daily 10am–6pm; Grand Cascade and Poison Garden closed in winter • Summer £12.10, winter £7; garden and castle £26.10 • ☎ 01665 511350, ⓦ alnwickgarden.com

The grounds of the castle are taken up by the huge and beautiful **Alnwick Garden**, designed by an innovative Belgian team and full of quirky features such as a bamboo labyrinth maze, a serpent garden involving topiary snakes, and the popular **Poison Garden**, filled with the world's deadliest plants. The heart of the garden is the computerized Grand Cascade, which shoots water jets in a regular synchronized display, while to the west is Europe's largest treehouse, which has a restaurant inside (see below). The walled Roots and Shoots community veg garden (no ticket required) is a delight.

Barter Books

Alnwick station, NE66 2NP • Daily 9am–7pm • ☎ 01665 604888, ⓦ barterbooks.co.uk

Housed in the Victorian train station on Wagonway Road, and containing visible remnants of the ticket office, passenger waiting rooms and the outbound platform, the enchanting **Barter Books** is one of the largest secondhand bookshops in England. With its sofas, murals, open fire, coffee and biscuits – and, best of all, a model train that runs on top of the stacks – it is definitely worth a visit.

ARRIVAL AND INFORMATION   ALNWICK

By bus The station is on Clayport St, a couple of minutes' walk west of the marketplace.
Destinations Bamburgh (Mon–Sat 7 daily; Sun 4 daily; 1hr 15min); Berwick-upon-Tweed (Mon–Sat 6 daily, Sun 3 daily; 1hr); Craster (Mon–Fri 7 daily, Sat 4 daily; 35min); Wooler (Mon–Sat 9 daily; 45min).

Tourist office 2 The Shambles, off the marketplace (April–June, Sept & Oct Mon–Sat 9.30am–5pm, Sun 10am–4pm; July & Aug daily 9am–5pm; Nov–March Mon–Fri 9.30am–4.30pm, Sat 10am–4pm; ☎ 01665 622152, ⓦ visitalnwick.org.uk).

ACCOMMODATION AND EATING

Alnwick Garden Treehouse Alnwick Gardens, NE66 1YU ☎ 01665 511852, ⓦ alnwickgarden.com. Glorious restaurant in the enormous treehouse in Alnwick Gardens (you don't have to pay the garden entry fee to visit). There's an open fire in the middle of the room and even tree trunks growing through the floor. A set menu is available at lunch and dinner (two courses £19.95/£28.50) with lots of local produce cooked to perfection (mains include English rack of lamb or stuffed field mushrooms). Booking essential. Mon & Tues noon–3pm, Wed–Sat noon–3pm & 6.30–9.15pm, Sun noon–8pm.
Station Buffet Barter Books Wagonway Road, NE66 2NP ☎ 01665 604888, ⓦ barterbooks.co.uk. Set in the old station waiting room at Barter Books, this unique café serves home-made food including cooked breakfasts (9–11.30am), hamburgers, sandwiches, salads and cakes

(meals around £7). Daily 9am–7pm.
Tate House 11 Bondgate Without, NE66 1PR ☎ 01665 660800, ⓦ stayinalnwick.co.uk. In a pretty Victorian house opposite Alnwick Gardens, the ten comfortable bedrooms are available on a "room only" basis, with spotless bathrooms and nice little touches such as hot-water bottles, iPod docks and DVD players. Ten percent off breakfast at *The Plough* across the road. **£65**
YHA Alnwick 4–38 Green Batt, NE66 1TU ☎ 01665 604661, ⓦ yha.org.uk/hostel/alnwick. A handsome Victorian courthouse nicely converted into a hostel with some private rooms. You're a stroll away from the gardens and castle, and there's a bus stop right outside the front door. Dorms **£18.50**, doubles **£39**

Craster and around

The tiny fishing village of **CRASTER** – known for its kippers – lies six miles northeast of Alnwick, right on the coast. It's a delightful little place, with its circular, barnacle-encrusted harbour walls fronting a cluster of tough, weather-battered little houses and the cheery *Jolly Fisherman* pub. Other villages worth visiting round here include

13

Newton-on-Sea and **Beadnell**, both exuding wind swept, salty charm. The **coastline** between Dunstanburgh and Beadnell is made up of the long sandy beaches that Northumberland is famous for.

Dunstanburgh Castle

Dunstanburgh Rd, NE66 3TT · April–Sept daily 10am–6pm; Oct daily 10am–4pm; Nov–March Sat & Sun 10am–4pm · £5; NT & EH · ☎ 01665 576231, ⓦ www.english-heritage.org.uk/visit/places/dunstanburgh-castle

Looming in the distance, about a thirty-minute walk northwards up the coast from Craster, is stunning **Dunstanburgh Castle**. Built in the fourteenth century, in the wake of civil war, its shattered remains occupy a magnificent promontory, bordered by sheer cliffs and crashing waves.

ARRIVAL   CRASTER AND AROUND

By bus Buses #X18 and #418 run to Alnwick (Mon–Sat 11 daily, Sun 3 daily; 35min).

ACCOMMODATION

Old Rectory Howick, NE66 3LE, 2 miles south of Craster ☎ 01665 577590, ⓦ oldrectoryhowick.co.uk. Just 400yd from the wind-whipped North Sea, this fantastic B&B sits in its own peaceful grounds and has extremely pretty bedrooms and comfortable sitting areas. Superb breakfasts feature plenty of cooked options, including Craster kippers. **£90**

EATING AND DRINKING

There's not much in the way of fine dining round these parts; most villages simply have a traditional pub serving decent meals. Craster's beloved **kippers** are smoked at L. Robson & Sons (☎ 01665 576223, ⓦ kipper.co.uk) in the centre of the village; they also sell salty oak-smoked salmon.

Jolly Fisherman 9 Haven Hill, NE66 3TR ☎ 01665 576461, ⓦ thejollyfishermancraster.co.uk. Located just above the harbour, this pub has sea views from its back window and a lovely summer beer garden. Not surprisingly for a pub opposite L. Robson & Sons, it serves plenty of fish – crab sandwiches, kipper pâté and a famously good crab-meat, whisky and cream soup. Mon–Sat 11am–11pm, Sun noon–11pm; kitchen Mon–Fri 11am–3pm & 5–8.30pm, Sun noon–7pm.

Ship Inn Low Newton-by-the-Sea, NE66 3EL, 5 miles north of Craster ☎ 01665 576262, ⓦ shipinnnewton.

co.uk. Great, rustic pub in a coastal hamlet serving dishes using ingredients from local suppliers – there's plenty of L. Robson smoked fish on the menu. Mains from £7. Ales are supplied by their own brewery next door. Dinner reservations essential in evening. April–Oct Mon & Tues 11am–10.30pm, Wed–Sat 11am–11pm, Sun & bank hols noon–10pm, Nov–March Mon–Wed 11am–5pm, Thurs–Sat 11am–11pm, Sun noon–6pm; kitchen April–Oct daily noon–2.30pm plus Wed–Sat 7–8pm, Nov–March daily noon–2.30pm plus Thurs–Sat 7–8pm.

Seahouses and the Farne Islands

Around ten miles north from Craster, beyond the small village of Beadnell, lies the fishing port of **SEAHOUSES**, the only place on the local coast that could remotely be described as a resort. It's the embarkation point for boat trips out to the wind swept **Farne Islands**, a rocky archipelago lying a few miles offshore.

The Farne Islands

Owned by the National Trust and maintained as a nature reserve, the **Farne Islands** (ⓦ nationaltrust.co.uk/farne-islands) are the summer home of hundreds of thousands of migrating seabirds, notably puffins, guillemots, terns, eider ducks and kittiwakes, and home to the only grey seal colony on the English coastline. A number of boat trips potter around the islands – the largest of which is Inner Farne – offering birdwatching tours, grey seal-watching tours and the Grace Darling tour, which takes visitors to the lighthouse on Longstone Island, where the famed local heroine (see page 619) lived.

ARRIVAL AND INFORMATION

By bus The bus stop is on King St, near the post office. The #X18 runs between Berwick (every 2hr; 1hr) and Alnwick (every 2hr; 1hr).

By boat Weather permitting, several operators in Seahouses run daily boat trips (2–3hr; from £15; National Trust landing fee £7–9) starting at around 10am. Wander down to the quayside, contact either the National Trust Shop or the tourist office (closed at time of research), or book online in advance at ⓦfarne-islands.com. During the breeding season (May–July) landings are restricted to morning trips to Staple Island and afternoons to Inner Farne.

Tourist information National Trust Shop, 16 Main St (☎01665 721099), by the Seahouses traffic roundabout. The tourist office is located in the main car park but was closed at the time of research. See ⓦseahouses.org for the latest information.

ACCOMMODATION

★ **St Cuthberts** 198 Main st, Seahouses, NE68 7UB ☎01665 720456, ⓦstcuthbertshouse.com. Award-winning B&B in a beautifully converted 200-year-old chapel a mile inland from the harbour. Rooms cleverly incorporate period features like the original arched windows with lovely modern touches such as wet rooms, flatscreen TVs, comfy dressing gowns and slippers. Breakfast is all locally sourced, from the sausages and the eggs to the kippers and the honey. **£105**

Bamburgh

One-time capital of Northumbria, the little village of **BAMBURGH**, just three miles from Seahouses, lies in the lee of its magnificent **castle**. Attractive stone cottages – holding the village shop, a café, pubs and B&Bs – flank each side of the triangular green, and at the top of the village on Radcliffe Road is the diminutive **Grace Darling Museum**. From behind the castle it's a brisk, five-minute walk to two splendid sandy **beaches**, backed by rolling, tufted dunes.

Bamburgh Castle

Half a mile from Bamburgh, NE69 7DF • Mid-Feb to Oct daily 10am–5pm; Nov to mid-Feb Sat & Sun 11am–4.30pm • £10.85 • ☎01668 214515, ⓦbamburghcastle.com

Solid and chunky, **Bamburgh Castle** is a spectacular sight, its elongated battlements crowning a formidable basalt crag high above the beach. Its origins lie in Anglo-Saxon times, but it suffered a centuries-long decline – rotted by sea spray and buffeted by winter storms, the castle was bought by Lord Armstrong (of Rothbury's Cragside; see page 612) in 1894, who demolished most of the structure to replace it with a hybrid castle-mansion. Inside there's plenty to explore, including the sturdy keep that houses an unnerving armoury packed with vicious-looking pikes, halberds, helmets and muskets; the King's Hall, with its marvellous teak ceiling that was imported from Siam (Thailand) and carved in Victorian times; and a medieval kitchen complete with original jugs, pots and pans.

Grace Darling Museum

Radcliffe Rd, NE69 7AE • Easter–Sept daily 10am–5pm; Oct–Easter Tues–Sun 10am–4pm • Free • ☎01668 214910, ⓦrnli.org.uk

The **Grace Darling Museum** celebrates the life of famed local heroine Grace Darling. In September 1838, a gale dashed the steamship *Forfarshire* against the rocks of the Farne Islands. Nine passengers struggled onto a reef where they were subsequently saved by Grace and her lighthouseman father, William, who left the safety of the Longstone lighthouse to row out to them. *The Times* trumpeted Grace's bravery, offers of marriage and requests for locks of her hair streamed into the Darlings' lighthouse home, and for the rest of her brief life Grace was plagued by unwanted visitors – she died of tuberculosis aged 26 in 1842, and was buried in Bamburgh, in the churchyard of the thirteenth-century St Aidan's.

13

ARRIVAL AND INFORMATION

By bus A regular bus service links Alnwick and Berwick-upon-Tweed with Bamburgh, stopping on Front St, by the green. Destinations Alnwick (Mon–Sat hourly; 1hr 10min);

Berwick-upon-Tweed (Mon–Sat every 2hr; 40min); Seahouses (Mon–Sat hourly; 10min). **Website** ⓦ bamburgh.org.uk

ACCOMMODATION AND EATING

Copper Kettle 21 Front St, NE69 7BW ☎01668 214315. Sweet little tearoom, with a sunny sitting area out the back, serving tasty cakes, teas and coffees – try the fruit loaf or the tempting carrot cake with icing. Also light meals such as sandwiches (£5), jacket potatoes (£6.50) and pies (£6). Daily 11am–6pm.

Victoria Hotel 1 Front St, NE69 7BP ☎01668 214431, ⓦ strhotels.co.uk/victoria-hotel. This smart boutique hotel has elegant rooms in a variety of sizes – one with lovely castle views – a couple of relaxing bars and a more expensive brasserie (dinner only). Pets are welcome for an additional charge of £7.50/night. **£90**

Holy Island

It's a dramatic approach to **HOLY ISLAND** – only accessible at low tide – past the barnacle-encrusted marker poles that line the three-mile-long causeway. Topped with a stumpy **castle**, the island is small (just 1.5 miles by 1), sandy and bare, and in winter it can be bleak, but come summer day-trippers clog the car parks as soon as the causeway is open. Even then, though, **Lindisfarne** (as the island was once known) has a distinctive, isolated atmosphere. Give the place time and, if you can, stay overnight, when you'll be able to see the historic remains without hundreds of others cluttering the views. The surrounding tidal mud flats, salt marshes and dunes have been designated a **nature reserve**.

Brief history

It was on Lindisfarne that St Aidan of Iona founded a monastery at the invitation of King Oswald of Northumbria in 634. The monks quickly established a reputation for scholarship and artistry, the latter exemplified by the **Lindisfarne Gospels**, the apotheosis of Celtic religious art, now kept in the British Library. The monastery had sixteen bishops in all, the most celebrated being the reluctant **St Cuthbert**, who never settled here – within two years, he was back in his hermit's cell on the Farne Islands, where he died in 687. His colleagues rowed the body back to Lindisfarne, which became a place of pilgrimage until 875, when the monks abandoned the island in fear of marauding Vikings, taking Cuthbert's remains with them.

Lindisfarne Priory

TD15 2RX • Feb daily 10am–4pm; March & Nov–Jan Sat & Sun 10am–4pm; April–Sept daily 10am–6pm; Oct daily 10am–5pm • £6.50; EH • ☎ 01289 389200, ⓦ www.english-heritage.org.uk/visit/places/lindisfarne-priory

Located just off the village green are the tranquil, pinkish sandstone ruins of **Lindisfarne Priory**, which dates from the Benedictine foundation. The **museum** next door displays a collection of incised stones that constitute all that remains of the first monastery.

Lindisfarne Castle

TD15 2SH • **Castle** Hours vary according to tide, but always include noon–3pm; generally Jan & Feb Sat & Sun, March–Oct daily, Nov & Dec occasional Sat & Sun • **Gardens** Daily dawn–dusk • £7.30; NT • ☎ 01289 389244, ⓦ nationaltrust.org.uk/lindisfarne-castle

Stuck on a small pyramid of rock half a mile away from the village, **Lindisfarne Castle** – which has just undergone major restoration work – was built in the middle of the sixteenth century to protect the island's harbour from the Scots. It was, however, merely a decaying shell when Edward Hudson, the founder of *Country Life* magazine, stumbled across it in 1901. He promptly commissioned Edwin Lutyens (1869–1944) to turn it into an Edwardian country house, and installed a charming walled garden in the castle's former vegetable gardens, to designs by Gertrude Jekyll.

ARRIVAL AND INFORMATION

By bus The #477 bus from Berwick-upon-Tweed to Holy Island (35min) is something of a law unto itself given the interfering tides, but basically service is daily in Aug and twice-weekly the rest of the year.

Crossing the causeway The island is cut off by tides for about 5hr a day. Consult tide timetables at a tourist office, in the local paper or at ⓦ holyisland.northumberland. gov.uk.

Castle shuttle A minibus trundles the half a mile to the castle from the main car park, The Chare (every 20min 10.20am–4.20pm; £1).

Website ⓦ lindisfarne.org.uk.

ACCOMMODATION AND EATING

Due to the size of the island and the small number of B&Bs, it's imperative to **book in advance** if you're staying overnight.

★**Bamburgh View** Fenkle St, TD15 2SR ☎01289 389212, ⓦ lindisfarne.org.uk/bamburghview. Sweet, friendly B&B very near the priory, with three airy, wood-floored rooms, good showers and generous breakfasts. **£90**

St Aidan's Winery TD15 2RX, in the modern building behind the green ☎01289 389230, ⓦ lindisfarne-mead.co.uk. If you're keen to sample some of the world-famous Lindisfarne mead, this is the place to come. They also sell home-made chutneys, biscuits and jams. Hours depend on tides.

The Ship Marygate, TD15 2SJ ☎01289 389311, ⓦ theshipinn-holyisland.co.uk. The best pub on the island; friendly and traditional, with open fires and wood-panelled walls. The ales are good, as is the inexpensive pub grub. They have four cosy, en-suite rooms upstairs. **£110**

Berwick-upon-Tweed

Before the union of the English and Scottish crowns in 1603, **BERWICK-UPON-TWEED**, twelve miles north of Holy Island, was the quintessential frontier town, changing hands no fewer than fourteen times between 1174 and 1482, when the Scots finally ceded the stronghold to the English. Interminable cross-border warfare ruined Berwick's economy, turning the prosperous Scottish port of the thirteenth century into an impoverished English garrison town. By the late sixteenth century, Berwick's fortifications were in a dreadful state and Elizabeth I, fearing the resurgent alliance between France and Scotland, had the place rebuilt in line with the latest principles of military architecture. Berwick was reborn as an important seaport between 1750 and 1820, and is still peppered with elegant **Georgian mansions** dating from that period.

Berwick's **walls** – one and a half miles long and still in pristine condition – are now the town's major attraction, but look out for panels that mark the **Lowry Trail**; L.S. Lowry (1887–1976) was a regular visitor to Berwick and his sketches and paintings of local landmarks are dotted about town.

Town walls

No more than 20ft high but incredibly thick, the Elizabethan **town walls** are protected by ditches on three sides and the Tweed on the fourth, and strengthened by immense bastions. It's possible to walk a mile-long circuit (45min) around Berwick, with wonderful views out to sea, across the Tweed and over the orange-tiled rooftops of the town.

Barracks

TD15 1DF • April–Sept Mon–Fri 10am–6pm; Oct 10am–4pm • £4.90; EH • ☎01289 304493, ⓦ www.english-heritage.org.uk/visit/places/berwick-upon-tweed-barracks-and-main-guard

The town's finely proportioned **Barracks**, designed by Nicholas Hawksmoor (1717) functioned as a garrison until 1964, when the King's Own Scottish Borderers regiment decamped. Inside there's the rather specialist **By the Beat of the Drum** exhibition, tracing the lives of British infantrymen from the Civil War to World War I, as well as the **King's Own Scottish Borderers Museum** and the **Berwick Museum and Art Gallery**, which has a collection of works donated by Sir William Burrell.

13

ARRIVAL AND DEPARTURE

By train From the train station it's a 10min walk down Castlegate and Marygate to the town centre.

Destinations Durham (every 30min; 1hr 10min); Edinburgh (hourly; 45min); Newcastle (hourly; 45min).

By bus Most buses stop on Golden Square (where Castlegate meets Marygate), though some also stop by

the train station.

Destinations Bamburgh (Mon–Sat every 2hr; Sun 3 daily; 45min); Holy Island (Aug 2 daily, rest of the year 2 weekly; 35min); Newcastle (Mon–Sat hourly; 2hr 15min); Wooler (Mon–Sat 6 daily; 1hr).

INFORMATION AND TOURS

Tourist office Berwick TIC and Library, Walkergate (Mon–Fri 9am–5pm, Sat 10am–5pm; ☎01670 622155).

Tours The tourist office can book you onto a walking tour (Easter–Oct Mon–Fri 11am; £7; ⓦexplore-

northumberland.co.uk) which includes the walls and an eighteenth-century gun bastion not usually open to the public.

ACCOMMODATION

Marshall Meadow Hotel 3 miles north of Berwick-Upon-Tweed, TD15 1UT ☎01289 331133, ⓦmarshallmeadowshotel.co.uk. An eighteenth-century country house set in delightful grounds. The 19 en-suite guest rooms are traditional – but without chintz – and very clean. The oak-panelled restaurant has a menu of comforting seasonal dishes, featuring local produce. £109

Queen's Head 6 Sandgate, TD15 1EP ☎01289 307852, ⓦqueensheadberwick.co.uk. One of the best

pubs in town has six snug rooms, including a family room. Great evening meals and breakfasts, too (mains around £15). £99

YHA Berwick Dewars Lane, TD15 1HJ ☎0845 371 9676, ⓦyha.org.uk/hostel/berwick. Set in a remarkable eighteenth-century granary building which, thanks to a fire in 1815, has a lean greater than that of the Leaning Tower of Pisa. Thirteen en-suite rooms, some private and family, plus a bistro and gallery. Dorms £18, doubles £78

EATING AND DRINKING

Barrel's Alehouse 59–61 Bridge St, TD15 1ES ☎01289 308013, ⓦfacebook.com/TheBarrelsAle House. Atmospheric pub specializing in (frequently changing) cask ales, lagers and stouts. It's also a great music venue, hosting an eclectic mix of jazz, blues, rock and indie bands. Daily noon–midnight.

The Maltings Eastern Lane, TD15 1AJ ☎01289 330999, ⓦmaltingsberwick.co.uk. Berwick's arts centre has a year-round programme of music, theatre, comedy, film and dance and a licensed café, the *Maltings Kitchen*. Café Mon–Wed 9.30am–4pm, Thurs–Sat 9.30am–4pm & 5.45–7.30pm.

Durham

The handsome city of **DURHAM** is best known for its beautiful Norman **cathedral** – there's a tremendous view of it as you approach the city by train from the south – and for its flourishing university, founded in 1832. Together, these form a little island of privilege in what's otherwise a moderately sized, working-class city. It's worth visiting for a couple of days – there are plenty of attractions, but it's more the overall atmosphere that captivates, enhanced by the omnipresent golden stone, slender bridges and the glint of the river. The heart of the city is the **marketplace**, flanked by the Guildhall and St Nicholas Church. The cathedral and church sit on a wooded peninsula to the west, while southwards stretch narrow streets lined with shops and cafés.

Brief history

Durham's history revolves around its cathedral. Completed in just forty years, the cathedral was founded in 1093 to house the shrine of **St Cuthbert**, arguably the Northeast's most important and venerated saint (see page 624). Soon after Cuthbert was laid to rest here, the bishops of Durham were granted extensive powers to control the troublesome northern marches of the Kingdom (a rabble of invading

Picts from Scotland and revolting Norman earls, ruling as semi-independent **Prince Bishops**, with their own army, mint and courts of law. At the peak of their power in the fourteenth century, the office went into decline, especially in the wake of the Reformation), yet the bishop's clung to the vestiges of their authority until 1836, when they ceded them to the Crown. The bishops abandoned Durham Castle for their palace in Bishop Auckland (see page 627) and transferred their old home to the fledgling Durham University, England's third-oldest seat of learning after Oxford and Cambridge.

Durham Cathedral

DH1 3EH • Mon–Sat 9.30am–6pm, Sun 12.30–5.30pm • Donation requested; Open Treasure ticket (£7.50) covers entry to the Monks' Dormitory, the Great Kitchen and the Treasures of St Cuthbert • **Tours** April–Oct Mon–Sat 2–3 daily; 1hr • £5 • ☎ 0191 386 4266, ⓦ durhamcathedral.co.uk

From the marketplace, it's a five-minute walk up Saddler Street to **Durham Cathedral**, considered a supreme example of the Norman-Romanesque style. The awe-inspiring **nave** used pointed arches for the first time in England, raising the vaulted ceiling to new and dizzying heights. The weight of the stone is borne by massive pillars, their heaviness relieved by striking Moorish-influenced geometric patterns. A door on the western side gives access to the **tower**, from where there are beautiful views. Separated from the nave by a Victorian marble screen is the **choir**, where the dark Restoration stalls are overshadowed by the 13ft-high **bishop's throne**. Beyond is the **Chapel of the**

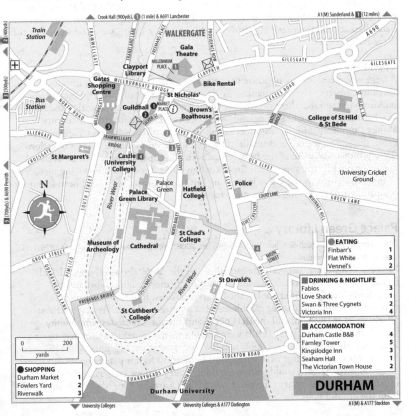

13

> ## ST CUTHBERT
>
> Born in North Northumbria in 653, **Cuthbert** spent most of his youth in Melrose Abbey
> in Scotland, from where he moved briefly to Lindisfarne Island, which was at that time
> a well-known centre of religious endeavour. Preferring the peace and rugged solitude
> of the Farne Islands, he lived on Inner Farne for thirty years. News of his piety spread,
> however, and he was head-hunted to become Bishop of Lindisfarne, a position he
> accepted reluctantly. Uncomfortable in the limelight, he soon returned to Inner Farne,
> and when he died his remains were moved to Lindisfarne before being carted off to
> **Durham Cathedral**.

Nine Altars, which dates from the thirteenth century. Here, and around the **Shrine
of St Cuthbert**, much of the stonework is of local Weardale marble, each dark shaft
bearing its own pattern of fossils. Cuthbert himself lies beneath a plain marble slab,
his shrine having gained a reputation over the centuries for its curative powers. The
legend was given credence in 1104, when the saint's body was exhumed in Chester-
le-Street for reburial here, and was found to be completely uncorrupted, more than
four hundred years after his death on Lindisfarne. Almost certainly, this was the result
of his fellow monks having (unintentionally) preserved the body by laying it in sand
containing salt crystals.

Back near the entrance, at the west end of the church, is the **Galilee Chapel**; begun
in the 1170s, its light and exotic decoration is in imitation of the Great Mosque
of Córdoba. The chapel contains the simple tombstone of the **Venerable Bede** (see
page 606), the Northumbrian monk credited with being England's first historian.
Bede died at the monastery of Jarrow in 735, and his remains were transferred to the
cathedral in 1020.

Open Treasure

A large wooden doorway opposite the cathedral's main entrance leads into the
spacious cloisters, which are flanked by the most intact set of medieval monastic
buildings in the UK. These now house **Open Treasure**, a display exploring the history
of Christianity in northeast England, which kicks off in the fourteenth-century
Monks' Dormitory with its magnificent oak-beamed ceiling, where interactive displays
evoke the sights, sounds and smells of life in a medieval monastery. The **Collections
Gallery** showcases some of the most precious manuscripts from the cathedral's
collections; while the spectacular **Great Kitchen** – one of only two surviving medieval
monastic kitchens in the UK – is a setting for The Treasures of St Cuthbert, featuring
beautifully preserved Anglo-Saxon artefacts.

Palace Green Library

Palace Green, DH1 3RN • Mon noon–5pm, Tues–Sun 10am–5pm • Free, although entry fee for changing exhibitions • ☎ 0191 334 2972,
🌐 dur.ac.uk/palace.green/whatson

Palace Green Library, between the cathedral and the castle, shows off a wonderful
collection of the university's treasures, including medieval manuscripts and
incunabula – early printed books. The library is divided into four separate galleries,
two of which host permanent exhibitions that are free to view: **Living on the Hills:
10,000 years of Durham**; and the **DLI Collection: Courage, Comrades, Community**.
The Durham Light Infantry (DLI) were one of the most famous county regiments
in the British Army and the exhibit tells the story from their beginnings in 1181, via
World War I (when it lost twelve thousand soldiers) to its last parade in 1968. Other
exhibitions change but could feature anything from Japanese enamel pots to Chinese
imperial textiles and ancient Egyptian relics. The *Courtyard Café* (daily 9.30am–4pm)
is on the ground floor.

Durham Castle

DH1 3RW • Tours daily: Easter & July–Sept 10am, 11am, noon, 2pm, 3pm, 4pm & 5pm; rest of the year 2pm, 3pm & 4pm; 50min • £5 • ☎ 0191 334 3800, Ⓦ durhamworldheritagesite.com

13

Durham Castle lost its medieval appearance long ago, as each successive Prince Bishop modernized the building according to the tastes of the time. The university was bequeathed the castle in the nineteenth century and subsequently renovated the old keep as a hall of residence. It's only possible to visit the castle on a **guided tour**, departing from outside Palace Green Library, highlights of which include the enormous hanging staircase and the underground Norman chapel, one of the few surviving interiors from the period. It's notable for its lively Romanesque carved capitals, including a green man, and what may be the earliest surviving depiction anywhere of a mermaid. Note that out of term time you can stay here (see below).

Crook Hall

Frankland Lane, Sidegate, DH1 5SZ • Mon–Wed & Sun 10am–5pm • April–Oct £7.50, Nov–March £5.50 • ☎ 0191 384 8028, Ⓦ crookhallgardens.co.uk

Around half a mile north of the centre, **Crook Hall** is a hidden gem. A rare mix of medieval, Jacobean and Georgian architecture, with origins dating from the twelfth century, it's said to be one of the oldest inhabited houses in the area. You can explore its rambling rooms, complete with period furniture and rickety staircases, as well as a series of beautifully tended, themed gardens, including the ethereal Silver and White garden, the Shakespeare Garden, planted with herbs used in Elizabethan times, and the delightful Secret Walled Garden. Book **afternoon tea** in the manor house tearooms in advance (£24.50) or drop in at the **Garden Gate Café and shop** at the gatehouse (sandwiches from £5).

ARRIVAL AND INFORMATION

DURHAM

By train Durham's train station is on North Rd, a 10min walk from the centre of the city.

Destinations Berwick-upon-Tweed (every 30min; 1hr 10min), Darlington (frequent; 20min); London (every 30min–1hr; 3hr); Newcastle (frequent; 15min); York (frequent; 50min).

By bus It's a 5min walk to the city centre from the bus station on North Rd.

Destinations Bishop Auckland (frequent; 30min); Darlington

(every 20min; 1hr 10min); Middlesbrough (every 30min; 55min); Newcastle (Mon–Sat every 30min, Sun 4–6 daily; 50min); Stanhope (Mon–Fri 4 daily; 45min).

Tourist information There are visitor information points dotted around the city. From mid-April to mid-Sept volunteer "pointers" on Market Square give out information (Ⓦ durhampointers.co.uk).

Website Ⓦ thisisdurham.com.

GETTING AROUND

By bus The Cathedral Bus is a minibus service running two routes around Durham via the train station, the bus station, the marketplace and the cathedral. Tickets cost £1 and are valid all day (Mon–Sat).

ACCOMMODATION

Durham Castle B&B DH1 3RW ☎ 0191 334 4106, Ⓦ dur.ac.uk; map p.623. Out of term time you can have the unique experience of staying in Durham Castle. Accommodation ranges from standard rooms with shared bathrooms to two grand "state rooms" (£250), one with a four-poster and seventeenth-century tapestries. Breakfast is served in the thirteenth-century Great Hall. **£100**

Farnley Tower The Avenue, DH1 4DX ☎ 0191 375 0011, Ⓦ farnley-tower.co.uk; map p.623. A 10min walk up a steep hill west from the centre, this fine stone Victorian house

has thirteen comfortable rooms with bright, coordinated fabrics. The best rooms have sweeping city views. **£95**

Kingslodge Inn Waddington St, DH1 4BG ☎ 0191 370 9977, Ⓦ kingslodgeinn.co.uk; map p.623. The 23 en-suite rooms at this newly reopened inn aren't spacious, but they are comfortable and clean. The pub-restaurant is usually fairly quiet. Free on-site car park, a rarity in central Durham. **£95**

Seaham Hall Lord Byron's Walk, Seaham, SR7 7AG, 12 miles northeast of Durham ☎ 0191 516 1400,

13

ⓦseaham-hall.co.uk; map p.623. Perched on a clifftop overlooking the sea, this hip, exclusive hotel makes a great coastal base for city sightseeing – Durham is only a 20min drive away. It's known for its luxurious spa and pampering treatments and has a wonderful restaurant; spa, dinner, bed and breakfast packages are available. **£195**

The Victorian Town House 2 Victoria Terrace, DH1 4RW ☎0191 370 9963, ⓦdurhambedandbreakfast. com; map p.623. This friendly and tranquil B&B features three en-suite rooms: one twin, one double and one family room. It's located on a quiet and attractive backstreet backed by gardens and is a 5min walk from the station. **£95**

EATING

Finbarrs Aykley Heads House, HH1 5TS ☎0191 307 7033, ⓦfinbarrsrestaurant.co.uk; map p.623. This chic restaurant with crisp white tablecloths serves anything from full English breakfasts and banana pancakes to dinners of Moroccan lamb with golden raisins; the sweet cherry and pistachio sundaes are delicious. Mains from £15. Mon–Sat noon–2.30pm & 6–9.30pm, Sun noon–2.30pm & 6–9pm.

Flat White 21a Elvet Bridge, DH1 3AA ☎07936 449291, ⓦflatwhitekitchen.com; map p.623. Durham's hippest café, serving barista-standard coffee and hearty sandwiches

served on wooden boards (£5). Sit outside in the sun, or inside at tables made from old sewing machines. It has a fancier sister restaurant on Saddler St, too. Mon–Sat 8am–4pm, Sun 10am–6pm.

Vennel's 71 Saddler's Yard, Saddler St, DH1 3NP ☎0191 375 0571; map p.623. Named after the skinny alley or "vennel" where it stands – near the junction with Elvet Bridge – this café serves generous sandwiches, salads, quiche (£5–6) and tasty cakes in its sixteenth-century courtyard. Mon–Sat 9.30am–5.30pm, Sun 10.30am–5.30pm.

DRINKING AND NIGHTLIFE

Walkergate is the area to head for if you're after loud, lively bars and mainstream nightclubs pumping out cheesy music, but there are also plenty of quieter establishments and more traditional, laidback pubs. Durham's **clubs**, frequented by students during the week and locals at the weekends, don't generally have a dress code, but the locals tend to make an effort.

Fabios 66 Sadler St, DH1 3NP ☎0191 383 9290, ⓦfabiosdurham.com; map p.623. Just above *La Spaghettata* pizzeria, *Fabios* occupies a series of rooms filled with comfy, rug-draped sofas and chalked-up blackboards offering drinks from around £3. The atmosphere is cool and relaxed, with music a melange of rap, r'n'b and dance. Daily 6pm–2am.

Love Shack Walkergate, DH1 1WA ☎0191 384 5757, ⓦloveshackdurham.com; map p.623. Large, popular club with two bars, snug booths and a sleek dancefloor. Music is an energetic mix of contemporary club tunes and cheesy classics. Wed–Fri 10pm–2am, Sat 8pm–2am.

Swan & Three Cygnets Elvet Bridge, DH1 3AF ☎0191

384 0242; map p.623. Sitting proudly at the end of Elvet Bridge overlooking the River Wear, this loud and cheery pub serves cheap drinks and is filled with a mixed crowd of locals and students. Mon–Sat 11am–11pm, Sun noon–10.30pm.

Victoria Inn 86 Hallgarth St, DH1 3AS ☎0191 386 5269, ⓦvictoriainn-durhamcity.co.uk; map p.623. With its three open fires and rickety wooden stools, this cosy, traditional pub specializes in local ales – try the creamy Tyneside Blonde or the hoppy Centurion Bitter – and stocks more than thirty Irish whiskeys. Mon–Sat noon–3pm & 6–11pm, Sun noon–3pm & 7–11pm.

ENTERTAINMENT

In addition to shows at the Gala Theatre, you can catch regular **classical concerts** at venues around the city, including the cathedral. Ask the tourist office for more details.

Gala Theatre Millennium Place, DH1 1WA ☎0191 332 4041, ⓦgaladurham.co.uk A modern venue staging

music of all kinds, plus theatre, cinema, dance and comedy.

SHOPPING

As well as the indoor market, Durham has a monthly **farmer's market** in the Market Place (third Thurs of the month 9am–4pm; ⓦthisisdurham.com).

Durham Market Market Place, DH1 3NJ ⓦdurham markets.co.uk; map p.623. Durham's Indoor Market holds a variety of stalls including a haberdashers, sweet

shop and fishmongers. Mon–Sat 9am–5pm.

Fowlers Yard Silver St, DH1 3RA ⓦfowlersyarddurham. co.uk; map p.623. A series of workshops behind the marketplace showcasing local trades and crafts. Drop by to watch the craftspeople at work, commission a piece or buy off the cuff. Opening hours vary.

Riverwalk DH1 4SL ⓦ theriverwalk.co.uk; map

p.623. Shopping development undergoing a much-needed revamp, but stores including vintage Ding Dong and gentleman's outfitters Woven remain open.

Around Durham

The county of Durham has shaken off its grimy reputation in recent years and recast itself as a thriving tourist area. The well-to-do market towns of **Bishop Auckland** and **Barnard Castle** make great day-trips from Durham, and there's plenty of excellent walking and cycling in the wilds of the two Pennine valleys, **Teesdale** and **Weardale**. You'll find some top-class museums in the area, too, including **Beamish**, **Locomotion** and the **Bowes Museum**.

Beamish Museum

10 miles north of Durham, DH9 0RG • Daily: April–Oct 10am–5pm; Nov–March 10am–4pm • £19, under-17s £11 • ☎ 0191 370 4000, ⓦ beamish.org.uk • Waggonway #28/28A runs from Newcastle (every 30min Mon–Sat, hourly Sun); from Durham catch a bus to Chester-le-Street to connect with the #28/28A

The open-air **Beamish Museum** spreads out over three hundred acres, with buildings taken from all over the region painstakingly reassembled in six main sections linked by restored trams and buses. Complete with costumed shopkeepers, workers and householders, four of the sections show life in 1913, before the upheavals of World War I, including a **colliery village** complete with drift mine (regular tours throughout the day) and a large-scale recreation of the high street in a **market town**. Two areas date to 1825, at the beginning of the northeast's industrial development, including a **manor house**, with horse yard, formal gardens, vegetable plots and orchards. You can ride on the beautifully restored steam-powered carousel, the **Steam Galloper**, which dates from the 1890s, and the **Pockerley Waggonway**, which is pulled along by a replica of George Stephenson's *Locomotion* (see page 628), the first passenger-carrying steam train in the world.

Bishop Auckland

BISHOP AUCKLAND, a busy little market town eleven miles southwest of Durham, grew up slowly around its showpiece building, **Auckland Castle**, and became famous throughout England as the homeland of the mighty Prince Bishops. Today the town has paled into lesser significance but still offers enough for a pleasant hour or two's wander.

Auckland Castle

DL14 7NR • **Castle and Market Place buildings** Sections closed until 2020 for extensive restoration work; see online for times and charges • **Deer park** Daily 7am–dusk • Free • ☎ 01388 602576, ⓦ aucklandcastle.org

Looking more like an opulent Gothic mansion than a traditional fortress, **Auckland Castle** served for 900 years as a private palace for the Prince Bishops of Durham, who stood second in power only to the King of England. The castle is one of the most important and best-preserved medieval bishops' palaces in Europe and today it's being transformed into an arts, faith and heritage destination; an extension will house the UK's first **Faith Museum**, the original seventeenth-century walled garden is being revamped, and a mining art gallery (which includes works by prominent local mining artists Tom McGuinness and Norman Cornish), Spanish gallery and welcome building are opening in the adjoining Market Place. These are opening in stages between 2017 and 2020, with Auckland Castle itself

13

reopening in December 2018. Meanwhile, you can stroll around the 200-acre **Deer Park**, or book tickets for the summer spectacular open-air show, **Kynren** (ⓦelevenarches.org), which features the castle as a backdrop to a reenactment of 2000 years of history.

Binchester Roman Fort

1.5 miles north of Bishop Auckland, DL14 8DJ • Daily: Easter–June & Sept 11am–5pm; July & Aug 10am–5pm • £2.55 • ☎ 0191 370 8712, ⓦ durham.gov.uk

From the town's marketplace, it's a pleasant twenty-minute walk along the banks of the River Wear to the remains of **Binchester Roman Fort**. While most of the stone fort and a civilian settlement that occupied the area remain hidden beneath surrounding fields, the bathhouse with its sophisticated underground heating system (hypocaust) is visible. Excavations are ongoing.

ARRIVAL   BISHOP AUCKLAND

By train Bishop Auckland is the end of the line for trains from Darlington (26min); the station is on Newgate St.

By bus Buses terminate at Saddler St. There are frequent services to Durham (40min) and Newcastle (1hr 25min).

Locomotion (National Railway Museum Shildon)

Shildon, DL4 2RE, 12 miles south of Durham • Daily 10am–5pm • Free • ☎ 01388 777999, ⓦ nrm.org.uk • Trains from Durham and Darlington to Bishop Auckland stop at Shildon station, a 2min walk from the museum. Buses #1 and 1B (to Crook and Tow Law) run from Darlington (Mon–Sat every 30min), stopping at Dale Rd, a 15min walk from the museum

The first passenger train in the world left from the station at Shildon in 1825 – making this the world's oldest railway town. It's a heritage explored in the magnificently realized **Locomotion** (also known as NRM Shildon), the regional outpost of York's National Railway Museum. It's less a museum and more an experience, spread out around a 1.5-mile-long site, with the attractions linked by free bus from the reception building. Depots, sidings, junctions and coal drops lead ultimately to the heart of the museum, **Collection** – a gargantuan steel hangar containing an extraordinary array of seventy locomotives, dating from the very earliest days of steam. With interactive children's exhibits, summer steam rides, rallies and shows, it makes an excellent family day out.

Barnard Castle

Affectionately known as "Barney", the honey-coloured market town of **BARNARD CASTLE** lies fifteen miles southwest of Bishop Auckland. The middle of the town is dominated by the splendid octagonal **Market Cross**; built in 1747 and formerly functioning as a market for dairy and butter, it now serves a more mundane purpose as a roundabout.

The castle

Galgate, DL12 8PR • Daily: April–Sept 10am–6pm; Oct 10am–5pm; Nov–March Sat & Sun 10am–4pm • £5.40; EH • ☎ 01833 638212, ⓦ www.english-heritage.org.uk/visit/places/barnard-castle

The skeletal remains of the town's **castle** sit high on a rock overlooking the River Tees. It was founded in 1125 by the powerful Norman baron Bernard de Balliol – thus the town's name – and later ended up in the hands of Richard III. Richard's crest, in the shape of a boar, is still visible carved above a window in the inner ward.

Bowes Museum

Half a mile east of the town centre, DL12 8NP • Daily 10am–5pm • £10.50, under-16s free • ☎ 01833 690606, ⓦ bowesmuseum.org.uk

Castle aside, the prime attraction in town is the grand French-style chateau that constitutes the **Bowes Museum**. Begun in 1869, the chateau was commissioned by John and Josephine Bowes, a local businessman and MP and his French actress wife, who

TRAILS AND CYCLEWAYS

Coast-to-Coast (C2C) ⓦ c2c-guide.co.uk. This demanding cycle route runs 140 miles from Whitehaven to Sunderland.

Hadrian's Wall Path ⓦ hadrianswallcountry.co.uk. An 84-mile waymarked trail allowing you to walk the length of this atmospheric Roman monument.

National Route 72 ⓦ hadrian-guide.co.uk. Cycle path that starts in the Lake District and heads to the Northumberland coast, running the length of Hadrian's Wall.

Pennine Way ⓦ thepennineway.co.uk. This 270-mile-long footpath starts in the Peak District National Park, runs along the Pennine ridge through the Yorkshire Dales, up into Northumberland, across the Cheviots, and finishes in the Scottish Borders.

spent much of their time in Paris collecting ostentatious treasures and antiques. Don't miss the beautiful **Silver Swan**, a life-size musical automaton dating from 1773 – every afternoon at 2pm it puts on an enchanting show, preening its shiny feathers while swimming along a river filled with jumping fish.

Egglestone Abbey

A mile southeast of Barnard Castle, DL12 9TN • Daily 10am–6.30pm • Free; EH • ⓦ www.english-heritage.org.uk/visit/places/egglestone-abbey

It's a fine mile-long walk from the castle, southeast (downriver) through the fields above the banks of the Tees, to the lovely shattered ruins of **Egglestone Abbey**, a minor foundation dating from 1195. A succession of wars and the Dissolution destroyed most of it, but you can still see the remnants of a thirteenth-century church and the remains of the monks' living quarters, including an ingenious latrine system.

ARRIVAL AND INFORMATION
BARNARD CASTLE

By bus Buses stop either side of Galgate.
Destinations Bishop Auckland (Mon–Sat 6 daily; 50min); Darlington (Mon–Sat every 30min; Sun hourly; 45min); Middleton-in-Teesdale (Mon–Sat hourly; 35min); Raby

Castle (Mon–Sat hourly; 15min).
Tourist information There's a visitor information point at The Witham arts centre, 3 Horsemarket (Tues–Sat 10am–4pm).

ACCOMMODATION

Homelands 85 Galgate, DL12 8ES ☎ 01833 638757, ⓦ homelandsguesthouse.co.uk. An assortment of pretty rooms with floral soft furnishings and comfortable beds.

The owners are very knowledgeable about the area and can recommend plenty of good walks. Breakfast is great, with delicious fruit salads and generous cooked options. **£85**

EATING AND DRINKING

Blagraves House 30–32 The Bank, DL12 8PN ☎ 01833 637668, ⓦ blagraves.com. Supposed to be the oldest house in Barnard Castle, dating back 500 years, this refined restaurant – oozing atmosphere, with its low oak wooden beams, open log fires and plush furnishings – specializes in traditional British cuisine. Dishes such as pan-fried fillet of beef cost from £23. Tues–Sun 7–10pm.

Fernaville's Rest Whorlton, DL12 8XD ☎ 01833 627341, ⓦ fernavilles.com. Cosy country pub, with open fires and flagstone floors, in a picturesque village four miles east of Barnard Castle. The food is traditional pub grub which changes seasonally – try the shepherd's pie with red cabbage, apple and kale (£12.90). Daily 5–10pm; kitchen daily 5.30–8.30pm.

Teesdale

TEESDALE extends twenty-odd miles northwest from Barnard Castle, its pastoral landscapes on the lower reaches beginning calmly enough but soon replaced by wilder Pennine scenery. Picturesque little villages like **Middleton-in-Teesdale** and Romaldkirk pepper the valley, while natural attractions include the stunning **Cow Green Reservoir** in Upper Teesdale, home to the indigenous Teesdale violet and the blue spring gentian.

13

Raby Castle

Staindrop, DL2 3AH, 8 miles northeast of Barnard Castle · **Castle** Easter to Sept Mon–Wed & Sun 12.30–4.30pm (weekdays by guided tour only) · £12 (includes park & gardens) · **Park & gardens** Easter to Sept Mon–Wed & Sun 11am–5pm · £7 · ☎ 01833 660202, ⓦ rabycastle.com

Eight miles from Barnard Castle, up the A688, beckon the splendid, sprawling battlements of **Raby Castle**, reflecting the power of the Neville family, who ruled the local roost until 1569. The Neville estates were confiscated after the "Rising of the North", the abortive attempt to replace Elizabeth I with Mary Queen of Scots, with Raby subsequently passing to the Vane family in 1626, who still own it today. You can explore the interior, with its lavish bedrooms, dining room, kitchen and drawing rooms, which are filled with furniture and artwork dating from the sixteenth and seventeenth centuries.

Middleton-in-Teesdale

Surrounded by magnificent, wild countryside laced with a myriad of public footpaths and cycling trails, the attractive town of **MIDDLETON-IN-TEESDALE** is a popular base for walkers and cyclists. A relaxed little place, it was once the archetypal "company town", owned lock, stock and barrel by the London Lead Company, which began mining here in 1753. Just a few miles out of town is a famous set of waterfalls, **Low Force** and **High Force**.

High Force

DL12 0XH · Daily: Easter–Oct 10am–5pm; Nov–Easter 10am–4pm · £1.50 · ⓦ highforcewaterfall.com

Heading on the B6277 northwest out of Middleton-in-Teesdale, you'll first pass the turning off to the rapids of **Low Force**. Another mile up the road is the altogether more spectacular **High Force** (from the Norse "foss", meaning waterfall), a 70ft cascade that tumbles over an outcrop of the Whin Sill ridge and into a deep pool. The waterfall is on private Raby land (see above) and is reached by a short woodland walk.

ARRIVAL AND INFORMATION

By bus There are hourly bus services to Middleton-in-Teesdale from Barnard Castle (35min).

MIDDLETON-IN-TEESDALE

Tourist office Market Place (restricted hours, though usually daily 10am–1pm; ☎ 01833 641001).

ACCOMMODATION AND EATING

★ **The Old Barn** 12 Market Place, DL12 0QG ☎ 01833 640258, ⓦ theoldbarn-teesdale.co.uk. In a very central location next to the tourist office, this sympathetically converted barn has three attractive B&B rooms with rustic furniture, elegant iron beds and Egyptian cotton sheets. There's a little patio garden to chill out in after a hard day's walking. **£75**

Rose & Crown Romaldkirk, DL12 9EB, 4 miles southwest of Middleton-in-Teesdale ☎ 01833 650213,

ⓦ rose-and-crown.co.uk. Beautiful ivy-clad eighteenth-century coaching inn set on the village green and next to a pretty Saxon church. Beneath the tastefully decorated rooms is a refined restaurant (mains from £16), serving accomplished dishes such as pan-fried wood pigeon with juniper-berry sauce and grilled pancetta, plus a cosy bar with a wood fire. Restaurant Mon–Sat 6.30–9pm, Sun noon–2.30pm; bar meals daily noon–2.30pm and 6.30–9pm. **£140**

Weardale

Sitting to the north of Teesdale, the valley of **WEARDALE** was once hunting ground reserved for the Prince Bishops, but was later transformed into a major centre for lead mining and limestone quarrying; this industrial heritage is celebrated at the excellent **Killhope Lead Mining musueum** and the **Weardale Museum** near Irehopesburn. The main settlement is **Stanhope**, a small market town with a pleasant open-air heated swimming pool (£4; times at ⓦ stanhopehosting.co.uk/pool), perfect for cooling off after a long walk in the hills. Just to the east is the village of **Wolsingham**, a renowned pilgrimage centre in the Middle Ages, and neighbouring **Frosterley** which features the remnants of an eleventh-century chapel.

13

Weardale Museum

Ireshopeburn, DL13 1HD, 9 miles west of Stanhope • Easter, May, June, Sept & Oct Wed–Sun 1.30–4.30pm; July & Aug daily
1.30–4.30pm • £3 • ☎ 01388 517433, ⓦ www.weardalemuseum.co.uk

At Ireshopeburn, west of Stanhope, the **Weardale Museum** tells the story of the dale, in
particular its lead mining and the importance of Methodism (the faith of most of the
county of Durham's lead miners). There's a reconstructed miner's house as well as the
"Wesley Room", dedicated to the founder of Methodism, John Wesley, and filled with
his writings, books and belongings.

Killhope Lead Mining Museum

5 miles west of Ireshopeburn and 12 miles east of Stanhope, DL13 1AR • April–Oct daily 10.30am–5pm • £8.60 (includes mine visit) •
☎ 01388 537505, ⓦ www.killhope.org.uk • Request stop on bus #101 (see below), contact Weardale Travel (☎ 01388 528235,
ⓦ weardale-travel.co.uk)

If you're keen to learn about Weardale's mining past, a visit to **Killhope Lead Mining
Museum**, five miles west of Ireshopeburn, is an absolute must. After many successful
years as one of the richest mines in Britain, Killhope shut for good in 1910, and
now houses a terrific, child-friendly museum that brings to life the difficulties
and dangers of a mining life. The site is littered with preserved machinery and
nineteenth-century buildings, including the Mine Shop where workers would
spend the night after finishing a late shift. The highlight of the visit comes when
you descend Park Level Mine – you'll be given wellies, a hard hat and a torch – in
the company of a guide who expounds entertainingly about the realities of life
underground, notably the perils of the "Black Spit", a lung disease which killed
many men by their mid-forties.

ARRIVAL AND INFORMATION   WEARDALE

By bus Bus #101 runs roughly hourly (Mon–Sat) between
Bishop Auckland and Stanhope, calling at Wolsingham
and Frosterley.
Information Durham Dales Centre, Stanhope, houses

the tourist office (daily: April–Oct 9am–5pm; Nov–March
9am–4pm; ☎ 01388 527650, ⓦ durhamdalescentre.co.uk)
and a café.

GETTING AROUND

By bus Apart from #101, buses are relatively irregular
and sporadic round these parts. Contact the Weardale Bus
Company (☎ 01388 528235, ⓦ weardale-travel.co.uk).
By train Weardale Railway is a volunteer-run steam line

which chugs along from Bishop Auckland (see page 627)
to Stanhope, stopping at Wolsingham and Frosterley on
request. For timetables and fares see ⓦ weardale-railway.
org.uk.

ACCOMMODATION AND EATING

★ **Black Bull** Frosterley, DL13 2SL ☎ 01388 527784,
ⓦ blackbullfrosterley.com. Hop off the Weardale
Railway (see above) and into this traditional pub with
beams, ranges, oak tables and flagstone floors. The ales
are excellent, as is the food, which is hearty and delicious;
mains, like herb-crusted lamb shoulder with apricot and
walnut stuffing, start at £10. Thurs–Sat 11am–11pm,
Sun 11am–5pm; food served Thurs–Sat noon–3pm &

7–9pm, Sun noon–2.30pm.
★ **Dowfold House** Crook, DL15 9AB, 6 miles east of
Wolsingham ☎ 01388 762473, ⓦ dowfoldhouse.co.uk.
Wonderful, relaxed B&B in a Victorian house surrounded by
lush gardens and with splendid views out over Weardale.
Breakfast, served in the elegant dining room, is the
highlight, with lashings of free-range eggs, locally sourced
sausages and bacon, home-made bread and jams. **£90**

Tees Valley

Admittedly not much of a tourist hotspot in comparison to Northumberland or
Durham, the **Tees Valley** – once an industrial powerhouse and birthplace of one of
the greatest developments in Britain, the public steam railway – nevertheless has some
enjoyable attractions. **Darlington**, with its strong railway heritage, is a pleasant place

13

to spend a day, while Middlesbrough's **MIMA** and Hartlepool's **Maritime Experience** (daily: April–Oct 10am–5pm; Nov–March 11am–4pm; £9.25, under-16s £7; ☎01429 860077, ⍟hartlepoolsmaritimeexperience.com) are all worthwhile, the latter particularly if you have children to entertain.

Darlington

Abbreviated to "Darlo" by the locals, the busy market town of **DARLINGTON** hit the big time in 1825, when George Stephenson's "Number 1 Engine", later called *Locomotion*, hurtled from here to nearby Stockton-on-Tees at the terrifying speed of fifteen miles per hour. The town subsequently grew into a rail-engineering centre, and it didn't look back till the closure of the works in 1966. The origins of the rest of Darlington lie deep in Saxon times. The monks carrying St Cuthbert's body from Ripon to Durham (see page 622) stopped here, the saint lending his name to the graceful riverside church of **St Cuthbert**. The market square, one of England's largest, spreads beyond the church up to the restored and lively **Victorian covered market** (Mon–Sat 8am–5pm).

Head of Steam

North Rd Station, a 20min walk up Northgate from the marketplace, DL3 6ST • April–Sept Tues–Sun 10am–4pm, Oct–March Wed–Sun 11am–3.30pm • £4.95 • ☎01325 460532, ⍟www.darlington.gov.uk

Darlington's railway history is celebrated at the wonderful little **Head of Steam** museum, which is actually the restored 1842 passenger station on the original Stockton and Darlington railway route. The highlight is Stephenson's *Locomotion No. 1*, a tiny wood-panelled steam engine, the first-ever steam train to carry fare-paying passengers. Other locomotives jostle for space alongside, including the shiny, racing-green *Derwent*, the oldest surviving Darlington-built steam train. These, along with a collection of station and line-side signs, uniforms, luggage, a reconstructed ticket office and carriages, successfully bring to life the most important era in Darlington's existence.

ARRIVAL AND INFORMATION

DARLINGTON

By train The train station is on Bank Top, a 10min walk from the central marketplace: from the train station walk up Victoria Rd to the roundabout and turn right down Feethams.
Destinations Bishop Auckland (frequent; 25min); Durham (frequent; 20min); Newcastle (frequent; 35min).
By bus Most buses stop outside the Town Hall on Feethams.

Destinations Barnard Castle (Mon–Sat every 30min, Sun hourly; 45min); Bishop Auckland (Mon–Sat every 30min, Sun hourly; 1hr); Durham (every 20min; 1hr 10 min).
Information Leaflets on the region are available at the library on Crown St (Mon & Tues 9am–6pm, Thurs 10am–6pm, Wed & Fri 9am–5pm, Sat 9am–4pm; ☎01325 462034).

ACCOMMODATION AND EATING

★ **Bay Horse** 45 The Green, Hurworth, 5 miles south, DL2 2AA ☎01325 720663, ⍟thebayhorsehurworth. com. This exquisite pub has a roaring fire, exposed wooden beams, comfy bar stools and chalked-up menus. Tuck into delicious bar meals like braised daube of beef (£22) and be sure to leave room for pud; the sticky toffee pudding with salted caramel sauce (£7) is fabulous. Mon–Sat 11am–11pm, Sun noon–10.30pm; kitchen Mon–Sat noon–2.30pm & 6–9.30pm, Sun noon–4pm & 6.30–8.30pm.

Clow Beck House Croft-on-Tees, 2 miles south, DL2 2SP ☎01325 721075, ⍟clowbeckhouse.co.uk. Very

welcoming B&B with thirteen individually decorated rooms named after flowers and set round a pretty landscaped garden. The owner is also an accomplished chef, creating delicious breakfasts – the Skipton sausage is very tasty – and evening meals (mains from £17). **£140**

Rockliffe Hall Hurworth-on-Tees, 5 miles south, DL2 2DU ☎01325 729999, ⍟rockliffehall.com. Swanky hotel in a red-brick Victorian Gothic pile between the villages of Croft-on-Tees and Hurworth, which lays claim to having the UK's longest golf course. The rooms are cool and luxurious, and there's a spa, as well as three restaurants. **£175**

Middlesbrough Institute of Modern Art

Centre Square Middlesbrough, TS1 2AZ, 15 miles east of Darlington • Tues, Wed, Fri & Sat 10am–4.30pm, Thurs 10am–7pm, Sun noon–4pm • Free • ℗ 01642 726720, Ⓦ visitmima.com • 10min walk from the train station

The stunning **Middlesbrough Institute of Modern Art (MIMA)** is one of the few tourist draws in the industrial town of Middlesbrough. Bringing together its municipal art collections, changing exhibitions concentrate on fine arts and crafts from the early twentieth century to the present day, with a heavy emphasis on ceramics and jewellery. The collection features work by David Hockney, L.S. Lowry and Tracey Emin, among others.

Saltburn

South of the Tees estuary along the coast, it's not a difficult decision to bypass the kiss-me-quick tackiness of Redcar in favour of **SALTBURN**, twelve miles east of Middlesbrough, a graceful Victorian resort in a dramatic setting overlooking extensive sands and mottled red sea-cliffs. Soon after the railway arrived in 1861 to ferry Teessiders out to the seaside on high days and holidays, Saltburn became a rather fashionable spa town boasting a hydraulic **inclined tramway**, which still connects upper town to the pier and promenade, and ornate **Italian Gardens** that are laid out beneath the eastern side of town.

ARRIVAL AND INFORMATION
SALTBURN

By train There are regular train services from Newcastle (1hr 40min) and Durham (1hr 30min) via Darlington (50min) and Middlesbrough (25min).

By bus Frequent buses from Middlesbrough stop outside the train station (40min).

Information Some tourist information is available at the library on Windsor Rd (Mon & Wed–Fri 9am–12.30pm, 1.30–6.30pm, Tues 1.30–6.30pm, Sat 10am–12.30 & 1.30–4pm, Sun noon–4pm; ℗ 01287 622422)

Website Ⓦ redcar-cleveland.gov.uk.

South Wales

PEMBROKESHIRE COAST PATH

South Wales

The most heavily populated part of Wales, and by far the most anglicized, is the south. This is a region of distinct character, whether in the resurgent seaport cities of Cardiff and Swansea, the mine-scarred Valleys or the dramatically beautiful Glamorgan and Pembrokeshire coasts. Monmouthshire, Wales' easternmost county, abuts the English border and contains the bucolic charms of the River Wye and Tintern Abbey. To the west and north, although the coal mines no longer operate, the world-famous Valleys retain their tight-knit towns and a rich working-class heritage, and some excellent museums and colliery tours, including Big Pit at Blaenavon and the Rhondda Heritage Park in Trehafod.

The Valleys course down to the great ports of the coast, which once shipped Wales' products all over the world. The greatest of them all was **Cardiff**, now Wales' upbeat capital and an essential stop. Further west is Wales' second city, **Swansea** – rougher, tougher and less anglicized than Cardiff, it sits on an impressive arc of coast that shelves round to the delightful **Gower peninsula**, replete with grand beaches, rocky headlands, bracken heaths and ruined castles.

Carmarthenshire, often missed out, is well worth visiting: of all the routes radiating from the county town of Carmarthen, the most glorious is the winding road to **Llandeilo** along the **Tywi Valley**, past ruined hilltop forts and two of the country's finest gardens. Immediately east sits Wales' most impressively sited castle at **Carreg Cennen**, high on a dizzy rock-plug on the edge of the Black Mountain. The wide sands fringing Carmarthen Bay stretch towards the popular seaside resort of **Tenby**, a major stop on the 186-mile **Pembrokeshire Coast Path**. The rutted coastline of **St Bride's Bay** is the most glorious part of the coastal walk, which leads north to brush past the impeccable mini-city of **St Davids**, whose exquisite cathedral shelters in a protective hollow. Nearby are plenty of opportunities for spectacular coast and hill walks, boat crossings to nearby islands, wildlife-watching and numerous outdoor activities.

GETTING AROUND
SOUTH WALES

By car Southeast Wales is by far the easiest part of the country to travel around. Swift dual carriageways connect with the M4, bringing all corners of the region into close proximity.

By bus and train This is the only part of Wales with a half-decent train service, and most suburban and rural services interconnect with Cardiff, Newport or Swansea. Bus services fill in virtually all of the gaps, though often rather slowly, while Sun services are often dramatically reduced.

Cardiff and around

Official capital of Wales since only 1955, buoyant **CARDIFF** (Caerdydd) grew swiftly into its new role. A number of massive developments, not least the shiny Welsh

Highlights

❶ Wales Millennium Centre, Cardiff Bay
A symphony of opposites – industry and art, grandeur and intimacy – the WMC is a bold and brilliant asset to the capital. See page 643

❷ Blaenavon Industrial heritage at its finest, thanks to a thrilling deep-mine museum and the fascinating ironworks town. See page 653

❸ National Waterfront Museum, Swansea A celebration of Welsh innovation and industry – one of the best museums in Wales. See page 659

❹ The Gower Holding some of the country's most inspirational coastal and rural scenery, culminating in the stunning Rhossili Bay. See page 661

❺ Carreg Cennen The most magnificently sited castle in Wales, this fantasy fortress offers splendid views and endless possibilities for exploration. See page 666

❻ The Pembrokeshire Coast Path A narrow ribbon of mainly cliff-top footpath that winds its way through some magnificent coastal scenery. See page 670

❼ St Davids Inspirational city (little more than a village, in fact) with a splendid cathedral and heart-racing boat trips out to offshore islands. See page 674

HIGHLIGHTS ARE MARKED ON THE MAP ON PAGE 638

National Assembly and Millennium Centre on the rejuvenated Cardiff Bay waterfront, and a fabulous city-centre sports stadium, give the city the feel of an international capital, if not always with a very Welsh flavour.

Cardiff's sights are clustered in fairly small, distinct districts. The compact commercial centre is bounded by the **River Taff**, which flows past the tremendous **Principality Stadium**; in this rugby-mad city, the atmosphere in the pubs and streets when Wales have a home match – particularly against the old enemy, England – is charged with good-natured, beery fervour. Just upstream, the Taff is flanked by the wall of Cardiff's extraordinary **castle**, an amalgam of Roman remains, Norman keep and Victorian fantasy. North of the castle is a series of white Edwardian buildings grouped around **Cathays Park**: the City Hall, Cardiff University and the superb **National Museum**. A mile south of the centre, **Cardiff Bay**, once a bustling port, now a classy waterside development, houses the stunning Welsh National Assembly and Millennium buildings, and a stack of bars and restaurants. A number of sights within striking distance of Cardiff warrant a visit: **Llandaff Cathedral**, with its strange clash of Norman and modern styles; the thirteenth-century fairy-tale castle of **Castell Coch**, on a hillside in the woods; the massive **Caerphilly Castle**; and the hugely popular **National History Museum** at St Fagans.

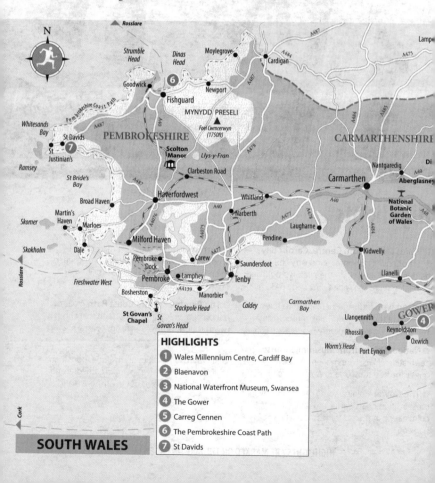

HIGHLIGHTS

1. Wales Millennium Centre, Cardiff Bay
2. Blaenavon
3. National Waterfront Museum, Swansea
4. The Gower
5. Carreg Cennen
6. The Pembrokeshire Coast Path
7. St Davids

SOUTH WALES

Brief history

The second Marquess of Bute built Cardiff's first dock in 1839, opening others in swift succession. The Butes owned massive swathes of the rapidly industrializing South Wales Valleys and insisted that all coal and iron exports use the family docks in Cardiff, which became one of the world's busiest ports. The twentieth century saw varying fortunes: the dock trade slumped in the 1930s and the city suffered heavy bombing in World War II, but with the creation of Cardiff as capital in 1955, optimism and confidence in the city blossomed. Many government and media institutions have since moved here from London, and the development of the dock areas around the modern Assembly building in Cardiff Bay has given a largely positive boost to the cityscape.

14

Central Cardiff

Cardiff **centre** forms a rough square bounded by the castle, Queen Street and Central stations and the River Taff. Dominating the skyline is the magnificent **Principality Stadium**.

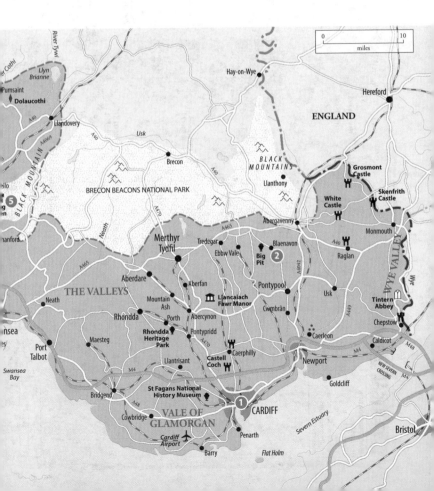

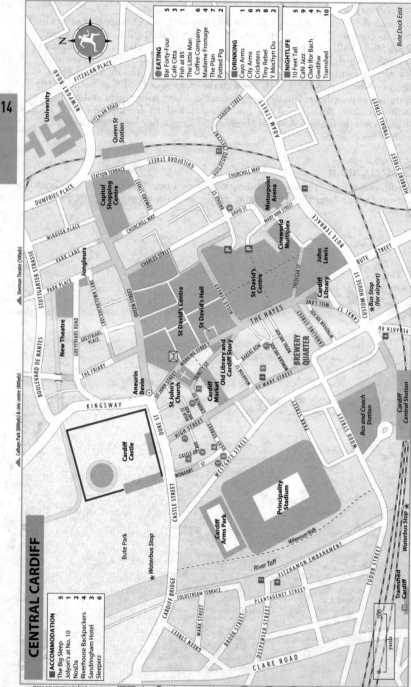

CENTRAL CARDIFF

ACCOMMODATION
The Big Sleep	5
Jolyon's at No. 10	1
NosDa	2
Riverhouse Backpackers	4
Sandringham Hotel	3
Sleeperz	6

● **EATING**
Bar Forty-Four	5
Café Citta	3
Fish at 85	1
The Little Man Coffee Company	6
Madame Fromage	4
The Plan	7
Potted Pig	2

● **DRINKING**
Cayo Arms	1
City Arms	6
Cricketers	3
Tiny Rebel	8
Y Mochyn Du	2

● **NIGHTLIFE**
10 Feet Tall	5
Café Jazz	9
Clwb Ifor Bach	4
Gwdihw	7
Tramshed	10

Principality Stadium

Westgate St, CF10 1NS • Guided tours only (starting from the WRU store): hourly Mon–Sat 10am–5pm, Sun 10am–4pm; 1hr • £12.50 • ☏ 029 2082 2432, ⓦ principalitystadium.wales

Dominating the city from all angles is the **Principality Stadium**, built as the Millennium Stadium for the 1999 Rugby World Cup and renamed in 2016. With its trademark retractable roof, and seating for 74,500 people, it has hosted sporting matches of every description – including the 2017 Champion's League final – as well as an array of huge rock gigs and other spectaculars. The very worthwhile **stadium tours** take you into the press centre, dressing rooms, VIP areas, players' tunnel and pitchside.

14

Cardiff arcades

Secreted away between The Hayes and St Mary Street and High Street are some half a dozen renovated arcades, a series of Victorian and Edwardian galleries where you'll find many alluring little independent shops and cafés. Particularly impressive are the **High Street** and **Castle arcades**, packed with great clothes shops, quirky gift stores, independent little coffeehouses and a range of esoteric emporia where you can pick up fliers for clubs and events. A few yards further down towards Central Station is the elegant Edwardian **indoor market** and further still the **Royal** and **Morgan arcades**, linking St Mary Street with the lower end of The Hayes.

The Old Library and Cardiff Story

The Hayes, CF10 1BH • Mon–Sat 10am–4pm • Free • ☏ 029 2034 6214, ⓦ cardiffstory.com

At the top of the Hayes is the beautifully colonnaded frontage of the **Old Library**, home to the **Cardiff Story**. Using artefacts, hands-on gizmos and audiovisual displays, it's an enlightening romp through the city's colourful history, with emphasis on how Cardiff has been shaped by the docks and the local coal industry. Don't miss the stunning **tiled corridor**; this was the original library entrance, its ornate floor-to-ceiling tiles produced by Maw & Co in 1882.

Cardiff Castle

Castle St, CF10 3RB • Daily: March–Oct 9am–6pm; Nov–Feb 9am–5pm • £12.50 • **House tours** Same days, hourly on the hour; 50min • £3.25 • **Clock tower tours** April–Oct Sat & Sun hourly 11.30am–2.30pm; 30min • £4.25 • ☏ 029 2087 8100, ⓦ cardiffcastle.com

The political, geographical and historical heart of the city is **Cardiff Castle**. An intriguing hotchpotch, the fortress hides inside a vast walled yard corresponding roughly to the outline of the original fort built by the Romans. The neat Norman motte and **keep** look down onto the turrets and towers of the **Castle Apartments**, which date in part from the fourteenth and fifteenth centuries, but were much extended in Tudor times, when residential needs began to overtake military priorities. In the late nineteenth century, the third Marquess of Bute lavished a fortune on upgrading his pile, commissioning architect and decorator William Burges to aid him. With their passion for the religious art and symbolism of the Middle Ages, they transformed the crumbling interiors into palaces of vivid colour and intricate design.

Castle apartments

A self-guided tour of the house allows you to visit the **library**, whose richly stocked bookcases are carved with cheeky animal friezes (beavers, possums, platypuses), the **Drawing Room**, notable for its wall-length portraits of the Butes and, upstairs, the grand **Banqueting Hall**, originally from 1428, which was transformed by Bute and Burges with a riotously kitsch fireplace and a church-like ceiling. Two **guided tours** are available for an additional charge. The house tour includes all of the above, plus the fabulous **Winter Smoking Room**, the **Nursery** – with hand-painted tiles and silhouette lanterns depicting contemporary nursery rhymes – and, in the Bute Tower, **Lord Bute's bedroom**, with a mirrored ceiling, and the **Roof Garden**, awash with Sicilian marble. The clocktower tour also takes in the **Clock Chamber**, **Bachelor's Bedroom** and, above that, the **Summer Smoking Room**, the latter two decorated in rich patterns of gold, maroon and cobalt, with many of the images inspired from medieval myths and beliefs.

Cathays Park and the civic centre

On the northern edge of the city centre is **Cathays Park**, a large rectangle of lawns and flowerbeds that forms the focus for the impressive buildings of the **civic centre**. Dating from the early twentieth century, the gleaming white buildings are arranged with pompous Edwardian precision, and speak volumes about Cardiff's self-confidence a full half-century before it was officially declared capital of Wales. The dragon-topped, domed **City Hall** is the magnificent centrepiece, an exercise in every cliché of ostentatious civic self-glory, with a roll call of statues of male Welsh heroes including Llywelyn ap Gruffydd, St David, Giraldus Cambrensis and Owain Glyndŵr.

National Museum

Cathays Park, CF10 3NP • Tues–Sun 10am–5pm • Free • ☎ 0300 111 2333, ⓦ museum.wales/cardiff

The fine **National Museum** starts with the epic **Evolution of Wales** exhibition, a natural-history exhibition packed with high-tech gizmos and spectacular big-screen visuals. The most intriguing exhibit is the fossilized remains of a Jurassic-era dinosaur discovered at Lavernock Point near Penarth in 2014 following a rock fall; this remarkable specimen – parts recovered included the skull, claws, teeth and foot bones – was subsequently given the title *Dracoraptor hanigani* – the first part translating as "Dragon Robber", the second part named in honour of the brothers who found the dinosaur.

The first floor is given over to the museum's extraordinary **art collection**. Galleries one to ten feature a substantial number of works by the three great eighteenth-century Welsh artists – Richard Wilson, William Parry and Thomas Jones, Of the fine landscapes, look out for Wilson's *Caernarfon Castle* and *Dolbadarn Castle*, and Jones's *A View from Radnorshire* along with the memorable *The Bard*. There's a nod to Wales' mining heritage too, courtesy of Lowry's evocative *Six Bells Abertillery*.

Galleries eleven to fifteen begin with nineteenth-century French art and include Millet (the haunting, unfinished *Peasant Family* and lovely, pastoral *Goose Girl at Gruchy*), Boudin and Manet. Gallery twelve concentrates on **Art in Britain after 1930**, with some terrific pieces by Welsh supremo Ceri Richards, and a typically raw and bizarre *Study for Self Portrait* by Francis Bacon. Gallery fourteen, **Art in Europe after 1900**, features *Nature Morte au Poron* by Picasso and Magritte's *The Empty Mask*, while in gallery fifteen the emphasis is very much on **British art around 1900**, with the likes of Walter Sickert, Sylvia Gosse and Gwen John, and Harold Gilman's colourful London scenes (*Café Royal* and *Mornington Crescent*).

Best of all, though, is gallery sixteen, which has a fabulous collection of **Impressionists** and **Post-Impressionists**. Dominating the room are several pieces by Monet, including a smog-bound *Charing Cross Bridge*, alongside Cézanne, Sisley (with his views of Penarth and Langland Bay), Pissarro and Renoir, whose coquettish *La Parisienne* is a standout. The centrepiece here, though, is Van Gogh's magnificent *Rain at Auvers*, painted just weeks before his suicide. Look out, too, for the wonderful **sculpture collection** in the Rotunda, including many by the one-man Victorian Welsh statue industry, Goscombe John.

Cardiff Bay

A thirty-minute stroll from the city centre, **Cardiff Bay** has become one of the world's biggest regeneration projects, the downbeat dereliction of the old docks having been almost completely transformed into a designer heaven. In years gone by, when the docks were some of the busiest in the world, the area was better known by the evocative name of **Tiger Bay**, immortalized by local lass Shirley Bassey.

Ever-expanding, the bay area now comprises four distinct parts, situated either side of **Roald Dahl's Plass**, the main square, named after the Cardiff-born children's author: on the eastern side lie the swanky civic precincts around the glorious **Wales Millennium Centre**, while to the west is **Mermaid Quay**, an airy jumble of shops, bars and restaurants. South of here is the **BBC Drama Village** – where both *Doctor Who* and *Casualty* are shot – and finally, set back from the water's edge in the north, the somewhat down-at-heel, but increasingly gentrified, Taff-side suburb of **Butetown**.

Wales Millennium Centre

Bute Place, CF10 5AL · ☎ 029 2063 6464, Ⓦ wmc.org.uk

14

Dominating Cardiff Bay is the mesmerizing **Wales Millennium Centre**, a vibrant performance space for theatre and music, and home to many of Wales' premier arts organizations. Likened by critics to a copper-plated armadillo or a great snail, the WMC soars gracefully over the rooftops, its exterior swathed in Welsh building materials, topped with a stainless-steel shell tinted with a bronze oxide to resist salty air. The grace and style continue throughout the interior, fashioned from materials that hark back to Wales' mineral-extracting past, from the native oak, ash, beech, sycamore, alder, birch, chestnut and cherry woods to the riveted steel and coal-like pillars. The ground floor houses the main box office, music and souvenir shop, tourist office and the excellent *ffresh* bar and brasserie.

The Pierhead

Cardiff Bay, CF10 4BZ · Daily 10.30am–4.30pm · Free · ☎ 0300 200 6565, Ⓦ pierhead.org

Down by the water's edge is the magnificent red-brick **Pierhead**, a typically ornate neo-Gothic terracotta pile that was built for the Cardiff Railway Company, formerly the Bute Dock Company. It now houses an enjoyable **exhibition** documenting the rise and fall of the local coal-exporting industry, although its most striking exhibit is the binnacle from the *Terra Nova*, which set sail from the bay in June 1910 ahead of Captain Scott's ill-fated polar expedition.

The Senedd

Cardiff Bay, CF10 4BZ · Mon–Fri 9.30am–4.30pm, Sat & Sun 10.30am–4.30pm; guided tours (1hr) daily 11am, 2pm & 3pm; plenary sessions in the debating chamber Tues & Wed 1.30pm · Free · ☎ 0300 200 6565, Ⓦ assembly.wales

Home of the Welsh National Assembly, the **Senedd** is distinguished by its wraparound glass facade and soaring wooden roof. Daily guided tours explain more about the building, which was constructed using traditional Welsh materials, notably slate and Welsh oak, and it's possible to attend plenary sessions in the debating chamber. Otherwise, you can always pop in to the perky **café**, which affords marvellous views of the bay.

Norwegian church

Harbour Drive, CF10 4PA · Daily 10.30am–4pm; hours can vary depending on events · ☎ 029 2087 7959, Ⓦ norwegianchurchcardiff.com

The lovely white, stumpy-spired **Norwegian church** is an old seamen's chapel that once served the needs of thousands of Scandinavian sailors, though it's better known as the place where Roald Dahl was christened (his parents were Norwegian). It's now a convivial café and performance and exhibition space.

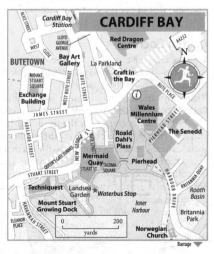

CARDIFF BAY

14

Cardiff Bay Barrage

Cardiff Bay, CF10 4PA · Daily 7am–10pm · Free · ☎ 029 2087 7900, Ⓦ cardiffharbour.com · Waterbuses run between the waterfront and the southern end of the barrage daily 10.30am–4.30pm (£4 return)

Central to the whole Bay project is the **Cardiff Bay Barrage**, built right across the Ely and Taff estuaries, transforming a vast mud flat into a freshwater lake and creating eight miles of useful waterfront. It's a fine bit of engineering, and it's well worth a wander along the embankment to see the lock gates and sluices; there's a great kids' play area and skate park here too. For something more strenuous, you could tackle the 6.2-mile **Bay Trail**, a circular path for walkers and cyclists that wends its way around the bay and across to Penarth.

Butetown

The area immediately inland from the bay is the salty old district of **Butetown**, whose inner-city dereliction still peeps through the rampant gentrification. James Street is the main commercial focus, while to its north are the old buildings around the **Exchange Building**, built in the 1880s as Britain's central Coal Exchange, but which has been revamped into one of the city's plushest hotels.

Llandaff Cathedral

Cathedral Rd, Llandaff, 2 miles northwest of the city centre, CF5 2LA · Cathedral: Mon–Sat 9am–7pm, Sun 7am–7pm; walled garden daily 24hr · Free · ☎ 029 2056 4554, Ⓦ llandaffcathedral.org.uk · Bus #33 or #33A from Cardiff bus station (frequent; 15min)

The small, quiet suburb of **Llandaff** is home to a church that has now grown up to become the city's **cathedral**. Believed to have been founded in the sixth century by St Teilo, it was rebuilt in Norman style in around 1120, and was used well into the thirteenth century. From the late fourteenth century it fell into an advanced state of disrepair, and one of the twin towers and the nave roof eventually collapsed. Restoration only began in earnest in the 1840s, when **Pre-Raphaelite** artists such as Edward Burne-Jones, Dante Gabriel Rossetti and William Morris were commissioned to make colourful new windows and decorative panels. Their work is best seen in the south aisle.

The fusion of different styles and ages is evident from outside, especially in the mismatched western towers. Inside, the nave is dominated by Jacob Epstein's overwhelming *Christ in Majesty*, a concrete parabola topped with a soaring Christ figure. At the west end of the north aisle, the **St Illtyd Chapel** features Rossetti's cloying triptych *The Seed of David*. In the south presbytery is a tenth-century Celtic cross, the only survivor of the pre-Norman cathedral.

Castell Coch

Tongwynlais, 4 miles north of Llandaff, CF15 7JS · March–June, Sept & Oct daily 9.30am–5pm; July & Aug daily 9.30am–6pm; Nov–Feb Mon–Sat 10am–4pm, Sun 11am–4pm · £6.50, including audio guide · ☎ 029 2081 0101, Ⓦ cadw.gov.wales/daysout/castell-coch · Bus #26 from Westgate St in Cardiff (every 30min; 25min)

Rising mysteriously out of a steep wooded hillside above the village of Tongwynlais is **Castell Coch**, a ruined thirteenth-century fortress rebuilt into a fantasy castle in the late 1870s by William Burges for the third Marquess of Bute. With its working portcullis and drawbridge, Castell Coch is pure medieval fantasy, and shares many similarities with Cardiff Castle, notably the lavish decor, culled from religious and moral fables.

An excellent audio guide leads you around, beginning in the banqueting hall, with its striking painted timber ceiling and Burges-designed furnishings. From here you enter the octagonal drawing room, its walls and domed ceiling decorated with murals depicting Aesop's Fables. Above the winch room is Lord Bute's bedroom, with a typically ostentatious bronze-plated bed, though this is relatively staid compared to Lady Bute's bedroom, incorporating a mirrored, double-dome ceiling around which 28 panels depict frolicking monkeys.

CAERPHILLY: THE BIG CHEESE

In addition to its castle, Caerphilly is also known for its crumbly white cheese, which has inspired the vibrant **Big Cheese Festival** (ⓦcaerphilly.gov.uk/bigcheese), held over three days in late July in the shadow of the castle. It's a hoot, with concerts, street theatre, historical re-enactments, a funfair, falconry and, naturally, a cheese race.

Caerphilly Castle

14

Castle St, Caerphilly, 7 miles north of Cardiff, CF83 1JD • March–June, Sept & Oct daily 9.30am–5pm; July & Aug daily 9.30am–6pm; Nov–Feb Mon–Sat 10am–4pm, Sun 11am–4pm • £7.95; CADW • ☎ 029 2088 3143, ⓦ cadw.gov.wales/daysout/caerphilly-castle • Trains (every 15–20min; 20min) and buses (every 15–20min; 25min) depart from Cardiff; from the stations it is a 5min walk up Cardiff Rd to the centre of town and the castle

Now almost a suburb of Cardiff, the town of **CAERPHILLY** (Caerffili) has a particularly staggering town-centre **castle**, the first in Britain built concentrically, with an inner system of defences overlooking the outer ring. Looming out of its vast surrounding moat, the medieval fortress with its cock-eyed tower occupies more than thirty acres, presenting an awesome promise that the interior does not entirely fulfil. The castle was begun in 1268 by Gilbert de Clare as a defence against Llywelyn the Last. For the next few centuries Caerphilly was little more than a decaying toy, given at whim by kings to their favourites. By the turn of the twentieth century, it was in a sorry state, sitting amid a growing industrial town that saw fit to build in the then-dry moat and castle precincts. Houses and shops were demolished in order to allow the moat to be reflooded in 1958. The most interesting section of the castle is the massive eastern gatehouse, which includes an impressive upper hall and oratory and, to its left, the wholly restored and re-roofed **Great Hall**.

St Fagans National History Museum

St Fagans, 4 miles west of Cardiff, CF5 6XB • Daily 10am–5pm • Free • ☎ 0300 111 2333, ⓦ museum.wales/stfagans • Bus #32A (every 25min; 20min) from Westgate St in Cardiff

ST FAGANS (Sain Ffagan) has a rural feel that is only partly disturbed by the busloads of tourists rolling in to visit the excellent **National History Museum**, built around **St Fagans Castle**, a country house erected in 1580 and now furnished in early nineteenth-century style.

Beyond the castle lies the **open-air museum**, an outstanding assemblage of buildings from all corners of Wales that have been carefully dismantled and rebuilt on this site. The superb Rhyd-y-car **ironworkers' cottages**, from Merthyr Tydfil, were originally built in around 1800; each of the six houses are furnished in the style of a different period, stretching from 1805 to 1985.

ARRIVAL AND DEPARTURE   CARDIFF

By plane Cardiff Airport (☎01446 711111, ⓦcardiff-airport.com) is 10 miles southwest of the city on the other side of Barry. The most direct way to reach the city centre is by Express bus #T9 (every 20–30min; 30min; £5). A taxi from the airport to the centre of Cardiff will cost around £30. Getting to the airport, buses currently leave from Custom House St; they also call in at Cardiff Bay, by the Red Dragon Centre.

By train Cardiff Central train station is served by all intercity services as well as many suburban and Valley Line services. Queen St station, at the eastern edge of the centre, is for local trains only.

Destinations from Cardiff Central Abergavenny (every 45min; 40min); Bristol (every 30min; 50min); Caerphilly (every 15min; 20min); Carmarthen (hourly; 1hr 45min);

Chepstow (every 30min–1hr; 40min); Haverfordwest (9 daily; 2hr 30min); London Paddington (2 hourly; 2hr); Newport (every 15–30min; 15min); Swansea (every 30–45min; 1hr).

By bus Pending the (much delayed) construction of a new bus station in front of Cardiff Central train station, buses currently depart from all over the city – check ⓦ cardiffbus. com for details. National Express buses currently leave from Bute Park.

Destinations Abergavenny (Mon–Sat hourly; 1hr 45min); Brecon (Mon–Sat 8 daily; 1hr 35min); Bristol (8 daily; 1hr 20min); Caerphilly (every 20min; 40min); Chepstow (Mon–Sat every 30min–1hr, Sun 5, 1 change; 1hr 20min); London (6 daily; 3hr 20min); Newport (Mon–Sat every 30min, Sun hourly; 40min); Swansea (hourly; 1hr 20min).

14

GETTING AROUND

Cardiff is compact enough to walk around, and even Cardiff Bay is just a 30min stroll from Central station. Otherwise, you can take a **train** (every 20min) from Queen Street station to Cardiff Bay station, or Baycar **bus** #6.

By bus Cardiff Bus (Bws Caerdydd; ⓦ cardiffbus.com) runs an extensive and reliable bus network, with buses generally operating between 5.30am and 11.30pm. A one-way fare anywhere in the city costs £1.80 (payable on the bus, exact money only). Various travel passes offer good savings: a "Day to Go" ticket (£3.60) gives unlimited bus travel around Cardiff and Penarth for a day, which can be extended to Barry and the Vale of Glamorgan with the "Day to Go Plus" ticket (£4.90). The Network Dayrider ticket (£8) covers all the above plus much of the rest of southeast Wales. All are available from the customer service centre in the library on the Hayes (Mon–Fri 10am–6pm, Sat 9am–4.30pm; ☎ 029 2066 6444), at Paypoint outlets throughout the city, or on board buses themselves; you can also buy the "Day to Go" tickets from the tourist office.

By waterbus A scenic waterbus service (hourly 10.30am–4.30pm; £4 one-way; ☎ 029 2034 5163, ⓦ aquabus .co.uk) operates between Bute Park, near Cardiff Castle, to Mermaid Quay in the bay, though occasionally (depending on the river flow), the service will only run as far as Taff's Mead Embankment, diagonally across from the Principality Stadium.

INFORMATION

Tourist office There's no tourist office in the city centre, but you can get lots of information, both on Cardiff and further afield, at the Wales Millennium Centre in Cardiff Bay (Mon–Sat 10am–6pm, Sun 10am–4pm; ☎ 029 2087 3573, ⓦ visitcardiff.com). *Buzz*, a free monthly guide to arts and events in the city, is worth seeking out.

ACCOMMODATION

The Big Sleep Bute Terrace, CF10 2FE ☎ 029 2063 6363, ⓦ thebigsleephotel.com; map p.640. Snazzy, if somewhat soulless, budget(ish) option occupying a former 1960s office block turned retro designer hotel. The colourful rooms – doubles, triples and family – are well furnished, their dual-aspect windows affording panoramic city views. Breakfast £7.95. __£70__

Jolyon's at No. 10 10 Cathedral Rd, CF11 9LJ ☎ 029 2009 1900, ⓦ jolyons10.com; map p.640. There's no scrimping on style at this gorgeous boutique hotel, which accommodates 21 handsomely presented rooms (eight of which are larger suites; £129) with Italian-/French-inspired furnishings. __£99__

NosDa 53–59 Despenser St, CF11 6AG ☎ 029 2037 8866, ⓦ nosda.co.uk; map p.640. Hip hostel/budget hotel on the riverbank opposite the Principality Stadium, with singles, doubles (some en suite) and four- to ten-bed dorms, some with flip-down beds. There's a kitchen and comfy lounge, though most folk just decamp to the popular *Tafarn* bar. Dorms __£12.50__, doubles __£32__

★ **Riverhouse Backpackers** 59 Fitzhamon Embankment CF11 6AN ☎ 029 2039 9810, ⓦ riverhousebackpackers. com; map p.640. Cosy, contemporary backpackers' hostel in a Victorian villa with mixed and female-only dorms and twin rooms, as well as a self-catering kitchen, a welcoming dining/lounge area and a sunny wraparound garden-terrace. Dorms __£18__, twins __£40__

Sandringham Hotel 21 St Mary St, CF10 1PL ☎ 029 2023 2161, ⓦ sandringham-hotel.com; map p.640. Pleasantly old-fashioned, family-run hotel – rooms may be careworn and bathrooms antiquated, but it is friendly, convenient and very cheap. Better still, it's just a short stumble up the stairs from the excellent *Café Jazz* (see page 649). __£40__

★ **Sleeperz** Station Approach, CF10 1RH ☎ 029 2047 8747, ⓦ sleeperz.com; map p.640. Cleverly utilizing the architectural space between the train line and two roads, this funky hotel has light-filled rooms (all doubles, all the same price) in white/orange and black/grey colour schemes. The corner cabin bunk rooms are particularly neat. Terrific value. Breakfast £9.45. __£55__

EATING

Cardiff has a great mix of places serving innovative **Welsh cuisine** and ethnic food, though the best restaurants are just outside the centre up in Pontcanna; you'll also find a plethora of places down on Mermaid Quay in Cardiff Bay.

Bar Forty-Four 15–23 Westgate St, CF10 1DD ☎ 03333 444049, ⓦ bar44.co.uk; map p.640. From the colourful tiled entrance to the low-brick-vaulted ceiling, there's an understated elegance about this glamorous tapas bar. Perch yourself on a high stool and peruse a lengthy menu featuring the likes of *fabada Asturiana* (white bean stew with chorizo and smoked *morcilla*), *pulpo* (octopus with capers and red wine) and exclusively Spanish wines. The express weekday lunch menu (three courses £11) is a good deal. Mon–Thurs 11.30am–11.30pm, Fri & Sat 11.30am–midnight.

14

Café Citta 4 Church St, CF10 1BG ☎029 2022 4040, ⓦcafecitta.com; map p.640. A friendly, laidback pizzeria straight out of Italy, with a fine little log-burning oven knocking out freshly cooked pizzas (£9–10) using dough and sauces made on the premises, and locally sourced ingredients. Mon 4–11pm, Tues–Sat noon–11pm.

★ **Fish at 85** 85 Pontcanna St, CF11 9HS ☎029 2023 5666, ⓦfish85.co.uk; map p.640. Wholesalers, fishmongers and restaurant all in one, and quite brilliant it is too. The "catch menu" allows you to pick something from the counter, which could be, for example, brill, snapper or red mullet, along with a sauce, and then have it cooked just the way you like it. Alternatively, select something from the menu, perhaps roast monkfish with *boulangère* potatoes and creamy curried mussels (£22.50). Tues–Sat noon–2.30pm & 6–9pm.

★ **The Little Man Coffee Company** Ivor House, Bridge St, CF10 2EE ☎07933 844234, ⓦlittlemancoffee. co.uk; map p.640. This erstwhile post office and bank has been superbly repurposed into one of the city's most stylish coffeehouses, whose easy-going retro vibe owes much to the stripped-back wooden flooring, 70s armchairs and pew-style seating – it's the kind of place you could quite happily laze around in all afternoon. The staff really do know their beans and the beautifully crafted coffee (there are typically two espressos on the go each day) tastes superb, particularly with a slice of sticky homemade ginger cake. Mon–Fri 7am–9pm, Sat & Sun 8am–5pm.

Madame Fromage 21–25 Castle Arcade, CF10 1BU ☎029 2064 4888, ⓦmadamefromage.co.uk; map p.640. A small slice of Paris at this delightful corner café-cum-deli where cheese is king – the menu offers a lot more, however, from quiche to lamb cawl and charcuterie platters. Check out, too, the shop's tempting stock of jams, pickles and chutneys. Mon–Fri 10am–5.30pm, Sat 9.30am–5.30pm.

The Plan 28–29 Morgan Arcade, CF10 1AF ☎029 2039 8764; map p.640. This great-looking, two-storey artisan coffee bar has been around for ages and remains *the* place in Cardiff to come for a caffeine shot; it also offers a super range of light meals, including breakfasts, home-made burgers and quiches (£7–8), all made using locally sourced organic produce. Mon–Sat 8.45am–5pm, Sun 9.45am–5pm.

Potted Pig 27 High St, CF10 1PU ☎029 2022 4817, ⓦthepottedpig.com; map p.640. This venue – in the reconditioned vaults of a former bank – is a terrific spot to tuck into all things porcine, from crispy pig's ear with black pudding salad to roast belly of pork with pomme purée (£18). The wine list complements the food brilliantly. Tues–Sat noon–2pm & 7–10pm, Sun noon–2.30pm.

DRINKING

The **pub** scene is lively, with a number of wonderful Edwardian palaces of etched, smoky glass and deep red wood, where you'll find Cardiff's very own Brains bitter; some of the most enjoyable places to drink are on Cathedral Road.

Cayo Arms 36 Cathedral Rd, CF11 9LL ☎029 2039 1910, ⓦcayopub.co.uk; map p.640. Within a six of the cricket ground, this large, busy and proudly Welsh pub, in two conjoined Victorian townhouses, offers Tomos Watkin beers, decent food and a happy crowd. Mon–Sat noon–11pm, Sun noon–10.30pm.

City Arms 10 Quay St, CF10 1EA ☎029 2064 1913; map p.640. Near the Principality Stadium, this no-nonsense boozer is always popular, especially on international match days and before gigs at *Clwb Ifor Bach* around the corner. Brains beers and some choice guest ales. Mon–Thurs 11am–11pm, Fri & Sat 11am–2.30am, Sun noon–10.30pm.

Cricketers 66 Cathedral Rd, CF11 9LL ☎029 2034 5102, ⓦcricketerscardiff.co.uk; map p.640. Set in a gorgeous Victorian townhouse, the beautiful-looking *Cricketers* combines a sunny interior with lively beer gardens front and back. The cask-conditioned Welsh beers are some of Cardiff's best and the food is creditable. Daily noon–11pm.

★ **Tiny Rebel** 25 Westgate St, CF10 1DD ☎029 2039 9557, ⓦtinyrebel.co.uk; map p.640. Cool craft beer bar owned by the Newport-based brewery of the same name. There's a bewildering choice of cask and keg beers – mostly their own – so if deciding is too onerous, try a flight of thirds. Brilliant themed nights include Americana, Bring Your Own Vinyl and, on Mon, board games. Daily noon–2am.

Y Mochyn Du Sophia Close, off Cathedral Rd, CF11 9HW ☎029 2037 1599, ⓦymochyndu.com; map p.640. This old gatekeeper's lodge is a fine place to sup a Welsh-brewed pint, either in the conservatory or outside among the greenery. Popular with Welsh-speakers. Mon–Fri noon–11pm, Sat noon–midnight, Sun noon–10.30pm.

NIGHTLIFE

Cardiff is renowned for its rumbustious **nightlife**, with one of the best **live music scenes** in the UK.

10 Feet Tall 11a Church St, CF10 1BG ☎029 2022 8883, ⓦ10feettall.co.uk; map p.640. Perenially popular tapas-cum-cocktail bar. IT rocks hard most nights of the week, but the vibe is ramped up a notch when the basement *Undertone* club – hosting gigs and various themed nights – clicks into gear. Mon–Wed 3pm–midnight, Thurs, Fri &

CARDIFF ROCKS

Welsh music has a fantastically strong pedigree, and Cardiff has spawned its fair share of great **bands**, not least the wonderful Super Furry Animals whose lead singer, Gruff Rhys, has also made several solo Welsh-language albums. Hailing from the nearby mining town of Blackwood, pop/rock champions the Manic Street Preachers have been making thrilling records for more than twenty years; more recently bands such as Los Campesinos! have taken up the baton. Great places to catch live music include the *Tramshed* (see below) and the inimitable *Clwb Ifor Bach* (see below), which has long been a bastion of Welsh-language bands. Cardiff is also home to the world's oldest record shop, **Spillers** (Morgan's Arcade; Mon–Sat 10am–6pm; ⓦ spillersrecords.co.uk), founded in 1894; you could easily spend a couple of hours leafing through its hard-to-find records of all genres.

14

Sun 3pm–3am, Sat noon–3am.

Café Jazz 21 St Mary St, CF10 1PL ☎ 029 2038 7026, ⓦ cafejazzcardiff.com; map p.640. Unassuming but popular venue, below the *Sandringham Hotel*, hosting a diverse range of concerts – electric blues, funk, swing, gypsy jazz and the like – nightly between Tues and Fri, with the house band on Sat. Entrance typically £4–6. Tues–Sat, times vary.

★ **Clwb Ifor Bach** Womanby St, CF10 1BR ☎ 029 2023 2199, ⓦ clwb.net; map p.640. Cardiff's premier venue for Welsh-language bands (hence the "Welsh Club" moniker), this is a sweaty and enjoyable live music venue and club with nightly gigs and sessions. Mon–Wed & Sun 7–10.30pm, Thurs–Sat 7pm–4am.

★ **Gwdihw** 6 Guildford Crescent, CF10 2HJ ☎ 029 2039 7933, ⓦ gwdihw.co.uk; map p.640. Pronounced "goody-hoo" (meaning Owl), this is a wonderful little corner café/bar, its exterior painted bright orange and the interior decked out with stripped wood flooring, odd bits of furniture and retro bits and bobs. Daily happenings include alternative movies, poetry recitals, micro-festivals and regular bouts of live music on the dinky stage. Mon–Wed 3pm–midnight, Thurs–Sat noon–2am, Sun 4pm–midnight.

Tramshed Clare Rd, Grangetown, CF11 6QP ☎ 029 2023 5555, ⓦ tramshedcardiff.com; map p.640. Occupying Cardiff's old red-brick tram depot in the southern suburb of Grangetown, this atmospheric one-thousand-capacity space fills the gap between the city's smaller, niche venues and the behemoth that is the Motorpoint. Expect a top quality roster of gigs. Days and times vary.

ENTERTAINMENT

Cardiff's **theatre** scene encompasses everything from the radical and alternative at the smaller venues to big, blowsy productions and West End spectaculars at the Wales Millennium Centre. The WMC and St David's Hall are the main venues for **classical music**.

Chapter Arts Centre Market Rd, Canton, CF5 1QE ☎ 029 2030 4400, ⓦ chapter.org. Although best known for its arthouse movies, this superb multifunctional arts complex also hosts comedy, local and touring theatre and dance companies, and exhibitions; there's invariably a strong Welsh theme to events.

St David's Hall The Hayes, CF10 1AH ☎ 029 2087 8444, ⓦ stdavidshallcardiff.co.uk. Part of the massive St David's shopping centre, this large venue is home to visiting orchestras and musicians from jazz to opera to folk, and is frequently used by the excellent BBC National Orchestra of Wales.

Sherman Theatre Senghennydd Rd, Cathays, CF24 4YE ☎ 029 2064 6900, ⓦ shermantheatre.co.uk. Excellent two-auditorium rep theatre hosting a mixed bag of new and translated classic Welsh-language pieces, stand-up comedy, children's entertainment, drama, music and dance.

Wales Millennium Centre Bute Place, Cardiff Bay, CF10 5AL ☎ 029 2063 6464, ⓦ wmc.org.uk. Stunning performance space home to the Welsh National Opera (ⓦ wno.org.uk), along with other music and dance companies. Also used for touring West End and other mega-productions.

Wye Valley

The **Wye Valley** (ⓦ visitwyevalley.com), along with the rest of Monmouthshire, was finally recognized as part of Wales in the local government reorganization of 1974. Before then, the county was officially included as part of neither England nor Wales, so that maps were frequently headlined "Wales and Monmouthshire". Most of the rest of Monmouthshire is undoubtedly Welsh, but the woodlands and hills by the meandering River Wye have more in common with the landscape over the border. The two main centres are **Chepstow**, with its massive castle, and the spruce, old-fashioned town of **Monmouth**, sixteen miles upstream. Six miles north of Chepstow lie the atmospheric ruins of the Cistercian **Tintern Abbey**.

INFORMATION
WYE VALLEY

Tourist information The excellent Old Station visitor centre (daily: April–Sept 10.30am–5.30pm; Oct 10am–4pm; ☎01291 689566) is in the former Tintern station; two refurbished carriages house an exhibition on the valley, while you can pick up leaflets on local walks, including the surrounding wildflower meadows and cliff rambles above the river. For kids, there's a play area and a miniature railway (generally Sat; £1). Bus #69 between Chepstow and Monmouth stops outside.

Chepstow

Of all the places that call themselves "the gateway to Wales", **CHEPSTOW** (Cas-Gwent), sitting on the western bank of the River Wye, has probably the best claim. Although lacking the immediate charm of many other Welsh market towns, there is, nonetheless, an identifiably medieval street-plan hemmed in by the thirteenth-century **Port Wall**.

Chepstow Castle

Bridge St, NP16 5EY • March–June, Sept & Oct daily 9.30am–5pm; July & Aug daily 9.30am–6pm; Nov–Feb Mon–Sat 10am–4pm, Sun 11am–4pm • £6.50; CADW • ☎01291 624065, ⓦcadw.gov.wales/daysout/chepstow-castle

Strategically sited within a tight loop of the River Wye, **Chepstow Castle** was the first stone castle to be built in Britain, with its first Norman incarnation, the Great Tower keep, rising in 1067. The largest of the three enclosures is the Lower Ward, where you'll find the modest **Great Hall** and the colourful Earl's chamber. Twelfth-century defences separate the Lower Ward from the Middle Ward, which is dominated by the imposing ruins of the **Great Tower**, an immense hall-like structure that still bears some fantastic ornamentation. Beyond this, the far narrower Upper Ward leads up to the Barbican **watchtower** from where there are superb views down to the estuary.

Chepstow Museum

Bridge St, NP15 5EZ • Daily 11am–4pm • Free • ☎01291 625981

Housed in a handsome Georgian townhouse, **Chepstow Museum** contains a wealth of nostalgic photographs and paintings of the trades once supported by the River Wye, as well as records of the town's brief life as a shipbuilding centre in the early twentieth century. Take a look, too, upstairs at the rather fine eighteenth-century topographical prints of Chepstow Castle.

ARRIVAL AND INFORMATION
CHEPSTOW

By train The train station is a 5min walk south of High St. Destinations Cardiff (every 30min–1hr; 40min); Gloucester (every 30min–1hr; 30min); Newport (every 30min–1hr; 25min).

By bus The bus station is on Thomas St, just beyond the West Gate. Destinations Bristol (Mon–Sat hourly, Sun 5; 50min); Monmouth (Mon–Sat hourly, Sun 5; 50min); Newport (Mon–Sat every 30min, Sun 5; 25min–1hr); Tintern (Mon–Sat hourly, Sun 5; 20min).

Tourist office Castle car park, off Bridge St (daily: July & Aug 10am–5pm; Sept–June 10am–3pm; ☎01291 623772, ⓦvisitmonmouthshire.com).

WALKS FROM CHEPSTOW

Chepstow is the starting point for three of Wales' most popular long-distance walks: the famous Offa's Dyke Path, the Wye Valley Walk, and the **Wales Coast Path**; this path begins in Riverside Gardens, near the Old Wye Bridge, before cutting inland across fields and then meeting up with the Severn estuary. Guides and maps for all three paths can be obtained from the tourist office (see above).

ACCOMMODATION

Castle View Hotel 16 Bridge St, NP16 5EZ ☎ 01291 620349, ⍟ wyevalleyaccommodation.com. Bags of charm in this seventeenth-century building, with a grand oak spiral staircase leading off to thirteen cosy rooms featuring crooked floors, thick oak beams and exposed stone walls; some have Nespresso machines and castle views. **£80**

Greenman Backpackers 13 Beaufort St, NP16 5EP ☎ 01291 626773, ⍟ chepstowbackpackers.com. A cut above your average hostel, this lovingly restored building on the main square has a handful of single-sex dorms (sleeping four or six) with wide bunks and chunky mattresses (bottom bunks have curtains too), plus en-suite twins. Guests gather around the farmyard-like table for continental breakfast (included), while there's also a rather smart lounge bar (guests only). Dorms **£22**, twins **£55**

14

EATING AND DRINKING

★ **Queens Head** 12 Moor St, NP16 5DD ☎ 07793 889613. You wouldn't give this place a second glance from the outside, but step inside and you'll find a minute single-room pub with a bar culled from an old church altar, locals chatting merrily on pew seating, and no TV, music or wi-fi in sight. Not only that, but the microbrewed ales and ciders are terrific; a flight of three thirds costs £3.20. Tues–Fri 5–11pm, Sat noon–11pm, Sun 2–8pm.

Riverside Wine Bar 18a The Back, NP16 5HH ☎ 01291 628300, ⍟ theriversidewinebar.co.uk. Cracking location aside, this handsome riverside restaurant offers super tapas (green lip mussels, salt'n'pepper squid, stilton mushrooms, all around £4.95) and modern Mediterranean cuisine, such as paella (£12.95). Mon–Thurs & Sun noon–11pm, Fri & Sat noon–midnight.

Tiffin 8 St Mary's St, NP15 5EW. This engaging vintage tearoom, with the requisite mix'n'match furnishings, floral formica tablecloths and bunting, is loved above all for its griddled crumpets, whether with lashings of butter or smoked salmon and cream cheese. Spanish omelettes, home-made cakes and much more, too. Mon–Sat 10am–4pm.

Tintern Abbey

Six miles north of Chepstow, NP16 6SE • March–June, Sept & Oct daily 9.30am–5pm; July & Aug daily 9.30am–6pm; Nov–Feb Mon–Sat 10am–4pm, Sun 11am–4pm • £6.50; CADW • ☎ 01291 689251, ⍟ cadw.gov.wales/daysout/tinternabbey • Bus #69 (Mon–Fri hourly, Sat 6, Sun 4) between Chepstow and Monmouth stops by the abbey

Spectacularly located on one of the most scenic stretches of the River Wye are the roofless ruins of **Tintern Abbey**. The abbey and its valley have inspired writers and painters for more than two centuries – Wordsworth and Turner among them. The abbey was founded in 1131 by Cistercian monks from Normandy, though most of the remaining buildings date from the massive rebuilding and expansion of the fourteenth century, when Tintern was at its mightiest. Its survival after the Dissolution is largely due to its remoteness, as there were no nearby villages ready to use the abbey stone for rebuilding.

The centrepiece of the complex is the magnificent Gothic **church**, whose remarkable tracery and intricate stonework remain intact. Around the church are the less substantial ruins of the monks' domestic quarters and cloister, mostly reduced to one-storey rubble. The course of the abbey's waste-disposal system can be seen in the Great Drain, an irregular channel that once linked kitchens, toilets and the infirmary with the nearby Wye. The **Novices' Hall** lies handily close to the Warming House, which together with the kitchen and infirmary would have been the abbey's only heated areas.

Monmouth

Enclosed on three sides by the rivers Wye and Monnow, **MONMOUTH** (Trefynwy), fifteen miles north of Chepstow, retains some of its quiet charm as an important border post and county town, and makes a good base for a drive – or a long hike – around the **three castles** of the pastoral border country to the north (see page 653). The centre of town is **Agincourt Square**, a handsome open space at the top of the wide, shop-lined Monnow Street. The street narrows to squeeze through the 700-year-old **Monnow Bridge**, crowned with its hulking stone gate of 1262.

14

Shire Hall

3 Agincourt Square, NP25 3DY • April–Sept daily 10am–4pm; Oct–March Mon–Sat 10am–4pm • Free • ☎ 01600 775257, ⓦ shirehallmonmouth.org.uk

The arched, Georgian **Shire Hall**, built in 1724 as a law court, was where, in 1839, the three ringleaders of the Chartists – Frost, Williams and Jones – were sentenced to death (though this was later commuted to transportation). The Chartists were responsible for drafting the 1838 People's Charter, which called for widespread political and social reform throughout the UK, and demanded, among other things, a vote for every man aged over 21 and secret ballots. The hall continued to function as a court until 1992, and you can still see the original courtrooms and the holding cells. Embedded in the facade is an eighteenth-century statue of the Monmouth-born King Henry V, victor of the Battle of Agincourt in 1415, and just in front is the pompous statue of another local, the Honourable Charles Stewart Rolls, co-founder of Rolls-Royce and, in 1910, the first man to pilot a double flight over the English Channel.

Nelson Museum and Local History Centre

Priory St, NP25 3XA • 11am–4pm: March–Oct daily; Nov–Feb Mon, Tues & Thurs–Sun • Free • ☎ 01600 710630

The market hall complex is home to the **Nelson Museum and Local History Centre**, containing a voluminous display of Nelson memorabilia accumulated by Lady Llangattock (Charles Rolls' mother), who was an ardent admirer of the admiral. Among the many personal artefacts are letters and medals, and his epaulette, book and bible; here, too, is the logbook from HMS *Boreas*, which he captained between 1784 and 1787, and the breakfast table that he dined at when visiting the town in 1802.

ARRIVAL AND INFORMATION · MONMOUTH

By bus The bus station is at the bottom of Monnow St.
Destinations Abergavenny (Mon–Sat 7 daily, Sun 4; 1hr); Chepstow (Mon–Sat hourly, Sun 5; 50min); Raglan (Mon–Sat hourly, Sun 7; 25min); Tintern (Mon–Fri hourly, Sat 6, Sun 4; 35min).

Tourist office In the foyer of the Shire Hall (Mon–Sat 10am–4pm; ☎ 01600 775257, ⓦ visitmonmouthshire.com).

ACCOMMODATION AND EATING

#7 Church Street 7 Church St, NP25 3BX ☎ 01600 712600, ⓦ numbersevenchurchstreet.co.uk. Eight individual, tightly packed rooms in a cosy B&B above the town's finest restaurant, a sprightly bistro; Scandinavian wood furnishings, pastel-painted walls and anglepoise lamps are all standard, and there's a resident's lounge. Daily noon–2.30pm & 6.30–9.30pm. **£90**

Gate House Old Monnow Bridge, NP25 3EG ☎ 01600 713890, ⓦ the-gate-house.com. Occupying an enviable spot by the medieval bridge, and with a veranda perched over the water, the *Gate House* is one of the best spots in town for a pint on a sunny day. Mon–Fri 11am–11pm, Sat & Sun 11am–midnight.

Monnow Bridge Campsite Drybridge St, NP25 5AD ☎ 01600 714004. Simple, clean and convenient town-centre site with no facilities other than toilets and showers; to get there, cross Monnow Bridge, turn right and it's behind the *Three Horseshoes* pub. **£11**

Punch House 4 Agincourt Square, NP25 3BT ☎ 01600 713855, ⓦ sabrain.com/punchhouse. The generous rooms above this popular, Tudor-looking tavern have grey-painted timber beams, contemporary furnishings and mirrored walls, with uneven floors and doors lending further character. Good for a morning coffee or an afternoon beer, too. Mon–Fri 8.30am–11pm, Fri & Sat 8.30am–midnight. **£70**

Raglan Castle

Castle Rd, Raglan, 7 miles west of Monmouth, NP15 2BT • March–June, Sept & Oct daily 9.30am–5pm; July & Aug daily 9.30am–6pm; Nov–Feb Mon–Sat 10am–4pm, Sun 11am–4pm • £6.50; CADW • ☎ 01291 690228, ⓦ cadw.gov.wales/daysout/raglancastle • Bus #60 (every 45min; 20min) from Monmouth to Newport, via Usk

Unassuming **RAGLAN** (Rhaglan) is known for its glorious **castle**, whose fussy and comparatively intact style distinguishes it from so many other crumbling Welsh fortresses. The last medieval fortification built in Britain, designed to combine practical strength with ostentatious style, Raglan was begun by Sir William ap Thomas

THE THREE CASTLES

The fertile, low-lying land between the Monnow and Usk rivers was important for easy access into the agricultural lands of South Wales, and in the eleventh century the Norman invaders built **three castles** here to protect their interests. In 1201, **Skenfrith** (Ⓦnationaltrust.org.uk/skenfrith-castle), **Grosmont** (Ⓦcadw.gov.wales/daysout/grosmontcastle) and **White** (Ⓦcadw.gov.wales/daysout/whitecastle) **castles** were presented by King John to Hubert de Burgh, who employed sophisticated new ideas on castle design to replace the earlier, square-keeped structures. In 1260, the advancing army of Llywelyn ap Gruffydd began to threaten the king's supremacy in South Wales, and the three castles were refortified in readiness. Gradually, the castles were adapted as living quarters and royal administration centres, and the only return to military usage came in 1404–05, when Owain Glyndŵr's army pressed down to Grosmont, only to be defeated by the future King Henry V. The castles slipped into disrepair and were finally sold separately in 1902, the first time since 1138 that the three had fallen out of single ownership.

in 1435 on the site of a Norman motte. The **gatehouse**, still the main entrance, houses fantastic examples of the castle's decoration in its heraldic shields, intricate stonework edging and gargoyles. In the mid-fifteenth century, ap Thomas's grandson, William Herbert II, built two courts around the original gatehouse, hall and keep: the cobbled **Pitched Stone Court** – designed to house the kitchen and servants' quarters – and to the left, the grass-covered **Fountain Court**, once surrounded by opulent residences that included grand apartments and state rooms. The most impressive element, though, is the moated yellow ashlar **Great Tower** (aka the Yellow Tower of Gwent), two sides of which were blown up by Cromwell's henchman, Fairfax, after an eleven-week onslaught against the Royalist castle in 1646. Climbing its five floors gives you marvellous views of the complex and the three peaks of Blorenge, Skirrid Fawr and Sugar Loaf in the distance.

The Valleys

No other part of Wales is as instantly recognizable as the **Valleys**, a generic name for the strings of settlements packed into the narrow gashes in the mountainous terrain to the north of Newport and Cardiff. Each of the Valleys depended almost solely on coal mining which, although nearly defunct as an industry, has left its mark on the staunchly working-class towns: row upon row of brightly painted terraced housing, tipped along the slopes at incredible angles, are broken only by austere chapels, the occasional remaining pithead and the dignified memorials to those who died underground.

This may not be traditional tourist country, but it's one of the most interesting and distinctive corners of Wales, with a rich social history. Some former mines have reopened as gutsy museums – **Big Pit** at Blaenavon and the **Rhondda Heritage Park** at Trehafod are the best – while other excellent civic museums include those at **Aberdare** and **Pontypridd** (which is probably the best place to base yourself in the region). There's also a more traditional visitor attraction in the form of **Llancaiach Fawr Manor**.

Blaenavon

Fourteen miles north of Newport, the valley of the Llwyd opens out at the airy iron and coal town of **BLAENAVON**, a UNESCO World Heritage Site. A spirited and evocative place, its population today stands at around five thousand, a third of its size in the nineteenth century.

14

WORKING THE BLACK SEAM

The land beneath the inhospitable South Wales Valleys had some of the most abundant and accessible natural seams of **coal and iron ore** to be found, and were readily milked in the boom years of the nineteenth and early twentieth centuries. Wealthy, predominantly English capitalists came to Wales and ruthlessly stripped the land of its natural assets, while simultaneously exploiting those who risked life and limb underground. The mine owners were in a formidably strong position as thousands flocked to the Valleys in search of work and some sort of sustainable life.

In 1920, there were 256,000 men working in the 620 mines of the South Wales coalfields, providing a third of the world's coal. Vast Miners' Institutes jostled for position with Nonconformist chapels, whose muscular brand of Christianity was matched by the zeal of the region's politics – trade-union-led and avowedly left-wing. Great socialist orators rose to national prominence, cementing the Valleys' reputation as a world apart from the rest of Britain, let alone Wales. Even Britain's pioneering National Health Service, founded by a radical Labour government in the years following World War II, was based on a Valleys' community scheme devised by local politician **Aneurin Bevan**. More than half of the original pits closed in the harsh economic climate of the 1930s, as coal seams became exhausted and the political climate changed. In the 1980s, further closures threatened to bring the number of men employed in the South Wales coalfields down to four figures, and the miners went on strike from 1984–85. The last of the deep pits closed in 2008.

Blaenavon ironworks

North St, NP4 9RQ • April–Oct daily 10am–5pm; Nov–March Thurs–Sat 10am–4pm • Free; CADW • ☎ 01495 792615, ⓦ cadw.gov.wales/daysout/blaenavonironworks

The town's boom kicked off at the **Blaenavon ironworks**, just off the Brynmawr road, founded in 1789. Limestone, coal and iron ore – ingredients for successful iron-smelting – were abundant locally, and the Blaenavon works was one of the largest in Britain until it closed in 1900. This remarkable site contains three of the five original Georgian blast furnaces, one with its cast house still attached, and the immense water-balance lift. Also here are the workers' cottages, some unchanged and others converted into a museum offering a thorough picture of the process and the lifestyle that went with it.

Big Pit National Mining Museum

Signposted on west side of town, off the B4246, NP4 9XP • Jan & Dec call for tour times; Feb–Nov daily 9.30am–5pm, hourly tours (1hr) 10am–3.30pm • Free • ☎ 0300 111 2333, ⓦ museum.wales/bigpit • #30 bus (hourly; 40min) from Cwmbran stops outside the entrance

Guided tours at the evocative **Big Pit National Mining Museum** involve you being kitted out with a lamp, helmet and heavy battery pack, and then lowered 300ft into the labyrinth of shafts and coalfaces. The guides – mostly ex-miners – lead you through explanations and examples of the different types of coal mining, while streams of rust-coloured water flow by. The dank and chilly atmosphere must have terrified the small children who were once paid twopence for a six-day week pulling the coal wagons along the tracks. Back on the surface, the old pithead baths – one of the last remaining in the country – now holds a compelling, and very moving, museum documenting the lives and times of the miners and their families.

ARRIVAL AND INFORMATION

BLAENAVON

By bus Buses from Newport (every 15min; 1hr) stop at the top of High St, which runs parallel to Broad St, the main focus of activity (such as it is) in town.

Tourist information The Blaenavon Heritage Centre, Church Rd (Tues–Sun 10am–5pm; ☎ 01495 742333, ⓦ visitblaenavon.co.uk), has an enlightening exhibition on the history of the town's coal-mining and ironworking industries, as well as a café.

ACCOMMODATION AND EATING

Coffi Bean 1860 76 Broad St, NP4 9NF ☎ 01495 790127. There are very few places to eat or drink in Blaenavon, but this charmingly staffed coffee shop more than compensates; park yourself at a stripped wooden table under the original green and cream tiling and enjoy a home-made pastry and a steaming cup of coffee. Tues–Sun 8am–3pm.

Lion Hotel 41 Broad St, NP4 9NH ☎ 01495 792516, ⓦ thelionhotelblaenavon.co.uk. The town's one hotel is a bright affair, its twelve deep-burgundy rooms boasting warm, fluffy carpets, cool fabrics and sparkling, marble- tiled bathrooms; perhaps surprisingly, there's a sauna and steam room, too. **£85**

The Taff and Cynon valleys

The River Taff flows into the Bristol Channel at Cardiff, after passing through a couple of dozen miles of industry and population. The first town in the Taff vale is **Pontypridd**, one of the cheeriest in the Valleys. Continuing north, valleys meet at **Abercynon**, where the River Cynon flows in from **Aberdare**, site of the excellent **Cynon Valley Museum**. Just outside Abercynon is the enjoyable sixteenth-century **Llancaiach Fawr** manor house.

14

Pontypridd

PONTYPRIDD, twelve miles north of Cardiff, is built up around its quirky arched **bridge**. This was once the largest single-span stone bridge in Europe, built in 1775 by local amateur stonemason William Edwards. Wednesdays and Saturdays are good days to be here, with the old-fashioned **market** spilling out onto Market Street and the surrounding squares.

Ponty Lido

Ynysangharad Park, CF37 4PE • May–Sept daily 7.30am–7.15pm • £1; children free; booking advised • ☎ 0300 004 0000, ⓦ rctcbc.gov. uk/EN/Resident/SportsandLeisure/Lido

On the far side of the river from the town centre is **Ynysangharad Park**, established after World War I as a memorial park, but now the town's popular green space. The focal point here is the beautifully restored **Ponty Lido**, a grade II-listed building constructed in 1927 but which closed in 1991. Re-opened in 2015, it comprises three heated pools (main, activity and splash pools), heated changing facilities and a superb café.

Pontypridd Museum

Bridge St, CF37 4PE • Mon–Sat 10am–4.30pm • Free • ☎ 01443 490748, ⓦ pontypriddmuseum.cymru

A lovingly restored church by the bridge houses the illuminating **Pontypridd Museum**, a treasure-trove of photographs, videos, models and exhibits that paints a warm picture of the town and its outlying valleys, as well as paying homage to the town's famous sons, singer Tom Jones and opera star Sir Geraint Evans.

ARRIVAL AND INFORMATION   PONTYPRIDD

By train The train station is a 10min walk south of the old bridge on High St.
Destinations Abercynon (every 15min; 10min); Aberdare (every 30min; 35min); Cardiff (every 20–30min; 30min).
By bus The bus station is directly above the old bridge on the western bank.
Destinations Abercynon (every 15min; 10min); Aberdare (every 15min; 50min); Cardiff (every 15min; 35min).
Tourist office Pontypridd Museum, Bridge St (Mon–Sat 10am–4.30pm; ☎ 01443 490748).

THE ABERFAN DISASTER

North of Abercynon, the Taff Valley contains one sight that's hard to forget. Two neat lines of distant arches mark the graves of 144 people killed in October 1966 by an unsecured slag heap collapsing on Pantglas primary school in the village of **Aberfan**. Among the dead were 116 children, who died huddled in panic at the beginning of their school day. A humbling and beautiful valediction can be seen on one of the gravestones, that of a 10-year-old boy, who, it simply records, "loved light, freedom and animals". Official enquiries all told the sorry tale that this disaster was almost inevitable, given the cavalier approach to safety so often displayed by the coal bosses. Gwynfor Evans, then newly elected as the first Plaid Cymru (Welsh Nationalist) MP in Westminster, spoke with well-founded bitterness when he said: "Let us suppose that such a monstrous mountain had been built above Hampstead or Eton, where the children of the men of power and wealth are at school". But that, of course, would never have happened.

ACCOMMODATION AND EATING

Blueberry Inn Market St, CF37 2ST ☎ 01443 485331, ⓦ blueberryinn-pontypridd.co.uk. An appropriately appealing name for this sparkling little hotel, whose nine rooms are fashioned in one of two styles: cool, crisp white-on-white, or classic French. Breakfast £11. **£74**

Bunch of Grapes Ynysangharad Rd, CF37 4DA ☎ 01443 402934, ⓦ bunchofgrapes.org.uk. On a residential street beyond the park and A470 flyover, this is a terrific combination of restaurant/pub, whose imaginative menu (pan-fried guinea fowl with home-smoked new potato and caramelized pumpkin, say; £15) is the best for miles around. The beer's great too, with typically more than half a dozen real ales on at any one time. Daily 11am–11pm; kitchen Mon–Sat noon–9.30pm, Sun noon–2.30pm.

Llancaiach Fawr Manor

Gelligaer Rd, Nelson, 7 miles northeast of Pontypridd, CF46 6ER • Tues–Sun 10am–5pm (last admission 4pm) • £8.50 • ☎ 01443 412248, ⓦ your.caerphilly.gov.uk/lancaiachfawr • Bus #X38 from Pontypridd (Mon–Sat hourly; 15min)

Llancaiach Fawr Manor, a Tudor house built around 1530, has been transformed into a living-history museum. Set in 1645, the time of the Civil War, with guides dressed as house servants and speaking seventeenth-century English, it's all very deftly done, with authentic period colour and many fascinating anecdotes. Special tours include seventeenth-century evenings, and, from October to March, candlelit and ghost tours.

The Cynon Valley Museum & Gallery

Depot Rd, Aberdare, CF44 8DL • Wed–Sat 11am–4pm • Free • ☎ 01685 886729, ⓦ cynonvalleymuseum.org

Eight miles northwest of Abercynon, towards the top of the Cynon Valley, is the spacious town of **ABERDARE** (Aberdâr), built on the local iron, brick and brewing industries. The main reason to come here is for the **Cynon Valley Museum & Gallery**, in an old tram depot next to the Tesco superstore. Exhibits portray the valley's social history, from the appalling conditions of the mid-nineteenth century, when nearly half of all children born here died by the age of 5, to stirring memories of the 1926 General Strike and the 1984–85 miners' strike. Alongside are some fun videos and exhibits on Victorian lantern slides, teenage life through the ages, the miners' jazz bands and Aberdare's role as a centre of early Welsh-language publishing. There's also a bright art gallery and decent café.

Rhondda Fawr

Pointing northwest from Pontypridd, the **Rhondda Fawr** – sixteen miles long and never as much as a mile wide – is undoubtedly the most famous of all the Welsh Valleys, as well as being the heart of the massive South Wales coal industry. For many it immediately conjures up Richard Llewellyn's 1939 book – and subsequent Oscar-winning weepie – *How Green Was My Valley*, although this was, strictly speaking, based on the author's early life in nearby Gilfach Goch, outside the valley. Between 1841 and 1924 the Rhondda's population grew from under a thousand to 167,000, squeezed into ranks of houses grouped around sixty or so pitheads. The Rhondda, more than any other of the Valleys, became a self-reliant, hard-living, chapel-going, poor and terrifically spirited breeding ground for radical religion and firebrand politics – for decades, the Communist Party ran the town of Maerdy (nicknamed "Little Moscow" by Fleet Street in the 1930s). The last pit in the Rhondda closed in 1990, but what was left behind was not some dispiriting ragbag of depressing towns, but a range of new attractions, cleaned-up hillsides and some of the friendliest pubs and communities to be found anywhere in Britain.

Rhondda Heritage Park

Coed Cae Rd, Trehafod, CF37 2NP • Tues–Sat 9am–4.30pm • Free • **Tours** Same days, hourly 9am–3pm; 1hr 15min • £5.95 • ☎ 01443 682036, ⓦ rctcbc.gov.uk • Trehafod train station is a 5min walk from the Heritage Park; bus #130 (every 20–30min; 10min) runs here from Pontypridd

The best attraction hereabouts is the **Rhondda Heritage Park** at **TREHAFOD**. The site was opened in 1880 by William Lewis (later Lord Merthyr), and by 1900 some five thousand men were employed here, producing more than a million tonnes of coal a year. Wandering around the yard, you can see the 140ft-high chimney stack, which

MALE VOICE CHOIRS

Fiercely protective of its reputation as a land of song, Wales demonstrates its fine voice most affectingly in its ranks of **male voice choirs**. Although found all over the country, it is in the southern, industrial heartland that they are loudest and strongest. Their roots lie in the Nonconformist religious traditions of the seventeenth and eighteenth centuries, when Methodism in particular swept the country, and singing was a free and potent way of cherishing the often persecuted faith. Classic hymns like *Cwm Rhondda* and the Welsh national anthem, *Hen Wlad Fy Nhadau* (*Land of My Fathers*), are synonymous with the choirs. Each Valleys town still has its own choir, most of whom welcome visitors to sit in on rehearsals. Ask at the local tourist office or library, and take the chance to hear one of the world's most distinctive choral traditions in full, roof-raising splendour.

fronts two iconic latticed shafts, named Bertie and Trefor after Lewis's sons. **Guided tours** take you through the engine-winding houses, lamp room and fan house, and give you a simulated "trip underground", with stunning visuals and sound effects re-creating 1950s' life through the eyes of colliers.

Upstairs in the main building, the illuminating **Black Gold exhibition** recalls the history of mining in the Rhondda, largely through informative wall panels, but there are some wonderful photos too, including a handful showing staff and miners working the last days of the Lewis Merthyr colliery. Inevitably, disaster looms large and the sad facts reveal that fatalities from pit explosions were an annual occurrence up until World War II – the worst disaster at the Lewis colliery was in 1956 when nine men perished; among the few exhibits on display is the pocket watch belonging to Gildas Jones, one of the victims.

Swansea

Dylan Thomas called **SWANSEA** (Abertawe) – his birthplace – an "ugly, lovely town", which fellow poet Paul Durcan updated to "pretty, shitty city". Both ring true. Sprawling and boisterous, with around 200,000 people, Swansea may be only the second city of Wales, but it's the undoubted Welsh capital of attitude, coated in a layer of chunky bling. The city centre was massively rebuilt after devastating bomb attacks in World War II, and a jumble of tower blocks now dot the horizon. But closer inspection reveals Swansea's multifarious charms: some intact old corners of the city centre, the spacious and graceful suburb of **Uplands**, a wide **seafront** overlooking Swansea Bay and a bold marina development around the old docks. Spread throughout are some of the best-funded **museums** in the country, including the stunning **National Waterfront Museum**.

Brief history

Swansea's Welsh name, Abertawe, refers to the mouth of the **River Tawe**, a grimy ditch that is slowly recovering after centuries of abuse by heavy industry. The city itself dates back to 1099 when William the Conqueror's troops built a castle here. A settlement grew around this, later exploiting its location between the coalfields and the sea to become a shipbuilding centre, and then, by 1700, the largest coal port in Wales. Copper smelting took over as the area's dominant industry in the eighteenth century, and this attracted other metal trades, developing the region into one of the world's most prolific metal-bashing centres.

Glynn Vivian Art Gallery

Alexandra Rd, SA1 5DZ • Tues–Sun 10am–5pm • Free • ☎ 01792 516900, ⓦ swansea.gov.uk/glynnvivian

The **Glynn Vivian Art Gallery** is a delightful Edwardian venue named after the philanthropist. The main exhibition, on Vivian himself, is slated to run until 2019, though it may be extended beyond this date. In 1869 he embarked upon an epic two-year journey to the Far East, during which time he amassed a wealth of extraordinary items, including Chinese vases and Japanese fans. Vivian was also an inveterate collector of European porcelain, though most pieces here were produced locally.

The museum also houses an inspiring collection of **Welsh art**, which tends to rotate, but expect works by Gwen John, her brother Augustus (his mesmerizing portrait of Caitlin Thomas, Dylan's wife, is a highlight), Kyffin Williams and Ceri Richards, Wales' most respected twentieth-century painter.

14

Swansea Museum

Victoria Rd, SA1 1SN • Tues–Sun 10am–4.30pm • Free • ☎ 01792 653763, ⓦ swanseamuseum.co.uk

The city's old South Dock features the enticingly old-fashioned **Swansea Museum**, whose highlight is the Cabinet of Curiosities, a roomful of glass cases stuffed with everything from offbeat household items and memento mori – miniature shrines containing photos and models of the deceased – to intriguing local photos, including several of Winston Churchill during his visit to Swansea in World War II. There's also a marble bust of a Gower boy, Edgar Evans, who perished with Scott in Antarctica in 1912.

Dylan Thomas Centre

Somerset Place, SA1 1RR • Daily 10am–4.30pm • Free • ☎ 01792 463980, ⓦ dylanthomas.com

In the nineteenth-century former guildhall is the **Dylan Thomas Centre**, where a superb exhibition offers a compelling insight into the poet's life and times. Unique archive material includes a love letter to his wife, Caitlin, written on a cheque stub, bar tabs, a tweed jacket borrowed from Jorge Fick during a stay at New York's *Chelsea Hotel*

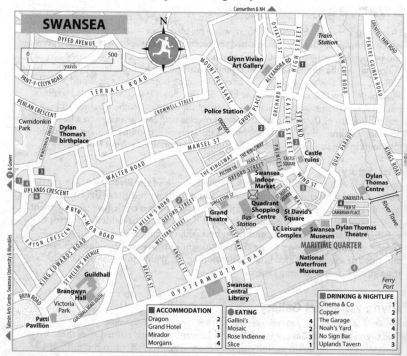

in 1953, and the last photos of Thomas taken in a New York bar just days before his death. The original doors of the shed in which Thomas wrote at Laugharne (see page 666) front a mocked-up version here that contains original manuscripts, doodles and some of the books and poems that inspired him.

National Waterfront Museum

Oystermouth Rd, SA1 3RD • Daily 10am–5pm • Free • ☎ 0300 111 2333, ⓦ museum.wales/swansea

Swansea's superb **National Waterfront Museum** houses a breathtakingly varied set of exhibitions dealing with Wales' history of innovation and industry. The museum is divided into fifteen zones, looking at topics such as energy, landscape, coal, genealogy, networks and money, and each section is bursting with interactive technology. Look out for the many superb heritage pieces, such as the 1907 Robin Goch (Redbreast) monoplane, one of the very few pre-World War I planes still in existence.

14

Dylan Thomas's birthplace

5 Cwmdonkin Drive, SA2 0RA • Daily 10.30am–4.30pm • £8 • ☎ 01792 472555, ⓦ dylanthomasbirthplace.com

A thirty-minute walk from the city centre, leafy avenues rise past the sharp terraces of **Cwmdonkin Park**, at the centre of which is a memorial to Dylan Thomas inscribed with lines from *Fern Hill*, one of his best-known poems. On the eastern side of the park, a blue plaque at 5 Cwmdonkin Drive denotes this solid Victorian semi as **Dylan Thomas's birthplace**. Born in 1914, Thomas lived here until he was twenty, and while nothing remains from his time, the house has been sympathetically restored to re-create the atmosphere of early twentieth-century Swansea. **Guided tours** of the surprisingly spacious interior include the grand lounge, his father's study, the kitchen and Thomas's boxy bedroom. There isn't always someone in attendance, so it's best to call in advance.

ARRIVAL AND DEPARTURE
SWANSEA

By train Swansea is the main interchange for trains out to the west of Wales, and for the slow line across to Shrewsbury in England. The station is at the top end of High St.

Destinations Cardiff (every 30min; 55min); Carmarthen (hourly; 50min); Haverfordwest (9 daily; 1hr 30min); Llandrindod Wells (4 daily; 2hr 20min); London (hourly; 3hr); Newport (every 30min; 1hr 20min); Pembroke (5 daily; 2hr 5min); Tenby (6 daily; 1hr 40min).

By bus Swansea's enormous bus station is in the centre of the city next to The Quadrant shopping centre.

Destinations Brecon (Mon–Sat 7 daily, Sun 4; 1hr 45min); Cardiff (every 30min; 1hr); Carmarthen (Mon–Sat every 30min; 1hr 45min); Mumbles (every 10min; 15min); Oxwich (8 daily, 1 change; 1hr); Port Eynon (8 daily, 1 change; 1hr 15min); Rhossili (10 daily; 1hr).

ACCOMMODATION

For a reasonably large city, Swansea is not exactly bursting with great **accommodation**. That said, there are some inexpensive hotels and B&Bs lining the seafront Oystermouth Road, and it's just a stone's throw to the Gower, where there are more options. There are no hostels in Swansea, and the nearest campsite is west of the city towards Mumbles.

Dragon Kingsway Circle, SA1 5LS ☎ 01792 657100, ⓦ dragon-hotel.co.uk; map p.658. Despite its officious-looking facade, this landmark central hotel is an elegant and modern establishment with plush, a/c rooms coloured vivid red. Amenities include a gym, indoor pool, lounge and piano bar and restaurant. Book early for good rates. __£75__

Grand Hotel Ivey Place, High St, SA1 1NX ☎ 01792 645898, ⓦ thegrandhotelswansea.co.uk; map p.658. Accomplished yet pleasingly informal hotel next to the train station, with softly coloured, a/c rooms with large flatscreen TVs and sparkling bathrooms with fantastic showers. Convivial café/sports bar downstairs. __£60__

Mirador 14 Mirador Crescent, Uplands, SA2 0QX ☎ 01792 466976, ⓦ themirador.co.uk; map p.658. Swansea's most enjoyable accommodation, a family-run townhouse in the Uplands area with seven fun rooms, each themed on a theme (African, Oriental, Egyptian, Roman and so on) and furnished accordingly. __£89__

★ **Morgans** Somerset Place, SA1 1RR ☎ 01792 484848, ⓦ morganshotel.co.uk; map p.658. Swansea's showpiece boutique hotel, split between the sumptuously converted old Port Authority HQ and

14

the beautiful Regency terrace townhouse opposite. The superbly appointed rooms boast hardwood flooring, polished wood fittings, Egyptian-cotton bed linen and goosedown duvets. **£110**

EATING

Gallini's 3 Fishmarket Quay, SA1 1UP ☎01792 456285, ⊛gallinisrestaurant.co.uk; map p.658. This somewhat ordinary-looking but cheery restaurant offers terrific flavour combinations such as venison steak in a gin and cranberry sauce (£15.95). The downstairs coffee shop is a relaxing spot to kick back with a cup of fresh coffee and take in the view across the marina. Great value two-course lunch menu £9.95. Daily: restaurant noon–2.30pm & 6pm–midnight; coffee shop 10am–5pm.

Mosaic 11 St Helen's Rd, SA1 4AB ☎01792 655225, ⊛mosaicswanseauk.com; map p.658. Modern industrial design and understated cool mark this café-cum-restaurant out as something a little different from most places in Swansea; the tapas-style menu comprises delicious light bites such as salt cod croquettes or chorizo with fig and goat's cheese (£7.50) – a great accompaniment to the occasional live music. Wed–Fri 6–11pm, Sat noon–3pm & 6–11pm.

Rose Indienne 73–74 St Helen's Rd, SA1 4BG ☎01792 467000, ⊛rose-indienne.co.uk; map p.658. Comfortably the best of Swansea's many Indian restaurants, the beautifully appointed *Rose Indienne* offers exciting and unusual dishes such as Goan duck curry (£12.95) and a spicy fish masala, in addition to a dozen or so lentil- and vegetable-based options. Charming staff, too. Mon–Thurs 5.30pm–midnight, Fri & Sat noon–2pm & 5.30pm–1am, Sun noon–midnight.

Slice 73–75 Everley Rd, Sketty, SA2 9DE ☎01792 290929, ⊛sliceswansea.co.uk; map p.658. Out in the Sketty area, 2 miles west of the centre, the diminutive *Slice* – so named because of the quirkily shaped building – offers a level of cuisine unmatched anywhere in the city, with confident contemporary dishes such as wild boar loin with pickled red cabbage, celeriac fondant and apple. Two-course lunch menu £29, three-course evening menu £42. Booking essential. Thurs 6.15–10pm, Fri–Sun 12.30–2pm & 6.15–10pm.

DRINKING AND NIGHTLIFE

Swansea has a proliferation of **pubs** and **bars**; most of the action centres on Wind Street – not a place for the faint-hearted on a Friday or Saturday evening – though the Uplands area, to the west of the city centre, has its fair share of good-time party places. The **club** scene is extremely diverse, and many places double up as live music venues, showcasing a varied and exciting range of bands and other entertainment.

Cinema & Co 17 Castle St, SA1 1JF ☎07982 626959, ⊛cinemaco.co.uk; map p.658. Secreted away behind its cheery chipboard-designed coffee shop/bar is a brilliant cinema, with seating crafted from wheel-mounted pallets that can be removed to accommodate other events, such as live music and art exhibitions. Screenings – typically classics, independent movies and foreign films – are at 8pm and cost £8. Tues–Sun 6pm–midnight.

Copper 38–39 Castle St, SA1 1HZ ☎01792 456689; map p.658. Groovy artisan coffeehouse/craft-beer bar serving superb locally roasted coffee alongside ales from its own Boss brewery. The decor's great, with tables carved from pallets and stools culled from copper kegs. There's also a free jukebox, but if it all gets too raucous upstairs (and it can), head downstairs for a game of ping-pong. Mon–Thurs & Sun 10am–10pm, Fri & Sat 10am–midnight.

The Garage 47 Uplands Square, SA2 0NP ☎01792 475147, ⊛whitez.co.uk; map p.658. The city's premier live music venue, by virtue of its quality (and wonderfully varied) acts and understatedly cool atmosphere; rock predominates, but there's much else besides. It's tricky to find; the entrance is through Whitez pool club. Mon, Tues & Sun 8.30am–8pm, Wed–Sat 8.30am–11pm.

Noah's Yard 38 Uplands Crescent, SA2 0PG ☎01792 447360; map p.658. Classy wine bar with big bay windows, bare brick walls, Art Deco lighting, Chesterfield sofas and trunks for tables, as well as lots of contemporary artwork including a piece by Banksy. Live jazz Mon 8.30pm (£3) and an ace pop-up kitchen on Wed at 6.30pm. Daily 2pm–midnight.

No Sign Bar 56 Wind St, SA1 1EG ☎01792 465300, ⊛nosignwinebar.com; map p.658. If you deign/dare to visit one place on Wind St, make it *No Sign*, one of the oldest hostelries in town. A narrow frontage leads into a long, warm pub interior with bare brick walls, pale wood flooring and squishy sofas, while down in the vaulted cellar, you'll catch live music most weekends. Mon–Thurs 11am–midnight, Fri & Sat 11am–1am, Sun noon–11pm.

Uplands Tavern 42 Uplands Crescent, SA2 0PG ☎01792 458242, ⊛uplandstavern-uplands.co.uk; map p.658. Despite looking a little tired these days, this former haunt of Dylan Thomas – the walls of the Dylan snug corner are plastered with fabulous photos – remains a bastion of local live music, especially rock and blues, usually from Thurs to Sat. Open mic on Mon. Mon–Thurs & Sun 11am–11pm, Fri & Sat 11am–midnight.

ENTERTAINMENT

Brangwyn Hall The Guildhall, Guildhall Rd South, SA1 4PE ☏01792 635432, ⓦswansea.gov.uk/brangwyn hall. This vastly impressive music hall in the Art Deco civic centre hosts regular concerts by the BBC National Orchestra of Wales and others.

Dylan Thomas Theatre Dylan Thomas Square, Maritime Quarter, SA1 1TY ☏01792 473238, ⓦdylan thomastheatre.org.uk. Thriving community operation staging reruns of Thomas's classics, alongside modern works, in the Little Theatre.

Taliesin Arts Centre Swansea University, SA2 8PZ ☏01792 602060, ⓦtaliesinartscentre.co.uk. Welsh, English and international visiting theatre, film, dance and music (jazz, world), including offbeat and alternative offerings.

14

Gower peninsula

A nineteen-mile-long finger of undulating sandstone and limestone, **Gower** (Gŵyr) is a world of its own, pointing into the Bristol Channel to the west of Swansea. The area is fringed by sweeping yellow bays and precipitous cliffs, with caves and blowholes to the south and wide, flat marshes and cockle beds to the north. Bracken heaths dotted with prehistoric remains and tiny villages lie between, and there are numerous castle ruins and curious churches. Out of season, the winding lanes afford wonderful opportunities for exploration, but in high summer – July and August especially – they can be horribly congested. Frequent buses from Swansea serve the whole peninsula.

Gower starts in Swansea's western suburbs, following the curve of Swansea Bay to the pleasantly old-fashioned resort of **Mumbles** and finishing at **Rhossili Bay**. West of Port Eynon, the coast becomes a wild, frilly series of inlets and cliffs, topped by a five-mile path that stretches all the way to the peninsula's glorious westernmost point, **Worms Head**. The northern coast merges into the tidal flats of the Loughor estuary.

Mumbles

At the far westernmost end of Swansea Bay and on the cusp of Gower, **MUMBLES** (Mwmbwls) is a lively and enjoyable alternative base to Swansea – the name is derived from the French word *mamelles*, or "breasts" (a reference to the twin islets off the end of Mumbles Head). The seafront, an unbroken curve of stylish B&Bs, cafés and restaurants, leads down to the refurbished pier and the rocky plug of Mumbles Head. Around the headland, reached either by the longer coast road or by a short walk over the hill, is the district of **Langland Bay**, whose sandy beach is popular with surfers.

Oystermouth Castle

Castle Ave, SA3 4BA · April–Sept daily 11am–5pm · £3.50 · ⓦswansea.gov.uk/oystermouthcastle

The hilltop above town is crowned by the ruins of **Oystermouth Castle**, founded as a Norman watchtower and strengthened to withstand attacks by the Welsh, before being converted for residential purposes during the fourteenth century. A sensitive long-term restoration project has now returned the castle to something like its former glory. The keep, hall and Great Chamber form the earliest part of the castle (roughly late twelfth and early thirteenth centuries), with the remainder (including the chapel block) later additions. Inside the chapel, stairs lead up to a glass bridge platform, from where you can see the superb traceried east window, which frames magnificent views of the bay. The ramparts, too, afford lush vistas over the Mumbles headland, Swansea and its sweeping bay.

ARRIVAL AND DEPARTURE

MUMBLES

Frequent **buses** from Swansea (every 10min; 15min) stop at various points along the seafront.

ACCOMMODATION

Coast House 708 Mumbles Rd, SA3 4EH ☏01792 368702, ⓦthecoasthouse.co.uk. Welcoming seafront guesthouse with four fresh-looking rooms, two of which have glorious sea views. Closed Jan and Dec. **£80**

14

Langland Road B&B 17 Langland Rd, SA3 4ND ☎01792 361170, ⓦ langlandroad.co.uk. LGBT-friendly bed and breakfast providing five smart rooms with DVD players and iPod docking stations. To get there, head to the top of Newton Rd and turn left by the church. **£85**

Tides Reach 388 Mumbles Rd, SA3 5TN ☎01792 404877, ⓦ tidesreachguesthouse.com. Seven spacious and immaculate rooms in this elegant, cheerfully run guesthouse, where you can also enjoy the homely lounge and delightful courtyard garden bursting with roses and honeysuckle. **£75**

EATING AND DRINKING

Café 93 93 Newton Rd, SA3 5TW ☎01792 368793, ⓦ cafe93.co.uk. Cheery, two-floored pink-and-white café at the top of the road, with tea, coffee and cakes plus crisp pizzas and juicy burgers/veggie burgers. Mon 9am–5pm, Tues 9am–8pm, Wed–Sat 9am–11pm.

The Front Room 618 Mumbles Rd, SA3 4EA ☎01792 362140. Homely spot for a light lunch (Welsh cheddar and onion tartlet, perhaps; £5.20), afternoon high tea for two (£17) or, on the first Thurs evening of each month, a three-course menu (£20.95). It's great for kids too, with a "munchkins" menu and boxes of toys to play with. Tues–Fri 10am–4.30pm, Sat & Sun 10am–5pm.

★ **P.A.'s Wine Bar** 95 Newton Rd, SA3 4BN ☎01792

367723. Mumbles' most rewarding restaurant, whose myriad seafood possibilities (around £20) and meaty treats perfectly complement its outstanding repertoire of wines; there's a big Sun lunch too. The vine-covered terrace is a fine spot in warmer weather. Mon–Sat noon–2.30pm & 6–11pm, Sun noon–2.30pm.

Verdi's Knab Rock, SA3 4EE ☎01792 369135, ⓦ verdis-café.co.uk. Overlooking the sea near the pier, this Welsh/Italian institution is well regarded for its superb pizzas and ice creams, sorbets and sundaes; the coffee's not half bad, either. Mid-March to mid-Oct daily 10am–9pm; mid-Oct to mid-March Mon–Thurs 10am–6pm, Fri–Sun 10am–9pm.

Rhossili and around

The spectacularly located village of **RHOSSILI** (Rhosili), at the western end of Gower, is a centre for walkers and beach lovers alike. Dylan Thomas wrote of the "rubbery, gull-limed grass, the sheep-pilled stones, the pieces of bones and feathers" to the west of the village, and you can follow his footsteps to **Worms Head**, an isolated string of rocks, accessible for only five hours at low tide.

Rhossili Bay

Below Rhossili, a great curve of white sand stretches into the distance, a dazzling coastline vast enough to absorb the crowds, especially if you are prepared to head north towards **Burry Holms**, an islet that is cut off at high tide. The northern end of the beach can also be reached by the small lane from Reynoldston, in the middle of the peninsula, to **Llangennith**, on the other side of the towering **Rhossili Down** (633ft).

ARRIVAL AND INFORMATION

RHOSSILI AND AROUND

By bus Buses drop off in Rhossili by the car park near the *Worm's Head Hotel*.

Tourist information The National Trust Centre, at the head of the road beyond Rhossili village, stocks plenty

of literature, excellent local walking maps and a tide timetable (Jan & Feb Tues–Sun 10.30am–4pm; March–May & Sept–Dec daily 10.30am–4.30pm; June–Aug 10.30am–5pm; ☎01792 390707, ⓦ nationaltrust.org.uk).

ACCOMMODATION

Blas Gwyr Llangennith, by the roundabout on the lane towards the beach, SA3 1HU ☎01792 386472, ⓦ blasgwyr.co.uk. An old farmhouse with four cottagey-style rooms set away from each other around a little courtyard; stripped back stone walls, colourful Welsh fabrics and large wet rooms are standard, while Dafydd, the affable proprietor, will whip you up a cracking breakfast at the same time as regaling you with entertaining stories. **£115**

Hillend Near the hamlet of Hillend, SA3 1JD ☎01792 386204, ⓦ hillendcamping.com. Large, fabulously

located campsite behind the dunes and with direct access to the glorious beach. Two of the four fields are set aside for families and couples. Shop and on-site café/bar. Closed Nov–March. There's a surfing school on site (see page 663). **£20**

King Arthur Hotel Reynoldston, SA3 1AD ☎01792 390775, ⓦ kingarthurhotel.co.uk. The village's convivial pub has half a dozen comfortable en-suite rooms upstairs, though the annexe offers larger, more attractive options with French windows and cast-iron beds and tables (£105). **£90**

SURFING ON GOWER

Gower has some of the finest surf in Britain, the best of which is to be had around the bays and beaches of **Langland**, **Caswell**, **Oxwich** and **Rhossili**, though the most consistent is at **Llangennith**, which is also suitable for beginners. The website ⓦ gowerlive.com has live webcams and tide times.

COURSES AND EQUIPMENT RENTAL

PJ's Surfshop Llangennith ☎ 01792 386669, ⓦ pjsurfshop.co.uk. The best place for equipment rental, with a wide range of surfboards (£11/day), boogie boards (£6/day) and wetsuits (£11/day). Daily 9am–5pm.

Sam's Surf Shack Rhossili ☎ 01792 390519, ⓦ rhossilileisure@hotmail.com. Equipment rental and lessons (£20/hr). Daily 9am–5pm, though erratic.

Welsh Surfing Federation's Surf School Hillend campsite ☎ 01792 386426, ⓦ surfschool.wsf.wales. The Welsh Surfing Federation's Surf School runs half- and full-day courses (£25/£45) year-round.

14

King's Head Llangennith, SA3 1HX ☎ 01792 386212, ⓦ kingsheadgower.co.uk. The most prominent accommodation in the village is in this sixteenth-century pub, offering rooms of a fairly high standard (some with sea views) in the pub annexe and, better still, in a newer stone building across the car park. **£99**

YHA Port Eynon By the beach, SA3 1NN ☎ 0345 371 9135, ⓦ yha.org.uk/hostel/port-eynon. In a tremendous beachside location, this Victorian-era lifeboat station has been converted into a super hostel, with four- to eight-bedded dorms and double rooms. Shared shower facilities, self-catering kitchen and lounge. Groups only Nov–March. Dorms **£18**, doubles **£40**

EATING AND DRINKING

Bay Bistro Rhossili, SA3 1PP ☎ 01792 390519, ⓦ thebaybistro.co.uk. Easy-going café serving light meals, including terrific burgers (Welsh wagyu £13.95) and home-made cakes; park yourself inside on one of the sunken armchairs or out on the windy terrace, where you can admire the glorious coastal views. Daily: June–Sept 10am–5pm & 7–9pm; Oct–May 10am–5pm.

King Arthur Hotel Reynoldston, SA3 1AD ☎ 01792 390775, ⓦ kingarthurhotel.co.uk. The hotel's restaurant is fine, but better is the lovely wood-lined bar, where you can chomp on succulent Welsh rump washed down with one of the superb guest ales; in fine weather, though, most locals head out to the green and drink among the sheep. Daily 10am–11pm; kitchen noon–2.30pm & 6–9pm.

Carmarthenshire

Frequently overlooked in the stampede towards the resorts of Pembrokeshire, **Carmarthenshire** is a quiet part of the world. Dramatically set **Kidwelly Castle** is the only reason to stop before **Carmarthen**, which sadly fails to live up to its status as regional capital. Better to press on up the bucolic Tywi Valley, visiting the **National Botanic Garden** and the more intimate **Aberglasney** on the way to **Llandeilo**. The wonderfully sited **Carreg Cennen** castle is well worth a stop-off, while the delightful coastal village of **Laugharne** is a place of pilgrimage for Dylan Thomas devotees.

Kidwelly Castle

Just north of the town centre, SA17 5BQ • March–June, Sept & Oct daily 9.30am–5pm; July & Aug daily 9.30am–6pm; Nov–Feb Mon–Sat 10am–4pm, Sun 11am–4pm • £4; CADW • ☎ 01554 890104, ⓦ cadw.gov.wales/daysout/kidwellycastle • Kidwelly train station, 0.5 mile west of the town centre down Station Rd, is on the main line between Swansea (15 daily; 30min) and Carmarthen (15 daily; 15min)

The sleepy little town of **KIDWELLY** (Cydweli) is dominated by its imposing castle, established around 1106 by Henry I's minister Roger, Bishop of Salisbury. **Kidwelly Castle** is strategically sited overlooking the River Gwendraeth and vast tracts of coast. Entering through the massive gatehouse, completed in 1422, you can still see portcullis slats and the murder holes through which noxious substances could be tipped onto intruders. This forms the centrepiece of the impressively intact outer ward walls, which give great views over the grassy courtyard and rectangular inner ward to the river.

Carmarthen

In the early eighteenth century **CARMARTHEN** (Caerfyrddin) was Wales' largest town and it remains the regional hub, a solid, if hardly thrilling, commercial centre best known as the supposed birthplace of the wizard Merlin.

The most picturesque part of town is around Nott Square, where the handsome eighteenth-century **Guildhall** sits at the base of Edward I's uninspiring **castle**. The most picturesque eighteenth- and nineteenth-century part of town lies along King Street, heading northeast from Nott Square towards **St Peter's Church**.

Carmarthen County Museum

Abergwili, 2 miles east of Carmarthen, SA31 2JG • Tues–Sat 10am–4.30pm • Free • ☎ 01267 228696, ⓦ carmarthenmuseum.org.uk • Served by Carmarthen–Llandeilo buses (6 daily; 12min from Carmarthen)

The severe grey Bishop's Palace in Abergwili, the seat of the Bishop of St Davids between 1542 and 1974, now houses the **Carmarthen County Museum**. The interesting exhibitions include the history of Welsh translations of the New Testament and Book of Common Prayer – both first translated here, in 1567.

ARRIVAL AND INFORMATION

CARMARTHEN

By train Trains between Swansea and Pembrokeshire stop at the station on the south side of the River Tywi.
Destinations Cardiff (20 daily; 1hr 45min–2hr); Fishguard (4 daily; 1hr); Haverfordwest (11 daily; 40min); Kidwelly (15 daily; 15min); Pembroke (9 daily; 1hr 10min); Swansea (26 daily; 50min); Tenby (9 daily; 50min).
By bus The bus station is on Blue St, north of the river.

Destinations Aberystwyth (hourly; 2hr 20min); Haverfordwest (3 daily; 1hr); Kidwelly (every 30min; 25min); Laugharne (5 daily; 30min); Llandeilo (10 daily; 40min); Swansea (every 30min; 1hr 20min); Tenby (1 daily; 1hr 10min).
Tourist office Castle House, between the castle's ring walls (Mon–Sat 9.30am–4.30pm; ☎ 01267 231557).

ACCOMMODATION AND EATING

Diablo's on the Quay Coracle Way, SA31 3JP ☎ 01267 223000, ⓦ diablos.co. Lively bar by the river that's ideal for the two-course lunch (£15) or full meals (mains such as beef pie, steaks or pan-roasted sea-bass; mains £12.50–24). There's an outside deck for cocktails. Daily noon–late; kitchen noon–3pm & 6–9pm.
Falcon Hotel 111 Lammas St, SA31 3AP ☎ 01267 234959, ⓦ falconcarmarthen.co.uk. The best town-centre option, this well-established family-run hotel has fresh individually styled rooms, a good restaurant and attentive service. **£75**

Y Dderwen Fach 98 Priory St, SA31 1NB ☎ 01267 234193, ⓦ ydderwenfach.co.uk. The best of the central budget B&Bs, in a simple seventeenth-century house. Some rooms have bathtubs; others have shared showers. **£50**
The Warren 11 Mansel St, SA31 1PX ☎ 01267 236079, ⓦ warrenmanselst.co.uk. This café-bar promises craft beers and gins, interesting starters (£3.50–7) such as spicy dips or vegetable fritters, and mains (£11–16) from veggie burgers to lamb moussaka. Thurs–Sat 11am–3pm & 6–9.30pm, Sun 11am–3pm.

Tywi Valley

The **River Tywi** curves and darts its way east from Carmarthen through some of the most magical scenery in south Wales as well as passing a couple of fine gardens: the **National Botanic Garden of Wales** and the faithful reconstruction of the walled gardens around the long-abandoned house of **Aberglasney**. The twenty-mile trip to Llandeilo is punctuated by gentle, impossibly green hills topped with ruined castles, notably the wonderful **Carreg Cennen**: it's not hard to see why the Merlin legend has taken such a hold in these parts.

National Botanic Garden of Wales

Seven miles east of Carmarthen, SA32 8HN • Daily: April–Oct 10am–6pm; Nov–March 10am–4.30pm • April–Oct £9.55; Nov–March £8.86; half price for visitors arriving by bike • ☎ 01558 668768, ⦿ gardenofwales.org.uk • Bus #279 runs daily from Carmarthen train station (25min)

Opened in 2000, the great glass "eye" of the **National Botanic Garden of Wales** quickly became the centrepiece of the Tywi Valley. Its central walkway leads past lakes, sculpture and geological outcrops from all over Wales, with walks down towards slate-bed plantings and wood and wetland habitats. A double-walled garden has been teased back to life (providing vegetables for the excellent café/restaurant), and enhanced with a small, exquisite Japanese garden, a tropical house and a bee garden that's home to a million bees. At the top of the hill is Norman Foster's stunning oval **glasshouse**, packed with endangered plants from South Africa, Chile, California and the Mediterranean. The whole complex is sustainably managed, and the surrounding land has been turned over to either organic farming or the restoration of typical Welsh habitat.

14

Aberglasney

Five miles northeast of the National Botanic Garden of Wales, 0.5 mile south of the A40, SA32 8OH • Daily: April–Oct 10am–6pm; Nov–March 10.30am–4pm • £8 • ☎ 01558 668998, ⦿ aberglasney.org

While a partly ruined manor house is the centrepiece of the **Aberglasney** estate, interest is focused on the stunning **gardens** where archeologists have peeled back half a century's neglect to reveal interlinking walled gardens mostly constructed between the sixteenth and eighteenth centuries. A walkway leads around the top of what is thought to be Britain's only secular cloister garden, giving access to a set of six Victorian aviaries from where there are great views over the Jacobean pool garden. Look out for the **yew tunnel**, planted around three hundred years ago. The house's glassed-in atrium shelters subtropical plants.

Llandeilo

Fifteen miles east of Carmarthen, the handsome market town of **LLANDEILO** is heading upmarket, with a growing group of chichi cafés and shops on and near the main Rhosmaen Street.

Dinefwr Park

One mile west of Llandeilo, SA19 6RT • Dinefwr Park Daily 24hr • Free • **Newton House** Mid-March to Oct daily 10am–6pm; Nov to mid-March Fri–Sun 10am–4pm • £7.27; NT • ⦿ nationaltrust.org.uk/dinefwr

There's little to see in town, but to the west is the gorgeous **Dinefwr Park**, where the tumbledown shell of the largely thirteenth-century **Dinefwr Castle** sits on a wooded bluff above the Tywi. The owners, the Rhys family, aspired to something a little more luxurious, and in 1523 built a "new" castle, half a mile away, now named **Newton House**. Today the interiors are arranged just as they were a hundred years ago.

ARRIVAL AND DEPARTURE   LLANDEILO

By train Llandeilo train station, on the scenic Heart of Wales Line from Swansea to Shrewsbury, is just east of the centre. Destinations Shrewsbury (4 daily; 2hr 50min); Swansea (5 daily; 1hr 10min).

By bus Buses stop on New Rd. Destinations Carmarthen (8 daily; 40min); Swansea (6 daily; 90min).

ACCOMMODATION AND EATING

★ **Angel Hotel** 62 Rhosmaen St, SA19 6EN ☎ 01558 822765, ⦿ angelbistro.co.uk. Convivial pub serving real ales and great bar meals (mains £12–20), with a slightly more formal restaurant at the rear (£10 for one course, £14 for two, £16 for three). Mon–Sat 11.30am–3pm & 6–11pm; kitchen 11.30am–3pm & 6–9pm.

The Cawdor 70 Rhosmaen St, SA19 6EN ☎ 01558 823500, ⦿ thecawdor.com. Llandeilo's focal point, this former coaching inn has been given a modern makeover with delightful, simply decorated rooms (all different) and stunning attic suites (£200). __£85__

Ginhaus 1 Market St, SA19 6AH ☎ 01558 823030,

ⓦginhaus.co.uk. In addition to the best coffee, breads, cheese, charcuterie, antipasti and wines in town, this deli also offers baguettes and wraps, quiches and pies, and specials such as chilli con carne to take away or eat at the tables in front. Oh, and they stock 250 gins too. Mon–

Thurs 8am–6pm, Fri & Sat 8am–10pm.

Plough Inn Rhosmean, SA19 6NP ⓣ01558 823431, ⓦploughrhosmaen.com. Just a mile north of town, this well-established pub/restaurant has a modern extension with large, comfortable rooms, gym and sauna. **£100**

14

Carreg Cennen Castle

Four miles southeast of Llandeilo, SA19 6UA • Daily: April–Oct 9.30am–6pm; Nov–March 9.30am–5pm • £5.50; CADW • ⓣ01558 822291, ⓦcarregcennencastle.com

Isolated in the rural hinterland, in the far western extremes of the Brecon Beacons National Park (see page 686), **Carreg Cennen Castle** is one of the country's most magnificently positioned castles. Urien, one of King Arthur's knights, is said to have built his fortress on the fearsome rocky outcrop, although the first known construction dates from 1248. Carreg Cennen fell to the English King Edward I in 1277, and was largely destroyed in 1462 by the Earl of Pembroke for being a rebel base. The castle's most astounding aspect is its commanding position, 300ft above a sheer drop down into the green valley of the River Cennen. After the views, the highlight of a visit is the long, damp descent into a pitch-black **cave** that served as a shelter in prehistoric times. Torches (which can be rented for £1.50 from the excellent tearoom near the car park) are essential; continue as far as possible and then turn them off to experience absolute darkness.

Laugharne

The village of **LAUGHARNE** (Talacharn) is a delightful spot, with its ragged castle looming over reeds and tidal flats, and narrow lanes snuggling in behind. Come in high season, though, and you're immediately aware that Laugharne is increasingly being taken over by the legend of the poet **Dylan Thomas**. The village plays its Thomas connections with curiously disgruntled aplomb – nowhere more so than his old boozing hole, **Brown's Hotel**, on the main street (see page 667). The poet is buried in the graveyard of the parish church just north of the centre, his grave marked by a simple white cross.

Dylan Thomas Boathouse

Dylan's Walk, SA33 4SD • Daily: April–Sept 10am–5pm; Oct–March 10.30am–3pm • £4.20 • ⓣ01994 427420, ⓦdylanthomasboathouse.com

Down a narrow lane (no cars) by the estuary is the **Dylan Thomas Boathouse**, the simple home of the Thomas family from 1949 until the writer's death in 1953. It's an enchanting museum, with views of the peaceful, ever-changing water and light of the estuary and its "heron-priested shore". Along the narrow lane, you can peer into the green garage where he wrote: curled photographs of literary heroes, a pen collection and scrunched-up balls of paper suggest that he could return at any minute.

Laugharne Castle

Wogan St, SA33 4SA • April–Oct daily 10am–5pm • £4; CADW • ⓣ01994 427906, ⓦcadw.gov.wales/daysout/laugharnecastle

At the bottom of the main street, the gloomy hulk of **Laugharne Castle** broods over the estuary. Built in the twelfth and thirteenth centuries, most of the original buildings were obliterated in Tudor times when it was transformed into a splendid mansion, largely destroyed in the Civil War. The Inner Ward is dominated by two original towers, one of which you can climb for sublime views from the domed roof over the huddled town. This is now surrounded by an attractive formal garden with fine mature trees.

ARRIVAL AND INFORMATION   LAUGHARNE

By bus Laugharne is a stop on the bus route from Carmarthen (Mon–Sat 5 daily; 30min) to Pendine.

Tourist information Corran Books, opposite *Brown's*

Hotel on King St (April–Oct Mon–Sat 10am–5pm; ⓣ01994 427444).

DYLAN THOMAS

Dylan Thomas (1914–53), born into a snugly middle-class family in Swansea, was the quintessential Celt – fiery, verbose, richly talented and habitually drunk. His first glimmers of of literary talent came after joining the *South Wales Evening Post* as a reporter, a period that inspired some of the most popular tales in his *Portrait of the Artist as a Young Dog*.

Rejecting Swansea's provincialism, Thomas arrived in London as a broke 20-year-old in 1934, weeks before the publication of his first volume of poetry. Another volume followed shortly afterwards, cementing the engaging young Welshman's reputation. Marrying in 1937, he returned to Wales and settled in the hushed backwater of Laugharne. Short stories – crackling with rich and melancholy humour – tumbled out as swiftly as poems, further widening his base of admirers, though, like so many other writers, Thomas only gained star status posthumously.

Perhaps better than anyone, Thomas wrote with a rhythmic, identifiably Welsh, cadence. Especially in public, he liked to adopt the persona of an archetypal stage Welshman, as he saw it: sonorous tones, loquacious, romantic and inclined towards a stiff tipple. This went down particularly well in the United States, where he made lucrative lecture tours. It was on one of these that he died, in 1953, supposedly from a massive whisky overdose, although it now seems likely he was a victim of pneumonia or diabetes and incompetent doctors. Just a month earlier, he had put the finishing touches to what many see as his masterpiece: *Under Milk Wood*, a "play for voices", describing the dreams, thoughts and lives of a village rather like Laugharne.

14

ACCOMMODATION

Tiny Laugharne has only limited **accommodation**, so book ahead in season.

Ants Hill Caravan Park A4066, 1 mile north, SA33 4QN ☎ 01994 427293, ⓦ antshill.co.uk. The nearest campsite to Laugharne has an outdoor heated swimming pool (summer only). Closed Nov–Feb. **£20**

Boat House Inn 1 Gosport St, SA33 4SY ☎ 01994 427263, ⓦ theboathousebnb.co.uk. Stylish, comfortable four-room B&B right in the centre. Great breakfasts might include vanilla waffles or smoked salmon. **£85**

Brown's Hotel King St, SA33 4RY ☎ 01994 427688, ⓦ browns.wales. Thomas' old boozing hole, built in 1752, is now a "bar-with-rooms" – and the "genuine" Dylan Thomas dartboard has been reinstated. Rooms are in a retro 1950s style, but with modern gadgets. There's a good breakfast and a basic menu for lunch and dinner, with a soup of the day (£6.50), toasties, pizzas and curries (£8–9). Daily 11am–11pm; kitchen noon–3pm & 6–8.30pm. **£95**

EATING AND DRINKING

Arthur's Bistro 6 Grist Square, SA33 4SS ☎ 01994 427422. This friendly café serves breakfasts (until 11.30am) then soups, sandwiches, rarebit, pizza, fish and chips. Four evenings a week there's a choice of antipasti followed by fairly standard mains (£8–14). Mon & Wed 10am–3pm, Thurs–Sun 10am–3pm & 6.30–9pm.

New Three Mariners Victoria St, SA33 4SE ☎ 01994 427426, ⓦ newthreemarinersinn.co.uk. Cheery pub that offers the best drinking in town, as well as bar meals and pizzas. Mon–Fri 3–11pm, Sat & Sun noon–11pm.

Southern Pembrokeshire

Anyone exploring the far southern reaches of Pembrokeshire will pass through **Tenby**, the quintessential British seaside resort built high on cliffs with views across to monastic **Caldey Island**. The coast zigzagging west from Tenby is a strange mix of caravan parks, Ministry of Defence shooting ranges, spectacularly beautiful bays and gull-covered cliffs. The coastal road passes idyllic coves, the lily ponds at **Bosherston** and the remarkable and ancient **St Govan's Chapel**, squeezed into a rock cleft above the crashing waves. The ancient town of **Pembroke** really only warrants a visit to its impressive castle and the fine Bishop's Palace in neighbouring **Lamphey**.

14

Tenby

On a natural promontory of great strategic importance, beguilingly old-fashioned **TENBY** (Dinbych-y-Pysgod) is everything a seaside resort should be. Narrow streets wind down from the medieval centre past miniature gardens facing the afternoon sun, and steps lead down to dockside arches where fishmongers sell the morning's catch.

First mentioned in a ninth-century bardic poem, Tenby grew under the twelfth-century Normans, who erected a castle on the headland in their attempt to colonize South Pembrokeshire and create a **"Little England beyond Wales"**. Three times in the twelfth and thirteenth centuries the town was ransacked by the Welsh before the stout town walls – largely still intact – were built. Tenby prospered as a port between the fourteenth and sixteenth centuries, and although decline followed, the arrival of the railway renewed prosperity as the town became a fashionable resort.

Today, wandering the medieval streets is one of Tenby's delights. The town is triangle-shaped, with two sides formed by the coast meeting at Castle Hill, and the third by the 20ft-high town **walls**, built in the late thirteenth century and massively strengthened by Jasper Tudor in 1457. The only town gate still standing is the **Five Arches**, a semicircular barbican that combined day-to-day practicality with hidden lookouts and angles acute enough to surprise invaders.

St Mary's Church

Between St George's St and Tudor Square, SA70 8AP • Usually open • Free • ☎ 01834 845484

The centre's focal point is the 152ft-high spire of the largely fifteenth-century **St Mary's church**. Its pleasantly light interior shows the elaborate ceiling bosses in the chancel to good effect, and fifteenth-century tombs attest to Tenby's mercantile tradition.

Tudor Merchant's House

Quay Hill, SA70 7BX • 11am–5pm: Feb half-term & Aug daily; March, Nov & Dec Sat & Sun; April–Oct Mon & Wed–Sun • £5; NT • ☎ 01834 842279, Ⓦ nationaltrust.org.uk/tudor-merchants-house

Wedged in a corner of Quay Hill is the fifteenth-century **Tudor Merchant's House**. A compact building on three floors, it has been filled with reproduction Tudor furniture that visitors are welcome to sit on. The rear herb garden gives a good view of the huge Flemish chimney.

ARRIVAL AND INFORMATION   **TENBY**

By train Tenby's station is just west of the town centre, at the foot of Warren St.

Destinations Carmarthen (9 daily; 50min); Pembroke (9 daily; 20min); Swansea (8 daily; 1hr 45min).

CALDEY ISLAND

Celtic monks first settled **Caldey Island** (Ynys Pŷr), a couple of miles off Tenby, in the sixth century. This community may have been wiped out in Viking raids, but in 1136 a Benedictine priory was founded here. After the Dissolution of the Monasteries in 1536, the island was bought and sold until 1906, when it returned to monastic use – it is now home to fifteen members of a Reformed Cistercian order.

A short woodland walk from the jetty leads to the main settlement: a tiny post office, the popular tea garden and a **perfume shop** selling fragrances distilled by the monks from Caldey's herbs. The narrow road to the left leads past the abbey to the heavily restored **chapel of St David**, whose most impressive feature is the round-arched Norman door.

A lane leads south from the village to the old **priory**, and the remarkable, twelfth-century **St Illtud's church**, where one of the most significant pre-Norman finds in Wales, the sandstone **Ogham Cross**, stands on the south side of the nave. It bears a sixth-century runic inscription, added to, in Latin, during the ninth. The lane continues to the gleaming white **lighthouse**, built in 1828.

Caldey Island is accessible by **boat** from Tenby Harbour, or Castle Beach when the tide is out (10am–5pm, every 20min: Easter–May & Oct Mon–Fri; May–Sept Mon–Sat; 20min each way; £12 return; ☎ 01834 844453, Ⓦ caldey-island.co.uk). Tickets are sold at the kiosk at the harbour.

By bus Some buses stop at South Parade, at the top of Trafalgar Rd, although most (including National Express coaches) call at the bus shelter on Upper Park Rd.
Destinations Carmarthen (1 daily; 1hr); Haverfordwest (hourly; 1hr); Manorbier (hourly; 20min); Pembroke (hourly; 45min).

Tourist office Upper Park Rd (June–Aug Mon–Fri 9am–5pm, Sat 10am–5pm, Sun 10am–4pm; Sept–May Mon–Fri 9am–1pm & 1.45–5pm, Sat 10am–1pm & 1.45–5pm; ☏ 01437 775603).

ACCOMMODATION

Atlantic The Esplanade, SA70 7DU ☏ 01834 842881, ⊛ atlantic-hotel.uk.com. The best hotel along the South Beach, with fine rooms (some with sea views), a decent restaurant and a pool and spa. Watch out for good off-season specials. £115

Langdon Villa Guest House 3 Warren St, SA70 7JU ☏ 01834 849467, ⊛ langdonguesthousetenby.co.uk. Handy for the station, this four-star B&B has a range of double and twin rooms and puts on a hearty breakfast. £70

Meadow Farm Northcliffe, SA80 8AU ☏ 01834 844829, ⊛ meadowfarmtenby.co.uk. Under a mile north of Tenby on the coastal path, this campsite in a grassy field has limited facilities but long views over the town towards Caldey Island. Closed Nov–March. Per person £9

Roch Villa 1 Harding Villas, SA70 7LL ☏ 01834 843096, ⊛ rochvillabandb.com. Budget accommodation with three rooms with shared bathrooms and video or DVD player. Limited parking, but it's near the train station. £50

YHA Manorbier Skrinkle Haven, SA70 7TT ☏ 0345 371 9031, ⊛ yha.org.uk/hostel/manorbier. Modern hostel in an old MoD building overlooking the cliffs 5 miles west of Tenby, near the Manorbier bus route. Meals and camping facilities available. Closed Nov–Feb. Dorms £19, doubles £59

EATING AND DRINKING

Caffè Vista 3 Crackwell St, SA70 7HA ☏ 01834 849636. Great little licensed Greek-/Australian-run café with excellent panini, espresso and cakes, plus a small selection of hot dishes such as beef or butterbean stew. Good harbour views from the terrace and free wi-fi. Summer school hols Mon–Wed & Sun 9am–5pm, Thurs–Sat 9am–10.30pm; rest of year daily 9am–5pm.

Coach and Horses Upper Frog St, SA70 7JD ☏ 01834 842704. Animated, wooden-beamed pub (said to be the oldest in Tenby) with good beer, well-prepared bar meals and tasty Thai dishes. Daily noon–11pm; kitchen daily noon–3pm & 6–9pm.

Lifeboat Tavern St Julian's St, SA70 7AD ☏ 01834 844948. Popular and welcoming pub, with a young clientele and family-friendly food such as steaks, burgers and fish and chips; live music Tues and Sun. Daily noon–midnight, kitchen Mon–Fri noon–9pm, Sat & Sun noon–7pm.

★ **The Plantagenet** Quay Hill, SA70 7BX ☏ 01834 842350, ⊛ plantagenettenby.co.uk. For a splurge, try this cosy and thoroughly enjoyable restaurant in one of Tenby's oldest houses – ask for a table inside the massive tenth-century Flemish chimney. Dinner mains go for £21–27 (£16 for vegetarian), but lunch is cheaper (£8–13). Daily noon–2.30pm & 5–10pm.

West of Tenby

The coastal path south and west of Tenby skirts the gorgeous long beach of **Penally**, then hugs the clifftop for a couple of miles to **Lydstep Haven** (fee charged for the sands). A mile further west is the cove of **Skrinkle Haven**, and above it the excellent *Manorbier* hostel (see above).

Manorbier

A couple of miles beyond Skrinkle Haven, the quaint village of **MANORBIER** (Maenorbŷr), pronounced "manner-beer", was the birthplace in 1146 of the Welsh-Norman historian, writer and ecclesiastical reformist Giraldus Cambrensis (Gerald of Wales).

Manorbier Castle

Off the B485, 1.2 miles south of Manorbier train station, SA70 7SY • Feb & Oct half-terms & April–Sept daily 10am–4pm • £5.50 • ☏ 01834 871394, ⊛ manorbiercastle.co.uk • Buses run hourly to the village from Haverfordwest (1hr 15min), Lamphey (15min), Pembroke (20min) and Tenby (20min)

Founded in the early twelfth century, the baronial residence of **Manorbier Castle** sits above the village and its beach on a hill of wild gorse. Strong Norman walls surround gardens and a grassy courtyard in which the remains of chapel and staterooms jostle for position with the nineteenth-century domestic residence. Views from the ramparts are wonderful,

> ## THE PEMBROKESHIRE COAST NATIONAL PARK AND COAST PATH
>
> The **Pembrokeshire Coast** is Britain's only predominantly sea-based national park (Ⓦpembrokeshirecoast.wales), hugging the rippled coast around the entire southwestern section of Wales. Established in 1952, the park is not one easily identifiable mass, rather a series of occasionally unconnected coastal and inland scenic patches.
>
> Following almost every wriggle of the coastline, the **Pembrokeshire Coast Path** winds 186 miles from Amroth, just east of Tenby, to its northern terminus at St Dogmael's near Cardigan. For the vast majority of the way, the path clings precariously to cliff-top routes, overlooking seal-basking rocks, craggy offshore islands, unexpected gashes of sand and shrieking clouds of seabirds. The most popular and ruggedly inspiring segments of the coast path are the stretch along the southern coast from the castle at Manorbier to the tiny cliff chapel at Bosherston; either side of St Bride's Bay, around St David's Head and the Marloes peninsula; and the generally quieter northern coast either side of Fishguard, past undulating contours, massive cliffs, bays and old ports.
>
> For **information**, the national park's free newspaper *Coast to Coast* details guided walks, boat trips and other events; published every spring, it can be found in local visitor centres. Check also the park's general site and Ⓦnt.pcnpa.org.uk.

taking in the corrugated coastline, bushy dunes, deep-green fields and smoking chimneys of the village houses. There's a warren of dark passageways to explore, occasionally opening out into little cells populated by lacklustre wax figures, including Gerald himself.

Stackpole Estate

The #387/#388 Coastal Cruiser bus (generally summer daily; rest of year Thurs & Sat only) makes various loops from Pembroke, calling at Bosherton (3 daily; 15min–1hr), Stackpole village (2 daily; 30–40min), Stackpole Quay (2 daily; 35–55min) and St Govan's (1 daily, Sat or Sun only; 30min)

The tiny rocky harbour at **Stackpole Quay**, reached by a small lane lane from East Trewent and part of the National Trust's **Stackpole Estate**, is a good starting point for walks along the breathtaking cliffs to the north. Another walk leads half a mile south to one of Wales' finest beaches, **Barafundle Bay**, its soft sands fringed by wooded cliffs at either end. The path continues around the coast, through the dunes of **Stackpole Warren**, to **Broadhaven South**, where a pleasant little beach overlooks several rocky islets. Road access is through the village of **BOSHERSTON** where three beautifully landscaped fingers of water known as **Bosherston Lakes** (NT; free) were created in the late eighteenth century. The westernmost lake is the most scenic, especially in late spring and early summer when the lilies that carpet much of its surface are in full bloom.

A lane from Bosherston (often closed Mon–Fri, due to military use) dips south across the MoD training grounds to a spot overlooking the cliffs where tiny **St Govan's Chapel** (daily; free) is wedged: it's a remarkable building, at least eight hundred years old. Steps descend straight into the sandy-floored chapel, now empty save for the simple stone altar.

Pembroke

The old county town of **PEMBROKE** (Penfro) sits below its fearsome castle on the southern side of Pembroke River. It's a restful place, with one long main street of attractive Georgian and Victorian houses and some intact stretches of medieval town wall, but little else to keep you.

Pembroke Castle

Westgate Hill, SA71 4LA · Daily: March, Sept & Oct 10am–5pm; April–Aug 9.30am–5.30pm; Nov–Feb 10am–4pm · £6 · ☎01646 681510, Ⓦpembrokecastle.co.uk

Pembroke's history is inextricably bound up with that of its **castle**, founded by the Normans as the strongest link in their chain of fortresses across south Wales.

During the Civil War, Pembroke was a Parliamentarian stronghold until its military governor suddenly switched allegiance to the king, whereupon Cromwell's troops sacked it after a 48-day siege. Yet despite this battering, and centuries of subsequent neglect, the castle still inspires awe with its sheer, bloody-minded bulk. The soaring gatehouse, housing some excellent history displays, leads into the large, grassy courtyard around the vast Norman **keep**, 75ft high and with walls 18ft thick. Beyond this, steps lead far down into **Wogan Cavern**, a huge natural cave, dank and slimy, where light beams in through a barred hole in the wall facing out over the waterside path.

14

ARRIVAL AND INFORMATION
PEMBROKE

By train Pembroke's train station lies at the eastern end of Main St.

Destinations Lamphey (9 daily; 3min); Manorbier (9 daily; 12min); Pembroke Dock (9 daily; 10min); Swansea (8 daily; 2hr 10min); Tenby (9 daily; 20min).

By bus Buses stop near the castle on Main St. The Coastal Cruiser hikers' bus takes a loop from Pembroke to Angle via Bosherston and Stackpole; journey times depend on whether you take the #387 (anticlockwise) or #388 (clockwise).

Destinations Bosherston (May–Sept 3 daily; Oct–April Mon, Thurs & Sat 2 daily; 35min–1hr); Haverfordwest (hourly; 55min); Manorbier (hourly; 20min); Pembroke Dock (every 20min; 10min); Stackpole (May–Sept 2 daily; Oct–April Mon, Thurs & Sat 2 daily; 30–55min); Tenby (hourly; 40min).

By ferry Irish Ferries (☎0870 517 1717, ⓦirishferries.com) sail twice daily from Rosslare in Ireland to Pembroke Dock, 2 miles northwest of Pembroke and starting point for trains to Carmarthen and Swansea.

Tourist office In the library, Commons Rd (Easter–Oct Mon–Wed, Fri & Sat 10am–1pm & 2–5pm, Thurs 10am–1pm & 2–7pm; Nov–Easter Tues–Sat 10am–1pm; ☎01646 776499).

ACCOMMODATION AND EATING

Cornstore Café North Quay, SA71 4NG ☎01646 684290, ⓦthecornstore.com/cafe. Attached to the eclectic Cornstore furnishings shop, with riverside seating, this serves good espresso, light meals and fantastic homemade cakes. Mon–Sat 10am–5pm.

Food at Williams 18 Main St, SA71 4NP ☎01646 689990, ⓦfoodatwilliams.co.uk. A stylish, licensed café, serving fine coffee and cakes, breakfasts till noon and light lunches such as Glamorgan sausages or mackerel pâté (£6.50), sandwiches and daily specials. Mon–Fri 9am–4.30pm, Sat 9am–4pm, Sun 10am–3pm.

Old King's Arms 13 Main St, SA71 4JS ☎01646 683611, ⓦoldkingsarmshotel.co.uk. Good pub grub, tapas and more substantial restaurant dishes; they also have four decent en-suite rooms. Daily 11am–11pm; kitchen noon–2.15pm & 6.30–9.15pm. £80

Penfro 111 Main St, SA71 4DB ☎01646 682753, ⓦfacebook.com/Penfro-BB-239277051946. Three large rooms in a fine Georgian townhouse, some without bathroom or TV; there's a lovely spacious garden at the rear. £75

Tregenna 7 Upper Lamphey Rd, SA71 5JL ☎01646 621525, ⓦtregennapembroke.co.uk. If Penfro is full, try one of the four en-suite rooms here, about 900yd beyond the train station. £70

Lamphey

The pleasant village of **LAMPHEY** (Llandyfai), two miles east of Pembroke and accessible on **buses** and **trains** between Tenby and Pembroke, is best known for the ruined **Bishop's Palace**, off a quiet lane to the north of the village. There's also a handful of good **places to stay** nearby.

Bishop's Palace

Off the A4139, SA71 5NT • Daily 10am–4pm • April–Oct £3.50; Nov–March free; CADW • ☎01646 672224, ⓦcadw.gov.wales/daysout/lampheybishopspalace

Once a country retreat for the bishops of St Davids, Lamphey's **Bishop's Palace** dates from around the thirteenth century, but was abandoned following the Reformation. Stout walls surround the scattered ruins and grassy banks under which other buildings have long been lost. Most impressive are the remains of the Great Hall, at the complex's eastern end, topped by fourteenth-century arcaded parapets.

14

ARRIVAL AND DEPARTURE

By train The station is central, on Station Rd just off A4139. Destinations Carmarthen (every 2hr; 1hr 10min); Pembroke (every 2hr; 5min); Pembroke Dock (every 2hr; 15min); Swansea (every 2hr; 2hr); Tenby (every 2hr; 20min).

By bus Buses stop at the church, south of the lane to th Bishop's Palace.
Destinations Haverfordwest (hourly; 1hr); Pembrok (hourly; 8min); Tenby (hourly; 40min).

ACCOMMODATION

Lamphey Court Hotel & Spa Opposite Bishop's Palace, SA71 5NT ☎ 01646 672273, ⓦ lampheycourt. co.uk. Grand, if slightly over-the-top, accommodation, with spa, opposite the palace ruins. **£98**

Portclew House B&B 2 miles south, SA71 5LA

☎ 01646 672800, ⓦ portclewhouse.co.uk. Just 0.5 mil from the superb beach of Freshwater East, this Grade I listed Georgian house, in two acres of grounds, offers seve spacious rooms and good, hearty breakfasts. **£98**

Carew Castle and Tidal Mill

Carew, SA70 8SL • Castle & mill April–Oct daily 10am–5pm; Nov–March castle only Mon–Fri 11am–3pm • April–Oct £5.50; Nov–March £4 • ⓦ carewcastle.com • Buses from Pembroke (4 daily; 10min) and Tenby (9 daily; 30min)

Tiny **CAREW**, four miles northeast of Pembroke, is a pretty place beside the River Carew. By the main road just south of the river crossing stands a 13ft **Celtic cross**, the graceful taper of the shaft covered in fine tracery of ancient Welsh designs. Nearby, an Elizabethan walled garden houses the ticket office for **Carew Castle and Tidal Mill**. Little remains of the castle, a hybrid of defensive necessity (c.1100) and Elizabethan whimsy, but its large, impressive bare walls give a good sense of scale. A few hundred yards west is the **Tidal Mill**, used commercially until 1937 and now the only tide-powered mill in Wales. The impressive eighteenth-century exterior belies the pedestrian displays inside.

Mid- and northern Pembrokeshire

The most westerly point of Wales is one of the country's most enchanting. Just ten miles or so north of Tenby is **Narberth**, with its charming shopping; another ten or so miles west the region's chief town, **Haverfordwest** is rather soulless, but it's the jumping-off point for stunning **St Bride's Bay**. The coast here is broken into rocky outcrops, islands and broad, sweeping beaches curving between two headlands that sit like giant crab pincers facing out into the warm Gulf Stream. The southernmost headland winds around every conceivable angle, offering calm, east-facing sands at **Dale** and sunny expanses of south-facing beach at **Marloes**. At **Martin's Haven**, boats depart for the offshore islands of **Skomer**, **Skokholm** and **Grassholm**. To the north, there's spectacularly lacerated coast around **St Davids peninsula**, with towering cliffs interrupted only by occasional strips of sand. The tiny city of **St Davids** is a highlight: rooks and crows circle above the impressive ruins of the huge Bishop's Palace and the delicate bulk of the cathedral, the most impressive in Wales.

The wild, rugged coast that forms the very southern tip of Cardigan Bay is breathtakingly beautiful, and noticeably less commercialized and far more Welsh than the shores of south and mid-Pembrokeshire. From the crags and cairns above St David's Head, the coast path perches precariously on cliffs where only the thousands of seabirds have access. Hidden coves and secluded beaches slice into the rocky headlands, at their most magnificent around **Strumble Head**, where a picturesque lighthouse stands on a tiny islet. From here, there's only wilderness to detain you en route to charming **Newport** – unless you're heading for **Fishguard** and the Irish ferry.

Narberth

According to legend, **NARBERTH** (Arberth) was the court of Pwyll, and its castle was probably home to the Welsh princes. Today, it is Pembrokeshire's prime boutique **shopping** destination, with a dozen or so delis, galleries and independent shops along High Street, and a lively farmer's market on Thursday afternoons.

ARRIVAL AND GETTING AROUND
NARBERTH

By train The train station is a mile east from High St; bus #381 (every hour or so; 4min) will take you to the centre. Destinations Carmarthen (every 2hr; 30min); Pembroke (every 2hr; 45min); Swansea (every 2hr; 1hr 25min); Tenby (every 2hr; 30min).

By bus Buses stop at the top of High St. Destinations Cardigan (3 daily; 1hr); Carmarthen (3 daily; 40min); Haverfordwest (hourly; 20min); Tenby (hourly; 45min).

ACCOMMODATION AND EATING

Plas Hyfryd Country Hotel Moorfield Rd, SA67 7AB ☏ 01834 869006, ⓦ plashyfrydhotel.com. Comfortable hotel at the top of town, in a former rectory with fourteen rooms (including family and executive suites), bar and restaurant, with terrace dining. £90

★ **Ultracomida** 7 High St, SA76 7AR ☏ 01834 861491, ⓦ ultracomida.co.uk. Perfect for lunch, this little slice of Spain has hams hanging from the ceiling, large shared tables, delicious authentic tapas or larger *raciones* (£4–7), as well as salads and sandwiches, with Iberian wines or sherries to wash them down. Mon–Sat: deli & takeaway 10am–6pm; restaurant 10am–5pm.

Haverfordwest

In the seventeenth and eighteenth centuries, **HAVERFORDWEST** (Hwlffordd), ten miles north of Pembroke, prospered as a port and trading centre. Today it is scarcely a place to linger, though as the main transport hub and shopping centre for western Pembrokeshire, you are likely to pass through.

ARRIVAL AND DEPARTURE
HAVERFORDWEST

By train Trains stop a 10min walk east of the Old Bridge. Destinations Cardiff (7 daily; 2hr 25min); Carmarthen (10 daily; 40min); Swansea (7 daily; 1hr 30min).
By bus The bus station is at the end of the Old Bridge. Destinations Broad Haven (6 daily; 20min); Cardigan (hourly; 1hr 20min); Carmarthen (3 daily; 1hr); Fishguard (hourly; 40min); Manorbier (hourly; 1hr 10min); Newport, Pembrokeshire (hourly; 1hr); Pembroke (hourly; 55min); St Davids (hourly; 45min); Tenby (hourly; 1hr).

INFORMATION AND GETTING AROUND

Tourist office Dew St, behind the library (Mon, Wed & Fri 10am–5pm – also Thurs during summer holidays – Tues 10am–7pm, Sat 10am–1pm; ☏ 01437 775244).
By bike Mike's Bikes, 17 Prendergast, a quarter of a mile northeast of the bus station (Mon–Sat 9am–5.30pm; ☏ 01437 760068, ⓦ mikes-bikes.co.uk). The region's best bike rental, supplying mountain bikes and hybrid tourers (both £12/day) with panniers, lock and helmet, and tagalongs for kids.

ACCOMMODATION AND EATING

Boulston Manor 3 miles southeast, SA62 4AQ ☏ 01437 764600, ⓦ boulstonmanor.co.uk. On a stunning site overlooking the Western Cleddau, this top-end B&B has just three rooms, all furnished in Georgian style but with modern comforts. £75
College Guest House 93 Hill St, SA62 1QL ☏ 01437 763710, ⓦ collegeguesthouse.com. One of several decent B&Bs near the Leisure Centre (free parking) at the top of Hill St. £80
The Creative Common 11 Goat St, SA61 1PX ☏ 01437 779397, ⓦ thecreativecommon.co.uk. Linked to a co-working space, this attractive coffee shop has great coffee and tea (served with a timer), delicious cakes and enthusiastic staff. Mon–Fri 8am–2.30pm, Sat 10am–3pm.
The George's 24 Market St, SA61 1NH ☏ 01437 766683, ⓦ thegeorges.uk.com. A great option for lunch, taking a wholefood approach to delicious peasant dishes. You can eat in a lovely walled garden if the weather allows, or the cellar bistro if not. Tues–Sat 10am–5.30pm.

14

Dale

DALE, fourteen miles west of Haverfordwest, has a sheltered east-facing shore; it's excellent for bathing and **watersports**, but it can be unbearably crowded in peak season. West Wales Wind, Surf and Sailing gives instruction in power-boating, windsurfing, surfing, sailing and kayaking (April–Oct; £35–70/half-day; ☎01646 636642, ⓦsurfdale.co.uk), and rents gear.

ARRIVAL AND DEPARTURE   DALE

By bus There are various bus stops, including on the seafront (B4327). The village is served by buses from/ to Haverfordwest (3 daily; 55min) and Milford Haven (3 daily; 30min).

ACCOMMODATION

Allenbrook Castle Way, SA62 3RN ☎01646 636254, ⓦallenbrook-dale.co.uk. A luxurious, charming, somewhat timewarped country house; all rooms have sea views across the lawns. No children. **£80**

Griffin Inn Waterfront, SA62 3RB ☎01646 636227, ⓦgriffininndale.co.uk. This traditional waterfront pub, with a modern extension and open deck above, has built a strong reputation for its fish specials (mostly perfectly fresh and lightly steamed), but is also a real village pub where you can relax and chat freely. May–Sept daily noon–11pm; Oct–April Tues–Sun noon–11pm; kitchen same days noon–2.30pm & 6–8.30pm.

Marloes

MARLOES, a mile north of Dale, is an unexciting little place, but the broad, deserted beach is magnificent, offering safe swimming as well as fine views of the island of Skokholm. The coast path and a narrow road continue for two miles to the National Trust-owned **Deer Park**, the grassy far tip of the southern peninsula of St Bride's Bay – and **Martin's Haven**, from where you can take a **boat** out to the islands of Skomer (where you can disembark), Skokholm and Grassholm (see below).

ARRIVAL AND DEPARTURE   MARLOES

The Puffin Shuttle **bus** runs from St Davids (May–Sept 3 daily; Oct–April 3 Thurs & 3 Sat; 1hr 30min).

St Davids

ST DAVIDS (Tyddewi) is one of the most enchanting spots in Britain. This miniature city – really just a large village – sits at Wales' very westernmost point in bleak, treeless countryside, above its purple- and gold-flecked **cathedral**, the country's spiritual heart. Supposedly founded by the Welsh patron saint himself in 550 AD, the shrine of St David has drawn pilgrims for a millennium and a half – William the Conqueror included – and by 1120, Pope Calixtus II decreed that two journeys to St Davids

---

SKOMER, SKOKHOLM AND GRASSHOLM ISLANDS

Weather permitting, Dale Sailing operates **boats** (April–Oct Tues–Sun & bank hols 10am, 11am & noon; £21; no booking required) from Martin's Haven to **Skomer**, a 722-acre flat-topped island whose rich birdlife and spectacular carpets of wild flowers make it perfect for birdwatching and walking.

Though no landings are permitted, Dale also offers fast cruises that loop around **Skokholm** (daily 10.30am, 1pm, 3.30pm & 6.30pm; 2hr; £45; booking essential; ☎01646 603109, ⓦpembrokeshire-islands.co.uk), a couple of miles south of Skomer and far smaller, more rugged and remote, noted for its cliffs of warm red sandstone. Britain's first bird observatory was founded here in 1933, and there are still huge numbers of petrels, gulls, puffins, oystercatchers and Manx shearwaters.

The same company also offers cruises out to the tiny outpost of **Grassholm Island**, five miles west of Skomer (daily 11.30pm; 2hr; £45; booking essential). Some eighty thousand or so screaming gannets nest here, and though you cannot land boats stop to watch the wildlife.

were the spiritual equivalent of one to Rome. Today, with so many historical sites, outdoor-pursuit centres, surf beaches, good cafés, superb walks, bathing and climbing, St Davids and its peninsula are a must-visit.

From the central **Celtic cross**, the main street runs under the thirteenth-century **Tower Gate**, forming the entrance to the serene **Cathedral Close**, backed by a windswept landscape of treeless heathland. The cathedral lies down to the right, hidden in a hollow by the River Alun. This apparent modesty is explained by reasons of defence, as a towering cathedral, visible from the sea on all sides, would have been vulnerable to attack. On the other side of the babbling Alun stand the ruins of the **Bishop's Palace**.

14

St Davids Cathedral

The Close, SA62 6RD • Mon–Sat 8.30am–5.30pm, Sun 12.45–5.30pm • £3 donation requested • Guided tours (1hr) Aug Mon 11.30am & Fri 2.30pm, other times by appointment; arranged at the bookshop in the nave • £4 • ☎ 01437 720202, ⊛ stdavidscathedral.org.uk

Entering **St Davids Cathedral**, you at once have a full view of its most striking feature, the intricate, latticed oak **roof** of the low, twelfth-century nave, added to hide emergency restoration work in the sixteenth century. The nave floor still has a pronounced slope and the support buttresses inserted in the northern aisle look incongruously new and temporary. The choir stalls include a unique **monarch's stall**, complete with royal crest, for, unlike any other British cathedral, the Queen is an automatic member of the St Davids Cathedral Chapter. Separating choir and presbytery is an unusual **parclose screen** of finely traced woodwork; beyond this is the tomb of Edmund Tudor, father of King Henry VII. The back wall of the **presbytery** was once the eastern end of the cathedral, as can be seen from the two lines of windows. The upper row remains intact, while the lower three were filled with delicate gold mosaics in the nineteenth century. On the south side are two thirteenth-century bishops' tombs, facing the disappointingly plain tomb of St David, largely destroyed in the Reformation. Behind the filled-in lancets at the back of the presbytery is **Bishop Vaughan's chapel**, its exquisite fan tracery roof built in 1508–22. A peephole looks back into the presbytery, over a casket reputedly containing some of the intermingled bones of St David and his friend, St Justinian.

Bishop's Palace

The Close, SA62 6PE • March–June, Sept & Oct daily 9.30am–5pm; July & Aug daily 9.30am–6pm; Nov–Feb Mon–Sat 10am–4pm, Sun 11am–4pm • £4; CADW • ☎ 01437 720517, ⊛ cadw.gov.wales/daysout/stdavidsbishopspalace

The splendid fourteenth-century **Bishop's Palace** has a huge central quadrangle fringed by a neat jigsaw of ruined buildings built in extraordinarily richly tinted stone. The **arched parapets** that run along the top of most of the walls were a favourite feature of Bishop Gower. Two ruined but still impressive halls – the **Bishop's Hall** and the enormous **Great Hall**, with its glorious rose window – lie off the main quadrangle; beneath the Great Hall, dank vaults contain an interesting exhibition on the palace and the indulgent lifestyles of its occupants. The destruction of the palace is largely due to sixteenth-century Bishop Barlow, who supposedly stripped the buildings of their lead roofs to provide dowries for his five daughters' marriages to bishops.

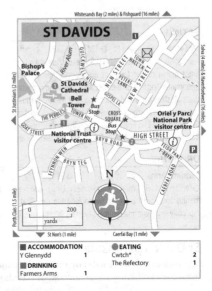

ST DAVIDS

■ ACCOMMODATION		● EATING	
Y Glennydd	1	Cwtch*	2
		The Refectory	1
■ DRINKING			
Farmers Arms	1		

14

OUTDOOR ACTIVITIES AROUND ST DAVIDS

Several local companies run **boat trips** to the outlying islands (see page 674), and there are all manner of activities from **biking** to **rock climbing**.

Ma Simes Surf Hut 28 High St, St Davids, SA62 2SD ☎01437 720433, ⓦmasimes.co.uk. The place to rent surfboards (£12/day) or book lessons (£35/half-day).

Preseli Venture 10 miles east of St Davids, near Mathry, SA62 5HN ☎01348 837709, ⓦpreseli venture.co.uk. Coasteering, sea kayaking, surfing, walking and biking (all half-day £52; £98/day).

TYF 1 High St, SA62 6SA ☎01437 721611, ⓦtyf.com. TYF pioneered coasteering, an exhilarating combo that involves scrambling over rocks, jumping off cliffs and swimming across the narrow bays of St Davids peninsula. It's possible for just about anyone (even non-swimmers) and is available all year, along with surfing, kayaking and rock climbing (all £58/half-day, £99/day). Also multiday sessions and courses.

Oriel y Parc Landscape Gallery

National Park visitor centre, High St, SA62 6NW · Daily 10am–4pm · Free · ☎01437 720392, ⓦpembrokeshirecoast.org.uk

The **Oriel y Parc Landscape Gallery** features paintings by Graham Sutherland plus rotating loans from the National Museum of Wales. The thoughtfully curated displays aim to interpret the landscape and natural world of the National Park.

ARRIVAL AND INFORMATION
ST DAVIDS

By bus From mid-April to Sept, the Celtic Coaster bus (#403) connects the Grove car park (by the tourist office) and the centre of St Davids with Whitesands Bay, St Justinians and Porth Clais. Buses from Haverfordwest stop on the High St; buses to and from Fishguard and Whitesands Bay stop on New St (when arriving) and Nun St (when leaving).

Destinations Broad Haven (3 daily; 45min); Fishguard (7

daily; 50min); Haverfordwest (hourly; 45min); Marloes (3 daily; 1hr 20min).

National Park visitor centre East end of the High St (daily; March–Oct 9.30am–5pm; Nov–Feb 10am–4.30pm; ☎01437 720392, ⓦstdavids.co.uk).

National Trust visitor centre Captain's House, Cross Square (Mon–Sat 9am–5pm, Sun 9am–4pm; ☎01437 720385, ⓦnationaltrust.org.uk/st-davids-visitor-centre-and-shop).

ACCOMMODATION

Y Glennydd 51 Nun St, SA62 6NU ☎01438 870487 or ☎01437 720576, ⓦglennyddhotel.co.uk; map p.675. Welcoming two-star hotel (built for coastguard

officers in the 1880s) with eleven rooms (some with shared bathrooms) and a restaurant (£17 for two courses, £20 for three). __£65__

EATING

★**Cwtch*** 22 High St ☎01437 720491, ⓦcwtch restaurant.co.uk; map p.675. Some of Pembrokeshire's finest dining can be found at the award-winning *Cwtch* * (pronounced "cutsh"), an intimate and easy-going restaurant that's all slate and wood and blackboard menus, featuring top-quality local ingredients. You'll pay £27/£33 for two/ three courses; £23/£27 if you arrive within 45min of opening. Booking recommended. Mid-Feb to Easter, Nov & Dec

Wed–Sat 6–9.30pm (last orders), Sun noon–2.30pm; Feb half-term, Easter & Oct Mon–Sat 6–9.30pm, Sun noon–2.30pm; Easter–Sept daily 5/6pm–9.30pm.

The Refectory St Davids Cathedral, SA62 6PE ☎01437 721760; map p.675. The beautiful St Mary's Hall is a great spot for tea and cakes, classy sandwiches (£6) and mains such as burgers, faggots or fish skewers (all £10). Daily: Nov–Easter 11am–4pm; Easter–Nov 10.30am–4.30pm.

DRINKING

Farmers Arms Goat St, SA62 6RF ☎01437 721666, ⓦfarmersstdavids.co.uk; map p.675. Lively and very friendly local, with a terrace overlooking the cathedral – especially enjoyable on a summer's evening. Decent pub grub

also available (summer only). Easter–Sept daily 11am–midnight; Oct–Easter Mon–Thurs 4pm–midnight, Fri 3pm–midnight, Sat & Sun 11am–midnight; kitchen Easter–Sept daily noon–2.30pm & 6–9.30pm.

St Davids peninsula

Surrounded on three sides by inlets, coves and rocky stacks, St Davids is an easy base for some excellent walking around **St Davids peninsula**. A mile south, the popular

Caerfai Bay provides a sandy beach in the purple sandstone cliffs – rock which was used in the construction of the cathedral.

St Non's Bay and Porth Clais

Immediately south of St Davids (reached by Goat St), the craggy indentation of **St Non's Bay** is where St Non reputedly gave birth to St David during a tumultuous storm around 500 AD. The bay has received pilgrims for centuries, resulting in the foundation of a tiny, isolated **chapel** in the pre-Norman age; the ruins of the later thirteenth-century chapel now lie in a field near the sadly dingy well and coy shrine marking the birthplace of the nation's patron saint.

14

Just west of St Non's, **Porth Clais** is supposedly where St David was baptized by a bishop with the unlikely name of St Elvis. This was the city's main harbour from Roman times, its remains still visible at the bottom of the turquoise creek. Today, commercial traffic has long gone, replaced by fishing boats and dinghies.

Whitesands Bay

From **St Justinians**, two miles west of St Davids, the coast path leads north over another lowly headland to the magnificent **Whitesands Bay** (Porth Mawr), a narrow arc of dune-backed sand that's popular with both surfers and families alike, and is also accessible by road from St Davids. From here though, there's no further road access to the coast for some distance, giving this section of the coast path a thoroughly untamed feel, and making it perfect for wildlife-watching.

ACCOMMODATION   ST DAVIDS PENINSULA

★ **Crug Glâs** Abereiddi, 4 miles northeast of St Davids off the A487, SA62 6XX ☎01348 831302, ⓦcrug-glas.co.uk. Luxurious country house on a working farm. Breakfasts are excellent (great bacon) and dinners are very classy, with starters such as Abercastle crab cake and mains such as cannon of lamb, plus a good long wine list. **£150**

Glan-Y-Mor Caerfai Rd, 0.5 mile south of St Davids, SA62 6QT ☎01437 721788, ⓦglan-y-mor.co.uk. The nearest campsite to town, with bookings and transfers offered for surfing lessons. Closed Oct–March. **£14**

Ramsey House Lower Moor, on the road from St Davids to Porth Clais, SA62 6RP ☎01437 720321, ⓦramseyhouse.co.uk. Quality B&B with six boutique-style rooms and excellent breakfasts (featuring eggs from their own hens and ducks). They also have a bar. Closed Dec–Feb. **£100**

YHA St Davids Llaethdy, 2 miles northwest of St Davids near Whitesands Bay, SA62 6PR ☎0345 371 9141, ⓦyha.org.uk/hostel/st-davids. Large, renovated hostel in a former farmhouse. Daytime lockout and 11pm curfew. Closed Nov–March. Dorms **£15**, doubles **£50**

EATING

Grub Kitchen Dr Beynon's Bug Farm, Lower Harglodd Farm, a mile northeast of St Davids, SA62 6BX ☎07986 698169, ⓦgrubkitchen.co.uk. As flagship of the movement for entomophagy, or eating insects (as part of a drive to reduce the global environmental impact of producing more and more meat), this quirky restaurant serves dishes such as cricket-flour cookies and bug burgers, as well as more standard offerings – vegetarian, vegan and sustainable, local lamb and beef. There's also a fun museum and bug zoo. Bookings required for dinner. School hols Mon–Thurs & Sun 10.30am–4.30pm, Fri & Sat 10.30am–4.30pm & 6–9.30pm; rest of year Sat & Sun 10.30am–4.30pm & 6–9.30pm.

RAMSEY ISLAND

The harbour at St Justinians has a ticket hut for the boats over to **Ramsey Island**. This enchanting dual-humped plateau, less than two miles long, has been under the RSPB's able stewardship since 1992. Birds of prey circle above the island, but it's better known for the tens of thousands of seabirds that noisily crowd the cliffs on its western side and the seals lazing sloppily about. Thousand Islands Expeditions **boat trips** (April–Oct daily; £18; ☎01437 721721, ⓦthousandislands.co.uk) allow up to six hours on Ramsey. During the springtime nesting season you actually see more from boats that circle the island but don't land: try Voyages of Discovery (daily; £25; ☎01437 721911, ⓦramseyisland.co.uk).

Fishguard

From St Davids peninsula the main road runs northeast, parallel to numerous small and less-commercialized bays, to the wild and windswept **Strumble Head**, perhaps the best place in Wales for watching seabirds. This protects **FISHGUARD** (Abergwaun), an attractive, hilltop town mainly of interest as the port for the **ferries** to and from Rosslare in Ireland. It's often grouped into one community with neighbouring **GOODWICK**, where Fishguard Harbour ferry terminal is actually located.

In the centre of town is the **Royal Oak Inn**, where a bizarre Franco-Irish attempt to conquer Britain in 1797 at nearby Carregwastad Point is remembered. Having landed in the wrong place and then got hopelessly drunk, the hapless forces surrendered after two days. This was supposedly triggered by the sight of a hundred local women marching towards them. Due to their stovepipe hats and red flannel shawls they mistook them for British infantry and instantly capitulated. Even if this is not true, it is undisputed that 47-year-old cobbler's wife Jemima Nicholas, the "Welsh Heroine", single-handedly captured fourteen French soldiers with nothing but a pitchfork. Her grave can be seen next to the uninspiring Victorian church, **St Mary's**, behind the pub. The fabulous **Fishguard Tapestry**, telling the story of this ramshackle invasion, hangs in the town hall across the road (April–Sept Mon–Wed & Fri 9.30am–5pm, Thurs 9.30am–6pm, Sat 9.30am–4pm; Oct–March closes 1pm on Sat; free).

ARRIVAL AND INFORMATION

By train Trains call at Fishguard & Goodwick station on Station Hill in Goodwick and terminate at Fishguard Harbour on Quay Rd.
Destinations Cardiff (6 daily; 2hr 40min); Carmarthen (7 daily; 50min); Swansea (7 daily; 1hr 50min).
By bus Buses stop in the central Market Square, right outside Fishguard's tourist office, and on Station Hill in Goodwick, 0.5 mile from the ferry terminal.

Destinations Cardigan (hourly; 40min); Haverfordwest (hourly; 40min); Newport, Pembrokeshire (hourly; 15min); St Davids (6–8 daily; 45min).
By ferry Fishguard Harbour, for ferries to Rosslare, Ireland (2 daily; 3hr 30min), is on Quay Rd in Goodwick.
Tourist office Town hall, Market Square (June–Aug Mon–Fri 9am–5pm, Sat 10am–4pm; Sept–May Mon–Fri 9am–1pm & 1.45–5pm; ☎01347 776636).

GETTING AROUND

By bus Occasional buses to Fishguard (Mon–Sat) stop across the road from Fishguard & Goodwick station.

By taxi A taxi (☎01348 873075) into Fishguard costs about £4 from the harbour.

ACCCOMMODATION

Cefn-y-Dre A mile south, along Hamilton St, SA65 9QS ☎01348 875663, ⓦcefnydre.co.uk. There's a relaxed and understated elegance to this lovely country house. Just three rooms, attractive grounds, tasty breakfasts, and superb home-cooked meals (reserve in advance; not high season) prepared by wonderful hosts. **£90**

Hamilton Lodge 21–23 Hamilton St, SA65 9HL ☎01348 874797, ⓦhamiltonbackpackers.co.uk. Cosy, very central and well-set-up hostel with rooms for two, three and four (light breakfast included), a private double and self-catering for groups in the old chapel next door. Bed linen provided; towels can be rented. Dorms **£20**, double **£49**

EATING AND DRINKING

Pepper's aka Café Celf 16 West St, SA65 9AE ☎01348 873867, ⓦpeppers-hub.co.uk. Arty café that's great for tapas or a bistro meal. Mains (£15–18) might include lamb meatballs or chicken with saffron, almonds, raisins and spices. They offer popular music nights, too. Mon–Sat 10am–10.30pm.
Royal Oak Market Square, SA65 9HA ☎01348 872514, ⓦfacebook.com/trofishguard. Historic pub with real ales and good pub lunches. There's a long-established folk

night on Tues – participants very welcome. Mon–Thurs & Sun 11am–12.30am, Fri & Sat 11am–1.30am; kitchen daily noon–4pm.
Ship Inn 3 Newport Rd, Lower Town, SA65 9ND ☎01348 874033. Eccentric, unmissable pub with interesting clutter all over the walls and ceiling, including black-and-white photos of the filming of *Under Milk Wood* and *Moby Dick* in Fishguard. Daily noon–midnight.

14

Newport

NEWPORT (Trefdraeth) is an ancient and proud little town set on a gentle slope leading down to the Nevern estuary. There's little to do except stroll around, but you'd be hard pressed to find a better place to do it. The footpath that runs along the river either side of the bridge is marked as the Pilgrims' Way; follow it east for a delightful riverbank stroll to Nevern, a couple of miles away. Another popular local walk is up to the craggy and magical peak of **Carn Ingli**, the Hill of Angels, behind the town.

Newport's nearest beach, the **Parrog**, is complete with sandy stretches at low tide. On the other side of the estuary is the vast dune-backed **Traeth Mawr beach**. Newport also makes a good jumping-off point for **Pentre Ifan**, a couple of miles south, with its massive, 4000-year-old capstone.

14

ARRIVAL AND INFORMATION

NEWPORT

By bus Buses stop on Bridge St in the centre of town. Destinations Cardigan (hourly; 20min); Fishguard (hourly; 15min); Haverfordwest (hourly; 1hr).

Tourist office The National Park tourist office is on Long St (☎ 01239 820912), but was closed at the time of research.

ACCOMMODATION

The Globe Upper St Mary St, SA42 0PS ☎ 01239 820296, ⓦ theglobebedandbreakfast.co.uk. About the cheapest around, with shared bathroom and a pleasant garden; continental breakfast included. **£73**

Morawelon The Parrog, 300yd northwest of town, SA42 0RW ☎ 01239 820565, ⓦ campsite-pembrokeshire.co.uk. Seaside campsite nicely set in pleasant gardens and with its own café overlooking the beach, and coin-op showers. Closed Nov–Feb. **£18**

YHA Newport Lower St Mary St, SA42 0TS ☎ 0345 371 9543, ⓦ yha.org.uk/hostel/newport-pembrokeshire. This classily converted school has dorms and a couple of private rooms; self-catering only. Closed Oct–March. Dorms **£15**, doubles **£78**

EATING AND DRINKING

Golden Lion East St, SA42 0SY ☎ 01239 820321, ⓦ goldenlionpembrokeshire.co.uk. Nice old pub with bare stone walls and timber beams; along with real ales, they serve a superb menu of carefully prepared pub meals (£12) and fancier restaurant-style dishes (£13–22), either in the bar or more formally at the back. Daily noon–midnight; kitchen noon–2pm & 6–9pm.

★ **Llys Meddyg** East St, SA42 0SY ☎ 01239 820008, ⓦ llysmeddyg.com. A Georgian dining room, a cellar bar and a partly walled kitchen garden (July & Aug) provide settings for exquisite dinners, which might start with crab with green apple and fennel (£9) followed by fish stew or local lamb with asparagus (£16). Lunches are no less appealing. April–Sept Tues–Sat noon–3pm & 6–9pm, Sun noon–3pm; Oct–March Wed–Sat noon–3pm & 6–9pm.

Mid-Wales

BRECON BEACONS NATIONAL PARK

Mid-Wales

Mid-Wales is a huge, beautiful region, crisscrossed by mountain passes, dotted with characterful little towns and never far from water – whether sparkling rivers, great lakes or the sea of the Cambrian coast. This is the least-known part of Wales, and it's here that you'll find Welsh culture at its most authentic, folded into the contours of the land as it has been for centuries. By far the most popular attraction is the Brecon Beacons National Park, stretching from the dramatic limestone country of the Black Mountain (singular) in the west through to the English border beyond the Black Mountains. The best bases are the tiny city of Brecon or the market towns of Abergavenny and Hay-on-Wye, the former a foodie paradise, the latter a must for bibliophiles.

15

North of the Beacons lie the old spa towns of Radnorshire, the most enjoyable of which are **Llanwrtyd Wells**, known throughout the land for its eccentric events, and **Llandrindod Wells**. The quiet countryside to the north, crossed by spectacular mountain roads such as the **Abergwesyn Pass** from Llanwrtyd, is barely populated, dotted with ancient churches and introspective villages. In the east, the border town of **Knighton** is the home of the flourishing **Offa's Dyke Path** industry. Like many country towns in Mid-Wales, beautiful **Llanidloes** has a healthy stock of old hippies among its population, contributing to a thriving arts and crafts community and a relaxed atmosphere. **Montgomeryshire** is the northern portion of Powys, similarly underpopulated and remote. Its largest town, **Welshpool**, is home to Powis Castle, one of the country's finest fortresses.

The enduringly popular **Cambrian coast** stretches from Cardigan up to Harlech, starting off with cliff-top paths and small sandy coves that give way to wide sandy beaches around higgledy-piggledy **New Quay** and neat, Georgian **Aberaeron**. The beguiling "capital" of Mid-Wales, **Aberystwyth**, is a great mix of seaside resort, university city and market town backed by the Vale of Rheidol Railway to **Devil's Bridge**. Further north, **Machynlleth** revels in beaches, mountains and the showpiece **Centre for Alternative Technology**. Beyond the great mountain massif of **Cadair Idris**, the beautiful **Mawddach estuary** leads to Dolgellau, a base for mountain biking in **Coed-y-Brenin** and the first of the huge North Wales castles at **Harlech**.

GETTING AROUND

By train Services are restricted to the Heart of Wales line from Shrewsbury to Swansea via Knighton, Llandrindod Wells, Llanwrtyd Wells and smaller stops in between; and the Cambrian line, from Shrewsbury to Machynlleth via Welshpool. At Machynlleth, the line splits, with one heading south to Aberystwyth, the other going north along the coast to Llŷn.

By bus Buses plug virtually all of the gaps not covered by train, though you'll find just a few daily services between some towns, and occasionally none at all on Sun. One of the most useful long-distance buses is the #T4 (Mon–Sat), which runs from Cardiff up through the heart of Powys, calling in at Brecon and Llandrindod Wells along the way. Along the coast, the most useful route is the

BOG SNORKELLING, LLANWRTYD WELLS

Highlights

❶ Brecon Beacons National Park Trek to your heart's content among these wild, rambling moors, with dozens of thundering waterfalls. See page 686

❷ Abergavenny food Some of Wales' finest restaurants, along with a lip-smacking food festival. See page 691

❸ Llanwrtyd Wells Bizarre events galore, notably the Man versus Horse Marathon, the World Bog Snorkelling Championships and the Real Ale Wobble. See page 693

❹ New Quay Follow Dylan Thomas's footsteps through the salty seaside town that inspired *Under Milk Wood*. See page 704

❺ Aberaeron Even if you're not in town for Aberaeron's Seafood Festival, stroll around its colourful Georgian harbour lined by great places to sleep and eat. See page 704

❻ Aberystwyth A lively, seaside university town, steeped in Welsh culture. See page 705

❼ Bwlch Nant yr Arian Visit mid-afternoon to see dozens of red kites squabbling over a heap of beef and lamb; it's a remarkable sight. See page 709

❽ Harlech Castle The glorious views across to the Llŷn peninsula are as good a reason as any to visit Harlech's hulking castle. See page 713

HIGHLIGHTS ARE MARKED ON THE MAP ON PAGE 684

MID-WALES

HIGHLIGHTS

1. Brecon Beacons National Park
2. Abergavenny food
3. Llanwrtyd Wells
4. New Quay
5. Aberaeron
6. Aberystwyth
7. Bwlch Nant yr Arian
8. Harlech Castle

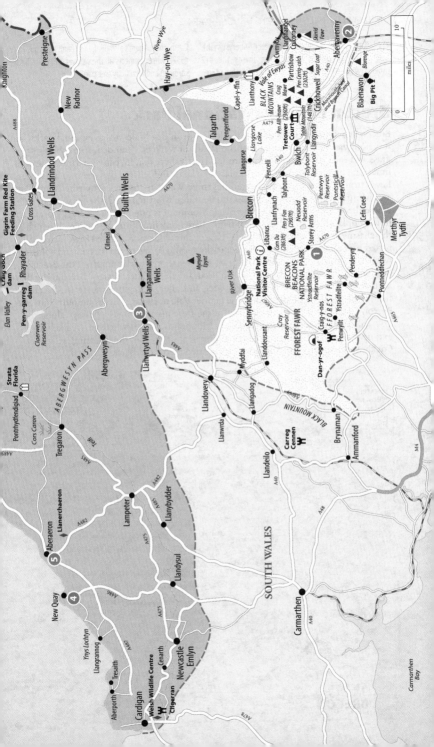

#T1 (Carmarthen–Lampeter–Aberaeron–Aberystwyth), while heading up into North Wales there's the #T2 (Aberystwyth–Machynlleth–Dolgellau–Porthmadog–Caernarfon). There's also the handy Cardi Bach bus (service #552), which connects all the villages and coves between Cardigan and New Quay (see page 704).

Brecon Beacons National Park

Brecon Beacons National Park has the lowest profile of Wales' three national parks, but it is nonetheless the destination of thousands of walkers. Rounded, spongy hills of grass and rock tumble and climb around river valleys that lie between sandstone and limestone uplands, peppered with glass-like lakes and villages that seem to have been hewn from one rock. The park straddles three Welsh counties: Carmarthenshire, Powys and Monmouthshire, covering 520 square miles. Most remote is the far western side, where the vast, open terrain of the Black Mountain is punctuated by craggy peaks and hidden upland lakes. The southern flanks bare bony limestone ribs, beneath which are the chasms of the **Dan-yr-ogof caves**. East of this wilderness, **Fforest Fawr** forms miles of tufted moorland tumbling down to a rocky terrain of rivers, deep caves and spluttering waterfalls around **Ystradfellte**. The heart of the national park comprises the **Brecon Beacons** themselves, a pair of 2900ft hills and their satellites. East of Brecon, the **Black Mountains** stretch over the English border, and offer the region's most varied scenery, from rolling upland wilderness to the gentler **Vale of Ewyas**. The **Monmouthshire and Brecon Canal** defines the eastern limit of the Beacons and forges a passage along the Usk Valley between them and the Black Mountains. This is where you're likely to end up staying, in towns such as the county seat of **Brecon**, the charming village of **Crickhowell**, or sprightly **Abergavenny**, nestled below the Black Mountains.

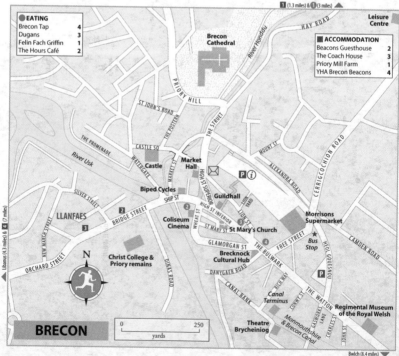

THE CENTRAL BEACONS NEAR BRECON

Popular for walking and pony trekking, the central **Brecon Beacons**, grouped around the two highest peaks in the national park, are easily accessible from Brecon, which lies just six miles to the north. The panorama fans out from the **Brecon Beacons National Park Visitor Centre** (Mon–Thurs 9.30am–4.30pm, Fri–Sun 9.30am–5pm; ☎01874 623366, ⊚breconbeacons.org), on a windy ridge just off the A470 turn-off at Libanus, six miles southwest of Brecon. **Pen y Fan** (2907ft) is the highest peak in the Beacons. Together with **Corn Du** (2863ft), a mile or so to the west, they form the most popular ascents in the park. **The Brecon Beacons Park Society** (⊚breconbeaconsparksociety.org) organizes walks and events each summer; particularly useful if you don't fancy going it solo.

Brecon

A handsome county town at the northern edge of the central Beacons, **BRECON** (Aberhonddu) offers a proliferation of fine Georgian buildings, while its proximity to the hills and lakes of the national park make it a popular stopping-off place and a good base for day-walks in the well-waymarked hills to the south.

15

Regimental Museum of the Royal Welsh

The Watton, LD3 7EB • April–July & Sept Mon–Fri 10am–5pm, Sat 10am–4pm; Aug Mon–Fri 10am–5pm, Sat & Sun 10am–4pm; Oct–March Mon–Fri 10am–5pm • £5 • ☎01874 613310, ⊚royalwelsh.org.uk

Beyond the foreboding frontage of the South Wales Borderers' **barracks** is the **Regimental Museum of the Royal Welsh**, packed with mementos from the regiment's 330 years existence. As well as an extraordinary stash of guns and medals, there's comprehensive coverage of campaigns in Burma, the Napoleonic and Boer wars and both World Wars, as well as more recent operations in Northern Ireland, Iraq and Afghanistan. More absorbing, though, is the room devoted entirely to the 1879 Zulu War when 140 Welsh soldiers faced an attack by four thousand Zulu warriors at Rorke's Drift.

Brecon Cathedral

Cathedral Close, Priory Hill, LD3 9DP • Daily 8.30am–6.30pm; lunchtime recitals Mon 1pm • Free • ☎01874 623857, ⊚breconcathedral.org.uk

From the town centre crossroads, High Street Superior goes north, becoming The Struet, running alongside the rushing waters of the Honddu. Off to the left, a footpath climbs up to the **Brecon Cathedral**, whose lofty interior, framed by a magnificent timber roof, is graced with a few Norman features from the eleventh century, including a hulking font. More impressive is the **Cresset Stone**, a concrete boulder indented with thirty scoops in which to place oil or wax candles. The mid-sixteenth-century **Games Monument**, in the southern aisle, is made of oak and depicts a woman whose identity remains uncertain; her hands are clasped in prayer but her arms and nose appear to have been unceremoniously hacked off.

ARRIVAL AND INFORMATION

BRECON

By bus Buses stop above the car park on Heol Gouesnou. Destinations Abergavenny (Mon–Sat hourly; 40min–1hr); Cardiff (Mon–Sat 7 daily; 1hr 50min); Craig-y-nos/Dan-yr-ogof (Mon–Sat hourly, Sun 5; 40min); Crickhowell (Mon–Sat hourly; 30–50min); Hay-on-Wye (7 daily; 40min); Libanus (Mon–Sat hourly, Sun 2; 15min); Llandrindod Wells (Mon–Sat 7 daily, Sun 1; 1hr).

Tourist office In the car park off Lion St (Mon–Sat 9.30am–5pm, Sun 10am–4pm; ☎01874 622485, ⊚breconbeacons.org); its vast stock of material includes a good range of walking maps.

ACCOMMODATION

Beacons Guesthouse 16 Bridge St, Llanfaes, LD3 8AH • ☎01874 623339, ⊚thebreconbeacons.co.uk; map p.686. Converted townhouse concealing a large number of run-of-the-mill, but fairly priced, rooms (some with shared showers), all leading off a central spiral staircase. **£63**

The Coach House 12/13 Orchard St, Llanfaes, LD3 8AN ☎01874 620043, ⦿coachhousebrecon.com; map p.686. High-class and very hospitable guesthouse with rooms furnished with designer accessories. Great Welsh breakfasts, including vegetarian options. **£80**

Priory Mill Farm Hay Rd, LD3 7SR ☎01874 611609, ⦿priorymillfarm.co.uk; map p.686. Lovely, low-key riverside campsite, with wooden cabins for showers and trays for log fires. It's on the northern edge of town, reached by a 10min walk along the riverbank. Closed Nov– Feb. Per person **£8**

YHA Brecon Beacons 7 miles southwest of Brecon, near Libanus, LD3 8NH ☎01874 624261, ⦿yha.org. uk/hostel/brecon-beacons; map p.686. Traditional farmhouse hostel surrounded by woodland and overlooking the River Tarell, just off the A470 and main bus route to Merthyr. Variously sized dorms, en-suite doubles and, up behind the hostel, two wooden pods sleeping four, as well as a wild woodland campsite. Nov–Feb closed Mon & Tues. Camping/person **£11**, dorms **£13**, doubles **£50**, pods **£89**

EATING

Brecon Tap 6 Bulwark, LD3 7LB ☎01874 623888, ⦿breconinns.co.uk; map p.686. Cheerfully informal restaurant/bar owned by the local Brecon Brewing company. As well as a superb range of beers, including the core keg ales Golden Brecon and Three Beacons, they've got scrummy pies (Moroccan lamb, for example), which you get with a choice of two sides, perhaps mustard mash and roasted root veg (£9.75). Mon–Sat 11am–11pm, Sun noon–11pm; kitchen daily noon–3pm & 6–9pm.

Dugans 7 Pegasus Lane, LD3 7BH ☎01874 623113, ⦿dugans.co.uk; map p.686. Cracking patisserie with a home-spun interior of oak flooring, kitchen-style tables and chairs and artwork splashed across the whitewashed walls. The food, be it savoury (leek, cheese and walnut quiche £7.50) or sweet (salted caramel and pear tart, or rolled apple and cinnamon strudel, £2.80), tastes just as good as it looks. Mon 10am–5pm, Tues–Sat 9am–5pm.

★ **Felin Fach Griffin** Felin Fach, A470, 3 miles northwest, LD3 0UB ☎01874 620111, ⦿eatdrinksleep. ltd.uk; map p.686. Super pub/restaurant offering some of the finest Modern Welsh cuisine anywhere in the region; scrumptious dishes might include silver mullet with confit potato and Savoy cabbage, or smoked ox tongue with pickled red cabbage, horseradish and beetroot. Three-course set menu £29. Beyond the restaurant is the pubby bit, a tiny bar fronting a couple of farmhouse tables laden with newspapers, crumpled leather sofas and a crackling log fire. Daily 11am–11pm; kitchen noon–2.30pm & 6–9pm.

The Hours Café 15 Ship St, LD3 9AD ☎01874 622800, ⦿the-hours.co.uk; map p.686. Cheerful daytime café-cum-bookshop, with sloping floors and black timber beams, where you can enjoy warm salads and toasted sandwiches, hearty soups, cakes and a good range of Fairtrade coffees. Tues–Sat 10am–5pm.

Fforest Fawr

Covering a vast expanse west of the central Brecon Beacons, the **Fforest Fawr** (Great Forest) seems something of a misnomer for an area of largely unforested sandstone hills dropping down to a porous limestone belt in the south. The name, however, refers to its former status as a hunting area. The hills rise up to the south of the A40, west of Brecon, with the dramatic A4067 defining the western side of the range and the A470 dividing it from the central Beacons.

Ystradfellte and around

In the heart of the Brecon Beacons, a twisting mountain road crosses a bleak plateau and descends into one of Britain's classic limestone landscapes. The hamlet of **YSTRADFELLTE** is hugely popular for its walks over great pavements of bone-white rock next to cradling potholes, disappearing rivers and crashing **waterfalls**. At **Sgwd Clun Gwyn** (White Meadow Fall), the river crashes 50ft over two large, angular steps of rock before hurtling down the course for a few hundred yards to two more falls – the impressive **Sgwd Isaf Clun Gwyn** (Lower White Meadow Fall) and, around the wooded corner, the **Sgwd y Pannwr** (Fall of the Fuller). A little further along the Hepste is **Sgwd yr Eira** (Fall of Snow), whose rock below the main tumble has eroded, allowing access behind a dramatic 20ft curtain of water.

Dan-yr-ogof Showcaves

Glyntawe, just west of A4067, SA9 1GJ • April–Oct daily 10am–3.30pm • £15 • ☎01639 730284, ⦿showcaves.co.uk

Six miles of upland forest and grass-covered mountains lie between Ystradfellte and the **Dan-yr-ogof Showcaves** to the west. Discovered in 1912, they are claimed to form the largest system of subterranean caverns in northern Europe. The path leads you into the **Dan-yr-ogof** cave, framed by stalactites and frothy limestone deposits, from where you'll be steered around a circular route of about a mile and a half. Back outside, you pass a re-created Iron Age "village" and walk past some of the many life-size fibreglass dinosaurs lurking within the forested hillside to reach **Cathedral Cave**, an impressive 150ft-long, 70ft-high cave inside of which are two 65ft-high waterfalls. Reached via a precarious path is **Bone Cave**, the third and final cavern, known to have been inhabited by Bronze Age tribes.

Penderyn Welsh Whisky Distillery

Penderyn, CF44 0SX • Guided tours only (hourly; 1hr) daily 9.30am–5pm • £8.50, prebooking advised • ☎ 01685 810650, ⓦ penderyn.wales

On the southern fringes of the national park, in the village of **PENDERYN, Penderyn Welsh Whisky Distillery** is the only working distillery in the country. Today it produces three single malt whiskies, matured in bourbon barrels and finished in Madeira wine casks. **Guided tours** take in an exhibition on the working of the distillery, an explanation of the distillation and bottling processes and, of course, a taster at the end. Uniquely, the process here involves the use of a single copper pot still – as opposed to the conventional two or three – before the whisky is matured for between four and seven years.

15

Black Mountains

The easternmost section of the national park centres on the **Black Mountains**, far quieter than the central belt of the Brecon Beacons and skirted by the wide valley of the River Usk to the south and the Wye to the north. The only exception to the range's unremitting sandstone is an isolated outcrop of limestone, long divorced from the southern belt, that peaks north of Crickhowell at Pen Cerrig-calch. The Black Mountains have the feel of a landscape only partly tamed by human habitation: tiny villages, isolated churches and enchanting lanes are folded into an undulating green landscape that levels out to the south around the village of **Crickhowell**.

Crickhowell

Compact **CRICKHOWELL** (Crug Hywel) lies on the northern bank of the wide and shallow Usk. Apart from a grand seventeenth-century **bridge**, with thirteen arches visible from the eastern end and only twelve from the west, spawning many a local myth, there's not much to see in town. That said, it is a hugely popular destination for walkers, especially at the end of February during the annual **Walking Festival** (ⓦ crickhowellfestival.com); it's also the setting for the country's premier music gathering, the **Green Man Festival** (ⓦ greenman.net).

Table Mountain (1481ft) provides a spectacular northern backdrop, topped by the remains of the 2500-year-old hillfort (*crug*) of Hywel, accessed on a path past The Wern, off Llanbedr Road. Many walkers follow a route north from Table Mountain, climbing two miles up to the plateau-topped limestone hump of **Pen Cerrig-calch** (2302ft) and on to **Pen Allt-mawr** (2360ft) from where a circular route can be completed.

ARRIVAL AND INFORMATION

CRICKHOWELL

By bus Buses run from the main square at the top of the High St.
Destinations Abergavenny (Mon–Sat hourly; 20min); Brecon (Mon–Sat hourly; 30–50min).

Tourist office The Crickhowell Resource and Information Centre on Beaufort St (Mon–Sat 10am–5pm, Sun 10am–1.30pm; ☎ 01873 811970, ⓦ visitcrickhowell.co.uk) also has a café and a gallery selling quality local art.

ACCOMMODATION AND EATING

Bear Hotel Beaufort St, NP8 1BW ☎ 01873 810408, ⓦ bearhotel.co.uk. A grand old coaching inn whose

architectural quirks have lent themselves to some idiosyncratic rooms. Those in the hotel itself possess more character, while those in the old courtyard stables are a touch more polished. **£107**

★ **Book-ish** 18 High St, NP8 1BD ☎ 01873 811256, ⓦ book-ish.co.uk. If you like books and coffee, this enthusiastically run indie bookshop-cum-café should be your first port of call. Once done browsing head through to the rear and the light-filled mezzanine, where you can kick back with a book and a brew, or perhaps a glass of wine. Lots of literary and musical events, too. Mon–Sat 9am–5.30pm, Sun 10am–4pm.

Bridge End Inn Bridge St, NP8 1AR ☎ 01873 810338, ⓦ thebridgeendinn.com. Comprising part of the town's former tollhouse, this is a truly old-fashioned pub with flagstone flooring, a stone fireplace and brass, copper pots hanging from the walls and ceilings, and a sweet riverside garden. Daily 11am–11.30pm.

Dragon Inn 47 High St , NP8 1BE ☎ 01873 810362, ⓦ dragoninncrickhowell.com. Salmon-pink building at the quieter, far end of the High St, with sharply furnished rooms sporting silver and grey trimmings, wall-length mirrors and Welsh art. Relaxing, friendly and great for families. **£85**

Abergavenny

Flanking the Brecon Beacons National Park, **ABERGAVENNY** (Y Fenni), seven miles southeast of Crickhowell, is a busy and breezy market town which people flock to primarily for its outstanding cuisine – this reaches its zenith during the September **Food Festival**. The town is also a useful base for walkers bound for the local mountains: **Sugar Loaf**, the **Blorenge** and the legendary **Skirrid Mountain** (Ysgyryd Fawr). Stretching north from town, the **Vale of Ewyas** runs along the foot of the Black Mountains, where the astounding churches at Partrishow and Cwmyoy are lost in rural isolation.

The castle and Abergavenny Museum

Castle St, NP7 5EE • 10am–4pm: July–Sept daily; Oct–June Mon, Tues & Thurs–Sun • Free • ☎ 01873 854282, ⓦ abergavennymuseum.co.uk

From the train station, Monmouth Road rises gently, eventually becoming High Street, off which you'll find the fragmented remains of the medieval **castle**. Entrance is through the sturdy, though now roofless, gatehouse, to the right of which stands an extensive portion of the curtain wall. The old Victorian keep now houses the **Abergavenny Museum**, which displays ephemera from the town's history. Glorious views aside, the grounds are a lovely spot for a picnic.

Church of St Mary

Monk St, NP7 5ND • Mon–Sat 9am–4pm • Free • ☎ 01873 858787, ⓦ stmarys-priory.org

Abergavenny's **Church of St Mary** contains some superb detail, not least the **Jesse Tree**, one of the finest late medieval sculptures in Britain. Tombs here span the entire medieval period, including those of Sir William ap Thomas, founder of Raglan Castle, and Dr David Lewis (died 1584), the first Principal of Jesus College, as well as effigies of members of the notorious de Braose family.

Tithe Barn

Monk St, NP7 5ND • Mon–Sat 9am–4pm • Free • ☎ 01873 858787, ⓦ stmarys-priory.org

Adjacent to the church is the splendidly restored fourteenth-century **Tithe Barn**, which in times past has variously functioned as a coach house, a theatre for travelling actors and even a disco. It's now a heritage centre, with a good exhibition on the history of Abergavenny; star sight is the **Abergavenny Tapestry**, an expansive, brightly coloured visual record of the town's past.

ARRIVAL AND INFORMATION

By train The station is a 5min walk southeast of town on Station Rd.

Destinations Cardiff (every 30min–1hr; 45–55min); Hereford (every 30–45min; 25min); Newport (every 30min–1hr; 30min).

By bus Buses depart from Swan Meadows bus station, at the bottom of town on Cross St.

Destinations Brecon (Mon–Sat hourly; 40min–1hr); Cardiff (Mon–Sat hourly, Sun 2; 1hr 40min–2hr 30min); Crickhowell (Mon–Sat hourly; 20min); Llanfihangel Crucorney (Mon–Sat 7 daily; 15min); Monmouth (Mon–Sat 7 daily, Sun 4; 45min); Raglan (Mon–Sat 7 daily, Sun 4; 35min).

Tourist office Tithe Barn, Monk St (Mon–Sat: April–Oct 10am–4pm; Nov–March 10am–2pm; ☎01873 853254, ⓦvisitabergavenny.co.uk).

Bike rental Hopyard Cycles in Govilon, a couple of miles west (☎01873 830219, ⓦhopyardcycles.co.uk; mountain bikes from £15/day), can deliver bikes (for a small charge) throughout the area.

ACCOMMODATION

★ **Angel Hotel** 15 Cross St, NP7 5EN ☎01873 857121, ⓦangelhotelabergavenny.com. Occupying an old coaching inn, Abergavenny's premier central hotel is a warren of corridors with a range of very classy rooms fitted out in soft beige, with plush carpets, big comfy beds and large bathrooms replete with posh toiletries. **£105**

Black Sheep Backpackers 24 Station Rd, NP7 5HS ☎01873 859125, ⓦgreatwesternabergavenny.com. A few paces down from the station, this converted railway hotel has accommodation in four- to ten-bed dorms (with shared showers), as well as en-suite doubles. There are self-catering facilities and a laundrette across the road. Continental breakfast included. Dorms **£17.50**, doubles **£60**

Kings Arms 29 Neville St, NP7 5AA ☎01873 855074, ⓦkingsarmsabergavenny.co.uk. Limewash beams, bare, sloping wood floors and low, crooked doorways are all quirky features of this pleasing, sixteenth-century coaching inn. The neatly conceived pod-like bathrooms, meanwhile, feature roll-top or jacuzzi baths. **£105**

Pyscodlyn Farm Llanwenarth Citra, 2 miles west of town off A40, NP7 7ER ☎01873 853271, ⓦpyscodlyncaravanpark.com. Easy to reach – all Brecon and Crickhowell buses pass by – this is primarily a caravan site, but there is one sheltered field for campers, with separate shower blocks for males and females. Closed Nov to mid-March. **£14**

EATING AND DRINKING

★ **Art Shop & Chapel** Market St, NP7 5EH ☎01873 736430, ⓦartshopandgallery.co.uk. Occupying the basement of an old nineteenth-century chapel, this artistically decorated gallery-cum-café makes for a splendid late breakfast or lunch stop; try Turkish eggs with chorizo and yoghurt, or Welsh rarebit with leek and rhubarb ketchup on sourdough (£7.80). They also serve terrific homemade cordials, craft ales and biodynamic wines. Tues–Sat 10am–5pm.

The Foxhunter Nantyderry, 7 miles southeast of town, NP7 9DN ☎01873 881101, ⓦthefoxhunter. com. Named after a locally bred, 1952 Olympic-gold-medal winning horse, this lovingly restored former stationmaster's house is now a comely pub and restaurant; it's nothing flash or fiery, but dishes such as sirloin with stilton sauce and roasted field mushrooms (£19) are tremendously satisfying. Pub Mon 5.30–11pm, Tues–

Thurs 11.30am–3pm & 5.30–11pm, Fri–Sun 11.30am–11pm; kitchen Mon 6–9pm, Tues–Sat noon–3pm & 6–9pm, Sun noon–4pm.

The Hardwick Old Raglan Rd, 2 miles east of town, NP7 9AA ☎01873 854220, ⓦthehardwick.co.uk. Headed up by chef Stephen Terry, this fabulous-looking pub offers a choice of brilliantly simple but fantastically presented dishes such as deep-fried pork belly and black pudding with pickled fennel and apple and mustard sauce (£18). The Sun three-course lunch is superb value at £28. Pub daily 11am–11pm; kitchen noon–3pm & 6.30–10pm.

Trading Post 14 Neville St, NP7 5AD ☎01873 855448, ⓦtradingpostcatering.co.uk. The former eighteenth-century *Cow Inn* – cast your eyes up to the row of cows' heads on the front of the building – is now a sprightly café, and an ideal spot for poring over the paper while sipping a cappuccino or tucking into Welsh rarebit. Mon–Sat 9am–5pm.

Vale of Ewyas

The main A465 Hereford road leads six miles north out of Abergavenny to Llanfihangel Crucorney, where the B4423 diverges off to the north into the enchanting **Vale of Ewyas** along the banks of the Honddu river. In **LLANFIHANGEL CRUCORNEY**, the reputedly haunted **Skirrid Inn** was first mentioned in 1110 and is thus thought to be the oldest pub in Wales. It's said that some 180 people were hanged here during the seventeenth century; you can still see the beam that bears the scorch marks of the rope. It's an atmospheric spot for a drink.

Llanthony Priory

Llanthony, NP7 7NN • Daily 10am–4pm • Free • ☎01443 336000, ⓦcadw.gov.wales/daysout/llanthonypriory

Four miles from Llanfihangel Crucorney stand the wide-open ruins of **Llanthony Priory**. The priory was founded in around 1100 by the Norman knight William de Lacy, who, it is said, was so captivated by the spiritual beauty of the site that he renounced worldly living and founded a hermitage, attracting like-minded recluses and forming Wales' first Augustinian priory. The roofless church, with its pointed transitional arches and squat tower, was constructed in the latter half of the twelfth century and retains a sense of spirituality and peace.

Hay-on-Wye

Straddling the Anglo-Welsh border some twenty miles west of Hereford, the hilly little town of **HAY-ON-WYE** has an attractive riverside **setting** and narrow, winding streets lined with an engaging assortment of old stone houses, but is known to most people for one thing – **books**. Hay saw its first bookshop open in 1961; today it has more than thirty, many of which are highly specialized, focusing on areas like travel, poetry or murder mystery. The prestigious **Hay Festival** of literature and the arts (ⓦhayfestival.com), is held over ten days at the end of May, when it seems like the entire literary world decamps here en masse. Running concurrently, the innovative **HowTheLightGetsIn** (ⓦhowthelightgetsin.org) greets some of the world's leading thinkers in music and philosophy.

15

ARRIVAL AND INFORMATION

By bus Buses stop on Oxford Rd, just along from the tourist office.
Destinations Brecon (Mon–Sat 7 daily; 45min); Hereford (Mon–Sat 7 daily, Sun 3; 1hr).
Tourist office Chapel Cottage, Oxford Rd (daily: Easter–

Oct 10am–4.30pm; Nov–Easter 11am–3pm; ☎01497 820144, ⓦhay-on-wye.co.uk). The free booklet *Hay-on-Wye Booksellers, Printsellers & Bookbinders* details the town's bookshops, galleries, restaurants and bars.

ACCOMMODATION

Hay has plenty of accommodation, though prices are a little higher here than in places nearby, and there are no hostels. Everywhere gets **booked up** months in advance for the festival.

Old Black Lion Lion St, HR3 5AD ☎01497 820841, ⓦoldblacklion.co.uk. Very well regarded thirteenth-century inn which has charming en-suite rooms above the pub and in the neighbouring annexe, which are slightly more appealing. **£79**
Radnors End A 10min walk from town across the Hay Bridge on the road to Clyro, HR3 5RS ☎01497 820780, ⓦhay-on-wye.co.uk/radnorsend. Small but neat camping field in a beautiful setting overlooking Hay, with on-site showers and laundry facilities. Closed Nov–Feb. Per person **£7**
Seven Stars 11 Broad St, HR3 5DB ☎01497 820886, ⓦtheseven-stars.co.uk. Former town pub near the clocktower, with eight modest, cosy rooms, some with original oak beams and window frames. There's also an

indoor swimming pool and sauna. **£94**
The Start Hay Bridge, HR3 5RS ☎01497 821391, ⓦthe-start.net. Neatly renovated Georgian house on the riverbank, with three rooms boasting antique furnishings and hand-made quilts. The vegetable garden provides many of the ingredients for the scrummy breakfasts. **£80**
Swan at Hay Church St, HR3 5DQ ☎01497 821188, ⓦswanathay.co.uk. This graceful, pale grey stone Georgian hotel has undergone a recent, impeccable renovation, resulting in nineteen light-filled rooms with beautifully upholstered furnishings and sparkling bathrooms; some rooms have garden views. A lounge and bistro, alongside a couple of snugs and a pretty garden, completes this classy ensemble. **£125**

EATING AND DRINKING

Blue Boar Castle St, HR3 5DF ☎01497 820884. Tasteful, wood-panelled real-ale pub centred around a gently curving bar and two stone fireplaces, with a separate dining area to one side. Daily 9.30am–11pm.
The Granary Broad St, HR3 5DB ☎01497 820790. This unpretentious café-bistro offers a wide range of excellent meals (around £10), with good veggie options. Save space for the wonderful desserts and espresso. Daily

9am–5.30pm.
The Old Stables Tearooms Bear St, HR3 5AN ☎07796 484766, ⓦoldstablestearooms.co.uk. Barely half a dozen tables are crammed into this delightful place, with chalked-up boards listing superb Welsh produce and a fantastic array of teas and home-made tarts. On a warm day, eat in the flower-filled yard. Tues–Sat 11am–5pm.
Shepherd's Ice Cream 9 High Town, HR3 5AE ☎01497

821898. Popular Georgian-style café/ice-cream parlour doling out local ice cream made from sheep's milk; flavours include raspberry cheesecake and banana toffee crunch. Mon–Fri 9am–5.30pm, Sat 9.30am–6pm, Sun 10.30am–5.30pm.

★ **St John's Place** 3 Lion St, HR3 5AA ☎07855 783799, ⓦstjohnsplacehay.tumblr.com. Occupying an old chapel, *St John's* is just a bit special. The menu is essentially whatever takes the fancy of chef Julia Robson, but there are usually three options for each course: to start you might have ox heart with red chilli and coriander, followed by a main of sea trout with shrimp, hispi cabbage and seaweed and, to finish, jasmine pannacotta with strawberries and shortbread. Expect to pay around £30 for three courses. Booking essential. Fri & Sat 6–10pm.

SHOPPING

Hay Cinema Bookshop Old town cinema, Castle St, HR3 5DF ☎01497 820071, ⓦhaycinemabookshop.co.uk. Secondhand, antiquarian and remaindered books across all subjects and at very low prices. Mon–Sat 9am–6pm, Sun 10am–5.30pm.

Richard Booth's Bookshop 44 Lion St, HR3 5AA ☎01497 820322, ⓦboothbooks.co.uk. Just beyond the main square, High Town, this slicked-up, three-storey emporium (despite the name, no longer owned by Booth) offers unlimited browsing potential – every conceivable subject is covered. Incorporated into the rear is the wonderful little Bookshop Cinema, screening arthouse movies at weekends. Mon–Sat 9.30am–5.30pm, Sun 10.30am–5.30pm.

15

The Wells towns

The **spa towns** of Mid-Wales, strung out along the Heart of Wales train line between Swansea and Shrewsbury, were once all obscure villages, but with the arrival of the great craze for spas in the early eighteenth century, anywhere with a decent supply of apparently healing water joined in on the act. Royalty and nobility spearheaded the fashion, but the arrival of the railways opened them to all. Today, the best of the bunch is undoubtedly the westernmost spa of **Llanwrtyd Wells**, hunkered down beneath stunning mountain scenery and renowned for its bizarre special events. **Llandrindod Wells**, the most famous spa, attracted the international elite in its Victorian heyday, and has two excellent museums. In between, the larger town of **Builth Wells** was very much the spa of the Welsh working classes and there's no real reason to stop, except in mid-July when it hosts the absorbing **Royal Welsh Show**, Britain's biggest rural jamboree.

Llanwrtyd Wells

Twenty miles northwest of Brecon, **LLANWRTYD WELLS** was where the Welsh – Dyfed farmers along with Nonconformist middle classes from Glamorgan – flocked to the great eisteddfodau (festivals of Welsh music, dance and poetry) in the valley of the River Irfon; today, it's the Welsh capital of eccentric events.

Llanwrtyd District Heritage and Arts Centre

3 Ffos Rd, LD5 4RG • Thurs–Sun 10am–4pm • Free • ☎01591 610067, ⓦllanwrtydhistorygroup.webs.com

Just up from the main square, and occupying the former chapel (which functioned as such until 2009), the wonderful **Llanwrtyd District Heritage and Arts Centre** recalls the town's colourful past through a chronological timeline from the spa years via World War II through to more recent traditions – including, of course, its wacky sports events (see page 694).

ARRIVAL AND INFORMATION   LLANWRTYD WELLS

By train The train station is a 5min walk east of town on Station Rd.
Destinations Builth Wells (Mon–Sat 4 daily, Sun 2; 20min); Knighton (Mon–Sat 4 daily, Sun 2; 1hr 10min); Llandrindod Wells (Mon–Sat 4 daily, Sun 2; 30min); Shrewsbury (Mon–Sat 4 daily, Sun 2; 2hr 10min);

Swansea (Mon–Sat 4 daily, Sun 2; 1hr 50min).
By bus Buses stop on the main square and serve Builth Wells (5 daily; 25min).
Tourist information There's no official tourist office, but the heritage centre (see before) has plentiful information.

WACKY WALES: LLANWRTYD WELLS

Belying its appearance as a sleepy kind of place, Llanwrtyd Wells has its distinctly zany moments. Although a host of events take place here throughout the year, three in particular take precedence. In mid-June, the **Man versus Horse Marathon** is a punishing 22-mile endurance test between man (and woman) and beast over various types of terrain. At the end of August, it's the turn of the **World Bog-Snorkelling Championships**, in which competitors must complete two lengths of a water-filled trench cut through a peat bog – the current world record, posted in 2014, is one minute and 22 seconds. Then, in November, there's the wonderfully named **Real Ale Wobble**, two days of combined mountain biking and beer drinking for the somewhat less serious-minded cyclist. Visit ⓦ green-events.co.uk for full listings.

A fourth major event takes place bi-annually (every even-numbered year); in the wake of the 2012 Olympic Games in London, organizers decided to set up their own **World Alternative Games** (ⓦ worldalternativegames.co.uk), two weeks of more than sixty madcap events including belly flopping, gravy wrestling and husband dragging.

15

ACCOMMODATION

★ **Ardwyn House** Station Rd, LD5 4RW ☎ 01591 610768, ⓦ ardwynhouse.co.uk. Stunning turn-of-the-twentieth-century period piece with three, richly detailed en-suite rooms, including roll-top baths, cast-iron fireplaces and antique light fittings. Downstairs, guests can avail themselves of a marvellous book-lined billiards room and honesty bar. **£80**

Lasswade Station Rd, LD5 4RW ☎ 01591 610515, ⓦ lasswadehotel.co.uk. A few paces down from *Ardwyn House*, this is a lovely Edwardian residence overlooking lush fields with eight tranquil, florally decorated rooms. There's a five percent discount for visitors arriving by train. **£85**

Stonecroft Lodge Dolecoed Rd, LD5 4RA ☎ 01591 610332, ⓦ stonecroft.co.uk. This self-catering guesthouse, adjoining the inn of the same name, looks fairly grubby from the outside, but it has a perfectly acceptable selection of three-, four- and six-bed rooms, though all are with shared shower facilities. There's also a lounge and fully equipped kitchen. Dorms **£16**

EATING AND DRINKING

Carlton Riverside Irfon Crescent, LD5 4SP ☎ 01591 610248, ⓦ carltonriverside.com. The food at this well-regarded restaurant is traditional Welsh, prepared with flair and imagination – pan-fried venison with potato fondant, punchnep (root vegetables) and a port *jus*, for example (£21) – with a wine list to match. The restaurant itself has just half a dozen well-spaced, crisply laid tables offering river views. Mon–Sat 6.30–10pm.

★ **Drover's Rest Riverside Restaurant** The Square, LD5 4RA ☎ 01591 610264, ⓦ food-food-food.co.uk. Bric-a-brac fills this warm, cottage-like restaurant, where wholesome traditional Welsh dishes are the order of the day; Brecon venison in red wine (£17.50), or braised lamb rump in a Madeira and redcurrant sauce, are typical. On a warm day, it's lovely to be able to dine out on the wooden deck perching precariously over the Irfon river. Reservations essential. Wed–Sun 10.30am–3.30pm & 7.30–10pm.

Neuadd Arms The Square, LD5 4RB ☎ 01591 610236. Lively place home to the Heart of Wales Brewery, which currently produces eight fabulous ales plus lots of seasonal offerings. It was here, in 1980, that the Man versus Horse race was conceived, hence the many wonderful photos of the town's various crazy events lining the walls. Daily 11am–midnight; kitchen noon–2.30pm & 6–9.30pm.

Llandrindod Wells

Following the 1864 arrival of the railway, **LLANDRINDOD WELLS** (Llandrindod; locally referred to as "Llandod" or simply "Dod") was once Wales' most elegant spa resort. Its Victorian heyday is a distant memory, however, although many of the fine buildings from the era still stand, and it's well worth a stop to admire the faded glamour of its ornate architecture. There are a couple of worthwhile **museums**, too, and a fantastic Victorian **park**.

Radnorshire Museum

Temple St, LD1 5DL • April–Sept Tues–Sat 10am–4pm; Oct–March Tues–Fri 10am–4pm, Sat 10am–1pm • £1 • ☎ 01597 824513, ⓦ powys.gov.uk/radnorshiremuseum

The small but entertaining **Radnorshire Museum** evokes the area's history with exhibits ranging from archeological finds to items from Victorian spa days. Among the pick of these is a Sheela-na-gig, a typically explicit and remarkably well-preserved carved relief of a figure displaying its vulva, which was found in the local parish church, and a log-boat dredged up from the Ifor river in 1929 and thought to date from around 1200 AD.

National Cycle Collection

Temple St, LD1 5DL · Tues, Wed & Fri 10am–4pm · £5 · ☎ 01597 825531, ⓦ cyclemuseum.org.uk

The **National Cycle Collection** is a nostalgic exhibition showcasing more than 280 bikes, ranging from a reproduction 1818 hobbyhorse to relatively modern folding bikes and choppers, including some contraptions that look far too uncomfortable to have been a success. The museum holds some notable machinery, not least a bike belonging to the prolific, if little-known, George Nightingale, the first man to ride 25 miles in under an hour (in 1938).

Rock Park

Quietly tucked away on the southwest side of town, and accessed via several paths, **Rock Park** (ⓦ therockpark.org) is a delightful spot for a leisurely ramble. Part Victorian arboretum (including Douglas fir and Japanese red cedar), part native woodland, it's also the site of numerous mineral-rich springs, such as the Chalybeate spring, consisting of an ornate pink marble fountain and drinking basin. At the heart of the park, the once-lavish **spa pump room** is now, somewhat more prosaically, a conference centre, though the iron-and-glass-framed pavilion, connecting the pump room and old treatment centre, remains impressive. From here, a path leads to "**Lovers' Leap**", a Victorian fake cliff overlooking the river.

15

ARRIVAL AND INFORMATION

LLANDRINDOD WELLS

By train The station is a 5min walk east of town on Station Rd. Destinations Knighton (Mon–Sat 5 daily, Sun 2; 40min); Llanwrtyd Wells (Mon–Sat 4 daily, Sun 2; 30min); Shrewsbury (Mon–Sat 5 daily, Sun 2; 1hr 30min); Swansea (Mon–Sat 4 daily, Sun 2; 2hr 30min).
By bus Buses pull in by the train station.

Destinations Brecon (Mon–Sat 8 daily, Sun 1; 1hr); Builth Wells (Mon–Sat hourly; 20–30min); Newtown (Mon–Sat 6 daily, Sun 1; 50min); Rhayader (Mon–Sat 7 daily; 30min).
Tourist office Inside the town council building in front of the Radnorshire Museum on Temple St (Mon–Fri 10am–1pm; ☎ 01597 822600, ⓦ llandrindod.co.uk).

ACCOMMODATION AND EATING

Arvon Ale House Temple St, LD1 5DL ☎ 07477 627267. Occupying an old shop premises, this small, neat pub is great, typically offering five real ales as well as a two or three real ciders and perrys, plus an impressive selection of gins. The interior is fun, too, with old postcards plastered over the walls and ceilings, while evenings of folk and acoustic music add to the general air of bonhomie. Wed, Thurs & Sun 4–10pm, Fri & Sat 4–11pm.

The Cottage Spa Rd, LD1 5EY ☎ 01597 825435, ⓦ thecottagebandb.co.uk. Handsome Edwardian property

with seven differently configured rooms, all laden with period-style furnishings. No TVs in the rooms, but guests are welcome to use the lounge. **£68**

Herb Garden Café 5 Spa Centre, LD1 5BB ☎ 01597 823082, ⓦ herbgardencafe.co.uk. Delightful community-run café/diner with squashy sofas and big windowsills heaving with greenery; the accent here is on fresh, organically grown (mostly) veggie food, such as salads and platters (mango and avocado salad £7.90), and juicy house burgers. Mon–Sat 9.30am–5pm.

THE ABERGWESYN PASS

A lane from Llanwrtyd meets up with another road from Beulah at the riverside hamlet of **ABERGWESYN**, five miles north. From here, you can drive the quite magnificent winding thread of an ancient cattle-drovers' road – the **Abergwesyn Pass** – up the perilous **Devil's Staircase** and through dense conifer forests to miles of wide, desolate valleys where sheep graze unhurriedly. At the little bridge over the tiny Tywi river, a track heads south past an isolated, gas-lit hostel at **DOLGOCH**. Remote paths lead from the hostel through the forests and hillsides to the exquisitely isolated chapel at **Soar-y-Mynydd** and over the mountains to the next hostel at **TYNCORNEL**, five miles from Dolgoch.

Elan Valley and around

From the workaday market town of **RHAYADER**, ten miles northwest of Llandrindod Wells, the B4518 heads southwest four miles to the gorgeous **Elan Valley**. It was here that the poet Shelley spent his honeymoon in buildings now submerged by the waters of the valley's reservoirs, a nine-mile-long string of four lakes built between 1892 and 1903 to supply water to the rapidly growing industrial city of Birmingham, 75 miles east.

Frequent guided **walks** head off from the valley's visitor centre, and a road tucks in along the first reservoir, Caban Coch, to the **Garreg Ddu** viaduct, where it winds along for four spectacular miles to the vast, rather chilling 1952 dam on **Claerwen Reservoir**. More remote and less popular than the Elan lakes, Claerwen is a good base for a serious **walk** from the far end of the dam across eight or so harsh but beautiful miles to the monastery of Strata Florida. Alternatively, you can follow the path that skirts around the northern shore of Claerwen to the lonely **Teifi Pools**, glacial lakes from which the River Teifi springs.

Back at the Garreg Ddu viaduct, a more popular road continues north along the long, glassy finger of Garreg Ddu reservoir, before doubling back on itself just below the awesome **Pen-y-garreg** dam and reservoir; if the dam is overflowing, the vast wall of foaming water is mesmerizing. At the top of Pen-y-garreg lake, it's possible to drive over the final dam on the system, at **Craig Goch**. Thanks to its gracious curve, elegant Edwardian arches and neat little cupola, this is the most photographed of all the dams.

Gigrin Farm Red Kite Feeding Station

Off South Rd (the A470 from Builth) on the outskirts of Rhayader, LD6 5BL · Tues–Sun 12.30–4pm · £6 · ☎ 01597 810243, ⓦ gigrin.co.uk

One of the best places in Europe to watch **red kites feeding** is at **Gigrin Farm**. Each day at 3pm (2pm in winter), these magnificent birds are lured here (ravens and buzzards join in the frenzy too), with as many as five hundred descending at any one time – it's a fantastic sight. There's also a scenic 1.5-mile-long **nature trail**, and a small café/shop.

ARRIVAL AND INFORMATION
ELAN VALLEY AND AROUND

There is no **public transport** to the Elan Valley, so you will require a car or a bike, or you can hike.

Tourist information Just below the dam of the first reservoir, Caban Coch, the Elan Valley visitor centre (daily 9.30am–4.30/5pm; ☎ 01597 810898, ⓦ elanvalley.org.uk) has useful leaflets on walks around the valley, a permanent exhibition about the history and ecology of the area, a tearoom and bike rental (£6/hr, £24/day). The centre also runs a series of excellent ranger-led events, most of which are free to attend.

Bike rental Clive Powell Mountain Bikes, West St, Rhayader (daily 9am–5.30pm; £6/hr, £24/day; ☎ 01597 811343, ⓦ clivepowell-mtb.co.uk). They also offer servicing and repairs.

ACCOMMODATION, EATING AND DRINKING

Crown Inn North St, Rhayader, LD6 5BU ☎ 01597 811099. The most agreeable of the town's several boozers, with lots of small, dark wooden tables gathered under a large stone fireplace, and Brains beer. Daily noon–11pm.

Ty Morgans East St, Rhayader, LD6 5BH ☎ 01597 811666, ⓦ tymorgans.com. Superb building housing nine effortlessly cool rooms, most of which still feature their original red or grey bare brick walls and oak-beamed ceilings. The buzzy bar/bistro offers a mouthwatering burger menu in addition to more sophisticated dishes (braised rabbit with potatoes and leeks, for example, for £13.95). The bistro leads to the bustling *Strand* coffeehouse and deli. Daily: bar/bistro 8am–9pm (kitchen 8am–2.30pm & 5–9pm); coffeehouse 8am–7pm. **£80**

Wyeside Immediately north of Rhayader off the A470, LD6 5LB ☎ 01597 810183, ⓦ wyesidecamping.co.uk. On the banks of the Wye, this is a smart site with separate camping and caravan areas and clean, modern amenities. Closed Nov to Feb. **£17**

Montgomeryshire

The northern part of Powys is made up of the old county of **Montgomeryshire** (Maldwyn), an area of enormously varying landscapes and few inhabitants. The solid little town of **Llanidloes** is a base for ageing hippies on the banks of the infant River Severn (Afon Hafren). To the east, the muted old county town of **Montgomery**, with its fine Georgian architecture, perches amid gentle, green hills above the border and Offa's Dyke. Further north, **Welshpool**, the only major settlement, is packed in above the wide flood plain of the Severn; with its pubs and hotels it's a fair base for Montgomeryshire's unmissable sight, the sumptuous **Powis Castle** and its terraced gardens.

Llanidloes

The small market town of **LLANIDLOES**, twelve miles north of Rhayader, has developed from a rural village to a weaving town, and is now an arty, alternative-lifestyle kind of place. One of Mid-Wales' prettiest towns, it centres on four main streets, which all meet at the market hall – the main thoroughfare is Great Oak Street, a wide, handsome road framed by well-proportioned, two- and three-storey buildings variously accommodating shops, restaurants and tenements.

15

Old Market Hall

Great Oak St, SY18 6HU • Late May to Sept Tues–Sun 11am–4pm • Free • ☎ 01686 412388

At the junction of the town's four main streets is the black-and-white **Old Market Hall**, built on timber stilts around 1600, allowing the market – now long since moved – to take place on the cobbles underneath. The only surviving timber-framed market hall in Wales, it's also known as the Booth Hall, and remained a popular trading place until the early twentieth century. At one time or another it has also functioned as a law court, a meeting place for the Quakers, a flannel store and the local Working Men's Institute. Today it houses a fascinating **exhibition** on other similarly timbered buildings in Llanidloes and further afield; you can pick up a free trail leaflet outlining the finest.

St Idloes church

Church St, off Bridge St, SY18 6EE • Daily 10.30am–3.30pm • ⓦ llanidloes.com/saint-idloes

The glory of **St Idloes church** is its impressive fifteenth-century hammerbeam roof (also known as the "Angel Roof"). Recent tree-ring dating refutes the previously held theory that it was poached from the village of Abbeycwmhir, some fourteen miles south of Llanidloes; the pillars and arches, though, were most certainly taken from the abbey following its dissolution in 1536. The adjoining mid-fourteenth-century tower, meanwhile, is typical of those found in the county, a massive square block crowned by a wooden belfry and pyramidal roof.

ARRIVAL AND INFORMATION
LLANIDLOES

By bus China St curves down to the car park where all buses arrive and depart.
Destinations Aberystwyth (Mon–Sat 3 daily; 1hr); Newtown (Mon–Sat 8 daily; 30min); Ponterwyd (3 daily; 40min); Shrewsbury (Mon–Sat 6 daily; 2hr); Welshpool (Mon–Sat 6 daily; 1hr 10min).

Tourist information There's no tourist office, but the Llani Leisure shop, 16 Long Bridge St (Tues–Sat 10am–5pm; ☎ 01686 414893, ⓦ llanidloes.com), stocks lots of literature on the town and surrounds.

ACCOMMODATION AND EATING

Dol-llys Farm Trefeglwys Rd, SY18 6JA ☎ 01686 412694, ⓦ dolllyscaravancampsite.co.uk. Large site around a 15min walk north of town. Choose from a pitch on the level field near the facilities, or a more secluded spot down by the river, where campfires are permitted. Closed Nov to Easter. Per person **£7.50**

Unicorn Hotel 4 Long Bridge St, SY18 6EE ☎01686 411171. A small hotel of considerable charm and quality, hosting six crisp, generous and impeccably clean rooms; there's a substantial breakfast to look forward to as well.

The fabulous daytime bistro/evening restaurant offers delicious dishes such as roasted duck leg with Cointreau and orange gravy (£13.75). Tues–Sat 6–9.30pm. **£90**

DRINKING

Red Lion 8 Long Bridge St, SY18 6EE ☎01686 412270. The most agreeable of the town's pubs; the main lounge bar has comfy leather seating huddled around an imposing

stone fireplace festooned with brass, while the noisier other room is principally for bar games. Daily 11am– midnight.

Montgomery

Tiny **MONTGOMERY** (Trefaldwyn), around twenty miles northeast of Llanidloes, is Montgomeryshire at its most anglicized. From the mound of its **castle**, situated just on the Welsh side of Offa's Dyke, there are wonderful views over the lofty church tower and the handsome Georgian streets, notably the impressively symmetrical main road – appropriately named Broad Street – which swoops up to the little red-brick **town hall**, crowned by a pert clocktower. Montgomery is within striking distance of one of the best-preserved sections of **Offa's Dyke** (see page 700), traced by the long-distance footpath that runs on either side of the B4386.

Old Bell Museum

Arthur St, SY15 6RA • April–July & Sept Wed–Fri & Sun 1.30–5pm, Sat 10.30am–5pm; Aug Mon–Fri & Sun 1.30–5pm, Sat 10.30am– 5pm • £1 • ☎01686 668313, ⓦ oldbellmuseum.org.uk

The **Old Bell Museum**, formerly a temperance house and butcher's, is now an unusually enjoyable local history collection. Crammed into every nook and cranny of this marvellous little building are artefacts from excavations, scale models of local castles, mementos from Montgomery civic life and displays on the region's various trades, with due prominence given to the likes of clogmakers, clockmakers, carpenters and tanners.

Cloverlands Model Car Museum

Arthur St, SY15 6RA • Thurs 10am–1pm, Fri 2–5pm, Sat 9.30am–1pm, Sun 2–4.30pm • £2.50 • ☎01686 668004, ⓦ cloverlandsmuseum.org.uk

The **Cloverlands Model Car Museum** holds the remarkable collection of Gillian Rogers, a local motoring fanatic who started acquiring miniature cars as a young girl in the 1950s – the result is in excess of 1500 models, including classics, sports cars, fire engines, trams and much more. Rogers worked in the automotive industry (which was extremely rare for a woman in those days) and built model cars – on display is a 1:4 scale model of the 1935 Singer Le Mans she owned for forty years and which she regularly drove down to Le Mans.

ARRIVAL AND DEPARTURE   MONTGOMERY

By bus Buses pick up and drop off in front of the Town Hall at the bottom of Broad St.
Destinations Newtown (Mon–Sat 8 daily; 30min);

Shrewsbury (Mon–Sat 4 daily; 50min); Welshpool (Mon–Sat 5 daily; 25min).

ACCOMMODATION AND EATING

Brynwylfa 4 Bishops Castle St, SY15 6PW ☎01686 668555, ⓦ brynwylfa.co.uk. There are just two rooms in this beautiful townhouse, off the main square, one with exposed brick walls, the other with a gorgeous roll-top bath. Closed June–Aug. **£80**

Castle Kitchen 8 Broad St, SY15 6PH ☎01686 668795, ⓦ castlekitchen.org. Sociable café/deli with an open

kitchen doling out savoury (soups, quiches and tarts) and sweet (cakes and pastries) delights. The busy downstairs area extends to a vine-covered terrace, while upstairs is all wonky flooring and stripey walls. Mon–Sat 9.30am– 4.30pm, Sun 11am–4.30pm.

★**The Checkers** Broad St, SY15 6PN ☎01686 669822, ⓦ checkerswales.co.uk. The five stylish rooms

> **OFFA'S DYKE**
>
> **Offa's Dyke** has provided a potent symbol of Welsh–English antipathy ever since it was created in the eighth century as a demarcation line by King Offa of Mercia, ruler of central England. George Borrow, in his classic book *Wild Wales*, notes that, once, "It was customary for the English to cut off the ears of every Welshman who was found to the east of the dyke, and for the Welsh to hang every Englishman whom they found to the west of it".
>
> The earthwork – up to 20ft high and 60ft wide – made use of natural boundaries like rivers in its run north to south, and is best seen in the sections near **Knighton**. Today's England–Wales border crosses the dyke many times, although the basic boundary has changed little since Offa's day. A glorious, 177-mile **long-distance footpath** (ⓦ nationaltrail.co.uk/offas-dyke-path) runs the length of the dyke from Prestatyn in the north to Chepstow, and is one of the most rewarding walks in Britain.

15

of this erstwhile coaching inn are characterized by higgledy-piggledy beams and low ceilings and doorways. The Michelin-starred restaurant is an inviting setting for classically French seasonal menus – roasted breast of Gressingham duck with *pain d'epices* (spiced bread), pak choi and pineapple is typical. Six-course menu £65. Booking essential. Tues–Sat 7.15–10pm. £125

Welshpool

Eastern Montgomeryshire's chief town of **WELSHPOOL** (Y Trallwng), seven miles north of Montgomery, was formerly known as just Pool, its prefix added in 1835 to distinguish it from the English seaside town of Poole in Dorset. Lying in the valley of the River Severn, just three miles from the English border, it's an attractive place, with fine Tudor, Georgian and Victorian buildings in the centre, and the fabulous **Powis Castle** nearby.

Powysland Museum

Canal Wharf, SY21 7AQ · June–Aug Mon–Fri 10.30am–1pm & 2–5pm, Sat 10.30am–3pm; Sept–May Mon, Tues, Thurs & Fri 11am–1pm & 2–5pm, Sat 11am–2pm · £1 · ☎ 01938 554656

A humpback bridge over the **Montgomery Canal** hides the canal wharf and a wharfside warehouse that has been carefully restored as the **Powysland Museum**. The impressive local history collection includes archeological nuggets such as those from an old local woodhenge, and displays medieval remains from the now-obliterated local Cistercian abbey of Strata Marcella.

Welshpool & Llanfair Light Railway

Raven Square, SY21 0SF · Generally 3–5 trains on operating days: April & Oct hols & weekends only; May, June & Sept Tues–Thurs, Sat & Sun; July & Aug daily · £13.50 rover ticket · ☎ 01938 810441, ⓦ wllr.org.uk

Broad Street changes name five times as it rises up the hill towards the tiny Raven Square station of the **Welshpool & Llanfair Light Railway**. The eight-mile narrow-gauge rail line was open to passengers for less than thirty years prior to its closure in 1931. Now, scaled-down engines once more chuff their way along to the peaceful little village of **Llanfair Caereinion**, a good base for daytime walks; the round journey takes two hours.

Powis Castle

A mile southwest of town up Park Lane, SY21 8RF · **Castle** Daily: March 12.30–4pm; April–Sept 11am–5pm; Oct–Dec 11am–4pm· £12.50 (includes gardens); NT · **Garden** Daily: March 11am–4pm; April–Sept 10am–6pm; Oct–Dec 10am–4pm · £9.25; NT · ☎ 01938 551944, ⓦ nationaltrust.org.uk/powis-castle-and-garden

In a land of ruined castles, the sheer scale and beauty of **Powis Castle** is quite staggering. On the site of an earlier Norman fort, the castle was started in the reign of Edward I by the Gwenwynwyn family; in 1587, Sir Edward Herbert bought it and began to transform the complex into the Elizabethan palace that survives today.

The sumptuous period rooms are impressive, from the vast and kitsch frescoes by Lanscroon above the balustraded staircase to the mahogany bed, brass and enamel toilets and decorative wall hangings of the state bedroom. Many rooms throughout the castle were remodelled in the Jacobean style in the early 1900s, hence the proliferation of oak panelling and elaborate plasterwork ceilings. The former ballroom houses the **Clive Museum** – named after the diplomat Robert Clive (aka Clive of India on account of his political and military deeds in the country during the mid-eighteenth century), and his son Edward, who married into the family in 1784; it's a remarkable collection of diaries, notes, letters, paintings, tapestries, weapons and jewels.

The **gardens**, designed by Welsh architect William Winde, are spectacular. Dropping down from the castle in four huge, stepped terraces, the design has barely changed since the seventeenth century, with a charming orangery and trim topiary.

ARRIVAL AND INFORMATION

By train The station is at the bottom of Severn St, behind the neo-Gothic turrets of the old Victorian station.
Destinations Aberystwyth (9–10 daily; 1hr 30min); Birmingham (6–8 daily; 1hr 30min); Machynlleth (9–10 daily; 1hr); Newtown (9–10 daily; 15min); Shrewsbury (9–10 daily; 25min).
By bus Buses use the Old Station on Severn Rd.
Destinations Llanidloes (Mon–Sat 6 daily; 1hr 20min); Llanfyllin (Mon–Sat 4 daily; 35min); Llanymynech (Mon– Sat 5 daily; 30min); Montgomery (Mon–Sat 7 daily; 25min); Oswestry (Mon–Sat 5 daily; 45min); Shrewsbury (Mon–Sat 6 daily; 50min).

Tourist office Just off Church St in the Vicarage Gardens car park (Mon–Sat 9.30am–5pm, Sun 10am–4pm; ☎01938 552043, ⓦvisitwelshpool.org); they've got stacks of information and a National Express bus- and train-booking service.

ACCOMMODATION AND EATING

The Bay Tree 5–6 Church St, SY21 7DL ☎01938 555456. Eccentrically decorated café featuring, among many things, a telephone box, seating culled from a Waltzer and a room themed on Alice in Wonderland – once you've digested all that, settle back with a cuppa and a sandwich. Mon–Thurs 9am–5pm, Fri & Sat 9am–midnight.

Royal Oak The Cross, SY21 7DG ☎01938 552217, ⓦroyal oakwelshpool.co.uk. Traditional Georgian coaching inn with spruce rooms in three sizes. The restaurant offers a cracking grazing menu (try the honey and mustard mini-sausages, £6) and a fuller menu of seasonal dishes (rump of lamb with creamed potatoes and rosemary gravy, for example, £16). The adjoining café/bar is a relaxing spot to kick back with a coffee or glass of wine. Daily: restaurant noon–3pm & 6–10pm; café/bar 9am–11pm. **£99**

Trefnant Hall Farm Four miles southwest, beyond Powis Castle, SY21 8AS ☎01686 640262, ⓦtrefnanthall.co.uk. You'll need your own transport to get to this isolated Georgian farmhouse, whose three flowery rooms have delightful views of sloping green fields. Guests are free to use the lounge with its gorgeous fireplace. **£65**

The Cambrian coast

Cardigan Bay (Bae Ceredigion) takes a huge bite out of the west Wales coast, leaving behind the Pembrokeshire peninsula in the south and the Llŷn in the north. Between them lies the **Cambrian coast**, a loosely defined mountain-backed strip periodically split by tumbling rivers, which stretches from Cardigan up to Harlech. Large sand-fringed sections are peppered with low-key coastal resorts, peopled in the summer by families from the English Midlands.

The southern Ceredigion coast is broken by some spirited little ports, all soaked in a relaxed, upbeat and firmly Welsh culture: the old county town of **Cardigan**; higgledy-piggledy **New Quay**; and pretty Georgian **Aberaeron**. Ceredigion's main town is ebullient **Aberystwyth**, a great base for the waterfalls and woods of the **Vale of Rheidol**.

To the north, the flat river plain and rolling hills of the **Dyfi Valley** lay justifiable claim to being one of the greenest corners of Europe. Their focal point is the genial town of **Machynlleth**, a candidate for the Welsh capital in the 1950s and site of Owain Glyndŵr's embryonic fifteenth-century Welsh parliament. Machynlleth looks up at one of Wales' most inspirational mountains, **Cadair Idris** (2930ft), incised by the Talyllyn Valley (with its toy railway) and the delightful Dysynni Valley. On its northern flank, the beautiful **Mawddach estuary** snakes its way seaward from grey-stone **Dolgellau**, springboard for the mountain biking and forest pursuits at **Coed-y-Brenin**. The coast begins to feel more like North Wales at hilltop fortress of **Harlech** where the castle overlooks the dunes and the Llŷn.

Cardigan and around

An ancient former port of **CARDIGAN** (Aberteifi), which sits at the lowest bridging point of the **River Teifi**, was founded by the Norman lord Roger de Montgomery in 1093 around a castle, itself recently reopened after a decade-long renovation programme. From the castle, Bridge Street sweeps up to the turreted oddity of the **Guildhall**, through which you access the town's **covered market**, an eclectic mix of fresh food, local crafts and secondhand stalls.

15

Cardigan Castle

Green St, SA43 1JA • Daily: April–Sept 10am–4pm; Oct–March 11am–3pm • £4.50 • ☎ 01239 614131, ⓦ cardigancastle.com

Just a stone's throw from Cardigan's **medieval bridge**, is **Cardigan Castle**, originally constructed in 1093 but which, in 1171, was the first Welsh castle to be made of stone. Despite the presence of four of the seven original towers, it doesn't much resemble a castle at all these days – though that's not to detract from its charm.

At the heart of the complex is **Castle Green House**, a handsome Georgian pile dating from 1808 that now accommodates several superb exhibitions, one of which focuses on the castle's last resident, **Barbara Wood**, who lived here from 1940 until 1999, by which time the place was virtually uninhabitable – on display is her rather bashed-up doll's house, rusting typewriter and items of correspondence. Other rooms are devoted to the Welsh **eisteddfod** (Cardigan was the site of the first eisteddfod in 1176) and the town's history, in particular its prestigious **shipbuilding** heritage. Between 1792 and 1840, more than 140 vessels were built here. Fronting the house are the perfectly manicured lawns of the **Regency Gardens**, around which are dotted various objects of interest, including an oversized replica of the eisteddfod chair from 1176 and a World War II pillbox, positioned here in the event of a German offensive emanating from Ireland.

Welsh Wildlife Centre

Teifi Marshes, SA43 2TB • Daily: Easter–Oct 10am–5pm; Nov–Easter 10am–4pm • Free • ☎ 01239 621600, ⓦ welshwildlife.org

An elegant, modern, timber-and-glass structure in the centre of the Teifi Marshes, the **Welsh Wildlife Centre** is home to informative displays and an airy café with expansive views over the reserve, plus an adventure playground to keep kids entertained. You can easily spend half a day here exploring the four themed trails, the shortest of which is an easy ten-minute stroll around the meadow, and the longest a 45-minute walk through the wetlands. There are also seven observation hides (including an otter hide) dotted around the reserve, with binocular rental available. This area is best explored, however, on **canoe trips** run by Heritage Canoes (☎ 01239 613961, ⓦ heritagecanoes.squarespace.com), based in Slate Cottage just below the wildlife centre; they offer tours of the river and Cilgerran Gorge (2hr 30min; £35/person), with an emphasis on spotting local wildlife.

Cilgerran Castle

Cilgerran, a couple of miles up the Teifi River from Cardigan • Daily: April–Oct 10am–5pm; Nov–March 10am–4pm • April–Oct £3.20; Nov–March free; CADW • ☎ 01239 621339, ⓦ cadw.gov.wales/daysout/cilgerran-castle

The attractive village of **CILGERRAN** clusters behind the bulk of its **castle**, on a high wooded bluff above the river. This is the site of an attack in 1109 that culminated in the abduction of Nest (the "Welsh Helen of Troy") by a love-struck Prince Owain of Powys. Her husband, Gerald of Pembroke, escaped the attack by slithering down a oilet waste chute through the castle walls. The two massive drum towers still dominate he castle, and the outer walls are traced by vertiginously high walkways. The outer ward is a good example of the keepless castle that evolved in the thirteenth century.

Tresaith

The best destination on the lovely south Ceredigion coast is tiny **TRESAITH**, eight miles northeast of Cardigan, which staggers down impossibly narrow lanes to a delightful beach and the *Ship Inn*. A few yards around the rocks to the right, a refreshing small waterfall cascades right onto the beach.

Llangrannog

Four miles north of Tresaith, **LLANGRANNOG** comes wedged between bracken- and gorse-beaten hills, the streets winding to the tiny seafront. The beach can become horribly congested in midsummer, when it's better to follow the cliff path to **Cilborth Beach** and on to the glorious National Trust-owned headland, **Ynys Lochtyn**.

15

ARRIVAL AND INFORMATION   CARDIGAN AND AROUND

By bus Buses to Cardigan stop on Finch Square.
Destinations Aberaeron (Mon–Sat hourly, Sun 3; 1hr); Aberystwyth (Mon–Sat hourly, Sun 3; 1hr 45min); Cenarth (Mon–Sat hourly; 15min); Cilgerran (5 daily; 15min); Llangrannog (2 daily; 15min); New Quay (Mon–Sat hourly,

Sun 5; 45min); Tresaith (2 daily; 10min).
Tourist office Theatr Mwldan, Bath House Rd (term time Tues–Sat 10am–1pm & 2–4pm; hols Mon–Sat same times; ☎ 01239 613230, ⓦ visitcardigan.com).

ACCOMMODATION

Caemorgan Mansion Caemorgan Rd, a mile northeast of Cardigan just off the A487, SA43 1QU ☎ 01239 613297, ⓦ caemorgan.com. An outstanding level of comfort and hospitality awaits at this marvellous guesthouse, whose five rooms have been appointed to the highest order, and include, among other things, luxury Egyptian cotton, underfloor heating and smart drinks stations with fresh milk. You won't find better cooked Welsh breakfasts anywhere. **£120**

Ffynnon Fendigaid Rhydlewis, 3 miles south of Llangrannog, SA44 5SR ☎ 01239 851361, ⓦ ffynnonf. co.uk. Eclectically decorated rural B&B in six acres of semi-wild grounds – they've also got a beautifully furnished circus wagon sleeping two and a Swedish lodge with a 1960s, retro-inspired interior (sleeping four). Walkers and cyclists are particularly welcome, with pick-ups and drop-offs possible. B&B **£80**, wagon **£80**, lodge **£85**

Llety Caravan Park Tresaith, SA43 2ED ☎ 01239 810354, ⓦ lletycaravanpark.co.uk. Amid the static caravans there's a wonderful (if significantly sloping) cliff-top field for tents and tourers with a pretty footpath that descends straight to the beach. Friendly, and with excellent shower blocks. **£17**

Llety Teifi Pendre, SA43 1JU ☎ 01239 615566, ⓦ lletyteifi-guesthouse.co.uk. A raspberry-pink boutique guesthouse with ten contemporary rooms in a Victorian townhouse with its own restaurant/bar. Breakfast is taken in the conservatory. **£75**

YHA Poppit Sands 4 miles northwest of Cardigan, SA43 3LP ☎ 01239 612936, ⓦ yha.org.uk/hostel/poppit-sands. Remote hostel on the northern end of the Pembrokeshire Coast Path, with great views; male and female dorms, all with six beds and shared shower facilities, plus doubles, and a self-catering kitchen. The #407 bus stops within half a mile. Closed Nov–Feb. Dorms **£15**, doubles **£50**

EATING

Ferry Inn St Dogmaels, just over a mile west of Cardigan, SA43 3LF ☎ 01239 615172, ⓦ ferry-inn. co.uk. Enviably sited right beside the Teifi, this rambling delight of a pub offers loads of seating areas (including upper and lower alfresco decks) where you can enjoy a range of tasty meals such as the house bouillabaisse or fish pie (£14.95). Great beer, too. Daily noon–11.30pm; kitchen noon–3pm & 6–9pm.

Pendre Art Gallery and Café 35 Pendre, Cardigan, SA43 1JL ☎ 01239 615151. Formerly a minor shopping complex, this place is heaps of fun, from the 70s retro

tables and sofas at the front, through to the back room arranged with furnishings culled from pallets, coffee sacks and the like. Fri nights are given over to an evening of tapas, while Sat is cocktail night. Mon–Sat 10am–5pm, plus Fri & Sat 6.30pm–late.

Pizzatipi 1 Cambrian Quay, Cardigan, SA43 1EZ ☎ 01239 612259, ⓦ pizzatipi.co.uk. The main reason to visit this easy-going waterside café is to dine on wood-fired pizza (£8) and craft beer under the ingeniously conceived pizza tepee. Occasional live music and events. June–Sept daily noon–9.30pm.

DOLPHIN-SPOTTING FROM NEW QUAY

One of only two pods in Britain, the Cambrian coast's **bottlenose dolphins** are among New Quay's major attractions, and can often be seen frolicking by the harbour wall, particularly when the tide is full and the weather calm. A mile-wide strip of the coastal waters forms the Ceredigion Marine Heritage Coast, in summer plied by boat trips geared around sightings. The best trips are those run by **Dolphin Survey Boat Trips** (part of the CBMWC; April–Oct daily; £17.50 for 90min, £20 for 2hr, £38 for 4hr, £60 for 8hr; ☎01545 560032, ☻dolphinsurveyboattrips.co.uk). Your fee goes towards marine mammal research, partly undertaken by the on-board ranger.

New Quay and around

NEW QUAY (Cei Newydd) lays claim to being the original Llareggub in Dylan Thomas's *Under Milk Wood*. Certainly, it has the little tumbling streets, prim Victorian terraces, cobbled stone harbour and air of dreamy isolation that Thomas evoked in his play. Although there is a singular lack of excitement in town, it's a pleasant base for good beaches, dolphin-spotting and walks along the rocky promontory of **New Quay Head**, where the invigorating coast path steers along the top of aptly named **Bird Rock**.

Cardigan Bay Marine Wildlife Centre

Glanmor Terrace, SA45 9PS • April–Oct daily 9am–5pm • Free • ☎01545 560224, ☻cbmwc.org

Tucked away down the slipway above New Quay's beach, the **Cardigan Bay Marine Wildlife Centre** (CBMWC) has excellent interactive and interpretative displays on the dolphins, seals and seabirds of Cardigan Bay. They also organize (weather permitting) daily whale- and dolphin-watching boat trips (see above).

ARRIVAL AND INFORMATION

NEW QUAY

By bus Buses stop at the top of Church St.
Destinations Aberaeron (Mon–Sat hourly, Sun 3; 20min); Aberystwyth (Mon–Sat hourly, Sun 3; 1hr); Cardigan (Mon–Sat hourly, Sun 5; 50min).

Tourist office On the corner of Church St and Wellington Place (Easter & summer holidays only Mon–Sat 10am–1pm & 2–4pm; ☎01545 560865, ☻discoverceredigion. co.uk).

ACCOMMODATION, EATING AND DRINKING

The Black Lion Glanmor Terrace, SA45 9PT ☎01545 561144, ☻blacklionnewquay.co.uk. Dylan Thomas's favourite New Quay watering hole has been smartened up considerably, with nine rooms (five with superlative sea views) characterized by high ceilings, sash windows and stripy, boldly coloured curtains. **£75**

Hungry Trout 2 South John St, SA45 9NG ☎01545 560680, ☻thehungrytrout.co.uk. A couple of delightful rooms, both with sea views, above New Quay's finest seafood restaurant, where you might try smoked Teifi sewin (sea trout) with asparagus (sorrel) and capers. Outside seating for summer evenings. Daily 9am–3pm & 6–9pm. **£95**

The Lime Crab South John St, SA45 9NP ☎01545 561400, ☻limecrab.com. Eye-catching fish-and-chip shop that offers a slightly more refined take on your average chippie, with the likes of scallops, salt-and-pepper squid and mackerel goujons, all for around £7–8. Daily noon–8pm.

Seahorse Inn Margaret St, SA45 9QJ ☎01545 560736. This fine, traditional local, a world away from the holiday bustle down the street, is little more than one room with exposed stonework, fake beams, pool table and a limited range of good ales. Known to Dylan Thomas as the *Commercial*, it was the model for the *Sailor's Arms* in *Under Milk Wood*. Daily 11am–11.30pm.

Aberaeron

ABERAERON, seven miles northeast of New Quay, comes as something of a surprise. This little nugget of Georgian architecture was built by the Reverend Alban Gwynne, who spent his wife's inheritance dredging the Aeron estuary and constructing a planned town around it as a new port for Mid-Wales. The colourful terraces of quoin-edged buildings around **Alban Square** and along **Quay Parade** are undeniably pretty, though the moneyed weekenders from Cardiff (and even London) are more interested in the excellent array of places to stay as well as the good restaurants. Aberaeron's beach is unappealing, so head out along the coast path or just amble around the streets and waterfront and graze in its cafés and pubs.

Llanerchaeron

Ciliau Aeron, A482, 3 miles east of Aberaeron, SA48 8DG • House April–Oct daily 11.30am–4pm; parkland daily 10.30am–5pm • March–Oct £7.45; Nov–March £3.75 (parkland only); NT • ☎ 01545 570200, ⓦ nationaltrust.org.uk/llanerchaeron • Bus #T1 stops on the main road, 1 mile from the site

Aberaeron's one essential sight, **Llanerchaeron** is the substantially restored remains of a late eighteenth-century Welsh country estate, which today boasts exquisite kitchen gardens and a pristine, Nash-designed main house. The original, mostly Edwardian set-piece rooms only hint at the fact that this was someone's home little more than two decades ago. This is much more apparent in the servants' quarters and the serviced courtyard which acted as laundry, dairy, salting room and home brewery.

ARRIVAL AND INFORMATION   ABERAERON   **15**

By bus The main bus stop is on the north side of Alban Square, from where it's a walk across the road down towards the harbour area.

Destinations Aberystwyth (Mon–Sat every 30min, Sun 3; 40min); Cardigan (Mon–Sat hourly, Sun 3; 1hr);

Carmarthen (Mon–Sat hourly, Sun 3; 1hr 30min); New Quay (Mon–Sat hourly, Sun 3; 20min).

Tourist office Down by the harbour at 3 Pen Cei (Mon–Wed, Fri & Sat 10am–4pm; school summer hols daily 10am–4pm; ☎ 01545 570602, ⓦ discoverceredigion.co.uk).

ACCOMMODATION AND EATING

Cadwgan 10 Market St, SA46 0AU ☎ 01545 570149. Unpretentious local that's like walking into someone's living room: someone who serves a rotating roster of real ales and a few bar snacks, that is. Daily noon–11.30pm.

★ **Harbourmaster Hotel** 1 Pen Cei, SA46 0BT ☎ 01545 570755, ⓦ harbour-master.com. Wonderful hotel with ultra-modern rooms with crisp white linen softened by Welsh wool throws. The restaurant (£35 for three courses) serves the likes of Cardigan Bay crab cake with pink grapefruit and ginger mayo, or you might plump for crispy cockles with chilli vinegar salt in the bistro, which also serves breakfast until 11.45am. Daily: bistro 8am–late; restaurant noon–2.30pm & 6–9pm. **£145**

The Monachty Market St, SA46 0AS ☎ 01545 570389, ⓦ monachtyaberaeron.co.uk. A respectable semi-budget option in a town full of otherwise pricey establishments. Seven light-filled rooms come with big dollops of colour, and despite being above a pub, are well insulated. It's dog-friendly, too. **£80**

Naturally Scrumptious 18 Market St, SA46 0AX ☎ 01545 574733. Excellent deli groaning with Welsh cheese, pies, posh sausages and panini; otherwise, content yourself with the best cakes in town (hazelnut and amaretti, raspberry and almond) and a freshly brewed coffee in the breezy café to the rear. Mon–Sat 9.30am–4.30pm.

Aberystwyth

The liveliest seaside resort in Wales, **ABERYSTWYTH** is an essential stop. With two long, gentle bays curving around between rocky heads, its position is hard to beat, and being rooted in all aspects of Welsh culture, it is possibly the most enjoyable and relaxed place to gain an insight into the national psyche. As the capital of sparsely populated Mid-Wales, and with one of the most prestigious university colleges in the country, it offers plenty of things to do, and has a nice array of Victorian and Edwardian seaside trappings. Politics here are firmly radical Welsh – in a country that still struggles with its inherent conservatism, Aberystwyth is a blast of fresh air.

Constitution Hill

Railway Cliff Terrace, SY23 2DN • April–June, Sept & Oct daily 10am–5pm; July & Aug daily 10am–6pm; winter hours are unpredictable, so check in advance • £5 return • **Camera obscura** April–Oct daily 11am–4pm • £1 • ☎ 01970 617642, ⓦ aberystwythcliffrailway.co.uk

The 430ft-high **Constitution Hill** (Y Graig Glais) rises sharply from the rocky beach at the long Promenade's northern end. It's accessible on foot, though if you don't fancy the invigorating but stiff walk up, you can take the clanking 1896 **Cliff Railway**, which creeps up the crooked tracks at scarcely more than walking pace from the grand terminus building at the top of Queen's Road, behind the Promenade. On a clear day, the views of Cardigan Bay are fantastic.

At the top of Constitution Hill you'll find a café, picnic area, telescopes and an octagonal **camera obscura**, a device popular in the pre-TV era using a mirror and hefty lens to project close-up and long-shot views over the town, the surrounding mountains and bays. The existing structure was built in 1985 on the ground plan of the Victorian original, but with its scale expanded to make it the largest of its type in the world.

Ceredigion Museum

Terrace Rd, SY23 2AQ • Mon–Sat: Easter–Oct 10am–5pm; Nov–Easter noon–4.30pm • Free • ☎ 01970 633088, ⓦ ceredigion.gov.uk

From the bottom of Constitution Hill, the **Promenade** – officially Marine Terrace – arcs away to the south, past ornate benches decorated with snakes, a continuous wall of hotels and guesthouses, a prim bandstand and a shingle beach.

The **Ceredigion Museum** is atmospherically housed over three floors in the ornate Edwardian Coliseum music hall, which functioned as a variety theatre until the 1930s and then as a **cinema** until 1977; much to the delight of the locals, screenings resumed here in 2016, with fortnightly showings (typically, and fittingly, old

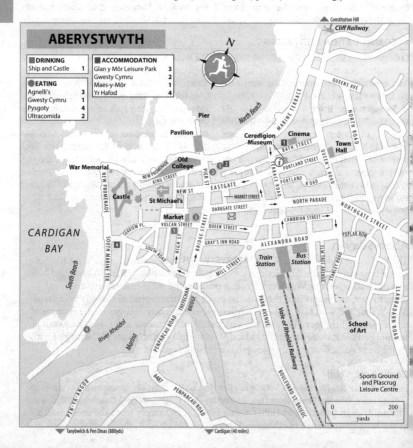

classics). Mementos of the building as a theatre and cinema give a sense of place to an otherwise wonderfully disparate collection. A fascinating section charts the seafaring exploits in the bay, where more than a thousand ships were built during the eighteenth and nineteenth centuries – look out for the barometer designed by Robert Fitzroy, captain of HMS *Beagle* during Darwin's voyage to Tierra del Fuego.

National Library of Wales

Penglais Rd, SY23 3BU · Mon–Fri 9.30am–6pm, Sat 9.30–5pm · Free · **Guided tours** Mon 11am & Wed 2.15pm; 1hr · £5 · ☎ 01970 632800, ⓦ llgc.org.uk · Bus #03 (Mon–Sat every 20min; Sat & Sun hourly) from the bus station

In the lively university area, east of town, the massive white-stone Edwardian **National Library of Wales** possesses fine manuscripts including the oldest extant Welsh text – the twelfth-century *Black Book of Carmarthen* – and the earliest manuscript of *The Mabinogion*. Occasionally these form part of the typically excellent temporary exhibitions. Displays from the permanent collection of books, manuscripts and papers include the **World of the Book**, which looks at the history of the written word and publishing in Wales. Also here is the **Nanteos Cup**, an ancient mazer bowl, or chalice, discovered at Strata Florida around 1880. Actually little more than a fragment of wood, albeit one with alleged healing properties, the cup (named after the nearby mansion in which it was kept, by a group of monks, for many years) is believed by some to be the holy grail, though it more likely dates from the fourteenth or fifteenth century; regardless, its mythological status ensures a steady stream of devotees.

15

ARRIVAL AND INFORMATION ABERYSTWYTH

By train Vale of Rheidol and mainline trains (to Machynlleth: 10–12 daily; 30min) use the same station on Alexandra Rd, a 10min walk from the seafront.

By bus The main bus station is adjacent to the train station on Alexandra Rd.

Destinations Aberaeron (Mon–Sat every 30min, Sun 3; 40min); Cardigan (Mon–Sat every 30min, Sun 3; 1hr 45min); Machynlleth (hourly; 40min); New Quay (Mon–Sat every 30min, 3 on Sun; 1hr).

Tourist office Sharing the entrance with the Ceredigion Museum, Terrace Rd (Mon–Sat 10am–5pm; ☎ 01970 612125, ⓦ discoverceredigion.gov.uk).

ACCOMMODATION

Glan y Môr Leisure Park Clarach Bay, 3 miles north, SY23 3DT ☎ 01970 828900, ⓦ sunbourne.co.uk; map p.706. On the other side of Constitution Hill, with on-site caravans and tent pitches, plus a superb range of leisure facilities including (for a fee) a heated indoor pool and gym. **£25**

★ **Gwesty Cymru** 19 Marine Terrace, SY23 2AZ ☎ 01970 6122252, ⓦ gwestycymru.com; map p.706. This classy guesthouse offers eight colour-themed, artfully designed rooms (four with sea view), each with hand-crafted oak furnishings inlaid with slate, crisp white cotton sheets and applestone-tiled bathrooms. They also have an

excellent restaurant (see below). **£90**

Maes-y-Môr 25 Bath St, SY23 2NN ☎ 01970 639270, ⓦ maesymor.co.uk; map p.706. Brightly painted and very central guesthouse with nine rooms (seven twins, a double and a family room), though bathrooms are shared; there's a kitchen for guest use, as well as laundry facilities. Breakfast not included. **£50**

Yr Hafod 1 South Marine Terrace, SY23 1JX ☎ 01970 617579, ⓦ yrhafod.co.uk; map p.706. Good-value seafront accommodation, with spacious, well-maintained and tastefully decorated rooms (some en-suite and several with sea views). **£70**

EATING

Agnelli's 3 Bridge St, SY23 1PY ☎ 07969 959466; map p.706. You'll find the best espresso for miles around at this warm and welcoming Italian-run deli/café. Hot drinks go down a treat with a slice of Sicilian cannoli with vanilla; there's more substantial food too, such as grilled Tuscan sausages with pancetta (£8) or baked aubergines in a parmesan crust. Mon–Sat 10am–8pm.

Gwesty Cymru 19 Marine Terrace, SY23 2AZ ☎ 01970 6122252, ⓦ gwestycymru.com; map p.706. The

accomplished slate-floored restaurant of this hotel (see above) offers an exciting, thoroughly modern Welsh menu featuring the likes of Welsh lamb rump with sautéed kale, leeks and Parmentier potatoes (£19.50), and Welsh honey and lavender crème brûlée. Mon–Sat noon–2.30pm & 6–9pm, Sun noon–2.30pm.

★ **Pysgoty** The Harbour, South Promenade, SY23 1JY ☎ 01970 624611, ⓦ pysgoty.co.uk; map p.706. Located in a former public convenience, the "Fish House"

15

fully deserves its many plaudits. A tiny space, with just four tables inside and half a dozen outside, the restaurant serves more or less whatever comes in off the boat that day, so you might end up with wild turbot with chorizo mash or fillet of John Dory with pea and mint risotto (£18), but you'll usually find a couple of house staples such as Cardigan Bay lobster with herb butter (£18.50). Tues & Wed 10am–5pm, Thurs–Sat 10am–10pm.
Ultracomida 31 Pier St, SY23 2LN ☎ 01970 630686, ⓦ ultracomida.co.uk; map p.706. Spain comes to Aber

in this fabulous deli, its walls lined with Iberian wines and meats, alongside Welsh cheeses and all manner of other goodies. You can sample tapas (£4–5), like *croquetas* with Welsh cheddar and chilli jam, or deep-fried Basque peppers in tempura batter, in the casual restaurant/bar at the rear, which is also a cool spot to kick back with a coffee. Deli Mon–Sat 10am–6pm, Sun noon–5pm; restaurant Mon 10am–5pm, Tues–Sat 10am–10pm, Sun noon–4pm.

DRINKING

Ship and Castle Corner of Vulcan and High sts, SY23 1JG ☎ 01970 612334; map p.706. Much smarter inside than out, this nicely refurbished pub offers a pool table and

a great jukebox, and takes considerable pride in having the best selection of real ales in town. Mon 4pm–midnight, Tues–Sun 2pm–midnight.

ENTERTAINMENT

Aberystwyth Arts Centre The University, Penglais, SY23 3DE ☎ 01970 623232, ⓦ aberystwythartscentre. co.uk. The town's main venue for arthouse cinema, touring theatre, classes, events and wide-ranging temporary exhibitions.

Côr Meibion Aberystwyth Aberystwyth Rugby Cub, Plascrug Ave, SY23 1HL ☎ 01970 202980, ⓦ aberchoir. co.uk. Visitors are welcome to attend rehearsals of the local male voice choir, which take place every Thurs 7–8.30pm.

Vale of Rheidol

Inland from Aberystwyth, the River Rheidol winds its way up to a secluded, wooded **valley**, where old industrial workings have sometimes moulded themselves into the contours, rising up past waterfalls and hamlets to **Devil's Bridge**. The latter is best accessed by narrow-gauge railway; otherwise you need your own transport.

Vale of Rheidol Railway

Park Ave, Aberystwyth, SY23 1PG • April–Oct 2–4 trains most days • £21 return • ☎ 01970 625819, ⓦ rheidolrailway.co.uk

Steam trains on the narrow-gauge **Vale of Rheidol Railway** wheeze their way along steep hillsides from the Aber terminus to Devil's Bridge, some twelve miles distant. It was built in 1902, ostensibly for the valley's lead mines but with a canny eye on its tourist potential as well, and has run ever since. The trip takes one hour each way (though you can break your journey at any of the seven intermediate stations), and is most enjoyable from the comfortable first-class observation carriage (£3 extra each way) or the open-sided "summer car".

Devil's Bridge

Devil's Bridge, A4120, 12 miles east of Aberystwyth, SY23 3JW • ☎ 01970 890233, ⓦ devilsbridgefalls.co.uk

Folk legend, incredible scenery and travellers' lore combine at **DEVIL'S BRIDGE** (Pontarfynach), a tiny settlement that can be reached by road or, far more scenically, via the Vale of Rheidol Railway, whose upper terminus is here (see above). The **bridge** spanning the chasm of the churning River Mynach is actually three stacked bridges: the eleventh-century original, a stone arch from 1753 and the modern road bridge.

Punch Bowl and Mynach Falls

Easter–Oct daily 9.30/9.45am–5/6pm • Punch Bowl £1 in the turnstile; Mynach Falls £3.75 at the ticket office by the entrance to the walks – outside office hours, and Nov–Easter, pay £2 in the turnstile

Beyond the turnstile on Devil's Bridge, head down slippery steps to the deep cleft for a remarkable view of the **Punch Bowl**, where the water pounds and hurtles through the gap crowned by the bridges. Across the road from the Punch Bowl the trails around the rashing **Mynach Falls** offer even more dramatic sights as the path tumbles down into he valley below the bridges. The scenery here is magnificent: sharp, wooded slopes rise way from the frothing river and distant mountain peaks surface on the horizon.

Bwlch Nant yr Arian

A44, 9 miles east of Aberystwyth, SY23 3AB • Visitor centre daily 10am–5pm • Free • ☎ 01970 890453, ⓦ naturalresources.wales/bwlchnantyrarian • Bus #525 (Mon–Sat; 20min) from Aberystwyth stops outside

Bwlch Nant yr Arian is a prominent activity centre, as well as being one of the country's most important red kite feeding centres. From the **visitor centre**, which has a decent café with a lovely deck, three well-marked walking trails (30min, 1hr & 2hr) head out into the evergreen forest and among the abandoned lead-mining detritus. The easiest and shortest trail loops around a lake past the kite hide, a superb spot for watching the daily red kite feeding (3pm, 2pm in winter) when 20lb of beef and lamb lure up to two hundred kites. The woods also offer top-class **mountain biking**, with three dedicated trails: two red (5.6 miles and 11 miles) and one black (22 miles; 4–5hr); pick up a trail map from the shop. There are no rentals.

15

Machynlleth and around

Eighteen miles northeast of Aberystwyth is **MACHYNLLETH** (pronounced "ma-hun-thleth"), a bustling little place with a great vibe, as well as being the undisputed centre of all things New Age, thanks in large part to the nearby **Centre for Alternative Technology**. The wide main street, **Heol Maengwyn**, is busiest on Wednesdays, when a lively market springs up; **Heol Penrallt** intersects this at the fussy clocktower.

Owain Glyndŵr Centre

Heol Maengwyn, SY20 8EE • Easter–Sept Mon–Sat 11am–3pm • Free • ☎ 01654 702932, ⓦ canolfanglyndwr.org

The **Owain Glyndŵr Centre**, in the partly fifteenth-century **Parliament House**, charts the course of Glyndŵr's life, his military campaigns, his downfall, and the 1404 parliament in the town, when he controlled almost all of what is now known as Wales and even negotiated international recognition of the sovereign state (see below).

Museum of Modern Art, Wales

Heol Penrallt, SY20 8AJ • Mon–Sat 10am–4pm • Free • ☎ 01654 703355, ⓦ moma-machynlleth.org.uk

The **Museum of Modern Art, Wales**, housed in a beautifully serene old chapel, hosts temporary exhibitions. It also has a peaceful, arty **café**, and is the place to go for films,

---

OWAIN GLYNDŴR, WELSH HERO

Owain Glyndŵr has remained a potent figurehead of Welsh nationalism since he rose up against the occupying English in the early fifteenth century. He was born into an aristocratic family, and studied English in London, where he became a distinguished soldier of the English king. When he returned to Wales to take up his claim as Prince of Wales, he became the focus of a rebellion born of discontent with the English rulers.

Glyndŵr garnered four thousand supporters and attacked Ruthin, Denbigh, Rhuddlan, Flint and Oswestry, before finally encountering English resistance at Welshpool. In a vain attempt to break the spirit of the rebellion, England's Henry IV drew up severely punitive laws, even outlawing Welsh-language bards and singers. Even so, by the end of 1403, Glyndŵr controlled most of Wales. In 1404, he was crowned king of a free Wales and assembled a parliament at Machynlleth, where he drew up mutual recognition treaties with France and Spain. Glyndŵr made plans to carve up England and Wales into three as part of an alliance against the English king, but started to lose ground before eventually being forced into hiding (where he died). The anti-Welsh laws remained in place until the coronation of Henry VII, who had Welsh origins, in 1485, and Wales was subsequently subsumed into English custom and law.

theatre, comedy and concerts. The **Gŵyl Machynlleth festival** (ⓦmachynllethfestival.co.uk) is held here in August, which combines classical and folk music with theatre and debate.

Centre for Alternative Technology

A487, 3 miles north of Machynlleth, SY20 9AZ • Daily: April–Oct 10am–5pm; Nov–March 10am–4pm; guided tours (1hr; free) daily 2pm in the school hols • April–Oct £8.50; Nov–March free • ☎ 01654 705950, ⓦ cat.org.uk • Bus #34 (Mon–Sat hourly–every 2hr) from Machynlleth

After the oil crisis of 1974, seven acres of a once-derelict slate quarry were turned into the **Centre for Alternative Technology** (**CAT**), an almost entirely sustainable community. At one stage, eighty percent of the power was generated from wind, sun and water, but this is no back-to-the-land hippy commune. Much of the on-site technology was developed and built here, though with the rise of eco-consciousness the emphasis has shifted more towards promoting its application in urban situations. CAT's water-balanced **cliff railway** (Easter–Oct) whisks visitors 200ft up from the car park to the beautiful main site, sensitively landscaped using local slate and wood, and you can easily spend half a day sauntering around. There's plenty for kids, a good wholefood restaurant and an excellent shop.

Corris Mine Explorers

Corris Craft Centre, Corris, 6 miles north of Machynlleth, SY20 9RE • Tours all year on demand, book ahead • Taster (50min) £12.50, Explorer (2hr) £27, Expedition (4hr) £52 • ☎ 01654 761244, ⓦ corrismineexplorers.co.uk • The #X27 from Machynlleth to Dolgellau runs to the craft centre (Mon–Sat every 45min–1hr, Sun 2; 15min)

In **CORRIS**, a small former slate-quarrying settlement north of Machynlleth, **Corris Mine Explorers** takes adventure enthusiasts – kitted out in climbing harnesses and helmets – deep into a cool, dark, disused slate mine that has been barely touched since it closed in 1970. Ancient tallow candles are stuck to the walls, hand drills lie scattered along the passageways and winch flywheels still spin at the slightest touch. Adventurous parties might be clipped into safety wires in order to sidle along the steeply shelving walls of a vast slate cavern, while others might just want to hear fascinating stories about mining life. Wear something warm.

ARRIVAL AND DEPARTURE

By train The station is a 5min walk up Heol Penrallt from the town's central clocktower.

Destinations Aberdyfi (8 daily; 20min); Aberystwyth (10–12 daily; 30min); Harlech (8 daily; 1hr 25min); Porthmadog (8 daily; 2hr).

By bus Buses stop close to Machynlleth's central

MACHYNLLETH AND AROUND

clocktower, and many also call at the train station.

Destinations Aberdyfi (Mon–Sat 7 daily, Sun 2; 25min); Aberystwyth (Mon–Sat hourly, Sun 3; 45min); Corris (Mon–Sat every 45min–1hr, Sun 2; 15min); Dolgellau (Mon–Sat hourly, Sun 2; 30min); Tywyn (Mon–Sat 7 daily, Sun 2; 35min).

ACCOMMODATION AND EATING

Maenllwyd Newtown Rd, SY20 8EY ☎ 01654 702928, ⓦ maenllwyd.co.uk. Comfortable eight-room B&B in a former manse, one of which is a good-sized family option. There is also a large garden, plus off-street parking. **£65**

Quarry Café Heol Maengwyn, SY20 8EB ☎ 01654 702624, ⓦ thequarrycafemachynlleth.co.uk. This popular wholefood café offers a cracking veggie menu featuring the likes of chilli with Welsh yoghurt and the "Big Mach" burger (lentil patty, soya mayonnaise and a wholesome salad; £5.75). Mon–Fri 9am–4pm, Sat & Sun 10am–3pm.

Wynnstay Arms Heol Maengwyn, SY20 8AA ☎ 01654 702941, ⓦ wynnstay.wales. Some rooms in this former coaching inn have heavy beams, creaky floors and a four-

poster, others are relatively modern. While the classic slate-floored restaurant itself is justifiably popular (try grilled plaice with capers and mint butter; £14.50), most people come for the superb pizzeria in an adjoining building to the rear. The bar is a fine place for a beer. Restaurant daily noon–2pm & 6.30–9pm; pizzeria Wed–Sun 4.30–9.30pm; bar daily 11am–11pm. **£95**

★**Ynyshir Hall** A487, 6 miles southwest of Machynlleth beside the Ynys-hir Nature Reserve, SY20 8TA ☎ 01654 781209, ⓦ ynyshir.co.uk. This sublime country-house hotel in expansive manicured grounds has ten gorgeous rooms, but it's the Michelin-starred restaurant that really stands out. Dishes such as pollock with black bean, crab with elderflower and wild strawberry, or sheep's oghurt with olive oil and wood sorrel are listed on a nine-course lunch menu (£55), eighteen-course dinner menu (£110) or, for the ultimate gastronomic experience, the

Chef's Table (£130). Booking essential. Tues 6.30–9pm, Wed–Sat noon–2pm & 6.30–9pm. **£210**

Aberdyfi and around

The proud maritime heritage of **ABERDYFI** (Aberdovey) has largely been replaced by its reincarnation as a well-heeled resort. With its south-facing aspect across the Dyfi estuary, it's a lovely base for exploring the Talyllyn and Dysynni valleys to the north. There's not much in the way of activities – though you can swim at **Cemetery Beach**, about a mile and a half north.

Talyllyn Railway

Station Rd, Tywyn, 5 miles north of Aberdyfi, LL36 9EY • April–Oct 2–7 trains daily; also some winter weekends (check website for details) • £17.50 unlimited one-day travel • ☎ 01654 710472, ⓦ talyllyn.co.uk

Experience the lower Talyllyn Valley aboard the cute 27-inch gauge **Talyllyn Railway**, the inspiration for Thomas the Tank Engine. The railway tootles seven miles inland from **TYWYN** through the delightful wooded valley to the old slate quarries at Nant Gwernol. From 1866 to 1946, the rail line hauled slate to Tywyn Wharf station. Five years after the quarry closed, rail enthusiasts took over the running of services, making this the world's first volunteer-run railway. The round trip takes just over two hours, but you can get on and off as frequently as the schedule allows, taking in some fine broadleaf forest walks (best at Dolgoch Falls station), or the small village of **Abergynolwyn**.

15

ARRIVAL AND INFORMATION

ABERDYFI

By train Aberdyfi is served by two train stations: the request-only Penhelig, 0.5 mile east (the most convenient for the centre of town); and Aberdyfi, 0.5 mile west of the tourist office.

Destinations Machynlleth (9 daily; 20min); Porthmadog (8 daily; 1hr 30min); Tywyn (8 daily; 15min).

By bus The #28 and #X29 from Machynlleth and Tywyn stop close to the tourist office.

Destinations Machynlleth (8 daily; 20min); Tywyn (8 daily; 10min).

Tourist office Wharf Gardens (Easter–Oct daily 9.30am–5pm; ☎ 01654 767321, ⓦ aberdovey.org.uk).

ACCOMMODATION AND EATING

Britannia Inn 13 Seaview Terrace, LL35 0EF ☎ 01654 767426, ⓦ britannia-aberdovey.co.uk. There is usually a lively atmosphere at this town centre pub, especially when the sun comes out and everyone piles onto the deck for the sunset with a pint of real ale. Meals are a significant cut above the usual pub standard and might include Aberdyfi crab (£12.95). Mon–Wed 11am–midnight, Thurs–Sat 11am–

1am, Sun noon–midnight; kitchen daily noon–9pm.

Llety Bodfor 1 Bodfor Terrace, LL35 0EA ☎ 01654 767475, ⓦ lletybodfor.co.uk. The fairly typical frontage of this Aberdyfi townhouse hides the town's swankiest accommodation; singles, doubles and suites, all with sea views. The guest lounge is equipped with a piano, games, DVDs and a stack of vintage vinyl. Breakfast £12. **£80**

Dolgellau and around

The handsome former county town of **DOLGELLAU** still maintains an air of unhurried importance, never more so than when the area's farmers pile into town for market. With the lofty crags of **Cadair Idris** framing the grey squares and streets, Dolgellau feels as Welsh as it is possible to be.

Coed-y-Brenin

A470, 8 miles north of Dolgellau, LL40 2HZ • **Forest** Daily 24hr • Free • **Visitor Centre** April–Oct daily 9.30am–5pm; Nov–March Mon–Fri 9.30am–4.30pm, Sat & Sun 9am–5pm • ☎ 01341 440747, ⓦ naturalresources.wales/coedybrenin

The vast **Coed-y-Brenin** forest park is home to some of Wales' finest **mountain biking**, with miles of old trackways, roads and eight purpose-built trails crisscrossing the hillsides,

WALKS AROUND DOLGELLAU

There are some great **walks** and beautiful cycle trails around Dolgellau. Here are a couple of the best:

Mawddach Trail (10 miles from Dolgellau to Barmouth; flat). Follow this beautiful combined walking and cycle route along a disused rail line beside the Mawddach estuary's broad sands.

Precipice Walk (3–4 miles; 2hr; negligible ascent). Easy-going loop with great views to the 1000ft ramparts of Cadair Idris and along the Mawddach estuary – best in late afternoon or early morning sun.

Cadair Idris: Pony Path (9 miles; 4–5hr; 2800ft ascent). If the weather is fine, don't miss this classic and enjoyable ascent of Cadair Idris. Early views to the craggy flanks of the massif are tremendous, but they disappear as you climb steeply to the col, where you turn left on a rocky path to the summit shelter on Penygadair (2930ft).

offering lung-busting uphill rides and adrenalin-pumping descents. They're all graded like ski runs: black for experts, red and blue for intermediates and green for family riders. Here, too, is the UK's first bespoke trail-running centre, with five waymarked routes ranging from a mile-long shoe-test route to a half-marathon distance; there are also superb walking trails, orienteering and geocaching courses, and innovative kids' play areas. You can rent bikes (£25/3hr, £30/day), buy a pack of trail maps (£2.50; or download free from the website), take a shower (£1) and recover in the very decent café.

ARRIVAL AND INFORMATION

By bus Buses pull into Eldon Square. Most northbound services head inland past Coed-y-Brenin.
Destinations Bala (Mon–Sat 10 daily, Sun 5; 40min); Machynlleth (Mon–Sat hourly, Sun 3; 30min); Porthmadog (Mon–Sat 7 daily, Sun 4; 50min).

DOLGELLAU AND AROUND

Bike rental Dolgellau Cycles, Smithfield St (March–Oct daily 9.30am–5pm; Nov–Feb Tues–Sat 9.30am–5pm; ☎01341 423332, ⓦdolgellaucycles.co.uk), rents bikes (£13/half-day, £20/day) suitable for the Mawddach Trail (see page 712) and offers repairs and servicing.

ACCOMMODATION

Ffynnon Love Lane, LL40 1RR ☎01341 421 774, ⓦffynnontownhouse.com. Six impeccable rooms in this large house, variously furnished with mahogany beds, slipper baths and French chandeliers, but all with separate sitting areas and great views. Rates include afternoon tea on arrival and daily newspapers, and there's an honesty bar in the lounge. Two-night minimum stay at weekends. **£150**

Graig Wen A493, 5 miles west of Dolgellau near Arthog, LL39 1YP ☎01341 250482, ⓦgraigwen.co.uk. Access is steep but the Mawddach estuary views make it all worthwhile at this wonderfully tranquil campsite with B&B. There's camping in both the upper and lower (car-free) fields, the latter offering a wilder camping experience with compost toilets and campfires. Camping/person **£9**, doubles **£110**

★ **Tan y Gader** Meyrick St, LL40 1LS ☎01341 421102, ⓦtanygader.co.uk. This sociable guesthouse offers three startlingly original rooms crammed with playful elements alongside a host of thoughtful touches like fresh coffee and shortbread, bedside hand cream and eye masks. Guests are encouraged to use the cosy drawing room, chock-full of books and games, which is also where tea and home-made cake are served upon arrival. **£85**

Y Meirionnydd Smithfield Square, LL40 1ES ☎01341 422554, ⓦthemeirionnydd.com. This solid stone Georgian townhouse has been refashioned as a chic five-roomed hotel with light tones and blond woods offset by feature cushions and curtains; the retro Roberts radios are a great addition. **£85**

EATING AND DRINKING

Gwin Dylanwad Smithfield St, LL40 1ET ☎01341 422870, ⓦdylanwad.com. Part café, part bar, this charmingly run establishment is highly respected for the quality of its wines, which go down a treat with the small plates (around £6–8) – herring with mustard mayonnaise, for example, or goat's cheese with apple and Welsh honey. The place oozes atmosphere, above all in the adjoining glass conservatory. Tues & Wed 10am–6pm, Thurs–Sat 10am–11pm

★ **Siop Coffi T.H.** Bridge St, LL40 1BD ☎01341 423573. This large, perennially busy café was once the town's ironmongers, as the old fixtures and fittings testify: a long, raised wooden table where folk tap away on laptops, and the former glassed-in office, which is now a snug. Come for freshly made baguettes and paninis, sumptuous cakes and freshly roasted coffee. Mon–Sat 9am–5.30pm, Sun 10am–4pm.

15

Harlech

Charming **HARLECH**, twenty miles northwest of Dolgellau, is one of the highlights of the Cambrian coast, with its time-worn castle dramatically clinging to its rocky outcrop and the town cloaking the ridge behind, commanding one of Wales' finest views over Cardigan Bay to the Llŷn.

Harlech Castle

Castle Square, LL46 2YH • March–June, Sept & Oct daily 9.30am–5pm; July & Aug daily 9.30am–6pm; Nov–Feb Mon–Sat 10am–4pm, Sun 11am–4pm • £6.50; CADW • ☎ 01766 780552, ⓦ cadw.gov.wales/daysout/harlechcastle

The substantially complete **Harlech Castle** sits on a 200ft-high bluff, a site chosen by Edward I to create one more link in his magnificent chain of fortresses. Begun in 1285, it was built of a hard Cambrian rock, known as Harlech grit, hewn from the moat. Harlech withstood a siege in 1295, but was taken by Owain Glyndŵr in 1404. The young Henry VII held out against a seven-year siege at the hands of the Yorkists until 1468, when the castle was again taken. It fell into ruin, but was put back into service for Charles I during the Civil War; in March 1647, it was the last Royalist castle to fall. The first defensive line comprised the three successive pairs of gates and portcullises built between the two massive half-round towers of the **gatehouse**. Much of the castle's outermost ring has been destroyed, leaving only the 12ft-thick curtain walls rising up 40ft to the exposed **battlements**. Only the towering gatehouse prevents you from walking the full circuit. The entrance is through a new **visitor centre**, linked to the castle by an impressive curving pedestrianized bridge suspended over the moat.

ARRIVAL AND INFORMATION
HARLECH

By train The train station is on the A496 below the castle. **Destinations** Barmouth (8 daily; 25min); Machynlleth (8 daily; 1hr 20min); Porthmadog (8 daily; 20min).

By bus Buses generally call both at the train station and at the southern end of High St.

Destinations Barmouth (Mon–Sat hourly, Sun 3; 30min); Porthmadog (Mon–Sat 7 daily; 25min).

Tourist information There's no tourist office in town, but the castle's visitor centre (see above) can provide all the information you need on the town and area.

ACCOMMODATION AND EATING

As.Is Castle Square, LL46 2YH ☎ 01766 781208, ⓦ asis-harlech.com. Marvellous little bistro next to the castle with tables culled from pallets and filament bulbs strung across the ceiling. Refreshingly original food combinations might include radish, mustard and red pepper strudel with kale and walnut puree (£11.50), or lamb Henri with parmesan polenta and salsa verde. Mon, Tues & Thurs–Sat 5.30–9pm.

★ **Castle Cottage** Pen Llech, LL46 2YL ☎ 01766 780479, ⓦ castlecottageharlech.co.uk. Established "restaurant with rooms" with a contemporary yet cosily informal feel. The seven rooms are natural-toned and very well appointed, many with massive weathered beams and slate floors. In the gorgeous restaurant, meanwhile, you can choose from a two- or three-course menu (£35/£40), which gets you canapés followed by the likes of pan-seared scallops with avocado and poppy seed dressing. Daily 7–10pm. **£130**

Cemlyn Tea Shop Stryd Fawr, LL46 2YA ☎ 01766 780425, ⓦ cemlynteashop.co.uk. Upmarket café serving the best loose-leaf teas and espresso coffees around, plus home-made gluten- and dairy-free cakes, and afternoon tea (£6.20). If you can, grab a table on the sunny terrace and soak up the marvellous coastal views. Mid-March to Dec Wed–Sun 9.30am–5pm.

Pen Y Garth Old Llanfair Rd, LL46 2SW ☎ 01766 781352, ⓦ pen-y-garth.co.uk. High-quality and super-friendly B&B in a former YHA with three, mostly all-white, rooms, each with a view of either the castle or coast. It's popular with cyclists, golfers and walkers – they can provide packed lunches. **£75**

15

North
Wales

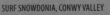

SURF SNOWDONIA, CONWY VALLEY

North Wales

The A55 motorway makes the North Wales coast easily accessible, but it hasn't tamed the wild interior of this stunningly beautiful area. No question, Snowdonia is the crowning glory of the region. A cluster of jagged peaks and soaring cliffs, broad glacial valleys and waterfalls, the area measures little more than ten miles by ten but has enough mountain paths to keep the most experienced hiker happy for weeks. The folds of the mountains reveal atmospheric Welsh castle ruins, while the lowlands are perfect for lakeside rambles and rides on heritage steam trains. And meanwhile, a string of innovative launches have seen the region stake a claim to be the adventure capital of Great Britain.

Snowdonia is the heart of the massive **Snowdonia National Park** (Parc Cenedlaethol Eryri) which falls within the county of **Gwynedd** and extends north and south, beyond the bounds of Snowdonia itself (and beyond the bounds of this chapter, into Chapter 15), to encompass the Rhinogs, Cadair Idris (see page 702) and 23 miles of superb coastal scenery. One of the best approaches to Snowdonia is along the **Dee Valley**, a fertile landscape historically much fought over by the Welsh and the English. There's a tangibly Welsh feel to **Llangollen**, a great base for a variety of ruins, rides and rambles, as well as the venue for the colourful **International Music Eisteddfod**. Pressing on along the A5 – the region's second main road – you hit the fringes of Snowdonia at **Betws-y-Coed**, which is slightly twee but great for gentle walks and mountain biking. As you head deeper into the park, old mining and quarry towns such as **Beddgelert** or **Llanberis** make good bases for walks or adrenaline activities in former slate capital **Blaenau Ffestiniog**, while on the eastern fringes of Snowdonia, **Bala** tempts with whitewater rafting down the Tryweryn.

West of Snowdonia, the former slate port of **Porthmadog** is home to the eccentric "village" folly of **Portmeirion** and two superb narrow-gauge steam railways: the **Ffestiniog Railway** and **Welsh Highland Railway**. Beyond lies the **Llŷn peninsula**, a rural wellspring of Welsh language where Wales ends in a flourish of small coves and former fishing villages. Roads loop back along the Llŷn to **Caernarfon**, which is overshadowed by its stupendous castle.

Separated from the mainland by the Menai Strait, the island of **Anglesey** is a largely flat patchwork of fields, beautiful beaches, ancient sites and Edward's final castle in the handsome town of **Beaumaris**. Back on the mainland is the university and cathedral city of **Bangor**, and **Conwy**, where a picturebook castle and narrow streets huddle above a scenic quay. Victorian **Llandudno** is easily the best of the north coast's seaside resorts, with the cultural sights of **Bodelwyddan Castle** and the cathedral of **St Asaph** within day-trip distance.

GETTING AROUND

By train Fast services along the north coast run all the way to the Irish ferries at Holyhead on Anglesey, while the delightful Conwy Valley line threads inland to link up with the narrow-gauge Ffestiniog Railway at Blaenau Ffestiniog. From here you can continue on the tourist Ffestiniog Railway to Porthmadog and then the Welsh

16

CAERNARFON CASTLE

Highlights

❶ Llangollen Small but substantial, this enjoyable riverside town features a romantic house, an impressive aqueduct and lovely castle ruins. See page 719

❷ Snowdon Scale Wales' highest mountain, with six hiking paths and a cog railway converging on the summit-top café and bar. See page 728

❸ Llŷn peninsula This heartland of the Welsh language is a pastoral drop off the radar, with a gorgeous coastline, especially around Aberdaron. See page 731

❹ Portmeirion Spend the day at this surreal seaside "village", the setting for the cult TV series *The Prisoner*. See page 732

❺ Caernarfon Castle One of the greatest of Edward I's "Iron Ring" of thirteenth-century castles. See page 736

❻ Beaumaris A fine castle and Georgian townscape make this a splendid base for exploring Anglesey's beaches and Neolithic remains. See page 738

❼ Conwy The pick of North Wales' towns, with its imposing castle and intact ring of medieval walls enclosing a fascinating centre. See page 742

❽ Llandudno The British Victorian seaside resort par excellence, with one of the finest period piers in the country, and the limestone hummock of Great Orme a cable car ride away. See page 745

HIGHLIGHTS ARE MARKED ON THE MAP ON PAGE 718

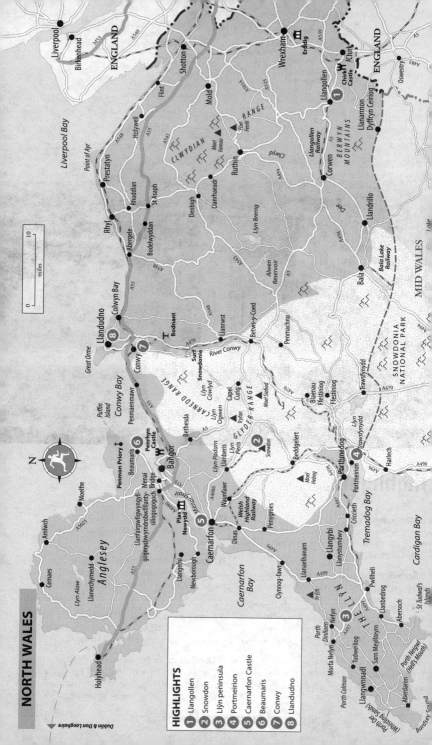

Highland Railway from there through Beddgelert and across the southern flanks of Snowdon to Caernarfon.

By bus Buses plug the gaps, especially the Snowdon Sherpa services, which provide hiker access all around

Snowdon and the Ogwen Valley. There is no useful bus or train service linking Llangollen with Snowdonia along the A5: instead head along the north coast to either Llandudno Junction or Bangor then inland from there.

Llangollen and around

LLANGOLLEN, just six miles from the English border, is the embodiment of a Welsh town, clasped in a narrow valley where a weighty Gothic bridge straddles the River Dee. This was an important town long before the early Romantics arrived at the end of the eighteenth century. Turner came to paint the swollen river and the Cistercian ruin of **Valle Crucis**; John Ruskin found the town "entirely lovely in its gentle wildness"; and George Borrow made Llangollen his base for the early part of his 1854 tour detailed in *Wild Wales*. The rich and famous also came to visit the "Ladies of Llangollen" at **Plas Newydd**. But by this stage some of the town's rural charm had been eaten up by the works of one of the century's finest engineers, Thomas Telford, who squeezed both his London–Holyhead trunk road and the **Llangollen Canal** alongside the river.

Plas Newydd

Butler's Hill, LL20 8AW • **House** April, May & Sept Mon & Wed–Sun 10.30am–5.30pm; June–Aug daily 10.30am–5.30pm; Oct Mon & Wed–Sun 10.30am–4pm • £6 • **Grounds** Daily 9am–dusk (until 9pm in summer) • Free • ☎ 01978 862834, ⓦ plasnewyddllangollen.co.uk

Set in twelve acres of formal gardens, the mock-Tudor **Plas Newydd** was, for almost fifty years, home to the **Ladies of Llangollen**. Lady Eleanor Butler and Sarah Ponsonby were a lesbian couple, from Anglo-Irish aristocratic backgrounds, who tried to elope at the end of the eighteenth century. After two botched attempts dressed in men's clothes, they were grudgingly allowed to leave their respective ancestral homes in Ireland in 1778 with enough allowance to settle in Llangollen, where they became celebrated hosts. Despite their desire for a "life of sweet and delicious retirement", they didn't seem to mind the constant stream of guests. Walter Scott was well received, though he found them "a couple of hazy or crazy old sailors", and like "two respectable superannuated clergymen" in their mode of dress. Visitors' gifts of sculpted **wood panelling** formed the basis of the riotous friezes of woodwork that cover the walls; this is set off by a mixed bag of furniture in a style similar to that owned by the ladies.

Llangollen Railway

Llangollen station, Abbey Rd, LL20 8SN • April–Sept Mon–Fri 3 services daily (usually steam), plus most Sat & Sun year-round up to 7 steam and diesel services daily • £15 return • ☎ 01978 860979, ⓦ llangollen-railway.co.uk

The hills around Llangollen echo to the shrill cry of steam engines easing along the **Llangollen Railway**, shoehorned into the north side of the valley. From Llangollen's time-warped station ancient carriages proudly sporting the liveries of their erstwhile owners are hauled along ten miles of the old Ruabon–Barmouth line to Corwen.

Castell Dinas Brân

Above town, LL20 8DY • Daily 24hr • Free • Follow signs from Llangollen Wharf

The panoramic view, especially at sunset, justifies the 45-minute slog up to **Castell Dinas Brân** (Crow's Fortress Castle), a few evocative stumps of masonry perched on a hill 750ft above town. This was once the district's largest and most important fortress, built in the 1230s by the ruler of northern Powys, Prince Madog ap Gruffydd Maelor. Edward I captured it as part of his first campaign against Llywelyn ap Gruffydd, and it was then left to decay.

16

> ### THE LLANGOLLEN INTERNATIONAL MUSIC EISTEDDFOD
>
> Llangollen is heaving all summer, especially in early July, when for six days the town explodes in a frenzy of music, dance, poetry and colour. Unlike the National Eisteddfod, which is a purely Welsh affair, the **Llangollen International Eisteddfod** (ⓦ international-eisteddfod.co.uk) draws amateur performers from fifty countries, all competing for prizes inside the six-thousand-seat Royal International Pavilion and at several other venues. The eisteddfod has been held in its present form since 1947, when forty choirs from fourteen countries performed. Today, more than four thousand participants lure up to 150,000 visitors, and there is an irresistible *joie de vivre* as brightly costumed dancers stroll the streets and fill the restaurants. When the day's competition is over, headlining stars often pack out the Pavilion; the final Sunday is the all-day party known as Llanfest.
>
> The eisteddfod is followed by the less frenetic **Llangollen Fringe** (ⓦ llangollenfringe.co.uk), which sees a number of more alternative acts in the town hall.

Valle Crucis Abbey

A542, 1.5 miles north of Llangollen, LL20 8DD • Daily: April–Oct 10am–5pm; Nov–March 10am–4pm • April–Oct £4; Nov–March free; CADW • ☎ 01978 860326, ⓦ cadw.gov.wales/daysout/vallecrucisabbey

The gaunt ruin of **Valle Crucis Abbey** greets you with its largely intact west wall, pierced by the frame of a rose window. Though one of the last Cistercian foundations in Wales, and Britain's first Gothic abbey, it is no match for Tintern Abbey (see page 651), but nevertheless stands majestically in a pastoral – and much-less-visited – setting. After the Dissolution in 1535, the church fell into disrepair and the monastic buildings were used as farm buildings. Now they hold displays on monastic life, reached by a detour through the mostly ruined cloister and past the weighty vaulting of the chapter house.

Llangollen Canal

Built in 1806, Thomas Telford's **Llangollen Canal** remains one of Britain's finest feats of canal engineering. Passing without locks through fourteen miles of hilly terrain, it starts at **Horseshoe Falls**, a crescent-shaped weir two miles west of Llangollen, which diverts water from the River Dee into the canal. The eleven miles from here via the spectacular **Pontcysyllte Aqueduct** and Chirk Aqueduct to the English border are a UNESCO World Heritage Site (ⓦ pontcysyllte-worldheritage.co.uk).

Pontcysyllte Aqueduct

Four miles east of Llangollen, LL20 7TP • **Boat tours** Easter–Oct daily noon, 1pm, 2pm & 3pm; 45min • £7.50 • ☎ 01978 824166, ⓦ canaltrip.co.uk

The 1000ft-long **Pontcysyllte Aqueduct**, rising almost 127ft above the Dee, is still the world's highest navigable aqueduct. Telford's design, positioning long cast-iron troughs on nineteen great stone piers, was bold for its time. You can take a vertiginous walk along the **towpath** across the top or a leisurely **narrowboat ride** across and back.

Erddig Hall

Off the A483, 10 miles northeast of Llangollen, LL13 0YT • Daily: house late March to July, Sept & Oct 12.30–3.30pm; Aug 10am–5pm; Nov to late March 11am–2.30pm; garden, shop and restaurant late March to Oct 10am–5pm; Nov to late March 11am–4pm • Late March to Oct £11.80, garden only £7.60; Nov to late March £5.60 (kitchens, outbuildings only), garden only £3.70; NT • ☎ 01978 355314, ⓦ nationaltrust.org.uk/erddig

Ancestral home of the Yorke family, the seventeenth-century **Erddig Hall** has now been restored to its 1922 appearance: the State Rooms have their share of fine furniture and portraits, but the real interest lies below in the servants' quarters. Eighteenth- and early nineteenth-century portraits of staff still hang in the Servants' Hall, each with a verse written by one of the Yorkes. You can also see the blacksmith's shop, lime yard, stables, laundry, kitchen, still-used bakehouse and the lovely walled garden.

ARRIVAL AND INFORMATION

By train Trains stop 5 miles east at Ruabon, which is served by Llangollen–Wrexham buses.

By bus Buses from Bala (9 daily; 1hr) and Dolgellau (9 daily; 1hr 45min) stop on Parade St (as do daily National Express coaches on the Wrexham–Llangollen–Birmingham–London run: tickets are sold at the tourist office).

Tourist office Y Capel, Castle St (Mon–Sat 9.30am–5pm, Sun 9.30am–4pm; ☎01978 860828, ⓦllangollen.org.uk).

ACCOMMODATION

Cornerstones 15–19 Bridge St, LL20 8PF ☎01978 861569, ⓦcornerstones-guesthouse.co.uk. The over-the-top exuberance of this luxury B&B, spread across three sixteenth-century houses, can easily be forgiven when you see the river views. Amenities include DVD library, well-appointed guest lounges and an extensive breakfast. Midweek deals are available. **£120**

★ **Glasgwm** Abbey Rd, LL20 8SN ☎01978 861975, ⓦglasgwm-llangollen.co.uk. Relaxed B&B with plenty of books, a piano and engaging hosts whose good taste is reflected in the decor of the doubles, twin and single (which has its own deep bath). They'll do Offa's Dyke pick-ups and drop-offs, as well as packed lunches and dinners. **£70**

Llangollen Hostel Berwyn St, LL20 8NB ☎01978 861773, ⓦllangollenhostel.co.uk. A Victorian townhouse with modernized rooms (mostly en suite, with four to six bunks), a well-equipped kitchen and a comfy lounge. Dorms **£18**, doubles **£45**

★ **Tyddyn Llan Country House** Llandrillo, 15 miles southwest, LL21 0ST ☎01490 440264, ⓦtyddynllan. co.uk. A dozen individually designed, en-suite rooms (and a suite) above an excellent, Michelin-starred restaurant (see below). B&B or dinner, bed and breakfast rates available – and well worth doing when the food's this good. **£190**

Wern Isaf Farm Wern Rd, LL20 8DU ☎01978 860632, ⓦwernisaf.co.uk. Simple but lovely farmhouse campsite almost a mile up the steep Wern Rd (turn right over the canal on Wharf Hill). Closed Nov–March. **£15**

EATING

★ **The Corn Mill** Dee Lane, LL20 8PN ☎01978 869555, ⓦbrunningandprice.co.uk/cornmill. Superb conversion of a town-centre mill, with a sunny riverside deck. Good all day for coffee, fine ales, sandwiches (£6) and café-bar food. Mains (£11–19) might include crispy harissa lamb with couscous and felafels; seabass with mussels and samphire; or spinach and ricotta tortellini with roasted butternut squash. Mon–Sat 11am–11pm, Sun 11am–10.30pm; kitchen Mon–Sat noon–9.30pm, Sun noon–9pm.

★ **Gales Wine Bar** 18 Bridge St, LL20 8PF ☎01978 860089, ⓦgalesoflllangollen.co.uk. Old church pews, wooden floors, delicious bistro-style food and a good raange of wines from around the world make this chilled-out place a local favourite. Dishes come as starter or main portions (£6–8/£11–19); there's also a two-course set lunch (£10). Mon–Sat noon–2pm & 6–9.30pm, Sun noon–2pm.

Tyddyn Llan Country House Llandrillo, 15 miles southwest, LL21 0ST ☎01490 440264, ⓦtyddynllan. co.uk. Elegant Georgian restaurant-with-rooms (see above), where the emphasis is on Bryan Webb's Michelin-starred, Modern British food. Two-/three-course lunches £29/£36; three-course dinner £65, six-/nine-course tasting menus £75/£90. Mon–Thurs 7–9pm, Fri–Sun 1–2pm & 7–9pm.

DRINKING AND NIGHTLIFE

Sun Inn 49 Regent St, LL20 8HN ☎01978 860079. Convivial, slate-floored locals' pub with a wide range of well-kept beers and live bands (of just about any stripe) most nights. Tues–Fri 7pm–2am, Sat & Sun 5pm–2am.

16

WHITEWATER RAFTING AT BALA

The little town of **BALA** (Y Bala), on the border of Snowdonia National Park, twenty miles southwest of Llangollen, sits at the northern end of Wales's largest natural lake, **Llŷn Tegid**. Nearby, waters crash down the Tryweryn River, perfect for **whitewater rafting**. Water is released around two hundred days a year at the **National White Water Centre** (Jan to mid-Oct & Dec daily 9am–dusk; ☎01678 521083, ⓦukrafting.co.uk), crashing down a mile and a half of Grade III rapids where numerous rafting options include the Taster (40min–1hr; £35) involving two runs down the course. The 2hr session (£66) typically gives you four runs, or you can step up a notch to the Orca Adventure (half-day; £88) involving two runs down in a normal raft followed by a chance to tackle the rapids in a more challenging two-person inflatable.

Ruthin

Strategically set in the middle of the Vale of Clwyd, fifteen miles northwest of Llangollen, charming **RUTHIN** (Rhuthun) boasts some of the area's finest food and lodging. An attractive knot of half-timbered buildings centres on **St Peter's Square**.

Nantclwyd y Dre

Castle St, LL15 1DP • April, May & Sept Mon & Sun 11am–3pm, Sat 11am–5pm; June–Aug Mon & Wed 11am–4pm, Tues & Sun 11am–3pm, Sat 11am–5pm • £5 • ☎ 01824 709822, ⓦ nantclwydydre.co.uk

Dating from 1435, **Nantclwyd y Dre** is Wales' oldest hall-house, a wonderfully higgledy-piggledy place, with wonky oak floors and interesting nooks and crannies. Extended over five centuries, its major phases are re-created in seven rooms including Jacobean and Georgian bedrooms, a Stuart study, a Victorian schoolroom and an entrance hall of 1942.

Ruthin Gaol

Clwyd St, LL15 1HP • April–Sept Mon & Wed–Sun 10am–5pm • £5 • ☎ 01824 708281, ⓦ ruthingaol.co.uk

Although **Ruthin Gaol** has been a prison site since 1654, visits focus on the Victorian cell block intended to improve living conditions and penal correction, with one prisoner per cell and the requirement to work while incarcerated. You can poke around freely, following the life of a fictional prisoner on a free audio guide.

ARRIVAL AND DEPARTURE   RUTHIN

By bus Buses stop at the corner of Market St and Wynnstay Rd.

Destinations Chester (3 daily; 1hr); Rhyl (hourly; 75min); Wrexham (hourly; 45min).

ACCOMMODATION AND EATING

★ **Leonardo's Deli** 4 Well St, LL15 1AH ☎ 01824 707161, ⓦ leonardosdeli.co.uk. Great Welsh/German deli/bakery where quality is paramount. April–Oct Mon–Fri 8.30am–5pm, Sat 8.30am–4.30pm; Nov–March Mon–Thurs 9am–3.30pm, Fri 9am–4.30pm, Sat 9am–3pm.

★ **Manorhaus** 10 Well St, LL15 1AH ☎ 01824 704830, ⓦ manorhausruthin.com. Georgian house with boldly themed boutique rooms plus a fine restaurant (£25/£30 for two/three courses). Tues–Sat 6.30–9pm. **£95**

Snowdonia

The mountains of **Snowdonia** present Wales at its grandest – a fantastic landscape of glacial valleys and ridges as sharp as dragon's backs. Such is its grandeur it comes as a surprise to learn that the tallest peaks only just top 3500ft. It was to this mountain fastness that Llewelyn ap Gruffydd, the last true prince of Wales, retreated in 1277 after his first war with Edward I. It was also here that Owain Glyndŵr held on most tenaciously to his dream of regaining for the Welsh the title of Prince of Wales. Centuries later, the English slate barons built huge fortunes from slate and reshaped the patterns of Snowdonian life forever, as men seeking steady work in the quarries left the hills and moved to the towns.

Thousands of hikers arrive every weekend to walk up **Snowdon** massif (Eryri) over steep and constantly varying terrain. Several of the ascent routes are superb, and you can also take the cog railway to the summit café from **Llanberis**. But the other mountains are just as good and far less busy, giving unsurpassed views of Snowdon. The **Glyderau** and **Tryfan** – best tackled from the **Ogwen Valley** – are particular favourites for more experienced walkers.

Small settlements dot in the valleys, usually coinciding with some former mine or quarry. Foremost among these are **Blaenau Ffestiniog**, Wales' former slate capital now turned activities town, and **Beddgelert**, both of which have mines open to the public.

SNOWDONIA **NORTH WALES** | 723

The only place of any size not associated with slate mining is **Betws-y-Coed**, a largely Victorian resort away from the higher peaks.

Betws-y-Coed and around

BETWS-Y-COED (pronounced "betoos-e-coyd"), sprawled around the confluence of the Conwy, Llugwy and Lledr valleys, overlooked by the conifer-clad slopes of the **Gwydyr Forest Park**, and centred on the low cataract of **Pont-y-Pair Falls**, is almost totally devoted to the needs of holidaymakers. Walkers and mountain bikers are the focus – there are a lot of outdoor gear retailers, but no decent grocery shop – but the town has the best choice of accommodation in the region and most visitors use it as a base. Serious mountain walkers, however, might want to head west instead to Snowdon and the Glyderau range. For everyone else there are delightful, easy strolls to the local beauty spots of the **Conwy** and **Swallow** falls.

Fairy Glen

Signposted off A470, 2 miles south of Betws-y-Coed, LL24 0SH • Daily 24hr • Car park £1, turnstile 50p

Southeast of town, after negotiating a series of rapids, the waters of the Conwy River follow a staircase of drops and enter **Fairy Glen**, a lovely cleft in a small wood; it is named after the Welsh fairies, the Tylwyth Teg, once believed to live here. Bring your swimming costume in summer – the narrow gorge is idyllic when waters are slow, especially in a pool where two rivers meet.

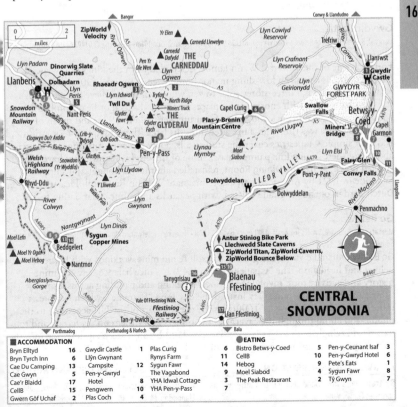

■ ACCOMMODATION					● EATING				
Bryn Elltyd	16	Gwydir Castle	1	Plas Curig	6	Bistro Betws-y-Coed	5	Pen-y-Ceunant Isaf	3
Bryn Tyrch Inn	6	Llŷn Gwynant		Rynys Farm	11	CellB	10	Pen-y-Gwryd Hotel	6
Cae Du Camping	13	Campsite	12	Sygun Fawr	14	Hebog	9	Pete's Eats	1
Cae Gwyn	5	Pen-y-Gwryd		The Vagabond	9	Moel Siabod	4	Sygun Fawr	8
Cae'r Blaidd	17	Hotel	8	YHA Idwal Cottage	3	The Peak Restaurant	2	Tŷ Gwyn	7
CellB	15	Pengwern	10	YHA Pen-y-Pass	7				
Gwern Gôf Uchaf	2	Plas Coch	4						

> ### BETWS-Y-COED BIKING
>
> There's good trail riding in the **Gwydyr Forest Park**, north and west of Betws-y-Coed. The classic route is the **Marin Trail** (15 miles; 2–4hr) near Llanrwst – single-track heaven with big climbs and swooping descents, ridgelines and deep forest, plus great scenery. Other trails include **Dolen Eryri** and **Dolen Machno** near Penmachno. You can rent bikes at Beics Betws (hardtails from £32/day; ☎01690 710766, ⓦbikewales.co.uk) behind the post office.

Conwy Falls

A5, 3 miles south of Betws-y-Coed, LL24 0PN • Daily 24hr • £1

South of Betws-y-Coed the river plunges 50ft over the **Conwy Falls** into a deep pool. After paying the fee, you can view the falls on the right and a series of rock steps to the left; these were cut in 1863 as a kind of primitive fish ladder so spawning fish could swim up the waterfall, but are now superseded by a tunnel through the rock on the far side.

Swallow Falls

A5, 2 miles west of Betws-y-Coed towards Capel Curig, LL24 0DW • Daily 24hr • £1.50 via turnstile

Swallow Falls is one of the region's most visited sights, but it's really no more than a pretty cascade. You can pay to view or catch a glimpse from the **Llugwy Valley Walk** (3 miles; 400ft ascent; 1hr 30min), a forested path from the north side of Pont-y-Pair Falls which follows the twisting river upstream towards Capel Curig. Along the way you pass the steeply sloping **Miners' Bridge**, below which are a series of plunge pools, perfect for swimming.

Gwydir Castle

Llanrwst, 3.5 miles north of Betws-y-Coed via B5106, LL26 0PN • April–Oct Wed–Sun 10am–4pm • £6 • ☎01492 641687, ⓦgwydir-castle.co.uk

Former home of the powerful Wynn family, descended from the kings of Gwynedd, **Gwydir Castle** is actually a low-slung manor house begun around 1490 with later additions. Its core is a three-storey solar tower, whose windows relieve the gloom of the great halls, each with enormous fireplaces and stone-flagged or heavy timber floors. Most of the original fittings and Tudor furniture were sold in 1921, and much of the rest of the house was ruined in a fire a few months later. The subsequent restoration was kept simple – tapestries cover the stone walls, a few pieces of furniture are scattered about and there's some fine painted glass. Some of the original furnishings have been tracked down, as has the **Dining Room**, reinstalled after it was bought and shipped Stateside in 1921 by American newspaper magnate William Randolph Hearst. The **Dutch Garden** outside is Grade I-listed, with peacocks and a fine cedar dating to 1625.

Go Below

Meet at Conwy Falls Café, 3 miles southeast of Betws-y-Coed, LL24 0PN • Times vary; reservations required • ☎01690 710108, ⓦwww.go-below.co.uk

Go Below tours take you underground to explore old **mine workings** with harness, helmet and headlamp. The "Challenge" trip (£49) is a nice balance between mine history and activity tour, involving zip lines, abseiling and paddling across a small subterranean lake. Too tame? Try instead the day-long "Extreme", which explores a mine at Blaenau Ffestiniog; at 1600ft it's the deepest part of the UK accessible to the public. You climb through the caverns as the miners knew them on via ferrata and too-narrow, dizzyingly high ledges (you're harnessed on) before a steep zip-line ride into the void. There's one version for over-14s and another for over-18s (£79/£89).

ARRIVAL AND INFORMATION

By train Trains from Llandudno Junction arrive via the gorgeous Conwy Valley.

Destinations Blaenau Ffestiniog (5 daily; 30min); Llandudno (4 daily; 40–50min); Llandudno Junction (6

daily; 30min); Llanrwst (6 daily; 5min).
By bus Buses (including the Snowdon Sherpa) fan out from near the train station.
Destinations Bangor (3 daily; 50min); Blaenau Ffestiniog (5 daily; 25min); Capel Curig (10 daily; 12min); Llyn Ogwen (3 daily; 20min); Llanberis/Pen-y-Pass (10 daily; 35min); Llandudno (6 daily; 50min); Llanrwst (every 2hr; 10min); Penmachno (4 daily; 30min).

INFORMATION AND ACTIVITIES

Tourist information The region's largest National Park information centre is in Royal Oak Stables off Station Rd (daily: Easter to mid-Oct 9.30am–5pm; mid-Oct to Easter 9.30am–4pm; ☎01690 710426).
Plas y Brenin: The National Mountain Sports Centre A4086 Capel Curig, 6 miles west of Betws-y-Coed, LL24 0ET ☎01690 720214, ⓦpyb.co.uk. Built around a former coaching inn, this centre runs well-regarded multi-day skills training courses in hiking, mountaineering, kayaking, skiing and rock climbing. There's also a small artificial ski slope (Tues–Fri 1–9pm, Sat–Sun 10.30am–6pm; £10 first hour, then £5/hr).

ACCOMMODATION

Bryn Tyrch Inn Capel Curig, 6 miles west of Betws-y-Coed, LL24 0EL ☎01690 720223, ⓦbryntyrchinn.co.uk; map p.723. Sensitively modernized small inn with a relaxed, informal style and tasteful rooms, some with old stone walls. It also has four-bunk en-suite dorms (minimum three in one room) plus a good restaurant and bar offering local ales and tasty food (mains mostly £15–19) Two-night minimum at weekends. Closed mid-Dec to mid-Jan. Pub and kitchen mid-Jan–Easter & Oct to mid-Dec Fri–Sun noon–3pm & 5.30–9pm; Easter–Sept pub daily noon–11pm, kitchen noon–3pm & 5.30–9.30pm. Dorms £25, doubles £90
Gwydir Castle Llanwrst, 3 miles north of Betws-y-Coed, LL26 0PN ☎01492 641687, ⓦgwydir-castle.co.uk; map p.723. A chance to stay in a Tudor manor – former guests include King George V and Queen Mary (albeit as Duke and Duchess of York) – that feels like a family home. Two bedrooms have been fitted in baronial style, with four-posters, deep baths and nicely eclectic decor. TVs are anathema. No children under 12. Minimum two nights at weekends. Reservations required. £95
Pengwern Allt Dinas, 1.5 miles east of Betws-y-Coed on the A5, LL24 0HF ☎01690 710480, ⓦsnowdonia accommodation.co.uk; map p.723. There are slate floors and art on the walls in this elegant, three-room B&B, formerly the residence of a Victorian artists' colony. Great views down the valley, too; book the Richard Gay Somerset room for a bath with a view. In summer they also have a sweet self-contained cottage for two with a wood-burner (three nights minimum; from £80/night). £84

★**Plas Curig** A5, Capel Curig, LL24 0EL ☎01690 720225, ⓦsnowdoniahostel.co.uk; map p.723. Wales' only independent five-star hostel is as stylish as a boutique B&B: the public areas are beautiful, with slate floors and reclaimed wood, and dorms are splendid – custom-built bunks with privacy curtains and bed lights. Choose between four- and eight-bed dorms, doubles, twins and family rooms (no en-suites), plus a luxury self-catering cottage for up to six (five nights minimum; from £138). Two-night minimum at weekends. Dorms £25, doubles £55
★**Rynys Farm** A5, 3 miles southeast of Betws-y-Coed near the Conwy Falls, LL24 0PN ☎01690 710218, ⓦrynys-camping.co.uk; map p.723. Pure rural bliss on a National Trust-listed farm campsite with plenty of flat sites tucked behind trees or against dry-stone walls, great valley views, good facilities and eco principles. The charming owners will sell you farm eggs. There's also a bell tent, yurt and shepherd's hut, all sleeping two, plus a static caravan that sleeps four. Camping/person £8, bell tent £40, caravan £40, hut £45, yurt £50
The Vagabond Craiglan Rd, LL24 0AW ☎01690 710850, ⓦthevagabond.co.uk; map p.723. A small independent hostel with four- to eight-bunk dorms and family rooms, plus facilities including secure bike lock-up and off-street parking. Though there's a self-catering kitchen they serve breakfasts (£5) and maintain an inexpensive bar. Bookings recommended at weekends when B&B is obligatory. Dorms £20

16

EATING

Bistro Betws-y-Coed Holyhead Rd, LL24 0AY ☎01690 710328, ⓦbistrobetws-y-coed.co.uk; map p.723. Owner-chef Gerwyn Williams offers modern and traditional food in his casual bistro. Either way, the seasonal dishes have a Welsh bias and showcase regional produce. Lunches are light; dinners, such as local lamb marinated in Snowdonian honey (£16.25), up the ante. March–May Wed–Sun 11.30am–2.30pm & 6–9pm; June–Sept daily 11.30am–2.30pm & 6–9pm; Oct–Feb Wed–Fri 6.30–9pm, Sat & Sun 11.30am–2.30pm & 6–9pm.
Moel Siabod A5, Capel Curig, LL24 0EL ☎01690 720429, ⓦmoelsiabodcafe.co.uk; map p.723. Preparing to go out? Hard day in the hills? This hangar-like café is your place for big breakfasts (£6.95), fresh home-made mains (around £12) like chilli con carne, and home-made cake. With maps and old climbing magazines to browse, it's the best outdoors

enthusiasts' caff in the area. Mon–Fri & Sun 7.30am–6pm (summer hols Mon–Fri till 8pm), Sat 7.30am–8pm.

Tŷ Gwyn A5, 0.5 mile southeast of Betws-y-Coed, LL24 0SG ☎01690 710383, ⓦtygwynhotel.co.uk; map p.723. First choice for historic atmosphere is this former coaching inn, which positively creaks with old oak furniture. Traditional dishes (mains £13–19) including cottage pie, halibut with creamed leeks and slow-braised lamb are served in the bar or a snug restaurant. Reservations recommended. Daily noon–2pm & 6–9pm (Jan closed Mon–Wed).

Ogwen Valley

Northwest of Capel Curig, the A5 forges through the **Ogwen Valley**, which separates the Carneddau massif from the rock-strewn summits of the **Glyderau** range and triple-peaked **Tryfan,** perhaps Snowdonia's most demanding mountain. West of Tryfan, the road follows the shores of **Llyn Ogwen**, to the YHA hostel, the start of some of the UK's finest walks.

ZipWorld Velocity

Signposted off A5 south of Bethesda, LL57 4YG · Booking centre daily 9am–6pm · £70 · ☎01248 601444, ⓦzipworld.co.uk

Who would've imagined a disused quarry could be so much fun? **ZipWorld Velocity**, the world's fastest zip wire (and Europe's longest single span, at just over a mile) was strung above a former slate quarry in 2013 to provide a ride at speeds of up to 70mph. Reservations are essential and there are restrictions on weight, height and age. Note too that the weather can affect your ride and that ZipWorld offers rescheduling, not refunds.

ARRIVAL AND DEPARTURE   OGWEN VALLEY

By bus From mid-April to Oct the #S6 Snowdon Sherpa runs between Bethesda and Capel Curig (Sat & Sun 3 daily; 30min), continuing either to Betws-y-Coed (20min) or Bangor (30min).

ACCOMMODATION

★ **Gwern Gôf Uchaf** A5, 4 miles west of Capel Curig, LL24 0EU ☎01690 720294, ⓦtryfanwales.co.uk; map p.723. Superbly located campsite right at the base of Tryfan with a decent shower block, and a good fourteen-berth bunkhouse with a fully equipped kitchen and drying room. Bring a sleeping bag and food. Camping/person **£5**, dorms **£12**

YHA Idwal Cottage A5, 5 miles west of Capel Curig, LL57 3LZ ☎0345 371 9744, ⓦyha.org.uk/hostel/ idwal; map p.723. Perfectly sited for walkers, this former quarry manager's house was opened as one of Wales' first hostels in 1931. Well refurbished since, it offers mostly four-bunk dorms, a double, a single, family rooms and an alcohol licence, but no meals. Opens 5pm for check-in. Limited opening Nov–March (mostly weekends); check the website. Camping **£13**, dorms **£25**, doubles **£59**

Llanberis and around

LLANBERIS is the nearest you'll get in Wales to an alpine climbing village. Its single main street is thronged with walkers and climbers – people march out with rucksacks around 9am, leaving the place quiet during the day, and then return from the hills from mid-afternoon. Miraculously, it also survives as a Welsh rural community. Most visitors come for **Snowdon**, to which Llanberis is inextricably linked, not least because of the five-mile **Snowdon Mountain Railway** ride to the summit (page 728). If you plan to walk up, most routes start from **Pen-y-Pass**, 5.5 miles east.

Dinorwig Power Station

Tours start from the Electric Mountain complex on the A4086, LL55 4UR · Underground tours (1hr) 4 daily, or 7 daily in the school holidays: Easter–May, Sept & Oct 10am–4pm; June–Aug 9.30am–5.30pm · £8.50 · ☎01286 870636, ⓦelectricmountain.co.uk

Views north from Llanberis are dominated by the entrance to the **Dinorwig Power Station**, hollowed out of the ground in the mid-1970s and visitable on a subterranean bus tour. It actually consumes more electricity than it produces, but benefits the national grid by being able to instantly supply electricity to cope with surges in demand.

WALKS FROM THE OGWEN VALLEY

Tourists hike up Snowdon (see page 729), but mountain connoisseurs prefer the sharply angled peaks of **Tryfan** and the **Glyderau**, with their challenging terrain, cantilevered rocks and fantastic views back to Snowdon. If you're going to attempt the walks, arm yourself with either the 1:50,000 OS *Landranger* #115 or the 1:25,000 OS *Explorer* OL17 map.

Cwm Idwal (1.5 miles return; 1hr; 200ft ascent). An easy hike on a well-graded path leading up to Llŷn Idwal, nestled in the magnificent cirque of Cwm Idwal. The area was designated Wales' first nature reserve in 1954, after botanists discovered rare arctic-alpine plants growing here. Tackling the rough, rocky paths right around the lake can turn this into a half-day outing, partly beneath huge sloping cliffs – the Idwal Slabs.

Tryfan Miners' Track (5 miles; 4–6hr; 2000ft ascent). The easiest route up Tryfan, from the car park at Idwal Cottage. You'll need to use your hands for the final section up the South Ridge of Tryfan, past the Far South Peak to the summit. You can then tackle the 5ft jump between Adam and Eve, the two chunks of rhyolitic lava that crown the mountain. Don't underestimate the seriousness of the leap: it's only when you see the mountain dropping away on all sides that it hits home quite how disastrous it would be to overshoot.

Padarn Country Park

Gilfach Ddu, LL55 4TY • Daily 24hr • Free

At **Padarn Country Park**, beside Lake Padarn, 0.5 miles northeast of Llanberis centre, lakeside oak woods are gradually recolonizing the discarded workings of the defunct **Dinorwig Slate Quarries**, formerly one of the largest slate quarries in the world. Equipment and engines that once hauled materials up inclined tramways punctuate the paths that link levels chiselled from the hillside.

National Slate Museum

Gilfach Ddu, LL55 4TY • Easter–Oct daily 10am–5pm; Nov–Easter Mon–Fri & Sun 10am–4pm • Free • ☎ 01286 870630, Ⓦ museumwales.ac.uk

The former quarry's maintenance workshops now house Wales' **National Slate Museum**, where a 50ft-diameter water wheel that once powered cutting machines still turns. Most of the equipment was still in use until the quarries closed in 1969 and is familiar to the former quarry workers who demonstrate how to split an inch-thick slab of slate into perfectly smooth slivers. The slate was delivered to the slate-dressing sheds by means of a maze of tramways, cranes and rope lifts, all kept in good order in the fitting and repair shops. Look out for the slate workers' cottages, furnished in the styles of 1861, 1901 and 1969.

ARRIVAL AND INFORMATION
LLANBERIS AND AROUND

By bus Buses stop along High St. Frequent Sherpa #S1 buses travel up daily to Pen-y-Pass, 5.5 miles east of Llanberis. It can be a good approach even if you're travelling by car, since the Pen-y-Pass car park is usually full at weekends and school holidays; if so use the park-and-ride car park at the bottom of the pass, near the *Vaynol Arms*.
Destinations Bangor (9 daily; 45min); Betws-y-Coed (10 daily; 50min); Caernarfon (Mon–Sat every 30min, Sun 8; 25min); Capel Curig (10 daily; 35min); Pen-y-Pass (roughly every 30min; 10min).

Tourist information There's no dedicated tourist office, but the Electric Mountain (see page 726) doubles as an information point, with leaflets.

ACCOMMODATION

Cae Gwyn Nant Peris, 2 miles southeast, LL55 4UF ☎ 01286 870718; map p.723. Climbers and bikers make up the bulk of the clientele in this basic field campsite and very primitive bunkhouse (bring everything). It's handy for the *Vaynol Arms* pub opposite and the Pen-y-Pass park-and-ride. Camping/person __£6__, bunkhouse __£12__

★ **Pen-y-Gwryd Hotel** 6.5 miles east of Llanberis, LL55 4NT ☎ 01286 870211, Ⓦ pyg.co.uk; map p.723. Wonderfully rustic hotel where the 1953 Everest expedition stayed while training; there are plenty of mementos. Rooms (some en suite) are priced per person; some share magnificent Edwardian bathrooms. __£90__

16

Plas Coch High St, LL55 4HB ☎01286 872122, ⊛plas cochsnowdonia.co.uk; map p.723. Beautifully refurbished B&B with seven en-suite rooms plus an extra bathroom with a tub for post-hike soaks. The owners are going the extra mile, and offer packed lunches to hikers. **£80**

YHA Pen-y-Pass Pen-y-Pass LL55 4NY ☎0345 371 9534, ⊛yha.org.uk/hostel/snowdon-pen-y-pass; map p.723. The only accommodation at Pen-y-Pass had a £1.3m renovation in 2015 to transform what was long a popular walkers' hostel – George Mallory's ill-fated Everest team stayed here – into a modern option. There are a few private twins (some en suite), a café-bar, a laundry and drying room, but no wi-fi. Access 7am–10.30pm. Dorms **£24**, doubles **£60**

EATING

The Peak Restaurant 86 High St, LL55 4SU ☎01286 872777, ⊛peakrestaurant.co.uk; map p.723. This unflashy open-kitchen restaurant has long been the best place to eat in Llanberis, championing home-made, seasonal and fresh food long before it became fashionable. Seabass with leek and dill potato cake (£18) typify a Modern British menu which usually finds space for a daily curry and a pie. Booking advised. Wed–Sun 7–10pm.

Pen-y-Ceunant Isaf Snowdon Path, LL55 4UW ☎01286 872606, ⊛snowdoncafe.com; map p.723. An eighteenth-century cottage café, 400yd up the Llanberis Path, that's been serving Welsh teas and home-baked cakes for decades. There are no meals, but you're welcome to eat your own sandwiches here if you buy a cuppa. Daily: April–Oct 9am–10pm; Nov–March 10am–6pm.

Pen-y-Gwryd Hotel 6.5 miles east of Llanberis, LL55 4NT ☎01286 870211, ⊛pyg.co.uk; map p.723. Non-guests are welcome at the restaurant at this hotel (see above) – plain, mid-priced, home-cooking – or to pop in for a pint. March to mid-Nov daily noon–2pm & 7.30pm (set dinnertime); mid-Nov to Dec Fri & Sat noon–2pm & 7.30pm, Sun noon–2pm.

Pete's Eats 40 High St, LL55 4EU ☎01286 870117; map p.723. A Llanberis legend for walkers, climbers and bikers for its cheap unpretentious grub – full breakfasts (£5), lamb burgers or fish and chips (£7) – in large portions. There are heaps of magazines and maps to browse and free wi-fi, so it's always busy when the weather turns bad. Daily: summer 8am–9pm; rest of year 6am–8pm.

Snowdon

Hardened walkers sometimes dismiss **Snowdon** (3560ft) as overcrowded. It can certainly be busy; in summer there are bottlenecks on the more popular footpaths to the summit and a thousand visitors a day press into the postbox-red carriages of the **Snowdon Mountain Railway**. But this fine mountain massif sports some of the finest walking and scrambling in the national park (see page 729): hike early, late or in shoulder seasons if you want a bit more solitude. Summer crowds aside, the target of some walking purists' disdain is the licensed summit café and gift shop, *Hafod Eryri* (mid-May to Oct). Still, you try resisting a cuppa – or perhaps a beer – by the time you reach it.

Snowdon Mountain Railway

Victoria Terrace (on A4086), Llanberis, LL55 4TT • Mid-March to Oct daily 9am–2.30pm (roughly three ascents): Clogwyn Station mid-March to May; summit May–Oct • Clogwyn Station return £16 (no singles); summit return £29, one-way £22; booking fee £3.50; £6 discount if reserving in advance for 9am train • ☎01286 870223, ⊛snowdonrailway.co.uk

The **Snowdon Mountain Railway** is Britain's only rack-and-pinion railway, completed in 1896. Trains (sometimes pushed by 70-year-old steam locos) still climb to the summit in just under an hour from the eastern end of Llanberis. Times, type of locomotive and final destination vary – summit or Clogwyn Station, halfway up – according to demand and conditions at the top. Be warned: it's popular – buy tickets in advance during settled summer weather.

Beddgelert

A huddle of grey houses around a bridge, **BEDDGELERT** is arguably the prettiest village in the area. A sentimental tale tells how the town got its name: **Gelert's Grave** (*bedd* means burial place) is supposedly the final resting place of a local prince's faithful dog, Gelert, slain by his master by mistake. In truth, the sentimental yarn is a Victorian fabrication dreamed up by a publican to lure tourists – the full tale is related by the enclosed "grave" just south of town.

16

ASCENDING SNOWDON

The following are justifiably the most popular of the seven accepted **walking** routes up Snowdon. All are easy to follow in good weather, but you should still carry the 1:25,000 OS *Explorer* OL17 map. If you're not equipped or confident enough to get out on the mountain by yourself, a number of companies offer bespoke **guided trips**, featuring everything from straightforward hillwalking to scrambling, rock climbing (for all abilities), navigation and winter climbing. Try Paul Poole Mountaineering (Ⓦ paulpoolemountaineering.co.uk) or Raw Adventures (Ⓦ raw-adventures.co.uk). Expect to pay around £160 a day for a couple.

Llanberis Path (5 miles to summit; 3200ft ascent; 3hr). The easiest and longest route up Snowdon, following the rail line, which gets gradually steeper, to the "Finger Stone" at Bwlch Glas (Green Pass). This marks the arrival of the routes coming up from Pen-y-Pass to join the Llanberis Path for the final ascent to Yr Wyddfa, the summit.

Miners' Track (4 miles to summit; 2400ft ascent; 2hr 30min). The easiest of the three routes up from Pen-y-Pass, a broad track leading south then west to the dilapidated remains of the former copper mines in Cwm Dyli. Skirting around the right of a lake, the path climbs more steeply to the lake-filled Cwm Glaslyn, then again to Upper Glaslyn, followed by a switchback ascent to the junction with the Llanberis Path.

Pig Track (3.5 miles to summit; 2400ft ascent; 2hr 30min). A steeper and stonier variation on the Miners' Track, leaving from the western end of the Pen-y-Pass car park and climbing up to Bwlch y Moch (the Pass of the Pigs) before meeting the Miners' Track prior to the zigzag up to the Llanberis Path.

Snowdon Horseshoe (8 miles round trip; 3200ft ascent; 5–7hr). One of the UK's finest ridge walks starts up the knife-edge ridge of Crib Goch before a full circuit around three glacier-graven cwms. It's not to be taken lightly: take advice before you travel and take all the relevant OS maps.

Sygun Copper Mine

1 mile northeast of Beddgelert on A498, LL55 4NE • Self-guided audio tours (45min) daily: summer 9.30am–5pm; rest of year 10am–4pm; closed mid-Nov to Dec except Christmas; last admission 1hr before closing • £8.95 • ☎ 01766 890595, Ⓦ syguncoppermine.co.uk

Copper ore was first mined here by the Romans, then by nineteenth-century prospectors. The **Sygun Copper Mine** showcases what was once the valley's main source of income on a family-oriented self-guided **tour** through the multiple levels of restored tunnels and galleries (cool at 9°C). It's more interesting than exciting, featuring costumed mannequins and a disembodied voice of a miner describing his working life.

Aberglaslyn Gorge

A few hundred yards downstream from Beddgelert, the river crashes down the picturesque **Aberglaslyn Gorge** towards Porthmadog. You can walk past Gelert's Grave, then cross over the bridge onto a path along the left bank for a mile, affording a closer look at the river's course through chutes and channels. Return the same way; the round trip takes around an hour.

Welsh Highland Railway

23 Oberon Woods, LL55 4YW • Late March to Oct 2–4 trains daily • Sample return fares: to Caernarfon £30.50; to Porthmadog £21.90 ; one child under 16 travels free with an adult • ☎ 01766 516000, Ⓦ festrail.co.uk

Beddgelert is linked to Caernarfon and Porthmadog by the **Welsh Highland Railway** (see page 732). You could just ride through the Aberglaslyn Gorge to Nantmor (£4.50), then walk back to Beddgelert along the Fisherman's Path (1hr) or walk the Lon Gwyrfai path and cycle track to Rhyd Ddu (4.5 miles; £7.50) then catch the train back. Bikes can be rented in Beddgelert from beside the station.

ARRIVAL AND INFORMATION	BEDDGELERT

By bus Beddgelert is on two bus routes: the #S4 Snowdon Sherpa from Caernarfon and the #S97 between Pen-y-Pass and Porthmadog.

Destinations Caernarfon (Mon–Sat 7 daily; 30min); Pen-y-Pass (2 daily; 20min); Porthmadog (Mon–Sat 8 daily, Sun 3; 30–50min).

Tourist information There's a national park visitor centre on the A498 in the village centre (Easter–Oct daily 9.30am–5pm; ☎ 01766 890615, ⓦ beddgelerttourism. com).

ACCOMMODATION

★ **Cae Du Camping** A498, 0.5 mile north, LL55 4NE ☎ 01766 890345, ⓦ caeducampsite.co.uk; map p.723. Spacious and peaceful site that is immaculately maintained without affecting the natural beauty of the area; there are a few lovely stream-side pitches. Good facilities include hot showers, some power hook-ups and a small shop. Closed Oct–Feb. **£21**

Llŷn Gwynant Campsite A498, 5 miles northeast, LL55 4NW ☎ 01766 890853, ⓦ gwynant.com; map p.723. A lakeside site, in a gorgeous valley beneath Snowdon, which can host more than three hundred tents yet still retain its natural appeal. You can access the Watkin Path directly from here, and they rent out kayaks and canoes (June–Sept). Hot showers are free, mobile phones don't work. Closed Nov to mid-March. Per person **£10**

Sygun Fawr 1 mile northeast off A498, LL55 4NE ☎ 01766 890258, ⓦ sygunfawr.co.uk; map p.723. The smartest of the local hotels, offering comfy rooms in a seventeenth-century country house with beams and stone walls. The big draws here are the peace (no TVs in rooms) and, from some rooms, the views across to Snowdon. Closed Dec to mid-Feb. **£89**

EATING

Hebog Caernarfon Rd, LL55 4UY ☎ 01766 890400, ⓦ hebog-beddgelert.co.uk; map p.723. This rustic-chic bistro ticks all the boxes. Alongside jacket potatoes and the now requisite gourmet burgers more ambitious dishes include traditional game pie or lamb with local samphire (£19). There are a few tables beside the river – great on warm days. Daily noon–10pm.

Sygun Fawr 1 mile northeast off A498, LL55 4NE ☎ 01766 890258, ⓦ sygunfawr.co.uk; map p.723. The restaurant at this country house hotel (see above), open to non-residents, serves the likes of slow-cooked Welsh lamb shank with red wine *jus* (mains £13–16). Tues–Sun 6–10pm.

Blaenau Ffestiniog

BLAENAU FFESTINIOG sits at the head of the Vale of Ffestiniog, hemmed in by bare slopes strewn with splintered slate. Thousands of tonnes of the stuff were once hewn from the underground caverns until the last subterranean mine closed in 1951. For some years the town was only kept alive by a rather tired slate-cavern tour and the splendid, narrow-gauge **Ffestiniog Railway** (see page 732). Today, a revamped tour and a series of new attractions in the old quarries have seen Blaenau rebrand itself as an adrenaline-sports capital. Despite such recent shifts towards tourism, however, it remains a gritty, scruffy and utterly genuine place.

Slate Caverns

A470, 1 mile north of Blaenau Ffestiniog, LL41 3NB • Tours daily 9.30am–5.30pm, last tour 4.30pm; 1hr 15min; reservations recommended • Each tour £20, combined ticket £30 • ☎ 01766 830306, ⓦ llechwedd-slate-caverns.co.uk

In 1898, as housing demand boomed during the Industrial Revolution, Snowdonia's quarries were producing half a million tonnes of dressed slate a year. For a sense of what slate meant to Blaenau Ffestinog, visit the **Slate Caverns**. The **Llechwedd Deep Mine Tour** uses a steeply inclined railway to descend into the deepest part of the mine – a labyrinth of impressive tunnels that angle back into the gloom. The natural partner to the subterranean trip is the **Quarry Explorer**, an off-road adventure in a 4WD truck that grinds uphill among the shattered slate tailings.

ZipWorld Caverns and ZipWorld Bounce Below

Daily 9.30am–5.30pm; 3–5 tours, up to 1hr (Bounce Below) and 3hr (Caverns); reservations required • Bounce Below £25, ZipWorld Caverns £60 • ☎ 01248 601444, ⓦ zipworld.co.uk

In the mine, but operated by a different company, the two ZipWorld adventures re-interpret the caverns as huge playgrounds. **ZipWorld Caverns** is the most intrepid of the pair; an Indiana Jones-style adventure that combines the thrill of zip lines (including the steepest in the UK) with rope bridges. **ZipWorld Bounce Below** lets you explore via a series of slides and huge suspended trampolines. Kids love it.

16

Antur Stiniog Bike Park

A470, 1 mile north of Blaenau Ffestiniog, LL41 3NB · Thurs–Sun 9am–5.30pm; daily during school hols · Mon–Fri £29; Sat & Sun £32.50; daily £20 for a half-day · ☎ 01766 238007, ⓦ anturstiniog.com

Launched in 2012, **Antur Stiniog Bike Park** – an ambitious downhill and free-ride park – is almost as popular as the slate mine next door. There are five trails – a family friendly blue-grade trail for novices, plus three red and two black and a double-black run – and bike transport back up to the trailheads. While walk-in visitors are accommodated, it's worth booking ahead to guarantee a slot. Bike rental is available, and there's a small café.

ZipWorld Titan

A470, 1 mile north of Blaenau Ffestiniog, LL41 3NB · Generally every 30min: April–June & Oct to early Nov 10am–3pm; June to early Sept 9am–5pm; reservations required · £50 · ☎ 01248 601444, ⓦ zipworld.co.uk

ZipWorld Titan, occupying a former slate quarry, is not only categorized as the longest zip-line course in the world –it has three tracks (2930ft, 2060ft and 1476ft) – but also the only one which allows you to fly downhill alongside family or friends at speeds up to 70mph. Reservations are essential and there are restrictions on weight, height and age. Note, too, that the weather can affect your ride and that ZipWorld offers rescheduling, not refunds.

ARRIVAL AND INFORMATION

BLAENAU FFESTINIOG

By train The central train station serves both the Ffestiniog Railway (see page 732) and mainline services. Destinations Betws-y-Coed (6 daily; 30min); Llandudno (6 daily; 1hr 20min); Llandudno Junction (6 daily; 1hr).
By bus Buses stop outside the train station or along High St. Destinations Barmouth (3 daily; 1hr 10min); Betws-y-Coed (Mon–Sat 8 daily; 25min); Harlech (Mon–Sat 3 daily; 40min); Llandudno (Mon–Sat 8 daily; 1hr 10min); Porthmadog (Mon–Sat hourly; 30min).
Tourist information The Antur Stiniog mountain bike information centre (Easter & June–Sept Mon–Sat 10am–5pm; Oct–Easter Wed–Sat 10am–4pm; ☎ 01766 832214), on Church St in the heart of the town centre, doubles as a tourist office.

ACCOMMODATION

★ **Bryn Elltyd** Tanygrisiau, 1 mile southwest, LL41 3TW ☎ 01766 831356, ⓦ accommodation-snowdonia. com; map p.723. The former slate mine manager's house, beside the Ffestiniog Railway, is now Wales' only carbon-neutral B&B thanks to the efforts of its passionate (and helpful) environmentalist owner – if you want to know about eco living this is the place. Accommodation is in homely rooms or sweet cabins in the garden. **£90**
Cae'r Blaidd A470, 3 miles south, LL41 4PH ☎ 01766 762765, ⓦ caerblaidd.com; map p.723. Spacious Victorian country house set in four acres of woodland with just three country-style rooms, two with fabulous views of the Moelwyn mountains. Sustaining breakfasts and *table d'hôte* dinners (£19.50 for three courses) are excellent, and the hosts run guided hiking, climbing and scrambling trips. **£90**
CellB Park Square, LL41 3AD ☎ 01766 832001, ⓦ cellb. org; map p.723. This community arts centre, in a former police station (see below), also features a two-room, nine-bed hostel. **£22**

EATING

CellB Park Square, LL41 3AD ☎ 01766 832001, ⓦ cellb. org; map p.723. Occasional gigs, a cinema (Wed–Sun) and an informal bar-restaurant serving cheap, gutsy home cooking: pasta bakes, lamb burgers and shepherds pie. Bar/coffee Mon & Tues 4–10pm, Wed–Sun 8am–11.45pm; restaurant Wed–Sun noon–2.30pm & 6–9.30pm.

West into the Llŷn

The most westerly part of North Wales, the staunchly Welsh **Llŷn** forms a cliff- and cove-lined finger of land that juts out south and west from Snowdonia, separating Cardigan and Caernarfon bays. Its hills taper along its spine, carrying an ancient route to Aberdaron, where pilgrims once sailed for **Ynys Enlli** (Bardsey Island). Most people come for its beaches, especially at **Abersoch** and **Aberdaron**, and for escapism. The

16

peninsula's main town, **Pwllheli**, is the terminus for Cambrian Coast **trains** and a hub for local **buses**. The Llŷn is reached through either **Porthmadog** – home to the private "dream village" of **Portmeirion** and terminus of the **Ffestiniog Railway** – or **Caernarfon**, where a magnificent fortress guards the mouth of the Menai Strait.

Keen walkers have cottoned on to the **Llŷn Coastal Path**, which, resembling a quieter Pembrokeshire coast path, can be completed in a week; the full 110-mile route tracks along two coasts from Caernarfon to Porthmadog.

Porthmadog and around

In a region crammed with wonderful views, **PORTHMADOG**, at the crook of the Cambrian coast and the Llŷn, has some of the finest – up the Vale of Ffestiniog and across the estuary of the Glaslyn river to the mountains of Snowdonia. Yet the town – formerly North Wales' busiest slate port and large by regional standards – makes little of its position, and nor is it any great beauty itself. It's best used as a gateway to surrounding sights, from the superb **Ffestiniog** and **Welsh Highland railways** to the eccentric Italianate folly of **Portmeirion**.

Ffestiniog Railway

Harbour Station, Glaslyn Bridge, LL49 9NF • March–Oct 4–6 services daily; Nov–March services depending on maintenance, check website • Sample fares: all-day Rover £24; return to Tan-y-Bwlch £15.50; single fares two-thirds of a return; one child under 16 travels free with an adult • ☎ 01766 516024, ⊛ festrail.co.uk

The **Ffestiniog Railway** ranks as Wales' finest narrow-gauge rail line, twisting up 650ft from the wharf at Porthmadog to the slate mines at Blaenau Ffestiniog, thirteen miles away. The gutsy little engines make light of the steep gradients and chug through stunning scenery, from broad estuarine expanses to the deep greens of the Vale of Ffestiniog and then the slate-shattered slopes of the upper terminus at Blaenau Ffestiniog. In the late nineteenth century the rail line carried 100,000 tonnes a year of Blaenau Ffestiniog slate, but after the collapse of the slate-roofing industry the line was abandoned in 1946 and fell into disrepair. Reconstruction of the tracks was complete by 1982. After Porthmadog, trains stop at **Minffordd**, a mile from Portmeirion (see below).

Welsh Highland Railway

Harbour Station, Glaslyn Bridge, LL49 9NF • March–Oct 2–4 trains daily; Nov–Feb services depending on maintenance, check website • Sample return fares: to Beddgelert £21.90; to Caernarfon £39.80; one child under 16 travels free with an adult; single fares are two thirds of a return • ☎ 01766 516000, ⊛ festrail.co.uk

One of the most scenic lines in a land packed with charming railways, the restored narrow-gauge **Welsh Highland Railway** connects Porthmadog with Caernarfon, 25 miles away, rising from sea level to 650ft along the southern flank of Snowdon and passing gorgeous scenery. The full Porthmadog–Caernarfon round trip gives you five hours on the train and an hour in Caernarfon.

Portmeirion

Minffordd, 3 miles east of Porthmadog, LL48 6ER • Daily 9.30am–7.30pm; guided tours Easter–Oct daily 10am–3.30pm (20min) • £12; guided tours free; free entry for guests of both hotels; free afternoon entry if you prebook Sun lunch at *Hotel Portmeirion* or lunch at *Castell Deudraeth* • ☎ 01766 770000, ⊛ portmeirion-village.com • Either walk there in an hour from Porthmadog; catch the #1B bus to the gate; or take either the mainline or Ffestiniog trains to Minffordd, from where it's a signposted 25min walk

Famous as "The Village" in the 1960s cult British TV series *The Prisoner*, the Italianate private village of **PORTMEIRION** in Tremadog Bay was the brainchild of eccentric architect Clough Williams-Ellis. In the 1920s, he devised the site as a "Home for Fallen Buildings" – endangered structures from all over Britain and abroad were dismantled then rebuilt here around a Mediterranean piazza. The idea was to create an ideal village

using a "light-opera sort of approach", and the result is certainly theatrical: a stage set with a lucky dip of buildings arranged to distort perspectives and reveal glimpses of the seascape behind.

In September Portmeirion fills up for **Festival No. 6** (ⓦfestivalnumber6.com), a celebration of leftfield music, culture and literature.

Criccieth Castle

Castle St, Criccieth, 5 miles west of Porthmadog, LL52 0DP • April–Oct daily 10am–5pm; Nov–March Mon–Sat 9.30am–4pm, Sun 11am–4pm • April–Oct daily & Nov–March Fri–Sun £5; Nov–March Mon–Thurs free; CADW • ☎01766 522227, ⓦcadw.gov.wales/ daysout/criccieth-castle • Buses from Porthmadog (every 30min–1hr; 10min)

Battle-worn **Criccieth Castle**, with its distinctive twin-towered gatehouse, was an irresistble subject for painter J.M.W. Turner, who captured it in several works. It was started by Llywelyn ap Iorwerth in 1230, strengthened by Edward I around 1283, and razed by Owain Glyndŵr in 1404. It's a great spot to sit and look over Cardigan Bay to Harlech, backed by mountains.

ARRIVAL AND DEPARTURE

By train Porthmadog's mainline train station is at the north end of the High St; the Ffestiniog and Welsh Highland station is by the harbour about half a mile to the south.

Destinations Aberdyfi (8 daily; 1hr 30min–1hr 40min); Barmouth (8 daily; 50min); Criccieth (8 daily; 7min); Harlech (8 daily; 20min); Machynlleth (8 daily; 1hr 55min); Pwllheli (8 daily; 25min).

By bus National Express buses stop outside Tesco in

PORTHMADOG AND AROUND

between Porthmadog's two heritage train stations; local buses stop on High St beside the central park.

Destinations Beddgelert (8 daily; 25min); Blaenau Ffestiniog (Mon–Sat hourly; 30min); Borth-y-Gest (Mon–Sat 9 daily; 3min); Caernarfon (Mon–Sat 6 daily; 40min); Criccieth (Mon–Sat every 30min, Sun 7; 15min); Dolgellau (3–4 daily; 50min); Harlech (Mon–Sat 6 daily; 20min); Pwllheli (Mon–Sat every 30min, Sun 7; 40min).

ACCOMMODATION

Castell Deudraeth A 10min walk north of Portmeirion centre, LL48 6ER ☎01766 772400, ⓦportmeirion-village.com. While the standard modern rooms are smart rather than glamorous, all are spacious, with mod-cons, and provide a comfortable stay. You're here most of all for the joy of staying in a remodelled Victorian "castle" where you're free to roam and use the heated outdoor pool. **£174**

Golden Fleece Inn Market Square, Tremadog, 1 mile north of Porthmadog, LL49 9RB ☎01766 512421, ⓦgoldenfleeceinn.com. This former coaching inn offers mid-range accommodation across three buildings. Choose from simply furnished rooms above the pub and a

neighbouring house or larger, rather theatrical, "Executive King" rooms and King suites (£90) in the Royal Madoc annexe nearby. **£65**

★ **Hotel Portmeirion** Portmeirion, LL48 6ER ☎01766 770000, ⓦportmeirion-village.com. The spirit of Clough Williams-Ellis lives on in styling that's equal parts grand and eccentric; the main waterside hotel and cottages throughout Portmeirion village abound in quirky decorative detail. Though lacking the wow factor of public areas, rooms are excellent, many with beautiful views. Former guests include H.G. Wells, George Bernard Shaw and Noël Coward. Breakfast £20. **£204**

EATING AND DRINKING

The Australia 35 High St, LL49 9LR ☎01766 510931. What was once a shabby boozer has been gutted by Porthmadog's Purple Moose brewery and revived as a spacious, welcoming pub. A wide range of its award-winning beers are on tap, from pale ales to interesting seasonal offerings. Daily noon–11pm.

★ **Dylans** Maes y Mor, Criccieth, LL52 0HU ☎01766 522773, ⓦdylansrestaurant.co.uk. Criccieth's Art Deco beach pavilion is now the buzziest place in town. Come for coffee, cocktails or meals such as seafood linguini (mains £13–24), all served in a bright dining room with wraparound views of castle, coast and Cambrian

mountains. Daily 11am–11pm; kitchen noon–10pm.

★ **Moorings Bistro** 4 Ivy Terrace, Borth-y-Gest, 1 mile south of Porthmadog, LL49 9TS ☎01766 513500, ⓦmooringsbistroborthygest.com. Great little bistro specializing in local seafood (£14–18). Lunches (£6–11) are lighter – falafel wraps, perhaps, or seafood chowder. It's hugely popular, not least for the estuary views from its terrace; reservations recommended. April–Sept Mon, Tues & Thurs 11am–3pm & 6–11pm, Fri & Sat 9am–3pm & 6–9pm, Sun 9am–4pm; Oct–March Wed–Sun 11am–3pm plus some evenings (call ahead).

Y Sgwar The Square, Tremadog, 1 mile north of

16

WATERSPORTS ON THE LLŶN PENINSULA

Abersoch is a hub for aquatic activities in the region, whether you want **lessons** or simply prefer to **rent** equipment.

Abersoch Sailing School North end of Main Beach, LL53 7DP ☎01758 712963, ⓦabersochsailingschool. com. Runs lessons and rents laser dinghies, catamarans, kayaks and pedalos on the town's main beach (dinghies from £45 for 2hr). March–Oct.

Llyn Adventures ☎07751 826714, ⓦllynadventures. com. Coasteering lessons around the peninsula's superb coastline as well as kayaking and surfing trips (all £40 for 3hr). March–Oct.

Offaxis Town centre, where road turns left behind harbour, LL53 7HP ☎01758 713407, ⓦoffaxis.co.uk. A paddleboarding, kitesurfing, wakeboarding and surfing academy (£30/lesson) and gear rental (from £10/day). Summer only.

West Coast Surf Lôn Pen Cei, LL53 7AP ☎01758 713067, ⓦwestcoastsurf.co.uk. Rents out surfing gear (boards £10, wetsuits £8), offers lessons (£30 for 2hr) and provides paddleboarding rental (£20/2hr, £30/day). Open year-round.

orthmadog, LL49 9RB ☎01766 515451, ⓦysgwar-estaurant.co.uk. A menu of quick lunches (average 10) – BLT sandwiches, burgers, Menai mussels cooked in white wine – ramps up into well-prepared restaurant dishes in the evening, when local beef and lamb star (mains £18–23). Daily noon–2pm & 6–9pm.

Abersoch

The former fishing village of **ABERSOCH**, pitched in the middle of two bays of fine white sand, is a rather glossy, anglicized resort, catering to affluent yachties and holidaying families from England's northwest. It's just a five-minute walk to the closest beach, **Abersoch Bay**, a beautiful strand lined by beach huts that are as colourful as they are expensive – one sold for £153,000 in 2015. **Porth Neigwl** (Hell's Mouth), two miles southwest, is the finest **surf** beach in North Wales – though beware of the undertow if you're swimming.

16

ARRIVAL AND DEPARTURE

ABERSOCH

By bus Buses from Pwllheli (Mon–Sat 10–11 daily, Sun 4; 20–30min) loop through the middle of Abersoch, stopping on Lôn Pen Cei. To continue to Aberdaron by bus, you must take a Pwllheli-bound service as far as Llanbedrog, then change onto the #17. Between April and Oct the Llŷn Coastal Bus shuttles on a hail-and-ride basis along the coastline between Abersoch and Nefyn via Aberdaron and Porth Neigwl (Thurs–Sun 4 daily; ⓦbwsarfordirllyn.co.uk).

ACCOMMODATION AND EATING

Angorfa Lôn Sarn Bach, LL53 7EB ☎01758 712967, ⓦangorfa.com. Bare boards and white linen characterize this superior budget B&B, the closest to central Abersoch (by 70yd or so). All rooms are en suite; the two attic rooms have the best views. Breakfast is served in the daytime café downstairs. Closed Oct to early March. **£85**

Coconut Kitchen Lôn Pont Morgan (main road opposite harbour), LL53 7AN ☎01758 712250, ⓦcoconutkitchen.co.uk. It's been going for ages and remains the best Thai place for miles. As well as classics like beef Massaman or green chicken curry (around £12), it features interesting daily dishes – Aberdaron crab, for example. Takeaway available. Daily 5.30–10pm.

★ **Venetia** Lôn Sarn Bach, LL53 7EB ☎01758 713354, ⓦvenetiawales.com. Metro-chic in a boutique B&B with five bold rooms with plush bathrooms – the baths could hold a hippo. It also has an award-winning modern restaurant serving the likes of linguini with local crab and fish fresh off the boat. Note there was talk of the business being put for sale at the time of research. Most mains £13–17. Food served Wed–Sun 6.30–10pm **£108**

Aberdaron

You really feel you're at the end of Wales at the lovely lime-washed fishing hamlet of **ABERDARON**, two miles short of the tip of the Llŷn. For the best part of a thousand years up until the sixteenth century the inn and church here were the last stops on a pilgrim trail to **Ynys Enlli**, around the headland.

Porth y Swnt

Village centre, at the car park beside the bridge, LL58 8BE • Daily: March & Oct–Dec 10am–4pm; April–June & Sept 9am–5pm; July & Au
9am–6pm • £2; NT • ☎ 01758 703814, ⓦ nationaltrust.org.uk/porth-y-swnt

The art and traditional crafts displays at **Porth y Swnt** take second place to audio guides
with interviews with local geologists, artists, gardeners, walkers, poets and farmers. The
result is an oral history that subtly reveals something of the unique character of the
Llŷn peninsula.

Ynys Enlli (Bardsey Island)

Ynys Enlli (The Island of the Currents) or **Bardsey Island** is separated from the tip
of the Llŷn by two miles of churning, unpredictable water – it looks brilliant from
Mynydd Mawr, two miles southwest of Aberdaron. This national nature reserve has
been an important pilgrimage site since the sixth century: three visits were proclaimed
equivalent to one pilgrimage to Rome. You can still see the ruins of the thirteenth-
century abbey, but most visitors come to watch **birds** – Manx shearwaters, fulmars and
guillemots – plus the **seals** lazed over rocks at low tide.

Crossings are dependent on sea conditions and a viable load of passengers:
you will need to be flexible. Bardsey Boat Trips (£30 return; ☎ 07971 769895,
ⓦ bardseyboattrips.com) sails from Porth Meudwy, a tiny cove a mile south of
Aberdaron (sat nav LL53 8DA), in around fifteen minutes; you get around four hours
on Enlli. The Aberdaron village shop serves as an unofficial office.

ARRIVAL AND DEPARTURE   **ABERDARON**

16

By bus The #17 bus operates year-round from Pwllheli
(Mon–Sat 8 daily; 40min). Between April and Oct the
Llŷn Coastal Bus calls en route to Abersoch or Nefyn on the
north coast (Thurs–Sun 4 daily; ⓦ bwsarfordirllyn.co.uk)
It operates on a hail-and-ride basis.

ACCOMMODATION AND EATING

Mynydd Mawr Llanllawen Fawr, 2 miles southwest,
LL53 0BY ☎ 01758 760223. A couple of peaceful grassy
fields in which to pitch your tent right by Mynydd Mawr –
the hill overlooking Bardsey Sound – with views across to
Ynys Enlli. Hot showers and electricity hook-up available.
You'll need your own transport. Closed Nov–Feb. **£18**

Tŷ Newydd Village centre, LL53 8BE ☎ 01758 760207,
ⓦ gwesty-tynewydd.co.uk. A modernized hotel right on
the beach with sea views from front rooms (£115); the best
have mini-balconies. Nice touches including iPod dock
and superking beds make up for the slightly bland decor
It's a good choice for eating, with a terrace over the beach –
offerings include lobster and herb-crusted cod (£13) plus
pub favourites like Glamorgan bangers and mash (£10.95).
Daily noon–2.30pm & 6–8.30pm. **£110**

Caernarfon

CAERNARFON, superbly set at the southern entrance to the Menai Strait, has a lot going
for it. Its polygonal-towered **castle** is an undoubted highlight, the **Welsh Highland
Railway** connects the town with the slopes of Snowdon (see page 729) and Porthmadog
(see page 732), and the modern marina development adds **Galeri Caernarfon**, a modest
but interesting arts centre, to the mix. There is some appealing accommodation nearby,
making this a possible base for exploring both sides of Snowdon and the Llŷn.

Caernarfon Castle

Entrance on Castle Ditch, LL55 2AY • March–June, Sept & Oct daily 9.30am–5pm; July & Aug daily 9.30am–6pm; Nov–Feb Mon–Sat
10am–4pm, Sun 11am–4pm • £8.95; CADW • ☎ 01286 677617, ⓦ cadw.gov.wales/daysout/caernarfon-castle

In 1283, Edward I started work on **Caernarfon Castle**, the strongest link in his Iron
Ring, a decisive hammer-blow to any Welsh aspirations to autonomy and the ultimate
symbol of Anglo-Norman military might – it withstood two sieges by Owain Glyndŵr
with a garrison of just 28 men-at-arms. As you enter through the **King's Gate**, the
castle's strength is immediately apparent. Embrasures and murder holes between the

octagonal towers face in on no fewer than five gates and six portcullises, and that's once you have crossed the moat. Inside, the huge lawn gives a misleading impression as the wall dividing the two original wards, and all the buildings that filled them, crumbled away long ago. The towers are in a much better state, linked by an exhausting honeycomb of wall-walks and tunnels. Don't miss the **Eagle Tower**, the castle's highest, with the best views of the town.

ARRIVAL AND DEPARTURE | CAERNARFON

By train There's no national rail link – though you can connect to one in Bangor – but the West Highland Railway heritage tourist route (see page 732) ends here on its journey from Porthmadog via Beddgelert and Snowdon.
By bus National Express and local buses stop on Pool Side,

northeast of central Y Maes (Castle Square).
Destinations Bangor (every 30min at least; 30min); Beddgelert (Mon–Sat 7 daily; 30min); Llanberis (Mon–Sat every 30min, Sun 8; 25min); Porthmadog (Mon–Sat 14 daily; 50min); Pwllheli (Mon–Sat roughly hourly, Sun 3; 55min).

ACCOMMODATION

Cadnant Valley Llanberis Rd, 1km east of Y Maes, LL55 2DF ☎01286 673196, ⓦ www.cwmcadnantvalley.

co.uk; map p.737. Pleasant wooded campsite that feels more rural than the location – 15min walk east of the

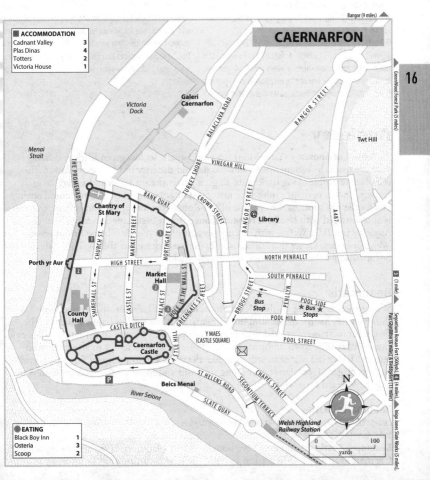

CAERNARFON

Bangor (9 miles)

Victoria Dock

Galeri Caernarfon

Menai Strait

THE PROMENADE

BALACLAVA ROAD

BANGOR STREET

Twt Hill

VINEGAR HILL

TURKEY SHORE

BANK QUAY

CROWN STREET

BANGOR STREET

A487

Chantry of St Mary

@ Library

CHURCH ST.

MARKET STREET

NORTHGATE ST.

NORTH PENRALLT

Porth yr Aur

HIGH STREET

Market Hall

SOUTH PENRALLT

SHIREHALL ST.

CASTLE ST.

PALACE ST.

HOLE IN THE WALL ST.

GREENGATE STREET

BRIDGE STREET

PENLLYN

Bus Stop

POOL SIDE

Bus Stops

County Hall

CASTLE DITCH

POOL HILL

Y MAES (CASTLE SQUARE)

POOL STREET

Caernarfon Castle

CASTLE HILL

P

Beics Menai

River Seiont

ST HELENS ROAD

SEGONTIUM TERRACE

SLATE QUAY

CHAPEL STREET

N

Welsh Highland Railway Station

0 — 100
yards

GreenWood Forest Park (5 miles)

16

3 (1 mile) / Segontium Roman Fort (500yds); Parc Glynllifon (6 miles) & Beddgelert (13 miles) / Inigo Jones Slate Works (5 miles)

centre, near the start of the A4086 to Llanberis – suggests. Closed Nov–Feb. **£20**

Plas Dinas Bontnewydd, 2 miles south, LL54 7YF ☎01286 830214, ⓦplasdinas.co.uk; map p.737. Understated luxury in an elegant ten-room country house. Very much the "historic home" (it was the ancestral home of Lord Snowdon), it retains a personal feel thanks to attentive hosts amd furnishings pieced together with an eye for romantic glamour. One for a splurge. **£119**

★**Totters** 2 High St, LL55 1RN ☎01286 672963, ⓦtotters.co.uk; map p.737. Excellent, central hostel with lovely communal spaces, including a fourteenth-century cellar kitchen. There's also a great attic en-suite double with sea views and a separate self-contained house for groups of up to six (£20–25/person). Rates include continental breakfast. Dorms **£18.50**, doubles **£44**

Victoria House 13 Church St, LL55 1SW ☎01286 678263; map p.737. Our favourite B&B in Caernarfon has a large balcony suite with a private deck beside the town walls (£110) plus immaculate Victorian-style (but modern) en-suites with flatscreen TV/DVD and complimentary drinks in the lounge. A shared town-wall terrace has views over the Menai Strait. **£90**

EATING

Black Boy Inn Northgate St, LL55 1RW ☎01286 673604, ⓦblack-boy-inn.com; map p.737. Ancient hostelry with two low-beamed bars and the best pub meals in town; lamb shank with mash or pan-fried plaice are typical (£12–16). Daily 11am–11pm; kitchen noon–2pm & 7–9pm.

Osteria 26 Hole in the Wall St, LL55 1RF ☎01286 674343; map p.737. With a Tuscan chef-owner, this sweet little restaurant offers a short menu of genuine, fresh Italian cuisine – *bruschette*, excellent grazing platters (£10), *carpaccio* and authentic pasta dishes that make a virtue of their simplicity (£10). Tues–Thurs 6–9.30pm, Fri & Sat noon–2.30pm & 6–9.30pm.

Scoops 8 Palace St, LL55 1RR ☎01286 673604, ⓦscoopscaernarfon.com; map p.737. Artisan ice cream (£1.95 a cone) made on site, with the likes of honey and quinoa, sea buckthorn or apple and mango frozen yoghurt alongside plain vanilla or chocolate. The owner's Dutch mother prepares excellent savoury and sweet crêpes. Tues–Sun 10.30am–4pm; daily Easter and school holidays.

16

Anglesey

The island of **Anglesey** (Ynys Môn) is a world apart. Its low green fields and farms are a far cry from the mountains of Snowdonia, and the pace of life is even slower. This is a place to amble along backroads, lingering over the sea views and superb coastal scenery, and to perhaps explore the many **restaurants** that have seen the island emerge as a foodie hot spot. As the crucible of pre-Roman druidic activity in Britain, the area is also scattered with **Neolithic remains** from a pagan past. Linguistically and politically, Anglesey is solidly Welsh, with seventy percent of the islanders being first-language Welsh-speakers. Other than the coastline, the main draws are the ancient castle town of **Beaumaris** and the Whistler mural at **Plas Newydd**.

Beaumaris

With its lovely setting on the Menai Strait, its air of relaxed prosperity and wealth of things to see, handsome **BEAUMARIS** (Biwmares) is the stuff of happy holidays. The first inhabitants were evicted by Edward I to make way for the construction of his new castle and bastide town, dubbed "beautiful marsh" in an attempt to attract English settlers. Today the place can still seem like the small English outpost Edward intended, with its elegant Georgian terrace along the front and more English accents than you may have heard for a while.

Beaumaris Castle

Castle St, LL58 8AP • March–June, Sept & Oct daily 9.30am–5pm; July & Aug daily 9.30am–6pm; Nov–Feb Mon–Sat 10am–4pm, Sun 11am–4pm • £6.50; CADW • ☎01248 810361, ⓦcadw.gov.wales/daysout/beaumaris-castle

Beaumaris Castle might never have been built had Madog ap Llywelyn not captured Caernarfon in 1294. When asked to build the new castle, Edward I's favourite architect, James of St George, abandoned the Caernarfon design for a concentric plan, developing it into a highly evolved symmetrical octagon. Located at the edge of town, the castle lacks the majesty of Caernarfon or Harlech. Indeed, its low outer walls appear almost welcoming – it's only when you discover the concentric defences protected by massive towers, the moat linked to the sea and the staggered entries through two gatehouses, that you grasp its defensive design. You can explore a number of inner and outer **wall walks**, and wander through internal passages in the walls.

Beaumaris Gaol

Bunker's Hill, LL58 8EP • Easter–Sept Mon–Thurs, Sat & Sun 10.30am–5pm; Oct & half-terms Sat & Sun 10.30am–5pm • £7 • ☎ 01248 810921, ⓦ visitanglesey.co.uk

The English rulers made a habit of rough justice for local Welsh miscreants; many were unfairly tried in the Jacobean **Beaumaris Courthouse** opposite the castle. While some of the covicted were transported to the colonies for their crimes, others wound up in the **Beaumaris Gaol**, which was considered a model prison when built in 1829, with running water and toilets in each cell, and an infirmary. Still, it's a gloomy place: witness the windowless punishment cell, the yard for stone-breaking and the treadmill water-pump operated by the prisoners.

Puffin Island

Beaumaris Pier, LL58 8BS • Easter–Oct 4 daily 10am–5pm • £9 • ☎ 01248 810251, ⓦ starida.co.uk and ⓦ seacoastsafaris.co.uk

One of the best excursions hereabouts on a fine day is the cruise to **Puffin Island**, five miles northeast. Two operators sell tickets from booths at the pier for hour-long excursions around – but not onto – the island, spotting nesting razorbills, guillemots and puffins. Outside peak season you should be able to hop aboard the next service.

16

ARRIVAL AND DEPARTURE
BEAUMARIS

By bus Timetables for the #53, #57 and #58 services from Beaumaris to Bangor are facing reduced services; visit ⓦ anglesey.gov.uk for up-to-date information. Currently buses arrive from Bangor (every 20–30min; 20–35min) and Menai Bridge (every 30min; 15min).

ACCOMMODATION

★ **Cleifiog** Townsend, LL58 8BH ☎ 01248 811507, ⓦ cleifiogbandb.co.uk. A stay in one of the four rooms of this arty, Georgian B&B is the architectural equivalent of a hug. Best are the front rooms, with beautiful antique panelling and views across the Menai Strait to Snowdonia. Factor in a lovely lounge and charming host and it's a struggle to leave. **£100**

Victoria Cottage Victoria Terrace, LL58 8DA ☎ 01248 810807, ⓦ victoriacottage.net. Good boutique B&B with two spacious en-suite rooms and two cheaper loft rooms that share a bathroom with a big bath. **£95**

Ye Olde Bull's Head Inn 18 Castle St, LL58 8AP ☎ 01248 810329, ⓦ bullsheadinn.co.uk. This ancient coaching inn, which once hosted Dr Johnson and Charles Dickens, still offers accommodation – in the main building, where many of the chic rooms have original features, and in the generally more spacious *Townhouse*. **£110**

EATING

Pier House Bistro The Front, LL58 8BS ☎ 01248 811055, ⓦ pierhousebistro.com. This café-bistro is the place to be on a sunny day – there are great views across the Strait to Snowdonia from the terrace. Menus featuring largely local ingredients list breakfasts, snacks and larger mains such as Menai mussels or fish and chips with gin-and-tonic batter (£12.95). Daily 9am–9pm.

Red Boat Ice Cream Parlour 34 Castle St, LL58 8BB ⓦ redboatgelato.com. Cheerful little café with an ever-changing selection of gelati and sorbets all freshly made on the premises, from standard vanilla to sea buckthorn – the owner trained at a prestigious Italian ice-cream academy. Daily 10am–5pm.

★ **Ye Olde Bull's Head Inn** 18 Castle St, LL58 8AP ☎ 01248 810329, ⓦ bullsheadinn.co.uk. Two choices: posh pub food – slow-cooked lamb or risotto of wild mushrooms and pine nuts, say – at *The Coach* brasserie (mains around £13), and seasonal, locally sourced Modern British fine dining at *Loft* (three courses £47.50). The Coach: Mon–Sat noon–2pm & 6–9pm, Sun noon–3pm & 6–9pm; Loft: Wed & Thurs 7–9pm, Fri & Sat 6.30–9pm.

Llanfairpwllgwyngyllgogerychwyrndrobwllllantysiliogogogoch (Llanfairpwll)

In the 1880s a local tailor invented the longest place name in Britain in a successful attempt to draw tourists. It still does, but most visitors will be disappointed when they arrive at **Llanfairpwllgwyngyllgogerychwyrndrobwllllantysiliogogogoch**, which translates as "St Mary's Church in the hollow of white hazel near a rapid whirlpool and the Church of St Tysilio near the red cave" – commonly shortened to **LLANFAIRPWLL**. There's little here but a train station – the stop for the obligatory town-name photo. The nearby house of **Plas Newydd**, however, is worth a visit.

Plas Newydd

A4080, 1.5 miles southwest of Llanfairpwll, LL61 6DQ • **House** Mid-Feb to early Nov daily 11am–4.30pm • £11 including gardens; NT • **Gardens** Early Nov to Easter 11am–3pm; Easter to early Nov daily 10.30am–5pm • £8.65; NT • ☎ 01248 715272 or ☎ 01248 714795, ⓦ nationaltrust.org.uk/plas-newydd-country-house-and-gardens • Bus #42 (Llagefni–Bangor via Llanfairpwll) stops outside Plas Newydd (Mon–Sat 11 daily, Sun 2 daily)

Plas Newydd, a modest three-storey mansion with incongruous Tudor caps on slender octagonal turrets, has been the ancestral home of the marquesses of Anglesey since the eighteenth century. Corridors of oil paintings and period rooms lead to the highlight, a 58ft-long wall with a trompe l'oeil painting by artist **Rex Whistler**, who spent a couple of years here in the 1930s. As you walk alongside his imaginary seascape, the mountains of Snowdonia and a whimsical composite of elements, drawn from Italy as well as Britain, change perspective. Portmeirion is there, as is the Round Tower from Windsor Castle, and Whistler appears both as a gondolier and as a gardener in one of the two right-angled panels at either end. Also worth a look is the **Cavalry Museum** a few rooms further on, its prize exhibit the world's first articulated false leg, designed for the first marquess, who lost his at Waterloo.

ARRIVAL AND DEPARTURE

By train The station is beside the main road (A5) in central Llanfairpwll.
Destinations Bangor (8 daily; 25min); Holyhead (8 daily; 30min).

By bus Buses stop along the A5 through road.
Destinations Bangor (every 30min; 15min); Holyhead (hourly; 1hr).

Holyhead and around

Drab **HOLYHEAD** (Caergybi; pronounced in English "holly-head") is Anglesey's largest town and the terminus for ferry routes to Ireland. It isn't somewhere you'll want to spend any time, but the coastline nearby is fantastic; the sea cliffs two miles west at **South Stack** (Ynys Lawd) are excellent for birdwatchers (no public transport), and there are lovely beaches at **Trearddur** and **Rhoscolyn**.

Ellin's Tower Seabird Centre

South Stack, LL65 1YH • Tower Easter–Sept daily 10am–5pm; visitor centre daily 10am–5pm • Free • ☎ 01407 762100, ⓦ rspb.org.uk/wales

The views of the high sea cliffs at the tip of Anglesey are best from the RSPB's **Ellin's Tower Seabird Centre**, where binoculars and closed-circuit TV give an unrivalled opportunity to watch some three thousand birds – razorbills, guillemots and a few puffins – nesting on the nearby sea cliffs while choughs and peregrines wheel outside the windows.

South Stack Lighthouse

South Stack, LL65 1YH • Previously Easter–Sept Sat–Thurs 10.30am–5pm • Previously £5.80

If the seabird centre teetering on cliffs seems precarious, it's nothing compared to the pepper-pot **South Stack Lighthouse**, built in 1809. Visits had been suspended at the time of research; seek current information at the seabird centre. Even if it's not open for

isits, it's worth taking the four hundred steps down to a suspension bridge across, once
he keeper's only access, for close-up views of the cliffs and birds beneath.

rearddur and Rhoscolyn

us #23 from Holyhead stops at Trearddur (Mon–Sat 5 daily; 7–15min) and Rhoscolyn (Mon–Sat 3 daily; 15min)

f Anglesey can be said to have a smart beach resort, it's **Trearddur**, 2.5 miles south
f Holyhead. Though the village centre is grey pebbledash, the **beach** is a beauty; a
leeply indented bay with a white-sand beach and, beyond it, rocky coves. Sunsets can
ie magical. A couple of miles south, tiny **Rhoscolyn** is less chic but has a couple of
xquisite beaches notched in a wild ragged coast.

ARRIVAL AND DEPARTURE   HOLYHEAD AND AROUND

By train Holyhead's central station is linked by Arriva trains
o North Wales and by intercity Virgin trains as far as London.
Destinations Bangor (22 daily; 30–40min); Chester (23
aily; 1hr 30min–2hr); Conwy (11 daily; 1hr); Llandudno
18 daily; 1hr 20min); Llanfairpwll (9 daily; 30min); London
5 daily; 3hr 45min).
By bus Local and National Express buses stop by the

passenger ferry terminal.
Destinations Bangor (hourly; 1hr 15min); Llanfairpwll
(Mon–Sat hourly; 1hr).
By ferry Irish Ferries (ⓦ irishferries.com) and Stena Line
(ⓦ stenaline.com) run to Dublin and Dun Laoghaire using
ferries (4hr) and fast catamarans (2hr). The two operate
around eight ferries between them, 24 hours a day.

EATING

★ The White Eagle Rhoscolyn, 5 miles south of
lolyhead, LL65 2NJ ☏ 01407 860267, ⓦ white-eagle.
o.uk. Excellent gastropub offering the best eating on
loly Island – cuisine such as pan-seared hake with basil
r braised ox cheek (mains £10–16) – and a selection of

cask ales. The huge deck with long views of the indented
coastline is a great spot for a pint or two beforehand. Be
warned: it's busy and reservations are for large groups only.
Mon–Sat noon–11pm, Sun noon–10.30pm.

16

The north coast

Anglesey connects with the mainland at the university town of **Bangor** – missable
except as a springboard for **Penrhyn Castle** or Snowdonia. Heading east you encounter
the **north coast** proper, where the castle town of **Conwy** and elegant **Llandudno** are the
essential stops.

Bangor and around

BANGOR, across the bridge from Anglesey, is not big, but as the largest town in
Gwynedd county and home to Bangor University, it passes for cosmopolitan in these
parts. Though the staunchly Welsh town makes a dramatic contrast from the English-
speaking north-coast resorts, for the visitor there's little to see.

Penrhyn Castle

landygai, off A5, 2 miles east of central Bangor, LL57 4HN • House: March–Oct daily noon–5pm; grounds & Industrial Railway Museum:
March–Oct 11am–5pm, Nov–Feb 11am–3pm • £11.80, grounds & Industrial Railway Museum only £7.90; NT • ☏ 01248 363219,
ⓦ nationaltrust.org.uk/penrhyn-castle • Buses #5, #6, #67 and #75 run frequently from Bangor to Penrhyn's gates, from where it is a mile
o the house

Built on the profits of a Welsh slate mine, **Penrhyn Castle** – a nineteenth-century fancy,
dripping with luxury in its three hundred opulent rooms – is testament to the Anglo-
Welsh gentry's oppression of the rural Welsh.

The house was built by Caribbean sugar plantation owner, slave trader and vehement
anti-abolitionist Richard Pennant, First Baron Penrhyn, who built a port on the
northeastern edge of Bangor in order to ship his Bethesda slate to the world. But it
was his self-aggrandizing great-great-nephew, George Dawkins, who inherited the

40,000-acre estate and transformed the neo-Gothic hall. With the aid of architect Thomas Hopper, Dawkins spent thirteen years from 1827 encasing his inheritance in a Norman-style fortress with a five-storey keep.

The decoration is glorious, and fairly true to Romanesque style. Three-foot-thick oak doors separate the rooms, ebony is used to dramatic effect, and a slate bed was built for the visit of Queen Victoria. The family also amassed Wales' largest private painting collection, including a Gainsborough landscape, Canaletto's *The Thames at Westminster* and a Rembrandt portrait. You can also see the Victorian kitchen and servants' quarters.

ARRIVAL AND DEPARTURE

By train Bangor's station is at the south end of Holyhead Rd. Destinations Chester (roughly every 30min; 1hr 10min); Conwy (12 daily; 17min); Holyhead (22 daily; 30–40min); Llandudno Junction (roughly every 30min; 20min).

By bus National Express and local buses stop in the centre.

BANGOR AND AROUND

Destinations Beaumaris (every 30min; 20–35min); Caernarfon (every 15min; 30min); Conwy (every 15min; 30min); Holyhead (hourly; 1hr 15min); Llanberis (hourly; 30–45min); Llandudno (every 15min; 1hr)

ACCOMMODATION

Treborth Hall Farm A487, 1.8 miles southwest of upper Bangor between the two Menai Strait bridges ☎01248 364104, ⓦtreborthleisure.co.uk. The nearest campsite is a well-kept, relaxed spot, partly enclosed in an old walled garden. Coin-op showers. Bus #5 passes the entrance. Closed Nov–March. **£13**

Y Garth Garth Rd, LL57 2RT ☎01248 362277, ⓦthe garthguesthouse.co.uk. This decent B&B, with te rooms – en-suite doubles/twins and family options – and big breakfasts, is probably the best value in the tow centre. **£65**

EATING

★ **Blue Sky** Rear of 236 High St, LL57 1PA (passage beside G Williams butcher) ☎01248 355444, ⓦblueskybangor.co.uk. Bangor's finest by a long shot, with superb food, mostly created from local and organic ingredients and often gluten-free, in a hall-like space. Dishes (£5–15) include sharing platters, daily soups and blackboard specials such as Welsh lamb meatballs with

fusilli. Occasional gigs and films. Mon–Sat 9.30am–5.30pm; ; kitchen 9.30am–4pm.

Kyffin 129 High St, LL57 1NT ☎01248 355161. A sweet littl vegetarian and vegan café serving tasty home-made lunche often with Middle Eastern flavours – spicy lentil lasagne perhaps – at low prices (most plates are under £10). Som gluten-free and non-dairy options. Mon–Sat 9.30am–5pm.

Conwy and around

CONWY, twenty miles east of Bangor, is wonderfully set on the Conwy estuary. The key sights are its fine medieval **castle** – the town's raison d'être – and the complete belt of 30ft-high **walls** that encircle the compact, predominantly Victorian core. It's an extremely easy place to potter around, and though you'll see everything you need to in a day, you may well find yourself lingering longer. There's a lot in the surrounding area to warrant a stay, not least **Bodnant Garden** and artificial surf-break **Surf Snowdonia**.

Conwy Castle

Rose Hill St, LL32 8LD · Daily: March–June, Sept & Oct 9.30am–5pm; July & Aug 9.30am–6pm; Nov–March 10am–4pm · £8.95; joint ticket with Plas Mawr (see below) £10.95; CADW · ☎01492 592358, ⓦcadw.gov.wales/daysout/conwycastle

Conwy Castle is the toughest-looking link in Edward I's fortresses around North Wales. With 1500 men, James of St George took just five years to construct eight massive **towers** in a rectangle around the two wards on a strategic knoll near the mouth of the river. In 1401, on Good Friday, when the fifteen-strong castle guard were at church, two cousins of Owain Glyndŵr took the castle and razed the town for Glyndŵr's cause. It was re-fortified for the Civil War then stripped of all its iron, wood and lead, and was left substantially as it is today.

The outer ward's 130ft-long **Great Hall** and the **King's Apartments** are both well preserved, but the only part of the castle to have kept its roof is the **Chapel Tower**, named for the small room built into the wall. Also worth a look is Thomas Telford's slender **suspension bridge** (ⓦnationaltrust.org.uk/conwy-suspension-bridge), anchored to the castle walls as if it were a drawbridge, and with crenellations to match.

Aberconwy House

▪ Castle St, LL32 8AY • March–June, Sept & Oct daily 11am–5pm; July & Aug daily 10am–5pm; Nov & Dec Sat–Sun noon–3pm • £3.40; NT • ☎ 01492 592246, ⓦ nationaltrust.org.uk/aberconwy-house

Aberconwy House is the oldest in Conwy, built about 1300 and variously used as a bakery, antique shop, sea captain's house and temperance hotel. Its incarnations are re-created in rooms furnished with a simple yet elegant collection of rural furniture.

Plas Mawr

20 High St, LL32 8DE • April–Sept daily 9.30am–5pm; Oct Tues–Sun 9.30am–4pm • £6.90, joint ticket with Conwy Castle (see page 742) £10.95; CADW • ☎ 01492 580167, ⓦ cadw.gov.wales/daysout/plasmawr

The Dutch-style **Plas Mawr** is among the best-preserved Elizabethan townhouses in Britain, built in 1576 for Robert Wynn, one of the first Welsh people to live in the town. Much of the dressed stonework was replaced during renovations in the 1940s and 1950s, but the interior sports more original features, in particular the friezes and superb moulded-plaster ceilings depicting fleurs-de-lis, griffons, owls and rams.

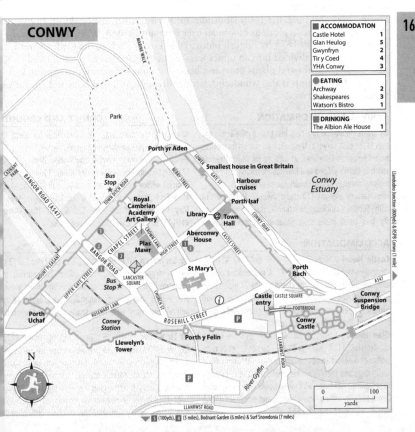

CONWY

16

◼ ACCOMMODATION	
Castle Hotel	1
Glan Heulog	5
Gwynfryn	2
Tir y Coed	4
YHA Conwy	3

● EATING	
Archway	2
Shakespeares	3
Watson's Bistro	1

◼ DRINKING	
The Albion Ale House	1

Park

MARINE WALK

Porth yr Aden

LOWER GATE ST

Smallest house in Great Britain

BERRY STREET

Bus Stop ★

TOWN DITCH ROAD

Harbour cruises

Conwy Estuary

CADNANT PARK

BANGOR ROAD (A547)

Royal Cambrian Academy Art Gallery

Library @

Porth Isaf

CONWY QUAY

CHAPEL STREET

CROWN LANE

Town Hall

Aberconwy House

BANGOR ROAD

Plas Mawr

HIGH STREET

CASTLE STREET

Porth Bach

MOUNT PLEASANT

St Mary's

LANCASTER SQUARE

Bus Stop ★

UPPER GATE STREET

CHURCH ST

ⓘ

Castle entry CASTLE SQUARE

Conwy Suspension Bridge

A547

Porth Uchaf

ROSEMARY LANE

Conwy Station

ROSEHILL STREET

P

FOOTBRIDGE

Conwy Castle

Llewelyn's Tower

Porth y Felin

LLANRWST ROAD

River Gyffin

P

N

0   100
yards

LLANRWST ROAD

Llandudno Junction (800yds) & RSPB Conwy (1 mile)

▼ ⑤ (100yds), ④ (5 miles), Bodnant Garden (6 miles) & Surf Snowdonia (7 miles)

Smallest house in Great Britain

Lower Gate St (Conwy Quay), LL32 8BE • Easter to mid-Oct daily 10am–5pm • £2 • ☎ 01492 573965, ⓦ thesmallesthouse.co.uk

The two tiny rooms of the **smallest house in Great Britain** are together only 9ft high and 6ft wide. You'll have to duck to get in, a problem that by all accounts vexed the last resident, a 6ft 3in fisherman, until he left in around 1900.

Surf Snowdonia

Dolgarrog, 7 miles south of Conwy, LL32 8QE • Daily 10am–sunset • Freesurf from £40/hr, lessons from £45/hr (both beginners, includes equipment); Crash & Splash £25/hr (wetsuit rental £5) • ☎ 01492 353123, ⓦ surfsnowdonia.com • #19 bus from Conwy (roughly hourly; 20min)

The world's first public surfing lagoon, **Surf Snowdonia** is an audacious project that has turned the Conwy Valley into an unlikely surfing destination. Generated by a sort of underwater snowplough, the waves in the 1000ft-pool range from waist-high for beginners to head-high for advanced surfers. Equipment rental and lessons are available, and there's an aquatic adventure playground, Crash & Splash, plus **accommodation** in camping pods (£70). Even if you're not into surfing it's worth a visit simply to sit in the **café** and watch the waves roar by.

Bodnant Garden

Tal-y-Cafn, off the A470, 8 miles south of Conwy, LL28 5RE • March to mid-Oct daily 10am–5pm (till 8pm Wed May–Aug); late Oct–Feb daily 10am–4pm • £12; NT • ☎ 01492 650460, ⓦ nationaltrust.org.uk/bodnant-garden • #25 bus from Llandudno and Llandudno Junction (Mon–Sat 5 daily; 25min)

During May and June, the 160ft laburnum tunnel flourishes and banks of rhododendrons are in glorious bloom all over **Bodnant Garden**, Wales' finest formal garden. Laid out in 1875 by English industrialist Henry Pochin, the garden spreads over eighty acres, divided into an upper terraced garden and lower pinetum and wild garden. Shrubs and plants provide a blaze of colour throughout late spring and summer, but autumn is also wonderful, with hydrangeas still in bloom and fruit trees shedding their leaves.

ARRIVAL AND INFORMATION

By train Llandudno Junction, less than a mile across the river to the east, serves as the main train station for services from Chester to Holyhead, as well as for trains heading south to Betws-y-Coed and Blaenau Ffestiniog. Only slow, regional services stop in Conwy itself (on request).

Destinations Bangor (10 daily; 20min); Holyhead (10 daily; 50min); Llandudno Junction (12 daily; 4min).

By bus Local buses stop either on Lancaster Square or outside the town walls on Town Ditch Rd. Head to Llandudno to pick up National Express coaches.

Destinations Bangor (every 15min; 40min); Betws-y-Coed (7 daily; 50min); Llandudno (every 30min; 15min).

Tourist office Near the castle on Rosehill St (June–Aug Mon–Fri 9.30am–5.30pm, Sat & Sun 10am–5pm; Sept–May Mon–Fri 9.30am–5pm, Sat & Sun 10am–4pm ☎ 01492 577566, ⓦ visitllandudno.org.uk).

CONWY AND AROUND

ACCOMMODATION

Castle Hotel 5 High St, LL32 8DB ☎ 01492 582800, ⓦ castlewales.co.uk; map p.743. A modernized central coaching inn that creaks with character. The 27 rooms have been renovated with flamboyance without abandoning historic appeal. Free central parking for guests and a great restaurant. Book online for best rates. **£140**

Glan Heulog Llanrwst Rd, 0.5 mile out on B5106 to Trefriw, LL32 8LT ☎ 01492 593845, ⓦ conwy-bedandbreakfast.co.uk; map p.743. Modern floral wallpapers and friendly owners make this one of Conwy's best small guesthouses; a Victorian house with six en suites (from £68), including family rooms, and one room with a private adjacent bathroom. **£65**

★ **Gwynfryn** 4 York Place, LL32 8AB ☎ 01492 576733 ⓦ gwynfrynbandb.co.uk; map p.743. Two options in a central B&B: five eclectic en suites in the main house, plus slightly smaller rustic minimalist rooms in the *Vestry* behind. "Superiors" have more space, views and bathtubs (£88). **£78**

★ **Tir y Coed** Rowen, 5 miles south of Conwy, LL32 8TP ☎ 01492 650219, ⓦ tirycoed.com; map p.743. In a pretty mountainside hamlet, this small hotel has bags of style, whether in spacious doubles – some classic, some offering quietly modern glamour – or the large Rowen Suite (£185), yet it remains as relaxed as you'd hope of a small country five-star. The in-house restaurant is

16

xcellent. No children under 14. **£135**

HA Conwy Lark Hill, LL32 8AJ ☎ 0345 371 9732, ⓦ yha.org.uk/hostel/conwy; map p.743. Spacious hostel in a 1970s' block 15min walk uphill from the centre, with great views to the castle and inland plus bright two- and four-bunk rooms, and family rooms, all en suite. Reservations recommended. Check-in afternoons only. Dorms **£21.99**, twins **£70**

EATING

Archway 12 Bangor Rd ☎ 01492 592458; map p.743. Quality eat-in and take-out fish and chip restaurant also doing pizza and pies. On a fine evening take your haul to the quay and wash it down with a pint from the *Liverpool Arms*. Mon–Thurs 11.30am–2pm & 4.30–8pm, Fri–Sun 11.30am–8.30pm.

Shakespeares Castle Hotel, High St, LL32 8DB ☎ 01492 582800, ⓦ castlewales.co.uk; map p.743. Smart bar and restaurant where the emphasis is on quality ingredients cooked well and served without too much fuss; expect the likes of Conwy musssels in a white wine, garlic and herb sauce (£12.95). The bar, *Dawson's*, has cheaper meals. Daily: restaurant 6–11pm; bar noon–11pm.

★ **Watson's Bistro** Chapel St, LL32 8BP ☎ 01492 596326, ⓦ watsonsbistroconwy.co.uk; map p.743. Conwy's best food, in a relaxed bistro with outside seating beneath the town walls: expect filo of chestnut mushrooms, leeks and puy lentils in brandy cream (£16) or pan-roasted hake with prawns and samphire (£18). Early dinner set menus cost £11 for two courses. Wed, Thurs & Sun noon–2pm & 5.30–8.30pm, Fri & Sat noon–2pm & 5.30–9pm.

DRINKING

★ **The Albion Ale House** Cnr Uppergate St, LL32 8RF ☎ 01492 582484, ⓦ albionalehouse.weebly.com; map p.743. Four local breweries, including the excellent Conwy Brewery, joined forces to run this Grade II-listed pub. There's no muzak and no TV, just eight ales on tap, bar snacks (including local pies), open fires and the charm of a 1920s wooden interior. Mon–Thurs noon–11pm, Fri & Sat noon–midnight. Mon–Thurs & Sun noon–11pm, Fri & Sat noon–midnight

16

Llandudno

Bill Bryson, writing in *Notes from a Small Island*, named **LLANDUDNO** his favourite British beach town, calling it "a fine and handsome place". And so it remains. This is one of Britain's best examples of the genteel Victorian resort, and on a sunny day it offers quintessential seaside charm; there's a splendid, 700ft-long **pier** and an increasingly sophisticated range of accommodation and restaurants.

Llandudno spreads behind the beach beneath **Great Orme** headland, where St Tudno built a monastic cell in the sixth century that gave the town its name. Little changed here until a local landowner, Edward Mostyn, exploited the growing craze for sea-bathing in the early nineteenth century and built a resort for the upper-middle classes.

Oriel Mostyn

12 Vaughan St, LL30 1AB • Tues–Sun 10am–4pm • Free • ☎ 01492 879201, ⓦ mostyn.org

The elaborate brick facade gives little clue to the rough-cast bare concrete interior of the refurbished **Oriel Mostyn** gallery, named after Lady Mostyn, for whom it was built in 1901. The five rooms almost always show something of interest, much of it by leading Welsh artists. There's also a good arts shop on site, and the bare-bones *Café Lux*.

Great Orme

Though low by local standards, the view from the top of **Great Orme** (Y Gogarth) ranks alongside any from a Snowdonian mountain, combining the seascapes east towards Rhyl and west over the sands of the Conwy estuary with the northern limit of the Carneddau range where Snowdonia crashes into the sea. This huge lump of carboniferous limestone was subject to some of the same stresses that folded Snowdonia, producing fissures filled by molten mineral-bearing rock.

Great Orme Tramway

Church Walks, LL30 2NB • Daily every 20min: late March & Oct 10am–5pm; April–Sept 10am–6pm • £6 single, £7.50 return • ☎ 01492 879306, ⊛ greatormetramway.co.uk.

The best way to ascend for the views and heath on top of the Orme is by the heritage **Great Orme Tramway**, which creaks up from the bottom of Old Road, much as it has done since 1902. Note that the journey is interrupted at the Halfway Station, where you change to a second tram.

Great Orme Aerial Cable Car

North Parade (Happy Valley Rd), LL30 2LP • Easter–Sept daily, roughly 10am–5pm, depending on the weather • £9 single, £9.50 return • ☎ 01492 877205

Near the base of the pier and close to the start of Marine Drive, a **cable car** lifts people up to the summit – when it isn't too windy – in open four-seater cabins that glide above the formal gardens of **Happy Valley**.

Great Orme Bronze Age Mines

Bishop's Quarry Rd, 430yd west of Halfway Station and 550yd east of visitor centre, LL30 2XG • Mid-March to Oct daily 10am–5pm • £7 • ☎ 01492 870447, ⊛ greatormemines.info

A Bronze Age settlement developed around what are now the **Great Orme Bronze Age Mines**, accessed via the tramway. Hard hats and miners' lamps are provided for the self-guided **tour** through a small portion of the tunnels, just enough to give you a feel for the cramped working conditions and the dangers of falling rock.

16

ARRIVAL AND INFORMATION

LLANDUDNO

By train Direct services to Llandudno's train station arrive from Betws-y-Coed and Chester; for all other services change at Llandudno Junction, near Conwy.

Destinations Bangor (26 daily; 16–25min); Betws-y-Coed (4 daily; 45min); Blaenau Ffestiniog (6 daily; 1hr); Chester (roughly hourly; 1hr 10min); Holyhead (18 daily; 1hr 20min); Llandudno Junction (roughly every 30min; 10min).

By bus Local buses stop on either Mostyn St or Gloddaeth St opposite the *Palladium* pub, while National Express buses from Chester, Bangor and Pwllheli (bookings at the tourist office) stop at the Coach Park on Mostyn Broadway. Alpine runs an open-top double-decker bus (May–Oct 10am–4pm hourly; £10 for 24hr; ☎ 0800 043 2452) that loops between Llandudno and Conwy – it's useful for a day-trip.

Destinations Bangor (every 40min; 1hr); Betws-y-Coed (13 daily; 50min); Blaenau Ffestiniog (5 daily; 1hr 10min); Conwy (every 30min; 20min).

Tourist office Library, Mostyn St (Easter–Sept Mon–Sat 9am–4.30pm, Sun 9.30am–4pm, ☎ 01492 577577, ⊛ visitllandudno.org.uk).

ACCOMMODATION

There's plenty of accommodation in Llandudno. Nevertheless **booking ahead** is wise. Most of the **budget places** congregate along St David's Rd, just west of the station, and on Deganwy Ave.

★ **The Cliffbury** 34 St Davids Rd, LL30 2UH ☎ 01492 877224, ⊛ thecliffbury.co.uk. Stylish wallpapers, sparkling bathrooms and dedicated hosts define this smart B&B on a quiet street with six individually decorated rooms. The two bigger front suites (£80) come with DVD players. Breakfast ingredients are locally sourced where possible. Generally two-night minimum stay. **£72**

★ **Escape** 48 Church Walks, LL30 2HL ☎ 01492 877776, ⊛ escapebandb.co.uk. One of the most celebrated B&Bs in North Wales, this pioneered the boutique B&B experience in Llandudno. Its nine individually styled rooms are playful, offering clean-lined modernism, retro chic or feminine vintage style. Lovely hosts and a guest lounge with honesty bar complete the package. **£110**

Glenthorne 2 York Rd, LL30 2EF ☎ 01492 879591, ⊛ glenthorne-guesthousellandudno.co.uk. Traditional Welsh-speaking guesthouse with hosts who go the extra mile. With seven rooms, it's a relaxing home from home; evening meals available on request. Minimum two-night stay. **£70**

Llandudno Hostel 14 Charlton St, LL30 2AA ☎ 01492 877430, ⊛ llandudnohostel.co.uk. Central, family-run, forty-bed hostel with dorm beds, doubles, a family room and a friendly atmosphere. Sheets, towels and a continental breakfast are supplied, but there's no self-catering. Often full with school groups during term time, so call ahead. Dorms **£25**, twins **£60**

★ **Ty Carthen** 12 Abbey Rd, LL30 2EA ☎ 01492

375886, ⓦtycarthenbandb.co.uk. This Grade II-listed Georgian house, on a quiet street, provides an elegant, relaxing stay. The style is arty and distinctly Welsh: there's Welsh art on the walls and Welsh blankets in beautifully furnished guest bedrooms. Lovely hosts, too. Reservations recommended. Closed Dec. <u>£75</u>

EATING AND DRINK

Bodysgallen Hall A470, 3 miles south, LL30 1RS ⓣ01492 584466, ⓦbodysgallen.com. There's a modern bistro in the old coach house, *1620*, but really you're here for formal fine dining in the hall of a seventeenth-century manor; expect the likes of slow-cooked local lamb with fennel pollen and smoked red pepper purée at £45 for two courses; or £25.50 on Mon, when the atmosphere is more relaxed. It's a grand spot for afternoon tea, too (Mon–Sat 3.30–5.30pm, Sun 4–5.30pm; £24). Reservations and smart(ish) dress required. Daily 12.30–1.45pm & 7–9pm.

Cottage Loaf Market St, LL30 2SR ⓣ01492 870762, ⓦthe-cottageloaf.co.uk. A slice of the country in the heart of Llandudno, all beams and fireplaces in the front and a bright back room decorated with nautical paintings and old maps. It has the best gastropub menu in town (mains £12–17) and the cask ales are local. Daily 11am–11pm; kitchen noon–9pm.

Home Cookin 139 Upper Mostyn St, LL30 2PE ⓣ01492 876585, ⓦhomecookin-llandudno.co.uk. A small modern bistro that's highly rated by locals because it does what it says. Light lunches, classics, bistro dishes (grilled salmon with a creamy tarragon Hollandaise sauce, say) and good veggie dishes such as sweet potato and spinach curry (£9.35) are all freshly cooked and competitively priced. Daily 10.30am–9.30pm.

Osborne's 17 North Parade, LL30 2LP ⓣ01492 860330, ⓦosbournehouse.co.uk. Opulent café and restaurant lit by chandeliers, serving the likes of slow-roast lamb or sea bass with garlic and crushed peas (£14.95). Come early for a cocktail. Lunch menus are lighter, and afternoon teas (Mon–Sat 3.30–5.30pm, Sun 4–5.30pm) splendid. Mon–Thurs & Sun 10.30am–9.30pm, Fri & Sat 10.30am–10pm.

16

St Asaph Cathedral

High St, St Asaph, LL17 0RD • Daily 9am–6.30pm • Free • ⓦstasaphcathedral.org.uk

ST ASAPH (Llanelwy) is home to Britain's smallest **cathedral**, founded around 570 by St Kentigern and no bigger than many village churches. From 1601 until his death in 1604, the bishopric was held by **William Morgan**, who was responsible for the translation of the first Welsh-language Bible, without which the language may have died out. A thousand Morgan bibles were printed, of which only nineteen remain, one of them displayed in the south transept along with notable prayer books and psalters.

Edinburgh and the Lothians

ROYAL MILE, EDINBURGH

17 Edinburgh and the Lothians

Venerable, dramatic Edinburgh, the showcase capital of Scotland, is a historic, cultured and ever more dynamic and cosmopolitan city. Of course, the locals have always known as much, savouring a skyline perched on a series of extinct volcanoes and rocky crags that rise from the generally flat landscape of the Lothians, with the sheltered shoreline of the Firth of Forth to the north. "My own Romantic town", Sir Walter Scott called it, although it was another Edinburgh-born author, Robert Louis Stevenson, who perhaps best captured the feel of his "precipitous city", declaring that "No situation could be more commanding for the head of a kingdom; none better chosen for noble prospects."

Along with its beauty, Edinburgh is blessed by its size: this is a wonderfully compact city, perfect for walking. The centre has two distinct parts: the unrelentingly medieval **Old Town**, with its tortuous alleys and tightly packed closes, and the dignified, eighteenth-century Neoclassical **New Town**. Dividing the two are **Princes Street Gardens**, which runs roughly east–west under the shadow of **Edinburgh Castle**. Set on the hill that rolls down from the fairytale castle to the royal **Palace of Holyroodhouse**, the Old Town preserves all the key landmarks from its time as a historic capital, augmented by the dramatic and unusual **Scottish Parliament** building, opposite the palace, and the attendant redevelopment of both Holyrood Road and the area around Market and New Streets just off the **Royal Mile**. A few hundred yards away, a tantalizing glimpse of the wild beauty of Scotland's scenery can be had in **Holyrood Park**, an extensive and unique wilderness area bang in the centre of the city, dominated by **Arthur's Seat**, the largest and most impressive of the city's nine extinct volcanoes. Among Edinburgh's many museums, the exciting **National Museum of Scotland** houses ten thousand of Scotland's most precious artefacts, while the **National Gallery of Scotland** and its offshoot, the **Scottish National Gallery of Modern Art**, have two of Britain's finest painting collections.

Beyond the centre, Edinburgh's liveliest area is **Leith**, the city's medieval port, whose seedy edge is softened by a series of great bars and restaurants, along with the presence of the former royal yacht *Britannia*. The wider rural surroundings of Edinburgh, known as the **Lothians**, mix rolling countryside and attractive country towns with impressive historic ruins.

Brief history

It was during the Dark Ages that the name Edinburgh first appeared. Built upon the Castle Rock volcano, at the heart of today's city, the strategic fort served as Scotland's **southernmost border post** until 1018, when King Malcolm I established the River Tweed as the permanent frontier. Under King James IV (1488–1513), the city enjoyed a short but brilliant **Renaissance era**, which saw the construction of a new

Highlights

❶ The Old Town The haunted heart of old Edinburgh, with tenements, closes and catacombs piled up cheek-by-jowl. See page 753

❷ Edinburgh Castle Perched on an imposing volcanic crag, the castle dominates Scotland's capital, its ancient battlements protecting the Crown Jewels. See page 753

❸ Scottish Parliament An architectural one-off that still divides opinion; squeeze in among the tourist hordes and decide for yourself. See page 761

❹ Holyrood Park Wild moors, rocky crags and an 800ft peak (Arthur's Seat), all slap in the middle of the city. See page 762

❺ National Museum of Scotland The treasures of Scotland's past housed in a dynamic and superbly conceived building. See page 763

❻ The Shore Leith's medieval port and surrounds are a foodie paradise of Michelin stars, foraged produce and ethnic eats. See page 770

❼ The Edinburgh Festival The whole world descends on Edinburgh come August for the famed festival – or rather festivals. The mother of all arts extravaganzas. See page 772

❽ Rosslyn Chapel *Da Vinci Code* fever may have cooled but this gothic masterpiece is as mesmerising as ever. See page 783

HIGHLIGHTS ARE MARKED ON THE MAPS ON PAGES 752 & 754

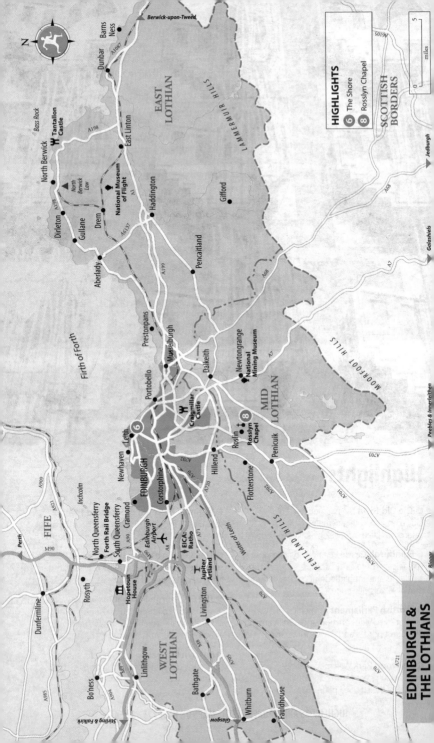

palace alongside Holyrood Abbey. This period came to an abrupt end in 1513 with the calamitous defeat at the Battle of Flodden and in the 1540s, English king Henry VIII's attempt to force a royal union with Scotland led to the sacking of Edinburgh, prompting the Scots to turn to France: French troops arrived to defend the city, while the young Scottish queen Mary was dispatched to Paris. While the French occupiers succeeded in removing the English threat, they themselves antagonized the locals, who had become increasingly sympathetic to the ideals of the **Reformation**. When the radical preacher John Knox returned from exile in 1555, he quickly won over the city to his Calvinist message.

James VI's rule saw the foundation of the University of Edinburgh in 1583, but following the **Union of the Crowns** in 1603, when James assumed the throne of England in addition to that of Scotland, the city was upstaged by London. The **Union of the Parliaments** of 1707 dealt a further blow to Edinburgh's political prestige, though guaranteed preservation of the national church and the legal and educational systems ensured that it was never relegated to a purely provincial role. On the contrary, it was in the second half of the eighteenth century that Edinburgh achieved the height of its intellectual influence, led by natives such as David Hume and Adam Smith. Around the same time, the city began to expand beyond its medieval boundaries, laying out the **New Town**, a masterpiece of the Neoclassical style and grand town planning. Edinburgh's urban expansion continued throughout the nineteenth and twentieth centuries annexing, among many other small burghs, the large port of **Leith** and the coastal village of **Cramond**. Following World War II Edinburgh was chosen to host the great **International Festival**, a symbol of the new peaceful European order; despite some hiccups, it has flourished ever since, in the process helping to make tourism a mainstay of the local economy.

The Old Town

Edinburgh's **Old Town**, although only about a mile long and 400 yards wide, represented the total extent of the twin burghs of Edinburgh and Canongate for the first 650 years of their existence, and its general appearance and character remain indubitably medieval. Containing the majority of the city's most famous tourist sights, the Old Town is compact enough to explore in a single day, though a thorough visit requires a bit longer. No matter how pressed you are, make sure you spare time for at least a taste of the wonderfully varied scenery and breathtaking vantage points of **Holyrood Park**, an extensive tract of open countryside on the eastern edge of the Old Town that includes **Arthur's Seat**, the peak of which rises so distinctively above the city.

Edinburgh Castle

Castlehill, EH1 2NG • Daily: April–Sept 9.30am–6pm; Oct–March 9.30am–5pm; last entry 1hr before closing; guided tours (30min) every 15min–1hr • £17, audio guides £3.50; guided tours free • ☎ 0131 225 9846, ⓦ edinburghcastle.gov.uk

Edinburgh Castle, which dominates the skyline from a lofty seat atop an extinct volcanic rock, is inextricably linked with the city's history. It requires no great imaginative feat to comprehend the strategic importance that underpinned the castle's – and hence Edinburgh's – pre-eminence in Scotland. From Princes Street, the north side rears high above an almost sheer rock face; the southern side is equally formidable, and the western, where the rock rises in terraces, only marginally less so. Would-be attackers, like modern tourists, were forced to approach the Castle from the narrow ridge to the east – today's **Royal Mile**. The disparate styles of the fortifications reflect the change in its role from defensive citadel to national monument, and today, as well as attracting more paying visitors than anywhere in the country, the castle is still a military barracks and home to Scotland's Crown Jewels.

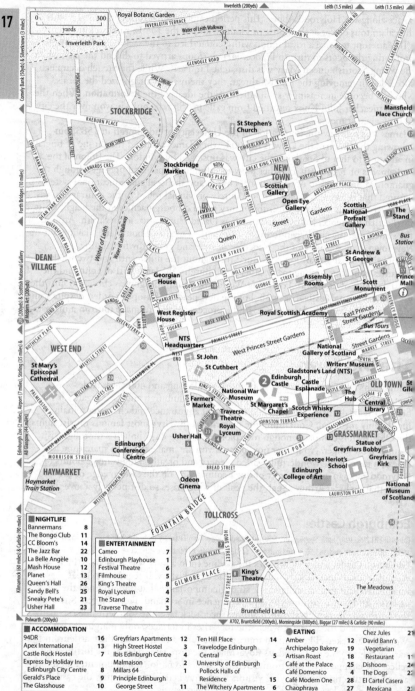

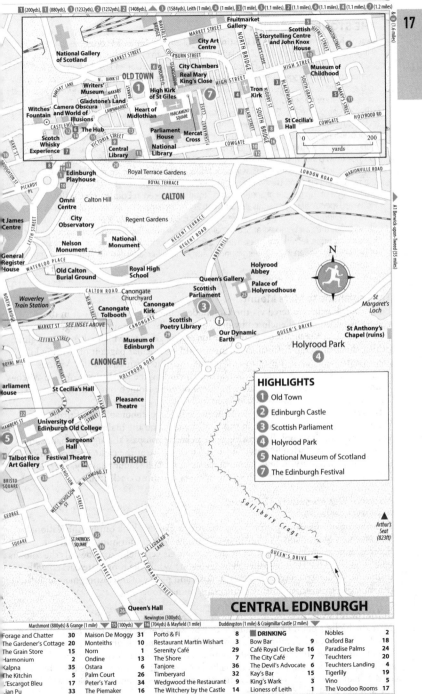

CENTRAL EDINBURGH

17

THE STONE OF DESTINY

Legend has it that the **Stone of Destiny** (also called the **Stone of Scone**) was "Jacob's Pillow", on which he dreamed of the ladder of angels from earth to heaven. Its real history is obscure, but it's known to have been moved from Ireland to Dunadd by missionaries, and thence to Dunstaffnage, from where Kenneth MacAlpine, king of the Dalriada Scots, brought it to the abbey at Scone, near Perth, in 838. There it remained for almost five hundred years, used as a coronation throne on which all kings of Scotland were crowned.

In 1296, an over-eager Edward I stole what he believed to be the Stone and installed it at Westminster Abbey, where, apart from a brief interlude in 1950 when it was removed by Scottish nationalists and hidden in Arbroath for several months, it remained for seven hundred years. All this changed in December 1996 when, after an elaborate ceremony-laden journey from London, the Stone returned to Scotland, in one of the doomed attempts by the Conservative government to win back Nationalist converts. Much to the annoyance of the people of Perth and the curators of Scone Palace (see page 859), and to the general indifference of the people of Scotland, the Stone was placed in **Edinburgh Castle**. However, speculation surrounds the authenticity of the Stone, for the original is said to have been intricately carved, while the one seen today is a plain block of sandstone. Many believe that the canny monks at Scone palmed this off onto the English king (some say that it's nothing more sacred than the cover for a medieval septic tank), and that the real Stone of Destiny lies hidden in an underground chamber, its whereabouts a mystery to all but the chosen few.

The Esplanade to Mill's Mount

Edinburgh Castle is entered via the **Esplanade**, a parade ground laid out in the eighteenth century and enclosed by ornamental walls. In the summer huge grandstands are erected for the **Edinburgh Military Tattoo** (see page 773), which takes place nightly during the Edinburgh Festival. A shameless and spectacular pageant of swirling kilts and massed pipe bands, the tattoo makes full use of its dramatic setting. Various memorials are dotted around the Esplanade, including the pretty Art Nouveau **Witches' Fountain** commemorating the three hundred or more women burnt at this spot on charges of sorcery, the last of whom died in 1722.

The castle is entered via a 10ft-wide opening in the **gatehouse**, one of many Romantic-style additions made in the 1880s; you'll find the main ticket office on your right. Continue uphill, showing your ticket as you pass through the handsome sixteenth-century **Portcullis Gate**, and you'll soon arrive at the eighteenth century six-gun **Argyle Battery**. A few further steps west, on **Mill's Mount Battery**, a well-known Edinburgh ritual takes place – the daily firing of the **one o'clock gun**.

National War Museum of Scotland

Entry included in Castle entry fee

Continuing on the main path beyond the Argyle Battery, look out for the **National War Museum of Scotland** on your right. Covering the last four hundred years of Scottish military history, the slant of the museum is very definitely towards the soldiers who fought for the Union, rather than against it. While the rooms are packed with uniforms, medals, paintings of heroic actions and plenty of interesting memorabilia, the museum manages to convey a reflective, human tone.

St Margaret's Chapel

Near the highest point of the citadel is tiny **St Margaret's Chapel**, the oldest surviving building in the castle, and probably in Edinburgh. Although once believed to have been built by the saint herself, and mooted as the site of her death in 1093, its architectural style suggests that it actually dates from about thirty years later. In front of the chapel you'll see the famous fifteenth-century siege gun, **Mons Meg**, which could fire a 500lb stone nearly two miles.

Crown Square

The historic heart of the Castle, **Crown Square** is the most important and secure section of the entire complex. The eastern side is occupied by the **Palace**, a surprisingly unassuming edifice begun in the 1430s which owes its Renaissance appearance to King James IV. You can visit a few rooms, including the tiny panelled bedchamber where Mary, Queen of Scots gave birth to James VI. The Palace also houses a detailed audiovisual presentation on the nation's **Crown Jewels**, known as the **Honours of Scotland**, a potent image of Scotland's nationhood; the originals are in the Crown Room at the very end of the display. The glass case containing the Honours has been rearranged to create space for the incongruously plain **Stone of Destiny**, a coronation throne on which all kings of Scotland were crowned from AD838 until Edward I stole it in 1296 (see page 756). On the south side of Crown Square is James IV's hammerbeam-ceilinged **Great Hall**, used for meetings of the Scottish Parliament until 1639.

The Royal Mile

The **Royal Mile** was described by Daniel Defoe in 1724, as "the largest, longest and finest street for buildings and number of inhabitants, not in Britain only, but in the world". Today, its tight, foreboding closes dwarfed by soaring rubble-stone merchant houses and grand neo-Grecian sandstone buildings make it a veritable feast of architectural heritage. Scratch the surface and it gets even more interesting, as many of the structures here sit atop a medieval **subterranean world** of caverns, rooms and closes; some can be visited on tours, while others are yet to be rediscovered.

Comprising a row of **four streets** (Castlehill, Lawnmarket, High Street and Canongate) and bookended by the castle and the Palace of Holyroodhouse, the Royal Mile possesses an enviable number of sights and attractions only exceeded (and somewhat detracted) by the inexhaustible knitwear, tartan and shortbread outlets that, along with the bagpipers on a rota, draw tourists here in their droves.

Camera Obscura and World of Illusions

549 Castlehill, EH1 2ND • Daily: April–June, Sept & Oct 9.30am–7pm; July & Aug 9.30am–9pm; Nov–March 10am–6pm • £15 • ☎0131 226 3709, ⓦ camera-obscura.co.uk.

Housed in a domed black-and-white turret, Edinburgh's **Camera Obscura** – a small, darkened room with a white wooden table onto which a periscope reflects live images of prominent buildings and folk walking on the streets below – has been a tourist attraction since 1853. Today, it is greatly overshadowed by **World of Illusions**, a labyrinth of family-friendly exhibits of optical illusions, holograms and clever visual trickery spread across five floors beneath the camera itself. Many are playfully interactive, like the Maze of Mirrors or the Vortex, where you attempt to walk across a static ramp surrounded by a rotating tunnel – much harder than you might think. There's also the Big-Small room where photos taken from the viewing window reveal giant children towering over their shrunken parents.

Scotch Whisky Experience

354 Castlehill, EH1 2NE • Tours (50min–1hr 30min) every 20min daily: April–Aug 10am–6pm; Sept–March 10am–5pm • From £15 • ☎0131 220 0441, ⓦ scotchwhiskyexperience.co.uk

The **Scotch Whisky Experience** mimics the kind of tours offered at distilleries in the Highlands, and while it can't match the authenticity of the real thing, the centre does offer a thorough introduction to the "water of life" (*uisge beatha* in Gaelic). On the ground floor, a well-stocked shop gives an idea of the sheer range and diversity of the drink, while downstairs there's a pleasant whisky bar and restaurant, *Amber* (see page 776).

17 Gladstone's Land

477b Lawnmarket, EH1 2NT · April–Dec daily 10am–5pm · £7; NTS · ☏ 0131 458 0200, ⓦ nts.org.uk/Visit/Gladstones-Land

Doing its best to maintain its dignity among a sea of cheap tartan gifts and discounted woolly jumpers, Gladstone's Land is the Royal Mile's best surviving example of a typical seventeenth-century tenement. The tall, narrow building – not unlike a canal-side house in Amsterdam – would have been home to various families living in cramped conditions. The arcaded and wooden-fronted ground floor is home to a reconstructed cloth shop; pass through this to encounter a warren of tight staircases, creaking floorboards and tiny rooms, the finest of which is on the first floor, where a marvellous Renaissance painted ceiling was only discovered in the 1930s after the building was saved from demolition.

EDINBURGH: UNESCO CITY OF LITERATURE

While Edinburgh's stunning skyline, world-renowned festivals, art galleries and architectural heritage draw in an exponentially increasing number of visitors every year, it is arguably **literary tourism** that is having the city's most impressive renaissance. A new breed of writers, like the classic novelists of the past, have found inspiration among Edinburgh's ancient howfs (Scots for pub), tight closes and grand Georgian buildings; their readers meanwhile, keen to discover their favourite real-life book locations, are flocking to the city in droves.

It's no surprise that **Harry Potter** is the main draw: take a stroll down Victoria Street, J.K. Rowling's inspiration for Diagon Alley, where there's a dedicated Potter shop, and then enter Greyfriars Kirkyard to look for the final resting place of Thomas Riddell, which may well have inspired the author when she created Lord Voldemort. Yet another tombstone displays the name William McGonagall, perhaps inspiration for the Hogwarts' Professor played in the film adaption by Maggie Smith. (Coincidentally, Smith performed a scene in this very kirkyard when she starred in the 1969 movie version of Muriel Spark's novel *The Prime of Miss Jean Brodie*.)

Inevitably, cult fiction has more than its fair share of pilgrims, and it doesn't get much more cult than Irvine Welsh's **Trainspotting**. The 1996 film adaption famously included several of Edinburgh's more iconic cityscapes while also introducing some of her less savoury localities such as Leith's notorious Banana flats (used as Sick Boy's drug den). On a more salubrious note, fans of **Alexander McCall Smith** will inevitably want to wander down Scotland Street in the New Town, just as **Inspector Rebus** diehards will want to sink a pint in Ian Rankin's famous boozer of choice, the *Oxford Bar* (see page 779).

If you were to go on statuary and novelistic references alone, however, you'd inevitably conclude that Edinburgh reserves most of its literary acclaim for hopeless-Romantic-cum-arch-Unionist **Sir Walter Scott**. Not many writers can claim to have inspired both a train station (Waverley) and football team (Heart of Midlothian), while the thrusting Scott Monument (see page 765) is the largest dedication to an author in the world. You might also want to head to Arthur's Seat, where a more infamous alfresco scene is played out in *Confessions of a Justified Sinner*, the seminal Gothic novel by the Ettrick Shepherd (and Scott confidant), **James Hogg**.

While Hogg's prose is as claustrophobic as it gets, the city's passion for literature is anything but insular. The **Scottish Storytelling Centre** (see page 759) and the **Scottish Poetry Library** (see page 760), relatively recent additions to the Royal Mile, widened the focus internationally, helping Edinburgh earn the world's very first UNESCO City of Literature designation in 2004.

TOP 5 BOOKISH SIGHTS

Literary tours See page 774
Rosslyn Chapel See page 783
The Scott Monument See page 765
Scottish Poetry Library See page 760
Writers' Museum See page 759

Writers' Museum

17

Lady Stair's Close, EH1 2PA • Wed–Sat 10am–5pm, Sun noon–5pm • Free • ☎ 0131 529 4901, ⓦ edinburghmuseums.org.uk

Situated within the seventeenth-century Lady Stair's House, the **Writers' Museum** is dedicated to Scotland's three greatest literary lions: Sir Walter Scott, Robert Louis Stevenson and Robert Burns. It's a small affair, with displays of first-edition copies, original manuscripts and personal effects. Highlights include Burns's original writing desk, a pair of riding boots given to Stevenson by a Samoan chief – note the engraved word Tusitala, meaning "teller of tales" – and the original press used to print Scott's Waverley novels. The house's tight, winding stairs and poky, wood-panelled rooms offer an authentic and attractive flavour of the medieval Old Town.

High Kirk of St Giles

High St, EH1 1RE • May–Sept Mon–Fri 9am–7pm, Sat 9am–5pm, Sun 1–5pm; Oct–April Mon–Sat 9am–5pm, Sun 1–5pm • Free • ☎ 0131 226 0674, ⓦ stgilescathedral.org.uk

The dominant building on the High Street – the central section of the Royal Mile – is the **High Kirk of St Giles**, dating back to 1485. Its resplendent crown spire is formed from eight flying buttresses, while four massive piers support the tower (originally part of a Norman church built here around 1120). The original parish church of medieval Edinburgh, from where John Knox launched and directed the Scottish Reformation, it's often referred to as a cathedral, although it has only been the seat of a bishop on two brief and unhappy occasions in the seventeenth century. According to one of the city's best-known legends, the attempt here in 1637 to introduce the English Prayer Book, and thus episcopal government, so incensed a humble stallholder named Jenny Geddes that she hurled her stool at the preacher, prompting the rest of the congregation to chase the offending clergy out of the building. A tablet in the north aisle marks the spot from where she let rip.

Real Mary King's Close

2 Warriston's Close, High St, EH1 1PG • Tours (1hr) daily every 15min: April–Oct daily 10am–9pm; Nov–March Mon–Thurs & Sun 10am–5pm, Fri & Sat 10am–9pm • £14.75 • ☎ 0131 225 0672, ⓦ realmarykingsclose.com

Subterranean **Real Mary King's Close** is one of Edinburgh's most unusual attractions. When work on the City Chambers began in 1753, the tops of the existing houses on the site were simply sliced through at the level of the High Street and the new building constructed on top of them. Because the tenements had been built on a steep hillside, this process left parts of the houses, together with the old streets (or closes) that ran alongside them, intact but entirely enclosed among the basement and cellars of the chambers. You can visit this rather spooky "lost city" on **tours** led by costumed actors.

Scottish Storytelling Centre and John Knox House

43–45 High St, EH1 1SR • July & Aug Mon–Sat 10am–6pm, Sun noon–6pm; Sept–June Mon–Sat 10am–6pm • Storytelling Centre free; John Knox House £5 • ☎ 0131 556 9579, ⓦ scottishstorytellingcentre.co.uk

There are two distinct parts to the **Scottish Storytelling Centre**. One half is a stylish contemporary development based around an airy Storytelling Court, with a small permanent exhibition about Scottish stories from ancient folk tales to *Harry Potter*. By contrast, the **John Knox House** is a fifteenth-century stone-and-timber building that, with its distinctive external staircase, overhanging upper storeys and busy pantile roof, is a classic example of the Royal Mile in its medieval heyday. Regular performances and events, often aimed at a younger audience, take place in the centre.

17 Canongate

For more than seven hundred years, the **Canongate** district, through which the eastern section of the Royal Mile runs, was a burgh in its own right, separated from the capital by a tollbooth at the foot of High Street. Although now demolished, the Tolbooth was nicknamed the "World's End" back in the sixteenth century because most of Edinburgh's residents were too poor to pass through it and thus lived their entire lives within the city walls. Canongate itself was also notoriously poor; a slum area even into the 1960s, it has been the subject of some of the most ambitious restoration programmes in the Old Town, though the lack of harmony between the buildings renovated in different decades is fairly obvious. Construction has particularly gained pace in recent years and while many controversial modern developments have helped rejuvenate the area, the arguably unsympathetic style of the changes have raised eyebrows at UNESCO who have threatened to withdraw Edinburgh's prized World Heritage status.

Canongate Kirk

153 Canongate, EH8 8BN • Mon–Sat 10.30am–4.30pm, Sun 12.30–4.30pm, depending on volunteer staff and church services • Free • ☎ 0131 556 3515, ⓦ canongatekirk.org.uk

Built to house the congregation expelled from Holyrood Abbey when the latter was commandeered by James VII (James II in England), **Canongate Kirk** is the church used by the Queen when she's at Holyrood and was the location for Britain's "other royal wedding" of 2011, when Prince William's cousin Zara Philips married England rugby player Mike Tindall. The kirk has a modesty rarely seen in churches built in later centuries, with a graceful curved facade and a bow-shaped gable to the rear. The surrounding churchyard provides an attractive and tranquil stretch of green and affords fine views of Calton Hill; it also happens to be one of the city's most exclusive **cemeteries** – well-known internees include the political economist Adam Smith, Mrs Agnes McLehose (better known as Robert Burns's "Clarinda") and Robert Fergusson. Fergusson's headstone was donated by Burns, a fervent admirer, and a statue of the young poet can be seen just outside the kirk gates.

Museum of Edinburgh

142–146 Canongate, EH8 8DD • Mon & Thurs–Sat 10am–5pm, Sun noon–5pm • Free • ☎ 0131 529 4143, ⓦ edinburghmuseums.org.uk

The **Museum of Edinburgh** is the city's principal collection devoted to local history, and is as interesting for the labyrinthine network of wood-panelled rooms as for its rather quirky array of artefacts. These include a number of items of real historical significance, in particular the National Covenant, the petition for religious freedom drawn up on a deerskin parchment in 1638, and the original plans for the layout of the New Town drawn by James Craig (see page 764).

Scottish Poetry Library

5 Crichton's Close, EH8 8DT • Tues–Fri 10am–5pm, Sat 10am–4pm • Free • ☎ 0131 557 2876, ⓦ scottishpoetrylibrary.org.uk

A sweet note of modern architectural eloquence amid a cacophony of large-scale developments, the **Scottish Poetry Library** incorporates a section of an old city wall, and the attractive, contemporary design harmoniously combines brick, oak, glass, Caithness stone and blue ceramic tiles. The library contains Scotland's most comprehensive collection of native poetry, and visitors are free to read the books, periodicals and leaflets found on the shelves, or to listen to recordings of poetry in English, Scots and Gaelic.

Holyrood

At the foot of Canongate lies **Holyrood**, with its ruined thirteenth-century abbey and the **Palace of Holyroodhouse**, the residence of the Queen and other royals when they're in town. The area has been transformed by Enric Miralles' highly controversial **Scottish Parliament**, a love-it-or-loathe-it concrete monolith "almost surging out of the rock" – as Miralles put it – of adjacent **Arthur's Seat**, a slumbering volcano in the adjacent wilderness of **Holyrood Park**.

Palace of Holyroodhouse

Canongate, EH8 8DX • Daily: April–Oct 9.30am–6pm; Nov–March 9.30am–4.30pm; last admission 1hr 30min before closing • £12.50, £17.50 joint ticket with the Queen's Gallery • ☎ 0303 123 7306, ⓦ royalcollection.org.uk

In its present form the **Palace of Holyroodhouse** is largely a seventeenth-century creation, planned for Charles II. Audio tours guide you through a series of royal **reception rooms** featuring some outstanding encrusted plasterwork. On the northern side of the internal quadrangle, the **Great Gallery** is dominated by portraits of 96 Scottish kings, painted by Jacob de Wet in 1684 to illustrate the lineage of Stewart royalty: the result is unintentionally hilarious, as it's clear that the artist's imagination was taxed to bursting point in his commission to paint so many different facial types without having an inkling as to what the subjects actually looked like. As you then move into the oldest part of the palace, known as **James V's tower**, the formal, ceremonial tone gives way to dark medieval history, with a tight spiral staircase leading to the chambers used by Mary, Queen of Scots. These contain various relics, including jewellery, associated with the queen, but most compelling of all is a tiny supper room from where, in 1566, Mary's Italian secretary, David Rizzio, was dragged by conspirators – including her jealous husband, Lord Darnley – to the outer chamber and stabbed 56 times. A brass plaque on the wall points out what are rather unconvincingly identified as the consequent bloodstains on the wooden floor.

Holyrood Abbey

Canongate, EH8 8DX • Free as part of palace tour

The evocative ruins of **Holyrood Abbey**, some of which date from the thirteenth century, lie next to the palace. The roof tumbled down in 1768, but the melancholy scene has inspired artists down the years, among them Felix Mendelssohn, who in 1829 wrote "Everything is in ruins and mouldering … I believe I have found the beginning of my Scottish Symphony there today."

Queen's Gallery

Canongate, EH8 8DX • Daily: April–Oct 9.30am–6pm; Nov–March 9.30am–4.30pm; last admission 1hr before closing • £7, £17.50 joint ticket with Palace of Holyroodhouse • ☎ 0303 123 7306, ⓦ royalcollection.org.uk

Essentially an adjunct to the Palace of Holyroodhouse, the **Queen's Gallery** is located in the shell of a former church between the palace and the parliament. It's a compact space with just two principal viewing rooms that display changing exhibitions from the **Royal Collection**, a vast array of art treasures held by the Queen on behalf of the British nation. Because the pieces are otherwise exhibited only during the limited openings of Buckingham Palace and Windsor Castle, the exhibitions tend to draw quite a lot of interest.

Scottish Parliament

Horse Wynd, EH99 1SP • Mon, Fri & Sat 10am–5pm, Tues, Wed & Thurs 9am–6.30pm; guided tours (1hr) leave depending on demand; last entry 30min before closing • Free (booking recommended for tours) • ☎ 0800 092 7600, ⓦ visitparliament.scot

By far the most controversial public building to be erected in Scotland since World War II, the **Scottish Parliament** houses the country's directly elected assembly. A separate

17

parliament to look after the running of internal Scottish affairs was reintroduced to the British constitution in 1999, nearly two hundred years after the previous Scottish parliament had joined the English assembly at Westminster as part of the Union of the two nations in 1707. The home of the directly elected parliament was eventually opened in 2004, late and dramatically over budget – initial estimates for the building's cost were tentatively put at £40 million; the final bill was more than £400 million. Made up of various linked elements rather than one single building, the complex was designed by Catalan architect **Enric Miralles**, whose death in 2000, halfway through construction, caused ripples of uncertainty as to whether he had in fact set down his final draft. However, the finished product is an impressive – if imperfect – testament to the ambition of Miralles, and it has won over the majority of the architectural community, scooping numerous awards including Britain's prestigious Royal Institute of British Architects (RIBA) Stirling Prize in 2005.

There's free access into the **entrance lobby** where a small **exhibition** provides some historical, political and architectural background. If parliament is in session, it's normally possible to watch proceedings in the **debating chamber**. Grand yet intimate, the chamber is flooded with light through high windows and features a complex network of thick oak beams, lights and microphone wires. The European-style layout is a deliberate move away from the confrontational Westminster model, though some have been quick to point out that while the traditional inter-party insults still fly, the quality of the parliamentarians' rhetoric rarely matches that of the soaring new arena. To see the rest of the interior properly you'll need to join one of the regular **guided tours**, which give you a more detailed appreciation of the building's design.

Our Dynamic Earth

112 Holyrood Rd, EH8 8AS • April–June, Sept & Oct daily 10am–5.30pm; July & Aug daily 10am–6pm; Nov–March Wed–Sun 10am–5.30pm; last entry 1hr 30min before closing • £15 • ☎ 0131 550 7800, ⓦ dynamicearth.co.uk

Beneath a pincushion of white metal struts that make it look like a miniature version of London's O2, **Our Dynamic Earth** is a high-tech attraction aimed at children aged between 5 and 15. Galleries cover the formation of the Earth and continents with crashing sound effects and a shaking floor, while the calmer grandeur of glaciers and oceans is explored through magnificent large-screen landscape footage. Further on, the polar regions – complete with a real iceberg – and tropical jungles are imaginatively re-created.

Holyrood Park

Information centre Holyrood Lodge, Horse Wynd, EH8 8HG • Daily 9.30am–3pm • Free • ☎ 0131 652 8150

Comprising a dazzling array of landscapes – hills, crags, moorland, marshes, glens, lochs and fields – packed into 650 acres, **Holyrood Park** is Scotland in miniature. Once a royal hunting estate, it was given park status in the sixteenth century by King James V. While

---

ASCENDING ARTHUR'S SEAT

The usual starting point for the ascent of **Arthur's Seat**, which at 823ft above sea level towers over Edinburgh's numerous high points, is Dunsapie Loch, reached by following the tarred Queen's Drive in a clockwise direction from the information centre in Holyrood Park (30–40min walk). The Seat is part of a volcano that last saw action 350 million years ago, and its connections to the legendary king are fairly sketchy: the name is more likely to be a corruption of the Gaelic **Ard-na-said**, or "height of arrows". From Dunsapie Loch it's a twenty-minute climb up grassy slopes to the rocky summit. On a clear day, the views might just stretch to the English border and the Atlantic Ocean; more realistically, the landmarks that dominate are Fife, a few Highland peaks and, of course, Edinburgh itself laid out on all sides.

old photographs of the park show crops growing and sheep grazing, it's now used mostly by outdoor enthusiasts. A single tarred road, **Queen's Drive**, loops through the park, perfect for a circular cycle route. The park's information centre is a good starting point for a hike; as well as details on the park's geology and flora, you can pick up a **map** of suggested routes up Arthur's Seat and Salisbury Crags.

17

Grassmarket and around

Tucked in below the castle's high southern edifice is an open, partly cobbled area known as **Grassmarket**, which was used as the city's cattle market from 1477 to 1911 and was also the site of Edinburgh's public gallows – the spot is marked by a tiny garden. Despite the height of many of the surrounding buildings, Grassmarket offers an unexpected view up to the precipitous walls of the castle and, come springtime, it's sunny enough for cafés to put tables and chairs along the pavement.

The pubs and restaurants here are busy by night, while by day you can admire the architectural quirks and interesting shops, in particular the string of offbeat boutiques on curving **Victoria Street**, an unusual two-tier thoroughfare, with arcaded shops below and a pedestrian terrace above. Southeast of Grassmarket, near the old city boundary, the fondly remembered hound **Greyfriar's Bobby** is commemorated outside his master's kirkyard home, while across the road the **National Museum of Scotland** is an essential stop.

Surgeons' Hall

Nicolson St, EH8 NDW • Daily 10am–5pm • £6.50 • ☎ 0131 527 1711, ⓦ museum.rcsed.ac.uk

Inside the stately **Surgeons' Hall**, a handsome Ionic temple built by William Henry Playfair (1790–1857) as the headquarters of the Royal College of Surgeons, is one of the city's most unusual and morbidly compelling museums. In the eighteenth and nineteenth centuries Edinburgh developed as a leading centre for medical and anatomical research, nurturing world-famous figures such as James Young Simpson, pioneer of anaesthesia, and Joseph Lister, the father of modern surgery. The building holds **three museums** covering pathology, surgery and dentistry, with exhibits ranging from early surgical tools to a pocketbook covered with the leathered skin of serial killer, William Burke.

National Museum of Scotland

Chambers St, EH1 1JF • Daily 10am–5pm • Free • ☎ 0300 123 6789, ⓦ nms.ac.uk

The **National Museum of Scotland** fuses a grand Victorian building with an extension built in the 1990s. The recently refurbished older section, known as the **Royal Museum**, exhibits an extensive collection covering natural history, indigenous cultures, science, crafts and textiles. Alongside it, the clean lines and imaginatively designed interior of the **Museum of Scotland** offer a fresh perspective on the nation's history.

Royal Museum

Centred on a soaring, three-storey atrium, the **Royal Museum** is a dignified Venetian-style structure with a cast-iron interior modelled on London's Crystal Palace. There's much to appreciate simply in the building itself, with the main **Grand Gallery** flooded by natural light and encircled by two levels of balcony. The main exhibits are found in rooms off the Grand Gallery, the most notable (particularly for younger visitors) being the **natural history** collection with stuffed animals, dinosaur skeletons and numerous models of sea creatures suspended from the ceiling among giant plasma screens showing wildlife in action. An area dedicated to **science and technology** features everything from robots and space ships to a stuffed model of Dolly the sheep.

17

GREYFRIARS BOBBY AND GREYFRIARS KIRK

The statue of **Greyfriars Bobby** at the southwestern corner of George IV Bridge, just across the road from the Museum of Scotland, must rank as Edinburgh's most sentimental tourist attraction. According to the legend – no doubt embellished down the years – Bobby was a Skye terrier acquired as a working dog by a police constable named John Gray. When Gray died in 1858, Bobby was found a few days later sitting on his grave, a vigil he maintained until his death fourteen years later. Bobby's legendary dedication was picked up by Disney, whose 1960 feature film of the story ensured that streams of tourists have paid their respects ever since.

The grave Bobby mourned over is in the yard of nearby **Greyfriars Kirk**, which has a fine collection of seventeenth-century gravestones and mausoleums and is visited regularly by ghost tours. It was renowned for grave-robbing in the early 1800s, when freshly interred bodies were exhumed and sold to the nearby medical school. Greyfriars Kirk itself was built in 1620 on land that had belonged to a Franciscan convent, though little of the original late Gothic-style building remains.

Museum of Scotland

The seven-floor **Museum of Scotland** is Scotland's premier historical museum. The nation's beginnings and earliest peoples are covered in the basement, with artefacts including the **Cramond Lioness**, a sculpture from a Roman tombstone found recently in the Firth of Forth, along with carved stones and jewellery from Pictish times. Moving up through the museum, look out for the famous **Lewis chessmen**, idiosyncratic twelfth-century pieces carved from walrus ivory, along with pieces relating to the more significant periods of Scotland's past, including the Highland uprisings under Bonnie Prince Charlie (whose silver travelling canteen is on display). **Industry and Empire** covers the era of heavy industry and mass emigration, while **Scotland: A Changing Nation** traces the different experiences of people living and working in contemporary Scotland, through film, objects and personal stories.

From the small **roof garden**, accessed by a lift, sweeping views open out to the Firth of Forth, the Pentland hills and across to the Castle and Royal Mile skyline. Other fine views can be enjoyed from the museum's stylish *Tower* restaurant.

The New Town

The **New Town**, itself well over two hundred years old, stands in total contrast to the Old Town: the streets are broad and straight, and most of the buildings are Neoclassical. Originally intended to be residential, the entire area, right down to the names of its streets, is something of a celebration of the Union, which, at the time building began in 1767, was nevertheless far from universally popular. Today, the main streets form the bustling hub of the city's commercial, retail and business life. In many ways, the layout of the greater New Town is its own most remarkable sight, an extraordinary grouping of squares, circuses, terraces, crescents and parks that display a restrained symmetry. Predominantly Georgian, it does however contain assorted Victorian additions, notably the **Scott Monument** on Princes Street, the **Royal Botanic Garden** on its northern fringe and two of the city's most important public collections – the **National Gallery of Scotland** and, further afield, the **Scottish National Gallery of Modern Art**.

Brief history

The existence of the New Town is chiefly due to the vision of **George Drummond**, who made schemes for the expansion of the city soon after becoming Lord Provost in 1725. Work began on the draining of the Nor' Loch below the castle in 1759, a job that took some sixty years. The North Bridge, linking the Old Town with the main road leading to the port of Leith, was built between 1763 and 1772 and, in 1766, following a public competition, a plan for the New Town by 22-year-old architect **James Craig** was chosen. Its gridiron pattern was perfectly matched to the site: central **George Street**, flanked by showpiece squares, was laid out along the main ridge, with parallel **Princes Street** and **Queen Street** on either side, built up on one side only, so as not to block the spectacular views of the Old Town and Fife.

Princes Street

Although only allocated a subsidiary role in the original plan of the New Town, **Princes Street** had developed into Edinburgh's principal thoroughfare by the middle of the nineteenth century, a role it has retained ever since. Its unobstructed views across to the castle and the jagged silhouette of the Old Town are undeniably magnificent. Indeed, without them, Princes Street would lose much of its appeal; its northern side, dominated by large outlets of the familiar national chains, is almost always crowded with shoppers, and few of the original eighteenth-century buildings remain.

Princes Street Gardens

Princes St, EH2 2HG • **Gardens** Dawn to dusk • Free • **Ferris wheel** July, Aug & late Nov to early Jan daily 10am–10pm • £9 • ☎ 0131 529 7921, ⓦ edinburgh.gov.uk

It's hard to imagine that **Princes Street Gardens**, which flank nearly the entire length of the street, were once the stagnant, foul-smelling **Nor' Loch**, into which the effluent of the Old Town flowed for centuries. The railway has since replaced the water, and today a sunken cutting carries the main lines out of Waverley Station. The gardens were originally the private domain of Princes Street residents and their well-placed acquaintances, only becoming a public park in 1876. The larger and more verdant western section has a floral clock and the Ross Bandstand, a popular Festival venue, while at Christmas the eastern section is home to numerous funfair attractions including a towering **Ferris wheel**.

The Scott Monument

East Princes Street Gardens, EH2 2EJ • Daily: April–Sept 10am–7pm; Oct–March 10am–4pm • £5 • ☎ 0131 529 4068, ⓦ edinburghmuseums.org.uk.

Erected in memory of the prolific author and patriot Sir Walter Scott within a few years of his death, the 200ft sandstone **Scott Monument** is closely modelled on the writer's beloved Melrose Abbey (see page 793), while the rich sculptural decoration shows sixteen Scottish writers and 64 characters from his famous *Waverley* novels. On the central plinth at the base of the monument is a statue of Scott with his deerhound Maida, carved from a thirty-tonne block of Carrara marble. Inside the memorial a tightly winding spiral staircase climbs 287 steps to a narrow platform near the top: from here, you can enjoy inspiring vistas of the city below, and hills and firths beyond.

National Gallery of Scotland

The Mound EH2 2EL • Mon–Wed & Fri–Sun 10am–5pm, Thurs 10am–7pm • Free, charge for some temporary exhibitions • ☎ 0131 624 6200, ⓦ nationalgalleries.org

Built as a "temple to the fine arts" in 1850 by William Henry Playfair (1790–1857) the **National Gallery of Scotland** houses the nation's finest array of European and Scottish art from the early 1300s to the late 1800s. Its modest size makes it a manageable place to visit in a couple of hours and affords a pleasantly unrushed atmosphere. The vast collection, one of the finest in the world, is shared between the National Portrait

17

Gallery (see page 767) and the Scottish National Gallery of Modern Art (see page 768); consequently many of the great masterpieces are displayed on rotation.

Early works

Among the **early works**, one highlight is a superb painting by **Botticelli**, *The Virgin Adoring the Sleeping Christ Child* which, along with Raphael's graceful tondo *The Holy Family with a Palm Tree*, has undergone careful restoration to reveal a striking luminosity and depth of colour. Of the four mythological scenes by **Titian**, the sensuous *Three Ages of Man* is one of his most accomplished early compositions. Alongside the Titians, **Bassano's** *Adoration of the Kings* and a dramatic altarpiece, *The Deposition of Christ*, by Tintoretto, as well as several other works by Veronese, complete the fine Venetian section.

European works

The gallery has a number of important **European works**, including **Rubens'** *The Feast of Herod*, an archetypal example of his sumptuously grand manner. Among the four **Rembrandt** canvases are a poignant *Self-Portrait Aged 51* and the ripely suggestive *Woman in Bed*. *Christ in the House of Martha and Mary* is the largest and probably the earliest of the thirty or so surviving paintings by **Vermeer**.

Impressionist masters have a strong showing, including a collection of **Degas'** sketches, paintings and bronzes, **Monet's** *Haystacks* (*Snow*) and **Renoir's** *Woman Nursing Child*. Representing the Post-Impressionists are three exceptional works by **Gauguin**, including *Vision After the Sermon*, set in Brittany, **Van Gogh's** *Olive Trees* and **Cézanne's** *The Big Trees* – a clear forerunner of modern abstraction.

Scottish and English works

Scottish and English works are, naturally, well represented. Of **Sir Henry Raeburn's** large portraits, the swaggering masculinity of *Sir John Sinclair in Highland Dress* shows the artist's technical mastery, though he was equally confident when working on a smaller scale, as seen in one of the gallery's most popular pictures, *The Rev Robert Walker Skating on Duddingston Loch*. The gallery also owns a brilliant array of watercolours by **Turner**, faithfully displayed each January when damaging sunlight is at its weakest; at other times two of his fine Roman views are displayed in a dim gallery.

George Street and around

Parallel to Princes Street, and originally designed as the central thoroughfare of the New Town, **George Street** leads along the crest of the hill that sweeps down to the Forth. At the western end is **Charlotte Square**, designed by Robert Adam in 1791, a year before his death. Generally regarded as the epitome of the New Town's elegant simplicity, the square was once the most exclusive residential address in Edinburgh,

---

EDINBURGH'S ART SCENE

With such an aesthetic backdrop, it seems fitting that Edinburgh's **art scene** thrives not only in the main galleries, but also on the streets through market sales and in independent outlets. If your visit to the city coincides with the end of the academic year then the huge Degree show at the prestigious **College of Art** (74 Lauriston Place; ☎0131 651 5800, ⓦeca.ed.ac.uk) is well worth a good couple of hour's inspection; the college also stages its Masters degree show in August. Earlier in the year you should check out the **Hidden Door** alternative arts festival (ⓦhiddendoorblog.org), a volunteer-run bonanza of art installations, music and various creative activities. For more established exhibitions, the best place to go is **Dundas Street** in the New Town, where you'll find a cluster of reputable independent galleries within feet of one another.

nd though much of it is now occupied by offices, the imperious dignity of the rchitecture is still evident. Indeed, the north side is once again the city's premier ddress, with the official residence of the First Minister of the Scottish Government at o. 6 (Bute House), the Edinburgh equivalent of 10 Downing Street. In August each ear, the gardens in the centre of the square are colonized by the temporary tents of the dinburgh International Book Festival (see page 773).

Georgian House

Charlotte Square, EH2 4DR • March & Nov daily 11am–4pm; April–Sept daily 10am–5pm; early Dec Thurs–Sun 11am–4pm • £7.50; TS • ☎ 0131 225 2160, ⓦ nts.org.uk/Visit/Georgian-House

The **Georgian House** provides a revealing sense of well-to-do New Town living in the arly nineteenth century. The rooms are impressively decked out in period furniture – ook for the working barrel organ that plays a selection of Scottish airs – and hung with ine paintings, including portraits by Ramsay and Raeburn. In the basement are the riginal wine cellar and a kitchen complete with an open fire.

Scottish National Portrait Gallery

Queen St, EH2 1JD • Mon–Wed & Fri–Sun 10am–5pm (6pm in Aug), Thurs 10am–7pm • Free, entrance charge for some temporary xhibitions • ☎ 0131 624 6200, ⓦ nationalgalleries.org

Housed in a fantastic, red sandstone Gothic-Revival palace, the **Scottish National Portrait Gallery** makes an extravagant contrast to the New Town's prevailing Neoclassicism. The exterior is encrusted with statues of national heroes, a theme reiterated in the stunning two-storey entrance hall by William Hole's tapestry-like frieze and mural, carefully restored during the building's revamp. The collection extends to more than thirty thousand images, with seventeen exhibition spaces exploring the differing characteristics of Scotland as a nation and a people. Inevitably oil paintings of the likes of Mary, Queen of Scots and Robert Burns form the backbone of the collection, but there's a lot to be said for the contemporary portraits that often show a country in cultural flux.

Royal Botanic Garden

Arboretum Place EH3 5NZ • Daily: Feb & Oct 10am–5pm; March–Sept 10am–6pm; Nov–Jan 10am–4pm • Free; glasshouses £6.50 • **Guided tours** April–Oct 11am & 2pm; 1hr 30min • £6 • ☎ 0131 248 2909, ⓦ rbge.org.uk

Just beyond the northern boundaries of the New Town, the seventy-acre **Royal Botanic Garden**, with origins as far back as the seventeenth century, rivals Kew (see page 110) as a must-see botanical attraction. Filled with mature trees and a huge variety of native and exotic plants and flowers, the "Botanics" (as they're commonly called) are most popular simply as a place to stroll and lounge around on the grass. The main entrance is the West Gate on Arboretum Place, through the contemporary, eco-designed **John Hope Gateway**, where you'll find interpretation areas, a shop and a restaurant. Towards the eastern side of the gardens, a series of ten **glasshouses**, including a soaring 1850s Palm House, shows off a steamy array of palms, ferns, orchids, cycads and aquatic plants. Pride of the collection here in recent years has been the titan arum plant which around June produces the world's largest flower. A notoriously stubborn plant to bloom, Edinburgh's specimen has been named Auld Reekie (Edinburgh's nickname) thanks to its fly-attracting, rotting-flesh scent. Outside, gardens are planted on different themes: the large Chinese-style garden, for example, has a bubbling waterfall and the world's largest collection of Asian wild plants outside China, while in the northwest corner there's a Scottish native woodland which very effectively evokes the wild unkemptness of parts of the Scottish Highlands and west coast.

17

Calton Hill

Edinburgh's tag as the "Athens of the North" is nowhere better earned than on **Calton Hill**, the volcanic peak that rises up above the eastern end of Princes Street. The hill an its odd collection of grandiose buildings aren't just for looking *at*: this is also one of th best viewpoints from which to appreciate the whole city and the sea beyond.

Nelson Monument

32 Calton Hill, EH7 5AA • April–Sept Mon–Sat 10am–7pm, Sun noon–5pm; Oct–March Mon–Sat 10am–4pm • £5 • ☎ 0131 556 2716

Robert Louis Stevenson reckoned that Calton Hill was the best place to view Edinburgh, "since you can see the Castle, which you lose from the Castle, and Arthur's Seat, which you cannot see from Arthur's Seat". Though the panoramas from ground level are spectacular enough, those from the top of the **Nelson Monument**, perched near the summit with an appearance like a giant sandstone ches rook, are even better. Before the fourteen-step ascent you'll pass a small ground-level **exhibition** with details of the structure's maritime connections and a model of Nelson's flagship, *Victory*.

National Monument

The **National Monument** is often referred to as "Edinburgh's Disgrace", yet many locals admire this unfinished and somewhat ungainly attempt to replicate the Parthenon atop Calton Hill. Begun as a memorial to the dead of the Napoleonic Wars, the project's shortage of funds led architect William Henry Playfair to ensure that it would still serv as a striking landmark, despite having only twelve completed columns. With a bit of effort and care you can climb up and around the monument, sit and contemplate from one of the huge steps or meander around the base of the mighty pillars.

West End and Dean Village

Much of Edinburgh's wealth is concentrated in its **West End**, where embassies and lawyers occupy many of the huge Georgian townhouses west of Charlotte Square. On the main thoroughfares and in the pretty cobbled lanes of **West End village** attractive pubs, cafes and restaurants thrive on the affluent footfall from locals and office workers. Further prosperity can be found nearby; Edinburgh's theatre and financial districts, which occupy the area south of Princes Street's western tip, have seen major developments in recent times and gentrification has followed.

On the West End's northern fringe the gradient drops sharply towards the Water of Leith, where the old milling settlement of **Dean Village** is an unexpected delight, and a good place to begin exploring the city's lesser touristed treasures.

Scottish National Gallery of Modern Art

Belford Rd, EH4 3DR • Daily 10am–5pm, till 6pm in Aug • Free, entrance charge for some temporary exhibitions • ☎ 0131 624 6200, Ⓦ nationalgalleries.org

The first collection in Britain devoted solely to post-1800s painting and sculpture is housed across two distinctive Neoclassical buildings – **Modern One** and **Modern Two**. The grounds serve as a **sculpture park**, featuring works by Jacob Epstein, Henry Moore, Barbara Hepworth and, most strikingly, Charles Jencks, whose *Landform*, a swirling mix of ponds and grassy mounds, dominates the area in front of the gallery.

17

Modern One

Modern One, on the western side of Belford Road, divides its display spaces between temporary exhibitions and selections from the gallery's own holdings; the latter are arranged thematically, but are almost constantly moved around. The collection starts with early twentieth-century Post-Impressionists, then moves through the Fauvists, German Expressionism, Cubism and Pop Art, with works by **Lichtenstein** and **Warhol** establishing a connection with the extensive holdings of Eduardo Paolozzi's work in Modern Two. There's a strong section on living **British artists**, from Gilbert & George to **Britart stars**, while modern **Scottish** art ranges from the Colourists to the distinctive styles of contemporary Scots including John Bellany, a portraitist of striking originality, and the poet-artist-gardener Ian Hamilton Finlay.

Modern Two

Modern Two was refurbished to make room for the huge collection of work of Edinburgh-born sculptor **Sir Eduardo Paolozzi**, described by some as the father of Pop Art. There's an impressive introduction to Paolozzi's work in the form of the huge *Vulcan*, a half-man, half-machine that squeezes into the Great Hall immediately opposite the main entrance – view it both from ground level and the head-height balcony to appreciate the sheer scale of the piece. In the rooms to the right of the main entrance Paolozzi's London studio has been expertly re-created, right down to the clutter of half-finished casts, toys and empty pots of glue.

The ground floor holds a world-renowned collection of **Dada** and **Surrealist** art; Marcel Duchamp, Max Ernst and Man Ray are represented. Look out for Dalí's *The Signal of Anguish* and *Magritte's Magic Mirror* along with work by Miró and Giacometti – all hung on crowded walls with an assortment of artefacts and ethnic souvenirs. Elsewhere, look out for 2009 Turner Prize-winner Richard Wright's major wall-painting *The Stairwell Project*, his most complex and ambitious work to date in Britain.

Out from the centre

Just over a mile northeast of the city centre is **Leith**, one of the capital's fine-dining hot spots; it's a fascinating mix of cobbled streets and new developments, with the vibrant, picturesque old port at its heart. To the centre's west, Britain's only pandas draw in the crowds at Edinburgh's **zoo**.

Leith

Although **Leith** is generally known as the port of Edinburgh, it developed independently of the city up the hill, its history bound up in the hard graft of fishing, shipbuilding and trade. The presence of sailors, merchants and continental traders also gave the place a cosmopolitan – if slightly rough – edge, which is still obvious today. While the standalone attractions are few, Leith is an intriguing place, not just for the contrasts to central Edinburgh, but also for its nautical air and its excellent cafés, pubs and restaurants.

Leith's initial revival from down-and-out port to des-res waterfront began in the 1980s, around the area known as **the Shore**, the old harbour at the mouth of the Water of Leith. More recently, the massive **dock areas** beyond are being transformed at a rate of knots, with landmark developments including a vast building housing civil servants from the Scottish Government, and Ocean Terminal, a shopping and entertainment complex beside which the former royal yacht **Britannia** has settled into her retirement.

The Royal Yacht Britannia

Ocean Terminal, EH6 6JJ • Daily: April–Sept 9.30am–4.30pm; Oct 9.30am–4pm; Nov–March 10am–3.30pm • £15.50 • ☎ 0131 555 5566, ⓦ royalyachtbritannia.co.uk • Tour buses leave from Waverley Bridge; otherwise, take buses #11 or #22 from Princes St, or #35 from the Royal Mile

Launched in 1953, **Britannia** was used by the royal family for 44 years for state visits, diplomatic functions and royal holidays. Video clips of the vessel's most famous moments are shown in the **visitor centre** (within Ocean Terminal) along with royal holiday snaps, and you can roam around the yacht itself, which has been largely kept as she was while in service, with a well-preserved 1950s dowdiness – a far cry from the opulent splendour that many visitors expect.

Edinburgh Zoo

134 Corstorphine Rd, EH12 6TS • Daily: March & Oct 9am–5pm; April–Sept 9am–6pm; Nov–Feb 9am–4.30pm; penguin parade April–Sept daily 2.15pm, plus sunny days in March & Oct • £17 in advance, £19 on the door • ☎ 0131 334 9171, ⓦ edinburghzoo.org.uk • Buses #12, #26 & #31 from town

A couple of miles west of the city centre, **Edinburgh Zoo**, established in 1913, has a reputation for preserving rare and endangered species. With its imaginatively designed habitats and viewing areas, the place is permanently packed with kids. Historically, the zoo's most famous attraction was its **penguin parade**, though a pair of **pandas** – the only ones in the UK – nabbed the top spot after their arrival in 2011. If you want to see them, book a time slot on the website before you arrive. Beyond the pandas it's a bit of an uphill hike to the far end of the zoo, but once there you can admire the city views, then wander back down passing under the reinforced glass tiger tunnel, past the Asiatic lions and sun bears, to arrive at the enormous dedicated chimpanzee research centre.

ARRIVAL AND DEPARTURE

EDINBURGH

By plane Edinburgh International Airport (☎ 0844 448 8833, ⓦ edinburghairport.com) is at Turnhouse, 7 miles west of the city centre, close to the start of the M8 motorway to Glasgow. Trams (every 8–15min 6am–11pm; 35min; £5) connect with Murrayfield Stadium and Haymarket train station en route to the centre, terminating at York Place. Airlink shuttle buses (#100; every 10–15min 4am–midnight; every 30min midnight–4am; 30min; £4.50) connect with Waverley Station in the centre of town. Taxis charge £20–26 for the same journey, which takes about 25min.
Destinations Belfast (3–5 daily; 50min); Dublin (8–10 daily; 1hr 10min); Kirkwall (3 daily; 1hr 15min); London City (Mon–Fri & Sun 7–15 daily, Sat 1; 1hr 35min); London Gatwick (5–9 daily; 1hr 30min); London Heathrow (Mon–Fri 10–17 daily; 1hr 30min); London Luton (1–4 daily; 1hr 20min); London Stansted (2–8 daily; 1hr 10min); Stornoway (Mon–Fri & Sun 2 daily, Sat 1; 1hr 10 min); Sumburgh (Shetland) (Mon–Fri & Sun 4 daily, Sat 2; 1hr 30min); Wick (Mon–Sat 1 daily; 1hr 55min).
By train Waverley Station (☎ 0345 711 4141) is the main arrival point for all mainline trains. The other mainline

train stop, Haymarket Station is just under 2 miles west of Waverley on the lines from Waverley to Glasgow, Fife and the Highlands, and is only really of use if you're staying nearby.
Destinations from Waverley Station Aberdeen (hourly; 2hr 20min); Birmingham (hourly; 5hr); Dunbar (10–17 daily; 19min); Dundee (hourly; 1hr 45min); Falkirk (every 15min; 25min); Fort William (change at Glasgow, 3 daily; 4hr 55min); Glasgow (every 15–30min; 50min); Inverness (6 daily direct; 3hr 50min); London (hourly; 4hr 30min); Manchester (3 daily; 4hr); Newcastle upon Tyne (hourly; 1hr 30min); North Berwick (hourly; 30min); Oban (change at Glasgow, 2–3 daily; 4hr 10min); Perth (6 daily; 1hr 15min); Stirling (every 30min; 45min); York (hourly; 2hr 30min).
By bus The terminal for local and intercity services is on the east side of St Andrew Square, a 2min walk from Waverley Station.
Destinations Aberdeen (hourly; 3hr 50min); Birmingham (2–3 daily; 6hr 50min); Dundee (hourly; 1hr 45min–2hr); Glasgow (every 15min; 1hr 10min); Inverness (hourly; 3hr 30min–4hr 30min); London (10 daily; 7hr 50min); Newcastle upon Tyne (5 daily; 2hr 45min); Perth (hourly; 1hr 20min).

INFORMATION

Main tourist office Princes Mall, 3 Princes St, near the northern entrance to Waverley train station (June 3–June 30 Mon–Sat 9am–6pm, Sun 10am–6pm; July–Sept 8 9am–7pm, Sun 10am–7pm; Sept 9–June 2 Mon–Sat 9am–5pm,

Sun 10–5pm; ☎ 0131 473 3868, ⓦ visitscotland.com).
Airport tourist office Arrivals concourse, towards the trams (Mon–Fri 7.30am–7.30pm, Sat & Sun 7.30am–9pm; ☎ 0131 473 3690).

17

GETTING AROUND

By bus The city is generally well served by buses; the white-and-maroon Lothian Buses provide the most frequent and comprehensive coverage (timetables and passes from offices on Waverley Bridge, Haymarket or Hanover St; ☎0131 555 6363, ⓦlothianbuses.co.uk); all buses referred to in this chapter are run by Lothian unless otherwise stated. Tickets cost £1.60 single or £4 for a day-pass, payable to the driver (who cannot provide change). Children pay half, and a family day-ticket is £8.50.

By tram One solitary route connects the airport with Murrayfield Stadium, Haymarket, Princes St and St Andrew Square (☎0131 4750177, ⓦedinburghtrams.com). Ticket can be bought from vending machines at the tram stop and will cost £1.60 single (or £5.50 single to the airport Bus day-tickets are also valid on the tram.

By bike Although hilly, Edinburgh is a reasonably bike friendly city, with several cycle paths along disused railway and waterside paths. In parts of the centre it's a different story, with very few dedicated cycle ways although plan to introduce a network of Copenhagen-style cycle lane are in the pipeline. The local cycling action group, Spoke (☎0131 313 2114, ⓦspokes.org.uk), publishes a

---

THE EDINBURGH FESTIVAL

For all its appeal as a historic and attractive capital city, Edinburgh is perhaps best known for its incredible annual **Festival**, which takes place every August and transforms the place into an overwhelming mass of cultural activity. To even attempt to get a handle on what's going on, it's worth appreciating that the "Edinburgh Festival" is an umbrella term that encompasses several different festivals. The principal events are the **Edinburgh International Festival** and the much larger **Edinburgh Festival Fringe**, but there are also **Book**, **Jazz and Blues** and **Art** festivals going on, as well as a **Military Tattoo** on the Castle Esplanade.

The sheer volume of the Festival's output can be bewildering: virtually every branch of arts and entertainment is represented, and world-famous stars mix with pub singers in the daily line-up. It can be a struggle to find **accommodation**, get hold of the **tickets** you want, book a table in a **restaurant** or simply get from one side of town to another; you can end up seeing something truly dire, or something mind-blowing; you'll inevitably try to do too much, stay out too late or spend too much – but then again, most Festival veterans will tell you that if you don't experience these things then you haven't really "done" the Festival.

Dates, venues, names, star acts, happening bars and burning issues change from one year to the next. This **unpredictability** is one of the Festival's greatest charms, so be prepared for – indeed, enjoy – the unexpected.

THE EDINBURGH INTERNATIONAL FESTIVAL

The original **Edinburgh Festival**, sometimes called the "Official Festival", was conceived in 1947 when, after decades of war, poverty and racism, a handful of wise civic leaders sought to embrace cultural diversity and "provide a platform for the flowering of the human spirit". Initially dominated by opera, other elements such as theatre, ballet, dance and classical music were gradually introduced, and it's still very much a highbrow event. That said, the festival has widened its cultural horizons in recent years, with P.J. Harvey, Mogwai and a Joe Boyd-directed Incredible String Band tribute all making it on to the programme. Performances take place at the city's large venues such as the Usher Hall and the Festival Theatre (see page 781), and tickets cost £10–95. The festival culminates in a classical **Fireworks Concert** beside the castle, visible from various points in the city.

THE EDINBURGH FESTIVAL FRINGE

"Welcome to the Alliance of Defiance". So ran the headline on the **Edinburgh Festival Fringe** website (ⓦedfringe.com) during their seventieth anniversary year in 2017. Seven decades earlier, eight theatre companies had turned up uninvited to the Edinburgh International Festival (see below) and were refused entry; undaunted they proceeded to perform their shows in alternative venues on what critics and commentators dubbed "the fringe" of the official festival. The idea caught on: now indisputably the "largest platform on earth for creative freedom", the Fringe sees more than fifty thousand performances of more than three thousand shows, in almost three hundred venues, with performers – and audiences – hailing from every corner of the globe. While the headlining names at the International Festival reinforce its cultural credibility, it is the dynamism, spontaneity and sheer exuberance of the Fringe that dominate Edinburgh every August, giving the city its

excellent map. For rental, try Biketrax, 13 Lochrin Place (☎0131 228 6633, ⓦbiketrax.co.uk), in Tollcross.

By car It can be a very bad idea to take a car into central Edinburgh, due to the phenomenally high cost of parking. Illegally parked cars are very likely to be fined £30 within minutes by one of the countless patrolling inspectors.

By taxi Edinburgh is well endowed with taxi ranks, and you can also hail black cabs on the street. All taxis are metered and costs are reasonable – from the city centre to Leith, for example, costs around £9. Try Capital Cars (☎0131 777 7777, ⓦcapitalcarsscotland.co.uk) or City Cabs (☎0131 228 1211, ⓦcitycabs.co.uk). Uber (ⓦuber.com) users will have little trouble finding a ride as the city is comprehensively covered.

ACCOMMODATION

Already a tourism hotspot, Edinburgh's recent upsurge in traveller numbers – thanks to its expanding airport and elevated world standing – has seen a growth in the number of hotels and aparthotels in the city. This, together with Airbnb's seemingly untameable march, has resulted in a bewildering choice of places to stay. **Bargains** are always there to be

unique atmosphere and doubling its population. These days, the most prominent and ubiquitous aspect of the Fringe is **comedy**, having overtaken theatre as the largest genre in 2008.

At the same time, the Fringe's **theatre** programme shows no signs of dying out, with hundreds of brand-new cutting-edge and often controversial works airing alongside offbeat classics and familiar Shakespearean tragedies. The whole thing kicks off and winds up on the same days as the International Festival, and usually runs for a little over three weeks.

INFORMATION

International Festival Box Office The Hub, Castlehill EH1 2NE ☎0131 473 2000, ⓦeif.co.uk. Mon–Fri 10am–5pm; during the Festival Mon–Sat 9am–7.30pm, Sun 10am–7.30pm.

Festival Fringe Office 180 High St, EH1 1QS ☎0131 226 0026, ⓦedfringe.com. Fringe tickets (generally £5–18) available from here, online or at venues. June to mid-July Mon–Sat noon–3pm; mid- to end July daily 10am–6pm; Aug 10am–9pm.

Half Price Hut Mound Precinct, by the National Gallery of Scotland, EH2 2EL ⓦtickets.edfringe.com/box-office/virgin-money-half-price-hut. Sells half-price tickets for some shows during the Fringe. During the festival daily 10am–9pm.

Useful website For up-to-date information at any time of year, visit ⓦedinburghfestivals.co.uk, which has links to the home pages of most of the main festivals.

Publications Each festival produces its own programme well in advance and during the Festival various publications are widely available. Local what's-on guide *The List* comes out weekly during the Festival and manages to combine comprehensive coverage with an on-the-pulse sense of what's hot. Of the local newspapers, *The Scotsman* carries a dedicated daily Festival supplement with an events diary and respected reviews, while various freebie newspapers are also available – the best is *Fest*, which mixes news with pithy reviews and yet more listings.

THE OTHER FESTIVALS

Edinburgh Art Festival ☎0131 226 6558, ⓦedinburghartfestival.com. A relative newcomer on the scene, held throughout August and including high-profile exhibitions by internationally renowned contemporary artists as well as retrospectives of work by pioneering twentieth-century artists. Virtually every gallery in the city participates, from small private concerns to blockbuster shows at the National Gallery of Scotland's five venues.

Edinburgh International Book Festival ☎0845 373 5888, ⓦedbookfest.co.uk. Held in mid-August, this is the world's largest celebration of the written word. It's held in a tented village in Charlotte Square and offers talks, readings and signings by a star-studded line-up of visiting authors and politicians, as well as panel discussions and workshops.

Edinburgh Jazz and Blues Festival ☎0131 473 2000, ⓦedinburghjazzfestival.com. Mid- to end of July festival with highlights including nightly jam sessions and a colourful New Orleans-style Mardi Gras street parade.

The Military Tattoo ☎0131 225 1188, ⓦedintattoo.co.uk. Staged in the spectacular stadium of the Edinburgh Castle Esplanade every night during August, the Tattoo is an unashamed display of pomp and military pride. The programme of choreographed drills, massed pipe bands, historical tableaux, energetic battle re-enactments, national dancing and pyrotechnics has been a feature of the Festival for more than half a century, its emotional climax provided by a lone piper on the Castle battlements. Followed by a quick fireworks display, it's a successful formula barely tampered with over the years. Tickets (£25–300 depending on seat location and day, plus a £5 booking fee if bought online) should be booked well in advance.

SIGHTSEEING TOURS AND GUIDED WALKS

Year round, a fleet of state-of-the-art open-top double-deckers run by **Edinburgh Bus Tours** (daily roughly 9am–6pm; every 10–15min; 1hr; £15; ☎0131 556 2244, ⊛edinburghtour.com) line up on Waverley Bridge, hoovering up the tourists pouring out of Waverley Station and the Airlink bus (see page 771). Several themed tours are available, covering most of the major sights, as well as a summer option to South Queensferry (see page 786) combined with a cruise on the Firth of Forth (3hr; £35).

Unsurprisingly for such an atmospheric city, Edinburgh is served by countless **walking tours**. As well as traditional historical tours (for which the family-run **Edinburgh Guided Tour** have one of the best reputations: ☎07927 904695, ⊛edinburghguidedtour.com), there are myriad – and often highly acclaimed – specialist variations covering almost every conceivable theme from the inevitable **ghosts** to **Harry Potter** (☎07977 934274, ⊛edinburghwalkingtour.co.uk/harry-potter-walk.html), gourmet **food and drink** (☎07740 869359, ⊛eatwalkedinburgh.co.uk;), small-group **photography** (☎07795 337778, ⊛jameschristiephotography.com/edinburgh- photography-tours-2), Inspector **Rebus** (⊛rebustours.com) and, of course, **Outlander** (☎0131 225 5445, ⊛mercattours.com/tours/history-walks/view-tour/edinburgh-outlander-experience). Tours last anything from an hour or two to a whole day, and while many are priced in the £10–30 range, some of the specialist options can cost double that. If you're on a budget, opt for one of the numerous cheap and cheerful **free tours** (⊛edinburghfreetour.com, ⊛neweuropetours.eu/edinburgh).

found, usually by way of a last-minute booking or a promotion, while budget travellers can choose between plenty of hostels, particularly around the Old Town. Making **reservations** is worthwhile at any time of year, and is essential during the Festival and around Hogmanay when prices swell considerably and spaces get booked months in advance.

OLD TOWN AND SOUTH EDINBURGH

94DR 94 Dalkeith Rd, EH16 5AF ☎0131 662 9265, ⊛94dr.com; map p.754. A boutique guesthouse with three luxurious rooms, great breakfasts from a trained chef and free bike rental. Front-facing rooms have a view of Arthur's Seat. **£130**

★ **Apex International** 31–35 Grassmarket, EH1 2HS ☎0131 300 3456, ⊛apexhotels.co.uk; map p.754. This ex-university building turned 175-bed business-oriented hotel has comfortable rooms, some with unencumbered views to the Castle and balconies that peer down onto Grassmarket below. Up top there's a double rosette rooftop restaurant with a dramatic – especially after dark – skyline view, while downstairs you'll find a small pool and gym. **£145**

★ **Castle Rock Hostel** 15 Johnston Terrace, EH1 2PW ☎0131 225 9666, ⊛castlerockedinburgh.com; map p.754. Tucked below the Castle ramparts, with two hundred or so beds arranged in large, bright dorms, as well as triple and quads and some doubles. Communal areas include a games room with pool and table tennis and a sunny patio. Dorms **£11**, doubles **£45**

Greyfriars Apartments Just off the Royal Mile or nearby ☎07794 875 890, ⊛greyfriars-apartments.com; map p.754. Among the best value in town, the moderately spacious apartments offered by Greyfriars – including Grassmarket, a one-bed apartment for two – are stylish and superbly located. You'll need to book early, especially if you're planning a weekend trip. **£125**

High Street Hostel 8 Blackfriars St, EH1 1NB ☎0131 557 3984, ⊛highstreethostel.com; map p.754754 Lively and popular hostel in an attractive sixteenth-century building just off the Royal Mile, with dorms of up to eighteen beds and twin rooms. Communal facilities include a kitchen, a quiet room and a large party dining lounge with piano and pool table. Dorms **£12**, twins **£54**

Ibis Edinburgh Centre 6 Hunter Square, EH1 1QW ☎0131 619 2800, ⊛ibis.com; map p.754. Probably the best-located chain hotel cheapie in the Old Town, within sight of the Royal Mile. Rooms are modern and inexpensive, but there are few facilities other than a rather plain bar. **£125**

Ten Hill Place 10 Hill Place, EH8 9DS ☎0131 662 2080, ⊛tenhillplace.com; map p.754. A contemporary efficient hotel linked to the historic Royal College of Surgeons, with 78 sleek and smartly styled bedrooms, all run according to an environmentally conscious policy. **£170**

Travelodge Edinburgh Central 33 St Mary's St, EH1 1TA ☎0871 984 6137, ⊛travelodge.co.uk; map p.754. There's more than a hint of concrete brutalism in the look of this chain hotel, but it's well priced and centrally located, 100yd from the Royal Mile near some excellent restaurants. At weekends it tends to fill up with stag and hen parties but the rooms are quiet enough, if a little grungy. **£91**

★ **The Witchery Apartments** Castlehill, EH1 2NF ☎0131 225 5613, ⊛thewitchery.com; map p.754. Nine riotously indulgent suites grouped around this famously spooky restaurant, just downhill from the castle:

expect antique furniture, big leather armchairs, tapestry-draped beds, oak panelling and huge roll-top baths, as well as ultramodern sound systems and complementary champagne. **£365**

★ **University of Edinburgh Pollock Halls of Residence** 18 Holyrood Park Rd, EH16 5AY ☎ 0131 651 2007, ⓦ edinburghfirst.com; map p.754. Unquestionably the best located of any of the city's university accommodation, right beside Holyrood Park, just southeast of the Old Town. It provides single rooms, doubles and large studio self-catering apartments (sleeping two) mostly available at Easter and from June to mid-Sept, though some rooms are available year-round. Singles **£48**, apartments **£75**, doubles **£112.50**

NEW TOWN

Express by Holiday Inn Edinburgh City Centre Picardy Place, EH1 3JT ☎ 0131 558 2300, ⓦ ihg.com; map p.754. It's by a busy roundabout, but otherwise in a good location in an elegant old Georgian tenement near the top of Broughton St, with 161 rooms featuring neat but predictable chain-hotel decor and facilities. **£148**

★ **Gerald's Place** 21b Abercromby Place, EH3 6QE ☎ 0131 558 7017, ⓦ geraldsplace.com; map p.754. A homely taste of New Town life at an upmarket but wonderfully hospitable and comfy basement B&B. The rustic decor is tasteful, with some fine artwork and old books to catch your eye, while the generous breakfasts feature many home-made components. **£150**

The Glasshouse 2 Greenside Place, EH1 3AA ☎ 0131 525 8200, ⓦ theglasshousehotel.co.uk; map p.754. Incorporating the castellated facade of the former Lady Glenorchy's Church, this ultra-hip hotel has 65 chi-chi rooms with push-button curtains and sliding doors opening onto a huge, lush roof garden scattered with Philippe Starck furniture. Perfect if you're in town for a weekend of flash indulgence. **£250**

Principle Edinburgh George Street 19–21 George St, EH2 2PB ☎ 0131 225 1251, ⓦ phcompany.com/principle/edinburgh-george-street; map p.754. A beautiful example of a prime Georgian building, inside and out, thanks to its Neoclassical frontage and sympathetically harmonious decor. The suites are luxurious from top to tail and many come with lofty views north to the firth of forth. **£220**

LEITH AND NORTH EDINBURGH

Malmaison 1 Tower Place, EH6 7BZ ☎ 0131 285 1478, ⓦ malmaison.com; map p.754. Chic, modern hotel set in the grand old seamen's hostel just back from the wharfside. Bright, bold original designs in each room, as well as a stereo and satellite TV. Also has a gym, room service, a Parisian-style brasserie and a café-bar serving lighter meals. **£105**

Millars 64 64 Pilrig St, EH6 5AS ☎ 0131 454 3666, ⓦ millars64.com; map p.754. An award-winning B&B striving for perfection in every way. Spotlessly clean from top to bottom, with beautifully cooked breakfasts and home-made shortbread on the hospitality tray. **£90**

EATING

As you'd expect for a capital city, Edinburgh's **dynamic** eating scene offers Scotland's very best choice. Here you will find everything from cheapie cosmopolitan pies to fresh-from-the-quayside seafood, via hipster pop-ups, seasonally foraged feasts and a kaleidoscopic array of ethnic eats, with plenty of Michelin stars to go round. **Prices** aren't necessarily high, either, especially at lunchtime, when you can often dine on a gourmet quality, two- or even three-course meal for around a tenner. While lunch is generally served between noon and 2pm, and in the evening restaurants start filling up from around 7pm and serve till around 10/11pm, the sheer weight of Edinburgh's tourist numbers means that many places serve food round the clock, seven days a week. Many places are perpetually packed, so it's a good idea to make a **reservation**; don't ever assume you can simply turn up and get a table. Generally, the **Old Town** remains the focus of traditional, pricey Scottish and French-influenced cuisine, with local sourcing on the increase, while **Leith**, naturally, is home to the most renowned seafood, and, increasingly, the most exciting and creative new ventures.

OLD TOWN AND SOUTHSIDE

CAFÉS AND SNACKS

Café at the Palace Canongate, EH8 8DX ☎ 0131 652 3685; map p.754. The rarefied setting of the glass-roofed Palace Mews and Courtyard at Holyroodhouse makes for a suitably genteel backdrop to a classic afternoon tea (£18.95), served in specially commissioned china; if you're feeling particularly regal, treat yourself to the champagne option (£27). Daily: April–Oct 9.30am–6pm; Nov–March 9.30am–4.30pm; afternoon tea daily 1–4pm.

Maison De Moggy 17–19 West Port, EH1 2JA ☎ 0131 629 5530, ⓦ maisondemoggy.com; map p.754. Edinburgh's

contribution to the cat café craze, this niche redoubt allows you to pass one therapeutic hour – the length of each session – with a clowder of pedigree pussycats and a cup of locally produced coffee. Reservations strongly advised; entry £7; children under 10 not allowed. Daily 10.45am–6.30pm.

Peter's Yard 27 Simpson Loan, EH3 9GG ☎ 0131 228 5876, ⓦ petersyard.com; map p.754. A Swedish outfit with the bread ovens on view and baskets of delicious loaves out front. Set on the edge of The Meadows, it's popular with flush-feeling students and professionals drawn by the excellent coffee and cardamom buns. Mon–Fri 7.30am–6pm, Sat & Sun 9am–6pm.

17

The Piemaker 38 South Bridge, EH1 1LL ☎0131 558 1728, ⓦthepiemaker.co.uk; map p.754. Possibly the cheapest place to fill up in town, with a mightily impressive range of pies from carnivore to vegan plus a few sweet options. Prices hover around £2.50 each. Mon–Wed 9am–8.15pm, Thurs & Fri 9am–10.45, Sat 10am–10.45pm, Sun 10.30am–7.45pm.

Serenity Café 8 Jacksons Entry, EH8 8PJ ☎0131 556 8765, ⓦserenitycafe.co.uk; map p.754. Sitting snug between the Canongate and Holyrood Rd, this pioneering community café was the first of its kind when it opened in 2009, set up and run by recovering addicts, with all profits ploughed back into helping others. A uniquely welcoming vibe and delicious, great-value food (mains under a fiver) has made it a favourite with both locals and ethically minded visitors. Daily 9am–5pm.

RESTAURANTS

Amber Scotch Whisky Heritage Centre, 354 Castlehill, EH1 2NE ☎0131 477 8477, ⓦamber-restaurant.co.uk; map p.754. Connected to The Scotch Whisky Experience (see page 757), this restaurant offers national specialities on a "Taste of Scotland" menu, featuring a trio of starters and mains including haggis bonbons, for £33.50. There's also a "whisky sommelier" on hand to suggest accompanying drams for each course. Mon–Thurs & Sun 10am–8.30pm, Fri & Sat noon–9pm.

David Bann's Vegetarian Restaurant 56–58 St Mary's St, EH1 1SX ☎0131 556 5888, ⓦdavidbann.com; map p.754. Fine dining, vegetarian style, with a tried and tested menu. There are a few unconventional dishes on offer, such as the quinoa chilli and tortilla chips with chocolate sauce or the beetroot, apple and blue cheese pudding – both main courses – for £13 and £14 respectively. Mon–Thurs noon–10pm, Fri noon–10.30pm, Sat 11am–10.30pm, Sun 11am–10pm.

The Grain Store 30 Victoria St, EH1 2JW ☎0131 225 7635, ⓦgrainstore-restaurant.co.uk; map p.754. Decades-long Victoria St fixture and a haven amid the bustle of the Old Town, with intimate stone walls and soft lighting. Combines top-quality modern Scottish and French cuisines; lunches (three courses £16) offer the likes of red mullet with mussel velouté and pomme pureé. Mon–Sat noon–2.30pm & 6–9.45pm, Sun 6–9.30pm.

Kalpna 2–3 St Patrick's Square, EH8 9EZ ☎0131 667 9890, ⓦkalpnarestaurant.com; map p.754. Outstanding vegetarian family restaurant that's been serving authentic Gujarati dishes for more than 25 years, with an unfussy interior that has barely changed in all that time. The primary focus is always on the food, with an "all you can eat" lunch for £8.50. Especially popular with students and Edinburgh University academics. Mon–Sat noon–2pm & 5.30–10.30pm.

Lian Pu 14 Marshall St, EH8 9BU ☎0131 662 8895; map p.754. Thoroughly hip fast food restaurant popular with Edinburgh's surging Chinese student community, thanks to its true home-from-home cooking and palatable prices. Try the tofu noodle stir-fry for £6.70 with a side order of the deeply savoury spicy shredded cabbage. Daily noon–10pm.

Monteiths 61 High St, EH1 1SR ☎0131 557 0330, ⓦmonteithsrestaurant.co.uk; map p.754. Entered through an enticing vennel adorned with fairy lights and twisted willow canes, *Monteiths* is a sophisticated part restaurant/part cocktail bar. Not great for vegetarians, its focus is heavily on melt-in-the-mouth permutations of venison and beef. Mains start at £18. Daily noon–midnight.

★ **Ondine** 2 George IV Bridge, EH1 1AD ☎0131 226 1888, ⓦondinerestaurant.co.uk; map p.754. Tucked in next to the swanky *G & V Hotel*, this seafood restaurant and oyster bar from Edinburgh chef Roy Brett, once Rick Stein's main chef in Padstow, turns out sublime dishes using native shellfish and fish from sustainable sources. Two-course lunch and pre-theatre menus cost £19. Mon–Sat noon–3pm & 5.30–10pm.

Tanjore 6–8 Clerk St, EH8 9HX ☎0131 478 6518, ⓦtanjore.co.uk; map p.754. South Indian cuisine's finest ambassador on these shores, offering all the regional standards including *vadai* (crunchy lentil doughnuts), *idli* (rice and lentil cakes) and *sambar* – a distinctly rich, savoury curry with fragrant, bittersweet curry leaves. The freshly made *dosai* (lentil and rice crêpes) are among the lightest and crispiest you'll ever taste, and come with a wide variety of fillings for around £7. Mon–Fri noon–2.30pm & 5–10pm, Sat & Sun noon–3.30pm & 5–10pm.

Timberyard 10 Lady Lawson St, EH3 9DS ☎0131 221 1222, ⓦtimberyard.co; map p.754. This swanky yet rustic old workshop makes for a genial atmosphere with its shared, candlelit benches indoors and sunny courtyard garden. The food focuses on high-quality Scottish produce, where unfamiliar bedfellows like mackerel, nasturtium and buttermilk come together harmoniously on one plate as part of a four-course £55 menu. Kitchen Tues–Sat noon–2pm & 5.30–9.30pm; bar stays open until 1am.

★ **Wedgwood the Restaurant** 267 Canongate, EH8 8BQ ☎0131 558 8737, ⓦwedgwoodtherestaurant.co.uk; map p.754. This small, award-winning fine-dining restaurant, complete with in-house forager, creatively plates all the best of Scotland's land, rivers and seas. There's so much choice on the à la carte menu that they offer "deciding time" – canapés and champagne – while you peruse the menu. The mains begin at £16, although the £15 lunch deal is the best value. Seasonal freshness guaranteed. Mon–Sat noon–3pm & 6–10pm.

The Witchery by the Castle Castlehill, EH1 2NF ☎0131 225 5613, ⓦthewitchery.com; map p.754. An upmarket restaurant set in magnificently over-the-top medieval surroundings full of Gothic panelling, tapestries and heavy stonework, all a mere broomstick-hop from the Castle. The à la carte menu is as ostentatious as the surroundings with wallet-draining lobster and lamb Wellington on offer; however, there are good-value set menus from £22 for two courses. Daily noon–11.30pm.

NEW TOWN AND AROUND

CAFÉS AND SNACKS

Archipelago Bakery 39 Dundas St, EH3 6QQ ☎07932 462715, ⓦarchipelagobakery.co.uk; map p.754. Serving some of Edinburgh's crustiest loaves. You can sit and drink coffee here while marvelling at the mouth-watering breads, pies and pastries thrust out of the ovens in full view. Mon–Sat 9am–5pm.

Artisan Roast 57 Broughton St, EH1 3RJ ☎07526 236 615, ⓦartisanroast.co.uk; map p.754. A seemingly unstoppable force in the connoisseur coffee roasters' market, *Artisan Roast* offers sweet, nutty brews that are found in independent cafés all over town. This narrow, grungy shop, with hessian beans bags for decor and obligatorily bearded baristas, is where their revolution started. Mon–Thurs 8am–6.30pm, Sat & Sun 9am–6.30pm.

★ **Café Modern One** Scottish National Gallery of Modern Art One, Belford Rd, Dean Village, EH4 3DR ☎0131 624 6200, ⓦnationalgalleries.org/visit/café; map p.754. One of the nicest cafes in all Edinburgh, thanks to its delightful walled garden around the back of the Modern One gallery. The canteen serves up superb healthy lunches, including a range of vibrant home-made salads; three/person (£6) should suffice. Mon–Fri 9am–4.30pm, Sat & Sun 10am–4.30pm.

Palm Court Balmoral Hotel. 1 Princes St, EH2 2EQ ☎0131 556 2414, ⓦroccofortehotels.com; map p.754. The ultimate afternoon tea experience; within the *Balmoral* hotel complex the oval-shaped Palm Court, with its glass cupola, Grecian pillars and tall potted palms, has somehow struck a balance between decadence and tasteful understatement. Pinkies aloft, sup the hotel's signature tea blend with the exquisite handmade pastries while a harpist recites from the balcony. Afternoon tea £37.50. Afternoon tea daily noon–5pm.

RESTAURANTS

Chaophraya 33 Castle St, EH2 3DN ☎0131 226 7614, ⓦchaophraya.co.uk; map p.754. Thai restaurant with a rooftop location that gives diners who sit in the "Glassbox" section a near 360-degree view of the city. The menu is stunning too, and reasonably priced; if you go veggie, there's a set meal for £25. Mon–Sat noon–10.30pm, Sun noon–10pm.

Chez Jules 109 Hanover St, EH2 1DJ ☎0131 226 6992, ⓦchezjulesbistro.com; map p.754. Run by the former boss of the once mighty *Pierre Victoire* bistro chain. The

formula is much the same: cheap and generous set menus, good table wine and an informal setting. Your two-course lunch (£7.90) might include French onion soup and beef bourguignon with fries. Mon–Thurs & Sun noon–11pm, Fri & Sat noon–midnight.

Dishoom 3a St Andrew Square ☎0131 202 6406, ⓦdishoom.com; map p.754. Set up to evoke the feel of the Persian cafés of Old Bombay, this bustling Indian restaurant has an exciting and extensive menu that requires repeated visits. For a good introduction try the *pau bhaji* for £4.50 – curry and a roll – and the gunpowder potatoes for £6.50. Mon–Wed 8am–11pm, Thurs–Sat 8am–noon, Sun 9am–11pm.

The Dogs 110 Hanover St, EH2 1DR ☎0131 220 1208, ⓦthedogsonline.co.uk; map p.754. British gastropub cooking taken to a whole new level with confident use of traditional ingredients paired with thoroughly modern flavours such as the ox cheek burger with skirlie (oats and onions fried in lard) and barbecue sauce for £7. Mon–Fri noon–2.30pm & 6–10pm, Sat noon–4pm & 5–10pm, Sun noon–4pm & 6–10pm.

El Cartel Casera Mexicana 64 Thistle St, EH2 1EN ☎0131 226 7171, ⓦelcartelmexicana.co.uk; map p.754. Mexican *antojitos* (tapas-sized street food; £4–10) served with funky margaritas in a cool setting that draws heavily from the Día de los Muertos festival. Tacos, street corn (charred sweet corn) and quesadillas feature on the menu as well as oddities like shredded ox patties. Mon–Thurs & Sun noon–10pm, Sat noon–midnight.

★ **Forage and Chatter** 1A Alva St, EH2 4PH ☎0131 225 4599, ⓦforageandchatter.com; map p.754. Showcasing the best produce sourced within a 25-mile radius, this concept restaurant garners more accolades than any other in town. Be it foraged, farmed or fished, it's all about the ingredients; Scotland's larder brought to bear on Scots-French cuisine with accomplished plates like hay-smoked and braised pork belly with sage, cavolo nero and Jerusalem artichoke – part of the £18 three-course lunch. Tues–Sat noon–2.30pm & 6–11pm.

The Gardener's Cottage 1 Royal Terrace Gardens, London Rd, EH7 5DX ☎0131 558 1221, ⓦthegardeners cottage.co; map p.754. In an achingly beautiful little cottage, uniquely locatedd in a parkland setting. Dining is intimate, in two small rooms with communal long tables, while the open kitchen is stamp-sized. There's no choice, just eight outstanding courses of Scottish design for £50. Mon & Wed–Sun noon–2.30pm & 5–10pm.

L'Escargot Bleu 56 Broughton St ☎0131 557 1600, ⓦlescargotbleu.co.uk; map p.754. Classic French country cooking brought to bear on a range of locally sourced produce from Barra snails to Orkney beef. Two-course lunch and pre-theatre menus are a snip at £13 and £15. Mon–Thurs noon–2.30pm & 5.30–10pm, Fri & Sat noon–3pm & 5.30–10.30pm.

17

LEITH AND NEWHAVEN

With some of the city's top restaurants, specializing in seafood and haute cuisine, as well as backstreet brunch stops and well-worn, friendly pubs, Leith and the neighbouring harbour district of Newhaven are among the best places to eat and drink in Edinburgh.

CAFÉS AND SNACKS

★ **Ostara** 52 Coburg St, EH6 6HJ ☎ 0131 261 5441, ⓦ ostaracafe.co.uk; map p.754. Brunch specialists serving some of the city's most vibrant plates of food. There are lots of healthy options, including smashed avocado on sourdough and fruity porridge, while anyone in need of an umami hit should target the potato *bravas*, mushroom salt, smoky ketchup, halloumi and fried egg for £8. Daily 8am–4pm.

Porto & Fi 47 Newhaven Main St, EH6 4NQ ☎ 0131 551 1900, ⓦ portofi.com; map p.754. A bright daytime/early-evening café-restaurant not far from Newhaven's old stone harbour, with tempting cakes alongside a serious menu that includes fish pie and haddock kedgeree (both £12). Mon–Thurs 8am–8pm, Fri & Sat 8am–10pm, Sun 10am–6pm.

The Shore 3 The Shore, EH6 6QW ☎ 0131 553 5080, ⓦ fishersbistros.co.uk; map p.754. Well-lived-in bar-restaurant with huge mirrors, wood panelling and aproned waiters who serve up good seafood and land food from £13.50. Live jazz and folk music and a general hubbub float through from the adjoining bar, where you'll find a wide selection of snacks on offer including trout and herb croquettes for £4.50. Mon–Sat noon–late, Sun 12.30pm–late; kitchen daily noon–10.30pm.

RESTAURANTS

Café Domenico 30 Sandport St, EH6 6EP ☎ 0131 467 7266, ⓦ cafedomenico.co.uk; map p.754. A superb-value, authentic backstreet Italian restaurant (not a café) that dishes up damn fine Italian fast food and takeaway sandwiches. Slurp down a spaghetti *alle vongole* for just £6. Mon–Thurs 10am–2.30pm & 5–10pm, Fri 10am–

2.30pm & 5–10.30pm, Sat 10.30am–10.30pm, Sun 11am–10pm.

Harmonium 60 Henderson St, EH6 6DE ☎ 0131 55? 3160, ⓦ facebook.com/harmoniumbar; map p.754. From the team behind Glasgow's infamous music bar *Mono*, *Harmonium* is pushing the boundaries of the vegan cause with its cutting-edge gastro-bar food. Oysters, crab caviar, quarter pounders and even black pudding feature on their menus – in interpretive plant form – and the young professionals and local intellectuals that frequent this thriving bar can't seem to get enough, especially at lunchtime, when specials are only a fiver. Daily noon–1am.

The Kitchin 78 Commercial Quay, EH6 6LX ☎ 0131 55? 1755, ⓦ thekitchin.com; map p.754. Opened in 2006 by celebrity chef Tom Kitchin and the winner – less than six months later – of a Michelin star, the motto here is "from nature to plate", a philosophy that ensures the freshest ingredients. This is particularly well demonstrated on their "Celebration of the Season" menu, where you might find lobster with snail butter or grouse with girolles. Menus from £33 (lunch) to £85. Tues–Sat noon–2.30pm & 6–9.30pm.

★ **Norn** 50-54 Henderson St, EH6 6DE ☎ 0131 629? 2525, ⓦ nornrestaurant.com; map p.754. Set to give its Michelin-starred neighbours a good run for their money, Leith's newest and most exciting fine-dining restaurant takes the best of Scotland's larder – foraged, farmed and fished; whatever comes in that day – and delivers some of the most creative, confident dishes you're ever likely to encounter. There's no menu; you just choose either four (£40) or seven (£60) courses. Book well ahead. Tues & Wed 7pm to late, Thurs–Sat 5.30pm–late.

Restaurant Martin Wishart 54 The Shore, EH6 6RA ☎ 0131 553 3557, ⓦ martin-wishart.co.uk; map p.754. The eponymous chef is one of the leading lights of the Scottish culinary scene, and was the first Michelin-star holder in Edinburgh. Expect highly accomplished and exquisitely presented dishes featuring Scottish-sourced fish and meat. A two-course lunch (Tues–Fri) is £32, while a six-course evening tasting menu costs £85. Tues–Thurs noon–1.30pm & 7–9pm, Fri & Sat noon–1.30pm & 6.30–9.30pm.

DRINKING

Many of Edinburgh's pubs, especially in the **Old Town**, have histories that stretch back centuries, while others, particularly in the **New Town**, are unaltered Victorian or Edwardian period pieces. Add a plentiful supply of trendy modern bars, and there's enough to cater for all tastes. Note that the opening hours quoted below may well be extended during August's festivals.

THE ROYAL MILE AND AROUND

★ **Bow Bar** 80 West Bow, EH12HH ☎ 0131 226 7667; map p.754. Wonderful old wood-panelled bar that is one of the most pleasant, convivial drinking spots in the city centre. Choose from among nearly 150 whiskies or a changing selection of first-rate Scottish and English cask beers. Mon–Sat noon–midnight, Sun noon–11.30pm.

The City Café 19 Blair St, EH1 1QR ☎ 0131 2200125, ⓦ citycafeedinburgh.co.uk; map p.754. The American-diner-cum-minimalist *grande dame* of Edinburgh's style bars, and a home from home for fashionistas, wannabes and DJs in the late 80s and 90s. The competition may be much stiffer these days, but it's still a pre-club fixture. Daily 9am–1am.

The Devil's Advocate 9 Advocates Close, EH1 1ND ☎ 0131

225 4465, ⓦ devilsadvocateedinburgh.co.uk; map p.754. Great modern bar in a converted Victorian pump house hidden halfway down a close. Specializing in exotic whisky, it tends to fill at the end of the working day with young office workers sipping cocktails. Daily noon–1am.

Paradise Palms 41 Lothian St, EH1 1HB ☎0131 225 4186, ⓦ theparadisepalms.com; map p.754. In a location that has seen countless bars come and go over the decades, *Paradise Palms* has firmly established itself as perhaps the capital's hippest outpost. A tropical-thriftstore-cum-cabaret-lounge theme, vegan and veggie takes on Deep South soul food and even a vinyl store and electronica-oriented record label are all part of the appeal. Daily noon–3am; kitchen noon–9pm.

Vino 27 East Market St, EH7 9AB ☎0131 629 4282, ⓦ vinowines.co.uk; map p.754. Independent wine bar and shop in the attractively renovated arches under Jeffrey St. A great stop before heading out to a BYOB restaurant. Mon–Thurs & Sun 10am–10pm, Sat & Sun 10am–midnight.

NEW TOWN AND WEST END

Café Royal Circle Bar 17 West Register St, EH2 2AA ☎0131 556 1884, ⓦ caferoyaledinburgh.co.uk; map p.754. Worth a visit for its Victorian decor alone, notably the huge elliptical island bar and tiled portraits of renowned inventors. The beer and food are good, too. The *Café* is a better bet than its equally venerable, but much more staid, neighbouring *Oyster Bar* restaurant. Mon–Wed 11am–11pm, Thurs 11am–midnight, Fri & Sat 11am–1am, Sun 12.30pm–11pm.

★ **Kays Bar** 39 Jamaica St, EH3 6HF ☎0131 225 1858, ⓦ kaysbar.co.uk; map p.754. Tucked away in a New Town side street, this former Georgian coaching house was remodelled in the Victorian era as a wine and spirit merchant. Thankfully it has retained its Victorian charm and now operates as a cosy little pub serving real ale and plenty of whiskies. Mon–Thurs 11am–midnight, Fri & Sat 11am–1pm, Sun 12.30pm–11pm.

Oxford Bar 8 Young St, EH2 4JB ☎0131 539 7119, ⓦ oxfordbar.co.uk; map p.754. Unpretentious, unspoilt, no-nonsense city bar – which is why local crime writer Ian Rankin and his Inspector Rebus like it so much. Fans duly make the pilgrimage, but fortunately not all the regulars have been scared off. Mon–Thurs noon–midnight, Fri & Sat 11am–1am, Sun 12.30–11pm.

Teuchters 26 William St, EH3 7NH ☎0131 225 2973, ⓦ teuchtersbar.co.uk; map p.754. The more traditional of the three-pub cluster in William St, and at times the most lively. It's a free house with a good range of Scottish cask ales and a menu of honest Scottish pub grub – haggis

stovies cost £8.25. Mon–Sat 10.30am–1am; kitchen Mon–Sat 10.30am–10pm.

Tigerlily 125 George St, EH2 4JN ☎0131 225 5005, ⓦ tigerlilyedinburgh.co.uk; map p.754. The daddy of all George St's decadent destination bars, where the locals come to see and be seen. Can be lots of fun – but only if you're wearing the right outfit. Daily 7am–1am.

The Voodoo Rooms 19a West Register St, EH2 2AA ☎0131 556 7060, ⓦ thevoodoorooms.com; map p.754. Glamorous and stylish Victorian bar, dining room and events space that attracts a dressed-up crowd, especially at the weekend. Frequent live music, performance and club nights, including Edinburgh's legendary Vegas! (ⓦ vegasscotland.co.uk). Mon–Thurs 4pm–1am, Fri–Sun noon–1am; kitchen Mon–Thurs 4–10pm, Fri–Sun noon–10pm.

LEITH

King's Wark 36 The Shore, EH6 6QU ☎0131 554 9260, ⓦ kingswark.co.uk; map p.754. Restored fifteenth-century harbourside pub with attached restaurant. Its picturesque interior – stone walls and corniced ceilings – provides an ambience that's little changed since the days of the old sea dogs telling tales at the bar. Mon–Thurs & Sun 10am–midnight, Fri & Sat 10am–1am.

Lioness of Leith 21–25 Duke St, EH6 8HH ☎0131 629 0580, ⓦ thelionessofleith.co.uk; map p.754. With Pop Art on the walls, an arcade machine in the corner and a table made out of a pinball machine, this Victorian boozer certainly looks young for its age. There's regular live music at weekends, a good kitchen and a loyal local following. Mon–Thurs noon–1am, Fri–Sun 11am–1am.

Nobles 44a Constitution St, EH6 6RS ☎0131 629 7215, ⓦ noblesbarleith.co.uk; map p.754. Handsome Victorian bar with more than its fair share of stained glass, chandeliers and wood panelling, this is a good place to sup a posh cocktail or two. The kitchen heads into gastropub territory, with a particularly fine dessert to look out for: green tea pannacotta with poached rhubarb (£7). Mon–Wed 11am–midnight, Thurs & Fri 11am–1am, Sat & Sun 10am–1am; kitchen noon–10pm.

★ **Teuchters Landing** 1 Dock Place, EH6 6LU ☎0131 554 7427, ⓦ teuchtersbar.co.uk; map p.754. Spilling out onto a bespoke pontoon, with seductive harbour views, *Teuchters'* beer garden is the ideal place to while away a braw, bricht summer's afternoon. The pub itself, converted from a waiting room for the decommissioned Leith-to-Aberdeen steamboat, is a delightful, traditional-style free house carved into a genial collection of nooks and snugs with an overcrowded bar and a superfluously large whisky selection. Daily 10.30am–1am.

NIGHTLIFE

Inevitably, Edinburgh's **nightlife** is at its best during the August festivals (see page 772), which can make the other 49 weeks of the year seem like an anticlimax. However, at any time the city has plenty to offer, especially in the realm of

17

theatre and **music**. The best way to find out what's on is to pick up a copy of *The List* (ⓦ list.co.uk), a free monthly listings magazine covering Edinburgh and Glasgow. The entry fee to clubs usually depends on the night. Friday and Saturday nights range from £10 to £15 for the main venues while weeknights average around a fiver.

CLUBS

The Bongo Club 66 Cowgate, EH1 1JX ☎0131 558 8844, ⓦthebongoclub.co.uk; map p.754. This is the current home of this iconic, peripatetic Edinburgh club and arts venue; its line-up is routinely eclectic, experimental and always worth checking out. Look out for the monthly grime and dubstep night Electrikal, funk and Latin fixture Soulsville and immortal reggae institution and "original roots advertiser", Messenger Sound System, which has outlasted (by decades!) almost every other club night in the city. Daily 11pm–3am, opens earlier on occasion.

La Belle Angèle 11 Hasties Close, Cowgate, EH1 1HJ ☎0131 225 8382, ⓦla-belleangele.com; map p.754. A legendary 90s venue which rose from the ashes, quite literally, after it was infamously burned to the ground in a 2002 fire. Radiohead, Oasis and some of the city's best club nights graced it back in the day; in its new incarnation, the likes of Craig Charles and Leftfield have shown up for DJ sets, while midweek bass frenzy Loco Kamanchi is one of the most credible student nights around. Free. Club nights 10pm–3am.

Mash House 37 Guthrie St (entrance up Hastie's Close from the Cowgate), EH1 1JQ ☎0131 220 2514, ⓦthemashhouse.co.uk; map p.754. Sequestered away in a sidestreet hidey-hole just off the Cowgate, this is regarded as one of the best venues in the city among bands, promoters, DJs and punters alike, and has hosted the likes of Andrew Weatherall. The downstairs dancefloor is just the right size for working up a sweat, especially when Samedia are in town (usually first Fri of month) with their trademark blend of tropical bass. Daily 10pm/11pm–3am.

Sneaky Pete's 73 Cowgate, EH1 1JW ☎0131 225 1757, ⓦsneakypetes.co.uk; map p.754. Condensed sweat and a fiercely eclectic roster characterize this one-hundred-capacity Cowgate perennial, often cited as the soul of the capital's grass roots scene. Club nights such as Wasabi Disco and Teesh are solid fixtures, while the tiny stage has hosted everyone from seminal DJ Bill Brewster to veteran Japanese psych-rockers Acid Mothers Temple. Daily 11pm–3am.

LGBT+ CLUBS AND BARS

CC Bloom's 23–24 Greenside Place, EH1 3AA ☎0131 556 9331, ⓦfacebook.com/ccbloomsbar; map p.754. Edinburgh's most enduring gay bar/club, with a big dancefloor, stonking rhythms and a young, friendly crowd and free entry all night. Daily 11am–3am; club nights start at 11pm.

Planet 6 Baxter's Place, EH1 3AF ☎0131 556 5551, ⓦfacebook.com/gaybar.edinburgh; map p.754. Loud and outrageous bar with lots going on, from drag queens to karaoke sessions. Daily 1pm–3am.

LIVE MUSIC VENUES

Bannermans 212 Cowgate, EH1 1NQ ☎0131 556 3254, ⓦbannermanslive.co.uk; map p.754. Indefatigable granddaddy of Edinburgh's live music scene, with a labyrinth of caves and musky warrens located at the base of South Bridge. The most atmospheric joint in town in which to discover local indie bands hoping for a big break. Mon–Sat noon–1am, Sun 12.30pm–1am.

The Jazz Bar 1a Chambers St, EH1 1HR ☎0131 220 4298, ⓦthejazzbar.co.uk; map p.754. There's been a subterranean jazz bar on this site for decades, more or less, and the current incarnation (set up by the late jazz drummer Bill Kyle in 2005) hosts up to five performances a day, every day, with an eclectic roster and a generous definition of jazz seeing soul, funk, blues and electronica getting a look-in. All door money (usually around £4) goes directly to the musicians. Daily 11pm–3am, opens earlier on occasion.

Queen's Hall 85–89 Clerk St, EH8 9JG ☎0131 668 2019, ⓦthequeenshall.net; map p.754. There's nothing quite like an intimate jazz or classical performance in the hushed

---

SHOPPING IN EDINBURGH

While Edinburgh has traditionally been outdone on the designer clothing front by Glasgow, the early noughties opening of **Multrees Walk** and its showpiece Harvey Nichols store redressed the balance. If labels are your thing, you'll find enough here and in nearby **George Street** to blow your entire travel budget in a couple of hours. For vintage gear, independent designers, comics, antiquarian books and even fossils, the **Old Town** is your oyster, especially Candlemaker Row, Victoria Street, the Grassmarket and West Port. **Stockbridge** (especially St Stephen Street) and **Newington** are also good bets for quirky boutiques and antique shops. For delis and artisan **food** shopping, again the Old Town and Stockbridge come up trumps, as does Marchmont, Bruntsfield and Morningside. And last but not least, it may not surprise you to learn that the **Royal Mile** is the place to load up on malt whisky and get kilted-out with some tartan.

17

HOGMANAY

Like most of the capital's festivals, Edinburgh's **Hogmanay** has recently taken on a life of its own, with the focus on Princes Street – ticket numbers have been restricted to sixty thousand after the legendary 1996–97 event clocked in at almost half a million revellers.

Regularly cited by travel experts and bucket-listers as one of the globe's must-experience events, the party has grown from a drunken, stranger-snogging celebration of the midnight bells to a six-hour marathon including the Ceilidh under the Castle, the Concert in the Gardens (featuring A-list pop, rock and indie bands), flash mobs, fire eaters and dramatic pyrotechnics. The high point is, of course, midnight, when hundreds of tonnes of fireworks are let off above the Castle, and Edinburgh joins the rest of the world singing "Auld Lang Syne", an old Scottish tune with lyrics by Robert Burns, Scotland's national poet. For information go to ⓦedinburghshogmanay.com.

environs of this former church, one of Edinburgh's best-loved live music venues. Most shows start 7.30pm.

Sandy Bell's 25 Forrest Rd, EH1 2QH ☎0131 225 2751, ⓦsandybellsedinburgh.co.uk; map p.754. A truly legendary, richly atmospheric and strictly traditional folk music bar that's been doing its thing since the 1940s. Famous for fine ales, malt whiskies and a good old sing-song, it's one of the last of its kind in the capital. Mon–Sat noon–1am, Sun 12.30pm–midnight.

Usher Hall Lothian Rd, EH1 2EA ☎0131 228 1155, ⓦusherhall.co.uk; map p.754. Reopened after a major refurbishment with a strikingly contemporary extension, Edinburgh's main civic concert hall frequently features choral and symphony concerts, as well as legends of country, jazz, world and pop. Most shows start 7.30pm.

ENTERTAINMENT

THEATRE, DANCE AND COMEDY

Edinburgh Playhouse 18–22 Greenside Place, EH1 3AA ☎0844 871 3014, ⓦedinburgh-playhouse.co.uk; map p.754. The largest theatre in Britain, formerly a cinema. Used largely for extended runs of popular musicals and occasional rock concerts and comedy shows.

Festival Theatre Nicolson St, EH8 9FT ☎0131 529 6000, ⓦfctt.org.uk; map p.754. The largest stage in Britain, principally used for Scottish Opera and Scottish Ballet's appearances in the capital, but also for everything from the children's show *Singing Kettle* to Engelbert Humperdinck concerts.

King's Theatre 2 Leven St, EH3 9LQ ☎0131 529 6000, ⓦedtheatres.com/kings; map p.754. Edwardian civic theatre majoring in pantomime, touring West End plays and the occasional drama or opera performance. The interior is surprisingly luxurious, with marble staircases, carved mahogany doors and a sumptuously regal auditorium.

Royal Lyceum 30 Grindlay St, EH3 9AX ☎0131 248 4848, ⓦlyceum.org.uk; map p.754. A fine Victorian civic theatre and leading venue for mainstream drama. The theatre commissions around seven plays annually as well as hosting travelling productions.

The Stand 5 York Place, EH1 3EB ☎0131 558 7272, ⓦthestand.co.uk; map p.754. The city's undisputed top comedy spot, with different acts every night and some of the UK's top comics headlining at the weekends. Be sure to arrive early to secure a good table. Entry ranges wildly from £3 to £17.50.

Traverse Theatre 10 Cambridge St, EH1 2ED ☎0131 228 1404, ⓦtraverse.co.uk; map p.754. One of Britain's premier venues for new plays and avant garde drama from around the world. Going from strength to strength in its custom-built home beside the Usher Hall, with a great bar downstairs.

ARTHOUSE CINEMAS

Cameo 38 Home St, EH3 9LZ ☎0131 228 2800, ⓦpicturehouses.co.uk; map p.754. A treasure of an arthouse cinema, screening the more challenging mainstream releases and cult late-nighters. Quentin Tarantino has been here and he thinks it's great.

Filmhouse 88 Lothian Rd, EH3 9BZ ☎0131 228 2688, ⓦfilmhousecinema.com; map p.754. Three-screen cinema, home to the city's international film festival, which shows an eclectic programme of independent, arthouse and classic films.

DIRECTORY

Hospital Royal Infirmary, Little France (☎0131 536 1000), has a 24hr casualty department. There's also a minor injuries clinic at the Western General, Crewe Rd South (daily 8am–9pm; ☎0131 537 1000).

Left luggage Counter by platform 1 at Waverley Station (daily 7am–11pm; from £6/ item; ☎0131 558 3829).

17 East Lothian

East Lothian consists of the coastal strip and hinterland immediately east of Edinburgh, bounded by the Firth of Forth to the north and the Lammermuir Hills to the south. All of it is within easy day-trip range from the capital, though there are places you can stay overnight if you're keen to explore. Often mocked as the "home counties" of Edinburgh, there's no denying its well-ordered feel, with prosperous farms and large estate houses dominating the scenery. The main attractions are on or near the coast, with the trip east from Edinburgh taking you past wide sandy beaches by **Aberlady** and famous golf courses at **Gullane**. The town of **North Berwick** is the main focal point on the coast, with dramatic cliff-top ruins at **Tantallon** and the supersonic draw of Concorde at the **Museum of Flight** both within easy reach.

North Berwick and around

NORTH BERWICK has a great deal of charm and a somewhat faded, old-fashioned air, its guesthouses and hotels extending along the shore in all their Victorian and Edwardian sobriety. The town's small harbour is set on a headland which cleaves two crescents of sand, though it is the two volcanic heaps, the offshore **Bass Rock** – resembling a giant molar – and 613ft-high **North Berwick Law**, which are the town's defining features.

Scottish Seabird Centre

Harbour Lodge, 7 Beach Rd, EH39 4AB • Feb, March, Sept & Oct Mon–Fri 10am–5pm, Sat & Sun 10am–5.30pm; April–Aug daily 10am–6pm; Nov–Jan Mon–Fri 10am–4pm, Sat & Sun 10am–5pm • £8.95 • ☎ 01620 890202, ⓦ seabird.org

Housed in an attractively designed new building by the harbour, the **Scottish Seabird Centre** offers access to gannets and puffins that thrive on the rocky outcrops in the sea before North Berwick. There are live links from the centre to cameras mounted on the islands showing close-up pictures of the nesting sites. At the risk of getting wet (and cold) you can also hop aboard one of the thrilling speedboat rides to the islands (weather permitting). Contact the centre to see what trips are available on any given day.

Tantallon Castle

Three miles east of North Berwick on the A198, EH39 5PN • April–Sept daily 9.30am–5.30pm; Oct–March daily 10am–4pm • £6; HES • ☎ 01620 892 727, ⓦ historicenvironment.scot/visit-a-place/places/tantallon-castle • From North Berwick's High St take the Dunbar bus (Eves Coaches #120; Mon–Sat 6 daily, Sun 2; 6min), or walk along the cliffs in around 1hr

With a sheer drop down to the sea on three sides and a sequence of moats and ditches on the fourth, the desolate invincibility of **Tantallon Castle**'s melodramatic ruins is daunting, especially when the wind howls over the remaining battlements and the surf crashes on the rocks far below.

National Museum of Flight

Five miles south of North Berwick on the B1347, EH39 5LF • April–Oct daily 10am–5pm; Nov–March Sat & Sun 10am–4pm • £12 • ☎ 0300 123 6789, ⓦ nms.ac.uk/flight • First Bus runs the #121 service from North Berwick to Haddington via the museum (Mon–Sat 5 daily; 25min)

Standing on an old military airfield by East Fortune, the **National Museum of Flight** is home to *Alpha Alpha*, British Airways' first Concorde. The supersonic passenger jet, one of only twenty such planes built, has been reassembled to show how she looked when decommissioned in 2003. A visit on board is restricted to a slightly stooped wander through the forward half of the aircraft, while a display follows the Concorde project as a whole, from the early days of Anglo-French bickering to the tragic Paris crash of 2000. In and around the restored hangars on the site, you can see more than fifty vintage aircraft including a Vulcan bomber, a Comet airliner, a Spitfire and a Tigermoth.

17

ARRIVAL AND DEPARTURE   NORTH BERWICK

By train North Berwick is served by trains (hourly; 30min) from Edinburgh Waverley, with discount deals for those heading for the Seabird Centre. From the station it's a 10min walk east to the town centre.

By bus First Group buses #X24 and #X25 depart from Edinburgh's Leith St, just outside the St James Centre (every 30min; 1hr 30min) and run along the coast via Aberlady, Gullane and Dirleton stopping near North Berwick's seafront.

ACCOMMODATION AND EATING

The Glebe House B&B Law Rd, EH39 4PL ☎ 01620 892 608, ⓦ glebehouse-nb.co.uk. A grand eighteenth-century manse in secluded grounds 100yd inland but still overlooking the sea. With decor befitting of its period, the rooms are spacious yet homely. Breakfast choices swing from healthy yoghurt and muesli to a hearty Scottish fry-up, all served on vintage crockery. **£140**

Lobstershack The Harbour, EH39 4JL ☎ 07910 620480, ⓦ lobstershack.co.uk. Get lobster, langoustine and mackerel straight from the boats at this licensed harbourside hut with a handful of outdoor tables and chairs. The menu is more sophisticated than you might think, with offerings such as seafood scotch eggs for £10

and crab/prawn cocktail for £6. Best of all, though, is the garlic-and-herb-butter-grilled lobster for £16/half or £27/ whole. April & May Sat & Sun noon–6pm; June–Sept daily noon–6pm; closes in bad weather.

★ **Osteria** 71 High St, EH39 4HQ ☎ 01620 890 589, ⓦ osteria-no1.co.uk. Run by a highly successful father-and-daughter team, this is one of the country's top Italian restaurants. Their intelligent use of herbs adds a subtle Mediterranean fragrance to the dishes. Prices hover around £8 for *primi* courses while meaty *secondi piatti* rise steeply from £15. Booking recommended. Mon 6–10pm, Tues–Sat 12.30–2pm & 6–10pm.

Midlothian

Immediately south of Edinburgh lies the old county of **Midlothian**. It's one of the hilliest parts of the Central Lowlands, with the Pentland chain running down its western side, and the Moorfoots defining its boundary with the Borders to the south.

Roslin

The tranquil village of **ROSLIN**, seven miles south of the centre of Edinburgh, has two claims to fame: it was near here, at the Roslin Institute, that the world's first cloned animal, Dolly the sheep, was created in 1997, and it's also home to the mysterious, richly decorated, late Gothic **Rosslyn Chapel**.

Rosslyn Chapel

Chapel Loan, EH25 9PU • June–Aug Mon–Sat 9.30am–6pm, Sun noon–4.45pm; Sept–May Mon–Sat 9.30am–5pm, Sun noon–4.45pm • £9 • ☎ 0131 440 2159, ⓦ rosslynchapel.org.uk • Roslin can be reached by bus #15 westbound from Edinburgh's Princes St (every 30min; 50min)

Revered for its sublime stone carvings – some of the finest in the world – and subject of intrigue and mystery for its alleged Crusader connections, fifteenth-century **Rosslyn Chapel** is more like a cathedral than a chapel in its dimensions. Its exterior bristles with pinnacles, gargoyles, flying buttresses and canopies, while inside the stonework is, if anything, even more intricate. Among the carvings are representations of cacti and Indian corn, compounding the legend that the founder's grandfather, the daring sea adventurer Prince Henry of Orkney, did indeed set foot in the New World a century before Columbus. The rich and subtle figurative sculptures have given Rosslyn the nickname of "a bible in stone", though they're more allegorical than literal, with portrayals of the Dance of Death, the Seven Acts of Mercy and the Seven Deadly Sins. The greatest and most original carving of all is the extraordinary knotted **Apprentice**

17

> ### ROSSLYN'S SECRETS
>
> The imagery of certain carvings found in Rosslyn Chapel, together with the history of the family, the St Clairs, which owns the chapel, leave little doubt about its links to the **Knights Templar** and **Freemasonry**. The Masonic connection was said to have saved the chapel from the armies of Oliver Cromwell, himself a Freemason, which destroyed the surrounding area but spared Rosslyn. More intriguing still are claims that, because of such connections, the chapel has been the repository for items such as the lost Scrolls of Solomon's Temple in Jerusalem, the true Stone of Scone and, most famously, the Holy Grail. Rosslyn Chapel has been regularly drawn into conspiracy theories on these themes, most famously through Dan Brown's bestseller *The Da Vinci Code*; the chapel's appearance in the 2006 film of the same name precipitated a huge surge in visitor numbers.

Pillar at the southeastern corner of the Lady Chapel. According to local legend, the pillar was made by an apprentice during the absence of the master mason, who killed him in a fit of jealousy on seeing the finished work.

National Mining Museum

Lady Victoria Colliery, Newtongrange, 8 miles southeast of Edinburgh on the A7, EH22 4QN • Daily: April–Oct 10am–5pm; Nov–March 10am–4pm • £9 • **Tours** (1hr–1hr 30min): summer hourly; winter 11am, 12.30pm & 2pm • £4.50–9 • ☏ 0131 663 7519, ⓦ nationalminingmuseum.com • Trains leave Edinburgh for Newtongrange (every 30min; 22min), or you can take bus #29 or #33 southbound from Princes St (50min)

Closed in 1989, this Victorian colliery, now the **National Mining Museum**, is one of the best preserved in the world. A variety of exhibits show numerous engineering innovations throughout the years, including the largest steam engine in Scotland, originally used to haul men up and down the pit shaft. The site is truly vast, and much of the colliery will remain in the renovation queue for years to come, which gives the place an atmospheric ambience of decay. Ex-minor tour guides offer real insight into what it was like to work here while you absorb the sights, smells and sounds of the working pit.

West Lothian

To many, **West Lothian** is a poor relative to the rolling, rich farmland of East and Midlothian, with a landscape dominated by motorways, industrial estates and giant hillocks of ochre-coloured mine waste called "bings". However, in the royal palace at **Linlithgow**, the area boasts one of Scotland's more magnificent ruins. Nearby, the village of **South Queensferry** lies under the considerable shadow of the rail and road bridges that traverse the **Firth of Forth**, though it's an interesting enough place in its own right, with a historic high street and the stately home of **Hopetoun** nearby.

Jupiter Artland

Wilkieston, 11 miles west of the centre of Edinburgh on the B7015, EH27 8BB • 10am–5pm: May, June & Sept Thurs–Sun; July & Aug daily • £8.50 • ☏ 01506 889 900, ⓦ jupiterartland.org • First bus #27 from Princes St (40min)

Fulfilling the dreams of its art collector owners, **Jupiter Artland**, a 100-acre country pile, has been transformed since the turn of the century into a remarkable sculpture park. Its appeal as a virgin project, an unparalleled blank canvas, has drawn in many of the heavyweights of outdoor installation – including **Charles Jencks**, whose signature swirling grassy hillocks and ponds also feature outside the Scottish National

17

Gallery of Modern Art. Here his landscape *Cells of Life* interprets the biological process of mitosis using large grassy Walnut-Whip-shaped mounds dissected by a driveable causeway. **Andy Goldsworthy** contributes a number of installations, too, including a complete dry stone cottage and a clay tree, while Sam Durant's *Scaffold*, a protest interpretation of a gallows, has an unlikely secondary function as a children's climbing frame.

Linlithgow

Fifteen miles west of Edinburgh is the ancient royal burgh of **LINLITHGOW**. The town itself has largely kept its medieval layout, but development since the 1960s has, sadly, stripped it of some fine buildings, notably around the Town Hall and Cross – the former marketplace – on the long High Street.

Linlithgow Palace

Kirkgate, just off High St, EH49 7AL • Daily: April–Sept 9.30am–5.30pm; Oct–March 10am–4pm • £6; HES • ☎ 01506 842 896, ⓦ historicenvironment.scot/visit-a-place/places/linlithgow-palace

The splendid fifteenth-century lochside ruins of **Linlithgow Palace** are renowned for their strong royal connections: from the top of the northwest tower, Queen Margaret looked out in vain for the return of James IV from the field of Flodden in 1513 (the views from her bower, six storeys up from the ground, are exceptional). The ornate octagonal fountain in the inner courtyard, with its intricate figures and medallion heads, flowed with wine for the wedding of James V and Mary of Guise; their daughter Mary was born here on 8 December 1542 and just six days later began her reign as the famous Queen of Scots.

ARRIVAL AND INFORMATION   LINLITHGOW

By train Linlithgow is on the main train routes from Edinburgh to Glasgow Queen Street and Stirling; the station lies at the southern end of town.

Destinations Edinburgh Waverley & Haymarket (4 hourly; 20min); Glasgow (2 hourly; 30min); Stirling (2 hourly; 30min).

ACCOMMODATION AND EATING

Champany Inn Champany, EH49 7LU ☎ 01506 834 532, ⓦ champany.com. West Lothian's unexpected gourmet oasis, the *Champany Inn* – a one-time Michelin-star holder – serves seriously expensive steaks and seafood as well as top-notch South African wines. There's also a less formal chop-and-ale-house attached. Two-course lunches start at £27.50. Mon–Fri 12.30–2pm & 7–10pm, Sat 7–10pm.

Court Residence 1 Court Square, High St, EH49 7EQ ☎ 01506 538 687, ⓦ courtresidence.com. Beautiful old hotel conversion in the heart of the historic centre, with a sleek and modern interior. There's free parking and a range of rooms from studios to suites (from £89) with kitchen facilities and additional capacity. **£69**

Taste 47 High St, EH49 7ED ☎ 01506 844445, ⓦ taste-deli-cafe.co.uk. A former bakery with its original cast-iron ovens on show, this café sells takeaway soups and sandwiches: good for a picnic in the delightful grounds of the palace. A lunch should cost in the region of £7. Mon–Wed 8.30am–4.30pm, Thurs & Fri 8.30am–5.30pm, Sat 9am–5.30pm, Sun 10am–4.30pm.

Edinburgh International Climbing Arena (EICA)

Ratho, 5 miles west of Edinburgh Airport, signposted just beyond the Newbridge junction of the M8 and M9, EH28 8AA • Mon–Fri 8am–10pm, Sat & Sun 9am–6pm • £10.80 plus equipment rental; "clip n climb" £9 • ☎ 0131 333 6333, ⓦ eica-ratho.co.uk • Take the tram from Princes St (every 7 min; 18min) to Hermiston Gate and change for Lothian bus #20 to Ratho (every 30min; 13min), then follow canal path west for 2min from The Bridge Inn

The **Edinburgh International Climbing Arena** is Europe's largest, built into the remnants of a disused quarry on the banks of the Union Canal. The place is truly gigantic and the some of the climbs challenge not only your skills and stamina but also your head for heights. You'll need to bring a partner to belay with, and ideally that person will

17

have completed a short belaying course. For the kids' "clip n climb"course belaying is automated. If you don't have your own harness, any necessary equipment can be bought or rented from the shop within the complex. There are also a number of rope-free boulders on which you can practice specific techniques with a crash mat below to break your fall.

South Queensferry

Eight miles northwest of Edinburgh city centre is the small town of **SOUTH QUEENSFERRY**, located at the southern end of the three mighty bridges that traverse the Firth of Forth. It's an attractive old settlement, with a narrow, cobbled High Street lined with tightly packed buildings, most of which date from the seventeenth and eighteenth centuries. From the pier you can catch a sailing to the exquisite twelfth-century abbey on **Inchcolm** island.

Queensferry Museum

53 High St, EH30 9HP • Mon & Thurs–Sat 10am–1pm & 2–5pm, Sun noon–5pm • Free • ☎ 0131 331 5545

Giving insight into the construction of the bridges that dominate the townscape, the small **Queensferry Museum** exhibits photos and relics of the town's history, showing its importance as a ferry port from the eleventh century until September 3, 1964, after which the first road bridge was opened.

Hopetoun House

Hopetoun Estate, 3 miles west of Queensferry, EH30 9SL • Mid-April to Sept daily 10.30am–5pm • £9.85 house and grounds, £4.55 grounds only • ☎ 0131 331 2451, ⓦ hopetoun.co.uk • On foot, follow the coastline west from Queensferry for 3 miles; by car, take M90 turn off onto the A904 from where it is signposted

Ranking as one of the most impressive stately homes in Scotland, **Hopetoun House** was built at the turn of the eighteenth century for the first Earl of Hopetoun by Sir William Bruce, the architect of Holyroodhouse. A couple of decades later, William Adam carried out an enormous extension, engulfing the structure with a curvaceous main facade and two projecting wings – superb examples of Baroque pomp and swagger. The grounds include a long, regal driveway, lovely walks along woodland trails and the banks of the Forth, and plenty of picnic spots.

Inchcolm

Five miles northeast of South Queensferry, near the Fife shore • **Sailings from South Queensferry: Maid of the Forth, Hawes Pier** April–Oct times vary, more regular in high season; check website for timetables • £20 for 1hr 30min landing trip • ☎ 0131 331 5000, ⓦ maidoftheforth.co.uk • **Departures by bus and then boat from Edinburgh: Forth Boat Tours, Waverley Bridge** Easter–Oct 2–5 daily; winter some weekend sailings • £26 for 1hr 30min landing trip, including bus from Waverley Bridge • ☎ 0870 118 1866, ⓦ forthtours.com

The island of **Inchcolm** is home to the best-preserved medieval abbey in Scotland, founded in 1235 after King Alexander I was stormbound here. Although the structure as a whole is half-ruined today, the tower, octagonal chapter house and echoing cloisters are intact and well worth exploring. The ninety minutes you're given ashore allows time for a picnic on the abbey's lawns or the chance to explore Inchcolm's old military fortifications.

ARRIVAL AND DEPARTURE

SOUTH QUEENSFERRY

By train From Edinburgh Waverley take the train to Dalmeny (every 30min; 20min). From there it's a mile to South Queensferry's centre: head west on Station Rd then turn right on The Loan.

By bus First bus #X38 connects with Edinburgh (every 20min; 1hr) and Stirling (every 20min; 1hr 5min).

ACCOMMODATION AND EATING

The Boathouse 19b High St, EH30 9PP ☎0131 331 5429, ⓦtheboathouse-sq.co.uk. A popular bistro in a great location with outside tables and sea views towards the three magnificent bridges. It's very much a seafood institution, with a menu of safe favourites like fish and chips for £11 and smoked haddock in cheese sauce for £13.45. Daily 10am–11.30pm.

Orocco Pier 17 High St, EH30 9PP ☎0131 331 1298, ⓦoroccopier.co.uk. A stylish contemporary drinking spot on South Queensferry's medieval High St, boasting unbeatable views over the water to the Forth bridges and serving pleasant bistro food such as crab linguine with chilli, garlic and parsley sauce for £14. They also have smart guest rooms and serviced apartments. Daily 9am–1am; kitchen Mon–Fri noon–3pm & 6–10pm, Sat & Sun 8am–10pm. Rooms **£115**, apartments **£185**

Southern
Scotland

GALLOWAY FOREST PARK

Southern Scotland

Dominated by the Southern Uplands, a chain of bulging round-topped hills, southern Scotland divides neatly into three regions: the Borders, Dumfries and Galloway, and Ayrshire. Although none of them has the highest of tourist profiles, those visitors who whizz past on their way north to Edinburgh, Glasgow or the Highlands are missing out on a huge swathe of Scotland that is in many ways the very heart of the country. Over the centuries, its inhabitants, particularly in the Borders, bore the brunt of long, brutal wars with the English; its farms have fed Scotland's cities since industrialization; and two of the country's greatest literary icons, Sir Walter Scott and Robbie Burns, lived and died here.

North of the inhospitable Cheviot Hills, which separate Scotland from England, the **Borders** region is dominated by the meanderings of the **River Tweed**. The towns here have provided inspiration for countless folkloric ballads telling of bloody battles with the English and clashes with the notorious Border Reivers, who conducted raids on border settlements. The delightful small town of **Melrose** is the most obvious base, and has the most impressive of the four **Border abbeys** founded by the medieval Canmore kings, all of which are now reduced to romantic ruins.

Dumfries and Galloway, in the southwestern corner of Scotland, gets even more overlooked than the Borders. If you do make the effort to get off the main north–south highway to Glasgow, you'll find more ruined abbeys, medieval castles, forested hills and dramatic tidal flats and sea cliffs ideal for birdwatching. The key resort is the modest, charming town of **Kirkcudbright**; it sits halfway along the Solway coast, which is indented by sandy coves.

Ayrshire is rich farming country, with fewer sights than its neighbours; almost everything of interest is confined to the coast. The **golf courses** along its gentle coastline are among the finest links courses in the country, while fans of **Robert Burns** could happily spend several days exploring the author's old haunts, especially at **Ayr**, the county town, and the nearby village of **Alloway**, the poet's birthplace.

GETTING AROUND
SOUTHERN SCOTLAND

By train The Borders has two lines running south from Edinburgh: one along the east coast en route to London and another that runs inland stopping a couple of miles shy of Melrose. A reasonable network connects Ayrshire with Dumfries and Galloway and Glasgow.

By bus Buses will get you practically everywhere mentioned in this chapter, although there is no link between the Borders and the rest of the region.

The Borders

The **Borders** region is sandwiched between the Cheviot Hills on the English border and the Pentland and Moorfoot ranges to the south of Edinburgh. The finest section of the lush **Tweed Valley** lies between **Melrose** and **Peebles**, where you'll find a string of

MELROSE ABBEY

Highlights

❶ Melrose Abbey Border abbey with superbly preserved sculptural detail. See page 793

❷ Traquair House The oldest continuously inhabited house in Scotland, virtually unchanged since the fifteenth century. See page 797

❸ Caerlaverock One of Scotland's most photogenic moated castles, set beside a superb site for waterfowl and waders. See page 802

❹ Kirkcudbright One-time artists' colony, and the best-looking town on the "Scottish Riviera". See page 804

❺ Galloway Forest Park Go mountain biking along remote forest tracks, or hiking on the Southern Upland Way. See page 805

❻ Alloway The village where poet Robert Burns was born, and the best of many Burns pilgrimage spots in the region. See page 807

❼ Culzean Castle Stately home with a fabulous cliff-edge setting, surrounded by acres of gardens and woods reaching down to the shore. See page 808

❽ Dumfries House An eighteenth-century architectural masterpiece, designed by the Adam brothers and decked out by Thomas Chippendale. See page 809

❾ Ailsa Craig Take a boat out to this volcanic lump and watch baby gannets learn the art of flying and diving for fish. See page 809

HIGHLIGHTS ARE MARKED ON THE MAP ON PAGE 792

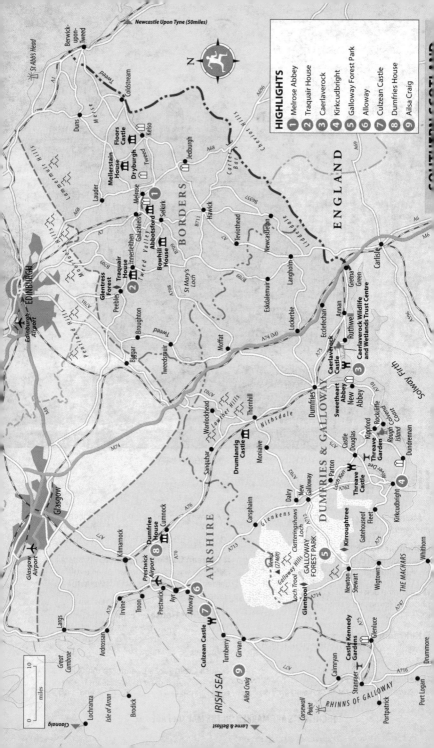

attractions, from Sir Walter Scott's eccentric mansion at **Abbotsford** to the ancient seat of **Traquair House**, along with the region's famous **abbeys**, founded in the reign of King David I (1124–53).

Melrose and around

Minuscule **MELROSE**, tucked in between the Tweed and the gorse-backed Eildon Hills, is the most beguiling of towns, its narrow streets trimmed by a harmonious ensemble of styles, from pretty little cottages and tweedy shops to high-standing Georgian and Victorian facades. Its chief draw is its ruined **abbey**, but it's also well positioned for exploring the Tweed Valley, with the Scott-related attractions of **Abbotsford** and **Dryburgh** nearby.

Melrose Abbey

Abbey St, TD6 9LG · Daily: April–Sept 9.30am–5.30pm; Oct–March 10am–4pm · £6; HES · ☎ 01896 822562, ⓦ historicenvironment.scot/visit-a-place/places/melrose-abbey

The pink- and red-tinted stone ruins of **Melrose Abbey** soar above their riverside surroundings. Founded in 1136, Melrose was the first Cistercian settlement in Scotland and grew rich selling wool and hides to Flanders. The English repeatedly razed the abbey, most viciously in 1385 and 1545, and most of the remains date from the intervening period. The site is dominated by the **Abbey Church**, which has lost its west front, and whose nave is reduced to the elegant window arches and chapels of the south aisle. Amazingly, however, the stone **pulpitum** (screen), separating the choir monks from their lay brothers, is preserved. Beyond, the **presbytery** has its magnificent perpendicular window, lierne vaulting and ceiling bosses intact, with the capitals of the surrounding columns sporting the most intricate of curly kale carving. Look out, too, for the Coronation of the Virgin on the east end gable, and the numerous mischievous **gargoyles**, such as the pig playing the bagpipes on the roof on the south side of the nave.

Abbotsford

Two miles west of Melrose, TD6 9BQ · **Visitor centre** Daily: April–Oct 10am–5pm; Nov–March 10am–4pm · Free · **House and gardens** Daily: April–Oct 10am–5pm; Nov & March 10am–4pm · House and gardens £9.60; gardens only £5 · ☎ 01896 752043, ⓦ scottsabbotsford.co.uk · The fast, frequent Melrose–Galashiels bus provides easy access to Abbotsford: ask for the Tweedbank island on the A6091, from where the house is a 10min walk

Abbotsford was designed to satisfy the Romantic inclinations of **Sir Walter Scott**, who lived here from 1812 until his death. The building took twelve years to evolve, with the fanciful turrets and castellations of the Scots Baronial exterior incorporating copies of medieval originals. Despite all the exterior pomp, the interior is surprisingly small and poky, with just six rooms open for viewing on the upper floor. Visitors start in the wood-panelled study, with its small writing desk made of salvage from the Spanish Armada, at which Scott banged out the Waverley novels at a furious rate. The wood-panelled library boasts his extraordinary assortment of memorabilia, including Napoleon's pen case and blotting book, Rob Roy's purse and *skene dhu* (knife), and the inlaid pearl crucifix that accompanied Mary, Queen of Scots, to the scaffold. Henry Raeburn's famous portrait of Scott hangs in the drawing room.

Dryburgh Abbey

Five miles southeast of Melrose, TD6 6RQ · Daily: April–Sept 9.30am–5.30pm; Oct–March 10am–4pm · £6; HES · ☎ 01835 822381, ⓦ historicenvironment.scot/visit-a-place/places/dryburgh-abbey · There is no public transport to the abbey, though it's just a mile's walk north of St Boswells on the A68, and a pleasant 5 miles from Melrose

Hidden away in a U-bend in the Tweed, the remains of **Dryburgh Abbey** occupy an idyllic position against a hilly backdrop. Founded in the twelfth century by the Premonstratensians, virtually nothing survives of the nave of the **Abbey Church**, though the transepts have fared better, their chapels now serving as private burial

18

SIR WALTER SCOTT

As a child, **Walter Scott** (1771–1832), disabled by polio, was sent to recuperate at his grandfather's farm in Smailholm, where his imagination was fuelled by his relative's tales of the old, violent troubles in the Borders. Throughout the 1790s he transcribed hundreds of old Border ballads, publishing a three-volume collection entitled *Minstrelsy of the Scottish Borders* in 1802. An instant success, *Minstrelsy* was followed by Scott's own *Lay of the Last Minstrel*, a narrative poem whose strong story and rose-tinted regionalism proved very popular. More **poetry** was to come, most successfully *Marmion* (1808) and *The Lady of the Lake* (1810).

However, despite having two paid jobs, his finances remained shaky. He had become a partner in a printing firm, which put him into debt, not helped by the enormous sums he spent on his mansion, **Abbotsford** (see page 793). From 1813, writing to pay the bills, Scott thumped out a flood of historical novels, producing his best work within the space of ten years: *Waverley* (1814), *The Antiquary* (1816), *Rob Roy* and *The Heart of Midlothian* (both 1818), as well as two notable novels set in England, *Ivanhoe* (1819) and *Kenilworth* (1821).

In 1825 Scott's money problems reached crisis proportions after an economic crash bankrupted his printing business. Attempting to pay his creditors in full, he found the quality of his writing deteriorating with its increased speed. His last years were plagued by illness; in 1832 he died at Abbotsford and was buried within the ruins of Dryburgh Abbey.

grounds for, among others, Sir Walter Scott and Field Marshal Haig, the infamous World War I commander. The night stairs, down which the monks stumbled in the early hours of the morning, survive in the south transept, and lead even today to the monks' dormitory. Leaving the church via the east processional door in the south aisle, with its dog-tooth decoration, you enter the cloisters, the highlight of which is the barrel-vaulted **Chapter House**, complete with low stone benches and blind interlaced arcading.

ARRIVAL AND INFORMATION

By bus Buses stop on Buccleuch St; just south of the abbey ruins.

Destinations Edinburgh (Mon–Sat every 30min, Sun hourly; 2hr 20min); Galashiels (Mon–Sat every 15–30min,

MELROSE AND AROUND

Sun hourly; 20min); Jedburgh (Mon–Sat 8 daily, Sun 1; 30min); Kelso (Mon–Sat 7 daily, Sun 5; 30min); Selkirk (Mon–Sat hourly, Sun 3; 20–30min).

ACCOMMODATION

Braidwood Buccleuch St, Melrose, TD6 9LB ☎01896 822488, ⍟braidwoodmelrose.co.uk. A comfortable, early Victorian cottage guesthouse ideally located between the town centre and its abbey. Cheaper rooms have private facilities in the hall; £5 extra gets you an en-suite upgrade. **£65**

Dunfermline House 3 Buccleuch St, Melrose, TD6 9LB ☎01896 822411, ⍟dunfermlinehouse.co.uk. Solid townhouse B&B with en-suite rooms that look on to the garden or across to the abbey. The decor might be a bit 1980s, but everything's clean and in good order. **£65**

★ **Old Bank House** 27 Buccleuch St, Melrose, TD6

9LB ☎01896 823712, ⍟oldbankhousemelrose.co.uk. Tastefully furnished Victorian B&B with charming hosts and three pristinely maintained and comfy en-suite rooms. The fine Scottish or vegetarian cooked breakfasts are served on Spode crockery in the former bank manager's office. **£70**

The Townhouse Market Square, Melrose, TD6 9PQ ☎01896 822645, ⍟thetownhousemelrose.co.uk. Small, smart hotel on the main square, with eleven stylish en-suite doubles with contemporary furnishings. To ensure a peaceful night's sleep, avoid the street-facing suites. Good bar/brasserie and restaurant, too (see below). **£138**

EATING AND DRINKING

★ **Abbey Fine Wines & The Cellar Coffee Shop** 17 Market Square, Melrose, TD6 9PL ☎01896 823224, ⍟abbeyfinewines.co.uk. This long-established wine merchant turns its hand to coffee and cakes in a good little café

at the back of their generously stocked shop. Light lunches are also served (from £6 for soup and bread) and sample wine bottles are always open – nice with their £9 cheese board. Mon–Sat 9.30am–4.30pm; shop closes 5pm.

Hoebridge Inn Hoebridge Rd East, Gattonside, 500yd past Melrose Abbey and across the old suspension bridge, TD6 9LZ ☎ 01896 823082, ⓦ thehoebridge. com. Once a bobbin mill, this family restaurant retains a timeless charm thanks to its deep rubble walls and simple furnishings. The focus on the seasonal menu is on French- and Italian-influenced fine dining using local produce. Mains include the likes of beef shin, pork ragù and home-made pappardelle (£17). April–Sept Wed–Sat 5.30–9.30pm.

Marmion's Brasserie Buccleuch St, Melrose, TD6 9LB ☎ 01896 822245, ⓦ marmionsbrasserie.co.uk. While this popular all-day bistro might have overdone it a bit with pine cladding, it still manages to conjure up a peppy atmosphere in the evening. The menu is strong on bistro classics – *moules frites* for £10.25; beer-battered haddock and chips £12.50 – but also has a vegetarian roast

cauliflower curry for £13. Mon–Sat 9am–9pm.

Ship Inn East Port, Melrose, TD6 9RA ☎ 01896 822190, ⓦ shipinnmelrose.co.uk. The liveliest pub in town, especially on Sat afternoons when the Melrose rugby team have played at home. While it could certainly do with some redecoration, its saving grace is the beer garden out back. Mon–Thurs 11am–11pm, Fri & Sat 11am–1am, Sun noon–11pm.

The Townhouse Market Square, Melrose, TD6 9PQ ☎ 01896 822645, ⓦ thetownhousemelrose.co.uk. This smart hotel (see above) has an excellent bar/brasserie and a restaurant; they share the same menu. French-style dishes made with Scottish produce include seared venison with confit of carrot and juniper *jus* for £17, and there's an early bird (pre-7pm) two-course menu for £17. Both daily noon–2pm & 6–9.30pm.

ENTERTAINMENT

The Wynd Buccleuch St, Melrose, TD6 9LD ☎ 01896 820028, ⓦ sites.google.com/site/thewyndtheatre. Melrose's very own pint-sized theatre, tucked away down

an alleyway north of the main square, hosts films, gigs and dramatic performances, plus special shows for young kids.

Kelso and around

KELSO, ten miles or so downstream from Melrose, grew up in the shadow of its now-ruined Benedictine **abbey**, once the richest and most powerful of the Border abbeys. Sadly, very little survives today, although at first sight it looks pretty impressive, with the heavy Norman west end of the abbey church almost entirely intact at the end of Abbey Row. Little remains otherwise, though it is possible to make out the two transepts and towers that gave the abbey the shape of a double cross, unique in Scotland.

Kelso town is centred on **The Square**, a large cobbled expanse presided over by the honey-hued Ionic columns, pediment and oversized clock bell tower of the elegant **Town Hall**. Leaving the Square along Roxburgh Street, take the alley down to the **Cobby Riverside Walk**, where a brief stroll leads to Floors Castle. En route, but hidden from view by the islet in the middle of the river, is the spot where the Teviot meets the Tweed. Known as The Junction, this section has long been famous for its **salmon fishing**, with permits booked sometimes years in advance.

Floors Castle

A mile northwest of Kelso, TD7 5SF · Castle Easter–Sept daily 10.30am–5pm, Oct Sat & Sun 10.30am–5pm; gardens & grounds daily 10.30am–4pm · Castle, gardens & grounds £11.50; garden & grounds only £6.50 · ☎ 01573 223333, ⓦ floorscastle.com · From the town centre, follow Roxburgh St to its northern end and bear left at the fork

Stand on Kelso's handsome bridge over the Tweed and you can easily make out the pepper-pot turrets and castellations of **Floors Castle**, a vast, pompous mansion to the northwest. The bulk of the building was designed by William Adam in the 1720s and, despite its Victorian modifications, the interior still demonstrates his uncluttered style. However, you won't see all that much of it – Floors is still home to the Duke of Roxburghe, with just ten rooms and a basement open to the public. The duke's imperious features can be seen in portraits around the house, where highlights include paintings by Matisse, Augustus John and Odilon Redon, and some fine Brussels and Gobelin tapestries. The surrounding grounds include a verdant walled garden, forest paths and a modern interpretation of a formal garden.

18

Mellerstain House

Six miles northwest of Kelso off the A6089, TD3 6LG · May–Sept Mon & Fri–Sun house 12.30–5pm, gardens 11am–5pm · £8.50; gardens only £5 · ☎ 01573 410225, ⓦ mellerstain.com

Mellerstain House represents the very best of the Adam family's work – William designed the wings in 1725, and his son Robert the castellated centre fifty years later. Robert's love of columns, roundels and friezes culminates in a stunning sequence of plaster-moulded, pastel-shaded ceilings: the **library** is the high point for admirers of his work, with four unusual, long panels in plaster relief of classical scenes that relegate the books to second place. The art collection, which includes works by Constable, Gainsborough, Ramsay and Veronese, is also noteworthy. After a visit you can wander the formal Edwardian gardens, which slope down to the lake.

ARRIVAL AND INFORMATION KELSO

By bus Buses arrive and depart from Woodmarket, a brief walk from The Square.
Destinations Edinburgh (Mon–Sat every 2hr, Sun 2; 2hr); Melrose (Mon–Sat 7 daily, Sun 5; 30min).

Tourist office Town House, The Square (July & Aug Mon–Sat 10am–5pm; Sept & Oct Mon–Sat 10am–3.30pm; ☎ 01573 221119).

ACCOMMODATION AND EATING

★ **Cobbles Inn** 7 Bowmont St, TD5 7JH ☎ 01573 223548, ⓦ thecobbleskelso.co.uk. One of Scotland's eight best real ale pubs, according to CAMRA. This place has a formidable reputation locally, not just for beer, supplied by the proprietor's own brewery, Tempest – try the Jalepeño IPA! – but also for its top-notch food. With an emphasis on red meat and game, the menu uses regional country produce in dishes like chargrilled lamb belly, shank and piperade. Mains from £10; four-course gourmet menu

£45. Mon–Thurs 11.30am–11pm, Fri & Sat 11am–late, Sun noon–11pm; kitchen daily noon–2.30pm & 7.45–9pm.
The Old Priory Woodmarket, TD5 7JF ☎ 01573 223030, ⓦ theoldpriorykelso.com. A tasteful Georgian townhouse, just off The Square, with a very pretty garden. Rooms are spacious and light, with lovely wooden furniture, and there's a shared sitting room where guests are free to relax. **£85**

Selkirk and around

The royal burgh of **SELKIRK** lies just five miles southwest of Melrose. The old town sits high up above the river of Ettrick Water; down by the riverside, the imposing grey-stone woollen mills are mostly boarded up now, an eerie reminder of a once prosperous era. Situated on the edge of some lovely countryside, the town serves as the gateway to the picturesque, sparsely populated valleys to the west.

At the centre of Selkirk you'll find the tiny **Market Square**, overlooked by a statue of Sir Walter Scott; the former Town House, now dubbed **Sir Walter Scott's Courtroom** (March–Sept Mon–Fri 10am–4pm, Sat 11am–3pm; Oct Mon–Sat noon–3pm; free), is where he served as sheriff for 33 years. Just off Market Square to the south is **Halliwell's House Museum** (April–Oct Mon–Sat 11am–4pm, Sun noon–3pm; free), an old-style hardware shop with an informative exhibit on the industrialization of the Tweed Valley.

Bowhill House

Three miles west of Selkirk off the A708, TD7 5ET · **House** Guided tours (1hr 15min) every 30min 12.30–3pm: July daily, also on selected weekends and bank hols (see website) · £10, including country estate · **Country estate** April–June Tues–Fri 10am–4pm, Sat & Sun 10am–5pm; July & Aug daily 10am–5pm; Sept Mon & Fri 10am–4pm, Sat & Sun 10am–5pm · £4.50, £10 including house · ☎ 01750 22204, ⓦ bowhillhouse.co.uk · Walk (1hr) from Selkirk along the north bank of Ettrick Water and cross over General's Bridge and into the estate, or take a taxi from Selkirk (£10)

A pleasant three-mile walk from Selkirk, **Bowhill House** is the property of the seriously wealthy Duke of Buccleuch. Beyond the grandiose mid-nineteenth-century mansion's facade of dark whinstone is an outstanding collection of French antiques and European **paintings**: in the dining room, for example, are portraits by Reynolds and Gainsborough, and a Canaletto cityscape, while the drawing room features Boulle furniture, Meissen tableware, paintings by Ruysdael, Leandro Bassano and Claude Lorraine, and two more family portraits by Reynolds. Look out also for the Scott Room, which features a splendid portrait of Sir Walter by Henry Raeburn, and the Duke of Monmouth's execution shirt.

The wooded hills of Bowhill's **country estate** are crisscrossed by scenic footpaths and cycle trails. The woods also shelter the 72-seat **Bowhill Theatre**, in the house's former game larder, which hosts the occasional production.

18

ARRIVAL AND INFORMATION
SELKIRK

By bus Buses arrive in the Market Square from Edinburgh (hourly; 1hr 45min) and Melrose (Mon–Sat hourly, Sun 5; 20min).

Tourist office Halliwell's House, off Market Square (April–Oct Mon–Sat 11am–4pm, Sun noon–3pm; ☎01750 20054).

ACCOMMODATION

Heatherlie House Hotel Heatherlie Park, TD7 5AL ☎01750 721200. A large Victorian mansion set within wooded grounds on the west side of Selkirk. Inside, the hotel is tastefully presented with six spacious en-suite rooms; the best have bay windows overlooking the garden. **£69**

Peebles and around

Fast, wide, tree-lined and fringed with grassy banks, the Tweed looks at its best at **PEEBLES**, a handsome royal burgh that sits on the north bank, fifteen miles northwest of Selkirk. The town itself has a genteel, relaxed air, its wide, handsome High Street bordered by houses in a medley of architectural styles, mostly dating from Victorian times, that accommodate a profusion of independent retailers, tearooms and restaurants.

Tweedale Museum & Gallery

High St, EH45 8AJ • Mon–Fri 10.30am–12.30pm & 1–4pm, Sat 9.30am–12.30pm • Free • ☎01721 724820

Halfway down the High Street is the **Tweedale Museum & Gallery**, stuffed with casts of the world's most famous sculptures. It also features two handsome friezes: one a copy of the Elgin marbles taken from the Parthenon; the other of the **Triumph of Alexander**, originally cast in 1812 to honour Napoleon.

Traquair House

Seven miles southeast of Peebles on the B7062, EH44 6PW • April–Sept daily 11am–5pm; Oct daily 11am–4pm; Nov Sat & Sun 11am–3pm • £8.80, grounds only £4.50 • ☎01896 830323, ☺traquair.co.uk • The regular Peebles to Melrose bus stops in Innerleithen, from where it's a 10min signposted walk south to Traquair

The Maxwell Stuarts have lived in **Traquair House** since 1491, making it the oldest continuously inhabited house in Scotland. The whitewashed facade is strikingly handsome, with narrow windows and trim turrets surrounding the tiniest of front doors – in other words it's a welcome change from other grandiose stately homes. Inside, you can see original vaulted cellars, where locals once hid their cattle from raiders; the twisting main staircase and the earlier medieval version, later a secret escape route for persecuted Catholics; a carefully camouflaged priest's hole; and even

---

MOUNTAIN BIKING IN GLENTRESS

One of seven forest biking centres in southern Scotland – known collectively as the 7 Stanes (☺7stanesmountainbiking.com) – **Glentress Forest**, two miles east of Peebles on the A72, has some of the best mountain biking in Scotland. There are numerous carefully crafted purpose-built trails, colour-coded according to difficulty, and a helpful bike rental centre, Alpine Bikes (from £25/day; ☎01721 724522, ☺tweedvalleybikehire.com).

a **priest's room** where a string of resident chaplains lived in hiding. In the **museum room** there is a wealth of treasures, including a fine example of a Jacobite Amen glass, a rosary and crucifix owned by Mary, Queen of Scots, and the cloak worn by the Earl of Nithsdale during his dramatic escape from the Tower of London.

Spare time for the surrounding **grounds**, where you'll find a **hedge maze**, several craft workshops and the **Traquair House Brewery**, which claims to be the only British brewery that still ferments totally in oak. There's a café serving snacks in an estate cottage on the redundant avenue that leads to the locked **Bear Gates**; Bonnie Prince Charlie left the house through these gates, and the then-owner promised to keep them locked till a Stuart should ascend the throne.

ARRIVAL AND INFORMATION
PEEBLES AND AROUND

By bus Buses, which arrive in the car park just north of the eastern end of the main shopping street, include services from Edinburgh (Mon–Sat every 30min, Sun hourly; 1hr) and Melrose (Mon–Sat every 30min, 1hr 15min).

Tourist office 23 High St (July & Aug Mon–Sat 9am–5.30pm, Sun 11am–4pm; Sept–June Mon–Sat 9am–5pm, Sun 11am–4pm; ☎ 01721 728095).

ACCOMMODATION, EATING AND DRINKING

★ **Bridge Inn** 72 Port Brae, Peebles, EH45 8AW ☎ 01721 720589. With its attractive mock-Tudor, dormer frontage, this traditional pub cuts a fine figure in the Peebles skyline. Inside, its classic decor and cosy seating arrangements complement the wide range of real ales and whiskies on offer. There's a sunny terrace out back, looking on to the river. Mon–Wed 11am–midnight, Thurs–Sat 11am–1am, Sun noon–midnight.

Glentress Forest Lodges The Peel Gateway, entrance to Glentress, 2 miles east of Peebles on the A72, EH45 8NA ☎ 01721 721007, ⓦ glentressforestlodges.co.uk. Simple but attractive wooden huts (sleeping five) arranged in clusters, with basic accommodation; benches to sit/sleep on, a door and a window. There's also a communal kitchen

and a generous firewood supply. **£48**

★ **Leaven Deli** 6 Newby Court, Peebles, EH45 8AL ☎ 01721 721088, ⓦ leavendelipeebles.wix.com/leavendeli. Hidden in a tiny courtyard near the tourist office, this not-for-profit social enterprise offers fresh loaves, artisan cheeses and a few deli treats as well as light lunches and coffees that can be enjoyed in the suntrap outside. Tues–Sat 9am–4pm.

Traquair 7 miles southeast of Peebles on the B7062, EH44 6PW ☎ 01896 830323, ⓦ traquair.co.uk. Most visitors come to Traquair as a day-trip from Peebles (see page 797), but if you're really taken by the place, you can stay in one of its three double guest rooms, exquisitely decked out with antiques and four-posters. **£190**

Jedburgh

JEDBURGH nestles in the lush valley of the Jed Water, ten miles southeast of Melrose. During the interminable Anglo-Scottish Wars, this was the quintessential frontier town, a heavily garrisoned royal burgh incorporating a mighty castle and abbey. Though the castle was destroyed by the Scots in 1409 to keep it out of the hands of the English, the abbey survived, albeit in ruins. Today, Jedburgh is the first place of any size that you come to on the A68, having crossed over Carter Bar from England, and as such gets quite a bit of passing tourist trade.

Jedburgh Abbey

Abbey Bridge End, TD8 6JQ • Daily: April–Sept 9.30am–5.30pm; Oct–March 10am–4pm • £6; HES • ☎ 01835 863925, ⓦ historicenvironment.scot/visit-a-place/places/jedburgh-abbey

Founded in the twelfth century as an Augustinian priory, **Jedburgh Abbey** is the best preserved of all the Border abbeys, its vast church towering over a sloping site right in the centre of town beside the Jed Water. Entry is through the **visitor centre** at the bottom of the hill, where you can view Jedburgh's most treasured archeological find, the **Jedburgh Comb**, carved around 1100 from walrus ivory and decorated with a griffin and a dragon. Enter the **Abbey Church** itself via the west door to fully appreciate the three-storey nave's perfectly proportioned parade of columns and arches.

Jedburgh Castle Jail

Castlegate, TD8 6AS · Easter–Oct Mon–Sat 10am–4.30pm, Sun 1–4pm · Free · ☎ 01835 864750

At the top of Castlegate stands **Jedburgh Castle Jail**, an impressive castellated nineteenth-century pile built on the site of the old royal castle. As well as detailed information about Jedburgh's history, there's a fascinating insight into conditions in jail, deportation, crime and punishment. The cells themselves are, for the period, remarkably comfortable, reflecting the influence of reformer John Howard.

Mary, Queen of Scots' Visitor Centre

Queen St, TD8 6EN · March–Nov Mon–Sat 10am–4.30pm, Sun noon–4.30pm · Free · ☎ 01835 863331

Located in a sixteenth century tower house, the **Mary, Queen of Scots' Visitor Centre** offers a rather cursory insight into Mary's complex life through its assortment of paintings, textiles and associated objects including Mary's own death mask.

18

ARRIVAL AND INFORMATION   JEDBURGH

By bus Buses pick up and drop off at Canongate just east of the Market Place.
Destinations Edinburgh (Mon–Sat every 2hr, Sun 4; 1hr 50min); Melrose (Mon–Sat every 2hr, Sun 1; 30min).

Tourist office Murray's Green (April–June, Sept & Oct Mon–Sat 9am–5pm, Sun 10am–4pm; July & Aug Mon–Sat 9am–5.30pm, Sun 10am–5pm; Nov–March Mon–Sat 10am–4pm; ☎ 01835 863170).

ACCOMMODATION AND EATING

Border Meringues Unit 1, Old Station Yard, Edinburgh Rd, TD8 6EE ☎ 01835 863383, ⓦ bordermeringues.com. An unlikely setting for a café/cake shop in an anonymous industrial estate building on the northern outskirts of town, but locals go out of their way for this place. There are all manner of cakes and tray bakes here, starting at £2. Mon–Fri 9am–4pm, Sat 10am–4pm.

★ **The Capon Tree Town House** 61 High St, TD8 6DQ ☎ 01835 869596, ⓦ thecapontree.com. Part fine dining restaurant, part wine bar, this place conjures up the best plates in town – the Dijon-crusted lamb with mint pea purée and haggis bonbons (£26.50) is typical. Mon–Fri 2–11pm, Sat noon–late; kitchen Mon–Sat 7–9.30pm.

Meadhon House 48 Castlegate, TD8 6BB ☎ 01835 862504, ⓦ meadhon.co.uk. Pronounced "mawn", this is the finest of several B&Bs among Castlegate's row of seventeenth-century houses, with tasteful en-suite rooms overlooking the town. **£72**

Dumfries and Galloway

The southwest corner of Scotland, **Dumfries and Galloway** has stately homes, deserted hills and ruined abbeys to compete with the best of the Borders. It also has the **Solway coast**, a long, indented coastline of sheltered sandy coves that's been dubbed the "Scottish Riviera" – it's certainly Scotland's warmest, southernmost stretch of coastline.

Dumfries is the largest town in the region, and only really a must for those on the **Robert Burns** trail. Some 27 miles southwest lies enticing **Kirkcudbright**, once a bustling port thronged with sailing ships, later an artists' retreat, and now a tranquil, well-preserved little town. Contrasting with the essentially gentle landscape of the Solway coast is the brooding presence of the **Galloway Hills** to the north, their beautiful moors, mountains, lakes and rivers centred on the **Galloway Forest Park**, a hillwalking and mountain-biking paradise.

Dumfries

On the wide banks of the River Nith a short way inland from the Solway Firth, **DUMFRIES** is the largest town in southwest Scotland. Long known as the "Queen of the South" (as is its football club), the town flourished as a medieval seaport and trading centre. Enough remains of the original, warm red sandstone buildings to distinguish Dumfries from other towns in the southwest, though its main appeal is its associations with **Robert Burns** (see page 801).

Dumfries Museum

Rotchell Rd, DG2 7SW• April–Sept Tues–Sat 10am–1pm & 2–5pm • Free; camera obscura £3 • ☎ 01387 253374

On the hill above the Robert Burns Centre (see page 801) the **Dumfries Museum** affords great views over the town. The museum is housed partly in an eighteenth-century windmill, which was converted into the town's observatory in the 1830s, and features the world's oldest working **camera obscura** on its top floor. On the floors below the focus is on local history and prehistory with a good collection of tools and weaponry from the region's earliest peoples as well as some nice carved masonry from the early Christians.

Old Bridge House Museum

Mill Rd, DG2 7BE • April–Sept Mon–Sat 10am–5pm, Sun 2–5pm • Free • ☎ 01387 256904

Devorgilla Bridge, built in 1431, is one of the oldest bridges in Scotland. Attached to its southwestern end is Dumfries's oldest house, built in 1660 and now home to the tiny, quirky **Old Bridge House Museum**. Now stuffed full of Victorian bric-a-brac, including a teeth-chattering range of dental gear, the house was once an inn, which Burns would undoubtedly have visited.

ARRIVAL AND INFORMATION   DUMFRIES

By train The station is a 5min walk northeast of the town centre.
Destinations Carlisle (Mon–Sat hourly, Sun 5; 40min); Glasgow Central (Mon–Sat hourly, Sun 2; 1hr 45min).
By bus Buses stop at Whitesands beside the River Nith.
Destinations Castle Douglas (Mon–Sat hourly, Sun 6; 45min); Edinburgh (Mon–Sat 6 daily, Sun 2; 2hr 50min);

Kirkcudbright (Mon–Sat hourly, Sun 2; 1hr 40min); New Abbey (Mon–Sat 12 daily, Sun 3; 15min); Newton Stewart (Mon–Sat hourly, Sun 4; 1hr 30min).
Tourist office 64 Whitesands (April–Oct Mon–Sat 9.30am–5pm, Sun 11am–4pm; Nov–March Mon–Sat 9.30am–4.30pm; ☎ 01387 253862).

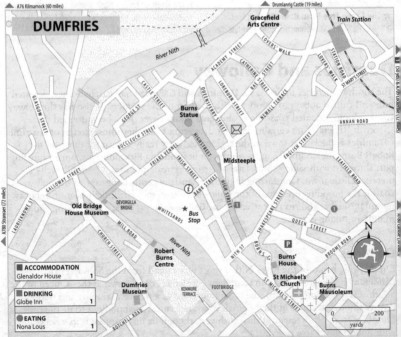

DUMFRIES

■ ACCOMMODATION	
Glenaldor House	1

■ DRINKING	
Globe Inn	1

● EATING	
Nona Lous	1

ON THE BURNS TRAIL IN DUMFRIES

Robert Burns, posthumously titled Scotland's National Poet, spent the last five years (1791–96) of his short life in Dumfries, working as an excise man by day and fraternizing at the *Globe Inn* (see below) by night. Today Dumfries is a popular tourist destination for fans of the poet, thanks to its high concentration of Burns sights.

Burns' House Burns St, DG1 2PS ☎01387 255297. Simple sandstone building where the poet died of rheumatic heart disease in 1796, a few days before the birth of his youngest son, Maxwell. Inside, one of the bedroom windows bears his signature, scratched with his diamond ring. Free. April–Sept Mon–Sat 10am–5pm, Sun 2–5pm; Oct–March Tues–Sat 10am–1pm & 2–5pm.

Burns Statue Northern end of High St. Presiding over a roundabout, this sentimental piece of Victorian frippery in white Carrara marble features the great man holding a posy. His faithful hound, Luath, lies curled around his feet.

Midsteeple High St, EH1 2BH. Burns' body lay in state here in Dumfries' most singular building, a wonky hotchpotch of a place built in 1707 to fulfil the multiple functions of prison, clock tower, courthouse and arsenal.

Robert Burns Centre (**RBC**) Mill Rd, DG2 7BE ☎01387 264808, ⓦrbcft.co.uk. A free exhibition on the poet's years in Dumfries; in fact, though, perhaps the most interesting item on display is the scale model of the town from the 1790s. There's a good audiovisual presentation on Burns in the small cinema, which also shows a mixture of Hollywood, children's and arthouse films (Tues–Sat). April–Sept Mon–Sat 10am–5pm, Sun 2–5pm; Oct–March Tues–Sat 10am–1pm & 2–5pm.

St Michael's Parish Church St Michael's St, DG1 2PR ⓦstmichaelschurchdumfries.org. Originally buried in a simple grave near St Michael's Church, in 1815 Burns was dug up and moved across the graveyard to a purpose-built mausoleum, a Neoclassical eyesore that houses a statue of him being accosted by the Poetic Muse. Daily 10am–4pm.

18

ACCOMMODATION

Glenaldor House 5 Victoria Terrace, DG1 1NL ☎01387 264248, ⓦglenaldorhouse.co.uk; map p.800. A light and bright Victorian house near the station, with four comfortably spacious en-suite bedrooms. Wake up to a full Scottish breakfast, made with local produce; there's also a wide choice from pastries to porridge. **£75**

EATING

Nona Lous Brooke St, DG1 2JL ☎07989 031491; map p.800. Located in a converted primary school among a cluster of arts and beauty-related businesses, this contemporary tearoom bakes exceedingly attractive cakes (around £2 a slice) – try the colourful seven-layer rainbow cake. Old crockery and knitted teapot- and cup-cosies give the place a personal touch. Light breakfasts and lunches, too. Mon–Wed & Sat 10am–4pm, Thurs 10am–5pm, Fri 10am–4pm.

DRINKING

★**Globe Inn** 56 High St, DG1 2JA ☎01387 252335, ⓦglobeinndumfries.co.uk; map p.800. If you're on Burns's trail (see above), make sure you duck down the alleyway to the seventeenth-century *Globe Inn*, just beyond the ornate red and gold Victorian fountain. Burns had a fling with Annie Park, a barmaid in this pub, and the resultant child was taken into the Burns household by his long-suffering wife, Jean Armour. Beyond the main bar you can enter the beautifully panelled snug and sit in the very chair used by the poet. Although if you do, by tradition, you'll be expected to recite a Burns poem or else buy everyone in the bar a drink. Mon–Wed 10am–11pm, Thurs–Sat 10am–midnight, Sun noon–midnight.

Around Dumfries

Notable sights around Dumfries include grand **Drumlanrig Castle** with its fine paintings, moated **Caerlaverock** and the picturesque ruins of thirteenth-century **Sweetheart Abbey**; the **Caerlaverock Wetland Centre** is a good destination for twitchers.

18

Drumlanrig Castle

Eighteen miles north of Dumfries, DG3 4AQ • **House** Guided tours only (1hr), every 20min: July & Aug daily 11am–4pm; occasional weekends throughout the year (check website) • £10 • **Country park** April–Sept daily 10am–5pm • £6 • ☎ 01848 331555, ⓦ drumlanrigcastle.co.uk • Bus #102 from Dumfries (Mon–Sat 2 daily, Sun 1; 20min) runs to Drumlanrig along the A76

Drumlanrig Castle is not a castle at all, but the grandiose stately home of the Duke of Buccleuch and Queensberry. Approached by an impressive driveway that sweeps along an avenue of lime trees, the seventeenth-century sandstone "Pink Palace" bristles with cupolas, turrets and towers. The highlights of the richly furnished interior are the **paintings** by the great masters, most notably Rembrandt, van Dyck, Holbein and Gainsborough. As well as the house, Drumlanrig has a host of other attractions, including formal **gardens** and a forested **country park**.

Caerlaverock Castle

Caerlaverock, 8 miles southeast of Dumfries, DG1 4RU • Daily: April–Sept 9.30am–5.30pm; Oct–March 10am–4pm • £6; HES • ☎ 01387 770244, ⓦ historicenvironment.scot/visit-a-place/places/caerlaverock-castle • Bus #6A from Dumfries (Mon–Sat 3 daily, Sun 2; 30min) runs to Caerlaverock along the B725

Caerlaverock Castle is a picture-perfect, thirteenth century ruined castle, moated, built from rich local red sandstone, triangular in layout and with a mighty double-towered gatehouse. The most surprising addition, however, lies inside, where you're confronted by the ornate Renaissance facade of the **Nithsdale Lodging**, erected in the 1630s by the first earl of Nithsdale. The decorated tympana above the windows feature lively mythological and heraldic scenes. Sadly, six years later Nithsdale and his garrison were forced to surrender after a thirteen-week siege and bombardment by the Covenanters, who wrecked the place. It was never inhabited again.

Caerlaverock Wildlife and Wetlands Trust Centre

Eastpark Farm, Caerlaverock, 8 miles southeast of Dumfries, DG1 4RS • Daily 10am–5pm • £8.45 • ☎ 01387 770200, ⓦ wwt.org.uk • Bus #6A from Dumfries to Caerlaverock (Mon–Sat 3 daily, Sun 2; 30min) runs past the start of the 2-mile lane leading off the B725 to the wetlands

One mile east, as the crow flies, of Caerlaverock Castle, the **Caerlaverock Wildfowl and Wetlands Trust Centre** spreads across 1400 acres of protected salt marsh and mud flat edging the Solway Firth,. Famous for the 25,000 or so Svalbard barnacle geese that winter here between September and April, it also has wild whooper swans and regular osprey sightings.

Sweetheart Abbey

Main St, New Abbey, DG2 8BU • April–Sept daily 9.30am–5.30pm; Oct daily 10am–4pm; Nov–March Mon–Wed, Sat & Sun 10am–4pm • £5; HES • ☎ 01387 850397, ⓦ historicenvironment.scot/visit-a-place/places/sweetheart-abbey • From Dumfries, bus #372 runs to New Abbey (Mon–Sat 12 daily, Sun 3; 15min), stopping outside the post office

Sweetheart Abbey, lying romantically ruined to the east of the village of **NEW ABBEY**, takes its name from its founder, Devorgilla de Balliol, who carried the embalmed heart of her husband, John Balliol (of Oxford college fame) for the last 22 years of her life – she is buried with the casket, in the presbytery. The last of the Cistercian abbeys to be founded in Scotland – in 1273 – Sweetheart is dominated by the red sandstone abbey church, which remains intact, albeit minus its roof. Its grassy nave is flanked by giant compound piers supporting early Gothic arches, and above them a triforium. The other great survivor is the precinct wall, a massive structure made from rough granite boulders.

ACCOMMODATION AND EATING
AROUND DUMFRIES

Abbey Cottage Tearoom 26 Main St, New Abbey, DG2 8BY ☎ 01387 850377, ⓦ abbeycottagetearoom.com. Enjoying an unrivalled view over Sweetheart Abbey, this tearoom is renowned for its coffee, teas and home-made cakes. The meals are excellent too, exemplified by the formidable ploughman's lunch at £7.65. Mid-Feb to Oct 10am–5pm; Nov to mid-Dec Wed–Sun 11am–4pm.

Caerlaverock Wildfowl and Wetlands Trust (WWT) Centre Eastpark Farm, Caerlaverock, DG1 4RS ☎ 01387 770200, ⓦ wwt.org.uk. Large parties can rent the centre's homely five bedroom farmhouse, which has a fantastic observation tower and appropriately proportioned living space. £180

Colvend coast

The **Colvend coast**, twenty miles or so southwest of Dumfries, is one of the finest stretches of coastline along the so-called "Scottish Riviera". The best approach is via the A710, which heads south through New Abbey before cutting across a handsome landscape of rolling farmland to **ROCKCLIFFE**, a beguiling little place of comfortable villas around a rocky sand-and-shell bay, sheltered beneath wooded hills.

For vehicles, Rockcliffe is a dead end, but it's the start of a pleasant thirty-minute walk along the Jubilee Path to neighbouring **KIPPFORD** a tiny, lively yachting centre strung out along the east bank of the Urr estuary. At low tide you can walk over the Rough Firth causeway from the shore below across the mud flats to **Rough Island**, a humpy twenty-acre bird sanctuary owned by the National Trust for Scotland – it's out of bounds in May and June during the nesting season.

ARRIVAL AND GETTING AROUND   COLVEND COAST

By bus One of the more useful bus services in the area is the frequent #372, which links Dumfries with Sandyhills (Mon–Sat 8 daily, Sun 3; 55min) and New Abbey (Mon–

Sat 11 daily, Sun 3; 14min). The #372A is also handy, continuing on from Sandyhills to Kippford and Rockcliffe (Mon–Sat 5 daily, Sun 3; 20–30min).

ACCOMMODATION AND EATING

Anchor Hotel Kippford, DG5 4LN ☎ 01556 620205, ⓦ anchorkippford.co.uk. Right on Kippford's waterfront, the popular *Anchor* is a good reward for the gentle stroll required to get here from Rockcliffe. The place serves local fish (mains around £11) and good ale; there's also a real fire in winter. Daily 11am–midnight; kitchen Mon–Thurs noon–2pm & 6–8pm, Fri noon–2pm & 5.30–8.30pm, Sat & Sun noon–8.30pm.

Castle Point Caravan Site Just south of Rockcliffe, DG5 4QL ☎ 01556 630248, ⓦ castlepointcc.com. Secluded

campsite, with free wi-fi, just south of Rockcliffe village and a stone's throw from the seashore (there are three sandy beaches within walking distance). Closed mid-Oct to late March. **£25**

Millbrae House Rockcliffe, DG5 4QG ☎ 01556 630217, ⓦ millbraehouse.co.uk. Excellent B&B in a whitewashed cottage near the bay. Rooms are bright and elegantly furnished and breakfast is served in the conservatory. A couple of self-catering options are also available. **£78**

Castle Douglas and around

Most folk come to **CASTLE DOUGLAS**, eighteen miles southwest of Dumfries, in order to visit the nearby attractions of **Threave Garden** and **Threave Castle**. A small, low-rise town of painted cottages lining grid-like streets, with a relatively vibrant high street and its own pint sized loch (Carlingwark), Castle Douglas is pleasant for an evening stroll.

Threave Garden

1.5 miles southwest of Castle Douglas, DG7 1RX • Daily: Jan & Feb 11am–3pm; March–Oct 10am–5pm; Nov & Dec 10am–4pm • £7.50; NTS • ☎ 01556 502575, ⓦ nts.org.uk/Visit/Threave

Threave Garden is a pleasant mile or so's walk southwest of Castle Douglas along the shores of Loch Carlingwark. The garden features a magnificent spread of flowers and woodland, sixty acres divided into more than a dozen areas from the bright, old-fashioned blooms of the Rose Garden to the brilliant banks of rhododendrons in the Woodland Garden. In springtime, thousands of visitors turn up for the flowering of more than two hundred types of daffodil.

Threave Castle

Around 2 miles west of Castle Douglas, DG7 1TJ • Daily: April–Sept 10am–4.30pm; Oct 10.30am–3.30pm • £5, including boat fare; HES • ☎ 07711 223101, ⓦ historicenvironment.scot/visit-a-place/places/threave-castle • From Castle Douglas the gardens are a very pleasant 30min walk around Carlingwark Loch from the southern edge of town

A visit to **Threave Castle** begins with a ten-minute walk from the car park to the River Dee, where you ring a brass bell for the boat to take you over to the flat and grassy island on which the stern-looking castle stands.

18

Built in around 1370 for one of the Black Douglases, Archibald the Grim, first Lord of Galloway and third Earl of Douglas, the fortress was among the first of its kind, a sturdy, rectangular structure completed shortly after the War of Independence. The rickety curtain wall to the south and east is all that remains of the **artillery fortifications**, hurriedly constructed in the 1450s by the ninth earl in a desperate – and unsuccessful – attempt to defend the castle against James II's new-fangled cannon. The castle was partially dismantled in the 1640s, but enough remains of the interior to make out its general plan.

ARRIVAL AND INFORMATION   CASTLE DOUGLAS

By bus Buses stop on the main shopping street, King St. Destinations Dumfries (Mon–Sat hourly, Sun 6; 45min); Kirkcudbright (Mon–Sat hourly, Sun 6; 20min).

Tourist office King St (April–June Mon–Sat 10am–5pm, Sun 11am–3pm; July & Aug Mon–Sat 9.30am–6pm, Sun 10am–4pm; Sept & Oct Mon–Sat 10am–5pm; ☎ 01556 502611).

ACCOMMODATION AND EATING

Designs Gallery and Café 179 King St, DG7 1DZ ☎ 01556 504552. Capacious gallery, craft shop and café with tables spilling out onto a delightful walled garden out back. Light lunches, including salads and chicken wraps and a wide range of home baking, cost around £7. Mon–Sat 9.30am–5pm.

Lochside Caravan Site Loch Carlingwark, DG7 1EZ ☎ 07824 528467. Immaculate waterside campsite on the southern fringe of Castle Douglas that welcomes caravans (pitches £24) and tents. Facilities include electrical hookup, play areas, a putting green, boat rental and free fishing in the loch. **£11.50**

Kirkcudbright

KIRKCUDBRIGHT – pronounced "kir-coo-bree" – hugging the muddy banks of the River Dee ten miles southwest of Castle Douglas, is the only major town along the Solway coast to have retained a working harbour. In addition, it has a ruined **castle** and an attractive town centre, a charming medley of simple two-storey cottages and medieval pends, Georgian villas and Victorian townhouses, all brightly painted.

MacLellan's Castle

Castle St, DG6 4JD • Daily: April–Sept 9.30am–5.30pm; Oct 10am–4pm • £4; HES • ☎ 01557 331856, ⓦ historicenvironment.scot/visit-a-place/places/maclellan-s-castle

The most surprising sight in Kirkcudbright is **MacLellan's Castle**, a pink-flecked sixteenth-century tower house sitting at one end of the high street by the harbourside. Part fortified keep and part spacious mansion, the castle was built in the 1570s for the then Provost of Kirkcudbright, Sir Thomas MacLellan of Bombie. Its interior is well preserved, from the kitchen (complete with bread oven) to the spyhole known as the "**laird's lug**", behind the fireplace of the Great Hall.

Broughton House

12 High St, DG6 4JX • Daily: Feb & March (garden only) 11am–4pm; April–Oct noon–5pm • Feb & March entry by donation; April–Oct £6.50; NTS • ☎ 01557 330437, ⓦ nts.org.uk/Visit/Broughton-House

Broughton House, a smart Georgian townhouse and former home of the artist **Edward Hornel** (1863–1933), stands on the L-shaped High Street, near the castle. Hornel, an important member of the late nineteenth-century Scottish art scene, spent his childhood a few doors down the street, and returned in 1900 to establish an artists' colony with some of the "Glasgow Boys" (see page 823). At the back of the house Hornel added a studio and a vast gallery, now filled with the mannered, vibrant paintings of girls at play that he churned out in the latter part of his career. Hornel's trip to Japan in 1893 imbued him with a lifelong affection for the country, and his densely packed, rambling **gardens** have a strong Japanese influence.

GALLOWAY FOREST PARK

Galloway Forest Park (ⓦscotland.forestry.gov.uk) is Britain's largest forest park, with a spectacularly varied landscape of mountain peaks, lochs, coast and moorland, cut through by the Southern Uplands Way. It has **visitor centres** (generally March–Oct daily 10.30am–4.30pm) at Clatteringshaws Loch, Glentrool and Kirroughtree. Each has a tearoom, several waymarked walks and information on activities and events. The only **tarmacked road** to cross the park is the desolate twenty-mile stretch of the A712 between Newton Stewart and New Galloway, known as the **Queen's Way**.

Both Glentrool and Kirroughtree visitor centres have **mountain bike trails**, which form part of southern Scotland's outstanding mountain-biking facilities, known as the 7 Stanes (ⓦ7stanesmountainbiking.com). Of the two, Kirroughtree, three miles east of the town of Newton Stewart, is by far the most varied and fun, with lots of exciting single track trails for all abilities and good bike-rental facilities at The Break Pad in the visitor centre (rental from £17; ☏01671 401303, ⓦthebreakpad.com).

About seven miles east of Newton Stewart, at the **Grey Mare's Tail Bridge**, various **hiking trails** delve into the pine forests beside the tarmacked road, crossing gorges, waterfalls and burns. **Clatteringshaws Loch**, meanwhile, a reservoir surrounded by pine forest at the eastern side of the park, has a fourteen-mile footpath running right around it. Serious hikers should head for **Glentrool**, at the western edge of the park, about ten miles north of Newton Stewart, where a narrow lane twists the five miles over to Loch Trool.

The entire park has been designated a "dark sky park", with a couple of panoramic spots reserved for **stargazing** (ⓦforestry.gov.uk/darkskygalloway).

18

Tolbooth Art Centre

High St, DG6 4JL • Mid-April to Sept Mon–Sat 11am–4pm • Free • ☏01557 331556

For background information on Kirkcudbright, visit the imposing, church-like **Tolbooth**, with its stone-built clock tower and spire. Built in the 1620s, the building now houses the **Tolbooth Art Centre**, which has a small display of paintings including S.J. Peploe's Colourist view of the Tolbooth as well as a contemporary art and craft gallery on the top floor and a small café.

ARRIVAL AND INFORMATION
KIRKCUDBRIGHT

By bus Buses to and from Dumfries (Mon–Sat hourly, Sun 2; 1hr 40min) pull up in the harbour car park, next to the tourist office.

Tourist office Harbour Square (Feb, March & Nov Mon–Sat 11am–4pm; April–June & Sept–Oct Mon–Sat 10am–5pm Sun 11am–3pm; July & Aug Mon–Sat 9.30am–6pm, Sun 10am–5pm; ☏01557 330494, ⓦkirkcudbright.co.uk).

ACCOMMODATION AND EATING

Baytree House 110 High St, DG6 4JQ ☏01557 330824, ⓦbaytreekirkcudbright.co.uk. An old-fashioned Georgian B&B with four spacious rooms and a guests' drawing room. There's also a self-catering garden studio for two with its own conservatory and garden (minimum stay usually three days). Double __£88__, studio __£82__

Castle Restaurant 5 Castle St ☏01557 330569, DG6 4JA ⓦthecastlerestaurant.net. An intimate contribution to Kirkcudbright's small fine dining scene, offering Scots-French cuisine in tasteful surroundings overlooking the castle. The menu might include smoked duck two ways, pairing breast meat with smoked apple duck pâté and honey; three-course menus £20. Mon–Sat 6–9pm.

Mulberries Coffee Shop and Chocolatiers 11 St Cuthbert St, DG6 4DJ ☏01557 330961. The town's finest coffee, cakes and chocolates are served in this cosy little café near the harbour car park. The cream tea for £5 offers excellent quality and value, and coffee comes with free refills. Mon–Thurs 10am–6pm, Fri & Sat 10am–7pm, Sun 11am–6pm.

Wigtown

WIGTOWN, seven miles south of Newton Stewart, is a tiny place with a remarkable main square, a vast, triangular affair laid out as it was in medieval times. Overlooking and dominating the square and its central bowling green are the gargantuan **County**

Buildings, built in French Gothic style. Wigtown styles itself as "Scotland's national book town", with a highly rated **literary festival** (ⓦwigtownbookfestival.com) in late September and more than a dozen **bookshops** occupying some of the modest houses that line the square, and more dotted around town.

By bus Buses from Newton Stewart (Mon–Sat 16 daily, Sun 4; 15min) and Stranraer (Mon–Sat 2 daily; 1hr 50min) stop on the main square.

ACCOMMODATION AND EATING

Hillcrest House Maidland Place, DG8 9EU ☎01988 402018, ⓦhillcrest-wigtown.co.uk. This extended stone Victorian villa on the south side of town provides plenty of space. Champions of slow food, the owners turn out a substantial three-course menu (£23) each night that might include roast venison or a caramelized onion and cheese tart. The restaurant is open to non-guests, but booking is essential. Dinner daily 7pm. **£75**

The Rhinns of Galloway

The hilly, hammer-shaped peninsula at the western end of the Solway coast is known as the **Rhinns of Galloway**. The Gulf Stream dominates the climate here and subtropical plants grow in abundance throughout the area's gardens, linked by an official, signposted route (ⓦscotlandsgardenroute.co.uk). Each has its own personality, with colourful seasonal displays, palm trees and many coastal views. If you only have time to visit one, aim for **Castle Kennedy Gardens**.

Castle Kennedy Gardens

Castle Kennedy, 3 miles east of Stranraer, DG9 8SL • 10am–5pm: Feb & March Sat & Sun; April–Oct daily • £5 • ☎01776 702024, ⓦcastlekennedygardens.co.uk • From Stranraer, bus #430 stops at the gatehouse to the gardens (Mon–Sat hourly, Sun 4; 10min)

The approach to **Castle Kennedy Gardens** passes along a tree-lined avenue that frames the ruined medieval fortress of Castle Kennedy beyond, and then across a palm-fringed canal. The **castle** forms the centrepiece of the gardens, on a hill squeezed between two lochs, though its ruins can no longer be visited. The 75-acre landscaped gardens stretch west as far as nearby Lochinch Castle, seat of the earl of Stair (and also inaccessible), via a giant lily pond and a stupendous avenue of monkey puzzle trees.

Portpatrick

The old seafaring port of **PORTPATRICK**, on the Rhinns of Galloway, is the nicest place to stay on the peninsula, with an attractive pastel-painted seafront that wraps itself round a small rocky bay sheltered by equally rocky cliffs.

By bus Buses leave from South Crescent, next to the sandy bay, for Stranraer (Mon–Sat 11 daily, Sun 3; 22min).

ACCOMMODATION AND EATING

The Crown 9 North Crescent ☎01776 810261, ⓦcrown portpatrick.com. Right on the seafront, this cosy inn is a good bet for fresh seafood, hand-pulled ales and live music in front of an open fire. Highlight of the menu is the seafood pancake gratin for £13. There are also a few en-suite rooms, some of which have sea views. Mon–Thurs & Sun noon–11pm, Fri & Sat noon–midnight; kitchen daily noon–9.15pm. **£75**

Mull of Galloway

The **Mull of Galloway**, twenty miles south of Portpatrick, is a precipitous headland. Crowned by a classic whitewashed Stevenson lighthouse, it really feels like the end of the road. It's the southernmost point in Scotland, and a favourite nesting spot for guillemots, razorbills and kittiwakes. You can climb the **lighthouse** for views of the Isle of Man (10am–4pm: April–June, Sept & Oct Sat & Sun; July & Aug Mon–Wed, Sat & Sun; £2.50).

ARRIVAL AND DEPARTURE   MULL OF GALLOWAY

By bus The nearest bus stop is 4 miles north at Drummore, with services to Port Logan (Mon–Sat 4 daily; 10min).

EATING

★ **Gallie Craig Café** Drummore ☎ 01776 840558, ⓦ galliecraig.co.uk. Perched on the cliff edge, roofed with turf and with a panoramic glass wall and terrace looking out to the sea, Scotland's southernmost building provides armchair birdwatching while you enjoy tea, home baking and well-priced hot food (soup and crusty bread £3.75). Feb & March Mon–Wed, Sat & Sun 11am–4pm; April–Oct daily 10am–5.30pm; Nov Sat & Sun 11am–4pm.

18

Ayrshire

Ayrshire's main appeal lies along its coastline, with visitors attracted by the wide, flat sandy **beaches** and numerous **golf** courses. Inland, cattle and sheep grazing form the backbone of the economy while the relentlessly charmless settlements give little incentive to visit. That said, to the east of **Ayr**, the county town, is the delightful Palladian country pile, **Dumfries House**, recently bought by a consortium headed by Prince Charles. South of Ayr, the more obvious points of interest are **Culzean Castle**, with its Robert Adam interior and extensive wooded grounds, and the offshore islands of **Ailsa Craig**, while to the north is **Irvine**, home to the Scottish Maritime Museum.

Ayr

AYR is by far the largest town on the Firth of Clyde coast. It was an important seaport and trading centre for many centuries, and rivalled Glasgow in size and significance right up until the late seventeenth century. Nowadays, it pulls in the crowds for the Scottish Grand National and the Scottish Derby (ⓦ ayr-racecourse.co.uk), and for the fact that Robbie Burns was born in the neighbouring village of **Alloway** (see below).

ARRIVAL AND INFORMATION   AYR

By plane Ayr is the nearest large town to Glasgow Prestwick Airport (☎ 08712 230700, ⓦ glasgowprestwick. com), which lies 3 miles north of town and is connected by frequent trains to Ayr and Glasgow.

By train The station is a 5min walk southeast of the town centre on Station Rd.

Destinations Glasgow Central (up to every 15min; 50min); Irvine (up to every 15min; 15–20min); Prestwick Airport (up to every 15min; 7min); Stranraer (Mon–Sat 6 daily,

Sun 3; 1hr 20min).

By bus The station is at the foot of Sandgate, near the tourist office.

Destinations Glasgow (every 15min; 1hr 15min); Stranraer (9 daily; 1hr 40min–2hr).

Tourist office 22 Sandgate (April–Sept daily 9am–5pm; Oct–March Mon–Sat 9am–5pm, Sun 10am–5pm; ☎ 01292 290300).

ACCOMMODATION AND EATING

Savoy Park Hotel 16 Racecourse Rd, KA7 2UT ☎ 01292 266112, ⓦ savoypark.com. Impressive Scots Baronial building with a delightful secluded guests' garden at the back. Inside are plenty of traditional characteristics – check out the open fire and wood panelling in the lounge – but, save for the lofty ceilings, the bedrooms look more like standard modern hotel rooms. **£95**

Stage Door Café 12 Carrick St, KA7 1NU ☎ 01292 280444, ⓦ stagedoorcafe.co.uk. Aptly named (it's part of the Gaiety Theatre), this place draws in the crowds with fresh, reasonably priced dishes such as crispy chicken tempura with a honey mustard dressed salad. Three courses £24 after 7pm; slightly less before. Daily 10am–11pm; kitchen 10am–9pm.

Alloway

ALLOWAY, formerly a small village but now on the southern outskirts of Ayr, is the birthplace of Robert Burns (1759–96), Scotland's national poet. The several places associated with the writer have been linked together under the auspices of the **Robert Burns Birthplace Museum**.

18

ROBERT BURNS

The eldest of seven children, **Robert Burns** was born in Alloway on January 25, 1759. His tenant-farmer father's bankruptcy had a profound effect on the boy, leaving him with an antipathy towards authority. After the death of his father, Robert, now head of the family, moved them to a farm at Mossgiel where he began to write in earnest: his first volume, *Poems Chiefly in the Scottish Dialect*, was published in 1786. The book proved immensely popular with ordinary Scots and Edinburgh literati alike, with *Holy Willie's Prayer* attracting particular attention. The object of Burns' poetic scorn was the kirk, whose ministers had condemned him for fornication.

Burns spent the winter of 1786–87 in Edinburgh, but despite his success he felt financially trapped, unable to leave farming. His radical views also landed him in a political snare, his recourse being to play the unlettered ploughman-poet who might be excused impetuous outbursts and hectic womanizing. He made useful contacts in the capital, however, and was recruited to write songs set to traditional Scottish tunes: works including *Auld Lang Syne* and *Green Grow the Rushes, O*. At this time, too, he produced *Tam o' Shanter* and a republican tract, *A Man's a Man for a' That*.

Burns fathered several illegitimate children, but in 1788 married **Jean Armour**, a stonemason's daughter with whom he already had two children, and moved to Ellisland Farm, near Dumfries. The following year he was appointed excise officer and was able to give up farming. But his years of labour, allied to a rheumatic fever, damaged his heart, and he died in Dumfries in 1796, aged 37.

Burns' work, inspired by romantic nationalism and tinged with wry wit, has made him a potent symbol of "Scottishness". Today, Burns Clubs all over the world mark the poet's birthday with the Burns' Supper, complete with haggis, piper and whisky – and a ritual recital of *Ode to a Haggis*.

Robert Burns Birthplace Museum

Murdoch's Lone, KA7 4PQ, plus other locations • Daily 10am–5pm • Museum and cottage £9; NTS • ☎ 01292 443700, ⓦ burnsmuseum.org.uk

The **Robert Burns Birthplace Museum** on Murdoch's Lone displays original manuscripts and some of Burns' personal belongings, adding a good dash of technology and interactive elements. The writer was born in what is now known as **Burns Cottage**: a low, whitewashed, single-room thatched cottage half a mile north of the museum on Alloway (the B7024), where animals and people lived under the same roof.

Other Burns sights

You can still see the plain, roofless ruins of **Alloway Kirk**, two minutes walk west of the Burns Museum, where Robert's father William is buried, and where Burns set much of *Tam o' Shanter*. Down the road, the **Brig o' Doon**, the picturesque thirteenth-century humpback bridge over which Tam is forced to flee for his life, still stands, curving gracefully over the river. High above the river and bridge towers stands the **Burns Monument** (daily: April–Sept 9am–5pm; Oct–March 10am–4pm; free), a striking Neoclassical temple in a small, carefully manicured garden.

ARRIVAL AND DEPARTURE   ALLOWAY

By bus To reach Alloway from Ayr town centre, take bus #8 or #361 from Sandgate (Mon–Sat hourly). Both services stop on The Loaning, a short walk east of the museum.

Culzean Castle

Maybole, 10 miles south of Ayr, KA19 8LE • **Castle** Easter–Oct daily 10.30am–5pm (last admission 4pm) • £15.50, includes country park; NTS • **Country park** Daily 9.30am to dusk • £10.50; NTS • ☎ 01655 884455, ⓦ nts.org.uk/Visit/Culzean-Castle-and-Country-Park

Sitting on the edge of a sheer cliff, looking out over the Firth of Clyde to Arran, **Culzean Castle** (pronounced "Cullane") couldn't want for a more impressive situation. The current castle is actually a grand, late eighteenth-century stately home, designed by Scottish Neoclassical architect **Robert Adam**. Adam's most brilliantly conceived work is the Oval Staircase, where tiers of classical columns lead up to a huge glazed cupola. Other highlights include a portrait of Napoleon by Lefèvre, a superb Chippendale four-poster bed and a boat-shaped cradle. Many folk come here purely to stroll and picnic in the castle's 500-acre **country park**, mess about by the beach, or have tea and cakes.

Dumfries House

Just north of Cumnock, 13 miles east of Ayr, KA18 2NJ • Prebooked guided tours only (1hr–1hr 30min): April–Oct Mon–Fri & Sun 10.45am & 3.30pm, Sat 10.45am & noon; Nov–March Sat & Sun 12.15pm & 1.45pm • £9 • ☎ 01290 421742, ⓦ dumfries-house.org.uk • From Ayr take the #42 bus to Barony Rd, Auchinleck, just before Cumnock (every 30min; 30min); the house is signposted and 1.5 miles to the south

Rescued from exponential dilapidation by a consortium led by Prince Charles, the handsome Palladian villa of **Dumfries House** is an essential stop for anyone with an interest in domestic architecture. Lively tours illuminate the beauty of the furnishings: the house was built and decked out swiftly – between 1756 and 1760 – meaning its Rococo decorative scheme is in perfect harmony with the graceful sandstone exterior. Chief among the treasures is a huge collection of **Chippendale furniture**.

Irvine

IRVINE, twelve miles north of Ayr, was once the principal port for trade between Glasgow and Ireland, and later for coal from Kilmarnock. Its halcyon days are recalled in an enjoyable living-history **museum**, spread across several locations around the town's restored old harbour.

Scottish Maritime Museum

The Linthouse, Gottries Rd, Irvine KA12 8QE • Daily 10am–5pm • £7.50 • ☎ 01294 278283, ⓦ scottishmaritimemuseum.org

The **Scottish Martime Museum** is sread across several locations down at Irvine's carefully restored harbour. The **main exhibition** is in the late nineteenth-century **Linthouse Engine Shop**, on Gottries Road, housing everything from old sailing dinghies and lifeboats to giant ship's turbines. Free guided tours (1hr 15min) set off regularly for the nearby **Shipyard Worker's Tenement Flat**; it has been restored to its appearance in 1910, when a family of six to eight plus a lodger would have occupied its two rooms and scullery. Moored at the **pontoons** on Harbour Street is an assortment of craft that you can board, including the oldest seagoing steam yacht in the country.

ARRIVAL AND DEPARTURE   IRVINE

By train and bus Trains (from Glasgow roughly every 15min; 30–40min) and buses (from Ayr Mon–Sat every 30min, Sun hourly; 55min) arrive at New St; from here it is a 5min walk southwest to the harbour.

AILSA CRAIG

If the weather's half decent, it's impossible to miss **Ailsa Craig**, ten miles off the south Ayrshire coast in the middle of the Firth of Clyde. The island's name means "Fairy Rock" in Gaelic, though it actually looks more like an enormous muffin. It would certainly have been less than enchanting for the persecuted Catholics who escaped here during the Reformation. The island's granite has long been used for making curling stones, and in the late nineteenth century 29 people lived here, either working in the quarry or at the Stevenson lighthouse. With its volcanic, columnar cliffs and 1114ft summit, Ailsa Craig is now a **bird sanctuary** – home to some forty thousand gannets. The **best time** to make the trip is at the end of May and in June when the fledglings are learning to fly. Several companies in the town of **GIRVAN** offer **cruises** round the island, but only Mark McCrindle, who also organizes sea-angling trips, is licensed to land (May to late Sept 1–2 daily; ☎ 01465 713219, ⓦ ailsacraig.org.uk). It takes about an hour to reach the island. Timings and prices depend on the length of trip, tides and weather; booking ahead is essential.

Glasgow and the Clyde

KELVINGROVE ART GALLERY AND MUSEUM

Glasgow and the Clyde

Set on the banks of the mighty River Clyde, Glasgow, Scotland's largest city, is a former industrial giant. It changed its image irrevocably in 1990, however – when it energetically embraced its status as European City of Culture – and has continued to transform itself ever since, with the most recent feather in its cap being the hosting of the Commonwealth Games in 2014. The cityscape has been spruced up, proudly showing off its handsome buildings from long rows of sandstone terraces to the fantastical spires of the Kelvingrove Museum. Glasgow is without doubt, in its own idiosyncratic way, a cultured, vibrant and irrepressibly sociable place that's well worth getting to know.

19

The city has some of the best-financed and most imaginative museums and galleries in Britain – not least the palatial **Kelvingrove Art Gallery and Museum** – nearly all of which are free. Glasgow's **architecture** is some of the most striking in the UK, from the restored eighteenth-century warehouses of the **Merchant City** to the hulking Victorian prosperity of **George Square**. Most distinctive of all is the work of local luminary Charles Rennie Mackintosh, whose elegant Art Nouveau designs appear all over the city. Development of the old shipyards of the Clyde, notably in the space-age shapes of the **Glasgow Science Centre** and the dynamic **Riverside Museum**, hint at yet another string to the city's bow: cleverly combining design with innovation. The metropolis boasts thriving live music venues, distinctive places to eat and drink, busy theatres, concert halls and an opera house.

Despite all the upbeat energy, however, it is true that the gentrification has passed by deprived inner-city areas such as the **East End**, home of the staunchly change-resistant **Barras market** and some forbidding pubs. Indeed, even in the more stylish quarters, there's a gritty edge that reinforces the city's peculiar mix of grime and glitz.

Glasgow makes an excellent base from which to explore the **Clyde Valley and coast**, easily accessible by a reliable train service. Chief among the draws is the remarkable eighteenth-century **New Lanark** mills and workers' village, a World Heritage Site, while other day-trips might take you towards the scenic Argyll sea lochs, past the old shipbuilding centres on the Clyde estuary.

Brief history

Glasgow's earliest history, like so much else in this surprisingly romantic city, is obscured in a swirl of myth. Its name is said to derive from the Celtic *Glas-cu*, which loosely translates as "the dear, green place". It is generally agreed that the first settlers arrived in the sixth century to join Christian missionary **Kentigern** – later to become St Mungo – in his newly founded monastery on the banks of the tiny Molendinar Burn.

William the Lionheart granted the town an official charter in 1175, after which it continued to grow in importance, peaking in the mid-fifteenth century when the **university** was founded on Kentigern's site – the second in Scotland after St Andrews.

NECROPOLIS, GLASGOW

Highlights

❶ Rennie Mackintosh architecture The visionary architect left an extraordinary legacy, manifest in masterpieces such as the Scotland Street School. See pages 820

❷ Necropolis Elegantly crumbling graveyard on a city-centre hill behind the ancient cathedral, with great views giving a different perspective on the city. See page 821

❸ Kelvingrove Art Gallery and Museum Splendid civic collection in a magnificent red sandstone building in the West End; a regular Sunday outing for Glaswegians. See page 822

❹ Hit the West End Wander the laneways of the West End on a Friday or Saturday night, and see Glasgow at its glammed up, exuberant best. See page 822

❺ Clydeside The river that made Glasgow: walk or cycle along it, take a boat on it, cross a bridge over it, or get a view of it from the absorbing Riverside Museum. See page 824

❻ New Lanark Fascinating, UNESCO-recognized eighteenth-century planned mill village set within a dramatic gorge that offers superb woodland walks. See page 835

HIGHLIGHTS ARE MARKED ON THE MAPS ON PAGES 814, 816 & 818

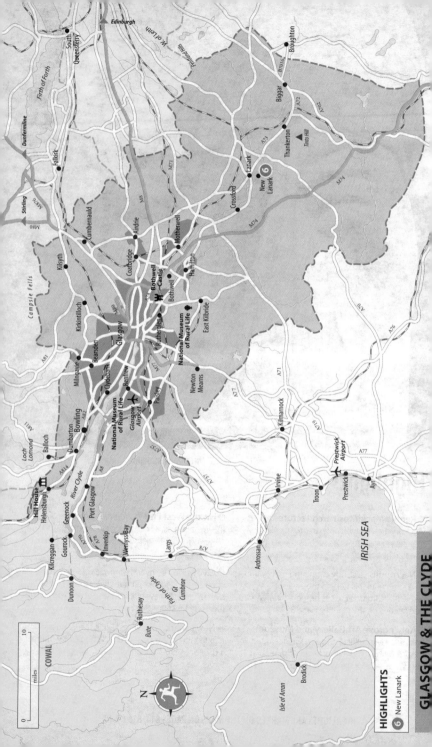

GLASGOW & THE CLYDE

HIGHLIGHTS

6 New Lanark

This led to the establishment of an archbishopric, and hence city status, in 1492, and, due to its situation on a large, navigable river, Glasgow soon expanded into a major industrial **port**. The first cargo of tobacco from Virginia offloaded in Glasgow in 1674, and the 1707 Act of Union between Scotland and England – despite demonstrations against it in Glasgow – led to a boom in trade with the colonies. Following the **Industrial Revolution** and James Watt's innovations in steam power, coal from the abundant seams of Lanarkshire fuelled the ironworks all around the Clyde, worked by the cheap hands of the Highlanders and, later, those fleeing the Irish potato famine of the 1840s.

Shipbuilding and decline

The **Victorian** age transformed Glasgow beyond recognition. The population boomed from 77,000 in 1801 to nearly 800,000 at the end of the century, and new tenement blocks swept into the suburbs in an attempt to cope with the choking influxes of people. By the turn of the twentieth century, Glasgow's industries had been honed into one massive **shipbuilding** culture. Everything from tugboats to transatlantic liners were fashioned out of sheet metal in the yards that straddled the Clyde. In the 1930s, however, unemployment spiralled, and Glasgow could do little to counter its popular image as a city dominated by inebriate violence and (having absorbed vast numbers of Irish emigrants) sectarian tensions. The city's image has never been helped by the depth of animosity between its two great rival football teams, Catholic **Celtic** and Protestant **Rangers** (see page 827).

The city reinvented

Shipbuilding, and many associated industries, died away almost completely in the 1960s and 1970s, leaving the city depressed and directionless. Then, in the 1980s, the self-promotion campaign began, snowballing towards the year-long party as European City of Culture in 1990, before Glasgow became **UK City of Architecture and Design** in 1999. This was followed in 2002 by hosting the Champions' League Final, and then the staging of the **Commonwealth Games** in 2014. These various titles have helped Glasgow break the industrial shackles of the past and evolve into a city of stature, confidence and style.

The city centre

Glasgow's large **city centre** is ranged across the north bank of the River Clyde. At its geographical heart is **George Square**, a nineteenth-century municipal showpiece crowned by the enormous **City Chambers** at its eastern end. To the southeast lies the **Merchant City**, an area that blends magnificent Victorian architecture with yuppie conversions. The grand buildings and trendy cafés cling to the borders of the run-down **East End**, a strongly working-class district that chooses to ignore its rather showy neighbour. The oldest part of Glasgow, around the **Cathedral**, lies immediately north of the East End.

George Square

Now hemmed in by the city's grinding traffic, the imposing architecture of **George Square** reflects the confidence of Glasgow's Victorian age. The wide-open square has an almost continental airiness about it, although there isn't much subtlety about the 80ft column at its centre. It's topped by a statue of Sir Walter Scott, even though his links with Glasgow are, at best, sketchy. Haphazardly dotted around the great writer's plinth are a number of dignified statues of assorted luminaries, ranging from Queen Victoria to Scots heroes such as James Watt and wee Robbie Burns.

19

City Chambers

George Square, G2 1DU • Guided tours only Mon–Fri 10.30am & 2.30pm; 30–45min • Free • ☎ 0141 287 4018 • Buchanan Street underground

The florid splendour of the **City Chambers**, opened by Queen Victoria in 1888, occupies the entire eastern end of the square. Built from wealth gained by colonial trade and heavy industry, it epitomizes the aspirations and optimism of late-

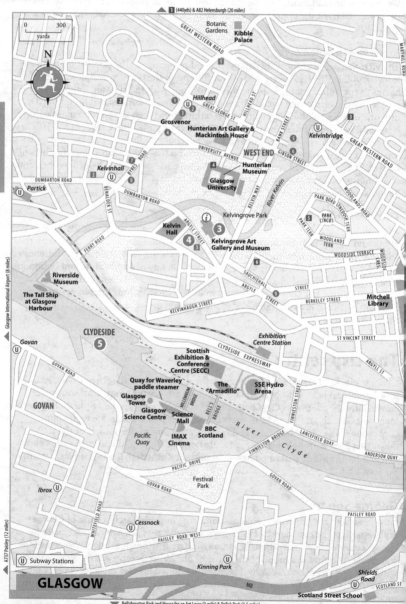

Victorian city elders. The only way to see the labyrinthine interior is to join a **guided tour**, where (depending upon council business), you get to see the ground floor, with its domed mosaic ceilings and two mighty Italian-marble stairwells, and the council chamber, richly furnished in Spanish dark mahogany and embossed leather.

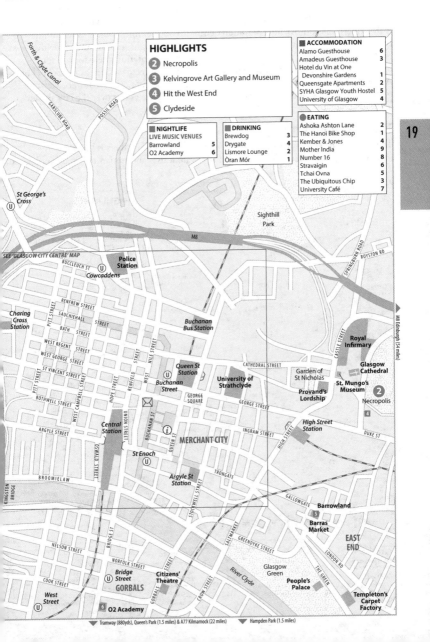

HIGHLIGHTS

- ❷ Necropolis
- ❸ Kelvingrove Art Gallery and Museum
- ❹ Hit the West End
- ❺ Clydeside

■ ACCOMMODATION

Alamo Guesthouse	6
Amadeus Guesthouse	3
Hotel du Vin at One Devonshire Gardens	1
Queensgate Apartments	2
SYHA Glasgow Youth Hostel	5
University of Glasgow	4

■ NIGHTLIFE

LIVE MUSIC VENUES

Barrowland	5
O2 Academy	6

■ DRINKING

Brewdog	3
Drygate	4
Lismore Lounge	2
Òran Mór	1

● EATING

Ashoka Ashton Lane	2
The Hanoi Bike Shop	1
Kember & Jones	4
Mother India	9
Number 16	8
Stravaigin	6
Tchai Ovna	5
The Ubiquitous Chip	3
University Café	7

19

The Lighthouse

11 Mitchell Lane, G1 3NU • Mon–Sat 10.30am–5pm, Sun noon–5pm • Free • ☎ 0141 276 5365, ⓦ thelighthouse.co.uk • St Enoch underground

A spectacularly converted Charles Rennie Mackintosh building, **the Lighthouse** has found new life as Scotland's **Centre for Design and Architecture**. The 1895 building was Mackintosh's first public commission, and housed the offices of the *Glasgow Herald* newspaper until 1980, after which it lay derelict until 1999. The building's star attraction is the superb **Mackintosh Interpretation Centre** up on the third floor. It's an illuminating trawl through the great man's work, with plans, photographs, models and video displays exploring many of the themes behind his buildings and interiors; here too are some original items, including an armchair designed for the director's room at the School of Art and a gorgeous cabinet for the manager's office at *Herald*. The sixth-floor viewing platform and the Lighthouse Tower itself give fantastic views out over the city skyline.

19

The Merchant City

The grid of streets that lies immediately east of the City Chambers is known as the **Merchant City**, an area of eighteenth-century warehouses and homes that was sandblasted

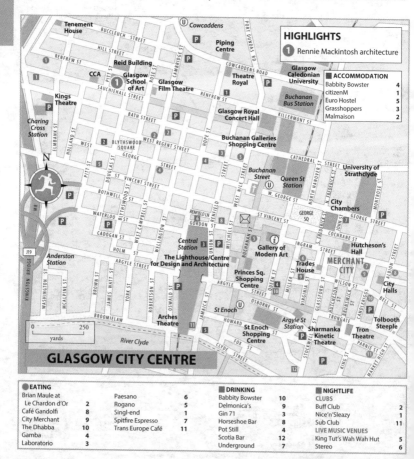

GLASGOW CITY CENTRE

●EATING		■DRINKING		■NIGHTLIFE	
Brian Maule at		Paesano	6	Babbity Bowster	10	CLUBS	
Le Chardon d'Or	2	Rogano	5	Delmonica's	9	Buff Club	2
Café Gandolfi	8	Singl-end	1	Gin 71	3	Nice'n'Sleazy	1
City Merchant	9	Spitfire Espresso	7	Horseshoe Bar	8	Sub Club	11
The Dhabba	10	Trans Europe Café	11	Pot Still	4	LIVE MUSIC VENUES	
Gamba	4			Scotia Bar	12	King Tut's Wah Wah Hut	5
Laboratorio	3			Underground	7	Stereo	6

and swabbed clean with greater enthusiasm and municipal money than any other part of Glasgow in an attempt to bring residents back into the city centre. The expected flood of yuppies was more of a trickle, but the expensive designer shops, cool bars and bijou cafés continue to flock here, giving the area a pervasive air of sophistication.

Sharmanka Kinetic Theatre

Trongate 103, G1 5HD • Shows Wed 5pm, Thurs 5pm & 7pm, Fri 1pm, Sat 3pm, Sun 3pm & 5pm • 45min (1hr 10min for Thurs 7pm & Sun 5pm shows); £8 (£10 for 1hr 10min show) • ☏ 0141 552 7080, Ⓦ sharmanka.com • St Enoch underground

Founded by Russian émigrés Eduard Bersudsky and Tatyana Jakovskaya, the **Sharmanka Kinetic Theatre** is like a mad inventor's magical workshop, with dozens of allegorical contraptions, made from old wheels, levers, lights, carved wooden figures and scrap metal, which spark into life during performances. A unique art form, Sharmanka (Russian for barrel organ or hurdy-gurdy) is at once hypnotic, playful and deeply poignant, with its mechanical sculptures, or "kinemats" imprisoned in their relentless routine.

19

Glasgow School of Art

167 Renfrew St, G3 6RF • **Guided tours (exterior and Reid building)** Check status online; booking advised • £7, when running • **Window on Mackintosh Visitor Centre** Closed at time of going to print; usually daily 10am–4.30pm • Free • ☏ 0141 353 4526, Ⓦ gsa.ac.uk • Cowcaddens underground

Rising above Sauchiehall Street is one of the city centre's steepest hills, where you'll find Charles Rennie Mackintosh's **Glasgow School of Art**, among the most prestigious art schools in the UK. Tragically, in May 2014, a fire – which started in the basement – took hold in the west wing, destroying studios, archival stores and, worst of all, the library. Scaffolding was quickly erected, and restoration work begun. However, in June 2018 the building suffered yet another devastating fire. At the time of going to print, the future of the site was unclear; tours had been suspended, and there was no access to any part of the building.

Widely considered to be the pinnacle of Mackintosh's work, the school is a characteristically angular building of warm sandstone that, due to financial constraints, had to be constructed in two stretches (1897–99 and 1907–09). There's a clear change in the architect's style from the earlier severity of the mock-Baronial east wing to the softer lines of the western half. All over the school, from the roof to the stairwells, Mackintosh introduced unique touches – Japanese lantern shapes, images of seeds and roses and stylized Celtic illuminations.

When running (check online to see if they've been resumed), the student-led **tours** focus on the exterior and the **Reid building** opposite. The Reid building, venue for the school's design courses, also houses the **Furniture Gallery**, which shelters an Aladdin's cave of Mackintosh's original designs – numerous tall-backed chairs, a semicircular settle designed for the (now closed) *Willow Tea Rooms* and a chest of drawers with highlighted silver panels. There are also a couple of pieces by his wife, Margaret, notably a magnificent gesso panel. The building is also home to the **Window on Mackintosh Visitor Centre**, which includes an enlightening timeline tracing the work of the school's students over the years, plus drawers stuffed with plans, programmes and flyers.

Tenement House

145 Buccleuch St, G3 6QN • April–June, Sept & Oct daily 1–5pm; July & Aug Mon–Sat 11am–5pm, Sun 1–5pm • £6.50; NTS • ☏ 0141 333 0183, Ⓦ nts.org.uk/Visit/Tenement-House • Cowcaddens underground

On the first floor of a typical tenement block still inhabited today, the fascinating **Tenement House** holds the perfectly preserved home of one Agnes Toward, who moved here with her mother in 1911, changing nothing and throwing very little out until she was hospitalized in 1965. The flat gives every impression of still being lived in, with a

19

CHARLES RENNIE MACKINTOSH

The work of the architect **Charles Rennie Mackintosh** (1868–1928) is synonymous with the image of Glasgow. Historians may disagree over whether his work was a forerunner of the Modernist movement or merely the sunset of Victorianism, but he undoubtedly created buildings of great beauty, idiosyncratically fusing Scots Baronial with Gothic, Art Nouveau and modern design. Since the postwar years Mackintosh's ideas have become particularly fashionable, giving rise to a certain amount of ersatz "**Mockintosh**" in his home city, with his distinctive lettering and design details used time and again. Fortunately, there are also plenty of examples of the genuine article, making the city a pilgrimage centre for art and design students.

As a young child Mackintosh began to cultivate his interest in drawing from nature during walks in the countryside taken to improve his health. This talent was to flourish when he joined the Glasgow School of Art in 1884: here Mackintosh met Herbert MacNair and the sisters Margaret and Frances MacDonald, whose work was in sympathy with his, fusing the organic forms of nature with a linear, symbolic, Art Nouveau style. Nicknamed "**The Spook School**", the four created a new artistic language, using extended vertical design, stylized abstract organic forms and muted colours, reflecting their interest in Japanese design and the work of Whistler and Beardsley. However, it was **architecture** that truly challenged Mackintosh.

His big break came in 1896, when he won the competition to design a new home for the **Glasgow School of Art** (see page 819). This is his most famous work, but a number of smaller buildings document the development of his style. In the 1890s Glasgow went wild for tearooms, and Miss Cranston, who dominated the Glasgow teashop scene and ran the most elegant establishments, gave Mackintosh great freedom of design. In 1896 he started to plan the interiors for her growing business and, over the next twenty years, designed articles from teaspoons to furniture and, finally, as in the case of the **Willow Tea Rooms**, the structure itself (sadly, the tearoom itself has now closed, though you can still see the exterior).

Despite his success, the spectre of limited budgets was to haunt Mackintosh. These constraints didn't manage to dull his creativity, though his forceful personality and originality did not endear him to construction workers: he would frequently change his mind or add details at the last minute, often over-stretching budgets. This lost him the support of local builders and architects and prompted him to move to Suffolk in 1914 to escape the "philistines" of Glasgow. World War I curtailed building projects and effectively ended Mackintosh's career; from 1923 he lived in the south of France where he gave up architectural work in favour of painting. For more on Mackintosh, see ⓦcrmsociety.com.

cluttered hearth and range, kitchen utensils, recessed beds, framed religious tracts and sewing machine all untouched. There's also a gorgeous walnut and rose piano, which it is believed both Miss Toward and her mother played. Take time, too, to view the fascinating display on the development of the humble tenement block, with a poignant display of relics – ration books, letters, bills, holiday snaps and so forth – from Miss Toward's life.

The East End

East of Glasgow Cross, down Gallowgate beyond the train lines, lies the **East End**, the district that perhaps most closely corresponds to the old perception of Glasgow. Hemmed in by Glasgow Green to the south and the old university to the west, this densely packed industrial area essentially created the city's wealth. Today, isolated pubs, tatty shops and cafés sit amid the dereliction, in sharp contrast to the gloss of the Merchant City just a few blocks west. You're definitely off the tourist trail here, though it's not as threatening as it may feel. Between London Road and the River Clyde are the wide and tree-lined spaces of **Glasgow Green**. Reputedly Britain's oldest public park, the Green has been common land since at least 1178, and has been a popular spot for Sunday afternoon strolls for centuries.

People's Palace

Glasgow Green, G40 1AT • Tues–Thurs & Sat 10am–5pm, Fri & Sun 11am–5pm; Winter Gardens daily 10am–5pm • Free • ☎ 0141 276 0788, ⓦ glasgowlife.org.uk • St Enoch underground

A squat, red sandstone Victorian structure, built as a museum back in 1898, **People's Palace** offers a wonderfully haphazard evocation of the city's history. Throughout, various themes with a particular resonance in Glasgow are explored, including alcohol – look out for the Drunk's Barrow in which the most inebriated were carted off to jail for the night – and crime and punishment, where you'll find the bell from the notorious Duke Street Prison, which rang when someone was hanged on the Green. On a more cheerful note, the section on the Barras recalls evenings of dancing and merriment at the nearby Barrowland and there's some guidance to understanding "the Patter" – Glaswegians' idiosyncratic version of the Queen's English. The Victorian glasshouse at the back of the palace contains the **Winter Gardens**, which has assorted tropical plants and shrubs, a water garden and a café.

Glasgow Cathedral

19

Castle St, G4 0QZ • April–Sept Mon–Sat 9.30am–5.30pm, Sun 1–5pm; Oct–March Mon–Sat 10am–4pm, Sun 1–4pm • Free • ☎ 0141 552 8198, ⓦ glasgowcathedral.org.uk • Buchanan Street underground

Built in 1136, destroyed in 1192 and rebuilt soon after, stumpy-spired **Glasgow Cathedral** was not completed until the late fifteenth century. Dedicated to the city's patron saint and reputed founder, St Mungo, the cathedral is effectively on two levels, the crypt being part of the lower church. On entering, you arrive in the impressively lofty nave of the **upper church**, with the lower church entirely hidden from view. Beyond the nave, the **choir** is concealed by the curtained stone pulpit, making the interior feel a great deal smaller than might be expected from outside. In the choir's northeastern corner, a small door leads into the gloomy **sacristy**, in which Glasgow University was first founded more than five hundred years ago. Two sets of steps from the nave lead down into the **lower church**, where you'll find the dark and musty **chapel** surrounding the tomb of St Mungo. The saint's relics were removed in the late Middle Ages, although the tomb still forms the centrepiece. The chapel itself is one of the most glorious examples of medieval architecture in Scotland, best seen in the delicate fan vaulting rising up from the thicket of cool stone columns.

The Necropolis

Behind the Cathedral • ⓦ glasgownecropolis.org • Buchanan Street underground

Inspired by the Père Lachaise cemetery in Paris, the atmospheric **Necropolis** is a grassy mound covered in a fantastic assortment of crumbling and tumbling gravestones, ornate urns, gloomy catacombs and Neoclassical temples. Paths lead through the rows of eroding, neglected graves and from the summit, next to the column topped with an indignant John Knox, there are superb **views** of the city and its trademark mix of grit and grace.

> ## GLASGOW TENEMENTS
>
> Originally conceived as a convenient way to house the influx of workers in the late 1800s, the **Glasgow tenement** design became more refined as the wealthy middle classes began to realize its potential. Mainly constructed between 1860 and 1910, these tenements, decked out with bay windows, turrets and domes, were home to the vast majority of Glaswegians for much of the twentieth century, and developed a culture and vocabulary all of their own: the "hurley", for example, was the bed on castors which was kept below the box bed in an alcove of the kitchen; a "single end" tenement comprised just one room; and the "dunny" was the secluded bottom end of the "close" (entrance way), the perfect spot for games of hide and seek as well as romantic and nefarious encounters.

The West End

The urbane **West End** seems a world away from Glasgow's industrial image and the bustle of the centre. In the 1800s, wealthy merchants established huge estates here away from the soot and grime of city life, and in 1870 the ancient university was moved from its cramped home near the cathedral to a spacious new site overlooking the River Kelvin. Elegant housing swiftly followed, the Kelvingrove Art Gallery and Museum was built to house the 1888 International Exhibition and, in 1896, the Glasgow District Subway – today's underground – started its circuitous shuffle from here to the city centre.

The hub of life hereabouts is **Byres Road**, running between Great Western Road and Dumbarton Road past Hillhead underground station. Shops, restaurants, cafés, some enticing pubs and hordes of students give the area a sense of style and vitality, while glowing red-sandstone tenements and graceful terraces provide a suitably upmarket backdrop.

The main sights straddle the banks of the River Kelvin, which meanders through the gracious acres of the **Botanic Gardens** and the slopes, trees and statues of **Kelvingrove Park**. Overlooked by the Gothic towers and turrets of **Glasgow University**, Kelvingrove Park is home to the pride of Glasgow's civic collection of art and artefacts, **Kelvingrove Art Gallery and Museum**, off Argyle Street.

Kelvingrove Art Gallery and Museum

Argyle St, G3 8AG • Mon–Thurs & Sat 10am–5pm, Fri & Sun 11am–5pm • Free • ☎ 0141 276 9599, ⊛ glasgowlife.org.uk • Kelvinhall underground

Founded on donations from the city's Victorian industrialists and opened at an international fair held in 1901, the huge, red sandstone fantasy castle of **Kelvingrove Art Gallery and Museum** is a brash statement of Glasgow's nineteenth-century self-confidence. Intricate and ambitious both in its riotous exterior detailing and within, Kelvingrove offers an impressive and inviting setting for its exhibits. The displays are organized under two principal headings: **Life**, in the western half of the building, encompassing archeology, local history and stuffed animals, and **Expression**, in the eastern half, which houses much of the superb art collection. Here, most visitors are drawn to Salvador Dalí's stunning *St John of the Cross*, though there are other big hitters such as Monet, Gaugin, Pissarro, Cezanne and Van Gogh (*The Blute-Fin Windmill*). You can also acquaint yourself with significant **Scottish art** including works by the Glasgow Boys and the Scottish Colourists (see page 823). There's a special section of paintings, furniture and murals devoted to Charles Rennie Mackintosh and the "**Glasgow Style**" he and his contemporaries inspired.

Glasgow University

University Ave, G12 8QQ • **University Visitor Centre & Shop** Mon–Sat 9.30am–5pm, Sun 11am–4pm • **Guided tours** From the Visitor Centre, bookings advised; 1hr • Tues–Sun 2pm • £10 • ☎ 0141 330 5360, ⊛ gla.ac.uk/tours • Kelvinhall/Hillhead underground

Dominating the West End skyline, the gloomy turreted tower of **Glasgow University**, designed by Sir George Gilbert Scott in the mid-nineteenth century, overlooks the glades edging the River Kelvin. Student-led guided tours of the campus begin at the **University Visitor Centre & Shop**, in the dark neo-Gothic pile under the tower; no buildings are entered, but the tour focuses on the university's history, taking in the grounds, notable statues, tombstones and the like.

Hunterian Museum

University Ave, G12 8QQ • Tues–Sat 10am–5pm, Sun 11am–4pm • Free • ☎ 0141 330 4221, ⊛ gla.ac.uk/hunterian • Kelvinhall/Hillhead underground

Beside Glasgow University's Visitor Centre is the **Hunterian Museum**, Scotland's oldest public museum, dating back to 1807. The collection was donated to the university by

THE GLASGOW BOYS AND THE COLOURISTS

In the 1870s a group of Glasgow-based painters formed a loose association that was to imbue Scottish art with a contemporary European flavour far ahead of the rest of Britain. Dominated by five men – Guthrie, Lavery, Henry, Hornel and Crawhall – "**The Glasgow Boys**" came from very different backgrounds, but all rejected the eighteenth-century conservatism that spawned little other than sentimental, anecdotal renditions of Scottish history peopled by "poor but happy" families.

Sir James Guthrie, taking inspiration from the *plein air* painting of the Impressionists, spent his summers in the countryside, observing and painting everyday life. Instead of happy peasants, his work shows individuals staring out of the canvas, detached and unrepentant, painted with rich tones but without undue attention to detail or the play of light. Typical of his finest work during the 1880s, *A Highland Funeral* (in the Kelvingrove collection; see page 822) was hugely influential for the rest of the group, who found inspiration in its restrained emotional content, colour and unaffected realism. Seeing it persuaded **Sir John Lavery**, then studying in France, to return to Glasgow. Lavery was eventually to become an internationally popular society portraitist, his subtle use of paint revealing his debt to Whistler, but his earlier work, depicting the middle class at play, is filled with light and motion.

An interest in colour and decoration united the work of friends **George Henry** and **E.A. Hornel**. The predominance of pattern, colour and design in Henry's *Galloway Landscape*, for example, is remarkable, while their joint work *The Druids* (both part of the Kelvingrove collection; see page 822), in thickly applied *impasto*, is full of Celtic symbolism. In 1893 both artists set off for Japan, funded by Alexander Reid and later William Burrell, where their work used vibrant tones and texture for expressive effect and took Scottish painting to the forefront of European trends. Newcastle-born **Joseph Crawhall** was a reserved and quiet individual who combined superb draughtsmanship and simplicity of line with a photographic memory to create watercolours of an outstanding naturalism and originality.

The Glasgow Boys school reached its height by 1900 and did not outlast World War I, but the influence of their work cannot be underestimated, shaking the foundations of the artistic elite and inspiring the next generation of Edinburgh painters, who became known as the "**Colourists**". Samuel John Peploe, John Duncan Fergusson, George Leslie Hunter and Francis Cadell shared an understanding that the manipulation of colour was the heart and soul of a good painting. All experienced and took inspiration from the avant garde of late nineteenth-century Paris as well as the landscapes of southern France. **J.D. Fergusson**, in particular, immersed himself in the bohemian, progressive Parisian scene, rubbing shoulders with writers and artists such as Picasso. Some of his most dynamic work, which can be seen in the Fergusson Gallery in Perth (see page 859), displays elements of Cubism, yet is still clearly in touch with the Celtic imagery of Henry, Hornel and, indeed, Charles Rennie Mackintosh. The work of the Scottish Colourists has become highly fashionable and valuable, with galleries and civic collections throughout the country featuring their work prominently.

ex-student William Hunter, a pathologist and anatomist whose eclectic tastes form the basis of a diverting zoological and archeological jaunt. The highlight is an exhibition entitled *The Antonine Wall: Rome's Final Frontier*; the shorter counterpart to Hadrian's Wall further south, this highly developed wall was built around AD142 and ran from Clyde to the Firth of Forth. On display are sixteen distance slabs (it's thought that there were nineteen), carved stones that document the work of the legions, alongside funerary monuments and sculptural stones – a quite unique ensemble from the Roman Empire.

Hunterian Art Gallery

University Ave, G12 8QQ • Tues–Sat 10am–5pm, Sun 11am–4pm • Free • ☎ 0141 330 4221, ⓦ gla.ac.uk/hunterian • Kelvinhall/Hillhead underground

Opposite the Hunterian Museum, across University Avenue, is Hunter's more frequently visited bequest, the **Hunterian Art Gallery**. It's best known for its wonderful works by James Abbott McNeill Whistler; only Washington, DC, has a larger collection. The gallery's other major collection is of nineteenth- and twentieth-century Scottish art, including the quasi-Impressionist Scottish landscapes of William McTaggart, a forerunner of the Glasgow Boys movement (see page 823), itself represented here by Guthrie and Hornel. Finally, the monumental dancing figures of J.D. Fergusson's *Les Eus* preside over a small collection of work by the Scottish Colourists.

Mackintosh House

82 Hillhead St, G12 8QQ • Tues–Sat 10am–5pm, Sun 11am–4pm; guided tours (30min) Tues–Fri every 30min 10am–12.30pm • £5 • ☎ 0141 330 4221, ⒲ gla.ac.uk/hunterian • Kelvinhall/Hillhead underground

A side gallery off the Hunterian Art Gallery leads to the **Mackintosh House**, a re-creation of the interior of the now-demolished Glasgow home of Margaret MacDonald and her husband Charles Rennie Mackintosh. Its exquisitely cool interior contains more than sixty pieces of Mackintosh furniture on three floors. The first room is the dining room, complete with three-dimensional fireplace and a half a dozen chairs considered so futuristic that they have been used in episodes of *Babylon 5* and *Dr Who*. The studio drawing room – a startlingly modern design for that period – contains Mackintosh's ebony writing desk, while the standout items in the white-painted oak bedroom are a pair of stunning dove wardrobes and a slimming mirror. There are plenty of contributions from MacDonald, not least several impressive gesso panels.

Botanic Gardens

730 Great Western Rd, G12 0UE • Daily 7am–dusk; glasshouses 10am–6pm, till 4.15pm in winter • Free • ☎ 0141 276 1614, ⒲ glasgowbotanicgardens.com • Hillhead underground

At the northern, top end of Byres Road is the main entrance to the **Botanic Gardens**. The best-known glasshouse here, the hulking, domed **Kibble Palace**, houses lush ferns, exotic blooms and swaying palms from around the world. Nearby, in the **Main Range Glasshouse**, stunning orchids, cacti, ferns and tropical fruit luxuriate in the humidity. In addition to the area around the main glasshouses, there are some beautifully remote paths in the gardens that weave along the closely wooded banks of the deep-set River Kelvin, linking up with the walkway running alongside the river all the way down to Dumbarton Road, near its confluence with the Clyde.

Clydeside

"The **Clyde** made Glasgow and Glasgow made the Clyde" runs an old saying, full of sentimentality for the days when the river was the world's premier shipbuilding centre, and when its industry lent an innovation and confidence that made Glasgow a major city of the British Empire. Despite the hardships heavy industry brought, every Glaswegian would follow the progress of the skeleton ships under construction in the riverside yards, cheering them on their way down the Clyde as they were launched. The last of the great liners to be built on **Clydeside** was the *QE2* in 1967. Such events are hard to visualize today: shipbuilding is restricted to a couple of barely viable yards. However, the river is once again becoming a focus of attention, with striking new buildings including the titanium-clad **Armadillo** concert hall, **Glasgow Science Centre** and the Zaha Hadid-designed **Riverside Museum**.

Glasgow Science Centre

50 Pacific Quay, G51 1EA • **Science Mall** Daily 10am–5pm • £11 • **Glasgow Tower** April–Nov daily 10am–5pm • £6.50 • ☎ 0141 420 5000, ⒲ glasgowsciencecentre.org • Cessnock or Ibrox underground

On the south bank of the Clyde, linked to the Scottish Exhibition and Conference Centre (SECC) by pedestrian Bell's Bridge, are the three space-age, titanium-clad constructions that make up the **Glasgow Science Centre**. Of the three buildings, the largest is the curvaceous, wedge-shaped **Science Mall**. Behind the vast glass wall facing the river, four floors of interactive exhibits range from lift-your-own-weight pulleys to thermograms. The centre covers almost every aspect of science, from simple optical illusions to cutting-edge computer technology, including a section on moral and environmental issues – all good fun, although weekends and school holidays are a scrum. Meanwhile, a bubble-like **IMAX theatre** shows science- and nature-based documentaries, while the 416ft-high **Glasgow Tower** has a viewing tower offering panoramic vistas of central Glasgow.

19

Riverside Museum

100 Pointhouse Place, G3 8RS · Mon–Thurs & Sat 10am–5pm, Fri & Sun 11am–5pm · Free · 📞 0141 287 2720, 🌐 glasgowlife.org.uk · Partick underground; the #100 Riversider bus runs every 30min from George Square via the Kelvingrove Art Gallery and Museum

The wave-like titanium-clad building on the north bank of the river houses the magnificent **Riverside Museum**, Scotland's old Museum of Transport and Travel. Designed by the late Zaha Hadid, and a recent winner of the prestigious European Museum of the Year, its cathedral-like interior is home to a huge, dramatically displayed collection of trains, boats, trams, bikes and cars, and the intricate models on which full-scale ships were based. Among the highlights is a formidable South African Class 15F locomotive, the bike on which Graham Obree twice broke the one-hour world record and the motorbike ridden by Ewan McGregor during his 22,000-mile road trip through eighteen countries in 2004, recorded in the television documentary *Long Way Round*.

Berthed alongside the museum is the **Tall Ship**, a square-rigger called *Glenlee*. A 245ft-long, three-masted barque launched on the river in 1896, she circumnavigated the globe four times before being put to use as a sail training vessel – it's now one of only five large sailing vessels built on Clydeside that are still afloat.

The Southside

The section of Glasgow south of the Clyde is generally described as the **Southside**, though within this area there are a number of recognizable districts, including the notoriously deprived **Gorbals** and Govan, which are sprinkled with new developments but still derelict and tatty in many parts. There's little reason to venture here unless you're making your way to one of the revived architectural gems of Charles Rennie Mackintosh – the **Scotland Street School** and the **House for an Art Lover**, or the famously innovative **Citizens' Theatre** (see page 832).

Scotland Street School Museum

225 Scotland St, G5 8QB · Tues–Thurs & Sat 10am–5pm, Fri & Sun 11am–5pm · Free · 📞 0141 287 0500, 🌐 glasgowlife.org.uk · Shields Road underground

The wonderfully designed **Scotland Street School Museum** is another of the city's Charles Rennie Mackintosh treasures, and the one to head for if time is limited.

The school, which opened in 1906 and closed in 1979, was Mackintosh's second commission for the School Board and the last individual building he designed in Glasgow. The most immediately striking elements are the twin towers (one of Mackintosh's favoured design features): one an entrance for boys, the other for girls. Entering via the light-filled Drill Hall and its superb geometrically patterned, green-and-white-tiled columns, you continue up to the mezzanine, where blue tiles are employed along with leaded pane windows.

There are reconstructed classrooms from the Victorian era, World War II and the 50s and 60s, when classes of 45 pupils were the norm; if you visit on a weekday during term-time, you're likely to stumble on local schoolkids enjoying a period-style lesson, struggling with their ink blotters, gas masks and archly unsympathetic teachers. One room is given over to exhibiting Mackintosh's designs, while another fondly recalls the school's history, with books, photos and a rather grand roll-top desk belonging to William Davidson, the first headmaster.

19

House for an Art Lover

10 Dumbreck Rd, Bellahouston Park, G41 5BW • Daily 10am–5pm, though it's best to call ahead as the building is often used for public functions • £5.50 • ☎ 0141 353 4770, ⓦ houseforanartlover.co.uk • Dumbreck station

Tucked just inside Bellahouston Park is Charles Rennie Mackintosh's **House for an Art Lover**, designed in 1901 for a German competition. It wasn't until 1987 that civil engineer Graham Roxburgh conceived the idea of actually building the house (he just happened to be running past the site one day), and it eventually opened in 1996; however, few original drawings for the structure remained, so its design was largely based on other Mackintosh buildings.

The house is entered via the **Main Hall**, a deliberately grand, high space where massive windows cast a cool light upon an area designed for large parties. The delicate **Oval Room** was intended for women to retire to after dinner; not only is the room itself oval, but so is everything within it, such as the windows, stained glass ceiling light and chair motifs. Next door, the dazzling white **Music Room** has bow windows opening out to a large balcony; it is designed to symbolize a forest glade, with floor-to-ceiling pillars, teardrop leaves, clusters of lanterns and rose stencils above the hearth – the room's most theatrical piece, though, is a piano enclosed within a four-poster bed. In complete contrast, the **Dining Room** is decorated with darkened stained wood and enhanced by beautiful gesso tiles. While here, it'd be remiss not to have a bite to eat or drink in the lovely ground-floor **café**.

ARRIVAL AND DEPARTURE

GLASGOW

By plane Glasgow International Airport (☎ 0844 481 5555, ⓦ glasgowairport.com) is at Abbotsinch, 8 miles southwest of the city. The 24hr Glasgow Shuttle bus (every 10–15min; £7.50, open return £10) runs to the Buchanan St bus station, also stopping at Bothwell St/Hope St and Queen St train station; tickets can be purchased from the Visit Scotland information desk (see below) or on the bus. Taxis charge around £22 to the city centre.

By train Above Argyle St, one of the city's main shopping thoroughfares, Central Station is the terminus for trains to Ayrshire and the Clyde coast, as well as nearly all trains from England. The walk between Glasgow Central and Queen St station takes less than 10min; otherwise, bus #398 from the front entrance on Gordon St shuttles every 10min to Queen St station.

Destinations from Glasgow Central Ardrossan for Arran ferry (every 20–30min; 40–50min); Ayr (every 20–30min; 50min); East Kilbride (hourly; 30min); Gourock (every 20–30min; 45min); Greenock (every 20–30min; 45min); Lanark (every 20–30min; 50min); London Euston (hourly; 4hr 30min); Paisley (every 10min; 10min); Queen's Park (every 10min; 6min); Stranraer (4 daily; 2hr 15min); Wemyss Bay (hourly; 50min).

Destinations from Glasgow Queen St Aberdeen (6 daily; 3hr 10min); Balloch (every 30min; 45min); Dumbarton (every 15min; 35min); Dundee (hourly; 1hr 20min); Edinburgh (every 15min; 1hr 10min); Fort William (2–3 daily; 3hr 40min); Helensburgh (every 30min; 45min); Inverness (Mon–Sat 6 daily, Sun 3; 3hr 45min); Milngavie (every 30min; 25min); Oban (Mon–Sat 5 daily, Sun 3; 3hr 10min); Perth (hourly; 1hr); Stirling (every 20min; 25–40min).

THE OLD FIRM

Football, or *fitba'* as it's pronounced locally, is one of Glasgow's great passions – and one of its great blights. While the city can claim to be one of Europe's premier footballing centres, it's known above all for one of the most bitter rivalries in any sport, that between **Celtic** and **Rangers**. Two of the largest clubs in Britain, with weekly crowds regularly topping sixty thousand, the **Old Firm**, as they're collectively known, have dominated Scottish football for a century.

The roots of Celtic, who play at Celtic Park in the eastern district of Parkhead (☎0871 226 1888, ⓦcelticfc.net), lie in the city's immigrant Irish and **Catholic** population, while Rangers, based at Ibrox Park in Govan on the Southside (☎0871 702 1972, ⓦrangers.co.uk), have traditionally drawn support from local **Protestants**: as a result, sporting rivalries have been enmeshed in a sectarian divide, and although Catholics do play for Rangers, and Protestants for Celtic, sections of supporters of both clubs seem intent on perpetuating the feud. While large-scale violence on the terraces and streets has not been seen for some time – thanks in large measure to canny policing – Old Firm matches often seethe with bitter passions, and sectarian-related assaults do still occur in parts of the city.

However, there is a less intense side to the game, found not just in the fun-loving "Tartan Army" which follows the (often rollercoaster) fortunes of the Scottish national team, but also in Glasgow's smaller clubs, who actively distance themselves from the distasteful aspects of the Old Firm and plod along with home-grown talent in the lower reaches of the Scottish league. All-important reminders that football is, after all, only a game.

By bus Buchanan St bus station is the arrival point for regional and intercity coaches.

Destinations Aberdeen (hourly; 3hr); Campbeltown (5 daily; 4hr 15min); Dundee (every 30min; 1hr 50min); Edinburgh (every 15min; 1hr 10min); Fort William (4 daily; 3hr); Glen Coe (4 daily; 2hr 30min); Inverness (4 daily; 3hr 20min); Kyle of Lochalsh (3 daily; 5–6hr); Loch Lomond (hourly; 45min); Oban (5 daily; 3hr); Perth (hourly; 1hr–1hr 40min); Portree (3 daily; 6–7hr); Stirling (hourly; 45min).

INFORMATION

Tourist office There are currently two branches of the tourist office: one in the basement of the Gallery of Modern Art on Royal Exchange Square (Mon–Wed & Sat 10am–4.45pm, Thurs 10am–6.45pm, Fri & Sun 11am–4.45pm; ⓦpeoplemakeglasgow.com) and another inside the Kelvingrove Art Gallery and Museum (Mon–Thurs & Sat 10am–4.45pm, Fri & Sun 11am–4.45pm). There's also a Visit Scotland desk in the domestic arrivals hall at the airport (Mon–Sat 7.30am–5pm, Sun 8am–3.30pm; ☎0141 848 4440, ⓦvisitscotland.com).

GETTING AROUND

The best way to explore any one part of the city is to **walk**. However, as the main sights are scattered – the West End, for example, is a good 30min walk from the centre – you'll probably need to use the comprehensive **public transport** system, which includes an underground network. If you're travelling beyond the city centre or the West End, or to the main sights on the Southside, you may need to use the bus and train networks. For information on all transport within the city and further afield, check Traveline (ⓦtravelinescotland.com); otherwise, you can get information and pick up timetables at the **Travel Centre** (Mon–Sat 6.30am–10.30pm, Sun 7am–10.30pm) in Buchanan Street bus station.

By underground The best way to get between the city centre and the West End is to use the underground (Mon–Sat 6.30am–11.45pm, Sun 10am–6.15pm), whose stations are marked with a large orange U. There's a flat fare of £1.65, or you can buy a day-ticket for £4.

By bus The array of different bus companies and the routes they take is perplexing even to locals; pick up individual timetables at the Travel Centre (see above). A flat fare costs £2.20 while a FirstDay pass, allowing unlimited travel throughout Glasgow, costs £4.50; tickets can be bought on the bus (have the exact change ready).

By train The suburban train network is swift and convenient. Suburbs south of the Clyde are connected to Central Station, either at the mainline station or the subterranean low-level platforms, while trains from Queen St (which also has mainline and low-level stations) head into the northeast suburbs. The train is an excellent way to link to points west and northwest of Glasgow, including Milngavie (for the start of the West Highland Way), Balloch (for Loch Lomond) and Helensburgh.

By taxi You can hail a black cab from anywhere in the city centre, day or night. There are also ranks at Central and

Queen St train stations and Buchanan St bus station. Expect to pay around £6–7 for a journey from the city centre to the West End. If you're calling in advance, try Glasgow Taxi Ltd (☎0141 429 7070, ⓦglasgowtaxis.co.uk) or West En Radio Cars (☎0141 954 2000, ⓦwestendradiocars.co.uk)

ACCOMMODATION

Glasgow has plentiful accommodation, and while many hotels are business-oriented, there is an increasing number c fashionable (though fairly priced) design hotels. The majority of the best guesthouses and B&Bs can be found in the **Wes End**, while there's also a reasonable, though not particularly exciting, spread of hostels across the city.

CITY CENTRE

Babbity Bowster 16–18 Blackfriars St, off High St, G1 1PE ☎0141 552 5055, ⓦbabbitybowster.com; map p.818. Best known as a pub (see page 830), *Babbity Bowster* also features six plain but serviceable rooms that provide visitors with a great, and decently priced, Merchant City location; a simple breakfast is included. **£70**

citizenM 60 Renfrew St, G2 3BW ☎0141 404 9485, ⓦcitizenm.com; map p.818. This modern European chain offers a luxury experience that won't break the bank; check in via computer then head to your room to enjoy the innovative mood lighting, hip decor and rain shower. After that, you could do a lot worse than hang around in the cool *CanteenM*, a homely breakfast-bar-cum-lounge area that's open around the clock – indeed, you're quite likely to spend more time in this hotel than out of it. **£75**

Euro Hostel 318 Clyde St, G1 4NR ☎08455 399956, ⓦeurohostels.co.uk; map p.818. Enormous, seven-storey hotel smack in the centre with a mix of en-suite rooms (sleeping from two to fourteen) and suites, the latter with a small lounge/TV area. there's also a self-catering kitchen, laundry and adjoining bar, which is where breakfast (£5) is taken. Dorms **£12**, suites/person **£14**, doubles **£50**

★ **Grasshoppers** 87 Union St, G1 3TA ☎0141 222 2666, ⓦgrasshoppersglasgow.com; map p.818. Occupying the sixth (top) floor of the former Caledonian Railway Company building, this medium-sized hotel is a real gem, from the artwork-lined corridors to the rooms themselves, which have an understatedly cool, urban feel: oak flooring, bespoke, Scandinavian-style furnishings and pod-like bathrooms. **£78**

Malmaison 278 West George St, G2 4LL ☎0141 572 1000, ⓦmalmaison.com; map p.818. Glasgow's version of the sleek, chic mini-chain, an austere Grecian-temple frontage masking a superbly comfortable designer hotel whose rooms are dominated by various shades of greys and purples, and come with deep, inviting beds and big fluffy pillows. **£95**

WEST END

★ **Alamo Guesthouse** 46 Gray St, G3 7SE ☎0141 33 2395, ⓦalamoguesthouse.com; map p.816. Good value, family-run boarding house next to Kelvingrov Park, with ten rooms, each completely different in size an character variously featuring stucco plasterwork, Frenc oak beds, slate-tile sinks and cast-iron chandeliers, c perhaps a free-standing tub. **£80**

Amadeus Guesthouse 411 North Woodside Rd, G20 6N ☎0141 339 8257, ⓦamadeusguesthouse.co.uk; ma p.816. Handily located near Great Western Rd, but on quiet street opposite the River Kelvin, this place offers stylis en-suite rooms in a welcoming Victorian townhouse. **£80**

★ **Hotel du Vin at One Devonshire Gardens** Devonshire Gardens, Great Western Rd, G12 0U ☎0141 378 0385, ⓦhotelduvin.com; map p.816 Glasgow's most exclusive and exquisite small hotel, a 10min walk up the Great Western Rd from the Botani Gardens. Rooms are grandly furnished in rich colours, some with four posters and jacuzzis. **£140**

Queensgate Apartments 107 Downhill St, G12 9E ☎07796 651451, ⓦqueensgateapartments.com; map p.816. A choice of attractive and cosy flats in traditiona tenement buildings. Three apartments are within walkinc distance of the West End's vibrant Byres Rd, and all have TVs, wi-fi and other mod cons. A good option for families o groups. One-week minimum stay. **£57**

SYHA Glasgow Youth Hostel 7–8 Park Terrace, G 6BY ☎0141 332 3004, ⓦsyha.org.uk/where-to-stay lowlands/glasgow; map p.816. This popular, well-equipped hostel occupies a wonderful townhouse in one of the West End's grandest terraces. All the dorms (from singles up to eight-bed) are en suite. Kelvinbridge underground station or bus #44 from the city centre. Breakfast £4.95. Dorms **£24**, doubles **£68**

University of Glasgow ☎0141 330 4116, ⓦcvso.co.uk; map p.816. Low-priced, self-catering accommodation in single rooms only; mostly in the West End. Closed mid-Sept to May. **£26**

EATING

Glasgow's restaurant scene has improved dramatically over the past few years and can now hold its own with the best cities in Britain. Although the greatest concentration of places is in the city centre itself, the best restaurants are out in the trendy **West End**. Originally brought up on the culinary skills of the long-established **Italian** community and later waves of **Indian** and **Chinese** immigrants (the city has some of the best Indian restaurants in the UK), the city has recently seen a more studied move towards great **Scottish produce**. Many menus now contain at least one seasonal and Modern Scottish component, offering a new take on the country's culinary traditions.

CITY CENTRE AND THE MERCHANT CITY
CAFÉS AND COFFEEHOUSES

★ **Laboratorio** 93 West Nile St, G1 2SH ☎0141 353 1111; map p.818. The "Lab" is a terrific little bolt-hole with cement board walls and recycled wood panelling, and super-friendly baristas who really do know their beans. There's typically a single-origin espresso and a guest espresso on the go at any one time. Sit-down and takeaway. Mon–Fri 7.30am–5.30pm, Sat 9am–5pm, Sun 11am–5.30pm.

Singl-end 265 Renfrew St, G3 6TT ☎0141 353 1277, ⓦthesingl-end.co.uk; map p.818. An engaging, below-street-level café and bakehouse with pretty, blue-shuttered windows and, inside, blue-painted steel girders and glass-topped tables laden with postcards and photos of Glasgow. It's a great spot to kick back with a cup of coffee and a slice of apple-and-olive-oil cake, or something more substantial like spicy baked eggs with toasted sourdough. Mon–Fri 9am–5pm, Sat & Sun 10am–5pm.

Spitfire Espresso 127 Candleriggs St, G1 1NP ☎07578 250105, ⓦspitfireespresso.com; map p.818. Another fine addition to the city's roster of artisan coffeehouses, this cool, light and airy space, with marine-blue-painted walls and window frames, offers a short but enticing coffee menu alongside a delicious all-day egg menu, among other treats. Mon & Tues 8am–6pm, Wed–Sat 8am–10pm, Sun 10am–3pm.

★ **Trans Europe Café** 25 Parnie St, G1 5RJ ☎0141 552 7999; map p.818. Named after the legendary Kraftwerk album, this fun, railway-style diner – with 80s-style bus seating – takes culinary inspiration from various European capitals. Thus you will find gourmet sandwiches like the Madrid (chorizo sausage, pesto and mozzarella) and the Monte Carlo (tuna melt with cheddar and mayonnaise; £6.95). On weekend evenings they serve bistro-style dishes. Mon–Wed & Sun 10am–5pm, Thurs–Sat 10am–10pm.

RESTAURANTS

Brian Maule at Le Chardon d'Or 176 West Regent St, G2 4RL ☎0141 248 3801, ⓦbrianmaule.com; map p.818. Owner-chef Maule, who worked with the Roux brothers at *Le Gavroche* in London, turns out fancy yet unpretentious French-influenced food along the lines assiette of pork with creamed potatoes and truffle *jus* (£26). Tues–Sat noon–2.30pm & 5–10pm.

Café Gandolfi 64 Albion St, G1 1NY ☎0141 552 6813, ⓦcafegandolfi.com; map p.818. *Gandolfi* serves a wonderful selection of Scottish-inspired dishes such as Stornoway black pudding, peat-smoked salmon or haggis-stuffed pork belly (£18). The snappy little attic bar offers

the same food plus a cracking pizza menu; there's a great gin list, too. Daily: café 8am–midnight; bar and bar kitchen 11am–midnight.

City Merchant 97 Candleriggs, G1 1NP ☎0141 553 1577, ⓦcitymerchant.co.uk; map p.818. Warm, classy brasserie that blazed the Merchant City trail and which offers plenty of fresh Scottish produce, from Ayrshire lamb to the house speciality: collops of fillet steak with oatmeal-encrusted haggis in a whisky *jus*. Well-priced lunch (£11.50) and pre-theatre menus (£12.50). Mon–Sat noon–10.30pm.

The Dhabba 44 Candleriggs, G1 1LD ☎0141 553 1249, ⓦthedhabba.com; map p.818. Prices are higher and portions are smaller here, but the menu has some truly interesting options and uses fresh ingredients that place it steps above most others. The tandoor dishes are cooked with North Indian spices in a clay oven: whole black bream with carom and tandoori masalas, for example (£18). Mon–Fri noon–2pm & 5–11pm, Sat & Sun 1–11pm.

★ **Gamba** 225a West George St, G2 2ND ☎0141 572 0899, ⓦgamba.co.uk; map p.818. Continental contemporary sophistication prevails in this super basement restaurant where fish is king: once you've devoured the signature fish soup (Portland crabmeat and prawn dumplings), perhaps try some crisp-fried red mullet and crayfish tails with melon and goat's cheese (£18.50). A beautifully refined interior and outstanding service. Mon–Sat noon–2.30pm & 5–10pm, Sun 5–9pm.

★ **Paesano** 94 Miller St, G1 1DT ☎0141 258 5565, ⓦpaesanopizza.co.uk; map p.818. In a city bursting with great Italian restaurants, this authentic Neopolitan pizzeria is a real standout. Rustled up in wood-fired ovens made in Naples, there are eight different pizzas to choose from (£6–8), each made using a hybrid yeast and sourdough recipe and with the freshest ingredients from Campania. Daily noon–midnight.

Rogano 11 Exchange Place, G1 3AN ☎0141 248 4055, ⓦroganoglasgow.com; map p.818. A Glasgow institution since 1935, this Art Deco fish restaurant is wearing its age well and the food is still top drawer, from the legendary fish soup (£6.50) to dishes like crusted venison loin with roasted salsify and rosemary *jus* (£23). *Café Rogano*, in the basement, is slightly cheaper; better still, park yourself at the bar and indulge in a half dozen oysters for £11. Daily noon–10.30pm.

WEST END
CAFÉS AND COFFEEHOUSES

Kember & Jones 134 Byres Rd, G12 8TD ☎0141 337 3851, ⓦkemberandjones.co.uk; map p.816. This stylish café and deli more than holds its own in the ultra-

19

19

competitive Byres Rd area, thanks to its freshly made salads and sandwiches and its irresistible cakes and pastries. Better still, they roast their own coffee – very enjoyable with a warm waffle breakfast. Mon–Fri 8am–10pm, Sat 9am–10pm, Sun 9am–6pm.

Tchai Ovna 42 Otago Lane, G12 8PB ☎0141 357 4524, ⓦtchaiovna.com; map p.816. A low-key bohemian hangout overlooking the Kelvin river, offering savoury vegetarian options (try the red dhal curry at £5.90), cakes, snacks and a selection of teas from around the world. Daily 11am–11pm.

★ **University Café** 87 Byres Rd, G11 5HN ☎0141 339 5217; map p.816. This institution dates back to the 1910s and has been adored by at least three generations of students and West End residents, with its formica tables in snug booths, etched glass partitions and cinema-style pull down seating. The favourites are fish'n'chips or mince'n'tatties rounded off with an ice-cream cone – you won't spend more than a tenner. Mon–Thurs 9am–10pm, Fri & Sat 9am–10.30pm, Sun 10am–10pm.

RESTAURANTS

Ashoka Ashton Lane 19 Ashton Lane, G12 8SJ ☎0141 337 1115, ⓦashokarestaurants.com; map p.816. Lively curry house with franchises across the west of Scotland; all offer consistent quality and reasonable prices (mains from £8). Mon–Thurs noon–midnight, Fri & Sat noon–1am, Sun 5pm–midnight.

The Hanoi Bike Shop Ruthven Lane, G12 9BG ☎0141 334 7165, ⓦhanoibikeshop.co.uk; map p.816. This enthusiastically run Vietnamese place just off the busy Byres Rd might not have much to do with bicycles (though there are wheels on the walls), but it is just the ticket for a quick hit of freshly prepared street food – sesame chicken livers, say, or black pepper tofu. It's all very reasonably priced at £6–8. Mon–Thurs noon–11pm, Fri noon–12.30am, Sat 11am–12.30pm, Sun 11am–11pm.

Mother India 28 Westminster Terrace, off Sauchiehall St, G3 7RU ☎0141 221 1663, ⓦmotherindia.co.uk; map p.816. Still setting the standard for Indian cuisine in Glasgow, with some original specials (ginger crab and prawn dosa) alongside old favourites (monkfish kebab, lamb pasanda), all at affordable prices (mains around £12). Mon–Thurs 5.30–10.30pm, Fri noon–11pm, Sat 1–11pm, Sun 1–10pm.

Number 16 16 Byres Rd, G11 5JY ☎0141 339 2544, ⓦnumber16.co.uk; map p.816. Intimate, wood-beamed establishment covering two floors, offering daily menus of Scottish produce from seared fillet of Shetland mackerel with beetroot gazpacho (£6.95) to roast haunch of Highland venison (£19.50). Mon–Sat noon–2.30pm & 5.30–10pm, Sun 1–2.30pm & 5.30–9pm.

★ **Stravaigin** 28–30 Gibson St, G12 8NX ☎0141 334 2665, ⓦstravaigin.co.uk; map p.816. This gorgeous basement restaurant and hip street-level café-bar combination offers exciting dining. In both, a host of unexpected ingredients results in unusual and wildly inventive combinations such as sea bream with mussel croquettes and pistachio (£17.95). Restaurant Mon–Fri 5–11pm, Sat 11am–11pm, Sun 11am–10pm; café-bar Mon–Fri 10am–1am, Sat & Sun 11am–1am.

The Ubiquitous Chip 12 Ashton Lane, G12 8SJ ☎0141 334 5007, ⓦubiquitouschip.co.uk; map p.816. Opened in 1971, *The Chip* led the way in headlining upmarket Modern Scottish cuisine and it's still up there among the best in the city; expect mouth-watering plates such as Eyemouth crab with apple and elderflower yoghurt, and guinea fowl with Arran pumpkin and truffle cream (£24). Mon–Sat noon–2.30pm & 5–11pm, Sun 12.30–3pm & 5–10pm.

DRINKING

Most drinking dens in the **city centre**, the **Merchant City** and the **West End** are places to experience real Glaswegian bonhomie, with a good selection of atmospheric pubs featuring folk music, as well as more upscale bar/clubs.

CITY CENTRE AND THE MERCHANT CITY

Babbity Bowster 16–18 Blackfriars St, off High St, G1 1PE ☎0141 552 5055, ⓦbabbitybowster.com; map p.818. Lively place with an unforced and kitsch-free Scottish feel that features music on Wed and Sat (including traditional and gypsy jazz), as well as spontaneous folk sessions at other times. Mon–Sat 11am–midnight, Sun 12.30pm–midnight.

Delmonica's 68 Virginia St, G1 1TX ☎0141 552 4803, ⓦdelmonicas.co.uk; map p.818. One of Glasgow's liveliest and largest LGBT+ bars, in a popular area with a mixed, hedonistic crowd. Nightly entertainment and events. Mon–Sat noon–midnight, Sun 12.30pm–midnight.

Drygate 85 Drygate, G4 0UT ☎0141 212 8815, ⓦdrygate.com; map p.816. Injecting a welcome dollop of life into the East End, this small but progressive brewery has a ground-floor restaurant and bar and an upstairs beer hall leading to a rooftop terrace. It offers five of its own craft beers on tap plus a dozen or so guest ales, and a regular programme of live music and comedy. Well worth the short trek from the city centre. Daily 11am–midnight; kitchen noon–10pm.

★ **Gin 71** 71 Renfield St, G2 1LP ☎0141 353 2959, ⓦgin71.com; map p.818. This gorgeous, glamorous gin bar occupies the old Bank of India building, hence the lavishly coloured tiles and dazzling mosaic flooring. There are gins of every persuasion here, 71 in fact: fruity, floral, trus, spiced, you name it, and all with superb tasting notes. But if it's all still too confusing, have a cheeky bash at a gin flight (three gins for £15). Mon–Thurs & Sun –11pm, Fri & Sat 5pm–midnight.

Horseshoe Bar 17 Drury St, G2 5AE ☎ 0141 248 6368, ⊛ thehorseshoebarglasgow.co.uk; map p.818. An original "Gin Palace" and, with the longest continuous bar in the UK, reputedly Glasgow's busiest drinking hole; it's no less renowned for its nightly karaoke sessions. A must for pub aficionados. Mon–Sat 10.30am–midnight, Sun 2.30pm–midnight.

Pot Still 154 Hope St, G2 2TH ☎ 0141 333 0980, ⊛ thepotstill.co.uk; map p.818. Whisky galore – in excess of seven hundred different single malts are found in this traditional pub, which also offers a decent ale selection. Daily 11am–midnight.

Scotia Bar 112 Stockwell St, G1 4LW ☎ 0141 552 8681, ⊛ scotiabar-glasgow.co.uk; map p.818. Dating from 1792, which (allegedly) makes it the city's oldest pub, this happily careworn place has a cracking atmosphere, thanks in no small part to its programme of semi-pro live folk, blues and rock sessions, typically on Fri evenings and Sun at 5pm. Mon–Sat 11am–midnight, Sun 12.30pm–midnight.

Underground 6a John St, G1 1JQ ☎ 0141 553 2456; map p.818. This welcoming, low-key LGBT+ basement bar is geared more towards the art of conversation than dance, although Tues (karaoke) and Sat (Drag Queen) see things perk up a bit. Men and women welcome. Daily noon–midnight.

WEST END

★ **Brewdog** 1397 Argyle St, G3 8AN ☎ 0141 334 7175, ⊛ brewdog.com; map p.816. Dedicated, and quite brilliant, craft beer bar with fourteen ales on tap (around half of which are Brewdog's own creations), plus dozens more bottled possibilities. Tricky choices await, but if you're completely stumped, try guzzling a beer flight (£5.70 for four "third" pints). Daily noon–midnight.

Lismore Lounge 206 Dumbarton Rd, G11 6UN ☎ 0141 576 0103; map p.816. Decorated with specially commissioned stained-glass panels depicting the Highland Clearances, this bar is a meeting point for the local Gaels, who come to chat, relax and enjoy impromptu music sessions. Daily 11am–midnight.

Òran Mór Byres Rd, corner of Great Western Rd, G12 8QX ☎ 0141 357 6200, ⊛ oran-mor.co.uk; map p.816. Capacious bar, club venue and performance space, all within the tastefully restored Kelvinside parish church; perhaps the best reason to visit, though, is for the perennially popular *A Play, A Pie and A Pint* lunchtime theatre programme (Mon–Sat; £12.50). Mon–Sat 9am–3am, Sun 10am–3am.

19

NIGHTLIFE

The liveliest area for nightlife remains the **West End**, with students mixing with locals around Byres Road, as well as in the nearby Woodlands and Kelvingrove districts. The city's **clubbing** scene is rated among the best in the UK, attracting top DJs from around the world and also breeding a good deal of local talent. Glasgow has long had one of the most exciting **music** scenes in the UK, producing the likes of Franz Ferdinand, Primal Scream and Mogwai, and on any given night you can catch a raft of top-class gigs. For detailed listings on what's on, check out *The List* (⊛ list.co.uk) or visit ⊛ theskinny.co.uk, both of which cover other cities in the UK.

CLUBS

Buff Club 142 Bath Lane ☎ 0141 248 1777, ⊛ thebuffclub.com; map p.818. The playlist of vintage disco, funk and northern soul here draws an eclectic crowd of clubbers. Mon, Tues & Thurs–Sat 11pm–3am.

Nice'n'Sleazy 421 Sauchiehall St, G2 3LG ☎ 0141 333 0900, ⊛ nicensleazy.com; map p.818. Don't be put off by the name – this Glasgow institution is a great venue, with DJs on the decks most nights, playing everything from garage and punk to indie and techno. It also hosts the occasional alternative and indie-oriented act in the performance space below the funky bar.

Sub Club 22 Jamaica St, G1 4QD ☎ 0141 248 4600, ⊛ subclub.co.uk; map p.818. Near-legendary venue and base for the noteworthy Optimo club night as well as Sat night's Subculture, this is the home for house and techno lovers in the west of Scotland. Tues–Sun 11pm–3am.

LIVE MUSIC VENUES

Barrowland 244 Gallowgate, G4 0TT ☎ 0141 552 4601, ⊛ glasgow-barrowland.com; map p.816. Legendary East End ballroom accommodating around two thousand people. Come here to see big-time acts who return to it as their favourite venue in Scotland, as well as bands on the rise.

King Tut's Wah Wah Hut 272a St Vincent St, G2 5RL ☎ 0141 221 5279, ⊛ kingtuts.co.uk; map p.818. Famous as the place where Oasis was discovered, and still presenting one of the city's best live music programmes. It's also a good bar, with an excellent jukebox.

O2 Academy 121 Eglinton St, G5 9NT ☎ 0870 771 2000, ⊛ glasgow-academy.co.uk; map p.816. With a capacity of 2500, this is the city's principal mid-sized venue. Less atmosphere than *Barrowland*, but gets reliably big names.

Stereo 22–28 Renfield Lane, G2 6PH ☎0141 222 2254, ⓦstereocafebar.com; map p.818. Housed inside the Mackintosh-designed former *Daily Record* office, this cool café-cum-bar is now the place to track down up-and-coming local bands. Mon–Thurs & Sun noon–midnight, Fri & Sat noon–3am.

ENTERTAINMENT

Glasgow is no slouch when it comes to the **performing arts**: it's home to Scottish Opera, Scottish Ballet and the Royal Scottish National Orchestra. Most of the larger theatres, multiplexes and concert halls are in the city centre, while the West End and the Southside are home to several innovative venues.

THEATRE

Citizens' Theatre 119 Gorbals St, G5 9DS ☎0141 429 0022, ⓦcitz.co.uk. The "Citz" has evolved from its 1960s working-class roots into one of Britain's most respected and innovative contemporary theatres; it's also home to the well-regarded Vanishing Point theatre company. Three stages, concessions for students and free preview nights.

Theatre Royal 282 Hope St, G2 3QA ☎0141 332 9000, ⓦglasgowtheatreroyal.org.uk. This late nineteenth-century playhouse was revived in the mid-1970s as the opulent home of Scottish Opera, whose repertoire features large-scale and adventurous productions. It also hosts visiting theatre groups, including the Royal Shakespeare Company, and orchestras.

Tramway 25 Albert Drive, off Pollokshaws Rd, G41 2PE ☎0845 330 3501, ⓦtramway.org. Based in a converted tram terminus, whose lofty proportions make it a remarkable venue for experimental productions by directors such as Peter Brook and Robert Lepage. It has also played a significant role in promoting visual art by figures such as David Mach, Douglas Gordon and Christine Borland.

Tron Theatre 63 Trongate, G1 5HB ☎0141 552 4267, ⓦtron.co.uk. Critically acclaimed venue staging a varied repertoire of mainstream, as well as more challenging, productions from leading local companies. Also folk music performances and Sun jazz in the theatre's Victorian bar.

CONCERT HALLS

City Halls Candleriggs, G1 1NQ ☎0141 353 8000, ⓦglasgowconcerthalls.com. This Merchant City venue in completely renovated Victorian halls, is home to the BBC Scottish Symphony Orchestra and hosts many of the annual Celtic Connections concerts.

Glasgow Royal Concert Hall 2 Sauchiehall St, G2 3NY ☎0141 353 8000, ⓦglasgowconcerthalls.com. One of Glasgow's less memorable modern buildings, though with great acoustics, this is the venue for big-name touring orchestras and the home of the Royal Scottish National Orchestra. Also features major rock and r'n'b stars. Box office Mon–Sat 10am–6pm.

ARTHOUSE CINEMAS

Glasgow Film Theatre 12 Rose St, G3 6RB ☎0141 332 6535, ⓦglasgowfilm.org. Dedicated art, independent and rep cinema with a history going back to 1939. The glamorous Art Deco *Café Cosmo* is an excellent place for pre-show drinks.

Grosvenor 24 Ashton Lane, G12 8SJ ☎0845 166 6002, ⓦgrosvenorwestend.co.uk. Two-screen neighbourhood filmhouse with a bar and sofas that you can reserve for screenings of mostly mainstream films.

DIRECTORY

Hospital There is a 24hr casualty department at the Royal Infirmary, 84 Castle St near Glasgow Cathedral (☎0141 211 4000).

Left luggage Buchanan St bus station has left-luggage facilities (£5/24hr), and there are lockers at Central and Queen St train stations.

Police The main police station is at 50 Stewart St. For emergencies, dial ☎999.

Post office The most central post offices are at 135 West Nile St (Mon–Sat 9am–5.30pm); 177 Sauchiehall St (Mon–Sat 9am–5.30pm, Sun 10.30am–2.30pm); 59 Glassford St (Mon–Sat 8.30am–5.30pm).

SHOPPING IN GLASGOW

The main area for spending money in the city centre is formed by the Z-shaped and mostly pedestrianized circuit of **Argyle**, **Buchanan** and **Sauchiehall** streets. Along the way you'll find **Princes Square**, a stylish and imaginative shopping centre hollowed out of the innards of a soft sandstone building. The interior, all recherché Art Deco and ornate ironwork, holds lots of pricey, fashionable shops. Otherwise, make for the **West End** or the **Merchant City**, which have more eccentric and individual offerings. The latter is the place for secondhand and antiquarian **bookshops** as well as quirky vintage and one-off fashion stores on the lanes off Byres Road.

FERRIES: GOUROCK AND WEMYSS BAY

Northwest of Glasgow on the coast lies the dowdy old resort of **GOUROCK**, once a holiday destination for generations of Glaswegians, but today only of real significance as a **ferry terminal**: both CalMac (☎0800 066 5000, ⓦcalmac.co.uk) and the more frequent Western Ferries (☎01369 704452, ⓦwestern-ferries.co.uk) ply the twenty-minute route across the Firth of Clyde to Dunoon on the Cowal peninsula (£4.50 single; car plus passenger £17.10), while a passenger-only ferry runs from Gourock to Kilcreggan (15min) on the north bank of the Clyde (Mon–Sat 13 daily; £2.60 single; ⓦspt.co.uk/kilcreggan-ferry). Immediately south of Gourock, **WEMYSS BAY**, where thousands of Glaswegians used to alight for their steamer trip "doon the watter", is today of note only for its splendid 1903 train station and the CalMac **ferry** connection to Rothesay on Bute (see page 872).

The Clyde

The **River Clyde** is the dominant physical feature of Glasgow and its environs, an area that comprises the largest urban concentration in Scotland, with almost two million people living in the city and satellite towns. Little of this hinterland can be described as beautiful, with crisscrossing motorways and grim housing estates dominating much of the landscape. Beyond the sprawl, however, rolling green hills, open expanses of water and attractive countryside eventually begin to dominate, holding promises of wilder country beyond.

West of the city, regular trains and the M8 motorway dip down from the southern bank of the Clyde to **Paisley**, where the distinctive cloth pattern gained its name, before heading back up to the edge of the river again as it broadens into the **Firth of Clyde**. North of Glasgow trains terminate at tiny **Milngavie** (pronounced "Mill-guy"), which acts as the start of Scotland's best-known long-distance footpath, the **West Highland Way** (see page 847).

Southeast of Glasgow, the industrial landscape of the **Clyde valley** eventually gives way to far more attractive scenery of gorges and towering castles. Here lies the stoic town of **Lanark**, where eighteenth-century philanthropists built their model workers' community around the mills of **New Lanark**.

Paisley

Founded in the twelfth century as a monastic settlement around an abbey, **PAISLEY** expanded after the eighteenth century as a linen-manufacturing town, specializing in the production of highly fashionable imitation Kashmiri shawls. These days, it more than merits a visit courtesy of its quite superb **abbey** and a **museum** packed with terrifically varied exhibits.

Paisley Museum and Art Gallery

High St, PA1 2BA • Tues–Sat 11am–4pm, Sun 2–5pm • Free • ☎0141 618 2598

Housed inside an attractive civic building, **Paisley Museum and Art Gallery** embraces several engaging collections from archeology and natural history to local history. In the last of these, local tragedies dominate: specifically, a boat sign and newspaper cuttings from the Paisley Canal disaster of 1810, in which a barge capsized and killed 85 people; and the Glen Cinema fire in 1929, which resulted in the deaths of 71 children. Most people, though, come to see the **Shawl Gallery**, which traces the familiar pine-cone (or teardrop) pattern from its simple beginnings to elaborate later incarnations. The **Upper Gallery** houses a small art collection including works by Glasgow Boys Hornel, Guthrie and Lavery (see page 823).

19

Paisley Abbey

Abbey Close, PA1 1JG · Mon–Sat 10am–3.30pm; guided tours (1hr) Tues & Thurs 2pm · Free · ☎ 0141 889 7654, ⓦ paisleyabbey.org.uk

Paisley Abbey was established by Cluniac monks in 1163, and became an abbey in 1219, before being massively overhauled in the Victorian age. Inside the squat grey building, the elongated choir – the longest of any medieval abbey in Scotland – is illuminated by jewel-coloured stained glass from a variety of ages and styles. Elsewhere, take a look inside the St Mirin chapel, whose superb, though incomplete, frieze depicts the life of the saint to whom the original priory was dedicated. Don't miss the exhibition in the sacristy, which displays finds from a section of the monastery's **Medieval Drain**, an arched tunnel dating from the fourteenth century that was discovered in 1990; among the extraordinary items recovered are copper alloy tweezers, a bone dice and a fragment of lead slate with script.

ARRIVAL AND INFORMATION

By train Regular trains from Glasgow Central (every 10min; 10min) connect with Paisley's Gilmour St station in the centre of town.

By bus McGills bus #38 departs from Renfield St in Glasgow (every 15min; 35min), stopping on Gilmour St, while bus #757 leaves Gilmour St (stand 7) every 10–15min for Glasgow International Airport, 2 miles north of town.

Hill House

Upper Colquhoun St, Helensburgh, 20 miles northwest of Glasgow, G84 9AJ · April–Oct daily 11.30am–5pm · £10.50; NTS · ☎ 01436 673900, ⓦ nts.org.uk/Visit/Hill-House · Train to Helensburgh Central (every 30min; 45min) from where it's a 20min uphill walk; alternatively take a taxi (£5) from Helensburgh Central station

In 1902 Charles Rennie Mackintosh was commissioned by the Glaswegian publisher Walter Blackie to design the iconic **Hill House** in Helensburgh. Without doubt the best surviving example of Mackintosh's domestic architecture, the house is stamped with his very personal, elegant interpretation of Art Nouveau – right down to the light fittings and fire irons – characterized by his sparing use of colour and stylized floral patterns. Various upstairs rooms are given over to interpretive displays on the architect's use of light, colour, form and texture, while changing exhibitions on contemporary domestic design from around Britain are a testament to Mackintosh's ongoing influence and inspiration. After exploring the house, head for the **tearoom** in the kitchen quarters, or wander round the beautifully laid out **gardens**.

The Clyde valley

Mostly following the course of the Clyde upstream, the journey southeast of Glasgow along the **Clyde valley** into Lanarkshire is dominated by endless suburbs, industrial parks and wide strips of concrete highway. The principal road here is the M74, though you'll need to get off the motorway to find the main points of interest, which tend to lie on or near the banks of the river. The **National Museum of Rural Life**, set on a historic farm, offers an in-depth look at the history of agriculture in Scotland, while further south lies the remarkable eighteenth-century planned village of **New Lanark**.

National Museum of Rural Life

Philipshill Rd, East Kilbride, 7 miles southeast of Glasgow, G76 9HR · Daily 10am–5pm · £7 · ☎ 0300 123 6789, ⓦ nms.ac.uk/national-museum-of-rural-life · Bus #31 from Glasgow's St Enoch Centre to East Kilbride takes you past the museum (Stewartfield Way), or you can get the train from Glasgow Central to East Kilbride (every 30min; 35min) from where you can walk – or take a taxi (☎ 01355 241212) – for the final 3 miles

Situated on the edge of **EAST KILBRIDE** new town, the **National Museum of Rural Life** is an unexpected union of historic farm and modern museum. The 170-acre farm, **Kittochside**, avoided the intensive farming that came to dominate agriculture in Britain after World War II, and today showcases traditional methods. On its edge, the custom-built museum uses light and space extremely well to explore the Scots' relationship with the land over centuries. A tractor and trailer shuttles visitors the half-mile up to the eighteenth-century **farmhouse**, which is furnished much as it would have been in the 1950s, the crucial decade just before traditional methods using horses and hand-tools were replaced by tractors and mechanization.

New Lanark

Visitor Centre New Lanark, ML11 9DB • April–Oct 10am–5pm; Nov–March 10am–4pm • Passport ticket £12.50 • ☎ 01555 661345, ⓦ newlanark.org

A UNESCO-designated World Heritage Site, the eighteenth-century planned village of **NEW LANARK** lies a mile below the neat little market town of **Lanark**. The first sight of the place, hidden away down in the gorge, is unforgettable: large, broken, curving walls of honeyed warehouses and tenements, built in Palladian style, are lined up along the turbulent river's edge. The community was founded by David Dale and Richard Arkwright in 1785 to harness the power of the Clyde waterfalls in their cotton-spinning industry, but it was Dale's son-in-law, Robert Owen, who revolutionized the social side of the experiment in 1798, creating a "village of unity". Believing the welfare of the workers to be crucial to industrial success, Owen built adult educational facilities, the world's first day-nursery and playground, and schools in which dancing and music were obligatory and there was no punishment or reward.

While you're free to wander around the village, which is still partially residential, you need to buy a passport ticket to get into the **exhibitions**. The Neoclassical building that now houses the visitor reception was opened by Owen in 1816 under the utopian title of **The Institute for the Formation of Character**. The multitude of fascinating on-site attractions include the **Annie McCleod Experience**, an "immersive" ride that whisks visitors on a chairlift through a social history of the village through the eyes of the eponymous millworker; reconstructed **Millworker's Houses** from both the 1820s and the 1930s; the **Historic Classroom**; and the stunningly designed **Roof Garden**, complete with water features and animal sculptures. You can also poke around the domestic kitchen, study and living areas of **Robert Owen's House**, which contains his desk. Beyond the visitor centre, a riverside path leads you the mile or so to the major **Falls of the Clyde**, where the river plunges 90ft in three tumultuous stages.

19

ARRIVAL AND INFORMATION

NEW LANARK

By train Trains run from Glasgow Central to Lanark (every 30min; 50min); from there either walk (it's 1.5 miles away) or take one of the hourly buses, which depart from next to the train station.

Tourist information In the Horsemarket, 100yd west of the station (May–Sept daily 10am–5pm; Oct–April Mon–Sat 10am–5pm; ☎ 01555 661661).

Central Scotland

CULROSS PALACE, FIFE

Central Scotland

Central Scotland, the strip of mainland north of the densely populated Glasgow–Edinburgh axis and south of the main swathe of Highlands, has been the main stage for some of the most important events in Scottish history. Stirling, its imposing castle high above the town, was historically the most important bridging point across the River Forth. From the castle battlements you can see the peaks of the forested Trossachs region, with its archetypal, wild and wonderful Scottish scenery. Popular for walking and, in particular, cycling, much of the Trossachs, together with the attractive islands and "bonnie, bonnie banks" of Loch Lomond, form the core of Scotland's first national park.

To the east, between the firths of Forth and Tay, lies the county of **Fife**, a Pictish kingdom that boasts a fascinating coastline sprinkled with historic fishing villages and sandy beaches, as well as the university town of **St Andrews**, famous worldwide for its venerable golf courses. A little to the north, the ancient town of **Perth** has as much claim as anywhere to be the gateway to the Highlands. Spectacular **Highland Perthshire** begins north and west of the city – an area of glorious wooded mountainsides and inviting walks, particularly around Rannoch Moor.

20

GETTING AROUND
CENTRAL SCOTLAND

While Stirling, Falkirk and Perth are well served by **trains** from all over Scotland, the rest of the region is only accessible on sporadic local **bus** services so you may find it easier to have your own transport. In rural areas, Stirling Council provides a **DRT** (Demand Responsive Transport) service, which connects places like Balquhidder, Callander, Killin and the Trossachs where there are few or no conventional bus services. Trip requests must be booked 24hr in advance, with fares costing no more than a regular bus ticket (☎01786 404040, ⦿stirling.gov.uk). Many people opt to explore the Trossachs by **mountain bike**.

Stirling and around

Straddling the River Forth a few miles upstream from the estuary at Kincardine, **STIRLING** looks, at first glance, like a smaller version of Edinburgh. With its crag-top castle, steep, cobbled streets and mixed community of locals, students and tourists, it's an appealing if parochial place.

Stirling was the scene of some of the most significant developments in the evolution of the Scottish nation. It was here the Scots under William Wallace defeated the English at the **Battle of Stirling Bridge** in 1297, only to fight – and win again – under Robert the Bruce just a couple of miles away at the **Battle of Bannockburn** in 1314. The town enjoyed its golden age in the fifteenth to seventeenth centuries, most notably when its castle was the favoured residence of the Stuart monarchy and the setting for the coronation in 1543 of the young Mary, future Queen of Scots. By the

FALKIRK WHEEL

Highlights

❶ Stirling Castle Impregnable, impressive and resonant with history. If you see only one castle in Scotland, make it this. See page 842

❷ Falkirk Wheel The most remarkable piece of modern engineering in Britain, this fascinating contraption lifts boats 100ft between two canals. See page 844

❸ The Trossachs Pocket Highlands with shining lochs, wooded glens and noble peaks. Great for hiking and mountain biking. See page 847

❹ Himalayas putting course, St Andrews The world's finest putting course, right beside the world's finest golf course; a snip at £3 a round. See page 852

❺ The gin and whisky revival Fife is the original home of Scotch and a number of new outfits are leading a revival. See page 853

❻ The East Neuk Buy trap-to-table lobster from the wooden shack at Crail's historic stone harbour or dine in style at *The Cellar* restaurant in the fishing town of Anstruther. See page 855

❼ Forth bridges The Forth Rail bridge is an icon of Victorian engineering, while its shiny new partner – the Queensferry Crossing – is a world-beating record breaker. See page 858

❽ Rannoch Moor One of the most inaccessible places in Scotland, where hikers can discover a true sense of isolation. See page 864

HIGHLIGHTS ARE MARKED ON THE MAP ON PAGE 840

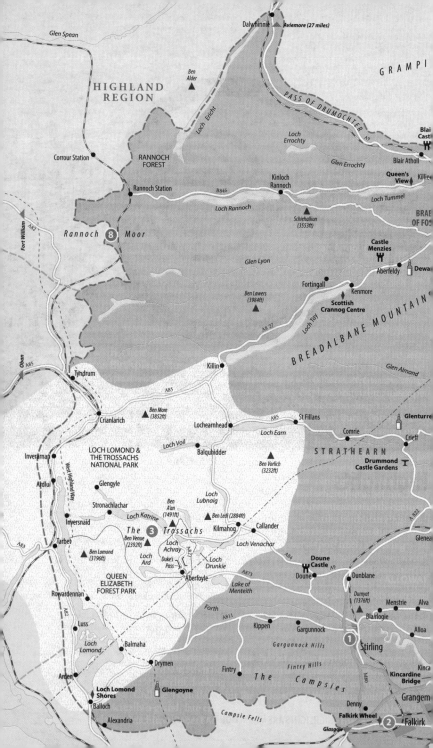

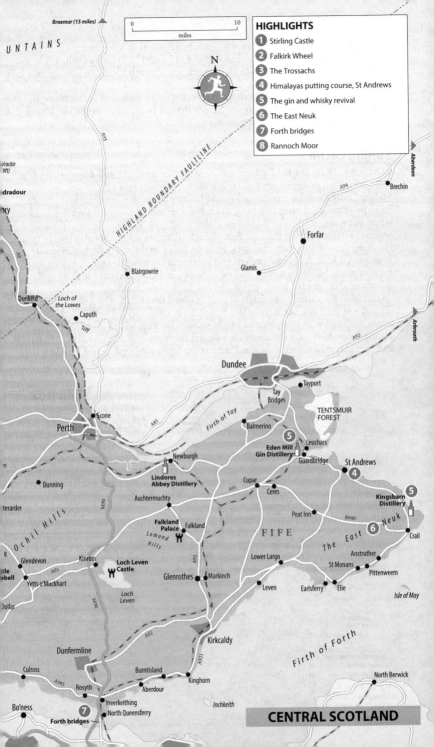

Braemar (15 miles)

HIGHLIGHTS

1. Stirling Castle
2. Falkirk Wheel
3. The Trossachs
4. Himalayas putting course, St Andrews
5. The gin and whisky revival
6. The East Neuk
7. Forth bridges
8. Rannoch Moor

0   miles   10

N

MOUNTAINS

HIGHLAND BOUNDARY FAULTLINE

Aberdeen

dradour
ncy
Vrackie
(9ft)

A93

Brechin

A94

Forfar

Blairgowrie

Glamis

Dunkeld
Loch of
the Lowes
Caputh
Tay

A9

Arbroath

A92

Scone

Perth

A85

Firth of Tay

Dundee

Tay
Bridges

Tayport

TENTSMUIR
FOREST

Balmerino

Newburgh

5 Eden Mill
Gin Distillery

Leuchars

Guardbridge

St Andrews

4

Dunning

Lindores
Abbey Distillery

Cupar

Ceres

Kingsbarn
Distillery

5

terarder

Auchtermuchty

A91

M90

Peat Inn

B940

6 Neuk

Crail

Ochil Hills

Falkland
Palace

Falkland

Lomond
Hills

FIFE

The East

Glendevon

Kinross

A91

Loch Leven
Castle

A92

Lower Largo

Anstruther

le
bell

Yetts o'Muckhart

Glenrothes

Markinch

St Monans

Pittenweem

Dollar

Loch
Leven

M90

Leven

Earlsferry

Elie

Isle of May

Kirkcaldy

Firth of Forth

Dunfermline

A92

Culross

A985

Burntisland

North Berwick

Rosyth

Aberdour

Kinghorn

Bo'ness

Inverkeithing

Inchkeith

7
Forth bridges

North Queensferry

CENTRAL SCOTLAND

early eighteenth century the town was again besieged, its location being of strategic importance during the Jacobite rebellions of 1715 and 1745. Today Stirling is known for its **castle** and the lofty **Wallace Monument**, a mammoth Victorian homage to a hero high on Abbey Craig.

Nearby, the region's historic heritage is reflected in the cathedral at **Dunblane** and the imposing castle at **Doune** (an icon to Monty Python fans), while the **Falkirk Wheel** is undisputed marvel of modern engineering.

Stirling Castle

Upper Castle Wynd, FK8 1EJ • Daily: April–Sept 9.30am–6pm; Oct–March 9.30am–5pm • £15; HS • **Guided tours** Same days, every 30min; 45min; last tour 3pm • Free with entry fee; HS • ☏ 01786 450000, ⊕ stirlingcastle.gov.uk

Stirling Castle must have presented would-be invaders with a formidable challenge. Its impregnability is most daunting when you approach the town from the west, from where the vision of the sheer 250ft drop down the crag is spine-tingling. The rock was first fortified during the Iron Age, though what you see today dates largely from the fifteenth and sixteenth centuries. Built on many levels, the main buildings are interspersed with delightful gardens and patches of lawn, while endless battlements, cannon ports, hidden staircases and other nooks and crannies make it thoroughly absorbing. Free **guided tours** start at the well in the Lower Square.

Central to the castle is the magnificently restored **Great Hall**, which dates from 1501–03 and was used as a barracks by the British army until 1964. The building stands out across Stirling for its controversial bright yellow cladding, added after the discovery during renovations of a stretch of the original sixteenth-century limewash. Inside, the hall has been restored to its original state as the finest medieval secular building in

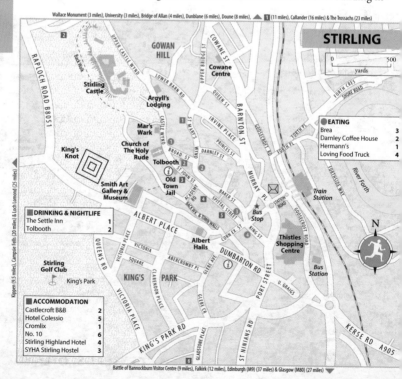

Wallace Monument (3 miles), University (3 miles), Bridge of Allan (4 miles), Dunblane (6 miles), Doune (8 miles), (11 miles), Callander (16 miles) & The Trossachs (23 miles)

STIRLING

GOWAN HILL

Cowane Centre

Stirling Castle

Argyll's Lodging

Mar's Wark

Church of The Holy Rude

King's Knot

Tolbooth

Old Town Jail

Smith Art Gallery & Museum

ALBERT PLACE

Albert Halls

Thistles Shopping Centre

Train Station

Bus Stop

Stirling Golf Club

King's Park

KING'S PARK

Bus Station

Kippen (9.5 miles), Campsie Fells (20 miles) & Loch Lomond (25 miles)

EATING

Brea	3
Darnley Coffee House	2
Hermann's	1
Loving Food Truck	4

DRINKING & NIGHTLIFE

The Settle Inn	1
Tolbooth	2

ACCOMMODATION

Castlecroft B&B	2
Hotel Colessio	5
Cromlix	1
No. 10	6
Stirling Highland Hotel	4
SYHA Stirling Hostel	3

Battle of Bannockburn Visitor Centre (9 miles), Falkirk (12 miles), Edinburgh (M9) (37 miles) & Glasgow (M80) (27 miles)

Scotland, complete with five gaping fireplaces and an impressive hammer-beam ceiling of rough-hewn wood. A major restoration of the **Palace**, with specially commissioned tapestries and furniture, returned the rooms to something like their appearance in the mid-sixteenth century.

On the sloping upper courtyard of the castle, the **Chapel Royal** was built in 1594 by James VI for the baptism of his son. The interior is charming, with a seventeenth-century fresco of elaborate scrolls and patterns. Go through a narrow passageway beyond the Chapel Royal to get to the **Douglas Gardens**, reputedly the place where the eighth Earl of Douglas, suspected of treachery, was thrown to his death by James II in 1452. It's a lovely, quiet corner of the castle, with mature trees and battlements over which there are splendid views of the rising Highlands beyond, as well as a bird's-eye view down to the **King's Knot**, a series of grassed octagonal mounds that were planted with box trees and ornamental hedges in the seventeenth century.

The old town

Stirling evolved from the top down, starting with its castle and gradually spreading south and east onto the low-lying flood plain. In the eighteenth and nineteenth centuries, as the threat of attack decreased, the centre of commercial life crept towards the River Forth, with the modern town growing on the edge of the plain over which the castle had stood guard.

Leaving the castle, head downhill into Stirling's **old town**, fortified behind the massive, whinstone boulders of the **town walls**, built in the mid-sixteenth century and intended to ward off the advances of Henry VIII, who had set his sights on the young Mary, Queen of Scots, as a wife for his son, Edward. The walls now constitute some of the best-preserved town defences in Scotland, and can be traced by following the path known as **Back Walk**, which leads right under the castle, taut along the edge of the crag. Though a little overgrown in places, the path does afford panoramic views.

20

National Wallace Monument

1.5 miles north of the old town, Abbey Craig, FK9 5LF • Daily: March 10am–5pm; April–June 9.30am–5pm; July & Aug 9.30am–6pm; Sept & Oct 9.30am–5pm; Nov–Feb 10.30am–4pm • £10.50 • ☏ 01786 472140, ⓦ nationalwallacemonument.com • First Bus #62A & #63A from the town centre

The prominent **National Wallace Monument** is a 220ft tower built in the 1860s as a tribute to Sir William Wallace, the freedom fighter who led Scottish resistance against Edward I, the "Hammer of the Scots", in the late thirteenth century. The crag on which the monument is set was the scene of his greatest victory, when he sent his troops charging down the hillside onto the plain to defeat the English at the Battle of Stirling Bridge in 1297. Exhibits inside the tower include Wallace's long steel sword and a life-sized "talking" model of the Scottish hero, who tells visitors about his battle preparations. The climb to the top – up 246 spiral steps – rewards you with superb views across to Fife and Ben Lomond.

Battle of Bannockburn Visitor Centre

Two miles south of Stirling centre, on the A872, FK7 0LJ • Daily: March–Oct 10am–5.30pm; Nov–Feb 10am–5pm • £11.50; NTS • ☏ 01786 812664 • ⓦ battleofbannockburn.com • Buses #2A, #39, #54A, #54 from Stirling bus station or Murray Place

All but surrounded by drab social housing, the **Battle of Bannockburn Visitor Centre** commemorates the most famous battle in Scottish history, when King Robert the Bruce won his mighty victory over the English on June 24, 1314. It was this battle, the climax of the Wars of Independence, which united the Scots under Bruce and led to independence from England; Bruce employed brilliantly innovative tactics in mustering his army to defeat a much larger English force.

The actual site of the main battle is still a matter of debate: most agree that it didn't take place near the present visitor centre, but on a boggy plain a mile or so to the west. The centre itself, rebooted for the seven hundredth anniversary of the battle in 2014, is largely devoid of the kind of artefacts that bring Culloden (see page 920) so movingly to life, and the centre relies on interactive displays and a 3D military video game. That said, it's popular, so be sure to book ahead.

Dunblane Cathedral

The Cross, Dunblane, 5 miles north of Stirling, FK15 0AQ • April–Sept Mon–Sat 9.30am–5.30pm, Sun 2–5pm; Oct–March Mon–Sat 10am–4pm, Sun 2–4pm • Free; HS • ☎ 01786 825388, ⓦ dunblanecathedral.org.uk • Regular trains connect Dunblane with Stirling and points north

The attractive small town of **DUNBLANE** has been an important ecclesiastical centre since the seventh century, when the Celts founded the Church of St Blane here. **Dunblane Cathedral** dates mainly from the thirteenth century, and restoration work carried out a century ago has returned it to its Gothic splendour. Inside, note the delicate blue-purple stained glass, and the exquisitely carved pews, screen and choir stalls, all crafted in the early twentieth century.

Doune Castle

Eight miles west of Stirling, FK16 6EA • Daily: April–Sept 9.30am–5.30pm; Oct–March 10am–4pm • £6; HS • ☎ 01786 841742, ⓦ historicenvironment.scot/visit-a-place/places/doune-castle • From Stirling bus station, take bus #1 to Callander to Doune's main street

Standing on a small hill in a bend of the River Teith in the parish of **DOUNE**, the stern-looking, fourteenth-century **Doune Castle** is a marvellous semi-ruin. Perhaps its greatest claim to fame is as the setting for the 1970s cult movie *Monty Python and the Holy Grail*; the shop by the gatehouse keeps a scrapbook of stills from the film, as well as a selection of souvenirs including bottles of Holy Grail Ale. Today another fifteen minutes of fame beckons, as hit series *Game of Thrones* and *Outlander* have also been filmed here.

Falkirk Wheel

Lime Rd, 2 miles west of Falkirk, which is 10 miles southeast of Stirling on the M9 to Edinburgh, FK1 4RS • **Visitor Centre** Daily 10am–5.30pm • Free • **Boat tours** Every 30min: April–Oct daily 9.30am–4.30pm; Nov–March Wed–Sun 11am–4pm • 50min • £12.95 • ☎ 0870 0500208, ⓦ thefalkirkwheel.co.uk • There are buses from Stirling (every 30min; 15min), and trains to Falkirk from Edinburgh (every 15–30min; 30min), Glasgow Queen St (every 15–30min; 25min) and Stirling (every 30min; 15min) – taxis can take you the 2.5 mile journey from the train station to the wheel

The town of **FALKIRK** has a good deal of visible history, going right back to the remains of the Roman Antonine Wall. A massive transformation came in the eighteenth century with the construction of canals connecting Glasgow and Edinburgh; within a few years, however, the trains arrived, and the canals gradually fell into disuse. While Falkirk's canals were a very visible sign of the area's industrial heritage, it was only recently that their leisure potential was realized, thanks to British Waterway's £84.5 million **Millennium Link** project to restore them and re-establish a navigable link between east and west coasts.

The icon of this project is the remarkable **Falkirk Wheel**. The giant grey wheel, the world's first and only rotating boat-lift, scoops boats in two giant buckets, or caissons, and moves them the 100ft between the levels of the Forth & Clyde and Union canals linked to Glasgow and Edinburgh respectively. Beneath the wheel, the **visitor centre** sells tickets for the **boat trip** from the lower basin into the wheel, along the Union Canal, and back again.

ARRIVAL AND INFORMATION	STIRLING AND AROUND
By train The train station is in the centre of town on Goosecroft Rd.	55min); Edinburgh (every 30min; 1hr); Falkirk (every 30min; 15min); Glasgow Queen St (every 20min; 30min); Inverness
Destinations Aberdeen (hourly; 2hr 5min); Dundee (hourly;	(3–5 daily; 2hr 55min); Perth (hourly; 30min).

By bus The bus station, on Goosecroft Rd, can be accessed from the Thistles Shopping Centre.

Destinations Aberfoyle (4 daily; 45min); Bridge of Allan (hourly–every 2hr; 15min); Callander (40min–1hr; 45min); Dollar (every 2hr; 35min); Doune (40min–1hr; 25min); Dunblane (hourly; 20min); Dundee (hourly; 1hr 30min); Edinburgh (hourly; 1hr); Falkirk (hourly; 30min); Glasgow (hourly; 50min); Inverness (every 2hr; 3hr 20min); Perth (hourly; 40min); St Andrews (every 2hr; 1hr 55min).

Tourist office The Old Town Jail, St John St (daily 10am–5pm; ☎01786 475019, ⓦdestinationstirling.com).

ACCOMMODATION

Castlecroft B&B Ballengeich Rd, FK8 1TN ☎01786 474933, ⓦcastlecroft-uk.com; map p.842. Modern guesthouse with six en-suite rooms on the site of the King's Stables just beneath the castle rock, with terrific views north and west and a very friendly welcome. **£70**

Hotel Colessio 33 Spittal St, FK8 1DX ☎01786 448880, ⓦhotelcolessio.com; map p.842. Bling, with a cheeky self-knowing wink, this born-again Victorian building is the closest Stirling gets to five-star luxury. Its forty rooms are unashamedly glam (sleek monochrome interiors, widescreen TVs, marble bathrooms), but the wow factor really comes with the Scotch beef and cracked lobster at the *Grill Room* restaurant (mains from £14). **£90**

★ **Cromlix** Kinbuck, 11 miles north of Stirling, FK15 9JT ☎01786 822125, ⓦcromlix.com; map p.842. It's rare for a tennis superstar to own a luxury country-house hotel, but then Sir Andy Murray's not your average sports personality. This venture, close to his hometown of Dunblane, is set in 34 acres of beautiful woodland and comes with traditional Victorian paintings and furnishings, a restaurant (courtesy of London-based Michelin gourmand Michel Roux) and – surprise, surprise – perfectly trimmed tennis courts. **£220**

No. 10 10 Gladstone Place, FK8 2NN ☎01786 472681, ⓦcameron-10.co.uk; map p.842. Modernized Victorian home with neat, uncluttered decor providing friendly and pleasant B&B accommodation. It's close to the city centre, but on a quiet and elegant King's Park street. **£60**

Stirling Highland Hotel Spittal St, FK8 1DU ☎01786 272727, ⓦthecairncollection.co.uk; map p.842. Built in 1854 as the city's original grammar school, this Victorian Gothic hotel is a charmer on all fronts, with a health club, pool, an on-site whisky shop and a working observatory on the top floor. Make sure to visit the bar in the old French classroom. **£100**

SYHA Stirling Hostel St John St, FK8 1EA ☎01786 473442, ⓦsyha.org.uk/where-to-stay/lowlands/stirling; map p.842. Located at the top of the town (a strenuous trek with a backpack) in a converted church with an impressive 1824 Palladian facade. All rooms have en-suite showers and toilets, and facilities include a games room. Dorms **£15**, doubles **£35**

EATING

Brea 5 Baker St, FK8 1BJ ☎01786 446277, ⓦbrea-stirling.co.uk; map p.842. A great little bistro with exposed brick walls and pop-art interiors that delves deep into Scotland's larder with west coast seafood, steak burgers and fresh-from-the-farm salads. Also specializes in craft beers and gins of the month (mains from £13.95). Mon–Thurs & Sun noon–9pm, Fri & Sat noon–10pm.

Darnley Coffee House 18 Bow St, FK8 1BS ☎01786 474468; map p.842. Named after Mary Queen of Scots' lover, this vaulted café is a tartan throwback with plenty of Old Town atmosphere and bargain lunches, soups, teas, home-made cakes and fruit cordials (lunch from £6). Daily 11am–4pm.

★ **Hermann's** 58 Broad St, FK8 1EF ☎01786 450632, ⓦhermanns.co.uk; map p.842. Stirling's classiest eating option, set in the historic Mar Place House towards the top of the Old Town. Run by affable Tirolean expat Hermann Aschaberlt, it offers an upmarket Austrian-Scottish hybrid with dishes such as *Jagerschnitzel* (veal) or smoked Scottish duck with Speck (bacon). Mains from £11.50. Daily noon–2pm & 6–9pm.

Loving Food Truck King's Park Pavilion ☎07788 567113, ⓦloving-food.com; map p.842. When it's open for business, this vintage green-and-white Citroen van is easy to spot around town. It's run by a DIY food crew who love nothing better than creative street food combos, which includes everything from meatloaf flatbreads to veggie haggis tacos (from £6). They're looking around for a permanent HQ. Mon–Fri only.

DRINKING AND NIGHTLIFE

The Settle Inn 91 St Mary's Wynd, FK8 1BU ☎01786 474609, ⓦtwitter.com/settleinn; map p.842. An old-school, no-frills boozer that's big on local ales, folk music nights and history. It's Stirling's oldest pub, in business since 1736, and was once commandeered by Bonnie Prince Charlie during a brief occupation of the town. Daily noon–11pm.

Tolbooth Jail Wynd, FK8 1DE ☎01786 274000, ⓦculturestirling.org/tolbooth; map p.842. Built on the site of Stirling's medieval prison, the *Tolbooth* is by far the best option for a night out, with a high-ceilinged bar and eclectic live music programme. Look out for their boisterous ceilidhs in July & Aug. Open daily.

20

Loch Lomond

The largest stretch of fresh water in Britain (23 miles long and up to five miles wide), **Loch Lomond** is thought of as the epitome of Scottish scenic splendour, thanks in large part to the ballad that fondly recalls its "bonnie, bonnie banks". In reality, however, the peerless scenery of the loch can be tainted by the sheer numbers of day-trippers.

Designated Scotland's first national park in 2002, the **Loch Lomond and the Trossachs National Park** (Ⓦlochlomond-trossachs.org) covers a large stretch of scenic territory from the lochs of the Clyde estuary to Loch Tay in Perthshire, with the centrepiece being Loch Lomond. The most popular gateway into the park is the town of **Balloch**, nineteen miles from Glasgow city centre. Both Balloch and the western side of the loch around Luss are often packed with tour coaches, though the loch's eastern side, abutting the Trossachs, is very different in tone, with wooden ferryboats puttering out to a scattering of tree-covered islands off the village of **Balmaha**.

Balloch

Little more than a suburb of the much larger factory-town of Alexandria to the south, **BALLOCH**, on the southwestern corner of Loch Lomond, has few redeeming features. However, its road and train links with Glasgow ensure that it remains the focal point of the national park.

ARRIVAL AND DEPARTURE

BALLOCH

By train Balloch has good train connections with Glasgow (every 30min; 45min).

By bus Buses connect with Balmaha (every 2hr; 30min) and Luss (hourly; 20min).

ACCOMMODATION AND EATING

Cameron House 2 miles north of Balloch, G83 8QZ · ☎01389 310777, Ⓦcameronhouse.co.uk. The ultimate in lochside luxury, this romantic country house and spa hosted A-list movie stars, heads of state and royal dignitaries and was home to Michelin-starred *Restaurant Martin Wishart*. At the time of writing, the hotel had suffered a devastating fire and was closed until further notice; check the website for the latest news. **£197**

Loch Lomond Shores

National Park Gateway Centre Ben Lomond Way, G83 8QL · Daily 10am–6pm · Free · ☎01389 751031 · Ⓦlochlomondshores.com ·
Drumkinnon Tower Daily 10am–5pm · £13.95 · ☎01389 721500, Ⓦvisitsealife.com/loch-lomond

Signposted from miles around, **Loch Lomond Shores** contains the **National Park Gateway Centre**, which has background and tourist information outlining all waterbuses, loch cruises and transport links within the park, as well as a number of shops, including an outpost of Edinburgh department store Jenners and the Edinburgh Woollen Mill. Alongside, **Drumkinnon Tower** is a striking cylindrical building housing an aquarium.

THE ISLANDS OF LOCH LOMOND

Many of Loch Lomond's 22 **islands** and 27 **islets** are privately owned, and, rather quaintly, an old wooden mail-boat still delivers post to four of them. It's possible to join the **mail-boat cruise**, which is run by Macfarlane & Son from the jetty at Balmaha (May–Oct Mon, Thurs & Sat 11.30am, returns 2pm; July & Aug daily 11.30am, returns 2pm; £10; ☎01360 870214, Ⓦbalmahaboatyard.co.uk). There's time for a stop on Inchmurrin Island, the largest and most southerly of the islands, with a permanent population of just ten people. If you're looking for an island to explore, however, a better bet is **Inchailloch**, the closest to Balmaha. Owned by Scottish Natural Heritage (Ⓦsnh.gov.uk) it has a two-mile, signposted nature trail. You can row here yourself using a boat hired from Macfarlane & Son (from £10/hr or £40/day), or use their on-demand ferry service (£5 return).

THE WEST HIGHLAND WAY

Opened in 1980, the spectacular **West Highland Way** was Scotland's first long-distance footpath, stretching 96 miles from Milngavie (pronounced "mill-guy") six miles north of central Glasgow to Fort William, where it reaches the foot of Ben Nevis, Britain's highest mountain. Today, it is by far the most popular such footpath in Scotland, and while for many the range of scenery, relative ease of walking and nearby facilities make it a classic route, others find it a little too busy in high season.

The route runs along the eastern shores of Loch Lomond, over the Highland Boundary Fault Line, then round Crianlarich, crossing the open heather wilderness of **Rannoch Moor**. It passes close to **Glen Coe**, notorious for the massacre of the MacDonald clan, before reaching **Fort William**. Apart from one stretch halfway along when the path is within earshot of the main road, this is wild, remote country, and you should be well prepared for sudden and extreme weather changes.

While this is emphatically not the most strenuous of Britain's long-distance walks, a moderate degree of fitness is required as there are some steep ascents. You might choose to walk individual sections of the Way (the eight-mile climb from Glen Coe up the Devil's Staircase is particularly spectacular), but to tackle the whole thing you need to set aside at least seven days; avoid a Saturday start from Milngavie and you'll be less likely to be walking with hordes of people. Most walkers tackle the route from south to north, and manage between ten and fourteen miles a day, staying at hotels, B&Bs and bunkhouses en route. Camping is permitted at recognized sites.

For further details on the Way, including a comprehensive accommodation list and various tour options, see ⓦ west-highland-way.co.uk.

Balmaha

The tranquil **eastern shore** of Loch Lomond is far better for walking and appreciating the loch's natural beauty than the overcrowded western side. The dead-end B837 road from Drymen will take you halfway up the east bank, as far as you can get by car or bus, while the West Highland Way (see page 847) sticks close to the shores for the entire length of the loch, beginning at the tiny lochside settlement of **BALMAHA**, which stands on the Highland Boundary Fault, the geological fault that separates the Highlands from the Lowlands.

ARRIVAL AND INFORMATION   BALMAHA

By bus The #309 bus from Balloch and Drymen runs to Balmaha every 2hr.

National Park Centre Next to the large car park, with great information on forest walks (daily 9.30am–4pm; ☎01360 722100, ⓦ lochlomond-trossachs.org).

ACCOMMODATION AND EATING

Cashel Rowardennan, 2 miles north of Balmaha, G63 0AW ☎01360 870234, ⓦ campingintheforest.co.uk. A lovely, secluded campsite on the loch shore, with a decent loo block. Campers can launch craft from here onto the loch, while the West Highland Way passes right past its door. Closed Nov–Feb. **£18.25**

Oak Tree Inn Balmaha, G63 0JQ ☎01360 870357, ⓦ theoaktreeinn.co.uk. This corker of an inn is set back from the boatyard, and offers en-suite doubles and bunk-bed quads. There's also a convivial pub with an all-day food menu. Daily noon–9pm. **£100**

The Trossachs

Often described as the Highlands in miniature, the **Trossachs** area has a magnificent diversity of scenery, with dramatic peaks and mysterious, forest-covered slopes that live up to all the images of Scotland's wild land. It is country ripe with stirring tales of brave kilted clansmen, a role fulfilled by **Rob Roy Macgregor**, the seventeenth-century outlaw whose name seems to attach to every second waterfall, cave and barely discernible path.

> **CENTRAL SCOTLAND: TOP 5 PLACES TO WALK**
> **Ben Lawers** See page 862
> **Loch Lomond** See page 846
> **Pass of Killiecrankie** See page 864
> **Queen Elizabeth Forest Park** See page 849
> **Rannoch Moor** See page 864

The Trossachs' high tourist profile was largely attributable in the early days to the novels of Sir Walter Scott, several of which are set in the area. Since then, neither the popularity nor beauty of the region have waned, and in high season the place is jam-packed with tourist coaches, as well as walkers and mountain bikers enjoying the easily accessible scenery. Add to this the 2017 bicentenary of the publication of Scott's historical novel *Rob Roy* and the park is now busier than ever. Autumn is the best time to come, when the hills are blanketed in rich, rusty colours and the crowds thin out.

Aberfoyle

Each summer the little holiday town of **ABERFOYLE**, twenty miles west of Stirling, dusts itself down for its annual influx of tourists. Though of little appeal itself, Aberfoyle's position in the heart of the Trossachs is ideal. From here, the A821 road to **Loch Katrine** winds its way into the **Queen Elizabeth Forest Park**, snaking up the roller coaster **Duke's Pass** (so called because it once belonged to the Duke of Montrose). For a mini Scottish road-trip, it's unrivalled.

Lake of Menteith

About 4 miles east of Aberfoyle towards Doune, FK8 3RA • To rent fishing gear contact Lake of Menteith Fisheries ☎ 01877 385664, ⓦ mentieth-fisheries.co.uk

The **Lake of Menteith** is a superb **fly-fishing** centre and Scotland's only lake (as opposed to loch), so named due to a historic mix-up with the word *laigh*, Scots for "low-lying ground". From the northern shore, you can take a little ferry out to **Inchmahome** in order to explore the island's lovely ruined Augustinian priory.

Inchmahome Priory

Daily: April–Sept 10am–4.15pm; Oct 10am–3.15pm • £7.50, including ferry; HS • ☎ 01877 385294, ⓦ historicenvironment.scot/visit-a-place/places/inchmahome-priory

Founded in 1238, **Inchmahome Priory** is the most beautiful island monastery in Scotland, its remains rising tall and graceful above the trees. A refuge for the young Mary Queen of Scots in late 1547, the priory is thought to have been built by the same masons responsible for Dunblane Cathedral (see page 844).

ARRIVAL AND INFORMATION
ABERFOYLE

By bus Buses connect with Callander (#504; 25min) and Port of Menteith (#C11 towards Stirling, or #504 towards Callander; 10min).

Tourist information The excellent Queen Elizabeth Forest Park Visitor Centre at the David Marshall Lodge is a mile north of Aberfoyle on the A821. Helpful guides dispense maps of the walks and cycle routes in the forest, and there is a nice café with splendid views over the treetops (daily: Jan & Feb 10am–3pm; March, April & Oct–Dec 10am–4pm; May, June & Sept 10am–5pm; July & Aug 10am–6pm; ☎ 0300 067 6615, ⓦ scotland.forestry.gov.uk/forest-parks/queen-elizabeth-forest-park/the-lodge-forest-visitor-centre).

ACCOMMODATION AND EATING

Lake of Menteith Hotel Port of Menteith, FK8 3RA ☎ 01877 385258, ⓦ lake-hotel.com. A beautiful place to stay, with spacious, glamorous rooms: the hotel enjoys a lovely waterfront setting next to Port of Menteith's Victorian Gothic parish church, and also has a classy restaurant. Ask – of course – for a room with a lake view. Daily noon–2.30pm & 5.30–9pm. **£138**

Loch Katrine

Heading down the northern side of the Duke's Pass you first come to **Loch Achray**, tucked under Ben A'an. At the head of the loch, a road leads the short distance to the southern end of **Loch Katrine** at the foot of Ben Venue (2392ft).

Cruises on Loch Katrine

Trossachs Pier, FK17 8HZ • March–Nov daily • £16.50 return; shorter 1hr cruises with no stops £13.50 • ☎ 01877 376315, Ⓦ lochkatrine.com

An elegant Victorian passenger **steamer**, the SS *Sir Walter Scott*, has been plying the waters of Loch Katrine since 1900, chugging up to the wild country of Glengyle. It offers various cruises each day, but only the first run in summer (June–Oct 10.30am) stops at Stronachlachar. Afternoon trips on the fleet's more modern cruiser *Lady of the Lake* follow the same route, departing at 1.30pm and 4.15pm (subject to numbers and weather). A popular combination is to **rent a bike** from the Katrinewheelz hut by the pier (☎01877 376366, Ⓦkatrinewheelz.co.uk; £20/day), take the steamer up to Stronachlachar, then cycle back along the north side of the loch.

EATING
LOCH KATRINE

★ **Venacher Lochside** 5 miles west of Callander, FK17 8HP ☎01877 330011, Ⓦvenacher-lochside.com. Once an unloved café, this sensational boathouse restaurant on the north shore of Loch Venacher has been reborn following a change in ownership. The menu proposes a Scottish greatest hits (Perthshire short rib, Shetland mussels, Venacher-caught trout; mains from £13), but it's equally worth a stop for coffee or for a look at their local arts and crafts (available to buy). Mon–Thurs & Sun 10am–4pm, Fri & Sat 10am–4pm & 5–7pm.

20

Callander

CALLANDER, on the eastern edge of the Trossachs, sits on the banks of the River Teith at the southern end of the **Pass of Leny**, one of the key routes into the Highlands. Significantly larger than Aberfoyle, eleven miles west, it is a popular summer holiday base and suffers in high season for being on the main tourist trail from Stirling through to the west Highlands.

ARRIVAL AND GETTING AROUND
CALLANDER

By bus The local bus service has been replaced by a Demand Responsive Transport (DRT; ☎ 01786 404040 Ⓦ stirling.gov. uk) system. Trip requests must be booked 24hr in advance; fares cost no more than a regular bus ticket.
Bike rental Handily located in the centre of Callander, Wheelology, 4 Ancaster Square (☎01877 331052, Ⓦcycle hirecallander.co.uk), offers bike rental, sales, repairs and accessories. However, Wheels Cycling Centre, 1.5 miles southwest of Callander, is the best bike rental place in the area, with front- or full-suspension models, as well as baby seats and children's cycles (☎01877 331100, Ⓦscottish-cycling.com).

HIKING AND BIKING IN THE TROSSACHS

The Trossachs is ideal for exploring **on foot** or on a **mountain bike**. This is partly because the terrain is slightly more benign than the Highlands proper, but much is due to the excellent management of the **Queen Elizabeth Forest Park**, a huge chunk of the national park between Loch Lomond and Loch Lubnaig. The main visitor centre for the area, David Marshall Lodge, is just outside Aberfoyle (see page 848).

For **hill-walkers**, the prize peak is Ben Lomond (3196ft), best accessed from Rowardennan on Loch Lomond's east shore. Other highlights include Ben Venue (2392ft) and Ben A'an (1491ft) on the shores of Loch Katrine, as well as Ben Ledi (2884ft), just northwest of Callander, which all offer relatively straightforward but rewarding climbs and, on clear days, stunning views. Walkers can also choose from any number of waymarked routes through the forests and along lochsides; pick up a map at the visitor centre.

The area is also popular with **mountain bikers**, with a number of useful rental shops (see above), a network of forest paths and one of the more impressive stretches of the National Cycle Network cutting through the region from Loch Lomond to Killin.

ACCOMMODATION

★ **Monachyle Mhor Hotel** Balquidder, 17 miles north of Callander, FK19 8PQ ☎01877 384622, ⓦmonachylemhor.net. Run by Welsh brothers Tom and Dick Lewis, both champions of the local food scene, this refined eighteenth-century farmhouse turned lochside boutique hotel is part of the Mhor mini hotel and restaurant empire – and deserves all its plaudits. Choose from luxurious courtyard or stylish farmhouse rooms, a kitsch backwoods cabin (£140) or a wacky glamping wagon with wood-burning stove (£125). The family-sty motel *Mhor84* is nearby. **£195**

Roman Camp Country House Hotel 182 Main S FK17 8BG ☎01877 330003, ⓦromancamphotel.co.u The town's most upmarket option is this romantic, turrete seventeenth-century hunting lodge, built for the Dukes Perth, in twenty-acre gardens on the River Teith. The co *Whyte Bar* has a sleek grand piano and offers more tha forty single malts. **£160**

EATING AND DRINKING

Lade Inn Kilmahog, 1 mile west of Callander, FK17 8HN ☎01877 330152, ⓦtheladeinn.com. Top-notch Scottish gastropub food is the draw at this hospitable inn where the owners are particularly keen on real ales; an on-site shop sells bottled beers from all over Scotland, including their very own refreshing amber ale Ladeback. Mains from £9.75. Restaurant: Mon–Sat noon–9pm, Sun 12.30–9pm. Bar: Mon–Thurs noon–11pm, Fri &

Sat noon–1am, Sun 12.30–10.30pm.

★ **Mhor Fish** 75–77 Main St, FK17 8DX ☎0187 330213, ⓦmhorfish.net. Brothers Tom and Dick Lew (see above) are at it again with their new breed of fis and chip shop – a sustainable fish policy, daily specia and everything from takeaway suppers (from £5.50) bistro-style seafood dishes (mains around £10). Dail noon–9pm.

20 Fife

The ancient Kingdom of **Fife** is a small area, barely fifty miles at its widest point, but one that has a definite identity, inextricably linked with the waters that surround it on three sides – the Tay to the north, the Forth to the south and the cold North Sea to the east. Despite its size, Fife encompasses several different regions, with a marked difference between the rural north and the semi-industrial south. Fishing still has a role to play, but ultimately most visitors are drawn to **St Andrews**, the home of the world-famous Royal and Ancient Golf Club. South of St Andrews, the tiny stone harbours, pubs and restaurants of the **East Neuk** fishing villages are an appealing extension to any visit to this part of Fife.

Inland from St Andrews is the absorbing village of **Falkland** with its impressive ruine palace. To the **south**, the perfectly preserved town of **Culross** is the most obvious draw with its cobbled streets and historic buildings.

St Andrews and around

Confident, poised and well groomed, if a little snooty, **ST ANDREWS**, Scotland's oldest **university town** and a pilgrimage centre for **golfers** from all over the world, is situated on a wide bay on the northeastern coast. Of all Scotland's universities, St Andrews is the most often compared to Oxford or Cambridge, both for the dominance of gown over town, and for the intimate, collegiate feel of the place. In fact, the university attracts a significant proportion of English undergraduates, among them Prince William, who spent four years studying here, where he met fellow student and future wife Kate Middleton.

According to legend, the town was founded, pretty much by accident, in the fourth century. **St Rule** – or Regulus – a custodian of the bones of St Andrew in Patras in southern Greece, had a vision in which an angel ordered him to carry five of the saint's bones to the western edge of the world, where he was to build a city in his honour. The conscientious courier set off, but was shipwrecked on the rocks close to the present harbour. Struggling ashore with his precious burden, he built a shrine to the saint on what subsequently became the site of the **cathedral**; St Andrew became Scotland's patron saint and the town its ecclesiastical capital.

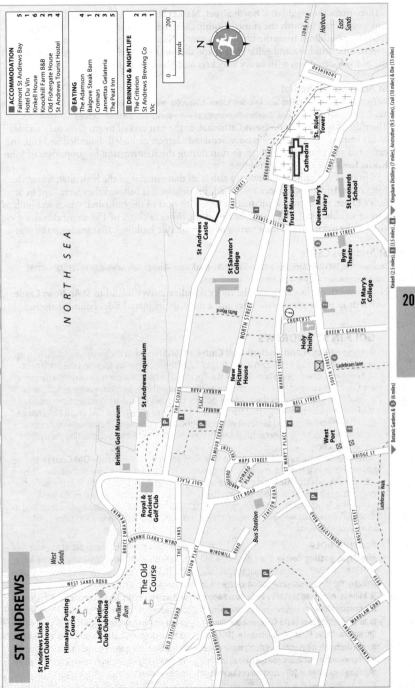

ST ANDREWS

West Sands

NORTH SEA

Harbour

East Sands

Long Pier

SHOREHEAD

0 — 200 yards

N

St Andrews Castle

St Rule's Tower

Cathedral

GREGORY PLACE

PENDS ROAD

St Leonards School

Queen Mary's Library

Preservation Trust Museum

EAST SCORES

CASTLE STREET

ABBEY STREET

Byre Theatre

St Mary's College

Holy Trinity

CHURCH ST

QUEEN'S GARDENS

Ladebraes lane

SOUTH STREET

BELL STREET

MARKET STREET

GREYFRIARS GARDENS

West Port

BRIDGE ST

St Salvator's College

Burns Wynd

NORTH STREET

New Picture House

St Andrews Aquarium

THE SCORES

MURRAY PARK

MURRAY PLACE

PILMUR TERRACE

ABBOTSFORD CRESCENT

HOWARD PLACE

HOPE STREET

CITY ROAD

MARY'S PLACE

STATION ROAD

Bus Station

ARGYLE STREET

DOUBLEDYKES ROAD

WARDLAW GDNS

KENNEDY GARDENS

A918

British Golf Museum

Royal & Ancient Golf Club

GOLF PLACE

LINKS ROAD

THE LINKS

GIBSON PLACE

WINDMILL ROAD

GUARDBRIDGE ROAD

OLD STATION ROAD

The Old Course

Swilken Burn

Ladies Putting Club Clubhouse

Himalayas Putting Course

St Andrews Links Trust Clubhouse

BRUCE EMBANKMENT

GRANNIE CLARK'S WYND

WEST SANDS ROAD

Ladebraes Walk

20

Kinkell (2.5 miles), **5** (3.5 miles), **6** ▶ Kingsbarn Distillery (7 miles), Anstruther (9.5 miles), Crail (10 miles) & Elie (13 miles) ▶

Botanic Gardens & **5** (6 miles) ▶

◀ **1** (1.5 miles), Eden Mill Gin Distillery, Leuchars (6 miles), Dundee (14 miles) & Falkland Palace (20 miles) | **3** (5 miles), **2**

Three main thoroughfares, **North Street**, **Market Street** and **South Street** – which run west to east towards the ruined Gothic cathedral – feature several of the original university buildings from the fifteenth century. Narrow alleys connect the cobbled streets, attic windows and gable ends shape the rooftops, and here and there you'll see the old wooden doors with heavy knockers and black iron hinges.

St Andrews Cathedral

The Pends, KY16 9QL • **Visitor centre** Daily: April–Sept 9.30am–5.30pm; Oct–March 10am–4pm • £5, with castle £9; HS • **Grounds** Daily 9am–5.30pm • Free • ☎ 01334 472563, ⊕ historicenvironment.scot/visit-a-place/places/st-andrews-cathedral

The ruin of the great **St Andrews Cathedral**, at the east end of town, gives only an idea of the importance of what was once Scotland's largest cathedral. Founded in 1160, the cathedral was plundered and left to ruin during the Reformation by supporters of John Knox, fresh from a rousing meeting.

In front of the cathedral window a slab is all that remains of the high altar, where the relics of St Andrew were once enshrined. Previously, it is believed they were kept in **St Rule's Tower**, the austere Romanesque monolith next to the cathedral, which was built as part of an abbey in 1130. From the top of the tower (a climb of 157 steps) there's a good view of the town, and of the remains of the monastic buildings that made up the priory.

St Andrews Castle

The Scores, KY16 9AR • Daily: April–Sept 9.30am–5.30pm; Oct–March 10am–4pm • £6, with cathedral £9; HS • ☎ 01334 477196, ⊕ historicenvironment.scot/visit-a-place/places/st-andrews-castle

Not far north of the cathedral, the rocky coastline curves inland to **St Andrews Castle**, with a drop to the sea on two sides and a moat on its inland side. Founded around

20

GOLF IN ST ANDREWS

St Andrews **Royal and Ancient Golf Club** (or "R&A") has been the international governing body for golf since 1754, when a meeting of 22 of the local gentry founded the Society of St Andrews Golfers, being "admirers of the ancient and healthful exercise of golf". The game itself has been played here since the fifteenth century. Those early days were instrumental in establishing Scotland as the home of golf, for the rules were distinguished from those of the French game by the fact that participants had to manoeuvre the ball into a hole, rather than hit an above-ground target. It was not without its opponents, however – particularly James II who, in 1457, banned his subjects from playing since it was distracting them from archery practice.

The approach to St Andrews from the west runs adjacent to the famous **Old Course**, the oldest course in the world, and just one of seven in the immediate vicinity of the town. The R&A's strictly private **clubhouse**, a stolid, square building dating from 1854, is at the eastern end of the Old Course overlooking both the 18th green and the long strand of the West Sands. The British Open Championship was first held here in 1873, having been inaugurated in 1860 at Prestwick in Ayrshire, and since then it has been held at St Andrews regularly, pulling in enormous crowds.

PLAYING GOLF

Himalayas putting course The Links, KY16 9JD ☎ 01334 475196, ⊕ standrewsputtingclub.com. Arguably the most pleasurable golfing experience in St Andrews, even if you can't tell a birdie from a bogey, this fantastically lumpy eighteen-hole putting course is in an ideal setting next to the Old Course and the sea. Officially the Ladies' Putting Club, founded in 1867, with its own clubhouse, it has grass as perfectly manicured as the championship course, and you can have all the thrill of sinking a six-footer in golf's most famous location, at

the bargain price of £3. March Sat 11am–4pm, Sun noon–4pm; April–Sept Mon–Fri 10.30am–6.30pm, Sat 10.30am–6pm, Sun noon–6.30pm; Oct daily 11am–3pm (weather permitting).

St Andrews Links Trust Alongside the fairway of the first hole of the Old Course ⊕ standrews.org.uk. To play on the venerated Old Course itself you'll need a valid handicap certificate and must enter a daily ballot for tee times; the green fees are £175 in summer. For full details contact the trust, which looks after all the courses in town.

1200 and extended over the centuries, it was built as part of the Palace of the Bishops and Archbishops of St Andrews. There's not a great deal left of the castle, since it fell into ruin in the seventeenth century – apart from the fourteenth-century Fore Tower, most of what can be seen dates from the sixteenth century.

British Golf Museum

Bruce Embankment, KY16 9AB · April–Oct Mon–Sat 9.30am–5pm, Sun 10am–5pm; Nov–March daily 10am–4pm · £8 · ☎ 01334 460046, ⓦ britishgolfmuseum.co.uk

Pictures of golfing greats from Tom Morris to Tiger Woods, along with clubs and a variety of memorabilia donated by famous players, are displayed in the admirable **British Golf Museum**. Telling the story of British golf from its beginnings to the present day, it is rather appropriately located on the waterfront below the Royal and Ancient Golf Club clubhouse.

The beaches

St Andrews has two great **beaches**: West Sands, which stretches for two miles from just below the R&A Clubhouse, and the shorter, more compact, East Sands, which curves from the harbour beyond the cathedral. West Sands was featured in the opening sequences of the Oscar-winning film *Chariots of Fire*. The blustery winds, which are the scourge of golfers and walkers alike, do at least make it a great place to **fly kites**.

Eden Mill Gin Distillery

Main St, Guardbridge, 5 miles northwest of St Andrews, KY16 0US · Daily tours at various times 9am–5pm; 1hr · £10 · ☎ 01334 834038, ⓦ edenmill.com · Take bus #99 towards Dundee (10min)

Forget the craft beer movement: the last few years have been all about Scottish craft gin, with St Andrews' **Eden Mill Gin Distillery** in the vanguard. The first to distil gin in the area for more than 150 years, it has revived the city's lost art on a historic site once owned by the Haig family, one of the country's oldest whisky dynasties. As well as **gin**, Eden Mill has expanded into **whisky** and **beer**; lip-smacking tours are available to see each process come to life. Highly recommended is the **gin tour**, where after learning about locally sourced botanicals you can try tipples such as a bourbon-aged oak gin or – playing to the crowds – a cannily marketed golf gin. Serious connoisseurs should also venture farther down the coast to Crail to see the recently converted **Kingsbarn Distillery** (tours £10; ☎ 01333 451300, ⓦ kingsbarndistillery.com).

Falkland Palace

Falkland, KY15 7BY · March–Oct Mon–Sat 11am–5pm, Sun noon–5pm · £12.50; NTS · ☎ 01337 857397, ⓦ nts.org.uk/Visit/Falkland-Palace · Buses #59, #64 or #94 (hourly) from St Andrews stop on New Rd, just east of the palace

A 35-minute drive southwest of St Andrews, the village of Falkland grew up around **Falkland Palace**, which stands on the site of an earlier castle, home to the Macduffs, the earls of Fife. James IV began the construction of the present palace in 1500; it was completed and embellished by James V, and became a favoured country retreat for the royal court. The palace was completely restored by the third Marquess of Bute, and today it is a stunning piece of architecture, complete with parapets, mullioned windows, round towers and massive walls. Free audioguides lead you through a cross section of public and private rooms in the south and east wings. Outside, the **gardens** are worth a look, their well-stocked herbaceous borders lining a pristine lawn. Don't miss the high walls of the oldest real (or Royal) tennis court in Britain – built in 1539 for James V and still used.

ARRIVAL AND INFORMATION ST ANDREWS AND AROUND

By train St Andrews' nearest train station (on the Edinburgh–Dundee line) is 5 miles northwest at Leuchars, across the River Eden, from where regular buses make the 10min trip into town. When you buy your train ticket back to Leuchars, ask for a St Andrews rail-bus ticket, which includes the bus fare.

20

Destinations Aberdeen (hourly–every 2hr; 1hr 50min); Dundee (hourly–every 2hr; 35min); Edinburgh (hourly–every 2hr; 1hr20min).

By bus The bus station is on Station Rd, just off City Rd and near the town centre.

Destinations Anstruther (every 30min; 25min); Crail (hourly; 30min); Dundee (every 10min; 35min); Dunfermline (hourly; 1hr 30min); Edinburgh (hourly–every

2hr; 1hr 55min); Glasgow (hourly; 2hr 25min); Glenroth (every 30min; 45min); Kirkcaldy (every 30min; 1hr30min; Stirling (every 2hr; 2hr).

Tourist office 70 Market St (April–June, Sept & Oct Mon Sat 9.15am–5pm, Sun 10am–5pm; July & Aug Mon–S 9.15am–6pm, Sun 10am–5pm; Nov–March Mon–S 9.15am–5pm; ☎ 01334 472021, ⓦ visitstandrews.com).

ACCOMMODATION

There's no shortage of accommodation both in town and around, although average **prices** in all categories vie wit Edinburgh's as the highest in Scotland. Rooms often fill up in summer, when you should book in advance.

Fairmont St Andrews Bay 2 miles south of town, KY16 8PN ☎ 01334 837000, ⓦ standrewsbay.com; map p.851. Five-star golf hotel wedged between two of the area's championship courses – the Torrance and the Kittocks. Unlike the majority of the city's more traditional hotels, this is big and brash, with roomy corridors and staircases, and just enough splashes of tartan throughout its two hundred or so rooms to keep international golfers happy. **£160**

★ **Hotel Du Vin** 40 The Scores, KY16 9AS ☎ 01334 845313, ⓦ hotelduvin.com; map p.851. With the air of a Victorian clubhouse, this fabulous 36-room wine hotel knows its audience. Sweeping fairway views, tweed furnishings and golf memorabilia complement the modern rooms and, of course, the first tee of the world's oldest golf course is just a 2min stroll away. **£129**

Kinkell House 2 miles south of town, off the A917, KY16 8PN ☎ 01334 472003, ⓦ kinkell.com; map p.851. Countryside B&B in a lovely family farmhouse near the beach; the house is furnished with antiques, and

breakfast includes eggs from their own hens. **£100**

Knockhill Farm B&B 4 miles west of town, KY16 9X ☎ 01334 850313, ⓦ knockhillfarm.co.uk; map p.851 A converted farmstead on a working farm with views ove the Eden estuary. Choose from the former stable, tackroom granary or hayloft, all spruced up with king-size bed walk-in showers, TVs and private access. **£120**

Old Fishergate House 35 North Castle St ☎ 0133 470874, ⓦ oldfishergatehouse.co.uk; map p.851. On of the oldest townhouses in the oldest part of St Andrew with two spacious twin rooms brimming with perio features. It's full of character without being clutterd breakfast options include smoked haddock omelette an Scotch pancakes. Plus, free home-made shortbread! **£125**

St Andrews Tourist Hostel St Mary's Place, KY1 9UY ☎ 01334 479911, ⓦ hostelstandrews.com; ma p.851. Superbly located backpackers in a converte townhouse above *The Grill House* restaurant, with five seven- and eight-bed dorms, but no doubles. The cheapes option in town, but not the quietest. **£11**

EATING

The Adamson 127 South St, KY16 9UH ☎ 01334 479191, ⓦ theadamson.com; map p.851. Named after John Adamson, the pioneer photographer whose family lived in the building in the 1800s, this stylish see-and-be-seen bistro is where the St Andrews jet set come for exceptional mains (pork belly with black pudding or halibut with fennel, for example). If the sun shines, grab a people-watching spot out the front. Mains £10–28 at dinner, with an oyster happy hour (Mon–Thurs & Sun). Mon–Fri noon–3pm & 5–10pm, Sat & Sun noon–10pm.

★ **Balgove Steak Barn** Strathtyrum Farm, 1 mile north of town, KY16 9SF ☎ 01334 479475, ⓦ balgove. com; map p.851. This former sawmill, a patchwork of stacked potato boxes, timber beams and communal beechwood tables, is an inspired setting for eating fire-pit barbecue steaks and burgers made using free-range cuts from the butcher next door. Sticking to the farm-to-table philosophy, there's a farm shop and a flower shed and the team run butchery classes and night markets, too. Keeping

it casual, there's a no bookings policy. Mains from £8.95 Wed–Sun noon–8.30pm.

Cromars 11 Union St, KY16 9PQ ☎ 01334 47555 ⓦ cromars.co.uk; map p.851. It's some accolade, bu this terrific restaurant and takeaway has been voted th best fish and chip shop in Scotland twice since openin in 2013. The reason is its sustainably sourced pokes o mussels, scallops and cod, plus home-made fishcakes classic scampi and crispy whitebait. You're not dreaming this takeaway serves its chips with truffle oil and parmesan Mains from £8.95. Daily 11.30am–10pm.

Jannettas Gelateria 31 South St, KY16 9QR ☎ 0133 479475, ⓦ jannettasgelateria.co.uk; map p.851. In Fife, some say Scotland, there is only one place to go fo ice cream. *Jannettas* has been in business for one hundre years, producing artisan gelatos with seasonal flavour including rhubarb and ginger, peaches and cream, an Scottish tablet. Patience is key: there's always a queue a the weekend. Mon–Sat 9am–10pm, Sun 10am–10pm.

20

★ **The Peat Inn** Cupar, 6 miles southwest of town, KY15 5LH ☎ 01334 840206, ⊛ thepeatinn.co.uk; map p.851. Maintaining its reputation as one of Scotland's best restaurants for some 25 years, *The Peat Inn* excels at fine dining using top local produce – East Neuk wood pigeon, Baldinnie quail eggs and St Andrews Bay lobster, for example. Chef Geoffrey Smeddle's menus range from a three-course set lunch (£22) to a six-course tasting menu (£70). They also have eight plush, if pricey, rooms. Tues–Sat 12.30–2pm & 6.30–9pm.

DRINKING AND NIGHTLIFE

The Criterion 99 South St, KY16 9QW ☎ 01334 474543, ⊛ criterionstandrews.co.uk; map p.851. As traditional and creaky as a St Andrews boozer gets, this well-aged Victorian relic is renowned for its whisky selection (160 bottles at the last count) and its "Cri" pies (£8.50). Locals and tourists love it, particularly the in-demand pavement tables out front. Mon–Wed & Sun 10am–midnight, Thurs–Sat 10am–1am.

St Andrews Brewing Co 177 South St, KY16 9EE ☎ 01334 471111, ⊛ standrewsbrewingcompany.com; map p.851. Craft beer fans rejoice! This brewpub has eighteen taps of cask and keg ales, including as many local drops as they can fit behind the bar, plus comfort-food burgers and board games for rainy day sessions. Order a Crail Ale or Fife Gold to fit right in. Daily 11am–midnight.

★ **Vic** 1 St Marys Place, KY16 9UY ☎ 01334 476964; map p.851. A Xanadu for craft beer drinkers and gourmet-burger lovers, this chilled-out pub and kitchen is Ground Zero for the town's hipster scene. It gets packed out for the DJ nights and pub quizzes, and there's a social club with ping pong and Wii. Mon, Tues & Sun 10am–1am, Wed–Sat 10am–2am.

ENTERTAINMENT

Byre Theatre Abbey St, KY16 9LA ☎ 01334 475000, ⊛ byretheatre.com. Occupies a stylish modern building, with a pleasant bar and bistro. Productions range from Scottish drama to musicals; if anything is happening in St Andrews at the weekend it's happening here. Box office Mon–Sat 10am–4pm.

20

The East Neuk

Extending south of St Andrews as far as Largo Bay, the **East Neuk** is famous for its stopped-clock fishing villages replete with crow-stepped gables and red pan-tiled roofs, the Flemish influence indicating a history of strong trading links with the Low Countries. The area is dotted with blustery **golf courses**, and there are plenty of bracing coastal paths, including the waymarked **Fife Coastal Path**: tracing the shoreline between St Andrews and the Forth Rail Bridge, it's at its most scenic in the East Neuk stretch.

Crail

CRAIL is the archetypally charming fishing village, its maze of rough cobbled streets leading steeply down to a tiny stone-built harbour surrounded by piles of lobster creels, and with fishermen's cottages tucked into every nook and cranny. Though often populated by artists at their easels and camera-toting tourists, it is still a working harbour, and if the boats have been out you can buy fresh lobster and crab cooked to order from a small wooden shack on the harbour edge (see below). To trace the history of the town, visit the **Crail Museum and Heritage Centre**, 62 Marketgate (Mon–Sat, 11am–4pm, Sun 1.30pm–4pm; free; ☎ 01333 450869). Also worth a look is **Crail Pottery**, 75 Nethergate (Mon–Fri 9am–5pm, Sat & Sun 10am–5pm), which has a wide range of ceramics.

ARRIVAL AND INFORMATION
CRAIL

By bus Bus #95 runs hourly to St Andrews (30min) and Leven (for connections to Edinburgh; 1hr) from the High St.

Tourist information Crail Museum and Heritage Centre (see above).

EATING

Crail Harbour Gallery and Tearoom Shoregate, KY10 3SU ☎ 01333 451896, ⊛ crailharbourgallery.co.uk. Tucked into a wee seventeenth-century cottage on the way down to the harbour, with a terrace overlooking the Isle of May. They serve Fairtrade coffees, hot chocolate and paninis, plus local crab (£12), smoked salmon and herring (snacks from £6). Daily 10.15am–5.30pm (4.30pm in winter).

★ **Reilly Shellfish** 34 Shoregate, KY10 3SU ☎01333 450476. This tiny lobster and crab shack offers boat-fresh, zero-miles seafood with beach views, and is the best place in town for a sunset supper. A half lobster costs £12. Mid-April to early Oct Tues–Sun noon–4pm.

Anstruther

ANSTRUTHER, four miles south along the coast from Crail, is the largest of the East Neuk fishing harbours. With an attractively old-fashioned air and no shortage of character in its houses and narrow streets, it is also home to the wonderfully unpretentious **Scottish Fisheries Museum**.

Scottish Fisheries Museum

Harbourhead, KY10 3AB · April–Sept Mon–Sat 10am–4.30pm, Sun 11am–5pm; Oct–March Mon–Sat 10am–4.30pm, Sun noon–4.30pm · £9 · ☎01333 310628, ⓦ scotfishmuseum.org

Set in an atmospheric complex of sixteenth- to nineteenth-century buildings with timber ceilings and wooden floors, the **Scottish Fisheries Museum** chronicles the history of the fishing and whaling industries with ingenious displays, including a series of exquisite ships' models built on site by a resident model-maker.

Isle of May

Boat trips Anstruther Harbour · One trip daily at varying times according to the tides; 4hr 30min–5hr for a round trip with 2hr 30min–3hr on the island · £26 · ☎07957 585200, ⓦ isleofmayferry.com

Located on the rugged **Isle of May**, several miles offshore from Anstruther, is a lighthouse erected in 1816 by Robert Louis Stevenson's grandfather, as well as the remains of Scotland's first lighthouse, built in 1636. The island is now a **nature reserve** and bird sanctuary; as well as puffins, guillemots, shags and kittiwakes, **boat trippers** have the chance to see dolphins, seals and, if you get lucky, even the odd passing whale.

ARRIVAL AND INFORMATION

ANSTRUTHER

By bus Buses stop at the harbour and serve Edinburgh (hourly; 2hr 15min) and St Andrews (hourly; 25min).
Tourist information Scottish Fisheries Museum, Harbourhead (April–Sept Mon–Sat 10am–4.30pm, Sun 11am–5pm; Oct–March Mon–Sat 10am–4.30pm, Sun noon–4.30pm; ☎01333 310628).

ACCOMMODATION AND EATING

★ **The Cellar** 24 East Green, KY10 3AA ☎01333 310378, ⓦ thecellaranstruther.co.uk. Tucked in behind the Scottish Fisheries Museum in one of the village's oldest buildings, once a cooperage and smokehouse, this fantastic restaurant serves classy dishes such as Anstruther crab with squid and partridge with cherry. Five courses £60. Wed 6.30–9pm, Thurs–Sun 12.30–1.45pm & 6.30–9pm.

★ **The Ship Tavern** Elie, 6 miles south of Anstruther, KY9 1DT4 ☎01333 330246, ⓦ shipinn.scot. A maritime pub with a restaurant and six rooms, this storming harbourfront inn is definitely worth the ten-minute trip south from Anstruther to stay overnight. The white and sky-blue wood-clad rooms are straight from a Scandinavian interiors catalogue, while the seafood in the restaurant is worth getting shipwrecked for. Mains from £13.50. Bar Mon–Thurs & Sun 10.30am–11pm, Fri & Sat 10.30am–midnight. Restaurant daily noon–3pm & 5–9pm. **£150**

Southern Fife

Although the coast of **southern Fife** is predominantly industrial – with everything from cottage industries to the refitting of nuclear submarines – mercifully, only a small part has been blighted by insensitive development. Thanks to its proximity to the early coal mines, the charming village of **Culross** was once a lively port that enjoyed a thriving trade with Holland, the Dutch influence obvious in its lovely gabled houses. It was from nearby **Dunfermline** that Queen Margaret ousted the Celtic Church from Scotland in the eleventh century; her son, David I, founded an abbey here in the twelfth century. Southern Fife is linked to Edinburgh by the three **Forth bridges**, the red-painted girders of the Rail Bridge representing one of Britain's great engineering spectacles.

20

Culross

CULROSS (pronounced "Coorus") is one of Scotland's most picturesque settlements, owing to the work of the National Trust for Scotland, which has been renovating its whitewashed, pan-tiled buildings since 1932. For an excellent introduction to the burgh's history, head to the **National Trust Visitor Centre**, in the **Town House** facing Sandhaven, where goods were once unloaded from ships (times vary, check website; free; ☎01383 880359, ⓦnts.org.uk/Visit/Culross). Of particular note is the remains of **Culross Abbey**, founded by Cistercian monks on land given to the church in 1217 by the Earl of Fife. More recently, the entire village was recast as post-WWII Inverness for historic American TV soap *Outlander*.

Culross Palace

April, May & Sept Mon, Sat & Sun 11am–5pm; June Mon & Wed–Sun 11am–5pm; July & Aug daily 11am–5pm; Oct Mon & Fri–Sun 11am–4pm • £10.50; NTS • ☎01383 880359, ⓦnts.org.uk/Visit/Culross

The most impressive building in the village is the ochre-coloured **Culross Palace**, built by wealthy coal merchant George Bruce in the late sixteenth century; it's not a palace at all but a grand and impressive house, with lots of small rooms and connecting passageways. Inside, well-informed staff point out the wonderful painted ceilings, pine panelling, antique furniture and curios; outside, dormer windows and crow-stepped gables dominate the walled court in which the house stands.

ARRIVAL AND DEPARTURE   CULROSS

By bus Stagecoach bus #8 from Dunfermline train station runs to Culross (hourly; 25min).

20

Dunfermline

Scotland's capital until the Union of the Crowns in 1603, **DUNFERMLINE** lies inland seven miles east of Culross, north of the Forth bridges. Ringed by shabby development, the town is not initially charismatic, but the **abbey** and surrounds make it worth the trip.

Dunfermline Abbey

Dunfermline, KY12 7PE • April–Sept daily 9.30am–5.30pm; Oct daily 10am–4pm; Nov–March Mon–Wed, Sat & Sun 10am–12.30pm & 1.30–4pm • £5; HS • ☎01383 724586 ⓦdunfermlineabbey.com

The oldest part of **Dunfermline Abbey** is attributable to Queen Margaret, who began building a Benedictine priory in 1072, the remains of which can still be seen beneath the nave of the present church; her son, **David I**, raised the priory to the rank of abbey in the following century. In 1303, during the first of the **Wars of Independence**, the English king Edward I occupied the palace and ordered the destruction of most of the monastery buildings. **Robert the Bruce** helped rebuild the abbey, and when he died of leprosy 25 years later was buried here, although his body went undiscovered until construction began on a new parish church in 1821. Inside, the stained glass is impressive, and the columns are artfully carved into chevrons, spirals and arrowheads.

ARRIVAL AND DEPARTURE   DUNFERMLINE

By train Dunfermline has two train stations: Queen Margaret and Dunfermline Town. The latter is the most convenient; it's on the south side of the centre, with its main entrance off St Margaret's Drive.
Destinations Edinburgh (every 30min; 40min); Kirkcaldy (hourly; 1hr).

By bus The bus station is on Queen Anne St, between Carnegie Drive and High St.
Destinations Culross (hourly; 25min); Edinburgh (every 30min; 1hr); Glasgow (every 30min; 1hr 20min); Kirkcaldy (hourly; 50min); North Queensferry (every 30min; 30min); Stirling (every 2hr; 1hr 30min).

North Queensferry

The highlight of Fife's **south coast** is the trilogy of Scotland's finest man-made structures (ⓦtheforthbridges.org): the impressive Forth Rail Bridge, the Forth Road

Bridge and the newly opened Queensferry Crossing, all of which join Fife at **NORTH QUEENSFERRY**. Until the opening of the road bridge, this small fishing village was the northern landing point of the ferry from South Queensferry (see page 786).

Forth Rail Bridge

The cantilevered **Forth Rail Bridge**, built from 1883 to 1890 by Sir John Fowler and Benjamin Baker, ranks among the supreme achievements of Victorian engineering, with some fifty thousand tonnes of steel used in the construction of a design that manages to express grace as well as might. The only way to cross the rail bridge is on a train heading to or from Edinburgh, but this doesn't allow much of a perspective of the spectacle itself. For the best **panorama**, use the pedestrian and cycle lanes on the east side of the road bridge.

Forth Road Bridge

Derived from American models, the suspension format chosen for the **Forth Road Bridge**, alongside the rail bridge, once made an interesting modern complement to the older structure. Erected between 1958 and 1964 it finally killed off the 900-year-old ferry, but dogged by maintenance problems and overused by commuter traffic this slate-gray "Golden Gate" has been usurped in the engineering stakes by the 1.7 mile-long Queensferry Crossing to the west (see page 786). It is now only open to public buses, cyclists and pedestrians.

Queensferry Crossing

Opened in August 2017 by Queen Elizabeth II, 53 years to the day after she opened the adjacent Forth Road Bridge, this engineering behemoth is the biggest infrastructure project in Scotland in a generation. Costing £1.35bn, the **Queensferry Crossing** is the longest three-tower, cable-stayed bridge in the world, absorbing the vast bulk of traffic from the Forth Road Bridge. Unlike its predecessor, the new crossing affords no access to pedestrians or cyclists.

ARRIVAL AND DEPARTURE
NORTH QUEENSFERRY

By train Trains connect North Queensferry with Edinburgh every 15min (25min).

By bus There are hourly services to Dunfermline (30min from the main road.

Perthshire

Genteel, attractive **Perthshire** is, in many ways, the epitome of well-groomed rural Scotland. An area of gentle glens, mature woodland, rushing rivers and peaceful lochs, it's the long-established domain of Scotland's well-to-do country set. First settled more than eight thousand years ago, it was ruled by the Romans and then the Picts before Celtic missionaries established themselves.

The ancient town of **Perth** occupies a strategic position at the mouth of the River Tay; salmon, wool and, by the sixteenth century, whisky, were exported, while a major import was Bordeaux claret. At nearby **Scone**, Kenneth MacAlpine established the capital of the kingdom of the Scots and the Picts in 846. When this settlement was washed away by floods in 1210, William the Lion founded Perth as a royal burgh.

North and west of Perth, **Highland Perthshire** is made up of gorgeous and mighty woodlands, particularly along the banks of the River Tay. The area is dotted with neat, confident towns and villages like **Dunkeld**, with its mature trees and lovely ruined cathedral, and **Aberfeldy** set deep among farmland east of Loch Tay. Farther north, the countryside becomes more sparsely populated and spectacular, with some wonderful walking country, especially around **Pitlochry**, **Blair Atholl** and the wild expanses of **Rannoch Moor** to the west.

ACTIVITY OPERATORS IN PERTHSHIRE

In Perthshire, **outdoor activities** range from gentle strolls through ancient oak forests to white-knuckle rides down frothing waterfalls.

Highland Safaris Aberfeldy, PH15 2JQ ☎01887 820071, ⦿highlandsafaris.net. An inspiring introduction to wild Scotland in which you're taken by 4WD to search for golden eagle eyries, stags and pine martens.

Nae Limits Dunkeld and Ballinluig, PH9 0LG ☎01796 482600, ⦿naelimits.co.uk. An everything-but-the-kitchen-sink operator for adrenalin junkies: canyoning, cliff-jumping, bungee jumping, river tubing and gorge walking.

National Kayak School Aberfeldy, PA34 5SG ☎01631 565310, ⦿nationalkayakschool.com. Based out of Oban on the west coast as well as in Aberfeldy, this outfit offers a multitude of whitewater kayaking courses and kayaking holidays.

Splash Aberfeldy, PH15 2AQ ☎01887 829706, ⦿rafting.co.uk. Rafting on larger craft through the best rapids on the Tay at Grandtully, plus accredited rafting courses.

Perth and around

Surrounded by fertile agricultural land and beautiful scenery, the bustling market town of **PERTH** was Scotland's capital in the fifteenth century, and expanded in the eighteenth. Today, with the whisky and insurance trades employing significant numbers, it remains an important town. Two large areas of green parkland, known as the North and South Inch, flank the **centre**; the city's main shopping areas are **High Street** and **South Street**, along with St John's Shopping Centre on King Edward Street. Perth is at its most attractive along **Tay Street**, with a succession of grander buildings along one side and the attractively landscaped riverside embankment on the other.

20

Fergusson Gallery

Corner of Tay St and Marshall Place, PH2 8NS • Tues–Sat 10am–5pm, Sun noon–4.30pm • Free • ☎01738 783425, ⦿pkc.gov.uk/museums

Perth's artistic highlight is the **Fergusson Gallery**, occupying a striking Victorian sandstone water tower, and home to an extensive collection of work by J.D. Fergusson, foremost artist of the Scottish Colourist movement (see page 823). Greatly influenced by Impressionist and Post-Impressionist artists, he created a distinctive approach that marries both movements' freedom of style with bold use of colour and lighting – shown, for example, in his portrait of Elizabeth Dryden, *The Hat with the Pink Scarf*. In addition to oils, the collection includes sketches, notebooks and sculpture.

Scone Palace

A couple of miles north of Perth on the A93, PH2 6BD • April & Oct daily 9am–4pm; May–Sept daily 9.30am–5pm; Nov–March Fri–Sun (grounds only) 10am–4pm • £11.50, grounds only £6.80 (grounds free in winter) • ☎01738 552300, ⦿scone-palace.co.uk • Bus #3 (towards Scone) or #58 (towards Blairgowrie) from Perth

Scone Palace (pronounced "skoon") is one of Scotland's finest historical country homes. Owned and occupied by the Earl and Countess of Mansfield, the two-storey building on the eastern side of the Tay is stately but not overpowering, more a home than an untouchable monument. The rooms, although full of priceless antiques and lavish furnishings, feel lived-in.

The abbey that stood here in the sixteenth century was where all Scottish kings until James IV were crowned. Long before that, Scone was the capital of Pictavia, and it was here that Kenneth MacAlpine brought the famous Coronation **Stone of Destiny**, or Stone of Scone, now to be found in Edinburgh Castle, and where he ruled as the first king of a united Scotland. A replica of the (surprisingly small) stone can be found on Moot Hill, opposite the palace. In the **grounds** you'll also find a beech-hedge maze in the pattern of the heraldic family crest and avenues of venerable trees. Scone was the birthplace of botanist and plant collector **David Douglas**, and following the trail named after him brings you to a fragrant pinetum planted in 1848 with many of the exotic species he discovered in California and elsewhere.

Lindores Abbey Distillery

Newburgh, 12 miles southeast of Perth, KY14 6HH • Distillery tours (45min) 10.30am, 12.30pm & 2pm: April–Sept daily; Oct–March Wed–Sun • £12.50 • ☎ 01337 842547, ⓦ lindoresabbeydistillery.com

Whisky's spiritual home – or at least the site of the earliest written reference to Scotch production, in 1494 – the sleek **Lindores Abbey Distillery** and visitor centre, opened in October 2017, heralds a revival for central Scotland whisky. A £5 million investment has seen the once-derelict Lindores Abbey, in ruin since it was sacked during the Reformation by John Knox, reborn with the addition of a new distillery, shop and café. Though located in Fife, it's best accessed from Perth – it's a fifteen-minute drive east along the banks of the River Tay.

ARRIVAL AND INFORMATION

PERTH

By train The station is in the southwest of town on Leonard St.

Destinations Aberdeen (hourly; 1hr 35min); Blair Atholl (every 1hr 30min; 47min); Dundee (every 30min; 25min); Dunkeld (3–7 daily; 35min); Edinburgh (hourly; 1hr 25min); Glasgow Queen St (every 30min; 1hr); Inverness (4–9 daily; 2hr 15min); Pitlochry (4–9 daily; 30min); Stirling (hourly; 30min).

By bus The bus station is opposite the train station on Leonard St.

Destinations Aberfeldy (10 daily; 1hr 20min); Crieff (hourly; 55min); Dundee (every 30min; 45min); Dunkeld (hourly; 55min); Edinburgh (hourly; 1hr 45min); Glasgow (hourly; 1hr 30min); Gleneagles (hourly; 45min); Inverness (hourly; 2hr 45min); Pitlochry (hourly; 1hr 15min); Stirling (hourly; 45min).

Tourist information Visit Scotland iCentre, 45 High St (Mon–Sat 9.30am–5pm, Sun 11am–4pm; ☎ 01738 450600, ⓦ visitscotland.com/info/services/perth-icentre-p234431).

ACCOMMODATION

★ **Gleneagles** Auchterarder, 16 miles southwest of Perth, PH3 1NF ☎ 01764 662231, ⓦ gleneagles.com. Scotland's most luxurious hotel bar none. There's a polished spa, three eighteen-hole championship golf courses and opportunities aplenty to act like a monarch of the glen while trout fishing, shooting or visiting the gun dog school. New arrivals following a multimillion pound reboot include the Art Deco *American Bar*, the excellent *Birnam Brasserie* and laidback *Garden Café*. The dress code may scream Barbour jacket and Hunter Wellingtons, but with a spectacular two-Michelin-star restaurant from top Scots chef Andrew Fairlie to boot, who cares? **£325**

Parklands Hotel 2 St Leonards Bank, PH2 8EB ☎ 01738 622451, ⓦ theparklandshotel.com. Of the numerous central hotels, aim for the fifteen-bedroom *Parklands* close to the train station, which has a dash of contemporary styling and touches of luxury behind its Victorian facade. Restaurant *63@Parklands* is sister to the highly recommended *63 Tay Street* (see below). **£69.50**

The Townhouse 17 Marshall Place, PH2 8AG ☎ 01738 446179, ⓦ thetownhouseperth.co.uk. Lovely Georgian B&B overlooking South Inch Park run by a Scots-French couple who traded St Barts in the Caribbean for Perth. Rooms come with generous touches (antique furnishings, rainforest showers, home-made biscuits), and the hosts are as helpful as they come. **£120**

EATING AND DRINKING

★ **63 Tay Street** 63 Tay St, PH2 8NN ☎ 01738 441451, ⓦ 63taystreet.com. At the top end of the market in Perth, serving wild game and seafood with a Scots-Mediterranean twist. It's pricey (dinner mains from £19), but the four-course surprise lunch menu is a bargain £22. Tues & Wed 5.45–8.45pm, Thurs–Sat noon–1.45pm & 6–9pm.

The Bothy 33 Kinnoull St, PH1 5EN ☎ 0845 659 5907, ⓦ bothyperth.co.uk. More Scottish than Billy Connolly or the Loch Ness Monster, *The Bothy*'s menu is a tour de force of Scottish produce. From Isle of Arran haggis and Barra scallops to Inverlochy goats' cheese and Orkney ribeye, provenance and seasonality is the order of the day. Mains from £12.95 Tues–Thurs 6–9.30pm, Fri 6–10pm, Sat 6–10.30pm.

Pig'Halle 38 South St, PH2 8PG ☎ 01738 248784, ⓦ pighalle.co.uk. The decor may be kitsch, but the food at Paula and Herve Tabourel's French brasserie is impeccable. Dishes such as confit pig's trotters (£14) and garlicky *moules marinière* (£13) set the culinary mood. Tues & Wed noon–3pm & 5.30–9.30pm, Thurs–Sat noon–3pm & 5.30–10.30pm, Sun noon–3pm & 5.30–9pm.

Strathtay

North of Perth, both the railway and main A9 trunk road speed through some of Perthshire's most attractive countryside before heading into the Highlands.

Magnificent woodland spreads around the valley – or "strath" – of the River Tay, as it heads towards the sea from attractive **Loch Tay**. On the eastern side of the loch, the Tay calmly glides past the attractive country town of **Aberfeldy**. The loch itself, meanwhile, is set up among the high Breadalbane mountains, which include the striking peak of **Ben Lawers**, Perthshire's highest, and the hills that enclose the long, enchanting **Glen Lyon**.

Dunkeld

Twelve miles north of Perth, **DUNKELD** was proclaimed Scotland's ecclesiastical capital by Kenneth MacAlpine in 850. The town is one of the area's most pleasant communities, with handsome whitewashed houses, appealing arts and crafts shops, a picturesque cathedral and a vibrant folk music venue.

Dunkeld Cathedral

10 Cathedral St, PH8 0AW • Daily: April–Sept 9.30am–5.30pm; Oct–March 10am–4pm • Free • ☏ 01350 727249, ⊕ dunkeldcathedral.org.uk

The partly ruined **Dunkeld Cathedral** is on the northern side of town, in an idyllic setting amid lawns and trees on the east bank of the Tay. The present structure consists of the fourteenth-century choir and the fifteenth-century nave; the choir, restored in 1600 (and several times since), now serves as the parish church, while the nave remains roofless apart from the clocktower.

ARRIVAL AND INFORMATION   DUNKELD

By train Dunkeld station is served by fast and frequent services from Perth (10 daily; 20min).
Tourist office The Cross, town centre (April–June & Sept Mon–Sat 10.30am–4.30pm, Sun 11am–4pm; July & Aug

Mon–Sat 9.30am–6.30pm, Sun 10am–4pm; Oct–March Fri–Sun 11am–4pm; ☏ 01350 727688, ⊕ visitscotland. com/info/services/dunkeld-icentre-p333361).

EATING AND DRINKING

★ **Taybank Hotel** Tay Terrace, PH8 0AQ ☏ 01350 727340, ⊕ thetaybank.co.uk. Despite the name, this characterful beacon for music fans – who come for the regular live sessions (every Wed & Thurs) in the convivial

bar – isn't a hotel but a pub. Decent bar meals, too (the Dunkeld smoked salmon is a speciality). Mains from £9. Mon–Thurs & Sun 11am–11pm, Fri & Sat 11am–midnight.

Aberfeldy

A prosperous settlement of large stone houses and 4WDs, **ABERFELDY** acts as a service centre for the wider Loch Tay area. The town's main attraction is **Dewar's Aberfeldy Distillery**, where tours, which incude a dram, describe the whisky-making process (tours every 30min: Mon–Sat 10am–4pm, Sun noon–2pm; 1hr 30min; from £9.50; ⊕ dewars.com). The rest of the town centre is a mixture of craft and tourist shops, the most interesting being **The Watermill** on Mill Street (Mon–Sat 10am–5pm, Sun 11am–5pm; ⊕ aberfeldywatermill.com), an inspiring bookshop, café and art gallery in a restored, early nineteenth-century mill.

ARRIVAL AND INFORMATION   ABERFELDY

By bus Buses connect Aberfeldy with Perth (6–9 daily; 1hr 25min), stopping at Chapel St.
Tourist office The Square (April–Oct Mon–Sat 10am–

5pm, Sun 10.30am–3.30pm; Nov–March Mon–Wed & Sat 10am–4pm; ☏ 01887 820276).

Loch Tay

A fourteen-mile-long stretch of fresh water, **Loch Tay** virtually hooks together the western and eastern Highlands. Guarding the northern end of the loch is **KENMORE**, a cluster of whitewashed estate houses and well-tended gardens. The main draw here is living heritage museum, the **Scottish Crannog Centre**.

20

Scottish Crannog Centre

Kenmore, PH15 2HY · April–Oct daily 10am–5.30pm · £10 · ☏ 01887 830583, ⓦ crannog.co.uk

Crannogs are Iron Age loch dwellings built on stilts over the water. Originally they would have had a gangway to the shore; upon the approach of hostile intruders, whether animal or human, the gangway would quickly be raised. At the **Scottish Crannog Centre** visitors can walk out over the loch to a superbly reconstructed, thatched, wooden crannog set up to look as it would have 2500 years ago.

Ben Lawers

Dominating the northern side of Loch Tay is spectacular **Ben Lawers** (3984ft), Perthshire's highest mountain; from the top there are incredible views towards Argyll and the Highlands. The ascent – which should not be tackled unless you're properly equipped for hillwalking – takes around three hours and can be reached via a winding hill road off the A827.

ARRIVAL AND DEPARTURE LOCH TAY

By bus The convenient hop-on, hop-off Ring of Breadalbane Explorer bus that once connected Aberfeldy, Kenmore, Killin, Comrie and Crieff has been cancelled until further notice. Consider a taxi or a rental car.

ACCOMMODATION

Comrie Croft 5 miles east of Crieff, Braincroft, PH7 4JZ ☏ 01764 670140, ⓦ comriecroft.com. Hillwalking and glamping eco-nirvana with Nordic *katas* (wigwams), tent pitches and a farmhouse hostel ideal for an off-grid wilderness experience. Discount if arriving by public transport. Camping **£8**, dorms **£25**, katas **£99**

Highland Perthshire

North of the Tay Valley, Perthshire doesn't discard its lush richness immediately, but there are clear indications of the more rugged, barren influences of the Highlands proper. The principal settlements of **Pitlochry** and **Blair Atholl**, both off the A9, are separated by the narrow gorge of Killiecrankie, once a crucial strategic spot for anyone seeking to control movement of cattle or armies from the Highlands to the Lowlands. Greater rewards, however, are to be found farther from the main drag, most notably in the winding westward road along the shores of **Loch Tummel** and **Loch Rannoch** past the distinctive peak of **Schiehallion**, which eventually leads to the remote wilderness of **Rannoch Moor**.

Pitlochry

PITLOCHRY has a lot going for it, not least the backdrop of Ben Vrackie and the River Tummel slipping by. While there's little charm to be found on the main street, filled with shops selling cut-price woollens, it has plenty of castle hotels and is the jumping-off point for hiking and biking adventures in the surrounding countryside.

Edradour Distillery

A couple of miles east of Pitlochry on the A924, PH16 5JP · Tours (1hr) hourly: April–Oct Mon–Sat 10am–5pm; Nov–March Mon–Fri 10am–4.30pm · £7.50 · ☏ 01887 830583, ⓦ edradour.co.uk

In an idyllic position tucked into the hills, **Edradour Distillery** is Scotland's smallest. Although the tour itself isn't out of the ordinary, the fact that the whole grain-to-glass process is done on site gives Edradour more personality than many of its rivals.

Pitlochry Dam and Fish Ladder

Armoury Rd, PH16 5AP · Daily 9.30am–5.30pm · Free · ☏ 01796 484111, ⓦ pitlochrydam.com

Home to a salmon ladder, where fish can be seen acrobatically leaping up the gushing river from a series of viewing windows, the family-friendly **Pitlochry Dam and Fish Ladder** has an innovatively designed visitor centre with breathtaking views down the glen. As well as interactive exhibits on the history of hydroelectricity and the salmon life cycle, there is a café and shop.

ARRIVAL AND DEPARTURE | PITLOCHRY

By train Pitlochry is on the main line to Inverness (hourly; 1hr 40min). The station is on Station Rd, just south of the centre.

By bus Regular buses from Perth (hourly–every 2hr; 1hr 25min) and Inverness (7 daily; 2hr 10min) stop near the train station.

INFORMATION AND GETTING AROUND

Tourist office 22 Atholl Rd (April–June Mon–Sat 9am–5pm, Sun 10am–5pm; July & Aug Mon–Sat 9am–6pm, Sun 10am–6pm; Sept & Oct Mon–Sat 9.30am–5.30pm, Sun 10am–4pm; Nov–March Mon–Sat 10am–4pm; ☎01796 472215, ⓦvisitscotland.com/info/services/pitlochry-icentre-p234421).

Cycling Escape Route, 3 Atholl Rd (☎01796 473859, ⓦescape-route.co.uk), can provide advice on local cycling routes, bike rental (£24/day) and general outdoor gear.

ACCOMMODATION

Knockendarroch Hotel Higher Oakfield, PH16 5HT ☎01796 473473, ⓦknockendarroch.co.uk. One of the buzziest wee hotels in the country, the *Knockendarroch* benefits from close ties to the Pitlochry Festival Theatre across the river, good pre-theatre menus in the (evening only) restaurant and a great whisky lounge with a log fire. Daily 5.30–9.30pm **£150**

Pitlochry Backpackers Hotel 134 Atholl Rd, PH16 5AB ☎01796 470044, ⓦpitlochrybackpackershotel. com. This central hostel, based in a renovated Victorian hotel, offers dorms along with around ten en-suite twins and doubles. Dorms **£19.50**, doubles **£52.50**

EATING AND DRINKING

20

Pitlochry is the domain of the tearoom; you have to look to the **hotels** for a fine three-course meal.

Moulin Inn Moulin, on Pitlochry's outskirts along A924, PH16 5EW ☎01796 472196, ⓦmoulinhotel. co.uk. A great bet for traditional pub grub (mains from £10), this award-winning inn is handily placed at the foot of Ben Vrackie. The original building dates back to 1695, but the microbrewery is shiny new. Daily noon–9.30pm.

The Old Mill Inn Mill Lane, PH16 5BH ☎01796 474020, ⓦtheoldmillpitlochry.co.uk. If after all that fresh air you need some real ale, head to this popular family-run inn for its superb selection of local IPAs and stouts. The food menu is a great calorific companion to a pint, with sandwiches, pastas, steaks and Buckie-caught haddock and chips. Mains from £13.95. Daily 8am–9pm.

ENTERTAINMENT

Pitlochry Festival Theatre Port Na Craig, PH16 5DR ☎01796 484626, ⓦpitlochry.org.uk. On the western edge of town, Scotland's renowned "Theatre in the Hills" stages a variety of productions – mostly mainstream theatre from the resident rep company, along with regular music events – during the summer season and on ad hoc dates the rest of the year.

Loch Tummel

West of Pitlochry, the B8019/B846 makes a memorably scenic, if tortuous, traverse of the shores of **Loch Tummel** and then **Loch Rannoch**. These two lochs and their adjoining rivers were much changed by massive hydroelectric schemes built in the 1940s and 1950s, yet this is still a spectacular stretch of countryside. **Queen's View** at the eastern end of Loch Tummel is an obvious vantage point, looking down the loch to the misty peak of **Schiehallion** (3553ft), whose name comes from the Gaelic meaning "Fairy Mountain". One of Scotland's few freestanding hills, it's a popular, fairly easy and inspiring climb, with views on a good day to both sides of the country. The path up starts at Braes of Foss, just off the B846: allow three to four hours to the top and back.

Loch Rannoch

Beyond Loch Tummel, at the eastern end of Loch Rannoch, the small community of **KINLOCH RANNOCH** doesn't see a lot of passing trade other than fishermen and

RANNOCH MOOR

Rannoch Moor occupies roughly 150 square miles of uninhabited peat bogs, lochs, heather hillocks, strewn lumps of granite and a few gnarled Caledonian pine, all of it more than 1000ft above sea level. Perhaps the most striking aspect is its inaccessibility: one road, between Crianlarich and Glen Coe, skirts its western side, while another struggles west from Pitlochry to reach its eastern edge at Rannoch Station. The only regular form of transport is the **West Highland railway**, which stops at Rannoch and, a little to the north, Corrour line, which has no road access at all. From Rannoch station it's possible to catch the train to Corrour and walk the nine miles back; it's a longer slog west to the eastern end of Glen Coe (see page 847), the dramatic peaks of which poke up above the moor's western horizon.

Corrour Lodge 5 miles from Corrour train station on the shores of Loch Ossian, PH30 4AA ☎ 01397 707070, ⓦ corrour.co.uk. Part James Bond lair, part Narnia castle, this remote seven-bedroom wilderness lodge for stalking and walking is a triumph of modern architecture and as far from the clichéd Highland country house as you can get. It needs to be booked on an exclusive basis (price on request), but there are a variety of great cottages to pick from. **£320**

SYHA Loch Ossian A mile from Corrour train station on the shores of Loch Ossian, PH30 4AA ☎ 01397 732207, ⓦ syha.org.uk/where-to-stay/highlands/loch-ossian. This comfortable, cosy – and remote – eco-hostel is a great place for hikers seeking somewhere genuinely off the beaten track. Good wildlife-watching opportunities, too. **£19**

hillwalkers. Otherwise, the only real destination here is **Rannoch station**, a lonely outpost on the Glasgow–Fort William West Highland train line, sixteen miles farther on at the end of the road.

ARRIVAL AND DEPARTURE

LOCH RANNOCH

By train Rannoch station sees trains to Corrour (3–4 daily; 12min); Fort William (3–4 daily; 1hr); Glasgow Queen St (3–4 daily; 2hr 45min) and London Euston (sleeper service; Sun–Fri daily; 11–12hr 40min).

By bus Buses run to Kinloch Rannoch from Pitlochry (Mon, Wed & Fri 4 daily; 55min); Broons Bus runs #DRT2, an on-demand Dial-A-Bus service to Rannoch Station (40min, ☎ 01882 632418).

ACCOMMODATION

Dunalastair Hotel Suites Kinloch Rannoch, PH16 5PW ☎ 01882 580444, ⓦ dunalastairhotel.com. Historic stone venue at the heart of loch life, given a multimillion-pound overhaul by new owners. Deluxe suites feature contemporary furnishings, a splash of art and humungous beds. **£159**

Moor of Rannoch Rannoch Station, PH17 2QA ☎ 01882 633238, ⓦ moorofrannoch.co.uk. Pleasant, small hotel in a handsome whitewashed building. Despite a friendly welcome, there's still a feeling of isolation in this empty landscape. Closed Nov to mid-Feb. **£140**

Pass of Killiecrankie

Four miles north of Pitlochry, the A9 cuts through the **Pass of Killiecrankie**, a sigh-triggering wooded gorge that falls away to the River Garry below. This dramatic setting was the site of the **Battle of Killiecrankie** in 1689, when the Jacobites quashed the forces of General Mackay. Legend has it that one soldier of the Crown, fleeing for his life, made a miraculous jump across the 18ft **Soldier's Leap**, an impossibly wide chasm halfway up the gorge. Exhibits at the slick **NTS visitor centre** on the east side of the Pass (April–Nov daily 10am–5pm; ☎ 01796 473233, ⓦ nts.org.uk/Visit/Killiecrankie) recall the battle and examine the gorge in detail.

Blair Atholl

Three miles north of Killiecrankie, the village of **BLAIR ATHOLL** makes for a much quieter and more idiosyncratic stop than Pitlochry. You can wander around the still functioning **Watermill** on Ford Road (April–Oct daily 9.30am–4.30pm; free; ⓦ blairathollwatermill.co.uk), which dates from 1613, and witness flour being milled. The mill also has a great bakery and tearoom (see page 865).

Blair Castle

Blair Atholl, PH18 5TL · April–Oct daily 9.30am–5.30pm (last admission 4.30pm); Nov–March occasional weekends – see website for details · £11; grounds only £6.50 · ☎ 01796 481207, ⓦ blair-castle.co.uk

By far the most important and eye-catching building in these parts is **Blair Castle**, seat of the Atholl dukedom for more than seven hundred years. This whitewashed, turreted Hogwarts looks particularly impressive as you sweep along the driveway leading from the centre of Blair Atholl village, especially if a piper is playing. The pipers belong to the Atholl Highlanders, a select group retained by the duke as his private army – a unique privilege afforded to him by Queen Victoria, who stayed here in 1844. Highlights are the soaring **entrance hall** and the vast **ballroom**, with its timber roof, antlers, and mixture of portraits.

ARRVAL AND INFORMATION

BLAIR ATHOLL

By train Trains from Pitlochry heading north arrive at Blair Atholl station (every 2–3hr; 9min).

By bus There are Citylink bus services from Edinburgh (daily; 2hr 40min), Glasgow (daily; 3hr), Perth (daily; 1hr) and Inverness (daily; 2hr) to the *Atholl Arms* in Blair Atholl.

Atholl Estates Information Centre Opposite the Blair Castle Caravan Park, just off A9 (April–Oct daily 9am–4.45pm; ☎ 01796 481355, ⓦ athollestatesrangerservice.co.uk).

EATING

Blair Atholl Watermill Ford Rd, PH18 5SH ☎ 01796 481321, ⓦ blairathollwatermill.co.uk. Lovely little working mill (see page 864) where you can enjoy home-baked scones, cakes and light lunches in its timber-beamed tearoom. Daily 9.30am–4.30pm.

20

Argyll

BAILE MÒR, IONA

21 Argyll

Cut off for centuries from the rest of Scotland by the mountains and sea lochs that characterize the region, Argyll remains remote and sparsely populated, its scatter of offshore islands forming part of the Inner Hebridean archipelago. Geographically and culturally, this is a transitional area between Highland and Lowland, boasting a rich variety of scenery from subtropical gardens warmed by the Gulf Stream to flat, treeless islands on the edge of the Atlantic. The strengths and beauties of mainland Argyll lie in the folds and twists of the countryside, the interplay of land and water and the views out to the islands – the one area of man-made sights you shouldn't miss, however, is the cluster of Celtic and prehistoric sites near Kilmartin.

The eastern duo of **Bute** and **Arran** are the most popular of Scotland's more southerly islands, the latter – now, strictly, part of Ayrshire – justifiably so, with spectacular scenery ranging from the granite peaks of the north to the Lowland pasture of the south. Of the Hebridean islands covered in this chapter, mountainous **Mull** is the most visited, and large enough to absorb the crowds, many of whom are only passing through en route to the tiny isle of **Iona**, a place of spiritual pilgrimage for centuries. **Islay**, best known for its malt whiskies, is fairly quiet even in the height of summer, as is neighbouring **Jura**, which offers excellent walking. And, for those seeking further solitude, there are the more remote islands of **Tiree** and **Coll**, which, although swept with fierce winds, have more sunny days than anywhere else in Scotland.

GETTING AROUND   ARGYLL

Argyll's **public transport** options are minimal, though buses do serve most major settlements, and the train line reaches Oban. In the remoter parts and on the islands, you'll have to rely on walking, shared taxis and the postbus. If you're planning to take a **vehicle** across to one of the islands, make sure to reserve both your outward and return journeys as early as possible, as the ferries get very booked up.

Bute

The island of **BUTE** is in many ways simply an extension of the Cowal peninsula, from which it is separated by the narrow Kyles of Bute. Thanks to its mild climate, big sandy beaches and a **ferry link** with Wemyss Bay, Bute has been a popular holiday and convalescence spot for Clydesiders for more than a century.

ARRIVAL AND DEPARTURE   BUTE

By ferry Regular CalMac ferries (⑩ calmac.co.uk) run from Wemyss Bay, 30 miles west of Glasgow, to Rothesay (every 45–60min; 35min). There's also a small CalMac ferry crossing from Colintraive, 25 miles south of Inveraray, to Rhubodach, 6 miles north of Rothesay (every 30min; 5min).

Hiking up Goat Fell p.884
Islay whisky p.887

Geese on Islay p.888
George Orwell on Jura p.889

TOBERMORY, MULL

Highlights

● **Mount Stuart, Bute** An architecturally overblown aristocratic mansion, set in the most beautiful grounds in the region. See page 872

● **Tobermory, Mull** The archetypal picturesque fishing village, ranged around a sheltered harbour and backed by steep hills. See page 875

● **Iona** A centre of Christian culture since the sixth century, the isle of Iona is, despite the crowds, a very special place. See page 878

● **Golden beaches** Argyll abounds in stunning sandy beaches, with lovely stretches at Coll, Tiree and Islay. See pages 879 and 886

❺ **Gigha** The ideal island-scape: sandy beaches, friendly folk and the azaleas of Achamore Gardens. See page 882

❻ **Goat Fell, Arran** Spectacular views over north Arran's craggy mountain range and the Firth of Clyde. See page 884

❼ **Whisky distilleries, Islay** With a generous scattering of often beautifully located distilleries to choose from, Islay is the ultimate whisky-lover's destination. See page 887

HIGHLIGHTS ARE MARKED ON THE MAP ON PAGE 870

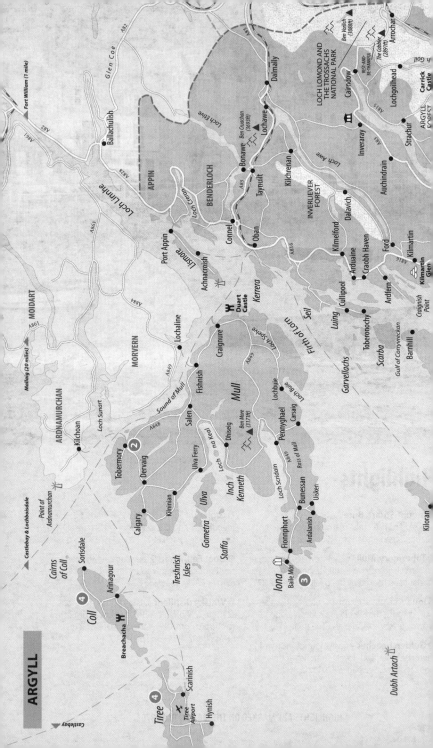

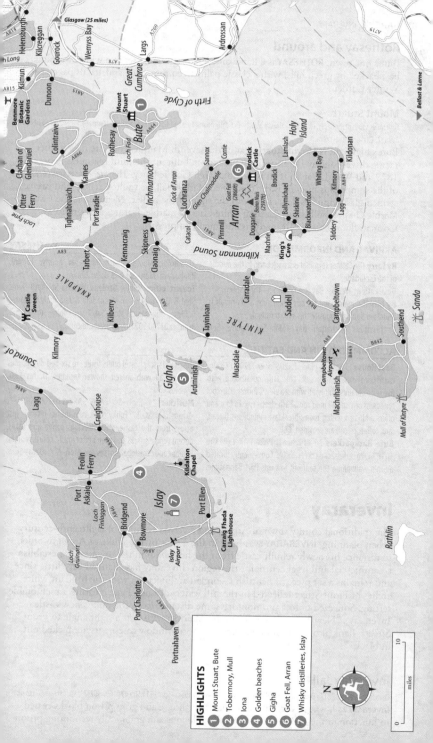

Glasgow (25 miles)

Firth of Clyde

Belfast & Larne

Mount Stuart 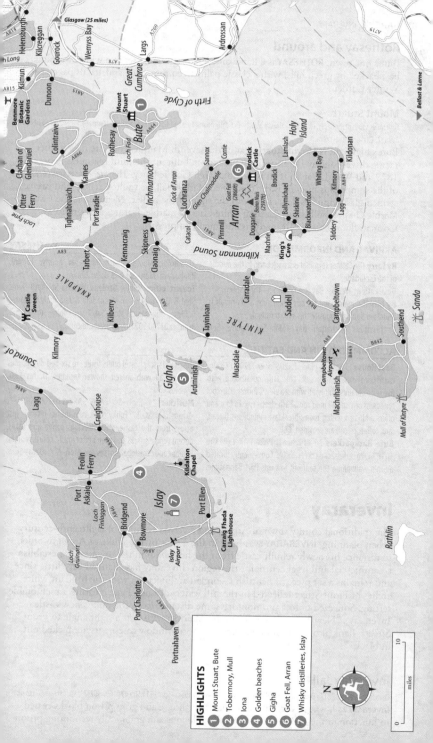 ①
Bute
Loch Fad

Rothesay

A846

Great Cumbrae

Wemyss Bay

Largs

Ardrossan

A78

A719

A760

Helensburgh

Gourock

Kilcreggan

Kilmun

Dunoon

A815

Benmore Botanic Gardens

Colintraive

A886

Clachan of Glendaruel

Kames

Otter Ferry

Tighnabruaich

Portavadie

Loch Fyne

Inchmarnock

Skipness

Claonaig

Kennacraig

Tarbert

KNAPDALE

Kilberry

Castle Sween

Kilmory

Sound of Jura

Lagg

Craighouse

A846

Feolin Ferry

Port Askaig

Islay

Loch Finlaggan

Loch Gruinart

Bridgend

Bowmore

Loch Indaal

A846

Port Charlotte

Portnahaven

A847

Kildalton Chapel

Port Ellen

Islay Airport ✈

Carraig Fhada Lighthouse

④ ⑦

Rathlin

Cock of Arran

Lochranza

Glen Chalmadale

Catacol

Pirnmill

Machrie

King's Cave

Arran

Goat Fell (2866ft) ▲ ⑥

Dougarie

Beinn Nuis (2597ft)

Sannox

Corrie

Brodick Castle

Brodick

Lamlash

Holy Island

Whiting Bay

Ballymichael

Shiskine

Blackwaterfoot

Sliddery

Kilmory

Lagg

A841

Kilmory

Kildonan

Kilbrannan Sound

Carradale

Saddell

B842

Campbeltown

Gigha ⑤

Ardminish

Tayinloan

Muasdale

KINTYRE

A83

Campbeltown Airport ✈

Machrihanish

B843

Southend

B842

Sanda

Mull of Kintyre

HIGHLIGHTS

① Mount Stuart, Bute
② Tobermory, Mull
③ Iona
④ Golden beaches
⑤ Gigha
⑥ Goat Fell, Arran
⑦ Whisky distilleries, Islay

N

0   10
miles

21

Rothesay and around

Bute's one town, **ROTHESAY** is a handsome Victorian resort set in a wide, sweeping bay, backed by green hills, with a classic palm-tree promenade and 1920s pagoda-style Winter Gardens.

Mount Stuart

Four miles south of Rothesay, PA20 9LR • **House** March–Oct daily noon–4pm • £11.50 • **Gardens** Daily 10am–6pm • £6.50 • ☎ 01700 503877, ⊛ mountstuart.com

Bute's highlight is **Mount Stuart**, seat of the seventh Marquess of Bute (aka former racing driver Johnny Dumfries). The mansion, built for the third marquess between 1879 and World War II, is an incredible High Gothic fancy. The *pièce de resistance* of the sumptuous interior is the columned **Marble Hall**, its vaulted ceiling and twelve stained-glass windows decorated with the signs of the zodiac. Meanwhile, the vast **Marble Chapel**, built from dazzling white Carrara marble, features a magnificent Cosmati floor pattern. The gardens are equally impressive.

ARRIVAL AND INFORMATION
ROTHESAY

By ferry The CalMac terminal is smack bang in the middle of the Esplanade.

Destinations Wemyss Bay (every 45min–1hr; 35min).

By bus The main point for bus departures and arrivals is Guildford Square, opposite the ferry terminal.

Destinations Kilchattan Bay (Mon–Sat hourly, Sun 3; 30min); Mount Stuart (Mon–Sat hourly; 15min); Rhubodach (Mon–Sat 2–3 daily; 20min).

Tourist office Winter Gardens, Victoria St (April–June, Sept & Oct daily 10am–5pm; July & Aug daily 9.30am–5.30pm; Nov–March Mon–Sat 10am–4pm, Sun 11am–3pm; ☎ 01700 502151, ⊛ visitbute.com).

ACCOMMODATION AND EATING

Boat House 15 Battery Place, PA20 9DP ☎ 01700 502696, ⊛ theboathouse-bute.co.uk. Chic little guesthouse with five self-contained suites, all with sea views, furnished in cool tones and offering all mod cons. Each sleeps two to four and offers a kitchen-dining room; breakfast ingredients (bread, jam, coffee, cereal) are provided. **£80**

Bute Backpackers 36 Argyle St, PA20 0AX ☎ 01700 501876, ⊛ butebackpackers.co.uk. Conveniently located a 5min walk along the seafront towards Port Bannatyne,

the island's sole hostel offers three- to six-bed dorms, plus doubles, all with shared shower facilities. Dorms **£20**, doubles **£50**

Musicker 11 High St, PA20 9AS ☎ 01700 502287, ⊛ musicker.co.uk. Funky café-cum-music retailer just across from the castle, with delicious coffee and cakes, decent veggie snacks and even better music, courtesy of the jukebox and occasional jam session. Mon–Sat 10am–5pm

Inveraray

The traditional county town of Argyll, and a classic example of eighteenth-century urban planning, **INVERARAY** was built in the 1770s by the Duke of Argyll in order to distance his newly rebuilt castle from the hoi polloi in the town and to establish a commercial and legal centre for the region. Inveraray has changed very little since and remains a set piece of Scottish Georgian architecture, with the brilliant white arches of Front Street reflected in the still waters of Loch Fyne creating a memorable setting. Squeezed onto a promontory some distance from the duke's new castle, Inveraray's "New Town" has a distinctive **Main Street** (set at a right angle to Front Street), flanked by whitewashed terraces whose window casements are picked out in black.

Inveraray Jail

Church Square, PA32 8TX • Daily: April–Oct 9.30am–6pm; Nov–March 10am–5pm • £11.50 • ☎ 01499 302381, ⊛ inverarayjail.co.uk

Inveraray Jail, whose attractive Georgian courthouse and grim prison blocks ceased to function in the 1930s, is now an enjoyable museum graphically recounting prison conditions from medieval times to the twentieth century. You can check out the minute "Airing Yards" where the prisoners got to exercise for an hour a day and, in the semicircular courthouse with its great views over the loch, listen to a re-enactment of a trial of the period.

Inveraray Castle

A 10min walk north of Main St, PA32 8XE • April–Oct daily 10am–5.45pm • £11 • ☎01499 302203, ⓦ inveraray-castle.com

Inveraray Castle remains the family home of the Duke of Argyll. Built in 1745, it was given a touch of the Loire in the nineteenth century with the addition of dormer windows and conical corner spires. Inside, the most startling feature is the armoury hall, where the displays of weaponry – supplied to the Campbells by the British government to put down the Jacobites – rise through several storeys. Otherwise, the interior is pretty unremarkable, though the small exhibition on Rob Roy, complete with his belt, sporran and dirk handle, is worth poring over.

ARRIVAL AND INFORMATION INVERARAY

By bus Buses pick up and drop off on Front St, opposite the tourist office.
Destinations Glasgow (4–6 daily; 2hr); Oban (4 daily; 1hr 5min); Tarbert (2–3 daily; 1hr 30min).

Tourist office Front St (daily: April–June, Sept & Oct 10am–5pm; July & Aug 9am–6pm; Nov–March 10am–4pm; ☎01499 302263, ⓦ inveraray-argyll.com).

ACCOMMODATION, EATING AND DRINKING

The George Main St East, PA32 8TT ☎01499 302111, ⓦ thegeorgehotel.co.uk. The rambling, and very convivial, restaurant/bar of *The George* feels like a proper pub with its flagstone flooring, log fires and dimly lit nooks and. Daily 11am–11pm; kitchen noon–9pm.
Inverary Hostel Dalmally Rd, PA32 8XD ☎01499 302454, ⓦ inverarayhostel.co.uk. Small, low-key hostel in a low, wood-and-stone chalet-type building a short walk up the A819 to Oban (just beyond the petrol station). The rooms (twins and quads) all have shared shower facilities, and there's a communal lounge and kitchen. Breakfast £3.50. Closed Nov–March. **£17**
★ **Loch Fyne Oyster Bar and Shop** 8 miles east of Inveraray, PA26 8BL ☎01499 600482, ⓦ lochfyne.com.

On the shores of Loch Fyne, this oyster bar spawned the *Loch Fyne* restaurant chain. The food is delicious and beautifully thought through, from Makar gin-cured salmon (£9) to whole sea bream curry (£20); or you can tuck into oysters (six for £12) at the superb marble-topped oyster bar. The gorgeous on-site shop/deli is a great place to assemble a gourmet picnic. Restaurant daily 9am–10pm; shop Mon–Sat 9am–6pm, Sun 10am–5pm.
★ **Newton Hall** Shore Rd, PA32 8UH ☎01499 302484, ⓦ newtonhallguesthouse.co.uk. A 5min walk from town, this former church accommodates an outstanding ensemble of seven rooms, each in a different style and boasting splendid views across the Loch. Closed Jan & Dec. **£70**

Oban

The solidly Victorian resort of **OBAN** enjoys a superb setting, distinguished by a bizarre granite amphitheatre, dramatically lit at night, on the hilltop above the town. Despite a small population it's by far the largest port in northwest Scotland, and the main departure point for **ferries** to the Hebrides.

Oban's main landmark is **McCaig's Tower**, a stiff ten-minute climb from the quayside. Built in 1902 in imitation of Rome's Colosseum, it was the brainchild of a local businessman who wanted both to alleviate off-season unemployment among Oban's stonemasons and to create a museum, art gallery and chapel. In his will, McCaig gave instructions for the lancet windows to be filled with bronze statues of the family, though no such work was ever undertaken. Instead, the folly has been turned into a sort of walled garden, and provides a wonderful seaward panorama, particularly at sunset.

21

Oban Distillery

Stafford St, PA34 5NH • Tours (1hr) Jan & Feb daily 12.30–3.15pm; March–June, Oct & Nov daily 9.30am–3.45pm; July–Sept Mon–Fri 9.30am–6.15pm, Sat & Sun 9.30am–3.45pm; Dec daily noon–3.15pm • £10 • ☎ 01631 572004, ⊛ malts.com

Oban Distillery is one of Scotland's oldest, founded in 1794 by the Stevenson brothers, and today it produces in excess of a million bottles a year of its lightly peaty malt, which is acknowledged to be a touch easier on the palate than many other whiskies produced hereabouts. Excellent **tours** take in the Mash House, with four massive Scandinavian larch washbacks, and the Still House, with its beautifully proportioned copper stills – and ends, as is the custom, with a generous dram.

ARRIVAL AND INFORMATION   OBAN

By ferry The CalMac terminal is on Railway Pier, close to the train and bus stations.
Destinations Achnacroish, Lismore (Mon–Sat 4 daily, Sun 2; 50min); Coll (daily except Wed & Fri; 2hr 40min); Colonsay (daily; 2hr 15min); Craignure, Mull (9 daily; 50min); Tiree (1 daily; 3hr 40min).
By train Trains from Glasgow Queen St (4 daily; 3hr 15min) pull up on Station Square.

By bus On Station Rd, next to the train station.
Destinations Fort William (3 daily; 1hr 30min); Glasgow (5 daily; 3hr); Inveraray (4 daily; 1hr 10min).
Tourist office 3 North Pier (April, May, Sept & Oct Mon–Sat 9am–5pm, Sun 10am–5pm; June daily 9am–6pm; July & Aug daily 9am–7pm; Nov–March 10am–5pm; ☎ 01631 563122, ⊛ oban.org.uk).

ACCOMMODATION AND EATING

Coast 104 George St, PA34 5NT ☎ 01631 569900, ⊛ coastoban.com. A slick place with a metropolitan atmosphere, serving acclaimed and original fish dishes such as pan-fried fillet of red gurnard with anchovy and parsley fritters (£17.50). Mon–Sat noon–2.30pm & 5.30–10pm, Sun 5.30–9.30pm.
Oban Backpackers Breadalbane St, PA34 5NZ ☎ 01631 562107, ⊛ obanbackpackers.com. Large, friendly and colourful hostel with a range of dorms; the largest have twelve beds. The big, open lounge-dining area has mismatched sofas, a pool table and a real fire. Breakfast £2. £17.50
The Old Manse Guest House Dalraich Rd, PA34 5JE ☎ 01631 564886, ⊛ obanguesthouse.co.uk. There are few more welcoming places in town than this spotless Victorian villa whose five rooms (two with sea views) offer thoughtful touches all round, including CD players,

complimentary sherry and great toiletries. The breakfast is top-notch. Closed Nov to mid-Feb. £92
Original Green Shack Railway Pier, PA34 4DB. Longstanding and hugely popular seafood shack serving langoustine sandwiches, scallops in hot garlic butter (£6.95), mussels in white wine (£3.95), oysters, prawns, cockles and loads more. Wooden benches available for seating. Mon–Fri & Sun 10am–6pm, Sat 10am–8pm.
Waterfront Fishouse Restaurant 1 Railway Pier, PA34 4LW ☎ 01631 563110, ⊛ waterfrontfishouse. co.uk. Upstairs in the old Fishermen's Mission, and enjoying lovely views over the bay, this elegant restaurant rustles up impressive dishes primarily using scallops (chargrilled Isle of Mull scallops with a parmesan and basil mash), langoustine (crispy tails) and the best of the daily catch; the two-course lunch and early evening menu is a steal at £13.99. Daily noon–2pm & 5.30–10pm.

Mull

Just forty minutes from Oban by ferry, **MULL** is by far the most accessible of the Hebrides. As so often, first impressions largely depend on the weather – it's the wettest of the group (and that's saying something) – and without the sun the large tracts of moorland, particularly around the island's highest peak, **Ben More** (3196ft), can appear bleak and unwelcoming. There are, however, areas of more gentle pastoral scenery around **Dervaig** in the north, and the indented west coast varies from the sandy beaches around **Calgary** to the cliffs of Loch na Keal.

ARRIVAL AND GETTING AROUND   MULL

By ferry There are frequent daily car ferries from Oban to Craignure (booking advisable), plus a smaller and less expensive daily car ferry from Lochaline on the Morvern

peninsula to Fishnish, 6 miles northwest of Craignure. Another, even smaller, car ferry connects Kilchoan on the Ardnamurchan peninsula (see page 934) with Tobermory, Mull's capital.

y bus The two main bus routes are the #95 (#495) between Craignure and Tobermory, and the #96 (#496) between Craignure and Fionnphort, with a third route (#494) from Tobermory to Dervaig and Calgary.

Craignure and around

CRAIGNURE is little more than a scattering of cottages with a small shop, a bar, toilets and a CalMac ticket and **tourist office**. However, there is plenty of accommodation here, as well as a few places to eat and drink, so it's a useful base.

Duart Castle

848, 3 miles southeast of Craignure, PA64 6AP • April Mon–Thurs & Sun 11am–4pm; May–Oct daily 10.30am–5pm • £6.50 • 01680 12309, duartcastle.com

On a picturesque spit of rock, **Duart Castle** makes for a striking landmark viewed from the Oban–Craignure ferry. Headquarters of the once-powerful MacLean clan from the thirteenth century, it was burnt down by the Campbells and confiscated after the 1745 rebellion. Finally, in 1911, the 26th clan chief, Fitzroy MacLean (1835–1936), bought it back and restore it. You can peek at the dungeons, climb up to the ramparts, study the family photos, and learn about the world scout movement – the 27th clan chief became Chief Scout in 1959.

ARRIVAL AND INFORMATION

CRAIGNURE AND AROUND

By ferry The ferry terminal dominates the village centre, with the CalMac office directly opposite.
Destinations Oban (9 daily; 50min).
By bus Buses pick up and drop off by the main road by the ferry terminal.
Destinations Fionnphort (Mon–Sat 3–5 daily, Sun 1; 1hr

10min); Fishnish (2–3 daily; 15min); Tobermory (4–6 daily; 45min).
Tourist office Opposite the ferry terminal in shared premises with CalMac (April–June, Sept & Oct daily 9am–5pm; July & Aug daily 9am–7.30pm; Nov–March Mon–Sat 9am–5pm, Sun 10am–noon & 2–5pm; 01680 812377).

ACCOMMODATION AND EATING

Craignure Bunkhouse 350m up the road towards Fionnphort, PA65 6AY 01680 812043, craignure-bunkhouse.co.uk. Super-smart eco-hostel with four en-suite bunk rooms, each with four or six beds, plus a homely lounge with woodburner, sofas and a library. They also have a self-catering kitchen, laundry and drying room. **£20**
Craignure Inn 400m up the road towards Fionnphort, PA65 6AY 01680 812305, craignure-inn.co.uk. A snug pub for a pint in the bar or a meal in the adjoining

restaurant; venison loin saddle (£14.95) is a popular dish. Daily 11.30am–11pm; kitchen noon–9pm.
Shieling Holidays 0.5 mile up the road towards Fionnphort, PA65 6AY 01680 812496, shielingholidays.co.uk. Quiet and very appealing family-run campsite offering tent pitches and cool accommodation in "shielings" (large, sometimes furnished, hard-top tents), sleeping between two and six; some are en suite. Closed Nov–Feb. **£18.50**, shielings **£37**

Tobermory

Mull's chief town, **TOBERMORY**, at the northern tip of the island, is easily the most attractive fishing port on the west coast of Scotland, with its clusters of brightly coloured houses and boats sheltering in a bay backed by a steep bluff. The harbour – known as **Main Street** – is one long parade of multicoloured hotels, guesthouses, restaurants and shops.

Mull Museum

Main St, PA75 6NY • Easter to mid-Oct Mon–Fri 10am–4pm, Sat 10am–1pm • Free • 01688 301100, mullmuseum.org.uk

A good wet-weather retreat is the one-room **Mull Museum**, packed with fascinating local information and artefacts. Among these are a handful of objects salvaged from the *San Juan de Sicilia*, a ship from the Spanish Armada that sank in 1588 and now lies at the bottom of Tobermory harbour; even today, it remains subject to repeated salvage attempts by locals still, somewhat optimistically, seeking gold.

21

Mull Aquarium

Harbour Building, Ledaig car park, PA75 6NR • April–Oct daily 9.30am–5pm • £5 (day ticket) • ☎ 01688 302876, ⓦ mullaquarium.co.uk

An absolute delight, the small, community-owned **Mull Aquarium** is the first catch-and-release aquarium in Europe, meaning that all marine life – caught by local divers, fishermen and anyone else willing to head out to sea – is released back into the waters within four weeks. So, for example, you might get to see dogfish, jellyfish, sea scorpion or velvet swimming crabs in the half a dozen or so tanks, alongside all manner of weird and wonderful creatures.

ARRIVAL AND INFORMATION
TOBERMORY

By ferry The CalMac terminal is at the far end of Main St, in the northernmost part of the bay.

Destinations Kilchoan (5–7 daily; 35min).

By bus The bus station is in the main Ledaig car park, by the distillery.

Destinations Calgary (Mon–Fri 4 daily, Sat 2; 45min); Craignure (4–6 daily; 45min); Dervaig (Mon–Fri 4 daily, Sat 2; 25min); Fishnish (2–4 daily; 40min).

Tourist office Privately run Explore Mull, in a cabin in the Ledaig car park (April–Oct daily 9am–6pm; ☎ 01688 302875, ⓦ isle-of-mull.net), has plenty of information and can arrange accommodation and wildlife tours.

ACCOMMODATION AND EATING

Fisherman's Pier Fish & Chip Van Fisherman's Pier, PA75 6PU ☎ 01688 301109. The friendly proprietors of this venerable takeaway van serve traditional fish suppers, though most venture here for their scrumptious scallops and chips (£9.50). June–Sept daily 12.30–9pm; Oct–May Mon–Sat 12.30–9pm.

★ **Highland Cottage** Breadalbane St, PA75 6PD ☎ 01688 302030, ⓦ highlandcottage.co.uk. Super-luxurious B&B run by a welcoming couple in a quiet street high above the harbour; the six modestly sized but gorgeously furnished rooms, each one named after an Argyll island, are fashioned with home comforts firmly in mind, such as shelves rammed with books. **£155**

SYHA Tobermory Hostel Main St, PA65 6NU ☎ 01688 302 481, ⓦ syha.org.uk/where-to-stay/islands/tobermory.aspx. Small, friendly and superbly located hostel on the harbourfront, with two- to five-bed rooms, plus shared shower facilities, kitchen, TV lounge and laundry. Closed Mid-Oct to mid-March. Dorms **£19**, doubles **£50**

Tobermory Hotel 53 Main St, PA75 6NT ☎ 01688 302091, ⓦ thetobermoryhotel.com. The highly creditable restaurant conjures up tempting dishes such as home-made crab cakes with lemongrass, chilli and roasted garlic mayonnaise, and grilled Isle of Mull langoustines (£23.95). Pleasant, warming atmosphere and first-rate service. Mon–Sat 6–10pm, Sun 1–3pm & 6–10pm.

Staffa and the Treshnish Isles

Seven miles off the west coast of Mull, the isle of **STAFFA** is the most romantic and dramatic of Scotland's many uninhabited islands. On its south side, the perpendicular rock face features an imposing series of black basalt columns, known as the Colonnade, which have been cut by the sea into cathedralesque caverns, most notably **Fingal's Cave**. Turner painted it, Wordsworth explored it, but Mendelssohn's *Die Fingalshöhle*, inspired by the sounds of the sea-wracked caves he heard on a visit here in 1829, did most to popularize the place – after which Queen Victoria gave her blessing, too. The polygonal basalt organ-pipes were created by a massive subterranean explosion some sixty million years ago, when a huge mass of molten basalt burst forth and, as it cooled, solidified into what are essentially crystals.

Treshnish Isles

Northwest of Staffa lie the **Treshnish Isles**, an archipelago of uninhabited volcanic islets, none more than a mile or two across. The most distinctive is **Bac Mór**, shaped like a Puritan's hat and popularly dubbed the Dutchman's Cap. **Lunga**, the largest island, is a summer nesting-place for hundreds of seabirds, in particular guillemots, razorbills and puffins, the last of which are by far and away the main reason for visiting; it's also a major breeding ground for seals.

ARRIVAL AND DEPARTURE   **STAFFA AND THE TRESHNISH ISLES**

Boat tours From April to Oct several operators offer boat trips to Staffa and the Treshnish Isles. Best is long-established Turus Mara, based in Penmore (☎ 01688 400242, ⓦ turusmara.com), which sets out from Ulva

Ferry. They offer a round trip (£65) to Staffa and the Treshnish Isles – typically including 1hr on Staffa and 2hr on Lunga – and a 3hr 30min trip to Staffa (£32).

Iona

Less than a mile off the southwest tip of Mull, the isle of **IONA** (ⓦ welcometoiona.com), just three miles long and little more than a mile wide – has been a place of pilgrimage for several centuries, and a site of Christian worship for more than 1400 years. It was to this flat Hebridean island that **St Columba** fled from Ireland in 563 and established a monastery, compiling a vast library of illuminated manuscripts and converting more or less all of pagan Scotland as well as much of northern England. This history and the island's splendid isolation have lent it a peculiar religiosity; in the much-quoted words of Dr Johnson, who visited in 1773, "That man is little to be envied … whose piety would not grow warmer among the ruins of Iona". Today, however, the island can barely cope with the flood of day-trippers, so in order to appreciate the atmosphere and to have time to see the whole island, including the often-overlooked west coast, you should stay at least one night.

Baile Mòr

The passenger ferry from Fionnphort drops you off at the island's main village, **BAILE MÒR** (literally "large village"), which is in fact little more than a single terrace of cottages facing the sea. Just inland lie the extensive pink-granite ruins of the **Augustinian nunnery**, built around 1200 but disused since the Reformation; these, if nothing else, give an idea of the state of the present-day abbey before it was restored. Just south of the manse and church stands the fifteenth-century **MacLean's Cross**, a fine, late medieval example of the distinctive, flowing, three-leaved foliage of the Iona school.

Iona Abbey

A 5min walk from the Heritage Centre, PA76 6SQ • Daily: April–Sept 9.30am–5.30pm; Oct–March 10am–4pm • £7.50; HES • ☎ 01681 700512, ⓦ historicenvironment.scot/visit-a-place/places/iona-abbey-and-nunnery

Although no buildings remain from Columba's time, the present **Iona Abbey** dates from the arrival of the Benedictines in around 1200, was extensively rebuilt in the fifteenth and sixteenth centuries, and restored virtually wholesale early last century. Adjoining the facade is a small steep-roofed chamber, believed to be St Columba's grave; it's now a small chapel. The three high crosses in front of the abbey date from the eighth to tenth centuries, and are decorated with the Pictish serpent-and-boss and Celtic spirals for which Iona's early Christian masons were renowned. The cloisters were placed, contrary to the norm, on the north side of the church (where running water was available); entirely reconstructed in the late 1950s, they now shelter a historical account of the abbey's development.

ARRIVAL AND DEPARTURE   IONA

By ferry Passenger-only ferries run from Fionnphort to Iona (summer daily every 15–30min; less frequent in winter; 10min; £3.40 return, bicycles free).

ACCOMMODATION AND EATING

As demand far exceeds supply you should book **accommodation** well in advance. If you want to stay with the **Iona Community**, contact the MacLeod Centre (☎ 01681 700404, ⓦ iona.org.uk).

Argyll Near the jetty, Baile Mòr, PA76 6SJ ☎01681 700334, ⓦargyllhoteliona.co.uk. Inviting, stone-built hotel in the village's terrace of cottages overlooking the Sound of Iona, with sixteen sweet, somewhat boxy, rooms. The restaurant is first class (try braised Mull beef cheek with roast shallots and wild garlic butter; £16); you could also simply sup a pint from the bar, taking it out onto the trim, sea-facing lawn. Closed Jan, Nov & Dec. Daily: bar 11am–11pm; restaurant noon–2pm & 6–9pm. **£99**

Iona Hostel Lagandorain, about a mile north of Iona Abbey, PA76 6SW ☎01681 700781, ⓦionahostel. co.uk. In the north of the island, this simple but attractive hostel has five rooms sleeping two to six, and a living space with lovely wooden furniture, a wood-burning stove and views out to the Treshnish Isles. They've also have a delightful shepherd's bothy (sleeping two) tucked on a rocky outcrop just behind the hostel. Dorms **£21**, bothy **£60**

Martyrs' Bay Restaurant By the jetty, Baile Mòr, PA76 6SJ ☎01681 700382, ⓦmartyrsbay.co.uk. A self-service canteen by day, a fully fledged restaurant come evening; either way, the tourist hordes invariably pack this place out for steaks and seafood. Lunches such as haddock and chips (£9.95) or baked potato with haggis are worth a punt, too. Mon & Sun 11am–9pm, Tues–Sat 11am–11pm.

Coll

The fish-shaped rocky island of **COLL** (ⓦvisitcoll.co.uk), with a population of around a hundred, lies less than seven miles off the coast of Mull. The CalMac ferry drops off at the only real village, **ARINAGOUR**, whose whitewashed cottages dot the western shore of Loch Eatharna. Half of Coll's population lives here, where you'll find the island's hotel and pub, post office, churches and a couple of shops.

On the southwest coast are two edifices, both confusingly known as **Breachacha Castle**. The older is a restored fifteenth-century tower house, and now a training centre for overseas aid volunteers. The less attractive "new castle", to the northwest, is made up of a central block built around 1750 and two side pavilions added a century later, and has been converted into holiday homes. Much of the area around the castles is owned by the RSPB, with the aim of protecting the island's small corncrake population. A vast area of **giant sand dunes** lies to the west of the castles, with two glorious, golden, sandy bays stretching for more than a mile on either side.

ARRIVAL AND DEPARTURE COLL

By ferry In summer, the CalMac ferry from Oban calls daily at Coll (2hr 40min) and Tiree (3hr 40min).

Destinations Barra (Wed 1 daily; 4hr); Oban (daily except Tues & Wed; 2hr 40min).

ACCOMMODATION AND EATING

Coll Hotel Arinagour, PA76 6SZ ☎01879 230334, ⓦcollhotel.com. Small, family-run hotel offering refined accommodation in six rooms, four of which overlook the bay. The place also doubles as Coll's social centre, with creel-caught seafood forming the mainstay of a mouthwatering menu. Daily noon–2pm & 6–9pm. **£100**

Garden House In the west of the island, near Breachacha beach, PA78 6TB ☎01879 230374. Basic campsite in the shelter of an old walled garden surrounded by the RSPB reserve and 5min from Breachacha beach. Closed Nov–March. **£16**

Island Café Shore St, Arinagour, PA78 6SY ☎01879 230262. In the old harbour stores overlooking the bay, offering hot meals all day. Sun is most popular for the superb two-course late lunches, comprising a roast and a dessert (£18), for which reservations are advised. Wed–Sat 11am–2pm & 5–9pm, Sun noon–6pm.

Tiree

TIREE (ⓦisleoftiree.com) as its Gaelic name *tir-iodh* ("land of corn") suggests, was once known as the breadbasket of the Inner Hebrides, thanks to its acres of rich machair (sandy, grassy, lime-rich land). Nowadays crofting and tourism are the main sources of income for the small resident population. One of the most distinctive features of the island is its architecture, in particular the large numbers of "pudding" or "spotty" houses, where only the mortar is painted white. The sandy beaches attract large numbers of windsurfers for the **Tiree Wave Classic** every October (ⓦtireewaveclassic.co.uk).

An Turas and Scarinish

The **ferry** calls at Gott Bay Pier, now best known for **An Turas** (The Journey), Tiree's award-winning artistic "shelter": two parallel white walls connected via a black felt section to a glass box which punctures a stone dyke and frames a sea view. Just up the road is the village of **SCARINISH**, home to a post office, public toilets, a supermarket, a butcher's and a bank, with a petrol pump back at the pier, as well as **An Iodhlann** (July & Aug Mon–Fri 11am–5pm; Sept–June Mon, Wed & Thurs 9am–1pm; free; ⓦaniodhlann.org.uk) – "haystack" in Gaelic – which has an enlightening exhibition on the islands' history.

Hynish

Below the higher of Tiree's two landmark hills is **HYNISH**, with its restored **harbour**, designed by Alan Stevenson in the 1830s to transport building materials for the magnificent 157ft-tall **Skerryvore Lighthouse**, which lies on a sea-swept reef some twelve miles southwest of Tiree. Up on the hill behind the harbour stands a stumpy granite signal tower, whose signals used to be the only contact the lighthouse keepers had with civilization. Occupying a converted smithy on Lower Square, the **Skerryvore Lighthouse Exhibition** (Easter to mid-Oct daily 9am–5pm; free, but suggested £3 donation; ☏01879 220045, ⓦhebrideantrust.org) recalls the herculean effort required to erect the lighthouse, alongside many intriguing items gathered along the way.

ARRIVAL AND GETTING AROUND
TIREE

By plane Flights connect Tiree with Glasgow (2 daily; 1hr) and Oban (Mon & Wed 2 daily; 1hr); the airport (☏01879 220456, ⓦhial.co.uk) lies 3 miles west of Scarinish.

By ferry Car ferries arrive in Scarinish from Barra (summer 1 on Wed; 2hr 45min) and Oban (summer 1 daily; 3hr

40min).

By minibus The useful Ring'n'Ride service will take you anywhere on the island (Mon–Sat 7am–6pm, Tues 7am–10pm; ☏01879 220419); costs vary between £1.25 and £3.

ACCOMMODATION

Millhouse Hostel Near Loch Bhasapol, in the northwest of the island, PA77 6XY ☏01879 220892, ⓦtireemillhouse.co.uk. Great hostel in a snugly converted barn dating from the early 1900s, with two dorms sleeping six, a couple of doubles and a triple. The kitchen/lounge opens onto a patio from where you can watch the sunset. Dorms £24, doubles £54

Wild Diamond Near Loch a'Phuill, 6 miles southwest of Scarinish, PA77 6XA ☏01879 220399, ⓦwilddiamond. co.uk. The island's only formal campsite is operated by Wild Diamond Watersports, and is well equipped with showers, toilets, a self-catering kitchen and washing/drying facilities. £24

Mid-Argyll

Mid-Argyll is a vague term that loosely describes the central wedge of land south of Oban and north of Kintyre. The highlights of this gently undulating scenery lie along the sharply indented west coast, in particular the rich Bronze Age and Neolithic remains in the **Kilmartin** valley. Separating **Kilmartin Glen** from the Knapdale peninsula is the **Crinan Canal**, a shortcut for boats disinclined to round the Mull of Kintyre, which ends in the pint-sized, picturesque port of Crinan.

Kilmartin Glen

The **Kilmartin Glen** is the most important prehistoric site on the Scottish mainland, whose most remarkable relic is the **linear cemetery**, where several cairns are aligned for more than two miles to the south of the village of Kilmartin. These are thought to represent the successive burials of a ruling family or chieftains, but nobody can be sure. The best view of the cemetery's configuration is from the Bronze Age **Mid-Cairn**, but the Neolithic **South Cairn**, dating from around 3000 BC, is by far the oldest and the most impressive, with its large chambered tomb roofed by giant slabs. Close to the Mid-Cairn, the two **Temple Wood stone circles** appear to have been the architectural focus of burials in the area from Neolithic times to the Bronze Age. Visible to the south are the impressively cup-marked **Nether Largie standing stones** (no public access), the largest of which looms more than 10ft high.

Kilmartin Museum

Kilmartin village, PA31 8RQ • Daily: March–Oct 10am–5.30pm; Nov–Christmas 11am–4pm • £6.50 • ☎ 01546 510278, ⓦ kilmartin.org

Housed within the old manse next to Kilmartin's village church is the superb **Kilmartin Museum**. Among the many remarkable exhibits is an eagle bone flute, a bronze sword from Shuna, a carved slab from the Nether Largie north cairn and decorated querns (stones used for making flour from grain) from Barnasluagan. At 2pm on Wednesdays, museum staff run a superb (free) two-hour guided walk of the cairns.

Dunadd

South of Kilmartin, beyond the linear cemetery, PA31 8SU • Daily 24hr • Free • ⓦ historicenvironment.scot/visit-a-place/places/kilmartin-glen-dunadd-fort

The raised peat bog of Moine Mhòr (Great Moss) is best known as home to the Iron Age fort of **Dunadd**, one of Scotland's most important Celtic sites, occupying a distinctive 176ft-high rocky knoll once surrounded by the sea, but currently stranded beside the winding River Add. It was here that Fergus, the first king of Dalriada, established his royal seat, having arrived from Ireland in around 500 AD. Its strategic position, the craggy defences and the view from the top are all impressive, but it's the **stone carvings** (albeit now fibreglass copies) between the twin summits that make Dunadd so remarkable: several lines of Pictish inscription in *ogam* (an ancient alphabet of Irish origin), the faint outline of a boar, a hollowed-out footprint and a small basin.

ARRIVAL AND DEPARTURE   KILMARTIN GLEN

By bus Bus #423 between Oban and Ardrishaig runs through the glen (Mon–Fri 4 daily, Sat 2).

ACCOMMODATION AND EATING

★ **Dunchraigaig House** A mile south of Kilmartin village, PA31 8RG ☎ 01546 605300, ⓦ dunchraigaig. co.uk. A large detached Victorian house opposite the Ballymeanoch standing stones. The five spotless en-suite rooms have either woodland or Jura island views, though its star attraction is the local pine marten, who appears at the feeding table most mornings. **£80**

Kilmartin Museum Café Kilmartin Museum, Kilmartin village, PA31 8RQ ☎ 01546 510278, ⓦ kilmartin.org. Looking out across to Glebe Cairn, this is a lovely spot at which to refuel after examining the local treasures, with the likes of wild venison burger (£8.95), as well as lots of delicious home-baked dishes, to feast on. Daily: March–Oct 10am–5.30pm; Nov & Dec 11am–4pm.

Crinan Canal

In 1801 the nine-mile-long **Crinan Canal** opened, linking Loch Fyne at Ardrishaig, south of Lochgilphead, with the Sound of Jura, thus cutting out the long and treacherous journey around the Mull of Kintyre. The canal runs parallel to the sea for quite some way before hitting a flight of locks either side of **CAIRNBAAN** (there are fifteen in total); a walk along the towpath is picturesque and none too strenuous. There are usually one or two yachts passing through the locks, but the most relaxing place from which to view the action is **CRINAN**, a pretty little fishing port at its western end.

21

ARRIVAL AND DEPARTURE

By bus Bus #926 connects Glasgow with the Crinan Canal, via Lochgilphead (3 daily).

ACCOMMODATION AND EATING

Cairnbaan Hotel Cairnbaan, PS31 8SQ ☎01546 603668, Ⓦ cairnbaan.com. An eighteenth-century coaching inn overlooking the canal at Lock 5, with twelve accomplished, well-designed rooms. The lively restaurant-cum-bar deservedly does well from lots of passing trade from the canal, with dishes such as smoked haddock on chive mash with Kintyre cheddar (£14.50). Otherwise, just grab a pint and watch the boats pass by. Bar daily 11am–10pm; food kitchen daily noon–2.30pm & 6–9.30pm. **£90**

Crinan Hotel Crinan, PS31 8SR ☎01546 830261, Ⓦ crinanhotel.com. Reward yourself after the long canalside walk with steamed mussels or an Arbroath smokie (£13) washed down with a pint, and enjoy one of Scotland's most beautiful views – especially at sunset. As gorgeous as the rooms here are, you're really just paying a fortune for amazing views. Bar daily noon–2.30pm & 6–8.30pm. **£230**

Kintyre

But for the mile-long isthmus between West Loch Tarbert and the much smaller East Loch Tarbert, the little-visited peninsula of **KINTYRE** (Ⓦ kintyre.org) – from the Gaelic *Ceann Tire*, "land's end" – would be an island. Despite its relative proximity to Scotland's Central Belt, Kintyre remains quiet and unfashionable; its main towns, **Tarbert** and **Campbeltown**, have few obvious attractions, but that's part of their appeal. In many ways, it's a peninsula in a time warp, where you can hole up in perfect solitude; there's some splendid walking, too.

Tarbert

A distinctive rocket-like church steeple heralds the fishing village of **TARBERT** (in Gaelic *An Tairbeart*, meaning "isthmus"), sheltering an attractive little bay backed by rugged hills. Tarbert's harbourfront is pretty, and is best appreciated from the rubble of Robert the Bruce's fourteenth-century **castle** above the town to the south. A good time to be here is early July for the superb **Tarbert Seafood Festival**, which is when traditional boats also hit town.

ARRIVAL AND INFORMATION

By ferry Regular ferries connect Tarbert with Portavadie (hourly; 25min). The ferry terminal is on Pier Rd, a 10min walk along Harbour St.

By bus Buses arrive in the centre of town on Campbeltown Rd and Barmore Rd.

Destinations Campbeltown (5 daily; 1hr 15min); Claonaig (Mon–Sat 3 daily; 30min); Glasgow (5 daily; 3hr 10min);

Kennacraig (5 daily; 15min); Tayinloan (Mon–Fri 3 daily; 30min).

Tourist office Harbour St (April–June, Sept & Oct Mon–Sat 10am–5pm, Sun 11am–5pm; July & Aug Mon–Sat 9am–6pm, Sun 10am–5pm; Nov–March Tues–Sat 10am–2pm; ☎01880 820429, Ⓦ tarbertlochfyne.com).

ACCOMMODATION AND EATING

Starfish Castle St, PA29 6UH ☎01880 820733, Ⓦ starfishtarbert.com. Sparkling, informal seafood restaurant where scallops are king, literally – a plate will set you back £18, as will the *Starfish* stew, comprising mussels, queen scallops and the catch of the day. Mon–Thurs & Sun 6–10pm, Fri & Sat noon–2pm.

Struan House Harbour St, PA29 6UD ☎01880 820190, Ⓦ struan.biz. Opposite the Harbour Authority building up towards the ferry terminal, this charming six-room guesthouse has bespoke furnishings, grand wooden bedsteads, books and wall-mounted artwork. **£75**

Gigha

Gigha (Ⓦ gigha.org.uk) – pronounced "geeya" – is a low-lying, fertile island three miles off the west coast of Kintyre, reputedly occupied for five thousand years. Like many of the smaller Hebrides, Gigha was bought and sold numerous times after its original lairds, the MacNeils, sold up in 1865, and was finally bought by the islanders themselves in 2002. The island is so small – six miles by one – that most visitors come here for the day. The real draw, apart from the peace and quiet, is the white sandy **beaches**.

The ferry from Tayinloan, 23 miles south of Tarbert, deposits you at Gigha's only village, **ARDMINISH**, where you'll find the post office and shop, and a lovely beach. A mile and a half south, the **Achamore Gardens** (daily 9am–dusk; £6) were established by the first postwar owner, Sir James Horlick (of hot-drink fame). Their spectacularly colourful display of azaleas is best seen in early summer.

ARRIVAL AND ACTIVITIES
GIGHA

By ferry Regular CalMac ferries connect Gigha with Tayinloan (hourly; 20min).

Bike rental Next to the ferry slip, Gigha Boats Activity Centre (Easter–Sept daily 10am–6pm; ☎07876 506520,

ⓦ gighaboatsactivitycentre.co.uk) rents bikes (£10/half day, £15/day), kayaks (£10/hr), stand-up paddle-boards (£10/hr) and rowing boats (£20/hr).

ACCOMMODATION AND EATING

★ **The Boathouse** Ardminish, PA41 7AA ☎01583 505123, ⓦ boathouseongigha.co.uk. Gorgeous little restaurant in a converted boathouse perched above a white sandy bay rustling up treats like dressed crab salad (£16) or seared scallops with ginger, chilli and lime. They've also got a small but perfectly located campsite overlooking the

beach. April–Oct daily noon–10pm. £9

Gigha Hotel Ardminish Bay, PA41 7AA ☎01583 505254, ⓦ gighahotel.com. Just 200m from the ferry terminal, this is the island's social hub and a very welcoming place to stay; its twelve, largely pinewood-furnished rooms are inviting and spotless. £85

Campbeltown

CAMPBELTOWN's best feature is its setting, in a deep bay sheltered by Davaar Island and the surrounding hills. With a population of around five thousand, it's Kintyre's largest town and its shops are by far the best for supplies. Campbeltown's heyday was the Victorian era, when shipbuilding was going strong; coal was shipped by canal from Drumlemble, the fishing fleet was vast and the town had 34 whisky distilleries – today only three remain.

Springbank distillery

85 Longrow, but sign up at Cadenhead's whisky shop at 30–32 Union St, PA28 6HY • Tours (1hr) Mon–Fri 10am, 11.30am, 1.30pm & 3pm; Sat 10am & 2pm • £7 • ☎01586 551710, ⓦ springbankwhisky.com

A deeply traditional, family-owned business founded in 1828, **Springbank distillery** is the only distillery in Scotland to carry out the full production process on one site, from the malting to the bottling. Tours take you first to the malting floor, before continuing down to the peat stacks and kiln, the magnificent copper stills and the capacious warehouse. At the end, you return to **Cadenhead's** whisky shop on Union St to collect your free miniature.

ARRIVAL AND INFORMATION
CAMPBELTOWN

By plane Flights from Glasgow connect with Campbeltown (Mon–Fri 2 daily; 40min); the airport is 3 miles northwest of town towards Machrihanish.

By bus The main terminal is in front of the swimming pool on the Esplanade.

Destinations Glasgow (5 daily; 4hr 15min); Tarbert (5 daily; 1hr 10min).

By ferry The ferry terminal is on the south side of the harbour; it's a 5min walk into the centre.

Destinations Ardrossan (Thurs, Fri & Sun 1 daily; 2hr 40min).

Tourist office Old Quay (April–June & Sept Mon–Sat 10am–5pm, Sun noon–4pm; July & Aug Mon–Sat 9am–6pm, Sun 11am–5pm; Oct–March Mon–Fri 10am–4pm; ☎01586 556162).

ACCOMMODATION AND EATING

Ardshiel Hotel Kilkerran Rd, PA28 6JL ☎01586 552133, ⓦ ardshiel.co.uk. Well-run hotel in a former

whisky distiller's Victorian mansion on a lovely leafy square. The rooms are functional; more impressive is the hotel's

21

> ### HIKING UP GOAT FELL
>
> The desolate north half of Arran – effectively the Highland part – features bare granite peaks, the occasional golden eagle and miles of unspoilt scenery, within reach only to those prepared to do some serious hiking. Arran's most accessible peak is also the island's highest, **Goat Fell** (2866ft), which can be ascended in just three hours from Brodick, though it's a strenuous hike. You can also hike up Goat Fell from Corrie, Arran's prettiest little seaside village, six miles north of Brodick, where a procession of pristine cottages lines the road to Lochranza and wraps itself around an exquisite little harbour and pier.

glamorous, grown-up whisky bar, stocking more than seven hundred malts. Daily 11am–11pm. £85
Café Bluebell 6 Hall St, PA28 6BU ☏01586 552800. Simple, warm and welcoming café opposite the tourist office, offering a terrific selection of light snacks (soups, sandwiches, sausage rolls), as well as a gut-busting all-day breakfast (£7.95). Tues–Sat 9am–4.30pm, Sun 11am–4pm.

Arran

Shaped like a kidney bean and occupying centre stage in the Firth of Clyde, **ARRAN** is the most southerly (and therefore the most accessible) of all the Scottish islands. The Highland–Lowland dividing line passes through its centre; the northern half is sparsely populated, mountainous and bleak, while the lush southern half enjoys a much milder climate. The population, of around five thousand, tends to stick to the southeastern quarter of the island, leaving the west and the north relatively undisturbed.

ARRIVAL AND GETTING AROUND

By ferry CalMac ferries run from Ardrossan, 14 miles north of Ayr, to Brodick (6–8 daily; 55min), and from Claonaig, 8 miles south of Tarbert, to Lochranza (8–9 daily; 30min).

By bus Daily buses circle the island while the Arran Day Rider (£5.60) allows you to hop on and off as you please. Buses also link in with the two ferry services.

Brodick

The island's capital and main communication hub, **BRODICK** (from the Norse *breidr vik*, "broad bay") is the busiest town on Arran. Although the resort is a place of only moderate charm, it does at least have a grand setting in a wide, sandy bay set against a backdrop of granite mountains.

Brodick Castle

2.5 miles north of town, just off the A841, KA27 8HY • **Castle** Daily: April–Sept 11am–4pm; Oct 11am–3pm • £12.50; NTS • **Gardens** Daily 9.30am to sunset • £7; NTS • ☏ 0844 493 2152, ⊛ nts.org.uk/Visit/Brodick-Castle-and-Country-Park

Former seat of the duke of Hamilton, **Brodick Castle** is set on a steep bank on the north side of Brodick Bay. The interior is comfortable if undistinguished, but the **walled garden** and extensive **country park** contain a treasury of exotic plants and trees and command a superb view across the bay. Hidden in the grounds is a bizarre Bavarian-style summerhouse lined entirely with pine cones, one of three built by the eleventh duke to make his wife, Princess Marie of Baden, feel at home.

ARRIVAL AND INFORMATION

By ferry The ferry terminal is a 5min walk south of the resort.

By bus Island buses connect Brodick with Blackwaterfoot (Mon–Sat 8–10 daily, Sun 4; 30min); Lamlash (Mon–Sat hourly, Sun 4; 10–15min) and Lochranza (Mon–Sat 7 daily, Sun 4; 45min).

Tourist office By the CalMac pier (April–Sept Mon–Sat 9am–5pm, Sun 10am–5pm; Oct–March Mon–Sat 10am–4pm; ☏01770 303774, ⊛ visitarran.com).

ACCOMMODATION AND EATING

Fiddlers' Shore Rd, KA27 8AJ ☎01770 302579, ⓦfiddlersmusicbar.com. The fabulous music bar, with performances on Tues, Fri and Sat at 8pm, is actually more restaurant than drinking den, offering succulent dishes like chargrilled swordfish steak or Texan spiced black and blue burger (£12.95). Diners are given preference (and keep their table for the evening), but if you just fancy a pint, pop along after 9pm. Daily 11am–midnight; kitchen noon–2pm & 7–9pm.

Glenartney Guest House Mayish Rd, KA27 8BX ☎01770 302220, ⓦglenartney-arran.co.uk. Tucked away just uphill from the post office, this is the pick of the town's guesthouses, with a dozen or so immaculately presented, albeit not overly spacious, rooms, plus two homely lounges and an evening bar. **£90**

Glen Rosa Campsite 2 miles from the town centre, off the B880 to Blackwaterfoot, KA27 8DF ☎01770 302380, ⓦarrancamping.co.uk. Very basic, almost wild, campsite (no showers; cold water only) enjoying a wonderful setting beside a burn, with superb views across the glen. Campfires allowed. Per person **£4**

Lamlash

The southern half of Arran is less spectacular and less forbidding than the north; it's more heavily forested, the land is more fertile and the vast majority of the population lives here. With its distinctive Edwardian architecture and mild climate, **LAMLASH** epitomizes the sedate charm of southeast Arran.

Holy Island

The Holy Island boat (May–Sept daily, more or less hourly; 15min) is subject to cancellations in windy weather · £12 return · ☎01770 700463, ⓦholyisland.org

From Lamlash you can take a boat out to the slug-shaped hump of **Holy Island**, which shelters the bay, and where a group of Tibetan Buddhists have established a retreat. Providing you don't dawdle, it's possible to scramble up to the top of **Mullach Mòr** (1030ft), the island's highest point, and still catch the last ferry back.

ARRIVAL AND DEPARTURE   LAMLASH AND AROUND

By bus Lamlash is served by buses from Brodick (Mon–Sat hourly, Sun 4; 10–15min).

ACCOMMODATION AND EATING

Drift Inn Shore Rd, KA27 8JN ☎01770 600608, ⓦdriftinnarran.com. Despite its undistinguished exterior, the well-regarded food at this seafront pub – including mussels in chilli sauce, and Arran venison haunch with a herb and hazelnut risotto (£15.50) – and its convivial beer garden, make the *Drift Inn* a fun place to hang out. Daily noon–11pm; kitchen noon–9pm.

Glenisle Hotel & Restaurant Lamlash, KA27 8LY ☎01770 600559, ⓦglenislehotel.com. High-end, and expensive, option, with thirteen gorgeous rooms painted and furnished in colours that reflect those of the island itself; around half have a sea view. **£145**

Lochranza

The ruined castle that occupies the mud flats of the surrounding bay, and the brooding north-facing slopes of the mountains which frame it, provide **LOCHRANZA** with one of the most spectacular settings on the island. Despite being the only place of any size in this sparsely populated area, Lochranza attracts far fewer visitors than other Arran resorts. The **castle** is worth a brief look inside, but Lochranza's main tourist attraction is the **distillery** (mid-March to Oct daily 10am–5.30pm; Nov–Feb daily 10am–4pm; £8; ☎01770 830264, ⓦarranwhisky.com), distinguished by its pagoda-style roofs.

ARRIVAL AND DEPARTURE   LOCHRANZA

By ferry CalMac ferries arrive and depart from the pier, a 10min walk north of Lochranza distillery. A small ferry runs from Claonaig, 8 miles south of Tarbert, to Lochranza (8–9 daily; 30min).

21

Lochranza Camping By the golf course, KA27 8HL 01770 830273, w arran-campsite.com. Relaxed and scenically placed campsite which has three two-man pods with heating and lighting. Facilities include modern shower blocks, laundry and a camper's lounge. Reception is basically the hut that doubles up as the golf clubhouse. Closed Nov–Feb. Camping/pitch **£18**, pods **£60**

Stags Pavilion By the golf course, KA27 8HL 01770 830600, w stagspavilion.com. Accomplished restaurant in an attractive pavilion at the entrance to the campsite, with sumptuous dishes such as slow-roasted honey and rosemary Arran lamb (£12.75). It's not licensed, but you can bring your own bottle (no corkage fee) Reservations advised. Mon, Tues & Thurs 5.30–10pm, Fri–Sun 11am–2.30pm & 5.30–10pm.

Islay

The fertile, largely treeless island of **ISLAY** (w islayinfo.com) is famous for one thing – single malt **whisky**. The smoky, peaty, pungent quality of Islay whisky is unique, recognizable even to the untutored palate, and most of the distilleries offer fascinating guided tours (see page 887). In medieval times, Islay was the political centre of the Hebrides, with **Loch Finlaggan**, near **Port Askaig**, the seat of the MacDonalds, lords of the Isles. The picturesque, whitewashed villages you see on the island today, however, date from the planned settlements founded by the Campbells in the late eighteenth and early nineteenth centuries. Apart from whisky and solitude, the other great draw is the **birdlife** – not least the scores of white-fronted and barnacle geese who winter here in their thousands.

By plane Islay's airport, 6 miles north of Port Ellen in Glenegedale, has flights from Glasgow (Mon–Fri 2 daily, Sat 1 daily; 40min).

By ferry CalMac ferries from Kennacraig, 12 miles south of Tarbert on Kintyre, go either to Port Ellen or Port Askaig (3–4 daily; 2hr 5min). There's also a ferry that makes the short trip across to Jura.

Port Ellen and around

Laid out as a planned village in 1821 by Walter Frederick Campbell, and named after his wife, **PORT ELLEN** is the chief port on Islay, with the island's largest fishing fleet and main CalMac ferry terminal. The neat whitewashed terraces that overlook the bay of golden sand are pretty enough, but the view is dominated by the modern maltings, whose powerful odours waft across the town.

The only reason to pause in this part of the island is to head off east along a dead-end road that passes three **distilleries** in as many miles (see page 887). Another six miles down the track and you eventually come to the simple thirteenth-century **Kildalton Chapel**, which has an eighth-century Celtic ringed cross made from the local "bluestone". The exceptional quality of the scenes matches any to be found on the crosses carved by the monks in Iona.

By ferry CalMac ferries arrive on the west side of the bay from Kennacraig (3–4 daily; 2hr 20min).

By bus Buses connect Port Ellen with Bowmore (Mon–Sat 8 daily; 25min) and Port Askaig (Mon–Sat 3 daily; 50min). The bus stop is on Charlotte St in the centre of the village.

ACCOMMODATION

★ **Kintra Farm campsite** 3 miles northwest of Port Ellen, PA42 7AT 01496 302051, w kintrafarm.co.uk. Enjoying a stunning situation at the southern tip of sandy Laggan Bay among the grassy dunes, this is not far off wild camping at its best. Facilities are basic, but there are showers and running water as well as laundry. Once settled in, you're unlikely to bother exploring anywhere else. Closed Oct–April. **£16**

ISLAY WHISKY

It goes without saying that Islay's **whisky distilleries** are a major tourist attraction. Nowadays, every distillery offers **guided tours**, which usually last an hour and traditionally end with a generous dram. Most also offer more comprehensive tours with more tastings, and some even do warehouse tours: here are some of our favourites. Phone ahead to make sure there's a tour running, as times do change.

Ardbeg Port Ellen, PA42 7EA ☎01496 302244, ⓦardbeg.com. Ardbeg is traditionally considered the saltiest, peatiest malt on Islay (and that's saying something). It's a relatively small distillery by Islay's standards, yet it has bags of character and the tour is one of the best. The *Old Kiln Café* is excellent (daily 10am–4.30pm). Tours £6. Daily 11am & 3pm.

Bowmore Bowmore, PA43 7JS ☎01496 810441, ⓦbowmore.com. Bowmore is the most touristy of the Islay distilleries, and by far the most central; it is also one of the few still doing its own malting and kilning. Tours £7. April–Sept Mon–Sat 9.30, 10.30am, 1.30pm & 2.30pm, Sun 12.30pm & 2pm; Oct–March Mon–Fri 10.30am & 3pm, Sat 9.30am.

Bruichladdich Port Charlotte, PA49 7UN ☎01496 850190, ⓦbruichladdich.com. Progressive and innovative, this is one distinctly cool distillery; moreover, they also produce the island's only gin, the scrumptious Botanist. Tours £6. April–Sept Mon–Fri 10am, 11.30am, 1pm, 2pm & 4pm, Sat 10am, 11am, 1pm & 2pm, Sun 1pm & 2pm; Oct Mon–Sat 10am, 11am,

1pm & 3pm, Sun 1pm & 2pm; Nov–March Mon–Fri 10am, 11am & 2pm, Sat 10am & 2pm.

Kilchoman Rockside Farm, PA49 7UT ☎01496 850011, ⓦkilchomandistillery.com. Kilchoman is a very welcoming, tiny, farm-based enterprise that grows its own barley, as well as distilling, maturing and bottling its whisky on site. Tours £7. April–Oct daily 9.45am, 11am, 2pm & 3pm; Nov–March Mon–Fri 9.45am, 11am, 2pm & 3pm.

Lagavulin Port Ellen, PA42 7DZ ☎01496 302749, ⓦmalts.com. Lagavulin is the classic, all-round Islay malt, with lots of smoke and peat. The distillery enjoys a fabulous setting. Tours £6. April–Sept daily 9.30am, 11.30am & 3.30pm; March & Oct Mon–Fri 9.30am & 12.30pm, Sat & Sun 12.30pm.

Laphroaig Port Ellen, PA42 7DU ☎01496 302418, ⓦlaphroaig.com. Another classic smoky, peaty Islay malt, and another great setting – you also get to see the malting and see and smell the peat kilns. It also has a great little museum. Tours £6. March–Oct Mon–Fri 10.30am, 2pm & 3.15pm; Nov–Feb Mon–Fri 10am & 2pm.

Lach Mhara The Oa, PA42 7AZ ☎01496 302666, ⓦlach-mhara.co.uk. Enviably sited near the Carraig Fhada lighthouse, the "Sea Duck" bed and breakfast offers as restful a stay as you could imagine; two comely, sea-facing rooms with glass doors that open up onto a patio, and underfloor heated bathrooms (not en suite). Breakfast is taken upstairs in the open-plan living area, which offers tremendous views across to Port Ellen. **£90**

Bowmore

BOWMORE, Islay's administrative capital, lies on the north side of the monotonous peat bog of Duich Moss, on the southern shores of the tidal Loch Indaal. It's a striking place, laid out in 1768 on a grid plan rather like Inveraray, with the whitewashed terraces of Main Street climbing up the hill in a straight line from the pier on Loch Indaal to the town's crowning landmark, the **Round Church**. Built in the round so that the devil would have no corners in which to hide, it has a plain, wood-panelled interior, with a lovely tiered balcony and a big central mushroom pillar.

ARRIVAL AND INFORMATION   BOWMORE

By bus Buses stop on the main square – The Square. Destinations Port Askaig (Mon–Sat 5–6 daily; 25min); Port Charlotte (Mon–Sat 6 daily; 25min); Port Ellen (Mon–Sat 9 daily; 25min).

Tourist office The Square (April–Sept Mon–Sat 9.30am–5.30pm, Sun noon–3pm; Oct–March Mon–Fri 10am–3pm; ☎01496 305165).

ACCOMMODATION AND EATING

Harbour Inn Main St, PA43 7RJ ☎01496 810330, ⓦbowmore.com/harbour-inn. Smart harbourside restaurant with lovely views, serving sumptuous plates of food such as squid ink risotto with pickled crab meat

21

GEESE ON ISLAY

If you're visiting Islay between mid-September and the third week of April, it's impossible to miss the staggeringly large wintering population of **Greenland barnacle and White-fronted geese**. During this period, the geese dominate the landscape, feeding incessantly off the rich pasture, strolling by the shores, and flying in formation across the winter skies. You can see the geese just about anywhere on the island – there are an estimated five thousand white-fronted and forty thousand barnacles here – though in the evening, they tend to congregate in the tidal mud flats and fields around **Loch Gruinart**.

(£19.50). You can also warm yourself by the peat fire in the adjoining pub, where they offer lunchtime bar snacks. They also have seven elegant rooms. Daily; restaurant noon–2pm & 6–10pm; pub noon–11pm. **£135**

Lambeth Guesthouse Jamieson St, PA43 7HL ☎ 01496 810597, ✉ lambethguesthouse@tiscali.co.uk. Just off Main St, this is a jovially run guesthouse with six, modestly sized but impeccably prepared en-suite rooms. **£96**

Port Charlotte

PORT CHARLOTTE, with its immaculate whitewashed cottages clustered around a sandy cove overlooking Loch Indaal, is Islay's prettiest village. On the northern fringe of the village, in a whitewashed former chapel, the imaginative **Museum of Islay Life** (April–Oct Mon–Fri 10.30am–4.30pm; £3.50; ☎ 01496 850358, ⊕ islaymuseum.org) is crammed to bursting with local memorabilia, including tantalizing snippets about eighteenth-century illegal whisky distillers. The **Islay Natural History Trust** (May–Sept Mon–Fri 10.30am–4.30pm; £3.50; ☎ 01496 850288, ⊕ islaynaturalhistory.org), housed in the former distillery warehouse, is also worth a visit for anyone interested in the island's fauna and flora.

ARRIVAL AND DEPARTURE
PORT CHARLOTTE

By bus Buses run from Bowmore to Port Charlotte (Mon–Sat 6 daily; 25min), stopping outside the *Port Charlotte Hotel*.

ACCOMMODATION AND EATING

Port Charlotte Hotel Main St, PA48 7TU ☎ 01496 850360, ⊕ portcharlottehotel.co.uk. Beautifully appointed whitewashed stone hotel. The ten rooms have their original exposed stone walls – they're all thoughtfully designed and decorated in bold, beautiful colours. **£230**

Port Mòr Campsite Just outside the village on the road to Portnahaven, PA48 7UE ☎ 01496 850441, ⊕ islandofislay.co.uk. Community-run campsite with glorious sea views and tip-top modern facilities, including hot showers and a café. Closed Dec–Feb. **£19**

SYHA Port Charlotte hostel Main St, PA48 7TX ☎ 01496 850385, ⊕ syha.org.uk/where-to-stay/islands/port-charlotte.aspx. Capacious modern hostel in an old bonded warehouse next to the Islay Natural History Trust centre with a mix of differently sized dorms as well as doubles. Dorms **£18.50**, doubles **£45**

Yan's Kitchen Main St, PA43 7UD ☎ 01496 850230, ⊕ yanskitchen.co.uk. Opposite the museum in a former croft kitchen, this convivial place offers a clever mix of seafood, grilled meats and tapas (garlic chicken in scallops, chorizo *con patatas*), the latter coming in at round £3.50 a pop. Daily 10am–3pm & 5–10pm.

Loch Finlaggan

Just beyond Ballygrant, on the road from Bowmore to Port Askaig, a narrow road leads north to **Loch Finlaggan**, site of a number of prehistoric crannogs (artificial islands) and, for four hundred years from the twelfth century, headquarters of the Lords of the Isles, semi-autonomous rulers over the Hebrides and Kintyre. Duckboards allow you to walk out across the reed beds of the loch and explore the main crannog, **Eilean Mòr**, where several carved gravestones are displayed under cover in the chapel. These seem to support the theory that the Lords of the Isles buried their wives and children there, while having themselves interred on Iona.

GEORGE ORWELL ON JURA

In April 1946, Eric Blair (better known by his pen name of **George Orwell**), suffering badly from TB and intending to give himself "six months' quiet" in which to write his new novel *The Last Man in Europe* (later to become *1984*), moved to a remote farmhouse on the northern tip of Jura. He lived out a spartan existence in Barnhill for two years, but due to ill health was forced to return to England shortly before his death. The house, 23 miles north of Craighouse, up an increasingly poor road, is as remote today as it was in Orwell's day, and is now let out as a **self-catering cottage** (☏ 01786 850274).

Jura

The long, whale-shaped island of **JURA** is one of the wildest and most mountainous of the Inner Hebrides, its entire west coast uninhabited and inaccessible except to dedicated walkers. Jura's distinctive **Paps** – so called because of their smooth breast-like shape, though there are in fact three of them – seem to dominate every view off the west coast of Argyll, their glacial rounded tops covered in a light dusting of quartzite scree. The island's name is commonly thought to derive from the Norse *dyr-oe* (deer island) and, appropriately enough, the current deer population of around five thousand far outnumbers the 190 or so humans. With just one road, which sticks to the more sheltered eastern coast, one hotel and a smattering of B&Bs, Jura is an ideal place to go for peace, quiet and great walking.

Anything that happens here happens in the only real village, **CRAIGHOUSE**, eight miles up the road from Feolin Ferry. The village enjoys a sheltered setting, overlooking Knapdale on the mainland – so sheltered, in fact, that there are even a few palm trees thriving on the seafront. There's a shop/post office, hotel and a tearoom, plus the tiny **Isle of Jura distillery**, which offers guided tours (☏ 01496 820385, ⟐ jurawhisky.com; £6).

ARRIVAL AND DEPARTURE   JURA

By ferry The main car ferry departs from Port Askaig on Islay to Feolin (Mon–Sat every 45min–1hr, Sun 7; 10min), 8 miles west of Craighouse. Between April and Sept there's also a passenger ferry from Tayvallich, on the Argyll mainland, to Craighouse (Mon & Wed–Sat 2 daily, Sun 1; 1hr; ☏ 07768 450000, ⟐ jurapassengerferry.com).

ACCOMMODATION AND EATING

Jura Hotel Craighouse, PA60 7XU ☏ 01496 820243, ⟐ jurahotel.co.uk. Not much to look at from the outside, but warm and friendly within, with good rooms. Campers are welcome to pitch tents in the field fronting the hotel; there's a shower block and laundry facilities at the back. Unsurprisingly, it's also the centre of the island's social scene, with a restaurant, lounge-bar and pub. Daily: restaurant noon–2.30pm & 6–9pm; pub 11am–11pm. Camping/pitch **£5**, doubles **£100**

Northeast Scotland

DUNNOTTAR CASTLE

Northeast Scotland

22

A large triangle of land thrusting into the North Sea, northeast Scotland comprises the area east of a line drawn roughly from Perth north to the fringe of the Moray Firth at Forres. The area takes in the county of Angus, the city of Dundee and, beyond the Grampian Mountains, the counties of Aberdeenshire and Moray and the city of Aberdeen. Geographically diverse, the landscape in the south of the region is comprised predominantly of undulating farmland, but as you travel further north of the Firth of Tay this gives way to wooded glens, mountains and increasingly harsh land fringed by a dramatic coast of cliffs and long, sandy beaches.

The long-depressed city of **Dundee** is shedding its postindustrial image with a reinvigorated cultural scene and an impressive £1 billion waterfront development centred around the show-stopping **V&A Museum of Design**, a Titanic swoosh of curved concrete and stone on the harbour. A little way up the Angus coast lie the historically important towns of **Arbroath** and **Montrose**, which are linked by an especially inviting stretch of coastline, with scarlet cliffs and sweeping bays. Further south towards Dundee, these are replaced by gentler dunes and long, sandy beaches, while inland the long fingers of the **Angus Glens** – heather-covered hills tumbling down to rushing rivers – are overlooked by the southern peaks of the Grampian Mountains. **Glen Shee** is one of the most popular, while handsome market towns such as **Blairgowrie** are good bases. Extravagant **Glamis Castle** is also well worth a visit.

The northeast was the southern kingdom of the **Picts**, reminders of whom are scattered throughout the region in the form of beautifully carved stones found in fields churchyards and museums, such as the one at **Meigle**. The area never grew particularly prosperous, and a handful of feuding and intermarrying families grew to wield disproportionate influence, building many of the region's **castles** and developing and planning its towns.

Many of the most appealing settlements are along the coast, but while the fishing industry is but a fondly held memory in many parts, a number of the northeast's ports were transformed by the discovery of **oil** in the North Sea in the 1960s – particularly **Aberdeen**, Scotland's third-largest city.

North of the glens and west of Aberdeen is **Deeside**, a fertile, ruggedly attractive area made famous by the Royal Family: **Balmoral** has been a royal residence since Victoria's time. Beyond are the eastern sections of the **Cairngorms National Park** and travelling north into Moray brings you to Scotland's most productive whisky-making area, **Speyside**. For connoisseurs, a pilgrimage here is unmissable.

GETTING AROUND

By train Trains from Edinburgh and Glasgow connect with Dundee, Aberdeen and other coastal towns, while an inland line from Aberdeen heads northwest to Elgin and on to Inverness.

By bus The region has a reasonably comprehensive scheduled bus service; only in the most remote and mountainous parts does public transport disappear altogether.

By car Northeast Scotland is well served by an extensive road network, with fast links between Dundee and Aberdeen.

Skiing at Glen Shee p.903
Aberdeenshire's castle trail p.904

The malt whisky trail p.912
The Findhorn Foundation p.913

ARBROATH SMOKIES

Highlights

❶ Dundee's design scene The unparalleled McManus Art Galleries and Museum, the place to come for ceramics, fine art and photography, is now joined by the buzz-worthy V&A Museum of Design. See page 897

❷ Arbroath smokies A true Scottish delicacy: succulent haddock best eaten when still warm from the oak smoker. See page 900

❸ Pictish stones Fascinating carved relics of a lost culture, standing alone in fields, or protected from the elements in museums – Meigle's is particularly good. See page 903

❹ Dunnottar Castle The moodiest clifftop ruin in Europe, built in the ninth century and surrounded by crashing seas. See page 907

❺ Speyside's whiskies See the distilleries and landscapes of places such as Glenfiddich, Glenlivet and Glen Grant by bike, foot or bus – visits give you ample opportunities to taste the amber bead. See page 912

❻ Museum of Scottish Lighthouses, Fraserburgh Lights, lenses and legends at one of the quirkiest and most intriguing small museums in the country. See page 912

HIGHLIGHTS ARE MARKED ON THE MAP ON PAGE 894

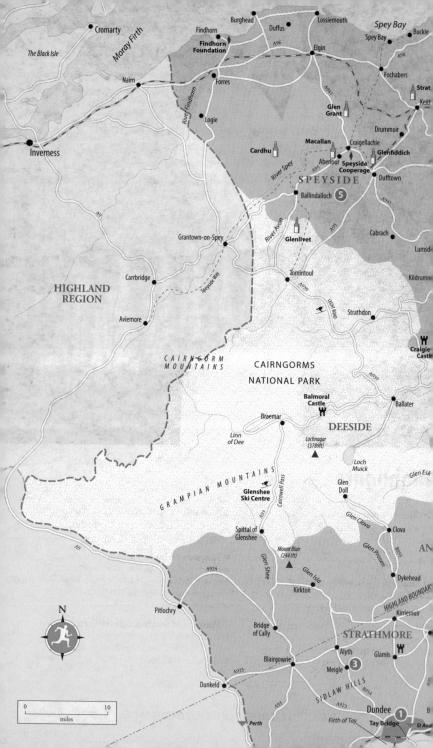

Portsoy • Macduff • Gardenstown • Crovie • Pennan • **6** Fraserburgh
Banff • **Duff House** B9031
A97
Turrif A947 A98 A950 Mintlaw A90 Peterhead
Fyvie A952 **Slains Castle**
A96 Cruden Bay
Insch Pitmedden Collieston
Bennachie (1733ft) ▲ Inverurie Newburgh A92
River Don
Aberdeen Airport ✈
A96
A944 **Aberdeen**
A93
A980 **Drum Castle**
Crathes Castle
River Dee Banchory
Stonehaven
4 **Dunnottar Castle**
B9074 Catterline
Fasque B967 Kinneff
Fettercairn Arbuthnott Inverbervie
Fettercairn
Edzell A92
HOWE OF THE MEARNS St Cyrus
House of Dun 🏛 R. North Esk
A935
Aberlemno Brechin
Montrose Basin Wildlife Centre 🦆 Montrose
B9113 Lunan Bay
St Vigeans Auchmithie
2 Arbroath

Carnoustie
fieth

NORTH
SEA

↗ Orkney & Shetland

HIGHLIGHTS
1 Dundee's design scene
2 Arbroath smokies
3 Pictish stones
4 Dunnottar Castle
5 Speyside's whiskies
6 Museum of Scottish Lighthouses, Fraserburgh

NORTHEAST SCOTLAND

Dundee

The decline of manufacturing wasn't kind to **DUNDEE** but, rising like a phoenix, the city is having a moment. Historically, its heyday was in the 1800s, when its train and harbour links made it a major centre for shipbuilding, whaling and the manufacture of **jute**, the world's most important vegetable fibre after cotton. However, this, along with jam and **journalism** – the three Js that famously defined the city – has all but disappeared. Only local publishing giant D.C. Thomson, which makes the *Beano* comic, among other publications, still plays a meaningful role in the city.

Nowadays, any talk of print is more likely to focus on design, especially as Dundee was named the first **UNESCO City of Design** in the UK in 2014 for its diverse contributions to fields including medical research, comics and video games. And with the arrival of the **V&A Museum of Design**, the city seems set to grow and grow as a destination to be reckoned with.

City centre

Dundee's city centre, dominated by large shopping malls, is focused on the pedestrianized **City Square**, a couple of hundred yards north of the Tay. Where Reform Street meets City Square, look out for a couple of statues to Dundee heroes: **Desperate Dan** and **Minnie the Minx**, from the *Dandy* and *Beano* comics.

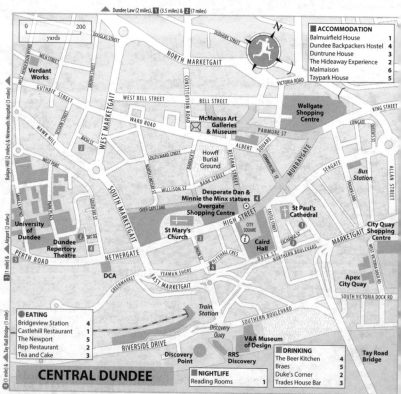

CENTRAL DUNDEE

■ ACCOMMODATION
Balmuirfield House	1
Dundee Backpackers Hostel	4
Duntrune House	3
The Hideaway Experience	2
Malmaison	6
Taypark House	5

● EATING
Bridgeview Station	4
Castlehill Restaurant	1
The Newport	5
Rep Restaurant	2
Tea and Cake	3

■ NIGHTLIFE
Reading Rooms	1

■ DRINKING
The Beer Kitchen	4
Braes	5
Duke's Corner	2
Trades House Bar	3

McManus Art Galleries and Museum

Albert Square, DD1 1DA • Mon–Sat 10am–5pm, Sun 12.30–4.30pm • Free • ☎ 01382 307200, ⓦ mcmanus.co.uk

The **McManus Art Galleries and Museum**, Dundee's most impressive Victorian structure, makes for an unbeatable afternoon for art lovers. The ground-floor rooms explore the nature of museums, the surrounding landscape and the making of modern Dundee, while upstairs an impressive collection by masters including Rossetti and Henry Raeburn cover the curved red walls of the splendid Victoria gallery. The rest of this floor is equally engrossing, holding an eclectic ethnographic collection, work by the Scottish Colourists, historic and modern ceramics, and a number of fine art acquisitions including contemporary photography.

22

Verdant Works

West Henderson Wynd, Blackness, DD1 5BT • April–Oct Mon–Sat 10am–6pm, Sun 11am–6pm; Nov–March Wed–Sat 10.30am–4.30pm, Sun 11am–4.30pm • £9.25, joint ticket with Discovery Point (see below) £16 • ☎ 01382 309060, ⓦ verdantworks.com

The award-winning **Verdant Works** tells the story of jute from its harvesting in India to its arrival in Dundee on clipper ships. The museum, set in a beautifully refurbished old jute mill, makes a lively attempt to re-create the turn-of-the-century factory floor, the highlight being the chance to watch jute being processed on fully operational quarter-size machines.

The Cultural Quarter

Immediately west of the city centre, High Street becomes Nethergate and passes into Dundee's **Cultural Quarter**. As well as the university and the highly respected **Rep Theatre**, the area is home to some of the city's most charming pubs and cafés.

DCA

152 Nethergate, DD1 4DY • Complex daily 10am–midnight; galleries Mon–Wed & Fri–Sun 10am–6pm, Thurs 10am–8pm; print studio Tues–Thurs 11am–9pm, Fri & Sat 11am–6pm • Free • ☎ 01382 909900, ⓦ dca.org.uk

The **DCA**, or Dundee Contemporary Arts, is a stunningly designed five-storey complex incorporating galleries, a print studio, a cool design shop and an airy café-bar. It's worth visiting for the stimulating temporary and touring exhibitions of contemporary art, as well as its eclectic programme of art-house films and cult classics.

Discovery Point

Discovery Quay, DD1 4XA • April–Oct Mon–Sat 10am–6pm, Sun 11am–6pm; Nov–March Mon–Sat 10am–5pm, Sun 11am–5pm • £9.25, joint ticket with Verdant Works (see above) £16 • ☎ 01382 309060, ⓦ rrsdiscovery.com

The waterfront area is currently undergoing a massive thirty-year £1 billion transformation. Here you'll find the domed **Discovery Point**, an impressive development focused on the Royal Research Ship Discovery. Something of an icon for Dundee's renaissance, *Discovery* is a three-mast steam-assisted vessel built here in 1901 to take Captain Robert Falcon Scott on his polar expeditions. A combination of brute strength and elegance, she has been beautifully restored, with polished wood panels and brass trimmings giving scant indication of the privations suffered by the crew. In the Antarctic, temperatures on board would plummet to -28°C and turns at having a bath came round every 47 days. Before you step aboard, there are a series of interactive displays about the construction of the ship and Scott's journeys, including the chill-inducing "Polarama", about life in Antarctica.

V&A Museum of Design

Discovery Quay, DD1 4QB • Check website for opening times • Free • ☎ 01382 305665, ⓦ vandadundee.org

Just east of *Discovery*, and shaped like a futuristic ocean liner, the **V&A Museum of Design** is the first museum of its kind in Scotland and the only other V&A anywhere in the world outside London. A homage to the untold story of a nation of designers and a catalyst for the next generation, the galleries showcase hundreds of historically significant objects, including inventions such as Charles Macintosh's waterproof fabric and the pioneering work of Patrick Geddes in improving urban living. The centrepiece of the **Scottish Design Galleries** is an evocative reconstruction of Charles Rennie Mackintosh's **Oak Room,** unseen for fifty years and one of the world-famous architect's most important interiors. It's spectacularly ambitious on all counts; the building itself, a masterwork of design by renowned Japanese architect Kengo Kuma, is his first in Britain and has been labelled "Dundee's new living room".

ARRIVAL AND INFORMATION   DUNDEE

By plane Dundee Airport (ⓦhial.co.uk/dundee-airport), west of the city centre, is served by flights from London Stansted (Mon–Fri 2 daily, Sun 1; 1hr 30min). There are no buses to the centre; the 5min taxi ride will cost around £8.

By train Trains stop south of the city centre near Riverside Drive.

Destinations Aberdeen (every 20–30min; 1hr 15min); Arbroath (every 30min; 20min); Edinburgh (every 30min–1hr; 1hr 30min); Glasgow (every 30min–1hr; 1hr 30min); Montrose (every 30min–1hr; 30min).

By bus Most long-distance buses are operated by Stagecoach Strathtay (ⓣ01382 313700) and arrive at the station on Seagate, a couple of hundred yards east of the centre. Local buses leave from High St or nearby Union St (ⓣ01382 201121). Destinations Aberdeen (hourly; 2hr 20min); Arbroath (every 30min; 30–50min); Blairgowrie (hourly; 1hr); Glamis (2–5 daily; 35min); Kirriemuir (hourly; 55min); Meigle (hourly; 40min); Montrose (hourly; 1hr).

Tourist office 16 City Square (Mon–Sat 9.30am–5pm; ⓣ01382 527527, ⓦangusanddundee.co.uk).

ACCOMMODATION

Balmuirfield House 3 miles north of centre, Harestane Rd, DD3 0NU ⓣ01382 819655, ⓦbalmuirfieldhouse. com; map p.896. This rip-roaring B&B has bags of personality. Rooms are designed with subtle themes – one has a French colonial style, another is a homage to Charles Rennie Mackintosh – and with Dundee marmalade and Arbroath Smokies on the breakfast menu it far outweighs any downtown place. **£95**

Dundee Backpackers Hostel 71 High St, DD1 1SD ⓣ01382 224646, ⓦhoppo.com; map p.896. Dundee's premier hostel, with dorm beds spread around a warren-like former merchant's house that dates back to 1560. Private rooms are also available and there's 24hr access – ideal, because the city's best bars are moments away. Dorms **£18.50**, doubles **£40**

Duntrune House 5 miles northeast of the city centre, Duntrune, DD4 0PJ ⓣ01382 350239, ⓦduntrunehouse. co.uk; map p.896. Few B&Bs can claim country house status, but this squeaky-clean grand manse can, with three double rooms in the building's main wing. The rooms have beds fit for a king (they're king-size, at least), there are rambling gardens and it claims its very own ghost. **£100**

★ **The Hideaway Experience** 7 miles north of Dundee, Auchterhouse, DD3 0RA ⓣ01382 320 707,

ⓦthehideawayexperience.co.uk; map p.896. For something completely different, this collection of stargazing cottages and honeymooners' cabins hidden in the barley fields north of the city offers up country living for the Airbnb generation. Each hideaway comes with private hot tub, sauna and garden, and the creative team can stock the kitchen with local goodies in advance. Complimentary pickup from Dunde. **£270**

Malmaison 44 Whitehall Crescent, DD1 4AY ⓣ01382 339715, ⓦmalmaison.com; map p.896. Don't let the fact that it's part of a UK-wide chain put you off. This boutique bolthole promises luxury "dun' differently" and it's true to its word. Aside from the swoon-worthy Victorian facade and wrought-iron staircase, rooms and suites are the swishiest in town, with soft furnishings, bubble lamps and rolltop baths. **£85**

Taypark House 1 mile west of the centre, 484 Perth Rd, DD2 1LR ⓣ01382 643777, ⓦtayparkhouse.co.uk; map p.896. Taking pride of place in Dundee's affluent West End is this 150-year-old baronial mansion. It's a respite from the city centre, with beautiful grounds and views of the nearby botanical gardens. There are a variety of deluxe rooms and suites (the stand-out is the Turret Suite; £160) and it's home to a chi-chi gin bar. **£90**

EATING

The **west end** of Dundee, around the main university campus and Perth Road, is the best area for eating and drinking. The suburb of **Broughty Ferry** (a 20min bus ride away) and **Newport-on-Tay** are pleasant alternatives, with a good selection of pubs and waterfront restaurants that get particularly busy on summer evenings.

Bridgeview Station Riverside Drive, DD1 4DB ⓣ01382 660066, ⓦbridgeviewstation.com; map p.896. Housed within a historic railway station, this gastronomic all-rounder benefits from great views across the Tay estuary and a menu that plays to local strengths. Breakfast includes organic porridge and home-made breads (£2.50–6.95), while dinner sees dishes such as Angus grouse and cured Perthshire venison (three-course dinner menu £23). Mon, Tues & Sun 8am–6pm, Wed–Sat 8am–late.

Castlehill Restaurant 22–26 Exchange St, DD1 3DL ☎01382 220008, ⓦcastlehillrestaurant.co.uk; map p.896. Stalwart of the city's fine-dining scene, with a focus on local produce with dishes such as Crieff hare, Atlantic cod and Angus beef from just down the road. Chef Graham Campbell was the youngest in Scotland to receive a Michelin star, aged 25. Dinner tasting menu £55. Wed–Fri 5.30–10pm, Sat 12–2.30pm & 5.30–10pm.

★ The Newport Across the Tay Rd Bridge, 1 High St, Newport-on-Tay, DD6 8AB ☎01382 541449, ⓦthe newportrestaurant.co.uk; map p.896. The current talk-of-the-Tay, this gourmet treat is the brainchild of chef Jamie Scott, a recent winner of BBC TV cookery show, *Masterchef: The Professionals*. Expect creative kitchen flair, belly-hugging takes on asparagus, mutton loin and hake, and a smile on your face when you leave. Tasting menu £45. Tues 6–9.30pm, Wed–Sat 12–2.30pm & 6–9.30pm, Sun 10am–3.30pm.

Rep Restaurant Tay Square, Dundee Rep Theatre, DD1 1PB ☎01382 206699, ⓦdundeereprestaurant.co.uk; map p.896. Location, location, location. Slap bang in the heart of the action, this super-friendly bistro keeps the critics happy with a great pre-theatre menu (two courses £16.25) and hearty dishes like Dundee Law haddock, veg risottos and steaks (mains from £12.25). The latest addition is *Upstairs at The Rep*, a deli stocked with soups, salads, quiches and frittatas. Mon & Tues 12–2.30pm, Wed–Sat 12–2.30pm & 5pm–late.

Tea and Cake 27 Exchange St, DD1 3DJ ☎01382 203950, ⓦteaandcakedundee.co.uk; map p.896. Cute and popular little café under new ownership in the city centre, doing a brisk trade with great coffee, tasty vegan bakes, gluten-free cakes, flatbreads and sandwiches (from £4.70). At the very least, pop in for a slice of delicious coconut bread (£2.25). Tues–Fri 10am–5pm, Sat 10am–4pm.

DRINKING

The Beer Kitchen 10 South Tay St, DD1 1PA ☎01382 202070, ⓦinnisandgunn.com/bars; map p.896. Outpost of Edinburgh brewer Innis & Gunn's ever-expanding craft beer empire. Popular with a mix of locals and visitors, this place is a cut above the rest because of its 500-litre tank of unpasteurized beer and hop-mad menu, with dishes such as IPA-battered haddock and beer beef curry. Mon–Thurs & Sun 10am–midnight, Fri & Sat 10am–1am; kitchen daily 10am–10pm.

Braes 14–18 Perth Rd, DD1 4LN ☎01382 226344, ⓦsocialsquirrel.com/braesdundee; map p.896. Quirky and colourful cask beer and cocktail bar with a side serving of American-style burgers, ribs, southern fried chicken and nachos. It's first and foremost a pub, so come for a snack, then stay for the tap take-overs and tin can cocktails. Mon–Thurs & Sun 10am–midnight, Fri & Sat 10am–1am; kitchen daily 10am–9pm.

Duke's Corner 13 Brown St, DD1 5EG ☎01382 205052, ⓦdukescorner.com; map p.896. The catch-all slogan says it in a nutshell: beers, eats, tunes. Located in a former school, this airy beer hall has an entire backwall of thirty shiny pumps, and a suntrap garden perfect for summer barbecues. Charcoal-grilled meats, hot dogs and burgers are around £8–14, but it also has cheap-as-chips favourites for £5 (Mon–Thurs & Sun before 5pm). Mon & Tues noon–midnight, Wed–Sun noon–2.30am; kitchen daily noon–midnight.

Trades House Bar 40 Nethergate, DD1 4ET ☎01382 229494, ⓦtrades-housedundee.co.uk; map p.896. A converted bank fronted with bright stained-glass windows and Victorian timber-framed snugs for friendly boozing in the heart of the city. They serve simple pub meals for around £9. Daily 10/11am–midnight; kitchen Mon–Sat 10/11am–3pm, Sun 10/11am–5.45pm.

NIGHTLIFE

Reading Rooms 57 Blackscroft, DD4 6AT ☎01382 228496, ⓦreadingroomsdundee.com; map p.896. From rock 'n' roll and disco to soul, blues and punk, you'll find it at this former Edwardian library. The schedule, available online, is mostly taken up by DJs, dancehall and club nights, but rappers and indie bands play too. Thurs–Sat, typically 10.30pm–3.30am.

ENTERTAINMENT

DCA 152 Nethergate, DD1 4DY ☎01382 909900, ⓦdca.org.uk. As well as two art galleries and a print studio (see page 897), the *DCA* has two cinema screens showing a range of foreign and arthouse movies, alongside more challenging mainstream releases. It is also home to the popular *Jute Bar Café*. 10am–midnight.

Dundee Repertory Theatre Tay Square, DD1 1PB ☎01382 223530, ⓦdundeereptheatre.co.uk. Right at the heart of the Cultural Quarter is the prodigious Rep, home to an indigenously produced contemporary theatre and the only permanent rep company in Scotland.

The Angus coast

Two roads link Dundee to Aberdeen and the northeast coast of Scotland. By far the more pleasant option is the slightly longer A92 coast road, which joins the inland A90 at Stonehaven, just south of Aberdeen. Intercity **buses** follow both roads, while the coast-hugging train line from Dundee is one of the most picturesque in Scotland, passing attractive beaches and impressive cliffs, and stopping in the old seaports of **Arbroath** and **Montrose**.

22

Carnoustie

Just north of Dundee, **CARNOUSTIE** and its historic **Carnoustie Golf Links** course (☎01241 802270, ⑩carnoustiegolflinks.co.uk), with its thick rough and devilish bunkers, is one of the world's most challenging 18-holers. A close second in Scotland to St Andrews' Old Course (see page 852), its fairways and greens are a magnet for players and it is a regular host of **The Open**, the most prized competition in golf. A new visitor centre is being built, but it's still possible for visitors to play one of the three seafront courses (green fees on the Championship course cost £175, but a 50 percent discount applies Nov–March).

Arbroath

Since it was settled in the twelfth century, local fishermen have been landing their catches at **ARBROATH**, about fifteen miles northeast of Dundee. The town's most famous product is the **Arbroath smokie** – line-caught haddock, smoke-cured over smouldering oak chips and still made here in a number of family-run smokehouses around the harbour. One of the most atmospheric is **M&M Spink's** tiny whitewashed premises at 10 Marketgate (☎01241 875287, ⑩arbroathsmokies.co.uk); chef and food writer Rick Stein described the fish here, warm from the smoke, as "a world-class delicacy".

Arbroath Abbey

Abbey St, DD11 1EG • Daily: April–Sept 9.30am–5.30pm; Oct–March 10am–4pm • £6; HS • ☎01241 878756, ⑩ historicenvironment.scot/visit-a-place/places/arbroath-abbey

Arbroath's real glory days came with the completion in 1233 of **Arbroath Abbey**, whose rose-pink sandstone ruins were described by Dr Johnson as "fragments of magnificence". Founded in 1178, but not granted abbey status until 1285, it was the scene of one of the most significant events in Scottish history when, on April 6, 1320, a group of barons drew up the **Declaration of Arbroath**, asking Pope John XXII to reverse his excommunication of Robert the Bruce and recognize him as king of a Scottish nation independent from England. The wonderfully resonant language of the document still makes for a stirring expression of Scottish nationhood: "For so long as one hundred of us remain alive, we will never in any degree be subject to the dominion of the English, since it is not for glory, riches or honour that we do fight, but for freedom alone, which no honest man loses but with his life". It was duly dispatched to the Pope in Avignon, who in 1324 agreed to Robert's claim. The **visitor centre** at the Abbey Street entrance offers in depth background on these events and other aspects of the history of the building.

ARRIVAL AND INFORMATION	ARBROAT▶
By train The train station is on Keptie St in the town centre. Destinations Aberdeen (every 30min; 1hr); Dundee (every 30min; 20min); Montrose (roughly every 30min; 15min).	**By bus** Buses stop on Catherine St, near the train station Destinations Aberdeen (hourly; 1hr 55min); Dunde (every 30min; 40min); Forfar (hourly; 45min); Montros (every 30min; 25min).

ACCOMMODATION

★ **Brucefield Boutique B&B** Cliffburn Rd, DD11 5BS ☎ 01241 875393, ⊛ brucefieldbandb.com. Rooms at this renovated 1920s manor house – a mix of French revival and hip Scots – are as good as those in the region's best hotels, with high-end bathroom amenities and plush beds. Downstairs there is a sitting room with a free minibar, and outside seats overlook a croquet lawn. **£125**

Harbour Nights Guest House 4 Shore, DD11 1P ☎ 01241 434343, ⊛ harbournights.co.uk. Close enough that you can breathe in the salt-tang of the sea, this simple four-room B&B has a great perch overlooking the harbour with an eclectic mix of furnishings. The breakfast staple, naturally, is an Arbroath smokie landed across the road. **£65**

Montrose and around

A seaport and market town since the thirteenth century, **MONTROSE** sits on the edge of a virtually landlocked two-mile-square lagoon of mud known as the Basin. It's a great little town to visit, with a pleasant old centre.

Montrose Basin Wildlife Centre

Two miles west of Montrose along the A92 • Mid-Feb to Oct daily 10.30am–5pm; Nov to mid-Feb Mon & Fri–Sun 10.30am–4pm • £4 • ☎ 01674 676336, ⊛ montrosebasin.org.uk

On the south side of the Basin, the well-run **Montrose Basin Wildlife Centre** has binoculars, high-powered telescopes, bird hides and remote-control webcams. Arctic terns often make an appearance during the summer, and there's a good chance of seeing wood pigeons and great crested grebes throughout the year.

House of Dun

Four miles west of Montrose, DD10 9LQ • House April–Sept Mon–Wed, Sat & Sun 10.30am–4.30pm; Oct & Nov Sat & Sun 11am–2.30pm; garden and estate daily 9am–dusk • £10.50; NTS • ☎ 01674 810264, ⊛ nts.org.uk/Visit/House-Of-Dun • Accessible on the Montrose–Brechin bus #30 (hourly; 25min)

The Palladian **House of Dun**, crammed full of period furniture and *objets d'art*, was built in 1730 for David Erskine, Laird of Dun, to designs by renowned Georgian architect William Adam. Inside, the ornate relief plasterwork is the most impressive feature, extravagantly emblazoned with Jacobite symbolism. The buildings in the courtyard – a hen house, gamekeeper's workshop and potting shed – have been renovated, and it is surrounded by wildlife-rich woodlands and gardens.

ARRIVAL AND DEPARTURE
MONTROSE

By train The train station overlooks the River South Esk basin, a block back from High St on Western Rd.
Destinations Aberdeen (every 30min–hourly; 40min); Arbroath (every 20min; 15min); Dundee (every 20min; 30min); Stonehaven (every 30min–hourly; 20min).

By bus Most buses stop on the High St or at the railway station.
Destinations Aberdeen (hourly; 1hr 30min); Stonehaven (hourly; 50min).

ACCOMMODATION

36 The Mall The Mall, towards the north of town, DD10 8SS ☎ 01674 673646, ⊛ 36themall.co.uk. Attractive Georgian four-bedroom B&B townhouse with en-suite

facilities and a conservatory. Ask nicely and they may order in Arbroath smokies for breakfast. **£80**

The Angus Glens and around

Immediately north of Dundee, the low-lying Sidlaw Hills divide the city from the rich agricultural region of **Strathmore**, whose string of tidy market towns lies on a fertile strip along the southernmost edge of the heather-covered lower slopes of the Grampian mountains. These towns act as gateways to the **Angus Glens** (⊛ visitcairngorms.com/angus-glens), a series of tranquil valleys penetrated by single-

SKIING AT GLEN SHEE

Scotland's **ski resorts** make for a fun day out for anyone from beginners to experienced skiers and, given that **Glen Shee** is arguably the most accessible of Scotland's ski areas, close to Aberdeen and Dundee – and around 2hr 30min from both Glasgow and Edinburgh – it's as good an introduction as any to the sport.

For information, contact **Glenshee Ski Centre** (☎01339 741320, ⓦ ski-glenshee.co.uk), which also offers ski rental and can connect you with ski instructors. Ski rental starts at around £22 a day, and lessons cost £75 for two hours. Lift passes cost £30/day or £120 for a five-day (Mon–Fri) ticket. For the latest **weather conditions**, phone the centre or visit the Ski Scotland website (ⓦ ski.visitscotland.com).

22

track roads and offering some of the most rugged and majestic landscapes in northeast Scotland. It's a rain-swept, wind-blown area, whose roads become impassable with the first snows, sometimes as early as October, and where the summers see clouds of ferocious midges. The most attractive road through the glens is the stunning A93, which cuts through **Glen Shee**, linking Blairgowrie to Braemar on Deeside (see page 910). It's pretty dramatic stuff, threading its way over Britain's highest main road, the **Cairnwell Pass** (2199ft).

Blairgowrie

The upper reaches of **Glen Shee**, the most dramatic and best known of the Angus Glens, are dominated by its **ski fields**, ranged over four mountains above the Cairnwell mountain pass. To get to Glen Shee from the south, you'll pass through the well-heeled little town of **BLAIRGOWRIE**, set among raspberry fields on the glen's southernmost tip and a good place to pick up information and plan your activities.

ARRIVAL AND INFORMATION   BLAIRGOWRIE

By bus Buses #57 & #58 bus connect Blairgowrie with Perth (every 30min–1hr; 50min), while #59 goes to Dundee (hourly; 1hr).
Tourist office 26 Wellmeadow (an–March & Nov Mon–Sat 10am–4pm; April–June Mon–Sat 9.30am–5.30pm,

Sun 10am–4pm; July & Aug Mon–Sat 9am–6pm, Sun 9.30am–5.30pm; Sept & Oct Mon–Sat 10am–5pm, Sun 10.30am–3.30pm; Dec Mon–Sat 10am–4pm, Sun 11am–3pm; ☎01250 872960, ⓦ visitscotland.com).

ACCOMMODATION

Gulabin Lodge Outdoor Centre Spittal of Glenshee, 20 miles north of Blairgowrie, PH10 7QE ☎01250 885 255, ⓦ gulabinoutdoors.co.uk. Adventure centre in a wild, spectacular location with hostel-style doubles, twins (£50) and family rooms (£80). The helpful team can organize everything from skiing to biking, hiking and climbing. **£55**

Kinloch House Blairgowrie, PH10 6SG ☎01250 884732, ⓦ kinlochhouse.com. This Relais & Chateaux-affiliated country house has 25 acres, an oak-panelled hall and a portrait gallery, making it worthy of a wannabe laird. A whisky bar, regal lounge and fine-dining restaurant complete the perfect Highland fling. **£250**

Meigle Sculptured Stone Museum

Meigle, 15 miles north of Dundee on the B954, PH12 8SB • Daily: April–Sept 9.30am–5.30pm; Oct 10am–4pm • HS • £5, including free guided tour • ☎ 01828 640612, ⓦ historicenvironment.scot/visit-a-place/places/meigle-sculptured-stone-museum • Take bus #57 from Dundee's Seagate Bus Station (hourly; 40min)

The tiny settlement of **MEIGLE** is home to Scotland's most important collection of early Christian and **Pictish inscribed stones**. The exact meaning and purpose of the stones and their enigmatic symbols is obscure, as is the reason why so many of them were found here. The most likely theory is that Meigle was once an important ecclesiastical centre that attracted secular burials of prominent Picts. Housed in a modest former schoolhouse, the **Meigle Sculptured Stone Museum** displays some 26 pieces dating from

22

ABERDEENSHIRE'S CASTLE TRAIL

One of the most compelling driving routes in Scotland – and with good reason – is **Aberdeenshire's Castle Trail**, a looping six-day coast-to country itinerary taking in some nineteen dramatic castles, clifftop keeps and one or two claiming resident ghosts. While it is a blessing for history buffs, it's also an unrivalled way to slip off the beaten track. Big hitters like **Glamis Castle** (see below) and **Dunnottar Castle** (see page 907) are undeniably spectacular, but there are also some under-the-radar national treasures like **Fyvie Castle,** near Turriff, and **Cragievar Castle,** in many ways the quintessential Scottish baronial tower house. Of particular help when planning a trip is Visit Scotland's online guide which can help tailor a route from A to B (🌐ebooks.visitscotland.com/scotlands-castle-trail/). Who knew castle-bagging could be so addictive?

the seventh to the tenth centuries, all found in and around the nearby churchyard. The majority are either gravestones that would have lain flat, or cross slabs inscribed with the sign of the cross, usually standing. Most impressive is the 7ft-tall great cross slab, said to be the gravestone of Guinevere, wife of King Arthur.

Glamis Castle

Dundee Rd, 5 miles south of Kirriemuir, DD8 1RJ • April–Oct daily 10am–5.30pm (last admission 4.30pm) • £12.50 • ☎01307 840393, 🌐 glamis-castle.co.uk • Various bus options to Glamis are available; see Stagecoach Strathtay's website for details (stagecoachbus.com)

The wondrously over-the-top, five-storey pink-sandstone **Glamis Castle** is set in an extensive landscaped park complete with Highland cattle and pheasants beside the picturesque village of **GLAMIS** (pronounced "glahms"). One of the country's most famous chateau castles, featuring in *Macbeth* and with **royal connections** (it was the childhood home of the late Queen Mother and birthplace of the late Princess Margaret), it's an essential stop on any Scottish circuit.

Obligatory guided tours take in the fifteenth-century **crypt**, where the 12ft-thick walls enclose a haunted "lost" room, the family **chapel** and **Duncan's Hall**, a fifteenth-century guardroom, the – inaccurate – setting for Duncan's murder by Macbeth. Glamis' **grounds**, including the Italian Gardens, are worth a few hours in their own right, with verdant walks out to Earl John's Bridge and through the woodland.

J.M. Barrie's Birthplace

9 Brechin Rd, Kirriemuir, DD8 4BX • April–June & Sept Mon, Sat & Sun 11am–4pm; July & Aug Mon & Thurs–Sun 11am–4pm; last entry 3.30pm • £6.50 • ☎01575 572646, 🌐 nts.org.uk/Visit/J-M-Barries-Birthplace • Bus #20 from Dundee's Seagate Bus Station (hourly; 1hr)

Giving a remarkable insight into the early life of the author behind the much-loved character Peter Pan, **J.M. Barrie's Birthplace** – where the author was born on 9 May, 1860 – has been turned into a carefully rendered tribute. Furniture and personal items belonging to Barrie help tell the story, while two rooms have been re-created to show the house as it was when he was a boy.

Aberdeenshire and Moray

Aberdeenshire and Moray cover a large chunk of northern Scotland – some 3500 square miles. Much of it is open and varied country, dotted with historic and archeological sights from neat NTS properties and eerie prehistoric standing stones to quiet kirkyards and dramatic castles. Geographically, the counties break down into two distinct areas: the **hinterland**, once barren and now a patchwork of fertile farms, rising towards high mountains, sparkling rivers and gentle valleys; and the **coast**, a classic stretch of rocky cliffs, remote fishing villages and long, sandy beaches.

For visitors, the city of **Aberdeen** is the obvious focal point, and while it's not a place to keep you for long, it does have some intriguing architecture, attractive museums and a lively social scene born from a hefty student population. From here, it's a short hop west to **Deeside**, visited annually by the British royal family, where the trim villages of **Ballater** and **Braemar** act as a gateway to the spectacular Cairngorms National Park. Further north, the "malt whisky country" of **Speyside** has less impressive scenery, but numerous distilleries, while the **coast** beyond features dramatic cliffs and beaches punctuated by picturesque fishing villages.

22

Aberdeen and around

The third-largest city in Scotland, **ABERDEEN**, commonly known as the "Granite City", lies 120 miles northeast of Edinburgh on the banks of the rivers Dee and Don, smack in the middle of the northeast coast. Based around a working harbour, it's a place that people either love or hate. Certainly, while some extol the tones and colours of Aberdeen's **granite** buildings – and the architecture is stunning – others see only uniform grey. The weather doesn't help: Aberdeen lies on a latitude north of Moscow and the cutting wind and driving rain is the epitome of the Scots' word "dreich", meaning dreary. But when the sun shines, all that granite shimmers and sparkles silver.

In the twelfth century, Alexander I noted "Aberdon" as one of his principal towns, and by the thirteenth century it had become a centre for **trade and fishing**. A century or so later Bishop Elphinstone founded the Catholic university in the area north of town known today as **Old Aberdeen**, while the rest of the city developed as a mercantile centre and important port. By the mid-twentieth century, Aberdeen's traditional industries were in decline, but the discovery of **oil** in the North Sea transformed the place from a depressed port into a boom town. In the decades followiing the 1970s, Aberdeen became a wealthy and self-confident, swaggering place once more, only to fall on hard times again in recent years as the price per barrel has plummeted.

Castlegate

Any exploration of the **city centre** should begin at the open, cobbled **Castlegate**, where Aberdeen's long-gone castle once stood. At its centre is the late seventeenth-century **Mercat Cross**, or market cross, carved with a unique gallery of Stewart sovereigns alongside some fierce gargoyles. The view along gently rising Union Street – a jumble of grey spires, turrets and jostling double-decker buses – is quintessential Aberdeen. A quick stroll can take in **Marischal College**, the city's most imposing granite edifice, as well as **St Andrew's Cathedral**, where America's first bishop was ordained.

Aberdeen Art Gallery

Schoolhill, AB10 1FQ · Check website for opening times · Free · ☏ 03000 200293, ⓦaagm.co.uk/Visit/AberdeenArtGallery/aag-overview.aspx

The engrossing **Aberdeen Art Gallery**, purpose-built in 1884 and closed for refurbishment until late 2018, is one of the UK's best regional galleries. The main body of the collection remains the superb works of **Victorian Narrative Art**, some decent twentieth-century British painting and Impressionist art, including works by Boudin, Courbet, Sisley, Monet, Pissarro and Renoir.

Maritime Museum & Provost Ross's House

Shiprow, AB11 5BY · Mon–Sat 10am–5pm, Sun noon–3pm · Free · ☏ 01224 337700, ⓦaagm.co.uk

Just off cobbled Shiprow, peering towards the harbour through a striking glass facade, the engrossing **Maritime Museum** combines a modern, airy museum with the aged, labyrinthine corridors of **Provost Ross's House**. Inside the entrance, you'll see a blackboard updated daily with the price of a barrel of crude oil, and suspended above the foyer, visible from five different levels, is a spectacular 27ft-high model of an oil rig. The older industries of herring fishing, whaling, shipbuilding and lighthouses also have their place, with well-designed displays, many drawing heavily on personal reminiscences.

Gordon Highlanders Museum

St Luke's Viewfield Rd, AB15 7XH • Feb–Nov Tues–Sat 10am–4.30pm • £7.50 • ☎ 01224 311200, ⊛ gordonhighlanders.com • Bus #11 or #X17 from Union St (every 15min; 20min)

For anyone interested in military history, the award-winning **Gordon Highlanders Museum** is a must-see. Some two miles east of the city centre, it tells the extraordinary 200-year story of the regiment described by Sir Winston Churchill as "the finest in the world", charting the soldiers' exploits from the Napoleonic Wars to campaigns in India, Afghanistan and South Africa right up until the Cold War.

Old Aberdeen

Nearly 2 miles north of Aberdeen centre • Buses leave from the city centre (frequent; 10min)

An independent burgh until 1891, tranquil **Old Aberdeen** has maintained a village-like identity. Dominated by **King's College** and **St Machar's Cathedral**, its medieval cobbled streets, wynds and little lanes are beautifully preserved.

King's College Chapel

King's Campus, University of Aberdeen, AB24 3FX • Mon–Fri 10am–3.30pm • Free • ☎ 01224 272137, ⊛ abdn.ac.uk/chaplaincy/chapel

King's College Chapel, the first and finest of Aberdeen's college buildings, was completed in 1495, with a chunky Renaissance spire. The highlights of the interior, which, unusually, has no central aisle, are the ribbed, arched wooden ceiling and the rare and lovely examples of medieval Scottish woodcarving in the screen and the stalls.

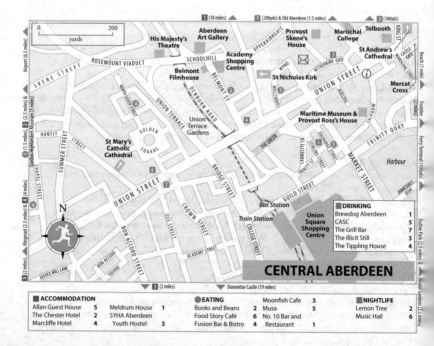

CENTRAL ABERDEEN

■ DRINKING	
Brewdog Aberdeen	1
CASC	5
The Grill Bar	7
The Illicit Still	3
The Tippling House	4

■ ACCOMMODATION				● EATING		Moonfish Cafe	3	■ NIGHTLIFE	
Allan Guest House	5	Meldrum House	1	Books and Beans	2	Musa	5	Lemon Tree	2
The Chester Hotel	2	SYHA Aberdeen		Food Story Café	6	No. 10 Bar and		Music Hall	6
Marcliffe Hotel	4	Youth Hostel	3	Fusion Bar & Bistro	4	Restaurant	1		

St Machar's Cathedral

18 The Chanonry, AB24 1RQ • Daily: April–Oct 9.30am–4.30pm; Nov–March 10am–4pm • Free • ☎ 01224 485988, ⓦ stmachar.com

St Machar's Cathedral overlooks leafy Seaton Park and the River Don. The site was reputedly founded in 580 AD by Machar, a follower of Columba, when he was sent by the latter to find a grassy platform near the sea, overlooking a river shaped like the crook on a bishop's crozier. This setting fitted the bill perfectly, and the cathedral, a huge fifteenth-century fortified building, became one of the city's first great granite edifices.

The beach

22

Aberdeen can surely claim to have the best sandy **beach** of all Britain's large cities. Less than a mile east of Union Street is a great two-mile sweep of clean sand, broken by groynes and lined with an esplanade, where most of the city's population gathers on sunny days. Further north, most of the beach's hinterland is devoted to golf links.

Dunnottar Castle

Fifteen miles south of Aberdeen, 2 miles south of Stonehaven, AB39 2TL • Daily: March & Oct 10am–4.30pm; April–Sept 9am–5.30pm; Nov–Feb 10am–2.30pm or later, depending on weather • £7 • ☎ 01569 762173, ⓦ dunnottarcastle.co.uk • Bus #X7 or 107 from Aberdeen bus station (hourly; 55min)

South of Aberdeen, the A92 and the main train line follow the coast to the pretty harbour town of **STONEHAVEN**. Two miles south, the stunningly capricious **Dunnottar Castle** is one of Scotland's finest ruined castles, a huge ninth-century fortress set on a three-sided sheer cliff jutting into the sea – a setting striking enough to be chosen as the backdrop for Zeffirelli's 1990 film version of *Hamlet* and the inspiration for Walt Disney and Pixar's Scottish cartoon *Brave*. Once the principal fortress of the northeast, the ruins are worth a good roam around, and there are many dramatic views out to the crashing sea. Bloodstained drama splatters the castle's past – not least in 1297, when the entire English Plantagenet garrison was burned alive here by William Wallace.

ARRIVAL AND INFORMATION

ABERDEEN AND AROUND

By plane Aberdeen's International Airport (ⓦ aberdeen airport.com) lies 7 miles northwest of town, connecting with more than fifty destinations, including dozens in the UK such as Belfast, Bristol, Newcastle, London and Manchester, plus regular flights to Wick, Kirkwall (for Orkney) and Sumburgh (for Shetland). Frequent buses (up to every 10min) run from the airport to Union Square. The flagship link is Jet Service #727 (£3.20 single; £4.80 return), while First Bus runs #16 to Guild St in the centre (40min).

By train The main station is on Guild St, in the city centre.
Destinations Arbroath (every 30min; 55hr); Dundee (every 30min; 1hr 15min); Edinburgh (every 30min–1hr; 2hr 35min); Elgin (every 2hr; 1hr 30min); Glasgow (hourly; 3hr); Inverness (every 2hr; 2hr 25min); London (2–3 daily; 7hr 35min–12hr; sleeper service Mon–Fri & Sun 1 daily; 10hr); Montrose (every 30min; 40min); Nairn (every 1hr 30min; 2hr); Stonehaven (every 30min; 15min).

By bus The terminal is beside the train station.
Destinations Ballater (every 30min–1hr; 2hr 20min); Banff (every 30min; 1hr 55min); Braemar (hourly–every 2hr; 3hr 20min); Cullen (hourly; 2hr 30min); Elgin (hourly; 2hr 30min); Fraserburgh (hourly; 1hr 30min); Macduff (every 30min; 1hr 50min); Stonehaven (every 30min; 40min).

By ferry Aberdeen has links to Lerwick in Shetland and Kirkwall in Orkney, with regular crossings from Jamieson's Quay in the harbour (☎ 0845 600 0449, ⓦ northlinkferries. co.uk).
Destinations Kirkwall, Orkney (April–Oct Tues, Thurs, Sat & Sun; Nov–March Thurs, Sat & Sun; 6hr); Lerwick, Shetland (daily; 12hr 30min overnight).

Tourist office 23 Union St (Jan–March Mon–Sat 9.30am–5pm; April, May & Sept–Dec Mon–Sat 9.30am–5pm, Sun 11am–4pm; July & Aug Mon–Sat 9am–6.30pm, Sun 10am–4pm; ☎ 01224 269180).

ACCOMMODATION

Allan Guest House 56 Polmuir Rd, AB11 7RT ☎ 01224 584484, ⓦ theallan.co.uk; map p.906. Attractive three-storey Victorian townhouse in a peaceful spot near Duthie Park, just 5min from the city centre on bus #17. There are eight rooms – a mix of singles, doubles and a luxury suite. Rates include a hearty breakfast. **£80**

The Chester Hotel 59–63 Queens Rd, AB15 4YP ☎ 01224 327777, ⓦ chester-hotel.com; map p.906. Aberdeen's hardest-working boutique hotel, *The Chester* knows its audience, targeting business travellers, golfers and weekend breakers. Rooms have a characteristically Aberdonian granite-grey colour scheme, while the star

22

of the show is award-winning chef Kevin Dalgleish's *IX Restaurant*. **£18**

Marcliffe Hotel North Deeside Rd, Pitfodels, 4 miles west of the centre, AB15 9YA ☏01224 861000, ⓦmarcliffe.com; map p.906. This 42-room hotel is by far the most luxurious and tasteful option in the immediate Aberdeen area. There's a drawing room, featuring originals by Scottish artists, and a fine-dining restaurant. They also specialize in organizing salmon fishing trips. **£170**

★ **Meldrum House** Oldmeldrum, 18 miles northwest of Aberdeen, AB51 0AE ☏01651 872294, ⓦmeldrum house.com; map p.906. Fresh from a chic renovation,

this lavish country house, spa and golf course is one of the northeast's most sought after addresses. It has a storied history, with the thirteenth-century tower – an eyrie from which to view the surrounding 240-acre estate – forming the nucleus of the property. There is also a spa and fine restaurant with a suitably upmarket ambience. **£105**

SYHA Aberdeen Youth Hostel 8 Queen's Rd, AB15 4ZT ☏01224 646988, ⓦsyha.org.uk/where-to-stay/highlands/aberdeen.aspx; map p.906. Clean hostel in a grand stone mansion a 15min walk from the High St, with dorms and private rooms. It's recently undergone a major renovation and has a giant self-catering kitchen and free parking. Dorms **£17**, doubles **£31**

EATING

Books and Beans 22 Belmont St, AB10 1JH ☏01224 646438, ⓦbooksandbeans.co.uk; map p.906. As the name suggests, bumper-to-bumper secondhand books provide the perfect companion for great coffee, fresh soups, toasted paninis, couscous salads and an encyclopaedic kids menu. Mains around £5. Mon–Sat 7.45am–4.30pm, Sun 9.45am–4pm.

★ **Food Story Café** 13–15 Thistle St, AB10 1XZ ⓦfoodstorycafe.co.uk; map p.906. Funded by a Kickstarter campaign, this pine-clad health-food café has become a strong community force for great coffee, cakes, music and events: expect organic porridge, veg-packed salads, hotpot chilli and gluten-free scones. Dinner mains from £6.50. Mon–Thurs 8am–9pm, Fri 8am–10pm, Sat 9am–9pm, Sun 11am–3pm.

Fusion Bar & Bistro 10 North Silver St, AB10 1RL ☏01224 652959, ⓦfusionbarbistro.com; map p.906. As much a style-conscious evening hangout as a classy dining affair, this place wows with a succession of creative starters (cured salmon with quail eggs, for example) and butcher's block steaks (from £18). Or go the whole hog and splurge on an entire lobster (£33.50). Tues–Thurs 5pm–midnight, Fri 5pm–1am, Sat noon–midnight.

Moonfish Cafe 9 Correction Wynd, AB10 1HP ☏01224 644166, ⓦmoonfishcafe.co.uk; map p.906. Sensationally creative Modern British menu with a choice of two, three or four courses for dinner, all served in the intriguing Merchant Quarter. An extensive gin menu rounds things off nicely. Lunch mains £11; three-course dinner £30. Tues–Fri noon–2pm & 6–9pm, Sat noon–2.30pm & 6–9pm.

Musa Exchange St, AB11 6PH ☏01224 571771, ⓦmusa aberdeen.com; map p.906. Based in an old church and banana warehouse, this good-value café, gallery and music venue has a terrific vibe, with live music and fabulous, if pricey, fine dining with a few curveballs on the menu – haggis spring roll, anyone? Mains from £17. Mon–Sat 11am till late.

No. 10 Bar and Restaurant 9 & 10 Queens Terrace, AB10 1XL ☏01224 631928, ⓦno10aberdeen.co.uk; map p.906. An Aberdeen institution in a granite building dating back to 1877. Great veggie options, steak and seafood, plus a bar menu and a lunchtime express menu. The name is a bit misleading: its popularity has seen it expand into No. 9 next door. Mains from £14. Mon–Fri noon–2.30pm & 5–11pm, Sat & Sun noon–3.30pm & 5–11pm.

DRINKING

Brewdog Aberdeen 17 Gallowgate, AB25 1EB ☏01224 631223, ⓦbrewdog.com; map p.906. Where it all started for the Fraserburgh brewer that's gone global. The chain's flagship, this hipster-friendly bar sets itself apart from the copycats with exposed brickwork, dangly light bulbs and a cracking selection of Aberdeenshire ales (bottles around £4.50). Mon–Thurs noon–midnight, Fri & Sat noon–1am, Sun 12.30pm–midnight.

★ **CASC** 7 Stirling St, AB11 6ND ☏01224 212373, ⓦcasc bar.co.uk; map p.906. An Aladdin's Cave of craft beers, single malts and cigars, this novel boozer and bottle shop is all about the numbers. There are 24 rotating drafts, 250 beers in the fridge (colour coded by flavour) and more than five hundred whiskies served in a canteen-style setting.

Mon–Thurs & Sun 11am–midnight, Fri & Sat 11am–1am.

The Grill Bar 213 Union St, AB11 6BA ☏01224 573530, ⓦthegrillaberdeen.co.uk; map p.906. Opposite the *Music Hall* (see page 909), this 1870s-era boozer is where you'll find old Aberdeen stubbornly clinging to life. It has an unrivalled selection of some six hundred single malts on the shelves, so you may feel as much a part of the warp and weft of the place by the time you leave. Mon–Thurs 10am–midnight, Fri & Sat 10am–1am, Sun 12.30pm–midnight.

The Illicit Still Netherkirkgate, Broad St, AB10 1AU ☏01224 623123, ⓦillicit-still.co.uk; map p.906. Follow the stairs down past sneering gargoyles to this

Gothic bar-cum-speakeasy that resembles an illegal distilling den. Beautifully designed, it is packed with leather armchairs and pool tables. Mon–Thurs 11am–midnight, Fri & Sat 11am–1am, Sun 12.30pm–midnight.

The Tippling House 4 Belmont St, AB10 1JE ☎01224 631640, ⓦthetipplinghouse.com; map p.906. Late-night drinking den that doubles as a time-warp back to 1920s prohibition-era New York. Despite the air of a gentleman's club, it draws a mixed, glammed-up crowd who come to drink cocktails such as Ageing Pornstars (vodka and passionfruit). For more of the same, see *Rye and Soda* on Belmont St, which is run by the same savvy crew. Mon–Thurs & Sun 4pm–2am, Fri 4pm–3am, Sat 1pm–3am.

NIGHTLIFE

Lemon Tree 5 West North St, AB24 5AT ☎01224 337688, ⓦboxofficeaberdeen.com; map p.906. The fulcrum of the city's arts scene, with a great buzz and regular live music, club nights and comedy, as well as decent theatre.

Music Hall Union St, AB10 1QS ☎01224 641122, ⓦboxofficeaberdeen.com; map p.906. Following a £7 million renovation, this nineteenth-century concert hall – favourite venue of home-grown pop sensation Emile Sandé – is back with a bang, with better acoustics and performance spaces.

ENTERTAINMENT

His Majesty's Theatre Rosemount Viaduct, AB25 1GL ☎01224 641122, ⓦboxofficeaberdeen.com. The city's main theatre resides in a beautiful Edwardian building, with an extensive programme ranging from serious drama and opera to panto.

Deeside

More commonly known as **Royal Deeside**, the land stretching west from Aberdeen along the River Dee revels in its connections with the royal family, who have regularly holidayed here, at **Balmoral**, since Queen Victoria bought the estate. Eighty thousand Scots turned out to welcome her on her first visit in 1848, but some weren't so charmed: one local journalist remarked that the area was about to be "desolated by cockneys and other horrible reptiles". Today, most locals are fiercely protective of the royal connection.

Deeside is undoubtedly handsome in a fierce, craggy way, and the royal presence has helped keep a lid on unattractive mass development. The villages strung along the A93, the main route through the area, are well heeled, with an old-fashioned air, and visitor facilities are first class. It's an excellent area for **outdoor activities**, with hiking routes into the Grampian and Cairngorm mountains and good mountain biking, horseriding and skiing.

Crathes Castle

Fifteen miles southwest of Aberdeen, AB31 5QJ • April–Oct daily 10.30am–5pm; Nov–March Sat & Sun 11am–4pm • £12.50; NTS • ☎01330 844525, ⓦnts.org.uk/Visit/Crathes-Castle • Buses #201, #202 and #203 from Union St, Aberdeen, stop opposite (hourly; 45min)

Crathes Castle is a splendid sixteenth-century granite tower house adorned with flourishes such as overhanging turrets, gargoyles and conical roofs. Its thick walls, narrow windows and tiny rooms loaded with heavy old furniture make it all rather claustrophobic, but it's well worth visiting for some wonderful painted ceilings, either still in their original form or sensitively restored; the earliest dates from 1602.

Ballater

The neat and ordered town of **BALLATER** stands attractively hemmed in by the river and fir-covered mountains. It was here that Queen Victoria first arrived in Deeside by train from Aberdeen back in 1848; she wouldn't allow a station to be built any closer to Balmoral, eight miles further west. Although the line has long been closed, the town's rather self-important royalism is much in evidence with oversized "By Appointment" crests above the doorways of most businesses.

Ballater is an excellent base for local **walks** and **outdoor activities**. There are numerous hikes from Loch Muik (pronounced "mick"), including the well-worn but strenuous all-day trek up and around Lochnagar (3789ft), the mountain much painted and written about by Prince Charles.

Balmoral Castle

Eight miles west of Ballater, off the A93, AB35 5TB · April–July daily 10am–5pm · £11.50 · ☎013397 42534, ⓦ balmoralcastle.com · Bus #201 or from Ballater (around 8 daily; 15min) stops at Crathie – a 10min walk east of the castle

Originally a sixteenth-century tower house built for the powerful Gordon family, **Balmoral Castle** has been a royal residence since 1852. The royal family traditionally spend their summer holidays here each August, but despite its fame is still very much in use by Her Majesty The Queen, and it can be something of a disappointment even for a dedicated royalist – only the ballroom, an exhibition room in the stables and the grounds are open to the public.

ARRIVAL AND INFORMATION   BALLATER

By bus Buses stop at the northern end of Golf Rd, near the A93. Destinations Aboyne (hourly; 20min); Banchory (hourly; 40min); Braemar (roughly hourly; 30min).

Tourist office In the renovated former train station (daily 10am–5pm; ☎013397 55306).

ACCOMMODATION AND EATING

Ballater Hostel Bridge Square, AB35 5QJ ☎01339 753752, ⓦ ballater-hostel.com. Formerly *Habitat@ Ballater*, this excellent and well-equipped 28-bed hostel has changed ownership but has benefited from a new lease of life. Choose between a bunk bed with private locker, or one of the doubles. Dorms £22, doubles £33

Hilton Grand Vacations at Craigendarroch Suites Braemar, AB35 5XA ☎01339 755858, ⓦ hilton.com. Unlike most of this international hotel chain's cookie-cutter city hotels, this one is a treat. A Hogwarts for grown-ups in the foothills of the Cairngorms National Park, it can organize fishing, highland safaris, golf and skiing. Choose

between deluxe rooms or family suites with balconies and kitchenettes. £140

Rothesay Rooms 3 Netherley Place, AB35 5QE ☎01339 753816, ⓦ rothesay-rooms.co.uk. Many places have the royal seal of approval in Ballater, but only one can claim to being set up by Prince Charles, or the Duke of Rothesay as he is known in Scotland. A charitable restaurant, it's given a new lease of life to an empty building, offering a sensational, locally sourced seasonal menu. Book ahead. Mains around £20. Thurs–Sat noon–2pm & 6–9pm, Sun noon–2.30pm, Wed 6–9pm.

Braemar

At 1100ft above sea level, the village of **BRAEMAR** is an invigorating, outdoor kind of place, well patronized by committed hikers, but probably best known for its Highland Games, the annual **Braemar Gathering**, on the first Saturday of September (ⓦ braemargathering.org). Since Queen Victoria's day, successive generations of royals have attended and the world's most famous Highland Games have become rather an overcrowded, overblown event. Definitely book tickets in advance.

ARRIVAL AND INFORMATION   BRAEMAR

By bus Buses arrive and depart from the Mar Rd roundabout, just west of the village centre. Destinations Ballater (roughly hourly; 30min); Spittal of Glenshee (1 daily; 40min).

Tourist office The Mews, in the middle of the village on Mar Rd (daily: April–June 9.30am–5pm; July & Aug 9.30am–6pm; Sept–March 9.30am–4.30pm; ☎01339 741600).

ACCOMMODATION AND EATING

The Gathering Place Invercauld Rd, AB35 5YP ☎01339 741234, ⓦ the-gathering-place.co.uk. Bistro in the heart of the village with Scottish dishes such as Cullen Skink, smoked salmon, haggis and steak walked

in from the butcher along the street. Mains from £11.95. Daily 5.30pm–late.

Ivy Cottage Braemar Cluniebank Rd on Glenshee Rd, AB35 5ZP ☎01339 741642, ⓦ ivycottagebraemar.

co.uk. As central as you can get in Braemar, this well-presented B&B has a lovely garden and a cosy mixture of doubles and twins overlooking the hills. A self-catering cottage (£200) and studio (£160) – both with a minimum three-night stay – are also available. **£80**

Speyside

Strictly speaking, the term **Speyside** refers to the entire region surrounding the River Spey, but to most people the name is synonymous with the **whisky triangle**, stretching from just north of Craigellachie down towards Tomintoul in the south and east to Huntly. There are more whisky distilleries and famous brands (including Glenfiddich and Glenlivet) concentrated in this small area than in any other part of the country. Running through the heart of the region is the River Spey, whose clean, clear, fast-flowing waters not only play such a vital part in the whisky industry, but also make it one of Scotland's finest angling locations. At the centre of Speyside, the quiet market town of **Dufftown** makes a good base for a single malt tour.

Dufftown and around

The cheery community of **DUFFTOWN**, founded in 1817 by James Duff, the fourth Earl of Fife, proudly proclaims itself "Malt Whisky Capital of the World" with good reason – it produces more of the stuff than any other town in Britain and hosts two annual whisky festivals (one at springtime and another in the autumn). There are seven active distilleries around Dufftown, as well as a cooperage; an extended stroll around the outskirts gives a good idea of the density of whisky distilling going on, with glimpses of giant warehouses filled with barrels of the heady liquid, and whiffs of fermenting barley or peat smoke lingering on the breeze.

On the edge of town along the A941 is the town's largest working distillery, **Glenfiddich** (see page 912), as well as the old Dufftown train station, which has been restored by enthusiasts and is now the departure point for the **Keith & Dufftown Railway** (three trips daily May–Sept; £11 return; ☎01340 821181, ⓦkeith-dufftown-railway. co.uk), which uses restored diesel locomotives to chug through whisky country to Keith, home of the Strathisla distillery, the world's oldest working distillery (see page 912).

ARRIVAL AND INFORMATION   DUFFTOWN AND AROUND

By bus Buses run from Aberlour (Mon–Sat hourly; 15min) and Elgin (Mon–Sat hourly; 50min), stopping near the clock tower in the middle of Dufftown.

By train Trains plying the Keith & Dufftown Railway (see above) stop at the station a mile north of town on the A941.

ACCOMMODATION AND EATING

Glenlivet House Ballindalloch, AB37 9DJ ☎01807 590376, ⓦglenlivethouse.com. Once a shooting lodge, this combo of a B&B and self-catering cottage is deep in whisky country. The Glenlivet Distillery is just a short stroll away. **£110**

Highland Spirit B&B 51 Fife St, Dufftown, AB55 4AP ☎01340 821136, ⓦhighlandspiritbandb.co.uk. Run by a pair of savvy single malt connoisseurs, this beautifully designed three-bedroom guesthouse is a great option, with a breakfast that comes with optional whisky porridge. **£139**

The Seven Stills 30 Fife St, AB55 4AL6 ☎01340 821534, ⓦsevenstills.co.uk. Family-run pub and restaurant with a locally sourced menu (Tain blue cheese, Portsoy seafood, Moray smoked salmon). Offers quirky foodie experiences, including a whisky and chocolate pairing, plus an impressive 200-bottle single malt bar. Mains around £15. Daily noon–11pm.

The Moray coast

The **Moray coast** from Aberdeen to Inverness has a rugged, sometimes bleak, fringe with pleasant if undramatic farmland rolling inland. If the weather is good, it's well worth spending a couple of days meandering through the various little fishing villages and along the miles of deserted beaches.

22

THE MALT WHISKY TRAIL

There are nine attractions on the **Malt Whisky Trail** (ⓦmaltwhiskytrail.com), a clearly signed seventy-mile meander around Speyside. All the distilleries offer a tour with a tasting to round it off; if you're driving you may be offered a miniature to take away. You could cycle or walk parts of the route, using the Speyside Way (see page 913). The following are selected highlights.

Cardhu On the B9102 at Knockando, AB38 7RY ⓣ01479 874635, ⓦdiageo.com. Established more than a century ago, when the founder's wife would raise a red flag to warn crofters if the authorities were on the lookout for their illegal stills. With attractive, pagoda-topped buildings, it sells rich, full-bodied whisky with distinctive peaty flavours that comes in an attractive bulbous bottle. Tours £5. Hourly: April Mon–Fri 10am–5pm; May–Sept Mon–Sat 10am–5pm, Sun 11am–4pm; Oct–March Mon–Fri 10am–4pm.

Glenfiddich On the A941 just north of Dufftown, AB55 4DH ⓣ01340 820373, ⓦglenfiddich.com. The biggest and slickest of the Speyside distilleries, still owned by the same Grant family who founded it in 1887. It's a light, sweet whisky, in triangular bottles – unusually, the bottling is still done on the premises and can be seen as part of the tours. Tours £10. Daily: April–Oct 9.30am–4.30pm; Nov–March 11am–3pm.

Glen Grant Rothes, AB38 7AF ⓣ01340 820373, ⓦglengrant.com. The highlight here is the attractive Victorian gardens, a combination of well-tended lawns and mixed, mature trees; there's a tumbling waterfall and a hidden whisky safe. Tours £5. April–Oct daily 9.30am–5.30pm; Nov–March Mon–Sat 9.30am–5pm, Sun noon–5pm.

Glenlivet On the B9008 to Tomintoul, AB37 9DB ⓣ01340 821720, ⓦtheglenlivet.com. A famous name in a lonely hillside setting. This was the first licensed distillery in the Highlands, following the 1823 act that aimed to reduce illicit distilling and smuggling. The Glenlivet 12-year-old malt is a floral, fragrant, medium-bodied whisky. Tours £10. March–Nov daily 9.30am–6pm (last tour 4.30pm).

Speyside Cooperage Dufftown Rd, Craigellachie, AB38 9RS ⓣ01340 871108, ⓦspeysidecooperage. co.uk. The only stop on the trail that isn't a distillery, with fascinating glimpses into how coopers make casks – a highly skilled job and a vital part of the industry. Tours £3.50. Mon–Fri 9am–5pm (last tour 3.30pm).

Strathisla Seafield Ave, Keith, AB55 5BS ⓣ01542 783044, ⓦchivas.com. A small, attractive distillery in business since 1786. Inside there's an old-fashioned mash tun and brass-bound spirit safes. You can arrive here via the Keith & Dufftown Railway (see page 911). Tours £7.50. March–Nov Mon–Sat 9.30am–5pm, Sun 12.30–5pm; Nov–Feb Mon–Fri 10am–4pm.

The largest coastal towns are **Peterhead** and **Fraserburgh**, both dominated by sizeable fishing fleets; the latter's **Museum of Scottish Lighhouses** is one of the most attractive small museums in Scotland. Most visitors, however, are more drawn to the quieter spots, including the charming villages of **Pennan**, **Gardenstown**, **Portsoy** and nearby **Cullen**. The other main attractions are **Duff House** in Banff, a branch of the National Gallery of Scotland, and the **Findhorn Foundation** near Forres.

Museum of Scottish Lighthouses

Kinnaird Head, Stevenson Rd, Fraserburgh, AB43 9DU • April–Oct daily 10am–5pm; Nov–March Tues–Sun 10am–4.30pm • £7.70 • ⓣ01346 511022, ⓦlighthousemuseum.org.uk • The #69 bus from Peterhead towards Fraserburgh (hourly; 55min) and less frequent services from Macduff (3 daily; 1hr) stop at the bus station on Hanover St; the museum is a 10min walk north

Large and severe-looking **FRASERBURGH** is home to the excellent **Museum of Scottish Lighthouses**. Here you can see a collection of huge lenses and prisms gathered from decommissioned lighthouses, and a display on various members of the famous "Lighthouse" Stevenson family (including the father and grandfather of author Robert Louis Stevenson), who designed many of them. The highlight is the tour of Kinnaird Head **lighthouse** itself, preserved as it was when the last keeper left in 1991.

Banff

Heading farther west along the coast from Fraserburgh brings you to **Macduff** and its neighbour **BANFF**, separated by the beautiful seven-arch bridge over the River Deveron. Banff's mix of characterful old buildings and boarded-up shops give little clue to the extravagance of **Duff House**, the town's main attraction.

Duff House

Just south of the town centre, AB45 3SX • April–Oct daily 11am–5pm; Nov–March Thurs–Sun 11am–4pm • £7.50; HS • ☎ 01261 818181, ⓦ duffhouse.org.uk

A tale of two Williams, **Duff House** was built to William Adam's design in 1730 for William Duff, the former owner, now painstakingly restored and reopened as an outpost of the **National Gallery of Scotland**. While the emphasis inside the four-storey Georgian Baroque house is on period artwork rather than any broader selection of the gallery's paintings, temporary exhibitions from the collections are regular highlights.

22

ARRIVAL AND INFORMATION   BANFF

By bus Buses run from Fraserburgh to Banff (Mon–Sat 2–4 daily; 1hr) and from Aberdeen (Mon–Sat hourly; 1hr 55min).
Tourist office Collie Lodge, in the town centre, close to

where Carmelite St, Low St and Strait Path meet (April–Sept Mon–Sat 10am–5pm; Oct Mon–Sat 10am–4pm; ☎ 01261 812419).

Cullen to Spey Bay

CULLEN, twelve miles west of Banff, is strikingly situated beneath a superb series of arched viaducts. The town is made up of two sections: Seatown, by the harbour, and the new town on the hillside. The local delicacy, **Cullen Skink** – a soup made from milk (or cream), potato and smoked haddock – is available at local hotels and bars.

West of Cullen, the scruffy, working fishing town of **BUCKIE** marks one end of the **Speyside Way** long-distance footpath which follows the coast west for five miles to windy **Spey Bay**. It's a remote spot bounded by sea, river and sky; it's here you'll find the charitable **Scottish Dolphin Centre** (10.30am–5pm: March Sat & Sun; April–Oct daily; free; ☎ 01343 820339, ⓦ dolphincentre.whales.org), whose main mission is researching the Moray Firth dolphin population (see page 924).

Findhorn

Located at one end of a wide sweep of sandy beach, **FINDHORN** is a tidy village with some neat fishermen's cottages and a delightful harbour dotted with moored yachts. Findhorn is best known, however, for the controversial **Findhorn Foundation** (see below), based beside the town's caravan park about a mile before you reach the village.

ARRIVAL AND INFORMATION   FINDHORN

By bus Findhorn is served by the #31 bus from Elgin (hourly; 45min) and Forres (hourly; 20min). The bus stop is a mile north of the Findhorn Foundation.

THE FINDHORN FOUNDATION

In 1962, Eileen and Peter Caddy, their three children and friend Dorothy Maclean settled on a caravan site at **Findhorn**. Dorothy believed she had a special relationship with what she called the "devas … the archetypal formative forces of light or energy that underlie all forms in nature – plants, trees, rivers", and from the uncompromising sandy soil they built a remarkable garden filled with plants and vegetables, far larger than had ever been seen in the area. A few of those who came to see the phenomenon stayed to help out and tune into the spiritual aspect of the nascent community. With its emphasis on inner discovery and development, but unattached to any doctrine or creed, the **Findhorn Foundation** has today blossomed into a permanent community of a few hundred people, with a well-developed series of courses and retreats on subjects ranging from astro-shamanic healing to organic gardening, drawing another eight thousand or so visitors each year. But the reputation of the place is such that it attracts visitors both sympathetic and sceptical – yet both find something to feed their preconceptions.

The Findhorn Foundation's **visitor centre** (see website for opening times; ☎ 01309 690311, ⓦ findhorn.org) has information on staying within the community, either as part of an introductory "Experience Week", or simply overnighting; there are a number of eco-houses nearby offering B&B. Guided tours of the park cost £8/person.

The Highland region

LOCH TORRIDON

The Highland region

Scotland's Highland region, covering the northern two-thirds of the country, holds much of the mainland's most spectacular scenery. You may be surprised at just how remote much of it still is: the vast peat bogs in the north, for example, are among the most extensive and unspoilt wilderness areas in Europe, while a handful of the west coast's isolated crofting villages can still be reached only by boat. The only major city, Inverness, is best used as a springboard for more remote areas where you can soak in the Highlands' classic combination of mountains, glens, lochs and rivers, surrounded on three sides by a magnificently pitted and rugged coastline.

23

South of Inverness, the **Strathspey** region, with a string of villages lying along the River Spey, is dominated by the dramatic **Cairngorm mountains**, an area brimming with attractive scenery and opportunities for outdoor activity. The Monadhliath mountains lie between Strathspey and **Loch Ness**, the largest and most famous of the necklace of lochs that make up the **Great Glen**, an ancient geological faultline which cuts southwest across the region from Inverness to the town of **Fort William**. From Fort William, beneath Scotland's highest peak, Ben Nevis, it's possible to branch out to some fine scenery – most conveniently the beautiful expanses of **Glen Coe**, but also in the direction of the appealing **west coast**, notably the remote and tranquil **Ardnamurchan peninsula**, the "Road to the Isles" to **Mallaig**, and the lochs and glens that lead to **Kyle of Lochalsh** on the most direct route to Skye. Between Kyle of Lochalsh and **Ullapool**, the main settlement in the northwest, lies **Wester Ross**, home to quintessentially west-coast scenes of sparkling sea lochs, rocky headlands and sandy beaches set against some of Scotland's most dramatic mountains, with Skye and the Western Isles on the horizon.

The **north coast**, stretching from wind-lashed **Cape Wrath**, at the very northwest tip of the mainland, east to **John O'Groats**, is even more rugged, with sheer cliffs and sand-filled bays bearing the brunt of frequently fierce Atlantic storms. The main settlement on this coast is **Thurso**, jumping-off point for the main ferry service to Orkney.

On the fertile **east coast**, stretching north from Inverness to the old herring port of **Wick**, green fields and woodland run down to the sweeping sandy beaches of the **Black Isle** and the **Cromarty and Dornoch firths**. This region is rich with historical sites, including the **Sutherland Monument** by Golspie, **Dornoch**'s fourteenth-century sandstone cathedral and a number of places linked to the Clearances, a poignantly remembered chapter in the Highland story.

GETTING AROUND   THE HIGHLAND REGION

Getting around the **Highlands**, particularly the remoter parts, can be tricky without your own transport. **Bus services** are sporadic and often cease entirely on Sunday. Most sizeable villages have a petrol station or 24hr fuel supply (typically card payment only), although these are few and far between in the west and north, so fill up early and be prepared for higher prices. Bear in mind, too, that the Highlands' single-track roads are far from fast; remember to pull in to let drivers behind overtake.

THE OLD FORGE PUB, KNOYDART

Highlights

❶ West Highland Railway From Glasgow to Mallaig via Fort William: the further north you travel, the more spectacular it gets. See page 920

❷ The Cairngorms Scotland's grandest mountain massif, a place of rare plants, wild animals, inspiring vistas and challenging outdoor activities. See page 924

❸ Glen Coe Stunning, moody, poignant and full of history – a glorious place for hiking or to simply admire. See page 931

❹ Knoydart Only accessible by boat or a two-day hike over the mountains, this peninsula also boasts mainland Britain's most isolated pub, the welcoming *Old Forge*. See page 935

❺ Wester Ross Scotland's finest scenery – a heady mix of high mountains, rugged sea lochs, sweeping bays and scattered islands. See page 937

❻ Ceilidh Place, Ullapool The best venue for modern Highland culture, with evenings of music, song and dance. See page 940

❼ Cromarty Set on the fertile Black Isle, this charming small town boasts beautiful vernacular architecture and dramatic east-coast scenery. See page 946

HIGHLIGHTS ARE MARKED ON THE MAP ON PAGE 918

23

THE WEST HIGHLAND RAILWAY

A fixture in lists of the world's most scenic train journeys, the brilliantly engineered **West Highland Railway** runs from Glasgow to Mallaig via Fort William. The line is in two sections: the southern part travels from **Glasgow** Queen Street station, up the banks of Loch Lomond to **Crianlarich**, then around Beinn Odhar on a horseshoe of viaducts to cross **Rannoch Moor**, where the track had to be laid on a mattress of tree roots, brushwood and thousands of tons of earth and ashes. You're out in the wilds here, the line long having diverged from the road. The route then swings into Glen Roy, passing through the **Monessie Gorge** to enter **Fort William**.

Leg two, from Fort William to Mallaig, is even more spectacular. Shortly after leaving Fort William the railway crosses the Caledonian Canal beside Neptune's Staircase at **Benavie**, before travelling along Locheil and crossing the 21-arch viaduct at **Glenfinnan**, where passengers get to live out *Harry Potter* fantasies. Then it's on to the coast, with views of the Small Isles and Skye before journey's end at **Mallaig**. You can book tickets through ⓦscotrail.co.uk. Between late April and October, this leg of the route is also served by the **Jacobite Steam Train** (ⓦwestcoastrailways.co.uk).

Inverness and around

Straddling a nexus of road and rail routes, **INVERNESS** is the hub of the Highlands, and an inevitable port of call if you're exploring the region by public transport: **buses** and **trains** leave for communities right across the far north of Scotland. Though it has few conventional sights, the city has an appealing setting on the banks of the River Ness.

Inverness Museum and Art Gallery

Castle Wynd, IV2 3EB • April–Oct Tues–Sat 10am–5pm; Nov–March Tues–Thurs noon–4pm, Fri & Sat 11am–4pm • Free • ☎ 01463 237114, ⓦhighlifehighland.com

Below **Inverness Castle**, the **Inverness Museum and Art Gallery** offers an insight into the social history of the Highlands, with treasures from the times of the Picts and Vikings, taxidermy exhibits such as "Felicity" the puma, caught in Cannich in 1980, and interactive features including an introduction to the Gaelic language. Though the **castle** itself is closed to the public, there are various plaques and statues in the grounds, including a small plinth marking the start of the 73-mile Great Glen Way, and a 360-degree viewpoint offers views of the city.

Culloden

Six miles east of Inverness off the B9006, IV2 5EU • Visitor centre daily: April, May, Sept & Oct 9am–5.30pm; June & July 9am–6pm; Aug 9am–7pm; Nov, Dec, Feb & March 10am–4pm • £11; entrance includes an audioguide; NTS • ☎ 01463 796090, ⓦnts.org.uk/culloden

The windswept moorland of **CULLODEN** witnessed the last-ever battle on British soil when, on April 16, 1746, the Jacobite cause was finally subdued – a turning point in the history of the Scottish nation (see page 922). Today, this historic site attracts more than 200,000 visitors annually. Your first stop should be the superb **visitor centre**, which hosts costumed actors and state-of-the-art audiovisual and interactive technology, all employed to tell the tragedy of Culloden through the words, songs and poetic verse of locals and soldiers who experienced it. The *pièce de résistance* is the powerful "battle immersion theatre" where visitors are surrounded by lifelike cinematography and the sounds of the raging, bloody fight.

Every April, on the Saturday closest to the date of the battle, there's a small commemorative service here.

Cawdor Castle

Cawdor, 14 miles northeast of Inverness, IV12 5RD · May–Oct daily 10am–5.30pm · £11.20; £6.50 for gardens & nature trails only · ☎ 01667 404401, ⓦ cawdorcastle.com · Trains and buses from Inverness to Nairn (frequent; 20–45min), then pick up a taxi for the final 6 miles

Cawdor Castle, in the pretty village of **CAWDOR**, is intimately linked to Shakespeare's *Macbeth*: the fulfilment of the witches' prediction that Macbeth was to become thane of Cawdor sets off his tragic desire to be king. Though visitors arrive in their droves each summer, the castle, which dates from the early fourteenth century, could not have witnessed the grisly eleventh-century events on which the Bard's drama was based. However, the immaculately restored monument – a fairy-tale affair of towers, turrets, hidden passageways, dungeons, gargoyles and crenellations whimsically shooting off from the original keep – is well worth a visit. Outside is a 1620 walled kitchen garden, a formal flower garden and a rambling 1960s wild garden.

Fort George

Thirteen miles northeast of Inverness, near Ardersier, IV2 7TD · Daily: April–Sept 9.30am–5.30pm; Oct–March 10am–4pm · £9; HES · ☎ 01667 460232, ⓦ historicenvironment.scot/visit-a-place/places/fort-george

Fort George, an old Hanoverian bastion with walls a mile long, is considered by military architectural historians to be one of the finest fortifications in Europe. Crowning a sandy spit that juts into the middle of the Moray Firth, it was built between 1747 and 1769 as a base for George II's army, in case the Highlanders should

23

THE DEFEAT OF THE JACOBITES

It didn't take long for Scottish opinion to turn against the **Union** between Scotland and England, signed in 1707, after it failed to bring Scots any tangible economic benefits. The first Jacobite rebellion of 1715, led by John Erskine, fell flat when his troops failed to take military advantage at the Battle of Sheriffmuir. A few decades later, tensions continued to simmer.

The **second Jacobite rebellion** had begun on August 19, 1745, with the raising of the Stuarts' standard at Glenfinnan on the west coast (see page 934). Shortly after, Edinburgh fell into Jacobite hands, and Bonnie Prince Charlie began his march on London. The ruling Hanoverians had appointed the ambitious young Duke of Cumberland to command their forces, which included troops from the Lowlands and Highlands. The duke's pursuit, together with bad weather and lack of funds, eventually forced the Jacobite forces – mostly comprised of Highlanders – to retreat north. They ended up at **Culloden**, where, ill fed and exhausted after a pointless night march, they were hopelessly outnumbered by the government forces. The open, flat ground of Culloden Moor was totally unsuitable for the Highlanders' style of courageous but undisciplined fighting, which needed steep hills and lots of cover to provide the element of surprise, and they were routed.

After the battle, in which 1500 Highlanders were slaughtered (many of them as they lay wounded on the battlefield), Bonnie Prince Charlie fled west to the hills and islands, where loyal Highlanders sheltered and protected him. He eventually escaped to France, leaving his supporters to their fate – and, in effect, ushering in the end of the clan system. The clans were disarmed, the wearing of tartan and playing of bagpipes forbidden, and the chiefs became landlords greedy for higher and higher rents. The battle also unleashed an orgy of violent reprisals on Scotland, as unruly government troops raped and pillaged their way across the region; within a century, the Highland way of life had changed beyond all recognition.

attempt to rekindle the Jacobite flame. By the time of its completion, however, the uprising had been firmly quashed and the fort has been used ever since as barracks; note the armed sentries at the main entrance and the periodic crack of live gunfire from the nearby firing ranges. Walking on the northern, grass-covered casemates, which look out into the estuary, you may be lucky enough to see a pod of bottle-nosed **dolphins** (see page 924) swimming in with the tide.

ARRIVAL AND INFORMATION
INVERNESS

By plane Inverness Airport (☎ 01667 464000, ⊛ hial. co.uk/inverness-airport) is at Dalcross, 7 miles east of the city. Taxis to the centre cost around £14 (try Tartan Taxis on ☎ 01463 222777).
Destinations Belfast (6 weekly; 1hr 5min); Birmingham (Mon–Fri & Sun 1 daily; 1hr 25min); Bristol (1–2 daily; 1hr 20min); Kirkwall (Mon–Sat 1–2 daily; 45min); London Gatwick (4–5 daily; 1hr 50min); Luton (1 daily; 1hr 20min); Manchester (Mon–Fri 2 daily, Sat & Sun 1 daily; 1hr 30min); Stornoway (Mon–Fri 3–4 daily, Sat & Sun 1 daily; 40min).
By train The station lies just off Academy St, northeast of the centre.
Destinations Aberdeen (Mon–Sat 11 daily; Sun 6; 2hr 10min); Aviemore (Mon–Sat 12 daily, Sun 7; 35min); Edinburgh (Mon–Sat 9 daily, Sun 5; 3hr 30min); Glasgow Queen St (Mon–Sat 3 daily; Sun 3; 3hr 20min); Kyle of

Lochalsh (Mon–Sat 4 daily, Sun 2; 3hr); London King's Cross/ Euston (1 daily; 8–11hr); Thurso (Mon–Sat 4 daily, Sun 1; 3hr 45min); Wick (Mon–Sat 4 daily, Sun 1; 4hr 15min).
By bus The main bus station is just north of the train station, close to the public library.
Destinations Aberdeen (hourly; 3hr 50min); Aviemore (every 30min; 45min); Drumnadrochit (at least hourly; 30min); Fort Augustus (up to 9 daily; 1hr); Fort William (up to 9 daily; 2hr); Glasgow (5 daily; 3hr 25min–4hr); Kyle of Lochalsh (3 daily; 2hr); Nairn (every 20–30min; 45min); Perth (7 daily; 2hr 50min); Portree (3 daily; 3hr 15min); Thurso (Mon–Sat 5 daily, Sun 3; 3hr); Ullapool (2–4 daily; 1hr 25min).
Tourist office Castle Wynd (July & Aug Mon–Sat 9am– 6.30pm, Sun 9.30am–6pm; outside peak season shorter hours; ☎ 01463 252401, ⊛ visitscotland.com).

ACCOMMODATION

Bazpackers 4 Culduthel Rd, IV2 4AB ☎ 01463 717663, ⊛ bazpackershostel.co.uk; map p.921. The most cosy and relaxed of the city's hostels, with more than thirty

beds, including three doubles and two twins. Good location in an 1826 townhouse, with great views and a garden that is used for barbecues. Dorms **£18**, doubles **£50**

23

CRUISES FROM INVERNESS

Inverness is the departure point for **day-tours** and **cruises** to nearby attractions like Loch Ness and the Moray Firth. **Loch Ness cruises** typically incorporate a visit to a monster exhibition at **Drumnadrochit** and **Urquhart Castle** – try Jacobite Cruises (from £32; ☎01463 233999, ⓦjacobite.co.uk) or **Cruise Loch Ness** (from £14.50; ☎01320 366277, ⓦcruiselochness.com).

Bught Caravan and Camping Site Bught Park, a mile south, IV3 5SR ☎01463 236920, ⓦinvernesscaravanpark. com; map p.921. Inverness's main campsite, on the west bank of the river near the sports centre. Good facilities, but can get crowded in peak season. Closed Nov–March. Per person **£10**

Furan Guest House 100 Old Edinburgh Rd, IV2 3HT ☎01463 712094, ⓦfuran.co.uk; map p.921. Good-value B&B a mile south of the centre, run by former hoteliers. There is a good choice of spotless rooms and a friendly resident cat. Book direct for the best rates. **£85**

Glenmoriston Town House Hotel 20 Ness Bank, IV2 4SF ☎01463 223777, ⓦglenmoristontownhouse.com; map p.921. A smart contemporary hotel by the riverside just a few minutes' walk from the town centre, with muted decor and good dining at *Contrast Brasserie*. **£181**

Inverglen Guest House 7 Abertarff Rd, IV2 3NW ☎01463 716350, ⓦinverglenguesthouse.co.uk; map p.921. Supremely cosy and colourful rooms in a handsome villa. Smoked Scottish salmon is on the breakfast menu, and they run photography workshops, with trips to nearby glens and castles (£180/day). **£95**

Loch Ness Country House Hotel 3 miles southwest of central Inverness, off A82 (Fort William Rd), IV3 8JN ☎01463 230512, ⓦlochnesscountryhousehotel. co.uk; map p.921. Luxurious country-house offering Modern Scottish food, fine wines and more than two hundred malts, as well as very comfortable and spacious rooms. **£86**

★ **Rocpool Reserve** Culduthel Rd, IV2 4AG ☎01463 240089, ⓦrocpool.com; map p.921. Just a 10min walk south of the castle, this acclaimed hotel and restaurant has minimal but luxurious rooms (white cotton bedsheets, subtle splashes of colour and jacuzzis in the high-end rooms), plus a swanky, French-inspired restaurant. **£270**

EATING

★ **Leakey's Bookshop** Church St, IV1 1EY ☎01463 239947; map p.921. Prise yourself away from the old books and maps at Scotland's largest used bookshop to enjoy a cup of tea or a warming bowl of soup (£3.30) in the upstairs café. Mon–Sat 10am–5.30pm.

The Mustard Seed 16 Fraser St, IV1 1DW ☎01463 220220, ⓦmustardseedrestaurant.co.uk; map p.921. Airy, welcoming restaurant with great-value Mediterranean-style lunches and tasty, à la carte dining (mains around £16). Daily noon–3pm & 5.30–10pm.

Number 27 27 Castle St, IV2 3DU ☎01463 241999, ⓦfacebook.com/number27inverness; map p.921. Skinny bar/restaurant with a wide range of beers (there's a new guest ale every Sun) and hearty main meals such as baked potato with haggis and whisky sauce (£4.95). Mon–

Sat noon till late, Sun 11am–11pm.

Rocpool Restaurant 1 Ness Walk, V3 5NE ☎01463 717274, ⓦrocpoolrestaurant.com; map p.921. Another of the city's excellent, smart-ish dining options, with a contemporary setting, attentive staff and deliciously rich food. Roast rump of lamb with rose harissa is £22.95. Mon–Sat noon–2.30pm & 5.45–10pm.

★ **Velocity** 1 Crown Ave, IV2 3NF ☎01463 419956, ⓦvelocitylove.co.uk; map p.921. A must for cycling enthusiasts (or anyone with a taste for good coffee and organic cakes), this café-cum-bicycle-workshop sits in a quiet and leafy part of town. They sell doorstep sandwiches (£4), have maps covering local cycling routes and run beer-tasting evenings. Mon–Wed, Fri & Sat 9am–5pm, Thurs 9am–9pm, Sun 11am–5pm.

DRINKING AND NIGHTLIFE

Blackfriars 93–95 Academy St, IV1 1LU ☎01463 233881, ⓦblackfriarshighlandpub.co.uk; map p.921. Lively pub, dating back to the late eighteenth century, where you can enjoy live folk or ceilidh music while supping a pint of real ale. Daily 11am–9pm.

Hootananny 67 Church St, IV1 1ES ☎01463 233651, ⓦhootananny.co.uk; map p.921. You can enjoy excellent

free ceilidhs (Sat 2.30–4.30pm) at this popular pub, plus real ale and simple bar meals (fish and chips £8.95). Mon–Thurs & Sun noon–1am, Fri & Sat noon–3am.

The Ironworks 122b Academy St, IV1 1LX ☎08717 894173, ⓦironworksvenue.com; map p.921. This large live venue is the place to come for touring bands, tribute acts, stand-up and the occasional club night.

ENTERTAINMENT

Eden Court Theatre Near the cathedral, IV3 5SA ☎01463 234234, ⓦeden-court.co.uk. A major arts

venue and hub for dance and theatrical performances in the Highlands. Hollywood films are also screened.

23

23

THE DOLPHINS OF THE MORAY FIRTH

The **Moray Firth**, a great wedge-shaped bay forming the eastern coastline of the Highlands, is one of just three areas of UK waters that support a resident population of **dolphins**. More than a hundred of these beautiful, intelligent marine mammals live in the estuary, the most northerly breeding-ground in Europe for this particular species – the bottle-nosed dolphin (*Tursiops truncatus*) – and you stand a good chance of spotting a few, either from the shore or a boat.

One of the best places in Scotland, if not in Europe, to look for them is **Chanonry Point**, on the Black Isle (see page 946) – a spit of sand protruding into a narrow, deep channel, where converging currents bring fish close to the surface, and thus the dolphins close to shore; a rising tide is the most likely time to see them. **Kessock Bridge**, a mile north of Inverness, is another prime dolphin-spotting location, or you can go all the way down to the beach at the small village of North Kessock, underneath the road bridge.

Several companies run dolphin-spotting **boat trips** around the Moray Firth. However, researchers claim that the increased traffic is causing the dolphins unnecessary stress. If you decide to go on a cruise to see the dolphins – and perhaps minke whales, porpoises, seals and otters – make sure the operator is a member of the Dolphin Space Programme's **accreditation scheme** (see ⓦ dolphinspace.org for a list). Trips (April–Oct) are very popular, so book well in advance.

The Cairngorms and Strathspey

Rising high in the heather-clad hills above remote Loch Laggan, forty miles south of Inverness, the **River Spey**, Scotland's second longest river, drains northeast towards the Moray Firth through one of the Highlands' most spellbinding valleys. Famous for its ancient forests, salmon fishing and ospreys, the area around the upper section of the river, known as **Strathspey**, is dominated by the sculpted **Cairngorms**, Britain's most extensive mountain massif, unique in supporting subarctic tundra on its high plateau. Outdoor enthusiasts flock to the area to take advantage of the superb hiking, watersports and winter snows, aided by good road and rail links from central Scotland and Inverness. A string of villages along the river provide useful bases for setting out into the wilder country, principal among them **Aviemore**.

Aviemore and around

AVIEMORE was first developed as a ski- and tourist resort in the mid-1960s and, over the years, fell victim to profiteering developers with scant regard for the needs of the local community. Although a facelift has removed some of the architectural eyesores of that era, the settlement remains dominated by a string of soulless shopping centres and sprawling housing estates surrounding a Victorian railway station. That said, Aviemore is well equipped with visitor facilities, and is the most convenient base for the Cairngorms.

Strathspey Steam Railway

Aviemore Station, Dalfaber Rd, PH22 1PY • July & Aug 3 daily; less regular service at other times; return trip 1hr 30min • £14.25 return • ⓣ 01479 810725, ⓦ strathspeyrailway.co.uk

The main attractions of Aviemore are its **outdoor pursuits**, though train enthusiasts are drawn to the restored **Strathspey Steam Railway**, which chugs the short distance (around ten miles) between Aviemore and Broomhill, just beyond Boat of Garten village.

Cairngorm Ski Area

Nine miles southeast of Aviemore, PH22 1RB • Ski season generally Dec–April, but varies depending on snowfall • ⓣ 01479 861261, ⓦ cairngormmountain.org • **Cairn Gorm Mountain Railway** Leaves from the base station by the Coire Cas car park • Daily every 20min:

May–Oct 10am–4.30pm; Nov–April 9am–4.30pm; last train up 4pm • £13.50 • **Ranger office** Accessed via the Coire Cas car park • Daily: April–Oct 8.30am–5pm; Nov–March 8.30am–4.30pm • Free • Buses from Aviemore wind past Inverdruie, stopping at the Coire Cas car park

Though it's on a tiny scale by continental European and North American standards, occasionally snow and sun coincide at the **Cairngorm Ski Area**, high above Loch Morlich in Glenmore Forest Park, to offer beginners and experts alike a great day on the pistes. The controversial (bitterly opposed by conservationists) **Cairn Gorm Mountain Railway**, a two-car funicular system, runs to the top of the Cairngorm Ski Area (3600ft), not far from the summit of Cairn Gorm mountain (4085ft). At the top is an exhibition/interpretation area and a café/restaurant giving spectacular views on clear days. There is no access beyond the confines of the top station unless you're embarking on a winter skiing trip or a guided walk; anyone wanting to explore the subarctic Cairngorm plateau has to trudge up from the car park at the bottom. The base station also houses a **ranger office** where you can find out about various trails, check the latest weather report and – on fine days between May and October – join guided walks.

23

RSPB Abernethy National Nature Reserve

12 miles northeast of Aviemore, PH25 3HA • **Reserve** Daily 24hr; **observation centre** April–Aug daily 10am–6pm • £5 • **Guided walks** Late May to early Aug Wed 9.30am; 3hr • £6 • ☎ 01479 831476, ⓦ rspb.org.uk • From Aviemore, cross the Spey then take the Grantown road; the reserve is signposted to the right

The **RSPB Abernethy National Nature Reserve**, on the northeastern edge of **Loch Garten**, is famous as the nesting site of the **osprey**. Having completely disappeared from Britain, a single pair of these exquisite white-and-brown raptors mysteriously reappeared in 1954 and built a nest in a tree half a mile or so from the loch; the birds are now well established here and elsewhere across the Highlands. The best time to visit is between April and August, when the RSPB opens an **observation centre**, complete with telescopes and CCTV monitoring the nest.

ARRIVAL AND INFORMATION

AVIEMORE AND AROUND

By train Aviemore's train station is on Grampian Rd, just south of the tourist office.

Destinations Edinburgh (6 daily; 3hr); Glasgow (5 daily; 2hr 50min); Inverness (Mon–Sat 12 daily, Sun 7; 35min).

By bus Buses depart from outside the train station.

Destinations Cairngorm ski area (hourly; 35min); Edinburgh (8 daily; 3–4hr); Glasgow (5 daily; 2hr 40min–3hr 20min); Grantown-on-Spey (Mon–Sat every 30min–1hr, Sun 4; 30min); Inverness (at least 11 daily; 45min).

Tourist office 7 The Parade, Grampian Rd (July & Aug Mon–Sat 9.30am–6.30pm, Sun 9.30am–6pm; outside peak season shorter hours; ☎ 01479 810930).

ACTIVITIES

Alvie Stables 5 miles south of Aviemore, near Kincraig, PH22 1NE (call Ingrid on ☎ 07831 495397, ⓦ alvie-estate.co.uk). Family-friendly riding centre set in superb countryside a short drive from Aviemore, offering 30min lessons and longer guided rides (£27/hr).

G2 Outdoor Plot 10, Dalfaber Industrial Estate, Aviemore, PH21 1NE ☎ 01540 651784, ⓦ g2outdoor. co.uk. The experts here provide tuition in the art of telemarking or ski touring (£220 for 3 people) and summer kayaking and canyoning trips.

Glenmore Lodge National Outdoor Training Centre East end of Loch Morlich, 8 miles east of Aviemore, PH22 1QZ ☎ 01479 861256, ⓦ glenmorelodge.org.uk. For a crash course in surviving Scottish winters, try a week at this superbly equipped and organized centre (complete with cosy après-ski bar). Winter and summer courses in hillwalking, mountaineering, alpine ski-mountaineering, avalanche awareness and much more.

Loch Insh Watersports Centre 6 miles up-valley near Kincraig, PH22 1RH ☎ 01540 651272, ⓦ lochinsh. com. Sailing, windsurfing and canoeing trips; also rents mountain bikes (£18/day) and boats for fishing, and offers accommodation.

Mountain Spirit 98 Grampian Rd, PH22 1RH ☎ 01479 811788, ⓦ bit.ly/mountainspiritaviemore. This friendly, well-stocked shop in Aviemore centre sells and rents out equipment from ski boots and poles to mountaineering gear. Daily 9am–5.30pm.

Rothiemurchus Estate Inverdruie, PH22 1QH ☎ 01479 810703, ⓦ rothiemurchus.net. Success is

CAIRNGORMS NATIONAL PARK

The **Cairngorms National Park** (ⓦcairngorms.co.uk) covers some 1500 square miles and incorporates the **Cairngorms massif**, the UK's largest mountainscape and only sizeable plateau over 2500ft. While Aviemore and the surrounding area is the main point of entry, particularly for those planning outdoor activities, it's also possible to access the eastern side of the park from both Deeside and Donside in Aberdeenshire. There are 52 summits higher than 2953ft in the park, as well as a quarter of Scotland's native woodland, and a quarter of the UK's threatened wildlife species. Vegetation ranges from one of the largest tracts of ancient **Caledonian pine and birch forest** remaining in Scotland at Rothiemurchus to subarctic tundra on the high plateau, where **alpine flora** such as starry saxifrage and the star-shaped pink flowers of moss campion peek out of the pink granite in the few months of summer when the ground is free of snow. **The bird of prey** you're most likely to see is the **osprey**, especially at Loch Garten's osprey observation centre (see above), or fishing on the lochs around Aviemore.

23

virtually guaranteed at their stocked rainbow trout-fishing loch. A 1hr lesson followed by an hour's fishing costs £49.
The Ski School Day Lodge, near the funicular railway base station in the Cairngorm Ski Area, PH22 1RB

ⓣ01479 811066, ⓦtheskischool.co.uk. A good bet for ski/board rental and lessons, not least because of its proximity to the funicular, which whizzes skiers up to the slopes. Courses mid-Dec to early April.

ACCOMMODATION

Aviemore Bunkhouse Dalfaber Rd, next to the Old Bridge Inn, PH22 1PU ⓣ01479 811181, ⓦaviemore-bunkhouse.com. A large modern place beside a cosy pub and walking distance from the station, with six- and eight-bed dorms, plus private rooms. Dorms £19, doubles £50
Glenmore Lodge 8 miles east of Aviemore, PH22 1QZ ⓣ01479 861256, ⓦglenmorelodge.org.uk. Specialist outdoor pursuits centre with excellent accommodation in en-suite twin rooms and self-catered lodges – guests can make use of the superb facilities, which include a pool, weights room, sauna and indoor climbing wall. Twins £83

Rothiemurchus Caravan Park Coylumbridge, 2 miles southeast of Aviemore, PH22 1QU ⓣ01479 812800, ⓦrothiemurchus.net. Relaxed site for tents and caravans, nestled among tall pine trees on the way to Loch Morlich. Per person £12
SYHA Aviemore 25 Grampian Rd, PH22 1PR ⓣ01479 810345, ⓦsyha.org.uk/where-to-stay/highlands/aviemore. Aviemore's large SYHA hostel, with its own bike store and drying room, has rather plain rooms but is within easy walking distance of the town centre. Dorms £26, twins £62

EATING AND DRINKING

★ **Mountain Café** 111 Grampian Rd, PH22 1RH ⓣ01479 812473, ⓦmountaincafe-aviemore.co.uk. Above the Cairngorm Mountain Sports shop in the centre of town, Kiwi-run *Mountain Café* is reasonably priced, serving an all-day menu of wholesome snacks and freshly prepared meals for around £10. Specializes in wheat- and gluten-free food. Mon, Thurs & Fri 8.30am–5pm, Sat & Sun 8.30am–5.30pm.

Old Bridge Inn Dalfaber Rd, PH22 1PU ⓣ01479 811137, ⓦoldbridgeinn.co.uk. Fire-warmed pub that hosts regular live music sessions and serves decent dinners; the menu includes Shetland hake with braised haricot and mussel *suquet* for £18. Mon–Thurs & Sun noon–midnight, Fri & Sat noon–1am; kitchen daily noon–3pm & 5.30–9pm.

The Great Glen

The **Great Glen**, a major geological faultline cutting diagonally across the Highlands from Fort William to Inverness, is the defining geographic feature of the north of Scotland. A huge rift valley was formed when the northwestern and southeastern sides of the fault slid in opposite directions for more than sixty miles, while the present landscape was shaped by glaciers that retreated only around 8000 BC. The glen is impressive more for its sheer scale than its beauty, but the imposing barrier of loch

nd mountain means that no one can travel into the northern Highlands without
assing through it. With the two major service centres of the Highlands at either end
t makes an obvious and rewarding route between the west and east coasts.

Of the Great Glen's four elongated lochs, the most famous is **Loch Ness**, home to
he mythical monster; lochs **Oich**, **Lochy** and **Linnhe** (the last of these a sea loch) are
ess renowned, though no less attractive. All four are linked by the Caledonian Canal.
The southwestern end of the Great Glen is dominated by **Fort William**, the second-
argest town in the Highland region. Situated at the heart of the Lochaber area, it's a
useful base and an excellent hub for outdoor activities. Dominating the scene to the
south is **Ben Nevis**, Britain's highest peak (4406ft), best approached from scenic **Glen
Nevis**. The most famous glen of all, **Glen Coe**, lies on the main A82, half an hour's
drive south of Fort William. Nowadays the whole area is unashamedly given over to
tourism, and Fort William is swamped by bus tours throughout the summer, but, as
ever in the Highlands, within a thirty-minute drive you can be totally alone.

Loch Ness

Twenty-three miles long, unfathomably deep, cold and often moody, **Loch Ness** is
bounded by rugged heather-clad mountains rising steeply from a wooded shoreline
with attractive glens opening up on either side. Its fame is based overwhelmingly on
its legendary inhabitant **Nessie**, the "Loch Ness monster", who ensures a steady flow of
hopeful visitors to the settlements dotted along the loch, in particular **Drumnadrochit**.
Nearby, the impressive ruins of **Urquhart Castle** – a favourite monster-spotting
location – perch atop a rock on the lochside and attract a deluge of bus parties in
summer. Almost as busy in high season is the village of **Fort Augustus**, at the more
scenic southwest tip of Loch Ness, where you can watch queues of boats tackling one
of the Caledonian Canal's longest flights of locks.

NESSIE

The world-famous **Loch Ness monster**, affectionately known as **Nessie** (and by aficionados
as *Nessiteras rhombopteryx*), has been a local celebrity for some time. The first mention of
a mystery creature crops up in St Adamnan's seventh-century biography of **St Columba**,
who allegedly calmed an aquatic animal that had attacked one of his monks. In 1934, the
Daily Mail published London surgeon R.K. Wilson's sensational photograph of the head and
neck of the monster peering up out of the loch, and the hype has hardly diminished since.
Encounters range from glimpses of ripples by anglers to the famous occasion in 1961 when
thirty hotel guests saw a pair of humps break the water's surface and cruise for about half a
mile before submerging.

Photographic evidence is showcased in the two monster exhibitions at Drumnadrochit, but
the most impressive images – including the famous black-and-white movie footage of Nessie's
humps moving across the water, and Wilson's original head and shoulders shot – have now
been exposed as fakes. Indeed, in few other places on earth has watching a rather lifeless and
often grey expanse of water seemed so compelling, or have floating logs, otters and boat
wakes been photographed so often and with such excitement. Yet while even high-tech
sonar surveys carried out over the past two decades have failed to come up with conclusive
evidence, it's hard to dismiss Nessie as pure myth. After all, no one yet knows where the
unknown layers of silt and mud at the bottom of the loch begin and end: best estimates say
the loch is more than 750ft deep, deeper than much of the North Sea, while others point
to the possibilities of underwater caves and undiscovered channels connected to the sea.
Technological advances have also expanded the scope for Nessie-watching: the slightly
barmy ⊚lochness.co.uk offers round-the-clock **webcams** for views across the loch, while
⊚lochnessinvestigation.org is packed with research information. The local tourist industry's
worst fear – dwindling interest – is about as unlikely as an appearance of the mysterious
monster herself.

Drumnadrochit and around

Situated above a verdant, sheltered bay of Loch Ness, fifteen miles southwest of Inverness, touristy **DRUMNADROCHIT** is the southern gateway to remote Glen Affric and the epicentre of Nessie hype, complete with a rash of tacky souvenir shops and two rival monster exhibitions.

Loch Ness Centre & Exhibition

On the main A82, IV63 6TU • Daily: Easter–June, Sept & Oct 9.30am–5pm; July & Aug 9.30am–6pm; Nov–Easter 10am–3.30pm • £7.95 • ☎ 01456 450573, ⊛ lochness.com

Of the two major monster hubs in Drumnadrochit (the other being the Nessieland Monster Centre), the **Loch Ness Centre & Exhibition** is the better bet, offering an in-depth rundown of eyewitness accounts and information on various Nessie research projects. It does a good job, mixing "evidence" of the monster's existence with frank appraisals of pictures and sightings that turned out to be hoaxes. **Nessie-spotting cruises** on the loch aboard *Deepscan* run from here; the *Nessie Hunter* can be booked at the nearby Nessieland Monster Centre.

Urquhart Castle

Beside Loch Ness, 2 miles southeast of Drumnadrochit and just off the A82, IV63 6XJ • Daily: April–Sept 9.30am–6pm; Oct 9.30am–5pm; Nov–March 9.30am–4.30pm • £9; HES • ☎ 01456 450551, ⊛ historicenvironment.scot/visit-a-place/places/urquhart-castle

Most photographs allegedly showing the monster have been taken a couple of miles southeast of Drumnadrochit, around the thirteenth-century ruined lochside **Urquhart Castle**. It's one of Scotland's classic picture-postcard ruins, crawling with tourists by day but particularly splendid when floodlit at night after the crowds have gone. In the small visitor centre, a short film highlights the turbulent history of the castle.

ARRIVAL AND INFORMATION

By bus Buses stop near the post office, on the A82. Destinations Fort Augustus (up to 10 daily; 35min); Fort William (up to 9 daily; 1hr 30min); Inverness (at least hourly; 30min).

DRUMNADROCHIT AND AROUND

Tourist information In the middle of the main car park (July & Aug Mon–Sat 9am–6pm, Sun 10am–4pm; outside peak season shorter hours; ☎ 01456 459086).

ACCOMMODATION AND EATING

The Benleva Kilmore Rd, Kilmore, IV63 6UH ☎ 01456 450080, ⊛ benleva.co.uk. Small, basic hotel in Kilmore, a 15min walk from the monster centres of Drumnadrochit, with six en-suite rooms. **£110**

Fiddlers' Just south of the village green on A82, IV63 6TU ☎ 01456 450678, ⊛ fiddledrum.co.uk. Busy, friendly bar with plenty of outside seating and, it's claimed, more than five hundred single malt whiskies. Meat-focused menu, with a couple of veggie options including a mushroom and brie burger (£12.95). Daily 12.30–2.30pm & 6–9pm.

Glenkirk B&B 330yd west of Nessieland Monster Centre along A831, IV63 6TZ ☎ 01456 450802, ⊛ loch nessbandb.com. Bright, friendly B&B in a former church just a few minutes' walk from the centre, with simple, smartly decorated bedrooms. **£95**

Loch Ness Backpackers Lodge Coiltie Farmhouse, Lewiston, 1 mile south of the centre of Drumnadrochit, IV63 6UJ ☎ 01456 450807, ⊛ lochness-backpackers. com. For a cheap bed, head for this immaculate and friendly hostel, which has dorms, rooms and good facilities including a bar and two lounges. Coming from Drumnadrochit, follow the signs to the left. Dorms **£20**, doubles **£52**

Glen Affric

A vast area of high peaks, remote glens and few roads lies west of Drumnadrochit, including **Glen Affric**, generally held as one of Scotland's most beautiful landscapes and heaven for walkers, climbers and mountain-bikers. The approach is through the small settlement of **CANNICH**, fourteen miles west of Drumnadrochit on the A831.

Hemmed in by a string of Munros, Glen Affric is great for picnics and pottering, particularly on a calm and sunny day, when the still water reflects the islands and surrounding hills. From the car park at the head of the singletrack road along the glen, ten miles southwest of Cannich, there's a selection of **walks**: the trail around Loch Affric will take you a good five hours but captures the glen, its wildlife and Caledonian pine and birch woods in all their remote splendour.

ARRIVAL AND DEPARTURE
GLEN AFFRIC

By bus From July to Sept, Ross's Minibuses (☎01463 761250, ⓦross-minibuses.co.uk) runs scheduled services to the car park at Glen Affric from Cannich (Mon, Wed & Fri 4 daily; 30min); Drumnadrochit (Mon, Wed & Fri 3 daily; 1hr 35min) and Inverness (Mon, Wed & Fri 2 daily; 2hr 10min). Its vehicles will also carry bikes if given notice.

ACCOMMODATION AND EATING

Cannich Caravan & Camping Park Cannich centre, IV4 7LN ☎01456 415364, ⓦhighlandcamping.co.uk. Mountain bikes can be rented (£17/day) at this pretty, shaded campsite; good facilities include a TV room. Camping pods available. Camping/person **£8.50**, pods **£34**

Fort Augustus

FORT AUGUSTUS, a tiny, busy village at the scenic southwestern tip of Loch Ness, was named after George II's son, the chubby lad who later became the "Butcher" Duke of Cumberland of Culloden fame; today, the village is dominated by comings and goings along the Caledonian Canal, which leaves Loch Ness here. From its berth near the swing bridge, **Cruise Loch Ness** (2 daily; 1hr; £14.50; ☎01320 366277, ⓦcruiselochness.com) sails five miles up Loch Ness, using sonar technology to provide impressive, live 3D imagery of the deep.

23

ARRIVAL AND INFORMATION
FORT AUGUSTUS

By bus Frequent buses ply the A82, linking Fort Augustus with Drumnadrochit (35min) and Inverness (1hr) to the north, and Fort William, 30 miles south (1hr).
Tourist office In the car park north of the canal (July & Aug Mon–Sat 9am–6pm, Sun 10am–4pm; outside peak season shorter hours; ☎01320 366779). Very helpful office, with useful maps of the Great Glen Way (see page 920) and free walking leaflets.

ACCOMMODATION

Corrie Liath Market Hill, 0.5 mile south of the centre along A82, PH32 4DS ☎01320 366409, ⓦcorrieliath. co.uk. Small, thoughtfully managed B&B whose comfortable rooms have books and DVDs for guests to enjoy. The garden has a barbecue hut for summer. **£75**

Morag's Lodge Bunoich Brae, on the Loch Ness side of town, PH32 4DG ☎01320 366289, ⓦwww.moragslodge. com. The atmosphere at this well-equipped hostel – with four- and six-bed dorms – livens up with the daily arrival of backpackers' minibus tours. Dorms **£24**, doubles **£60**

Fort William

With its stunning position on Loch Linnhe, tucked in below the snow-streaked bulk of Ben Nevis, the important regional centre of **FORT WILLIAM** (often known as "Fort Bill"), should be a gem. Sadly, the same lack of taste that nearly saw the town renamed "Abernevis" in the 1950s is evident in the ribbon bungalow development and dual carriageway – complete with grubby pedestrian underpass – that have wrecked the waterfront. The main street and the little squares off it are more appealing, though occupied by some decidedly tacky tourist giftshops. On Cameron Square, the idiosyncratic **West Highland Museum** (Jan–April & Oct–Dec Mon–Sat 10am–4pm; May, June & Sept Mon–Sat 10am–5pm; July & Aug Mon–Sat 10am–5pm, Sun 11am–5pm; free; ☎ 01397 702169, ⓦwesthighlandmuseum.org.uk) covers virtually every aspect of Highland life through traditional, well-done, exhibits.

ARRIVAL AND INFORMATION
FORT WILLIAM

By train Fort William is a stop on the scenic West Highland Railway from Glasgow. The train station is just across the A82 dual carriageway from the north end of the high street. **Destinations** Crianlarich (Mon–Sat 4 daily, Sun 3; 1hr 45min); Glasgow Queen St (4 daily; 3hr 45min); London (1 nightly; 12hr); Mallaig (4 daily; 1hr 20min).

By bus Intercity coaches from Glasgow and Inverness stop outside the train station on MacFarlane Way.
Destinations Drumnadrochit (9 daily; 1hr 25min); Edinburgh (1 daily; 4hr); Fort Augustus (9 daily; 50min); Glasgow (8 daily; 3hr); Inverness (Mon–Sat 9 daily, Sun 6; 2hr); Mallaig (Mon–Fri 3 daily; 1hr 20min); Oban (Mon–

Sat 3 daily; 1hr 30min); Portree, Skye (4 daily; 3hr).
Tourist office 15 High St (July & Aug Mon–Sat 9am–6.30pm, Sun 9am–6pm; outside peak season shorter hours; ☎01397 701801, ⓦvisitscotland.com). Busy and very helpful tourist office stocking an excellent selection of maps and guidebooks on the Great Glen.

ACCOMMODATION

Calluna Connochie Rd, PH33 6JX ☎01397 700451, ⓦfortwilliamholiday.co.uk. Well-run self-catering and hostel accommodation a 10min walk from the centre of town, configured for individual, family and group stays. Also has laundry facilities and a bouldering wall. The owners can also organize mountaineering trips. Dorms **£20**, doubles **£44**

Great Glen Yurts 3 miles northeast of Fort William off A82 (signposted from Torlundy), PH33 6SP ⓦgreat glenyurts.com. Rotund and spacious, these luxury yurts

occupy a magnificently peaceful setting with views of Ben Nevis. There's also a shepherd's hut and wooden cabins, and an open-sided kitchen that's great for sociable evening meals. Closed Nov–March. Shepherd's hut **£70**, yurts **£90**, cabins **£100**

★ **The Grange** Grange Rd, PH33 6JF ☎01397 705516, ⓦgrangefortwilliam.com. Top-grade accommodation in a striking old stone house, with log fires, views towards Loch Linnhe and luxurious en-suite doubles. Closed Nov–March. **£180**

EATING AND DRINKING

Crannog at the Waterfront Town pier, just off the bypass on entering Fort William, PH33 6DB ☎01397 705589, ⓦcrannog.net. Red-roofed restaurant with lochside views and fresh seafood, including Mallaig langoustine, plus a reasonable wine list (two-course lunch £15.95). The neighbouring shack sells super-cheap Cullen skink and oysters. Daily noon–2.30pm & 6–9pm.

Lime Tree Restaurant The Old Manse, Achintore Rd, PH33 6RQ ☎01397 701806, ⓦlimetreefortwilliam. co.uk. This restaurant serves an excellent selection of contemporary Scottish food; moorland pheasant breast, say (£19.95). They also have rooms (from £100). Daily 6–9pm.

Glen Nevis

A ten-minute drive south of Fort William, **GLEN NEVIS** is among the Highlands' most impressive glens: a U-shaped glacial valley hemmed in by steep bracken-covered slopes and swathes of blue-grey scree. Herds of shaggy Highland cattle graze the valley floor, where a sparkling river gushes through glades of trees.

A great **low-level walk** (six miles round-trip) runs from the far end of the road at the top of Glen Nevis. The rocky path leads through a dramatic gorge with impressive falls and rapids, then opens out into a secret hanging valley, carpeted with wild flowers and featuring a high waterfall at the far end. Of all the walks in and around Glen Nevis, however, the **ascent of Ben Nevis** (4406ft), Britain's highest summit, inevitably attracts the most attention. Despite the fact that it's quite a slog up to the summit, and it's by no means the most attractive mountain in Scotland, in high summer the trail is teeming with hikers, whatever the weather. It can snow round the summit any day of the year, so take the necessary precautions; in winter, of course, the mountain should be left to the experts. The most obvious **route** to the summit, a Victorian pony path up the whaleback south side of the mountain, built to service the observatory that once stood on the top, starts from the helpful **Glen Nevis Visitor Centre** (see below): allow a full day for the climb (8hr).

ARRIVAL AND INFORMATION   GLEN NEVIS

By bus Bus #42 runs from the high street in Fort William, past the Glen Nevis Visitor Centre, campsite and SYHA hostel to the Lower Falls car park (2 daily; 25min) 3 miles up the Glen Nevis road.

Glen Nevis Visitor Centre 1.5 miles southeast of Fort William along the Glen Nevis road (daily 8.30am–6pm; ☎01397 705922). Staff can give good advice on climbing the mountain; grab a free leaflet.

THE NEVIS RANGE

Seven miles northeast of Fort William by the A82, on the slopes of **Aonach Mòr**, one of the high mountains abutting Ben Nevis, the **Nevis Range** (T 01397 705825, W nevis-range.co.uk) is Scotland's highest winter ski area. Bus #41 runs from Fort William (Mon–Sat 4 daily, Sun 2 daily) to the base station of the country's only **gondola** system (daily: Easter–June, Sept & Oct 10am–5pm; July & Aug 9.30am–6pm; early Nov & late Dec–Easter 9am–sunset; £14 return). The 1.5-mile gondola trip, rising 2000ft, gives an easy approach to some high-level walking as well as spectacular views from the terrace of the self-service restaurant at the top station. From the top of the gondola station, you can experience Britain's only World-Cup-standard **downhill mountain-bike course** (mid-May to mid-Sept 10.15am–3.45pm; £14.50 includes gondola one way), a hair-raising 3km route that's not for the faint-hearted. There are also 25 miles of waymarked off-road bike routes, known as the Witch's Trails (open all year), on the mountainside and in the Leanachan Forest, ranging from gentle paths to cross-country scrambles. At the entrance to the lower gondola station, Nevis Cycles (daily 9am–5.30pm; T 01397 705825, W neviscycles.com/bike-hire) rents general mountain bikes (from £30) as well as full-suspension models for the downhill course.

ACCOMMODATION AND EATING

★ **Ben Nevis Inn** Achintee, across the river from the visitor centre, PH33 6TE T 01397 701227, W ben-nevis-inn.co.uk. A basic and cosy bunkhouse (booking advised) in the basement of a lively 250-year-old pub at the start of the Ben Nevis footpath. The pub has a terrific atmosphere, and the menu – with ale-battered North Sea haddock for £11.50 – is especially tempting after a day on the mountain. Daily noon–11pm; kitchen noon–9pm. £17

SYHA Glen Nevis 1 mile past the visitor centre along the Glen Nevis road, PH33 6SY T 01397 702336, W syha.org.uk/where-to-stay/highlands/glen-nevis. This friendly hostel is an excellent base for walkers and has full catering, as well as a decent kitchen. It gets very busy in summer, so book ahead. Dorms £24, doubles £62

Glen Coe

Sixteen miles south of Fort William on the A82, breathtakingly beautiful **Glen Coe** (literally "Valley of Weeping") is the best known of the Highland glens: a spectacular mountain valley between velvety-green conical peaks, their tops often wreathed in cloud, their flanks streaked by cascades of rock and scree. In 1692 it was the site of a notorious massacre, in which the MacDonalds were victims of a long-standing government desire to suppress the clans. When clan chief **Alastair MacDonald** missed the deadline of January 1, 1692, to sign an oath of allegiance to William III, a plot was hatched to make an example of "that damnable sept". **Campbell of Glenlyon** was ordered to billet his soldiers in the homes of the MacDonalds, who for ten days entertained them with traditional Highland hospitality. In the early morning of February 13, the soldiers turned on their hosts, slaying between 38 and 45, and causing more than three hundred to flee.

Beyond the small village of **GLENCOE** at the western end of the glen, the glen itself (a property of the National Trust for Scotland since the 1930s) is virtually uninhabited, and provides outstanding climbing and walking.

ARRIVAL AND INFORMATION — GLEN COE

By bus To get to the NTS visitor centre or chairlift station from Fort William's bus station, hop on one of the Glasgow-bound Scottish Citylink coaches (up to 8 daily; 30–45min). Bus #44 from Fort William also stops at least 8 times a day (4 on Sun) at Glencoe village en route to Kinlochleven.

Tourist information The NTS visitor centre is a mile southeast of Glencoe village, with a balanced account of the massacre that took place here (Feb–Easter & Nov–Jan Thurs–Sun 10am–4pm; Easter–Oct daily 9.30am–5.30pm; T 01855 811307, W nts.org.uk). Book ahead for guided walks (Easter & June–Sept; £6.50).

ACCOMMODATION AND EATING

★ **Clachaig Inn** 2.5 miles south of Glencoe on the minor road off A82, PH49 4HX ☎ 01855 811252, ⓦ clachaig.com. The liveliest, best-known hotel in the area is a great place to reward your exertions with cask-conditioned ales and heaped plates of food (Highland game pie, perhaps, for £13.95); they also have 23 comfy en-suite rooms. Mon–Thurs & Sun 8am–11pm, Fri 8am–midnight, Sat 8am–11.30pm. £55

Glencoe Independent Hostel North of the river, PH49 4HX ☎ 01855 811906, ⓦ glencoehostel.co.uk.

Cheap and excellent independent hostel and bunkhouse in rustic whitewashed buildings, offering hot showers and a laundry service. £14

Red Squirrel 150m south of the turn-off to Glencoe Independent Hostel, PH49 4HX ☎ 01855 811256, ⓦ redsquirrelcampsite.co.uk. Sylvan year-round campsite just south of the SYHA hostel on the road to *Clachaig Inn*. Campfires and pets permitted. £12

The west coast

23

The Highlands' starkly beautiful **west coast** – stretching from the **Morvern peninsula** (opposite Mull) in the south to wind-lashed **Cape Wrath** in the far north – is arguably the finest part of Scotland. Serrated by fjord-like sea lochs, the long coastline is scattered with windswept white-sand beaches, cliff-girt headlands and rugged mountains sweeping up from the shoreline. When the sun shines, the sparkle of the sea, the richness of colour and the clarity of the views out to the scattered Hebrides are simply irresistible. This is the least populated part of Britain, with just two small towns and yawning tracts of moorland and desolate peat bog between crofting settlements.

Within easy reach of Inverness, the popular stretch of the coast between Kyle of Lochalsh and Ullapool features the region's more obvious highlights: the awe-inspiring mountainscape of **Torridon**, **Gairloch**'s sandy beaches, the famous botanic gardens at **Inverewe** and **Ullapool** itself, a picturesque and bustling fishing town from where ferries leave for the Outer Hebrides. However, press on further north, or south, and you'll get a truer sense of the isolation that makes the west coast so special. Traversed by few roads, the remote northwest corner of Scotland is wild and bleak, receiving the full force of the North Atlantic's frequently ferocious weather. The scattered settlements of the far southwest, meanwhile, tend to be more sheltered, but they are separated by some of the most extensive wilderness areas in Britain – lonely peninsulas with evocative Gaelic names like **Ardnamurchan** and **Knoydart**.

GETTING AROUND
THE WEST COAST

By car Without your own vehicle, transport can be a problem. Driving is much simpler: the roads aren't busy, though they are frequently singletrack and scattered with sheep.

By train There's a direct train from Inverness to Kyle of Lochalsh and from Fort William to Mallaig.

By bus D&E Coaches offers a useful summer-only bike-carrying Inverness–Durness bus service via Ullapool and Lochinver (May & June Mon & Thurs–Sun; July–Sept Mon–Sat; ☎ 01463 222444).

The "Rough Bounds"

The remote and sparsely populated southwest corner of the Highlands, from the empty district of **Morvern** to the isolated peninsula of **Knoydart**, is a dramatic, lonely region of mountain and moorland fringed by a rocky, indented coast whose stunning white beaches enjoy wonderful views to Mull, Skye and other islands. Its Gaelic name, *Garbh-chiochan*, translates as the "**Rough Bounds**", implying a region geographically and spiritually apart. Even if you have a car, you should spend some time here exploring on foot; there are so few roads that some determined hiking is almost inevitable.

Ardnamurchan peninsula

A nine-mile drive south of Fort William down Loch Linnhe, the five-minute ferry crossing at **Corran Ferry** (every 20–30min; Mon–Sat 6.30am–9.30pm, Sun 8.45am– 9.30pm; car £8.20; foot passengers and bicycles free) provides the most direct point of entry for Morvern and the rugged **Ardnamurchan peninsula**. The most westerly point on the British mainland, the peninsula lost most of its inhabitants during the infamous Clearances and is now sparsely populated, with just a handful of tiny croftin settlements clinging to its jagged coastline. It boasts some beautiful, pristine, empty beaches – especially about three miles north of the **Ardnamurchan Lighthouse** at Sanna Bay, a shell-strewn strand and series of dunes that offers unforgettable vistas of the Small Isles to the north, circled by gulls, terns and guillemots. The coastal hamlet of **Salen** marks the turn-off for Ardnamurchan Point: from here it's a further 25 miles of slow, scenic driving along the singletrack road which follows the northern shore of Loch Sunart. **Kilchoan**, a modest crofting settlement that straggles along the Sound of Mull, is Ardnamurchan's main village.

23

ARRIVAL AND DEPARTURE

ARDNAMURCHAN PENINSUL

By ferry A CalMac (ⓦ calmac.co.uk) car ferry operates between Tobermory (Mull) and Kilchoan (Mon–Sat 7 daily, plu May–Aug Sun 5 daily; 35min).

ACCOMMODATION

★ **Ardnamurchan Campsite** Ormsaigbeg, 0.5 mile beyond the Ferry Stores, PH36 4LL ☎ 01972 510766, ⓦ ardnamurchanstudycentre.co.uk. Cracking views and campfires on the beach at this laudably back-to-basics

campsite behind the loch – pure magic at sunset an usually spared summer midges by a breeze. Closed Oct Easter. Per person **£9**

The Road to the Isles

The "**Road to the Isles**" (ⓦ road-to-the-isles.org.uk) from Fort William to Mallaig, followed by the West Highland Railway and the narrow, winding A830, traverses the mountains and glens of the Rough Bounds before breaking out onto a spectacularly scenic coast of sheltered inlets, white beaches and wonderful views to the islands of Rùm, Eigg, Muck and Skye. The area is associated with **Bonnie Prince Charlie**, whose adventures of 1745–46 began and ended on this stretch of coast with his first, defiant gathering of the clans at **Glenfinnan**, nineteen miles west of Fort William at the head o lovely **Loch Shiel**.

Glenfinnan

Glenfinnan Monument , PH37 4LT • Daily: April–June, Sept & Oct 10am–5pm; July & Aug 9.30am–5pm • £3.50; NTS • ☎ 01397 722250, ⓦ nts.org.uk/Visit/Glenfinnan-Monument

GLENFINNAN is a poignant place, a beautiful stage for the opening scene in a brutal drama that was to change the Highlands forever. One of Scotland's most iconic structures, the 60ft **Glenfinnann Monument** is crowned with a Highland clansman in full battle dress. The **visitor centre** (with café) opposite gives an account of the 1745 uprising through to the rout at **Culloden** eight months later (see page 920). Nowadays just as many visitors come to see the imposing arched viaduct nearby, crossed by the *Hogwarts Express* in the *Harry Potter* films.

ACCOMMODATION AND EATING

GLENFINNA

Sleeping Car Glenfinnan station, PH37 4LT ☎ 01397 722295, ⓦ glenfinnanstationmuseum.co.uk. A restored 1958 train coach is now a (very) mini-bunkhouse with three twin compartments (bunk beds), a family compartment

and a kitchen, lounge and bathroom. The adjacent *Dinin Car* is open for light meals, and the owners also run th neighbouring Station Museum. April–Sept daily 9am 5pm; phone ahead for evening meals. Per person **£15**

Arisaig

ARISAIG, scattered round a sandy bay at the west end of the Morar peninsula, makes a good base for exploring the coast. A **bypass** whizzes cars (and, more importantly, fish lorries) on their way to Mallaig, but you shouldn't miss the slower "Alternative Coastal Route", which runs alongside a string of stunning **beaches** backed by flowery machair, with barren granite hills and moorland rising up behind and wonderful seaward views of Eigg and Rùm.

Mallaig

MALLAIG, 47 miles west of Fort William, is seen as somewhere to go through, not to. Before the railway arrived in 1901 it consisted of a few cottages. Now, as the main embarkation point for ferries to Skye, the Small Isles and Knoydart, it's full of visitors in season. While not especially pretty, it is a solid town given a workaday honesty by its local **fishing** industry – it once had one of Europe's busiest herring ports and the harbour remains the source of its wealth.

ARRIVAL AND DEPARTURE
MALLAIG

23

By ferry The CalMac ticket office (☎01687 462403), serving passengers for Skye and the Small Isles, is near the tourist office on the harbour. Car reservations are essential in peak season. For Knoydart, Western Isles Cruises (☎01687 462233, ⓦ westernislescruises.co.uk) sails to Inverie, on the Knoydart peninsula. Times listed are for peak season (April–Oct); check online for reduced winter timetables.

Destinations Armadale, Skye (Mon–Sat 8 daily, Sun 6; 30min); Canna (Mon, Wed & Fri–Sun 1 daily; 2hr 30min); Eigg (Mon, Thurs, Sat & Sun 1 daily; 1hr 15min); Inverie (April–Oct Mon–Fri 5 daily, Sat 4, Sun 3; 25–40min); Muck (Tues & Thurs–Sun 1 daily; 1hr 40min–2hr); Rùm (Mon, Wed & Fri–Sun 1 daily; 1hr 20min).

ACCOMMODATION AND EATING

Cornerstone Main St, PH41 4PU ☎01687 462306, ⓦ seafoodrestaurantmallaig.com. This simple first-floor restaurant is the locals' choice for classic seafood – expect a daily soup and a menu of fresh fish, simply but excellently prepared and fairly priced at around £11–25. March to mid-Oct daily noon–2.45pm & 4.45–9pm.

Mallaig Backpackers Main St, PH41 4PU ☎01687 462764, ⓦ mallaigbackpackers.co.uk. There are two mixed dorms, a small kitchen and a lounge in this relaxed, independent modern hostel. "Reception" is in the *Tea Garden* restaurant opposite the harbour. **£20**

Seaview Main St, PH41 4QS ☎01687 462059, ⓦ seaviewguesthousemallaig.com. Snug dimensions and surprisingly smart decor – with a leaning towards modest boutique – set the tone in this central B&B with harbour views from the front. Closed Nov–Feb. **£80**

Knoydart peninsula

Flanked by **Loch Nevis** ("Loch of Heaven") in the south and the fjord-like inlet of **Loch Hourn** ("Loch of Hell") to the north, **Knoydart peninsula**'s knobbly green peaks – three of them Munros – sweep straight out of the sea, shrouded for much of the time in a pall of grey mist. To get to the heart of the peninsula, you must catch a **boat** from Mallaig, or else **hike** for a couple of days across rugged moorland and mountains and sleep rough in old stone bothies (most of which are marked on Ordnance Survey maps).

At the end of the eighteenth century, around a thousand people eked out a living from this inhospitable terrain through crofting and fishing. These days the peninsula supports around seventy, most of whom live in the hamlet of **INVERIE**. Nestled beside a sheltered bay on the south side of the peninsula, it has a pint-sized post office, a shop and mainland Britain's most remote pub.

ARRIVAL AND DEPARTURE
KNOYDART PENINSULA

By ferry Western Isles Cruises (☎01687 462233, ⓦ westernislescruises.co.uk) sails to Inverie from Mallaig (April–Oct Mon–Fri 5 daily, Sat 4, Sun 3; 25–40min).

ACCOMMODATION AND EATING

Knoydart Foundation Bunkhouse 0.5 mile east of Inverie pier, PH41 4PL ☎01687 462163, ⓦknoydart-foundation.com. The community hostel is on an old farm near Long Beach. Dorms are large, facilities include a kitchen and laundry, and a comfy lounge with a woodburner. **£18**

★ **The Old Forge** Inverie, PH41 4PL ☎01687 462267, ⓦtheoldforge.co.uk. Britain's most isolated pub remains one of Scotland's finer boozers, fuelled by a convivial atmosphere and wonderful sense of remoteness. The menu is all about the seafood, including hand-dived seared Loch Nevis scallops for £19.95. Easter–Oct Mon, Tues & Thurs–Sun noon–midnight.

Kyle of Lochalsh and around

As the main gateway to Skye, **KYLE OF LOCHALSH** used to be an important transit point for tourists and locals. However, with the building of the **Skye Bridge** in 1995, Kyle was left as merely the terminus for the train route from Inverness, with little else to offer. Of more interest is nearby **Eilean Donan Castle**, perched at the end of a stone causeway on the shores of **Loch Duich**. A few miles north of Kyle of Lochalsh is the delightful village of **Plockton**, a refreshing alternative to its utilitarian neighbour, with cottages grouped around a yacht-filled bay and Highland cattle wandering the streets.

ARRIVAL AND DEPARTURE

KYLE OF LOCHALSH

By train It's a glorious journey from Inverness to Kyle of Lochalsh (Mon–Sat 4 daily, Sun 2; 2hr 35min); trains stop at Plockton (15min from Kyle) en route.
By bus Reservations are recommended for all services (☎0870 550 5050, ⓦcitylink.co.uk). Buses stop on the waterfront at the old slipway.
Destinations Fort William (7 daily; 1hr 55min); Glasgow (daily; 5hr 15min); Inverness (8 daily; 2hr); Kyleakin, Skye (6 daily; 5min).

Eilean Donan Castle

Beside A87 near the village of Dornie, IV40 8DX • Daily: Feb–Easter 10am–4pm; Easter–Oct 10am–6pm; Nov & Dec 10am–4pm • £7.50 • ☎01599 555202, ⓦeileandonancastle.com

After Edinburgh's fortress, **Eilean Donan Castle** has to be the most photographed monument in Scotland. The forbidding crenellated tower rises from the water's edge, joined to the shore by a narrow stone bridge and with sheer mountains as a backdrop. The original castle was established in 1230 by Alexander II to protect the area from the Vikings. Later, during a Jacobite uprising in 1719, it was occupied by troops dispatched by the king of Spain to help the "**Old Pretender**", James Stuart. However, when King George heard of their whereabouts, he sent frigates to take the Spaniards out, and the castle was blown up with their stocks of gunpowder. Thereafter, it lay in ruins until John Macrae-Gilstrap had it rebuilt between 1912 and 1932. Three floors, including the banqueting hall, the bedrooms and the troops' quarters, are open to the public, with various Jacobite and clan relics also on display. You can also see one of the few working portcullises in Scotland in action (10.45am & 2.45pm).

Plockton

At the seaward end of islet-studded Loch Carron lies the unbelievably picturesque village of **PLOCKTON**: a chocolate-box row of neatly painted cottages ranged around the curve of a tiny harbour and backed by a craggy landscape of heather and pine. It's packed in high season with yachties – a popular regatta fills the bay over a fortnight from late July – artsy second-home owners with easels in tow, and visiting families squelching over the seabed at low tide to take a turn around the small island.

ARRIVAL AND DEPARTURE

PLOCKTON

By train Trains from Inverness stop in Plockton (2hr 20min; Mon–Sat 4 daily, Sun 2) before continuing on to Kyle of Lochalsh (15min).

ACCOMMODATION AND EATING

Plockton Hotel 41 Harbour St, IV52 8TN ☎01599 544274, ⓦplocktonhotel.co.uk. This friendly, small hotel has rooms with cosy, contemporary-cottage decor – the best come with a view at the front. A four-room annexe on the harbour appeals for its shared kitchen as much as its cheaper rates (which still include breakfast). There's a well-stocked pub downstairs, with a grassy beer garden overlooking the bay. Pub daily noon–midnight; kitchen Mon–Sat noon–2.15pm & 6–9pm, Sun 12.30–2.15pm

& 6–9pm. Annexe £90, doubles £140

Plockton Shores 30 Harbour St, IV52 8TN ☎01599 544263. Metropolitan-styled café-restaurant that starts the day as a relaxed coffee and lunch stop, then shifts up a gear for Modern Scottish dishes like scallops in a lime, ginger and honey glaze (£15.95). Rotating exhibitions of local art adorn the walls. Tues–Sat 5.30–9pm, Sun 5.30–9pm; closed Tues in winter.

Wester Ross

The western seaboard of the old county of Ross-shire, **Wester Ross** blends all the classic elements of Scotland's **coastal scenery** – dramatic mountains, sandy beaches, whitewashed crofting cottages and shimmering island views – in spectacular fashion. Though popular with generations of adventurous Scottish holiday-makers, only one or two places feel blighted by tourist numbers, with places such as **Applecross** and the peninsulas north and south of **Gairloch** maintaining an endearing simplicity and sense of isolation. There's some tough but wonderful **hiking** in the mountains around **Torridon** and **Coigach**, while **boat trips** out among the islands and the prolific sea- and birdlife of the coast are another draw. The main settlement is the attractive fishing town of **Ullapool**, port for ferry services to Stornoway in the Western Isles, but a pleasant enough place to use as a base, not least for its active social and cultural scene.

23

Applecross peninsula

The most dramatic approach to the **Applecross peninsula** (the English-sounding name is a corruption of the Gaelic *Apor Crosan*, meaning "estuary") is from the south, up a glacial U-shaped valley and over the infamous **Bealach na Bà** (literally "Pass of the Cattle"). Crossing the forbidding hills behind Kishorn, and rising to 2053ft, with a gradient and switchback bends worthy of the Alps, this route – a popular cycling piste – is hair-raising in places, and the panoramic views across the Minch to Raasay and Skye augment the experience.

Applecross

The sheltered, fertile coast around **APPLECROSS** village, where the Irish missionary monk Maelrhuba founded a monastery in 673 AD, comes as a surprise after the bleakness of the moorland approach. Maybe it's the journey, but Applecross feels like an idyllic place: you can wander along lanes banked with wild iris and orchids, and explore beaches and rock pools on the shore.

Loch Torridon

Loch Torridon marks the northern boundary of the Applecross peninsula, its awe-inspiring setting enhanced by the appealingly rugged mountains of **Liathach** and **Beinn Eighe**, hulks of reddish 750-million-year-old Torridonian sandstone tipped by streaks of white quartzite. Some 15,000 acres of the massif are under the protection of the National Trust for Scotland, you can learn about the local geology, flora and fauna at their **Countryside Centre**, by Torridon village at the head of the loch (Easter–Oct Sun–Fri 10am–5pm; free).

ARRIVAL AND DEPARTURE

APPLECROSS PENINSULA

By bus Lochcarron Garage (☎01520 722205) operates a twice-weekly service from Applecross to Inverness (Wed & Sat; full journey 3hr 15min), with stop-offs in Lochcarron,

Shieldaig and Kishorn. Services skirt the southern edge of Loch Torridon and stop off at Achnasheen. Book ahead.

23

ACCOMMODATION AND EATING

★ **Applecross Inn** On the waterfront, Applecross, IV54 8LR ☎01520 744262, ⓦapplecross.uk.com/inn. This old, family-run inn beside the sea has rooms upstairs, and a lively bar that serves divine seafood including Applecross Bay prawns (£22) or king scallops (£18). Outside, the *Applecross Innside Out* food cart serves quality fish and chips and ice cream in summer. Reservations recommended in season. Daily noon–11pm; kitchen noon–9pm. **£130**

Applecross Walled Garden Signposted northeast of the bay, Applecross, IV54 8ND ☎01520 744440, ⓦapplecrossgarden.co.uk. Head here to enjoy delicious food in the laidback atmosphere of a Victorian walled garden. Try the decent full Scottish breakfasts (£10) or generous slices of divine home-made cake; evenings see

the likes of bouillabaisse (£20) and chickpea, feta and spinach parcels (£12). March–Oct daily 8.30am–8.30pm

SYHA Torridon Torridon village, 100yd northwest of junction with A896, IV22 2EZ ☎01445 791284, ⓦsyha.org.uk/where-to-stay/highlands/torridon. Though the Seventies-vintage municipal building is no looker, this hostel is spacious and a popular choice with hikers and bikers thanks to its location beneath the peaks. Kitchen, laundry and drying room, plus very cheap meals daily. Closed three weeks in Jan. Dorms **£21.50**, twins **£55**

Torridon Hotel On the A896, 1.5 miles south of Torridon village, IV22 2EY ☎01445 791242, ⓦthetorridon.com. hotel. On the south side of Loch Torridon stands one of the area's grandest hotels, a smart, rambling Victorian building set amid well-tended lochside grounds. **£265**

Loch Maree

About eight miles north of Loch Torridon, **Loch Maree**, dotted with Caledonian pine-covered islands, is one of the west's scenic highlights. It's best visited by car and viewed from the A832 road that skirts the loch's southern shore, passing the **Beinn Eighe Nature Reserve**, the UK's oldest wildlife sanctuary. Parts of the reserve are forested with Caledonian pinewood, which once covered the whole of the country, and it is home to pine martens, wildcats, buzzards and golden eagles. A mile north of Kinlochewe, the well-run **Beinn Eighe Visitor Centre** (March–Oct daily 10am–5pm) on the A832, offers excellent information on the area's rare species.

Gairloch and around

GAIRLOCH spreads around the northeastern corner of the wide sheltered bay of Loch Gairloch. During the summer, Gairloch thrives as a low-key holiday resort, with several tempting sandy beaches and excellent coastal walks within easy reach. The main supermarket and **tourist office** (see page 939) are in Achtercairn, right by the **Gairloch Heritage Museum** (Easter–Oct Mon–Fri 10am–5pm, Sat 11am–3pm; £4), which has eclectic, appealing displays covering geology, archeology, fishing and farming.

The Gairloch coast

The area's main attraction is its beautiful **coastline**, easily explored on a wildlife-spotting **cruise**: several operators, including Gairloch Marine Life Centre & Cruises (Easter–Oct 3 daily; ☎01445 712636, ⓦporpoise-gairloch.co.uk; from £20), run informative and enjoyable trips across the bay from Gairloch in search of dolphins, seals and even the odd whale. One of the most impressive stretches of coastline is around the north side of the bay, along the singletrack B8021, at **BIG SAND**, which has a cleaner and quieter beach than Gairloch. Three miles beyond stands the **Rubha Reidh lighthouse**.

Three miles south of Gairloch, a narrow singletrack lane winds west to **BADACHRO**, a sleepy former fishing village in a very attractive setting with a wonderful **pub**. Beyond Badachro, the road winds for five more miles along the shore to **REDPOINT**, a straggling hamlet with beautiful beaches of peach-coloured sand and great views to Raasay, Skye and the Western Isles.

Inverewe Gardens

Half a mile north of Poolewe on A832, IV22 2LG • **Gardens** Daily: Jan–March & Oct–Dec 10.30am–4pm; April 10.30am–5pm; May–Aug 9.30am–5.30pm; Sept 10am–5pm • **Visitor Centre** Daily: April 10.30am–5pm; May–Aug 9.30am–5.30pm; Sept 10am–5pm; Oct 10.30am–4pm • **House** April–Oct daily 11am–4pm • £10.50; NTS • ☎0844 493 2225, ⓦnts.org.uk/Visit/Inverewe

Most visitors arrive in Poolewe for **Inverewe Gardens**, a subtropical-style oasis of foliage that is riotously colourful compared to the wild coast. A network of paths and walkways wanders through more than a dozen gardens featuring exotic plant collections from as far afield as Chile, China, Tasmania and the Himalayas. Free **guided walks** set off from the visitor centre, and *Osgood's* and the *Bothy Café* serve refreshments. Visitors can also explore the opulent **Inverewe House** and the Sawyer Gallery, which hosts exhibitions on the gardens and the surrounding area of Wester Ross.

ARRIVAL AND INFORMATION

By bus Public transport is minimal and requires careful planning. Bus stops for all services are at the *Old Inn*, Charlestown, as well as Achtercairn and Strath.
Destinations Inverness (Mon–Sat 1 daily; also ScotBus June–Sept Mon–Sat 1 daily; 2hr 45min); Poolewe (Mon,

GAIRLOCH AND AROUND

Wed & Sat 1 daily; 15min); Ullapool (Mon, Wed, Thurs & Sat 1 daily; 1hr 10min).
Tourist information In the community centre, Gale Centre, in Achtercairn (Mon–Sat 9.30am–6pm, Sun 10.30am–5pm; ☎01445 712071, ⓦgaleactionforum.co.uk).

ACCOMMODATION AND EATING

Gairloch has a good choice of accommodation, but you might prefer to stay out along the road north to **Melvaig** or south to **Redpoint** (see page 938).

★ **Badachro Inn** Badachro, IV21 2AA ☎01445 741255, ⓦbadachroinn.filmdesign.org.uk. Settle onto the terrace with a plate of fresh seafood (around £11–16) at this pub by the old harbour. Inside are real ales and around fifty malts. April–Oct Mon–Sat noon–midnight, Sun noon–11pm; Nov–March Wed–Sat noon–midnight, Sun noon–11pm; kitchen April–Oct Mon–Fri noon–3pm & 6–9pm, Sat & Sun noon–3pm; Nov–March Wed–Fri noon–3pm & 6–9pm, Sat & Sun noon–3pm.
Mountain Coffee Company Achtercairn, IV21 2BX ☎01445 712316. Here's an unusual find for a small Highlands town – a relaxed café with a global backpacker vibe. Try the coffees, mammoth scones and toasted bagels with fresh fillings, and check out the good on-site bookshop. Daily: Easter–Nov 9am–5.30pm; Dec–Easter Mon–Sat 10am–4pm.

Old Inn Charlestown, IV21 2BD ☎01445 712006. Flagstone floors and stone walls provide the character in this modernized coaching inn; posh-pub specials such as game casserole (£14.95), plus beers from the on-site microbrewery, provide the sustenance. Mains average £13. Easter–Nov daily 11am–11pm; kitchen 11am–9.30pm.
Sands Caravan and Camping B8021, 3.5 miles west of Gairloch, IV21 2DL ☎01445 712152, ⓦsandscaravanandcamping.co.uk. The best of the area's campsites, with pitches behind the dunes for sea views. Also rents "wigwams" – actually Scandi-style cabins, sleeping up to five, with a fire-pit. Laundry facilities, plus kayak and bike rental. The cosy on-site *Barn Café* serves brekkie, lunch and evening meals (reserve ahead). Closed Dec–Feb. Camping £19, wigwams £42

Ullapool

ULLAPOOL, northwest Scotland's principal centre of population, was founded at the height of the herring boom in 1788 by the British Fisheries Society, on a sheltered arm of land jutting into Loch Broom. The grid-plan town is still an important fishing centre, though the **ferry** link to Stornoway on Lewis (see page 966) ensures that in high season it's swamped with visitors. Though busy, Ullapool remains a hugely appealing place and a good base for exploring the northwest Highlands.

By day, Ullapool's attention focuses on the comings and goings of the ferry, fishing boats and smaller craft, while in the evening, yachts swing on the current, shops stay open late, and drinkers line the sea wall. In summer, trips head to the **Summer Isles** (see page 941).

The only formal attraction in town is the award-winning **Ullapool Museum**, in the old parish church on West Argyle Street (Easter–Oct Mon–Sat 11am–4pm; ☎01854 612987; £4), which provides an insight into life in a Highland community, including crofting, fishing, local religion and emigration.

23

ARRIVAL AND DEPARTURE

By bus Buses stop near Ullapool's ferry terminal and run to Durness (May, June & Sept Mon–Sat 1 daily; July & Aug 1 daily; 3hr) and Inverness (1–3 daily; 1hr 30min).

By ferry From the ferry dock along Shore St, CalMac (☎0870 565 0000, ⓦcalmac.co.uk) sails to Stornoway on Lewis (Mon–Sat 2 daily, Sun 1; 2hr 45min).

ACCOMMODATION

Broomfield Holiday Park West Shore St, IV26 2UT ☎01854 612020, ⓦbroomfieldhp.com; map p.940. Large, good-value campsite, conveniently located within walking distance of the harbour. It's exposed to the wind off Loch Broom, but offers great views and warm showers. **£15**

SYHA Ullapool Shore St, IV26 2UJ ☎01854 612254, ⓦyha.org.uk/where-to-stay/highlands/ullapool; map p.940. Busy hostel bang on the seafront, where prints and murals of seaside scenes add a cheerful holiday atmosphere. There are dorms of various sizes, doubles, twins, two lounges and laundry plus lots of good information about local walks. Closed Nov–March. Dorms **£20**, doubles **£45**

★**Tanglewood House** 1 mile south off A835, IV26 2TB ☎01854 612059, ⓦtanglewoodhouse.co.uk; map p.940. Charm and character in an extraordinary, curved house full of art and antiques. Rooms are individually furnished; the best (the Green Room), with a terrace to enjoy the position above Loch Broom, is worth its extra £14. Factor in a rocky beach beneath for a dip and this is a truly memorable stay. Closed Nov–April. **£96**

EATING

★**The Ceilidh Place** 14 West Argyle St, IV26 2TY ☎01854 612103, ⓦtheceilidhplace.com; map p.940. A popular spot for lunch, snacks and dinners – home-made burgers and fish casseroles, for example (£11.50–20) – in a pleasant bistro. They are famed for theri ceilidhs and music nights. Also has dorms (£23) and double rooms (£124). Daily 8am–1am.

The Seafood Shack West Argyle St, IV26 2TY ☎07876 142623, ⓦseafoodshack.co.uk; map p.940. Much-hyped new takeaway shack serving super-fresh, beautifully prepared seafood; from *moules marinières* (£4.50) to tempura monkfish bites (£8.50). Tues–Sat noon–8pm, Sun noon–3pm.

West Coast Delicatessen Argyle St, IV26 2UB ☎01854 613450; map p.940. Fine-food deli serving proper coffees, home-made hummus and fresh salads, tarts and cakes, plus unmissable "pakora Fridays". For a proper fry-up, the *Tea Store* over the road will do the job. Mon–Sat 8.30am–5pm.

DRINKING AND NIGHTLIFE

Ferry Boat Inn Shore St, IV26 2UJ ☎01854 612366; map p.940. Popular with locals and their dogs, the *FBI* remains a choice spot to swig a pint of ale at the lochside (midges permitting) and watch the boats. You can enjoy live music here and at sister pub *The Argyle* round the corner. Daily 11am–11pm.

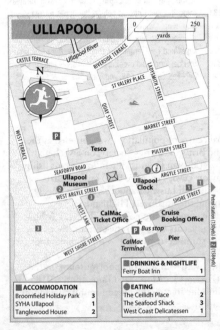

Assynt

If you've travelled to the northwest of Scotland and come as far as Ullapool, it's worth continuing further north into the ever more dramatic, remote and highly distinctive hills of **Assynt,** which marks the transition from Wester Ross into Sutherland. One of the least populated areas in Europe, this is a landscape not of mountain ranges but of extraordinary peaks rising from the moorland.

Kylesku

Until a road bridge swept over the mouth of lochs Glencoul and Glendhu, **KYLESKU**, 33 miles north of Ullapool, was the embarkation point for a ferry that was the only link from the west Highlands to north Scotland. Off the main road since the bridge's construction in 1984, it's now a beautiful, soporific spot, where interlocking slopes plunge into the deep waters. Marking a last hurrah before Assynt's sharp sandstone gives way to rounded quartzite, Kylesku is popular with walkers due to its proximity to **Quinag** (2651ft), less a single peak than several peaks reached by a **ridge walk**. The easiest ascent is from a car park on the A894 a few miles south of Kylesku. Also in the area is Britain's highest waterfall, **Eas a' Chual Aluinn** (650ft), at the head of **Loch Glencoul**. It's a five-mile return walk that heads east from a car park two miles south of Kylesku, or a full-day walk on a track around the north side of both lochs. Alternatively, boat tours run from the wharf in Kylesku.

INFORMATION AND ACTIVITIES KYLESKU

Tourist office The new North West Highlands Geopark visitor centre and café, *The Rock Stop* (daily 9am–5pm; ☎01971 488765, ⓦnwhgeopark.com), is based in Kylesku's old Unapool School Building. It has information on the region, plus hot drinks and sandwiches.
Kylesku Boat Tours Gentle cruises into lochs Glendhu and Glencoul (April–Sept 2 daily, round trip 1hr 45min; £25; ☎01971 502231, ⓦkyleskuboattours.com).

ACCOMMODATION AND EATING

Kylesku Hotel Kylesku centre, IV27 4HW ☎01971 502231, ⓦkyleskuhotel.co.uk. This small hotel, in a crisp, modern style, provides by far the best food in the area, all sourced locally – from the vegetables to the shellfish. Expect the likes of Kylesku langoustines (£20.95) or hogget curry (£17.50). The smart new wing, *Willy's Hoose*, is named after a local – some rooms have a private balcony and loch views. Closed Dec & Jan. Daily noon–2.30pm & 6–9pm. **£110**

Achiltibuie

North of Loch Broom, and accessible via a slow, winding singletrack road off the A835, is the old crofting village **ACHILTIBUIE**. It's the main settlement on the **Coigach Peninsula**, a narrow spit of land that juts out into the sea just north of Ullapool. The village is scattered across the hillside above a series of white-sand coves and rocks, from where a fleet of small fishing boats carries sheep, and tourists, to the enticing pastures of the **Summer Isles**, a cluster of islets a couple of miles offshore. Right now they are uninhabited by humans, but there are plenty of seabirds, dolphins and porpoises in residence. The largest, Tanera Mòr, made news in 2013 when it was put up for sale at £2.5m – in the end, it was bought by a hedge fund tycoon for under £2m in 2017.

ARRIVAL AND DEPARTURE ACHILTIBUIE

By bus Scotbus #811 connects Ullapool's ferry terminal with Achiltibuie (Mon–Sat 2 daily, Sun 1; 1hr 10min). Cruises to the Summer Isles (summer only, Mon–Sat; ⓦsummerqueen.co.uk) run from the waterfront in Ullapool.

Lochinver and around

Sixteen miles north of Ullapool (although more than thirty by road), **LOCHINVER** is one of the busiest fishing harbours in Scotland, from where large trucks head off for the continent. The potholed and narrow road that leads here from Achiltibuie, passing through Inverkirkaig on the way, is unremittingly spectacular. It threads its way through a tumultuous landscape of heaving valleys, moorland and bare rock, past the distinctive, mound-shaped **Suilven** (2398ft).

The first village worthy of a detour on the road north is **ACHMELVICH**, three miles northwest of Lochinver, where a tiny bay cradles a stunning white-sand beach lapped by startlingly turquoise water. However, for total peace and quiet, head to other, equally seductive beaches beyond the headlands.

By bus Lochinver has connections with Inverness (May, June & Sept Mon–Sat 1 daily; July & Aug 1 daily; 2hr 45min) and Ullapool (July & Aug 1–3 daily; Sept–June Mon–Sat 1–3 daily; 1hr).

EATING

★ **The Caberfeidh** Main St, near the bridge, IV27 4JZ ☎ 01571 844321, ⓦ thecaberfeidh.co.uk. Run by the same owners as the nnearby, Michelin-starred *Albannach*. Small plates and wine by the glass bring the same superb quality but for a fraction of the price; think wild venison meatballs (£6.95) and straight-from-the-boat bouillabaisse (£5.95). River views and a roaring fire top this off as one of the Highlands' best dining pubs. Mon 5–11pm, Tues–Sun noon–11pm; kitchen Mon 6–9pm, Tues–Sun noon–2.30pm & 6–9pm.

Lochinver Larder Main St, near bridge, IV27 4JY ☎ 01571 844356, ⓦ lochinverlarder.co.uk. Sensational home-made pies, featuring exotic ingredients like wild boar and saag paneer, have made this fine bistro famous, but it offers other food too: smoked fish linguini or home-made fishcakes, perhaps (both £13.95), or langoustine in lime, ginger and chilli butter (£20). Takeaway available. Easter–Oct Mon–Sat 10am–7.45pm, Sun 10am–5.30pm; Nov–March daily 10am–4pm.

23

The north coast

Until a few years ago, relatively few visitors travelled the length of the Highlands' **north coast**; its least interesting corner, **John O'Groats**, has always borne the brunt of the tourists. However, with the launch of the **North Coast 500** tourism initiative (ⓦnorthcoast500.com), this remote stretch of coast is now welcoming flocks of visitors from around the world, making it necessary to start planning a trip several months in advance to avoid having to sleep in your car – something which, according to locals, happens a fair amount these days.

Pounded by one of the world's most ferocious seaways, Scotland's rugged northern shore is backed by barren mountains in the west, and in the east by lochs and open rolling grasslands. Between its far ends, miles of crumbling cliffs and sheer rocky headlands shelter bays whose perfect white beaches are nearly always deserted, even in the height of summer – though, somewhat incongruously, they're also home to Scotland's best **surfing** waves.

Durness is a good jumping-off point for nearby **Balnakeil beach**, one of the area's most beautiful sandy strands, and for rugged **Cape Wrath**, the windswept promontory at Scotland's northwest tip. **Thurso**, the largest town on the north coast, is really only visited by those en route to Orkney. More enticing are the huge seabird colonies clustered in clefts and on remote stacks at **Dunnet Head** and **Duncansby Head**, east of Thurso.

Durness and around

Scattered around a string of sheltered sandy coves and grassy clifftops, **DURNESS** is the most northwesterly village on the British mainland. It straddles the turning point on the main A838 road as it swings east from the inland peat bogs of the interior to the north coast's fertile strip of limestone machair. Durness village sits above its own sandy bay, Sango Sands, while half a mile to the east is **SMOO**, formerly an RAF station. Between Durness and Smoo is the village hall, whose windblown and rather forlorn community garden harbours a memorial commemorating the Beatle **John Lennon**, who used to come to Durness on family holidays as a child (and revisited the place in the 1960s with Yoko Ono). It's worth pausing at Smoo to see the 200ft-long **Smoo Cave** (free to access; though tours deeper into the cave run Easter–Sept; £4), a gaping hole in a sheer limestone cliff formed partly by the action of the sea and partly by the small burn that flows through it.

ARRIVAL AND DEPARTURE   DURNESS

By bus Public transport to Durness is sparse; the key service is the D&E Coaches link (May, June & Sept Mon–Sat 1 daily; July & Aug 1 daily; 5hr 20min) from Inverness via Ullapool and Lochinver.

ACCOMMODATION AND EATING

Cocoa Mountain Balnakeil Craft Village, a mile northwest of Durness, IV27 4PT ☎01971 511233, ⓦcocoamountain.co.uk. A bright modern café linked to a chocolatier – a rich bittersweet hot chocolate topped with white chocolate is the speciality. They offer snacks (£5–7), too, plus their own chocolates and truffles. Easter–Oct daily 9am–6pm.

Lazy Crofter Bunkhouse Centre of Durness, IV27 4PN ☎01971 511202, ⓦvisitdurness.com/bunkhouse. Run by *Mackay's* hotel next door, this is the finest bunkhouse on the north coast, sleeping twenty. There's a snug cabin atmosphere and it gets extra marks for individual reading lights in the two dorms and compact (bunk-bed) twins. The terrace has sea views. Dorms __£20__, twins __£40__

Cape Wrath

Two miles southwest of Durness at **KEOLDALE**, a foot-passenger **ferry** (April–Sept daily 11am, plus June–Aug 9am; £6.50 return; ☎01971 511246 or ☎07719 678729) crosses the spectacular Kyle of Durness estuary. The ferry, which only runs when the tides allow, links with a **minibus** (£12 return; ☎07742 670196) that travels the eleven miles out to **Cape Wrath**, mainland Britain's most northwesterly point. Note that nearby Garvie Island (An Garbh-eilean) is an air bombing range, and the military regularly closes the road to Cape Wrath. The headland takes its name not from the stormy seas that crash against it for most of the year, but from the Norse word *hvarf*, meaning "turning place" – a throwback to the days when Viking warships used it as a navigation point during raids on the Scottish coast.

23

Tongue and around

Arriving from the west, the road to the pretty crofting village of **TONGUE** takes a wonderfully slow and circuitous route around Loch Eriboll and east over the top of A' Mhoine moor. The village is dominated by the ruins of **Castle Varrich** (Caisteal Bharraich), a medieval stronghold of the Mackay clan – it's a three-mile return walk from the centre.

Tongue itself is strewn above the east shore of the **Kyle of Tongue**, which you can either cross via a new causeway or by following the longer and more scenic singletrack road around its southern side. When the tide recedes, this shallow estuary becomes a mass of golden sand flats, superb on sunny days, with the sharp profiles of **Ben Hope** (3040ft), the most northerly Munro, and **Ben Loyal** (2509ft) looming like twin sentinels to the south.

ARRIVAL AND DEPARTURE   TONGUE AND AROUND

By bus Stagecoach bus #73 connects Tongue with Thurso (Mon–Fri 1 daily, Sat 2; 1hr 50min) and Bettyhill (Mon–Sat 2 daily; 35min). The buses pull up outside the *Tongue Hotel*, on A838.

ACCOMMODATION

Kyle of Tongue Hostel & Holiday Park East of Kyle of Tongue Bridge, IV27 4XH ☎01847 611789, ⓦtonguehostelandholidaypark.co.uk. The Duke of Sutherland's old shooting lodge has been repurposed as a large, well-equipped hostel with spacious dorms and family rooms, plus great mountain views. It's SYHA-affiliated, with plans to expand as a caravan park and campsite. Closed Oct to mid-April. Dorms __£18__, twins __£39__

Bettyhill and around

BETTYHILL is a major crofting village set among rocky green hills 25 miles east of Tongue. The village's splendid, sheltered **Farr beach** forms an unbroken arc of pure white sand between the Naver and Borgie rivers. Even more visually impressive is the River Naver's narrow tidal estuary, west of Bettyhill, and **Torrisdale beach**, which ends in a smooth white spit that forms part of the **Invernaver Nature Reserve**.

Flow Country

At a junction around fifteen miles west of Thurso you can head forty miles or so south towards Helmsdale on the A897, through the fascinating blanket bog of the **Flow Country**, whose name comes from *flói*, an Old Norse word meaning "marshy ground". At the train station at **FORSINARD**, fourteen miles south of Melvich and easily accessible from Thurso, Wick and the south, there is an **RSPB visitor centre** (Easter–Oct daily 9am–5pm; free; ☎01641 571225, ⓦrspb.org.uk/forsinard), which acts as the gateway to the so-called **Forsinard Flows** – a surprisingly rich and diverse nature reserve covering vast tracts of boggy peatland. Here you have a good chance of spotting dunlin, dippers and wading greenshanks, who use the boggy environment as a breeding ground.

Thurso

Approached from the isolation of the west, **THURSO** feels like a metropolis. In reality, it's a relatively small service centre visited mostly by people passing through to the adjoining port of **Scrabster** to catch the ferry to Orkney, or by increasing numbers of surfers attracted to the waves on the north coast. There's little to see, but the grid-plan streets have some rather handsome Victorian architecture in the local, greyish sandstone. If you're coming to **surf**, want a lesson or need to rent a board and wet suit (£20/day), head for *Café Tempest* on Riverside Road (see below).

Caithness Horizons

High St, KW14 8AJ • May–Aug Mon–Fri 10am–6pm, Sat 10am–5pm, Sun noon–5pm; Sept–April Mon–Fri 10am–6pm, Sat 10am–5pm • Free (donations welcome) • ☎ 01847 896508, ⓦ caithnesshorizons.co.uk

Caithness Horizons, a local museum in a revamped Victorian town hall, is more modern than any other museum on the north coast, with artefacts relating to the Dounreay Nuclear Power Plant, the Vikings and the Picts, as well as a paleontology collection featuring 380 million-year-old fish fossils. The centre also has a temporary exhibition gallery, a café and a gift shop.

ARRIVAL AND DEPARTURE   THURSO

By train Thurso station is near the town centre on Princes St.

Destinations Dingwall (Mon–Sat 4 daily, Sun 1; 3hr); Inverness (Mon–Sat 4 daily, Sun 1; 3hr 40min); Lairg (Mon–Sat 4 daily, Sun 1; 2hr); Wick (Mon–Sat 4 daily, Sun 1; 35min).

By bus Buses pass through the middle of town, stopping on the A9.

Destinations Inverness (up to 8 daily; 3–4hr); John O' Groats (Mon–Sat every 1–2hr; 1hr); Wick (Mon–Sat every 30min–1hr, Sun 5; 35min).

By ferry Buses run from the A9 in the centre of town to the Scrabster ferry terminal, roughly 2 miles northwest of town, every hour or so. From there, ferries cross to Stromness on Orkney Mainland (2–3 daily; 90min).

ACCOMMODATION AND EATING

Café Tempest Riverside Rd, KW14 8DE ☎01847 892500. Home baking, toasties and home-made burgers (£5–8) served in a harbourside café with a laidback surf-shack vibe. Bring-your-own drinks on Sat evenings during the summer (£3 corkage). Jan–March daily 10am–4pm; April–Dec Mon–Fri 10am–6pm, Sat 10am–8pm, Sun 10am–4pm.

Captain's Galley The Harbour, Scrabster, KW14 7UJ ☎01847 894999, ⓦcaptainsgalley.co.uk. This former ice-house and salmon bothy serves the best seafood in the area; a four-course dinner, with mains including the likes of hake with saffron potatoes, costs £54. Also takeaway fish and chips using the freshest catch. Restaurant Wed–Sat 7–9pm; takeaway Tues–Sat 12.30–6.30pm.

The Marine 38 Shore St, KW14 8BN ☎01847 890676, ⓦthemarinethurso.co.uk. Modern furnishings and tweed headboards make for a relaxed, contemporary style. More appealing than the rooms is the small conservatory off the gorgeous breakfast room, with sea views – surfers take note. **£99**

Dunnet Head

Despite the publicity given to John O'Groats, the most northerly point of mainland Britain is actually **Dunnet Head** four miles north of the sleepy village of **DUNNET**. It's an evocative spot up at the Head, covered in heather and bog and with high red cliffs at the headland, marked by a Stevenson lighthouse – on a clear day, you'll see the whole north coast spread out before you from Cape Wrath to Duncansby Head. There's not a great deal to do in Dunnet itself, beyond popping in to Britain's northernmost micro-distillery, the **Dunnet Bay Distillers**, on the A836 (May–Oct Mon–Fri 10am–4pm; tours 45min with tasting session; £6; ☎01847 851287, ⓦdunnetbaydistillers.co.uk).

ARRIVAL AND INFORMATION   DUNNET HEAD

By bus Bus #80 between Thurso and John O'Groats passes through Dunnet and Mey (Mon–Fri 8 daily, Sat 5).
Tourist information You can pick up information on local history and nature walks at the unmanned

information centre at the northeast end of the bay (Mon–Fri & Sun: April, May & Sept 2–5.30pm; July & Aug 10.30am–5.30pm; free).

Castle of Mey

6.5 miles west of John O'Groats, KW14 8XH • **Castle** May–July & mid-Aug to Sept daily 10.20am–4pm • £11.50 • **Grounds** May–July & mid-Aug to Sept daily 10am–5pm • £6.50 • ☎ 01847 851473, ⓦ castleofmey.org.uk

The Queen Mother's former Scottish home, the **Castle of Mey**, is the most northerly castle on the UK mainland. It's a modest little place, hidden behind high flagstone walls, with great views north to Orkney, and a herd of the Queen Mother's beloved Aberdeen Angus grazing out front. She used to spend every August here, and unusually for a royal palace, it's remarkably unstuffy inside, the walls hung with works by local amateur artists and watercolours by Prince Charles (who still visits late July/early August, when it's closed for two weeks).

John O'Groats and around

Snap-happy tourists, windswept pilgrims and exhausted cyclists convene at **JOHN O'GROATS**, the most northeasterly settlement on mainland Britain. Consisting of a car park, a souvenir village and not much else, the place has never quite lived up to its folkloric reputation, although a recent regeneration project has brought new life to the place with the opening of a technicolour seafront hotel and a sparkly café. There are plenty of prettier places to view the sea in north Scotland, but as one end of the Land's End to John O'Groats tour, there's always a happy flow of people either starting or ending a life-affirming journey here. A couple of miles to the east, **Duncansby Head** is a much more stimulating place to visit than John O'Groats, with its lighthouse, dramatic cliffs and well-worn coastal path.

The east coast

The **east coast** of the Highlands, between Inverness and Wick, is nowhere near as spectacular as the west, with gently undulating moors, grassland and low cliffs where you might otherwise expect to find sea lochs and mountains. While many visitors speed up the main A9 road through this region in a headlong rush to the Orkneys' prehistoric sites, those who choose to dally will find a wealth of brochs, cairns and standing stones, many in remarkable condition. The area around the Black Isle and the Tain was a Pictish heartland, and has yielded many important finds. Further north, from around the ninth century AD onwards, the **Norse** influence was more keenly felt than in any other part of mainland Britain, and dozens of Scandinavian-sounding names recall the era when this was a Viking kingdom.

23

The fishing heritage is a recurring theme along this coast, though there are only a handful of working boats scattered around the harbours today; the area remains one of the country's poorest, reliant on relatively thin pickings from sheep farming, fishing and tourism. The one stretch of the east coast that's always been relatively rich, however, is the **Black Isle** just over the Kessock Bridge heading north out of Inverness, whose main village, **Cromarty**, is the region's undisputed highlight. Beyond the golfing resort of **Dornoch**, the ersatz-Loire chateau **Dunrobin Castle** is the main tourist attraction, a monument as much to the iniquities of the Clearances as to the eccentricities of Victorian taste.

The Black Isle

Sandwiched between the Cromarty Firth to the north and, to the south, the Moray and Beauly firths which separate it from Inverness, the **Black Isle** is not an island at all, but a fertile peninsula whose rolling hills, prosperous farms and stands of deciduous woodland make it more reminiscent of Dorset or Sussex than the Highlands. It probably gained its name because of its mild climate: there's rarely frost, which leaves the fields "black" all winter; another explanation is that the name derives from the Gaelic word for black, *dubh* – a possible corruption of St Duthus. On the south side of the Black Isle, near Fortrose, **Chanonry Point** juts into a narrow channel in the Moray Firth and is an excellent place to look for **dolphins** (see page 924).

Cromarty

An appealing jumble of handsome Georgian townhouses and pretty workers' cottages knitted together by a cat's-cradle of lanes, **CROMARTY**, the Black Isle's main settlement, is a joy to wander around. An ancient ferry crossing on the pilgrimage trail to Tain, became a prominent port in 1772, fuelling a period of prosperity that gave Cromarty some of the Highlands' finest Georgian houses. The railways poached that trade in the nineteenth century – a branch line to the town was begun but never completed – but the flip side of stagnation is preservation. Be sure to drop into **Hugh Miller's Birthplace Cottage and Museum** (Church St; late March to Sept daily noon–5pm; free, donations welcome; NTS; ☎01381 600418, ⊛nts.org.uk/visit/hugh-millers-birthplace), the thatched home of Cromarty's celebrated social reformer.

ARRIVAL AND DEPARTURE   CROMARTY

By bus Stagecoach buses #23 and #26 run from Inverness main bus station (Mon–Sat every 30min, Sun 5; 1hr).

By ferry The tiny four-car Nigg–Cromarty ferry (every 30min; June & Sept Mon–Sat 8am–6pm, Sun 9am–

6.10pm; July & Aug Mon–Sat 8am–7.10pm, Sun 9am–7.10pm; £4.50, £9.50 with a car) is one of Britain's smallest. Embark from the jetty near the lighthouse.

ACCOMMODATION AND EATING

★ **The Factor's House** Denny Rd, IV11 8YT ☎01381 600394, ⊛thefactorshouse.com. King-size beds, roll-top baths and fluffy bathrobes await in the three rooms of this B&B – the Urquhart is our pick – while the lounge is a peaceful spot for a drink by the fire. The dinner menu (three courses £37.50) features fresh Scottish cuisine and home-baked delights. **£125**

★ **Sutor Creek** 21 Bank St, IV11 8YE ☎01381 600855, ⊛sutorcreek.co.uk. There are few more satisfying, down-to-earth restaurants in the Highlands than this. It serves organic wines, delicious seafood and fresh wood-fired pizza cooked. Light lunches £6–10. May–Sept daily noon–9pm; Oct–April Wed 5–9pm, Thurs–Sun 11am–9pm.

The Dornoch Firth and around

North of the Cromarty Firth, the hammer-shaped **Fearn peninsula** can still be approached from the south by the ancient ferry crossing from Cromarty to Nigg, though to the north the link is a causeway over the **Dornoch Firth**, the inlet that marks the northern boundary of the peninsula.

Tain

On the southern edge of the Dornoch Firth the A9 bypasses **TAIN**, an attractive, old-fashioned small town of grand, whisky-coloured sandstone buildings that was the birthplace of **St Duthus**, an eleventh-century missionary who inspired great devotion in the Middle Ages. The main attraction is the **Glenmorangie whisky distillery**, where the highly rated malt is produced (☎01862 892477; tours April, May, Sept & Oct Mon–Sat 10am–3pm hourly; June–Aug daily 10am–4pm every 30min; Nov–March 10am or 2pm by appointment; £7; book ahead); it lies beside the A9 on the north side of town.

Dornoch

DORNOCH, a genteel and appealing town eight miles north of Tain, lies on a flattish headland overlooking the **Dornoch Firth**. A middle-class holiday resort, with solid Edwardian hotels, trees and flowers in profusion and miles of sandy beaches giving good views across the estuary to the Fearn peninsula, Dornoch is renowned for its championship **golf course**, Scotland's most northerly first-class course.

ARRIVAL AND DEPARTURE

DORNOCH

By bus Stagecoach's Inverness–Thurso service (via Helmsdale) stops at Dornoch.

Destinations Inverness (5 daily; 1hr 10min); Thurso (Mon–Sat 4 daily, Sun 3; 1hr 45min).

ACCOMMODATION AND EATING

Dornoch Castle Hotel Castle St, IV25 3SD ☎01862 810216, ⓦdornochcastlehotel.com. This fifteenth-century hotel, in the Bishop's Palace on the main square, has a decent restaurant and a cosy old-fashioned bar with a roaring log fire. Choose from comfy but bland rooms facing the "Old Courtyard"; spacious superior rooms (from £185) with pillow chocolates and whisky miniatures; or a deluxe room in the turreted tower (from £235). Daily 6–9pm. __£120__

Golspie

The straggling red-sandstone town of **GOLSPIE**, whose status as an administrative centre does little to relieve its dullness, sits ten miles north of Dornoch on the A9. It is, however, the jumping-off point for some brilliant **mountain biking**: the fabulous Highland Wildcat Trails (ⓦhighlandwildcat.com) are within the forested hills just half a mile to the west. The easy to severe (colour-coded) trails include a huge descent from the summit of Ben Bhraggie to sea level and a ride past the **Sutherland monument**, erected in memory of the landowner who oversaw the eviction of thousands of his tenants during the **Clearances**.

Dunrobin Castle

A9, 1 mile north of Golspie, KW10 6SF • March–May, Sept & Oct Mon–Sat 10.30am–4.30pm, Sun noon–4.30pm (no falconry Sun); June–Aug daily 10.30am–5pm (falconry daily) • £11 • ☎01408 633177, ⓦdunrobincastle.co.uk • Dunrobin Castle is a summer stop on the Inverness–Thurso line (April–Oct Mon–Sat 3 daily; 2hr 15min from Inverness, 1hr 35min from Thurso)

Mountain biking aside, the main reason to stop at Golspie is to look around **Dunrobin Castle**, overlooking the sea north of town. This fairy-tale confection of turrets and pointed roofs – modelled by the architect Sir Charles Barry (designer of the Houses of Parliament) on a Loire chateau – is the seat of the infamous Sutherland family, at one time Europe's biggest landowners, with a staggering 1.3 million acres, and the principal driving force behind the Clearances in this area. The castle has 189 furnished rooms, but as a visitor you'll only be able to see a fraction of them. Staring up at the pile from its elaborate **formal gardens**, it's worth remembering that such extravagance was paid for by uprooting literally thousands of crofters from the surrounding glens.

23

By bus Stagecoach's Inverness–Thurso service stops at Golspie.

Destinations Inverness (Mon–Sat 5 daily, Sun 4; 1hr 25min); Thurso (Mon–Sat 5 daily, Sun 4; 1hr 35min).

Helmsdale

HELMSDALE, eleven scenic miles north along the A9 from Golspie, is an old herring port, founded in the nineteenth century to house the evicted inhabitants of Strath Kildonan, which lies behind it. The Strath was the unlikely location of a gold rush in the 1860s, and a few determined prospectors still pan the Kildonan Burn. The story of the area's gold hunters is told in the **Timespan Heritage Centre**, beside the river (daily: April–Oct 10am–5pm; Nov–March reduced hours; £4; ☎ 01431 821327, ⊛ timespan.org.uk), along with tales of Viking raids, witch-burning, Clearances and fishing.

Just north of Helmsdale, the A9 begins its long haul up the **Ord of Caithness**, a busy, winding pass. Once over the pass, the landscape changes dramatically as heather-clad moors give way to miles of treeless green grazing lands, peppered with derelict crofts and latticed by long dry-stone walls. As you come over the pass, look out for signs to the ruined village of **Badbea**, a ten-minute walk from the car park at the side of the A9. Built by tenants cleared from nearby Ousdale, the settlement entered a slow decline and is now abandoned, its ruined hovels showing what hardship the crofters had to endure: the cottages stood so near the windy cliff edge that children had to be tethered to prevent them from being blown into the sea.

By bus From Golspie, buses run to a stop beside the roundabout in the centre of the town, right near the river (Mon–Fri 3 daily; 30min).

Wick

Since it was founded by Vikings as *Vik* (meaning "bay"), **WICK** has lived by the sea. It's actually two towns: Wick proper and, south across the river, **Pultneytown**, created by the British Fisheries Society in 1806 to encourage evicted crofters to take up fishing. By the mid-nineteenth century, Wick was the busiest herring port in Europe, with a fleet of more than 1100 boats exporting fish to Russia, Scandinavia and the West Indian slave plantations. The demise of its fishing trade has left Wick down at heel, reduced to a mere transport hub. Yet the huge harbour in Pultneytown and a walk around the surrounding area – scruffy rows of fishermen's cottages, derelict net-mending sheds and stores – gives an insight into the scale of the former fishing trade.

Wick Heritage Centre

Bank Row, Pultneytown, KW1 5EY • Easter–Oct Mon–Sat 10am–5pm, last entry 3.45pm • £4 • ☎ 01955 605393, ⊛ wickheritage.org

The volunteer-maintained **Wick Heritage Centre** is the best place to learn about Wick's fishing heyday. Deceptively labyrinthine, it contains a fascinating array of artefacts, including fully rigged boats, models of the sea-faring vessels and reconstructed period rooms, plus a superb archive of photographs captured by three generations of a local family between 1863 and 1975.

By plane Wick John O'Groats Airport (☎ 01955 602215, ⊛ wickairport.com), just north of town, has flights to and from Edinburgh (Mon, Wed–Fri & Sun 1 daily; 1hr) and Aberdeen (Mon–Fri 3 daily; 35min) with Flybe/Loganair and Eastern Airways respectively.

By train The train station is immediately south and west of the central bridge. Trains from Inverness (Mon–Sat 3 daily; 4hr 20min) make a long but scenic journey via Lairg, Helmsdale and then the Flow Country inland.

By bus Local buses depart from just south and west of the central bridge. They run to John O'Groats then Thurso; long-distance routes to and from Inverness involve a coordinated change at Dunbeath.

Destinations Inverness (Mon–Sat 6 daily, Sun 4; 3hr); John O'Groats (Mon–Fri 7 daily, Sat 5; 35min); Thurso (Mon–Sat approx hourly, Sun 5; 30–35min).

ACCOMMODATION AND EATING

Bord de l'Eau Market St, KW1 4AR ☎01955 604400. This riverside bistro offers a little slice of France, with a changing menu of Gaelic and seafood dishes, plus some French classics (£16–20). The best seats are in the airy conservatory. Tues–Sat noon–2pm & 6–9pm, Sun 6–9pm.

Mackays Union St, KW1 5ED ☎01955 602323, ⓦmackayshotel.co.uk. The oversized headboards, streamlined oak furnishings and iPod docks make this Wick's prime accommodation option. The first- and second-floor rooms are best. Its acclaimed *No.1 Bistro* serves the likes of lemon- and garlic-roasted chicken with Moroccan spices, plus superb fish and chips (mains average £14). Daily 8am–9pm. **£122**

23

Skye
and the
Western
Isles

THREE CHIMNEYS, DUNVEGAN

Skye and the Western Isles

A procession of Hebridean islands, islets and reefs off the northwest shore of Scotland, Skye and the Western Isles between them boast some of Britain's most alluring scenery. It's here that the turbulent seas of the Atlantic smash against an extravagant shoreline hundreds of miles long, a geologically complex terrain of rough rocks and mighty sea cliffs interrupted by a thousand sheltered bays and, in the far west, a long line of sweeping sandy beaches. The islands' interiors are equally dramatic, a series of formidable mountain ranges soaring high above great chunks of boggy peat moor, a barren wilderness enclosing a host of lochans, or tiny lakes.

Each island has its own character, though the grouping splits quite neatly into two. **Skye** and the **Small Isles** – the improbably named **Rùm**, **Eigg**, **Muck** and **Canna** – are part of the Inner Hebrides. Beyond Skye, across the unpredictable waters of the Minch, lie the Outer Hebrides or **Western Isles**, a 130-mile-long archipelago stretching from **Lewis** and **Harris** in the north to **Barra** in the south. There are four obvious areas of outstanding natural beauty to aim for: on Skye, the harsh peaks of the **Cuillin** and the bizarre rock formations of the **Trotternish** peninsula; on the Western Isles, the mountains of **North Harris** and the splendid sandy beaches that string along the seaboard of **South Harris** and the **Uists**.

Brief history

Skye and the Western Isles were first settled by Neolithic farming peoples in around 4000 BC. They lived along the coast, where they are remembered by scores of remains, most famously at **Callanish** (Calanais) on Lewis. Viking colonization gathered pace from 700 AD onwards and it was only in 1266 that the islands were returned to the Scottish Crown. James VI (James I of England), a Stuart and a Scot, though no Gaelic-speaker, was the first to put forward the idea of clearing the Hebrides. However, it wasn't until after the Jacobite uprisings in the eighteenth century, in which many Highland clans backed the losing side, that the **Clearances** began in earnest.

The isolation of the Hebrides exposed them to the whims and fancies of the various merchants and aristocrats who bought them up. Time and again, from the mid-eighteenth century to the present day, the land and its people were sold to the highest bidder. Some proprietors were well-meaning, others simply forced the inhabitants onto ships bound for North America. Despite this, their language survived, ensuring a degree of cultural continuity, especially in the Western Isles, where even today the first language of the majority remains **Gaelic** (pronounced "gallic").

ARRIVAL AND DEPARTURE | SKYE AND THE WESTERN ISLES

Skye Most visitors reach Skye via the Skye Bridge, which sweeps across the sea from Kyle of Lochalsh, itself linked to Inverness by train. The more scenic approach is via Armadale on the Sleat peninsula, linked by CalMac car ferry (☎ 0800 066 5000, ⓦ calmac.co.uk) with Mallaig, at the end of the train line from Fort William. A third option is to arrive at Kylerhea, also on the Sleat peninsula, via the tiny car ferry (ⓦ skyeferry.co.uk) that leaves from Glenelg, south of Kyle of Lochalsh.

The Western Isles If you're heading for the Western Isles, note that it's 57 miles from Armadale and 49 miles from Kyleakin to Uig, from where ferries leave for Tarbert on Harris and Lochmaddy on North Uist.

Bonnie Prince Charlie p.960
Gaelic in the Western Isles p.965
Harris tweed p.970
Whisky Galore! p.974

GARENIN (GEARRANNAN), LEWIS

Highlights

❶ Skye Cuillin These jagged peaks dominate and define Skye's landscape – they also contain twelve Munros and a challenging eight-mile ridge trail. See page 957

❷ Loch Coruisk, Skye Few sights in Scotland prepare you for the drama of this beautiful, remote glacial loch in the Cuillin – the boat ride there from Elgol just adds to the fun. See page 958

❸ Kinloch Castle, Rùm Visit this frankly bonkers Edwardian pile and enjoy a slice of old-school landed gentry decadence. See page 963

❹ Garenin (Gearrannan), Lewis An abandoned crofting township of thatched blackhouses that have been restored as self-

catering cottages and a café – with a couple left as they were when last inhabited. See page 968

❺ Callanish (Calanais), Lewis Scotland's Stonehenge, backed by a serene sea loch on the west coast of Lewis. See page 968

❻ Beaches The western seaboard of the Outer Hebrides is scattered with stunning, mostly deserted, golden strands backed by flower-strewn machair. See pages 969, 971 and 972

❼ Barra Airport Situated on the wide, shallow bay of Cockle Strand, the world's only beach airport with scheduled landings is an unbeatable introduction to the island known as the "Hebrides in miniature". See page 974

HIGHLIGHTS ARE MARKED ON THE MAP ON PAGE 954

Skye

Jutting out from the mainland like a giant butterfly, the bare and bony promontories of **Skye** fringe a deeply indented coastline. The island's most popular destination is the **Cuillin** ridge, whose jagged peaks dominate the island during clear weather. More accessible and equally dramatic are the rock formations of the **Trotternish** peninsula in the north, from which there are inspirational views across to the Western Isles. Of the two main settlements, **Portree** is the only one with any charm, and a useful base for exploring the Trotternish.

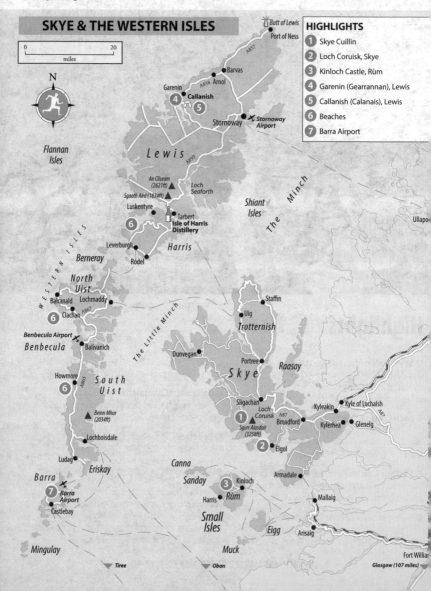

SKYE & THE WESTERN ISLES

0 ——— 20
miles

N

HIGHLIGHTS

1. Skye Cuillin
2. Loch Coruisk, Skye
3. Kinloch Castle, Rùm
4. Garenin (Gearrannan), Lewis
5. Callanish (Calanais), Lewis
6. Beaches
7. Barra Airport

Butt of Lewis
Port of Ness

A857

Barvas

Garenin
4
Callanish
5
Arnol
A858

Stornoway
Stornoway
Airport
A859

Flannan
Isles

Lewis

An Cliseam
(2621ft)
Sgaoth Aird (1834ft)
Loch
Seaforth

Shiant
Isles

The Minch

Ullapo

Luskentyre
Tarbert
Isle of Harris
Distillery
6

Leverburgh
Rodel
Harris

Berneray

North
Uist
Lochmaddy

Balranald
Clachan
6
A867

Benbecula Airport

Benbecula
Balivanich

WESTERN ISLES

The Little Minch

Staffin

Uig

Trotternish

Dunvegan

Portree
Raasay

Skye

Howmore
6
South
Uist

Beinn Mhor
(2034ft)

Lochboisdale

Sligachan
Loch
Coruisk
1
A87
Broadford

Kyleakin
Kyle of Lochalsh

Kylerhea
Glenelg

Sgurr Alasdair
(3258ft)
2
Elgol

Ludag
Eriskay

Barra
7
Barra
Airport

Castlebay

Canna

Sanday
3
Kinloch

Harris
Rùm

Armadale

Mallaig

Small
Isles

Eigg
Arisaig

Muck

Mingulay

Fort William
Glasgow (107 miles)

Tiree
Oban

By bus Bus services peter out in more remote areas and don't run on Sun. Skye Dayrider tickets for unlimited one-day travel cost £8.85 (☎ 0871 200 2233, ⓦ stagecoachbus.com).

The Sleat peninsula

Thanks to the CalMac ferries from Mallaig to **ARMADALE** (Armadal), many people's introduction to Skye is the uncharacteristically fertile **Sleat** (pronounced "Slate") **peninsula**, on Skye's southern tip.

Clan Donald Skye

On A851, 0.5 mile north of Armadale , IV45 8RS • Late March to Oct: garden 9.30am–5.30pm, museum 10am–5.30pm • £8.50 • ☎ 01471 844305, ⓦ clandonald.com

Branded as **Clan Donald Skye**, the ancestral home of the MacDonald clan is centred on the shell of the neo-Gothic **Armadale Castle** which houses a café and a library, for those who want to chase up their ancestral Donald connections. The gardens' slick, purpose-built **Museum of the Isles** has a good section on the Jacobite period and its aftermath and one or two top-notch works of art by Angelika Kaufmann and Henry Raeburn. Just as appealing is the castle's forty-acre wooded **garden**, where you can try your hand at archery and clay-pigeon shooting.

ARRIVAL AND DEPARTURE   THE SLEAT PENINSULA

By ferry Reservations are essential in peak season (ⓦ calmac.co.uk) for the Mallaig–Armadale crossing (Mon–Sat 9 daily, Sun 6 daily; 35min).

By bus All bus services from/to Armadale are via Broadford.

Destinations Broadford (Mon–Fri 5 daily, Sat 2; 25min); Portree (Mon–Fri 2 daily; 1hr 10min); Sligachan (Mon–Fri 2 daily; 55min).

24

ACCOMMODATION AND EATING

Ardvasar Hotel Ardvasar, 0.5 miles south of Armadale, IV45 8RS ☎ 01471 844223, ⓦ ardvasarhotel.com. This pretty little inn – one of the oldest on Skye – has benefited from refurbishment to create comfortable, contemporary accommodation as well as a smart restaurant specializing in local seafood – scallops and crab, plus Speyside beef for around £15. **£145**

★ **Eilean Iarmain** Isleornsay, IV43 8QR ☎ 01471 833332, ⓦ eileaniarmain.co.uk. This small hotel in a whitewashed hamlet is a charmer, romantically furnished in cosy country style. The restaurant offers fine dining such as venison with garlic and white truffle mash (two courses £35), and there's informal eating in the *Am Praban* bar

(sandwiches from £7.50). Daily 7am–9.30am, noon–2.30pm & 5.30–9pm. **£200**

Rubha Phoil Entry at ferry terminal, Armadale, IV45 8RS ☎ 07393 830403, ⓦ skyeforestgarden.com. Twelve pitches, four wooden bothies and a tepee (sleeping two) set in a labyrinthine 16-acre woodland campsite. Alongside green credentials, you get eggs from free-range hens, communal campfires and, for early risers, astounding sunrises. The woodland walk, beach cave and otter hide make this a good stop-off for families. Camping/person **£7.50**, bothies **£40**, tepee **£40**

Kyleakin

The **Skye Bridge** rendered the ferry crossing from Kyle of Lochalsh redundant, leaving the tiny port of **KYLEAKIN** (Caol Acain – pronounced "Kalakin") well and truly bypassed, but bizarrely it's since become something of a backpackers' hangout. The bridge has been less kind to **Eilean Bàn**, an island from which the bridge leapfrogs to cross Loch Alsh. In 1968, the lighthouse keeper's cottage on the island briefly became the home of writer and naturalist Gavin Maxwell, author of *Ring of Bright Water*. The island now serves as a nature reserve and can be visited on tours (11am & 2pm; £7), booked through the **Bright Water Visitor Centre** (Easter–Sept Mon–Fri 10am–4pm; ☎ 01599 530040, ⓦ eileanban.org) in Kyleakin.

ARRIVAL AND DEPARTURE

By bus Buses depart from the Shorefront Bus Shelter. Destinations Broadford (Mon–Sat hourly, Sun 3; 15min); Kyle of Lochalsh (Mon–Sat hourly, Sun 3; 10min); Portree (Mon–Sat 7 daily, Sun 6; 1hr); Uig (Mon–Sat 2 daily; 1hr 30min).

ACCOMMODATION

Skye Backpackers Kyleakin, IV41 8PH ☎01599 534510, ⓦskyebackpackers.com. The quirkier and better-equipped of Kyleakin's two hostels was totally refurbed in 2017. Dorms, doubles, and a couple of caravans offer a basic night's sleep. The Groove Lounge has a log burner and board games. Caravan dorms £14, dorms £19.50, doubles £52

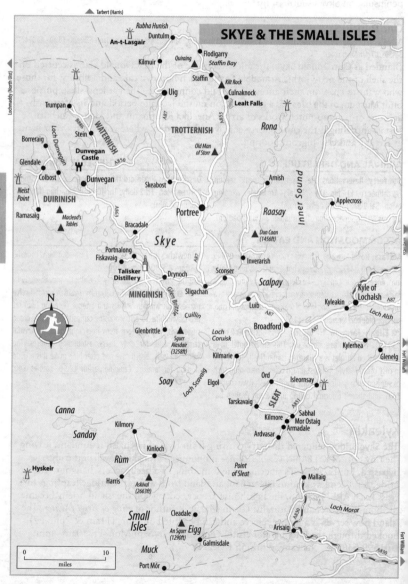

SKYE & THE SMALL ISLES

Broadford

Skye's second-largest village, **BROADFORD** (An t-Àth Leathann), strung out along the main road, has a traffic problem and a charm bypass. It's handy for its facilities – not least a large supermarket and 24-hour fuel – but you won't want to hang around for too long. Fill the tank, load up the boot with supplies and go explore the island.

ARRIVAL AND INFORMATION   BROADFORD

By bus Local buses serve Kyle of Lochalsh (Mon–Sat 6–7 daily; 25min), Kyleakin (Mon–Sat hourly, Sun 3; 15min) and Portree via Sligachan (Mon–Sat 4–6 daily; 50min).

Tourist information There's a friendly independent info point by the 24hr garage and supermarket in the centre (May–Oct daily 8.30am–6pm).

ACCOMMODATION AND EATING

Café Sia On the A87, IV49 9AB ☎ 01471 822616, ⓦ cafesia.co.uk. The best pizzas on Skye, wood-fired to perfection, and probably among the best coffees too. They also serve breakfast, and the outdoor deck has views out to the Red Cuillin. Daily 8.30am–9.30pm.

★ **Tigh an Dochais** 13 Harrapool, IV49 9AQ ☎ 01471 820022, ⓦ skyebedbreakfast.co.uk. Jaw-dropping views down Broadford Bay through walls of glass are the draw at this striking B&B, which has a streamlined contemporary style and a calm, grown-up vibe. Closed Dec–Feb. **£105**

Isle of Raasay

Despite lying less than a mile offshore, the fourteen-mile long, hilly island of **Raasay** (Ratharsair) sees few visitors. Yet, in many ways, it's the ultimate Skye escape, with plenty of walks and that thrill of being cast away. For much of its history, Raasay belonged to a branch of the Jacobite MacLeods of Lewis. When the last laird sold up in 1843 and moved to Tasmania, the Clearances began. In 1921, several ex-servicemen and their families from neighbouring **Rona** were imprisoned after they squatted in crofts on Raasay. The public outcry led to both islands being bought by the government, and since then they have remained in state hands. Raasay's population continues to fall and is currently around 160. The ferry docks in Churchton Bay, near **INVERARISH** – the island's tiny village set within thick woods on the southwest coast.

The most obvious spot to head for in the island's interior is the curiously flat-topped volcanic plug of **Dun Caan** (1456ft) – the trail to the top of the peak is fairly easy to follow, a splendid five-mile trek up through the forest and along the burn behind Inverarish. In 2017, the new **Isle of Raasay Distillery** opened its doors to the public; you can check out the visitor centre for free or take a 1hr tour (tours coincide with ferry arrivals; £10; ⓦ raasaydistillery.com).

24

ARRIVAL AND DEPARTURE   ISLE OF RAASAY

By ferry CalMac ferries from Sconser arrive at Churchton Bay (Mon–Sat 8–10 daily, Sun 2; 25min).

ACCOMMODATION AND EATING

Raasay House Short walk from ferry pier, IV40 8PB ☎ 01478 660300, ⓦ raasay-house.co.uk. The MacLeods' rebuilt manor offers everything from four-star deluxe options with balconies and views to the Cuillins to modern bunkrooms. This is also the only place to eat or drink on the island, in the convivial bar/restaurant (mains £12–18). Among activities on offer (Easter–Oct, weather-dependent other months; £15–60) are fast boat trips, archery, coasteering, kayaking and sailing. Bike/electric bike rental available (£15/£35 half-day). April–Oct daily 9.30am–11pm; kitchen 9.30am–8.30pm; Nov–March call for hours. Dorms **£20**, doubles **£95**

The Cuillin and the Red Hills

For many people, the **Cuillin** (An Cuiltheann), whose sharp peaks rise mirage-like from the flatness of the surrounding terrain, are Skye's raison d'être. When – if – the clouds disperse, they are the dominating feature of the island, visible from every other peninsula.

There are three **approaches** to the Cuillin: by foot or by boat from **Elgol** to the south; from the **Sligachan Hotel** to the north; or from **Glen Brittle** to the west of the mountains The second route, down Glen Sligachan, divides the granite of the round-topped **Red Hills** (sometimes known as the Red Cuillin) to the east from the dark, coarse-grained, jagged-edged gabbro of the real Cuillin (also known as the Black Cuillin) to the west. With some twenty Munros between them, these are mountains to be taken seriously, and many routes through the Cuillin are for experienced climbers only.

Elgol and Loch Coruisk

The road to **ELGOL** (Ealaghol), at the tip of the Strathaird peninsula, is one of the most dramatic on the island, with a stunning view from the top down to Elgol pier. Weather permitting, you can take a **boat** from Elgol across Loch Scavaig, past a seal colony, to a jetty near the entrance to the glacial **Loch Coruisk** (April–Oct; £26 return). A needle-like shaft of water nearly two miles long, but only a couple of hundred yards wide, Loch Coruisk lies in the shadow of the highest peaks of the Black Cuillin, a wonderfully overpowering landscape. The journey from Elgol takes about an hour and passengers are dropped to spend time ashore before returning to Elgol. **Walkers** can jump ship and hike amid the Red Hills, or over the pass into **Glen Sligachan**.

Glen Brittle

Six miles along the A863 to Dunvegan from the *Sligachan Hotel*, a turning signed "Carbost and Portnalong" quickly leads to the entrance to stony **Glen Brittle**, edging the most spectacular peaks of the Cuillin; at the end of the glen, idyllically situated by the sea, is the village of **GLENBRITTLE**. Climbers and serious walkers tend to congregate at the SYHA **hostel** or the beautifully situated **campsite**, both of which have the only grocery stores for miles.

From the valley a score of difficult and strenuous trails lead east into the **Black Cuillin**, a rough semicircle of peaks, rising to about 3000ft, which surround Loch Coruisk. One of the easiest walks is the five-mile round-trip (3hr) from the campsite up **Coire Làgan** to a crystal-cold lochan squeezed in among the sternest of rock faces. Above the lochan is Skye's highest peak, **Sgùrr Alasdair** (3258ft), one of the more difficult Munros; Sgurr na Banachdich (3166ft), to the northwest, is considered the most easily accessible Munro in the Cuillin.

ARRIVAL AND DEPARTURE   THE CUILLIN AND THE RED HILLS

By bus Elgol is accessed by bus from Broadford (Mon–Fri 2 daily, Sat 1; 1hr), Glenbrittle is connected to Portree (Mon–Fri 2 daily; 50min) and Sligachan is a stop on the Broadford–Portree route (Mon–Sat 4–6 daily; 50min).

ACCOMMODATION AND EATING

★ Coruisk House Elgol, IV49 9BL ☎01471 866330, ⓦcoruiskhouse.com. A taste of Skye on super-fresh menus – fillet of cod with Orbost Iron Age pork belly, or roast loin of venison with port and juniper sauce – with two courses around £40. Above are two beautiful cottage rooms of understated luxury: expect dinner, a relaxing night and an awesome breakfast. Perfect. Reservations essential. Daily noon–2pm & 7–10pm. **£150**

Glenbrittle Campsite End of road, Glenbrittle, IV47 8TA ☎01478 640404. With sea views and the beach in front, and mountains behind, this spacious, remote site offers the best of both worlds. The bad news – midges. Thousands of them, though they vanish with a breeze. The on-site shop and café sells camping essentials and proper coffee. Closed Oct–March. Camping/person **£9**

Glenbrittle SYHA Glenbrittle, IV47 8TA ☎01478 640278, ⓦsyha.org.uk/where-to-stay/islands/glen brittle. There's a mountain chalet vibe in this recently modernized hostel, with excellent facilities and an open lounge. Its old wood panelling and leather sofas combine into a sort of rugged Scandi chic. A favourite among climbers. Basic meals offered. Closed Oct–March. Dorms **£21.50**, doubles **£61**

Sligachan Bunkhouse On A87, IV47 8SW ☎01478 650458, ⓦsligachanselfcatering.com. There are peaks just beyond the back door from this modern, clean, no-frills bunkhouse next to the *Sligachan Hotel*. Within are large dorm rooms plus a laundry, a spacious kitchen and a small lounge with a fireplace. Dorms without linen **£18**, dorms with linen **£22**

ligachan Hotel and Campsite On A87, IV47 8SW ☎01478 650204, ⓦsligachan.co.uk. This long-standing launchpad for hikers (closed Nov to Easter) lies in the shadows of the Cuillin's peaks. Alongside dated but comfy enough en-suite rooms, it maintains the barn-like *Seumas' ar* which serves dishes like venison stew or rib of beef with haggis (£10–15), and which is stocked with more than four hundred whiskies and serves beer from the on-site Cuillin Brewery. A year-rounnd campsite is over the road (no telephone) – the midges in summer are as famous as the view. Easter–Oct daily: bar noon–11pm; kitchen noon–9pm. Camping/person **£7.50**, doubles **£140**

Dunvegan

After the Portnalong and Glen Brittle turning on the A863, the road slips north across bare rounded hills to skirt the bony sea cliffs and -stacks of the west coast. Twenty miles on, it reaches **DUNVEGAN** (Dùn Bheagain), an unimpressive place, but a good base for exploring the interesting Duirinish peninsula.

Dunvegan Castle

April to mid-Oct daily 10am–5.30pm • £13, gardens only £11 • ☎01470 521206, ⓦwww.dunvegancastle.com

Dunvegan's conventional tourist attraction is **Dunvegan Castle**, which sprawls on top of a rocky outcrop, sandwiched between the sea and several acres of beautifully maintained gardens. Seat of the Clan MacLeod since the thirteenth century, the present greying, rectangular fortress dates from the 1840s. Inside, you don't get a lot of castle for your money, and the contents are far from stunning; most intriguing are the battered remnants of the **Fairy Flag** which was allegedly carried back to Skye by Norwegian king Harald Hardrada's Gaelic boatmen after the Battle of Stamford Bridge in 1066. Weather-dependent seal-spotting **excursions** (25min; £7.50) and fishing trips (2hr; £45) into Loch Dunvegan depart from the gardens.

24

ARRIVAL AND INFORMATION

By bus Dunvegan sees regular buses from Portree (Mon–Sat 3–6 daily; 45min).

DUNVEGAN

Tourist information St Kilda Shop, Dunvegan Castle (April to mid-Oct daily 10am–5.30pm; ☎01470 521287).

ACCOMMODATION

Carter's Rest 8/9 Upper Milovaig, 9 miles west of Dunvegan, IV55 8WY ☎01470 511272, ⓦcarters restskye.co.uk. This luxury four-star B&B has super-king beds and a residents' lounge with a wood-burning stove; the main draw, though, is the astonishing view over Little Minch and Loch Pooltiel. Look out for seals and dolphins from the dining room. **£125**

Roskhill House Roskhill, 3 miles south of Dunvegan, IV55 8ZD ☎01470 521317, ⓦroskhillhouse.co.uk. Stone walls and home-made cake bring charm to this old crofthouse, whose modern oak furnishings, throws and crisp white linen lend understated style. Great breakfasts, too. **£94**

EATING AND DRINKING

Jann's Cakes 46 Kilmuir, Dunvegan, IV55 8GU ☎01470 592298. This tiny place on the high street is a Skye legend for its cakes and home-made soups. Not cheap at £5 a slice of cake, but the quality is high and they do great sandwiches and scallop chowder, too. Daily 11am–5pm.

Stein Inn Stein, 8 miles north of Dunvegan, IV55 8GA ☎01470 592362, ⓦsteininn.co.uk. This eighteenth-century waterfront inn – the oldest on Skye – is as traditional as you would hope. Come for an impressive array of malts and uncomplicated dishes like beer-battered Mallaig haddock and chips (average £12). Above are five cheerful en-suite rooms with sea views. Mon–Thurs 11am–11pm/midnight, Fri & Sat 11am–midnight/1am; kitchen Easter–Oct noon–4pm & 6–9pm; Oct–Easter Tues–Sun noon–2.30pm & 5.30–8pm. **£77**

Three Chimneys 5 miles west of Dunvegan, IV55 8ZT ☎01470 511258, ⓦthreechimneys.co.uk. A world-famous gourmet restaurant at the vanguard of Skye's foodie revolution, serving dishes such as Skye venison with ash-baked celeriac and elderberry sauce. Lunch is £40/person and in the evening you can try the "Skye, Land and Sea" tasting menu for £90. Reservations essential. Daily: Easter–Nov 12.15–1.30pm & 6.30–9pm; Nov–Easter 6.30–9pm.

BONNIE PRINCE CHARLIE

Prince Charles Edward Stewart – better known as **Bonnie Prince Charlie** or the "Young Pretender" – was born in Rome in 1720 where his father, the "Old Pretender", claimant to the British throne, was living in exile. At the age of 25, having little military experience, no knowledge of Gaelic, an imperfect grasp of English and a strong attachment to the Catholic faith, the prince set out for Scotland with two French ships. He arrived on the Hebridean island of **Eriskay** on July 23, 1745, and went on to raise the royal standard at Glenfinnan, gather a Highland army, win the Battle of Prestonpans, march south into England and reach Derby before finally (and foolishly) agreeing to retreat. Back in Scotland, he won one last victory, at Falkirk, before the final disaster at **Culloden** in April 1746.

The prince spent the following five months in hiding, with a price of £30,000 on his head. He endured his share of cold and hunger while on the run, but the real price was paid by the Highlanders who risked, and sometimes lost, their lives by aiding, abetting, or even simply just supporting him. The most famous of these was 23-year-old **Flora MacDonald**, whom Charles met on South Uist in June 1746. Flora was persuaded – either by his beauty or her relatives, depending on which account you believe – to convey Charles "over the sea to Skye", disguised as a servant. She was arrested later in Portree, and held in the Tower of London until July 1747. She went on to marry a local man, had seven children, and in 1774 emigrated to America, where her husband was taken prisoner during the American War of Independence. Flora returned to Scotland and was reunited with her husband on his release; they resettled in Skye and she died aged 68.

Charles eventually boarded a ship back to France in September 1746, but never returned to Scotland; nor did he see Flora again. After mistreating a string of mistresses, he eventually got married at the age of 52 to the 19-year-old Princess of Stolberg, in an effort to produce a Stewart heir. They had no children, and she eventually fled from his violent drunkenness; in 1788, a none-too-"bonnie" Prince Charles died in the arms of his illegitimate daughter in Rome.

Portree

PORTREE is the only real town on Skye, with a population of around 2500. It's also one of the most attractive fishing ports in northwest Scotland with its deep, cliff-edged harbour filled with fishing boats and circled by multicoloured restaurants and guesthouses. Above the harbour is the spick-and-span town centre, spreading out from **Somerled Square**, which was built in the late eighteenth century and now houses the bus station and car park. The **Royal Hotel** on Bank Street occupies the site of *McNab's Inn* where Bonnie Prince Charlie took leave of Flora MacDonald (see above), and where, 27 years later, Boswell and Johnson had "a very good dinner, porter, port and punch".

ARRIVAL AND INFORMATION

By bus Portree is the hub of all transport on the island and has mainland connections from Glasgow with CityLink.

Destinations Broadford via Sligachan (Mon–Sat 4–6 daily; 50min); Dunvegan (Mon–Sat 3–6 daily; 45min); Glasgow (Mon–Sat 3 daily; 6hr 15min); Glenbrittle (Mon–Sat 2 daily; 50min); Trotternish circuit via Old Man of Storr, Staffin and Uig (Mon–Sat 6 daily; 2hr total circuit).

Tourist office Just off Bridge St (April Mon–Sat 9am–5pm, Sun 10am–4pm; May–Oct Mon–Sat 9am–6pm, Sun 10am–4pm; Nov–March Mon–Sat 9am–5pm; ☎01478 612992). The best tourist office on the island can book accommodation and has internet terminals.

ACCOMMODATION

★ **Ben Tianavaig** 5 Bosville Terrace, IV51 9DG ☎01478 612152, ⍟ben-tianavaig.co.uk. The best B&B in the centre, with a warm welcome and four cottagey en-suites that are modern and bright, with unrestricted harbour views from the top-floor rooms. Reservations essential. Closed Nov–March. **£80**

Portree SYHA Centre of town, Bridge Rd, IV51 9EW ☎01478 612231, ⍟syha.org.uk/where-to-stay/islands/portree. Sparkling new, this SYHA hostel is one of the best equipped on the island. Some 55 beds across bunk dorms and private en-suite doubles. Dorms **£26**, doubles **£82**

Viewfield House Signposted off A87, IV51 9EU ☎01478 612217, ⓦviewfieldhouse.com. The last word in Scots Baronial style is this pile on the southern edge of town. It's almost eccentric in its Victorian grandeur, all fabulous floral wallpaper, hunting trophies, stuffed polecats and antiques. Rooms are individually furnished; some tranquil, some gloriously over the top. Closed Nov to Easter. **£180**

EATING AND DRINKING

Café Arriba Quay Brae, IV51 9DB ☎01478 611830, ⓦcafearriba.co.uk. This local institution packs in the punters, who come for a gossip over coffee or tea served in large china pots as much as for the changing lunch menu of home-made soups, wraps, pastas or creative fast food like wild-boar hot dogs (mains around £7). Good veggie options. **Easter–Oct daily 7am–6pm.**

Dulse and Brose Bosville Hotel, IV51 9DG ☎01478 612846, ⓦbosvillehotel.co.uk. The name translates as "seaweed and oatmeal" and the menu is as varied as this suggests; everything from smoked halloumi with puy lentil vinaigrette (£9.95) for lunch, to pork and scallops with apple remoulade (£22.50) for dinner, all served in chic surroundings. **Daily noon–3pm & 6–10pm; shorter hours in winter.**

★ **Scorrybreac** Bosville Terrace, IV51 9DG ☎01478 612069, ⓦscorrybreac.com. Just eight tables in what could be somebody's front room, but is in fact Skye's most exciting new restaurant. Chef Calum Munro serves the likes of coffee-seared venison or smoked haddock with curried egg (two courses £33; three courses £39) in charmingly intimate quarters. **Feb–Nov Tues–Sun 5–9.30pm.**

Trotternish peninsula

Protruding twenty miles north from Portree, the **Trotternish peninsula** boasts some of the island's most bizarre scenery, particularly on the east coast, where volcanic basalt has pressed down on the softer sandstone and limestone underneath, causing massive landslides. These, in turn, have created pinnacles and pillars, at their most eccentric in the **Quiraing**, above **Staffin Bay**, on the east coast.

The east coast

The first geological eccentricity on the Trotternish peninsula, six miles north of Portree along the A855, is the **Old Man of Storr**, a 165ft column of rock, shaped like a willow leaf, which, along with its neighbours, is part of a massive landslip. Huge blocks of stone still occasionally break off the cliff face of the Storr (2358ft) above and slide downhill. From the woods beside the car park it's a half-hour trek up a footpath to the foot of the column.

Further north, **Staffin Bay** is spread out before you, dotted with whitewashed and "spotty" houses. A singletrack road cuts across the peninsula from the north end of the bay, allowing access to the **Quiraing**, a spectacular forest of mighty pinnacles and savage rock formations. There are two car parks: from the first, beside a cemetery, it's a steep half-hour climb to the rocks; from the second, on the saddle, it's a longer but more gentle traverse.

Skye Museum of Island Life

On the A855, 2 miles southwest of Duntulm, IV51 9UE • Easter–Oct Mon–Sat 9.30am–5pm • £2.50 • ☎01470 552206, ⓦskyemuseum.co.uk

The **Skye Museum of Island Life** is an impressive cluster of thatched blackhouses on an exposed hill overlooking the Western Isles. The museum gives a fascinating insight into a way of life that was commonplace on Skye a century ago. Behind the museum, in the cemetery up the hill, are the graves of **Flora MacDonald** (see page 960) and her husband. Thousands turned out for her funeral in 1790, creating a procession a mile long – so widespread was her fame that the original family mausoleum fell victim to souvenir hunters and had to be replaced.

Uig

Skye's chief ferry port for the Western Isles is **UIG** (Uige), which curves its way round a dramatic, horseshoe-shaped bay on the west coast of the Trotternish peninsula.

24

There's a lovely, gentle **walk** up Glen Uig, better known as the **Faerie Glen**, a Hobbity landscape of miniature hills at the east end of the bay.

ARRIVAL AND DEPARTURE
TROTTERNISH PENINSULA

By ferry CalMac sails between Uig and Tarbert on the Isle of Harris (1–2 daily; 1hr 40min).

By bus A circular bus route (service #57A and #57C) loops around the peninsula from Portree via Old Man of Storr, Staffin and Uig (Mon–Sat 6 daily; 2hr total circuit).

ACCOMMODATION AND EATING

★ **Cowshed Bunkhouse** Just south of Uig, off the A87, IV51 9YD ☎07917 536820, ⓦskyecowshed. co.uk. Skye's first "boutique bunkhouse", with underfloor heating and all, is far closer to chic hotel than banged-up bothy, with sophisticated dorms and glamping pods. The relaxed, open-plan living and dining area is kitted out with log-burner and Space Invaders gaming table, and offers panoramic views of Uig harbour. Dorms **£16**, pods **£60**

Ferry Inn On the A87, Uig, IV51 9XP ☎01470 543200. This sophisticated, luxury inn has four en-suite doubles – the front two with bay views – above one of Skye's cosiest pubs. The long, impressive bar was made from elm wood salvaged from the Clan Donald estate, and the cask Isle of Skye Brewing Co ales are brewed just a few hundred yards away. Tues–Sat: bar 5–10pm; kitchen 6–9pm. **£170**

Skye Pie Café 3 miles south of Staffin, IV51 9JH ☎01470 562248, ⓦskyepiecafe.co.uk. Hands down the best pies on Skye, with classics like apple crumble or innovative combinations like pulled mutton with harissa, apricot and coriander (all around £5). Upstairs, three spacious, king-sized rooms are decorated in quirky, vintage style. Easter–Oct Tues–Fri noon–4pm. **£95**

24 The Small Isles

Seen from Skye or the west coast of Scotland, the **Small Isles** – **Rùm**, **Eigg**, **Muck** and tiny **Canna** – lie scattered in a silver-grey sea like a siren call to adventure. After centuries of being passed between owners, most islands have stabilized into tight-knit communities of crofters and incomers. While Muck is privately owned, Eigg was bought out by the islanders in 1997, and the other two islands have been bequeathed to national agencies: Rùm, by far the largest and most-visited of the group, belongs to Scottish Natural Heritage; Canna is in the hands of the National Trust for Scotland.

Many people come on a day-trip from Mallaig, yet the Small Isles deserve longer. They grant an opportunity to experience off-grid island life while walking, birdwatching or simply admiring the seascapes. Staying overnight requires **forward planning** and public transport is nonexistent, but the regular ferry service links all the islands: a boon for anyone wishing to island-hop.

ARRIVAL AND DEPARTURE
THE SMALL ISLES

By ferry CalMac ferries sail to the Small Isles from Mallaig (Easter to mid-Oct daily; mid-Oct to Easter Mon–Sat only; ☎0800 066 5000, ⓦcalmac.co.uk), although not to each island every day – day-trips are only possible on Sat. The *Sheerwater* sails from Arisaig (see page 935) to Rùm, Eigg and Muck (late April to late Sept; ☎01687 450224, ⓦarisaig.co.uk); it doubles as a wildlife cruise so, while enjoyable, it's more expensive than travelling with CalMac.

Rùm

Like Skye, **Rùm** is dominated by its Cuillin, which, despite only reaching a height of 2663ft at the summit of Askival, rises up with comparable drama straight from the sea in the south of the island. The majority of the island's twenty or so inhabitants live in **KINLOCH**, the only village, overlooking the large bay on the sheltered east coast, and are employed by Scottish Natural Heritage (SNH), which runs the island as a National Nature Reserve.

The island's best beach is at **KILMORY** to the north, though check with the reserve manager, Lesley Watt, about public access (☎01687 462026). The hamlet of **HARRIS** on the southwest coast once housed a large crofting community; all that remains now are several ruined blackhouses and the extravagant **Bullough Mausoleum**, which was built in the style of a Greek Doric temple by Sir George to house the remains of his father, and overlooks the sea.

Kinloch Castle

Kinloch, signposted 15min walk from ferry, PH43 4RR • March–Oct Mon–Sat guided tours (45min) coincide with the ferry • £9 • ☎ 01687 462026

Most day-trippers to Rùm head straight for **Kinloch Castle**, a squat, red-sandstone edifice. Built at huge expense in 1900 – the red sandstone was shipped in from Dumfriesshire and the soil for the gardens from Ayrshire – its interior is sheer Edwardian decadence. It's also appealingly bonkers. From the galleried hall, with its tiger rugs, stags' heads and giant Japanese incense burners, to the Soho snooker table in the Billiard Room, the interior is packed with technical gizmos accumulated by **Sir George Bullough** (1870–1939), the spendthrift son of self-made millionaire, Sir John Bullough, who bought the island as a sporting estate in 1888. In 2017 Scottish National Heritage suggested the building could be demolished if it fails to raise the £20 million needed for restoration.

ARRIVAL AND DEPARTURE | RÙM

By ferry The longest day-trip on CalMac from Mallaig is on Sat (11hr). In summer the following services operate: Mallaig–Rùm (Mon, Wed & Fri–Sun; 1hr 20min–2hr 30min); Rùm–Eigg (Mon & Sat; 1hr–3hr 30min); Rùm–

Muck (Sat; 1hr 10min) and Rùm–Canna (Mon, Wed, Fri & Sat; 55min). The Sheerwater boat runs from Arisaig (April, May & Sept Tues & Thurs; June–Aug Tues, Thurs & Sat; 1hr 45min–2hr 30min).

ACCOMMODATION

Ivy Cottage Kinloch, PH43 4RR ☎ 01687 462744, ⊕ ivycottageisleofrum.co.uk. Delivers loch views from two pleasant en-suite rooms and the conservatory where you have breakfast. Its young owners prepare dinners for guests (included in the price) and non-residents on request. Bikes to rent, and a cute craft shop next door. **£150**

Kinloch Village Campsite Kinloch, PH43 4RR ☎ 01687 460328. A community-run campsite with an appealing location spread along the shore on the south side of Kinloch Bay. Also on site are four tiny, insulated

camping cabins with four beds each. Closed Nov–March. Camping/person **£6**, cabins for two **£22**

Rum Bunkhouse Kinloch Kinloch, PH43 4RR ☎ 01687 460318, ⊖ bunkhouse@isleofrum.com. This impressive bunkhouse is the most comfortable option on the island, particularly for walking groups who don't want to brave the bothies. Twenty beds (one twin, three four-bedders and a six-bed dorm), plus a large living area with sofas and a wood-burning stove. **£23**

24

Eigg

From a distance, **Eigg** is the most easily distinguishable of the Small Isles, since the island is mostly made up of a basalt plateau reaching 1000ft above sea level, and a great stump of columnar pitchstone lava, known as **An Sgùrr**, rising 1290ft out of the plateau. It's also the most vibrant, populous and welcoming of the Small Isles, with a strong sense of community among its hundred or so residents. With An Sgùrr watching over you wherever you go, many folk feel duty-bound to climb it, and enjoy the wonderful views over to Muck and Rùm (3–4hr round trip). For a longer, easier stroll, head three miles up the road to the northwest coast and the **Singing Sands**, so called because the quartz grains squeak underfoot.

ARRIVAL AND DEPARTURE | EIGG

By ferry CalMac summer timetables are: Mallaig–Eigg (Mon, Tues & Thurs–Sun; 1hr 15min–2hr 25min); Muck–Eigg (Tues & Thurs–Sat; 35min); Rùm–Eigg (Mon & Sat;

1hr–3hr 30min) and Canna–Eigg (Mon & Sat; 2hr 15min). The *Sheerwater* runs from Arisaig (April–Sept daily).

ACCOMMODATION AND EATING

Galmisdale Bay Harbour, PH42 4RL ☎ 01687 482487, ⊕ almisdale-bay.com. Island ingredients go into home-

made soups, quiche, pizza, lamb or venison burgers, plus blackboard specials such as fishcakes – all for under £10.

There's a craft shop and well-stocked mini-supermarket in the same complex. Easter–Oct Mon, Wed, Thurs & Sat 10am–11pm, Tues 10am–5pm, Sun 11.30am–5pm; Nov–Easter open around ferry schedules.

Glebe Barn Galmisdale, PH42 4RL ☎01687 482417, ⓦglebebarn.co.uk. Eigg's hostel on the hill above the harbour has a spacious lounge with awesome coast views and pleasant wee dorm rooms and twins. Better still is the self-contained cottagey annexe *Glebe Apartment* – a superb option for up to five people (from £60). Closed Nov–March. Dorms **£20**, twins **£45**

★ **Lageorna** Cleadale, PH42 4RL ☎01687 460081, ⓦlageorna.com. Beautiful, modern rooms full of contemporary crafts – think rustic wooden beds and knitted throws – and astonishing views, plus a lovely vintage cottage that sleeps four (£650). The owner also prepares hearty dishes (£30 non-guests, £25 for guests) such as venison with spicy puy lentils; reservations recommended. Closed over Christmas and New Year, open by arrangement over winter months. **£110**

Sue Holland's Croft Cleadale, PH42 4RL ☎01687 482480, ⓦeiggorganics.co.uk. On an organic croft, this is the island's only designated campsite and it's a belter, with views and sunsets to inspire poetry. The old cowshed is now a basic bothy for up to four; for more comfort choose a yurt. Sue also runs crofting tours and courses on growing vegetables. Camping/person **£5**, yurts **£55**, bothy for four **£55**

Muck

The smallest and most southerly of the Small Isles, **Muck** is low-lying, mostly treeless and extremely fertile. You'll arrive at **PORT MÒR**, the village on the southeast corner of the island. A road, a little more than a mile long, connects Port Mór with the island's main farm, **GALLANACH**, which overlooks the rocky seal-strewn skerries on the north side of the island; to the east lies the nicest sandy beach, **Camas na Cairidh**. In the southwest corner of the island, it's worth climbing **Beinn Airein**, despite it being only 453ft above sea level, for the 360-degree panoramic view (2hr round trip).

ARRIVAL AND INFORMATION

MUCK

By ferry CalMac ferries' (·0800 066 5000, ⓦcalmac.co.uk) summer timetables are: Mallaig–Muck (Tues & Thurs–Sun; 1hr 40min–4hr 20min); Eigg–Muck (Thurs, Sat & Sun; 35min) and Rùm–Muck (Sat; 2hr 45min). The *Sheerwater* boat also sails to Muck from Arisaig (April–Sept Wed & Fri–Sun).

Tourist information The *Craft Shop* in Port Mòr (see below), which springs into life when day-trippers arrive, is a de facto information centre.

ACCOMMODATION AND EATING

The Craft Shop Port Mòr, PH41 2RP ☎01687 462990, ⓦisleofmuck.com. The only shop on the island prepares daily soups and sandwiches made from fresh home-baked bread, plus afternoon teas and dinners of tasty Scottish home-cooking prepared on request. April, May & Sept hours vary; June–Aug daily 11am–4pm.

Gallanach Lodge Gallanach Bay, PH41 2RP ☎01687 462365, ⓦisleofmuck.com. A purpose-built luxury lodge that takes full advantage of a superb position above the beach to provide fantastic views of Rùm. The style is island boutique – rustic, handmade beds in rooms with hotel-style mod cons. Full board only. **£180**

Isle of Muck Bunkhouse Port Mòr, PH41 2RP ☎01687 462042, ⓦisleofmuck.com. Despite the name, the island's characterful, wood-panelled bunkhouse near the port has beds, not bunks – two twins and a double – and is heated by an oil-fired Raeburn stove. Not luxurious, but full of character. **£20**

Canna

Measuring just five miles by one, **Canna** (ⓦnts.org.uk/visit/canna) is run as a single farm and bird sanctuary by the National Trust for Scotland, with a dwindling population now down to single figures. For visitors, the chief pastime is walking – you can circuit the entire island in a long day's hike (twelve miles; 10hr). For a shorter stroll, it's about a mile from the dock across a grassy basalt plateau to the bony sea cliffs of the north shore, which rise to a peak around **Compass Hill** (458ft) – so called because its high metal content distorts compasses – in the northeastern corner of the island, from where you get great views across to Rùm and Skye. The cliffs of the buffeted western half of the island are a breeding ground for Manx shearwater, razorbill and puffin.

ARRIVAL AND DEPARTURE   **CANNA**

By ferry Summer timetables are: Eigg–Canna (Mon & Sat; 1 daily; 2hr 20min); Mallaig–Canna (Mon, Wed, Fri & Sun 1 daily, Sat 2; 2hr 30min–3hr 45min); Muck–Canna (Sat 1; 1hr 35min); Rùm–Canna (Mon, Wed & Fri–Sun 1 daily; 1hr 5min).

ACCOMMODATION

Tighard 15min walk from the pier, PH44 4RS ☎ 01687 462474, ⓦ tighard.co.uk. The Sanday room is the pick – spacious, traditional and with sweeping sea views – in the only B&B on Canna. The other two smaller and simpler twins also enjoy sea views. Friendly hosts Colin and David also offer packed lunch and dinner with prior arrangement. **£120**

The Western Isles

Beyond Skye, across the unpredictable waters of the Minch, lie the wild and windy Outer Hebrides or **Western Isles**, a 130-mile-long archipelago stretching from Lewis and Harris in the north to the Uists and Barra in the south. An elemental beauty pervades the two hundred or so islands; only a handful are inhabited, and the total population hits around 28,000 people.

The interior of the northernmost island, **Lewis**, is mostly peat moor, a barren and marshy tract that gives way to the bare peaks of **North Harris**. Across a narrow isthmus lies **South Harris**, presenting some of the finest scenery in Scotland, with wide beaches of golden sand trimming the Atlantic, in full view of a rough boulder-strewn interior. Across the Sound of Harris, to the south, a string of tiny, flatter isles – **North Uist**, **Benbecula** and **South Uist** – are linked by causeways, offering breezy beaches, fine sands and a narrow band of boggy farmland, mostly bordered by a range of hills to the east. Finally, tiny **Barra** contains all these landscapes in one small Hebridean package, and is a spectacular introduction to the region.

In direct contrast to their wonderful landscapes, villages in the Western Isles are seldom picturesque, usually made up of scattered, relatively modern crofts dotted around the elementary road system. **Tarbert** on Harris and **Castlebay** on Barra are the exceptions, offering seafood stops, cafés and one or two attractions; **Stornoway**, meanwhile, is the Outer Hebrides' urban centre and its cultural heart.

24

GETTING AROUND   **THE WESTERN ISLES**

By car/ferry A series of causeways makes it possible to travel by road from one end of the Western Isles to the other with just two interruptions – the CalMac ferries from Harris to Berneray, at the very tip of North Uist, and from Eriskay to Barra (☎ 0800 066 5000, ⓦ calmac.co.uk).

By bus The islands have a decent bus service, though there are no buses on Sundays. For up-to-date schedules visit the Outer Hebrides council website (ⓦ cne-siar.gov.uk/travel/busservice/current/indexu.asp).

By bike The popular Hebridean Cycling Way Route, a 185-mile ride of a lifetime across the archipelago's ten islands, sees bikers heading south to north to catch the prevailing winds.

Lewis (Leodhas)

Shaped like the top of an ice-cream cone, **Lewis** is the largest and most populous of the Western Isles. Nearly half of the inhabitants live in the crofting and fishing villages strung out along the northwest coast, between **Callanish** (Calanais) and **Port of Ness** (Port Nis), in one of the country's most densely populated rural areas. On this

---

GAELIC IN THE WESTERN ISLES

The Outer Hebrides remains the heartland of **Gaelic** culture, with the language spoken by the majority of islanders. Many **road signs** in the Western Isles are almost exclusively in Gaelic; bilingual **maps** are available at most tourist offices. We've used the English names first throughout this chapter, with the Gaelic in parentheses.

coast, you'll also find the best-preserved **prehistoric remains** – including the Callanish standing stones. The landscape is mostly flat peat bog – hence the island's Gaelic name, from *leogach* (marshy) – but the shoreline is more dramatic, especially around the Butt of Lewis in the north. The rest of the island's population lives in **Stornoway** on the east coast, the only real town in the Western Isles. In the south, where Lewis is joined with Harris, the land rises to more than 1800ft, providing an exhilarating backdrop for the unrivalled beaches that hug the isolated west coast.

Stornoway (Steornabhagh)

In these parts, **STORNOWAY** is a buzzing metropolis, with around nine thousand inhabitants and all the trappings of a large town. Aesthetics are not its strong point, and the urban pleasures on offer are limited, but in July the town hosts the **Hebridean Celtic Festival** (W hebceltfest.com). Stornoway's best-looking civic building is the old **Town Hall** on South Beach, a splendid Scots Baronial pile from 1905, its rooftop interspersed with conical towers, above which a central clocktower rises. One block east along South Beach, you'll find **An Lanntair** – Gaelic for "lantern" – Stornoway's modern cultural centre.

Lews Castle

Across the bay from the town centre, HS2 0XS • **Museum nan Eilean** April–Sept Mon–Wed, Fri & Sat 10am–5pm; Oct–March Mon–Wed, Fri & Sat 1–4pm • Free • **Grounds** Daily 24hr • ☎ 01851 822746, W lews-castle.co.uk

The castellated pomposity of **Lews Castle**, surrounded by mature woodland, was built by Sir James Matheson in 1863 after resettling the crofters who used to live here. As the former laird's pad, it has long been seen as a symbol of oppression by many. After lying abandoned for more than 25 years, the building has had an extensive £14 million makeover to transform it into luxury accommodation (see below) while the excellent new **Museum nan Eilean** tells the story of the islands' geology, its Gaelic culture and the struggles of the nineteenth century. Before leaving, make sure to stop by the fantastic **Storehouse Café**, selling paninis, soups and salads (daily 9.30am–6pm), and the **Outfitters** store, with souvenirs and knits from across the islands.

ARRIVAL AND INFORMATION

By plane Stornoway Airport (☎ 01851 702256, W hial.co.uk/stornoway-airport) is 4 miles east of the town centre: there are buses (Mon–Sat hourly; 15min) and taxis (around £6).

By ferry CalMac ferries to Ullapool (Mon–Sat 2 daily, Sun 1–2; 2hr 30min; ☎ 01851 307470, W calmac.co.uk) run from the octagonal CalMac ferry terminal on South Beach, near the bus station.

By bus The bus station (☎ 01851 704327) is on South Beach in the town centre.

Destinations Callanish (Mon–Sat 4–6 daily; 32min); Carloway (Mon–Sat 4–6 daily; 45min); Garenin (Mon–Sat 2–4 daily; 1hr); Leverburgh (Mon–Sat 4–5 daily; 1hr 50min); Port of Ness (Mon–Sat hourly; 1hr); Tarbert (Mon–Sat 5 daily; 1hr), Uig (Mon–Sat 4–6 daily; 1h 30min).

Tourist office 26 Cromwell St (May–Aug Mon–Sat 9am–5.45pm; Sept–March Mon–Sat 9am–4.45pm; ☎ 01851 703088, W visithebrides.com).

ACCOMMODATION

Heb Hostel 25 Kenneth St, HS1 2DR ☎ 01851 709889, W hebhostel.co.uk. A clean, central, Victorian-era terrace house in salmon pink, converted into a simple hostel, with laundry, kitchen facilities and breakfast. It's run by friendly resident warden Christine, who ropes in her extended family to help. **£18**

Jannel 5 Stewart Drive, HS1 2TU ☎ 01851 705324, W jannel-stornoway.co.uk. A short walk from the town centre, this B&B, run by a delightful landlady, offers five spacious, immaculate en-suite rooms. She serves Stornoway's famous black pudding for breakfast, too **£89**

★ **Lews Castle by Natural Retreats** Overlooking the harbour, HS2 0XS ☎ 01625 416430, W naturalretreats.com. This 27-room Gothic Revival keep offers the most luxurious stay in the Hebrides. Choose from deluxe suites with design catalogue furnishings, or chi-chi self-catering apartments (£180). **£140**

Royal Hotel Stornoway Cromwell St, HS1 2DG ☎ 01851 702109, W royalstornoway.co.uk. Lewis' most historic property, a few steps away from the town centre. There's a pick of singles, twins and doubles, plus two great eating options – *The Boatshed Restaurant*, a safe bet for fresh-off-the-boat seafood, and *HS-1* (see below). Handily, the marina is across the road. **£105**

EATING AND DRINKING

An Lanntair Kenneth St, HS1 2DS ☎01851 708490, ⓦlanntair.com. Popular café-restaurant in the arts centre, celebrating local produce with ingredients such as steamed Leurbost mussels and home-made haggis (both meat and veggie). A great breakfast and kids' menu, plus steak night every Wed. Mains from £10.95. Mon–Sat 10am–8pm.

The Criterion 32 Point St, HS1 2XF ☎01851 701990. A wee, authentic, no-frills Stornoway pub, staging regular informal music sessions– if nothing's going down here, try nearby *McNeill's*. Mon–Thurs 11am–11pm, Fri & Sat 11am–1am.

★ **Digby Chick** 5 Bank St, HS1 2XG ☎01851 700026, ⓦdigbychick.co.uk. Arguably the best restaurant on Lewis, this buzz-worthy bistro impresses with the kind of fine dining you'd expect in Edinburgh or Glasgow. The early-evening menu is a bargain (three courses; £23.50), while stand-outs include smoked haddock, fillet of Minch cod and a taster of partridge breast. Dinner mains from £18. Mon–Sat noon–2pm & 5.30–9pm.

HS-1 27 Cromwell St, HS1 2QN ☎01851 702109, ⓦroyalstornoway.co.uk. Located in the *Royal Hotel Stornoway* (see above), this family-friendly café-pub specializes in burgers, wraps, curries and light meals, using meats farmed on local estates. Mains around £11.95. Daily noon–9pm.

The road to Port of Ness (Port Nis)

Northwest of Stornoway, the A857 crosses the barren **peat bog** of the interior, an empty, undulating wilderness, riddled with stretchmarks formed by peat cuttings and pockmarked with freshwater lochans. For the people of Lewis, the peat continues to serve as a valuable energy resource, its pungent smoke one of the most characteristic smells of the Western Isles.

Twelve miles across the peat bog, near Barvas (Barabhas), the road divides, heading southwest towards Callanish (see page 968), or northeast through a string of scattered settlements to the fishing village of **PORT OF NESS** (Port Nis). Shortly before Port of Ness, a narrow road twists northwest to the blustery northern tip of the island, *Rubha Robhanais* – known to devotees of the BBC shipping forecast as the **Butt of Lewis** – where a lighthouse sticks up above a series of sheer cliffs and stacks, alive with seabirds.

24

ARRIVAL AND DEPARTURE · THE ROAD TO PORT OF NESS

By bus There's a regular bus service from Stornoway to Port of Ness (Mon–Sat hourly; 1hr).

ACCOMMODATION AND EATING

The Decca Lionel A few minutes from the Butt of Ness Lighthouse, HS2 0XB ☎01851 810571, ⓦthedecca. co.uk. Born from the ashes of an old radio navigation station, this homely B&B has a mix of singles, doubles and twins (one of which has a jacuzzi). Evening meals are available, for non-residents too (£25 for three courses), and there are folk sessions on Wed throughout summer. **£100**

Galson Farm South Galson (Gabhsann Bho Dheas), HS2 0SH ☎01851 850492, ⓦgalsonfarm.co.uk. An attractive converted eighteenth-century farmhouse on a working croft, which offers generous home-cooked meals – dinner and B&B are available, and they run a six-bunk bunkhouse close by. Bunkhouse **£20**, doubles **£92**

Westside

Heading southwest from the crossroads near Barvas brings you to the **Westside** (An Toabh Siar), an area where several villages meander towards the sea, and which is home to the **Callanish** stone circle.

Arnol Blackhouse

Arnol, HS2 9DB · Mon–Sat: April–Sept 9.30am–5.30pm; Oct–March 10am–4pm · £5; HS · ☎01851 710395, ⓦhistoricenvironment. scot/visit-a-place/places/the-blackhouse-arnol

In **ARNOL**, the remains of traditional farmsteads – or blackhouses – lie abandoned by the roadside. Ay the north end of the village, no. 42 has been preserved as the **Arnol Blackhouse**. The dark interior is lit and heated by a small peat fire, which is kept alight in the central hearth of bare earth. As there's no chimney, smoke drifts through the thatch, helping to kill any creepy crawlies, keep out the midges and turn the heathery sods and oat-straw thatch itself into next year's fertilizer.

Garenin

5a Garenin, HS2 9AL · Mon–Sat 9.30am–5.30pm · £2.50 · ☎ 01851 643416, ⓦ gearrannan.com

A mile-long road leads north off the A858 to the beautifully remote coastal settlement of **GARENIN** (Gearrannan). Here, rather than re-create a single museum-piece blackhouse as at Arnol, a whole cluster of nine thatched crofters' houses – the last of which was abandoned in 1974 – have been restored and put to a variety of uses: a café, a museum, self-catering cottages and a hostel. Like walking into a time-warp, the ensemble gives a great impression of what life in a blackhouse village – or *baile tughaidh* – must have been like.

Dun Carloway (Dùn Charlabhaigh)

Carloway, HS2 9AZ · Daily 24hr · Free

Just beyond Carloway village, **Dun Carloway** (Dùn Charlabhaigh) perches on top of a conspicuous rocky outcrop overlooking the sea. This is one of Scotland's best-preserved brochs – or prehistoric stone fort – its dry-stone circular walls reaching a height of more than 30ft. The broch consists of two concentric walls, the inner one perpendicular, the outer one slanting inwards, the two originally fastened together by roughly hewn flagstones, which also served as lookout galleries reached via a narrow stairwell.

Callanish (Calanais) standing stones

Loch Roag, HS2 9DY · **Standing stones** Daily 24hr · Free · **Callanish Visitor Centre** April, May, Sept & Oct Mon–Sat 10am–6pm; June–Aug Mon–Sat 9.30am–8pm; Nov–March Tues–Sat 10am–4pm · £3.50 · ☎ 01851 621422, ⓦ callanishvisitorcentre.co.uk

Overlooking the sheltered, islet-studded waters of Loch Roag (Loch Ròg), on the west coast, are the islands' most dramatic prehistoric ruins, the **Callanish standing stones**. These monoliths – nearly fifty slabs of gnarled and finely grained Lewissian gneiss up to 15ft high – were transported here between 3000 and 1500 BC, but their exact function remains a mystery. No one knows for certain why the ground plan resembles a colossal Celtic cross, nor why there's a central burial chamber. It's likely that such a massive endeavour was prompted by the desire to predict the seasonal cycle upon which these early farmers were dependent, and indeed many of the stones are aligned with the positions of the sun and the stars. Whatever the reason, there's no denying its powerful primeval presence, not to mention the sheer beauty, of the stones. Within striking distance a mile along the road are two smaller, quieter stone circles, imaginatively named **Callanish II** and **Callanish III**.

ARRIVAL AND DEPARTURE
CALLANISH

By bus There are regular buses between Stornoway and Arnol (Mon–Sat 6–8 daily; 30min); Callanish (Mon–Sat 4–6 daily; 32min); Carloway (Mon–Sat 4–6 daily; 45min); and Garenin (Mon–Sat 2–4 daily; 1hr).

ACCOMMODATION

Leumadair 7a Callanish, HS2 9DY ☎ 01851 621706, ⓦ leumadair.co.uk. A purpose-built modern guesthouse near the Callanish stones, owned by a friendly couple who cure and smoke their own bacon, keep hens and have four pet Harris hawks. Dinner can be provided, for guests only, on request (£25 for three courses). **£86**

Loch Roag Guest House 22a Breascletea, HS2 9EF ☎ 01851 621 771, ⓦ lochroag.com. Two miles from Callanish, with sea and mountain views, this four-star, six-bed B&B whips up great breakfasts and three-course evening meals (residents only) for £25 (Lewis lamb and Stornoway black pudding are a given). **£80**

Harris (Na Hearadh)

Hillier, more dramatic and arguably more appealing than its northern neighbour, **Harris** has boulder-strewn slopes descending to aquamarine bays of dazzling white sand. While the "island" shares the same land mass as Lewis, it remains clearly divided itself by a minuscule isthmus into the wild, inhospitable mountains of **North Harris** and the gentler landscape and sandy shores of **South Harris**.

North Harris (Ceann a Tuath na Hearadh)

If you're coming from Stornoway on the A859, mountainous **North Harris** is a spectacular introduction to Harris, its bulging, pyramidal mountains of gneiss looming over the dramatic, fjord-like **Loch Seaforth** (Loch Shìphoirt). You weave your way over a boulder-strewn saddle between mighty **Sgaoth Aird** (1834ft) and **Clisham** (An Cliseam), the highest peak in the Western Isles, at 2621ft. This wild terrain, littered with debris left behind by retreating glaciers, offers but the barest of vegetation, with an occasional cluster of crofters' houses sitting in the shadow of a host of pointed peaks.

Tarbert (An Tairbeart)

Sheltered in a green valley on the narrow isthmus, **TARBERT** is the largest place on Harris and a wonderful place to arrive by boat. The port's mountainous backdrop is impressive, and the town is attractively laid out on steep terraces sloping up from the dock. Taking pride of place at the apex of the harbour is the **Isle of Harris Distillery**, which as well as producing (legally) the first whisky in the Outer Hebrides since 1829, shares the secret to its sugar kelp-infused gin during **tours** (summer Mon–Sat 10am–5pm; rest of year Tues, Wed & Fri noon & 2pm; £15; 1hr 15min; ☏01859 502212 ⍟harrisdistillery.com).

ARRIVAL AND INFORMATION　　　　　　　　　　　　　　　　　　　　TARBERT

By ferry There are CalMac ferries to and from Uig on Skye (1–2 daily; 1hr 40min).

By bus Tarbert is served by regular buses from Leverburgh via the west coast (Mon–Sat 6–8 daily; 45min) and via the east coast (Mon–Sat 2–4 daily; 1hr 5min) and Stornoway (Mon–Sat 5 daily; 1hr). Buses stop at the pier.

Tourist office Tarbert has Harris's only tourist office (April, Sept & Oct Mon–Sat 9.15am–4.45pm; May–Aug Mon, Wed & Fri 9am–6pm, Tues, Thurs & Sat 9am–8.30pm; ☏01859 502011).

ACCOMMODATION AND EATING

Harris Hotel Scott Rd, HS3 3DL ☏01859 502154, ⍟harrishotel.com. A 5min walk from the harbour, this is Tarbert's longest-established and largest hotel. A family-run affair, it's a solid choice, with 23 en-suite rooms and a restaurant (mains around £20) where they even serve food on Sun (a rarity in these parts). The village's liveliest pub – the *Isle of Harris Inn* – is just across the road. Daily noon–9pm. **£110**

No. 5 Hostel Dinishader (Drinisiadar), 3 miles south of Tarbert, HS3 3DX ☏01851 511255, ⍟number5.biz. A converted cottage offering canoes, kayaks and cycles for rent. There's a shared croft, chalet and cottage hostel with dorms, all with stunning sea views. There is no phone signal or wi-fi – perfect for a digital detox. Dorms **£22**, twins **£50**

The Pierhouse Restaurant Pier Rd, HS3 3DG ☏01859 502364, ⍟hotel-hebrides.com. Tucked inside the *Hotel Hebrides* on the harbourfront, this seafood specialist is Tarbert's classiest option, with hand-dived scallops, rope-grown Lewis mussels and local-cured smoked salmon (mains £13–25). The *Mote Bar* next door has bar food, local ales and easier to swallow prices. Daily: restaurant noon–3pm & 6–9pm; bar noon–9pm.

Rhenigdale Hostel Rhenigdale (Reinigeadal), HS3 3BD ⍟gatliff.org.uk. Simple twelve-bed hostel in an isolated coastal hamlet. There's a request-only bus service or else it's a magnificent six-mile hike (3hr) over the rocky landscape from Tarbert – ask at the tourist office for directions. Camping permitted. No advance bookings. Dorms **£15**

South Harris (Ceann a Deas na Hearadh)

The mountains of **South Harris** are less dramatic than in the north, but the scenery is equally sigh-triggering. There's a choice of routes from Tarbert to the ferry port of **Leverburgh**, which connects with North Uist: the east coast, known as **The Bays** (Na Baigh), is home to a couple of **Harris Tweed** designer showrooms, while the **west coast** is endowed with some of the finest stretches of sandy **beaches** in the UK. Most stunning of all is the vast golden strand of **Luskentyre Bay** (Tràigh Losgaintir), with the islet-studded turquoise sea to the west – even on the dullest day the sand glows beneath the waves. Paradoxically, most people on South Harris live along the harsh eastern coastline. But not by choice – they were evicted from their original crofts to make way for sheep-grazing in the nineteenth century.

24

HARRIS TWEED

Far from a cottage industry, **Harris Tweed** production is vital to the local economy, and involves a well-organized and unionized workforce. Traditionally, the tweed was made by women to provide clothing for their families, using a 2500-year-old process. They first plucked the wool by hand, washed and scoured it, dying it with lichen, heather flowers or ragwort, before carding, spinning and weaving the material.

In the mid-nineteenth century, Catherine Murray, Countess of Dunmore, who owned large parts of Harris, began to sell surplus cloth to her aristocratic friends, helping kick-start the modern industry. To earn the official **Harris Tweed Authority** trademark today, the fabric has to be hand-woven on the Outer Hebrides from pure new Scottish wool, while the manufacturing process must take place in local mills – currently in Shawbost, Carloway and Stornoway in Lewis. A number of **designer showrooms** sell tweed suits, waistcoats and jackets, the best of which are The Harris Tweed Company (☎01859 511108, ⓦharristweedco.co.uk) and Harris Tweed (☎01859 502040, ⓦharristweedisleofharris.co.uk), both in South Harris.

Leverburgh (An t-Ob)

The west-coast road veers to the southeast to trim the island's south shore, eventually reaching the sprawling settlement of **LEVERBURGH**, named after Lord Leverhulme, who planned to turn the place into the largest fishing port on the west coast of Scotland. The main reason to come is to catch the CalMac **ferry** service to Berneray and the Uists (see below).

Rodel (Roghadal)

A mile or so from Renish Point (Rubha Reanais), the southern tip of Harris, is the old port of **RODEL** (Roghadal), where a smattering of ancient stone houses lies among the hillocks. On top of one of these grassy humps is **St Clement's Church** (Tur Chliamainn), burial place of the MacLeods of Harris and Dunvegan in Skye. Dating from the 1520s, the church's bare interior is distinguished by its wall tombs; look out, too, for the *Sheela-na-gig* (a naked pre-Christian fertility goddess) halfway up the south side of the tower.

ARRIVAL AND DEPARTURE
SOUTH HARRIS

By ferry The CalMac ferry zigzags its way through the shallows between Berneray and Leverburgh (3–4 daily; 1hr).

By bus Buses from Tarbert run to Leverburgh via the west coast (Mon–Sat 6–8 daily; 45min) and via the east coast (Mon–Sat 2–4 daily; 1hr 5min). Buses stop at the pier.

ACCOMMODATION

Am Bothan Ferry Rd, Leverburgh, HS5 3UA ☎01859 520251, ⓦambothan.com. Quirky, bright red, timber-clad bunkhouse that makes for a pretty luxurious, welcoming hostel, close to the ferry. A lovely kitchen-living room combo, plus laundry and drying facilities. **£25**

Beul Na Mara 12 Seilbost, HS3 3HP ☎01859 550205, ⓦbeulnamara.co.uk. This B&B can rightly claim the most sweeping views of the golden sands of Luskentyre Beach – they're right outside the front window. One of the first guesthouses on the island, it's now complemented by two self-catering cottages (from £660/week), with the magical hills of North Harris as a backdrop. **£95**

★ **Horgabost Campsite** South of Seilebost on the west coast, HS3 3HR ☎01859 550386. Lewis and Harris have a number of stunning campsites, but judged by location alone this one is unbeatable. It's sheltered on a curving beach overlooking Luskentyre Beach and the North Harris hills, wedged between an undulating strip of machair and the A859. The facilities are basic (shower-block washroom and communal kitchen), but on a long summer's night, it's pinch-yourself-you're-dreaming stuff. **£14**

Lickisto Blackhouse Camping Lickisto (Liceasto), HS3 3EL ☎01859 530485, ⓦfreewebs.com/vanvon. A beautiful, rugged spot overlooking the sea, offering home-baked bread and eggs, a peat fire to warm you in the blackhouse and toilets in the byres. Yurts also available. Closed Nov–Feb. Camping/pitch **£20**, yurts **£70**

24

EATING

Croft 36 Northton, HS3 3JA ☎01859 520779, ⓦcroft36.com. The first sign that this low-key takeaway is the best in the Hebrides is the crab-stuffed pasta, rabbit stew and venison pie on the menu. It's run out of a simple white timbered shack and arranges deliveries to campsites in season. Mains around £10. Mon–Fri 10am–4.30pm & 6–9pm.

★ **The Machair Kitchen** South of Seilebost on the west coast, HS3 3HR ☎01859 520225, ⓦhotel-hebrides.com. A west-coast must-see, this community-owned cultural centre and restaurant with architecturally stunning design and cracking Atlantic views is a revelation. The menu lists local lamb, monkfish and potted crab, and they host art and photography exhibitions and folk nights. Very cool indeed. Mon–Sat 10am–4.30pm & 6–9pm.

The Temple Café Northton (Taobh Tuath), HS3 3JA ☎07876 340416, ⓦfacebook.com/TheTempleCafe. Down a remote road on the west coast, this fabulously funky stonehouse café is an absolute treat. Pick from delicious cakes, coffee, sandwiches and takeaway pizza. Closed in winter. Tues, Wed & Sat 10.30am–5pm, Thurs, Fri & Sun 10.30am–5pm & 6.30–8pm.

North Uist (Uibhist a Tuath)

Compared to the mountainous scenery of Harris, **North Uist** – seventeen miles long and thirteen miles wide – is much flatter and, for some, comes as something of an anticlimax. More than half the surface area is covered by water, creating a distinctive peaty-brown lochan-studded "drowned landscape". Most visitors are here for the trout and salmon **fishing** and the deerstalking, both of which (along with poaching) are critical to the island's economy. Others come for the smattering of **prehistoric sites**, the **birds**, or the sheer peace and solitude of North Uist's vast sandy **beaches**, which extend – almost without interruption – along the north and west coasts.

Lochmaddy

Despite being on the east coast, some distance away from any beach, the ferry port of **LOCHMADDY** (Loch Nam Madadh, or "Loch of the Hounds") makes a good base for exploring the island.

Taigh Chearsabhagh

Lochmaddy, HS6 5AA · **Museum** Mon–Sat 10am–5pm · Free · ☎01870 603970, ⓦtaigh-chearsabhagh.org

A converted eighteenth-century merchant's house, **Taigh Chearsabhagh** is now home to a vibrant community arts centre that houses a café (Mon–Sat 10am–4pm), post office and shop as well as an excellent museum. The arts centre was a prime mover behind the commissioning of a series of seven **sculptures** dotted about the Uists – ask for directions to those in and around Lochmaddy, the most interesting of which is the **Both Nam Faileas** (Hut of the Shadow), roughly half a mile north of town.

Berneray (Bhearnaraigh)

The ferry connection with Harris arrives and departs from the southeasternmost point of **Berneray** (ⓦisleofberneray.com), a low-lying island immediately north of North Uist and connected to the latter via a causeway. Two miles by three, with a population of around 140, the island has a superb three-mile-long sandy **beach** on the west and north coast, backed by rabbit-free dunes and machair.

Balranald RSPB Reserve

Western tip of the island, HS6 5DL · Daily 24hr · **Visitor centre** April–Aug daily 9am–6pm · Free · ☎01870 560287, ⓦrspb.org

North Uist's **Balranald RSPB Reserve** is best known for its population of corncrakes: there are usually one or two making a loud noise right outside the **visitor centre**, where you can pick up a leaflet outlining a two-hour walk along the headland, marked by posts. A wonderful carpet of flowers covers the machair in summer, and there are usually corn buntings and arctic terns inland and gannets, Manx shearwater and skuas out to sea.

ARRIVAL AND INFORMATION — NORTH UIST

By ferry CalMac car ferries run from Leverburgh to Berneray (3–4 daily; 1hr) and from Uig to Lochmaddy (1–2 daily; 1hr 45min).

By bus There are services between Lochmaddy and Balivanich (Mon–Sat 6–7 daily; 30–45min), Balranald (Mon–Sat 3 daily; 50min), Berneray (Mon–Sat 8 daily; 20min) and Lochboisdale (Mon–Sat 5–6 daily; 1hr 30min).

Tourist office Pier Rd, Lochmaddy (April–Oct Mon–Wed, Fri & Sat 10am–4.30pm, Tues & Thurs 10.15am–4.45pm; ⊕01876 500321).

ACCOMMODATION AND EATING

Bagh Alluin 21 Baleshare (Baile Sear), HS6 5HG ⊕01876 580370, ⊛jacvolbeda.co.uk. A secluded, beautifully designed modern B&B with fantastic views over the island, run by a warm and friendly Dutch artist. £85

Berneray Hostel Berneray (Bhearnaraigh), HS6 5BQ ⊛gatliff.org.uk. Berneray's wonderful 21-bed hostel, occupying a pair of thatched blackhouses, is in a lovely beachside spot, beyond the main village on the north side of Bays Loch (Loch a Bhàigh). No advance bookings. £15

Hamersay House Lochmaddy, HS6 5AE ⊕01876 500700, ⊛hamersayhouse.co.uk. This hotel is what North Uist is all about. It's homely, comfortable, and has eye-popping sea views and a bistro heavy on seafood and game. Nearby, *Langass Lodge*, an old hunting lodge to the south overlooking Locheport, is run by the same husband-and-wife team. Mon–Sat 11am–11pm, Sun 12.30pm–11pm. £135

The Tractor Shed Paible, HS6 5DZ ⊕0795 216308, ⊛northuistbunkhouse.co.uk. A no-frills bunkhouse appealing to hikers and cyclists, with unique turf-roofed sheds and family castaway huts. Also has laundry, peat fires, a BBQ and secure parking for bikes. Closed Nov–March. £36

Westford Inn Claddach Kirkibost (Cladach Chireboist), HS6 5EP ⊕01876 580653, ⊛facebook.com/WestfordInn. North Uist's only pub is housed in an eighteenth-century factor's house. There's a wood-panelled bar and several smaller rooms with real fires, Skye ales on tap and standard pub food. May–Sept Mon–Thurs noon–11pm, Fri noon–midnight, Sat noon–1am, Sun 12.30pm–11pm; kitchen until 9pm.

24

Benbecula (Beinn na Faoghla)

Blink and you could miss the pancake-flat island of **Benbecula** (stress on the second syllable), sandwiched between North Uist and South Uist. Most visitors simply trundle along the main road that cuts across the middle of the island in less than five miles – not such a bad idea, since the island is scarred from the postwar presence of the Royal Artillery who, until recently, made up half the local population.

The legacy of Benbecula's military past is only too evident in barracks-like **BALIVANICH** (Baile a Mhanaich), the grim, grey island capital. The only reason to come here is if you happen to be flying into or out of **Benbecula Airport**, or need an ATM or a supermarket.

ARRIVAL AND DEPARTURE — BENBECULA

By plane Benbecula Airport (⊕01851 602051, ⊛hial.co.uk/benbecula-airport) is a 10–15min walk north of Balivanich. There's a small café inside the airport building.

By bus Buses to and from North and South Uist stop outside the post office. For onward bus connections from the airport, check the Outer Hebrides council website (⊛cne-siar.gov.uk/travel/busservice/current/indexu.asp). Destinations Berneray (Mon–Sat 5–7 daily; 1hr 10min); Eriskay (Mon–Sat 5–7 daily; 1hr 30min); Lochboisdale (Mon–Sat 7–8 daily; 1hr); Lochmaddy (Mon–Sat 6–7 daily; 30min).

South Uist (Uibhist a Deas)

South Uist is the largest and most varied of the southern chain of islands. The west coast boasts some of the region's finest machair and **beaches** – a necklace of gold and grey sand strung twenty miles from one end to the other – while the east coast features a ridge of high mountains rising to 2034ft at the summit of Beinn Mhòr. However, the chief settlement and ferry port, **LOCHBOISDALE**, occupying a narrow, bumpy promontory on the southeast coast, is only worth visiting to catch the ferry.

Howmore (Tobha Mòr)

One of the best places to gain access to the sandy shoreline is at **HOWMORE** (Tobha Mòr), a pretty little crofting settlement with a fair number of restored houses, many still thatched. Close by are the shattered, lichen-encrusted remains of no fewer than four medieval churches and chapels, and a burial ground harbouring just a few scattered graves. From the village church, it's an easy walk across the flower-strewn machair to the **beach**.

Kildonan Museum (Taigh Tasgaidh Chill Donnain)

Five miles south of Howmore, HS8 5RZ • April–Oct daily 10am–5pm • £2 • ☎ 01878 710343, ⊕ kildonanmuseum.co.uk

A little museum with a lot of heart, the **Kildonan Museum** includes mock-ups of Hebridean kitchens through the ages, two lovely box beds and an impressive selection of old photos. Pride of place goes to the sixteenth-century **Clanranald Stone**, carved with the arms of the clan who ruled over South Uist from 1370 to 1839. There is also a small exhibit on Bonnie Prince Charlie and Flora Macdonald, who was born in Kildonan.

ARRIVAL AND INFORMATION   **SOUTH UIST**

By ferry A CalMac ferry connects Lochboisdale to Mallaig on the mainland (3hr 30min) and Oban (5hr 30min). As the schedule varies in summer and winter, check online first (⊕ calmac.co.uk).

By bus There are buses between Lochboisdale and Balivanich (Mon–Sat 7–8 daily; 1hr), Eriskay (Mon–Sat 6–7 daily; 35min) and Lochmaddy (Mon–Sat 6–7 daily; 1hr 30min).

Tourist office Pier Rd, Lochboisdale (April–Oct Mon–Sat 9am–5pm; ☎ 01878 700286, ⊕ southuist.com).

ACCOMMODATION AND EATING   **24**

Howmore Hostel Howmore, HS8 5SH ⊕ gatliff.org.uk. Opened in 1966, this simple Gatliff Trust hostel is still going strong. It occupies a lovely thatched crofthouse next to a ruined thirteenth-century monastery, and is just a short walk from the beach. No advance bookings. **£15**

Uist Storm Pods Lochboisdale, HS8 5TH ☎ 01878 700845, ⊕ uiststormpods.com. Something completely different, these three Hobbit bunkers offer Uist-style glamping in timber-framed huts located on a working croft. Sea views and creature comforts, including a mini-kitchenette with microwave, complete the cosy picture. **£70**

Orasay Inn Lochcarnan (Loch a' Charnain), HS8 5PD ☎ 01870 610298, ⊕ orasayinn.co.uk. A modern, purpose-built hotel off the main road, in the north of the island. The rooms are standard, but the location and restaurant make it one of the most popular in the Uists – if you're looking for a decent meal of Hebridean lamb, game, crab cakes or enormous scallops, book ahead (mains around £13). Daily noon–2pm & 6–9pm. **£99**

★ **Polochar Inn** Polochar (Poll a' Charra), HS8 5TT ☎ 01878 700215, ⊕ polocharinn.com. One of the most scenic places to hole up in, overlooking the Sound of Barra and with its own sandy beach close by. The rooms all have sea views and on the ground floor is a genuine tartan-carpeted pub, serving decent bar meals (mains around £14). Service is as friendly as can be. Kitchen daily 12.30–2.30pm & 5.30–9pm. **£95**

Eriskay (Eiriosgaigh)

Famous for its patterned jerseys and a diminutive breed of pony, the hilly island of **Eriskay** is connected to South Uist by a causeway built in 2001. The island, measuring just two miles by one, shelters a population of about 150, and makes a great day-trip either from South Uist or Barra; look out for the ponies, who roam free on the hills but tend to graze around Loch Crakavaig, the island's freshwater source. History lovers take note: the main beach on the west coast, the **Prince's Cockle Strand** (Coilleag a' Phrionnsa), was where **Bonnie Prince Charlie** landed on Scottish soil on July 23, 1745 – the sea bindweed that grows there to this day is said to have sprung from the seeds the Young Pretender brought with him from France.

ARRIVAL AND DEPARTURE   **ERISKAY**

By ferry CalMac runs a small car ferry between Barra and the southwest coast of Eriskay (5 daily in summer; 2–5 daily in winter; 40min).

By bus There's a regular service between Eriskay and Lochboisdale (Mon–Sat 4–6 daily; 40min).

WHISKY GALORE!

Eriskay's greatest claim to fame came in 1941 when the 8000-tonne **ss Politician** – or *Polly* as it's fondly known – sank on its way from Liverpool to Jamaica, along with its cargo of bicycle parts, £3 million in Jamaican currency and 264,000 bottles of whisky. The aftermath inspired Compton MacKenzie's book **Whisky Galore!** – and the Ealing comedy (filmed here in 1948), as well as a 2016 remake. The real story was somewhat less romantic, especially for the 36 islanders charged with illegal possession by the Customs and Excise officers, nineteen of whom were found guilty and imprisoned in Inverness for helping themselves to the booty. The ship's stern can sometimes be seen to the northwest of Calvey Island at low tide, and there's a collection of memorabilia on show in the island's only pub, *Am Politician*.

ACCOMMODATION AND EATING

Am Politician 3 Balla, HS8 5JL ☏ 01878 720246, ⓦ facebook.com/Am-Politician. The island's purpose-built pub, near the two cemeteries on the west coast, offers an extensive seafood-heavy bar menu (scallops, salmon, fish and chips; mains around £12) as well as home-made cakes and coffee, plus great Sound of Barra views from its conservatory. Summer only; kitchen daily noon–8pm.

An Taigh Mor 15b Balla, HS8 5JL ☏ 01878720717, ⓦ antaighmor.com. Named the "Big House" in Gaelic, this modern B&B has a fabulous location looking towards Barra. It's dog friendly, great for families and offers full Scottish breakfasts. Like everything in Eriskay, everything you may need is just a 10min walk away. **£95**

Barra (Barraigh)

24

Four miles wide and eight miles long, **Barra** is the Western Isles in miniature, characterized by sandy beaches backed by machair, mountains of Lewissian gneiss, prehistoric ruins, a strong Gaelic culture and a laidback, welcoming population of around 1200.

Castlebay

The only settlement of any size on Barra is **CASTLEBAY** (Bàgh a Chaisteil), which curves around the barren rocky hills of a wide inlet on the south side of the island. All eyes on arriving fall on the majestic **Kisimul Castle** perched on a rocky outcrop in the middle of the bay. The view is also framed by the large Catholic church, Our Lady, Star of the Sea, which overlooks the harbour, and **Sheabhal** (1260ft), the largest peak on Barra.

Kisimul Castle

Castlebay Harbour, HS9 5UZ • April–Sept daily 9.30am–5.30pm • £4.80; HS • ☏ 01871 810313, ⓦ historicenvironment.scot/visit-a-place/places/kisimul-castle

As its name suggests, Castlebay has an impressive fortification in its harbour; the three-story medieval islet-fortress of Caisteal Chiosmuil, or **Kisimul Castle**, ancestral home of the MacNeil clan. The castle burned down in the eighteenth century, but in 1937 the 45th MacNeil chief bought back the island and set about restoring his heritage. At the time of writing restoration work meant the ticket price was reduced (normally £5.50), but the whole experience remains fun – head down to the slipway at the bottom of Main Street, where the ferry skipper will take you over (weather permitting).

Cockle Strand (Barra Airport)

Oddly enough, one of Barra's most interesting sights is its **airport**, on the northern tip of the island, where planes land and take off from the crunchy shell sands of Tràigh Mhòr, better known as **Cockle Strand**. The exact timing of the flights depends on the sea – at high tide the beach (and therefore the runway) is covered in water – but, nevertheless, it draws crowds of onlookers and plane-spotters who come to see this unusual aviation one-off. To meet demand, the terminal is home to a bustling **café** serving great coffee, sandwiches and hot meals, including – perhaps a world first from an airport – takeaway fish and chips.

ARRIVAL AND INFORMATION

By plane Barra Airport (☎ 01871 890212, ⓦ hial.co.uk/barra-airport) has daily direct flights to and from Glasgow (1hr 10min).

By ferry The main ferry terminal is in Castlebay; coming from Eriskay (summer 5 daily; winter 2–5 daily; 40min), you arrive at an uninhabited spot on the island's northeast. Destinations from the main terminal Coll & Tiree (Wed; 3hr); Lochboisdale (Mon & Tues; 1hr 30min); Oban (1 daily; 4hr 45min).

By bus Buses run between Castlebay, the airport and the Eriskay ferry dock (Mon–Sat 4–6 daily; 35–45min).

Tourist office Main St, Castlebay, just round from the pier (April–Oct Mon–Sat 9.30am–5pm; ☎ 01871 810336).

ACCOMMODATION AND EATING

Café Kisimul Main St, Castlebay, HS9 5XD ☎ 01871 810645, ⓦ cafekisimul.co.uk. As well as offering Italian comfort food, the *Kisimul* cooks some of the best seafood curries in northwest Scotland – try its original scallop pakora or monkfish masala. Mains around £15. Mon–Sat 10am–10pm, Sun 5–9pm.

Castlebay Hotel Castlebay, HS9 5XD ☎ 01871 810223, ⓦ castlebay-hotel.co.uk. The more welcoming of the town's two hotels – a solid Victorian manse from 1880, with spectacular views from the restaurant as well as the locals' favourite pub. Grab a table outside for a pint with a stellar view. Kitchen daily: summer noon–2pm & 6–9.30pm; rest of year 6–8.30pm. **£135**

Dunard Hostel & Lodge Castlebay, HS9 5XD ☎ 01871 810443, ⓦ dunardhostel.co.uk. A relaxed, family-run place just west of the ferry terminal that has dorm beds, twins and a family room in the adjoining lodge. Hebridean sea kayaking specialist *Clearwater Paddling* also has its HQ here. Dorms **£20**, twins **£45**

Isle of Barra Beach Hotel Tangasdale Beach, HS9 5XW ☎ 01871 810383, ⓦ isleofbarrahotel.co.uk. The most westerly hotel in the UK, this lovely, if pricey, nautical-themed escape is a 5min drive along the west coast from Castlebay, overlooking a prime strip of beach real estate. There's a bar and restaurant, plus the helpful team can arrange car rental and electric bikes. Closed Oct–April. Kitchen May–Sept daily 7–9.30am, 11.30am–3pm & 6–8.45pm. **£165**

24

Orkney and Shetland

SKARA BRAE, ORKNEY

25 Orkney and Shetland

Reaching up towards the Arctic Circle, the Orkney and Shetland islands gather into two distinct and very different clusters. Orkney lies just north of the Scottish mainland, but with the exception of hilly Hoy, its islands are mostly low-lying, gently sloping and richly fertile. Sixty miles further north, Shetland is a complete contrast. Ice-sculpted sea inlets cut deep into the land that rises straight out of the water to rugged, heather-coated hills. With little fertile ground, Shetlanders have traditionally been crofters rather than farmers, scratching an uncertain living in fishing and whaling or the naval and merchant services.

Orkney boasts a bevy of well-preserved Stone Age settlements, such as **Skara Brae**, standing stones and chambered cairns. The **Norse** heritage is also apparent in Shetland, where there are many unique prehistoric sites, such as **Mousa Broch** and **Jarlshof**. It's impossible to underestimate the influence of the **weather** up here. More often than not, it'll be windy and rainy, though you can have all four seasons in one day. The wind-chill factor is not to be taken lightly either, and there's frequently a dampness or drizzle in the air, even when it's not raining.

Orkney

Orkney is a captivating and fiercely independent archipelago of seventy or so mostly low-lying islands, with a population of around twenty thousand. For an Orcadian, **Mainland** means the largest island in Orkney rather than the rest of Scotland, and their history is inextricably linked with Scandinavia. Orkney Mainland has two chief settlements: the old port of **Stromness**, an attractive fishing town in the southwest, and the central capital of **Kirkwall**.

Mainland is relatively heavily populated and farmed, and is joined by causeways to a string of southern islands, the largest being **South Ronaldsay**. South of Mainland, **Hoy** presents a superbly dramatic landscape, boasting some of Britain's highest sea cliffs. Hoy, however, is atypical: Orkney's smaller, much quieter **northern islands** are flat, elemental but fertile outcrops of rock and sand.

ARRIVAL AND DEPARTURE   **ORKNEY**

By plane Flybe (⊛flybe.com) offers direct flights to Kirkwall airport from Sumburgh in Shetland, Inverness, Aberdeen, Edinburgh and Glasgow.

By car ferry Northlink Ferries (☎01856 885500, ⊛northlinkferries.co.uk) offers services to Stromness from Scrabster (2–3 daily; 1hr 30min), which is connected to nearby Thurso by shuttle bus, and ferries from Aberdeen to Kirkwall (3–4 weekly; 6hr) and Lerwick in Shetland (daily; 12hr 30min). Pentland Ferries (☎01856 831226, ⊛pentlandferries.co.uk) runs catamarans from Gills Bay,

near John O'Groats (linked by bus to Wick and Thurso) to St Margaret's Hope on South Ronaldsay (3–4 daily; 1hr).

By passenger ferry John O'Groats Ferries (☎01955 611353, ⊛jogferry.co.uk) runs a passenger ferry from John O'Groats to Burwick on South Ronaldsay (May–Sept 2–3 daily; 40min); departures connect with the Orkney Bus from Inverness, and there's a free shuttle service from Thurso train station. The ferry is small, and, except in fine weather, is only recommended for travellers with strong stomachs.

ST MAGNUS CATHEDRAL, KIRKWALL

Highlights

❶ Maes Howe Europe's finest Neolithic chambered tomb is sealed in a grassy mound in the centre of Orkney's Mainland. See page 982

❷ Skara Brae Mesmerizing Neolithic village, crammed with domestic detail. See page 983

❸ St Magnus Cathedral, Kirkwall Orkney's cathedral is a miniature masterpiece built in red sandstone by the Vikings. See page 984

❹ Rackwick Experience splendid isolation, a rumbling rocky beach and the famous Old Man of Hoy in this remote village. See page 986

❺ Scapa Flow Visitor Centre & Museum, Lyness Learn about the rich wartime history of Orkney's natural harbour. See page 986

❻ Westray Thriving island with seabird colonies, beaches, a ruined castle, a prehistoric fertility symbol and top fish and chips. See page 988

❼ Noss National Nature Reserve island where you're guaranteed seals, puffins and dive-bombing "bonxies". See page 996

❽ Mousa Offshore Shetland islet with Scotland's finest-preserved 2000-year-old broch and nesting storm petrels (in season). See page 997

❾ Jarlshof Impressive archeological site mingling Iron Age, Bronze Age, Pictish, Viking and medieval settlements. See page 997

HIGHLIGHTS ARE MARKED ON THE MAPS ON PAGES 980 & 993

25

GETTING AROUND

By ferry Getting to the other islands by ferry from Mainland is easy enough, but travel between individual islands isn't straightforward. Ask Orkney Ferries (☎ 01856 872044, ⓦ orkneyferries.co.uk) about summer Sunday sailings, which make useful interisland connections. Tickets are expensive and you should book ahead if you've a vehicle.

By plane Flights from Kirkwall to the outer isles are operated by Loganair (☎ 01856 872494, ⓦ loganair.co.uk), using an eight-seater plane, with discounted fares to North Ronaldsay and Papa Westray and between the islands if you stay over.

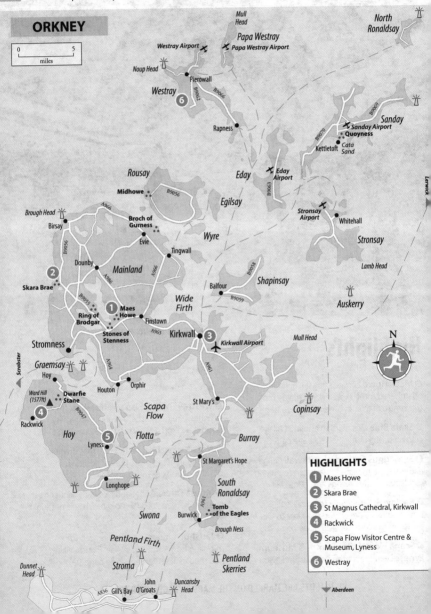

ORKNEY

HIGHLIGHTS

1 Maes Howe
2 Skara Brae
3 St Magnus Cathedral, Kirkwall
4 Rackwick
5 Scapa Flow Visitor Centre & Museum, Lyness
6 Westray

ORKNEY FESTIVALS AND EVENTS

Kirkwall's chief cultural bash is the week-long **St Magnus Festival** (ⓦstmagnusfestival. com), a superb arts festival held in the middle of June, with some events in Stromness. July is peppered with several island regattas and agricultural shows, culminating in the agricultural **County Show** held in Kirkwall in the middle of August.

To find out **what's on** (and the weather forecast), tune in to Radio Orkney on 93.7FM, buy a copy of *The Orcadian*, which comes out on Thursdays, or log on to ⓦorkneynewstoday.co.uk.

By bus Bus services (☎01856 870555, ⓦstagecoachbus. com) on Mainland are good during the week, but skeletal on Sundays – except in Stromness and Kirkwall, there are no scheduled bus stops, so just stand at a safe visible spot and flag the bus down. On the smaller islands, a minibus usually meets the ferry and will take you to your destination.

By bike Cycling is feasible if the weather holds, with few steep hills and modest distances, though the wind can make it hard going.

Stromness

STROMNESS is one of the most enchanting ports at which to arrive by boat, its picturesque waterfront a procession of tiny sandstone jetties and slate roofs. An important harbour town since the eighteenth century, it's well worth half a day's exploration, and in many ways is a better base than Kirkwall, especially during the popular four-day **Orkney Folk Festival** (ⓦorkneyfolkfestival.com) in May.

Pier Arts Centre

Victoria St, KW16 3AA • Feb to mid-June & Sept–Christmas Tues–Sat 10.30am–5pm; mid-June to Aug Mon–Sat 10.30am–5pm • Free • ☎01856 850209, ⓦpierartscentre.com

A warehouse on one of the old jetties forms half of the **Pier Arts Centre**; the other half is a modern glass-and-steel structure that offers views of the harbour framed like pictures. The gallery features a remarkable collection of twentieth-century British art, most notably members of the Cornish school such as Barbara Hepworth, Ben Nicholson and the self-taught Alfred Wallis. Contemporary works, many by northern and Scandinavian artists, continue the marine themes.

Stromness Museum

52 Alfred St, KW16 3DH • April–Sept daily 10am–5pm; Oct–March Mon–Sat 11am–3.30pm • £5 • ☎01856 850025, ⓦorkneycommunities.co.uk/stromnessmuseum

The intriguing **Stromness Museum**, built in 1858, has a wonderfully old-fashioned natural-history collection – don't miss the pull-out drawers of birds' eggs, butterflies and moths – and an early inflatable like the one used by John Rae, the Stromness-born Arctic explorer, whose fiddle, octant and shotgun are also on display. Look out, too, for the barnacle-encrusted crockery from the German High Seas Fleet that was sunk in Scapa Flow in 1919.

ARRIVAL AND INFORMATION   STROMNESS

By ferry Car ferries from Scrabster on the Scottish mainland (2–3 daily; 1hr 30min) arrive in the centre of Stromness. A passenger ferry sails from the old harbour to Moaness Pier on Hoy (Mon–Fri 4–5 daily, Sat & Sun 2 daily; 25min).

By bus Buses depart from Stromness ferry terminal.

Destinations Houton (Mon–Fri 2 daily; 20min); Kirkwall (Mon–Sat hourly, Sun every 2hr; 30min); Skara Brae (Mon, Thurs & Sat 1 daily; 20min).

Tourist office In the ferry terminal (Mon–Sat: June–Aug 10am–4pm; Sept–May 10am–3pm; ☎01856 850716, ⓦvisitorkney.com).

ACCOMMODATION

Brinkies Guest House Innertown, KW16 3JN ☎01856 851881. A substantial double-bay-fronted Victorian guesthouse 10min walk up from the town. Rooms enjoy fantastic views, the residents' lounge has loads of reading matter. **£70**

★ **Burnside Farm** North End Rd, KW16 3LJ ☎01856

25

850723, ⓦburnside-farm.com. A cracking B&B run by a local couple on a working farm about a mile out of town on the road to Kirkwall. The views are great, and the furnishings and facilities are top-notch: en-suite wet-rooms and *bere bannocks* for breakfast. **£80**

Hamnavoe Hostel 10a North End Rd, KW16 3JR ☎01856 851202, ⓦhamnavoehostel.co.uk. A good 10min walk from the ferry terminal and no beauty from the outside, but inside it's welcoming and well equipped, with thirteen beds in six rooms ranging from a single to to four-bed dorm. **£20**

Point of Ness Campsite A mile south of the ferry terminal, KW16 ☎01856 873535. Busy council-run campsite in a superb (though extremely exposed) setting, with views over to Hoy. Facilities include a TV lounge and a washing machine. Closed Oct–March. **£12.20**

EATING

Hamnavoe Restaurant 35 Graham Place, KW16 3BY ☎01856 850606. The town's most ambitious cooking, concentrating on local produce such as grilled sole or peppered monkfish (mains from £15). Booking essential. May–Sept Tues–Sun 7–10pm.

Julia's Café and Bistro 20 Ferry Rd, KW16 3AE ☎01856 850904, ⓦjuliascafe.co.uk. Right opposite the ferry terminal, with a sunny conservatory and tables outside when the weather's good. It's comfort food for the most part; you can get a decent fish pie for under £10. Mon–Sat 9am–5pm, Sun 10am–5pm.

West Mainland

The great bulk of **West Mainland** – west of Kirkwall, that is – is fertile farmland, fenced off into a patchwork of fields, used for cattle grazing. Fringed by a spectacular western coastline, West Mainland is littered with some of the island's most impressive prehistoric sites, such as the village of **Skara Brae**, the standing **Stones of Stenness** and the chambered tomb of **Maes Howe**.

Stones of Stenness

4.5 miles northeast of Stromness, KW16 3JZ • Daily 24hr; guided tours (1hr) June–Aug Mon, Wed & Fri • Free; HS • ☎01856 841732, ⓦhistoricenvironment.scot/visit-a-place/places/stones-of-stenness-circle-and-henge

The most visible part of the ceremonial complex between the twin lochs of Stenness (which is tidal) and Harray (which is freshwater) is the **Stones of Stenness**. From an original circle of twelve rock slabs, four remain standing; the tallest is a real monster at more than 16ft high and remarkable for being so slender. A broken table-top lies within the circle, surrounded by a much-diminished henge (a circular bank of earth and a ditch) with a couple of entrance causeways.

Ring of Brodgar

Less than a mile northwest of the Stones of Stenness, KW16 • Daily 24hr; guided tours (1hr) June–Aug daily 1pm • Free; HS • ☎01856 841732, ⓦhistoricenvironment.scot/visit-a-place/places/ring-of-brodgar-stone-circle-and-henge

Beyond the huge **Watch Stone**, which stands more than 18ft high beside the road, the **Ring of Brodgar** is a much wider circle than the Stones of Stenness, dramatically sited on raised ground on the thin strip of land between two lochs. There were originally sixty stones, 27 of which still stand; of the henge, only the ditch survives. At the height of summer, get here early (or late) to avoid the coach parties – or arrive in time for one of the guided tours.

Maes Howe

Less than a mile northeast of the Stones of Stenness, KW16 3LB • Guided tours only (1hr) from visitor centre (daily, hourly: April–Sept 10am–5pm; Oct–March 10am–4pm); advance booking essential • £6; HS • ☎01856 761606, ⓦhistoricenvironment.scot/visit-a-place/places/maeshowe-chambered-cairn

Maes Howe, one of Europe's most impressive Neolithic burial chamber complexes, dates from around 3000 BC. Its excellent state of preservation is partly due to the massive slabs of sandstone from which it was constructed, the largest of which weighs more than thirty tonnes. Perhaps its most extraordinary aspect is that the tomb is aligned so that the rays of the winter solstice sun reach right down the passage to the ledge of one of the three cells built into the walls of the tomb. The Vikings entered in the twelfth century, leaving large amounts of runic graffiti, cut into the walls of the main chamber and still visible today.

Skara Brae

Seven miles north of Stromness, KW16 3LR • Daily: April–Sept 9.30am–5.30pm; Oct–March 10am–4pm • £7.50; HS • ☎ 01856 841815, ⓦ historicenvironment.scot/visit-a-place/places/skara-brae

The extensive remains of a small Neolithic fishing and farming village, dating back to 3000 BC, were discovered at **Skara Brae** in 1850 after a fierce storm ripped off the dunes covering them. The village is amazingly well preserved, its huddled houses connected by narrow passages originally covered with turf. The houses themselves consist of a single, spacious living room, stuffed with Neolithic mod cons including fireplaces, cupboards, beds and boxes, all ingeniously constructed from slabs of stone. The visitor centre houses a good café and an introductory exhibition, while beyond is a full-scale replica of the best-preserved house; it's a bit neat and tidy, but gives you the idea and makes up for the fact that you can only look down on the village from the outer walls.

Birsay

The parish of **BIRSAY**, in northwest Mainland, was the centre of Norse power in Orkney for several centuries before the earls moved to Kirkwall and built the cathedral. Today a tiny cluster of homes is gathered around the sandstone ruins of the **Earl's Palace**, built in the sixteenth century by Robert Stewart, Earl of Orkney, using the forced labour of the islanders. The palace appears to have lasted barely a century before falling into rack and ruin, though the crumbling walls and turrets retain much of their grandeur.

Brough of Birsay

Just over 0.5 mile northwest of Birsay village, KW17 2LX • Accessible 2hr either side of low tide; tide times available at Stromness and Kirkwall tourist offices (see pages 981 & 985) and on Radio Orkney (93.7FM; Mon–Fri 7.30–8am) • ⓦ historicenvironment.scot/visit-a-place/places/brough-of-birsay

The focus of the **Brough of Birsay**, a substantial Pictish settlement on a small tidal island, was – and still is – the sandstone-built twelfth-century **St Peter's Church** (mid-June to Sept daily 9.30am–5.30pm; £5). Close by, a large complex of Viking-era buildings includes several houses, a sauna and some sophisticated stone drains.

Broch of Gurness

Evie, KW17 2NH • April–Oct daily 9.30am–5.30pm • £6; HS • ☎ 01856 751414, ⓦ historicenvironment.scot/visit-a-place/places/broch-of-gurness

The **Broch of Gurness** is the best-preserved broch on an archipelago replete with them, and is still surrounded by a remarkable complex of later buildings. As at Birsay, the sea has eaten away half the site, but the broch itself, dating from 100 BC, still stands, its walls up to 12ft in places, its inner cells still intact. The compact group of homes huddled around the broch have also survived amazingly well, with much of their original and ingenious stone shelving and fireplaces still *in situ*.

ACCOMMODATION
WEST MAINLAND

Birsay Outdoor Centre Birsay, KW17 2LY ☎ 01856 873535 ext 2415, ⓦ orkney.gov.uk. A large refurbished hostel with a fully equipped kitchen and a drying room; there's also a campsite alongside. Camping **£12.20**, dorms **£16**

Mill of Eyrland Stenness, off the A964 towards Orphir, KW16 3HA ☎ 01856 850136, ⓦ millofeyrland.com. Lovingly converted watermill in a delightful spot by a trout-filled stream. Rooms are filled with antiques and old mill equipment, and breakfasts are enormous. **£80**

25

Kirkwall

KIRKWALL, Orkney's capital, has one great redeeming feature – its sandstone **cathedral**, the finest medieval building in the north of Scotland. The town itself divides into two focal points: the old **harbour**, to the north, where interisland ferries come and go, and the flagstoned **main street**, which changes its name four times as it twists its way south from the harbour past the cathedral. Kirkwall's chief cultural bash is the week-long **St Magnus Festival** (ⓦstmagnusfestival.com), a superb arts festival in June.

St Magnus Cathedral

Broad St, KW15 1NX • April–Sept Mon–Sat 9am–6pm, Sun 2–5pm; Oct–March Mon–Sat 9am–1pm & 2–5pm; guided tours of the upper level (1hr 15min) Tues & Thurs 11am & 2pm – book in advance • Free; guided tours £8 • ☎ 01856 874894, ⓦ stmagnus.org

Standing at the heart of Kirkwall, **St Magnus Cathedral** is the town's most compelling sight. This beautiful red-sandstone building was begun in 1137 by the Viking Earl Rognvald in honour of his uncle Magnus, killed on the orders of his cousin Håkon in 1117. Today much of the detail in the soft sandstone has worn away – the capitals around the main doors are reduced to gnarled stumps – but it's still immensely impressive, its shape and style echoing the great cathedrals of Europe. Inside, the atmosphere is surprisingly intimate, the bulky sandstone columns drawing your eye up to the exposed brickwork arches, while around the walls is a series of mostly seventeenth-century tombstones, many carved with a skull and crossbones and other emblems of mortality.

Bishop's and Earl's palaces

Palace Rd, KW15 1PD • April–Sept daily 9.30am–5.30pm • £5; HS • ☎ 01856 871918, ⓦ historicenvironment.scot/visit-a-place/places/bishop-s-and-earl-s-palaces-kirkwall

The ruined remains of the **Bishop's Palace**, residence of the Bishop of Orkney since the twelfth century, lie to the south of the cathedral. Most of what you see, however, dates from the time of Bishop Robert Reid, sixteenth-century founder of Edinburgh University. A narrow spiral staircase takes you to the top for a good view over the cathedral and Kirkwall's rooftops.

The **Earl's Palace**, on the other side of Watergate, was built by the infamous Earl Patrick Stewart around 1600, using forced labour. With its grand entrance, fancy oriel windows, dank dungeons, massive fireplaces and magnificent central hall, it's reckoned to be one of the finest examples of Renaissance architecture in Scotland. The roof may be missing, but many domestic details remain, including a set of toilets and the stone shelves used by the clerk.

Orkney Museum

Broad St, KW15 1DH • Mon–Sat: May–Sept 10.30am–5pm; Oct–April 10.30am–12.30pm & 1.30–5pm • Free • ☎ 01856 873191

The sixteenth-century Tankerness House, a former home for the clergy, opposite the cathedral, is now home to the **Orkney Museum**. A couple of rooms have been restored as they would have been in the 1820s when it was a private house. The rest houses some of the islands' most treasured finds, including a witch's spell box and a lovely whalebone plaque from a Viking boat grave discovered on Sanday, plus a section on the town's peculiarly physical annual "football" game, the Ba'.

ARRIVAL AND INFORMATION

By plane Kirkwall Airport (☎ 01856 886210, ⓦ hial.co.uk) is about 3 miles southeast of town on the A960 – take the bus (Mon–Sat every 30min; 15min) or a taxi (£6).

By bus The bus station is behind the Kirkwall Travel Centre, West Castle St.

Destinations Birsay (Mon–Sat 2 daily; 30–40min); Burwick (2–3 daily; 40min); Houton (5–6 daily; 25min); Skara Brae (June–Aug Mon, Thurs & Sat 1 daily; 50min); St Margaret's Hope (Mon–Sat hourly; 35min); Stromness (Mon–Sat hourly, Sun every 2hr; 30min); Tingwall (Mon–Sat 4–5 daily; 25min).

By ferry NorthLink (☎ 01856 885500, ⓦ northlinkferries. co.uk) ferries from Shetland and Aberdeen (and all cruise ships) dock at the Hatston terminal, a mile or so northwest of town; buses will take you into Kirkwall. Orkney Ferries (☎01856 872044, ⓦorkneyferries.co.uk) leave from Kirkwall harbour in the centre of town.

Destinations within Orkney Eday (2–3 daily; 1hr 15min–2hr 25min); North Ronaldsay (Tues & Fri 1 daily; 2hr 40min); Sanday (2 daily; 1hr 25min); Stronsay (1–3 daily; 1hr 40min–2hr); Westray (2–3 daily; 1hr 25min).

Tourist office The Kirkwall Travel Centre, West Castle St (daily 9am–5pm; ☎01856 872856, ⓦvisitorkney.com).

ACCOMMODATION

2 Dundas Crescent 2 Dundas Crescent, KW15 1JQ ☎01856 874805. Just behind the cathedral, this former manse, run by an Orcadian couple is a grand and tastefully decorated Victorian house, with four spacious rooms and period fittings. **£80**

Avalon House Carness Rd, KW15 1UE ☎01856 876665, ⓦavalon-house.co.uk. Don't judge it on the drab, modern exterior; this is a comfortable, purpose-built guesthouse run efficiently by a very welcoming couple, and situated a pleasant 20min coastal walk from the town centre. **£80**

Peedie Hostel 1 Ayre Houses, KW15 1QX ☎01856 875477, ⓦstayinkirkwall.co.uk. Centrally located, overlooking the old harbour and out to sea, this is a clean and comfortable hostel with three singles, three twins and two four-bed dorms. Laundry facilities available. Closed Nov–March. Dorms **£15**, twins **£35**

Pickaquoy Campsite Ayre Rd, KW15 1LR ☎01856 879900, ⓦpickaquoy.net. Well-equipped and -maintained place behind (and run by) the local leisure centre. Not the prettiest of spots. Closed Jan and Feb. **£20**

EATING AND DRINKING

Helgi's 14 Harbour St, KW15 1LE ☎01856 879293, ⓦhelgis.co.uk. Popular modern pub on the harbourfront, serving nicely presented bar food (around £10) from burgers or fish and chips to fajitas. Free wi-fi. No children allowed. Mon–Wed 11am–midnight, Thurs–Sat 11am–1am, Sun 12.30pm–midnight; kitchen Mon–Sat 11am–9pm, Sun 12.30–9pm.

Lucano 31 Victoria Rd, KW15 1DN ☎01856 875687, ⓦlucanokirkwall.com. Busy, bright, modern Italian – the family hail from Basilicata – offering 10-inch pizzas, fresh pasta and risotto with an Orcadian angle, all for around £10. It's popular, so book ahead. Daily 11am–9pm.

★ **The Reel** 6 Broad St, KW15 1NX ☎01856 871000, ⓦwrigleyandthereel.com. The old customs house near the cathedral is now a laidback, self-service café run by the musical Wrigley sisters, serving great coffee, sandwiches, toasties, panini and cakes, and offering free wi-fi and regular live music (Wed, Thurs & Sat). Mon–Fri 8.30am–6pm, Sat 9am–1am; summer also Sun 10am–5pm.

South Ronaldsay

At the southern end of the Churchill Barriers (see page 987) is **South Ronaldsay**, the largest of the islands linked to Mainland. Its main settlement is **ST MARGARET'S HOPE** – or "The Hope" – a pleasing little gathering of stone-built houses overlooking a sheltered bay. Once a thriving port, the Hope is now a peaceful place, despite the nearby presence of the **Pentland Ferries terminal**.

Tomb of the Eagles

Liddle, KW17 2RW • Daily: March 10am–noon; April–Sept 9.30am–5.30pm; Oct 9.30am–12.30pm • £7.50 • ☎01856 831339, ⓦtomboftheeagles.co.uk

One of the most enjoyable archeological sights on Orkney is the Isbister chambered burial cairn at the southeastern corner of South Ronaldsay, known as the **Tomb of the Eagles**. Discovered, excavated and still owned by local farmer Ronald Simpson, the tomb makes a refreshing change from the usual interpretative centre. First, you get to look round the family's private museum of prehistoric artefacts; then you get a guided tour of a nearby Bronze Age **burnt mound**, which is basically a Neolithic rubbish dump; and finally you walk the mile or so to the **chambered cairn** by the cliff's edge, where human remains were found alongside talons and carcasses of sea eagles. To enter the cairn, you must lie on a trolley and pull yourself in using an overhead rope.

ARRIVAL AND DEPARTURE   SOUTH RONALDSAY

By ferry Car ferry catamarans run from Gills Bay, near John O'Groats, to St Margaret's Hope (3–4 daily; 1hr), while passenger ferries run from John O'Groats to Burwick, 7 miles from St Margaret's Hope (May–Sept 2–3 daily; 40min).

25

ACCOMMODATION AND EATING

Bankburn House St Margaret's Hope, KW17 2TG ☏ 01856 831310, ⓦ bankburnhouse.co.uk. Solid Victorian sea captain's house just outside The Hope, with a variety of rooms, some en suite, all with high ceilings and period features. **£56**

The Creel Front Rd, St Margaret's Hope, KW17 2SL ☏ 01856 831311, ⓦ thecreel.co.uk. There are just three lovely sea-view rooms at this quality B&B, all beautifully furnished with light pine fittings. The breakfasts are superb and non-residents can usually drop in for tea and cakes (evening meals too, if booked in advance). **£110**

Skerries Bistro Banks, Cleat, KW17 2RW ☏ 01856 831605, ⓦ skerriesbistro.co.uk. Ultra-modern bistro, with its own chambered cairn nearby, overlooking the Pentland Firth. Dine on local fish and king scallops as big as steaks (evening mains around £15), plus delicious home-made puddings and cakes. April–Oct Mon, Wed, Fri & Sat noon–4pm & 6–9.30pm, Tues, Thurs & Sun noon–4pm.

Wheems Eastside, KW17 2TJ ☏ 01856 831556, ⓦ wheemsorganic.co.uk. Rambling old crofthouse and organic farm, with a couple of wooden glamping pods, a stone cottage and a yurt, plus a sloping field for tents. Closed Nov–March. Camping **£12**, pods **£40**, yurt **£50**, cottage **£60**

Hoy

Hoy, Orkney's second-largest island, rises sharply out of the sea to the southwest of Mainland. Its dramatic landscape is made up of great glacial valleys and mountainous moorland rising to more than 1500ft, dropping into the sea off the red sandstone cliffs of St John's Head.

Rackwick

RACKWICK is an old crofting and fishing settlement squeezed between towering sandstone cliffs on the west coast. A small farm building beside the hostel (see page 987) serves as a tiny **museum** (daily 24hr; free), with a few old photos and a brief rundown of Rackwick's rough history. Despite its isolation, the village has a steady stream of walkers and climbers passing through en route to the **Old Man of Hoy**, a sandstone column some 450ft high, perched on an old lava flow protecting it from the erosive power of the sea. The well-trodden footpath from Rackwick is an easy three-mile walk (3hr return). Halfway along the road between Hoy village and Rackwick, duckboards head across the heather to the **Dwarfie Stane**, Orkney's most unusual chambered tomb, cut from a solid block of sandstone and dating back to 3000 BC.

Scapa Flow Visitor Centre & Museum

Lyness, opposite the ferry terminal, KW16 3NT • March, April & Oct Mon–Sat 10am–4.30pm; May–Sept daily 10am–4.30pm • Free • ☏ 01856 791300, ⓦ scapaflow.co.uk

Hoy was a key site for the Royal Navy during both world wars and the harbour and hills around Lyness are scarred with the scattered remains of concrete structures that served as hangars and storehouses during World War II. The old oil pump house has been turned into the **Scapa Flow Visitor Centre & Museum**, a fascinating insight into wartime Orkney. The pump house itself retains much of its old equipment – you can ask for a working demo of an oil-fired boiler – used to pump oil off tankers moored at Lyness into sixteen tanks, and from there into underground reservoirs cut into the neighbouring hillside. Even the café has an old NAAFI feel about it. The museum is closed from 2018, possibly until 2020, for redevelopment.

ARRIVAL AND GETTING AROUND HOY

By ferry A passenger ferry runs from Stromness to Moaness pier, by Hoy village (Mon–Fri 4–6 daily, Sat & Sun 2 daily; 25min; ☏ 01856 850624), and a car ferry runs from Houton on Mainland to Lyness (Mon–Fri 6 daily, Sat & Sun 2–5 daily; 35min–1hr; ☏ 01856 811397).

By minibus/bus A minibus usually meets the Stromness ferry and will take folk over to Rackwick or further afield. A seasonal Hoy Hopper bus service (mid-May to mid-Sept Wed–Fri) departs from Kirkwall Travel Centre and drives onto the ferry to Lyness.

SCAPA FLOW AND THE CHURCHILL BARRIERS

The presence of a huge naval base in **Scapa Flow** during both world wars presented an irresistible target to the Germans, and protecting the fleet was always a nagging problem for the Allies. During World War I, blockships were sunk to guard the eastern approaches, but just weeks after the outbreak of World War II, a German U-boat managed to manoeuvre past the blockships and torpedo the battleship HMS *Royal Oak*, which sank with the loss of 833 lives.

The sinking of the *Royal Oak* convinced the First Lord of the Admiralty, Winston Churchill, that Scapa Flow needed better protection, and in 1940 work began on a series of barriers – known as the **Churchill Barriers** – to seal the waters between Mainland and the string of islands to the south. Special camps were built to accommodate the 1700 men involved in the project; their numbers were boosted by the surrender of Italy in 1942, when Italian POWs were sent to work here.

Besides the barriers, the Italians also left behind the beautiful **Italian Chapel** (June–Aug daily 9am–6pm; Sept–May shorter hours; £3) on the first of the islands, Lamb Holm. This, the so-called "miracle of Camp 60" is made from two Nissen huts, concrete, barbed wire and parts of a rusting blockship. It has a great false facade, and colourful trompe l'oeil decor, lovingly restored by the chapel's principal architect, Domenico Chiocchetti.

ACCOMMODATION AND EATING

HOY

Beneth'ill Café Moaness, KW16 3NJ ☎01856 851116, ⓦbenethillcafe.co.uk. Friendly, simple café, a short walk from Moaness Pier, offering sandwiches and salads, home-made puddings and proper coffee. April–Sept daily 10am–4.30pm – some evening openings and occasional closures.

Burnside Bothy By the beach, KW16 3NJ ☎01856 791316. You can camp in the dry-stone wall field beside this beautiful, but basic, heather-thatched bothy– toilets,

cold water and a driftwood fire available inside. Donations welcome.

Rackwick Outdoor Centre Rackwick, KW16 3NJ ☎01856 873535, ext 2417, ⓦvisitorkney.com/accommodation/hostels/rackwick-outdoor-centre. There are eight dorm beds in Rackwick's tiny little former schoolhouse. Be warned, though, North Hoy is probably the worst place on Orkney for midges. Closed Oct–March. **£13**

Rousay

The hilly island of **Rousay**, one of the more accessible northern isles, is also home to a number of intriguing prehistoric sites. A whole parade of archeological remains are spread out on and off the road that leads west from the ferry terminal. **Midhowe Cairn**, four miles along the road, comes as something of a surprise, both for its immense size – it's nearly 100ft long and known as "the great ship of death" – and because it's now entirely surrounded by a stone-walled barn with a corrugated roof. You can't actually explore the roofless communal burial chamber, dating back to 3500 BC, but you can look down from the overhead walkway. A couple of hundred yards beyond is Rousay's finest archeological site, **Midhowe Broch**, whose compact layout suggests that it was originally built as a fortified family house, surrounded by a complex series of ditches and ramparts. The interior is divided into two rooms, each with their own hearth, water tank and quernstone, all of which date from the final phase of occupation around the second century AD.

ARRIVAL AND GETTING AROUND

ROUSAY

By ferry Rousay makes a good day-trip from Mainland, with car ferries from Tingwall (5–6 daily; 30min; ☎01856 751360).

By bus A bus service runs on request every Thurs (☎01856 821360) and, in season, on-demand minibus tours connect with ferries (☎01856 821234, ⓦrousaytours.co.uk; £30).

ACCOMMODATION AND EATING

The Pier Ferry terminal, KW17 2PY ☎01856 821359. Simple pub serving basic bar meals (all under £10) and

Orkney beers; they can serve lobster or make fresh crab sandwiches if you phone in advance. May–Sept Mon,

25

Tues & Thurs 11am–11pm, Wed 11am–6.30pm, Fri & Sat 11am–1am, Sun 11am–7pm; Oct–April Mon & Tues 11am–2pm & 4.30–11pm, Thurs 10am–2pm & 4.30–11pm, Fri 11am–2pm & 4.30pm–1am, Sat 11am–1am, Sun 4.30–11pm.

The Taversoe 3 miles west of the ferry terminal, KW17 2PT ☎01856 821325, ⓦ taversoehotel.co.uk. Unpretentious accommodation in four rooms (all with sea views), and classic pub meals – fish and chips, scampi and

burgers – for less than £10. May–Sept Mon 11am–5pm, Tues–Sat 11am–11pm, Sun 11am–10.30pm; Oct–April Wed–Sat noon–2pm & 5–11pm, Sun noon–7.30pm. **£80**

Trumland Farm 0.5 mile west of the ferry terminal, KW17 2PU ☎01856 821252, ⓔ trumland@btopen world.com. Working organic farm with a couple of dorms and a family room – you can also camp here, and they rent bikes. Camping/person **£6**, dorms **£14**

Westray

Although exposed to the full force of the Atlantic weather in the far northwest of Orkney, **Westray** shelters one of the most tightly knit and prosperous island communities.

The main village and harbour is **PIEROWALL**, set around a wide bay in the north. Here the **Westray Heritage Centre** (May–Sept Mon 11.30am–5pm, Tues–Sat 9am–noon & 2–5pm, Sun 1.30–5pm; £3) is a great place to gen up on the Westray Wife or **Orkney Venus**, a remarkable, miniature Neolithic female figurine found in 2009 in the nearby dunes. Above the village to the west is the sandstone hulk of **Noltland Castle**, begun around 1560 by Gilbert Balfour, Master of the Household to Mary, Queen of Scots, who was implicated in the murder of Mary's husband Lord Darnley. To explore, pick up the key at the nearby farm.

The northwestern tip of Westray rises sharply, culminating in the dramatic sea cliffs of **Noup Head**. In early summer, the guano-covered rock ledges are packed with more than 100,000 nesting seabirds, primarily guillemots, razorbills, kittiwakes and fulmars, with puffins as well – an awesome sight, sound and smell. For a closer view of puffins, head for **Castle o' Burrian**, a sea stack in the southeast of the island.

ARRIVAL AND GETTING AROUND   WESTRAY

By plane You can fly from Kirkwall (Mon–Fri 2 daily, Sat & Sun 1 daily; 15min) and go on the world's shortest scheduled flight between Westray and the neighbouring island of Papa Westray (Mon–Sat 1 daily; 2min).

By ferry Westray is served by car ferry from Kirkwall (2–3 daily; 1hr 25min; ☎01856 872044) and there's a passenger

ferry between Pierowall (Westray) and Papa Westray (3–6 daily; 25min; ☎01857 8677216).

By bus A minibus (May–Sept; at other times phone ☎07789 034289) meets the ferry and connects with the Papa Westray ferry from Pierowall.

ACCOMMODATION AND EATING

★**The Barn** Chalmersquoy, Pierowall, KW17 2BZ ☎01857 677214, ⓦ thebarnwestray.co.uk. A converted farm hostel at the southern edge of Pierowall; it's luxurious inside, with family rooms and twin bunks available. It also has a small campsite adjacent to it, a games room – run by a genuinely friendly Westray family. Camping **£12**, dorms **£22**

No. 1 Broughton Pierowall, KW17 2DA ☎01857 677726, ⓦ no1broughton.co.uk. Top-notch, good-value

B&B in a renovated mid-nineteenth-century house with views across the bay, a lovely conservatory and even a small sauna. **£60**

Pierowall Hotel Pierowall, KW17 2BZ ☎01857 677472, ⓦ pierowallhotel.co.uk. Pierowall's social hub is unpretentious and very welcoming – the cheaper rooms have shared facilities. The popular bar has excellent fish and chips, fresh off the boats (mains under £10). Daily noon–11pm. **£82**

Papa Westray

Across Papa Sound from Westray is the island of **Papa Westray**, known locally as "Papay". With a population of around ninety, Papay has had to fight hard to keep itself viable over the last couple of decades, helped by a hefty influx of outsiders. With one of

25

Orkney's best-preserved Neolithic settlements, and a large nesting seabird population, it's worth an overnight stay or a day-trip.

A road leads down from Holland House, in the centre of the island, to the western shore, where the **Knap of Howar** stands. Dating from around 3500 BC, this Neolithic farm building makes a fair claim to being the oldest standing house in Europe. Half a mile north along the coast is **St Boniface Kirk**, a restored pre-Reformation church, with a bare flagstone floor, dry-stone walls, a little wooden gallery and just a couple of surviving box pews.

ARRIVAL AND GETTING AROUND
PAPA WESTRAY

By plane You can fly direct from Kirkwall (Mon–Sat 2–3 daily, Sun 1; 25min) for £15 return if you stay overnight. The island is also connected to Westray (Mon–Sat 1 daily; 2min).

By ferry On Tues, the car ferry goes from Kirkwall to Papa Westray via North Ronaldsay (more than 4hr); on Fri, the car ferry from Kirkwall to Westray continues to Papa Westray (2hr 15min). At other times, you must book a

bus to connect with the Papa Westray ferry from Pierowall (ⓦwestraybusservice.com, ☎07789 034289); the bus accepts a limited number of bicycles.

By bus The Papay Ranger offers Papay Peedie Tours by minibus (☎01857 252028) – full days with lunch (May–Aug Wed, Thurs & Sat; £40) or half-days (£25) – you can even do it from Kirkwall as a 12hr day-trip. You can also arrange bespoke tours with the ranger.

ACCOMMODATION AND EATING

Papay Co-op Beltane House, east of Holland House, KW17 2BU ☎01857 644224, ⓦpapawestray.co.uk. The Papay Co-op offers B&B, a two-room, sixteen-bed hostel, a place to camp and a shop, all within the old estate workers'

cottages. The Co-op also runs an ad hoc self-service café for all island visitors and a weekly "bar cupboard", when bar meals are available (Sat from 9pm). Camping/person £8, dorms £15, doubles £44

Eday

A long, thin island, **Eday** is dominated by a great block of heather-covered upland, with farmland confined to a narrow strip of coastal ground. The chief points of interest are all in the northern half of the island, beyond the community shop on the main road. Clearly visible from the road is the 15ft **Stone of Setter**, Orkney's most distinctive standing stone, weathered into three thick, lichen-encrusted fingers. From here you can climb the hill to the **Vinquoy Chambered Cairn**, which has a similar structure to that of Maes Howe (see page 982). You can crawl into the tomb through the narrow entrance: a skylight inside lets light into the main, beehive chamber – now home to some lovely ferns – but not into the four side-cells.

ARRIVAL AND DEPARTURE
EDAY

By plane You can make a day-trip by plane from Kirkwall to Eday (1 on Mon, 2 on Wed; 10min).

By ferry Eday is served by regular car ferries from Kirkwall (2–3 daily; 1hr 15min–2hr). The terminal is at Backaland

pier in the south, although you should be able to get a lift to the north of the island with someone from the ferry if you ask around.

GETTING AROUND AND TOURS

Eday's Minibus (May to mid-Sept Mon, Wed & Fri or by appointment; 2hr 30min; £15; ☎01857 622206) will collect you from the ferry, take you on a tour of the island

and deposit you wherever you want. In addition, every Thurs it will simply take you wherever you wish to go (without the tour).

ACCOMMODATION AND EATING

Eday SYHA Hostel 3 miles north of Backaland by the airport, KW17 2AB ☎07776 281084, ⓦsyha.org.uk/where-to-stay/islands/eday. An SYHA-affiliated, community-run hostel, in an exposed spot – phone ahead,

as there's no resident warden. They offer laundry facilities, bike rental and – unusually in this part of the world – free wi-fi, and you can camp, too. Camping £7.50, dorms £16
Roadside B&B Backaland, KW17 2AA ☎01857 622303.

25

day's only pub is in a pleasant old building overlooking the erry terminal, and offers B&B in two en-suite rooms and vening meals on request (mains under £10). **£50**

Swenstay Bothy 3 miles southwest of the airport,

KW17 2AA ☎01857 622262. Recently renovated, snug, wood-panelled self-catering bothy with flagstone floors and a traditional box bed – it can be rented out on a nightly basis. **£50**

Stronsay

A beguiling combination of green pastures, white sands and clear turquoise bays, Stronsay was a centre for the curing of herring from the 1840s to the 1930s. WHITEHALL is the island's only real village, made up of rows of stone-built fishermen's cottages set between two large piers. Wandering along the tranquil harbourfront today, it's hard to believe that the village once supported five thousand people in the fishing industry during the summer, as well as a small army of coopers, coal merchants, butchers, bakers, several Italian ice-cream parlours and a cinema. **Papa Stronsay**, the tiny island that shelters Whitehall from the north, is home to the multimillion-pound **Golgotha Monastery** belonging to the Sons of the Most Holy Redeemer – they're happy to take visitors across to (and around) the island by boat, by prior arrangement (☎01857 616210, ⍵papastronsay.com).

ARRIVAL AND GETTING AROUND   STRONSAY

By plane Day-trips are possible from Kirkwall (Mon–Fri 2 daily, Sat & Sun 1 daily; 25min) and regular flights depart from Sanday (Mon–Fri 1 daily; 6min).

By ferry Stronsay is served by a regular car ferry from

Kirkwall to Whitehall (1–3 daily; 1hr 40min–2hr).
By taxi/car There's no bus service, but D.S. Peace (☎01857 616335) operates taxis and offers car rental.

ACCOMMODATION AND EATING

Storehouse Whitehall, KW17 2AR ☎01857 616263, ⍵facebook.com/Storehouse-BB-345981345506957. A good alternative to the *Stronsay Hotel* is this welcoming little B&B with en-suite rooms, a guest lounge and full board on request. **£65**

Stronsay Fish Mart By the ferry terminal, Whitehall, KW17 2AR ☎01857 616401, ⍵stronsayfishmart. uk. The old fish market has been refurbished as a hostel,

a heritage centre and a cheap and cheerful daytime café serving tea, sandwiches and delicious home-made cakes. Free wi-fi. Mon–Wed & Fri–Sun 11am–3pm. Dorms **£20**
Stronsay Hotel By the ferry terminal, Whitehall, KW17 2AR ☎01857 616213, ⍵stronsayhotelorkney. co.uk. Stronsay's only hotel has modern en-suite rooms and a bar serving generous portions of home-cooked pub food (mains under £10). **£80**

Sanday

Despite being the largest of the northern isles, **Sanday** is the least substantial, a great low-lying, drifting dune strung out between several rocky points. The island's sweeping aquamarine bays and vast stretches of clean white sand are the finest in Orkney, and in dry, clear weather it's a superb place to spend a day or two. The coastline offers superb walks, with particularly spectacular sand dunes to the south of Cata Sand. The most impressive archeological sight is **Quoyness Chambered Cairn**, on the fertile farmland of Els Ness peninsula, dating from before 2000 BC, and partially reconstructed to a height of around 13ft.

ARRIVAL AND GETTING AROUND   SANDAY

By plane The airfield, in the centre of the island, sees regular flights to Kirkwall (Mon–Fri 2 daily, Sat & Sun 1 daily; 10min) and a daily connection to Stronsay (Mon–Fri 1 daily; 6min).

By ferry Ferries from Kirkwall (2 daily; 1hr 25min) arrive at Loth Pier, at Sanday's southern tip.

By bus or minibus All sailings are met by the Sanday Bus (☎01857 600438), which will take you to most points on Sanday. The Sanday Ranger (☎01857 600341, ⍵sandayranger.org) organizes occasional activities, and there's a regular Sanday Bus Tour (☎01857 600438; May–Sept Wed; £35).

25

ACCOMMODATION AND EATING

Ayre's Rock 6 miles northeast of ferry terminal, KW17 2AY ☎01857 600410, ⓦayres-rock-sanday-orkney. com. A great budget option with a well-equipped eight-bed hostel, a couple of caravans and a small campsite (with several wooden camping pods) overlooking the sea. They offer washing and laundry facilities, a chip shop (every Sat) and bike rental. Camping £12, pods £18.50, dorms £19.50, caravans £50

Backaskaill Farmhouse 5 miles northeast of ferry terminal, KW17 2BA ☎01857 600305, ⓦbedandbreakfastsandayorkney.com. Lovely, solid, stone-built farmhouse overlooking Backaskaill Bay – check out the views from the conservatory – run by a very welcoming Manx couple and a couple of goats. Full board available. £75

Belsair Hotel Kettletoft, KW17 2BJ ☎01857 600206 One of two pubs in Kettletoft, Sanday's original fishing port, offering decent pub food (fish and chips, burgers and the like; under £10). Daily; hours vary – check ahead.

North Ronaldsay

Measuring just three miles by one and rising only 66ft above sea level, **North Ronaldsay** is almost overwhelmed by the huge sky, the strength of wind and the ferocity of the sea. The island's **sheep** are a unique, tough, goat-like breed, feeding mostly on seaweed, giving their flesh a dark tone and a rich, gamey taste, and making their thick wool highly prized. A high **dry-stone dyke**, running the thirteen miles around the edge of the island, keeps the sheep off the farmland, except during lambing season. The most frequent visitors to the island are ornithologists, who come to catch a glimpse of the rare birds that land here briefly on their spring and autumn migrations. The only features to interrupt the flat horizon are two **lighthouses** in the north, the newer of which you can visit (May–Aug daily 10am–5pm; £6).

ARRIVAL AND GETTING AROUND — NORTH RONALDSAY

By plane Your best bet is to catch a flight from Kirkwall (Mon–Sat 3 daily, Sun 2; 15min): if you stay the night on the island, you're eligible for a bargain £21 return fare.

By ferry The ferry from Kirkwall to North Ronaldsay runs just once a week (usually Fri; 2hr 40min), though there are also summer sailings via Papa Westray (usually Tues; 3hr 10min), and day-trips are possible on occasional Suns between late May and early Sept (☎01856 872044).

By minibus A minibus usually meets the ferries and planes (☎01857 633244) and will take you off to the lighthouse, but phone ahead to make sure.

ACCOMMODATION AND EATING

Bird Observatory Twingness, KW17 2BE ☎01857 633200, ⓦnrbo.co.uk. You can stay at the ecofriendly bird observatory, which has an en-suite guest room, dorms and camping space. The *Obscafé* serves decent evening meals (around £15 for two courses) – try the mutton and a Dark Island beer. Daily noon–2pm & evenings by arrangement. Camping £5, dorms £18.50, doubles £65

Lighthouse North Ronaldsay, KW17 2BG ☎01857 633297, ⓦnorthronaldsay.co.uk. Great little café in the old lightouse-keepers' cottages, serving snacks and (by arrangement) evening meals. May–Aug daily 10am–4pm; Sept–April phone ahead.

Shetland

Shetland is surprisingly different from neighbouring Orkney: while Orkney lies within sight of the Scottish mainland, Shetland lies beyond the horizon, closer to Bergen in Norway than Edinburgh, and nearer the Arctic Circle than Manchester. The 23,000 islanders refer to themselves as Shetlanders first, and, with the Shetland flag widely displayed, they regard Scotland as a separate entity. As in Orkney, when they refer to Mainland they are speaking of the landmass in their own archipelago, not the Scottish mainland. And while Shetland experiences occasional spells of dry, sunny weather, it's the **simmer dim** – the twilight that lingers through the small hours at this latitude – which makes the summers here so memorable.

The capital, **Lerwick**, is a busy little port and the only town of any size; many parts of Shetland can be reached from here on a day-trip. **South Mainland** is a narrow finger of land that runs 25 miles from Lerwick to **Sumburgh Head**, an area particularly rich in archeological remains, including the Iron Age **Mousa Broch** and the ancient settlement of **Jarlshof**. A further 25 miles south of Sumburgh Head is the remote but thriving **Fair Isle**, synonymous with knitwear and exceptional birdlife. Even more remote are the distinctive peaks and precipitous cliffs of the island of **Foula**, fourteen miles west of Mainland. Shetland's three **North Isles** bring Britain to a dramatic, windswept end: **Yell** has the largest population of otters in the UK; **Fetlar** is home to

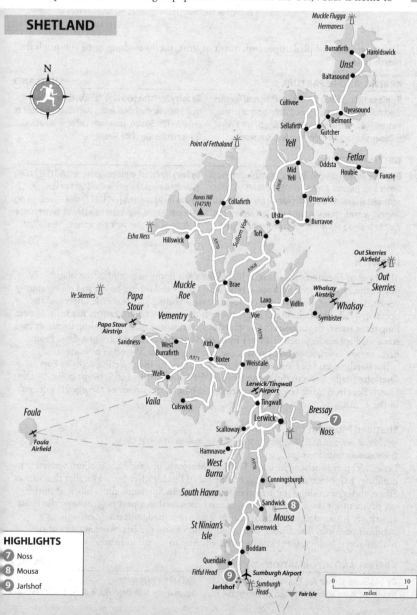

SHETLAND

N

Muckle Flugga
Hermaness
Burrafirth
Haroldswick
Unst
Baltasound
Cullivoe
Uyeasound
Belmont
Sellafirth
Gutcher
Yell
Oddsta
Fetlar
Houbie
Funzie
Point of Fethaland
Mid
Yell
Otterswick
Ronas Hill
(1475ft)
Collafirth
Ulsta
Burravoe
Esha Ness
Hillswick
Toft
Out Skerries
Airfield
Sullom Voe
*Out
Skerries*
Ve Skerries
*Muckle
Roe*
Brae
*Papa
Stour*
Laxo
Whalsay
Airstrip
Whalsay
Vementry
Voe
Vidlin
Symbister
Papa Stour
Airstrip
Sandness
West
Burrafirth
Aith
Bixter
Weisdale
Vaila
Walls
Lerwick/Tingwall
Airport
Bressay
Culswick
Tingwall
Noss
Foula
Lerwick
Scalloway
Foula
Airfield
Hamnavoe
*West
Burra*
Cunningsburgh
South Havra
Sandwick
Mousa
St Ninian's
Isle
Levenwick
Boddam
Quendale
Fitful Head
Jarlshof
Sumburgh Airport
Sumburgh
Head
Fair Isle

0   10
miles

HIGHLIGHTS

7 Noss

8 Mousa

9 Jarlshof

UP HELLY-AA

On the last Tuesday in January, Lerwick plays host to **Up Helly-Aa** (ⓦuphellyaa.org), the largest of the fire festivals held in Shetland (Jan–March). Around nine hundred torchbearing participants, all male and in extraordinary costumes, march in procession before throwing their torches into a longship. A firework display follows, then the squads to do the rounds of a dozen "halls" (including the Town Hall), giving comic performances at each.

Up Helly-Aa dates from Victorian times, and although it's essentially a community event with entry by invitation only, visitors are welcome at the Town Hall – contact the tourist office for details.

the rare red-necked phalarope; and, north of **Unst**, there's nothing until you reach the North Pole.

ARRIVAL AND DEPARTURE   SHETLAND

By plane Flybe (☎0871 7002000, ⓦflybe.com) operates direct flights to Sumburgh Airport, 25 miles south of Lerwick, from Inverness, Aberdeen, Edinburgh, Glasgow and Kirkwall in Orkney, plus summer flights from Bergen in Norway.

By ferry Northlink (☎01856 885500, ⓦnorthlinkferries. co.uk) runs overnight car ferries daily from Aberdeen to Lerwick (12hr 30min), sometimes calling in at Kirkwall in Orkney on the way (14hr 30min).

GETTING AROUND

By plane Airtask (☎01595 840246, ⓦairtask.com) runs flights from Tingwall Airport (☎01595 745745), 5 miles northwest of Lerwick, to the more remote islands. To reach Tingwall Airport, there's a dial-a-ride taxi service that must be booked a day in advance by calling the airport.

By ferry The council-run interisland ferries (☎01595 743970, ⓦshetland.gov.uk) are excellent and fares are very low.
By bus The bus network (☎01595 744868, ⓦzettrans.org. uk) is pretty good, with buses from Lerwick to every corner of Mainland, and even via ferries across to Yell and Unst.

Lerwick

The focus of Shetland's commercial life, **LERWICK** is home to a third of the islands' population. Its sheltered **harbour** is busy with ferries and fishing boats, and oil-rig supply vessels. In summer, the quayside comes alive with visiting yachts, cruise liners and the occasional tall ship. Behind the old harbour is the compact town centre, made up of one long main street, flagstone-clad **Commercial Street**, whose narrow, winding form, set back from the Esplanade, provides shelter from the elements even on the worst days. From here, narrow lanes, known as **closses**, rise westwards to the Victorian new town.

The northern end of Commercial Street is marked by the towering walls of **Fort Charlotte** (daily dawn to dusk; free), begun for Charles II in 1665, burnt down by the Dutch fleet in August 1673 and repaired and named in honour of George III's queen in the 1780s.

Shetland Museum

Hay's Dock, off Commercial Rd, ZE1 0WP • Mon–Sat 10am–5pm, Sun noon–5pm • Free • ☎01595 695057,
ⓦshetlandmuseumandarchives.org.uk

Lerwick's chief tourist sight is the **Shetland Museum**, in a stylishly modern waterfront building. Exhibits include replicas of a hoard of Pictish silver found locally; the Monks Stone, thought to show the arrival of Christianity in Shetland; and a block of butter, tax payment for the King of Norway, found preserved in a peat bog. Among the boats artistically suspended in the Boat Hall is a sixareen, used, amazingly enough, as a mailboat to Foula. The Upper Gallery concentrates on the last two centuries of the islands' social history, from knitting and whaling to the oil industry.

ARRIVAL AND INFORMATION   LERWICK

By bus Buses stop on the Esplanade, close to the old harbour, or at the Viking bus station on Commercial Rd,

north of the town centre.
Destinations Brae (Mon–Sat 8 daily; 45min); Hillswick

(Mon–Sat 3 daily; 1hr 40min); Levenwick (Mon–Sat 6–8 daily, Sun 5; 30min); Scalloway (Mon–Sat hourly, Sun 2; 25min); Sumburgh Airport (Mon–Sat 5–6 daily, Sun 4; 45min); Tingwall (Mon–Fri 7 daily, Sat 4; 10min); Toft (Mon–Sat 5–6 daily; 50min); Voe (Mon–Fri 5 daily, Sat 3; 35min).

By ferry Ferries from Aberdeen and Orkney arrive at Lerwick's ferry terminal, about a mile north of the town centre. Ferries to other Shetland islands leave from the town harbour.
Tourist office Market Cross, Commercial St (April–Oct Mon–Sat 9am–5pm, Sun 10am–4pm; Nov–March Mon–Sat 9am–4pm; ☎ 01595 6693434, ⓦ visitshetland.com).

ACCOMMODATION

Brentham House 7 Harbour St, ZE1 0LR ☎ 01950 460201, ⓦ brenthamhouse.com; map p.995. Spacious rooms in a Victorian, bay-fronted terrace. There's no proper breakfast, and no reception – pick up the keys from the Chinese restaurant a couple of doors down. **£75**
Rockvilla Guest House 88 St Olaf St, ZE1 0ES ☎ 01595 695804, ⓦ rockvillaguesthouse.com; map p.995. Recently refurbished, spotless guesthouse in one of the handsome Victorian houses in the upper part of town. The very hospitable owners serve a top-notch breakfast. **£80**

SYHA Islesburgh House King Harald St, ZE1 0EQ ☎ 01595 692114, ⓦ syha.org.uk/where-to-stay/islands/lerwick; map p.995. Spacious Victorian hostel offering well-worn but comfortable dorm beds, family rooms, a café, wi-fi and laundry facilities. Closed Oct–March. **£21**
Woosung 43 St Olaf St, ZE1 0EN ☎ 01595 693687, ⓦ vshetlandvisitor.com/woosung; map p.995. Family-run B&B, up on the hill above the harbour, run by a genuinely friendly, local landlady. The whole place is sparklingly clean, but not all rooms are en suite. **£60**

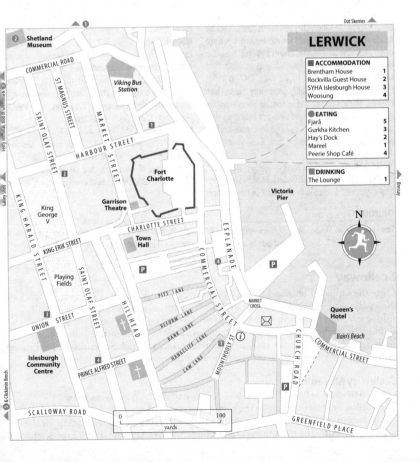

25

NOSS

Inhabited until World War II, and now a National Nature Reserve, **Noss** is a popular day-trip from Lerwick. Sloping gently into the sea at its western end, and plunging vertically for more than 500ft at its eastern end, the island has the dramatic outline of a half-sunk ocean liner. The cliffed coastline is home to vast colonies of gannets, puffins, guillemots, shags, razorbills and fulmars. As Noss is only one mile wide, it's easy enough to do an entire circumference in one day. If you do, keep close to the coast, since otherwise you're likely to be dive-bombed by the great skuas (locally known as "bonxies"). Shetland Seabird Tours offers **boat trips** from Lerwick to Noss (May–Oct daily 9.45am & 2.15pm; 3hr return; £45; ☎07767 872020, ⓦshetlandseabirdtours.com). It's also possible to take a ferry to Maryfield on **Bressay** (every 30min–1hr; 7min; ☎01595 743974); from here it's three miles by foot, bike, bus or car to the landing stage where a Scottish Natural Heritage RIB can take you to Noss (May–Aug Tues, Wed & Fri–Sun; £3 return; call ☎0800 107 7818 before setting off).

EATING

Fjarå Sea Rd, ZE1 0ZJ ☎01595 697388, ⓦfjaracoffee.com; map p.995. In an unlikely location (by the big Tesco), 15min walk from town, this buzzy bistro is a hit with the locals – it's right by the shoreline, so the views are great, and the sandwiches and salads (under £10) are imaginative. Booking advised for the evening when the menu gets more adventurous (mains £10–16). Tues–Sat 8am–10pm, Sun 10am–10pm; kitchen until 8pm.

Gurkha Kitchen 33 North Rd, ZE1 0NQ ☎01595 690400; map p.995. Reliably good curry house, with cheerful, efficient service and reasonable prices – try the Nepalese roti or the the mixed balti and mop it up with garlic naan (mains under £10), or go for the all-day Sun buffet (£10). Mon–Sat noon–2pm & 5–11pm, Sun 1–11pm.

★ **Hay's Dock** Shetland Museum, Hay's Dock, ZE1 0WP ☎01595 741569, ⓦhaysdock.co.uk; map p.995. Bright, modern, licensed café-restaurant in the museum,

with a great view over the north bay. Sandwiches, bagels and simple lunches are all £10 or under; the evening menu features local salmon and lamb (mains £13–20). Mon 10.30am–5pm, Tues–Sat 10.30am–9pm, Sun noon–5pm.

Mareel North Ness, ZE1 0WQ ☎01595 745555, ⓦmareel.org; map p.995. Come to Lerwick's modern cultural complex for films and gigs – and to sink into a leather sofa and enjoy views over the north bay while tucking into burger and chips, ciabatta sandwiches and salads (until 4pm) or nachos and bar snacks. Mon–Wed & Sun 10am–11pm, Thurs–Sat 10am–1am.

Peerie Shop Café Esplanade, ZE1 0LL ☎01595 692816, ⓦpeerieshop.co.uk; map p.995. Designer shop/gallery/café in an old waterside warehouse, with a good range of cakes, soup and sandwiches (all under £5), and probably Britain's northernmost latte. Mon–Sat 9am–6pm.

DRINKING

The Lounge 4 Mounthooly St, ZE1 0BJ ☎01595 692231; map p.995. The friendliest pub in town is this

upstairs bar where local musicians often gather for a session – Thurs night is quiz night. Daily 11am–1am.

Scalloway

Once the capital of Shetland, **SCALLOWAY** waned in importance as Lerwick grew. Nowadays it's fairly sleepy, though the harbour remains busy enough, with a small fishing fleet and the North Atlantic Fisheries College on the far side. The town is dominated by the imposing shell of **Scalloway Castle**, a classic fortified tower-house built using forced labour in 1600 by the infamous Earl Patrick Stewart, who held court here and gained a reputation for cruelty and corruption.

Scalloway Museum

Castle St, ZE1 0TP · Easter–Sept Mon–Sat 11am–4pm, Sun 2–4pm · £3 · ☎01595 880734, ⓦscallowaymuseum.org

The **Scalloway Museum**, next to the castle, covers everything from Neolithic finds to the impact of modern aquaculture, with a replica wheelhouse and a longship for the kids to play with. The most interesting section, however, tells the story of the **Shetland**

25

MOUSA BROCH

The island of **Mousa** boasts the most amazingly well-preserved broch in Scotland. Rising to more than 40ft, and looking rather like a Stone Age cooling tower, **Mousa Broch** has a remarkable presence, and even makes an appearance in the Norse sagas. The low entrance-passage leads through two concentric walls to a central courtyard, divided into separate beehive chambers. Between the walls, a rough (very dark) staircase leads to the top parapet; a torch is provided. Mousa is just a mile wide, but if the weather's not too bad it's easy enough to spend the whole day here. From late May to late July, thousands of **storm petrels** breed in and around the broch walls, fishing out at sea during the day and returning to the nests after dark.

A small **passenger ferry** runs to Mousa from Sandwick (April–Sept; £16 return; ☏07901 872339, ⒲mousa.co.uk). The ferry runs special late-night trips (late May to mid-July Mon, Wed & Sat; £25), setting off in the "simmer dim" twilight around 11pm.

Bus – the link between Shetland and Norway that helped to sustain the Norwegian resistance in World War II.

ARRIVAL AND DEPARTURE   SCALLOWAY

There are regular **buses** to Scalloway from Lerwick (Mon–Sat hourly, Sun 4; 20min).

ACCOMMODATION AND EATING

The Cornerstone Burn Beach, ZE1 0TR ☏01595 880346, ⒲thecornerstonebandb.com. Bright, modern café and B&B on the corner of the main street, with five rooms. The café serves fry-ups until 11.30am, comfort food until 2pm, scones and cakes after that. Mon–Sat 9.30am–5pm, Sun noon–5pm. **£80**

Da Haaf Port Arthur, ZE1 0UN ☏01595 772480, ⒲nafc. uhi.ac.uk/facilities. Unpretentious restaurant in the NAFC, with views over Scalloway harbour. Simple, super-fresh grilled fish dishes (£10–15), high-quality fish and chips

and home-made puddings (£5–6). Mon–Thurs 8.30am–4pm, Fri 8.30am–4pm & 5.30–9pm, Sat 5.30–9pm.

Scalloway Hotel Main St, ZE1 0TR ☏01595 880444, ⒲scallowayhotel.com. Hotel on the harbour – ask for a room with a view. The restaurant serves up pretty impressive dishes (mains around £20), but you can also eat well in the bar (mains £12–16) – both menus feature lots of local fish and seafood. Kitchen Mon–Sat noon–3pm & 5–9pm, Sun noon–8pm. **£130**

South Mainland

Shetland's **South Mainland** is a long, thin finger of land, three or four miles wide and 25 miles long, ending in the cliffs of **Sumburgh Head** and **Fitful Head**. It's a beautiful area with wild undulating landscapes, lots of good green farmland, fabulous views out to sea and the mother of all brochs on the island of **Mousa**, off the east coast. Most points of interest are the southern end of the peninsula, where you'll find seabird colonies, a crofting museum and **Jarlshof**, Shetland's most impressive archeological treasure.

Jarlshof

One mile south of Sumburgh airport ZE3 9JN • Daily: April–Sept 9.30am–5.30pm; Oct–March restricted hours (call for details) • £6; HS • ☏01856 841815, ⒲historicenvironment.scot/visit-a-place/places/jarlshof-prehistoric-and-norse-settlement

Jarlshof is the largest and most impressive of Shetland's archeological sites. Only half of the original broch survives, and its courtyard is now an Iron Age aisled roundhouse with stone piers. It's difficult to distinguish the original broch from the later Pictish **wheelhouses** that now surround it, but it's great fun to explore as you're free to roam around the cells, checking out the in-built stone shelving, water tanks, beds and so on. Inland, a maze of grass-topped foundations marks out the **Viking longhouses**. Towering over the complex are the ruins of the laird's house, built by Robert Stewart, Earl of Orkney and Lord of Shetland, in the late sixteenth century, and the **Old House of Sumburgh**, built by his son, Earl Patrick.

25

Sumburgh Head Lighthouse

2.5 miles south of Sumburgh airport, ZE3 9JN · Daily: April–Sept 11am–5.30pm · £6; lighthouse tour (Fri–Sun only) £3 · ☎ 01595 694688, ⊛ sumburghhead.com

Shetland's Mainland comes to a dramatic end at **Sumburgh Head** (262ft), with its clifftop **lighthouse** and **visitor centre**. The road up to the lighthouse is also the perfect place to watch nesting seabirds such as kittiwakes, fulmars, shags, razorbills and guillemots, not to mention gannets diving for fish. Sumburgh Head is also the easiest place in Shetland to get close to **puffins** during the nesting season (May to early Aug).

ARRIVAL AND DEPARTURE
SOUTH MAINLAND

There are regular **buses** from Lerwick to Levenwick (Mon–Sat 6–8 daily, Sun 5; 30min), Sandwick (Mon–Fri 10 daily, Sat & Sun 5–6 daily; 25min) and Sumburgh (Mon–Sat 6–7 daily, Sun 5; 45min).

ACCOMMODATION

Levenwick Campsite Levenwick, 18 miles south of Lerwick, ZE2 9HX ☎ 01950 422320, ⊛ levenwick.shetland.co.uk. Small, terraced campsite run by the local community, with hot showers, a tennis court, friendly Shetland ponies and a superb view over the east coast. Closed Oct–April. **£8**

★ **Mucklehus** Levenwick, 18 miles south of Lerwick, ZE2 9HX ☎ 01950 422370, ⊛ mucklehus.plus.com A lovely B&B run by a local artist in a former Master Mariner's house built in 1890 near Levenwick's sandy beach. Rooms are small, but stylish. **£80**

Setterbrae Scousburgh, 22 miles south of Lerwick, ZE2 9JE ☎ 01950 460468, ⊛ setterbrae.co.uk. There's a homely feel to this B&B, just a stone's throw from Spiggie Loch – the residents' lounge has lots of books on Shetland and the conservatory has views over the loch. **£80**

Fair Isle

Fair Isle is marooned in the sea halfway between Shetland and Orkney. By the late 1940s, the population had tumbled from 400 to 44, at which point George Waterston set up a bird observatory and rejuvenation began. Although crofting still takes place in the south of the island, the focus for many visitors remains the **Bird Observatory**, just above the sandy bay of North Haven where the ferry from Shetland arrives. It's one of Europe's major centres for ornithology and its work in watching, trapping, recording and ringing resident and migrant birds goes on all year. Fair Isle is even better known for its **knitting** patterns, still produced with great skill by the local knitwear cooperative – there are samples on display at the island's **museum** (Mon 2–4pm, Wed 10.30am–noon, Fri 2–4pm; free; ☎ 01595 760244), next door to the Methodist chapel.

ARRIVAL AND DEPARTURE
FAIR ISLE

By plane Airtask (☎ 01595 840246, ⊛ airtask.co.uk) flies from Tingwall to Fair Isle (Mon–Sat 1–3 daily) and from Sumburgh (Sat only) for around £85 return.
By ferry The passenger ferry connects Fair Isle with either Lerwick (alternate Thurs; 4–5hr) or Grutness in Sumburgh (Tues, alternate Thurs & Sat; 3hr) – it's advisable to book in advance (☎ 01595 760363).

ACCOMMODATION

Fair Isle Bird Observatory Lodge 1 mile east of the airport ZE2 9JU ☎ 01595 760258, ⊛ fairislebirdobs.co.uk. Full-board accommodation is available at the observatory in en-suite doubles/twins and singles. FIBO is the island's social hub and offers tea, coffee and good home-cooking to guests and visitors alike. Closed Nov–March. **£140**
South Lighthouse 2 miles south of the airport, ZE2 9JU ☎ 01595 760355, ⊛ southlightfairisle.co.uk. This B&B is not literally in the lighthouse, but in the adjacent keepers' cottages – bathrooms are shared. Full board only. **£120**

Foula

Foula is without a doubt the most isolated inhabited island in Britain, separated from the nearest point on Mainland Shetland by about fourteen miles of often turbulent ocean. Its western **cliffs**, the second highest in Britain after those of St Kilda, rise at

The Kame to some 1220ft above sea level; a clear day at The Kame offers a magnificent panorama stretching from Unst to Fair Isle. On a bad day, the exposure is complete and the cliffs generate blasts of wind known as "flans", which rip through the hills with tremendous force. In addition to its forty or so human inhabitants, the island is home to a quarter of a million **birds**, including a colony of **great skuas** or "bonxies", which you can't fail to notice in the breeding season.

ARRIVAL AND DEPARTURE
FOULA

By plane Airtask (☎01595 840246, ⓦairtask.com) flies from Tingwall (Mon 1, Tues, Wed & Fri 2 daily; 15min).

By ferry Be sure to book and reconfirm your journey by ferry (Tues, Thurs & Sat; 2hr; ☎01595 5840208, ⓦbkmarine.

org); ferries leave from Walls (Tues, Sat & alternate Thurs; 2hr) or Scalloway (alternate Thurs; 3hr 30min) and arrive at Ham, in the middle of Foula's east coast.

ACCOMMODATION

Leraback Near Ham, ZE2 9PN ☎01595 753226, ⓦoriginart.eu/leraback/leraback.html. Foula's only accommodation, unless you camp, is this modern croft-

house B&B. It's simple, but very welcoming; they'll collect you from the airstrip or pier. Full board only. **£80**

North Mainland

North Mainland, stretching more than thirty miles north from Lerwick, is wild even for Shetland. The tiny, picturesque fishing port of **VOE** is well worth visiting – not so **BRAE**, built hastily during the 1970s oil boom. **HILLSWICK**, the main settlement in the northwest peninsula of **Northmavine**, was once a centre for deep-sea or haaf fishing, and later a herring station. By the harbour is **Da Böd**, founded by a Hanseatic merchant in 1684, which later became Shetland's oldest pub and is now a seal and wildlife sanctuary (☎01806 503348, ⓦhillswickwildlifesanctuary.org).

A side road leads west to the exposed headland of **Esha Ness** (pronounced "Aysha Ness"), celebrated for its red sandstone cliffs, stacks, blowholes and its lighthouse. A mile or so south off the main road, the **Tangwick Haa Museum** (Easter–Sept daily 11am–5pm; free) tells the moving story of this remote corner of Shetland and its role in the dangerous trades of deep-sea fishing and whaling.

ARRIVAL AND DEPARTURE
NORTH MAINLAND

By bus From Lerwick there are buses to Brae (Mon–Sat 8 daily; 45min), Hillswick (Mon–Sat 3 daily; 1hr 40min) and Voe (Mon–Fri 5 daily, Sat 3; 35min).

ACCOMMODATION AND EATING

★ **Busta House** Brae, ZE2 9QN ☎01806 522506, ⓦbustahouse.com. A laird's house with stepped gables that sits across the bay from Brae. Even if you're not staying the night, it's worth coming for afternoon tea in the Long Room, for a stroll around the wooded grounds, or for a drink and a meal in the hotel's pub-like bar (mains £10– 12). Kitchen daily noon–2.30pm & 6–9pm. **£115**

Frankie's 200yd south of the main crossroads, ZE2 9QJ ☎01806 522700, ⓦfrankiesfishandchips.com. Brae's best food option, aside from *Busta House*, is this very popular fish-and-chip café with great views over Busta Voe. As well as fish straight off the boats, you can get king scallops, smoked haddock and mussels. Mon–Sat 9.30am–8pm, Sun noon–8pm.

St Magnus Bay Hotel Hillswick, ZE2 9RW ☎01806 503372, ⓦstmagnusbayhotel.co.uk. Large, distinctive

hotel with large, high-ceilinged public spaces and guestrooms ranging from spacious to cosy. The restaurant serves generous portions – the Sunday lunch is particularly popular. Mon–Sat 11am–2.30pm & 4–8.30pm, Sun 12.30–3.30pm. **£130**

Sail Loft By the loch, ZE2 9PX ☎01595 694688, ⓦcamping-bods.co.uk. Originally a giant storeroom, this enormous camping böd (like a hostel but with no mattresses, and solid fuel heating) has hot showers and a kitchen. Bring £1 coins for the electricity meter. Closed Nov–Feb. **£12**

Westayre Muckle Roe, ZE2 9QW ☎01806 522368, ⓦwestayre-shetland.co.uk. A modern crofthouse B&B in a tranquil position, overlooking a red sandy bay at the end of the road on the peaceful island of Muckle Roe, linked to the mainland by a bridge. **£80**

25

The North Isles

Many visitors never make it out to Shetland's trio of remote **North Isles**, which is a shame, as the ferry links are frequent and inexpensive, the roads fast, and with Lerwick that much further away, the spirit of independence and self-sufficiency is much more keenly felt. **Yell**, best-known for its otter population, is often overlooked, while **Fetlar**, famed for its phalaropes, is the smallest and most fertile, but it's **Unst** that has the widest appeal, partly because it's the most northerly landmass in the British Isles, and partly for its nesting seabirds.

Yell

The interior of **Yell** features a lot of peat moorland, but the coastline is gentler and greener and provides an ideal habitat for a large population of **otters**. The only sight as such is at **BURRAVOE**, in the island's southeastern corner. Here there's a lovely whitewashed laird's house, dating from 1672, with crow-stepped gables, which now houses the **Old Haa Museum** (April–Sept Mon–Thurs & Sat 10am–4pm, Sun 2–5pm; free). Stuffed with artefacts, the museum has lots of material on the history of the local herring and whaling industry and there's a pleasant wood-panelled café on the ground floor.

ARRIVAL AND DEPARTURE   YELL

By ferry ☎01595 745804, ⦿shetland.gov.uk. Ferries to Ulsta (Yell) from Toft (Mainland) are frequent (every 30min–1hr; 20min).

By bus There's an integrated bus and ferry service from Lerwick that goes all the way to Gutcher (Mon–Sat 1 daily; 2hr 10min). On Yell, buses from Ulsta run to Gutcher (Mon–Sat 3–4 daily; 30min).

ACCOMMODATION AND EATING

Gutcher Goose Café Gutcher, ZE2 9DF ☎01957 744382. A café in a prefab at Gutcher offering soup, baked tatties and filled bannocks for those waiting for the ferry to Unst. Mon–Sat 9am–5pm.

Quam West Sandwick, ZE2 9BH ☎01957 766256, ⦿quambandbyellshetland.co.uk. Large, kit-built Scandinavian-style working croft with sheep, ducks, hens and Shetland ponies. There are wonderful sea views across Yell Sound and dinner is available for an extra £15/head. **£70**

Windhouse Lodge Mid Yell, ZE2 9BJ ☎01595 694688, ⦿camping-bods.co.uk. The Windhouse gatehouse, on the main road near Mid Yell, is a camping böd (see page 999) with a wood- and peat-fired heater and hot showers. Bring £1 coins for the electricity meter. Closed Nov–Feb. **£12**

Fetlar

Fetlar is the most fertile of the North Isles, much of it covered by grassy moorland and lush green meadows with masses of summer flowers. At the main settlement, **HOUBIE**, you can learn more about the island from the welcoming **Fetlar Interpretive Centre** (May–Sept Mon–Sat 11am–4pm, Sun 12.30–4pm; £2; ☎01957 733206, ⦿fetlar. com). Fetlar is also one of the very few places in the UK where you'll see graceful **red-necked phalarope** (late May to early Aug): a hide overlooks the marshes (or mires) to the east of the **Loch of Funzie** (pronounced "finny").

ARRIVAL AND DEPARTURE   FETLAR

By ferry Ferries to Fetlar (Mon–Sat 7–9 daily; 25–40min) depart regularly from Gutcher (Yell) and Belmont (Unst), and dock at Hamar's Ness, 3 miles northwest of Houbie.

By bus There's a service from Funzie to Hamar's Ness (Mon–Sat 3–4 daily), and a dial-a-ride electric minibus – book the day before (☎01595 745745, ⦿fetlar.org).

ACCOMMODATION

Aithbank Böd A mile east of Houbie, ZE2 9DJ ☎01595 694688, ⦿camping-bods.com. A cosy wood-panelled cottage with two rooms, sleeping a total of seven. There's hot water, a kitchen and a solid fuel stove. Bring £1 coins for the electricity meter. Closed Nov–Feb. Per person **£12**

Gord Houbie, ZE2 9DJ ☎01957 733227, ✉gordbandb@ btinternet.com. The modern house attached to the island shop is also a B&B, with great sea views from all the rooms. Full board only, with meals for non-residents by arrangement. **£100**

Unst

Much of **Unst** is rolling grassland but the coast is more dramatic: a fringe of cliffs relieved by some beautiful sandy beaches. As Britain's most northerly inhabited island, there is a surfeit of "most northerly" sights. Most visitors head straight for **Hermaness**, to see the seabirds and look out over Muckle Flugga and the northernmost tip of Britain, to the North Pole beyond.

On the south coast, not far from **UYEASOUND**, lie the ruins of **Muness Castle**, a diminutive defensive structure with matching bulging bastions and corbelled turrets at opposite corners. The castle was built in 1598 by the Scots incomer, Laurence Bruce, stepbrother and chief bullyboy of the infamous Earl Robert Stewart. As you leave Unst's main settlement, **BALTASOUND**, heading north, be sure to look out for **Bobby's Bus Shelter**, an eccentric, fully furnished, award-winning bus shelter on the edge of the town. The **Keen of Hamar**, east of Baltasound, and signposted from the main road, is one of the largest expanses of serpentine debris in Europe, home to an extraordinary array of plant life.

Unst Boat Haven and Unst Heritage Centre

Haroldswick, ZE2 9EQ • Both May–Sept Mon–Sat 11am–4pm, Sun 2–4pm • £3 each

Near the shore at **HAROLDSWICK**, the **Unst Boat Haven** displays a beautiful collection of historic boats with many tools of the trade and information on fishing. The nearby **Unst Heritage Centre**, housed in the old school building by the main crossroads, puts on activities such as spinning, knitting and potting.

Hermaness Nature Reserve

The bleak headland of **Hermaness Nature Reserve**, home to more than 100,000 nesting seabirds (May–Aug), lies northwest of Haroldswick. There's an excellent **visitor centre** in the former lighthouse-keeper's shore station, where you can pick up a leaflet showing the marked routes across the heather to the view over to **Muckle Flugga** lighthouse and **Out Stack**, the most northerly bit of Britain. The views from here are marvellous, as is the birdlife; there's a huge gannetry on one of the stacks, and puffins burrow all along the clifftops.

ARRIVAL AND DEPARTURE UNST

By ferry Ferries (☎01595 745804) shuttle regularly across Bluemull Sound from Gutcher on Yell to Belmont on Unst (every 30min–1hr; 10min).

By bus An integrated bus and ferry service goes from Lerwick to Baltasound on Unst (Mon–Sat 1 daily; 2hr 40min). From Belmont, Unst's ferry terminal, buses run to Uyeasound (Mon–Sat 3–4 daily; 5min), Baltasound (Mon–Sat 3–4 daily; 15min) and Haroldswick (Mon–Sat 3–4 daily; 30min).

ACCOMMODATION AND EATING

Baltasound Hotel Baltasound, ZE2 9DS ☎01957 711334, ⒲baltasoundhotel.co.uk. Wherever you stay, it's a good idea to book yourself in for dinner or self-cater, as the only other option is the basic bar food here (mains £10–18). Kitchen daily 5–8pm.

Gardiesfauld Hostel Uyeasound, ZE2 9DW ☎01957 755279, ⒲gardiesfauld.shetland.co.uk. A large, clean and modern hostel, with sheltered camping and bike rental. Closed Oct–March. Camping/person £6, dorms £15

Prestegaard Uyeasound, ZE2 9DL ☎01957 755234, Ⓔprestegaard@postmaster.co.uk. This attractive, whitewashed Victorian B&B, with just three rooms, has great sea views – they offer dinner for residents and non-residents, as well as a bargain room for those who just want a bed for the night. £60

LAURENCE OLIVIER IN SHAKESPEARE'S HENRY V (1944)

Contexts

History

Britain's history is long and densely woven, its protagonists influential in western Europe from Anglo-Saxon times and globally during the days of the British Empire from the eighteenth century onwards. What follows is a necessarily brief introduction.

From the Stone Age to the Bronze Age

Britain has been inhabited for the best part of half a million years. The earliest archeological evidence is scant, but **Old Stone Age (Paleolithic)** bones and flint tools have been found in several different parts of the country. The comings and goings of these migrant peoples were dictated by successive **Ice Ages**, the most recent of which lasted for the ten thousand years up to 5000 BC. This final thawing caused the British Isles to separate from the European mainland, but the **sea barrier** did little to hinder further influxes of nomadic hunters, drawn by the game that inhabited Britain's forests.

Around 3500 BC, a new wave of colonists reached Britain, probably via Ireland, bringing a **New Stone Age (Neolithic)** culture based on farming and livestock. These tribes were the first to impact upon the environment and their most profuse relics are **graves**, usually stone-chambered, turf-covered mounds called long barrows, cairns or cromlechs, such as those at Belas Knap in Gloucestershire, Barclodiad y Gawres in Anglesey, and Maes Howe on Orkney.

The next transition, to the **Bronze Age**, began around 2500 BC, with the importation from continental Europe of artefacts attributed to the **Beaker Culture** – named after the distinctive cups found at many burial sites. Spreading along established trade routes, this stimulated the development of a well-organized social structure with an established aristocracy. Many of Britain's **stone and timber circles** were completed at the tail end of the Neolithic period, including **Stonehenge** in Wiltshire and Calanais on the Isle of Lewis, while others belong entirely to the Bronze Age, including the Nine Maidens on Cornwall's Bodmin Moor.

Iron Age progress

By 500 BC, the British **Iron Age** comprised a sophisticated farming economy with a social hierarchy dominated by a druidic priesthood. Most farmers grew wheat and barley, and kept cattle, sheep and pigs; chickens arrived later, with the Romans. These early Britons gradually developed better methods of **metal-working**, favouring iron and gold rather than bronze, from which they forged not just weapons but also coins and ornamental works, thus creating the first recognizable indigenous art. A network of **hillforts** or brochs and other defensive works now stretched over the entire country, the greatest being at **Maiden Castle** in Dorset and **Mousa** in the Shetland Islands. These earthworks suggest endemic tribal warfare, a situation further complicated by the appearance of bands of **Celts**, who arrived in numbers from central Europe around 600 BC, though some historians dispute the notion of

5000 BC	2500 BC	55 BC	43 AD
As the ice sheets retreat, the sea floods in, separating Britain from continental Europe.	The start of the Bronze Age – and the construction of dozens of stone and timber circles.	Chickens reach England for the first time – courtesy of Julius Caesar.	The Roman Emperor Claudius invades Britain – and he means business.

a Celtic "invasion", arguing that change and conflict were triggered by trade rather than conquest.

The Romans

The **Roman** invasion of Britain began hesitantly, when **Julius Caesar** led small cross-Channel incursions in 55 and 54 BC. A century later, the Romans arrived in force, principally because of anti-Roman collaboration between the Britons of southern England and their Celtic cousins in Gaul (France). The subtext was that the **Emperor Claudius**, who led the invasion, owed his power to the army and needed a military triumph. In 43 AD, a substantial force landed in Kent, then fanned out to establish a base along the Thames estuary. Joined by elephants and camels for major battles, the Romans soon reached Camulodunum (Colchester), and within four years were dug in on the frontier of south Wales.

By 80 AD the Roman governor, **Agricola**, felt secure enough in the south of Britain to begin an invasion of the **north**, stringing forts across the Clyde–Forth line and defeating the Scottish tribes at Mons Graupius. The long-term effect, however, was slight and in 123 AD, the Emperor Hadrian sealed the frontier against the northern tribes by building **Hadrian's Wall** from the Solway Firth to the Tyne.

The written history of Britain begins with the Romans, whose rule lasted nigh on four centuries. For the first time, most of England was absorbed into a unified political structure, in which commerce flourished and cities prospered, and **Londinium** assumed a pivotal role in commercial and administrative life. Although Latin became the language of the Romano-British ruling elite, local traditions were allowed to coexist, so that British gods were often worshipped at the same time as Rome's. **Christianity** was introduced during the third century, and became entrenched after its official recognition across the Roman Empire in 313.

The Anglo-Saxons arrive

By the middle of the fourth century AD, Roman England was subject to regular **raids** by Germanic Saxons from the east and, as central authority collapsed, so a series of military commanders usurped local authority. By the early fifth century, England had become irrevocably detached from what remained of the Roman Empire and shortly thereafter the **Saxons** – and the **Angles**, also from northern Germany – were settling England and parts of Scotland themselves. Romano-British resistance was led by such semi-mythical figures as **King Arthur**, said to have held court at Caerleon in Wales, but crumbled after the **Battle of Dyrham** (near Bath) in 577. By the end of the sixth century, Romano-British culture was all but eliminated in England, which was divided into the **Anglo-Saxon kingdoms** of Northumbria, Mercia, East Anglia, Kent and Wessex. Even today, some ninety percent of English place names have an Anglo-Saxon derivation. Meanwhile, those native Britons who had not been absorbed by the invaders were dispersed into Wales, the far southwest of England, and Scotland, which was a real mix, with Angles on the east coast, Irish-Celtic **Scotti** on the west, the Picts, descended from Iron Age tribes, to the north, and Romano-Britons in between. The Scotti spoke **Goidelic** (or Q-Celtic), the precursor of modern Gaelic, while **Brythonic** (P-Celtic) was spoken in Wales and Cornwall.

60 AD	**313**	**c. 500**	**597**
An affronted and enraged Boudicca and her Iceni sack Roman Colchester.	The Emperor Constantine makes Christianity the official religion of the Roman Empire.	St David, the patron saint of Wales, is born on a clifftop during a violent storm.	St Augustine lands in Kent with instructions to convert Britain to Christianity.

Christian epiphany

In England, the revival of **Christianity** was driven by **St Augustine**, who landed in Kent in 597 at the behest of the pope, accompanied by forty monks. His mission to convert the pagan Anglo-Saxons went relatively smoothly and was continued by a long succession of monkish missionaries; the last part of England to become Christian was Sussex in 680. Meanwhile, on what might be called the Celtic fringe, a Christian Church had survived from Roman times, winning new converts and promoting a hermetical vision of holiness exemplified by St David, ultimately Wales's patron saint, and **St Columba**, who founded several Christian outposts in Scotland, including one on the island of Iona. Liturgical differences between this "Ionan Church" and the "Roman Church" of St Augustine were resolved when the **Synod of Whitby** determined in 663 that the English Church should follow the rule of Rome.

Arrival of the Vikings

In the eighth century, the kingdom of **Mercia**, occupying what is today the Midlands, became the dominant power in England. Its most talented ruler was Offa, who was responsible for **Offa's Dyke**, an earthwork stretching from the River Dee to the Severn, marking the border with Wales. After Offa's death, **Wessex** gained the upper hand and, by 825, its King Egbert had conquered or taken allegiance from all the other English kingdoms. Elsewhere, in Scotland, **Kenneth MacAlpine** united the Scotti and the Picts into one kingdom in 843. His successors extended their fiefdoms by marriage and force of arms until, by 1034, almost all of modern Scotland was under their rule. The supremacy of Wessex coincided with the first large-scale **Viking** (or Norse) raids, which began with coastal attacks, but grew into a migration. By 871, a substantial **Viking (Danish) army** had conquered Northumbria, Mercia and East Anglia. The new king of Wessex, however, **Alfred the Great** (reigned 871–99), successfully resisted the Danes, and signed a truce that fixed an uneasy border between Wessex and Danish territory – the **Danelaw** – to the north and east. While the Danes soon succumbed to internal warfare, Alfred modernized his kingdom and strengthened its defences. His successor, **Edward the Elder**, reaped the benefits, establishing Saxon supremacy over the Danelaw and becoming the de facto overlord of all England. The relative calm continued under Edward's son, **Athelstan** (925–40), who extended his sway over much of Scotland and Wales, and his son, **Edgar** (959–75), crowned as the first **king of England** in 973. However, this was but a lull in the Viking storm. Returning in force, the Vikings milked Edgar's son **Ethelred the Unready** (978–1016) for all the money they could, but the ransom (the Danegeld) paid brought only temporary relief and Ethelred hot-footed it to Normandy, leaving the Danes in command.

England: Danish dominance and defeat

The first Danish king of England, the ever-so shrewd **Cnut** (1016–35), constructed an Anglo-Scandinavian empire, but the Saxons regained the initiative from his two disreputable sons, and placed Ethelred's son, **Edward the Confessor** (1042–66), on the throne. It was a poor choice. More suited to be a priest than a king, Edward allowed power to drift into the hands of his most powerful subject, Godwin, Earl of Wessex,

793	796	1066	1085
In a surprise attack, Viking raiders destroy the monastery at Lindisfarne.	Death of King Offa, the most powerful king in England and long-time ruler of Mercia.	King Harold, the last Saxon king of England, catches an arrow in the eye at the Battle of Hastings.	The Normans start work on the Domesday Book, detailing who owns what, does what and lives where.

and his son Harold. On Edward's death, the Witan – a sort of council of elders – confirmed **Harold** (1066) as king, thereby ignoring several rival claims, including that of **William, Duke of Normandy.** William's claim was a curious affair, but he always insisted that the childless Edward the Confessor had promised him his crown. Unluckily for Harold, his two main rivals struck at the same time. First to do so was his alienated brother Tostig and his ally King Harald of Norway, reliably reckoned to be seven feet tall. They landed with a Viking army in Yorkshire and Harold hurriedly marched north to meet them. Harold won a crushing victory at **Stamford Bridge**, but then heard that William of Normandy had invaded the south. Rashly, Harold dashed south without mustering more men. William famously routed the Saxons – and killed Harold – at the **Battle of Hastings** in 1066. On Christmas Day, William the Conqueror was installed as king in Westminster Abbey.

England: Normans and Plantagenets (1066–1399)

William I (1066–87) imposed a **Norman** aristocracy on his new subjects, bolstering his rule by constructing a network of castles, including the Tower of London. His most effective measure, however, was the compilation of the **Domesday Book** in 1086. Recording land ownership, type of cultivation, the number of inhabitants and their social status, it afforded William an unprecedented body of information, providing the framework for taxation, the judicial structure and feudal obligations. William was succeeded by his son **William Rufus** (1087–1100), an ineffectual ruler who died in mysterious circumstances, killed by an unknown assailant's arrow while hunting in the New Forest. The throne then passed to **Henry I** (1100–35), William I's youngest son, who spent much of his time struggling with his unruly barons, but at least he proved conciliatory in his dealings with his Anglo-Saxon subjects, even marrying into one of their leading families.

A long-winded civil war followed the death of Henry I, ending when **Henry II** (1154–89), the first of the **Plantagenets** secured the throne. Energetic and far-sighted, Henry kept his barons in check and instigated profound administrative reforms, including the introduction of trial by jury. However, his attempt to subordinate Church to Crown went terribly awry in 1170, when he sanctioned the murder in Canterbury Cathedral of his erstwhile drinking companion **Thomas Becket**, whose canonization three years later created an enduring Europe-wide cult. Henry had other troubles too: his inheritance had bequeathed him great chunks of France and the struggle to conquer more (or hold on to what he had) was to drain the royal treasury until the fifteenth century.

Henry II was succeeded by his eldest son, **Richard I** (or Lionheart; 1189–99), who spent most of his reign crusading in the Holy Land. Neglected, England fell prey to Richard's scheming brother **John** (1199–1216), the villain of the Robin Hood tales, who became king in his own right after Richard's death. John's failure to hold on to many of his French possessions alienated the English barons, who in 1215 forced him to sign a charter guaranteeing their rights and privileges, the **Magna Carta**, at Runnymede, on the Thames.

Edward I to Edward III

Edward I (1272–1307) was a great law-maker, but he became obsessed with military matters, spending years subduing Wales and imposing English jurisdiction over

1102	1190	1237
By the terms of the Synod of Westminster, clergy are forbidden to marry.	King Richard complains that in England it is "cold and always raining", and joins the Third Crusade.	The Treaty of York, signed by Henry III of England and Scotland's Alexander II, sets the Anglo-Scottish border.

THE CONQUEST OF WALES (1272–1415)

William the Conqueror installed a gang of landholding barons, the **Lords Marcher**, along the border with Wales (The Marches) rather than attempting conquest. His successor, **Edward I**, decided to conquer Wales instead, provoked in part by a Welsh chieftain, **Llywelyn the Last**, who failed to attend his coronation and refused to pay him homage. Aided by the skilful use of sea power, Edward had little trouble in forcing Llywelyn into the mountains of Snowdonia, and, by the **Treaty of Aberconwy** in 1277, Llywelyn was robbed of almost all his land and left the hollow title of "Prince of Wales". Five years later, Llywelyn's brother **Dafydd** rose against Edward and Llywelyn felt obliged to help. It was a disaster: Edward crushed the revolt with relative ease and both brothers were killed. The **Treaty of Rhuddlan** in 1284 set down the terms by which the English king was to rule Wales: those parts of the country not given to the Lords Marcher were divided into administrative and legal districts similar to those in England. Often seen as a symbol of English subjugation, the treaty in fact respected much of Welsh law and provided an embryonic basis for civil rights and privileges. Many Welsh accepted Edward's rule, but after he brutally crushed a 1294 rebellion led by **Madog ap Llywelyn**, a number of those privileges were rescinded. Thereafter, the Anglo-Welsh aristocracy took firm hold of Wales, but one of their number, the charismatic Welsh hero **Owain Glyndŵr**, rose in revolt in 1400, declaring himself "Prince of Wales" in defiance of his English overlord, **Henry IV**. The key fortress of Conwy Castle was captured in 1401 and three years later Glyndŵr summoned a parliament in Machynlleth, and had himself crowned. He then demanded independence for the Welsh Church from Canterbury and set about securing alliances with disaffected English noblemen. However, Glyndŵr's allies deserted him, and the rebellion fizzled out, though Glyndŵr was never captured and disappeared into the mountains. It's believed he died in 1415 or 1416, but his body was never found – cue lots of mystical ruminations.

Scotland. Fortunately for the Scots, the next king of England, **Edward II** (1307–27), proved completely hopeless. After Robert the Bruce inflicted a huge defeat on his guileless army at the Battle of Bannockburn in 1314 (see page 843), Edward ended up being murdered by his wife Isabella and her lover Roger Mortimer in 1327.

After sorting out the Scottish imbroglio, **Edward III** (1327–77) turned his attention to his (essentially specious) claim to the throne of France. Starting in 1337, the ensuing **Hundred Years' War** began with several English victories, principally Crécy in 1346 and Poitiers in 1356, but was interrupted by the outbreak of the **Black Death** in 1349. The plague claimed about a third of the population – and in England the resultant scarcity of labour gave the peasantry great economic clout. Predictably, the landowners attempted to restrict the concomitant rise in wages, provoking widespread rioting that culminated in the **Peasants' Revolt** of 1381. The rebels marched on London hoping to appeal to the king – **Richard II** (1377–99) – for fair treatment. The monarch agreed to meet their spokesman, **Wat Tyler**, but his bodyguards killed Tyler instead and dispersed his followers amid mass slaughter.

Medieval Scotland (1040–1329)

In 1040, **Macbeth** famously killed King Duncan and usurped the Scottish throne. In 1057, however, Duncan's son, **Malcolm III**, returned to Scotland and defeated Macbeth. His long reign was to transform Scottish society. Malcolm established a secure dynasty –

1266	1277	1295
Alexander III, the king of Scotland, buys the Western Isles from the Norwegians.	Well-armed and well-organized, Edward I of England embarks upon the conquest of Wales.	France and Scotland sign a treaty of mutual assistance – the start of the "Auld Alliance".

the **Canmores** ("Bigheads") – based on succession through the male line, and replaced the old Gaelic system of blood ties with **feudalism**: the followers of a Gaelic king were his kindred, whereas those of a feudal king were his vassals. However, while the Canmores successfully feudalized much of southern and eastern Scotland by making grants to their Norman, Breton and Flemish followers, traditional clan-based social relations persisted to the north and west, a division which was to define much of Scotland's later history.

The Canmores also set about reforming the Church. Malcolm III's English wife **Margaret** brought Scottish religious practices into line with the rest of Europe, while **David I** (1124–53) imported monks to found monasteries, principally in the Borders at Kelso, Melrose, Jedburgh and Dryburgh. By 1200 the country was covered by eleven bishoprics, although church organization remained weak within the Highlands. Similarly, the dynasty founded **royal burghs**, recognizing towns such as Edinburgh, Stirling and Berwick as centres of trade. Their charters usually granted a measure of self-government, which the monarchy hoped would encourage loyalty and increase prosperity. Scotland's Gaelic-speaking clans had little influence within the burghs, and by 1550 Scots – a northern version of Anglo-Saxon – had become the main language throughout the Lowlands.

Anglo-Scottish wars

Scotland's progress as an independent nation was threatened by the hotly contested succession following the death of **Alexander III** in 1286. Edward I, king of England, muscled in, presiding over a conference in which the rival claimants to the Scottish throne presented their cases. Edward chose John Balliol, in preference to **Robert the Bruce**, and forced John to pay him homage, thus turning Scotland into a vassal kingdom. Bruce's refusal to accept this decision prolonged the conflict, and in 1295 Balliol switched his allegiance from England to **France** – the start of what is known as the "Auld Alliance". In the ensuing warfare, Balliol was defeated and imprisoned, and Edward seized control of almost all of Scotland. However, Edward's cruelty provoked a truly national resistance that focused on **William Wallace**, a man of relatively lowly origins who forged a proto-nationalist army of peasants, lesser knights and townsmen that was determined to expel the English. Yet Wallace never received the support of the nobility and after ten bitter years he was betrayed, captured and executed in London.

Feudal intrigue now resumed. In 1306 **Robert the Bruce** defied Edward and had himself crowned king of Scotland. Edward died the following year, but the turbulence dragged on until 1314, when Bruce decisively defeated an English army under Edward II at the **Battle of Bannockburn**. At last Bruce was firmly in control, and in 1320 the Scots asserted their right to independence in a successful petition to the pope, now known as the **Arbroath Declaration**.

England: the houses of Lancaster and York (1399–1485)

In 1399, **Henry IV** (1399–1413), the first **Lancastrian** king, supplanted the weak and indecisive Richard II. His son and successor, the bellicose **Henry V** (1413–22), promptly renewed the Hundred Years' War. A comprehensive victory at **Agincourt** forced the French king to acknowledge Henry as his heir in the Treaty of Troyes of 1420, but Henry died just two years later and his son, **Henry VI** (1422–61 & 1470–1471) – or

1314	1349	1380s
At the Battle of Bannockburn, Robert the Bruce's Scots destroy an English army.	The Black Death reaches England and moves on into Scotland the year after.	Geoffrey Chaucer begins work on *The Canterbury Tales* and transforms the face of English literature.

rather his regents – easily succumbed to a French counterattack inspired by **Joan of Arc**; by 1454, only Calais was left in English hands.

When it became obvious that Henry VI was mentally unstable, two aristocratic factions fought for the throne – the **Yorkists**, whose emblem was the white rose, and the **Lancastrians**, represented by the red rose. At first, in the **Wars of the Roses**, the Lancastrians had the upper hand, but the Yorkist **Edward IV** seized the Crown in 1461. Edward IV then proceeded to over-reach himself and was driven into exile with **Henry VI** returning for a second term as king – but not for long. In 1471, Edward IV came back and Henry was captured and dispatched when the Yorkists crushed the Lancastrians at the Battle of Tewkesbury.

Edward IV (1461–70 & 1471–83) proved to be a precursor of the great Tudor princes – licentious, cruel and despotic, but also a patron of Renaissance learning. In 1483, his 12-year-old son succeeded as **Edward V** (1483), but his reign was cut short after only two months, when he and his younger brother were murdered in the Tower of London – allegedly by their uncle, the Duke of Gloucester, who was crowned **Richard III** (1483–85). Richard was himself killed at the battle of **Bosworth Field** in 1485 and Henry Tudor, Earl of Richmond, took the throne as **Henry VII**.

England: the Tudors (1485–1603)

The start of the **Tudor** period brought radical transformation. A Lancastrian through his mother's line, **Henry VII** (1485–1509) promptly reconciled the Yorkists by marrying Edward IV's daughter Elizabeth, a shrewd gambit that ended the Wars of the Roses at a stroke. By marrying his daughter off to James IV of Scotland and his son to Catherine, the daughter of Ferdinand and Isabella of Spain, Henry also began to establish England as a major European power.

Henry's son, **Henry VIII** (1509–47) is best remembered for separating Anne Boleyn from her head and the English Church from Rome, thereby establishing the independent Protestant **Church of England**. His schism with the pope was triggered not by doctrinal issues but by the failure of his wife **Catherine of Aragon** – his elder brother's widow – to produce male offspring. When Pope Clement VII refused to grant a decree of nullity, Henry dismissed his chancellor Thomas Wolsey and turned to **Thomas Cromwell**, who helped make the English Church recognize Henry as its head. One consequence, the **Dissolution of the Monasteries**, enabled both king and nobles to get their hands on a vast chunk of monastic property. In his later years Henry became a corpulent, syphilitic wreck, six times married but at last furnished with an heir, **Edward VI** (1547–53), who was only nine years old when he ascended the throne. His short reign saw Protestantism established on a firm footing, with churches stripped of their icons and Catholic services banned.

Despite the spread of Protestantism, most of the country accepted **Mary** (1553–58), daughter of Catherine of Aragon and a fervent Catholic, as queen upon Edward's death. Returning England to the papacy, Mary married the future Philip II of Spain, forging an alliance that provoked war with France – and the loss of Calais, England's last French possession. The marriage was unpopular and so was Mary's persecution of Protestants: the leading lights of the English Reformation, Hugh Latimer, Nicholas Ridley and Thomas Cranmer, the archbishop of Canterbury, were all executed, hence the queen's rebranding as "Bloody Mary".

1485	**1559**	**1567**
Battle of Bosworth Field ends the Wars of the Roses. Richard III does not say "A horse, a horse, my kingdom for a horse".	Religious reformer John Knox returns to Scotland, where he leads the Protestant Reformation.	Mary, Queen of Scots, implicated in the murder of her second husband – pandemonium ensues.

Elizabeth I

When she came to the throne on the death of her half-sister, **Elizabeth I** (1558–1603) looked vulnerable. The country was divided by religion and threatened from abroad by Philip II of Spain, the most powerful man in Europe. Famously, Elizabeth eschewed marriage and, although a Protestant herself, steered a delicate course in relations with the Catholic Church. Her prudence rested well with the burgeoning English merchant class, who were mostly opposed to foreign military entanglements. An exception was, however, made for the piratical activities of English seafarers like Walter Raleigh, Martin Frobisher, John Hawkins and Francis Drake, who made a fortune raiding Spain's American colonies. Inevitably, Philip II's irritation took a warlike turn, but his **Spanish Armada** was defeated in 1588. Elizabeth's reign also saw the efflorescence of a specifically English Renaissance, especially in the field of literature, with **William Shakespeare** (1564–1616) pre-eminent.

Wales under the Tudors

Welsh allegiance during the Wars of the Roses lay broadly with the Lancastrians, who had the support of the ascendant **Tewdwr** (or Tudor) family of northern Wales. Nevertheless, Wales benefited little from the Tudors – at least until a uniform administrative structure was implemented under Henry VIII. The latter also passed two **Acts of Union**, in 1536 and 1543, formalizing English sovereignty. As for the **Church**, Protestantism made rapid headway in Wales, supplanting Catholicism during Henry VIII's reign, and the Bible was translated into Welsh. In addition, new landownership laws hastened the emergence of the **Anglo-Welsh gentry**, both eager to claim a Welsh pedigree and promote the English language and legal system. Landless peasants remained poor, only gaining slightly from the increase in cattle trade with England and the development of mining and ore smelting.

Scotland's Bruces and Stewarts (1329–1603)

After the death of Robert the Bruce in 1329, the Scottish monarchy hit the skids. The last of the Bruce dynasty died in 1371, to be succeeded by the "Stewards", hence **Stewarts** (known as Stuarts in England), though power remained in the hands of the nobility – or at least those nobles who were **regents** during the minority of a series of child kings. **James IV** (1488–1513), the most talented of the early Stewarts, might have restored the authority of the Crown, but his invasion of England ended in a calamitous defeat – and his own death – at the **Battle of Flodden Field** in Northumberland.

The reign of **Mary, Queen of Scots** (1542–87), typified the problems of the Scottish monarchy. Just one week old when she came to the throne, Mary immediately caught the attention of the English king, Henry VIII, who sought, first by persuasion and then by force of arms, to secure her hand in marriage for his 5-year-old son, Edward. The Scottish nobility resisted and turned instead to the **"Auld Alliance"** with the French king promising military assistance in return for marriage between Mary and the Dauphin Francis. The alliance reaffirmed, the child queen sailed for France in 1548, leaving her loyal nobles and their French allies in control. Six years later, **Mary of Guise**, the French mother of the absent Mary, became regent of Scotland, but although she had some

1588	c. 1592	1603	1605
Spanish Armada fails to reach England – Elizabeth I relieved.	First performance of Shakespeare's *Henry VI, Pt 1*, at the Rose Theatre, Bankside, London.	King James unites the crowns of Scotland and England.	Gunpowder Plot: Guy Fawkes plans to blow up the Houses of Parliament, but fails.

TOIL AND TUMULT: THE TRAVAILS OF MARY, QUEEN OF SCOTS

A devout(ish) Catholic, **Mary, Queen of Scots** (1542–87), returned to Scotland in 1561 after the death of Francis, her French husband. It was a country she barely knew and certainly did not understand, although, in fairness, she did try to avoid an open breach with her Protestant subjects. She might have pulled it off too, but for her disastrous second marriage to **Lord Darnley**. A cruel man, Darnley's jealousy led to his involvement in the murder of Mary's favourite, **David Rizzio**, who was dragged from the queen's chambers and stabbed 56 times. Outraged Scottish Protestants were even more horrified when Darnley himself was murdered in 1567, and Mary married the **Earl of Bothwell**, widely believed to be the murderer. The Scots rose in rebellion, driving Mary into exile in England at the age of just 25. The queen's illegitimate half-brother, the **Earl of Moray**, became regent and her son, the infant **James**, was left behind to be raised a Protestant prince. Mary, meanwhile, was such a threat to the English throne that Queen Elizabeth I had little choice but to imprison and ultimately execute her – despite her profound reservations as to the wisdom of executing a fellow royal.

success in keeping the English at bay and quelling her nobles, her French – specifically Catholic – connection was out of sympathy with the times as **Protestantism** took root.

Scotland's Protestants ascendant

In 1557, a group of Protestant nobles banded together to form the **Lords of the Congregation** and they proceeded to depose Mary of Guise with English military backing. In 1560, the Scottish Parliament asserted the primacy of Protestantism, the culmination of the fast-moving **Scottish Reformation**, a complex social process speeded by the weakness of the established Church, the unpopularity of the Catholic Mary of Guise, and the tireless efforts of Protestant reformers like **John Knox** (1514–1572). Protestant proceedings were temporarily interrupted by the return of Mary, Queen of Scots (see page 1011), but with Mary chased into exile, Knox could concentrate on the organization of the reformed Church, or **Kirk**, which he envisaged as a body empowered by God to intervene in the daily lives of the people. **Andrew Melville** proposed the abolition of all traces of episcopacy – the rule of the bishops in the Church – and suggested instead a **presbyterian** structure, administered by a hierarchy of assemblies, part elected and part appointed. In 1592, the Melvillian party achieved a measure of success when presbyteries and synods were accepted as legal church courts and the office of bishop was suspended.

United Kingdom: 1603–60

James VI of Scotland, the son of Mary, Queen of Scots, succeeded Elizabeth as **James I of England** (1603–25), thereby **uniting** the English and Scottish crowns. James quickly moved to end hostilities with Spain and adopted a policy of toleration to the country's embattled Catholics. Both initiatives offended many Protestants, whose fears were confirmed in 1605 when **Guy Fawkes** and his Catholic co-conspirators were discovered preparing to blow up the Houses of Parliament in the **Gunpowder Plot**: Fawkes was tortured and then hung, drawn and quartered for his pains. Elsewhere, **Puritan** sentiment and commercial interests converged with the founding of the first

1642	1660	1669
The Civil War begins when Charles I raises his standard in Nottingham, but has to do it three times – he should have taken the hint.	The Restoration: Charles II takes the throne – and digs up the body of Oliver Cromwell to hammer home his point.	Samuel Pepys gives up his diary, after nine years of detailed, sometimes saucy/sordid jottings.

permanent **colony in North America**, Virginia, in 1608. Twelve years later, the **Pilgrim Fathers** landed in New England, establishing a colony that absorbed a hundred thousand Puritan immigrants by the middle of the century.

Meanwhile, James restored the Scottish bishops, much to the chagrin of the Presbyterians and assorted Protestants, and alienated England's landed gentry. His absolutist vision of the monarchy – the **divine right of kings** – was out of step with the Protestant leanings of his subjects, and he also relied heavily on court favourites, especially the much reviled George Villiers, Duke of Buckingham. It was a recipe for disaster, but it was his successor, **Charles I**, who reaped the whirlwind.

Charles I

Inheriting James's dislike of Protestants and approval of absolutism, **Charles I** (1625–49) ruled without Parliament from 1629 to 1640, but overreached himself when he tried to impose a new Anglican prayer book on the (Scottish) Kirk. Scottish reformers organized the **National Covenant** in religious indignation; lack of finance stopped Charles from responding with an effective military campaign, but the well-financed Covenanters assembled a proficient army under Alexander Leslie. In desperation, Charles summoned the English Parliament hoping it would pay for an army to fight the Scots, but they refused their support. Indeed, the **Long Parliament**, as it became known, impeached several of Charles's allies, and compiled its grievances in the Grand Remonstrance of 1641.

Civil War and Commonwealth

Confronted by this concerted hostility, the king withdrew to Nottingham where, in 1642, he raised his standard, the first act of the **Civil War**. The Royalist forces ("Cavaliers") were initially successful, but in response **Oliver Cromwell** overhauled part of the Parliamentary army ("Roundheads"), to create the formidable, ideologically committed **New Model Army**, which cut its teeth at the battle of Naseby and thereafter simply brushed the Royalists aside. In defeat, Charles surrendered to the Scots, who handed him over to the English Parliament, by whom he was ultimately executed in 1649. The following year, Charles's son, the future Charles II, returned from exile, landing in Scotland. To secure Scottish support, he was obliged to sign the Covenant; however, the New Model Army proved too good for the Royalists and, after several defeats, Charles had to flee into exile yet again.

For the next eleven years the whole of Britain was a **Commonwealth** – at first a true republic, then, after 1653, a **Protectorate** with **Oliver Cromwell** as Lord Protector and commander-in-chief. He reformed the government, secured commercial treaties with foreign nations and put the fear of God into his enemies. After Cromwell died in 1658, his son **Richard Cromwell** ruled briefly and ineffectually until 1660, when **Charles II** regained the throne: the aristocracy and much of the gentry were relieved and delighted; Milton, amongst many, was distraught.

The Restoration and the later Stuarts (1660–1714)

A Stuart was back on the throne, but **Charles II** (1660–85) had few absolutist illusions – the terms of the **Restoration** were closely negotiated and included a general amnesty for

1678	1684	1703
John Bunyan, the Protestant preacher and reformer, writes his *Pilgrim's Progress*.	Isaac Newton observes gravity – but is probably not hit on the head by an apple.	"The Great Storm", a week-long hurricane, blasts through southern England.

most of those who had fought against the Stuarts, with the exception of the regicides – those who had signed Charles I's death warrant. Nonetheless, there was a sea change in public life with the re-establishment of a royal court and the foundation of the **Royal Society**, whose scientific endeavours were furthered by Isaac Newton (1642–1727). The low points of Charles's reign were the **Great Plague** of 1665 and the 1666 **Great Fire of London**. Politically, underlying tensions persisted between the monarchy and Parliament, though the latter was more concerned with the struggle between the **Whigs** and **Tories**, factions representing, respectively, the low-church gentry and the high-church aristocracy. There was a degree of religious toleration too, but its brittleness was all too apparent in the anti-Catholic riots of 1678.

The Glorious Revolution

The succession of the Catholic **James II** (1685–88), brother of Charles II, provoked much opposition, though the response was indifferent when the Protestant **Duke of Monmouth**, the favourite among Charles II's illegitimate sons, raised a rebellion in the West Country. Monmouth was defeated at Sedgemoor, in Somerset, in July 1685; nine days later he was beheaded at Tower Hill, and, in the subsequent **Bloody Assizes** of Judge Jeffreys, hundreds of rebels and suspected sympathizers were executed or deported. More important for James's popularity was his **Declaration of Indulgence**, which removed anti-Catholic restrictions, and the birth of his son, which threatened to secure a Catholic succession. Alarmed, powerful Protestants sent for **William of Orange**, the Dutch husband of Mary, the Protestant daughter of James II, to save them from "popery". William landed in Devon and, as James's forces simply melted away, speedily took control of London in the **Glorious Revolution** of 1688. This was the final postscript to the Civil War – although it was another couple of years before James and his remaining Jacobites were finally defeated in Ireland at the **Battle of the Boyne.**

William, Mary and Anne

William and Mary (1688–94) became joint sovereigns after they agreed to a **Bill of Rights** defining the limitations of the monarch's powers and the rights of subjects, thereby making Britain a **constitutional monarchy**, in which the roles of legislature and executive were separate and interdependent. The model was broadly consistent with that outlined by the philosopher and political thinker **John Locke** (1632–1704), whose essentially Whig doctrines of toleration and social contract were gradually embraced as the new orthodoxy.

After Mary's death, **William** (1694–1702) ruled alone; during his reign the **Act of Settlement of 1701** barred Catholics, or anyone married to one, from succession to the English throne. This Act did not, however, apply in Scotland, and the English feared that the Scots would invite James II's son, **James Edward Stuart**, back from France to be their king. These fears were allayed when Scotland passed the **Act of Union** uniting the English and Scottish parliaments in 1707, though neither the Scottish legal system nor the Presbyterian Kirk were merged with their English equivalents.

After William's death the crown passed to Mary's sister **Anne** (1702–14). A string of British military victories on the continent now began with the Duke of Marlborough's triumph at Blenheim in 1704, followed the next year by the capture of Gibraltar, establishing a British presence in the Mediterranean. These military outings were part

1707	1715	1745
The Act of Union merges the Scottish Parliament into the English Parliament.	First Jacobite Rebellion: James Stuart ("The Old Pretender") raises a Scottish army, but is defeated.	Second Jacobite Rebellion: Charles Stuart (Bonnie Prince Charlie) invades England with a Scots army, but is defeated at Culloden.

of the Europe-wide **War of the Spanish Succession**, a long-winded dynastic squabble that rumbled on until the **Treaty of Utrecht** in 1713 all but settled the European balance of power for the rest of the century.

The Hanoverians (1714–1815)

On Anne's death, the crown passed to the Protestant Elector of Hanover, who became **George I** (1714–27). During his lacklustre reign, power leached into the hands of a Whig oligarchy led by a chief minister – or prime minister – the longest serving of which was **Robert Walpole** (1676–1745). In the meantime, plans were being hatched for a **Jacobite Rebellion** in support of **James Edward Stuart**, the "Old Pretender". Its timing appeared perfect: Scottish opinion was moving against the Union, which had failed to bring Scotland tangible economic benefits, and many English Catholics supported the Jacobite cause too, toasting the "king across the water". In 1715, the Earl of Mar raised the Stuart standard at Braemar Castle, and just eight days later he captured Perth, where he gathered an army of more than ten thousand men. Mar's rebellion took the government by surprise. They had only four thousand soldiers in Scotland, but Mar dithered until he lost the military advantage. There was an indecisive battle at Sheriffmuir, but by the time the Old Pretender landed in Scotland in December 1715, six thousand veteran Dutch troops had reinforced government forces. The rebellion disintegrated rapidly and James slunk back to exile in France.

Thirty years later, with **George II** (1727–60) on the throne and England embroiled in yet another dynastic squabble, the War of the Austrian Succession (1740–48), the Jacobites tried again – this time led by the **Young Pretender**, **Charles Stuart** (Bonnie Prince Charlie) – but the Stuarts were defeated once more. With the rebellion crushed, it was back to normal in London, where the political tussles between king and Parliament were enlivened by **John Wilkes**, the first of an increasingly vociferous line of parliamentary radicals.

Empire and colonies

At the tail end of George II's reign, the **Seven Years' War** (1756–63) harvested England yet more overseas territory in India and Canada at the expense of France; and, in 1768, with **George III** (1760–1820) now on the throne, **Captain James Cook** stumbled upon New Zealand and Australia, thereby extending Britain's empire still further. The fly in the ointment was the deteriorating relationship with the thirteen colonies of North America, which came to a head with the **American Declaration of Independence** and Britain's subsequent defeat in the **Revolutionary War** (1775–83). The British government was not, however, directly involved in the momentous events across the Channel, where the **French Revolution** convulsed Britain's most consistent foe. Out of the turmoil emerged one of Britain's most daunting enemies, **Napoleon** (1769–1821), whose stunning military progress was interrupted by Nelson at **Trafalgar** in 1805 and finally halted in 1815 by the Duke of Wellington (and the Prussians) at **Waterloo**.

The Industrial Revolution

Britain's triumph over Napoleon was underpinned by its financial strength, which was itself born of the **Industrial Revolution**, the switch from an agricultural to a

1781	1783	1819
Opening of the Iron Bridge – the first iron bridge the world has ever seen – over the River Severn.	End of the American War of Independence – the American colonies break from Britain.	Peterloo Massacre: in Manchester, the cavalry wade into a huge crowd who are demanding parliamentary reform. Many are killed.

manufacturing economy that transformed the face of the country within a century. The earliest mechanized production was in the Lancashire and Derbyshire **cotton mills**, where cotton spinning progressed from a cottage industry to a highly productive factory-based system. Initially, the cotton mills were powered by water, but in 1781 James Watt patented his **steam engine**. As Watt's engines needed **coal**, the population shifted towards the Midlands, central Scotland and the north of England, where the great coal reserves were mined. The industrial economy boomed and diversified, and regional towns mushroomed at an extraordinary rate. Sheffield was a steel town, Manchester possessed huge cotton warehouses, and Liverpool had the docks, where raw materials from India and the Americas flowed in and manufactured goods went out. Commerce and industry were also served by improving transport facilities, such as the construction of **canals**. A second major leap forward arrived with the **railway**, heralded by the Stockton–Darlington line in 1825, followed five years later by the Liverpool–Manchester railway, where George Stephenson's *Rocket* made its first outing. Industrialisation needed an expanded work force and Britain's **population** rose from eight and a half million to more than fifteen million during George III's reign, boosted by a vast influx of Jewish, Irish, French and Dutch workers.

The Chartists – and social reform

In their hundreds, workers threatened by mechanization joined the **Chartist movement**, which demanded parliamentary reform – the most important industrial boom-towns were unrepresented in Parliament – and the repeal of the **Corn Laws**, which kept the price of bread artificially high. Social tensions ran high, but judicious parliamentary acts helped quieten things down: the **Reform Act** of 1832 established the principle (if not always the practice) of popular representation; the **Poor Law** of 1834 improved the condition of the most destitute; and the **Corn Laws** were repealed in 1846. Significant sections of the middle class supported progressive reform, as evidenced by the immense popularity of **Charles Dickens** (1812–70), whose novels railed against poverty and injustice. **John Wesley** (1703–91) and his **Methodists** had pre-empted these social concerns by leading the anti-slavery campaign. As a result of their efforts, **slavery** was banned in Britain in 1772 and throughout the British Empire in 1833.

Victorian Britain

In 1820, a blind and insane George III died. His two sons, **George IV** (1820–30) and **William IV** (1830–37), were succeeded in turn by his niece, **Victoria** (1837–1901), whose long reign witnessed the zenith of British power. The economy boomed, and the British trading fleet was easily the mightiest in the world. Victoria became the symbol of both the nation's success and the imperial ideal. There were extraordinary intellectual achievements too – as typified by the publication of **Charles Darwin**'s *On the Origin of Species* in 1859. Britain's industrial and commercial prowess was embodied by the engineering feats of **Isambard Kingdom Brunel** (1806–1859) and by the **Great Exhibition** of 1851, a display of manufacturing achievements without compare. During the last third of the century, Parliament was dominated by the duel between **Disraeli** and the Liberal leader **Gladstone**. While Disraeli eventually passed the Second Reform Bill in 1867, further extending the electoral franchise, Gladstone's first ministry of

1824	**1858**	**1865**
Charles Dickens' father is imprisoned as a debtor; his son never forgets.	English engineer Isambard Kingdom Brunel builds the iron-hulled SS Great Eastern, the largest ship in the world.	William Booth from Nottingham founds the Salvation Army, in the East End of London.

1868–74 created such far-reaching legislation as compulsory education, and the full legalization of trade unions.

As for foreign entanglements, troops were sent in 1854 to protect the Ottoman Empire against the Russians in the **Crimea**, an inglorious debacle whose horrors reached the public via the first-ever press coverage of a military campaign, and the revelations of **Florence Nightingale** (1820–1910), who was appalled by the lack of medical care for the soldiers. The **Indian Mutiny** of 1857 exposed the fragility of Britain's hold over the Asian subcontinent, though the imperial status quo was brutally restored and Victoria took the title Empress of India after 1876. Thereafter, the British army fought various minor wars against poorly armed Asian and African opponents, but came unstuck when it faced the better armed Dutch settlers of South Africa in the **Boer War** (1899–1902). The British ultimately fought their way to a sort of victory, but the discreditable conduct of the war prompted a military shake-up at home that proved significant in the coming European war.

World War I and its aftermath (1914–39)

Victoria was succeeded by her son, **Edward VII** (1901–10), whose leisurely lifestyle has often been seen as the epitome of the complacent era to which he gave his name. It wasn't to last. On August 4, 1914, with **George V** (1910–36) now on the throne, the Liberal government declared war on Germany, thereby honouring the Entente Cordiale signed with France in 1904. Hundreds of thousands volunteered for the army, but their enthusiastic nationalism could not ensure a quick victory, and **World War I** dragged on for four miserable years. Britain and her allies eventually prevailed, but the number of dead beggared belief, undermining deference for the ruling class, whose generals had displayed a startling combination of incompetence and indifference to the plight of their men. Many Britons looked admiringly towards the Soviet Union, where Lenin and his Bolsheviks had rid themselves of the Tsar and seized control in 1917. After the war ended in 1918, the sheer weight of public opinion pushed Parliament into extending the **vote** to all men 21 and over and to women over 30. The liberalization of women's rights owed much to the efforts of the radical **Suffragettes**, led by Emmeline Pankhurst and her daughters Sylvia and Christabel, but the process was only completed in 1929 when women were at last granted the vote at 21. The royal family itself was shaken in 1936 by the **abdication of Edward VIII** (1936), following his decision to marry a twice-divorced American, Wallis Simpson, but in the event, the succession passed smoothly to his brother **George VI**.

Hard times

By the late 1920s, the **Labour Party** had supplanted the Liberals as the main force on the left of British politics, its strength founded on an alliance between the working-class trade unions and middle-class radicals. Labour formed its first government in 1923 under **Ramsay MacDonald**, but the publication of the Zinoviev Letter, a forgery in which the Soviets supposedly urged British leftists to promote revolution, undermined his position and the Conservatives were returned with a large parliamentary majority in 1924. Two years later, a bitter dispute between coal miners and mine-owners escalated into a **General Strike**, which quickly spread to the railways, the newspapers

1888	**1909**	**1912**	**1926**
First football game between Celtic and Rangers in Glasgow.	Lord Baden-Powell forms the "British Boy Scouts".	Bad news: the Titanic sinks and Captain Scott and his men die on the ice in the Antarctic.	Britain's first-ever General Strike: a nine-day walkout in support of the coal miners. The workers lose (again).

and the iron and steel industries. Involving half a million workers, the strike lasted nine days before it was broken when the government called in the army. The economic situation deteriorated further after the **crash** of the New York Stock Exchange in 1929 precipitated a worldwide depression. Unemployment topped 2.8 million in 1931, generating mass demonstrations that peaked with the 1936 **Jarrow March** from the Northeast of England to London.

World War II

When Hitler set about militarizing Germany in the mid-1930s, the British government adopted a policy of appeasement. Consequently, when Britain declared war on Germany after Hitler's invasion of Poland in September 1939, the country was poorly prepared. After embarrassing military failures during the first months of **World War II**, the discredited government was replaced in May 1940 by a national coalition headed by the charismatic **Winston Churchill** (1874–1965) – days before the British army made a forced evacuation from Dunkirk. These were bleak and uncertain days for Britain, but the war turned when the Germans invaded the Soviet Union in 1941 – and Churchill found he had a new and powerful ally. Further reinforcements arrived in December 1941, when the United States declared war on both Germany and Japan after the Japanese had made a surprise attack on Pearl Harbor. The involvement of both the United States and the USSR swung the military balance and by early 1943 the Germans were doomed to defeat – though it took two more years to finish Hitler off. In terms of casualties, World War II was not as calamitous as World War I, but its impact upon British civilians was much greater. In its first wave of **bombing** of the UK, the Luftwaffe caused massive damage to industrial and supply centres such as London, Glasgow, Swansea, Coventry, Manchester, Hull, Liverpool, Southampton and Plymouth. Later raids, intended to shatter morale rather than factories and docks, battered the cathedral cities of Canterbury, Exeter, Bath, Norwich and York. Germany surrendered in May 1945 and Japan followed in September, but although the British were overjoyed by the Allied victory, the country's finances were in a parlous state and its infrastructure had been badly damaged.

Postwar Britain: from Attlee to Callaghan (1945–79)

Hungry for change (and demobilization), voters in 1945's immediate postwar election replaced Churchill with the Labour Party under **Clement Attlee** (1883–1967), who set about a radical programme to **nationalize** the coal, gas, electricity, iron and steel industries, as well as the inland transport services. The early passage of the **National Insurance Act** and the **National Health Service Act** gave birth to what became known as the **welfare state**. However, despite substantial American aid, the rebuilding of the economy was a huge task and austerity became the keynote, with food and fuel rationing enduring for several years.

Meanwhile, Britain, the USA, Canada, France and the Benelux countries defined their postwar international commitments in 1949's **North Atlantic Treaty**, a counterbalance to Soviet power in Eastern Europe. Nevertheless, there was continuing confusion over Britain's imperial – or rather post-imperial – role and this bubbled

1950	1951	1962	1967
Soap rationing ends in Britain – a general clean-up follows.	Britain's first supermarket opens, in south London. Shopping trolleys become a new traffic hazard.	The Beatles hit the big time with their first single, *Love Me Do*.	First withdrawal from a cash dispenser (ATM) in Britain – at a branch of Barclays.

to the surface in both the incompetent **partition of India** in 1947 and the **Suez Crisis** of 1956, when Anglo-French and Israeli forces invaded Egypt to secure control of the Suez Canal, only to be hastily recalled following international (American) condemnation; the resignation of the Conservative prime minister, **Anthony Eden** (1897–1977) followed. His replacement, the pragmatic, silky-tongued **Harold Macmillan** (1894–1986), accepted the end of empire, but was still eager for Britain to play a leading international role – and the country kept its nuclear arsenal, despite the best efforts of the Campaign for Nuclear Disarmament (CND).

The dominant political figure in the 1960s was **Harold Wilson** (1916–95), a witty speaker and skilled tactician who was Labour prime minister from 1964 to 1970 – and again from 1974 to 1976. The 1960s saw a boom in consumer spending, pioneering social legislation (primarily on homosexuality and abortion), and a corresponding cultural upswing, with London becoming the hippest city on the planet. But the good times lasted barely a decade: the Conservatives returned to office in 1970 and although the new prime minister, the ungainly **Edward Heath**, led Britain into the brave new world of the **European Economic Community (ECC)**, the 1970s were a decade of recession and industrial strife. In 1975, with Labour back in power, Heath was usurped by **Margaret Thatcher** (1925–2013). Four years later, to the amazement of many pundits, Thatcher defeated **James Callaghan**'s Labour Party in the general election; as events proved, she was primed and ready to break the unions and anyone else who crossed her path.

Thatcher and Major (1979–97)

Thatcher pushed the UK towards sharp social polarization. While taxation policies and easy credit fuelled a consumer boom for the professional classes, the erosion of manufacturing and the weakening of the welfare state impoverished a great swathe of the population. Nevertheless, Thatcher won a second term of office in 1983, partly thanks to the recapture of the **Falkland Islands**, a remote British dependency in the South Atlantic, retrieved from the Argentine military in 1982. Social and political tensions surfaced in sporadic urban rioting and also in the year-long **miners' strike** (1984–85) against colliery closures, a bitter dispute in which the police were given unprecedented powers to restrict the movement of citizens. Violence in Northern Ireland also intensified, and in 1984 IRA bombers almost blew up the entire Cabinet, who were staying in a Brighton hotel during the Conservatives' annual conference.

The divisive politics of Thatcherism reached their apogee when the desperately unpopular **Poll Tax** led to her overthrow by Conservative colleagues who feared defeat if she led them into another election. Her uninspiring successor, **John Major**, somehow managed to win the Conservatives a fourth term of office in 1992, but the political writing was on the wall.

Blair and Brown (1997–2010)

The new and dynamic leader of the Labour Party, **Tony Blair**, swept to power in 1997 on a wave of genuine popular optimism. There were immediate improvements in public services and progress in the Irish peace talks, but Blair's re-election in 2001 was

1985	1994	1999	2009
The bitter, year-long miners' strike is crushed by Margaret Thatcher.	The Channel Tunnel opens to traffic.	The Scottish Parliament and the national assemblies for Wales and Northern Ireland take on devolved powers.	Financial crisis prompts the Bank of England to reduce interest rates to a record low of 0.5%: misery for savers; indulgence for spenders.

accompanied by little of the previous optimism: few voters fully trusted Blair, and his administration had by then developed a reputation for "**spin**" – laundering events to present the government in the best possible light.

The terrorist attacks of **September 11, 2001** downgraded Blair's domestic agenda in favour of a rush to support President Bush in his assaults on Afghanistan and then **Iraq**, in 2003. In the event, Saddam Hussein was deposed with relative ease, but neither Bush nor Blair had a coherent exit strategy, and back home Blair was widely seen as having "spun" Britain into the war by exaggerating the danger presented by Saddam. Even so, Blair managed to win a third general election in 2005, though only after promising to step down before the next one. He was succeeded in June 2007 by his Labour colleague and arch-rival, **Gordon Brown**, who proved to be a clumsy prime minister with a tin ear for the public mood. Indeed, Brown even managed to secure little credit for his one major achievement, staving off a banking collapse during the worldwide **financial crisis** that hit the UK hard in the autumn of 2007.

In the build-up to the **general election of 2010**, both main political parties, as well as the Liberal Democrats, spoke of the need to **cut public spending** more or less drastically, manoeuvring the electorate away from blaming the bankers for the crash. Although no party managed to secure a majority, an impasse was avoided when the Liberal Democrats swapped principles for power to join a **Conservative–Liberal Democrat coalition**, which took office in May 2010 with Conservative David Cameron as prime minister.

The Cameron years (2010–2016)

David Cameron made a confident and sure-footed start as prime minister, keeping his ideological cards well hidden (if indeed he had any), while his government limbered up for a prolonged attack on the public sector under the guise of reducing the national debt – with "austerity" as the watch word. The principal threat to the established political order came from **Alex Salmond**, the wily leader of the **Scottish Nationalists**, who galvanized support for his vision of an independent Scotland in the **referendum of September 18, 2014**. The Nationalists came within a hair's breadth of victory, but the most remarkable feature of the referendum was the high turnout, an astounding 84 percent.

Surprisingly, Cameron managed to win an overall majority in the **general election of 2015** by promising strong fiscal management – and yet more austerity. The Conservative election manifesto also committed to a referendum on the UK's membership of the EU – partly as a sop to the Eurosceptics within the Conservative party and partly to head off an emergent UKIP, an EU-hating, right-wing party led by the shrewd and jokey **Nigel Farage**. Cameron, who wanted to stay in the EU, seems to have been quietly confident that the "remainers" would win by a country mile, but in the **European Union membership referendum** of June 23, 2016, almost 52% of voters wanted to leave the EU; Cameron was toast – and promptly resigned.

Into the future

After Cameron's departure, **Theresa May** was elected the new Prime Minister from within the ranks of the Conservative Party. Initially, it seemed a sound choice, but it

2012	2013	2014
London hosts the Olympic Games.	Same-sex marriage legalized in England and Wales; Scotland follows in 2014.	By a pip and a squeak, the Scots reject independence and remain part of the United Kingdom in the Scottish referendum.

soon became obvious that the **Brexit** negotiations with the EU would both strain the resources of the British government and sharpen divisions within the Tories about the speed of leaving the EU – and what, exactly, leaving meant. Still, the Tories thought, they were in no electoral danger as the unexpected new leader of the Labour Party, **Jeremy Corbyn**, was far too left-wing to gain any traction – and many more right-wing Labour MPs agreed, whispering away in corners to plot Corbyn's downfall.

And so it was that May called the **general election of June 2017**, which she presumed would be a romp. It wasn't. May's campaign was extraordinarily inept, but rather more surprisingly a fair chunk of the population warmed to the much-maligned Labour leader – social media buzzed with photos of a young Corbyn being arrested for protesting South Africa's apartheid policies. Somehow, suddenly, there seemed to be a sea-change in the popular mood and although the Conservatives actually won the election by a nose (albeit with the help of a controversial confidence-and-supply deal with Northern Ireland's populist, right-wing **DUP**) austerity, their key policy plank, may well be dead in the water – though it's still too early to tell.

2015	2016	2017
Conservatives win the general election under David Cameron.	British narrowly votes to leave the EU (51.9 percent). Many leave voters express "Regrexit"; remainers unimpressed.	Conservative PM, Theresa May, calls a snap election – disaster for her, but an unexpected boost for Labour; a hung parliament.

Books

The bibliography we've given here is necessarily selective, and entirely subjective. Most of the books listed below are in print and, and any which are out of print should be easy to track down. Titles marked with the ★ symbol are especially recommended.

TRAVEL AND JOURNALS

★ **Bill Bryson** *Notes from a Small Island.* Bryson's best-selling and highly amusing account of an extended journey around Britain in the 1990s.

William Cobbett *Rural Rides.* First published in 1830, Cobbett's account of his various fact-finding tours bemoaned the death of the old rural England and its customs, while decrying both the growth of cities and the iniquities suffered by the exploited urban poor.

David Craig *On the Crofter's Trail.* Using anecdotes and interviews with descendants, Craig conveys the hardship and tragedy of the Highland Clearances without being mawkish.

Olivia Laing *To the River.* This acclaimed account of the author's midsummer walk along Sussex's River Ouse from source to sea is beautifully written and observed, interweaving nature writing, history and folklore.

★ **Jan Morris** *The Matter of Wales.* Prolific half-Welsh travel writer Jan Morris immerses herself in the country that she evidently loves. Highly partisan and fiercely nationalistic, the book combs over the origins of the Welsh character, and describes the people and places of Wales with precision and affection. Published in the mid-1980s.

J.B. Priestley *English Journey.* Quirky account of the Bradford-born author's travels around England in the 1930s.

GUIDEBOOKS

★ **Simon Jenkins** *England's Thousand Best Churches; England's Thousand Best Houses.* A lucid, witty pick of England's churches and houses, divided by county and with a star rating. Sales were so good that Jenkins has had further stabs in the same format with *England's 100 Best Views* (2014) and *England's Best Cathedrals* (2016) and even *Britain's 100 Best Railway Stations* (2017).

A. Wainwright *A Pictorial Guide to the Lakeland Fells* (7 vols). These beautifully produced small-format volumes of handwritten notes and sketches (1952 to 1966) have led generations up the Lake District's mountains and down through its dales. The originals have now been revised to take account of changing routes and landscapes.

★ **Ben Weinreb and Christopher Hibbert** *The London Encyclopaedia.* More than a thousand pages of concisely presented and well-illustrated information on London past and present – the most fascinating single book on the capital.

HISTORY, SOCIETY AND POLITICS

John Campbell *The Iron Lady: Margaret Thatcher.* Campbell has been mining the Thatcher seam for several years now and this abridged paperback version, published in 2012, hits many political nails right on the head. By the same author, and equally engaging, is his 1987 *Aneurin Bevan and the Mirage of British Socialism* as well as his latest work, a biography of *Roy Jenkins.*

Tom Devine *The Scottish Nation: A Modern History.* Scotland's pre-eminent historian cuts a well-researched and well-considered swathe through his home country's recent history – from 1700 to 2007. Devine has also written a string of more specific titles – on the Lowland Clearances for one – as well as an exploration of Scotland's current constitutional pickle, *Independence or Union: Scotland's Past and Scotland's Present.*

Christopher Hill *The World Turned Upside-Down; God's Englishman: Oliver Cromwell and the English Revolution.* A pioneering Marxist historian, Hill (1912–2003) transformed the way the story of the English Civil War and the Commonwealth was related in a string of superbly researched, well-written texts – among which these are two of the best.

★ **Eric Hobsbawm** *Industry and Empire.* Ostensibly an economic history of Britain from 1750 to the late 1960s, charting Britain's decline and fall as a world power, this book's great skill lies in its detailed analysis of the effects on ordinary people. By the same author, *Captain Swing* focuses on the labourers' uprisings of nineteenth-century England; *Age of Extremes: The Short Twentieth Century 1914–1991* has at its heart an examination of the collapse of Communism; and his magnificent trilogy, *The Age of Revolution 1789–1848, The Age of Capital 1848–1875,* and *The Age of Empire: 1875–1914;* there is nothing better.

Philip Jenkins *A History of Modern Wales 1536–1990.* Splendidly thorough book, placing Welsh history in its British and European context. Unbiased and rational appraisal of events and the struggle to preserve Welsh consciousness.

Owen Jones *Chavs: The Demonization of the Working Class*. A trumpet blast from the political left – and a yell of moral/political outrage at the way the media treat the working class. You'll do more howling if you follow up with Jones's equally trenchant *The Establishment: And how they get away with it*.

★ **David Kynaston** *Austerity Britain, 1945–51*. Comprehensive vox pop that gives the real flavour of postwar England. Everything is here, from the skill of a Dennis Compton cricket innings through to the dangers of hewing coal down the pit, all in a land where there were "no supermarkets, no teabags, no Formica, no trainers ... and just four Indian restaurants". Also recommended is Kynaston's follow-up volumes *Family Britain, 1951–1957* and *Modernity Britain, 1957–1959*.

★ **Andrew Rawnsley** *The End of the Party*. Arguably Britain's most acute political journalist, Rawnsley cross- examines and dissects New Labour under Blair and Brown to withering effect. Different target, same approach – *In It Together: The Inside Story of the Coalition Government*.

Simon Schama *A History of Britain* (3 vols). British history, from 3000 BC to 2000 AD, delivered at pace by the TV-famous historian and popularizer, Simon Schama. The prolific Schama can't half bang it out – even in his seventies, he's showing no signs of slowing down.

★ **E.P. Thompson** *The Making of the English Working Class*. A seminal text – essential reading for anyone who wants to understand the fabric of English society. Traces the tribulations of England's emergent working-class between 1780 and 1832.

Wynford Vaughan-Thomas *Wales*. Working chronologically from the pre-Celtic dawn to the aftermath of the 1979 devolution vote, this masterpiece is a warm and spirited history of Wales, offering perhaps the clearest explanation of the evolution of Welsh culture.

ART, ARCHITECTURE AND ARCHEOLOGY

Owen Hatherley *A Guide to the New Ruins of Great Britain*. No good news here from this angry rant of a book, which rails against – and describes in detail – the 1990s architectural desecration of a string of British cities in the name of speculation masquerading as modernization.

★ **Duncan MacMillan** *Scottish Art 1460–2000* and *Scottish Art in the Twentieth Century*. The former is a lavish overview of Scottish painting with good sections on landscape, portraiture and the Glasgow Boys, while the latter covers its period (till 2000) in splendid detail.

Francis Pryor *Home: A Time Traveller's Tales from Britain's Prehistory*. The often arcane discoveries of working archeologists are given fascinating new exposure in Pryor's lively archeological histories of Britain. This latest book concentrates on family life, but other Pryor titles include *Britain in the Middle Ages*; *Britain BC* and *Britain AD: A Quest for Arthur, England and the Anglo-Saxons*.

Brian Sewell *Naked Emperors: Criticisms of English Contemporary Art*. Trenchant, idiosyncratic, reviews – often attacks – on contemporary art from this leading critic and arch debunker of pretension, who died in 2015. Few would want to plough through all 368 pages of the assembled reviews – but dip in and yelp with glee, or splutter with indignation.

FICTION BEFORE 1900

★ **Jane Austen** *Pride and Prejudice*; *Sense and Sensibility*; *Emma*; *Persuasion*. All-time classics on manners, society and provincial life; laced with bathos and ever-so-subtle twists of plot.

James Boswell *The Life of Samuel Johnson*. England's most famous man of letters and pioneer dictionary-maker displayed – warts and all – by his engagingly low-life Scottish biographer.

★ **Emily Brontë** *Wuthering Heights*. Set on the Yorkshire Moors, this is the ultimate English melodrama, complete with volcanic passions, craggy landscapes, ghostly presences and gloomy Yorkshire villagers/villages.

John Bunyan *Pilgrim's Progress*. Simple, allegorical tale of hero Christian's struggle to achieve salvation. Prepare to feel guilty.

Thomas De Quincey *Confessions of an English Opium-Eater*. Tripping out with the most famous literary drug-taker after Coleridge – *Fear and Loathing in Las Vegas* it isn't, but neither is this a simple cautionary tale.

Charles Dickens *Bleak House*; *David Copperfield*; *Little Dorrit*; *Oliver Twist*; *Hard Times*. Many of Dickens' novels are set in London, including *Bleak House*, *Oliver Twist* and *Little Dorrit*, and these contain some of his most trenchant pieces of social analysis; *Hard Times*, however, is set in a Lancashire mill town, while *David Copperfield* draws on Dickens' own unhappy experiences as a boy, with much of the action taking place in Kent and Norfolk.

George Eliot *Scenes of Clerical Life*; *Middlemarch*; *Mill on the Floss*. Eliot (real name Mary Ann Evans) wrote mostly about the county of her birth, Warwickshire, the setting for the three searing tales that comprise her fictional debut, *Scenes of Clerical Life*. *Middlemarch* is a gargantuan portrayal of English provincial life prior to the Reform Act of 1832, while the exquisite *Mill on the Floss* is based on her own childhood experiences.

Thomas Hardy *Far from the Madding Crowd*; *The Mayor of Casterbridge*; *Tess of the D'Urbervilles*; *Jude the Obscure*. Hardy's novels contain some famously evocative descriptions of his native Dorset, but originally it was Hardy's defiance of conventional pieties that attracted most attention: *Tess*, in which the heroine has a baby out of wedlock and commits murder, shocked his contemporaries while his bleakest novel, the Oxford-set *Jude the Obscure*, provoked such a violent response that Hardy gave up novel-writing altogether.

Walter Scott *Waverley*. Swirl the tartan, blow the pipes, this is the first of the novels by Scott that did much to create a highly romanticized version of Scottish life and history. Others include *Rob Roy*, a rich and ripping yarn that transformed the diminutive brigand into a national hero.

Lawrence Sterne *Tristram Shandy*. Anarchic, picaresque eighteenth-century ramblings based on life in a small English village; full of bizarre textual devices – like an all-black page in mourning for one of the characters.

★ **Robert Louis Stevenson** *Dr Jekyll and Mr Hyde*; *Kidnapped*; *The Master of Ballantrae*; *Treasure Island*; *Weir of Hermiston*. Superbly imagined and pacily written nineteenth-century tales of intrigue and derring-do.

Anthony Trollope *Barchester Towers*. Trollope was an astonishingly prolific novelist who also, in his capacity as a postal surveyor, found time to invent the letterbox. The "Barsetshire" novels, of which *Barchester Towers* is the best known, are set in and around a fictional version of Salisbury.

TWENTIETH-CENTURY CLASSICS

Joseph Conrad *The Secret Agent*. Spy story based on the 1906 anarchist bombing of Greenwich Observatory, exposing the hypocrisies of both the police and anarchists.

E.M. Forster *Howards End*. Bourgeois angst in Hertfordshire and Shropshire, by one of the country's most intense modern novelists.

Lewis Grassic Gibbon *A Scots Quair*. A landmark trilogy, set in northeast Scotland during and after World War I, the events are seen through the eyes of Chris Guthrie, "torn between her love for the land and her desire to escape a peasant culture". Strong, seminal work.

Robert Graves *Goodbye to All That*. Horrific and humorous memoirs of public school and World War I trenches, followed by postwar trauma (Graves had been badly wounded). Graves hit the literary big time in 1934 with an erudite Roman soap opera, *I, Claudius*.

D.H. Lawrence *Sons and Lovers*; *Lady Chatterley's Lover*. Lawrence's less-than-flattering take on working-class life in a Nottinghamshire pit village never went down well with the locals. His *Sons and Lovers*, a fraught, autobiographical novel, contains some of his finest writing, as does *Lady Chatterley's Lover*, which pushes sex and class hard (and harder) together.

Laurie Lee *Cider with Rosie*. Beautifully written reminiscences of adolescent frolics in the rural Cotswolds of the 1920s.

Richard Llewellyn *How Green Was My Valley*; *Up into the Singing Mountain*; *Down Where the Moon is Small*; *Green, Green My Valley Now*. Vital tetralogy in eloquent and passionate prose, following the life of Huw Morgan from his youth in a South Wales mining valley through emigration to the Welsh community in Patagonia and back to 1970s Wales. The pick, *How Green Was My Valley*, captured a longing for a simple if tough life, and steered clear of cloying sentimentality.

Daphne du Maurier *Rebecca*. Long derided as a popular piece of fluff, this darkly romantic novel has come to be appreciated as a Gothic meditation on sexual inequality and obsession, focused around the brooding mansion of Manderley, on du Maurier's beloved Cornish coast. See also the same author's *Frenchman's Creek* and *Jamaica Inn*.

George Orwell *Down and Out in Paris and London*; *The Road to Wigan Pier*. Famous more than anything else for *1984*, which was published in 1949, Orwell had warmed up in the 1930s with these angry denunciations of inequity, giving respectively a tramp's-eye view of the world and an examination of the brutal effects of the Great Depression on industrial communities in Lancashire and Yorkshire.

Alan Sillitoe *Saturday Night and Sunday Morning*. Gritty account of factory life and sexual shenanigans in Nottingham in the late 1950s.

★ **Dylan Thomas** *Under Milk Wood*; *Collected Stories*; *Collected Poems: 1934–1953*. *Under Milk Wood* is Thomas's most popular piece, telling the story of a microcosmic Welsh seaside town over a 24-hour period. *Collected Stories* contains all of Thomas's classic prose pieces, including the compulsive, crackling autobiography, *Portrait of the Artist as a Young Dog*. Thomas's beautifully wrought and inventive poems carry a deep, pained concern with mortality and the nature of humanity.

Evelyn Waugh The *Sword of Honour* trilogy. A brilliant satire of the World War I officer class laced with some of Waugh's funniest set pieces. The best-selling *Brideshead Revisited* is possibly his worst book, rank with snobbery, nostalgia and love of money.

P.G. Wodehouse *Thank You, Jeeves; A Damsel in Distress*. For many, Wodehouse (1881–1975) is the quintessential English humorist and his deftly crafted tales – with their familiar cast of characters, primarily Bertie Wooster and Jeeves – have remained popular for decades.

CONTEMPORARY FICTION

Peter Ackroyd *English Music*. A typical Ackroyd novel, constructing parallels between interwar London and distant epochs to conjure a kaleidoscopic vision of English culture. His other novels, such as *Chatterton, Hawksmoor*, *The House of Doctor Dee* and, most recently the crime-ridden *Limehouse Golem*, are variations on his preoccupation with the English psyche's darker depths.

★ **Julian Barnes** *The Sense of an Ending*; *Levels of Life*.

One of the UK's most versatile writers, Barnes seems to be able to turn his hand to just about anything. These two novels, perhaps his best, touch on themes of sex and inhibition, regret and false recollection, but most of all death and bereavement.

George Mackay Brown *Beside the Ocean of Time*. A child's journey through the history of an Orkney island, and an adult's effort to make sense of the place's secrets.

William Golding *The Spire*. Atmospheric albeit complex novel centred on the building of a cathedral spire, taking place in a thinly disguised medieval Salisbury. Also, if you ever wondered what it was like to be at sea in an early nineteenth-century British ship, try the splendid *Rites of Passage* trilogy.

Alasdair Gray *Lanark*. Gray's first novel was twenty-five years in the writing and remains his most influential, leading Anthony Burgess to hail him as "the most important Scottish writer since Sir Walter Scott". This challenging, loosely autobiographical work – part science fiction, part *bildungsroman* – relates, in sometimes hallucinatory style, the journey of a man who hankers to create great art.

Alan Hollinghurst *The Stranger's Child*. Hollinghurst excels in pin-sharp and often very funny observations of British society. This particular work, from 2011, starts with a pre-World War I encounter in a country house, by turns bucolic, edgy and romantic. The focus of attention is a young poet who is killed in the war, and the narrative that follows develops into a satire on the uncertain art of biography.

★ **P.D. James** *Original Sin*. James wrote skilful tales of murder and mystery; of her umpteen novels featuring poet/Police Commander Adam Dalgliesh, this is one of the best. The novels *An Unsuitable Job for a Woman* and *The Skull Beneath the Skin* are also worth reading, featuring London private detective Cordelia Gray.

James Kelman *The Busconductor Hines; How Late It Was, how late*. The first is a wildly funny story of a young Glasgow bus conductor with an intensely boring job and a limitless imagination. *How Late It Was* is Kelman's award-winning and controversial look at life from the perspective of a blind Glaswegian drunk. A disturbing study of personal and political violence, with language to match.

Hilary Mantel *Wolf Hall; Bring up The Bodies*. Best-selling Mantel has made an enormous literary splash with her sharply observed, superbly crafted historical novels – and these are two of the best, set in the troubled days of Henry VIII and focused on his loyal enforcer, Thomas Cromwell.

★ **Ian McEwan** *Atonement; On Chesil Beach*. One of Britain's finest contemporary novelists, McEwan's dark and unsettling works are punctuated by the unforeseen and the accidental. *Atonement* is possibly his most masterful book, tracing the course of three lives from a sweltering country garden in 1935 to absolution in the new century, while *On Chesil Beach* is a tale of innocence and loss, misunderstanding and tenderness between two newlyweds in a hotel on the Dorset coast in the early 1960s.

Ian Rankin *Knots and Crosses; The Falls*. One of Britain's most popular crime authors, Rankin introduced John Rebus in 1987 and since then the hard-drinking, anti-authoritarian, emotionally scarred detective has featured in almost twenty novels. He inhabits the mean streets of Edinburgh – streets the tourists rarely see – though visitors can rub shoulders with him in cherished locations like the *Oxford Bar*.

Ruth Rendell/Barbara Vine *From Doon With Death; Gallowglass; King Solomon's Carpet; Grasshopper; The Birthday Present*. Rendell wrote brilliantly and disturbingly of contemporary dysfunction in all its guises. Her long-standing Inspector Wexford series was set in the fictional West Sussex town of Kingsmarkham, but it's when writing as Barbara Vine that Rendell excelled in creating memorable fictions and a sense of place, namely London.

Zadie Smith *White Teeth*. Smith explores mixed families, mixed races, mixed religions and mixed England in this zeitgeist-capturing debut novel, finished in her final year at Cambridge University. Among her other excellent work is the more experimental *NW*, which follows the lives of four people in northwest London (where Smith was born).

Film

Britain has produced a wealth of great films as well as some of the world's finest actors, producers and directors, but for all that it's well-nigh impossible to get critics to agree on what exactly constitutes a British film (or indeed, where "British" film stops and Scottish, Welsh and Irish film starts). Take sci-fi-horror classic *Alien* – a 20th Century Fox movie that launched the career of New York's Sigourney Weaver, but was filmed at London's Shepperton Studios, was directed by Tyne and Wear-born Ridley Scott and featured English RADA-trained classical actor John Hurt. The films reviewed below all depict a particular aspect of British life, whether reflecting the experience of immigrant communities, investigating its rippling class tensions or having a self-deprecatory laugh. The ★ symbol indicates films that are especially recommended.

THE 1930S AND 1940S

★ **Brief Encounter** (David Lean, 1945). Wonderful weepie in which Trevor Howard and Celia Johnson teeter on the edge of adultery after a chance encounter at a railway station. Noël Coward wrote the clipped dialogue; the flushed, dreamy soundtrack features Rachmaninov's *Piano Concerto No. 2*.

Brighton Rock (John Boulting, 1947). A fine adaptation of Graham Greene's novel, featuring a young, scary Richard Attenborough as the psychopathic Pinkie, who marries a witness to one of his crimes to ensure her silence. Beautiful cinematography and good performances, with a real sense of film noir menace.

★ **Great Expectations** (David Lean, 1946). Another early film by one of Britain's finest directors (see above), this superb rendition of a Dickens novel features magnificent performances by John Mills (as Pip) and Finlay Currie (as Abel Magwitch). The scene in the graveyard will (should) make your hair stand on end. Lean was also to be responsible for *Lawrence of Arabia* and *Bridge on the River Kwai*.

Henry V (Laurence Olivier, 1944). With dreamlike Technicolor backdrops, this rousing piece of wartime propaganda is emphatically cinematic rather than "theatrical", the action spiralling out from the Globe Theatre itself. Olivier is a brilliantly charismatic king, and the atmospheric pre-battle scene where he goes disguised amongst his men is heartachingly muted.

I Know Where I'm Going! (Michael Powell and Emeric Pressburger, 1945). Powell and Pressburger made some of the finest British films of all time (see also *A Matter of Life and Death*, *The Life and Death of Colonel Blimp*, *Black Narcissus*, *The Red Shoes* and *A Canterbury Tale*), all of which expose the peculiarities of the British character and reveal hidden depths and longings. In this delightful romance, Wendy Hiller's modern young woman, who knows what she wants and how to get it, is stymied in her goals by the mysterious romanticism of the Scottish islands and their inhabitants.

Jane Eyre (Robert Stevenson, 1943). Joan Fontaine does a fine job of portraying Jane, and Orson Welles is a suavely sardonic Rochester – the scene where he is thrown from his horse in the mist hits the perfect melodramatic pitch. With the unlikely tagline "A Love Story Every Woman Would Die a Thousand Deaths to Live!", it briefly features a young Elizabeth Taylor as a dying Helen Burns.

★ **Rebecca** (Alfred Hitchcock, 1940). Hitchcock does du Maurier: Laurence Olivier is wonderfully enigmatic as Maxim de Winter, and Joan Fontaine glows as his meek second wife, living in the shadow of her mysterious predecessor.

The Thirty-Nine Steps (Alfred Hitchcock, 1935). Hitchcock's best-loved British movie, full of wit and bold acts of derring-do. Robert Donat stars as innocent Richard Hannay, inadvertently caught up in a mysterious spy ring and forced to flee both spies and Scotland Yard. In a typically perverse Hitchcock touch, he spends a generous amount of time handcuffed to Madeleine Carroll – before the action returns to London for the film's great music-hall conclusion.

★ **Wuthering Heights** (William Wyler, 1939). The version of Emily Brontë's novel that everyone remembers, with Laurence Olivier as the dysfunctional Heathcliff and Merle Oberon as Cathy. It's tense, passionate and wild, and lays proper emphasis on the Yorkshire landscape, the best of all possible places for doomed lovers.

1950 TO 1970

Billy Liar! (John Schlesinger, 1963). Tom Courtenay is Billy, stuck in a dire job as an undertaker's clerk in a northern town, spending his time creating extravagant fantasies. His life is lit up by the appearance of Julie Christie, who holds out the glamour and promise of swinging London.

Carry On Screaming (Gerald Thomas, 1966). One of the best from the Carry On crew, with many of the usual suspects (Kenneth Williams, Charles Hawtrey, Joan Sims) hamming it up with the usual nudge-nudge merriment in a Hammer Horror spoof. Great one-liners too, but not the best – for this you have to watch *Carry on Cleo* (as in Cleopatra; 1964) with Julius Caesar (Kenneth Williams) announcing "Infamy, infamy… they've all got it in for me".

Far From the Madding Crowd (John Schlesinger, 1967). An imaginative adaptation of Hardy's doom-laden tale of the desires and ambitions of wilful/wishful Bathsheba Everdene. Julie Christie is a radiant and spirited Bathsheba, Terence Stamp flashes his blade to dynamic effect, Alan Bates is quietly charismatic as dependable Gabriel Oak, and the West Country setting is sparsely beautiful.

Kes (Kenneth Loach, 1969). The unforgettable story of a neglected Yorkshire schoolboy who finds solace and liberation in training his kestrel. As a still-pertinent commentary on poverty and an impoverished school system, it's bleak but idealistic. Pale and pinched David Bradley, who plays Billy Casper, is hugely affecting. Loach at the top of his game.

★ **The Ladykillers** (Alexander Mackendrick, 1955). Alec Guinness is fabulously toothy and malevolent as "Professor Marcus", a murderous con man who lodges with a sweet little old lady, Mrs Wilberforce (Katie Johnson), in this skewed Ealing comedy.

A Man for All Seasons (Fred Zinnemann, 1966). Sir Thomas More takes on Henry VIII in one of British history's great moral confrontations. Robert Bolt's wry screenplay, muted visuals and a heavenly host of theatrical talent (including Orson Welles as Cardinal Wolsey) add to the spectacle if not the tension, which is where the film dithers.

★ **Night and the City** (Jules Dassin, 1950). Great film noir, with Richard Widmark as an anxious nightclub hustler on the run. It's gripping and convincingly sleazy, and the London streetscapes have an Expressionist edge of horror.

Saturday Night and Sunday Morning (Karel Reisz, 1960). Reisz's monochrome captures all the grit and dead-end grind of Albert Finney's life working in a Nottingham bicycle factory – and his anarchic rejection of pretty much everything that surrounds him. The way out: heavy drinking and heavy petting (if not more).

★ **This Sporting Life** (Lindsay Anderson, 1963). One of the key British films of the 1960s, and a classic of the gritty "kitchen sink" genre. It's the story of a Northern miner turned Rugby League star with the young Richard Harris giving a great (and singularly muscular) performance as the inarticulate antihero, able only to express himself through physical violence.

THE 1970S AND 1980S

★ **Babylon** (Franco Rosso, 1980). A moving account of black working-class London life. We follow the experiences of young Blue through a series of encounters that reveal the nation's insidious racism. Good performances and a great reggae soundtrack: an all too rare example of Black Britain taking centre stage in a British movie.

Distant Voices, Still Lives (Terence Davies, 1988). Beautifully realized autobiographical tale of growing up in Liverpool in the 1940s and 1950s. The mesmeric pace is punctuated by astonishing moments of drama, and the whole is a very moving account of how a family survives and triumphs, in small ways, against the odds.

★ **Get Carter** (Mike Hodges, 1971). Vivid British gangster movie, featuring a hard-nosed, hard-case Michael Caine as the eponymous hero-villain, returning to his native Newcastle to avenge his brother's death.

Great use of its Northeastern locations and a fine turn by playwright John Osborne as the local godfather.

My Beautiful Laundrette (Stephen Frears, 1985). A slice of Thatcher's Britain, with a young, on-the-make Asian, Omar, opening a ritzy laundrette in London. His lover, Johnny (Daniel Day-Lewis), is an ex-National Front glamour boy, angry and inarticulate when forced by the acquisitive Omar into a menial role in the laundrette. The racial, sexual and class dynamics of their relationship mirror the tensions in the city itself.

Withnail and I (Bruce Robinson, 1986). Richard E. Grant is superb as the raddled, drunken Withnail, a "resting" actor with a penchant for drinking lighter fluid. Paul McGann is the "I" of the title – a bemused spectator of Withnail's wild excesses, as they abandon their grotty London flat for a remote country cottage, and the attentions of Withnail's randy Uncle Monty (Richard Griffiths).

THE 1990S

Bhaji on the Beach (Gurinder Chadha, 1993). An Asian women's group takes a day-trip to Blackpool in this issue-laden but enjoyable picture. A lot of fun is had contrasting the seamier side of British life with the mores of the Asian aunties, though the male characters are cartoon villains all.

Braveheart (Mel Gibson, 1995). Enjoyable cod-Highland camp, with a shaggy-haired Mel Gibson wielding his claymore as thirteenth-century Scottish nationalist William Wallace. The English are thieving effete scum, the cots all warm-blooded noble savages, and history takes a back seat. Filmed largely in Ireland.

Breaking the Waves (Lars von Trier, 1996). A lyrical, moving drama set in a devout community in the north of Scotland. An innocent young woman, Bess (Emily Watson), falls in love with Danish oil-rig worker Jan Stellan Skarsgård). Blaming herself for the injury that cripples him, she embarks on a masochistic sexual odyssey, which rapidly takes her into uncharted waters.

East is East (Damien O'Donnell, 1999). Seventies Salford is the setting for this lively tragi-comedy, with a Pakistani chip-shop owner struggling to keep control of his seven children as they rail against the strictures of Islam and arranged marriages. Inventively made, and with some delightful performances.

Elizabeth (Shekhar Kapur, 1998). Cate Blanchett is stunning in this visually beautiful, gothic production, where the young, innocent Elizabeth slowly adapts to the role of the "Virgin Queen" to secure her survival. It's better than its sequel *Elizabeth: The Golden Age* (2007), which also stars Blanchett, and focuses on the defeat of the Spanish Armada – but don't take it as historical gospel.

The Full Monty (Peter Cattaneo, 1997). Set in Sheffield, where six unemployed former steel-workers throw caution to the wind and become male strippers, their boast being that all will be revealed in the "full monty". Unpromising physical specimens all, they score an unlikely hit with the locals. The film was itself an unlikely hit worldwide and the long-awaited striptease is a joy to behold (well, almost).

Howards End (James Ivory, 1992). A superb Anthony Hopkins leads the way in this touching re-creation of E.M. Forster's celebrated novel. From the prolific Merchant Ivory team, who produced a string of exquisite period films, renowned for their elegiac settings.

Lock, Stock and Two Smoking Barrels (Guy Ritchie, 1998). Ritchie may be much derided for his marriage to Madonna and his mockney accent, but this – his breakout film – was a witty and inventive comedy-meets-heist movie that gave gangland heavies a "geezer" reboot.

The Madness of King George (Nicholas Hytner, 1994). Adapted from a witty Alan Bennett play, this royal romp is handsomely staged, with the king's loopy antics (a wonderfully nuanced performance from Nigel Hawthorne) played out against a cartoon-like court and its acolytes. Rupert Everett is superb as the Prince Regent.

★ **Nil by Mouth** (Gary Oldman, 1997). With strong performances by Ray Winstone as a brutish South Londoner and Kathy Burke as his abused wife, this brave and bleak picture delves deep into domestic violence and drug/drink addiction. Brace yourself.

The Remains of the Day (James Ivory, 1993). Kazuo Ishiguro's masterly novel of social and personal repression translates beautifully to the big screen. Anthony Hopkins is the overly decorous butler who gradually becomes aware of his master's fascist connections, Emma Thompson the housekeeper who struggles (unsuccessfully) to bring his deeply suppressed feelings to the surface. Call a counsellor.

Richard III (Richard Loncraine, 1995). A splendid film version of a renowned National Theatre production, which brilliantly transposed the action to a fascist state in the 1930s. The infernal political machinations of a snarling Ian McKellen as Richard are heightened by Nazi associations, and the style of the period imbues the film with the requisite glamour, as does languorously drugged Kristin Scott-Thomas as Lady Anne.

Secrets and Lies (Mike Leigh, 1996). Serious-minded, slice-of-life ensemble drama charting a dysfunctional family's hidden secrets, from infidelity to reconciliation – and all seen through the prism of class. Mike Leigh at his most penetrating.

Sense and Sensibility (Ang Lee, 1995). Ah, the English and their period dramas. They are all here – Rickman, Winslett, Thompson, Grant, Robert Hardy et al – in this tone-perfect re-creation of Jane Austen's sprightly story of love, money and, of course, manners.

Small Faces (Gillies MacKinnon, 1995). A moving little saga about the lives of three brothers growing up in 1960s Glasgow amid feuding gangs of local teenagers. We follow the rough education of young Lex, torn between the excitement and real danger of a life of fighting, and the artistic ambitions of his older brother.

★ **Trainspotting** (Danny Boyle, 1996). High-octane dip into the heroin-scarred world of a group of young Scotsmen both at home and in London; includes what might be the best cinematic representation of a heroin fix ever.

Wonderland (Michael Winterbottom, 1999). One Bonfire Night in London as experienced by three unhappy sisters. Winterbottom's use of real locations, natural light and 16mm film gives it a naturalistic air that's also dreamlike, an effect heightened by Michael Nyman's haunting score.

THE 2000S

24 Hour Party People (Michael Winterbottom, 2002). Steve Coogan plays the entrepreneurial/inspirational Tony Wilson (1950–2007) – the man of many quotes – in this fast-moving re-creation of the early days of Manchester's Factory Records. Stunning soundtrack, too.

Atonement (Joe Wright, 2007). This adaptation of Ian McEwan's highly literary novel of misunderstanding and regret benefits from strong performances from Keira Knightley and James McAvoy, as well as fluent plotting.

Bend It Like Beckham (Gurinder Chadha, 2003).

Immensely successful film focusing on the coming of age of a football-loving Punjabi girl in a suburb of London. Both socially acute and comic.

★ **Bronson** (Nicolas Winding Refn, 2009). The subject matter may seem unappetizing – Welsh criminal Bronson (Tom Hardy) is reputed to be the most violent man ever locked up in a British prison – and it's not easy viewing, but Refn's take on this unusual antihero is inventive, creative and insightful. Notable also for the appearance of a Rough Guide author as an extra – but blink and you'll miss him.

Control (Anton Corbijn, 2007). Ian Curtis, the lead singer of Joy Division, committed suicide in 1980 at the age of 23. This biopic tracks his life in and around Manchester, based on the account provided by his wife, Deborah. Some have raved over Sam Riley's portrayal of Curtis, others have been less convinced, but as an evocation of the Northwest – and pioneering Factory Records – it's hard to beat.

Dirty Pretty Things (Stephen Frears, 2003). A tumbling mix of melodrama, social criticism and black comedy, this forceful, thought-provoking film explores the world of Britain's illegal migrants.

Fish Tank (Andrea Arnold, 2009). Arnold delves deep into working class life in this searing coming-of-age tale in which a volatile teenager struggles to make sense of things – and the attentions of her mum's boyfriend. Arnold's breakthrough movie, which used CCTV to tell a story of obsession in Glasgow, was *Red Road* (2006), and there's also her excellent *Wuthering Heights* (2011), revealing a lyrical eye for the natural world in an arty, elemental reworking of Emily Brontë's romantic tragedy.

Gosford Park (Robert Altman, 2001). Astutely observed upstairs-downstairs murder mystery set in class-ridden 1930s England. The multilayered plot is typical of the director; the script, from Julian Fellowes, is more nuanced than some of his later TV work; and the who's who of great British actors is led by the superb Maggie Smith.

Harry Potter and the Philosopher's Stone (Chris Columbus, 2001). The first film adaptation of J.K. Rowling's world-conquering series, eight films in all. They are all enjoyable romps (which get progressively darker) with excellent ensemble casts – Spall, Gambon, Rickman et al. The series did wonders for the English tourist industry, and boosted the pension pots of a platoon of British actors.

In the Loop (Armando Iannucci, 2009). Look what we have to put up with from our politicians, screams Iannucci, in this satire on the opaque and corrupt meanderings of our leaders and their assorted advisors.

★ **Sexy Beast** (Jonathan Glazer, 2000). Gangster thriller distinguished by the performances of Ray Winstone and more especially Ben Kingsley, who plays one of the hardest, meanest criminals ever. Delightful cameos by an evil Ian McShane and a debauched James Fox, too.

Shaun of the Dead (Edgar Wright, 2004). Shuffling and shambolic zombies roam and groan on the streets of London in this zom-com, horror-romp that made a name for Simon Pegg. Wright and Pegg's "Cornetto Trilogy" was completed with buddy-cop movie homage *Hot Fuzz* (2007) and pub-crawl/apocalyptic sci-fi flick *The World's End* (2013).

This is England (Shane Meadows, 2006). British cinema rarely ventures into the East Midlands, but this is where Shane Meadows is at home. Set in the early 1980s, this thoughtful film deals with a young working-class lad who falls in with skinheads – the good-hearted ones to begin with, the racists thereafter.

★ **Vera Drake** (Mike Leigh, 2004). Moving story of a 1950s working-class woman, who performs illegal abortions from the goodness of her heart – and without thought for either money or the legal consequences. Her actions eventually threaten to destroy her and her close-knit family, and serve as a powerful counterblast to the anti-abortion lobby.

2010 ONWARDS

★ **Catch me Daddy** (Daniel Wolfe, 2014). Rippling and gripping tale of a young British-Pakistani woman, who breaks family convention by running away with her white boyfriend. Bleak Yorkshire moorland settings add to the gloom as she is hunted down by her male relatives – with a bitter, tragic ending. No sentimental get-out clause here.

Dreams of a Life (Carol Morley, 2011). Haunting drama-doc on the life and unnoticed death of Joyce Carol Vincent – heartbreakingly portrayed by Zawe Ashton – whose body was found in her London flat two years after her death. How did it happen? How could a life of promise end so sadly? No conclusions, but so very moving.

I, Daniel Blake (Ken Loach, 2016). Hear Loach's howl of rage as unemployed Daniel, the epitome of a decent man,

is scuppered and skewered by a benefits system seemingly designed to crush him. How Loach hates the Tories – and what their austerity policies have done.

The King's Speech (Tom Hooper, 2010). Colin Firth is suitably repressed as the vocally challenged King George VI, who is given the confidence to become king by Geoffrey Rush's exuberant Australian speech therapist. Superb performances also from Helena Bonham Carter as his imperious wife (later to become the Queen Mother) and Guy Pearce as the spoiled, self-indulgent Edward VIII.

Made in Dagenham (Nigel Cole, 2010). Good-hearted, good-natured film about the struggle for equal pay in the car industry in 1960s Britain. Sweet packaging for a tough industrial message.

Mr Nice (Bernard Rose, 2010). Picaresque tale of one-time drug king and (supposedly) very good egg, Howard Marks (Mr Nice himself) from baffled beginnings to stoned (very stoned) fame and fortune via imprisonment and hostile drug cartels. Rhys Ifans is perfect as the drug-addled hero, Chloë Sevigny as his wife.

Mr Turner (Mike Leigh, 2014). One of Leigh's most ambitious films, elbowing into the last years of the eponymous artist's life. The curmudgeonly Turner (1775–1851) is played by Timothy Spall with consummate skill.

A talented supporting cast – Dorothy Atkinson, Marion Bailey et al – add pace and vigour.

Prevenge (Alice Lowe, 2016). Reckless romp and gory goings-on in this comedy-slasher – the foetus must have revenge. Filmed in Cardiff.

★ **Sightseers** (Ben Wheatley, 2012). Murder, mayhem, sadism and psychosis on a caravan holiday in the Midlands and the North. Never, but never before, has Crich Tramway Village seemed so dangerous. This is horror with ironic flair – so avert your eyes strategically or prepare to grimace.

Small print and index

A ROUGH GUIDE TO ROUGH GUIDES

Published in 1982, the first Rough Guide – to Greece – was a student scheme that became a publishing phenomenon. Mark Ellingham, a recent graduate in English from Bristol University, had been travelling in Greece the previous summer and couldn't find the right guidebook. With a small group of friends he wrote his own guide, combining a contemporary, journalistic style with a thoroughly practical approach to travellers' needs.

The immediate success of the book spawned a series that rapidly covered dozens of destinations. And, in addition to impecunious backpackers, Rough Guides soon acquired a much broader readership that relished the guides' wit and inquisitiveness as much as their enthusiastic, critical approach and value-for-money ethos. These days, Rough Guides include recommendations from budget to luxury and cover more than 120 destinations around the globe, from Amsterdam to Zanzibar, all regularly updated by our team of roaming writers.

Browse all our latest guides, read inspirational features and book your trip at **roughguides.com**.

Rough Guide credits

Editors: Samantha Cook, Natasha Foges, Rebecca Hallett, David Leffman
Cartography: Katie Bennett, Carte, Rajesh Chhibber, Richard Marchi
Picture editor: Aude Vauconsant

Managing editors: Rachel Lawrence, Mani Ramaswamy
Cover photo research: Nicole Newman
Senior DTP coordinator: Dan May
Head of DTP and Pre-Press: Rebeka Davies

Publishing information

This 10th edition published in 2018 by
Rough Guides Ltd

Distribution
UK, Ireland and Europe
Apa Publications (UK) Ltd; sales@roughguides.com
United States and Canada
Ingram Publisher Services; ips@ingramcontent.com
Australia and New Zealand
Woodslane; info@woodslane.com.au
Southeast Asia
Apa Publications (SN) Pte; sales@roughguides.com
Worldwide
Apa Publications (UK) Ltd; sales@roughguides.com
Special Sales, Content Licensing and CoPublishing
Rough Guides can be purchased in bulk quantities
at discounted prices. We can create special editions,
personalised jackets and corporate imprints tailored to
your needs; sales@roughguides.com.
roughguides.com

Help us update

We've gone to a lot of effort to ensure that the 10 edition of **The Rough Guide to Great Britain** is accurate and up-to-date. However, things change – places get "discovered", opening hours are notoriously fickle, restaurants and rooms raise prices or lower standards. If you feel we've got it wrong or left something out, we'd like to know, and if you can remember the address, the price, the hours, the phone number, so much the better.

Please send your comments with the subject line "**Rough Guide Great Britain Update**" to mail@ uk.roughguides.com. We'll credit all contributions and send a copy of the next edition (or any other Rough Guide if you prefer) for the very best emails.

Readers' updates

Thanks to all the readers who have taken the time to write in with comments and suggestions (and apologies if we've inadvertently omitted or misspelt anyone's name):

Amy Adams; Chris Allen; Sandra Ball; Vanessa Bennett; Claudia Berettoni; Mary Birch; Finnian Brewer; Matt Burrows; Chris Bush; Lorenza Canepa; Will Carey; Peter Carney; Georgina Church; Leanne Cromie; Matthew Crowther; Sam Dalley; Peter and Carol Delbridge; Tom Edwards; Fergus Ewbank; Rachel Faulkner; Heather Finlay; Helen Gibbons; Heather Gifford-Jenkins; Kitty Gilbert; Laura Hampton; Sam Hanson; James Harrison; James Horrocks; Dave Hough; Jo Hudson-Cook; Helen Hughes; Jerry Hyde; Ashley Jackson; Margaret Jailler; Gary Jenkins; Matthew Johnson; Feroza Kassam; Hayley Kitto; Trina King; Belinda Kirk; Rachel Knott; Lewis Lawson; Clare Leedale; Adam Legg; Shy Lewis; Alice Lowe; Gigi Mann; Alex Manners; Sophie Mason; Thomas Maxwell; John Bury Meaker; Belinda Mercer; Jamie Milton; Cheryl Morris; Shadyn Nikzad; Harley Nott; Zennor Pascoe; Allie Pinder; Sophie Pitt; Sara Priddle; Nicky Primavesi; Gabriel Quiro; Joe Rodriguez; Lucy Sambrook; Ben Selvaratnam; Alan Sharp; Samantha Sims; Robin Simpson; Gary Snapper; Owen Stephen; Diana Stoica; Koji Takeuchi; Jake Tibbits; Michael Tracey; Rachel White; Jacqui Wieksza; Anna Wilson-Barnes; Geoff Wisher; Jen Workers.

ABOUT THE AUTHORS

Rob Andrews has written or contributed to the Rough Guides to Devon & Cornwall; Italy; Sardinia; Sicily; Bath, Bristol & Somerset; and England. He lives in Bristol.

Tim Burford studied languages at Oxford University and worked briefly in publishing. In 1991 he began writing hiking guides to east-central Europe and then Latin America. Somewhat randomly, he also works on the Rough Guides to Romania and Alaska, and leads hiking groups in Europe's mountains. He lives in Cambridge, loves train travel in Europe, and flies as rarely as possible.

Samantha Cook was born in London and has lived in the city all her life. In addition to the London and Southeast chapters of this guide, she has written, edited and contributed to many other Rough Guides, including London; Kent, Sussex and Surrey; and Best Places to Stay in Britain on a Budget.

Greg Dickinson has edited guidebooks at Bradt Travel Guides, DK Eyewitness and Rough Guides, and has written about his travels for The Independent and The Telegraph. He is happiest when he can't feel his cheeks atop a hill somewhere in Sutherland.

Matthew Hancock is co-author of *The Rough Guide to Dorset, Hampshire and the Isle of Wight*, *The Rough Guide to Portugal* and *The Rough Guide to Porto*, and is author of *The Rough Guide to Lisbon* as well as being a contributor to *The Rough Guide to Spain*.

Rob Humphreys has spent some part of every year in Scotland since he was nowt but a lad in rural Yorkshire. One day he hopes to sail round the islands, but in the meantime can be found steering the Puppet Theatre Barge through the waterways of London.

Phil Lee has been writing for Rough Guides for well over twenty years. His other books in the series include Norway, Norfolk & Suffolk, Amsterdam, Mallorca & Menorca and The Netherlands. He lives in Nottingham, where he was born and raised.

David Leffman has been writing guidebooks for Rough Guides, Dorling Kindersley and others since 1992, and has lived in the UK, Australia and China.

Norm Longley is a regular visitor to Wales from his home in Somerset, and has a particular fondness for the Brecons and the Gower. He is also author of *The Rough Guide to Slovenia* and co-author of the Rough Guides to Romania, Budapest, Wales, Scotland and Ireland.

Mike MacEacheran is an Edinburgh-based travel journalist and guidebook author who writes for Rough Guides, *The Guardian*, *The Sunday Times*, Lonely Planet, *CN Traveler*, *The Wall Street Journal*, *The Independent* and the BBC. He also recently co-authored the update to *The Rough Guide to the Philippines*.

Rachel Mills is a freelance writer and editor based on the Kent coast, or in her campervan somewhere in the UK. She is a co-author to Rough Guides to New Zealand, Vietnam and Ireland, as well as England and Great Britain.

Keith Munro has been a freelance writer since 2010 after a stretch working in London's music industry as a record label manager. A keen traveller, he spent a year in the French Pyrenees before returning to his childhood home of Edinburgh, and has since contributed to the Rough Guides to France and Scotland, as well as other travel-related publications.

Alice Park is a freelance editor and writer. She has edited numerous guidebooks and has written about Switzerland, Austria and Germany as well as her native South London.

Claire Saunders grew up in Brighton and now lives in nearby Lewes, where she works as a freelance editor and writer. She updated the Sussex sections of this book, and is the co-author of *The Rough Guide to Kent, Sussex and Surrey*.

James Stewart is a freelance journalist who has covered Wales for the *Sunday Times*, *Telegraph* and *Guardian* newspapers among others. He is the author of more than fifteen guides, and has written about Wales in *The Rough Guide to Camping* and *The Best Places to Stay in Britain on a Budget*.

Matthew Teller is a writer, journalist and broadcaster. He writes for media worldwide, is the author of *The Rough Guide to the Cotswolds*, among other titles, and produces and presents documentaries for BBC Radio.

Amanda Tomlin is a Dorset-based freelance author and travel editor. She is co-author of *The Rough Guide to Dorset, Hampshire and the Isle of Wight*, and *The Rough Guide to Porto*, and a contributor to *The Rough Guide to Portugal*.

Acknowledgements

Rob Andrews I'd like acknowledge the huge assistance given by Evelina at Visit England, Claire Pickup at Bath Tourism, Lesley Gillilan at Destination Bristol and Rosa Pedley at Visit Cornwall, and to thank Becca Hallett for expert editing.

Tim Burford Thank you to Freddie, Robbie and Katy, and to Jane Harris and all at Visit Wales.

Samantha Cook Thanks to Natasha and Becca for diligent editing; to Alice and Claire, great co-authors both; and to Greg Ward for everything.

Greg Dickinson Thanks to everyone in the north and northwest Highlands, Skye and the Small Isles for your remarkable warmth in cold conditions, and huge thanks to Victoria Wainwright for being the most wonderful co-updater I could ask for. Last, but not least, thanks to the "Class of 80 Strand" Rough Guides crew for your support, beers, friendship – may the fires in your bellies continue to burn strong.

Matthew Hancock and Amanda Tomlin Thanks to Olivia and Alex Hancock-Tomlin for their additional research.

Rob Humphreys Thanks to Val for company and for staying in the odd place that will never make it into the guide for good reasons. And thanks to the Wrigley Sisters for a cracking gig in the Hope.

Phil Lee Thank you to my editor, Rebecca Hallett, for the fine quality of your editing – hard to beat. Special thanks also to Simon Gribbon in Leicester; Kerry McGinty in Stratford-upon-Avon; Rabia Raza in Birmingham; and Lydia Rusling in Lincoln.

David Leffman Thanks to Becca for her editorial work, and to Rajesh and Richard for the excellent cartography.

Norm Longley Thank you to Rebecca and Sam for diligent editing. Thanks also to Jane Harris at Visit Wales, but most importantly to Christian, Anna, Luka and Patrick.

Mike MacEacheran Thanks to all those who helped out and provided assistance along the way, in particular Laura Mitchell at Visit Scotland, and Leanne Cromie at Bunk Campers and CalMac Ferries. Thanks also to my fellow authors and ever-patient editor Samantha Cook. Huge thanks and love, as always, to my wife Katalin (Traveller No.2) and one-year-old son Kyle (Traveller No.3) for their love, support and patience during research.

Rachel Mills Thank you to Ed Aves, Becca Hallett and David Leffman in the RG editorial team; Andy Parkinson at Visit Manchester; Joe Keggin at Visit Liverpool; Ubiquity PR; YHA youth hostels; Hope and Glory PR; NewcastleGateshead Initiative; Visit Blackpool; Visit Hull and East Yorkshire; Mark Hibbert PR; Visit Northumberland; and Visit Yorkshire.

Alice Park Many thanks to my fellow London guide authors for their contributions: Samantha Cook, Matt Norman and Neil McQuillian. At Rough Guides, huge thanks to the editorial supergroup of Edward Aves, Rebecca Hallett and Natasha Foges.

Claire Saunders Thank you to Becca, for another smooth and stress-free edit, and to my splendid Southeast co-author Sam, and (as ever) to Ian, Tom and Mia.

Index

Main references are in **bold** type

Map symbols

The symbols below are used on maps throughout the book

International boundary	★ Bus stop	Nature reserve	Bridge
County boundary	Boat	Wildfowl area	Waterfall
Chapter boundary	P Parking	Tin mine	Cave
Motorway	@ Internet access	Viewpoint	Castle
Main road	(i) Information office	Lighthouse	Battlefield
Minor road	Hospital	Swimming pool	▲ Mountain peak
Pedestrian road	Post office	Surfing	Mountain range
Steps	Public gardens	Distillery	Gorge
Path	Point of interest	Ski area	Standing stones
Wall	Golf course	Arboretum	Cairn
Ferry	Vineyard/winery	Cider farm	Building
Railway	Ferris wheel	Synagogue	Church (town maps)
Funicular railway	Gate	Mosque	Mosque
Cable car	Ruin	Hindu temple	Stadium
Airport	Museum	Church (regional maps)	Market
Local airport/airstrip	Memorial/statue	Abbey	Beach
London underground station	Country park	Stately/historic house	Park
London DLR station	Zoo	Swamp	Cemetery
London Overground station			

Listings key

- Accommodation
- Eating
- Drinking/nightlife
- Shopping